ENVIRONMENTAL LAW

Fourth Edition

By

Frank P. Grad
J. P. Chamberlain Professor Emeritus of Legislation
Columbia University School of Law

Joel A. Mintz
Professor of Law
Nova Southeastern University Law Center

CASEBOOK SERIES

LEXIS Publishing™

LEXIS®·NEXIS® · MARTINDALE-HUBBELL®
MATTHEW BENDER® · MICHIE™ · SHEPARD'S®

Library of Congress Cataloging-in-Publication Data

Grad, Frank P.
Environmental law / by Frank P. Grad, Joel A. Mintz.—4th ed.
p. cm.—(Casebook series)
Includes bibliographical references and index.
ISBN 0-8205-4133-8
1. Environmental law—United States—Cases. I. Mintz, Joel A., 1949- II. Title. III. Series.
KF3775.A7 G73 2000
344.73'046—dc21

00-039131

Editorial Offices
2 Park Avenue, New York, NY 10016-5675 (212) 448-2000
201 Mission Street, San Francisco, CA 94105-1831 (415) 908-3200
701 East Water Street, Charlottesville, VA 22902-7587 (804) 972-7600
www.lexis.com

(Pub.328)

PREFACE

The fourth edition, prepared for publication in mid-2000, reflects the further development of the field, noted first in the first edition which appeared in 1971. The first edition was the first coursebook in general use in environmental law in what was then a novel field. It is interesting to recall the problem faced in the collection of materials for the first edition because there was so little environmental law around at the time. The first edition did not contain a single federal case that dealt with the enforcement of pollution standards—there weren't any! Subsequent editions increasingly faced an embarrassment of riches, reflected in the growth of the field into new areas, an ever greater flood of judicial decisions, and an ever expanding universe of secondary descriptive and analytical materials.

The fourth edition is the work of two authors, Frank P. Grad at Columbia Law School and Joel A. Mintz at Nova Southeastern University Law Center. We believe that the insights of two practicing law professors, both with significant teaching and writing experience, have contributed to the insights provided in the work. Both of the writers have done a great deal of work in the field, much of it reflected and cited in the materials that follow. Because the writers have known each other and worked together for many years, the book is the result not only of two insightful and experienced academics, but demonstrates, in the integration of its parts, a close collaboration and a broadening of points of view which we acknowledge and are grateful for.

The fourth edition is thus a very old and a very new book—it has been available in its earlier editions for almost 30 years and reflects both old experiences and knowledge and new insights.

The fourth edition contains the latest decisions of the U.S. Supreme Court and other appellate tribunals, reflecting the latest pronouncements on standing to sue, citizen suits, the application of NEPA, and recent developments in land use controls and the application of the Fifth Amendment to regulatory takings. The work also reflects recent developments in Superfund law, in the new field of environmental justice, and in references to new modes of environmental enforcement not relying entirely on command and control. The work also deals with such new environmental concerns as control of ozone layer destroying gases, control of acid deposition, and other newly emerging problems in the control of air toxics.

While the field of environmental law has achieved some maturity and stability, it will probably continue to be a field in progress as new legislation is passed and old legislation is revised to keep pace with new insights and scientific growth. Environmental law still reflects older environmental conservation concerns with ever newer and stronger concerns for the protection of public health, as demonstrated in the revision of national ambient air quality standards for nitrogen oxide and particulate matter pollution, as well as in the constant update of the regulation of air toxics. Similar developments may be noted in the field of water pollution control, where there is a growing concern for pollution from nonpoint sources as well as a growing concern for the protection of entire river basins and wetlands.

The work retains certain successful features of earlier editions, such as significant references to earlier common law materials and to very early municipal legislation addressing environmental concerns. Modern environmental law, however, is a statutory field, which involves the application of complex statutes to complex facts, often of a technical and scientific nature. This is especially true in cases reviewing the setting of ambient and emission standards under the intricate schemes of the pollution control laws. Thus, it is impossible to gain a full understanding of the field without substantial exposure to this complicated law-fact relationship, a relationship which is reflected in the length and complexity of the judicial decisions. The fourth edition retains the classic cases in the field and it reproduces them, usually with most of the judicial text, so as to provide not only the substance of the case, but also the court's mode of expression and the full ambience of the decision in its original legal context. This is particularly true in the materials that address environmental litigation and enforcement, which retain their primary significance for the development of the field.

We have chosen a sequence of chapters that proved most useful to us, but this should not prevent our colleagues from rearranging the sequence of major topics in any way that is most helpful. Topics are frequently cross-referred to Grad's *Treatise on Environmental Law*, in the hope that these references may be useful to teachers and students who wish to pursue them in greater detail. There is no need to do so, however, because we have tried to be as complete in each of the subject areas as a work of this nature permits. For every part of the course it is strongly recommended that students have available—and read—the statutes referred to; most of them readily available in collections of environmental legislation.

The work intentionally avoids any dominant doctrine or point of view in its presentation. While we are committed to environmental protection and to the protection of public health, the purpose is to familiarize students with the major areas of environmental law and to provide them with a sound basis for analyzing and finding their way in the complex legislation and other legal materials in the field. We have avoided casting the work in any particular theoretical perspective. The book is not a tract for public choice theory, law and economics, pragmatism, civic republicanism or law and biology. We have also tried to avoid the straightjacket of both green theory and anthropocentrism. In other words, the book invites teachers to use the work in teaching environmental law in any way that suits their own legal and philosophical convictions.

We are pleased to acknowledge our debt to many friends, colleagues and students who contributed to this work by their encouragement, comments, and criticism. We are pleased also to acknowledge the help of Susan Silvey, Leslie Deckelbaum and Jesse Monteagudo, who prepared and assembled the manuscript.

Frank P. Grad
Columbia Law School

Joel A. Mintz
Nova Southeastern
University Law Center

March 2000

SUMMARY TABLE OF CONTENTS

TABLE OF CONTENTS

Page

CHAPTER 5

THE NATIONAL ENVIRONMENTAL POLICY ACT OF 1969

CHAPTER 6

PUBLIC LANDS AND CONSERVATION POLICIES

Page

CHAPTER 7

LAND USE PLANNING AND ITS ENVIRONMENTAL IMPLICATIONS

Chapter 1

INTRODUCTION TO ENVIRONMENTAL LAW: ITS BEGINNINGS, ITS MAJOR CONCERNS AND SOME OF ITS RECURRING PROBLEMS

§ 1.01 A Brief Account of the Beginnings of the Field

The beginnings of modern environmental law can be found in the 1960s, when the growth of industry that had taken place during and after World War II began to have a noticeable impact on the environment. Little attention could be paid to adverse environmental impacts during the war; nor was there much emphasis on environmental protection in the early post-war years, although a nascent interest in the field may be noted. The first federal law to deal with water pollution (aside from the earlier River and Harbors Act of 1899, which primarily addressed obstructions to navigation) was passed in 1948, although permanent federal water pollution legislation was not enacted until 1956. The first federal air pollution legislation was enacted in 1955, but again, broader, more permanent measures did not become law until 1963.

The impact of major disasters on the development of pollution control law must also be kept in mind. The air pollution disaster in Donora, Pennsylvania in 1948, resulting from smoke emissions and temperature inversion, and the recurring smog incidents in Los Angeles beginning around that time, provided an impetus for concern and action for air pollution control. So, too, the 1967 break-up of the oil tanker Torrey Canyon off the southern coast of England, the 1968 break-up of the tanker Ocean Eagle near the coast of Puerto Rico, and the 1969 blow-out of an offshore oil drilling operation near Santa Barbara, California, gave rise to concerns about major oil spills in the western world. These concerns reinforced public awareness of other water pollution problems, such as those relating to increasing urbanization, and the reliance on sewer systems that emptied human wastes into rivers with little or no treatment.

An alarm regarding the environmental and public health impact of new chemicals and pesticides, originally considered benign and necessary, was sounded by Rachel Carson's book Silent Spring, published in 1962. The book energized conservationists and environmentalists. Its full contribution to the environmental movement is difficult to measure. In dramatically reporting on the disappearance of butterflies, and the widespread destruction of living things caused by DDT and other pesticides, Carson called attention to the price we pay for the use of substances heretofore considered benign and useful in the growing and protection of crops. The impact on plants and birds, and on animal life, became even more frightening when it became clear that man, too, could be hurt by pesticides, and that man was endangered because, standing at the very end of the food chain, man's pesticide intake was likely to be greater as a result of bioconcentration.

It is apparent that actual catastrophes and the fear of imminent catastrophes have brought about significant developments in environmental law and have boosted the impact of the environmental movement. Many of these incidents, having broad if not worldwide consequences, have advanced the national and international efforts at environmental control, encouraging advances in national law as well as initiatives leading to international covenants and agreements, which in turn are then reflected in additional national legislation. Such potentially catastrophic events included the 1985 Chernobyl disaster in the Soviet Union, involving a runaway nuclear power plant, which caused vast emissions of radioactive materials over many parts of Europe, destroying many crops and making milk unfit to drink by children because cattle had grazed on land covered with significant residues of nuclear particulates. The nuclear fallout also affected produce as far away as northern Italy and in the northern part of Europe, destroying herds of reindeer in Scandinavia that had ingested foliage and grass covered with radioactive fallout materials. Aside from the vast human toll in the immediate area of Chernobyl, and other areas in close proximity, the consequences of which will continue for many years, the incident gave rise to major international concerns leading to the tightening of controls over nuclear power plants worldwide, and leading also to the adoption, within a year of the incident, of two international agreements relating to nuclear safety. This was record time, compared to the time normally taken for the adoption of significant international agreements.[1]

Similar far-reaching international and national consequences resulted from the worldwide fear following the discovery of the destruction of the ozone layer over the South Pole. Clear scientific evidence led to the well founded fear that the destruction of the ozone layer would result in a vast increase in the number of melanomas or skin cancers, as well as a major increase of eye injuries and cataracts. In addition to such human injuries, the destruction of the ozone layer was likely to lead to the vast destruction of biota and unicellular organisms in the oceans. This well founded and documented fear led to the adoption of the Vienna and Montreal agreements on the control of ozone destroying gases, most particularly hydrochlorofluorocarbons (HCFCs) and similar gases destructive of the stratospheric ozone layer.[2] In addition to several international agreements and their technical protocols, the worldwide control effort led to the legislative adoption of controls in the United States and elsewhere. In the United States, the 1990 Amendment of the Clean Air Act placed controls on the use of hydrochlorofluorocarbons, including controls on their use as refrigerants, particularly in motor vehicle air

1 IAEA Convention on Early Notification of a Nuclear Accident. Concluded at Vienna and New York, September 26, 1986. Entered into force October 27, 1986, 25 I.L.M. 1369 (1986). IAEA Convention on Assistance in the Case of a Nuclear Accident or Radiological Emergency. Concluded at Vienna and New York, September 26, 1986. Entered into force September 26, 1987, 25 I.L.M. 1377 (1986).

2 Vienna Convention for the Protection of the Ozone Layer. Concluded at Vienna, March 22, 1985. Entered into force September 22, 1988. UNEP Doc. IG.53/5, 26 I.L.M. 1529 (1987). *See also*, Helsinki Declaration on the Protection of the Ozone Layer, May 2, 1989. 28 I.L.M. 1335 (1989); Montreal Protocol on Substances That Deplete the Ozone Layer, September 26, 1987. 28 I.L.M. 1550 (1987). Helsinki Declaration on the Protection of the Ozone Layer, May 2, 1989. 28 I.L.M. 1335. London Amendments to the Montreal Protocol on Substances that Deplete the Ozone Layer with Annexes, June 29, 1990. UNEP/OzL.Pro, 2/3.

conditioning systems. These far-reaching controls include regulating the replacement of exhausted coolant canisters by automobile and garage mechanics.

Another major occurrence, involving improper use of hazardous chemicals in the workplace, was the Bhopal disaster in India in 1987, which caused thousands of deaths, led to mega-international lawsuits, and gave rise to significant demands for toxic substance control—in the workplace and in general. The increased attention to hazardous air pollutants under the Clean Air Act can be attributed at least in part to the worldwide impact of the Bhopal disaster.

Regardless of the year chosen to represent the "beginning" of environmental law, it has clearly been around long enough so as not to be regarded as a new field. It is a field which is forever developing, in response to natural events, public disasters and the discoveries of new hazards, sometimes resulting from long existing conditions. Thus, in 1997, several fish kills in Chesapeake Bay led to the discovery that a heretofore little recognized organism, pfiesteria piscicida, probably generated from the waste of pig farms, had begun to cause major health problems.

A momentous current issue is global warming, a matter on which there is substantial scientific agreement, but not as yet full consensus. The consequences of global warming include changes in climate, changes in the ecology and fruitfulness of different parts of the world, and the likelihood of resulting sequential changes in demography. The warming of our world has been the subject of international attention for some time, leading to several international agreements.

The discovery of new risks from old conditions is a recurring phenomenon. Operating under existing legal authority, EPA in 1997 began to work on new controls on emission of particulate matter. It had been noted by air pollution specialists, and by physicians working with persons afflicted with pulmonary disease, that smaller particulates designated as P-10, approximately one-tenth the size of particulates which had been subject to regulation previously, caused a great deal more damage than previously had been recognized. EPA began work on new P-10 regulations in mid-1997, and regulations will be fully effective in due course.

While we may place the beginnings of modern environmental law, and of the modern environmental movement, in the 1960s, one part of the field had its genesis during the era of President Theodore Roosevelt in the last part of the nineteenth and continuing into the early twentieth century. Roosevelt was enormously effective in advancing conservationist interests by reserving major parts of the national forests, totaling 125 million acres, thus keeping them from development. Roosevelt's impact is hard to overstate. Had he not been successful in protecting national forests during his term, there would be little to protect in our time, considering the rapaciousness of timber interests and others seeking access to the exploitation of the country's natural resources.

The environmental movement, with modern beginnings in the early 1960s, and which continues to this day, reflects the confluence of two separate interests, each with its own history and well-respected agenda. One of these was essentially conservationist, outdoor oriented, intent on protecting our scenic resources and natural heritage for ourselves and future generations. The concern for "quality of life" (a term hard to limit or define) has been most strongly associated with that part of the environmental movement. It includes the protection of forests and other open areas, terrestrial and marine wildlife, endangered species, wild and scenic rivers, wetlands and other threatened habitats, and the rich scenic resources of the nation. Perhaps we may think of the advocates of this broad range of conservationist interests as "high-road environmentalists," as distinct from "low-road environmentalists," who form the other part of the confluence. This group, espousing more immediate and practical concerns, has a primary interest in public health, in protecting people in our cities and highly populated areas against the pervasive impact of environmental pollution—water pollution, air pollution, pollution from hazardous and conventional waste, as well as noise, radiation, and the other polluting effects of our modern, highly industrialized world. This concern for the protection of public health has an ancient history of its own, much of it reflected in the early common law of nuisance as well as in the common law protections of riparian interests. It began very early in the history of American law, and much of it is reflected in early nuisance cases involving excessive smoke from chimneys, and other interferences with the use and enjoyment of land. These early cases, some based on common law and some on early local law and municipal legislation are referred to in this book as early controls of air and water pollution and the disposal of waste materials.

It has become clear that the two concerns—for nature and for humankind—are indivisible. The control of pollution is necessary for the protection of human health as much as for the protection of the environment. The same pollutants that hurt man also hurt forests and animals that live on land or in the sea. The integrity and interconnection of our biosphere, the singularity of our ecosystem is brought home to us again and again when harm inflicted on other parts of the ecosystem ultimately also harms man. In the classic example, the threat of DDT to the peregrine falcon served as a signal of harm to man.

Early environmental legislation was paced by early environmental litigation, much of it addressed at developmental ventures—primarily the building of roads and dams—that threatened existing scenic values and natural resources. In the protection of the natural heritage, the epochal *Scenic Hudson*[3] case in 1965 provided a basis for later environmental litigation efforts, by deciding that plaintiffs with demonstrable environmental interests had standing sue, and by permitting expert testimony on scenic values to be balanced against evidence of economic and developmental concerns.

---

[3] Scenic Hudson Preservation Conference v. Federal Power Commission, 354 F.2d 608 (2d Cir. 1965), *cert. denied,* 384 U.S. 941 (1966). The litigation prevented the destruction of Storm King Mountain, a scenic and historical treasure, by the construction of a proposed storage electrical power plant.

§ 1.02 Early Environmental Litigation and Legislation

[1] Roots in Litigation

Common law litigation in the 1950s and'60s sought to create new legal remedies for environmental violations. Unfortunately, quite early in the game, environmental litigators discovered that they had run out of plausible common law causes of action.[1] When that occurred, environmental litigators began to seek opportunities to base environmental rights on statutory provisions that had originally been conceived for other purposes. The Rivers and Harbors Act[2] is one such example. The law, initially aimed at protecting navigation by preventing the obstruction and silting of waterways and channels, was later discovered to have environmental protection against water pollution as its true aim.[3] The first great environmental law decision, the *Scenic Hudson* case,[4] provides another example. The Federal Power Act was initially intended to support the construction of reservoirs and dams for the generation of electric power. In *Scenic Hudson* the Act was found to provide the beginnings of environmental protection for rivers, based on the fact that the statutory provision governing reservoirs and waterworks designed for power production also required them to serve recreational purposes. "Recreational purposes" in the statutory language was imaginatively read in 1965 by Judge Paul R. Hays and his law clerk Harvey Goldschmidt to include the concept of environmental protection. *Scenic Hudson* was also the first case to give standing to intervenors based on their environmental, rather than economic, interest. The extent to which then existing legislation could be used for environmentally protective purposes was limited because in environmental law, as well as in other fields, courts have always been reluctant to imply individual rights of action from general statutory prohibitions. Even though individuals injured by the violation of the statute may be clearly within the group sought to be protected, such violations have rarely afforded such individuals causes of action for negligence or other torts.

[2] The Emergence of Legislation

Although the field of environmental law may have started with the efforts of inventive litigators involved in common law litigation, and while the common law still plays a role in environmental litigation,[5] environmental law clearly became a separate field of law with the emergence of federal legislation, reaching its full momentum in the late 1960s.[6]

The basis for protection against pollution, like most other interests in public health, was essentially statutory. There was a good deal of early state and

---

[1] Frank P. Grad and Laurie R. Rocket, *Environmental Litigation: Where the Action Is?*, 10 Nat. Resources J. 742 (1970).

[2] Rivers and Harbors Act (Refuse Act), 33 U.S.C. § 407 *et seq.*, 30 Stat. 1152 *et seq.*

[3] New Jersey v. New York, 283 U.S. 336, 342 (1931) ("a river is a treasure . . ." to Justice Holmes). *See also* United States v. Standard Oil Company, 384 U.S. 224 (1966).

[4] Scenic Hudson Preservation Conference v. Federal Power Comm'n, 354 F.2d 608 (2d Cir. 1965), *cert. denied*, 384 U.S. 941 (1966).

[5] *See* Frank P. Grad, Treatise on Environmental Law, Chapter 18.

[6] *See* Chapter 2, *infra*.

local water and smoke pollution legislation,[7] but permanent federal water pollution legislation was not passed until 1956, and the first permanent federal air pollution legislation did not become law until 1963. With the confluence of environmental interests, the pace quickened. 1965 saw the first federal solid waste law; 1970, the Clean Air Act; 1972, the Federal Water Pollution Control Act Amendments and the Noise Control Act; 1976, the Toxic Substance Control Act (TOSCA) and the Resource Conservation and Recovery Act (RCRA), and 1977, substantial revision of both the Clean Air Act and the Clean Water Act. In the meantime, on the other side of environmental concerns, the National Environmental Policy Act (NEPA), which was passed in 1969, would assure the consideration of environmental values before the federal government could proceed with any project with significant impact on the human environment.

In the 1970s, evidence of the overwhelming dangers of pollution by hazardous waste led to the enactment of RCRA, with emphasis by the federal government on the passage of Subtitle C to regulate hazardous waste. This was followed in 1980 by the enactment of the Comprehensive Environmental Response, Compensation and Liability Act (CERCLA), the Superfund legislation, to achieve the cleanup of abandoned "orphan" hazardous waste disposal sites. It is fair to say that the dangers of hazardous waste—dramatized by the Love Canal disclosures and litigation—served to emphasize the public health concerns of environmental law.

Other significant legislation includes the Federal Insecticide, Fungicide and Rodenticide Act (FIFRA), and the Safe Drinking Water Act, both with significant cross references to the control of food safety under the Federal Food, Drug and Cosmetic Act. The Occupational Safety and Health Act (OSHA) also has close connections with hazardous substance controls.

[3] Contributions to Other Fields of Law

Decisional law, soon followed by statutory law, thus contributed to the establishment of the field of environmental law. In the course of its development, environmental law made reciprocal contributions to other fields of law. The efforts of citizens and citizen groups to participate in the enforcement of pollution control laws and regulations led to the institutionalization of the private attorney general in citizen suit provisions in the 1970 and 1972 air and water pollution legislation. The general gain for public interest litigation was immeasurable because there are now scores of citizen suit provisions in protective legislation, environmental and otherwise. Environmental law has made major contributions, too, to the general area of administrative law. Involving, as it does, standard setting and rulemaking of a sophisticated technical nature by government agencies, as well as administrative determination of controversies and the issuance of administrative orders and their enforcement, environmental law involves every important aspect of administrative law. Because of the high level of activity in the field, and the complex nature of the area, decisions with environmental implications now make up the

[7] *See* Grad, Rathjens and Rosenthal, Environmental Control: Priorities, Policies and the Law, Chapter 2 at 47 (Columbia University Press 1971).

majority of administrative law decisions in the federal courts, and, in consequence, the leading coursebooks on administrative law could probably be adapted quite easily to teach a course in environmental law. Thus, recent developments relating to the applications and interpretation of the Administrative Procedures Act generally occurred in the course of environmental litigation.

Other contributions of environmental law to the public interest law area might also be noted. The allowance of legal fees to persons who succeed in citizen suits created an expansion of fee awards to successful public litigators generally, ending with the enactment of the Equal Access to Justice Act. Thus the field of environmental law not only benefitted from the general concern for public interest law in the 1960s, but made substantial reciprocal contributions to public interest law generally.

§ 1.03 The Ethics of Environmental Protection and Law

Perhaps the concern for ethical aspects of environmentalism and environmental law is evidence of the maturity of the field. Broad ethical issues were rarely articulated at the beginning. Early environmental concerns were very immediate, addressing crisis situations that needed to be resolved in order to prevent the destruction of resources that, once lost, could not be recovered. In the early 1960s particular threats called for rapid responses, usually by immediate recourse to litigation, without much opportunity to ponder broad philosophical issues. By now, however, the ethical dimensions of environmentalism have been examined, and although today, as before, major philosophical issues may not be articulated in environmental litigation or environmental legislation, their presence underlies a great deal of current thinking and activity.

We have noted that the two concerns, for nature and for man, may be considered indivisible. But some ethicists would not necessarily agree. Some ethicists have been troubled by the issue of anthropocentrism, the notion that man is central to creation, finding its beginning in Judeo-Christian religious sources. The phrase often relied on is from the book of *Genesis* where mankind is told to "Be fruitful and multiply, and fill the earth and subdue it, and have dominion over the fish of the sea and over the birds of the air and over every living thing."[1]

In the nineteenth century, in a different context, the issue of man's relation to nature had been a subject for discussion. George Perkins Marsh took the position that the earth was given to man not for consumption but only for usufruct and that usufruct did not include profligate waste.[2] The stewardship

[1] Genesis I-28. For different views on the religious basis of environmental ethics, see Lynn White, Jr., *The Historical Roots of Our Ecologic Crisis*, 155 Science 1203 (1967); Rene Dubos, *A Theology of the Earth*, reprinted in Western Man and Environmental Ethics 43 (Ian Barbour, ed., 1973). *See also* Arnold Joseph Toynbee, *The Religious Background of the Environmental Crisis,* 3 Int'l J. Envtl. Stud. 143 (1972), comparing classical, pre-Christian attitudes with Judeo-Christian attitudes toward the environment.

[2] George Perkins Marsh, *Man and Nature; or Physical Geography Modified as Human Action* 35 (1869).

notion was more recently developed by John Passmore in a work entitled *Man's Responsibility for Nature*, published in 1974.

It should be noted that the ethical discussion of anthropocentrism and the relationship of man to nature generally does little to differentiate conservationist from basic public health concerns. While the anthropocentrism issue may well play a role in ranking our values with relation to conservational issues, it can hardly play a role when dealing with harmful pollution and the protection against the impact of toxic effluents and emissions. In pollution control, the anthropocentric view that we must protect human beings, *i.e.*, the primacy of public health concerns, is clearly the guiding light. In dealing with the protection of human beings against insects and rodent pests, we rarely surrender our anthropocentric stance in order to protect the roaches and the rats. We note that although environmental protection against harmful emissions and effluents primarily protects man, in consequence, the rest of the environment is protected as well.

Ethical concerns over the environment have sometimes expanded into other areas of controversy. It is true that the modern environmental movement was in some respects a response to the burst of technological developments in the twentieth century, accelerated to a great extent by the impact of wartime technology. World War II, in particular, propelled science and technology in service of the war effort. Clearly the development of the atomic and hydrogen bombs were momentous developments for which we are still paying the price in the disposal of nuclear wastes, still left over from urgent wartime developments when there was little time to clean up the messes created in the process. The preparation for possible chemical warfare ultimately saw some peacetime impacts in the development of more effective pesticide substances. The development of herbicidal agents such as Agent Orange left chemical residues in the process of their development which we also are still cleaning up, largely through our Superfund law.

The rapid growth of the chemical industry, energized by war, has changed our mode of life, but in the process has also given us new kinds of waste materials never previously encountered. Wartime also led to the development of new medical and pharmaceutical substances, including penicillin and the sulfur drugs which put soldiers back into the front lines more rapidly, but which also changed the character of modern medicine. Many more examples could, of course, be cited. Suffice to say that this coursebook does not glorify technology nor does it demonize it. Modern technology and modern science are tools. It does not help environmental protection to sentimentalize the past. While primitive societies may have worshipped aspects of nature, many of them, with their slash and burn mode of cultivation, also did an enormous amount of damage. The cedars of Lebanon are no more. We have gained the historical insight that earlier civilizations were quite efficient in managing deforestation and the devastation of their resources. While today's chain saws and giant earth-moving machinery can do the work of devastation more quickly and effectively, earlier civilizations managed their own means of devastation well enough. That they did no worse was not for lack of trying.

This coursebook will try to steer a middle course on the subject of technology, avoiding the view held by some that technology is evil per se. It is true that the automobile has contributed greatly to the waste of resources and has encouraged the devastation of natural environments by unnecessary highway development. But it has also provided more mobility than was known by any other age, and geographic mobility has sometimes brought desirable social mobility as well. Disposable diapers have created significant problems of waste disposal, but they have also eased the burden of child care and helped to keep babies healthier. Technology is not the problem, but how it is used and how intelligently choices are made are the challenges we must face.

§ 1.04 Branches of Environmental Law

[1] Pollution Control

A major branch of the field of environmental law is that of pollution control. While excessive smoke and the fouling of water by human and animal excrement, notably from feed lots and pig farms, had long been a problem, it is the vast development of industry that has produced the pollution problems of recent years. Air and water are regarded as free goods, and not being paid for, they are used prodigally in industrial production and in the production of power, and they suffer the adverse consequences of pollution and abuse. Modern agriculture, with its reliance on chemical pesticides and fertilizers, and modern methods of animal husbandry also add their share to the pollution load.

The primary interest which must be protected through pollution control is public health. In this respect, recent legislation and recent legal developments reflect characteristic and traditional exercises of the police power. Pollution can produce chronic and deteriorative diseases. In addition to their immediate impact, some forms of pollution may damage generations to come through their teratogenic and mutagenic effects.

Aside from the protection of public health, and very important to civilized life, there is an interest in protecting the esthetic quality of the environment. Smog, in addition to its demonstrably adverse health effects, also imposes esthetic injury in that it does not permit the normal enjoyment of sunlight and fresh air. Odors, though they may not always be harmful to health, create annoyance and lessen the enjoyment of our surroundings. A substantial noise level, though below the range of injury to hearing, nonetheless interferes with repose and the orderly conduct of human activities.

The need for regulatory controls to protect health and esthetic values is sharpened by the need to protect a variety of property interests. Pollution may adversely affect plant life and may interfere with the development of crops and livestock. It may severely damage and shorten the useful life span of buildings, machinery, means of transportation, and the like. Pollution also affects interests in the maintenance of historical and artistic values. Indeed, when reckoning the costs of pollution, damage to property is often stressed to a greater extent--because it is more easily measurable in monetary terms—than the effects on health and well-being, which may be delayed and which may be difficult to attribute to particular pollutants and hard to measure in terms of money damages.

Whether agricultural or industrial in origin, the problem of pollution arises from the well-known physical and ecological principle of the persistence and indestructibility of matter. It is impossible to dispose of "matter" permanently. All we can do is to turn matter from one form into another—we cannot make it disappear. In the course of industrial manufacture, or of advanced agriculture, we produce pollutants which will be emitted into the atmosphere, onto the land, or into the waters.

Anything emitted into the air will eventually come down onto the land or the oceans. Anything placed on the land may either undergo chemical changes, deteriorate or degrade, or it may remain inert. In either event, it may have adverse effects on the land. Pollution on land is likely to get into underground water, or it may run off into rivers. Sooner or later it will end up in the ocean. Whether polluting substances land on the earth's land surface or in the oceans, they are very likely to be absorbed into the bodies of living organisms, which in turn may be ingested by other living organisms, until this food chain conducts them into the body of man. Many pollutants are relatively harmless, others range from causing minor irritations to outright toxicity. Many are carcinogenic, some are teratogenic, and a few are likely to be mutagenic. Some pollutants are nonpersistent, combining rapidly with other substances into harmless chemical compounds. So, for instance, carbon monoxide, which in its undiluted form is a nerve gas, in unconfined space will rapidly combine into harmless carbon dioxide and will no longer create any immediate danger. Other pollutants, such as lead, mercury, and cadmium, or beryllium and other heavy metals, are likely to degrade only over long periods of time, or for practical regulatory purposes, never. Such persistent pollutants which may accumulate as a result of new industrial or agricultural processes are among the most troublesome, and should become the subject of stringent regulations. On the other hand, the large quantity of degradable, nonpersistent pollutants may create serious short-term problems that may well make them an important subject of legal regulation as well.

Human and animal wastes are readily degradable, yet even over the short term they present dangers to health. When present in substantial quantities, they may result in major and adverse consequences to the water quality of rivers and lakes and may result in the death of rivers and lakes through "overfeeding"—eutrophication—which, though reversible, may have a major adverse impact on an entire region. Thus, the need for regulatory controls may be as great for nonpersistent pollutants as for persistent ones. To be sure, highly toxic and persistent pollutants may require immediate and stringent regulation, lest a source of such pollutants create major irreversible consequences for the future. Though water pollution is a serious problem that needs constant regulation and control, the threatened emission of any substantial quantity of radioactive substances with possibly mutagenic effect and with a half-life of thousands of years may require immediate and drastic action.

It is the task of the environmental lawyer to deal with the legal control of pollution, and to participate in the working of the administrative process, and if possible, to improve it legislatively or in the representation of clients. The pollution control branch of environmental law shares the complexity of other modern regulatory fields, and their need for legal as well as technical expertise.

[2] Conservation of Natural and Environmental Resources: Scenic, Esthetic Values and the Quality of Life

The traditional law of conservation emphasizes the need to conserve and protect natural resources, such as the renewable resources of the range and the forests, and such non-renewable resources as minerals, including coal, oil and gas. The environmentalists' primary emphasis has not been on the conservation of natural resources to protect the national economy, but rather on keeping the natural environment intact and maintaining it for its contributions to the quality of life in our time and for future generations. A sound policy of resource conservation will contribute to maintaining the natural environment in satisfactory shape; but whereas an environmentalist might wish to protect resources because of a general opposition to waste and resource depletion, the primary legislative emphasis is on protecting the natural system against destructive changes. Thus, the agenda of recent legislation includes protecting the public lands, wild and scenic rivers, the national forests, national parks, wildlife refuges, unique scenic features, and endangered species. The legal basis for protection is established in the laws governing the public lands and the rivers of the nation. The National Environmental Policy Act (NEPA) also provides a special tool in the protection of environmental values against developmental incursions. It should be noted that the examination of environmental impacts is required not only when government itself undertakes developmental projects, but also when government affords an opportunity for private development through a grant of a necessary license or permit.

While the control of pollution and the protection of conservational values provide a general division of the field, there are numerous situations in which the essential unity of the field becomes evident. The control of air pollution, for instance, includes in certain situations measures to prevent interference with visibility. Likewise, offshore oil drilling calls into question conservational and scenic environmental values as well as a serious concern over the polluting effect of a disastrous blowout during drilling operations.

[3] Land Use Control

An element that unites the branches of environmental law is the pervasive extent of land use control. Both the protection of environmental and scenic resources, and the control of pollution involve the question of the permissible uses of land—whether to keep it open or to develop it, and what kind of development, industrial or otherwise, is to be allowed by law.

Land use planning and control are the key to future growth and resource preservation. In the urban context, zoning and subdivision regulation are the mechanisms for controlling urban growth, assuring sound residential patterns, and protecting public health in the cities by separating incompatible uses, such as residential uses and heavy industry. Land use planning has also sought to regulate and manage suburban development and the growth of cities at their periphery, so as not to encroach on open land that should be preserved for agricultural uses, as well as for uses of an environmentally protective nature.

Land use regulations interrelate with pollution control, which defines the limits of the uses of industrial land in determining what pollution and how much of it may be produced by particular businesses and factories on such lands. In addition, the concerns of land use control in the environmental context include the protection of environmental and scenic resources, the protection of particular areas of special ecological value, and the maintenance of particular aspects of biodiversity. Such special areas may be places where particular fragile ecologies are at risk, such as wetlands, forests and range, or areas which form the habitat of certain endangered or hazarded species.

[4] Population Growth and Power Needs

An area closely related to environmental law, though not given a special place in this coursebook, is that of population control. An increasing population has a greater need for power and food and puts increasing demands on natural resources. Most environmental and resource problems will not be resolved until we control the growth of population—worldwide and particularly in the developing countries. Even in highly developed countries, such as the United States, population pressures and resulting power needs have a significant impact on our ability to conserve resources and protect the natural environment.

The projection of future population growth and its impact on power and resource needs, based on an analysis of past experience, is necessary, although its uncertainties must be acknowledged. Many high-growth projections made in the mid-seventies—such as for nuclear energy and the need for oil and gas resources—were not realized because market forces and energy conservation measures combined to undermine the futurists' calculations.

Working in the area of conservation of environmental resources involves the environmental lawyer in the task of preventing—or of advancing—certain developmental interests. Valuable environmental resources are protected by reviewing the work of government agencies that have a duty to protect them, and by litigation to prevent the development of areas with significant scenic, historic, open land or other resource value, or to modify such development into less harmful directions. It is in this aspect of environmental law that the lawyer often works in the shadow of the bulldozer, because, unless intervention is timely, there may be nothing left to protect.

§ 1.05 The Locus of Government Responsibility for Environmental Control

The federal government clearly has the dominant role in the control of the environment and in the enforcement of environmental law. To be sure, the states and local governments play a significant part in the regulatory process, but it is clear that the federal legislation relating to pollution control and the management of the public lands sets the pattern for the entire protective effort. The protection of state-owned lands, on the other hand, remains the obligation of the several states.

Federal involvement in environmental regulation was slow and reluctant in earlier years, but the dominant federal role emerged in the seventies, with the passage of the 1970 Clean Air Act and the 1972 Clean Water Act Amendments, and the coming into effect of NEPA in 1969.

The incremental growth of federal involvement mirrors the incremental growth of environmental problems. In the early part of this century, the terms environmental protection and environmental pollution had not been coined, and the minimal controls on the fouling of the air by smoke and of water by human waste and incipient industrial effluents was handled by state law, or, more often, by municipal ordinances, as an exercise of the police power. In addition, there was considerable reliance on private tort litigation, seeking to vindicate the right to be free from invasions of private land or disturbing nuisances which interfere with the enjoyment of one's land. The public environmental benefit was incidental, and was not the purpose of the litigation. With respect to the pollution of rivers, primary concern involved the private right to the use of the waters, rather than any public notion of environmental protection.

The earlier federal legislation in the fields of environmental pollution was largely based on the federal power to tax and spend—it relied on federal grants-in-aid to state and local efforts, generally requiring the states to adopt and enforce certain minimum standards, in return for federal funding of their administrative and management efforts. The setting of ambient standards—as well as the determination of effluent standards in the water pollution field was the responsibility of the states. In the air pollution field, too, the federal involvement was through grants-in-aid. The first assertion of direct federal regulatory power, the exercise of the constitutional commerce power, did not occur until the federal government undertook to regulate motor vehicles, instrumentalities clearly in interstate commerce, in 1965. It should be noted that early federal legislation in the air and water field clearly stated that air and water pollution control was a state or local matter, and that all the Congress was doing was to aid the states in carrying out their job.

The problem with the early regulatory scheme that relied on state regulation was that it simply did not work. It failed, particularly, in dealing with interstate pollution problems, which are common because the place of emission or discharge is often in a different state from the place of fallout. Early federal legislation established some interstate enforcement procedures that were so complex as to delay enforcement against interstate polluters for many years (twelve years, to be exact, in the instance of the only single case against an interstate polluter that was actually tried.) The grant-in-aid scheme did not work to reduce air and water pollution in the intrastate situation, either, and congressional impatience and frustration at the states' failure to manage the problem are clearly apparent in the legislative history of the federal legislation, as well as in the hard technology-forcing language of the laws themselves. Later federal expansion of power, in part through the grant-in-aid power, in part through exercise of the commerce power, reflect increasing perceptions of the need for such measures. Greater awareness of the problem of hazardous pollutants in air and water then led to more legislation in the hazardous waste area and in the area of control of toxic substances. Later, in 1980 it led to an effort to undo the consequences of the ignorant or profligate practices of the past in the disposal of hazardous waste, through Superfund cleanup efforts.

The accretion of federal power resulted in part from the realization that smaller units of government were unable to cope effectively with problems national in scope, and in part from the slow response of state governments to the emerging problems. While political trends change, and while the return of programs to the states may be part of a political agenda, it seems that the greater federal involvement was a response to real national needs. The question whether state and local governments can effectively deal with problems that are national in scope in terms of their impact, geographic and otherwise, is difficult. It is a question that applies to many other regulatory fields as well as the environment.

§ 1.06 Recurring Problems in Environmental Law and Enforcement

[1] Jurisdictional Constraints

The recurring problem of interjurisdictional pollution control is not only an interstate problem, but also a problem on an interlocal level, because enforcement personnel, inspectors and persons engaged in monitoring activities normally cannot operate outside their own limited jurisdiction--there is no hot pursuit rule for environmental pollution. The interlocal enforcement problem, like the interstate one, is made more difficult by the fact that the place where an industrial emission or discharge originates enjoys the employment and tax benefit of having the polluter at its location, and has less interest in enforcement than does the place of fallout.

[2] Disparity in Resources for Litigation

Another recurring problem is that of the disparity of means in many litigation situations. In the pollution control area, the laws commonly provide for technology-based standards—*i.e.*, standards based on best available technology or the like. The laws also generally provide for pre-enforcement review of regulations in the Court of Appeals. The review of standards involves highly sophisticated questions of science and technology. The regulated industries are generally very large and have almost unlimited means to litigate. They also employ large numbers of highly trained specialists as part of their regular staff. Government litigators may find it difficult to match the available economic means for litigation, and will sometimes find it difficult to match the massive array of expert witnesses industry is ready to field. The disparity of resources is even greater for environmental groups using the citizen suit provisions to initiate litigation, or seeking review of standards in the Court of Appeals. Groups such as the Sierra Club, Environmental Defense Fund, Natural Resources Defense Council and others have limited means, and must constantly choose where to intervene, determining which threatened injuries to the environment are of sufficient importance to warrant the expenditure of their limited means. The vast disproportion of means faced by environmental interest groups in actions against major chemical, steel, cement and paper companies, is hardly equalized by the provision of attorneys' and expert witness' fees under the citizen suit provisions or under the Equal Access to

Justice Act. This inequality is not restricted to pollution control litigation, but also extends to litigation in the environmental conservation area, where major mining companies, oil companies and developmental interests litigate NEPA or public land issues. The recurring pattern of litigation, pitting large corporate developmental interests against slimly funded government or public interest litigators is a noteworthy aspect of the environmental law field that will not emerge in the text of reported cases. To note the fact of disparity of means may be taken as a tendentious comment, because there are many other fields of law where this disparity recurs. It is fair to say that in our system, the disparity of means is not necessarily determinative of the outcome, but it may make a difference when technical issues are complex and expert witnesses are expensive. Furthermore, the playing field has not been leveled significantly by the continuing public support of environmental interests, including the perennial solicitation of contributions by environmental organizations.

[3] Problems of Sanctions and Remedies

The circumstances which give rise to the inequality of means in litigation are related to another problem of environmental law, namely the difficulty in assessing effective sanctions and remedies. Few small businesses are the targets of environmental enforcement. To be sure, relatively small-scale enforcement actions are conducted at the state and local level, seeking to compel compliance by the imposition of relatively small fines, or even by injunctive relief. But the significant enforcement actions are likely to involve major industrial complexes, owned and operated by large corporate enterprises.

The recurring problem in enforcement against large corporations has traditionally been the difficulty of pinpointing personal responsibility. Corporate responsibility of large companies for the payment of fines is not very meaningful, because the larger the company, the less the impact of the fine on individual shareholders. The purpose of the imposition of sanctions in environmental enforcement is not punitive—it is to bring about compliance. Fines and even criminal convictions for corporate activities were not effective to secure compliance, and the change in the Clean Air Act to establish a penalty based on the economic gain attributable to the company's non-compliance indicates the failure of earlier sanction approaches. Significant change did not occur until changes in the law and in prosecutorial practice in the mid 1980s, with concerted efforts to hold corporate officers and other corporate employees civilly and criminally responsible for environmental violations in which they had a part. This new approach of prosecuting environmental violations as white collar crimes has made a significant change in the field, raising many questions of prosecutorial discretion as well as ethical issues raised by the reliance on criminal sanctions in an originally administrative field of law.

[4] Technical and Scientific Problems in Environmental Law

Another recurring issue in environmental law is scientific and technological uncertainty. Whether a particular ambient level of air or water pollution is "safe," whether a particular standard provides "an ample margin of safety," whether a particular standard is "achievable" by a certain date, and many other mixed questions of law and fact of this nature make environmental law a field which is both challenging and frustrating. Lawyers like to think that scientists have clear and definite answers to certain factual questions—is this level of pollution harmful, and precisely what damage will it produce? The answer is likely to reflect a judgment, rather than a statement of fact. It is not surprising that judges faced with scientific questions invariably confess a sense of unease, and do not insist upon a showing that the agency answer is right, but that it was arrived at in a procedurally sound manner and that the agency did not exclude data or factors that should have been taken into consideration. Thus, it is evident that many environmental questions are difficult to answer. Is Storm King Mountain such a beautiful and scenic resource that other interests—such as an interest in electric power—ought to yield to the interest in preserving it? Is clear cutting a defensible and available alternative for forest management? Many similar questions concerning environmental conservation or pollution control can be asked, and are asked quite often. In environmental litigation, questions which appear simple on the surface may have major, even awesome policy implications.

The need to resolve such mixed questions of law and fact is one of the earmarks of environmental law. It is also one of the reasons why government agencies seem to lag in the promulgation of standards. The impatience with agencies may be justified, but some recurring delays in regulation and adjudication understandably result from the complexity of the field. Particularly in certain areas, such as hazardous wastes and toxic substances, there are sometimes not yet clear answers to the many good questions lawyers and administrators want to ask the scientists.

§ 1.07 Some Comments on Environmental Law as Reflected in This Coursebook

The entire field of environmental law has clear economic implications, and many of these are referred to in the pages that follow. The field of pollution control may be discussed as a problem of externalities, and the field of environmental conservation may be treated as exemplifying a variety of opportunity costs. Indeed, there are works that treat the entire field of environmental law as a subset of economic studies. While no consideration of environmental protection or environmental law can ignore economic considerations, they are not the main emphasis of this work. Nevertheless, the question of how clean and how beautiful an environment we want is invariably followed by the question of how clean and how beautiful an environment we can afford. The answers to these questions may not reflect an economic judgment, but a judgment of values. Clearly there are values in our society that ought to have precedence over environmental values--such as civil liberties, the prevention of nuclear war, the prevention of hunger, the provision of shelter, and a variety of other needed social welfare benefits. But the question in recent years has rarely been how to balance values, but rather how to cut costs. Economics can help cut the cost of environmental protection and it can compare the cost of different kinds of protection. The coursebook touches on the questions of whether and how it can do more.

Except for the vindication of the private right to a clean environment in private tort litigation, the field of environmental law is entirely statutory, reflecting its recent and modern origins. This characteristic of environmental law has several consequences. It is imperative that persons with an interest in the field acquire sound familiarity with the basic legislation. It also follows that decisions in the field cannot be read and understood without reference to the legislation which they interpret or enforce, and a knowledge of how this legislation came to be adopted.

Chapter 2

AIR POLLUTION

§ 2.01 Sources of Air Pollution and its Health and Economic Impact

[1] In General

Council on Environmental Quality
First Annual Report 61-70
(transmitted to Congress August 1970)

We tend to view air pollution as a recently discovered phenomenon. But since the dawn of the Industrial Revolution, people in many communities have endured levels of smoke pollution that would be held intolerable today. In the last half of the nineteenth century, a surprising number of aroused citizen groups protested the smoke-laden air of London. But their protests were lost in the overwhelming clamor for industrial development at any price.

Progress in the United States was no more heartening. Chicago and Cincinnati passed smoke control laws in 1881. By 1912, 23 of the 28 American cities with populations over 200,000 had passed similar laws. But still there was little dent made in air pollution.

In the 1930s, 1940s, and 1950s smoke pollution reached its zenith in the United States, especially in Eastern and Midwestern industrial cities. The public outcry against these conditions resulted in the enactment of improved smoke pollution legislation, its partial enforcement, and a visible improvement in the air of some industrial cities. These local control efforts focused primarily on cutting down smoke from fossil fuels, particularly coal. The fortunate advent of diesel engines in place of steam locomotives and the increased use of gas as a fuel for space heating also helped cut back air pollution in that era.

The Donora disaster in Pennsylvania in 1948 pricked the conscience of the nation, but the experience of Los Angeles beginning in that same decade was a more certain sign of the complex air pollution problem which now confronts cities throughout the world. When the citizens of Los Angeles began to complain of smog, few people suspected that air pollution was a great deal more than just smoke. Los Angeles used virtually none of the fuels primarily responsible for the smoke problems of cities elsewhere, yet smog appeared and worsened. Dr. Arie J. Haagen-Smit, of the California Institute of Technology, finally pinpointed the principal sources of photochemical smog in Los Angeles—hydrocarbons and nitrogen oxides from automobile exhausts. Smog was at first thought to be a phenomenon amplified by local weather conditions and limited to Los Angeles. Today, however, most major cities are afflicted to some degree by photochemical smog as well as by other forms of air pollution.

Air pollution is for the most part a phenomenon of urban living that occurs when the capacity of the air to dilute the pollutants is overburdened. Population and industrial growth and a high degree of dependence on the motor vehicle cause new gaseous and particulate emissions to complement, interact with, and further complicate the traditional ones.

When the first federal air pollution control legislation was passed in 1955, there were no viable ongoing state programs at all. There was little interest in the scientific community, and the public, by and large, equated air pollution with coal smoke and considered smog a problem unique to Los Angeles. It is no wonder that air pollution is regarded as a recently discovered phenomenon.

POLLUTANTS AND THEIR SOURCES

Five main classes of pollutants are pumped into the air over the United States, totaling more than 200 million tons per year. . . .

Transportation—particularly the automobile—is the greatest source of air pollution. It accounts for 42% of all pollutants by weight. It produces major portions not only of carbon monoxide but of hydrocarbons and nitrogen oxides . . . .

Almost two-thirds of the carbon monoxide emitted comes from internal combustion engines, and the overwhelming bulk of that comes from gasoline-powered motor vehicles.

WHAT AIR POLLUTION DOES

Air pollution adversely affects man and his environment in many ways. It soils his home and interferes with the growth of plants and shrubs. It diminishes the value of his agricultural products. It obscures his view and adds unpleasant smells to his environment. Most important, it endangers his health.

The extent of air pollution depends heavily on how weather disposes of the pollutants. The ability of the atmosphere to dilute and disperse them is limited to two factors—wind speed and the depth in the atmosphere to which air near the surface can be mixed. Although considerable variation occurs from day to day in the extent to which these factors disperse air pollution, the same patterns tend to repeat themselves over months or years. On some few days in a year, strong winds and highly unstable atmospheric conditions may disperse even the heaviest blanket of pollution. On many other days, weak winds and highly stable conditions let small quantities of pollutants accumulate and build up to serious proportions. Between these extremes, variations in weather conditions create varying levels of pollution over a given area.

Many cities lie in natural basins at the confluence of rivers, around bays, or in flat areas backed against mountains. Such basins are natural gathering places for low-lying masses of warm air, which trap pollutants in the familiar phenomenon known as an "inversion." However, even communities more favorably located increasingly find that atmospheric conditions limit the amount of air available as a dumping place for pollutants.

. . . to Human Health

The most important effect of air pollution is its threat to human health. Acute episodes of pollution in London, New York, and other cities have been marked by dramatic increases in death and illness rates, especially among the elderly and those with preexisting respiratory or cardiac conditions.

The incident most familiar to Americans occurred in 1948 in Donora, an industrial town in the mountains of western Pennsylvania. Almost half of the town's 14,000 inhabitants fell ill; 20 died. The worst air pollution disaster of modern times struck in London in 1952 when its famous "killer smog" increased the number of deaths in London to 1,600 more than would have normally occurred. Both of those episodes occurred when, under conditions lasting for several days, unusual weather prevented the dispersal of pollutants.

Such major disasters are cause for concern. However, of much greater significance for the American population are the subtle, long-range effects on human health of exposure to low-level, long-lasting pollution.

The causes of chronic diseases which constitute the major public health problems of our time are difficult to determine. Assessing the contribution of particular pollutants to these conditions is complicated by the seemingly infinite variety of pollutants to which persons, particularly those in urban areas, are exposed from the day of their birth. And it is difficult to separate pollution from the other biological and physical stresses to which people are subjected.

Nonetheless, it is well established that air pollution contributes to the incidence of such chronic diseases as emphysema, bronchitis, and other respiratory ailments. Polluted air is also linked to higher mortality rates from other causes, including cancer and arteriosclerotic heart disease. Smokers living in polluted cities have a much higher rate of lung cancer than smokers in rural areas.

The incidence of chronic diseases has soared sharply during this century, while the infectious diseases which were the primary public health concern in the past have been brought under control. Heart and blood vessel diseases caused more than half the deaths in the United States in 1962. Lung cancer, once a rarity, now kills more persons than all other cancer types combined. Emphysema has doubled every five years since World War II. Air pollution has been linked to asthma, acute respiratory infections, allergies, and other ailments in children. Such childhood diseases may well underlie chronic ills developed in later life.

Knowledge of the health effects of specific contaminants present in the air is far from complete. However, the more overt health effects of several major classes of pollutants are beginning to be defined. Those pollutants are found almost everywhere in the United States. . . .

The findings relating to particulate matter, as a class of pollutants, amply justify measures to reduce their level in the air. Included in this class of pollutants are a number of substances which are potential health hazards at much lower concentrations and which will require even more stringent controls.

Beryllium, for example, which may be emitted from industrial sources and from rocket fuel, can cause lesions in the lung, producing serious respiratory damage and even death. Since the sources of this pollutant are limited, however, it may be a problem only in specific localities.

Asbestos, long recognized as an occupational hazard, is increasingly present in the ambient air because of its use in construction materials, brake linings, and other products. Long exposure in industry produces the lung-scarring disease, asbestosis. On the other hand, mesothelioma, a type of lung cancer associated almost exclusively with asbestos exposure, does not appear to be associated only with heavy or continued exposure.

Many other particulate pollutants are a growing public health worry even though they may not constitute such an immediate and direct threat. Current studies suggest that lead levels now found in the blood and urine of urban populations—although well below those associated with classic lead poisoning—may interfere with the ability of the human body to produce blood. As air pollution becomes more widespread, increased numbers of people are being exposed to airborne lead, chiefly from automotive emissions, at levels formerly found only in congested areas.

. . . to Vegetation and Materials

Air pollution inflicts widespread and costly damage on plant life and buildings and materials. Some experiences of the past warned of the effects of air pollution on plant life. Sulfur dioxide fumes from a large copper smelting plant set up after the Civil War in Copper Basin, Tenn., damaged 30,000 acres of timberland. Much of this originally forested mountain land is still barren. Today, the damage to plant life is less dramatic than in the days of unrestricted smelter operations. But the slower, chronic injury inflicted on agricultural, forest, and ornamental vegetation by increasing quantities and varieties of air pollutants has now spread to all parts of the country.

Smog in the Los Angeles basin contributes to the slow decline of citrus groves south of the city and damages trees in the San Bernardino National Forest 50 miles away. Fluoride and sulfur oxides, released into the air by phosphate fertilizer processing in Florida, have blighted large numbers of pines and citrus orchards. Livestock grazing on fluoride-tainted vegetation develop a crippling condition known as fluorosis. In New Jersey, pollution injury to vegetation has been observed in every county and damage reported to at least 36 commercial crops.

At sulfur oxide levels routinely observed in some of our cities, many plants suffer a chronic injury described as "early aging." Nitrogen dioxide produces similar injury symptoms and seems to restrict the growth of plants even when symptoms of injury are not visible. Ozone, a major photochemical oxidant, is a significant threat to leafy vegetables, field and forage crops, shrubs, and fruit and forest trees—particularly conifers. The damage from ozone in minute quantities can be great. Extended ozone exposure to 0.05 parts per million can reduce a radish yield 50 percent. Tobacco is sensitive to ozone at a level of 0.03 parts per million.

Air pollutants also damage a wide variety of materials. Sulfur oxides will destroy even the most durable products. Steel corrodes two to four times faster in urban industrial areas than it does in rural areas where much less sulfur-bearing coal and oil are burned. When particulate matter is also present in the air, the corrosion rates multiply. One-third of the replacement cost of steel rails in England is estimated to be caused by sulfur pollution. The rise of sulfur oxides levels in the air is accelerating the erosion of statuary and buildings throughout the world, and in some cities, works of art made of stone, bronze, and steel must be moved indoors to preserve them from deterioration. Particulate matter in the air not only speeds the corrosive action of other pollutants but by itself is responsible for costly damage and soiling. Clothes and cars must be washed, houses painted, and buildings cleaned more often because of the particulates in the air. Ozone damages textiles, discolors dyes, and greatly accelerates the cracking of rubber.

. . . to Visibility

Air pollution dims visibility, obscures city skylines and scenic vistas, interferes with the safe operation of aircraft and automobiles, and disrupts transportation schedules. In one recent year, low visibility from smoke, haze, and dust was the suspected cause of 15 to 20 plane crashes. In Los Angeles, visibility in the smog frequently lowers to less than three miles. . . . The Federal Aviation Administration's visibility safety factor for airplane operation without instruments is 5 miles. Nitrogen dioxide, which reaches peak levels during morning rush-hour traffic, is responsible for the whiskey-brown haze that stains the sky over many cities. Particulates, however, are the major villain in reducing visibility. Particles (ash, carbon, dust, and liquid particles) discharged directly to the air scatter and absorb light, reducing the contrast between objects and their backgrounds. Particles are also formed in the atmosphere by photochemical reactions and by the conversion of sulfur dioxide to sulfuric acid mist. Wherever sulfur pollution is significant—which is wherever large amounts of coal and oil are burned—visibility diminishes as relative humidity rises.

. . . to Climate

Air pollution alters climate and may produce global changes in temperature.

. . . in Damages

The total costs of air pollution in the United States cannot be precisely calculated, but they amount to many billions of dollars a year. Economic studies are beginning to identify some of the more obvious costs. . . .

NOTES AND QUESTIONS

The preceding account of air pollution and its impacts was prepared in 1970 as part of the first report of the Council on Environmental Quality. It provides some of the background that led to the enactment of the 1970 Clean Air Act. How much of this more than 25-year-old account is still accurate today, and how much of it has undergone significant changes? How much of a changed account would reflect new insights of a scientific nature, and how much of it would document the success of environmental legislation and enforcement efforts? This may be a useful question to keep in mind in later discussions. Note also that the five main categories of pollutants mentioned in 1970 have since increased to six major categories.

[2] NAAQS (National Ambient Air Quality Standard) Pollutants[1]

Over the past decade, air quality levels in the United States have shown continued improvement. The six pollutants for which EPA sets an NAAQS are carbon monoxide, lead, nitrogen dioxide, ozone, particulates and sulfur dioxide. Tracking by monitoring stations documents progress in reducing air levels for each pollutant.

[a] Carbon Monoxide

Carbon monoxide (CO) is a colorless, odorless, and poisonous gas, produced by the incomplete burning of carbon in fuels. Elevated carbon monoxide levels can enter the human bloodstream and reduce normal delivery of oxygen to organs and tissues. In areas where levels exceed the NAAQS, the health threat is most serious for persons who suffer from cardiovascular disease, particularly those with angina or peripheral vascular disease, although healthy individuals also can be affected. Such exposure is associated with impairment of visual perception, manual dexterity, learning ability and performance of complex tasks.

Two-thirds of the nationwide emissions of carbon monoxide are from transportation sources, with the largest contribution coming from highway motor vehicles (such as light-duty gas vehicles and motorcycles, light-duty and heavy-duty gas trucks, and diesels). Long-term trends indicate that emissions for all types of highway vehicles nearly tripled from 1940 through 1970. From 1970 to 1980, emissions from highway vehicles increased only 11 percent, largely because of the national implementation of the Federal Motor Vehicle Control Program, regulating emissions from new vehicles. This program has resulted in widespread use of catalytic converters on automobiles to reduce carbon monoxide, nitrogen oxides, and volatile organic compound emissions. Another benefit has been the use of unleaded gasoline for vehicles with these converters. Since 1980, carbon monoxide emissions have decreased 37% as a result of pollution control and retirement of older vehicles without converters.

Ambient atmospheric concentrations of carbon monoxide have recorded a general long-term improvement. The ten year period, 1983-1992, showed a 34% improvement, which comports with the estimated 30% reduction in highway vehicle emissions. These reductions, largely attributable to vehicle emission controls, occurred despite a 37% increase in vehicle miles of travel in the United States during the reporting period. The environmental and

[1] Council on Environmental Quality, Environmental Quality Annual Report (1993).

transportation communities are concerned that rising vehicle miles of travel could overtake the emission improvements realized over the last decade.

Despite these improvements EPA designated 42 areas as nonattainment for carbon monoxide in November, 1993. These areas failed to meet the carbon monoxide NAAQS of 9 parts per million (ppm) in an 8-hour period. Based upon the magnitude of carbon monoxide concentrations, 41 areas were classified as moderate, with Los Angeles alone classified as serious.

Air Quality Success Stories

Prior to 1993, EPA had designated Syracuse, New York, as "moderate nonattainment" for carbon monoxide; Knoxville, Tennessee, as "marginal nonattainment" for ozone; and Greensboro, North Carolina, as "moderate nonattainment" for ozone. EPA in 1993 was able to redesignate these areas as "attainment."

To do so, the EPA Administrator had to determine that the areas had attained the national ambient air quality standard, and that the improvement in air quality was the result of permanent and enforceable reductions in emissions. In addition, other NAAQS criteria had to be met. Each area was required to have an approved "applicable implementation plan," describing the measures used to reduce emissions and achieve attainment, and a maintenance plan showing that the ambient air standard would be maintained for at least ten years after redesignation. These plans are designed for a particular area, but draw on national guidance as to applicable controls for certain types of pollution sources.

Syracuse was able to achieve "attainment" status under the carbon monoxide standard through a combination of measures. These include a traffic management plan for major events in the downtown area (such as concerts and athletic events), and institution of a ride-share program. Knoxville applied reasonably available control technology (RACT) to major emission sources in its efforts to attain the ozone standard. Greensboro, in addition to applying RACT for major sources, adopted an inspection/maintenance (IM) program in two counties in the nonattainment area.

In September, 1993, Syracuse became the first area in the nation to be redesignated by EPA as "attainment."

[b] Lead

The major sources of atmospheric lead emissions are lead gasoline additives, nonferrous smelters, and battery plants. Transportation contributes more emissions than any other sector of the U.S. economy. Exposure to lead can occur through multiple pathways, including inhalation of air and ingestion of lead in food, water, soil or dust. Lead accumulates in the body in blood, bone and soft tissue. Because it is not readily excreted, lead also affects the kidneys, nervous system and blood-forming organs. Exposure in adults to lead levels exceeding the NAAQS can cause seizures, mental retardation and behavioral disorders. Fetuses, infants and children are most susceptible to lead and the associated central nervous system damage; however, adults may be affected as well. Studies show that lead may be a factor in high blood pressure and subsequent heart disease in middle-aged white males.

Lead emissions from highway sources decreased sharply from 1970 to 1986 as a result of the Federal Motor Vehicle Control Program. Gasoline consumption increased 16% between 1970 and 1975, but because of the reduced lead content of gasoline, lead emissions from highway vehicles actually decreased 24%. Since 1984, lead emissions from transportation sources have decreased 96%, brought about by increased use of unleaded gasoline in catalytic converter-equipped cars, which made up 99% of the gasoline market in 1993. In 1984, the unleaded share of the gasoline market was about 60%. In addition to the use of unleaded gasoline, the decrease can be attributed to the reduced lead content in leaded gasoline, which went from an average of 1.0 grams per gallon to 0.1 grams per gallon in January, 1986.

Programs are also in place to control lead emissions from stationary sources. Lead emissions from fuel combustion by industry and lead smelters, which contribute to total lead emissions, have decreased over the past two decades. The reductions reflect utility and industrial lead-emission controls and some plant closures.

Ambient lead concentrations in urban areas, where most lead-monitoring stations are located, have decreased 89% since 1984. This improvement has been evenly distributed over the entire network of 204 monitoring sites. Over the past decade, ambient lead concentrations at 66 monitoring sites near such industrial sources of lead as smelters and battery plants improved 63%. Most areas in the United States meet national air quality standards for lead. Those that do not are industrial areas impacted by point sources of lead. In 1993, these areas were Cleveland, Ohio; Indianapolis, Indiana; Memphis, Tennessee, and nearby parts of Alabama and Mississippi; Omaha, Nebraska, and parts of Iowa; Philadelphia, Pennsylvania, and parts of New Jersey; and St. Louis, Missouri, and parts of Illinois.

[c] Nitrogen Dioxide

Nitrogen dioxide is a yellowish brown, highly reactive gas present in the urban atmosphere. Formed by the oxidation of nitrous oxide, it is emitted when fuels burn at high temperatures. Nitrogen dioxide plays a major role, together with volatile organic compounds, in the atmospheric reactions that produce harmful, ground level ozone. It is also a precursor to acidic deposition and contributes to environmental nitrogen loading that can affect both aquatic and terrestrial ecosystems.

Nitrogen dioxide can irritate the lungs, cause bronchitis and pneumonia, and lower resistance to respiratory infections such as influenza. Continued or frequent exposure to concentrations exceeding the NAAQS can cause pulmonary edema.

The two main sources of nitrogen dioxide are transportation and stationary fuel combustion from electric utilities and industrial boilers. Emissions from all sources have increased since the turn of the century. Since 1984, reductions have occurred in emissions from many sources, although total 1993 emissions were one percent higher than 1984 figures. Fuel combustion emissions have remained relatively constant during the last five years. Most decreases in mobile source emissions occurred in urban areas. The Federal Motor Vehicle Control Program and the New Source Performance Standards recently set by EPA have helped reduce the growth of nitrogen dioxide emissions from electric utilities and highway sources.

Ambient concentrations of nitrogen dioxide increased significantly during the first two-thirds of the century as a result of increased fuel consumption. Since 1984, however, concentrations have declined by 12%. Los Angeles, the only urban area in the past ten years with recorded violations of the annual average nitrogen dioxide standard, in 1992, for the first time, had air quality levels that met this standard, and the air quality continued to improve in 1993.

[d] Ozone

Tropospheric (ground-level) ozone is a major component of smog. While ozone in the upper atmosphere (stratosphere) benefits life by shielding the earth from ultraviolet radiation from the sun, concentrations of ozone at ground level in excess of the NAAQS (National Ambient Air Quality Standards) are a major health and environmental concern. Ozone is not emitted directly into the atmosphere but is formed through complex chemical reactions between precursor emissions of volatile organic compounds and nitrogen oxides in the presence of sunlight. These reactions are stimulated by light intensity and temperature, so that peak ozone levels typically occur during the warmer times of the year, especially under dry, stagnant conditions.

The reactivity of ozone causes health problems because it damages lung tissue, reduces lung function, and sensitizes the lungs to other irritants. Ambient levels of ozone affect not only persons with impaired respiratory systems, but healthy adults and children as well. Several hours of exposure to ozone in doses that exceed the NAAQS can reduce lung function in normal, healthy people during exercise. This decrease in lung function generally is accompanied by symptoms that may include chest pain, sneezing, and pulmonary congestion. Ozone also can damage forests and crops.

Transportation and industrial sources emit volatile organic compounds (VOCs) and nitrogen dioxide, which are the precursor chemicals of ozone. Emissions of VOCs from fuel combustion have declined steadily since 1900, with the exception of a recent peak caused by residential wood combustion. Emissions from industrial processes increased from 1900 to 1970, but emission control devices and process changes have helped limit these increases. Decreases in emissions after 1970 are also attributed to the substitution of water-based emulsified asphalt for asphalt liquefied with petroleum distillates.

Emissions from transportation sources increased from 1900 to 1970, first from railroads, and later from highway vehicles. By 1970, railroads were contributing only one percent of total emissions, while highway emissions had risen to 41%. Since then highway emissions from diesel and gasoline-powered vehicles have declined by 50% from the 1970 level, as a result of the Federal Motor Vehicle Control Program and national limits on fuel volatility. Overall total emissions of VOCs are estimated to have declined by 9% since 1984.

Ambient concentrations of ozone improved nationally by 12% from 1983 to 1992. The 1993 composite average is higher than the 1992 level, but it is noteworthy that 1992 ozone levels were the lowest of the past ten years. Since 1984, the expected number of exceedances of the ozone NAAQS also has decreased by 60%.

[e] Particulates

Air pollutants called particulates include dust, dirt, soot, smoke and liquid droplets. Particulates are emitted directly into the air by sources such as factories, power plants, cars, construction activity, fires, and natural wind-blown dust. Particles also form in the atmosphere from the condensation or transformation of emitted gases such as sulfur dioxide and volatile organic compounds.

The major effects on human health from concentrations of particulates that exceed the NAAQS often are associated with sulfur dioxide. They include breathing and respiratory symptoms, aggravation of existing respiratory and cardiovascular disease, alterations in the body's defense systems against foreign materials, damage to lung tissues, carcinogenesis, and premature mortality. Individuals with chronic obstructive pulmonary or cardiovascular disease, influenza, or asthma, as well as children and the elderly, are most likely to be sensitive to the effects of particulates. Particulate matter also soils and damages building materials and impairs visibility in many parts of the country.

In 1987, EPA promulgated annual and 24-hour standards for particulate matter, using a new indicator, PM-10, which includes only those particles with aerodynamic diameter smaller than 10 micrometers. These smaller particles are more likely to be responsible for adverse health effects because of their ability to reach the lower thoracic region of the respiratory tract. The new standards specify an expected annual arithmetic mean not to exceed 50 micrograms per cubic meter. They also specify that expected 24-hour concentrations greater than 150 micrograms per cubic meter per year may not exceed one occurrence per year.

PM-10 particulates are emitted by point and nonpoint sources:

Point Sources. These include fuel combustion of electric utilities and industry; industrial processes involving chemicals, metals and petroleum; and transportation.

Nonpoint Sources. Among these are fugitive dust from agriculture, construction, mining, quarrying, paved and unpaved roads, and wind erosion.

Over the 9-year period, 1985-1993, total PM-10 emissions from point sources decreased almost 3%. PM-10 emissions by highway vehicles and off-highway vehicles decreased by 7% during that period, while emissions from a category entitled Fuel Combustion decreased 14%. Emissions in this category are produced predominantly by residential wood combustion—the in-home use of fireplaces and wood stoves. Several innovative approaches to controlling residential wood combustion are responsible for the large decrease in this emission category.

Fugitive dust contributes six to eight times more PM-10 particulates than point sources; it is consistently emitted by construction activity and unpaved roads. Among road types, emissions from unpaved roads have remained fairly steady, while emissions from paved roads are estimated to have increased 30% since 1985, most likely due to increased vehicular traffic. Emissions from construction sites have decreased an estimated 13% since 1985. Mining and quarrying, sources estimated to be a relatively small contributor to total fugitive particulate matter emissions at the national level, can be major factors in local areas.

A minor contributor to the national total, agricultural tilling is a major source of particulates in specific regions of the country, such as the Great Lakes, Upper Midwest, and Pacific Northwest. Over the 9-year period, 1985-1993, fugitive dust emissions showed no significant change in these areas. PM-10 emissions caused by wind erosion are very sensitive to regional soil conditions and year-to-year changes in total precipitation. Accordingly, estimated emissions from wind erosion were extremely high for the drought year of 1988.

Measured ambient air PM-10 concentrations decreased by 20% between 1988 and 1993. Declines in particulate levels are attributable to the installation of pollution control devices in electric utilities and to reduced activity in some industrial sectors, such as iron and steel.

Note that in 1998, EPA strengthened the controls on particulate emission by focusing its regulations on smaller particulates than PM-10.

[f] Sulfur Dioxide

Ambient sulfur dioxide results largely from stationary source coal and oil combustion, steel mills, refineries, pulp and paper mills, and from nonferrous smelters. The largest and most consistent source of these emissions has been coal-burning electric power plants.

Human exposure to concentrations of sulfur dioxide exceeding the NAAQS can affect breathing and aggravate existing respiratory and cardiovascular disease. Sensitive populations include asthmatics, individuals with bronchitis or emphysema, children and the elderly. Sulfur dioxide is a primary contributor to acidic deposition (acid rain), causing acidification of lakes and streams and damaging trees, crops, historic structures, and statues. In addition, sulfur compounds in the air contribute to visibility degradation in large parts of the country, including national parks. The conversion of sulfur dioxide to sulfate aerosols in the atmosphere could impact global climate change.

Historic emissions of sulfur dioxide from fuel combustion and industrial processes increased steadily from 1900 until 1925 and then decreased during the 1930s primarily because of the Great Depression, only to increase sharply from 1940 to 1970. During the 1970s and early 1980s, emissions decreased by 25% as a result of several factors:

Coal cleaning and lower sulfur coal blending by electric utilities;

Reduction in coal burning by industrial, commercial and residential consumers;

Increased use of emission control devices by industry, especially sulfuric acid manufacturing plants; and

Byproduct recovery of sulfuric acid at nonferrous smelters.

Emissions have declined slightly in recent years. Nationally, the long-term trend in ambient sulfur dioxide concentration shows a 26% reduction over the 10-year period, 1984-1993, although the annual rate of decline has slowed over the last few years. Currently there are 47 areas in the United States that do not meet national air quality standards for sulfur dioxide.

[3] Air Quality Population Estimates

Although ambient air quality improvements in the 1984-1993 period are encouraging, population estimates suggest that 59 million Americans live in counties where pollution levels failed to meet one or more air quality standards in 1993. Such estimates provide a relative measure of the extent of the problem for each pollutant. As an indicator, however, they have limitations. For example, an individual living in a county that violates an air quality standard may not actually be exposed to unhealthy air.

[a] Smog

Urban, ground-level ozone (smog) continued to be the most pervasive air quality problem in 1993, with an estimated 44.6 million people living in counties that did not meet the ozone standard. This figure, however, was the lowest for the 10-year period, and represents a substantial decrease compared to the 112 million people thought to live in areas that did not meet ozone NAAQS in 1988, when hotter, drier meteorological conditions prevailed and contributed to more ozone formation. The decrease is also partly because of new emission control programs.

[b] Pollution Standards Index (PSI)

EPA developed the Pollution Standards Index (PSI) as an air quality indicator for describing urban air trends. The PSI has found widespread use in the air pollution field for reporting daily air quality to the general public. The index integrates information from many pollutants across an entire monitoring network into a single number that represents the worst daily air quality experienced in an urban area. It is computed for carbon monoxide, nitrogen dioxide, ozone, particulates (PM-10), and sulfur dioxide. The index is based on short-term National Ambient Air Quality Standards, Federal Episode Criteria, and Significant Harm Levels.

Index Range Health Effects Categories:

0 to 50 Good

51 to 100 Moderate

101 to 199 Unhealthful

200 to 299 Very Unhealthful

300 and Above Hazardous

The impact of hot dry summers in 1983 and 1988 in the eastern United States can be measured by examining total PSI data along with PSI data for selected metropolitan areas. Pittsburgh is the only city where a significant number of PSI days greater than 100 is caused by pollutants other than carbon monoxide or ozone; the Pittsburgh pollutants are sulfur dioxide and PM-10 particulates.

[c] Sulfur Dioxide/Nitrogen Dioxide

The year 1992 marked the first time since EPA began making population estimates that the agency recorded no monitoring violations of either sulfur dioxide or nitrogen dioxide NAAQS.

[d] Health Effects

The effects of air pollution on health are not necessarily limited to respiratory diseases, such as chronic bronchitis, pulmonary emphysema, bronchial asthma, and the like. A causal connection has been established between certain particulate emissions and diseases, including carcinomas, of other than respiratory organs. Though particulates may be ingested into the system through the respiratory apparatus, the effects may appear in other parts of the body. Thus, for instance, cadmium has been identified as a causative agent in the development of hypertension, and contamination by zinc and cadmium show a marked correlation with heart disease. A number of chemical pollutants of the air have been identified as inducing potential genetic damages and operating as mutagens. For brief and early data on health impacts of air pollution, see Sub-Report: Air Quality Criteria, 90th Cong. (2d Sess. 1968). For general health and other background data, consult World Health Organization, Air Pollution (1961), and Goddard, *Health Protection*, in Jones, ed., The Health of Americans (American Assembly 1970), p. 121. Other useful information may also be found in Cassell, *The Health Effects of Air Pollution and the Implications for Control*, 33 Law and Contemp. Probs. 197 (1968), and Ludwig, *Air Pollution Control Technology: Research and Development on New and Improved Systems*, 33 Law and Contemp. Probs. 217 (1968).

NOTES AND QUESTIONS

(1) There is a lively question, of some consequence in setting regulatory priorities, as to whether the fossil-fuel burning power plant or the internal combustion engine is the prime culprit in the pollution of the air of cities. Examine the data earlier referred to. Which of the two sources produces "more" pollution? Which produces the more dangerous pollutants?

(2) It has been said that concern for an unpolluted environment is largely a middle-class preoccupation, because the slum dweller who lives in an unheated apartment cares little whether the fuel in the furnace is high sulfur or low sulfur fuel—as long as there is *some* kind of fuel. Even granting the validity of the narrow premise, are there persuasive arguments—related in part to the availability of health services—that environmental protection, particularly with respect to air pollution, may have an even greater impact on the underprivileged part of the population than on all the rest? For evidence

that the poorer part of the population is likely to live in the more highly polluted parts of the city, see D. Harrison, Jr., Who Pays for Clean Air? 103-105 (1975).

[4] Control Methods

Air pollution can be controlled in three ways: (1) preventing the pollutants from forming in the process or operation; (2) dispersing the pollutants into the atmosphere in such a way that their strength is satisfactorily dissipated; and (3) collecting the pollutants after they have formed but before they reach the outdoor air. Often, all three methods must be used to meet air quality requirements.[2]

[a] Prevention

Sometimes the formation of a pollutant may be prevented by taking one or several of these courses:

Replacing or Altering the Fuel or Raw Materials Used. For example, hydrocarbon emissions from paint manufacture can be reduced by reformulating the paint. The new formula is made with little or no highly reactive solvent.

Changing the Production Process. For instance, kraft pulping (an operation in paper manufacture) involves cooking wood chips in a chemical solution, and then treating the spent ("black") liquor to recover the expensive chemicals for reuse. The gaseous sulfur compound emissions have a repellent odor. Changing to what is known as a black liquor oxidation recovery process converts the sulfur compounds to less odorous ones by oxidizing them before the liquor is sent into evaporators.

Changing the Equipment. Metallurgical processes, for example, can be very high in the production of aerosols—particulate matter under a micron in diameter. But replacing an open-hearth melting furnace with an electric-arc one reduces these emissions. Electric-arc furnaces use electrical energy for melting and so are inherently cleaner than fuel-burning furnaces.

Improving Operation and Maintenance Practices. One example: All industrial furnaces and boilers are designed for specific loads and temperatures. Operating within the specifications minimizes the particulate and carbon monoxide pollution.

Enclosing the Operation. For instance, refineries handle many hydrocarbons that are highly volatile: that is, they evaporate readily at normal temperatures. Tanks with floating roofs and vapor recovery systems prevent the escape of these volatile products to the atmosphere. Vapor recovery systems also prevent losses during tank truck loading.

---

[2] American Lung Association, Controlling Air Pollution: A Primer on Stationary Source Control Techniques (1974).

[b] Dispersal

Although it is possible to dilute the concentration of a pollutant by raising the smokestack height, or by moving the plant where its emissions will not affect neighboring inhabited areas, dispersal is no longer an acceptable alternative under the Clean Air Act, particularly as amended in 1977. As noted, the Clean Air Act emphasizes and requires emission controls, and prohibits dispersal techniques in most situations. Tall stacks are now stringently regulated under § 123 of the Clean Air Act, and moving a plant out of range is not feasible when available evidence indicates that some pollutants, particularly sulfur dioxide, are carried for thousands of miles, adding to acid rain in remote areas. *See* F. Grad, Treatise on Environmental Law, §§ 2.03[7][a][ii], 2.09[2], [4], and 12.03[4][d][ii], [e], [j].

[c] Collection

A pollutant may be trapped, changed, or destroyed before it reaches the atmosphere. The methods of doing this are often called *tail-end* techniques, since they are put to use after the pollutant is formed in the industrial process or the combustion equipment. These tail-end methods involve a multitude of considerations, although the categories of equipment are relatively limited.

[i] Control Equipment for Particulates

Some equipment is designed especially to trap particulates. Other equipment is designed for gas (and odor) elimination. And some can be used for both gaseous and particulate matter. The devices to remove particulates may involve either dry or wet techniques; that is, they may or may not use a liquid in the removal process.

[A] Dry Collectors

Among the dry collectors are:

Settling Chambers. These work very simply according to the law of gravity. The chamber is large and the inlet duct, by comparison, small. The particulate-laden gas stream is sent through the duct into the chamber. (In the language of air pollution technology, no distinction is made between air and other gases: all are referred to as "gas.") The gas travels swiftly through the narrow duct, but when it arrives at the larger settling chamber, it slows down. At this relaxed pace, large particles fall to the bottom.

Settling chambers can be expected to remove only large particles—nothing less than 40 microns in diameter. Smaller, lighter dusts and droplets settle too slowly—if at all—for the short time the air stream remains in the limited space of the chamber. This kind of equipment needs a lot of space. But a settling chamber can be useful for certain applications, such as rock-crushing, where the crusher would be enclosed by a hood. The dust-filled gas stream would be exhausted through a settling chamber in order to reduce the load on a second, more efficient collector of particulate matter.

Inertial collectors. These rely on inertial force as well as gravity for their operation. The most common in the cyclone collector. Here, the gas stream is rushed into a cylindrical chamber through a tangential inlet duct (one set at an angle to the chamber wall) at the top of the cylinder. This combination of shapes sets the stream whirling downward with increasing rapidity toward a cone-shaped base. Centrifugal force throws the entrained particles out of the spinning gas stream onto the wall of the chamber. From there they fall into a collecting hopper while the air stream then swirls upward through a tube in the center.

Depending on design, cyclone collectors can remove particles as small as three microns, although high-efficiency collection cannot be expected for particles under 15 microns, and efficiency is also affected by variable loads. (The efficiency of a collector is rated according to the percentage of pollutants removed. A high-efficiency particulate collector can remove over 95%, by weight, of the particles.) Multiple cyclones—that is, several low-capacity units in place of a single large one—are popular because they can increase collection efficiency without using more power.

Another form of inertial collector is the dynamic precipitator. Here the particle-laden gas stream is driven against a series of fan blades, so shaped that the particles are caught on the blades and deposited in a hopper while the cleaned air continues up, around, and out. These units remove particles over ten microns.

Inertial separators are widely used as preliminary collectors for dry particulates. Depending on the fineness of the particles, these collectors can achieve an efficiency of from 85 to 95 percent. Among the many processes in which they are used are phosphate fertilizer production, limestone crushing, and chemical and rubber manufacture.

Both inertial and gravitational separators, called mechanical collectors, are relatively inexpensive both to buy and run. Buying and installing a dry centrifugal collector could cost a quarter of what a cloth filter collector (described below) would run and a ninth of what a high-voltage electrostatic precipitator (also described below) might come to, to process the same amount of dirty air. To operate them, though, the costs would be least for the precipitator and about equal for centrifugal and cloth filter collectors.

Cloth filter collectors. These work on the same principle as a vacuum cleaner bag. The bags for industrial collectors, though, may be 30 or more feet in length. In operation, the gas stream that carries a burden of particles passes through a woven fabric in which the particles themselves are caught. These widely used, very versatile collectors come in a variety of materials, including cotton, wool, asbestos, glass fiber, and any of a number of synthetics; the choice of fabric is based on the temperature and chemical composition of the gas and the physical and chemical characteristics of the particulate matter.

Cloth filter collectors are used for fine particles; some can remove close to 100% of particles as fine as 0.4 micron. Cloth filter collectors are used to trap particulate emissions from Portland cement kilns, iron foundry cupolas, primary steel production furnaces, and many other sources. The most common types are mounted in banks of multiple units, called *baghouses*. Custom-designed installations can be as big as a good-sized building.

Fabric collectors, good as they are, have their disadvantages. Even with the most carefully chosen fabric, very hot gases have to be cooled first: and the bags are affected by humidity and chemicals and have to be replaced after, at the most, five years.

And they are expensive. In order to improve the dust and fume control system for the lead blast furnace at a Herculaneum, Missouri plant (the country's largest lead smelter, to be sure), $4 million was spent to design and build a baghouse and the concomitant facilities. These facilities treat 550,000 cubic feet of gas a minute, collected from the blast furnace hoods, and they include, in addition to the baghouse, an improved fume collection system, gas cooling equipment, duct work, and the necessary fans, motors, and instrumentation.

Electrostatic precipitators. These capture particles electrically, through the use of electrodes. (Electrodes conduct an electric current through the nonmetallic part of a circuit.) Electrostatic precipitators entail a small-diameter negative electrode—usually a wire—and a grounded positive electrode plate. In operation, a strong electric charge from the negative electrode sets up a one-directional electric field. The particles passing through the field pick up the charge and are then drawn to the positive collecting surface where they are neutralized and either fall or are shaken into a collection hopper.

Electrostatic precipitators can remove many different kinds of particles as small as 0.1 micron with as much as 99.9% efficiency. In spite of the drawbacks—among them, a sensitivity to the composition and electrical properties of the substances passing through them—they are used in a great many plants, including those producing power, sulfuric acid, paint, plastics, chemicals, and automobile tires.

Their efficiency is costly. Jones & Laughlin Steel Corporation paid over $8 million for a system purchased for one of their steelmaking shops, a system that included two new electrostatic precipitators. Of course this price was for a "turnkey" contract (one that includes everything from design to delivery of the installation in full working order), which involved, in addition to providing the two new electrostatic precipitators, modifying existing ones so that they all performed at a guaranteed emission collection efficiency of 99.9%. The total system was capable of processing 1.5 million cubic feet of gas a minute.

[B] Wet Collectors

All wet collectors present a dilemma. As they eliminate air pollution, they can create water pollution. So, when designing or selecting a wet collector, an engineer has to figure out how to dispose of the resultant contaminated liquid or sludge. Other problems exist too—including corrosion and freezing in cold weather. Nevertheless, wet collectors are used. Among them are:

Electrostatic precipitators. As wet collectors, they remove particles by washing them off the electrode plate.

Dynamic precipitators. Wet dynamic collectors constantly spray a film of water on a moving surface, such as the blades of a fan. They are moderately efficient on particles from 15 to 50 microns in diameter.

Gravity spray towers. In a gravity spray tower, as particles ride upward on a gas stream, they are trapped by much larger drops of water (500 to 1,000 microns) sprayed from above. A gravity spray tower is not very effective for particles smaller than two microns, but it does work with large particles, especially liquid ones.

Scrubbers. (The term *scrubber* is used by some authorities to mean any device employing a liquid to separate out an unwanted substance.) There are many kinds of scrubbers, using either water or some other liquid, and they may combine a number of techniques to pick up and dissolve or wash out solid or liquid pollutants.

One of the many varieties of scrubbers is the centrifugal spray scrubber. Here the gas stream is sent spinning—one scrubber type uses a tangential inlet duct—through the scrubbing chamber, while a liquid is sprayed against the stream, wetting the gas and the chamber walls. The centrifugal force of the swirling gas throws the wetted particles against the walls and from there they are washed down. Efficiencies as high as 96% are possible for two-and three-micron particles.

Another popular type is the Venturi scrubber, in which the gas stream passes through a Venturi tube (a short tube with flaring ends and a constricted middle—the constriction forces an increase in a gas streams' speed and a decrease in its pressure). A coarse spray of water is injected at the throat of the tube through radial jets. The spray is atomized by the speed of the gas to drops about 50 microns in size. These collide with and trap the dust particles. Venturi scrubbers can collect from 97 to over 99 percent of particles as small as 0.5 microns.

Scrubbers, though they answer many needs and are widely used, have serious drawbacks. Like all wet collectors, they can create severe problems in treating the resulting waste water. Their power requirements are high, for they cool the gas stream, which is difficult to disperse into the atmosphere. They are noisy. And they are generally less effective than filters or electrostatic precipitators in removing very fine particles.

Nor are they inexpensive. In an Eagle Mountain, California iron ore pelletizing plant (where iron ore dust is agglomerated to make more easily manageable pellets), a scrubber that treats 60,000 cubic feet of dust-laden air a minute and recirculates the water was manufactured and installed at a cost of $180,000.

[ii] Control Equipment for Gases

The removal of unwanted gases poses a greater problem than that of particulates. There are four different processes to solve the problem: (1) absorption, (2) adsorption, (3) incineration, and (4) condensation.

[A] Absorption

In this process, the gas stream passes through a liquid—the absorbent—that collects and sometimes modifies one or more of the constituents of the stream. The absorbent may be recirculated, or it may have to be discarded after a single use, or it may be regenerated; that is, reused after treatment. If it is to be discarded, the problem of water pollution comes up again.

There are a number of different kinds of absorbers:

Scrubbers. Scrubbers are often used as absorbers, sometimes with a liquid other than water. In Los Angeles, the sulfur oxide and hydrocarbon gases are removed from asphalt processing by a Venturi scrubber using sea water.

Packed towers. The tower, a vertical structure, is packed with some chemically inert material; the liquid absorbent enters from the top and trickles down through the packing; and the gas stream to be treated enters at the bottom and is absorbed by the liquid as it rises.

In a sulfuric acid plant, for example, in order to reduce the sulfur oxide emissions (and to increase the production of sulfuric acid), the potentially polluting sulfur dioxide is first converted to sulfur trioxide by the addition of oxygen and then sent into a packed tower, where a circulating stream of sulfuric acid absorbs enough of the gas to meet control regulations. Actually, this is just more of the same—sending sulfur trioxide through a multi-stage absorber is how the sulfuric acid product is made in the first place. In an effort to meet emission standards, engineers have added an extra, slightly altered absorption stage to convert additional sulfur dioxide.

Plate or tray towers. In these towers, a series of plates with a number of openings allow the gas to bubble slowly upward through the liquid that covers each plate. In most designs, the force of the gas keeps the liquid from coming through the openings. Instead, the absorbent makes its way down slowly, layer by layer, through tubes at the side.

[B] Adsorption

In adsorption, the gas is attracted and adheres to the multi-surfaces of a porous solid. In dry-cleaning plants, activated carbon adsorption units can be added to the discharge of the ventilating system to trap the vapor of the dry-cleaning solvent. The vapor is collected during the cleaning process and is passed through the adsorber, from which all the solvent can be recovered.

Regenerating an adsorbent, however, may cause erosion, and it is so costly that it is usually done only when some valuable product can be recovered. Synthetic dry cleaning solvent, usually perchloroethylene, *is* expensive—so expensive that its recovery can pay for the adsorption unit within a year or two. So the solvent is recovered by sending a stream at low pressure through the carbon and then cooling and condensing the steam-vapor mixture and decanting the solvent.

[C] Incineration

Waste organic—that is, carbon-containing—gases and vapors can be eliminated by burning. This can be accomplished in a number of ways:

Direct-fired afterburners. Shunting a polluted gas stream through a direct-fired afterburner, or firebox, before the steam is vented to the atmosphere is the most commonly used control method for combustible gases, and for aerosols and odors as well. Afterburners are designed to provide high enough temperatures (1100° to 1600° F.), thorough enough mixing, and sufficient retention time to achieve complete combustion.

Because such high temperatures are needed, fuel and operating costs are high, and direct-fired afterburners are not cost-effective except with relatively small volumes of air. They can be efficient, however. For example, the organic vapors emitted from varnish cookers (so called because the major part of varnish manufacture consists of heating the ingredients in huge kettles) are most effectively destroyed in a direct-fired afterburner to which the polluting emissions are vented.

Catalytic afterburners. The catalyst, usually a platinum alloy, adsorbs the gases to be burned along with large amounts of oxygen that have been injected; the gases interact with each other on the catalyst; and oxidation products, carbon dioxide and water, are released.

To make proper use of a catalyst, the gas stream has to be relatively free of dusts and mineral ash (which requires additional cleaning costs). Many substances are catalyst poisons. If there is a lot of inorganic particulate matter, a coating is formed on the catalyst and the effectiveness of these afterburners is reduced.

Using a catalyst in an afterburner, however, is preferred in a number of circumstances. Catalytic afterburners are often chosen when treating volumes of cool gas so large that the costs of fuel for heating it would be prohibitive; catalytic afterburners require less fuel than open-flame ones. Catalytic afterburners are also used when there is not enough of the pollutant in the gas stream to catch fire; they can destroy low concentrations of gases and droplets. And when lower operating temperatures are needed for the production process involved, an oxidizing catalyst would again be the choice; it requires lower temperatures than a direct-fired afterburner to destroy unwanted gases. Catalytic combustion of most organic gases can take place at about 500° F.

Catalytic afterburners are most often used in connection with organic solvent and vapor emissions from industrial ovens. For example, the manufacture of ethylene, a chemical product of petroleum with many uses, produces waste vapor that is successfully burned in a catalytic afterburner. As a bonus, once the vapor begins oxidizing, it produces a great deal of heat that can be put to other use.

Flares. Flares are used primarily to control hydrocarbon gases released intermittently in certain refinery and petrochemical processes. Flares are designed to provide for smokeless combustion of gases that keep changing in composition and rate of flow. Since it is difficult to maintain high efficiency and smokeless combustion, many communities ban big flares as nuisances.

There are two kinds of flares, Venturi and steam injection. Venturi flares mix air with the gas stream before it is ignited; they are usually used at ground level. Steam-injection flares mix steam with exhaust gases at the top of the stack. The steam separates the hydrocarbon molecules and reduces unwanted polymerization (a chemical reaction in which two or more similar molecules combine and form a very stable substance).

[D] Condensation

Condensation may be part of a collection and recovery system designed to prevent the escape of gases and vapors into the atmosphere at any point in a production process. Emissions are vented to a condenser where the temperature of the gas stream is lowered to the condensation point of the substance to be collected.

There are two types of condensers:

Contact condensers. In these, the gas is condensed by mixing it with a cooling liquid. For example, rendering animal matter for tallow and for livestock and poultry feed produces very offensive gases. These gases can be partially controlled by being vented into a contact condenser and mixed with cold water. In this case, the resulting mixture—the condensate—is disposed of as sewage.

Surface condensers. In these, vapor is condensed by contact, not directly with the cooling liquid, but instead with a cooling surface, behind which is the liquid. The surface is usually the outside of a metal tube through which the coolant runs. In resin manufacture, for example, containers of volatile liquids are often equipped with cooling coils. Low concentrations of vapors cannot be efficiently removed by condensers, but these devices are useful as a preliminary step to afterburners or adsorbers.

[d] Control Selection

The selection and design of a control system—especially a tail-end one—is no easy matter. It is the work of highly skilled engineers. They have to consider long lists of factors, such as the limitations imposed by the product manufacturing process, the space available, and all the physical and chemical properties of the pollutant and the carrier gas. Among the properties that must be considered are temperature, pressure, humidity, reactivity, solubility, reaction products, corrosiveness, flammability, stickiness, and—if particulate matter—shape, size range, and density. Plus, of course, the emission standards to be met and the cost of it all. It's quite a task.

§ 2.02 Private Common Law Rights to a Healthful Atmosphere: Trespass and Nuisance Theories

MARTIN v. REYNOLDS METALS CO.

Supreme Court of Oregon (1959)
221 Or. 86, 342 P.2d 790, cert. denied, 362 U.S. 918

O'CONNELL, JUSTICE

This is an action of trespass. The plaintiffs allege that during the period from August 22, 1951 to January 1, 1956 the defendant, in the operation of its aluminum reduction plant near Troutdale, Oregon caused certain fluoride compounds in the form of gases and particulates to become airborne and settle upon the plaintiffs' land rendering it unfit for raising livestock during that period. Plaintiffs allege that their cattle were poisoned by ingesting the fluorides which contaminate the forage and water on their land. They sought damages in the amount of $450,000 for the loss of use of their land for grazing purposes and for the deterioration of the land through the growth of brush, trees and weeds resulting from the lack of use of the premises for grazing purposes. The plaintiffs also sought punitive damages in the amount of $30,000.

The plaintiffs and the defendant each moved for a directed verdict, whereupon the trial court found that the plaintiffs had suffered damage in the amount of $71,500 in the loss of use of their land and $20,000 for the deterioration of their land and entered judgment accordingly. The trial court rejected the plaintiffs' claim for punitive damages.

In the course of the pleadings the defendant raised the issue as to whether the complaint alleged a cause of action in trespass. The defendant contended that at most a cause of action in nuisance was stated. The trial court accepted the plaintiffs' theory of the case. The principal assignments of error rest upon the defendant's contention that the trial court was mistaken in identifying the defendant's invasion of the plaintiffs' land as a trespass; that there was not sufficient evidence to establish a cause of action under any theory, but that if the court should find the evidence sufficient to give rise to liability the defendant's conduct constituted a nuisance and not a trespass.

Through appropriate pleadings the defendant set up the two-year statute of limitations applicable to nontrespassory injuries to land (ORS 12.110). If the defendant's conduct created a nuisance and not a trespass the defendant would be liable only for such damage as resulted from its conduct during a period of two years immediately preceding the date upon which plaintiffs' action was instituted. On the other hand, if the defendant's conduct resulted in a trespass upon plaintiffs' land the six-year statute of limitations provided for in ORS 12.080 would be applicable and plaintiffs would be entitled to recover damages resulting from the trespasses by defendant during the period from August 22, 1951 to January 1, 1956.

The gist of the defendant's argument is as follows: a trespass arises only when there has been a "breaking and entering upon real property," constituting a direct, as distinguished from a consequential, invasion of the possessor's interest in land; and the settling upon the land of fluoride compounds consisting of gases, fumes and particulates is not sufficient to satisfy these requirements.

Before appraising the argument we shall first describe more particularly the physical and chemical nature of the substance which was deposited upon plaintiffs' land. In reducing alumina (the oxide of aluminum) to aluminum the alumina is subjected to an electrolytic process which causes the emanation of fluoridic compounds consisting principally of hydrogen fluoride, calcium fluoride, iron fluoride and silicon tetrafluoride. The individual particulates which form these chemical compounds are not visible to the naked eye. A part of them were captured by a fume collection system which was installed in November, 1950; the remainder became airborne and a part of the uncaptured particles eventually were deposited upon plaintiffs' land.

There is evidence to prove that during the period from August 1951 to January 1956 the emanation of fluorides from defendant's plant averaged approximately 800 pounds daily. Some of this discharge was deposited upon the plaintiffs' land. There is sufficient evidence to support the trial court's finding that the quantity of fluorides deposited upon plaintiffs' land was great enough to cause $91,500 damage to the plaintiffs in the use of their land for grazing purposes and in the deterioration of their land as alleged.

We must determine, however, whether all or only a part of this damage may be shown; all, if the invasion constitutes a trespass, a part only (i. e., the damage which resulted within the two-year period of the statute of limitations) if the invasion was a nuisance and not a trespass.

Trespass and private nuisance are separate fields of tort liability relating to actionable interference with the possession of land. They may be distinguished by comparing the interest invaded; an actionable invasion of a possessor's interest in the exclusive possession of land is a trespass; an actionable invasion of a possessor's interest in the use and enjoyment of his land is a nuisance. 4 Restatement, Torts 224, Intro. Note Chapter 40.

The same conduct on the part of a defendant may and often does result in the actionable invasion of both of these interests, in which case the choice between the two remedies is, in most cases, a matter of little consequence. Where the action is brought on the theory of nuisance alone the court ordinarily is not called upon to determine whether the conduct would also result in a trespassory invasion. In such cases the courts' treatment of the invasion solely in terms of the law of nuisance does not mean that the same conduct could not also be regarded as a trespass. Some of the cases relied upon by the defendant are of this type; cases in which the court holds that the interference with the plaintiff's possession through soot, dirt, smoke, cinders, ashes and similar substances constitute a nuisance, but where the court does not discuss the applicability of the law of trespass to the same set of facts.

However, there are cases which have held that the defendant's interference with plaintiff's possession resulting from the settling upon his land of effluents emanating from defendant's operations is exclusively nontrespassory. Although in such cases the separate particles which collectively cause the invasion are minute, the deposit of each of the particles constitutes a physical intrusion and, but for the size of the particle, would clearly give rise to an action of trespass. The defendant asks us to take account of the difference in size of the physical agency through which the intrusion occurs and relegate entirely to the field of nuisance law certain invasions which do not meet the dimensional test, whatever that is. In pressing this argument upon us the defendant must admit that there are cases which have held that a trespass results from the movement or deposit of rather small objects over or upon the surface of the possessor's land.

Thus it has been held that causing shot from a gun to fall upon the possessor's land is a trespass.

The dropping of particles of molten lead upon the plaintiff's land has been held to be a trespass. *Van Alstyne v. Rochester Telephone Corp.*, 163 Misc. 258, 296 N.Y.S. 726. And the defendant was held liable in trespass where spray from a cooling tower on the roof of its theater fell upon the plaintiffs land. *B & R Luncheonette, Inc. v. Fairmont Theatre Corp.*, 278 App. Div. 133, 103 N.Y.S.2d 747.

The deposit of soot and carbon from defendant's mill upon plaintiff's land was held to be a trespass in *Young v. Fort Frances Pulp and Paper Co.*, Canada 1919, 17 Ont. Wkly. Notes 6.

And liability on the theory of trespass has been recognized where the harm was produced by the vibration of the soil or by the concussion of the air which, of course, is nothing more than the movement of molecules one against the other. . . . The view recognizing a trespassory invasion where there is no "thing" which can be seen with the naked eye undoubtedly runs counter to the definition of trespass expressed in some quarters. I Restatement, Torts § 158, Comment h (1934); Prosser, Torts § 13 (2d Ed. 1955). It is quite possible that in an earlier day when science had not yet peered into the molecular and atomic world of small particles, the courts could not fit an invasion through unseen physical instrumentalities into the requirement that a trespass can result only from a *direct* invasion. But in this atomic age even the uneducated know the great and awful force contained in the atom and what it can do to a man's property if it is released. In fact, the now famous equation $E = mc^2$ has taught us that mass and energy are equivalents and that our concept of "things" must be reframed. If these observations on science in relation to the law of trespass should appear theoretical and unreal in the abstract, they become very practical and real to the possessor of land when the unseen force cracks the foundation of his house. The force is just as real if it is chemical in nature and must be awakened by the intervention of another agency before it does harm.

If, then, we must look to the character of the instrumentality which is used in making an intrusion upon another's land we prefer to emphasize the object's energy or force rather than its size. Viewed in this way we may define trespass as any intrusion which invades the possessor's protected interest in exclusive possession, whether that intrusion is by visible or invisible pieces of matter or by energy which can be measured only by the mathematical language of the physicist.

We are of the opinion, therefore, that the intrusion of the fluoride particulates in the present case constituted a trespass.

The defendant argues that our decision in *Amphitheaters, Inc. v. Portland Meadows*, 1948, 184 Or. 336, 198 P.2d 847, 851, 5 A.L.R.2d 690, requires a contrary conclusion. In discussing the distinction between trespass and nuisance the court referred to a difference between "a cannon ball and a ray of light" indicating that the former but not the latter could produce a trespassory invasion. The court also said "The mere suggestion that the casting of light upon the premises of a plaintiff would render a defendant liable without proof of any actual damage, carries its own refutation." 184 Or. 336, 343, 198 P.2d 847, 850. We do not regard this statement as a pronouncement that a trespass can *never* be caused by the intrusion of light rays or other intangible forces; more properly the case may be interpreted as stating that the conduct of the defendant in a particular case may not be actionable if it does not violate a legally protected interest of the plaintiff. The court states that the defendant is not liable *without proof of actual damage.* In that case the plaintiff contended that he had suffered damage in the form of a less efficient cinema screen due to the defendant's lights. In denying recovery the court found that there was no damage, apparently because whatever harm the plaintiff suffered was damnum absque injuria.

In every case in which trespass is alleged the court is presented with a problem of deciding whether the defendant's intrusion has violated a legally protected interest of the plaintiff. In most cases the defendant's conduct so clearly invades the well established possessory interest of the plaintiff that no discussion of the point is called for. But where neither the defendant's conduct nor the plaintiff's use fall within the familiar trespass pattern of the past the courts are faced with a preliminary inquiry as to whether the plaintiff has a protectible interest under the law of trespass. This in turn calls for the inquiry as to whether the defendant's conduct was such as to constitute an invasion of that interest.

. . . .

As stated earlier, normally no inquiry is made in the trespass cases as to whether the plaintiffs' interest in making a particular use of his property is within the protection provided for under the law of trespass, because traditionally the interest has been regarded as one clearly entitled to protection in the trespass field. There are adjudicated cases which have refused to find a trespass where the intrusion is clearly established but where the court has felt that the possessor's interest should not be protected. Thus it has been held that the flight of aircraft over the surface of plaintiffs land does not constitute a trespass unless the intrusion interferes with the present enjoyment of property. *Hinman v. Pacific Air Transport*, 9 Cir., 1936, 84 F.2d 755. The same result would seem to follow if the intrusion interfered with the present use of the land but where such use was not entitled to legal protection as against the socially desirable conduct of the defendant. Here it is apparent that the law of trespass and the law of nuisance come very close to merging. This is so because when inquiry is made as to whether the plaintiff's interest falls within the ambit of trespass law the courts look at the interference with the plaintiffs *use and enjoyment* of his land to determine whether his interest in *exclusive possession* should be protected and thus the two torts coalesce.

. . . .

The scope of the possessor's legitimate interest in the exclusive possession of land is broad and difficult to define specifically. Once recognizing that actual damage need not be shown in making out an actionable invasion, the plaintiff's right to insist upon freedom from interference with his possession seems almost limitless.

But there are limits and they can be found, if only vaguely, in the reasons for protecting the possessory interest of the landholder where no actual damage is suffered. It is sometimes said that the plaintiff is permitted to recover in order to prevent a loss of interest by the running of the statute of limitations. 1 Harper & James, Torts, § 1.8, pp. 25 and 26; *Whittaker v. Stangvick, supra*; *Bragg v. Laraway*, 1893, 65 Vt. 673, 27 A. 492. But this is not a respectable reason because the statute could be made inapplicable by holding that no cause of action arose for the harmless invasion. The modern law of trespass can be understood only as it is seen against its historical background. Originally all types of trespass, including trespass to land, was punishable under the criminal law because the trespasser's conduct was regarded as a breach of the peace. When the criminal and civil aspect of trespass were separated, the civil action for trespass was colored by its past, and the idea that the peace of the community was put in danger by the trespasser's conduct influenced the courts' ideas of the character of the tort. Therefore, relief was granted to the plaintiff where he was not actually damaged, partly at least as a means of discouraging disruptive influences in the community. Winfield on Torts (4th ed.) p. 305 expresses the idea as follows:

> "The law, on the face of it, looks harsh, but trespass was so likely in earlier times to lead to a breach of the peace that even unwitting and trivial deviations on to another person's land were reckoned unlawful. At the present day there is, of course, much greater respect for the law in general and appreciation of the security which it affords, and the theoretical severity of the rules as to land trespass is hardly ever exploited in practice."

The idea is similarly expressed in 1 Harper & James, Torts, § 1.8, p. 25:

> "In the early law, emphasis was placed upon the criminal aspect of willful trespasses, as a breach of the peace or a wrong to the state. Compensation to the injured victim was regarded as of secondary importance. It came about, therefore, that the rule developed that the plaintiff might recover nominal damages even though he sustained no actual pecuniary loss as a result of the trespass."

If then, we find that an act on the part of the defendant in interfering with the plaintiff's possession, does, or is likely to result in arousing conflict between them, that act will characterize the tort as a trespass, assuming of course that the other elements of the tort are made out. The importance of this consideration in describing a trespass to land is evident in many of the modern cases.

Probably the most important factor which describes the nature of the interest protected under the law of trespass is nothing more than a feeling which a possessor has with respect to land which he holds. It is a sense of ownership; a feeling that what one owns or possesses should not be interfered with, and that it is entitled to protection through law. This being the nature of the plaintiff's interest, it is understandable why actual damage is not an essential ingredient in the law of trespass. As pointed out in 1 Harper & James, Torts, § 1.8, p. 26, the rule permitting recovery in spite of the absence of actual damages "is probably justified as a vindicatory right to protect the possessor's proprietary or dignitary interest in his land."

We think that a possessor's interest in land as defined by the considerations recited above may, under the appropriate circumstances, be violated by a ray of light, by an atomic particle, or by a particulate of fluoride and, contrariwise, if such interest circumscribed by these considerations is not violated or endangered, the defendant's conduct, even though it may result in a physical intrusion, will not render him liable in an action of trespass. *Amphitheaters, Inc. v. Portland Meadows, supra.*

We hold that the defendant's conduct in causing chemical substances to be deposited upon the plaintiff's land fulfilled all of the requirements under the law of trespass.

. . . .

The trial court found that the fluoride compounds emitted from the defendant's plant between August 22, 1951 and January 1, 1956 rendered plaintiffs' land and the drinking water on the land unfit for consumption by livestock grazing thereon. The defendant contends that there is no substantial evidence to support this finding. In support of this contention the defendant points to the effectiveness of the fume control system which was installed in 1950 prior to August 22, 1951, the beginning of the period during which the plaintiffs alleged that the damage occurred. The evidence is conflicting but there is substantial evidence from which the trial court could have connected the emanation of the fluorides with the damage alleged. We cannot, therefore, disturb the trial court finding.

It is also urged that the trial court erred in failing to enter a special finding requested by the defendant. The requested finding in effect stated that it was impossible in the operation of an aluminum reduction plant to capture all fluorides which are created in the manufacturing process; that the fume collection system was in operation during the period in question; and that it was the most efficient of the systems known in aluminum reduction plants in the United States. . . .

The issue thus raised, as to the character of defendant's conduct in making the intrusion upon plaintiffs' land, would be material only with respect to the claim for punitive damages which, as we have already indicated, was rejected by the trial court. Since we hold that the intrusion in this case constituted a trespass it is immaterial whether the defendant's conduct was careless, wanton and willful or entirely free from fault. Therefore, the refusal to enter the requested finding is not error.

The judgment of the lower court is affirmed.

McALLISTER, Chief Justice (specially concurring).

I concur in the result of the above opinion but dissent from that portion thereof that attempts to reconcile the holding in this case with the holding in the case of *Amphitheaters, Inc. v. Portland Meadows*, 184 Or. 336, 198 P.2d 847.

NOTE

In *Fairview Farms, Inc. v. Reynolds Metal Co.*, 176 F. Supp. 178 (D. Or. 1959), the court had before it a situation substantially similar on its facts. Plaintiff sought injunctive relief, damages for depreciation of its lands, punitive damages, and compensatory damages for injury to its dairy herd and for loss of milk production. The court denied injunctive relief, on the grounds that legal remedies, *i.e.*, compensatory damages, sufficed to make plaintiff whole. It also rejected the claim for depreciation of the value of the plaintiff's lands, for failure of proof, and the claim for punitive damages on the grounds that though the fluoride pollution constituted an "intentional" trespass, it did not amount to a "willful" tort. Compensatory damages, for injury to the land and for loss of milk production, were allowed.

RENKEN v. HARVEY ALUMINUM CO.

United States District Court, District of Oregon (1963)
226 F. Supp. 169

KILKENNY, District Judge

Plaintiffs seek to enjoin the defendant from operating its plant in such a manner as to permit the escape therefrom of excessive quantities of the element, fluorine, which is carried by air currents to plaintiffs' lands. Defendant is a corporation, incorporated under the laws of the State of California. Since July 28, 1958, it has been and still is the operator of a certain aluminum reduction plant located near the city of The Dalles in Wasco County, Oregon. Since said date the plant has been continuously operated and, as an integral part of said operation, has emitted and still emits into the atmosphere quantities of matter chemically composed of various elements, including fluorides. The said matter in the form of particles, particulates, solids and gasses has been and is spread by currents of air and wind and, from time to time, such material has been deposited on plaintiffs' lands and fruit trees.

. . . .

The initial fume control apparatus at the Harvey plant consisted of a cast iron skirt surrounding the anode, which collected a portion of the fumes at the source and directed them to burners mounted at both ends of each anode. To these burners were connected fume exhaust ducts which led the fumes to a main collector pipe carrying them to the dust collector and a fan. The fan created a suction which pulled the fumes from the cells and the burners, through the ducts. From the fans the fumes are directed to a humidifying and bubbling chamber before entering the scrubber tower. The fumes are washed in the tower by multiple layers of water sprayers placed 10 feet apart. At the top of the towers is a mist eliminator.

Tests made, from time to time, indicate that the fume control system, thus described, operated at 95% efficiency, or better, during the test periods on the portion of the fumes caught and delivered to the system. The amount of equivalent fluoride ion leaving the scrubbing towers into the atmosphere from this control apparatus is calculated at 300 pounds per day. This system treats approximately 80% of the fumes released from the cells. The remaining 20% of the fumes escape into the open building, and rise to the top where they pass into roof monitors located at the top of each of the buildings housing the cells. In the spring of 1962, a system of sprayers and screens were installed in the roof monitor and this system has been operating at full capacity since the beginning of 1963. These sprayers and screens collect a portion of the fluorides reaching the roof monitor. Since this latest installation the roof monitor sprays and screens have been between 67 and 70% effective in collecting the fluorides reaching the roof monitors. The amount of equivalent fluoride ion leaving the roof monitors into the atmosphere is calculated at 1,000 pounds per day. Overall, the combination of the original fume control system, as it has been added to and improved from time to time, and the roof monitor sprays and screens has achieved approximately 90% effectiveness with respect to collecting the fluorides released from the aluminum cells.

The record is undisputed that approximately 1,300 pounds of fluoride ion escape from the roof monitors and scrubbing towers into the atmosphere each day. Although the prevailing wind is southwesterly, the record clearly shows that on numerous days each month and on many hours of each day, the area is without measurable wind. At such times, a blanket of smoke from defendant's plant covers the area, including plaintiffs' lands and orchards. This blanket was observed by the Court, not only on the day of inspection of the plant, but also on many occasions since that time. There is no doubt in my mind but that better controls can be exercised over the escape of the material in question. No sound reason has been advanced by defendant why hoods, similar to those employed by Reynolds, should not be installed. While it is true that a substantial portion of the gasses and particulates escape at the time when the new aluminum ore is being introduced into the pot or the liquid metal is removed, I am convinced that such an escape could be prevented by a properly designed hood over the open area. I agree with the expert, that after the installation of the hood, the small amount of gasses which might escape on the introduction of ore or the removal of liquid metal would be inconsequential.

Likewise, the record convinces me of the feasibility of the introduction of electrostatic precipitators for the removal of the minute or small particulates which are not removed by the other processes. The multicyclone dust collector now used in the plant at The Dalles is efficient in collecting the large or heavy particulates, but is of little value in removing the smaller variety. All of the experts agree that this is the field in which the electrostatic precipitators are at their best. The great weight of the evidence points to the conclusion that the installation of the cell hoods and the employment of electrostatic precipitators would greatly reduce, if not entirely eliminate, the escape of the excessive material now damaging the orchards of the plaintiffs.

While the cost of the installations of these additional controls will be a substantial sum, the fact remains that effective controls must be exercised over the escape of these noxious fumes. Such expenditures would not be so great as to substantially deprive defendant of the use of its property. While we are not dealing with the public as such, we must recognize that air pollution is one of the great problems now facing the American public. If necessary, the cost of installing adequate controls must be passed on to the ultimate consumer. The heavy cost of corrective devices is no reason why plaintiffs should stand by and suffer substantial damage.

DAMAGES TO PLAINTIFFS

It is my considered opinion that the evidence on damage to cherries is so conflicting and controversial it would be difficult to hold that the cherry crops were severely damaged by the gasses or particulates emitted from defendant's plant. The evidence clearly shows that the year 1960, the one in which plaintiffs claim their principal cherry damage, was an exceptionally light cherry crop, not only in Wasco County, but throughout the States of Oregon and Washington. I am convinced that the light cherry crop in 1960 was due to factors other than the fluorides escaping from the plant of the defendant. However, the evidence is convincing that the deposit of this material on the trees at blossom time creates damage.

On the other hand, I find that the evidence is clear and convincing that peaches and apricots and peach and apricot trees were damaged by the escape of the fluorine and fluorides from defendant's plant, and, that each plaintiff owning a peach or apricot orchard, sustained a substantial damage from said source to his crops and trees during each year since 1958. This fact is not seriously contested by the defendant. The defendant recognized this damage and voluntarily dispatched its crews to different peach orchards in the area to ascertain the amount and settle for the damages caused to the orchard owners. Defendant agrees that it settled the damage claims of plaintiffs Ellett, Feling, Fleck, Weston, Meyer, W. H. Meyers, Jr., Wachter and Polehn for loss of prune and apricot crops and damage to peaches and damage to or loss of peach, prune or apricot trees occurring as a result of the operation of the defendant's aluminum plant prior to January 1, 1962. I find that said damage to each of said landowners was substantial, although not approaching $10,000.00 as to each plaintiff, or group of plaintiffs, interested in one tract of land. On the other hand, I find that each of said plaintiffs or group of plaintiffs, owning one particular tract of land, in good faith, alleged damage in excess of $10,000.00 in the Pre-Trial Order, that there is a diversity of citizenship and that the Court has jurisdiction.

REMEDY

Defendant concedes that plaintiffs repeatedly warned it of the emissions, damages to and alleged trespasses on plaintiffs' property. The evidence supports, and I find, that the emissions from defendant's plant continued to settle on plaintiffs' land and orchards to and including the time of the trial. That the continued settling of the fluorides from defendant's plant on plaintiffs' property constituted a continuing trespass, as a matter of law, is beyond question. *Martin v. Reynolds Metals Co.*, 221 Or. 86, 342 P.2d 790 (1959); *Fairview Farms, Inc. v. Reynolds Metals Co., supra*; *Reynolds Metals Co., et al, v. Lampert*, 316 F.2d 272 (9 Cir. 1963), re-hearing denied November 15, 1963, 324 F.2d 465.

That equity will intervene to prevent a continuing trespass is well recognized. . . .

Plaintiffs [Defendants?] rely on *Fairview Farms, Inc. v. Reynolds Metals Co., supra*, and in particular on that portion of the opinion in which it is indicated that an award of compensatory damages for past trespasses and future trespasses would adequately compensate the plaintiffs. The basic reason the Court did not grant an injunction in the Fairview case was that there was no evidence the acts or conduct of Reynolds were reasonably certain to be repeated in the future. Here, of course, the evidence is entirely to the contrary. Here, Harvey has taken the position that it has done everything possible to eliminate the problem, and that it must continue to operate with its present control system. The 1962-1963 improvement by Harvey was of no particular significance.

Also wide of the mark is *Reynolds Metals Co. v. Wand*, 308 F.2d 504 (9 Cir. 1962). The opinion in Wand makes a point of the fact that the company had recently installed a new system for the minimizing of the escape of the gasses, fumes and particulates, at a cost of $2,139,185.00, and that there was nothing in the record to show that any further lessening of the escape of such materials was possible. The record before me contains clear and convincing evidence that the defendant has yet to install a hood system over and around the cells, similar to that installed by Reynolds.

. . . .

I find I that the injury in this case is irreparable to each of said plaintiffs and that they would be relegated to pursuing a judicial merry-go-round in actions at law, if they were required to seek a remedy in a Court of Law.

BURDEN OF PROOF

Throughout, I have taken the position that the burden of proof was on the plaintiffs on all issues. I find they have sustained that burden. I am now convinced that once the plaintiffs established that fluorides were deposited on their lands from the plant of the defendant, the burden of going forward with the evidence was on the defendant to show that the use of its property, which caused the injury, was unavoidable or that it could not be prevented except by the expenditure of such vast sums of money as would substantially deprive it of the use of its property. This seems to be the general rule. *Herring v. H. W. Walker Co.*, 409 Pa. 126, 185 A.2d 565 (1962).

. . . .

It is an obvious fact that defendant made no attempt to carry the burden of going forward with the evidence. On the other hand, the plaintiffs called experts, whose testimony was clear and convincing to the effect that the amount of the emitted material could be substantially reduced, or almost eliminated, without an expenditure which would substantially deprive defendant of the use of its property. Frankly stated, there is no good reason why the defendant company, like other companies similarly situated, should not make a reasonable expenditure in the erection of hoods, or like devices, over or around its pots or cells. To require less would be placing a premium on air pollution. What's good for Reynolds should be good for Harvey, even though the cost of the new system might exceed $2,000,000.00, as it did in the case of Reynolds.

. . . .

Defendant's contention that the Oregon Air Pollution Law[1] pre-empts this field is without foundation. Specifically recognized by ORS 449.820 is the right by an individual to prosecute a suit to abate a private or public nuisance. The

[1] ORS 449.765 *et seq.*

record in this case is sufficiently broad to be viewed as a suit to abate a nuisance, as well as a suit to enjoin a continuing trespass. For that matter, a continuing trespass could well be a nuisance. The York cases recognize that the deposit of smoke screenings and particulates on the lands of another amounts to a nuisance. The rule of construction *"expressio unius est exclusio alterius"*, for which defendant contends, is not a rule of law, but is a mere guide in determining intent and such a rule must be harmonized with all other rules of construction. *In re Moore's Estate*, 210 Or. 23, 307 P.2d 483, 65 A.L.R.2d 715, mandate recalled 210 Or. 23, 308 P.2d 180. It is a rule which should be applied with caution and merely as an auxiliary rule to determine the legislative intention.

Although recognizing a distinction between a trespass and a private nuisance, *Martin v. Reynolds Metals Co., supra*, involving the same type of affluents as here presented, also recognizes that the words are used interchangeably. The first mention, by the Legislature, of abatement of a nuisance, relating to the pollution of air, was in the enactment of 1959, Chapter 357, Oregon Laws 1959, Section 11.

In common parlance, a nuisance includes a continuing trespass; a nuisance is defined in Webster's New International Dictionary, 2d Edition, page 1672, as ". . . 2. Law. An offensive, annoying, unpleasant, or obnoxious thing or practice; a cause or source of annoyance, *especially a continuing or repeated invasion or disturbance of another's right*. . . . Anything that works a hurt, inconvenience or damage. Blackstone." In construing a statute, words of common use are to be given their natural, plain and obvious meaning. Words of common use are to be taken in their natural and obvious meaning and signification. *Superior Oil & Refining Syndicate v. Handley*, 99 Or. 146, 195 P. 159. Thus, it is seen, that the common ordinary definition of nuisance includes the continued or repeated invasion or disturbance of a right, such as a continuing trespass. Surely, the Oregon Legislature employed the word in that sense when enacting ORS 449.820. Furthermore, all statutes which encroach on personal or property rights of an individual are to be construed strictly, and in the absence of express words or necessary implication, it will be presumed that such statute is not intended to interfere with or prejudice a private right or title.

We must assume that the Oregon Legislature was familiar with this rule of construction and that it never intended, by this legislation, to deprive individuals, such as plaintiffs, of their common law right to enjoin a flagrant violation of those rights nor to pursue their right to enjoin a continuing trespass in a proper Court.

Pinpointing the ever increasing problem of air pollution is the great concern of our national and state legislatures as expressed in the Air Pollution Control Act of 1955, 42 U.S.C. §§ 1857-1857g, as supplemented by the Clean Air Act of 1963, and the Oregon legislation to which I have previously referred.

The defendant will be required to install proper hoods around the cells and electrostatic precipitators in usual, advantageous and proper places in the plant, within one year of the date of the decree. Otherwise, an injunction will issue as prayed for by plaintiffs.

There is no room for application of the doctrine of balancing of the equities at this time. The required improvements should entirely eliminate the problem.

Conforming findings and decree shall be prepared, served and presented by counsel for plaintiffs.

LUDLOW v. COLORADO ANIMAL BY-PRODUCTS CO.

Supreme Court of Utah (1943)
104 Utah 221, 137 P.2d 347

McDONOUGH, Justice

Plaintiffs instituted suit against defendant to permanently enjoin the reconstruction of defendant's rendering plant near Benjamin in the vicinity of plaintiffs' properties. The trial court found that the plant as operated was a nuisance, but denied injunctive relief and permitted plaintiffs to file amended pleadings to recover damages for depreciation of their properties occasioned by the maintenance of the nuisance. Defendant appeals from the judgment and decree wherein the plaintiffs are severally awarded damages for impairment of market value of their properties.

About 1933 the defendant corporation acquired the property of a brick manufacturing plant. For a while it used the property as a receiving station for dead animals, slaughterhouse offal, etc., preliminary to shipment to its rendering plants elsewhere. In the latter part of 1934 defendant installed some machinery and equipment, together with a cooker, to render animals. The cooker went into operation early in 1935. Dead animals were collected not only from the surrounding area, but from other parts of Utah. Defendant occasionally purchased a dead animal from one of the plaintiffs. No action was taken by plaintiffs to enjoin operation of the plant, and no complaint was made about the stench carried into the atmosphere from its operations, until after the old plant was destroyed by fire on April 8, 1937.

For a while after the plant burned, defendant reverted to the practice of using the premises as a receiving station for shipment of animals and animal products to other rendering plants. Shortly thereafter it began the reconstruction of the plant as a fireproof structure on a somewhat larger scale. Residents and property owners in the vicinity of the plant filed protests with the county commissioners, requesting that defendant be prohibited form rebuilding the plant, on the ground it constituted a stench nuisance. The manager of defendant corporation attended the meeting with the residents and property owners on at least two occasions, and on June 8, 1937, he assured the board of county commissioners that the type of plant in the process of construction would be modern and sanitary, and that it would not be offensive in the least. Two months later, before the plant was completed, plaintiffs commenced this suit to enjoin operation and maintenance of the plant on the ground it would constitute a nuisance by reason of the "unwholesome smoke, gases, vapors, and stenches arising and resulting" from the rendering of carcasses.

The temporary restraining order granted by the court was subsequently lifted to enable the defendant to demonstrate that all objectionable features of the old plant had been abated and remedied. At the trial even witnesses for defendant admitted there was a stench from the operation of both the old and new plants which permeated the atmosphere and reached the properties of some of the plaintiffs intermittently, depending on the direction of wind and air currents.

There was ample evidence that the air was frequently befouled from the operation of the rendering plant. Various witnesses for plaintiffs testified that the odors from cooking carcasses went off into the atmosphere and reached the various properties of plaintiffs; that such odors were obnoxious to such a degree it was impossible to enjoy a meal when the wind carried the stench over to the homes of witnesses; that such condition existed both before the old plant was destroyed by fire and after the new plant was put into operation; that they were awakened at nights and rendered sleepless by the nauseous smell; and that the clothing of men working in the fields emitted an offensive odor for hours after exposure to the fetid air from the vicinity of the plant. Nearly all of the witnesses for plaintiffs testified that the stench was just as bad from the new plant as from the old one.

At the conclusion of the original trial the court entered a written memorandum of decision in which it found that the operation of the plant constituted a nuisance, but held that plaintiffs should not have injunctive relief by reason of delay in applying for an injunction; and that in lieu of an injunction plaintiffs should be permitted to file supplemental pleadings to obtain damages for depreciation of their properties by reason of such nuisance. A supplemental complaint was filed, in which parties as to whom the action previously had been dismissed, were joined as plaintiffs. Plaintiffs alleged depreciation of the value of their properties by reason of the existence of the nuisance created by defendant's rendering plant. In the final judgment and decree, damages were awarded to all except one of plaintiffs.

. . . .

We shall first consider the contention that there was no competent evidence that the operation of defendant's rendering plant created a nuisance either before or after the new plant was built. Among other things counsel for appellant argue that the evidence was undisputed that within a radius of several miles from the plant there were in existence at the time of the trial or there had been in existence several years previously, the following facilities and industries which defendant claims rendered the area an industrial rather than agricultural one: (1) A sugar factory; (2) a pea vinery; (3) two railroads; (4) a flour mill; (5) an alfalfa feed mill; (6) beet storage and loading chutes adjoining each railroad; (7) wool loading platforms; (8) a local brickyard; (9) livestock feeding yards; and (10) livestock loading pens on both railroads. On this appeal it is strenuously urged by defendant that such facilities made the region an industrial area, and potentially valuable chiefly for industrial purposes, and not for residential or agricultural purposes; that smells and odors emanating from defendant's plant are not the only obnoxious odors, there being the smell of decaying pea vines at the pea vinery and the odor of beet pulp at the sugar factory during certain months of the year; and that such smells constitute mere incidents of an industrial area. Defendant argues that plaintiffs could not be injured any more than the general public, and that neither the odors from its plant nor its method of operation could constitute a nuisance.

Appellant points out that the trial court found that defendant's plant performs a useful service in disposing of carcasses in an efficient manner instead of allowing them to rot in the fields or to create a menace to health by shallow burial; that a plant of such character properly located is beneficial to the public. They contend, therefore, that the plant could not be located to serve a useful purpose except in an industrial area along a railroad where it could have proper shipping facilities; and that the conclusion of the trial court to the effect that the rendering plant was and is a nuisance as operated, is inconsistent with the aforesaid finding of fact.

Such contentions are untenable. The mere fact that an area is not incorporated in a city or town with zoning regulations does not warrant establishment of commercial institutions which emit the described stenches in such region where life thereby will be rendered unpleasant to the residents thereof. Nor does the fact that an industry may serve a useful purpose or produce commercial commodities warrant its location at a place which merely suits the convenience of the owner or operator, in utter disregard for the effect it has on the value or enjoyment of other properties.

We also must reject the argument that the existence of some of the facilities pointed out by counsel for defendants, made the region an industrial rather than an agricultural area; although in view of what we have said, the fact that a region actually may be industrial does not justify the creation with impunity of odors or stenches to an excessive degree which unreasonably annoy others in the legitimate use of their properties or in their occupations, especially when such conditions depreciate the value of other properties in such area. The evidence shows that the sugar factory, pea vinery, stock-feeding yards and loading platforms are essential to the marketing of agricultural products and livestock. The region consists principally of farms on which there are homes and other buildings characteristic of rural life. In most instances the farms and livestock raisers reside on their farms.

Section 104-56-1, R. S. U. 1933 (same, U. C. A. 1943), defines the term "nuisance" and provides for injunction or damages:

> "Anything which is injurious to health, or indecent, or *offensive to the senses,* or an obstruction to the free use of property, *so as to interfere with the comfortable enjoyment of life or property, is a nuisance and the subject of an action.* Such action may be brought by any person whose property is injuriously affected, or whose personal enjoyment is lessened by the nuisance; and by the judgment the nuisance may be enjoined or abated, and damages may also be recovered." (Italics added.)

Section 103-41-1 provides in part:

> "Whatever is dangerous to human life or health, and whatever renders soil, air, water and food impure or unwholesome, are declared to be nuisances and to be illegal. . . ."

It could hardly be urged that the maintenance of a condition which is rendered illegal by legislative enactment under the police power of the state, could be said to be lawful merely because it is a result of the operation of an industry which in itself is lawful to operate when done in a lawful manner and at the proper place. When an industry is of such a character that it produces foul odors, those who are responsible for its operation have the duty to place it where it will not result in injury to the property of others. The mere fact that there may already exist in the area a condition which may be obnoxious to some persons, does not create a license for establishment of other more offensive conditions.

There can be no doubt about the fact that the operation of defendant's plant, by reason of the nauseating odors and stenches thereby produced, constituted an intermittent but frequently recurring nuisance within the meaning of our statutes. . . .

In connection with its contention that there was a misjoinder of parties plaintiff, defendant apparently concedes that if the suit had been maintained solely for purposes of determining whether or not plaintiffs should have a decree enjoining operations of the plant as a nuisance, and the trial court had not permitted the injection of damages into the case, all of the plaintiffs as property owners whose properties were affected by the plant operations, might properly be joined as plaintiffs. Appellant takes the position that when the trial court denied injunctive relief it should have made findings of fact, conclusions of law and decree in favor of defendant, without prejudice to the right of each plaintiff to bring a separate action for damages. Appellant claims it was error for the court to allow the case to be reopened by filing a supplemental complaint. It argues that in the supplemental pleadings there are eleven separate causes of action for damages, no two of which are alike, and that as a result there is a misjoinder of parties plaintiff such as precluded defendant from having a fair trial as to each plaintiff.

The court decided there had been unnecessary delay in seeking injunctive relief after the nuisance was abated by the fire, and until after defendant had spent considerable sums of money in reconstruction and enlargement of the plant facilities. However, as soon as plaintiffs discovered there was any intention to reconstruct the plant they filed protests with the county commissioners, and defendant assured the commissioners all of the objectionable features of the old plant would be eliminated. Plaintiffs did not cross-appeal, so we are not required to determine whether the court abused its discretion in denying an injunction. The court took the position that the case was not concluded upon determination of whether the nuisance should be enjoined. It expressly retained jurisdiction for purposes of final adjudication to afford complete relief between the parties and to avoid a multiplicity of suits. The practical effect of the court's ruling was that inasmuch as injunctive relief was within the discretion of the court, some other appropriate relief in lieu thereof might be granted. The trial court considered a proper solution would be just compensation by way of allowing each plaintiff the amount his property was depreciated by the recurrence of the nuisance.

. . . .

In an equity action where the prayer is for both specific and general relief, such as for an injunction and "any further or other relief which the court shall deem appropriate in the premises," having once acquired jurisdiction of the parties and the subject matter, the court will retain that jurisdiction until full justice has been achieved between the parties, even if equitable relief is denied. This is especially true in this state where we have only one form of civil action, and various kinds of relief can be administered in the same action. Where a number of persons join in an action to restrain the operation of a plant or business as a nuisance, and also request general relief, if for some cause equitable relief is denied although the court finds there is actually a recurring nuisance; notwithstanding the nuisance would warrant each plaintiff in maintaining a separate action for damages for depreciation of his property, and the only separate issue is the amount of compensation due each plaintiff in lieu of injunction, it is proper for the court to allow plaintiffs so joined in the action to amend their pleadings or file supplemental pleadings and proceed to trial for determination of what compensation each plaintiff is entitled to receive, without requiring them to institute separate actions.

Defendant further complains that the supplemental pleadings in effect constituted initiation of a new action in which there was misjoinder of plaintiffs, each having a separate cause of action for damages; for the suit was dismissed as to several of the plaintiffs when the court denied a permanent injunction, but they joined in the supplemental complaint and thereby came back into the case. Some of them were awarded compensation. In view of the language in the *Kinsman* case, and the fact the other parties similarly situated might have intervened by leave of court, we do not see how defendant was prejudiced in any manner. There is no contention that a defense materially different from the defense to the claims asserted by any of the other plaintiffs had to be prepared by defendant. . . .

Appellant also assigns as error the trial court's refusal to hold that action was barred by the pleaded statutes of limitations. Its position is that the nuisance, if it ever existed, was a continuing and a permanent one, and that the right of action arose immediately upon its creation and consequently it was barred at the date this suit was instituted. However, such argument overlooks the fact that the rendering plant did not commence operations as such until the early part of 1935. The plant was destroyed by fire a little over two years later. The shortest period of limitations pleaded was three years. Not only was the nuisance effectually abated by the fire, but before the plant was reconstructed and placed in operation again this suit was commenced, which was within three years of the time the rendering of animals originally began. Furthermore, the trial court properly held that the nuisance was a recurring rather than a continuing one, and therefore very properly held that the statutes of limitations were inapplicable. *Thackery v. Union Portland Cement Co.,* 64 Utah 437, 231 P. 813.

There is considerable argument to the effect that the wrong method of computing damages was employed. The measure of damages for the maintenance of a recurrent nuisance is the depreciation of market value of the property affected. *Thackery v. Union Portland Cement Co., supra.* The same measure of damages applies to permanent uninterrupted nuisances. *See Lewis v. Pingree National Bank*, 47 Utah 35, 151 P. 558, L. R. A. 1916C, 1260. It appears to be the view of appellant that the rule of diminution of market value was not properly applied. It is claimed that witnesses for plaintiffs made valuations from which they computed depreciation on some theory of absence of the plant structure and without reference to other existing industries, activities and facilities. However, at least one witness indicated he took into consideration the surrounding conditions, and he based depreciation solely on the odors emanating from defendant's plant. It appears that the trial court based depreciation on the frequent recurrence of stench, not on any assumption that the building and other physical structures of appellant as located constituted a nuisance. The findings and conclusions of the court indicate that in assessing damages the trial judge used the proper criterion—the difference in market value of each tract with its improvements without the stench nuisance existing, as compared with the value as affected by such odors.

It is claimed that the damages awarded are excessive in the light of all the evidence. For instance, it is pointed out that one witness testified that he depreciated all structures and other improvements on several tracts 100 per cent, and on other tracts 75 per cent, although such improvements so depreciated included pig pens, corrals and chicken coops. The findings of fact indicate that any extravagant assertions of any witness as to valuations or depreciation were disregarded by the court.

. . . .

On cross-examination counsel for defendant directed attention of witnesses to the railroad tracks, the sugar factory, the pea vinery and other facilities and industries, so there does not appear to be any substance to the argument that such other industries or facilities were disregarded in arriving at valuations by the court. The trial judge viewed the premises and the area. There was ample evidence at the two trials to support the conclusion of the court that the region at that time was in fact an agricultural and cattle raising area, and depended on the facilities of the pea vinery as well as beet pulp from the sugar factory. Most of the witnesses testified that while on their own properties they could not detect any odor coming from the beet pulp plant or the pea vinery, so it may well be that it was not necessary to take such odors into consideration. The stench from the rendering plant was declared to be so much worse and so much more offensive than any other odor, that there was little if any possibility that the witnesses were actually confused as to the source of the offensive odors which made living or working on their properties so uncomfortable.

. . . .

Counsel for appellant point out that on the premises of some of the plaintiffs there were filthy corrals, manure piles, rotting carcasses and other offensive conditions which produced disagreeable odors. Counsel claim that as a result, such plaintiffs were precluded from complaining about any stench created by the operations of defendant's plant. Inexcusable as such conditions might have been, there is no proof that they resulted in any damage to any other property or generally depreciated the neighborhood. Naturally such conditions would have a hearing on market value, and such conditions were called to the attention of the court. All of such objectionable features and unsanitary conditions could be remedied by the owners or occupants, while the stench from defendant's plant could not be abated by the individual plaintiffs. Furthermore, there was testimony that the odors produced on some of plaintiffs' properties did not surcharge the atmosphere, while the stench from the rendering plant was worse than any odor and permeated the atmosphere for a considerable distance.

In view of the fact that defendant's own witnesses valued the properties less than 10 per cent under the valuations determined by the court, absent the nuisance, it is not likely that the trial court failed to recognize depreciation resulting from the remediable conditions on plaintiffs' lands. The court had to determine the market value of the properties of each plaintiff as they existed with reference to all conditions other than the stench nuisance, and then determine the margin of depreciation which resulted from the frequent recurrence of the obnoxious odors from defendant's plant. Considering the relatively small margin of difference between the values fixed by defendant's witnesses and the values determined by the court, absent the stench, it does not appear the court yielded to any excessive appraisals nor overlooked any of the elements which affect market value. As indicated by the United States Supreme Court in *United States v. Miller et al.*, 317 U. S. 369, 63 S. Ct. 276, 87 L. Ed 336 . . . exactitude in determining market value cannot be attained.

. . . .

The evidence clearly shows that the new plant did produce obnoxious odors, whether or not to the same degree as the old plant. When defendant built a fire-proof structure it manifested an intention to operate permanently. After defendant failed to make good its promises, and placed in full operation its new plant on a permanent basis, it became apparent that defendant would continue at frequent intervals to create such stench nuisance, and the court very properly determined depreciation as of the time when the new plant was in operation.

. . . .

BOOMER v. ATLANTIC CEMENT CO.

New York Court of Appeals (1970)
26 N. Y. 2d 219, 309 N.Y.S.2d 312, 257 N.E.2d 870

BERGAN, Judge

. . . .

The public concern with air pollution arising from many sources in industry and in transportation is currently accorded ever wider recognition accompanied by a growing sense of responsibility in State and Federal Governments to control it. Cement plants are obvious sources of air pollution in the neighborhoods where they operate.

But there is now before the court private litigation in which individual property owners have sought specific relief from a single plant operation. The threshold question raised by the division of view on this appeal is whether the court should resolve the litigation between the parties now before it as equitably as seems possible, or whether, seeking promotion of the general public welfare, it should channel private litigation into broad public objectives.

A court performs its essential function when it decides the rights of parties before it. Its decision of private controversies may sometimes greatly affect public issues. Large questions of law are often resolved by the manner in which private litigation is decided. But this is normally an incident to the court's main function to settle controversy. It is a rare exercise of judicial power to use a decision in private litigation as a purposeful mechanism to achieve direct public objectives greatly beyond the rights and interests before this court.

Effective control of air pollution is a problem presently far from solution even with the full public and financial powers of government. In large measure adequate technical procedures are yet to be developed and some that appear possible may be economically impracticable.

It seems apparent that the amelioration of air pollution will depend on technical research in great depth; on a carefully balanced consideration of the economic impact of close regulation, and of the actual effect on public health. It is likely to require massive public expenditure and to demand more than any local community can accomplish and to depend on regional and interstate controls.

A court should not try to do this on its own as a by-product of private litigation, and it seems manifest that the judicial establishment is neither equipped in the limited nature of any judgment it can pronounce nor prepared to lay down and implement an effective policy for the elimination of air pollution. This is an area beyond the circumference of one private lawsuit. It is a direct responsibility for government and should not thus be undertaken as an incident to solving a dispute between property owners and a single cement plant—one of many—in the Hudson River valley.

The cement making operations of defendant have been found by the court at Special Term to have damaged the nearby properties of plaintiffs in these two actions. That court, as it has been noted, accordingly found defendant maintained a nuisance, and this has been affirmed at the Appellate Division. The total damage to plaintiffs' properties is, however, relatively small in comparison with the value of defendant's operation and with the consequences of the injunction which plaintiffs seek.

The ground for the denial of injunction, notwithstanding the finding both that there is a nuisance and that plaintiffs have been damaged substantially, is the large disparity in economic consequences of the nuisance and of the injunction. This theory cannot, however, be sustained without overruling a doctrine which has been consistently reaffirmed in several leading cases in this court and which has never been disavowed here, namely that where a nuisance has been found and where there has been any substantial damage shown by the party complaining an injunction will be granted.

The rule in New York has been that such a nuisance will be enjoined although marked disparity be shown in economic consequence between the effect of the injunction and the effect of the nuisance.

The problem of disparity in economic consequence was sharply in focus in Whalen v. Union Bag & Paper Co. (208 N.Y. 1). A pulp mill entailing an investment of more than a million dollars polluted a stream in which plaintiff, who owned a farm, was "a lower riparian owner." The economic loss to plaintiff from this pollution was small. This court, reversing the Appellate Division, reinstated the injunction granted by the Special Term against the argument of the mill owner that in view of "the slight advantage to plaintiff and the great loss that will be inflicted on the defendant" an injunction should not be granted (p. 2). "Such a balancing of injuries cannot be justified by the circumstances of this case," Judge Werner noted (p. 4). He continued: "Although the damage to the plaintiff may be slight as compared with the defendant's expense of abating the condition, that is not a good reason for refusing an injunction" (p. 5).

Thus the unconditional injunction granted at Special Term was reinstated. The rule laid down in that case, then, is that whenever the damage resulting from a nuisance is found not "unsubstantial," viz., $100 a year, injunction would follow. This states a rule that had been followed in this court with marked consistency (*McCarty v. Natural Carbonic Gas Co.*, 189 N.Y. 40; *Strobel v. Kerr Salt Co.*, 164 N.Y. 303; *Campbell v. Seaman,* 63 N.Y. 568).

There are cases where injunction has been denied. McCann v. Chasm Power Co. (211 N.Y. 301) is one of them. There, however, the damage shown by plaintiffs was not only unsubstantial, it was non-existent. Plaintiffs owned a rocky bank of the stream in which defendant had raised the level of the water. This had no economic or other adverse consequence to plaintiffs, and thus injunctive relief was denied. Similar is the basis for denial of injunction in Forstmann v. Joray Holding Co. (244 N.Y. 22), where no benefit to plaintiffs could be seen from the injunction sought (p. 32). Thus if, within Whalen v. Union Bag & Paper Co. (*supra*), which authoritatively states the rule in New York, the damage to plaintiffs in these present cases from defendant's cement plant is "not unsubstantial," an injunction should follow.

Although the court at Special Term and the Appellate Division held that injunction should be denied, it was found that plaintiffs had been damaged in various specific amounts up to the time of the trial and damages to the respective plaintiffs was awarded for those amounts. The effect of this was, injunction having been denied, plaintiffs could maintain successive actions at law for damages thereafter as further damage was incurred.

The court at Special Term also found the amount of permanent damage attributable to each plaintiff, for the guidance of the parties in the event both sides stipulated to the payment and acceptance of such permanent damage as a settlement of all the controversies among the parties. The total of permanent damages to all plaintiffs thus found was $185,000. This basis of adjustment has not resulted in any stipulation by the parties.

This result at Special Term and at the Appellate Division is a departure from a rule that has become settled; but to follow the rule literally in these cases would be to close down the plant at once. This court is fully agreed to avoid that immediately drastic remedy; the difference in view is how best to avoid it.[2]

One alternative is to grant the injunction but postpone its effect to a specified future date to give opportunity for technical advances to permit defendant to eliminate the nuisance; another is to grant the injunction conditioned on the payment of permanent damages to plaintiffs which would compensate them for the total economic loss to their property present and future caused by defendant's operations. For reasons which will be developed the court chooses the latter alternative.

If the injunction were to be granted unless within a short period, *e.g.*, 18 months, the nuisance be abated by improved methods, there would be no assurance that any significant technical improvement would occur.

The parties could settle this private litigation at any time if defendant paid enough money and the imminent threat of closing the plant would build up the pressure on defendant. If there were no improved techniques found, there would inevitably be applications to the court at Special Term for extensions of time to perform on showing of good faith efforts to find such techniques.

Moreover, techniques to eliminate dust and other annoying by-products of cement making are unlikely to be developed by any research the defendant can undertake within any short period, but will depend on the total resources of the cement industry nation-wide and throughout the world. The problem is universal wherever cement is made.

For obvious reasons the rate of the research is beyond control of defendant. If at the end of eighteen months the whole industry has not found a technical solution a court would be hard put to close down this one cement plant if due regard be given to equitable principles.

On the other hand, to grant the injunction unless defendant pays plaintiff such permanent damages as may be fixed by the court seems to do justice between the contending parties. All of the attributions of economic loss to the properties on which plaintiffs' complaints are based will have been redressed.

The nuisance complained of by these plaintiffs may have other public or private consequences, but these particular parties are the only ones who have sought remedies and the judgment proposed will fully redress them. The limitation of relief granted is a limitation only within the four corners of these actions and does not foreclose public health or other public agencies from seeking proper relief in a proper court.

It seems reasonable to think that the risk of being required to pay permanent damages to injured property owners by cement plant owners would itself be a reasonably effective spur to research for improved techniques to minimize nuisance.

The power of the court to condition on equitable grounds the continuance of an injunction on the payment of permanent damages seems undoubted (*see, e.g.*, the alternatives considered in *McCarty v. Natural Carbonic Gas Co., supra*, as well as *Strobel v. Kerr Salt Co., supra*).

---

[2] Respondent's investment in the plant is in excess of $45,000,000. There are over 300 people employed there.

The damage base here suggested is consistent with the general rule in those nuisance cases where damages are allowed. "Where a nuisance is of such a permanent and unabatable character that a single recovery can be had, including the whole damage past and future resulting therefrom, there can be but one recovery" (66 C.J.S., Nuisances, sec. 140, p. 947). It has been said that permanent damages are allowed where the loss recoverable would obviously be small as compared with the cost of removal of the nuisance (Kentucky-Ohio Gas Co. v. Bowling, 95 S.W.2d 1, 5).

The present cases and the remedy here proposed are in a number of other respects rather similar to Northern Indiana Public Service Co. v. W. J. & M. S. Vesey (200 N.E. 620) decided by the Supreme Court of Indiana. The gases, odors, ammonia and smoke from the Northern Indiana company's gas plant damaged the nearby Vesey greenhouse operation. An injunction and damages were sought, but an injunction was denied and the relief granted was limited to permanent damages "present, past, and future" (p. 634).

Denial of injunction was grounded on a public interest in the operation of the gas plant and on the court's conclusion "that less injury would be occasioned by requiring the appellant [Public Service] to pay the appellee [Vesey] all damages suffered by it . . . than by enjoining the operation of the gas plant, and that the maintenance and operation of the gas plant should not be enjoined" (p. 625).

The Indiana Supreme Court opinion continued: "When the trial court refused injunctive relief to the appellee upon the ground of public interest in the continuance of the gas plant, it properly retained jurisdiction of the case and awarded full compensation to the appellee. This is upon the general equitable principle that equity will give full relief in one action and prevent a multiplicity of suits" (p. 627).

It was held that in this type of continuing and recurrent nuisance permanent damages were appropriate (*see also City of Amarillo v. Ware*, 120 Tex. 456, 40 S.W.2d 57, 61) where recurring overflows from a system of storm sewers were treated as the kind of nuisance for which permanent depreciation of value of affected property would be recoverable.

There is some parallel to the conditioning of an injunction on the payment of damages in the noted "elevated railway cases" (*Pappenheim v. Metropolitan El. Ry Co.*, 128 N.Y. 436, and others which followed). Decisions in these cases were based on the finding that the railways created a nuisance as to adjacent property owners, but in lieu of enjoining their operation, the court allowed permanent damages.

Judge Finch reviewing these cases in Ferguson v. Village of Hamburg (272 N.Y. 234, 239-240), said: "The courts decided that the plaintiffs had a valuable right which was being impaired, but did not grant an absolute injunction or require the railway companies to resort to separate condemnation proceedings. Instead they held that a court of equity could ascertain the damages and grant an injunction which was not to be effective unless the defendant failed to pay the amount fixed as damages for the past and permanent injury inflicted."

Thus it seems fair to both sides to grant permanent damages to plaintiffs which will terminate this private litigation. The theory of damage is the "servitude on land" of plaintiffs imposed by defendant's nuisance. (*See United States v. Causby*, 328 U.S. 256, 261, 262, 267, where the term "servitude" addressed to the land was used by Justice Douglas relating to the effect of airplane noise on property near an airport.)

The judgment, by allowance of permanent damages imposing a servitude on land, which is the basis of the actions, would preclude future recovery by plaintiffs or their grantees (*See Northern Indiana Public Service Co. v. W. J. & M. S. Vesey, supra*, p. 623).

This should be placed beyond debate by a provision of the judgment that the payment by defendant and the acceptance by plaintiffs of permanent damages found by the court shall be in compensation for a servitude on the land.

Although the Special Term has found permanent damages as a possible basis of settlement of the litigation, on remission the court should be entirely free to re-examine this subject. It may again find the permanent damage already found; or make new findings.

The orders should be reversed, without costs, and the cases remitted to Special Term to grant an injunction which shall be vacated upon payment by defendant of such amounts of permanent damage to the respective plaintiffs as shall for this purpose be determined by the court.

JASEN, J. (dissenting)—I agree with the majority that a reversal is required here, but I do not subscribe to the newly enunciated doctrine of assessment of permanent damages, in lieu of an injunction, where substantial property rights have been impaired by the creation of a nuisance.

It has long been the rule in this state, as the majority acknowledges, that a nuisance which results in substantial continuing damage to neighbors must be enjoined (*Whalen v. Union Bag & Paper Co.*, 208 N.Y. 1; Campbell v. Seaman, 63 N.Y. 568; *see also Kennedy v. Moog*, 21 N.Y.2d 966). To now change the rule to permit the cement company to continue polluting the air indefinitely upon the payment of permanent damages is, in my opinion, compounding the magnitude of a very serious problem in our state and nation today.

In recognition of this problem, the Legislature of this state has enacted the Air Pollution Control Act (Public Health Law, secs. 1264-1299-m) declaring that it is the state policy to require the use of all available and reasonable methods to prevent and control air pollution (Public Health Law, sec. 1265).

The harmful nature and widespread occurrence of air pollution have been extensively documented. Congressional hearings have revealed that air pollution causes substantial property damage, as well as being a contributing factor to a rising incidence of lung cancer, emphysema, bronchitis and asthma.

The specific problem faced here is known as particulate contamination because of the fine dust particles emanating from defendant's cement plant. The particular type of nuisance is not new, having appeared in many cases for at least the past sixty years (*See Hulbert v. Calif. Portland Cement Co.*, 161 Cal. 239, 1911). It is interesting to note that cement production has recently been identified as a significant source of particulate contamination in the Hudson Valley. This type of pollution, wherein very small particles escape and stay in the atmosphere, has been denominated as the type of air pollution which produces the greatest hazard to human health. We have thus a nuisance which not only is damaging to the plaintiffs, but also is decidedly harmful to the general public.

I see grave dangers in overruling our long-established rule of granting an injunction where a nuisance results in substantial continuing damage. In permitting the injunction to become inoperative upon the payment of permanent damages, the majority is, in effect, licensing a continuing wrong. It is the same as saying to the cement company, you may continue to do harm to your neighbors so long as you pay a fee for it. Furthermore, once such permanent damages are assessed and paid, the incentive to alleviate the wrong would be eliminated, thereby continuing air pollution of an area without abatement.

[The dissent by Jasen J. asserts that the kind of inverse condemnation here established is not constitutionally permissible under the New York State Constitution because, in effect, it takes property for a public use without just compensation. The dissent suggests that the Court follow earlier precedents and issue an injunction effective within 18 months unless in the interim the cement company finds a method of control to abate the nuisance.]

In each action:

Order reversed, without costs, and the case remitted to Supreme Court, Albany County, for further proceedings in accordance with the opinion herein. Opinion by *Bergan, J.* All concur except *Jasen, J.*, who dissents in part and votes to reverse in an opinion. *Breitel and Gibson, JJ.*, taking no part.

NOTES

For a recommendation that in actions for damages based on air pollution, the causes of action in nuisance be combined into a single private tort of air pollution so as to avoid conflicting statutes of limitations and difficulties, see F. Grad, Treatise on Environmental Law, § 2.02[1][d]. For a discussion of the role of common law remedies today, even in the age of environmental statutes, see F. Grad, Treatise on Environmental Law, Ch. 18.

A detailed analysis of private causes of action and their underlying legal theories may be found in Prosser, Torts, pp. 592-633 (3d ed. 1964); Prosser, *Private Action for Public Nuisance*, 52 Va. L. Rev. 997 (1966). *Also see* Juergensmeyer, *Control of Air Pollution Through Assertion of Private Rights*, 1967 Duke L.J. 1126.

§ 2.03 Government Regulation of Air Pollution

[1] Exercise of State and Local Police Power for "Smoke Control"—Old Law with Current Implications

Digest of Health Laws, 143
Boston 1904
Regulation Adopted by the Board of Health, August 22, 1901

Sieving, screening, etc., regulated.

No substance in any way liable to be distributed or blown about by wind or air currents shall be sieved, screened, agitated, or otherwise handled or exposed in any street or public place, nor elsewhere in such a manner that particles or portions of such substances are scattered, blown or otherwise pass into or upon any such street or public place, or into or upon any inhabited buildings. This shall not apply to the delivery of coal, provided suitable precautions for dampening are taken.

Beating of carpets, etc., regulated.

No carpets, rugs, mats or similar articles shall be beaten in any street or public place, and no carpets, rugs, mats, old garments, or similar articles shall be beaten or cleaned upon or near inhabited buildings unless reasonable precaution is taken to prevent dust particles or portions of said articles from being blown, scattered or otherwise passing from the place where such beating or cleaning is carried on.

Prevention of dust blowing about during work on buildings.

No work shall be done upon any building or other structure while in course of erection, alteration or demolition, unless every reasonable precaution is taken to prevent dust or fragments of lime, mortar and other similar material from being blown or carried into or upon any street, public place or inhabited buildings.

PEOPLE v. CUNARD WHITE STAR, LTD.

New York Court of Appeals (1939)
280 N.Y. 413, 21 N.E.2d 489

LEHMAN, J. Informations charging the defendant with three violations of section 211 of the Sanitary Code of the City of New York (New York Code of Ordinances, ch. 20, art. 12) were tried together. One information alleges that the defendant, on the 20th day of October, 1937, "did unlawfully cause, suffer and allow dense smoke to be discharged from the smoke stack of steamship *Queen Mary* while tied up at Pier 90, North River, in the City, County and State of New York." Another information contains similar allegations concerning smoke from the steamship *Laconia* while tied up at Pier 54, North River. The third information alleges that dense smoke was discharged from a chimney located on Pier 90. The defendant was convicted on all three charges. Appeals taken to the Appellate Division from the judgments of conviction were heard and decided together. The appellant has appealed from the judgment of the Appellate Division, affirming the three judgments of conviction, but states in its brief that it desires "to present for the decision of this court only the questions involved in the application of the New York City Smoke Ordinance to steamships." It does not challenge the conviction upon the charge that it permitted dense smoke to be discharged from the chimney on Pier 90.

The evidence establishes that dense smoke was discharged on the days specified in the informations from the steamships *Queen Mary* and *Laconia.* The *Queen Mary* was under observation by an inspector of the Health Department from seven a.m. to eight-forty a.m. The discharge of dense smoke was not continuous but was noticed during five short periods aggregating twenty-four minutes. At that time the steamship was being prepared for a voyage which started at ten-thirty that morning. The same inspector observed a discharge of smoke on the *Laconia* for a period of five minutes not long before that ship left port.

The validity of the ordinance is not challenged, if its scope is limited to prohibition of the discharge of smoke, avoidable by the use of modern appliances and of methods which are practicable. So limited, the ordinance is reasonably calculated to protect the health and comfort of residents and visitors in the city of New York, and the Legislature has delegated to city officers the power to pass such ordinances. The defendant is engaged in foreign commerce which, though subject to regulation by the Congress of the United States, is not immune from the police power. The defendant does not claim such immunity. It asks the court to reverse the conviction for violation of the ordinance, on the ground that the ordinance is unreasonable and the police power does not justify unreasonable obstruction of its business as carrier in foreign commerce.

The defendant was convicted in spite of an offer to prove that "all due and reasonable precautions were taken on board the ships at the time of each of these charges with respect to the reduction of smoke, and that such smoke as may have been created was only such smoke as is absolutely unavoidable under the conditions prevailing on those ships." It says that the court excluded such evidence on the ground that it would be immaterial because any discharge of smoke, even if unavoidable, would constitute a violation of the ordinance, stating: "I will hold that the smoke came out of those funnels and in the other case from the structure, therefore, you were guilty from the testimony given by Inspector Kirchner and your own testimony on the entire case, I find the Defendant guilty as charged." The defendant had previously shown that its steamships are provided with oil burning boilers and with up-to-date and efficient smoke prevention appliances, and the court stated that it so found. The defendant admits, however, that at times smoke is discharged from its steamships, especially when cold boilers are being "lighted up" and when a ship is entering or leaving port and the demands for steam fluctuate.

Great cities depend for existence upon industry and commerce there conducted; but industry and commerce, if conducted in manner which will produce the greatest economic return, may create conditions which injure the public health and welfare. In the exercise of the police power, the State may require industry and commerce to be carried on in a manner which will promote the public health and welfare, though such requirement may increase the cost of doing business. Conflicting considerations of business advantage and the public health and welfare must be weighed by the Legislature, and the court may not interfere unless interference with lawful business is manifestly unreasonable. None the less, there is a point beyond which the Legislature may not go and the courts must refuse to enforce a statute, ordinance or regulation in those rare cases where a legislative body has transcended the constitutional restrictions upon its power. Even in the exercise of the police power the State may not obstruct or directly burden interstate or foreign commerce. (Di Santo v. Pennsylvania, 273 U.S. 34.) If the prohibition against the discharge of dense smoke is so applied that a steamship company may be found guilty of a violation because, in the operation of great liners with up-to-date equipment, dense smoke is discharged for a few minutes while a vessel is being prepared for departure, though it is shown that, even in the exercise of the greatest care, it would be impossible or impractical to avoid such smoke, then it seems to me clear beyond question that the ordinance is unreasonable, obstructs foreign commerce and exceeds the power of the State.

Perhaps the evidence, quoted in the opinion of Judge O'BRIEN, which was elicited upon cross-examination of defendant's witnesses, might, if unexplained, be sufficient to sustain a finding that the emission of the dense smoke might have been avoided without undue interference with the operation of the steamship. Read with the testimony given by the same witness on direct, these admissions are at most equivocal and certainly were subject to explanation or even contradiction through other proof, but here offer of such proof was, as I have pointed out, rejected. In my opinion, the colloquy of court and counsel leaves no question that the offer of such proof was made and rejected and that the ruling of the trial court was unambiguous and may be reviewed by this court. I do not, however, labor that point by argument or attempt demonstration by quotation of the full colloquy; for affirmance of the judgment of conviction, if it is based on the ground that the offer of proof was insufficient and that the court was justified in passing judgment upon the evidence actually presented, would have no consequences other than the payment by the defendant of small fines.

The important questions which the appellant seeks to bring up for review would even then be presented upon the appeal from a judgment of the Appellate Division, affirming a conviction of the same defendant for the discharge of smoke from the steamship *Carinthia,* which has been argued here at the same time as the judgment affirming conviction in the *Queen Mary* and *Laconia* cases, though the information was tried after the conviction in the earlier cases had been affirmed by the Appellate Division. In the *Carinthia* case the inspector testified that he observed smoke being discharged from the steamship *Carinthia* from ten-forty-eight to ten-fifty-three a.m. on October 22, 1937. The vessel had arrived that morning. By testimony which is not challenged the defendant showed that an hour after a vessel has arrived at the dock and the passengers have left, there is need for less steam. Then there is change to smaller burners and the change causes smoke for about five minutes. The defendant also showed by its chief engineer that the steamship had proper equipment and that smoke is unavoidable when the burners are changed. There is no evidence or even contention by the People that smoke could be avoided if the steamship company allows any burner or boiler to become cool while the vessel is in dock and less steam is required. A witness testified without contradiction or even cross-examination that if the change to smaller burners were not made, the reduced demand for steam "would necessitate us putting fires out and lighting them up again frequently, which would cause smoke."

In the *Carinthia* case the People argue that the conviction must be sustained because "It is no defense to a violation of a public health law that a particular steamship has been so constructed and is so operated as to make continued violations a 'necessary incident' to the defendant's carrying on his business." That might be true if construction or operation is improper or if change there were practical. Here, however, there is no suggestion that either operation or construction is not in conformity with the highest standards or that occasional emission of smoke, for a few minutes on the day a vessel enters or leaves port, could be avoided by change which would not unreasonably obstruct the operation of the steamship. The defendant's witnesses were not even cross-examined on those matters by the Corporation Counsel, and the record is bare of evidence like that quoted by Judge O'BRIEN upon the appeal in the other cases. The case was tried and decided on the theory that a carrier engaged in foreign commerce may be convicted of violation of the ordinance whenever dense smoke is discharged even for a brief period, though such discharge is unavoidable by any means which are practicable.

The judgments of the Appellate Division and of the Court of Special Sessions of the City of New York (Municipal Term) convicting the defendant for the discharge of smoke from the steamship should be reversed and new trials ordered.

The judgment of the Appellate Division affirming the judgment of the Court of Special Sessions of the City of New York (Municipal Term) convicting the defendant for the discharge of smoke from the chimney on Pier 90 should be affirmed.

O'BRIEN, J. (dissenting). Three violations by defendant of the provisions of section 211 of the Sanitary Code of the City of New York are charged. The first alleges that steamship *Queen Mary,* while docked at Pier 90, North river, discharged dense smoke; the second that steamship *Laconia,* while docked at Pier 54, North river, also discharged dense smoke; the third that dense smoke was discharged from a chimney owned by defendant on Pier 90, North river.

Section 211 provides: "No person shall cause, suffer or allow dense smoke to be discharged from any building, vessel, stationary or locomotive engine or motor vehicle, place or premises within the city of New York or upon the water adjacent thereto, within the jurisdiction of said city. . . ."

The People proved the emission of dense smoke from both the ships and from the chimney on the pier. This fact is not denied. On the trial defendant's counsel stated in respect to the ships: "I have not denied that we get smoke. We know we do. We cannot help it. We always do. The discharge of smoke, under those circumstances, was from our point of view unavoidable and accidental in the sense that it simply could not be prevented by the exercise of the greatest amount of care."

The *Queen Mary* and the *Laconia* are both oil burners. The boilers on the *Queen Mary* were started about five o'clock in the morning, according to the testimony of defendant's witness, and the ship was still tied to the pier as late as eight-forty that morning. She sailed that day at ten-thirty. Heavy black smoke was discharged, according to the observation of the People's witness, from seven-twenty-two to eight-thirty-five. Here is testimony by defendant's witness: "Q. You cannot actually control the fire so as not to have smoke? A. *We do that.* Q. How do you do it? A. By lighting up one at a time. Q. And with only one or two boilers lit up, you do not have dense smoke, is that right, under normal conditions? A. No, we do not. But when she is getting ready for sea, there will come a time when you have a great demand for steam, that is the time when she is leaving port. Q. And how many boilers do you light up then? A. *Every one of them.* Q. And all at about the same time, isn't that right? A. *About the same time* . . . Q. Suppose you only started one boiler at a time, you wouldn't have as much dense smoke coming from those stacks as if you started them all at the same time, would you? A. No. Q. So, therefore, to that extent, you can control it? A. *We can control the quantity that would be emitted at that time.*" The same witness testified that the ship starts getting up steam three or four hours before it sails. Another witness for defendant testified that, after the boilers on *Queen Mary* are steamed, his duty is to watch the smoke and that he did see smoke that day, sometimes black and sometimes thick brown. He reported to his superior that the funnel was "smoking heavily." The People are correct in their argument that the emission of this dense smoke was not unavoidable but could have been controlled. The practice pursued by defendant is admitted to be cheaper and more convenient. In respect to steamship *Laconia,* the evidence is clear in respect to the emission of dense, black smoke between nine-thirteen and nine-eighteen a.m. The practice regarding the lighting of the burners on this ship is the same as that prevailing on the *Queen Mary.*

Appellant's brief presents no argument respecting the correctness of the conviction in connection with the emission of smoke from the chimney on the pier.

The argument that this enactment tends to burden foreign commerce to such an extent as to render it unconstitutional cannot be sustained. First of all, it is a health ordinance and, in respect to such matters and many others, a State possesses extensive police power, even though interstate or foreign commerce may be directly involved.

The judgment should be affirmed.

CRANE, Ch. J., HUBBS and RIPPEY, JJ., concur with LEHMAN, J.; O'BRIEN, J., dissents as to the steamships in opinion in which LOUGHRAN and FINCH, JJ., concur.

Judgment accordingly.

HURON PORTLAND CEMENT CO. v. CITY OF DETROIT

United States Supreme Court (1960)
362 U.S. 440, 80 S. Ct. 813, 4 L. Ed. 2d 825

MR. JUSTICE STEWART delivered the opinion of the Court.

This appeal from a judgment of the Supreme Court of Michigan draws in question the constitutional validity of certain provisions of Detroit's Smoke Abatement Code as applied to ships owned by the appellant and operated in interstate commerce.

The appellant is a Michigan corporation, engaged in the manufacture and sale of cement. It maintains a fleet of five vessels which it uses to transport cement from its mill in Alpena, Michigan, to distributing plants located in various states bordering the Great Lakes. Two of the ships, the *S. S. Crapo* and the *S. S. Boardman,* are equipped with hand-fired Scotch marine boilers. While these vessels are docked for loading and unloading it is necessary, in order to operate deck machinery, to keep the boilers fired and to clean the fires periodically. When the fires are cleaned, the ship's boiler stacks emit smoke which in density and duration exceeds the maximum standards allowable under the Detroit Smoke Abatement Code. Structural alterations would be required in order to insure compliance with the Code.

Criminal proceedings were instituted in the Detroit Recorder's Court against the appellant and its agents for violations of the city law during periods when the vessels were docked at the Port of Detroit. The appellant brought an action in the State Circuit Court to enjoin the city from further prosecuting the pending litigation in the Recorder's Court, and from otherwise enforcing the smoke ordinance against its vessels, "except where the emission of smoke is caused by the improper firing or the improper use of the equipment upon said vessels." The Circuit Court refused to grant relief, and the Supreme Court of Michigan affirmed, 355 Mich. 227, 93 N. W. 2d 889. An appeal was lodged here, and we noted probable jurisdiction, 361 U. S. 806.

In support of the claim that the ordinance cannot constitutionally be applied to appellant's ships, two basic arguments are advanced. First, it is asserted that since the vessels and their equipment, including their boilers, have been inspected, approved and licensed to operate in interstate commerce in accordance with a comprehensive system of regulation enacted by Congress, the City of Detroit may not legislate in such a way as, in effect, to impose additional or inconsistent standards. Secondly, the argument is made that even if Congress has not expressly preempted the field, the municipal ordinance "materially affects interstate commerce in matters where uniformity is necessary." We have concluded that neither of these contentions can prevail, and that the Federal Constitution does not prohibit application to the appellant's vessels of the criminal provisions of the Detroit ordinance.[1]

The ordinance was enacted for the manifest purpose of promoting the health and welfare of the city's inhabitants. Legislation designed to free from pollution the very air that people breathe clearly falls within the exercise of even the most traditional concept of what is compendiously known as the police power. In the exercise of that power, the states and their instrumentalities may act, in many areas of interstate commerce and maritime activities, concurrently with the federal government.

The basic limitations upon local legislative power in this area are clear enough. The controlling principles have been reiterated over the years in a host of this Court's decisions. Evenhanded local regulation to effectuate a legitimate local public interest is valid unless preempted by federal action, or unduly burdensome on maritime activities or interstate commerce.

In determining whether state regulation has been preempted by federal action, "the intent to supersede the exercise by the State of its police power as to matters not covered by the Federal legislation is not to be inferred from the mere fact that Congress has seen fit to circumscribe its regulation and to occupy a limited field. In other words, such intent is not to be implied unless the act of Congress fairly interpreted is in actual conflict with the law of the State." *Savage v. Jones*, 225 U. S. 501, 533.

In determining whether the state has imposed an undue burden on interstate commerce, it must be borne in mind that the Constitution when "conferring upon Congress the regulation of commerce, . . . never intended to cut the States off from legislating on all subjects relating to the health, life, and safety of their citizens, though the legislation might indirectly affect the commerce of the country. Legislation, in a great variety of ways, may affect commerce and persons engaged in it without constituting a regulation of it, within the meaning of the Constitution." *Sherlock v. Alling*, 93 U. S. 99, 103. But a state may not impose a burden which materially affects interstate commerce in an area where uniformity of regulation is necessary.

Although verbal generalizations do not of their own motion decide concrete cases, it is nevertheless within the framework of these basic principles that the issues in the present case must be determined.

---

1 The Detroit legislation also contains provisions making it unlawful to operate any combustion equipment in the city without a certificate, § 2.16, providing for an annual inspection of all such equipment used in the city, § 2.17, and further providing for the sealing of equipment in the event that the inspection requirements are repeatedly ignored, § 2.20. There is nothing in the record to indicate that the city has at any time attempted to enforce these provisions with respect to the appellant's ships. Accordingly, we do not reach the question of the validity of the inspection sections as they might be applied to appellant, but limit our consideration solely to what is presented upon this record—the enforcement of the criminal provisions of the Code for violation of the smoke emission provisions.

I

For many years Congress has maintained an extensive and comprehensive set of controls over ships and shipping. Federal inspection of steam vessels was first required in 1838, 5 Stat. 304, and the requirement has been continued ever since. Steam vessels which carry passengers must pass inspection annually, 46 U.S. C. § 391 (a), and those which do not, every two years. 46 U. S. C. § 391 (b). Failure to meet the standards invoked by law results in revocation of the inspection certificate, or refusal to issue a new one, 46 U. S. C. § 391 (d). It is unlawful for a vessel to operate without such a certificate. 46 U. S. C. § 390c (a).

These inspections are broad in nature, covering "the boilers, unfired pressure vessels, and appurtenances thereof, also the propelling and auxiliary machinery, electrical apparatus and equipment, of all vessels subject to inspection. . . ." 46 U. S. C. § 392 (b). The law provides that "No boiler . . . shall be allowed to be used if constructed in whole or in part of defective material or which because of its form, design, workmanship, age, use, or for any other reason is unsafe." 46 U. S. C. § 392 (c).

As is apparent on the face of the legislation, however, the purpose of the federal inspection statutes is to insure the seagoing safety of vessels subject to inspection. Thus 46 U. S. C. § 392 (c) makes clear that inspection of boilers and related equipment is for the purpose of seeing to it that the equipment "may be safely employed in the service proposed." The safety of passengers, 46 U.S.C. § 391 (a), and of the crew, 46 U. S. C. § 391 (b), is the criterion. The thrust of the federal inspection laws is clearly limited to affording protection from the perils of maritime navigation.

By contrast, the sole aim of the Detroit ordinance is the elimination of air pollution to protect the health and enhance the cleanliness of the local community. Congress recently recognized the importance and legitimacy of such a purpose, when in 1955 it provided:

> "[I]n recognition of the dangers to the public health and welfare, injury to agricultural crops and livestock, damage to and deterioration of property, and hazards to air and ground transportation, from air pollution, it is hereby declared to be the policy of Congress to preserve and protect the primary responsibilities and rights of the States and local governments in controlling air pollution, to support and aid technical research to devise and develop methods of abating such pollution, and to provide Federal technical services and financial aid to State and local government air pollution control agencies and other public or private agencies and institutions in the formulation and execution of their air pollution abatement research programs." 69 Stat. 322; 42 U. S. C. § 1857.

Congressional recognition that the problem of air pollution is peculiarly a matter of state and local concern is manifest in this legislation. Such recognition is underlined in the Senate Committee Report:

> "The committee recognizes that it is the primary responsibility of State and local governments to prevent air pollution. The bill does not propose any exercise of police power by the Federal Government and no provision

in it invades the sovereignty of States, counties or cities." S. Rep. No. 389, 84th Cong., lst Sess. 3.

We conclude that there is no overlap between the scope of the federal ship inspection laws and that of the municipal ordinance here involved. For this reason we cannot find that the federal inspection legislation has preempted local action. To hold otherwise would be to ignore the teaching of this Court's decisions which enjoin seeking out conflicts between state and federal regulation where none clearly exists.

An additional argument is advanced, however, based not upon the mere existence of the federal inspection standards, but upon the fact that the appellant's vessels were actually licensed, 46 U. S. C. § 263, and enrolled, 46 U. S. C. §§ 259-260, by the national government. It is asserted that the vessels have thus been given a dominant federal right to the use of the navigable waters of the United States, free from the local impediment that would be imposed by the Detroit ordinance.

The scope of the privilege granted by the federal licensing scheme has been well delineated. A state may not exclude from its waters a ship operating under a federal license. *Gibbons v. Ogden,* 9 Wheat. 1. A state may not require a local occupation license, in addition to that federally granted, as a condition precedent to the use of its waters. *Moran v. New Orleans,* 112 U. S. 69. While an enrolled and licensed vessel may be required to share the costs of benefits it enjoys, *Huse v. Glover,* 119 U. S. 543, and to pay fair taxes imposed by its domicile, *Transportation Co. v. Wheeling,* 99 U.S. 273, it cannot be subjected to local license imposts exacted for the use of a navigable waterway, *Harman v. Chicago,* 147 U. S. 396. *See also Sinnot v. Davenport,* 22 How. 227.

The mere possession of a federal license, however, does not immunize a ship from the operation of the normal incidents of local police power, not constituting a direct regulation of commerce. Thus, a federally licensed vessel is not, as such, exempt from local pilotage laws, *Cooley v. Board of Wardens of Port of Philadelphia,* 12 How. 299, or local quarantine laws, *Morgan's Steamship Co. v. Louisiana Board of Health,* 118 U. S. 455, or local safety inspections, *Kelly v. Washington,* 302 U. S. 1, or the local regulation of wharves and docks, *Packet Co. v. Catlettsburg,* 105 U. S. 559. Indeed this Court has gone so far as to hold that a state, in the exercise of its police power, may actually seize and pronounce the forfeiture of a vessel "licensed for the coasting trade, under the laws of the United States, while engaged in that trade." *Smith v. Maryland,* 18 How. 71, 74. The present case obviously does not even approach such an extreme, for the Detroit ordinance requires no more than compliance with an orderly and reasonable scheme of community regulation. The ordinance does not exclude a licensed vessel from the Port of Detroit, nor does it destroy the right of free passage. We cannot hold that the local regulation so burdens the federal license as to be constitutionally invalid.

II

The claim that the Detroit ordinance, quite apart from the effect of federal legislation, imposes as to the appellant's ships an undue burden on interstate commerce needs no extended discussion. State regulation, based on the police power, which does not discriminate against interstate commerce or operate to disrupt its required uniformity, may constitutionally stand.

It has not been suggested that the local ordinance, applicable alike to "any person, firm or corporation" within the city, discriminates against interstate commerce as such. It is a regulation of general application, designed to better the health and welfare of the community. And while the appellant argues that other local governments might impose differing requirements as to air pollution, it has pointed to none. The record contains nothing to suggest the existence of any such competing or conflicting local regulations. *Cf. Bibb v. Navajo Freight Lines*, 359 U. S. 520. We conclude that no impermissible burden on commerce has been shown. *The judgment is affirmed.*

MR. JUSTICE DOUGLAS, with whom MR. JUSTICE FRANKFURTER concurs, dissenting.

The Court treats this controversy as if it were merely an inspection case with the City of Detroit supplementing a federal inspection system as the State of Washington did in *Kelly v. Washington*, 302 U. S. 1. There a state inspection system touched matters "which the federal laws and regulations" left "untouched." *Id.*, at 13. This is not that type of case. Nor is this the rare case where state law adopts the standards and requirements of federal law and is allowed to exact a permit in addition to the one demanded by federal law. *California v. Zook,* 336 U. S. 725, 735. Here we have a criminal prosecution against a shipowner and officers of two of its vessels for using the very equipment on these vessels which the Federal Government says may be used. At stake are a possible fine of $100 on the owner and both a fine and a 30-day jail sentence on the officers.

Appellant has a federal certificate for each of its vessels—S.S. John W. Boardman, S.S.S.T. Crapo and others. The one issued on March 21, 1956, by the United States Coast Guard for S.S.S.T. Crapo is typical. The certificate states "The said vessel is permitted to be navigated for one year on the Great Lakes." The certificate specifies the boilers which are and may be used—"Main Boilers Number 3, Year built 1927, Mfr. Manitowoc Boiler Wks." It also specifies the fuel which is used and is to be used in those boilers—"Fuel coal."

Appellant, operating the vessel in waters at the Detroit dock, is about to be fined criminally for using the precise equipment covered by the federal certificate because, it is said, the use of that equipment will violate a smoke ordinance of the City of Detroit.

The federal statutes give the Coast Guard the power to inspect "the boilers" of freight vessels every two years,[2] and provides that when the Coast Guard approves the vessel and her equipment throughout, a certificate to that effect shall be made.[3]

The requirements of the Detroit smoke ordinance are squarely in conflict with the federal statute. Section 2.2A of the ordinance prohibits the emission of the kind of smoke which cannot be at all times prevented by vessels

[2] 46 U.S.C. § 392.

[3] 46 U.S.C. § 399provides in part: "When the inspection of a steam vessel is completed and the Secretary of the Department in which the Coast Guard is operating approves the vessel and her equipment throughout, he shall make and subscribe a certificate to that effect."

equipped with hand-fired Scotch marine boilers such as appellant's vessels use. Section 2.16 of the ordinance makes it unlawful to use any furnace or other combustion equipment or device in the city without a certificate of operation which issues only after inspection. Section 2.17 provides for an annual inspection of every furnace or other combustion equipment used within the city. Section 2.20 provides that if an owner has been previously notified of three or more violations of the ordinance within any consecutive 12-month period he shall be notified to show cause before the Commissioner why the equipment should not be sealed. At the hearing, if the Commissioner finds that adequate corrective means have not been employed to remedy the situation, the equipment shall be sealed. Section 3.2 provides for a fine of not more than $100 or imprisonment for not more than 30 days or both upon conviction of any violation of any provision of the ordinance, and each day a violation is permitted to exist constitutes a separate offense.

Thus it is plain that the ordinance requires not only the inspection and approval of equipment which has been inspected and approved by the Coast Guard but also the sealing of equipment, even though it has been approved by the Coast Guard. Under the Detroit ordinance a certificate of operation would not issue for a hand-fired Scotch marine boiler, even though it had been approved by the Coast Guard.[4] In other words, this equipment approved and licensed by the Federal Government for use on navigable waters cannot pass muster under local law.

If local law required federally licensed vessels to observe local speed laws, obey local traffic regulations, or dock at certain times or under prescribed conditions, we would have local laws not at war with the federal license, but complementary to it. In *Kelly v. Washington, supra,* at 14-15, the Court marked precisely that distinction. While it allowed state inspection of hull and machinery of tugs over and above that required by federal statutes, it noted that state rules which changed the federal standards "for the structure and equipment of vessels" would meet a different fate:

> "The state law is a comprehensive code. While it excepts vessels which are subject to inspection under the laws of the United States, it has provisions which may be deemed to fall within the class of regulations which Congress alone can provide. For example, Congress may establish standards and designs for the structure and equipment of vessels, and may prescribe rules for their operation, which could not properly be left to the diverse

[4] The trial court in its opinion said:

"It is agreed it is impossible to prevent emission of the kind of smoke prohibited by the smoke ordinance if the vessel is equipped with handfired scotch marine boilers. The Boardman has two boilers each with two doors and one steam air jet over each door. The Crapo has three boilers, each with two doors and one steam air jet over each door. The steam jets being installed at the suggestion of Benjamin Linsky, former Chief of the Bureau of Smoke Abatement for the City.

"Testimony showed also that the plaintiff used a chemical in an attempt to reduce the smoke. plaintiff urges it has done everything that it could possibly do with the equipment it has to prevent the emission of smoke. It was shown on trial that the fleet is subject to periodic inspection by the coast guard, which issues a search [sic] of inspection. The Crapo in 1955, docked at Detroit twenty-two times for an average docking time of 23.9 hours and the Boardman docked at Detroit 25 times that year with an average stay of 16.2 hours. Both vessels were constantly engaged in interstate and foreign commerce during this period."

action of the States. The State of Washington might prescribe standards, designs, equipment and rules of one sort, Oregon another, California another, and so on. But it does not follow that in all respects the state Act must fail."

. . . .

Here the Coast Guard would be entitled to insist on different equipment. But it has not done so. The boats of appellant, therefore, have credentials good for any port; and I would not allow this local smoke ordinance to work in derogation of them. The fact that the Federal Government in certifying equipment applies standards of safety for seagoing vessels, while Detroit applies standards of air pollution seems immaterial. Federal pre-emption occurs when the boilers and fuel to be used in the vessels are specified in the certificate. No state authority can, in my view, change those specifications. Yet that is in effect what is allowed here.

. . . .

What we do today is in disregard of the doctrine long accepted and succinctly stated in the 1851 Term in *Pennsylvania v. Wheeling & Belmont Bridge Co.*, 13 How. 518, 566, "No State law can hinder or obstruct the free use of a license granted under an act of Congress." The confusion and burden arising from the imposition by one State of requirements for equipment which the Federal Government has approved was emphasized in *Kelly v. Washington*, *supra*, in the passage already quoted. The requirements of Detroit may be too lax for another port. *Cf. People v. Cunard White Star, Ltd.*, 280 N. Y. 413, 21 N. E. 2d 489. The variety of requirements for equipment which the States may provide in order to meet their air pollution needs underlines the importance of letting the Coast Guard license serve as authority for the vessel to use, in all our ports, the equipment which it certifies.

NOTES AND QUESTIONS

(1) Is there any evidence from early smoke and dust regulations that their primary purpose was to protect health? Is there any evidence in any materials that early regulations based enforcement on any objectively measurable standards? In view of the fact that these early regulations rely primarily on the subjective impression of an inspector, could any of these regulations have been invalidated on due process grounds because they were too vague to provide a reasonable guide for conduct? Note that the issue of standards that rely on subjective judgment is still alive; see the discussion of the opacity standards under current federal regulations, enforceable by visual reference to the "Ringelmann Chart," in *Portland Cement Association v. Ruckelshaus*, *infra* p. 191.

(2) Under the statues involved in the preceding cases, is it a defense to claim that the emission of dense smoke—or the scattering of dust and other materials—could not be avoided in carrying on a particular economically and socially useful activity even in the exercise of due care, or even in the exercise

of more than ordinary care? Do these cases provide a precedent for the doctrine that there is no absolute liability for failure to live up to environmental standards but merely liability for failure to live up to standards which may be attained by reasonable efforts? Compare *People v. Savage*, 1 Misc. 2d 337, 148 N.Y.S.2d 191, *aff'd mem.* 309 N.Y. 941, 132 N.E.2d 313 (1955), and *Department of Health v. Owens-Corning Fiberglas Corp.*, 242 A.2d 21 (N.J. Super. 1968). The doctrine here involved has generally been referred to as the defense of "unavoidable necessity." It is a direct antecedent of the more contemporary defense of "technological and economic infeasibility" which has been raised in a variety of contexts to challenge standards set under the current federal Clean Air Act. *See, e.g., Portland Cement Association v. Ruckelshaus, infra* p. 191, and *Union Electric Co. v. EPA, infra* p. 135.

(3) The *Huron Portland Cement Co.* case resulted in a more favorable holding for local and state air pollution controls than the *Cunard White Star* case. The more recent case was aided in its holding by the legislative finding of the first federal air pollution act, passed in 1955. Examine the most recent legislative policy expressed in federal law, § 2.03[2] *infra,* and consider whether the court in *Huron Portland Cement Co.* would reach a different result today, on the basis of the present federal legislative policy.

(4) Based on your knowledge of the sources of air pollution and its impact, consider whether effective air pollution control today could rely exclusively on the exercise of state and local police power. Consider also whether effective air pollution control would be possible today *without* the exercise of state and local police power.

[2] Federal Laws and Regulations from 1955 to 1990

In 1955, Congress enacted the first air pollution law, entitled Air Pollution Control—Research and Technical Assistance, Ch. 360, 69 Stat. 322, providing for grants-in-aid for state and local air pollution control agencies for research, training and demonstration projects. It was based on the federal taxing and spending powers. Subsequent federal legislation moved closer to asserting federal regulatory powers based on the Commerce Clause, notably in the Motor Vehicle Air Pollution Control Act of 1965 (Pub. L. No. 89-272, 79 Stat. 992), which was clearly based on the interstate commerce power. The succession of laws culminated in the Clean Air Act of 1970, which provided the statutory scheme federal air pollution control has followed ever since (Clean Air Amendments of 1970, Pub. L. No. 91-664, 89 Stat. 1676). For a detailed account of the assumption of regulatory power over air pollution control by the federal government, see F. Grad, Treatise on Environmental Law, § 2.03[1]. Air pollution control functions previously lodged in the Department of Health, Education and Welfare, which controlled public health concerns generally, were transferred to the Administrator of the Environmental Protection Agency newly established under Reorganization Plan No. 3 of 1970.

[3] The Clean Air Act[5]

[a] Clean Air Act—A Primer

The Clean Air Act, first passed in 1970, was significantly amended in 1977 and underwent a very major revision in 1990. As noted, although the basic scheme of the law, particularly with reference to stationary sources, has not changed significantly, its revisions now make it one of the longest environmental control laws on the books and one of the more complex ones. This very brief overview is intended to provide a schematic guide, which ought to make the detailed treatment which follows more easily understandable. For a full treatment, also see F. Grad, Treatise on Environmental Law, Ch. 2.

The law divides the regulation of sources of air pollution into two categories, from stationary sources, including mostly factories, and from mobile sources, including mostly automobiles.

For stationary sources of air pollution, the Clean Air Act provides for federal and state participation in the regulatory process. The federal government, and particularly the Administrator of EPA, is charged with the promulgation of national ambient air quality standards (NAAQS) of two kinds—primary air quality standards to protect health, and secondary air quality standards to protect welfare. These national ambient air quality standards have been set for so-called "criteria pollutants," sometimes also referred to as "NAAQS pollutants," *i.e.,* the most significant air pollutants with known adverse health effects. The Administrator, in setting ambient air quality standards, must rely on the "criteria" for each pollutant which he has promulgated earlier. "Criteria" in this instance means collected data on health effects and on methods of control. The Administrator, with the participation of the states, also divides the nation into "air quality control regions," with each state consisting of at least one region, and with some regions covering interstate areas.

The national ambient air quality standards for the "criteria pollutants" carbon monoxide, sulfur oxides, nitrogen oxides, hydrocarbons, particulate matter, photochemical oxidants (or ozone) and lead, apply to the nation as a whole. They are to be achieved in each of the air quality control regions through the adoption and enforcement of "state implementation plans (SIPs)."

Each of the several states is required to adopt a state implementation plan for its air quality control regions. The Clean Air Act prescribes the contents of the state implementation in some detail, and requires that a public hearing be held before its adoption and submission by the state. When the plan has been submitted, and has been published in the Federal Register, it is subject

[5] The Clean Air Amendments of 1970, Pub. L. No. 91-604, 84 Stat. 1676 were the last in a series of amendments of the Clean Air Act of 1963. Citations below are to the Clean Air Act of 1963, Pub. L. No. 88-206, 77 Stat. 392 as amended Pub. L. No. 89-272, 79 Stat. 992 (1965), as amended Pub. L. No. 89-675, 80 Stat. 953 (1966), as amended Pub. L. No. 90-148, 81 Stat. 485 (1967), as amended Pub. L. No. 91-604, 84 Stat. 1676 (1970), as amended by the Clean Air Act Amendments of 1977, Pub. L. No. 95-95, 91 Stat. 685 (Aug. 7, 1977), with Technical Amendments, Pub. L. No. 95-190, 91 Stat. 1399 (Nov. 16, 1977), 42 U.S.C. § 7401 *et seq.*, as amended by the Clean Air Act Amendments of 1990, Pub. L. No. 101-549, 104 St. 2399 (Nov. 15, 1990). Citations below are to the current section of the Clean Air Act as last amended, and to the appropriate section of the U.S. Code.

to approval by the Administrator. When it is approved, it has the dual character of state law and of enforceable federal regulation.

The state implementation plan commonly consists of state law and regulations aimed at reducing air pollution so as to attain the national ambient air quality standards. In the main, the states are required to rely on emission controls, rather than on dispersion and other intermittent control devices, to improve air quality. Other requirements for state implementation plans may involve the reduction of pollution from automobiles through transportation plans and voluntary indirect source controls.

A valid state implementation plan must meet certain conditions which are contained in § 110 of the Act. Section 110 has become more detailed with each amendment of the statute. As additional requirements were included in the Act, they were generally worked into § 110 as additional matters to be included in the state implementation plan. The original timetable in the 1970 Act had called for the attainment of primary national ambient air quality standards no later than 1977. Starting with the 1977 amendment, regions with air quality better than required by law were required to adopt in the state implementation plan measures for the "prevention of significant deterioration (PSD)," while those regions which had not attained the standard were required to adopt special requirements applicable to non-attainment areas. While the requirements for PSD areas and nonattainment areas differ, they are both complex and require the states to place restrictions on the construction of new sources of air pollution. All of these requirements are subsumed under the states' implementation plans, subject to federal approval and both state and federal enforcement.

When a state fails to adopt a state implementation plan, or fails to adopt a plan that meets the requirements of the law, the Administration may, after public hearing, adopt a plan for the state, with the same force and effect under federal law as a state-adopted plan.

Under the state implementation plan scheme, ambient standards are set by the federal EPA, and emissions standards for stationary sources are set by the states (or, by delegation, by local governments). However, the federal government retains the power to set emissions standards for certain kinds of stationary sources. These include "new source performance standards" for major new sources of air pollution, listed by category in the law. The Administrator also sets standards for the listed hazardous air pollutants, enunciated in Section 112. Although the emission standards for such sources are set by the Administrator, the states may take on the enforcement of such standards as part of their implementation plans.

The Clean Air Act provides for the pre-enforcement review in the circuit courts of standards set by EPA, including ambient air quality standards, new source performance standards, and hazardous air pollutant emission standards. Thus, standards set by EPA can only be reviewed during the time set for such review. They cannot thereafter be challenged during the enforcement process. Other administrative decisions subject to judicial review include the approval of state implementation plans.

The Clean Air Act is enforced both by the state and the federal EPA. To the extent that state implementation plans incorporate state law and regulation, they are enforceable, like other state enactments, by the state agencies, under state laws which generally provide for administrative enforcement and for enforcement in the courts. Available state sanctions usually include both civil and criminal penalties, as well as injunctive relief. The violation of the law and regulations is subject to federal sanctions, including administrative compliance orders, and judicial enforcement proceedings leading to civil penalties, and criminal fines and imprisonment. The failure to comply with the provisions of an Administrator-approved SIP is a violation of the Clean Air Act, and can lead to federal enforcement in the same manner as other violations. The dual character of SIPs—as state law or federal regulation—has been noted earlier.

In addition to the established methods of enforcement, the 1970 Clean Air Act brought about a veritable revolution in public interest litigation. For the first time in any federal law, it authorized citizen suits, establishing a new cause of action and granting standing to public interest litigants without regard to the earlier, difficult to meet, standing rules. The citizen suit provision authorized any citizen to sue any other party (except a state) to compel compliance with the Act. This includes a suit against the Administrator to compel him to carry out any nondiscretionary duty under the Act, much in the manner of a writ of mandamus.

Another sanction provided since the 1977 amendment is an economic enforcement sanction, a non-compliance penalty measured in amount by moneys saved by the polluter by not installing pollution control equipment. The purpose is to make non-compliance at least as costly as compliance.

The Clean Air Act has a different scheme for the control of pollution from automotive sources. The automobile has always been a product in interstate commerce, and from the Air Quality Act of 1965 on, the federal government has exercised control of new automobiles by regulating the manufacture and sale of the new car as a product. The regulation of new automotive sources has always been preemptive—*i.e.*, the states have not had any part in framing the requirements, and have been barred from setting or enforcing product standards of their own. (This statement is not qualified by the well known California "exception." Because California preceded Congress in its regulations, California was authorized to have more stringent requirements than the federal ones, subject to annual approval, however, by the Administrator.)

Federal law sets or authorizes detailed requirements for new vehicles to make sure that no vehicles are sold which exceed the set emission standards for carbon monoxide, nitrogen oxides, and hydrocarbons. These standards have become progressively more stringent, in an effort to force automotive technology and to achieve a roll-back of automotive emissions.

The law authorizes the imposition of requirements on the configuration of devices to fuel automobiles so as to prevent the use of improper fuels which would interfere with the functioning of catalysts or other pollution control devices. Detailed provision is made for the testing of motor vehicles and their engines for compliance with the law, and the manufacturer is required to provide certain warranties to the purchaser relating to compliance with emission standards, including warranties of the control devices for the useful life of the vehicle, as defined by law. Stringent prohibitions apply to tampering with pollution control devices. Fuel controls and controls on fuel additives are also provided for.

A separate part of the law on moving sources authorizes the preemptive establishment of standards for emissions from aircraft.

The provisions of the Clean Air Act relating to judicial review and citizen suits apply to the regulation of automotive pollution. While automotive pollution is subject to separate enforcement sanctions and penalties, motor vehicles in actual use clearly affect ambient air quality and are also covered by the general provisions. State implementation plans must therefore deal with the automobile in actual use as a source of pollution subject to state and local regulation, and subject, therefore, to the general SIP scheme of federal and state regulations.

[b] The Clean Air Act Amendments of 1990

In October 1989, following lengthy legislative proceedings, the House and the Senate adopted the Conference Committee Report on S. 1630[6] which contained the full text of the Clean Air Act Amendments of 1990.[7]

The Clean Air Act Amendments of 1990 extend the Clean Air Act by another 314 pages, probably making it one of the longest environmental laws on the books. The law is not only exceptionally long, but it is also highly complex and contains a great deal of material which previously would have been committed to Regulations. The complexity of the law indicates an appreciation of the complexity of the subject, but its detail also indicates the Congressional distrust of the executive, and particularly of EPA. The 1990 Amendments seek to deal with a number of subjects which had been left undone in the earlier administration of the Act.

Title I of the Act leaves intact the basic structure, calling for the setting of ambient air quality standards, and the system of state implementation plans to attain them. However, Title I is more stringent in dealing with attainment and maintenance of the standards. Instead of the broad categories of attainment and non-attainment, each NAAQS pollutant area in non-attainment is now categorized as *Marginal, Moderate, Serious, Severe* or *Extreme*. The Act also imposes on virtually all air quality control regions the obligation to prepare new implementation plans, particularly when there are more stringent standards applicable to areas in which attainment is as yet in the distant future. Different requirements are then imposed depending on the nature of non-attainment and the kind of pollutant involved. Some of the attainment dates, depending on the anticipated difficulty in achieving the goal, may be well into the 21st century. Deadlines for the accomplishment of ozone standards, for instance, are set for some areas for three years after enactment of the Clean Air Act Amendments of 1990, and for Extreme Areas of nonattainment, for 20 years from enactment. In areas which are not close to attainment, new provisions are set for new sources, imposing new offset requirements. Moreover, sanctions are provided for failure to attain, including

[6] Conference Report (H. Rept. 101-952), 136 Cong. Rec., 2d Sess., H 13101 *et seq.* (daily edition, October 26, 1990)

[7] Pub. L. No. 101-549, signed into law November 15, 1990.

excess emission fees for certain major sources, and penalties on the states by way of reduction of grants for air pollution control.

Title II of the Clean Air Act Amendments of 1990 likewise imposes far more stringent standards for new mobile sources. For light duty vehicles and light duty trucks, new emission standards were set to be phased in beginning with the 1994 model year and providing for further tightening of the standards beginning with model year 2004. New standards are set, also, for buses and trucks. The useful life of a vehicle for which the standards are set is extended to 10 years and 100,000 miles. New standards are also established for vehicles in use, including standards relating to evaporative controls from automotive engines as well as requirements for the recapture of evaporative losses. Each vehicle is required to have a warning device to let the operator know when the emission control system is not functioning properly. The new provisions, moreover, add specific requirements relating to automotive fuels. Provision is made for reformulated gasoline to be sold in areas of the country with the worst ozone problems. The provision also requires the development and use of vehicles operating on alternative fuels, particularly in high ozone areas. Such less polluting vehicles relying on alternative fuels are required for fleet vehicles in California. The California-developed less polluting vehicles may then be phased in in other states.

Title III provides for the control of hazardous air pollutants, also referred to as air toxics. Instead of allowing the Administrator to designate hazardous air pollutants by regulation, the law lists 189 substances and requires the Administrator to provide regulations to limit emissions to the level of the "maximum available control technology (MACT)." The standards under the newly amended and enlarged § 112 of the Act are largely technology based, but the law continues to rely on risk assessment by insisting that standards provide an ample margin of safety, as under earlier law. In addition to providing for control of hazardous emissions, the law also seeks to regulate accidental releases of toxic chemicals requiring the publication of a list of 100 or more extremely hazardous air pollutants and mandating owners of plants to take certain precautions against accidental releases. A Chemical Safety and Hazard Identification Board is created to investigate chemical accidents and to make recommendations for accident prevention.

Title IV of the Act addresses the acid deposition or acid rain problem. In very detailed and highly technical provisions, it targets—by name—111 power generating units in 22 states, imposing a two-phase regulatory scheme to reduce sulfur dioxide and nitrogen oxide emissions. The emission controls for such units are set to reduce the year 2000 sulfur dioxide emissions by 10 million tons below the 1980 levels. The title establishes an elaborate scheme allocating marketable pollution allowances to generating units, providing for the negotiability of such allowances. The provisions utilize market forces in the service of pollution control, making it possible for a utility to decide whether to purchase additional emission allowances, or to reduce pollution from a particular source, without affecting the sum total of emissions. This is accomplished by limiting the allocation of allowances and by limiting the number of allowances that may be provided, so that the total amount of emissions to be covered by allowances will remain constant in accordance with the requirements of the law. There are provisions in the law to lessen reliance on low sulfur coal and to encourage other devices so as not to unfairly disadvantage coal producers and miners in high sulfur coal areas.

Title V establishes a permit program, phased in during three years following the date of the amendment. The law shifts the granting of permits to state permitting agencies. The new permit program establishes a substantial fee structure, which will in effect compel permittees—*i.e.*, practically everyone regulated under the Clean Air Act—to pay for the costs of administration. Title V seeks to parallel in many respects the provisions of the NPDES (National Pollution Discharge Elimination System) program under the Clean Water Act, except that under the Title V provisions, much of the administrative burden seems to pass from EPA to the states. This in turn may create some problems for judicial review because parties may be limited to seek judicial review in the state courts.

Title VI deals with stratospheric ozone protection. Recognizing the global nature of the impact of air pollution, it implements agreements reached in the Montreal Protocol by international treaty to phase out production of many ozone destructive chemicals by the year 2000. Different degrees of control are asserted over chemicals with different destructive impacts on the ozone layer. Provisions are made for the recycling of ozone depleting chemicals, and there are stringent provisions controlling the use of such chemicals in automobile air conditioners and in other refrigeration equipment.

Title VII of the Act strengthens many of the Clean Air Act enforcement provisions. In particular, it changes the citizen suit provisions to allow citizen plaintiffs to recover civil penalties against violators, similar to the provisions of the Clean Water Act. In addition, Title VII significantly enhances the criminal penalties against knowing violators of the Act. The law also creates a new administrative penalty structure, which allows EPA to collect penalties from minor violators on the basis of administrative "field citations."

Titles VIII and IX of the Act provide for a variety of authorities relating to investigations and researches of different causes of air pollution and of different air pollution impacts. In Title VIII, there is an important provision authorizing the control of air pollution from Outer Continental Shelf activities such as oil drilling. Section 816 authorizes the investigation of the causes of haze in parks and wilderness areas and authorizes the promulgation of regulations to carry out the findings. It also authorizes the investigation of greenhouse gases. Title VIII also includes the all important authorization of appropriations to carry out the Act, which includes funding for a variety of planning activities. Title IX emphasizes clean air research, relating to air pollutant monitoring analysis modeling and inventory research; environmental health effects research; and including also the continuation of the National Acid Precipitation Assessment Program. Other research is to deal with clean alternative fuels and the assessment and comparison of international air pollution control technologies.

Title X seeks to secure fair treatment for disadvantaged business concerns in providing funding for environmental research.

Title XI provides for "clean air employment transition assistance." The title amends the Job Training Partnership Act to provide funding for grants to states, employers, employer associations, and representatives of employees to provide monies for persons who have been dislocated or displaced by new Clean Air Act requirements. Provision is made for adjustment assistance by way of job search allowances and relocation allowances. The provision is addressed particularly to the needs of miners and others who may be dislocated as a result of sulfur dioxide emission controls which may produce adverse economic consequences in parts of the country producing high sulfur coal.

The Clean Air Act Amendments of 1990 also add to the Congressional findings and purposes. A finding has been added that air pollution prevention, *i.e.*, the reduction or elimination of the amount of pollutants produced or created at the source, is a primary responsibility of states and local governments.[8] A newly stated goal of the Act is to encourage federal, state and local governmental actions for pollution prevention.[9]

Note that the Clean Air Act Amendments of 1990 place considerable emphasis on utilizing market forces in the service of pollution control by providing for negotiable emission permits. Noteworthy too, is the fact that although the 1990 Amendments provide for very stringent standards, the law is immediately effective only in requiring the Administrator to amend regulations and provide guidance documents. In many of its provisions, however, the law will not become fully effective and its impact will not be felt for several years. Indeed, many of the provisions of the law will not become effective until sometime in the first quarter of the 21st century.

[c] Air Quality Control Regions

The regulatory scheme following the adoption of the 1970 Clean Air Amendments provides for a division of roles between the federal and state governments. Primary responsibility for general standard setting is clearly lodged on the federal level, while day-to-day responsibility for enforcement activities clearly remains with the states, subject to direct state control, or control delegated to the municipalities and local governments. There are, however, far-reaching provisions that enhance the federal Administrator's direct enforcement powers.

Every state is divided into two or more air quality control regions designated by the state with the approval of the Administrator.[10] The governor of each state must make the following designations for each air quality control region within the state. He must designate an area (1) nonattainment, for any area that does not meet national primary or secondary ambient air quality standards for a pollutant, or that contributes to the ambient air quality in a nearby area that does not meet such standards; (2) attainment, designating any area that meets the national primary or secondary ambient air quality standard for that pollutant; or (3) unclassifiable, designating any area that cannot be classified on the basis of available information as meeting or not meeting the national primary or secondary ambient air quality standard for that pollutant.

[8] CAA § 101(a)(3), as amended by Clean Air Act Amendments of 1990, § 108(k)(1).

[9] CAA § 101(c), as added by Clean Air Act Amendments of 1990, § 108(k)(3).

[10] CAA § 107(b); 42 U.S.C. § 7407(b).

The governor is to make such designations when requested by the Administrator but in any event no later than one year after the promulgation of a new or revised national ambient air quality standard for any criteria pollutant. The governor may also submit such designations at other times, whenever he deems appropriate. The Administrator may not require the governor to submit his designations sooner than 120 days after the promulgation of a new or revised national ambient air quality standard.[11]

Area designation is very significant because it triggers the applicable controls under the state implementation plan to manage the area's attainment of the National Ambient Air Quality Standards, including the special requirements of the Act for the regulation of nonattainment areas as well as for the prevention of significant deterioration. The importance of the designation of areas makes this a subject of state-Administrator coordination, with the final determination the clear responsibility of the Administrator.

The Administrator must promulgate the final designation of all area designations submitted by the governors no later than two years from the date of promulgation of new or revised ambient air quality standards. The Administrator may postpone their promulgation up to one year if he has insufficient information to promulgate the designations.[12]

The Administrator may modify the area designations submitted by the governor, but he must allow the state to show why the proposed modification is inappropriate. If the governor fails to submit the list of designations, the Administrator may himself promulgate designations for any area not designated by the state.

When the governor of a state has submitted the list of nonattainment, attainment, or unclassifiable areas, the designation remains in effect until the area is redesignated, pursuant to § 107(d)(3) or (4). Designations made under prior law are left intact under the 1990 Amendments until redesignated. This applies as well to areas designated as attainment areas by operation of law under such earlier law.

All designations and redesignations must be published by notice in the Federal Register, but such notice or designation does not give rise to notice and comment proceedings under the Administrative Procedure Act, even though the section states that public notice and comment is not precluded whenever possible.[13]

The law provides for mutual notification from the Administrator to the governor and from a governor to the Administrator relating to the revision of an earlier designation. The law also provides for the effect of a redesignation on the effectiveness and enforceability of an earlier state implementation plan.[14]

The Administrator may not redesignate a nonattainment area to attainment unless the area has attained the national ambient air quality standard and

---

[11] CAA § 107(d)(1)(A); 42 U.S.C. § 7407(d)(1)(A), as last amended by the Clean Air Act Amendments of 1990.

[12] CAA § 107(d)(1)(B)(i); 42 U.S.C. § 7407(d)(1)(B)(i).

[13] CAA § 107(d)(2)(B); 42 U.S.C. § 7407(d)(2)(B).

[14] CAA § 107(d)(3)(D); 42 U.S.C. § 7407(d)(3)(D).

unless the Administrator has fully approved the applicable implementation plan for the area under § 110(k). In order to make such a designation, the Administrator must determine that the improvement in air quality is due to permanent and enforceable reductions in emissions resulting from the implementation of the applicable state implementation plan and other applicable federal regulations. For such a redesignation, the Administrator must fully approve a maintenance plan for the area meeting the requirements of § 175(a), and the state must have met all the requirements applicable of the state implementation plan under § 110 and under the prevention of significant deterioration provisions (Part D) of the Act.[15] The Administrator may not promulgate a redesignation of any area from "nonattainment" to "unclassifiable."

The Act makes special provisions for the nonattainment designations for ozone, carbon monoxide and particulate matter (PM-10). When the Administrator makes modifications in the designation of such areas, he must give the governor 60 days notice of his intention to modify. If the governor does not submit an area designation, then the Administrator must promulgate the appropriate designation.[16]

Special provision is made for ozone or carbon monoxide nonattainment areas which are located within a metropolitan statistical area or consolidated metropolitan statistical area which is classified under Part D of the Clean Air Act as a Serious, Severe, or Extreme Area. The boundaries of the area are revised by operation of law to include the entire metropolitan statistical area or consolidated statistical area, effective 45 days after such classification. The law provides a 45-day period for the governor to notify the Administrator that a formal evaluation is necessary to undertake a study to determine whether the entire metropolitan statistical area is to be included within the nonattainment area. Upon a proper showing, the Administrator may approve the governor's request to exclude a portion from the area.[17] Certain similar designations apply with respect to nonattainment for particulate matter (PM-10) which may also be designated as nonattainment for PM-10 by operation of law. This applies to any area containing a site for which air quality monitoring data show a violation of the national standard before January 1, 1989.[18] The Administrator may also designate areas for nonattainment with respect to the national ambient air quality standard for lead in effect at the date of enactment of the 1990 amendments.[19]

[15] CAA § 107(d)(3)(E); 42 U.S.C. § 7407(d)(3)(E).

[16] CAA § 107(d)(4)(A)(ii); 42 U.S.C. § 7407(d)(4)(A)(ii).

[17] CAA § 107(d)(4)(v); 42 U.S.C. § 7407(d)(4)(v).

[18] CAA § 107(d)(4)(B); 42 U.S.C. § 7407(d)(4)(B).

[19] CAA § 107(d)(5); 42 U.S.C. § 7407(d)(5).

[d] National Ambient Air Quality Standards

Council on Environmental Quality
Twelfth Annual Report, 25
(transmitted to Congress 1981)

[The text which follows the table in the 1981 CEQ Report at 25-30 analyzes the attainment status for each of the criteria pollutants, and shows considerable progress for all pollutants in certain parts of the country.]

NAAQS (National Ambient Air Quality Standard) Pollutants Table

NATIONAL AMBIENT AIR QUALITY STANDARDS

PRIMARY STANDARDS			SECONDARY STANDARDS	
Pollutant	Averaging Time	Concentration	Averaging Time	Concentration
Carbon Monoxide	8 hr	9 ppm (10 μg/m³)	No secondary standard	
	1 hr	35 ppm (40 μg/m³)		
Lead	Maximum quarterly average	1.5 μg/m³	Same as primary	
Nitrogen Oxide	Annual arithmetic mean	0.053 ppm (100 μg/m³)	Same as primary	
Ozone	8 hr	0.08 ppm	Same as primary	
Particulates	Annual arithmetic mean	15 μg/m³	Same as primary	
	24 hr	150 μg/m³		
PM 2.5	Annual arithmetic mean	15 μg/m³ 65 μg/m³		
Sulfur Dioxide	Annual arithmetic mean	(0.03 ppm)		
	24 hr	(0.14 ppm)	3 hr	1300 μg/m³ (0.50 ppm)

KENNECOTT COPPER CORP. v. EPA

U.S. Court of Appeals, D.C. Circuit (1972)
462 F.2d 846

[One of the earliest decisions interpreting the 1970 Clean Air Act, the case addressed the relationship of air quality criteria promulgated under § 109 of the Clean Air Actwith national ambient air quality standards. Plaintiffs complained that the national secondary ambient air quality standards for sulfur oxides promulgated by EPA on April 30, 1971 were not based on the underlying air quality criteria, also issued by EPA. It was also asserted that the air quality criteria did not meet the requirement of a concise general statement of their basis and purpose, as required by § 4(c) of the Administrative Procedure Act, and necessary to insure adequate judicial review. As usual in such early cases, the court outlined the general legislative scheme. It noted the special meaning of "air quality criteria" not as a standard, but as a document that accurately reflects the latest scientific knowledge useful in indicating identifiable effects on public health and welfare which may be expected from the presence of such a pollutant in the ambient air. Here the quality criteria were properly published and reflected pertinent scientific knowledge. The standard—reportedly set on the basis of the criteria—required the limitation of 60 micrograms of sulfur dioxide per cubic meter, while the data supplied in the criteria document referred to no adverse effects at a level below 85 micrograms per cubic meter. The statement and purpose of the regulation focused on the basis for primary standards, which were simultaneously adopted with the secondary standards. With respect to the secondary standards the Administrator said only

> National secondary ambient air quality standards are those which, in the judgment of the Administrator, based on the air quality criteria, are requisite to protect the public welfare from any known or anticipated adverse effects associated with the presence of air pollutants in the ambient air.

As justification for the higher standard than the one supported in the criteria document, EPA asserted that the resume in the criteria document is not conclusive and, in the alternative, that the 85 figure in the criteria document supports a 60 standard, on the basis of the Administrator's judgment as to anticipated effects and a margin necessary to avoid the adverse effects noted at the 85 level.

Relying on earlier decisions, the court noted that judicial review rests on the premise that the agency and court "together constitute a partnership in furtherance of the public interest" and collaborate in the achievement of justice. "Inherent in the responsibility entrusted to this court is a requirement that we be given sufficient indication of the basis on which the Administrator reached the 60 figure so that we may consider whether it embodies an abuse of discretion or error of law." Without disclosure of the basis of the agency's action, the court cannot fully dispose of the issue. The court's decision by Judge Leventhal is one of the early decisions which insists that statutory judicial review requires the disclosure of the basis for the agency's action. While justification may not need to be as detailed as is required for orders or regulations issued after formal rulemaking hearings, there must be some data for the court to work on. The court noted the emphasis on expedition in making air pollution controls effective, as clearly provided in the statute. It emphasized its desire to avoid any delay in the accomplishment and enforcement of clean air standards. While the Clean Air Act requires no hearings on proposed national ambient air quality standards, such hearings are required in the adoption of state implementation plans. The court therefore avoided the imposition of detailed standards in the general statement of support required in the Administrative Procedure Act. However, it reiterated the necessity for the submission of the factual data considered by the Administrator in support of the standard promulgated, and remanded the case for expeditious disposition, requiring the Administrator to supply an implementing statement to enlighten the court as to the basis on which he reached the 60 standard based on the material in the criteria. The court states its intention that the remand not halt or delay the ongoing proceedings for state adoption of implementation plans to meet and maintain the national standard. The Administrator was given freedom by the court to revise the criteria on the basis of material in his hand, without requiring any additional submissions.

The *Kennecott* decision provides a strong direction for the future course of environmental litigation in setting pollution standards. The court characterized its role in the standard-setting process and emphasized judicial insistence on adequately reasoned and clearly articulated data to support the standards arrived at. A frequently recurring theme is also reflected in the court's desire not to have administrative procedures delay the process unduly, insisting however on a record that the court can use in the judicial review of the promulgated standards.]

LEAD INDUSTRIES ASSOCIATION, INC. v. EPA

United States Court of Appeals, D.C. Circuit (1980)
647 F.2d 1130
cert. denied, 101 S. Ct. 621 (1980)

Before WRIGHT, Chief Judge, and ROBINSON and MacKINNON, Circuit Judges.

J. SKELLY WRIGHT, Chief Judge:

This is the third occasion on which this court has been asked to review Environmental Protection Agency (EPA or Agency) regulations promulgated under authority of the Clean Air Act, as amended, 42 U.S.C. § 7401 *et seq.* (Supp. I 1977) (the Act), and specifically designed to deal with the health problems associated with lead in the ambient air. In *Amoco Oil Co. v. EPA*,

501 F.2d 722 (D.C.Cir.1974), we upheld regulations prohibiting the sale of leaded gasoline for use in automobiles equipped with "catalytic converter" devices for controlling exhaust emissions and requiring widespread retail marketing of at least one grade of unleaded gasoline. And in *Ethyl Corp. v. EPA*, 541 F.2d 1 (D.C.Cir.) *(en banc), cert. denied,* 426 U.S. 941, 96 S.Ct. 2663, 49 L.Ed.2d 394 (1976), we affirmed an EPA order requiring annual reductions in the lead content of leaded gasoline. In the present consolidated cases we are asked to review EPA regulations establishing national ambient air quality standards for lead. These air quality standards prescribe the maximum concentrations of lead that will be permitted in the air of our country. We must decide whether EPA's Administrator acted within the scope of his statutory authority in promulgating these regulations and, if so, whether the evidence adduced at the rulemaking proceeding supports his final determinations. In addition, we must examine the petitioners' claims that infirmities in the procedures employed by EPA in this rulemaking warrant remand of the regulations to the Agency. Petitioners are the Lead Industry Association, Inc. (LIA), a nonprofit trade association whose 78 members include most of the country's producers and commercial consumers of lead (No. 78-2201), and St. Joe Minerals Corporation (St. Joe) (No. 78-2220).[20]

I. BACKGROUND

Man's ability to alter his environment to achieve perceived goals has undoubtedly made an enormous contribution to his economic and social well-being. This undertaking is not, however, without attendant costs. One of these costs is the toll that these alterations may exact on the environment itself and, in turn, the dangers that this may pose for the public health and welfare. Unfortunately, man's ability to alter the environment often far outstrips his ability to foresee with any degree of certainty what untoward effects these changes may bring. The issues presented by these cases illustrate this sad fact.

Lead's environmental significance is a consequence of both its abundance and its utility. The relative abundance of lead in the earth's crust makes it unique among the toxic heavy metals. EPA's "Air Quality Criteria For Lead" (hereinafter cited as CD) 1-1, Joint Appendix (JA) 1105. And centuries of mining and smelting, and the use of lead in a variety of human activities, have increased the natural background concentration of lead in the environment. *Id.* But it is only since the industrial age and the use of lead as a gasoline additive that lead has become pervasive. *Id.* at 1-2-1-3, JA 1106-1107. Today lead is ubiquitous. It is found in almost every medium with which we come into contact-food, water, air, soil, dust, and paint, *id.* 1-1, JA 1105, each of which represents a potential pathway for human lead exposure through ingestion or inhalation. The widespread presence of this toxic metal in the environment poses a significant health risk. Lead is a poison which has no known beneficial function in the body, *id.* 1-12, JA 1116, but when present in the body in sufficient concentrations lead attacks the blood, kidneys, and

[20] The Bunker Hill Company is an intervenor, and the Natural Resources Defense Council, Inc. and the Air Resources Board of the State of California were granted permission to participate as *amici curiae*.

central nervous and other systems and can cause anemia, kidney damage, severe brain damage, and death. *Id.* 1-6-1-9, JA 1110-1113.[21]

There are three major sources of the body's lead burden. In most people the largest source is diet. CD 7-9, JA 1179.[22] Another source, particularly in children, is the habit of placing hands, objects, and materials in the mouth.[23] The third major source is the ambient air; airborne lead is deposited in the respiratory tract as a person breathes lead-contaminated air and is subsequently absorbed into the bloodstream. CD 1-5, JA 1108. Once the lead is in the bloodstream its source is immaterial; total lead intake is the sum of the intake from all these sources. The multiplicity of sources of lead intake increases the difficulty of controlling human lead exposure. Much of the protective activity in this area has focused on limiting the amount of lead in the ambient air, the most controllable source of lead exposure. In this country, by far the largest source of lead emissions—accounting for 88 percent of total lead emissions according to EPA estimates—is the exhaust of motor vehicles powered by gasoline containing lead additives. CD 5-3, JA 1140. Another eight percent of lead emissions is the result of solid waste incineration and combustion of waste oil. *Id.* Industrial facilities account for the remaining four percent of total lead emissions. *Id.*

Acting pursuant to authority conferred on it by Congress in the Clean Air Act, as amended, 42 U.S.C. § 7401 *et seq.*, EPA has been involved in regulation of lead emissions almost since the Agency's inception.[24] Its initial approach to controlling the amount of lead in the ambient air was to limit lead emissions from automobiles by restricting the amount of lead in gasoline. To this end it promulgated the regulations which we upheld in *Amoco Oil Corp. v. EPA, supra,* and *Ethyl Corp. v. EPA, supra.* However, in 1975 the Natural Resources Defense Council, Inc. (NRDC) and others brought suit against EPA claiming that the Agency was required by Section 108 of the Clean Air Act, 42 U.S.C. § 7408, to list lead as a pollutant for which an air quality criteria document would be prepared, and for which national ambient air quality standards should be promulgated under Section 109 of the Act, 42 U.S.C. § 7409. The District Court agreed with NRDC and directed the Administrator to list lead as a pollutant under Section 108 of the Act, by March 31, 1976. *Natural Resources Defense Council, Inc. v. Train,* 411 F. Supp. 864 (S.D.N.Y. 1976). The Second Circuit affirmed, 545 F.2d 320 (2d Cir. 1976), and EPA initiated the proceedings outlined in the statute which are under review here.

. . . .

---

21 *See generally* EPA's "Air Quality Criteria For Lead" (hereinafter cited as CD), Chapter 11, JA 1223-1276.

22 Estimates of daily lead intake from diet in adult males range between 100 to 500 grams/day. Only a fraction of the lead ingested is actually absorbed. CD 7-9, 10-1—10-4, JA 1179, 1212-1215.

23 Pica, the habitual ingestion of nonfood substances, is a particularly important source of lead exposure for children who live in urban areas. CD 1-5, JA 1109.

24 EPA and other federal agencies, including the Department of Housing and Urban Development, the Occupational Health and Safety Administration, and the Consumer Product Safety Commission, are involved in a variety of regulatory efforts aimed at controlling other sources of lead exposure. *See* 43 Fed. Reg. 46256-46257, JA 2958-2959.

III. THE LEAD STANDARDS RULEMAKING PROCEEDINGS

As required by statute, EPA's first step toward promulgating air quality standards for lead was to prepare a criteria document. The Lead Criteria Document was the culmination of a process of rigorous scientific and public review, and thus is a comprehensive and thoughtful analysis of the most current scientific information on the subject. The Lead Criteria Document went through three major drafts, and three separate reviews, including public meetings by the Subcommittee on Scientific Criteria for Environmental Lead of EPA's Science Advisory Board (SAB Lead Subcommittee). The Agency reviewed over 280 public comments, most of a sophisticated scientific nature, before it issued the final Criteria Document. Members of the public, industry (including the petitioners in these cases), environmental groups, the scientific community, and state and federal government agencies actively participated in the review of the drafts. Notice of the meetings of the SAB Lead Subcommittee was published in the *Federal Register,* and the drafts of the Criteria Document which were to be reviewed were available before the meetings. A formal record and a transcript of the proceedings were kept, and a review of the transcript shows that scientists with differing views could—and did—exchange ideas with each other as well as agency staff, and that all were questioned by the members of the Subcommittee.

A. The Lead Criteria Document[25]

EPA released its "Air Quality Criteria For Lead" on December 14, 1977. 42 Fed. Reg. 63076, JA 1480. The document was "prepared to reflect the current state of knowledge about lead—specifically, those issues that are most relevant to establishing the objective scientific data base that will be used to recommend an air quality standard for lead that will adequately safeguard the public health." CD 1-1, JA 1105. Accordingly, the Criteria Document examined a large number of issues raised by the problem of lead in the environment. One of these was the effects of lead exposure on human health. The Criteria Document concluded that, among the major organ systems, the

[25] The first draft of the Criteria Document was released for public comment on November 18, 1976. This draft was severely criticized for its lack of scholarship, poor analysis, and low overall quality by most of the experts who reviewed it. By a 4-3 vote the SAB Subcommittee adopted a resolution that the draft's fundamental flaws made it an inadequate basis for future drafts and recommended that EPA prepare an entirely new draft. JA 268-270. The second draft of the Criteria Document was released on May 27, 1977 and, while the reaction to it was slightly more favorable, the SAB Subcommittee concluded that the draft was inadequate as a basic scientific support document for development of health-related air quality standards. JA 821-824. The third draft of the Criteria Document was released on August 22, 1977, and this time the consensus of the SAB Subcommittee was that the draft was basically sound and represented a vast improvement over the previous drafts. JA 935, 1069-1073. The Subcommittee agreed that another meeting to review the final draft of the Criteria Document was unnecessary. Instead, each individual member would submit written comments, if any, on the final draft. In his final report to the Agency the chairman of the Subcommittee stated that on the whole the final draft "accurately reflect[ed] the available scientific literature and provid[ed] an adequate scientific basis for promulgation and issuance of a standard for airborne lead." JA 913-914. The only other comments on the final draft were from two consultants retained by the Subcommittee who found the draft sound on many points but declined to endorse it because they disagreed with some of its conclusions. JA 915-920, 2107-2114.

hematopoietic (blood-forming) and neurological systems are the areas of prime concern. CD 1-12, JA 1116. Its discussion of the effects of lead on these two organ systems is central to our review of the lead standards.[26]

The Criteria Document identified a variety of effects of lead exposure on the blood-forming system. We will discuss only the effects that played an important role in the Administrator's analysis. Anemia, which can be caused by lead induced deformation and destruction of erythrocytes (red blood cells) and decreased hemoglobin synthesis,[27] is often the earliest clinical manifestation of lead intoxication. CD 11-7, 11-8, 11-13, JA 1229-1230, 1235. Symptoms of anemia include pallor of the skin, shortness of breath, palpitations of the heart, and fatigability.[28] The Criteria Document concluded, after a review of various studies, that in "children, a threshold level for anemia is about 40 u[g] Pb/dl, whereas the corresponding value for adults is about 50 ug Pb/dl." CD 11-13, JA 1235. (The concentration of lead in the blood is measured in micrograms of lead per decaliter of blood-ug Pb/dl.)

The Criteria Document also examined other more subtle effects on the blood-forming system, associated with lower levels of lead exposure. The most pertinent of these "subclinical"[29] effects for purposes of these cases is lead-related elevation of erythrocyte protoporphyrin (EP elevation).[30] According to the Criteria Document, this phenomenon must, for a number of reasons, be regarded as an indication of an impairment of human health. CD 11-11, JA 1233. First, EP elevation indicates an impairment in the functioning of the mitochondria, the subcellular units which play a crucial role in the production of energy in the body, and in cellular respiration. CD 11-6, 11-11, 11-14, 13-5, JA 1110, 1233, 1236, 1335. Second, it indicates that lead exposure has begun to affect one of the basic biological functions of the body—production of heme within the red blood cells.[31] Heme is critical to transporting oxygen

26 Lead also affects the renal, reproductive, endocrine, hepatic, cardiovascular, immunologic, and gastrointestinal systems. CD Chapter 11, JA 1223-1276.

27 Hemoglobin is the protein which transports life-sustaining oxygen from the respiratory system to all cells in the body. CD 11-8, JA 1230. It consists of a combination of heme and globin, and lead interferes with hemoglobin synthesis by inhibiting synthesis of the globin moiety and affecting several steps in synthesis of the heme molecule. *See* CD 11-13—11-14, JA 1235-1236.

28 Stedman's Medical Dictionary 94 (Unabridged Lawyers' Edition 1961).

29 According to the Criteria Document, "subclinical" effects "are disruptions in function, which may be demonstrated by special testing but not by the classic techniques of physical examination; using the term 'subclinical' in no way implies that those effects are without consequences to human health." CD 13-4, JA 1334. Stedman's Medical Dictionary, *supra* note 10, defines "subclinical" as "[d]enoting a period prior to the appearance of manifest symptoms in the evolution of a disease." *Id.* at 1433.

30 A major function of the hematological system is the production of red blood cells (erythrocytes) which carry oxygen to the cells of the body by chemically binding oxygen to the protein hemoglobin, one of the components of erythrocytes. *See* note 9 *supra*. Heme, one of the components of hemoglobin, is formed through a series of biochemical steps (heme synthesis), the final step in which is incorporation of iron into the protein protoporphyrin IX. This process takes place in the mitochondria of the cell, and one of the ways in which lead affects heme synthesis is by interfering with this final step. The result is that protoporphyrin IX, without iron, is incorporated in the hemoglobin molecule in the erythrocytes. This phenomenon is detected as an elevation of protoporphyrin in the erythrocyte, *i.e.*, EP elevation. CD 11-7—11-14, JA 1229-1236.

31 *See* note 12 *supra*. Lead also interferes with heme synthesis by inhibiting production of an enzyme which acts as a catalyst in an

to every cell in the body. Third, EP elevation may indicate that any reserve capacity there may be in the heme synthesis system has been reduced. CD 11-11, JA 1233. Finally, the Criteria Document noted that lead's interference with the process of heme synthesis in the blood may suggest that lead interferes with production of heme proteins in other organ systems, particularly the renal and neurological systems. CD 11-11, JA 1233. The Criteria Document reported that the threshold for EP elevation in children and women is at blood lead levels of 15-20 ug Pb/dl, and 25-30 ug Pb/dl in adult males. CD 13-8 (Table 13-2), JA 1338 (Table 13-2). While suggesting that some of the initial hematological effects of lead exposure may constitute relatively mild effects at low blood lead levels, the Criteria Document concluded that "they nevertheless signal the onset of steadily intensifying adverse effects as blood lead elevations increase. Eventually, [these] . . . effects reach such magnitude that they are of clearcut medical significance as indicators of undue lead exposure." CD 11-13, JA 1117. The Criteria Document did not identify a particular blood lead level at which regulatory response was appropriate, but it did note with approval the 1975 guidelines issued by the Center For Disease Control, which use elevated EP at blood lead levels of 30 ug Pb/dl as the cut-off point in screening children for lead poisoning. CD 13-5, JA 1335.

The Criteria Document also examined the effects of lead exposure on the central nervous system. Among the most deleterious effects of lead poisoning are those associated with severe central nervous system damage at high exposure levels. The Criteria Document noted that neurological and behavioral deficits have long been known to be among the more serious effects of lead exposure, but it pointed out that there is disagreement about whether these effects are reversible, and about what exposure levels are necessary to produce specific deleterious effects. CD 11-14, JA 1236. Much of the impetus for the debate on these questions has been provided by the continual emergence of new information suggesting that lead exposure levels previously thought to be harmless actually cause significant neurological damage. *Id.* The more severe neurological effects of high level lead exposure are the clinical syndrome of lead encephalopathy. Early symptoms include dullness, restlessness, irritability, headaches, muscular tremor, hallucinations, and loss of memory. These symptoms rapidly progress (sometimes within 48 hours) to delirium, mania, convulsions, paralysis, coma, and death. *Id.* at 11-15, JA 1237. The Criteria Document expressed particular concern that the onset of these serious symptoms can be quite abrupt, even in the absence of prior overt or clinical symptoms of disease. *Id.* at 13-6, JA 1336. After a review of various studies, the Criteria Document concluded that the blood lead threshold for these neurological effects of high level exposure is 80-100 ug Pg/dl in children, and 100-200 ug Pb/dl in adults. *Id.* at 11-13, 11-18, 11-25, 13-6, JA 1117, 1240, 1247, 1336.

The Criteria Document also went on to consider the evidence on whether lower level lead exposures can affect the central nervous system, particularly

early step in production of heme. *See* CD 11-8—11-10, JA 1230-1232. Although the threshold for detection of inhibition of this enzyme is about 10 ug Pb/dl, the Criteria Document concluded that this effect should not be considered a physiological impairment until blood lead concentrations reach levels of 40 ug Pb/dl. CD 11-6, 11-10, JA 1110, 1232.

in children. It acknowledged that the issue is unsettled and somewhat controversial, but it was able to conclude, after a careful review of various studies on the subject,[32] that "a rather consistent pattern of impaired neural and cognitive functions appears to be associated with blood lead levels below those producing the overt symptomatology of lead encephalopathy." CD 11-7, JA 1111. The Criteria Document reported that "[t]he blood lead levels at which neurobehavioral deficits occur in otherwise asymptomatic children appear to start at a range of 50 to 60 ug/dl, although some evidence tentatively suggests that such effects may occur at slightly lower levels for some children." *Id.*[33]

In addition to examining the health effects of lead exposure, the Criteria Document also discussed other issues critical to the task of setting air quality standards for lead. One of these issues is the relationship between air lead exposure and blood lead levels —a relationship commonly referred to as the air lead/blood lead ratio. The Criteria Document acknowledged that derivation of a functional relationship between air lead exposure and blood lead levels is made difficult by the fact that the relationship is not a linear one; rather, the ratio tends to increase as air lead levels are reduced, CD 12-24, JA 131 11. The Document was nevertheless able to conclude, after a detailed examination of the relevant studies, CD 12-22—12-29, JA 1309-1316, that air lead/blood lead ratios fall within a range of 1:1 to 1:2 (ug Pb/m^3 air):(ug Pb/dl blood) at the levels of lead exposure generally encountered by the population, *i.e.*, blood lead levels increase by between 1 and 2 ug Pb/dl of blood for every 11 ug Pb/m^3 of air. (Air lead content is measured in micrograms of lead per cubic meter of air—ug Pb/m^3.) CD 12-38, JA 1325. The Criteria Document reported that the studies indicate that the ratio for children is at the upper end of this range or even slightly above it. *Id.*

Finally, the Criteria Document also examined the distribution of blood lead levels throughout the population, concluding that there is a significant variability in individual blood lead responses to any particular level of air lead exposure. It further found that this variability is consistent and predictable, and that the application of established statistical techniques to the distribution of individual blood lead levels would make it possible to predict what proportion of the population would be above or below any particular blood lead level at a given level of air lead exposure.[34] The Criteria Document looked into the question whether any sub-groups within the population are particularly vulnerable to the effects of lead exposure. It concluded that preschool-age

[32] *See* CD 11-18—11-26, JA 1240-1248. Some of these studies suggested that low level lead exposure may cause central nervous system deficits, resulting in impaired concept formation and altered behavioral profiles, may interfere with the normal intellectual development of lead-exposed children, and may cause subtle neurological damage. *Id.*

[33] The Criteria Document also discussed the possibility that adverse health effects, including neurobehavioral deficits, may be induced by *in utero* exposure of the human fetus to lead. It pointed out that the potential for deleterious health effects from lead exposure in the areas of reproduction and development is particularly large, but felt that the paucity of information and confirmatory studies precluded any firm conclusions about threshold blood lead levels, CD 11-45—11-58, JA 1267-1270.

[34] The statistical distribution of individual blood lead levels in a homogeneous population was found to be lognormal; *i.e.*, the log values of blood lead levels would fall in the familiar bell-shaped curve. CD 12-1, JA 1288. This means that for any given level of air lead exposure the population will have a range of blood lead levels rather than a single level, with about half the population having blood lead levels above the geometric mean and the other half below it.

children and pregnant women are particularly sensitive to lead exposure, the latter mainly because of the risk to the unborn child. CD 13-11—13-14, JA 1341-1344.

B. The Proposed Standards

Simultaneously with the publication of the Lead Criteria Document on December 14, 1977, the Administrator proposed a national primary ambient air quality standard for lead of 1.5 ug Pb/m^3 monthly average. 42 Fed. Reg. 63076, JA 1480. He also proposed that the secondary air quality standard be set at the same level as the primary standard because the welfare effects associated with lead exposure did not warrant imposition of a stricter standard. 42 Fed. Reg. 63081-63082, JA 1485-1486. In the preamble to the proposed standards the Administrator explained the analysis EPA had employed in setting the standards.

The Administrator first pointed out that a number of factors complicate the task of setting air quality standards which will protect the population from the adverse health effects of lead exposure. First, some subgroups within the population have a greater potential for, or are more susceptible to the effects of, lead exposure. *Id.* at 63077, JA 1481. Second, there are a variety of adverse health effects associated with various levels of lead exposure. *Id.* Third, the variability of individual responses to lead exposure, even within particular sub-groups of the population, would produce a range of blood lead levels at any given air lead level. *Id.* at 63079, JA 1483. Fourth, airborne lead is only one of a number of sources of lead exposure and the relative contribution from each source is difficult to quantify. *Id.* at 63080, JA 1484. Finally, the relationship between air lead exposure and blood lead levels is a complex one. *Id.* at 63079, JA 1483.

In response to the first problem the Administrator began by noting that protection of the most sensitive groups within the population had to be a major consideration in determining the level at which the air quality standards should be set. And he determined that children between the ages of 1 and 5 years are most sensitive to the effects of lead exposure both because the hematologic and neurologic effects associated with lead exposure occur in children at lower threshold levels than in adults, and because the habit of placing hands and other objects in the mouth subjects them to a greater risk of exposure. *Id.* at 63077-63078, JA 1481-1482. Next, the Administrator examined the various health effects of lead exposure and proposed that EP elevation should be considered the first adverse health effect of lead exposure because it indicates an impairment of cellular functions, and should be the pivotal health effect on which the lead standards are based. *Id.* at 63078, JA 1482. Accordingly, he proposed that the air lead standards be designed to prevent the occurrence of EP elevation in children. In order to accomplish this, and to address the problem of variable responses to lead exposure, the Administrator selected 15 ug Pb/dl, the lowest reported threshold blood lead level for EP elevation in children, as the target mean population blood lead level.[35] He reasoned that setting the target mean population blood lead level at the lowest reported threshold blood lead level for EP elevation would ensure that most of the target population would be kept below blood lead levels at which adverse health effects occur. *Id.* at 63078, JA 1483. The Administrator also discussed the alternative approaches of basing the standard on more severe effects such as anemia, or attempting to decide the actual level of EP elevation which represents an adverse effect on health, and then making an adjustment to allow a margin of safety. *Id.* He specifically invited comments on these alternative approaches. *Id.* Finally, the Administrator outlined another approach to calculating the target mean population blood lead level involving the use of statistical techniques discussed in the Criteria Document. *Id.*[36]

Having selected a target mean population blood lead level, the Administrator's next step was to allow for the multiplicity of sources of lead exposure. He thus had to estimate the amount of blood lead that should be attributed to non-air sources. The Administrator admitted that any amount he selected could be no more than a theoretical national average, and on the basis of the evidence available he proposed that the lead standards should be based on the general assumption that 12 ug Pb/dl of blood lead should be attributed to non-air sources. *Id.* at 63080-63081, JA 1484-1485. Given the target mean population blood lead level of 15 ug Pb/dl and the assumed contribution from non-air sources of 12 ug Pb/dl, the maximum allowable contribution from ambient air is 3 ug Pb/dl, The final step in his analysis was to determine what air lead level would prevent the ambient air contribution to blood lead levels from exceeding 3 ug Pb/dl. This step required determining the relationship between air lead exposure and blood lead levels, *i.e.*, the air lead/blood lead ratio. On the basis of the information in the Criteria Document, the Administrator selected a ratio of 1:2 as appropriate for calculating the effect of air lead exposure on blood lead levels in children. *Id.* at 63079, JA 1483.

Thereafter, calculation of the air quality standard was a mathematical exercise as shown in the following table.

1.	Target mean blood lead level	15 ug Pb/dl
2.	Assumed non-air contribution	− 12 ug Pb/dl
3.	Allowable air contribution	= 3 ug Pb/dl
4.	Permissible air lead concentration given assumed air lead/blood lead ratio	

[35] The target mean population blood lead level is the blood lead level that will ensure that the great majority of the target population is protected from the adverse health effects of lead. Given the variability in individual blood lead responses to lead exposure, a population with a mean blood lead level of 15 ug Pb/dl will have individuals with blood lead levels higher and lower than 15 ug Pb/dl, but since 15 ug Pb/dl is the lowest blood lead level at which EP elevation has been detected, most children will be kept below blood lead levels at which adverse health effects occur.

[36] *See* CD 12-1—12-3, 12-38, JA 1288-1290, 1325. This alternative approach would use lognormal statistical procedures to determine what mean population blood lead levels would keep a specified percentage of the population below a blood lead level chosen to represent the safe blood lead level for the average individual. The Administrator pointed out that he had misgivings about this approach because it might overestimate the degree to which the mean population level should be below the threshold lead level, particularly since 15 ug Pb/dl is the lowest reported threshold blood level for EP elevation. 42 Fed. Reg. 63079, JA 1483.

$$3 \text{ ug Pb/dl} \times \frac{1 \text{ ug Pb/m3 air}}{2 \text{ ug Pb/dl blood}} = 1.5 \text{ ug Pb/m}^3$$

The Administrator concluded, on the basis of available information, that the averaging period for the lead standard should be a calendar month. *Id.* at 63081, JA 1485.

C. Public Comments

The public comment period ran from December 14, 1977 to March 17, 1978, and public hearings on the proposed standards were held on February 15 and 16, 1978. 43 Fed. Reg. 46246, JA 2948. The comments on the proposed standards were sharply divided. The comments submitted by the lead industry and its experts uniformly opposed the proposed standards, and many endorsed a standard of 5 ug Pb/m^3, the standard proposed in the discredited first draft of the Criteria Document, see note 7 *supra,* as adequate to protect the public health. 43 Fed. Reg. 46248, JA 2950. On the other hand, environmental groups, medical experts, and state, local, and federal agencies either endorsed the proposed standards or called for even stricter standards. *Id.* None of the comments seriously questioned the selection of children between the ages of 1 and 5 years as the target population group, or the estimate of a contribution from non-air sources of 12 ug Pb/dl. The major areas of controversy were the Administrator's choice of EP elevation as the pivotal adverse health effect and his conclusion that the threshold blood lead level for EP elevation in children is 15 ug Pb/dl, the selection of an appropriate air lead/blood lead ratio, the appropriate allowance for an adequate margin of safety, and the averaging time period for the standards. *Id.* [37]

A number of comments challenged the selection of EP elevation as the pivotal adverse health effect, insisting that EP elevation merely indicates a biological change or response which is in no way harmful to health,[38] and in addition they criticized the Administrator's determination that the blood lead threshold for EP elevation in children is 15 ug Pb/dl.[39] These comments suggested that a decrease in hemoglobin levels, which begins at blood lead levels no lower than 40 ug Pb/dl, should be the pivotal adverse health effect on which the standards are based.[40] Other experts, however, agreed with the Administrator's conclusion that EP elevation must be considered an adverse health effect of lead exposure, and argued that using EP elevation as the pivotal adverse health effect would, in addition, allow an adequate margin of safety in protecting against the more serious health effects associated with higher levels of lead exposure.[41] Finally, several industry experts appeared to

[37] A summary of the significant comments that were submitted and EPA's responses to them can be found in the preamble to the final regulations. 43 Fed. Reg. 46248-46252, JA 2950-2954.

[38] *See, e.g.,* JA 2176, 2193-2194 (statement of St. Joe Minerals Corp.); JA 1843 (statement of E. Jacobs, Dupont Corp.); JA 2067 (statement of G. Ter Haar, Ethyl Corp.); JA 2388-2390, 2393 (statement of J. Jandl, LIA); JA 1773-1774 (J. Chisholm, LIA).

[39] *See, e.g.,* JA 1775-1779 (J. Chisholm, LIA); JA 2362-2366 (comments of LIA); JA 2492-2498 (E. Jacobs, Dupont Corp.); JA 1843-1845 (statement of E. Jacobs, Dupont Corp.)

[40] *See, e.g,,* JA 2193-2194 (statement of St. Joe Minerals Corp.); JA 2263-2271 (Asarco); JA 1774-1775 (J. Chisholm, LIA); JA 1831-1832 (J. Cole, LIA).

[41] *See, e.g.,* JA 2161-2167 (D. Schoenbrod,

indicate a preference for the lognormal statistical procedures that the Administrator had, in the proposed standards, suggested as an alternative method for determining the target mean population blood lead level.[42]

D. The Final Air Quality Standards for Lead

The Administrator promulgated the final air quality standards on October 5, 1978, prescribing national primary and secondary ambient air quality standards for lead of 1.5 ug Pb/ml, averaged over a calendar quarter. 43 Fed. Reg. 46246, JA 2948. Although the final standards were the same as the proposed standards (with the exception of the change in the averaging period from 30 to 90 days), the Administrator arrived at the final standards through somewhat different analysis. The preamble to the final standards reveals that the comments on the proposed standards had led the Administrator to reconsider his analysis. In particular, he seemed to feel that legitimate questions had been raised concerning the health significance of the early stages of EP elevation and about the threshold blood lead level for this condition. 43 Fed. Reg. 46248, 462539 JA 2950t 2955. The Administrator's reexamination focused on two key questions: (1) What is the maximum safe individual blood lead level for children? and (2) What proportion of the target population should be kept below this blood lead level? *Id.* at 46249, 46252-46253, JA 2951, 2954-2955. Addressing the first issue required a review of the health effects of lead exposure discussed in the Criteria Document. The Administrator concluded that, although EP elevation beginning at blood lead levels of 15-20 ug Pb/dl is potentially adverse to the health of children, only when blood lead concentration reaches a level of 30 ug Pb/dl is this effect significant enough to be considered adverse to health. *Id.* at 46253, JA 2955. Accordingly, he selected 30 ug Pb/dl as the maximum safe individual blood lead level for children. *Id.* The Administrator based this choice on three mutually supporting grounds. First, it is at this blood lead level that the first adverse health effect of lead exposure—impairment of heme synthesis—begins to occur in children. Second, a maximum safe individual blood lead level of 30 ug Pb/dl would allow an adequate margin of safety in protecting children against more serious effects of lead exposure—anemia, symptoms of which begin to appear in children at blood lead levels of 40 ug Pb/dl, and central nervous system deficits which start to occur in children at blood lead levels of 50 ug Pb/dl. Third, the Administrator reasoned that the maximum safe individual blood lead level should be no higher than the blood lead level used by the Center for Disease Control in screening children for lead poisoning—30 ug Pb/dl. *Id.*

Having determined the maximum safe individual blood lead level for the target population, the Administrator next focused on the question of what percentage of children between the ages of 1 and 5 years the standard should attempt to keep below this blood lead level. According to the 1970 census, there are approximately 20 million children under the age of 5 years in the United

---

NRDC); JA 2168-2169 (H. Needleman); JA1563-1564 (P. Landrigans Center for Disease Control); JA 2499-2508 (S. Piomelli); JA 2580-2588 (H. Needleman and S. Piomelli); JA 2612-2614 (E. Silbergeld).

[42] *See* text and note at note 18 *supra*. *See* JA 2100-2101 (J. Chisholm, LIA); JA 2223 (St. Joe); JA 2368-2369 (LIA); JA 1831-1832 (J. Cole, LIA).

States, 12 million of them in urban areas and 5 million in inner cities where lead exposure may be especially high. The Administrator concluded that in order to provide an adequate margin of safety, and to protect special high risk sub-groups, the standards should aim at keeping 99.5% of the target population below the maximum safe individual blood lead level of 30 ug Pb/dl.[43] *Id.* at 46253t 462559 JA 2955, 2957. The next step in the analysis was to determine what target mean population blood lead level would ensure that 99.5% of the children below the age of 5 years would be kept below the maximum safe individual blood lead level of 30 ug Pb/dl. Using the lognormal statistical technique he had alluded to in the proposed standards,[44] he calculated that a target mean population blood lead level of 15 ug Pb/dl (the same number as in the proposed standards, but arrived at through different analysis), would accomplish this task.[45] *Id.* at 46253, 46254, JA 2955, 2956. Thereafter, the Administrator used the same estimate of the contribution from non-air sources, 12 ug Pb/dl, and the same air lead/blood lead ratio, 1:2, that he had used in calculating the proposed standards,[46] to compute the final ambient air quality standards for lead. The result was an ambient air quality standard of 1.5 ug Pb/m^3, the same as the proposed standard. *Id.* at 46254, JA 2956. The Administrator did, however, change the averaging period for the standards from one calendar month to one calendar quarter, *id.* at 46255, JA 2957, because he felt that this change would significantly improve the validity of the data to be used in monitoring the progress toward attainment of the standards without rendering the standards less protective. *Id.*

On December 8, 1978 LIA petitioned EPA for reconsideration and a stay of the lead standards. JA 2980-3000. The Administrator denied the petition on February 2, 1979. JA 3001-3007. These petitions for review of the lead standards regulations followed. Before examining the petitioners' challenges to the regulations, we consider the limits of our reviewing function.

IV. STANDARD OF REVIEW

. . . .

[The Court applied the "arbitrary, capricious, etc." standard under § 307(d) of the CAA,citing particularly the reference to setting aside any action found "without observance of procedure required by law" under § 307(d)(8), and relying also on the *Overton Park* standard, including an inquiry into the consideration of "relevant factors" and an examination into the "rational basis" for every decision. The Court noted that it was called upon to do more than decide technical issues, second guessing the technically expert agency.]

[43] Some of the industry comments on the proposed standards had, in calculating alternative standards, also chosen to protect 99.5% of the target population. *See* JA 2223 (St. Joe); JA 2368 (LIA).

[44] *See* text and note at note 18 *supra.*

[45] The procedure involved determining the geometric mean blood lead level that would place 99.5% of the target population below a blood lead level of 30 ug Pb/dl (*i.e.*, given the variability in individual responses to lead exposure, *see* text and note at note 16 *supra,* it was necessary to base the standards on a blood lead level of 15 ug Pb/dl in order to ensure that 99.5% of the children below the age of 5 years are kept under a blood lead level of 30 ug Pb/dl). In performing the calculation the Administrator used a geometric standard deviation of 1.3. 43 Fed. Reg. 46253, JA 2955.

[46] *See* 647 F.2d at 1142 *supra.*

It is also important to note that although the pertinent sections of the Clean Air Act outline the policy objectives to be sought and the procedural framework to be followed in promulgating ambient air quality standards, Congress left the formulation of the specific standards to EPA's Administrator. This task presents complex questions of science, law, and social policy under the Act. The record is lengthy—approximately 10,000 pages—and it is highly technical. The Administrator's task required both "a legislative policy determination and an adjudicative resolution of disputed facts." *Mobile Oil Corp. v. FPC*, 483 F.2d 1238, 1257 (D.C.Cir.1973).

These are conceptually distinct types of decisions, and it is important that we keep this in mind in reviewing the Administrator's decisions. *See Industrial Union Dep't, AFL-CIO v. Hodgson*, 499 F.2d 467, 474-475 (D.C.Cir.1974). Where factual determinations were necessary the Administrator often had to make decisions in the face of conflicting evidence. In some instances this merely required that he draw conclusions from the evidence in the record. In reviewing these conclusions we can examine the record to ascertain whether there is substantial evidence in the record when considered as a whole which supports the Administrator's determinations. *Id.* at 474. Other questions involved in the standard-setting process, however, are at the very "frontiers of scientific knowledge." Consequently, the information available may be insufficient to permit fully informed factual determinations. In such instances the Administrator's decisions necessarily had to rest largely on policy judgments. Policy choices of this sort "are not susceptible to the same type of verification or refutation by reference to the record as are [other] factual questions." 499 F.2d at 475. While we will indeed scrutinize such judgments carefully, we must adopt a different mode of judicial review. *Id.* accord, *Nat'l Asphalt Pavement Ass'n v. Train*, 539 F.2d 775, 783-784 (D.C.Cir. 1976); *Automotive Parts & Accessories Ass'n, Inc. v. Boyd*, 407 F.2d 330, 336, 338 (D.C.Cir.1968). As this court has previously stated:

> What we are entitled to . . . is a careful identification by the [Administrator], when his proposed standards are challenged, of the reasons why he chooses to follow one course rather than another. Where that choice purports to be based on certain determinable facts, [he] must, in form as well as substance, find those facts from evidence in the record. By the same token, when the [Administrator] is obliged to make policy judgments where no factual certainties exist or where facts alone do not provide the answer, he should so state and go on to identify the considerations he found persuasive.

Industrial Union Dep't, AFL-CIO v. Hodgson, supra, 499 F.2d at 475-476. In short, "[t]he paramount objective is to see whether the agency, given an essentially legislative task to perform, has carried it out in a manner calculated to negate the dangers of arbitrariness and irrationality in the formulation of rules for general application in the future." *Automotive Parts & Accessories Ass'n, Inc. v. Boyd, supra,* 407 F.2d at 338.

. . . .

V. STATUTORY AUTHORITY

The petitioners' first claim is that the Administrator exceeded his authority under the statute by promulgating a primary air quality standard for lead which is more stringent than is necessary to protect the public health because it is designed to protect the public against "sub-clinical" effects which are not harmful to health. According to petitioners, Congress only authorized the Administrator to set primary air quality standards that are aimed at protecting the public against health effects which are known to be *clearly harmful* They argue that Congress so limited the Administrator's authority because it was concerned that excessively stringent air quality standards could cause massive economic dislocation.

In developing this argument St. Joe contends that EPA erred by refusing to consider the issues of economic and technological feasibility in setting the air quality standards for lead. St. Joe's claim that the Administrator should have considered these issues is based on the statutory provision directing him to allow an "adequate margin of safety" in setting primary air quality standards. In St. Joe's view, the Administrator must consider the economic impact of the proposed standard on industry and the technological feasibility of compliance by emission sources in determining the appropriate allowance for a margin of safety. St. Joe argues that the Administrator abused his discretion by refusing to consider these factors in determining the appropriate margin of safety for the lead standards, and maintains that the lead air quality standards will have a disastrous economic impact on industrial sources of lead emissions.

This argument is totally without merit. St. Joe is unable to point to anything in either the language of the Act or its legislative history that offers any support for its claim that Congress, by specifying that the Administrator is to allow an "adequate margin of safety" in setting primary air quality standards, thereby required the Administrator to consider economic or technological feasibility. To the contrary, the statute and its legislative history make clear that economic considerations play no part in the promulgation of ambient air quality standards under Section 109.

. . . .

Furthermore, we agree with the Administrator that requiring EPA to wait until it can conclusively demonstrate that a particular effect is adverse to health before it acts is inconsistent with both the Act's precautionary and preventive orientation and the nature of the Administrator's statutory responsibilities. Congress provided that the Administrator is to use his judgment in setting air quality standards precisely to permit him to act in the face of uncertainty.[47] And as we read the statutory provisions and the legislative

[47] The House Report on the 1977 Amendments discussed the significance of the provision that the Administrator is to use his judgment in making the decisions required under the Act. It explained that the purpose is:

> To reflect awareness of the uncertainties and limitations in the data which will be available to the Administrator in the foreseeable future to enable him to execute his rulemaking duties under this act, because of the limitations on research resources and the fact that decision making about the risks to public health from air pollution falls on "the frontiers of scientific and medical knowledge"; to provide for adequate judicial review of the reasonableness of the Administrator's judgment in assessing risks, while restraining the courts from attempting to act "as the equivalent of a combined Ph.D. in chemistry, biology, and statistics" or from applying a standard of review which is appropriate only to review of adjudications or formal fact finding.

H.R. Rep. No.95-294, at 50. Although this

history, Congress directed the Administrator to err on the side of caution in making the necessary decisions. We see no reason why this court should put a gloss on Congress' scheme by requiring the Administrator to show that there is a medical consensus that the effects on which the lead standards were based are *"clearly harmful to health."* All that is required by the statutory scheme is evidence in the record which substantiates his conclusions about the health effects on which the standards were based.[48] Accordingly, we reject LIA's claim that the Administrator exceeded his statutory authority and turn to LIA's challenge to the evidentiary basis for the Administrator's decisions.

VI. HEALTH BASIS FOR THE LEAD STANDARDS

[The Court reviewed the standards and the supporting data in considerable detail, and concluded that the standards—including standards based on "sub-clinical effect"—were based on sound decisions concerning health effects, and did not exceed the adequate margin of safety required by the statute. The Court's discussion refers to expert scientific opinion relating to threshold effects, and subclinical impacts. The Court concluded that in its judgment and choice of methods, the Administrative standard-setting had not been arbitrary or capricious. Relying on the *Vermont Yankee* case, the Court also rejected a procedural challenge based on the Administration's refusal to allow cross-examination of experts. The Court rejected an effort by the petitioner to cloak this procedural maneuver in the assertion of a denial of constitutional due process. The Court also rejected the effort to overturn the standard on grounds that EPA Assistant Administrator David Hawkins had participated in the rulemaking proceeding, because he had been involved in advocating lead standards as staff attorney for the Natural Resources Defense Council prior to joining EPA. The Court failed to find any conflict of interest, and noted that the Lead Industry Association objection was untimely, because it had failed to raise it during the public comment period.]

---

discussion specifically relates to the use of the phrase "in [the Administrator's] judgment" in sections of the Act other than § 109(b), the discussion undoubtedly also illuminates Congress' intentions with regard to its use in § 109(b).

[48] We find nothing in the portions of the legislative history cited by LIA that supports the claim that Congress limited the Administrator's authority in the manner LIA suggests. The passage in the Senate Report which describes the national air quality standards as "minimum standards" merely refers to the fact that the states are free to adopt air quality standards which are more stringent than the national standards. S. Rep. No.91-1196, 91st Cong., 2d Sess. 10 (1970). *See* 42 U.S.C. § 7416. Moreover, it is difficult to see how the suggestion that the national standards are "minimum standards" implies that the Administrator must wait until there is a consensus among medical experts that certain effects are clearly adverse to health before he can base air quality standards on these effects. And the suggestions by Senator Muskie and the 1977 House Report that the air quality standards should not be set at zero or background levels by no means imply that the standards may only be based on effects which all the experts agree are clearly harmful to health. The Administrator has not suggested that he has the authority to protect against all effects of air pollution, whether or not they are adverse to health. Indeed, he specifically noted that the health effects of lead exposure begin at blood lead levels of 15-20 ug Pb/dl, and concluded that these effects are not significant enough to be regarded as adverse to health until blood lead concentrations reach a level of 30 ug Pb/dl. 43 Fed. Reg. 46253, JA 2955. As should be evident from the numerous references we have made to it, the House Report on the 1977 Amendments provides support for the Administrator's interpretation of the Act, not LIA'S.

[The Court denied LIA's motion for leave to supplement the administrative record.]

IX. THE SECONDARY AIR QUALITY STANDARD

The final challenge to the Administrator's actions that we must consider is LIA's objection to his decision to promulgate a national secondary ambient air quality standard for lead of 1.5 ug Pb/m^3, the same level as the primary standard. The Administrator explained that this decision was based on his conclusion that the evidence on the "welfare effects" of lead exposure did not justify promulgation of a secondary standard more stringent than the primary standard. LIA argues that the Administrator had no authority to adopt the secondary standard without making supporting findings showing that the standard is necessary to protect the public welfare. It contends that this court's decision in *Kennecott Copper Corp. v. EPA*, 462 F.2d 846 (D.C.Cir. 1972), mandates remand of the secondary standard. In that case we remanded the national secondary air quality standard for sulphur dioxide because the Administrator had failed to "enlighten the court as to the basis on which he reached the . . . standard from the material in the Criteria [Document]." *Id.* at 850. LIA argues that the Administrator should have considered whether the welfare effects of lead exposure would permit him to set a secondary air quality standard higher than the primary standard. Pointing out that the primary standards are supposed to protect public health and that they are based on a 90-day averaging period, LIA argues that it follows that primary standards need be met only in inhabited areas, whereas the secondary standards must also be met in uninhabited areas. Consequently, LIA contends, the Administrator's failure to consider the possibility of setting a higher secondary standard will impose an additional burden on industrial sources located in uninhabited areas which may not be justified by the requirements of protecting the public welfare.

LIA's complaint is based on a misconception about the reach of the primary standard. As EPA notes, the primary standard must be met in all parts of the country, whether inhabited or uninhabited. Thus by setting the secondary standard at the same level as the primary standard, the Administrator imposed no additional burdens on the industry, and he properly concentrated his attention on whether the welfare effects of lead exposure justified promulgation of a more stringent secondary standard. Our decision in *Kennecott Copper,* on which LIA relies, involved an attempt by the Administrator to set a secondary standard which was *more stringent* than the primary standard without explaining the basis for this decision, *see* 36 Fed. Reg. 8187, and it is therefore inapposite to the instant case. Furthermore, LIA did not object to the Administrator's proposal to set the secondary standard at the same level as the primary standard either in the comments that it filed on the proposed standards or at any other time during the public comment period. Indeed, so far as we have been able to determine, none of the participants in the rulemaking proceedings commented on the proposal. Accordingly, LIA is precluded from raising this objection by the timeliness requirement of the Act.

. . . .

We have accorded these cases the most careful consideration, combining as we must careful scrutiny of the evidence in the record with deference to the Administrator's judgments. We conclude that in this rulemaking proceeding the Administrator complied with the substantive and procedural requirements of the Act, and that his decisions are both adequately explained and amply supported by evidence in the record. Accordingly, we reject petitioners' claims of error. The regulations under review herein are

Affirmed.

NOTES AND QUESTIONS

(1) The Clean Air Act provides for primary and secondary ambient air quality standards for so-called "criteria pollutants." How is the determination made to add more pollutants to the list of substances for which ambient air quality standards are to be promulgated? *See, e.g.,* the litigation that caused lead to be added, *Natural Resources Defense Council v. Train,* 411 F. Supp. 864, 8 E.R.C. 1695 (S.D.N.Y. 1975). What other pollutants might be "graduated" to criteria status?

(2) National primary ambient air quality standards are intended to protect "health," while the secondary standards are to protect "welfare." What is the distinction between the two? Which is the stricter of the two? Do elements of technical and economic feasibility have a greater impact in setting secondary standards?

(3) About eight years separate the *Kennecott Copper* decision from the *Lead Industries* case. There had been no change in the relevant provisions of the CAA, yet there seems to be a considerable difference in the general tone of the two decisions. Is there a difference, what is it, and how can it be explained?

[e] State Implementation Plan

[i] Adoption and Variances

TRAIN v. NATURAL RESOURCES DEFENSE COUNCIL

United States Supreme Court (1975)
421 U.S. 60, 95 S. Ct. 1470, 43 L. Ed. 2d 73

MR. JUSTICE REHNQUIST delivered the opinion of the Court.

We granted certiorari in this case, 419 U.S. 823 (1974), to review a judgment of the Court of Appeals for the Fifth Circuit which required petitioner Administrator of the Environmental Protection Agency to disapprove a portion of the implementation plan submitted to him by the State of Georgia pursuant to the Clean Air Act Amendments of 1970. The case presents an issue of statutory construction which is illuminated by the anatomy of the statute itself, by its legislative history, and by the history of congressional efforts to control air pollution.

Within nine months after the Agency's promulgation of primary and secondary air quality standards, each of the 50 States was required to submit to the Agency a plan designed to implement and maintain such standards within its boundaries. § 110(a)(11) of the Clean Air Act. The Agency was in turn required to approve each State's plan within four months of the deadline for submission, if it had been adopted after public hearings and if it satisfied eight general conditions set forth in § 110(a)(2). Probably the principal of these conditions, and the heart of the 1970 Amendments, is that the plan provide for the attainment of the national primary ambient air quality standards in the particular State "as expeditiously as practicable but . . . in no case later than three years from the date of approval of such plan." § 110(a)(2)(A). In providing for such attainment, a State's plan must include "emission limitations, schedules, and timetables for compliance with such limitations"; it must also contain such other measures as may be necessary to insure both timely attainment and subsequent maintenance of national ambient air standards. § 110(a)(2)(B).

. . . .

Georgia chose the Agency's preferred approach. Its plan provided for immediately effective categorical emission limitations, but also incorporated a variance procedure whereby particular sources could obtain individually tailored relief from general requirements. This variance provision, Ga. Code Ann. § 88-912(1971), was one of the bases upon which the Agency's approval of the Georgia plan was successfully challenged by respondents in the Court of Appeals. It is the only aspect of that court's decision as to which the Agency petitioned for certiorari.

. . . .

The Agency is plainly charged by the Act with the responsibility for setting the national ambient air standards. Just as plainly, however, it is relegated by the Act to a secondary role in the process of determining and enforcing the specific, source-by-source emission limitations which are necessary if the national standards it has set are to be met. Under § 110(a)(2), the Agency is *required* to approve a state plan which provides for the timely attainment and subsequent maintenance of ambient air standards, and which also satisfies that section's other general requirements. The Act gives the Agency no authority to question the wisdom of a State's choices of emission limitations if they are part of a plan which satisfies the standards of § 110(a)(2), and the Agency may devise and promulgate a specific plan of its own only if a State fails to submit an implementation plan which satisfies those standards. § 110(c). Thus, so long as the ultimate effect of a State's choice of emission limitations is compliance with the national standards for ambient air, the State is at liberty to adopt whatever mix of emission limitations it deems best suited to its particular situation.

This analysis of the Act's division of responsibilities is not challenged by respondents insofar as it concerns the process of devising and promulgating an initial implementation plan. Respondents do, however, deny that the States have such latitude once the initial plan is approved. Yet the third paragraph of § 110(a), and the one immediately following the paragraphs which specify that States shall file implementation plans and that the Agency shall approve them if they satisfy certain broad criteria, is the section which *requires* the Agency to "approve any revision of an implementation plan" if it "determines that it meets the requirements" of § 110(a)(2). On its face, this provision applies *to any* revision, without regard either to its breadth of applicability, or to whether it is to be effective before or after the attainment date; rather, Agency approval is subject only to the condition that the revised plan satisfy the general requirements applicable to original implementation plans. Far from evincing congressional intent that the Agency assume control of a State's emission limitations mix once its initial plan is approved, the revision section is to all appearances the mechanism by which the States may obtain approval of their developing policy choices as to the most practicable and desirable methods of restricting total emissions to a level which is consistent with the national ambient air standards.

. . . .

We believe that the foregoing analysis of the structure and legislative history of the Clean Air Amendments shows that Congress intended to impose national ambient air standards to be attained within a specific period of time. It also shows that in §§ 110(e) and (f) Congress carefully limited the circumstances in which timely attainment and subsequent maintenance of these standards could be compromised. We also believe that Congress, consistent with its declaration that "[e]ach State shall have the primary responsibility for assuring air quality" within its boundaries, § 107(a), left to the States considerable latitude in determining specifically how the standards would be met. This discretion includes the continuing authority to revise choices about the mix of emission limitations. We therefore conclude that the Agency's interpretation of §§ 110(a)(3) and 110(f) was "correct," to the extent that it can be said with complete assurance that any particular interpretation of a complex statute such as this is the "correct" one. Given this conclusion, as well as the facts that the Agency is charged with administration of the Act, and that there has undoubtedly been reliance upon its interpretation by the States and other parties affected by the Act, we have no doubt whatever that its construction was sufficiently reasonable to preclude the Court of Appeals from substituting its judgment for that of the Agency. *Udall v. Tallman,* 380 U. S. 1, 16-18 (1965); *McLaren v. Fleischer*, 256 U. S. 477, 480-481 (1921). We are not persuaded to the contrary by any of the arguments advanced by respondents or by the courts of appeals which have rejected § 110(a)(3) as authority for granting variances. To these various arguments we now turn.

[The Court addressed the question of the difference between a "postponement" and a "revision," and differed with the view of the 5th Circuit that § 110(f)—now obsolete—governed postponements or variances, while § 110(a)(3) governed general revisions. The court concluded, as noted earlier, that variances are revisions to be accommodated under § 110(a)(3). The issue is no longer a significant one, in view of the repeal of the original § 110(f).]

VI.

For the foregoing reasons, the Court of Appeals for the Fifth Circuit was in error when it concluded that the postponement provision of § 110(f) is the sole method by which may be obtained specific ameliorative modifications of state implementation plans. The Agency had properly concluded that the revision mechanism of § 110(a)(3) is available for the approval of those variances which do not compromise the basic statutory mandate that, with carefully circumscribed exceptions, the national primary ambient air standards be attained in not more than three years, and maintained thereafter. To the extent that the judgment of the Court of Appeals for the Fifth Circuit was to the contrary, it is reversed and the cause is remanded for further proceedings consistent with this opinion.

It is so ordered.

Mr. JUSTICE DOUGLAS dissents.

Mr. JUSTICE POWELL took no part in the consideration or decision of this case.

VIRGINIA v. ENVIRONMENTAL PROTECTION AGENCY

United States Court of Appeals, D.C. Circuit (1997)
323 U.S. App. D.C. 368, 108 F.3d 1397, 27 ELR 20718

RANDOLPH, Circuit Judge:

These are consolidated petitions for review of a final rule issued by the Environmental Protection Agency under the Clean Air Act ("CAA"). The rule is aimed at reducing ozone pollution in the northeastern United States. It requires the twelve states in the region and the District of Columbia to adopt what is essentially California's vehicle emission program. Opposing the rule, and appearing here as petitioners, are the Commonwealth of Virginia, and three associations representing automobile manufacturers and dealers. Intervening to defend the rule are the Commonwealth of Massachusetts, the States of New York, Connecticut, Rhode Island and Vermont, the City of New York, and two associations.

Petitioners believe EPA's rule is unsupported by the record, contrary to the statute, and constitutionally defective. The evidence regarding ozone pollution, they maintain, does not support EPA's demand for region-wide emission reductions and, in any event, the means EPA has chosen for realizing those reductions—mandating that these states prohibit the sale of new cars that do not satisfy California's standards—is something Congress has barred the Agency from imposing. A majority of the governors of the twelve northeastern states recommended, over the objection of Virginia and other states, that EPA impose this solution. The group operated as a regional commission under a new section of the Clean Air Act, a section petitioners say is unconstitutional because it gave the commission significant legislative and executive powers without regard to the Appointments Clause of the Constitution, the non-delegation doctrine, the Joinder and Compact Clauses and other constitutional limitations. Furthermore, in petitioners' view EPA's interpretation of the Act renders it unconstitutional under the Tenth Amendment because it compels the states to enact and administer a federal regulatory program.

I

A

EPA believed that if the states in the Northeast passed legislation adopting the California car program this would help alleviate the ozone hazard. Ozone (O sub3) in the upper atmosphere was not the problem. There it absorbs harmful ultraviolet rays. Ozone at ground level is another matter entirely. It is one of the primary constituents of smog. Ozone's three-atom arrangement is highly unstable: the third oxygen atom, in a process called oxidation, has an aggressive tendency to react with whatever substance is available. Ozone's high reactivity, evident in the stratosphere where ozone reacts with chlorofluorocarbons, has harmful effects at ground level. Much of the ozone inhaled reacts with sensitive lung tissues, irritating and inflaming the lungs, and causing a host of short-term adverse health consequences including chest pains, shortness of breath, coughing, nausea, throat irritation, and increased susceptibility to respiratory infections. Final Rule, 60 Fed. Reg. 4712, 4712-13 (1995). "The mechanisms of ozone-induced impairment of lung function are only partly understood," but "the effects of a single exposure to" ozone "are reversible and last up to 48" hours. Editorial, Ozone: Too Much in the Wrong Place, The Lancet, July 27, 1991, at 221. On the other hand, "[c]hronic effects that have resulted from recurrent seasonal exposure to ozone have been studied only to a limited degree. Most of the current evidence is derived from animal responses to chronic ozone exposure." Committee on Tropospheric Ozone Formation and Measurement, National Research Council, Rethinking the Ozone Problem in Urban and Regional Air Pollution 33 (1991) [hereinafter National Research Council]. In addition to its direct effect on humans, excessive ozone can also damage forests and food crops.

Exactly how ozone is created and transported in the lower atmosphere, and how it decays, is a matter of extreme complexity. Ozone is not a direct pollutant. Vehicles do not emit it, and it does not billow out of smokestacks. Instead, it is formed mostly from the mixture of two chemical precursors emitted by automobiles and industry: nitrogen oxides (NOx) and a large group of hydrocarbon pollutants called volatile organic compounds (VOCs).[49] National Research Council, *supra*, at 153. These precursors cook in the sun—they cook best in a "sea" of warm stagnant air—and produce ozone through a complex chain of reactions. The creation of ozone can thus be seen as a seasonal phenomenon, with concentrations peaking in the summer, and as a diurnal occurrence, with concentrations peaking during the afternoon and falling during the night. The precursor-and ozone-laden air slowly moves downwind, and as the air mass moves, ozone levels often continue to increase, in part because the ozone has more time to develop, in part because the air mass picks up more precursors along the way. Ultimately, this process can bring high ozone levels to areas hundreds of miles downwind of the pollution

[49] "Major sources of" volatile organic compounds "in the atmosphere include motor vehicle exhaust, emissions from the use of solvents, and emissions from the chemical and petroleum industries. In addition, there is now a heightened appreciation of the importance of reactive" volatile organic compounds "emitted by vegetation." National Research Council, *supra*, at 1. Nitrogen oxides come "mainly from the combustion of fossil fuels; major sources include motor vehicles and electricity generating stations." *Id.*

sources. *See id.* at 100. Therein lies the source of much of the difficulty in controlling it.

At the moment, dozens of areas throughout the United States have not attained the national ambient air quality standard for ozone. The standard permits a maximum one-hour average ozone concentration of 0.12 parts per million. 40 C.F.R. § 50.9. If the ambient air exceeds this standard more than once per year averaged over three years, the area is considered in "nonattainment." *Id.* The ozone season of 1994 was a good one; EPA estimated that there was twelve percent less ozone than in 1985. EPA Air Quality Trends Brochure 1994 (EPA-454/F-95-003) (1995). But the warmer 1995 season was worse, with national ozone concentrations increasing four percent from 1994. EPA Air Quality Trends Brochure 1995 (EPA-454/F-96-008) (1996). According to press reports, New Jersey and Maryland each exceeded the ambient air standard fourteen times. *See* Northeast Ozone Problems Continue, Show Long-Term Gain, Octane Wk., Oct. 9, 1995, at 2.

Because of the ozone transport phenomenon, an area in nonattainment may be unable to do much about it. Even if the state implements the strictest practicable control measures, it might still fail to satisfy the ambient air standard. Across the country there are what one might call interstate ozone transport regions: around Chicago; in the region from Cleveland to Erie, Pennsylvania; in the Texas-Louisiana area; and in the northeast from Virginia to Maine, an area that became subject to special legislation in 1990.

B

The "Northeast Ozone Transport Region," defined in the 1990 amendments to the Clean Air Act, consists of Connecticut, Delaware, Maine, Maryland, Massachusetts, New Hampshire, New Jersey, New York, Pennsylvania, Rhode Island, Virginia, Vermont, and the District of Columbia.[50] To decrease ozone pollution in this "Region," EPA promulgated the rule we have before us. Each of these states had an implementation plan, adopted after public hearings, containing measures to control air pollution, and approved by EPA under section 110. CAA § 110(a)(1), 42 U.S.C. § 7410(a)(1). EPA's rule declared all of these implementation plans "substantially inadequate" and therefore in need of revision. Final Rule, 60 Fed. Reg. 4712, 4736 col. 2 (1995). The plans were inadequate, according to EPA, because nitrogen oxide and volatile organic compound emissions had to be reduced by 50% to 75% from a 1990 baseline "throughout" this densely populated Region to attain the national ambient air quality standard for ozone in "serious and severe areas." *Id.* at 4720 col. 1. EPA acknowledged that it was "enormously complicated to

[50] 42 U.S.C. § 7511c(a). While Virginia is not among the specifically enumerated States in § 7511c(a), it is considered part of "the Consolidated Metropolitan Statistical Area that includes the District of Columbia." *Id.* Accordingly, Virginia's participation is limited to that portion of Virginia in the Washington, D.C., metropolitan area. *See* Supplemental Notice of Proposed Rulemaking, 59 Fed. Reg. 48,664, 48,685 col. 3 (1994) [hereinafter Supplemental Notice]. *See generally* U.S. Bureau of the Census, Population Estimates for Metropolitan Areas (MAs) Outside of New England: July 1, 1990 to July 1, 1995 (Mar. 8, 1996) <http://www.census.gov/estimates/metro-city/metal95.txt> (listing counties comprising the Washington-Baltimore consolidated metropolitan statistical area).

determine which reductions" were needed where. *Id.* col. 2. But, it said, "wind trajectory data" supported the following conclusions. *Id.* col. 3. During the summer, ozone and emissions of precursors in the Washington, D.C. area contribute to the ozone problem in Baltimore, which lies to the northeast. Baltimore and the rest of Maryland contribute to ozone pollution in the Philadelphia area, which contributes to the problem in New York, which contributes to the problem in Boston, and so on up the Eastern seaboard from one metropolitan area to another. *Id.* at 4720-21. (Of course the northeastern section of the country is not some isolated island; and there are indications that western Pennsylvania receives ozone from Ohio and West Virginia.)

Congress, too, had found the entire subject very complex. In the 1990 amendments it ordered EPA, "in conjunction with the National Academy of Sciences, [to] conduct a study on the role of ozone precursors in tropospheric ozone formation and control. The study shall examine the roles of NOx and VOC emission reductions, the extent to which NOx reductions may contribute (or be counterproductive) to achievement of attainment in different nonattainment areas. . . ." CAA § 185B, 42 U.S.C. § 7511f. One part of the study, completed in 1991, found that reducing NOx emissions can sometimes increase, rather than decrease, ambient ozone levels. *See* National Research Council, *supra*, at 11. "This seemingly contradictory prediction, that lowering NOx can, under certain conditions, lead to increased ozone, results from the complex chemistry involved in ozone formation in VOC-NOx mixtures. . . ." *Id.* at 167.

Nonetheless, having declared the state plans inadequate, EPA required the states to revise their plans and enact a Low Emission Vehicle program, or LEV as the parties call it. In EPA's words, the final rule orders "all of the northeastern states to adopt the California car program to reduce significantly the pollution emitted by new cars and light-duty trucks." Final Rule, 60 Fed. Reg. at 4713 col. 1. To appreciate the rationale of this order one must understand that there are two, and only two, permissible sets of regulations limiting emissions from new cars sold in the United States. There are the California regulations; and there are the federal regulations, which preempt the laws of the other 49 states. CAA §§ 202, 209(a), 42 U.S.C. §§ 7521, 7543(a). The California standards—the "Low Emission Vehicle" standards— are considerably more restrictive than the federal standards and include ceilings on motor vehicle emission of nitrogen oxides, see 13 Cal. Admin.Code § 1960.1(f)(2), (g)(1), and volatile organic compounds, see 13 Cal. Admin.Code § 1960.1(f)(2), (g)(1), (g)(2), the two chief ozone precursors.

C

In finding the twelve state plans inadequate, and in requiring the states to adopt the California solution, EPA acted on the recommendation of the "Northeast Ozone Transport Commission," a body established by section 184 of the Act. CAA § 184, 42 U.S.C. § 7511c. As part of the 1990 amendments, section 184 set up a panel consisting of the governors of the twelve states (and the Mayor of the District of Columbia) or their delegates. This panel, or Ozone Commission as we shall call it, was to develop, through majority vote, proposals for additional control measures for ozone pollution in the Region "necessary to bring any area in such region into attainment." *Id.* § 7511c(c)(1).[51]

After EPA receives a Commission proposal, EPA must "publish in the Federal Register a notice stating that the recommendations are available and provide an opportunity for public hearing within 90 days beginning on the receipt date"; "commence a review of the recommendations to determine whether the control measures in the recommendations are necessary to bring any area into attainment" with national standards; and "consult with members of the commission" and take into account data and comments received during the notice and comment process. *Id.* § 7511c(c)(2), (c)(3).

From the time of receiving the Commission's recommendations, EPA has nine months: to "determine whether to approve, disapprove," or approve in part and disapprove in part, the recommendation; to "notify the commission in writing" of the Administrator's determination; and to "publish such determination in the Federal Register." *Id.* § 7511c(c)(4). Absent complete approval, EPA must explain "why any disapproved additional control measures are not necessary to bring any area in such region into attainment . . . or are otherwise not consistent with" the remainder of the Act, and must recommend "actions that could be taken by the commission to conform the disapproved portion of the recommendations to the requirements" of section 184. *Id.* § 7511c(c)(4)(i) & (c)(4)(ii).

If EPA approves the recommendation, it must declare each state's implementation plan inadequate and it must order the states to include the approved control measures in their revised plans pursuant to section 110(k)(5). CAA § 184(c)(5), 42 U.S.C. § 7511c(c)(5). Failure to heed EPA's order unleashes a panoply of sanctions upon the noncomplying state. We will have more to say on the subject of sanctions later in the opinion. EPA's final rule in this case resulted from the section 184 process just described. In August 1993, Maine, Maryland, and Massachusetts petitioned the Ozone Commission to adopt a recommendation calling for the application of the California Low Emission Vehicle program throughout the Region. *See* Notice of Availability, 59 Fed. Reg. 12,914, 12,915 col. 1 (1994). After holding several "public forums," and a hearing, the Commission voted on February 1, 1994, "to recommend that EPA mandate the California" vehicle program "throughout the" Region. *Id.* A minority of Ozone Commission members—those from Virginia, Delaware, New Jersey, and New Hampshire—voted against the recommendation. *See id.* On February 10,1994, the Commission submitted the recommendation to EPA. *Id.* at 12,914 col. 1.

[51] Another provision, also added in 1990, allows EPA (or the states) to establish interstate transport regions elsewhere in the country. CAA § 176A(a), 42 U.S.C. § 7506a(a). These regions may recommend strategies and plans to EPA and "may request" the agency to issue findings that a member state's implementation plan is substantially inadequate. *Id.* § 7506a(a) & (b)(2). An individual state, or the subdivision of a state, has the same ability to petition EPA with respect to the State Plan of a neighboring state. *See* CAA § 126(b), 42 U.S.C. § 7426(b). For that matter, any interested person has "the right to petition" EPA "for the issuance, amendment, or repeal" of any rule. 5 U.S.C. § 553(e). Section 184 is different. EPA must review the Ozone Commission's recommendation, it must do so on an expedited timetable, and it must order the states to include the additional control measures in their plans if EPA approves the recommendation. CAA § 184(c)(5), 42 U.S.C. § 7511c(c)(5).

In its final rule, EPA approved the Commission's recommendation. 60 Fed. Reg. at 4713 col. 1. Therefore, as section 184(c)(5) required, EPA found "that the State Implementation Plans" for the twelve states in the Region "are substantially inadequate to comply with the requirements of section 110(a)(2)(D) of the Clean Air Act, 42 U.S.C. § 7410(a)(2)(D), and to mitigate adequately the interstate pollutant transport described in section 184 of the Clean Air Act, 42 U.S.C. § 7511c, to the extent that they do not provide for emission reductions from new motor vehicles in the amount that would be achieved by the" Low Emission Vehicle program. Final Rule, 60 Fed. Reg. at 4736 col. 2 (to be codified at 40 C.F.R. § 51.120(a)).

D

EPA purported to offer the states an alternative to enacting the California program. Instead of restricting the type of new cars sold within its jurisdiction, a state may choose its own mix of programs. To be an acceptable "Substitute Program," however, it must reduce ozone precursors anywhere from 3.5 to 6.5 times more than would the California program. *See infra* part II.A.[52]

II

Of petitioners' many challenges to EPA's rule, one is aimed at something known in Clean Air Act parlance as a "SIP call"—EPA's declaration that a state's implementation plan is substantially inadequate and must be revised. Virginia maintains that the record does not support the SIP call to it. If Virginia is correct, EPA's regulation requiring Virginia to adopt the California car program would fall. However, the issues raised by the other petitioners—the automobile manufacturers and dealers—reach beyond Virginia. If the states implement the California program in response to EPA's rule, these petitioners claim their members will be adversely affected throughout the Northeast Region as new car price increases take effect.[53] Furthermore, it is not clear whether EPA would have issued a SIP call to any state if EPA knew it lacked a legal basis for requiring the California program. We therefore think it best to start our analysis with questions other than the SIP call, questions relating mainly to EPA's statutory authority.

---

[52] EPA mentioned one other acceptable way for these states to reduce ozone precursors. The idea is to have automakers voluntarily opt into a program to meet higher emissions standards in the 49 states outside California (the "Equivalent Program"). These "national" standards would be less onerous than California's and would enable automakers to enjoy economies of scale in their production processes. Final Rule, 60 Fed. Reg. at 4714 cols. 1-2. The program is voluntary because section 202 of the Clean Air Actforbids EPA from itself modifying motor vehicle emission standards "before the model year 2004." CAA § 202(b)(1)(C), 42 U.S.C. § 7521(b)(1)(C).

The northeastern states also would have to agree to opt into the Equivalent Program, and in so doing, to abandon the California program, or any such program an individual state had itself independently enacted. *See* Final Rule, 60 Fed. Reg. at 4724 col. 3; Notice of Proposed Rulemaking, 60 Fed. Reg. 52,734, 52,740 col. 2 (1995).

Because the Equivalent Program is merely a proposal, we will not consider it further.

[53] Neither EPA's final rule nor either of its notices of proposed rulemaking reach any conclusion about how EPA's ozone reduction rule will affect the price of new cars. Still, there are some estimates floating around. [Estimates varied widely—from $186.50 to $2,000 per car.]

We will discuss those questions in this order and explain why we have reached the following conclusions. First, did EPA condition its approval of a state's revision of its implementation plan on the state's adoption of the California program? We think the answer is yes. Second, does section 110 give EPA the authority to condition approval of a state's plan on the state's adoption of control measures EPA has chosen? We conclude that section 110 does not give EPA this authority. Third, does section 184 authorize EPA to so condition its approval of plan revisions? We believe the answer is yes. Fourth, did other provisions of the Clean Air Act nevertheless bar EPA from ordering states to enact the California program? We hold that EPA was so barred and that this portion of its final rule is therefore invalid.

A

Did EPA condition approval of a state's revised implementation plan on the state's adoption of the California car program? EPA tells us it did not because it offered the states a choice—they could either enact the California program or submit a "Substitute Program." It turns out, however, that EPA's alternative is no alternative at all.

Having determined that, at a minimum, 50 percent reductions of each precursor are necessary to bring each northeastern state into ozone attainment, 60 Fed. Reg. at 4718 col. 3, EPA required any Substitute Program to reduce precursor emissions by the difference between that 50 percent and the percentage reduction "achievable through implementation of all of the Clean Air Act-mandated and potentially broadly practicable control measures," *id.* at 4737 col. 2 (to be codified at 40 C.F.R. § 51.120(d)(1) & (d)(2)). The phrase "potentially broadly practicable control measures" refers to other options—"those control measures that could potentially render the" California program "unnecessary in the" Northeast. Since none of those options (taken individually or cumulatively) could produce the necessary 50 percent reduction for precursors, EPA takes the position that all the measures are necessary, and presupposes that those measures will be included in state implementation plans submitted sometime in the future. *Id.* at 4723 col. 3.

Thus, a state that chooses not to adopt the California program must legislate a state implementation plan containing measures to make up this "shortfall"—the difference between the 50 percent reductions EPA says is necessary and the 35.9 percent and 37 percent that it has already targeted for nitrogen oxides and volatile organic compounds, respectively. Virginia or any other state seeking to implement a program not involving California vehicles, therefore, must pass legislation or issue regulations or orders reducing nitrogen oxide production in the year 2005 by 14.1 percent (50 percent minus 35.9 percent), and volatile organic compound production by 13 percent (50 percent minus 37 percent).

In contrast, the California program, by 2005, reduces nitrogen oxides by 4 percent, and volatile organic compounds by 2 percent. Supplemental Notice, 59 Fed. Reg. at 48,683 col. 1. States adopting the California program need legislate nothing more.[54] Virginia, therefore, must reduce nitrogen oxides 3.5 times (14.1%/4%) and volatile organic compounds 6.5 times (13%/2%) more than do states that pass legislation incorporating the California program, and Virginia must do so by means EPA has already concluded are not practicable.[55] In sum, the Substitute Program is expected to solve a shortfall EPA itself has no idea how to remedy, a shortfall states enacting the California program are not expected to make up.

Of course, only a very foolish state would see EPA's offer to accept this Substitute Program as a real alternative. EPA conceded as much. No state, EPA recognized, "would seriously entertain unreasonable or impracticable measures to adopt in place of the" California program "in order to achieve the necessary emissions reductions." Supplemental Notice, 59 Fed. Reg. at 48,672 col. 2. As a practical matter, then, EPA "require[d] all the northeastern states to adopt the California car program." Final Rule, 60 Fed. Reg. at 4713 col. 1. And that is how we shall treat the rule.

B

Does section 110 give EPA the authority to condition approval of a state's plan on the state's adoption of control measures EPA has chosen? EPA's discovery that section 110 gave it this authority came late in the rulemaking proceedings. The Ozone Commission, acting pursuant to section 184, started the ball rolling. It forced ozone pollution in the Northeast to the forefront of EPA's agenda. In EPA's Notice of Proposed Rulemaking, the agency therefore naturally treated section 184 as the sole source of its authority to approve or disapprove the Commission's recommendation. *See* 59 Fed. Reg. 21,720, 21,720-21 (1994).

The agency shifted its position after automobile manufacturers and dealers began questioning the constitutionality of section 184. *See* Supplemental Notice, 59 Fed. Reg. at 48,670 col. 1 & n.11. In response to the proposed rule, some argued that EPA deference to the Ozone Commission's technical and policy judgments would violate the Appointments Clause of the Constitution and the nondelegation doctrine. Commenters also complained that the Joinder and Compact Clauses prevented a multi-state alliance such as the Ozone Commission from exercising significant power. And they maintained that the proposed rule forcing the California program on the states would violate the Tenth Amendment because it would " 'commandeer' state governments into the service of federal regulatory purposes, and would for this reason be inconsistent with the Constitution's division of authority between federal and

[54] EPA asserts that states choosing the California program are expected to make up the shortfall, that the California program will be complemented by "other measures that may be promulgated thereafter." Final Brief for Respondent at 35. . . . Since EPA offers nothing more than wishful promises—and promises without deadlines, no less—we examine the reductions created by the measures actually undertaken by states choosing the California program.

[55] The disparity is greater still if instead of a 50 percent minimum total reduction, we use the 65 percent minimum for nitrogen oxides, the percentage EPA reported as necessary "for attainment in the serious and severe nonattainment areas of the region." Using this figure, a state choosing a Substitute Program would be required to legislate solutions 7.3 times as great (29.1%/4%) for nitrogen oxides as would states implementing the California program.

state governments." *New York v. United States*, 505 U.S. 144, 175, 112 S.Ct. 2408, 2428, 120 L.Ed.2d 120 (1992).

In response to these comments, EPA issued a supplemental notice stating that the arguments against section 184's constitutionality lacked "merit," and that "in any case, given EPA's independent authority under section 110(k)(5), any constitutional question regarding the validity of section 184 would not affect the validity of the" proposed rule. Supplemental Notice, 59 Fed. Reg. at 48,670 col. 1. And so, not only section 184, but also section 110 supposedly provided the legal basis for EPA's action.

C

Enacted more than a quarter of a century ago, section 110 has gone through many changes, but its basic structure has survived. The provision has been the subject of dozens of appellate court decisions. Yet we are aware of no case (EPA has cited none) supporting the proposition EPA now urges upon us, namely, that under section 110 EPA may condition approval of a state's implementation plan on the state's adopting a particular control measure, here the California Low Emission Vehicle program. Despite the volumes of legislative history on the Clean Air Act and its amendments, EPA has offered no committee reports, no statements on the floor of either house, suggesting that anyone in Congress ever shared its view of section 110. Nor has EPA given us reason to believe that it has followed any consistent, long-standing practice of using section 110 to force states to adopt control measures of EPA's choosing. The final rule provides no explanation of why EPA read section 110 as it did. The rule contains only this bare conclusion: "EPA disagrees with comments claiming that EPA lacks" authority "because section 110 does not authorize EPA to require states to adopt specific measures. . . ." Final Rule, 60 Fed. Reg. at 4717 col. 1. EPA's brief offers little more. We are told the "plain language" of the statute gives EPA this authority, and even if the language is not so plain, EPA's reading is reasonable and deserves our deference. Final Brief for Respondent at 34. We are not persuaded, and therefore do not reach Virginia's contention that EPA's interpretation would render section 110 unconstitutional, in violation of the Tenth Amendment.

Congress added section 110 to the Clean Air Act in 1970. *See* Clean Air Amendments of 1970, Pub. L. No. 91-604, § 4, 84 Stat. 1676, 1680-81 (1970). It has remained one of the key provisions of the Act. The Act authorizes EPA to promulgate national ambient air quality standards for ozone and five other pollutants. CAA §§ 108 & 109, 42 U.S.C. §§ 7408 & 7409. Areas that do not meet the minimum level of air quality mandated by these national standards are considered to be "nonattainment areas." CAA §§ 107(d) & 171(2), 42 U.S.C. §§ 7407(d) & 7501(2). The degree of nonattainment is classified as marginal, moderate, serious, severe, or extreme. CAA § 181(a), 42 U.S.C. § 7511(a).

If a state has an area within it that EPA has classified as being in nonattainment with respect to ozone (or one of the five other regulated pollutants), the state must devise and implement a "state implementation plan" ("State Plan"). Section 110 governs the interplay between the states and

EPA with respect to the formulation and approval of such State Plans. 42 U.S.C. § 7410. The basic procedure is that "each state determines an emission reduction program for its nonattainment areas, subject to EPA approval, within deadlines imposed by Congress." *Natural Resources Defense Council, Inc. v. Browner*, 57 F.3d 1122, 1123 (D.C.Cir.1995).

Should a state fail to submit an implementation plan, or should its plan fail to provide the required reductions in air pollution, certain penalties—some mandatory, others at EPA's discretion—may follow. *See generally Commonwealth of Virginia v. United States*, 74 F.3d 517, 520 (4th Cir.1996); Natural Resources Defense Council, 57 F.3d at 1123-25 & n. 5. The noncomplying state may, for instance, be prevented from spending federal highway money in nonattainment areas. *See* CAA §§ 110(m), 176(c) & 179(b)(1); 42 U.S.C. §§ 7410(m), 7506(c) & 7509(b)(1). This sanction becomes mandatory if the state fails to implement an adequate State Plan within 24 months of EPA's finding that the state's proposed plan is deficient. CAA § 179(b)(1), 42 U.S.C. § 7509(b)(1). At that same point, EPA must impose a "federal implementation plan" ("Federal Plan") on those areas of the state in nonattainment. CAA § 110(c), 42 U.S.C. § 7410(c). The Federal Plan "provides an additional incentive for state compliance because it rescinds state authority to make the many sensitive and policy choices that a pollution control regime demands." Natural Resources Defense Council, 57 F.3d at 1124.

Section 110(a)(2), the predecessor to the current section 110(k)(5), spelled out the extent of EPA's authority over state implementation plans within this structure. When enacted in 1970, the relevant portion of section 110(a)(2) read:

> The Administrator shall, within four months after the date required for submission of a plan under paragraph (1), approve or disapprove such plan, or each portion thereof. The Administrator shall approve such plan, or any portion thereof, if he determines that it was adopted after reasonable notice and hearing and that—
>
> * * * * * *
>
> (H) *it provides for revision, after public hearings, of such plan* (i) from time to time as may be necessary to take account of revisions of such national primary or secondary ambient air quality standard or the availability of improved or more expeditious methods of achieving such primary or secondary standard; or (ii) *whenever the Administrator finds on the basis of information available to him that the plan is substantially inadequate to achieve the national ambient air quality primary or secondary standard which it implements.* 42 U.S.C. § 1857c-5(a)(2)(H)(1970) (emphasis added).

At the time, section 110(a)(3) required EPA to review a state's revisions to its plan—which is what EPA is calling for here—by the same criteria EPA used to judge the original plan. 42 U.S.C. § 1857c-5(a)(3)(1970). In 1970 as now, if a state failed to submit a plan, or if the plan did not satisfy section 110(a)(2), EPA had a non-discretionary duty to implement the Act through a federal implementation plan. CAA § 110(c), 42 U.S.C. § 1857c-5(c)(1970).

In 1975, the Supreme Court analyzed section 110's "division of responsibilities" between the states and the federal government. *Train v. Natural*

Resources Defense Council, 421 U.S. 60, 79, 95 S.Ct. 1470, 1482, 43 L.Ed.2d 731 (1975). . . . A state could, the Court held, use section 110(a)(3) [to revise an SIP] so long as the revised plan would still enable the state to attain and maintain national ambient standards. Train, 421 U.S. at 72, 95 S.Ct. at 1478.

A "broader issue," the Court thought, was at stake in the case—namely, "whether Congress intended the States to retain any significant degree of control over the manner in which they attain and maintain national standards." *Id.* at 78, 95 S.Ct. at 1481. The Act expressly gave the states initial responsibility for determining the manner in which air quality standards were to be achieved. *See id.* at 64, 95 S.Ct. at 1474-75. . . . In light of section 107(a), the Court construed section 110: The Act gives the Agency no authority to question the wisdom of a State's choices of emission limitations if they are part of a plan which satisfies the standards of § 110(a)(2), and the Agency may devise and promulgate a specific plan of its own only if a State fails to submit an implementation plan which satisfies those standards. § 110(c). Thus, so long as the ultimate effect of a State's choice of emission limitations is compliance with the national standards for ambient air, the State is at liberty to adopt whatever mix of emission limitations it deems best suited to its particular situation. Train, 421 U.S. at 79, 95 S.Ct. at 1482. . . .To be sure, if EPA rejected a State Plan because it would not achieve or maintain ambient air quality standards, EPA could promulgate a federal implementation plan. But even then, as EPA admitted in confessing error in the Supreme Court, section 110 did not permit the agency to require the state to pass legislation or issue regulations containing control measures of EPA's choosing. *EPA v. Brown*, 431 U.S. 99, 103, 97 S.Ct. 1635, 1636-37, 52 L.Ed.2d 166 (1977) (per curiam).

In 1977 Congress again amended the Act, changing some parts of section 110. But these changes did not modify the "division of responsibilities" Train had discerned in the Act. EPA's later administrative efforts to alter the balance were therefore firmly rebuffed. *Bethlehem Steel Corp. v. Gorsuch*, 742 F.2d 1028 (7th Cir.1984), held that EPA could not, under the guise of partially approving a state implementation plan, render the plan more stringent than the state intended. If EPA wanted to impose stricter regulations, the Clean Air Act gave it the option of implementing a federal plan. The court explained:

> [T]he Clean Air Act creates a partnership between the states and the federal government. The state proposes, the EPA disposes. The federal government through the EPA determines the ends—the standards of air quality— but Congress has given the states the initiative and a broad responsibility regarding the means to achieve those ends through state implementation plans and timetables of compliance. . . . The Clean Air Act is an experiment in federalism, and the EPA may not run roughshod over the procedural prerogatives that the Act has reserved to the states, . . . especially when, as in this case, the agency is overriding state policy.

Id. at 1036-37.

. . . .

Thus, as section 110 stood in 1975 when the Supreme Court decided Train and as it stood after the 1977 amendments, the provision did not confer upon

EPA the authority to condition approval of Virginia's implementation plan, or the plan of any other state, on the state's adoption of a specific control measure. EPA "identifies the end to be achieved, while the states choose the particular means for realizing that end." *Air Pollution Control Dist. v. USEPA*, 739 F.2d 1071, 1075 (6th Cir.1984). The validity of EPA's argument that it now has broader authority depends, therefore, on whether the 1990 Clean Air Act Amendments eliminated the "liberty" every state had under the earlier legislation "to adopt whatever mix of emission limitations it deems best suited to its particular situation." *Train*, 421 U.S. at 79, 95 S.Ct. at 1482.

The 1990 amendments were the most comprehensive since 1970, but the changes to section 110, at least as they concern EPA's approval of State Plans, were predominantly of syntax, not substance. Section 110(a)(2)(H)(ii), as amended, requires each State Plan to "provide for revision" not only when EPA finds the plan "substantially inadequate to attain" national ambient standards, but also when EPA finds that the plan does not "otherwise comply with any additional requirements established under this chapter." CAA § 110(a)(2)(H)(ii), 42 U.S.C. § 7410(a)(2)(H)(ii).

Also in the 1990 law, Congress repealed section 110(a)(3)(A), a provision requiring the Administrator to approve a State Plan revision meeting the (a)(2) criteria. The language of the repealed subsection was moved to a new subsection (k), so that the new section 110(k)(3) imposed the same obligation upon the Administrator to approve plans satisfying the (a)(2) requirements: "In the case of any" State Plan submission or revision, "the Administrator shall approve such submittal as a whole if it meets all of the requirements of this chapter." *Id.* § 7410(k)(3).

The main differences between this portion of subsection (k)(5) and the original section 110(a)(2)(H)(ii) are that EPA may set the timetable for a state to revise its plan, and that a plan's failure "to mitigate adequately the interstate pollution transport described in" sections 176A or 184 may trigger the need for revision. Neither of these differences, however, amounts to a new grant of authority to EPA to require states to insert in their plans control measures EPA has selected.

EPA apparently thinks the "as necessary" language in section 110(k)(5) altered the division of responsibilities between the states and the agency. We suppose the idea is that because section 110(k)(5) empowers EPA to "require the State to revise the plan as necessary to correct" inadequacies, it empowers EPA to require the state to include particular control measures in the revised plan. There is nothing to this.

The Supreme Court's decision in Train provides the starting point, and is itself the endpoint for interpreting section 110, unless an "intervening development of the law has 'removed or weakened the conceptual underpinnings from the prior decision, or . . . the later law has rendered the decision irreconcilable with competing legal doctrines or policies.' " *Neal v. United States*, 516 U.S. 284, 294-295, 116 S.Ct. 763, 768-69, 133 L.Ed.2d 709 (1996). Congress' insertion of "as necessary" in section 110(k)(5) does not affect the underpinnings of Train, nor is the Train interpretation irreconcilable with those two words. All this additional language does is keep EPA within bounds. If a state plan is inadequate—that is, if the state is not achieving an ambient air quality standard—EPA can call only for revisions "as necessary" to correct that problem. EPA cannot, in other words, require the state to go through a wholesale revision of its entire plan.

We therefore hold that the 1990 amendments did not alter the division of responsibilities between EPA and the states in the section 110 process. It was with this understanding that we recently summarized the statutory system: "The states are responsible in the first instance for meeting the" national ambient standards "through state-designed plans that provide for attainment, maintenance, and enforcement of the" national standards "in each air quality control region. Thus, each state determines an emission reduction program for its nonattainment areas, subject to EPA approval, within deadlines imposed by Congress." *Natural Resources Defense Council, Inc. v. Browner*, 57 F.3d 1122, 1123 (D.C.Cir.1995).

Because section 110 does not enable EPA to force particular control measures on the states, EPA's authority to promulgate the rule under review must be derived from section 184 alone.

D

Does section 184 give EPA the authority to condition approval of a state's plan on the state's adoption of particular control measures? The language of this statute, unlike section 110, answers with an emphatic yes. By a majority vote, the Ozone Commission recommends "additional control measures" for all or part of the Region. CAA § 184(c)(1), 42 U.S.C. § 7511c(c)(1). If EPA approves the recommendation, section 184(c)(5) requires it to issue a "finding" that the implementation plans of the affected states are inadequate. "Such finding shall require each such State to revise its implementation plan to include the approved additional control measures within one year after the finding is issued." *Id.* We think the only possible reading of section 184(c)(5) is that a state must revise its plan to include whatever "additional control measures" EPA has approved, or it must suffer the consequences of losing its federal highway funds, of having new factories and other "major stationary sources" of air pollution restricted, and of having the federal government impose an implementation plan in the state. *See Commonwealth of Va. v. Browner*, 80 F.3d 869, 881-83 (4th Cir.1996).

Virginia and the other petitioners do not quarrel with this reading of section 184. But, they say, section 184 is unconstitutional in light of the role of the Ozone Commission. We would not have to reach the constitutional questions if, as Virginia also argues, sections 202 and 177 of the Clean Air Actbarred EPA from ordering states to implement the California car program. It is an old principle that if a case may be decided on statutory grounds "it will be unnecessary, and consequently improper, to pursue any inquiries, which would then be merely speculative, respecting the power of Congress in the case." Cohens v. Virginia, 19 U.S. (6 Wheat.) 264, 441, 5 L.Ed. 257 (1821) (Marshall, C.J.); Ashwanderv. Tennessee Valley Auth., 297 U.S. 288, 347, 56 S.Ct. 466, 483, 80 L.Ed. 688 (1936) (Brandeis, J., concurring). And so we turn to those two sections.

E

Does section 177, read together with section 202, forbid EPA from conditioning its approval of a state's implementation plan on the state's adoption of the California program to limit motor vehicle emissions? We hold that this provision did so bar EPA and that, in this respect, the final rule is invalid.

Section 202 of the Clean Air Act,codified at 42 U.S.C. § 7521, regulates emission standards for new motor vehicles or new motor vehicle engines. The standards, covering all air pollutants that may endanger public health or welfare, preempt the laws of every state except California. CAA § 209(a) & (b), 42 U.S.C. § 7543(a) & (b). Why Congress exempted California, and how, is explained in *Motor Vehicle Manufacturers Ass'n v. New York State Department of Environmental Conservation*, 17 F.3d 521, 524-28 (2d Cir.1994). We will not go into the subject here.

With respect to the federal "Phase I" standards applicable to all the states except California, subparagraph (b)(3)(C) of section 202 provides: "It is the intent of Congress that the numerical emission standards specified in subsections (a)(3)(B)(ii), (g), (h), and (i) of this section shall not be modified by the Administrator after November 15, 1990, for any model year before the model year 2004." CAA § 202(b)(3)(C), 42 U.S.C. § 7521(b)(3)(C). Section 202(b)(3)(C) thus prevents EPA from prescribing, before the model year 2004, emissions standards for motor vehicles more restrictive than those already written into the statute. Accord *id.* § 202(i)(1), (i)(3)(A)(ii), (i)(3)(B)(ii), (i)(3)(C), (i)(3)(E). The proviso just quoted resolved a debate in the Senate about whether there should be any future rounds of heightened emission standards. *See, e.g.*, 136 CONG. REC. S250 (daily ed. Jan. 24, 1990) (statement of Sen. Baucus), reprinted in Legislative History of the Clean Air Act Amendments of 1990, at 4941 (1993) [hereinafter 1990 Legislative History]. Senator Wirth, one of the sponsors of the bill, explained: "We do not know if the second round is going to be needed. This compromise was reached. Let us have a jump ball on the situation. Defer the question until the late 1990's; have EPA do a study. If that study points out a second round is needed" then "in effect we in the U.S. Congress can vote it up or down." 136 CONG. REC. S2739 (daily ed. Mar. 20, 1990), reprinted in 1990 Legislative History, *supra*, at 5864.

In the meantime, section 202 required EPA to conduct a study of the "need for, and cost effectiveness of, obtaining further reductions in emissions from [cars and certain trucks], taking into consideration alternative means of attaining or maintaining the national ambient air quality standards pursuant to State implementation plans." CAA § 202(i)(2)(A)(ii), 42 U.S.C. § 7521(i)(2)(A)(ii). EPA must report to Congress on its study no later than June 1, 1997. Based on the study, EPA must then determine by December 31, 1999, whether there is a need for new, stricter standards, and whether new standards would be cost effective. CAA §§ 202(i)(2)(B) & (i)(3), 317(a)(5), 42 U.S.C. §§ 7521(i)(2)(B) & (i)(3), 7617(a)(5).

To the extent EPA's final rule can be viewed as setting emissions standards for new motor vehicles in the northeastern states stricter than those contained in section 202, the rule is inconsistent with the statute.[56] EPA nevertheless denies that it violated § 202. States may voluntarily choose to adopt the California standards, pursuant to section 177.[57] And so, EPA's argument goes, it is the northeastern states, not EPA, who will be deciding to impose the California program on their citizens.

There is more than a bit of inconsistency in EPA's stance. On the one hand, in responding to Virginia's constitutional arguments, EPA denies that the Ozone Commission has any real power. EPA tells us that it and it alone has the final say under section 184. Any resulting orders of the sort section 184(c)(5) contemplates—orders, in the statute's words, "requir[ing] each such State to revise its implementation plan to include the approved additional control measures"—are EPA's, not the Commission's. But when it comes to sections 202 and 177, EPA asks us to believe that the states who implement the California program in response to EPA's section 184 order will be doing so voluntarily. Perhaps this is true with respect to states whose governors voted for the Commission's recommendation, although the legislatures in those states might have something to say on the subject. But no one can suppose that Virginia, whose governor voted against the recommendation, will be freely enacting these restrictive emission standards.

It is time to examine section 177 more closely. It provides that "any State . . . may adopt and enforce . . . standards relating to control of emissions from new motor vehicles or new motor vehicle engines" if the state standards "are identical to the California standards" and if the standards are adopted "at least two years before" they take effect. CAA § 177, 42 U.S.C. § 7507. As EPA has acknowledged, section 177 gives states the discretion to pass laws containing certain emission standards, laws that would otherwise be preempted. Supplemental Notice, 59 Fed. Reg. at 48,761 col. 1. In other words, a state may decide to follow California's lead, or it may not.

EPA's rule takes this choice from the states. To say, as EPA has, that it is "requiring the states to exercise their own independent authority under section 177" is to admit that EPA is depriving the states of that authority. Final Rule, 60 Fed. Reg. at 4718 col. 1. Independence signifies freedom from the dictates of a federal agency. EPA's rule does not respect the states' independent authority; it removes it. At several points in its final rule EPA made no bones about this. EPA said its rule would "mandate state action that

---

[56] EPA ordered the states to enact California's standards contained in 13 Cal. Admin.Code § 1960.1(g)(1), which sets emissions requirements for each class of California-certified cars; and § 1960.1(g)(2), which prescribes fleet averages for hydrocarbon emissions that must be met by selling a mix of the classes of cars certified in subpart (g)(1). Together these California provisions impose emissions limitations significantly more restrictive for non-methane hydrocarbon emissions—of which volatile organic compounds, ethane, and some exotic hydrocarbons are the constituents, see 40 C.F.R. § 51.100(s)—and nitrogen oxide emissions than those under existing federal Phase I standards. Compare 13 Cal. Admin.Code § 1960.1(g)(1) & (g)(2) with CAA § 202(g), Table G. *See generally* 60 Fed. Reg. at 4736 col. 3 (implementing the California provisions as part of 40 C.F.R. § 51.120(c)(1)(iii) and (c)(1)(iv)).

For example, under the California regulations, model year 2001 cars may emit, as a fleet average, 0.070 grams of non-methane compounds per mile driven, 13 Cal. Admin.Code § 1960.1(g)(2). Under federal Phase I standards, cars may not emit more than 0.25 grams per mile driven, 42 U.S.C. § 7521(g), Table G.

[57] New York, Massachusetts, and Connecticut did so before EPA issued its rule.

would otherwise be discretionary," *id.* at 4718 col. 2, and that it was "requir-[ing] all the northeastern states to adopt the California car program," *id.* at 4713 col. 1. And if EPA has chosen those emission standards and mandated their implementation, as it admits it has, the standards are effectively federal standards, in violation of section 177 in light of section 202.

There is another way of approaching this subject. One might treat EPA's action, not as a requirement that each northeastern state adopt the California standards, but merely as a condition on EPA's approval of the state's revised implementation plan. We do not think putting the matter this way changes the outcome. For one thing, the effect of EPA's rule remains the same despite the difference in formulation. For another, the House Committee Report on section 177 stated: "Finally, the Committee intends these provisions as grants of authority to the States. They are not intended as requirements. Nor may the Administrator require the States to utilize the authorities contained in this section as a condition of approval of a State's implementation plan." H.R.Rep. No. 95-294, at 311 (1977), reprinted in 1977 U.S.C.C.A.N. 1077, 1390; *see also* 123 Cong. Rec. 16,675 (1977) (statement of Rep. Rogers) ("No one will force the State to make a judgment. It is left up to the State. They can either do it or not do it. . . . If a State decides to make that change to clean up the air, clean up the automobile, it can adopt and enforce the California standards which are more strict than the Federal."); *id.* at 16,677 (statements of Reps. Wirth and Waxman).

EPA would have us disregard this legislative history because it is pre-1990, when the Act was amended. True enough, the report is old, but so is section 177. The 1990 amendments did not affect the substance of section 177. Congress simply added language preventing the states from prohibiting the sale or manufacture of California-certified vehicles and from taking "any action of any kind to create, or have the effect of creating, a [different type of] motor vehicle." CAA § 177, 42 U.S.C. § 7507. As explained by Senator Baucus, the author of the Senate bill: "The new language placed in Section 177 . . . neither adds to nor detracts from the present authority of the states under Section 177 to adopt, administer and enforce motor vehicle standards that are identical to those adopted by the state of California. The new language simply codifies, in effect, Congress' understanding of the authority originally" granted "to states by section 177 as expressed in the legislative history of section 177 when it was adopted in 1977." 136 Cong. Rec. S16,976 (daily ed. Oct. 27, 1990), reprinted in 1990 Legislative History, *supra*, at 1021-22.

EPA has another defense against the charge that it has violated section 202 and section 177. The argument is that in enacting section 184 and giving the agency the authority to order states to include control measures in their plans, Congress did not "exclude motor vehicle standards from the measures available to achieve attainment," Final Brief for Respondent at 41. But this proves much too much. The fact is that section 184 excludes no sort of control measures, of which there are many, some more effective than others. A state might ration gasoline; impose tougher emission standards for boilers, gas turbines, and large internal combustion engines, Supplemental Notice, 59 Fed. Reg. at 48,679 col. 2; encourage carpooling; develop "a comprehensive system of fees and incentives designed to affect driving habits and vehicle usage," *id.* at 48,680 col. 2; require "California reformulated gasoline", *id.*; enhance "vehicle inspection and maintenance" programs, CAA § 182(c)(3), 42 U.S.C. § 7511a(c)(3); encourage "the voluntary removal from use and the marketplace of pre-1980 model year light duty vehicles and pre-1980 model year light duty trucks," CAA § 108(f)(1)(A)(xvi), 42 U.S.C. § 7408(f)(1)(A)(xvi).

But among the universe of possible control measures, Congress specifically barred EPA from imposing one particular type—stricter emissions limitations on motor vehicles than those set forth in section 202. And "when a conflict arises between specific and general provisions of the same legislation, the courts should give voice to Congress' specific articulation of its policies and preferences." *Ohio Power Co. v. FERC*, 954 F.2d 779, 784 (D.C.Cir.1992). Here Congress' policy and preference is loud and clear. It "is the intent of Congress that" EPA not modify the "numerical emission standards" for "any model year before . . . 2004." CAA § 202(b)(1)(C), 42 U.S.C. § 7521(b)(1)(C). EPA therefore may not require, mandate, order, or impose conditions demanding that any state enact particular motor vehicle emission standards, even if those standards are identical to California's. The time will come when EPA can make its case for tougher emission limitations on motor vehicles. But that time is years from now and, under section 202, the case must be made to Congress.

III

This brings us to the issue we postponed at the beginning of part II of this opinion—whether the record supported EPA's "SIP call." In its final rule EPA declared that each of the state's implementation plans were "substantially inadequate to comply with the requirements of section 110(a)(2)(D) . . . and to mitigate adequately the interstate pollution transport described in section 184 . . . to the extent that they do not provide for emissions reductions from new motor vehicles in the amount that would be achieved by the" California "low emission vehicle . . . program." Final Rule, 60 Fed. Reg. at 4736 col. 2 (to be codified at 40 C.F.R. § 51.120(a)).

EPA's decision to declare the state plans inadequate depended on its view that it could order the California remedy. Section 184 limits EPA to requiring the control measures the Ozone Commission proposes as "necessary" to cure the problem the Commission identifies. Upon finding the California program "necessary," EPA became obligated to declare, pursuant to section 110(k)(5), that the states' plans were inadequate under section 110(a)(2)(D). *See* CAA § 184(c)(5), 42 U.S.C. § 7511c(c)(5). Section 110(a)(2)(D) provides that state plans must prohibit "emissions activity"—such as driving cars—if this will produce air pollution in amounts that "contribute significantly to nonattainment" in any other state. CAA § 110(a)(2)(D), 42 U.S.C. § 7410(a)(2)(D). EPA's reasoning was that if the California program is necessary, then the failure of a state to have that program equals a failure (under section 110(a)(2)(D)) to prohibit "significant contribution" to nonattainment in another state. *See* Final Rule, 60 Fed. Reg. at 4718 col. 3; *see also* Geoffrey L. Wilcox, New England and the Challenge of Interstate Ozone Pollution Under the Clean Air Act of 1990, 24 B.C. Envtl. Aff. L.Rev. 1, 49 (1996). This explains why

EPA framed the SIP call as it did—the state implementation plans are inadequate "to the extent they do not provide for reductions from new motor vehicles in the amount that would be achieved" by the California program. 60 Fed. Reg. at 4736 col. 2 (to be codified at 40 C.F.R. § 51.120(a)); *see also id.* at 4718 col. 3, 4719 col. 1. In short, since the particular measure recommended to EPA is not one the agency can mandate, EPA's finding of inadequacy—its SIP call—cannot survive.

Furthermore, throughout the rulemaking process, EPA operated on the belief that it had discretion to decide whether to issue a SIP call under section 110, but had no such discretion under section 184. Section 184 forced EPA to review the Ozone Commission's recommendation, to decide if it was "necessary," and if it was, to declare all the state plans inadequate. EPA had "no discretion"; it had to find each state plan lacking the measure deficient. But the agency viewed section 110(k)(5) in a different light. As EPA put it, "if the Administrator were to determine . . . that a particular measure is necessary to attain" the National Ambient Standards, "she might exercise her authority under section 110(k)(5) to find that a" State Plan "lacking such measure is substantially inadequate, but she might also refrain from doing so." Final Brief for Respondent at 64. Thus, although EPA purported to make an independent finding under section 110(k)(5), it is doubtful whether the agency would have exercised the discretion it finds in that provision if section 184 had not been triggered and if the agency had realized that section 110 gave it no power to choose this particular control measure for the states.

Virginia is the only state that has challenged EPA's rule and we have therefore considered whether to vacate the SIP call only with respect to Virginia. No one has argued for such a ruling. Furthermore, such limited relief would be inconsistent with EPA's approach and would threaten to further complicate this proceeding. EPA's modeling was based on an important and, it turns out, invalid assumption: that it could order each northeastern state to adopt the California program. Even if only Virginia's SIP call were stricken, any findings under section 110 would still have to be revised. If the ozone problem does in fact snowball as it moves up the Eastern seaboard, Virginia's lack of participation will necessarily affect all areas in the Region downwind of it, namely the rest of the entire Region. The SIP call requires states to "revise" their State Plans "as necessary to correct" them when the "Administrator finds that the applicable implementation plan . . . is substantially inadequate to attain or maintain the relevant national ambient air quality standard," or "to mitigate adequately the interstate pollutant transport described in" sections 176A or 184. CAA § 110(k)(5), 42 U.S.C. § 7410(k)(5). In the absence of applicable modeling, no such agency finding could be made. Thus, there is no existing basis for these SIP calls.

Seven states plus the District of Columbia voted for the California program; only three states (New York, Massachusetts, and Connecticut) have enacted it. It is foreseeable that should the SIP call to other states remain in effect, some will be pressured to adopt the California program. They are, of course, free to do so on their own. But they may not be pushed into that step on the basis of an EPA order that is no longer factually supported. The automobile manufacturers and dealers, who would make and sell different and more expensive cars under the California program, would thus be harmed if we allowed the remaining SIP calls to remain in effect on what is an inadequate record.

Finally, we notice that EPA's 1996 deadline for areas in moderate nonattainment has passed and that its 1999 deadline for areas in serious nonattainment is drawing near. *See* CAA § 181(a)(1)Table 1, 42 U.S.C. § 7511(a)(1)Table 1. If EPA considers it appropriate to reexamine state implementation plans in the Northeast, and if EPA requires the states to make revisions in order to bring about further reductions in ozone precursors, it must take these now-passed and rapidly approaching deadlines into account.

IV

In sum, we hold that EPA may not, under section 110, condition approval of a state's implementation plan on the state's adoption of a particular control measure. We also hold that EPA may not, under section 184, circumvent section 177, as we interpret it in light of section 202. For the reasons given, we hold that the SIP call EPA issued with respect to each state and the District of Columbia cannot stand.

The petitions for review are granted and the rule is vacated in its entirety.

So ordered.

NOTES AND QUESTIONS

(1) The decision in *Train v. Natural Resources Defense Council* legitimizes the concept of "variances" from strict adherence to standards. The decision holds firm to the idea that variances may not interfere with the attainment or maintenance of national ambient air quality standards. Why was the decision so roundly denounced by environmentalists? For an instance of the troublesome experience with variances on the state level, see Norwell & Bell, *Air Pollution Control in Texas*, 47 Tex. L. Rev. 1086 (1969).

(2) Does *Train v. Natural Resources Defense Council* have any implications on the policy of nondegradation or on significant deterioration? *See, e.g.*, Note, *Considerations of Technological and Economic Factors in Air Pollution Control*, 44 U. Cin. L. Rev. 573 (1975); Comment, *Train v. Natural Resources Defense Council, Inc.: A Judicial Restraint on the Clean Air Act Amendments of 1970*, 10 Urb. L. Ann. 297, 311 (1976). Does *Sierra Club v. EPA*, 540 F.2d 1114 (1976), fully dispose of the issue?

[ii] Compliance of State with "Approval Criteria"

NATURAL RESOURCES DEFENSE COUNCIL v. EPA

U.S. Court of Appeals, Fifth Circuit (1974)
489 F.2d 390

WISDOM, Circuit Judge:

The petitioners in this case are two non-profit corporations, Natural Resources Defense Council (NRDC) and Save America's Vital Environment (SAVE), and two individual citizens. They seek review of an order of the Administrator of the Environmental Protection Agency (EPA), approving the State of Georgia's plan for achieving the federal ambient air quality standards under the Clean Air Act Amendments of 1970. Petitioners raise four objections to the Administrator's action on the Georgia Plan. These concern (1) a provision of that Plan guaranteeing the confidentiality of secret trade information supplied to Georgia pollution control officials; (2) a provision allowing Georgia officials to grant variances from particular requirements of the Plan; (3) Georgia's adoption of a "control strategy" allowing "sources" of sulfur dioxide and particulate matter emissions, e. g. manufacturing plants, to avoid the necessity of installing emission reduction equipment by increasing the height of their smokestacks; and (4) provisions of the Plan directing Georgia officials to take into account economic impact and technological feasibility in the discharge of their duties under the state's air pollution control statutes.

We conclude that in approving each of the challenged provisions of the Georgia Plan, the Administrator exceeded his authority under the Clean Air Act Amendments, and order him to take appropriate corrective action.

We begin with a necessary discussion of the provisions of the Clean Air Act Amendments of 1970 relevant to the issues in this case.

. . . .

II.

The petitioners' first objection concerns a Georgia statute requiring the agencies responsible for Georgia's air quality program to keep confidential "any information" they obtain relating to "secret processes, devices, or methods of manufacture or production."[58] Ga.Code Ann. § 88-908 (1971). The petitioners contend that the Administrator's approval of this provision was prohibited by 42 U.S.C. § 1857c-5(a)(2)(F)(iii), (iv)[as amended § 114(c)]. Those two clauses require that the state implementation plan provide "for periodic reports on the nature and amounts of [stationary source] emissions" from all sources covered by the plan, and "that such reports shall be correlated by the State agency with any emission limitations or standards established pursuant to this Act, which reports shall be available . . . for public inspection." The petitioners contend that Georgia's section 88-908 should have been disapproved because that statute, with its blanket protection of "any information" relating to trade secrets, would direct Georgia officials to block public access to emission data where such data could qualify as "trade secret" information, and that this violates section 1857c-5(a)(2)(F)(iii), (iv) [as amended § 114(c)].

We agree. The public information and disclosure requirements of section 1857c-5(a)(2)(F)(iii), (iv) [as amended § 114(c)] have an important function under the 1970 Amendments. The Amendments embraced the concept of "citizen enforcement" of antipollution laws. 42 U.S.C. § 1857h-2permits "any

---

58 Ga.Code Ann. § 88-908 provides in full: Any information relating to secret processes, devices, or methods of manufacture or production obtained by the board, department or their employees in the administration of this Act shall be kept confidential.

person" to bring civil action in the federal district courts to enforce compliance with "any emission standard or limitation" promulgated under the Clean Air Act. The public information requirements play a crucial role in assuring effective citizen enforcement. They are designed to ensure that "citizen enforcers" will have access to any and all information they will need in prosecuting enforcement suits or in deciding whether to bring them.

Georgia's section 88-908 would hamper the operation of the public information and disclosure requirements in Georgia. The statute directs officials to ignore their duty under the federal statute to assure the disclosure of *all* emission data if some emission data touches upon trade secrets. And the dictates of section 88-908 may be stern indeed, for a separate provision of the Georgia air pollution code threatens criminal penalties to an official who violates section 88-908. In addition, section 88-908 could invite private parties to litigate questions whether emission data is "information relating to secret processes, devices, or methods of manufacture or production," and could thereby further impede the prompt and full disclosure of emission data.

In holding as we do, we are not insensitive to private interests in protecting confidential trade information. We view that interest, however, as subordinate to the public interest in full disclosure of emission data. This was the balance Congress itself struck in the 1970 Amendments. The Amendments provide for the confidentiality of trade secrets contained in information supplied to *federal* officials, but expressly state that emission data is not entitled to trade secret protection. *See* 42 U.S.C. § 1857c-9(c)[as amended § 114(c)]. The statute is not similarly explicit where information supplied to state officials is concerned, but there is no reason to strike the balance differently in that context.

The Administrator has himself disapproved provisions in fourteen state plans virtually indistinguishable from the provision in question here. The EPA has presented no persuasive reason for distinguishing the situation here from the fourteen other situations in which the Administrator disapproved over inclusive confidentiality provisions. . . .We hold that this provision, like the fourteen others, violated section 1857c-5(a)(2)(F)(iii), (iv) [as amended § 114(c)], and should have been disapproved.

Accordingly, we order the Administrator to publish forthwith his disapproval of section 88-908.

. . . .

IV.

The third objection the petitioners raise concerns Georgia's "control strategy" for meeting the national ambient air quality standards for particulate matter and sulfur dioxide. Georgia's implementation plan, as submitted to the Administrator and approved by him in May 1972, made the permissible amounts of particulates and sulfur dioxide emissions dependent on the heights of the smokestacks at the sources; the higher its smokestack, the more a source was permitted to emit. Georgia Rules and Regulations for Air Quality Control § 270-5-24-.02(2)(g) (SO_2), -(m) (particulates). This "tall stack" approach represents a form of "dispersion enhancement technique." Dispersion enhancement techniques are techniques to reduce concentrations of pollutants not by reducing the quantities emitted into the air —the objective of so-called "emission limitation" techniques —but rather by altering the conditions under which substances are emitted, in order to enhance their dispersion throughout the atmosphere.

The petitioners contend that Georgia's choice of such a strategy is in conflict with 42 U.S.C. § 1857c-5(a)(2)(B)[as amended § 110(a)(2)(A)]. That subparagraph requires that state implementation plans "includ[e] emission limitations, schedules, and timetables for compliance with such limitations, and such other measures as may be necessary to insure attainment and maintenance of such primary or secondary standard." The petitioners contend that the directive to use "emission limitations," coupled with the reference to "other measures . . . *necessary,*" means that "other measures," including any and all dispersion techniques, may be employed only when "necessary" in the sense that all available emission limitation has been first achieved. And they suggest that Georgia had not adopted controls capable of achieving the maximum possible emission limitation before it adopted the tall stack controls.

. . . .

B.

42 U.S.C. § 1857c-5(a)(2)(B)provides:

"The Administrator shall approve such [state implementation] plan, or any portion thereof, if he determines that . . .

. . . .

"(B) it includes emission limitations, schedules, and timetables for compliance with such limitations and such other measures as may be necessary to insure attainment and maintenance of such primary or secondary standard, including, but not limited to, land-use and transportation controls." [*See* section as amended, § 110(a)(2)(A).]

The issue before this Court, in interpreting this provision, is well framed in an EPA staff paper, now published in the Congressional Record. In framing the issue, we take the liberty of quoting at length from that paper:

It should be clear . . . that the intent of Congress in the Clean Air Act is that the State Implementation Plans must include emission limitations. It is also clear that the words "and such other measures as may be necessary" exclude the interpretation that emission reduction is the only acceptable means of meeting [national ambient air quality standards]. Between these two boundaries to interpretation there is a broad, unexplored territory.

. . . .

[The court concluded that it was the Congressional intent to rely primarily on emission controls rather than on tall stack dispersion technology.] [For current reference to Tall Stacks, see C.A.A. § 123, Stack Heights.]

V.

The petitioners' final challenge is to the Administrator's approval of portions of section 88-906 of the Georgia Code. That provision, entitled "Factors to be considered in exercising powers and responsibilities related to air quality," sets out a list of factors the Board of Health and Department of Public Health are to consider in exercising their responsibilities under the Georgia air quality code. The petitioners object to the inclusion of five of these factors. These are:

> (h) The availability of air-cleaning devices
>
> (i) Economic feasibility of air-cleaning devices
>
> . . . .
>
> (k) Effect on efficiency of industrial operations from use of air-cleaning devices
>
> . . . .
>
> (o) The economic and industrial development of the State and the social and economic value of the source of air contaminants
>
> . . . .
>
> (q) Other factors which the Department may find applicable.

The petitioners contend that the inclusion of these factors in the list undermines the intent of Congress that considerations of public health should always take precedence over considerations of economic impact or technical feasibility under the Clean Air Act.

We agree that the Administrator's approval of the challenged portions of this Georgia statute violated the Amendments. The statute implies that consideration of economic factors be limited in two respects. First, Congress made it clear that considerations of economic cost or technical feasibility were *always* to be subordinate to considerations of public health. Second, and as a corollary to this, Congress made it clear that cost and feasibility were not to be considered in meeting the three-year deadlines for attaining national primary standards. Those standards are set in terms of what is required for the protection of public health.

The legislative history of the Amendments, fortified by statements made by some of the draftsmen of the Amendments since the enactment of the Amendments, supports this conclusion. The House version of the Amendments included the phrase "giving due consideration to the economic and technological feasibility of compliance." The phrase was removed in the House-Senate Conference, after what Senator Thomas F. Eagleton remembers as "hours" of debate. The Senate Report on the Amendments states the essential position of the Amendments with respect to cost and feasibility factors:

> "The Committee determined that 1) the health of the people is more important than the question of whether the early achievement of ambient air quality standards protective of health is technically feasible; and 2) the growth of the pollution load in many areas, even with the application of available technology, would be deleterious to public health. Therefore, the Committee determined that existing sources of pollutants should meet the standard of law or be closed down. . . ."

S.Rep. No. 91-1196 at 2-3 (1970). The Senate Subcommittee on Air and Water Pollution, which had been responsible for drafting the Senate version of the

Amendments, sent a briefing paper to the Administrator in early 1972. In that paper, the Subcommittee stated its understanding of the matter:

> "Inclusion of a test of social and economic feasibility of compliance with those control requirements necessary to achieve protection of public health as part of implementation plan guidelines compromises the intention of the Act . . . ."

Hearings Before the Subcomm. on Air and Water Pollution of the Senate Comm. on Public Works on the Implementation of the Clean Air Act Amendments of 1970, 92nd Cong., 2d Sess. at 308 (1972).

The vice in section 88-906 is similar to the vice in Georgia's trade secrets provision: it is over inclusive. The provision does not distinguish between situations where cost and feasibility considerations compete with other considerations and those where they do not. It is, of course, appropriate for state air pollution control officials to take into account cost and feasibility factors in most circumstances; their doing so is proscribed only when those considerations are in conflict with considerations of public health. As it stands, the provision may deflect state officials from properly discharging their duties under the state implementation plan. And like the trade secrets provision, it may invite time-consuming litigation brought by private parties, litigation which could impede the progress of the state's implementation plan.

In support of the Administrator's approval of the statute, the EPA notes that consideration of economic factors is proper in the context of the attainment of the national *secondary* standards, and asserts that section 88-906(h)-(i), (k), (o), and (q) will be applied only in that context. We cannot accept this argument. The language of the statute still exists on the statute books, and still, on its face, directs officials to weigh these considerations against considerations of public health. As long as this is the case there will remain a danger that state officials will be influenced by the statute.

Thus we conclude that the Administrator's approval of the statute exceeded his authority, and direct him to publish forthwith his disapproval of section 88-906(h)-(i), (k), (o), and (q).

NOTE

The opinion in *National Resources Defense Council v. EPA* (Georgia Plan) includes an early effort to deal with the issue of the permissibility of the so-called "tall stack" strategy—to meet ambient air quality standards not by reducing emissions, but by dispersing emissions more widely and therefore more thinly. The tall stack issue has remained a problem even after the express regulation of tall stacks and other dispersion techniques in CAA § 123added in 1977. Section 123 and earlier regulations approached the issue by not allowing a reduction resulting from so much of the height of tall stacks as exceeds good engineering practice. For an opinion on the post-1977 tall stack regulations, see *Sierra Club v. EPA,* 719 F.2d 436, 13 E.L.R. 21001 (D.C. Cir. 1983), *cert. denied,* 468 U.S. 1204 (1984).

NATURAL RESOURCES DEFENSE COUNCIL v. EPA

U.S. Court of Appeals, First Circuit (1973)
478 F.2d 875

CAMPBELL, Circuit Judge.

Petitioners seek review of decisions by the Administrator of the Environmental Protection Agency (E.P.A.) approving portions of the Rhode Island and Massachusetts air pollution implementation plans.

[The court recited the scheme of the Clean Air Act and recounted the states' obligation to adopt implementation plans.]

Petitioners raise eight objections to the Administrator's approval of the Rhode Island plan, and four to the Massachusetts plan.

THE RHODE ISLAND PLAN

. . . .

III.

Petitioners assert that the Administrator erred in approving the Rhode Island plan since it does not provide for revisions, as required by 42 U.S.C. § 1857c-5(a)(2)(H)[as amended 42 U.S.C. § 7410(a)(2)(H)].

The statutory language is clear:

> "[The Administrator shall approve the plan if he determines that] it provides for revision, after public hearings, of such plan (i) from time to time as may be necessary to take account of revisions of such national primary or secondary ambient air quality standard or the availability of improved or more expeditious methods of achieving such primary or secondary standard; or (ii) whenever the Administrator finds on the basis of information available to him that the plan is substantially inadequate to achieve the national ambient air quality primary or secondary standard which it implements."

We think the plan must expressly provide for revision after public hearings on the occasions and under the circumstances described in the federal statute. Congress did not indicate merely that the state, or some state authority, should have a power of amendment. Compare G.L.R.I. §§ 23-25-5(l) and 23-25-5(n). The plan was to be approved only if *"it provides* for revision after public hearings" in two sets of circumstances where revision is mandatory, not merely optional. (emphasis supplied). The Administrator erred in approving a plan which sets forth something less. We see no reason, when Congress has spoken precisely, for the Administrator or us to try to decide whether the state's informal substitute is, in the long run,.just or almost as good. Presumably the necessary revision undertaking could be in regulations promulgated by the state director of health or, if more convenient, the Administrator could promulgate his own regulations as a part of the state plan. § 1857c-5(c).

IV.

Petitioners claim that the Rhode Island plan failed to provide the "necessary assurances that the State will have adequate personnel, funding, and authority to carry out such implementation plan" required by 42 U.S.C. § 1857c5(a)(2)(F)[as amended 42 U.S.C. § 7410(a)(2)(E)]. Respondent counters that the Rhode Island Plan complied with EPA regulation 40C.F.R. § 51.20:

> "Each plan shall include a description of the resources available to the State and local agencies at the date of submission of the plan and of any additional resources needed to carry out the plan during the 5-year period following its submission. Such description, which shall be provided in a form similar to that in Appendix K to this part, shall include projections of the extent to which resources will be acquired at 1-, 3-, and 5-year intervals."

The Rhode Island Plan *described* the available resources and projected further resource acquisition. The question becomes whether 40 C.F.R. § 51.20is consistent with the statute. An assurance is "the act of assuring . . . something that inspires or tends to inspire confidence . . . the quality or state of being sure or certain: freedom from doubt: CERTAINTY . . ." (Webster's Third New International Dictionary). At first glance, a description does not seem to inspire confidence or provide certainty that the state will have adequate personnel, funding and authority to carry out its plan. Yet given the mechanics of state-federal relations, it is difficult to imagine what sort of guarantee the current Rhode Island executive or legislature could give the E.P.A. to insure that adequate resources would be devoted to the Plan. Petitioner speaks of a "commitment . . . to use all reasonable efforts to obtain these resources from the legislature or from other programs . . . The Governor [should] give his assurance that he will do everything possible to obtain adequate resources, including filing special acts before the state legislature, or if necessary making available the necessary resources from other programs under his control." Such assurances might have a symbolic effect; however, they would have little more, since a governor or even a present session of the legislature cannot make binding commitments on behalf of their successors, nor would such representations seem to be enforceable.

We believe that Congress has left to the Administrator's sound discretion determination of what assurances are "necessary." The Administrator has required the states to describe their resources, doubtless reasoning that review of such an inventory is the best practical "assurances" he can obtain. The Administrator can determine whether the itemized resources together with such federal funds as the Administrator may himself channel to Rhode Island (*see* 42 U.S.C. § 1857c) will enable the state to carry out the plan. The Administrator might also have asked for a promise by the Governor to use his "best efforts." But we are not prepared to fault the Administrator for deciding that such a gesture would be so lacking in enforceability as to be meaningless. The "necessary assurances" clause seems to us to call less for rhetoric than for the Administrator's reasoned judgment as to the adequacy of resources.

V.

Petitioners say the Administrator erred in approving that portion of the Rhode Island plan which permits the state to grant variances.

. . . .

THE MASSACHUSETTS PLAN

Petitioners' first three objections to the Massachusetts plan raise substantially the same issues as those discussed above with regard to the Rhode Island plan.

. . . .

XII.

We agree with petitioners that the Massachusetts plan failed to comply with 42 U.S.C. § 1857c-5(a)(2)(F)[as amended 42 U.S.C. § 7410(a)(2)(F)], which requires each plan to provide,

> ". . . (ii) requirements for installation of equipment by owners or operators of stationary sources to monitor emissions from such sources; (iii) for periodic reports on the nature and amounts of such emissions; (iv) that such reports shall be correlated by the State agency with any emission limitations or standards established pursuant to this chapter, *which reports shall be available at reasonable times for public inspection. . . .*" [Emphasis supplied.]

This section, particularly important to insure public participation in the enforcement process, is implemented by E.P.A. regulations 40C.F.R. §§ 51.10(e) and 51.11(a)(6).[59]

Regulation 14 of the Massachusetts Department of Public Health Air Pollution rules states:

> "Upon request by the Department through direct communication or public notice, any person who owns or operates a stationary emission source . . . (b) shall make periodic reports to the Department on the nature and amounts of emissions from said such source which the Department shall review and correlate for its use in emissions control and exhibit for public information."

As petitioners point out, Regulation 14 does not *require* periodic reports. If the Department does not request such reports, they need not be made. We

[59] "Each plan shall provide for public availability of emission data reported by source owners or operators or otherwise obtained by a state or local agency. Such emission data shall be correlated with applicable emission limitations or other measures. . . ." 40 C.F.R. § 51.10(e).

"Each plan shall show that the State has legal authority to carry out the plan, including authority to . . . (6) Require owners or operators of stationary sources to install, maintain, and use emission monitoring devices and to make periodic reports to the State on the nature and amounts of emissions from such stationary sources; also authority for the State to make such data available to the public as reported and as correlated with any applicable emission standards or limitations." 40 C.F.R. § 51.11(a)(6).

agree that this discretionary aspect of the Regulation is in conflict with the Act, and should have been disapproved.

There is a further problem with this aspect of the Massachusetts plan. G.L. c.111 § 142D is enabling legislation for the Department to implement federal air pollution requirements. § 142D provides, in part, that "The powers, duties and rights of the department in the exercise of air pollution control in districts established under this section . . . shall be as provided in section one hundred and forty-two B." § 142B states:

> "Personnel of the department may in the performance of their duties under this section, enter and inspect any property, premise, or place, . . . *Any information relating to secret processes, methods of manufacture, or production obtained in the course of such inspection shall be kept confidential upon request.*" [Emphasis supplied.]

G.L. c. 111 § 2B contains similar language regarding information obtained during inspections to uncover violations of air pollution emergency orders:

> "Information relating to trade secrets, secret processes or methods of manufacture or production shall be confidential and shall not be disclosed or received during the course of any such investigation; nor shall such information be used or disclosed in any public hearing under this section."

These statutes suggest that Massachusetts does not have authority to compel public disclosure of emission data.

That the federal statute specifically intended emission data to become public knowledge is clear from 42 U.S.C. § 1857c-9(c)[as amended 42 U.S.C. § 7414(a)]:

> "Any records, reports or information obtained under subsection (a) of this section [permitting the Administrator access to emission records] shall be available to the public, except that upon a showing satisfactory to the Administrator by any person that records, reports, or information, or particular part thereof, *(other than emission data)* to which the Administrator has access under this section if made public, would divulge methods or processes entitled to protection as trade secrets of such person, the Administrator shall consider such record, report, or information or particular portion thereof confidential in accordance with the purposes of section 1905 of Title 18, except that such record, report, or information may be disclosed to other officers, employees, or authorized representatives of the United States concerned with carrying out this chapter or when relevant in any proceeding under this chapter." [Emphasis supplied.]

The Administrator should have disapproved so much of the Massachusetts statutes and regulations forming a part of the state's implementation plan as allow emission reports to be held confidential.

. . . .

NOTES AND QUESTIONS

(1) For a similar decision, see *Natural Resources Defense Council v. EPA* (Iowa Plan), 483 F.2d 690 (8th Cir. 1973).

(2) The Supreme Court in *Train v. Natural Resources Defense Council* reversed the decision in *Natural Resources Defense Council v. EPA* relating to the Georgia plan only with respect to the variance issue. The other issues in that case were not before the Supreme Court. But the Supreme Court did indicate that so long as the ultimate effect of the state's choice of emission limitations is to comply with national ambient standards, a state is at liberty to adopt whatever mix of emission limitations it deems best suited to its own situation. Section 124 of the Clean Air Act,adopted in 1977, imposes a limit on stack height. Does it affect the Court's cited holdings? *See also* EPA's Final Stack Height Regulations, 40 C.F.R. Part 100; 50 Fed. Reg. 27892 (1985). *See also* F. Grad, Treatise on Environmental Law § 2.03[7][a][ii].

(3) Is the argument that tall stack strategies merely disperse pollutants rather than reducing them—thereby contributing to degradation of air quality—entirely sound? EPA had issued "Stack Height Increase Guidelines," 41 Fed. Reg. 7450 (Feb. 18, 1976), allowing increases in stack height for supplementary control systems. What is the purpose of a supplementary control system? If tall stacks are good enough for "supplementary" controls, why aren't they generally acceptable? In its discussion, the court in the Georgia plan case treats fuel regulations relating to permissible sulfur content as a species of "emission limitations." Is this an appropriate way to view such regulations?

(4) In the Georgia plan case, the court rejects the reference to technological and economic infeasibility as factors to be considered in exercising the state's powers to control air quality. Yet in the case of *Union Electric Co. v. EPA, infra,* the Supreme Court indicated that such factors could be taken into account at the state level when preparing a state implementation plan. Are these views consistent?

(5) It is clear that ultimately effective air pollution control through state implementation plans depends on meeting the "necessary assurances that the state will have adequate personnel, funding and authority" required as part of the plan. "Authority" is a matter of having necessary laws and regulations, but adequate personnel and funding is not nearly as readily ascertainable. "Adequate" for what? Does EPA provide a measure for adequacy in its regulations? Suppose the state does not provide enough of a budget and does not authorize enough personnel to do a reasonable job of enforcement. What, as a constitutional and legal matter, can the Administration or the federal government do about it? Is a citizen suit effort likely to be more effective in accomplishing the goal of the federal requirement?

[iii] Technological and Economic Infeasibility

UNION ELECTRIC CO. v. EPA

United States Supreme Court (1976)
427 U.S. 246, 96 S. Ct. 2518, 49 L. Ed. 2d 474

Mr. JUSTICE MARSHALL delivered the opinion of the Court.

After the Administrator of the Environmental Protection Agency (EPA) approves a state implementation plan under the Clean Air Act, the plan may be challenged in a court of appeals within 30 days, or after 30 days have run if newly discovered or available information justifies subsequent review. We must decide whether the operator of a regulated emission source, in a petition for review of an EPA-approved state plan filed after the original 30-day appeal period, can raise the claim that it is economically or technologically infeasible to comply with the plan.

I.

We have addressed the history and provisions of the Clean Air Act Amendments of 1970, Pub L 91-604, 84 Stat 1676, in detail in Train v. Natural Resources Defense Council (NRDC), 421 US 60, 43 L Ed 2d 731, 95 S Ct 1470 (1975), and will not repeat that discussion here. Suffice it to say that the Amendments reflect congressional dissatisfaction with the progress of existing air pollution programs and a determination to "tak[e] a stick to the States," *id.*, at 64, 43 L Ed 2d 731, 95 S Ct 1470, in order to guarantee the prompt attainment and maintenance of specified air quality standards. The heart of the Amendments is the requirement that each State formulate, subject to EPA approval, an implementation plan designed to achieve national primary ambient air quality standards—those necessary to protect the public health—"as expeditiously as practicable but . . . in no case later than three years from the date of approval of such plan." § 110(a)(2)(A) of the Clean Air Act,as added, 84 Stat 1680, 42 U.S.C. § 1857c-5(a)(2)(A). The plan must also provide for the attainment of national secondary ambient air quality standards—those necessary to protect the public welfare—within a "reasonable time." *Ibid.* Each State is given wide discretion in formulating its plan, and the Act provides that the Administrator "shall approve" the proposed plan if it has been adopted after public notice and hearing and if it meets eight specified criteria. § 110(a)(2).

On April 30, 1971, the Administrator promulgated national primary and secondary standards for six air pollutants he found to have an adverse effect on the public health and welfare. 40 C.F.R. pt 50 (1975). *See* § 108(a) of the Act, as added, 84 Stat 1678, 42 U.S.C. § 1857c-3(a). Included among them was sulfur dioxide, at issue here. 40 C.F.R. §§ 50.4-50.5(1975). After the promulgation of the national standards, the State of Missouri formulated its implementation plan and submitted it for approval. Since sulfur dioxide levels exceeded national primary standards in only one of the State's five air quality regions—the Metropolitan St. Louis Interstate region, 40 C.F.R. § 52.1321—the Missouri plan concentrated on a control strategy and regulations to lower emissions in that area. The plan's emission limitations were effective at once, but the State retained authority to grant variances to particular sources that could not immediately comply.[60] § 203.110, Rev Stat Mo (1969). The Administrator approved the plan on May 31, 1972. *See* 40 C.F.R. § 52.1320 *et seq.*

Petitioner is an electric utility company servicing the St. Louis metropolitan area, large portions of Missouri, and parts of Illinois and Iowa. Its three coal-fired generating plants in the metropolitan St. Louis area are subject to the

---

[60] The plan was designed to attain primary and secondary air quality standards in the Metropolitan St. Louis Interstate region by July 1975. *See* 40 C.F.R. § 52.1332.

sulfur dioxide restrictions in the Missouri implementation plan. Petitioner did not seek review of the Administrator's approval of the plan within 30 days, as it was entitled to do under § 307(b)(1) of the Act, as added, 84 Stat 1708, 42 U.S.C. § 1857h-5(b)(1), but rather applied to the appropriate state and county agencies for variances from the emission limitations affecting its three plants. Petitioner received one-year variances, which could be extended upon reapplication. The variances on two of petitioner's three plants had expired and petitioner was applying for extensions when, on May 31, 1974, the Administrator notified petitioner that sulfur dioxide emissions from its plants violated the emission limitations contained in the Missouri plan.[61] *See* 40 Fed Reg 3566 (1975). Shortly thereafter petitioner filed a petition in the Court of Appeals for the Eighth Circuit for review of the Administrator's 1972 approval of the Missouri implementation plan.

Section 307(b)(1) allows petitions for review to be filed in an appropriate court of appeals more than 30 days after the Administrator's approval of an implementation plan only if the petition is "based solely on grounds arising after such 30th day." Petitioner claimed to meet this requirement by asserting, inter alia, that various economic and technological difficulties had arisen more than 30 days after the Administrator's approval and that these difficulties made compliance with the emission limitations impossible.[62] The Court of Appeals ordered briefing on the question of its subject-matter jurisdiction to hear the case and, after argument, granted the motions of the EPA and intervenor-respondents, the Attorney General of Missouri and the Missouri Air Conservation Commission, to dismiss the petition for review for lack of jurisdiction.

The Court held that "only matters which, if known to the Administrator at the time of his action [in approving a state implementation plan], would

[61] The notice included all three plants, even though the variance on one of them had not yet expired, because the one variance still in effect had not been submitted to EPA as a plan revision under § 110(a)(3)(A), as amended, 88 Stat 256, 42 U.S.C. § 1857c-5(a)(3)(A), and therefore was not part of the applicable implementation plan. *See* n. 15, *infra*.

[62] Petitioner also claimed that the presence of sulfur dioxide in the ambient air should no longer be regarded as a health hazard and that compliance with the Missouri implementation plan was not necessary for attainment of national primary or secondary air quality standards. The Court of Appeals found that these claims were not sufficient to establish jurisdiction under § 307(b)(1).

The Court held that the challenge to the validity of regulating sulfur dioxide was not properly before it because the alleged new information had not previously been presented to the Administrator for action, a procedure the Court held was necessary for the exercise of its jurisdiction. 515 F2d 206, 220. *See also* Oljato Chapter v. Train, 169 US App DC 195, 515 F2d 654 (1975). In any case, the Court held, the challenge was to a national air quality standard and as such could be brought only in the Court of Appeals for the District of Columbia Circuit under § 307(b)(1). 515 F2d, at 220. While petitioner sought certiorari on this ruling, our grant of the writ was limited to the question whether claims of economic or technical infeasibility could be raised in a challenge to a state implementation plan. 423 US 821, 46 L Ed 2d 38, 96 S Ct 35 (1975).

The Court of Appeals also found that no claim was stated by petitioner's assertion that the Missouri standards exceeded those necessary for compliance with the national standards because, the Court held, the States are free to adopt stricter standards than the national standards under § 116 of the Clean Air Act,as amended, 84 Stat 1689 and 88 Stat 259, 42 U.S.C. § 1857d-1(Supp 1975). 515 F2d, at 220. While certiorari was not sought on this question, it has been briefed for us and we find it necessary to resolve it in deciding this case.

justify setting aside that action are properly reviewable after the initial 30 day review period." 515 F2d 206, 216 (1975). Since, in the Court's view, claims of economic and technological infeasibility could not properly provide a basis for the Administrator's rejecting a plan, such claims could not serve—at any time—as the basis for a court's overturning an approved plan. Accordingly, insofar as petitioner's claim of newly discovered or available information was grounded on an assertion of economic and technological infeasibility, the court held itself to be without jurisdiction to consider the petition for review, and so dismissed the petition. In so holding the Court of Appeals considered and rejected the contrary or partially contrary holdings of three other circuits. . . . We granted certiorari to resolve the conflict among the circuits, 423 US 821, 46 L Ed 2d 38, 96 S Ct 35 (1975), and we now affirm.

II.

A

We reject at the outset petitioner's suggestion that a claim of economic or technological infeasibility may be considered upon a petition for review based on new information and filed more than 30 days after approval of an implementation plan even if such a claim could not be considered by the Administrator in approving a plan or by a court in reviewing a plan challenged within the original 30-day appeal period. In pertinent part § 307(b)(1) provides:

> "A petition for review of the Administrator's action in approving or promulgating any implementation plan under section 110 . . . may be filed only in the United States Court of Appeals for the appropriate circuit. Any such petition shall be filed within 30 days from the date of such promulgation or approval, or after such date if such petition is based solely on grounds arising after such 30th day."

Regardless of when a petition for review is filed under § 307(b)(1), the court is limited to reviewing "the Administrator's action in approving . . . [the] implementation plan . . ." Accordingly, if new "grounds" are alleged, they must be such that, had they been known at the time the plan was presented to the Administrator for approval, it would have been an abuse of discretion for the Administrator to approve the plan. To hold otherwise would be to transfer a substantial responsibility in administering the Clean Air Act from the Administrator and the State agencies to the federal courts.

B

Since a reviewing court—regardless of when the petition for review is filed—may consider claims of economic and technological infeasibility only if the Administrator may consider such claims in approving or rejecting a state implementation plan, we must address ourselves to the scope of the Administrator's responsibility. The Administrator's position is that he has no power whatsoever to reject a state implementation plan on the ground that it is economically or technologically infeasible, and we have previously accorded great deference to the Administrator's construction of the Clean Air Act. *See* Train v NRDC, 421 US at 75, 43 L Ed 2d 731, 95 S Ct 1470. After surveying the relevant provisions of the Clean Air Act Amendments of 1970 and their legislative history, we agree that Congress intended claims of economic and technological infeasibility to be wholly foreign to the Administrator's consideration of a state implementation plan.

As we have previously recognized, the 1970 Amendments to the Clean Air Act were a drastic remedy to what was perceived as a serious and otherwise uncheckable problem of air pollution. The Amendments place the primary responsibility for formulating pollution control strategies on the States, but nonetheless subject the States to strict minimum compliance requirements. These requirements are of a "technology-forcing character," Train v NRDC, 421 US, at 91, 43 L Ed 2d 731, 95 S Ct 1470, and are expressly designed to force regulated sources to develop pollution control devices that might at the time appear to be economically or technologically infeasible.

The approach is apparent on the face of § 110(a)(2). The provision sets out eight criteria that an implementation plan must satisfy, and provides that if these criteria are met and if the plan was adopted after reasonable notice and hearing, the Administrator "shall approve" the proposed state plan. The mandatory "shall" makes it quite clear that the Administrator is not to be concerned with factors other than those specified, Train v NRDC, 421 US, at 71 n 11, 79, 43 L Ed 2d 731, 95 S Ct 1470, and none of the eight factors appears to permit consideration of technological or economic infeasibility.[63] Nonetheless, if a basis is to be found for allowing the Administrator to consider such claims, it must be among the eight criteria, and so it is here that the argument is focused.

It is suggested that consideration of claims of technological and economic infeasibility is required by the first criterion—that the primary air quality standards be met "as expeditiously as practicable but . . . in no case later than three years . . . " and that the secondary air quality standards be met within a "reasonable time." § 110(a)(2)(A). The argument is that what is "practicable" or "reasonable" cannot be determined without assessing whether what is proposed is possible. This argument does not survive analysis.

Section 110(a)(2)(A)'s three-year deadline for achieving primary air quality standards is central to the Amendments' regulatory scheme and, as both the language and the legislative history of the requirement make clear, it leaves no room for claims of technological or economic infeasibility. The 1970 congressional debate on the Amendments centered on whether technology forcing was necessary and desirable in framing and attaining air quality standards sufficient to protect the public health, standards later termed primary standards. The House version of the Amendments was quite moderate in approach, requiring only that health-related standards be met "within a reasonable time." HR 17255, 91st Cong, 2d Sess, § 108(c)(1)(C)(i) (1970). The

[63] . . . Comparison of the eight criteria of § 110(a)(2) with other provisions of the Amendments bolsters this conclusion. Where Congress intended the Administrator to be concerned about economic and technological infeasibility, it expressly so provided. Thus, §§ 110(e), 110(f), 111(a)(1), 202(a), 211(c)(2)(A), and 231(b) of the Amendments all expressly permit consideration, *e.g.*, "of the requisite technology, giving appropriate consideration to the cost of compliance." § 231(b), as added, 84 Stat 1703, 42 U.S.C. § 1857f-9(b). *See also* 42 U.S.C. §§ 1857c-5(e), 1857c-5(f), 1857c-6(a)(1), 1857f-1(a), 1857f-6c(c)(2)(A). Section 110(a)(2) contains no such language.

Senate bill, on the other hand, flatly required that, possible or not, health-related standards be met "within three years." S 4358, 91st Cong, 2d Sess, § 111(a)(2)(A) (1970).

The Senate's stiff requirement was intended to foreclose the claims of emission sources that it would be economically or technologically infeasible for them to achieve emission limitations sufficient to protect the public health within the specified time. As Senator Muskie, manager of the Senate bill, explained to his chamber:

> "The first responsibility of Congress is not the making of technological or economic judgments—or even to be limited by what is or appears to be technologically or economically feasible. Our responsibility is to establish what the public interest requires to protect the health of persons. This may mean that people and industries will be asked to do what seems to be impossible at the present time." 116 Cong Rec 32901-32902 (1970).

See also id., at 32919 (remarks of Sen. Cooper); 33115 (remarks of Sen. Prouty). This position reflected that of the Senate committee:

> "In the Committee discussions, considerable concern was expressed regarding the use of the concept of technical feasibility as the basis of ambient air standards. The Committee determined that 1) the health of the people is more important than the question of whether the early achievement of ambient air quality standards protective of health is technically feasible; and 2) the growth of pollution load in many areas even with application of available technology, would still be deleterious to public health.
>
> "Therefore, the Committee determined that existing sources of pollutants either should meet the standard of the law or be closed down. . . ." S Rep No. 1196, 91st Cong, 2d Sess, 2-3 (1970).

The Conference Committee and, ultimately, the entire Congress accepted the Senate's three-year mandate for the achievement of primary air quality standards, and the clear import of that decision is that the Administrator must approve a plan that attains the primary standards in three years even if attainment does not appear feasible. In rejecting the House's standard of reasonableness, however, the Conferees strengthened the Senate standard. The Conference Committee made clear that the States could not malinger until the deadline approached. Rather, the primary standards must be met in less than three years if possible; they must be met "as expeditiously as practicable." § 110(a)(2)(A). Whatever room there is for considering claims of infeasibility in the attainment of primary standards must lie in this phrase, which is, of course, relevant only in evaluating those implementation plans that attempt to achieve the primary standard in less than three years.

It is argued that when such a state plan proceeds more rapidly than economics and the available technology appears to allow, the plan must be rejected as not "practicable." Whether this is a correct reading of § 110(a)(2)(A) depends on how that section's "as expeditiously as practicable" phrase is characterized. The Administrator's position is that § 110(a)(2)(A) sets only a minimum standard that the States may exceed in their discretion, so that he has no power to reject an infeasible State plan that surpasses the minimum federal requirements —a plan that reflects a state decision to engage in technology forcing on its own and that proceeds more expeditiously than is practicable. On the other hand, petitioner and its amici argue that § 110(a)(2)(A) sets a mandatory standard that the States must meet precisely, and conclude that the Administrator may reject a plan for being too strict as well as for being too lax. Since the arguments supporting this theory are also made to show that the Administrator must reject a state plan that achieves more than the secondary air quality standards require, we defer consideration of this question in order to outline the development and content of the secondary standards provision of § 110(a)(2)(A).

Secondary air quality standards, those necessary to protect the public welfare, were subject to far less legislative debate than the primary standards. The House version of the Amendments treated welfare-related standards together with health-related standards, and required both to be met "within a reasonable time." HR 17255, 91st Cong, 2d Sess, §§ 107(e)(1), 108(c)(1)(C)(i) (1970). The Senate bill, on the other hand, treated health-and welfare-related standards separately and did not require that welfare-related standards be met in any particular time at all, S 4358, 91st Cong, 2d Sess, §§ 110(a)(3), 110(b), 111(a)(2)(A) (1970), although the Committee Report expressed the desire that they be met "as rapidly as possible." S Rep No. 91-1196, 91st Cong, 2d Sess, 11 (1970). The final Amendments also separated welfare-related standards from health-related standards, labeled them secondary air quality standards, and adopted the House's requirement that they be met within a "reasonable time." §§ 109(b), 110(a)(2)(A). Thus, technology forcing is not expressly required in achieving standards to protect the public welfare.[64]

It does not necessarily follow, however, that the Administrator may consider claims of impossibility in assessing a state plan for achieving secondary standards. As with plans designed to achieve primary standards in less than three years, the scope of the Administrator's power to reject a plan depends on whether the State itself may decide to engage in technology forcing and adopt a plan more stringent than federal law demands.[65]

Amici Appalachian Power Co. et al. argue that the Amendments do not give such broad power to the States. They claim that the States are precluded from submitting implementation plans more stringent than federal law demands by § 110(a)(2)'s second criterion—that the plan contain such control devices "as may be necessary" to achieve the primary and secondary air quality standards. § 110(a)(2)(B). The contention is that an overly restrictive plan is not "necessary" for attainment of the national standards and so must be rejected by the Administrator.[66]

---

[64] The Administrator appears to take this position in his guidelines for attaining secondary standards. *See* 40 C.F.R. § 51.13(b)(1975).

[65] A different question would be presented if the Administrator drafted the plan himself pursuant to § 110(c). Cf. District of Columbia v. Train, 172 US App DC 311, 521 F2d 971 (1975); South Terminal Corp. v. EPA, 504 F2d 646 (CA1 1974). Whether claims of economic or technical infeasibility must be considered by the Administrator in drafting an implementation plan is a question we do not reach.

[66] Amici not only argue that the Administrator must reject state plans that attempt to attain the primary standards more rapidly than "practicable" or the secondary standards in less than a "reasonable time," but also that he must reject state implementation plans that call for more quantitative emission controls than those necessary to meet the national

Amici's principal support for this theory lies in the fact that while the House and Senate versions of § 110(a)(2) both expressly provided that the States could submit for the Administrator's approval plans that were stricter than the national standards required, see HR 17255, 91st Cong, 2d Sess, § 108(c) (1970); S 4358, 91st Cong, 2d Sess, § 111(a)(1) (1970), the section as enacted contains no such express language. Amici argue that the Conference Committee must have decided to require state implementation simply—and precisely—to meet the national standards. Amici's argument proves too much. A Conference Committee lacks power to make substantive changes on matters about which both Houses agree. Here the Conference Report expressly notes that both the Senate and House bills would allow States to submit plans more stringent than the national standards demand, and offers no suggestion that the Conference bill intended to change that result, even if it could. HR Rep No. 91-1783, 91st Cong, 2d Sess, 45 (1970). And while the final language of § 110(a)(2)(B) may be less explicit than the versions originally approved by the House and the Senate, the most natural reading of the "as may be necessary" phrase in context is simply that the Administrator must assure that the minimal, or "necessary," requirements are met, not that he detect and reject any state plan more demanding than federal law requires.[67]

This reading is further supported by practical considerations. Section 116 of the Clean Air Act,as added, 84 Stat 1689, 42 USC § 1857d-1, provides that the States may adopt emission standards stricter than the national standards.[68] Amici argue that such standards must be adopted and enforced independently of the EPA-approved state implementation plan. This construction of §§ 110 and 116, however, would not only require the Administrator to expend considerable time and energy determining whether a state plan was precisely tailored to meet the federal standards,[69] but would simultaneously

primary and secondary standards. This argument adds nothing to deciding whether claims of economic or technological infeasibility can be raised. If quantitatively stiffer standards are barred, all plans containing them must be rejected, whether infeasible or not. In any case, as we make clear below, the States may adopt such more rigorous emission standards, and the Administrator must approve plans containing them if the minimum federal requirements are satisfied.

67 Subsequent legislation confirms that this was Congress' original intent. In response to the fuel shortages of late 1973, Congress enacted the Energy Supply and Environmental Coordination Act of 1974, Pub L 93-319, 88 Stat 246. The Act allows the Administrator to review state implementation plans and notify the State if their restrictions on fuel-burning stationary sources may be relaxed without interfering with timely attainment and maintenance of national air quality standards. The decision whether to relax restrictions, however, is left to the States. The Act shows congressional awareness and approval of the fact that federally approved implementation plans may be stricter than necessary for . . . subattainment of national standards.

68 Section 116, 42 USC § 1857f-6a, provides:

> "Except as otherwise provided in sections 209, 211(c)(4), and 233 (preempting certain State regulation of moving sources) nothing in this Act shall preclude or deny the right of any State or political subdivision thereof to adopt or enforce (1) any standard or limitation respecting emissions of air pollutants or (2) any requirement respecting control or abatement of air pollution; except that if an emission standard or limitation is in effect under an applicable implementation plan or under section 111 or 112, such State or political subdivision may not adopt or enforce any emission standard or limitation which is less stringent than the standard or limitation under such plan or section."

69 This burden would be particularly onerous in view of the facts that Congress gave the Administrator only four months in which to evaluate each plan submitted, § 110(a)(2), and that all state plans are submitted at approximately the same time. § 110(a)(1).

require States desiring stricter standards to enact and enforce two sets of emission standards, one federally approved plan and one stricter state plan. We find no basis in the Amendments for visiting such wasteful burdens upon the States and the Administrator, and so we reject Amici's argument.

We read the "as may be necessary" requirement of § 110(a)(2)(B) to demand only that the implementation plan submitted by the State meet the "minimum conditions" of the Amendments.[70] Train v. NRDC, 421 US, at 71 n 11, 43 L Ed 2d 731, 95 S Ct 1470. Beyond that, if a State makes the legislative determination that it desires a particular air quality by a certain date and that it is willing to force technology to attain it—or lose a certain industry if attainment is not possible—such a determination is fully consistent with the structure and purpose of the Amendments, and § 110(a)(2)(B) provides no basis for the EPA Administrator to object to the determination on the ground of infeasibility.[71] *See* Train v NRDC, 421 US, at 79, 43 L Ed 2d 731, 95 S Ct 1470.

In sum, we have concluded that claims of economic or technological infeasibility may not be considered by the Administrator in evaluating a state requirement that primary ambient air quality standards be met in the mandatory three years. And, since we further conclude that the States may submit implementation plans more stringent than federal law requires and that the Administrator must approve such plans if they meet the minimum requirements of § 110(a)(2), it follows that the language of § 110(a)(2)(A) provides no basis for the Administrator ever to reject a state implementation plan on the ground that it is economically or technologically infeasible. Accordingly, a court of appeals reviewing an approved plan under § 307(b)(1) cannot set it aside on those grounds, no matter when they are raised.

III.

Our conclusion is bolstered by recognition that the Amendments do allow claims of technological and economic infeasibility to be raised in situations where consideration of such claims will not substantially interfere with the primary congressional purpose of prompt attainment of the national air quality standards. Thus, we do not hold that claims of infeasibility are never of relevance in the formulation of an implementation plan or that sources unable to comply with emission limitations must inevitably be shut down.

Perhaps the most important forum for consideration of claims of economic and technological infeasibility is before the state agency formulating the

[70] Economic and technological factors may be relevant in determining whether the minimum conditions are met. Thus, the Administrator may consider whether it is economically or technologically possible for the state plan to proceed more rapidly than it does. If he determines that it is, he may reject the plan as not moving "as expeditiously as practicable" in achieving primary standards or as failing to attain secondary standards within a "reasonable time."

[71] In a literal sense, of course, no plan is infeasible since offending sources always have the option of shutting down if they cannot otherwise comply with the standard of the law. Thus, there is no need for the Administrator to reject an economically or technologically "infeasible" state plan on the ground that anticipated noncompliance will cause the State to fall short of the national standards. Sources objecting to such a state scheme must seek their relief from the State.

implementation plan. So long as the national standards are met, the State may select whatever mix of control devices it desires, Train v NRDC, 421 US, at 79, 43 L Ed 2d 731, 95 S Ct 1470, and industries with particular economic or technological problems may seek special treatment in the plan itself. Cf. 40 CFR §§ 51.2(b), (d)(1975); S Rep No. 91-1196, 91st Cong, 2d Sess, 36 (1970). Moreover, if the industry is not exempted from, or accommodated by, the original plan, it may obtain a variance, as petitioner did in this case, and the variance, if granted after notice and a hearing, may be submitted to the EPA as a revision of the plan,[72] § 110(a)(3)(A), as amended, 88 Stat 256. Lastly, an industry denied an exemption from the implementation plan, or denied a subsequent variance, may be able to take its claims of economic or technological infeasibility to the state courts. *See, e.g.*, § 203.130 Rev Stat Mo (1969); Ann Cal Code, Health & Safety § 39506 (1966); 71 Pa Stat § 1710.41 (1962).[73]

While the State has virtually absolute power in allocating emission limitations so long as the national standards are met, if the state plan cannot meet the national standards, the EPA is implicated in any postponement procedure. There are two ways that a State can secure relief from the EPA for individual emission sources, or classes of sources, that cannot meet the national standards. First, if the Governor of the State so requests at the time the original implementation plan is submitted, and if the State provides reasonable interim controls, the Administrator may allow a two-year extension of the three-year deadline for attainment of primary air quality standards if he finds, inter alia, that it is technologically infeasible for the source to comply. § 110(e).[74] Second, again upon application of the Governor of the State, the Administrator may allow a one-year postponement of any compliance date in an implementation plan if he finds, inter alia, that compliance is technologically infeasible and that "the continued operation of [the emission source] is essential to national security or to the public health or welfare . . ." § 110(f). *See* Train v NRDC, 421 US, at 81, 43 L Ed 2d 731, 95 S Ct 1470.

Even if the State does not intervene on behalf of an emission source, technological and economic factors may be considered in at least one other circumstance. When a source is found to be in violation of the state implementation plan, the Administrator may, after a conference with the operator, issue a compliance order rather than seek civil or criminal enforcement. Such an order must specify a "reasonable" time for compliance with the relevant standard, taking into account the seriousness of the violation and "any good

[72] A variance approved as a revision of a plan under § 110(a)(3)(A) will be honored by the EPA as part of an applicable implementation plan, § 110(d), a matter of no little import to those granted variances. *See* n 3, *supra*.

[73] Of course, the Amendments do not *require* the States to formulate their implementation plans with deference to claims of technological or economic infeasibility, to grant variances on those or any other grounds, or to provide judicial review of such actions. Consistent with Congress' recognition of the primary role of the States in controlling air pollution, the Amendments leave all such decisions to the States, which have typically responded in the manner described in the text. Cf. 40 CFR §§ 51.2(b), (d)(1975).

[74] Section 110(e) itself convincingly demonstrates that the statutory scheme did not contemplate the Administrator's rejecting state implementation plans as infeasible. There would be little purpose in providing noncomplying sources with § 110(e)'s limited mechanism for postponing infeasible plans—dependent upon the cooperation of the State—if the sources had the option of going to court instead and freeing themselves entirely of the plan by having it struck down as infeasible.

faith efforts to comply with applicable requirements." § 113(a)(4) of the Clean Air Act,as added, 84 Stat 1686, 42 USC § 1857c-8(a)(4). Claims of technological or economic infeasibility, the Administrator agrees, are relevant to fashioning an appropriate compliance order under § 113(a)(4). Brief for Respondent 36 n 34.[75]

In short, the Amendments offer ample opportunity for consideration of claims of technological and economic infeasibility. Always, however, care is taken that consideration of such claims will not interfere substantially with the primary goal of prompt attainment of the national standards. Allowing such claims to be raised by appealing the Administrator's approval of an implementation plan, as petitioner suggests, would frustrate congressional intent. It would permit a proposed plan to be struck down as infeasible before it is given a chance to work, even though Congress clearly contemplated that some plans would be infeasible when proposed. And it would permit the Administrator or a federal court to reject a State's legislative choices in regulating air pollution, even though Congress plainly left with the States, so long as the national standards were met, the power to determine which sources would be burdened by regulation and to what extent. Technology forcing is a concept somewhat new to our national experience and it necessarily entails certain risks. But Congress considered those risks in passing the 1970 Amendments and decided that the dangers posed by uncontrolled air pollution made them worth taking. Petitioner's theory would render that considered legislative judgment a nullity, and that is a result we refuse to reach.[76]

Affirmed.

Mr. JUSTICE POWELL, with whom The CHIEF JUSTICE joins, concurring.

I join the opinion of the Court because the statutory scheme and the legislative history, thoroughly described in the Court's opinion, demonstrate irrefutably that Congress did not intend to permit the Administrator of the Environmental Protection Agency to reject a proposed state implementation plan on the grounds of economic or technological infeasibility. Congress adopted

[75] If he chooses not to seek a compliance order, or if an order is issued and violated, the Administrator may institute a civil enforcement proceeding. § 113(b). Additionally, violators of an implementation plan are subject to criminal penalties under § 113(c) and citizen enforcement suits under § 304, as added, 94 Stat 1706, 42 USC § 1857h-2. Some courts have suggested that in criminal or civil enforcement proceedings the violator may in certain circumstances raise a defense of economic or technological infeasibility. *See* Buckeye Power, Inc. v EPA, 481 F2d 162, 173 (CA6 1973); Indiana & Michigan Electric Co. v EPA, 509 F2d 839, 847 (CA7 1975). We do not address this question here.

[76] Petitioner has briefed its contention that the Due Process Clause of the Fifth Amendment demands that at some time it be afforded the opportunity to raise before a court claims of economic and technological impossibility. This claim was neither presented to, nor considered by, the Court of Appeals, and we declined to grant certiorari on the question. 423 US 821, 46 L Ed 2d 38, 96 S Ct 35 (1975). In any case, we could not resolve petitioner's claim here, for there has been no showing that a § 307(b)(1) appeal would be the only opportunity for petitioner to raise before a court its claims of economic and technological impossibility.

this position despite its apparent awareness that in some cases existing sources that cannot meet the standard of the law must be closed down.[77]

The desire to impose strong incentives on industry to encourage the rapid development and adoption of pollution control devices is understandable. But it is difficult to believe that Congress would adhere to its absolute position if faced with the potentially devastating consequences to the public that this case vividly demonstrates.

Environmental concerns, long neglected, merit high priority, and Congress properly has made protection of the public health its paramount consideration. *See* S Rep No. 91-1196, pp 2-3 (1970). But the shutdown of an urban area's electrical service could have an even more serious impact on the health of the public than that created by a decline in ambient air quality. The result apparently required by this legislation in its present form could sacrifice the well being of a large metropolitan area through the imposition of inflexible demands that may be technologically impossible to meet and indeed may no longer even be necessary to the attainment of the goal of clean air.

I believe that Congress, if fully aware of this draconian possibility, would strike a different balance.

NOTES AND QUESTIONS

(1) The issue of technological and economic infeasibility has been widely discussed both before and after the *Union Electric* case. *See, e.g.,* D. Currie *Federal Air Quality Standards and Their Implementation*, 1976 A.B. Found. Res. J. 365, 378-379; G. Newcombe, *Impossibility: A Viable Defense Under the Clean Air Act*, I Colum. J. Envtl. L.147 (1974); Note, *Economic and Technological Feasibility Under the Clean Air Act Amendments of 1970*, 51 Notre Dame Law. 849 (1976); Note, *Considerations of Technological and Economic Factors in Air Pollution Control*, 44 U. Cin. L. Rev. 573. *See also* F. Grad, Treatise on Environmental Law, § 2.03[6][b][i], [8].

(2) The *Union Electric* case was decided prior to the amendment of the law in 1977. If the case had arisen in 1999, would there be the same set of "draconian" possibilities referred to in the concurrence? Which provisions of the

---

[77] The record is clear beyond question that at least the sponsors and floor leaders of the Clean Air Act intended that industries unable to comply with approved state implementation plans, whether because of economic or technological infeasibility, would be "closed down." This is explicit in the Senate Report. S Rep No. 91-1196, p 3 (1970). It is repeated quite candidly in the statements of various members of the Senate and is described in detail in the EPA's brief in this case. Brief for the United States, at 20-32. Indeed, remarkable as it may seem, it is clear from the legislative history that even total technological infeasibility is "irrelevant." *See id.*, at 16, 19-23.

What this means in this case, if the allegations of Union Electric Company prove to be correct, is that—in the interest of public health—the utility will be ordered to discontinue electric service to the public. As one cannot believe this would be allowed, I suppose that the State or Federal Government will find some basis for continuing to operate the company's facilities to serve the public despite noncompliance. But no such contingency program or authority therefor is found in the statute, and we must decide the case on the record before us.

current law would allow the plant to continue power production, and under what conditions?

(3) The court's opinion gives some comforting indications of how technological and economic infeasibility can be taken into account at the enforcement level under the Act before its amendment in 1977. The Court's advice, which left a good deal to the Administration's discretion, was not designed to reassure industry or the public that their particular interest would be reflected in the process. What provisions in current law meet the problem, at least to some extent? *See* §§ 110 and 120 of the Act for a likely answer.

(4) The Clean Air Act as amended does allow technological and economic considerations to be taken into account in situations other than in the approval of state implementation plans. Compare these other situations and determine why the state implementation plan is so strongly emphasized so as not to permit any relaxation.

(5) Supposing a state fails to adopt a state implementation plan of its own and the Administrator must adopt a plan for the state. In this situation, may he or she consider technological and economic feasibility in spite of the *Union Electric* case?

[iv] State Implementation Plan; Prevention of Significant Deterioration

SIERRA CLUB v. RUCKELSHAUS

United States District Court, District of Columbia (1972)
344 F. Supp. 253 , aff'd per curiam, 2 ELR 20656,
4 E.R.C. 1815 (D. C. Cir. 1972), aff'd by an equally
divided court sub nom. Fry v. Sierra Club, 412 U.S. 541 (1973)

PRATT, J.

Initially, this matter came before the Court on plaintiffs' motion for temporary restraining order wherein they sought to enjoin the Administrator of the Environmental Protection Agency from approving certain portions of state air pollution control plans—implementing the national primary and secondary standards—which had been submitted to the Administrator pursuant to Section 110 of the Clean Air Act of 1970, 42 U.S.C. § 1857c-5(1970). Having been informed that the Administrator would not be approving the plans until May 31, 1972, we denied the motion for temporary restraining order and scheduled a hearing on the preliminary injunction for May 30. At the conclusion of the May 30 hearing, having considered the pleadings and memoranda and the arguments of counsel, we announced our findings and conclusions and granted plaintiffs' motion for preliminary injunction. We now set down those findings and conclusions in memorandum form.

Standing

Although the Administrator does not question plaintiffs' standing to bring this action, it is clear to us that under the allegations of the complaint each of the four environmental groups who are parties plaintiff has the requisite standing, even under the limitations expressed in the most recent Supreme Court case on the subject, Sierra Club v. Morton, 405 U.S. 727, 92 S.Ct. 1361 (1972).

Jurisdiction

The Administrator challenges the jurisdiction of this Court to hear this case on the theory that the plaintiffs should wait until the Administrator approves the plans and then appeal the approval under 42 U. S. C. § 1857h-5. We disagree. It is our judgment that plaintiffs have the right to bring the action in this Court at this juncture under 42 U.S.C. § 1857h-2(a)[as amended 42 U.S.C. § 7604(a)] which provides in pertinent part that:

> "any person may commence a civil action on his own on behalf—
>
> . . . .
>
> "(2) against the Administrator where there is alleged failure of the Administrator to perform any act or duty under this chapter which is not discretionary with the Administrator.
>
> "The district courts shall have jurisdiction without regard to the amount in controversy or the citizenship of the parties, . . . to order the Administrator to perform such act or duty, as the case may be."

The Administrator, in recent testimony before Congress, indicated that he had declined to require state implementation plans to provide against significant deterioration of the existing clean air areas—*i.e.*, areas with levels of pollution lower than the secondary standard—because he believed that he lacked the power to act otherwise. Unpublished transcript of Hearings Before the Subcomm. on Public Health and the Environment of the House Comm. on Interstate and Foreign Commerce, 92d Cong., 2d Sess. at 351-52 (remarks delivered on Jan. 27-28, 1972).

Previously, the Administrator had promulgated a regulation permitting states to submit plans which would allow clean air areas to be degraded, so long as the plans were merely "adequate to prevent such ambient pollution levels from exceeding such secondary standard." 40 C.F.R. § 51.12(b)(1972).

Plaintiffs claim that the Administrator's interpretation of the extent of his authority is clearly erroneous and that his declination to assert his authority, evidenced in his remarks before Congress and his promulgation of a regulation that is contrary to the Clean Air Act, amounts to a failure to perform a non-discretionary act or duty.

It would appear that such an allegation is precisely the type of claim which Congress, through 42 U.S.C. § 1857h-2(a)[as amended 42 U.S.C. § 7604(a)], intended interested citizens to raise in the district courts. In view of this clear jurisdictional grant, the Administrator's assertion that plaintiffs should await his approval of the state plans (formulated, in part, pursuant to his allegedly illegal regulation) and then proceed to appeal his approval under 42 U.S.C. § 1857h-5is, in our opinion, untenable.

In discussing the merits of the present action —*i.e.*, the extent of the Administrator's authority and the validity of the questioned regulation—we turn to the stated purpose of the Clean Air Act of 1970, the available legislative history of the Act and its predecessor, and the administrative interpretation of the Act.

Purpose of the Act

In Section 101(b) of the Clean Air Act,Congress states four basic purposes of the Act, the first of which is

> "to protect and enhance the quality of the Nation's air resources so as to promote the public health and welfare and the productive capacity of its population." 42 U.S.C. § 1857(b)(1).

On its face, this language would appear to declare Congress' intent to improve the quality of the nation's air and to prevent deterioration of that air quality, no matter how presently pure that quality in some sections of the country happens to be.

Legislative History

The administrative guidelines promulgated by the National Air Pollution Control Administration (NAPCA) of the Department of Health, Education and Welfare (HEW), which at that time had the responsibility of carrying out the directives of the Air Quality Act of 1967, point up the significance of the "protect and enhance" language as follows:

> "[A]n explicit purpose of the Act is 'to *protect and enhance* the quality of the Nation's air resources' (emphasis added). Air quality standards which, even if fully implemented, would result in significant deterioration of air quality in any substantial portion of an air quality region clearly would conflict with this expressed purpose of the law." National Air Pollution Control Administration, U.S. Dept. of HEW, *Guidelines for the Development of Air Quality Standards and Implementation Plans,* Part I § 1.51, p. 7 (1969).

Turning now to the legislative history of the 1970 Act, we note at the outset that both Secretary Finch and Under Secretary Veneman of HEW testified before Congress that neither the 1967 Act nor the proposed Act would permit the quality of air to be degraded. Hearings on Air Pollution Before the Subcomm. on Air and Water Pollution of the Senate Public Works Comm., 91st Cong., 2d Sess., at 132-33, 143 (1970); Hearings on Air Pollution and Solid Waste Recycling Before the Subcomm. on Public Health and Welfare of the House Interstate and Foreign Commerce Comm., 91st Cong., 2d Sess., at 280, 287 (1970).

More important, of course, is the language of the Senate Report accompanying the bill which became the Clean Air Act of 1970. The Senate Report, in pertinent part, states:

"In areas where current air pollution levels are already equal to or better than the air quality goals, the Secretary shall not approve any implementation plan which does not provide, to the maximum extent practicable, for the continued maintenance of such ambient air quality." S. Rep. No. 1196, 91st Cong., 2d Sess., at 2 (1970).

The House Report, although not as clear, does not appear to contradict the Senate Report. *See* H. Rep. No.1146, 91st Cong., 2d Sess., at 1, 2 and 5 (1970).

Administrative Interpretation

As we noted under our discussion of the legislative history of the 1967 Act, the 1969 guidelines promulgated by HEW's NAPCA emphasized that significant deterioration of air quality in any region would subvert the "protect and enhance" language of the 1967 Act. We also pointed out that Secretary Finch and Under Secretary Veneman applied this same administrative interpretation to the very same language found in the proposed 1970 Act.

On the other hand, the present Administrator, in remarks made in January and February of 1972 before certain House and Senate Subcommittees, has taken the position that the 1970 Act allows degradation of clean air areas. Several Congressional leaders voiced their strong disagreement with the Administrator's interpretation. Unpublished transcript of Hearings Before the Subcomm. on Public Health and the Environment of the House Comm. on Interstate and Foreign Commerce, 92nd Cong., 2d Sess., at 352 (remarks of Congressman Paul Rogers, Chairman of the Subcommittee); Unpublished transcript of Hearings Before the Subcomm. on Air and Water Pollution of the Senate Comm. on Public Works, 92d Cong., 2d Sess. at 33-34, 260 *et seq.* (remarks of Senator Thomas Eagleton, Vice-Chairman of the Subcommittee, presiding over the hearings at the time).

The Administrator's interpretation of the 1970 Act, as disclosed in his current regulations, appears to be self-contradictory. On the one hand, 40 C.F.R. § 50.2(c)(1970) provides:

"The promulgation of national primary and secondary air quality standards shall not be considered in any manner to allow significant deterioration of existing air quality in any portion of any State."

Yet, in 40 C.F.R. § 51.12(b), he states:

"In any region where measured or estimated ambient levels of a pollutant are below the levels specified by an applicable secondary standard, the State implementation plan shall set forth a control strategy which shall be adequate to prevent such ambient pollution levels from exceeding such secondary standard."

The former regulation appears to reflect a policy of nondegradation of clear air but the latter mirrors the Administrator's doubts as to his authority to impose such a policy upon the states in their implementation plans. In our view, these regulations are irreconcilable and they demonstrate the weakness of the Administrator's position in this case.

Initial Conclusions

Having considered the stated purpose of the Clean Air Act of 1970, the legislative history of the Act and its predecessor, and the past and present administrative interpretation of the Acts, it is our judgment that the Clean Air Act of 1970 is based in important part on a policy of non-degradation of existing clean air and that 40 C.F.R. § 51.12(b), in permitting the states to submit plans which allow pollution levels of clean air to rise to the secondary standard level of pollution, is contrary to the legislative policy of the Act and is, therefore, invalid. Accordingly, we hold that plaintiffs have made out a claim for relief.

Injunctive Relief

Whether this Court may properly grant injunctive relief depends on whether the plaintiffs have met the four criteria set forth in Virginia Petroleum Jobbers Ass'n v. Federal Power Commission, 104 U.S. App. D.C. 106, 259 F.2d 921 (1958) and such later authorities as A Quaker Action Group v. Hickel, 137 U.S. App. D.C. 176, 421 F.2d 111 (1969).

First, have the plaintiffs made a strong showing that they are likely to prevail on the merits? It appears to us, from our foregoing discussion, that the plaintiffs have made such a showing in this case.

Second, have the plaintiffs shown that without such relief they would suffer irreparable injury? In view of the nature and extent of the air pollution problem, once degradation is permitted the range of resulting damages could well have irreversible effects. Thus, we hold that plaintiffs have made the requisite showing of irreparable injury.

Third, will the issuance of a stay cause any significant harm or inconvenience to the Administrator or other parties interested in the proceedings? We are persuaded that no substantial harm or inconvenience will result from our order granting the preliminary injunction. The order is a very limited one. It was submitted by plaintiffs' counsel after consultation with counsel for the Administrator and, in our view, it provides the Administrator with sufficient time and flexibility so that he may exercise his expertise and carry out his duties under the Act with as little inconvenience as possible.

Fourth, and finally, where lies the public interest? It seems to us that the public interest in this case strongly supports the legislative policy of clean air and the non-degradation of areas in which clean air exists.

Conclusion

Having separately considered the four criteria for injunctive relief, and having found that plaintiffs have met each of these criteria, we conclude that we can and should grant the requested relief. The order effecting such relief is attached hereto.

Prevention of Significant Deterioration (PSD)

As a philosophical matter, it is easy to subscribe to the idea of nondegradation. When the ambient quality of the air and of water are wholesome, it's not difficult to assert that we ought to keep them in that condition. This is no more difficult a decision than to assert that when air and water quality are inadequate to preserve or protect health, then we must do everything possible to improve ambient quality to make them wholesome so as not to endanger human health. But the answer is not that simple. In many parts of the world and of the United States air quality is good because there is no pollution, and there is no pollution because there is no industry. To assert that we must not worsen the condition of the air or water may well amount to saying that this area's excellent air quality is so good that the area should be debarred from economic development, because economic development and industrial development will, inevitably, worsen air quality. Thus, it is clear that nondegradation raises issues of the appropriate balance between ambient air quality and the economic development of the area. The problem is illustrated by the eventual development of the federal regulations which did not provide for "nondegradation" but rather provided for the "prevention of *significant* deterioration." What the EPA regulations and, later, the 1977 amendment of the Clean Air Act did was to provide for the classification of areas with clean air, allowing some degradation of air quality in each classified area, depending on the nature of the area and the exact quality of its air. In effect these regulations prohibited "significant" deterioration, defining in some detail how much deterioration would be considered significant. The pre-1977 regulations were eventually incorporated into the 1977 amendment of the Clean Air Act.[78] These early regulations are discussed in Note, *Review of EPA's Significant Deterioration Regulations: An Example of Difficulties of the Agency Court Partnership in Environmental Law*, 61 Va. L. Rev. 1115 (1975).

Under § 107(d)(1) of the CAA,each state had to submit information to EPA, listing each air quality control region and reporting on compliance with national ambient air quality standards for certain criteria pollutants.[79] This report is used by the Administrator to determine the applicability of Part C of the 1977 Act, relating to Prevention of Significant Deterioration (PSD) of Air Quality, or the applicability of Part D, setting requirements for Nonattainment Areas.[80]

Part C, Prevention of Significant Deterioration of Air Quality, was added by amendment in 1977. This was the first time in the history of federal air pollution control legislation that non-degradation or the prevention of significant deterioration of air quality had become an articulated policy of federal law, though the House Committee report relating to the 1977 amendment placed great stress on the lengthy history of concern for non-degradation in

[78] *See* F. Grad, Treatise on Environmental Law § 2.03[9][a].

[79] 42 U.S.C. § 7407(d)(1)

[80] *See* p. 156 *et seq. infra*.

federal legislation.[81] Non-degradation had previously remained implicit in federal air pollution control legislation, and had found direct expression only in judicial opinions which discerned the Congressional intent of non-degradation from air pollution control legislation generally, and from regulations of EPA.

When an area has excellent air quality, exceeding the requirements of ambient air quality for each criteria pollutant, it does not get a prize in recognition of its fine air quality, but instead becomes subject to the additional obligations of Part C of the Clean Air Act which adds significant new requirements to its state implementation plan. Thus, the designation of an area as a "PSD" (prevention of significant deterioration) area has a great many consequences for the area and imposes significant additional burdens. These burdens are enumerated in Part C.

Section 160 of the Clean Air Actspells out what these additional burdens seek to achieve. In certain special areas such as national parks, national wilderness areas, and other areas of special natural, recreational, scenic or historical value, maintenance of high air quality is clearly emphasized. The section rather blandly states that another purpose of Part C is to insure that economic growth be consistent with the preservation of clean air resources. This clearly calls for a balance in the regulations, even though this may not be articulated. In addition, the prevention of significant deterioration from sources outside the state must also be guarded against, and each state is under an obligation not only to protect its own air quality, but also not to interfere with the air quality of neighboring states. The provision also requires that if any increases of air pollution are permitted, they may only be permitted after the consequences of such a decision has been evaluated, sufficient safeguards have been provided and the public has had an opportunity to participate in the decision making process. The ambient air quality standards for sulfur oxides and particulates are cited as a special concern in measuring deterioration. In addition, strategies for controlling photochemical oxidants on a regional or multistate basis must also be considered in order to implement Part C and § 110 of the Act.

Part C provides for the initial classification of air quality regions and provides three classifications for areas with air qualities cleaner than required by ambient air quality standards. All clean air areas have an initial designation of Class II and some areas will be designated Class I, the best air quality, in which the least deterioration is permitted. Class I areas include international parks, national wilderness areas and national memorial parks exceeding 5,000 acres in size, and all national parks which exceed 6,000 acres in size and which were in existence at the time of the 1977 Clean Air Act Amendments. A mandatory Class I designation of such areas has been judicially upheld.

The prevention of significant deterioration is accomplished by setting forth in the law a maximum allowable increase in the concentration of sulfur dioxide

---

[81] House Report (Interstate and Foreign Commerce Committee) No. 95-294, May 12, 1977, to accompany H.R. 6161, 103-178 95th Cong., 1st Sess. (1977). For a fine analysis of the non-degradation issue, see N.W. Hines, *A Decade of Nondegradation Policy in Congress and the Courts: The Erratic Pursuit of Clean Air and Clean Water*, 62 Iowa L. Rev. 643 (1977).

and particulate matter in Class I, II, and III regions over certain baseline concentrations. Implementation plans must contain measures to assure that in PSD regions allowable increases are not exceeded.

While redesignation of areas from one classification to another is provided for, the downgrading of areas—which would allow for more pollution—is not encouraged and is prohibited in certain areas, particularly the mandatory Class I areas. Redesignation of areas is subject to approval by the Administrator.

The most significant control on the prevention of significant deterioration —*i.e.*, the increase of pollution—is a system of preconstruction permits in classified areas, requiring that no major emitting facility may be constructed in an area for which Part C applies unless a permit has been issued for such a proposed facility which contains emission limitations conforming to the Part C requirements. Very stringent conditions are imposed on the grant of such construction permits and the permit application must show that the proposed facility is subject to the best available control technology (BACT) for each regulated pollutant produced by the facility. In addition, stringent monitoring requirements are imposed on such new facilities so as to determine the effect of emissions from such a facility on air quality in any area which may be affected.

The preconstruction permit requirements are particularly detailed and stringent for Class I areas, where air quality related values, including visibility, are given special protection. Variances from these requirements are limited to specific conditions. Thus, for instance, in the case of Class I areas, ultimate authority for the grant of variances in the national interest is the President of the United States—*i.e.*, EPA.

State and local governments are involved in the permit review for major emitting facilities in PSD areas. Public hearings to review applicable data, including monitoring data, are provided for and the Administrator is authorized to conduct studies and to promulgate regulations to prevent the significant deterioration of air quality resulting from the emission of hydrocarbons, carbon monoxide, photochemical oxidants, and nitrogen oxides. Stringent enforcement measures are also provided, which include injunctive relief to prevent the construction of major emitting facilities not conforming to the requirements of Part C or to an implementation plan.

Mention has been made of the visibility protections contained in § 169(a) of the law, addressing aesthetics of wide open spaces in highly protected, mandatory Class I areas. Provisions protecting against adverse visibility impacts include the requirement of the "best available retrofit technology" in the State Implementation Plan (SIP).[82]

In summary, it should be noted that the provisions of Part C, with their inherent limitations on new development in an area, are incorporated in the state implementation plan requirements. Thus, air quality regions which are

[82] For detailed analysis of the protection of aesthetic resources, see Ostrow, J., *Visibility Protection under the Clean Air Act: Preserving Scenic and Background Areas in the Southwest*, 10 Ecology L.Q. 397 (1982). The protection of visibility may also involve control of automotive emissions at high altitudes.

subject to Part C requirements must follow the developmental controls in Part C. These have also been incorporated in § 110(A)(2)(J) of the Clean Air Act.[83]

NOTES AND QUESTIONS

(1) Is it possible for an air quality control region to be a PSD area and a nonattainment area at the same time? In its preconstruction permit review, would it be possible to limit the review to sulfur dioxide and to particulate matter? Does *Alabama v. Costle*, 606 F. 2d 1068, 10 E.L.R. 20001 (D.C. Cir. 1979), cast any light on this issue? *See* Floy, *Preventions of Significant Deterioration of Air Quality—The Regulations After Alabama Power*, 9 Envtl. Aff. L. Rev. 13, 55 (1981); 40 C.F.R. §§ 51.24(i)(3), 52.21(i)(3).

(2) The target of much PSD regulation is the "major emitting facility" as defined in CAA § 169(1), falling into particular categories, which "emit or have the potential to emit" 100 TPA (tons per year) or 250 TPA respectively. Does "potential to emit" mean with or without pollution control equipment? *See Alabama Power Co. v. Costle*, 10 E.L.R. at 20007. Does the Court's reading enlarge or limit the number of sources controlled?

(3) In preventing the use of excessive increments, *i.e.*, in preventing the increase of emissions beyond the permissible increase applicable to an area in a given classification, does the Administration have controls other than preconstruction review?

(4) An air quality control area in State A is a PSD area. A major emitting facility is planned across the state line in an area which is not a PSD area. CAA § 165(a)provides that a PSD permit is required before a major facility "may be constructed in any area to which this part applies." Is a preconstruction review and permit required in this instance? *See Alabama Power*, 10 E.L.R. at 20014. Consider the impact of CAA §§ 1110(a)(2)(E)(i) and 126. Compare *Connecticut v. EPA*, 656 F.2d 902 (2d Cir. 1981).

(5) The PSD provisions establish maximum allowable increase, or "increments" of pollution measured against a baseline concentration defined in CAA § 169(4). As of what time is the baseline established, what facilities are included or excluded in establishing the baseline, and how is it actually arrived at? *See Alabama Power*, 10 E.L.R. at 20020-21.

(6) The term "stationary source" is not defined in the PSD provisions, though it is part of the definition of "major emitting facility." What is encompassed in the term "source" as used in the PSD provisions? Is the application of the "bubble concept" required in this instance? *See* § 2.03[3][g], *infra*. *See also Alabama Power*, 10 E.L.R. at 20033. *See also Chevron, U.S.A., Inc. v. Natural Resources Defense Council, Inc.*, 104 S. Ct. 2778, 13 E.L.R. 20507 (June 25, 1984), at 223, *infra*.

---

[83] For discussion of the requirements of Part C of the Clean Air Act, see F. Grad, Treatise on Environmental Law § 2.03[9].

(7) Two developers file applications for preconstruction review with the proper pollution control agency to construct substantial new plants in a PSD area. Each plant will emit similar pollutants in similar amounts. Who has first call on the permissible increments? Does it depend on who files first? Suppose one will produce more emissions than the other, or one applicant's emissions are likely to be less difficult to control than the other's? Suppose one will employ many more people than the other, or will meet a particular local economic need—how will it affect the allocation of permissible increments? *See* Terziev, *PSD: New Regulations and Old Problems*, 5 Harv. Envtl. L. Rev. 130, 142-144 (1980); Kontnick, *Who Is Allowed to Pollute*, 74 Nw. U. L. Rev. 936 (1980).

[v] State Implementation Plan Requirements for Nonattainment

Nonattainment Area; Designation

The Clean Air Act passed in 1970 ambitiously anticipated the attainment of national primary ambient air quality standards by mid-1977. The target was not attained by many air quality control regions, and both the 1977 amendment and the 1990 major revision of the Act provided for additional and ever more stringent measures to attain ambient air quality standards as soon as possible. For many areas this postpones the attainment of standards well into the third millennium.

The attainment of ambient air quality standards was, and still is, the task of the state implementation plans which have been amended continuously, and have become more detailed and stringent. The provisions have also become more sophisticated in their technical requirements and in their categorization of what is to be accomplished at different times in the future.

Somewhat similar to the requirements of the PSD provisions, the requirements for nonattainment areas seek to advance attainment, *i.e.*, seek to promote ambient air quality by reducing emissions from new sources. Thus, again balancing the interest of economic and industrial developments against healthful air, nonattainment area provisions rigidly control air pollution sources by following an "offset policy" which allows the construction of new sources or the expansion of existing sources only if emissions from such new or expanded sources are more than offset by emission reductions at existing facilities in the area. The base line to be used for the determination of appropriate emission offset is the applicable standard under the implementation plan of the state in effect at the time an application is made for a permit for a proposed major stationary source. The proposed major source must then adopt at a minimum the "LAER" standard, *i.e.*, it must meet the "lowest achievable emission rate."[84]

A nonattainment area to which Part D applies is defined in CAA § 171as an area which is shown by monitoring data or which is calculated by air

[84] Pub. L. No. 95-95, CAA § 129(a)(2). *See* comment, *Emission Offsets: EPA Rules Clean Air Act Arouse New Sources in Nonattainment Areas*, 7 E.L.R. 10029 (1977). For a definition of "lowest achievable emission rate," see CAA § 171(3), 42 U.S.C. § 7501. For permit requirements, see CAA § 173, 42 U.S.C. § 7503.

quality modeling to exceed any national ambient air quality standard. The term "nonattainment area" includes any area so identified under subparagraphs (a) to (c) of § 107(d)(1), which requires the state to make appropriate designations. In designating nonattainment areas, the state may not consider pollution control systems that do not rely on continuous emission controls. A state may base its designation on proper air quality modeling.[85]

In addition to ambient air quality data, the EPA used other criteria in the designation of the attainment status for each pollutant. For example, since almost every urban area in the United States for which data are available experiences photochemical oxidant levels above NAAQS, the EPA presumed nonattainment status for the urban areas that were unable to collect the relevant data.[86] With regard to designation for total suspended particulates (TSP), EPA found, under earlier law, that general area size criteria were impossible because of the spatially limited nature of TSP violations. Thus, TSP designations were calculated along political boundaries which were practical from an air quality management point of view. Another problem peculiar to TSP is that fugitive dust in urban areas is usually contaminated with man-made toxic pollutants, while rural windblown dust is not. Thus, the EPA designated rural areas—defined as having low population density and as lacking major industries with significant industrial particulate emissions—experiencing TSP violations because of fugitive dust as having attained the NAAQS for TSP.[87]

EPA designated small urban core areas as nonattainment areas for carbon monoxide, even though larger designations were more desirable. The rationale for this designation was that carbon monoxide violations are most pervasive in downtown areas of high traffic density. Finally, designations for sulfur dioxide were made in accordance with the areas substantiated by the monitoring data.[88]

---

[85] 42 U.S.C. § 7501. *See* Dow Chemical Co. v. EPA, 635 F.2d 559, 11 E.L.R. 20001 (6th Cir. 1981). The U.S. Court of Appeals for the Sixth Circuit held that the Clean Air Act (CAA), 42 U.S.C. § 7401 *et seq.*, does not allow the EPA to take into account the effects of "supplemental pollution control systems" when designating nonattainment areas. Dow Chemical argued that supplemental controls should be allowed if it's proven that continuous controls are "economically or technologically infeasible." The court rejected this argument, stating that the CAA clearly requires a decrease of pollutants on a steady basis. For reliance on air quality modeling in the designation of nonattainment areas, see Republic Steel v. Costle, 621 F.2d 797 (6th Cir. 1980); PPG Industries, Inc. v. Costle, 630 F.2d 462 (6th Cir. 1980); Cincinnati Gas & Electric Co. v. Costle, 632 F.2d 14 (6th Cir. 1980); Columbus & Southern Ohio Electric Co. v. Costle, 638 F.2d 910, 10 E.L.R. 20, 895 (6th Cir. 1980).

[86] 43 Fed. Reg. at 8962-63.

[87] 43 Fed. Reg. at 8963.

[88] 43 Fed. Reg. at 8963. *See* PPG Industries v. Costle, 630 F.2d 462 (6th Cir. 1980). Four companies with industrial plants petitioned for review of the Environmental Protection Agency's designation of part of the county in which the plants were located as a nonattainment area for sulfur dioxide. The Court of Appeals granted the petitions, and remanded the cases for development of an administrative record. The court held that projected future violations of national primary ambient air quality standards may provide the basis for a nonattainment designation in a currently clean area, and that a nonattainment designation may be based on modeling if the accuracy of the model is proved by the EPA. In the instant case, however, the EPA's designation was not supported by the administrative record. Since the promulgation of attainment designations is a procedure subject to the Administrative Procedures Act, and since the record did not support the agency's designation, the court remanded to the agency for development of the record.

The states, under Part C of the CAA, were to consider the attainment status designations only as a point of departure in correcting existing air quality problems and in implementing programs. In addition, states must consider (1) the impact of new sources on nearby areas, as well as on the area in which they would locate, (2) prevention of significant deterioration (PSD) rules, which must apply to every area that shows attainment for at least one pollutant, and (3) case-by-case new source review to account for the possibility that an area with a particular designation may encompass "pockets" which do not fit that designation. The implementation of Section 107 is an ongoing process, with further promulgation of amplifying regulations to be expected.

Nonattainment SIP; Application of RACT

All nonattainment plans shall "provide for the implementation of all reasonably available control measures as expeditiously as practicable," and shall "require in the interim, reasonable further progress (as defined in section 171(1)) including such reductions in emissions from existing sources in the area as may be obtained through the adoption, at a minimum, of reasonably available control technology." (RACT)[89]

Nonattainment SIPs must make provisions for a permit system for new or modified stationary sources. These provisions, in addition to requiring data on existing sources of emission and on projected emissions from the new source, must also evidence the involvement of local and state authorities under the planning procedures of § 174, and their commitment to the implementation of the plan.

Construction Permits; Application of LAER

New sources in nonattainment areas may be constructed only in accordance with a permit issued under § 173 in accordance with the offset policy—a permit will be issued only if the permitting agency determines that when the new facility commences operations, the sum of emissions from all existing sources and from the new source will be less than the total emissions under the SIP prior to the application for such permit so as to represent reasonable further progress. Reasonable further progress is defined as an annual incremental reduction in emissions of the applicable air pollutant which is sufficient, in the opinion of the Administrator, to attain the applicable ambient

[89] CAA § 172(b)(2), (3), 42 U.S.C. § 7502(b)(2), (3). The requirement of the adoption of "RACT"—of reasonably available control technology—was interpreted in National Steel Corp. v. Gorsuch, 700 F.2d 314, 13 E.L.R. 20295 (6th Cir. 1983). Industry challenged the approval or conditional approval of a state implementation plan, which Michigan had adopted for certain nonattainment areas. The challenged SIP was upheld because EPA's application of RACT to the area was neither unreasonable nor capricious under the usual standard of review, even though RACT alone was not likely to bring the state into compliance. The obligation to set RACT standards under the SIP is that of the state in the first instance, but EPA may measure the state's compliance against its own RACT guidelines. The court held that the imposition of RACT standards on a given source does not require a prior showing that the source contributed to the nonattainment, since there is no precise way of determining the extent to which each source contributes. The court also rejected technical and economic infeasibility as a basis for challenge, relying on Union Electric v. EPA, 427 U.S. 246 (1976).

standard by the target date. As amended in 1990, in applying emission offsets as required in § 173 to new or modified sources or emission units for which a permit is required, the rule is that the ratio of emission reductions to increased emissions must be at least two to one. CAA § 179(b)(2)as amended.

The proposed source is required to comply with the lowest achievable emission rate (LAER), which is defined as reflecting the most stringent emission limitation which is contained in the state implementation plan of any state for such class or category or source, or the most stringent emission limitation which is achieved in practice, whichever is the more stringent. One of the requirements relating to the issuance of permits relates to other sources owned or operated by the owner or operator of the proposed new source. Such owner or operator must demonstrate that all major stationary sources owned or operated by him or by any entity controlling, controlled by, or under common control with him in the state are subject to emission limitations and are in compliance or on a schedule of compliance with applicable emission limitations and standards under the Act.

An additional requirement in applying emissions offsets of § 173 to new or modified sources or emissions units for which a permit is required under Part D is that the ratio of emission reductions to increased emissions must be at least two to one.[90] Within six months after the attainment date for a nonattainment area, the Administrator must determine whether the area has actually attained the standard by that date. The notice of determination must be published in the *Federal Register* and must identify each area that has failed to attain. Based on more complete information or analysis of the area's air quality as of the attainment date, the Administrator may revise or supplement his determination at any time.[91] Within a year after the Administrator publishes the notice, the state containing a nonattainment area must submit a revision of the applicable implementation plan, which must meet the requirements of § 110 and § 172, *i.e.*, the requirements relating to state implementation plans generally and the requirements applicable to plans in nonattainment areas. The revision should also include additional measures that the Administrator may prescribe. These may be measures that can be feasibly implemented, in light of related health and environmental impacts. The attainment date for such revised implementation plan follows the requirements of § 172(a)(2), *i.e.*, as expeditiously as feasible, but no later than five years, except that the period of five years runs from the date of the notice under § 179(c)(2), *i.e.*, from the date of notice of nonattainment.[92]

Special Provisions; Planning; Planning Grants; Motor Vehicle Standards

Section 174 provides for detailed planning procedures in nonattainment areas and gives a major and significant role to local governments and to interstate or regional agencies in the planning process. In the air quality control regions which have not attained ozone, carbon monoxide or PM-10

[90] CAA § 179(b)(2), as added by the Clean Air Act Amendments of 1990 § 102.

[91] CAA § 179(c), as added by the Clean Air Act Amendments of 1990 § 102.

[92] CAA § 179(d), as added by the Clean Air Act Amendments of 1990 § 102.

standards, state and local governments must agree to divide the responsibility for the implementation of the revised SIP.[93]

The nonattainment provisions call for some specific measures to deal with the problem of automotive pollutants. Section 177 makes special provision for new motor vehicle emission standards in nonattainment states—*i.e.*, such states may adopt the higher California standards. Special requirements are also imposed with respect to transportation planning—no project, federal or other, relating to transportation, may be funded unless it complies with the nonattainment SIP. A state that fails to comply with SIP requirements will lose U.S. highway funds under Title 23. The Administrator has issued a policy memorandum summarizing the elements that must be included in SIP revisions for nonattainment areas,[94] with certain specific requirements for automotive sources—such as vehicle inspection and maintenance programs, and the expansion of public transportation facilities.

In *Dow Chemical Company v. EPA*, 635 F.2d 559 (6th Cir. 1980), Dow sought the review of an EPA designation of Midland County as a "nonattainment area," and EPA's refusal to approve a state-approved revision of Michigan's State Implementation Plan. In anticipation of eventually meeting its power needs through nuclear power, Dow put in operation an alternative to burning of high sulphur coal in its power plants in the form of a "supplementary control system" for the temporary use of low sulfur oil on occasions when its emissions of SO_2 would otherwise cause air pollution in Midland County to exceed national air quality standards. The system clearly worked, but it violated the prohibition of the Clean Air Act of intermittent, temporary system of air quality control, in that CAA § 302(k), 42 U.S.C. § 7602(k)defines emission limitation and emission standards to refer to continuous emission controls. The Court also referred to H.Rep. No. 95-294 which accompanied H.R. 6161, and which dealt with the problems created by intermittent pollution controls. Hence, the designation of Midland County as a nonattainment area was proper because its attainment of the national ambient air quality standard depended on an intermittent control technology, rather than on a long-range reduction of pollution.

PPG Industries, Inc. v. Costle, 630 F.2d 462 (6th Cir. 1980), addressed the question whether EPA could, by regulation, provide that "projected future violations may provide the basis for nonattainment designations in currently clean areas." 43 Fed. Reg. 45998 (1978). The court upheld the regulation based on its own decision in *Republic Steel v. Costle*, 621 F.2d 797 (6th Cir. 1980), holding that EPA's use of computer modeling in making attainment designations was not itself arbitrary and capricious. The court held that basing a nonattainment designation on hypothetical future circumstances rather than on actual August 7, 1977 air quality was valid if the determination and the

93 CAA § 174(a), 42 U.S.C. § 7504(a). New regulations have been promulgated for requirements for preparation, adoption and submittal of implementation plans relating to intergovernmental consultation for a variety of purposes under the Act as well as under Section 174 of the Act which requires intergovernmental cooperation with particular reference to nonattainment areas for carbon monoxide, ozone, or PM-10.

94 Criteria for Preparing Approval of Revision to Plans for Non-Attainment Areas, 43 Fed. Reg. 21673 (May 19, 1978). 40 C.F.R. Pt. 51.

modeling had a rational basis. Upon reviewing the actual modeling data, however, the court found that the administrative record did not support the designation. The review was based on the Overton Park standard—consideration of the relevant factors and clear error of judgment, as tested under the arbitrary and capricious rule of the APA. The court remanded, but indicated that the agency could properly base its designation on proper modeling and is not required to rely on monitoring to establish air quality. To the same effect, on the proper reliance on modeling, see *Cincinnati Gas & Electric Co. v. Costle*, 632 F.2d 14 (6th Cir. 1980).

Nonattainment—Sanctions for Failure to Attain

The Clean Air Act Amendments of 1990 added a new section 179, Sanctions and Consequences of Failure To Attain. The section authorizes sanctions if the Administrator (1) finds that the state has not submitted a plan for a nonattainment area, or that the plan submitted fails to meet minimum requirements, or if the submission has been disapproved because it does not meet the minimum criteria of § 110(k); or (2) determines that a state has failed to make another submission required under the Act (*e.g.*, a maintenance plan) that satisfies the minimum criteria established under § 110(k)(1)(A), or disapproves such a submission in whole or in part; or (3) finds that any requirement or part of an approved plan is not being implemented. Penalties apply unless the particular deficiency has been corrected within 18 months after the initial finding, disapproval or determination of inadequacy. The sanctions remain in force until the Administrator determines that the state has come into compliance. If the Administrator finds that there has been a lack of good faith, then both highway sanctions and offsets apply (under subsections 179(b)(1) and (2)) until compliance is established. In addition to imposing the other sanctions provided for, the Administrator may withhold all or part of the grants for support of air pollution planning and control programs that may be awarded under § 105.[95]

So-called highway sanctions allow the Administrator, with the Secretary of Transportation's approval, to prohibit any projects or the awarding of grants by the Secretary under Title 23 of the U.S. Code in the nonattainment area. This prohibition does not apply to projects or grants whose principal purpose is to resolve a demonstrated safety problem and that will result in a significant reduction of accidents. Also, despite sanctions, the Secretary may approve capital programs for public transit and a variety of projects that improve traffic flow and achieve a net emission reduction. In general, the purpose is to allow transportation-related programs that the Administrator, in consultation with the Secretary of Transportation, finds would improve air quality and

[95] CAA § 179(a), as added by the Clean Air Act Amendments of 1990 § 102. The House Committee Report noted that mandatory sanctions are intended to provide a clear incentive to states for the adoption and implementation of approvable state plans. The Committee noted its intention to send a strong message that Congress is very serious about the effort to achieve clean air, and will require full compliance by the states. The Committee stressed that states not making a good faith effort be sanctioned severely, but it also noted that the objective is clean air and not punishment. House Committee on Energy and Commerce, Report on H.R. 3030, Rep. 101-490, Pt. I at 228 (May 17, 1990).

would discourage single occupancy vehicle capacity. An additional purpose of such permitted measures is to ensure adequate access to downtown and other commercial and residential areas, and to avoid increasing or relocating emissions and congestion rather than reducing them.[96]

SOUTHWESTERN PENNSYLVANIA GROWTH ALLIANCE v. BROWNER

United States Court of Appeals, Sixth Circuit (1998)
144 F.3d 984, 28 E.L.R. 21251

MERRITT, Circuit Judge

This case arises under the Clean Air Act, 42U.S.C. §§ 7401-7671q, as amended. The petitioner, the Southwestern Pennsylvania Growth Alliance, appeals the decision of the Administrator of the United States Environmental Protection Agency directly to this Court under 42 U.S.C. § 7607(b)(1). The petitioner argues that EPA's decision to redesignate the Cleveland-Akron-Lorain, Ohio area as an "attainment" area for ozone was arbitrary and capricious because EPA failed to take into account the "regional" effect of ozone pollution—specifically the effect of the airborne transport of ozone and its precursors across from Ohio into Pennsylvania. EPA counters that the petitioner does not have standing to bring this case and that the petitioner's claims fail on the merits because EPA acted reasonably in making the redesignation. It argues that it is handling the regional transport problem separately in a comprehensive study and set of proposals. We find that the actions of EPA were reasonable and within its administrative authority, and therefore we affirm the decision of EPA.

I.

. . . .

Before EPA designates an area for ozone attainment, EPA follows a two-step system. First, EPA determines whether an area has met the applicable technical, chemical standards for attainment of the correct level of ozone in the area. Second, EPA determines whether the area has met the additional requirements for redesignation to attainment.

In the first step, EPA determines whether the area has met the attainment standard for ozone, called the "national primary standard." EPA regulations define the standard for ozone as.12 parts per million. The "standard is attained when the expected number of days per calendar year with maximum hourly average concentrations above.12 parts per million . . . is equal to or less than 1, as determined by appendix H." 40 C.F.R. Pt. 50. An area will have attained the standard if three or fewer instances over the standard are recorded over a three year period at any of the monitoring sites within the area.

---

[96] CAA§ 179(b)(1), as added by the Clean Air Act Amendments of 1990 § 102.

In the second step, after an area has met the applicable standard for attainment, EPA determines whether the area has met the additional four criteria for redesignation from nonattainment to attainment: (1) EPA must fully approve the applicable State Implementation Plan; (2) EPA must determine that improvement in air quality is due to permanent reductions in emissions; (3) EPA must fully approve a maintenance plan adopted by the state which demonstrates that the area will maintain the standard for at least 10 years after redesignation; and (4) the state has met all the requirements applicable to the area under § 7410 (requirements of State Implementation Plans) and part D. 42 U.S.C. § 7407(d)(3)(E).

In 1991, the Cleveland-Akron-Lorain, Ohio area was designated as a moderate ozone nonattainment area. On November 15, 1994, the governor of the state of Ohio submitted a request to the EPA to redesignate the area to attainment.

On June 15, 1995, EPA published a Notice of Proposed Rulemaking, proposing to approve Ohio's redesignation request for the area contingent on final approval by EPA of several elements of Ohio's State Implementation Plan. 60 Fed. Reg. 31,433 (1995). As part of this proposal, EPA included the following section:

> Transport of Ozone Precursors to Downwind Areas
>
> Preliminary modeling results utilizing USEPA's [United States Environmental Protection Agency] regional oxidant model (ROM) indicate that ozone precursor emissions from various states west of the ozone transport region (OTR) in the northeastern United States contribute to increases in ozone concentrations in the OTR. The state of Ohio has provided documentation that VOC and Nox emissions in the CAL [Cleveland-Akron-Lorain] nonattainment area are predicted to remain below attainment levels for the next ten years. Should emissions exceed attainment levels, the contingency plan will be triggered. In addition, eight years after redesignation to attainment, Ohio is required to submit a revision to the maintenance plan which demonstrates that the NAAQS [National Ambient Air Qualitiy Standards] will be maintained until the year 2105. The USEPA is currently developing policy which will address long range impacts of ozone transport. The USEPA is working with the states and other organizations to design and complete studies which consider upwind sources and quantify their impacts. The USEPA intends to address the transport issue through § 110 based on a domain-wide modeling analysis. 60 Fed.Reg. at 31,439.

The proposed rule stated that the comment period on redesignation closed on July 17, 1995. The petitioner did not submit comments on redesignation by the close of the comment period.

On June 29, 1995, EPA published a direct Final Rule on attainment. In the rule, EPA determined that the Cleveland, Toledo, Dayton and Cincinnati-Hamilton areas had achieved attainment. 60 Fed.Reg. 33,742 (1995). The action was based on Ohio's demonstration that the areas achieved the standards for ozone during the three year period from 1992 through 1994. The rule stated that the action would become effective on August 14, 1995, unless

EPA received adverse comments by July 31, 1995. On July 28, 1995, the petitioner submitted comments directed at the determination of attainment in a letter captioned "Adverse Comments on Determination of Attainment of Ozone Standard by Cleveland, Toledo, Dayton, and the Cincinnati-Hamilton Interstate Ozone Attainment Areas, as published in the June 29, 1995 Federal Register." J.A. at 861. In the letter, the petitioner claimed that there was "strong evidence" that the ozone problem in southwestern Pennsylvania is caused by emissions of ozone precursors from states to its west, particularly Ohio and West Virginia. J.A. at 862. EPA also received a comment on the attainment rule from the New York State Department of Environmental Conservation. After receiving adverse comments on the direct final notice of attainment determination, EPA issued a notice on August 25, 1995, withdrawing the direct final notice and announcing that EPA would summarize and respond to the comments in a subsequent final rule. 60 Fed. Reg. 44,277 (1995).

On May 7, 1996, EPA took action on both the attainment and the redesignation, responding to comments on both actions. 61 Fed. Reg. 20,458 (1996). The interstate transport issue was raised as a comment to the attainment determination. EPA responded that interstate transport is not relevant to the narrow issue of attainment of air quality standards but that it is relevant in a determination of redesignation.

EPA has been separately studying the regional ozone transportation problem. In November 1997, EPA issued a new proposed rule based in part on the technical work and recommendations generated by the Ozone Transport Assessment Group. 62 Fed. Reg. 60,318 (1997). The Ozone Transport Assessment Group is an informal advisory committee formed to assess the regional ozone transport problem and develop solutions. The Group includes representatives from EPA, 37 states in the midwestern and eastern portions of the country (including Ohio), and industry and environmental groups. Based in part on the Group's recommendations, EPA's new proposed rule would require 22 states, including Ohio, to adopt and submit revised State Implementation Plans containing control measures that will mitigate the transport of ozone to other states. Under the new rule, Ohio would be required to reduce its emissions of oxides of nitrogen by approximately 40% from otherwise expected levels. 62 Fed. Reg. at 60,361.

The petitioner, Southwestern Pennsylvania Growth Alliance, is an organization of major manufacturers and local governments in the Pittsburgh-Beaver Valley area. *See Southwestern Pennsylvania Growth Alliance v. Browner,* 121 F.3d 106, 111, 27 ELR 21540 (3d Cir. 1997) (same petitioner). On July 8, 1996, the petitioner filed this case in the Court of Appeals, as permitted by statute. . . . [The court here examined EPA's decision under the "arbitrary and capricious" standard and applied the *Chevron* standard of statutory interpretation.]

II.

EPA argues that this Court should dismiss the petitioner's case because the petitioner has no standing to challenge the EPA rule redesignating Ohio from nonattainment to attainment. Constitutional standing requires a showing of three elements: (1) an "injury in fact" that is concrete and particularized; (2) a connection between the injury and the conduct at issue—the injury must be fairly traceable to the defendant's action; and (3) likelihood that the injury would be redressed by a favorable decision of the Court. *Lujan v. Defenders of Wildlife*, 504 U.S. 555, 560-61, 22 ELR 20913 (1992).

EPA argues that the petitioner has not shown standing because the petitioner fails to show that emissions transported from the newly redesignated Cleveland-Akron-Lorain area are greater than they would have been if EPA had denied Ohio's redesignation application. The petitioner also asserts two other injuries, however, that provide standing. The petitioner argues that it is injured by EPA's process of dealing with the regional transport of ozone. It says that this appeal is the only way it can attack the separation of the attainment decision from the regional transport decision. This fact together with its next argument establishes standing.

The petitioner also argues that southwestern Pennsylvania is at an economic disadvantage as a result of the Cleveland-Akron-Lorain redesignation. The redesignation enables Ohio businesses to pay less for ozone controls, while businesses in southwestern Pennsylvania are required to pay the higher costs for nonattainament areas. EPA concedes that areas designated as attainment are subject to different requirements than nonattainment areas. Attainment areas are subject to the less costly New Source Review requirements under Part C of Title I, and the nonattainment areas are subject to the more costly New Source Review requirements under Part D of Title I. In addition, EPA conceded during oral argument that if the Cleveland-Akron-Lorain area had not been redesignated to attainment, the area would have been subject to additional emissions controls.

If EPA incorrectly redesignated the Cleveland-Akron-Lorain area as attainment, then that area has an economic advantage over its neighbors in southwestern Pennsylvania because businesses in the Ohio area unfairly pay less for ozone control measures. Thus, the southwestern Pennsylvania area, which is designated as nonattainment, suffers an economic disadvantage compared to its Ohio neighbor. This economic disadvantage is an alleged "injury in fact" directly caused by the EPA's decision, an injury that would be redressed if the decision were overturned by this Court. . . .

III.

The petitioner argues that EPA's decision to redesignate the Cleveland-Akron-Lorain area as an attainment area for ozone was arbitrary and capricious and should be overturned by this Court. As already discussed, once an area has satisfied the technical requirements of attainment, it must also meet four additional requirements before it is redesignated to attainment. One of these requirements is that EPA approve Ohio's State Implementation Plan. The Act provides that each State Implementation Plan shall:

> contain adequate provisions—
>
> (i) prohibiting, consistent with provisions of this subchapter, any source or other type of emissions activity within the state from emitting any air pollutant in amounts which will—

> (I) contribute significantly to attainment in, or interfere with maintenance by, any other state with respect to any such national primary or secondary ambient air quality standard. . . . 42 U.S.C. § 7410(a)(2)(D)(i)(I).

The petitioner argues that the Ohio State Implementation Plan should not have been approved because it did not contain a provision prohibiting sources of pollution in one state from emitting pollutants in amounts which contribute significantly to nonattainment in another state.

EPA argues that Congress left to EPA the method of determining whether interstate transport is a problem and it says that it has properly addressed the problem in this case. Obviously, most land areas are upwind of some areas and downwind of others. According to EPA, it is addressing the interstate transport problem by using a regional approach to consider the broad and complex regional nature of ozone transport with the limited resources of the agency. This approach is being implemented through the Ozone Transport Assessment Group, which has studied the problem and recently made recommendations to address the problem. Based in part on these recommendations, EPA issued a new proposed rule in November 1997. 62 Fed. Reg. 60,318 (1997). One portion of this rule requires Ohio to submit a revised State Implementation Plan that will reduce its emissions of oxides of nitrogen by approximately 40% from otherwise expected levels. 62 Fed.Reg. at 60,361.

At the time that EPA approved the Ohio State Implementation Plan, the Ozone Transport Assessment Group had not yet made its recommendations. EPA argues that while it was waiting for the Group to finish its studies and make recommendations, EPA reasonably relied on its earlier approval of an Ohio State Implementation Plan which complied with the interstate transport requirement. EPA presented in its exhibits a memorandum which confirms its position that it has consistently interpreted § 7607(d)(3)(E) as permitting EPA to rely on prior approvals of State Implementation Plans when reviewing redesignation requests. The memorandum, which was written by John Calcagni, Director of Air Quality Management Division to the Directors of various Air Divisions, J.A. at 801, states: "Regions should not reconsider those things that have already been approved and for which the Clean Air Act Amendments did not alter what is required." In addition, Congress explicitly codified the same principle in 42 U.S.C. § 7401(n)(1).

The petitioner counters that EPA should have reconsidered the ozone transport issue because the previous Ohio State Implementation Plan was approved in 1980, before the 1990 amendments, and the 1990 amendments made the requirements for interstate transport more stringent. EPA argues that the 1990 amendments did not change the standard for interstate transport. Rather, EPA requested the change in the law because prior to 1990 EPA had enforced the stricter standards and wanted Congress to codify EPA's longstanding interpretation of the earlier provision. EPA's explanation is confirmed in 57 Fed.Reg. 13,556 n.34, which provides:

> The pre-amended 110(a)(2)(E) required SIPs to contain a provision prohibiting stationary sources from emitting an air pollutant in amounts which will "prevent attainment" in another state. The amended version of this language requires a SIP provision that prohibits emissions that

will "contribute significantly to nonattainment" in another state. However, EPA interpreted the pre-amended language in the manner that Congress expressed in the amended Act.

We find that EPA's approach to the regional transport problem is reasonable and not arbitrary and capricious. We therefore will not disturb the decision of EPA to redesignate the Cleveland-Akron-Lorain area as an attainment for ozone.

NOTES AND QUESTIONS

(1) The nonattainment construction permits under § 173 involve the emission offset policy. This affords an opportunity for trades in emission credits. Is there any evidence that this part of the control system is working in a satisfactory fashion? *See, e.g.*, National Commission on Air Quality, *To Breathe Clean Air*, 135-138 (1981).

(2) The question of the achievement of an effective offset requires a comparison with the sum of emission "under the applicable implementation plan prior to the application for such permit . . ." How much "prior"? Is it possible to manipulate the "prior" data so as to achieve a more favorable baseline? *See, e.g., Citizens Against the Refinery's Effects (CARE) v. EPA*, 643 F.2d 183 (4th Cir. 1981).

(3) Part of the emphasis in nonattainment areas is on automotive emissions which are subject to transportation planning. How effective are available remedies against state failure of compliance likely to be? *See* "Transportation Control Plans . . .," subsection [vi], immediately *infra*.

(4) The trading of offsets in nonattainment areas suggests the application of the "bubble concept" to sources in the area. Is it permissible to apply the bubble concept to *new* sources planned for such an area? *See* § 2.03[3][g], *infra*. *See also* Note, *New Source Netting in Nonattainment Areas Under the Clean Air Act*, 11 Ecology L. Q. 343 (1984).

[vi] Transportation Control Plans—and Federal Power

BROWN v. EPA

United States Court of Appeals, Ninth Circuit (1975)
521 F.2d 827

Before WRIGHT, KILKENNY and SNEED, Circuit Judges.

SNEED, Circuit Judge:

This is a proceeding growing out of numerous petitions for review of certain regulations of the Environmental Protection Agency. Petitioners included the Governor of the State of California, Trustees of the California State University and Colleges, the California Air Resources Board, numerous California cities and counties, private business concerns, and others. Certain of these petitioners filed consolidated briefs in which certain constitutional questions were raised. In due course, the Agency moved to expedite the hearing with respect to these constitutional issues. This motion was granted. Those petitioners seeking to present constitutional issues thereafter were directed to appear at a preheating conference pursuant to Rule 33, Fed. R. App. P., at which the issues sought to be raised were identified and the time to be allowed for oral argument was fixed. At this preheating conference, the petitioners were informed that this Court contemplated entering a judgment regarding the constitutional issues pursuant to Rule 54(b), Fed. R. Civ. P., prior to a hearing on, or disposition of, such other issues as were raised by the petitioners. Oral argument on the constitutional issues has been heard and our disposition of them is set forth herein. Our jurisdiction to hear these petitions is based on Section 307(b) of the Clean Air Act.

I.

The Background of This Proceeding

The controversy between the petitioners and the Administrator has its roots in the Clean Air Amendments of 1970. Under these Amendments, California was required to submit for the approval of the Administrator a state plan providing for the implementation, maintenance, and enforcement of national ambient air quality standards, including, if necessary, land-use and transportation controls. California complied by submitting its plan on February 21, 1972. The Administrator approved this plan in part and disapproved it in part on May 31, 1972. Following a further revision by California and partial approval by the Administrator, there were promulgated rules by the Administrator on September 22, 1972, applicable to certain aspects of air pollution control. These rules, however, did not purport to control photochemical oxidants.

This omission led to *City of Riverside* v. *Ruckelshaus*, 4 E.R.C. 1728 (C.D.Cal. 1972), a suit in the District Court for the Central District of California, in which the Administrator was ordered to promulgate regulations to control photochemical oxidants, including all necessary transportation controls and land-use controls, not later than January 15, 1973. The Administrator thereafter issued such regulations but, pursuant to discretion recognized by the court in *City of Riverside*, extended the time within which the national primary standard for photochemical oxidants in California could be attained for two years.

Such extensions were held impermissible under the terms of the Clean Air Act in *National Resources Defense Council, Inc. v. Environmental Protection Agency*, 154 U.S. App.D.C. 384, 475 F.2d 968 (1973). The court directed the Administrator to inform the states which had not submitted an implementation plan enabling them to meet the primary standard by May 31, 1975 to submit such plans, including but not limited to land-use and transportation controls, not later than April 15, 1973. California failed to submit the required plan and the Administrator disapproved its previous plan because it did not provide for attainment and maintenance of the national standards for photochemical oxidants. Thereafter, the Administrator promulgated a transportation control plan for California which, together with the regulations promulgated pursuant to the mandate of the court in *City of Riverside, supra*, covered all of California's Air Quality Control Regions.

After concluding that attainment of the required ambient air quality standard for photochemical oxidants and carbon monoxide must be deferred until 1977 because the necessary technology or other alternatives are not available, the Administrator's plan contemplated among other things, the reduction of gasoline sold within the Los Angeles, San Francisco, Sacramento Valley, San Joaquin Valley and San Diego Regions; the operation by the State of California of an inspection and maintenance program designed to reduce emissions from automobiles; limitations to be imposed by the State on the use of motorcycles; the institution by the State of an oxidizing catalyst retrofit program; control of dry cleaning solvent vapor losses; the imposition of surcharges on parking spaces; the development of a procedure of review and approval of construction or modification of parking facilities; the establishment by the State of a computer-aided carpool matching system; and the fixing by the State of certain preferential bus and carpool lanes.[97] This plan specifically directed the State of California to undertake those tasks assigned to it, to report its compliance to the Agency, and, in the case of the inspection and maintenance program, to report the date by which the State would recommend any needed legislation and to submit "[a] signed statement from the Governor and State Treasurer identifying the sources and amounts of funds for the program" and the "text of needed legislation" if existing legislation does not authorize the funds which the program will require. Other miscellaneous duties were imposed upon the State. The Agency has made it clear that it believes it has the legal authority to bring civil actions or seek penalties against the states which fail to comply with its regulations.

At least 208 parties petitioned this Court for a review of these actions within the 30-day period allowed by the Clean Air Act. Many of these have been dismissed, but a large number are currently pending. In addition to certain revisions, the Administrator has suspended indefinitely the regulations pertaining to management of parking supply and has withdrawn all parking surcharge regulations. The indefinite suspension of the parking management regulations has enabled us to dismiss without prejudice a number of petitions which were directed to the validity of these regulations.

Nonetheless the Administrator insists that the remainder of his regulations constitute a valid exercise of his authority and that his directions to the State of California contained therein must be obeyed. In keeping with this view, the Administrator on April 11, 1975 dispatched to California a "Notice of Violation" pursuant to Section 113(a)(1) of the Clean Air Actfor failure "to submit the compliance schedule or the adopted regulations establishing the inspection and maintenance program" required by the Administrator's regulations.

The Administrator, however, suggests that a determination regarding his authority under the Clean Air Act and the Constitution is not ripe at the present time because he has not instituted as yet the procedures necessary

---

[97] 38 Fed.Reg. 31232-55 (1973). The Agency's requirements are codified at 40 C.F.R. §§ 52.220-52.226(1974).

to invoke sanctions against the State of California. The sanctions include, the Administrator insists, injunctive relief, imposing a receivership on certain state functions, holding a state official in civil contempt with a substantial daily fine until compliance is secured, and requiring a state to allocate funds from one portion of its budget to another in order to finance the undertakings required by the Agency. The Agency disclaims any authority to seek criminal penalties against state legislators. It also indicates that in the final analysis the fashioning of sanctions is within the discretion of the appropriate court. We do not believe any doctrine of ripeness or exhaustion of administrative remedies should preclude our determination of the issues raised in this proceeding by the State of California and others regarding the authority to impose the regulations with respect to which these petitions for review were filed. Such issues must be determined in this proceeding for it is unlikely they could be raised "in a civil or criminal proceeding for enforcement."[98] Moreover, the orderly administration of the Clean Air Act requires that the serious questions to which the parties have addressed themselves be resolved as expeditiously as possible.

The position of the State of California and the other petitioners in this proceeding is simply that the Clean Air Act does not authorize the Administrator to impose sanctions on the State or its officials for failure to comply with the regulations here being reviewed, and that any such attempt based on the Commerce Power would be unconstitutional. While we do not feel it necessary to embrace fully California's position, we do believe that the meaning of the Clean Air Act, insofar as the imposition[s] of sanctions is concerned, is sufficiently ambiguous to permit us to interpret it in a fashion that avoids the constitutional issues. Accordingly, we hold that the Clean Air Act does not authorize the imposition of sanctions on a state or its officials for failure to comply with the Administrator's regulations which direct the state to regulate the pollution-creating activities of those other than itself, its instrumentalities and subdivisions, and the municipalities within its borders. Specifically, we hold that the Clean Air Act does not authorize the imposition of sanctions for any failure of the State of California to comply with the directions contained in 40 C.F.R. § 52.22(a)(growth plans for maintenance of national standards); 40 C.F.R. § 52.242(inspection and maintenance program); 40 C.F.R. § 52.243(motorcycle limitation); 40 C.F.R. § 52.244(oxidizing catalyst retrofit); 40 C.F.R. § 52.245(control of oxides of nitrogen, hydrocarbon, and carbon monoxide emissions from in-use vehicles); 40 C.F.R. § 52.257(computer carpool matching); 40 C.F.R. § 52.258(mass transit priority-exclusive bus use); 40 C.F.R. § 52.259(ramp metering and preferential bus/carpool lanes); 40 C.F.R. § 52.261(preferential bus/carpool lanes, San Francisco Bay Area); 40 C.F.R. § 52.263(priority treatment for buses and carpools, Los Angeles Region); 40 C.F.R. § 52.264(mass transit priority strategy and planning); 40 C.F.R. § 52.265(mass transit and transit priority planning); and 40 C.F.R. § 52.266(mass transit and transit priority planning). It follows that we consider 40 C.F.R. § 52.23(violations and enforcement) invalid to the extent it is contrary to this holding.

---

[98] *See* Clean Air Act § 307(b)(2), 42 U.S.C. § 1857h-5(b)(2)(1970).

Our holding recognizes that the pollution-creating activities of the State of California, its instrumentalities and subdivisions, and its municipalities, are subject to valid regulations promulgated by the Administrator. We also recognize that the State must avoid impeding any enforcement of valid regulations which the Administrator undertakes. We reject, however, the view that the Clean Air Act authorizes the imposition of sanctions against the State for its failure to administer and enforce a system of regulations promulgated by the Administrator which are designed to control the pollution-creating activities of the citizens of the State and others subject to its jurisdiction. Tersely put, the Act, as we see it, permits sanctions against a state that pollutes the air, but not against a state that chooses not to govern polluters as the Administrator directs.

In support of this proposition, we shall examine those portions of the Clean Air Act upon which the Administrator relies and demonstrate that the Act does not unambiguously vest him with the powers he here asserts. Thereafter, we shall examine the constitutional difficulties which the Administrator's view encounters and which induce us to reject his interpretation of his powers.

II.

Interpretation of the Act

The Clean Air Act as amended is both lengthy and complex. . . . As already indicated, the controversy between the Administrator and the State of California before us grows out of section 110(c)(1) of the Act, which empowers the Administrator to promulgate an implementation plan if the plan submitted by a state is not "in accordance with the requirements of this section." The Administrator contends that having promulgated such a plan the Act empowers him to impose sanctions on the State, or at least on the administrative officials of the State, should it or they fail to administer and enforce the plan. It is clear that the Administrator's regulation, 40 C.F.R. § 52.23, so provides.[99]

The statutory authority for this regulation is by no means apparent. The most likely place in the Act for such authority to be found would seem to be section 113 of the Clean Air Act,which deals with "Federal enforcement procedures." More particularly, this authority should appear in subsection (a)(2) which deals with the situation in which violations of implementation plans "appear to result from a failure of the State in which the plan applies to enforce the plan effectively." It does not unambiguously so appear. The subsection first provides that if the "Administrator finds such failure extends

[99] 40 C.F.R. § 52.23(1974) provides:

Failure to comply with any provisions of this part shall render the person or Governmental entity so failing to comply in violation of a requirement of an applicable implementation plan and subject to enforcement action under Section 113 of the Clean Air Act. With regard to compliance schedules, a person or Governmental entity will be considered to have failed to comply with the requirements of this part if it fails to timely submit any required compliance schedule, if the compliance schedule when submitted does not contain each of the elements it is required to contain, or if the person or Governmental entity fails to comply with such schedule. [38 Fed. Reg. 30633 (1973).]

beyond the 30th day after such notice, he shall give public notice of such finding." Thereafter, it provides that during the period of the State's recalcitrance or neglect, "the Administrator may enforce any requirement of such plan with respect to any person—(A) by issuing an order to comply with such requirement, or (B) by bringing a civil action under subsection (b) of this section." The Administrator contends that, inasmuch as the term "person" is defined in subsection 302(e) to include a state, municipality, or political subdivision, subsection 113(a)(2) authorizes a civil action against a recalcitrant state. Moreover, he contends that subsections (b) and (c) of section 113 which impose sanctions also are applicable to states because of their use of the term "person."

We disagree. While we are not prepared to say that under no circumstances should the term "person" be read to include a state when used in connection with a sanction-imposing provision of the Act, we are convinced that section 113(a)(2) is designed to provide the Administrator with power to enforce against polluters provisions of an implementation plan not being enforced by the state. Moreover, we are not convinced that the section is designed to equip the Administrator with power to sanction the non-enforcing state.

Our lack of conviction on this point primarily is grounded in our belief that Congress would not have intended in this obscure manner to take such a step in the light of the delicacy with which federal-state relations always have been treated by all branches of the Federal government. In addition, we should be reluctant to interpret expansively a provision such as subsection 113(a)(2) when by doing so we encounter fundamental constitutional questions. We also find comfort in the fact that in subsection 113(a)(1), as well as within subsection 113(a)(2), the term "State" is employed in a manner that distinguishes it from the term "person." That is, in subsection 113(a)(1) the Administrator must notify both the "person" in violation of a plan and the "State" in which the plan being violated applies. In subsection 113(a)(2) when a "State" fails to enforce the plan effectively, the Administrator may enforce it against "any person." . . . The Administrator had no difficulty in making clear his intention to impose sanctions on states not enforcing effectively implementation plans. Congress can be expected to have no less capacity for clarity.

As we see it, subsections 113(a)(1) and (a)(2) are designed to vest the Administrator with power to enforce a state implementation plan should the state fail to do so. This parallels the Administrator's power to promulgate an implementation plan for a state which fails to prepare a suitable plan. A diligent search of the sections of the Clean Air Act fails to reveal a single instance in which Congress explicitly has vested in the Administrator power to compel the states to administer and enforce regulations promulgated by him designed to govern polluters, potential or actual, other than the state, municipality, or political subdivision of the state. Counsel for the Administrator also have been unable to guide us to such a provision. This strengthens our belief that the function of subsections 113(a)(1) and (a)(2) is as we perceive it to be.

Viewed generally, the structure of the Clean Air Act reflects a genuine effort to develop an elaborate form of cooperative federalism in which both the

Federal government and the states are assigned vital roles. Techniques such as preemption, total and partial, delegations to the states of federal authority, and the creation of opportunities for states to participate in the task of controlling air pollution are employed. We find this complex structure incompatible with the view that buried within section 113 is the Congressional intent to make the states departments of the Environmental Protection Agency no less obligated to obey its Administrator's command than are its subordinate officials.

We readily acknowledge that our reading of section 113 and our perception of the structure of the Act is not unambiguously supported by the applicable legislative history. On the other hand, we have found nothing that marks our interpretation as plainly erroneous. An important example of the ambiguity that characterizes the relevant history is the following colloquy between Senator Eagleton of Missouri and Senator Muskie of Maine following the presentation by Senator Muskie of the Conference Report on the Clean Air Amendments of 1970. Senator Eagleton, in commenting on "the significance and the parameters of this noteworthy piece of legislation," said,

> I think we should also pause to record that this bill also marks a very significant step forward in the continuing development of more responsive and responsible relationships among the Federal Government and the State and local governments of our country. . . . Would the Senator from Maine agree that this bill has very broad significance in the area of Federal-State relations?

Senator Muskie's reply was imprecise:

> Yes. May I say to the Senator that during the deliberations on this bill I have been very much interested in preserving "local option" features. . . . In my judgment, the bill will give State and local authorities sufficient latitude in selecting ways to prevent and control air pollution.

116 Cong. Rec. 42386 (1970).

. . . .

While the House version was significantly different from section 113 as enacted, it is by no means clear that section 113 intended to lump ineffectively-enforcing states with polluters and subject each of them to the same far-ranging set of remedies provided by that section. To so intend indicates an insensitivity to the delicacy of federal-state relations which neither is reflected in other portions of the Act nor is worthy of Congress. . . . Enough has been said to demonstrate why we do not feel compelled by the language of the Act to reach the serious constitutional issues which the Administrator's interpretation raises. Validation of our interpretation, however, requires that we set forth these issues and, by suggesting our evaluation of them, reveal the intensity of our desire to avoid confronting them. To this task we now turn.

III.

Constitutional Issues

The Administrator contends that his interpretation encounters no constitutional barriers. Planting himself on Chief Justice Marshall's expansive definition of the power of Congress to regulate commerce set forth in *Gibbons v. Ogden*, 22 U.S. (9 Wheat.) 1, 6 L.Ed. 23 (1824), he then points to that Chief Justice's classic statement of the Necessary and Proper Clause: "Let the end be legitimate, let it be within the scope of the constitution, and all means which are appropriate, which are plainly adapted to that end, which are not prohibited, but consistent with the letter and spirit of the constitution, are constitutional." *McCulloch v. Maryland*, 17 U.S. (4 Wheat.) 316, 4 L.Ed. 579 (1819). On these foundations, the Administrator correctly asserts, were built the decisions in *Wickard v. Filburn*, 317 U.S. 111, 63 S.Ct. 82, 87 L.Ed. 122 (1942), *Heart of Atlanta Motel v. United States*, 379 U.S. 241, 85 S.Ct. 348, 13 L.Ed.2d 258 (1964), and *Katzenbach v. McClung*, 379 U.S. 294, 85 S.Ct. 377, 13 L.Ed.2d 290 (1964), in which activities, otherwise local in scope and character, which exert a "substantial effect on interstate commerce" were held subject to regulation under the Commerce Power.

The emission of air pollutants without regard to their source, the Administrator asserts, has been found by Congress to exert the requisite effect on interstate commerce. This finding, moreover, cannot be said to be without a "rational basis." Having the power to regulate air pollution, the Administrator continues, Congress, under the Necessary and Proper Clause, has the power to direct that state officials either incorporate in the law of their state or administer and enforce on behalf of the Federal Government those regulations designed to control air pollution which are properly promulgated by the Administrator. The end (abatement of air pollution) is legitimate; it (the power to regulate air emissions) is within the scope of the Constitution; and the means (state administration and enforcement) are appropriate, plainly adapted to the end, which is not prohibited, and consistent with the letter and spirit of the Constitution.

States by reason of their position under the Constitution are not immune from federal regulation under the Commerce Power, continues the Administrator. This has been established, he points out, by *United States* v. *California*, 297 U.S. 175, 56 S.Ct. 421, 80 L.Ed. 567 (1936), *Maryland* v. *Wirtz*, 392 U.S. 183, 88 S.Ct. 2017, 20 L.Ed.2d 1020 (1968), *Fry* v. *United States*, 421 U.S. 542, 95 S.Ct. 1792, 44 L.Ed.2d 363 (1975). It was put in *Maryland* v. *Wirtz*, *supra*, as follows:

> But while the commerce power has limits, valid general regulations of commerce do not cease to be regulations of commerce because a State is involved. If a State is engaging in economic activities that are validly regulated by the Federal Government when engaged in by private persons, the State too may be forced to conform its activities to federal regulation.

392 U.S. at 196, 197, 88 S.Ct. at 2024. This regulation includes the power to direct that a state either enact such laws to control air pollution as the Administrator might require, or administer and enforce such regulations as the Administration might properly promulgate. The state, as a builder of roads, maker of traffic laws, licensor of vehicles, is no more immune from this form of coercion, says the Administrator, than is a state-owned railroad exempt from the duty to comply with Federal safety regulations.[100] *See United States v. California*, 297 U.S. 175, 56 S.Ct. 421, 80 L.Ed. 567 (1936).

---

[100] For an exposition of this view by the Administrator, *see* 38 Fed.Reg. 30632-33 (1973).

The petitioners sharply challenge this reading of the Commerce Power. Their fundamental contention is that the Commerce Power does not extend to requiring a state to undertake such *governmental* tasks as might be assigned to it by Congress, or its proper delegate, with respect to activities which admittedly are within the reach of the Commerce Power. The Constitution's Tenth Amendment and Article IV, Section 4, which obligates the United States to guarantee to every state a Republican Form of Government, precludes such an extension of the Commerce Power, assert the petitioners. Moreover, insofar as the Necessary and Proper Clause is concerned, the petitioners contend that the means, compulsory state administration and enforcement, is inappropriate and inconsistent with the letter and spirit of the Constitution.

We do not view these contentions as frivolous. Moreover, we are certain that neither *Maryland* v. *Wirtz* nor *Fry* v. *United States* passed upon the precise issues raised by the petitioners. These cases establish that the payment of wages by states to certain types of state employees is an economic activity that substantially affects interstate commerce and is thus subject to those regulations imposed by Congress which were then before the Court. Neither of these cases holds or even suggests that a state's exercise of its police power with respect to an economic activity which affects interstate commerce is itself an economic activity or "species of commercial intercourse" subject to regulation by Congress. *See Gibbons* v. *Ogden*, 22 U.S. (9 Wheat.) 1 (1824). Nor do we believe that it is proper to equate the operation by a state of a railroad, an *economic activity* indistinguishable from that of private parties, with its *governance* of the use of highways and automobiles, an exercise of its police power with respect to commerce.[101]

. . . .

To treat the governance of commerce by the states as within the plenary reach of the Commerce Power would in our opinion represent such an abrupt departure from previous constitutional practice as to make us reluctant to adopt an interpretation of the Clean Air Act which would force us to confront the issue. Such treatment, for example, would authorize Congress to direct the states to regulate any economic activity that affects interstate commerce in any manner Congress sees fit. While such an interpretation might not

[101] We recognize that our views both with regard to the interpretation of the Clean Air Act and the constitutional issues here discussed differ from those expressed in Pennsylvania v. Environmental Protection Agency, 500 F.2d 246 (3d Cir. 1974). With regard to the latter issues, we believe with all deference that the Third Circuit failed to recognize the difference between a state engaging in commerce, as all states must under the Supreme Court's interpretation of the Commerce Power, and a state's regulation of the commerce of others. This failure is reflected in the following passage, at 261:

> This reasoning indicates that the basis for the Court's decision in *Maryland v. Wirtz*, *supra*, is the principle that the constitutionality of federal regulation of state activities is subject to the same analyses as that of private activities; *viz.* the determinative factor is simply whether they have an impact on interstate commerce. Following this principle, we believe that the Administrator acted within the federal commerce power in requiring the Commonwealth to enforce its transportation plan.

The conclusion is a non sequitur. The principle deduced from *Maryland v. Wirtz* far exceeds its holding in our respectful opinion. We cannot believe that a careful craftsman like Mr. Justice Harlan intended in *Maryland v. Wirtz* to announce a principle so clearly inconsistent with the history of our federal structure.

enable Congress to direct the enactment or enforcement of a federal probate code, there is sufficient doubt about even that to illumine the breadth of the sweeping claim here being made by the Administrator. To make *governance* indistinguishable from *commerce* for the purposes of the Commerce Power cannot be equated to the "unintrusive" regulation of economic activities of the states upheld by the Supreme Court in *Maryland* v. *Wirtz* and *Fry* v. *United States.* A Commerce Power so expanded would reduce the states to puppets of a ventriloquist Congress. We will not attribute to Congress any such intent unless it is expressed unequivocally. As we have already pointed out, that was not done in the Clean Air Act.

[The Court here continued with an extensive discussion of the difficulties the federal system would suffer if the Commerce Clause were construed to allow the imposition of affirmative duties upon the states, particularly if such affirmative orders were backed by sanctions. The court placed reliance on Professor Hart's distinction between prohibition of state activity, leaving outside the scope of its prohibition a wide range of alternatives, and the unusual situation of a direct order to "Do This Thing," leaving no other choice but to go ahead. Hart, *The Relations Between State and Federal Law,* 54 Colum. L. Rev. 515-16 (1954).]

It is our task, where possible, to avoid a statutory interpretation which would require us to decide whether the extensive control of state expenditures, which the Administrator's view would permit, does either threaten "the utter destruction of the State as a sovereign political entity," or "impair the States' integrity or their ability to function effectively in a federal system." As we have made abundantly clear, we are sufficiently apprehensive about the ability of states "to function effectively in a federal system" under the Administrator's interpretation to justify our strong preference for an interpretation that puts our concerns at rest. In addition, we reject as a means of allaying our fears the assumption that the prospect of "utter destruction of the State as a sovereign political entity" is confronted only when Congress asserts the power to regulate *all* aspects of state and local government. Only the mischievous would contend that not until then is the issue ripe.

All efforts by the Administrator to impose sanctions on the State of California are stayed to the extent indicated in this opinion. To that extent the petitions for review are granted.

Pursuant to Rule 54(b), Fed.R.Civ.P., to the extent that there remain unresolved claims presented by the petitioners, the disposition of the issues set forth herein shall be treated as a final judgment with respect to fewer than all the claims presented by the petitioners and we expressly determine that there is no just reason for delay in entering such final judgment with respect to the claims of which this opinion disposes.

Petitions for review granted in part.

ENVIRONMENTAL PROTECTION AGENCY v. BROWN

United States Supreme Court (1977)
431 U.S. 99, 97 S. Ct. 1635, 52 L. Ed. 2d 166

PER CURIAM.

These cases arise under the Clean Air Act, as amended in 1970, 42 U.S.C. § 1857, and raise questions concerning the authority of the Administrator of petitioner Environmental Protection Agency to compel various types of implementation and enforcement actions by the States. Three separate decisions in the Court of Appeals reviewed transportation control plans promulgated by the Administrator for several States which had previously failed to submit adequate plans of their own. Four petitions have been filed seeking review of those decisions which, with limited exceptions, invalidated the Administrator's transportation control plans which had been adopted in the form of regulations.

Those transportation control plans have a variety of aspects which need not be discussed in great detail to explain our disposition of the case. In general, they imposed upon the States the obligations (1) to develop an inspection and maintenance program pertaining to the vehicles registered in the affected Air Quality Control Regions, and to submit to the Administrator, by fixed deadlines, both a schedule of compliance and the operative regulations by which the program was to be run; (2) to develop various retrofit programs pertaining to several classes of older vehicles, in order to minimize several different types of emissions; (3) to designate and enforce preferential bus and carpool lanes, on streets sometimes specifically identified in the regulations and sometimes left to be chosen by the State; (4) to develop a program to monitor actual emissions as affected by the foregoing programs; and to adopt certain other programs which varied from State to State.

The critical fact about all of the foregoing obligations was that they were imposed on the States, under 40 CFR § 52.23, as elements of an applicable implementation plan. The State's failure to carry out any of them would therefore not merely allow the Administrator to step in and carry them out himself under § 113(a)(2), but would, in the view of each of the Courts of Appeals, render the State "in violation of a requirement of an applicable implementation plan" and therefore apparently subject to direct enforcement actions against it under the provisions of § 113(a)(1):

> "Whenever, on the basis of any information available to him, the Administrator finds that any person is in violation of any requirement of an applicable implementation plan, the Administrator shall notify the person in violation of the plan and the State in which the plan applies of such finding. If such violation extends beyond the 30th day after the date of the Administrator's notification, the Administrator may issue an order requiring such person to comply with the requirements of such plan or he may bring a civil action in accordance with subsection (b)."

Under dual challenges by the States that these regulations were not within the mandate of the Act, and that if they were they were in violation of the Constitution, the United States Courts of Appeals for the Ninth, Fourth, and District of Columbia Circuits struck them down. All of the courts rested on statutory interpretation, but noted also that serious constitutional questions might be raised if the statute were read as the United States argued it should be. *Brown v. EPA*, 521 F.2d 827 (CA9 1975); *Arizona v. EPA*, 521 F.2d 825 (CA9 1975); *District of Columbia v. EPA*, — U.S. App. D.C. —, 521 F.2d 971 (1975); *Maryland v. EPA*, 530 F.2d 215 (CA4 1975). The only substantial variation in the outcome of these decisions was that the District of Columbia Circuit affirmed regulations requiring the creation of bus lanes, the purchase by the affected jurisdictions of a fixed number of new buses, and the denial of registration to a vehicle whose owner is unable to produce a federal certificate of compliance, should a federal inspection program be instituted.

The Solicitor General's petitions from all three Courts of Appeals challenged them only insofar as they invalidated the regulations requiring state inspection and maintenance programs. In addition we granted the petition for certiorari of the State of Virginia on its challenge to the regulations which the District of Columbia Circuit had upheld. Prior to argument, the Solicitor General informed the Court that repeal of the bus purchase regulations was imminent, Government Reply Brief at 25,[102] and that issue was thereby effectively removed from the case. Thus the case has undergone a great deal of shrinkage since the decisions below due to the Government's exercise of its prerogative not to seek review of the invalidation of certain regulations.

But the Government has not merely renounced an intent to pursue certain specified regulations; it now appears to admit that those remaining in controversy are invalid unless modified in certain respects.

> "The Administrator . . . concedes the necessity of removing from the regulations all requirements that the States submit legally adopted regulations; the [Administrator's] regulations contain no requirement that the State adopt laws." Government Brief, at 20, n. 14.

The Government's position now appears to be that, while the challenged transportation plans do not require the enactment of state *legislation*, they do now contain, and must be modified to eliminate, certain requirements that the State promulgate *regulations*. *See* Government Reply Brief, at 14 n. 22.

We decline the Government's invitation to pass upon the EPA regulations, when the only ones before us are admitted to be in need of certain essential modifications. Such action on our part would amount to the rendering of an advisory opinion. For this Court to review regulations normally required to be first reviewed in the Court of Appeals, before such review is had, is extraordinary. *See Youngstown Sheet & Tube Co.* v. *Sawyer*, 343 U.S. 579, 584-585 (1952). For it to review regulations not yet promulgated, the final form of which has only been hinted at would be wholly novel. *See, generally, CBS* v. *United States*, 316 U.S. 407, 417-419 (1942); *United States* v. *Los Angeles & Salt Lake Railroad Co.*, 273 U.S. 299, 309-310 (1927).

---

102 The regulations were officially rescinded on February 8, 1977. 42 Fed.Reg. 7957.

The judgments of the respective Courts of Appeals are vacated, and the cases are remanded for consideration of mootness and such other proceedings as may be consistent with this opinion.

It is so ordered.

Mr. JUSTICE STEVENS, dissenting.

The action the Court takes today is just as puzzling as the Government's position. Unless and until the Environmental Protection Agency rescinds the regulations in dispute, it is perfectly clear that the litigation is not moot. Moreover, an apparent admission that those regulations are invalid unless modified is not a proper reason for vacating the Court of Appeals judgments which invalidated the regulations.

If the Court is satisfied that the Government will modify the regulations regardless of the outcome of the litigation, the writs of certiorari should be dismissed as improvidently granted. On the other hand, if the survival of the regulations is dependent on our disposition of these cases, we should address the merits and resolve the issues which have been fully briefed and argued. By vacating the judgments below, the Court hands the Government a partial victory as a reward for an apparent concession that its position is not supported by the statute. I respectfully dissent.

DELAWARE VALLEY CITIZENS' COUNCIL FOR CLEAN AIR v. PENNSYLVANIA

United States District Court, Eastern District of Pennsylvania (1982)
12 E.L.R. 2019

Memorandum and Order

These two consolidated cases arose under the Clean Air Act, as amended, 42 U.S.C. § 7401, *et seq.* On August 29, 1978, the Commonwealth of Pennsylvania ("Commonwealth") and two of its administrative agencies voluntarily entered into a consent decree with the United States of America ("United States") and the Delaware Valley Citizens' Council for Clean Air ("DVCCCA"). In that consent decree, the Commonwealth defendants agreed to establish an automobile emissions inspection and maintenance program ("I/M program") for the Philadelphia and Pittsburgh areas. On October 5, 1981, the Pennsylvania General Assembly enacted a statute prohibiting the expenditure of public funds for the establishment of the I/M program. Presently before the Court are the motion of the Commonwealth defendants for a stay and a modification of the consent decree and the motion of the DVCCCA to declare defendants in civil contempt and to establish sanctions, both filed as a result of the General Assembly's action.

[The court here recounts the initial inclusion of an I/M program in the Pennsylvania SIP, and its approval in *Commonwealth of Pennsylvania v. EPA*, 500 F.2d 246 (3d Cir. 1974).]

The I/M program was never implemented by the Commonwealth. On June 29, 1976, DVCCCA instituted a citizen's action, pursuant to 42 U.S.C. § 7604, against the Commonwealth of Pennsylvania, the Secretary of the Pennsylvania Department of Transportation ("PennDOT"), the Secretary of the Pennsylvania Department of Environmental Resources ("PennDER"), and the Administrator and Regional Administrator of the EPA to enforce the Pennsylvania SIP requirement for the implementation of an I/M program in the Philadelphia and Pittsburgh areas. On September 23, 1976, the EPA issued notices of violation to the Governor of Pennsylvania and the Secretary of PennDOT, pursuant to § 113(a)(1) of the Clean Air Act,as amended, 42 U.S.C. § 7413(a)(1), because of Pennsylvania's failure to implement the I/M program by May 1, 1975. On February 18, 1977, the United States instituted its own suit against the Commonwealth of Pennsylvania and certain of its departments and officers, pursuant to § 113(b) of the Clean Air Act,as amended, 42 U.S.C. § 7413(b), to enforce the Pennsylvania SIP requiring the implementation of an I/M program.

Meanwhile, on August 7, 1977, Congress passed the Clean Air Act Amendment of 1977, Pub. L. 95-95, tit. I-IV, 91 Stat. 685. This amendment added a new Part D to the Clean Air Act requiring states to submit revised SIPs for areas which had not yet attained the national ambient air quality standards. 42 U.S.C. § 7501 *et seq.* These revised SIPs must meet specific requirements outlined in Part D of the Act and must provide for attainment of national ambient air quality standards by December 31, 1982. If a state cannot attain certain air quality standards in certain areas by December 31, 1982, § 172(a)(2) of the Act allows the EPA to grant an extension of the attainment deadline to December 31, 1987. 42 U.S.C. § 7502(a)(2). In the event that such an extension is granted, a state is required by § 172(b)(11) to submit "a specific schedule for implementation of a vehicle emission control inspection and maintenance program" in any area with an extended attainment deadline. 42 U.S.C. § 7502(b)(11).

On August 29, 1978, after extensive negotiations, the Commonwealth of Pennsylvania, and two of its departments, PennDOT and PennDER, voluntarily entered into a consent decree with both the DVCCCA and the United States by agreeing to implement an I/M program for ten counties in the Philadelphia and Pittsburgh areas by August 1, 1980. . . .

. . . On May 20, 1981, the Court denied the Commonwealth's motion for a further modification and postponement of the implementation deadline and ordered that the I/M program commence operations "without further delay." *Memorandum and Order* (May 20, 1981). In its order, the Court declared the Commonwealth to be in violation of the consent decree and directed the Commonwealth to file, by June 1, 1981, a proposed plan for the immediate implementation of the I/M program in the Philadelphia and Pittsburgh areas. On June 16, 1981, the Court denied the Commonwealth's motion for reconsideration and approved a Court modified version of the Commonwealth's Proposed Emission Inspection and Maintenance Program I to commence operations on May 1, 1982. *Memorandum and Order* (June 16, 1981).

Following the Court's decision in June, 1981, the Pennsylvania General Assembly passed House Bill No. 456, § 2 ("H.B. 456"), which prohibited the expenditure of state funds by the executive branch for the implementation of the I/M program. On July 10, 1981, the Governor of Pennsylvania vetoed H.B. 456 and returned it to the General Assembly. Nevertheless, on October 5, 1981, the General Assembly overrode the Governor's veto and enacted H.B. 456 into law as an amendment to the Administrative Code of 1929. Section 2 of H.B. 456 provides:

> Section 2013. *Prohibition on Expenditures for Emission Inspection Program*
>
> Neither the department nor any other department or agency of the Executive Branch of State Government shall expend any public funds for the establishment and administration of any system for the periodic inspection of emissions or emission system of motor vehicles.

Act of October 5, 1981, No. 99, § 2, 1981 Pa. Legis. Serv. 312 (to be codified at PA. STAT. ANN. tit. 71, § 523). PennDOT and the executive branch immediately ceased operations in the implementation of the I/M program following the passage of this law. Nevertheless, on October 10, 1981, final regulations pertaining to the standards for the emission analyzers to be purchased by the private garage owners wishing to participate in the I/M program were published in the Pennsylvania Bulletin. 11 Pa. Bull. 3519 (Oct. 10, 1981). Moreover, $36,118,000.00 had previously been appropriated without restriction by the General Assembly to PennDOT "for the salaries, wages and all necessary expenses for the administration of the traffic safety program and the administration and operation of the operator and vehicle registration programs." The current law prohibits the expenditure of these appropriated funds for the implementation of the I/M program agreed to by the Commonwealth when it entered into the consent decree. On December 2, 1981, a notice of deficiency was issued to the Commonwealth by the EPA because of the lack of funding assurances required by §§ 172(b)(7) and 110(a)(2)(F) under the Clean Air Act due to the passage of H.B. 456. 46 Fed. Reg. 58593 (1981).

II.

Presently before the Court are two motions: (1) the motion of state defendants, Commonwealth of Pennsylvania and PennDOT, for a stay and a modification of the consent decree, and (2) the motion of DVCCCA to declare the defendants in civil contempt and to establish sanctions. In addition, in response to the Court's Order of October 20, 1981, the United States has filed a brief taking the position that defendants' motion for a stay and a modification should be denied and that the Court should postpone a ruling on the motion for civil contempt and defer to the EPA for the initiation of administrative procedures and remedies available under the Clean Air Act, 42U.S.C. § 7401, *et seq.* We will now address each parties' contentions.

A.

The Commonwealth urges the Court to stay further implementation of the I/M program until such time that the Pennsylvania legislature decides to fund the program. Defendants argue that since H.B. 456 prohibits the expenditure of public funds for the implementation of an I/M program, the executive branch is now disabled from complying with the requirements of the consent decree and the Court's orders despite its continued willingness to do so. *See, generally, Shapp v. Sloan* 480 Pa. 449, 391 A.2d 595 (1978). Moreover, defendants argue that the legislature's passage of H.B. 456 constitutes "changed circumstances" which warrant a stay or modification of the consent decree.

Paragraph 13 of the August 29, 1978 consent decree specifically provides:

> Jurisdiction is retained by this Court for the purpose of enabling any party to apply to the Court at any time for such further orders and directions as may be necessary or appropriate for carrying out of this Consent Decree, *for the modification or termination of any of the provisions herein upon a showing of changed circumstances and good cause*, or for the enforcement of compliance therewith and the punishment of violations thereof.

(Emphasis added.) Indeed, even in the absence of such a clause, a federal district court may, in its discretion, modify a consent decree in the interests of justice as reflected by changed circumstances. *Mayberry v. Maroney*, 529 F.2d 332, 335 (3d Cir. 1976). Nevertheless, in *United States v. Swift & Co.*, 286 U.S. 106 (1932), the Supreme Court stated that a modification of a consent decree would only be appropriate where the decree "has been turned through changing circumstances into an instrument of wrong," *id.* at 115; and that "[n]othing less than a clear showing of grievous wrong evoked by new and unforeseen conditions should lead us to change what was decreed by years of litigation with the consent of all concerned." *Id.* at 119.

A party should not be permitted, however, to obtain a modification of a consent decree because of changed circumstances of its own creation. *See Mayberry v. Maroney*, 558 F.2d 1159, 1164 (3d Cir. 1977). This is especially true where the change in circumstances does not render continued compliance with the consent decree oppressive but merely a party's act disabling itself from carrying out its part of its own judicially sanctioned agreement. Such "changed circumstances" simply do not fall within the realm of those recognized by courts in the past. . . .

B.

Next, the United States contends that the Court should defer to the EPA to allow for the initiation of administrative procedures and remedies available to the EPA under the Clean Air Act where, as here, a SIP is deficient, before deciding the questions of constitutionality and contempt raised by the Pennsylvania General Assembly's passage of H.B. 456 prohibiting the expenditure of public funds for the implementation of the I/M program. Pursuant to the Act, the EPA can impose a moratorium on all future construction or modification of major stationary sources of pollution, *see* 42 U.S.C. §§ 7410(a)(2)(I) and 7503(4), and withhold future Clean Air Act planning and pollution control funds. *See* 42 U.S.C. § 7506(b). . . .

After considering these views, the Court holds that it is not required to defer to the EPA before taking action on the motions presently pending and that it has jurisdiction over the present dispute. First, the issues raised concern a consent decree which was voluntarily entered by the Commonwealth and two of its agencies after a citizens' action was filed in the district court by the DVCCCA pursuant to § 304(a) of the Clean Air Act, 42 U.S.C. § 7604(a), and an enforcement action was filed by the United States pursuant to § 113(b), 42 U.S.C. § 7413(b). The notion of primary jurisdiction does not apply where the parties have already properly resorted to the remedies available in the federal district court and have entered a consent decree in settlement of their dispute. Of course, judicial action to enforce the consent decree does not prevent the EPA from taking contemporaneous administrative action, where authorized, to enforce compliance. Nevertheless, where, as here, the parties are already properly, lawfully and voluntarily before the Court as parties to the consent decree, no purpose would be served by deferring to an administrative agency. Accordingly, the Court declines to adopt the suggestion of the United States.

C.

The Court now turns to the motion of plaintiff DVCCCA to declare the defendants in civil contempt and to establish sanctions. DVCCCA's motion essentially seeks four items of relief: (1) a declaration that defendants are in civil contempt for failure to comply with the modified consent decree and the Court's orders on May 20 and June 16, 1981; (2) a declaration that § 2 of H.B. 456 is unconstitutional and without effect; (3) an order directing defendants forthwith to comply with the modified consent decree and the Court's orders; and (4) the establishment of coercive and compensatory civil penalties, primarily consisting of fines of $50,000.00 per day for continued violations. The first two items of relief sought raise substantive legal questions. The remaining items are merely matters of remedy which must be addressed only if the Court first holds that defendants are in civil contempt, and then only to determine whether they constitute appropriate relief. Therefore, the Court will begin by addressing DVCCCA's first two items of requested relief.

1. Constitutionality of H.B. 456.

Plaintiff DVCCCA argues that H.B. 456 violates the Supremacy Clause of the Federal Constitution, U.S. CONST., art. VI, cl. 2, in two respects: first, by having the effect of nullifying the Court's orders and the consent decree; and secondly, by directly conflicting with the requirements of the Clean Air Act, 42U.S.C. § 7401, *et seq.* Upon full consideration, the Court has concluded that H.B. 456 cannot be declared unconstitutional on either ground.

a. Interference with a Consent Decree.

It is well settled that a state law which purports to nullify or prevent compliance with a federal judicial decree is unconstitutional and without effect. *Washington v. Washington State Commercial Passenger Fishing Vessel Association*, 443 U.S. 658, 692-696 [9 ELR 20517] (1979); *Cooper v. Aaron*, 358 U.S. 1, 18-19 (1958); *Ableman v. Booth*, 62 U.S. (21 How.) 506, 523-524 (1858); *United States v. Peters*, 9 U.S. (5 Cranch) 115, 136 (1809). Moreover, by preventing the Commonwealth defendants from fulfilling their obligations under the consent decree, H.B. 456 clearly interferes with the realization of a federal judicial decree. Nevertheless, there are serious limits not reached by the cases cited above on the power of the federal government to require action on the part of state government. The Supreme Court has held that Congress, in enacting legislation otherwise within its authority, may not impose burdens on states which impair essential attributes of state sovereignty. *National League of Cities v. Usery*, 426 U.S. 833 (1976). This principle is not only embodied in the language of the Tenth Amendment, but is also implicit in the concept of federalism underlying the structure of our government.

[The Court cannot] countermand the decision of a state legislature not to expend state funds on the establishment of an I/M program.

b. Conflict with the Clean Air Act.

Plaintiff DVCCCA also claims that H.B. 456 is unconstitutional because it conflicts directly with the Clean Air Act, as amended. In particular, plaintiff DVCCCA relies upon those provisions of the Clean Air Act which require that a SIP provide for an I/M program where necessary. *See* 42 U.S.C. §§ 7410(b)(2)(G), 7502(b)(11)(B). Plaintiff argues that, since an I/M program is required under the Act, and H.B. 456 effectively prohibits the establishment of such a program, H.B. 456 is unconstitutional. The Courts of Appeals of several circuits have considered this argument, however, and the majority have concluded that the Clean Air Act does not require states to establish and fund I/M programs or authorize the EPA to so require. Indeed, those same opinions suggest that Congress lacks the power to do so because of the Tenth Amendment and principles of federalism. The Court agrees . . . and accordingly concludes that H.B. 456 does not conflict with the Clean Air Act, as amended.

For these reasons, the Court holds that H.B. 456 cannot be declared unconstitutional because of the Tenth Amendment prohibitions on the reach of the Commerce Clause and legislation enacted pursuant to that provision.

2. Motion for Civil Contempt.

a. Defendants' Conduct as Contempt.

It is well established that a consent decree, although negotiated by the parties, is a judicial act. . . .

It is well settled that civil contempt consists of a party's failure to comply with a judicial order where the party has knowledge of the order and the ability to comply. . . .

. . . In this regard, it is important to note that H.B. 456 is not a legal disability imposed upon the Commonwealth from without; rather, it is a disability imposed from within the sovereignty itself reflecting a decision of the legislative arm of that government that the I/M program shall not go forward as agreed to by the executive arm even though that very executive arm had previously been lawfully empowered to enter into the program by that same legislative arm.

In this regard, the Court cannot accept the Commonwealth defendants' argument that for the purposes of the present proceeding the conduct of the state's executive branch should be considered separately form that of its legislative branch. . . .

. . . The Commonwealth of Pennsylvania and its two agencies are party defendants. The fact that these defendants that are before the Court have been prevented by a part of the Commonwealth that is not before the Court from carrying out the decree does not insulate the parties before the Court from the consequences of a self-imposed failure to fulfill the obligations of the judgment that is before the Court and represented by the decree. Accordingly, the Court finds that the Commonwealth of Pennsylvania and the other Commonwealth defendants that are part of that Commonwealth are in civil contempt for failing to comply with the judgment of the Court.

b. The Appropriate Remedy.

Having determined the Commonwealth defendants to be in civil contempt of the consent decree, the Court must decide upon an appropriate remedy, bearing in mind that a sanction for civil contempt should be designed either to coerce the contumacious party into compliance, or to compensate the aggrieved party for loss, if any, or for both purposes. . . .

A remedy that appears to meet the present need is suggested by the Clean Air Act itself. In the 1977 amendments to the Act, Congress sought to induce states to establish I/M programs by including provisions which, if invoked, could lead to the termination of certain related federal benefits. Most important among these federal funds are those for highway construction. It was for this purpose that Congress enacted, as one means of inducement, § 176(a) of the Act, which provides in relevant part:

(a) The Administrator shall not approve any projects or award any grants authorized by this chapter and *the Secretary of Transportation shall not approve any projects or award any grants under Title 23 other than for safety, mass transit, or transportation improvement projects related to air quality improvement or maintenance, in any air quality control region—*

(1) in which any national primary ambient air quality standard has not been attained,

(2) where transportation control measures are necessary for the attainment of such standard, and

(3) *where the Administrator finds after July 1, 1979, that the Governor has not submitted an implementation plan which considers each of the elements required by § 7502 of this title or that reasonable efforts toward submitting such an implementation plan are not being made (or, after July, 1982, in the case of an implementation plan revision required under § 7502 of this title to be submitted before July 1, 1982).*

42 U.S.C. § 7506(emphasis added). The coercive purpose of § 176(a) is clear from the legislative history of the 1977 amendments.

. . . .

With the foregoing in mind, under the auspices of the Court's inherent equitable process, the Court will enjoin the United States Secretary of Transportation from approving any projects or awarding any grants to the Commonwealth of Pennsylvania for highway projects in the Philadelphia and Pittsburgh areas as defined in the consent decree, other than those grants required for safety, mass transit, or transportation improvement projects related to air quality improvement or maintenance in those same Philadelphia and Pittsburgh areas. In refusing to comply with the provisions of the consent decree through the passage of H.B. 456 which prohibits the expenditure of state funds for the implementation of an I/M program, Pennsylvania has indirectly but with calculated effectiveness rescinded the state SIP revisions submitted for the Philadelphia and Pittsburgh non-attainment areas as required under 42 U.S.C. § 7502. For this reason, Pennsylvania's adoption of H.B. 456 is tantamount to no SIP revision having ever been submitted before, which would, thus, trigger the invocation of the sanctions prescribed by Congress in 42 U.S.C. § 7506(a). Moreover, this remedy, under all the circumstances, serves to promote the underlying goal of the consent decree and the philosophies behind the enactment of the Clean Air Act and subsequent amendments since the further construction of highways encourages the further use of motor vehicles which thereby results in an increase in air pollutants and a decrease in air quality. Finally, the aforementioned remedy will not interfere with state sovereignty since it permits the state's action to stand as long as the state chooses to remain adamant in its refusal to establish the I/M program it agreed to, while it also encourages the state to reconsider its position and comply with the consent decree. For these reasons the Court is of the view that a cut-off of federal highway funds serves all of the Court's remedial objectives.

III.

To summarize, the enactment of H.B. 456 by the Pennsylvania legislature does not constitute a change in circumstances warranting a stay of the consent decree, nor does it require the Court to defer to the EPA for the resolution of its effects. At the same time, the Court has concluded that there is nothing in the Federal Constitution which prohibits the state from enacting such a measure. Nevertheless, since the effect of H.B. 456 is that the Commonwealth defendants are no longer complying with the provisions of the consent decree of which they are parties, the Court holds that the defendants are in civil contempt. As a remedy, and as applied to the Philadelphia and Pittsburgh Areas covered by the decree, the Secretary of the United States Department of Transportation will be enjoined from approving and awarding grants of federal highway funds unless they are for safety, mass transit, or transportation projects related to air quality improvement and maintenance.

An appropriate Order will be entered.

NOTES AND QUESTIONS

(1) The issues of federalism involved in the *Brown* case, and in the other Court of Appeals cases that came to the Supreme Court with *Brown*, were

widely discussed in the 1970s, with a variety of views expressed on the relative powers of the nation and the states in the situation. The discussion was cast in terms of reviewing EPA regulations under Tenth Amendment strictures, as described by the Court in *National League of Cities v. Usery*, 426 U.S. 833, 96 S. Ct. 2465, 49 L. Ed. 2d 245 (1976). The decision of the Supreme Court in *Brown*, and the later amendment of the Clean Air Act in 1977, have relieved the situation of much of its tension and immediacy. For comments, *see* D. Currie, *Federal Air Quality Standards and Their Implementation*, 1976 A.B.A. Found. Res. J., 365, 391 *et seq.*; D. Salmon, *The Federalist Principle: The Introduction of the Commerce Clause and the Tenth Amendment in the Clean Air Act*, 2 Colum. J. Env. L. 290 (1976); Note, *The Clean Air Act Amendments of 1970: A Threat to Federalism?* 76 Colum. L. Rev. 990 (1976); Note, *The Federal Government May Require a State to Adopt and Enforce Penal Regulations Relating to State Activity that Affects Interstate Commerce*, 53 Tex. L. Rev. 38 (1975); Note, *Transportation Control: An Urban Reality*, 12 Hous. L. Rev. 689, 696 (1975). Regarding decision on transportation plans generally, see F. Grad, Treatise on Environmental Law, § 2.03[11]. For an analysis of the effectiveness of transportation planning, see F. Grad, A. Rosenthal, et al., The Automobile and the Regulation of Its Impact on the Environment, 151 *et seq.* (Ch. 5 by G. Ingram) (1975).

(2) Must every state prepare a transportation plan as part of its state implementation plan under the statutory requirements? For a discussion of the earlier view of the role of land use planning in air pollution control, see Mandelker & Rothschild, *The Role of Land Use Controls in Combatting Air Pollution Under the Clean Air Act of 1970*, 2 Ecol. L.Q. 235 (1973). What elements of land use control remain in § 110 of the Clean Air Actafter its 1977 and 1990 amendments? What is the impact on transportation planning for air pollution control of the 1977 amendments of the Clean Air Act?

(3) Was anything resolved by the Supreme Court decision in *Brown*? Was the issue merely postponed and is it likely to emerge in the foreseeable future? What precisely was the interference with state sovereignty alleged—ordering the state to pass certain laws; EPA adopting state implementation plans for the states; or EPA ordering the states and state officers to comply with EPA-adopted implementation plans? Has there been a clear resolution of the constitutional issue?

(4) Does the decision in the *Brown* case limit the power of the Administrator to impose duties on the states by way of transportation plan requirements which fit normally into state law requirements—such as a requirement for regular motor vehicle emissions inspections that ties into a state's normal vehicle safety inspection and registration program? *See* Comment, "Federalism and Clean Air: In Dubious Battle," 1975 Utah L. Rev. 969. *See also Testa v. Katt*, 330 U.S. 386 (1948). Compare *City of Santa Rosa v. EPA*, 534 F.2d 150, 8 E.R.C. 1929 (9th Cir. 1976) which upheld EPA's authority to impose gas rationing in some areas of California.

(5) In the *Delaware Valley Citizen's Council* case, did Pennsylvania suffer any special or unusual sanctions as a result of the court's imposition of a penalty for civil contempt?

(6) Does it matter from the constitutional point of view whether the mandate from EPA to the state requires a substantial or a minimal performance? When EPA promulgates a transportation plan for a state, requiring the state to deny registration to vehicles which have not passed the I/M test required in the SIP, can the EPA proceed directly against the state in the district court to require enforcement? If the state highway is regarded as the "source" in violation, can it be said that the purpose of the registration ban is to require the state to modify the management of a polluting facility—all the more since the state has long used vehicle registration as a means of controlling the use of the highway, as well as raising revenue for its maintenance. *See United States v. Ohio Dept. of Highway Safety*, 635 F.2d 1195 (1980). What new sanctions are currently imposed on states for nonattainment and other failures to comply following the 1990 revision of the Clean Air Act?

(7) Issues of federal-state relations abound in the field of pollution control. The transportation plans cases indicate that there are limits on the power of EPA under the Clean Air Act to order the states and their officers to take certain affirmative steps to carry out and enforce federal law or regulation. It is also clear that a state can be treated as a polluter when the state itself causes the emission of air pollution (state vehicles, for instance, are not immune from federal enforcement). On the other hand, must the federal government comply with the requirements of a state implementation plan that has been duly approved by EPA? The question is not merely theoretical. The federal government owns over 20,000 and leases approximately 60,000 facilities, ranging from small post offices to large office buildings and Defense Department installations. In a state with a large number of federal facilities, it may be difficult for the state to attain and maintain national ambient air quality standards unless the federal facilities comply with the state implementation plan. What can the state do if federal facilities fail to comply? Consider CAA § 118as amended in 1977 following the decision in *Hancock v. Train*, 426 U.S. 167, 96 S. Ct. 2006, 48 L. Ed. 2d 578 (1976), and the companion case in water pollution, *EPA v. California*, 426 U.S. 200, 96 S. Ct. 2022, 48 L. Ed. 2d 578 (1976), and as further amended in 1990. Under § 118, can the federal government assert an absolute right to pollute when the facility is involved in national defense?

[f] National Emission Standards; New Source Performance Standards

The Clean Air Act authorizes the Administrator to issue two separate kinds of emission standards for emissions from stationary sources. One authorization deals with "standard of performance" for new stationary sources,[103] the other with national emission standards for hazardous air pollutants.[104] With respect to new sources, the law requires the Administrator to issue a list of categories of stationary sources, this list to be revised from time to time.[105]

[103] CAA § 111, 42 U.S.C. § 7411.

[104] CAA § 112, 42 U.S.C. § 7412.

[105] CAA § 111(b), 42 U.S.C. § 7411(b). EPA has promulgated the list of major source categories for which standards of performance for new stationary sources were to be promulgated by August 1982, pursuant to § 111(f) of the Clean Air Actas amended in 1977. The section provides that the Administrator publish a list of the categories of major stationary sources

This list is to include categories of sources which, the Administrator determines, may contribute significantly to air pollution that endangers public health or welfare.[106] Within one year after the inclusion of a category of stationary sources in such a list, the Administrator must propose regulations establishing federal "standards of performance" for new sources within such category.[107]

The term "standard of performance" is used somewhat misleadingly in the law. A standard of performance is a federal emission standard, set for certain designated major sources. The term "standard of performance" means a standard for emissions of air pollutants which reflects the degree of emission limitation achievable through the application of the best system of emission reduction which (taking into account the cost of achieving such reduction and any nonair quality health and environmental impact and energy requirements) the Administrator determines has been adequately demonstrated.[108] This standard of performance is to apply to any "new source." "New source" is defined as follows:

> The term "new source" means any stationary source, the construction or modification of which is commenced after the publication of regulations (or, if earlier, proposed regulations) prescribing a standard of performance under this section which will be applicable to such source.[109] When a new standard of performance has been proposed, interested persons may submit written comments[110] and after considering such comments, the Administrator may promulgate the new regulation within one year after publication.

The regulations may be revised from time to time, after publication and submission for review in the same manner as the original standards.[111] In connection with the issuance of such regulations, the Administrator may distinguish among "classes, types and sizes" within a category of new sources[112] and, as in the case of air quality criteria, he must also issue

---

which had not been listed previously as source categories for which standards of performance were to be established. The promulgated list reflects the Administrator's determination that emissions from the list of source categories contribute significantly to air pollution. The standards promulgated for categories on the list apply only to new or modified stationary sources in the categories designated. The list appears at 40 C.F.R. § 60.16, 44Fed. Reg. 49222 (August 21, 1979).

[106] CAA § 111(b)(1)(A), 42 U.S.C. § 7411(b)(1)(A).

[107] CAA § 111(b)(1)(B), 42 U.S.C. § 7411(b)(1)(B).

[108] CAA § 111(a)(1), 42 U.S.C. § 7411(a)(1).

[109] CAA § 111(a)(2), 42 U.S.C. § 7411(a)(2).

[110] CAA § 111(b)(1)(B), 42 U.S.C. § 7411(b)(1)(B).

[111] CAA § 111(b)(1)(B), 42 U.S.C. § 7411(b)(1)(B).

[112] CAA § 111(b)(2), 42 U.S.C. § 7411(b)(2). *See* PPG Industries, Inc. v. Harrison, 660 F.2d 628 (5th Cir. 1981) where the owner and operator of a chemical manufacturing plant appealed an action of the EPA subjecting the "waste heat" boilers of its newly constructed power plant to new source performance standards for fossil fuel-fired steam generating units. On remand from the Supreme Court, 64 L.Ed. 2d 525, the Court of Appeals held that petitioners' waste heat boilers, which used a combination of waste heat gases and fossil fuel, did fall within the § 111 definition of fossil fuel-fired steam generating units, but that the applicable new source performance standard was not drawn to apply to boilers using a combination of fossil fuel and waste heat. The court remanded, holding that by applying the new source standard to petitioner's boilers, EPA acted inconsistently with its prior position on the use of high sulfur fuel in combination with other sources.

information on pollution control techniques for categories of new sources.[113] When the new source regulations have been promulgated, it is unlawful for the owner or operator of any new source to operate in violation of any standard of performance applicable to such source.[114] The regulations adopted by the Administrator under the "new source" provisions of the law only apply to stationary sources of major size. The stationary new sources for which Administrative approval must be sought include fossil fuel steam generators,[115] incinerators,[116] Portland cement plants,[117] nitric acid plants,[118] and sulfuric acid plants.[119] The coverage of the regulations for fossil-fueled steam generators is limited, for example, to generators of more than 250 million B.T.U. per hour heat input.[120]

The new source regulations, which also apply to "modifications" of existing sources, exclude from coverage mere routine maintenance, repair and replacement, as well as any change in operation which merely increases production to the existing operating design capacity of the facility, or increases the hours of operation, or changes in fuel or process material if appropriate design changes for such alternatives have been made.[121] Provision is made for plan review by the Administrator upon request of the owner or operator of the new source[122] and such owner or operator may also ask for the Administrator's determination as to whether the planned construction or modification will bring the facility within the new source regulations.[123]

The regulations require the owner of the new source to give 30 to 60 days notice to the Administrator of the date of planned initial startup, as well as notice of the actual startup date within 15 days.[124] Written reports of performance test must be submitted within 60 days after achieving maximum production rate, and not later than 180 days after initial startup, and the Administrator must also be given prior notice of the performance test to afford opportunity for the presence of an observer.[125] The regulations also require the new source facility to provide adequate performance testing facilities, including sampling ports, sampling platforms, and adequate access.[126]

New source performance standards are intended to operate primarily through the instrumentality of each state's implementation plan. Each state may develop and submit to the Administrator a plan for the implementation and enforcement for new sources located in the state. If the state procedure is found adequate by the Administrator, he shall delegate his authority to implement and enforce such standards to the state. However, the Administrator retains the authority to enforce applicable standards of performance regardless of this delegation.[127] The Clean Air Act also provides for the

113 CAA § 111(b)(3), 42 U.S.C. § 7411(b)(3).

114 CAA § 111(c), 42 U.S.C. § 7411(e).

115 40 C.F.R. § 60.40 *et seq.* (1972)

116 40 C.F.R. § 60.50 *et seq.*

117 40 C.F.R. § 60.60 *et seq.*

118 40 C.F.R. § 60.70 *et seq.*

119 40 C.F.R. § 60.80 *et seq.*

120 40 C.F.R. § 60.40.

121 40 C.F.R. § 60.2(h).

122 40 C.F.R. § 60.6.

123 40 C.F.R. § 60.5.

124 40 C.F.R. § 60.7(d).

125 40 C.F.R. § 60.8(a), (d). EPA has improved and eased the application of its so-called "reference method" to measure emissions from sources required to comply with standards of performance. 42 Fed. Reg. 41754 (Aug. 18, 1977).

126 40 C.F.R. § 60.8(e).

127 CAA § 111(c), 42 U.S.C. § 7411(b).

establishment of standards of performance for existing sources. Parallel to § 110 of the Act, the Administrator must prescribe a procedure under which each state must submit to the Administrator a plan to establish standards of performance for existing sources for any air pollutant for which air quality criteria have not been issued or which is not included on the list under § 108(a) or emitted from a source category regulated under § 112 (Hazardous Air Pollutants) of the law to which a standard of performance under § 110 would apply if such existing source were a new source, and the Administrator must provide for the implementation and enforcement of such standards of performance. The Administrator's regulation under this provision must allow the state in applying a standard of performance to consider the remaining useful life of the source.[128] When a state fails to submit a plan, the Administrator may prescribe a plan for the state, as in the case of a state's failure to submit an implementation plan. So, too, the Administrator may enforce such standards as in the case of a state failure to enforce a state implementation plan.[129]

The Administrator may grant waivers from the application of new source performance standards.[130] Such waivers are strictly conditioned and limited and may not be granted if they would prevent the attainment and maintenance of any national ambient air quality standard.[131]

EPA revised the new source performance standards in 1990 when the amendments of the Act became effective. The amendments allowed certain modifications to reflect both experience and results achieved under earlier standards imposed. The new standards, however, required the Administrator to catch up with the promulgation and new source performance standards which had not yet been adopted prior to the 1990 amendment of the law. The new standards are to be based on best available technology ("BAT"), skipping the "BPT," the best practicable standard for new sources. It is an example of technology forcing that also serves an important economic purpose because it is a great deal more expensive to retrofit old equipment to meet a more advanced standard than it is to impose the new, higher standard from the very beginning. Thus, new sources must attain the higher standard more quickly than older sources, but are saved the substantial expense of retrofitting older environmental equipment.

Decisions Under the 1970 Act

The new source standard requirement of the Clean Air Act, as enacted in 1970, differed from the 1977 amendment in some detail though not in its major requirements. The original standard was interpreted in *Portland Cement Association v. Ruckelshaus*[132] and *Essex Chemical Corporation v. Ruckelshaus.*[133] In both of these cases, the court first had to dispose of the assertion that the Administrator was under an obligation to file an environmental impact statement under NEPA before he could promulgate new source standards. This

[128] CAA § 111(d)(1), 42 U.S.C. § 7411(d)(1).

[129] CAA § 111(d)(2), 42 U.S.C. § 7411(d)(2).

[130] CAA § 111(j).

[131] *See* F. Grad, Treatise on Environmental Law, § 2.03[14][a].

[132] 486 F.2d 375 (D.C. Cir. 1973).

[133] 486 F.2d 427 (D.C. Cir. 1973).

assertion was rejected on the basis of an examination of the legislative history and a consideration of the purposes to be met by an environmental impact statement. In both of the cases, decided by the District of Columbia Circuit, the challenge to the new source regulations promulgated by the Administrator was based in part on the allegation that he had failed to take into account the costs of achieving the emission reductions he had prescribed, as required by § 111 of the Clean Air Act. In *Portland Cement Association,* it appeared that the Administrator had in fact found that in a wet process plant with a capacity of 2.5 million barrels per day, the total investment for air pollution control equipment required by the new standards would represent approximately 12% of the investment of the total facility. In addition, the Administrator had found that operating costs for the control equipment would be approximately 7% of total plant operating costs if a so-called "bag house" was used on the kiln, and 5% if an electrostatic precipitator was used. Petitioner cement companies argued that the Administrator, under the law, did not merely have to determine the costs but that he was also obliged to prepare a quantified cost-benefit analysis showing the benefit to ambient air measured against the cost of pollution control devices. In both instances, the court ruled that the Administrator had adequately taken economic costs into account and that the kind of detailed, sophisticated cost-benefit analysis sought by petitioners was not required under the Act, particularly in light of the time constraints imposed upon the Administrator in the promulgation of the regulations.

Other questions raised by the petitioner relating to costs included the possible effect of the standards on the future of wet process plants generally, the use of electrostatic precipitators as a control device, and the possible unfair discrimination between standards set for cement plants and those set for power plants and incinerators. As to the issue of the effect of the standards on future establishment of cement factories and the exclusion of electrostatic precipitators, the court, though not basing its remand on this issue, declared that the Administrator should consider as a matter of economic costs the allegation that the standards as adopted had an adverse effect on the supply of cement and had an adverse effect as to certain qualities, areas, or low-cost supplies. On the issue of the comparison of standards between cement plants and power plants and incinerators, the court noted that the standards set for cement plants were indeed more stringent than those set for power plants and incinerators but concluded that the Administrator is not under any obligation to provide justifications for setting different standards for different industries. In the court's view, Congress had not anticipated such an inter-industry comparison and, moreover, the court noted that the technology for the control of pollution from cement plants was considerably more advanced than the control technology for power plants and incinerators. The court noted, however, that there was a proper scope for inter-industry comparisons in the case of industries producing substitute or alternative products, since such a comparison would have a bearing on the issue of economic costs.

On the economic issue, *Essex Chemical* relied on and followed the *Portland Cement* case.

Another issue dealt with in both cases involved the achievability of the proposed emission standard. Section 111 of the Clean Air Actrequires the standard of performance to reflect the degree of emission limitation achievable through the best system of emission reduction (taking cost into account) which the Administrator determines has been adequately demonstrated. The Portland Cement Company contended that the standard had not been adequately demonstrated, challenging both the procedures followed by the agency in arriving at its standards and the scientific evidence on which it was based. In *Portland Cement Association,* the court undertook a detailed review of the manufacturing processes, both wet and dry, in the cement industry and examined the question of the achievability of the Administrator's emission standards in light of available technology. Relying on legislative history, and particularly on the relevant Senate Committee Report, the court indicated that the technology need not be "in actual routine use somewhere" in order to be considered achievable. In the court's view, "the essential question was whether the technology would be available for installation in new plants."[134] Relying on a standard of proof analogous to the one examined in *International Harvester,*[135] the court held that the Administrator may make a projection based on existing technology, which projection, however, is subject to restraints of reasonableness and cannot be based on "crystal ball"[136] inquiry. The court also showed awareness that availability is oftentimes a matter of the lead-time to make existing technology available for actual use. In light of this analysis, it becomes essential that the petitioner have access to test results and procedures which formed the basis for the Administrator's standards. Moreover, it becomes essential that the petitioner have access to the assumptions and theoretical projections on which the Administrator's standard-setting was based.

The court found that the Administrator had not given adequate access to test results and methodology to the petitioner and had therefore failed to give the petitioner any realistic, adequate opportunity to comment although some of the test results had indeed been made available so late in the process as to deny them any realistic opportunity to respond. In one instance, in which the court had, on earlier remand, ordered the agency to include the testimony of one of petitioner's experts in its record, the Administrator had in fact done so, but had failed to respond to this expert's testimony in any way. While refusing to establish the principle that EPA must respond to every comment made by manufacturers on the validity of its standards or on the methodology and scientific basis for their formulation, the court nonetheless indicated that in this instance its prior remand reflected the potential significance of this witness's testimony, and that in this instance there was indeed a burden on the Administrator to review this very significant scientific information, particularly since the witness, on the basis of extensive mathematical calculations, had stated that the emissions from a particular plant reported by the Administrator were grossly erroneous.

The court then proceeded to examine in considerable detail the tests made to support the new source standards for cement plants promulgated by the Administrator. Included in the court's review were the question of the adequacy of the number of tests performed, the details of the sampling

[134] 486 F.2d at 391.

[135] International Harvester v. Ruckelshaus, 478 F.2d 615 (D.C. Cir. 1973).

[136] 486 F.2d at 391.

technique used and the accuracy of the measurement process. Other matters considered were the concern of the manufacturer for start-up and upset conditions due to plan or emission device malfunctioning which, in the petitioner's view, had not been properly taken into account. The court, moreover, indicated that EPA had failed to cite specifically any findings in the literature of the field that are relied upon in its promulgation of standards.

Another significant issue on which remand to the agency was based was the promulgation by the Administrator of a 10% opacity standard. The petitioner challenged the standard on the grounds that such 10% opacity measurements cannot be made with any reasonable accuracy. The court remanded on this issue for a showing and explanation that such measurements can be made, particularly in light of the fact that states which maintain opacity standards for emissions set the opacity standard at least at a 20% standard, corresponding to No. 1 on the Ringelman smoke chart. The court's question on the opacity issue is most significant, because many state laws rely on visual observation and the use of the Ringelman smoke chart in the enforcement of air pollution control standards.

In remanding, the court reiterated the standard of judicial review which it had first articulated in the *International Harvester*[137] case. Though asserting that it would not substitute its judgment for that of the technically expert agency, and though asserting its diffidence in approaching problems of technical complexity, the court nonetheless asserts that it is under an obligation to consider whether the agency's decision was based on a consideration of the relevant factors and whether there had been a clear error of judgment. The court acknowledges that it "requires enough steeping in technical matters" to determine whether the agency has indeed exercised a reasoned discretion. Thus it appears that the burden is on the Administrator, upon a challenge by the petitioner, to show that his procedure and technical basis for determination support his conclusion as an exercise of reasoned discretion.

The *Essex Chemical*[138] case largely followed *Portland Cement Association* with respect to the issue of costs and the further issue of the adequacy of the opacity standard. In dealing with the standards set by the Administrator for sulfuric acid plants and coal-fired steam generators, the court again reviewed the technical evidence submitted in considerable detail, and concluded that with some exceptions the standards set met the requirement of reasoned discretion. The court, however, remanded for further examination of the reasonableness of the opacity standard and for the consideration of an absolute standard which was never to be exceeded, in light of problems of start-up, shut-down and equipment malfunction, when lesser standards should properly apply.

Another issue giving rise to remand was the question whether § 111 of the Clean Air Actrequires the Administrator, when he makes his "best system" and "achievable limitation" determination, to take into account counterproductive environmental effects. The record, in the court's view, did not show

[137] International Harvester v. Ruckelshaus, 478 F.2d 615 (D.C. Cir. 1973).

[138] Essex Chemical Corp. v. Ruckelshaus, 486 F.2d 427 (D.C. Cir. 1973).

whether the Administrator had indeed taken such counterproductive environmental effects into account in the case of recycled-acid plants. It had been shown that a major sulfuric acid plant of this kind operating at capacity would produce a very substantial amount of waste in even a single day of operation, and while a scrubber would effectively cut air emissions, it would have very considerable water pollution effects. The court relied on the dictum in *Portland Cement Association* that "we cannot imagine that Congress intended that 'best' would apply to a system which would do more damage to water than it prevented to air."[139] A similar problem with respect to lack of consideration of counterproductive environmental consequences was noted, and caused the remand of the case to the Administrator for further consideration, in the instance of the coal-fired steam generation standards.

After the Administrator's response to the remand order, the Portland Cement Association petitioned the court to determine whether the Administrator had complied with the remand order and whether the standards should be affirmed or set aside. Upon remand, EPA had reconsidered the use of opacity standards and concluded that they are a reliable, inexpensive and useful means of insuring that control equipment is properly maintained and operated at times when performance tests are not being conducted. EPA also made certain changes in the general provisions and opacity test method to minimize the possibility that a plant which meets applicable emission or concentration standards and is properly maintained and operated may nonetheless violate the applicable opacity standard. The changes were made applicable to new fossil fuel-fired steam generators and all other sources for which opacity standards have been promulgated or proposed under § 111. The court found that the Administrator had complied with the remand order and upheld the use of plume opacity as a measure of pollution or as an aid in controlling emissions.[140]

---

[139] 486 F.2d at 439, quoting from 486 F.2d at 386.

[140] Portland Cement Ass'n v. Ruckelshaus, 513 F.2d 506 (D.C. Cir. 1975). "EPA reviewed its standards for these plants pursuant to the remand and tentatively concluded that the standards other than the opacity standard should not be revised." Draft response to remand order, 40 Fed. Reg. 42045 (Sept. 10, 1975). As to the opacity standards, EPA considered only those aspects not covered in the Portland Cement response which are specifically addressed to fossil fuel-fired steam generators. As a result of these court actions, the regulations in 40 C.F.R. Part 60 were revised as follows: (a) Method 9 (the opacity test method) has been changed to base compliance on the average of one or more sets of 24 consecutive observations; (b) Method 9 now defines the possible error associated with a set of opacity observations; and (c) § 60.11(e) has been added to provide a generally applicable mechanism allowing any owner or operator to petition the Administrator for a higher opacity standard for any facility that demonstrates compliance with the mass emission standard concurrent with failure to attain the promulgated opacity standard.

NATIONAL LIME ASSOCIATION v. EPA

United States Court of Appeals, D.C. Circuit (1980)
627 F.2d 416

[The D.C. Circuit closely followed the methodology of *Portland Cement Association* in the first review of new source performance standards for particulate emissions under the 1977 Act. The court noted that the 1977 Act stressed "achievability" as did the 1970 law (adding only the requirements of *continuous* emission reduction and consideration of non-air health and environmental impact). The court, in a lengthy and technically detailed opinion, remanded to EPA because it had not demonstrated achievability in the variety of plants and technological settings of the lime industry, as to different control systems—bag house, precipitators, wet scrubbers—and as to such factors as particle size, depending on the nature of the feedstock and the nature of the heat source. The court found that the industry's failure to cooperate in the standard setting process, though regrettable, did not relieve EPA's burden to demonstrate achievability.]

IV. ASSESSMENT OF THE OBJECTIONS RAISED BY THE INDUSTRY

Our review has led us to conclude that the record does not support the "achievability" of the promulgated standards for the industry as a whole.[141]

---

[141] An achievable standard need not be one already routinely achieved in the industry. *Essex Chemical*, 486 F.2d at 433-34, *citing Portland Cement I*. But, to be achievable, we think a uniform standard must be capable of being met under most adverse conditions which can reasonably be expected to recur and which are not or cannot be taken into account in determining the "costs" of compliance.

The statutory standard is one of achievability, given costs. Some aspects of "achievability" cannot be divorced from consideration of "costs." Typically one associates "costs" with the capital requirements of new technology. *See e.g., AFL-CIO v. Marshall*, 617 F.2d 636, 659 (D.C.Cir. 1979). However, certain "costs" (*e.g.*, frequent systemic shutdown to service emissions control systems or use of feedstock of a certain size or composition in order to meet the new emissions standards) are more intimately intertwined with "achievability" than are the capital costs of new technology. In this case the lime industry attacks the standards as "unachievable." When questioned at oral argument, counsel for petitioner disclaimed any attack upon the expense of implementation, stating that he attacked the achievability of the standard "on any reliably repetitive basis," "because of the very variables in the production of lime." This necessarily asserts that a standard which does not account for certain routine variations in conditions is "unachievable." We agree, where, as here, there is no evidence in the record that the "costs" of adjusting for such routine variations (assuming such adjustments be possible) were considered by the Agency in promulgating its standard.

The EPA has expressly built some flexibility into the enforcement end of the new source performance standards, 40 C.F.R. § 60.8(c)(1979) (relating to startup, shutdown and malfunction) and is vested with a more general enforcement discretion, but the flexibility appropriate to enforcement will not render "achievable" a standard which cannot be achieved on a regular basis, either for the reasons expressly taken into account in compliance determination regulations (here startup, shutdown and malfunction), or otherwise. *Cf. Portland Cement I*, 486 F.2d at 398 n.91 and see discussion *infra* text

This conclusion is a cumulative one, resulting from our assessment of the many points raised by the industry at the administrative level and in this court;[142] no one point made is so cogent that remand would necessarily have followed on that basis alone.[143] In the analysis that follows, common threads

at notes 111-15. In this connection the Congress' new concern that emissions control systems operate continuously, *see* 42 U.S.C. § 7411(a)(1)(Supp. I 1977) and discussion *infra*, note 54, is pertinent.

Because we remand for the development of a more adequate rationale for the promulgated standards we do not now specify the kinds of variations in conditions—not accounted for in the Agency's cost analysis—which might render a uniform standard "unachievable" or so "unachievable" as to represent an arbitrary or capricious exercise of the Administrator's discretion under the Act.

142 A myriad of objections were raised by the industry to the Agency's test methodology, analysis of data and conclusions. Our scrutiny of the record has revealed that some of these objections have merit. Those objections we consider meritorious are incorporated in the analysis that follows. The remainder are not discussed.

143 In addition to the points made in connection with the achievability of the standard, NLA disputes EPA's determination that lime manufacturing plants "may contribute significantly to air pollution which causes or contributes to the endangerment of public health or welfare." 42 U.S.C. § 1857c-6(b)(1)(A)(1976) (repealed 1977).

EPA considers the significant production of particulate emissions itself to cause or contribute to air pollution (which may reasonably be anticipated to endanger public health or welfare). The Agency has made this determination for purposes of establishing national primary and secondary ambient air quality standards under § 109 of the Clean Air Act,now codified at 42 U.S.C. § 7408(Supp. I 1977), and without regard to the harmful or beneficial effect of the material of which the particulate is composed. 36 Fed.Reg. 1502, 8137, 8138 (1971). When ambient air quality standards for particulate were first proposed, the Agency described some of the health effects of particulate matter:

> Particulate matter of technological origin is pervasive in its distribution and is associated with a variety of adverse effects on public health and welfare. Particulate matter in the respiratory tract may produce injury by itself, or it may act in conjunction with gases, altering their sites or their mode of action. Particles cleared from the respiratory tract by transfer to the lymph, blood, or gastrointestinal tract may produce effects elsewhere in the body.
>
> Detailed information on particulate matter is presented in the document "Air Quality Criteria for Particulate Matter" (NAPCA Publication No. AP-49), which provided a basis for the development of the standards set forth below.

36 Fed.Reg. 1502 (1971). . . .

The MRI [Midwest Research Institute, Particulate Pollutant System Study] Report, considered by EPA in developing the proposed standard, observes that lime dust can raise the pH of water bodies. MRI Report 22. However, EPA does not appear to have relied on this effect of the lime emissions in support of its standard. It focused instead on the sheer quantity of dust generated by lime plants. 42 Fed.Reg. 22507 ("A study performed for EPA in 1975 by the Research Corporation of New England ranked the lime industry twenty-fifth on a list of 112 stationary sources categories which are emitters of particulate matter"); SSEIS 8-2 ("In a study performed for EPA by Argonne National Laboratory in 1975, the lime industry ranked seventh on a list of the 56 largest particulate source categories in the U.S.").

The industry's argument rests on the asserted nontoxicity of lime dust.

> In spite of a few expressed opinions, maybe more than a few, that lime dust under certain unspecified conditions might be suspect or might be harmful to the respiratory system, there is overwhelming counter evidence that lime is not toxic or unhealthy, except under extremely concentrated conditions. It is simply a nuisance dust.

R. 139, 18, App. 200. *See also* R. 140, 56, App. 301. NLA argues the innocuousness or even benign effect of lime emissions and concludes that "the statement that lime endangers health should be stricken from this EPA document." R. 139, 19, App. 201. The fact that lime dust reacts with and traps SO_2 emissions leads NLA to continue, "A more plausible case could be made that the presence of a low concentration of lime particles in the air could actually be beneficial in minimizing so-called acid rains, neutralizing molecules of airborn acid gases, will be discerned in our discussions of individual points. Chief among these common threads is a concern that the Agency consider the representativeness for the industry as a whole of the tested plants on which it relies, at least where its central argument is that the standard *is* achievable because it *has* been achieved (at the tested plants). The Agency's failure to consider the representativeness—along various relevant parameters—of the data relied upon is the primary reason for our remand. The locus of administrative burdens of going forward or of persuasion may shift in the course of a rulemaking proceeding, but we think an initial burden of promulgating and explaining a non-arbitrary, non-capricious rule rests with the Agency and we think that by failing to explain how the standard proposed is achievable under the range of relevant conditions which may affect the emissions to be regulated, the Agency has not satisfied this initial burden.

Bearing this initial burden will involve first, identifying and verifying as relevant or irrelevant specific variable conditions that may contribute substantially to the amount of emissions, or otherwise affect the efficiency of the emissions control systems considered. And second, where test results are relied upon, it should involve the selection or use of test results in a manner which provides some assurance of the achievability of the standard for the

---

like SO_2 and NO_x into harmless compounds." R. 139, 19, App. 201.

We think the danger of particulate emissions' effect on health has been sufficiently supported in the Agency's (and its predecessor's) previous determinations to provide a rational basis for the Administrator's finding in this case. *See* Air Quality Criteria for Particulate Matter, *supra*. Moreover, whatever its impact on public health, we cannot say that a dust "nuisance" has no impact on public welfare. Congress has provided that with respect to the Clean Air Act:

> All language referring to effects on welfare includes, but is not limited to, effects on soils, water, crops, vegetation, manmade materials, animals, wildlife, weather, visibility, and climate, damage to and deterioration of property, and hazards to transportation, as well as effects on economic values and on personal comfort and well-being.

42 U.S.C. § 7602(h)(Supp. I 1977); 42 U.S.C. § 1857h(h)(1976) (repealed 1977) (same). Thus, we could not say that the Administrator's determination is arbitrary, even if the dust were shown innocuous to public health.

The Administrator's assessment of a pollutant's danger to public health or welfare

> involves questions which are "particularly prone to uncertainty," and as a result "the statute accords the [Administrator] flexibility to assess [those] risks and make essentially legislative policy judgments. . . ." *Ethyl Corp. v. EPA*, 176 U.S.App.D.C. 373, 541 F.2d 1, 24, 26 (1976), *cert. denied*, 426 U.S. 941, 96 S.Ct. 2663, 49 L.Ed.2d 394 (1976). These policy choices "are not susceptible to the same type of verification or refutation by reference to the record as are some factual questions," *Industrial Union Department, AFL-CIO v. Hodgson*, 162 U.S.App.D.C. 331, 499 F.2d 467, 475 (1974), and consequently are not subject to review with the "substantive rigor proper for questions of fact," *Ethyl Corp. v. EPA, supra*, 541 F.2d 1 at 24. Instead, our "paramount objective is to see whether the agency, given an essentially legislative task to perform, has carried it out in a manner calculated to negate the dangers of arbitrariness and irrationality in the formulation of rules for general application in the future." *Automotive Parts and Accessories Ass'n, Inc. v. Boyd*, 132 U.S.App.D.C. 200, 407 F.2d 330, 338 (1968).

Nat'l Asphalt, 539 F.2d at 783-84. Our conclusion in *Nat'l Asphalt* is equally applicable here:

> Particulate matter poses enough of a threat to public health to warrant the promulgation of air quality standards—which are aimed at reducing existing levels of particulate matter—and we have no basis on this record to dispute the Administrator's decision that there is a need to prevent further deterioration of "clean air" by establishing additional national standards of performance for particulate matter.

Id. at 784.

industry as a whole, given the range of variable factors found relevant to the standards' achievability.

EPA itself acknowledged in this case that "standards of performance . . . must . . . meet these conditions for *all variations of operating conditions being considered* anywhere in the country." SSEIS 2-6 (emphasis supplied). As set forth in the standards support statement, EPA's guidelines require data to be assessed with consideration of the "representativeness" of the source tested, including the "feedstock, operation, size and age" of the source. SSEIS at 2-7. Furthermore, the record strongly suggests other factors that may affect the particulate emissions from lime plants. Yet at no point does EPA evaluate the relevance or irrelevance of such factors to regulable emissions; nor does the Agency explain how such factors might have been taken into account in choosing test plant sites or in analyzing the data from the sites it chose.

The critical question presented here is whether the regulated industry, through its trade association, should have borne the entire burden of demonstrating the unreliability for the industry as a whole of the conclusions drawn by the EPA. In this connection we are candidly troubled by the industry's failure to respond, at a crucial juncture in the standards development process, to the Agency's invitation to submit data supporting a fundamental industry objection to the achievability of the standard. We would have expected the industry to have been eager to supply supporting data for its position, assuming the "cost" of obtaining such data were less than the "cost" of compliance with a standard that was argued to be unachievable on any reliably repetitive basis for the industry as a whole. We cannot help but wonder if the industry's failure to supply such data means that the data available or obtained would not be favorable to the industry's position. Nevertheless we remand because we think, on balance, EPA must affirmatively show that its standard reflects consideration of the range of relevant variables that may affect emissions in different plants.

The showing we require does not mean that EPA must perform repeated tests on every plant operating within its regulatory jurisdiction.[144] It does, however, mean that due consideration must be given to the possible impact on emissions of recognized variations in operations and some rationale offered for the achievability of the promulgated standard given the tests conducted and the relevant variables identified. To facilitate public comment,[145] we think this rationale should have appeared in the Agency's initial standards support statement.

[144] It is one thing to generalize from a sample of one when one is the only available sample, or when that one is shown to be representative of the regulated industry along relevant parameters. *See, e.g., Essex Chemical*, 486 F.2d at 438. It is another thing altogether to generalize from an extremely limited sample when a broader sample (both different conditions at the same plant and conditions at different plants) can be readily obtained and when no showing of the representativeness of the sample is made. *See, e.g., Ethyl Corp. v. EPA*, 541 F.2d 1, 38 (D.C.Cir.) (*en banc*), *cert. denied*, 426 U.S. 941, 96 S.Ct. 2663, 49 L.Ed.2d 394 (1976); *Int'l Harvester Co. v. Ruckelshaus*, 478 F.2d at 625, 642.

[145] *See Portland Cement I*, 486 F.2d at 394: "In order that rule-making proceedings to determine standards be conducted in orderly fashion, information should generally be disclosed as to the basis of a proposed rule at the time of its issuance."

We must remand to the Agency for a more adequate explanation or, if necessary, for supplementary data to justify the standard in terms of the "representativeness" of the sources tested. The specific doubts generated by our review of the record in light of the lime industry's attack on the standard are more fully explained below.[146]

A. *The Particulate Emission Standards*

1. *Rotary Kilns*

EPA tested emissions at six plants[147] before it proposed its mass emission standard for rotary lime kilns. These six plants were selected for testing on the basis of visits to thirty-nine plants, during which the visibility of emission was observed and information obtained on the emissions control systems employed.[148] The thirty-nine plants were themselves selected because they

[146] Our review of the 1977 Clean Air Act Amendments has generated additional doubts. For example, in the development of these NSPS, EPA appears to have given no consideration to the new requirement that NSPS be achievable under systems of *continuous* emission control. 42 U.S.C. § 7411(Supp. I 1977). Addition of the word "continuous" in 1977 was meant to ban the use of "intermittent" controls. H.R.Rep. No. 294, 95th Cong., 1st Sess. 190 (1977), *reprinted in* 4 Legislative History at 2657. (House intent to ban intermittent control measures for new stationary sources under § 111); H.R. Conf.Rep. No. 564, 95th Cong., 1st Sess. 129 (1977), *reprinted in* 3 Legislative History at 509 (same); *Id.* at 130, 3 Legislative History at 510 (Senate concurrence in House intent). The "intermittent" controls that concerned Congress were any of those which entailed temporary reductions in emissions when weather conditions were poor. H.R.Rep. No. 294, 95th Cong., 1st Sess. 81 (1977), *reprinted in* 4 Legislative History at 2548 (speaking of intermittent controls as those which temporarily reduce or defer emissions when meteorological conditions adversely affect emissions dispersion); *Id.* at 86, 4 Legislative History at 2553 (describing an intermittent control system which reduced the load of a generator during peak pollution periods); *Kennecott Copper Corp. v. Train*, 526 F.2d 1149, 1155 (9th Cir. 1975), *cited in* H.R.Rep. No. 294, 95th Cong., 1st Sess. 82 (1977), *reprinted in* 4 Legislative History at 2549 (characterizing temporary use of low sulfur fuel during adverse conditions as "intermittent"). But it is not clear that in requiring systems of "continuous" emission reduction the Congress banned only deliberate reductions in emissions when weather conditions were poor.

There are some indications that the 1977 Amendments were intended to prohibit *all* averaging to determine compliance where continuous emission reduction systems were specified. *See* H.R.Rep. No. 294, 95th Cong., 1st Sess. 92, *reprinted in* 4 Legislative History at 2559, U.S. Code Cong. & Admin. News 1977, p. 1170 ("Any emission limitation under the Clean Air Act, therefore must be met on a constant basis, not on an 'averaging' basis. . . . The 'averaging' method is not allowable, precisely because it cannot provide assurances that the emission limitation will be met at all times."); 123 Cong.Rec. H8662, H8664 (daily ed. Aug. 4, 1977) (statement of intent with respect to Conference Committee substitute, referring to NSPS for fossil-fuel fired boilers) ("No averaging in fuel content or in emissions content or levels [will be] allowed in determining whether the prescribed performance standard will be met by a source."). . . .

[147] The plants are identified in the support statement only by letter. The plants (and the methods of emissions control they employ) are as follows: Plant A (baghouse); Plant B (baghouse); Plant C (ESP); Plant D (ESP); Plant E (baghouse); Plant F (scrubber).

The tests were conducted under EPA's "Method 5" for the measurement of particulate emissions. Method 5 consists of withdrawal of sample emissions by means of a probe inserted into the wall of a smokestack, through which sample emissions are withdrawn by means of a pump set to correspond to the velocity of the air within the stack. 40 C.F.R. Part 60, App. A (1979).

[148] The six rotary kiln plants selected for testing were those "deemed to employ best systems of emission reduction." SSEIS A-1. This determination was based both on informa-

had been identified as effectively controlled after a review of the literature and contact with industry representatives. SSEIS A-1. The results of the tests of one plant (Plant A) which could not meet the proposed standard were excluded from consideration because the plant was thought not to represent best technology.[149] From what we can gather from the record, three plants were able to meet the standard consistently.[150]

Our doubts about the representativeness of the data relied upon are grouped under three subheadings below: *Variations in Quantity of Particulate Generated in the Kiln; Variations in Controllability of Particulate Generated;* and *Explanation of Discarded Data from Plants A and F.* Under the subheading *Variations in Quantity of Particulate Generated in the Kiln*, we discuss the possible impact on the standard's achievability of composite dust levels generated by the tested plants and two factors (feedstock variations and gas velocity) that may contribute to composite dust levels. Under the subheading *Variations in Controllability of Particulate Generated*, we discuss two factors—apart from sheer quantity of dust—that may affect emissions control: coal usage and particulate size. Finally under the subheading *Explanation of Discarded Data from Plants A and F*, we discuss the EPA's handling of the results of two tested plants that were unable to meet the standards proposed.

. . . .

B. *The Opacity Standard and Continuous Monitoring Requirement*

1. *The Opacity Standard*

"Opacity" is defined by regulation to mean "the degree to which emissions reduce the transmission of light and obscure the view of an object in the background." 40 C.F.R. § 60.2(j)(1979). EPA explains that "[t]he opacity level of visible emissions is an indication of the mass concentration of a particular pollutant" and that "[v]arious studies have shown that opacity varies directly with mass concentrations of particulate matter." SSEIS 8-19. EPA considers opacity standards to be "a necessary supplement to particulate mass emission standards" basically because "[o]pacity test methods are quicker, easier to

---

tion obtained during the initial visit "on the process and the equipment used to control emissions," *id.*, and on an evaluation of the visibility of emissions. *Id.* That emission visibility factored into the selection of plants for more thorough testing seems clear from EPA's explanation at oral argument of the reasons why Plant A was selected for testing. Counsel for the Agency explained: "I believe . . . that it was reported to the Agency that A was a well-controlled plant and that persons had observed no visible emissions at all from the Plant A stacks, which seemed to be an indication it was well controlled."

[149] SSEIS 8-17. The Plant A test results and the rationale for their exclusion from consideration are discussed below, text at note 91. One of the five considered (Plant F) was, like Plant A, thought not to represent best technology, 42 Fed.Reg. 22507 (1977), but the results of these tests were presented, if not treated, differently in the Standards Support Statement. *See* SSEIS C-12 (Table C-1 including Plant F data but excluding data from Plant A).

[150] Plant D did not consistently meet the standard. The Plant F test results did not meet the standard at all. EPA concluded that Plant F, controlled by a low-pressure scrubber, did not represent best technology but that a higher pressure scrubber would be able to meet the proposed standard. 42 Fed. Reg. 22507 (1977). Plant A, excluded from consideration in standard development, was also unable to meet the standard. SSEIS 8-17.

apply, and less costly than concentration/mass tests for particulate matter." SSEIS 8-19.

The performance standards prescribed by EPA for rotary lime kilns consist of both a mass emission standard (grams of particulate emission per gram of feed) and an opacity standard (ten percent). 43 Fed. Reg. 9453 (1978). Only those kilns using dry methods of emissions control are subject to the ten percent opacity standard. As previously noted, no opacity standard was promulgated for lime hydrators (which almost never employ dry control methods) and rotary kilns using wet scrubbers have been exempted from compliance with the opacity standard.

We have considered the various arguments made by the NLA and conclude that EPA's apparent failure to consider in this case some variables which were (1) given more careful consideration in the promulgation of earlier opacity standards and (2) given inadequate consideration in the companion mass emission standard requires us to remand the opacity standard to the Administrator for additional explanation or for revision.[151]

a. *Variables Considered in the Promulgation of Earlier Opacity Standards*

On remand from *Portland Cement I*, 486 F.2d 375, the Administrator undertook extensive reconsideration of both the opacity standard proposed for portland cement plants and the methodology (EPA's "Method 9," 40 C.F.R. Part 60, App. A (1979)) of opacity measurement.[152] In the year and a half that followed, the methodology was revised and the standard set for portland cement plants was raised from ten to twenty percent.[153] EPA has explained its relaxation of the portland cement standard as an effort to accommodate the complete range of available data obtained in that case, having adjusted the data for stack diameter. SSEIS II, 13. Stack diameter was thus a variable

151 NLA makes a three-pronged attack on the opacity standard. First, it argues the inherent inaccuracy of opacity testing. Second, it points to the discrepancies between the 10% standard promulgated here and the 20% standard promulgated for portland cement and asphalt concrete plants. Third, it notes EPA's failure to abide by its stated methodology in standard-development testing.

Our conclusion to remand the standard derives in part from our examination of the materials drawn to our attention by the industry in connection with the first two prongs of the industry's attack and in part from our conclusion with respect to the mass emission standard above.

We reject the third prong of the industry's attack—EPA's failure to abide by its own "Method 9" in obtaining the test results on which the standard is based. The articles concerning opacity testing submitted by the NLA themselves demonstrate that in most cases the alleged failure to abide by the standards would have had the effect of overestimating rather than underestimating opacity. That is, EPA's mistakes would have laid the basis for a standard which was easier, not harder, to achieve by the industry.

152 EPA, Response to Remand, 85-125.

153 *See* 38 Fed.Reg. 28564 (1973) (opacity standards will not apply to emissions during periods of startup, shutdown and malfunction); 39 Fed.Reg. 39872 (1974) (raising opacity standard from 10% to 20% for portland cement plants, providing some weight may be given in enforcement to discrepant transmissometer readings, adding sort of variance procedure for plants that meet performance but not opacity standards, providing that accuracy of method must be taken into account in enforcement, specifying average of 24 readings at 15 second intervals for enforcement purposes and specifying observer position with respect to both sun and plume).

for which EPA made adjustments in the portland cement case but it was not the only variable considered in formulating that standard. It is clear that the possible impact of other variables were also taken into account on remand, including: particle size and shape, EPA Response to Remand 112;[154] and stack gas exit velocities, *id.* 116.

The impact of variations in particle size and shape were also considered by EPA in evaluating an opacity standard for asphalt concrete plants.[155] It is this difference in Agency methodology underlying the various new source opacity standards and not the difference in the standards themselves that gives us most pause.[156] No attention to particle size and shape appears to

---

[154] In responding to the contentions of the Portland cement industry on remand from *Portland Cement I*, EPA stated a general principle that plume opacity varies with the size of the particles emitted. The industry there argued

> that opacity varies with particle size and shape, so that a given mass concentration of particles—which could be composed of various combinations of different size and shape particles—could result in differing opacities. *EPA agrees that this correctly states the theory of plume transmittance (opacity) as it relates to particle dimensions.*

Id. (emphasis supplied). Having conceded this principle, EPA supported its standard as follows:

> In typical high efficiency collector exhaust gases there are generally few particulates larger than 40 microns diameter. The predominant number of particles are between 0.5 and 10 microns with the average size being about 2-4 microns. Maximum light scattering is generally acknowledged to be caused by particles in the size range of 0.2 to 2.0 microns. Available data indicate that the size distribution of particulates released from well controlled cement kilns are similar within a narrow range (approximately 2 to 6 microns) from one kiln to another, and therefore from one plant to another.
>
> What the above data and studies indicate, in short, is that the size of particles emitted by plants with such control equipment varies only within a very narrow range. This variability in average size is theoretically not sufficient to cause more than a ± 5 percent variation in opacity for typical cement kilns.

Id. at 113 (footnotes omitted).

Variations in particle size were thus considered and found not to warrant a change in the opacity standard. Whether such variations were attributable to different *feed composition* is not clear.

[155] *See* EPA, Reevaluation of Standards of Performance for Asphalt Concrete Plants 4 (Nov. 1974):

> The opacity standard applicable to asphalt concrete plants has been established at a level (less than 20 percent) such that, taking into account all of the variations in particle size, shape and stack size encountered by asphalt concrete plants, violation of the opacity standard is indicative of a violation of the mass standard.

(The opacity standard for asphalt concrete plants, originally promulgated in March 1974, 39 Fed.Reg. 9307 (1974), was affirmed by this court in *Nat'l Asphalt*, 539 F.2d 775 (1976).)

[156] That different industries may be subject to different standards and that the Administrator need not bear the burden of explaining those differences is clear.

> [T]he Administrator is not required to present affirmative justifications for different standards in different industries. Inter-industry comparisons of this kind are not generally required, or even productive; and they were not contemplated by Congress in this Act. The essential question is whether the mandated standards can be met by a particular industry for which they are set, and this can typically be decided on the basis of information concerning that industry alone. This is not to say that evidence collected about the functioning of emission devices in one industry may not have implications for another. Certainly such information may bear on technological capability. But there is no requirement of uniformity of specific standards for all industries. The Administrator applied the same general approach, of ascertaining for each industry what was feasible in that industry. It would be unmanageable if, in reviewing the cement standards, the court should have to consider whether or not there was a mistake in the incinerator standard, with all the differences in parties, practice, industry procedures, and

have been given by EPA in the preparation of opacity standards for lime plants.[157]

b. *Variables Inadequately Considered in Mass Emission Standard*

Opacity standards are intended to operate in tandem with mass emission standards, notwithstanding their independent enforceability. Ideally, a violation of an opacity standard should indicate a violation of a mass emission standard. *See* SSEIS 8-19. For this reason the Agency relies on data from the same test plants to support both the opacity and the mass emission standard; but for this reason when the representativeness of data relied upon for one standard is inadequately shown, the representativeness of data relied upon for the other standard is drawn in question.

As discussed above, the Agency failed to consider the representativeness of the particle size produced at its tested plants. This failure is particularly striking in connection with the opacity standard because variations in particle size have been given careful consideration in the development of earlier opacity standards.

We have already noted that the emissions control systems favored by the standards and by prevailing economic and technological trends may operate more efficiently when the predominant size of particulate emissions is large. As it happens, large particulate is also likely to appear less opaque. Thus, it is possible that a plant would meet both standards only because the particles emitted are uniformly large and we cannot ascertain how the plants tested here "measure up."[158]

c. *EPA's Arguments*

Both in this court and at the administrative level EPA emphasizes the overwhelming extent to which the plants tested were able to meet the ten percent opacity standard.[159] But without knowing the representativeness of

record for decision. Of course, the standard for another industry can be attacked, as too generous, and hence arbitrary or unsupported on the record, by those concerned with excessive pollution by that industry. There is, therefore, an avenue of judicial review and correction if the agency does not proceed in good faith to implement its general approach. But this is different from the supposition that a claim to the same specific treatment can be advanced by one who is in neither the same nor a competitive industry.

Portland Cement I, 486 F.2d at 389-90.

157 EPA contends that NLA did not make such an objection at the administrative level. Brief for Respondent at 28. EPA's contention is refuted by the record. EPA's failure to consider particle size and shape was raised both in connection with the opacity standard, R. 139, 14, App. 196, and in connection with the mass emission standard.

158 It is possible that the plants tested here were in effect selected for their large particle size. Thirty-nine plants thought to be "well controlled" were visited by EPA and six were selected from among these for testing because of their low level of visible emissions. As already noted, larger particles produce less visible emissions.

159 Of six-minute average readings "normalized" for stack diameter, "[o]ver 67 percent of the six-minute averages were equal to zero and over 82 percent of the averages were less than or equal to five percent opacity. Only 0.4 percent of the normalized averages exceeded 10 percent opacity. The highest single average read was 10.6 percent opacity." SSEIS 8-20; Brief for Respondent at 27. Like EPA, we are puzzled by the NLA's assertion (Brief for Petitioner at 36) that the opacity standard is based

the plants tested or of test conditions, we cannot say that the standard is neither arbitrary nor capricious. Certainly the fact that virtually all plants tested were able to meet the standard is an important consideration, but our doubts are sufficient, when coupled with our doubts concerning the mass emissions standard (discussed above), to remand to the Agency for amplification of the record.

EPA has committed itself to take the possibility of inaccurate opacity measurement into account in the enforcement of the standard.[160] It has also provided a type of "variance" mechanism under which new sources which meet the mass emission standard but which cannot meet the opacity standard may petition the Administrator to establish a separate opacity standard for that facility. 40 C.F.R. § 60.11(e)(1979), 39 Fed.Reg. 39872 (1974). The variance mechanism, however, seems clearly to have been intended to be narrowly construed.[161]

The Agency relies upon the flexibility built into the regulatory scheme to support the rationality of its standards.[162] The wisdom of such flexibility has been applauded on earlier occasions by this court,[163] but the statutory scheme prescribes "achievable" standards and there is a limit to the flexibility with which the Agency is or should be endowed.[164]

We recognize the usefulness of opacity standards as an enforcement tool.[165] Opacity can be monitored by the Agency with little advance warning or costly preparation.[166] We also realize that "[o]pacity standards are not novel . . .

on the test results of only one plant. We presume NLA seeks by this assertion to pin the Agency to its final support statement, SSEIS II at 13, where it examines the test results from Plant D (from which the worst readings were obtained). But it is clear that the Agency does not rely on the results obtained from this one plant in support of its standard. SSEIS 8-19—8-20.

160 Brief for Respondent at 27 n.18; 40 C.F.R. Part 60, App. A (Method 9) (1979): "The accuracy of the method must be taken into account when determining possible violations of applicable opacity standards." The regulations also allow for "excursion" from the standards during periods of startup, shutdown or malfunction. 40 C.F.R. § 60.8(c)(1979).

161 As described when the mechanism was first announced in connection with the portland cement remand:

> This provision is intended primarily to apply to cases where a source installs a very large diameter stack which causes the opacity of the emissions to be greater than if a stack of the diameter ordinarily used in the industry were installed. Although this situation is considered to be very unlikely to occur, this provision will accommodate such a situation. The provision could also apply to other situations where for any reason an affected facility could fail to meet opacity standards while meeting mass emission standards, although no such situations are expected to occur.

39 Fed.Reg. 39872-73 (1974).

162 SSEIS 8-19 (referring to the "variance" mechanism); SSEIS II, 13 (referring to enforcement discretion to accommodate method inaccuracy); Brief for Respondent at 27 n.18 (same).

163 *Portland Cement I*, 486 F.2d at 399; *Int'l Harvester Co. v. Ruckelshaus*, 478 F.2d at 641.

164 *Portland Cement I*, 486 F.2d at 399 n.91: "Companies must be on notice as to what will constitute a violation. Moreover, an excessively broad theory of enforcement discretion might endanger securing compliance with promulgated standards." *Cf. E.I. duPont de Nemours & Co. v. Train*, 430 U.S. 112, 137-39, 97 S.Ct. 965, 51 L.Ed.2d 204 (1977) (variance authority will not be implied in statutory provision for new source effluent discharge standards under Federal Water Pollution Control Act). *But cf. Weyerhaeuser Co. v. Costle*, 590 F.2d 1011, 1056-58 (D.C.Cir. 1978) (Agency may handle "upset" conditions for effluent limitations for existing sources under Federal Water Pollution Control Act by exercising enforcement discretion rather than through "excursion" regulations).

165 *Portland Cement I*, 486 F.2d at 400.

166 *See* 39 Fed.Reg. 9309 (1974).

opacity standards have been upheld previously by this court[167] under closely analogous circumstances . . . [and that] Congress . . . has expressed concern for opacity values in measuring air pollution under the Clean Air Act. . . ." *Alabama Power Co. v. Costle*, No. 78-1006, slip op. at 32, (D.C. Cir. Dec. 17, 1979) (Wilkey, J.), and we do not wish to imply that the Agency cannot justify their use. We remand to the Agency because on this record the reasonableness of the standard has not been demonstrated.

2. *Continuous Monitoring*

On the opacity monitoring requirement, the petitioner's argument is simple: there is no adequately demonstrated technology for monitoring opacity.[168] One company operating affected facilities (Dow Chemical) commented, "We have tried several continuous monitoring systems in the past and have been unable to find an instrument that will suitably do the job and can be maintained in operation." R. 148, App. 327-28. The company cited high opacity readings attributable to instrument malfunctioning "as frequently as twice a day" and also remarked that "[t]he opacity readings [of the monitor] do not relate to the actual stack conditions as measured by visual observers."

EPA answers that the continuous monitoring data would not be used to determine compliance with the opacity standard but "to keep a check on the operation and maintenance of the control equipment," and to trigger performance checks by trained observers. Brief for Respondents at 12-13, *citing* SSEIS 8-24 and standard as proposed (42 Fed.Reg. 22506, 22509 (1977)). The Agency argues that if the equipment gives any "indication" of changed opacity it is enough to justify a continuous monitoring requirement. Brief for Respondents at 29. It dismisses the industry's contention that reliable monitoring equipment is not available to perform this limited a function and shifts the burden to the industry to show "by supporting data," SSEIS II, 13, that it is not.

EPA states that it now routinely requires continuous monitoring of opacity in new source performance standards.[169] Brief for Respondents at 14-15. Opacity

---

[167] *E.g., Portland Cement II*, 513 F.2d at 507, 508-09 (upholding 20% opacity standard against petitioner's arguments that "pollution and plume opacity cannot be reliably correlated and evaluations of the same plume by several qualified observers will vary substantially"); *Nat'l Asphalt*, 539 F.2d at 787 (upholding against challenge to reliability 20% opacity standard for asphalt concrete plants in light of *Portland Cement II's* decision with respect to similar standards).

[168] NLA does not take issue with the quite different continuous monitoring requirements for scrubber-controlled systems. Scrubber-controlled systems are monitored not for opacity but for liquid supply pressure and pressure drop in the scrubber.

[169] 40 C.F.R. § 60.13(1979) governs continuous monitoring requirements. Performance specifications for continuous monitoring equipment are set forth in Appendix B to 40 C.F.R. Part 60 (1979). EPA explained that in this case:

> The visible emissions monitoring systems that are adequate for other stationary sources, such as steam generators, covered by performance specifications contained in Appendix B of 40 C.F.R. [Part] 60 (Federal Register, October 6, 1975) should also be applicable to lime plants, except where condensed moisture is present in the exhaust stream.

SSEIS D-8. Equipment and installation costs for visible emissions monitoring were estimated at $18,000 to $20,000 per site. *Id.* Annual operating costs, including recording of data, were estimated at $8,000 to $9,000 per site. *Id.*

monitoring was first required and performance specifications for monitoring systems prescribed in connection with the NSPS for fossil-fuel fired steam generators and petroleum refineries.[170] As of the date the lime standard was proposed, five other promulgated NSPS included a requirement for the continuous monitoring of opacity.[171] Since the lime standard's proposal, at least one other standard has been promulgated that contains such a requirement.[172] In answer to NLA's observation that no continuous opacity monitoring is required of portland cement plants, R. 139, 14 App. 196, EPA informs the court that the Agency is now reviewing the Portland cement standards pursuant to § 111(b)(1)(B), 42 U.S.C. § 7411(b)(1)(B)(Supp. I 1977) to see if the same requirement should be imposed there. Brief for Respondents at 15.[173]

EPA maintains that it has had considerable experience with the use of continuous monitoring devices and that in its experience a monitor will show if an emissions control device is being properly operated and maintained and the opacity standards met. SSEIS II, 14; SSEIS 8-24. Thus monitoring will act as a needed warning alarm when the control system is out of kilter. SSEIS 8-24.

The industry itself admits there is some value to a continuous monitoring requirement. Dow Chemical took a critical stance (adopted by NLA, Brief for Petitioner at 52) but also acknowledged that monitoring equipment "gives an indication of whether the opacity is increasing or decreasing." R. 148, 2, App. 328. Given this concession, we cannot find the continuous monitoring requirement arbitrary as an adjunct to a non-arbitrary, non-capricious opacity standard. We have today remanded the opacity standard for lime plants. If on remand an opacity standard is retained, EPA may continue to require continuous monitoring.

V. THE STANDARD OF REVIEW AS APPLIED

Our requirement that the EPA consider the representativeness of the test data relied upon in the development and justification of its standard does not presage any new or more stringent standard of judicial review. The rigorousness of the review in which this court has engaged in previous NSPS decisions—known to some as the "hard look" standard[174] —has already been described.

---

[170] 40 Fed.Reg. 46250, 46255, 46256, 46257 (1975).

[171] *See* 40 C.F.R. § 60.165(b)(1)(1979) (primary copper smelters); 40 C.F.R. § 60.175(a)(1)(1979) (primary zinc smelters); 40 C.F.R. § 60.185(a)(1)(1979) (primary lead smelters); 40 C.F.R. § 60.264(a)(1979) (ferroalloy production facilities); 40 C.F.R. § 60.273(a)(1979) (electric arc furnaces in steel mills).

[172] *See* 40 C.F.R. § 60.284(a)(1)(1979) (kraft pulp mills). None of these monitoring requirements has been the subject of judicial review.

[173] On October 22, 1979, EPA announced an intention to require continuous opacity monitoring at portland cement plants, 44 Fed.Reg. 60761 (1979), but the requirement was not then formally proposed.

[174] *E.g.*, Rodgers, *A Hard Look at* Vermont Yankee: *Environmental Law Under Close Scrutiny*, 67 Geo. L.J. 699, 704 (1979) [hereinafter cited as *A Hard Look at* Vermont Yankee]; Breyer, Vermont Yankee *and the Courts' Role in the Nuclear Energy Controversy*, 91 Harv.L.Rev. 1833, 1834 (1978); W. Rodgers, Environmental Law 19 (1977).

The phrase "hard look" derives from Judge

In enacting the Clean Air Act Amendments of 1977, Congress expressly approved the rigorous standard of review which the courts had theretofore applied to Agency decisions under the Clean Air Act.[175] Although the judicial

Leventhal's opinions in *Greater Boston Television Corp. v. FCC*, 444 F.2d 841 (D.C.Cir. 1970), *cert. denied*, 403 U.S. 923, 91 S.Ct. 2229, 29 L.Ed.2d 701 (1971), and *Pike's Peak Broadcasting Co. v. FCC*, 422 F.2d 671 (D.C.Cir.), *cert. denied* 395 U.S. 979, 89 S.Ct. 2134, 23 L.Ed.2d 767 (1969). As originally articulated the words "hard look" described the agency's responsibility and not the court's. However, the phrase subsequently evolved to connote the rigorous standard of judicial review applied to increasingly utilized informal rulemaking proceedings or to other decisions made upon less than a full trial-type record. Judge Leventhal himself used the phrase in this sense in *Maryland-Nat'l Capital Park and Planning Comm'n v. United States Postal Serv.*, 487 F.2d 1029, 1037-38 and n.4 (D.C.Cir. 1973).

The etymological evolution of the phrase "hard look" and of other capsule descriptions of standards stated on judicial review of administrative decisions is in no small part attributable to the shifting meaning of "informal rulemaking." The transformation in informal rulemaking proceedings in turn can be traced to the more rigorous standards of review applied.

As originally conceived, "notice and comment" rulemaking provided a scant "record" for review. The statutorily required rationale consisted merely in "a concise general statement of [the rule's] basis and purpose." 5 U.S.C. § 553(c)(1976). The cumbersomeness of rulemaking "on the record" and its attendant delays prompted increased provision for the more flexible and expedient "notice and comment" rules in areas in urgent need of regulation. *See* Pedersen, *Formal Records and Informal Rulemaking*, 85 Yale L.J. 38, 39 (1975) [hereinafter cited as Pedersen].

The sheer massiveness of impact of the urgent regulations issued under the new rulemaking provisions and the diffidence of judges in the face of highly technical regulatory schemes prompted the courts to require the agencies to develop a more complete record and a more clearly articulated rationale to facilitate review for arbitrariness and caprice. *See Kennecott Copper Corp. v. EPA*, 462 F.2d 846, 849-50 (D.C.Cir. 1972) (remand of national secondary ambient air quality standards to EPA for additional rationale); K. Davis, Administrative Law of the Seventies, § 29.01-6 (1976); Steward, Vermont Yankee *and the Evolution of Administrative Procedure*, 91 Harv.L.Rev. 1805; 1812-13 (1978); Nathanson, *Probing the Mind of the Administrator: Hearing Variations and Standards of Judicial Review Under the Administrative Procedure Act and Other Federal Statutes*, 75 Colum. L.Rev. 721, 746-70 (1975). (Indeed, a section of the Clean Air Act Amendments of 1977 not applicable to the instant proceedings expressly codified much of prior law and the suggestions made in Pedersen concerning the "formalization" of records in informal rulemaking. 42 U.S.C. § 7607(d)(Supp. I 1977); H.R.Rep.No.294, 95th Cong., 1st Sess. 320 (1977), *reprinted in* 4 Legislative History at 2787.)

As these newly-required records and rationales became more routinely available, the "hard look" taken began to appear more judicial than administrative, blurring the original meaning of that phrase. The availability for judicial review of substantial administrative records has also generated both confusion and controversy over the applicable standard of review under the Administrative Procedure Act. *See generally* DeLong, *Informal Rulemaking and the Integration of Law and Policy*, 65 Va.L.Rev. 257, 284-89 (1979); Auerbach, *Informal Rulemaking: A Proposed Relationship Between Administrative Procedures and Judicial Review*, 72 Nw.U.L.Rev. 15 (1977); Pedersen, at 46-49.

175 H.R.Conf.Rep.No. 564, 95th Cong., 1st Sess. 178 (1977), *reprinted in* 3 Legislative History 558, U.S. Code Cong. & Admin.News 1977, p. 1559:

> With respect to the "arbitrary and capricious" scope of review retained in these amendments, the conferees intend that the courts continue their thorough, comprehensive review which has characterized judicial proceedings under the Clean Air Act thus far.

The conferees also recognized the convergence in practice of the "substantial evidence" and the "arbitrary and capricious" standards of review. *Id.* (reinstating "arbitrary and capricious" standard of review):

> In changing the scope of review as contained in the House bill, the conferees were aware that there may be little practical difference between the "substantial evidence" scope of review and the "arbitrary and capricious" scope of review and that the two tests tend to converge as described by recent court

review provisions of the 1977 Amendments do not apply to this rulemaking proceeding, Congress' express affirmance of the standards already developed fortifies our adherence to the learning of our earlier Clean Air Act decisions in reviewing the new source performance standards currently before us.

We think these decisions amply support our conclusion that a remand is appropriate in this case. Both decisions reviewing the NSPS and those reviewing other administrative determinations under the Clean Air Act evince a concern that variables be accounted for,[176] that the representativeness of test conditions by ascertained,[177] that the validity of tests be assured[178] and the statistical significance of results determined.[179] Collectively, these concerns have sometimes been expressed as a need for "reasoned decision-making"[180] and sometimes as a need for adequate "methodology." . . .

Our opinion should not suggest the necessity of "ninety-five percent certainty"[181] in all the "facts" which enter into the Agency's decision. We would

decisions. [Referring to *Assoc. Indus. v. Dep't of Labor*, 487 F.2d 342 (2d Cir. 1973)].

[176] *Ethyl Corp. v. EPA*, 541 F.2d at 25 (*en banc*) (review of regulations under Clean Air Act requiring reduction of lead content of gasoline).

Congress has authorized the Administrator to "distinguish among classes, types and sizes within categories of new sources for the purpose and establishing . . . standards [under § 7411]," 42 U.S.C. § 7411(b)(2)(Supp. I 1977). But the Administrator has not availed himself of the discretion to account for variations in conditions covered by the standard here. *Compare* the extensive exercise of analogous discretion (with respect to *existing* facilities) under the Federal Water Pollution Control Act, 33U.S.C. § 1251 *et seq.* (Supp. I 1977). *Weyerhaeuser Co. v. Costle*, 590 F.2d at 1053 (300 pulp and paper plants classified into 16 subcategories and 66 subdivisions, with different limitations for each subdivision). *See also* Judge Leventhal's concurring opinion in *ASARCO, Inc. v. EPA*, 578 F.2d 319, 330 (D.C. Cir. 1978) (noting the Administrator's discretion to classify under § 111 of the Clean Air Act).

[177] *Portland Cement I*, 486 F.2d at 396 (Agency must explain generalization of standard based on tests of dry-process kilns to wet-process kilns). *Cf. AFL-CIO v. Marshall*, 617 F.2d at 656-657 (D.C. Cir. 1979) (challenge to technical feasibility of OSHA cotton dust regulation upheld where mills meeting the standard ran the "dustiest variety" of cotton); *Weyerhaeuser Co. v. Costle*, 590 F.2d at 1055-60 (D.C. Cir. 1978) (Agency gave adequate consideration to claimed variables in climate and hydraulic flow in establishing effluent limitations under the Federal Water Pollution Control Act). *See Nat'l Asphalt*, 539 F.2d at 786-87 (particulate standard upheld against claim that Agency "ignored a number of variables which should have been taken into account (including variations in the size, shape, and smoothness of particles in the feed aggregate, type of fuel, atmospheric conditions, and start up/shut down [of] plant operations)" when "Administrator's statements indicate an awareness of and a willingness to adjust for such factors"). *See also Ethyl Corp. v. EPA*, 541 F.2d at 38 (only rarely will single study or bit of evidence suffice) ("By its nature, scientific evidence is cumulative: the more supporting, albeit inconclusive, evidence available, the more likely the accuracy of the conclusion."); *Portland Cement I*, 486 F.2d at 396 (significance of single test doubted); *Int'l Harvester Co. v. Ruckelshaus*, 478 F.2d at 625 (noting that only one of 384 test vehicles was able to meet the standard).

[178] *Portland Cement I*, 486 F.2d at 396-97 (use of faulty or discrepant testing procedures "raises serious questions about the validity of the standard" based on the data thereby obtained)

[179] *Portland Cement I*, 486 F.2d at 396:

> "It would . . . seem incumbent on the Administrator to estimate the possible degree of error [inherent] in his prediction,"

quoting Int'l Harvester Co. v. Ruckelshaus, 478 F.2d at 647.

[180] *Portland Cement I*, 486 F.2d at 402; Ethyl Corp. v. EPA, 541 F.2d at 35-36 (*citing* several decisions of Judge Leventhal).

[181] *Ethyl Corp. v. EPA*, 541 F.2d at 28 n. 58:

> Petitioners demand sole reliance on *scientific* facts, on evidence that reputable scientific techniques certify as certain. Typically, a scientist will not so certify evidence unless the probability of error, by standard statisti-

require only that the Agency provide sufficient data to demonstrate a systematic approach to problems, not that it adduce vast quantities of factual data. However, where the facts pertinent to the standard's feasibility are available and easily discoverable by conventional technical means, there is somewhat less reason for so limited a data base. Nothing in the record suggests the relevant facts are not readily accessible to the Agency; the number of plants is large,[182] use of the control methods found by the Agency to represent the "best systems" is widespread,[183] and stack emission measurement techniques have been known and applied for many years.[184]

With respect to the standard's achievability we are thus not presented with the question how much deference is owed a judgment predicated on limited evidence when additional evidence cannot be adduced or adduced in the near future.[185] We do not depart from some of the most carefully considered and closely reasoned decisions of this court which permit an agency latitude to exercise its discretion in accordance with the remedial purposes of the

cal measurement, is less than 5%. That is, scientific fact is at least 95% certain.

Such certainty has never characterized the judicial or the administrative process. It may be that the "beyond a reasonable doubt" standard of criminal law demands 95% certainty. *Cf. McGill v. United States*, 121 U.S. App.D.C. 179, 185 n. 6, 348 F.2d 791, 797 n. 6 (1965). But the standard of ordinary civil litigation, a preponderance of the evidence, demands only 51% certainty. A jury may weigh conflicting evidence and certify as adjudicative (although not scientific) fact that which it believes is more likely than not. Since *Reserve Mining* [*Co. v. EPA*, 514 F.2d 492 (8th Cir. 1975)] was adjudicated in court, this standard applied to the court's fact-finding. Inherently, such a standard is flexible; inherently, it allows the fact-finder to assess risks, to measure probabilities, to make subjective judgments. Nonetheless, the ultimate finding will be treated, at law, as fact and will be affirmed if based on substantial evidence, or, if made by a judge, not clearly erroneous.

The standard before administrative agencies is no less flexible. Agencies are not limited to scientific fact, to 95% certainties. Rather, they have at least the same fact-finding powers as a jury, particularly when, as here, they are engaged in rule-making.

Looking to the future, and commanded by Congress to make policy, a rule-making agency necessarily deals less with "evidentiary" disputes than with normative conflicts, projections from imperfect data, experiments and simulations, educated predictions, differing assessments of possible risks, and the like.

Amoco Oil Co. v. EPA, . . . 163 U.S. App.D.C. at 175, 501 F.2d at 735.

182 EPA estimated 179 lime plants were operating in 1975. SSEIS 3-1.

183 According to the MRI Report, one study showed that 24% of 85 rotary kiln lime plants were controlled by baghouses. *Id.* at 8-9. None of the emissions control systems found by the EPA to be capable of meeting the promulgated standard utilizes a newly developed or little-used technology. All have been widely used in the industry for many years. *See* R. Boynton, Chemistry and Technology of Lime and Limestone 267-68 (1966).

184 EPA's "Method 5" was established as a reference method in 1971. 36 Fed.Reg. 24876, 24888 (1971).

185 *Cf. Ethyl Corp. v. EPA*, 541 F.2d at 28:

> Where a statute is precautionary in nature, the evidence difficult to come by, uncertain, or conflicting because it is on the frontiers of scientific knowledge, the regulations designed to protect the public health, and the decision that of an expert administrator, we will not demand rigorous step-by-step proof of cause and effect. Such proof may be impossible to obtain if the precautionary purpose of the statute is to be served. Of course, we are not suggesting that the Administrator has the power to act on hunches or wild guesses. *Amoco* makes it quite clear that his conclusions must be rationally justified.

(footnote omitted) (*citing Amoco Oil Co. v. EPA*, 501 F.2d 722 (D.C. Cir. 1974)).

controlling statute where relevant facts cannot be ascertained or are on the frontiers of scientific inquiry.[186]

A systematic approach may not necessarily require a conclusion grounded in actual test results. We do not intend to bridle the Agency's discretion to make well-founded assumptions even where the assumption could be replaced by valid test results, but we think first, the assumption should be stated and second, where test data *could* have verified the assumption, a reason for not testing or relying on such data should be given.

We recognize, for example, that the finding of facts, especially through elaborate testing, is costly[187] and the costs of additional testing may be added by the Agency to the costs of delay in issuing the proposed rule and the sum of these costs weighed against the benefit of proposing a rule without additional data.[188]

We leave to the Agency on remand the decision whether additional Agency-conducted testing is appropriate in this case. Data may already be available to the Administrator which would support the achievability of these standards for the industry as a whole. If so, satisfaction of the concerns we have expressed in this opinion may be fairly simple matter.

To ensure that the Agency has engaged in reasoned decisionmaking, we remand. We have outlined our substantive misgivings; the Agency may choose the appropriate method of response.

Remanded.

NOTES

In supporting its conclusion that the standards required remand, the court provided massive detail and significant support from earlier decisions. It reviewed earlier unsuccessful efforts by EPA to set capacity standards for Portland cement plants, including the impact of the size of the particles omitted on plume opacity, noting that EPA had not found it necessary to change the standard because of particle size, both in the instance of Portland cement plants or in the case of asphalt concrete plants. The standards had been affirmed in the asphalt plant situation but the court noted that different industries may have different standards, and the Administrator does not have a burden to explain those differences if the different standards were arrived

[186] *Ethyl Corp. v. EPA*, 541 F.2d 1; *Amoco Oil Co. v. EPA*, 501 F.2d at 738-39; *Indus. Union Dep't v. Hodgson*, 499 F.2d 467, 474 (D.C. Cir. 1974). *See generally* McGarity, *Substantive and Procedural Discretion in Administrative Resolution of Science Policy Questions: Regulating Carcinogens in EPA and OSHA*, 67 Geo. L.J. 729 (1979).

[187] EPA here estimated: "Sampling costs for performing a test consisting of three Method 5 runs [are] estimated to range from $5,000 to $9,000. If in-plant personnel are used to conduct tests, the costs will be somewhat less." SSEIS D-8.

[188] *Cf. AFL-CIO v. Marshall*, 617 F.2d at 657-658 (D.C. Cir. 1979) (OSHA might have improved quality of record with more extensive studies at different mills and over different periods of time, but OSH Act, although requiring best available evidence, does not require administration to incur these costs).

at in good faith. The court noted that opacity standards are intended to operate in tandem with mass emission standards, even though they are independently enforceable. It found that the Administrator had failed to consider the representativeness of particle size produced at its various test plants. The early opacity standards, variation in particle size had indeed been considered. EPA had emphasized both in court and at the administrative level that most of the plants tested were indeed able to meet the 10% opacity standard. The court found that without knowing the representativeness of the plants tested or of test conditions, it could not say whether the test was arbitrary or capricious. Combined with the court's doubts concerning the mass emission standard, the court's problem with the opacity standard was adequate to remand to the agency for amplification of the record. The court seemed to believe that the grant of a variance in this instance would not be appropriate since there were no questions in this case relating to stack capacity, which may have an impact on opacity of emissions. Noting the usefulness of opacity standards for enforcement, the court noted that such standards had been upheld earlier. The court remanded because, on this record, the reasonableness of the standard had not been demonstrated. On the issue of the use of continuous monitoring data to determine compliance with the opacity standard, the court noted that EPA now required continuous monitoring as part of all new source performance standards. The court noted that continuous monitoring requirements had recently been imposed on a number of other industries. Relying on the fact that it had considerable experience with the use of continuing monitoring devices, EPA maintained that a monitor will show if an emission control device is being properly operated and maintained and the opacity standards met. Monitoring acts as a needed warning alarm when the system is out of kilter. There was an industry concession that monitoring shows whether opacity is increasing or decreasing, and in the light of this concession the court found that a continuous monitoring requirement was not an arbitrary requirement as an adjunct to non-arbitrary, non-capricious opacity standards. It held that if on remand an opacity standard were to be retained, EPA could continue to require continuous monitoring.

With respect to the issue of the representativeness of the data used by EPA in establishing the standard, the court noted that it had applied the "hard look" standard, which Judge Leventhal had so named in one of his early opinions. The hard look standard is now applied both to agency determinations as well as in judicial informal rulemaking proceedings. The court commented on the increasing complexity of the highly technical regulatory schemes covered by informal rulemaking. This requires greater detail and formalization of records in such proceedings, and the hard look requirement was a response to the greater complexity of issues in informal rulemaking. Reviewing the legislative history of the Clean Air Act with respect to rulemaking issues, the court noted that Congress has accepted the convergence in practice of the "substantial evidence" and the "arbitrary and capricious" standards of review. The court used these analytical comments as a basis for its conclusion to remand, noting that decisions reviewing new source performance standards and other Clean Air Act determinations show a concern that variables be accounted for. The court noted earlier examples when courts have required the agency to explain the generalization and variation of standards based on different kinds of industrial processes and different kinds of raw materials involved. In accounting for variables, the agency must account, for instance, on the generalization of standard based on tests of dry process kilns to wet process kilns, or the different application of standards to different kinds of cotton in OSHA regulations. Similar variations may require the adjustment of standards for such factors as the type of fuel, atmospheric conditions, and start up and shut down of plant operations. Altogether, these considerations call for a reflection of the factual and scientific basis of the rule in the record, as well as the representativeness of the test conditions, all collectively fulfilling the need for reasoned decisionmaking. In relying on Judge Leventhal's assertions of the need for adequate "methodology," substantive concerns for adequate rulemaking have always been coupled with the requirement that the assumptions on which the rules are based are stated. Rejecting the necessity of "95% certainty" expressed in some earlier decisions, the court rejected the 95% certainty rule as appropriate for scientists, but not for the judicial process. The court noted that agencies, like juries, are not tied to a 95% certainty test but they have the same fact finding powers as a jury when engaged in rulemaking.

The court required that the agency provide sufficient data to demonstrate a systematic approach to the problems, not that they adduce vast quantities of factual data. The relevant data are accessible to the agency and must be supplied. In the situation before the court, the technology used was well established and thus, with respect to the standard's achievability, the court was not presented with the question whether deference is owed to a judgment predicated on limited evidence when additional evidence cannot be adduced now or in the near future. While a systematic approach may not require a conclusion grounded in actual test results, and the court did not intend to limit the agency's discretion to make well founded assumptions where these assumptions could be replaced by valid test results, the assumption nevertheless should be stated, and where test results have verified the assumption, a reason for not testing or relying on such data should be given. The finding of facts through elaborate testing is very expensive, and the requirement of best available evidence does not require that such costs be incurred. On remand, the court left to the agency the decision whether additional agency-conducted testing would be appropriate in this case. If data were available to support the achievability of the new standards for the industry as a whole, it ought to be a fairly simple matter for the Administrator to satisfy the court's concerns. "To ensure that the agency has engaged in reasoned decisionmaking, we remand. We have outlined our substantive misgivings; the agency may choose the appropriate method of response."[189]

QUESTIONS

(1) In setting "standards of performance" (*i.e.*, emission standards) for new sources, the Administrator must take certain technological and cost factors into account. On the economic side, how and to what extent are costs to be considered—and is there any guidance in the *Portland Cement Association* case on how costs are to be balanced against greater technological advances?

[189] 627 F.2d at 455.

On the technological side, the Court holds that an available technology, or an adequately demonstrated technology, need not be in routine use somewhere. Acknowledging that standard setting under these circumstances is an exercise in projection, how is the line to be drawn between mere crystal ball prophecy and reasonable judgment? *See also International Harvester v. Ruckelshaus*, 478 F.2d 615 (D.C. Cir. 1973), at p. 304, *infra*.

(2) How does the Administrator determine what categories of sources are to be covered by new source performance standard requirements? *See National Asphalt Pavement Ass'n v. Train*, 539 F.2d 775, 9 E.R.C. 1109 (D.C. Cir. 1976).

(3) How do new source performance standards mesh with the state implementation plan requirements?

[g] The Bubble Concept and Other Options for Compliance

ASARCO, INC. v. EPA

United States Court of Appeals, D.C. Circuit (1978)
578 F.2d 319

J. SKELLY WRIGHT, Circuit Judge:

These cases involve challenges by ASARCO Incorporated, Newmont Mining Corporation, and Magma Copper Company (hereinafter referred to collectively as ASARCO) and the Sierra Club (Sierra) to regulations issued by the Environmental Protection Agency (EPA). The challenged provisions modify previous regulations implementing Section 111 of the Clean Air Act, 42 U.S.C. § 1857c-6(1970 & Supp. V 1975), *as amended*, Pub.L.No. 95-95 § 109, 91 Stat. 685, 697-703 (1977), which mandates national emission standards for new stationary sources of air pollution, by introducing a limited form of what the parties call the "bubble concept." This court has jurisdiction over these petitions under Section 307(b)(1) of the Act, 42 U.S.C. § 1857h-5(b)(1)(1970 & Supp. V 1975), *as amended*, Pub.L.No. 95-95 § 305, 91 Stat. 772-777.

I

A. *Section 111 and the "Bubble Concept"*

. . . .

. . . The New Source Performance Standards (NSPSs) established under Section 111 are designed to force new sources to employ the best demonstrated systems of emission reduction. Since the NSPSs are likely to be stricter than emission standards under State Implementation Plans, plant operators have an incentive to avoid application of the NSPSs.

The basic controversy in the cases before us concerns the determination of the units to which the NSPSs apply. Under the Act the NSPSs apply to "new sources." A "new source" is defined as "*any stationary source*, the *construction or modification* of which" begins after the NSPS covering that type of source is published. Section 111(a)(2), 42 U.S.C. § 1857c-6(a)(2)(1970) (emphasis added). Further statutory definitions explain the terms used in this one. A " 'stationary source' means any building, structure, facility, or installation which emits or may emit any air pollutant." Section 111(a)(3), 42 U.S.C. § 1857c-6(a)(3)(1970). A " 'modification' means any physical change in, or change in the method of operation of, a stationary source which increases the amount of any air pollutant emitted by such source or which results in the emission of any air pollutant not previously emitted." Section 111(a)(4), 42 U.S.C. § 1857c-6(a)(4)(1970). The statute thus directs that the NSPSs are to apply to any building, structure, facility, or installation which emits or may emit any air pollutant and which is either (1) newly constructed or (2) physically or operationally changed in such a way that *its* emission of any air pollutant increases.

The "bubble concept" is based on defining a *stationary source* as a *combination* of facilities, such as an *entire plant*, and applying the NSPSs only when a new *plant* is constructed or when an existing *plant* is physically or operationally changed in such a way that *net* emissions of any pollutant form the *entire plant* increase. If applied consistently, the bubble concept would allow the operator of an existing plant to avoid application of the strict NSPSs by offsetting any increase in pollution caused by a change in the plant (*e.g.*, modification or replacement of an existing facility, or even addition of a new facility) against a decrease in pollution from other units within the plant as a whole.

B. *History of the EPA Regulations*

EPA's original regulations interpreting Section 111, promulgated in 1971, repeated the statutory definitions of "stationary source" and "modification" almost word for word[190] and did not contain any version of the "bubble concept." *See* 36 Fed. Reg. 24877 (1971), *codified at* 40 C.F.R. §§ 60.2(d) & (h)(1975). EPA acknowledges in its brief that it originally "defined the term *new source* as 'an affected *facility*' which in turn was defined as any apparatus to which a standard of performance is specifically applicable." Brief for EPA at 10 (emphasis added). Affected facilities, and thus new sources, were clearly not synonymous with entire plants. For example, the regulations setting the NSPSs for sources in portland cement plants identify the following "affected facilities" in such plants: "kiln, clinker cooler, raw mill system, finish mill system, raw mill dryer, raw material storage, clinker storage, finished product storage, conveyor transfer points, bagging and bulk loading and unloading systems." 40 C.F.R. § 60.60(1975).[191]

---

[190] The definition of "modification" in the regulations differed in several respects from the statutory definition. The regulations specified that "[r]outine maintenance, repair, and replacement" would not constitute "physical changes" and that "change[s] in the method of operation" would not include an increase in the production rate up to the "operating design capacity" of a facility, "[an] increase in the hours of operation," or "[u]se of an alternative fuel or raw material" that the facility was previously designed to accommodate. 40 C.F.R. § 60.2(h)(1975). These provisions have been slightly amplified and carried over into the new regulations, 40 C.F.R. § 60.14(e)(1976), but they are not challenged by the petitioners here. *See* br. for petitioner Sierra Club at 7 & n.4.

[191] An entire plant is an awkward unit to set standards for. Indeed, even under the new regulations EPA sets standards for *facilities* rather than entire plants. *See, e.g.*, 40 C.F.R. §§ 60.2(d), 60.120-60.122(1976). A single standard applies to an entire plant only when the plant contains a single facility. *See, e.g.*, 40

The "bubble concept" appeared first in proposals from the nonferrous smelting industry and the Department of Commerce (DOC) beginning in December 1972. The industry and DOC urged that a stationary source be defined as an entire plant so that no "modifications" of the source would occur unless the total emissions of some pollutant from the plant increased.

In response to industry proposals and demands form DOC, EPA prepared draft regulations in May and July 1974 "clarifying" the previous regulations. EPA made some concessions to the industry in these drafts,[192] but did not accept the industry's position that an entire plant should be defined as a single source.[193] EPA continued to resist the bubble concept in meetings with industry representatives, DOC, and the Office of Management and Budget through August 1974. *See* JA 8-9, 30-34.

Then, in September 1974, the agency again revised its position, making further concessions and proposing new regulations incorporating a limited version of the bubble concept. After an additional concession further extending the bubble concept in response to a submission by DOC, the proposed regulations were adopted by EPA.

The new regulations would classify an entire plant as a single stationary source by embellishing the statutory definition of a stationary source as follows:

> "Stationary source" means any building, structure, facility, or installation which emits or may emit any air pollutant *and which contains any one or combination of the following:*
>
> (1) Affected facilities.
>
> (2) Existing facilities.
>
> (3) Facilities of the type for which no standards have been promulgated in this part.

C.F.R. § 60.90(1976) (NSPS for asphalt concrete plants). Even ASARCO does not argue that EPA should set a single NSPS for an entire plant. *See* br. for petitioner ASARCO at 6-7; reply br. for ASARCO at 3-4. Yet the Act's direction that NSPSs are to be set "for *sources*" indicates that the units for which standards are set are *sources.* 42 U.S.C. § 1857c-6(b)(1)(B)(Supp. V 1975), *as amended,* Pub.L.No. 95-95 § 109(c)(2), 91 Stat. 700 (emphasis added).

192 The draft regulations defined a single "stationary source" as containing a "combination of facilities." *See* May Meeting Minutes, *supra* note 11, Appendix F at 13. At this stage, however, a "combination of facilities" was not intended to refer to an entire plant. EPA intended to "limit[] the scope of a combined emission system to a group of facilities whose emissions can be controlled by an existing common control system." *Id.* at 13. Furthermore, the combined emissions approach was to be applied only to "those facilities where a high-quality control system already exists and where substantial savings of control costs or energy could be achieved." *Id.*

193 EPA's major objection to the bubble concept was that it would make emission standards extremely difficult to enforce. *See, e.g.,* May Meeting Minutes, *supra* note 11, at 13; Draft Memorandum, "Proposed Rulemaking to Clarify the Modification Provisions of Section 111 of the Clean Air Act—ACTION MEMO," July 12, 1974, Tab D at 2. The agency was also concerned that an approach based on maintaining existing levels of pollution would reward those operators who were presently using the fewest controls and use up air that would otherwise be available for new construction complying with NSPS. *See, e.g.,* Minutes of Meeting: National Air Pollution Control Techniques Advisory Committee, Jan. 8-10, 1974, Doc. No. 130, at 7-8; Public Comment Summary, Revised April 1976, at 12-14, JA 110-112 (response to Comment 24).

40 C.F.R. § 60.2(d)(1976) (emphasis added). The italicized language is not included in the statutory definition of "stationary source" ("any building, structure, facility, or installation which emits or may emit any air pollutant"), nor was it included in the prior regulations. *See* 40 C.F.R. § 60.2(d)(1975). Thus the present regulations, instead of limiting the definition of "stationary source" to one "facility" as the statute does, make it cover "any one or combination of" facilities.[194] The preamble to the new regulations makes it clear that the purpose of this change is to define a statutory source as an entire plant.[195]

Relying on this new definition of a statutory source, EPA applies the bubble concept to allow a plant operator who alters an existing facility in a way that increases its emissions to avoid application of the NSPSs by decreasing emissions from other facilities within the plant. The regulations provide that "[a] modification shall not be deemed to occur" unless the change in an existing facility results in a net increase in the emission of a pollutant from the whole "source."[196]

In spite of strong comments from the nonferrous smelting industry, represented here by ASARCO,[197] the new regulations do not consistently apply the bubble concept to treat an entire plant as a single stationary source. EPA continues to apply NSPSs to all *newly constructed* facilities, even when the emission increases from the new facilities are offset by emission decreases from other facilities in the same plant. Newly constructed facilities are thus

[194] The EPA's definition of a "facility," which this court accepts, is "any apparatus to which a standard of performance is specifically applicable." *See* 188 U.S. App. D.C. at —, 578 F.2d at 323 *supra*. This definition is clearly designed to designate as "facilities" those units of equipment—be they individual machines, combinations of machines, or even entire plants—that the agency finds to be appropriate units for separate emission standards. A cursory review of the EPA's regulations indicates that the units designated as "facilities" under this definition are usually larger than individual machines or single pieces of equipment, and are sometimes whole plants. *See* text and note at note 9 *supra*. In designating what will constitute a facility in each particular industrial context, EPA is guided by a reasoned application of the terms of the statute it is charged to enforce, not by an abstract "dictionary" definition. This court would not remove this appropriate exercise of the agency's discretion. *See Union Electric Co. v. EPA*, 427 U.S. 246, 256, 96 S.Ct. 2518, 49 L.Ed.2d 474 (1976): *Train v. Natural Resources Defense Council, Inc.*, 421 U.S. 60, 75, 87, 95 S.Ct. 1470, 43 L.Ed.2d 741 (1975); *Ethyl Corp. v. EPA*, 176 U.S. App. D.C. 373, 541 F.2d 1, 12 n. 16, 31 n.64 (*en banc*), cert. denied, 426 U.S. 941, 96 S.Ct. 2663, 49 L.Ed.2d 394 (1976).

[195] "Generally speaking, 'sources' are entire plants, while 'facilities' are identifiable pieces of process equipment or individual components which when taken together would comprise a source. . . ." 40 Fed. Reg. 58416 (1975), JA 99.

[196] [40 C.F.R. § 60.14(d)(1976)]:

> A modification shall not be deemed to occur if an existing facility undergoes a physical or operational change where the owner or operator demonstrates to the Administrator's satisfaction . . . that the total emission rate of any pollutant has not increased from all facilities within the stationary source to which appropriate reference, equivalent, or alternative methods . . . can be applied. An owner or operator may completely and permanently close any facility within a stationary source to prevent an increase in the total emission rate regardless of whether such reference, equivalent or alternative method can be applied, if the decrease in emission rate from such closure can be adequately determined by any of the procedures prescribed under paragraph (b) of this section. The owner or operator of the source shall have the burden of demonstrating compliance with this section.

[197] *See, e.g.*, Comments of American Smelting & Refining Co., Newmont Mining Corp., and Magma Copper Co. on Proposed Rules, Nov. 27, 1974, at 42-50, JA 79-87.

treated as independent stationary sources. In order to draw a line defining when the bubble concept will be applied, the regulations classify any changes in existing facilities that cost more than a fixed percentage of the value of the changed facility as "reconstruction." 40 C.F.R. § 60.15(1976). "Reconstructed" facilities, like new facilities, are subject to NSPSs regardless of whether emissions from the plant of which they are a part increase.

In its petition for review ASARCO argues that the bubble concept must be applied to allow emission increases from reconstruction and new construction to be offset. Sierra argues that the Act defines a "source" as an *individual* facility, as distinguished from a combination of facilities such as a plant, and that the bubble concept must therefore be rejected *in toto.* For the reasons stated below we agree with Sierra and remand to EPA for further proceedings consistent with this opinion.

II

A. *Scope of Review*

The proper scope for judicial review of EPA's regulations interpreting the Clean Air Act is defined in Section 10(e) of the Administrative Procedure Act,which requires a reviewing court to "decide all relevant questions of law, interpret . . . statutory provisions, and . . . hold unlawful and set aside agency action, findings, and conclusions found to be . . . in excess of statutory jurisdiction, authority, or limitations, or short of statutory right. . . ." 5 U.S.C. § 706(2)(C)(1970). . . .

. . . .

B. *Sierra's Challenge to the Regulations*

The Sierra Club's basic contention is that the new regulations are inconsistent with the plain language of Section 111. The statute defines a *stationary source* as "any building, structure, *facility*, or installation which emits or may emit any air pollutant." Section 111(a)(3), 42 U.S.C. § 1857c-6(a)(3)(1970) (emphasis added). In contrast, the new regulations define stationary source to include "any . . . *combination* of . . . facilities. . . ." 40 C.F.R. § 60.2(d)(1976) (emphasis added).

This change in the definition of a stationary source is essential to EPA's adoption of the bubble concept. By treating a combination of facilities as a single source, the regulations allow a facility whose emissions are increased by alterations to avoid complying with the applicable NSPS as long as emission decreases from other facilities within the same "source" cancel out the increase from the altered facility.[198] Sierra argues forcefully that this result is incompatible with the statute's mandate that NSPSs should be applied to "*any* structure, building, facility, or installation" that undergoes "any physical change . . . or . . . change in the method of operation . . . which increases the amount of any air pollutant emitted by such [structure, building,

[198] *See* text and note at note 19 *supra.*

facility, or installation]." 42 U.S.C. §§ 1857c-6(a)(3), 1857c-6(a)(4)(1970) (emphasis added). *See* brief for petitioner Sierra Club at 25-33.

EPA responds that the "broad" statutory definition of *stationary source* gives it "discretion" to define a *stationary source* as either a single facility or a combination of facilities. Brief for EPA at 13-16. We find this response unpersuasive.[199] The regulations plainly indicate that EPA has attempted to change the basic unit to which the NSPSs apply from a *single* building, structure, facility, or installation—the unit prescribed in the statute—to a *combination* of such units. The agency has no authority to rewrite the statute in this fashion.

Our conclusion that the regulations incorporating the bubble concept must be rejected as inconsistent with the language of the Act is reinforced when we consider the purpose of the Clean Air Act and Section 111, the confusion generated by the present regulations, and the weakness of EPA's arguments in favor of the bubble concept.

"[T]he goal of the Clean Air Act," as EPA admits in its brief, "is to *enhance* air quality and not merely to *maintain* it." Brief for EPA at 17 (emphasis added). *See* Clean Air Act § 101(b)(1), 42 U.S.C. § 1857(b)(1)(1970). Section 111's provisions mandating New Source Performance Standards were passed because Congress feared that the system of state plans designed to keep air pollution below nationally determined levels, was insufficient by itself to achieve the goal of protecting and *improving* air quality. The New Source

[199] The Act's definition of a "stationary source" as "any building, structure, facility, or installation which emits or may emit any air pollutant" is a broad and comprehensive one that cannot be reconciled with the regulations' restrictive definition of a source as an entire plant. In its briefs as intervenor and petitioner ASARCO attempts to justify the definition of a stationary source as an entire plant by pointing to passages in the legislative history that contain lists of the types of polluters Congress sought to regulate: *e.g.*, "refineries, steel mills, primary smelting plants. . . ." S. Rep. No. 91-1196, 91st Cong., 2d Sess. 16, *in* Senate Comm. on Pub. Works, 91st Cong., 2d Sess., 1 Legislative History of the Clean Air Act Amendments of 1970, at 416 (Comm. Print 1974) (hereinafter cited as Legislative History); "power plants, steel mills, and cement plants. . . ." 116 Cong. Rec. 42384 (1970) (remarks of Sen. Muskie), *in* 1 Legislative History at 130. Br. for petitioner ASARCO at 22. EPA itself, however, points out that the legislative history contains lists mentioning "numerous other terms which refer to operations rather than entire plants as physical entities." Br. for EPA at 14 & n.12. Sierra argues further that these lists were not intended to be exclusive, that these larger "sources" are in fact regulated when their components are regulated, and that the Senators mentioned whole plants as sources because they lacked the familiarity with various industries to mention smaller units. Br. for *amicus curiae* Sierra Club at 16-17. We find the legislative history on this point a much less reliable guide than the words of the statute itself.

EPA attempts to base its "discretion" to redefine the term "stationary source" on § 111(b)(2), 42 U.S.C. § 1857c-6(b)(2)(1970):

> The Administrator may distinguish among classes, types, and sizes within categories of new sources for the purpose of establishing [New Source Performance] standards.

This language on its face merely allows the Administrator to set different standards for different classes, types, and sizes of sources. It does not give the Administrator authority to rewrite the definition of a stationary source, or to use different and inconsistent definitions when considering modification and new construction.

Finally, EPA claims that § 111 is aimed primarily at *new construction*, br. for EPA at 19-20, and candidly admits that it intended "to develop a modification regulation . . . which minimizes that impact on existing sources." May Meeting Minutes, *supra* note 11, at 11. The Act's language, however, is aimed at *new sources*, not just *new construction*, and defines existing sources that are altered so that their emissions increase as *new sources*.

Performance Standards are designed to enhance air quality by forcing all newly constructed *or modified* buildings, structures, facilities, or installations to employ pollution control systems that will limit emissions to the level "achievable through application of the best technological system of continuous emission reduction which . . . the Administrator determines has been adequately demonstrated." 42 U.S.C. § 1857c-6(a)(1)(1970), *as amended*, Pub.L.No. 95-95 § 109(c)(1), 91 Stat. 699-700. The bubble concept in the challenged regulations would undercut Section 111 by allowing operators to avoid installing the best pollution control technology on an altered facility as long as the emissions from the entire plant do not increase. For example, under the bubble concept an operator who alters one of its facilities so that its emission of some pollutant increases might avoid application of the NSPS by simultaneously equipping other plant facilities with additional, but inferior, pollution control technology or merely reducing their production. Applying the bubble concept thus postpones the time when the best technology must be employed and at best maintains the present level of emissions.

Moreover, the challenged regulations are internally inconsistent and create confusion by defining a *stationary source* one way (as an entire plant) when determining whether a "source" has been "modified," and another way (as an individual facility) when determining whether a "source" has been newly constructed or "reconstructed." This inconsistency is apparently the result of a "compromise" between EPA's original regulations, which followed the Act in treating a single facility as a source, and the industry position presented by ASARCO that a source must be defined as an entire plant. We are unable to understand why EPA should find it necessary to compromise by adopting a position that it admits is contrary to both the language and the basic purpose of the Act.

EPA's main argument in support of its regulations is that its version of the bubble concept is necessary to provide flexibility in applying the NSPSs to modified facilities because the cost of bringing *existing* facilities into compliance with NSPSs is allegedly much greater than the cost of bringing *new* facilities into compliance. This argument does not survive analysis. The record does not show that any version of the bubble concept is needed to provide flexibility to the operators of existing facilities. Under provisions of the regulations that are not challenged in this litigation, the operator of an existing facility can make any alterations he wishes in the facility without becoming subject to the NSPS *as long as the level of emissions from the altered facility does not increase.* Thus the level of emissions before alterations take place, rather than the strict NSPS, effectively defines the standard that an altered facility must meet. The record does not indicate why more flexibility than this is necessary or even appropriate. Even if flexibility were a problem, the statute on its face allows for cost considerations to be taken into account in setting NSPSs, rather than in determining whether the standards will apply to whole plants or to individual facilities within those plants.

Finally, the record indicates that the bubble concept has been supported by examples drawn from circumstances peculiar to the nonferrous smelting industry. As EPA itself recognizes in its brief, the proper place to consider the problems a particular industry will have in meeting the NSPSs is in proceedings dealing with the standards for that particular industry, not in regulations setting standards for all industries.

We therefore agree with the Sierra Club that EPA's regulations incorporating the bubble concept are inconsistent with the language and purpose of the statute and cannot be justified by any alleged need for flexibility.

C. *ASARCO's Challenge to the Regulations*

The dispute between ASARCO and EPA centers on how far the bubble concept should extend. ASARCO asserts that a *stationary source* must be defined as an entire plant for *all purposes* and that the NSPSs should therefore never apply to an existing plant, even if new facilities are built or old ones are "reconstructed," unless the net emissions of some pollutant from the entire plant increase. ASARCO argues that the inconsistency in EPA's present definition of a stationary source—an inconsistency created by EPA's partial concessions to ASARCO's position—should be resolved by doing away with all limitations on the bubble concept. Brief for petitioner ASARCO at 18-23.

Since we find that *any* version of the bubble concept is incompatible with the language of the Act and contrary to its purpose, ASARCO's position is clearly untenable. Our holding therefore resolves the inconsistency in the challenged regulations by eliminating its source: the bubble concept.

Accordingly, we remand to the EPA for further proceedings not inconsistent with this opinion.

So ordered.

[Concurring opinion by Leventhal, J. and opinion by MacKinnon, J. concurring in part and dissenting in part, have been omitted.]

State Implementation Plan; "Bubble Concept"— Alternative Options Within State Implementation Plans

Application to New Sources and in PSD Context

The "bubble concept" addresses the question of how to minimize the costs of pollution control without adverse impact on the attainment and maintenance of national ambient air quality standards. The crucial consideration in the bubble concept is the definition of a "source" of emissions. As defined in Section 111(a)(3) for purposes of the regulation of new source performance standards, a stationary source is "any building, structure, facility, or installation which emits or may emit any air pollutant." The definition of "stationary source" does not say whether more than one building, structure, etc. can be regarded as a single "source". In 1975, EPA proposed such a broad reading of the statute,[200] which has been dubbed the "bubble concept" because it treats

[200] 40 Fed. Reg. 58416 (Dec. 16, 1975), 40 C.F.R. § 60.2(d), (h), (aa), (bb); 60.5; 60.7; 60.14; 60.15 (1976).

a number of points of emission as if they were all emitting into a single bubble which has a single stack through which all of the combined emissions are ventilated. The concept is an attractive one to industry, because a plant or factory complex with a number of emission points could offset poorly controlled emissions against highly controlled emissions, thus offsetting, for instance, older less highly controlled parts of the plant against newer, more efficiently controlled ones, potentially reducing the total cost of pollution control.

The "bubble concept" was originally proposed in 1975 for new source performance standards under Section 111.[201] As interpreted by EPA, the definition of stationary source for Section 111 purposes was to include a *combination of facilities*, applied only, however, to newly constructed plants or to modification of a plant that would result in an increase of total pollution. In *ASARCO, Inc. v. EPA*, the D.C. Circuit Court of Appeals burst the bubble, however, holding that "any version of the bubble concept is incompatible with the language of the Act and contrary to its purposes."[202]

Undismayed by the rejection of the bubble in *ASARCO*, EPA reintroduced the concept in its Prevention of Significant Deterioration Regulations (PSD).[203] This time, the same D.C. Court of Appeals upheld the concept in *Alabama Power Co. v. Costle*,[204] laboriously distinguishing *ASARCO* and finding that the concept—and the acceptance of a combination of sources—could be supported under the Congressional policies reflected in Part C, the PSD provisions of the 1977 Amendments.

The discussion begins with EPA's December 1979 policy statement, "Recommendation for Alternative Emission Reduction Options Within State Implementation Plans," which adopted the "bubble concept" approach to air pollution control by existing sources. Thus, the policy statement encouraged revisions of state implementation plans that enable sources to adopt different, more economically efficient controls on their various emission points, subject to EPA approval to be granted upon the fulfillment of a number of conditions.

It should be noted that the court's distinction of the *ASARCO* holding in *Alabama Power Co. v. Costle*[205] left that holding undisturbed. Thus, the bubble concept was not applicable to new source performance standards. It has been clearly upheld as applicable to the PSD regulations. As far as existing sources are concerned, the new policy had not as yet been tested in the courts by mid-1980, though its policy seems clearly sustainable under *Train v. Natural Resources Defense Council*,[206] because it affords the state another alternative in its state implementation plans, which seems permissible if it does not interfere with the attainment or the maintenance of the national ambient air quality standards.

National Resources Defense Council, Inc. v. Gorsuch[207] challenged the fate of the bubble concept, and with it the fate of a variety of emission reduction

---

201 43 Fed. Reg. 26388 (June 19, 1978), 40 C.F.R. § 52.21(1978).

202 578 F.2d 319, 329 (D.C. Cir. 1978). *See* text *supra*.

203 44 Fed. Reg. 71780 (Dec. 11, 1979), 40 C.F.R. Pt. 52.

204 606 F.2d 1068, 10 E.L.R. 20001 (D.C. Cir. 1979).

205 636 F.2d 323 (D.C. Cir. 1979).

206 421 U.S. 60, 95 S. Ct. 1470, 43 L. Ed. 2d 73 (1975).

207 685 F.2d 718, 12 ELR 20942 (D.C. Cir. 1982).

credits, emission reduction banking systems, and other related notions set forth at large in the materials that follow. The precise question there determined was whether the so-called bubble concept applied to the new source review requirements in nonattainment areas. The problem arose because EPA had changed the definition of the word "source" in its October 14, 1981 bubble regulation[208] to mean an entire plant. Under earlier regulations, "source" referred to an individual piece of process equipment within a plant. EPA's purpose in changing the definition of "source" was to cut back substantially the coverage of nonattainment area new source review, *i.e.*, the more that is included within one "source," the fewer sources need to be covered for nonattainment review purposes. In a very perceptive opinion, subsequently reversed, Ginsburg J., writing for a unanimous court, neatly reconciled *Alabama Power Co. v. Costle*[209] with *ASARCO Inc. v. EPA.*[210] In *Alabama Power* the court held that EPA *must* employ the bubble concept in the Prevention of Significant Deterioration scheme to *maintain* air quality in clean air areas; in *ASARCO* the court *ruled out* the application of the concept to national new source performance standards (NSPS) which EPA must set under the law so as to *enhance* air quality. Thus, the court said, the bubble concept is impermissible when the Congressional purpose is improvement of air quality, but it is particularly well suited to the Congressional purpose of preserving existing air quality. In the challenged situation of standard setting for nonattainment areas, which clearly calls for improvement of air quality, the use of the concept is impermissible, and the regulation was invalidated.

The Supreme Court, on June 25, 1984, reversed the holding by Ginsburg J. in *Chevron, U.S.A. v. NRDC*, which provided the Court's full endorsement of the bubble policy.

CHEVRON, U.S.A., INC. v. NATURAL RESOURCES DEFENSE COUNCIL, INC.

United States Supreme Court (1984)
467 U.S. 837, 104 S. Ct. 2778, 81 L. Ed. 2d 694, 13 E.L.R. 20507

JUSTICE STEVENS delivered the opinion of the Court.

In the Clean Air Act Amendments of 1977, Pub. L. 95-95, 91 Stat. 685, Congress enacted certain requirements applicable to States that had not achieved the national air quality standards established by the Environmental Protection Agency (EPA) pursuant to earlier legislation. The amended Clean Air Act required these "nonattainment" States to establish a permit program regulating "new or modified major stationary sources" of air pollution. Generally, a permit may not be issued for a new or modified major stationary source unless several stringent conditions are met. The EPA regulation promulgated to implement this permit requirement allows a State to adopt

---

208 46 Fed. Reg. 50766 (1981).

209 636 F.2d 323 (D.C. Cir. 1979).

210 578 F.2d 319 (D.C. Cir. 1978).

a plantwide definition of the term "stationary source." Under this definition, an existing plant that contains several pollution-emitting devices may install or modify one piece of equipment without meeting the permit conditions if the alteration will not increase the total emissions from the plant. The question presented by this case is whether EPA's decision to allow States to treat all of the pollution-emitting devices within the same industrial grouping as though they were encased within a single "bubble" is based on a reasonable construction of the statutory term "stationary source."

I

. . . .

The court observed that the relevant part of the amended Clean Air Act "does not explicitly define what Congress envisioned as a'stationary source,' to which the permit program . . . should apply," and further stated that the precise issue was not "squarely addressed in the legislative history." 685 F. 2d, at 723. In light of its conclusion that the legislative history bearing on the question was "at best contradictory," it reasoned that "the purposes of the nonattainment program should guide our decision here." 685 F. 2d, at 726, n. 39. Based on two of its precedents concerning the applicability of the bubble concept to certain Clean Air Act programs, the court stated that the bubble concept was "mandatory" in programs designed merely to maintain existing air quality, but held that it was "inappropriate" in programs enacted to improve air quality. 685 F. 2d, at 726. Since the purpose of the permit program—its "*raison d'etre*," in the court's view—was to improve air quality, the court held that the bubble concept was inapplicable in this case under its prior precedents. *Ibid.* It therefore set aside the regulations embodying the bubble concept as contrary to law. We granted certiorari to review that judgment, and we now reverse.

The basic legal error of the Court of Appeals was to adopt a static judicial definition of the term stationary source when it had decided that Congress itself had not commanded that definition. Respondents do not defend the legal reasoning of the Court of Appeals. Nevertheless, since this Court reviews judgments, not opinions, we must determine whether the Court of Appeals' legal error resulted in an erroneous judgment on the validity of the regulations.

II

When a court reviews an agency's construction of the statute which it administers, it is confronted with two questions. First, always, is the question whether Congress has directly spoken to the precise question at issue. If the intent of Congress is clear, that is the end of the matter; for the Court, as well as the agency, must give effect to the unambiguously expressed intent of Congress. If, however, the Court determines Congress has not directly addressed the precise question at issue, the Court does not simply impose its own construction on the statute, as would be necessary, in the absence of an administrative interpretation. Rather, if the statute is silent or ambiguous with respect to the specific issue, the question for the Court is whether the agency's answer is based on a permissible construction of the statute. . . .

In light of these well-settled principles it is clear that the Court of Appeals misconceived the nature of its role in reviewing the regulations at issue. Once it determined, after its own examination of the legislation, that Congress did not actually have an intent regarding the applicability of the bubble concept to the permit program, the question before it was not whether in its view the concept is "inappropriate" in the general context of a program designed to improve air quality, but whether the Administrator's view that it is appropriate in the context of this particular program is a reasonable one. Based on the examination of the legislation and its history which follows, we agree with the Court of Appeals that Congress did not have a specific intention on the applicability of the bubble concept in these cases, and conclude that the EPA's use of that concept here is a reasonable policy choice for the agency to make.

III

. . . .

Nonattainment

The 1970 legislation provided for the attainment of primary NAAQS's by 1975. In many areas of the country, particularly the most industrialized States, the statutory goals were not attained. In 1976, the 94th Congress was confronted with this fundamental problem, as well as many others respecting pollution control. As always in this area, the legislative struggle was basically between interests seeking strict schemes to reduce pollution rapidly to eliminate its social costs and interests advancing the economic concern that strict schemes would retard industrial development with attendant social costs. The 94th Congress, confronting these competing interests, was unable to agree on what response was in the public interest: legislative proposals to deal with nonattainment failed to command the necessary consensus.

In light of this situation, the EPA published an Emissions Offset Interpretative Ruling in December 1976, see 41 Fed. Reg. 55524, to "fill the gap," as respondents put it, until Congress acted. The Ruling stated that it was intended to address "the issue of whether and to what extent national air quality standards established under the Clean Air Act may restrict or prohibit growth of major new or expanded stationary air pollution sources." *Id.*, at 55524-55525. In general, the ruling provided "that a major new source may locate in an area with air quality worse than a national standard only if stringent conditions can be met." *Id.*, at 55525. The Ruling gave primary emphasis to the rapid attainment of the statute's environmental goals. Consistent with that emphasis, the construction of every new source in nonattainment areas had to meet the "lowest achievable emission rate" under the current state of the art for that type of facility. *See Ibid.* The 1976 Ruling did not, however, explicitly adopt or reject the "bubble concept."

IV

The Clean Air Act Amendments of 1977 are a lengthy, detailed, technical, complex, and comprehensive response to a major social issue. A small portion of the statute—91 Stat. 745-751 (Part D of Title I of the amended Act, 42 U.S.C. § 7501-7508)—expressly deals with nonattainment areas. The focal point of this controversy is one phrase in that portion of the Amendments.

Basically, the statute required each State in a nonattainment area to prepare and obtain approval of a new SIP by July 1, 1979. In the interim those States were required to comply with the EPA's interpretative ruling of December 21, 1976. 91 Stat. 745. The deadline for attainment of the primary NAAQS's was extended until December 31, 1982, and in some cases until December 31, 1987, but the SIP's were required to contain a number of provisions designed to achieve the goals as expeditiously as possible.

Most significantly for our purposes, the statute provided that each plan shall:

> "(6) require permits for the construction and operation of new or modified major stationary sources in accordance with section 173. . . ." 91 Stat. 747.

Before issuing a permit, § 173 requires the state agency to determine that (1) there will be sufficient emissions reductions in the region to offset the emissions from the new source and also to allow for reasonable further progress toward attainment, or that the increased emissions will not exceed an allowance for growth established pursuant to § 172(b)(5); (2) the applicant must certify that his other sources in the State are in compliance with the SIP; (3) the agency must determine that the applicable SIP is otherwise being implemented; and (4) the proposed source complies with the lowest achievable emission rate (LAER).

The 1977 Amendments contain no specific reference to the "bubble concept." Nor do they contain a specific definition of the term "stationary source," though they did not disturb the definition of "stationary source" contained in § 111(a)(3), applicable by the terms of the Act to the NSPS program. Section 302(j), however, defines the term "major stationary source" as follows:

> "(j) Except as otherwise expressly provided, the terms 'major stationary source' and 'major emitting facility' mean any stationary facility or source of air pollutants which directly emits, or has the potential to emit, one hundred tons per year or more of any air pollutant (including any major emitting facility or source of fugitive emissions of any such pollutant, as determined by rule by the Administrator)." 91 Stat. 770.

V

The legislative history of the portion of the 1977 Amendments dealing with nonattainment areas does not contain any specific comment on the "bubble concept" or the question whether a plantwide definition of a stationary source is permissible under the permit program. It does, however, plainly disclose that in the permit program Congress sought to accommodate the conflict between the economic interest in permitting capital improvements to continue and the environmental interest in improving air quality. Indeed, the House Committee Report identified the economic interest as one of the "two main purposes" of this section of the bill. It stated:

> "Section 117 of the bill, adopted during full committee markup establishes a new section 127 of the Clean Air Act. The section has two main purposes:

(1) to allow reasonable economic growth to continue in an area while making reasonable further progress to assure attainment of the standards by a fixed date; and (2) to allow States greater flexibility for the former purpose than EPA's present interpretative regulations afford.

"The new provision allows States with nonattainment areas to pursue one of two options. First, the State may proceed under EPA's present 'tradeoff' or 'offset' ruling. The Administrator is authorized, moreover, to modify or amend that ruling in accordance with the intent and purposes of this section.

"The State's second option would be to revise its implementation plan in accordance with this new provision." H.R. Rep. No. 95-294, p. 211 (1977).

The portion of the Senate Committee Report dealing with nonattainment areas states generally that it was intended to "supersede the EPA administrative approach," and that expansion should be permitted if a State could "demonstrate that these facilities can be accommodated within its overall plan to provide for attainment of air quality standards." S. Rep. 95-127, p. 55 (1977). The Senate Report notes the value of "case-by-case review of each new or modified major source of pollution that seeks to locate in a region exceeding an ambient standard," explaining that such a review "requires matching reductions from existing sources against emissions expected from the new source in order to assure that introduction of the new source will not prevent attainment of the applicable standard by the statutory deadline." *Ibid.* This description of a case-by-case approach to plant additions, which emphasizes the net consequences of the construction or modification of a new source, as well as its impact on the overall achievement of the national standards, was not, however, addressed to the precise issue raised by this case.

Senator Muskie made the following remarks:

"I should note that the test for determining whether a new or modified source is subject to the EPA interpretative regulation [the Offset Ruling]—and to the permit requirements of the revised implementation plans under the conference bill—is whether the source will emit a pollutant into an area which is exceeding a national ambient air quality standard for that pollutant—or precursor. Thus, a new source is still subject to such requirements as 'lowest achievable emission rate' even if it is constructed as a replacement for an older facility resulting in a net reduction from previous emission levels.

"A source—including an existing facility ordered to convert to coal—is subject to all the nonattainment requirements as a modified source if it makes any physical change which increases the amount of any air pollutant for which the standards in the area are exceeded." 123 Cong. Rec. 26847 (1977).

VI

As previously noted, prior to the 1977 Amendments, the EPA had adhered to a plantwide definition of the term "source" under a NSPS program. After adoption of the 1977 Amendments, proposals for a plantwide definition were considered in at least three formal proceedings.

In January 1979, the EPA considered the question whether the same restriction on new construction in nonattainment areas that had been included in its December 1976 ruling should be required in the revised SIP's that were scheduled to go into effect in July 1979. After noting that the 1976 ruling was ambiguous on the question "whether a plant with a number of different processes and emission points would be considered a single source," 44 Fed. Reg. 3276 (1979), the EPA, in effect, provided a bifurcated answer to that question. In those areas that did not have a revised SIP in effect by July 1979, the EPA rejected the plantwide definition; on the other hand, it expressly concluded that the plantwide approach would be permissible in certain circumstances if authorized by an approved SIP. It stated:

> "Where a state implementation plan is revised and implemented to satisfy the requirements of Part D, including the reasonable further progress requirement, the plan requirements for major modifications may exempt modifications of existing facilities that are accompanied by intrasource offsets so that there is no net increase in emissions. The agency endorses such exemptions, which would provide greater flexibility to sources to effectively manage their air emissions at least cost." *Ibid.*

In April, and again in September 1979, the EPA published additional comments in which it indicated that revised SIP's could adopt the plant-wide definition of source in nonattainment areas in certain circumstances. *See id.*, at 20372, 20379, 51951, 51924, 51958. On the latter occasion, the EPA made a formal rulemaking proposal that would have permitted the use of the "bubble concept" for new installations within a plant as well as for modifications of existing units. It explained:

> " *'Bubble' Exemption*: The use of offsets inside the same source is called the 'bubble.' EPA proposes use of the definition of 'source' (see above) to limit the use of the bubble under nonattainment requirements in the following respects:
>
> "i. Part D SIPs that include all requirements needed to assure reasonable further progress and attainment by the deadline under section 172 and that are being carried out need not restrict the use of a plantwide bubble, the same as under the PSD proposal.
>
> "ii. Part D SIPs that do not meet the requirements specified must limit use of the bubble by including a definition of 'installation' as an identifiable piece of process equipment."

Significantly, the EPA expressly noted that the word "source" might be given a plantwide definition for some purposes and a narrow definition for other purposes. It wrote:

> "Source means any building, structure, facility, or installation which emits or may emit any regulated pollutant. 'Building, structure, facility or installation' means plant in PSD areas and in nonattainment areas except where the growth prohibitions would apply or where no adequate SIP exists or is being carried out." *Id.*, at 51925.

The EPA's summary of its proposed ruling discloses a flexible rather than rigid definition of the term "source" to implement various policies and programs:

"In summary, EPA is proposing two different ways to define source for different kinds of NSR programs:

"(1) For PSD and complete Part D SIPs, review would apply only to plants, with an unrestricted plantwide bubble.

"(2) For the offset ruling, restrictions on construction, and incomplete Part D SIPs, review would apply to both plants and individual pieces of process equipment, causing the plant-wide bubble not to apply for new and modified major pieces of equipment.

"In addition, for the restrictions on construction, EPA is proposing to define 'major modification' so as to prohibit the bubble entirely. Finally, an alternative discussed but not favored is to have only pieces of process equipment reviewed, resulting in no plant-wide bubble and allowing minor pieces of equipment to escape NSR regardless of whether they are within a major plant." *Id.*, at 51934.

In August 1980, however, the EPA adopted a regulation that, in essence, applied the basic reasoning of the Court of Appeals in this case. . . .

In 1981 a new administration took office and initiated a "Government-wide reexamination of regulatory burdens and complexities." 46 Fed. Reg. 16281. In the context of that review, the EPA reevaluated the various arguments that had been advanced in connection with the proper definition of the term "source" and concluded that the term should be given the same definition in both nonattainment areas and PSD areas.

In explaining its conclusion, the EPA first noted that the definitional issue was not squarely addressed in either the statute or its legislative history and therefore that the issue involved an agency "judgment as how to best carry out the Act." *Ibid.* It then set forth several reasons for concluding that the plant-wide definition was more appropriate. It pointed out that the dual definition "can act as a disincentive to new investment and modernization by discouraging modifications to existing facilities" and "can actually retard progress in air pollution control by discouraging replacement of older, dirtier processes or pieces of equipment with new, cleaner ones." *Ibid.* Moreover, the new definition "would simplify EPA's rules by using the same definition of 'source' for PSD, nonattainment new source review and the construction moratorium. This reduces confusion and inconsistency." *Ibid.* Finally, the agency explained that additional requirements that remained in place would accomplish the fundamental purposes of achieving attainment with NAAQ's as expeditiously as possible. These conclusions were expressed in a proposed rulemaking in August 1981 that was formally promulgated in October. *See id.*, at 50766.

VII

In this Court respondents expressly reject the basic rationale of the Court of Appeals' decision. That court viewed the statutory definition of the term "source" as sufficiently flexible to cover either a plantwide definition, a narrower definition covering each unit within a plant, or a dual definition that could apply to both the entire "bubble" and its components. It interpreted the policies of the statute, however, to mandate the plantwide definition in programs designed to maintain clean air and to forbid it in programs designed to improve air quality. Respondents place a fundamentally different construction on the statute. They contend that the text of the Act requires the EPA to use a dual definition—if either a component of a plant, or the plant as a whole, emits over 100 tons of pollutant, it is a major stationary source. They thus contend that the EPA rules adopted in 1980, insofar as they apply to the maintenance of the quality of clean air, as well as the 1981 rules which apply to nonattainment areas, violate the statute.

Statutory Language

The definition of the term stationary source in § 111(a)(3) refers to "any building, structure, facility, or installation" which emits air pollution. *See supra*, at 8. This definition is applicable only to the NSPS program by the express terms of the statute; the text of the statute does not make this definition applicable to the permit program. Petitioners therefore maintain that there is no statutory language even relevant to ascertaining the meaning of stationary source in the permit program aside from § 302(j), which defines the term major stationary source. *See supra*, at 12. We disagree with petitioners on this point.

The definition in § 302(j) tells us what the word "major" means—a source must emit at least 100 tons of pollution to qualify—but it sheds virtually no light on the meaning of the term "stationary source." It does equate a source with a facility—a "major emitting facility" and a "major stationary source" are synonymous under § 302(j). The ordinary meaning of the term facility is some collection of integrated elements which has been designed and constructed to achieve some purpose. Moreover, it is certainly no affront to common English usage to take a reference to a major facility or a major source to connote an entire plant as opposed to its constituent parts. Basically, however, the language of § 302(j) simply does not compel any given interpretation of the term source. . . .

. . . .

We are not persuaded that parsing of general terms in the text of the statute will reveal an actual intent of Congress. We know full well that this language is not dispositive; the terms are overlapping and the language is not precisely directed to the question of the applicability of a given term in the context of a larger operation. To the extent any congressional "intent" can be discerned from this language, it would appear that the listing of overlapping, illustrative terms was intended to enlarge, rather than to confine, the scope of the agency's power to regulate particular sources in order to effectuate the policies of the Act.

Legislative History

In addition, respondents argue that the legislative history and policies of the Act foreclose the plantwide definition, and that the EPA's interpretation is not entitled to deference because it represents a sharp break with prior interpretations of the Act.

Based on our examination of the legislative history, we agree with the Court of Appeals that it is unilluminating.

. . . .

More importantly, that history plainly identifies the policy concerns that motivated the enactment; the plantwide definition is fully consistent with one of those concerns—the allowance of reasonable economic growth—and, whether or not we believe it most effectively implements the other, we must recognize that the EPA has advanced a reasonable explanation for its conclusion that the regulations serve the environmental objectives as well. *See supra*, at 19-20, and n. 29; *see also supra*, at 17, n. 27. Indeed, its reasoning is supported by the public record developed in the rulemaking process, as well as by certain private studies.

Our review of the EPA's varying interpretations of the word "source"—both before and after the 1977 Amendments—convince us that the agency primarily responsible for administering this important legislation has consistently interpreted it flexibly—not in a sterile textual vacuum, but in the context of implementing policy decisions in a technical and complex arena. The fact that the agency has from time to time changed its interpretation of the term source does not, as respondents argue, lead us to conclude that no deference should be accorded the agency's interpretation of the statute. An initial agency interpretation is not instantly carved in stone. On the contrary, the agency, to engage in informed rulemaking, must consider varying interpretations and the wisdom of its policy on a continuing basis. Moreover, the fact that the agency has adopted different definitions in different contexts adds force to the argument that the definition itself is flexible, particularly since Congress has never indicated any disapproval of a flexible reading of the statute. . . .

. . . We conclude that it was the Court of Appeals, rather than Congress or any of the decisionmakers who are authorized by Congress to administer this legislation, that was primarily responsible for the 1980 position taken by the agency.

Policy

The arguments over policy that are advanced in the parties' briefs create the impression that respondents are now waging in a judicial forum a specific policy battle which they ultimately lost in the agency and in the 32 jurisdictions opting for the bubble concept, but one which was never waged in the Congress. Such policy arguments are more properly addressed to legislators or administrators, not to judges.

In this case, the Administrator's interpretation represents a reasonable accommodation of manifestly competing interests and is entitled to deference: the regulatory scheme is technical and complex, the agency considered the matter in a detailed and reasoned fashion, and the decision involves reconciling conflicting policies. Congress intended to accommodate both interests, but did not do so itself on the level of specificity presented by this case. Perhaps that body consciously desired the Administrator to strike the balance at this level, thinking that those with great expertise and charged with responsibility for administering the provision would be in a better position to do so; perhaps it simply did not consider the question at this level; and perhaps Congress was unable to forge a coalition on either side of the question, and those on each side decided to take their chances with the scheme devised by the agency. For judicial purposes, it matters not which of these things occurred. . . .

We hold that the EPA's definition of the term "source" is a permissible construction of the statute which seeks to accommodate progress in reducing air pollution with economic growth. "The Regulations which the Administrator has adopted provide what the agency could allowably view as . . . [an] effective reconciliation of these twofold ends. . . ." *United States v. Shimer*, 367 U.S., at 383.

The judgment of the Court of Appeals is reversed.

It is so ordered.

JUSTICE MARSHALL and JUSTICE REHNQUIST did not participate in the consideration or decision of these cases.

JUSTICE O'CONNOR did not participate in the decision of these cases.

QUESTIONS

(1) What, exactly, did the Court hold in the *Chevron* case? Did it hold that the use of the bubble policy is always available in nonattainment areas, or that it may be flexibly applied, depending on the definition of "stationary source" that the EPA applies or chooses to adopt?

(2) Is the *Chevron* decision consistent with *Asarco* and *Alabama Power Co. v. Costle*, 636 F.2d 323 (D.C. Cir. 1979)? *See* L. Rhinelander, *The Proper Place for the Bubble Concept Under the Clean Air Act*, 13 E.L.R. 10406 (1983).

(3) Is the *Chevron* case dispositive of the propriety of applying such other "alternative emission reduction options" as trading in, or banking emission reduction credits, netting, etc. Since none of these are mentioned in the Clean Air Act, can the Court's reasoning be extended to them, too?

NOTES

When an agency changes its earlier interpretation of a statute, the later conflicting interpretation is not given the same degree of deference as a "consistently held agency view." *I.N.S. v. Cardoza Fonseca,* 480 U.S. 421, N.30, relying on *Watt v. Alaska,* 451 U.S. 125, 143 (1981). The policy of statutory interpretation put forth in the *Chevron* case, which places reliance on administrative interpretation and forecloses judicial interpretation, did not follow *Fonseca* and has been widely commented on and criticized. *See, e.g.,* Dyk, *The Supreme Court's Role in Not Shaping Administrative Law,* 42 Admin. L. Rev. 429 (1992); Sunstein, *Judicial Review of Administrative Action in a Conservative Era,* 39 Admin. L. Rev. 353 (1987). Professor Sunstein is particularly critical of situations in which an agency needs to determine the scope of its own authority. To let the agency interpret its own authority under *Chevron* lets the foxes guard the hen houses. *See also* Sunstein, *Law and Administration After Chevron,* 90 Colum. L. Rev. 2071 (1990), where the author notes not only the frequent application of *Chevron,* but also the fact that the *Chevron* approach has been rejected by the courts in a number of significant cases. *See also* Schuck & Elliott, *To the Chevron Station: An Empirical Study of Federal Administrative Law,* 1990 Duke L. J. 984. The authors found that *Chevron* led to many more affirmances of administrative agency decisions post-*Chevron* than before, and that reversals of agency decisions had declined most particularly for agencies charged with the protection of health, safety, and environmental concerns. It has also been noted, rather oddly, that the current Supreme Court emphasis on textualism in statutory interpretation has led to a greater reliance on verbal analysis of statutory texts and has, in consequence, diminished reliance on *Chevron* interpretation. Merrill, *Textualism and the Future of the Chevron Doctrine,* 72 Wash. U. L.Q. 351 (1994).

The Bubble and Market Mechanisms as Regulatory Alternative

For articles supporting the use of market mechanisms, such as transferrable pollution credits and the bubble policy, see Bruce Ackerman & Richard Stewart, *Reforming Environmental Law: The Democratic Case for Market Incentives,* 13 Colum. Envtl. L.J. 171 (1988); Robert Stavins & Bradley Whitehead, *Dealing with Pollution: Market Based Incentives for Environmental Protection,* 34 Env't 7 (1992). For critical analysis, see Howard Latin, *Ideal Versus Real Regulatory Efficiency: Implementation of Uniform Standards and "Fine Tuning" Regulatory Reform,* 37 Stan. L. Rev. 1267 (1985); Kelman, *Cost-Benefit Analysis: An Ethical Critique,* Regulation 33 (Jan/Feb 1981). *See also* Mark Sagoff, The Economy of the Earth (Cambridge U.P. 1988); Joel Mintz, *A Brief Comment on a Recent Debate*, 15 Harv. Envtl. L. Rev. 149 (1991). For another critical view, see Michael C. Blumm, *The Fallacies of Free Market Environmentalism*, 15 Harv. J.L. & Pub. Pol'y 371 (1992).

The bubble concept first proposed in 1975 was eventually upheld in *Chevron* and was followed by an EPA policy statement in December of 1979, "Recommendation for Alternative Emission Reduction Options Within State Implementation Plans," 44 Fed. Reg. 71780 (Dec. 11, 1979). That policy statement encouraged revisions of state implementation plans that enabled sources to adopt different, more economically efficient controls on their various emission points, subject to EPA approval to be granted upon the fulfillment of a number of conditions. After several years of experience with the policy, EPA adopted a final policy statement in 1986.

EPA promulgated its final bubble policy in 1986, *Emissions Trading Policy Statement; General Principles for Creation, Banking and Use of Emission Reduction Credits* (51 Fed. Reg. 43814 *et seq.*, Dec. 4, 1986). It must be noted that there is no requirement that anyone engage in emissions trading. Emissions trading is not a requirement but a compliance option. The lengthy emissions trading policy describes various forms of emissions trading and sets out general principles EPA will use to evaluate emission trades under the Clean Air Act and applicable regulations

Emissions trading that is covered in the policy includes bubbles, netting, and offsets, as well as banking (storage) of emission reduction credits (ERCs)

for future use. These alternatives do not alter air quality requirements. They merely give states and industry greater flexibility to meet the requirements. While EPA endorses emissions trading and encourages its sound use by states and industry to help meet the goals of the Clean Air Act more quickly and inexpensively, it is left to each state to decide whether it wants to provide the option of emissions trading to meet its state implementation plan requirements.

[h] Sanctions and Remedies; Judicial Review

Introductory Note

This section of the air pollution materials deals with matters of enforcement and judicial review. As amended in 1977 and 1990, the Clean Air Act provides for noncompliance penalties measured by the economic advantage of noncompliance to the polluter, as well as for the utilization of certain market mechanisms to achieve compliance. As amended, too, the Act (as interpreted) provides for a broader scope of judicial review of agency rulemaking. In providing for an ample record for judicial review of the promulgation of standards, the law moves in the direction of requiring "hybrid rulemaking," which is also discussed in Chapter 8, Environmental Litigation.

It should be noted that the Clean Air Act in its citizen suit provision, § 304, and its provision for federal enforcement, both civil and criminal, § 113, as well as its general scheme of pre-enforcement judicial review, § 307(b)(1), largely set the pattern for pollution control legislation generally.

[i] Noncompliance Penalty: *Duquesne Light Co. v. EPA*

Clean Air Act § 120provides for penalties geared to delayed compliance with the law. As adopted in 1977, the section provides a new kind of civil penalty for certain violations of the Clean Air Act, keyed into pre-1990 § 113 and designed to deprive the polluter of any financial savings realized as a result of delayed compliance with the law. The section requires the Administrator, or alternatively the states, to assess and collect a noncompliance penalty, fixed and determined by regulation, and calculated on the basis of the cost a noncomplying source avoids by delaying compliance.[211]

The noncompliance penalty regulations were promulgated in 1980[212] after lengthy periods for comment, nearly a year and a half after the statutory deadline. The implementing regulations were challenged by industry in twenty separate cases, and the challenges were consolidated and disposed of by the D.C. Circuit in *Duquesne Light Co. v. EPA*[213] With one exception, the court upheld the validity of the regulations.

The first challenge went to the scope of applicability of § 120, which the regulations had interpreted broadly. Section 120 provides that noncompliance penalties are to be assessed against "every person who owns or operates" one of three categories of non-complying sources: (1) a major stationary source not

[211] CAA § 120(a)(1)(A), 42 U.S.C. § 7420(a)(1)(A).

[212] 45 Fed. Reg. 50, 086, codified at 40 C.F.R. §§ 66.1 to 66.43.

[213] 698 F.2d 456 (D.C. Cir. 1983).

complying with an emission limitation or standard, or with a compliance schedule under any applicable implementation plan, "whether or not such source is subject to a Federal or State consent decree";[214] (2) a stationary source not complying with an emission limitation or standard, a standard of performance or another requirement established under federal new source performance requirements or federal standards for hazardous pollutants;[215] and (3) a source failing to comply with the interim emission control requirements or schedule of compliance of any applicable extension, order, suspension or consent decree.[216] In implementing these requirements, the regulations specify that a notice of noncompliance—the first step in the penalty assessment process—is to be sent to the owner or operator of any source in violation of "applicable legal requirements."[217]

In general, owners and operators as defined in the Act are subject to the compliance penalty in instances where their sources are "major" as defined. "Applicable legal requirements" as related to the compliance penalty include emission limitations under an approved state implementation plan, whether or not subject to a court ordered consent decree. In general, the legislative history of § 120, relied on in EPA's regulations, emphasized the goal of removing the benefits derived by sources from any delayed compliance with the Act. Delays encompassed by a consent decree will not exempt the source from a compliance penalty.

The *Duquesne* court disposed of constitutional objections, noting that Congress has the power to impose a penalty on continuing activities, and ruling that imposition of the penalty does not result in the revision of any consent order, and does not require another hearing or factual finding. The court also rejected the assertion that the penalty was an unconstitutional deprivation of property without due process of law, noting that there was no constitutional deprivation from the date of the notice of noncompliance and continuing throughout the period of administrative and judicial review. The court of appeals however upheld petitioners' objection based on the delay which resulted when EPA exceeded the statutory time limit for a revision of the SIP, thus extending the time of noncompliance.

The court upheld the definition of what constitutes a major source by reference to the source's potential to emit. Thus, potential to emit involves the capability of emitting pollutants at maximum design capacity of the source after the application of air pollution control equipment. A stationary source is "major" if it emits or has the potential to emit 100 tons per year or more of any air pollutant. The court also held that the inclusion of fugitive emissions in the definition of potential to emit was proper because it is limited to those sources for which fugitive emissions are regulated by the SIP. In this fashion, the court followed the decision in the *Alabama Power* case.[218]

In its regulations, EPA also implemented five mandatory exemptions from the delayed compliance penalty. EPA listed seven events causing delays that

[214] CAA § 120(a)(2)(A)(i), U.S.C. § 7420(a)(2)(A)(i).

[215] CAA § 120(a)(2)(A)(ii), 42 U.S.C. § 7420(a)(2)(A)(ii).

[216] CAA § 120(a)(2)(A)(iii), 42 U.S.C. § 7420(a)(2)(A)(iii).

[217] 40 C.F.R. § 66.11(a)(1981). The applicability requirements track those of the applicability requirements set forth in CAA § 120. *See* 40 C.F.R. § 66.3(c)(1)-(4)(1981).

[218] 606 F.2d 1068 (D.C. Cir. 1979).

it will consider as beyond the control of the source. These were (1) act of God, (2) fire, (3) embargo, (4) strike, (5) inability to obtain capital—in effect, inability as a result of temporary market conditions, (6) failure of equipment to perform as designed, assuming that performance expectations were reasonable, and (7) the complete inability of a supplier or contractor to furnish labor or materials. Industry petitioners objected both to the absence of a factor concerning technological impossibility and to EPA's promulgation of an exclusive list. The court upheld EPA's action with respect to technological impossibility because EPA had made provisions to calculate the penalties to ensure that sources doing their best to surmount existing technology would not be assessed any penalties. EPA's regulations provided that where existing technology had not yet demonstrated compliance, the penalty would be based upon the cost of installing the best available controls as determined on a case by case basis, as well as a commitment to appropriate research and development. Finding that this provision complies with the technology forcing purposes of the act, the court upheld it. Based on legislative history, the court noted that the sponsor of the bill, Senator Muskie, had stated that the exemption was not intended to cover a claim of technological impossibility.

In connection with exemption based on inability to comply, the court upheld EPA's definition of the word "control," so as to leave it to the finders of fact in each instance whether the source or an affiliated entity fully used its powers to comply. The court also affirmed EPA's stated condition that in order to be eligible for an exemption from a compliance penalty, the source must have passed through the procedures leading to, and must have obtained, a delayed compliance order under § 113 of the Act.

Another mandatory exemption from § 120 arises when the failure to comply is due solely to "the conditions by reason of which a temporary emergency suspension is authorized under §§ 110(f) or (g), which provides for temporary suspension by a governor or by the President due to energy or economic emergency." The court of appeals also upheld EPA's determination of a number of procedural issues, as well as some issues relating to penalty calculations. The court likewise upheld EPA's determination that it was not required to provide for individualized variances from the requirements of § 120, since the statute provides adequately for exemptions and for statutorily provided adjustments.

Despite the detailed regulations to amplify and explain the noncompliance penalties provided under § 120[219] and the persuasive precedent set by the *Duquesne* case[220] there has been little enforcement activity applying the compliance penalty section.[221]

See also American Cyanamid Co. v. EPA, 810 F.2d 493 (5th Cir. 1987), which differs from the Duquesne decision with respect to the commencement of a § 120 proceeding while a SIP revision is pending. Unlike *Duquesne*, the case held that EPA must dispose of the SIP revision first, *i.e.*, it must reject the SIP before it can start a § 120 proceeding.

---

219 45 Fed. Reg. 50,086, codified at 40 C.F.R. §§ 66.1-66.43.

220 698 F.2d 456 (D.C. Cir. 1983).

221 For additional discussion of the *Duquesne* case and the § 120 noncompliance penalty, see F. Grad, Treatise on Environmental Law § 2.03[16][a][ii].

QUESTIONS

(1) Does the noncompliance penalty in CAA § 120meet the requirements of a soundly conceived economic emission charge (later discussed in the water pollution context)? Describe which features of it are sound, and which fail to meet the objective of cost internalization and of cost equalization through transfer payments.

(2) Does the collection of the noncompliance penalty result in cleaner air? Who benefits from the payment—when the payment is made to EPA, and when the penalty is collected, as authorized, by the state?

[ii] Scope of Review Under the Clean Air Act

HARRISON v. PPG INDUSTRIES, INC.

United States Supreme Court (1980)
446 U.S. 578, 100 S. Ct. 1889, 64 L. Ed. 2d 525

Mr. Justice STEWART delivered the opinion of the Court.

Section 307(b)(1) of the Clean Air Act (Act) provides for direct review in a federal court of appeals of certain locally and regionally applicable actions taken by the Administrator of the Environmental Protection Agency (EPA) under specifically enumerated provisions of the Act, and of "*any other final action* of the Administrator under [the] Act . . . which is locally or regionally applicable." (Emphasis added.) The issue in this case is whether the Court of Appeals for the Fifth Circuit was correct in concluding that it was without jurisdiction under § 307(b)(1) to entertain a petition for review in which PPG Industries, Inc. (PPG) and Conoco, Inc. (Conoco), the respondents here, challenged a decision of the Administrator concerning the applicability of EPA's "new source" performance standards to a power generating facility operated by PPG. More specifically, we must decide whether the Administrator's decision falls within the ambit of "any other final action" reviewable in a court of appeals under § 307(b)(1).

I

The dispute underlying this jurisdictional question involves a decision of the Administrator under § 111 of the Act, 42 USC § 7411(1976 ed, Supp II). That provision requires the Administrator to publish, and from time to time to revise, a list of categories of stationary sources that he determines "cause, or may contribute significantly to, air pollution which may reasonably be anticipated to endanger public health or welfare," § 111(b)(1)(A), and to promulgate regulations establishing standards of performance for "new sources" within the list of those categories, § 111(b)(1)(B). The Act defines a "new source" as "any stationary source, the construction or modification of which is commenced after the publication of regulations (or, if earlier, proposed regulations) prescribing a standard of performance under this section which will be applicable to such source." § 111(a)(2).

In 1971, the Administrator included "fossil fuel-fired steam generators" in his list of stationary sources. 36 Fed. Reg 5931. Later that year, pursuant to his mandate to promulgate "new source" performance standards, the Administrator established certain emission limits for any "fossil fuel-fired steam generating unit" of more than 250 million BTU's per hour heat input, the construction or modification of which was commenced after August 17, 1971, the date on which the standards were proposed. 40 CFR §§ 60.1-60.15, 60.40-60.46(1979). These "new source" regulations define the term, "fossil fuel-fired steam generating unit," *id.*, § 60.41(a), and also create a procedure under which the Administrator, upon request, will determine whether any action taken or planned by the owner or operator of a facility constitutes or will constitute "construction" or "modification" of the facility for purposes of triggering the applicability of the performance standards. *Id.*, at § 60.5.

Sometime in 1970, the respondent PPG, a chemical manufacturing corporation, began the planning and preliminary construction of a new power generating facility at its plant in Lake Charles, Louisiana. That facility, designed to take advantage of fuel-efficient "cogeneration" technology, was to consist of two gas turbine generators, two "waste-heat" boilers, and a turbo-generator. The dispute between EPA and PPG concerns the applicability of the "new source" performance standards to the waste-heat boilers of this facility. This controversy first arose in 1975, when the respondent Conoco, PPG's fuel supplier, informed EPA that Conoco was switching the supply of fuel to the Lake Charles facility from natural gas to fuel oil. An exchange of correspondence ensued, initiated by EPA's request that PPG submit additional information bearing on whether the waste-heat boilers were covered by the "new source" standards. PPG's submissions revealed that although assembly of the waste-heat boilers had not begun until 1976, the new power facility itself, of which the boilers were an integral component, had been originally designed and partially ordered in 1970, a year before the proposed date of the "new source" performance standards.

On the basis of PPG's submissions, the Regional Director for Enforcement of the EPA notified PPG of his conclusion that the boilers were subject to the "new source" standards, since construction of the boilers themselves had not begun until long after January 14, 1971, the date on which the standards had been proposed. In response, PPG took the position that the boilers were part of an integrated unit, the construction of which had begun in 1970, before the proposed date of the standards. The Regional Director, nevertheless, reaffirmed his initial decision.

Pursuant to the procedure outlined in the "new source" regulations, 40 CFR § 60.5(1979), PPG then submitted a formal request for an EPA determination that (1) the "new source" standards for "fossil fuel-fired steam generators" do not apply to the type of boilers in question, and (2) in any event, since construction of the facility of which the boilers were a part began before the date on which the standards were proposed, the boilers were not "new sources" and thus not subject to the performance standards. In the event that EPA determined that PPG's waste-heat boilers were subject to the standards, PPG also requested a clarification as to how those standards would apply.

Responding to PPG's request, the Regional Administrator notified PPG by letter that he had concluded that the waste-heat boilers were, indeed, subject to the "new source" standards for "fossil fuel-fired steam generators," and rejected PPG's argument that construction of the boilers had begun with the construction of other facets of the Lake Charles facility. Thus, the Regional Administrator affirmed the previous EPA determination that the waste-heat boilers were subject to the "new source" performance standards. With regard to the manner in which those standards were to apply to the waste-heat boilers, the Regional Administrator indicated that since PPG's gas turbine generators were not subject to the "new source" standards, PPG would be held accountable only for those emissions from the waste-heat boilers attributable to the combustion of fossil fuel, not those emissions attributable to waste heat from the gas turbine generators.[222]

PPG then filed a petition in the Court of Appeals for the Fifth Circuit, seeking review of EPA's decision concerning the applicability of the "new source" standards to its waste-heat boilers. Because of its uncertainty regarding the proper forum for judicial review, PPG also filed a complaint for injunctive relief against the Administrator in the United States District Court for the Western District of Louisiana. That suit has been stayed pending the disposition of the present case.

PPG's uncertainty, and the issue in this case, stem from conflicting views as to the proper interpretation of § 307(b)(1) of the Act, 42 USC § 7607(b)(1)(1976 ed., Supp II). Before 1977, § 307(b)(1) provided for exclusive review in an appropriate court of appeals of certain locally or regionally applicable actions of the Administrator under several specifically enumerated provisions of the Act. Actions of the Administrator under provisions not specifically enumerated in § 307(b)(1) were reviewable only in a district court under its federal-question jurisdiction, 28 USC § 1331. Congress expanded the ambit of § 307(b)(1) in 1977. The Clean Air Amendments of 1977, Pub L 95-95, 91 Stat 776, added to the list of locally or regionally applicable actions reviewable exclusively in the appropriate court of appeals both (1) actions of the Administrator under another specifically enumerated provision of the Act, and (2) "*any other final action* of the Administrator under [the] Act which is locally or regionally applicable." (Emphasis added.) Later in 1977, in enacting

[222] In a request for clarification, PPG expressed its understanding that the "new source" standards would not be applicable during the normal course of operation of the boilers, but only during performance tests or other periods when the boilers were operating on 100% fossil fuel. EPA by letter confirmed PPG's understanding. This position, however, was inconsistent with both the Regional Administrator's earlier ruling and with EPA's position in similar cases. Accordingly, an EPA representative notified PPG by telephone that the letter was incorrect. In a subsequent letter, the Director of the Division of Stationary Source Enforcement of EPA reiterated that the "new source" standards would be applicable during the normal operation of the waste-heat boilers, but only to the extent that the boilers were operating on fossil fuel, rather than waste heat. The Director also indicated that, pursuant to the standards, PPG would be required to operate the boilers at all times with fuel containing less than a certain specified content of sulfur. He further noted that PPG would be required to install and operate opacity monitors in the stacks of the boilers and to perform alternative monitoring tests.

the Clean Air Act Technical and Conforming Amendments, Pub L 95-190, 91 Stat 1404, Congress added several more provisions to those listed in § 307(b)(1) under which a locally or regionally applicable action of the Administrator is reviewable in the appropriate court of appeals.

It was under § 307(b)(1), as amended, that PPG filed a petition for review in the Court of Appeals for the Fifth Circuit. Despite having filed its petition there, PPG, and Conoco as intervenor, argued that that court was without jurisdiction, since the Administrator's decision was not an action taken under one of the provisions specifically enumerated in § 307(b)(1), and could not be properly characterized as "any other final action of the Administrator." The latter phrase, they argued, referred only to other locally or regionally applicable final actions under the provisions of the Act specifically enumerated in § 307(b)(1). In response, EPA argued that the phrase, "any other final action," should be read literally to mean *any* final action of the Administrator.

The Court of Appeals concluded that the Administrator's decision did not fall within the meaning of "any other final action" under § 307(b)(1). *PPG Industries v Harrison*, 587 F2d 237. It was the court's view that "[i]f Congress intended . . . to cast the entire responsibility for reviewing all EPA action under the Act into the courts of appeals, the numeration of specific sections would appear to be redundant." *Id.*, at 243. The "most revealing" aspect of the legislative history of § 307(b)(1), the court thought, was the complete absence of any discussion of such a "massive shift" in jurisdiction. Moreover, the court found it unlikely that Congress could have intended a shift of jurisdiction that would require the courts of appeals to review decisions of the Administrator that simply applied or interpreted his regulations, as in this case. Such a decision, the court noted, is often based on a "skeletal record" that may leave the reviewing court unable to perform meaningful judicial review. Since an appellate court is ill-suited to augment such a record, especially when compared to a trial court in which the tools of discovery are available, the court concluded that "[w]hatever addition to the jurisdiction of the courts of appeals Congress may have contemplated by adding the'any other final action' language to § 307(b)(1), we assume that section was drafted with the mechanical limitations of the courts of appeals in mind." *Id.*, at 245. Accordingly, the Court of Appeals dismissed PPG's petition for lack of jurisdiction under § 307(b)(1). *Ibid.* We granted certiorari because of the importance of determining the locus of judicial review of the actions of EPA.

II

It is undisputed that the Administrator's decision concerning the applicability of the "new source" performance standards to PPG's waste-heat boilers was locally applicable action under a provision of the Act not specifically enumerated in § 307(b)(1). The question at issue is whether the Administrator's decision falls within the scope of the phrase, "any other final action of the Administrator," so as to make that decision reviewable in a federal court of appeals under § 307(b)(1).

At the outset, we note that the parties are in agreement that the Administrator's decision was "final action" as that term is understood in the context of the Administrative Procedure Act and other provisions of federal law. It is undisputed that the Administrator's ruling represented EPA's final determination concerning the applicability of the "new source" standards to PPG's power facility. Short of an enforcement action, EPA has rendered its last word on the matter. The controversy thus is not about whether the Administrator's decision was "final," but rather about whether it was "*any other* final action" within the meaning of § 307(b)(1), as amended in 1977.

A

The petitioners argue that the phrase, "any other final action," should be construed in accordance with its literal meaning so as to reach *any* action of the Administrator under the Act that is "final" and not taken under a specifically enumerated provision in § 307(b)(1). The respondents argue that the statutory language should be construed more narrowly. Relying on the familiar doctrine of ejusdem generis, they assert that the phrase, "any other final action," should be read not to reach all final actions of the Administrator, but rather only those similar to the actions under the specifically enumerated provisions that precede that catch-all phrase in the statute. The similarity that the respondents discern among the actions under the specifically enumerated provisions in § 307(b)(1) is that those actions must be based on what the respondents refer to as "a contemporaneously compiled administrative record," by which they mean a record "based on administrative proceedings reflecting at least notice and opportunity for hearing." Since the Administrator's informal decision in this case was not based on such a record, the respondents argue that his decision was not "other final action" within the meaning of § 307(b)(1) and thus not within the jurisdiction of the Court of Appeals.

The respondents' reliance on the rule of ejusdem generis is, we think, misplaced in two respects. Under the rule of ejusdem generis, where general words follow an enumeration of specific items, the general words are read as applying only to other items akin to those specifically enumerated. Applying this rule to § 307(b)(1), the respondents argue that "any other final action" must refer only to final actions based on an administrative record reflecting at least notice and opportunity for a hearing. The flaw in this argument is that at least one of the specifically enumerated provisions in § 307(b)(1), namely, § 112(c) of the Act, 42 USC § 7412(1976 ed, Supp I) does not require the Administrator to act only after notice and opportunity for a hearing. In fact, the respondents themselves recognize that an action by the Administrator under § 112(c) would be based on an administrative record not unlike that involved in this case. Thus, even if the rule of ejusdem generis were applied, it would not significantly narrow the ambit of "any other final action" under § 307(b)(1).

. . . .

B

We have found nothing in the legislative history to support a conclusion that the phrase, "any other final action," in § 307(b)(1) means anything other than what it says.

. . . .

The respondents infer from this scant legislative history that Congress never intended the addition of the phrase, "any other final action," to § 307(b)(1) to enlarge the jurisdiction of the courts of appeals to include the review of cases based on an administrative record reflecting less than notice and an opportunity for a hearing. But, insofar as the respondents rely on what the Committee said in its Report, we fail to see how the Committee's observations on venue have any bearing at all on the jurisdictional issue now before the Court.[223] Moreover, since the Administrative Conference had not proposed that the jurisdiction of the courts of appeals be expanded to include "any other final action," the fact that the Committee expressly disclaimed an endorsement of the recommendations of the Administrative Conference on matters other than venue would appear wholly irrelevant.

The respondents also rely on what the Committee and the Congress did *not* say about the 1977 amendments to § 307(b)(1). It is unlikely, the respondents assert, that Congress would have expanded so radically the jurisdiction of the courts of appeals, and divested the district courts of jurisdiction, without some consideration and discussion of the matter. We cannot accept this argument. First, although the number of actions comprehended by a literal interpretation of "any other final action" is no doubt substantial, the number would not appear so large as ineluctably to have provoked comment in Congress. Secondly, it would be a strange cannon of statutory construction that would require Congress to state in committee reports or elsewhere in its deliberations that which is obvious on the face of a statute. In ascertaining the meaning of a statute, a court cannot, in the manner of Sherlock Holmes, pursue the theory of the dog that did not bark.[224]

C

The respondents finally argue that, as a matter of policy, the basic purpose of § 307(b)(1)—to provide prompt pre-enforcement review of EPA action—would be better served by providing for judicial review of cases such as this in a district court rather than a court of appeals. It is the respondents' view that since agency action predicated on neither formal adjudication nor informal rulemaking is apt to be based on a record too scant to permit informed judicial review, the district court is the preferable forum, since the tools of discovery are there available to augment the record, whereas in a court of appeals a time-consuming remand to EPA might be required.

This is an argument to be addressed to Congress, not to this Court. It is not our task to determine which would be the ideal forum for judicial review

[223] That the Committee intended the phrase, "any other final action," to result in at least some expansion of the jurisdiction of the courts of appeals is evident in the fact that the Committee Report expressly indicated that several types of nationwide action under provisions not specifically enumerated in § 307(b)(1) would be reviewable in the District of Columbia Circuit. *See* HR Rep No. 95-294, *supra*, at 323-324 (*e.g.*, regulations to carry out the nonattainment policy set out in § 117 of the Act). Thus, as even the respondents concede, the issue here is not whether Congress intended any expansion of the jurisdiction of the courts of appeals, but rather the extent to which Congress intended to expand that jurisdiction. As to that issue, the legislative history is silent.

[224] Arthur Conan Doyle, The Silver Blaze, in The Complete Sherlock Holmes (1938).

of the Administrator's decision in this case. See, e. g., Currie & Goodman, Judicial Review of Federal Administrative Action: Quest for the Optimal Forum, 75 Colum L Rev 1 (1975). Rather, we must determine what Congress intended when it vested the courts of appeals with jurisdiction under § 307(b)(1) to review "any other final action." The language of the statute clearly provides that a decision of the sort at issue here is reviewable in a court of appeals, and nothing in the legislative history points to any different conclusion.[225]

We add only that, as a matter of policy, this conferral of jurisdiction upon the courts of appeals is not wholly irrational. The most obvious advantage of direct review by a court of appeals is the time saved compared to review by a district court, followed by a second review on appeal. It may be seriously questioned whether the overall time lost by court of appeals remands to EPA of those cases in which the records are inadequate would exceed the time saved by foregoing in every case initial review in a district court. But whatever the answer to this empirical question, an appellate court is not without recourse in the event it finds itself unable to exercise informed judicial review because of an inadequate administrative record. In such a situation, an appellate court may always remand a case to the agency for further consideration.[226]

For the reasons stated, we hold that the Court of Appeals erred in dismissing the petition for want of jurisdiction. Accordingly, the judgment is reversed, and the case is remanded to the Court of Appeals for further proceedings consistent with this opinion.

It is so ordered.

Mr. Justice POWELL, concurring. [omitted]

Mr. Justice BLACKMUN, concurring in the result.

For the reasons stated in my Brother Stevens' dissent, I accept the Court's conclusion that the Agency's determination in this case constituted "final" action. The opaque language of § 307(b)(1) and the scant attention it received by Congress, however, leave me in doubt concerning Congress' true intention with respect to the scope of direct appellate review. Like my dissenting Brethren, I find it difficult to believe that Congress would undertake such a massive expansion in the number of Agency actions directly reviewable by the courts of appeals without some palpable indication that it had given thought to the consequences. Nonetheless, I agree with the Court that the dearth of evidence to the contrary makes its broad interpretation of the statute inescapable. On this legislative record, we must leave to Congress, should it be so inclined, the task of introducing some clear limitation on appellate jurisdiction over review of informal Agency determinations like the one now before us.

225 The dissenting opinions would modify the language of § 307(b)(1) so as to read either (1) any other final action similar to that under the specifically enumerated provisions other than those added in the Clean Air Act Technical & Conforming Amendments, ante, at [446 U.S.] 600-602, or (2) any other final action expressly, but not impliedly, authorized under the sections of the Act not specifically enumerated in § 307(b)(1), ante, at [446 U.S.] 607. But neither the language of the statute nor its legislative history supports either of these proposed readings of § 307(b)(1).

226 Whether the present administrative record in this case is adequate to permit informed judicial review is a question that the Court of Appeals must determine.

Mr. Justice REHNQUIST, dissenting.

The effort to determine congressional intent here might better be entrusted to a detective than to a judge. The court rejects the application of the traditional canon of ejusdem generis to the phrase "any other final action" on the grounds that (1) there is no uncertainty as to the meaning of that phrase, *ante*, at [446 U.S.] 588, and (2) at least one of the provisions now included in § 307(b)(1), 42 USC § 7607(b)(1)(1976 ed, Supp II)—*i.e.*, § 112(c), 42 USC § 7412(c)(1976 ed, Supp II)—does not require the Administrator to act after notice and opportunity for comment or hearing, *ante*, at [446 U.S.] 588. While I agree with the court that the phrase "any other final action" may not by itself be "ambiguous," I think that what we know of the matter makes Congress' additions to § 307(b)(1) in the Clean Air Act Technical & Conforming Amendments of 1977 no less curious than was the incident in the Silver Blaze of the dog that did nothing in the nighttime. If I am correct in this, we must look beyond the language of the phrase "any other final action" in ascertaining congressional intention. The Court did just that in *Chemehuevi Tribe of Indians v Federal Power Commission*, 420 US 395, 43 L Ed 2d 279, 95 S Ct 1066 (1975).

. . . .

In my view, absent any clear indication to the contrary, the statute should not be construed as creating a broad expansion of the jurisdiction of the federal courts of appeals. Such an approach is quite appropriate in this case because the jurisdictional expansion wrought by the Court is thoroughly inconsistent with the traditional role of appellate courts. Indeed, I think it is difficult to believe that Congress would adopt a massive shift in jurisdiction from the district courts to the courts of appeals without any comment whatsoever. The sketchy legislative history here indicates that Congress considered the Administrative Conference's recommendations and that the principal purpose of the 1977 amendment was to effect the change in venue that was recommended by the Administrative Conference. The change would be far less substantial than the jurisdictional shift that according to the Court Congress adopted sub silentio. . . . Thus, I think the most sensible way to interpret the phrase "any other final action" is to do so by reference to § 307(b)(1) at the time that phrase was enacted, rather than at the subsequent time at which the technical amendments were added.

If the phrase "any other final action" is interpreted by reference to § 307(b)(1) at the time the phrase was added, this case is clearly a proper one in which to apply the rule of ejusdem generis. . . . This interpretation offers the most satisfactory explanation for Congress' curious failure to provide any indication that it intended to effect a major jurisdictional change in the manner of reviewing EPA actions such as the one before us, a change that is inconsistent with the traditional role of appellate courts. In a case where the construction of legislative language such as this makes so sweeping and so relatively unorthodox a change as that made here, I think judges as well as detectives may take into consideration the fact that a watchdog did not bark in the night.

Mr. Justice STEVENS, dissenting.

From May 1976 through June 1977, respondent PPG Industries, Inc. ("PPG") exchanged a series of letters with various officials of the Environmental Protection Agency concerning the applicability of certain federal performance standards to PPG's waste-heat boilers at its Lake Charles, La., plant. PPG took the position that its boilers were not required to meet these standards, first, because construction had begun on them prior to the effective date of the standards and, second, because waste-heat boilers are not within the category of sources to which the standards in question apply.[227]

In April 1977 PPG submitted a formal request, pursuant to 40 CFR § 60.5(a), for a definitive determination on these issues. Although § 60.5(a) provides for such determinations only with respect to the first issue raised by PPG,[228] EPA's Regional Administrator apparently rejected both arguments in his June 1977 response, unequivocally stating that PPG's boilers were subject to the standards in question.

After a few more "clarifying" letters were exchanged, PPG brought two separate petitions for review of EPA's determination, filing in both the District Court for the Western District of Louisiana and the Court of Appeals for the Fifth Circuit. The Fifth Circuit dismissed the petition on the ground that review was properly had, if at all, in the District Court.

There are two issues before us today: first, whether EPA's determination constitutes "final" agency action such that any review is appropriate and, second, if so, whether that review must be had in the Court of Appeals because the determination constituted "any other final action" within the meaning of § 307(b)(1) of the Clean Air Act, 42 USC § 7607(b)(1). While I accept the Court's holding that the Agency's determination constituted "final" action as that term is ordinarily used under the Administrative Procedure Act, Iam not persuaded that Congress intended exclusive review of this type of action in the courts of appeals.

In *Abbott Laboratories v Gardner*, 387 US 136, 149-156, 18 L Ed 2d 681, 87 S Ct 1507, this Court set out three tests that informal agency action must meet in order to be considered final agency action that is ripe for judicial review. First, the action must involve an issue that is appropriate for judicial review, such as a purely legal question. Second, it must be a definitive statement of the Agency's position and not merely a tentative view or the opinion of a subordinate official. Finally, the party seeking review of the action must be faced with serious hardship if he is not allowed to obtain preenforcement review. In Abbott Laboratories itself the third requirement was satisfied by the fact that the affected companies either had to expend substantial amounts of money to comply with the regulation or not comply and risk serious criminal and civil penalties.

Although informal advice by agency personnel as to how the agency is likely to react to a particular set of circumstances will not ordinarily be subject to

[227] PPG also had questions about compliance in the event that the standards were found to apply.

[228] 40 CFR § 260.5(a)provides:

"When requested to do so by an owner or operator, the Administrator will make a determination of whether action taken or intended to be taken by such owner or operator constitutes construction (including reconstruction) or modification or the commencement thereof within the meaning of this part."

judicial review under the Abbot Laboratories tests, this case would seem to be an exception. As EPA argues, the only issue to be decided is whether certain regulations apply under the facts submitted to the Agency by PPG. Second, the Regional Administrator of EPA himself signed the letter rejecting PPG's position; thus, it appears to be, as the Court suggests, the Agency's "last word" on the issue. *Ante*, at [p. 241], 64 L Ed 2d 534.[229] And finally, although the parties have not informed us of the magnitude of PPG's estimated compliance costs, it appears that PPG would have to risk sizeable penalties under 42 USC §§ 7413(b), (c) and 7420in order to challenge EPA's determination in enforcement proceedings.

Assuming that EPA's letter in this case would constitute "final agency action" under the APA, the second question is whether we are compelled by the language of § 307(b)(1) to hold that the Court of Appeals had exclusive jurisdiction to review that action. As Mr. Justice Rehnquist points out in his dissent, such a construction of the statute will greatly increase the burdens currently borne by the courts of appeals, both in terms of numbers of cases and difficulty of issues presented.[230] *Ante*, at 64 L Ed 2d 540-541, 542-543. In my view, it will also distort the concept of final agency action by giving EPA virtually unlimited discretion to transform its informal advice into final agency action subject to court of appeals review.

Under § 307(b)(2) of the Clean Air Act,any agency action that was reviewable in the courts of appeals cannot be challenged in an enforcement proceeding, whether or not review was actually sought.[231] Under § 307(b)(1), a petition for review must be filed within 60 days of the publication of the agency action in the Federal Register. Although EPA apparently did not publish letters like its letter to PPG in the Federal Register prior to the Clean Air Act Amendments of 1977, it is now embarking on a program to do so.[232]

229 The Court relies exclusively on this factor, along with the fact that the parties agree that the action is "final." I would not place much reliance on the parties' agreement, however, since they share a common interest in having the threshold jurisdictional question resolved in the affirmative. Thus, it serves PPG's interests to treat EPA's letter as a final action because PPG wants judicial review as soon as possible. It also serves EPA's interests because broadening the category of agency actions that are final and reviewable only in the courts of appeals increases the number of agency actions that cannot be challenged in enforcement proceedings under the Act. 64 L Ed 2d 546.

230 Whether or not the record in this case was sufficiently developed for purposes of court of appeals' review (an issue on which the parties differ), it is clear that there will be many cases involving informal EPA action in which the "record" on which the agency relied in making its determination will be minimal.

231 Section 307(b)(2) of the Clean Air Actprovides:

"Actions of the Administrator with respect to which review could have been obtained under paragraph (1) shall not be subject to judicial review in civil or criminal proceedings for enforcement."

232 In EPA's brief in the Court of Appeals, it took the position that, by adding "any other final action" to § 307(b)(1), Congress intended to require the agency to give notice in the Federal Register of each and every "final action" it takes, contrary to its prior practice. Although the Agency noted that it had not yet begun complying with this obligation, it stated that it intended to begin publication in the near future of all final agency actions taken since the 1977 amendments. Brief, at 27-29. EPA's interpretation of the Federal Register clause as a requirement that notice of final determinations be given seems backwards to me. I think a more plausible interpretation of the statute is that Congress intended the term "final agency action" to refer only to the types of actions that EPA was accustomed to publishing in the Federal Register prior to the 1977 amendments.

Because publication may give the Agency the benefit of the preclusive effect of § 307(b)(2), it has every incentive to notice a wide range of actions in the Federal Register.

Once notice of an action has been published in the Federal Register, it would be difficult to argue that it was not "final" agency action. Most of the determinations would, like this one, concern applications of particular regulations to undisputed fact situations. Second, the very fact that the agency had published its position would indicate that it was a definitive statement of agency policy. And finally, the requirement that an aggrieved person show some hardship entitling him to pre-enforcement review would also seem to be satisfied by mere publication, since the failure to raise the issue might well foreclose future review entirely.[233]

I find it difficult to believe that Congress intended this highly undesirable result. Although I do not share Mr. Justice Rehnquist's interpretation of the statute, I would construe it as drawing a line short of allowing EPA complete discretion to turn anything it chooses into final action reviewable only in the courts of appeals.

Section 307(b)(1) mandates exclusive review in the courts of appeals of the Administrator's actions under certain specific subsections of the Act. Those subsections contain specific grants of authority to the Administrator to make certain determinations. Thus, §§ 110 and 111(d), 42 USC §§ 7410 and 7411(d)empower the Administrator to approve state implementation plans; §§ 111(j), 112(c), 113(d) and 119, 42 USC §§ 7411(j), 7412(c), 7413(d) and 7419, empower the Administrator to grant (and by necessary implication to deny) waivers to companies that are unable to comply with the applicable standards; and § 120, 42 USC § 7420, sets up a procedure through which the Administrator is to assess noncompliance penalties, after notice and hearing on the record. Each of these types of agency action has an immediate impact on the legal rights of the affected party.

By contrast, agency advice as to whether or not particular sources are subject to previously promulgated regulations does not, in itself, change any party's legal status; nor is there anything in the statute that specifically requires or permits the Administrator to give such advice. This does not mean that it is beyond the Administrator's power to do so or to set up his own procedures, as he has done in 40 CFR § 60.5(a), for giving advice in a formalized manner. But I do not believe Congress intended the review provisions of the statute to cover this type of "agency action" as well as those types specifically contemplated by the statute. In making reviewable "any other final action of the Administrator under this chapter," Congress must have been thinking of actions it had specifically directed or authorized the Administrator to take under sections of the Act not specifically enumerated in § 307(b)(1). This interpretation is consistent with both an ejusdem generis construction of the statute and its plain language. It is also supported by

[233] The hardship determination, of course, becomes circular, since there is no preclusion unless there is "final" agency action and no finality unless there is some hardship in not according pre-enforcement review. Under these circumstances, the courts are likely to emulate the Court's approach in this case, ignoring the hardship component entirely and making reviewable any action that constitutes a definitive statement of the agency's position.

Congress' apparent belief that it was extending court of appeals review only to the types of actions that EPA had been accustomed to publishing in the Federal Register. *See* n 7, *supra*.

Accordingly, I respectfully dissent.

QUESTIONS

(1) The case of *Harrison v. PPG Industries* addresses a problem of legislative interpretation. No one wishes to spoil the fun the members of the Court were having with Conan Doyle's dog that did not bark, but isn't Congressional silence often taken as a sign that Congress did *not* wish to change the earlier legal situation?

(2) Does the decision in *Harrison v. PPG Industries* allow EPA to determine what is and what is not a "final action" by publishing its opinion, advice, policy statement or other written expression in the federal register? Would any person potentially affected by the publication then be under an obligation to file an appeal under § 307(b) in order not to be foreclosed from objecting?

(3) What, if any, advantage is it to EPA to have won the case? Does the Court's decision make it easier or more difficult for environmental defense groups to participate effectively in the rulemaking process?

[i] Hazardous Air Pollutants

[i] Air Toxics

Title III of the Clean Air Act Amendments of 1990 made major changes in the regulation of hazardous air pollutants, also referred to as air toxics. In the main, Title III involves a major expansion of § 112 of the Clean Air Act. As amended, § 112 is a reaction to the frustrations environmentalists—and Congress—experienced with EPA's enforcement under § 112 as contained in the original 1970 Clean Air Act. The original law had authorized EPA to regulate hazardous air pollutants, and to select specific pollutants for regulation, but standards for such pollutants during the past 20 years had only been promulgated for seven substances. The 1990 amendment relieved EPA of the selection responsibility by listing 172 chemicals and 17 compounds as hazardous air pollutants in the law itself. There is authority to revise the list when appropriate. The original revisions of § 112 required EPA to set standards with an ample margin of safety. There is a question whether the original standards sought to achieve zero risk, but it is clear that the standards were primarily based on a risk evaluation. The reliance on a risk-based approach in such cases as the vinyl chloride decision in *NRDC v. EPA,*[234] and in the subsequent benzene decisions, caused problems for the further development of hazardous air pollution standards, persuading both EPA and environmentalists that a technology-based approach would better protect the public health.

---

[234] 824 F.2d 1146 (D.C. Cir. 1987).

The law provides that the substances listed be regulated by categories of facilities which emit the particular air toxics, somewhat reminiscent of the promulgation of New Source Performance Standards. EPA was required to promulgate the list of categories and subcategories one year after the enactment of the Clean Air Act Amendments of 1990, namely by November 15, 1991. A major source of air toxics is a facility which emits 10 tons per year of any single substance on the list, or 25 tons per year of any combination of substances on the list. In addition to major sources, the amendments also regulate "area sources," such as dry cleaners, gas stations, bakeries, etc. EPA must regulate 90% of the 30 most serious toxic pollutants emitted by such area sources.

The law requires that emissions of air toxics be reduced to the level attained by the "maximum achievable control technology" (MACT). It provides for process changes, control equipment, changes in work practices, and training of operators and their certification. Emissions of the 189 toxic chemicals from major industrial sources must be reduced to the average level of the cleanest 12% of the industries in the category. Although the primary reliance in the statute is on a technology-based approach, each source is nevertheless required to reduce emissions to provide an ample margin of safety for persons exposed. Such an ample margin of safety is defined as a 1:10,000 risk of cancer to the most exposed person. When EPA promulgated its list of categories and subcategories by November 15, 1991, it also had to promulgate standards for the first 40 source categories.

Control of hazardous air pollution was also a target of the revisions of Title V of the Clean Air Act Amendments of 1990, in that by 1993, all major industrial sources were required to obtain permits under Title V. Reductions in emissions for major sources are phased in to become effective by 1992 to 2005. Coke oven emissions reductions are to begin in the year 2003 and to be phased in successively until the year 2020, requiring certain interim reductions. The new provisions require that major sources achieve compliance within three years after the promulgation of the standards. A one year extension is also provided for. Thus, the new hazardous air pollution controls were to become effective by 1995 or 1996.

Special incentives are provided for facilities that reduce emissions prior to the promulgation of standards. A six-year extension is provided for any facility which achieves a 90% reduction before the Administrator proposes the standards for the source category.

Special provisions are made in the law for accidental releases of hazardous air pollutants. By November 15, 1992, EPA had to publish a list of 100 or more extremely hazardous air pollutants and plant owners must develop plans to deal with the risk of accidental releases. A Chemical Safety and Hazard Identification Board is created to make recommendations for accident prevention and to investigate chemical accidents to determine their causes. Formal safety reviews are to be made available to the public, and EPA must set safety standards for plants which use toxic chemicals in bulk.

[ii] Ample Margin of Safety

Major issues in the regulation of hazardous air pollution had arisen even prior to the amendment of § 112 of the Clean Air Actin the 1990 revision. One recurring issue in the regulation of hazardous materials is invariably the question of the meaning of "ample margin of safety" in § 112. This issue was significantly addressed in *National Resources Defense Council, Inc. v. United States Environmental Protection Agency*. That case is generally referred to as the vinyl chloride decision.[235]

In the *National Resources Defense Council* case, the issue of what constitutes an "ample margin of safety" for pollutants that present an unqualified health risk at any level of exposure was before the D.C. Circuit Court in an en banc panel reviewing the standard for vinyl chloride emissions. An opinion by Judge Bork rejected NRDC's contention that as a matter of statutory construction of the Act, prior to its amendment in 1990, cost and technological feasibility could never be considered. In its determination the court stated that cost and technological feasibility were permissible factors in determining the margin of safety to be provided; it nevertheless concluded that the vinyl chloride standards as promulgated constituted an abuse of discretion because the Administrator "had simply substituted technological feasibility for health as the primary consideration under § 112."[236] While the court expressly stated that "safe" did not mean "risk-free" "the Congressional mandate to provide an 'ample margin of safety' to protect the public health requires the Administrator to make an initial determination of what is 'safe.' " This determination must be based exclusively on the Administrator's determination of the risk to health at a particular emission level. While the court refused to bind the Administrator to any specific method of determining what is "safe" or "an adequate margin," it did state that cost and technological feasibility are improper factors to use in determining what is "safe."

The court also found that fugitive dust was not to be included in determining whether a source was major or not, and that "major emitting facility" may be defined differently for § 112 purposes than for other purposes, such as the control of sources for the prevention of significant deterioration. The court further held that a source's "potential to emit" is not limited to "federally enforceable" controls in determining what are major sources; the statute referred to governmental regulations generally, and therefore state or local regulations are properly to be included within the controls to be accounted for in determining what is a major source under § 112(a)(1).

The benzene case, *AFL-CIO v. Occupational Safety and Health Administration,*[237] referred to an issue in the vinyl chloride case under somewhat similar language in the Occupational Safety and Health Act with respect to worker exposure to benzene. The court reviewed provisions under OSHA designed to reduce occupational exposure from 10 ppm to 1 ppm, apparently the lowest

[235] 824 F.2d 1146 (D.C. Cir. 1987). A similar issue was discussed and dealt with by the U.S. Supreme Court in the so-called "benzene decision" in AFL-CIO v. American Petroleum Institute, 448 U.S. 607, 100 S. Ct. 2844, 65 L. Ed. 2d 1010 (1980).

[236] NRDC v. EPA, 824 F.2d 1146, 1163 (D.C. Cir. 1987), 27 ELR at 21042.

[237] AFL-CIO v. American Petroleum Institute, 448 U.S. 607, 100 S. Ct. 2844, 65 L. Ed. 2d 1010 (1980).

feasible exposure in a workplace. Like vinyl chloride, benzene exposure was not safe at any level and hence OSHA did not find itself required to undertake a risk assessment, since there was no threshold. Justice Stevens in his opinion stated:

> OSHA's rationale for lowering permissible exposure limit to 1 ppm was based not on any finding that leukemia has ever been caused by exposure to 10 ppm of benzene and that it will not be caused by exposure to 1 ppm, but rather on a series of assumptions indicating that some leukemias might result from exposure to 10 ppm and that the number of cases might be reduced by reducing that exposure level to 1 ppm.[238]

The court apparently concluded that the language requiring a safe standard in OSHA did not mean that the standard set had to be completely risk free. The court apparently relied on the conclusion that something is "unsafe" when it threatens humans with a "significant risk of harm." The judgment of what is a significant risk of harm is apparently left to the expert knowledge and decision of the administrative agency which must be granted a fair measure of sound discretion in the matter, taking into account the acceptable risks in what may be an important and economically significant activity.[239]

Another issue, which was disposed of after the 1990 amendment of the Clean Air Act, was the issue of the full scope of the application of § 112, in particular, the question of what "major sources" of hazardous emissions would be covered, including the question as to whether fugitive emissions were to be included in the determination of major emitting facilities.

In *National Mining Association v. U.S. Environmental Protection Agency,*[240] an electric company, mining trade association, paper trade association, industrial chemical trade association, and petroleum trade association sought review of the EPA rule implementing the 1990 amendments to the Clean Air Act (CAA) with respect to the definition of "major sources" of hazardous air emissions, subject to stricter emissions controls, challenging three aspects of EPA's implementation of the definition of "major source."

First, the mining trade association and the electric company questioned EPA's requiring the aggregation of all hazardous air emissions within a plant site, instead of only those emissions from equipment in similar industrial categories, in a § 112 major source determination. Second, the mining trade association challenged EPA's requiring the inclusion of "fugitive emissions" in a source's aggregate emissions in determining whether the source is major. Third, the industrial chemical trade association and the petroleum trade

[238] 448 U.S. 634.

[239] For an effort to define what constitutes a significant risk, see Cross, Byrd & Lave, *Discernible Risk: A Proposed Standard for Significant Risk in Carcinogen Regulation,* 43 Admin. L. Rev. 61 (1991). The article cites such examples as OSHA's asbestos standard, holding a risk of 40-45 extra cancer deaths per thousand would be significant, and the OSHA ethylene oxide standard providing 12-23 excess deaths per ten thousand to be significant. 2.2 excess deaths per thousand resulting from the arsenic standard was noted to substantially exceed the excess risk of one per thousand that the Supreme Court stated that a reasonable person might well consider significant. The article suggests that a significant risk lies somewhere between one in one million and one in one thousand. The broad range of discretion this leaves to the agency is also noted.

[240] 59 F.3d 1351, 25 ELR 21390 (D.C. Cir. 1995).

association contended that EPA overstepped its regulatory authority by permitting a source to reduce its "potential to emit" only with "federally enforceable" emission controls and limitations.

The D.C. Circuit upheld EPA's definition of "major sources" in its 1994 rule governing the procedures and criteria for implementing emission standards for hazardous air pollutants (HAPs) under § 112, but held that EPA failed to explain why otherwise effective state or local controls must be "federally enforceable" to be considered in determining a source's potential to emit under § 112(a)(1).

The court first held that the EPA rule reasonably interpreted the CAA to require aggregation of all hazardous air emissions within a plant site, instead of only those emissions from equipment in the same EPA source categories or the same standard industrial classification (SIC) code, in determining whether a site was a "major source." The court held that the EPA's definition of "major source" is faithful to the language of § 112(a)(1), which states that a "group of stationary sources" need meet only three conditions to be termed a "major source," and says nothing about combining emissions only from sources within the same source categories or SIC codes.

The court also held that the other provisions of § 112, when read in full and in context, support the EPA's implementation of the major source definition without reference to source category. The court rejected the petitioner's contention that because several provisions of the CAA use the terms "major source" and "category" in the same sentence, EPA must read a source category restriction into § 112(a)(1)'s definition of "major source." The court further held that EPA's definition of "major source" would not lead to anomalous and unreasonable results when other parts of § 112 are implemented, and that EPA's implementation of § 112(a)(1) was not at odds with other aspects of the CAA.

The D.C. Circuit then rejected the petitioner's argument that the EPA's implementation of § 112(a)(1) was procedurally flawed. EPA sufficiently addressed the definition's effect on various aspects of the HAP program and was sufficiently explicit about the definition's binding effect on future action, and, thus, any procedural errors in the promulgation of the rule were not so serious as to create a substantial likelihood that the rule would have been significantly changed.

The court next held that EPA reasonably defined "major source," as used in the rule-implementing provision of CAA limiting nationwide emissions of hazardous air pollutants, to require aggregating of all hazardous air emissions within a plant site, even though EPA used a different definition of the term, dependent on SIC codes, for the purposes of controlling emissions of volatile organic compounds in serious, severe and extreme ozone nonattainment areas, under CAA § 182 (c) through (e), and for the Title V permitting program (CAA § 501(2)), as the different programs had different objectives and structures. The court then rejected the petitioner's argument that EPA's definition of "major source" is inconsistent with the legislative history of the 1990 CAA amendments. It held that contrary to the petitioner's contention that the legislative history compels a conclusion that Congress intended that a source-based limitation, such as the SIC limitation, apply to all definitions of "major source," the sections of the House and Senate Reports that specifically discussed this definition contradict that interpretation. The court concluded that at most, the legislative history leaves unresolved whether the agency must define "major source" with reference to SIC codes; thus, applying *Natural Resources Defense Council v. EPA*, 22 F.3d 1125, 1141 (D.C. Cir. 1994), the EPA's interpretation of "major source" is reasonable.

The court further ruled that EPA reasonably required inclusion of fugitive emissions in a site's aggregate hazardous air emissions for the purposes of determining whether the site was a "major source," without requiring any special rulemaking on fugitive emissions, pursuant to § 302(j), as required for other CAA purposes, since the only statutory qualification governing which emissions may be aggregated was that they emanated from a contiguous site under common control. The court rejected the petitioner's argument that this situation is indistinguishable from that in *Alabama Power Co. v. Costle,* 636 F.2d 323 (D.C. Cir. 1979), which held that EPA could not, without rulemaking, include fugitive emissions of air pollutants in a facility's aggregate emissions for purposes of determining whether the facility was a "major emitting facility" within § 169(1), distinguishing *Alabama Power* as pre-*Chevron,* and holding that there are significant differences between § 112(a)(1) and § 302(j). Section 302(j) speaks of sources that "directly" emit air pollutants on the one hand, and fugitive emissions on the other, suggesting that emissions of the fugitive variety are not direct. In contrast, § 112(a)(1) does not contain the modifier "directly," and it does not mention fugitive emissions as a separate category of emissions. Additionally, title V of the Act explicitly draws a distinction between the nomenclature of § 112 and that of § 302, defining "major source" for permitting purposes as either a major source as defined in § 112 or a major stationary source as defined in § 302. The court concluded that EPA may require the inclusion of fugitive emissions without conducting any special rulemaking, even if "major source" and "major stationary source" mean the same thing.

The court lastly addressed the petitioners' contention that the EPA's limitation of the controls to be considered in determining a source's "potential to emit" to "federally enforceable" controls, disregarding emissions limitations imposed by state or local regulations not deemed "federally enforceable," is contrary to the language of § 112(a)(1). The EPA was accused of interpreting the statute so as to pressure states—through the ministrations of sources eager to have local controls counted in determining their capacity to emit under § 112—to seek EPA approval of state emissions policies. The court noted that Congress meant "controls" to refer to governmental regulations and to stand for effective controls, and that in drafting § 112, Congress specifically directed EPA to consider controls in determining which producers should be classified as "major sources," but conspicuously did not limit controls to those that are federally enforceable.

Though the government correctly argued that since Congress did not specify what kind of controls would qualify, EPA was free to answer that question, which it did by requiring that they had to be "federally enforceable," for each of the regulatory approaches through which states can impose restraints and have them deemed "federally enforceable," the EPA had proposed conditions for achieving such enforceability that went beyond the mere effectiveness of particular constraints as a practical matter. The court held that EPA had not explained how its refusal to consider limitations other than those that are "federally enforceable" serves the statute's directive to consider controls imposed by a state or locality even if they are unquestionably effective, and why it is essential that a control be included in an SIP. The court rejected EPA's argument that its interpretation of § 112 was supported by legislative history, reasoning that the fact that Congress rejected the Senate version of the bill, which focused exclusively on the actual operating conditions, did not necessarily suggest that it implicitly delegated to EPA the authority to limit the class of governmentally imposed restraints that could be taken into account to those that are "federally enforceable."

Further, Congress did not implicitly ratify EPA's past treatment of non-federally enforceable controls when it enacted the 1990 amendments. Throughout the 1980s, the EPA vacillated on the degree of federal involvement required, and when Congress voted in 1990, the EPA's 1989 regulations requiring federal enforceability as a prerequisite to recognition were the subject of litigation.

For further consideration of air toxics, see F. Grad, Treatise on Environmental Law, § 2.03[15].

UNITED STATES v. BUCKLEY

United States Court of Appeals, Sixth Circuit (1991)
934 F.2d 84, 21 ELR 21113

RYAN, Circuit Judge.

A jury convicted Paul J. Buckley of violating 42 USC §§ 7412(c)(1)(B), 7413(c)(1)(C), Clean Air Act provisions regulating the release of asbestos into the environment. The jury also convicted him of violating 42 U.S.C. § 9603(b)(3), a CERCLA[241] provision requiring notification to authorities of any release of a reportable quantity of asbestos. Appealing both convictions, Buckley places two issues before this court. The first is whether the jury instructions offended due process by misstating the level of scienter required for conviction under the statutes. The second is whether the district court abused its discretion in denying Buckley's motion for a mistrial, in view of the government's efforts to elicit testimony concerning certain unduly prejudicial physical evidence.

We conclude that the jury instructions accurately stated the law, and that the trial court did not abuse its discretion in declining to grant a mistrial.

---

[241] Comprehensive Environmental Response, Compensation and Liability Act of 1980, 42 U.S.C. 9601 *et seq.*

I

A grand jury indicted Buckley and other parties on several counts related to the release of asbestos into the environment in the course of a demolition project. This appeal concerns only counts 4 and 5. Count 4 charged that Buckley violated 42 U.S.C. §§ 7412(c)(1)(B), 7413(c)(1)(C)by knowingly emitting certain amounts of asbestos into the environment in the process of demolishing a stationary source. Count 5 charged that Buckley violated 42 U.S.C. § 9603(b)(3)by failing to notify the appropriate federal agency of a known release of a reportable quantity of asbestos.

At trial, with respect to count 4 and related counts, the district court charged the jury in part as follows:

> "Counts . . . 4, . . . are alleged violations of the Clean Air Act.'
>
> "The Clean Air Act prohibits the emission of a hazardous air pollutant in violation of any emission standard set by the EPA.
>
> . . . .
>
> "Before any defendant may be found guilty of a violation of the Clean Air Act, you must find beyond a reasonable doubt that . . . he *knowingly* failed or caused any other person or employee to fail to comply with any of the work practice standards set forth. . . ." (Emphasis added).

With respect to count 5 and related counts, the district court charged the jury in part as follows:

> "Counts 3 and 5 of the Indictment charge specific defendants with failure to notify the appropriate agency of the United States that one [1] pound or more of asbestos had been released into the environment from a facility, in violation of CERCLA.
>
> . . . .
>
> "In order to prove a defendant guilty of this charge, the government must prove each of the following elements beyond a reasonable doubt:
>
> . . . .
>
> "*Second*: That the defendant *knew* of the release of more than one [1] pound of asbestos into the environment from the facility.
>
> . . . .
>
> "CERCLA's reporting requirements are not extended to all employees involved in a release. The term 'person in charge' is deliberately designed to cover only supervisory personnel who have the responsibility for the particular facility. The reporting requirements of CERCLA apply to any person—even if of relatively low rank—who, because he was in charge of a facility, was in a position to detect, prevent, and abate a release of hazardous substances.
>
> "The defendant's control over a facility need not be sole or exclusive. He need not be the only one in charge. There may be several persons in charge of the same facility.
>
> "All that is necessary is that the individual have or share such control of the facility where the release occurred.

> . . . .
>
> "*Knowledge ordinarily may not be proved directly*, because there is no way of fathoming or scrutinizing the operations of the human mind. But *you may infer the defendant's knowledge* from the surrounding circumstances.
>
> "You may consider any statement made and done or omitted by the defendant, and all other facts and circumstances in evidence which indicate his state of mind.
>
> "*All the government must prove is that the defendant knew the general nature of the asbestos material* on pipes or other facility components being demolished. The *government does not have to show that the defendant knew the legal status of the asbestos materials or that he was violating the law.*
>
> . . . .
>
> "*The government is not required to prove a wrongful intent or awareness of wrongdoing*. The question whether the defendant acted in *good faith is not material*. It is the responsibility of persons who voluntarily associate themselves with asbestos demolition operations as supervisors or persons in charge to comply with the law." (Emphasis added).

On the element of "knowledge," the district court instructed generally as follows:

> "The law provides that *an individual cannot avoid knowledge by deliberately closing his eyes to what would otherwise be obvious or by failing to investigate if he is in possession of facts which cry out for investigation.*
>
> "Consequently, if you find beyond a reasonable doubt that the defendant acted with a conscious purpose to avoid learning the truth about the presence of asbestos, or *consciously avoided investigating even though he was in possession of facts which demanded investigation*, then you may find that the government has satisfied its burden of establishing knowledge.
>
> "If you find that the defendant was aware of a high probability that asbestos was present and that the defendant acted with deliberate disregard of the facts, you may find that the defendant acted knowingly. However, *if you find that the defendant actually believed that there was no asbestos on pipes or in stoves, he may not be convicted.*
>
> "It is entirely up to you whether you find that the defendant *deliberately closed his eyes* and any inferences to be drawn from the evidence on this issue." (Emphasis added.)

Buckley objected to these instructions on the ground that they created a strict-liability criminal offense. The jury found Buckley guilty of counts 4 and 5. The court imposed a $5000 fine and sentenced Buckley to three years of probation and 300 hours of community service.

II

A

Buckley contends that the instructions violated due process by eliminating knowledge as an element of the crimes. He also seems to contend that due process requires the courts to define "knowledge" as awareness of wrongdoing, not awareness of the occurrence of the prohibited acts or omissions.

"The standard on appeal for a court's charge to the jury is whether the charge, taken as a whole, fairly and adequately submits the issues and applicable law to the jury." *United States v. Martin*, 740 F.2d 1352, 1361 (6th Cir. 1984). The question is "what a reasonable juror could have understood the charge as meaning." *California v. Brown*, 479 U.S. 538, 541, 107 S.Ct. 837, 83 9, 93 L.Ed. 2d 934 (1987). Even if an instruction proves impermissible viewed in isolation, the reviewing court upholds the instruction if it takes on a permissible meaning in the context of surrounding instructions. *Id.* Where, in formulating instructions, the "district court engages in statutory construction as a matter of law, . . . [the Sixth Circuit] review[s] [the] conclusions de novo." *United States v. Brown*, 915 F.2d 219, 223 (6th Cir. 1990).

1. Clean Air Act Violation

As effective at the time of asbestos emissions, the Clean Air Act, 42U.S.C. § 7401 *et seq.*, provided in pertinent part, "No air pollutant [such as asbestos] to which [an established emission] standard applies may be emitted from any stationary source in violation of [the established] standard. . . . Any person who knowingly violates . . . [this prohibition] . . . shall be punished by a fine . . . or . . . imprisonment . . . or . . . both." 42 U.S.C. §§ 7412(c)(1)(B), 7413(c)(1)(C)(1986).

The statutory language makes knowledge an element of the crime of violating emission standards; however, the statute requires knowledge only of the emissions themselves, not knowledge of the statute or of the hazards that emissions pose. "[W]here a statute does not specify a heightened mental element . . ., general intent is presumed to be the required element." Brown, 915 F.2d at 225. Indeed, in the phrase "knowingly violates . . . section 7412(c)," "section 7412(c)" serves as a shorthand expression for the specific acts that 7412(c) forbids in detail. Cf. *United States v. Int'l Minerals and Chemical Corp.*, 402 U.S. 558, 562-63, 91 S.Ct. 1697, 1700-01, 29 L.Ed. 2d 178 (1971). Such phrases do "not signal an exception to the rule that ignorance of the law is no excuse." *Id.*

Because of the very nature of asbestos and other hazardous substances, individuals dealing with them have constitutionally adequate notice that they may incur criminal liability for emissions-related actions. *See id.* at 565, 91 S.Ct. at 1701. "[W]here . . . dangerous or deleterious . . . products or obnoxious waste materials are involved, the probability of regulation is so great that anyone who is aware that he is in possession of them or dealing with them must be presumed to be aware of the regulation." Id. . . .

Here the district court properly instructed the jurors that they could not find Buckley guilty unless he "knowingly failed . . . to comply with

. . . standards." The district court also explained the meaning of "knowledge" for the jurors. The court noted that under the law, the government could establish Buckley's knowledge by showing that Buckley closed his eyes to obvious facts or failed to investigate when aware of facts which demanded investigation. Finally, near the end of its explanation of knowledge, the district court noted that the jury could not convict Buckley if it found that he actually believed that the pipe and stove coverings contained no asbestos.

Accordingly, we hold that whether evaluated separately or together, these instructions accurately state the law and do not offend due process.

2. CERCLA Violation

At the time of the asbestos emissions, CERCLA provided in pertinent part:

> Any person . . . in charge of a facility from which a hazardous substance is released, other than federally permitted release, in a quantity equal to or greater than that determined pursuant to § 9602 of this title [that is, more than one pound of asbestos] who fails to notify immediately the appropriate agency of the United States Government as soon as he has *knowledge* of such release . . . shall . . . be fined . . . or imprisoned . . . or both. . . . 42 U.S.C. § 9603(b)(3)(1986) (emphasis added).

As we explained above, "knowledge" as used in such regulatory statutes means knowledge that one is doing the statutorily proscribed acts, not knowledge that the statutes or potential health hazards exist. As we noted, the very nature of hazardous substances such as asbestos puts individuals controlling the substances on notice that criminal statutes probably regulate the handling and release of the substances.

The district court properly charged jurors that to prove Buckley guilty of failure to notify, the government needed to prove that Buckley "knew of the release of more than one [1] pound of asbestos. . . ." The district court also correctly informed jurors that the government needed to establish only knowledge of the presence of the asbestos, not knowledge of the asbestos's legal status. Buckley takes particular exception to the following instruction:

> The government is not required to prove a wrongful intent or awareness of wrongdoing. The question whether the defendant acted in good faith is not material. It is the responsibility of persons who voluntarily associate themselves with asbestos demolition operations as supervisors or persons in charge to comply with the law.

Perhaps, viewed in isolation, this instruction might lead a juror to conclude that the statute did not specify knowledge as an element of the offense. However, immediately prior to reading this instruction, the district court unequivocally foreclosed such a misinterpretation by stating that the government needed to prove that Buckley knew of the presence of asbestos at the demolition site.

Accordingly, we hold that taken as a whole, the instruction accurately states the law.

. . . .

III

For the foregoing reasons, Buckley's convictions are AFFIRMED.

NOTES

See also United States v. Walsh, 8 F.3d 659, 24 ELR 20030 (6th Cir. 1993), in which individual liability was found against an employee and officer of an asbestos removal service. The defendant was held liable, suffered a substantial civil penalty, and was enjoined from performing further asbestos related projects for a two-year period without complying with the Act and without notifying EPA. The defendant was an "operator" because he was the person who had the necessary control and who was therefore responsible for the failure to wet down friable asbestos. Thus, he could be held liable, although he was never on the job site while the work was being performed. His defense of being "singled out" for the penalty action was rejected, although the firm itself had entered bankruptcy without paying any civil penalties and the owner of the business had entered into a consent decree resolving all claims against them.

Another civil penalty action involved asbestos violations by a break shoe rehabilitation business, which fabricated friction products containing commercial asbestos. The regulatory requirement that the emissions be visible to the naked eye was held to apply to emissions generally from the process and did not require that asbestos emissions—which are microscopic—be visible to the naked eye. The court held that EPA's emission standard applied to such break shoe rehabilitation operations. *United States v. Midwest Suspension & Brake*, 49 F.3d 1197, 25 ELR 20651 (6th Cir. 1995).

QUESTION

In the above cases, all of which dealt with asbestos violations under § 112 of the Clean Air Act,is there any indication why the *Buckley* case led to a criminal indictment while the other two cases referred to ended with the imposition of civil penalties, following civil investigation and a civil trial?

[j] Stratospheric Ozone Protection

The Clean Air Act Amendments of 1990 included a new Title VI to address stratospheric ozone protection. This new title, replacing some earlier provisions on ozone protection contained in the Clean Air Act prior to its 1990 amendment, regulates discharge of substances that deplete the ozone layer. In large part, federal action in this area was in response to an international initiative, under the aegis of the United Nations Environment Programme [UNEP], to prevent and control the damage and depletion of stratospheric ozone. The initiative was a response to the publication of the discovery of the Antarctic Ozone Hole in May 1985, which added a measure of urgency. With the onset of spring, a hole opens up each year in the ozone layer over Antarctica. As deep as Mount Everest and as vast as the United States, this hole has been growing since 1979. Elsewhere the ozone layer is also thinning. The average concentration of ozone over a wide belt of the northern hemisphere, from the Arctic Circle to the Sahara, has decreased by 1% in summer and 4% in winter in the last 20 years. Moreover, there are now reports of ozone holes over northern Europe.[242] Another ozone hole over Switzerland requires further confirmation. There is also some evidence of Arctic ozone destruction.[243]

Stratospheric ozone is essential to life on earth. Acting as a shield, stratospheric ozone absorbs harmful ultraviolet radiation and thus protects life on this planet from its harmful effects. Any modification or depletion of this ozone layer would have adverse effects, including an increase in squamous, basal and melanoma skin cancers; the weakening of the human immune system, exacerbating the severity of such diseases as herpes, leishmaniasis and other infectious cutaneous diseases; an increase in cataract cases; the alteration of competition among plant species and a reduction in crop yields; changes in aquatic ecosystems and possible effects on aquatic food chains; a potential increase in hydrogen peroxides, an acid rain precursor; and contributions to "greenhouse warming" until ozone depletion becomes substantial, at which point it would reduce temperature.[244] According to a National Academy of Science estimate, a one percent drop in ozone levels could result in an additional 10,000 cases of skin cancer each year—a two percent increase—in the United States alone.[245] Theoretically, the total elimination of stratospheric ozone would lead to extinction of life on earth.

Unfortunately, human activity is disturbing the natural balance between the creation and destruction of stratospheric ozone. The introduction into the atmosphere of certain manmade chemicals, namely halogens, which include chlorofluorocarbons (CFCs), is responsible for ozone destruction. Produced first in 1928 by General Motors, CFCs are inert gases with several industrial uses. They are used extensively as coolants in the refrigeration of air conditioning, as solvents in the production of plastic foam, in medical equipment sterilization and as aerosol propellants, a use now banned in the United States since 1978 except for certain specified essential uses.[246] On percolating into the stratosphere, CFCs react with ultraviolet rays to release stray chlorine atoms which, in a further catalytic chemical reaction, break down ozone molecules. Each chlorine atom released into the atmosphere is estimated to result in the destruction of 100,000 ozone molecules. The link between CFCs and ozone destruction was conclusively established in 1988 while it was first suggested in 1974 by two atmospheric scientists, Dr. Rowland and Dr. Molina.[247] Recognized by the United Nations Environmental Programme, the problem was addressed in an international Agreement on Monitoring of the Stratosphere and following a number of international working group efforts, the first "umbrella treaty," the Vienna Convention, was signed in 1985 by

---

[242] *Ozone Hole Found Over Europe*, New Sci., October 16, 1986 at 21.

[243] Kerr, *Evidence of Arctic Ozone Destruction*, 240 Science 1144 (1988).

[244] Office of Air and Radiation, Environmental Protection Agency, *An Assessment of the Risks of Stratospheric Modification* 6 (final draft, 1986).

[245] Lemonick, *The Heat Is On: Chemical Wastes Spewed into the Air Threaten the Earth's Climate*, Time, October 19, 1987 at 58, 59-60.

[246] 21 CFR § 2.125(1978) and Toxic Substances Control Act, 15U.S.C. § 2601(1982).

[247] *See* M. Molina and F.S. Rowland, *Stratospheric Sink for Chlorofluoromethanes: Chlorine Atom-Catalyzed Destruction of Ozone*, 249 Nature No. 5460 at 810-812 (1976).

some 20 countries and the European Community (E.C.). This was the first convention to address a clear global threat. The Vienna Convention was followed by a number of protocols, most notably the Montreal Protocol on Substances That Deplete the Ozone Layer, which by 1990 had been signed by a total of 62 countries and the European Community.[248]

The provisions on stratospheric ozone protection were briefly summarized in the conference committee report on the Clean Air Amendments.[249]

As required by the Montreal Protocol, EPA lists the regulated substances into two classes, with different phaseout schedules. The purpose is to limit and eventually totally phase out the production and use of ozone destructive substances. The production of Class I substances was to be banned by January 1, 2000, and in the case of listed CFCs, halons, and carbon tetrachlorides, and by January 1, 2002, in the case of methyl chloroform.[250] The production of Class II hydrochlorofluorocarbons (HCFCs) which are less destructive than CFCs will be frozen by January 1, 2020. The production of HCFCs will be totally prohibited by January 1, 2030.[251] Beginning in 1992, EPA was required to issue regulations to reduce the use and emissions of Class I and Class II substances and requiring the recapturing and recycling of such substances. The knowing venting, release or disposal of a Class I or Class II

---

[248] For an account of international developments relating to protection of the ozone layer, see F. Grad, Treatise on Environmental Law § 13.03[4][g].

[249] Joint Explanatory Statement of the Committee of Conference, 136 Cong. Rec. 2d Sess. H. 13197-13201 (daily ed. Oct. 26, 1990):

"The conference agreement includes phase out schedules for CFCs, halons, carbon tetrachlorides, and methyl chloroform. Key provisions include:

—HCFC production freeze in 2015 and elimination in 2030, coupled with use limitations beginning in 2015 and, for use as a refrigerant in appliances, 2020;

—recapture, recycling, and safe disposal regulations to be phased in beginning January 1, 1992;

—a July 1, 1992 prohibition on venting during appliance service, repair, and disposal;

—effective January 1, 1992, a requirement to use certified recycling equipment when servicing motor vehicle air conditioners;

—restrictions on the sale of small cans of class I and class II refrigerants;

—a ban on nonessential uses of ozone depleting chemicals;

—labeling requirements;

—a safe alternatives policy to promote the transition to safe substitutes;

—a requirement for federal agencies to modify procurement regulations in accordance with the requirements and policies of this title;

—a prohibition on the export of technologies to produce class I substances and on investments to produce class I or class II substances to nations that are not parties to the Montreal Protocol;

—domestic and international trading of production allowances (industrial rationalization);

—authorization for the U.S. contribution to the international fund that has been established to assist developing countries; and

—studies on sources of and options for controlling emissions of methane.

"The conference agreement does not include a requirement to construe the term 'production' 'in a manner consistent with the Protocol.' The Protocol's exclusion for manufactured substances that are subsequently destroyed is too broad and does not include adequate safeguards to preclude abuse. In the course of implementing this Act, however, EPA shall consider whether an exclusion will be allowed on a case-by-case basis for the manufacturer of controlled substances that are (1) coincidental, unavoidable by-products of a manufacturing process and (2) immediately contained and destroyed by the producer using maximum available control technologies."

[250] CAA § 602, § 604.

[251] CAA § 605.

refrigerant from household appliances, refrigerators and air conditioners during servicing, repair or disposal were prohibited as of July 1, 1992.[252] EPA is also authorized to restrict the production and use of certain specified products. Only repair shops using certified recycling equipment can service motor vehicles and air conditioners as of January 1, 1992.[253] EPA regulations also prohibit the distribution and sale of nonessential CFC-containing products including consumer goods like plastic party streamers, noise horns and cleaning fluids for electronic and photographic products.[254] Starting on January 1, 1994, it became unlawful to sell or distribute aerosol products or other pressurized dispensers or any plastic foam product containing Class II substances.[255] Medical devices, however, are exempted from this requirement.

Containers for storage and transport of such substances must meet certain labeling requirements[256] and such ozone depleting substances are to be replaced by chemicals, product substitutes, or alternative manufacturing processes that reduce the risks to human health and the environment.[257] All federal agencies must conform their procurement regulations to the policies and requirements of Title VI.[258]

Provision is made to prohibit the export of technology used in producing Class I substances and to ban direct and indirect investment in facilities producing Class I and II substances and to ban financial aid to countries that are not party to the Montreal Protocol.[259] Production allowances can be transferred to or received by the U.S. from other protocol parties as long as the protocol limits are observed.[260] Title VI also authorizes studies under Title VI, and the President is authorized to enter into international agreements promoting cooperation or research on studies made under Title VI and to develop standards for protecting the stratosphere in accordance with regulations applicable within the U.S.[261] In order to promote universal participation in the Protocol, provision is made for financial and technical assistance to developing countries that are parties to the Montreal Protocol.[262]

OZ TECHNOLOGY INCORPORATED v. EPA

United States Court of Appeals, D.C. Circuit (1997)
129 F.3d 631, 28 ELR 20224

HARRY T. EDWARDS, Chief Judge:

Section 612(c) of the Clean Air Act("CAA" or "Act") instructs the Administrator of the Environmental Protection Agency ("EPA" or "agency") to promulgate

[252] CAA § 608.

[253] CAA § 609(c).

[254] CAA§ 610(b).

[255] CAA § 610(d).

[256] CAA § 611.

[257] CAA § 612.

[258] CAA § 613.

[259] CAA § 614(c).

[260] CAA § 616.

[261] CAA § 617(a).

[262] CAA § 617(b). For additional detail, *see also* F. Grad, Treatise on Environmental Law, § 2.03[20] and § 13.03[g][v].

rules that prohibit the replacement of ozone-depleting compounds with substances "which [she] determines may present adverse effects to human health or the environment." 42 U.S.C. § 7671k(c)(1994). In the instant case, EPA designated Petitioner OZ Technology Inc.'s ("OZ") product HC-12a as an unacceptable substitute for CFC-12 (an ozone-depleting substance commonly known as "freon") for end-uses other than industrial process refrigeration. 60 Fed. Reg. 31092, 31098 (1995). In so doing, EPA effectively banned HC-12a for those end uses. *See* 40 CFR § 82.174(1996). Subsequently, EPA rejected a request by OZ, filed pursuant to regulations implementing § 612(d) of the Act, seeking to remove HC-12a from the list of unacceptable substitutes and add it to the list of acceptable substitutes. 61 Fed. Reg. 51018 (1996). OZ then petitioned for review, challenging EPA's initial decision to put HC-12a on the unacceptable list and the agency's subsequent refusal to amend the list.

On the record at hand, we must reject the petition for review. As EPA found, OZ failed in this case to submit valid data supporting its claim that HC-12a should be added to the list of acceptable substitutes. In light of OZ's acknowledgment that HC-12a was flammable, and EPA's previous decision prohibiting a very similar compound manufactured by OZ for the same end uses, EPA's actions banning HC-12a reasonably satisfied its obligation under § 612 to reduce overall risk to human health and the environment.

I. BACKGROUND

A. *The Statutory and Regulatory Regime*

Title VI of the CAA, as amended in 1990, requires the phase out of CFC-12 and other substances that have the capability of depleting the stratospheric ozone layer. 42 USC §§ 7671-7671q(1994). Section 612 of the Act instructs EPA to regulate replacement substances to reduce overall risk to human health and the environment. 42 USC § 7671k(c). Section 612(c) requires EPA to publish a list of the substitutes prohibited for specific uses and a list of the substitutes that are safe alternatives for specific uses. *Id.* Section 612(d) of the Act grants any person the right to petition EPA to add a substance or to delete a substance from either of the lists published pursuant to § 612(c). 42 USC § 7671k(d).

EPA promulgated regulations to implement § 612, known as the Significant New Alternatives Policy ("SNAP") program. 59 Fed. Reg. 13044, 13147 (1994) (codified at 40 CFR pt. 82). Under the SNAP program, any person who has developed a substitute for an ozone-depleting substance must notify EPA before introducing the substitute into interstate commerce. 40 CFR § 82.176(a). The person must submit information concerning, among other things, the likely end uses and flammability of the proposed substitute. *Id.* § 82.178(a)(3), (9). With respect to flammability, the submitter must provide the flash point and flammability limits of the product, as well as information on the procedures used for determining the flammability limits. *Id.* § 82.178(a)(9). If a substitute is flammable, "the submitter must analyze the risk of fire resulting from the use of [the] substitute and assess the effectiveness of measures to minimize such risk." *Id.* "For substitutes that will be used in consumer applications, documentation of testing results conducted by independent laboratories should be submitted, where available." *Id.*

Once the information submitted to EPA is "adequate to support analysis of the submission," *id.* § 82.180(a)(3), the agency decides, based on the information submitted and any other information available to EPA, whether the substitute is acceptable, unacceptable, or acceptable subject to certain use restrictions for the proposed end uses. *Id.* § 82.180(b). Where EPA proposes to list a substitute as unacceptable for certain end uses, EPA follows notice-and-comment rulemaking procedures. *Id.* § 82.180(a)(8)(ii). If EPA then determines that a substitute is unacceptable for a specific end use, the SNAP program prohibits replacing ozone-depleting substances with the substitute proposed for that end use. *Id.* § 82.174(b)-(d). Under § 612(d) of the Act, any person may petition EPA to amend existing listing decisions or to add a new substance to any of the SNAP lists. *Id.* § 82.184.

B. *EPA's Designation of HC-12a as Unacceptable*

OZ has developed a substance called HC-12a as a substitute for CFC-12. HC-12a has end use applications in refrigeration and air conditioning, including motor vehicle air conditioning systems and household refrigerators and freezers. In March 1994, OZ began marketing HC-12a. Petitioner's Br. at 13. Soon thereafter, EPA informed OZ that it was required under SNAP to submit a notice of intent to introduce HC-12a into interstate commerce. *Id.* at 14. OZ sent documentation to EPA in a purported effort to comply with the SNAP notice requirement. Joint Appendix ("J.A.") 853-76. In September 1994, however, EPA formally proposed to list HC-12a (identified as Hydrocarbon Blend B) as an unacceptable substitute for CFC-12 for end uses other than industrial process refrigeration. 59 Fed. Reg. 49108, 49112 (1994).

OZ subsequently submitted comments to EPA, along with documentation to initiate a petition under § 612(d). The gist of OZ's position was that EPA should delete HC-12a from the "proposed unacceptable" list and add it to the list of acceptable substitutes. Because EPA had not promulgated a final rule on HC-12a, the documentation submitted by OZ to support a 612(d) petition was accepted as an additional comment on the proposal. *See* EPA's Supplemental Response To Comments on the Proposal To Find HC-12a Unacceptable, July 18, 1996 ("July 1996 Decision Doc."), J.A. 766. Later in the comment period, other documents concerning the flammability risks of HC-12a were submitted to EPA, either by OZ or by other parties on its behalf. *See* Letter from Charles B. Lempesis to EPA, June 5, 1995, J.A. 897-99 (listing submissions); Attachment to Letter from EPA to OZ, August 30, 1996 ("August 1996 Decision Doc."), J.A. 784 (identifying additional submissions). On June 13, 1995, EPA took final action listing HC-12a as an unacceptable substitute for end uses other than industrial process refrigeration, citing concern about flammability. 60 Fed. Reg. at 31098.

Prior to the action on HC-12a, EPA had designated as unacceptable a very similar product of OZ, namely OZ-12. OZ-12 (identified as Hydrocarbon Blend A) was included on the unacceptable list because of concerns over flammability and the lack of an adequate risk assessment showing that OZ-12 could be used in end uses other than industrial process refrigeration. 59 Fed. Reg. 13044, 13082, 13122-24 (1994). In processing the application for OZ-12, EPA officials explained to OZ, in at least one meeting, four letters, and a phone conversation what was required in a valid risk assessment. J.A. 811-15, 819-20, 825-26.

EPA's decision to designate HC-12a as unacceptable coincided with the agency's rejection of a § 612(d) petition submitted by OZ for OZ-12, requesting that EPA delete OZ-12 from the unacceptable list and add it to the acceptable list. 60 Fed. Reg. 49407 (1995). On July 25, 1995, EPA wrote a letter to OZ stating that the company's submissions regarding the flammability risks of HC-12a were inadequate for the same reasons that the company's submissions for OZ-12 were inadequate. J.A. 770. In an attachment to another letter which EPA sent to OZ that same day, EPA explained at length why the company's submissions regarding the flammability risks of OZ-12 were insufficient to warrant listing the compound as an acceptable substitute. Response to OZ Technology, Inc. Petition To Find OZ-12 Acceptable ("July 1995 Decision Doc."), J.A. 772-79. EPA's communications with OZ in July 1995 did not explain why additional documentation submitted by OZ for HC-12a but not for OZ-12 also was insufficient to warrant listing HC-12a as acceptable.

On August 14, 1995, OZ petitioned the United States Court of Appeals for the Ninth Circuit for judicial review of EPA's June 13, 1995 action listing HC-12a as an unacceptable substitute. The petition was transferred to this court, which granted EPA's motion to remand the administrative record. *See* Order Granting Motion for Voluntary Remand of the Record (Apr. 23, 1996). During the remand period, EPA addressed some of the documentation that had been submitted by OZ for HC-12a but not for OZ-12. *See* July 1996 Decision Doc., J.A. 766-69 (addressing Exhibits T through Z of OZ's November 1994, § 612(d) petition for HC-12a).

C. *EPA's Denial of OZ's § 612(d) Petition Regarding HC-12a*

In December 1995, after OZ sought judicial review of EPA's final rule designating HC-12a as an unacceptable substitute, OZ submitted another petition to the agency pursuant to § 612(d), requesting that EPA list HC-12a as acceptable. ("1995 Petition"). EPA rejected the 1995 Petition, 61 Fed. Reg. 51018 (1996), and issued a full response to the many documents submitted by OZ covering HC-12a. *See* August 1996 Decision Doc., J.A. 784-810. EPA concluded that OZ had not submitted a "scientifically valid, comprehensive risk assessment" that would justify changing the designation of HC-12a from unacceptable to acceptable. EPA Letter, August 1996, J.A. 780. OZ petitioned for judicial review of this determination, and this court granted the parties' joint motion to consolidate the two petitions for review. *See* Order Granting Joint Motion To Consolidate (Oct. 29, 1996).

II. DISCUSSION

This court may grant a petition challenging an action of EPA under § 612 of the Act if it is "arbitrary, capricious, an abuse of discretion, or otherwise not in accordance with law." 42 U.S.C. § 7607(d)(9)(A)(1994). This provision commands essentially the same standard of review as the analogous provision contained in the Administrative Procedure Act, 5U.S.C. § 706(1994). *Ethyl Corp. v. EPA*, 51 F.3d 1053, 1064 (D.C. Cir. 1995). And, as the Supreme Court has made clear, the arbitrary and capricious standard has certain clear parameters:

> The scope of review under the "arbitrary and capricious" standard is narrow and a court is not to substitute its judgment for that of the agency. Nevertheless, the agency must examine the relevant data and articulate a satisfactory explanation for its action including a "rational connection between the facts found and the choice made." In reviewing that explanation, we must "consider whether the decision was based on a consideration of the relevant factors and whether there has been a clear error of judgment." Normally, an agency rule would be arbitrary and capricious if the agency has relied on factors which Congress had not intended it to consider, entirely failed to consider an important aspect of the problem, offered an explanation for its decision that runs counter to the evidence before the agency, or is so implausible that it could not be ascribed to a difference in view or the product of agency expertise. The reviewing court should not attempt itself to make up for such deficiencies; we may not supply a reasoned basis for the agency's action that the agency itself has not given. We will, however, "uphold a decision of less than ideal clarity if the agency's path may reasonably be discerned."

Motor Vehicle Mfrs. Ass'n v. State Farm Mut. Auto. Ins. Co., 463 U.S. 29, 43, 103 S.Ct. 2856, 2866-67, 77 L.Ed. 2d 443 (1983) (citations and footnote omitted). It is also well understood that "[t]he rationale for deference is particularly strong when the EPA is evaluating scientific data within its technical expertise." *International Fabricare Inst. v. U.S. EPA*, 972 F.2d 384, 389 (D.C. Cir. 1992).

OZ contends that EPA acted arbitrarily and capriciously in initially designating HC-12a as an unacceptable substitute for CFC-12 for all end uses other than industrial process refrigeration, and in rejecting OZ's 1995 Petition. Petitioner's Br. At 24. According to OZ, EPA's decision was contrary to the documentation submitted in support of HC-12a. *Id.* at 24-25. OZ also argues that EPA acted unlawfully in failing to provide guidance on the kind of data or risk analysis that the company was required to submit, beyond the documentation that was offered, in order for EPA to decide that HC-12a was safe under the CAA. *Id.* at 26-28.

EPA responds that OZ had the burden of demonstrating through a scientifically valid risk analysis that HC-12a did not pose unacceptable flammability risks under CAA § 612(c). EPA also asserts that it reasonably determined that OZ failed to submit an adequate risk analysis, and that the agency therefore justifiably declined to decide whether the risks posed by HC-12a in fact were acceptable under the Act. Respondent's Br. At 16-22. We substantially agree with EPA on both counts. Given OZ's acknowledgment that its product is flammable, as well as EPA's mandate to regulate under § 612 to reduce overall risk to human health, EPA's actions with respect to HC-12a were reasonable.

Documents submitted on behalf of OZ to EPA recognized the flammability of HC-12a. *See* Draft Test Protocol Phase I, J.A. 886 ("OZ . . . produces a propane-based flammable refrigerant designated as HC-12a."). Moreover, before considering OZ's submissions for HC-12a, EPA already had designated a very similar compound, OZ-12, as unacceptable because of flammability concerns. Given these circumstances, OZ was required to submit data on HC-12a, analyzing "the risk of fire resulting from the use of such a substitute and assess[ing] the effectiveness of measures to minimize such risk." 40 C.F.R. §§ 82.178(a)(9), 82.184(c). The regulations make it clear that EPA was fully justified in rejecting OZ's § 612(d) petition when the company failed to supply adequate data to support that petition:

> If the petition is inadequately supported, the Agency will query the petitioner to fill any data gaps before the 90-day review period begins, or may deny the petition because data are inadequate. *Id.* § 82.184(d)(4).

OZ claims that EPA was obligated to conduct its own tests on HC-12a before determining that it was unacceptable for OZ's intended end uses. This position finds no support in the statute. OZ sought to introduce into the market a product with known risks to human health and the environment. In light of the statutory mandate of § 612, it is hardly surprising that EPA's regulations require the company to submit data defining the risk and assessing the effectiveness of measures to minimize the known dangers.

Arguably, during the proceedings involving OZ's products, EPA officials could have been more forthcoming in responding to OZ's requests for clarification on the contents of the required documentation. However, it is clear from the record that EPA stated in no uncertain terms that OZ was obligated to quantify data on the flammability of HC-12a, and to use scientifically valid studies, in order to enable the agency to consider listing the compound as an acceptable substitute for all end uses. *See, e.g.*, July 1995 Decision Doc., J.A. 772-79. Moreover, OZ was put on notice of the requirement of a comprehensive risk analysis, as well as the contents of such an analysis, from the company's prior efforts to have the agency designate OZ-12 an acceptable substitute. EPA officials met with OZ about OZ-12, J.A. 811-13, and sent several letters to OZ outlining the contents of a risk analysis. *Id.* at 811-15, 819-20, 825-26. For particular proposed end uses for OZ-12, EPA referred OZ to testing guidelines produced by the Society of Automotive Engineers, which the agency stated were acceptable. *Id.* at 811, 814. Thus, EPA did not leave OZ completely without direction.

In addition, a private consultant recommended to OZ the contents of what might have constituted an acceptable risk analysis for OZ-12. Letter from Bryant Consulting to Gary Lindgren, President, OZ Technology, Inc., October 12, 1993, J.S. 816. OZ conceded at oral argument that it did not undertake the procedures recommended by the consultant and did not ask EPA whether the recommended risk analysis would suffice to allow the agency to make an affirmative decision about any of its products under SNAP and the CAA. Although OZ may at times have felt stonewalled by EPA, OZ had only itself to blame for not pursuing leads offered by EPA officials and the outside consultant.

Thus, the principal focus of our inquiry is on EPA's contention that it reasonably determined that OZ failed to submit a valid risk analysis of HC-12a. During the course of its dealings with OZ, EPA produced three documents that, in increasing detail, explained why the data submitted by OZ were insufficient. *See* July 1995 Decision Doc., J.A. 772-79; July 1996 Decision Doc., J.A. 766-69; August 1996 Decision Doc., J.A. 780-810. For example, EPA pointed out that OZ's submissions analyzed refrigerants that were less flammable than HC-12a, or used a smaller charge of refrigerant than would be used in actual practice, or both. J.A. 773, 791; that the submissions failed to analyze all of the risks posed by the end uses in question, *id.* at 773, 790-91; and that the submissions failed to quantify risks at all, or attempted to do so with unrealistically low assumptions unsupported by empirical data. *Id.* at 776-78, 795, 805-06.

Given the comprehensive scope of EPA's responses to OZ's submissions and OZ's utter lack of explanation as to how EPA's responses might be inaccurate or unfounded, we hold that EPA's determination that OZ failed to carry its burden under SNAP was justified. *See Ethyl Corp.*, 51 F.3d at 1059 (holding, under another provision of the CAA, that "[t]here is no doubt that [EPA] has the authority to make the factual determination of whether an applicant has submitted enough data . . . to satisfy the applicable standards, and a reviewing court must respect this role") (citing *Ethyl Corp. v. EPA*, 541 F.2d 1, 36-37 (D.C. Cir. 1976) (en banc)). Under the circumstances in this case, EPA was not required to render an affirmative decision that HC-12a was either safe or unsafe under the Act. It was enough for the agency to find that the company had failed to address the known risk of flammability in a scientifically valid, comprehensive risk analysis.

In short, we hold that EPA did not act arbitrarily and capriciously in designating Petitioner's product HC-12a an unacceptable substitute to CFC-12 for end uses other than industrial process refrigeration under CAA § 612(c) and SNAP. We also hold that EPA did not act arbitrarily and capriciously in rejecting Petitioner's subsequent request under CAA § 612(d) and SNAP to remove HC-12a from the unacceptable list for the above-mentioned end uses and add the compound to the acceptable list.

III. CONCLUSION

For the reasons discussed above, OZ's petitions for review are denied.

[k] Acid Deposition

Added in the 1990 revision of the Clean Air Act, Title IVdeals with the subject of acid deposition in a number of novel and unusual ways. In considering the following general account of the system of acid deposition controls, it should be noted that these controls, which affect American sources of the precursor gases to acid deposition, are in part the result of international policy considerations. Acid deposition is a problem of recurring transfrontier pollution, as well as interstate pollution. The fallout of acid deposition is commonly hundreds if not thousands of miles distant from its source. In addition, these provisions include a novel aspect of control, with federal law listing the power plant sources of the pollution by name, in effect regulating individual plants for pollution control ends, both within and without the United States.

Another notable aspect of the controls is their unusual structure, utilizing market mechanisms in the service of pollution controls. The law operates by distributing to each source a number, set by law, of tradeable pollution allowances. Since the number of allowances is limited, sources which cannot meet the pollution control target must purchase additional allowances from utilities that can meet the targets and consequently may have allowances to spare—allowances which they then may sell at a profit.

The following account provides a basic outline of the control system. For greater detail on the formation, scope and effects of acid rain, a description of the geographic scope of the acid rain problem, greater detail on the nature of acid rain damages and on the nature of the impact of acid rain on public health, as well as more detailed analysis of the market mechanisms used in this control system, see F. Grad, Treatise on Environmental Law, § 2.09.

Title IV is based on a significant statement of Congressional findings and purposes. Congress found that the presence of acidic compounds in the atmosphere and in deposition from the atmosphere represents a threat to natural resources, ecosystems, materials, visibility, and public health. Congress further found that the principal sources of the acidic compounds and of their precursors are emissions of sulfur and nitrogen oxides from the combustion of fossil fuels. It noted that the problem of acidic deposition (generally referred to as "acid rain") is of national and international significance. Yet, strategies and technologies to control acid depositions exist, and are economically feasible. Improved methods are also expected to become increasingly available.

Congress also found that delays in controlling the problem will adversely affect current and future generations of Americans, while a reduction of nitrogen oxides and sulfur oxides in the atmosphere will enhance the protection of the public health and welfare and of the environment. Congress concluded that control measures to reduce precursor emissions from steam electric generating units should be initiated without delay. The purpose of the new title is to reduce the adverse effect of acid deposition through reductions in annual emissions of sulfur dioxide of 10 million tons from 1980 emission levels, and of nitrogen oxide emissions of approximately two million tons from 1980 emission levels in the 48 contiguous states and the District of Columbia.

> "It is the intent of this Title to effectuate such reductions by requiring compliance by affected sources with prescribed emission limitations by specified deadlines, which limitations may be met through alternative methods of compliance provided by an emission allocation and transfer system. It is also the purpose of this Title to encourage energy conservation, use of renewal and clean alternative technologies, and pollution prevention as a long-range strategy, consistent with provisions of this Title, for reducing air pollution and other diverse impacts of energy production and use."[263]

The acid deposition title establishes an emission limitation program that focuses exclusively on power plant sulfur dioxide (SO_2) and nitrogen oxide (NOx) emissions. It operates by setting annual allowances for each of 111 specific generating units in 22 states. This annual allowance listed for each

263 Title IV, Acid Deposition Control, § 401, as added by Clean Air Act Amendments of 1990, § 401, CAA § 601, 42 U.S.C. § 7671 *et seq.*

unit reflects the annual across-the-board cap on emissions, calculated as specifically provided in the different sections of the law. The law provides for Phase I limitations reflected in Phase I allowance allocations. Allowances were established by references to the SO_2 emissions generated by burning the average fuel consumed during the 1985 to 1987 base line period, at an emission rate of 2.5 lbs/mm BTU (*i.e.* millions of British Thermal Units). The more stringent Phase II allowance allocations for each of the units subject to the Act starts on January 1, 2000 so as to allow emissions at the rate of 1.2 lbs/mm BTU. The system of allowances allocated under this Title provides an opportunity to transfer allowances not used to other units. Normally, the trading of allowances is for units of the same pollutant, but there are provisions in the law to provide for the investigation of the possibility of trading sulfur dioxide allowances for nitrogen oxide allowances. Special provisions are made too for the acquisition of allowances by new utility units. In general, the allocation of allowances creates a limited authorization, somewhat akin to a permit system, to emit a particular pollutant such as sulfur dioxide in accordance with the provisions of the Title. The law provides that it is a violation to emit sulfur dioxide in excess of allowances, and it is also unlawful to acquire allowances except in accordance with the provisions of the law. The amount of permissible emission of sulfur dioxide is set for Phase I which limits emissions after January 1995. The maximum emission is set by reference to the unit's baseline, based on the annual average quantity of mm BTUs consumed during calendar years 1985, 1986 and 1987, generally as recorded at the level specified for the unit in the 1985 National Acid Precipitation Assessment Program (NAPAP) emissions inventory. The law provides for an application by the owner or operator of the unit to challenge the baseline determination, and to rely on a substitute measure allowing the Administrator to decide the issue.

The law provides a table listing each of the affected sources and units, and for Phase I prescribes their sulfur dioxide allowance in tons per year. Title IV also requires that every affected source employ a continuous emission monitoring system (CEMS) to measure and provide a continuous and permanent record of emissions from each unit.

Title IV grants allowances for emissions avoided through the use of energy conservation and renewable energy sources. The underlying basis for the grant of such allowances is that qualified energy conservation measures and the use of renewable energy sources avoid sulfur dioxide emissions.

For Phase II, more stringent sulfur dioxide requirements are provided, to become applicable after January 1 of the year 2000. A system of allowances is also applied for Phase II, except that fewer allowances are provided during Phase II than for Phase I. The law also sets annual tonnage emission limitations for units that commenced operation between 1986 and December 31, 1995. Special measures are provided for oil and gas fired units whose annual average fuel consumption during the period 1980 through 1989 consisted 90% or more of natural gas, on a BTU basis. Special provisions are also made for Phase II allowance allocations to units in high growth states. Special provisions for the allocation of allowances are also made for states with low emission rates, *i.e.*, emission rates at or below 0.80 lbs. per mm BTU.

Title IV provides separately for nitrogen oxide emission reductions. On the date that a coal fired utility unit becomes an affected unit under Title IV or must meet the SO_2 reduction, such unit also becomes an affected unit for purposes of emission limitations for nitrogen oxides. The Administrator must establish annual allowable emission limitations for nitrogen oxides for utility boilers as listed in the statute. The kind of emission standards for NOx for different units may differ on the basis of the technology used. The statute permits the Administrator to set different kinds of emissions standards for certain kinds of boilers from which there are known technological problems in the control of NOx. The statute also allows the application of the bubble concept, *i.e.*, the averaging of emissions from two or more units of the same owner or operator that may be subject to different applicable emission limitations.

Administratively, emissions are controlled through a permit program with each unit having to apply and submit a compliance plan for its operation. The Administrator issues permits when he approves the compliance plan.

The Title also provides for second phase permits, with the Administrator required to provide related regulations. The states are required to administer the program and to issue permits. Provision is also made for the reallocation of allowances to units that would be repowered with a qualifying clean coal technology to comply with the requirements of § 405.

Penalties for excess emissions are calculated on the basis of the number of tons emitted in excess of the unit's emissions limitation requirement, or, in the case of sulfur dioxide, in excess of the allowances the operator holds for use of the unit for that year. The penalties are to be adjusted by the Administrator, pursuant to regulation, for inflation based on the Consumer Price Index on the date of enactment of the Clean Air Act Amendments of 1990 and annually thereafter. Since the entire system depends on the knowledge of performance of different units, there are detailed monitoring, reporting and recordkeeping requirements. Provision is also made for federally supported demonstration projects to advance clean cold technology.

Title IV requires the Administrator to build up a Special Allowance Reserve, by withholding a small percentage of the allocation of allowances for each year from 1995 through 1999, and by withholding the same percentage of allowances beginning in the year 2000 from Phase II allocations. The Administrator is authorized to offer allowances for sale at $1,500 per ton in designated years. Certain preferences are to be given in the purchase of such allowances to independent power producers who are in the process of establishing a new independent pilot production facility. The law provides for certain eligibility requirements for the purchase of allowances. The Administrator must also establish an Auction Subaccount in the special reserve. The auction subaccount is to contain allowances to be sold at auction in the amount of 150,000 tons per year for each year 1995 through 1999, inclusive, and 250,000 tons per year for each year beginning in the calendar year 2000. The law provides the number of allowances available for auction in each year starting with the year 1993. The proceeds from an auction must be transferred on a pro rata basis to the owners or operators of affected units from whom allowances were withheld, who were unable to purchase allowances on direct sale.

ALLIANCE FOR CLEAN COAL v. BAYH

United States Court of Appeals, Seventh Circuit (1995)
72 F.3d 556, 26 ELR 20557

CUMMINGS, Circuit Judge.

Plaintiff Alliance for Clean Coal ("Alliance") is a trade association whose members market and transport coal produced from western United States mines. Alliance sued the governor of Indiana and members of the Indiana Utility Regulatory Commission ("Commission") challenging the portions of the Indiana Environmental Compliance Plans Act ("ECPA") (IC 8-1-27-6(b)(6), 8-1-27-8(1)(D) and 8-1-27-20) (Appendix, *infra*).[264] The challenged sections of the ECPA are virtually identical to those sections of the Illinois Coal Act that we recently held were unconstitutional in Alliance for Clean Coal v. Miller, 44 F.3d 591 (7th Cir. 1995). For the reasons more fully discussed below, we hold that the ECPA discriminates against interstate commerce just as did the Illinois Coal Act and thus violates the Commerce Clause of the United States Constitution.

Background

Coal remains a vital source of fuel for this country's electrical utilities. As of 1992, 409 of the 998 million tons of coal produced in the United States were produced in 17 states west of the Mississippi River. Energy Information Administration, Coal Production 1992 (Oct. 1993). Almost all of the coal produced in these western states is sold and shipped to utilities for electricity generation. Alliance members market and transport coal produced from Wyoming, Colorado, Montana and Utah mines ("western coal") and represent the major participants in interstate commerce in western coal.

Because of the sulfur contained in the coal they burn, coal fired generating plants are a principal source of atmospheric sulfur dioxide emissions. The sulfur content of coal burned by utilities depends upon the geological origin of the coal: whereas coal mined in the western United States has the lowest sulfur content, almost all of the coal mined in the "Illinois Basin," including most of Illinois and parts of Indiana and western Kentucky, has a relatively high sulfur content.

Congressional enactment of the Clean Air Act Amendments of 1970 required newly constructed generating units to use systems of emissions control approved by the Environmental Protection Agency ("EPA"). The EPA initially provided two methods for controlling sulfur dioxide emissions: (1) the use of low sulfur coal; and (2) the installation of a device to scrub high sulfur coal emissions before they reach the atmosphere. Because scrubbing was costlier

---

[264] Originally Alliance attacked the entire ECPA (App. 54) but later limited its attack to certain portions of the statute (App. 8).

than using low sulfur western coal, states producing high sulfur coal suffered competitively.

In 1990 the Clean Air Act was amended again to require drastic reductions in industrial sulfur dioxide emissions by the year 2000. 42 U.S.C. §§ 7401-7571q. The 1990 Act implemented an innovative market driven approach to emissions regulation, allowing for the free transfer of emissions "allowances." The Act is aimed at reducing emissions efficiently and allows utilities to meet the standards in the cheapest manner possible. To comply with the new emissions limitations, utilities now have a choice of the following strategies: (1) installing pollution control devices; (2) using low sulfur coal; (3) purchasing allowances to emit sulfur dioxide; (4) switching to another fuel; (5) closing down certain units; (6) offsetting emissions at one plant by over-complying at another; or (7) adopting some combination. According to Alliance, because of the high costs associated with installing pollution devices, the 1990 amendments should result in a decline in demand for the Illinois Basin's high sulfur coal.

High sulfur coal mining states like Indiana considered legislation responsive to the foregoing federal acts. Thus in 1991 Indiana adopted its ECPA. IC §§ 8-1-27-1 to 8-1-27-23. This statute permits electric utilities to avail themselves of early prudency review by submitting plans for complying with the federal legislation to the Commission. In order to approve a utility's plan, the Commission must find that the plan (A) meets the Clean Air Act Amendments of 1990; (B) constitutes a reasonable and least cost strategy over the life of the investment consistent with providing reliable, efficient, and economical electrical service; (C) is in the public interest; and (D) either:

> (i) provides for continued or increased use of Indiana coal in the coal-consuming electric generating units owned or operated by the public utility and affected by the Clean Air Act Amendments of 1990; or
>
> (ii) if the plan does not provide for continued or increased use of Indiana coal, such nonprovision is justified by economic considerations including the effects in the regions of Indiana in which the mining of coal provides employment and in the service territory of the public utility. IC § 8-1-27-8(1).

A plan that has a negative impact on Indiana coal is subject to continuing annual surveillance. IC § 8-1-27-20 ("The commission shall annually review each environmental compliance plan, the implementation of which has resulted in the displacement or diminished use of Indiana coal and determine whether a different compliance measure would more fully satisfy the requirements of § 8 of this chapter."). Those utilities whose plans are approved can include in their rate bases the cost of capital projects constructed under the plan and can recover approved costs so incurred. IC § 8-1-27-12 & 19.

In the court below Alliance moved for summary judgment on the ground that the ECPA unjustifiably discriminated against interstate commerce. The district court concluded that the ECPA was intended to promote high sulfur coal at the expense of western coal and unconstitutionally burdens interstate commerce.[265]

---

[265] Intervenor PSI Energy, Inc. sided with plaintiff whereas intervenor United Mine Workers of America agreed with defendants. The former has filed a brief urging affirmance.

As Judge Tinder explained (App. 24, 25):

> The ECPA clearly imposes a facial and patent burden on interstate commerce. It is plainly protectionist to the extent that it requires the [Commission] to consider the effects a utility's 1990 CAAA compliance plan may have on the Indiana coal industry and imposes restrictions on approval of the plan based upon the plan's effects on the Indiana coal industry.
>
> . . . .
>
> The obvious intent of the challenged portions of the ECPA was to limit or eliminate the use of western coal in Indiana generating plants with an eye toward promoting instead the use of high sulfur coal, preferably that mined in Indiana. This is exactly the type of statute the dormant Commerce Clause prohibits.

As a result, certain provisions of the ECPA were held to be unconstitutional in a well-reasoned 30-page opinion of the district court issued on March 27, 1995 (App. 4-33).

A few months after the district court decided this case, the Court of Appeals of Indiana reached the same conclusion in General Motors v. Indianapolis Power & Light, 654 N.E.2d 752 (Ind. App. 1995).[266] There the court approved Judge Tinder's reasoning that Indiana could not escape the reality that the statute is patently protectionist. *Id.* at 764-766. It stated that individual states are not granted "the right to discriminate legislatively in favor of in-state industry." *Id.* It further rejected the argument that the phrase "Indiana coal" in the statute does not truly mean coal from the state of Indiana because the plain language of the statute itself provides that Indiana coal "means coal from a mine whose coal deposits are located in the ground fully or partially in Indiana, regardless of the location of the mine's tipple." *Id.* at 766 n.4. The court further concluded that a fault of the challenged provisions is that "plans that do not provide for continued or increased use of Indiana coal may be rejected on that basis alone." *Id.* at 766.

Discussion

The United States Supreme Court has repeatedly held that "[a]lthough the Commerce Clause is phrased merely as a grant of authority to Congress to 'regulate Commerce . . . among the several States,' Art. I, § 8, cl. 3, it is well established that the Clause also embodies a negative command forbidding the States to discriminate against interstate trade." Associated Industries of Missouri v. Lohman, 511 U.S. 641, 646, 114 S.Ct. 1815, 1820, 128 L.Ed. 2d 639 (1994). "When a state statute clearly discriminates against interstate commerce, it will be struck down . . . unless the discrimination is demonstrably justified by a valid factor unrelated to economic protectionism." Wyoming v. Oklahoma, 502 U.S. 437, 454, 112 S.Ct. 789, 800, 117 L.Ed. 2d 1 (1992). The threshold inquiry we must make in deciding whether the ECPA violates the Commerce Clause is whether it "is basically a protectionist measure, or if it can fairly be viewed as a law directed to legitimate local concerns with

[266] In addition to the three sections of the ECPA declared unconstitutional by Judge Tinder, the Indiana Court of Appeals found three additional sections to be unconstitutional, but they are not before us.

effects upon interstate commerce that are only incidental." Oregon Waste Systems, Inc. v. Dept. of Environmental Quality, 511 U.S. 93, 99, 114 S.Ct. 1345, 1350, 128 L.Ed. 2d 13 (1994).

As the district judge recognized, the outcome of the case is controlled by Alliance for Clean Coal v. Miller, 44 F.3d 591 (7th Cir. 1995) (App. 10-12). There we invalidated the Illinois Coal Act, also enacted on the heels of the Clean Air Act Amendments of 1990, on the ground that it was repugnant to the Commerce Clause of the United States Constitution. The Illinois Coal Act provided that in preparing and approving compliance plans, the Illinois Commerce Commission and utilities were required to "take into account . . . the need to maintain and preserve as a valuable State resource the mining of coal in Illinois." *Id.* at 593-594. The Act also encouraged implementing scrubbers to allow the continued use of high sulfur coal by guaranteeing utilities the ability to recover the installation costs of scrubbers by including such costs in their rate base. *Id.* We stated "[t]he Illinois Coal Act is a none-too-subtle attempt to prevent Illinois electric utilities from switching to low sulfur western coal as a Clean Air Act compliance option." *Id.* at 595. Therefore, we concluded that the Act was "repugnant to the Commerce Clause and the principle of a unitary national economy which that clause was intended to establish." *Id.*

The ECPA contains provisions that are virtually identical to the sections of the Illinois Coal Act discussed above. First, in determining whether to approve a plan that includes a compliance option calling for a decrease in the use of Indiana coal, the ECPA requires the Commission to take into account "the effects in the regions of Indiana in which the mining of coal provides employment and in the service territory of the public utility." IC § 8-1-27-8(1). The ECPA also provides incentives for utilities to install scrubbers to continue to use high sulfur fuel by guaranteeing a recoupment of the implementation costs. IC § 8-1-27-12 & 19.

We agree with the district court that, just as in *Miller*, the ECPA discriminates against interstate commerce based solely upon geographic origin, and thus violates the Commerce Clause. The clear intent of the statute is to benefit Indiana coal at the expense of western coal. The fact that the ECPA does not explicitly forbid the use of out-of-state coal or require the use of Indiana coal, but "merely encourages" utilities to use high-sulfur coal by providing economic incentives does not make the ECPA any less discriminatory. As we stated in *Miller*:

> The Illinois Coal Act cannot continue to exist merely because it does not facially compel the use of Illinois coal or forbid the use of out-of-state coal. As recognized in *West Lynn Creamery*, even ingenious discrimination is forbidden by the Commerce Clause. 512 U.S. at 184, 114 S.Ct. at 2215. By "encouraging" the use of Illinois coal, the Act discriminates against western coal by making it a less viable compliance option for Illinois generating plants. *Miller*, 44 F.3d at 596.

The defendants attempt to distinguish the ECPA from the Illinois Coal Act by noting that the approval process provided under the ECPA is voluntary. They note that a utility is not required to obtain the prior approval allowed by the statute. Instead, a utility ostensibly can implement its compliance plan and seek approval at a later date for any increased rates that the plan requires. We agree with the district court that this argument is "particularly specious." As Judge Tinder correctly stated (App. 26):

> The problem with this system is obvious. A corporate officer charged with fiduciary duties toward the company would be virtually required to seek pre-approval of the utility's compliance plan. Failure to do so could result in the utility entering into a contract for the purchase of . . . western coal for which the [Commission] may refuse to provide a rate increase. The only way for the utility to ensure it will receive the necessary rate increases to finance its 1990 CAAA compliance plan is to avail itself of the procedures provided by the ECPA. . . . It is plain that the ECPA is "voluntary" in word alone.

Because the ECPA discriminates against interstate commerce, the burden lies with the defendants to prove that this discrimination is justified by a legitimate and compelling governmental interest. *Wyoming*, 502 U.S. at 456, 112 S.Ct. at 801. Defendants provide the following justification. They argue that a viable competitive Midwest high-sulfur coal market is a major component of low-cost electrical service by Indiana utilities and that the ECPA seeks only to ensure that market. [Def. Br. 12 ("The ECPA challenged provisions merely encourage the highly competitive interstate high sulfur coal market for the benefit of utilities/ratepayers and limit no benefit thereof to Indiana high sulfur coal producers.")]. However, ensuring such a regional market is not a proper justification for discriminating against interstate commerce. As the Supreme Court stated in *West Lynn Creamery, Inc.*:

> [R]espondent urges that "the purpose of the order, to save an industry from collapse, is not protectionist." . . . If we were to accept these arguments, we would make a virtue of the vice that the rule against discrimination condemns. Preservation of local industry by protecting it from the rigors of interstate competition is the hallmark of the economic protectionism that the Commerce Clause prohibits. West Lynn Creamery, Inc. v. Healy, 512 U.S. 186, 205, 114 S.Ct. 2205, 2217 [129 L.Ed. 2d 157]

While we do not doubt that a healthy Indiana mining industry and a fully employed workforce may aid Indiana in achieving a low cost electrical service, that is not a legitimate justification for discrimination against interstate commerce. Protection of local, or even regional, industry is simply not a legislative action that is consistent with the Commerce Clause.

Conclusion

Despite the fact that low sulfur western coal may be a more efficient compliance option, the ECPA clearly attempts to prevent Indiana electrical utilities from switching to low sulfur coal. This amounts to discriminatory state action that is forbidden by the Commerce Clause. *See Miller*, 44 F.3d at 596. The defendants have not discharged their burden of demonstrating that the statute serves a legitimate and compelling interest unrelated to economic protectionism. *Wyoming*, 502 U.S. at 454, 112 S.Ct. at 800. Judgment affirmed.

Appendix

The district court declared the following provisions of the Indiana Environmental Compliance Plans Act to be violative of the United States Constitution:

8-1-27-6. Voluntary submission of environmental compliance plan—Items required—

(b) An environmental compliance plan described in subsection (a) must include any information that the commission may reasonably require. The commission shall require a plan described in subsection (a) to include at least the following information:

. . . .

(6) For all compliance plans submitted to the commission after July 1, 1993, if an environmental compliance plan proposes a change of fuel type from the fuel type consumed in the public utility's generating units and that change of fuel type would result in the displacement or diminished use of Indiana coal from the quantity of Indiana coal consumed by the public utility during the calendar year 1990, or an average of the quantity of Indiana coal consumed by the utility in calendar years 1990, 1991, and 1992, whichever is submitted by the utility in the plan, the public utility shall submit the following as part of the environmental compliance plan:

(A) An analysis of the following:

(i) The economic and employment effects of the proposed change of fuel type on the regions of Indiana in which the mining of coal provides employment, and on the service territory of the public utility.

(ii) The effects of the proposed modification on the preservation of the mining of Indiana coal as a viable source of fuel. The analyses required under this clause must include a comparison of the effects likely to result from the alternative compliance measures identified under subdivision (5).

(B) Information describing the availability, the reliability, the current costs, and the projected future costs of the fuel type proposed for use in connection with the environmental compliance plan.

8-1-27-8. Requirements for approval of plan—The commission shall issue an order approving an environmental compliance plan if the commission:

(1) Finds that the environmental compliance plan:

. . . .

(D) Either:

(i) Provides for continued or increased use of Indiana coal in the coal-consuming electric generating units owned or operated by the public utility and affected by the Clean Air Act Amendments of 1990; or

(ii) If the plan does not provide for continued or increased use of Indiana coal, such nonprovision is justified by economic considerations including the effects in the regions of Indiana in which the mining of coal provides employment and in the service territory of the public utility.

8-1-27-20. Annual Review.—The Commission shall annually review each environmental compliance plan, the implementation of which has resulted in the displacement or diminished use of Indiana coal and determine whether a different compliance measure would more fully satisfy the requirements of section 8 [IC 8-1-27-8] of this chapter.

NOTES AND QUESTIONS

Alliance for Clean Coal v. Bayh reflects the post-1990 competition between the areas of the country which produce low sulfur coal—including several western states as well as the southern part of West Virginia and eastern Kentucky—and parts of the country that produce coal of high sulfur content. As a consequence of the Clean Air Act Amendments, high sulfur coal mines have closed, resulting in the loss of employment of many miners. Coal production in the west has increased, while it has decreased in the east. Are there provisions in the Clean Air Act to provide compensation for miners who have lost their jobs because of the change in the consumption of high sulfur coal?

See also B. Ackerman and W. Hassler, Clean Coal/Dirty Air (1981).

For comparison, also note the materials and comments on the Dormant Commerce Clause in Chapter 3, *infra*.

[1] Clean Air Permit System

The Clean Air Act Amendments of 1990 marked a change of direction in air pollution control enforcement. In significant part, the major purpose of the new approach is to shift enforcement to the states under a state permit program, inspired by the NPDES (National Pollutant Discharge Elimination System) under the Clean Water Act. Most requirements of the Clean Air Act are to be managed and enforced through the permit mechanism. The Administrator issues regulations that the states must meet in establishing their own state permit programs. These regulations were required to be in place some four years after the enactment of the 1990 Clean Air Act Amendments. In effect, the states are required to meet federal requirements in much the same way as state implementation plans must meet the requirements of federal ambient air quality standards. Indeed, the failure to have in place a state permit program as required results in sanctions under the law in the same manner that states are sanctioned for failure to meet ambient air quality attainment standards. Both kinds of nonattainment are subject to sanctions under § 179(b) of the Clean Air Act.

Another significant aspect of the permit program is that it is to be a pay-as-you-go program. In establishing the permit program, states must provide for the collection of fees calculated to cover the reasonable costs of permit administration. Permit fees moreover are to be indexed to the Consumer Price Index. They are paid into a special fund earmarked for the administration of the permit system. EPA has the authority to review the states' issuance of permits, but it may use the opportunity to waive the review of permits for certain small sources.

The permit system statute provides what the Congressional Conference Report refers to as a "permit shield." Compliance with a permit is deemed compliance with the requirement of the permit program as well as compliance with relevant provisions of the Clean Air Act, if the permit is issued in accordance with law and refers to the applicable provisions of the Clean Air Act.

Flexibility is provided in that facilities will be able to make changes in their operations without requiring a revision of the permit if certain conditions of the Act are met.

The permit program applies to affected sources as defined in Title IV and "major sources" as defined in § 112 and § 302, as defined in part D of Title I.

Section 502, as added by the Clean Air Act Amendments of 1990, provides the basic provisions of the permit program. After a permit program is approved or promulgated pursuant to Title V, it is unlawful for any person to violate the permit issued or to operate any affected source, major source or any source subject to the Clean Air Act, without or in violation of a permit. The law provides that certain designated activities or sources are now to be placed under permit. Thus the requirements of § 111 relating to new sources, or § 112 relating to hazardous air pollution now become permit requirements, and permits issued under Part C or D of Title I for any stationary source in a category designated by the Administrator's regulations must not operate except in compliance with a permit issued by a permitting authority under this Title. The Administrator may exempt one or more source categories from regulations if compliance is impracticable, infeasible or unnecessarily burdensome in such categories, but the Administrator may not exempt any major source from the requirements.

The law provides that the program must result in the collection in the aggregate of not less than $25 per pound of each regulated pollutant, or such other amount as the Administrator determines adequately reflects the reasonable costs of the permit program. The regulated pollutants for purposes of this bookkeeping entry means VOCs (Volatile Organic Compounds), pollutants regulated under § 111 or 112, and pollutants for which a national primary ambient air quality standard has been promulgated (except for carbon monoxide). Fees may be decreased or increased consistent with the need to cover the reasonable costs authorized.

In effect, § 502 provides for a kind of state implementation plan for the permit program. If the Administrator determines that the fee provisions do not meet the requirements of law or if the permitting authority is not enforcing an approved fee program, the Administrator may collect reasonable fees from the sources identified to cover the Administrator's cost in administering the provisions of the permit program promulgated by the Administrator. This is clearly analogous to the provisions relating to the SIP and applies the same sanctions to a state failing to comply with a permit program as it does for failing to comply with a state implementation plan requirement. Failure to pay the legally imposed fees results in penalties and penalty interest, computed in accordance with the provisions of the Internal Revenue Code. Fees collected, as well as penalties and interest, are to be earmarked and expended to carry out the agency's activities for which the fees were collected.

The state permit program must also include requirements for adequate personnel and funding, and the permitting authority must have adequate powers under state law to issue permits and to enforce the permit requirements. Permits are to be issued for a fixed term not to exceed five years and must assure that permits incorporate the emission limitations and other requirements in an applicable implementation plan. There must also be authority to terminate, modify, revoke or reissue permits for costs as well as the authority to recover civil penalties not less than $10,000 per day for each violation, providing also for appropriate criminal penalties. No permit may be issued by the state if the Administrator objects to its issuance in a timely manner.

There must be adequate procedures to determine when applications for permits are complete, as well as adequate opportunity for public comment and hearing and for review of permit actions. There must also be an opportunity for judicial review in a state court of the final permit action, by the applicant, by any person who participated in the public comment process, and by any other person who could obtain judicial review of that action under applicable law.

Section 502(e) provides for the prompt suspension of federal permits upon the publication of notice of approval of a state permit program.

Section 502 allows the state to impose permit requirements and conditions and it also provides for the notification of the Administrator and of contiguous states, under § 505 of the Act, of each permit application, permit modification and permit renewal. The permitting authority must notify all states whose air quality may be affected and that are contiguous to the state in which the emission originates, or that are within 50 miles of the source of each permit application or proposed permit forwarded to the Administrator under the section.

Under § 506 of the Act, a state or interstate permitting authority may establish additional permitting requirements not inconsistent with § 506. The Act in § 507 establishes a "small business stationary source technical and environmental compliance assistance program." Each state is required to adopt a plan for such a program, and the Administrator must establish a small business stationary source technical and environmental compliance assistance program to assist the states in developing and implementing their programs. The law defines the term "small business stationary source" for purposes of establishing eligibility under the program. A small business is one which employs 100 or fewer individuals; is a small business concern as defined in the Small Business Act; is not a major stationary source; does not emit 50 tons or more per year of any regulated pollutant; and emits less than 75 tons per year of all regulated pollutants.[267]

[267] For discussion of the state permit program generally, see F. Grad, Treatise on Environmental Law, § 2.03[16][c].

VIRGINIA v. BROWNER

United States Court of Appeals, Fourth Circuit (1996)
80 F.3d 869

M. BLANE MICHAEL, Circuit Judge:

The Commonwealth of Virginia petitions for review of the Environmental Protection Agency's final action disapproving Virginia's proposed program for issuing air pollution permits. Specifically, Virginia challenges EPA's finding that Virginia has failed to comply with Title V of the 1990 Amendments to the Clean Air Act (sometimes "CAA" or the "Act"), CAA §§ 501-507, 42 U.S.C. §§ 766-7661f, because Virginia's proposal lacks adequate provisions for judicial review of the Commonwealth's permitting decisions. Virginia also challenges the constitutionality of Title V and its sanctions provisions, CAA §§ 179(b) & 502(d), 42 U.S.C. §§ 7509(b) & 7661a(d). According to Virginia, these provisions improperly commandeer the legislative processes of the states, in violation of the Tenth Amendment and the Spending Clause, U.S. Const. art. I § 8, cl. 1. We have jurisdiction over all of Virginia's claims, see CAA § 307(b)(1), 42 U.S.C. § 7607(b)(1), and we find them to be without merit.

I.

A.

Because Virginia claims that the EPA has misinterpreted Title V and that Title V is unconstitutional as well, a brief discussion of the statute's structure and purposes is in order.

Title V's key provision, CAA § 502, 42 U.S.C. § 7661a, prohibits major stationary sources of air pollution from operating either without a valid permit or in violation of the terms of a permit.[268] The permit is crucial to the implementation of the Act: it contains, in a single, comprehensive set of documents, all CAA requirements relevant to the particular polluting source. Clean Air Act Amendments of 1990: Chafee-Baucus Statement of Senate Managers (Conf. Rep. No. 952, 101st Cong., 2d Sess.) ("*Chafee-Baucus Statement*"), reprinted in 136 Cong. Rec. S16933, S16983 (daily ed. Oct. 27, 1990). In a sense, a permit is a source-specific bible for Clean Air Act compliance.

Title V of the Act contemplates that states will administer and enforce the permitting program:

> The permit program is predicated on the principle that the primary responsibility for its day-to-day administration will rest squarely with

---

[268] A "stationary source" is defined in CAA §§ 112(a)(1), 182(b)(1)(A)(ii)(I), 182(c), 182(d), 182(e), 302(j), & 501(2); 42 U.S.C. §§ 7412(a)(1), 7511a(b)(1)(A)(ii)(I), 7511a(c), 7511a(d), 7511a(e), 7602(j), & 7661(2).

Stationary sources, such as power plants and factories, are distinguished from mobile sources, such as automobiles.

state and local air pollution agencies. While EPA has an important role of providing guidance and general oversight, the agency should not unduly interfere with states' implementation of the permit program. *Chafee-Baucus Statement* at S16983.

States are directed to submit for EPA approval their own programs for issuing permits. CAA § 502(d)(1), 42 U.S.C. § 7661a(d)(1). EPA may not approve a proposed permit program unless it meets certain minimum criteria set out in CAA § 502(b), 42 U.S.C. § 7661a(b). Among other things, states must design a standard permit application form (§ 502(b)(1)), adequately staff and fund the permit program (§ 502(b)(4)), develop a plan to ensure permit compliance (§ 502(b)(5)), provide public access to documents submitted in support of permit applications (§ 502(b)(8)), and provide for review in state courts of permitting decisions (§ 502(b)(6)).

If a state fails to submit a permit program, or submits a permit program that EPA disapproves for failure to comply with CAA § 502(b), the state becomes subject to sanctions designed to encourage compliance. CAA § 502(d), 42 U.S.C. § 7661a(d).[269]

One sanction deprives states of certain federal highway funds. CAA § 179(b)(1), 42 U.S.C. § 7509(b)(1). However, the state loses no funds that would be spent in regions that are in "attainment" within the meaning of the Act.[270] CAA § 179(b)(1)(A), 42 U.S.C. § 7509(b)(1)(A). And, even within "nonattainment" areas, funds remain available for highway projects that "resolve a demonstrated safety problem and likely will result in a significant reduction in, or avoidance of, accidents." *Id.* Finally, federal funds may be spent on many other types of transportation projects within nonattainment areas, including:

(i) capital programs for public transit;

(ii) construction or restriction of certain roads or lanes solely for the use of passenger buses or high occupancy vehicles;

(iii) planning for requirements for employers to reduce employee work-trip-related vehicle emissions;

(iv) highway ramp metering, traffic signalization, and related programs that improve traffic flow and achieve a net emission reduction;

(v) fringe and transportation corridor parking facilities serving multiple occupancy vehicle programs or transit operations;

(vi) programs to limit or restrict vehicle use in downtown areas or other areas of emission concentration particularly during periods of peak use,

---

[269] We discuss the timing of sanctions in greater detail in our opinion in a related case, *Virginia v. United States* (*Virginia I*), 74 F.3d 517 (4th Cir. 1996). Sanctions are mandatory, but they may be imposed earlier than mandated by the statute if EPA finds, after holding a notice-and-comment rulemaking proceeding, that early imposition of sanctions is necessary to encourage compliance. *See* CAA §§ 502(d) & (i), 42 U.S.C. §§ 7661a(d) & (i).

[270] We explain the concepts of "attainment" and "nonattainment" in greater detail in *Virginia I*. In brief, an area is in nonattainment with respect to a pollutant if levels of that pollutant in the ambient (breathable) air exceed a threshold level set by EPA. An ozone nonattainment area, for example, has what EPA has determined to be a sufficient amount of ozone in the air to cause health problems.

through road use charges, tolls, parking surcharges, or other pricing mechanisms, vehicle restricted zones or periods, or vehicle registration programs;

(vii) programs for breakdown and accident scene management, nonrecurring congestion, and vehicle information systems, to reduce congestion and emissions; and

(viii) such other transportation-related programs as the [EPA] Administrator, in consultation with the Secretary of Transportation, finds would improve air quality and would not encourage single occupancy vehicle capacity. In considering such measures, the State should seek to ensure adequate access to downtown, other commercial, and residential areas, and avoid increasing or relocating emissions and congestion rather than reducing them. CAA § 179(b)(1)(B), 42 U.S.C. § 7509(b)(1)(B).

A second sanction increases the pollution offset requirements already imposed on private polluters within ozone nonattainment areas. Normally, new major stationary sources of pollution may not be operated within nonattainment areas (and existing stationary sources may not be modified if the modification would increase emissions) unless pollution from other sources is reduced to offset increased pollution from the new or modified source. In regions of "marginal" nonattainment with respect to ozone, 110 tons of old pollution must be eliminated for every 100 additional tons of new pollution (a ratio of 1.1:1). CAA § 182(a)(4), 42 U.S.C. § 7511a(a)(4). In regions of "moderate" nonattainment, 115 tons of old pollution must be eliminated for every additional 100 tons of new pollution (a ratio of 1.15:1). CAA § 182(b)(5), 42 U.S.C. § 7511a(b)(5). In regions of "serious," "severe," or "extreme" nonattainment with respect to ozone, 120 tons of old pollution must be eliminated for every additional 100 tons of new pollution (a ratio of 1.2:1). CAA §§ 182(c)(10), (d), & (e); 42 U.S.C. § 7511a(c)(10), (d), & (e). In regions of "severe" and "extreme" nonattainment, higher ratios are mandated for certain pollutants. *See* CAA §§ 182(d)(2) & (e)(1); 42 U.S.C. §§ 7511a(d)(2) & (e)(1). The sanction supersedes these normal ratios by increasing the ratio in all ozone nonattainment areas to 2:1, requiring 200 tons of old pollutants to be eliminated for every 100 tons of new pollutants allowed. CAA § 179(b)(2), 42 U.S.C. § 7509(b)(2). The offset sanction, therefore, could slow the rate of industrial development within a noncomplying state.

A third sanction eliminates the state's ability to manage its own pollution control regime. If the state does not gain approval for its permit program, EPA develops and implements its own Title V permitting program within the noncomplying state. CAA § 502(d)(3), 42 U.S.C. § 7661a(d)(3). The state is not required to do anything to assist EPA in this effort; the federal government becomes wholly responsible.

B.

Virginia submitted a proposed Title V permit program to EPA on November 12, 1993, and January 14, 1994. EPA then opened a notice and comment period. EPA published notice of its intent to disapprove Virginia's proposal on June 17, 1994, 59 Fed. Reg. 31183, and Virginia responded to EPA's notice.

After considering Virginia's comments, as well as the comments of others, EPA took final action disapproving Virginia's proposed Title V program on December 5, 1994. 59 Fed. Reg. 62324.

EPA based its disapproval on five grounds:

(1) the proposed program contained inadequate judicial review provisions, in violation of CAA § 502(b)(6)(42 U.S.C. § 7661a(b)(6)) and 40 C.F.R. § 70.4(b)(3)(x) & 70.7(h);

(2) the proposed program would have allowed certain permits to be issued by default, in violation of § 505(b)(3) (42 U.S.C. § 7661d(b)(3)) and 40 C.F.R. § 70.8(e);

(3) the regulations that would have implemented the proposed program had expired without being re-promulgated;

(4) the proposed program did not "require issuance of permits to the proper universe of sources required by 40 CFR part 70"; and

(5) the proposed program did not "contain regulations meeting the requirements of 40 CFR part 70 to ensure issuance of permits that contain all applicable Federal requirements," and did not "correctly delineate provisions only enforceable by" Virginia.

See id. at 62324-25.

Virginia filed a petition for review in this Court on January 9, 1995. n4 Since that date Virginia has revised portions of its original proposal and now claims that it has corrected defects (2) through (5). EPA has not yet determined whether those defects have actually been corrected.

The claims in Virginia's petition to us fall into three broad categories. First, Virginia argues that because it has corrected defects (2) through (5) in its proposed permit program, we should remand the case to EPA for a new determination of whether the corrected version complies with the Act. Second, Virginia argues that EPA's disapproval of the originally proposed permit program was arbitrary and capricious. Third, Virginia argues that Title V of the CAA and its sanctions provisions are unconstitutional because the Act represents an attempt by Congress to coerce Virginia into exercising its sovereign legislative power. We consider each claim in turn.

II.

Virginia suggests that we must remand this case to EPA because four of the five defects in its originally proposed Title V state permit program have been corrected. We believe, however, that a remand would be inappropriate.

First, Virginia concedes that EPA properly disapproved its original submission on the basis of defects (2) through (5). We may affirm the agency on this basis, and this basis alone, if the CAA passes constitutional muster. Although the EPA "Administrator may approve a program [just] to the extent that the program meets the requirements of" the Act, she is not required to do so, and she has the authority to disapprove the entire program on the basis of one defect. CAA § 502(d)(1), 42 U.S.C. § 7661a(d)(1).

Second, EPA has not yet determined whether Virginia's new submission is adequate, because EPA has not completed the notice and comment rulemaking proceeding required by CAA § 502(d)(1). And absent any agency record, we have no way of knowing whether the new submission in fact complies with the CAA, as Virginia claims. . . .

A remand would serve no useful purpose here, and accordingly we reject Virginia's suggestion.

III.

Virginia claims that EPA erroneously determined that Virginia's permit program contained inadequate judicial review provisions (defect (1)). EPA's finding that Virginia submitted a deficient permit program must be upheld unless that finding is "arbitrary, capricious, or otherwise not in accordance with law." 5 U.S.C. § 706(2)(A). We find that EPA correctly determined that Virginia's proposed judicial review provisions do not comply with the Act. Therefore, even if EPA had based its disapproval solely on defect (1), such disapproval would not have been arbitrary and capricious.

A.

CAA § 502(b)(6), 42 U.S.C. § 7661a(b)(6), provides that a state permit program must contain:

> Adequate, streamlined, and reasonable procedures for expeditiously determining when applications are complete, for processing such applications, for public notice, including offering an opportunity for public comment and a hearing, and for expeditious review of permit actions, including applications, renewals, or revisions, and including *an opportunity for judicial review in State court of the final permit action by the applicant, any person who participated in the public comment process, and any other person who could obtain judicial review of that action under applicable law.*

(Emphasis supplied.)

The emphasized portion of this provision is at issue here. A state permit program will be disapproved unless the state submits a legal opinion stating that the proposed Title V program allows state court review of permitting decisions upon the request of "the [permit] applicant, any person who participated in the public participation process . . . and any other person who could obtain judicial review of such actions under State laws." 40 C.F.R. § 70.4(b)(3)(x). EPA interprets the statute and regulation to require, at a minimum, that states provide judicial review of permitting decisions to any person who would have standing under Article III of the United States Constitution. Notice of Proposed Disapproval, 59 Fed. Reg. 31183, 31184 (June 17, 1994).

Virginia law grants standing to seek judicial review of permitting decisions to "any owner aggrieved by" such decisions. Va. Code § 10.1-1318(A). This provision satisfies CAA § 502(b)(6)'s requirement that the permit "applicant" be allowed to seek judicial review. But § 502(b)(6) also requires that states grant certain standing rights to members of the public, and here is where Virginia's judicial review provision falls short of the mark. Under Virginia's provision, a member of the public "who is aggrieved by a final [permitting decision] who participated, in person or by submittal of written comments, in the public comment process" may only seek judicial review of a permitting decision if he can establish that

> (i) [he] has suffered an actual, threatened, or imminent injury; (ii) such injury is an invasion of an immediate, legally protected, *pecuniary and substantial* interest which is concrete and particularized; (iii) such injury is fairly traceable to the [permitting decision] and not the result of the action of some third party not before the court; and (iv) such injury will likely be redressed by a favorable decision of the court. Va. Code § 10.1-1318(B) (emphasis supplied).

According to EPA, this provision is too restrictive: limiting availability of review to those persons with "pecuniary and substantial" interests violates CAA § 502(b)(6). We agree with EPA.

B.

1.

Virginia argues that the text of CAA § 502(b)(6)does not require states to slacken their rules of judicial standing at all.

The critical language to be examined is: "an opportunity for judicial review in State court of the final permit action by the applicant, any person who participated in the public comment process, and any other person who could obtain judicial review of that action under applicable law."

As Virginia reads the statute, the final clause, "who could obtain judicial review of that action under applicable [state] law," modifies all three categories of persons earlier described as being allowed to seek judicial review: "the applicant," "any person who participated in the public comment process," and "any other person." Thus, according to Virginia, § 506(b)(6) requires states to grant standing to participants in the public comment process only if those persons would otherwise have standing under existing state law.

Virginia's proposed reading is contrary to ordinary principles of statutory construction and to the rules of English usage. The clause, "who could obtain judicial review of that action under applicable law," modifies only the immediately preceding category, "any other person." An elementary principle of statutory construction is the "last antecedent" rule, which holds that ordinarily a clause modifies only its nearest antecedent. *In re Grewe*, 4 F.3d 299, 302 (4th Cir. 1993), cert. denied, 127 L. Ed. 2d 377, 114 S. Ct. 1056 (1994). Furthermore, if the last antecedent rule does not apply, and the clause modifies all three categories, then there would have been no need for Congress to have included the first two categories. The statute could have been written simply to say that standing should be given to "any person" who complied with state standing rules. A court should not—and we will not—construe a statute in a manner that reduces some of its terms to mere surplusage. *See Arkansas*

Best Corp. v. Commissioner, 485 U.S. 212, 218, 99 L. Ed. 2d 183, 108 S. Ct. 971 (1988).

Properly read, the final clause simply allows the states to grant broader standing rights than those otherwise required under federal law.

> This provision ensures that existing provisions of law governing the availability of review of final actions on permit applications are in no way limited, and that interested persons who arguably are affected by permit decisions are guaranteed their day in court.

Chafee-Baucus Statement, 136 Cong. Rec. at S169941. In other words, the clause "who could obtain judicial review of that action under applicable law" creates a floor of rights, rather than a ceiling, and ensures that the CAA does not inadvertently diminish standing rights previously granted under state laws.

2.

A literal reading of the latter part of § 502(b)(6), then, would require that a state allow "any person who participated in the public comment process" to seek judicial review of permitting decisions. EPA, however, does not require that states go that far in providing for judicial review. EPA has determined that § 502(b)(6) is satisfied (and that therefore a state permit program may be approved) if a state grants standing only to those participants in the public comment process who would have Article III standing to sue in federal court.[271]

This determination is justified by analysis of the opening portion of § 502(b)(6), which requires that states provide "adequate, streamlined, and reasonable procedures for expeditiously" making permitting decisions. The two parts of the section must be harmonized, and EPA has done that by creating a safe harbor keyed to Article III standing.

But Virginia claims that because EPA agrees that § 502(b)(6), when read in its entirety, is ambiguous, the states may propose any Title V program that reasonably accommodates the statute's disharmonious provisions. Virginia claims that because its "pecuniary and substantial interest" requirement is a reasonable way to resolve the tension inherent in § 502(b)(6), EPA was arbitrary and capricious in its decision to reject Virginia's proposal.

We disagree. EPA's interpretation, if reasonable, must take precedence over any interpretation Virginia could offer or, indeed, even over any alternative interpretation we could formulate. *Chevron, U.S.A., Inc. v. Natural Resources Defense Council*, 467 U.S. 837, 844, 81 L. Ed. 2d 694, 104 S. Ct. 2778 (1984). We defer to EPA's definition of the bounds of the § 502(b)(6) safe harbor because "the power of an administrative agency to administer a congressionally created . . . program necessarily requires the formulation of policy and the making of rules to fill any gap left, implicitly or explicitly, by Congress."

[271] For Article III standing purposes, a potential litigant must show (1) actual or imminent injury that is concrete and particularized, (2) causal connection between the challenged conduct and the injury, and (3) likelihood that the injury would be redressed by favorable judicial action. *Lujan v. Defenders of Wildlife*, 504 U.S. 555, 112 S. Ct. 2130, 2136, 119 L. Ed. 2d 351 (1992).

Id. at 843 (quoting *Morton v. Ruiz*, 415 U.S. 199, 231, 39 L. Ed. 2d 270, 94 S. Ct. 1055 (1974)).

EPA's interpretation of the judicial review portion of CAA § 502(b)(6)harmonizes it with the portion that requires states to provide "adequate, streamlined, and reasonable procedures." We find EPA's importation of Article III principles to resolve the slight tension within CAA § 502(b)(6) to be reasonable. The Article III test is convenient to apply, primarily because a body of national caselaw interpreting Article III standing requirements already exists.

Virginia argues that *Chevron* deference is inappropriate because EPA's area of expertise is the environment, not jurisdictional rules. *See Hi-Craft Clothing Co. v. NLRB*, 660 F.2d 910, 914-15 (3d Cir. 1981). Again, we disagree. "Considerable weight should be accorded to an executive department's construction of a statutory scheme it is entrusted to administer." *Chevron*, 467 U.S. at 844.Congress has charged EPA with inducing the states to implement a permitting program that satisfies certain judicial review requirements, and if Congress has decided that EPA has sufficient expertise in the area, it is not our place to say otherwise. *See* Cass R. Sunstein, *Law and Administration After Chevron*, 90 Colum. L. Rev. 2071, 2097 (1990) ("an ad hoc inquiry into administrative competence would be an exceptionally poor way to handle the question whether *Chevron* applies").

Virginia also claims that *Gregory v. Ashcroft*, 501 U.S. 452, 115 L. Ed. 2d 410, 111 S. Ct. 2395 (1991), mandates a different result. Virginia is again mistaken. *Gregory* simply stands for the proposition that when congressional intent is unclear, a statute should be construed to avoid a constitutional question. That principle has no relevance in this case because here it is manifestly clear that Congress specifically intended that the states conform their judicial standing rules to meet the § 502(b)(6) standard. . . .

In *Gregory* the Supreme Court faced the question whether the Age Discrimination in Employment Act (ADEA), 29 U.S.C. §§ 621-34, applied to state judges. The ADEA contained no express reference to state courts or judges, and therefore the Court concluded that the statute did not apply. If the statute did apply to state judges, the Court reasoned, then an inquiry into key federalism concerns would be required. Specifically, could Congress, under the guise of an antidiscrimination statute, alter the qualifications for state judges, or would doing so violate the Tenth Amendment? The Court held that it would construe the ADEA in a manner that would allow it to avoid the constitutional question. Because the statute did not expressly say that it applied to state judges, and because a difficult constitutional question would have been presented if the statute did in fact apply to state judges, the statute was interpreted as not applying to state judges.

The Clean Air Act contains no ambiguity of the kind present in *Gregory*. Even if EPA's interpretation of CAA § 502(b)(6)can be said to implicate Tenth Amendment concerns by intruding upon what Virginia claims to be a core element of its sovereignty, see IV.A, *infra*, that interpretation is specifically authorized by the "plain statement" of Congress. *Gregory*, 501 U.S. at 461. In *Gregory*, the question was whether the ADEA applied to the state judiciary at all. Here, by contrast, Congress intended CAA § 502(b)(6) to apply to state courts, and Congress made "its intention unmistakably clear in the language of the statute." *Atascadero State Hosp. v. Scanlon*, 473 U.S. 234, 242, 87 L. Ed. 2d 171, 105 S. Ct. 3142 (1985). By its terms, § 502(b)(6) could apply to nothing but state courts.

Here, EPA resolved the slight tension within § 502(b)(6) by interpreting the section to require that states, at a minimum, extend judicial review rights to participants in the state public comment process who satisfy the standard for Article III standing. This resolution is both authorized by Congress and reasonable, and therefore we must reject Virginia's alternative interpretation.

3.

Virginia also argues that even if the Article III test is proper, Virginia's "pecuniary and substantial interest" requirement satisfies it. Again, we disagree. A plaintiff need not show "pecuniary" harm to have Article III standing; injury to health or to aesthetic, environmental, or recreational interests will suffice. *See, e.g.*, *United States v. Students Challenging Regulatory Agency Procedures (SCRAP)*, 412 U.S. 669, 68-87, 37 L. Ed. 2d 254, 93 S. Ct. 2405 (1973); *Sierra Club v. Morton*, 405 U.S. 727, 734, 31 L. Ed. 2d 636, 92 S. Ct. 1361 (1972).

In recent cases, Virginia courts have denied standing to plaintiffs who would have met Article III's standing requirements. For example, in *Fries v. State Water Control Bd.*, 13 Va. App. 213, 409 S.E.2d 634, 637 (Va. Ct. App. 1991), it was held that a town lacked standing to seek judicial review of the decision of the State Water Control Board to grant a permit, even though the permit allowed a sewage treatment plant to discharge waste directly upstream of the town. Standing also was denied to individual riparian landowners. The court held that "an anticipated public injury" was not "an immediate, pecuniary, and substantial interest" such that standing should be allowed. *Id.*; *see also Citizens for Clean Air v. Commonwealth* , 13 Va. App. 430, 412 S.E.2d 715, 719-21 (Va. Ct. App. 1991) (because unincorporated association was not an "owner aggrieved" under Virginia law, association was denied standing to challenge permitting decision of State Air Pollution Control Board, even though association members owned real estate near plant granted permit, were bothered by foul odors emitted by plant, and alleged decline in property values); *Environmental Defense Fund v. Virginia State Water Control Bd.*, 12 Va. App. 456, 404 S.E.2d 728, 731-32 (Va. Ct. App. 1991) (standing denied to association seeking review of water pollution permit decision, even though association represented both recreational users of a river and riparian landowners).

Virginia caselaw makes it clear that the "pecuniary and substantial interest" requirement is more stringent than Article III's requirement of concrete and particularized injury.

4.

Section 502(b)(6)'s requirement of broad availability of judicial review is necessary to ensure that the required public comment period serves its proper purpose. The comment of an ordinary citizen carries more weight if officials know that the citizen has the power to seek judicial review of any administrative decision harming him. EPA recently recognized this principle in another context:

> When citizens are denied the opportunity to challenge executive decisions in court, their ability to influence permitting decisions through other required elements of public participation, such as through public comments and public hearings on proposed permits, may be seriously compromised. If citizens perceive that a state is not addressing their concerns about [ ] permits because the citizens have no recourse to an impartial judiciary, that perception also has a chilling effect on all the remaining forms of public participation in the permitting process.

Amendment to Requirements for Authorized State Permit Programs Under Section 402 of the Clean Water Act, 60 Fed. Reg. 14588, 14589 (March 17, 1995) (notice of proposed rulemaking).

5.

Because Virginia's permit program did not provide the minimum judicial review rights required under § 506(b)(6), it was not arbitrary and capricious for EPA to disapprove Virginia's submission.

IV.

Having determined that EPA had a valid reason to disapprove Virginia's permit program, we now examine whether Title V and its sanctions provisions are constitutional. Virginia claims that Title V and its sanctions provisions are unconstitutional because they impinge upon a fundamental element of state sovereignty, the state's right to articulate its own rules of judicial standing. Even assuming arguendo the accuracy of Virginia's assertion that its standing rules are within the core of its sovereignty, we find no constitutional violation because federal law "may, indeed, be designed to induce state action in areas that otherwise would be beyond Congress' regulatory authority." *FERC v. Mississippi*, 456 U.S. 742, 766, 72 L. Ed. 2d 532, 102 S. Ct. 2126 (1982). As we explain below, we believe that if Virginia chooses to change its rules of judicial standing, it will make the change only because the CAA's sanctions provisions induce it to do so, not because they coerce it.

A.

We agree that Congress lacks power to impinge upon "the core of sovereignty retained by the States." *New York v. United States*, 505 U.S. 144, 112 S. Ct. 2408, 2419, 120 L. Ed. 2d 120 (1992). We also agree that an important aspect of a state's sovereignty is the administration of its judicial system. *See Gregory*, 501 U.S. at 460. Thus, a state cannot be required to create a court with power to decide federal claims, if no court otherwise exists. *Howlett v. Rose*, 496 U.S. 356, 372, 110 L. Ed. 2d 332, 110 S. Ct. 2430 (1990). Similarly, a state may apply neutral venue rules to require that federal claims be brought in a particular state court. *Herb v. Pitcairn*, 324 U.S. 117, 123, 89 L. Ed. 789, 65 S. Ct. 459 (1945), overruled in part on other grounds by *Michigan v. Long*,

463 U.S. 1032, 77 L. Ed. 2d 1201, 103 S. Ct. 3469 (1983). But the Supremacy Clause compels state judges to apply federal law, if such law is applicable. U.S. Const. art. VI, cl. 2. Furthermore, to require an existing state administrative body to adjudicate a dispute arising under federal law does not unreasonably interfere with state sovereignty. *FERC*, 456 U.S. at 760; *see also Testa v. Katt*, 330 U.S. 386, 91 L. Ed. 967, 67 S. Ct. 810 (1947) (state court must entertain civil action arising under federal Emergency Price Control Act); *E.A. v. State*, 623 P.2d 1210, 1215 n.13 (Alaska, 1981) (state court must exercise jurisdiction over actions brought pursuant to federal Indian Child Welfare Act); *cf. Mack v. United States*, 66 F.3d 1025, 1029-30 (9th Cir. 1995) (state law enforcement officials may be required to assist in operation of federal law enforcement scheme).

We need not decide whether judicial standing rules fall within the core of sovereignty identified in *Gregory* and *Howlett*, *supra*, because we find that the CAA does not compel the states to modify their standing rules; it merely induces them to do so.[272] The CAA is constitutional because although its sanctions provisions potentially burden the states, those sanctions amount to inducement rather than "outright coercion." *See New York*, 112 S. Ct. at 2423. We examine each sanction separately to explain how we reach this conclusion. *See id.* at 2425.

B.

Two sources of Congressional power allow use of the highway sanction. Because the elimination of air pollution promotes the general welfare, Congress may tie the award of federal funds to the states' efforts to eliminate air pollution. "The Congress shall have Power to lay and collect Taxes, Duties, Imposts and Excises, to pay the Debts and provide for the common Defence and general Welfare of the United States." U.S. Const. art. I § 8, cl. 1. Furthermore, the Commerce Clause, U.S. Const. art. I, § 8, cl. 3, gives Congress the power to regulate "activities causing air or water pollution, or other environmental hazards that may have effects in more than one State." *Hodel v. Virginia Surface Mining & Reclamation Ass'n*, 452 U.S. 264, 282, 69 L. Ed. 2d 1, 101 S. Ct. 2352 (1981).

---

[272] In its brief and during oral argument Virginia claimed that CAA § 113, 42 U.S.C. § 7413, exposes the state and its elected officials to civil and criminal liability for failure to promulgate a valid state permit program. A careful reading of this section, however, discloses that it provides for enforcement of an approved state permit program. Sanctions under § 113 may not be used to force Virginia to promulgate any state permit program, and EPA has not proposed invoking § 113 in this case. Sanctions under this section are available only to redress "violations of . . . an approved permit program under subchapter [Title] V." CAA § 113(a)(2), 42 U.S.C. § 7413(a)(2). EPA has not approved Virginia's proposed Title V program, so no "approved permit program" yet exists to trigger any § 113 sanctions against any Virginia official. In addition, EPA has expressed no intention to seek § 113 sanctions against Virginia officials in the future. For these reasons, a constitutional challenge to § 113 is unripe. *Renne v. Geary*, 501 U.S. 312, 321-22, 115 L. Ed. 2d 288, 111 S. Ct. 2331 (1991). The threat of such sanctions has not been "felt in a concrete way by" any Virginia official. *Reno v. Catholic Social Servs., Inc.*, 509 U.S. 43, 113 S. Ct. 2485, 2495, 125 L. Ed. 2d 38 (1993) (quoting *Abbott Labs., Inc. v. Gardner*, 387 U.S. 136, 148, 18 L. Ed. 2d 681, 87 S. Ct. 1507 (1967)); accord *Lujan v. National Wildlife Fed'n*, 497 U.S. 871, 891, 111 L. Ed. 2d 695, 110 S. Ct. 3177 (1990).

Generally, Congress may use the power of the purse to encourage states to enact particular legislation. *New York*, 112 S. Ct. at 2423. This power, however, is not limitless. Exercise of the power to the point of "outright coercion" violates the Constitution. *Id.* "In some circumstances the financial inducement offered by Congress might be so coercive as to pass the point at which 'pressure turns into compulsion.'" *South Dakota v. Dole*, 483 U.S. 203, 211, 97 L. Ed. 2d 171, 107 S. Ct. 2793 (1987) (quoting *Steward Machine Co. v. Davis*, 301 U.S. 548, 590, 81 L. Ed. 1279, 57 S. Ct. 883 (1937)). Also, it has been suggested that federal funds may be subject to conditions "only in ways reasonably related to the purpose for which the funds are expended." *South Dakota*, 483 U.S. at 213 (O'Connor, J., dissenting); *see also New York*, 112 S. Ct. at 2426. No court, however, has ever struck down a federal statute on grounds that it exceeded the Spending Power. *See Nevada v. Skinner*, 884 F.2d 445, 448 (9th Cir. 1989), cert. denied, 493 U.S. 1070, 107 L. Ed. 2d 1019, 110 S. Ct. 1112 (1990).

The highway sanction here does not rise to the level of "outright coercion." First, a state does not lose any highway funds that would be spent in areas of the state that are in attainment. CAA § 179(b)(1)(A), 42 U.S.C. § 7509(b)(1)(A). Second, even within nonattainment areas, federal highway funds may be spent on projects designed to promote safety or designed to reduce air pollution. CAA § 179 (b)(1), 42 U.S.C. § 7509(b)(1). More severe funding restrictions than those at issue here have been upheld. *See, e.g., New York*, 112 S. Ct. at 2426-27; *Skinner, supra* (virtually all highway funds); *Oklahoma v. Schweiker*, 210 U.S. App. D.C. 288, 655 F.2d 401 (D.C. Cir. 1981) (all Medicaid funds); *Nebraska, Dep't of Roads v. Tiemann*, 510 F.2d 446 (8th Cir. 1975) (broad category of highway funds).

Virginia concedes that it is allowed to spend federal money on safety projects, on projects that will reduce pollution, and on projects within areas that are in attainment. The Commonwealth contends, however, that because it is difficult to shift funds from one transportation project to another, these exemptions do not reduce the sanction's coercive effect. According to Virginia, it simply lacks the time to reallocate funds away from highway projects it has already planned for nonattainment areas. To this argument we can only say that Title V was enacted in 1990, and the states have had more than five years either to comply or to prepare themselves for the consequences of noncompliance.

And contrary to what Virginia claims, the conditions on spending are reasonably related to the goal of reducing air pollution. The CAA as a whole is a comprehensive scheme to cope with the problem of air pollution from all sources. Congress may ensure that funds it allocates are not used to exacerbate the overall problem of air pollution. It is therefore of no consequence that a highway sanction, which will have the effect of reducing emissions from mobile pollution sources, is being used to induce compliance with a portion of the Act designed to reduce emissions from stationary sources.

We hold that the highway sanction, CAA § 179(b)(1), is a valid exercise of the Spending Power. As a valid exercise of that power, it also comports with the requirements of the Tenth Amendment. *New York*, 112 S. Ct. at 2427. Congress has not overstepped its bounds here.

C.

The offset sanction, CAA § 179(b)(2), 42 U.S.C. § 7509(b)(2), which limits new construction or modification of major stationary sources of air pollution, is constitutional because it regulates private pollution sources, not states.

The burden of the offset sanction falls on private parties. The more stringent offset requirements will likely make it more difficult for individual pollution sources (manufacturers, utilities, and the like) to upgrade or modify existing plants and equipment or to open new plants. Thus, although the sanction may burden some Virginia citizens, it does not burden Virginia as a governmental unit. For this reason, the sanction does not violate the principles of federalism embodied in the Tenth Amendment. *New York*, 112 S. Ct. at 2427 (upholding a sanction because "any burden caused by a state's refusal to regulate will fall on" private citizens); *Hodel*, 452 U.S. at 288 (harm to citizens of states does not create Tenth Amendment violation, absent direct harm to state governmental entities). The offset sanction is constitutional.

D.

The final sanction, federal permit program implementation, CAA § 502(d)(3), 42 U.S.C. § 7661a(d)(3), also is constitutional. The essence of a Tenth Amendment violation is that the state is commanded to regulate. Here, Virginia is not commanded to regulate; the Commonwealth may choose to do nothing and let the federal government promulgate and enforce its own permit program within Virginia. Because "the full regulatory burden will be borne by the Federal Government," the sanction is constitutional. *Hodel*, 452 U.S. at 288. *Hodel*, in fact, is the mirror image of this case and controls our decision. In *Hodel* the federal government first implemented an environmental regulatory regime within each state but then gave each state the ability to end the federal program by implementing its own state environmental regulations that met certain criteria. In the present situation, the federal government gives the states the chance to enact their own regulations before the federal plan is imposed. For purposes of constitutional analysis, we cannot see how it makes a difference whether the federal plan is imposed first, or whether the states are given the chance to avoid imposition of the federal plan first. If anything, the CAA's method—to give the states a chance first to avoid imposition of any federal plan by promulgating satisfactory regulations—seems less coercive than the program upheld in *Hodel*. The CAA simply "establishes a program of cooperative federalism that allows the States, within limits established by federal minimum standards, to enact and administer their own regulatory programs, structured to meet their own particular needs." *Id.* at 289.

Because Congress may choose to preempt state law completely, it may also take the less drastic step of allowing the states the ability to avoid preemption by adopting and implementing their own plans that sufficiently address congressional concerns. *Id.* at 290; *Mack*, 66 F.3d at 1029 ("The federal government may offer to preempt regulation in a given area and permit the states to avoid preemption if they regulate in a manner acceptable to Congress.").

In *Maryland v. EPA*, 530 F.2d 215 (4th Cir. 1975), vacated and remanded for consideration of mootness sub nom. *EPA v. Brown*, 431 U.S. 99, 52 L. Ed. 2d 166, 97 S. Ct. 1635 (1977) (per curiam), this court examined regulations promulgated under the CAA that on their face would have directly required Maryland to enact statutes and to administer an EPA plan. *See also District of Columbia v. Train*, 172 U.S. App. D.C. 311, 521 F.2d 971, 983 (D.C. Cir. 1975), vacated and remanded for consideration of mootness sub nom. *EPA v. Brown*, 431 U.S. 99, 52 L. Ed. 2d 166, 97 S. Ct. 1635 (1977) (per curiam).

The regulations in Maryland provided that "the state of Maryland shall" establish and implement certain pollution control programs. 530 F.2d at 219. EPA argued that the regulations' use of the word "shall" meant that if Maryland did not comply, EPA could seek to impose civil and criminal penalties on the state for noncompliance. *Id.* at 224. We rejected that proposed interpretation as "astonishing," *id.*, and said it "would reduce the states to the puppets of a ventriloquist Congress." *Id.* at 226 (quoting *Brown v. EPA*, 521 F.2d 827, 839 (9th Cir. 1975), vacated and remanded for consideration of mootness, 431 U.S. 99 (1977) (per curiam)). Had we accepted EPA's proposed interpretation, Maryland's legislature would have been directly compelled to regulate, a result that would have offended the Tenth Amendment. *Maryland*, 530 F.2d at 224. Instead, we interpreted the regulations as authorizing EPA to implement a federal pollution control program directly. *Id.* at 227-28. This interpretation of the regulations did not offend the Tenth Amendment, even though Maryland was put under some pressure to pass laws satisfying federal criteria in order to avoid federal implementation. "Congress may induce a state to act by offering favors or exacting financial penalties." *Id.* at 226. *See also Train*, 521 F.2d at 984-85 (this procedure is "quite unremarkable"). In Maryland we sent Congress and EPA a signal that they could constitutionally use sanctions such as those at issue here.

Finally, the CAA's sanctions provisions maintain unity between regulation and political accountability. If sanctions are imposed, it will be "the Federal Government that makes the decision in full view of the public, and it will be federal officials that suffer the consequences if the decision turns out to be detrimental or unpopular." *New York*, 112 S. Ct. at 2424. The sanctions provisions are constitutional.

V.

In sum, we conclude (1) that EPA correctly disapproved Virginia's proposed state permit program because it did not satisfy the provisions of the Clean Air Act and (2) that the sanctions Virginia faces are constitutional. The petition for review is denied.

DENIED

WESTERN STATES PETROLEUM ASSOCIATION v. EPA

United States Court of Appeals, Ninth Circuit (1996)
87 F.3d 280, 26 ELR 21469

TASHIMA, Circuit Judge:

Title V of the 1990 Clean Air Act Amendments (Title V), 42 U.S.C. §§ 7601 *et seq.*, established a new operating permit program to be administered pursuant to rules developed by the states and approved by the Environmental Protection Agency (EPA). The State of Washington submitted for EPA approval a Title V program that would exempt "insignificant emissions units" (IEUs) from permit application requirements, as well as monitoring, reporting and recordkeeping requirements. The EPA granted only interim approval to Washington's program and conditioned final approval on the repeal of the IEU exemption. We reverse the EPA's decision as an abuse of discretion because it conflicts substantially with numerous EPA decisions in other states and localities.

Background

Title V instituted a centralized permitting program to be administered by the states subject to EPA oversight. Through the program, all Clean Air Act substantive and procedural requirements applicable to a pollutant emitter are written in the emitter's operating permit. 42 U.S.C. §§ 7661c(a)-(c). Each permit must include inspection, entry, monitoring, compliance certification, and reporting requirements to assure compliance with the Act. *Id.*

Title V directs the EPA to prescribe procedures for determining compliance, institute requirements for permit applications, and establish the minimum elements of a state permit program (including monitoring and reporting requirements). 42 U.S.C. §§ 7661a(b)(1), 7661a(b)(2), 7661c(b). 42 C.F.R. Part 70 sets forth the regulations that the EPA adopted to implement Title V. The Part 70 regulations set forth the criteria for EPA approval of state permit programs.

The EPA has allowed states to exempt insignificant activities and emissions levels from certain requirements in order to reduce the regulatory burdens on emitters. 40 C.F.R. § 70.5(c)(3). Subject to EPA approval, each state determines what activities and emissions levels may qualify as insignificant. 40 C.F.R. § 70.5(c)(3).

Pursuant to 42 U.S.C. § 7661a(d)(1), the State of Washington proposed a permit program to the EPA during November 1993. Washington's program designates a host of emissions as insignificant, *e.g.*, emissions from roof vents, vehicle exhaust from repair shops, and emissions from fire fighting equipment. Wash. Admin. Code § 173-401-532. Washington's program exempts IEUs from the permit application requirements of 40 C.F.R. § 70.5. The program also exempts IEUs from the permit compliance requirements of 40 C.F.R. § 70.6, including monitoring, testing, reporting, record keeping and compliance certification. Wash. Admin. Code § 173-401-530(2)(c).

On November 9, 1994, the EPA rejected Washington's IEU provisions, granting only interim approval to the program. 59 Fed. Reg. 55813 (1994). As a condition to final approval, the EPA required Washington to amend its IEU rules to disqualify any emissions unit subject to federally enforceable applicable requirements. 59 Fed. Reg. 55813, 55814, 55818. The EPA's interim approval allowed Washington to begin implementing its permit program while addressing the defects identified by the EPA. 40 C.F.R. § 70.4(e)(3).

Petitioners, five air pollutant emitters and two trade associations of pollutant emitters, filed a timely petition for judicial review on January 6, 1995.[273] The State of Washington Department of Ecology moved to intervene in support of its program.[274] On July 7, 1995, we granted the EPA's motion to vacate the portion of its decision that concerned IEUs and specifically retained jurisdiction of this matter.

On remand, the EPA adopted a final decision on November 15, 1995. 60 Fed. Reg. 62992, 62993 (1995). The EPA found that Part 70 allows states to exempt IEUs from Title V permit applications (40 C.F.R. § 70.5), but not from the permit content requirements of 40 C.F.R. § 70.6. *Id.* at 62993. Thus, the EPA disapproved Washington's exemption of IEUs from Title V monitoring, reporting and record keeping requirements. Petitioners seek review of this final agency decision.

We have jurisdiction to review the EPA's final action pursuant to § 307(b)(1) of the Clean Air Act, 42 U.S.C. § 7606(b)(1), and pursuant to our July 7, 1995 order retaining jurisdiction of this appeal.

Standard of Review

We review final administrative actions of the EPA pursuant to the Clean Air Act under the same standard as set forth in the Administrative Procedure Act. *Abramowitz v. United States EPA*, 832 F.2d 1071, 1074 (9th Cir. 1987). We will reverse the EPA's decision only if it is "arbitrary, capricious, an abuse of discretion, or otherwise not in accordance with law." 42 U.S.C. § 7607(d)(9)(A); *Ober v. United States EPA*, 84 F.3d 304, 307 (9th Cir. 1996).

Under this standard, we must give deference to the EPA's interpretation of its own regulations, if its interpretation is not unreasonable. *Id.*; *Citizens for Clean Air v. United States EPA*, 959 F.2d 839, 844 (9th Cir. 1992). However, if the EPA has abused its discretion in failing to follow its own prior standards, then we need not defer to the EPA's anomalous interpretation. *Oil, Chemical and Atomic Workers Int'l Union, Local 1-547 v. NLRB*, 842 F.2d 1141, 1143 n.1 (9th Cir. 1988).

---

[273] The EPA's 1994 interim approval decision mandated five changes in Washington's Title V program prior to final approval. 59 Fed. Reg. 55818. Petitioners do not challenge any of the approval conditions other than the requirement of repealing the IEU rules.

[274] That motion, which was referred to this merits panel, is now granted.

Discussion[275]

The EPA asserts that Part 70 allows IEUs to be exempted from permit application requirements, but not permit content requirements. Section 70.5, which addresses requirements for permit applications, reads, in relevant part: "The Administrator may approve as part of a State program a list of insignificant activities and emissions levels which need not be included in permit applications." 40 C.F.R. § 70.5(c). The EPA points out that § 70.6, which addresses permit content requirements, contains no such exemption for IEUs.

However, the EPA has identified only two Title V programs that in fact apply permitting requirements to IEUs—the Oregon and San Francisco Bay Area Quality Maintenance District programs. On the other hand, the EPA has condoned the exemption of IEUs from the permit content requirements of § 70.6 in at least eight other state and local programs. For example, the EPA has granted final, full approval to Title V programs from Ohio and Knox County, Tennessee, that omit IEUs entirely from permits. The EPA has also proposed to approve the programs of Jefferson County, Kentucky and Massachusetts despite their exemption of IEUs from permitting requirements. Although the EPA required revisions in the Title V programs of Florida, North Dakota, Hawaii, and North Carolina, the EPA's objections to those programs were based on grounds other than their general exemption of IEUs from the majority of permit content requirements.

The EPA urges this court to ignore the apparent inconsistency between its Washington decision and its approval of other state programs on the ground that the Washington decision represents the EPA's first thorough, well reasoned discussion of whether IEUs may be exempted from § 70.6's permitting requirements. Even so, the EPA's rejection of Washington's IEU rules is undeniably a change "in agency interpretation [which] must be supported by a 'reasoned analysis' over and above that required for an interpretation in the first instance." *Flagstaff Medical Center, Inc. v. Sullivan*, 962 F.2d 879, 886 (9th Cir. 1992) (citation omitted).

The EPA may have the power to adjust its policies and rulings in light of experience and to announce new principles in an adjudicatory proceeding. *California Trucking Ass'n v. ICC*, 900 F.2d 208, 212 (9th Cir. 1990). However, the EPA "may not depart, sub silentio, from its usual rules of decision to reach a different, unexplained result in a single case." *Id.* (citations omitted) To the contrary, the EPA must clearly set forth the ground for its departure from prior norms so that we may understand the basis of the EPA's action and judge the consistency of that action with the EPA's mandate. *Atchison, T. & S.F. Ry. v. Wichita Bd. of Trade*, 412 U.S. 800, 808, 93 S.Ct. 2367, 2375, 37 L.Ed. 2d 350 (1973); *Arizona Elec. Power Coop., Inc. v. United States*, 816 F.2d 1366, 1374 (9th Cir. 1987).

In this case, the EPA fails to provide any explanation at all for its anomalous Washington decision. Instead, it flatly denies the obvious inconsistency

[275] As a preliminary matter, the EPA contends that petitioners' failure to raise before the agency their current objections to EPA's decision forecloses this court's consideration of these arguments. However, we find that petitioners did in fact call their instant objections to EPA's attention either before the case was remanded for EPA's reconsideration or during the comment period below. Thus, petitioners' arguments are properly before us.

between its rejection of the Washington program and its approval of other state programs. 60 Fed. Reg. 62992, 629925 (1995) ("the commentators can point to no instance in which EPA has approved a state program which expressly exempts IEUs with applicable requirements from the permit content requirements of section 70.6.").

The EPA relies heavily on *Puerto Rican Cement Co. v. United States EPA*, 889 F.2d 292 (1st Cir. 1989), for the proposition that "[n]o large agency can guarantee that all its administrators will react similarly, or interpret regulations identically, throughout the United States." *Id.* at 299. In that case, the First Circuit found no significant, legally recognizable conflict that the EPA had to justify.

The EPA's reliance on *Puerto Rican Cement* is misplaced. Central to the holding in that case was the fact that the "deviant" interpretation occurred but once; EPA materials written both before and after the deviant letter were consistent with the EPA's position in the litigation. *Id.* Moreover, the deviant interpretation appeared in a letter written by a lower level official and did not reflect an unconscious change in established EPA policies. *Id.*

By contrast, there are at least eight EPA decisions published in the Federal Register that conflict with the Washington decision here. Further, the EPA issued the conflicting decisions both before and after the Washington decision. The EPA approved Ohio's IEU rules, which omit IEUs entirely from permits, on August 15, 1995. 60 Fed. Reg. 18790 (1995). The EPA then proposed to disapprove Washington's exemption of IEUs from § 70.6 permit content requirements on September 14, 1995. 60 Fed. Reg. 50166, 50173 (1995). Eleven days later, on September 25, EPA published its final interim approval of Florida's Title V program. 60 Fed. Reg. 49343 (1995). The EPA issued its final decision disapproving Washington's IEUs rules on November 15, 1995. 60 Fed. Reg. 62997. That same day, the EPA published its final interim approval of North Carolina's Title V program. 60 Fed. Reg. 57357 (1995). Ten days later, the EPA published its proposal to approve the Jefferson County, Kentucky program. 60 Fed. Reg. 58033 (1995). Finally, the EPA published interim approval of Massachusetts' program on February 2, 1996, 61 Fed. Reg. 3827 (1996), and full approval of the Knox County, Tennessee program on April 19, 1996. 61 Fed. Reg. 18966 (1996). The fact that the EPA changed its mind and course four times refutes its argument that the Washington decision marked a reflected, deliberate, or lasting change of policy.

In sum, the EPA has approved numerous state programs omitting IEUs from § 70.6's monitoring and compliance requirements, but rejected Washington's IEU rules on that very same basis. The EPA's reliance on its broad supervisory power over state Title V programs does not provide an adequate basis to support its otherwise arbitrary treatment of Washington's IEU rules. Cf. *Arizona Elec. Power Coop., Inc.*, 816 F.2d at 1374 (agency's "broad discretionary power" is not "an adequate basis to support its otherwise arbitrary treatment" of a single case). We need not defer to the EPA because the EPA has abused its discretion in departing from its own prior standards. *Oil, Chem. & Atomic Workers*, 842 F.2d at 1143 n.1. Because the EPA has failed to offer a sufficient explanation for its differential treatment of Washington's Title V program, we reverse EPA's decision on Washington's IEU rules.

McClaskey v. United States Dep't of Energy, 720 F.2d 583, 587 (9th Cir. 1983); *see also Motor Vehicle Mfrs. Ass'n v. State Farm Mut. Auto. Ins. Co.*, 463 U.S. 29, 43, 103 S.Ct. 2856, 2866-67, 77 L.Ed. 2d 443 (1983) (reviewing court must not supply a reasoned basis for agency's action that agency itself has not given).

Attorneys' Fees

Petitioners seek an award of attorneys' fees and costs on appeal pursuant to § 307(f) of the Clean Air Act,which provides:

> In any judicial proceeding under this section, the court may award costs of litigation (including reasonable attorney and expert witness fees) whenever it determines that such award is appropriate. 42 U.S.C. § 7607(f).

An award of attorneys' fees is "appropriate" where petitioners have: (1) attained some success on the merits; and (2) contributed substantially to the goals of the Clean Air Act in doing so. *Abramowitz*, 832 F.2d at 1079 (citing *Ruckelshaus v. Sierra Club*, 463 U.S. 680, 682-84, 103 S.Ct. 3274, 3276-77, 77 L.Ed. 2d 938 (1983); *Cason-Truckee Water Conservancy Dist. v. Secretary of the Interior*, 74 F.2d 523, 525-26 (9th Cir. 1984), cert. denied, 471 U.S. 1065, 105 S.Ct. 2139, 85 L.Ed. 2d 497 (1985)).

Because we reverse EPA's Washington Decision as an unexplained departure from precedent, petitioners have attained sufficient success on the merits to be eligible for attorneys' fees. *Ruckelshaus v. Sierra Club*, 463 U.S. at 682, 103 S.Ct. at 3276.

The second question—whether petitioners have contributed substantially to the goals of the Clean Air Act—is more difficult. We have yet to address whether a financially able, nongovernmental party having no more than its own economic interests at stake should be entitled to attorneys' fees under § 307(f).

The Fifth Circuit has answered this question in the affirmative. *Florida Power & Light Co. v. Costle*, 683 F.2d 941, 943 (5th Cir. 1982). However, we decline to adopt the approach of the Fifth Circuit. We agree with the District of Columbia Circuit that the legislative history of § 19(d) of the Toxic Substances Control Act, 15 U.S.C. § 2618(d), which uses the same "appropriate" standard as the Clean Air Act, reveals the clearest expression of congressional purpose in enacting statutes of this type. *Alabama Power Co. v. Gorsuch*, 672 F.2d 1, 7 n. 33 (D.C. Cir. 1982). During debate on the final version of § 19(d), Senator Magnuson, the ranking Senate Manager on the Conference Committee, stated:

> It is not the intention of these provisions to provide an award for an individual or a group if that individual or group may stand to gain significant economic benefits through participation in the proceeding. . . . It is not intended that the provisions support participation of persons, including corporations or trade associations, that could otherwise afford to participate. . . . Whether or not the person's resources are sufficient to enable participation would include consideration of . . . the likelihood that the person would seek to participate in the proceeding whether or not compensation was available.

112 Cong. Rec. 32855 (1976) (remarks of Senator Magnuson), as quoted in *Alabama Power Co.*, 672 F.2d at 7 n. 33. Thus, the legislative history indicates that Congress neither intended to subsidize all litigation under the Clean Air Act nor contemplated that § 307(f) would benefit financially able parties who, out of their own substantial economic interests, would have litigated anyway. For this reason, we hold that petitioners are ineligible for a fee award under § 307(f).

Moreover, petitioners do not assert, nor do we find, that their litigation of this case has served the public interest in assisting in the interpretation and implementation of the Clean Air Act. *Carson-Truckee*, 748 F.2d at 525. Petitioners' status as prevailing parties, by itself, does not automatically establish that they have assisted in the proper implementation of the Act. *Cf. id.* ("[a]lthough a complainant may have substantially prevailed in an action, the award of costs and attorney fees does not automatically follow."). The issue under the Act has been relatively narrow and concerns only the anomalousness of the EPA's Washington decision. Petitioners do not identify any other Title V programs that this litigation will affect. We are simply confronted with an anomalous decision which the agency should correct. Because petitioners, who are financially able to and would have litigated regardless of any potential for a fee award, have not contributed substantially to the goals of the Clean Air Act, for this further reason we do not find an award of attorneys' fees to be appropriate.

Conclusion

We reverse the EPA's decision with respect to Washington's proposed IEU regulations as an unexplained departure from precedent, and thus, as an abuse of discretion. On remand, the EPA shall grant full approval to Washington's proposed Title V program, as modified to correct the four other deficiencies identified in the EPA's November 9, 1994 notice. Petitioners' request for attorneys' fees is denied. Each party shall bear its or her own costs on appeal. PETITION FOR REVIEW GRANTED. REVERSED AND REMANDED.

QUESTIONS

(1) How does a state challenge to the imposition of the federal state implementation plan requirement differ from a state challenge to the federal requirement to establish a state permit plan? Are there any differences with respect to procedural, including standing requirements? Are there any differences in the substantive challenges that may be asserted in either case? Are there any differences in the sanctions a court may impose on a state for failure to meet the state implementation plan requirement or the requirement that the state prepare a satisfactory permit plan?

(2) In terms of compliance by the states and in terms of compliance by regulated industries and persons with the requirements of the Clean Air Act, are the requirements different after permit programs have been adopted by

the several states? What is the advantage, if any, to seeking compliance with the terms of a permit rather than with the terms of the earlier underlying legislation? What are the advantages of the permit program for EPA? for the several states? or for regulated industries and persons? What are the disadvantages for all of the regulatory agencies and affected persons and industries referred to earlier?

(3) In the *Western States* case, do you consider the Court's decision on attorneys' fees persuasive?

[4] Automotive Pollution

[a] The Regulation of Automotive Pollution: A General Overview

The automobile is the source of more than half of the weight of national air pollution, and the attainment of national ambient air quality standards is impossible without the stringent regulation of automotive pollutants, more particularly hydrocarbons (HCs), carbon monoxide (CO), and nitrous oxides (NOx). Prior to the banning of the sale of leaded gasoline, starting in 1996, automobiles were also the main source of lead in the atmosphere. The automobile is also one of the primary sources of ozone (bad ozone, not the good atmospheric ozone) formed by the catalytic action of sunlight on hydrocarbons and NOx as well as other photochemical oxidants.

Following five years of hearings and studies, triggered by the newly discovered connection between automobile emissions and photochemical smog, Congress in 1960 directed the Surgeon General of the Public Health Service to report on the effect of motor vehicle exhaust on human health through the pollution of air. After publication of the Surgeon General's Report in 1962, the Air Pollution Control Act, as then existing, was amended to deal with the nationwide problem of pollution from motor vehicles. The law required the study of the relationship between motor vehicle exhaust and human health as an ongoing requirement of federal law. The 1965 Air Pollution Control Act Amendments constituted the first Congressional departure from the attitude that primary responsibility for control of air pollution should rest with state and local governments. But the 1963 Clean Air Act had indicated the federal interest in automobile air pollution by directing the Secretary of HEW to encourage the development of emission control devices for motor vehicles through the appointment of a technical committee to serve as liaison among the manufacturers of automobiles, exhaust control devices and fuel. Throughout the 1960s, automobile manufacturers had continued to maintain that automobiles created no air pollution problem, and, indeed, manufacturers of automobiles "agreed" to abstain from the development of air pollution control devices.[276] Nonetheless, the Clean Air Act was amended in 1965 to require

[276] *See In re Multidistrict Private Civil Treble Damage Antitrust Litigation* involving motor vehicle air pollution control equipment. M.D.L. No. 31, United States District Court, Central District of California (1970). A conspiracy was charged under the Sherman Act which was enjoined in a consent decree to prevent, restrain or limit the development, manufacture, installation, distribution or sale of air pollution control equipment for motor vehicles.

the Secretary of HEW to set emission standards for new motor vehicles. The standards were to take technological feasibility and the economic cost of compliance into account. The sale of automobiles and violation of these regulations was made unlawful and a fine of $1,000 per vehicle that violated the standards was provided for.

The 1965 Act, though now long obsolete, set certain patterns which still prevail. Section 605 of the Act required the Secretary to test and certify vehicles submitted by manufacturers to determine whether they conformed to the standards. The law was limited in that only prototype vehicles submitted by the manufacturers were to be tested; compliance by the prototype then created a conclusive presumption that all production vehicles of the same model would also comply. At the time, no attempt was made to ensure that vehicles on the road would maintain the standards of the prototype certified.

Although the 1967 Air Quality Act further extended the federal role in providing air quality criteria, and in supporting more affirmative federal control of air quality, effective federal involvement began with the 1970 Clean Air Act, earlier discussed in the context of the control of stationary sources of air pollution. With respect to automotive sources, the full sweep of Congressional regulatory power did not begin until the 1970 Act. The 1970 Clean Air Act Amendments provided for federal control of the achievement of national ambient air quality standards by the states. The attainment of ambient air quality standards for automotive pollutants depends on the control of automobiles in the hands of their owners. Emission controls on motor vehicles cannot protect air quality if control devices are permitted to deteriorate in actual use. The Administrator therefore may not approve a plan which fails to provide for periodic motor inspection and testing where the Administrator determines such inspection and tests to be "necessary and practicable."

Thus, under the 1970 Act, the need for a dual system of control of pollution from automotive sources had become apparent and necessary. The two systems of automotive pollution control were and still are: (1) the control of the automobile at its source, *i.e.*, the control of the manufacture and sale of automobiles setting limits on the permissible pollution from each automobile produced; and (2) control of the automobile on the road, to assure that the pollution control devices will continue to function and will continue to be maintained in actual use so as to prevent vehicles that originally met emission standards from exceeding the emission limits. The controls of the vehicle on the road include such measures as programs of inspection and maintenance, as well as other kinds of periodic checks on the performance of emission controls.

The 1970 Amendment of the Clean Air Act and its amendments of Title II were the first instance of legislative "forcing" of technology to roll back the level of emissions for new vehicles. Emission roll back is a most important part of automotive pollution control. The national fleet of automobiles numbers about 140 million vehicles. About 10% of the vehicles are retired each year and are being replaced by more highly controlled vehicles, exchanging the oldest, most highly polluting vehicles for the newest, most highly controlled ones.

The 1970 Act sought to accelerate this roll back which provided for a 90% reduction of automotive pollution by 1975-76. At the time there was no technology to ensure that it could be done. Yet the law provided for substantial penalties for new non-complying vehicles and the one-year postponement provided in the Act provided the only protection in the law against the possibility of a major confrontation between EPA and the automobile industry. Such a confrontational scenario may seem unreal many years later, but the history of the automobile companies' efforts to meet the 1975-76 standards provides the clearest and most direct evidence of the implications of technology forcing.

The success of this technology forcing effort becomes even more impressive when it is realized that the 90% reduction was to be applied to automobiles that had already been required to meet earlier emission reduction standards. The first standards applied to the 1968 model required complete control of crank case hydrocarbons and partial control of exhaust hydrocarbons and carbon monoxide. In 1968, exhaust standards were tightened for 1970 and later models, and evaporative standards were set for the 1971 model year. Thus, the 90% reduction applied to automobiles that already had to meet what amounted to a 35% reduction in their emissions through crank case controls. From the point of view of the cost of controls, it may be well to recall the usual experience of incremental costs in pollution control where the cost of control goes up incrementally with every additional percent of control measures.

As noted earlier, the 1970 Act required that hydrocarbon and carbon monoxide emissions be reduced 90% from the 1970 standard by 1975, and that by 1976, nitrogen oxide emissions be reduced by 90% from their 1970 level. The forcing of automotive pollution technology was particularly unusual because when the 1970 amendments were passed, there was no known technology to achieve the new standards and there was no clear indication that the appropriate technology would, or could, be developed in time for the 1975-76 deadline. There is considerable evidence that the Congressional mandate that automobile emissions should be reduced by 90% from their 1970 and 1971 levels was based primarily on analyses performed in 1970 under the direction of Dr. Delbert Barth, then director of the Bureau of Criteria and Standards of the National Air Pollution Control Administration of the Department of Health, Education and Welfare. Barth and his colleagues sought to determine the automobile emission standards that would be required to ensure that ambient concentrations of all automobile-related air pollutants in 1990 would be below levels believed to have adverse effects on the health of at least some Americans. This determination, for each pollutant, began with a targeted ambient air quality standard then required by law, which in turn was based on an estimated threshold and the on conditions in the metropolitan areas subjected to the worst concentrations of this pollutant in 1990, assuming there were no controls. Barth then calculated for the worst case that would be required to meet the threshold concentration level in 1990, assuming that it takes about a decade to replace the automobile fleet. Barth concluded the automobile emission standards would have to be implemented in 1980 to achieve the ambient air quality goals by 1990. Though based on rather rough calculations, the projected Barth standards are quite close to the standards eventually promulgated by EPA.

The 1970 Act and its technology forcing effort to speed up major reductions in automotive emissions not only began a race among automobile companies to meet the standards, but it also resulted in a number of efforts to utilize and develop alternative automotive technologies, including efforts to develop a gas turbine engine, a steam engine and electric cars. The electric car has of course been revived more recently in efforts to develop a zero pollution vehicle. Another promising effort was a dual-carbureted stratified charge engine developed in Japan which reduced emissions very considerably. It was expected to meet the 1975 standards at least in small vehicles. This alternative seemed to have achieved some recognition from the National Academy in its legislatively required review of the effort.

American manufacturers however stayed with their earlier commitment to a dual-catalyst system, rather than the Japanese three-valve stratified charge engine. It is likely that this determination was made in light of the requirement of the Act that whichever company achieved the goal would have to issue a mandatory license to any other company in the field.

The grant of an extension of the 1975 deadline was conditioned, inter alia, on a report of the National Academy of Sciences to determine whether the technology was available to meet the 1975 standard. The Academy in its January 1, 1972 report concluded that the technology for mass production of vehicles meeting the 1975 standard was not available, although a few manufacturers might be able to certify a few of their models. They noted the technological problem in the deterioration in catalyst effectiveness. The Academy report noted however that the effect of a one-year suspension on air quality would be slight. Following the report of the National Academy of Sciences, the Administrator on March 12, 1972 denied the application for a suspension. This decision was promptly appealed by the automobile industry in *International Harvester v. Ruckelshaus.*[277] The Court of Appeals for the District of Columbia Circuit refused to uphold the Administrator's determination and remanded. In effect, the court's remand was based on its finding that the Administrator had failed to support his conclusion that technology would be available by 1975 with "reasoned presentation."[278]

The court reviewed the technical data before the Administrator in some detail and examined the extrapolations the Administrator had used in making his determination. Since no test vehicle had actually been driven for 50,000 miles and remained within the standards, and since vehicles on the road are not driven and maintained as carefully as test vehicles, the Administrator had made certain assumptions and interpretations which, his opinion had conceded, were necessarily somewhat controversial.[279] The court stated that for purposes of judicial review, the Administrator's determination rested on the determination that requisite technology was available to meet the 1975 standards, even though the Administrator had also placed his determination on "public interest" grounds, *i.e.*, that it would not, within the public interest

277 478 F.2d 615 (D.C. Cir. 1973).

278 478 F.2d at 648.

279 In re Applications for Suspension of 1975 Motor Vehicle Exhaust Emission Standards, Decision of the EPA Administrator (May 12, 1972) [hereinafter cited as 1975 Decision], in Hearings on Implementation of the Clean Air Act Amendments of 1970 Before the Subcomm. on Air and Water Pollution of the Senate Comm. on Public Works, 92d Cong., 2d Sess. 1358 (1972) at 1374-75.

criteria articulated in the statute, be in the public interest to grant the extension.

The case had first been argued before the court on December 12, 1972, and on that occasion the court remanded the record to the Administrator, directing him to supplement his decision by setting forth his consideration of the January 1, 1972 National Academy Report and the basis for his disagreement, if any, with the findings of that report relative to the technical feasibility of compliance with the 1975 standards.[280] Administrator Ruckelshaus, in a supplement to his initial decision, indicated his agreement with the initial NAS report. Although that report had indicated the technology to meet the 1975 standards was not then available, he nonetheless relied on the contents of the report to show that sufficient time was available to perfect the necessary technology to meet the deadline. He also indicated that two of the conditions for meeting the 1975 standards in the NAS report—catalytic converter replacement and the availability of gasoline with low lead levels—had been applied in his earlier determination.

The court rejected the automobile manufacturers' assertion that the question as to whether technology was "available" within the meaning of the law[281] had to be determined as of the time of the application for extension. The court found that neither the law nor the legislative history compelled such a conclusion and that there was sound basis for the Administrator's finding that the manufacturers could improve, test, and apply the technology during the lead-time period.

The court also rejected the contention that petitioners had been deprived of due process because they had not been able to engage the Administrator in cross-examination. The court held that the public hearing to be held in connection with an application for the suspension of the deadline was not a trial-type hearing, and that the absence of a general right of cross-examination was not a departure from basic considerations of fairness, in that prescreened questions, submitted in advance, had been used.

The court also found that it was not a denial of due process for the auto makers to have been unable to challenge the Administrator's methodology with respect to the Technical Appendix of the Administrator, issued almost three months after his decision, when judicial review had already been sought. Though the court was critical of EPA on this subject, it found no denial of due process under the Clean Air Act. The use of the procedure approved in *Smith v. Pollin*[282] was suggested, *i.e.,* remand to the agency for limited reconsideration during the course of judicial review so as not to conflict with the 60-day statutory time limit for hearing and decision.

The court weighed two major considerations in its decision. If suspension of the deadline is not granted and the Administrator's judgment that the 1975 deadline can be met is proved incorrect, grave economic consequences would follow, not only for the automobile manufacturers but for the country as a whole. If, on the other hand, the Administrator grants a one-year extension and it is found that the technology to meet the standards would indeed have

---

[280] 478 F.2d at 627.

[281] 1970 Act, § 202(b)(5)(D), 42 U.S.C. § 1857f-1(b)(5)(D)(1970). *See* 478 F.2d at 628.

[282] 194 F.2d 349 (D.C. Cir. 1952).

been available, there may be "irretrievable" ecological cost. Weighing the two considerations, the court found that ecological cost would not be irretrievable, in that, taking into account emissions from the vehicle population as a whole, the effect of a one-year suspension would be small, particularly in the light of the already substantial reduction in emissions from controlled vehicles on the road. On the other hand, the court suggested that if EPA erred in its assumption that the 1975 deadline could be met, then a relaxation of the standard might become necessary which would work great injustice on the manufacturers who came closest to meeting the deadline, because their very success would turn into a disadvantage—since the car with the most effective control system would use the most fuel per mile and would have lessened car performance in terms of drivability.

The Administrator's conception that enforcement of the 1975 standards could be permitted to restrict production of vehicles to that necessary to fill "basic demand" was examined in the context of a special issue presented by the International Harvester Company. The company had contended that the decision to deny the extension of the 1975 deadline had effectively ruled out production of its light-weight trucks and multi-purpose passenger vehicles for the 1975 model year because it could not meet the 1975 standards. This contention was not denied by the Administrator, who asserted, however, that International Harvester would have to alter the performance characteristics of its vehicles so as to meet the 1975 standards. The work-horse jobs for which these vehicles are designed, however, require higher than normal axle ratios and consequently greater power from the engine, thus producing higher exhaust temperatures—and more emissions—to attain any given speed. The International Harvester line could not be redesigned in the time remaining. The Administrator viewed the absence of International Harvester light-weight trucks in 1975 as an acceptable consequence under the Act, because the "new car demand" would be met by the production of the major auto companies. The court, however, found this conclusion unacceptable, and reviewed the applicability of the 90% reduction to "light duty vehicles." In the court's view, the legislative history indicates that light-duty vehicles means, simply, passenger cars.[283]

Thus, the court ruled that the definition in EPA regulations of the term "light duty vehicles" could not be sustained, insofar as it included light-weight trucks. These should properly be regulated under standards for trucks, buses, and other commercial vehicles. The court made no decision concerning the inclusion of multi-passenger vehicles that overlap in their use with passenger cars, leaving open the question of whether they should be granted a one-year suspension. The court added, however, that except with reference to the "basic demand" argument as applied to light-duty trucks, it agreed with the Administrator that as long as basic demands for new automobiles were generally met, it would not be concerned over the more limited choices a buyer might have in consequence of the effects of the imposition of the 1975 standards. However, the automobile makers argued that production and retooling capacity was not

[283] 478 F.2d 615, 639-40. The Court of Appeals relied on the distinctions made in the Senate committee report on S. 4358 between automobiles, buses, and other commercial vehicles. S. Rep. No. 1196, 91st Cong., 2d Sess. 23 (1970).

available to shift from pre-1975 models to models and engine types that could comply with the 1975 standards in sufficiently large numbers to meet the demand for new cars. The Administrator had made no finding on the issue—and the court held that "the statute requires such a finding, explaining how the Administrator estimates 'basic demand' and how this definition conforms to the statutory objective."[284] On the issue of technical feasibility, the court held, Congress had intended demand considerations to be taken into account.

Although the court approached the review of the Administrator's decision on available technology "with utmost diffidence"[285] and confirmed that it owed deference to the agency's expertise, it nonetheless felt itself constrained by the Congressional mandate of review to enter into technical matters which, in its view, were inextricably intermeshed with the legal issues. Without recounting the court's analysis in detail, it appears that in its view the Administrator's determination was deficient in that he had failed to articulate the assumptions used and the methodology applied in predicting—from the data supplied by the manufacturers—that the 1975 standards could be met. The court took issue with the Administrator's assertion that the companies did not submit sufficient evidence to enable him to make the requisite finding as to available technology. The court found that the companies had met their burden of proof by giving the Administrator all the data they had; they were not required to make a showing beyond a reasonable doubt. Since the automobile manufacturers must prove a negative averment, the reasonableness of the Administrator's methodology is an issue on which he bears the burden of proof, because that methodology alone offsets petitioners' data in support of suspension.

Examining EPA assumptions relating to prediction from manufacturers' data, the court found imprecise certain regulatory assumptions made by the Administrator relating, first, to maintenance to be performed on the 1975 model car during its "useful life" to meet the standards; second, to the result of catalyst replacement after 25,000 miles; and, third, to the effect of the projected availability of low lead gasoline for 1975 model cars. The court also examined engineering and scientific assumptions relating to extrapolation of emissions from cars after the first 4,000 miles, to adjustments necessary for translating emissions from cars run on practically lead-free gas to partly leaded gas, and to the disputed adjustment of certain unexplained high temperature readings resulting from the Chrysler cars. It also examined the methodology of the calculation of a deterioration factor; in particular, the unequal application of the deterioration factor considerably lower than that used by the National Academy of Sciences. The court also questioned the use of catalyst efficiency data from the advanced Ford catalyst and applied to the untreated emissions of other cars, notably GM vehicles, on the assumption that Ford's catalyst would work as efficiently on GM cars as it does on Fords. The court also drew attention to the admittedly low statistical reliability of the Administrator's predictions and called on him to "estimate the possible degree of error in his prediction."[286]

---

[284] 478 F.2d at 640.

[285] 478 F.2d at 641.

[286] 478 F.2d at 647.

> The number of unexplained assumptions used by the Administrator, the variance in methodology from that of the Report of the National Academy of Sciences, and the absence of an indication of the statistical reliability of the prediction, combine to generate grave doubts as to whether technology is available to meet the 1975 statutory standards. . . . We think the vehicle manufacturers established by a preponderance of the evidence, in the record before us, that technology was not available, within the meaning of the Act, when they adduced the tests on actual vehicles; that the Administrator's reliance on technological methodology to offset the actual tests raised serious doubts and failed to meet the burden of proof which in our view was properly assignable to him, in the light of accepted legal doctrine and the intent of Congress discerned, in part, by taking into account that the risk of an "erroneous" denial of suspension outweighed the risk of an "erroneous" grant of suspension. We do not use the burden of proof in the conventional sense of civil trials, but the Administrator must sustain the burden of adducing a reasoned presentation supporting the reliability of EPA's methodology.[287]

The opinion also placed heavy reliance on the differences of findings between the Administrator and the National Academy of Sciences Report.

The court remanded and required that limited cross-examination be made available to petitioners as to new lines of testimony, because the proceeding on remand is not subject to the same time constraints as the initial proceeding. Nevertheless, even with the cross-examination requirements, in the interest of justice and on the basis of Congressional intention that suspension proceedings be made timely in the light of the lead time required for 1975 model year production, the court ordered a decision to be made within another 60 days on all of the determinations which the statute requires as a condition of suspension. The court refused petitioners' request that it order the suspension, since the Administrator had not made the necessary determination under the statute as to public interest and good faith.[288] The court stressed that the law permits the Administrator to make a determination short of full suspension of the deadline, but consisting of "a conditional suspension that results in higher standards than an outright grant of applications for suspension"[289] by requiring compliance with interim standards.

The concurring opinion by Chief Judge Bazelon indicated that he would have preferred to proceed on more traditional grounds of judicial review of administrative determinations and showed some reluctance to enter into a detailed consideration of the technical issues discussed in the majority opinion. He indicated that he would have preferred simply to require procedures that "open the Administrator's decision to challenge and force him to respond,"[290] and in order to accomplish the benefits of unlimited cross-examination of the Administrator's position, he would have permitted an extension of the time limit for the making of the Administrator's determination on remand from 60 to "perhaps" 90 days. In his view, the 60-day time limitation in the Clean Air Act was not intended by Congress to be strictly enforced

---

287 478 F.2d at 648.

288 Under the statute, the Administrator had to find, as a basis for postponement, that the manufacturer had made a good faith effort to achieve the standards.

289 478 F.2d at 650.

290 478 F.2d at 652.

"so as to do major damage to the statute as a whole."[291] He further indicated that he would have preferred to make the determination on the public interest issue an independent reason for suspension, as required by the statute, rather than dealing with it through the device of burden of proof. He did, however, fully agree with the majority in the result of remand to the Administrator for such further examination of the issues as was indicated.

International Harvester v. Ruckelshaus was the high point of the effort to force technology in the automotive pollution area. The case reflects many of the legal difficulties that may arise in any technology forcing effort. The requirement for National Academy of Sciences review of changes in emission regulations is a continuing part of the law.[292]

[b] Emission Standards and Fuel Controls

The Clean Air Act Amendments of 1990 made substantial changes in Title II, Mobile Sources, of the Clean Air Act. While the changes are quite extensive, most of them are prospective and some of them do not become fully effective until the early 2000s. The report of the Conference Committee emphasizes the following changes in the law. Beginning in 1995, cleaner reformulated gasoline is required in the nine cities with the most severe ozone pollution. States could elect to have the requirement applied to other cities as well. Reformulated gasoline is required to have 15% lower emissions of volatile organic compounds (VOCs) and toxic chemicals by 1995 and greater reductions by 2000. There are also additional standards for oxygen, benzene and aromatics. The amendments also provide for the certification of fuel formulation by the Administrator. To provide flexibility, a credit program is provided with respect to the oxygen, aromatic hydrocarbon, and benzene content of reformulated gasoline. The credit program allows a person who is subject to these requirements—generally in a nonattainment area for VOCs or ozone—to pool gasoline sold in a given area for purposes of determining compliance with the requirements. Thus, a person may earn credit for gasoline with a higher oxygen content, lower aromatic hydrocarbon content or lower benzene than otherwise required. These credits, once earned, may be used in the same area in which they were earned to offset the sale or use of gasoline with a lower oxygen content, higher aromatic hydrocarbon content, or higher benzene content than otherwise required. EPA regulations, however, must require that use of credits will not result in an average content in a covered nonattainment area that is less stringent than without the application of a credit program. The reformulated gasoline requires a level of 2.7% of oxygen in 44 cities with carbon monoxide pollution, starting in 1992. The purpose of such provisions is to encourage the use of oxygen-containing additives, like ethanol or the natural gas derivative, MTBE.

Other major new requirements under the Clean Air Act Amendments of 1990 call for a reduction of 35% of tailpipe emissions of hydrocarbons and 60%

---

291 478 F.2d at 652.

292 For a full account of the development of the automotive emissions controls under the 1970 Act, see Grad, Rosenthal, Rockett *et al.*, The Automobile and the Regulation of Its Impact on the Environment (U. of Okla. Press 1975), prepared under a grant from the National Science Foundation by the Legislative Drafting Research Fund of Columbia University.

reduction of nitrogen oxides, beginning with 40% of the vehicles sold in 1994, and increasing to 100% of vehicles sold in 1998. Comparable reductions are required in the 1990 amendments for light trucks such as vans and pickups. An additional reduction in auto emissions, namely a 50% cut below the standards required in the mid-1990s, would be required after 2003, unless EPA finds that the new standard is not necessary, technologically feasible or cost effective.

The 1990 amendments require the installation of an alarm system to alert drivers when an emission control system is malfunctioning.

As amended in 1990, the law retains the language in § 177 which allows other states to adopt and enforce the California vehicle standards. Section 177 was amended to provide that states which exercise the California option may not create a "third vehicle" which meets neither the requirements of California nor of the other 49 states.

Another major development under the 1990 amendments is the program for fleet vehicles. The fleet program is applicable in Serious, Severe and Extreme nonattainment areas to fleets of ten or more vehicles that are capable of being centrally fueled. The program mandates California's low emission vehicle (LEV) standards by 1998 for light duty vehicles and light duty trucks below 6000 lbs. gross vehicle weight rating (GVWR) if such vehicles are offered for sale in California. By the year 2001, such vehicles will be required without regard to their availability in California. Heavy duty fleet vehicles from 8500 lbs. GVWR to 26,000 lbs. GVWR will be required to meet NOx and hydrocarbon emission standards that will provide a 50% reduction below emissions from a 1994 heavy duty diesel engine. If EPA determines that such a standard is not technically feasible for a clean diesel fueled engine, it may be modified to require a 30% reduction.

The Clean Air Act Amendments of 1990 also make significant changes in the warranty period. For all light duty vehicle and light duty truck emission control components, the warranty period is reduced to two years or 24,000 miles starting in 1995, but the applicable coverage for major components costing more than $200 (such as the catalytic converter, on-board diagnostics, and the electronic control system) is set at eight years or 80,000 miles.[293]

Other significant changes to be noted are the establishment of stricter standards for new vehicles for nonmethane hydrocarbons (NMHC), carbon monoxide (CO) and oxides of nitrogen (NOx). Two tiers are established. The initial tier requires standards for lightweight vehicles and very light trucks to be phased in for NMHC and CO between 1994 and 1998, and for NOx during 1994 and 1995. The following standards apply: 0.255 ppm for NMHC, 3.4 ppm for CO, and 0.4 ppm for NOx. Formaldehyde and benzene standards must also be set. EPA has the choice of establishing more stringent Tier 2 standards if it finds such standards to be necessary, technologically feasible, and cost effective. If such standards are set, they are to become effective between 2003 and 2006. If EPA does not act, the suggested standard of of the Tier 1 level will take effect by operation of law in 2003.

293 Joint Explanatory Statement of the Committee of Conference, 101 Cong. Rec., 2d Sess. (daily ed.), H. 13197, H. 13198, October 26, 1990.

New provisions required EPA to regulate evaporative emissions from the engine by 1994. Between 1995 and 1998, the law requires the phasing in of a requirement for on-board canisters to trap evaporative refueling emissions on new cars.

[c] Clean Fuel Vehicles

[i] In General

The Clean Air Act Amendments of 1990 added a new part C to Title II of the Clean Air Act to provide for clean fuel vehicles. Essentially, clean fuel vehicles are vehicles designed to run on clean alternative fuel, which is defined as any fuel including methanol, ethanol or other alcohols, and mixtures thereof, which contain 85% or more of such alcohol mixed with gasoline or other fuels, reformulated gasoline, diesel, natural gas, liquefied petroleum gas, and hydrogen, or another power source including electricity, used in a clean fuel vehicle that complies with the standards and requirements applicable to such vehicles, when using the designated alternative fuel or power source.[294]

[ii] Definitions

The Act defines "NMOG" or "non-methane organic gas" in terms of the sum of non-oxygenated and oxygenated hydrocarbons contained in a gas sample, providing its minimum contents. To demonstrate compliance with an NMOG standard, NMOG emissions must be measured in accordance with the California non-methane organic gas test procedures. Also defined is "base gasoline," including a considerably detailed specification of its contents. The definition section also provides that the Administrator shall modify the definition of NMOG, base gasoline, and the methods for making reactivity adjustments, to conform to the definitions and methods used in California under the Low Emission Vehicle and Clean Fuel Regulations of the California Air Resources Board, so long as the California definitions are in the aggregate at least as protective of public health and welfare as the definitions in this section.

[iii] Standards

Within two years after the enactment of the Clean Air Act Amendments of 1990, the Administrator was required to promulgate clean fuel vehicle standards for vehicles specified in the Act. Standards were required for light duty clean fuel vehicles and light duty trucks up to 3,750 lbs. LVW (loaded vehicle weight), and up to 6,000 lbs. GVWR (gross vehicle weight rating); clean fuel emission standards for light duty trucks greater than 6,000 lbs. GVWR; and standards for flexible and dual fuel vehicles. The Administrator was also required to set standards for heavy duty clean fuel vehicles (GVWR above 8,500 up to 26,000 lbs.).[295]

---

[294] CAA § 241(1) and (2), as added by the Clean Air Act Amendments of 1990 § 229.

[295] See discussion of CAA §§ 243, 244 and 245.

[iv] SIP Requirements Affecting Mobile Sources

Although the provision of part C for clean fuel vehicles imposes substantial obligations on the Administrator to set new vehicle standards, there is little in the chapter itself which compels the use of such vehicles, except § 246 which deals with centrally fueled fleets. The section requires that each state in which there is located all or part of a "covered area" submit a new implementation plan within 42 months after the enactment of the Clean Air Act Amendments of 1990 to establish a clean fuel vehicle program for fleets under the section. Covered areas in which such implementation plan revisions are necessary are ozone nonattainment areas classified as Serious, Severe or Extreme, based on calendar years 1987, 1988 and 1989, with a 1980 population of 250,000 or more. The Administrator was required to use the most recent interpretation methodology issued prior to the enactment of the Clean Air Act Amendments of 1990 in determining which ozone nonattainment area is to be treated as a covered area.[296] Also included in covered areas are carbon monoxide nonattainment areas with a 1980 population of 250,000 or more and a carbon monoxide design value above 16.0 parts per million based on the 1988 and 1989 calendar year data, again based on the most recent interpretation methodology issued prior to the Clean Air Act Amendments of 1990.

For ozone nonattainment areas reclassified as Serious, Severe or Extreme with a 1980 population of 250,000 or more, the state must submit a plan revision meeting the requirements of § 246(a) within one year after reclassification. The plan revision must implement the requirements applicable at the time of reclassification and thereafter, but the Administrator may adjust the deadlines for compliance where compliance within the deadline would be infeasible.[297] The state implementation plan revisions under § 246(a) must be developed in consultation with fleet operators, vehicle manufacturers, fuel producers and distributors and with other interested parties, taking into consideration such matters as operations range, specialty uses, vehicle and fuel availability, costs, safety, and resale value of vehicles.[298]

The state implementation plan revision must require that at least a portion of vehicles newly purchased by fleet operators in model year 1998 and thereafter within each covered area must be clean fuel vehicles using clean alternative fuels when operating within the area. For light duty trucks up to 6,000 lbs. GVWR and light duty vehicles in model year 1998, 30%, in model year 1999, 50% and in model year 2000,70% of new vehicles are to be phased in. For heavy duty trucks above 8,500 lbs. GVWR, in model year 1998, 50%, in model year 1999, 50%, and in model year 2000, 50% of new vehicles phased in are to be clean fuel vehicles.[299]

[v] Fleet Vehicles; Accelerated Standards

Subsection (c) of § 246 provides that for light duty vehicles and light duty trucks up to 6000 lbs. GVWR, the standards are to be accelerated for fleet

[296] CAA § 246(a)(2)(A), as added by Clean Air Act Amendments of 1990 § 229(a).

[297] CAA § 246(a)(3), as added by Clean Air Act Amendments of 1990 § 229(a).

[298] CAA § 246(a)(3), as added by Clean Air Act Amendments of 1990 § 229(a).

[299] CAA § 246(b), as added by Clean Air Act Amendments of 1990 § 229(a).

vehicles, so that notwithstanding the standards set for clean fuel vehicles in § 243, fleet vehicles manufactured in model years 1998 through model year 2000 are to be treated as clean fuel vehicles only if they comply with the standards applicable under § 243 for vehicles in the same class for model year 2001. The phase-in requirements under subsection (b) were to take effect either in the first model year after model year 1997 in which such new light duty vehicles and light duty trucks which comply with the model year 2001 standards under § 243 are offered for sale in California, or in model year 2001, whichever is earlier. Whenever the effective date of the phase-in requirements under subsection (b) is delayed by reason of the delay of the sale of such vehicles in California, then the phase-in requirement shall be modified to commence with the model year in which such vehicles are sold in California, in lieu of model year 1998.[300]

The section further provides that the choice of clean fuel vehicles and clean alternative fuels is to be made by the covered fleet operator in accordance with the requirements of the subsection. The plan revision must also require fuel providers to make clean alternative fuel available to covered fleet operators where covered fleet vehicles are centrally fueled.[301]

[vi] Pollution Reduction Credits

Section 246(f) provides for pollution reduction credits. The credit program is to follow regulations promulgated by the Administrator, but the state is to administer the program. The state plan revision is to provide credits to fleet operators who purchase more clean fuel vehicles than required under the section; who purchase clean fuel vehicles which meet more stringent standards as established by the Administrator under the section; who purchase vehicles in categories not covered by § 246 but which meet the standards established for such vehicles under the section. The credits provided may be used by the person holding them, or they may be traded or sold to other persons in the same nonattainment area. Credits may be held or banked for use at a later time and will retain the same value as if used earlier. However, credits issued with respect to vehicles of up to 8,500 lbs. GVWR may not be used by any other person to meet the requirements applicable to vehicles of more than 8,500 lbs. GVWR. So, too, credits issued with respect to the purchase of vehicles of more than 8,500 lbs. GVWR may not be used to demonstrate compliance with requirements applicable to vehicles weighing less than 8,500 lbs. A waiting system is also provided to adjust credits, to reflect the level of emission reduction achieved.[302]

Under § 246(f)(4), the Administrator is required, solely for purpose of issuing credits, to establish standards for Ultra-Low Emission Vehicles (ULEVs) and Zero Emission Vehicles (ZEVs). Such standards are to be more stringent than the standards otherwise applicable to clean fuel vehicles under this part. The Administrator must certify clean fuel vehicles as complying with the more stringent ULEV or ZEV standard, in the same manner as in the

[300] CAA § 246(c), as added by Clean Air Act Amendments of 1990 § 229(a).

[301] CAA § 246(d), as added by Clean Air Act Amendments of 1990 § 229(a).

[302] CAA § 246(f), as added by Clean Air Act Amendments of 1990 § 229(a).

case of other clean fuel vehicle standards. The standards established by the Administrator must conform as closely as possible to the standards established by California for ULEVs and ZEVs in the same class.[303]

Fleet operators that purchase vehicles meeting clean fuel vehicle standards at any time after approval of the plan revision and prior to the effective date of the fleet program under this section must also be granted credits.[304]

At facilities owned or operated by a department or agency of the United States where clean fuel vehicles are supplied with clean alternative fuel, such fuel must also be offered for sale "subject to national security concerns" to the public for use in other vehicles, unless such fuel is commercially available for vehicles in the vicinity of such federal facilities.[305]

Within one year of the Clean Air Act Amendments of 1990, the Administrator was to provide by regulation that certain transportation control measures, including restrictions on vehicles relating to time of day or day of week, do not apply to clean fuel vehicles that meet the requirements of § 246.[306]

[vii] Conversion of Engines

New § 247 applies the provisions of § 246, subject to the Administrator's regulations, to the *conversion* of existing gasoline or diesel powered engines to clean fuel vehicles by fleet operators. The section applies to voluntary conversions and states clearly that no fleet operator will be required to convert vehicles or to purchase converted vehicles. The Administrator's regulations relating to conversions must require that such converted vehicles meet the applicable standards to particular classes and categories of vehicles under §§ 242, 243, 244 and 245, with such modifications as the Administrator may find necessary. Persons who convert conventional vehicles to clean fuel vehicles are to be treated as manufacturers for purposes of §§ 206 and 207 and related enforcement provisions. The section also provides that such a conversion to clean fuel vehicles in compliance with the Administrator's regulations is not to be considered "tampering" for purposes of § 203(a)(3). If necessary, the Secretary of Transportation must promulgate rules relating to the safety of vehicles converted to clean fuel vehicles.[307]

[viii] Government Fleet Vehicles

Section 248 makes special provisions for the acquisition of covered fleet vehicles owned or operated by an agency, department or instrumentality of the United States. The section places certain limitations on appropriations for the acquisition of such vehicles, and for the acquisition, maintenance and operation of such vehicles, as well as for fuel storage and dispensing equipment. The section also carries a general appropriation to carry out the provisions of the section.[308]

---

303 CAA § 246(f)(4), as added by Clean Air Act Amendments of 1990 § 229(a).

304 CAA § 246(f)(5), as added by Clean Air Act Amendments of 1990 § 229(a).

305 CAA § 246(g), as added by Clean Air Act Amendments of 1990 § 229(a).

306 CAA § 246(h), as added by Clean Air Act Amendments of 1990 § 229(a).

307 CAA § 247, as added by Clean Air Act Amendments of 1990 § 229(a).

308 CAA § 248, as added by Clean Air Act Amendments of 1990 § 229(a).

[ix] California Pilot Program

Section 249, added by the Clean Air Act Amendments of 1990, creates a California pilot test program, which makes the state of California the major testing ground for the introduction of clean fuel technology. The Administrator must establish a pilot program in California "to demonstrate the effectiveness of clean fuel vehicles in controlling air pollution in ozone nonattainment areas."[309] The provisions of the test program apply only to light duty vehicles and light duty trucks and are limited to the state of California, except for an opt-in provision for other states. The Administrator was required to provide the necessary regulations applicable to the state of California within 24 months after the enactment of the Clean Air Act Amendments of 1990. The plan is to have 150,000 clean fuel vehicles sold and distributed in California in model years 1996, 1997 and 1998, and another 300,000 clean fuel vehicles in 1999 and thereafter. These numbers are also to include the covered clean fuel fleets provided for in § 246.

Within two years of the enactment of the Clean Air Act Amendments of 1990, the state of California was required to submit a revision of its implementation plan containing a clean fuel plan requiring that clean alternative fuels for the operation of clean fuel vehicles are to be produced and distributed by fuel suppliers and made available in California. Sufficient clean alternative fuels are to be produced and made available to assure that, to the fullest extent possible, all clean fuel vehicles required under this section would be able to operate exclusively on such fuels in California. The fuels must be offered for sale at an adequate number of geographically distributed locations so that all clean fuel vehicles can be conveniently refueled.[310]

The state of California may, by regulation, grant credits to a person for exceeding the requirements, and credits granted shall be transferable. In granting credits, the state may consider enforceability, environmental and economic factors, and may grant the credits on such conditions as it may find appropriate. The state may also establish specifications for any clean alternative fuel so as to reduce or eliminate unreasonable risks to public health, welfare or safety associated with its use, or to insure acceptable vehicle maintenance and maintenance characteristics.[311]

[x] Underground Storage Tank Replacement

The section also makes some special provisions with respect to the replacement of underground fuel storage tanks necessary to meet the requirements of this section. If a facility had to replace such a tank and accompanying piping in order to meet the requirements of Subtitle I of the Solid Waste Disposal Act prior to the Clean Air Act Amendments of 1990, it will not then be required to comply with the new requirements under this subsection until a period of seven years has passed from the date of the removal or replacement of the tank.[312]

---

[309] CAA § 249(a), as added by Clean Air Act Amendments of 1990 § 229(a).

[310] CAA § 249(b), (c)(1), (2)(A), as added by Clean Air Act Amendments of 1990 § 229(a).

[311] CAA § 249(c)(2)(B), (C).

[312] CAA § 249(c)(2)(D), as added by Clean Air Act Amendments of 1990 § 229(a).

It is noted that nothing in § 249 authorizes any state other than California to adopt clean alternative fuel provisions. If the state of California fails to adopt the clean fuel program that meets the requirements, then the Administrator may in accordance with § 110(c) establish a clean fuel program for the state of California.[313]

[xi] Credit for Clean Fuel Vehicles

The section also provides for credits to manufacturers towards the fulfillment of the manufacturer's share of the total number of clean fuel vehicles to be provided in model years 1996 through 1999 and thereafter. Such credits are to be granted for the sale of more clean fuel vehicles than required in any model year, and for the sale of clean fuel vehicles that meet more stringent standards than the clean fuel vehicle standards otherwise applicable. Such credits may then be transferred to other manufacturers. Credits are to be made available on terms and conditions as the Administrator finds appropriate, after considering enforceability, environmental and economic factors. The Administrator is to administer the credit program and is to promulgate regulations for it. The standards of issuing credits for cleaner vehicles established by the Administrator under the clean fuel vehicles fleet program under § 246(e) shall also apply here.[314]

The California program was to be evaluated in a report to Congress no later than June 30, 1994. The report was to evaluate the capability from a technological standpoint of motor vehicle manufacturers and motor vehicle fuel suppliers to comply with such programs and with the requirements of the California pilot program under this section. Another report was to be submitted to Congress no later than June 30, 1998, on the effectiveness of the California pilot program. The report had to evaluate the level of emissions reduction achieved under the program and the advantages and disadvantages of extending the program to other nonattainment areas and of continuing or expanding the program in California. The section provides that the program cannot be extended or terminated by the Administrator except by act of Congress.[315]

[xii] Opt-In Program; Incentives

The Administrator was to promulgate regulations within two years after the enactment of the Clean Air Act Amendments of 1990 to establish a voluntary opt-in program to provide that clean fuel vehicles and clean alternative fuels required to be sold in California may also be sold and used in other states which submit certain plan revisions. Such plan revisions may be submitted by any state in which there is an ozone nonattainment area classified as Serious, Severe or Extreme under Subpart D of Title I. The revision of the applicable implementation plan is to provide incentives for the sale in such an area of clean fuel vehicles as required in California, and of clean alternative fuels. Such a plan provision is not to take effect until a year

---

[313] CAA § 249(c)(2)(E), (F), as added by Clean Air Act Amendments of 1990 § 229(c).

[314] CAA § 249(d)(2), (3), as added by Clean Air Act Amendments of 1990 § 229(a).

[315] CAA § 249(e), as added by Clean Air Act Amendments of 1990 § 229(a).

after the state has given notice to motor vehicle manufacturers and fuel suppliers. The incentives provided may include a higher state registration fee for vehicles which are not clean fuel vehicles, with the proceeds of such fee to be used to provide for the financial incentives to purchasers of clean fuel vehicles and to clean fuel vehicle dealers. Other incentives include provisions to exempt clean fuel vehicles from high occupancy vehicle or trip reduction requirements and preferences in the use of existing parking spaces for clean fuel vehicles. However, these incentives are not to apply to covered fleet vehicles. Although the section provides for incentives, it also makes it clear that the plan revision is not to include any production or sales mandate for clean fuel vehicles or clean alternative fuels. Vehicle manufacturers and fuel suppliers may not be subjected to penalties or sanctions for failing to produce or sell clean fuel vehicles or clean alternative fuels.[316]

[xiii] Fuel Storage Safety

The section also provides that the Secretary of Transportation, in accordance with the National Motor Vehicle Traffic Safety Act of 1966, shall promulgate regulations regarding the safety and use of fuel storage cylinders and fuel systems, including provisions for the testing and retesting in conversions of motor vehicles. In carrying out his duties under the Act, the Administrator is to coordinate with the Secretaries of the Department of Energy and the Department of Transportation.[317]

Section 250 also provides that if a state implementation plan adopts a provision that existing state refueling facilities will be made available to the public for the purpose of clean alternative fuels, or that state operated refueling facilities for such fuels will be constructed and operated by the state and made available to the public, the Administrator, taking into consideration safety, cost, and other relevant factors, in approving such a plan under § 110 in Part D, may credit a state with the emission reductions for purposes of Part D attributable to such actions.[318]

The section also reaffirms that the Administrator has no authority under this part to mandate the production of clean fuel vehicles except under the California pilot test program, nor does he have authority to specify applicable models, line or marketing or price practices, policies or strategies for vehicles subject to this part. Nothing in this part is to be construed to give the Administrator the authority to mandate marketing or pricing practices, policies or strategies for fuel.[319]

[xiv] Standards for Clean Fuel Vehicles

As noted earlier, Part C of Title II, added by the Clean Air Act Amendments of 1990, set standards for clean fuel vehicle fleets, and requires the phase-in of such clean fuel vehicles in certain nonattainment areas in model years 1998, 1999 and 2000. A similar phase-in for light duty vehicles is required in the

[316] CAA § 249(f), as added by Clean Air Act Amendments of 1990 § 229(a).

[317] CAA § 250(c), (d), as added by Clean Air Act Amendments of 1990 § 229(a).

[318] CAA § 250(a), as added by Clean Air Act Amendments of 1990 § 229(a).

[319] CAA § 250(a), (b), as added by Clean Air Act Amendments of 1990 § 225(a).

California pilot test program under § 249. In addition to these phase-in requirements, new Part C establishes the emission standards for different types of vehicles. Thus, for light duty vehicles and light duty trucks of less than 3,750 lbs. loaded vehicles weight, Phase I standards are set, beginning with model year 1996. Emission standards are set for NMOG, CO, NOx, PM (particulate matter), and HCHO (formaldehyde). These very stringent standards are further upgraded in Phase II, beginning with model year 2001.[320]

Section 232 of the Clean Air ActAmendments of 1990 amended § 177 of the Clean Air Act to provide that nothing in this section or in Title II of the Act shall be construed as authorizing any state to prohibit or limit the manufacture or sale of a new vehicle that is certified in California as meeting the California standards, or to take any action which has the effect of creating a motor vehicle different from a motor vehicle certified in California, *i.e.*, to create a "third vehicle."[321]

[d] New Emissions Standards for Conventional Motor Vehicles

The Clean Air Act Amendments of 1990 added to § 202 a number of new provisions to prospectively set standards for conventional motor vehicles. Included in the section's coverage are light duty vehicles and light duty trucks up to 6,000 lbs. gross vehicle weight rating (GVWR). The standards apply to model years after 1993. Effective with model year 1994 and afterwards limits are set in table G for the emission of non-methane hydrocarbons, carbon monoxide and oxides of nitrogen. These standards must be phased in, in accordance with an implementation schedule, so that in 1994, 40% of each manufacturer's sales volume of such vehicles and trucks must comply; in 1995, 80% must comply; and after 1995, 100% must comply. The standards set in table G are set for emissions over five years and 50,000 miles and 10 years and 100,000 miles. The standards are set for certification as set forth in § 206.[322] The subsection also requires the setting of PM (particulate matter) standards for model year 1994 for light duty vehicles, and effective with model year 1995 and afterwards, for light duty trucks (LDTs) of up to 6,000 lbs. GVWR. The regulations under subsection (a) applicable to emissions of PM from such vehicles and trucks must provide that emissions from a percentage of each manufacturer's sales volume may not exceed levels specified in the table on PM standards for LDTs of up to 6,000 lbs. GVWR. For five years or 50,000 miles, the standard is to be 0.08 gpm and for 10 years or 100,000 miles, it will be 0.10 gpm. Again, the new standards are to be phased in between 1994 and 1996, in accordance with an implementation schedule provided.[323] Prospective standards for light duty trucks of more than 6,000 lbs. GVWR for model years after 1995 are also set in table H, which provides the standards for non-methane hydrocarbons, carbon monoxide, oxides of nitrogen and particulate matter. Again, the standards are to be phased in with 50%

[320] CAA § 243(a), as added by Clean Air Act Amendments of 1990 § 229(a).

[321] CAA § 177, as added by Clean Air Act Amendments of 1990 § 232.

[322] CAA § 202(g)(1), as added by the Clean Air Act Amendments of 1990, § 203.

[323] CAA § 202(g)(2), as added by the Clean Air Act Amendments of 1990, § 203.

of a manufacturer's sales volume to meet the standard in the year 1996 and 100% to meet the standard in model years after 1996.[324]

The 1990 amendments add a new subsection (i) to § 202, which, expressing an unusual degree of legislative optimism, provides that the Administrator, with the participation of the Office of Technology Assessment, should study whether or not further reductions in emissions should be undertaken, particularly whether, starting with model years after January 1, 2003, the standards and useful life period for gasoline and diesel fuel light duty vehicles and light duty trucks with a loaded vehicle weight of 3,750 lbs. or less should be as specified in table 3. Table 3 specifies a non-methane hydrocarbon emission level of 0.125 gpm, a NOx level of 0.2 gpm and a carbon monoxide level of 1.7 gpm, set for a useful life of 10years or 100,000 miles. The study should consider more stringent useful life requirements; the further need for emission reductions; the availability of technology, including its cost, for meeting more stringent standards after January 1, 2003 but no later than model year 2006; and the need for and cost effectiveness of obtaining further reductions in emissions, considering alternative means for attaining or maintaining national primary ambient air quality standards. The report of this study was to be submitted to Congress in about seven years, *i.e.*, no later than June 1997. Opportunity for public comment was to be provided. Based on the study, the Administrator must determine by rule within three calendar years after the report is submitted to Congress, but no later than December 31, 1999, whether there is a need for further emission reductions and whether the technology for meeting more stringent emission standards will be available for such light duty vehicles and light duty trucks, and whether further reductions in emissions will be needed and cost effective. If the Administrator makes negative determinations on any of these issues, he shall not then promulgate more stringent standards than those in effect under § 220(g) and (h). But if the Administrator determines that further reductions are necessary and that the technology for meeting the more stringent emission standards will be available and that obtaining such further reductions will be necessary and cost effective, the Administrator must then either promulgate the standards and useful life periods set forth in table 3 or promulgate alternative standards and useful life periods that are more stringent than those referred to in § 202(g) and (h). The standards and useful life periods promulgated by the Administrator will take effect no earlier than model year 2003 and no later than model year 2006, as determined by the Administrator. The section provides that nothing in this paragraph is to be construed as creating a presumption that any standards or useful life periods set forth in table 3 must be promulgated in the rulemaking required under this paragraph. The action required of the Administrator under this paragraph is to be treated as a non-discretionary duty for purposes of § 304(a)(2) (relating to citizen suits).

Unless the Administrator determines not to promulgate more stringent standards or to postpone the effective date of standards referred to in table 3, or to establish alternative standards, then starting with model years after January 1, 2003, the regulations under subsection (a) applicable to emissions of

---

324 CAA § 202(h), as added by the Clean Air Act Amendments of 1990, § 203.

non-methane hydrocarbons (NMHC), oxides of nitrogen (NOx) and carbon monoxide (CO) from motor vehicles and motor vehicle engines in the classes specified in table 3 must contain standards that provide that emissions may not exceed the pending emission levels specified in that table.

[e] Useful Life

The 1990 amendments also extended the definition of the useful life period of a motor vehicle or engine. The extension operates prospectively. For requirements that first become applicable after enactment, where the useful life period is not otherwise specified for a vehicle or engine, the period will be 10 years or 100,000 miles, whichever first occurs, with testing for purposes of in-use compliance under § 207, up to but not beyond seven years or 75,000 miles, whichever first occurs.[325]

Original equipment manufacturers whose projected sales in the United States for any model year will not exceed 300 are exempted from requirements to determine compliance with regulations relating to the useful life of the vehicle, subject, however, to such adjustment factors as the Administrator may deem appropriate, to assure that the vehicle will comply during its useful life.[326]

[f] Revised Emissions Standards

The 1990 amendments authorize the Administrator to promulgate regulations under subsection (a)(1) to revise any standard as needed to protect public health and welfare, taking costs, energy and safety into account. Though the amendment provides that any revision must require a reduction of emissions from previously applicable standards, and that any such revision may provide for a gradual phase-in, nonetheless the overall effect of the provisions is to freeze the newly established requirements for 14 years. "It is the intent of Congress that the numerical emission standards specified in subsections (a)(3)(B)(ii), (g), (h), and (i) shall not be modified by the Administrator after the enactment of the Clean Air Act Amendments of 1990 for any model year before the model year 2004."[327] An amendment of § 202(b)(2) required the Administrator to promulgate the emission standards that were not promulgated before enactment of the 1990 amendments to be so promulgated by regulations within 180 days after enactment.[328]

[g] Other, Miscellaneous Standards

Other controls in the 1990 revision include the regulation of carbon monoxide emissions at cold temperatures for different size engines and for different nonattainment areas.[329] Stringent controls are set also for evaporative

[325] CAA § 202(d), as amended by the Clean Air Act Amendments of 1990, § 202, 42 U.S.C. § 7521(d)(1).

[326] CAA § 206(a)(1), as amended by the Clean Air Act Amendments of 1990, § 208(b), 42 U.S.C. § 7525(a)(1).

[327] CAA § 202(b)(1)(C), as amended by the Clean Air Act Amendments of 1990, § 203(c), 42 U.S.C. § 7521(b)(1)(C).

[328] CAA § 202(b)(2), as amended by the Clean Air Act Amendments of 1990, § 203(d), 42 U.S.C. § 7521(b)(2).

[329] CAA § 202(j), 42 U.S.C. § 7521(j).

emissions of hydrocarbons from gasoline fueled motor vehicles during non-use of the vehicle.[330] Other controls are provided for the regulation of mobile source related air toxics.[331]

Emission control diagnostics must be installed for model year 1994 and beyond to be subject for inspection and for maintenance and repair of malfunctions.[332] A new provision also provides for standards of emission for particulate matter from buses from model year 1991 on.[333]

Another requirement is the adoption of a system of onboard vapor recovery following consultation with the Secretary of Transportation to assure the safety of such recovery systems. This requirement has special applicability for certain ozone nonattainment areas.[334]

The 1990 amendments provide for the revision of regulations relating to test procedures to determine whether 1994 model year cars and later model year light duty vehicles and light duty trucks will pass inspection methods and procedures established under § 207(b), when properly maintained and used, under conditions reasonably likely to be encountered during inspection and maintenance programs but that cannot be reasonably influenced or controlled by such I&M programs, such as fuel characteristics, ambient temperatures and less than 30 minute waiting periods.[335]

The 1990 amendment of the Clean Air Act also adjusted the duration of warranties provided under the Act, to reflect the changes in the law relating to the useful life of the vehicle as applied to specified major emission control components.[336] New intermediate in-use standards and final in-use standards have been set for light duty vehicles and for light duty trucks, which standards apply for model years 1994 and 1995, and for light duty trucks for model years 1996 and 1997, in lieu of the automotive pollution standards normally applicable.[337] In addition to other requirements relating to information that needs to be supplied by manufacturers, requirements for high altitude testing combined with a prohibition on leaded gasoline, and the authorization of new standards for urban buses, the law authorizes the collection of fees for the recovery of administrative costs, enabling the Administrator to recover the costs arising from new vehicle or engine certification, and new vehicle engine compliance monitoring.[338] The amended law also updates the inspection and testing requirements and continues the prohibition on the removal or rendering inoperative of any device installed in a motor vehicle in accordance with regulations.[339]

Violations of the certification of conformity is subject to a penalty of not more than $25,000, increased from the earlier penalty of $10,000. Each violation

[330] CAA § 202(j)(4), 42 U.S.C. § 7521(j)(4).

[331] CAA § 202(1), 42 U.S.C. § 7521(1).

[332] CAA § 202(m), 42 U.S.C. § 7521(m).

[333] CAA § 202(f)(should be (n)), 42 U.S.C. § 7521(f)(should be (n)).

[334] CAA § 202(a)(6), 42 U.S.C. § 7521(a)(6). *See* American Petroleum Inst. v. EPA, 846 F. Supp. 83, 24 ELR 21585 (D.C. Cir. 1994) which analyzes this requirement. *See also* Ethyl Corp. v. EPA, 25 F.3d 1241, 24 ELR 21591 (4th Cir. 1994).

[335] CAA § 206(a)(4)(A), 42 U.S.C. § 7525(a)(4)(A).

[336] CAA § 209(i)(1), 42 U.S.C. § 7541(i)(1).

[337] Clean Air Act § 207(c)(4), 42 U.S.C. § 7541(c)(4).

[338] Clean Air Act § 217. The provision was upheld in Engine Mfrs Ass'n v. EPA, 20 F.3d 1127, 24 ELR 20832 (D.C. Cir. 1994).

[339] CAA § 203(a)(2), 42 U.S.C. § 7522(a)(2) and (3).

by any motor vehicle is a separate offense. There are limits on where the action may be brought, and there are limitations on the imposition of the full penalty.[340] A new provision authorizes for the administrative assessment of certain civil penalties in lieu of commencing a civil action for certain designated violations of the Act. Such actions may be brought by the Attorney General for the amount of the penalty and interest and in such actions the validity, amount and appropriateness of the penalty is not subject to review. In addition, the violator will be required to pay the United States' enforcement expenses, including attorneys fees and costs in collection proceedings. Penalties are also applicable in the enforcement of automotive fuel regulations.[341]

[h] Testing of Uninstalled Aircraft Engines

Section 232 of the Clean Air ActAmendments of 1990 provides that the Administrator of EPA and the Secretary of Transportation, in consultation with the Secretary of Defense, are to commence a study of the testing of uninstalled aircraft engines in enclosed test cells to determine whether technology exists to control emissions of oxides of nitrogen from test cells, the effectiveness of such technologies, the cost of implementing such technologies, whether such technologies affect the safety, design, structure, etc. of aircraft engines, whether such technologies impair the effectiveness of aircraft engine safety design and the performance tests conducted in test cells, and the impact of not controlling such NOx emissions in the applicable nonattainment areas and on other sources, stationary and mobile, on oxides of nitrogen in such areas. A report of the result of the study had to be submitted to Congress no later than 24 months after the Clean Air Act Amendments of 1990. After the completion of the study, states may adopt or enforce standards for emission of oxides of nitrogen from such test cells, after issuing a public notice stating whether the standards are in accordance with the findings of the study.[342]

---

340 CAA § 205(a) and (b), 42 U.S.C. § 7524(a) and (b).

341 CAA § 205(c)(6).

342 CAA § 205(c)(6).

Chapter 3

WATER POLLUTION

The introductory materials which provide a general background for the discussion of water pollution are derived from the first report of the Council on Environmental Quality delivered to Congress in 1970. This report provides a snapshot in time of the nation's water pollution problem at the very beginning of modern environmental regulatory controls. The second set of materials, also prepared by the Council on Environmental Quality, consists of a description of environmental trends as viewed some 20 years later in 1989. These materials show that over the years, the problem of water pollution has been difficult to resolve. But a searching comparison also shows that though more work needs to be done, the first 20 years of environmental law and of public attention to the problems have resulted in major progress, in cleaner water, and in significantly improved public health.

In reviewing these materials, note the changes in the nature and dimension of the problem of clean water during the first 20 years of regulatory attention. There has been a shift from an emphasis on organic pollution to chemical pollution. Another noteworthy development that deserves attention is a changes in the regulatory environment itself. Environmental law and environmental regulation have become more complex as technological issues relating to the cleanup of sophisticated pollutants has become more necessary and pressing. Thus, while many effluents have decreased in quantity, they have become more difficult to deal with because of their complex chemical nature. Nonetheless, in spite of significant population increases, resulting in greater burdens on national waters, there has been a significant improvement in water quality in most parts of the nation.

The growth of population and increased urbanization have increased the burdens on water supply, particularly on certain aquifers, as well as on the need for improvements in the infrastructure of drainage and sewers.

The population increases and the burdens created by increased construction activities have also led to the loss of wetlands, affecting the habitat of many species. The developments reflected in the two CEQ reports also provide evidence of the coherence and interdependence of the human and natural environment. The needs of a larger population and the demands of urban growth have an immediate and direct impact on the natural environment. The human environment of cities is demonstrably linked with the natural environment through their common dependence on available and clean water.

§ 3.01 Sources of Water Pollution and Its Economic and Health Impact

Council on Environmental Quality First Annual Report, 29–42

(transmitted to Congress, August 1970)

Throughout history man has been ravaged by plague and epidemics visited on him by poor sanitation and polluted water. In more modern times, the great typhoid epidemics that swept London in the mid-19th century underscored the peril of water pollution and launched the first organized steps to combat it. And until very recent times this stress on preventing waterborne disease was the major thrust of efforts to stem the decline of the environment.

Americans have acted, until recently, as though their rivers and lakes had an infinite capacity to absorb wastes. Pollution was considered the price of progress. Not until 1948 was comprehensive Federal water pollution control legislation enacted, and the first permanent legislation was not passed until 1956. The original overriding concern was with human health, and almost all State water pollution programs were carried on by State health departments.

Water pollution control legislation and programs have now been broadened to embrace a host of environmental concerns, including recreation and esthetics. Epidemics due to waterborne causes are largely of the past, and our health efforts have moved to a more sophisticated concern for the effects of small amounts of toxic chemicals on humans and other forms of life.

Three reasons, besides the changed nature of the health problem, help explain the broader environmental concern of today: First, the growth of industries and cities has multiplied pollution in most waterways; second, demand for outdoor recreation has grown in a society increasingly affluent and leisure oriented; and third—a thread running through all the others—is man's inexplicable affinity to water. Whether it is the pleasure he derives from a fountain, the mood of a walk along the lake shore, the relaxation of fishing, or his identification with majestic water bodies—the Danube, the Great Lakes, or San Francisco Bay—man has found tranquility and inspiration in his appreciation of water. But, the current condition of many of our lakes and rivers makes appreciation impossible.

Pollution problems exist in all parts of the United States, particularly in the Northeast and in the Great Lakes region. In these areas, which have experienced tremendous urban and industrial growth over the past century, there was, at least until recently, inadequate investment in the construction of treatment plants. Now a big backlog of needed construction has accumulated. Specific sources of pollution, besides the ordinary municipal and industrial wastes, affect certain areas. Acid mine pollution is common in the coal mining States of Appalachia, and saline pollution occurs in the irrigation areas of Western States.

In some areas of the country, remedial programs have succeeded in raising the levels of water quality. However, population and industrial growth, higher water quality demanded by the public, and the increasing severity of certain types of pollution—for example, oil spills and increased algal blooms in lakes—all mean that we have only begun to tackle the problem.

NATURAL PROCESSES AND WATER POLLUTION

Several basic biological, chemical, and physical processes affect the quality of water.

Organic wastes decompose by bacterial action. Bacteria attack wastes dumped into rivers and lakes, using up oxygen in the process. Organic wastes are measured in units of biochemical oxygen demand (BOD), or chemical oxygen demand (COD), both measures of the amount of oxygen needed to decompose them. The COD measure is more inclusive than BOD, but BOD is much more commonly used. Fish and other aquatic life need oxygen. If the waste loads are so great that large amounts of oxygen are spent in their decomposition, certain types of fish can no longer live in that body of water. A pollution-resistant, lower order of fish, such as carp, replace the original fish population. The amount of oxygen in a water body is therefore one of the best measures of its ecological health.

If all the oxygen is used, an anaerobic (without air) decomposition process is set in motion with a different mixture of bacteria. Rather than releasing carbon dioxide in the decomposition process, anaerobic decomposition releases methane or hydrogen sulfide. In these highly polluted situations, the river turns dark, and odors—often overwhelming—penetrate the environment.

Heated water discharged into lakes and rivers often harms aquatic life. Heat accelerates biological and chemical processes, which reduce the ability of a body of water to retain dissolved oxygen and other dissolved gases. Increases in temperature often disrupt the reproduction cycles of fish. By hastening biological processes, heat accelerates the growth of aquatic plants—often algae. Finally, the temperature level determines the types of fish and other aquatic life that can live in any particular body of water. Taken together, these effects of excess heat operate to change the ecology of an area—sometimes drastically and rapidly.

One of the most serious water pollution problems is eutrophication—the "dying of lakes." All lakes go through a natural cycle of eutrophication, but normally it takes thousands of years. In the first stage—the oligotrophic—lakes are deep and have little biological life. Lake Superior is a good example. Over time, nutrients and sediments are added; the lake becomes more biologically productive and shallower. This stage—the mesotrophic—has been reached by Lake Ontario. As nutrients continue to be added, large algal blooms grow, fish populations change, and the lake begins to take on undesirable characteristics. Lake Erie is now in this eutrophic stage. Over time, the lake becomes a swamp and finally a land area.

Man greatly accelerates this process of eutrophication when he adds nutrients to the water—detergents, fertilizers, and human wastes. He has done this in Lake Erie and countless other lakes. Man's action can, in decades, cause changes that would have taken nature thousands of years.

WHERE WATER POLLUTION COMES FROM

Although water pollution comes from many sources, the major ones are industrial, municipal, and agricultural.

Industrial Wastes

The more than 300,000 water-using factories in the United States discharge three to four times as much oxygen-demanding wastes as all the sewered population of the United States. Moreover, many of the wastes discharged by industry are toxic. Table 1 shows the amount of water consumed by various industries and the pollution loads, before treatment, that they produce. The output of industrial wastes is growing several times faster than the volume of sanitary sewage.

TABLE 1.—Estimated Volume of Industrial Wastes Before Treatment, 1964[1]

Industry	Waste Water volume (billion gallons)	Process water intake (billion gallons)	BOD (million pounds)	Suspended solids (million pounds)
Food and kindred products	690	260	4,300	6,600
Meat products	99	52	640	640
Dairy products	58	13	400	230
Canned and frozen food	87	51	1,200	600
Sugar refining	220	110	1,400	5,000
All other	220	43	670	110
Textile mill products	140	110	890	N.E.
Paper and allied products	1,900	1,300	5,900	3,000
Chemical and allied products	3,700	560	9,700	1,900
Petroleum and coal	1,300	88	500	460
Rubber and plastics	160	19	40	50
Primary metals	4,300	1,000	480	4,700
Blast furnaces and steel mills	3,600	870	160	4,300
All other	740	130	320	430
Machinery	150	23	60	50
Electrical machinery	91	28	70	20
Transportation equipment	240	58	120	N.E.
All other manufacturing	450	190	390	930
All manufacturing	13,100	3,700	22,000	18,000
For comparison: Sewered population of United States	[2]5,300		[3]7,399	[4]8,800

[1]Columns may not add, due to rounding.
[2]120,000,000 persons times 120 gallons times 365 days.
[3]120,000,000 persons times 1/6 pound times 365 days.
[4]120,000,000 persons times 0.2 pound times 365 days.

Source: Data derived from T.J. Powers, National Industrial Waste Assessment, 1967.

Although there is as yet no detailed inventory of industrial wastes, indications are that over half the volume discharged to water comes from four major industry groups—paper, organic chemicals, petroleum, and steel.

The greatest volume of industrial wastes is discharged in the Northeast, the Ohio River Basin, the Great Lakes States, and the Gulf Coast States. Lesser, but significant volumes are discharged in some areas of the Southeast and the Pacific Coast States.

Most industrial water waste can be curbed—and much has been—by treatment and by designing production processes that minimize waste. For example, the average waste from modern sulfate pulp and paper plants is only 7 percent of what it was in the older sulfite process. Treatment processes are now available for most industrial wastes. Their total estimated costs, as a percentage of gross sales by all industry are well under 1 percent, although costs are much higher for some industries. Also, many industrial wastes—those from food processing, for example—can be treated efficiently (after pretreatment in some cases) in municipal waste treatment systems.

Some industrial pollution, however, presents difficult abatement problems. The trend toward using and shipping complex chemical products has greatly increased the possibility of releasing wastes in the environment. Many of these new chemicals are very difficult to detect and to control, and there is fear that too little caution and study preceded the processing and marketing of some of these materials.

Small amounts of heavy metals can be a problem. For example, until early this spring, little attention was given to mercury, although separate incidents of mercury poisoning had occurred in Japan and Sweden. Currently, levels of mercury above Food and Drug Administration standards have been discovered in more than 20 States with the result that in many of them, sport and commercial fishing has been curtailed. The Federal Government has collected data on the sources of mercury discharge—mainly chemical plants—and has sought court action against eight firms. The Council on Environmental Quality is coordinating long-term Federal agency efforts to spell out the danger and develop remedial programs.

Many authorities believe that waste heat looms as one of the most serious types of future water pollution. The chief source of thermal pollution today is the electric power industry, which requires tremendous amounts of water for cooling. Other sources include petroleum, chemical, steel, and pulp and paper processing. The heaviest users are listed in table 2.

The best single indicator of future potential for thermal pollution is the predicted increase in the generation of electricity. The electric power industry is growing at a rate of 7.2 percent annually, virtually doubling every 10 years. This trend is expected to continue, as table 3 shows.

TABLE 2.—Use of Cooling Water by U.S. Industry

Industry	Cooling water intake (billions of gallons)	Percent of total
Electric power	40,680	81.3
Primary metals	3,387	6.8
Chemical and allied products	3,120	6.2
Petroleum and coal products	1,212	2.4
Paper and allied products	607	1.2
Food and kindred products	392	0.8
Machinery	164	.3
Rubber and plastics	128	.3
Transportation equipment	102	.2
All others	273	.5
Total	50,065	100.0

Source: Federal Water Pollution Control Administration, "Industrial Waste Guide on Thermal Pollution," September 1968.

TABLE 3.—U.S. Electric Power—Past Use, Future Estimates

Year:	In billion kilowatt-hours
1912	12
1960	753
1965	1,060
1970	1,503
1975	2,022
1980	2,754
1985	3,639

Source: Federal Water Pollution Control Administration, "Industrial Waste Guide on Thermal Pollution," September 1968.

The principal use of water in steam-electric generating plants is for condenser cooling. The amount of water necessary depends on plant efficiency and the designed temperature rise within the condensers. The temperature rise of cooling water condensers is usually in the range of 10° to 20° F., with the average rise about 13° F. Large nuclear steam electric plants require about 50 percent more condenser water for a given temperature rise than late model fossil-fueled, steam-electric plants of equal size. However, the development of advanced reactors, such as the fast breeder, will essentially eliminate the difference between nuclear and fossil-fueled plants. It is estimated that by 1980, cooling operations by the electric power industry will require the equivalent of one-fifth of the total fresh water runoff of the United States.

Municipal Wastes

Municipal waste treatment plants handle more than just domestic wastes from homes and apartments. On a nationwide average, about 55 percent of the wastes processed by municipal treatment plants comes from homes and commercial establishments and about 45 percent from industries. Less than one-third of the Nation's population is served by a system of sewers and an adequate treatment plant. About one-third is not served by a sewer system at all. About 5 percent is served by sewers which discharge their wastes without any treatment. And the remaining 32 percent have sewers but inadequate treatment plants. Of the total sewered population, about 60 percent have adequate treatment systems. The greatest municipal waste problems exist in the areas with the heaviest concentrations of population, particularly the Northeast.

Three levels of treatment are employed in municipal treatment plants. Primary treatment is a simple gravity process that separates and settles solids in a big tank. Such primary plants provide BOD removal levels of 25 to 30 percent. Secondary treatment is a biological process that speeds up what nature does in natural water bodies. In the activated sludge process used by many large cities, bacteria and air are mixed with sewage to accelerate decomposition of wastes. The other secondary treatment process—the trickling filter—involves spraying wastes uniformly over a rock bed. Bacteria formed on the rocks, in the presence of air, accelerates decomposition of wastes. Good secondary treatment plants remove 90 percent of measured BOD. That does not mean that 90 percent of total oxygen-demanding wastes are removed, but only the part that is measured by certain laboratory tests.

Advanced waste treatment, often called tertiary treatment, involves a wide variety of processes tailored for specific treatment needs. For example, one advanced waste treatment process is lime-alum precipitation, which removes 80 percent of phosphates from waste water, compared to an average of 30 percent in normal secondary treatment. Other processes, using carbon adsorption and sand filtering, remove up to 99 percent of measured BOD.

The waste loads from municipal systems are expected to nearly quadruple over the next 50 years. Even if municipal and industrial waste loads are cut substantially through treatment, pollution problems will continue to plague densely populated and highly industrialized areas where the capacity to assimilate waste is exceeded.

Among other municipal waste problems that will grow more apparent as conventional treatment reduces gross pollution loads are those caused by storm or combined sewers and by nutrients. Many cities have combined sewers, which discharge raw sewage along with street runoff directly to streams when treatment systems become overloaded during storms or thaws. Even where sewers are separated, pollution from storm sewer discharges carrying a variety of wastes from the streets is possible. Although combined sewer problems exist in most regions of the country, the most severe are centered in the Northeast, Midwest, and to some degree, the Far West.

Municipal wastes contribute the major load of usable phosphates and significant amounts of nitrates to water bodies. Already nutrient pollution has led to a strict requirement for very high treatment levels for waste discharges to the Great Lakes and several other areas. Secondary treatment plants remove an average of 30 percent of the phosphorus and up to 20 percent of the nitrogenous materials, although with modifications higher levels of treatment are possible. In many places treatment levels approaching 100 percent will probably be necessary—especially if the phosphate content of detergents is not reduced.

Agricultural Wastes

Wastes from feedlots are a key source of agricultural pollution. The increasing number of animals and modern methods of raising them contribute to the worsening pollution of waters by animal wastes. Beef cattle, poultry, and swine feeding operations, along with dairy farms, are the major sources of actual or potential water pollution from animal wastes. In the United States today, the number of animals, their waste equivalents to humans, and the total waste equivalent are as follows:

	Animal population (in millions) (1)	Ratio of waste output of single animal to output of a human (2)	Total animal wastes expressed as equivalent number of humans (in millions of humans) (3)
Cattle	107	16.40	1,754.8
Horses	3	11.30	33.9
Hogs	53	1.90	100.7
Sheep	26	2.45	63.7
Chickens	375	0.14	52.5
Total[1]	564		2,005.6

[1]Col. 1 times col. 2 equals total in col. 3.
Source: Data derived from Federal Water Pollution Control Administration, "Cost of Clean Water," vol. 2, 1968.

Hence, animal wastes are estimated to be the equivalent of the wastes of 2 billion people. These figures should not be interpreted as an estimate of the potential pollution from feedlots, however, since most of these wastes never reach the water. But they are a measure of the total amount of animal wastes, part of which causes water pollution and solid waste problems.

Agricultural waste sources are scattered throughout the Nation. Large cattle herds are fed in the Midwest, West, and Southeast; poultry in the South and in the Middle Atlantic States; and hogs in the Midwest and South. If current consumption rates continue, animal wastes will increase significantly. The trend toward confined feeding and concentrated rations is bound to add to the pollution potential of feedlot wastes although better control methods are being developed.

Fertilizers contain nitrogen and phosphorus, two primary nutrients that nourish algae in water. Nitrates are the bigger problem since, unlike phosphates, which stick to soil, nitrates are very susceptible to runoff from rain. Also, nitrates leach into ground water. High nitrate concentrations in water cause infant methemoglobinemia or "blue baby." The use of chemical fertilizers has increased rapidly in the United States over the last decade and is expected to continue to rise, although at somewhat slower rates. In some areas, particularly in the West, water leached from irrigated lands has caused serious water pollution. In the Western United States, salt content in many rivers exceeds the levels considered acceptable for most types of crops. The problems resulting from use of pesticides, which pollute the air, the land, and the water, are covered in chapter VII.

Other Sources

Sediment and erosion—Sediments carried by erosion represent the greatest volume of wastes entering surface waters. The volume of suspended solids reaching U.S. waters is at least 700 times greater than the total sewage discharge loadings. Sediments are washed in from croplands, unprotected forest soils, overgrazed pastures, strip mines, roads, or bulldozed urban areas. Agricultural development increases land erosion rates four to nine times over what they are for natural cover. Construction may increase the rate a hundredfold. A 1969 report of the Federal Water Quality Administration estimated the average sediment yield during a rainstorm at highway construction sites at about 10 times that for cultivated land, 200 times that for grass areas, and 2,000 times that for forest areas—depending on the rainfall, land slope, and the exposure of the bank. Similar rates of sediment production occur from commercial and industrial construction in urban areas.

Oil and other hazardous substances—With the grounding of the *Torrey Canyon* in 1967, the breakup of the *Ocean Eagle* in Puerto Rican waters in 1968, and the Santa Barbara offshore oil leak in 1969, oil pollution has become recognized as a serious national and worldwide problem. An estimated 10,000 spills of oil and other hazardous materials annually pollute navigable waters of the United States. Although damages from other hazardous substances can be just as significant and diverse as those caused by oil pollution, the volume of oil transported and used makes it the most important single pollutant of this type.

Most oil spills exceeding 100 barrels come from vessels, although about one-third of the incidents involve pipelines, oil terminals, and bulk storage facilities. Vessel casualties are a prime source of oil pollution. Damage from several million gallons of oil entering the water at one time and place can be extensive.

TABLE 4.—Number of Reported Oil Spills in U.S. Waters (Over 100 Barrels)

	1968	1969
Vessels	347	532
Shore facilities	295	331
Unidentified	72	144
Total	714	1,007

Source: Federal Water Quality Administration, "Clean Water for the 1970's," June 1970.

Oil pollution may spring from several other sources. Gasoline service stations dispose of 350 million gallons of used oil per year, much of which was previously re-refined. Two hundred thousand miles of pipelines, carrying more than a billion tons of oil and hazardous substances, cross waterways and reservoirs and are subject to leakage. The blowout of offshore oil and gas wells, the dumping of drilling muds and oil-soaked wastes, the destruction of offshore drilling rigs by storms, and ship collisions—all are significant potential sources of pollution.

With more and more oil and hazardous materials being transported, the number of spills could grow. On the other hand, tightened regulations developed for oil exploration and production and sounder ship and pipeline construction could reduce this number.

Mine drainage—Mine drainage is one of the most significant sources of water pollution in Appalachia, in the Ohio Basin States, and in certain other areas of the country.

In Appalachia alone, where an estimated 75 percent of the coal mine pollution occurs, about 10,500 miles of stream are dropped below desirable quality levels by acid mine drainage. Similar drainage from other types of mining—such as phosphate, sand and gravel, clay, iron, gold, copper, and aluminum—pollutes other regions of the country. Acid formation occurs when water and air react with the sulfur-bearing minerals in the mines or in refuse piles to form sulfuric acid and iron compounds. Coal mines idle for 30 to 50 years may still discharge large quantities of acid waters. Mine drainage also contains copper, lead, zinc, and other metals toxic to aquatic life.

Watercraft wastes—About 46,000 federally registered commercial vessels, 65,000 unregistered commercial fishing vessels, 1,600 federally owned vessels, and 8 million recreational watercraft ply the navigable waters of the United States according to FWQA. The potential sewage pollution from these vessels is estimated to equal that from over 500,000 persons—comparable to the population of a city the size of San Diego. As a total source of pollution, it is insignificant, but it can be a major impediment to achieving clean water in some harbors and recreational areas. Further vessel pollution occurs when ships discharge bilge and ballast water heavy with oils and other substances.

Environmental Trends
Council on Environmental Quality
Executive Office of the President 31–38 (1989)

Water Quality

As water moves through the hydrologic cycle, it carries substances derived from both natural and human sources. These substances include dissolved salts, metals, organics, and radioactive materials, as well as suspended materials, such as bacteria, viruses, and sediments. Dissolved and suspended substances can become problems, or pollutants, when they reach concentrations that impair or destroy aquatic life, threaten human health, or foul water to the extent that its ability to support shellfish harvest, fish and wildlife habitat, swimming, boating, and other intended uses is lost.

Polluting substances enter surface water and ground water either at a discrete point, such as a pipe, ditch, or well, or in a diffused manner over a large area (nonpoint source). In surface-water systems, the major point sources of pollution are municipal sewage treatment plants, industrial facilities, and combined sewer overflows. These sources discharge a variety of substances, in different quantities and combinations, including sediments and other particulates, organic materials (which create biochemical oxygen demands), nutrients, and various caustic and toxic chemicals. Treatment of effluent waters can remove substantial quantities of these conventional and hazardous pollutants.

Nonpoint source pollution is carried in rainwater, runoff, and snowmelt over and through soil to surface water, or in water that percolates through soils to underground aquifers. The principal nonpoint sources of pollution to surface water are runoff from cropland, pasture, forest land, and animal feedlots; runoff from construction, mining, and logging areas; drainage from waste disposal sites and landfills; runoff from urban areas and roads; and atmospheric deposition. These sources contribute both conventional and hazardous pollutants. Non-point source pollutants are mobilized primarily during hydrologic events (rainfall, storms) rather than as continuous discharges.

With reference to ground-water quality, the most frequently cited sources of pollution are agricultural lands, faulty septic systems, and leaky underground storage tanks and pipes. Nitrates and pesticides are common contaminants from agricultural lands, whereas microorganisms, nitrates, and synthetic organic compounds are associated with faulty septic systems. Fuels, chemicals, solvents, and other toxic wastes are contaminants of concern from leaky underground storage tanks and pipes. Additional sources of groundwater contamination include municipal and industrial landfills, surface impoundments, abandoned mine sites, urban runoff, and groundwater mining.

Billions of gallons of wastewater are generated each day by municipalities and industries across the Nation. The types and amounts of wastewater pollutants that can be discharged are regulated according to national water quality standards.

Municipal sewage treatment facilities are the Nation's principal point source dischargers to surface water. These facilities treat and discharge wastewater from homes, public buildings, commercial establishments, storm water sewers, and some industries. Providing adequate municipal wastewater treatment to a growing population has been one of the major accomplishments of the past several decades. In addition, the level of sewage treatment has improved. Over the last 20 years, government spending on the construction and upgrading of sewage treatment facilities has increased and, concomitantly, contaminant levels in discharges have declined, even though population and industrial activity have increased. From 1972 to 1986, the total population served by secondary treatment or better increased from 85 million to 127 million people and the population served by less than secondary treatment declined from 5 million to less than 2 million (secondary treatment involves removal of at least 85% of several key conventional pollutants). By 1986, 15,587 wastewater facilities existed nationwide and, of these, more than one-half had secondary treatment or better. Advanced (tertiary) treatment is now mandated when secondary treatment is not adequate.

Upgrading the level of sewage treatment in the Nation has produced direct benefits by reducing pollution in surface water. The most widely used measure of municipal pollution is the extent to which the treated wastewater's organic content depletes the receiving water's oxygen. Oxygen depletion reduces the amount of oxygen available to fish and other aquatic life. As a result of improved wastewater treatment, municipal organic pollution has decreased dramatically and biological conditions around and downstream from treatment facilities have improved during the past decade. Components of major concern that still require attention and resolution include pretreatment of industrial wastes discharged into municipal sewage facilities, combined sanitary and storm sewers that occasionally overload treatment plant capacity, disposal of sludge produced during wastewater treatment, removal of excessive nutrients, that enrich receiving waters, and destruction or removal of disease-related microorganisms.

Industrial pollutants include conventional pollutants, such as suspended solids, organics, and nutrients, as well as hazardous substances, such as synthetic organic compounds, heavy metals, and other toxic chemicals. The thrust of industrial wastewater controls has been to require major industries to adequately treat their own wastewater rather than pipe it to municipal treatment plants. This is because most municipal facilities cannot adequately treat the more exotic contaminants found in industrial wastes. To comply with this requirement, industrial dischargers have invested heavily in best available technologies to reduce pollutant levels in wastewater discharged to surface water. One of the key measures of industries' cleanup efforts and progress is the greatly increased level of compliance with federal and state discharge limitations, especially for plants with the largest wastewater flows. A challenge for the future is the development of regulatory programs to assure pretreatment of industrial wastes before they are discharged into municipal treatment facilities.

Mineral and metal industries (for example, mines, iron and steel fabricators, metal finishers, and petroleum refineries) are the principal direct dischargers of suspended solids and heavy metals to surface water. Textile, pulp and paper, food, and beverage industries also discharge large quantities of suspended solids and are the principal sources of industry-generated organic materials that contribute to biochemical oxygen demands. Plastics molding and forming industries along with porcelain enameling and coil coating industries are the major industrial sources of phosphorus to surface water.

The pulp and paper industry provides an example of the progress made by industrial dischargers in controlling conventional pollutants through technology. Between 1973 and 1984, pulp and paper mills reduced biochemical oxygen demand and total suspended solids concentrations in effluent waters by approximately 500,000 tons per year and 490,000 tons per year, respectively. During this same time frame, production levels increased.

Trends in Water Quality

A commonly recurring question is whether the quality of the Nation's surface water and ground water is improving or deteriorating. Prior to landmark water pollution legislation of the late 1960s and early 1970s, industries and municipalities discharged poorly treated or raw wastes into rivers, lakes, and estuaries. Little or no consideration was given to controlling surface runoff. In addition, hazardous materials were dumped in landfills and dump sites without regard for environmental consequences, and the use of pesticides, such as DDT, was virtually unrestricted. The result was widespread degradation of surface water, loss of aquatic habitat and recreational uses of surface water in many areas, and contamination of ground water in some localities.

In 1972, the United States made an unprecedented commitment to the restoration and enhancement of the physical, chemical, and biological integrity of the Nation's water. Much progress has been made toward achieving this goal, but it has been expensive and has required major commitments from all levels of government, industry, and the private sector. Much of this progress has been accomplished by controlling the many municipal and industrial point sources of water pollution. Other reasons for observed water quality improvements include changes in agricultural practices to reduce nonpoint source pollution (including implementation of soil conservation methods and regulation of animal feedlot runoff), improvements in mine reclamation practices, and reductions in atmospheric emissions of lead, cadmium, and oxides of sulfur and nitrogen.

In 1972 and again in 1982, water quality conditions were evaluated to determine whether surface water was supporting the uses for which it had been designated. States reached their conclusions about water quality conditions using a combination of long-term trend monitoring records, short-term intensive surveys, and professional judgments. Uses were reported as being fully supported if monitoring indicated that no chemical pollution existed, biological communities were fully supported, and/or the most sensitive designated uses were observed to be supported. Uses were partially supported if there was minor chemical pollution, aquatic community health was uncertain, or the most sensitive uses were not supported at a maximum level. Uses were not supported if there was major chemical pollution, aquatic communities were stressed or absent, or the most sensitive designated uses were severely impaired or impossible.

States found that significant accomplishments in water quality had been achieved between 1972 and 1982. Much of the Nation's streams, lakes, and estuaries had maintained water quality, which was significant in itself because the population grew by 11% and water use increased dramatically over this decade. Yet, some of the Nation's water assessed in 1982 still had water quality problems that prevented full-use support.

In many parts of the Nation, pollutant loads from nonpoint sources continue to present water quality problems and prevent attainment of designated water uses. According to a 1985 survey, virtually all states in the Nation reported water in which uses were severely or moderately impaired by nonpoint sources or in which nonpoint sources threatened to impair designated uses. This included 11% of the Nation's total river miles, 30% of total lake acres, and 17% of total estuary square miles. The impacts are not uniform nationally, however.

In 1985, agriculture was reported by states as the primary nonpoint source in 64% of impacted river miles, 57% of impacted lake acres, and 19% of impacted estuary square miles. Animal wastes from livestock and poultry production, soil erosion from cropland and overgrazing, irrigation return flows, and pesticide and fertilizer application were the main agricultural sources. Mining was responsible for nonpoint pollution in 9% of impacted river miles and 1% of lake acres in 1985. This included pollution from past practices, such as abandoned mines, improperly sealed wells, and mining waste piles, as well as some existing mining practices, particularly oil and gas drilling and mineral mining. Other major nonpoint sources in the Nation's rivers were silviculture (impacting 6% of assessed river miles), urban runoff (5%), hydromodification (4%), construction (2%), and land disposal (1%). Hydromodification, urban runoff, land disposal, and construction-related nonpoint sources were more significant in lakes than rivers (impacting 13, 12, 5, and 4% of assessed lake acres, respectively), whereas mining and silviculture were less important (each contributing 1%).

States indicated worsening trends for some of the pollutants associated with nonpoint sources, particularly sediments, nitrate-nitrite, phosphorus, sodium, and chlorides. In 1985, sediments accounted for 47% of the nonpoint source pollutants in impacted river waters, nutrients accounted for 13%, pathogens and physical habitat alteration accounted for 9% each, and acidity, toxins, oxygen demand, pesticides, and salinity accounted for 7, 6, 4, 3, and 2%, respectively. In impacted lakes, nutrients and sediments were the major nonpoint source pollutants (accounting for 59 and 22% of the pollutants, respectively), followed by physical habitat alteration and acidity (4% each), oxygen demand, salinity, and toxins (3% each), pathogens (2%), and pesticides (less than 1%).

In a 1982 survey of the Nation's fishery biologists on the ability of perennial streams to support populations of sport fish and species of special concern,

3% of perennial streams ranked "0" (meaning they had no ability to support any fish populations). Five percent of perennial streams ranked "1" (ability to support a nonsport fish population only), and 17% ranked "2" (minimally able to support sport fish populations, species of special concern, or both). Forty percent of perennial streams were moderately able to support fish populations (ranks "3" and "4"), and only a small percentage of perennial streams (4%) were able to support sport fish, species of special concern, or both at a maximum level (rank "5"). The ability of the Nation's perennial streams to support sport fish or species of special concern did not change appreciably between 1977 and 1982.

The results of the 1982 fish survey indicate that 53% of the Nation's perennial streams have fish communities that are adversely affected by a variety of factors. The main problems were related to water quality, water quantity, usable fish habitat, and problems within the fish communities. The principal water quality factors were turbidity (affecting 29% of perennial stream miles), high water temperature (affecting 19%), excessive nutrient levels (11%), toxic substances (9%), and low concentrations of dissolved oxygen (8%). Agricultural and total nonpoint sources were probable contributors to water quality problems in 26 and 35% of perennial stream miles, respectively. . . .

River and Stream Water Quality

During the 1970s, several federal programs for nationally consistent water quality data collection were established as an adjunct to state and local monitoring. Only recently have sufficient data accumulated for a comprehensive analysis of longterm trends. Data for 30 regularly sampled water quality variables from more than 300 river locations for the period from 1974 to 1981, along with ancillary data on river basin characteristics and upstream pollution sources, are now available and, since 1981, continue to be collected.

Low dissolved oxygen levels were a pollution problem in streams and rivers 20 years ago but are rarely encountered today because of an overall reduction in point discharges of oxygen-demanding wastes. In the decade following 1972, municipal loads of biochemical oxygen demand decreased by an estimated 46%, and industrial loads decreased by at least 71%, nationally. Over roughly the same period, dissolved oxygen conditions improved, most frequently in the New England, Mid-Atlantic, Ohio, and Mississippi regional basins but declined most frequently in the Southeast. Runoff from urban areas remains a leading source of materials that have biochemical oxygen demands.

Fecal coliform and fecal streptococcal bacteria are contaminants associated with municipal sewage and agricultural runoff (principally livestock feedlots). Between 1974 and 1981, decreases in fecal coliform bacteria were especially common in parts of the Gulf Coast, central Mississippi, and the Columbia River Basins. Decreases in both types of bacteria were frequent in the Arkansas-Red River Basin and along the Atlantic Coast. Improved municipal treatment and better control of livestock wastes are reasons for improved water quality conditions. (Municipal loadings, cattle population density, and feedlot activity appear to be positively associated with fecal bacteria counts.)

Sediments in streams and rivers come from diffuse sources—as a natural consequence of geological erosion and from accelerated erosion of cropland, timbered forest land, surface mines, and construction sites. National trends in suspended sediment concentrations were nearly equally divided between increases and decreases during the period 1974-1981. Increasing concentrations occurred in basins where land uses historically have resulted in high rates of soil erosion, such as in the Columbia River Basin where logging is a predominant land use and in the Arkansas-Red River and Mississippi River Basins, where agriculture is the predominant land use. Increased sediment loads in the Columbia River Basin in 1980 and 1981 were also associated with the volcanic eruption of Mount St. Helens. Declining concentrations of suspended sediment in the Missouri River Basin have been traced to the effect of reservoir construction during the 1950s and 1960s.

Trends in total phosphorus concentrations are similar to those for suspended sediments. Decreases in total phosphorus concentration occurred frequently in the Great Lakes and Mississippi River Basins between 1974 and 1981. Where increases occurred, evidence suggests a link to non-point sources, particularly agriculture. Increases in total phosphorus concentrations are often associated with increases in fertilized acreage and cattle population density.

In contrast to trends for suspended sediments and phosphorus, total nitrogen concentrations increased more frequently and affected a larger area between 1974 and 1981. Increasing trends were most frequent east of the 100th meridian and were strongly associated with increased agricultural activity (particularly fertilizer use), livestock population density, and feedlot activity. Atmospheric deposition, on the other hand, is a suspected cause of increased nitrate concentrations in surface water in the Ohio, Mid-Atlantic, Great Lakes, and Upper and Mississippi River Basins during this time. Point source loads of nitrogen declined in many basins, supposedly as a result of improved wastewater treatment, but the magnitude of change nationally is poorly documented. Overall, total nitrogen trends appear to be related more to non-point sources than to point sources.

The differences in nitrogen and phosphorus trend patterns are also seen in recent changes in the delivery of nutrients to coastal waters. Nitrate loads to East Coast estuaries, the Great Lakes, and the Gulf of Mexico have increased significantly, whereas phosphorus loads to coastal areas have changed little or have even declined (with the exception of Gulf Coast and Pacific Northwest Basins, where phosphorus loads have increased in association with increases in sediment loads). These differences appear to result from three factors: atmospheric deposition of nitrates in the Midwest and East; moderation or delay in delivery of phosphorus by binding to sediment in stream channels; and point source pollution controls that have focused more heavily on phosphorus than nitrogen.

Trends in dissolved solids were also observed from 1974 to 1981. The major dissolved solids in streams and rivers are inorganic salts (sodium, potassium, calcium, magnesium, carbonate, bicarbonate, chloride, and sulfate ions). These salts come from a number of sources, including weathering of rocks and soil, atmospheric deposition, leaching by irrigation water (especially in semiarid basins of the West and Southwest), evaporation in reservoirs and other surface-water bodies, and runoff from highways where salt has been applied to control ice and snow (particularly in the Northeast, Mid-Atlantic, and North Central states). Between 1974 and 1981, increasing trends in chloride, sulfate, and sodium concentrations in surface water were frequent. The magnitude—an average increase of 30%—and wide distribution of' these trends represent a significant increase in the salinity of the Nation's rivers during the same period.

Several factors appear responsible for the general pattern of salinity increase. First, chloride trends were moderately correlated with basin population changes, which reflects the fact that human wastes are a major source of chloride in populated basins. Second, salt use on highways, which increased nationally by a factor of more than 12 between 1950 and 1980, was positively correlated with the regional pattern of sodium and chloride increases. Finally, increases in sulfate concentrations were especially frequent in the Missouri, Arkansas, and Tennessee Basins and highly correlated with changes in surface coal production from 1974 to 1981. In contrast with much of the rest of the Nation, salinity decreased in the upper Colorado River Basin, which has had a history of salt problems. These decreases were associated, in part, with salinity control efforts in agriculture and with the temporary effects of increasing reservoir storage during the early 1970s.

Trends in toxic element concentrations in surface water have remained largely unknown, despite increasing knowledge of the potential sources and fates of toxic substances in aquatic systems. Toxic waste pollution is associated with a variety of metals and organic chemicals produced by industry. Water quality records for the period 1974-1981 frequently showed increasing trends in the dissolved forms of two potentially toxic trace elements (arsenic and cadmium). The major environmental sources of these elements are fossil-fuel combustion, primary metals manufacturing, pesticide use, and use of phosphate-bearing commodities, such as fertilizers and detergents. Increasing concentrations of arsenic and cadmium occurred with greatest frequency in river basins of the industrial Midwest, and the evidence suggests that increased atmospheric deposition of fossil-fuel combustion products was the predominant cause of the trends in both elements. This conclusion was corroborated by finding increased trace element levels in lake sediments in regions with high deposition of fossil-fuel combustion products.

In contrast to arsenic and cadmium, dissolved lead concentrations decreased along the East and West coasts and on tributaries to the Missouri and Mississippi rivers between 1974 and 1981. The few increases in dissolved lead that did occur were clustered along the Texas Gulf Coast and in the lower Mississippi River Basin. Lead enters the aquatic environment via point and non-point sources, including atmospheric deposition. Declining environmental lead levels have been widely attributed to the nationwide reduction in lead content of fuels and consumption of leaded fuel since the mid-1970s (for example, automobile gasoline-lead consumption decreased nationally by 67% between 1975 and 1981). Decreases in lead concentrations in streams were significantly associated with both the level and rate of decline in gasoline-lead consumption in most basins with the exception of some with large urban and suburban populations, such as the Ohio River and Great Lakes Basins.

Pesticides in Rivers and Streams

Pesticides, which include insecticides and herbicides, are applied extensively to agricultural land throughout the Nation and, in urban areas, they are used on lawns and gardens and for exterminating household pests. Insecticide use has gradually decreased over the past two decades, whereas herbicide use has increased, though at a declining rate over time.

The long-term adverse effects of pesticides on aquatic ecosystems or human health are not fully understood. Different pesticides have markedly different chemical properties that behave differently in the environment. Furthermore, pesticides are difficult to measure in dilute surface water, and detection limits vary among the different pesticides and their metabolites. Some broad patterns have been recognized, however, in the relationships between application rates of certain pesticides, their chemical properties, and their detection in surface water and bed sediments.

A combination of increasing regulatory restriction on and decreasing effectiveness of organochlorine insecticides, such as DDT, chlordane, and dieldrin, has led to a dramatic decrease in their use since the mid-1960s and an erratic, but gradual, decrease in their occurrence in water and sediment samples since 1975. Most organochlorine insecticides are highly persistent in nature, have low solubility in water, and absorb strongly to sediment particles. Because of their resistance to decay, organochlorine insecticides continue to be found in sediments.

Detections of organochlorine insecticides in bed sediments are positively correlated with agricultural pesticide use. Detections are also frequent, however, in regions reporting low farm use (for example, in the highly populated and industrialized Northeast), which may indicate the importance of nonagricultural sources of these chemicals. There is no strong geographical relationship between pesticide use and detection in water, largely because of the small number of detections, which is due, in part, to the hydrophobic nature of organochlorine pesticides.

Chemicals in the organophosphate group of insecticides, such as malathion, parathion, and diazinon, are generally short lived (most persist in the soil for 1 to 12 weeks after application) and are highly soluble in water. Farm use of these chemicals declined steadily through the 1970s, although not as dramatically as for organochlorine insecticides. The geographic distribution of organophosphate insecticide use and detection are only weakly correlated, and no trends are evident in their detection on either a national or regional scale or at any individual station for either water or bed sediments. Because of their high solubility in water and their low persistence, no organophosphate chemicals were detected in bed sediments.

The use of atrazine and 2,4-D herbicides has accounted for most of the increase in herbicide use in the past 20 years, although the dominance of these chemicals had decreased somewhat by 1980. These herbicides are generally intermediate in persistence to organochlorine and organophosphate insecticides and are highly soluble in water. From 1975 to 1978, virtually no herbicides were detected in bed sediments and, except for atrazine, few were detected in water. The generally low rate of detections and the limited time span of data available make it impossible to evaluate trends in any herbicide concentrations in either bed sediments or water.

Water Quality Conditions in the Great Lakes

Over the past 10 years, water quality in the Great Lakes has generally improved. These improvements are attributed primarily to remedial action and reduced loadings of conventional pollutants from point sources (for example, nutrients, bacteria, suspended solids, oil and grease, and oxygen-consuming materials) as well as probable reduced loadings of phenols. . . .

§ 3.02 Private Water Rights and Their Relation to Pollution Control

Pollution control is connected with existing rights to use particular waters, especially when a dispute regarding the use of water develops between adjoining riparian owners or between different users of the particular waterway. Invariably related to the recognized uses of water for domestic, agricultural, and industrial purposes is the practical use of rivers and lakes for sewage disposal. Many rivers in industrial areas have indeed become open sewers whose major purpose is to receive and transport effluents.

The extent to which rivers and other waters may be used for sewage disposal was originally defined by the user's common-law rights to the waters. There are, basically, two systems of water law in the United States: One is the system of "riparian rights," which prevails primarily in the northeastern parts of the country; and the second system, which is considered to be an especially western-southwestern development, is that of "appropriation."

Riparian System

The riparian system, which has its roots in English common law, is identified with the abundant availability of water. Under that system, the right to use the waters of a river arises from the ownership of land which borders on that river. While riparian rights may be quite complex, they generally share the following incidents: The right is created by land ownership, and the owner continues to hold the right to use the waters whether or not he continues to use them. The right to use the water, on the other hand, is limited to uses connected with the land itself, *i.e.*, the owner may not use the water on another noncontiguous parcel which he owns, nor may he sell the water for use off the riparian property.

There are two different principles of allocation as between riparian owners along the same stream. One principle, that of "natural flow," holds that no riparian owner may affect the flow of the river in such a way as to impair or diminish it to the detriment of another riparian owner—the downstream owner is entitled to the waters exactly as if the river had remained in its original natural state. Normal use for domestic purposes is, usually, exempted from this concept. The natural flow principle is difficult to apply and, consequently, has become less useful. While, cases generally mention the "natural flow" principle, it is hardly ever relied on as a basis for decision. The more prevalent approach is that of "reasonable use." Each riparian owner may make reasonable use of the waters with due regard of the needs of other riparian owners. Reasonable use, therefore, involves the constant problem of balancing the needs of different users at a given time and place. In times of scarcity, a court may decree an apportionment of the waters or may prefer one use over another. Some uses have been traditionally preferred, *i.e.*, domestic and agricultural uses may simply reflect the preference of prior uses over new ones, although the riparian system does not generally involve a preference of prior uses. Sometimes the courts' decisions favoring agricultural and domestic uses over industrial uses involve an implicit judgment that the former are more "reasonable," *i.e.*, less damaging, than the latter. Since the riparian system, particularly under the reasonable use doctrine, is somewhat unpredictable, and because each use must be regarded on its own terms in the light of the particular circumstances, it is said to be more appropriate to parts of the country that do not generally suffer from water famines. It has been found to be unsuited to areas of the country where water scarcities are common and where availability of a minimal quantity of water must be assured by law.

Two aspects of riparian doctrine need emphasis as they relate to pollution actions. First, the riparian owner has the right to use the water because he owns land bordering the water course. Barring any special contractual arrangements, it is only the riparian owner who has a right to the flow of the water course, except as modified by other reasonable uses. Non-riparians complaining of injuries to water quality must rely on other doctrines, such as nuisance or negligence. Secondly, the idea of right to use the river's water held in common by all riparian owners requires the development of the doctrine of "reasonable use" earlier referred to. Since every water use involves some diminution of water or some deterioration of its quality, such common use involves the acceptance of the effects of "reasonable use" by others. Thus, there is judicial acceptance of the idea that it is the duty of upper riparians to return waters they have used to the stream bed in something close to—though not quite—their original condition. This may be described in some jurisdictions by the requirement that the upper riparian may not "materially corrupt" the returned waters to the "substantial injury" of the downstream riparian owners. Normally pollutants that occur "naturally" on the upper riparian land may relieve the upper riparian from responsibility for allegedly unreasonable use. In some jurisdictions, this may include even acid runoff from mines or from abandoned mines on the upper riparians' land. The issue of what is a reasonable use may give rise to a number of value judgments. For a long time, "balancing tests" have been applied although they may be time bound. In the 19th century, such tests were more likely to conclude that aesthetic or domestic use values had to yield to "reasonable" though polluting use of water by a plan that employed many workers. More recently the balancing of reasonable uses is more likely to emphasize conservational, rather than exploitative uses.[1]

---

[1] *See also* F. Grad, Treatise on Environmental Law, § 3.02, text at notes 29-50 and cases there cited.

There may be some confusion of doctrines between riparian rights and nuisance. The riparian owner's right to use of water, undiminished and unspoiled except for other riparian owners' reasonable uses, is not dependent on showing unreasonable interference with use and enjoyment, as in the case of nuisance, nor any kind of temporary invasion, as in an action in trespass. The riparian owner's right is, in a sense, absolute—*i.e.*, to vindicate it, he does not depend on a showing of a negligent or intentional invasion or interference, but merely on a showing that it has, in fact, been interfered with. Though an action between a non-riparian defendant and a riparian plaintiff in nuisance may be similar in many respects to an action between riparians, and there may be similar elements of proof, the doctrinal basis would be different.

The riparian owner's right to clean water has generally prevailed over attempts by municipal governments to assert some inherent right to use available water courses as open sewers. Even where municipalities have attempted to support their position by pointing to sewage disposal requirements imposed by state legislation, courts will not permit the rivers to be used in this fashion. The passage of state water pollution control statutes, it has been held, will not affect riparian owners' common law right to the substantially unpolluted and undiminished flow of water.[2]

State and federal pollution control laws may impose certain additional limitations on private riparian rights. So for instance, in *Ancarow v. City of Richmond*,[3] the plaintiff riparian landowner alleged that the continuing pollution of the James River due to discharges from the city's sewage treatment plant had rendered their property valueless for use as a marina, and constituted a "taking" in violation of the 14th Amendment. Reversing the lower court's decision, the court of appeals held that the plaintiffs had no riparian or other property interest in the James River which was "taken" by the city's discharge of treated wastes. The riparian interest which the plaintiff had claimed was the right to water of a particular purity, a right which under Virginia law is subject to the public's superior right to pollute public waters for sewage disposal. Since the sewage treatment plant's discharges concededly did not violate either state or federal pollution control laws, plaintiffs could not argue that the municipality's right to pollute the river in any way affected their riparian rights. Plaintiffs had contended that since the state's water quality statute regulates and limits the city's right to pollute, it constituted an intervening change in the law and by implication also created a new private riparian right superior to the public's right to pollute. The court rejected this contention both on the basis of the law's statutory language and because it would result in penalizing the city for complying with the state's pollution control standard.

Courts have generally refused to regard upstream riparian polluters as joint tort feasors, placing a practical burden on plaintiffs to ascertain and apportion the specific amounts of injury suffered by the downstream riparian from the pollutant of each specific defendant.[4]

[2] F. Grad, Treatise on Environmental Law, § 3.02, text at notes 55-57 and cases there cited.

[3] 600 F.2d 443 (4th Cir. 1979).

[4] F. Grad, Treatise on Environmental Law, § 3.02, text at notes 82 and 83 and cases there cited.

Appropriation System

The appropriation system, which prevails in the arid west and southwest, is an outgrowth of the water requirements for mining and irrigation needs that cannot be limited to riparian ownership. Had the use of western rivers been limited to riparian owners only, a major portion of the western United States would be unusable. Under the system of appropriation, ownership of riparian lands has nothing to do with the acquisition of the right to use the water. As the name implies, the right to use water is obtained by appropriating—*i.e.*, taking—the same and by making beneficial use of it. The right is retained only as long as it is used. Moreover, once the right is obtained, there is no limitation on where the water may be used, *i.e.*, it may be transported off the place of its origin for use elsewhere. As between riparian users of the water of the same river, priority of appropriation gives priority of right. When there is a shortage of water, the person who is last in time of appropriation may be entirely deprived of the use of the water in order to meet the needs of a prior appropriator.

The doctrine of appropriation first made substantial inroads during the mining discovery period in California in the mid-19th century. Much of the original mining and settling was done in ignorance of the laws of the United States, which had newly acquired the land as a result of the war with Mexico.[5] Land, minerals and water were distributed and apportioned according to the customs of the miners themselves, customs which reflected the simple rule of first come, first served. Actually, many of the miners and settlers were trespassers on the public lands, and could have been removed by the military. The government, however, did not interfere and Congress did not pass any act upon the subject until the "Proof of Custom Act of 1851" which admitted proof of custom with respect to water uses and mining claims. The 1966 act of Congress[6] vested rights to use of water for mining, agricultural, manufacturing or other purposes by priority of possession as recognized and acknowledged by local customs, laws and decisions of courts. It gave miners and others prior use of water even superior to homesteader grants and other grants by the United States. The courts relied on such laws as evidence of Congressional recognition of the whole appropriation system of water rights.[7]

The appropriation doctrine of water rights differs from the riparian doctrine in several respects in its impact on private rights to clean water. As noted, the basis of an appropriator's right is "beneficial use" rather than land ownership. The concept of "beneficial use" has expanded since the days of the 49ers when it generally meant "mining use." Whatever the specific statutory formulation, the idea that "capture," *i.e.*, appropriation, must be for a beneficial purpose is an idea that seeks to reconcile private use with public interest. The assertion of the quasi public nature of the sanctioned use, however, involves no real notion of public control and nurtured a laissez faire attitude concerning the duties owed to subsequent users of the appropriated waters. The effect of this attitude can be observed by examining the major differences between the two systems, namely the basis of allocation. Riparian owners take

[5] *See* Juan Kinney, The Law of Irrigation, § 596-598.

[6] 12 Stat. 253.

[7] F. Grad, Treatise on Environmental Law, § 3.02, text at notes 91-99.

their rights from the riparian land itself which is generally held to mean that all riparians have equal rights, barring any other intervening factor, to the use of the flow of the water. Appropriators, however, base their claim not on inalienable appurtenant rights, but on their need for water in regions where it is a scarce commodity. Once "beneficial use" is established, it provides an aura of public benefit, and is made on the basis of priority of use and the quantity of the water appropriated. The appropriator takes the quantity of water he diverts from the stream subject only to any prior vested rights in the water. This basis of allocation is not necessarily inconsistent with a private right to clean water. Clearly, subsequent upstream appropriators are barred from polluting a stream to the detriment of prior downstream appropriators. On the other hand, courts have been unwilling, generally, to restrict a prior appropriator's pollution to the quantity of water diverted, an interpretation consistent with priority which would allow a prior appropriator to pollute a stream only in proportion to the amount of water he may rightfully divert.[8] However, there have been few cases which impose such limitations on prior appropriators, and in general the only limit imposed has been that of "reasonableness."[9] A prior appropriator's right may, however, be limited in consequence of interests protected under the "public trust doctrine." The issue has been litigated extensively in California, in *National Audubon Society v. Superior Court.*[10]

Both the riparian and the appropriation systems have undergone a great many modifications in the several states that use them. The increased need for water and the recurrence of water shortages in the northeastern part of the country have given rise to proposals that would move northeastern states more closely in the direction of an appropriation system. It is likely that, eventually, a modified system of appropriation based on filed claims and apportionments may prevail.

For a detailed analysis of different water rights systems, see Clark, 1 Waters and Water Rights 29-36 (1967). For a briefer discussion of water rights, consult Beuscher, Water Rights 79-81 (1967).

PARKER v. AMERICAN WOOLEN CO.

Supreme Judicial Court of Massachusetts (1907)
195 Mass. 591, 81 N.E. 468

BILL IN EQUITY, filed in the Supreme Judicial Court on April 11, 1902, by the owner of a parcel of land through which runs a stream called Beaver Brook, in the town of Dracut, having thereon a paper mill operated by the plaintiff from 1883 continuously for a period of almost twelve years, and

[8] *See* Suffolk Gold Mining & Milling Co. v. San Miguel Consolidated Mining & Milling Co., *infra*, at p. 348.

[9] F. Grad, Treatise on Environmental Law, § 3.02, text at notes 110-119 and cases there cited.

[10] 33 Cal. 3d 419, *appeal denied, sub nom.* Los Angeles v. National Audubon Society, 464 U.S. 888, 14 ELR 10424 (1983).

thereafter operated by another paper manufacturer under a lease from the plaintiff until he was prevented from carrying on the business of manufacturing paper there by the acts of the defendant alleged in the bill, against a corporation manufacturing woollen and other cloths and owning since April, 1899, a large tract of land in Dracut situated on both sides of Beaver Brook and including the bed of the brook, about one and one half miles up the stream from the land and mill owned by the plaintiff, and having thereon large mill buildings, which, with the mill privileges and water rights appertaining thereto, constitute a manufacturing plant known as the Beaver Brook Mills, to restrain the defendant from emptying into Beaver Brook at any point above the premises of the plaintiff dyestuffs, chemicals, industrial or domestic sewage, scourings, acids, compounds of iron or of soap, or any other polluting matter, and from maintaining the height of the dam and flashboards upon its premises above the height at which they had been maintained previous to 1899, and from interfering with the natural flow of the water of Beaver Brook by holding back the water of the brook or otherwise; also praying that there might be an assessment of damages sustained by the plaintiff by reason of the quantities of dyestuffs, chemicals, industrial and domestic sewage, scourings, acids, compounds of iron and soap, and other polluting matter, which had been emptied into the brook from the defendant's premises since the defendant became the owner thereof, and by reason of the holding back of the water of Beaver Brook.

The case was referred to Charles P. Greenough, Esquire, as master. He made a report to which both the plaintiff and the defendant filed exceptions. The case was heard upon the master's report and the exceptions thereto by *Morton*, J., who sustained the exceptions of the plaintiff, and overruled those of the defendant. He ruled that upon the master's report and the evidence the plaintiff was entitled to an injunction restraining the defendant from discharging noxious substances into the stream which flows past the plaintiff's land and thereby corrupting its waters and rendering them unfit for drinking and domestic purposes and other uses. . . .

. . . .

SHELDON, J. It will be convenient in this case to consider first the questions raised by the plaintiff's exceptions to the master's report and to the ruling of the single justice thereon. That ruling was in substance that one riparian proprietor has no right to discharge into a stream substances which will corrupt and foul the waters thereof to the injury of a lower riparian proprietor; that a reasonable use of the waters of a stream by a riparian proprietor does not include the right to make the stream a sewer or to discharge into it such substances and things; and that upon the facts found by the master the plaintiff was entitled to an injunction restraining the defendant from discharging noxious substances into the stream and thereby corrupting its waters and rendering them unfit for drinking, and for domestic and other uses. The master on the other hand ruled (stating together the rulings set forth in his report and those given at the request of the defendant) that the right to discharge waste into a stream and to pollute it, either mechanically or chemically, to a reasonable extent, is one of the incidents to the ownership of land on the banks; that the general principles which govern the abstraction or diversion of water must govern in respect to the deposit of waste matter in a stream, resulting from the processes of manufacturing, that is, that a use of the water may be made which is reasonable under all the circumstances of the case; that what constitutes a reasonable use of water in a stream in respect to the deposit of waste matter therein is a question of fact to be determined from all the circumstances of the case; that every riparian proprietor on a stream has the right to have the water come to him in its natural condition except so far as it is affected by a reasonable use of their property by the owners or riparian proprietors above, and that in determining whether such use of water in a stream with respect to its pollution is reasonable all the circumstances should be considered, and more particularly the size and character of the stream, its condition, volume and rapidity, the density of the population on its banks; the use to which the stream has been, is and can be applied, the state of improvement of the country in regard to mills and machinery, and the use of water as a propelling power; the established usages of the country in similar cases and the needs, usages and wants of the community; the necessity or importance of the use claimed by the defendant; and the extent of the benefit to him as compared with the extent of the injury to the other party.

He also ruled that one who is asserting a right which at the time does no damage, but which may operate by long continuance to destroy or diminish the right of the plaintiff, even if that right is not then exercised by the plaintiff and there is no present intention of exercising it, will be restrained by injunction but that injunction will not be granted to restrain a nuisance when the result would be inequitable.

It is difficult, if not impossible, to reconcile all the decisions which have been made upon the question of the right of riparian proprietors to use the waters of streams flowing through or along their lands. This is a common right, and each must exercise it with all due regard to the rights of others, and each must submit to that degree of inconvenience and hardship in the exercise of his rights which results from the existence of like rights in others. In such cases, each proprietor is entitled to use the stream in such reasonable manner, according to the usages and wants of the community, as will not be inconsistent with a like use by other proprietors above and below him. Cases in which the proprietors of sawmills have been allowed to throw sawdust and similar refuse into the streams, frequently for the reason that the mills practically could not be run unless this was allowed to a reasonable extent, generally have been put upon the same ground. But permission to do this has been refused where it was found to make the water impure and unfit for drinking and domestic purposes; *Lewis v. Stein*, 16 Ala. 214; and the tendency of the later decisions is to restrict somewhat the liberality of the original rule. And in *Canfield v. Andrew*, *supra*, the court is careful to say in its opinion that no one is allowed to deposit any substance in a running stream that will pollute its waters to the injury of a lower riparian proprietor.

It is of course true that many of the uses which properly may be made of the water of a natural stream by the upper riparian proprietors will be likely to tend somewhat to defile the water. . . .

We regard it however as settled that no riparian proprietor has the right to use the waters of a natural stream for such purposes or in such a manner as will materially corrupt it to the substantial injury of a lower proprietor, or to cast or discharge into it noxious and deleterious substances which will tend to defile the water and make it unfit for use. . . .

The right to use the stream to carry away mere waste matter in a reasonable manner and to a reasonable extent is not so to be extended as to include a right to discharge into the stream noxious and deleterious matter to such an extent as sensibly and materially to foul the water and destroy its purity and fitness to be used by others.

It is true that there is in any large body of water a purifying principle which will, either by ordinary sedimentary deposit or by chemical change, obviate the evil effects which otherwise would arise from the deposit therein of some limited amount of noxious matter. Accordingly it is not for every small deposit of such matter that the law will give a remedy. . . . And it follows from what we have already said that the plaintiff is entitled to an injunction which will restrain the defendant from discharging into the stream any noxious or offensive substances to such an amount or in such a quantity as to affect noticeably or appreciably the purity of the water when it reaches the plaintiff's premises so as to render it materially less fit for drinking or for other uses than it was when it entered the defendant's premises. The court can fix no standard of reasonable use which will be more favorable to the defendant, or restrict any further the terms of the injunction to be issued. The defendant must at its peril see that it does not overpass this limit.

Nor can an injunction properly be refused on the ground of the magnitude of the defendant's interests and the importance of its business. . . .

SUFFOLK GOLD MINING & MILLING CO. v. SAN MIGUEL CONSOLIDATED MINING & MILLING CO.

Court of Appeals of Colorado (1897)
9 Colo. App. 407, 48 P.2d 828

BISSELL, J., delivered the opinion of the court.

This case presents an entirely new phase of what it well, though somewhat inaccurately, termed the "rights of riparian proprietors along the streams in this state." . . .

Two corporations attempted to acquire rights to water flowing in Howard's Fork of the San Miguel river, in San Miguel county. The Suffolk Gold Mining & Milling Company built a stamp mill on the creek, and diverted the water flowing in the creek, and applied it as power to run the stamps, jigs, and concentrators used in connection with their reduction works, as well as to furnish water under the stamps to flow the crushed metal over the amalgamating plates, the tables of the jigs, and through the concentrators; discharging the water, after its use, into a ditch, through which it ultimately returned into the creek. The evidence tended to show that this company had been using the mill for some years, though in their earlier operations it was very much smaller, and was not increased to its present size until about the years 1892 and 1893. . . .

. . . .

The rights of The San Miguel Consolidated Mining & Milling Company, so far as respects the water flowing in Howard's Fork, were initiated about the year 1890. This company was a corporation organized for the purpose of furnishing power and light to various mines in its neighborhood, and also to furnish light for the town of Telluride, near which the works of the company were situated. When this company first started its operations, it took its power and water from Lake Fork of the San Miguel river. In 1890, to extend and complete their plant, and for the purpose of enlarging its power and increasing its capacity, they built a dam at the headgate, and ran a pipe line to their plant, and took water from Howard's Fork. The plant was a very extensive one, and its construction involved the outlay of a very large amount of money. The pipe line ran several miles, and discharged the water onto a Pelton wheel, and thus furnished ample power to run the plant, and supply electric power and light to their customers and to the city. After this line had been running for some time, the San Miguel Company discovered that the nozzle at the end of the pipe line, through which the water was discharged onto the wheel, was being rapidly worn away, and that the buckets were being worn and destroyed, and that leakages were occurring at various points along the pipe line, which, being investigated, turned out to come from the wearing away and destruction of the connections in the pipe. Further investigations led the San Miguel Company to believe that all this danger and difficulty proceeded from the condition of the water as it was taken in at the headgate, and that the stamp mill which was located above them was causing all the damage. This whole subject was investigated during the progress of the trial, and the testimony tended to show that the Suffolk Company crushed the ore under its stamps, carried it over their plates and jigging tables, and into their concentrating mills, and that the tilings which resulted flowed off with the water, and down into Howard's creek and mingled with the general waters of the stream. The ore was crushed sufficiently fine to pass through screens of 45 or 55 mesh, and practically all the material crushed was ultimately discharged into the water of Howard's Fork, only an infinitesimal amount of the metal value of the ore being retained in the process.

The evidence disclosed that Howard's Fork was a very considerable stream; its volume at the point where the tailings were discharged into the stream amounting to 250 or 300 cubic feet per minute, while the amount used by the stamp mill to carry off the tailings rarely, if ever, exceeded 8 cubic feet per minute. When the cause of the damage was ascertained, the Milling Company were requested to remedy the difficulty and remove the cause. This they declined to do. It was insisted by them that they were the first comers on Howard's Fork, were appropriators, under the statute, of the waters in the stream, to the extent of their user, and they had a right to use the stream as they chose, and that the subsequent comer must take the water flowing down the fork as he found it when he came, and that he was without right to complain because of the pollution of the waters, or the method of use. Thereupon this action was begun by the San Miguel Company to restrain the

Suffolk Company from polluting the water. The case came on for hearing, was tried by the court, and a vast amount of testimony taken relative to the cause of the injury, the rights of the respective parties as prior and subsequent appropriators, and likewise on the proposition whether the Suffolk Company could impound the water as it was discharged from the mill, and thereby avoid the injury of which the plaintiff complained.

In stating these matters of fact, we follow the findings of the trial court. There is evidence in the record to sustain them, and we therefore treat them as conclusive. There was a great deal of evidence offered respecting the difficulty and expense of impounding the water, whereby the damage would be entirely, or at least substantially, avoided. The court found that this might easily and readily be done, and that, if the Suffolk Company should impound its water as it was discharged from the mill, it would very shortly settle, and all the grit, quartz, and fine sand, which had theretofore been discharged into Howard's Fork, would be retained, and the water used in the mill, subject to a very slight loss in quantity, would be returned in its original state of purity to the fork, along which it had been accustomed to run. . . .

. . . .

It thus becomes apparent that the pleadings and the proof present the very sharply-defined issue respecting the title which an appropriator of the waters of this state acquires by acts duly performed under the constitution and statutes regulating its acquisition, and the rights which he does or may acquire with reference to other appropriators along the line of the stream, though subsequent in time. This is the sole question argued in the briefs, and therefore the only one we need consider. . . .

. . . .

The question under consideration has not been made the subject of any judicial determination in this or any other state, and we are necessarily compelled to resort to those of a kindred and analogous character in order to determine whether therefrom we can derive the true principle by which the rights of these parties must be settled.

An "appropriator" (using this term in its full and absolute sense, and to include both a diverson and an application, both of which are essential to the completion of a title to water) acquires a right of property in that which he has appropriated. It is a right in one sense absolute, and in another qualified; at least, qualified as to its rights with respect to third persons. The supreme court decided in the *Strickler Case*, 16 Colo. 61, that what the appropriator acquires is "property," in the general signification of the term, and that the appropriator acquires a title and right which is in no sense appurtenant to the land to which the water has been applied, and probably not appurtenant to any use which he may make of it. It is capable of severance and transfer, may be applied by the appropriator to other lands and to other uses, and the purchaser may apply or use it on other lands and for other purposes than those to which it was originally put, and retain title, dating it as from the time of the original diversion and application. The court did not go so far as to hold that it was an absolute title and a complete right, subject to no limitations and conditions; nor did the court attempt to hold that this water right might be sold by the original appropriator, and diverted entirely from the stream, or its purity be destroyed. No such question was before the court, nor did it attempt to declare what the law would be under such circumstances. The opinion is equally silent as to the relative rights of the prior and subsequent locators on the stream. As we take it, the title to the waters of the state always remains, in a measurable sense, in the people, and any citizen has a right to use the waters flowing along the streams within our boundaries for any of the uses which the constitution recognizes. The appropriator may acquire title, but that title is necessarily subject to many conditions. This consideration shows it not to be the absolute title which one acquires to personal property either by original discovery or by purchase. For instance, it is subject to loss by abandonment. A party who locates on a stream, and diverts and applies the water, has a title, so long as he continues to use it, either for the purposes for which it was originally diverted, or for any legitimate purpose. Yet no one would dispute the proposition that if the appropriator abandons the use, whether it be the original or any subsequent one, he would thereby lose all title, and the right to the water would revert to the people, and would belong to whomsoever might thereafter appropriate it, and would likewise inure to the benefit of any subsequent locator on the stream who by reason of the abandonment might become both prior in time and prior in right. This demonstrates very conclusively that the title is not absolute, and that the appropriator's rights are relative. It must be conceded that the title is so far absolute that if the first appropriator runs the water onto his land, and devotes it to the purposes of husbandry, any diminution of the volume or amount of water would be an inconvenience to which subsequent locators must undoubtedly be subject. If some of it was devoted to manufacturing purposes, and in any wise the volume of water was diminished, and probably if its character was unavoidably affected by the nature of the use to which it had been put by the prior appropriator, when no question of preferential, constitutional or statutory rights arose between the parties, the subsequent locator further down the stream, or further up, must of necessity acquire his right subject to these modifications and conditions. In this sense, the appropriator's title may be regarded as a *quasi* absolute one, and his rights as superior to those of the late comer. For these reasons it is manifestly impossible to apply the law of riparian proprietors to the settlement of the legal status of two appropriators on the same stream. Riparian rights flow from, an are incident to, the ownership of the land through which the stream runs. The riparian proprietor is without title to the water. There was no known way at the common law whereby he could acquire title, unless it was by an actual grant, or by a prescription from which a grant would be presumed, whereby he would be entitled, perhaps, to a use freed from obligations with reference either to the property up or down the stream, as might happen to be the case. While this is true, and the title which the appropriator acquires comes from an observance of the constitutional and statutory requirements, and is not at all dependent on the ownership of riparian lands, yet since his title is a modified one, and his rights are, under some circumstances, subject to limitations and conditions with respect to prior and subsequent appropriators, we see no reason why some of the principles which have been thoroughly settled in many jurisdictions respecting riparian rights may not be applied to the determination of the relative rights of the appropriators along the line of the streams in Colorado. Take the present case, as a very apt illustration of a condition in which the rights of the appropriators should be deemed relative, and not absolute, even with reference to a subsequent locator further down the stream. In the present case the first appropriator neither undertook to appropriate, nor did he acquire by his acts an absolute title to, the entire stream. According to the findings of the court, the Suffolk Milling Company only utilized, in disposing of their tailings, about 8 cubic feet per minute. The total volume of the stream was from 250 to 300 cubic feet per minute at any stage of water which experience had found to run in Howard's Fork. Whatever title and whatever right the prior appropriator acquired which is here involved or under consideration related and extended only to the 8 cubic feet, and in no manner affected the balance of the water running in the stream. In other words, his title and his right covered only his necessary application for these purposes, and could neither be taken to control, limit, vary, or modify the rights of the subsequent locator as to the balance of the water in the stream. The unappropriated volume of water flowing down Howard's Fork was undoubtedly subject to subsequent appropriation, and after comers might, equally with the first, acquire a title to the waters thus unappropriated and left flowing in the stream. The subsequent appropriators must have some rights, and the prior appropriators must be subject to the rights wich the after locator may acquire; and in this sense, if in no other, the right and title of the first comer must be taken as subject to conditions and limitations. In this case we are to determine simply to what conditions and what limitations the prior appropriators' title was necessarily subject, under the evidence disclosed by the record. It plainly appears by the proof, and the court found, that the first appropriation was for the purpose of a stamp mill. The uses of such a mill, and its purposes, are well understood in this state. It is a mill erected for the reduction of ore. The quartz is put under the stamps, crushed to a fineness requisite to the general plan of reduction, and the whole mass and bulk is put into such a condition as by amalgamating plates, jigging tables, or concentrators, the valuable product may be extracted, and the refuse must necessarily flow from this reducing machinery, and pass off in the water, whether used as power to run the stamps, or as power to carry off the tailings. This was the use, this the purpose, and, as between these two litigants, there is no question of preferential rights. The Suffolk Company undoubtedly acquired a title, and likewise became possessed of the right to use what water they acquired by their diversion and appropriation, both for the purpose of furnishing power to run the machinery and power to dispose of the tailings.

The troublesome question still remains, whether this right was an absolute one, and whether the application of the water for the removal of the tailings extended so far as to permit them, at their will and pleasure, to discharge those tailings into the stream, whatever might be the effect on subsequent locators. We think the evidence destroyed this conclusion, for the court found that these tailings were composed of fine, quartz-like, gritty, cutting material, which, flowing into the main body of the stream through the ditch of the Milling Company, mixed with the general volume of the water which was not so used, flowed down the stream into the pipe line of the San Miguel Company, cut out the joints of the pipe, wore out the nozzles and the buckets of the wheel, and produced a constant and daily damage to the lower locators and subsequent appropriators. The question thus recurs, was this a damage for which there is a remedy, and are the rights of the prior appropriator subject to any limitation with respect thereto. It was the law with respect to riparian owners that their use was subject to certain limitations, among which was the preservation of the general volume of the stream for the lower riparian owners, who had the right to receive that volume of water unpolluted, and in its natural condition of purity. It must remain fit for the use of the lower riparian owner.

. . . .

Parties have been permitted to mine their own lands, but even thereon and therein they have been restrained from erecting pumping plants, hoisting water to the surface, discharging it into a stream, and letting it flow to their neighbors in such way as to injure the use and destroy the right which the lower owner had theretofore enjoyed. . . .

If this be the law with reference to riparian proprietors, the only remaining question is whether, in a case like the present one, prior appropriators of the waters of a stream in Colorado acquire a title subject to similar conditions with reference to subsequent locators. . . .

. . . .

Suffolk Company acquired title so far as regards a detrimental use to less than one thirtieth of the water of the stream. The balance of it was open to subsequent locators, who were, equally with the first comer, entitled to divert and apply it. Under these circumstances, we are quite of the opinion that the title and rights of the prior appropriating company were not absolute, but conditional, and they were obligated to so use the water that subsequent locators might, like lower riparian owners, receive the balance of the stream unpolluted, and fit for the uses to which they might desire to put it. This, of course, is subject to the condition that the circumstances and situation of the use and the application were such as to permit the preservation of the remaining volume of the stream in its original condition. We do not undertake to decide that, if the prior appropriator had put the property to a use under circumstances which rendered it impossible for him to enjoy it without some detriment to the unappropriated water, he might not have the right to thus use it. Such is not this case. The court found, as a matter of fact, that it was possible for the Suffolk Company to impound their water in settling basins, which the configuration of the country permitted, and thereafter discharge it, freed from its impurity, into the general body of the stream. The obligation and duty of the riparian proprietor in cases of this description has been recognized in many adjudications. As the books put it, it is a question of reasonable use, and the possibility of a fair and legitimate enjoyment of riparian rights, coupled with the preservation of the rights and title of the lower riparian owner. . . .

We see no reason why this same principle should not be applied in the settlement of the rights of appropriators of the public waters of this state. It undoubtedly carries out the intention and the purpose of our constitutional provision which in general terms reserves to the people of the state the right to all the waters of its streams for the purposes to which the citizens may apply them. We live in a region not blessed with rains, and where all our industries, whether agricultural, manufacturing, or mining, are dependent absolutely on the waters of our streams, as to those purposes for which water is a necessity. It is therefore quite consonant with the apparent purpose and declared will of the people to subject the rights of the appropriators of the public waters of the state to such limitations as shall tend not only to conserve the property interests which the appropriators may acquire, but to preserve the remaining unappropriated waters in their original condition for the use and benefit of late comers, who by their labors and industry may further develop our interests and resources. We believe the principle just, and we believe it applicable. . . .

NOTE

Suffolk Gold Mining has been cited and relied on for its general holding, but it does not appear to have been followed with respect to the point that an appropriation of a certain amount of water does not authorize the appropriator to return the water in such a condition as to cause the pollution of a significantly greater amount.

GLOBE AIRCRAFT CORP. v. THOMPSON

Texas Court of Civil Appeals, Fort Worth (1947)
203 S.W.2d 865

McDONALD, Chief Justice.

Appellee B.G. Thompson was plaintiff in the court below, and appellant Globe Aircraft Corporation was defendant.

The case made by plaintiff's pleadings, as narrowed by the issues submitted to the jury, is somewhat as follows: From the month of April, 1944, until the latter part of 1945, plaintiff occupied under lease a tract of land north of Fort Worth, on which he operated a dairy. From April of 1944 until June of 1945 some of plaintiff's cows died, and others depreciated in value, and plaintiff suffered a net loss in revenue derived from sale of milk, all as a result of the negligence of defendant in permitting chromic acid to escape from its manufacturing plant located near plaintiff's dairy. The case alleged is that the acid flowed into a creek on the land leased by plaintiff, and that his cows were poisoned by the polluted water in the creek.

Some of the jury findings will be noticed more in detail later in the opinion, but it may be said here that the findings were in part favorable to plaintiff, and that judgment was rendered on the verdict that plaintiff recover damages in the sum of $4,425. Defendant has appealed, relying on nine points of error.

. . . .

First, it is argued that the court should have instructed a verdict for defendant because there was no testimony showing that there was sufficient chromic acid in the waters of the creek to cause injury to plaintiff's cattle. Plaintiff undoubtedly tried the case in the court below, and still contends here, that his cattle began to suffer injury from the pollution of the creek within a short time after he moved onto the leased land in April of 1944. A sample of water was taken from the creek in April of 1945, and other samples were taken in June and later in the summer of that year. Those samples were analyzed by chemists, and found to contain chromic acid. The least chromic acid content shown by the analyses was 7.8 parts of acid to one million parts of water, the greatest content was 31 parts of acid to one million parts of water. Some of the expert witnesses testified that chromic acid was poisonous, but none of them testified as to the amount of acid which would be required to render the water injurious to the cattle. In other words, there is no expert testimony that water with chromic acid content of the amount shown by the chemical analyses would be injurious to cattle. Opposed to defendant's argument is the theory advanced by plaintiff to the effect that the poisonous nature of the polluted water may reasonably be inferred from the known fact that chromic acid was in the water, from the fact that the cattle suffered injury, and from the fact that the evidence excludes the likelihood of injury from any other cause. Since we have concluded that the judgment of the trial court must be reversed for other reasons, and since the proof may not be the same on another trial, we shall forego further discussion of this question except to say that we are unwilling, in view of the entire record, to render judgment for defendant on this ground.

Defendant also contends that there is no evidence showing that defendant was negligent in permitting chromic acid to escape from its plant onto plaintiff's premises. We overrule this contention. The proof is sufficient to show that defendant used chromic acid in a solution into which various metal parts were dipped in a cleaning process; that the metal parts were then dipped into a vat of rinsing water; that about once a day the water from the rinsing vat was emptied, and that this water would accumulate chromic acid; that the water from the rinsing vat was emptied into a roadside ditch, and then flowed a comparatively short distance into the creek in question. The evidence is sufficient to show that defendant knew of the polluted nature of the contents of the rinsing vat, and knew that it flowed into the creek and onto plaintiff's premises. The evidence was sufficient to raise a jury issue as to negligence vel non.

The fourth and fifth points of error will be considered together. Under the fourth it is contended that an instructed verdict should have been ordered, and under the fifth it is contended that judgment should have been rendered non obstante veredicto, for the reasons which will appear from our discussion of the points. As has been said, plaintiff moved onto the premises in question in April of 1944. He operated his establishment as a dairy until the month of January, 1945, when he ceased to sell milk. He continued to keep some cattle on the premises for several more months, finally selling the cattle he had left in or about the month of August. From the witness stand plaintiff declared that he did not seek recovery from defendant of any damages occurring after June 22, 1945, because the stream had then become polluted by oil escaping from the premises of another nearby industrial plant. Although plaintiff argues to the contrary in his brief, it is our opinion after a painstaking review of the record that the evidence shows without dispute that defendant did not begin the use of chromic acid in its plant, and did not permit the escape of such acid from its plant, prior to the month of November of 1944, or at the earliest, prior to the latter part of October, 1944. As we have said, plaintiff pleaded and tried his case on the theory that his cattle began to suffer damage from chromic acid poisoning within a short time after he moved onto the premises in April of 1944, and the evidence of damage offered by plaintiff related to the loss of and depreciation in value of cows, and the loss of milk production, before as well as after October of 1944. Defendant's theory is that, in view of the undisputed evidence as to the date when defendant first began the use of chromic acid, and in view of the fact that the evidence provides no basis for segregating the damages suffered before such date from the damages suffered afterwards, there is no basis for a finding by the jury nor for an award of partial damages for the injuries suffered after defendant began the use of the chromic acid and commenced the dumping of it in the roadside ditch which led to the creek. Defendant cites cases like *Pitzer & West v. Thigpen*, Tex.Civ.App., 68 S.W.2d 324, writ dismissed; and *Tucker Oil Co. v. Matthews*, Tex.Civ.App., 119 S.W.2d 606. In such cases it is held that where there is no basis for determining how much of the damages suffered resulted from the wrongful acts of the defendant, and how much resulted from other causes, a judgment would be based on mere conjecture, and could not be upheld. The rule is applicable in the present case. However, we cannot say that it appears from the record that plaintiff might not on another trial be able to segregate his damages by proper proof, and thus be entitled to recover such of his damages as occurred after defendant began to pollute the stream, provided, of course, it also be shown that such damages resulted from wrongful acts of the defendant. To quote from the language of the Supreme Court, in *Hall v. Rawls*, 141 Tex. 235, 171 S.W.2d 324, 327: "The cause will be remanded rather than rendered, because it appears that the justice of the case demands another trial." . . .

Issue No. 5 read as follows:

"Do you find from a preponderance of the evidence that as a direct result of chromic acid coming onto the lands in question, that the plaintiff's net revenue, if any, from the sale of milk from his cows was decreased?" Issue No. 6 inquired as to the amount of such loss. Other issues inquired as to the depreciation in value of certain cattle. It is seen that the court submitted the case to the jury on the theory that there was evidence to support a finding that chromic acid was escaping during the entire time plaintiff occupied the premises. We have held that the evidence shows without dispute that no acid escaped before October or November of 1944 (there may be some slight evidence that the escape of acid began in October). The verdict therefore, may include damages for injuries suffered before the date when defendant began the use of chromic acid. For reasons similar to those given in our discussion of the fourth and fifth points of error, we hold that the evidence was not sufficient to support the verdict. . . .

. . . .

The judgment of the trial court is reversed and the cause is remanded for another trial.

LANDERS v. EAST TEXAS SALT WATER DISPOSAL CO.

Texas Supreme Court (1952)
151 Tex. 251, 248 S.W.2d 731

MR. JUSTICE CALVERT delivered the opinion of the Court.

Suit by C.H. Landers, plaintiff, against East Texas Salt Water Disposal Company and Sun Oil Company, defendants, seeking a joint and several judgment of damages and injunctive relief was dismissed as to the damages feature by the trial court, when, after the defendants' plea in abatement asserting a misjoinder of parties and of causes of action had been sustained, the plaintiff declined to replead so as to assert several liability only against each of the defendants in separate suits. The Court of Civil Appeals affirmed. 242 S.W.2d 236.

In his petition plaintiff alleged that he was the owner of a small lake which he had drained, cleaned and stocked with fish at considerable expense; that defendant East Texas Salt Water Disposal Company was the owner of a pipe line which traversed land adjoining plaintiff's land on the west and into which the defendant pumped approximately 1500 barrels of salt water daily; that on or about April 1, 1949, such pipe line broke and the defendant Disposal Company negligently permitted some 10,000 to 15,000 barrels of salt water to escape from the line and to flow over plaintiff's land and into his lake, killing his fish and otherwise injuring and damaging him. Plaintiff further alleged that the defendant Sun Oil Company was the owner of an oil well, located a short distance from plaintiff's property line, from which the defendant pumped small quantities of oil and large quantities of salt water each day, the oil and salt water being carried off through a pipe line which for some distance ran parallel to a spring branch; that the branch crossed plaintiff's property and emptied into his lake; that on or about April 1, 1949, the pipe line broke and the defendant Sun Oil Company negligently permitted large quantities of oil and salt water to escape and run into the branch and thence into plaintiff's lake, killing his fish and otherwise injuring and damaging him.

When the trial judge sustained the plea in abatement he did not dismiss the suit as he would have done before the adoption of Texas Rules of Civil Procedure, but rather ordered a severance, leaving on the docket under the original cause number, 10472, that part of the suit seeking injunctive relief against both defendants, ordering that plaintiff's suit for damages against Sun Oil Company be docketed as Cause Number 10472A and that his suit for damages against East Texas Salt Water Disposal Company be docketed as Number 10472B. Plaintiff excepted to the action of the court and declined to replead his case. His cause of action for damages was thereupon dismissed.

Much of defendants' brief in this court is devoted to the general proposition that in refusing to replead the plaintiff lost his right to complain of the order of dismissal. It is the theory of respondents that orderly procedure required the plaintiff to replead when ordered to do so, proceed to trial in one of the severed cases of damages and appeal only when he had lost the case, assigning as error on such appeal the action of the court in ordering the severance and in requiring the repleader.

A plea of misjoinder, though sustained, can no longer in itself result in a dismissal. Rule 41, T.R.C.P., specifically so provides. Assuming that there was a misjoinder of parties and causes of action, the order entered by the trial court was in all respects in keeping with the provisions of Rule 41, and was perfectly proper. On the other hand, if there was no such misjoinder and it was error to order the severance and repleader, the plaintiff was within his rights in declining to replead and in declining to proceed through a futile and fruitless trial in order to test the correctness of the ruling. The plaintiff was asserting a joint and several cause of action for damages against the two defendants and when the trial court ordered a severance of the cause so that plaintiff's suit asserting joint and several liability of the two defendants could no longer be tried, the plaintiff's case was terminated just as effectively as if it had been dismissed. The plaintiff was not required under the circumstances of this case to replead and try a case wholly different from that asserted by him in order to obtain appellate review of his right to pursue to trial the case made by his pleadings.

Did the plaintiff in his pleading allege facts which, if established by evidence, made the defendants jointly and severally liable for plaintiff's damages? From the face of the petition it appears that there was no concert of action or unity of design between the defendants in the commission of their alleged tortious acts, an absence said by the court in the case of Sun Oil Co. et al v. Robicheaux et al, Tex. Com. App., 23 S.W. 2d 713 to be determinative of the nonexistence of joint liability. In that case the rule was thus stated:

"The rule is well established in this state, and supported by almost universal authority, that an action at law for damages for torts cannot be maintained against several defendants jointly, when each acted independently of the others and there was no concert or unity of design between them. In such a case the tort of each defendant is several when committed, and it does not become joint because afterwards its consequences, united with the consequences of several other torts committed by other persons in producing damages. Under such circumstances, each tort-feasor is liable only for the part of the injury or damages caused by his own wrong; that is, where a person contributes to an injury along with others, he must respond in damages, but if he acts independently, and not in concert of action with other persons in causing such injury, he is liable only for the damages which directly and proximately result from his own act, and the fact that it may be difficult to define the damages caused by the wrongful act of each person who independently contributed to the final result does not affect the rule. *Sun Co. v. Wyatt*, 48 Tex. Civ. App., 349, 107 S.W. 934; 38 Cyc. 484; 26 R.C.L. 766."

It may be noted that the opinion of the Commission of Appeals in the Robicheaux case was not adopted by the Supreme Court. Nevertheless, it has been generally recognized as having correctly stated the law of this state . . . and it was specifically cited and followed by the Court of Civil Appeals in deciding this case.

Undoubtedly the general rule adopted and followed in the Robicheaux case is adequately supported by respectable authority, though it may be doubted that it is as universally approved as is there indicated. A casual reading of the cited texts will demonstrate that different writers have different ways of stating the rule, each with somewhat different implications, and that they differ also in what constitutes majority sentiment. But with the exception of Oklahoma and Kansas, the courts of the country seem to be virtually unanimous in refusing to impose joint and several liability on multiple wrongdoers whose independent tortious acts interfere with a landowner's interest in the use and enjoyment of land by interfering with his air or water. Restatement of the Law of Torts, Vol. 4, p. 449, sec. 881; Cooley on Torts, 4th Edition, Vol. 1, pp. 283-287; 9 A.L.R. 947-952; 35 A.L.R. 412; 91 A.L.R. 763-765.

Much has been written on the need for re-examination of the rule approved in the Robicheaux case. *See* Wigmore in 17 Illinois Law Review 458; 27 Columbia Law Review 764, Gendel in 19 California Law Review 630; Prosser in 25 California Law Review 413; Jackson in 17 Texas Law Review 399; Robinson in 27 Texas Law Review 732. Thus far, however, but little has been achieved toward inducing the courts to re-examine the rule. Wigmore has suggested that the rule of joint and several liability in the field of torts had its inception in the need of the law, bent on justice, to relieve a plaintiff of the intolerable burden of proving what share each of two wrongdoers contributed to the plaintiff's injuries, and that the burden is just as intolerable and the need for relief therefrom is just as great when the independent tortious acts of multiple defendants contribute to a plaintiff's indivisible injuries as when the acts are done in concert and of common design. 17 Illinois Law Review 459.

The rule of the Robicheaux case, strictly followed, has made it impossible for a plaintiff, though gravely injured, to secure relief in the nature of damages through a joint and several judgment by joining in one suit as defendants all wrongdoers whose independent tortious acts have joined in producing an injury to the plaintiff, which, although theoretically divisible, as a practical matter and realistically considered is in fact but a single indivisible injury. As interpreted by the Courts of Civil Appeals the rule also denies to a plaintiff the right to proceed to judgment and satisfaction against the wrongdoers separately because in such a suit he cannot discharge the burden of proving with sufficient certainty, under pertinent rules of damages, the portion of the injury attributable to each defendant. [Citations omitted.] Thus at the time he filed his suit the plaintiff in this case was confronted with a declared status of the law in this state which effectively relieved the two defendants of the consequences of their wrongs and required the innocent plaintiff to suffer his injuries without recompense. Whether he insisted on standing on his joint and several suit against the defendants or bowed to the ruling of the trial court and proceeded against the defendants separately, he could not prevail. In other words, our courts seem to have embraced the philosophy, inherent in this class of decisions, that it is better that the injured party lose all of his damages than that any of several wrongdoers should pay more of the damages than he individually and separately caused. If such has been the law, from the standpoint of justice it should not have been; if it is the law now, it will not be hereafter. The case of *Sun Oil Co. v. Robicheaux* is overruled. Where the tortious acts of two or more wrongdoers join to produce an indivisible injury, that is, an injury which from its nature cannot be apportioned with reasonable certainty to the individual wrongdoers, all of the wrongders will be held jointly and severally liable for the entire damages and the injured party may proceed to judgment against any one separately or against all in one suit. If fewer than the whole number of wrongdoers are joined as defendants to plaintiff's suit, those joined may by proper cross action under the governing rules bring in those omitted. To permit the joinder as defendants of such wrongdoers without at the same time imposing joint liability upon them would not relieve the inequities of the situation nor cure the ills of the plaintiff. Simple procedural joinder of the defendants would put the plaintiff in no better position to produce the required proof of the portion of the injury attributable to each of the defendants. In most such cases, under the decisions heretofore cited, he would still be the victim of an instructed verdict. It would be of no comfort or advantage to the plaintiff that the instructed verdict relieved all of the defendants of liability in one suit at one time rather than in separate suits and one at a time.

Under the rule here announced, the allegations of plaintiff's petition were sufficient to assert a case of joint and several liability against the defendants. It follows that there was no misjoinder of either parties or causes of action. Rule 40, T.R.C.P.

. . . .

In spite of the rule announced in the Robicheaux case our courts have long since sanctioned the imposition of joint and several liability in negligent collision cases where there was neither concert of action nor unity of design. . . .

There is, of course, no joint liability for damages for the loss of trees and grass killed by the salt water escaping from the pipe line owned by East Texas Salt Water Disposal Company before such water entered the lake. It was not a misjoinder, however, to include this as an item of recovery sought in this suit.

The judgment of the Court of Civil Appeals and of the trial court are reversed and the cause is remanded to the trial court for further proceedings not inconsistent with this opinion.

[Dissenting opinion omitted]

SPRINGER v. JOSEPH SCHLITZ BREWING COMPANY

United States Court of Appeals, Fourth Circuit (1975)
510 F.2d 468

BUTZNER, Circuit Judge:

This North Carolina diversity case raises the question of the liability of an industry to downstream riparian owners when its wastes overload a city's treatment facilities and cause water pollution. The plaintiffs, David and Diana Springer, own an interest in a large farm on the Yadkin River. Seeking an injunction and compensatory and punitive damages, they contend that, beginning in late 1969, wastes from a new brewery owned by Joseph B. Schlitz Brewing Company in Winston-Salem, North Carolina, overloaded the city's sewage treatment plant, causing it to pollute the Yadkin and interfere with their riparian rights. The Springers introduced evidence, which, viewed in the light most favorable to them, showed that Schlitz knew, or in the exercise of reasonable care should have known, that the city sewage plant lacked the capacity to treat the brewery's waste; that in discussions with the city, Schlitz underestimated the quantity and harmfulness of the waste; and that the company violated the city sewage ordinance. The evidence also established that in the spring and summer of 1970, after Schlitz reached full production, inadequately treated sewage from the overloaded plant caused six unprecedented fish kills and otherwise impaired the quality of the Yadkin River.

At the close of the Springers' case, the court directed a verdict for Schlitz on the ground that North Carolina absolves the user of a municipal sewer system of liability for the city's failure to adequately treat its sewage. We reverse because we believe the case is controlled by exceptions to North Carolina's rule of immunity.

I.

In North Carolina, a riparian landowner has a right to the agricultural, recreational, and scenic use and enjoyment of the stream bordering his land, subject, however, to the rights of upstream riparian owners to make reasonable use of the water without excessively diminishing its quality. Though he does not own the fish in the stream, the riparian owner's rights include the opportunity to catch them. Interference with riparian rights is an actionable tort, and a riparian owner may join several polluters as joint tort-feasors. *See generally*, Aycock, Introduction to Water Use Law in North Carolina, 46 N.C.L. Rev. 1, 11-13 (1967).

Nevertheless, an industry that uses a municipal sewage system to dispose of its waste is not liable to a riparian landowner for the pollution caused by the city's failure to provide adequate treatment. . . .

The Springers claim that their proof is sufficient to invoke exceptions to the general rule of immunity. Specifically, they contend that Schlitz should be held liable if it violated the city sewage ordinance, or if Schlitz knew, or should have known, of the inability of the city to adequately treat the brewery's wastes. Since no North Carolina court has considered these exceptions, we must determine the common law of the state by examining the rationale for the established rule, developments on this point in other states, and analogous areas of the state's common law.

II.

In February 1970 the City of Winston-Salem enacted a comprehensive sewage ordinance to take effect in May. The ordinance requires every user of industrial sewers to have a discharge permit. Users may discharge only wastes containing 2500 ppm BOD or less, and they are forbidden to release sewage containing a wide variety of dangerous or difficult-to-treat substances. The ordinance imposes surcharges for BOD pound loadings caused by a concentration above 300 ppm. Originally, it allowed the city to furnish advice and technical assistance, but it did not provide for variances or exemptions. By state law, its violation is a misdemeanor.

Schlitz's effluent contained more than 2500 ppm BOD until April 1971. Beginning in May 1970, the city billed, and Schlitz paid, all BOD surcharges. The brewery and other industries, however, were allowed to operate in violation of the ordinance and without permits as long as they submitted schedules for compliance and conformed to them. It received its permit, one of the first issued to any industry, in May 1971.

The violation of a municipal sewage ordinance which is intended to protect downstream riparian owners can subject an industrial sewage source to private civil liability. *Hampton v. Spindale*, 210 N.C. 546, 548, 187 S.E. 775, 776 (1936), expressly restricts freedom from liability to those persons who use the sewers "in the way prescribed by law." Although this is dictum, it is consistent with the rationale for the private user's immunity. When an industry turns over the control of its sewage to the city, it can reasonably expect that the city will safeguard riparian property by effective treatment. But it is not reasonable for an industry to expect a city to safely treat prohibited sewage. Consequently, the reason for granting immunity does not then apply.

This reading of *Hampton* conforms to North Carolina's general law regarding the effect of regulatory legislation on civil liability. The state is firmly committed to the proposition that the "violation of a statute designed to protect persons or property is a negligent act, and if such negligence proximately causes injury, the violator is liable." *Murray v. Bensen Aircraft Corp.*, 259 N.C. 638, 131 S.E.2d 367 (1963) (federal aircraft safety statute); *accord*, *Bell v. Page*, 271 N.C. 396, 156 S.E.2d 711 (1967) (town ordinance regulating private swimming pools). The statute or ordinance, serving as a legislative declaration of a standard of care, creates a private right not to be harmed by its violation. *Bell v. Page*, supra; *King v. Pope*, 202 N.C. 554, 163 S.E. 447 (1932).

Schlitz's failure to obtain a permit until May 1971 does not afford the Springers a ground for recovery. The permit does not protect riparian owners. It is only an instrument of the city's enforcement program, and its absence does not pollute the stream. Moreover, the ordinance does not explicitly forbid the discharge of wastes containing more than 2500 ppm BOD. The ordinance is a criminal statute which must be construed in the defendant's favor in civil proceedings as well as in criminal ones. *Hinson v. Dawson*, 241 N.C. 714, 86 S.E.2d 585 (1955). Since the discharge of more than 2500 ppm BOD is not a crime, it does not constitute negligence *per se*.

In contrast, the discharge of sewage prohibited by Section 23-2(2) is a crime, and under North Carolina law it is actionable if it proximately causes damage to riparian property. Section 23-2(2) states in part:

> "(2) Except as hereinafter provided, it shall be unlawful for any person to discharge or cause to be discharged any of the following described materials, waters, liquids, or wastes into any public sanitary sewer:

. . . .

> "(g) Liquid wastes containing any toxic or poisonous substances in sufficient quantities to (i) interfere with the biological processes used in a sewage treatment plant, or (ii) which, in combination with other liquid wastes, upon passing through a sewage treatment plant will be harmful to persons, livestock, or aquatic life utilizing the receiving streams into which water from a sewage treatment plant is discharged."

In order to establish that Schlitz's violation of the ordinance was negligence, the Springers would have to prove that the brewery wastes had the characteristics forbidden by Section 23-2(2). Viewed in the light most favorable to them, the evidence showed that the brewery's wastes had a toxic or poisonous effect on bacteria that are essential to the sewage treatment process. The evidence also showed that after passing through the plant the wastes were harmful to aquatic life in the receiving stream. The jury should therefore be allowed to determine whether or not the discharge violated the ordinance. If it did, this was negligence, and the jury should then decide whether it proximately caused damage to the Springers' property.

Schlitz argues that its discharge of brewery wastes is not actionable because the city's officials did not require compliance with the ordinance until May 1971, except for the payment of surcharges. This contention lacks merit. Section 23-4(d) of the ordinance authorized the water and sewer officials to:

> "consult with and furnish technical assistance and advice to industrial users of the city's sewerage system in order to assist them in devising procedures and constructing equipment to reduce or eliminate from industrial wastes objectionable characteristics or properties which may not otherwise be discharged into the public sanitary sewers under Section 23-2."

While this provision recognized that compliance was not instantly attainable and allowed city officials to furnish technical assistance and advice, its terms gave them no power to affect the rights of third parties. A statute protecting life or property creates a private right not to be harmed by its violation unless the legislature specifically provides otherwise. *Carr v. Murrows Transfer Inc.*, 262 N.C. 550, 138 S.E.2d 228 (1964). Public officials have no more power to alter these private rights than the legislature chooses to give them. *Swaney v. Peden Steel Co.*, 259 N.C. 531, 542, 131 S.E.2d 601, 609 (1963); *Kotkins v. Seattle*, 119 Wash. 590, 206 P. 11 (1922).

It is argued, however, that the ordinance should not be read literally because the only reasonable construction is one which would allow city officials to dispense with its requirements. While it is true that the city's director of water and sewers believed that immediate, rigorous enforcement would be undesirable because it would "shut down just about every industry in Winston-Salem," there is no conflict between the public interest in keeping a factory open and the private right to recover damages for pollution. The two may be reconciled by requiring the source of pollution to pay damages while allowing it to operate. *See Boomer v. Atlantic Cement Co.*, 26 N.Y.2d 219, 309 N.Y.S.2d 312, 257 N.E.2d 870 (1970). Since the plain language of the ordinance does not authorize city officials to dispense with its requirements, their actions could not affect the Springers' rights. *Weingand v. City of North Platte*, 108 Neb.

17, 187 N.W. 90, 91 (1922); *Kotkins v. Seattle*, 119 Wash. 590, 206 P. 11, 13 (1922).

In addition, paying effluent surcharges did not relieve Schlitz from having to obey the rest of the ordinance. The city levies these charges "to cover some of the cost to the city of treating such wastes." They begin not at 2500 ppm but at 300 ppm, the approximate dividing line between domestic and industrial strength sewage. The charges are enumerated in the ordinance section which sets other fees, not in the one which describes prohibited uses. They are revenue measures rather than substitutes for civil liability.

III.

As an alternative ground of recovery, the Springers argued that Schlitz should be held liable if it knew, or in the exercise of reasonable care should have known, that the city could not adequately treat the brewery's waste. The validity of this claim depends on an analysis of the underlying reasons for the general rule of immunity.

In absolving the user of a municipal sewage system from liability, North Carolina follows the leading case of *Carmichael v. Texarkana*, 116 F. 845 (8th Cir. 1902). *See Hampton v. Spindale*, 210 N.C. 546, 187 S.E. 775, 776 (1936); *Clinard v. Town of Kernersville*, 215 N.C. 745, 748, 3 S.E.2d 267, 270 (1939). *Carmichael* involved a suit by a riparian owner against a city and its inhabitants. The court affirmed the dismissal of the complaint against the inhabitants, holding that the city alone was responsible for the nuisance created by its sewer system. It analogized the problem to a more familiar area of vicarious responsibility—the employer's liability for the torts of an independent contractor:

> "If [the inhabitants] had taken their own sewage to the creek, and poured it into its waters above the premises of the complainants, they would undoubtedly . . . have been liable . . . On the other hand, if they had made an agreement with an independent contractor . . . to remove all their sewage from their premises to a place where, and in a manner in which, it could do no unnecessary injury to any one, and their contractor had carelessly deposited it . . . in the stream above [complainants'] property, the [inhabitants] would not have been liable for these wrongful acts of their contractor. Their relation to the city and to its negligence is not of a different character." 116 F. at 849.

The city, in the court's view, undertook to dispose of the residents' wastes in a nuisance free manner, and they in turn consented to such conditions as the city might put on the use of the sewers. . . . The liability of the user of a municipal sewer system therefore appears to be limited in the same way as the liability of an independent contractor's employer.

A North Carolina employer is not liable for his contractor's negligence when he lacks the power to control the contractor's actions. He remains, though, responsible for negligent acts within his own control even when the contractor is also at fault. *State Highway Commission v. Diamond Steamship Transportation Corp.*, 226 N.C. 371, 38 S.E.2d 214 (1946); *Evans v. Rockingham Homes, Inc.*, 220 N.C. 253, 17 S.E.2d 125 (1941). Since the selection of the contractor is within the employer's control, "if it appears that the employer knew, or by the exercise of reasonable care might have ascertained that the contractor was not properly qualified to undertake the work, he may be held liable for the negligent acts of the contractor." *Page v. Sloan*, 12 N.C. App. 433, 183 S.E.2d 813, 817 (1971), aff'd, 281 N.C. 697, 190 S.E.2d 189 (1972).

The owner of a large industrial source of sewage, particularly one only planned or under construction, is similarly situated. A manufacturing company is in a position to know enough about its own operations to understand the nature of its wastes and the problems of treating them. If it has not yet selected a plant site, it may have a choice among cities and disposal systems. It may also be large enough to pre-treat or properly dispose of its own sewage. When the company represents a desirable source of jobs and tax revenues, the local authorities can be expected to provide it with technical information about the municipal sewers. In brief, a large industrial sewer user can make an informed decision whether to use a city sewer system to render its wastes nuisance free.

According to the Springers' evidence, Schlitz, which has more than a century of experience in brewing beer, considered several cities in the Southeast before selecting Winston-Salem for a brewery site. As part of its investigation, the company requested information about the city's sewage facilities, and its representatives toured the treatment plant. Had the company inquired, it would have learned that the plant was operating at or over its daily capacity of 18 million gallons of sewage containing 76,000 pounds of BOD. The city assured Schlitz that it would adequately treat its wastes after Schlitz advised the city to expect 15,000 pounds of BOD per day. Before the brewery had been open a year, however, it was discharging 56,000 pounds of BOD per day into a system which had previously reached its 76,000 pound capacity. Brewery wastes are known by sanitary engineers to be difficult to treat and to interfere with the treatment of other wastes because of their high concentration of BOD and fluctuating alkalinity.

These facts disclose that Schlitz knew the characteristics of its own sewage and that it exercised control over its selection of a site and of the sewage system which would dispose of its waste. The evidence also indicates that Schlitz could not rely on the city's acceptance of its sewage, because it had not furnished the city accurate information. Finally, the proof supports an inference that Schlitz knew, or in the exercise of reasonable care should have ascertained, that the city could not adequately treat its brewery wastes. The jury might reasonably have decided that Schlitz negligently selected the city of Winston-Salem to treat its sewage. Drawing upon North Carolina's common law principles governing the liability of an employer of an independent contractor, we conclude that Schlitz is not, as a matter of law, immune from liability. Accordingly, on remand, the district court should submit the issue of Schlitz's liability on the Springers' alternative theory.

IV.

The record discloses that after the 1970 fish kills, Schlitz expended more than $1,300,000 for sewage treatment facilities, and it is now in compliance with the effluent quality standards of the city ordinance. The city has doubled the size of its treatment plant, and it can now properly treat the waste from the brewery. In view of this evidence, it is unlikely that an injunction is appropriate under North Carolina law.

On remand, the court should instruct the jury that the Springers cannot recover if the evidence discloses only that Schlitz's waste, after passing through the Winston-Salem treatment plant, polluted the Yadkin, killed fish, and caused other damage to the Springers' riparian property. Under North Carolina's general rule of immunity, Schlitz cannot be held liable if the evidence discloses no more than those facts.

The jury should be told that in order for the Springers to recover they must prove by a preponderance of the evidence that Schlitz violated Winston-Salem's sewage ordinance by discharging sewage prohibited by § 23-2(2) or that Schlitz knew, or in the exercise of reasonable care should have ascertained, that the city's treatment plant could not adequately treat its sewage. In either event, the Springers must also prove that the brewery's waste proximately caused their injury; that is, that it was foreseeable that Schlitz's waste, alone, or in conjunction with other waste, would damage the Springers' riparian property. This outline of the elements of the plaintiffs' claim, of course, is not intended to preclude the court from charging the jury about defenses Schlitz may present when the case is fully tried.

NOTES AND QUESTIONS

(1) On the basis of the cases read thus far and on the basis of your general knowledge of law, do you conclude that private actions by injured parties against polluters can make a major contribution to water pollution control? Is the availability of private remedies dependent on the general water law, whether it be the riparian pattern prevailing in the northeast or the appropriation pattern prevailing in the west and southwest, or any other system that prevails in the jurisdiction? What sanctions and remedies are available to private litigants? Would it be sufficient for adequate water pollution control to strengthen these private remedies and to make private recoveries more certain? Why has it been said that courts are not the institutions best suited to administer effective pollution controls? *See generally*, Hines, *Nor Any Drop to Drink: Public Regulation of Water Quality, Part 1: State Pollution Control Programs*, 52 Iowa L. Rev. 186, 196-201 (1966). Compare dissenting opinion in *Town of Waterford v. Water Pollution Control Board*, 5 N.Y.2d 171, 182 N.Y.S.2d 789 (1959).

(2) McDonald owns farmlands in Rockland County, New York. He and his family have been using water from a small river which flows through their land for their farm and dairy operations. The entire area has in recent years become increasingly more industrialized, and, for the past year and one-half, the Foolscap Paper Company has been operating a plant upstream which has been emitting waste from its paper mills into the river, causing the same to become offensive to taste and smell and making it unfit for livestock and other

uses. McDonald employs one handyman year-round, and three migrant farm laborers during harvest time. The Foolscap Paper Company is an up-to-date, very efficient operation that regularly employs several hundred persons and is one of the major employers in the neighborhood. McDonald wants Foolscap to stop polluting the river or, failing to do that, he wants to stop the company from operating altogether. Will he succeed? *See Whelan v. Union Paper Bag Co.*, 208 N.Y. 1, 101 N.E. 805 (1913), and its effective overruling in *Boomer v. Atlantic Cement Co.*, 26 N.Y.2d 219, 25 N.E.2d 870, 309 N.Y.S.2d 312 (1970), § 2.02 *supra*. Would the result differ, depending on whether the court applied the "reasonable use doctrine" or the "natural floor doctrine"?

(3) Assume facts similar to those in Problem 2. There is evidence that Foolscap is not the only industrial enterprise that empties its waste into the river. Several factories, including one large tanning operation farther up the river, also add their share. However, it is clear that it was Foolscap's added wastes together with the wastes already in the river prior to Foolscap's appearance that made use of the water for domestic and farm purposes impractical for McDonald and his family. What are the prospects of an action by McDonald against Foolscap? Can he, or should he, join the other polluters upstream as defendants in his action, and will this improve his chances of recovery? Suppose McDonald finds other farmers downstream who are similarly affected. Would he improve his chances by having them join him in his action? Is a class action possible under the circumstances? If a single action is brought against all of the upstream polluters, is there any possibility that responsibility for the damage done may be apportioned among them? *See generally* F. Grad, Treatise on Environmental Law, § 3.02[4]. Analogous questions of liability and appropriation of damages have arisen in the area of hazardous waste. *See* F. Grad, Treatise on Environmental Law, § 4A.05[2][c], and Chapter 4 *infra*. Assume that these facts occurred in one of the western states—what are the relative rights of the parties under the doctrine of "prior appropriation" there prevailing?

(4) Should private industry use public waste treatment works, as in *Schlitz*, to dispose of its discharges? *See infra*, § 3.03[2][b][iii] at p. 403 on regulation of publicly owned waste treatment works (POTWs) and § 3.03[2][b][viii] at p. 474 on pretreatment requirements of the Clean Water Act.

(5) Discuss whether, from the point of view of the public interest in controlling water as a resource, the various doctrines referred to in Problem (2), such as the natural flow doctrine, the reasonable use doctrine, and the prior appropriation doctrine, as well as the usual weighing of economic factors, result in adequate public protections. Would a system of water pollution controls that is solely based on consideration of riparian rights make any sense from the broader policy point of view, and from the point of view of modern water pollution technology, in light of the fact that major elements of pollution are contributed by nonriparian users?

(6) For some years, the federal government and all of the states have enacted water pollution control laws. Assume that the kind of pollution involved in Problem (2) has been regulated so that Foolscap is now operating under appropriate effluent limitations and seeks a pollution permit (a NPDES permit under the Federal Water Pollution Control Act § 402). Is there any

point in continuing efforts to strengthen the law, both substantive and procedural, to allow private parties to bring lawsuits for harm suffered as a result of pollution?

§ 3.03 Government Regulation of Water Pollution

[1] Earlier Exercise of State and Local Police Powers

At an earlier and more primitive stage, environmental controls to maintain the purity of water were primarily concerned with the problem of disposal of human waste so as not to contaminate underground sources of drinking water. Reliance on a system of sewers—rather than on privies or other "private disposal systems"—is one of the earmarks of urbanization. With the development and growth of city sewer systems, concern shifts from the contamination of underground water to the contamination of the rivers, which inevitably become the sink into which the city sewers drain. Turn of the century health codes reflect both of these concerns. An examination of contemporary health codes demonstrates that the exercise of state and local police power, at its most basic level, has undergone little change. It is noteworthy, too, that the cities, which were the first to encounter the problem of pollution of their drinking water, were generally the first to enact anti-pollution regulations. Although a few states had enacted water pollution legislation in the latter part of the 19th century, most states did not enact such legislation until it had become apparent that isolated city action along a water course could not effectively cope with the total health problem. For a succinct history of early water pollution legislation, see Hines, *Nor Any Drop to Drink: Public Regulation of Water Quality, Part 1: State Pollution Control Programs*, 52 Iowa L. Rev. 186, 202-204 (1966). For an account of early efforts to control water purity by the development of sanitary sewers, see Murphy, Water Purity, 23-46 (1961).

The statutory materials that follow illustrate not only the early and continuing relationship between environmental law and public health, but also the recurring phenomenon that the solution of one problem is often the beginning of another. The water-flushed toilet of the nineteenth century was a response to the public health outrages of privies and cesspools, but it inevitably led to the major twentieth-century problem of sewer systems discharging untreated wastes into our rivers.

REVISED COMPENDIUM OF BUILDING, ETC.

(Regulations of the District of Columbia, 1905)

Privy Must Be Provided—

It shall be unlawful for any owner or owners to occupy, rent, or cause to be rented any dwelling houses or tenements without providing for each and every dwelling house or tenement a suitable privy for the use of the occupants of such dwelling house or tenement; and if any owner or agent shall neglect or refuse to provide such privy, he shall forfeit and pay a fine of five dollars for each and every week of such neglect or refusal; and it shall be unlawful for any person or persons to make any excavation under any privy within the city, under a penalty not to exceed ten dollars for each offense.

Drains Must Have Strainers—

In all cases where a drain shall be made from any lot, house, or other property into a public sewer constructed by this corporation, there shall be a good and sufficient copper or cast-iron strainer inside the basement or cellar wall of the property so drained, to prevent any vegetable matter or filth in a solid state from passing into the sewer; and such cellar or basement shall at all times be subject to the inspection of such person as may be authorized by the mayor or corporation to examine the same; and if at any time the strainer shall be found worn out or choked with filth, or if the drain itself shall be choked with filth, the owner or occupier of the premises, either or both of them, shall be fined not less than five dollars nor more than ten dollars for the first offense, and not less than ten dollars nor more than twenty dollars for the second or any subsequent offenses, and five dollars for every twenty-four hours during which the strainer or drain shall remain out of repair or be choked up; the said fines to be recovered as other fines of this corporation are recovered.

Regarding Excretia and Privies—

It shall be unlawful for any person or persons to maintain, upon any original lot or subdivided lot, situated on any street in the District of Columbia, where there is a public sewer and water main available for the use of such lot, any system of disposal of human excretia except by means of water-closets connected with such sewer and water main.

Sec. 2.—No privy shall be constructed or maintained in said District, every part of which is not at least five feet from the line of any adjoining lot, two feet from any street or public or private passageway, and ten feet from any building used for or intended to be used for dwelling purposes, or wherein persons are employed or intended to be employed in any trade or business; nor within fifty feet of any well or spring used or likely to be used by man as a source of water for drinking or domestic purposes.

Sec. 3.—Every privy in said District shall be constructed and maintained in such a manner and position as to afford ready means of access thereto for the purpose of cleaning the same, and to admit of the removal of the contents from the premises whereon such privy is situated to the public street without being carried through any dwelling house or building where persons are employed in any trade or business; and said privy shall be so constructed as to prevent undue exposure of the occupants thereof, and provided with a sufficient opening for ventilation, as near the top as practicable, communicating directly with the external air. The floor thereof shall be paved with some non-absorbent material, and constructed so that it shall be in every part at a height of no less than four inches above the level of the surface of the surrounding ground and have a fall or incline toward the door of the privy of half an inch to the foot. Said privy shall be provided with a suitable receptacle or suitable receptacles for filth, which may be movable or fixed, which shall have suitable covers and be kept closed therewith whenever practicable.

. . . .

SEC. 16.—The term privy shall be held to mean any building or part of a building used or intended to be used for the reception of human fecal matter or urine, and which is not connected with the public sewer or with some duly authorized system of sewage disposal, so as to immediately remove such material from such building; that the owner or owners of the premises on which any such privy is situated shall be held liable for its erection and maintenance in conformity to law, and for the removal of the contents thereof as may from time to time be necessary; and if such owner or owners can not be found in the District of Columbia a notice of the work required by this act to be done, specifying a reasonable time for the performance thereof, shall be left with the agent of such premises, or if no such agent can be found in said District, such notice shall be mailed to the last known address of such owner or owners; and if the work specified in said notice be not done within the time allowed therein, the Commissioners of the District of Columbia are hereby authorized to cause such work to be done and to assess the cost thereof as a tax against the property benefited, which tax shall be carried on the regular tax roll of the District of Columbia, and shall be collected in the manner provided for the collection of other taxes.

. . . .

NEW YORK CITY HEALTH CODE

(Adopted, as last revised, by the Board of Health in 1959)

ARTICLE 143. DISPOSAL OF SEWAGE

Introductory Notes

The article constitutes one part of the broad area of disposal of wastes. While Article 145, Water Pollution Control, deals with wastes entering the waters of the City, Article 143 is concerned with the specific problem of disposal of human, household, and commercial liquid wastes which do not involve immediate discharges into the waters of the City. Each of the two articles complements the other and takes cognizance of both the nuisance problem and the pollution problem. Thus, the issuance of a permit under the instant article or under Article 145 will be premised on the overriding goal of controlling sewage and other wastes both locally and at the point of ultimate discharge. The article takes cognizance of the activities and regulations of other public agencies, such as the office of the Borough President for each of the five boroughs of New York City and the Department of Public Works.

Compliance with the provisions of this article does not waive the requirements of any provision of State or local law or regulation, *e.g.*, a permit to construct a septic tank, when required by a Borough President, must be obtained in addition to complying with the permit requirements of this article.

The article contains a novel requirement that for subdivision realty developments involving 15 or more dwellings, a community private sewage disposal system be built rather than individual systems unless there are special circumstances such as cost or physical or engineering difficulties (section 143.11). This mandatory requirement will reduce the total financial burden to a home owner who is often forced to carry the construction charges for an individual private system, where there are no public systems, only to have to abandon such system when public sewers are later built, and for which he is assessed. Under the new provision, a single temporary system will be built. When the City extends its system, the sewers already installed can be connected to the new public sewers, and the temporary community system abandoned.

. . . .

§ 143.01 Definitions

When used in this article:

(a) Municipal sewage systems means the series of sanitary, combined and storm sewers, intercepting sewers and intercepting collecting sewers, sewage treatment plants or pollution control facilities, drains and other facilities, connections and equipment for the conveyance, treatment and disposal of sewage and drainage operated by departments and offices of the city of New York.

(b) Private sewage disposal system means a water-flushed facility for the disposition of sewage which does not connect either with the municipal sewage disposal system or with a sewer or other facility connecting with such municipal system.

(c) Privy means a facility for urinating or defecating which is not water-flushed and which does not connect, directly or otherwise, to a private sewage disposal system or the municipal sewage disposal system, and includes a chemical toilet.

(d) Sewage means human wastes, liquid kitchen wastes, waste water from wash basins, waste water from bathing facilities including a bathing establishment as defined in section 165.01, or liquid wastes resulting from any process of industry, manufacturing, trade or business or from the development or recovery of any natural resources.

§ 143.03 Disposal of sewage generally; use of private sewage disposal systems and privies

Sewage from any building or premises shall be discharged directly into the municipal sewage disposal system or into a facility connecting with such a municipal system, but if there is no public sewer or other part of the municipal sewage disposal system to which connection can be made from the building or premises concerned, or if it is impracticable to discharge sewage from such building or premises into the municipal system, a private sewage disposal system may be used. Privies shall not be used unless the Department, in writing, authorizes the construction and temporary use of a privy for a stated period, but temporary privies provided for workers during the construction of a building may be used without such authorization.

§ 143.05 Private sewage disposal systems; permit for construction; exception

(a) No private sewage disposal system shall be constructed without a permit issued by the Commissioner, [in accordance with standards established by the Commissioner, after he has approved the site and the subsoil] except that no permit is required by this section and this article shall not apply if a permit must be obtained for a disposal facility pursuant to section 145.03 of this Code or pursuant to Article 12 of the Public Health Law.

(b) [Provides for permit application showing that discharge into the municipal sewage disposal system is unavailable or impracticable; providing details relating to the site, its layout and topography; providing detailed information on the suitability and absorptive capacity of the soil; and providing pertinent geological data required by the department.]

. . . .

§ 143.09 Private sewage disposal systems; requirements for one and two family dwellings

[The section requires the system to have a capacity large enough so that it will not fail during maximum use. A septic tank with a minimum capacity of 750 gallons for a two-bedroom, single family home is required, of 900 gallons for a three bedroom house, and 1,000 for four bedrooms, with 250 gallons additional capacity required for each additional bedroom. These standards assume adequately absorptive soil quality. Following amendment in 1969, the standards reflect recommended standards of the U.S. Public Health Service.]

§ 143.11 Community private sewage disposal systems

(a) No permit shall be issued approving the site and sub-soil for the proposed construction of individual private sewage disposal systems in subdivision realty developments involving 15 or more dwellings, but application shall be made for a permit to construct and maintain a community private sewage disposal system for the disposal of sewage from all of the dwellings within the subdivision development. This provision shall not apply, however, if in the opinion of the Department, it is more practicable to construct individual systems rather than a community system, by reason of physical or engineering difficulties, estimated cost of construction or other pertinent considerations. . . .

[Note: This section is relatively new. The mandatory requirement for community systems for subdivision developments in areas of the City where there are no public sewers is an attempt to facilitate the eventual construction of public sewer systems and, meanwhile, relieve the private home owner from unnecessary costs for sewage disposal. At present, if a private sewage system is built because there are no public sewers, the home owner must bear the cost of such construction. Later, when public sewers are built, he must abandon the private sewer and pay an assessment for the construction of the public sewers. Thus, he pays twice: first for his private system, then for public sewer assessment. In requiring community systems, the home owner pays only for his proportionate share of the community system, which, after public sewers are constructed in the area concerned, may be tied in to the public sewer. It is hoped, in this way, to reduce overall cost to the home owner and, at the same time, assure adequate facilities for the disposal of sewage. In those instances where community systems would be impractical, by reason of engineering difficulties, or where, for example, the cost of construction of a community system would be more than the total cost of all the individual private systems in the subdivision development, the provision authorizes the Department to waive the mandatory requirement for a community system.]

ARTICLE 145. WATER POLLUTION CONTROL

Introductory Notes

The control and abatement of pollution of the waters of New York City has continued to be the concern of a host of government agencies. In 1936 New York and New Jersey, and later Connecticut, signed a Tri-State Compact for Pollution Abatement which established an interstate sanitation district and created the Interstate Sanitation Commission. Article 12 of the Public Health Law enacted in 1949 established the State Water Pollution Control Board. The City Department of Public Works has jurisdiction pursuant to City Charter § 683 over intercepting sewers and sewage disposal plants (pollution control projects), and Charter § 687 authorizes the Commissioner of Public Works to adopt regulations to require the discharge of sewage, refuse, factory waste or trade waste into the public sewers of the City, or to regulate, restrict or prohibit the use of the public sewers for the discharge of any material or substance, and allows him to prescribe civil penalties for their violation. The President of each of the five boroughs has jurisdiction over the construction and maintenance of public sewers, other than intercepting sewers. The Department of Sanitation is responsible for garbage disposal and the operation of incineration facilities and sanitary landfills. The Department of Parks, which is charged with the development of park and recreational facilities, is dependent in large measure on the success of pollution control measures and sanitary landfill operations. Thus, the vast Jamaica Bay area is presently being developed as a wildlife refuge, and for recreational, fishing and, eventually, bathing purposes, but this development is conditioned on the gradual decrease in pollution of the Bay area.

The Department of Health is concerned with pollution control from the broad viewpoint of health. It is the aim of this article to give the Department authority to control sources of pollution and to cooperate with other governmental agencies in the development of pollution abatement programs.

In order that the Department of Health may carry out its obligations under § 556(a) of the City Charter "to regulate all matter affecting health in the city," the provisions of this article of the Code require the Department of Health to pass on plans for all proposed pollution control facilities. It is hoped that this procedure will result in fruitful cooperation between the Department of Health and the Department of Public Works, as well as other departments, so that pollution control facilities, which represent a considerable capital expenditure on the part of the City, will prove of maximum benefit to the health of the people, in addition to meeting the necessary requirements of sound sanitary engineering. The Health Department's unique contribution to pollution control is its long experience in safeguarding health by controlling potential sources of disease.

NOTES AND QUESTIONS

(1) The excerpt from the New York City Health Code reflects the many governmental units that have a role to play in water pollution control. Consider the situation in your own jurisdiction. Which agencies share responsibilities? The materials also refer to the dependency of park development on water pollution control. What is the present situation of the Jamaica Bay case? Consider also the relationship of urban planning and building controls to water pollution. Have there been instances when the unavailability of public sewers on land suited for private sewage disposal has put a limit on development?

(2) Clapboard Home Builders, Inc., built a one-family residential development consisting of 300 units in the Borough of Queens in an unsewered part of the City of New York. In connection with its development operations, it caused to be incorporated the Clapboard Sewage Treatment Corp., for the purpose of collecting, treating, and disposing of the house sewage of the homes in the development. A sewer line leads from each of the homes to the main sewer line, which in turn flows into the corporation's sewage treatment plant. The sewage treatment plant discharges the liquid effluent of the treated sewage into a small natural stream which traverses the treatment company's property. This small stream empties into a small pond a couple of miles beyond. The Queens Motel Company owns a small motel which is separated from the pond by a road. The pond itself is owned by the city, which allows the public to use it for swimming, fishing, boating and other recreational purposes. One of the motel's main attractions is that it is conveniently located to the pond so that its guests have the full use of the pond's recreational opportunities.

The effluent from the treatment plant meets the requirements of the New York City Health Code and the established standards pursuant to state law for recreational waters. The discharge of effluent from the treatment plant can be observed from the motel and has had the unfortunate result of discouraging the recreational uses of the pond. Does the Queens Motel have an action against Clapboard Sewage Treatment Corp.? Does Clapboard

Sewage Treatment Corp. have a choice in the matter, *i.e.*, could it have built 300 separate septic tanks in connection with its 300 single family dwellings? From the point of view of water pollution control, would the situation be better or worse had 300 separate septic tanks been built instead of the sewage treatment plant? Would the Queens Motel's case be any better if, instead of being separated from the pond by a road, its property abutted on the pond or onto the small waterway which receives the effluent?

[2] Federal Laws and Regulations

[a] Rivers and Harbors Act of 1899—"Refuse Act" (30 Stat. 1152 *et seq.*, Title 33 U.S.C. § 401 *et seq.*)

§ 403. Obstruction of navigable waters generally; wharves; piers, etc.; excavations and filling in

The creation of any obstruction not affirmatively authorized by Congress, to the navigable capacity of any of the waters of the United States is prohibited; and it shall not be lawful to build or commence the building of any wharf, pier, dolphin, boom, weir, breakwater, bulkhead, jetty, or other structures in any port, roadstead, haven, harbor, canal, navigable river, or other water of the United States, outside established harbor lines, or where no harbor lines have been established, except on plans recommended by the Chief of Engineers and authorized by the Secretary of the Army; and it shall not be lawful to excavate or fill, or in any manner to alter or modify the course, location, condition, or capacity of, any port, roadstead, haven, harbor, canal, lake, harbor of refuge, or inclosure within the limits of any breakwater, or of the channel of any navigable water of the United States, unless the work has been recommended by the Chief of Engineers and authorized by the Secretary of the Army prior to beginning the same.

§ 407. Deposit of refuse in navigable waters generally

It shall not be lawful to throw, discharge, or deposit, or cause, suffer, or procure to be thrown, discharged, or deposited either from or out of any ship, barge, or other floating craft of any kind, or from the shore, wharf, manufacturing establishment, or mill of any kind, any refuse matter of any kind or description whatever other than that flowing from streets and sewers and passing therefrom in a liquid state, into any navigable water of the United States, or into any tributary of any navigable water from which the same shall float or be washed into such navigable water; and it shall not be lawful to deposit, or cause, suffer, or procure to be deposited material of any kind in any place on the bank of any navigable water, or on the bank of any tributary of any navigable water, where the same shall be liable to be washed into such navigable water, either by ordinary or high tides, or by storms or floods, or otherwise, whereby navigation shall or may be impeded or obstructed: *Provided*, That nothing herein contained shall extend to, apply to, or prohibit the operations in connection with the improvement of navigable waters or construction of public works, considered necessary and proper by the United

States officers supervising such improvement or public work: *And provided further*, That the Secretary of the Army, whenever in the judgment of the Chief of Engineers anchorage and navigation will not be injured thereby, may permit the deposit of any material above mentioned in navigable waters, within limits to be defined and under conditions to be prescribed by him, provided application is made to him prior to depositing such material; and whenever any permit is so granted the conditions thereof shall be strictly complied with, and any violation thereof shall be unlawful.

. . .

§ 411. Penalty for wrongful deposit of refuse; use of or injury to harbor improvements, and obstruction of navigable waters generally

Every person and every corporation that shall violate, or that shall knowingly aid, abet, authorize, or instigate a violation of the provisions of sections 407, 408, and 409 of this title shall be guilty of a misdemeanor, and on conviction thereof shall be punished by a fine not exceeding $2,500 nor less than $500, or by imprisonment (in the case of a natural person) for not less than thirty days nor more than one year, or by both such fine and imprisonment, in the discretion of the court, one-half of said fine to be paid to the person or persons giving information which shall lead to conviction.

. . .

§ 413. Duty of United States attorneys and other Federal officers in enforcement of provisions; arrest of offenders

The Department of Justice shall conduct the legal proceedings necessary to enforce the provisions of sections 401, 403, 404, 406, 407, 408, 409, 411, 549, 686, and 687 of this title; and it shall be the duty of United States attorneys to vigorously prosecute all offenders against the same whenever requested to do so by the Secretary of the Army or by any of the officials hereinafter designated, and it shall furthermore be the duty of said United States attorneys to report to the Attorney General of the United States the action taken by him against offenders so reported, and a transcript of such reports shall be transmitted to the Secretary of the Army by the Attorney General; and for the better enforcement of the said provisions and to facilitate the detection and bringing to punishment of such offenders, the officers and agents of the United States in charge of river and harbor improvements, and the assistant engineers and inspectors employed under them by authority of the Secretary of the Army, and the United States collectors of customs and other revenue officers shall have power and authority to swear out process, and to arrest and take into custody, with or without process, any person or persons who may commit any of the acts or offenses prohibited by the said sections, or who may violate any of the provisions of the same: *Provided*, That no person shall be arrested without process for any offense not committed in the presence of some one of the aforesaid officials: *And provided further*, That whenever any arrest is made under such sections, the person so arrested shall be brought forthwith before a commissioner, judge, or court of the United

States for examination of the offenses alleged against him; and such commissioner, judge, or court shall proceed in respect thereto as authorized by law in case of crimes against the United States.

. . .

UNITED STATES v. STANDARD OIL CO.

United States Supreme Court (1966)
384 U.S. 224, 86 S. Ct. 1427, 16 L. Ed. 2d 492

MR. JUSTICE DOUGLAS delivered the opinion of the Court.

The question presented for decision is whether the statutory ban on depositing "any refuse matter of any kind or description"[1] in a navigable water covers the discharge of commercially valuable aviation gasoline.

Section 13 of the Rivers and Harbors Actprovides:

> "It shall not be lawful to throw, discharge, or deposit . . . any refuse matter of any kind or description whatever other than that flowing from streets and sewers and passing therefrom in a liquid state, into any navigable water of the United States. . . ." 33 U.S.C. § 407(1964 ed.).

The indictment charged appellee, Standard Oil (Kentucky), with violating § 13 by allowing to be discharged into the St. Johns River "refuse matter" consisting of 100-octane aviation gasoline. Appellee moved to dismiss the indictment, and, for the purposes of the motion, the parties entered into a stipulation of fact. It states that the gasoline was commercially valuable and that it was discharged into the St. Johns only because a shut-off valve at dockside had been "accidentally" left open.

The District Court dismissed the indictment because it was of the view that the statutory phrase "refuse matter" does not include commercially valuable oil. The United States appealed directly to this Court under the Criminal Appeals Act (18 U.S.C. § 3731(1964 ed.)). We noted probable jurisdiction. 382 U.S. 807.

This case comes to us at a time in the Nation's history when there is greater concern than ever over pollution—one of the main threats to our free-flowing rivers and to our lakes as well. The crisis that we face in this respect would not, of course, warrant us in manufacturing offenses where Congress has not acted nor in stretching statutory language in a criminal field to meet strange conditions. But whatever may be said of the rule of strict construction, it cannot provide a substitute for common sense, precedent, and legislative history. We cannot construe § 13 of the Rivers and Harbors Actin a vacuum. Nor can we read it as Baron Parke[2] would read a pleading.

---

[1] 30 Stat. 1152, 33 U.S.C. § 407(1964 ed.).

[2] A man whose "fault was an almost superstitious reverence for the dark technicalities of special pleading." XV Dictionary of National Biography, p. 226 (Stephen and Lee ed. 1937-1938).

The statutory words are "any refuse matter of any kind or description." We said in *United States v. Republic Steel Corp.*, 362 U.S. 482, 491, that the history of this provision and of related legislation dealing with our free-flowing rivers "forbids a narrow, cramped reading" of § 13. The District Court recognized that if this were waste oil it would be "refuse matter" within the meaning of § 13 but concluded that it was not within the statute because it was "valuable" oil.[3] That is "a narrow, cramped reading" of § 13 in partial defeat of its purpose.

Oil is oil and whether usable or not by industrial standards it has the same deleterious effect on waterways. In either case, its presence in our rivers and harbors is both a menace to navigation and a pollutant. This seems to be the administrative construction of § 13, the Solicitor General advising us that it is the basis of prosecution in approximately one-third of the oil pollution cases reported to the Department of Justice by the Office of the Chief of Engineers.

Section 13 codified pre-existing statutes: . . .

The 1899 Act now before us was no more than an attempt to consolidate these prior Acts into one. It was indeed stated by the sponsor in the Senate to be "in accord with the statutes now in existence, only scattered . . . from the beginning of the statutes down through to the end" (32 Cong. Rec. 2296), and reflecting merely "[v]ery slight changes to remove ambiguities." *Id.*, p. 2297.

From an examination of these statutes, several points are clear. *First*, the 1894 Act and its antecedent, the 1888 Act applicable to the New York Harbor,[4] drew on their face no distinction between valuable and valueless substances. *Second*, of the enumerated substances, some may well have had commercial or industrial value prior to discharge into the covered waterways. To be more specific, ashes and acids were banned whether or not they had any remaining commercial or industrial value. *Third*, these Acts applied not only to the enumerated substances but also to the discharge of "any other matter of any kind." Since the enumerated substances included those with a pre-discharge value, the rule of *ejusdem generis* does not require limiting this latter category to substances lacking a pre-discharge value. *Fourth*, the coverage of these Acts was not diminished by the codification of 1899. The use of the term "refuse" in the codification serves in the place of the lengthy list of enumerated substances found in the earlier Acts and the catch-all provision found in the Act of 1890. The legislative history demonstrates without contradiction that Congress intended to codify without substantive change the earlier Acts.

The philosophy of those antecedent laws seems to us to be clearly embodied in the present law. It is plain from its legislative history that the "serious injury" to our watercourses (S. Rep. No. 224, 50th Cong., 1st Sess., p. 2) sought

[3] The District Court followed the decision of the United States District Court in United States v. The Delvalle, 45 F. Supp. 746, 748, where it was said: "The accidental discharge of *valuable, usable oil* . . . does not constitute . . . a violation of the statute." (Emphasis added.)

[4] The codification did not include the Acts of 1836 and 1888 which pertained only to New York. These remain in effect and are found at 33 U. S. C. §§ 441-451 (1964 ed.). The New York Harbor statute has been held to apply not only to waste oil which was unintentionally discharged (*The Albania*, 30 F. 2d 727) but also to valuable oil negligently discharged. *The Colombo*, 42 F.2d 211.

to be remedied was caused in part by obstacles that impeded navigation and in part by pollution—"the discharge of sawmill waste into streams" *(ibid.)* and the injury of channels by "deposits of ballast, steam-boat ashes, oysters, and rubbish from passing vessels." *Ibid.* The list is obviously not an exhaustive list of pollutants. The words of the Act are broad and inclusive: "any refuse matter of any kind or description whatever." Only one exception is stated: "other than that flowing from streets and sewers and passing therefrom in a liquid state, into any navigable water of the United States." More comprehensive language would be difficult to select. The word "refuse" does not stand alone; the "refuse" banned is "of any kind or description whatever," apart from the one exception noted. And, for the reasons already stated, the meaning we must give the term "refuse" must reflect the present codification's statutory antecedents.

The Court of Appeals for the Second Circuit in *United States v. Ballard Oil Co.*, 195 F. 2d 369 (L. Hand, Augustus Hand, and Harrie Chase, JJ.) held that causing good oil to spill into a watercourse violated § 13. The word "refuse" in that setting, said the court, "is satisfied by anything which has become waste, however useful it may earlier have been."[5] *Id.*, p. 371. There is nothing more deserving of the label "refuse" than oil spilled into a river.

That seems to us to be the common sense of the matter. The word "refuse" includes all foreign substances and pollutants apart from those "flowing from streets and sewers and passing therefrom in a liquid state" into the watercourse.

That reading of § 13 is in keeping with the teaching of Mr. Justice Holmes that a "river is more than an amenity, it is a treasure." *New Jersey v. New York*, 283 U.S. 336, 342. It reads § 13 charitably as *United States v. Republic Steel Corp., supra*, admonished.

We pass only on the quality of the pollutant, not on the quantity of proof necessary to support a conviction nor on the question as to what *scienter* requirement the Act imposes, as those questions are not before us in this restricted appeal.

Reversed.

MR. JUSTICE HARLAN, whom MR. JUSTICE BLACK and MR. JUSTICE STEWART join, dissenting.

Had the majority in judging this case been content to confine itself to applying relevant rules of law and to leave policies affecting the proper conservation of the Nation's rivers to be dealt with by the Congress, I think that today's decision in this criminal case would have eventuated differently. The best that can be said for the Government's case is that the reach of the provision of

[5] The decisions in the instant case below and in United States v. The Delvalle, *supra*, n. 3, are against the stream of authority. An unreported decision of a United States District Court in 1922 (*United States v. Crouch*), holding § 13 inapplicable to polluting but nonobstructing deposits, caused the Oil Pollution Act, 1924, 43Stat. 604, 33 U. S. C. § 431 *et seq.* (1964 ed.), to be passed. *See* S. Rep. No. 66, 68th Cong., 1st Sess.; H. R. Rep. No. 794, 68th Cong., 1st Sess. It is applicable to the discharge of oil by vessels into coastal waters but not to deposits into inland navigable waters; and it explicitly provides that it does not repeal or modify or in any manner affect other existing laws. 33 U. S. C. § 437 (1964 ed.).

§ 13 of the Rivers and Harbors Act of 1899, 30 Stat. 1152, 33 U.S.C. § 407(1964 ed.), under which this indictment is laid, is uncertain. This calls into play the traditional rule that penal statutes are to be strictly construed. In my opinion application of that rule requires a dismissal of the indictment.

I.

. . . .

Whatever might be said about how properly to interpret the 1890 and, more especially, the 1894 statutes, it is the 1899 Act that has been on the books for the last 67 years, and its purposes and language must guide the determination of this case. To the extent that there were some differences in scope between the 1890 and 1894 Acts, these were necessarily resolved in the 1899 codification, which, while embodying the essential thrust of both prior statutes, appears from its plain language to have favored the more restrictive coverage of the 1890 Act. Moreover, it is questionable to what extent the Court's speculation as to the meaning of a phrase in one of the prior statutes is relevant at all when the language of the present statute, which is penal in nature, is in itself explicit and unambiguous.

The purpose of § 13 was essentially to eliminate obstructions to navigation and interference with public works projects. This 1899 enactment, like the two preexisting statutes which it was intended to codify, was a minor section attached to a major appropriation act together with other measures dealing with sunken wrecks,[6] trespassing at public works sites,[7] and obstructions caused by improperly constructed bridges, piers, and other structures.[8] These statutes were rendered necessary primarily because navigable rivers, which the Congress was appropriating funds to improve, were being obstructed by depositing of waste materials by factories and ships.[9] It is of course true, as the Court observes, that "oil is oil," *ante*, p. 226, and that the accidental spillage of valuable oil may have substantially the same "deleterious effect on waterways" as the wholesale depositing of waste oil. But the relevant inquiry is not the admittedly important concerns of pollution control, but Congress' purpose in enacting this anti-obstruction Act, and that appears quite plainly to be a desire to halt through the imposition of criminal penalties the depositing of obstructing refuse matter in rivers and harbors.

The Court's construction eschews the everyday meaning of "refuse matter"—waste, rubbish, trash, debris, garbage, see Webster's New International Dictionary, 3d ed.—and adopts instead an approach that either reads "refuse" out of the Act altogether, or gives to it a tortured meaning. The Court declares,

[6] Rivers and Harbors Act of 1899, § 15, 30Stat. 1152, 33 U. S. C. § 409 (1964 ed.).

[7] Rivers and Harbors Act of 1899, § 14, 30Stat. 1152, 33 U. S. C. § 408 (1964 ed.).

[8] Rivers and Harbors Act of 1899, § 12, 30Stat. 1151, 33 U. S. C. § 406 (1964 ed.).

[9] Congress was presented, when considering one of the predecessors of the 1899 Act, with the representations of the Office of the Chief of Army Engineers that there had been "serious injury to navigable waters by the discharge of sawmill waste into streams. . . . In fair-ways of harbors, channels are injured from deposits of ballast, steam-boat ashes, oysters, and rubbish from passing vessels." S. Rep. No. 224, 50th Cong., 1st Sess., 2 (1888). *See also* H. R. Rep. No. 1826, 55th Cong., 3d Sess., 3-4 (1899). There is no support for the proposition that these statutes were directed at "pollution" independently of "obstruction."

at one point, that "The word 'refuse' includes all foreign substances and pollutants apart from those 'flowing from streets and sewers and passing therefrom in a liquid state' into the watercourse." *Ante*, p. 230. Thus, dropping anything but pure water into a river would appear to be a federal misdemeanor. At the same time, the Court also appears to endorse the Second Circuit's somewhat narrower view that "refuse matter" refers to any material, however valuable, which becomes unsalvageable when introduced into the water. *Ante*, pp. 229-230. On this latter approach, the imposition of criminal penalties would in effect depend in each instance on a prospective estimate of salvage costs. Such strained definitions of a phrase that is clear as a matter of ordinary English hardly commend themselves, and at the very least raise serious doubts as to the intended reach of § 13.

II.

Given these doubts as to the proper construction of "refuse matter" in § 13, we must reckon with a traditional canon that a penal statute will be narrowly construed. . . .

. . . .

In an area in which state or local law has traditionally regulated primary activity, there is good reason to restrict federal penal legislation within the confines of its language. If the Federal Government finds that there is sufficient obstruction or pollution of navigable waters caused by the introduction of commercial oil or other nonrefuse material, it is an easy matter to enact appropriate regulatory or penal legislation.[10] Such legislation can be directed at specific types of pollution, and the remedies devised carefully to ensure compliance. Indeed, such a statute was enacted in 1924 to deal with oil pollution in coastal waters caused by vessels, 43 Stat. 605, 33 U. S. C. §§ 433, 434 (1964 ed.).

To conclude that this attempted prosecution cannot stand is not to be oblivious to the importance of preserving the beauties and utility of the country's rivers. It is simply to take the statute as we find it. I would affirm the judgment of the District Court.

NOTES AND QUESTIONS

(1) The "Refuse Act," as the preceding case suggests, was enacted principally as an act to protect ships against floating refuse in the harbor. When and how did it become a pollution control law? Does *United States v. Republic Steel Corp.*, 362 U.S. 482 (1960) suggest the answer?

(2) The Rivers and Harbors Act has remained an environmental favorite even after the adoption of the broader Clean Water Act, and is relied on in

[10] *See, e. g.*, special message of the President dealing with new anti-pollution legislation, Preservation of Our National Heritage— Message from the President of the United States, H. Doc. No. 387, 89th Cong., 2d Sess., Cong. Rec., Feb. 23, 1966, pp. 3519-3522.

federal enforcement actions in wetlands and other pollution cases. *See, e.g.*, *United States v. Holland*, *infra*. What reasons are there for this reliance by environmental litigators? Does the Rivers and Harbors Act give a right to environmental litigators to enjoin the construction of a major water diversion facility by a state agency as violative of § 10 in creating an obstruction to navigation not authorized by Congress? *See California v. Sierra Club*, 451 U.S. 287, 11 E.L.R. 20357 (1981).

[b] Clean Water Act

[i] Historical and Introductory Note

The Federal Government has involved itself in environmental controls rather gradually, with reliance on the commerce power in the direct control of pollution being a fairly recent phenomenon of federal regulation; initially, it operated indirectly through the Federal Government's power to tax and spend for the general welfare (U.S. Constitution, Art. 1, § 8, Cl. 3). Thus, in most fields of pollution control, federal involvement begins not with an assertion of federal regulatory power under the Commerce Clause, but through sponsorship of federal grant-in-aid programs, with federal standards gradually being imposed as a condition of the receipt of federal funds for purposes of environmental control. This traditional, congressional approach to the pollution con trol problem is exemplified in the policy declaration of the Federal Water Pollution Act of 1948, the first major federal legislation on the subject:

> [I]t is hereby declared to be a policy of Congress to recognize, preserve, and protect the primary responsibilities and rights of the states in controlling water pollution. 62 Stat. 1155 (1948), 33 U.S.C. § 466(1964).

This limitation on the federal jurisdiction was almost entirely self-imposed. Its justification lies, in part, in a continued respect for the concept of federalism, and, again, in part, in a judgment, probably accurate in 1948, that some form of local control is a more effective means of combating water pollution than federal controls. Consequently, under early water pollution and air pollution control acts, the federal function was to operate in full cooperation with state and interstate agencies as well as with local and municipal governments. When pollution problems worsened rapidly, the wisdom of this secondary federal role was questioned. The new direction of the federal effort was first reflected in the declaration of policy of the Water Quality Control Act of 1965:

> The purpose of this act is to enhance the quality and value of our water resources and to establish a national policy for the prevention, control and abatement of water pollution. 79 Stat. 903 (1965); 33 U.S.C. § 466(1964 Supp. V).

Though the concept of a partnership with the states still remains, the unmistakable trend of federal programs has been to place the responsibility for any final decisions on water quality objectives, standards, and priorities in Washington.

The Federal Government asserted an interest in certain aspects of water pollution control as early as the late 19th century. The first such federal statute was enacted in 1886 and forbade the dumping of refuse in New York Harbor. (Act of August 5, 1886, Ch. 929, 24 Stat. 329.) The Rivers and Harbors Act of 1899 extended this prohibition to include the discharge of "waste materials" into any navigable waterway. Waste which flowed in a liquid state from streets or sewers was the only exception. While the Rivers and Harbors Act has seen recent and fairly frequent application as an antipollution measure, the obvious intent of early rivers and harbors legislation was simply to protect navigation against floating obstructions.

Later federal legislation dealt mainly with water pollution as a vector in the spread of communicable disease. The Public Health Services Act of 1912 authorized the investigation of the effect of pollution in navigable lakes and streams on public health. 37 Stat. 309 (1912), as amended 42 U.S.C. § 241(1964). Subsequent cooperation between the Public Health Service and state agencies resulted in the voluntary adoption of nationwide standards for the treatment of drinking water. The adoption of these standards has almost entirely eliminated waterborne diseases.

Oil pollution became a problem in the 1920s, and the Oil Pollution Control Act of 1924 was enacted to combat oil discharges that were causing damage to aquatic life, mainly shellfish, to recreational facilities, and to docks and harbors in coastal waters (Acts of June 7, 1924, Ch. 316, §§ 1-5, 7, 8, 43 Stat. 604-606 (repealed 1970 and replaced by new legislation *infra*)).

Between 1924 and 1948, several efforts were made to enlist the assistance of the Federal Government in water pollution control. Water pollution had increased drastically as a result of the wartime growth of industry, and, in 1947, a number of water pollution control bills were introduced in Congress. The first federal Water Pollution Control Act, which grew out of these legislative endeavors, was signed into law by President Truman on June 30, 1948 (Act of June 30, 1948, Ch. 758, § 2-13, as amended 33 U.S.C. §§ 1151-1160(1970)). The policy of this act—as has been noted—was one of cooperation with state and local authorities already engaged in water pollution control. Acknowledging the states' primary responsibility for water pollution control, Congress hoped that with federal support local programs would be able to handle pollution problems effectively. The federal role in enforcement under the 1948 Act was very narrow indeed. The Act was to expire in five years, and, in 1952, it was extended through 1956.

Comprehensive and permanent federal water pollution legislation was not enacted until 1956. The 1956 law, Federal Water Pollution Control Act, however, reaffirmed the standard congressional policy of acknowledging and protecting the state's primary responsibility in water pollution control. (Ch. 518, 70 Stat. 498.) In addition, the Act broadened and intensified the research and training aspects of the federal program by authorizing research grants to public and private agencies and to qualified individuals. It also authorized grants to the states and to interstate agencies for water pollution control activities. Moreover, it authorized a substantial annual appropriation for construction grants to states, cities, and other government agencies for the building of waste treatment works. Other aspects of the 1956 law were (1) provision of somewhat simpler procedures for federal abatement actions against interstate polluters and, (2) a strengthening of the Pollution Control Advisory

Board that had been created under the 1948 Act. The Act also established a program to control pollution emanating from federal installations. There was no further federal legislation during the Eisenhower years. In 1961, however, the Federal Water Pollution Control Act was amended so as to strengthen certain administrative aspects of the law and to strengthen both the grants-in-aid and the technical assistance features of the earlier program. (Act of July 20, 1961, 75 Stat. 204.) The 1961 amendment also extended the reach of federal abatement authority. Previously, the Federal Government had asserted authority to abate pollution only in "interstate waters," but this authority was extended to include all navigable waters, whether interstate or not.

In spite of these efforts, the quality of the nation's waters continued to deteriorate, and in April 1963, the Senate Committee on Public Works appointed a special Subcommittee on Air and Water Pollution. (109 Cong. Rec. 7304 (1963).) This subcommittee, under the chairmanship of Senator Edmund Muskie of Maine, became the leading force in water pollution control efforts. After three sessions of debate, Congress finally passed the Water Quality Act of 1965. (79 Stat. 903.) For the first time in any federal pollution statute, the declared purpose of the Act was to establish "a national policy" for the regulation of water pollution, language subsequently adopted in the 1967 Air Quality Act. Thus, the 1965 Water Quality Act marked the earliest assertion of federal leadership in the nation's antipollution efforts.

The Water Quality Act of 1965 assigned responsibility for the federal program to a newly created Federal Water Pollution Control Administration (FWPCA) in HEW. It also expanded the appropriations for construction grants for sewage treatment plants and provided more substantial funds for research into pollution problems. But most important was the enactment of a timetable for the establishment by the states of water quality standards for interstate waters; these standards were to be used by the federal agency in enforcing pollution abatement.

In 1966, shortly after the effective date of the new law, the President submitted a reorganization plan that proposed a transfer of the Federal Water Pollution Control Administration from HEW to the Department of the Interior. (Reorganization Plan No. 2 of 1966, 80 Stat. 1608.) The purpose of this transfer was to consolidate administrative responsibility for all phases of the Federal Government's water resources program into a single department. In 1970, the Administration was again transferred, this time to the Environmental Protection Agency, in a further consolidation of federal environmental programs.

There was considerable activity both in Congress and in the executive departments throughout 1966. Hearings and reports on water pollution followed in rapid succession. The result of all of this activity was the Clean Water Restoration Act of 1966.(80 Stat. 1246, *as amended* 33 U.S.C.A. §§ 1151 *et seq.* (1970).) This Act further increased authorizations for construction grants and for several existing and newly added research and training programs. It also provided added incentive to the states to adopt water quality standards and to contribute to the support of the construction of water treatment facilities. In addition, the 1966 law, as amended, (1) extended federal jurisdiction over enforcement to include international boundary waters as well as intrastate and interstate waters; (2) transferred responsibility for administration of the Oil Pollution Act to the Secretary of the Interior; and (3) extended the coverage of the Oil Pollution Act to include inland waters.

The contribution of the Water Quality Act of 1965 as amended by the Clean Water Restoration Act of 1966 was to provide for the establishment of nationally required quality standards for interstate waters as well as for raising standards of quality. The law did not provide, however, for the establishment of a single set of national standards. Congress established, instead, an elaborate procedure to ensure that the establishment of standards would be primarily a state responsibility, though one subject to federal approval. Under the Act, each state was given until June 30, 1967 to adopt water quality standards applicable to interstate waters within its borders. If a state failed to meet this deadline, or if the standards submitted to the Department of the Interior were rejected, the Department itself was authorized to establish water quality standards for interstate waters within that state.

In spite of apparent attempts to strengthen water pollution control, the federal efforts prior to the 1972 Amendment of the Federal Water Pollution Control Act resulted in little improvement in the quality of the country's rivers. One of the reasons for lack of success lay in the sluggish response of the states, which were slow in submitting their water quality standards and even slower in enforcing them, and where water pollution control boards or other standard-setting agencies were most frequently industry-dominated. Another reason for the lack of effective enforcement was to be found in the law itself, which provided for a very extended "conference procedure" requiring conferences among all of the control agencies in the region, a conference with the polluter, and a very informal hearing, all intended to resolve pollution problems by conciliation and coordination, rather than by enforcement sanctions. The conference procedure took at least two years until any enforcement action could be taken, and the only available enforcement action was injunctive relief, without any penalty for past violations—thus putting a premium on maximum delay. At the time the 1972 Amendment was passed, and for the 24 prior years in which the conference procedure was available, there had been some fifty informal conferences, four cases which proceeded to hearing, and only one, which involved St. Joseph, Missouri, in which court action was taken, ending in a consent decree! A second procedure, for abatement of violations of standards in interstate waters, was a considerable improvement because it required only 180 days' notice to the polluter. (For full discussion of procedures under the earlier FWPCA, see F. Grad, Treatise on Environmental Law § 3.03 [1][a].) The inadequacies and failures of past law explain some of the hard postures of the 1972 Amendments.

The Act was again amended in 1977, when Congress undertook some midcourse adjustments. Although the 1977 Act made some significant changes in areas to be noted, the structure and general scheme of the 1972 Act was retained. *See* Federal Water Pollution Control Act Amendments of 1972, Pub. L. No. 92-500, 86 Stat. 816, enacted over Presidential veto on October 16, 1972, as amended by Pub. L. No. 95-217, 91 Stat. 1566, 33 U.S.C. § 1251(a)(1977).

The Clean Water Act was again reauthorized and amended in February 1987. The 1987 enactment, like earlier water pollution control measures, was passed over a presidential veto. Significant amendments included changes in the amount of Federal grants in the POTW grant program, more stringent controls of toxic pollutants, a new system of controls of nonpoint sources, new regulation of industrial storm water discharges and sewage sludge controls. The new amendment also strengthened sanctions, both civil and criminal, adding a system of administratively imposed civil penalties, and heavier penalties for pollution which constitutes "knowing endangerment" of persons. Other changes included the treatment of Indian Tribes as states, particularly for purposes of POTW grants. Variances based on the "fundamentally different factors" (FDF) distinction were both legislatively authorized and limited. There were also changes in the NPDES program, and certain postponements in BAT compliance dates. New provisions also included an enhanced National Estuaries Program, a Clean Lakes Program, a Chesapeake Bay Program, and a program to enhance water quality in the Great Lakes.

[A] Changes in Regulatory Philosophy

The Clean Water Act in its main structure reflects the Federal Water Pollution Control Act Amendments of 1972 and includes the further amendments—midcourse adjustments—made in 1977 and the amendments of 1987. Although the 1977 and 1987 revisions made some important changes, the basic pattern and regulatory philosophy of the current law has remained essentially unchanged and a consideration of the regulatory philosophy must, therefore, begin with the 1972 Act.

The Federal Water Pollution Control Act Amendments of 1972 constituted a very far-reaching revision of the federal water pollution control legislation previously in force. The amendments not only attempted to resolve some of the earlier difficulties of water pollution control enforcement but, indeed, marked an entire change in regulatory philosophy. Under prior law, the main aim of federal legislation was to assist the states and localities in providing for water quality that was acceptable for particular, designated purposes.[11] In the main, the philosophy was that we ought to have the best water for designated classifications of water use at the most economical price.[12] The establishment of federal water quality standards—or actually water quality standards proposed by the states which then would, upon adoption, become the federally accepted standards—meant that the federal government would aim at the improvement of water quality, but would accept situations where waters would be kept in their present condition—*i.e.*, not be permitted to deteriorate any further—as long as their quality was adequate for particular designated purposes. In regard to actual improvement of water quality, the main provisions of the pre-1972 legislation relied less on regulatory efforts, and more on federal assistance, in a variety of ways, to the states and localities for research,

[11] Federal Water Pollution Control Act of 1948, 62 Stat. 1155, as amended; 33 U.S.C. § 1151 *et seq.* (1970); Water Quality Control Act of 1965, Pub. L. No. 89-234, 79 Stat. 903, as amended, 33 U.S.C. § 1151 *et seq.* (1970).

[12] *See, e.g.*, Hines, *Controlling Industrial Water Pollution: Color the Problem Green*, 9 B.C. Indus. & Comm. L. Rev. 553, 573 (1968).

establishment of water quality improvement programs, and primarily, for the construction of waste treatment plants.[13]

The 1972 legislation no longer relied on water quality standards established by the states as the primary standards for enforcement purposes. It has been pointed out that under the 1972 Act such water quality standards as are still required are essentially benchmarks to measure progress. They provide a means whereby the state's compliance with other, newer applicable federal standards can be measured,[14] rather than in themselves a part of the scheme of enforcement.

The most noteworthy aspect of the legislation, however, is what has been referred to as a "clean waters" approach. The declaration of goals and policies states that it is the objective of the legislation "to restore and maintain the chemical, physical and biological integrity of the Nation's waters."[15] It is stated as "the national goal that the discharge of pollutants into the navigable waters be eliminated by 1985,"[16] and that "wherever attainable, an interim goal of water quality which provides for the protection and propagation of fish, shellfish, and wildlife and provides for recreation in and on the water be achieved by July 1, 1983."[17] Another "national policy" is the prohibition of "the discharge of toxic pollutants in toxic amounts."[18]

Under prior law, water quality standards provided measures to which all other regulatory efforts were to be geared. It was each state's obligation to set effluent standards to make sure that the ambient water quality standards were not exceeded. It is very difficult to relate effluent standards to ambient water quality standards; perhaps it is even more difficult to do this in the water pollution control field than to relate emission standards to ambient standards in air pollution. In water pollution, the precise amount of effluent a given river can handle without deterioration of water quality depends not only on the amount of effluent emitted, but also on the temperature of the water, the speed at which the water is traveling, the general characteristics of the waterway, the time of the year, and the like. All of these factors play a considerable part in the amount of dissolved oxygen, for instance, which will be present in the river water at any given time. Relating effluent standards to ambient water quality standards presents significant difficulties, among other reasons, because the amount of effluent that a river can handle at different seasons of the year without exceeding water quality standards may differ quite considerably.

From the point of view of industry, a point of view reflected to some extent in the pre-1972 legislation, it was undesirable to require effluent limits that were excessive, that is, effluent limits that made the water "too clean"—because at a certain point effluent limits would no longer be economically cost

[13] Federal Water Pollution Control Act of 1948, c. 758, § 1, 62 Stat. 1155, as amended, 33 U.S.C. § 1151 *et seq.* (1970); Act of April 30, 1970, Pub. L. No. 91-224, Title I, § 105, 84 Stat. 113; 33 U.S.C. § 1156(1970).

[14] S. Rep. No. 414, 92d Cong., 1st Sess. 8 (1971) [hereinafter cited as S. Rep. No. 414].

[15] Federal Water Pollution Control Act as amended by the Federal Water Pollution Control Act Amendments of 1972, Pub. L. No. 92-500, Title I, § 101 (a), 86 Stat. 816, 33 U.S.C. § 1251(a), as further amended by Pub. L. No. 95-217, 91 Stat. 1566 (1977) [hereinafter cited as FWPCA].

[16] FWPCA § 101(a)(1), 33 U.S.C. § 1251(a)(1).

[17] FWPCA§ 101(a)(2), 33 U.S.C. § 1251(a)(2).

[18] FWPCA § 101(a)(3), 33 U.S.C. § 1251(a)(3).

effective. In other words, the incremental cost of making water cleaner than is demonstrably necessary for health or for downstream industrial uses would exceed the extra benefits to be achieved.[19] The 1972 legislation abandons this approach. The question is no longer how high must effluent standards be set in order to accomplish ambient water quality standards, but what technology can best be used, and how soon, to reduce water pollution to zero.[20]

The zero water pollution target, which was to be accomplished, if possible, by 1985, was severely criticized as potentially involving the nation in expenditures that are vastly excessive and unwarranted.[21] The question has been asked, too, whether the zero pollution policy is likely to require substantial expenditures at the expense of other social goals and purposes having equal or higher priority—such as social welfare or housing.[22]

The 1977 amendment of the law[23] retained the statement of policies and purpose of the 1972 Act, including the "zero pollution" target. It is fair to say, however, that the 1977 amendments show a partial relinquishment of that goal, both in the substantial postponement of standards mandated earlier, and particularly in dealing with so-called conventional pollutants, where the law accepts continuing pollution at some level.[24] Another, perhaps equally significant change is the emphasis in the repeated expression of the intent of Congress that the states bear responsibility for management and enforcement in the first instance, though leaving ultimate authority to the Administrator of EPA.[25]

The 1972 law is another example of legislative technology-forcing, following the pattern set by the 1970 Clean Air Amendments.[26] The 1972 Water Pollution Control Act is primarily based on the work of Senator Edmund Muskie's subcommittee,[27] which, indeed, had also been responsible for the clean air legislation some two years earlier. In the light of the stated intention "to restore and maintain the chemical, physical, and biological integrity of the

---

[19] *See* Testimony of Russel Train, Administrator of the EPA, in *A Legislative History of the Water Pollution Control Act Amendments of 1972* at 1116-1118 (Sen. Comm. Print 1973).

[20] S. Rep. No. 414 at 42.

[21] *See* Testimony of Russell Train, *supra* N. 9: "[T]he marginal costs of abatements increase greatly as higher levels of reductions are required. For example, EPA estimates that as a general proposition 85 percent reduction costs only 20 percent as much as 100 percent reduction. To go from 95 percent treatment to 98 percent treatment costs the same amount as going from 85 to 95 percent treatment. . . . The last percent of reduction often costs as much as the first 99 percent."

[22] *See* Testimony of Mr. Russell Train, N.9 at 1117: "If we insist that the public pay—through tax revenues and increased prices for manufactured goods—many billions of dollars for water cleanup beyond the point where added benefits can be demonstrated or even assumed . . . the public legitimately will question our wisdom on this and other environmental matters and perhaps feel that the measures needed to deal with environmental problems are being exaggerated. . . . [I]n both public and private sectors, pollution control is to a large extent regarded as a single major priority which must be weighed against other major priorities in allocating scarce resources." *See, also,* testimony of Paul V. McCracken, Chairman, Council of Economic Advisers, N.9, *supra* at 1122 *et seq.*

[23] Pub. L. No. 95-217, 91 Stat. 1566 (1977).

[24] *E.g.,* FWPCA § 301(b)(2)(F), § 304(b)(4), 33 U.S.C. § 1311(b)(4), § 1314(b)(4).

[25] *See, e.g.,* FWPCA § 101(b), (g), 33 U.S.C. § 1251(b), (g).

[26] Pub. L. No. 91-604, 84 Stat. 1676, 42 U.S.C. § 1857(1970).

[27] Subcommittee on Air and Water Pollution of the Senate Committee on Public Works.

nation's waters,"[28] the effort undertaken under the earlier legislation to establish a relationship between effluent standards and water quality standards will ultimately become irrelevant—though, indeed, the existing system is continued and relied upon to achieve the interim goal set for 1983.[29] Beyond that, however, it is no longer left to the states to determine the uses of water to be protected or the kinds and amounts of pollutants to be permitted. Moreover, states no longer have the power to determine the degree of pollution abatement to be required, nor the time to be allowed to a polluter for abatement. The entire thrust of the 1972 Act was to accomplish what the best water pollution control technology could accomplish in the shortest time. The stated objective of eliminating the discharge of pollutants by 1985 was explained by the House Public Works Committee as follows:

> The Administrator shall evaluate the level of effluent reduction that can be attained through the application of the best level of technology. Once he has evaluated what can be accomplished, the Administrator must set the standard at a particular volume of effluent or a particular percentage of effluent reduction. The Committee believes that the greatest public benefit can be achieved when each company in an industrial group is free to make its own engineering decisions on how to meet that standard. The Administrator should not attempt to dictate the use of specific processes or other methods of control to implement the standard of performance.[30]

However, though each industrial enterprise might be free to determine the best way of accomplishing the goal, the law made it clear that the precise degree of reduction was to be set by the Administrator and that it would be applicable nationwide and uniformly regardless of the differences in the absorptive capacities of different waters.[31]

In order to achieve the no-pollution objective, a two-phase program for applying effluent limits was created. In phase 1, all industrial point sources were required to apply the "*best practicable*" technology—this, in effect made secondary treatment the minimal requirement by July 1, 1977.[32] Communities were required to have secondary waste treatment construction programs no later than June 30, 1974. In phase 2, industries were required to utilize the "*best available*" technology, or the goal of no discharge could not be reasonably attained.[33] Any publicly owned treatment facility approved after the June, 1974 date was required to comply with the best available technology requirement. The Administrator had to require that, where appropriate, practices be adopted to recycle and reclaim water and to provide for the contained or confined disposal of pollutants. Thus, each applicant for federal support for the construction of a public waste treatment plant had to examine all waste management techniques, with the burden on the applicant to demonstrate compliance with national objectives.[34]

The Administrator could continue to apply effluent controls based on water quality standards where the relationship between effluent standards and

---

[28] FWPCA § 101(a), 33 U.S.C. § 1251(a).

[29] FWPCA § 303, 33 U.S.C. § 1313.

[30] S. Rep. No. 414 at 59.

[31] FWPCA § 306, 33 U.S.C. § 1316.

[32] FWPCA § 301(b)(1)(A), 33 U.S.C. § 1311(b)(1)(A); S. Rep. No. 414 at 43.

[33] FWPCA § 301(b)(2)(A), 33 U.S.C. § 1311 (b)(2)(B); S. Rep. No. 414 at 45.

[34] FWPCA § 301(b)(2), 33 U.S.C. § 1281(g)(2); S. Rep. No. 414 at 24.

water quality was established.[35] That relationship is no longer crucial, however, because it is not the improvement in water quality which measures compliance, but rather compliance is sought with federally issued effluent controls which take into account the "no-pollution" aims of the law.

The Senate Committee Report states the legislative intent that:

> [N]o one has the right to pollute . . . that pollution continues because of technological limits, not because of any inherent right to use the nation's waterways for the purpose of disposing of wastes.[36]

The Committee Report continues:

> The Administrator will have capability and the mandate to press technology and economics to achieve those levels of effluent reduction which he believes to be practicable in the first instance and attainable in the second.[37]

The law requires that all effluent limitations be reviewed at least every five years, and that industry reevaluate its control efforts, so as to apply the best control technology then available.[38] However, this is not to provide a permit to industry to pollute. Only if it is able to show that "no-discharge" is as yet unattainable, then, and only then, may it use the "best available control technology" approach.[39] The purpose, of course, is to approach zero-discharge as nearly as possible. Thus, while the pre-1972 law accepted pollution as inevitable and attempted to set regulations so as to reduce it to a relatively harmless limit, the 1972 legislation took the position that all pollution is unlawful and that some degree of pollution will be permitted only for as long as no technology is available to cope with it.

The movement in the direction of federal effluent standards, moreover, has been justified on a variety of grounds. The purpose of requiring the same stringent regulatory controls and the same stringent effluent standards in every part of the country is to discourage industries from shopping for locations in the state with the most lenient pollution control approach. It is also to discourage states from competing for new industries on the basis of relaxed standards.[40] The further requirement that any physical change in an existing plant or the construction of a new plant meet the best technology then available with respect to pollution control is justifiable since no expensive retrofitting of some plants would be needed.[41] This minimization strategy is not only "essential to the prevention of new pollution problems, and the eventual attainment of the goal of no discharge," but also tends towards national uniformity of enforcement which past experience has shown to be desirable.[42]

It is clear that the law gives the Administrator very considerable scope in determining what is the "best practicable" or the "best available" control technology at any given time. To this extent, the 1972 Federal Water Pollution Control Act Amendments present a parallel to the technology-forcing aspects

---

[35] FWPCA §§ 301, 302, 33 U.S.C. § 1281, 1312; S. Rep. No. 414 at 42, 46.

[36] S. Rep. No. 414 at 42.

[37] S. Rep. No. 414 at 42.

[38] FWPCA § 301(d), 33 U.S.C. § 1311(d); S. Rep. No. 414 at 42.

[39] FWPCA § 301(b)(2)(A), 33 U.S.C. § 1311(b)(2)(A); S. Rep. No. 414 at 42.

[40] FWPCA § 306, 33 U.S.C. § 1316.

[41] FWPCA § 306, 33 U.S.C. § 1316.

[42] S. Rep. No. 414 at 58.

of the automotive pollution controls, in the 1970 Clean Air Amendments.[43] The Administrator clearly has the power to compel industry to meet standards it cannot presently meet with known technology, *i.e.*, he may set regulations in such a way as to force the technology. In making the determination as to what is the "best available" control technology, the Administrator is instructed to:

> examine the degree of effluent control that has or can be achieved through the application of technology which is available or normally can be made available. This does not mean that the technology must be in actual routine use somewhere. It does mean that the technology must be available at a cost and a time which the Administrator determines to be reasonable, and the technology has been adequately demonstrated if not routinely applied.[44]

The targets and the deadlines for which the law aims clearly require a certain amount of technology forcing and, indeed, the Congress gave every indication of being aware of this fact, as is apparent from a number of comments on the floor of the Senate:

> Only under such conditions are we likely to press the technological threshold of invention into new and imaginative developments.[45] . . . some of these adjustments will be painful. It will require breakthroughs in science, in engineering, in economics and changes in our everyday lives as well.[46]
>
> . . . by setting a no discharge goal, we will direct research toward complete rather than partial solutions.[47]

In effect, "technology is to be directed towards solving some of the problems which have accompanied technological development."[48]

There was a substantial amendment of the Federal Water Pollution Control Act in 1987. These amendments did not reflect any significant change in regulatory philosophy but rather some new modalities of addressing the problem of pollution. Significantly, the 1987 amendment provides for the regulation of nonpoint source pollution, and for the submission of individualized control strategies for toxic pollutants. The 1987 act also broadened the law's area of control providing not only for pollution control in the Great Lakes, but also in estuarine bodies of water.

The most recent change in regulatory emphasis is the initiative begun in 1998 by the Clinton administration toward a new regime in water pollution control and enforcement. This new emphasis is a significant rediscovery of ambient water quality as the touchstone of the law. All of the water pollution control enforcement devices, effluent limitations, new source performance standards, and the elaborations of the permit system aim toward the same end: to make the waters of the nation fishable and swimmable. Viewed in this fashion, all enforcement techniques are designed to provide water of a quality which is wholesome and advances the life and health of the people. Together

---

43 *See* N. 16 *supra.*

44 S. Rep. No. 414 at 50.

45 117 Cong. Rec. 17407 (daily ed. Nov. 2, 1971) (remarks of Senator Montoya).

46 117 Cong. Rec. at 17406 (remarks of Senator Eagleton).

47 117 Cong. Rec. at 17402 (remarks of Senator Muskie).

48 117 Cong. Rec. at 17419 (remarks of Senator Cooper).

with efforts to enhance ambient water quality came a renewed insight that water quality depends not only on the amount of pollutants and effluents from point sources, but that even the successful application of point source pollution control measures will not result in good ambient water quality, unless the vast array of nonpoint sources, including agricultural pollutants, pollutants from the mining industry and the numerous pollutants from city and industrial sources that cannot be attributed to specific sources are adequately controlled. Thus, the new water quality control initiative addresses a long neglected part of the field, seeking to bring under regulatory control huge numbers of nonpoint sources that have contributed to the total pollutant load for many years. The control effort, only recently begun, will have to address a number of areas which have, for many years, been favored with a not so benign neglect, such as agricultural sources, including feedlots and other animal husbandry endeavors, sources managed by the mining industry, and sources managed by the timber industry, causing largely unregulated pollution on public and private lands. Nonpoint sources also include the building industry, in both the construction of highways and the construction of urban developments, both large and small. Thus, a new emphasis on ambient water quality control is likely to trigger a very substantial expansion of regulatory controls into many areas previously unregulated, calling for major new initiatives to deal with nonsource pollution in all of these areas in an effective manner.

[B] The Regulatory Scheme

The Clean Water Act, consisting of the 1972 Federal Water Pollution Control Act Amendments, as further amended in 1977,[49] is a very complex statute running well over 100 printed pages. Because of its length and complexity, a brief exposition of its regulatory scheme may be useful.

The statute may be viewed as containing several distinct, though interlocking regulatory schemes. To aid the schematic understanding of the statute, each of these regulatory schemes will be identified and the connections or bridges linking the separate schemes will be indicated. It should be noted that the separate schemes do not coincide fully with titles of the law, and the formal subdivision of the statute is thus of limited help.

Scheme 1: Construction of Waste Treatment Works and Area-Wide Waste Treatment Management. The first regulatory scheme, generally contained in Title II of the law,[50] provides for grants-in-aid for the construction of public waste treatment works.[51] However, the grant-in-aid provisions, though important in themselves, provide the framework for the requirement that states establish area-wide waste treatment management agencies with both regulatory and planning powers.[52] Thus, grants-in-aid for the construction of public waste treatment works are conditioned upon compliance by the states

[49] Federal Water Pollution Control Act as last amended by the Federal Water Pollution Control Act Amendments of 1972, Pub. L. No. 92-500, 86 Stat. 816, 33 U.S.C. § 1251 *et seq.*, as further amended by Pub. L. No. 95-217, 91 Stat. 1566 (1977), and the Water Quality Act of 1987, Pub. L. No. 100-4, 101 Stat. 60.

[50] FWPCA §§ 201-208, 211-212; 33 U.S.C. §§ 1281-1288, 1291-1292. For discussion, *see* § 3.03[3][b] *infra.*

[51] FWPCA §§ 201-208, 211-212; 33 U.S.C. §§ 1281-1288, 1291-1292.

[52] FWPCA § 208, 33 U.S.C. § 1288.

with requirements for far-reaching regional approaches and the preparation of area-wide waste treatment and management plans that include regulatory means for their accomplishment. In addition to providing for federal funds for the construction of waste treatment works, this part of the law requires that such treatment works be part of a regional plan for the integrated management of wastes.

The first scheme, which combines grants-in-aid for public waste treatment works with requirements for regional planning and management, is linked to other schemes in the law. There are significant linkages with the effluent standards scheme[53] through the requirements of Section 301 which imposes certain pretreatment effluent standards with respect to wastes discharged into waste treatment works. There are also significant connections with the permit system scheme, through Section 402(b)(8) which requires that discharges from publicly owned treatment works meet certain pretreatment requirements and special requirements of the law pertaining to the permit system.[54]

Scheme 2: Federal Effluent Standards. The second regulatory scheme forms part of Title III. The scheme is not unlike older state regulations in providing authorization for the setting and enforcement, in this instance, of *federal* effluent standards. These standards were required to reflect "best practical control technology currently available" by July 1, 1977 and under the 1972 Act, "best available technology economically achievable" by July 1, 1983. One of the mid-course corrections of the 1977 Act postponed the "best available" standard for most pollutants to July 1, 1984, including the standard of "best conventional pollutant technology" for the new category of "conventional pollutants."[55] The Administrator of EPA is to set effluent standards for point sources so as to meet these requirements of the law. In addition, the effluent standards scheme provides for the setting of special standards for toxic and other hazardous substances, for pretreatment standards of effluents that discharge into public treatment works, and for effluent standards for new sources of pollution.[56] In addition, the effluent standards scheme contains prohibitions on the discharges of chemical, biological and radiological warfare agents and on radioactive waste discharges.

The effluent standard scheme has linkages with the first scheme for area-wide waste treatment management, in that effluent limitations are applicable to public waste treatment plants and in that special pretreatment effluent standards are set for effluents that are discharged into public waste treatment plants.[57] The scheme also has linkages with the permit system in that permits may only be issued for the discharge of effluents that meet federal effluent standards.[58] The effluent standard scheme is also connected to the water quality standards scheme, in that federal effluent limitations must be adjusted and fine-tuned under the requirements of Section 302 of the Act which calls for relating effluent limitations to water quality—*i.e.* they must be made more

---

[53] *See* text at Ns. 7-11 *infra.*

[54] *See* text at Ns. 15-16 *infra.*

[55] FWPCA § 301(b)(1) and (2), 33 U.S.C. § 1311(b)(1) and (2). For discussion, *see* § 3.03[4][a] *infra.*

[56] FWPCA §§ 306, 307, 33 U.S.C. §§ 1316, 1317. For discussion, *see* § 3.03[4][a] and [b] *infra.*

[57] FWPCA § 108(b)(2)(C)(iii), 33 U.S.C. § 1288(b)(2)(C)(iii); FWPCA § 307(b), (c), (d), 33 U.S.C. § 1317(b), (c) and (d).

[58] FWPCA § 402(a), 33 U.S.C. § 1342(a).

stringent when that is necessary in order to meet the requirements of the water quality standard scheme.[59]

Scheme 3: Water Quality Standards and State Implementation Plans. The third scheme provided for in the law is the water quality standard scheme.[60] This regulatory scheme is a continuation of the main scheme of the prior law, whereby states establish water quality criteria and set ambient water quality standards for each of their rivers, subject to federal approval. The scheme continues the procedures under the prior law where the states submitted for federal approval their ambient water quality standards as well as state implementation plans, containing the machinery for enforcement, including the states' own effluent limitations designed to meet the ambient standards. The states are charged with the enforcement of their plans so as to meet the approved water quality standards.

Section 303 of the Clean Water Actimposes certain specific planning obligations on the states, and requires in some respects a parallel to the state implementation plan requirement in the Clean Air Act. It requires the states to examine its waters, and to determine the total maximum daily load (TMDL) of pollutants carried by the state's waters, to supply a basis for the state's plan to improve ambient water quality. The TMDL requirement was totally neglected for many years, but it has begun to form a significant part of the new Clinton administration national water quality initiative. At the end of the year 1999, the national effort to emphasize water quality is far from reaching fruition, but it is a significant effort with the important purpose of bringing nonpoint sources under control so that a liveable, fishable and swimmable ambient water quality can be achieved.[61]

The water quality standards scheme has linkages with the federal effluent standards scheme, in that—as has already been indicated—federal effluent standards must not be allowed to interfere with the achievement of the states' water quality standards, and if federal effluent standards are too low to achieve or maintain the water quality standards, more stringent requirements must be set.[62]

Scheme 4: Permit System. The fourth scheme is the pollution permit scheme known in the law as the "National Pollutant Discharge Elimination System." This scheme applies the device of licensure to the control of pollution, and requires that pollution sources obtain a permit from the Administrator before they discharge effluents. In effect, the pollution permit scheme is a check point for compliance with other schemes, and notably with the federal effluent standards scheme, because no permit may be issued unless the effluent to be discharged meets federal effluent standards.[63]

Thus, the permit system scheme is linked directly with the federal effluent standards scheme. It also has strong linkages with the area-wide waste treatment scheme in that the permit system requires public waste treatment works to obtain permits, and it is also used to regulate effluent discharges

---

59 FWPCA § 302, 33 U.S.C. § 1312.

60 FWPCA § 303, 33 U.S.C. § 1313.

61 *See also* Water Quality Standards, Nonpoint Solution Sources and Nondegradation Policy: New Life for an Old Theme, *infra* at (p. 545).

62 *See* text at Ns. 11-12, *supra*.

63 FWPCA § 402(a), 33 U.S.C. § 1342(a).

into public waste treatment works through the device of regulating the effluent from such waste treatment works.[64]

The four main regulatory schemes that have been identified are linked, too, by a variety of general provisions dealing with enforcement, citizen suits, judicial review, and the like.[65] In addition, there are a number of other, less general, schemes included in the Federal Water Pollution Control Act that rely on enforcement and administrative provisions of their own. These include a separate regulatory scheme for the regulation of oil and hazardous substances under Section 311,[66] a separate scheme for the regulation of marine sanitation devices under Section 312,[67] and a third scheme that deals with the problem of dumping refuse on the high seas under section 403 of the Act,[68] as further enhanced by the provisions of the Marine Protection, Research and Sanctuaries Act of 1972.[69]

[ii] Jurisdictional Scope

UNITED STATES v. HOLLAND

United States District Court, Middle District of Florida (1974)
373 F. Supp. 665

MEMORANDUM OPINION

KRENTZMAN, District Judge.

This is an action brought by the United States to enjoin allegedly unlawful landfilling operations in an area known as Harbor Isle, adjoining Papy's Bayou, St. Petersburg, Florida. The government contends that the defendants have begun filling the waters of the bayou with sand, dirt, dredged spoil and biological materials without the permits required by 33 U.S.C. §§ 403, 407 and 1311(a). For relief the government requests a stoppage of further filling and a restoration of some mangrove wetland.

[Following the grant of a temporary restraining order on December 26, 1973, the motion for a preliminary injunction was heard in early 1974. The court here recites findings that the area in question is a tidelands area frequently inundated by tides exceeding two feet above sea level, that the area is interlaced with artificial mosquito canals, that defendants, in the course of developing the area, are—without a permit—discharging sand, dirt, dredged spoil and biological materials in order to fill the area, and that continuing the fill would result in irreparable injury to the aquatic ecosystem, and to commercial and sport fisheries dependent on the Gulf of Mexico estuaries.]

The Court felt these facts established acts of sufficient scope to warrant federal jurisdiction under the Federal Water Pollution Control Act, and of sufficient magnitude to justify a preliminary injunction. The motion for such

64 *See* § 3.03[2][b][i][A], N. 9, *supra*.

65 *E.g.*, FWPCA §§ 505, 509, 33 U.S.C. §§ 1365, 1368.

66 33 U.S.C. § 1321.

67 33 U.S.C. § 1322.

68 33 U.S.C. § 1343.

69 Pub. L. No. 92-532, 86 Stat. 1051, 33 U.S.C. § 1401 *et seq.* (1972).

an injunction was granted at the hearing. A brief order of injunction and findings was signed January 11, 1974.

Since the courts have not yet been faced with the question of whether federal jurisdiction over water pollution encompasses intertidal wetlands by virtue of the relatively new Federal Water Pollution Control Act Amendments of 1972, 33U.S.C. § 1251 et seq., this opinion will offer the rationale for the grant of jurisdiction.

The Federal Water Pollution Control Act Amendments of 1972

The government charged the defendants with past and continuing violations of Section 301(a) of the Federal Water Pollution Control Act Amendments of 1972 (FWPCA). To sustain this allegation two showings had to be made. First it had to be established that the defendants' acts were such as to be prohibited if done in waters within federal jurisdiction, and second, that the waters receiving the impact of the prohibited conduct were indeed within that jurisdictional ambit.

Prohibited Activities

The FWPCA is an admirably comprehensive piece of legislation. It was designed to deal with all facets of recapturing and preserving the biological integrity of the nation's water by creating a web of complex interrelated regulatory programs. Section 301(a), the enforcement hub of the statute, however, is stated very simply. It provides that except as otherwise permitted within the Act "the discharge of any pollutant by any person shall be unlawful." The plainness of the prohibition is matched by the breadth given the definition of a "discharge of a pollutant":

> "(A) Any addition of any pollutant to navigable waters from any point source,
>
> "(B) Any addition of any pollutant to the waters of the contiguous zone or the ocean from any point source . . . other than a vessel or other floating craft." 33 U.S.C. § 1362(12).

"Pollutant" is in turn defined as

> ". . . *Dredged spoil*, solid waste, incinerator residue, sewage, garbage, sewer sludge, munitions, chemical wastes, *biological materials*, radioactive materials, heat, wrecked or discarded equipment, rock, *sand*, cellar dirt and *industrial*, municipal, and agricultural waste discharged into water. . . ." *Id.* § 1362(6) (emphasis added)

And "point source" is

> ". . . any discernible, confined and discrete conveyance, *including* but not limited to any *pipe, ditch*, channel, tunnel, conduit, well, discrete fissure, container, *rolling stock*, concentrated animal feeding operation, or vessel or other floating craft, from which pollutants are or may be discharged." *Id.* § 1362(14) (emphasis added)

The evidence substantiates the defendants' admission that without a permit they have discharged and would continue to discharge from point sources, including dump trucks, drag lines, and bulldozers, materials defined as pollutants. Whether these pollutants were discharged into waters within federal jurisdiction was the key issue.

Jurisdiction under the FWPCA

Throughout the course of this litigation there has been considerable discussion about whether the mosquito ditches that connect with Papy's Bayou are "navigable" and much testimony about whether certain discharges of pollutants were above or below the "mean high water line." Argument was heard on the issue of whether federal jurisdiction under the FWPCA was limited to activities taking place in navigable waters below the mean high water line. Because the terms "navigability" and "mean high water line" have played such important parts in determining federal jurisdiction over water pollution in the past, the contention that these terms should be used in arguing jurisdiction under the FWPCA was not surprising.

For years the mainstays of the federal water pollution effort were Sections 10 and 13 of Rivers and Harbors Act of 1899. Section 10 makes it illegal to fill, excavate, alter or modify the course, condition or capacity of waters within the boundaries of a navigable waterway without authorization from the Corps of Engineers. Section 13 prohibits the deposit of refuse in, or on the bank of, a navigable waterway without a Corps of Engineers' permit. Both of these laws are by their terms limited to waters that are deemed navigable. Because of this limitation past discussion of federal jurisdiction over water pollution was largely a question of the navigability of the waterway being affected.

. . . .

Although the reach of federal power under the commerce clause widened dramatically in the twentieth century, the nineteenth century legacy of "navigation" lingered to limit federal control over water pollution. Since Congress had clearly limited the Rivers and Harbors Act to navigation, any subsequent judicial broadening of jurisdiction under the statute of necessity had to be in the form of expanding the definition of "navigability."

Starting with the basic definition of waters that

> ". . . form in their ordinary condition by themselves, or by uniting with other waters, a continued highway over which commerce is or may be carried on with other States or foreign countries in the customary modes in which such commerce is conducted by water." (The Daniel Ball, 10 Wall. 557, 77 U.S. 557, 19 L. Ed. 999 (1870).)

The test of navigability was enlarged in 1874 to embrace waters that had the capability of commercial use, not merely those in actual use. The definition was again expanded in 1921 to bring in water bodies whose past history of commercial use made it navigable despite subsequent physical or economic changes preventing present use for commerce. In 1940 it was held that a waterway would be deemed navigable-in-fact if by "reasonable improvements" it could be made navigable. Thus the jurisdictional basis broadened until only the most insignificant body of water could escape one of the tests of navigability.

But the limitation of navigability still worked to impede efforts to forestall the degradation of the aquatic environment. Not only did small feeder streams and tributaries remain exempt from federal jurisdiction but, more importantly, the wetland areas adjoining the waterways did also.

Just as it was not surprising that Congress limited the Rivers and Harbors Act to navigable waters, it was not surprising to have limited enforcement under the statute to navigation-impeding activities taking place *in* the water. Those charged with enforcing the Act needed an easily discernible boundary for their jurisdictional power—*i. e.* the lateral extent of the water body. In tidal areas that boundary became the mean high water line.

The Mean High Water Line

Since the Rivers and Harbors Act was passed at a time when interstate commerce was thought of in a geographical sense, and since the Act was designed primarily to keep the navigable waters free of physical impediments, it was natural to draw on the property-law concept of the mean high water line to limit the scope of jurisdiction in tidal water areas. If an agency is responsible only for keeping a water body free of obstructions, there is little need to focus attention on activities beyond the ordinary reach of the water.

But because the mean high water line was, and is, used to demarcate authority in tidal zones does not necessarily mean that the line is an inviolate barrier to federal assumption of authority over activities landward of the line. Examining the history and use of the line underscores the point. . . . If the instant case involved only the question of federal jurisdiction over non-navigable streams and wetland areas under the Rivers and Harbors Act the Court might be compelled to deny jurisdiction by the sheer weight of precedent. But such is not the case. Here the Court is presented with a dispute brought pursuant to a new federal law not limited to the traditional tests of navigability.

On October 18, 1972, the Congress exercised its power under the commerce clause by enacting the FWPCA, establishing regulatory programs to combat pollution of the nation's waters. Even though it seems certain that Congress sought to broaden federal jurisdiction under the Act, it did so in a manner that appears calculated to force courts to engage in verbal acrobatics. Although using the term "navigable waters" in the prohibitory phase of the statute, the definition of "navigable waters" is stated to be "waters of the United States, including the territorial seas." 33 U.S.C. § 1362(7). The definition stands with no limiting language.

If indeed the Congress saw fit to define away the navigability restriction, the sole limitation on the reach of federal power remaining would be the commerce clause. Thus two questions emerge. Did Congress intend to define away the old "navigability" restriction? And does the Congress have such power?

The answer to the first question is in the affirmative. The Court is of the opinion that the clear meaning of the statutory definition may be ascertained on its face without having to rely on the well established judicial philosophy that "forbids a narrow, cramped reading" of water pollution legislation. United

States v. Ashland Oil and Transportation Co., 364 F. Supp. 349, 350 (W.D. Ky.1973). The legislative history of the FWPCA supports this clear meaning.

The bill submitted to the Senate as S. 2770 defined "navigable waters" to mean "navigable waters of the *United States*, portions thereof, and the tributaries thereof, including the territorial seas and the Great Lakes." Legislative History of the Water Pollution Control Act Amendments of 1972, Vol. 2, p. 1698 (hereinafter cited as "Legislative History"). The report of the Senate Committee on Public Works submitted with S. 2770 explained the definition:

> "The control strategy of the Act extends to navigable waters. The definition of this term means the navigable waters of the United States, portions thereof, tributaries thereof, and includes the territorial seas and the Great Lakes. Through narrow interpretation of the definition of interstate waters the implementation (of the) 1965 Act was severely limited. Water moves in hydrologic cycles and *it is essential that discharge of pollutants be controlled at the source.* Therefore, reference to the control requirements must be made to the navigable waters, portions thereof, and their tributaries." Legislative History, Vol. 2, p. 1495. (emphasis added)

The House of Representatives bill, H.R. 11896, contained a more restrictive definition: "The navigable waters of the United States, including the territorial seas." Legislative History, Vol. 1, p. 1069. Significantly, when the two bills went to the Committee of Conference, the word "navigable" was deleted from the House definition in creating the final standard. The reason for this change was stated in the Joint Explanatory Statement of the Committee of Conference:

> "The conferees fully intend that the term 'navigable waters' be given the broadest possible constitutional interpretation unencumbered by agency determinations which have been made or may be made for administrative purposes." Conference Report, Senate Report No. 92-1236, Sept. 28, 1972, page 144, U.S. Code Cong. & Admin. News 1972, p. 3822; Reprinted in Legislative History, Vol. 1, p. 327.

In presenting the Conference version to the House, Representative Dingell, a member of the Conference Committee, explained the Committee's intention on jurisdiction:

> "The Conference bill defined the term 'navigable waters' broadly for water quality purposes. (502(7)). It means 'all the waters of the United States' in a geographic sense. It does not mean 'navigable waters of the United States' in the technical sense as we sometimes see in some laws." Legislative History, Vol. 1, p. 250.

After a brief discussion of Court cases in which the judiciary has forced some expansion of the old navigability test for water quality purposes, Representative Dingell concluded:

> "Thus, this new definition clearly encompasses all water bodies, including main streams and their tributaries, for water quality purposes. No longer are the old, narrow definitions of navigability, as determined by the Corps of Engineers, going to govern matters covered by this bill." *Id.*

The foregoing compels the Court to conclude that the former test of navigability was indeed defined away in the FWPCA. The Court in United States v. Ashland Oil and Transportation Co., 364 F. Supp. 349 (W. D. Ky. 1973) reached the same conclusion when faced with a criminal prosecution brought under the Act. . . .

Clearly Congress has the power to eliminate the "navigability" limitation from the reach of federal control under the Commerce Clause. The "geographic" and "transportation" conception of the Commerce Clause which may have placed the navigation restriction in the Rivers and Harbors Act of 1899 has long since been abandoned in defining federal power. Now when courts are faced with a challenge to congressional power under the Commerce Clause a statute's validity is upheld by determining first if the general activity sought to be regulated is reasonably related to, or has an effect on, interstate commerce and, second, whether the specific activities in the case before the court are those intended to be reached by Congress through the statute.

It is beyond question that water pollution has a serious effect on interstate commerce and that the Congress has the power to regulate activities such as dredging and filling which cause such pollution. As stated by the Court in Zabel v. Tabb, 430 F.2d 199, 203 (5th Cir. 1970):

> "[T]he nation knows, if the Courts do not, that the destruction of fish and wildlife in our estuarine waters does have a substantial effect on interstate commerce . . . Nor is it challenged that dredge and fill projects are activities which may tend to destroy the ecological balance and thereby affect commerce substantially."

Congress and the courts have become aware of the lethal effect pollution has on all organisms. Weakening any of the life support systems bodes disaster for the rest of the interrelated life forms. To recognize this and yet hold that pollution does not affect interstate commerce unless committed in navigable waters below the mean high water line would be contrary to reason. Congress is not limited by the "navigable waters" test in its authority to control pollution under the Commerce Clause.

Having thus ascertained that Congress had the power to go beyond the "navigability" limitation in its control over water pollution and that it intended to do so in the FWPCA, the question remains whether the Congress intended to reach the type of activities involved in the instant case—the pollution of non-navigable mosquito canals and mangrove wetland areas.

As previously noted the defendants without a permit have filled and otherwise polluted various mosquito canals which connected with the waters of Papy's Bayou. The manmade canals were found to be non-navigable for the purposes of this action.

The conclusion that Congress intended to reach water-bodies such as these canals with the FWPCA is inescapable. The legislative history quoted *supra* manifests a clear intent to break from the limitations of the Rivers and Harbors Act to get at the sources of pollution. Polluting canals that empty into a bayou arm of Tampa Bay is clearly an activity Congress sought to regulate. The fact that these canals were manmade makes no difference. They were constructed long before the development scheme was conceived. That the defendants used them to convey the pollutants without a permit is the matter of importance.

The Court is of the opinion that the waters of the mosquito canals were within the definition of "waters of the United States" and that the filling of them without a permit was a violation of the FWPCA.

Whether the FWPCA was meant to reach activities such as those committed here in mangrove wetlands above the mean high water line is slightly less apparent. An examination of Congressional intent, however, leads this Court to the conclusion that such intertidal wetlands were indeed meant to be covered.

The first glimpse of Congressional intent comes from the FWPCA itself. Section 101(a) puts forth the purpose of the Act:

> "The objective of this Act is to restore and maintain the chemical, physical, and biological integrity of the Nation's waters. In order to achieve this objective it is hereby declared that, consistent with the provisions of this Act—
>
> (1) It is the national goal that the discharge of pollutants into the navigable waters be eliminated by 1985;
>
> (2) It is the national goal that wherever attainable, an interim goal of water quality which provides for the protection and propagation of fish, shellfish, and wildlife and provides for recreation in and on the water be achieved by July 1, 1983." 33 U.S.C. § 1251(a).

In Section 102(c) the Administrator of the Environmental Protection Agency is authorized to make grants for basin studies to provide comprehensive water quality control plans for a basin. "Basin" in that section is defined to include "rivers and their tributaries, streams, coastal waters, sounds, estuaries, bays, lakes, and portions thereof, as well as the lands drained thereby." 33 U.S.C. § 1252(c).

Section 404 of the Act establishes a program for permitting the discharge of dredged or fill materials into waters of the United States. Subsection (c) provides for careful consideration of whether or not such discharges will have "unacceptable adverse effect on municipal water supplies, shellfish beds, and fishery areas (including spawning and breeding areas), wildlife, or recreational areas." 33 U.S.C. § 1344(c).

These three sections do not by themselves prove conclusively that Congress sought to assume jurisdiction over activities taking place in wetlands above the mean high water line. What these sections do reveal is a sensitivity to the value of a coastal breeding ground.[70]

Composed of various interdependent ecological systems (*i.e.* marshes, mudflats, shallow open water, mud and sand bottoms, beach and dunes) the delicately balanced coastal environment is highly sensitive to human activities within its confines. *See* Cooper, Ecological Considerations, Coastal Zone Management 129 (J. Hite & J. Stepp ed. 1971).

[70] An ancillary statement of intent is found in the Coastal Zone Management Act of 1972, 16 U.S.C. § 1451which articulated the intent of Congress to preserve and protect the resources of the Coastal Zone. . . .

Congress realizes the coastal ecology is endangered by poorly planned development. It cannot be gainsaid that the discharge of pollutants into coastal, estuarine and adjacent waters have caused considerable damage to the marine environment. Estuaries, partially enclosed bodies of water within which there is a measurable dilution of sea water by fresh-water run off, and other breeding zones have suffered the most damage. Salt water marshes and other wetlands constitute a major component of the estuarine system.

Estuaries are not only highly productive in organic matter, but also are valuable in replenishing oxygen for the atmosphere. *See* Teclaff, The Coastal Zone—Control over Encroachments into the Tidewaters, 2 Environ. L.Rev. 618 (1971). Moreover, estuaries are vital to fish and shellfish. About two-thirds of all ocean animals either spend a part of their life there or feed upon a species that has lived there. The First Annual Report of the Council on Environmental Quality, 176 (1970). The FWPCA embodies the realization that pollution of these areas may be ecologically fatal.

In an attempt to combat these threats to the coastal environment, the Congress broadened its jurisdiction to encompass "all waters of the United States." In doing so Congress deemed it "essential that the discharge of pollutants be controlled *at the source.*" Legislative History Vol. 2, p. 1495. Getting at the source of pollution is going beyond the confines of a high water line. It cannot be doubted that most of the damage to marine life results from land-based and not sea-based activities.

One of the sources of pollution in the instant case was the discharge of sand, dirt and dredged spoil on land which, although above the mean high water line, was periodically inundated with the waters of Papy's Bayou. Defendants argue that such activities are beyond the reach of the FWPCA. This Court does not agree. Even the occasional lapping of the bayou waters has conveyed these pollutants into the waters of the United States. That the pollutants are not so conveyed every day is of no consequence. Pollutants have been introduced into the waters of the United States without a permit and the mean high water mark cannot be used to create a barrier behind which such activities can be excused. The environment cannot afford such safety zones.

The Court is of the opinion that the mean high water line is no limit to federal authority under the FWPCA. While the line remains a valid demarcation for other purposes, it has no rational connection to the aquatic ecosystems which the FWPCA is intended to protect. Congress has wisely determined that federal authority over water pollution properly rests on the Commerce Clause and not on past interpretations of an act designed to protect navigation. And the Commerce Clause gives Congress ample authority to reach activities above the mean high water line that pollute the waters of the United States.

The defendants' filling activities on land periodically inundated by tidal waters constituted discharges entering "waters of the United States" and, since done without a permit, were thus in violation of 33 U.S.C. § 1311(a).

. . . .

By determining that the defendants have violated the provisions of the FWPCA and by enjoining further unlawful activities, the Court has not permanently prohibited defendants from going forward with their plans. All the Court has said is that the activities cannot be continued without a federal permit.

NOTES AND QUESTIONS

The *United States v. Holland* case establishes a broad claim for federal jurisdiction over navigable waters. Does this claim of jurisdiction extend to manmade channels of all kinds? *See, e.g., BF-2 Properties, Inc. v. Train*, 393 F. Supp. 1370 (D.C. 1975). Is there an obligation on the Corps of Engineers to take jurisdiction over all navigable waters covered by the Act however the term navigable waters is defined? Is the Corps of Engineers under an obligation to issue regulations to cover the expanded jurisdiction over the waters of the nation even though in its own judgment it may prefer not to exercise regulatory powers? *See Natural Resources Defense Council v. Callaway*, 393 F. Supp. 685 (D.C. 1975). *See also* the Army Corps of Engineers Regulation issued subsequently, 40 C.F.R. § 209.120(1976), 40 Fed. Reg. 31520 (July 25, 1975). *See also United States v. Ashland Oil and Transportation Co.*, 364 F. Supp. 349 (W.D. Ky. 1973), *aff'd*, 504 F.2d 1317, 7 E.R.C. 1114 (6th Cir. 1974). Could a claim be made either that the definition of navigable waters as used in the Act is void for vagueness or, in the alternative, that the expansion of jurisdiction under the Federal Water Pollution Control Act Amendments violates the Tenth Amendment and impinges on state sovereignty?

[iii] Publicly Owned Waste Treatment Works (POTWs)

Council on Environmental Quality
Twelfth Annual Report, 75-78
(transmitted to Congress 1981)

Program Status

Since 1972, Congress has authorized $39.2 billion and appropriated $33.2 billion under the construction grants program to help municipalities meet their wastewater treatment needs (Table 3-9). As of September 30, 1981, $32.2 billion had been obligated (including over $1 billion for planning and over $1 billion for design), leaving $954 million unobligated. Tables 3-10 and 3-11 show the funding for completed and ongoing construction grants projects. Over 22,000 grants have been awarded for planning, design, and construction of municipal wastewater treatment facilities. Table 3-12 indicates the distribution of grants by community size.

By September 30, 1981, 10,573 planning, design, and construction projects had been completed since 1972. An estimated 4,000 wastewater treatment construction projects of the 1973-81 funding period are now physically complete and operating although some have final inspections and audits yet to be completed. In the next 2 years, approximately 6,200 projects, including many of the larger ones, are due to come on line and are expected to improve significantly the nation's water quality.

EPA's implementation of the 1981 Amendments emphasizes the fact that federal funds are limited and must be used to achieve maximum water quality benefits. Toward this goal, EPA is in the process of revising the secondary treatment regulations and the water quality standards regulations. The agency is also basing the national Needs Survey on the new eligibilities, streamlining the construction grants regulations, and encouraging the use of a water quality basis for state project priorities.

Performance of POTWs

A recent EPA survey of performance of publicly owned treatment works (POTWs) built with construction grants funding after 1972 found that about 1600 or 78 percent of major plants constructed to meet secondary standards were meeting or exceeding those standards in one or both of the last two quarters of 1980. Another study of 118 major plants in the Pacific southwest found that 85 percent of those plants were meeting NPDES permit limitations. Also, a survey of 161 plants conducted by the State of California indicated that nearly 85 percent of the plants there were operating satisfactorily and that only 8 percent had major problems.

Table 3-9

	Fiscal Year	Authorization	Allocation	Grants Made	
Funding	73	5.0	2.0	$1,532,000,000	
Availability Under	74	6.0	3.0	$1,444,000,000	
the Construction	75	7.0	4.0	$3,616,000,000	
Grants Program	76	—	9.0	$4,814,000,000	
(in billions)	77	0.7	1.42	$6,664,000,000	
	78	5.5	4.5	$2,301,000,000	
	79	5.0	4.2	$3,872,000,000	
	80	5.0	2.52	$4,376,000,000	
	81	5.0	2.55	$3,612,000,000	
		39.2	33.2	$32,231,000,000	(Rounded)

Source: U.S. Environmental Protection Agency, Office of Water Program Operations

Some plants developed prior to 1972 violate their permits because the plants were designed to meet treatment levels less stringent than those subsequently required by the 1972 Act. In many cases these projects were either under construction or just coming on line when the 1972 law was enacted. Permits issued to these projects reflected the most stringent 1972 requirements—requirements which were not in existence when the projects were designed. In many cases, these pre-1972 projects are meeting their design level of performance, but may not be in compliance with the statutory requirements reflected in their permits.

Other permit violations by municipal wastewater treatment plants result mostly from four major causes: (1) inadequate operation and maintenance of the plant, including chemical control and equipment upkeep; (2) infiltration-inflow of ground water or surface water which enters a sewage collection system increasing hydraulic capacity requirements and thereby causing plant upsets; (3) deficiencies in plant design and construction; and (4) influent which interferes with plant operation.

The full benefit of the public investment in the Construction Grants Program can be realized only if the facilities are properly operated and maintained. Even the best treatment plant will fail without proper operation and maintenance. Recognizing an urgent need to improve the performance of treatment plants, EPA has recently increased its efforts to assure that grantees are adequately prepared to assume the financial and administrative demands of successfully operating and maintaining their wastewater treatment facilities. EPA also assists the states with diagnostic inspection of major noncomplying plants to identify problems and possible remedial measures. EPA's role has shifted from a "hands on" project management function to that of providing program guidance, oversight, and evaluation. Strong, well-organized local operating agencies are the key to improved plant operation and maintenance.

Alternative Projects for Small Communities

Small rural communities have special problems in managing waste treatment. Many communities cannot afford to operate and maintain a conventional centralized wastewater treatment facility even if built without local funds. For some communities, even establishing a user charge system so that the facility can operate as a self-sustaining public utility is unrealistic because the charges to users would be too high. Concern for rural wastewater treatment problems is heightened by the fact that small communities with fewer than 3,500 people receive nearly half of the number of all wastewater treatment grants awarded.

To help these communities, the Clean Water Act requires that states with significant rural populations set aside 4 percent of their annual construction grants allotment to fund less costly alternatives to conventional treatment works. As of March 31,1981, about 83 rural small communities had been awarded $99 million in grants for design and construction of alternative technology systems. The use of one of these alternatives, land treatment, has grown substantially in recent years. Of 620 such projects funded since 1972, 250 were funded between October 1978 and April 1981. These land treatment projects, located in all regions of the country, include some large projects such as those in Clayton County, Georgia; Bakersfield, California; and Muskegon, Michigan.

Council on Environmental Quality
Sixth Annual Report, 72-74
(transmitted to Congress 1975)

Planning

Although delegating certification authority to the states may accelerate the rate at which grant monies are disbursed, it will not necessarily improve the economic efficiency or the environmental integrity of the program. EPA is attempting to deal with these problems through its project design guidelines. The revised guidelines provide more explicit instructions on cost effective design, environmental evaluations, and project review by the public and by state and local planning bodies. They also attempt to coordinate design of a facility with the three sections of the act having planning requirements.

Section 201 pertains to the planning of individual facilities. Section 303e pertains to statewide planning efforts and is designed to encourage the states to develop an overall strategy for water quality improvement, including industrial and municipal waste water discharges. And Section 208 calls for areawide waste treatment and water management plans that incorporate abatement facilities, land use, and economic growth considerations in covering metropolitan areas and other regions.

. . . .

NOTE

For comments on the planning requirements in § 208 of the Federal Water Pollution Control ActAmendments, see Phillips, *Developments in Water Quality and Land Use Planning: Problems in the Application of the Federal Water Pollution Control Act Amendments of 1972*, 10 Urb. L. Ann. 43 (1975); Comment, *Areawide Planning Under the Federal Water Pollution Control Act Amendments of 1972: Intergovernmental and Land Use Implications*, 54 Tex. L. Rev. 1047 (1976); Note, *Sewers, Clean Water, and Planned Growth: Restructuring the Federal Pollution Abatement Effort*, 86 Yale L.J. 733 (1977).

Natural Resources Defense Council, Inc. v. Train, 396 F. Supp. 1386 (D.C. 1975), held: FWPCA § 208 requires the state act as the planning agency for the nondesignated portions of the state in the same manner as planning organizations for designated areas. Waste treatment management planning is required for a state for portions not designated, and EPA is under an obligation to reflect this requirement in its regulations.

[iv] Effluent Limitations and Effluent Guidelines—Best Practicable Technology (BPT), Best Available Technology (BAT)

E. I. DU PONT DE NEMOURS & CO. v. TRAIN

United States Supreme Court (1977)
430 U.S. 112, 97 S. Ct. 965, 51 L. Ed. 2d. 204

Mr. Justice Stevens delivered the opinion of the Court.

Inorganic chemical manufacturing plants operated by the eight petitioners discharge various pollutants into the Nation's waters and therefore are "point sources" within the meaning of the Federal Water Pollution Control Act Amendments of 1972, 86Stat. 816, 33 U.S.C. § 1251 *et seq.* (Supp. IV) ("The Act"). The Environmental Protection Agency has promulgated industry-wide regulations imposing three sets of precise limitations on petitioners' discharges. The first two impose progressively higher levels of pollutant control on existing point sources after July 1, 1977, and after July 1, 1983, respectively. The third set imposes limits on "new sources" that may be constructed in the future.[71]

These cases present three important questions of statutory construction: (1) whether EPA has the authority under § 301 of the Act to issue industry-wide regulations limiting discharges by existing plants; (2) whether the Court of Appeals, which admittedly is authorized to review the standards for new sources, also has jurisdiction under § 509 to review the regulations concerning existing plants; and (3) whether the new source standards issued under § 306 must allow variances for individual plants.

As a preface to our discussion of these three questions, we summarize relevant portions of the statute and then describe the procedure which EPA followed in promulgating the challenged regulations.

The Statute

The statute, enacted on October 18, 1972, authorized a series of steps to be taken to achieve the goal of eliminating all discharges of pollutants into the Nation's waters by 1985, § 101(a)(1).

The first steps required by the Act are described in § 304, which directs the Administrator to develop and publish various kinds of technical data to provide guidance in discharging responsibilities imposed by other sections of the Act. Thus, within 60 days, 120 days, and 180 days after the date of

[71] The reasons for the statutory scheme have been described as follows: "Such direct restrictions on discharges facilitate enforcement by making it unnecessary to work backward from an overpolluted body of water to determine which point sources are responsible and which must be abated. In addition, a discharger's performance is now measured against strict technology-based effluent limitations—specified levels of treatment—to which it must conform, rather than against limitations derived from water quality standards to which it and other polluters must collectively conform." *EPA v. State Water Resources Control Board* 426 U.S. 200, 204-205, 96 S.Ct. 2022, 2024, 48 L.Ed.2d 578 (footnotes omitted).

enactment, the Administrator was to promulgate a series of guidelines to assist the States in developing and carrying our permit programs pursuant to § 402. §§ 304(h), (f), (g). Within 270 days, he was to develop the information to be used in formulating standards for new plans pursuant to § 306. § 304(c). And within one year he was to publish regulations providing guidance for effluent limitations on existing point sources. Section 304(b) goes into great detail concerning the contents of these regulations. They must identify the degree of effluent reduction attainable through use of the best practicable or best available technology for a class of plants. The guidelines must also "specify factors to be taken into account" in determining the control measures applicable to point sources within these classes. A list of factors to be considered then follows. The Administrator was also directed to develop and publish, within one year, elaborate criteria for water quality accurately reflecting the most current scientific knowledge, and also technical information on factors necessary to restore and maintain water quality. § 304(a). The title of § 304 describes it as the "information and guidelines" portion of the statute.

Section 301 is captioned "effluent limitations." Section 301(a) makes the discharge of any pollutant unlawful unless the discharge is in compliance with certain enumerated sections of the Act. The enumerated sections which are relevant to this case are § 301 itself, § 306, and § 402.[72] A brief word about each of these sections is necessary.

Section 402 authorizes the Administrator to issue permits for individual point sources, and also authorizes him to review and approve the plan of any State desiring to administer its own permit program. These permits serve "to transform generally applicable effluent limitations . . . into the obligations (including a timetable for compliance) of the individual discharger[s.] . . ." *EPA v. State Water Resources Control Board*, 426 U.S. 200, 205, 96 S.Ct. 2022, 2025, 48 L.Ed.2d 578. Petitioner chemical companies' position in this litigation is that § 402 provides the only statutory authority for the issuance of enforceable limitations on the discharge of pollutants by existing plants. It is noteworthy, however, that although this section authorizes the imposition of limitations in individual permits, the section itself does not mandate either the Administrator or the States to use permits as the method of prescribing effluent limitations.

Section 306 directs the Administrator to publish within 90 days a list of categories of sources discharging pollutants and, within one year thereafter, to publish regulations establishing national standards of performance for new sources within each category. Section 306 contains no provision for exceptions from the standards for individual plants; on the contrary, subsection (e) expressly makes it unlawful to operate a new source in violation of the applicable standard of performance after its effective date. The statute provides that the new source standards shall reflect the greatest degree of effluent reduction achievable through application of the best available demonstrated control technology.

---

72 There is no provision for compliance with § 304, the guideline section.

Section 301(b) defines the effluent limitations that shall be achieved by existing point sources in two stages. By July 1, 1977, the effluent limitations shall require the application of the best *practicable* control technology currently available; by July 1, 1983, the limitations shall require application of the best *available* technology economically achievable. The statute expressly provides that the limitations which are to become effective in 1983 are applicable to "categories and classes of point sources;" this phrase is omitted from the description of the 1977 limitations. While § 301 states that these limitations "shall be achieved," it fails to state who will establish the limitations.

Section 301(c) authorizes the Administrator to grant variances from the 1983 limitations. Section 301(e) states that effluent limitations established pursuant to § 301 shall be applied to all point sources.

To summarize, § 301(b) requires the achievement of effluent limitations requiring use of the "best practicable" or "best available" technology. It refers to § 304 for a definition of these terms. Section 304 requires the publication of "regulations, providing guidelines for effluent limitations." Finally, permits issued under § 402 must require compliance with § 301 effluent limitations. Nowhere are we told who sets the § 301 effluent limitations, or precisely how they relate to § 304 guidelines and § 402 permits.

The Regulations

The various deadlines imposed on the Administrator were too ambitious for him to meet. For that reason, the procedure which he followed in adopting the regulations applicable to the inorganic chemical industry and to other classes of point sources, is somewhat different from that apparently contemplated by the statute. Specifically, as will appear, he did not adopt guidelines pursuant to § 304 before defining the effluent limitations for existing sources described in § 301(b) or the national standards for new sources described in § 306. This case illustrates the approach the Administrator followed in implementing the Act.

EPA began by engaging a private contractor to prepare a Development Document. This document provided a detailed technical study of pollution control in the industry. The study first divided the industry into categories. For each category, present levels of pollution were measured and plants with exemplary pollution control were investigated. Based on this information, other technical data, and economic studies, a determination was made of the degree of pollution control which could be achieved by the various levels of technology mandated by the statute. The study was made available to the public and circulated to interested persons. It formed the basis of "effluent limitation guideline" regulations issued by EPA after receiving public comment on proposed regulations. These regulations divide the industry into 22 subcategories. Within each subcategory, precise numerical limits are set for various pollutants.[73] The regulations of each subcategory contain a variance

[73] Some subcategories are required to eliminate all discharges by 1977. *E.g.*, 40 C.F.R. §§ 415.70-415.76. Other subcategories are subject to less stringent restrictions. For instance, by 1977 plants producing titanium dioxide by the chloride process must reduce average daily discharges of dissolved iron to 0.72 pounds per thousand pounds of product. This limit is cut in half for existing plants in 1983 and for all new plants. 40 C.F.R. §§ 415.220-415.225.

clause, applicable only to the 1977 limitations.[74]

Eight chemical companies filed petitions in the United States Court of Appeals for the Fourth Circuit for review of these regulations.[75] The Court of Appeals rejected their challenge to EPA's authority to issue precise, single number limitations for discharges of pollutants from existing sources. It held, however, that these limitations and the new plant standards were only "presumptively applicable" to individual plants.[76] We granted the chemical compa nies' petitions for certiorari in order to consider the scope of EPA's authority to issue existing-source regulations. We also granted the Government's cross-petition for review of the ruling that new source standards are only presumptively applicable. 426 U.S. 947, 96 S.Ct. 3165, 49 L.Ed.2d 1183. For convenience, we will refer to the chemical companies as the "petitioners."

The Issues

The broad outlines of the parties' respective theories may be stated briefly. EPA contends that § 301(b) authorizes it to issue regulations establishing effluent limitations for classes of plants. The permits granted under § 402, in EPA's view, simply incorporate these across-the-board limitations, except for the limited variances allowed by the regulations themselves and by § 301(c). The § 304(b) guidelines, according to EPA, were intended to guide it in later establishing § 301 effluent limitation regulations. Because the process proved more time consuming than Congress assumed when it established this two-stage process, EPA condensed the two stages into a single regulation.[77]

In contrast, petitioners contend that § 301 is not an independent source of authority for setting effluent limitations by regulation. Instead, § 301 is seen as merely a description of the effluent limitations which are set for each plant on an individual basis during the permit-issuance process. Under the industry

---

[74] These limitations may be made "either more or less stringent" to the extent that "factors relating to the equipment or facilities involved, the process applied, or other such factors related to such discharges are fundamentally different from the factors considered" in establishing the limitations. *See, e.g.*, for the two subcategories discussed *supra*, n.9, 40 C.F.R. §§ 415.72 and 415.222, respectively.

[75] Because EPA's authority to issue the regulations is closely tied to the question whether the regulations are directly reviewable in the Court of Appeals, some of the companies also filed suit in District Court challenging the regulations. The District Court held that EPA had the authority to issue the regulations and that exclusive jurisdiction was therefore in the Court of Appeals. 383 F. Supp. 1244 (WD Va. 1974), aff'd, 4 Cir., 528 F.2d 1136.

[76] The Court of Appeals issued two separate opinions. In *DuPont I*, 528 F.2d 1136, the court held that it had exclusive jurisdiction to consider the validity of the regulations. It therefore affirmed the District Court's dismissal of a suit to set aside the regulations. *See* n.11, *supra*. In *DuPont II*, 541 F.2d 1018, the court held that EPA was authorized to issue "presumptively applicable" effluent limitations and new source standards. No. 75-978 is the companies' petition for certiorari in *DuPont I*, which we granted last Term, 425 U.S. 933, 96 S.Ct. 1662, 48 L.Ed.2d 174. No. 75-1473 is their petition in *DuPont II*. We granted that petition, consolidated it with EPA's cross-petition, No. 1705, and ordered that they be argued *in tandem* with the companies' petition in *DuPont I*. 426 U.S. 947, 96 S.Ct. 3165, 49 L.Ed.2d 1183.

[77] Section 304(b) calls for publication of guideline regulations within one year of the Act's passage. EPA failed to meet this deadline and was ordered to issue the regulations on a judicially imposed timetable. *National Resources Defense Council, Inc. v. Train*, 166 U.S.App. D.C. 312, 510 F.2d 692 (1975).

view, the § 304 guidelines serve the function of guiding the permit issuer in setting the effluent limitations.

The jurisdictional issue is subsidiary to the critical question whether EPA has the power to issue effluent limitation by regulation. Section 509(b)(1) provides that "[r]eview of the Administrator's action . . . (E) in approving or promulgating any effluent limitation . . . under section 301" may be had in the Courts of Appeals. On the other hand, the Act does not provide for judicial review of § 304 guidelines. If EPA is correct that its regulations are "effluent limitations under section 301," the regulations are directly reviewable in the Court of Appeals. If industry is correct that the regulations can only be considered § 304 guidelines, suit to review the regulations could probably be brought only in the District Court, if anywhere.[78] Thus, the issue of jurisdiction to review the regulations is intertwined with the issue of EPA's power to issue the regulations.[79]

---

[78] Although the Act itself does not provide for review of guidelines, the Eighth Circuit has held that they are reviewable in the District Court, apparently under the Administrative Procedure Act. *CPC International, Inc. v. Train*, 515 F.2d 1032, 1038 (1975). It has been suggested, however, that even if the EPA regulations are considered to be only § 304 guidelines, the Court of Appeals might still have ancillary jurisdiction to review them because of their close relationship with the § 301 effluent limitations, and because they were developed on the same record as the § 306 standards of performance for new plants, which are directly reviewable in the Court of Appeals.

[79] The Courts of Appeals have resolved these issues in various ways. Only the Eighth Circuit, the first to consider the issues, has accepted the industry position. In *CPC International, Inc. v. Train*, 515 F.2d 1032 (1975), it held that EPA lacked the authority to issue effluent limitation regulations and that jurisdiction to review the regulations as § 304 guidelines was in the District Court. The Fourth Circuit, in *DuPont II*, 541 F.2d 1018 (1976), and the Tenth Circuit, in *American Petroleum Institute v. EPA*, 540 F.2d 1023 (1976), held that EPA has the authority to issue effluent limitation regulations, but that these regulations are only presumptively applicable to individual sources. The majority position, adopted by the Third Circuit, *American Iron & Steel Institute v. EPA*, 526 F.2d 1027 (1975); the Seventh Circuit, *American Meat Institute v. EPA*, 526 F.2d 442 (1975); the District of Columbia Circuit, *American Frozen Food Institute v. Train*, 176 U.S. App.D.C. 105, 539 F.2d 107 (1976); and the Second Circuit, *Hooker Chemicals & Plastic Corp. v. Train*, 537 F.2d 620 (1976); is that EPA has the authority to issue regulations setting forth effluent limitations which individual plants may not exceed. Even these courts are not in complete agreement about the form the regulations should take. The commentators have also divided on the problem. *See* Parenteau & Tauman, The Effluent Limitations Controversy, 6 Ecology Law Quarterly 1 (1976); Note, Judicial Maelstrom in Federal Waters, 45 Fordham L. Rev. 625 (1976); Comment, The Application of Effluent Limitations and Effluent Guidelines to Industrial Polluters, 13 Hous. L.Rev. 348 (1976). Note, Effective National Regulation of Point Sources Under the 1972 Federal Water Pollution Control Act, 10Ga. L. Rev. 983 (1976).

The difference in opinion among the Circuits may be less significant than might appear. The Eighth Circuit has concluded that:

> "Under our ruling, the limitations written into individual permits for existing point sources should be substantially similar to those written into permits if the EPA's theory of the Act were to be adopted.
>
> "The only practical difference resulting from this Court's interpretation of the statute is that the § 304(b) guidelines for *existing* sources must be reviewed first in the District Court, while the § 306(b) standards of performance for *new* plants—often based on the same scientific research and conclusions—must be reviewed first in the Court of Appeals."

CPC International, Inc. v. Train, 540 F.2d 1329, 1331-1332 n.1 (C.A.8 1976) *(CPC II). See also American Meat Institute, supra*, 526 F.2d, at 449 n.14.

While this court has not had occasion to rule directly on this question, our discussion of the Act in a case decided last Term is suggestive of the answer. We then described § 402 permits as "serv[ing] to transform *generally applicable*

I.

We think § 301 itself is the key to the problem. The statutory language concerning the 1983 limitation, in particular, leaves no doubt that these limitations are to be set by regulation. Subsection (b) (2) (A) of § 301 states that by 1983 "effluent limitations *for categories and classes* of point sources" are to be achieved which will require "application of the best available technology economically achievable *for such category or class.*" (Emphasis added.) These effluent limitations are to require elimination of all discharges if "such elimination is technologically and economically achievable for a *category or class* of point sources." (Emphasis added.) This is "language difficult to reconcile with the view that individual effluent limitations are to be set when each permit is issued." *American Meat Institute v. EPA*, 526 F.2d 442, 450 (C.A.7 1975). The statute thus focuses expressly on the characteristics of the "category or class" rather than the characteristics of individual point sources.[80] Normally, such class-wide determinations would be made by regulation, not in the course of issuing a permit to one member of the class.[81]

Thus, we find that § 301 unambiguously provides for the use of regulations to establish the 1983 effluent limitations. Different language is used in § 301 with respect to the 1977 limitations. Here, the statute speaks of "effluent limitations for point sources," rather than "effluent limitations for categories and classes of point sources." Nothing elsewhere in the Act, however, suggests any radical differences in the mechanism used to impose limitations for the 1977 and 1983 deadlines. *See American Iron; & Steel Institute v. EPA*, 526 F.2d 1027, 1042 n.32 (C.A.3 1975). For instance, there is no indication in either § 301 or § 304 that the § 304 guidelines play a different role in setting 1977 limitations.

Moreover, it would be highly anomalous if the 1983 regulations and the new source standards[82] were directly reviewable in the Court of Appeals, while

---

effluent limitations . . . into the obligations (including a timetable for compliance) of the individual discharger. . . ." 426 U.S. 200, 205, 96 S.Ct. 2022, 2025, 48 L.Ed.2d 578 (emphasis added). This description clearly implied that effluent limitations of general application are to be established before individual permits are issued.

[80] The Court of Appeals noted that "[t]he 1983 and new source requirements are on the basis of categories." *DuPont II*, 541 F.2d, at 1029.

[81] Furthermore, § 301(c) provides that the 1983 limitations may be modified if the owner of a plant shows "that such modified requirements (1) will represent the maximum use of technology within the economic capability of the owner or operator; and (2) will result in reasonable further progress toward the elimination of the discharge of pollutants." This provision shows that the § 301(b) limitations for 1983 are to be established prior to consideration of the characteristics of the individual plant. *American Iron & Steel Institute v. EPA*, 526 F.2d 1027, 1037 n.15 (C.A.3 1975). Moreover, it shows that the term "best technology economically achievable" does not refer to any individual plant. Otherwise, it would be impossible for this "economically achievable" technology to be beyond the individual owner's "economic capability."

[82] Section 509(b)(1)(A) makes new source standards directly reviewable in the Court of Appeals. The Court of Appeals in this case did not believe that Congress "intended for review to be bifurcated," with the new source standards reviewable in a different forum than regulations governing existing sources. 528 F.2d at 1141. The Eighth Circuit has acknowledged the practical problems and potential for inconsistent rulings created by bifurcated review. *CPC II*, 540 F.2d 1329, 1332 n.1 (1976). We consider it unlikely that Congress intended such bifurcated review, and even less likely that Congress intended regulations governing existing sources to be reviewable in two different forums, depending on whether the regulations require compliance in 1977 or 1983.

the 1977 regulations based on the same administrative record were reviewable only in the District Court. The magnitude and highly technical character of the administrative record involved with these regulations makes it almost inconceivable that Congress would have required duplicate review in the first instance by different courts. We conclude that the statute authorizes the 1977 limitations as well as the 1983 limitations to be set by regulation, so long as some allowance is made for variations in individual plants, as EPA has done by including a variance clause in its 1977 limitations.[83]

The question of the form of § 301 limitations is tied to the question whether the Act requires the Administrator or the permit issuer to establish the limitations. Section 301 does not itself answer this question, for it speaks only in the passive voice of the achievement and establishment of the limitations. But other parts of the statute leave little doubt on this score. Section 304(b) states that "[f]or the purpose of adopting or revising effluent limitations . . . the Administrator shall" issue guideline regulations; while the judicial review section (§ 509(b) (1)) speaks of "the Administrator's action . . . in approving or promulgating any effluent limitation or other limitation under section 301. . . ." And § 101(d) requires us to resolve any ambiguity on this score in favor of the Administrator. It provides that "[e]xcept as otherwise *expressly* provided in this Act, the Administrator of the Environmental Protection Agency . . . shall administer this Act." (Emphasis added.) In sum, the language of the statute supports the view that § 301 limitations are to be adopted by the Administrator, that they are to be based primarily on classes and categories, and that they are to take the form of regulations.

The legislative history supports this reading of § 301. The Senate Report states that "pursuant to subsection 301(b) (1) (A), and Section 304(b)" the Administrator is to set a base level for all plants in a given category, and "[i]n no case . . . should any plant be allowed to discharge more pollutants per unit of production than is defined by that base level." Leg. Hist., at 1468;[84] U.S. Code Cong. & Admin. News 1972, pp. 3668, 3716. The Conference Report on § 301 states that "the determination of the economic impact of an effluent limitation [will be made] on the basis of classes and categories of point sources, as distinguished from a plant by plant determination." Leg.Hist., at 304; U.S. Code Cong. & Admin. News 1972, p. 3799. In presenting the Conference Report to the Senate, Senator Muskie, perhaps the Act's primary author, emphasized the importance of uniformity in setting § 301 limitations. He explained that this goal of uniformity required that EPA focus on classes or categories of sources in formulating effluent limitations. Regarding the requirement contained in § 301 that plants use the "best practicable control technology" by 1977, he stated:

> "The modification of subsection 304(b) (1) is intended to clarify what is meant by the term 'practicable.' The balancing test between total cost and effluent reduction benefits is intended to limit the application of technology

[83] We agree with the Court of Appeals, 541 F.2d, at 1028, that consideration of whether EPA's variance provision has the proper scope would be premature.

[84] All citations to the legislative history are to "A Legislative History of the Water Pollution Control Act Amendments of 1972," prepared by the Environmental Policy Division of the Congressional Research Service of the Library of Congress (Committee Print 1973).

only where the additional degree of effluent reduction is wholly out of proportion to the costs of achieving such marginal level of reduction for *any class or category* of sources.

"The Conferees agreed upon this limited cost-benefit analysis in order to maintain *uniformity within a class and category* of point sources subject to effluent limitations, and to avoid imposing on the Administrator any requirement to consider the location of sources within a category or to ascertain water quality impact of effluent controls or to determine the economic impact of controls on any individual plant in a single community." Leg. Hist., at 170 (emphasis added).

He added that:

"The Conferees intend that the factors described in section 304(b) be considered only within classes or categories of point sources and that such factors not be considered at the time of the application of an effluent limitation to an individual point source within such a category or class." Leg. Hist., at 72.

This legislative history supports our reading of § 301 and makes it clear that the § 304 guidelines are not merely aimed at guiding the discretion of permit issuers in setting limitations for individual plants.

What, then, is the function of the § 304(b) guidelines? As we noted earlier, § 304(b) requires EPA to identify the amount of effluent reduction attainable through use of the best practicable or available technology and to "specify factors to be taken into account" in determining the pollution control methods "to be applicable to point sources . . . within such categories or classes." These guidelines are to be issued "[f]or the purpose of adopting or revising effluent limitations under this Act."[85] As we read it, § 304 requires that the guidelines survey the practicable or available pollution control technology for an industry and assess its effectiveness. The guidelines are then to describe the methodology EPA intends to use in the § 301 regulations to determine the effluent

[85] Petitioners rely heavily on selected portions of the following passage from the Senate Report to support their view of § 301:

"It is the Committee's intention that pursuant to subsection 301(b) (1) (A) and Section 304(b) the Administrator will interpret the term 'best practicable' when applied to various categories of industries as a basis for specifying clear and precise effluent limitations to be implemented by January 1, 1976 [now July 1, 1977]. In defining the best practicable for any given industrial category, the Committee expects the Administrator to take a number of factors into account. These factors should include the age of the plants, their size and the unit processes involved and the cost of applying such controls. In effect, for any industrial category, the Committee expects the Administrator to define a range of discharge levels, above a certain base level applicable to all plants within that category. In applying effluent limitations to any individual plant, the factors cited above should be applied to that specific plant. In no case, however, should any plant be allowed to discharge more pollutants per unit of production than is defined by that base level.

"The Administrator should establish the range of best practicable levels based upon the average of the best existing performance by plants of various sizes, ages, and unit processes within each industrial category."

Leg. Hist. 1468: U.S. CODE Cong. & Admin. News 1972, p. 3716.

If construed to be consistent with the legislative history we have already discussed, and with what we have found to be the clear statutory language can be fairly read to allow the use of subcategories based on factors such as size, age and unit processes, with effluent limitations for each subcategory normally based on the performance of the best plants in that subcategory.

limitations for particular plants. If the technical complexity of the task had not prevented EPA from issuing the guidelines within the statutory deadline,[86] they could have provided valuable guidance to permit issuers, industry, and the public, prior to the issuance of the § 301 regulations.[87]

Our construction of the Act is supported by § 501(a), which gives EPA the power to make "such regulations as are necessary to carry out its functions, and by § 101(d), which charges the agency with the duty of administering the Act."

The petitioners' view of the Act would place an impossible burden on EPA. It would require EPA to give individual consideration to the circumstances of each of the more than 42,000 dischargers who have applied for permits (Respondent's Br., at 30 n.22), and to issue or approve all these permits well in advance of the 1977 deadline in order to give industry time to install the necessary pollution control equipment. We do not believe that Congress would have failed so conspicuously to provide EPA with the authority needed to achieve the statutory goals.

Both EPA and petitioners refer to numerous other provisions of the Act and fragments of legislative history in support of their positions. We do not find these conclusive, and little point would be served by discussing them in detail. We are satisfied that our reading of § 301 is consistent with the rest of the legislative scheme.[88]

---

[86] As the Court of Appeals held (541 F.2d, at 1027), EPA's response to this problem was within its discretion. Accord, *American Frozen Food Institute v. Train*, 176 U.S.App. D.C. 105, 539 F.2d 107, 130-131 (1967). Even if we considered this course to constitute a procedural error, it would not invalidate the § 301 regulations themselves since the purposes for issuing the guidelines were substantially achieved, see n.23, *infra*, and no prejudice has been shown.

[87] The guidelines could have served at least three functions. First, they would have provided guidance to permit issuers prior to promulgation of the § 301 effluent limitation regulations. Second, they would have given industry more time to prepare to meet the § 301 regulations. Third, they would have afforded a greater opportunity for public input into the final § 301 regulations, by giving notice of the general outlines of those regulations. These functions were substantially served by EPA's practice of obtaining public comment on the development document and proposed regulations. In addition, the guidelines could furnish technical guidance to companies lacking expertise in pollution control by informing them of appropriate control methods. *See* Leg. Hist. 1463. This function is served by the Development Document and supporting materials.

[88] *See American Iron & Steel Inst. v. EPA*, 526 F.2d 1027, 1037-1041 (C.A.3 1975); *American Meat Inst. v. EPA*, 526 F.2d 442, 450-452 (C.A. 7 1975); *American Meat Inst. v. Train*, 176 U.S.App.D.C. 105, 539 F.2d 107, 116-131 (1976). As these Courts have noted, a number of provisions of the Act seem to assume that § 301 effluent limitations have some existence apart from § 402 permits. Section 301(a) makes any discharge unlawful "[e]xcept as in compliance with this section and section[] . . . 402 . . . of this Act." Similarly, § 509(b), the judicial review provision, refers separately to the Administrator's action "(E) in approving or promulgating any effluent limitation or other limitation under section 301 . . . and (F) in issuing or denying any permit under section 402." Likewise, § 505(f), defines "effluent standard or limitation," for purposes of the citizen enforcement provision of the Act, to include "(2) an effluent limitation or other limitation under section 301 or 302 of this Act," and "(6) a permit or condition thereof issued under section 402 of this Act." The legislative history also recognizes a distinction between permit conditions and § 301 limitations. For instance: "The [House] Committee further recognizes that the requirements under [section] 301 . . . will not all be promulgated immediately upon enactment of this bill. Nevertheless, it would be unreasonable to delay issuing of permits until all the implementing steps are necessary." Leg.Hist., at 813.

These Court of Appeals decisions have also

Language we recently employed in another case involving the validity of EPA regulations applies equally to this case:

> "We therefore conclude that the Agency's interpretation . . . was 'correct,' to the extent that it can be said with complete assurance that any particular interpretation of a complex statute such as this is the 'correct' one. Given this conclusion, as well as the facts that the Agency is charged with administration of the Act, and that there has undoubtedly been reliance upon its interpretation by the States and other parties affected by the Act, we have no doubt whatever that its construction was sufficiently reasonable to preclude the Court of Appeals from substituting its judgment for that of the Agency." *Train v. Natural Resources Defense Council*, 421 U.S. 60, 87, 95 S.Ct. 1470, 1485, 43 L.Ed.2d 731.

When as in this case, the Agency's interpretation is also supported by thorough, scholarly opinions written by some of our finest judges, and has received the overwhelming support of the courts of appeals, we would be reluctant indeed to upset the Agency's judgment. In this case, on the contrary, our independent examination confirms the correctness of the Agency's construction of the statute.

Consequently, we hold that EPA has the authority to issue regulations setting forth uniform limitations for categories of plants.

II.

Our holding that § 301 does authorize the Administrator to promulgate effluent limitations for classes and categories of existing point sources necessarily resolves the jurisdictional issue as well. For, as we have already pointed out, § 509(b) (1) provides that "[r]eview of the Administrator's action . . . in approving or promulgating any effluent limitation or other limitation under section 301, 302, or 306, . . . may be had by any interested person in the Circuit Court of Appeals of the United States for the Federal judicial district in which such person resides or transacts such business. . . ."

Petitioners have argued that the reference to § 301 was intended only to provide for review of the grant or denial of an individual variance pursuant to § 301(c). We find this argument unpersuasive for two reasons in addition to those discussed in Part I of this opinion. First, in other portions of § 509, Congress referred to specific subsections of the Act and presumably would have specifically mentioned § 301(c) if only action pursuant to that subsection were intended to be reviewable in the Court of Appeals. More importantly, petitioners' construction would produce the truly perverse situation in which the Court of Appeals would review numerous individual actions issuing or denying permits pursuant to § 402 but would have no power of direct review of the basic regulations governing those individual actions. *See American Meat Institute v. EPA*, 526 F.2d 442, 452 (C.A. 7 1975).

We regard § 509(b)(1)(E) as unambiguously authorizing Court of Appeals review of EPA action promulgating an effluent limitation for existing point

thoroughly considered the arguments the Eighth Circuit found to be persuasive. . . .

sources under § 301. Since those limitations are typically promulgated in the same proceeding as the new source standards under § 306, we have no doubt that Congress intended review of the two sets of regulations to be had in the same forum.

III. NEW PLANTS

The remaining issue in this case concerns new plants. Under § 306, EPA is to promulgate "regulations establishing Federal standards of performance for new sources. . . ." § 306(b)(1)(B). A "standard of performance" is a "standard for the control of the discharge of pollutants which reflects the greatest degree of effluent reduction which the Administrator determines to be achievable through application of the best available demonstrated control technology, . . . including, where practicable, a standard permitting no discharge of pollutants." § 306(a)(1). In setting the standard, "[t]he Administrator may distinguish among classes, types, and sizes within categories of new sources . . . and shall consider the type of process employed (including whether batch or continuous)." § 306(b)(2). As the House Report states, the standard must reflect the best technology for "that category of sources, and for class, types and sizes within categories." Leg. Hist., at 798.

The Court of Appeals held that:

> "Neither the Act nor the regulations contain any variance provision for new sources. The rule of presumptive applicability applies to new sources as well as existing sources. On remand EPA should come forward with some limited escape mechanism for new sources." 541 F.2d, at 1028.

The Court's rationale was that "[p]rovisions for variances, modifications, and exceptions are appropriate to the regulatory process." *Ibid.*

The question, however, is not what a court thinks is generally appropriate to the regulatory process; it is what Congress intended for *these* regulations. It is clear that Congress intended these regulations to be absolute prohibitions. The use of the word "standards" implies as much. So does the description of the preferred standard as one "permitting *no* discharge of pollutants." (Emphasis added.) It is "unlawful for *any* owner or operator of *any* new source to operate such source in violation of any standard of performance applicable to such source." § 306(e) (emphasis added). In striking contrast to § 301(c), there is no statutory provision for variances, and a variance provision would be inappropriate in a standard that was intended to insure national uniformity and "maximum feasible control of new sources." Leg. Hist., at 1476.

That portion of the judgment of the Court of Appeals requiring EPA to provide a variance procedure for new sources is reversed. In all other aspects, the judgment of the Court of Appeals is affirmed.

It is so ordered.

MR. JUSTICE POWELL took no part in the consideration or decision of these cases.

NATURAL RESOURCES DEFENSE COUNCIL v. TRAIN

United States District Court, District of Columbia (1973)
6 E.R.C. 1033, 4 E.L.R. 20108

[The Administrator of EPA failed to publish effluent limitation guidelines within one year of the enactment of the Federal Water Pollution Control Act Amendments of 1972, pursuant to Section 304(b)(1)(A) of the Act. Upon action by NRDC for non-compliance, the court held that the Administrator had a "mandatory, non-discretionary duty" to publish such guidelines within the time limit, and issued an order imposing a detailed schedule for the final publication of all guidelines by November 29, 1974, so that the guidelines could be "applied meaningfully" in the permit program established under Section 402 of the Act.]

NOTES AND QUESTIONS

(1) The *du Pont* case resolved the question of the Administration's authority to issue uniform, national effluent limitations for different categories of sources. It also made clear that effluent guidelines would be applied in the issuance of NPDES permits. Since effluent limitations are to be uniform, there would be little point in mechanically "cranking in" the uniform effluent limitation into individual NPDES permits. What, then, is the function of the separate permits and how does the permit for one steel plant differ from the permit for another plant in the same category? What, in other words, does the "fine tuning" of individual permits consist of?

(2) A recurring theme in later cases is the issue of whether the quality of the receiving water must be considered in setting effluent limitations. Does *du Pont* give a clear answer to that question?

(3) What is the relationship of effluent limitations for 1977, for 1983, and for new sources as required under § 306(a)(1)? How does the Federal Water Pollution Control Act resolve the problem of the need to update effluent standards from time to time, and the need of industry to be relatively secure in the knowledge that newly acquired pollution control equipment will not be rendered permanently obsolete by rapid changes and increasingly strict requirements under EPA regulations?

[v] Best Conventional Technology Standards

AMERICAN PAPER INSTITUTE v. UNITED STATES EPA

United States Court of Appeals, Fourth Circuit (1981)
660 F.2d 954

Before WIDENER, PHILLIPS and ERVIN, Circuit Judges.

ERVIN, Circuit Judge:

The petitioners in these consolidated cases seek judicial review of the actions of the Administrator of the Environmental Protection Agency (EPA) in issuing regulations pursuant to section 304(b)(4)(B) of the Clean Water Act("the Act") promulgating effluent water limitations controlling conventional pollutants[89] from private industrial sources in accordance with section 301(b)(2)(E) of the Act. This court is vested with the responsibility and authority for making a pre-enforcement examination of the EPA guidelines by section 509(b)(1)(E) of the Act.

Although the petitioners challenge the best conventional technology (BCT) regulations issued pursuant to section 304(b)(4)(B), their primary objection is to the methodology used by the Administrator in promulgating the regulations. In particular, the petitioners contend that Congress in section 304(b)(4)(B) mandated that EPA incorporate two main factors in its methodology for determining BCT: an industry cost-effectiveness test and a test that compares the cost for private industry to reduce its effluent levels with that incurred by publicly owned treatment works (POTWs) for a similar purpose. The petitioners assert that EPA considered only the latter factor and that EPA's benchmark for this latter factor was arbitrary and capricious. Some of the other challenges that the petitioners raise are that EPA used statistically unreliable and internally inconsistent data, and that it deprived petitioners of their right to comment. We hold that all the regulations promulgated pursuant to section 301(b)(2)(E) must be invalidated on the ground that EPA did not consider all the factors mandated by section 304(b)(4)(B). The only other contention that has merit is that the data on which EPA relied in formulating its POTW benchmark are statistically unreliable.

I. BACKGROUND

In 1972, Congress amended the Federal Water Pollution Control Act to establish a timetable for achieving certain water pollution control objectives. Congress declared as its policy that the discharge of pollutants in our nation's navigable waters "be eliminated by 1985." 33 U.S.C. § 1251(a)(1). With respect to private industrial sources, such as these petitioners, this achievement was to be accomplished in two stages: an interim level of control effective in 1977, and a final level effective in 1983. The 1977 standard was designated "best

[89] Conventional pollutants are defined in the Act to include but not to be limited to, those "classified as biological oxygen demanding, suspended solids, fecal coliform, and pH." 33 U.S.C. § 1314(a)(4). The Administrator is required to "publish and revise as appropriate information identifying conventional pollutants." *Id.*

practicable technology" (BPT) and the more stringent 1983 standard was "best available technology" (BAT).

Five years later Congress undertook to re-examine these standards. Ultimately, the Federal Water Pollution Control Act was amended again, and the Act as amended became known as the Clean Water Act. Under the Clean Water Act, the 1977 requirements (BPT) were left intact, but changes were made in the 1983 requirements (BAT). As part of these changes, Congress established various standards and schedules for three classifications of pollutants: (1) conventional pollutants; (2) toxic substances; and (3) non-conventional non-toxic pollutants not otherwise classified. 33 U.S.C. § 1311. The strict BAT standards were retained for toxic pollutants known to be dangerous and for non-conventional non-toxic pollutants, the effects of which are uncertain, but the effective date for both categories was delayed.

While the parties disagree over precisely what Congress intended to do when it enacted the 1977 amendments to the Act and draw markedly different conclusions from the language of the amendments and the legislative history, it is clear that Congress felt that the results produced by the BPT had provided a high degree of water quality improvement, and that in some instances, BAT for conventional pollutants about which much was known might require treatment not deemed necessary to meet the 1983 water quality goals of the Act. Concern was expressed about requiring "treatment for treatment's sake," and there was much discussion about comparing the cost of treatment with the benefits obtained from the reductions achieved.

Out of this came the development of a new standard, best conventional pollutant control technology (BCT). The new requirement was described by one Senate-House conferee as "the equivalent of best practical technology or something a little bit better, even as far as best available technology in some circumstances."

In directing EPA to promulgate regulations concerning BCT standards, Congress passed section 304(b)(4)(B) of the Act, which provides in part:

> Factors relating to the assessment of best conventional pollutant control technology (including measures and practices) shall include consideration of the reasonableness of the relationship between the costs of attaining a reduction in effluents and the effluent reduction benefits derived, and the comparison of the cost and level of reduction of such pollutants from the discharge from publicly owned treatment works to the cost and level of reduction of such pollutants from a class or category of industrial sources, and shall take into account the age of equipment and facilities involved, the process employed, the engineering aspects of the application of various types of control techniques, process changes, non-water quality environment impact (including energy requirements), and such other factors as the Administrator deems appropriate. 33 U.S.C. § 1314(b)(4)(B).

In addition, in section 73 of the 1977 amendments, Congress directed EPA to "review every effluent guideline promulgated prior to the enactment of this Act which is final or interim final."[90] This required review of all outstanding

[90] 91 Stat. 1609.

At the time this action was filed, EPA had evaluated all the BAT regulations for the thirteen secondary industry categories having final

BAT limitations for conventional pollutants for all secondary industrial sources within 90 days after the effective date of the amendments.

Pursuant to this Congressional directive, EPA proceeded to carry out its duties. On August 23, 1978, proposed rules were published relating to 13 secondary industry categories. These rules also contained a methodology for determining the reasonableness of any proposed effluent limitation under the BCT criteria. Critical comments were received, and on April 2, 1979, a notice was published indicating that the use of two additional documents was being considered for the data contained therein and that such data might be used in the future for computing the costs and levels of pollutants from POTWs. EPA published its final BCT determinations on August 29, 1979 and the petitioners filed these petitions on May 9, 1980, thus presenting these final regulations for our review.

II. ANALYSIS

A. *COST EFFECTIVENESS TEST*

EPA's position is that Congress did not require it to utilize an industry cost-effectiveness test, but instead only mandated a POTW cost comparison standard in arriving at BCT regulations for industry. In interpreting section 304(b)(4)(B), EPA concludes that the proposed effluent guidelines are not required to pass two reasonableness tests. In support of its position, EPA reads the seemingly dual requirements of section 304(b)(4)(B) as one, commanding only a consideration of reasonableness. It contends that the second clause in the relevant portion of section 304(b)(4)(B) sets forth the benchmark of reasonableness—a comparison of the proposed BCT cost and level of effluent reduction for industry to the cost and level of reduction from the discharge of POTWs.[91]

---

or interim final BAT effluent guidelines. These thirteen categories include: dairy, grain mills, canned and preserved fruits and vegetables, canned and preserved seafoods, sugar processing, cement, feedlots, ferroalloys, glass, asbestos, meat products, fertilizer manufacturing, and phosphates industries. Although not all the subcategories of the thirteen categories were analyzed completely for reasons not relevant to our review, EPA did study 93 subcategories of the secondary industries extensively, using the methodology to which the petitioners object. Secondary industries were defined by the Administrator to include those industries not covered in the settlement agreement reached in *National Resources Defense Council, Inc. v. Train*, 8 E.R.C. 2120 (D.D.C. 1976). EPA made it clear in its final rules in which it used the contested methodology that it intended to use the same methodology when it reviewed conventional pollutant requirements for the primary industries, *i.e.*, those included in the above mentioned 1976 Consent Agreement. 44 Fed. Reg. 50,732 (1979).. . .

91 EPA has cited us to various comments in the legislative history that it claims supports its position. In particular, EPA relies on the statements of Senator Muskie in presenting the Conference Report to the Senate. Muskie commented:

> We are satisfied that he [the Administrator] has the capacity to relate cost of effluent reduction to the effluent reduction benefits, and we have provided him with some guidance. The bill provides as a basis comparison of the costs for industry to the costs for municipalities. Clearly, if the cost of achieving a certain level of reduction of conventional pollutants for industry is less than the cost of achieving a similar level of reduction for a community, it would be reasonable. 123 Cong.Rec. S19,637 (daily ed. Dec. 15, 1977).

EPA also points to the comments of Representative Roberts who, in explaining BCT, noted:

> Comparison of the costs and level of reduc-

We are unable to accept this suggested statutory interpretation. When faced with such a question, our starting point for discerning congressional intent is the words of the statute itself. *See American Textile Manufacturers Institute, Inc. v. Donovan*, 452 U.S. 490, 507-508, 101 S.Ct. 2478, 2489, 69 L.Ed.2d 185 (1981); *State Water Control Board v. Train*, 559 F.2d 921, 924-25 n.20 (4th Cir. 1977). The law which empowers EPA to act directs that EPA's effluent regulations "shall . . . specify factors to be taken into account in determining the best conventional pollutant control technology measures and practices to comply with section 1311(b)(2)(E) of this title to be applicable to any point source (other than publicly owned treatment works) within such categories or classes." 33 U.S.C. § 1314(b)(4)(B). Congress did not leave EPA free to select these factors. The statute continues:

> Factors relating to the assessment of best conventional pollutant control technology . . . *shall* include consideration of the reasonableness of the relationship between the costs of attaining a reduction in effluents and the effluent reduction benefits derived, *and* the comparison of the cost and level of reduction of such pollutants from the discharge from publicly owned treatment works to the cost and level of reduction of such pollutants from a class or category of industrial sources. *Id.* (emphasis added)

We find the language of this statute to be clear and straightforward. We thus find no reason to resort to additional rules of statutory construction or to rely on the legislative history, which has minimum probative value because of the numerous conflicts contained therein.

EPA's construction of section 304(b)(4)(B) is contrary to the plain meaning of the words contained therein. EPA ignores the mandatory language of the law ("shall"), disregards the conjunctive ("and"), and completely eliminates the first factor. By its own admission, the agency made no effort to determine what it would cost an affected industry to remove a pound of pollutant past the BPT level nor did it compare the cost of such removal with the benefits derived from the removal,[92] as specifically required by statute. *See American Textile*

> tion of such pollutants from the discharge of publicly owned treatment works to the cost and level of reduction of such pollutants from a class or category of industrial point sources is appropriate in making these determinations of reasonableness. 123 Cong. Rec. H12,928 (daily ed. Dec. 15, 1977).

Although these comments mention only the industry POTW comparison for determining reasonableness, it is not reasonable to conclude that their failure to point specifically to an industry cost-effectiveness test is indicative of Congress' intent to exclude such test when it is specifically provided for in the statute. Furthermore, Representative Roberts seems to make reference to an industry cost-effectiveness test in his statement preceding the one to which EPA directs our attention:

> In assessing the need for BCT, the Administrator is required to consider the reasonableness of the relationship between the costs of attaining a reduction in effluents and the effluent reduction benefits derived. Essentially, we are talking about removing additional "cheap pounds" of conventional pollutants. Stated another way, BCT imposes a level of control technology which anticipates and accepts the possibility of an increase in stringency beyond BPT, but not resulting in increased costs beyond the "knee of the curve," the take-off point where incremental costs begin to exceed incremental benefits. *Id.*

As evidenced by the above passages, the legislative history is conflicting and ambiguous at best.

[92] *See* 44 Fed. Reg. 50,733 (1979); 43 Fed. Reg. 37,571 (1978). We find that EPA is required by law to make such an industry cost-benefit comparison, and we do not think that it is contained within the industry-POTW comparison that EPA utilized.

Manufacturers Institute, Inc. v. Donovan, 452 U.S. 490, 507-508, & n.30, 101 S.Ct. 2478, 2489 & n.30, 69 L.Ed.2d 185 (1981).

This court has made it clear that EPA must be held to a standard of at least literal compliance with the language of a statute which it is authorized to implement. *Appalachian Power Co. v. Train*, 545 F.2d 1351, 1357 (4th Cir. 1976). Where, as here, the language of the Act is unambiguous and EPA has failed to comply with its directives, we must grant the petitions to set aside the regulations involved and remand the regulations to EPA for reconsideration. On remand EPA is to develop an industry cost-effectiveness test in accordance with the provisions of section 304(b)(4)(B), employ that test in a manner consistent with the statute, and re-examine all existing BCT regulations to ensure that they are not inconsistent with the proper employment of this industry cost-effectiveness test.

B. *POTW COMPARISON TEST*

The petitioners also challenge the action of EPA in the formation and application of the POTW comparison test. They argue that EPA erred in using an incremental approach, *i.e.*, one going beyond the cost of normal secondary treatment for POTWs, in arriving at a POTW benchmark. They also contend that even if EPA were permitted to use an incremental POTW comparison, it acted arbitrarily and capriciously because the increment was too large to comply with congressional intent. The petitioners also object to the POTW cost data as being inadequate and statistically unreliable. We reject each of these challenges, except the one directed to the errors in the cost data.

For rule making procedures conducted pursuant to Section 4 of the Administrative Procedure Act, 5 U.S.C. § 553, as these were, we must strike "agency action, findings, and conclusions" that we find to be "arbitrary, capricious, an abuse of discretion, or otherwise not in accordance with law."5 U.S.C. § 706(2)(A). In discussing the scope of judicial review under similar circumstances, this court has emphasized that "[t]he ultimate standard of review is narrow. This court is not empowered to substitute its judgment for that of the agency." *Consolidation Coal Co. v. Costle*, 604 F.2d 239, 243 (4th Cir. 1979), *rev'd on other grounds sub nom., EPA v. National Crushed Stone Association*, 449 U.S. 64, 101 S.Ct. 295, 66 L.Ed.2d 268 (1980). Our court has also stressed that "[i]n evaluating the course of conduct employed by the EPA, we must, of course, bear in mind that Congress vested that agency with the power to choose among alternative strategies." *Appalachian Power Co. v. Train*, 545 F.2d 1351, 1356 (4th Cir. 1976). Under the arbitrary and capricious standard of review, agency action is presumed to be valid, and we must uphold the agency's decision if it is rationally based. *Ethyl Corp. v. EPA*, 541 F.2d 1 (D.C.Cir.), *cert. denied*, 426 U.S. 941, 96 S.Ct. 2663, 49 L.Ed.2d 394 (1976).

1.

The petitioners specifically argue that EPA erred in concluding that it was appropriate to consider the cost of upgrading POTWs beyond secondary treatment.[93] The petitioners object to the POTW benchmark for several reasons because: (1) secondary treatment is the only specifically defined treatment level that POTWs are required by law to meet;[94] (2) advanced secondary treatment (AST),[95] the increment which EPA chose, was not in existence when Congress enacted section 304 of the Act; and (3) the legislative history indicates that the POTW benchmark should be based on the average cost of normal secondary treatment.

We reject the petitioners' contentions. Section 304(b)(4)(B) explicitly authorizes EPA in establishing BCT limitations to compare "the cost and level of reduction of such pollutants from the discharge from publicly owned treatment works to the cost and level of reduction of such pollutants from a class or category of industrial sources." This controlling statute unequivocally directs EPA to employ a POTW comparison test. Contrary to the suggestions, we find nothing on the face of the statute or in the legislative history to suggest that Congress intended for EPA to use a specific POTW benchmark.[96] Although Congress specifically directed the use of this comparison test, it did not issue any instructions as to how EPA was to structure or administer the test.

EPA considered a number of ways in which a POTW test could be formulated. 43 Fed. Reg. 37,572 (1978). One of the suggestions was that the POTW benchmark be based on the average pollutant removal costs for secondary treatment at POTWs, i. e., the increment from no treatment to secondary treatment. 43 Fed. Reg. 37,572 (1978). In addition to looking at average POTW costs for secondary treatment, EPA considered various incremental approaches below secondary treatment. EPA rejected these proposals primarily because it felt that a proper POTW benchmark should be one roughly paralleling that with which it is to be compared—the industrial increment from BPT to BAT. Whereas industry was required to be at a BPT level in 1977, POTWs were required to have met effluent limitations based upon secondary treatment by 1977. EPA believed that a relevant basis of comparison for POTWs would be at an incremental level beyond secondary treatment since

---

93 Secondary treatment is the level of treatment that POTWs were required to have achieved by July 1, 1977 unless granted an extension. 33 U.S.C. § 131(b)(1)(B). Secondary treatment has been broken down by the Administrator into three categories: biochemical oxygen demand (BOD), suspended solids (TSS), and pH. The parameters within each category are set forth in the Administrator's regulations. 40 C.F.R. § 133.102.

94 By 1983, POTWs are required to meet best practicable waste treatment technology over the life of the works, 33 U.S.C. § 1311(b)(2)(B), but such level of technology has not been specifically defined.

95 AST is not a technology-based limitation that is currently applicable to POTWs. Instead, AST was a term developed by EPA for a construction grant program for POTWs. AST is used to refer to a treatment facility that "can produce effluent of a higher quality than secondary, still using primarily secondary treatment technology." 44 Fed. Reg. 29,534(1979). AST facilities must meet effluent limits from 10 to 29 milligrams per liter (mg/1) for BOD and TSS. *Id.* AST has been set at a level of 10 mg/1 each for BOD and TSS for the POTW comparison at issue here. 44 Fed. Reg. 50,734 (1979).

96 We are not persuaded by the petitioners' citations to the legislative history. There is no reference to a specific POTW benchmark in either the Conference Report or in the House and Senate Reports. The references to the floor debates and to the other parts of the legislative history to which the petitioners direct our attention contain only minimal remarks concerning a POTW comparison from which we find it impossible to conclude that Congress intended EPA to use a specific POTW test. *See, e.g.*, 123 Cong.Rec. S19,637; 19,648 (daily ed. Dec. 15, 1977) (remarks of Sen. Muskie).

BCT would be at a level at least equal to BPT and in many cases beyond BPT. EPA considered several such increments. After a careful consideration of various alternatives, EPA adopted a test employing a comparison of the cost of upgrading POTWs from secondary treatment levels. The selection of this upgrade comparison does not do violence to the language of the statute, and we do not find it to be arbitrary or capricious.

2.

Not only do the petitioners object to an incremental POTW benchmark, but they also object specifically to the use of the increment from secondary to AST as being too costly. In essence, the petitioners contend that even if EPA were permitted to use an incremental POTW benchmark, it should have used a narrower increment, one that more closely straddles the marginal cost of secondary treatment.

We reject this contention. We cannot substitute our judgment for that of EPA and condemn EPA for not choosing what we may consider to be the best increment.

. . . .

EPA initially proposed comparing the incremental costs of removal from industrial plants with the incremental costs of removal from POTWs of a similar flow. EPA based its proposal on separate and distinct technologies for small and large POTWs and arrived at POTW cost-effectiveness ratios at an increment progressing from normal secondary treatment at 30 mg/1 each of BOD and TSS to better secondary treatment defined as 12 mg/1 each of BOD and TSS. 43 Fed. Reg. 37,571-72 (1978).

Both the Corn Refiners Association, Inc. (hereinafter the Corn Refiners) and the Council on Wage & Price Stability (CWPS) made suggestions on the calculation of an incremental POTW cost standard. . . .

As indicated by the above comments of the Corn Refiners and the CWPS, there may be any number of increments based on slightly different technology or slightly different sizes of a given technology that EPA could have used. It is clear from the record that EPA was not oblivious to these comments.[97] Instead of using POTW cost reasonableness figures based on specific separate and distinct technologies employed by small and large POTWs, as it had proposed initially, in its final rules, EPA used a single POTW cost reasonableness figure based on the average of all cost-effective technologies used by POTWs operating beyond secondary treatment, but employing basic secondary treatment technology.

---

[97] In an interagency memorandum, EPA specifically noted some of the alternative proposals for computing a POTW comparison figure that commentors such as CWPS had suggested. Memorandum: "BCT: The POTW Test," from Louis DuPuis from EPA's office of Analysis and Evaluation to BCT Work Group (February 22, 1979). App. at 3087-88. Although these recommendations related only to the flow basis of the comparison aspect of EPA's original proposal, EPA did have an outside consulting firm analyze and compare several of the alternatives to the flow basis. Booz-Allen and Hamilton, Inc., "An Analysis of Alternatives for Evaluating Existing Industrial Effluent Guidelines," 31, App. at 3056. In its final rules, EPA adopted a single figure cost test comparable to one that the CWPS had recommended. 43 Fed. Reg. 50,733-35 (1979).

We cannot conclude that EPA acted arbitrarily and capriciously in choosing AST as the increment beyond secondary treatment for the POTW benchmark. While EPA sought to use an increment that narrowly straddled secondary treatment, *i.e.*, one that closely approximated marginal cost, and although it admitted its failure to find the narrowest increment that would have more closely approximated marginal cost, there is no statutory mandate requiring EPA to use an increment that equals marginal cost.

EPA has rationally justified its use of the AST increment. AST is the "knee-of-the-curve" point, the maximum cost-effective level of control for POTWs. The increment from secondary treatment to AST for POTWs was also determined by EPA to be roughly analogous to the industrial increment from BPT to BAT. While comments received by EPA have suggested that there may have been a narrower increment that EPA could have used, the suggestions by the commentors imply that EPA would have had to limit itself to a specific POTW technology to arrive at a smaller increment.

We are unwilling to place a straitjacket on EPA to so limit its decision making process. We find that EPA made its decision on its POTW comparison after it fully considered various alternatives, and that its decision is rationally based. We thus conclude that EPA's choice of an increment for POTWs from secondary treatment to AST was neither arbitrary nor capricious.

3.

The petitioners also challenge the POTW benchmark on the grounds that the POTW cost data upon which it was based are inadequate, statistically unreliable, and internally inconsistent. Recently, we have been apprised that EPA confesses error in the date in the two documents on which it relied in formulating its POTW benchmark.[98] EPA has moved this court for a voluntary remand, and the petitioners do not contest the propriety of a remand solely to allow EPA to correct its data errors. Under these circumstances, therefore, we find it proper to remand this aspect of the case to EPA, but only for the purpose of allowing it to correct its data errors and to revise its BCT figures accordingly.[99]

III. CONCLUSION

We find no merit to the petitioners' other challenges. Accordingly, we vacate the regulations promulgated pursuant to section 304 of the Act. We remand this action to the agency with instructions to devise a cost-effectiveness test in accordance with the guidelines of this opinion and to correct its data errors.

---

[98] Dames and Moore, "Analysis of Operations and Maintenance Costs for Municipal Wastewater Treatment Systems," (Feb. 1980) (Report prepared for EPA); Dames & Moore, "Construction Costs for Municipal Wastewater Treatment Plants: 1973-1977" (Jan. 1978) (Report prepared for EPA).

[99] After it corrects its data errors. EPA may discover that the increment from secondary treatment to AST is not the best increment for its POTW benchmark.

AFFIRMED IN PART, REVERSED IN PART AND REMANDED.

PHILLIPS, Circuit Judge, concurring and dissenting:

I concur in the court's opinion save for Part II. A. dealing with the "cost effectiveness test." As to that I respectfully dissent.

The gist of the court's opinion on this point is that in 33 U.S.C. § 1314(b)(4)(B)Congress unambiguously required the Administrator to use a precise two-part test in formulating BCT regulations. The critical language of this statutory provision is characterized in the majority opinion as "clear and straightforward" and "unambiguous" on the point so that we need not resort to legislative history in divining its meaning and in holding EPA "to a standard of at least literal compliance" with its "plain meaning." I simply disagree with this threshold assessment of the clarity of the statutory directive.

To my reading it is instead at least sufficiently ambiguous to drive us first to the relevant if concededly inconclusive legislative history properly identified by the court and from that source to the standard of judicial review which compels us to give great respect and deference to contemporaneous agency interpretations of uncertain language in statutes defining agency powers and duties.

Attempting, as does the court, to divine the provision's plain meaning by parsing the convoluted key sentence only reveals, I suggest, that it will not effectively parse. It is true that the two critical clauses from which the two pronged test requirement is found by the court are phrased in the conjunctive, implying that they express parallel thoughts. But a look at their content reveals that they can only be made parallel in thought by importing into the first clause a phrase, "by means of an industry cost-effectiveness test," that is not literally or plainly there. Without that imported language—actually a construct out of whole cloth by the petitioners that has the happy effect of resolving the issue in their favor—the first clause simply lays down reasonableness of the cost/benefit relationship as a general standard for formulating the BCT regulations rather than positing, as the second clause surely does, a specific test by which reasonableness is to be gauged. This, of course, is the way EPA interpreted it; it seems obviously to have been Senator Muskie's understanding; and it is at least arguably that of Representative Roberts, based upon the extracts from the legislative history cited by the majority.

Indeed, were we compelled judicially to find plain meaning in the literal language one way or the other, the "plainer" meaning to me is that given it by the agency. The most internally consistent reading for me is this: EPA is directed in devising BCT regulations to take as its lodestar the imposition of no further requirements (beyond those imposed by BPT) than can be justified by demonstrating a reasonable relationship between the costs incurred and the benefits to be achieved through compliance, looking always to the end goal of total elimination of pollutant discharges by 1985. In testing reasonableness of the cost/benefit relationship, EPA must compare—because its affords a convenient and trustworthy cost/benefit relationship for comparison—the experience in effluent level reductions had by publicly owned treatment works, and must as well take into account such obvious factors as age of equipment, etc.

But of course we are not compelled to find a plain meaning, and as indicated, I do not believe it exists. As between alternative possible meanings, with legislative history inconclusive (though in my view favoring EPA's interpretation), I would defer to the agency's interpretation as a wholly reasonable, certainly not arbitrary or capricious, one. *See* 5 U.S.C. § 706(2)(A); *Unemployment Compensation Commission of Alaska v. Aragan*, 329 U.S. 143, 153-54, 67 S.Ct. 245, 250, 91 L.Ed. 136 (1946). On this basis I would remand solely for the purpose of correcting the confessed data errors in setting the POTW benchmark, and let the agency get on with a critical task entrusted to it in 1977 with an implicit mandate at that time to complete it within a ninety day period now long since passed.

[vi] Variances

ENVIRONMENTAL PROTECTION AGENCY v. NATIONAL CRUSHED STONE ASSOCIATION

ARE THERE VARIANCES IN BPT? NO.

United States Supreme Court (1980)
449 U.S. 64, 100 S. Ct. 295, 66 L. Ed. 2d 268

Justice WHITE delivered the opinion of the Court.

In April and July 1977, the Environmental Protection Agency (EPA), acting under the Federal Water Pollution Control Act Amendments of 1972 (Act), 33 U.S.C. § 1251 *et seq.*, promulgated pollution discharge limitations for the coal mining industry and for that portion of the mineral mining and processing industry comprising the crushed stone, construction and gravel categories.[100] Although the Act does not expressly authorize or require variances from the 1977 [BPT, best practicable technology] limitation, each set of regulations contained a variance provision.[101] Respondents sought review of the

[100] The coal mining standards were published at 42 Fed. Reg. 21380 *et seq.*, adopting 40 CFR Part 434. The mineral mining and processing standards were published at 42 Fed. Reg. 35843 *et seq.*, adopting 40 CFR Part 436.

[101] The variance provision reads as follows:

"In establishing the limitations set forth in this section, EPA took into account all information it was able to collect, develop and solicit with respect to factors (such as age and size of plant, raw materials, manufacturing processes, products produced, treatment technology available, energy requirements and costs) which can affect the industry subcategorization and effluent levels established. It is, however, possible that data which would affect these limitations have not been available and, as a result, these limitations should be adjusted for certain plants in this industry. An individual discharger or other interested person may submit evidence to the Regional Administrator (or to the State, if the State has the authority to issue NPDES permits) that factors relating to the equipment or facilities involved, the process applied, or other such factors related to such discharger are fundamentally different from the factors considered in the establishment of the guidelines. On the basis of such evidence or other available information, the Regional Administrator (or the State) will make a written finding that such factors are or are not fundamentally different for that facility compared to those specified in the Development Document. If such fundamentally different factors are found to exist, the Regional Administrator or the State shall establish for the discharger effluent limitations in the NPDES permit either more or less stringent than the limitations established herein, to the extent dictated by such fundamentally different factors. Such limitation must be approved by the Administrator of the Environmental Protection Agency. The

regulations in various courts of appeals, challenging both the substantive standards and the variance clause. All of the petitions for review were transferred to the Court of Appeals for the Fourth Circuit. In *National Crushed Stone Association v. EPA*, 601 F.2d 111 (CA4 1979), and in *Consolidation Coal Company v. Costle*, 604 F.2d 239 (CA4 1979), the Court of Appeals set aside the variance provision as "unduly restrictive" and remanded the provision to EPA for reconsideration.

To obtain a variance from the 1977 uniform [BPT] discharge limitations a discharger must demonstrate that the "factors relating to the equipment or facilities involved, the process applied, or other such factors relating to such discharger are fundamentally different from the factors considered in the establishment of the guidelines." Although a greater than normal cost of implementation will be considered in acting on a request for a variance, economic ability to meet the costs will not be considered.[102] A variance, therefore, will not be granted on the basis of the applicant's economic inability to meet the costs of implementing the uniform standard.

The Court of Appeals for the Fourth Circuit rejected this position. It required EPA to "take into consideration, among other things, the statutory factors set out in § 301(c)," which authorizes variances from the more restrictive pollution limitations to become effective in 1987 and which specifies economic capability as a major factor to be taken into account.[103] The court held that

> " 'if [a plant] is doing all that the maximum use of technology within its economic capability will permit and if such use will result in reasonable further progress toward the elimination of the discharge of pollutants . . . no reason appears why [it] should not be able to secure such a variance should it comply with any other requirements of the variance.' " 601 F.2d, at 124, quoting from *Appalachian Power Co. v. Train*, 545 F.2d 1351, 1378 (CA4 1976).

We granted certiorari to resolve the conflict between the decision below and *Weyerhaeuser Co. v. Costle*, 191 U.S.App.D.C. 309, 590 F.2d 1011 (1978), in which the variance provision was upheld.

Administrator may approve or disapprove such limitations, specify other limitations, or initiate proceedings to revise these regulations."

See 40 CFR 434.22(coal preparation plants); 40 CFR 434.32(acid mine drainage); 40 CFR 434.42(alkaline mine drainage); 40 CFR 436.22(crushed stone) and 40 CFR 436.32(construction sand and gravel).

[102] EPA has explained its position as follows:

"Thus a plant may be able to secure a BPT variance by showing that the plant's own compliance costs with the national guideline limitation would be X times greater than the compliance costs of the plants EPA considered in setting the national BPT limitation. A plant may not, however, secure a BPT variance by alleging that the plant's own financial status is such that it cannot afford to comply with the national BPT limitation." 43 Fed. Reg. 50042.

[103] Section 301(c), 33 U.S.C. § 1311(c)allows the Administrator to grant a variance [from best available technology, BAT standards] "upon a showing by the owner or operator . . . that such modified requirements (1) will represent the maximum use of technology within the economic capability of the owner or operator; and (2) will result in reasonable further progress toward the elimination of the discharge of pollutants."

Finally, the fact that the Court of Appeals for the Fourth Circuit held the variance provision to be invalid, while the Court of Appeals for the District of Columbia, in *Weyerhaeuser, supra*, upheld the same provision provides yet another reason for this Court to settle this controversy at this time. For all of these reasons, the issue is ripe for judicial review.

I

We shall first briefly outline the basic structure of the Act, which translates Congress' broad goal of eliminating "the discharge of pollutants into the navigable waters," 33 U.S.C. § 1251(a)(1), into specific requirements that must be met by individual point sources. . . .

II

The plain language of the statute does not support the position taken by the Court of Appeals. Section 301(c) is limited on its face to modifications of the 1987 BAT limitations. It says nothing about relief from the 1977 BPT requirements. Nor does the language of the Act support the position that although § 301(c) is not itself applicable to BPT standards, it requires that the affordability of the prescribed 1977 technology be considered in BPT variance decisions.

. . . .

[In a closely reasoned decision, the Court here finds that the variance provision in § 301(c) applies only to the BAT (best available technology) standards applicable to post-1987. The Court concludes that the best practicable standard sets the base standard under the Act and that the reference to maximum use of technology within the economic capability of the owner or operator and reasonable further progress toward the elimination of the discharge of pollutants refers to the progress required by BAT over the basic standard set by BPT. The requirements of the best practicable technology standard do not permit any variances, neither within the express terms of the statute nor within the logic of the Act. The Court notes that this interpretation is in line with the legislative history of the Act which clearly anticipated that some enterprises would be unable to meet the requirements, anticipating a small number of plant closings, and providing therefore for other means to accommodate some economic dislocations.]

More importantly, to allow a variance based on the maximum technology affordable by the point source, even if that technology fails to meet BPT effluent limitations, would undercut the purpose and function of BPT limitations. Rather than the 1987 requirement of the best measures economically and technologically feasible, the statutory provisions for 1977 contemplate regulations prohibiting discharges from any point source in excess of the effluent produced by the best practicable technology currently available in the industry. The Administrator was referred to the industry and to existing practices to determine BPT. He was to categorize point sources, examine control practices in exemplary plants in each category, and after weighing benefits and costs and considering other factors specified by § 304, determine and define the best practicable technology at a level that would effect the obvious statutory goal for 1977 of substantially reducing the total pollution produced by each category of the industry.

. . . .

Because the 1977 limitations were intended to reduce the total pollution produced by an industry, requiring compliance with BPT standards necessarily imposed additional costs on the segment of the industry with the least effective technology. If the statutory goal is to be achieved, these costs must be borne or the point source eliminated. In our view, requiring variances from otherwise valid regulations where dischargers cannot afford normal costs of compliance would undermine the purpose and the intended operative effect of the 1977 regulations.

III

The Administrator's present interpretation of the language of the statute is amply supported by the legislative history, which persuades us that Congress understood that the economic capability provision of § 301(c) was limited to BAT variances; that Congress foresaw and accepted the economic hardship, including the closing of some plants, that effluent limitations would cause; and that Congress took certain steps to alleviate this hardship, steps which did not include allowing a BPT variance based on economic capability.

[The legislative history clearly indicates that Congress did not intend foreseen economic impacts by providing for variances based on economic impact and this possibility was specifically considered and rejected. The provision for low cost loans to small businesses to help them meet the cost of technological improvement and certain employee protection provisions added to the statute indicate that variances were not an acceptable response to Congress in instances where certain plans could not meet the basic BPT standard. The Court reversed, holding that the Court of Appeals erred in not accepting EPA's interpretation of the Act and held that EPA is not required by the Act to consider economic capability in granting variances from its uniform BPT regulations.]

. . . .

NOTE

The matter of "FDF" (fundamentally different factors) variances was again before the Supreme Court in *Chemical Manufacturers Ass'n v. Natural Resources Defense Council, Inc.*, 470 U.S. 116, 105 S. Ct. 1102, 84 L. Ed. 2d 90, 15 ELR 20230 (1985). Subsequent to the *DuPont* case, the EPA promulgated regulations which authorized plant-specific variances in cases where national pretreatment standards as applied to a given source are either too lenient or too strict because of factors "fundamentally different" from those considered by the EPA in setting the standards.[104] An action was brought by the NRDC seeking a declaration that § 301(1) of the Clean Water Act, which prohibits the Administrator of the EPA from "modifying" any effluent limitations with respect to toxic pollutants, prohibited the EPA from issuing any "fundamentally different factor" variances to the extent that they would apply to toxic pollutants under the pretreatment standard for industry categories. Upholding the EPA, the U.S. Supreme Court stated that the agency charged with administering a statute is entitled to considerable deference and the

[104] 40 C.F.R. § 401.13(1985).

— CAME FROM CHEVRON CASE.

meaning of the word "modify" in § 301(1) is sufficiently ambiguous to preclude the court from substituting its judgment for that of the EPA.[105]

The dissenters, Marshall, Blackmun, Stevens, and O'Connor who dissented in part, differed with the majority in its assertion that § 301(1) has only the modifications expressly allowed by §§ 301 (a) and (g), and insisted that Congress had acted to disallow variances for toxic pollutants because of the increasingly evident toxic hazard. The dissenters also relied on the legislative history that emphasized the enforcement of uniform standards.

The view of the majority prevailed, however, in the 1987 amendment of the Clean Water Act, which expressly allows "modifications" for toxic pollutants in a newly enacted § 301(n). The new subsection, entitled "Fundamentally Different Factors," expressly provides for FDF variances for primary and secondary national effluent limitations, and for categorical pretreatment standards. Although the subsection seeks to limit the authority of the Administrator in granting variances, the conditions imposed generally track the earlier regulatory requirements referred to in *C.M.A. v. NRDC,* namely 40 C.F.R. § 125 30(1984) and 40 C.F.R. § 403 13(1983). A facility may be found to be fundamentally different based on factors identified in §§ 304(b)(2) and (g). These include age of equipment and facilities, the process employed, the engineering aspects of the types of control techniques, process changes, and other factors deemed appropriate by the Administrator. Costs, independent of the eligible factors, are not to be considered, and EPA must not replace a substantive and technical assessment with a test which emphasizes cost, *i.e.*, a major cost differential does not, by itself, point to fundamentally different factors. The alternative requirement imposed must be no less stringent than justified by the fundamental difference from the rest of the category, and may not result in a markedly more adverse non-water quality impact. An application for an FDF variance does not stay the application of the otherwise applicable standards during its pendency. CWA § 301(h), as added by Pub. L. No. 100-4, § 306, 101 Stat. 35 (1987).

[vii] Toxic Pollutants

NATURAL RESOURCES DEFENSE COUNCIL, INC. v. TRAIN

United States Court of Appeals, D.C. Circuit (1975)
519 F.2d 287, 5 E.L.R. 20578

ROBB, Circuit Judge:

Appellants, referred to here as plaintiffs, are four non-profit corporations interested in the implementation and enforcement of federal laws protecting the environment. They brought this suit in the District Court against the Administrator of the Environmental Protection Agency (EPA) "to review his implementation of Sections 101(a)(3) and 307(a)(1) of the Federal Water Pollution Control ActAmendments" of 1972 (FWPCA) 33 U.S.C. §§ 1251(a)(3),

105 *Chemical Manufacturers Association v. NRDC,* 470 U.S. 116, 15 ELR 20230 (1985). *See generally* Funk, *The Exception That Approves the Rule: FDF Variances Under the Clean Water Act,* 13 B.C. Envtl. Aff. L. Rev. 1 (1985).

1317(a)(1). The suit challenges the Administrator's action, pursuant to the statute, in publishing an initial list of toxic pollutants and in setting criteria for the inclusion of pollutants on the list. The District Court granted the Administrator's motion to dismiss the complaint on the merits.

The 1972 statute declares that "it is the national policy that the discharge of toxic pollutants in toxic amounts be prohibited." Section 101(a)(3), 33 U.S.C. § 1251(a)(3). In furtherance of this policy the Administrator is first directed to publish "and from time to time thereafter revise" a list of toxic pollutants or combination of pollutants, taking "into account the toxicity of the pollutant, its persistence, degradability, the usual or potential presence of the affected organisms in any waters, the importance of the affected organisms and the nature and extent of the effect of the toxic pollutant on such organisms." Section 307(a)(1), 33 U.S.C. § 1317(a)(1). The term "toxic pollutant" is defined in section 502(13), 33 U.S.C. § 1362(13).

Within 180 days after the publication of the list of toxic pollutants, the Administrator must propose effluent standards or prohibitions for the substances or combinations of substances on the list and must notice these proposed standards for public hearing. Within an additional six months after the publication of the proposed effluent standards or prohibitions, the Administrator must promulgate final effluent standards or prohibitions. Section 307(a)(2), 33 U.S.C. § 1317(a)(2). Final effluent standards or prohibitions established pursuant to Section 307(a)(2) must take effect no later than a year from the date of their promulgation. Section 307(a)(6), 33 U.S.C. § 1317(a)(6).

The complaint of the District Court is in two counts. The first count alleges that the selection criteria used by the Administrator in choosing pollutants for inclusion on his initial list "impose preconditions and restrictions upon the inclusion of pollutants and combinations of pollutants on the list that are unlawful and inconsistent with the provisions and policies of the Act"; that the "promulgation of these unlawfully restrictive selection criteria is arbitrary, is beyond defendant's statutory authority, and is in violation of the Act." The count further alleges that in omitting substances from the list the Administrator was "guided by certain selection criteria and other considerations and constraints that are neither authorized by nor consistent with the Act." Finally, it is alleged that the Administrator's action in rejecting candidate pollutants for inclusion on the list "was arbitrary, . . . an abuse of discretion and . . . in violation of the Act." In the second count the complaint lists twenty-five substances alleged to be "toxic within the meaning of the Act" and claims that the Administrator "was without direction to leave [these] substances . . . off the list of toxic pollutants." The omission of the twenty-five substances is alleged to have been "arbitrary and capricious, and in violation of the Act."

The complaint asks for a declaratory judgment and injunctive relief requiring the Administrator (1) to rescind and revoke the parts of the published selection criteria alleged to be unlawful for failure to reflect the relevant legislative factors; (2) to publish amended selection criteria reflecting the relevant legislative factors and those on which the Administrator relied; (3) to add to the list all substances satisfying the amended selection criteria, including the twenty-five substances alleged to have been wrongfully omitted.

Along with the complaint, the plaintiffs served on the Administrator a set of interrogatories and a request to produce documents. These requests were designed to elicit information as to what documents and materials were relied on by the Administrator in formulating his list of toxic pollutants—that is, what constituted the administrative record before the Agency. The plaintiffs also wished to determine what selection criteria were actually used by the Administrator in formulating his list, and whether and to what extent other considerations and constraints in addition to the published selection criteria were used in excluding substances from the list.

The Administrator did not answer the complaint or respond to the plaintiffs' requests for discovery. Instead he filed a number of documents which he characterized as the "administrative record" and moved to stay both discovery and answer pending resolution of a motion to dismiss. Thereafter, he filed a motion to dismiss, or in the alternative for summary judgment. The motion argued that the published selection criteria were lawful, and that the Administrator's action in publishing the list of toxic pollutants, as "reasoned decision-making" within the Administrator's discretion, was unreviewable. From these premises the Administrator argued that the complaint failed to state a claim upon which relief could be granted.

Countering the Administrator's motion for summary judgment the plaintiffs filed an affidavit from their counsel asserting that the documents filed with the court by the Administrator did not constitute the entire administrative record. Specifically, the affidavit listed several documents which had been relied upon by the Administrator and had come to the attention of counsel but which were not included among those filed with the court. One of these documents was a report or summary described as the "Administrator's Briefing Book, entitled 'Toxic Pollutants, § 307(a), P.L. 92-500, Prepared by "HATS" Task Force, Office of Water Programs, Environmental Protection Agency (June 1973).' " In response the Administrator filed two additional documents which he said constituted "parts of the record of the decision by the Administrator." He did not, however, file all the documents referred to in counsel's affidavit and in particular did not file the "Briefing Book" nor did he assert that the record as supplemented constituted the entire administrative record.

Holding there had been no showing that the Administrator had abused his discretion, the District Court granted the Administrator's motion to dismiss on the merits. The court pointed out that, pursuant to the statutory command that the list be revised from time to time, the Administrator was considering the inclusion of additional substances on his list. For this reason the court declined to "interject itself into an on-going and orderly administrative process." *Natural Resources Defense Council, Inc. v. Train*, 6 E.R.C. 1702, 1704 (D.D.C. 1974). The court did not deal with the plaintiffs' allegations that the entire administrative record was not before the District Court and that unstated and unpublished considerations were applied to exclude dangerous and toxic substances from the list.

Jurisdiction of the District Court

The complaint invokes the jurisdiction of the District Court under section 505 of the Federal Water Pollution Control Act Amendments of 1972, 33

U.S.C. § 1365; section 10 of the Administrative Procedure Act, 5 U.S.C. §§ 701-706; the General Federal Question Statute, 28 U.S.C. § 1331; Mandamus and Venue Act, 28 U.S.C. § 1361; and the Declaratory Judgment Act, 28 U.S.C. §§ 2201-2202. Although the Administrator questioned the jurisdiction of the District Court (*see* Memorandum in Support of Motion to Dismiss, pp. 29-35) the point apparently was not pressed, and as we have said the Administrator argued the case and the court decided it on the merits. On this appeal however the Administrator renews the jurisdictional argument, insisting that under Section 509(b)(1) of the FWPCA, 33 U.S.C. § 1369(b)(1), exclusive jurisdiction to review the Administrator's actions is in this court. We must therefore determine whether the District Court had jurisdiction over the subject matter.

Two provisions of the 1972 statute relate to judicial review of the Administrator's actions in promulgating Section 307(a) toxic pollutant lists and standards. Section 505, 33 U.S.C. § 1365provides in pertinent part:

> (a) Authorization; jurisdiction. Except as provided in subsection (b) of this section, any citizen may commence a civil action on his own behalf—
>
> . . . (2) against the Administrator where there is alleged a failure of the Administrator to perform any act or duty under this [Act] which is not discretionary with the Administrator.
>
> The district courts shall have jurisdiction, without regard to the amount in controversy or the citizenship of the parties, . . . to order the Administrator to perform such act or duty . . . .

Section 509(b)(1), 33 U.S.C. § 1369(b)(1)provides:

> Review of the Administrator's action . . . (C) *in promulgating any effluent standard* [*or*] *prohibition* . . . under Section [307] . . . may be had by any interested person in the Circuit Court of Appeals of the United States for the Federal judicial district in which such person resides or transacts such business upon application by such person. Any such application shall be made within ninety days from the date of such . . . promulgation, . . . or after such date only if such application is based solely on grounds which arose after such ninetieth day. [Emphasis supplied.]

The Administrator argues that since the use of selection criteria and the selection of substances to be listed are within his discretion Section 505(a)(2) could not confer jurisdiction on the District Court. Furthermore, says the Administrator, since there is an "inextricable connection" between "the listing stage and the standard-setting stage of the Section 307 process" any challenge to his actions at the listing stage must be made in a circuit court of appeals under Section 509. If this were not so, the argument runs, there would be "a real possibility of simultaneous suits in the district court and the court of appeals on the two stages of the same overall Section 307 process, with the attendant possible frustration of the actions of both courts."

We agree that when the Administrator has listed a substance and thereafter promulgated standards or prohibitions for that substance the listing and the promulgation of standards are interwoven; any challenge to the Administrator's action must then be in a court of appeals under Section 509 which provides for review of the Administrator's action "in promulgating any effluent standard [or] prohibition."

The problem comes when, as in this case, the Administrator has published a list of toxic substances, and it is alleged that the omission of certain substances from that list is arbitrary, capricious and unlawful. Unless a substance is listed no standard or prohibition reviewable under Section 509 will ever be promulgated. At the same time, if the decision not to list a substance is within the Administrator's discretion then it is not subject to review under Section 505. Absent a determination that listing is non-discretionary, an action like the present one, alleging that the failure of the Administrator to list certain substances is arbitrary, capricious and unlawful, would be consigned to jurisdictional limbo under FWPCA. Such a determination is not necessary here, however, for we have held that Section 505 is not an exclusive basis for jurisdiction in the District Court. *Natural Resources Defense Council, Inc. v. Train*, 510 F.2d 692, 698-703 (1974). The District Court has jurisdiction under the Administrative Procedure Act to review administrative action not expressly made unreviewable to determine whether there has been an abuse of discretion. 5 U.S.C. § 706(2)(A). We hold, therefore, that the District Court had jurisdiction in this case under 5 U.S.C. § 706(2)(A).

The Insufficiency of the Record Before the District Court

The Administrative Procedure Act and the cases require that the complete administrative record be placed before a reviewing court. Thus the Act provides that in reviewing agency action claimed to be "arbitrary, capricious, an abuse of discretion, or otherwise not in accordance with law" the court "shall review the whole record or those parts of it cited by a party. . . ." 5 U.S.C. § 706. In *Citizens to Preserve Overton Park, Inc. v. Volpe*, 401 U.S. 402, 91 S.Ct. 814, 28 L.Ed.2d 136 (1971), the plaintiffs challenged the decision of the Secretary of Transportation to authorize a highway through a public park. In the District Court the defendants introduced affidavits supporting the Secretary's decision. The plaintiffs filed counter affidavits and sought to take the deposition of a former federal highway administrator. The District Court refused to order the deposition and on the basis of the affidavits held that the Secretary had not exceeded his authority. The Circuit Court of Appeals affirmed, but the Supreme Court reversed on the ground that the affidavits "clearly do not constitute the 'whole record' compiled by the agency: the basis for review required by § 706 of the Administrative Procedure Act." The Court remanded the case for review "to be based on the full administrative record that was before the Secretary at the time he made his decision." 401 U.S. at 419-420, 91 S.Ct. at 825. The Court indicated that some discovery might be required if "additional explanation" of the Secretary's decision was necessary. *Id.* at 420-421, 91 S.Ct. 814. *See also Appalachian Power Co. v. EPA*, 477 F.2d 495, 507 (4th Cir. 1973).

As we have said the plaintiffs by way of an affidavit from their counsel made a substantial showing in the District Court that the Administrator had not filed the entire administrative record with the court. The affidavit specified several documents that had been omitted, including the Administrator's Briefing Book. Notwithstanding this showing the Administrator did not produce the Briefing Book nor did he ever claim that he had filed the entire administrative record; and the court proceeded with its review on the basis of a partial and truncated record. We think this was error.

. . . .

We think it in furtherance of sound judicial administration, 28 U.S.C. § 2106, to remand, rather than determine the validity of the Administrator's past course, having in mind that the remand will permit plaintiff to file a supplemental complaint. The Administrator will file the entire administrative record pertinent to the omissions identified in the complaint or supplemental complaint. With doubts as to the subject-matter jurisdiction set at rest, the District Court can proceed to consider issues of validity in their current context.

The judgment is reversed and remanded for further proceedings on the entire administrative record.

So ordered.

NICHOLS, Judge (dissenting):

Respectfully and reluctantly I dissent. It appears to me that the majority misconstrues the decision below, which I would affirm.

. . . .

Plaintiffs equated exclusion of a substance from the list of nine with a decision not to regulate it, effective in perpetuity. Yet it was not denied that the Act provided for amending and supplementing the list after initial publication, nor that defendant had numerous other toxic substances under serious study. The omission of a toxic substance from the initial list was in no sense intended as a final decision to take no action with respect to that substance. The position of the complainants manifestly was that defendant had no authority to pick and choose among toxic substances and list some of them according to a self-devised system of priorities. He had to publish all of them, no matter how much or little he knew about them nor how serious a peril they appeared to present, even though the statute required the publication to lead in a specified brief time to regulatory measures. Apparently, the defendant had to regulate, and whether the regulation was well or ill considered was no concern of the statute.

The opinion below dismissing the complaint, rejects this interpretation of the law and says that the law gives the Administrator discretion to select a short list of toxic substances for speedy action while continuing study of the others. In the circumstances, with rejection of no substance yet final, consideration by the court of what substances should be listed, other than the nine would be "to interject itself into an on-going and orderly administrative process. . . ." In this view of the case, the materials relating to individual toxic pollutants other than the nine, that defendant introduced voluminously into the record in support of its motion for summary judgment, were irrelevant to the motion to dismiss. Allowance of the latter motion pre-empted the summary judgment question. The court could not properly have considered these materials and did not do so. In effect, the court holds the suit to have been prematurely brought, and manifestly the decision, if affirmed, would not have been *res judicata* against a suit brought to obtain review of any final decisions to exclude, at a proper time, nor would appellants be left remediless in cases of unreasonable delay in deciding.

. . . .

NOTE

A settlement agreement in the case was approved in June 1976, 6 E.L.R. 20588; additional parties were allowed to intervene in *NRDC v. Costle*, 561 F.2d 904, 7 E.L.R. 20547 on June 15, 1977. Further litigation followed. *Environmental Defense Fund v. Costle*, 636 F.2d 1229, 10 E.L.R. 20808 (D.C. Cir. 1980), per J. Skelly Wright, C.J., upheld the settlement agreement and consent decree entered into by a number of industry associations and companies, environmental groups and EPA. The industry representatives had moved to vacate the consent decree and to modify the agreement on the grounds that the 1977 amendments of the FWPCA had superseded the settlement. The district court had denied the motion. On appeal, the D.C. Circuit affirmed. After a detailed review, it found that the 1977 amendments were not inconsistent with the settlement agreement and that Congress had not intended to supersede the consent decree. In its opinion, the Court notes that

> . . . Congress abandoned the requirement that EPA develop health-based standards regulating discharge of toxic pollutants on a pollutant-by-pollutant basis, substituting in its place an industry-by-industry, technology based BAT approach to controlling emission sources. In addition, Congress resolved the controversy over how many pollutants should be included in EPA's list of toxic pollutants by specifying 65 pollutants that had to be included in the list and granting EPA's administrator authority to add pollutants to or delete them from this list.

The Court rejected the assertion that certain cases included in the appeal relating to pretreatment and toxic criteria cases were moot, and denied reformation of the settlement agreement, but remanded to the District Court for the limited purposes of determining whether certain earlier modifications of the agreement, made in response to an NRDC motion seeking compliance with the agreement, impermissibly infringed on the discretion Congress committed to the Administrator to make certain decisions under the statute.

The settlement was again upheld in *NRDC v. Gorsuch*, 12 E.L.R. 20371 (1982) and a motion to modify the settlement was denied by the D.C. District Court, in May of 1982, 12 E.L.R. 20570.

In *Natural Resources Defense Fund, Inc. v. Gorsuch*, 12 E.L.R. 20570, 17 E.R.C. 2013 (D.C.D. May 17, 1982), the district court denied the petition of EPA to extend by 30 months its rulemaking schedule under FWPCA for toxic discharges by 23 industrial categories. Finding "insufficient justification" in EPA's arguments that the agency lacked sufficient staff and funds to meet the court-set deadlines, the district court ordered that rulemaking be completed by May, 1983.

The rulemaking schedule was set in the modified consent decree settling the litigation which began in 1973. The original consent decree provided for rulemaking to be completed by 1979 and industries to comply by 1983. The modified decree required industry to comply by 1984. *See NRDC v. Gorsuch*, 16 E.R.C. 2085 (Feb. 5. 1982).

HERCULES, INC. v. EPA

United States Court of Appeals, D.C. Circuit (1978)
598 F.2d 91

Before BAZELON, TAMM and ROBINSON, Circuit Judges.

TAMM, Circuit Judge:

We are called upon in these consolidated cases to review challenges to the Environmental Protection Agency's (EPA) first regulations limiting discharges into the nation's waterways of two toxic substances, toxaphene and endrin, under the Federal Water Pollution Control Act Amendments. For the reasons that follow, we uphold EPA's regulations.

I. FACTS AND PRIOR PROCEEDINGS

A. *Factual Background.*

Endrin is a chlorinated hydrocarbon first introduced about 1950.[106] It has been used as a pesticide for several decades, and is currently used for pest control on crops including cotton and sugar cane. At present, there is only one domestic manufacturer of endrin, Velsicol Chemical Corp. (Velsicol), which produces three to six million pounds a year. 42 Fed. Reg. 2595, 2600 (1977). Its endrin manufacturing plant is located at Memphis, Tennessee, and its discharges eventually reach the Mississippi River and are carried through the lower Mississippi to the Gulf of Mexico.

Evidence concerning the dangers of endrin to public health and the environment has been produced over the years since endrin was first introduced. In 1965, results from a study using rats suggested that it was carcinogenic. *See* 41 Fed. Reg. 31316 (1976).[107] EPA has found that endrin has caused fifty-two reported fish and wildlife kills, largely the result of leakage or runoff during agricultural use.[108] *Id.* at 31317. However, a massive fish kill in the lower Mississippi in 1963 was traced to discharges from Velsicol's Memphis plant. 42 Fed. Reg. 2591. Endrin is suspected in particular of threatening the brown pelican, an endangered species sensitive to endrin. 42 Fed. Reg. 2591; 41 Fed. Reg. 31317.

---

106 I Encyclopedia Britannica (Micropedia) 215 (1974) (definition of aldrin, a related substance).

107 *See Notice of Rebuttable Presumption Against Registration and continued Registration of Pesticide Products Containing Endrin*, 41 Fed. Reg. 31316 (1976).

108 The toxicity of endrin, and the fish kills caused by its agricultural use, are not a new phenomenon and are discussed in R. Carson, Silent Spring 26-27, 139-40 (1962).

Regulatory authorities have taken a number of steps to control endrin. The Food and Drug Administration has established a ceiling on endrin levels in food. 42 Fed. Reg. 2591. Velsicol discharged, on the average, approximately seven pounds of endrin per day in the mid-1960's, Joint Appendix (App.) I 182, but, under public and governmental pressure, it has taken steps to reduce this discharge. In June 1974, EPA issued Velsicol a National Pollutant Discharge Elimination System (NPDES) permit allowing an average daily discharge of no more than one pound of endrin.[109] Velsicol failed to reduce its endrin discharge below an average of 2.5 pounds per day in 1975, App. I 184, and it was found in violation of its permit and was subject to civil penalties. *United States v. Velsicol Chemical Corp.*, 9 ERC (BNA) 1723 (W.D. Tenn. 1976). Under the regulations now under review, Velsicol is required to limit its discharge to approximately.005 pounds of endrin per day. 42 Fed. Reg. 2594 & n.1.

Toxaphene is also a chlorinated hydrocarbon pesticide. It has been used for several decades, and is currently used for pest control on cotton and livestock. In the recent past, toxaphene was produced by four manufacturers. *See* 41 Fed. Reg. 23590 (1976). Hercules, Inc. (Hercules) contends that it is now the only manufacturer that discharges any toxaphene into waterways, and thus, the only manufacturer affected by these regulations.[110] In 1975, total domestic production of toxaphene was approximately one hundred million pounds. App. I 205-11. Hercules' toxaphene manufacturing plant is located at Brunswick, Georgia, and its discharge flows into the Brunswick Estuary, an arm of the Atlantic Ocean.

Evidence concerning the danger of toxaphene to public health and the environment, particularly to fish, has been produced in the years since the chemical was first introduced. Application of toxaphene to agricultural land surrounding several bird refuges resulted in massive bird kills in 1960-62. App. I 157. Toxaphene was identified as a cause of fish kills because of the characteristic "broken back" syndrome it produces in fish. In 1969, strobane, a pesticide closely related to toxaphene, was identified as a carcinogen in mice. App. I 148. Toxaphene has been frequently found in clarified and treated municipal drinking water. App. I 152.

Prior to 1970, Hercules' plant operated without a pollution treatment system; and, as Hercules concedes, its discharge "had an adverse effect upon the ecology" of local waters. Brief for Petitioner Hercules at 4. Subsequently, Hercules received an NPDES permit from the State of Georgia limiting its allowable toxaphene discharge. By 1975, Hercules reduced its average discharges of toxaphene to.27 pounds per day. App. I 206. Under the regulations now on review, Hercules is required to reduce its discharges to approximately.00375 pounds per day. 42 Fed. Reg. 2606 & n.2.

---

[109] Velsicol Chemical Corp. (Velsicol) appealed the terms of the permit. *Velsicol Chemical Corp. v. Train*, No. 76-2568 (6th Cir. filed Dec. 6, 1976).

[110] The Environmental Protection Agency (EPA) disputes Hercules, Inc.'s (Hercules) contention, but the issue is not one we need resolve. Hercules is the only manufacturer that has sought review of the toxaphene regulations.

B. *Proceedings.*

The early attempts of EPA to limit discharges of toxic substances are described in the opinion of this court in *EDF v. EPA [PCBs]*, 598 F.2d 62, at 68-70, (1978), decided today, and thus, there is no need to repeat that saga in detail. Endrin and toxaphene were on EPA's July 1973 proposed list of toxic substances and its September 1973 final list. 38 Fed. Reg. 18044, 24342 (1973). In December 1973, EPA proposed standards for endrin and toxaphene, 38 Fed. Reg. 35388 (1973); but after the 1974 hearings, EPA failed to issue final standards.

After the 1974 hearings, EPA subjected endrin and toxaphene to further investigation and analysis. EPA conducted its own experiments concerning the effects of endrin and toxaphene on a variety of species at its National Environmental Research Laboratory in Gulf Breeze, Florida.[111] Based on these experiments and on other studies, the Chief of the Criterion Branch of EPA's Office of Water Planning and Standards, Dr. Leonard J. Guarraia, prepared Criteria Documents summarizing the available information on endrin and toxaphene. On June 10, 1976, EPA proposed standards for endrin and toxaphene. 41 Fed. Reg. 23576 (1976). The standards were of two kinds: *concentration* limitations on the concentration of pollutant allowed in the discharges, and *mass* limitations on the amount of pollutant allowed in the discharges. For endrin, the proposed concentration limitation was 1.5 parts per billion, and the proposed mass limitation was 0.0003 kg/kkg (kilogram [kg.]/thousand [kilo] kilogram [kkg.]) of endrin produced. 41 Fed. Reg. 23595. For toxaphene, the proposed concentration limitation was 1.5 parts per billion, and the proposed mass limitation was 0.00001 kg/kkg of toxaphene produced. *Id.*

In July 1976, EPA commenced an evidentiary hearing on the proposed endrin and toxaphene standards before an administrative law judge (ALJ), which was concluded on October 12 after sixteen days of testimony. EPA presented the testimony of twelve witnesses. Velsicol presented the testimony of four witnesses concerning endrin, and Hercules presented the testimony of six witnesses concerning toxaphene. The Environmental Defense Fund (EDF) presented the testimony of one witness concerning the carcinogenic effects of endrin and toxaphene. 42 Fed. Reg. 2592, 2602. Three other parties participated in the hearing and twelve persons filed written comments. At the close of the hearing the record was furnished to the EPA Administrator (Administrator) for his consideration.[112]

On January 3, 1977, the Administrator filed his final decision concerning endrin and toxaphene with the EPA hearing clerk,[113] and on January 12, the decision was published. 42 Fed. Reg. 2588. The final decision adopted the proposed concentration limitations for endrin and toxaphene, but adopted

[111] Experiments on the effects of endrin on fresh water organisms were done at another EPA laboratory.

[112] The administrative law judge's function in this proceeding consisted of compiling a complete record for the EPA Administrator (Administrator), without making an initial decision or recommendation. *See* 42 Fed. Reg. 2588 (1977).

[113] There was no tentative decision. *Id.*

relaxed mass limitations of 0.0006 kg/kkg of endrin produced and 0.00003 kg/kkg of toxaphene produced.[114]

On the day the final standards were filed, the parties engaged in a customary "race to the courthouse." At 9:38 A.M., Hercules petitioned the United States Court of Appeals for the Fourth Circuit for review of the toxaphene regulations. However, the petition was premature as the standards were not filed until later in the day; Hercules filed a renewed petition for review two weeks later. At 11:13 A.M., the moment EPA filed its standards, EDF petitioned this court for review of the standards for both endrin and toxaphene. At 11:13 A.M., Velsicol also petitioned the United States Court of Appeals for the Sixth Circuit for review of the endrin regulations. Pursuant to motions by EPA, the Hercules and Velsicol petitions were transferred to this court. Subsequently, EDF's petition for review was dismissed on voluntary motion.[115] This court denied joint motions by Hercules and Velsicol for retransfer of their petitions and for expedition of the appeals.[116] Compliance with the standards was required by January 12, 1978.

II. APPLICABLE LAW.

EPA adopted the regulations now under review pursuant to authority conferred by the Federal Water Pollution Control Act Amendments of 1972 (1972 Act or the Act), 33 U.S.C. §§ 1251-1376(1976). Almost one year after EPA published its final regulations, while this case awaited oral argument in this court, Congress amended the toxics provision of the 1972 Act in section 53 of the Clean Water Act of 1977 (1977 Amendments or the Amendments), 33 U.S.C.A. § 1317(1977). Velsicol argues that the subsequent congressional action requires us to remand the toxic effluent standards for endrin for new proceedings under the 1977 Amendments. We do not agree. Courts apply the statutory law as it exists at the time of decision unless the intent of Congress is otherwise. *Bradley v. School Board*, 416 U.S. 696, 715-16 & n.21, 94 S.Ct. 2006, 40 L.Ed.2d 476 (1974). We conclude that this is a case in which it was intended that the new legislation not affect regulations that were awaiting judicial review prior to enactment of the legislation.

Congress passed the 1972 Act in an effort to deal with the regulatory problems that had hindered efforts to control water pollution. *EPA v. State Water Resources Control Board*, 426 U.S. 200, 202-03, 96 S.Ct. 2022, 48 L.Ed.2d 578 (1976). The 1972 Act solved some regulatory problems, but not others. By 1977, Congress concluded that the toxics provision of the 1972 Act,

[114] On the basis of information concerning the volume of water discharged during production of endrin and toxaphene, the Administrator determined that the appropriate mass limitations corresponding to the proposed (and final) concentration limitations were 0.0006 kg/kkg for endrin and 0.00003 kg/kkg for toxaphene. 42 Fed. Reg. 2594, 2606.

Mass limitations are expressed as kilograms of discharged toxic substance, per thousand kilograms of manufactured toxic substance. For example, a mass limitation of.01 kg/kkg requires that a manufacturer discharge no more than.01 kilogram for every thousand kilograms it manufactures. The mass limitation is expressed this way to allow manufacturers to produce as much or as little of the substance as they wish without affecting their proportionate duty to purify the discharge.

[115] *EDF v. EPA*, No. 77-1001 (D.C.Cir. June 17, 1977) (order granting unopposed motion for voluntary dismissal).

[116] Order of Sept. 28, 1977.

which provided for regulation based on health criteria, had been a failure.[117] As a reaction to inadequacy of the 1972 toxics provision, EPA commenced a new program to issue regulations under other provisions of the 1972 Act: it would regulate toxic discharges on an industry-by-industry basis and set standards based on the feasibility of control technology. EPA would also continue to issue health-based standards. EPA's new program was sanctioned by the judicial decree in *NRDC v. Train*, 8 ERC (BNA) 2120, 2122 (D.D.C.1976) ("Flannery decree"), *rev'd in part on other grounds sub nom. NRDC v. Costle*, 183 U.S.App.D.C. 11, 561 F.2d 904 (1977). In the 1977 Amendments, Congress remodeled the toxics provision based on the judicial decree in *NRDC v. Train.*[118]

In section 53(a) of the 1977 Amendments, 33 U.S.C.A. § 1317(a)(2)(1977), Congress directed EPA to take into account, in issuing health-based regulations, "the extent to which effective control is being or may be achieved under other regulatory authority," particularly EPA's authority to promulgate feasibility-based regulations. *See* 33 U.S.C.A. § 1311(b)(2)(C)(1977). Velsicol contends that this provision shows that Congress intended EPA to withdraw the health-based toxics regulations promulgated under the 1972 Act, particularly the endrin regulations, and to regulate endrin discharges using feasibility-based criteria.[119] EPA responds that the 1977 Amendments were intended to supplement its authority, and were not intended in any way to impede promulgation of health-based regulations.

On a question of statutory interpretation such as this one, involving legislation enacted with EPA's advice and cooperation, EPA's view of the legislative intent concerning its ongoing efforts deserves some deference.

Congress knew that EPA's health-based regulations were in effect and were awaiting judicial review. *See* 123 Cong. Rec. H12929 (daily ed. Dec. 15, 1977) (staff report). Moreover, its attitude was not that EPA had done too much and

---

[117] A number of Congressmen involved in the drafting of the amendments for the toxics provision commented on the inadequacy of the 1972 provision. 123 Cong.Rec. H12927 (remarks of Rep. Roberts), H12940 (Rep. Clausen), H12944 (Rep. Johnson) (daily ed. Dec. 15, 1977). Senator Muskie summed up the congressional mood:

> Toxics have not been dealt with effectively by this Congress under any piece of legislation we have eve[r] enacted into law. Never, never. . . .
>
> I am getting a little fed up myself, having written environmental laws for 15 years, to keep picking up the paper and reading about a new toxic that is killing more people, that is making more people ill because I have not done my job.

123 Cong.Rec. S13565 (daily ed. Aug. 4, 1977) (remarks concerning a related matter involving dredging).

[118] As Senator Randolph observed, "[t]he legislation follows the settlement agreement [in that case] in listing 65 pollutants and families of pollutants and declaring that each such pollutant is toxic." 123 Cong.Rec. S19663 (daily ed. Dec. 15, 1977).

[119] Velsicol contends that under the amended version of section 307(a), 33 U.S.C.A. § 1317(a)(1978):

> (1) the Administrator must first consider whether effective control can be obtained through the use of the best available technology economically achievable before promulgating a stricter standard; and
>
> (2) if a stricter standard than that obtained by use of the best available technology economically achievable is required to provide effective control, the Administrator must consider the technological feasibility of such stricter standard in determining the compliance data.

Supplemental Memorandum of Velsicol Chemical Corp. on the Clean Water Act Amendments of 1977 at 2-3.

should start all over, but rather that EPA had done too little. "Frankly, [Section 307(a)] has failed. . . . [O]nly six toxic chemicals—aldrin/dieldrin, endrin, DDT, toxaphene, benzidene and PCB's—*have been regulated.* Six chemicals in 5 years." *Id.* at H12927 (remarks of Rep. Roberts) (emphasis added). Congress's strong support for continuing health-based regulation is shown not only by its impatience with EPA's pace, but also by the great emphasis placed in the 1977 Amendments on making it *easier* for EPA to promulgate health-based regulations as a supplement to feasibility-based regulation. *See* 123 Cong.Rec. S19649 (daily ed. Dec. 15, 1977) (remarks of Sen. Muskie) ("these amendments reduce the evidentiary burden of establishing a toxic effluent standard"); S.Rep.No.370, 95th Cong., 1st Sess. 54 (1977); U.S. CODE Cong. & Admin.News 1977, p. 4378 (lifting of formal rulemaking requirement for health-based regulation). . . .

Thus, we conclude that the 1977 Amendments were intended to aid, not to impede, EPA's health-based regulation. In accordance with EPA's view that this intent would be frustrated if the regulations were nullified, we conclude that the applicable law in this proceeding is the 1972 Act and that no remand is necessary.

III. SUBSTANTIVE ISSUES CONCERNING TOXAPHENE.

A. *Claims of the Parties.*

In setting discharge standards, EPA's approach was to follow a procedure consisting in essence of determining, in the laboratory, which aquatic organisms were most vulnerable to toxaphene, measuring how much toxaphene they could take, and then, using these data, calculating a maximum tolerable discharge figure. Hercules challenges EPA's laboratory-based approach, as well as particular details of EPA's methodology.

EPA's approach may be viewed as consisting of six steps. In the first, EPA selected a half-dozen species of aquatic organisms for testing that were either important commercially in and of themselves (oysters), or important indirectly as food for other organisms (pinfish).[120]

Second, EPA conducted "bioassays" in the laboratory. In these bioassays, EPA exposed the organisms to toxaphene for ninety-six hours.[121] EPA derived, from the bioassay results, the concentration of toxaphene that kills one-half of a group of aquatic organisms. The short-term lethal dose for the tested organisms ranged from 16 parts per billion for oysters to 0.5 parts per billion for pinfish. These figures reflect the vulnerability of fish and other aquatic life to toxaphene. Third, EPA estimated from the short-term lethal dose the maximum tolerable long-term concentration of toxaphene for the tested species.[122] Fourth, EPA used the long-term tolerable concentration

---

[120] The species selected by EPA were the oyster, the longnose killifish, the pink shrimp, the grass shrimp, the sheepshead minnow, and the pinfish. 42 Fed. Reg. 2601. For reasons discussed at 106 of 598 F.2d *infra*, EPA did not limit its selection to species present or potentially present in Brunswick Estuary, or in other waters into which toxaphene is discharged, but used an array of important marine species.

[121] One of the species was exposed for twenty-eight days instead of ninety-six hours.

[122] Using a method developed by the Na-

level to set an "ambient water criterion." The ambient water criterion is intended to be the maximum concentration of the toxic substance allowed in the nation's waterways—a concentration low enough that even the most vulnerable important life in the water will be safe.[123]

Fifth, EPA translated the ambient water criterion into the effluent discharge standard, the standard controlling how much toxaphene a plant may discharge legally.[124] Finally, EPA set a "mass limitation" to supplement the effluent discharge limit. Whereas the effluent discharge limit is expressed in terms of a concentration of toxaphene, the mass limitation restates it in terms of the total amount of toxaphene produced. Such a supplemental figure compels a plant to meet the effluent discharge limit by removing toxaphene from its effluent. In the absence of such a mass limitation, a plant could meet the discharge limit simply by watering down its effluent until the effluent was diluted enough to meet the concentration limit.

Hercules' challenge to EPA's laboratory-based approach relies on alternative data using field studies. Starting in 1970, Dr. Robert Reimold, a Georgia biologist, conducted a field study of aquatic life in Terry Creek, the arm of Brunswick Estuary into which Hercules' plant discharges effluent. For six years, Dr. Reimold compared the variety of free-swimming species found in Terry Creek with the variety found in Duplin Estuary, a comparable nearby body of water not contaminated by toxaphene. Dr. Reimold believed that toxaphene was not harming the free-swimming aquatic life present in Terry Creek. The level of toxaphene in Terry Creek's waters was between 1 and 2 parts per billion, which is between 200 and 400 times EPA's "ambient water criterion" of.005 parts per billion. Accordingly, Hercules asserts that aquatic life can survive higher levels of toxaphene than EPA allows, and thus, that EPA's regulations are overly strict.

Hercules combines this frontal assault with several attacks on the specifics of EPA's methodology. It contends that EPA's use of the pinfish as a test species was misconceived, since the pinfish is not an important species in Brunswick Estuary. It also argues that EPA's toxicity tests were conducted improperly, that the tests failed to support the standard with substantial evidence, and that EPA should not have adopted a mass limitation precluding dilution.

---

tional Academy of Sciences in 1972, EPA estimated that an aquatic organism could tolerate, over the long term, about one one-hundredth of the dose of toxaphene that would kill it over the short term. By this estimation method, the long-term safe concentration of toxaphene ranged from.16 parts per billion for oysters to.005 parts per billion for pinfish. 42 Fed. Reg. 2603-04.

[123] Of the important species actually tested by EPA, the pinfish proved to be most sensitive. For water to be tolerable to pinfish over the long term, it must not contain more than.005 parts per billion of toxaphene. EPA employed the maximum safe toxaphene concentration for the pinfish as its ambient water criteria because the pinfish was the most sensitive species actually tested. Accordingly, the ambient water criteria was set at.005 parts per billion. *Id.*

[124] EPA set the discharge level on the assumption that, after discharge into a body of water, concentrated effluent is mixed naturally and quickly with water. EPA assumed that few aquatic organisms are exposed to the concentrated discharge, while most will face only a mixed, attenuated toxaphene solution. In this case, EPA considered it reasonable to expect that such post-discharge mixing would attenuate toxaphene effluent by a factor of 300. Therefore, EPA set an average daily effluent discharge limit of 1.5 parts per billion, since that would produce, after attenuation through mixing by a factor of 300, an ambient water level of.005 parts per billion. *Id.* at 2605-06.

EPA replies that its six-step approach was proper, since the toxics provision requires "categorical" standards for toxic pollutants, rather than standards based on local species and local receiving waters. EPA further responds that it was not required to give great weight to Hercules' evidence, and that its own tests furnished an adequate basis for regulation.

B. *Statutory Issues.*

The court has discussed the standards of section 307(a), 33 U.S.C. § 1317(a)(1976), in *EDF v. EPA* [*PCBs*], 598 F.2d at 79 81. As explained there, section 307(a)(2) of the 1972 Act lists six factors for EPA to "take into account" in proposing a toxic effluent standard: "the toxicity of the pollutant, its persistence, degradability, the usual or potential presence of the affected organisms in any waters, the importance of the affected organisms and the nature and extent of the effect of the toxic pollutant on such organisms." EPA is to set discharge standards that provide an "ample margin of safety." Section 307(a)(4). Under the "ample margin of safety" directive, EPA's standards must protect against incompletely understood dangers to public health and the environment, in addition to well-known risks. *See EDF v. EPA* [*PCBs*], 598 F.2d at 80-81.

TOXICS MUST MEET BAT STANDARDS NO VARIENCES

Hercules' challenge to the regulations concentrates on the last three factors in section 307(a): "the usual or potential presence of the affected organisms in any waters, the importance of the affected organisms and the nature and extent of the effect of the toxic pollutant on such organisms." Hercules argues that these factors preclude EPA from basing its calculations upon experiments performed on the pinfish, and require it to focus exclusively on organisms actually found in the particular receiving waters into which Hercules discharges. EPA's testing scheme, Hercules contends, is "contrary to the statutory requirement that EPA design its standards to fit the characteristics of *specific water bodies* in terms of 'the toxicity of the pollutant' *in those waters* and 'the importance of the affected organisms' *in those waters.*" Brief of Petitioner Hercules at 59 (emphasis added).

We agree with EPA's interpretation of the statute. *See, e.g., E.I. du Pont de Nemours & Co. v. Train,* 430 U.S. at 134-35, 97 S.Ct. 965. As reported, the House version of the 1972 Act, H.R. 11896, 92d Cong., 2d Sess. § 307(a)(1) & (2) (1972) (emphasis added), contained a factor for toxic standards related to local conditions, as Hercules would prefer: "the usual or potential presence of the affected organisms *in* [*the receiving*] *waters.*" The Senate version did not include any factors relating to "affected organisms." S. 2770, 92d Cong., 1st Sess. § 307 (1971). In conference, the House factors were accepted, but the phrase "in the receiving waters" was replaced by "in any waters." The Conference Report notes:

> Sections 307(a)(1) and (2) are the same as the comparable provisions of the House amendment, except that the Administrator is required to take into account the usual or potential presence of the affected organisms *in any water rather than in the receiving waters* as is provided in the House amendment.

1 Senate Comm. on Public Works, 93d Cong., 1st Sess., A Legislative History of the Water Pollution Control Act Amendments of 1972 (hereafter, Legislative

History) at 312 (Comm.Print 1973) (emphasis added). Senator Muskie, a conference manager, explained that the substitution was a compromise to preserve the "categorical determination" established by the Senate in lieu of the focus on particular "receiving waters" in the House version:

. . . .

The Conference Committee's focus on a "categorical determination" rather than on specific "receiving waters" reflected a drafters' leitmotif in the 1972 Act. Pre-1972 attempts at water pollution control had been based upon characteristics of local bodies of receiving water. For that reason, in part, they failed:

> The earliest version of the Federal Water Pollution Control Act was passed in 1948 and amended five times before 1972. Throughout that 24 year period, Congress attempted to use receiving water quality as a basis for setting pollution standards. W. Rodgers, Environmental Law 355-57 (1977). At the end of that period, Congress realized not only that its water pollution efforts until then had failed, but also that reliance on receiving water capacity as a crucial test for permissible pollution levels had contributed greatly to that failure. *EPA v. State Water Resources Control Board*, 426 U.S. 200, 202, 96 S.Ct. 2022, 48 L.Ed.2d 578 (1976).

Weyerhaeuser Co. v. Costle, 191 U.S.App.D.C. 309 at 340, 590 F.2d 1011 at 1042 (1978). . . .

Applying a categorical approach, EPA did not limit its study to the aquatic life found in receiving waters for toxaphene discharges. Instead, EPA tested six important marine species, and from the results of these tests, it inferred the likely sensitivity of other species. Specifically, it chose the most sensitive species actually tested (pinfish), and used the test results from that species to set the ambient water criterion.

The choice of the most sensitive species actually tested may be understood on at least two levels. Legally, section 307(a)(4)'s fundamental instruction is that EPA's standards should provide an "ample margin of safety." Basing the scheme upon the most sensitive species actually tested provides a margin of safety for less sensitive species. Scientifically, the scheme rests upon a statistical assumption:

> Reliable toxicity data exist for a relatively small percent of all organisms in the aquatic environment for any given substance. It seems a safe assumption to make, that as additional species are tested, some of them are going to be more resistant than those that have already been tested and some are going to be more sensitive. . . . If we consider the thousands of species of aquatic organisms which exist in our waterways and assume that only one hundred of these species are important enough to protect for the purpose of man's use; and if we further consider that perhaps only a half dozen species at most have been tested in most instances, it is highly probable that in any given water, species of greater sensitivity than those already tested, occur. Therefore, it would appear that the *use of the most sensitive species tested, to establish acceptable levels, may not be overly conservative*, since so few species have been tested and more sensitive important species surely exist. Furthermore, should one of the food chain species be sensitive and essential, an entire food pyramid would be jeopardized.

App. I 255-56 (Affidavit of Dr. Donald I. Mount) (emphasis added).

C. *Scope of Review.*

The applicable scope of review is discussed in *EDF v. EPA [PCBs]*, 598 F.2d at 82-83. EPA's determinations are subject to review under the "substantial evidence" test, which requires that EPA's conclusions be supported by "such relevant evidence as a reasonable mind might accept as adequate to support [the] conclusion[s]." *Consolidated Edison Co. v. NLRB*, 305 U.S. 197, 229, 59 S.Ct. 206, 217, 83 L.Ed. 126 (1938). When agency rulemaking is based on judgments "on the frontiers of scientific knowledge," this standard calls for deferential review of the agency's conclusions that "depend to a greater extent upon policy judgments." *Industrial Union Department, AFL-CIO v. Hodgson*, 162 U.S.App.D.C. 331, 338, 499 F.2d 467, 474-75 (1974).

In this case, we are called upon to review a *numerical standard* for discharge. In reviewing a numerical standard, we must ask whether the agency's numbers are within a "zone of reasonableness," not whether its numbers are precisely right.

A principal rationale for the "zone of reasonableness" concept is that it frees the court from the minutiae of particular calculations, and correspondingly, it allows an agency discretion to adapt a general formula or methodology to the aspects of a particular case.

Hercules argues that EPA failed to respond adequately to, or to rebut, its showing on particular issues. We shall discuss these issues individually. However, as a preliminary matter, we observe that the toxics provision places the burden of persuasion (in the agency hearing) on the person urging modification of the proposed standard. "*[U]nless* the Administrator finds, on the record, that a *modification* of such proposed standard (or prohibition) is justified based upon a preponderance of evidence adduced at such hearings, such standard (or prohibition) shall be promulgated." Section 307(a)(2) (emphasis added). Since Hercules urged EPA to modify the proposed standard (that is, to promulgate a more relaxed, revised standard), the burden of proof in the agency hearing was on Hercules, not EPA.

D. *Adequacy of the Basis for EPA's Regulations.*

1. EPA's policy judgments.

Although EPA's categorical focus led it to favor a laboratory approach, that focus did not preclude consideration of field data. Indeed, it considered past fish kills, bird kills, human poisonings, and other incidents, 42 Fed. Reg. 2602-03, as well as Dr. Reimold's Brunswick Estuary studies, *id.* at 2604-05. However, EPA concluded that, in this particular case, the Brunswick Estuary study should not be accorded much weight both because of the inherent limitations of such a study and because of the particular limitations on Dr. Reimold's technique. *Id.*

[The Court reviews the technical and expert testimony, and concludes that EPA was entitled to rely on its own data and experts.]

2. EPA's factual determinations leading to the numerical standard.

The Criteria Document prepared for EPA and affidavits presented by EPA and EDF summarized an array of studies and evidence concerning the toxicity (including carcinogenicity), persistence, and degradability of toxaphene. Toxaphene was shown to be toxic to phytoplankton, App. I 133, aquatic invertebrates, App. I 133-35, 292, fish, App. I 135-42, 293-345, fish-eating birds, App. I 142-43, and mammals, App. I 143-49.

Evidence was presented that toxaphene is carcinogenic. EPA summarized a study concluding that strobane, a substance related to toxaphene, causes cancer in mice. App. I 148. Preliminary data were presented indicating that toxaphene caused cancer in mice and rats. App. II 645-49. Toxaphene also was shown to cause enzyme induction. App. I 148. On this record, EPA cautiously refrained from declaring toxaphene to be a carcinogen, in part because the data were too recent to make a complete scientific analysis. However, EPA concluded that "the existence of these data underscores the Agency's concern that discharges of toxaphene be minimized." 42 Fed. Reg. 2602.

EPA also produced physical and chemical evidence that toxaphene is persistent, mobile, and adsorbed to sediments, and biological evidence that toxaphene is not degraded and tends to bioaccumulate in aquatic species. App. I 151-57, 249, 351.

Against this background, EPA conducted bioassays in order to derive a numerical discharge standard. Systematic comparable bioassays were conducted on six species, using a uniform methodology. App. I 346-54.

Hercules did not offer bioassays or other laboratory studies in opposition, but did criticize EPA's studies. Hercules contended in the administrative proceedings, as it does now, that the pinfish toxicity data were used to set the ultimate numerical standard, and that the pinfish bioassay was unreliable because the fish suffered artificial "stress," lowering resistance to toxaphene. EPA disputes the claim of artificial stress. Brief for Respondent in 77-1248 at 40-41. Hercules also objects to EPA's reference on appeal to evidence of toxaphene's carcinogenicity, since EPA's own decision declined to make a finding of human carcinogenicity.

We find EPA's determination of the effluent discharge and mass limitation standards supported by substantial evidence and within the zone of reasonableness. As this court stated in *Ethyl Corp. v. EPA*, 176 U.S.App.D.C. 373, 410, 541 F.2d 1, 38(en banc), *cert. denied*, 426 U.S. 941, 96 S.Ct. 2663, 49 L.Ed.2d 394 (1976), "[b]y its nature, scientific evidence is cumulative: the more supporting, albeit inconclusive, evidence available, the more likely the accuracy of the conclusion." Although the pinfish bioassay played a significant role in setting the numerical standard, it should not be viewed in isolation. Its persuasive value was enhanced by prior studies of the similarity of many other aquatic species to toxaphene, and by bioassays using five other species performed contemporaneously. Although the support that other tests and studies lend to the standard is not as direct as that provided by the pinfish data, those tests and studies are mostly decidedly part of the agency's cumulative evidence. With respect to the allegations that EPA's pinfish bioassay was itself flawed (*e.g.*, that the fish were under stress) these allegations were refuted by testimony. App. II 726-27.

Finally, we do not accept Hercules' contention that this court may not consider EPA's conclusion concerning carcinogenicity—that the data "underscore[] the Agency's concern that discharges of toxaphene be minimized." The record contains data concerning toxaphene's carcinogenicity for animals. Thus, EPA's limited conclusion, which articulates its "concern" about toxaphene's carcinogenicity, is supported in the record. Although EPA did not make an affirmative finding of carcinogenicity, its concern was relevant to the setting of a standard providing an "ample margin of safety," and therefore relevant in this appeal. *See EDF v. EPA* [*PCBs*], 598 F.2d at 80-81.

IV. SUBSTANTIVE ISSUES CONCERNING ENDRIN.

A. *Statutory Issues.*

Velsicol's principal argument for invalidating the endrin standard is that EPA was required to give consideration to the feasibility of achieving the standard with existing pollution control technology, but failed to do so adequately. It contends that consideration of feasibility is required by "reasoned decision making" and principles of "rational" consideration. Velsicol maintains that the standard under review is, in fact, not achievable. Velsicol refers to *Bunker Hill Co. v. EPA*, 572 F.2d 1286, 1301 (9th Cir. 1977), a case arising under the Clean Air Act, for the proposition that "[t]he record must establish that the required technology is feasible, not merely *possibly* feasible."

EPA defends its standard on alternative grounds. It contends that section 307(a) simply does not require it to give any consideration to economic and technological feasibility. Reviewing the factors listed in that section, it points out that "[a]bsent from the list is any requirement that the Administrator consider technological feasibility or economic impact." Brief for Respondent in No. 77-1349 at 41. *See also id.* at 53 & n. 30. EPA also contends that the endrin standard is, in fact, feasible. *Id.* at 53.

We agree with EPA's contention that section 307(a) does not require it to consider economic and technological factors.

. . . .

Section 307(a)(2) requires EPA to "take into account" six factors in proposing toxics standards that comprehensively cover the fate of toxic substances in the environment, their effects on living organisms in general, and their effects on some organisms present and important in particular. *EDF v. EPA* [*PCBs*], 598 F.2d at 79-80. None of the six factors speaks explicitly to the technical means used to control the discharge of substances, nor is there present any term commonly used to denote a feasibility consideration, *e.g.*, feasibility, achievability, practicability, economic impact, or cost. . . .

An examination of other provisions of the 1972 Act reinforces this interpretation of section 307(a). Section 307(a)(4) directs EPA to set standards providing "an ample margin of safety," without any mention of feasibility criteria. Further, we do not believe that section 307(a)(5) introduces feasibility criteria into the statutory scheme. Section 307(a)(5) states that "[w]hen proposing or promulgating any effluent standard (or prohibition) under this section, the Administrator shall designate the category or categories of sources to which the effluent standard (or prohibition) shall apply." The legislative history makes clear that categories would be differentiated not by the feasibility *vel non* of pollution control, but by the extent to which a toxic substance is present in the industrial process.

The legislative background explains why Congress focused on public and environmental protection, rather than discharge control technology, in the setting of toxic standards. . . .

Velsicol argues that, if feasibility is not considered, the regulations will be promulgated at an irrationally strict level. However, the congressional selection of factors is a legislative determination that the need of the public and the environment for protection from toxic chemicals is more important than the problems of stringent regulation. This congressional determination is a rational response to the dangers presented by toxic substances. The meaning of the statute being clear, it is not this court's prerogative to impose considerations of feasibility.

It may also be argued that, as a practical matter, it will prove very difficult to administer the statute without considering feasibility, because of the resistance of industry representatives and environmentalists to what will be perceived by them, respectively, as overly or underly stringent regulation. However, our interpretation, which follows in large part EPA's original interpretation of section 307(a), will not necessarily lead to great difficulty in administering the section, because it does not preclude EPA from gathering information about feasibility. Availability of information about feasibility may tend to induce industry and environmentalists to accept standards based on health criteria.

Velsicol points out that EPA did consider feasibility in the proceedings leading to the regulations in issue. Indeed, Velsicol contends that EPA first set its endrin standard in accordance with feasibility criteria and then justified it with evidence related to the section 307(a)(2) factors. This argument raises the possibility that we must remand the agency's standards on the grounds that EPA took an erroneous step in its deliberations. . . .

We have concluded that section 307(a) does not include feasibility as a factor for consideration. However, the fact that EPA considered evidence about feasibility does not require that the regulations be vacated. It is apparent that EPA calculated its endrin standards using health-based, not feasibility-related, evidence.[125] It conducted bioassays of aquatic species, determined the

---

[125] EPA stated in its final decision:

> Yet the statutory "ample margin" concept is an elastic one which, like the importance of the organism, allows for considerable exercise of judgment by the Administrator in setting the standards. In any case where a discharge is allowed, on the spectrum ranging from certain safety (a prohibition) to that uncertain point where harmful effects are caused and safety ends, a logical break point is struck where the very best that control technology can do is required.

42 Fed. Reg. 2597; 41 Fed. Reg. 23580. This language suggests EPA contemplated setting its standard, in some instances, not by the six-step procedure, but by determining what level was achievable and accepting that "logical break point" as to the standard. In this in-

maximum long-term dose of endrin that the most sensitive tested species could tolerate, set an ambient water criterion, and calculated effluent standards and mass limitations. Only then, upon calculating its standards, did it consider evidence about feasibility to provide an additional test. 42 Fed. Reg. 2597-600. It found that the standards were, in fact, feasible. Although consideration of feasibility is not contemplated by section 307(a), EPA's consideration of it did not affect its conclusions based on the factors specified by section 307(a), but constituted an attempt to confer additional legitimacy on its conclusions. The supererogatory consideration did not prejudice Velsicol in any way. Indeed, Velsicol actually gained an additional opportunity to press for relaxed standards by presenting evidence that the standards were not achievable.

. . . .

B. *Review of the Support for EPA's Policy Determinations.*

Velsicol contests two of EPA's determinations in calculating the endrin standards. We review the record, keeping in mind that, when issues are "on the frontiers of scientific knowledge," the "substantial evidence" test calls for deferential review of EPA's policy judgments. *Industrial Union Department, AFL-CIO v. Hodgson*, 499 F.2d at 474-75. Both of Velsicol's contentions concern EPA's alleged failure to deal adequately with local aquatic organisms and local receiving water conditions at the site of Velsicol's plant in Memphis, Tennessee. We reject Velsicol's contentions for the reasons underlying our rejection of Hercules' argument that EPA was required to focus on conditions at the site of its Brunswick plant.

1. Application factor.

EPA used the same six-step technique in setting its endrin standard that it used in setting its toxaphene standard. *See* App. I 355-59. In considering toxicity, it summarized studies showing that endrin was toxic to a broad range of invertebrates, fish, birds, and mammals. App. I 94-107. Evidence concerning the carcinogenicity of endrin in mice and rats had been produced, 41 Fed. Reg. 31316-17 (1976) (establishing "rebuttable presumption" against continued registration of endrin as a pesticide) and new evidence concerning this was presented in these proceedings, 42 Fed. Reg. 2591-93. Endrin was demonstrated to be persistent and mobile in some circumstances, and while it was sometimes degraded or eliminated, it was bioaccumulated in many organisms. App. I 108-17.

2. Mixing zone factor.

Once effluent is discharged, it mixes with the waters at the site of discharge. Having set an ambient water criteria for endrin of.004 parts per billion, EPA set an effluent discharge standard using a "mixing zone" factor. It employed a mixing factor of 375, anticipating that one part of effluent would be mixed

stance, however, EPA calculated its standard using the six-step procedure before it turned to consideration of feasibility. *See* 42 Fed. Reg. 2588-89 (describing overall procedure), 2590-94 (describing the derivation of the ambient water criterion), 2605-06 (describing application of the mixing zone factor).

with about 375 parts of water before aquatic organisms had significant contact with endrin. As a backstop, EPA also provided for a "tightening variance"—a smaller mixing zone factor for any discharges in waters where mixing is likely to be less thorough. 42 Fed. Reg. 2609, 2614-15. Velsicol contends that the evidence supports a larger mixing zone factor, up to 4,000 in view of the volume and flow of the Mississippi River, and that EPA must also provide for "loosening" variances (large mixing zone factors for thoroughly-mixed waters).

Having chosen a methodology, the compromise figure set by EPA was rational. A much higher figure for the mixing zone might well have frustrated two congressional policies: that the "margin of safety" provided by the standards be "ample" and that pollution concentration be controlled by treatment, not dilution. We find that the choice of 375 as the mixing zone factor was within the "zone of reasonableness" and, within that zone, the choice of a precise figure is left to EPA.

V. PROCEDURAL ISSUES.

Hercules and Velsicol challenge EPA's procedures in two basic respects. First, they contend that the Administrator and the judicial officer impermissibly relied on submissions from, and engaged in contacts with, EPA staff. Second, Hercules argues that EPA committed reversible error in not issuing a tentative decision after the close of the evidence and before the final decision.

A. *Applicable Standards Under the Administrative Procedure Act.*

Petitioners maintain that EPA was required to follow the procedure set forth in section 5 of the Administrative Procedure Act (APA), 5 U.S.C. § 554(1976). They support this contention basically by two arguments. First, section 307(a) states that the Administrator, after proposing standards, shall hold a "hearing" and that he shall make certain findings "on the record" of the hearing. Petitioners maintain that section 554 applies to all proceedings "on the record." *See* Reply Brief for Petitioner Hercules at 12-13. Second, petitioners argue that a "functional" analysis of these proceedings shows that EPA must follow section 554. We cannot agree. . . .

[The Court concludes that the setting of standards under § 307 is rule making, not adjudicatory, even though Velsicol is the sole domestic manufacturer of the affected toxic substances. EPA acquiesces in substantial evidence review, consistent with its formal rule making approach to § 307 regulations.]

B. *Reliance by the Administrator on Staff Assistance.*

[The Court upholds EPA.]

VI. COMPLIANCE TIME.

Under the 1972 Act's regulatory scheme, EPA sets discharge standards under the various statutory sections, and the standards are then incorporated into permits issued to dischargers which permit the maximum amount of pollutants that may be discharged. However, a special exception to this scheme is made in the area of toxic pollutant regulation. "Compliance with a permit issued pursuant to this section shall be deemed compliance [with the statutory standards] . . . except any standard imposed under [section 307] for a toxic pollutant *injurious to human health.*" Section 402(k) of the Act, 33 U.S.C. § 1342(k)(1976) (emphasis added). Thus, dischargers must meet newly established toxics standards even before their permits have been (or may be) revised to include them. EPA contends this provision applies to its toxaphene and endrin standards. Hercules responds that toxaphene is not "injurious to human health" within the meaning of the statute, because the current level of toxaphene discharges is not creating a human health hazard. Velsicol also argues that the one-year compliance period should be extended because section 53(b) of the Clean Water Act of 1977, 33 U.S.C.A. § 1317(a)(6)(1977) allows EPA to set a longer time for compliance than the maximum specified in the 1972 Act (if it determines that compliance within that time is technologically infeasible for a category of sources).

We reject petitioners' arguments and uphold EPA's requirement of swift compliance with the newly set toxics standards. The 1972 Act is replete with declarations that swift compliance with toxics standards is the normal, not the exceptional, circumstance that petitioners would make it. Section 307(a)(6) provides that "[a]ny effluent standard (or prohibition) established pursuant to this section shall take effect on such date or dates as specified in the order promulgating such standard, but in no case, more than one year from the date of such promulgation." As the legislative history of the 1972 Act explains:

> Because of the hazards posed by toxic substances, the committee considers the need for compliance with promulgated standards for toxic substances to be especially urgent. Language in section [307(a)(6)] is thus intended to convey that one year be an *absolute maximum time* allowed for compliance with standards promulgated under this section, and that compliance be required *as early as possible* within this limit.

2 Legislative History at 1479 (Senate Report) (emphasis added). . . .

. . . .

Hercules points out that the term "injurious to human health" must have been intended to distinguish some toxic substances that are "injurious" from others that are not. It contends that since all toxic substances are likely to be "injurious" in some amount, for the term to make a meaningful distinction, it must require proof that the toxic substance creates a human health hazard in the amount now being discharged. EPA concluded that a less restrictive view of the term would make it meaningful. As EPA interpreted the statute, the test should be whether the toxic substance would injure humans in "relatively small quantities." 42 Fed. Reg. 2601.

We adopt EPA's interpretation. Nowhere in the Act's approach to toxics is there any requirement that EPA determine what quantities of a toxic substance are now being discharged. Hercules' view would require EPA to investigate and determine local discharge conditions, while EPA's view allows a categorical approach to toxicity measurements similar to that used in section 307(a). *See* text accompanying notes 23-27 *supra.* Velsicol's argument based on the Clean Water Act of 1977 is similarly unpersuasive. The fact that the Clean Water Act of 1977 gave EPA discretionary authority to allow a longer compliance time does not necessarily imply or suggest that the pre-existing maximum one-year period was always to be considered excessively stringent.

VII. CONCLUSION.

For the foregoing reasons, we uphold EPA's regulations setting standards for discharges of endrin and toxaphene.

So ordered.

NOTE

The change from health based to technology based (BAT based) regulations for toxic pollutants was also reflected in the case which affirmed EPA's effluent limitations on the discharge of polychlorinated biphenols (PCBs) into waterways.[126] Industry petitioners challenged the regulations claiming that PCB controls under the Toxic Substances Control Act (TSCA) preempted EPA's authority under the Clean Water Act. The court held that EPA had a choice of regulatory authority and could use the most effective means to combat the unknown and potentially dangerous, including carcinogenic, risks from toxic substances. The court upheld EPA's authority to regulate the discharge of PCBs under the authority of § 307. The court also rejected the petitioner's claim that EPA lacked an adequate basis for the PCB regulations because the standards for highly chlorinated PCBs were extrapolated from knowledge about more highly chlorinated PCBs. The court held, however, that EPA is not required to demonstrate the toxicity of each chemical it seeks to regulate through studies demonstrating a clear line of causation between the particular chemical and harm to public health or the environment.[127] Rejecting the industry's objections, the court relied upon the "ample margin of safety" requirement of § 307(a)(4). When setting standards for toxic substances that presented incompletely understood risks, the court concluded that EPA could err on the side of overprotection with respect to known risks in order to provide safety from unknown dangers, deferring to EPA's judgment.

In general, EPA has set technology based standards since the 1977 amendment of the law. EPA has nonetheless extended more stringent regulations to cover health based standards going beyond the strict requirements of BAT, relying on the "ample margin of safety" language of the statute. Health based standards cover only six toxic pollutants, namely aldrin and dieldrin, DDT, endrin, toxaphene, benzidine, and PCBs. *See* 40 C.F.R. Pt. 129.

---

[126] Environmental Defense Fund v. EPA, 598 F.2d 62, 8 ELR 20765 (D.C. Cir. 1978).

[127] 598 F.2d 62 at 76-78, 8 ELR at 20772-73.

Individual Control Strategies for Toxic Pollutants

The 1987 amendment of the Clean Water Act projected a comprehensive program for the development of the so-called individual control strategies for toxic pollutants. The new program was slated to be in place three years from the enactment of the Water Quality Act of 1987, and until then, it did not affect the BAT requirements for toxic pollutants. The new provision modified §§ 303 and 304 of the Clean Water Act, to provide for the development of water quality based effluent limitations after BAT has been implemented.

Under this new provision, states are required to commence a program of toxic pollution load restrictions where BAT is not sufficient to meet state water quality standards, and to attain the public health and water quality objectives of the Act. The states must identify their water bodies that will not meet state water standards because of toxic pollutants *after* the implementation of BAT, new source performance standards and pretreatment standards. The state must also determine the specific point source discharging toxic pollutants which are believed to prevent the achievement of state water quality standards, and the amount of such pollutant discharged by such source. The state is to submit an individual control strategy (ICS), through the establishment of effluent limitations and water quality standards containing numerical criteria, to achieve the state water quality standards no later than three years after the establishment of the strategy. The Administrator must approve or disapprove the ICS, and if the state fails to submit a satisfactory control strategy, the Administrator, in cooperation with the state, must develop such a strategy. During state review, revision, or adoption of water quality standards, the state must adopt criteria for all priority toxic pollutants for which water quality criteria have been published under § 304(a). Criteria are to be based on specific numerical criteria, and if these are not available, then biological monitoring or assessment methods. Review of standards, and jurisdictional review of individual control strategies under § 509(b) are provided for.

The reviewability of submitted lists of impaired water hot spots to EPA for approval pursuant to § 304(l) was before the court in *Westvaco Corp. v. EPA*, 899 F.2d 1383, 20 ELR 20817 (4th Cir. 1990). The states of Maryland and Virginia had submitted lists of hot spots to EPA for approval, and the owner of several Kraft pulp and paper mills challenged EPA's decision requiring the two states to list the mills as point sources responsible for toxic pollutant discharges. The court reviewed the distinction between technology based controls, namely effluent limitations which are reflect in NPDES permits, and in addition noted that permits must also reflect limitations that are necessary to meet water quality standards developed by the states pursuant to § 303. If the state does not establish such standards, then EPA must do so. The court reviewed EPA supervision of the NPDES process, noting that the state may not issue a permit if the Administrator objects within 90 days. The 1987 amendment of the law, particularly the establishment of the § 304(l) program relating to "individual control strategies for toxic pollutant," requires EPA to approve or disapprove the state's submissions of ICSs by June 4, 1989. If the state fails to submit the list of toxic hot spots, referred to as the "B list," then EPA must develop such lists. For each water segment on the B list, the states must identify the point sources responsible for the discharge of the toxic pollutants, referred to as the "C list." For each point source on the C list, the state must develop an individual controls strategy. EPA has promulgated final regulations interpreting and implementing § 304(l). 54 Fed. Reg. 246-58 (Jan. 4, 1989). Under the regulations, in the event of a preliminary disapproval of the lists of ICSs, the procedure is similar to agency rulemaking in that public participation is sought. On the other hand, if EPA approves a state's lists and ICSs, the § 304(l) listing process is complete and constitutes final agency action. The court notes that exercising its agency discretion, EPA has defined an ICS to be a draft or final NPDES permit, with supporting documentation showing that effluent limits are sufficient to meet the applicable water quality standards. 40 C.F.R. § 123.46(c). In the instant case, plaintiff's petition for review challenged EPA's preliminary disapproval of Maryland's § 304(l) lists and associated ICSs developed by the Maryland Department of the Environment. Public comments on EPA's preliminary partial disapproval were taken, and similar action was taken with respect to the Virginia lists and ICSs. The court examined whether the agency action here involved was reviewable under § 509(b)(1). Plaintiff asserted that the action was reviewable under § 509(b)(1) because the agency action disapproving the list of hot spots and the failure to designate the mills as point sources for toxic pollutants was an implicit determination that the states had failed to perform their obligations imposed under § 302(a) to protect water quality, particularly with respect to the affected states' water quality standard. However, the court rejected the view that any decision taken by EPA that remotely relates to a state's administration of its NPDES program is reviewable under § 509(b)(1)(D). The court noted that all states must submit water quality standards and that the review of water quality standards is committed, where appropriate, to district courts because § 509(b)(1) confers no jurisdiction to review EPA approvals and disapprovals of water quality standards. The court also rejected the suggestion that preliminary disapproval of "B" and "C" lists constitutes a determination as to a state program submitted under § 402(b) as without merit. The court dismissed the petitions for review for lack of jurisdiction.

In the case that follows, *NRDC v. EPA*, the Ninth Circuit finds that it has jurisdiction to review EPA's regulation relating to individual control strategies under § 509(b)(1)(E). Note that in the *Westvaco* case, as well as in other similar cases, a number of circuits had held that the circuit court had no jurisdiction to review EPA's approval or disapproval of a state's lists and ICSs under § 509(b)(1)(E).

For an insightful analysis of toxic pollutant regulations, see Oliver A. Houck, *The Regulation of Toxic Pollutants under the Clean Water Act,* 23 ELR 10528 (1991). *Also see* F. Grad, Treatise on Environmental Law, § 3.03[4][g]. On the setting of ambient water quality standards for toxic pollutants, see *American Paper Institute v. EPA,* 996 F.2d 346, 23 ELR 20984 (D.C. Cir. 1993) *infra* at p. 505. The standard setting for ambient water quality for toxic pollutants is addressed in the context of requirements under the NPDES system.

NATURAL RESOURCES DEFENSE COUNCIL v. UNITED STATES ENVIRONMENTAL PROTECTION AGENCY

United States Court of Appeals, Ninth Circuit (1990)
915 F.2d 1314, 20 ELR 21372

Before LIVELY, FLETCHER and REINHARDT, Circuit Judges.

FLETCHER, Circuit Judge

The Natural Resources Defense Council (NRDC) petitions for review of a final rule issued by the Environmental Protection Agency (EPA). The rule provides that with regard to some, but not all, of the polluted waters listed pursuant to section 304(l) of the Clean Water Act, 33 U.S.C. § 1314(l), the states must identify the factories and other "point sources" responsible for discharging toxic pollutants into those waters and must develop strategies to control the pollution from those sources in an expedited manner. 40 C.F.R. §§ 123.46, 130.10. The NRDC argues that with regard to *all* of the listed waters, the states must identify "point source" toxic polluters and must develop strategies to control all the sources identified.

We grant the petition with respect to the claim that identification of toxic polluters must be made for all listed waters and remand for EPA to reconsider the question of individual control strategies.

I.

STATUTORY BACKGROUND

The Water Quality Act of 1987 (WQA), Pub. L. No. 100-4, 101 Stat. 7, amended the Clean Water Act (CWA), 33 U.S.C. §§ 1251 *et seq.*, adding a number of new provisions, including section 304(l), 33 U.S.C. § 1314(l), which is the focus of this petition. Section 304(l) refers to other provisions in the Clean Water Act; its proper construction requires a familiarity with the history, the structure, and, alas, the jargon of the federal water pollution laws.

A.

Prior to 1972, Congress attempted to control water pollution by focusing regulatory efforts on achieving "water quality standards," standards set by the states specifying the tolerable degree of pollution for particular waters. *See EPA v. State Water Resources Control Board*, 426 U.S. 200, 202-03, 48 L. Ed. 2d 578, 96 S. Ct. 2022 (1976). This scheme had two important flaws. First, the mechanism of enforcement was cumbersome. Regulators had to work backward from an overpolluted body of water and determine which entities were responsible; proving cause and effect was not always easy. Second, the scheme failed to provide adequate incentives to individual entities to pollute less; an entity's dumping pollutants into a stream was ignored if the stream met the standards. *Id.* The scheme focused on "the tolerable effects rather than the preventable causes" of pollution. *Id.* [The court here outlines the structure of the CWA.]

Congress, in passing the Clean Water Act, thus shifted the focus of the water pollution laws away from the enforcement of water quality standards and toward the enforcement of technological standards. But Congress recognized that even if all the firms discharging pollutants into a certain stream segment were using the best available technology, the stream still might not be clean enough to meet the water quality standards set by the states. To deal with this problem, Congress supplemented the "technology-based" limitations with "water-quality-based" limitations. *See* CWA §§ 302, 303, 33 U.S.C. §§ 1312, 1313.

The water quality standard for a particular stream segment was to be determined in the following manner. First, the state in which the stream segment was located was to designate the uses to which it wished to put the segment. The designations that the states had made prior to the 1972 Clean Water Act were deemed to be the initial designations under that Act; however, states were thereafter to review their designations at least once every three years. CWA § 303(c)(1), 33 U.S.C. § 1313(c)(1). Pursuant to the statute's policy that the designation of uses "enhance" the quality of water, CWA § 303(c)(2), 33 U.S.C. § 1313(c)(2), EPA enacted regulations setting limits on the states' ability to downgrade previously designated uses. If a state wished to redesignate a use so that the new use did not require water clean enough to meet the statutory goal of fishable, swimmable water, see CWA § 101(a)(2), 33 U.S.C. § 1251(a)(2), it had to conduct a "use attainability analysis" as a condition to federal approval of the redesignated use. CWA § 303(c)(3), 33 U.S.C. § 1313(c)(3); 40 C.F.R. §§ 131.10(j), 131.3(g)(1989). If the result of the "use attainability analysis" was that it was feasible to attain fishable, swimmable waters, EPA would reject the redesignated use.

Second, the state was to determine the "criteria" for each segment—the maximum concentrations of pollutants that could occur without jeopardizing the use. These criteria could be either numerical (*e.g.* 5 milligrams per liter) or narrative (*e.g.* no toxics in toxic amounts). The criteria, like the uses, were subject to federal review. The EPA was to reject criteria that did not protect the designated use or that were not based on a "sound scientific rationale." 40 C.F.R. § 131.11(1989).

Under sections 301(b)(1)(C) and 402(a)(1), 33 U.S.C. §§ 1311(b)(1)(C), 1342(a)(1), NPDES permit writers were to impose, along with the technology-based limitations, any more stringent limitations on discharges necessary to meet the water quality standards. Although ostensibly they were supposed to impose these more stringent limitations, in practice they often did not.

One explanation for this failure is that the criteria listed by the states, particularly for toxic pollutants, were often vague narrative or descriptive criteria as opposed to specific numerical criteria. These descriptive criteria were difficult to translate into enforceable limits on discharges from individual polluters. As one commentator put it:

> The descriptive criteria, in particular, call for both expert testimony and a receptive forum to transform, let us say, a general obligation to maintain

> 'recreational' uses into a specific obligation to reduce loadings of phosphorus or nitrogen from a particular source. The decision requires, among other things, judgments about the degree of algal bloom that interferes with 'recreational' uses such as swimming or boating, estimates of loadings from all contributing point and nonpoint sources, assumptions about degrees of control elsewhere, and predictions of how a water segment will respond to a hoped-for change of parameters.

Rodgers, 2 Environmental Law § 4.16 at 250-51 (1986). The Clean Water Act dealt with the difficulty of these decisions and judgments in various ways, for example by calling for the publication by the EPA of criteria documents spelling out causes and effects of various pollutant loads, see CWA § 304(a), 33 U.S.C. § 1314(a), and by requiring states to set total maximum daily loads for certain pollutants (but, notably, not for toxic pollutants) CWA § 303(d)(1), 33 U.S.C. § 1313(d)(1); however, the complexity of these decisions and judgments led many a permit writer to avoid making them altogether. Rodgers, § 4.18 at 283-84.

B.

In 1987 Congress reexamined the water pollution laws. It found that the requirement that individual polluters use the best available technology was not sufficient to solve the pollution problem, particularly the problem of toxic pollutants; a renewed emphasis on water quality-based standards was necessary. Congress enacted a number of new provisions. Three are relevant for our purposes.

CWA section 319, 33 U.S.C. § 1329, requires states to submit for federal approval nonpoint source reports and management programs by August 4, 1988, identifying specific nonpoint sources of pollution and setting forth a plan for implementing the "best management practices" to control such sources by 1992. Section 319 does not require states to penalize nonpoint source polluters who fail to adopt best management practices; rather it provides for grants to encourage the adoption of such practices.[128]

CWA section 303(c)(2)(B), 33 U.S.C. § 1313(c)(2)(B), requires states to adopt "specific numerical criteria" for toxics for which the EPA has published criteria pursuant to section 304(a), 33 U.S.C. § 1314(a). Those criteria are to be adopted when the state first reviews its water quality standards following the enactment of the 1987 amendments. The requirement of numerical criteria for toxics makes it easier for permit writers to incorporate the water quality standards into NPDES permits. Permit writers thus no longer have an excuse for failing to impose water-quality-based limitations on permit holders.

In addition to requiring the adoption of numerical criteria, Congress enacted new CWA section 304(l), 33 U.S.C. § 1314(l), the section directly at issue in

[128] The Water Quality Act also amended the Clean Water Act's declaration of goals and policy to state that "it is the national policy that programs for the control of nonpoint sources of pollution be developed and implemented to assure adequate control of sources of pollutants in each state." CWA § 101(a)(6), 33 U.S.C. § 1251(a)(6). Sections 101 and 319 reflect Congress' awareness that "the evidence of nonpoint pollution continues to grow" and that "it has been estimated that 50 percent of all water pollution comes from nonpoint sources." S. Rep. No. 50, 99th Cong., 1st Sess. at 8.

this petition. Certain aspects of section 304(l) are not in dispute. We briefly explain these background aspects to bring the disputed issues into sharper focus.

Section 304(l) provides:

(l) Individual Control Strategies for Toxic Pollutants. (1) State List of Navigable Waters and Development of Strategies. Not later than 2 years after the date of the enactment of this subsection [February 4, 1987], each State shall submit to the Administrator for review, approval, and implementation under this subsection:

(A) a list of those waters within the State which after the application of effluent limitations required under section 301(b)(2) of this Act cannot reasonably be anticipated to attain or maintain (i) water quality standards for such waters reviewed, revised, or adopted in accordance with section 303(c)(2)(B) of this Act, due to toxic pollutants, or (ii) that water quality which shall assure protection of public health, public water supplies, agricultural and industrial uses, and the protection and propagation of a balanced population of shellfish, fish and wildlife, and allow recreational activities in and on the water;

(B) a list of all navigable waters in such State for which the State does not expect the applicable standard under section 303 of this Act will be achieved after the requirements of sections 301(b), 306, and 307(b) are met, due entirely or substantially to discharges from point sources of any toxic pollutants listed pursuant to section 307(a);

(C) for each segment of the navigable waters included on such lists, a determination of the specific point sources discharging any such toxic pollutant which is believed to be preventing or impairing such water quality and the amount of each such toxic pollutant discharged by each such source; and

(D) for each such segment, an individual control strategy which the State determines will produce a reduction in the discharge of toxic pollutants from point sources identified by the State under this paragraph through the establishment of effluent limitations under section 402 of this Act and water quality standards under section 303(c)(2)(B) of this Act, which reduction is sufficient, in combination with existing controls on point and nonpoint sources of pollution, to achieve the applicable water quality standard as soon as possible, but not later than 3 years after the date of the establishment of such strategy.

(2) Approval or Disapproval. Not later than 120 days after the last day of the 2-year period referred to in paragraph (1), the Administrator shall approve or disapprove the control strategies submitted under paragraph (l) by any State.

(3) Administrator's Action. If a State fails to submit control strategies in accordance with paragraph (1) or the Administrator does not approve the control strategies submitted by such State in accordance with paragraph (1), then, not later than 1 year after the last day of the period referred to in paragraph (2), the Administrator, in cooperation with such State and

after notice and opportunity for public comment, shall implement the requirements of paragraph (1) in such State. In the implementation of such requirements, the Administrator shall, at a minimum, consider for listing under this subsection any navigable waters for which any person submits a petition to the Administrator for listing not later than 120 days after such last day.

Section 304(l) requires the preparation of three lists. The list required by section 304(l)(1)(B) (hereinafter the "B list") is the narrowest of the three lists. It consists only of waters that are not expected to meet water quality standards, even after the application of the technology-based limitations, due entirely or substantially to toxic pollution from point sources. The list required by section 304(l)(1)(A)(i) (hereinafter the "A(i) list") is broader; it includes most of the waters on the B list[129] plus waters expected not to meet water quality standards due to pollution attributable entirely or almost entirely to toxic pollution from nonpoint sources. The list required by section 304(l)(1)(A)(ii) (hereinafter the "A(ii) list") is the broadest. It includes all the waters on the other two lists plus any waters which, after the implementation of technology-based controls, are not expected to meet the water quality goals of the Act; since the goals of the Act are sometimes higher than the state standards, the A(ii) list includes even some waters expected to comply fully with applicable water quality standards.[130]

The effect of the individual control strategies is simply to expedite the imposition of water-quality-based limitations on polluters—limitations which otherwise would have had to be imposed when the polluters' NPDES permits expired. NPDES permits are issued for periods of no more than five years, although administrative delays can extend de facto the duration of the permits.

The EPA has promulgated a number of regulations interpreting the statute; two are particularly important for our purposes. The first regulation, codified at 40 C.F.R. § 130.10(d), interprets sections 304(l)(1)(A), (B), and (C).[131] The

---

129 The reason that some waters on the B list may not be on the A(i) list is that paragraph A(i) refers to section 303(c)(2)(B), which in turn refers only to waters whose water quality standards have been reviewed since the passage of the 1987 amendments, whereas paragraph B refers to all water quality standards, even if adopted before the 1987 amendments.

130 Since the states have a certain degree of flexibility in determining uses of their waters, not all states have set water quality standards based on the uses enumerated in paragraph A(ii).

131 40 C.F.R. § 130.10(d)provides in relevant part:

Not later than February 4, 1989, each State shall submit to EPA for review, approval, and implementation—

(1) a list of those waters within the State which after the application of effluent limitations required under section 301(b)(2) of the CWAcannot reasonably be anticipated to attain or maintain (i) water quality standards for such waters reviewed, revised, or adopted in accordance with section 303(c)(2)(B) of the CWA,due to toxic pollutants, or (ii) that water quality which shall assure protection of public health, public water supplies, agricultural and industrial uses, and the protection and propagation of a balanced population of shellfish, fish and wildlife, and allow recreational activities in and on the water;

(2) a list of all navigable waters in such State for which the State does not expect the applicable standard under section 303 of the CWAwill be achieved after the requirements of sections 301(b), 306, and 307(b) are met, due entirely or substantially to discharges from point sources of

first two subsections of that regulation, subsections 130.10(d)(1) and (2), simply track the language of subsections 304(l)(1)(A) and (B) respectively. The next subsection of the regulation, section 130.10(d)(3), does not, however, track subsection 304(l)(1)(C); rather it changes the word "lists" in the statute to "list." By referring to list in the singular, it excludes the A(i) and A(ii) lists from the requirement of section 304(l)(1)(C) that point sources of toxic pollution and the amount of pollution discharged for each source be identified. Only the B list is subject to the identification requirement.

The second regulation, codified at 40 C.F.R. § 123.46,[132] interprets section 304(l)(1)(D). It provides that individual control strategies (ICS's) must be prepared only for the point sources identified in section 304(l)(1)(C), as interpreted, of course, by the first regulation. Thus, under the regulations, ICS's are required only in connection with waters on the B list. The A(i) and A(ii) lists are not to be consulted in determining which segments require ICS's.

The NRDC petitioned for review of these regulations, arguing they are inconsistent with the statute. We have jurisdiction under CWA § 509(b)(1)(E), 33 U.S.C. § 1369(b)(1)(E).

II.

DISCUSSION

We review two separate regulations. The first one, 40 C.F.R. § 130.10(d)(3), interprets section 304(l)(1)(C). The second, 40 C.F.R. § 123.46, interprets section 304(l)(1)(D). We consider each regulation in turn.

A.

EPA argues that its interpretation of section 304(l)(1)(C) is entitled to special deference on review. In *Chevron U.S.A. v. Natural Resources Defense Council*, 467 U.S. 837, 843, 81 L. Ed. 2d 694, 104 S. Ct. 2778 (1984), the Supreme Court held:

> When a court reviews an agency's construction of the statute which it administers, it is confronted with two questions. First, always, is the question whether Congress has spoken directly to the precise question at issue. If the intent of Congress is clear, that is the end of the matter; for the court, as well as the agency, must give effect to the unambiguously expressed intent of Congress . . . . If the statute is silent or ambiguous with respect to the specific issue, the question for the court is whether the agency's answer is based on a permissible construction of the statute.

---

any toxic pollutants listed pursuant to section 307(a);

(3) for each segment of the navigable waters included on such list, a determination of the specific point sources discharging any such toxic pollutant which is believed to be preventing or impairing such water quality and the amount of each such toxic pollutant discharged by each such source.

[132] The regulation provides in relevant part:

Each state shall submit to the Regional Administrator for review, approval, and implementation an individual control strategy for each point source identified by the State pursuant to section 304(l)(1)(C) of the Act[.]

In this case, Congress has spoken directly, in unambiguous terms, to the question whether subsection 304(l)(1)(C) requires the identification of point sources discharging toxics into the waters identified on all three lists. By using the plural "lists," Congress foreclosed EPA from restricting the scope of paragraph C to waters on the B list. Since the language of paragraph C is unambiguous, there is no need to resort to extrinsic sources to interpret the statute. *Cf. Green v. Commissioner*, 707 F.2d 404, 405 (9th Cir. 1983). The EPA makes two arguments as to why paragraph C is ambiguous. First, it points to the caption of § 304(l)(1), which says, "State List of Navigable Waters and Development of Strategies." EPA argues that the use of the singular "List" in the caption creates an ambiguity, thus triggering *Chevron's* requirement of deference. While words in the title of a statute or the heading of a section can shed light on the meaning of an ambiguous word or phrase in the text of a statute, they cannot create an ambiguity where none otherwise would exist. *Brotherhood of Railroad Trainmen v. B. & O. Railroad*, 331 U.S. 519, 528-29, 91 L. Ed. 1646, 67 S. Ct. 1387 (1947). Since the text is not ambiguous, the caption does not aid our interpretation.

EPA attempts to distinguish *Trainmen* by arguing that it is not offering the caption as evidence of ambiguity but rather as evidence that Congress made a drafting error. But, other than the caption, EPA offers no evidence indicating that the text is the product of a drafting error. When the caption is the only evidence of a drafting error, there is no good reason to assume that it is the text and not the caption that is erroneous. The ordinary presumption is that Congress' drafting of the text is deliberate. *United States v. Motamedi*, 767 F.2d 1403, 1406 (9th Cir. 1985). Moreover in this case, even absent that presumption, there is good reason to believe that the use of the plural "lists" is not a drafting error. The conference committee which drafted section 304(l) fused elements of House and Senate bills containing similar provisions. The House version of section 304(l) required only one list to be prepared, corresponding to the B list. Cong. Research Service, *A Legislative History of the Water Quality Act of 1987*, Comm. Print No.1, 100th Cong., 2d Sess. at 1186. Since only one list had to be prepared, the House equivalent to section 304(l)(1)(C) required the identification of point sources for the waters on "such list." *Id.* The Senate version of section 304(l) required two lists, corresponding to the A(i) and A(ii) lists. *Id.* at 1557. The conferees determined that all three lists should be prepared. This change, in turn, necessitated changing the House version's phrase, "such list," since leaving that phrase intact would have created an ambiguity. Changing the phrase to "such lists" made clear that identification of point sources on all three lists was required. In these circumstances, it can hardly be argued that the change to the plural was inadvertent.

The EPA's next argument for its interpretation of section 304(l)(1)(C) is more complex. The EPA starts not with the language of paragraph C, but with the language of paragraph D. EPA asserts several propositions concerning paragraph D: that in referring to "effluent limitations under section 402 of this Act," paragraph D necessarily refers only to limitations imposed on point sources, since it is only point sources that are subject to the NPDES permitting process described in section 402; that paragraph D requires individual control strategies which will cause a reduction in toxic pollutants "sufficient, in combination with existing controls on point and nonpoint sources of pollution, to achieve the applicable water quality standard . . . not later than three years after the date of the establishment of such strategy"; and that since ICS's are not required under paragraph D when they cannot be expected to achieve water quality standards within the specified time, Congress must have intended ICS's to be required only for polluters discharging into streams whose failure to meet standards could be cured by eliminating discharges of toxics from point sources. From these propositions, the validity of which we do not now decide, EPA then arrives at two controversial conclusions: that ICS's are required only for polluters discharging into the streams on the B list, streams whose failure to meet water quality standards is due "entirely or substantially to discharges from point sources"; and that because only B list waters require ICS's under paragraph D, only those waters are subject to the identification requirement of paragraph C. EPA argues that the prepositional phrase introducing paragraph D, "for each such segment," compels these conclusions because the phrase must refer only to segments that will require ICS's.

We disagree. Even if EPA's interpretation of paragraph D is proper, which we do not decide here, its interpretation of paragraph C cannot stand. In using the phrase, "for each such segment," Congress was simply requiring the states to consult each segment before determining whether an ICS on that segment could achieve water quality standards within the relevant period of time. We acknowledge that if the use of the plural "lists" in paragraph C were treated as a drafting error, the phrase "for each segment" would make paragraphs B, C, and D flow together more smoothly. But a statute is not ambiguous simply because an agency can suggest a change in wording that would make the statute more elegant. Since paragraph C as drafted neither is ambiguous in its terms nor is incoherent when considered together with the other provisions of the statute to which it relates, we do not accord EPA's regulation redrafting paragraph C any special deference on review. *Cf. Chevron.*

Reviewing the regulation *de novo*, we conclude that EPA reached the wrong interpretation of paragraph C because it started with a faulty premise. EPA assumed that paragraph D, requiring individual control strategies for certain waters, was the only significant provision of section 304(l)(1) and that paragraphs B and C of that section had to be read as having one purpose and one purpose only—to effectuate paragraph D. This assumption has two flaws, one obvious and one more subtle. The obvious flaw is that the assumption utterly fails to account for the presence of paragraph A—especially paragraph A(ii). If Congress was interested only in individual control strategies for toxic pollutants, why would it have wanted a list of waters whose failure to meet the goals of the Act was not necessarily traceable to toxic pollutants? One readily can infer from the presence of paragraph A that Congress wanted certain information not necessarily because it would affect the ICS program but because it might subsequently be useful in formulating other statutory or regulatory programs. There are other provisions in the Clean Water Act which require the gathering of information but which do not necessarily require immediate action on the basis of the information. *See, e.g.*, CWA § 305, 33 U.S.C. § 1315; CWA § 303(d), 33 U.S.C. § 1313(d).[133]

The more subtle flaw in EPA's assumption is that it does not account for the purposes that paragraph C might serve. Like paragraph A, paragraph C will produce useful information. It requires the identification of point sources discharging toxic pollutants and the determination of the amount of such pollutants discharged. Such information may prove useful to regulators even if every point source identified does not require an ICS.

In sum, we hold that EPA erred in assuming that paragraph D and paragraph C of subsection 304(l)(1) must perfectly interlock. Since the provisions do not serve the identical purpose, there was no need to distort paragraph C in order to make it connect better with paragraph D.

B.

Our determination that EPA erred in interpreting section 304(l)(1)(C) does not settle the issue on which the parties have focused most of their attention: which waters are subject to the ICS's required by section 304(l)(1)(D)?

EPA's position is that only waters on the B list, *i.e.*, waters for which the state does not expect water quality standards to be achieved "due entirely or substantially to point sources of any toxic pollutants" are subject to the ICS requirement. EPA interprets "entirely or substantially" broadly:

> If a water meets either of the two conditions listed below the water must be listed [under paragraph B] on the grounds that the applicable standard is not achieved or expected to be achieved due entirely or substantially to discharges from point sources.
>
> (i) Existing or additional water quality-based limits on one or more point sources would result in the achievement of an applicable water quality standard for a toxic pollutant; or
>
> (ii) The discharge of a toxic pollutant from one or more point sources, regardless of any nonpoint source contribution of the same pollutant, is sufficient to cause or is expected to cause an excursion above the applicable water quality standard for the toxic pollutant. 40 C.F.R. § 130.10(d)(5)(1989).

Consider the hypothetical situation of a stream that can absorb a load of 100 pounds per day of a particular toxic substance without violating water quality standards. In June of 1992 (the date by which ICS's are required to achieve their purpose) after existing controls are implemented, it is expected that 105 pounds per day of the toxic will flow through the segment. If six of the expected 105 pounds are to come from point sources, the point source contribution is considered "substantial" under EPA's regulation and ICS's are

[133] EPA suggests that prior to the enactment of section 304(l), states already were required, albeit without a statutory deadline, to submit the information requested. It cites CWA § 303(d), but that section requires states to identify only those waters for which limitations based on the best practicable technology would not be stringent enough to implement the water quality standards. Those waters for which limitations based on the more demanding best available technology—the required level of technology to control toxics—were insufficient did not have to be listed.

required for the point sources. If three of the 105 pounds are expected to come from point sources, the contribution is considered "insubstantial" and no ICS's are required. The reason why the six pound contribution is considered substantial is that a reduction of six pounds would be "sufficient, in combination with existing controls on point and nonpoint sources of pollution, to achieve the applicable water quality standard." The language just quoted comes, of course, from paragraph D, which specifies when ICS's are required. EPA thus derived its interpretation of paragraph B essentially by beginning with its interpretation of paragraph D and working backward. That is the same method EPA used to interpret paragraph C. Since we are remanding to the agency to have it promulgate new regulations under paragraph C, we do not decide whether EPA's current interpretation of paragraph D is too restrictive. (It is not too inclusive.[134]) Rather we invite EPA to reconsider its interpretation on remand. In the meantime, until EPA promulgates new regulations, the program shall continue.

III.

CONCLUSION

We grant the petition for review in part and remand. On remand, EPA must, pursuant to CWA § 304(l)(1)(C), amend its regulations to require the states to identify all point sources discharging any toxic pollutant which is believed to be preventing or impairing the water quality of any stream segment listed under CWA §§ 304(l)(1)(A) and (B) and to indicate the amount of the toxic pollutant discharged by each source. EPA shall also reconsider its interpretation of CWA § 304(l)(1)(D).

REMANDED.

UNITED STATES OF AMERICA v. DAVID W. BOLDT

United States Court of Appeals, First Circuit (1991)
929 F.2d 35, 21 ELR 20998

Before BREYER, Chief Judge, CAMPBELL and TORRUELLA, Circuit Judges.

[134] EPA's regulations require ICS's not only for stream segments whose point source toxic problem, if eliminated, would bring the segment up to standards, but also for segments not meeting that description but whose point source contribution of a particular toxic is so severe that, standing alone, it would cause an excursion above the applicable water quality standard regardless of any nonpoint source contribution of the toxic. 40 C.F.R. § 130.10(d)(5)(ii). The inclusion of this latter type of stream segment in the ICS program has not been challenged. We note that EPA has ample authority, in addition to CWA § 304(l), to require expedited action on such stream segments. *See* CWA §§ 301(l), 402(k), 33 U.S.C. §§ 1311(l), 1342(k). To require such action is fully consistent with paragraph D's recognition that triage is necessary.

TORRUELLA, Circuit Judge

This is an appeal from a judgment of conviction, following a jury trial, of two counts relating to the discharge into a city sewer of industrial wastewater containing excessive metals. David Boldt raises five issues on appeal: (1) insufficiency of the evidence; (2) improper impeachment of a character witness; (3) improper comment in the prosecutor's closing argument; (4) prejudicial jury instruction; and (5) sentencing error. We affirm the conviction and sentence.

BACKGROUND

Boldt was one of four defendants named in a 52-count indictment charging numerous violations of the federal Clean Water Act, 33U.S.C. § 1251 *et seq.*, at Astro Circuit Corporation where defendants were management employees. Astro manufactured printed circuit boards using an electroplating process. Astro's manufacturing plant was located in Lowell, Massachusetts, until February 1988, when the company declared bankruptcy and went out of business.

The Clean Water Act and its implementing regulations require circuit board manufacturers to pretreat their industrial waste in order to remove toxic metals such as copper before discharging that waste into a city sewer system. 33 U.S.C. § 1317(b); 40 C.F.R. § 413.84(c); *see Chemical Mfrs. Ass'n v. Natural Resources Defense Council, Inc.*, 470 U.S. 116, 119, 84 L. Ed. 2d 90, 105 S. Ct. 1102 (1985). Astro's pretreatment facilities were completely inadequate. The system, installed in 1980, contained two components. One was a continuous flow system designed to treat 45 gallons per minute of wastewater. By 1987 the system was handling approximately 90 gallons per minute, twice the designed capacity. The company's routine practice when a failure occurred was to bypass the system, thus putting untreated wastewater directly into the city sewer.

Whereas the ordinary continuous flow treatment system handled the bulk of Astro's wastewater, the electroless copper waste was processed in a special batch system. When a large storage tank became full, the contents were treated by adding a caustic solution, which caused the copper to sink to the bottom so that the water could be drained off the top. The batch system usually, but not always, worked successfully.

David Boldt began working for Astro as Chemical Engineering Manager on June 26, 1987. Boldt's main responsibility was to keep the chemical production line running. Among his duties were supervision and management of Astro's pretreatment process, which was part of the company's pollution control department. Boldt worked for Astro for only six months; he was fired on January 8, 1988.

Boldt was charged with six counts of violating the Clean Water Act, 33U.S.C. § 1319(c), by knowingly discharging, into a municipal sewer, industrial wastewater which contained excessively high concentrations of toxic metals in violation of the federal industrial pretreatment standards. The court entered a judgment of acquittal on one count, which was based on a discharge on the day Boldt lost his job, and the jury acquitted Boldt of three counts.

The counts on which Boldt was convicted, numbered 8 and 12 in the indictment, involved two separate incidents. Count 8 charged that Boldt knowingly aided and abetted the discharge of pollutants on September 21, 1987, a date when the copper level in Astro's effluent exceeded the federal regulation by nearly four times. The high reading resulted from a failure of Astro's continuous flow wastewater treatment system, causing the company to bypass the system. It appears from the testimony that Boldt was informed of the bypass on this date and did not act to stop it. The company received a letter from the City of Lowell dated September 30 informing the company of the violation. Astro's president asked Boldt to respond. Boldt's reply to the city stated in part:

> On the date in question, we experienced a failure of two of our liquid transfer pumps, resulting in a serious flood (fully contained) in a portion of our waste treatment area. In order to remove the floodwaters so as to protect electrical equipment and controls and permit maintenance access, it was necessary to transfer these wastewaters into the treatment systems at a higher-than-normal rate. It is our belief that this clean-up effort caused a temporary overload of the system. Effluent analysis for copper performed later in the day showed normal values for copper, well within limits. Every effort is being made to prevent a recurrence of this problem.

The government alleged that this letter was misleading and false in that it failed to mention the almost daily bypassing of the pretreatment system at Astro, nor did it mention that the company had consistently found high amounts of copper in its effluent. Instead, the letter created the impression that the September 21 copper levels resulted from an unusual event.

Count 12 of the indictment, the other count on which Boldt was convicted, charged a violation of the Clean Water Act on January 7, 1988. On that evening, the lines feeding a caustic solution to a large batch treatment tank became clogged. Boldt's subordinate, James Swift, went to Boldt for advice. Boldt ordered Swift to add manually a caustic chemical to the tank. This treatment was unsuccessful. Boldt then ordered Swift to dump the entire contents of the tank—3,100 gallons of partially treated wastewater—into the city sewer.

According to Swift, Boldt then prepared a false written explanation concerning this incident and had Swift sign it. This memo, which was never located, was given to Astro's vice president. The next day, however, having second thoughts, Swift went to the vice president with an accurate statement of the event. Later that day Boldt was fired.

Boldt testified at trial that on January 7 he felt himself caught "between the devil and the deep blue sea." He had learned that the storage tank for the next batch of copper wastewater was full and would start overflowing soon, in which case the overflow would automatically be pumped directly to the sewer without any treatment at all. Under the circumstances, Boldt decided that it would be better to send the partially treated wastewater into the sewer rather than to allow the untreated solution to overflow. He denied that he had tried to cover up the dump.

Boldt's three co-defendants, his two supervisors and his predecessor at Astro, pled guilty, so Boldt was the only defendant to stand trial. The main issue at trial was the extent to which Boldt was culpable for admitted wastewater violations by Astro. Boldt's defense was that he was not directly responsible for discharging any of the illegal wastewater except on the January 7 occasion. The court gave Boldt's requested jury instruction of impossibility: that Boldt was not liable for violations if, despite exercising extraordinary care with respect to pollution, he was unable to prevent the violations because of the condition of the corporation or because of his relative power or position within the corporation. As to the January 7 count, Boldt took responsibility for the discharge, but used a defense of necessity. The court instructed the jury that Boldt was not liable if this discharge was necessary to avoid a worse harm.

SUFFICIENCY OF THE EVIDENCE

In reviewing the record for a sufficiency of the evidence appeal, it is well established:

> that the evidence must be examined in its entirety in the light most favorable to the Government to determine whether a rational trier of fact could have found guilt beyond a reasonable doubt and that the Government may prove its case by circumstantial evidence that need not exclude every reasonable hypothesis of innocence. [citations omitted]

Applying this standard, we conclude that although the evidence in this case was not over-whelming, it was sufficient to permit a reasonable jury to find guilt beyond a reasonable doubt.

The evidence showed that pollution control was part of Boldt's area of responsibility. On Count 8, the evidence showed that Boldt was aware of the practice of bypassing the pollution control system and had condoned it on the occasion at issue. He also authored a letter to the City of Lowell which could be construed as misleading. As to Count 12, there is no dispute that Boldt directly ordered his subordinate to dump the copper wastewater. There was also testimony from the subordinate that Boldt attempted to cover up the incident.

Boldt argues that the evidence did not support the verdict because there was no evidence that he could have avoided the violations by shutting down the plant. This contention is simply unsupported by the record. There was testimony from Robert McKiel, president of Astro, that Boldt was authorized to shut down the plant. Whether this court would credit McKiel's testimony is irrelevant; the jury apparently did, and rested its verdict on that ground.

Boldt's assertion of insufficient evidence boils down to a complaint that the jury did not accept his defenses of impossibility and necessity. The trial judge, in his denial of Boldt's motion for a new trial, stated: "The issues raised herein were presented to the jury. I would have resolved them differently, but I cannot say that the jury's determination was so irrational as to merit a new trial." We agree.

IMPEACHMENT OF A CHARACTER WITNESS

The defense called a character witness, Alan Hoye, who testified as to Boldt's efforts to prevent the illegal storage of drums of hazardous waste at Astro.

The defense asked Mr. Hoye his opinion of Boldt's honesty, credibility and law-abiding character. The witness replied, "I've never known Dave to be other than completely honest and above board in anything he's done."

On cross examination, the prosecutor asked Mr. Hoye, "Would it change your opinion if you knew that Mr. Boldt ordered subordinates to meter hazardous waste down the drain into a city sewer?" The defense objected and the prosecutor proffered at side bar: "I can offer, through Tom McNamara, Mr. Boldt's directing him to bring large barrels, some of which contain stickers, hazardous waste stickers, spent chemicals, solvents, and he directs him to put a meter pump on it and put it right in the third-stage reaction tank." The court allowed the question and Mr. Hoye admitted that knowing such additional information about Boldt would change his opinion regarding the defendant's law-abiding character.

Boldt now argues that the government failed to prove its proffer and in fact produced no evidence that Boldt had disposed of solvents as suggested or had improperly disposed of hazardous waste through the pollution control system. He charges that the government's tactic amounted to suggesting that Boldt had committed a serious crime not charged in the indictment, an implication which, coming from the prosecutor, may well have affected the jury.

The government's witness, McNamara, testified that Boldt had ordered him to dispose of items he believed to be formaldehyde, tin lead, and hydrogen peroxide, and that he also believed that "there might have been some acetones." Boldt testified in response that what McNamara was referring to was not *acetone*, a hazardous waste, but *acetane*, an unrelated chemical which may be properly disposed of through a pollution control system. Likewise the supposed tin lead was actually tin lead stripper, which may be disposed of through a waste treatment system, as may formaldehyde and hydrogen peroxide. Finally, Boldt stated that the materials were not dumped "down the drain," but were put into the third-stage reaction tank, which is the final step of the pre-treatment process.

Like the court below, we do not find much to favor with the government's approach in this line of questioning. The prosecutor seems over-disposed to throw around the highly significant—indeed, without intending any humor, explosive—term "hazardous waste." Nevertheless, we are not inclined to overturn the conviction on this ground. The defendant put his character into evidence. As the Supreme Court held long ago, "the price a defendant must pay for attempting to prove his good name is to throw open the entire subject which the law has kept closed for his benefit and to make himself vulnerable where the law otherwise shields him." [citations omitted]

Moreover, the defendant here had ample opportunity—and took advantage of that opportunity—to clarify and explain McNamara's damaging testimony, both by cross-examination of McNamara and during Boldt's own testimony. The points now raised by Boldt were also presented to the jury. We find no error here.

CLOSING ARGUMENT

In its initial closing argument, the government made the following statement: "Ladies and gentlemen, it's a favorite defense tactic to try to get you to focus on unnecessary facts or to get you emotionally wrapped up with the defendant." When defense counsel objected, the court sustained the objection and told the prosecutor: "I think you had better stick to your case." After the prosecutor's argument, defense moved for a mistrial, or in the alternative, a corrective instruction. The court gave this instruction:

> Members of the jury, the Assistant U.S. Attorney made a comment to which [defense counsel] Mr. Walker objected and which I sustained the objection, having to do with what may be a favorite defense tactic, tending to suggest that there was some standard and improper tactic that Mr. Walker had employed in his case. That was an improper comment by the Assistant U.S. Attorney and should be totally disregarded by you.
>
> Take the case as you find it. Make the decision on the basis of evidence as you've heard it, and counsel should avoid that kind of characterization of the defendant's efforts. You make the decision.

Boldt now argues that the "favorite defense tactic" remark requires a new trial. He maintains that the curative instruction was insufficient to cure the prejudice.

The remark was clearly improper. Although it is plain that a prosecutor may comment on a defense after it has been raised, this particular comment was made before the defense had established its theory of the case. More critical is the institutional nature of the comment, casting suspicion not merely on a defense possibly employed by this defendant but on the role of defense counsel in general.

Despite this impropriety, however, we do not find that a new trial is required. To make this determination we employ the following analysis:

> (1) whether the prosecutor's conduct was isolated and/or [less than] deliberate, (2) whether the trial judge's instructions were strong and explicit, and (3) whether it is likely that any prejudice that survived the judge's instructions could have affected the outcome of the case. [citations omitted]

On the final step of the inquiry, "perhaps the single most significant factor in weighing whether an error was harmful is the strength of the case against the defendant." 3A Wright, Federal Practice and Procedure § 854, at 305 (2d ed. 1982) (quoted in *Giry*, 818 F.2d at 134).

The comment here was plainly deliberate although also fairly isolated. The trial judge gave a very strong and thorough curative instruction, in addition to sustaining defense counsel's immediate objection. The last step is the most difficult to scale. As we have already noted, the evidence in this case, although sufficient to convict, was hardly overwhelming or even particularly strong. Nevertheless, we believe the curative instruction sufficed to dispel any prejudice from the improper comment. *See United States v. Savarese*, 649 F.2d 83, 88 (1st Cir. 1981). A new trial is not warranted.

JURY INSTRUCTION

During its instruction to the jury the court stated:

> The question of whether the only solution would have been to close this plant down is not an issue for you. If nothing can be done with a plant that is polluting in violation of the law other than to close it down, then the law says it must be closed down.
>
> The statute does not have any leeway. It is not a forgiving statute in any respect. It says this must not happen, so it is not enough to say: Well, if we comply with the statute, we will go out of business. Congress has said the pollution of the waterways takes precedence over all other considerations.

Boldt objected to the court's instruction, and now argues that this instruction was wrong as a matter of law, that it undermined the presumption of innocence, the requirement of proof beyond a reasonable doubt, and his two affirmative defenses, and that it sent the message that the court believed the law required a conviction. He argues that "no leeway" and "unforgiving" suggest that there are no affirmative defenses to the charge, whereas in fact both the defense of impossibility and necessity are available.

We disagree. During closing argument, Boldt's attorney attempted to assert that it was a defense if the jury found that shutting down the plant would unreasonably harm the business or put employees out of work. The Clean Water Act, however, does not appear to recognize a defense of *economic* or *business* necessity. The statute addresses cost concerns in a different context, by distinguishing between "best available technology" and "best practicable technology" in its compliance standards. [citations omitted] Negating Boldt's economic defense was the focus of the disputed instruction. The judge also adequately instructed the jury on Boldt's valid affirmative defenses, so there was no implication that they were not available. The court particularly emphasized that the burden of proof remained with the government at all times, so that once Boldt had raised an affirmative defense, it was up to the government to disprove it. Finally, the court repeatedly stressed the reasonable doubt standard of proof. For these reasons, we find no error in the instruction.

SENTENCE

The applicable sentencing statute states in part that knowing violators "shall be punished by a fine of not less than $5,000 nor more than $50,000 per day of violation, or by imprisonment for not more than 3 years, or by both." 33 U.S.C. § 1319(c)(2)(A),(B). At sentencing the court ruled that under the statute it was bound to impose either a fine or a committed prison sentence, or, in other words, that it had no power to give a suspended sentence or probation without a fine. Given the choice between imprisonment and a fine, Boldt requested the court not to impose a fine and the court accommodated that request by sentencing Boldt to a one-day committed sentence on each count. Neither party takes issue with the court's calculation under the sentencing guidelines, which applied only to Count 12 as Count 8 was an "old law" count not covered by the Sentencing Reform Act. Under the guidelines the range of imprisonment was zero to six months.

Boldt contends that the court erroneously concluded that where a statute requires a minimum fine or imprisonment, there must be a committed jail sentence if no fine is imposed. Boldt argues that there is no such requirement under the old law. Further, under current law, a sentence of probation is explicitly authorized except for Class A and Class B felonies. The violation here is a Class E felony.

Neither party has cited any law whatsoever supporting or refuting Boldt's contention regarding minimum sentence under the old law, and we have been unable to discover any case law on point. Even if a suspended sentence or probation would have been within the discretion of the court, however, so was the sentence actually imposed. Moreover, the court bent over backwards to accommodate Boldt by proceeding directly to the sentencing disposition rather than waiting for a presentence report (which would have been a requisite for probation), when the court clearly would have preferred to wait. Under the circumstances, we choose not to disturb the sentence.

Affirmed.

NOTES AND QUESTIONS

(1) What pollutants are covered under the Federal Water Pollution Control Act? The definition of pollutant under FWPCA § 502(6) includes "radioactive materials." Is the Administrator of EPA under an obligation to issue effluent limitations for radioactive materials emitted by nuclear powerplants? *See Train v. Colorado Public Interest Research Group, Inc.*, 426 U.S. 1, 86 S.Ct. 1938 (1976). For comment, *see* A. Murphy, *Old Maxims Never Die: The "Plain Meaning" Rule and Statutory Interpretation in the "Modern" Federal Courts*, 75 Colum. L. 1299 (1975).

(2) The FWPCA requires the Administrator of EPA to issue toxic and pretreatment effluent standards. What determines whether the Administrator chooses a particular substance for inclusion in the list of substances for which toxic effluent standards need to be promulgated? *See Natural Resources Defense Council v. Train, supra.*

(3) What is a "technology-based" standard and what is a "health-based" standard? Which is easier to formulate, and which is easier to enforce?

[viii] New Source Performance Standards

CPC INTERNATIONAL INC. v. TRAIN

- DO THEY MEET BPT & TYPE OF VARIENCE DO THEY GET.
- IS ABOUT BOD & TSS

United States Court of Appeals, Eighth Circuit (1975)
515 F.2d 1032

HEANEY, Circuit Judge.

The petitioners are engaged in the processing of corn into starch, syrup, dextrose, animal feed and corn oil. They file petitions for direct review of three distinct groups of regulations promulgated by the Administrator of the Environmental Protection Agency under the Federal Water Pollution Control Act Amendments of 1972. 33 U.S.C. §§ 1251 *et seq.* The regulations relate to the "Corn Wet Milling Subcategory" of the "Grain Mills Point Source Category," and consist of:

(1) Standards of performance for *new* plants, promulgated under § 306(b);

(2) Pretreatment standards for *new* plants which discharge wastes into municipal treatment plans, promulgated under § 307(c); and

(3) Effluent limitations guidelines for *existing* plants, promulgated under § 304(b).

[Part I of the opinion, which dealt with the promulgation of effluent limitations for existing plants, is omitted; it was overruled by the Supreme Court in *E.I. du Pont DeNemours & Co. v. Train, supra.*]

II. THE NATIONAL STANDARDS OF PERFORMANCE FOR NEW SOURCES.

Our review of the Administrator's action in promulgating the national standards of performance for new sources[135] is limited to a determination of whether the Administrator's decision was "arbitrary, capricious, an abuse of discretion, or otherwise not in accordance with law." 5 U.S.C. § 706(2)(A); Citizens to Preserve Overton Park v. Volpe, 401 U.S. 402, 416, 91 S.Ct. 814, 28 L.Ed.2d 136 (1971). *Cf.* Union Electric Co. v. Environmental Protection Agency, 515 F.2d 206, at 214 (8th Cir. 1975). As the Supreme Court noted in Citizens to Preserve Overton Park v. Volpe, *supra*, 401 U.S. at 416, 91 S.Ct. at 823, the scope of this review is a limited one:

> . . . [T]he court must consider whether the decision was based on a consideration of the relevant factors and whether there has been a clear error of judgment. . . . Although this inquiry into the facts is to be searching and careful, the ultimate standard of review is a narrow one. The court is not empowered to substitute its judgment for that of the agency.

The new source standards for the corn wet milling subcategory set maximum allowable discharge levels or "loads" for three pollutant measurements: five-day biochemical oxygen demand (BOD_5),[136] total suspended solids (TSS),[137] and pH.[138] The BOD_5 and TSS load levels are expressed in terms

[135] Section 306(a)(2) provides:

> The term "new source" means any source, the construction of which is commenced after the publication of proposed regulations prescribing a standard of performance under this section which will be applicable to such source, if such standard is thereafter promulgated in accordance with this section.

[136] While BOD is only a measure of organic pollution's effects, it is on occasion referred to as a pollutant. *See, e.g.* 40 C.F.R. § 128.121(1974). BOD measures the oxygen-consuming capabilities of organic matter which will be fulfilled as the matter decomposes. BOD_5 is a measure of the oxygen-demand of the organic matter after a five-day period, and is one of the most common measurements employed in the field of water quality.

By depressing the oxygen content of the receiving waters, an effluent with a high BOD measurement may drastically alter the aquatic environment, with ill effects on the inhabitants. Frequently, all of the oxygen in the receiving waters is exhausted by the BOD; in such instances, continued decay produces noxious gases and visible stagnation. BOD may also be an indicator of the presence of bacteria.

[137] Suspended solids include both inorganic and organic materials. While in a suspended state, they may inhibit light penetration and impair photosynthesis in aquatic plants. They also interfere with treatment processes used in purifying drinking water, and may render water unsuitable for certain industrial purposes. When they have settled to form a blanket on the beds of streams and lakes, they may adversely affect the aquatic environment by destroying normal fauna growth.

[138] Neither the new source standards for pH

of pounds per thousand standard bushels (MSBu) of corn processed.[139] For BOD_5, the new source standards permit a maximum average of daily values for thirty consecutive calendar days of 20 pounds per MSBu. For TSS, the standards permit a thirty-day average of 10 pounds per MSBu. The maximum allowable discharge level on any single day is three times the thirty-day average, or 60 pounds of BOD_5 and 30 pounds of TSS per MSBu. *See* 40 C.F.R. § 406.15.

The petitioners assert that the new source standards are arbitrary and capricious and are not in accordance with law, because there is no adequate basis in the record of the EPA's conclusion that the standards can be met by utilization of

> . . . the best available demonstrated control technology, processes, operating methods, or other alternatives. . . .

§ 306(a)(1).

Specifically, the petitioners contend that the new source standards are predicated on the existence and efficacy of technology which is neither "available" nor "demonstrated" within the meaning of the Act.

Initially, we must examine the EPA's justification for the new source standards. Those standards are identical to the 1983 guidelines for existing plants. 40 C.F.R. § 406.13. The 1983 guidelines assume the technology available to meet the 1977 guidelines will be supplemented by additional technology in 1983.[140]

The 1977 guidelines are predicated on a technology consisting essentially of recirculated cooling water, aerated equalization, activated sludge, and good housekeeping practices.[141] The EPA concluded that this technology would be

---

nor the existing source guidelines for pH are challenged by the petitioners. Our discussion of the new source standards, therefore, deals exclusively with the levels set for BOD_5 and TSS.

139 One difficulty encountered in reviewing the record stems from the fact that, in discussing the performance of existing plants, the EPA, its consultants, and industry spokesmen frequently recorded measurements solely in terms of milligrams per liter (mg/1), a measurement which reflects the concentration of the effluent. The EPA's decision not to set the standards in terms of mg/1 is proper, for any standard based on concentration may be met by diluting the effluent with large quantities of water. Nevertheless, the relationship of much of the backup data to the effluent/raw waste ratio ultimately selected was difficult to assess. To the extent that the agency is able to frame the backup data in the same terms as are used in the final standards, our task in reviewing the regulations would be facilitated.

140 The legislative history makes it clear that the Administrator is not to prescribe the technology which must be used, but is rather to set discharge levels which can be met if indicated technology is used. The choice of technology at each plant is left to the operator. *See* Conference Report in *Legislative History* at 311; Senate Report in *id.* at 1477.

141 We refer to these processes as the "1977 technology." The supporting document accompanying the corn wet milling regulations sets forth this technology as "Alternative B:"

> Alternative B includes 12 to 18 hours of aerated equalization ahead of the complete-mix activated sludge process and associated chemical feed, sedimentation, and sludge dewatering facilities proposed in Alternative A. . . .

Development Document for Effluent Limitations Guidelines and New Source Performance Standards for the Grain Processing Segment of the Grain Mills Point Source Category [hereinafter *Development Document*] (March 1974) at 93. "Alternative A," which is embraced by "Alternative B," is defined thus:

> This alternative provides for grit removal, pH adjustment, nutrient addition, com-

sufficient to permit compliance with the 1977 guidelines, which consist of 50 pounds each of BOD_5 and TSS per MSBu on a thirty-day average, with three times that amount permitted on any single day. *See* 40 C.F.R. § 406.12.

The 1983 guidelines/new source standards are predicated on the availability of 1977 technology plus the addition of deep bed filtration.[142] The EPA concluded that deep bed filtration will result in the removal of approximately 30 more pounds of BOD_5 and 40 more pounds of TSS per MSBu.[143]

The correctness of the EPA's conclusion that the new source standards can be met thus hinges on the validity of four intermediate conclusions: (1) that the 1977 technology is "demonstrated" and "available" for new plants; (2) that the 1977 technology will be sufficient to remove all but 50 pounds each of BOD_5 and TSS per MSBu; (3) that the incremental deep bed filter technology is "demonstrated" and "available" for new plants; and (4) that the incremental technology will be sufficient to remove an additional 30 pounds of BOD_5 and 40 pounds of TSS per MSBu.

The petitioners concede that the 1977 technology is available for implementation in new plants.[144] They contend, however, that it will not perform up to EPA expectations and that its use will not bring compliance with the 1977 guidelines. They rest their case on the premise that the CPC Plant at Pekin, Illinois, has not been able to meet the 1977 guidelines, despite its implementation of "most" of the 1977 technology. Their reliance is misplaced, for the record indicates that the Pekin Plan discharges 6,000 pounds of BOD_5 daily in once-through barometric cooling water without treatment—a practice

> pletemix activated sludge, secondary sedimentation, and centrifugation for solids dewatering. The treatment system does not include equalization or primary sedimentation. . . .

Id.

[142] We refer to these processes as the "1983/new source technology." The *Development Document* at 95 describes "Alternative D," which is the basis of the 1983 guidelines and new source standards:

> In this proposed system, deep bed filtration is added to the activated sludge system presented as Alternative B. . . .

Another portion of the *Development Document* indicates that the 1983/new source technology contains two additional increments to the 1977 technology: isolation and treatment of all process waste waters, and institution of "maximum water reuse." *Id.* at 120-121. These additions appear to be but a tightening up of controls already present in the 1977 technology. Nowhere has the EPA stated on the record the amount of BOD_5 and TSS reduction which is expected to result from these additions to the 1977 technology. However, the record as a whole indicates that deep bed filtration was expected to accomplish most of the 30 and 40 pound incremental reductions.

[143] [Footnote omitted.] [*Editor's Note*: In footnote 28, the court includes a table on BOD_5 reduction as well as on TSS reduction. The table shows the incremental reduction required, expressed in percentages, for BOD_5 and for TSS in Plant I, with the lowest waste load, and Plant II, with the highest waste load, as well as in the average plant. In Plant I, the incremental reduction required to achieve the 1983 New Source Limit is 25.2%, and for Plant II the incremental reduction is 4.3%. The average plant would need an incremental reduction of 7.2% in BOD_5. For TSS reduction, Plant I needs an incremental reduction of 65.5%, and Plant II, 5.5%, with the average plant requiring 14.2%. The percentage reduction to achieve the 1977 limit would be a lesser, but still quite substantial, reduction in each of the plants.]

[144] Except for the question of the performance capabilities of the 1977 technology, the principal objections raised by the petitioners to the 1977 guidelines relate to their implementation in existing plants and, therefore, need not be considered by us. For the same reason, what we say here with respect to the 1977 technology as it relates to new plants is not ultimately dispositive of the petitioners' challenge to the 1977 guidelines.

which does not square with the 1977 technology's requirement that cooling water be recirculated and treated. If the Pekin Plant recirculated this cooling water, treated it in accordance with approved technology, and maintained effective in-plant controls, it would, on the basis of the record, be able to meet 1977 discharge guidelines.

The EPA, on the other hand, based its conclusions as to the performance capabilities of the 1977 technology on the following reasoning:

(1) Data from existing plant operations indicates that the best existing plants have made substantial progress in reducing BOD_5 and TSS by using an activated sludge process plus some in-plant controls;

(2) The best existing plants fail to treat large quantities of BOD_5 and TSS because they use barometric condensers and discharge the waste from these condensers directly into receiving waters;

(3) By using surface condensers—a demonstrated technology—the raw effluent could be concentrated and subjected to activated sludge treatment thereby achieving significantly greater BOD_5 and TSS reductions;

(4) None of the best known in-plant controls are being used in combination in any one plant;

(5) By combining the best-known in-plant controls in one plant, greater reductions of BOD_5 and TSS would be achievable;

(6) There are no practical reasons which would preclude the implementation of the complete 1977 technology in a new plant.

We conclude that the data was sufficient, the projected results were reasonable, and the petitioners have not demonstrated that the EPA made a clear error of judgment in determining that the 1977 technology, when employed in a new plant, would enable it to comply with the 1977 guidelines.[145]

The remaining question, therefore, is whether the record supports the Administrator's conclusion that the technology necessary to achieve the incremental removal of 30 pounds of BOD_5 and 40 pounds of TSS per MSBu is available for use in new plants. We conclude that it does not.

The EPA's supporting documents concede that the deep bed filtration technology has not been "demonstrated" within the corn wet milling industry.[146]

---

145 The petitioners further contend that the single-day allowance of three times the thirty-day average is not sufficient to protect a new plant from the consequences of upsets or "shockloads." *Cf.* note 33, *infra.* They also contend that, in addition to the single-day "variability factor," the regulations must provide for statistically expected "excursions"—those rare occasions on which a well-run plant will exceed even the single-day limit.

There are an infinite number of ways in which the Administrator may approach the related questions of basic standards, variability, and excursions. For example, the industry itself agreed at one point in the rule-making process that an average of 90 pounds of BOD_5 and 30 pounds of TSS per MSBu "*might be* achievable," but urged that a maximum single-day allowance ought to be set at 2.5 times that amount. Statement by Robert C. Liebenow, President of Corn Refiners Association, to ES-QWIAC (April 30, 1973) at 5, 13. The ultimate question is not whether the variability factor selected is appropriate, but whether the 1977 guidelines can be achieved with the 1977 technology. We find no clear error in the Administrator's determination that they can.

146 The EPA expressed a belief that the Clin-

See Development Document at 87, 121. This does not end the inquiry, for new source standards may properly be based on a technology which has been demonstrated outside the industry, if that technology is transferable to it.[147] The EPA contends that deep bed filtration has been proven effective elsewhere and that it is readily transferable to corn wet milling.

To base its standards on transfer technology, the EPA must: (1) determine that the transfer technology—in this case, deep bed filtration—is available outside the industry; (2) determine that the technology is transferable to the industry; and (3) make a *reasonable* prediction that the technology, if used in the industry, will be capable of removing the increment required by the new source standards. *Cf.* Portland Cement Association v. Ruckelshaus, 158 U.S. App.D.C. 308, 486 F.2d 375, 391-392 (1973); International Harvester Co. v. Ruckelshaus, 155 U.S.App.D.C. 411, 478 F.2d 615, 628-629 (1973).

The petitioners concede that deep bed filtration has been successfully used in other industries and in municipal treatment works. They deny, however,

---

ton Corn Plant at Clinton, Iowa, which was then undergoing modifications, "*should demonstrate* the applicability of this level of technology to grain milling wastes." *Development Document* at 121 (Emphasis supplied). However, the Clinton Plant had not yielded test results and, accordingly, the EPA did not rely on data derived from its operation:

> . . .It should be emphasized that these design levels [for the Clinton Plant] are far below those which have been achieved by any other plant in the corn wet milling or related industries *and cannot yet be considered as demonstrated technology*. (Emphasis supplied.)

Id. at 87.

Subsequently, the EPA supplied information to this Court which indicated that the Clinton Plant had begun to achieve an effluent reduction sufficient to comply with the 1983 guidelines/new source standards. The petitioners responded to that data by submitting their own data indicating that the Clinton Plant was not even complying with the 1977 guidelines. In light of this factual dispute, the EPA retreated, and counsel informed the Court at oral argument that the Clinton Plant data was not being submitted for the purpose of showing that the technology there used would in fact result in the predicted effluent reduction. Hence, we need not decide whether post-promulgation data may properly be presented on judicial review to support the reasonableness of a prediction. *Compare* Amoco Oil Co. v. Environmental Protection Agency, 163 U.S.App.D.C. 162, 501 F.2d 722, 729, n.10 (1974), *with* Dry Color Manufacturers' Association, Inc. v. Department of Labor, 486 F.2d 98, 108 (3rd Cir. 1973).

We stress, however, that the EPA will be open, on remand, to consider any data obtained from the operation of the Clinton Plant or others, including such data as bears on the availability of the 1983/new source technology and the results which may be achieved thereby.

[147] Although the legislative history does not speak of "transferable technology," we think that it is consistent with this interpretation of the terms "demonstrated" and "available." The House Report stated:

> It will be sufficient, for the purposes of setting the level of control under available technology, that there be one operating facility which demonstrates that the level can be achieved or that there is sufficient information and data from a relevant pilot plant or semi-works plant to provide the needed economic and technical justification for such a new source.

Legislative History at 798.

The Senate Report declared:

> As used in this section, the term "available control technology" is intended to direct the Administrator to examine the degree of effluent reduction that has been or can be achieved through the application of technology which is available or normally can be made available. This does not mean that the technology must be in actual, routine use somewhere. Rather, it means that the technology must be available at a cost and at a time which the Administrator determines to be reasonable.

Id. at 1476, U.S.Code Cong. & Admin. News, 1972, p. 3724. *Cf.* Portland Cement Association v. Ruckelshaus, 158 U.S.App.D.C. 308, 486 F.2d 375, 391 (1973) (discussing the meaning of "available" in the new source provisions of the Clean Air Act Amendments of 1970).

that deep bed filtration is adaptable to the corn wet milling industry and deny that the use of such filters in the industry will result in the removal of the incremental 30 pounds of BOD_5 and 40 pounds of TSS per MSBu. The basis for their contention is the fact that corn wet milling industry effluent is subject to "shockloads,"[148] and contains such high concentrations of suspended solids that clogging of the filtration system is to be expected.[149]

Given the unique nature of the corn wet milling effluent, and the apparent relevance of its uniqueness of the efficacy of deep bed filtration,[150] the EPA cannot rely on a presumption of transferability of that technology.[151] Its conclusion that the technology is transferable, and its prediction that the use of the technology within the industry will result in removal of the 30 and 40 pound increments must be supported by evidence in the record.[152] The District

---

148 The record bears out this contention:

> It must be recognized that the treatment of high strength carbohydrate wastes is difficult. Upset conditions may occur that result in higher BOD_5 and suspended solids discharges than normal. While the in-plant modifications and controls and the treatment sequence defined as best practicable control technology currently available [the 1977 technology] will minimize these upsets, they may still occur.

Development Document at 117.

The EPA has elsewhere declared that upsets in the biological treatment facility may have a critical effect on deep bed filtration:

> The single most important factor affecting filter performance is the quality of the secondary effluent produced by the biological treatment. If consistently good performance is exhibited by the biological treatment system, good filter performance can be expected. Conversely, if the biological facility is subject to frequent upsets, filtration will be much more difficult.

EPA, Process Design Manual for Upgrading Existing Wastewater Treatment Plants [hereinafter *Process Design Manual*] (October 1974) at 7-17.

149 The 1977 technology includes the recirculation of cooling waters for the purpose of achieving more highly concentrated raw wastes, thus rendering them more susceptible to biological (activated sludge) treatment. Thus, the EPA has stated that the *treated* wastes pursuant to the 1977 technology will have TSS concentrations ranging from 50 to 200 mg/1, and that the higher values "are generally for new plants that practice maximum water recycling." *Development Document* at 113. It is biologically treated waste which will be sent to the deep bed filters. Moreover, the 1983 technology is predicated on even more water recirculation and "maximum water reuse," *see* note 27, *supra*, and hence even higher concentrations of TSS in the biologically treated wastes. In light of these facts, the EPA's conclusion in the *Development Document* at 122 that the effluent arriving at the deep bed filters will range from 30 to 50 mg/1 in TSS seems inexplicable.

By contrast, the effluent arriving at the filters in municipal treatment plants can normally be expected to be below 30 mg/1, and in discussing the capabilities of deep bed filtration elsewhere, the EPA does not discuss capability to handle concentrations above 50 mg/1 in TSS. *See Process Design Manual* at 7-18 to 7-22.

In a study completed for petitioner CPC International by consultant Roy F. Weston, Inc., in December of 1973, the consultant concluded that, for best results, waste with 100 mg/1 of TSS concentrations could only be fed to the filters at a rate of 1.7 gallons per minute foot. *See* Reply Brief for Petitioners, Appendix H at 10. This compares to a rate of 5 gallons per minute foot used by municipalities. *See Process Design Manual* at 7-17. Because the flow rate is so low, a huge filter would be required. In effect, the petitioners contend that the EPA's policy of *requiring* heavy concentrations of TSS by the 1977 technology has contributed to the unsuitability of deep bed filters to the industry.

150 *See* notes 33 and 34, *supra*.

151 Moreover, even if the EPA could rely on a presumption of transferability, the record is barren of any evidence as to what the performance of deep bed filters has been outside the industry.

152 The Administrator may, of course, predict results. *See* Portland Cement Ass'n v. Ruckelshaus, *supra*, at 401-402. But "[o]ne must distinguish between prediction and prophecy." International Harvester Co. v.

of Columbia Circuit, in examining new source standards under the Clean Air Act, has stated the matter well:

> . . . The Administrator may make a projection based on existing technology, though that projection is subject to the restraints of reasonableness and cannot be based on "crystal ball" inquiry. . . . [T]he question of availability is partially dependent on "lead time," the time in which the technology will have to be available. Since the standards here put into effect will control new plants immediately, as opposed to one or two years in the future, the latitude of projection is correspondingly narrowed. If actual tests are not relied on, but instead a prediction is made, "its validity as applied to this case rests on the reliability of [the] prediction and the nature of [the] assumptions." *International Harvester*, at 45 [155 U.S.App. at 438, 478 F.2d at 642.]

Portland Cement Ass'n v. Ruckelshaus, *supra*, at 391-392.

We conclude that the prediction as to the efficacy of deep bed filtration in the corn wet milling industry is not a reasonable one, because there is no support in the record for that prediction. The sum total of the evidence in the record as to the efficacy of deep bed filtration in or outside of the corn wet milling industry consists of the following.[153]

> (1) A statement that deep bed filtration has been used outside the industry for several years, and produces a "high quality effluent." *Development Document* at 121. This statement is not supported in the record and the degree of BOD_5 and TSS reduction obtained by other industries and municipalities is nowhere quantified.
>
> (2) Statements that:
>
> "It is *anticipated* that the technology of removing biological solids by filtration will improve rapidly. . . ." *Id.* at 120 (Emphasis supplied.)
>
> "Deep bed filtration will remove most of the remaining suspended solids. . . ." *Id.* at 121.
>
> "[I]t is . . . . *felt* that" the new performance standards can be met with the technology. *Id.* at 126 (Emphasis supplied.)
>
> The technology "*should* significantly reduce the raw waste loads" and the new source standards "*should* be achievable." *Id.* at 127 (Emphasis supplied.)
>
> The Clinton Plant "*should* demonstrate" the transferability of the technology to the industry.[154] *Id.* at 121 (Emphasis supplied.)

These statements are likewise not supported in the record. We can find no concrete data, test results, literature, or expert opinion tending to support the EPA's feelings, anticipation and prophecies.

Ruckelshaus, 155 U.S.App.D.C. 411, 478 F.2d 615, 642 (1973).

[153] The EPA in its presentation to this Court urges an additional basis for its conclusion: the fact that some municipalities are currently treating corn wet milling wastes and have found those wastes to be "compatible." This basis is not adequately developed, however, for there is nothing in the record to indicate that the municipal treatment plants which are currently handling corn wet milling wastes are able to comply or are in fact complying with the new source standards applicable to corn wet milling plants.

[154] *See* note 31, *supra*.

To the contrary, the EPA originally proposed a 1977 guideline of 35 pounds per MSBu of TSS, only to raise it to 50 pounds in the final regulations, with the following comment:

> . . .EPA believes that while the 30 lb limit might be attainable, the technology is not yet available to achieve this effluent level on a routine basis. . . .

39 Fed. Reg. 10512 (1974).[155]

Further doubt is cast on the achievability of the new source standards in a letter sent by the Department of Agriculture to the EPA on July 25, 1973:

> If the Level II (July 1, 1983) standards are to be applied immediately to any new construction, this would appear to delay any new construction by several years because of recognized lack of proven control and treatment technologies for economically achieving the proposed levels. Is such delay acceptable?

It follows that, on the basis of *this record*, we have no alternative but to reject the new source standards. There remains the question of remedy. The Act directs that the standards should have been promulgated more than one year ago. *See* § 306(b)(1). We believe that this mandate to proceed expeditiously would not be furthered if we simply held that the new source standards are unacceptable. Accordingly, we remand to the EPA with directions set forth below, and retain jurisdiction pending the remand. *See* South Terminal Corp. v. Environmental Protection Agency, 504 F. 2d 646, 665-667 (1st Cir. 1974); International Harvester Co. v. Ruckelshaus, *supra*, at 649; Kennecott Copper Corp. v. Environmental Protection Agency, 149 U.S. App.D.C. 231, 462 F.2d 846, 850-851 (1972). *Cf.* 28 U.S.C. § 2106.

The proceedings in the EPA on remand shall be conducted in accordance with the procedural requirements of the Act, except that the time periods shall be shortened so as to permit the EPA to enter its final order in the matter within 120 days. Within that time, the EPA shall either furnish support for the new source standards previously published, or establish new ones which can be achieved with the best available demonstrated control technology.[156] If the petitioners are satisfied with the Administrator's final action, they shall have ten days to file with this Court any objections to his final order. In that event, an accelerated briefing schedule shall be arranged with the clerk of this Court to review the Administrator's action.

On remand, we instruct the EPA to deal with one other matter which is not adequately covered in the record. Section 306(b)(1)(B) directs the

---

155 Similarly, the *Development Document* at 127 declared of the 1983 new source technology:

> . . .Inasmuch as this type of treatment has not been specifically applied to corn wet milling wastes, initial operating experience with such systems may not fully meet the expected . . . BOD_5 and suspended solids removals . . .

156 The EPA is not bound by its past indication that the best available demonstrated control technology would include deep bed filtration. If there are other methods which will result in reductions equal to or better than the amount required by the 1983 guidelines, or which will result in a no discharge level, the EPA can—and indeed should—promulgate new source standards based on such technology. *See* § 306(a)(1), requiring a no discharge standard where practicable. This freedom to change approach is but a specific application of the Act's provision that the Administrator shall revise the new source standards "from time to time." § 306(b)(1)(B).

Administrator to consider the issue of costs in adopting new source standards. This consideration is particularly important here, since the record indicates that capital and operating costs may be of more significance in this industry than in some others, due to low profit margins, the highly volatile nature of raw material prices, and competitive substitutes which make it difficult to pass on increased costs to consumers.[157] *Compare* Portland Cement Ass'n v. Ruckelshaus, *supra* at 387-388, 390.

The current record concerning costs for new sources is unsatisfactory in two major respects. First, the EPA has not projected separate operating and capital costs figures for new plants, but has relied on those prepared with respect to modifying existing plants to comply with the 1983 guidelines. It must correct this defect on remand. It may well be that these costs will be less for new plants than for modified ones, but we cannot assume this to be the case. Second, the EPA based its cost figures on 1971 prices, even though the *Development Document* and the regulations were published in March of 1974. More current figures than this are available, and should be used by the EPA in setting forth projected capital and operating costs for new plants.

III. THE PRETREATMENT STANDARDS FOR NEW SOURCES

Section 307(c) of the Act[158] provides that the Administrator shall promulgate pretreatment standards for new plants which introduce their pollutants into publicly owned treatment works. The pretreatment standards promulgated for new plants in the corn wet milling industry, 40 C.F.R. § 406.16, incorporate by reference a general set of pretreatment standards earlier promulgated in Part 128 of title 40 of the Code of Federal Regulations. *See* 38 Fed. Reg. 30982-84 (1973). Those standards split pollutants into two categories: "compatible" and "incompatible." Compatible pollutants include BOD, TSS and pH. *See* 40 C.F.R. § 128.121. Under the general pretreatment standards incorporated by the new source pretreatment standards, a plant is not required to pretreat its effluent for removal of compatible pollutants, except as required by 40 C.F.R. § 128.131or by state or municipality. *See id.* § 128.132. Since the corn wet milling effluent is a compatible one within the

---

[157] Costs become an increasingly important factor as pollution reduction enters the 95 to 100 percent range. *See, e.g., Legislative History* at 1127, 1147, 1150 (testimony of Paul V. McCracken, Chairman of the Council of Economic Advisers, before the House Subcommittee on Public Works); *id.* at 1222 (testimony of Mr. Ruckelshaus before the Subcommittee). The new source standards will require removal in this range for some plants, if past raw waste figures are predictive. *See* tables in note 28, *supra.*

[158] That section provides:

In order to insure that any source introducing pollutants into a publicly owned treatment works, which source would be a new source subject to section 306 of this title if it were to discharge pollutants, will not cause a violation of the effluent limitations established for any such treatment works, the Administrator shall promulgate pretreatment standards for the category of such sources simultaneously with the promulgation of standards of performance under section 306 of this title for the equivalent category of new sources. Such pretreatment standards shall prevent the discharge of any pollutant into such treatment works, which pollutant may interfere with, pass through, or otherwise be incompatible with such works.

meaning of the regulations,[159] new plants in the industry need worry only about the applicability of § 128.131. That section provides:

No waste introduced into a publicly owned treatment works shall interfere with the operation or performance of the works. Specifically, the following wastes shall not be introduced into the publicly owned treatment works:

(a) Wastes which create a fire or explosion hazard in the publicly owned treatment works.

(b) Wastes which will cause corrosive structural damage to treatment works, but in no case wastes with a pH lower than 5.0, unless the works is designed to accommodate such wastes.

(c) Solid or viscous wastes in amounts which would cause obstruction to the flow in sewers, or other interference with the proper operation of the publicly owned treatment works.

(d) Wastes at a flow rate and/or pollutant discharge rate which is excessive over relatively short time periods so that there is a treatment process upset and subsequent loss of treatment efficacy.

The petitioners complain that this standard is not really a standard, because it is too vague and uncertain. While their attack on § 128.131 is in the form of a general broadside, their only real complaint concerns subparagraph (d).[160] We conclude that the petitioners' objection to that subparagraph is well taken. The record clearly indicates that corn wet milling effluent is subject to shockloads.[161] A new operator whose shockload is determined to be "excessive over [a] relatively short time period . . . [causing] loss of treatment efficacy," would be subject under subparagraph (d) to substantial civil or criminal penalties. *See* § 309. This standard is too vague to warn the industry of the scope of prohibited conduct. On remand, therefore, the EPA shall review subparagraph (d) of § 128.131, as it applies to the corn wet milling industry, and shall amend the regulation so as to define in a reasonably specific manner what it considers to be an excessive discharge to a municipal plant over relatively short periods of time. We do not require, as the petitioners would have us do, that the regulations must be amended to provide that a new corn wet milling plant may discharge all compatible wastes into municipal treatment works without limitation.

We recognize that the Administrator's task in defining those shockloads which will upset municipal treatment works is a difficult one. Obviously such a definition is dependent on the size and capabilities of the particular works which is receiving the waste. Nevertheless, this is a difficulty with which the Administrator must grapple.

---

159 To the extent that there are any incompatible pollutants in corn wet milling effluent, the regulations clearly provide that they need not be pretreated. Section 406.16 provides that

. . .the pretreatment standard for incompatible pollutants introduced into a publicly owned treatment works shall be the standard of performance for new sources specified in 40 C.F.R. 406.15. . . .

The new source standards, of course, do not require treatment of any pollutants other than BOD, TSS and pH, all of which are compatible pollutants. The quoted portion of § 406.16, therefore, is reduced to gibberish.

160 The EPA conceded in its brief that normal corn wet milling effluent does not contain any of the characteristics of § 128.131(a), (b) or (c). *See* Respondent's Brief at 99.

161 *See* note 33, *supra*.

The pretreatment standards for new plants are remanded for reconsideration and amendment of the incorporated § 128.131(d), as it relates to new sources in the corn wet milling industry. The Administrator shall complete his action in that regard within the time limits and procedural requirements set forth in Part II of this opinion. This Court retains jurisdiction in the matter, and will hear objections to the Administrator's action on remand in accordance with the provisions of Part II of this opinion.

IV. SUMMARY

. . . The new source standards and the pretreatment standards for new sources are remanded to the Administrator of the EPA for proceedings consistent with this opinion. Each party to this proceeding shall bear its own costs.

NOTE

New source performance standards as provided for in § 306 are parallel both in wording and in intent to the new source performance standards in the Clean Air Act. In both situations, new source performance standards are the most stringent standards equaling or exceeding the requirements of the BAT (best available technology) standards, applicable directly to new sources. Since retrofit of plants and facilities is likely to be more costly than the original construction to meet higher standards, the purpose is clearly to force technology in a way that also makes sound economic sense. The speedup of the imposition of the higher standard is compensated by providing the regulated industry with the assurance that the standard will not be raised for ten years following its adoption, as provided in 33 U.S.C. § 1316(d).

The Third Circuit has long differed with the D.C. Circuit in the interpretation of the definition of "new source." The Third Circuit concluded on plain meaning grounds that new source was any source on which construction began after the proposal of an applicable new source performance standard. Such a source must then comply with the standard whenever it was published, acknowledging some question that a substantial lapse of time between proposal and promulgation may change the court's position. *Pennsylvania Dept. of Environmental Resources v. EPA*, 618 F.2d 991 (3d Cir. 1980). Consider the choice industry may have in taking advantage of either one of these judicial positions. In considering the commencement of construction, note the definition of "construction" in § 306(a)(5) of the Clean Water Act.

[ix] National Pollutants Discharge Elimination System (NPDES)

PERMITS, COMPLIANCE AND ENFORCEMENT

Council on Environmental Quality
Thirteenth Annual Report 81-82
(transmitted to Congress 1982)

Under the Clean Water Act, every public or private facility that discharges wastes directly into the waters of the United States must have a permit. These National Pollutant Discharge Elimination System (NPDES) permits are issued by an EPA regional office or by a state with an EPA-approved program. By August 1981, EPA had approved programs in 33 states and territories.

NPDES Permits

An NPDES permit generally states discharge limitations for specific pollutants, establishes compliance schedules for upgrading controls to meet such limits, and requires monitoring and periodic reports on compliance. As shown in Table 3-14, over 64,000 NPDES permits have been issued to municipal (mostly sewage treatment) and nonmunicipal (mostly industrial) dischargers.

Table 3-14

	EPA Region	Nonmunicipal	Municipal	Total
NPDES Permits[a] Issued as of September 17, 1981	1	2,039	578	2,617
	2	2,375	888	3,263
	3	6,712	1,605	8,317
	4	12,173	2,537	14,710
	5	11,691	4,204	15,895
	6	2,948	1,912	4,860
	7	4,561	2,154	6,715
	8	2,326	1,066	3,392
	9	1,539	457	1,996
	10	1,834	584	2,418
	Total	48,198	15,985	64,183

[a]Does not include federal facilities.

Source: Rosanne Light, U.S. Environmental Protection Agency, Office of Water Enforcement

Innovative Permitting

EPA has developed some innovative approaches to permitting. One such approach is the use of "general permits."

The general permit program was designed to regulate categories of point sources located within a designated geographic area which discharge the same types of wastes and which warrant similar pollution control measures. Under the original NPDES regulations, only individual permits could be issued to point sources. A single NPDES permit can now be written with limitations and conditions applicable to a defined category or subcategory of dischargers. Because individual permit applications are not required, the time spent in the processing and issuance of permits is significantly reduced. The issuance of general permits is optional; EPA regional offices and states retain the right to require individual permits for any and all point sources.

The states and EPA Regions began issuing general permits in 1981. As of August 1981, three general permits had been issued for oil and gas facilities operating in Bureau of Land Management lease sale areas in the Gulf of Mexico.

Enforcement

EPA can take several types of action against a municipality or firm found violating the conditions of an NPDES permit. As shown in Table 3-15, in fiscal year 1980, EPA issued 89 Notices of Violation and 569 Administrative Orders. EPA also referred 39 cases to the Department of Justice, most of which were in the nonmunicipal category. Referrals to Justice are frequently settled out of court. In 35 referral cases closed in fiscal year 1980, approximately $1.78 million in fines and penalties were levied, down from the 52 cases and $7.55 million in fiscal year 1979.

Table 3-15 EPA Enforcement Actions

	FY77		FY78		FY79		FY80	
	NM	M	NM	M	NM	M	NM	M
Notice of Violation	184	113	121	82	64	85	25	64
Administrative Order	495	633	489	241	347	169	351	218
Referrals to Department of Justice	75	23	122	27	61	10	32	7

NM = Nonmunicipal M = Municipal

Source: U.S. Environmental Protection Agency, Office Of Water Enforcement.

Introduction to the NPDES System

The National Pollution Discharge Elimination System (NPDES) was created under § 402 of the Federal Water Pollution Control Act of 1972.[162] The

[162] 33 U.S.C. § 1342. An earlier permit system established by regulation of the Army Corps of Engineers under the 1899 Rivers & Harbors Act was abandoned after the decision

NPDES system provides an exception to the provisions of § 301(a) of the Act which prohibits all pollution outright. Under the permit system, the Administrator, after opportunity for public hearing, may issue a permit for the discharge of any pollutant upon condition that the discharge will meet all the applicable effluent standards under the Act.[163] The NPDES system (and its offshoot, the SPDES system (State Pollutant Discharge Elimination System)), serves as one of the major pollution control elements under the law. It also serves as an important informational device, because prior to the establishment of the permit system, there was no information as to what pollutants were being discharged and who and which industries were discharging them. Without full knowledge of what was being discharged, no effective national system of pollution control was possible.

Because the permit system is a focal point for pollution control, and because the issuance of a permit is conditioned on the requirement that the discharge will meet all of the applicable effluent standards under the Federal Water Pollution Control Act, litigation involving challenges to permits and the enforcement of permits involve the full array of challenges to applicable effluent standards under § 301 of the Act. This includes challenges to (1) applicable BPT, BAT and BCPCT (best conventional pollutant control technology), (2) the application of variances and modification provisions of the Act, (3) new source performance standards and toxic and pretreatment effluent standards, and (4) plant-specific variances where national pretreatment standards as applied to a given source are either too lenient or too strict because of "fundamentally different" factors from those considered by the EPA in setting the standards. All of these issues may be included in challenges to permit standards because any of these may be the effluent standards which a particular permittee must meet.

The permit system is a dual system where the Administrator is in charge both of granting NPDES permits and of supervising qualified state agencies who issue SPDES permits as provided in the law.

The NPDES and SPDES systems therefore comprise a part of the law where the balance between national and state controls of water pollution must be worked out.

The cases that follow provide a basis for discussion of federal conditions on state permits and of the balance between state autonomy and federal controls in the grant of permits. *See also* F. Grad, Treatise on Environmental Law, at § 3.03[6].

---

in Kalur v. Resor, 335 F. Supp. 1 (D.D.C. 1971), which held that the Corps of Engineers had to prepare an environmental impact statement under NEPA before it could grant discharge permits.

163 FWPCA § 402(a)(1), 33 U.S.C. § 1342(a)(1).

NATURAL RESOURCES DEFENSE COUNCIL, INC. v. U.S. ENVIRONMENTAL PROTECTION AGENCY

United States Court of Appeals, D.C. Circuit (1988)
859 F.2d 156, 19 ELR 20016

[The case involves the revision of EPA NPDES regulations in 1979, 44 Fed. Reg. 32,854 (June 7, 1979) which was followed by numerous industry and environmental challenges. These challenges were consolidated in 673 F.2d 392 (D.C. Cir. 1980), cert denied, sub nom. *Chemical Manufacturers Ass'n v. EPA*, 459 U.S. 879 (1982). Upon remand, the Court reviews the challenges pursuant to § 509(b)(1) of the Clean Water Act, 33 U.S.C. § 1369(b)(1). Then followed two years of settlement negotiations between EPA and industry representatives. After a settlement agreement covering 27 of 47 issues raised, the court remanded the record to the agency to permit implementation of the agreement. After notice and comment, EPA promulgated final revisions to the NPDES regulations, 49 Fed. Reg. 37,997 (Sept. 26, 1984). Pursuant to the agreement industry signatories were free to renew their challenges and because the final regulations reflected various changes from the agreement, another flurry of petitions for review were filed and consolidated in this court.]

Before ROBINSON, STARR and WILLIAMS, Circuit Judges.

Opinion for the Court filed Per Curiam.

These consolidated cases arise out of the Environmental Protection Agency's issuance of regulations implementing the National Pollution Discharge Elimination System (NPDES) permit program, established under the Clean Water Act, 33U.S.C. §§ 1251 *et seq.* (1982). The events leading up to these challenges are set forth fully in our prior opinion, which disposed of several issues. *See NRDC v. EPA*, 261 U.S. App. D.C. 372, 822 F.2d 104 (D.C. Cir. 1987). This opinion addresses the remaining challenges, mounted by both environmental and industry petitioners.[164]

Although numerous issues are raised, they fall into eight general areas or categories. The first set of challenges involves regulations promulgated by EPA in furtherance of its obligations under the National Environmental Policy Act ("NEPA"), 42 U.S.C. §§ 4321 *et seq.* (1982).[165] Also challenged are regulations that (2) establish the rules for transfer of authority over the

[164] The environmental petitioners are the Natural Resources Defense Council, Inc. and Citizens For a Better Environment. The industry petitioners include the following: the American Iron and Steel Institute, the American Paper Institute, the National Forest Products Association, the American Petroleum Institute, the American Textile Manufacturers Institute, the American Wood Preservers Institute, the Chemical Manufacturers Association, the National Coal Association, Burlington Industries, Ford Motor Company, Kennecott, United Technologies Corporation, and Virginia Electric and Power Company.

[165] These NEPA issues include: (1) EPA's imposition of permit conditions unrelated to effluent limits based on its NEPA review; (2) the agency's refusal to adjust effluent limits as a result of this review; and (3) the admissibility of evidence in permit proceedings.

NPDES permitting program to the states and supervision of the state programs;[166] (3) permit the establishment of permit limits in terms of "toxicity"; (4) permit the use of non-adversary panel procedures ("NAPP" or "NAP procedures") for the issuance of initial permits and variances; (5) prohibit "backsliding" from permit limits when subsequent guidelines have become more lax;[167] and (6) define permit limits in "gross" terms, giving credit for pollutants in intake waters only in certain limited circumstances. Industry challenges EPA's refusal to provide an "upset defense" for noncompliance with water-quality-based permit limits; that is, a defense based on a showing that non-compliance was due to factors beyond the permittee's control. Finally, NRDC challenges on several fronts EPA's regulation providing for continuances of out-of-date permits pending renewal by the agency.

For the reasons that follow, we deny the petitions for review on all issues, save for those pertaining to the permit conditions unrelated to effluent limits and the upset defense.

II. THE NEPA-RELATEDREGULATIONS

As is well known, the National Environmental Policy Act ("NEPA"), 42 U.S.C. § § 4321 *et seq.*, requires environmental impact statements ("EISs") for "major Federal actions" affecting the environment, and normally authorizes the relevant agency to make some adjustment in its conduct as a result of what it learns from the necessary inquiry. 42 U.S.C. § 4332; *NRDC v. Berklund*, 197 U.S. App. D.C. 298, 609 F.2d 553, 558 (D.C. Cir. 1979). In the area of water quality regulation, § 511(c) of the CWA, 33 U.S.C. § 1371(c), structures and limits the role of NEPA. It makes clear that the provision of federal financial assistance for the construction of publicly owned treatment works and the issuance of discharge permits to new sources are the only actions taken by the Administrator under the CWA that will trigger a NEPA duty.

[The court here holds that EPA is not authorized to impose non-water quality permit conditions or to impose conditions involving non-water quality related environmental factors stressing the largely procedural nature of NEPA. The court invalidates the regulations which stray into this unauthorized territory.]

III. STATE PROGRAM REQUIREMENTS

Because of Congress's desire to "recognize, preserve, and protect the primary responsibilities and rights of States to prevent, reduce, and to eliminate pollution," 33 U.S.C. § 1251(b), the CWA provides for state assumption of the NPDES permit program. *Id.* § 1342(b). It specifies some prerequisites to states' assuming permitting responsibilities, *id.*, authorizes the Administrator

---

[166] This group of procedural issues includes challenges to the standards for (1) state allowance of public participation; (2) maximum penalties under state programs; and (3) EPA's veto of permits approved by states.

[167] This anti-backsliding controversy actually involves two separate issues. First, Industry challenges the propriety of prohibiting backsliding from permit limits based on new source performance standards ("NSPS"). Second, Industry contests the ban on backsliding from "BPJ" permit limits, which are those established, in the absence of a national guideline, according to the permit writer's best professional judgment.

to supplement them, *id.* §§ 1361(a), 1314(i) (2), and requires him to approve a state's application once satisfied that these standards have been met, *id.* § 1342(b). Through this mechanism the agency has thus far transferred its permitting authority to 39 of 50 states. EPA Brief on Ripeness at 12.

Environmentalist and industry petitioners attack different aspects of EPA's rules for transfer of authority and for supervision of the state programs. We find all these attacks ripe.

A. Penalties and Participation—Ripeness.

Environmental petitioners challenge two regulations clarifying the prerequisites for transfer of EPA's authority. Citizens for a Better Environment ("CBE") contests the agency's standards for state allowance of public participation, set forth in 40 C.F.R. § 123.27(d). It contends that 33 U.S.C. § 1251(e)requires states to provide for citizen suits and intervention rights just as the CWA does at the federal level. *See* 33 U.S.C. § 1365. NRDC complains that the agency's regulations for what a state must provide by way of penalties provision, 40 C.F.R. § 123.27, is illegal because it fails to require the states to set maximum penalties as high as those provided in the CWA itself. 33 U.S.C. § 1319, as amended.

We believe these challenges to be ripe. Both are pure issues of law: if the challengers' legal position be correct, the regulations are invalid. The agency position is final and the regulations' vulnerability to these attacks is not materially dependent upon further interpretations. . . .

B. Penalties and Participation—Merits.

A unique federal-state division of responsibilities is at the structural core of the Act. This is made crystal clear by the congressional declaration of the policy and goals pervading the Act:

> It is the policy of the Congress to recognize, preserve, and protect the primary responsibilities and rights of States to prevent, reduce, and eliminate pollution, to plan the development and use [] of land and water resources, and to consult with the Administrator in the exercise of his authority under this chapter.

Accordingly, the NPDES provides for state assumption of the permit program, and Congress repeatedly articulated its expectation that the states would play a major role in administering it. The Act specifies prerequisites for state assumption of the program, empowers the Administrator to further refine these standards, and commands the Administrator to approve the state permit system once he determines that the statutory requirements and administrative guidelines are met.

1. Regulatory Uniformity and State Autonomy.

Petitioners challenge two regulations implementing the Act's provisions on state assumption of the permit program. Citizens for a Better Environment (CBE) attacks the standards for minimum public participation at the state level. NRDC complains of the absence of state authority to impose a given maximum penalty. Both protests rest on the assumption that congressional emphasis on uniformity was directed to procedural as well as substantive standards, and that as a result federal requirements respecting public participation and penalties must be mirrored on the state level.

Uniformity is indeed a recurrent theme in the Act, a direct manifestation of concern that the permit program be standardized to avoid the "industrial equivalent of forum shopping" and the creation of "pollution havens" by migration of dischargers to areas having lower pollution standards. The desired uniformity, however, is spoken of almost exclusively in relation to effluent limitations. Moreover, Congress' quest for homogeneity is in tension with its independent emphasis on state autonomy, which is repeated throughout the legislative history of the Act, is enshrined in the Act as the basic policy to "recognize, preserve, and protect the primary responsibilities and rights of States," and is the very foundation of the permit program. Congress made even clearer its intent that the act be administered in such a manner that the abilities of the States to control their own permit programs will be developed and strengthened. [Members of Congress] look for and expect State and local interest, initiative, and personnel to provide a much more effective program than that which would result from control in the regional offices of the Environmental Protection Agency.

In fashioning its guidelines on both participation and penalties, EPA endeavored to reconcile the competing objectives of regulatory uniformity and state autonomy by establishing a floor for citizen participation and state enforcement authority, while ensuring that states have the maximum possible independence.[168] We are fully mindful of the rule that an agency is entitled to special deference when it harmonizes competing policies; "if this choice represents a reasonable accommodation of conflicting policies that were committed to the agency's care by the statute, we should not disturb it unless it appears from the statute or its legislative history that the accommodation is not one that Congress would have sanctioned." The regulations at issue are classic examples of such administrative balancing, and we find that they fall well within the permissible bounds of the agency's discretion.

2. *Public Participation.*

CBE assails on two grounds EPA's regulations specifying the minimum level of public participation that states must afford. CBE first claims that the regulations are inadequate because they do not include all of the protections built into the federal permit program. Alternatively, it contends that they fail to provide any meaningful right.

The requirement of public participation in efforts to control water pollution is established in the congressional declaration of policy and goals of the Act:

[168] *See* Consolidated Permit Regulations, 45 Fed. Reg. 33,290 (aim is to "ensure the benefits of public participation while intruding less into the States' management of their judicial and administrative systems") [hereinafter 1980 Regulations]; *id.* at 33,383 (regulations "set minimum levels of fines and penalties which States must have the authority to recover in order to ensure effective State enforcement programs," but "reduce [] the levels below those available to EPA based on the large volume of comments from States requesting such relief").

> Public participation in the development, revision, and enforcement of any regulation, standard, effluent limitation, plan, or program established by the Administrator or any State under this chapter shall be provided for, encouraged, and assisted by the Administrator and the States. The Administrator, in cooperation with the States, shall develop and publish regulations specifying minimum guidelines for public participation in such processes.

The statutory text does not, however, elaborate on the extent of public participation contemplated by Congress. The legislative history of the Act repeatedly echoes the desire "that its provisions be administered and enforced in a fishbowl-like atmosphere." CBE asserts that in Section 1365, which governs citizen suits, Congress spelled out the elements of the public participation envisioned. This contention is based on the characterization in the legislative history of that section as a "provision . . . that would provide citizen participation in the enforcement of control requirements and regulations." We find no indication, however, that these statements, made in the context of committee reports on Section 1365, were intended as definitional cross-references to Section 1251(e).

As CBE insists, Congress considered the citizen suit provision to be of dual importance, serving both as a method of prodding the agency, and as a backup means of enforcing the Act. On the other hand, Congress also expressed reservations about potential abuses of citizen suits, and expressly noted its concern "with protecting local government, industry, and individuals from harassing law suits while still keeping the courts open to responsible parties concerned with environmental protection." Nowhere in either the Act or its legislative history is there any express statement that the provisions of Section 1365 extend to states, nor do we find persuasive any equivocal intimation in that direction. It would have been very easy for Congress to say so if that was what it had in mind; instead, even intervention as of right was restricted to litigation in federal courts. It is difficult for us to believe that if Congress wanted the states simply to copy the federal minimum public participation requirements, it would limit the elaborate regulatory system to definition of federal-level public participation, and leave the specifications of the minimum acceptable state-level public participation for an exercise of the Administrator's rulemaking authority . . . .

CBE would also bootstrap a prescription for state-level citizen suits from the statutory mandate that "the permit program of the Administrator . . . shall be subject to the same terms, conditions, and requirements as apply to a State program . . . under subsection [1342(b)]." As the Seventh Circuit has noted, however, this provision on its face applies in only one direction: the federal program must meet specific requirements set out in subsection (b), such as a five-year fixed permit term and incorporation of effluent limitations.

Finally, we note that EPA maintains that "nothing in the Act or its legislative history indicates that Congress intended that states be required to provide identical rights to those Congress specified for citizens in Federal court." Because we have found that "Congress has not directly addressed the precise question at issue," and determined that "the agency's answer is based on a permissible construction of the statute," we defer to EPA's reading. We therefore hold that state-level citizen suits are not commanded by the Act, and find no impropriety in the Administrator's failure to require state programs to afford them.

CBE asks that, should we decide that state public participation specifications need not match the federal requirements, we hold that the present regulations are incapable of producing meaningful public involvement. We decline this invitation. The pertinent regulations read:

> Any state administering a program shall provide for public participation in the State enforcement process by providing either:
>
> (1) Authority which allows intervention as of right in any civil or administrative action . . . by any citizen having an interest which is or may be adversely affected; or
>
> (2) Assurance that the State agency or enforcement authority will:
>
> (i) Investigate and provide written responses to all citizen complaints . . . ;
>
> (ii) Not oppose intervention by any citizen when permissive intervention may be authorized by statute, rule, or regulation; and
>
> (iii) Publish notice of and provide at least 30 days for public comment on any proposed settlement of a State enforcement action.

Implementation of either of these options suffices, but it must be adequate enough to meet the "minimum guidelines for public participation." Congress contemplated that these regulations would do more than pay lip service to public participation; instead, "the public must have a genuine opportunity to speak on the issue of protection of its waters" on federal, state, and local levels. "Citizen groups," it was said, "are not to be treated as nuisances or troublemakers but rather as welcome participants in the vindication of environmental interests."

We might be somewhat more hospitable to CBE's claim, especially with regard to the second option, were it not for two statements by EPA in interpreting the regulations. First, in promulgating the regulations and again in its brief before this court, the agency indicated that the first option—provision of intervention as of right—called for state intervention rights similar to those accorded by the federal rules. Although, given the Act's confinement of mandatory intervention as of right to federal courts, we would not insist upon such a provision, its existence does undercut CBE's argument.

More importantly, however, EPA asserted at oral argument that the second option, to the extent that it is based on a state's agreement not to oppose permissive intervention, will not be available in states that do not provide some means of intervention. This interpretation is critical to our decision to uphold the agency. Were the second option open where permissive intervention is impossible, public participation would be limited to that flowing from the state's agreement to respond to citizen complaints and to entertain citizen comments on proposed settlements of state enforcement actions—rights dismissed by the Seventh Circuit as "no more than a legalistic articulation of a common courtesy and hardly . . . satisfaction of the EPA's statutory duty to issue regulations promoting public participation in state enforcement."

With this caveat, however, we conclude that the regulations, as interpreted, provide meaningful and adequate opportunity for public participation consistent with the statutory mandate. The regulations reasonably accommodate conflicting statutory prescriptions by "establish[ing] requirements which ensure the benefits of public participation, while intruding less into the States' management of their judicial and administrative systems." We accordingly reject CBE's challenge.

3. Maximum Penalties.

Section 1319, as amended by the Water Quality Act of 1987, specifies the penalties assessable on the federal level. A negligent violation is punishable by a penalty of "not less than $2,500 nor more than $25,000 per day of violation" for a first offense, and "not more than $50,000 per day" for any subsequently occurring. A knowing violation invites a fine of "not less than $5,000 nor more than $50,000 per day of violation" for a first offense, and "not more than $100,000" for additional offenses. A violator who knowingly places another person in imminent danger of death or serious bodily injury is subject to a fine of "not more than $250,000" if the violator is an individual and "not more than $1,000,000" if an organization. Falsification of reports, or monitoring devices or methods calls for a fine of "not more than $10,000" for a first offense, and "not more than $20,000 per day of violation" for recurring offenses. Civil penalties for permit violations are "not to exceed $25,000 per day for each violation."

States are required to have "adequate authority" "to abate violations of the permit or the permit program, including civil and criminal penalties and other ways and means of enforcement." The Administrator was charged with the responsibility of fashioning guidelines defining the minimum enforcement provisions deemed adequate. Pursuant to this mandate, the Administrator promulgated the regulations here in question, which require state authority to assess or sue to recover in court civil penalties and to seek criminal remedies, including fines, as follows:

> (i) Civil penalties . . . shall be assessable in at least the amount of $5,000 a day for each violation.
>
> (ii) Criminal fines [for permit or filing violations] . . . shall be assessable in at least the amount of $10,000 a day for each violation.
>
> (iii) Criminal fines [for falsification of reports or monitoring] . . . shall be recoverable in at least the amount of $5,000 for each instance of violation.

Petitioner NRDC contends that these regulations are invalid because they do not compel the states to provide authority to levy the maximum penalties assessable in federal enforcement programs.

Throughout its consideration of the Act, Congress reiterated the important role penalties play in enforcement of water pollution standards, and emphasized the need for substantial penalties, for example:

> Sanctions under existing law have not been sufficient to encourage compliance . . . . Therefore, the Committee proposes to increase significantly the penalties . . . . If the timetables established throughout the

> Act are to be met, the threat of sanction must be real, and enforcement provisions must be swift and direct.

In this articulation of congressional purpose, coupled with the congressional expectation that states would bear the primary enforcement burdens of the Act, NRDC would find a mandate for state ability and willingness to assess the federally required maximum penalties.

NRDC also relies on Section 1370, which provides that states "may not adopt or enforce any effluent limitation, or other limitation, effluent standard, prohibition, pretreatment standard, or standard of performance which is less stringent than the effluent limitation, or other limitation, effluent standard, prohibition, pretreatment standard, or standard of performance under this chapter." NRDC asserts that this means that states also may not adopt penalty provisions less stringent than those that the Act prescribes for federal enforcement. We note, however, that this section refers, not to enforcement powers, but only to effluent limitations and similar standards.

The Water Quality Act of 1987 contained a provision amending Section 1319 that weighs heavily against NRDC's contentions. The section laying out increased maximum civil penalties states:

> INCREASED PENALTIES NOT REQUIRED UNDER STATE PROGRAMS.—
>
> The Federal Water Pollution Control Act shall not be construed as requiring a State to have a civil penalty for violations described in section 309(d) of such Act which has the same monetary amount as the civil penalty established by such section, as amended by paragraph (1). Nothing in this paragraph shall affect the Administrator's authority to establish or adjudge by regulation a minimum acceptable State civil penalty.

NRDC concedes that this section relieves state programs from any obligation to match the maximum federal civil penalties set forth in the Water Quality Act. But, NRDC says, the quoted language should be read as a narrow exception applicable only to the federal penalties to which it expressly refers, with the result that state programs must adopt the federal civil penalties in force prior to the passage of the Water Quality Act and, more clearly than ever, must incorporate the maximum federal criminal penalties into their programs. EPA's reply is that the new provision should be understood as simply a confirmation of the broad authority the Administrator already enjoyed in crafting state program requirements. We accept EPA's position.

This challenge by NRDC exposes the same logical infirmity flawing the attack leveled by CBE. It presumes an unexpressed congressional intent that state requirements must mirror the federal ones, a presumption inconsistent with the elements of the statutory scheme limiting operation of the provisions to enforcement efforts at the national level and explicitly empowering the Administrator to set the prerequisites for state plans. Nothing in the Act or its legislative history supports a reduction of the Administrator's discretion to activity purely ministerial, as approval of NRDC's thesis would do, and the Administrator's conclusion to the contrary is eminently reasonable.

The Water Quality Act amendments to Section 1319 support this reasoning. The provision concerning federal civil penalties states specifically that "nothing in this paragraph shall affect the administrator's authority to establish or adjust by regulation a minimum acceptable State civil penalty." This language is indicative of the understanding that Congress was not enlarging the Administrator's authority for a narrowly defined purpose, as NRDC argues, but was confirming his existing authority. Surely the provision quoted is conclusive with respect to the treatment of federal civil penalties, and holding that federal civil penalties antedating the Water Quality Act must be included in state programs would run afoul of this clear intent.

Similarly, NRDC's contention that federal maximums for criminal violations must be incorporated into state programs must also be discarded here. NRDC maintains that congressional silence with respect to the applicability of federal criminal penalties to state programs, when contrasted with the treatment accorded civil penalties, should be read as a mandate for their adoption. We cannot agree. Absent any stronger indication to the contrary, it is patently unwise to assume that Congress intended sharply to limit the preexisting discretion of the Administrator in this area. Criminal penalties, even more than civil penalties, are traditionally under the control of the individual states. It is much more reasonable to assume that the Administrator would have far broader discretion to respect state autonomy in the criminal sector than in the civil area, and that Congress did not intend to divest the Administrator of this authority by its silence.

The rationale EPA offers for its disinclination to adopt the statutory maxima also buttresses this conclusion. The proposed regulations would have required the states to exert enforcement authority virtually identical with the federal, including the same levels of minimum and maximum fines. In final structure, however, the regulations, changed largely in response to state comments, reflect the balancing of uniformity and state autonomy contemplated by the Act:

> The Agency has determined that it is necessary to set specific minimum levels of fines and penalties which States must have the authority to recover in order to ensure effective State enforcement programs. Without such minimum levels, EPA would often be forced to take its own enforcement action in approved States because the State action imposed inadequate penalties. Such EPA action, while available as a backup, is not intended to be relied upon as the prime enforcement mechanism in approved States. Accordingly, the Agency has set minimum levels of fines and penalties. However, it has reduced the levels below those available to EPA based on the large volumes of comments from states requesting such relief.

We will not disturb this "reasonable accommodation of manifestly competing interests," and consequently we uphold the agency's penalty regulations.

[Finding the issue of EPA's veto authority ripe for decision, the court here reviews the legislative history and the structure of the legislation. It concludes:]

EPA persuasively argues that, although the States are to play a large role in administering the Act, section 1342(d)'s veto authority provides considerable evidence that Congress intended federal minima (even if crafted on the basis of BPJ [best professional judgment]) to take precedence. In short, the several States are to be centrally involved in the Act's administration, but their involvement is to be in the achievement of federal goals. By virtue of Congress' policy decision to allow EPA to approve federal permits based on the Administrator's best professional judgment, it is consonant with that policy to allow a similar power with respect to vetoing state permits. Rejection of a state permit in the latter situation represents no more an ad hoc judgment than approval of a federal permit in the former.

We are persuaded that the agency's interpretation is more in keeping with the Act's overall structure. But when the plain language of the Act is not clearly dispositive, and when respectable interpretive arguments are advanced in contradiction to the agency's view, we proceed out of an abundance of caution to Chevron's second step. In short, we cannot say with certainty that Congress' intent requires the interpretation EPA has adopted. To recap: The Act is, to be sure, pro-federalism in its operation; but the very existence of a veto authority cuts against Industry's rather absolutist view that all interpretive calls are to be made in favor of state authority. Still, we cannot say with confidence that Congress' intent is clear on the issue at hand. [The Court concludes by upholding EPA's regulation on its veto power.]

VI. THE ANTIBACKSLIDING CONTROVERSY

Although non-experts such as ourselves may picture water pollution controls becoming steadily more stringent over time, this is apparently not the case. In some instances new restrictions are more lax than old ones covering equivalent effluents. This raises the question of what happens when a permit holder asks, at the time of renewal or reissuance, to get the benefit of the new rule—to "backslide" as the parties call it.

In its original 1979 regulations, 44 Fed. Reg. 32,864, and in its 1984 promulgation, 40 C.F.R. § 122.44(1), EPA prohibited backsliding except under relatively narrow circumstances. In the initial phase of this suit, industry challenged two aspects of this rule. First, it objected to the ban on backsliding from "BPJ" limits (technology-based limitations set, in the absence of a national guideline, according to a permit writer's best professional judgment, pursuant to § 402(a)(2) of the CWA, 33 U.S.C. § 1342(a)(2)) when a more lenient federal guideline had taken effect. It attacked this rule on the grounds that the agency lacked statutory authority and had failed adequately to explain its decision to retain BPJ antibacksliding after proposing to shelve the rule in 1982. Second, industry challenged EPA's authority to prohibit permittees from backsliding from their original "new source performance standards" ("NSPS") under § 306 of the CWA, 33 U.S.C. § 1316. [The Court goes on to uphold EPA's antibacksliding regulation as reasonable and designed to advance the progress of the law.]

VIII. UPSET DEFENSE

A. Ripeness.

The agency's regulations provide an affirmative defense to an action for noncompliance with technology-based permit limitations where the source shows that the non-compliance was due to an "upset." Industry here objects to the agency's failure to extend this defense to noncompliance with water-quality-based limits.

The agency defines an "upset" as "an exceptional incident in which there is a temporary and unintentional noncompliance with permit effluent limitations because of factors beyond the reasonable control of the permittee." 49 Fed. Reg. at 38,038/1. Upsets may be caused by external events, such as power failures or storms, or by unpreventable failures of effluent treatment equipment; noncompliance due to operational error, improperly designed treatment facilities, inadequate treatment facilities, lack of preventive maintenance, or careless or improper operation is excluded. 40 C.F.R. § 122.41(n)(1). To qualify for the defense, a discharger must also perform any required remedial measures. § 122.41(n)(3)(iv).

In 1982 the agency proposed to extend the upset defense to violations of water-quality-based limits. 47 Fed. Reg. at 52,089/1. The defense would be available only to permittees who could demonstrate that despite the upset, instream water quality standards were maintained in all stream segments and for all parameters that could have been affected by the discharge. *Id.* Although EPA did not regard this extension as legally required, *id.* at 52,079/2, it offered the proposal on the view that there was no reason to punish a permittee for an upset if it could prove the absence of injury to water quality standards. *Id.*

In 1984, after reevaluating its proposal in light of various criticisms, the agency concluded that it would be impractical to extend the upset defense to violations of water quality-based effluent limitations. 49 Fed. Reg. at 33,038/2. It reasoned that "although the proposal would seemingly allow permittees to claim an upset defense, the costs, burdens, and technical difficulty of establishing that water quality standards were not violated would make the defense nearly impossible to establish." *Id.* at col. 3. Rather than leave in place an affirmative defense it believed "illusory," it decided to deny extension of the defense and to rely instead on case-by-case prosecutorial discretion. *Id.*

Industry's objections are two-fold. It contends first that the agency is legally required to provide for such a defense, at least where the discharge does not result in the violation of a water quality standard. Second, it maintains that the agency's decision to scrap its 1982 proposal was arbitrary and capricious because, even if the defense (as proposed) could not be met and was therefore "illusory," the agency failed to evaluate potential alternatives. It points to the curiosity of the agency's rejecting the defense on the ground that it was not good enough for the very interests that sought it.

We find the challenge ripe. The agency's position is clearly final. The issues raised may fairly be viewed as ones of law: whether the statute requires the proposed extension of the defense and, if not, whether the agency gave a reasoned explanation of its decision.

The agency's proposed exercise of prosecutorial discretion is not a close enough substitute for the defense to justify deferral of review. The agency would in no way be bound to exercise that discretion favorably. *See* 47 Fed. Reg. at 52,089/1. Moreover, even a firm agency commitment to exercise prosecutorial discretion would leave permittees without an affirmative defense in citizens' enforcement suits under § 505 of the Act, 33 U.S.C. § 1365. Further, unlike the net/gross dispute, the issue cannot be resolved at the time permits are issued; accordingly failure to resolve it now seems more likely to have an impact on dischargers' primary conduct. Even though such matters as "careless or improper operation" will disqualify a source for the defense, it seems probable that its absence will somewhat increase compliance expenditures.

B. Merits.

Lacking infallibility, no pollution control technology works perfectly all of the time. Occasionally, through no fault of the operator, the technology will fail, and pollution levels in the effluent will correspondingly rise. Current EPA regulations provide that when permit effluent limitations based on technological capabilities are briefly exceeded as the result of such an incident, the offending plant will nevertheless be deemed to be in compliance with the Act. This is the so-called "upset defense."

EPA, however, has refused to make this defense available to plants exceeding permit limitations predicated upon water quality standards. In the agency's view, the Act makes an important distinction between technology-based permit limitations and water quality-based permit limitations by requiring water quality standards to be observed at all times in all situations. On the other hand, because the technology used to satisfy water quality-based permit limitations is no more foolproof than that employed to meet technology-based permit limitations, industry petitioners contend that the rationale for the upset defense extends to water quality-based limitations as well. These petitioners further argue that a violation of a water quality-based permit limitation caused by an upset does not translate automatically into a violation of water quality standards in the body of water receiving the effluent. We disagree with industry petitioners that an upset defense for water quality-based permit limitations is required by the Act. We find meritorious, however, their claim that EPA acted arbitrarily when it declined to provide a limited form of the defense.

The need for an upset defense in connection with technology-based permit limitations was first recognized in 1977 by the Ninth Circuit in *Marathon Oil Co. v. EPA*, in connection with offshore oil and gas platforms. Prior to that decision, EPA refused to recognize such a defense under any circumstances. Typically, EPA's practice in formulating an effluent discharge standard for an industry was to collect data from plants in the industry applying the technology at an appropriate level in an exemplary fashion. EPA would then derive from the average of these data a standard for effluent discharge which these plants would be able to meet most of the time. The standard was purposefully not set at a level low enough to accommodate occasional failures of control technology at these plants, as this in EPA's view would have resulted in too lax a standard. This meant that a plant utilizing controls at a suitable level of technology in a commendable manner would invariably be in violation of the standard some of the time.

The court recognized that EPA was in effect holding dischargers to a higher standard of technology than that demanded by the Act:

> The Federal Water Pollution Control Act requires point sources of pollution to utilize the "best practicable control technology currently available" [BPCTCA] prior to 1983. The EPA cannot impose a higher standard without violating the Control Act. And yet the permits as currently written do exactly that. The permits on their face require petitioners to meet the standards 100 percent of the time. But platforms using BPCTCA can only be expected to achieve the effluent standards 97.5 percent of the time in the case of deck drainage and 99 percent of the time in the case of produced water. We, therefore, remand to the EPA with instructions to insert upset provisions into the permits.

Industry petitioners insist that a similar result should obtain in this case. A reasonable reading of the Act, they say, reveals no meaningful distinction between technology-based and water quality-based limitations for this purpose;[169] although limitations of the latter type may be more stringent than those grounded on technology, both are achieved through use of pollution control technology, and therefore are equally subject to upsets. They maintain that once limitations have been set and plant owners deploy appropriate pollution control equipment, they can be held responsible only for violations that could have been prevented.

In a second argument, industry petitioners contend that EPA's regulations obscure an important dissimilarity between permit limitations applicable to an individual plant and standards applicable to a body of water. An upset exceeding permit limitations at a single plant, they submit, does not always lead to infringement of water quality standards for the body of water receiving that plant's effluent. Because EPA has authority to enforce only those water quality permit limitations on effluents that are necessary to preserve water quality standards, they assert that EPA cannot penalize a plant for an upset that does not contravene these standards.

Industry petitioners' argument, however, overlooks the fundamental differences between the two types of permit limitations clearly envisioned by Congress. While Section 301(b)(1)(A) of the Act mandates merely the "application of the best practicable technology currently available," Section 301(b)(1)(C) requires satisfaction of "*any more stringent* limitation . . .

[169] Both the technology-focused provisions of § 301(b)(1)(A) and the water quality-focused language of § 301(b)(1)(C) require satisfaction of "limitations." Industry petitioners reason that because both types of limitations are to be met in the same manner, both types should be subject to the same exceptions. EPA counters with the argument that the water quality provision of § 301(b)(1)(C) calls for observance of "*any more stringent limitation* necessary *to meet* . . . water quality standards," 33 U.S.C. § 1311(b)(1)(A) & (C)(1982) (emphasis added), implying that water quality-standards are stricter and less compromising.

necessary to meet water quality standards." The import of this language is made clear by the legislative history:

> Any point source will be required to have effluent limitations which are consistent with the water quality standards and concomitant load limits for the receiving waters. Thus, if the best practicable control technology is inadequate to meet the water quality standards and load limits, a more stringent requirement would be imposed upon the given point source.

And

> the requirements of H.R. 11896, will assure that water quality standards are met, and that even if such "best practicable control technology currently available" is not sufficient to meet water quality standards, each point source will still be required to be so equipped to further enhance the quality of our waters. In other words we require the upgrading of our waters to a much greater degree than does S. 2770.

This evidence strongly supports EPA's position that Congress did not intend to tie compliance with water quality-based limitations to the capabilities of any given level of technology. A technology-based standard discards its fundamental premise when it ignores the limits inherent in the technology. By contrast, a water quality-based permit limit begins with the premise that a certain level of water quality will be maintained, come what may, and places upon the permittee the responsibility for realizing that goal.

In our view, the Act's differing treatment of water quality and technology-based standards provides persuasive evidence that the broad argument advanced by industry petitioners must fail. Nothing in the Act indicates suitably that individual technological failures may excuse violations of water quality-based limitations. Nor, contrary to industry petitioners' second argument, does the Act mandate that permit limitations properly established in accordance with water quality standards be ignored in favor of a direct measurement of water quality standards instream. The Act does not expressly provide for an upset defense, and, looking to the Act's structure and legislative history, we discern no clear congressional intent to confer one. While at first blush it seems odd to expect dischargers to go beyond the limits of extant technology, it becomes apparent that Congress had a deep respect for the sanctity of water quality standards and a firm conviction of need for technology-forcing measures.

In circumstances where, as here, congressional intent is unclear, it is our duty to uphold an agency's decision representing a permissible interpretation of its governing statute. We are satisfied that it does, and that the EPA's outcome reflects a reasonable accommodation of competing considerations. Indubitably, the Act requires overall water quality to be maintained, and even though an individual permit violation may not always produce an infringement of water quality standards for a particular body of water, the agency is at liberty to make the regulatory judgment not to allow permittees to assert an upset defense. EPA could reasonably view the impact to water quality under such a forgiving regime as potentially dangerous.

This conclusion does not, however, mark the end of the inquiry that we have been summoned to conduct. Although EPA is not statutorily compelled to provide an upset defense, we nevertheless must ask whether EPA acted arbitrarily in declining to allow it. Industry petitioners charge that it did when first it suggested the desirability of an upset defense for water quality permit limitations and later omitted it in the final regulations.

In its 1982 proposed regulations, EPA stated its belief that there is "no reason to penalize a discharger [able to] prove that an upset occurred and that water quality standards were met despite its non-complying [sic] discharge." EPA thus envisioned an extension of the upset defense to water quality-based permit limitations, with the added requirement that the permittee show that water quality standards were observed in all stream segments for all pollutants which the upset could have affected.

EPA never altered its interpretation of the statute that it had the statutory authority to establish an upset defense for water quality-based permit limitations. In its final regulations, however, EPA declined to extend the upset defense to water quality-based limitations, concluding that practical obstacles confronting a permittee attempting to establish the defense would be so great as to render the defense illusory. Our task is to ascertain whether this decision withstands scrutiny.

The scope of judicial review of agency decision making under the arbitrary-and-capricious standard is narrow. Nonetheless, the agency must "examine the relevant data and articulate a satisfactory explanation for its action including a 'rational connection between the facts found and the choice made.' " An agency rule normally must be overturned if the agency has "entirely failed to consider an important aspect of the problem, offered an explanation for its decision that runs counter to the evidence before the agency, or is so implausible that it could not be ascribed to a difference in view or the product of agency expertise." We cannot of course substitute our judgment for that of the agency. "What we do require is that the [agency] come to grips with the obvious ramifications of its approach and address them in a reasoned fashion."

EPA's explanation of its decision to deny an upset defense for water quality permit limitations falls short of these standards. In its final rule, EPA listed the elements it deemed satisfactory proof that water quality standards were maintained during an upset. But then, without discussing any record evidence, EPA noted several problems that would arise naturally during the course of an effort to demonstrate that fact, and summarily dismissed the defense as impracticable. There is no indication in the record before us that EPA made any serious effort to measure the intensity of these problems or to consider possible solutions to them.

EPA's decision rests upon its estimate that the defense would be virtually impossible to establish to its satisfaction. On this account, it felt that even to hold out the defense as a hope would be "illusory." EPA's only argument, in essence, is that the interests of the industry petitioners would be ill-served by the defense because EPA cannot envision circumstances under which petitioners would be able to make it out. Yet EPA offers no more than mere speculation to support its conclusion. These are not adequate grounds upon which to sustain an agency's action. Because it is elementary that agency action may be upheld only on grounds articulated by the agency, EPA must consider its position.

In so ruling, we do not mean to imply that EPA must permit the defense. EPA may decide to disallow it if, for example, it reasonably foresees a waste of agency resources in dealing with a complicated defense that can hope to succeed only rarely. Nor do we dispute EPA's position that it has authority to determine in the first instance what constitutes sufficient proof that water quality was maintained during an upset. Applying its technical expertise, EPA may, for instance, require monitoring schemes after an upset, establish standards for the promptness with which such monitoring must begin, and lay out procedures by which evidence derived from mathematical models may be used to supplement monitoring data. The agency's experience with water quality monitoring programs utilized for other purposes likely would be valuable in application of these techniques. Yet EPA, in delineating its final rule, failed even to mention efforts of this nature.

In summary, the Act, by virtue of the important differences between technology-based and water quality-based standards, does not require EPA to provide for an upset defense to water quality-based permit limitations violations. Because the agency reasonably could decide not to provide the defense, and the Act does not require it, the agency is at liberty to decide in its expert judgment not to allow the defense. Nevertheless, having included water quality-based permit violations in the proposed regulations, we find that EPA acted arbitrarily in eliminating the defense solely on the ground that it would be of little use to dischargers. EPA must therefore conduct further proceedings to determine whether to extend the upset defense to violations of water quality-based permit limitations. The existing upset regulation pertaining to noncompliance with technology-based permit limitations is to remain in force and effect. . . .

In sum, we hold that the following issues are not ripe for review: effluent-related permit conditions; admission of evidence in permit proceedings; three of the four challenges to EPA's regulations permitting the establishment of toxicity-based limits; backsliding from NSPS permit limits; and net/gross limits. On the merits, we find both the state program requirements established by EPA and the veto authority regulations to be within the permissible bounds of the agency's discretion. We reject Industry's argument that EPA lacks statutory authority to frame effluent limits in terms of toxicity; similarly without merit are those procedural challenges to EPA's toxicity regulations that we have concluded are ripe. We also hold that the non-adversary panel procedures permitted by EPA's regulations do not, on their face, infringe permit applicants' procedural rights, nor do the regulations violate the parties' 1982 settlement agreement. We further hold that EPA possessed authority under the Clean Water Act to prohibit backsliding from BPJ permit limits and that its decision to continue to do so in its 1984 regulations was fully explained and supported by the record. We also uphold the agency's regulation providing for continuances of out-of-date permits. We conclude, however, that EPA lacks authority to impose conditions in permits that are unrelated to effluent limits. Finally, we hold that although the CWA does not require EPA to provide for an upset defense to water quality-based permit limitations violations, the agency acted arbitrarily in eliminating that defense from its final regulations. Accordingly, the petitions for review are denied in part and granted in part.

Judgment accordingly.

AMERICAN PAPER INSTITUTE, INC. v. UNITED STATES ENVIRONMENTAL PROTECTION AGENCY

United States Court of Appeals, D.C. Circuit (1993)
996 F.2d 346, 23 ELR 20984

Before WALD, BUCKLEY and WILLIAMS, Circuit Judges.

Opinion for the Court filed by Circuit Judge WALD.

In these consolidated petitions for review, the American Paper Institute, Inc., the USX Corporation, Westvaco Corporation, the City of Akron, Ohio and a host of utilities contest several new Environmental Protection Agency ("EPA") regulations interpreting the Clean Water Act ("CWA" or the "Act") and its amendments. The petitioners primarily take issue with an EPA rule requiring writers of pollution discharge permits to use one of three methods to interpret state water quality standards containing so-called "narrative criteria" (*e.g.*, "no toxics in toxic amounts") so as to create precise chemical-specific effluent limitations in those permits. For the reasons discussed below, we find the regulation in question as well as other, related regulations challenged by petitioners to constitute reasonable, authorized attempts at necessary gap-filling in the CWA statutory scheme. Accordingly, we deny the petitions for review.

I.

In enacting the CWA, Congress sought to "restore and maintain the chemical, physical, and biological integrity of the Nation's waters." 33 U.S.C. § 1251 (a). Toward that end, Congress constructed a system in which discharges of pollutants into the waters of the United States from "point sources"— "discernable, confined and discrete conveyances," 33 U.S.C. § 1362(14), such as factory pipes—are normally permissible only if made pursuant to the terms of a National Pollution Discharge Elimination System ("NPDES") permit. *See* 33 U.S.C. §§ 1311(a), 1342. Under the Act, those licenses must be obtained from the EPA or, in the approximately 40 states the EPA has authorized to administer their own NPDES program, from a designated state agency. *See* 33 U.S.C. § 1342 (a)-(d); *see also* 57 FR 43,733, 43,734 -35 (1992) (listing states with permitting authority). In either case, section 301 of the Act mandates that every permit contain (1) effluent limitations that reflect the pollution reduction achievable by using technologically practicable controls, see 33 U.S.C. § 1311(b)(1)(A), and (2)any more stringent pollutant release limitations necessary for the waterway receiving the pollutant to meet "water quality standards." 33 U.S.C. § 1311(b)(1)(C).

Of primary importance in this case is section 301's second requirement—*i.e.*, that permits contain discharge limitations sufficient to assure that the receiving waterway satisfies water quality standards. Under the CWA, the water quality standards referred to in section 301 are primarily the states' handiwork. State water quality standards in effect at the time of the Act's passage in 1972 were deemed to be the initial water quality benchmarks for CWA purposes (so long as the standards passed an EPA review). *See* 33 U.S.C. § 1313 (a). The states were to revisit and, if necessary, revise those initial standards at least once every three years—a process commonly known as triennial review. *See* 33 U.S.C. § 1313(c)(1). Triennial reviews consist of public hearings in which current water quality standards are examined to assure that they "protect the public health or welfare, enhance the quality of water and serve the purposes" of the Act. 33 U.S.C. § 1313 (c)(2)(A). Additionally, the CWA directs states to consider a variety of competing policy concerns during these reviews, including a waterway's "use and value for public water supplies, propagation of fish and wildlife, recreational purposes, and agricultural, industrial, and other purposes." *Id.*

In accord with Congress' intent to cast the states in the featured role in the promulgation of water quality standards, the EPA may step in and promulgate water quality standards itself only in limited circumstances. It may act only where (1) it determines that a state's proposed new or revised standard does not measure up to CWA requirements and the state refuses to accept EPA-proposed revisions to the standard, or (2) a state does not act to promulgate or update a standard but, in the EPA's view, a new or revised standard is necessary to meet CWA muster. *See* 33 U.S.C. § 1313(c)(3)-(4).

The water quality standards that emerge from this state/federal *pas de deux* have two primary components: designated "uses" for a body of water (*e.g.*, public water supply, recreation, agriculture) and a set of "criteria" specifying the maximum concentration of pollutants that may be present in the water without impairing its suitability for designated uses. *See* 33 U.S.C. § 1313 (c)(2)(A). Criteria, in turn, come in two varieties: specific numeric limitations on the concentration of a specific pollutant in the water (*e.g.*, no more than.05 milligrams of chromium per liter) or more general narrative statements applicable to a wide set of pollutants (*e.g.*, no toxic pollutants in toxic amounts).[170] *See also Environmental Defense Fund, Inc. v. Costle*, 211 U.S. App. D.C. 313, 657 F.2d 275, 288 (D.C. Cir. 1981) (approving the use of narrative criteria). In deciding what criteria suit particular designated uses, the states are not left entirely to their own devices. As required by the CWA, *see* 33 U.S.C. § 1314(a)(1), the EPA has promulgated a set of recommended numeric criteria for certain listed pollutants that the states can, and quite often do, refer to in selecting appropriate criteria. *See* 57 FR 60,848, 60,874 (1992) (EPA notes that states generally rely on recommended criteria in establishing water quality standards).

Of course, the water quality standards by themselves have no effect on pollution; the rubber hits the road when the state-created standards are used

[170] There is one exception to this rule. Under the 1987 amendments to the CWA, discussed *infra* at pages 12-13, states were required to adopt, in their next triennial review, numeric criteria or criteria based on biological monitoring for certain specific toxic pollutants. *See* 33 U.S.C. § 1313(c)(2)(B).

as the basis for specific effluent limitations in NPDES permits. As noted above, once a water quality standard has been promulgated, section 301 of the CWArequires all NPDES permits for point sources to incorporate discharge limitations necessary to satisfy that standard. *See, e.g.*, *Westvaco Corp. v. EPA*, 899 F.2d 1383, 1385 (4th Cir. 1990). On its face, section 301 imposes this strict requirement as to all standards—*i.e.*, permits must incorporate limitations necessary to meet standards that rely on narrative criteria to protect a designated use as well as standards that contain specific numeric criteria for particular chemicals. The distinctive nature of each kind of criteria, however, inevitably leads to significant distinctions in how the two types of criteria are applied to derive effluent limitations in individual permits. When the standard includes numeric criteria, the process is fairly straightforward: the permit merely adopts a limitation on a point source's effluent discharge necessary to keep the concentration of a pollutant in a waterway at or below the numeric benchmark. Narrative criteria, however, present more difficult problems: How is a state or federal NPDES permit writer to divine what limitations on effluent discharges are necessary to assure that the waterway contains, for example, "no toxics in toxic amounts"? Faced with this conundrum, some permit writers threw up their hands and, contrary to the Act, simply ignored water quality standards including narrative criteria altogether when deciding upon permit limitations. *See* Natural Resources Defense Council v. EPA, 915 F.2d 1314, 1317 (9th Cir. 1990). Additionally, when standards containing narrative criteria were enforced—often through the device of whole effluent discharge limitations based on biological monitoring techniques,[171] see 48 Fed. Reg. 51,400, 51,402 (1983) (noting that biological monitoring is one method of testing compliance with narrative criteria)—the lack of standardized procedures made it impossible to even approximate consistency in the translation of criteria into permit limitations. *Cf.* 57 Fed. Reg. 60,848, 60,851 (1992). Moreover, the biological monitoring techniques relied on to enforce narrative criteria were better suited to assuring protection of aquatic life than human health. *See* 131 Cong. Rec. 15,324 (1985) (Statement of Senator Stafford). Thus, in the EPA's view, the lack of a required procedure for developing water-quality-based permit limits from narrative criteria hamstrung attempts to fulfill the statutory requirement that NPDES permits contain limitations necessary to meet all water quality standards. *See* 54 Fed. Reg. 23,868, 23,877 (1989) (noting that the EPA's legal obligation to assure that NPDES permits meet all applicable water quality standards could not be set aside until states promulgate numeric water quality criteria for all their standards).

II.

A. Interpreting Narrative Criteria to Create Chemical-specific Limitations

To address these difficulties, the EPA promulgated the regulation under attack here, 40 C.F.R. § 122.44(d)(1)(vi). That rule requires NPDES permit

[171] Biological monitoring, according to the EPA, includes such devices as "periodic sampling of the ecosystem, trend monitoring and/or periodic bioassays using the effluent." 48 Fed. Reg. at 51,402.

writers to use one of three mechanisms to translate relevant narrative criteria into chemical-specific effluent limitations. Specifically, the regulation provides that a permit writer must establish effluent limits from narrative criteria by using (1) a calculated numeric water quality criterion derived from such tools as a proposed state numeric criterion or an "explicit state policy or regulation interpreting its narrative water quality criterion"; (2) the EPA recommended numeric water quality criteria, but only on a "case-by-case basis" and "supplemented where necessary by other relevant information"; and/or (3) assuming certain conditions are met, limitations on the discharge of an "indicator parameter," *i.e.*, a different pollutant also found in the point source's effluent.

[After a detailed analysis of the regulation, the court upholds EPA's instructions on how to turn narrative criteria into chemical specific limitations. The court upholds the regulation, including the requirement that a federal permit writer is now charged with interpreting state standards].

NOTES

Distinguishing *Crown Simpson Pulp Co. v. Costle*, 642 F.2d 323 (9th Circuit 1981), the D.C. Circuit held in *District of Columbia v. Schramm*, 631 F.2d 854 (D.C. Cir. 1980), that EPA's decision not to veto a state permit is not subject to review under FWPCA. § 509(b)(1)(F), 33 U.S.C. § 1369(b)(1)(F)which authorizes the Court of Appeals to review the Administrator's action "in issuing or denying any permit under section 1342." The Court found, on the basis of the legislative history, that Congress intended to place the main regulatory burden on the states. It further found that the Agency's decision not to review or to veto a state action on an NPDES permit application is "committed to agency discretion by law," 5 U.S.C. § 701(a)(2). Finding that federal court review in such situations would upset the federal-state balance, the Court concluded that such a review is relegated to state law remedies in state courts. To the same effect, see *Montgomery Environmental Coalition v. Costle*, 646 F.2d 568 (D.C. Cir. 1980); *Chesapeake Bay Foundation v. Virginia State Water Control Board*, 495 F. Supp. 1229 (E.D. Va. 1980).

For a major case involving questions of sanctions for permit violations, see *Public Interest Research Group of New Jersey, Inc. v. Powell Duffryn Terminals, Inc.*, 913 F.2d 64, 20 ELR 21216 (3d Cir. 1990), *cert. denied,* 111 S. Ct. 1018 (1991). In this Clean Water Act citizens suit, the district court granted summary judgment to plaintiffs Public Interest Research Group of New Jersey and Friends of the Earth, finding that the defendant, Powell Duffryn Terminals, Inc., had violated its NPDES permit 386 times over a period of six years. After a bench trial on the issue of penalties, the district court enjoined the defendant from violating the terms of its permit and assessed $3,205,000 in civil penalties. On appeal by both parties, the Third Circuit reduced the penalty somewhat and provided that it be paid into the U.S. Treasury. It also limited the injunction to some extent, but affirmed in most major respects.

The CWA provides for another significant permit system in addition to NPDES. Section 404 of the Act provides for "dredge and fill" permits which serve the dual purpose of water pollution control and protection of ecologically crucial wetlands. The issue of wetlands protection, it will be recalled, was involved in *United States v. Holland*, which involved the jurisdictional reach of the 1972 FWPCA. Dredge and fill permits are issued under § 404 by the U.S. Army Corps of Engineers, and their issuance may also be delegated to the states having approved programs, except for discharges into coastal waters. Unlike the issuance of NPDES or SPDES permits which control the discharge of pollutants into publicly controlled waters, dredge and fill permits often involve control of the use of the permittee's own property. Although the law makes significant exception for agricultural or silvicultural activities, it often limits the owners' use of his own property—filling in his own mosquito ditches in the *Holland* case, or by filling in wetlands for a variety of development purposes. The grant of a permit involves notice and opportunity for hearing, and a determination that the disposal of dredged or fill materials will not have enumerated environmentally adverse effects. § 404(c). *See, e.g., Avoyelles Sportsmen's League v. Alexander*, 715 F.2d 897, 13 E.L.R. 20942 (5th Cir. 1983), reversing and affirming in part, 473 F. Supp. 525, 473 F. Supp. 525 (W.D. La. 1979). For general discussion, see F. Grad, Treatise on Environmental Law, § 3.03[6][b].

QUESTIONS

(1) Consider the relationship of the CWA permit requirements to NEPA. Under what circumstances is an EIS (environmental impact statement) necessary for the issuance of a NPDES permit, or for the issuance of a § 404 dredge and fill permit?

(2) *Costle v. Pacific Legal Foundation* defines the public hearing requirements for the issuance of an NPDES permit. Are similar requirements applicable to applications for § 404 permits? *See Buttrey v. United States*, 690 F.2d 1170, 13 E.L.R. 20085 (5th Cir. 1982).

NOTE ON OTHER LAWS WITH WATER POLLUTION CONTROL RELEVANCE

A variety of laws have been enacted by the Congress which affect water quality in a number of ways. Among these is the Resource Conservation and Recovery Act of 1976, discussed in § 4.02, *infra*. The relevance of this solid waste regulatory law lies in its regulation of disposal of solid wastes that will not affect water quality adversely. Another law with direct impact on water quality, which is also similar to the FWPCA in its regulatory scheme, is the Marine Protection, Research and Sanctuaries Act of 1972, 33 U.S.C. § 1401 *et seq.*, frequently referred to as the "Federal Ocean Dumping Act." The act is concerned with dumping of wastes, including solid wastes and sludge, in the ocean. Its regulatory scheme follows the FWPCA in requiring permits for ocean disposal. The act is administered by EPA and the Army Corps of Engineers with surveillance of dumping assigned to the U.S. Coast Guard. *See* § 4.02 *infra*. Other legislation affecting water pollution control includes the Fish and Wildlife Coordination Act, 16 U.S.C. §§ 661 *et seq.;* the Anadromous Fish Conservation Act, 16 U.S.C. §§ 757a *et seq.;* the Wild and Scenic Rivers Act, 16 U.S.C. §§ 1271 *et seq.;* and the Coastal Zone Management Act of 1972, 16 U.S.C. §§ 1451 *et seq.* For a discussion of the relevance of the laws referring to water pollution control, see F. Grad, Treatise on Environmental Law, § 3.03[13].

Another law which deserves special mention is the federal Safe Drinking Water Act, 42U.S.C. §§ 1401 *et seq.* This Act is specially concerned with the protection of public water systems and with the safeguarding of underground sources of drinking water. It is a significant law not only in filling a gap in the scope of federal regulatory powers relating to water pollution but also in marking a significant return to one of the original purposes of the regulation of water quality, namely the protection of public health. For discussion, see F. Grad, Treatise on Environmental Law, § 3.02[13][h].

[x] Protection of Wetlands

[A] Introduction

Section 404 of the Federal Water Pollution Control Actprovides for yet another permit system under the Clean Water Act—for discharge of dredged or fill material. The disposal of dredged or fill material into limited defined areas or bodies of water—or in wetlands—requires a permit system for a different kind of pollutant than those regulated under § 301 of the Act and permitted under the § 402 NPDES system. In addition to functioning as a system of permits for certain discharges and disposals, the section most importantly functions to provide protection for wetlands, a critical and frequently hazarded part of the ecology. The significance of the protections of § 404 has already been referred to in this coursebook in the discussion of the expansion of federal jurisdiction over the waters of the United States in the case of *United States v. Holland,* 373 F. Supp. 665 (M.D. Fla. 1974) at p. 395 *supra.* It will be recalled that the case involved the filling, without a permit, of manmade mosquito control ditches, which formed a part of Papy's Bayou in St. Petersburg, Florida. In effect, the holding read the navigability requirement out of the Federal Water Pollution Control Act.

The permit required under § 404 is jointly administered by the Army Corps of Engineers and EPA. While on its face a system of pollution control, § 404 is overwhelmingly important for the protection of an increasingly scarce environmental resource.

[B] General Definitions and Some Characteristics of Wetlands

Wetlands have been defined as "land where saturation with water is the dominant factor determining the nature of soil development and the types of plant and animal communities living in the soil and on its surface. The single feature that most wetlands share is soil or substrate that is at least periodically saturated with or covered with water."[172] Some wetlands dry out

[172] U.S. Fish & Wildlife Serv., Office of Biological Servs., Washington, DC, Cowardin, Carter, Golet & La Roe, *Classification of Wetland and Deepwater Habitats of the United States* 3 (Dec. 1979).

completely for some time each year. Complexity is a key factor in wetlands systems, which are dynamic and ever changing. They may be subject to cyclical change due to predictable fluctuations in climate, such as rainfall, or the regular rhythmic changes wrought by tidal action.[173]

The wetlands definition adopted by the Environmental Protection Agency (EPA) and the U.S. Army Corps of Engineers (the Corps) for use under the Clean Water Act (CWA)[174] was designed to provide a practical means of delimiting the wetlands system for regulatory purposes. Wetlands, under this definition, are described as:

> [T]hose areas that are inundated or saturated by surface or ground water at a frequency and duration sufficient to support, and that under normal circumstances do support, a prevalence of vegetation typically adapted for life in saturated soil conditions. Wetlands generally include swamps, marshes, bogs and similar areas.[175]

This definition stresses three observable and quantifiable aspects as the dominant elements of a wetland: its hydrological regime, its vegetation, and its soil. The definition recognizes that time is a critical element in a wetlands system, for it is the constant cyclical change which creates the conditions that give rise to the restorative forces at work in wetlands systems.

HAVE ONE OF THESE THREE CRITERIA

[C] Development of Wetlands Protection—Changing Attitudes; Balancing Conflicting Interests

In earlier times, wetlands were regarded as wastelands. In the mid-1800s, Congress passed legislation for the draining and filling of wetlands.[176] Fortunately, not all of the land targeted was "reclaimed," either because some of it was not in fact wetlands or because the states to which wetlands were transferred failed to fulfill their obligations.

Numerous studies chart the loss of wetland habitats in the United States. Wetland areas have been cleared and filled for a variety of purposes, including farmland, housing, airports, and recreational sites. Wetlands have been dramatically altered by developers who have used them to discharge pollutants, or who have mined them, among other things, for forest products and minerals. Similarly, wetlands have been polluted by oil and gas in the course of oil and gas exploration and exploitation. There were about 215 million acres of wetlands when the United States was first settled. There currently remain, exclusive of Alaska, 99 million acres.[177]

The major loss of wetlands has resulted from pursuit of economic interests, and a lack of appreciation for their ecological value and the need to protect

---

[173] These definitions and descriptions are ecological in their approach; the ecological definition tends to be the most comprehensive, since its author is usually searching to capture the living nature of a wetland—its populations of plants and animals interacting within its biological system in each period of climatic change.

[174] 33 U.S.C. § 1215 *et seq.* The primary legislation regulating the use of wetlands is § 404 of the Federal Water Pollution Control Act of 1972.

[175] 33 C.F.R. § 328.3(b) (Corps); 40 C.F.R.§ 232.2(r) (EPA).

[176] The Swamp Land Acts of 1849, 1850 and 1860 granted 15 western states nearly 65 million acres for swamp reclamation.

[177] U.S. Congress, Office of Technology Assessment, OTA-0-206, Washington, DC, *Wetlands: Their Use and Regulation* (Mar. 1984).

them. Wetlands are frequently located on privately owned land, necessitating balancing public interest in the ecological benefits of wetlands with the rights of the private owner. Real estate and business interests vie for construction rights on wetlands, which may be the only open lands remaining in some areas, making their protection even more critical to environmentalists and the public at large.

Certainly, attitudes about wetlands have changed: the road from nuisance swampland to protected "waters of the United States"[178] may almost be seen as dramatic, even though strewn, on occasion, with disheartened environmentalists and/or disappointed citizen advocates. Today, the functions of wetlands are generally understood and valued as fish and wildlife habitats which also serve: to purify water; maintain groundwater supplies; prevent flooding; provide essential wintering, feeding and resting grounds for migratory waterfowl, other water birds and song birds; and provide habitat for threatened and endangered plants and animals.[179] Additionally, studies have revealed some specific economic values of wetlands, including as a food source, spawning ground and nursery for commercially important fish and shellfish, and as a deterrent to flood damage because of wetlands' water-retentive characteristics. Rainwater retained by wetlands often percolates into aquifers, thus replenishing important groundwater supplies. Statutory regulation reflecting these altered attitudes has slowed, but not halted, the loss of the nation's wetlands.[180]

The nature of the shared jurisdiction over wetlands between the Army Corps of Engineers and EPA was ultimately resolved in a Memorandum of Understanding which determined that the Corps was to make the jurisdictional determination, that would be binding on EPA, as to whether a particular area was to be deemed a wetlands. The Corps, however, was required to consult with EPA in making determinations of geographic jurisdiction. EPA moreover has a veto authority under § 404(c) of the Act, and also has the power to promulgate environmental criteria for the issuance of § 404 permits. Some of these issues are reflected in the cases that follow.[181]

[D] Geographic Jurisdiction—Definitional Criteria

Congress, in drafting the Clean Water Act, in large part left to EPA and the Corps the responsibility for establishing by regulation which waters fall within the ambit of § 404. (The CWA limits federal jurisdiction to "navigable waters," which it then defines as "waters of the United States.")[182] Each agency has promulgated regulations[183] defining navigable waters under the

---

[178] Under the CWA, the word "wetlands" is not mentioned, but by an interpretive process wetlands are deemed to be included in the expression "navigable waters" as those two words are defined in the statute, *i.e.*, as "the waters of the United States, including the territorial seas." 33 U.S.C. § 1362(7).

[179] The number of such species relying on wetlands was found to be as high as 20% of those so identified. U.S. Congress, Office of Technology Assessment, OTA-0-206, Washington, DC, *Wetlands: Their Use and Regulation* 56 (Mar. 1984).

[180] *See also* F. Grad, Treatise on Environmental Law, § 3.03[6A][a] and [b].

[181] For a full discussion of the shared jurisdiction referred to, see F. Grad, Treatise on Environmental Law, § 3.03[6A][c].

[182] CWA §§ 404(a), 502(7); 33 U.S.C. §§ 1344(a), 1362(7).

[183] The Corps regulations are found generally at 33 C.F.R. pts. 320-330; EPA regulations are found generally at 40 C.F.R. pts. 230-233.

Clean Water Act; both EPA and the Corps use the same definition. The regulations defined the "waters of the United States" to include (1) the traditionally navigable waters,[184] as well as the following:

(2) All interstate waters, including interstate wetlands;

(3) All other waters such as intrastate lakes, rivers, streams (including intermittent streams), mudflats, sandflats, wetlands, sloughs, prairie potholes, wet meadows, playa lakes, or natural ponds, the use, degradation or destruction of which could affect interstate or foreign commerce;

– 33 CFR ARE USC.
– 40 CFR ARE EPA.

(4) All impoundments of waters otherwise defined as waters of the United States under the definition;

(5) Tributaries of waters identified in the preceding paragraphs;

(6) The territorial seas; and

(7) Wetlands adjacent to waters (other than waters that are themselves wetlands) identified in the preceding paragraphs.[185]

These far-reaching definitions, which include virtually all water bodies in the United States, expressly define waters of the United States to include interstate wetlands, wetlands adjacent to waters other than wetlands, and wetlands within the category of "other waters," degradation of which could affect interstate commerce. This last definition encompasses the so-called isolated wetlands—wetlands which are not adjacent to another body of water. Controversy over inclusion of isolated wetlands within the Corps' regulatory jurisdiction, as well as some other definitional questions relating to adjacency—what kind of barriers defeat (and do not defeat) a finding of adjacency—will be treated more fully below.[186]

Having defined the waters falling within the § 404 program, EPA and the Corps then defined wetlands to be "those areas that are inundated or saturated by surface or ground water at a frequency and duration sufficient to support, and that under normal circumstances do support, a prevalence of vegetation typically adapted for life in saturated soil conditions. Wetlands generally include swamps, marshes, bogs, and similar areas."[187] With the determinants of geographic jurisdiction established by the CWA's two administering agencies, the question, "what is a regulated wetland?" may be answered by determining, first, whether a wetland exists based on its physical characteristics, and second, whether that wetland is a water of the United States as defined under §§ 404(a) and 502(7) of the Clean Water Act.

In addition to the criteria referred to in the regulations, the characterization of an area as wetlands also depends on a variety of physical and

In addition to defining navigable waters, the two agencies' regulations relate to the administration of their regulatory policies in the areas over which they respectively have authority.

[184] "All waters which are currently used, or were used in the past, or may be susceptible to use in interstate or foreign commerce, including all waters which are subject to the ebb and flow of the tide[.]" 33 C.F.R. § 328.3(a)(1)(1992).

[185] 33 C.F.R. § 328.3(a)(2) through (7). Parallel EPA definitions are found in 40 C.F.R. § 232.2(q)(1) through (7).

[186] The term "adjacent" has been defined as "bordering, contiguous, or neighboring. Wetlands separated from other waters of the United States by man-made dikes or barriers, natural river berms, beach dunes and the like are 'adjacent wetlands'." 33 C.F.R. § 328.3(c); 40 C.F.R. § 230.3(b).

[187] 33 C.F.R. § 328.3(b); 40 C.F.R. §§ 230.3(t), 232.3(r).

biological/scientific factors. Wetlands are characterized by particular hydrological characteristics, by certain identifiable plant life, by certain specific characteristics of the soil, as well as by the circumstance that the parcel to be regulated is capable of supporting wetlands vegetation "under normal circumstances."[188] The enormous value of wetlands is reflected in the functions the wetland system fulfills. Tidal wetlands and estuaries, where a stream's fresh water mixes with the salt water of the sea, form a distinct ecosystem in which plants and animals exist with each other and with the nonliving environment in a complex interdependent system. Wetlands provide an important link in the food web and as detritus is carried through the marsh, it is consumed by microorganisms, by fiddler crabs, by the larvae of marsh insects, and by mussels, clams and other creatures which are then ingested by larger animals. The energy from the sun harnessed by marsh vegetation reaches human populations as we consume the oysters and fish which feed in the estuary or on the predators who live in the coastal waters. Wetlands too supply a useful environment for the growth and proliferation of bird life.

Wetlands also serve to provide the natural system in which energy circulates nutrients, in which animals feed on plants and on each other, and in which excess nutrients are washed out to feed organisms which live off shore. One of the primary measures of wetland productivity is fish yield including commercially valuable fish and shellfish.

Wetlands also provide very significant advantages in controlling pollution. They function as a pollution filtration system and as a natural flood control mechanism. Because wetland ecosystems hold nutrients, they simultaneously act as a pollution filtration system for water from such point sources as waste treatment plants, and from such nonpoint sources as runoff from agricultural fields and city streets, which carry a high level of pollutants, including excess levels of nitrogen and phosphorus. As the water circulates through a wetland, the plants take up and use these pollutants as nutrients; there are significant studies that show that heavily polluted water would be clean after passing through two or three miles of swamp forest—without the cost or technological complexity of water purification plants.

Though there is evidence that recent wetlands preservation efforts have significantly reduced the current loss of wetlands, a great many significant wetland losses need to be made up for. Between the mid-1950s and mid-1990s, total U.S. wetlands acreage was reduced from 107.45 million acres to 100.91 million acres. Of course, the more than 7 million acres loss of wetlands in the past 40 years was considerably smaller than the much larger loss of wetlands during the years from 1780 to 1980 when California lost 72% of its wetlands acreage and Colorado lost some 91%.[189]

---

188 33 C.F.R. § 328(b); 40 C.F.R. § 232.2(r). For discussion of these required wetlands characteristics, see F. Grad, Treatise on Environmental Law, § 3.03[6A][d][iii].

189 Council on Environmental Quality, *Along the American River,* Environmental Quality, 1998 report at page 304.

UNITED STATES v. RIVERSIDE BAYVIEW HOMES, INC.

United States Supreme Court (1985)
474 U.S. 121, 106 S. Ct. 455, 88 L. Ed. 2d 419, 16 ELR 20086

WHITE, J., delivered the opinion for a unanimous Court.

This case presents the question whether the Clean Water Act (CWA), 33 U. S. C. § 1251 *et seq.*, together with certain regulations promulgated under its authority by the Army Corps of Engineers, authorizes the Corps to require landowners to obtain permits from the Corps before discharging fill material into wetlands adjacent to navigable bodies of water and their tributaries.

I

The relevant provisions of the Clean Water Act originated in the Federal Water Pollution Control Act Amendments of 1972, 86Stat. 816, and have remained essentially unchanged since that time. Under §§ 301 and 502 of the Act, 33 U.S.C. §§ 1311 and 1362, any discharge of dredged or fill materials into "navigable waters"—defined as the "waters of the United States"—is forbidden unless authorized by a permit issued by the Corps of Engineers pursuant to § 404, 33 U. S. C. § 1344. After initially construing the Act to cover only waters navigable in fact, in 1975 the Corps issued interim final regulations redefining "the waters of the United States" to include not only actually navigable waters but also tributaries of such waters, interstate waters and their tributaries, and nonnavigable intrastate waters whose use or misuse could affect interstate commerce. 40 Fed. Reg. 31320 (1975). More importantly for present purposes, the Corps construed the Act to cover all "freshwater wetlands" that were adjacent to other covered waters. A "freshwater wetland" was defined as an area that is "periodically inundated" and is "normally characterized by the prevalence of vegetation that requires saturated soil conditions for growth and reproduction." 33 C.F.R. § 209.120(d)(2)(h)(1976). In 1977, the Corps refined its definition of wetlands by eliminating the reference to periodic inundation and making other minor changes. The 1977 definition reads as follows:

> "The term 'wetlands' means those areas that are inundated or saturated by surface or ground water at a frequency and duration sufficient to support, and that under normal circumstances do support, a prevalence of vegetation typically adapted for life in saturated soil conditions. Wetlands generally include swamps, marshes, bogs and similar areas." 33 C.F.R. § 323.2(c)(1978).

In 1982, the 1977 regulations were replaced by substantively identical regulations that remain in force today. *See* 33 C.F.R. § 323.2(1985).

Respondent Riverside Bayview Homes, Inc. (hereafter respondent), owns 80 acres of low-lying, marshy land near the shores of Lake St. Clair in Macomb County, Michigan. In 1976, respondent began to place fill materials on its property as part of its preparations for construction of a housing development. The Corps of Engineers, believing that the property was an "adjacent wetland" under the 1975 regulation defining "waters of the United States," filed suit in the United States District Court for the Eastern District of Michigan, seeking to enjoin respondent from filling the property without the permission of the Corps.

The District Court held that the portion of respondent's property lying below 575.5 feet above sea level was a covered wetland and enjoined respondent from filling it without a permit. Civ. No. 77-70041 (Feb. 24, 1977) (App. to Pet. for Cert. 22a); Civ. No. 77-70041 (June 21, 1979) (App. to Pet. for Cert. 32a). Respondent appealed, and the Court of Appeals remanded for consideration of the effect of the intervening 1977 amendments to the regulation. 615 F.2d 1363 (1980). On remand, the District Court again held the property to be a wetland subject to the Corps' permit authority. Civ. No. 77-70041 (May 10, 1981) (App. to Pet. for Cert. 42a).

Respondent again appealed, and the Sixth Circuit reversed. 729 F.2d 391 (1984). The court construed the Corps' regulation to exclude from the category of adjacent wetlands—and hence from that of "waters of the United States"—wetlands that were not subject to flooding by adjacent navigable waters at a frequency sufficient to support the growth of aquatic vegetation. The court adopted this construction of the regulation because, in its view, a broader definition of wetlands might result in the taking of private property without just compensation. The court also expressed its doubt that Congress, in granting the Corps jurisdiction to regulate the filling of "navigable waters," intended to allow regulation of wetlands that were not the result of flooding by navigable waters. Under the court's reading of the regulation, respondent's property was not within the Corps' jurisdiction, because its semiaquatic characteristics were not the result of frequent flooding by the nearby navigable waters. Respondent was therefore free to fill the property without obtaining a permit.

We granted certiorari to consider the proper interpretation of the Corps' regulation defining "waters of the United States" and the scope of the Corps' jurisdiction under the Clean Water Act, both of which were called into question by the Sixth Circuit's ruling. 469 U.S. 1206 (1985). We now reverse.

II

The question whether the Corps of Engineers may demand that respondent obtain a permit before placing fill material on its property is primarily one of regulatory and statutory interpretation: we must determine whether respondent's property is an "adjacent wetland" within the meaning of the applicable regulation, and, if so, whether the Corps' jurisdiction over "navigable waters" gives it statutory authority to regulate discharges of fill material into such a wetland. In this connection, we first consider the Court of Appeals' position that the Corps' regulatory authority under the statute and its implementing regulations must be narrowly construed to avoid a taking without just compensation in violation of the Fifth Amendment. We have frequently suggested that governmental land-use regulation may under extreme circumstances amount to a "taking" of the affected property. *See, e.g.*, *Williamson County Regional Planning Comm'n v. Hamilton Bank*, 473 U.S. 172 (1985); *Penn Central Transportation Co. v. New York City*, 438 U.S. 104 (1978). We have never precisely defined those circumstances, *see id.*, at 123-128; but our general approach was summed up in *Agins v. Tiburon*, 447 U.S. 255, 260 (1980), where we stated that the application of land-use regulations to a particular piece of property is a taking only "if the ordinance does not substantially advance legitimate state interests . . . or denies an owner economically viable use of his land." Moreover, we have made it quite clear that the mere assertion of regulatory jurisdiction by a governmental body does not constitute a regulatory taking. *See Hodel v. Virginia Surface Mining & Reclamation Assn.*, 452 U.S. 264, 293-297 (1981). The reasons are obvious. A requirement that a person obtain a permit before engaging in a certain use of his or her property does not itself "take" the property in any sense: after all, the very existence of a permit system implies that permission may be granted, leaving the landowner free to use the property as desired. Moreover, even if the permit is denied, there may be other viable uses available to the owner. Only when a permit is denied and the effect of the denial is to prevent "economically viable" use of the land in question can it be said that a taking has occurred. If neither the imposition of the permit requirement itself nor the denial of a permit necessarily constitutes a taking, it follows that the Court of Appeals erred in concluding that a narrow reading of the Corps' regulatory jurisdiction over wetlands was "necessary" to avoid "a serious taking problem." 729 F.2d, at 398. We have held that, in general, "[equitable] relief is not available to enjoin an alleged taking of private property for a public use, duly authorized by law, when a suit for compensation can be brought against the sovereign subsequent to a taking." *Ruckelshaus v. Monsanto Co.*, 467 U.S. 986, 1016 (1984) (footnote omitted). This maxim rests on the principle that so long as compensation is available for those whose property is in fact taken, the governmental action is not unconstitutional. *Williamson County, supra*, at 194-195. For precisely the same reason, the possibility that the application of a regulatory program may in some instances result in the taking of individual pieces of property is no justification for the use of narrowing constructions to curtail the program if compensation will in any event be available in those cases where a taking has occurred. Under such circumstances, adoption of a narrowing construction does not constitute avoidance of a constitutional difficulty, *cf. Ashwander v. TVA* , 297 U.S. 288, 341-356 (1936) (Brandeis, J., concurring); it merely frustrates permissible applications of a statute or regulation. Because the Tucker Act, 28 U. S. C. § 1491, which presumptively supplies a means of obtaining compensation for any taking that may occur through the operation of a federal statute, *see Ruckelshaus v. Monsanto Co., supra*, at 1017, is available to provide compensation for takings that may result from the Corps' exercise of jurisdiction over wetlands, the Court of Appeals' fears that application of the Corps' permit program might result in a taking did not justify the court in adopting a more limited view of the Corps' authority than the terms of the relevant regulation might otherwise support.

III

Purged of its spurious constitutional overtones, the question whether the regulation at issue requires respondent to obtain a permit before filling its property is an easy one. The regulation extends the Corps' authority under § 404 to all wetlands adjacent to navigable or interstate waters and their tributaries. Wetlands, in turn, are defined as lands that are "inundated *or saturated* by surface *or ground water* at a frequency and duration sufficient to support, and that under normal circumstances do support, a prevalence of vegetation typically adapted for life in saturated soil conditions." 33 C.F.R. § 323.2(c)(1985) (emphasis added). The plain language of the regulation refutes the Court of Appeals' conclusion that inundation or "frequent flooding" by the adjacent body of water is a *sine qua non* of a wetland under the regulation. Indeed, the regulation could hardly state more clearly that saturation by either surface or ground water is sufficient to bring an area within the category of wetlands, provided that the saturation is sufficient to and does support wetland vegetation.

The history of the regulation underscores the absence of any requirement of inundation. The interim final regulation that the current regulation replaced explicitly included a requirement of "[periodic] inundation." 33 C.F.R. § 209.120(d)(2)(h)(1976). In deleting the reference to "periodic inundation" from the regulation as finally promulgated, the Corps explained that it was repudiating the interpretation of that language "as requiring inundation over a record period of years." 42 Fed. Reg. 37128 (1977). In fashioning its own requirement of "frequent flooding" the Court of Appeals improperly reintroduced into the regulation precisely what the Corps had excised.[190]

Without the nonexistent requirement of frequent flooding, the regulatory definition of adjacent wetlands covers the property here. The District Court found that respondent's property was "characterized by the presence of vegetation that requires saturated soil conditions for growth and reproduction," App. to Pet. for Cert. 24a, and that the source of the saturated soil conditions on the property was ground water. There is no plausible suggestion that these findings are clearly erroneous, and they plainly bring the property within the category of wetlands as defined by the current regulation. In addition, the court found that the wetland located on respondent's property was adjacent to a body of navigable water, since the area characterized by

[190] The Court of Appeals seems also to have rested its frequent-flooding requirement on the language in the regulation stating that wetlands encompass those areas that "under normal circumstances do support" aquatic or semi-aquatic vegetation. In the preamble to the final regulation, the Corps explained that this language was intended in part to exclude areas characterized by the "abnormal presence of aquatic vegetation in a nonaquatic area." 42 Fed. Reg. 37128 (1977). Apparently, the Court of Appeals concluded that the growth of wetlands vegetation in soils saturated by ground water rather than flooded by waters emanating from an adjacent navigable water or its tributaries was "abnormal" within the meaning of the preamble. This interpretation is untenable in light of the explicit statements in both the regulation and its preamble that areas saturated by ground water can fall within the category of wetlands. It would be nonsensical for the Corps to define wetlands to include such areas and then in the same sentence exclude them on the ground that the presence of wetland vegetation in such areas was abnormal. Evidently, the Corps had something else in mind when it referred to "abnormal" growth of wetlands vegetation—namely, the aberrational presence of such vegetation in dry, upland areas.

saturated soil conditions and wetland vegetation extended beyond the boundary of respondent's property to Black Creek, a navigable waterway. Again, the court's finding is not clearly erroneous. Together, these findings establish that respondent's property is a wetland adjacent to a navigable waterway. Hence, it is part of the "waters of the United States" as defined by 33 C.F.R. § 323.2(1985), and if the regulation itself is valid as a construction of the term "waters of the United States" as used in the Clean Water Act, a question which we now address, the property falls within the scope of the Corps' jurisdiction over "navigable waters" under § 404 of the Act.

IV

A

An agency's construction of a statute it is charged with enforcing is entitled to deference if it is reasonable and not in conflict with the expressed intent of Congress. *Chemical Manufacturers Assn. v. Natural Resources Defense Council, Inc.*, 470 U.S. 116, 125 (1985); *Chevron U. S. A. Inc. v. Natural Resources Defense Council, Inc.*, 467 U.S. 837, 842-845 (1984). Accordingly, our review is limited to the question whether it is reasonable, in light of the language, policies, and legislative history of the Act for the Corps to exercise jurisdiction over wetlands adjacent to but not regularly flooded by rivers, streams, and other hydrographic features more conventionally identifiable as "waters."

On a purely linguistic level, it may appear unreasonable to classify "lands," wet or otherwise, as "waters." Such a simplistic response, however, does justice neither to the problem faced by the Corps in defining the scope of its authority under § 404(a) nor to the realities of the problem of water pollution that the Clean Water Act was intended to combat. In determining the limits of its power to regulate discharges under the Act, the Corps must necessarily choose some point at which water ends and land begins. Our common experience tells us that this is often no easy task: the transition from water to solid ground is not necessarily or even typically an abrupt one. Rather, between open waters and dry land may lie shallows, marshes, mudflats, swamps, bogs—in short, a huge array of areas that are not wholly aquatic but nevertheless fall far short of being dry land. Where on this continuum to find the limit of "waters" is far from obvious.

Faced with such a problem of defining the bounds of its regulatory authority, an agency may appropriately look to the legislative history and underlying policies of its statutory grants of authority. Neither of these sources provides unambiguous guidance for the Corps in this case, but together they do support the reasonableness of the Corps' approach of defining adjacent wetlands as "waters" within the meaning of § 404(a). Section 404 originated as part of the Federal Water Pollution Control Act Amendments of 1972, which constituted a comprehensive legislative attempt "to restore and maintain the chemical, physical, and biological integrity of the Nation's waters." CWA § 101, 33U. S. C. § 1251. This objective incorporated a broad, systemic view of the goal of maintaining and improving water quality: as the House Report on the legislation put it, "the word 'integrity' . . . refers to a condition in which the natural structure and function of ecosystems [are] maintained." H. R. Rep. No. 92-911, p. 76 (1972). Protection of aquatic ecosystems, Congress recognized, demanded broad federal authority to control pollution, for "[water] moves in hydrologic cycles and it is essential that discharge of pollutants be controlled at the source." S. Rep. No. 92-414, p. 77 (1972).

In keeping with these views, Congress chose to define the waters covered by the Act broadly. Although the Act prohibits discharges into "navigable waters," see CWA §§ 301(a), 404(a), 502(12), 33 U.S.C. §§ 1311(a), 1344(a), 1362(12), the Act's definition of "navigable waters" as "the waters of the United States" makes it clear that the term "navigable" as used in the Act is of limited import. In adopting this definition of "navigable waters," Congress evidently intended to repudiate limits that had been placed on federal regulation by earlier water pollution control statutes and to exercise its powers under the Commerce Clause to regulate at least some waters that would not be deemed "navigable" under the classical understanding of that term. *See* S. Conf. Rep. No. 92-1236, p. 144 (1972); 118 Cong. Rec. 33756-33757 (1972) (statement of Rep. Dingell).

Of course, it is one thing to recognize that Congress intended to allow regulation of waters that might not satisfy traditional tests of navigability; it is another to assert that Congress intended to abandon traditional notions of "waters" and include in that term "wetlands" as well. Nonetheless, the evident breadth of congressional concern for protection of water quality and aquatic ecosystems suggests that it is reasonable for the Corps to interpret the term "waters" to encompass wetlands adjacent to waters as more conventionally defined. Following the lead of the Environmental Protection Agency, see 38 Fed. Reg. 10834 (1973), the Corps has determined that wetlands adjacent to navigable waters do as a general matter play a key role in protecting and enhancing water quality:

> "The regulation of activities that cause water pollution cannot rely on . . . artificial lines . . . but must focus on all waters that together form the entire aquatic system. Water moves in hydrologic cycles, and the pollution of this part of the aquatic system, regardless of whether it is above or below an ordinary high water mark, or mean high tide line, will affect the water quality of the other waters within that aquatic system.
>
> "For this reason, the landward limit of Federal jurisdiction under Section 404 must include any adjacent wetlands that form the border of or are in reasonable proximity to other waters of the United States, as these wetlands are part of this aquatic system." 42 Fed. Reg. 37128 (1977).

We cannot say that the Corps' conclusion that adjacent wetlands are inseparably bound up with the "waters" of the United States—based as it is on the Corps' and EPA's technical expertise—is unreasonable. In view of the breadth of federal regulatory authority contemplated by the Act itself and the inherent difficulties of defining precise bounds to regulable waters, the Corps' ecological judgment about the relationship between waters and their adjacent wetlands provides an adequate basis for a legal judgment that adjacent wetlands may be defined as waters under the Act.

This holds true even for wetlands that are not the result of flooding or permeation by water having its source in adjacent bodies of open water. The

Corps has concluded that wetlands may affect the water quality of adjacent lakes, rivers, and streams even when the waters of those bodies do not actually inundate the wetlands. For example, wetlands that are not flooded by adjacent waters may still tend to drain into those waters. In such circumstances, the Corps has concluded that wetlands may serve to filter and purify water draining into adjacent bodies of water, see 33 C.F.R. § 320.4(b)(2)(vii)(1985), and to slow the flow of surface runoff into lakes, rivers, and streams and thus prevent flooding and erosion, see §§ 320.4(b)(2)(iv) and (v). In addition, adjacent wetlands may "serve significant natural biological functions, including food chain production, general habitat, and nesting, spawning, rearing and resting sites for aquatic . . . species." § 320.4(b)(2)(i). In short, the Corps has concluded that wetlands adjacent to lakes, rivers, streams, and other bodies of water may function as integral parts of the aquatic environment even when the moisture creating the wetlands does not find its source in the adjacent bodies of water. Again, we cannot say that the Corps' judgment on these matters is unreasonable, and we therefore conclude that a definition of "waters of the United States" encompassing all wetlands adjacent to other bodies of water over which the Corps has jurisdiction is a permissible interpretation of the Act. Because respondent's property is part of a wetland that actually abuts on a navigable waterway, respondent was required to have a permit in this case.

B

Following promulgation of the Corps' interim final regulations in 1975, the Corps' assertion of authority under § 404 over waters not actually navigable engendered some congressional opposition. The controversy came to a head during Congress' consideration of the Clean Water Act of 1977, a major piece of legislation aimed at achieving "interim improvements within the existing framework" of the Clean Water Act. H. R. Rep. No. 95-139, pp. 1-2 (1977). In the end, however, as we shall explain, Congress acquiesced in the administrative construction.

Critics of the Corps' permit program attempted to insert limitations on the Corps' § 404 jurisdiction into the 1977 legislation: the House bill as reported out of committee proposed a redefinition of "navigable waters" that would have limited the Corps' authority under § 404 to waters navigable in fact and their adjacent wetlands (defined as wetlands periodically inundated by contiguous navigable waters). H. R. 3199, 95th Cong., 1st Sess., § 16 (1977). The bill reported by the Senate Committee on Environment and Public Works, by contrast, contained no redefinition of the scope of the "navigable waters" covered by § 404, and dealt with the perceived problem of overregulation by the Corps by exempting certain activities (primarily agricultural) from the permit requirement and by providing for assumption of some of the Corps' regulatory duties by federally approved state programs. S. 1952, 95th Cong., 1st Sess., § 49(b) (1977). On the floor of the Senate, however, an amendment was proposed limiting the scope of "navigable waters" along the lines set forth in the House bill. 123 Cong. Rec. 26710-26711 (1977).

In both Chambers, debate on the proposals to narrow the definition of navigable waters centered largely on the issue of wetlands preservation. *See id.,* at 10426-10432 (House debate); *id.*, at 26710-26729 (Senate debate). Proponents of a more limited § 404 jurisdiction contended that the Corps' assertion of jurisdiction over wetlands and other nonnavigable "waters" had far exceeded what Congress had intended in enacting § 404. Opponents of the proposed changes argued that a narrower definition of "navigable waters" for purposes of § 404 would exclude vast stretches of crucial wetlands from the Corps' jurisdiction, with detrimental effects on wetlands ecosystems, water quality, and the aquatic environment generally. The debate, particularly in the Senate, was lengthy. In the House, the debate ended with the adoption of a narrowed definition of "waters"; but in the Senate the limiting amendment was defeated and the old definition retained. The Conference Committee adopted the Senate's approach: efforts to narrow the definition of "waters" were abandoned; the legislation as ultimately passed, in the words of Senator Baker, "[retained] the comprehensive jurisdiction over the Nation's waters exercised in the 1972 Federal Water Pollution Control Act."[191]

The significance of Congress' treatment of the Corps' § 404 jurisdiction in its consideration of the Clean Water Act of 1977 is twofold. First, the scope of the Corps' asserted jurisdiction over wetlands was specifically brought to Congress' attention, and Congress rejected measures designed to curb the Corps' jurisdiction in large part because of its concern that protection of wetlands would be unduly hampered by a narrowed definition of "navigable waters." Although we are chary of attributing significance to Congress' failure to act, a refusal by Congress to overrule an agency's construction of legislation is at least some evidence of the reasonableness of that construction, particularly where the administrative construction has been brought to Congress' attention through legislation specifically designed to supplant it. *See Bob Jones University v. United States* , 461 U.S. 574, 599-601 (1983); *United States v. Rutherford* , 442 U.S. 544, 554, and n. 10 (1979).

Second, it is notable that even those who would have restricted the reach of the Corps' jurisdiction would have done so not by removing wetlands altogether from the definition of "waters of the United States," but only by restricting the scope of "navigable waters" under § 404 to waters navigable in fact *and their adjacent wetlands.* In amending the definition of "navigable waters" for purposes of § 404 only, the backers of the House bill would have left intact the existing definition of "navigable waters" for purposes of § 301 of the Act, which generally prohibits discharges of pollutants into navigable waters. As the House Report explained: " 'Navigable waters' as used in section 301 includes all of the waters of the United States including their adjacent wetlands." H. R. Rep. No. 95-139, p. 24 (1977). Thus, even those who thought that the Corps' existing authority under § 404 was too broad recognized (1) that the definition of "navigable waters" then in force for both § 301 and § 404 was reasonably interpreted to include adjacent wetlands, (2) that the water quality concerns of the Clean Water Act demanded regulation of at least some discharges into wetlands, and (3) that whatever jurisdiction the Corps would retain over discharges of fill material after passage of the 1977 legislation should extend to discharges into wetlands adjacent to any waters over which

191 123 Cong. Rec. 39209 (1977); *see also id.*, at 39210 (statement of Sen. Wallop); *id.*, at 39196 (statement of Sen. Randolph); *id.*, at 38950 (statement of Rep. Murphy); *id.*, at 38994 (statement of Rep. Ambro).

the Corps retained jurisdiction. These views provide additional support for a conclusion that Congress in 1977 acquiesced in the Corps' definition of waters as including adjacent wetlands.

Two features actually included in the legislation that Congress enacted in 1977 also support the view that the Act authorizes the Corps to regulate discharges into wetlands. First, in amending § 404 to allow federally approved state permit programs to supplant regulation by the Corps of certain discharges of fill material, Congress provided that the States would not be permitted to supersede the Corps' jurisdiction to regulate discharges into actually navigable waters and waters subject to the ebb and flow of the tide, "including wetlands adjacent thereto." CWA § 404(g)(1), 33U. S. C. § 1344(g)(1). Here, then, Congress expressly stated that the term "waters" included adjacent wetlands.[192] Second, the 1977 Act authorized an appropriation of $ 6 million for completion by the Department of Interior of a "National Wetlands Inventory" to assist the States "in the development and operation of programs under this Act." CWA § 208(i)(2), 33U. S. C. § 1288(i)(2). The enactment of this provision reflects congressional recognition that wetlands are a concern of the Clean Water Act and supports the conclusion that in defining the waters covered by the Act to include wetlands, the Corps is "implementing congressional policy rather than embarking on a frolic of its own." *Red Lion Broadcasting Co. v. FCC*, 395 U.S. 367, 375 (1969).

C

We are thus persuaded that the language, policies, and history of the Clean Water Act compel a finding that the Corps has acted reasonably in interpreting the Act to require permits for the discharge of fill material into wetlands adjacent to the "waters of the United States." The regulation in which the Corps has embodied this interpretation by its terms includes the wetlands on respondent's property within the class of waters that may not be filled without a permit; and, as we have seen, there is no reason to interpret the regulation more narrowly than its terms would indicate. Accordingly, the judgment of the Court of Appeals is

Reversed.

---

[192] To be sure, § 404(g)(1) does not conclusively determine the construction to be placed on the use of the term "waters" elsewhere in the Act (particularly in § 502(7), which contains the relevant definition of "navigable waters"); however, in light of the fact that the various provisions of the Act should be read *in pari materia*, it does at least suggest strongly that the term "waters" as used in the Act does not necessarily exclude "wetlands."

BERSANI v. UNITED STATES ENVIRONMENTAL PROTECTION AGENCY

United States Court of Appeals, Second Circuit (1988)
850 F.2d 36, 18 ELR 20874

TIMBERS, Circuit Judge

Appellants John A. Bersani, the Pyramid Companies . . . appeal from a judgment entered October 23, 1987 in the Northern District of New York, Thomas J. McAvoy, District Judge, granting summary judgment in favor of appellees, the United States Environmental Protection Agency ("EPA"), the United States Army Corps of Engineers (the "Corps") . . . and denying Pyramid's motion for summary judgment. *Bersani v. United States EPA*, 674 F. Supp. 405 (N.D.N.Y. 1987).

This case arises out of Pyramid's attempt to build a shopping mall on certain wetlands in Massachusetts known as Sweedens Swamp. Acting under the Clean Water Act, 33U.S.C. § 1251 *et seq.* (1982), EPA vetoed the approval by the Corps of a permit to build the mall because EPA found that an alternative site had been available to Pyramid at the time it entered the market to search for a site for the mall. The alternative site was purchased later by another developer and arguably became unavailable by the time Pyramid applied for a permit to build the mall.

On appeal, the thrust of Pyramid's argument is a challenge to what it calls EPA's "market entry" theory, *i.e.*, the interpretation by EPA of the relevant regulation, which led EPA to consider the availability of alternative sites at the time Pyramid entered the market for a site, instead of at the time it applied for a permit. Pyramid argues principally (1) that the market entry approach is contrary to the regulatory language and past practice; and (2) that since the Corps, another agency which was jointly responsible with EPA for administering the program in question, interpreted the pertinent regulation in a different way than EPA had, and since the market entry issue does not involve environmental expertise, this Court should not defer to EPA's interpretation of the regulation. Other subordinate claims are raised by appellants as well as by two intervenors and the amicus curiae.

We hold (1) that the market entry theory is consistent with both the regulatory language and past practice; (2) that EPA's interpretation, while not necessarily entitled to deference, is reasonable; and (3) that EPA's application of the regulation is supported by the administrative record. We agree with the district court's conclusion that EPA's findings were not arbitrary and capricious. We also hold that Pyramid's other arguments, and the arguments of one intervenor and the amicus, lack merit.

We affirm.

I.

We shall summarize only those facts and prior proceedings believed necessary to an understanding of the issues raised on appeal.

A. Statutory and Regulatory Framework

One of the sections of the Clean Water Act (the "Act") relevant to the instant case is § 301(a), 33 U.S.C. § 1311(a)(1982), which prohibits the discharge of any pollutant, including dredged or fill materials, into the nation's navigable waters, except in compliance with the Act's provisions, including § 404. It is undisputed that Sweedens Swamp is a "navigable water," as defined in 33 U.S.C. § 1362(1982), and that Pyramid's shopping center proposal will involve the discharge of dredged or fill materials.

Section 404 of the Act, 33 U.S.C. § 1344(1982 & Supp. III 1985), focusing on dredged or fill materials, provides that the United States Army and EPA will share responsibility for implementation of its provisions. EPA and the Corps also share responsibility for enforcing the Act. 33 U.S.C. §§ 1311(1982), 1319 (1982), 1344(n) and (s) (1982). Section 404(a) authorizes the Secretary of the Army, acting through the Corps, to issue permits for the discharge of dredged or fill materials at particular sites. 33 U.S.C. § 1344(a)(1982). Section 404(b) provides that, subject to § 404(c), the Corps must base its decisions regarding permits on guidelines (the "404(b)(1) guidelines") developed by EPA in conjunction with the Secretary of the Army. 33 U.S.C. § 1344(b)(Supp. III 1985).

The 404(b)(1) guidelines, published at 40 C.F.R. Part 230 (1987), are regulations containing the requirements for issuing a permit for discharge of dredged or fill materials. 40 C.F.R. § 230.10(a)[193] covers "non-water dependent activities" (*i.e.*, activities that could be performed on non-wetland sites, such as building a mall) and provides essentially that the Corps must determine whether an alternative site is available that would cause less harm to the wetlands. Specifically, it provides that "no discharge of dredged or fill

---

193 Section 230.10(a)(2) and (3) provide:

"(a) Except as provided under section 404(b)(2) [pertaining to navigation] no discharge of dredged or fill material shall be permitted if there is a practicable alternative to the proposed discharge which would have less adverse impact on the aquatic ecosystem, so long as the alternative does not have other significant adverse environmental consequences. . . . .

(2) An alternative is practicable if it is available and capable of being done after taking into consideration cost, existing technology, and logistics in light of overall project purposes. If it is otherwise a practicable alternative, an area not presently owned by the applicant which could reasonably be obtained, utilized, expanded or managed in order to fulfill the basic purpose of the proposed activity may be considered.

(3) Where the activity associated with a discharge which is proposed for a special aquatic site [defined in Subpart E to include wetlands] does not require access or proximity to or siting within the special aquatic site in question to fulfill its basic purpose (*i.e.*, is not 'water dependent'), practicable alternatives that do not involve special aquatic sites are presumed to be available, unless clearly demonstrated otherwise. In addition, where a discharge is proposed for a special aquatic site, all practicable alternatives to the proposed discharge which do not involve a discharge into a special aquatic site are presumed to have less adverse impact on the aquatic ecosystem, unless clearly demonstrated otherwise."

material shall be permitted if there is a practicable alternative" to the proposal that would have a "less adverse impact" on the "aquatic ecosystem." It also provides that a practicable alternative may include "an area not presently owned by the applicant which could reasonably be obtained, utilized, expanded or managed in order to fulfill the basic purpose of the proposed activity." 40 C.F.R. 230.10(a)(2). It further provides that, "unless clearly demonstrated otherwise," practicable alternatives are (1) "presumed to be available" and (2) "presumed to have less adverse impact on the aquatic ecosystem." 40 C.F.R. 230.10(a)(3). Thus, an applicant such as Pyramid must rebut both of these presumptions in order to obtain a permit. Sections 230.10(c) and (d) require that the Corps not permit any discharge that would contribute to significant degradation of the nation's wetlands and that any adverse impacts must be mitigated through practicable measures.

In addition to following the 404(b)(1) guidelines, the Corps may conduct a "public interest review." 33 C.F.R. § 320.4(1987). This public interest review is not mandatory under § 404, unlike consideration of the 404(b) guidelines. In a public interest review, the Corps' decision must reflect the "national concern" for protection and use of resources but must also consider the "needs and welfare of the people." *Id.*

Under § 404(c) of the Act, 33 U.S.C. § 1344(c), EPA has veto power over any decision of the Corps to issue a permit. It is this provision that is at the heart of the instant case.

Specifically, § 404(c) provides that the Administrator of EPA may prohibit the specification of a disposal site "whenever he determines, after notice and opportunity for public hearings, that the discharge of materials into such area will have an unacceptable adverse effect" on, among other things, wildlife.[194] An "unacceptable adverse effect" is defined in 40 C.F.R. § 231.2(e)as an effect that is likely to result in, among other things, "significant loss of or damage to . . . wildlife habitat." The procedure under § 404(c) begins with the Regional Administrator ("RA") who, under § 231.3(a), must notify the Corps and the applicant when it is possible he will find an "unacceptable adverse effect." If within 15 days the applicant fails to satisfy the RA that no such effect will occur, the RA must publish his proposed determination to veto the grant of a permit. A period for public comment and an optional public hearing follows, after which the RA either withdraws the determination or submits a recommended determination to the national Administrator, whose decision to affirm, modify or rescind the RA's recommendation is the final determination of EPA for purposes of judicial review. The burden of proving that the

[194] Section 404(c), 33 U.S.C. § 1344(c), authorizes the Administrator:

> "to prohibit the specification (including the withdrawal of specification) of any defined area as a disposal site, and he is authorized to deny or restrict the use of any defined area for specification (including the withdrawal of specification) as a disposal site, whenever he determines, after notice and opportunity for public hearings, that the discharge of such materials into such area will have an unacceptable adverse effect on municipal water supplies, shellfish beds and fishery areas (including spawning and breeding areas), wildlife, or recreational areas. Before making such determination, the Administrator shall consult with the Secretary. The Administrator shall set forth in writing and make public his findings and his reasons for making any determination under this subsection."

discharge will have an "unacceptable adverse effect" is on EPA, 45 Fed. Reg. 85,336, 85,338 (1980); 44 Fed. Reg. 58,076, 58,080 (1979).

In short, both EPA and the Corps are responsible for administering the program for granting permits for discharges of pollutants into wetlands under § 404. The Corps has the authority to issue permits following the 404(b)(1) guidelines developed by it and EPA; EPA has the authority under § 404(c) to veto any permit granted by the Corps. The Corps processes about 11,000 permit applications each year. EPA has vetoed five decisions by the Corps to grant permits.

B. Factual Background of the Sweedens Swamp Project

Sweedens Swamp is a 49.5 acre wetland which is part of an 80 acre site near Interstate 95 in South Attleboro, Massachusetts. Although some illegal dumping and motorbike intrusions have occurred, these activities have been found to have had little impact on the site which remains a "high-quality red maple swamp" providing wildlife habitat and protecting the area from flooding and pollution.

The effort to build a mall on Sweedens Swamp was initiated by Pyramid's predecessor, the Edward J. DeBartolo Corporation ("DeBartolo"). DeBartolo purchased the Swamp some time before April 1982. At the time of this purchase an alternative site was available in North Attleboro (the "North Attleboro site"). Since Massachusetts requires state approval (in addition to federal approval) for projects that would fill wetlands, DeBartolo applied to the Massachusetts Department of Environmental Quality Engineering ("DEQE") for permission to build on Sweedens Swamp. DEQE denied the application in April 1982.

Pyramid took over the project in 1983 while the appeal of the DEQE denial was pending . . . .

One of the key issues in dispute in the instant case is just when did Pyramid begin searching for a suitable site for its mall. EPA asserts that Pyramid began to search in the Spring of 1983. Pyramid asserts that it began to search several months later, in September 1983. The difference is crucial because on July 1, 1983—a date between the starting dates claimed by EPA and Pyramid—a competitor of Pyramid, the New England Development Co. ("NED"), purchased options to buy the North Attleboro site. This site was located upland and could have served as a "practicable alternative" to Sweedens Swamp, if it had been "available" at the relevant time. Thus, if the relevant time to determine whether an alternative is "available" is the time the applicant is searching for a site (an issue that is hotly disputed), and if Pyramid began to search at a time before NED acquired options on the North Attleboro site, there definitely would have been a "practicable alternative" to Sweedens Swamp, and Pyramid's application should have been denied. On the other hand, if Pyramid did not begin its search until after NED acquired options on the North Attleboro site, then the site arguably was not "available" and the permit should have been granted. Of course it also is possible that the North Attleboro site remained "available" after NED's acquisition of the options, since Pyramid arguably could have purchased the options from NED.

Moreover, since the North Attleboro site indisputably was "available" when Pyramid's predecessor, DeBartolo, purchased Sweedens Swamp, one might argue, as EPA does, that Pyramid should be held to stand in its predecessor's shoes. The district court apparently agreed with Pyramid on the issue of when Pyramid entered the market, stating that "Pyramid initially became interested in developing a shopping mall in the Attleboro area in September 1983." *Bersani v. EPA*, 674 F. Supp. 405, 409 (N.D.N.Y. 1987).

In December 1983, Pyramid purchased Sweedens Swamp from DeBartolo. In August 1984, Pyramid applied under § 404(a) to the New England regional division of the Corps (the "NE Corps") for a permit. It sought to fill or alter 32 of the 49.6 acres of the Swamp; to excavate nine acres of uplands to create artificial wetlands; and to alter 13.3 acres of existing wetlands to improve its environmental quality. Later Pyramid proposed to mitigate the adverse impact on the wetlands by creating 36 acres of replacement wetlands in an off-site gravel pit.

During the review of Pyramid's application by EPA, by the Fish and Wildlife Service ("FWS") and by the Corps, Pyramid submitted information on "practicable alternatives," especially the North Attleboro site. In rejecting that site as an alternative, Pyramid asserted that building a mall there was not feasible, not that the site was unavailable. In the words of the district court, Pyramid claimed that

> "the site lacked sufficient traffic volume and sufficient access from local roads, potential department store tenants had expressed strong doubts about the *feasibility* of the site and previous attempts to develop the site had met with strong resistance from the surrounding community."

Bersani, supra, 674 F. Supp. at 410 (emphasis added).

In November 1984, EPA and FWS submitted official comments to the N.E. Corps recommending denial of the application because Pyramid's proposal was inconsistent with the 404(b)(1) guidelines. Pyramid had failed (1) to overcome the presumption of the availability of alternatives and (2) to mitigate adequately the adverse impact on wildlife. EPA threatened a § 404(c) review. Pyramid then proposed to create additional artificial wetlands at a nearby upland site, a proposal it eventually abandoned.

In January 1985, the N.E. Corps hired a consultant to investigate the feasibility of Sweedens Swamp and the North Attleboro site. The consultant reported that either site was feasible but that from a commercial standpoint only one mall could survive in the area. On February 19, 1985, the N.E. Corps advised Pyramid that denial of its permit was imminent. On May 2, 1985, the N.E. Corps sent its recommendation to deny the permit to the national headquarters of the Corps. Although the N.E. Corps ordinarily makes the final decision on whether to grant a permit, see 33 C.F.R. § 325.8(1982), in the instant case, because of widespread publicity, General John F. Wall, the Director of Civil Works at the national headquarters of the Corps, decided to review the N.E. Corps' decision. Wall reached a different conclusion. He decided to grant the permit after finding that Pyramid's offsite mitigation proposal would reduce the adverse impacts sufficiently to allow the "practicable alternative" test to be deemed satisfied. He stated:

> "In a proper case, mitigation measures can be said to reduce adverse impacts of a proposed activity to the point where there is no 'easily identifiable difference in impact' between the proposed activity (including mitigation) versus the alternatives to that activity."

Although he did not explicitly address the issue, Wall apparently assumed that the relevant time to determine whether there was a practicable alternative was the time of the application, not the time the applicant entered the market. In other words, Wall appears to have assumed that the market entry theory was not the correct approach. For example, while addressing the traditional "practicable alternatives" analysis as an alternative ground for his decision, Wall found that the North Attleboro site was unavailable "because it has been optioned by another developer." Since the site was *not* optioned at the time EPA argues Pyramid entered the market, this language suggests (to Pyramid at least) that Wall could not have been employing the market entry approach.

On May 31, 1985, Wall ordered the N.E. Corps to send Pyramid, EPA and FWS a notice of its intent to grant the permit. The N.E. Corps complied on June 28, 1985.

On July 23, 1985, EPA's RA initiated a § 404(c) review of the Corps' decision. Following the procedure set forth in 40 C.F.R. Part 231 (discussed above), EPA published notice of its intent to prohibit the project in the Federal Register; held a public hearing on September 26, 1985; and permitted a period for public comment which closed on October 4, 1985. A second hearing was held on November 18, 1985.

On March 4, 1986, the RA recommended that EPA veto the permit because of adverse impacts on wildlife and available "practicable alternatives." In particular, the RA found that Pyramid had not overcome the presumption that an alternative existed, in part because Pyramid had failed to provide information on the availability of the North Attleboro site. After first refusing to provide the information, Pyramid later had claimed "there is no further or more detailed information. It simply does not exist." The RA alternatively reasoned that the North Attleboro site had been available to DeBartolo, and that EPA should attribute this availability to Pyramid because Pyramid had benefitted from DeBartolo's application for state approval.

On May 13, 1986, EPA issued its final determination, which prohibited Pyramid from using Sweedens Swamp. It found (1) that the filling of the Swamp would adversely affect wildlife; (2) that the North Attleboro site could have been available to Pyramid at the time Pyramid investigated the area to search for a site; (3) that considering Pyramid's failure or unwillingness to provide further materials about its investigation of alternative sites, it was uncontested that, at best, Pyramid never checked the availability of the North Attleboro site as an alternative; (4) that the North Attleboro site was feasible and would have a less adverse impact on the wetland environment; and (5) that the mitigation proposal did not make the project preferable to other alternatives because of scientific uncertainty of success. In the second of these findings, EPA used what Pyramid calls the "market entry" approach.

On July 1, 1986, Pyramid commenced the instant action in the district court to vacate EPA's final determination as arbitrary and capricious. After the parties filed cross-motions for summary judgment, the newspapers reported that Pyramid intended to enter a joint venture with NED to build a mall at the North Attleboro site. Affidavits submitted concerning this development did not indicate whether Pyramid planned to continue the Sweedens Swamp project. Since the joint venture agreement was still in draft form, EPA did not take the position that the case was moot.

On October 6, 1987, the court granted EPA's motion for summary judgment. The court stated that, with regard to the market entry theory, EPA's interpretation of its regulations was entitled to deference. This appeal followed.

For the reasons which follow, we affirm.

II.

One of Pyramid's principal contentions is that the market entry approach is inconsistent with both the language of the 404(b)(1) guidelines and the past practice of the Corps and EPA.

A.

With regard to the language of the regulations, Pyramid reasons that the 404(b)(1) guidelines are framed in the present tense, while the market entry approach focuses on the past by considering whether a practicable alternative was available at the time the applicant entered the market to search for a site. To support its argument that the 404(b)(1) guidelines are framed in the present tense, Pyramid quotes the following language:

> "An alternative is practicable if it is available . . . . If it is otherwise a practicable alternative, an area not *presently* owned by the applicant which could reasonably be obtained, utilized, expanded or managed in order to fulfill the basic purpose of the proposed activity *may be* considered."

40 C.F.R. § 230.10(a)(2)(emphasis added). It then argues that EPA says "is" means "was." It cites *Gwaltney of Smithfield v. Chesapeake Bay Foundation*, 484 U.S. 49, 108 S. Ct. 376, 381, 98 L. Ed. 2d 306 (1987), to indicate that the Supreme Court believes that the "most natural" reading of present tense language in § 505(a) of the Act refers only to the present and future.

While this argument has a certain surface appeal, we are persuaded that it is contrary to a common sense reading of the regulations; that it entails an overly literal and narrow interpretation of the language; and that it creates requirements not intended by Congress.

First, while it is true that the language is in the present tense, it does not follow that the "most natural" reading of the regulations would create a time-of-application rule. As EPA points out, "the regulations do not indicate *when* it is to be determined whether an alternative 'is' available," (emphasis in original) *i.e.*, the "present" of the regulations might be the time the application is submitted; the time it is reviewed; or any number of other times. Based upon a reading of the language in the context of the controlling statute and the regulations as a whole, moreover, we conclude that when the agencies drafted the language in question they simply were not thinking of the specific issues raised by the instant case, in which an applicant had available alternatives at the time it was selecting its site but these alternatives had evaporated by the time it applied for a permit. We therefore agree with the district court that the regulations are essentially silent on the issue of timing and that it would be appropriate to consider the objectives of the Act and the intent underlying the promulgation of the regulations. *Bersani, supra*, 674 F. Supp. at 412.

Second, as EPA has pointed out, the preamble to the 404(b)(1) guidelines states that the purpose of the "practicable alternatives" analysis is "to recognize the special value of wetlands and to avoid their unnecessary destruction, particularly where practicable alternatives *were* available in non-aquatic areas to achieve the basic purpose of the proposal." 45 Fed. Reg. 85,338 (1980) (emphasis added). In other words, the purpose is to create an incentive for developers to avoid choosing wetlands when they could choose an alternative upland site. Pyramid's reading of the regulations would thwart this purpose because it would remove the incentive for a developer to search for an alternative site at the time such an incentive is needed, *i.e.*, at the time it is making the decision to select a particular site. If the practicable alternatives analysis were applied to the time of the application for a permit, the developer would have little incentive to search for alternatives, especially if it were confident that alternatives soon would disappear. Conversely, in a case in which alternatives were not available at the time the developer made its selection, but became available by the time of application, the developer's application would be denied even though it could not have explored the alternative site at the time of its decision.

Pyramid attacks this reasoning by arguing that few developers would take the risk that an available alternative site would become unavailable and that EPA's reading improperly considers the motives and subjective state of mind of the applicant. These arguments are wide of the mark. Whether most real-life developers would take such a risk is irrelevant. The point is that Pyramid's time-of-application theory is completely at odds with the expressed intent of the regulations to provide an incentive to avoid choosing wetlands. Similarly, EPA's interpretation does not require courts to investigate the subjective state of mind of a developer. EPA discusses state-of-mind issues only because it is discussing the *purpose* behind the regulations, which is concerned with incentives, and thus in fact is indirectly concerned with the developer's state of mind.

In short, we conclude that a common-sense reading of the statute can lead only to the use of the market entry approach used by EPA.

. . . .

III.

We turn next to the issue of whether EPA's interpretation of the 404(b)(1) guidelines is entitled to the deference usually accorded an agency with regard to its interpretation of regulations it is charged with administering, see *EPA v. National Crushed Stone Ass'n*, 449 U.S. 64, 83, 66 L. Ed. 2d 268, 101 S. Ct. 295 (1980), and participated in formulating. *See also United States v.*

Hescorp, Heavy Equip. Sales Corp., 801 F.2d 70, 76 (2 Cir.), cert. denied, 479 U.S. 1018, 107 S. Ct. 672, 93 L. Ed. 2d 723 (1986). The district court implied in its decision that it was according EPA such deference in examining its market entry approach.

Pyramid contends that such deference was unwarranted because two agencies—EPA and the Corps—developed and administered the regulations, and the Corps reached a different conclusion from that of EPA on the market entry issue.

Even if we are not thoroughly persuaded that EPA's interpretation was entitled to deference, however, we nevertheless conclude that the district court's decision in its favor must be upheld. As Pyramid itself points out (to the detriment of its argument), the issue of deference is separate from the issue of the standards of review of the district court and of our Court.

On appeal, we must subject the district court's judgment to plenary review . . . The standard of review for the district court in this case is that the court shall set aside EPA's findings, conclusions or actions only if they are "arbitrary, capricious, an abuse of discretion, or otherwise not in accordance with law." Administrative Procedure Act § 10(e), 5 U.S.C. § 706(2)(A)(1982). As stated by the Supreme Court in *Motor Vehicle Mfrs. Ass'n v. State Farm Mut. Auto. Ins. Co.*, 463 U.S. 29, 77 L. Ed. 2d 443, 103 S. Ct. 2856 (1983),

> "A reviewing court may not set aside an agency rule that is rational, based on consideration of the relevant factors, and within the scope of the authority delegated to the agency by the statute . . . . The scope of review under the 'arbitrary and capricious' standard is narrow and a court is not to substitute its judgment for that of the agency. Nevertheless, the agency must examine the relevant data and articulate a satisfactory explanation for its action including a 'rational connection between the facts found and the choice made.' "

Applying these standards, we are convinced that EPA's market entry interpretation was reasonable, and therefore was neither "arbitrary and capricious" nor "not in accordance with law." We therefore hold that the district court correctly found that EPA's interpretation of the regulations was reasonable.

IV.

. . . .

We affirm the district court's decision in all respects.

V.

To summarize:

We hold (1) that the market entry theory is consistent with both the regulatory language and past practice; (2) that EPA's interpretation, while not necessarily entitled to deference, is reasonable and its application of its rule is supported by the record; and (3) that Pyramid's other arguments lack merit.

Affirmed.

Dissent by PRATT, Circuit Judge, omitted.

AVOYELLES SPORTSMEN'S LEAGUE, INC. v. MARSH

United States Court of Appeals, Fifth Circuit (1983)
715 F.2d 897, 13 ELR 20942

Before CLARK, Chief Judge, THORNBERRY and RANDALL, Circuit Judges.

RANDALL, Circuit Judge:

This is an appeal from a district court judgment that enjoined the private defendants from any additional clearing, except by permit under 33 U.S.C. § 1344(Supp. V 1981), of certain lands determined by the district court to be wetlands. The federal defendants contend that the district court should have reviewed the Environmental Protection Agency's ("EPA") final wetlands determination (attached as an appendix to this opinion) on the basis of the administrative record, and that the court erred in adopting its own wetlands determination instead of reviewing the agency's determination under the arbitrary and capricious standard. The federal defendants also dispute the district court's conclusion that the mere removal of vegetation from wetlands constitutes a discharge of a pollutant under section 301(a) of the Clean Water Act("CWA"), 33 U.S.C. § 1311(a)(1976). The private defendants contest the validity of the district court's determination that approximately ninety percent of their land is a wetland, as well as the court's conclusion that their landclearing activities fall under the CWA's prohibition on the discharge of pollutants into waters of the United States.

For the reasons set forth below, to the extent that the district court's decision that ninety percent of the Lake Long Tract is a wetland is inconsistent with the EPA's determination, the decision of the district court is reversed. The court's determination that the private defendants' actual landclearing activities require permits is affirmed.

I. FACTUAL AND PROCEDURAL BACKGROUND.

This case concerns an approximately 20,000 acre tract of land (the "Lake Long Tract") in Avoyelles Parish, Louisiana. The tract lies within the Bayou Natchitoches basin, an area of approximately 140,000 acres, which, along with the Ouachita, Black and Tensas river basins, makes up the Red River backwater area. The Bayou Natchitoches basin is subject to flooding during the spring months, and it experiences an average rainfall of sixty inches per year.

Much of the basin had been cleared of forest before the private defendants began their landclearing activities, but 80,000 acres were still forested. The Lake Long Tract made up a quarter of this forested area. The topography of the tract itself is uneven, resulting in some areas with permanent water impoundments and other drier areas that support a variety of plant species.

The private defendants own the Lake Long Tract. They decided that the land could be put to agricultural use, specifically soybean production. Consequently, they began a program of large-scale deforestation in June of 1978. Using bulldozers with shearing blades that "floated" along the ground, the defendants cut the timber and vegetation at or just above ground level. The trees were then raked into windrows, burned, and the stumps and ashes were disced into the ground by other machinery. The shearing and raking caused some leveling of the tract, and the defendants dug one drainage ditch.

On August 25, 1978, the Vicksburg District of the Army Corps of Engineers ordered defendant Prevot to halt his activities pending a wetlands determination by the Corps. Thereafter, Dr. Donald G. Rhodes, an expert consultant employed by the Corps, undertook a comprehensive vegetative mapping of the Lake Long Tract and determined that thirty-five percent of it was a wetland. In October, 1978, the Fish and Wildlife Service wrote a letter to the Corps stating that the Service believed that the entire tract was a wetland. After Dr. Rhodes had made his determination, the landowners resumed their activities on the portion of the tract that the Corps had not designated as a wetland.

On November 8, 1978, the plaintiffs brought this citizens' suit against a number of Corps and EPA officials, as well as against the private landowners. The plaintiffs claimed, inter alia, that the landclearing activities would result in the discharge of dredged and fill material into the waters of the United States in violation of sections 301(a) and 404 of the CWA, 33 U.S.C. §§ 1311, 1344(1976 & Supp. V 1981), and also result in the discharge of pollutants into the waters of the United States in violation of section 402 of the CWA, 33 U.S.C. § 1342(1976 & Supp. V 1981). The plaintiffs requested a declaration that the tract was a wetland within the scope of the CWA, that the private defendants could not engage in their landclearing activities without obtaining a permit from the EPA or the Corps, and that the federal defendants had failed to exercise their "mandatory duty" to designate the tract a wetland and to order the private defendants to cease and desist from discharging pollutants and dredged materials. The plaintiffs also sought injunctive relief against the federal defendants to require them to exercise their jurisdiction over the property and to issue cease-and-desist orders until the private defendants obtained the requisite permits. The district court immediately issued a temporary restraining order, preventing the private defendants from engaging in landclearing activities pending the court's action on the plaintiffs' motion for a preliminary injunction.

On January 17, 1979, the district court granted the plaintiffs' motion for a preliminary injunction and ordered the federal defendants to prepare a final wetlands determination within sixty days. All of the private parties were to have the opportunity to participate in the administrative proceedings, and the federal defendants were to file a preliminary report within forty-five days. The court allowed the private defendants to engage in normal cultivation on the more than 10,000 acres that had been cleared, but ordered them to apply for a permit with respect to the area already designated by the government as a wetland and enjoined them for sixty days from engaging in landclearing activities on the remainder of the tract.

The parties complied with the court's preliminary order, and the EPA submitted its final wetlands determination on March 26, 1979. After examining the vegetation, soil conditions, and hydrology of the tract, the EPA concluded that approximately eighty percent of the land was a wetland. In a brief final paragraph, the EPA also offered its views of the types of activities that would require a section 404 permit.

At the private defendants' request, the district court agreed to bifurcate the consideration of the two major issues in the case: (1) how much of the Lake Long Tract was a wetland, and (2) which activities required a section 404 permit. After extensive trials on both issues, the court decided that a section 404 permit was required for the landclearing activities and that over ninety percent of the Lake Long Tract was a wetland. The court then enjoined the private defendants from engaging in any additional landclearing activities, without a section 404 permit, on the land that the court had determined to be a wetland, other than the land already cleared. The defendants timely appealed.

II. THE WETLANDS DETERMINATION.

. . . In deciding to give the federal defendants an opportunity to make a final wetlands determination, the district court recognized that the federal defendants bore the "primary responsibility" for the determination of which lands were wetlands:

> . . . In this instance one of the primary requests for relief made by the plaintiffs was that the agencies be directed to take up this matter of delineation of wetlands, the definition of what are wetlands, and then the enforcing of their order after it is so defined. Also, coupled with that was a prayer more directly to the merits; that is, that the Court itself makes such definitions and defines them. This is something which does not come up every day, and Congress has burdened and designated certain Government agencies with the responsibility for doing just what the prayer in this petition requests . . . . Whatever the reason, the matter of wetlands in this area, the definition of what is wetlands in that area is not now definite . . . Basically speaking, since this is a responsibility which Congress has designated the Corps and two other Government agencies to accomplish, it is their primary responsibility and they have the expertise to handle the question. And since in just about all cases that the Court has come into contact with, these cases have been cases in which the Court has the benefit of the consideration given by the agencies and is not called upon to be the agency of first impression, or to use its own initiative in making a definition or enforcing it. It has been asked to review a definition made by persons who are experts in that field and have accumulated expert testimony . . . . The Court ordinarily has the benefit of this consideration. And I feel that the Court in this instance should also have the benefit of this consideration, if it is possible to do so.

Preliminary Injunction Hearing Transcript at 34-36. After asking the federal agencies to use their expertise in making a final wetlands determination, however, the court proceeded to conduct a de novo trial on the wetlands issue and to substitute its judgment for the EPA's, without any explanation in its opinion of why it had found it necessary to go outside of the administrative record or of the standard that it was using to review the EPA's determination. Thus, while it may not be a sea that we have all been cast adrift upon, we have nevertheless been cast adrift.

The federal defendants maintain that the court's de novo review of the EPA's final wetlands determination was inappropriate. They contend that the district court should have reviewed the agency's determination on the basis of the administrative record, and that the agency's determination should have been upheld as long as it was not "arbitrary and capricious, an abuse of discretion, or otherwise not in accordance with law." 5 U.S.C. § 706(2)(B)(1976). We agree with the federal defendants that the district court's wetlands determination must be set aside because the court applied the wrong standard in reviewing the agency's determination.

A. Standard of Review.

[The Court here rejects the arbitrary/capricious standard as well as the "substantial evidence" standard, and further holds that "de novo" review, as referred to in *Citizens to Preserve Overton Park v. Volpe*, 401 U.S. 402, 91 S.Ct. 814, 28 L. Ed. 2d 136 (1971), is inappropriate. The court quoted the D.C. Circuit opinion in *Ethyl Corp. v. EPA*, 541 F.2d 1 at 36:]

> The enforced education into the intricacies of the problem before the agency is not designed to enable the court to become a superagency that can supplant the agency's expert decision-maker. To the contrary, the court must give due deference to the agency's ability to rely on its own developed expertise . . . .
>
> Thus, after our careful study of the record, we must take a step back from the agency decision. We must look at the decision not as the chemist, biologist or statistician that we are qualified neither by training nor experience to be, but as a reviewing court exercising our narrowly defined duty of holding agencies to certain minimal standards of rationality.

The basis for a court's review of an agency decision is subject to narrow limitations. Where an agency's decision is based on an administrative record, the decision should be reviewed in light of that record. *Camp v. Pitts*, 411 U.S. 138, 142-43, 93 S. Ct. 1241, 1244, 36 L. Ed. 2d 106 (1973); accord *Louisiana Environmental Society, supra*. If the agency decision is not sustainable on the basis of the administrative record, then "the matter should be *remanded* to [the agency] for further consideration." *Camp*, 411 U.S. at 143, 93 S. Ct. at 1244 (emphasis added); accord *Vermont Yankee Nuclear Power Corp. v. National Resources Defense Council, Inc.*, 435 U.S. 519, 549, 98 S. Ct. 1197, 1214, 55 L. Ed. 2d 460 (1978).

In "certain narrow, specifically limited situations," agency action may also be set aside if it is not supported by "substantial evidence," 5 U.S.C. § 706(2)(E), or, in "other equally narrow circumstances," a court may engage in de novo review of the action and set it aside if it is "unwarranted by the facts" 5 U.S.C. § 706(2)(F). *Overton Park*, 401 U.S. at 414, 91 S. Ct. at 822. De novo review under section 706(2)(F) is authorized only "when the action is adjudicatory in nature and the agency factfinding procedures are inadequate," or "when issues that were not raised before the agency are raised in a proceeding to enforce nonadjudicatory agency action."*Overton Park*, 401 U.S. at 415, 91 S. Ct. at 823. No one contends that the substantial evidence test applies to this case, nor is there any indication that de novo review was authorized by the presence of either of the circumstances mentioned in *Overton Park*.

Had this case commenced as a challenge to the Corps' decision to grant or deny a section 404 dredge-and-fill permit, the district court would clearly have been expected to review the agency's decision under the arbitrary and capricious standard on the basis of the administrative record. *See Buttrey v. United States*, 690 F.2d 1170, 1183-85 (5th Cir.1982), cert. denied, 461 U.S. 927, 103 S. Ct. 2087, 77 L. Ed. 2d 298 (1983) (Corps' denial of permit reviewed on administrative record under arbitrary and capricious standard); *Joseph G. Moretti, Inc. v. Hoffman*, 526 F.2d 1311, 1312 (5th Cir.1976) (discovery not improperly curtailed because challenge to Corps' denial of permit must be reviewed on basis of administrative record; Corps' decision was not arbitrary and capricious); *Di Vosta Rentals, Inc. v. Lee*, 488 F.2d 674, 678-79 (5th Cir.1973), cert. denied, 416 U.S. 984, 94 S. Ct. 2387, 40 L. Ed. 2d 761 (1974) (court's review of Corps' permit decision is limited to whether that decision is arbitrary and capricious in light of administrative record). The plaintiffs argue that the court's de novo review of the final wetlands determination was appropriate in this case because the EPA's determination was a jurisdictional decision. We disagree.

This is not a case where the parties have challenged the federal agency's jurisdiction to assert any authority over the tract. The landowners have conceded that thirty-five percent of the tract is a wetland subject to the federal defendants' regulatory jurisdiction under the CWA. We are not confronted with a situation where the court must determine whether the property falls under the agency's jurisdiction at all before it may determine whether the exercise of the agency's jurisdiction is appropriate. *See, e.g., United States v. Lee Wood Contracting, Inc.*, 529 F. Supp. 119 (E.D.Mich.1981) (enforcement action holding that land is "neighboring wetland" within Corps' jurisdiction); *Parkview Corp. v. Department of the Army Corps of Engineers*, 469 F. Supp. 217 (E.D.Wis.1979) (granting Corps' summary judgment motion that the land is a wetland under 1974 definition within Corps' jurisdiction); *P.F.Z. Properties, Inc. v. Train*, 393 F. Supp. 1370 (D.D.C.1975) (holding that Corps had jurisdiction over proposed building site).

The question in this case is the extent, not the existence, of agency jurisdiction. Since there is no assertion that the EPA's jurisdiction is conspicuously lacking, its findings with respect to the extent of its jurisdiction must be reviewed under the same standard as any other administrative findings. . . .

. . . .

At trial, the landowners objected to the EPA's reliance on the administrative record, claiming that it was not a true administrative record because it had been "prepared by order of the court, which was not in the ordinary course of administrative proceedings." 23 Record at 444-45. The administrative determination in this case is something of a hybrid since it was prepared in a sixty day period under a court order. In the absence of any indication that it was actually tainted by the nature of the proceedings, however, see *Overton Park*, 401 U.S. at 420, 91 S. Ct. at 825 (court may go outside of administrative record only upon showing of bad faith or improper behavior), the administrative record compiled by the agency should have served as the "focal point" for judicial review of the EPA's final wetlands determination. *See Camp, supra*, 411 U.S. at 142, 93 S. Ct. at 1244; *Louisiana Environmental Society, supra*, 707 F.2d at 119.

We hold that the district court erred in substituting its own wetlands determination for the EPA's instead of reviewing the agency's decision, as supported by the administrative record, under the arbitrary and capricious standard. Under different circumstances, we might end our review of the wetlands determination here and remand to the district court for review of the agency decision under the appropriate standard. This litigation has, however, already gone on long enough, particularly because it involves the type of project that may be killed by the delay. *See Sierra Club*, *supra*. Because the nature of the dispute over the EPA's wetlands determination is primarily a legal one, subject to our own independent review, and because the reasonableness of the EPA's decision turns on an analysis of documentary evidence, rather than on the credibility of witnesses appearing before a trial judge, we do not believe that anything could happen in the district court on remand that would change our view of whether the EPA's determination was arbitrary and capricious. Accordingly, we have decided to review the agency's determination ourselves. [citations omitted]

B. Methodology.

The private defendants claim that the EPA's decision to examine additional species of vegetation, as well as the soil and hydrology of the tract, in making its wetlands determination constituted rulemaking. Emphasizing the substantial difference between the Vicksburg District consultant's methodology and determination and the EPA's, and the probable impact of this change in methodology throughout the State of Louisiana, the landowners contend that the agencies could not make such a drastic change in their methodology without complying with the notice and comment procedures required by 5 U.S.C. § 553. The plaintiffs and federal defendants argue that the change in methodology was merely an interpretation of the Corps' existing wetlands definition, 33 C.F.R. § 323.2(c)(1982), and that therefore notice and comment proceedings were not required. 5 U.S.C. § 553(b)(A)(notice and comment requirements do not apply to "interpretative rules, general statements of policy, or rules of agency organization, procedure or practice."). All of the parties recognize that we must look beyond the label to the substance of an administrative action in order to determine whether rulemaking procedures were required. *CBS, Inc. v. United States*, 316 U.S. 407, 419, 62 S. Ct. 1194, 1201, 86 L. Ed. 1563

(1942). [The Court here rejects the private plaintiffs' attack on EPA's methodology in making the wetlands determination.]

1. Legislative or Interpretive Rule.

. . . .

While the landowners' challenge to the methodology is cast in procedural terms, their underlying contention is really nothing more than a challenge to the EPA's interpretation of the regulation. The EPA maintains that the 1977 amendments, not the methodology, expanded the Corps' wetlands definition. The landowners contend that the amendment was purely technical and was not intended to add facultative hydrophytes to the types of vegetation that would indicate the existence of wetlands. Because the landowners view the methodology as a significant expansion—or amendment—of the 1977 definition, they contend that rulemaking was required. We proceed, therefore, to consider whether the federal defendants' interpretation alters the regulation.

2. Vegetation Typically Adapted for Life in Saturated Soil Conditions.

In reviewing the federal defendants' interpretation, we must keep in mind that "the interpretation given [a] statute by the officers or agency charged with its administration" is entitled to substantial deference. [citations omitted] An agency's construction of its own regulations is entitled to even greater deference. [citations omitted] Regardless of whether the court would have arrived at the same interpretation, if the agency's interpretation is reasonable the court must respect it. [citations omitted]

A number of factors will influence the amount of deference due in a given case. These include: the degree of scientific or technical agency expertise necessarily drawn on in reaching the interpretation, "the consistency of the interpretation and the length of adherence to it, undisturbed by Congress; [and] the explicitness of the congressional grant of authority to the agency." Evaluation of these factors requires a high degree of deference in this case.

Congress has delegated substantial authority to the EPA administrator, and with respect to the dredge-and-fill permits, to the Corps, for the implementation of the CWA. *See, e.g.,* 33 U.S.C. §§ 1311, 1314, 1342, 1362(EPA responsible for setting effluent limitations, and water quality standards, issuing National Pollution Discharge Elimination System permits, and prescribing necessary regulations); 33 U.S.C. §§ 1344, 419(Corps responsible for issuing dredge-and-fill permits and is authorized to prescribe regulations under Rivers and Harbors Act). *See also E.I. Dupont de Nemours & Co. v. Train,* 430 U.S. 112, 134, 97 S. Ct. 965, 978, 51 L. Ed. 2d 204 (1977) (Supreme Court defers to EPA's interpretation of CWA because agency is charged with administering the Act, interpretation is reasonable and supported by scholarly opinion) (quoting *Train v. Natural Resources Defense Council, Inc.,* 421 U.S. 60, 87, 95 S. Ct. 1470, 1485-86, 43 L. Ed. 2d 731 (1976) (deferring to EPA's interpretation of Clean Air Act)). While the methodology used in this case had been recently established, the interpretation of the wetlands definition necessarily drew on the agencies' scientific expertise. The definition concerns the scope of the CWA, and with it the scope of the federal government's ability to control the discharge of pollutants into the waters of the United States. The EPA and the Corps were in the best position to determine precisely what property must come under federal control in order to protect the nation's waters.

The Corps' 1975 regulations defined "fresh water wetlands" as "those areas that normally are characterized by the prevalence of vegetation that requires saturated soil conditions for growth and reproduction." 42 Fed. Reg. 37128 (July 19, 1977) (emphasis added). In 1977, the Corps revised its regulations to define "wetlands" as

> The term "wetlands" means those areas that are inundated or saturated by surface or ground water at a frequency and duration sufficient to support, and that under normal circumstances do support, a prevalence of vegetation typically adapted for life in saturated soil conditions. Wetlands generally include swamps, marshes, bogs and similar areas.

33 C.F.R. § 323.2(c)(1982) (emphasis added). The Corps explained that this revision was intended to eliminate several problems and to achieve certain results:

> The reference to "periodic inundation" has been eliminated. Many interpreted that term as requiring inundation over a record period of years. Our intent under Section 404 is to regulate discharges of dredged or fill material into the aquatic system as it exists, and not as it may have existed over a record period of time. The new definition is designed to achieve this intent. It pertains to an existing wetland and requires that the area be inundated or saturated by water at a frequency and duration sufficient to support aquatic vegetation. This inundation or saturation may be caused by either surface water, ground water, or a combination of both.
>
> The use of the word "normally" in the old definition generated a great deal of confusion. The term was included in the definitions to respond to those situations in which an individual would attempt to eliminate the permit review requirements of Section 404 by destroying the aquatic vegetation, and to those areas that are not aquatic but experience an abnormal presence of aquatic vegetation. Several such instances of destruction of aquatic vegetation in order to eliminate Section 404 jurisdiction actually have occurred. However, even if this destruction occurs, the area still remains as part of the overall aquatic system intended to be protected by the Section 404 program. Conversely, the abnormal presence of aquatic vegetation in a non-aquatic area would not be sufficient to include that area within the Section 404 program.
>
> We have responded to the concern for the vagueness of the term "normally" by replacing it with the phrase ". . . and that under normal circumstances to [sic] support . . . ." We do not intend, by this clarification, to assert jurisdiction over those areas that once were wetlands and part of an aquatic system, but which, in the past, have been transformed into dry land for various purposes.

> Concerns were also expressed over the types and amount of vegetation that would be required to establish a "wetland" under this definition. We have again used the term "prevalence" to distinguish from those areas that have only occasional aquatic vegetation interspersed with upland or dry land vegetation.
>
> At the same time, we have changed our description of the vegetation involved by focusing on vegetation "typically adapted for life in saturated soil conditions." The old definition of "freshwater wetlands" provided a technical "loophole" by describing the vegetation as that which requires saturated soil conditions for growth and reproduction, thereby excluding many forms of truly aquatic vegetation that are prevalent in an inundated or saturated area, but that do not require saturated soil from a biological standpoint for their growth and reproduction. We intend to publish shortly vegetation guides to indicate the types of vegetation intended to be included in this definition, and to rely on the assistance of biologists, scientists and other technical experts from other Federal and State agencies to assist in delineating those wetland areas intended to be included in this definition.

42 Fed. Reg. 37128 (July 19, 1977).

. . . .

We are equally unpersuaded that the federal defendants' position is in error by the landowners' parsing of the definition itself. The landowners would read the words "vegetation typically adapted *for life* in saturated soil conditions" as limiting the wetlands indicators to species able to survive their entire life cycle in saturated soils. The federal defendants argue that "typically adapted *for life in*" these soil conditions means the ability to live in such conditions, although some of the species may require relief at certain points in their life cycles. A reading of the entire definition indicates that the agencies' interpretation is the more reasonable, since wetlands are not limited to areas that are permanently inundated.

Finally, we agree with the federal defendants that the decision to analyze the soil and hydrology flows from the language of the definition. The definition speaks of areas that are inundated or saturated "at a frequency and duration sufficient to support" the wetland indicators. We fail to understand how the agency may determine whether a tract is such an area without examining its hydrology. Similarly, the definition provides that a wetland is an area that "under normal circumstances [does] support" vegetation typically adapted for life in "saturated soil conditions." It would seem that the logical method for determining whether this requirement is met is to examine whether the soil is or is likely to be frequently saturated. Regardless of whether the agencies had engaged in an analysis of soil and hydrology in the past, no new burden not already contained in the definition was imposed on the landowners by this change in practice. [citations omitted] Since we conclude that the agencies' interpretation of the wetlands definition is reasonable, we are required to respect it. *Udall, supra*. A fortiori, we agree with the federal defendants that the methodology was not a significant alteration of the 1977 regulations, and therefore notice-and-comment procedures were not required.

3. Fairness.

There is an additional reason why we have concluded that the failure to engage in notice-and-comment procedures should not invalidate the EPA's final wetlands determination. As discussed above, in deciding whether such procedures are required, a court must keep in mind the underlying purpose of the APA: fairness to the affected parties. The landowners had, and took advantage of, the opportunity to argue about which species were wetlands indicators both at the administrative proceeding and at the trial. Further, while disclaiming the usefulness of the approach, Dr. Rhodes, on whose report the landowners rely heavily, conducted his own analysis of the Lake Long Tract's soil and hydrology conditions. Admin.Record, Tab 3.17. Therefore, the EPA's adoption of the methodology did not make the administrative proceedings less than fundamentally fair. . . .

We note further that even if we were to accept the landowners' contention that the methodology should have been adopted pursuant to notice-and-comment procedures, the same methodology would be required under the EPA's present regulations.

> Wetland vegetation consists of plants that require saturated soils to survive (obligate wetland plants) as well as plants, including certain trees, that gain a competitive advantage over others because they can tolerate prolonged wet soil conditions and their competitors cannot. In addition to plant populations and communities, wetlands are delimited by hydrological and physical characteristics of the environment. These characteristics should be considered when information about them is needed to supplement information available about vegetation, or where wetland vegetation has been removed or is dormant.

40 C.F.R. § 230.41(a)(3)(1982). Since an appellate court must apply the agency's current regulations, [citations omitted] the most that we could do would be to remand for reconsideration under the new regulations . . . . Here, there is no reason for a remand because the landowners have already had an adequate opportunity to present their evidence under the "new" regulations.

4. The Regulations and the Clean Water Act.

Having determined that the federal defendants' interpretation is consistent with the Corps' wetlands definition, we must consider whether the definition is consistent with the statute and the Constitution. Again in reviewing the statutory question, we must keep in mind the principle that an agency's interpretation of the statute that it administers is to be accorded significant deference. [The Court here holds that actual navigability of the waters is no longer a jurisdictional issue after the 1977 amendment of the Act.]

5. Constitutional Challenges to the Corps' Definition.

[The Court rejects challenges based on void-for-vagueness and improper-delegation grounds.]

The landowners also contend that if the CWA authorizes regulation to the extent proposed by the federal defendants, then the Act is unconstitutionally vague and an unlawful delegation of legislative power. We find no merit in either claim.

The CWA's delegation of authority to the EPA and the Corps clearly meets this test. Congress' goal—the restoration of the integrity of the nation's waters and the elimination of discharges of pollutants into those waters—is succinctly set forth in 33 U.S.C. § 1251(a). The agencies' jurisdiction under the CWA extends to all "waters of the United States," and the 1977 regulation provides specific criteria further defining the statutory term. In reviewing an application for a dredge-and-fill permit, the agencies are to consider any "unacceptable adverse effect on municipal water supplies, shellfish beds and fishery areas (including spawning and breeding wells), wildlife, or recreational areas," 33 U.S.C. § 1344(c), and the effect of the "disposal of pollutants on human health or welfare, . . . marine life, . . . esthetic, recreation and economic values . . . [and] the persistence and permanence of [these] effects . . . ." 33 U.S.C. § 1343(c)(1)(A)-(D). This is not the kind of standardless discretion condemned in *Schecter, supra*.

6. The Merits of the EPA's Wetlands Determination.

The essence of the landowners' challenge to the EPA's final wetlands determination concerned the legal issues described above, in particular the use of the new methodology. To a limited extent, the landowners have also disputed some of the agency's factual findings. Our review of the administrative record in this case does not indicate that the EPA's findings were arbitrary or capricious.

While the EPA found that approximately eighty percent of the Lake Long Tract was a wetland, the district court found that over ninety percent of the tract was a wetland. The court and the agency reached different conclusions because they held differing beliefs about whether Tensas and Dundee soils were wetlands soils. The EPA's conclusion that areas made up of these two soils should be excluded from the wetlands area was based on the report of the agency's soil expert, Dr. William H. Patrick, Jr. Dr. Patrick examined the site's soils for wetness, texture, color and extent of mottling and concluded that the Dundee and Tensas soils were less likely to remain saturated than the other wetlands soils. *See* Admin.Record, Tab 3.19. The district court found that all of these soils were wetlands soils because they drain poorly.

While there may have been room for a difference in opinion about the nature of these soils, such a difference does not mean that the agency's decision was arbitrary or capricious. The agency and its expert explained their reasons for concluding that the Dundee and Tensas soils were not wetlands, and their decision is not irrational. Since the courts may not require any more than that, *Overton Park, supra*, the district court erred in substituting its judgment about the character of the soils for the agency's.

The landowners emphasize that the EPA's determination that approximately eighty percent of the tract was a wetland does not correspond to the findings of any of its experts. In discussing percentages, it is all too easy to lose sight of the fact that we are discussing the characteristics of land, not the amount of octane required in gasoline or the amount of lead permitted in drainage pipes. We must not forget that these percentages are a mere shorthand for the map of wetlands that our pens and tongues cannot adequately describe.

The eighty-percent figure is based on Dr. Patrick's report about the area's soils. He opined that sixty percent of the tract was a wetland because he would have excluded from his calculations the Tensas-Sharkey soils, which he viewed as mixed and nonmixed wetlands soils, as well as the Dundee and Tensas soils. Admin.Record, Tab 3.19. The EPA decided not to exclude the Tensas-Sharkey soils because it was too difficult to separate these soils from the wetlands soils. Final Wetlands Determination at 6-7, 2 Record at 377-78; Admin. Record, Tab 3.38 (EPA Regional Administrator's Report). Since the Tensas-Sharkey soils accounted for approximately twenty percent of the tract, their inclusion explains the difference between the EPA's determination and its expert's.

Finally, the landowners dispute the EPA's findings with respect to which types of vegetation were wetlands indicators and the extent of the inundation of the tract. The vegetation dispute concerns whether the facultative hydrophytes should be considered wetlands indicators, not which types of vegetation were actually on the tract. We have already determined that the EPA's view of the matter was not irrational. While there were conflicting reports about the extent of flooding on the tract, both in the administrative record and at trial, this conflict was properly resolved by the agency.

In summary, we hold that the EPA's final wetlands determination was not arbitrary or capricious. Therefore, the district court's determination must be set aside to the extent that it is in conflict with the agency's, and the agency's determination should be reinstated.

III. ACTIVITIES REQUIRING A PERMIT.

. . . .

A. Factual Findings.

The district court found that the landowners had engaged in the following activities:

> Initially, bulldozers outfitted with shearing blades cut the timber and vegetation at or just above ground level. The shearing blades were v-shaped, had a serrated edge and flat bottom and were approximately 18-20 feet in length. The blades were adjusted to be free floating so that they would ride along the top surface of the ground. Occasionally, however, the blades would gouge the surface of the ground. Although the blades were adjusted to ride on the ground's surface, they did scrape the leaf litter and humus that overlaid the soil as they moved from tree to tree.
>
> After the shearing was completed in a section, bulldozers outfitted with rake blades pushed the felled trees into windrows. The upper portion of the raking blade was solid whereas the lower portion had tines that permitted soil to pass through the openings. The raking blades were also outfitted so that they generally operated on top of the soil. However, in

> the process of windrowing the trees and debris, soil and leaf litter was also scraped into the windrows. It is not clear whether the blades themselves or the broom-like action of the trees and brush that they were pushing actually scraped the soil and the overlying leaf litter. In any event the photographic evidence clearly demonstrated that soil and leaf litter was piled up during the windrowing process—this movement filled in low areas and along with the discing which followed, had a levelling effect on the surface of the land.
>
> The trees and other vegetation that had been windrowed were then burned. The remaining ashes were later disced into and across the tract. Some of the felled trees and other debris would not burn. This material was buried in four or five pits, each approximately 50 feet long and 6 feet deep that had been dug with backhoes by the private defendants.
>
> Tractors pulling chunk rakes would go over the areas that had been sheared and windrowed and rake together any remaining debris. Basically, the chunk rakes were sets of tines that were outfitted on cultivators that had had their blades removed. The chunk rakes gathered the small debris into piles where it was presumably burned. These ashes were also disced into the soil.
>
> After the shearing, windrowing and chunk raking the land was disced to prepare it for soybean cultivation. A disc is a bowl-shaped blade that cuts into the ground and fluffs the soil up. The disc's [sic] used on this tract were 24 inches in diameter and would cut into the ground approximately 9 inches. During discing, some soil would ride in front of the disc and would be redeposited in other areas of the tract, resulting in substantial displacement and redepositing of the soil itself.
>
> Defendants also dug a drainage ditch that was approximately three-quarters of a mile long. The earth excavated from the ditch was piled alongside the ditch and was to be spread over the adjacent area. Construction of at least four or five miles of additional ditches were contemplated for soybean cultivation.

Avoyelles Sportsmen's League v. Alexander (Avoyelles I), 473 F. Supp. 525, 528-29 (W.D.La.1979) (footnote omitted).

The private defendants are the only parties who challenge the district court's factual findings. While they have indicated portions of the record that support their contention that the landclearing activities did not result in any significant digging up of the earth or leveling of the land, the plaintiffs presented their own eyewitness testimony to the effect that large chunks of earth had been torn up, holes dug, and sloughs filed in. Resolution of this conflict in the evidence is properly left to the district court, who has had an opportunity to hear and observe the witnesses. We cannot say on the basis of this record that the trial court's factual findings were clearly erroneous.

B. The Discharge of Pollutants.

The district court held that the private defendants' landclearing activities constituted a "discharge of a pollutant" into the waters of the United States, and that engaging in those activities without a section 404 dredge-and-fill permit was a violation of section 301(a) of the CWA. 33 U.S.C. § 1311(a). As the district court did, we must look beyond section 301(a) itself, to the statutory and regulatory definitions, in order to determine whether the district court's holding was correct.

Section 502(12) defines the term "discharge of a pollutant" as "(a) any addition of any pollutant to navigable waters from any point source . . . ." 33 U.S.C. § 1362(12). A "point source" is defined in section 502(14) as "any discernible, confined and discrete conveyance, including but not limited to any . . . container, rolling stock, concentrated animal feeding operation, or vessel . . . from which pollutants are or may be discharged . . . ." 33 U.S.C. § 1362(14). Section 502(6) defines the term "pollutant" to mean "dredged spoil, solid waste, incinerator residue, sewage, garbage, sewage sludge, munitions, chemical wastes, biological materials, radioactive materials, heat, wrecked or discarded equipment, rock, sand, cellar dirt and industrial, municipal and agricultural waste discharged into water." 33 U.S.C. § 1362(6). The question in this case is whether the landclearing activities were (1) a discharge (2) of a pollutant (3) from a point source (4) into navigable waters. Further, we must determine whether the activities were "normal agricultural activities" exempted from the permit requirements by 33 U.S.C. § 1344(f).

As discussed in Part II, these activities did occur in navigable waters, as that term is defined in the statute. Further, we agree with the district court that the bulldozers and backhoes were "point sources," since they collected into windrows and piles material that may ultimately have found its way back into the waters. *See Sierra Club v. Abston Construction Co.*, 620 F.2d 41 (5th Cir.1980) (mining scrap piles may be point sources even though material may not be carried directly to waters from the piles); *United States v. Holland*, 373 F. Supp. 665, 668 (M.D.Fla. 1974) (bulldozers are point sources). The question then is whether these activities constituted a "discharge" of a "pollutant."

Emphasizing that the removal of all of the vegetation would destroy the vital ecological function of the wetlands, the district court concluded that the landclearing activities constituted a "discharge" within the meaning of the CWA. Both the federal and private defendants argue that the "mere removal" of wetlands vegetation was not a discharge because the term discharge is defined as the "addition" of pollutants, not the removal of materials. The district court rejected this argument as "untenable" because it believed that the federal defendants' interpretation would frustrate the ecological purposes of the CWA. 473 F. Supp. at 536. In the court's view, the federal defendants' argument implied that "the excavation of [a] ditch 6 feet deep and 100 feet long requires a § 404 permit (is destructive of wetlands) but that the clearing of 20,000 acres of forest wetlands by methods involving only de minimis movement of earth does not (is not destructive of wetlands)." *Id.* . . . .

A brief analysis of the district court's factual findings indicates that the dispute about whether the CWA covers the mere removal of vegetation is a false issue in this case. The EPA has explained on appeal that it agrees with the district court that "if vegetation or other materials are redeposited in the wetland, that activity is a discharge. [Their] point of disagreement with the district court was with its apparent conclusion that removal activities [were] covered by the Act even when nothing is redeposited on the land." Federal Defendants' Reply Brief at 2 n. 1. The district court's factual findings demonstrate that this is not a "mere removal" case. The court found that "during the clearing process small sloughs were filled in and larger ones partially filled thereby levelling the land." 473 F. Supp. at 536. The landowners' own witness admitted to burying logs in holes that he had dug, and the plaintiffs' witnesses testified that material that would not burn was buried. Since the landclearing activities involved the redeposit of materials, rather than their mere removal, we need not determine today whether mere removal may constitute a discharge under the CWA. Any suggestion made by the district court that the term "discharge" does cover removal is pure dicta.

The word "addition," as used in the definition of the term "discharge," may reasonably be understood to include "redeposit." As the district court recognized, this reading of the definition is consistent with both the purposes and legislative history of the statute. . . .

Similarly, we agree with the district court, the plaintiffs and the federal defendants that the material discharged in this case was "fill," if not "dredged," material and hence subject to the Corps' regulation under section 404, as long as the activities did not fall within the section 404(f) exemption. The term "fill material" is defined in the Corps' regulations as

> any material used for the primary purpose of replacing an aquatic area with dry land or of changing the bottom elevation of a waterbody. The term does not include any pollutant discharged into the water primarily to dispose of waste, as that activity is regulated under Section 402 of the Federal Water Pollution Control Act Amendments of 1972. 33 C.F.R. § 323.2(m).

As discussed above, the burying of the unburned material, as well as the discing, had the effect of filling in the sloughs on the tract and leveling the land. The landowners insist that any leveling was "incidental" to their clearing activities and therefore the material was not deposited for the "primary purpose" of changing the character of the land. The district court found, however, that there had been significant leveling. The plaintiffs' witnesses testified that sloughs that had contained rainwater in the past had been filled in; thus, the activities were "changing the bottom elevation of the waterbody." Certainly, the activities were designed to "replace the aquatic area with dry land." Accordingly, we hold that the district court correctly concluded that the landowners were discharging "fill material" into the wetlands.

The district court also found that removal of the vegetation constituted dredging. The regulations define "dredged material" as "material that is excavated or dredged from waters of the United States." 33 C.F.R. § 323.2(k). The district court reasoned that since the vegetation was part of the wetlands, it was also part of the "waters of the United States"; therefore, removal of the vegetation constituted dredging.

C. Statutory Exemptions.

Finally, the private defendants argue that their activities are normal farming activities exempt under section 404(f) of the Act. 33 U.S.C.

§ 1344(f)(Supp. V 1981). [The Court holds that the farming and silviculture exemptions do not apply to the private defendants' activities here.]

IV. OTHER CLAIMS.

A. Taking Without Just Compensation.

The private defendants claim that a determination that the Lake Long Tract is a wetland subject to the Corps' regulation constitutes a "taking" for which just compensation must be paid under the fifth amendment. The district court rejected this claim because it had not been shown that enforcement of the CWA was not "reasonable, legitimate and in the public interest." *Avoyelles II*, 511 F. Supp. at 287. *See, e.g., Andrus v. Allard*, 444 U.S. 51, 100 S. Ct. 318, 62 L. Ed. 2d 210 (1979); *Penn Central Transportation Co. v. New York City*, 438 U.S. 104, 123, 98 S. Ct. 2646, 2659, 57 L. Ed. 2d 631 (1978); *Deltona Corp. v. United States*, 228 Ct. Cl. 476, 657 F.2d 1184 (Ct.Cl.1981), cert. denied, 455 U.S. 1017, 102 S. Ct. 1712, 72 L. Ed. 2d 135 (1982). While we agree with the district court that there has as yet been no taking, we hold that the claim should have been dismissed because it was premature . . . .

. . . Since there has as yet been no determination whether the landowners may put their property to the uses that they desire, we hold that the consideration of their taking claim should have been delayed until after they had complied with the Corps' permit procedure.

. . . .

V. CONCLUSION.

With respect to the wetlands determination, we hold:

(1) that the district court erred in substituting its own wetlands determination for the EPA's final wetlands determination;

(2) that the district court should have reviewed the EPA's wetlands determination under the arbitrary and capricious standard and that the administrative record should have served as the focal point for that review;

(3) that notice and comment rulemaking procedures were not required before the EPA could apply its three-part methodology in determining the extent of wetlands on the property because the methodolody was an interpretation of the administrative regulations;

(4) that the federal defendants' interpretation of the 1977 wetlands definition is not inconsistent with the regulation, the Clean Water Act, or the United States Constitution;

(5) that the EPA's final wetlands determination was not arbitrary and capricious.

Accordingly, the district court's wetlands determination is reversed to the extent that it is inconsistent with the agency's, and the EPA's determination is reinstated.

With respect to the activities issue, we hold:

(1) that the bulldozers and backhoes were "point sources" within the meaning of the Clean Water Act;

(2) that in filling in the sloughs and leveling the land, the landowners were redepositing fill material into waters of the United States, and that therefore, these activities constituted a "discharge of a pollutant";

(3) that the landclearing activities were not exempt from the Corps' permit requirements under section 404(f)(1) of the CWAbecause those activities constituted a change in use of wetlands under section 404(f)(2). Accordingly, we affirm the district court's judgment that these landclearing activities may not be carried out without a section 404 dredge-and-fill permit; however, we note that should a section 404 permit application be filed, the Corps will be free to apply its expertise to that permit determination without any constraint from the district court's injunctive determinations except those we have expressly affirmed.

Finally, we hold that the district court should have dismissed the taking claim because it was premature, and that the district court's denial of the Louisiana Department of Agriculture's motion to intervene was proper because the filing of a notice of appeal nearly a month before the Department of Agriculture filed its motion deprived the district court of jurisdiction to entertain the department's motion.

The private defendants shall bear the costs of this appeal.

AFFIRMED in part and REVERSED in part.

QUESTIONS

On the basis of the leading cases you have just read, as well as on the basis of the wetlands legislation cited, discuss and answer the following questions:

(1) What factual determinations are necessary to establish that the lands in question are wetlands?

(2) Why is this factual determination a requirement precedent to the requirement that a permit must be obtained under § 404 for dredging, filling, or for any other activity or construction on wetlands?

(3) Once a determination has been made by the appropriate agency that the lands involved are wetlands, what other determination must be made in order to permit developmental activities, whether agricultural or building activities, to commence? Does it make a difference whether the land is to be used (a) for purely agricultural activities; (b) for the construction of a high-rise condominium building with a view across the bay; (c) for the construction of a major shopping center; (d) for the construction of a school; (e) for the construction of a major postal services building; (f) for the construction of an amusement park?

(4) Considering all of the earlier mentioned development projects, will the development require an environmental impact statement under the National Environmental Policy Act? If an environmental impact statement is required, will the consideration of alternatives under a NEPA environmental impact statement be parallel or will it displace the requirement of the consideration

of alternative sites under the provisions of the Clean Water Act wetlands provisions and regulations?

(5) In determining whether or not to grant a § 404 permit, to fill or develop a wetlands area, what other environmental impacts may be raised and will have to be considered? Consider, for instance, requirements under the Endangered Species Act, the Landmarks Preservation Act, and the Clean Air Act. Would all or some of these be included in considering alternative sites, or in considering alternatives in the course of preparing an environmental impact statement?

[xi] Sanctions and Remedies Particularly Applicable to Water Pollution

Introductory Note

This segment of the materials deals with selected sanctions and remedies with special relevance to water pollution control, except for remedies relating to oil and hazardous substance spills, and certain other remedies, such as those relating to marine sanitation devices. In particular, the materials involve remedial concerns regarding federal-state relations as well as the interaction between common law remedies and statutory requirements.

The Relationship Between Statutorily Authorized Citizen Suits and Law Suits for Damages

In *City of Evansville v. Kentucky Liquid Recycling, Inc.*, 604 F.2d 1008 (7th Cir. 1979), *cert. denied sub. nom. Louisville & Jefferson County Metro. Sewer Dist. v. City of Evansville*, 444 U.S. 1025 (1980) the court held that the plaintiffs' failure to comply with the notice requirement precluded reliance on § 505(a) as the basis for their action, distinguishing this case from others on the grounds that plaintiffs were attempting to assert a private cause of action under the Act. The court pointed out that even if proper notice had been given, the claim would not have been supported by § 505(a) because it does not authorize actions for past violations of effluent standards or for recovery of damages.[195]

The Supreme Court also reached this conclusion in *Middlesex County Sewerage Authority v. National Sea Clammers Association.*[196] Respondents, alleging damage to fishing grounds in the Atlantic Ocean caused by discharge and ocean dumping of sewage sludge and other waste, sought damages based on either federal common law or on the provisions of the FWPCA, as amended, 33 U.S.C. § 1251 *et seq.*, and the Marine Protection, Research and Sanctions Act of 1972 (MPRSA), 33 U.S.C. § 1401 *et seq.*

The District Court had rejected respondents' federal common law nuisance claim for injunctive and declaratory relief, $250 million in compensatory damages and $250 million in punitive damages, on the ground that such a

[195] The court's view finds support in the legislative history of § 505, see S. Rep. No. 92-414, 92d Cong., 1st Sess., 81, *reprinted in* [1972] U.S. Code Cong. & Ad. News 3746-3747.

[196] 453 U.S. 1, 101 S. Ct. 2615, 69 L. Ed. 2d 435 (1981).

cause of action is not available to private parties.[197] Also, because respondents had failed to comply with the 60-day notice requirement of the § 505 "citizen suit" provision, the District Court concluded that the claims based on the alleged FWPCA violations were unenforceable. The court applied the same reasoning with regard to the claims under the MPRSA. The court also rejected respondents' maritime tort claim because they had failed to include it in their pleadings.

The Court of Appeals reversed.[198] The court held that the § 505 citizen suit provision does not preclude suits under the Act, basing its conclusions on the savings clause in § 505(e), which preserves any right which any person (or class of persons) may have under any statute or common law to seek enforcement of any effluent standard or limitation or to seek any other relief. The court applied the same reasoning to the MPRSA. Concerning the federal common law nuisance claim, the Court of Appeals rejected the District Court's conclusion that private parties may not bring such claim and determined that respondents had alleged sufficient individual damage to permit them to recover damages. The Supreme Court granted certiorari to examine three questions:

(1) whether the FWPCA and MPRSA imply a private right of action independent of their citizen-suit provisions;

(2) whether all federal common law nuisance actions concerning ocean pollution now are preempted by the legislative scheme contained in the FWPCA and MPRSA; and

(3) if not, does a private citizen have standing to sue for damages under the federal common law of nuisance.

The Court held that there is no implied right of action under these statutes and that the federal common law of nuisance has been fully preempted in the area of ocean pollution.[199] It concluded: "In view of the elaborate enforcement provisions, it cannot be assumed that Congress intended to authorize by implication additional judicial remedies for private citizens suing under MPRSA and FWPCA." The Court noted that "[i]n absence of strong indicia of a contrary Congressional intent, we are compelled to conclude that Congress provided precisely the remedies it considered appropriate." Accordingly, the Court reversed the decision of the Court of Appeals. First, the Court found the language of the "savings clause" on which the Court of Appeals relied to be quite ambiguous regarding the intent of Congress to "preserve" remedies under the FWPCA. The Court expressed the view that it is doubtful that the phrase "any statute" of § 505(e) included the very statute in which the statement was contained. Second, the Court found in error the distinction which the Court of Appeals drew between "non-injured" plaintiffs, who may bring citizen suits to enforce provisions of the Act, and "injured" plaintiffs, who claim a right to sue under the Acts by virtue of the language of the savings clause. The Court stated that the citizen suit provisions apply only to persons who can claim some sort of injury and therefore there is no reason to infer the existence of a separate right of action for "injured" plaintiffs. The Court

[197] 101 S. Ct. at 2619.

[198] 616 F.2d 1222 (3d Cir. 1980).

[199] 101 S. Ct. at 2615.

noted that the Senate Conference Report indicates that § 505(g) was intended to allow suits by all persons possessing standing under *Sierra Club v. Morton*,[200] and that "[t]his broad category of potential plaintiffs necessarily includes both plaintiffs seeking to enforce these statutes as private attorneys general, whose injuries are'non-economic' and probably non-compensable, and persons like respondents who assert that they have suffered tangible economic injuries because of statutory violations."[201]

Finally, the court concluded that the Court of Appeals "failed to take account of the rest of the enforcement scheme expressly provided by Congress—including the opportunity for 'any interested person' to seek judicial review of a number of EPA actions within 90 days under § 509(b). The Court also reached the same decision with regard to the MPRSA because that "citizen suit" provision is in many respects almost identical. Therefore, the Court concluded, the structure of the Acts and their legislative history demonstrate that Congress intended that private remedies in addition to those expressly provided should not be implied.

After raising on its own the question of whether the Civil Rights Act, 42 U.S.C. § 1983(authorizing suits to redress violations by state officials of rights created by federal statutes) presented an alternate to express congressional authorization for private suits under the FWPCA and the MPRSA, the court concluded that it did not. It reasoned that the "existence of these express remedies demonstrates not only that Congress intended to foreclose implied private actions but also that it intended to supplant any remedy that otherwise would be available under § 1983."

Lastly, the Court determined that it need not decide whether a cause of action may be brought under the federal common law of nuisance by a private plaintiff seeking damages, since the Court had just recently held in *City of Milwaukee v. Illinois*,[202] that the federal common law of nuisance in the area of water pollution is entirely preempted by the more comprehensive scope of the FWPCA and MPRSA. This, the Court concluded, entirely disposed of respondents' federal common law claim.

Justice Stevens, dissenting, criticized the majority's decision, noting that the net effect of the Court's interpretation of the legislative history is that "Congress, by enacting the Clean Water Act and the MPRSA, deliberately deprived respondents of effective federal remedies that would otherwise have been available to them."[203] In his view, Congress did not intend the express remedies in the FWPCA and the MPRSA to be exclusive. Rather, Stevens interpreted § 505(e) to be a clear contrary indication. He argued that the majority had failed to uncover "a clear congressional mandate" to withdraw the § 1983 remedy otherwise available to respondents. Furthermore, while Stevens agreed with the majority that there is no implied private right of action for damages under FMPCA and MPRSA, he reached this conclusion because he reasoned that the statute was created to protect the general public, and not to provide private remedies.

---

[200] 405 U.S. 727, 92 S. Ct. 1361, 31 L. Ed. 2d 636 (1972).

[201] 101 S. Ct. at 2624.

[202] 451 U.S. 304, 101 S. Ct. 1784, 68 L. Ed. 2d 114 (1981).

[203] 101 S. Ct. at 2630.

QUESTIONS

(1) Does the Court in the *Sea Clammers* case follow the rule for implied rights of action in *Cort v. Ash*, 422 U.S. 66 (1975)? What is the determinative factor that persuades the Court that Congress did not intend to imply a private cause of action? Is the Court's rationale persuasive?

(2) Does the decision in *Sea Clammers* leave any room for a private damages action in the federal courts (other than on diversity of jurisdiction grounds)? The Court bases its rejection of any implied cause of action partially on the inclusion of provision for citizen suits, arguing that the provision of one "private" remedy by implication excludes another. In light of the language and purpose of the citizen suit provisions, is this a sound construction?

(3) Can a plaintiff injured as a result of defendant's violation of the CWA and who sues for damages in state court assert the violation of federal law as evidence of a *per se* violation, or as evidencing some breach of the duty of care?

Federal Common Law of Nuisance

In *Illinois v. City of Milwaukee* ("*Milwaukee I*") 406 U.S. 91 (1972), a unanimous Supreme Court upheld the right of the state of Illinois to invoke the Court's original jurisdiction under Article III, Section 2, Clause 2 of the Constitution in a case involving the pollution of Lake Michigan by sewage from Milwaukee and several other communities. The Court, finding that the pre-1972 Federal Waste Pollution Control Act could not provide prompt or effective remedies for such interstate pollution, held that remedies were available under federal common law. The Court added, "It may happen that new federal laws or new federal regulations may in time preempt the field of federal common law of nuisance." 406 U.S. at 91. Until such time, however, the Court found itself empowered to decide interstate cases of public nuisance by water pollution.

The 1972 Federal Water Pollution Control Act Amendments were enacted within a few months of *Milwaukee I*. In 1981 in *Illinois v. City of Milwaukee* ("*Milwaukee II*"), 451 U.S. 304, 101 S. Ct. 1784, the Court changed its earlier position, holding by a divided court, that in this instance, "Congress had not left the formulation of appropriate federal standards to the Courts through the application of often vague and indeterminate nuisance concepts and maxims of equity jurisprudence, but rather had occupied the field through the establishment of a comprehensive, regulatory program supervised by an expert administrative agency." 451 U.S. at 317. The dissenters, Blackmun J., with Marshall J. and Stevens J. concurring, were persuaded that §§ 505(e) and 510 of the Act were intended to save the federal common law of nuisance action from such preemption. For discussion of the federal common law of nuisance and its application, see F. Grad, Treatise on Environmental Law, § 3.03[12].

Another issue regarding occupancy of the field by the Clean Water Act resulted from the potential conflict between applicable standards in private tort actions and public enforcement actions under the Act.

In *International Paper Company v. Harmel Ouellette,*[204] the Supreme Court had to decide the preemptive reach of the Clean Water Act with respect to a private nuisance aciton brought in an affected (downstream) state against a polluter in an (upstream) source state:

> The question presented is whether the Act preempts a common law nuisance suit filed in a Vermont court under Vermont law, when the source of the alleged injury is located in New York.[205]

The polluter operated a paper mill on the New York side of Lake Champlain, and the plaintiffs, on the Vermont side of the lake, sued under Vermont nuisance law for substantial damages.

Writing for a divided court, Powell J. examined the reservation of state law and state actions in § 505(e) and in § 510 of the Act, and relied heavily on the Court's holding in *Milwaukee II* that Congress had intended to "establish an all-encompassing program of water pollution regulation."[206]

The Court held that the Clean Water Act prevents an affected state, here Vermont, from imposing liability on a point source in the source state, here New York. In the Court's opinion, to allow a different result could disrupt the application of the NPDES system, because it would lead to conflicting regulatory authority over a single source. The Court upheld the jurisdiction of the Vermont district court to entertain the action, and rejected the assertion that any such action must be brought in the source state. The Court held, however, that the governing law is the nuisance law of New York and not that of Vermont. The Court further indicated that the plaintiffs have the choice of suing in the courts of New York.

In a partial dissent, Brennan, J. and Marshall, J. agreed that Vermont was a proper forum, but disagreed that the Clean Water Act requires the application of the law of New York, the source state, asserting that the Clean Water Act left intact the affected state's right to apply its own law when its residents are injured by an out-of-state polluter. A partial dissent by Stevens, J., in which Blackmun, J. also joined, asserted that the choice of law issue is subject to the determination of the forum state and that the determination of the issue was premature because no such choice of law had as yet been made.

---

[204] 479 U.S. 481, 107 S. Ct. 805, 93 L. Ed. 2d 883 (1987).

[205] 479 U.S. at 483.

[206] 451 U.S. at 318.

ARKANSAS v. OKLAHOMA

United States Supreme Court (1992)
503 U.S. 91, 112 S. Ct. 1046, 117 L. Ed. 2d 239, 22 ELR 20552

STEVENS, J., delivered the opinion for a unanimous Court.

Pursuant to the Clean Water Act, 86Stat. 816, as amended, 33 U.S.C. § 1251 *et seq.*, the Environmental Protection Agency (EPA or Agency) issued a discharge permit to a new point source in Arkansas, about 39 miles upstream from the Oklahoma state line. The question presented in this litigation is whether the EPA's finding that discharges from the new source would not cause a detectable violation of Oklahoma's water quality standards satisfied the EPA's duty to protect the interests of the downstream State. Disagreeing with the Court of Appeals, we hold that the Agency's action was authorized by the statute.

I

In 1985, the city of Fayetteville, Arkansas, applied to the EPA, seeking a permit for the city's new sewage treatment plant under the National Pollution Discharge Elimination System (NPDES). After the appropriate procedures, the EPA, pursuant to § 402(a)(1) of the Act, 33 U. S. C. § 1342(a)(1), issued a permit authorizing the plant to discharge up to half of its effluent (to a limit of 6.1 million gallons per day) into an unnamed stream in northwestern Arkansas. That flow passes through a series of three creeks for about 17 miles, and then enters the Illinois River at a point 22 miles upstream from the Arkansas-Oklahoma border.

The permit imposed specific limitations on the quantity, content, and character of the discharge and also included a number of special conditions, including a provision that if a study then underway indicated that more stringent limitations were necessary to ensure compliance with Oklahoma's water quality standards, the permit would be modified to incorporate those limits.

Respondents challenged this permit before the EPA, alleging, inter alia, that the discharge violated the Oklahoma water quality standards. Those standards provide that "no degradation [of water quality] shall be allowed" in the upper Illinois River, including the portion of the river immediately downstream from the state line.

Following a hearing, the Administrative Law Judge (ALJ) concluded that the Oklahoma standards would not be implicated unless the contested discharge had "something more than a mere *de minimis* impact" on the State's waters. He found that the discharge would not have an "undue impact" on Oklahoma's waters and, accordingly, affirmed the issuance of the permit.

On a petition for review, the EPA's Chief Judicial Officer first ruled that § 301(b)(1)(C) of the Clean Water Act"requires an NPDES permit to impose any effluent limitations necessary to comply with applicable state water quality standards." *Id.*, at 116a-117a. He then held that the Act and EPA regulations offered greater protection for the downstream State than the ALJ's "undue impact" standard suggested. He explained the proper standard as follows:

> "[A] mere theoretical impairment of Oklahoma's water quality standards—*i.e.,* an infinitesimal impairment predicted through modeling but not expected to be actually detectable or measurable—should not by itself block the issuance of the permit. In this case, the permit should be upheld if the record shows by a preponderance of the evidence that the authorized discharges would not cause an actual *detectable* violation of Oklahoma's water quality standards." *Id.*, at 117a (emphasis in original).

On remand, the ALJ made detailed findings of fact and concluded that the city had satisfied the standard set forth by the Chief Judicial Officer. Specifically, the ALJ found that there would be no detectable violation of any of the components of Oklahoma's water quality standards. The Chief Judicial Officer sustained the issuance of the permit.

Both the petitioners in No. 90-1262 (collectively Arkansas) and the respondents in this litigation sought judicial review. Arkansas argued that the Clean Water Act did not require an Arkansas point source to comply with Oklahoma's water quality standards. Oklahoma challenged the EPA's determination that the Fayetteville discharge would not produce a detectable violation of the Oklahoma standards.

The Court of Appeals did not accept either of these arguments. The court agreed with the EPA that the statute required compliance with Oklahoma's water quality standards, see 908 F.2d 595, 602-615 (CA10 1990), and did not disagree with the Agency's determination that the discharges from the Fayetteville plant would not produce a detectable violation of those standards. *Id.*, at 631-633. Nevertheless, relying on a theory that neither party had advanced, the Court of Appeals reversed the Agency's issuance of the Fayetteville permit. The court first ruled that the statute requires that "where a proposed source would discharge effluents that would contribute to conditions currently constituting a violation of applicable water quality standards, such [a] proposed source may not be permitted." *Id.*, at 620. Then the court found that the Illinois River in Oklahoma was "already degraded," that the Fayetteville effluent would reach the Illinois River in Oklahoma, and that that effluent could "be expected to contribute to the ongoing deterioration of the scenic [Illinois R]iver" in Oklahoma even though it would not detectably affect the river's water quality. *Id.*, at 621-629.

The importance and the novelty of the Court of Appeals' decision persuaded us to grant certiorari. 499 U.S. 946 (1991). We now reverse.

II

Interstate waters have been a font of controversy since the founding of the Nation . . . .

Among these cases are controversies between a State that introduces pollutants to a waterway and a downstream State that objects. *See, e. g.*,

Missouri v. Illinois, 200 U.S. 496, 50 L. Ed. 572, 26 S. Ct. 268 (1906). In such cases, this Court has applied principles of common law tempered by a respect for the sovereignty of the States. Compare *id.*, at 521, with *Georgia v. Tennessee Copper Co.*, 206 U.S. 230, 237, 51 L. Ed. 1038, 27 S. Ct. 618 (1907). In forging what "may not improperly be called interstate common law," *Illinois v. Milwaukee*, 406 U.S. 91, 105-106, 31 L. Ed. 2d 712, 92 S. Ct. 1385 (1972) (*Milwaukee I*), however, we remained aware "that new federal laws and new federal regulations may in time pre-empt the field of federal common law of nuisance." *Id.*, at 107.

In *Milwaukee v. Illinois* , 451 U.S. 304, 68 L. Ed. 2d 114, 101 S. Ct. 1784 (1981) (*Milwaukee II*), we held that the Federal Water Pollution Control Act Amendments of 1972 did just that. In addressing Illinois' claim that Milwaukee's discharges into Lake Michigan constituted a nuisance, we held that the comprehensive regulatory regime created by the 1972 amendments pre-empted Illinois' federal common law remedy. We observed that Congress had addressed many of the problems we had identified in *Milwaukee I* by providing a downstream State with an opportunity for a hearing before the source State's permitting agency, by requiring the latter to explain its failure to accept any recommendations offered by the downstream State, and by authorizing the EPA, in its discretion, to veto a source State's issuance of any permit if the waters of another State may be affected. *Milwaukee II* , 451 U.S. at 325-326.

In *Milwaukee II* , the Court did not address whether the 1972 amendments had supplanted state common law remedies as well as the federal common law remedy. *See id.*, at 310. On remand, Illinois argued that § 510 of the Clean Water Act, 33 U. S. C. § 1370, expressly preserved the State's right to adopt and enforce rules that are more stringent than federal standards. The Court of Appeals accepted Illinois' reading of § 510, but held that that section did "no more than to save the right and jurisdiction of a state to regulate activity occurring within the confines of its boundary waters." *Illinois v. Milwaukee*, 731 F.2d 403, 413 (CA7 1984), cert. denied, 469 U.S. 1196 (1985).

This Court subsequently endorsed that analysis in *International Paper Co. v. Ouellette*, 479 U.S. 481, 93 L. Ed. 2d 883, 107 S. Ct. 805 (1987), in which Vermont property owners claimed that the pollution discharged into Lake Champlain by a paper company located in New York constituted a nuisance under Vermont law. The Court held the Clean Water Act taken "as a whole, its purposes and its history" pre-empted an action based on the law of the affected State and that the only state law applicable to an interstate discharge is "the law of the State in which the point source is located." *Id.*, at 493, 487. Moreover, in reviewing § 402(b) of the Act, the Court pointed out that when a new permit is being issued by the source State's permit-granting agency, the downstream State

> does not have the authority to block the issuance of the permit if it is dissatisfied with the proposed standards. An affected State's only recourse is to apply to the EPA Administrator, who then has the discretion to disapprove the permit if he concludes that the discharges will have an undue impact on interstate waters. § 1342(d)(2) . . . . Thus the Act makes it clear that affected States occupy a subordinate position to source States in the federal regulatory program. *Id.*, at 490-491.

Unlike the foregoing cases, this litigation involves not a state-issued permit, but a federally issued permit. To explain the significance of this distinction, we comment further on the statutory scheme before addressing the specific issues raised by the parties.

III

The Clean Water Act anticipates a partnership between the States and the Federal Government, animated by a shared objective: "to restore and maintain the chemical, physical, and biological integrity of the Nation's waters." 33 U. S. C. § 1251(a). Toward this end, the Act provides for two sets of water quality measures. "Effluent limitations" are promulgated by the EPA and restrict the quantities, rates, and concentrations of specified substances which are discharged from point sources. *See* §§ 1311, 1314. "Water quality standards" are, in general, promulgated by the States and establish the desired condition of a waterway. *See* § 1313. These standards supplement effluent limitations "so that numerous point sources, despite individual compliance with effluent limitations, may be further regulated to prevent water quality from falling below acceptable levels." *EPA v. California ex rel. State Water Resources Control Bd.*, 426 U.S. 200, 205, n. 12, 48 L. Ed. 2d 578, 96 S. Ct. 2022 (1976).

The EPA provides States with substantial guidance in the drafting of water quality standards. *See generally* 40 C.F.R. pt. 131 (1991) (setting forth model water quality standards). Moreover, § 303 of the Act requires, *inter alia* , that state authorities periodically review water quality standards and secure the EPA's approval of any revisions in the standards. If the EPA recommends changes to the standards and the State fails to comply with that recommendation, the Act authorizes the EPA to promulgate water quality standards for the State. 33 U. S. C. § 1313(c).

The primary means for enforcing these limitations and standards is the NPDES, enacted in 1972 as a critical part of Congress' "complete rewriting" of federal water pollution law. *Milwaukee II*, 451 U.S. at 317. Section 301(a) of the Act, 33 U. S. C. § 1311(a), generally prohibits the discharge of any effluent into a navigable body of water unless the point source has obtained an NPDES permit. Section 402 establishes the NPDES permitting regime, and describes two types of permitting systems: state permit programs that must satisfy federal requirements and be approved by the EPA, and a federal program administered by the EPA.

Section 402(b) authorizes each State to establish "its own permit program for discharges into navigable waters within its jurisdiction." 33 U. S. C. § 1342(b). Among the requirements the state program must satisfy are the procedural protections for downstream States discussed in *Ouellette* and *Milwaukee II. See* §§ 1342(b)(3), (5). Although these provisions do not authorize the downstream State to veto the issuance of a permit for a new point source in another State, the Administrator retains authority to block the issuance of any state-issued permit that is "outside the guidelines and requirements" of the Act. § 1342(d)(2).

In the absence of an approved state program, the EPA may issue an NPDES permit under § 402(a) of the Act. (In these cases, for example, because Arkansas had not been authorized to issue NPDES permits when the Fayetteville plant was completed, the permit was issued by the EPA itself.) The EPA's permit program is subject to the "same terms, conditions, and requirements" as a state permit program. 33 U. S. C. § 1342(a)(3). Notwithstanding this general symmetry, the EPA has construed the Act as requiring that EPA-issued NPDES permits also comply with § 401(a). That section, which predates § 402 and the NPDES, applies to a broad category of federal licenses, and sets forth requirements for "any applicant for a Federal license or permit to conduct any activity including, but not limited to, the construction or operation of facilities, which may result in any discharge into the navigable waters." 33 U. S. C. § 1341(a). Section 401(a)(2) appears to prohibit the issuance of any federal license or permit over the objection of an affected State unless compliance with the affected State's water quality requirements can be ensured.

IV

The parties have argued three analytically distinct questions concerning the interpretation of the Clean Water Act. First, does the Act require the EPA, in crafting and issuing a permit to a point source in one State, to apply the water quality standards of downstream States? Second, even if the Act does not *require* as much, does the Agency have the statutory authority to mandate such compliance? Third, does the Act provide, as the Court of Appeals held, that once a body of water fails to meet water quality standards no discharge that yields effluent that reach the degraded waters will be permitted? In these cases, it is neither necessary nor prudent for us to resolve the first of these questions. In issuing the Fayetteville permit, the EPA assumed it was obligated by both the Act and its own regulations to ensure that the Fayetteville discharge would not violate Oklahoma's standards. As we discuss below, this assumption was permissible and reasonable and therefore there is no need for us to address whether the Act requires as much. Moreover, much of the analysis and argument in the briefs of the parties relies on statutory provisions that govern not only federal permits issued pursuant to §§ 401(a) and 402(a), but also state permits issued under § 402(b). It seems unwise to evaluate those arguments in a case such as these, which only involve a federal permit.

Our decision not to determine at this time the scope of the Agency's statutory *obligations* does not affect our resolution of the second question, which concerns the Agency's statutory *authority*. Even if the Clean Water Act itself does not require the Fayetteville discharge to comply with Oklahoma's water quality standards, the statute clearly does not limit the EPA's authority to mandate such compliance. Since 1973, EPA regulations have provided that an NPDES permit shall not be issued "when the imposition of conditions cannot ensure compliance with the applicable water quality requirements of all affected States." 40 C.F.R. § 122.4(d)(1991); *see also* 38 Fed. Reg. 13533 (1973); 40 C.F.R. § 122.44(d)(1991). Those regulations—relied upon by the EPA in the issuance of the Fayetteville permit—constitute a reasonable exercise of the Agency's statutory authority.

Congress has vested in the Administrator broad discretion to establish conditions for NPDES permits. Section 402(a) (2) provides that for EPA-issued permits "the Administrator shall prescribe conditions . . . to assure compliance with the requirements of [§ 402(a)(1)] and *such other requirements as he deems appropriate.*" 33 U. S. C. § 1342(a)(2) (emphasis added). Similarly, Congress preserved for the Administrator broad authority to oversee state permit programs:

> "No permit shall issue . . . if the Administrator . . . objects in writing to the issuance of such permit as being outside the guidelines and requirements of this chapter." § 1342(d)(2).

The regulations relied on by the EPA were a perfectly reasonable exercise of the Agency's statutory discretion. The application of state water quality standards in the interstate context is wholly consistent with the Act's broad purpose "to restore and maintain the chemical, physical, and biological integrity of the Nation's waters." 33 U.S.C. § 1251(a). Moreover, as noted above, § 301(b)(1)(C) expressly identifies the achievement of state water quality standards as one of the Act's central objectives. The Agency's regulations conditioning NPDES permits are a well-tailored means of achieving this goal.

Notwithstanding this apparent reasonableness, Arkansas argues that our description in *Ouellette* of the role of affected States in the permit process and our characterization of the affected States' position as "subordinate," see 479 U.S. at 490-491, indicates that the EPA's application of the Oklahoma standards was error. We disagree. Our statement in *Ouellette* concerned only an affected State's input into the permit process; that input is clearly limited by the plain language of § 402(b). Limits on an affected State's direct participation in permitting decisions, however, do not in any way constrain the EPA's authority to require a point source to comply with downstream water quality standards.

Arkansas also argues that regulations requiring compliance with downstream standards are at odds with the legislative history of the Act and with the statutory scheme established by the Act. Although we agree with Arkansas that the Act's legislative history indicates that Congress intended to grant the Administrator discretion in his oversight of the issuance of NPDES permits, we find nothing in that history to indicate that Congress intended to preclude the EPA from establishing a general requirement that such permits be conditioned to ensure compliance with downstream water quality standards.

Similarly, we agree with Arkansas that in the Clean Water Act Congress struck a careful balance among competing policies and interests, but do not find the EPA regulations concerning the application of downstream water quality standards at all incompatible with that balance. Congress, in crafting the Act, protected certain sovereign interests of the States; for example, § 510 allows States to adopt more demanding pollution-control standards than those established under the Act. Arkansas emphasizes that § 510 preserves such state authority only as it is applied to the waters of the regulating State. Even assuming Arkansas' construction of § 510 is correct, *cf. id.*, at 493, that section only concerns state authority and does not constrain the EPA's authority to promulgate reasonable regulations requiring point sources in one State to comply with water quality standards in downstream States.

For these reasons, we find the EPA's requirement that the Fayetteville discharge comply with Oklahoma's water quality standards to be a reasonable exercise of the Agency's substantial statutory discretion. *Cf. Chevron U.S.A. Inc. v. Natural Resources Defense Council, Inc.*, 467 U.S. 837, 842-845, 81 L. Ed. 2d 694, 104 S. Ct. 2778 (1984).

V

The Court of Appeals construed the Clean Water Act to prohibit any discharge of effluent that would reach waters already in violation of existing water quality standards. We find nothing in the Act to support this reading.

The interpretation of the statute adopted by the court had not been advanced by any party during the Agency or court proceedings. Moreover, the Court of Appeals candidly acknowledged that its theory "has apparently never before been addressed by a federal court." 908 F.2d at 620, n. 39. The only statutory provision the court cited to support its legal analysis was § 402(h), *see id.*, at 633, which merely authorizes the EPA (or a state permit program) to prohibit a publicly owned treatment plant that is violating a condition of its NPDES permit from accepting any additional pollutants for treatment until the ongoing violation has been corrected. *See* 33 U. S. C. § 1342(h). Although the Act contains several provisions directing compliance with state water quality standards, *see, e.g.*, § 1311(b)(1)(C), the parties have pointed to nothing that mandates a complete ban on discharges into a waterway that is in violation of those standards. The statute does, however, contain provisions designed to remedy existing water quality violations and to allocate the burden of reducing undesirable discharges between existing sources and new sources. *See, e.g.*, § 1313(d). Thus, rather than establishing the categorical ban announced by the Court of Appeals—which might frustrate the construction of new plants that would improve existing conditions—the Clean Water Act vests in the EPA and the States broad authority to develop long-range, areawide programs to alleviate and eliminate existing pollution. *See, e.g.*, § 1288(b)(2).

To the extent that the Court of Appeals relied on its interpretation of the Act to reverse the EPA's permitting decision, that reliance was misplaced.

VI

The Court of Appeals also concluded that the EPA's issuance of the Fayetteville permit was arbitrary and capricious because the Agency misinterpreted Oklahoma's water quality standards. The primary difference between the court's and the Agency's interpretation of the standards derives from the court's construction of the Act. Contrary to the EPA's interpretation of the Oklahoma standards, the Court of Appeals read those standards as containing the same categorical ban on new discharges that the court had found in the Clean Water Act itself. Although we do not believe the text of the Oklahoma standards supports the court's reading (indeed, we note that Oklahoma itself had not advanced that interpretation in its briefs in the Court of Appeals), we reject it for a more fundamental reason—namely, that the Court of Appeals exceeded the legitimate scope of judicial review of an agency adjudication. To emphasize the importance of this point, we shall first briefly assess the soundness of the EPA's interpretation and application of the Oklahoma standards and then comment more specifically on the Court of Appeals' approach.

As discussed above, an EPA regulation requires an NPDES permit to comply "with the applicable water quality requirements of all affected States." 40 C.F.R. § 122.4(d)(1991). This regulation effectively incorporates into federal law those state-law standards the Agency reasonably determines to be "applicable." In such a situation, then, state water quality standards—promulgated by the States with substantial guidance from the EPA and approved by the Agency—are part of the federal law of water pollution control.

Two features of the body of law governing water pollution support this conclusion. First, as discussed more thoroughly above, we have long recognized that interstate water pollution is controlled by federal law. *See supra*, at 98-100. Recognizing that the system of federally approved state standards as applied in the interstate context constitutes federal law is wholly consistent with this principle. Second, treating state standards in interstate controversies as federal law accords with the Act's purpose of authorizing the EPA to create and manage a uniform system of interstate water pollution regulation. Because we recognize that, at least insofar as they affect the issuance of a permit in another State, the Oklahoma standards have a federal character, the EPA's reasonable, consistently held interpretation of those standards is entitled to substantial deference. *Cf. INS v. National Center for Immigrants' Rights*, 502 U.S. 183, 189-190, 116 L. Ed. 2d 546, 112 S. Ct. 551 (1991); *Chevron U. S. A. Inc. v. Natural Resources Defense Council, Inc.*, 467 U.S. 837, 81 L. Ed. 2d 694, 104 S. Ct. 2778 (1984). In these cases, the Chief Judicial Officer ruled that the Oklahoma standards—which require that there be "no degradation" of the upper Illinois River—would only be violated if the discharge effected an "actually detectable or measurable" change in water quality.

This interpretation of the Oklahoma standards is certainly reasonable and consistent with the purposes and principles of the Clean Water Act. As the Chief Judicial Officer noted, "unless there is some method for measuring compliance, there is no way to ensure compliance." (internal quotation marks omitted; citation omitted). Moreover, this interpretation of the Oklahoma standards makes eminent sense in the interstate context: If every discharge that had some theoretical impact on a downstream State were interpreted as "degrading" the downstream waters, downstream States might wield an effective veto over upstream discharges.

The EPA's application of those standards in these cases was also sound. On remand, the ALJ scrutinized the record and made explicit factual findings regarding four primary measures of water quality under the Oklahoma standards: eutrophication, esthetics, dissolved oxygen, and metals. In each case, the ALJ found that the Fayetteville discharge would not lead to a detectable change in water quality. He therefore concluded that the Fayetteville discharge would not violate the Oklahoma water quality standards. Because we agree with the Agency's Chief Judicial Officer that these findings are supported by substantial evidence, we conclude that the Court of Appeals should have affirmed both the EPA's construction of the regulations and the issuance of the Fayetteville permit.

In its review of the EPA's interpretation and application of the Oklahoma standards, the Court of Appeals committed three mutually compounding errors.

First, the court failed to give due regard to the EPA's interpretation of its own regulations, as those regulations incorporate the Oklahoma standards. Instead the court voiced its own interpretation of the governing law and concluded that "where a proposed source would discharge effluents that would contribute to conditions currently constituting a violation of applicable water quality standards, such [a] proposed source may not be permitted." 908 F.2d at 620. As we have already pointed out, that reading of the law is not supported by the statute or by any EPA regulation. The Court of Appeals sat in review of an agency action and should have afforded the EPA's interpretation of the governing law an appropriate level of deference. See generally *Chevron, supra*, at 842-844.

Second, the court disregarded well-established standards for reviewing the factual findings of agencies and instead made its own factual findings. The troubling nature of the court's analysis appears on the face of the opinion itself: At least four times, the court concluded that "there was substantial evidence before the ALJ to support" particular findings which the court thought appropriate, but which were contrary to those actually made by the ALJ. 908 F.2d at 620, 625, 627, 629. Although we have long recognized the "substantial evidence" standard in administrative law, the court below turned that analysis on its head. A court reviewing an agency's adjudicative action should accept the *agency's* factual findings if those findings are supported by substantial evidence on the record as a whole. The court should not supplant the agency's findings merely by identifying alternative findings that could be supported by substantial evidence.

Third, the court incorrectly concluded that the EPA's decision was arbitrary and capricious. This error is derivative of the court's first two errors. Having substituted its reading of the governing law for the Agency's, and having made its own factual findings, the Court of Appeals concluded that the EPA erred in not considering an important and relevant fact—namely, that the upper Illinois River was (by the court's assessment) already degraded.

As we have often recognized, an agency ruling is "arbitrary and capricious if the agency has . . . entirely failed to consider an important aspect of the problem." However, in these cases, the degraded status of the river is only an "important aspect" because of the Court of Appeals' novel and erroneous interpretation of the controlling law. Under the EPA's interpretation of that law, what matters is not the river's current status, but rather whether the proposed discharge will have a "detectable effect" on that status. If the Court of Appeals had been properly respectful of the Agency's permissible reading of the Act and the Oklahoma standards, the court would not have adjudged the Agency's decision arbitrary and capricious for this reason.

In sum, the Court of Appeals made a policy choice that it was not authorized to make. Arguably, as that court suggested, it might be wise to prohibit any discharge into the Illinois River, even if that discharge would have no adverse impact on water quality. But it was surely not arbitrary for the EPA to conclude—given the benefits to the river from the increased flow of relatively clean water and the benefits achieved in Arkansas by allowing the new plant to operate as designed—that allowing the discharge would be even wiser. It is not our role, or that of the Court of Appeals, to decide which policy choice is the better one, for it is clear that Congress has entrusted such decisions to the Environmental Protection Agency.

Accordingly, the judgment of the Court of Appeals is

Reversed.

[xii] Oil and Hazardous Substance Pollution

UNITED STATES v. THE CATHERINE

United States Court of Appeals, Fourth Circuit (1954)
212 F.2d 89

PARKER, Chief Judge.

This is an appeal from a judgment for defendant in a suit instituted against the S.S. Catherine to recover a penalty for alleged violation of the Oil Pollution Act of 1924, 33 U.S.C. §§ 431-437. It was conceded on the part of the vessel that a few barrels of fuel oil did escape while she was lying at a pier and taking on fuel in Baltimore harbor, but she claimed that this was the result of unavoidable accident within the meaning of the statute and that no penalty had been incurred. The trial judge so found; and the United States has appealed.

The facts are fully set forth in the opinion of the court below, see United States v. The Catherine, 116 F. Supp. 668, and may be briefly stated here. The Catherine was lying beside a grain elevator pier in Baltimore harbor and was bunkering fuel oil which was being pumped from a barge lying alongside her. The scuppers had been closed and other usual precautions taken before the pumping began; but after the double bottom tanks had been filled and the filling of the afterpeak tank had begun, it was discovered that oil was spilling on the deck. This occurred because a rag had been caught in the valve which closed the line leading to one of the tanks which had been filled, with the result that the complete closing of the valve was prevented and oil was allowed to escape therefrom. When the situation was discovered, the pumping was immediately stopped and everything was done that could reasonably have been done to prevent the oil from going overboard into the harbor. According to the government's witnesses, not over three to five barrels went overboard.

With respect to the presence of the rag in the valve, the trial judge said:

> "Subsequent examination by the chief engineer failed to disclose definitely where the rag had come from, or just how it happened to become lodged between the seat and disk of the valve. The only testimony on this point was that of the chief engineer to the effect that it is not uncommon to find that foreign matter of various kinds has been left in the bottom of the tanks of vessels, following their original construction, and that gradually, over a

period of time, it may work down to the suction line and be picked up when oil is pumped; that the rag must have come from the inside of the tank; and that the rag's presence in the valve was not capable of detection without taking the valve apart, which was later done, the rag's presence in the valve not being apparent by the mere opening and closing of the valve by the wheel provided for that purpose.

. . . .

"We are satisfied from the weight of the credible evidence that, as respects the question of the vessel's responsibility, presence of the rag in the valve was due to an unavoidable accident."

The findings of the trial judge were as follows:

"I find: (1) that the presence of the rag in the valve was an unavoidable accident; (2) that the resultant leak in the valve up through the sounding pipes was likewise an unavoidable accident; and (3) that there was no negligence on the part of those in charge of the vessel while the oil was being loaded into her tanks on the night in question, as respects sounding the tank; or not sooner detecting and stopping the flow of oil on to the deck; or as respects the means employed, or not employed to prevent discharge into the harbor, after the overflow on to the deck had been detected and stopped."

The pertinent portion of the statute, 33 U.S.C. § 433, for violation of which the penalty is asked is as follows:

"Except in case of emergency imperiling life or property, or unavoidable accident, collision, or stranding, and except as otherwise permitted by regulations prescribed by the Secretary as in sections 434 to 437 of this title inclusive, authorized, it shall be unlawful for any person to discharge, or suffer, or permit the discharge of oil by any method, means, or manner into or upon the coastal navigable waters of the United States from any vessel using oil as fuel for the generation of propulsion power, . . ."

This statute, which was enacted for the protection of the interest of the public in the navigable waters of the United States, is entitled to the liberal construction accorded remedial legislation. It is perfectly clear, we think, that it is not necessary to show willfulness or intent to establish a violation and that where the escape of oil from a vessel into navigable waters is shown, the burden rests upon those who would avoid liability therefor to bring themselves within one of the exceptions of the statute. . . .

We agree with the learned District Judge, however, that the vessel here has clearly shown that the escape of oil with which she is charged was the result of unavoidable accident within the exception of the statute. An unavoidable accident is one which could not have been avoided by that degree of prudence, foresight, care and caution which the law requires in the particular case. . . .

. . . .

The vessel here clearly carried the burden of showing that the escape of the oil was due to unavoidable accident when it showed that the escape resulted from the rag's being caught in the valve. No one could reasonably have foreseen a casualty of this sort, and the possibility of its occurring was so remote as not to require any special inspection to prevent it. There is no suggestion that the vessel was not properly inspected; and, if there had been any reasonably foreseeable danger of any such happening as occurred, or if any sort of inspection to guard against it had been customary or required in the exercise of ordinary care, it is a reasonable assumption that these would have been called to the attention of the court by the government engineers under whose direction the suit was prosecuted.

The government contends that the trial judge held that the burden of proof was on the government to establish negligence. We do not so interpret his opinion, and it was not so interpreted by those who reported it for publication, as shown by the headnotes. We need not go into this, however, since it is perfectly clear that, with the burden upon the vessel to negative negligence in the escape of the oil and establish that such escape was due to unavoidable accident, the burden has been met and unavoidable accident established.

Affirmed.

NOTE

When the case of *United States v. The Catherine* was decided, the original Oil Pollution Act of 1924 (43 Stat. 604) was still in effect. That act merely contained a prohibition against the discharge of oil "into or upon the coastal navigable water of the United States." There was, however, an exception in the law—discharges of oil were permitted "in case of emergency imperilling life or property, or unavoidable accident, collision, or stranding, and except as otherwise permitted by regulations prescribed by the Secretary. . . ." The law merely provided for misdemeanor penalties but did not deal with the subject of cleanup costs. The 1924 law was amended in 1966 (Pub. L. 89-753, 80 Stat. 1253). Its jurisdictional reach was extended to "navigable waters of the United States" and, in addition to earlier criminal penalties, the amendment provided that the person responsible for the discharge of the oil was to be responsible for the necessary cleanup operations. If he failed to undertake the cleanup, the Secretary of the Interior would arrange for the removal of the oil and would seek to collect from him all costs and expenses reasonably incurred in the cleanup of the navigable waters and adjoining shorelines. The cost of cleanup would remain a lien on the vessel until discharged. The 1966 amendment was passed largely to undo the narrow decision of the Supreme Court in *United States v. Standard Oil Co.*, 384 U.S. 224 (1966), which had held that the 1924 Act applied only to the discharge of oil into coastal waters, but not to discharges into inland navigable waters. The 1966 amendment resolved this problem but it created what developed into a far more substantial one, in that "discharge" was defined to include only "grossly negligent or willful" oil spills. This made the act almost impossible to enforce, in spite of its strengthened sanctions and remedies.

Three major incidents involving oil pollution of the sea and coastal waters occurred shortly after the passage of the 1966 amendment. In 1967, the

"Torrey Canyon" broke up off the southern coast of England, spilling thousands of tons of crude oil. In 1968 the "Ocean Eagle" broke up near the coast of Puerto Rico, again causing a major oil spill, and in 1969 there occurred a blowout of an off-shore drilling operation near Santa Barbara from a drilling platform operated by Union Oil Company. It is clear that the 1966 amendments of the Oil Pollution Act of 1924 would not have imposed liability on the owners of the tankers (had they been in U.S. waters) or on the drilling operations involved. The need for the 1970 Act must be viewed in this context. *See* Baldwin, "The Santa Barbara Oil Spill," in Baldwin & Page, Law and the Environment 5 (1970).

The hearings prior to the passage of the 1970 law (Pub. L. 91-224, Tit. I, § 102, 84 Stat. 91) provided ample evidence for the vast cleanup costs involved in restoring coastal areas and in restoring the ocean environment. The hearings also demonstrated that however effective the cleanup, vast damage to marine life and to the environment generally would be left from a massive oil spill even after cleanup operations are completed. *See, generally,* House Committee on Merchant Marine and Fisheries, Hearings on H.R. 6495, H.R. 6609, and H.R. 6794, and H.R. 7325 to Amend the Oil Pollution Act of 1924, 91st Cong., 1st Sess. (1969).

When the Federal Water Pollution Control Act was amended in 1972, the 1970 oil pollution controls were readopted without change, except that the provisions were expanded to cover not only oil, but also other hazardous substances. Since some of these substances are soluble and therefore not readily subject to the oil spill cleanup provision of the law, provisions were made in the law for alternative penalty sanctions in lieu of cleanup costs.

The 1977 amendment of the Act substantially increased the limits of liability under the law, but left intact its general structure. The 1978 amendment of § 311 strengthened EPA powers with regard to the setting of hazardous substance spill penalties, following the decision in *Manufacturing Chemists Association v. Costle, infra.*

In addition to § 311, another statute had to be considered in certain circumstances, namely 33 U.S.C. § 1001 *et seq.* (75 Stat. 402, last amended in 1966, 80 Stat. 372). This chapter was designed to implement the International Convention for the Prevention of the Pollution of the Sea by Oil. The special problems involved in control of oil pollution on the high seas is discussed in Utton, *Protective Measures and the Torrey Canyon*, 9 B.C. Ind. & Com. L. Rev. 613 (1971).

The 1970 amendment of the law was a response to the Torrey Canyon and Santa Barbara disasters. The next major development of water pollution law, namely the 1990 federal Oil Pollution Act, 33U.S.C. § 2701 *et seq.*, was a response to the 1989 Exxon Valdez oil spill into Prince William Sound in Alaska. This massive, disastrous oil spill, whose consequences have not as yet been eradicated ten years after the event, energized Congress into action after some 15 years of Congressional discussion of the regulation of oil spills and their resulting liabilities. The law is a broad measure which significantly enhances and enlarges the liabilities under § 311 of the Federal Water Pollution Control Act. The law creates a new range of civil liabilities, and includes a variety of provisions relating to the prevention of, response to, and cleanup of oil spills. It also provides for a one billion dollar Oil Spill Trust Fund, supported by a five cent per barrel tax on oil, to pay for cleanup and damage costs when the party responsible for the spill is unknown, has reached its liability limits, or is unable or refuses to pay. The fund limits spending on natural resource damage restoration and replacement to $500 million per spill, but provides for unlimited liabilities for gross negligence, willful misconduct, or the violation of federal operating or safety standards. The liability provisions clearly draw on and expand earlier § 311 provisions and parallel some of the provisions of the Superfund Law.

The Oil Pollution Act of 1990 has finally adopted the long-discussed double hull requirement for new tankers and barges of at least 5,000 gross tons. The double hull provisions also require the phasing out of single hull vessels between 1995 and 2010, unless they are converted.

The Act also requires contingency planning by federal, state and local governments, and imposes a clear responsibility on the federal government to take charge of the cleanup of major oil spills. Measures to increase navigation safety also include controls on the qualifications of the officers that operate tankers and on responsible pilots.

Although the Oil Pollution Act (OPA) is derived in large measure from § 311 of the Federal Water Pollution Control Act,it expands liabilities very extensively. Though many of the definitions of the Act are similar to the definitions originated in § 311, and although liability is defined as in the FWPCA, the standard, as in CERCLA, is that of strict, joint, and several liability. Moreover, limited defenses, such as act of god, act of war, and act of a third party, are provided. The third party defense has been limited substantially. Unlike earlier laws, the Oil Pollution Act provides for the recovery of damages by private parties, including damages for injury, for the destruction or loss of natural resources without regard to the ownership or management of such resources. OPA also provides for recovery for economic loss resulting from destruction of real or personal property or from the destruction of natural resources. Fishermen injured as a result of an oil spill thus can recover for their loss of livelihood under OPA.

Under the Act, the range of liability and of responsible persons is broadened considerably, and financial responsibility may be established by insurance, surety bond and other evidence of responsibility. Furthermore, the law provides that claims may be asserted directly against guarantors or insurers.

The Oil Pollution Act also contains a segment referred to as the "Oil Tanker Environmental Oversight and Monitoring Act of 1990" which is broadly designed to prepare for future oil spill emergencies and to involve not only a broad range of federal but also state and local agencies in the prevention and cleanup effort.

When an oil spill occurs, the prevention of major damage requires prompt notification of appropriate response mechanisms and agencies. If the spill occurs at night or in the contiguous zone, it may not be observed or detected unless there is prompt notification. Section 311(b)(5) of the Clean Water Actprovides that any person in charge of a vessel or an onshore or offshore facility who has knowledge of any discharge of oil or of a hazardous substance must immediately notify the U.S. Coast Guard, which in turn must notify the appropriate state agency of any state which may be reasonably expected to be affected by such a discharge. A person in charge of the vessel or facility who fails to provide such immediate notification shall, upon conviction, be fined in accordance with Title 18 of the U.S. Code or be imprisoned for not more than five years or both.

The giving of notice in accordance with the section results in use immunity regarding the information contained in the notice for purposes of prosecution under the Act, as well as under the Rivers and Harbors Act. Use immunity applies to criminal prosecution, but does not provide immunity from suit for civil penalties under the Act. The question had been raised as to whether the so-called civil penalties were in fact criminal in nature. The Supreme Court, following certiorari in *United States v. Ward*,[207] resolved disagreements between the circuits on this issue by holding that the civil penalties were remedial in nature, rather than criminal, thereby resolving the purported Fifth Amendment self incrimination problem.

The term "person in charge" was long interpreted to include both natural persons and corporations. When the Oil Pollution Act of 1990 amended § 311(b)(5), it limited the statutorily granted use immunity to natural persons, thus further limiting the immunity recognized by the Supreme Court in *United States v. Ward*.[208] The Act provides for substantial civil penalties for oil spill regulations following notice and hearing.[209]

One of the major contributions of the Oil Pollution Act of 1990 was that it did away with the totally unrealistic limitations on the imposition of cleanup costs. Section 311 of the Clean Water Act, 33 U.S.C. § 1321, provided for a limit of $150 per gross ton per vessel. In the case of the Exxon Valdez spill, Exxon's liability under § 311 would have been limited to $15-$31 million. The actual cleanup of that oil spill cost some $2 billion. The Oil Pollution Act of 1990 provides for a federal liability limit of $1,200 per gross ton which is eight times the earlier liability limit under § 311 of the FWPCA. The Oil Spill Liability Trust Fund under OPA provides for a billion dollar fund, all of which may be spent on a single oil spill. In addition, additional funding is likely to be available under state liability provisions pursuant to state oil spill funds. Pursuant to OPA § 1018, 33 U.S.C. § 2718, the state liability provisions and state laws relating to the regulation of state removal activities are not federally preempted. It will be noted in the materials that follow that state laws relating to oil spills are not limited by federal liability limits. Thus, violators may face unlimited state liabilities.

The Oil Pollution Act itself provides for unlimited liability when an incident that causes an oil spill is the result of gross negligence or wilful misconduct, or the result of the violation of federal safety, construction, or operating regulations. Also, liability limitations do not apply when the discharge has not been reported by the responsible party or when that party fails to cooperate or follow the orders of officials responsible for removal activities.

---

[207] 444 U.S. 1067, 100 S.Ct. 2636, 65 L.Ed.2d 742 (1980).

[208] *See also* F. Grad, Treatise on Environmental Law, § 3.03[8][b], text at note 74 *et seq.*

[209] FWPCA § 311(b)(6), 33 U.S.C. § 1321(b)(6).

In addition to the significant increase in cleanup liabilities for oil spills, the penalty provisions under the Oil Pollution Act are significantly steeper than under the Clean Water Act. The mandatory civil penalty is now $25,000 for each day of such offense or in the alternative $1,000 per barrel of oil discharged. The CWA § 311penalty had been $5,000 for each offense. Under the old law the gravity of the spill and the extent of the cleanup could increase the penalty to $50,000. Under the new Oil Pollution Act, the penalty is increased to not less than $100,000 and not more than $3,000 per barrel of oil discharged if there was gross negligence or wilful misconduct. Failure to report the discharge, subject to hearing requirements, may call for administrative penalties of up to $10,000 per violation to $125,000. As noted earlier, the failure to report a discharge formerly called for a fine of not more than $10,000 or imprisonment of not more than a year or both. Under the Oil Pollution Act, this has been raised to a fine of not more than $250,000 for an individual or $500,000 for a corporation, or by imprisonment of not more than three years—and five years for a subsequent conviction—or both. Discharging oil negligently now also results in criminal penalties of not less than $2,500 and not more than $25,000 per day of violation or by imprisonment for not more than one year or both. Knowing discharge now results in criminal penalties of not less than $5,000 nor more than $50,000 per violation or by imprisonment for not more than three years. Separate penalties may also be provided under state oil spill laws.

Whenever there is a spill of oil or hazardous substances into waters covered by the Federal Water Pollution Control Act, § 311(c)of the Act, as amended by § 4201 of the Oil Pollution Act of 1990requires the President, in accordance with the National Contingency Plan and any appropriate Area Contingency Plan, to ensure effective and immediate removal of the discharge, and mitigation or prevention of a substantial threat of a discharge (1) into or on the navigable waters; (2) on the adjoining shorelines to navigable waters; (3) into or on the waters of the exclusive economic zone; or (4) that may affect natural resources belonging to or under the exclusive management authority of the United States.

The section clearly places the President in charge of all response activities. In carrying out his obligations, the President may remove or arrange for the removal of a discharge and may mitigate or prevent a substantial threat of a discharge at any time. He may also direct or monitor all federal, state and private activities to remove a discharge, and may remove and, if necessary, destroy a vessel discharging or threatening to discharge, by whatever means are available. When a discharge, or the substantial threat of a discharge of oil or of a hazardous substance from a vessel, offshore facility, or onshore facility is of such a size or character as to be a substantial threat to the public health or welfare of the United States (including threats to fish, wildlife, other natural resources and the public and private beaches and shorelines), the President must direct all federal, state and private actions to remove the discharge or to mitigate or to prevent the threat. In carrying out this obligation, the President may act without regard to any provision of law governing contracting procedures or employment of personnel by the federal government.

The provision anticipates a fully coordinated effort in accordance with the National Contingency Plan. Each federal agency, state, owner or operator, or other person participating in efforts under the provision must act in accordance with the plan or as directed by the President. The section provides that there will be no removal costs or damages that result from actions taken or not taken in the course of rendering care, assistance or advice when such actions are consistent with the National Contingency Plan or the directives of the President. But this exemption from liability does not apply to (1) a responsible party (*i.e.*, the person who caused the spill); (2) a response under the Comprehensive Environmental Response Compensation and Liability Act of 1980; or (3) with respect to personal injury or wrongful death; or (4) if the person is grossly negligent or engages in wilful misconduct. Indeed, the section stresses that a responsible party is liable for any removal costs and for any damages that any other person would be relieved of under subparagraph (c)(3)(A). The section establishes that nothing in the response provisions affects the obligation of an owner or operator to respond immediately to a discharge or the threat of a discharge, nor does it affect the liability of a responsible party under the Oil Pollution Act of 1990. The term "responsible party" is defined in § 1001 of the Oil Pollution Act of 1990.

The Conference Committee Report calls attention to the immediate obligations of the President to see to the removal of the oil or hazardous substance, assuming responsibility and costs of these actions, subject to reimbursement from the responsible party. The President is to "federalize" the effort. The report also notes that the reference to the term "exclusive economic zone" is the zone established by Presidential Proclamation 5030 of March 10, 1983. And the report emphasizes the obligation to protect the public health or welfare of the United States including, but not limited to, fish, shellfish, wildlife, other natural resources, and public and private shorelines and beaches. It also notes that examples of spills that have posed such a substantial threat to the public health or welfare include the spills from the Exxon Valdez in Alaska's Prince William Sound and from the American Trader in California's coastal waters, and the spill and a substantial threat of a larger spill from the Mega Borg in the waters of the Gulf of Mexico. Commenting on the immunity from liability established under this section for those taking action in response to oil spills, the report notes that this provision reflects the Conferees' intention that responses to oil spills be immediate and effective.[210]

The requirement for the preparation of a National Contingency Plan and for compliance with the requirements of the plan is now to be found in § 311(d).[211]

Section 311(d) as amended requires the President to prepare and publish a National Contingency Plan for removal of oil and hazardous substances. The Plan must provide for efficient, coordinated, and effective action to minimize damages from oil and hazardous substance discharges, including containment, dispersal and removal of oil and hazardous substances. At a minimum, the plan must include the following:

---

[210] House Conf. Rep. No. 101-653 at 145-146.

[211] OPA § 4201, amending § 311(d) of the Federal Water Pollution Control Act, 33 U.S.C. § 1321(d).

(A) the assignment of duties and responsibilities among federal departments and agencies in coordination with state and local agencies and port authorities, including water pollution control and conservation and trusteeship of natural resources;

(B) the identification, procurement, maintenance and storage of equipment and supplies;

(C) the establishment or designation of Coast Guard strike teams consisting of properly prepared and trained personnel, adequate oil and hazardous substance pollution control equipment, and a detailed oil and hazardous substance pollution and prevention plan;

(D) a system of surveillance and notice to protect against, as well as to ensure the earliest possible notice of, oil and hazardous substance discharges or imminent threats of such discharges;

(E) the establishment of a national center to provide coordination and direction in carrying out the plan;

(F) procedures and techniques to be employed in identifying, containing, dispersing and removing oil and hazardous substances;

(G) a schedule prepared in cooperation with the states identifying dispersants, other chemicals and other spill-mitigating devices and substances, the waters in which the dispersants and other devices and substances may be used, and the quantities of such dispersants and other chemicals that can be used safely in such waters. The schedule must provide, in the case of any dispersant, chemical spill mitigating devices, or substance, or waters not specifically identified in the schedule, that the President (or his delegate) may on a case-by-case basis identify the dispersants, other chemicals and other spill mitigating devices that may be used, the waters in which they may be used, and the quantities that can be used safely in such waters;

(H) a system whereby the state or states affected by a discharge of oil or hazardous substance may act where necessary to remove the discharge and may then be reimbursed from the Oil Spill Liability Trust Fund in accordance with the Oil Pollution Act of 1990 for the reasonable costs incurred in that removal;

(I) the establishment of criteria and procedures to ensure immediate and effective federal identification of, and response to, a discharge or a threat of a discharge that results in a substantial threat to the public health or welfare of the United States, as required under § 311(c)(2);

(J) the establishment of procedures and standards for removing a worst case discharge of oil and for mitigating or preventing the threat of such a discharge;

(K) the designation of the federal official who will be the federal on-scene coordinator for each area for which an Area Contingency Plan must be prepared under § 311(j);

(L) the establishment of procedures for the coordination of the activities of Coast Guard strike teams under subparagraph (C); the federal on-scene coordinator designated under subparagraph (K); the district response groups established under subsection 311(j); and area committees established under subsection 311(j).

(M) a fish and wildlife response plan developed in consultation with the U.S. Fish and Wildlife Service, the National Oceanic and Atmospheric Administration, and interested parties (including state fish and wildlife conservation officials) for the immediate protection, rescue and rehabilitation of fish and wildlife resources and their habitats.

The President may from time to time revise and amend the National Contingency Plan as he deems advisable. After the Plan is published, the removal of oil and hazardous substances and actions to minimize damage from oil and hazardous substances must, to the greatest extent possible, be in accordance with the plan.

The amendments of § 311 of the Federal Water Pollution Control Actresulting from the 1990 Oil Pollution Act also established an elaborate national planning and response system with a central National Response Unit and Coast Guard District Response Groups in each Coast Guard district. In addition, area committees to effectuate Area Contingency Plans are also provided for making use of state and local instrumentalities and agencies. The requirements also include standards for equipment and requirements for periodic inspection of equipment suitable for oil removal. Note that the National Contingency Plan applies to oil removal and hazardous substance removal, thereby including national contingencies covered by CERCLA, the Comprehensive Environmental Response, Compensation, and Liability Act.[212] The National Contingency Plan is a very lengthy document of several hundred pages which defines responses and remedial activities under the Oil Pollution Act, § 311of the Federal Water Pollution Control Act, and under other hazardous waste laws. First established by Executive Order 12286 in January of 1981, the current version is found in 40 C.F.R. Pt. 300.

MANUFACTURING CHEMISTS ASSOCIATION v. COSTLE

United States District Court, Western District of Louisiana (1978)
455 F. Supp. 968

VERON, District Judge:

This action challenges certain regulations promulgated by the Environmental Protection Agency ("EPA") pursuant to Section 311 of the Federal Water Pollution Control Act,("the Act") 33 U.S.C. § 1321, as amended by the Clean Water Act of 1977, P.L. 95-217, 91 Stat. 1566. Published at 43 Fed. Reg. 10474 and promulgated as 40 C.F.R. Parts 116, 117, 118 and 119, these regulations identify some 271 chemicals as hazardous substances and thereby trigger a comprehensive reporting, liability and cleanup scheme for discharges of hazardous substances from offshore facilities, vessels and onshore facilities, including motor vehicles and rolling stock. (These regulations were originally intended to go into effect on June 12, 1978. However, on May 30, 1978, EPA

---

[212] *See also* F. Grad, Treatise on Environmental Law, § 4A.02[1][d].

amended the challenged regulations to delay their implementation until August 11 only insofar as they apply to chemical manufacturers whose operations are already regulated by the permit system established under § 402 of the Act.) Plaintiffs filed their complaint on May 11, 1978, and filed a motion on May 19 seeking a preliminary injunction against enforcement of the regulations pending the outcome of this litigation.

Plaintiff/Manufacturing Chemists Association ("MCA") is a nonprofit trade association of 196 member companies representing more than 90% of the production capacity of basic industrial chemicals in the United States. The individually-named plaintiffs are members of MCA and are engaged in the production of basic industrial chemicals throughout the country. (A number of facilities which will be affected by the challenged regulations are located in or near the city in which this court sits.) Intervenors/Association of American Railroads, et al ("AAR"), represent the interests of those involved in daily transportation of massive amounts of "hazardous substances" over the nation's railroad network. Intervenor/The Fertilizer Institute ("TFI") represents fertilizer manufacturing companies many of which, it is asserted, would be adversely affected should the challenged regulations be implemented. Defendants/Douglas M. Costle and the EPA have promulgated the regulations herein considered. Our jurisdiction in this matter is based on 28 U.S.C. §§ 1331(a), 1337 and 1361. Declaratory relief is sought under 28 U.S.C. §§ 2201 and 2202. The amount in controversy exceeds $10,000.

Plaintiffs, pursuant to Rule 65(a) of the Federal Rules of Civil Procedure,now move this court to grant a preliminary injunction barring enforcement of the challenged regulations. Plaintiffs urge that such an injunction should be granted because:

1. The regulations were promulgated in violation of certain clear legal requirements.

2. The immediate implementation of the challenged regulations on June 12, 1978, would inflict serious and irreparable injury on the plaintiffs.

3. The entry of an injunctive order to stay enforcement of the regulations pending this court's final decision on the merits would not be contrary to any public interests.

. . . .

I.

Plaintiffs contend that immediate implementation of the challenged regulations would cause them irreparable injury. They base this assertion on the fact that many chemical manufacturing facilities regularly discharge waste effluents containing some of the 271 substances designated as "hazardous" by the proposed EPA regulations even though these facilities are operating under and in conformance with the National Pollutant Discharge Elimination System ("NPDES") permit procedures authorized by Section 402 of the Act, since in most cases such permits do not limit the discharge of the newly-designated substances. Thus, should the new regulations be implemented immediately, many chemical manufacturers would be subject to severe penalties for violating the new standards. Two courses are therefore available to them. They would be forced either to cease operations completely or to spend millions of dollars (over an extended period of time) to purchase and install the new control systems necessary to bring the facilities into compliance with the regulations, even before a final determination on the actual validity of the regulations has been rendered. Defendants argue that the extension of the date of implementation until August 11, as well as the fact that a mere filing of a request for an amended NPDES permit by any chemical manufacturer will immediately shield the manufacturer from liability for discharges while his permit is being acted upon, mitigate against the claim of irreparable harm.

We do not agree with defendants' assertions. First, it is highly doubtful that even a 60-day extension will give plaintiffs enough time to monitor adequately their effluent, determine what hazardous substances are, in fact, being discharged, and prepare an application for an amended permit. Second, the filing of an application is an uncertain shield at best, since the EPA may decide to grant all such applications within days after receipt by simply applying the "hazardous substances" discharge limits developed as part of the challenged regulations directly to the permits being requested. The time limits for complying with the new permits are, as yet, undetermined. Finally, this extension has no effect on dischargers of hazardous substances who, for whatever reason, have no NPDES permit.

The specter of irreparable harm is especially frightening to Intervenors/AAR. As common carriers of goods by rail, intervenors are required by law to accept and transport all shipments offered in compliance with applicable tariffs. Interstate Commerce Act § 1(4), 49 U.S.C. § 1(4). At the same time, virtually all shipments tendered to a railroad are currently described according to the Standard Transportation Commodity Code (49 C.F.R. Part 1248), and a large percentage of the substances about to be designated as "hazardous" by the EPA would not be clearly identified by the STC Code. Moreover any attempt by a railroad to compel a shipper to provide specific identification of shipments containing substances designated as "hazardous" by the EPA would be subject to the requirements of Section 6(1) of the Interstate Commerce Act concerning the publication in tariff form of any rates, fares or charges for transportation (a lengthy and difficult process). As a result, many railroads would be in the perilous situation of not knowing whether the substances being carried are, in fact, subject to the constraints and penalties of the new regulations. It is possible under these challenged regulations that each individual railroad car may be taken as subjecting a carrier to separate potential liability for fines and penalties resulting from any discharges which may occur. Intervenors are thus in danger of being heavily penalized for discharges from "hazardous" cargoes even though (1) the composition of such cargoes may be unknown to them, and (2) they are statutorily prevented from refusing to ship such substances. Finally, the entire NPDES permit system (and the 60-day extension granted by the EPA to anyone applying for such permits) is in no way applicable to chemical carriers.

The court concludes, therefore, that plaintiffs and intervenors have met their burden of showing that immediate implementation of the new EPA regulations would result in their suffering irreparable harm. As a result, the first barrier in gaining the granting of a preliminary injunction has been surmounted.

II.

Next, plaintiffs and intervenors must show that the granting of a preliminary injunction will not significantly injure the interests either of the opposing party or of the public. The EPA's actions in promulgating the regulations now being challenged indicate that no such injuries could be expected in the case at bar. The history of these regulations indicates that Section 311 was enacted nearly six years ago. On August 22, 1974, the EPA announced its intention to promulgate regulations pursuant to that section (39 Fed. Reg. 30466). On December 30, 1975, the EPA published proposed regulations governing hazardous substances. Interested members of the public were given until March 1, 1976 to comment on the proposed regulations. On March 13, 1978 (more than two years later), the final hazardous substance regulations were issued, with final implementation to occur ninety days thereafter.

The languor that has characterized the entire process of developing the challenged regulations indicates that immediate implementation is by no means essential to protection of the environment or the public interest. This conclusion is supported by the continued enforcement of the NPDES permit system as well as by the fact that new regulations controlling discharges of toxic pollutants are to be developed within the framework of the existing permit structure by 1984.

Accordingly, the court finds that the granting of an injunction for the six or eight weeks it will take to reach a determination on the merits of this case would not result in significant injury to the defendants or to the interests of the public. While the court does not necessarily agree with plaintiff/MCA's contention that granting the desired relief would, in fact, be a positive step in forwarding the interests of the public (though it is inclined to agree with Intervenor/TFI's assertion that its products are essential to continued adequate food production in this country and that the interruption of producing such fertilizers would be a serious blow to the public welfare), such a conclusion is not essential to the decision in this case. Rather, the court need only find that the public will not be materially harmed if the regulations are not implemented until a decision on the merits of this case is rendered. The controlling considerations are clear and conclusive in the case at bar:

> "Where the questions presented by an application for an interlocutory injunction are grave, and the injury to the moving party will be certain and irreparable, if the application be denied and the final decree be in his favor, while if the injunction be granted the injury to the opposing party, even if the final decree be in his favor, will be inconsiderable . . . the injunction usually will be granted." *Ohio Oil v. Conway*, 279 U.S. 813, 815 (1929).

III.

The final and most important factor to be considered in determining whether a preliminary injunction should be granted is the likelihood that the moving parties will succeed when their claim is ultimately judged on its merits at a subsequent proceeding. While at the current stage of the judicial process the court need not make a binding determination as to the efficacy of each one of plaintiffs' assertions, it must apply much the same standards and reasoning here as it would in making a final decision on the merits.

. . . .

Plaintiffs attack EPA's selection of the one pound unit (and multiples thereof) for purposes of determining "hazardous quantities" as both contrary to the statutory mandate and arbitrary and capricious. Section 311(b)(3) of the Act prohibits discharges of hazardous substances "in harmful quantities" into navigable waters. Violations of this provision give rise to penalties, an obligation to notify the appropriate federal agency, and liability for the cost of removal under Sections 311(b)(5), (6) and (f). Determination of a "harmful quantity" is critical to the implementation of the remedial provisions. Section 311(b)(4) defines harmful quantities and directs the EPA to determine:

> "those quantities of . . . any hazardous substance the discharge of which, *at such times, locations, circumstances and conditions*, will be harmful to the public health or welfare." (Emphasis added).

The EPA's attempt to implement this directive is found in Part 118 of the final regulations. The list of 271 hazardous substances is divided into 5 categories based upon their relative toxicity. EPA then chooses one pound (the smallest common commercial container size) as the "harmful quantity" for all substances in the most toxic category. Larger multiples of the one pound unit are then applied to the remaining categories in ascending order as their toxicity decreases. Thus, a discharge of one pound of a substance in category "X" is deemed to be "harmful" for purposes of triggering the provisions regarding penalties and notification, while those who discharge 10 pounds of a substance in category "A" (that category of substances slightly less toxic than those in category "X") or 100 pounds of a substance in category "B" (a group of substances which are still less toxic) will find their actions subject to the same provisions. All such quantities must have been discharged within a 24 hour period.

The final regulations, on their face, do not appear to comport with the statutory mandate. Nowhere in Part 118 do we find reference to the considerations specifically required by Section 311(b)(4). Such factors as "times, locations, circumstances and conditions" are not mentioned, nor can their influence be found in the "one pound" rule. As counsel for the plaintiffs aptly noted, the choice of a "one pound bottle" as the basic unit of trade by the chemical industry was the result of many different considerations, none of which concerns the impact of the chemical within the container on the environment. Packaging, marketing, pricing and easy use of products (the factors normally taken into account by manufacturers) have no relationship to the purposes or intentions of the Act and regulations. It would appear then, that the EPA has not complied with the statutory requisites in promulgating the challenged regulations.

The considerations enumerated by Congress were prompted by what was thought to be a rational method for determining actual environmental harm.

If the challenged regulations fail to comply with that underlying purpose, they risk being found invalid because they are arbitrary and capricious. In the words of the EPA itself:

> "The harm produced by the introduction of any pollutant to water is dependent upon the resulting concentration of that material in the water and upon receiving water characteristics. Determining harmful quantities thus requires some evaluation of probabilistic damage or harm to representative water bodies." (Preamble to 1975 proposed EPA regs. 40 Fed. Reg. 59985.)

The harm that will result from the discharge of a given amount of a hazardous substance may be determined as much by characteristics of the receiving water body as by the toxicity of the substance itself. Conditions of the receiving body which will have an impact on the concentration of the pollutant include type, flow rate and size of the water body, and salinity, hardness, alkalinity, biological population and buffering capacity of the water.

In developing its proposed regulations, EPA employed Battelle Memorial Institute of Pacific Northwest Laboratories ("Battelle"). Battelle attempted to develop a system for determining the hazard presented by the discharging of various substances based on "critical concentrations" (concentrations at which substantial harm could be expected), "critical volumes" (referring to volumes of receiving waters that would be affected), and "harmful quantities" which would cause critical concentrations if discharged into a body of water. Different "harmful quantities" for each substance were determined depending on whether the receiving body was fresh water, an estuary, or coastal water. In making its determinations, Battelle attempted to develop a system which would be workable both for the EPA and for those being regulated. The EPA rejected the Battelle report in favor of its own "one pound" system. The EPA explained that it had rejected approaches such as the one proposed by Battelle because of their:

> "excessive complexity; incomplete or conflicting data; difficulty visualized in implementation." (40 Fed. Reg. 59985)

Counsel for the EPA argued that the harmful quantity test finally adopted by the regulations was chosen because it was "clear and easily comprehensible" and was therefore more easily understood by all interested parties. Counsel also urged that the "one pound" test would be an effective incentive for compliance with the notification requirements of Section 311. While it is conceivable that the test finally selected may accomplish the ends urged by the EPA, such goals should not be attained through totally arbitrary means. The Acting Chief of the U.S. Coast Guard Office of Marine Environment and Systems accurately described the "one pound" rule chosen by the EPA:

> "The method for determining harmful quantity of hazardous substances, while having some merit in its simplicity, ignores the relationship between quantity discharged and the receiving water and *has no sound technical basis*." (Letter from Capt. D.J. Riley to EPA on March 25, 1976, Plaintiffs' exhibit #14, emphasis added.)

In order for a statutory system intended to control pollution to have any reliability and legitimacy, the tests which form the underpinnings of that system must have some rational relationship to the harm sought to be prevented. It must also treat all citizens who discharge under similar circumstances with a certain degree of uniformity. Such is not the case in the challenged regulations. First, even the EPA itself does not contend that the values chosen for enforcement of the regulations represent discharges which are harmful in fact. It simply contends that the values are easier to use than any other test developed. Second, the regulations, as finally promulgated, draw an unreasonable distinction between chemical manufacturers operating with a valid NPDES permit and those without a permit. Under the regulations, a manufacturer who applies for an amended permit (or who has been granted a permit) may discharge hazardous substances in amounts far in excess of the quantities which the EPA has deemed to be hazardous without in any way triggering the notification and penalty provisions. On the other hand, a manufacturer discharging exactly the same amount of the same hazardous substances under exactly the same circumstances may be fined heavily if it has failed to apply for a permit or if its permit has expired. (It should be noted that this disparity in enforcement cannot be justified as an incentive to manufacturers to obtain valid permits since Section 402 contains its own penalty provisions covering failures to apply for or comply with a permit.)

. . . .

In essence, defendants urge that the "one pound" test was adopted because any more complicated test would raise insurmountable obstacles to uniform implementation and enforcement:

> "The discharger, particularly from a transportation source, is not equipped to differentiate between large and small streams, estuaries and rivers, or rivers and lakes. Adoption of such an approach using variable harmful quantities depending on water body type or size would place dischargers in the position of facing criminal penalties for failure to immediately notify without having the means to make the determination that a violation has occurred. . . . The proposed approach, identifying a single harmful quantity applicable to all waters, provides a clear and definitive threshold for activation of the reporting requirement. The inclusion of numerous variables which may accompany a particular discharge and modify the harmful quantity would create uncertainty in the notification requirement which is unacceptable in light of the criminal penalties provisions . . . and the importance of prompt activation of response activities through such notice." 43 Fed. Reg. 10491.

The court does not agree. The distinction between fresh water, estuaries, and coastal waters proposed by the Battelle report was a valid and workable first step in taking into consideration circumstances beyond the weight of the discharged substance. Further, the EPA could accomplish its avowed purpose of requiring compliance with the notification provisions for all substantial discharges by developing a two-stage process. Stage one could require notification after any discharges of hazardous substances in amounts exceeding the "hazardous quantities" now proposed as part of the "one pound" regulations. The second stage would trigger the penalty provisions based on an in-depth consideration of "times, locations, circumstances and conditions" in a manner which may or may not be similar to the methods recommended by Battelle. The court recognizes that its function in reviewing challenged administrative actions is not to suggest how the administrative body might have better attained its goals and implemented the underlying Congressional policies. However, the alternatives which are proposed here, when compared with the standards finally adopted by the EPA, indicate that the EPA's final regulations may well be arbitrary and capricious and have failed to carry out the policies of the statute under which they were promulgated.

CONCLUSION

The court now holds that plaintiffs and intervenors have overcome all obstacles in their effort to gain a preliminary injunction and that the injunction should therefore be granted. . . .

NOTE

Following the decision in *Manufacturing Chemists Association v. Costle*, § 311 was amended in what has often been referred to as a "quick legislative fix," by Pub. L. No. 95-576, 92 Stat. 2467. New EPA regulations on hazardous spills were promulgated promptly, 40 C.F.R. pt. 117, 44 Fed. Reg. 50766, adopted on August 29, 1979. The Regulations changed the term "harmful quantity" to "reportable quantity," reflecting the change in the law in § 311(b)(3), which no longer requires an assessment of actual harm. The same quantities were designated as "reportable quantities" which had previously been designated as "harmful." For comments and discussion of EPA's regulations of hazardous substance spills, see F. Grad, Treatise on Environmental Law, § 3.03[8][c]. The NPDES system is relied on for hazardous spill damages.

COUNCIL OF STATE GOVERNMENTS

1971 Suggested State Legislation 203 (1970)

Oil Discharge Control

The seacoast of our Nation provides a unique source for public and private recreation, fishing, and productive commercial activities. The preservation of such uses is a matter of highest priority that can only be attained by maintaining waters and land adjoining the seacoast in as close to a pristine condition as possible, considering necessary accommodations to public and private interests.

The transfer of oil, petroleum products and their by-products between vessels and between onshore facilities and vessels is a hazardous undertaking. Spills, discharges and escape of oil and petroleum products occurring as a result of procedures involved in the transfer and storage of such products pose threats of great danger and damage to the marine environment of the State, to owners and users of shorefront property, to public and private recreation, and to the beauty of the seacoast.

The following suggested legislation confers upon an appropriate state agency exclusive power to deal with the hazards posed by the transfer of oil and petroleum products. The act requires prompt containment and removal of pollution caused by such transfers and provides procedures whereby persons suffering damage from oil discharges may promptly be made whole from a specially created Coastal Protection Fund.

Based largely on a Maine Statute, Chapter 1835 of the 1970 Laws, the act applies specifically to coastal areas, and inland States must adapt this legislation to their own local situations.

The core of this draft is the prohibition against discharging oil, petroleum products or their by-products into or upon coastal waters and lands or into waters that drain into coastal waters. The term "discharge" includes spilling, leaking, pumping, pouring, emitting, emptying or dumping.

A further significant provision requires the annual licensing of operators of facilities which transfer, process or refine oil. License fees are credited to a Coastal Protection Fund. These fees are determined on the suggested basis of 1/2 cent per barrel of oil or petroleum products transferred by the applicant during the licensing period.

Any person discharging oil in an unlawful manner is required immediately to remove the discharge to the satisfaction of the state agency. Notwithstanding this requirement, the state agency may undertake the removal of the discharge. The removal of unexplained discharges is the responsibility of the state agency. Any expense involved in the removal of discharges, whether by the person causing them or by the State, is to be paid in the first instance from the Coastal Protection Fund. Costs incurred by the fund in abating prohibited discharges are recoverable against persons causing the discharge.

Persons claiming damages due to a prohibited discharge may apply to the state agency for recompense. A special Board of Arbitration is established to consider claims upon which the claimant, the negligent party, and the agency cannot agree.

Finally, in any suit to enforce claims of the State under this act, it is not necessary for the State to plead or prove negligence in any form or manner on the part of the licensee. The State need only plead and prove the fact of the prohibited discharge or other polluting condition and that it occurred at facilities under the control of the licensee or was attributable to carriers or others for whom the licensee is responsible.

. . . .

ASKEW v. AMERICAN WATERWAYS OPERATORS, INC.

United States Supreme Court (1973)
411 U.S. 325, 93 S. Ct. 1590, 36 L. Ed. 2d 280

Mr. JUSTICE DOUGLAS delivered the opinion of the Court.

This action was brought by merchant shipowners and operators, world shipping associations, members of the Florida coastal barge and towing industry, and owners and operators of oil terminal facilities and heavy industries located in Florida, to enjoin application of the Florida Oil Spill Prevention and Pollution Control Act, Fla. Laws 1970, c. 70-244 (hereinafter referred to as the Florida Act). Officials responsible for enforcing the Florida Act were named as defendants, but the State of Florida intervened as a party defendant, asserting that its interests were much broader than those of the named defendants. A three-judge court was convened pursuant to 28 U.S.C. § 2281.

The Florida Act imposes strict liability for any damage incurred by the State or private persons as a result of an oil spill in the State's territorial waters from any waterfront facility used for drilling for oil or handling the transfer or storage of oil ("terminal facility") and from any ship destined for or leaving such facility. Each owner or operator of a terminal facility or ship subject to the Act must establish evidence of financial responsibility by insurance or a surety bond.[213] In addition, the Florida Act provides for regulation by the State Department of Natural Resources with respect to containment gear and other equipment which must be maintained by ships and terminal facilities for the prevention of oil spills.

Several months prior to the enactment of the Florida Act, Congress enacted the Water Quality Improvement Act of 1970, 84 Stat. 91, 33 U.S.C. § 1161 *et seq.* (hereinafter referred to as the Federal Act).[214] This Act subjects ship owners and terminal facilities to liability without fault up to $14,000,000 and $8,000,000, respectively, for cleanup costs incurred by the Federal Government as a result of oil spills. It also authorizes the President to promulgate regulations requiring ships and terminal facilities to maintain equipment for the prevention of oil spills. It is around that Act and the federally protected tenets of maritime law evidenced by *Southern Pacific Co.* v. *Jensen*, 244 U.S. 205, and its progeny that the controversy turns. The District Court held that the Florida Act is an unconstitutional intrusion into the federal maritime domain. It declared the Florida Act null and void and enjoined its enforcement. 335 F. Supp. 1241.

---

213 At the hearing on plaintiffs-appellees' application for a temporary restraining order, it was indicated that none of the plaintiffs had attempted to comply with the Florida Act. Shipowners and operators had threatened to divert their vessels from Florida ports.

214 The Water Quality Improvement Act of 1970 was amended after this case was docketed by the Water Pollution Prevention and Control Act of 1972, 86 Stat. 816, 33 U.S.C. §§ 1251-1376. Since the sections of the 1970 Act cited in the opinion have not been substantially changed, references to the 1970 Act have been retained.

The case is here on direct appeal. We reverse. We find no constitutional or statutory impediment to permitting Florida, in the present setting of this case, to establish any "requirement or liability" concerning the impact of oil spillages on Florida's interests or concerns. To rule as the District Court has done is to allow federal admiralty jurisdiction to swallow most of the police power of the States over oil spillage—an insidious form of pollution of vast concern to every coastal city or port and to all the estuaries on which the life of the ocean and the lives of the coastal people are greatly dependent.

I.

It is clear at the outset that the Federal Act does not preclude, but in fact allows, state regulation. Section 1161 *(o)* provides that:

> "(1) Nothing in this section shall affect or modify in any way the obligations of any owner or operator of any vessel, or of any owner or operator of any onshore facility or offshore facility to any person or agency *under any provision of law for damages to any publicly-owned or privately-owned property* resulting from a discharge of any oil or from the removal of any such oil.
>
> "(2) Nothing in this section shall be construed as preempting any State or political subdivision thereof from imposing *any requirement or liability* with respect to the discharge of oil into any waters within such State.
>
> "(3) Nothing in this section shall be construed . . . to affect any State or local law not in conflict with this section." (Emphasis added.)

According to the Conference Report, "any State would be free to provide requirements and penalties similar to those imposed by this section or *additional requirements and penalties.* These, however, would be separate and independent from those imposed by this section and would be enforced by the States through its courts."[215] (Emphasis added.) The Florida Act covers a wide range of "pollutants," § 3(7), and a restricted definition of pollution. § 3(8). We have here, however, no question concerning any pollutant except oil.

The Federal Act, to be sure, contains a pervasive system of federal control over discharges of oil "into or upon the navigable waters of the United States, adjoining shorelines, or into or upon the waters of the contiguous zone." § 1161(b)(1). So far as liability is concerned, an owner or operator of a vessel is liable to the United States for actual costs incurred for the removal of oil discharged in violation of § 1161(b)(2) in an amount "not to exceed $100 per gross ton of such vessel or $14,000,000, whichever is lesser," § 1161(f)(1), except for discharges caused solely by an act of God, act of war, negligence of the United States, or act or omission of another party. With like exceptions the owner or operator of an onshore or offshore facility is liable to the United States for the actual costs incurred by the United States in an amount not to exceed $8,000,000. § 1161(f)(2)-(3). But in each case the owner or operator is liable to the United States for the full amount of the costs where the United States can show that the discharge of oil was "the result of willful negligence or willful misconduct within the privity and knowledge of the owner."

215 H.R. Conf. Rep. No. 91-940, p. 42.

Comparable provisions of liability spell out the obligations of "a third party" to the United States for its actual costs incurred in the removal of the oil. § 1161(g).

So far as vessels are concerned the federal Limited Liability Act, 46 U.S.C. §§ 181-189, extends to damages caused by oil spills even where the injury is to the shore. *Richardson v. Harmon*, 222 U.S. 96, 106. That Act limits the liabilities of the owners of vessels to the "value of such vessels and freight pending." 46 U.S.C. § 189.

Section 12 of the Florida Act makes all licensees[216] of terminal facilities "liable to the state for all costs of cleanup or other damage incurred by the state and for damages resulting from injury to others," it not being necessary for the State to plead or prove negligence.[217] There is no conflict between § 12 of the Florida Act and § 1161 of the Federal Act when it comes to damages to property interests, for the Federal Act reaches only costs of cleaning up. As respects damages, § 14 of the Florida Act requires evidence of financial responsibility of a terminal facility or vessel—a provision which does not conflict with the Federal Act.

The Solicitor General says that while the Limited Liability Act, *so far as vessels are concerned*, would override § 12 of the Florida Act by reason of the Supremacy Clause, the Limited Liability Act has no bearing on "facilities" regulated by the Florida Act. Moreover, § 12 has not yet been construed by the Florida courts and it is susceptible of an interpretation *so far as vessels are concerned* which would be in harmony with the Federal Act. Section 12 does not *in terms* provide for unlimited liability.

Moreover, while the Federal Act determines damages measured by the cost to the United States for cleaning up oil spills, the damages specified in the Florida Act relate in part to the cost to the State of Florida in cleaning up the spillage. Those two sections are harmonious parts of an integrated whole. Section 1161(c)(2) directs the President to prepare a National Contingency Plan for the containment, dispersal, and removal of oil. The plan must provide that federal agencies "shall" act "in coordination with State and local agencies." Cooperative action with the States is also contemplated by § 1161(e), which provides that "[i]n addition to any other action taken by a State or local government" the President may, when there is an imminent and substantial threat to the public health or welfare, direct the United States Attorney of the district in question to bring suit to abate the threat. The reason for the provision in § 1161*(o)*(2), stating that nothing in § 1161 pre-empts any State "from imposing any requirement or liability with respect to the discharge of oil into any waters within such State," is that the scheme of the Act is one which allows—though it does not require—cooperation of the federal regime with a state regime.

216 Those required to obtain a license are those who operate a terminal facility. § 6(1). But licenses to terminal facilities include "vessels used to transport oil, petroleum products, their by-products, and other pollutants between the facility and vessels within state waters." § 6(4).

217 Section 12 also provides that the pilot or the master of any vessel or person in charge of any licensee's terminal facility who fails "to give immediate notification of a discharge to the port manager and the nearest coast guard station" may be imprisoned for not more than two years or fined not more than $10,000.

If Florida wants to take the lead in cleaning up oil spillage in her waters, she can use § 12 of the Florida Act and recoup her costs from those who did the damage. Whether the amount of costs she could recover from a wrongdoer is limited to those specified in the Federal Act and whether in turn this new Federal Act removes the pre-existing limitations of liability in the Limited Liability Act are questions we need not reach here. Any opinion on them is premature. It is sufficient for this day to hold that there is room for state action in cleaning up the waters of a State and recouping, at least within federal limits, so far as vessels are concerned, her costs.

Beyond that is the potential claim under § 12 of the Florida Act for "other damage incurred by the state and for damages resulting from injury to others." The Federal Act in no way touches those areas. A State may have public beaches ruined by oil spills. Shrimp may be destroyed, and clam, oyster, and scallop beds ruined and the livelihood of fishermen imperiled. The Federal Act takes no cognizance of those claims but only of costs to the Federal Government, if it does the cleaning up.

We held in *Skiriotes* v. *Florida*, 313 U.S. 69, that while Congress had regulated the size of commercial sponges taken in Florida waters, it had not dealt with any diving apparatus that might be used. Florida had such a law and was allowed to enforce it against one of its citizens. Mr. Chief Justice Hughes, speaking for the Court, said: "It is also clear that Florida has an interest in the proper maintenance of the sponge fishery and that the statute so far as applied to conduct within the territorial waters of Florida, in the absence of conflicting federal legislation, is within the police power of the State," *Id.*, at 75.

Similarly, in *Manchester* v. *Massachusetts*, 139 U.S. 240, 266, we stated that if Congress fails to assume control of fisheries in a bay, "the right to control such fisheries must remain with the State which contains such bays."

Florida in her brief accurately states that no remedy under the Federal Act exists for state or private property owners damaged by a massive oil slick such as hit England and France in 1967 in the *Torrey Canyon* disaster. The *Torrey Canyon* carried 880,000 barrels of crude oil. Today not only is more oil being moved by sea each year but the tankers are much larger. . . .

Our Coast Guard reports that while in 1970 there were 3,711 oil spills in our waters, in 1971 there were 8,736. The damage to state interests already caused by oil spills, the increase in the number of oil spills, and the risk of ever-increasing damage by reason of the size of modern tankers underlie the concern of coastal States.

While the Federal Act is concerned only with actual cleanup costs incurred by the Federal Government, the State of Florida is concerned with its own cleanup costs. Hence there need be no collision between the Federal Act and the Florida Act because, as noted, the Federal Act presupposes a coordinated effort with the States, and any federal limitation of liability runs to "vessels," not to shore "facilities." That is one of the reasons why the Congress decided that the Federal Act does not pre-empt the States from establishing either "*any requirement or liability*" respecting oil spills.

Moreover, since Congress dealt only with "cleanup" costs, it left the States free to impose "liability" in damages for losses suffered both by the States and by private interests. The Florida Act imposes liability without fault. So far as liability without fault for damages to state and private interests is concerned, the police power has been held adequate for that purpose. State statutes imposing absolute liability on railroads for *all* property lost through fires caused by sparks emitted from locomotive engines have been sustained. *St. Louis & San Francisco R. Co. v. Mathews*, 165 U.S. 1. The Federal Act, however, while restricted to cleanup costs incurred by the United States, imposes limited liability for those costs and provides certain exceptions, unless willfulness is established. Where liability is imposed by §§ 1161(f)-(g), previously summarized, the United States may recover the full amount of the costs where the oil spillage was the result of "willful negligence or willful misconduct." If the coordinated federal plan in actual operation leaves the State of Florida to do the cleanup work, there might be financial burdens imposed greater than would have been imposed had the Federal Government done the cleanup work. But it will be time to resolve any such conflict between federal and state regimes when it arises.

Nor can we say at this point that regulations of the Florida Department of Natural Resources requiring "containment gear" pursuant to § 7(2)(a) of the Florida Act would be *per se* invalid because the subject to be regulated requires uniform federal regulation. *Cf. Huron Cement Co. v. Detroit*, 362 U.S. 440. Resolution of this question, as well as the question whether such regulations will conflict with Coast Guard regulations promulgated on December 21, 1972, pursuant to § 1161(j)(1) of the Federal Act, 37 Fed. Reg. 28250, should await a concrete dispute under applicable Florida regulations. Finally, the provision of the Florida Act requiring the licensing of terminal facilities, a traditional state concern, creates no conflict *per se* with federal legislation. Section 1171(b)(1) of the Federal Act provides that federal permits will not be issued to terminal facility operators or owners unless the applicant first supplies a certificate from the State that this operation "will be conducted in a manner which will not violate applicable water quality standards." And Tit. I § 102(b), of the recently enacted Ports and Waterways Safety Act of 1972, Pub. L. 92-340, 86 Stat. 424, provides that the Act does not prevent "a State or political subdivision thereof from prescribing for structures only higher safety equipment requirements or safety standards than those which may be prescribed pursuant to this title."

II.

And so, in the absence of federal pre-emption and any fatal conflict between the statutory schemes, the issue comes down to whether a State constitutionally may exercise its police power respecting maritime activities concurrently with the Federal Government.

The main barrier found by the District Court to the Florida Act are *Southern Pacific Co.* v. *Jensen*, 244 U.S. 205, and its progeny. *Jensen* held that a maritime worker on a vessel in navigable waters could not constitutionally receive an award under New York's workmen's compensation law, because the remedy in admiralty was exclusive. Later, in *Knickerbocker Ice Co.* v. *Stewart*, 253 U.S. 149, after Congress expressly allowed the States in such cases to grant a remedy, the Court held that Congress had no such power.

But those decisions have been limited by subsequent holdings of this Court. As stated by Mr. Justice Frankfurter in *Romero* v. *International Terminal Co.*, 358 U.S. 354, 373, *Jensen* and its progeny mark isolated instances where "state law must yield to the needs of a uniform federal maritime law when this Court finds inroads on a harmonious system." Mr. Justice Frankfurter added, however: "But this limitation still leaves the States a wide scope. State-created liens are enforced in admiralty. State remedies for wrongful death and state statutes providing for the survival of actions, both historically absent from the relief offered by the admiralty, have been upheld when applied to maritime causes of action. Federal courts have enforced these statutes. State rules for the partition and sale of ships, state laws governing the specific performance of arbitration agreements, state laws regulating the effect of a breach of warranty under contracts of maritime insurance—all these laws and others have been accepted as rules of decision in admiralty cases, even, at times, when they conflicted with a rule of maritime law which did not require uniformity." *Id.*, at 373-374.

Moreover, in *Just v. Chambers*, 312 U.S. 383, we gave our approval to *The City of Norwalk*, 55 F. 98, written by Judge Addison Brown, holding that a State may modify or supplement maritime law even by creating a liability which a court of admiralty would recognize and enforce, provided the state action is not hostile "to the characteristic features of the maritime law or inconsistent with federal legislation," 312 U.S., at 388. Mr. Chief Justice Hughes after citing *Steamboat Co. v. Chase*, 16 Wall. 522, and *Sherlock v. Alling*, 93 U.S. 99, went on to hold that, while no suit for wrongful death would lie in the federal courts under general maritime law, state statutes giving damages in such cases were valid. . . .

Mr. Chief Justice Hughes added that our decisions as of 1941, the date of *Just v. Chambers*, gave broad "recognition of the authority of the States to create rights and liabilities with respect to conduct within their borders, when the state action does not run counter to federal laws or the essential features of an exclusive federal jurisdiction." *Id.*, at 391.

Historically, damages to the shore or to shore facilities were not cognizable in admiralty. *See, e.g., The Plymouth*, 3. Wall. 20; *Martin v. West*, 222 U.S. 191. Mr. Justice Story wrote in 1813, "In regard to torts I have always understood, that the jurisdiction of the admiralty is exclusively dependent upon the locality of the act. The admiralty has not, and never (I believe) deliberately claimed to have any jurisdiction over torts, except such as are maritime torts, that is, such as are committed on the high seas, or on waters within the ebb and flow of the tide." *Thomas* v. *Lane*, 23 F. Cas. 957, 960 (No. 13,902) (CC Me.).

On June 19, 1948, Congress enacted the Admiralty Extension Act, 46 U.S.C. § 740. The Court considered the Act in *Victory Carriers, Inc.* v. *Law*, 404 U.S. 202. In that case, the Court held that the Admiralty Extension Act did not apply to a longshoreman performing loading and unloading services on the dock. The longshoreman was relegated to his remedy under the state workmen's compensation law. *Id.*, at 215. The Court said, "At least in the absence of explicit congressional authorization, we shall not extend the historic boundaries of the maritime law." *Id.*, at 214.

The Admiralty Extension Act has survived constitutional attack in the lower federal courts and was applied without question by this Court in *Gutierrez* v. *Waterman S.S. Corp.*, 373 U.S. 206. The Court recognized in *Victory Carriers*, however, that the Act may "intrude on an area that has heretofore been reserved for state law." *Id.*, at 212. It cautioned that under these circumstances, "we should proceed with caution in construing constitutional and statutory provisions dealing with the jurisdiction of the federal courts." *Ibid.* While Congress has extended admiralty jurisdiction beyond the boundaries contemplated by the Framers, it hardly follows from the constitutionality of that extension that we must sanctify the federal courts with exclusive jurisdiction to the exclusion of powers traditionally within the competence of the States. One can read the history of the Admiralty Extension Act without finding any clear indication that Congress intended that sea-to-shore injuries be exclusively triable in the federal courts.

Even though Congress has acted in the admiralty area, state regulation is permissible, absent a clear conflict with the federal law. Thus in *Kelly v. Washington*, 302 U.S. 1, it appeared that, while Congress had provided a comprehensive system of inspection of vessels on navigable waters, *id.*, at 4, the State of Washington also had a comprehensive code of inspection. Some of those state standards conflicted with the federal requirements, *id.*, at 14-15; but those provisions of the Washington law relating to safety and seaworthiness were not in conflict with the federal law. So the question was whether the absence of congressional action and the need for uniformity of regulation barred state action. Mr. Chief Justice Hughes, writing for the Court, ruled in the negative. . . .

It follows, *a fortiori*, that sea-to-shore pollution—historically within the reach of the police power of the States—is not silently taken away from the States by the Admiralty Extension Act, which does not purport to supply the exclusive remedy.

As discussed above, we cannot say with certainty at this stage that the Florida Act conflicts with any federal Act. We have only the question whether the waiver of pre-emption by Congress in § 1161(o)(2) concerning the imposition by a State of "any requirement or liability" is valid.

It is valid unless the rule of *Jensen* and *Knickerbocker Ice* is to engulf everything that Congress chose to call "admiralty," pre-empting state action. *Jensen* and *Knickerbocker Ice* have been confined to their facts, *viz.*, to suits relating to the relationship of vessels, plying the high seas and our navigable waters, and to their crews. The fact that a whole system of liabilities was established on the basis of those two cases, led us years ago to establish the "twilight zone" where state regulation was permissible. *See Davis* v. *Department of Labor*, 317 U.S. 249, 252-253. Where there was a hearing by a federal agency and a conclusion by that agency that the case fell within the federal jurisdiction, we made its findings final. *Ibid.* Where there were no such findings, we presumed state law, in terms applicable, was constitutional. *Id.*, at 257-258. That is the way the "twilight zone" has been defined.

Jensen thus has vitality left. But we decline to move the *Jensen* line of cases shoreward to oust state law from situations involving shoreside injuries by ships on navigable waters. The Admiralty Extension Act does not pre-empt state law in those situations. *See Nacirema Operating Co.* v. *Johnson*, 396 U.S. 212.

The judgment below is *reversed.*

NOTE

Thc Oil Pollution Act of 1990, § 1018, has expressly overcome obstacles to state oil pollution control laws, including the assertion of federal preemption. A number of states, mostly coastal states, make special provision for pollution by oil in their general water pollution statues. Some have adopted special provisions, including the creation of oil spill funds, in their law, generally following the pattern of the Suggested State Legislation, which follows the Maine statute. For an analysis of state oil pollution legislation, see F. Grad, Treatise on Environmental Law, § 3.04[3], and for materials on claims for private injury from oil pollution, § 3.03[8][d].

QUESTIONS

(1) Plaintiff Petroleum Corporation has oil tanks on its property. Vandals entered the company's property and opened valves on a railroad tank car recently loaded with oil from the plaintiff's tanks. A substantial quantity of oil spilled and flowed into a neighboring river. Plaintiff cleaned up its own property as well as the spill into the river, and now sues the United States in the Court of Claims for the recovery of the cleanup costs. The United States counterclaims for costs it incurred in completing the cleanup. What decision? *See Union Petroleum Corporation v. United States*, 11 E.L.R. 20755 (Ct. Claims, 1981).

(2) Should a claim for cleanup costs be subject to the Limited Liability Act? *See Complaint of Hokkaido Fisheries Co., Ltd.*, 506 F. Supp. 631 (D. Alaska 1981).

(3) When an oil spill is caused when a tanker is rammed by a tug boat that is towing it into port, can the owner defend against a claim for cleanup costs by the U.S. on the grounds that the spill was the responsibility of a "third party" under § 311(f)? *See United States v. Hollywood Marine, Inc.* , 11 E.L.R. 21001 (S.D. Tex. 1981), *cert. denied*, 101 S. Ct. 2336 (1981), with Justice Rehnquist dissenting, referring to *Tug Ocean Prince Inc. v. United States*, 436 F. Supp. 907 (S.D. N.Y. 1977), *affirmed in part and rev'd in part on other grounds*, 584 F.2d 1151 (2d Cir. 1978), *cert. denied*, 440 U.S. 959 (1979). What would the result be after 1990 under the Oil Pollution Act?

(4) When an oil spill is caused by the negligent operation of a third-party vessel which rams a tanker, the U.S. can clearly sue the responsible vessel for cleanup costs. What are the limits of the liability of the third party under the Oil Pollution Act? Can the U.S. nevertheless press for unlimited liability on negligence or maritime tort grounds?

(5) Examine the State Oil Discharge Control Law from the Council of State Governments' *1971 Suggested State Legislation.* Is the law consistent with

federal oil pollution control legislation and what gaps, if any, does it fill which the federal legislation leaves uncovered? Does a person who is damaged by an oil spill which is subject to federal as well as state regulation have any greater rights to recovery under the suggested state law than he has under the federal law? What is likely to determine the choice of court or the choice of law, to the extent that the plaintiff has such a choice?

[xiii] Water Quality Standards, Nonpoint Pollution Sources and the Nondegradation Policy: New Life for an Old Theme

Water Quality Requirements in the Clean Water Act

The 1972 Federal Water Pollution Control Act Amendments emphasized effluent limitation based primarily on technological feasibility. However, the earlier emphasis on ambient water quality standards, relying primarily on water quality standards set by the states, was not abandoned by the 1972 Act. Indeed, the various technological standards, best practicable technology (BPT) and best available technology economically achievable (BAT), had as their purpose to achieve the total elimination of all discharges of pollutants by 1985 and an interim 1983 standard of water quality which would provide for "protection and propagation of fish, shellfish, wildlife and provide for recreation in and on the water" the so-called fishable-swimmable standard.[218] The highly technical system of effluent limitations must therefore be viewed as a means of accomplishing a high level of ambient water quality. Both in water and in air what ultimately counts is the ambient quality we live in—the technological means of achieving it are important but they are merely the means toward that end. The water pollution control system is thus analogous to the system of air pollution control, where state implementation plans, consisting largely of emission controls, are designed to accomplish national ambient air quality standards—except that in the water quality system, water quality standards are set by the states.

As currently encompassed in § 303(c)(4) of the Clean Water Act,the water quality criteria set by each state are intended to be suitable for the designated uses of particular segments of the water. The designated uses may be for a public water supply, propagation of fish and wildlife, agriculture, or recreational purposes. The water quality standards then limit the concentrations of particular pollutants in defined classes of waters. Federal law requires the states to review their water quality standards every three years and these standards must then be submitted to EPA for its approval.[219] The standards are subject to EPA modification if they do not meet the requirements of the Act.[220] Under § 304, EPA must develop water quality criteria so that the states may then develop criteria for waters with certain designated uses. The setting of water quality criteria has been slow and has run into difficulties that the states have sometimes sought to resolve by relying on narrative rather than numerical criteria. These have been upheld, as for instance, in

---

218 33 U.S.C. § 1251(a)(2).

219 CWA § 303(c).

220 CWA § 303(c)(4).

the case of *American Paper Institute, Inc. v. EPA,* 996 F.2d 346 (D.C. Cir. 1993); *see* p. 505 *supra*.

Water quality standards have considerable consequences because whenever discharges of pollutants from a point source or group of point sources interfere with the achievement of water quality that will assure the protection of public water supplies, agricultural and industrial uses and the protection of shellfish, fish and wildlife, or the conduct of recreational activities, the Administrator may establish effluent limitations and other effluent control strategies which will contribute to the achievement or maintenance of the required water quality—even though such effluent may already meet the requirement of the best available technology economically achievable under § 301(b)(2) of the Act.[221] Such new limitations may be imposed after earlier notice and hearing to determine the relationship of the economic and social costs of achieving such limitations to the social and economic benefits to be obtained, including the attainment of the objectives of the Clean Water Act.

The triennial review of water quality standards must be preceded by public hearings in order to make necessary modifications. If required changes are not made, the Administrator, again following notice and hearing, may make such modifications for the state. Pursuant to federal requirements, each state must identify the waters within its boundaries wherein the application of the best practicable control technology currently available (BAT) are not stringent enough to implement any water quality standards applicable to such waters.[222] The states must establish priority rankings for such waters, taking the severity of the pollution and the uses to be made of the waters into account.

In accordance with the priority rankings, states are required to establish for the water so identified the total maximum load for pollutants for which such a daily maximum load can be calculated (TMDL).[223] The load to be established is to be at a level necessary to implement applicable water quality standards, taking into account seasonable variations and providing a margin of safety considering any lack of knowledge concerning the relationship between effluent limitations and water quality.[224] States must also identify waters for which thermal discharge controls promulgated as part of the effluent standards are not stringent enough for the protection of shellfish, fish and wildlife. Other matters to be taken into account include seasonable variations, existing sources of heat input and the capacity of the waters to dissipate such input and again the margin of safety required to take into account concerning the development of thermal water quality criteria.[225]

As noted earlier, the establishment of water quality criteria is also directly related to the establishment of the ICS (individual control systems) for criteria toxic pollutants. (*See* section on toxic water pollutants *supra* at p. 432.)

When a state fails to adopt water quality standards or when it fails to establish a total maximum daily load (TMDL) for pollutants for which a maximum daily load can be calculated, EPA has authority to adopt such standards

[221] FWPCA § 302(a), 33 U.S.C. § 1312(a).

[222] FWPCA § 303(d)(1)(A), 33 U.S.C. § 1313(d)(1)(A).

[223] FWPCA § 303(d)(1)(C), 33 U.S.C. § 1313(d)(1)(C).

[224] FWPCA § 303(d)(1)(C), 33 U.S.C. § 1313(d)(1)(C). On TMDLs, see F. Grad, Treatise on Environmental Law, § 3.03[4][j].

[225] FWPCA § 303(d)(1)(D), 33 U.S.C. § 1313(d)(1)(D).

or TMDLs for the state. The courts however have been slow to order EPA to do so. Courts have held that a lengthy failure by a state to submit TMDLs for a pollutant is equivalent to a constructive submission by the state of no limits and that if EPA does not act to approve such a submission, EPA is under a nondiscretionary duty to establish the TMDLs.[226]

The problem of inadequate enforcement of the state's duty to promulgate water quality standards and of the state's duty to adopt TMDLs has been chronicled in an insightful, analytical series of articles by Professor Oliver A. Houck.

Oliver A. Houck, "TMDLs: THE RESURRECTION OF WATER QUALITY STANDARDS-BASED REGULATION UNDER THE CLEAN WATER ACT"

27 ELR 10329, 10344 (1997)

Reflections on Water Quality Standards Legislation and Its Stakeholders

Water quality standards regulation has a 25-year history in federal law, and a longer history yet in some state programs. As national attention on water pollution intensified, states resisted federal supervision of their standards in 1965, and then fought a hard battle to retain these standards in the 1972 Amendments, which became the Clean Water Act. Water quality-based permitting was the last bastion of state authority in a program that was otherwise going rapidly to EPA. State governors, state agency heads, state water quality engineers, municipal authorities, and their representatives in Congress expressed their confidence—witness by witness, over and over—that states had the technology and the expertise to regulate by water quality standards. They could do this job, if only the federal government would let them.

Industry agreed with this position, although one suspects that industry may have been motivated less by confidence that water quality standards regulation would work than by confidence that it would not. Several administrations agreed, although one suspects they were motivated more by budget considerations, and by relief that this was one less chore for the federal government. Whatever their motives, both industry and federal administrators added their opinions that water quality regulation was something the states could and should be doing.

---

[226] *See, e.g., Scott v. City of Hammond*, 741 F.2d 992 (7th Cir. 1984); *Alaska Ctr for the Env't v. Reilly*, 762 F. Supp. 1422, 21 ELR 21305 (W.D. Wash. 1991), *aff'd sub nom. Alaska Ctr for the Env't v. Browner*, 20 F.3d 981, 24 ELR 20702 (9th Cir. 1994). *But see Sierra Club v. Browner*, 843 F. Supp. 1304, 24 ELR 21006 (D. Minn. 1993) where the court found a number of reasons why EPA was not required to prepare a TMDL for the state, even though the state had not acted for some 13 years. Courts are clearly reluctant to use their injunctive powers against states and to substitute their judgment for that of EPA.

Congress agreed, barely. It retained state water quality-based regulation, but in a fashion that has gone largely unnoticed in the literature and, until recently, almost equally unnoticed in practice. Congress did *not* simply retain the underperforming water quality program of the 1965 Act. In § 303(d), it completely rewrote the program, and in the rewrite spelled out a blueprint for compliance that is as specific in its detail as any other provision of the Act. While there was no debate on § 303(d), the provision was no sleeper to either the House or the Senate. Water quality standards were the House's major issue, and the House report describes the § 303(d) process with clarity and at some length. After that recitation, what was there really to debate? If a water quality-based program was going to be retained, this was, and remains, about the only way it could work.

For the next 25 years, states, industry, and various administrations have taken their runs at the Clean Water Act, and a consistent theme from these quarters has been the impropriety of "top down" controls, the wastefulness of "treatment for treatment sake," and the need to place more reliance on water quality-based regulation and provide more "flexibility" for state implementation based on the knowledge of local conditions. Whatever the merits of these arguments, they sidestep an important aspect of the Clean Water Act, which is its very explicit reservation of state authority to control water pollution more protectively than the federal program. Nothing in federal law prohibits a state from abating any discharge it wants, virtually any way it wants. This being so, and not surprisingly, the state arguments for greater flexibility invariably center on permission to *relax* criteria, use standards, testing, and monitoring requirements. Both implicit and explicit in these state, industry, and, at times, administration arguments are their representations that water quality-based regulatory programs make sense and that the states are well qualified, indeed uniquely qualified, to conduct them. Which brings this discussion to a great disconnect.

For the past 25 years, states and their adherents in and out of Congress have been arguing for recognition of their ability and authority to regulate based on water quality standards. And for the same 25 years states have had not only the authority under § 303 to do so, they have had a rather well-prescribed mandate to do so. They did not do so. By and large, they did not do anything called for under § 303(d): (1) they did not submit inventories of polluted waters, (2) they did not prioritize these waters for cleanup, (3) they did not promulgate TMDLs, and (4) they did not incorporate them into point source or nonpoint source discharge controls. They did not do it in the 1970s. They did not do it in the 1980s. They did not do it at the outset of the 1990s, nor did EPA—until a series of citizen suits rocked EPA and the states into a hasty rereading of § 303(d) and the current scramble to comply.

The compliance efforts are at an early stage, but they could have a dramatic impact on the course and future of the Clean Water Act. The § 303(d) litigation and its aftermath are the subject of an ensuing article.

Oliver A. Houck, "TMDLs, ARE WE THERE YET?: THE LONG ROAD TOWARD WATER QUALITY-BASED REGULATION UNDER THE CLEAN WATER ACT"

27 ELR 10391, 10399-10401 (1997)

Implementation

Implementation is of course where all public laws live or die, and environmental laws have, over time, accreted layers of overlapping responsibilities and enforcement mechanisms to ensure that, at day's end, something at least remotely like what Congress intended has happened. Section 303(d) muddies the issue because Congress plainly intended states to implement the program, and for EPA to backstop it only where the states failed to do their jobs. Two implementation issues arise. The first is the time frame within which TMDLs are to be established. The second is the mechanism by which they are to be carried out. Unfortunately, for these are critical issues to the success of the program, the language of the statute is not very helpful.

With regard to the time frame, § 303(d) provides only that states shall submit their WQLSs and TMDLs to EPA "from time to time,"[227] with the first submission due within six months of EPA's identification of the applicable pollutants, or June 26, 1979. It is obvious that Congress presumed a certain amount of good-faith effort here, a presumption that was not entirely borne out in EPA's regulations that called for one state submission and little more, or in state performance. As it turned out, this dilatory pace prompted courts to begin to impose their own deadlines, as short as five years for TMDLs on all of a state's listed waters.[228] EPA has subsequently proposed policy guidance that would require the submission of all TMDLs, from all states, within 8 to 13 years.[229] Whether even this pace can be maintained, and whether it will produce load allocations and plans of sufficient quality to be effective, are legitimate and difficult questions. Within them lie several issues of assessment and monitoring technology and of the accommodation of uncertainty. These issues pale, however, before the root question of this issue: do the resulting load allocations have to be implemented at all?

Once WQLSs and TMDLs are prepared, the language of § 303(d) ends. Section 303(e) proceeds to require a "continuing planning process" (CPP) with "plans" that "include" § 303(d)'s TMDLs.[230] While these sections authorize EPA to approve or disapprove a CPP on the basis, inter alia, of TMDLs, they do not authorize the Agency to implement them. The question is, at this point,

---

227 33 USC § 1313(d)(2), ELR Stat. FWPCA § 303(d)(2).

228 *See* Sierra Club v. Hankinson, No. 1:94-cv-2501-MHS, 1996 WL 534909 at *1 (N.D. Ga. Mar. 25, 1996).

229 Draft memorandum of Robert Perciasepe, Assistant Administrator of Water, EPA, *New Policies for Developing and Implementing Total Maximum Daily Loads (TMDLs)* 2 (Mar. 21, 1997).

230 33 USC § 1313(e)(1), ELR Stat. FWPCA § 303(e)(1).

has the statute run its string? Does all the work of TMDLs and their load allocations wind up as references in state plans, implemented if and as the states may wish? Or does the TMDL itself have to include the means of its own implementation in order to receive EPA's approval? EPA's authority to review and reject TMDLs[231] may succeed in securing the inclusion of those steps and commitments necessary to implement them, retaining some meaningful outcome for the process. Further, if these measures are inadequate, EPA may reject a TMDL and may then promulgate measures of its own in a federal TMDL.[232] But then what? For point sources, the Agency may ensure that those additional limitations imposed by a TMDL are actually implemented through its supervision of discharge permits under the NPDES program.[233] But for nonpoint sources, here is the rub: there are no federal controls over nonpoint sources under the Clean Water Act. For these sources, the § 303(d) program leads, ultimately, to a state prerogative.[234] If, as will next be discussed, it is found to cover point sources at all.

Nonpoint Sources

The big enchilada. As described in an earlier article, nonpoint source pollution has become the dominant water quality problem in the United States, dwarfing all other sources by volume and, in conventional contaminants, by far the leading cause of nonattainment for rivers, lakes, and estuaries alike. It is no secret to any observer of the Clean Water Act that the primary reason for this mushrooming problem is the fact that while other sources have been abated through required controls and their enforcement, no comparable controls or enforcement have been applied to agriculture, silviculture, and the rest of the nonpoint world. Enter, now, TMDLs, with the potential for specific, quantified load allocations (*i.e.*, reductions) from nonpoint sources. The nonpoint world quakes. And reacts.

From the outset of the FACA committee, agricultural interests made their view clear that § 303(d) does not apply to nonpoint sources.[235] In their reading of the Act, TMDLs are to be set after the exhaustion of emission limitations, and since emission limitations are only set for point sources, TMDLs are restricted to point sources as well.[236] An earlier article described the genesis of § 303(d) and its language and concluded that, while the section is entirely silent as to whether it applies to only point, only to nonpoint, or to both point and nonpoint sources, the members of the House Public Works Committee, where this section was born, were well aware that nonpoint sources contributed significantly to the failure to attain water quality standards, and that the most logical reading of the process they arrived at is to read nonpoint sources as included. Indeed, in both the context of that time and the present, TMDLs for point sources alone make no pollution control sense at all.

---

[231] *Id.* § 1313(d)(2), ELR Stat. FWPCA § 303(d)(2).

[232] *Id.*

[233] *Id.* § 1342(i), ELR Stat. FWPCA § 402(i) (EPA review of NPDES permits).

[234] EPA, of course, holds residual leverage that could be important in influencing a state to regulate nonpoint pollution, including direct funding assistance, related point-permit review, and approval of state-delegated programs. This leverage and its limits will be further explored in an ensuing article.

[235] Conversation with Richard Parrish, FACA committee member, March 11, 1997.

[236] *Id.*

This reading of the statute is bolstered by the fact that EPA has given the statute the same reading, consistently, from the issuance of its first regulations. As early as 1975, the Agency was calling for the allocation of nonpoint source loadings within TMDLs. It has continued to do so in its regulations, guidelines, and draft strategy through 1996, 20 years of consistent agency interpretation. Under the U.S. Supreme Court's ruling in *Chevron, U.S.A., Inc. v. Natural Resources Defense Council,*[237] and since,[238] on deference to an agency's interpretation of its statutory mandates, this regulatory history should be dispositive. Within the FACA committee, however, EPA has recognized the existence of the opposing view.[239] The opposing view, indeed, has taken the counteroffensive.

On April 29, 1997, the U.S. Forest Service wrote EPA to protest, and reject, the application of § 303(d) to nonpoint sources.[240] The section "was written with point sources in mind," it said, and EPA's approach "may not satisfy the requirements of the Act."[241] Getting to the point, the Forest Service wrote that EPA was "exposing all Federal and State agencies to additional litigation" over nonpoint source controls.[242] So much was, in fact, true; siltation from forest roads and washouts from clearcuts had eliminated trout and salmon from the then one mountain river[243] and, in the spring of 1997, wiped out quite a few human habitations as well.[244] The Forest Service, as many states, believed in the application of management practices without specific limits on pollution.[245] In support for this argument, the Forest Service pointed to § 319[246] of the Clean Water Act, adopted in 1987 specifically to address nonpoint sources of pollution.[247] Section 319, it wrote, was and should be the exclusive remedy.[248]

The argument is essentially political. As a legal argument, it is thin. In enacting § 303(d), Congress, at best, said nothing about whether nonpoint sources were in or out, and would have had to have been insane to, on the one hand, spell out the TMDL process, and on the other, exclude those nonpoint sources it recognized at the time were so much the cause of the problem. In enacting the 1987 Amendments with § 319, Congress likewise

---

[237] 467 U.S. 837, 14 ELR 20507 (1984) (deference to EPA's somewhat fluid policy on nonattainment under the Clean Air Act)

[238] *See, e.g.,* Babbitt v. Sweet Home Chapter of Communities for a Great Oregon, 115 S.Ct. 2407, 25 ELR 21194 (1994) (deference to U.S. Department of the Interior's interpretation of § 9 of the Endangered Species Act)

[239] EPA, Background Paper No. 2: Criteria for EPA Approval of State, Tribal TMDLs, FACA Committee Meeting 2 (Nov. 19-21, 1996) ("It has been suggested that since TMDLs do not have a direct regulatory effect (except through NPDES permits), they should not be a high priority, especially in watersheds impaired mainly by nonpoint sources. On the other hand, it has been argued that nonpoint source management programs should be guided by TMDLs and load allocations.").

[240] Letter of Arthur Bryant, Director, Watershed and Air Management, U.S. Forest Service, to Geoffrey H. Grubbs (Apr. 29, 1997).

[241] *Id.* at 1.

[242] *Id.* at 2.

[243] *See* National Wildlife Fed'n v. U.S. Forest Serv., 592 F. Supp. 931, 14 ELR 20755 (D. Or. 1984) (describing destruction of salmon streams by clearcutting and resultant landslides).

[244] *See* Hal Bernton, *Local Stories of Clearcuts & Mudslides,* Portland Oregonian, Feb. 2, 1997; Jeffrey St. Clair, *U.S. Environment: Logging Practices Unleash Lethal Landslides,* Inter Press Serv., Jan. 6, 1997.

[245] Letter of Arthur Bryant, *supra* note 161.

[246] 33 USC § 1329, ELR Stat. FWPCA § 319.

[247] Letter of Arthur Bryant, *supra* note 161.

[248] *Id.*

said nothing about TMDLs, pro or con, and whether nonpoint sources were included or excluded.[249] EPA's TMDL regulations including nonpoint sources had, by that time, been on the books for 11 years. The notion that Congress repealed a federal program without referring to it by enacting another is novel to environmental law. This argument has been considered and rejected with regard to a quite similar claim that § 303(d)'s application to toxic dischargers was preempted by Congress' subsequent enactment, also in the 1987 Amendments, of a separate water quality-based program for toxins.[250] In fact, Congress has, year after year, thrown program after program into the breach against specific environmental problems, often overlapping or duplicative programs, often without thinking through how the new and the old would mesh.[251] As of 1997, for example, it had enacted no fewer than six different strategies under the Clean Water Act to abate toxic pollution. All remain viable. There is rarely only one way in environmental law.

In practice, §§ 303(d) and 319's approaches to nonpoint source pollution are compatible and, indeed, mutually supportive. Within the statutory scheme, § 319 is the carrot, funding state programs for nonpoint source abatement statewide, for all waters whether they are currently above standard or below.[252] In keeping with its broad sweep, § 319's provisions are voluntary. States may choose to participate or not; participating states may choose regulatory approaches or not. Section 303(d), on the other hand, addresses a narrower and more nasty job: the chronically polluted waters of the United States. For this problem zone, enter a stick: qualified pollution load allocations. The nature of the allocations and of the implementing controls remain up to the states, but states do have to come up with them. The Clean Water Act is, after all, about restoring the nation's waters. In this context, the existence of both §§ 303 and 319 makes sense. Or at least as much sense as the multiple programs of the Clean Water Act, the Clean Air Act, and similar pollution control laws often do.

Nonetheless, given the stakes at issue and the vehemence with which the U.S. Department of Agriculture and its nonpoint source constituents will fight quantified abatement requirements, this question is far from resolved in the federal family. To say nothing of what a constituency-oriented Congress may do. At this juncture, the only safe observation from the fact and scale of nonpoint source pollution and its effect on achieving water quality standards is that, unless TMDLs include quantified restrictions on nonpoint sources, they are wasting everyone's time.

---

[249] *See* Senate Comm. on Environment & Public Works, 100th Cong., 2d Sess., A Legislative History of the Water Quality Act of 1987 (1987).

[250] Dioxin/Organochlorine Ctr. v. Rasmussen, 37 ERC 1845, 1848 n.3 (W.D. Wash. 1993), *aff'd sub nom.* Dioxin/Organochlorine Ctr. v. Clarke, 57 F.3d 1517, 25 ELR 21258 (9th Cir. 1995).

[251] For a discussion of the choice among several strategies under the Clean Air Act to control human exposure to lead, see Frederick R. Anderson et al., Environmental Protection: Law and Policy 174-181 (2d ed. 1990).

[252] 33 USC § 1329, ELR Stat. FWPCA § 319.

Oliver A. Houck, "TMDLs III: A NEW FRAMEWORK FOR THE CLEAN WATER ACT'S AMBIENT STANDARDS PROGRAM"

28 ELR 10415, 10436-10437 (1998)

TMDLs

At the end of § 303(d) and the long, contentious, and difficult road that leads to its implementation are the TMDLs themselves, the actual plans that identify pollution loadings, allocate them to sources, and present mechanisms for their abatement. Good plans and their execution in fact will vindicate the faith that at least some members of Congress, led by the House of Representatives, had in enacting these water quality-based requirements in 1972. Weak or unexecuted plans will confirm the skepticism of the Senate and others that this approach to water pollution control could ever work. We know enough from the process to date that this is an expensive and time-consuming courtship of state and regulated interests, particularly nonpoint discharge industries. What we don't know yet is whether what is coming out the end of the pipe is worth the effort.

But we do have some early data. Over the past few years, and in increasing numbers as the pressure of citizen suits is felt, states have begun submitting, and EPA approving, TMDLs for listed impaired waters. In the fall of 1997, this author sent Freedom of Information Act requests to each EPA region for five TMDLs illustrating the implementation of § 303 by their respective states. As of April 1998, 9 of the 10 regions had forwarded TMDLs; Region 7, as of that date, had no approved TMDLs. Additional TMDL summaries were obtained from EPA. In all, 55 TMDLs were reviewed in order to make very basic determinations of what pollutants, discharge sources, load calculations, and reductions were contained in these documents, as well as their inclusion of such regulatory criteria as margins for safety and for future development.

. . . .

The TMDLs reviewed reveal, and confirm, several features of the program that might have been predicted by its central conundrum: how to come to grips with nonpoint sources. These features include:

1. *Nonpoint sources are targets of last resort.* If at all possible, point sources will be identified as the sole source of even conventional pollution (*e.g.*, solids and oxygen demand) and the sole instrument of cleanup. Despite EPA guidance defining TMDLs as the combination of point source WLAs and nonpoint source WLAs and requiring both calculations for impaired waters, nearly 50% of the approved TMDLs (25 of a total of 55) did not even identify nonpoint source contributions. In effect, these documents described NPDES permit reductions, usually by municipal sewage treatment systems, that had taken place or would take place in the future.

2. *Even where identified, nonpoint source reductions will frequently not be calculated, and, where calculated, even more frequently will not be implemented through identified abatement plans.* Of the 30 TMDLs reviewed that acknowledged nonpoint contributions, 10 did not quantify these loadings, and only 13 projected actual, quantified reductions. Where projected, these reductions, further, were predicated in almost every case on unspecified BMPs contained in state nonpoint source or other documents and incorporated by reference. In only one case did it appear that nonpoint controls were going to be mandatory or enforceable.

3. *Statutory margins for safety and to accommodate future growth are honored more in the breach than the observance.* Only 20 documents contained margin of safety consideration, and only 6 made explicit provision for future growth. These conclusions, further, credit state assertions that margins of safety were provided not by allocating an increment for error but, rather, through the use of conservative estimates, assertions that might well be subject to question.

In sum, TMDLs have a long way to go before they contain the analysis or produce the results Congress intended in 1972. Taking the documents approved to date at face value, granting them the benefit of every doubt and making allowances for the fact that they are first efforts for many states and EPA regions, they provide little confidence that pollution sources are being addressed in any fashion beyond ratcheting down on NPDES permits where they are available and, where they are not, by passing the buck to unidentified and largely unenforceable nonpoint source BMPs. Congress, EPA, and citizen suits can lead this horse to water but it remains to be seen how much it is going to drink.

NOTE

See also Oliver A. Houck, *TMDL IV: The Final Frontier*, 29 ELR 10457, 10469 (1999) which presents a cautiously optimistic view of the future of TMDLs and ambient water quality developments, noting that "TMDLs hold the best prospect of those now available for coming to grips with the last major, unregulated sources of water pollution in this country" [at 29 ELR 10486 (1999)].

If Professor Houck, who is an acknowledged expert in the water quality law area, does not sound overly optimistic about the TMDL approach, which he himself helped to develop, it is because of the inherent difficulty of enforcing water quality standards, which unlike effluent limitations cannot be directly enforced against industrial and other polluters. This difficulty has been commented on in some judicial opinions including the opinion by Circuit Judge Wald, who is a very insightful judge, in *American Paper Institute, Inc., v. United States Environmental Protection Agency.*[253] The case involved the use

[253] 996 F.2d 346, 23 ELR 20984 (D.C. Cir. 1993), *supra* at p. 505.

of narrative criteria in writing pollution discharge permits in the context of maintaining water quality standards. Judge Wald comments as follows:

> Of course, the water quality standards by themselves have no effect on pollution; the rubber hits the road when the state-created standards are used as the basis for specific effluent limitations in NPDES permits. As noted above, once a water quality standard has been promulgated, § 301 of the CWArequires all NPDES permits for point sources to incorporate discharge limitations necessary to satisfy that standard. *See, e.g., Westvaco Corp. v. EPA*, 899 F.2d 1383, 1385 (4th Cir. 1990).

The difficulty which Professor Houck also refers to is not only the problem of relating effluent limitations to water quality standards, but also the problem of influencing water quality standards through raising effluent standards when there may be many polluters, including nonpoint source polluters, contributing to the unacceptable condition of ambient water quality.

The 1998 Clean Water Action Plan and New Life for Water Quality

President Clinton, on February 19, 1998, announced his administration's Clean Water Action Plan to protect and restore the nation's waters.[254] The emphasis on improving water quality was given a significant boost by the Plan, which signaled a major change in the administration of the federal Clean Water Act. The new initiative brought a significant departure from the sole emphasis on technology based effluent limitations, and is expected to change the approaches to water quality protection, requiring federal, state, tribal and local participation and cooperation in the effort.

The purpose of the plan is to establish cooperation and participation by federal and state agencies, tribes, communities, citizens and businesses to enhance existing water quality programs. Four key tools provide the basis for the plan: a watershed approach, strong federal and state standards, natural resource stewardship, and an information base for citizens and officials.[255] The plan anticipates a significant interagency effort, as decisions relating to the plan will involve EPA, the Army Corps of Engineers, and the Departments of Agriculture and Interior. The plan reflects an initial view of the water quality program of the future.

Without undercutting the established emphasis of the 1972 Clean Water Act on effluent limitations of point sources, the new plan expands the interpretation of statutory authorizations by focusing on nonpoint sources, such as runoff from urban and agricultural lands and facilities, including animal feeding operations and mines.[256]

---

[254] *See* statement by President Clinton on the Clean Water Action Plan, White House press release, February 19, 1998. 63 Fed. Reg. 14109 (March 24, 1998) Notice of Availability of Clean Water Action Plan.

[255] 63 Fed. Reg. at 14109.

[256] Brian R. Hanson, *Clean Water Action Plan: Dramatic New Approach to Water Quality Protection,* ABA Section of Natural Resources, Energy, and Environmental Law, Newsletter (March-April 1999) at p.1.

An early expression of the direction of the Clean Water Action Plan is the draft of the Unified Animal Feedlot Operations strategy.[257] Under this strategy, EPA and the Department of Agriculture establish a policy, referred to as a "National Performance Expectation" that the owners and operators of animal feedlot operations develop and apply "comprehensive nutrient management plans." EPA and USDA, pursuant to the plan, will also seek to minimize water quality and public health impacts of animal feeding operations. At this point, the draft strategy is largely voluntary, but EPA will provide regulatory programs to advance water quality. The NPDES system will provide an opportunity to control point source discharges at animal feeding operations. The total maximum daily load process (TMDL) will also be used to examine load allocations to AFO (Animal Feedlot Operations) sources, at streams that are impaired or threatened. The animal feedlot operation strategy may provide a prototype of how watershed protection will operate, and reference is made to examples of watershed-based initiatives currently being developed.[258]

The watershed-based approach of regulatory controls aims at the development of a "unified watershed assessment."[259] It is a part of the plan that EPA work with states, tribes, and communities to develop lists of impaired waters, and define drinking water source protection areas as part of the assessment. EPA released its Final Framework for Unified Watershed Assessment, Restoration Priorities, and Restoration Action Strategies on June 9, 1998.[260] The unified watershed assessment will be the basis for "watershed restoration action strategies." The purpose is to identify the most important causes of water pollution and resource degradation in order to take appropriate action to solve these problems. The plan is to gather and disperse information through the unified watershed assessments that will specify necessary local activities in each watershed. There is a promise to help fund local organizations by "watershed assistance grants" to help protect the watersheds.[261]

The entire program reflects an effort to make water quality protection more effective, following the extended earlier period of lack of attention to water quality standards. On July 7, 1998, EPA issued an unusual Advance Notice of Proposed Rulemaking (ANPRM) on the revision of federal water quality standards as well as on EPA policy on water quality issues generally.[262] EPA has also tried to assist federal, state, and tribal water quality programs by publishing a compilation of nationally recommended water quality criteria.[263]

The ANPRM clearly indicates EPA's new direction in a sound water quality based program. The notice not only discusses the past history of federal water quality standards but addresses numerous other issues, including water uses, water quality criteria, the implementation of antidegradation, mixing zones, the application of water quality standards to wetlands and the possibility of

[257] 63 Fed. Reg. 50192 (Sept. 21, 1998).

[258] Multimedia Strategy for Priority Persistent, Bioaccumulative, and Toxic Pollutants, 63 Fed. Reg. 63926 (Nov. 17, 1998); *see also* EPA and National Oceanic and Atmospheric Administration, Coastal Nonpoint Pollution Control Program Guidance, 63 Fed. Reg. 56146 (Oct. 21, 1998); both cited in Hanson, note 4 *supra* at 8.

[259] 63 Fed. Reg. at 14110.

[260] The final framework is available at www.epa.gov/cleanwater/uswfinal.

[261] 63 Fed. Reg. at 14111.

[262] 63 Fed. Reg. 36741 (July 7, 1998).

[263] 63 Fed. Reg. 67547 (Dec. 7, 1998).

the direct application of water quality standards. Thus, the ANPRM raises the leading issues of current Clean Water Act policies. As a current policy guidance, the ANPRM provides the direction for future EPA rulemaking.

While the outlines of future regulatory developments are firm and impressive, the ANPRM outlines a major work in progress in which water quality standards will play a significantly more important role than they have from the beginning of the Clean Water Act to 1998.

The Rationale for the Clinton Administration Clean Water Action Plan and Some of Its Problems

The new plan embraces a new emphasis on ambient water quality standards as well as considerable reliance on state activities and state enforcement to improve water quality. Emphasis on water quality and improvement of ambient water quality through state efforts was largely the state of the regulation of waters prior to the passage of the 1972 Federal Water Pollution Control Act Amendments. Indeed, the very reason for the enactment of the 1972 FWPCA was that the old approach had failed dismally and that the Clean Water Act with its emphasis on uniform water effluent standards set federally for categories of point sources was viewed as the only possible corrective for the dismal condition of the nation's waters. The effort has always been to regulate effluents through the best technology based controls. The view was then that if effluents from point sources were adequately controlled, water quality would inevitably improve. The approach was very successful and water quality has improved tremendously. Section 303 of the Clean Water Actrequires further technology based controls if earlier controls do not manage to achieve ambient water quality standards that still need to be set by the states.

To deal with the shortfall of adequate ambient water quality standards through technology based effluent limitation, EPA has rediscovered and reemphasized the Total Maximum Daily Load Program (TMDL). The TMDL program, a long dormant part of the Clean Water Act,[264] offers a method to deal directly with ambient water quality, though necessarily still placing some reliance on technology based limits with respect to point sources. The TMDL program is managed in part by controls operating through the NPDES program, *i.e.*, through the adjustments in the individual permitting of sources. The TMDL program, through the examination and management of total maximum daily loads, shows beyond question that a major shortfall in the accomplishment of good water quality depends not only on the control of point source effluents, but also on the control of nonpoint sources.

Failure to control nonpoint sources excludes from regulation variegated agriculture,[265] all agricultural storm water discharges,[266] animal feeding

---

[264] *See, generally*, Oliver A. Houck, *The Long Road Toward Water Quality Based Regulations under the Clean Water Act*, 27 ELR 10391 (1997); Oliver A. Houck, *TMDLs: The Resurrection of Water Quality Standards-Based Regulations under the Clean Water Act*, 27 ELR 10329 (1997).

[265] Pub. L. No. 95-217, § 33(b), 91 Stat. 1577 (1977).

[266] Pub. L. No. 100-4, § 503, 101 Stat. 75 (1987).

operations and concentrated animal feeding operations, except for exceptionally large major industrial feedlot operations. In addition, nonpoint sources include city storm water runoff which contains major sediment loadings from construction sites, typically exceeding ten to twenty times those from agricultural lands. Runoff rates may be as high as 100 times those of agricultural lands, and typically 1000 to 2000 times those of forest lands.[267]

Other major nonpoint sources, particularly from the public lands of the west, arise from grazing and harvesting of timber. To manage the TMDL process—meaning to reduce the total maximum daily load of pollution—will require massive regulatory efforts with respect to agricultural nonpoint sources, municipal sources and sources created by the exploitation of public lands.

Another major nonpoint source of pollution impacts directly on the coastal zone and on major river deltas. Nonpoint source pollution, for example, was sending more than 100 million tons of sediments into the Great Lakes every year, as Congress noted.[268] This massive deposit of sediments, as well as the creation of "dead zones" in some coastal waters resulting from fertilizer runoff from farms and lawns resulted in problem conditions, in such areas as the Gulf of Mexico, which contains so little oxygen that neither fish nor shrimp can survive in it. Sediments contribute more than half of the phosphorus, chromium, copper, lead, and zinc delivered to coastal waters.[269] It was these conditions that gave rise to the passage of the Coastal Zone Management Act[270] and to the passage of the Coastal Zone Amendments Reauthorization Act of 1990 (CZARA) to advance improvements of water quality standards in the coastal zone which had not been achieved under the Coastal Zone Management Act.

The Clean Water Action Plan, in undertaking a meaningful effort to improve water quality, must advance the control of nonpoint sources. The difficulties of this effort are substantial. Nonpoint sources involve enterprises and activities that have had a favored position and that for many years have escaped meaningful regulation. To avoid regulation, agriculture manages to project the protected image of the family farm; yet we live in an age when agriculture is a major industrial business and family farms are disappearing. So too, the folklore of the range and of the lumberjack and the lonesome miner and his burro have shielded these fields from the reality of regulations appropriate to large-scale cattle raising operations on the public lands and to major feedlots, as well as to mining operations and the massive clear cutting of lumber and the construction of access roads. These largely unregulated activities have contributed to massive runoffs of pollution and massive loss of surface and soil, resulting in major siltation and sedimentation in rivers and coastal zones.

The regulation of surface runoff from construction and building operations and from stormwater runoff in cities and towns cause massive additions to the pollution load; yet the infrastructure changes necessary to resolve the problem are likely to run into objections to federal interference with the resolution of local land use problems and controls. Furthermore, the expansion of

---

267 55 Fed. Reg. 47990, 47992 (Nov. 16, 1990).

268 H. Rep. No. 101-535, at 9 (1990).

269 H. Rep. No. 101-535, at 9 (1990).

270 16 U.S.C. §§ 1451-1465.

federal regulatory jurisdiction to cover the area of nonpoint source pollution will run into the modern anti-regulatory mood, and the pervasive objection, not to say abhorrence, for command and control regulations.[271]

The Role of the TMDL (Total Maximum Daily Load) Program in the 1998 Clean Water Action Plan

The Clinton administration's Clean Water Action Plan emphasizes a water quality approach within a watershed framework. As noted earlier, § 303 of the Clean Water Actcontinues the state water quality standards in effect prior to the 1972 adoption of the Federal Water Pollution Control Act.[272] The section requires the triennial review and update or modification of the state water quality standard; the state must submit the standard to the Administrator for review or for promulgation of revised standards if the state standards are not adequate.[273] Each state must then identify the waters within its boundaries where effluent limitations under § 301 of the Act are not sufficient to implement the applicable water quality standards. The state must identify the waters or parts of such waters for which the usual technology based standards are not stringent enough to assure protection of fish and wildlife. The state must establish a list of such areas in accordance with priority ranking and for each of the waters so identified the state must then prepare the total maximum daily load which the Administrator identifies under § 304 of the Act as suitable for such calculation. The TMDL must be established "to implement the applicable water quality standards with seasonable variations and a margin of safety which takes into account any lack of knowledge concerning the relationship between effluent limitations and water quality."[274] Section 303(d)(1)(D) requires the state to estimate for the waters identified the daily thermal load required to assure protection and propagation of fish and wildlife, concerning water temperatures, flow rates, seasonal variations and other aspects of thermal pollution.

Having identified and listed areas with insufficient controls, the state must submit to the Administration "from time to time, with the first such submission not later than 180 after the date of publication of the first identification of pollutants under § 304(a)(2)(D) for his approval the waters identified and the loads established" under the TMDL requirement.[275] The Administrator must either approve or disapprove the identification and the load not later than 30 days after the date of submission. If the Administrator approves such identification and load, the state must incorporate them into its "continuing planning process" provided for under § 303(e) of the statute. If the Administrator disapproves the identification and load, the Administrator must not later than 30 days after the date of disapproval identify such waters and establish such loads as he determines necessary to implement applicable water quality standards, and when the Administrator has done so, the state must then incorporate them into its planning process.

[271] For detailed reference to the new TMDL program, see F. Grad, Treatise on Environmental Law, § 3.03[4][j].

[272] CWA § 303(a), 33 U.S.C. § 1313(a).

[273] CWA § 303(b), (c), 33 U.S.C. § 1313(b), (c).

[274] CWA § 303(d)(1)(C).

[275] CWA § 303(d)(2).

"For the specific purpose of developing information," states must identify waters within their boundaries not identified earlier and must provide estimates for such waters of the total maximum daily load with seasonal variations and margins of safety for those pollutants which the Administrator has identified under § 304 as well as for thermal discharges, all at the level to assure protection and propagation of indigenous populations of fish and wildlife.

Although § 303 of the Clean Water Actcontains the outlines of an ambient water quality program, it was not a major agenda item for EPA and for the states until it was recognized in 1998 as a significant element of the new Clean Water Action Plan. In 1997, EPA issued a memorandum to "Regional Administrators Regional Water Division Directors." The subject of the memorandum, by Robert Perciasep, Assistant Administrator, was on the subject of "New Policies for Establishing and Implementing Total Maximum Daily Loads (TMDLs)." Its introduction reads as follows:

UNDER NEW LAWS MANY NP WILL BE REGULATED UNDER NPDES.

> Last August I issued a Healthy Watershed Strategy to advance the cause of clean water everywhere. A key component of the strategy was to "rapidly increase the development and implementation of total maximum daily loads to manage water quality on a watershed scale." Thanks to hard work by state and EPA managers and staffs, EPA now has received and taken action on all state lists required by § 303(d) of the Clean Water Act(CWA). It is now time to move towards the next stage of our strategy to achieve water quality standards—to make sure that TMDLs are established by all listed waters, and that the load allocations established by TMDLs are implemented by point and nonpoint sources alike.
>
> Almost 25 years after the passage of the CWA, the National Water Program is at a defining moment. We—meaning each of you, each of our state, local, and tribal partners and all of us in the Office of Water—are making the transition from a clean water program based primarily on technology-based controls to water quality based controls implemented on a watershed basis. Technology-based controls such as secondary treatment of sewage, effluent limitation guidelines for industrial sources, and management practices for some nonpoint sources, have dramatically reduced water pollution and laid the foundation for further progress.
>
> We must continue to preserve and protect the foundation we have worked so hard to put in place. If we are to achieve clean water everywhere, though, we must continue to build capacity to identify remaining problem areas and fix each problem on a watershed-by-watershed basis. The TMDL program is crucial to success because it brings rigor, accountability, and statutory authority to the process. These are the reasons the Administrator and I so strongly support the TMDL program in states, tribes and EPA regions.[276]

[276] Total Maximum Daily Load Program, p. 1 (1997).

Implementation of TMDLs for Water Impaired Solely or Primarily by Nonpoint Sources

After the States and the EPA have identified a water quality impairment on a section 303(d) list and have established the TMDLs for it, the next stage is implementation.

EPA has requested each State to describe its plan for implementing nonpoint Load Allocations, water segment by water segment, or by watershed, or statewide. These "implementation plans" were to be submitted as section 303(e)[277] plan revisions either "coupled with a proposed TMDL" or as part of an "equivalent" process. In the case of waters impaired by point sources only or by a blend of point and nonpoint sources in which point sources dominate, EPA regulations[278] require that effluent limits in NPDES permits for point sources be consistent with assumptions and requirements of wasteload allocations for the discharge contained in an EPA-approved TMDL. *The EPA Guidance for Water Quality Decisions: The TMDL Process* (April 1991)[279] broadly describes the process for deriving wasteload allocations for point sources and incorporating these allocations into NPDES permits. This guidance document also describes ways that load allocations are to be set and implemented for nonpoint sources, using available current state, local and tribal programs and authorities, including Section 319 of the CWA. Such programs may be regulatory, nonregulatory, or incentive based.

In watersheds impaired by a blend of point and nonpoint sources, if any wasteload load allocation to a point source is increased based on an assumption that loads from nonpoint sources will be reduced, the State must provide "reasonable assurances" that the nonpoint source load allocations will in fact be achieved.[280]

EPA's guidance on implementation of TMDLs does not yet address implementation of TMDLs for waters impaired only by nonpoint sources or by a blend of point and nonpoint sources in which nonpoint sources dominate. The Agency, faced with the realization that implementation of Load Allocations for nonpoint sources is essential if the goals of the CWA are to be met, recognized the voluntary measures of the section 319 program as the "primary implementation mechanism" for nonpoint sources.[281] However, it insisted that "all available federal, state and local programs and authorities" were to be used in order to achieve the TMDL load allocations for all nonpoint sources.[282] Nonpoint source implementation of Load Allocations within the TMDLs may be sought through regulatory, non regulatory, incentive-based programs or voluntary actions by committed citizens, individual land owners, public and private enterprises engaged in agriculture, forestry or urban development. Though EPA's flexibility is probably a last resort because of its lack of authority over nonpoint sources, the Agency can still make the flexible arrangement effective by the exercise of its authority to deny new point source

[277] 33 U.S.C. § 1313(e), State Continuing planning process.

[278] *See* 40 C.F.R. § 122.44(d)(1)(vii).

[279] Available at <http://www.epa.gov/owowwtrl/tmdl/decisions/index.html>.

[280] *See* 40 C.F.R. § 122.44(d)(1)(vii).

[281] *See* 1997 Schedule for Load Allocations.

[282] *See* 1997 Schedule for Load Allocations.

permits in water quality limited (*i.e.*, TMDL-required) waters;[283] modify permits for existing sources based on new information;[284] and revoke a state-delegated program for failure to develop, implement or enforce TMDLs.[285]

The difficulties with the regulation of nonpoint sources implicit in the "guidance" have been analyzed and articulated in elegant detail by Professor Houck, who suggests that citizen suits provide the best hope for enforcement in this area, as they have in the past.[286] Nevertheless, EPA is expected to pursue rule making that codifies the requirements of the program and provide the basis for citizen enforcement of the requirements.[287]

Unlike effluent limitations which are directly enforceable against point sources, water quality by its nature cannot be directly enforced against such sources, and it may be surmised that the adoption of the Federal Water Pollution Control Act in 1972 was the result of the inadequacy of the state water quality system which had not resulted in water quality improvements for many years prior to the 1972 enactment of federal law.

Antidegradation Policy

For purposes of comparison, consult the case of *Sierra Club v. Ruckelshaus* at § 2.03[3][e][iv], *supra* p. 147, which found that the Administrator of EPA had an affirmative duty not to approve state implementation plans which allowed the degradation of ambient air quality. When the Federal Water Pollution Control Act was enacted in 1972, lower courts had already decided *Sierra Club v. Ruckelshaus* and EPA determined that § 303 of FWPCA, which provided for the continuation of existing water quality standards, was a reflection of the nondegradation policy that EPA had earlier adopted as part of its guidance document, *Environmental Protection Agency, Guidelines for the Developing or Revising Water Standards under the Federal Water Pollution Control Act Amendments of 1972*. These guidelines, at pages 7 and 8, found that water quality standards must be designed to enhance the quality of the water and should not in any case provide for standards less than existing water quality. The nondegradation policy was finally published as Title 40, § 130.17(e) of the Code of Federal Regulations on November 28, 1975, following earlier threats of litigation and subsequent negotiations with NRDC. The mechanisms to implement the water pollution nondegradation policy were intended to be part of the revisions of state water quality standards under § 303, subject to EPA approval. The entire purpose of the effort was to speed

---

283 *See* 40 C.F.R. § 122.4(i)(1997) (No permit may be issued "to a new source or a new discharger, if the discharge from its construction or operation will cause or contribute to the violation of water quality standards.").

284 *See* 40 C.F.R. § 122.62(a)(2)(1997).

285 40 C.F.R. § 123.63(a)(5); *see also* Sierra Club v. Hankinson, 939 F. Supp. 865, 27 ELR 20280 (N.D. Ga. 1996) (citing with approval EPA's authorization under 40 C.F.R § 123.63(a)(5) to revoke a state program for failure to perform TMDLs).

286 Oliver A. Houck, *TMDLs III: A Framework for the Clean Water Act's Ambient Standards Program*, 28 ELR 10415, 10423, 10435 (1998).

287 This obligation is required of EPA by the basic principles of administrative law under the Administrative Procedure Act (APA), 5 U.S.C. § 553. However, the imposition of such generally applicable and detailed requirements calls for notice and comment rule making. United States v. Florida E. Coast Ry., 410 U.S. 224 (1973).

the achievement of the fishable/swimmable target of FWPCA. The relationship of the development of water pollution nondegradation standards to their counterparts in the Clean Air Act have significant similarities.[288]

[288] N.W. Hines, *A Decade of Nondegradation Policy in Congress and the Courts; the Erratic Pursuit of Clear Air and Clean Water*, 62 Iowa L. Rev. 643, 673-681 (1977). In connection with the nondegradation policy, see the provision against "backsliding" reviewed in the case of NRDC v. EPA, 859 F.2d 156, 19 ELR 20016 (D.C. Cir. 1988) on page 489, *supra*. Note that in that case the issue of nondegradation was raised in the context of regulations affecting the NPDES system.

Chapter 4

REGULATION OF SOLID WASTE, HAZARDOUS WASTE AND TOXIC SUBSTANCES

This chapter addresses some closely related and yet distinct areas. The regulation of solid waste had long been a subject of interest, concerned in part with resource conservation and in part with environmental sanitation, particularly in predominantly urban areas. Because the disposal of solid waste was likely to cause problems of air and water pollution, it became an increasingly serious national concern with increasing urbanization, and it first became the subject of federal legislation in 1965. With greater attention to the disposal of solid waste, and particularly the impact of land disposal on underground waters, a long-buried problem emerged—the problem of the disposal of hazardous waste and of the consequences of many years' improper disposal of such waste.

The problem of the disposal of conventional—domestic, municipal, agricultural and non-toxic industrial—waste is old and well-recognized. The problem of hazardous waste disposal, the result largely of developments in the chemical industry and in other industries that made use of numerous new materials during and following World War II, has received considerable attention because of its threat to health and safety. But while there may be a greater urgency to the consideration of hazardous waste, the long-range significance of the control of conventional waste must not be forgotten. The mechanized urban armies of sanitation workers that nightly and daily collect our waste not only serve to keep us healthy, but also to protect the most basic aspects of the quality of life in our cities.

The materials that follow first deal with the established area of conventional waste, and then address the field of hazardous waste, which had its modern beginning with the passage of the Resource Conservation and Recovery Act of 1976. Its special provisions signified major federal attention to that area. So too did the enactment in 1980 of the Comprehensive Environmental Response Compensation and Liability Act, a federal statute aimed at ameliorating the threats posed by past, haphazard disposal of toxic chemical wastes.

§ 4.01 Conventional Solid Waste: Background Materials

U.S. Environmental Protection Agency, Characterization of Municipal Solid Waste in the United States: 1996 Update

EPA 530-R-97-015 (May, 1997)

Municipal Solid Waste In 1995

Municipal solid waste (MSW) consists of both materials and products. Materials in MSW include paper and paperboard, yard trimmings, glass, metal, plastic, wood, and food wastes. Each material category (except for food wastes and yard trimmings) is madeup of many different products. MSW are grouped into three main categories: (1) durable goods (*e.g.*, appliances), (2) nondurable goods (*e.g.*, newspapers), and (3) containers and packaging. These product categories generally contain each type of MSW materials, with some exceptions. The durable goods category contains no paper and paperboard. The nondurable goods category includes only small amounts of metals and essentiallyglass or wood. The containers and packaging category includes only very small amounts of rubber, leather, and textiles.

Materials in MSW

In 1995, MSW generation totaled 208 million tons. Figure ES-1 provides a breakdown, by weight, of the MSW materials generated in 1995. Paper and paperboard products made up the largest component of MSW generated (30 percent), and yard trimmings comprised the second largest material component (14 percent). Glass, metals, plastics, wood, and food wastes each constitute between 6 and 10 percent of the total MSW generated. Other materials in MSW, such as rubber, leather, textiles, and miscellaneous wastes, made up approximately 10 percent of the MSW generated in 1995.

Figure ES-1. Materials generated in MSW by weight, 1995
(Total weight = 208.0 million tons)

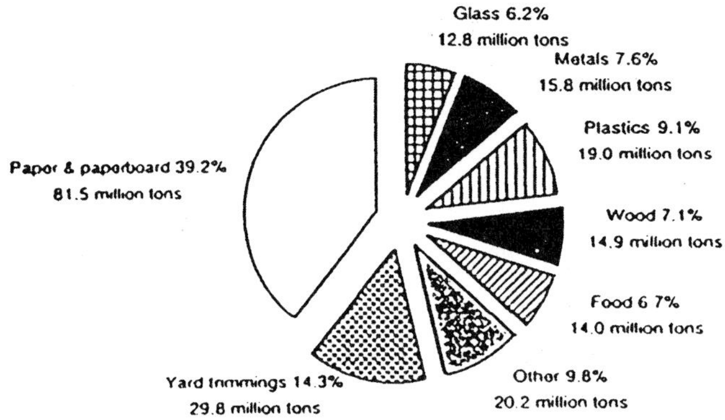

A portion of each material category in MSW was recycled (including being composted) in 1995, as illustrated in Table ES-1. It should be noted, however, that recovery rates for some products within a material category are higher than the overall recovery rate for the material category, because some products are not recovered at all. For example, aluminum cans are recovered at rates above 60 percent, but the overall recovery rate for aluminum is only 35 percent. Likewise, even though corrugated containers are recovered at rates above 64 percent, the overall recovery rate for paper and paperboard is 40 percent.

Table ES-1

GENERATION AND RECOVERY OF MATERIALS IN MSW, 1995
(In millions of tons and percent of generation of each material)

	Weight Generated	Weight Recovered	Recovery as a Percent of Generation
Paper and paperboard	81.5	32.6	40.0%
Glass	12.8	3.1	24.5%
Metals			
Ferrous metals	11.6	4.2	36.5%
Aluminum	3.0	1.0	34.5%
Other nonferrous metals	1.3	0.9	69.4%
Total metals	15.8	6.2	38.9%
Plastics	19.0	1.0	5.2%
Rubber and Leather	6.0	0.5	8.9%
Textiles	7.4	0.9	12.2%
Wood	14.9	1.4	9.6%
Other materials	3.6	0.8	23.1%
Total Materials in Products	161.1	46.6	28.9%
Other Wastes			
Food Wastes	14.0	0.6	4.1%
Yard Trimmings	29.8	9.0	30.3%
Miscellaneous Inorganic Wastes	3.2	Neg.	Neg.
Total Other Wastes	46.9	9.6	20.4%
TOTAL MUNICIPAL SOLID WASTE	208.0	56.2	27.0%

Includes wastes from residential, commercial, and institutional sources.
Neg. = Less than 50,000 tons or 0.05 percent.

Products in MSW

Figure ES-2 shows the breakdown, by weight, of MSW products generated in 1995. Containers and packaging comprised the largest portion of products generated, at 35 percent (73 million tons) of total MSW generation. Nondurable goods were the second largest fraction, comprising about 27 percent (57 million tons). The third main category of products is durable goods, which comprise 15 percent (31 million tons) of total MSW generation.

Figure ES-2. Products generated in MSW by weight, 1995
(Total weight = 208.0 million tons)

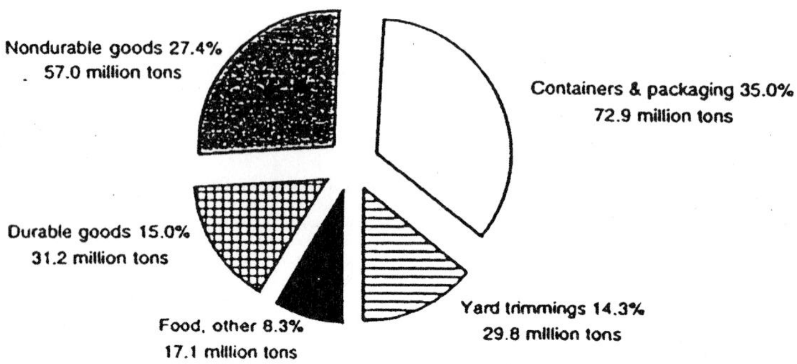

Table ES-2 shows the generation and recovery of the product categories in MSW. Recovery of containers and packaging was the highest of the three product categories—38 percent of containers and packaging generated in 1995 were recovered for recycling. About 52 percent of aluminum packaging was recovered (mostly aluminum beverage cans), while more than 54 percent of steel packaging (mostly cans) was recovered. Paper and paperboard packaging recovery was estimated at 52 percent; corrugated containers accounted for most of that figure. Approximately 27 percent of glass containers were recovered overall, while about 14 percent of wood packaging (mostly pallets) was recovered. About 10 percent of plastic containers and packaging was recovered in 1995, most of which was made up of soft drink, milk, and water bottles.

Table ES-2

GENERATION AND RECOVERY OF PRODUCTS IN MSW BY MATERIAL, 1995
(In millions of tons and percent of generation of each product)

	Weight Generated	Weight Recovered	Recovery as a Percent of Generation
Durable goods			
Ferrous metals	8.7	2.7	30.7%
Aluminum	0.8	Neg.	Neg.
Other non-ferrous metals	1.3	0.9	69.4%
Total metals	10.8	3.6	33.1%
Glass	1.3	Neg.	Neg.
Plastics	6.2	0.2	3.8%
Rubber and leather	5.2	0.5	10.3%
Wood	4.2	Neg.	Neg.
Textiles	2.3	0.1	5.0%
Other materials	1.1	0.8	77.8%
Total durable goods	31.2	5.3	17.0%
Nondurable goods			
Paper and paperboard	43.5	12.7	29.3%
Plastics	5.1	Neg.	<1%
Rubber and leather	0.8	Neg.	Neg.
Textiles	5.0	0.8	15.8%
Other materials	2.7	Neg.	Neg.
Total nondurable goods	57.0	13.5	23.7%
Containers and packaging			
Steel	2.8	1.6	54.6%
Aluminum	2.0	1.0	51.6%
Total metals	4.8	2.6	53.4%
Glass	11.5	3.1	27.3%
Paper and paperboard	38.1	19.9	52.3%
Plastics	7.7	0.7	9.7%
Wood	10.6	1.4	13.5%
Other materials	0.1	Neg.	Neg.
Total containers and packaging	72.9	27.8	38.1%
Other wastes			
Food wastes	14.0	0.6	4.1%
Yard trimmings	29.8	9.0	30.3%
Miscellaneous inorganic wastes	3.2	Neg.	Neg.
Total other wastes	46.9	9.6	20.4%
TOTAL MUNICIPAL SOLID WASTE	208.0	56.2	27.0%

Includes wastes from residential, commercial, and institutional sources.
Neg. = less than 50,000 tons or 0.05 percent.

Overall recovery of nondurable goods was almost 24 percent in 1995. Newspapers constituted the largest portion of this recovery, with 53 percent of newspapers generated being recovered for recycling. Office papers and magazines were also recovered in significant quantities in 1995, at 44 percent and 28 percent, respectively. Over 16 percent of clothing and other textile nondurable products also were recovered for recycling.

Residential and Commercial Sources of MSW

Sources of MSW, as characterized in this report, include both residential and commercial locations. Residential waste (including waste from multi-family dwellings) is estimated to be 55 to 65 percent of total MSW generation. Commercial waste (including waste from schools, some industrial sites where packaging is generated, and businesses) constitutes between 35 and 45 percent. Local and regional factors, such as climate and level of commercial activity, contribute to these variations.

. . . .

Management of Municipal Solid Waste Source Reduction

Source reduction is gaining more attention as an important solid waste management option. Source reduction, often called "waste prevention," is defined by EPA as "any change in the design, manufacturing, purchase, or use of materials or products (including packaging) to reduce the amount or toxicity before they become municipal solid waste. Prevention also refers to the reuse of products or materials." Thus, source reduction activities affect the waste stream before the point of generation. In this report, MSW is considered to have been generated if it is placed at curbside or in a receptacle such as a dumpster for pickup, or if it is taken by the generator to another site for disposal or other management alternative.

Source reduction measures encompass a very broad range of activities by private citizens, communities, commercial establishments, institutional agencies, and manufacturers and distributors. In general, source reduction activities include:

- Redesigning products or packages so as to reduce the quantity of materials or the toxicity of the materials used, by substituting lighter materials for heavier ones and lengthening the life of products to postpone disposal.
- Using packaging that reduces the amount of damages or spoilage to the product.
- Reducing amounts of products or packages used through modification of current practices by processors and consumers.
- Reusing products or packages already manufactured.
- Managing non-product organic wastes (food wastes, yard trimmings) through backyard compositing or other on-site alternatives to disposal.

. . . .

Since source reduction of products and packages can save money through reducing materials and energy costs, manufacturers and packaging designers have been pursuing these activities for many years. Design for source reduction can take several approaches.

Materials substitution can make a product or package lighter. For example, there has been a continuous trend of substitution of lighter materials such as plastics and aluminum for materials such as glass and steel. The substitution may also involve a flexible package instead of a rigid package. A product or package can be redesigned to reduce weight or volume. Toxic materials in products or packaging can be replaced with non-toxic substitutes. Considerable efforts have been made in this area in the past few years.

Lengthening product life delays the time when the products enter the municipal waste stream. The responsibility for lengthening product life lies partly with manufacturers and partly with consumers. Products can be designed to last longer and be easier to repair. Since some of these design modifications may make products more expensive, at least initially, manufacturers must be willing to invest in new product development and consumers must demand the products and be willing to pay for them to make the goal work. Consumers and manufacturers must also be willing to care for and repair products.

Combined with other source reduction measures, redesign can have a significant effect on material use and eventual discards.

. . . .

Modifying Practices to Reduce Materials Use

Business and individuals can often modify their current practices to reduce the amounts of waste generated. In a business office, electronic mail can replace printed memoranda and data. Reports can be copied on both sides of the paper (duplexed).

Individuals (and businesses) can request removal from mailing lists to reduce the amount of mail received and discarded. When practical, products can be purchased in large sizes or in bulk to minimize the amount of packaging per unit of product. Concentrated products can also reduce packaging requirements; some of these products, such as fabric softeners and powdered detergent, are designed to be used with refillable containers.

Modifying practices can be combined with other source reduction measures to reduce generation and limit material use.

. . . .

Reuse of Products and Packages

Similar to lengthening product life, reuse of products and packages delays the time when the items must finally be discarded as waste. When a product is reused, presumable purchase and use of a new product is delayed, although this may not always be true.

. . . .

Durable Goods

There is a long tradition of reuse of durable goods such as large and small appliances, furniture, and carpets. Often this is done informally as individuals pass on used goods to family members and friends. Other durable goods are donated to charitable organizations for resale or use by needy families. Some communities and other organizations have facilitated the exchange programs for citizens, and there are for-profit retail stores that deal in used furniture, appliances, and carpets. Other goods are resold by individuals at garage sales, flea markets, and the like. Borrowing and sharing items like tools can also reduce the number of products to be discarded ultimately. There is generally a lack of data on the volume of durable goods reused in the United States, and what the ultimate effect on MSW generation might be.

. . . .

Nondurable Goods

While nondurable goods by their very nature are designed for short term use and disposal, there is considerable reuse of some items classified as nondurable. In particular, footwear, clothing, and other textile goods are often reused. Much of the reuse is accomplished through the same types of channels as those described above for durable goods. That is, private individuals, charitable organizations, and retail outlets (consignment shops) all facilitate reuse of discarded clothing and footwear. In addition, considerable amounts of textiles are reused as wiping cloths before being discarded.

Another often-cited waste prevention measure is the use of washable plates, cups, napkins, towels, diapers, etc. instead of the disposable variety. (This will reduce solid waste but will have other environmental effects, such as increased water and energy use.) Other reusable items are available, for example: reusable air filters, reusable coffee filters, reconditioned printer cartridges, etc.

Containers and Packaging

Containers and packaging can be reused in two ways: they can be used again for their original purpose, or they can be used in other ways.

Glass bottles are a prime example of reuse of a container for its original purpose. Refillable glass beer and soft drink bottles can be collected, washed, and refilled for use again. Some years ago large numbers of refillable glass soft drink bottles were used, but these have largely been replaced by single-use glass bottles, plastic bottles, and aluminum cans. Considerable numbers of beer bottles are collected for refilling, often by restaurants and taverns, where the bottles can easily be collected and returned by the distributor. The Glass Packaging Institute estimates that refillable glass bottles achieve a rate of 8 trips (refillings) per bottle.

Another example in this category is the use of refurbished wood pallets for shipping pelletized goods. The National Wooden Pallet & Container Association estimates that over 50 percent of wood pallets produced are reusable.

Many other containers and packages can be recycled, but are not often reused. Some refillable containers (*e.g.*, plastic laundry softener bottles) have been introduced; the original container can be refilled using concentrate purchased in small packages. This practice can achieve a notable source reduction in packaging. As another example, some grocery stores will allow customers to reuse grocery sacks, perhaps allowing a refund for each sack brought back for reuse. Also, many parcel shippers will take back plastic packaging "peanuts" for reuse.

Many ingenious reuses for containers and packaging are possible in the home. People reuse boxes, bags, jars, jugs, and cans for many purposes around the house. There are no reliable estimates as to how these activities affect the waste stream.

Reuse Infrastructure

Many new industries are incorporating reuse concepts as a business practice. Reuse and repair of computers, durables, textiles, and pallets extend the life of products, delaying their disposal, and may curtail the production of new products, reducing material consumption.

. . . .

Management of Organic Materials

Food wastes and yard trimming combined made up 21.0 percent of MSW generation in 1995, so source reduction measures aimed at these products can have an important effect on waste generation. Composting is the usual method for recovering these organic materials. As defined in this report, composting of organic materials after they are taken to a central composting facility is a waste management activity comparable to recovery for recycling.

Composting or other reduction management measures that take place at the point of generation (*e.g.*, the yard of a home or business) is source reduction. Backyard composting of yard trimmings and some food discards is not a new practice, but in recent years publicity and education programs have encouraged more people to participate. There also is a trend toward leaving grass clippings on lawns, sometimes through the use of mulching mowers. Other actions that will complement the increase in yard trimmings management include establishment of variable rates, improved technology (mulching mowers), and legislative regulations.

Part of the impetus for source reduction of yard trimmings is the large number of state regulations discouraging landfilling or other disposal of yard trimmings. The Composting Council and other sources report that in 1992, 12 states (amounting to over 28 percent of the nation's population) had in effect legislation affecting management of yard trimmings. By 1997, nearly two dozen states (amounting to approximately 50 percent of the nation's population) were to have in effect legislation affecting disposal of yard trimmings. While data on amounts of yard trimmings received at disposal facilities is limited, there is considerable anecdotal evidence indicating that when these bans go into effect, people find ways to source reduce.

Recovery For Recycling (Including Composting)

Recycling Collection

Before recyclable materials can be processed and recycled into new products, they must be collected. Most residential recycling involves curbside recyclables collection, drop-off programs, buy-back operations, and/or container deposit systems. Most collection of commercial recyclables includes corrugated boxes and office-type papers.

. . . .

Commercial Recyclables Collection

The greatest quantity of recovered materials comes from the commercial sector. Old corrugated containers (OCC) and office papers are widely collected from commercial establishments. Grocery stores and other retail outlets that require corrugated packaging are part of an infrastructure that brings in the most recovered material. OCC is often baled at the retail outlet and picked up by a paper dealer.

Office paper (*e.g.*, white, mixed color, computer, etc.) is part of another commercial recyclables collection infrastructure. Depending on the quantities generated, businesses (*e.g.*, banks, institutions, schools, printing operations, etc.) can sort materials and have them picked up by a paper dealer, or self deliver the materials to the recycler. It should be noted that commercial operations also make recycling available for materials other than paper.

Multi-family residence recycling could be classified as either residential or commercial recyclables collection. Multi-family refuse is usually handled as a commercial account by waste haulers. It is also the same waste hauler that makes recycling available to multi-family dwellings (typically 5 or more units), which could resemble a drop-off center.

Recyclables Processing

Processing recyclable materials is performed at materials recovery facilities (MRFs), mixed waste processing facilities, and mixed waste composting facilities. Some materials are sorted at the curb and require less attention. Other materials are sorted into streams at the curb, such as a paper stream, and a container stream, with additional sorting at a facility (MRF). Mixed waste can also be processed to pull out recyclable and compostable materials.

. . . .

Combustion

Most of the municipal solid waste combustion currently practiced in this country incorporates recovery of an energy product (generally steam or electricity). The resulting energy reduces the amount needed from other sources, and the sale of the energy helps to offset the cost of operating the facility. In past years, it was common to burn municipal solid waste in incinerators as a volume reduction practice; energy recovery became more prevalent in the 1980s.

Total U.S. MSW combustion with energy recovery, referred to as waste-to-energy (WTE) combustion, had a 1995 design capacity of 99,000 tons per day. There were 112 WTE facilities in 1995. The Northeastern and Southern regions had most of the MSW combustion capacity in 1995. In addition to WTE combustion, 6,000 tons per day of refuse-derived fuel (RDF) were prepared, and there was an additional 3,500 daily tons of capacity for incineration without energy recovery.

In addition to facilities combusting mixed MSW (processed or unprocessed), there is a small but growing amount of combustion of source-separated MSW. In particular, there is considerable interest in using rubber tires as fuel in dedicated facilities or as fuel in cement kilns. In addition, there is combustion of wood wastes and some paper and plastic wastes, usually in boilers that already burn some other type of solid fuel. For this report, it was estimated that about 1.9 million tons of MSW were combusted in this manner in 1995, with tires contributing a majority of the total.

. . . .

The total throughput of MSW through all combustion facilities was an estimated 33.5 million tons, or 16 percent of MSW generation, in 1995.

Residues From Waste Management Facilities

Whenever municipal wastes are processed, residues will remain. For the purposes of this report, it is assumed that most of these residues are landfilled.

Materials processing facilities (MRFs) and compost facilities generate some residues when processing various recovered materials. These residues include materials that are unacceptable to end users (*e.g.*, broken glass, wet newspapers), other contaminants (*e.g.*, products made of plastic resins that are not wanted by the end user), or dirt. While residue generation varies widely, 5 to 10 percent is probably typical for a MRF. Residues from a MRF or compost facility are generally landfilled. Since the recovery estimates in this report are based on recovered materials purchased by end users rather than materials entering a processing facility, the residues are counted with other disposed materials.

When municipal solid waste is combusted, a residue (usually called ash) is left behind. Years ago this ash was commonly disposed of along with municipal solid waste, but combustor ash is *not* counted as MSW in this report because it generally must be managed separately. (There are a number of efforts underway to reuse ash.) As a general "rule of thumb," MSW combustor ash amounts to about 25 percent (dry weight) of unprocessed MSW input. This percentage will vary from facility to facility depending upon the types of waste input and the efficiency and configuration of the facility.

Landfill

Although the number of landfills is decreasing, the capacity has remained relatively constant. In 1995, there were about 2,500 landfills in the U.S. New landfills are now much larger than in the past.

. . . .

Summary of Historical And Current MSW Management

Municipal solid waste generation has grown steadily (except for occasional decreases during recession years) from 88.1 million tons in 1960 to 208 million tons in 1995. The data presented in this chapter and Chapter 2 [of the EPA 1996 Update] provide a perspective on the historical management of municipal solid waste. The study results are summarized in Table 37 and Figure 29.

This summary provides some historical perspective on municipal solid waste management practices in the U.S. In the 1960s and early 1970s a large percentage of MSW was burned. The remainder was not usually landfilled as we define landfill in the 1990s; that is, it was not compacted and buried in cells with cover material added daily. In fact, much of this waste was "dumped" and often it was burned at the dump to reduce its volume.

Table 37

GENERATION, MATERIALS RECOVERY, COMPOSTING, COMBUSTION, AND DISCARDS OF MUNICIPAL SOLID WASTE, 1960 TO 1995
(In thousands of tons and percent of total generation)

	Thousands of Tons								
	1960	1970	1980	1990	1991	1992	1993	1994	1995
Generation	88,120	121,060	151,640	197,300	196,880	202,210	205,400	209,630	208,050
Recovery for recycling	5,610	8,020	14,520	29,650	32,890	36,020	37,940	43,490	46,620
Recovery for composting*	Neg.	Neg.	Neg.	4,200	4,800	5,400	6,900	8,480	9,570
Total Materials Recovery	5,610	8,020	14,520	33,850	37,690	41,420	44,840	51,970	56,190
Discards after recovery	82,510	113,040	137,120	163,450	159,190	160,790	160,560	157,660	151,860
Combustion**	27,000	25,100	13,700	31,900	33,330	32,690	32,920	32,490	33,470
Discards to landfill, other disposal†	55,510	87,940	123,420	131,550	125,860	128,100	127,640	125,170	118,390

	Percent of Total Generation								
	1960	1970	1980	1990	1991	1992	1993	1994	1995
Generation	100.0%	100.0%	100.0%	100.0%	100.0%	100.0%	100.0%	100.0%	100.0%
Recovery for recycling	6.4%	6.6%	9.6%	15.0%	16.7%	17.8%	18.5%	20.7%	22.4%
Recovery for composting*	Neg.	Neg.	Neg.	2.1%	2.4%	2.7%	3.4%	4.0%	4.6%
Total Materials Recovery	6.4%	6.6%	9.6%	17.2%	19.1%	20.5%	21.8%	24.8%	27.0%
Discards after recovery	93.6%	93.4%	90.4%	82.8%	80.9%	79.5%	78.2%	75.2%	73.0%
Combustion**	30.6%	20.7%	9.0%	16.2%	16.9%	16.2%	16.0%	15.5%	16.1%
Discards to landfill, other disposal†	63.0%	72.6%	81.4%	66.7%	63.9%	63.3%	62.1%	59.7%	56.9%

* Composting of yard trimmings and food wastes. Does not include mixed MSW composting or backyard composting. MSW composting estimated to be less than 500 thousand tons per year.
** Includes combustion of MSW in mass burn or refuse-derived fuel form, incineration without energy recovery, and combustion with energy recovery of source separated materials in MSW.
† Discards after recovery minus combustion.
Details may not add to totals due to rounding.

Source: Franklin Associates, Ltd.

Historically, through the mid-1980s, incineration declined considerably and landfills became difficult to site, and waste generation continued to increase. Materials recovery rates increased very slowly in this time period, and the burden on the nation's landfills grew dramatically. As Figure 29 graphically shows, discards of MSW to landfill or other disposal apparently peaked in the 1986-87 period, then began to decline as materials recovery and combustion increased.

Figure 29. Municipal Solid Waste Management, 1960 to 1995

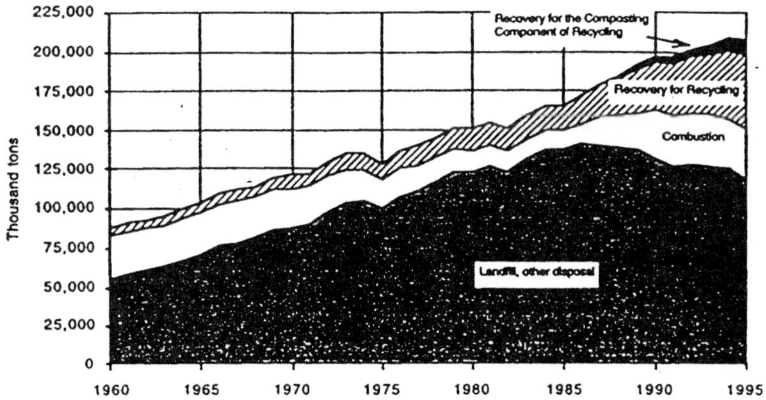

Generation of MSW declined in 1991 (a recession year), but then continued to increase until 1995, when it decreased again slightly. Recovery of products and yard trimmings increased steadily, while combustion stayed nearly constant. As a result, discards to landfills were lower each year from 1992 to 1995. Landfilling accounted for 118.4 million tons, or 56.9 percent of total generation in 1995. As a percent of total generation, landfilling has consistently decreased—from 83.2 percent of generation in 1986 to 56.9 percent in 1995.

. . . .

A Note on the Relationship of Solid Waste Disposal to Air and Water Pollution

An important aspect of the waste management problem involves the relationships among different forms of waste. Waste fiber from the production of paper may be discharged into a water-course as liquid waste. If stringent water pollution controls are imposed, it is more likely that such waste fibers will be incinerated, thereby being transformed into gaseous waste discharges with adverse impact on air quality. The consequence is that if both stringent water pollution and air pollution controls are imposed, the only remaining safe form for disposal of waste materials is the disposal of such waste materials in solid form in a sanitary landfill operation. It has also been suggested that it may be possible to transform one form of waste by the use of another. So, for instance, flue gas from catalytic cracking operations in petroleum refining may be used to strip sulfides from caustic treatment operations. The interrelationship among the three forms of waste is also evidence from waste disposal operations themselves. In incinerator operations, for instance, or in other fuel burning operations, it is likely that the so-called "wet scrubbers" will be used to reduce the amount of fly ash and other particulate wastes. This wet scrubbing method will result in either additional water use, with possible water pollution consequences, or, if the scrubbing water is retained, it will then settle out a solid residue which will itself require disposal. So, too, in waste water treatment operations such as, for instance, the processing of sanitary wastes, the residue, which may take on the form of sludge, may need to be disposed of, possibly as fertilizer material, in sanitary landfills, or in other forms of solid waste disposal.

If solid waste is deposited on the land by way of a sanitary landfill or otherwise, it may cause certain kinds of problems, such as the production of methane gas, the leaching of pollutants into underground waters, or the consequences of gradual settling of the sanitary landfill area. If it is to be disposed of by incineration, it will create air pollution control problems, and in addition it is likely to create problems of residue disposal when the resulting incinerator residue or the sludge from a wet scrubbing operation will need to be disposed of. If instead of incineration, the waste is in some way reduced to liquid form, it will then require treatment before it is released as an effluent into bodies of water. Essentially, the technical problems of waste disposal limit the choices in any given situation. A jurisdiction which has no such choice because of the unavailability of the land may well choose other forms, such as incineration. It is obvious, of course, that the more choices the jurisdiction can afford, the easier the solution of the problem. Thus, a region that includes broader areas will have a wider range of choices for disposal purposes than will a more narrow municipal or local jurisdiction. A regional rather than a narrowly local approach to the collection and disposal of waste may, in addition, provide economies of scale not otherwise available.[1]

QUESTIONS

(1) Though we speak of the interrelationship of solid waste and water and air pollution as if there were the possibility of a trade-off, what, realistically, are the choices open to a municipality? Does the city actually have a free choice between incineration and land disposal? What may determine or limit that choice? *See, e.g., Oriental Boulevard Co. v. Heller,* 58 Misc. 2d 920, 297 N.Y.S.2d 431 (Sup. Ct. Spec. Term, Kings Co. 1969). Consider a city's choices when it runs out of land disposal space.

(2) The interrelationship of air and water pollution permits choices to be made regarding waste disposal depending on whether water or air pollution consequences are easier to accommodate in a particular area. Why does this circumstance argue in favor of regional, rather than merely local, disposal arrangements? Are state laws imposing a ban on dumping out-of-state solid wastes a proper exercise of the state's police power, for instance? (*See Hackensack Meadowlands Development Commission v. Municipal Sanitary Landfill Authority,* 68 N.J. 451, 348 A.2d 506 (1975), remanded in *Philadelphia v. New Jersey,* 430 U.S. 141, 9 E.R.C. 1764 (1977), following the

[1] Technical Guidance Center for Environmental Quality, *Regionalized Solid Waste Management* (1972).

enactment of the Resource Conservation and Recovery Act of 1976.) Do such state prohibitions violate the "dormant commerce clause" of the Constitution of the United States? *See* p. 629, *infra*.

Private Litigation Relating to Solid Waste Collection and Disposal

Private litigation relating to solid waste problems is peculiar in that the solid waste *itself* generally does not give rise to injury or damage. Rather, such private injury or damage arises from the consequences of its improper disposal. These consequences consist mainly of air pollution,[2] especially odor pollution,[3] and of a variety of other environmental insults, such as water pollution,[4] and rodent and insect infestations.[5] Thus, private litigation involving solid waste disposal could properly be characterized as air pollution or water pollution litigation as well.

Much of the litigation with environmental significance in the area of solid wastes has considered whether a dump, incinerator, or landfill is a nuisance, public or private, and has weighed the remedies to correct the condition if a nuisance is found.[6] Since the problem of solid waste collection and disposal has traditionally been a matter of local concern, most frequently action is brought against a municipality, either to enjoin the establishment of a dump, incinerator, or landfill, or to enjoin the continued use of such facilities, with damages sought for past injuries incurred or for future reduction in the value of neighboring property.[7] Typically, the plaintiffs are owners or persons in possession of properties adjoining the actual or proposed municipal facility, or privately owned dumps and incinerators.[8]

---

[2] Bessemer v. Abbott, 212 Ala. 472, 103 So. 446 (1925); Wheaton v. City of Putnam, 126 Conn. 330, 11 A.2d 358 (1940); Gordy v. Armstrong, 190 Ga. 670, 10 S.E.2d 168 (1940); City of Chicago v. Fritz, 36 Ill. App. 2d 457, 184 N.E.2d 713 (1962); Keene v. City of Huntington, 79 W. Va. 713, 92 S.E. 119 (1917).

[3] Kobbe v. New Brighton, 23 A.D. 243, 48 N.Y.S. 990 (1897); Keene v. City of Huntington, 79 W. Va. 713, 92 S.E. 119 (1917); City of San Antonio v. Hamilton, 180 S.W. 160 (Tex. Civ. App. 1915).

[4] Yaffe v. City of Ft. Smith, 178 Ark. 406, 10 S.E.2d 886 (1928); Wheaton v. City of Putnam, 126 Conn. 330, 11 A.2d 358 (1940); Reinhart v. Lancaster Area Refuse Authority, 201 Pa. Super. 614, 193 A.2d 670 (1963); Acadian Heritage Realty, Inc. v. City of Lafayette, 446 So. 2d 375 (La. Ct. App. 1984); Sharp v. 251st St. Landfill, Inc., 925 P.2d 546 (Okla. 1996).

[5] Yaffe v. City of Ft. Smith, 178 Ark. 406, 10 S.E.2d 886 (1928); Lasko v. City of Akron, 109 Ohio App. 409, 166 N.E.2d 771 (1958); City of San Antonio v. Hamilton, 180 S.W. 160 (Tex. Civ. App. 1915); Harkes v. Skirving, 41 Wash. 2d 200, 248 P.2d 408 (1952).

[6] City of Chicago v. Fritz, 36 Ill. App. 2d 457, 184 N.E.2d 713 (1962); Sommers v. City of Detroit, 284 Mich. 67, 279 N.W. 767 (1938); Keene v. City of Huntington, 79 W. Va. 713, 92 S.E. 119 (1917).

[7] Sommers v. City of Detroit, 284 Mich. 67, 278 N.W. 767 (1938); Schulman v. City of Houston, 406 S.W.2d 219 (Tex. Civ. App. 1966); City of San Antonio v. Hamilton, 180 S.W. 160 (Tex. Civ. App. 1915).

[8] Wheaton v. City of Putnam, 126 Conn. 330, 11 A.2d 358 (1940); Sommers v. City of Detroit, 284 Mich. 67, 278 N.W. 767 (1938); Lasko v. City of Akron, 109 Ohio App. 409, 166 N.E.2d 771 (1958); Reinhart v. Lancaster Area Refuse Authority, 201 Pa. Super. 614, 193 A.2d 670 (1963).

The fact that a municipality is given authority by law to establish and maintain a disposal facility for its community does not protect it against actions asserting that such a facility does—or will—constitute a nuisance.[9] Similarly, the insistence that a private disposal facility is operating under a city or state license does not, as a matter of law, constitute a defense against an action based on nuisance.[10] Dumps, incinerators and landfill operations are clearly not nuisances *per se*,[11] but they may become nuisances[12] if improperly maintained and through the emission of noisome odors, ashes, smoke, and other substances, or by becoming a health hazard, as for instance, through rodent and insect infestations.

While a suit to enjoin the establishment of a facility may succeed, generally the mere apprehension that a nuisance will be created does not authorize an injunction, particularly if it can be shown that there is a public need for the facility and that plans call for its proper operation.[13]

Once the facility is in use, its operation may be enjoined as a nuisance, either permanently or pending certain preventive and curative measures.[14] In the case of a landfill, for instance, it may be enjoined unless the operator can give assurances that all wastes deposited on a given day will be covered with a proper layer of clean fill by a certain time on the day of deposit—*i.e.*, unless he can meet the accepted standards for a sanitary landfill.[15]

Damages for past injuries from neighboring dumps, landfills, or incinerators will generally consist of the reduction of useable or rental value of the property for the time the condition persisted, together with such special damages—including loss of business—as may be proved.[16] It has also been held, contrary to the general view, that in considering past damages for waste disposal nuisances, a court may also consider sickness and annoyance suffered by the owner or person in possession of the property and his family, since these impair his enjoyment of the property and depreciate its usable value.[17]

In instances where courts have found that there was a public necessity for the continued operation of the waste disposal facility, they have sometimes left the owner of adjoining property without any remedy on the grounds that he was not specifically affected and had to bear the burden like other members

---

[9] City of Selma v. Jones, 202 Ala. 82, 70 So. 476 (1918); Kirk v. McTyeire, 209 Ala. 125, 95 So. 361 (1923); Wilson v. City of Portland, 58 P.2d 257 (Or. 1936).

[10] *See* Heinl v. Pecher, 330 Pa. 232, 198 A. 797 (1938).

[11] Chenango, Inc. v. County of Chenango, 256 A.D.2d 793, 681 N.Y.S.2d 640 (1998); Kirk v. McTyeire, 209 Ala. 125, 95 So. 361 (1923); Wood v. Town of Wilton, 156 Conn. 304, 240 A.2d 904 (1968); Cullum v. Topps-Stillman's Inc., 1 Mich. App. 92, 134 N.W.2d 349 (1965); Sommers v. City of Detroit, 284 Mich. 67, 278 N.W. 767 (1938); Robert v. Lower Merion Tp., 333 Pa. 333, 5 A.2d 109 (1939).

[12] Brainard v. Town of West Hartford, 440 Conn. 631, 103 A.2d 135 (1954); Steifer v. City of Kansas City, 175 Kan. 794, 267 P.2d 474 (1954); Horn v. Commonwealth Refuse Disposal Inc., 186 Neb. 43, 180 N.W.2d 691 (1970); Webb v. Rye, 108 N.H. 147, 230 A.2d 223 (1967).

[13] Kirk v. McTyeire, 209 Ala. 125, 95 So. 361 (1923).

[14]

Steifer v. City of Kansas City, 175 Kan. 794, 267 P.2d 474 (1954).

[15] City of Birmingham v. Scogin, 115 So. 2d 505 (Ala. 1959).

[16] City of Warner Robins v. Holt, 220 Ga. App. 794, 470 S.E.2d 238 (1996); Milan v. Bethlehem, 372 Pa. 598, 94 A.2d 774 (1953).

[17] Miotke v. City of Spokane, 101 Wash. 2d 307, 678 P.2d 803 (1984); City of Louisville v. Hehemann, 161 Ky. 523, 171 S.W. 165 (1914).

of the community.[18] In some situations, courts have found that the adverse effects of a disposal facility constituted a form of condemnation, *i.e.,* a taking of property without just compensation. In this situation, the plaintiff may recover as damages the resulting reduction in the market value of his property, *i.e.,* the difference in value of the property with and without a neighboring disposal facility.[19]

§ 4.02 Government Regulation of the Disposal of Solid Wastes

State and Local Regulation: Arrangements for Collection or Transportation of Solid Wastes

State Legislation Relating to Solid Waste Collection

Until well into the sixties, both the collection and the disposal of solid waste were considered a function of local government. Indeed, in one of its studies, undertaken in 1963, the Advisory Commission on Intergovernmental Regulations concluded that there were so few regional spillover effects from solid waste management that it should remain a matter of exclusive local concern. Advisory Commission on Intergovernmental Relations, Performance of Urban Functions 183-192 (1963). In the interim, spillover effects have become more apparent as landfill areas have become increasingly scarcer and concerns for air pollution control have led to limitations on open burning and on incineration of wastes. Largely prompted by the 1965 Solid Waste Disposal Act, Pub. L. No. 89-272, 79 Stat. 992 as amended, there has been an increasing interest in the subject of solid waste management at the state level. However, collection of solid waste has still remained a predominantly local concern until very recently.

In the past, prior to the enactment of any significant state legislation, local governments discharged their solid waste collection and disposal functions in a variety of ways. In rural and sparsely settled suburban areas there were frequently no regulations on the subject at all, with each householder left to cope for himself. At most, there might be a local antidumping ordinance to prohibit dumping of wastes on vacant or municipally owned land. In more densely settled areas there were ordinances licensing or authorizing private garbage disposal services to collect solid wastes and to dispose of them in municipally or privately owned dumps. Some advanced ordinances had separate provisions for the disposal of refuse from households, businesses and industry. Only a few municipalities, and generally larger ones, provided by ordinance for refuse collection by municipal refuse collection services and for disposal in municipally owned facilities. Some early municipal ordinances also dealt with the householder's obligations in storing and sorting solid wastes and getting them ready for collection. Sanitary or health codes provided for

---

[18] Sommers v. City of Detroit, 284 Mich. 67, 278 N.W. 767 (1938).

[19] Hammond v. City of Warner Robins, 224 Ga. App. 684, 482 S.E.2d 422 (1997); City of Warner Robins v. Holt, 220 Ga. App. 794, 470 S.E.2d 238 (1996); Jacobs v. City of Seattle, 160 P.2d 299 (Wash. 1916).

the manner in which wastes were to be stored for collection—with galvanized iron cans, plastic cans, plastic bags or paper bags required at different times, with resistance to rodents, resistance to fire and ease of pickup by sanitation employees the major concerns, rather than an interest in environmental protection.

Thus, prior to the Federal Solid Waste Disposal Act of 1965 (as amended by the Resource Recovery Act of 1970) state governments exercised hardly any control or supervision over local governments in the collection and disposal of wastes, though a few state health departments promoted the use of sanitary landfills, and a few states prescribed minimum standards for the operation of disposal facilities.

State involvement in solid waste matters was greatly stimulated by the Federal Solid Waste Disposal Act of 1965 passed as Title II of the 1965 Amendments to the Clean Air Act. It was primarily the federal concern with disposal as an environmentally significant activity that caused the states to get involved in what had previously been a purely local or municipal concern. The states' response to federal legislation resulted in their taking, first, a more active role in waste disposal, and then a more direct interest in the collection of solid waste as well. The state involvement in solid waste matters was further stimulated as a result of the amendment of the Solid Waste Disposal Act by the Resource Recovery Act of 1970, Pub. L. No. 91-512, 84 Stat. 1227, which provided some grant-in-aid funds to the states if they met certain conditions of the federal law. The Solid Waste Disposal Act as amended in 1970 provided primarily for assistance to municipalities and states and for grants for research, development and planning. As was the case in earlier federal environmental legislation relating to air and water pollution, the law stressed the primary responsibility of state and local government for solid waste control, with the federal government assuming the role of provider of technical assistance and supporter of research and development. It recognized, however, that "problems of waste disposal . . . have become a matter national in scope and in concern and necessitate federal action through financial and technical assistance and leadership in the development, demonstration and application of new and improved methods and processes to reduce the amounts of waste and unsalvageable materials and to provide for proper and economical solid waste disposal practices."

A variety of grants for research and demonstration projects for energy and resource recovery were authorized. Grants were also authorized for state, interstate and local planning for solid waste disposal. The Administrator of EPA was required to promulgate "guidelines" for solid waste recovery, separation and disposal systems, as well as for collection. The guidelines were to be compatible with air and water quality standards and with appropriate land use plans. The guidelines encouraged state involvement in solid waste activities because no federal grants for research on resource recovery systems and improved solid waste disposal systems were to be made unless the recipients of the grants complied with the guidelines. The guidelines also applied to solid waste practices on federal lands. As a condition of federal grants, a single responsible agency had to be designated in each state to undertake the project, and each state had to have a well-developed state solid waste management plan, and the project was to be integrated into the planning for the entire area's solid waste management. In consequence of the 1970 federal legislation, virtually all of the states adopted new legislation in the early seventies to make it possible for themselves and for their municipalities to apply for federal grants under the Act. State laws, though frequently focused on disposal, also began to involve states in the regulation or management of the collection of wastes.

The states' greater involvement in solid waste matters was reflected in, and advanced by, the development of a Model "State Solid Waste Management and Resource Recovery Incentive Act" by the Council of State Governments as part of its 1972 Suggested State Legislation proposal. The Model has been extensively drawn on by the states in developing their own legislation. The Model Act includes the power to make and enforce regulations governing solid waste collection. It also deals extensively with the regulation of private haulers and with governments' contracts with private haulers. It also contains extensive provisions relating to environmentally sound means of solid waste disposal. The Model Act was developed by the National Symposium on State Environmental Legislation which includes a number of U.S. government agencies, such as the U.S. Council on Environmental Quality, EPA, and the Department of the Interior, among its sponsorship. Since 1965, and particularly after 1970, there has been a virtual explosion of state legislation relating to solid waste management. Almost all of the states have now enacted solid waste management statutes or have undertaken to draft solid waste management plans under appropriate regulatory powers, usually public health powers.

The matter of solid waste collection and its state regulation has ramifications relating to public health and to environmental controls. Few states have gone so far as to obligate municipalities to provide collection services. In most instances, collection services are encouraged and intergovernmental arrangements for the rendition of services are favored. The precise regulation of collection affects disposal because of the connection between collection and disposal through the sometimes lengthy trip that is necessary to move solid wastes from the collection point to the disposal facility. Most often, aside from regulations designed to control aspects of the business of private haulers, laws relating to collection add little to the old public health standard of trying to avoid conditions hazardous to public health or which create public health or safety hazards, odors, unsightly conditions or public nuisances. The regulations usually specify that containers used for storage must be strong, rust and leak proof, with tight-fitting lids to keep out insects and rodents. Similar provisions relating to disposable bags are often encountered.

State Legislation Relating to Solid Waste Disposal

As previously indicated, the federal Solid Waste Disposal Act of 1965, as amended by the Resource Recovery Act of 1970, indirectly stimulated state involvement in matters of solid waste collection which had previously been an entirely local or municipal matter. Every state has designated a state agency to be responsible for solid waste management and to deal with the federal government, and virtually all of the states had completed the solid waste management plans as required under federal law even prior to its amendment in 1976. Though federal guidelines on disposal under the 1965 act were not binding on the states, the adoption of state regulations prohibiting open dumping and open burning of solid wastes was required by EPA regulations relating to federal grants. Thus, all states had taken legislative or rulemaking action to regulate disposal sites by 1975.

In many states, counties or municipalities are now under a legal obligation to provide or arrange for solid waste disposal services as a matter of state law. In most state laws on solid waste disposal, provision is made for the selection of sites for landfill and for the issuance of licenses to persons engaged in disposal only upon evidence of compliance with environmental regulations. Most of the states' solid waste laws expressly require solid waste disposal to comply with air and water pollution control requirements, and about half of the states require municipal solid waste disposal plans to relate to, or to be consistent with, general state or local land use planning. In general, disposal sites or other disposal facilities must either be approved before they are established, or they may be placed under permit. The siting of disposal facilities and the issuance of permits for the operation of disposal facilities must meet appropriate environmental standards. In consequence of these requirements, the disposal of solid waste by dumping at open or unlicenced areas has now become illegal virtually nationwide. (This does not mean, however, that it has been stopped.)

The state's function under recent legislation has been primarily to regulate, rather than to manage directly, the disposal of solid wastes. Management authority is still in the local and municipal government in the first instance. A number of states, however, have advanced to the point where the states not only regulate but actively manage solid waste disposal.

The development of state legislation in response to federal initiatives, like other environmental protection legislation, has had far reaching economic consequences. The costs of disposing of solid wastes have been increased by legislation that bans the many open dumps and inadequate incinerators. A sanitary landfill operation is more expensive in requiring more manpower and more equipment than is the maintenance of an old-style open dump. A modern emission-controlled incinerator is more expensive than open burning. The concentration of disposal at a few properly maintained and approved or licensed sites, rather than at many small dumps, increases costs by increasing truck mileage from collection to disposal. Safety and health regulations affecting collection and disposal vehicles and other machinery also add to the cost of the disposal chore. In addition, the siting of newly approved disposal facilities is an expensive process in that it requires a thorough and detailed analysis of environmental conditions and a proper coordination with land use plans for the area as a whole. It is these added costs of disposal which lend greater urgency to efforts at reducing the amount of disposable waste by resource recovery and by other methods of bulk reduction as described in the EPA report excerpted above.

See F. Grad, Treatise on Environmental Law § 4.02[2].

NOTES AND QUESTIONS

(1) The position that solid waste disposal is a rather narrowly defined local function has had to yield to the scarcity of open land for landfill within the

economically sound reach of cities, as well as to the realities of the regional impact of air and water pollution from waste disposal facilities. The disposal of wastes as now clearly recognized is a matter of national concern, and one with broad regional land use planning implications. Although state waste disposal plans and federal guidelines mention the *collection* of wastes as well, the actual collection and the regulation of collection services is still a predominately local matter. To what extent can collection and disposal be separated and separately regulated? To what extent are they interrelated? What are the consequences of different kinds of modes on the collection process for the ultimate disposition of the wastes? Do certain waste collection processes, for instance, prevent certain resource recovery efforts? Does the collection process itself have significant environmental consequences on city life?

(2) The business of refuse collection, refuse hauling, and of certain aspects of refuse disposal have long had a reputation as racket-ridden. If in certain parts of the country private refuse collection and refuse disposal operations are indeed tainted by racket operations, sometimes under the protection of local political machines, what is the implication of this circumstance for the enforcement of adequate solid waste management controls on the local level?

(3) What land use implications are there in the siting of a waste disposal facility in terms of the surrounding community, traffic, and insect and pest problems? What are the implications of the designation of a site with respect to its future uses?

Federal Constitutional Considerations: The Dormant Commerce Clause and State and Local Solid Waste Disposal Regulations

The disposal of solid waste has become an active business of local governments who have disposal space or treatment facilities with capacity to spare and who want to make it available to other municipalities and other disposers in return for adequate consideration. To accomplish this goal, local governments may pass laws to assure the flow of waste into such facilities. They may also set tipping fees and other user charges. In so doing they may violate the U.S. Constitution's Commerce Clause, particularly its "negative" or dormant component.

In addition to the affirmative power to regulate commerce, the dormant component is the part of the Commerce Clause under which states may not erect barriers to interstate trade. The dormant Commerce Clause, under *Lewis v. BT Investment Managers, Inc.*,[1] applies whenever Congress "has not affirmatively acted to either authorize or forbid the challenged state activity." Thus, as several U.S. Supreme Court decisions have clarified, it applies when a state regulates the disposal of waste in a manner which burdens interstate commerce. Flow control statutes, and differential tipping charges for in-state or out-of-state waste impose such burdens.

---

[1] 447 U.S. 27, 35, 100 S. Ct. 2009, 2015, 64 L. Ed. 2d 702 (1980).

In *Fort Gratiot Sanitary Landfill, Inc. v. Michigan Dept. of Natural Resources,*[2] petitioner challenged the validity and sought to enjoin the enforcement of the waste import restrictions of Michigan's Solid Waste Management Act (SWMA), which provided that wastes generated in another county, state or country could not be accepted for disposal unless explicitly authorized in the receiving county's plan. The district court dismissed and the court of appeals affirmed, finding no facial discrimination against interstate commerce, as the statute did not treat out-of-county waste any differently than waste from other states.

Reversing, the Supreme Court held that the waste import restrictions unambiguously discriminated against interstate commerce and were appropriately characterized as protectionist measures that could not withstand the commerce clause scrutiny.

The Court held that the waste import restrictions clearly discriminated against interstate commere because they authorized each county to isolate itself from the national economy and afforded local waste producers complete protection from competition from out-of-state producers seeking to use local disposal areas unless a county acted affirmatively to authorize such use.

As the challenged provisions unambiguously discriminated against interstate commerce, the state bore the burden of proving that they furthered health and safety concerns that could not be adequately served by nondiscriminating alternatives. The respondents failed to meet this burden. They provided no valid health or safety reasons for limiting the amount of waste that a landfill operator could accept from outside the state, but not regulating the amount the operator could accept from inside the state.

In *Chemical Waste Management, Inc. v. Hunt,*[3] petitioner Chemical Waste Management, Inc. challenged an Alabama Act which imposed, *inter alia,* a hazardous waste disposal fee on hazardous wastes disposed of at in-state commercial facilities and an additional fee on hazardous wastes generated outside, but disposed of inside the state. The fee did not apply to such waste having a source in Alabama. The petitioner, an operator of a commercial hazardous waste land disposal facility in Emelle, Alabama that received both in-state and out-of-state wastes, sought declaratory and injunctive relief against respondent state officials and the enforcement of the Act, contending, *inter alia,* that the Act violated the commerce clause, and the due process, and equal protection clauses of the U.S. Constitution.

The trial court held that the additional fee, based only on the waste's origin, violated the commerce clause. The state supreme court, however, reversed, holding that the fee advanced legitimate local purposes that could not be adequately served by reasonable nondiscriminatory alternatives.

Reversing, the Supreme Court held that Alabama's differential treatment of out-of-state waste violated the commerce clause. No state may attempt to

---

[2] 437 U.S. 617, 626-627, 98 S. Ct. 2531, 2536-2537, 57 L. Ed. 2d 475 (1978).

[3] 504 U.S. 334, 112 S. Ct. 2009, 119 L. Ed. 2d 121 (1992). *See also* Chemical Waste Management, Inc. v. Templet, 967 F.2d 1058 (5th Cir. 1992) (involving Louisiana's prohibition on importation and disposal of waste generated in foreign nations).

isolate itself from a problem common to several states by raising barriers to the free flow of interstate commerce.[4]

The state Act's additional fee facially discriminated against hazardous waste generated outside Alabama, and the Act clearly discouraged the full operation of the petitioner's facility.

The Court further concluded that the state had not met its burden of showing the unavailability of adequate nondiscriminatory alternatives to preserve the local interests at stake.[5]

The state's concern about the volume of waste entering the facility could be met by less discriminatory means, *i.e.,* applying an additional fee on all hazardous waste disposed of within Alabama, such as a per-mile tax on all vehicles transporting such waste across state roads, or an evenhanded cap on the total tonnage landfilled at Emelle—which would curtail volume from all sources. Concerns regarding environmental conservation and Alabama citizens' health and safety did not vary with the wastes' point of origin. The prospective financial and environmental risks to be borne by the state did not vary with the waste's point of origin so as to allow foreign, but not local waste, to be burdened.

These decisions set the stage for the significant opinion that follows, in which the U.S. Supreme Court examined the constitutionality of a local "flow control ordinance" intended to channel all of a town's trash to a designated transfer station, where it would be sorted and shipped on for landfill, incineration or recycling.

C & A CARBONE, INC. v. CLARKSTOWN

United States Supreme Court (1994)
511 U.S. 383, 114 S. Ct. 1677, 128 L. Ed. 2d 399

[At issue in this case was an ordinance requiring that all solid waste be processed at a designated transfer station before leaving the municipality. The facility had been constructed by a private company to replace a local landfill. Bulk solid waste received by the station would be separated into recyclable and non-recyclable materials; recyclable materials would be baled for shipment to a recycling facility and un-recyclable materials would be disposed of at a suitable landfill or incinerator.

The private company that built the facility expended some $1.4 million and had an agreement with the municipality whereby the facility would charge a $1.81 tipping fee per ton, and if the facility received less than 120,000 tons of waste within a year, the town would make up the tipping fee deficit. The purpose of the arrangement was to amortize the cost of the transfer station, with the town financing the new facility with the income derived from tipping

[4] *See* Philadelphia v. New Jersey, 437 U.S. 617, 98 S. Ct. 2531, 57 L. Ed. 2d 475 (1978).

[5] *See* Hunt v. Washington Apple Advertising Comm'n, 432 U.S. 333, 353, 97 S. Ct. 2434, 2446-2447, 53 L. Ed. 2d 383 (1977).

fees. At the end of five years, the company would sell the plant to the town of Clarkstown for one dollar. Failure to comply with the regulation that all solid waste go through the receiving station was punishable by a $1,000 fine and up to 15 days in jail.

The plaintiff, Carbone, operated a recycling center in Clarkstown. There it received bulk solid waste, baled it and shipped it out to other processing facilities, in a manner similar to that of the receiving station in question. The ordinance permitted recyclers like Carbone to continue receiving solid waste, but it required them to bring non-recyclable residues to a transfer station. Thus, Carbone was prohibited from shipping the non-recyclable waste itself, moreover, the ordinance required Carbone to pay a tipping fee on trash that it has already sorted.

The town of Clarkstown sued Carbone in New York Supreme Court, seeking an injunction requiring Carbone to ship all unrecyclable waste to the transfer station. Carbone sued in federal district court to enjoin the flow control ordinance. The federal court, finding a sufficient likelihood that the ordinance violated the commerce clause, granted Carbone's injunction. The New York court granted summary judgment to Clarkstown, declared the flow control ordinance constitutional, and enjoined Carbone to comply with it. The federal court then dissolved its injunction. The New York Appellate Division affirmed, finding that the ordinance did not discriminate against interstate commerce because it applied evenhandedly to all solid waste processed within the town, regardless of the point of origin.

After granting certiorari, the U.S. Supreme Court reversed, for the reasons stated below.]

At the outset we confirm that the flow control ordinance does regulate interstate commerce, despite the town's position to the contrary. The town says that its ordinance reaches only waste within its jurisdiction and is in practical effect, a quarantine. It prevents garbage from entering the stream of interstate commerce until it is made safe. This reasoning is premised, however, on an outdated and mistaken concept of what constitutes interstate commerce.

While the immediate effect of the ordinance is to direct local transport of solid waste to a designated site within the local jurisdiction, its economic effects are interstate in reach. The Carbone facility in Clarkstown receives and processes waste from places other than Clarkstown, including from out of state. By requiring Carbone to send the nonrecyclable portion of this waste to the Route 303 transfer station at an additional cost, the flow control ordinance drives up the cost for out-of-state interests to dispose of their solid waste. Furthermore, even as to waste originating in Clarkstown, the ordinance prevents everyone except the favored local operator from performing the initial processing step. The ordinance thus deprives out-of-state businesses of access to a local market. These economic effects are more than enough to bring the Clarkstown ordinance within the purview of the Commerce Clause. . . .

The real question is whether the flow control ordinance is valid despite its undoubted effect on interstate commerce. For this inquiry, our case law yields two lines of analysis: first, whether the ordinance discriminates against interstate commerce, *Philadelphia,* 437 U.S. at 624 and second, whether the ordinance imposes a burden on interstate commerce that is "clearly excessive in relation to the putative local benefits." *Pike v. Bruce Church, Inc.,* 397 U.S. 137, 142 (1970). As we find that the ordinance discriminates against interstate commerce, we need not resort to the *Pike* test.

The central rationale for the rule against discrimination is to prohibit state or municipal laws whose object is local economic protectionism, laws that would excite those jealousies and retaliatory measures the Constitution was designed to prevent. We have interpreted the Commerce Clause to invalidate local laws that impose commercial barriers or discriminate against an article of commerce by reason of its origin or destination out of state.

Clarkstown protests that its ordinance does not discriminate because it does not differentiate solid waste on the basis of its geographic origin. All solid waste, regardless of origin, must be processed at the designated transfer station before it leaves the town. Unlike the statute in Philadelphia, says the town, the ordinance erects no barrier to the import or export of any solid waste but requires only that the waste be channeled through the designated facility.

Our initial discussion of the effects of the ordinance on interstate commerce goes far toward refuting the town's contention that there is no discrimination in its regulatory scheme. The town's own arguments go the rest of the way. As the town itself points out, what makes garbage a profitable business is not its own worth but the fact that its possessor must pay to get rid of it. In other words, the article of commerce is not so much the solid waste itself, but rather the service of processing and disposing of it.

With respect to this stream of commerce, the flow control ordinance discriminates, for it allows only the favored operator to process waste that is within the limits of the town. The ordinance is no less discriminatory because in-state or in-town processors are also covered by the prohibition. . . . In this light, the flow control ordinance is just one more instance of local processing requirements that we long have held invalid. . . . The essential vice in laws of this sort is that they bar the import of processing service. Out-of-state meat inspectors, or shrimp hullers, or milk pasteurizers, are deprived of access to local demand for their services. Put another way, the offending local laws hoard a local resource—be it meat, shrimp, or milk—for the benefit of local businesses that treat it.

The flow control ordinance has the same design and effect. It hoards solid waste, and the demand to get rid of it, for the benefit of the preferred processing facility. The only conceivable distinction from the cases cited above is that the flow control ordinances favor a single local proprietor. But this difference just makes the protectionist effect of the ordinance more acute. . . .

Discrimination against interstate commerce in favor of local business or investment is per se invalid, save in a narrow class of cases in which the municipality can demonstrate, under rigorous scrutiny, that it has no other means to advance a legitimate local interest. A number of *amici* contend that the flow control ordinance fits into this narrow class. They suggest that as landfill space diminishes and environmental cleanup costs escalate, measures like flow control become necessary to ensure the safe handling and proper treatment of solid waste.

The teaching of our cases is that these arguments must be rejected absent the clearest showing that the unobstructed flow of interstate commerce itself is unable to solve the local problem. The Commerce Clause presumes a national market free from local legislation that discriminates in favor of local interests. Here Clarkstown has any number of nondiscriminatory alternatives for addressing the health and environmental problems alleged to justify the ordinance in question. The most obvious would be uniform safety regulations enacted without the object to discriminate. These regulations would ensure that competitors like Carbone do not underprice the market by cutting corners on environmental safety.

Nor may Clarkstown justify the flow control ordinance as a way to steer solid waste away from out-of-town disposal sites that it might deem harmful to the environment. To do so would extend the town's police power beyond its jurisdictional bounds. States and localities may not attach restrictions to exports or imports in order to control commerce in other states.

The flow control ordinance does serve a central purpose that a non-protectionist regulation would not: It ensures that the town-sponsored facility will be profitable, so that the local contractor can build it and Clarkstown can buy it back at nominal costs in five years. In other words, as the most candid of *amici* and even Clarkstown admit, the flow control ordinance is a financing measure. By itself, of course, revenue generation is not a local interest that can justify discriminatory taxes against solid waste originating outside the State. . . .

. . . .

State and local governments may not use their regulatory power to favor local enterprise by prohibiting patronage of out-of-state competitors or their facilities. We reverse the judgment and remand the case for proceedings not inconsistent with this decision.

NOTES AND QUESTIONS

(1) Is *Carbone* a sound decision? Does it promote or obstruct environmental protection? Would its outcome have differed if the city had constructed the transfer station in question itself, with municipal funds, rather than buying the station from the private contractor which had built it and operated it privately for five years?

(2) Justice O'Connor concurred in the *Carbone* case. In her view, Clarkstown's ordinance was less facially discriminatory than other flow control measures which had been struck down previously because the benefit that was conferred upon the transfer station that the ordinance favored was achieved to the disadvantage of all other similar facilities, both within and outside New York State. Nonetheless, O'Connor voted with the *Carbone* majority because, as she saw it, the legitimate local benefits created by Clarkstown's ordinance could have been achieved by means which imposed less of an excessive burden on interstate commerce.

Justices Souter, Rehnquist and Blackmum dissented. In their opinion, through its ordinance "[t]he Town has found a way to finance a public improvement, not by transferring its cost to out-of-state economic interests but by spreading it among local generators of trash, an equitable result with tendencies that should not disturb the Commerce Clause and should not be disturbed by us."

(3) *Carbone* left open the question of whether the dormant commerce clause allows local governments to hire independent contractors to collect all of the solid waste generated in a city and to have that trash incinerated in a single incinerator. The U.S. Circuit Court of Appeals for the Second Circuit upheld such an arrangement in *USA Recycling, Inc. v. Town of Babylon,* 66 F.3d 1272 (2d Cir. 1995). Even though, in the court's view, the Town's law had created "monopolies" in the waste collection and disposal market by unilaterally providing trash services to everyone within its jurisdiction, the court concluded that the measure "neither discriminates against, nor imposes any incidental burdens on, interstate commerce." *USA Recycling* at 1275–1276.

Federal Legislation Relating to Solid Waste Disposal: Resource Conservation and Recovery Act of 1976

The Resource Conservation and Recovery Act of 1976 (RCRA)[6] took about two years to pass. With its passage, Congress advanced the federal involvement in the regulation of solid waste disposal and management to about the same stage as air and water pollution control. In form, RCRA is an amendment of the Solid Waste Disposal Act of 1965 (SWDA), but it greatly extends federal authority. RCRA was further amended and strengthened in some respects by the Solid Waste Disposal Act Amendments of 1980 (SWDAA).[7]

The statement of congressional findings and purposes in the new law[8] expands the earlier law in emphasizing the adverse impact of improper land disposal of wastes in wasting valuable land resources and in creating damage to health and the environment through air and water pollution. The findings also stress the dangers of improper disposal of hazardous wastes. They refer to the harmful consequences of the loss of valuable resources through wasteful disposal practices and find that better practices would contribute to meeting the country's energy needs and would result in lessening dependence on the importation of resources.

In the light of the broadened scope of the law, provision is made to coordinate the enforcement of the law with other federal pollution control legislation. The Resource Conservation and Recovery Act is not to apply to matters already subject to FWPCA, the Safe Drinking Water Act, the Marine Protection, Research and Sanctuaries Act of 1972, or the Atomic Energy Act "except to the extent that such application . . . is not inconsistent with the requirements of such Acts."[9]

---

[6] Pub. L. No. 94-580, 90 Stat. 2797, 42 U.S.C. § 6901.

[7] Pub. L. No. 96-482, 94 Stat. 2334.

[8] RCRA §§ 1002–1003, 42 U.S.C. §§ 6901–6902.

[9] RCRA § 1006, 42 U.S.C. § 6905.

The Administrator, moreover is instructed to "integrate" the provisions of the Act and to avoid enforcement and administrative duplication with the Acts referred to, as well as with the Clean Air Act and Federal Insecticide, Fungicide and Rodenticide Act.

The 1976 law also broadened the impact of the solid waste management guidelines. Under the law, the nature of the suggested guidelines is described more particularly and a two-year time table is established for their promulgation.

To assure greater emphasis on solid waste regulation, an Office of Solid Waste is established within EPA to carry out the Administrator's obligations under the Act. The Office has as one of its functions the provision of technical assistance on solid waste management, resource recovery and resource conservation. To carry out this function it is to establish "teams of personnel, including Federal, State and local employees or contractors"[10] known as "Resource Conservation and Recovery Panels." These panels are to receive not less than twenty percent of the total appropriation of funds for the enforcement of the Act generally.

In a development that closely parallels that of the Clean Air Act and the Federal Water Pollution Control Act, the Resource Conservation and Recovery Act provides for the establishment of state or regional solid waste plans in accordance with "guidelines for state plans" to be promulgated by the Administrator no later than eighteen months after the enactment of the law, after notice and hearing. The guidelines—and the state plans—must deal with "varying regional geologic, hydrologic, climactic, and other circumstances"[11] and with a variety of details relating to the character of the wastes, population characteristics, industry and transportation factors, appropriate resource recovery facilities, markets for recovered material, etc., and requires that public health and pollution control purposes be taken into account.

The state plans called for by the Resource Conservation and Recovery Act are analogous to state implementation plans mandated by the Clean Air Act. (*See* Chapter 2, *supra*). As in the Clean Air Act, such plans must meet stated requirements for approval. These include provisions for the closing or upgrading of open dumps, for necessary state regulatory powers, for authorization to local governments to enter into long-term contracts for the supply of solid wastes to resource recovery facilities, and for resource conservation and recovery, disposal in sanitary landfills, or other environmentally sound disposal practices. Provision is made for the designation of local or regional authorities to carry out the state plan or to coordinate with the state in carrying out the plan. Interstate regions may be established by the governors of the respective states, much in the manner of such regions under FWPCA § 208. If the state plans meets the requirements of the Act, the Administrator approves it within six months of submission and thereby renders the state eligible for federal assistance, both financial and technical, for as long as the state plan is implemented and remains an approved plan. Special provision is made for grants to assist small rural communities outside metropolitan areas.

---

[10] RCRA § 2003, 42 U.S.C. § 6913.

[11] RCRA § 4002(c), 42 U.S.C. § 6942(c).

To provide special emphasis on resource recovery, the Secretary of Commerce is given the duty to encourage "greater commercialization of power resource recovery technology" by assisting in the development (through the National Bureau of Standards) of specifications and standards for recovered materials. The Secretary of Commerce is also to identify markets for such materials, identify economic or technical barriers to their use, and to encourage the development of new uses. He is also to evaluate the commercial feasibility of resource recovery facilities, publish his evaluations, and develop a data base to assist persons in choosing such a system.

The Act also places a special obligation on federal procurement, in that purchasing agencies must purchase items "composed of the highest percentage of recovered materials practicable consistent with maintaining a satisfactory level of competition."[12] A number of exemptions based on availability, performance standards and price are provided for, however. The federal agencies are also required to recast procurement specifications so as to advance the purpose of greater reliance on recycled materials.

A variety of procedural and general provisions closely follow earlier air and water pollution control laws. This includes provisions on employee protection,[13] citizen suits,[14] judicial review of regulations, 90-day period for petition, following FWPCA,[15] and injunctive relief for imminent hazards.[16]

§ 4.03 Hazardous Waste: Its Regulation and Disposal

[1] Federal Regulation of Hazardous Wastes: Resource Conservation and Recovery Act of 1976 (RCRA)

Subtitle C of the Resource Conservation and Recovery Act (RCRA) deals with hazardous waste management.[1] This section describes the principal provisions of the 1976 version of RCRA (as amended in 1980) which established the essential framework for the present Act. The section that follows summarizes key provisions of the Hazardous and Solid Waste Amendments of 1984 (HSWA), a modification of the 1976/1980 statute that broadened its scope and impact in significant ways.

The provisions of the 1976 version of RCRA concerning the control of hazardous wastes generally follow the pattern of the air and water pollution control acts. They require publication by EPA of criteria eighteen months after enactment of the law in October 1976, and the publication of regulations based on those criteria, also within eighteen months of the enactment of the law.[2]

Hazardous waste under the Act is defined to mean:

> a solid waste or combination of solid wastes, which because of its quantity, or physical, chemical or infectious characteristics may—(A) cause, or significantly contribute to an increase in mortality or an increase in

[12] RCRA § 6002, 42 U.S.C. § 6962.

[13] RCRA § 7001, 42 U.S.C. § 6971.

[14] RCRA § 7002, 42 U.S.C. § 6972.

[15] RCRA § 4006, 42 U.S.C. § 6976.

[16] RCRA § 7003, 42 U.S.C. § 6973.

[1] RCRA § 3001 *et seq.*, 42 U.S.C. § 6921 *et seq.*

[2] RCRA § 3001(b), 42 U.S.C. § 6921(b).

serious irreversible, or incapacitating reversible illness; or (B) pose a substantial present or potential hazard to human health or the environment when improperly treated, stored, transported, or disposed of, or otherwise managed.[3]

The criteria promulgated after notice and opportunity for public hearing and after consultation with appropriate federal and state agencies are to list hazardous wastes and to identify their characteristics. The criteria should take into account toxicity, persistence and degradability in nature, potential for accumulation in tissue, and other such factors as flammability, corrosiveness, and other hazardous characteristics.[4]

The regulations to be promulgated are to identify the characteristics of hazardous wastes and to list particular hazardos wastes subject to provisions of the law.[5]

Following some initial delays and litigation,[6] the very compendious and detailed hazardous waste regulations were finally promulgated in February and May, 1980 with a general effective date of November, 1980.[7] The regulations are intended to track hazardous wastes from the point of generation to ultimate storage, treatment or disposal. The characteristics of hazardous wastes are identified, and particular wastes are listed as hazardous. Standards are established for generators, transporters, and disposers of hazardous wastes, and persons who handle hazardous wastes must comply with a manifest system and must file annual reports. All storage, treatment and disposal facilities are to be approved by EPA.

The regulations are broadly inclusive in their coverage and impose accountability on all parties that have any significant role in waste generation or management. Standards for waste management include groundwater monitoring within one year of a surface impoundment, closure and post-closure

---

[3] RCRA § 1004(5), 42 U.S.C. § 6903(5).

[4] RCRA § 3001(a), 42 U.S.C. § 6921(a). Prior to the issuance of final regulations, proposed regulations were issued. Solid Waste Disposal Facilities, Proposed Classification Criteria, 43 Fed. Reg. 4942 (February 6, 1978) to be codified at 40 C.F.R. pt. 257. The criteria regulations are intended to moderate the hazardous waste facility regulations proposed under § 3004 of the Act. They are also intended to be integrated with the regulations relating to surface impoundment under the Safe Drinking Water Act; *see* introduction to proposed regulations, 43 Fed. Reg. at 4944-45. Thus, the definition of the major terms used in the regulations follow the definition of related laws. The regulations propose to classify disposal facilities by reference to health and environmental risks. Proposed § 257.3 provides that for purposes of classification under RCRA §§ 4004(a) and 1008(a)(3)"a facility for the disposal of solid waste poses no reasonable probability of adverse effects on health, safety, or the environment if it is so located, designed, constructed, operated, completed, and maintained that it meets the following criteria." The regulations then set detailed criteria for "Environmentally Sensitive Areas," including wetlands, floodplains, permafrost areas, critical habitats of endangered species, and sole source aquifers. The aim of the criteria is clearly to protect surface waters from leachate from non-point sources, to protect groundwater and drinking water supplies, and to protect land used for the production of food crops. Air pollution and safety factors are also to be considered. *See also* EPA, Effective Hazardous Waste Management, Position Statement (issued before the enactment of RCRA) 41 Fed. Reg. 35050 (August 18, 1976).

[5] RCRA § 3001(a), 42 U.S.C. § 6921(a).

[6] The deadline under RCRA was initially April 21, 1978. By order of the D.C. District Court, following agreement on a settlement schedule when an action for injunction had been filed, the date was postponed to December 21, 1979.

[7] 40 C.F.R. Pt. 260, 45 Fed. Reg. 12722-12746, 33063-33588, 34560-34708 (February, May, 1980).

procedures to minimize public danger, maintenance requirements, and the use of containers closed and lined with nonreactive or compatible materials. Wastes may not be placed on land unless made less hazardous by biodegradation. Proper run-off must be ensured for landfill sites. In addition, extensive record keeping and manifest requirements will track shipments of waste.

Such manifests include the name, address, and EPA identification number of the generator, the designated storage or disposal facility, an alternate facility to be used in case of emergency, the volume and type of waste, and types of containers used. Signed, dated copies of these manifests must be given to every facility, transporter and generator. The waste itself must be packaged, labeled, marked and placarded in accordance with requirements set forth at 49 C.F.R. parts 172, 173, 178 and 179. The law requires such facilities to be properly designed and constructed to protect the environment and human health.

Section 3004 of RCRAdirects EPA to promulgate and enforce technical, administrative and financial standards, to be used for issuing permits to owners and operators of such facilities, and the exact laboratory protocol and equipment to be used in the extractor process toxicity test is specified in the regulations.

For states that wish to manage their own hazardous waste program, the Agency has issued guidelines under which they may seek authorization. The regulations cross-refer to relevant requirements of the Clean Air Act, the Federal Water Pollution Control Act, and Safe Drinking Water Act, with particular attention to the protection of ground water and drinking water supplies, surface waters, and air quality. Special provisions are made for emergencies and their prevention, including special personnel training, and for the protection of the environment after facilities have been closed. Specific security requirements are also outlined. The standards emphasize both protection of human health and environmental protection.

The governor of any state may petition the Administrator at any time (after eighteen months from the enactment of the Act) to list material as hazardous waste. The Administrator must act on such petition within 90 days and must notify the governor of his action or of his reasons for refusing to take action.[8]

Far-reaching regulations relating to the management of solid wastes are provided for. Regulations may include provisions on record keeping practices, identifying the quantities of hazardous wastes generated and their constituents.[9] Regulations on labeling are provided for, relating to containers used for the storage, transport or disposal of hazardous wastes and to identify such wastes accurately.[10]

The containers themselves may also be regulated.[11] The regulations may also require the furnishing of information on general composition of hazardous wastes to persons who transport, treat, store or dispose of such wastes.[12] Regulations are also provided for the establishment of a manifest system to assure that all hazardous wastes generated are designated for treatment,

[8] RCRA § 3001(c), 42 U.S.C. § 6921(c).

[9] RCRA § 3002(1), 42 U.S.C. § 6922(1).

[10] RCRA § 3002(2), 42 U.S.C. § 6922(2).

[11] RCRA § 3002(3), 42 U.S.C. § 6922(3).

[12] RCRA § 3002(4), 42 U.S.C. § 6922(4).

storage, or disposal in treatment, storage, or disposal facilities for which a permit has been issued as provided in the law (except in the case of disposal on the premises where the waste is generated).[13] The regulations may require the submission of reports to the Administrator or to the state agency where the state agency has assumed regulatory powers, and such reports may be required to set forth the quntities of hazardous wastes identified or listed under this provision of the law that have been generated during a particular time period and the disposition of all hazardous wastes reported as so identified.[14] The Act also sets forth an authorization for standards applicable to transporters of hazardous wastes. The regulations may contain provisions relating to record keeping on the hazardous wastes transported and their source and delivery points, the requirement that all wastes be transported only if properly labeled, and regulations relating to compliance with the manifest system previously authorized as part of the hazardous waste regulations.[15] The regulations may also provide the hazardous wastes may be transported only to hazardous waste treatment, storage or disposal facilities which the shipper has designated on the manifest form as a facility holding a permit issued under the Act.[16]

The section provides for coordination with the regulations of the Secretary of Transportation issued under the Hazardous Materials Transportation Act.[17] If hazardous wastes identified or listed under RCRA are also subject to the Hazardous Materials Transportation Act, the regulations promulgated by the Administrator must be consistent with the requirements of the Transportation Act and the regulations thereunder.[18] The Administrator may make recommendations to the Secretary of Transportation with respect to the regulation of hazardous wastes under the Hazardous Materials Transportation Act and for the addition of materials to be covered by such Act.[19]

Separate regulations and standards are authorized to be issued relating to owners and operators of hazardous waste treatment, storage and disposal facilities.[20] Again, these regulations are to be issued after opportunity for public hearings and after consultation with appropriate federal and state agencies.[21] Standards and regulations promulgated may include requirements relating to record keeping, satisfactory reporting, monitoring, inspection and compliance with the manifest system; treatment, storage or disposal of wastes received by the facility pursuant to methods and techniques and practices satisfactory to the Administrator; the location, design and construction of such facilities; contingency plans for effective action to minimize unanticipated damage from any treatment, storage or disposal of hazardous wastes; and regulations relating to the maintenance of the operation of such facilities. The regulations may also require additional qualifications as to

---

13 RCRA § 3002(5), 42 U.S.C. § 6922(5). As amended by Pub. L. No. 95-609 (Nov. 8, 1978), Quiet Communities Act of 1978, the section provides that regulations cover permits issued under RCRA or pursuant to Title I of the Marine Protection, Research and Sanctuaries Act, 33U.S.C. § 1412.

14 RCRA § 3002(6), 42 U.S.C. § 6922(b).

15 RCRA § 3002(6), 42 U.S.C. § 6922(b).

16 RCRA § 3002(6), 42 U.S.C. § 6922(b).

17 RCRA § 3003(b), 42 U.S.C. § 6923(b). *See* 49 U.S.C. § 1801 *et seq.*

18 RCRA § 3003(b), 42 U.S.C. § 6923(b).

19 RCRA § 3003(b), 42 U.S.C. § 6923(b).

20 RCRA § 3004, 42 U.S.C. § 6924.

21 RCRA § 3004, 42 U.S.C. § 6924.

ownership, continuity of operation, training of personnel, and financial responsibility.[22]

Regulations may also be issued relating to compliance with the requirements of § 3004 which provides for the issuance of permits for treatment, storage and disposal facilities.[23] The effectiveness of regulations relating to the maintenance and operation of such facilities and requirements of additional qualifications as to ownership, continuity of operation, training of personnel and financial responsibility is somewhat mitigated by the provision that no private entity "shall be precluded by reason of criteria established under paragraph 6 from the ownership or operation of facilities providing hazardous waste treatment, storage or disposal services, where such entity can provide assurances of financial responsibility and continuity of operation consistent with the degree and duration of risks associated with the treatment, storage, or disposal of specified hazardous wastes."[24]

The law establishes the permit system for the maintenance of facilities for the treatment, storage or disposal of hazardous wastes.[25] Regulations relating to permit applications are to be issued by the Administrator, but as a minimum provided for in the law, each application must contain information relating to estimates of the composition, quantities and concentrations of hazardous wastes to be managed at the particular facility, and the site at which such hazardous wastes or the product of treatment of such hazardous wastes will be disposed of, treated, transported, or stored.[26] Provision is made, too, for the interim status of owners or operators of facilities required to have a permit following the application for a permit and pending its issuance.[27]

The 1980 Amendment of the Act permits hazardous waste facilities which came into existence between the date of the 1976 Act and the final promulgation of the hazardous waste regulations under §§ 3001 and 3004 of the Act to qualify for "interim status." Thus, they were not immediately subject to prosecution for failure to have a permit.[28] The 1980 Amendment also provides that permits for coal mining wastes, issued under the Surface Mining control and Rehabilitation Act of 1977 are to be regarded as permits issued under § 3005, and the Administrator's regulations under § 3005 are not to be applicable to the treatment, storage or disposal of mining wastes.[29]

States are encouraged under the law to operate their own hazardous waste programs.[30]

---

[22] RCRA § 3004, 42 U.S.C. § 6924.

[23] RCRA § 3004, 42 U.S.C. § 6924.

[24] RCRA § 3004, 42 U.S.C. § 6924.

[25] RCRA § 3005, 42 U.S.C. § 6925.

[26] RCRA § 3005(b), 42 U.S.C. § 6925(b).

[27] RCRA § 3005(e), 42 U.S.C. § 6925(e).

[28] SWDAA § 9, 94 Stat. 2338 (1980), added to RCRA § 3004, 42 U.S.C. § 6924. The EPA had already issued "interim status" regulations pursuant to RCRA § 3005(e)on May 19, 1980, to become effective November 19, 1980. 40 C.F.R. Part 265 (1980).

[29] SWDAA § 11, 94 Stat. 2338 (1980), added to RCRA § 3005, a new subsection (f), 42 U.S.C. § 6925(f). For Surface Mining Control and Reclamation Act, *see* 30 U.S.C. § 1201 *et seq.*

[30] RCRA § 3006, 42 U.S.C. § 6926. In City of Philadelphia v. State, 73 N.J. 562, 376 A.2d 888 (1977), the New Jersey Supreme Court held that the subchapter dealing with hazardous wastes was an effort to achieve a degree of uniformity, setting minimum standards nationally, but that it did not prohibit more stringent state standards within a state's borders. The case was reversed on other grounds.

States that wish to operate their own authorized state hazardous waste programs must apply to the Administrator and within 90 days following the submission of the application, the Administrator must issue a notice whether or not he expects the program to be authorized, and within another 90 days following such notice and after opportunity for public hearing, he is to make his findings as to whether the state program meets the requirements of the law.[31] The state may then be authorized to carry out the program in lieu of the federal program and to issue and enforce permits for the storage, treatment and disposal of hazardous wastes. Bearing considerable similarity to the NPDES authorization to the states under the Federal Water Pollution Control Act and to state implementation plans under the Clean Air Act, the states are required to meet certain approval criteria.[32]

In order to turn down a state's application, the Administrator must find tha the state program is not equivalent to the federal program, that the program is not consistent with the federal or state programs applicable in other states, and that the program does not provide adequate enforcement of compliance with the requirements of the law.[33]

The Administrator may withdraw the authorization previously granted to a state to run a hazardous waste program whenever he determines after public hearing that the state is not carrying on the program in accordance with the requirements of the Act.[34] He may take such action only after first notifying the state and providing reasons for the withdrawal of authorization. As long as the state is operating an authorized hazardous waste program, however, any action taken by it has the same force and effect as actions taken by the Administrator under the Federal Hazardous Waste Management Program.[35]

Persons who generate, store, treat, transport, dispose of or otherwise handle hazardous wastes must allow inspection of their facilities and must allow access to all of their records relating to such wastes to the Administrator or to designated state officers if the state has an authorized hazardous waste program.[36] Such right to inspect facilities and records and to copy records may be exercised during all reasonable times and includes the right to inspect and obtain samples from any person of any such wastes or of any containers or labeling of such wastes.[37]

The provisions for federal enforcement of the hazardous waste management title (§ 3008) in general follow the enforcement provisions of the Federal Water Pollution Control Act.[38]

Criminal penalties are provided for persons who knowingly transport hazardous wastes covered by the subtitle to a facility which does not have a permit under the Act, or under Title I of the Marine Protection, Research and Sanctuaries Act, or who knowingly treat, store or dispose of any hazardous waste identified under the subtitle, either without having obtained a federal permit under § 3005 or a state permit under § 3006 pursuant to Title I of

[31] RCRA § 3006(b), 42 U.S.C. § 6926(b).

[32] *Compare* Clean Air Act, 42U.S.C. § 7410(1977), Federal Water Pollution Control Act, 33U.S.C. § 1342(1977).

[33] RCRA § 3006(b), 42 U.S.C. § 6926(b).

[34] RCRA § 3006(e), 42 U.S.C. § 6926(e).

[35] RCRA § 3006(d), 42 U.S.C. § 6926(d).

[36] RCRA § 3007(a), 42 U.S.C. § 6927(a).

[37] RCRA § 3007(a), 42 U.S.C. § 6927(a).

[38] RCRA § 3008, 42 U.S.C. § 6928. *Compare* FWPCA, 33 U.S.C. § 1320(1977).

the Marine Protection, Research and Sanctuaries Act, or in knowing violation of any material requirement or condition of such a permit. Criminal penalties are also to be imposed for knowingly making any false material statements or representation on any paper or document required to be filed, used or maintained in compliance with the subtitle, or for any person who "knowingly generates, stores, treats, transports, disposes of or otherwise handles any hazardous waste (whether such activity took place before or takes place after the date of the enactment of [the 1980 Amendment of the Act]) and who knowingly destroys, alters or conceals any record required to be maintained under regulations promulgated by the Administrator under this subtitle."[39]

The criminal penalty for either the knowing transportation or the treatment, storage or disposal of any hazardous waste without a permit or in violation of a permit is punishable by a fine of not more than $50,000 for each day's violation and by imprisonment of up to two years, or both. The knowing violation of the requirements relating to knowing misrepresentations and the destruction or concealment of records is subject to a fine of not more than $25,000 per day of violation, imprisonment of up to one year, or both. For any conviction subsequent to the first, the punishment is a fine of not more than $50,000, imprisonment of up to two years, or both.

The 1980 Amendment creates a new criminal violation for "knowing endangerment."[40]

Knowing endangerment consists of the knowing transportation, treatment, storage, or disposal of hazardous wastes in violation of the law, or having applied for a permit under §§ 3005 or 3006, knowingly failing to include in the application material information required to be included under the regulations, or knowingly failing to comply with the applicable interim status regulations and standards promulgated, under Subtitle C, "who knows at the time that he thereby places another person in imminent danger of death or serious bodily injury, and . . . if his conduct in the circumstances manifests an unjustified and inexcusable disregard for human life, or . . . if his conduct in the circumstances manifests an extreme indifference for human life." The crime is punishable by a fine of not more than $250,000, imprisonment for not more than two years or both. Where the violation manifests extreme indifference to human life, the prison term may be for no more than five years. A defendant that is an "organization," *i.e.,* a corporation or other form of business or organization (including a partnership!)[41] convicted of "knowing endangerment," is subject to a fine of not more than one million dollars.

The purpose is clearly to deal with the criminal and irresponsible dumper. It is very unlikely that any defendant will ever be convicted of knowing endangerment, because the "knowing" state of mind is defined in such a way that it presents an impossible burden of proof to the prosecutor. For a knowing state of mind for purposes of this crime, the defendant must be aware of the nature of his conduct; for knowledge with respect to an existing circumstance, he must be aware or he must believe that the circumstance exists; and for

[39] SWDAA § 13(5), 94 Stat. 2340 (1980), amended RCRA § 3008(d), 42 U.S.C. § 6928(d).

[40] SWDAA § 13(5), 94 Stat. 2340 (1980), added to RCRA § 3008a new subsection (e), 42 U.S.C. § 6928(e).

[41] SWDAA, § 13(5), 42 U.S.C. § 6928(f)(5).

knowledge with respect to the result of his conduct, he must be aware or believe that his conduct placed another person in imminent danger of death or serious bodily injury.[42] With respect to determining whether a defendant who is a natural person knew that his conduct placed another person in imminent danger of death or serious bodily harm, the defendant "is responsible only for actual awareness or actual belief that he possessed," and knowledge by a person other than the defendant may not be attributed to him. Circumstantial evidence may be used, and in particular, evidence that the defendant took steps to shield himself from relevant information.[43]

In addition to the difficulty of proving *knowing* endangerment, the statute also provides special, as well as general affirmative defenses. The special affirmative defenses are based on the so-called "consent" of the person endangered—*i.e.*:

> that the danger and conduct charged were reasonably foreseeable hazards of—(A) a business or profession; or (B) medical treatment or medical or scientific experimentation conducted by professionally approved methods and such other person had been made aware of the risks involved prior to giving consent.[44]

Unlike the heavy burden of proof on the prosecution, special affirmative defenses need be established only by a preponderance of the evidence. In addition, the statute provides that all general defenses, affirmative defenses and bars to prosecution may apply, and "shall be determined by the courts of the United States according to the principles of common law as they may be interpreted in light of reason and experience. Concepts of justification and excuse may be developed in the light of reason and experience."[45] It is unlikely that any natural person can be convicted under the knowing endangerment provision, and more significant for enforcement purposes, it is virtually impossible to convict a corporate defendant under it.

The 1980 Amendment also expands the applicability of civil penalties. Before the amendment, civil penalties of not more than $25,000 per day were provided for failure to obey a compliance order.[46] In addition, the amendment provided for a civil penalty of not more than $25,000 per day for any violation of Subtitle C.[47]

The Act provides that upon the effective date of regulations under the Hazardous Waste Management Subtitle, no state or political subdivision may impose requirements less stringent than those imposed under the regulations.[48]

Sections 3012 and 3013[49] provide for a state hazardous waste site inventory[50] and for the monitoring, analysis and testing of hazardous wastes at facilities.[51]

---

[42] 42 U.S.C. § 6928(f)(1).

[43] 42 U.S.C. § 6928(f)(2).

[44] 42 U.S.C. § 6928(f)(3).

[45] 42 U.S.C. § 6928(f)(4).

[46] RCRA § 3008(a)(3), 42 U.S.C. § 6928(a)(3).

[47] SWDAA, § 13(5), 42 U.S.C. § 6928(g).

[48] RCRA § 3009, 42 U.S.C. § 6929.

[49] SWDAA, § 17, 94 Stat. 2342 (1980), added RCRA §§ 3012 and 3013, 42 U.S.C. §§ 6933 and 6934.

[50] RCRA § 3012, 42 U.S.C. § 6933.

[51] RCRA § 3013, 42 U.S.C. § 6934.

Section 3012 requires each state, as expeditiously as practicable, to compile a continuous inventory of sites within the state at which hazardous waste has at any time been stored or disposed of. The inventory is to contain (1) the description of location of sites used prior to the date when permits under § 3005 are required for such storage and disposal; (2) information relating the amount, nature and toxicity of the hazardous waste at each site, as may be necessary to determine the extent of any health hazard presented by the site; (3) the name, address, or corporate headquarters of the owner of the site at the time of the inventory; (4) identification of the kind of waste treatment or disposal used at the site; and (5) information on the current use of the site, whether hazardous waste is currently treated or disposed of, and if not, when such activity ceased and what other use is currently made of the site.[52]

The Administrator is to help the states in compiling the necessary information, to the extent that he has the information or is able to obtain it from other federal agencies, and states may exercise the authority provided in § 3007, relating to inspections, to obtain the information.[53] This is particularly important in clarifying that inspection powers are not restricted to active disposal sites.

If the state program does not adequately provide the required information, the Administrator is to notify the state, and if, within ninety days following such notification, the state program has not been revised in such a manner as to provide the information, the Administrator is to carry out the state's inventory program, using the same powers as the state and utilizing the funds otherwise allocated to the state for inventory purposes. Moreover, no further grants are to be made to the state under the section until the Administrator determines the state is carrying out its inventory program and will continue to do so.[54]

A special grant program, with $20 million authorized for appropriation, is established to aid the states in carrying out the inventory program.[55]

The pendency of the inventory program, however, is not to postpone any enforcement or remedial action at hazardous waste sites.[56]

Section 3013 authorizes the Administrator to require the owner or operator of a facility to conduct monitoring, testing or analysis, when he determines upon receipt of information that the presence of any hazardous waste at a facility, or the release of any such waste from the facility, may present a substantial hazard to human health or the environment. The owner must report the results to the Administrator so that the nature and extent of the hazard may be ascertained.[57]

When the facility is not currently in operation, and the current owner cannot reasonably be expected to have the requisite knowledge, the Administrator may order the most recent owner or operator of the facility who can be

---

[52] RCRA § 3012(a), 42 U.S.C. § 6933(a). For a similar provision in the Comprehensive Environmental Response Compensation and Liability Act of 1980 ("Superfund"), Pub. L. No. 96-510, 94 Stat. 2767 (1980), 42 U.S.C. § 9601 *et seq., see* Superfund § 105(8), 42 U.S.C. § 9605(requiring national and state listings of priority hazardous substances release sites).

[53] RCRA § 3012(a), 42 U.S.C. § 6933(a).

[54] RCRA § 3012(b), 42 U.S.C. § 6933(b).

[55] RCRA § 3012(c), 42 U.S.C. § 6933(c).

[56] RCRA § 3012(d), 42 U.S.C. § 6933(d).

[57] RCRA § 3013(a), 42 U.S.C. § 6934(a).

reasonably expected to have the information to carry out the monitoring and testing obligations.[58]

When there is no present or previous owner or operator who can carry out the monitoring, etc., in a manner satisfactory to the Administrator, or when he finds that monitoring, testing, etc., is unsatisfactory, the Administrator may undertake it himself or may authorize a state or local agency to do it, in either event charging the owner for the cost, except that no reimbursement shall be required for monitoring, testing, etc., by the Administrator if it confirms the results of earlier monitoring by the owner or previous owner which have been ordered by the Administrator to carry out monitoring and testing activities. The Administrator and any person acting under this order may "exercise the authorities set forth in section 3007,"[59] *i.e.,* the powers of an inspector.

To secure compliance with his order under the section, the Administrator may commence a civil suit in district court, to obtain injunctive relief and to collect a civil penalty not to exceed $5,000 for each day of noncompliance.[60]

The significance of § 3013 can hardly be overstated. It provides the Administrator with the necessary power to order continuous monitoring and to obtain information from inactive (as well as active) disposal sites, a power which heretofore he could exercise only with the aid of the courts, following onerous litigation, most often under § 7003.[61] The protective element of the section involves the recognition of toxic waste problems in advance of their full damaging impact, thus providing an element of protection against more Love Canal incidents.

The subtitle authorizes the appropriation of $25 million for each of the fiscal years 1978 and 1979 to be used to make grants to the states for purposes of assisting them in developing and implementing state hazardous waste management programs.[62] The Administrator is to promulgate regulations to govern the allocation of appropriations among the several states, taking into account the extent of hazardous waste activities within each of the states and the extent of the exposure of human beings and the environment within each of the states to such wastes, and such other factors as he may deem appropriate.[63]

Other special study and demonstration projects are provided for to develop recommendations for legislative or administrative action to achieve such purposes.[64]

---

[58] RCRA § 3013(b), 42 U.S.C. § 6934(b).

[59] RCRA § 3013(d), 42 U.S.C. § 6934(d).

[60] RCRA § 3013(e), 42 U.S.C. § 6934(e).

[61] 42 U.S.C. § 6973.

[62] RCRA § 3001, 42 U.S.C. § 6931.

[63] RCRA § 3001, 42 U.S.C. § 6931. For regulations on Solid and Hazardous Waste Management Program Support Grants, *see* 40 C.F.R. Pt. 35, subpart 35.700 *et seq.,* 42 Fed. Reg. 56050 (Oct. 20, 1977). Supplemental to general grants under regulations set forth in 40 C.F.R. Pts. 30 and 35, the EPA grants are awarded to support an annual work program carried out in each state. The emphasis is on flexibility to meet the unique circumstances of each state. Each year states must develop and submit a draft work program by June 1 to be eligible for funding. EPA will approve the final work.

[64] 42 U.S.C. § 6985.

The Hazardous and Solid Waste Amendments of 1984

The early 1980s were a period of scandal and upheaval at the EPA that gave rise to a profound Congressional distrust of the Agency's willingness to regulate effectively in the area of hazardous waste.[65] One result of that distrust was the enactment in 1984, of the Hazardous and Solid Waste Amendments (HSWA), a far-reaching set of amendments to RCRA that expanded the reach of the Act at the same time as it restricted the EPA's regulatory discretion.[66] Among other things, HSWA contained specific directions to the Agency as to: new regulations it was required to publish, the content of those regulations, the number of RCRA permits it was to issue, and the substantive restrictions those permits were to contain.

The 1984 Amendments contained a preliminary finding that, "[C]ertain classes of land disposal facilities are not capable of assuring long-term containment of certain hazardous wastes, and to avoid substantial risk to human health and the environment, reliance on land disposal should be minimized or eliminated, and land disposal, particularly landfill and surface impoundment, should be the least favored method for managing hazardous wastes.[67] Consistent with that finding, HSWA prohibited the land disposal of certain hazardous wastes. Specifically, it required that (within 24 months for one category of wastes and within 32 months for another such category) hazardous wastes not be land disposed unless EPA determined that their land disposal need not be prohibited in order to "protect human health and the environment for as long as the waste remains hazardous." In making that determination, EPA was required to take into account, among other factors, the "long-term uncertainties associated with the land disposal" and the "persistence, toxicity, mobility and propensity to bioaccumulate of such hazardous wastes and their hazardous constituents."[68]

EPA was required to submit a schedule to Congress under which the Agency would review all hazardous wastes for possible prohibition from land disposal. If EPA missed those deadlines, disposal of hazardous wastes in a landfill or surface impoundment would only have been permitted where the facility in question complied with stringent RCRA requirements for new facilities, and the generator of the wastes certified to EPA that, after investigation of possible alternatives, the generator had determined that landfill or surface impoundment was the only "practical" disposal alternative that was available.[69]

Another thrust of HSWA was its attempt to expedite EPA's issuance of RCRA permits to hazardous waste management facilities. The amendments required EPA (as well as all authorized states) to issue final permits to all land disposal facilities within four years and to all other facilities within eight years.[70] Additionally, permits for new, replacement or expansion units at landfills and surface impoundments must require two or more liners, a leacheate collection system and extensive groundwater monitoring.[71] Moreover,

---

[65] For a detailed description of this period, see Mintz, *Agencies, Congress and Regulatory Enforcement*, 18 Envtl. L. 683 (1988), and Mintz, Enforcement at the EPA: High Stakes and Hard Choices (1995), at 40-59.

[66] *See* Pub. L. 98-616, 98 Stat. 3221 (1984).

[67] Pub. L. 98-616, 98 Stat. 3221 § 101.

[68] Pub. L. 98-616, 98 Stat. 3221 § 201.

[69] Pub. L. 98-616, 98 Stat. 3221 § 201.

[70] Pub. L. 98-616, 98 Stat. 3221 § 213.

[71] Pub. L. 98-616, 98 Stat. 3221 § 202.

within nine months following HSWA's enactment, each RCRA part B permit application had to be accompanied by a statement analyzing "the potential for the public to be exposed to hazardous waste or hazardous constituents through releases related to the unit."[72]

One important aspect of HSWA was its requirement that all RCRA permits require "corrective action" to halt all environmental releases of hazardous waste from any solid waste management unit subject to the permit, regardless of the time at which waste was placed in that unit.[73]

This corrective action must address problems of groundwater remediation beyond facility boundaries unless the owner of a leaking RCRA facility cannot obtain the permission of neighboring landowners to extend the cleanup in that fashion.[74]

Beyond that, HSWA also:

(1) expanded the applicability of RCRA by subjecting people, communities or firms that generate more than 100 kilograms per month of hazardous waste to RCRA generator standards;[75]

(2) created a new program for the regulation of underground storage tanks that contain an accumulation of regulated substances;[76]

(3) expanded RCRA's "citizen suit provision" to authorize the award of civil penalties and to allow citizen actions against past or present generators, transporters and disposers of hazardous waste who contributed to an "imminent hazard;"[77] and

(4) authorized EPA to promulgate standards that apply to people who produce, transport, distribute and/or use fuels which contain hazardous waste.[78]

---

[2] RCRA § 7003: A Significant Enforcement Tool

J. Mintz, "ABANDONED HAZARDOUS WASTE SITES AND THE RCRA IMMINENT HAZARD PROVISION: SOME SUGGESTIONS FOR A SOUND JUDICIAL CONSTRUCTION"

11 Harv. Envtl. L. Rev. 247 (1987)

. . . .

Section 7003 of RCRA,which is the focus of this article, represents one of RCRA's most powerful tools for redressing the legacy of the past dumping of

---

[72] Pub. L. 98-616, 98 Stat. 3221 § 247.

[73] Pub. L. 98-616, 98 Stat. 3221 § 206.

[74] Pub. L. 98-616, 98 Stat. 3221 § 207.

[75] Pub. L. 98-616, 98 Stat. 3221 § 221. The threshold level that had previously applied, under EPA regulations, was 1,000 kilograms/month.

[76] Pub. L. 98-616, 98 Stat. 3221 § 601.

[77] Pub. L. 98-616, 98 Stat. 3221 § 401.

[78] Pub. L. 98-616, 98 Stat. 3221 § 204.

hazardous waste, and has considerable importance as a supplement to the explicit and comprehensive liability scheme established under CERCLA. This provision, which is commonly referred to as the "imminent hazard" provision of RCRA, provides a statutory foundation for litigation to redress any imminent and substantial endangerments to public health or the environment resulting from past or present hazardous waste activities. Section 7003 authorizes the EPA Administrator to bring suit in U.S. District Court against past or present generators, transporters, operators of dump sites, or any party who has contributed or is contributing to an imminent and substantial endangerment to health or the environment by certain activities relating to hazardous wastes, to force necessary action in abatement of the problem.[79]

The federal government is not the only party who may bring a RCRA imminent hazard action. Under certain conditions, RCRA section 7002empowers "any person" to commence a civil action against parties whose past or present hazardous waste activities contribute to an imminent hazard, under a standard similar to that of section 7003.[80] This aspect of the statute thus represents a meaningful addition to the "citizen suit" authority existing under the Clean Air and Clean Water Acts.[81] It provides a potentially important complement to any governmental programs to seek judicially mandated cleanups of abandoned hazardous waste dumps.

Beyond its role as the legal basis for federal litigation, section 7003 is an important source of authority for EPA administrative orders. It authorizes the Agency Administrator, after notice to the affected state, to issue "such

---

[79] The relevant provision, 42 U.S.C. § 6973, provides:

> (a) Authority of Administrator
>
> Notwithstanding any other provision of this chapter, upon receipt of evidence that the past or present handling, storage, treatment, transportation or disposal of any solid waste or hazardous waste may present an imminent and substantial endangerment to health or the environment, the Administrator may bring suit on behalf of the United States in the appropriate district court against any person (including any past or present generator, past or present transporter, or past or present owner or operator of a treatment, storage, or disposal facility) who has contributed or who is contributing to such handling, storage, treatment, transportation or disposal, to restrain such person from such handling, storage, treatment, transportation, or disposal, to order such person to take such other action as may be necessary, or both. A transporter shall not be deemed to have contributed or to be contributing to such handling, storage, treatment, or disposal taking place after such solid waste or hazardous waste has left the possession or control of such transporter if the transportation of such waste was under a sole contractural (sic) arrangement arising from a published tariff and acceptance for carriage by common carrier by rail and such transporter has exercised due care in the past or present handling, storage, treatment, transportation and disposal of such waste. The Administrator shall provide notice to the affected State of any such suit. The Administrator may also, after notice to the affected State, take other action under this section including, but not limited to, issuing such orders as may be necessary to protect public health and the environment.

42 U.S.C. § 6973(Supp. II 1984) (footnote omitted).

[80] *See* 42 U.S.C. § 6972(a)(1)(B)(Supp. II 1984). This provision of RCRA confers on citizens a right to bring suit to abate an imminent and substantial endangerment pursuant to the standards of liability established under § 7003 of the Act. This right is limited, however, in the sense that it can be exercised only if the EPA Administrator, following advance notice by a citizen of intended litigation, fails to file an action under § 7003.

[81] *See* 42 U.S.C. § 7604(1977); 33 U.S.C. § 1365(1972).

orders as may be necessary to protect public health and the environment."[82] These orders may be enforced in the U.S. District Courts. Persons who willfully violate the terms of such orders may be fined up to $5,000 for each day the violation continues.[83]

Finally, section 7003 has significance as a potential source of public information. At section 7003(c), EPA's Administrator is required to provide "immediate notice" to "the appropriate local government agencies" where he or she has received information "that there is hazardous waste at any site which has presented an imminent and substantial endangerment to human health or the environment."[84] In addition, the Administrator must provide that notice of such an endangerment be "promptly posted" at the hazardous waste site.[85] Though less far-reaching than other aspects of RCRA's imminent hazard section, this "immediate notice" provision may provide vital information to private citizens who live, work, or play in proximity to a hazardous abandoned dump. It may also promote inter-governmental communication and coordination, a frequently overlooked aid to effective environmental enforcement.

. . . .

What Is an "Imminent and Substantial Endangerment?"

Although the legislative history of section 7003 of RCRAprovides only partial illuminations as to the meaning of the phrase "imminent and substantial endangerment," the legislative history of imminent hazard sections in other federal environmental legislation lends further support to the reading . . . . that the term establishes a substantive standard designed to prevent harm. For example, the House Committee Report on the imminent hazard provision of the Safe Drinking Water Act ("SDWA") indicates:

> Administrative and judicial implementation of this authority must occur early enough to *prevent* the potential hazard from materializing . . . . While the risk of harm must be "imminent" for the Administrator to act, the harm itself need not be. Thus, for example, the Administrator may invoke [Section 1431 of the SDWA] when there is an imminent likelihood of the introduction into drinking water of contaminants that may cause health damage after a period of latency (emphasis added).[86]

This interpretation is fully consistent with that presented in the Conference Report on the Toxic Substances Control Act. In explaining the provisions of the emergency response authority found in section 7 of the Act, the report states:

> The conferees wish to note that while the unreasonable risk of injury must be imminent, the physical manifestations of the injury itself need not be. Rather, an imminent hazard may be found at any point in the chain of events which may ultimately result in injury to health or the environment. The observance of actual injury is not essential to establish that

[82] 42 U.S.C. § 6973(a)(Supp. II 1984).

[83] 42 U.S.C. § 6973(b)(1982).

[84] 42 U.S.C. § 6973(c)(Supp. II 1984).

[85] 42 U.S.C. § 6973(c)(Supp. II 1984).

[86] H.R. Rep. No. 1185, 93d Cong., 2d Sess. 35-36, *reprinted in* 1974 U.S. Code Cong. & Admin. News 6454, 6488.

> an imminent hazard exists. The conferees intend that action under the imminent hazard section to be able to occur early enough to prevent the final injury from materializing.[87]

Similarly, the legislative history of the Clean Air Act provides an indication that the purpose of the imminent and substantial endangerment provisions of the Act is to prevent harm:

> The levels of concentration of air pollution agents or combination of agents which substantially endanger health are levels which should never be reached in any community. When the prediction can reasonably be made that such elevated levels could be reached even for a short period of time—that is that they are imminent—an emergency action plan should be implemented to reduce emissions of air pollution agents and prevent the occurrences of substantial endangerment.[88]

RCRA's imminent hazard provision authorizes the EPA Administrator to bring suit to redress the handling, storage, treatment, transportation or disposal of any solid or hazardous waste which "may present an imminent and substantial endangerment" to health or the environment.[89]

The phrase "imminent and substantial endangerment" is not defined in the statute itself. Nonetheless, the legislative history of the 1984 RCRA Amendments provides some indication as to its intended meaning. The House Energy and Commerce Committee, reporting on a bill which was ultimately enacted as a modification to RCRA, stated:

> Section 7003 has always provided the authority to require the abatement of present conditions of endangerment resulting from past disposal practices, whether intentional or unintentional. *These endangerments may be immediate or long-term problems* (emphasis added).[90]

This legislative history indicates that, as recently as November 1984, Congress looked favorably on the view that section 7003 requires the government to prove only that an existing dangerous condition creates the *risk* of harm—rather than actual, present harm—to the environment or human health.

This sound position has now been adopted by a number of courts in abandoned hazardous waste site cases. In *United States v. Vertac Chemical Corp.*,[91] the court ruled that proof of actual harm is not necessary to establish an imminent and substantial endangerment. In that case, the escape of the toxic chemical dioxin from a hazardous waste disposal area presented sufficient "risk" in the court's view, to make injunctive relief appropriate even in the absence of "conclusive" medical evidence of the harmful effect of dioxin on human health.[92] Similarly, in *United States v. Hardage*,[93] the court

---

87 Joint Explanatory Statement of the Conf. Comm., S. Rep. No. 1302, 94th Cong., 2d Sess., *reprinted in* R. Druley & G. Ordway, The Toxic Substances Control Act 147-48pp. B (1977).

88 Senate Public Works Comm., Clean Air Amendments of 1970, S. Rep. No. 1196, 91st Cong., 2d Sess. 36 (1970).

89 42 U.S.C. § 6973(a)(Supp. II 1984).

90 H.R. Rep. No. 198, 98th Cong., 2d Sess., pt. 1, at 48, *reprinted in* 1984 U.S. Code Cong. & Admin. News 5576, 5607.

91 489 F. Supp. 870 (E.D. Ark. 1980).

92 489 F. Supp. 870 (E.D. Ark. 1980).

93 No. 80-1031-W (W.D. Okla. 1980).

interpreted the phrase imminent and substantial endangerment to mean "that sort of emergency situation in which the application of the general provisions of the [Resource Conservation and Recovery] Act would be too time consuming to effectively ward off the threatened harm to health or the environment."[94] The court indicated that the imminence of a hazard does not depend on the proximity of the final harmful effect of improper hazardous waste disposal. To the contrary, such imminence may be proven by the setting in motion of a chain of events which could ultimately cause serious injury.[95]

Other courts have taken a similar approach to interpreting the imminent and substantial endangerment in section 7003 litigation. In *United States v. Price*,[96] the Third Circuit held that RCRA's endangerment provision has "enhanced the courts' traditional equitable powers by authorizing the issuance of injunctions when there is but a risk of harm, a more lenient standard than the traditional requirement of threatened irreparable harm."[97] Citing the *Price* opinion with approval, the Fourth Circuit in *United States v. Waste Industries* reversed as "unsupportable" a district court decision which held that the RCRA imminent hazard section was designed to control hazardous waste problems only in emergency situations.[98] Similarly, in *United States v. Reilly Tar & Chemical Corp.*,[99] the court rejected the proposition that section 7003 could only be invoked in a "disasterous emergency situation."[100] It concluded that an imminent and substantial endangerment could be demonstrated by proof that improperly disposed and carcinogenic wastes are entering groundwater and tha, unless preventive measures are taken, those contaminants will leach and migrate into an urban drinking water supply.[101]

This liberal interpretation of the phrase "imminent and substantial endangerment" finds additional support in judicial opinions giving similar readings of the imminent hazard provisions of other federal statutes. In *Reserve Mining Co. v. EPA*,[102] the Eighth Circuit addressed a provision of the Clean Water Act that allows the government to abate water pollution "which is endangering the health or welfare of persons." The court construed "endangering" as requiring only evidence of potential harm. It said: "In the context of this environmental legislation, we believe that Congress used the term 'endangering' in a precautionary or preventive sense, and therefore, evidence of potential harm as well as actual harm comes within the purview of that term."[103] The *Reserve Mining* court referred to the definition of "endanger" settled upon by the D.C. Circuit in an action brought under the Clean Air Act.[104]

---

[94] United States v. Hardage, No. 80-1031-W (W.D. Okla. 1980), at 3.

[95] United States v. Hardage, No. 80-1031-W (W.D. Okla. 1980), at 3-4. *Cf.* Mott, *Liability for Clean-up of Inactive Hazardous Waste Disposal Sites,* in Hazardous Waste Litigation 17018 (R. Mott ed. 1981) (contains an expression of skepticism as to whether nonsudden threats of chronic exposure to a hazardous chemical represents an "imminent" hazard). *See also* Skaff, *The Emergency Powers In The Environmental Protection Statutes: A Suggestion For A Unified Emergency Provision,* 3 Harv. Envtl. L. Rev. 298, 312-15 (1979).

[96] 688 F.2d 204 (3d Cir. 1982).

[97] 688 F.2d at 211.

[98] United States v. Waste Indus., 734 F.2d 159 (4th Cir. 1984), *rev'g* 556 F. Supp. 1301 (E.D. N.C. 1982).

[99] 546 F. Supp. 1100 (D. Minn. 1982).

[100] 546 F. Supp. at 1109.

[101] 546 F. Supp. at 1110.

[102] 514 F.2d 492 (8th Cir. 1975).

[103] 514 F.2d at 528.

[104] 514 F.2d at 529.

The D.C. Circuit opinion, *Ethyl Corp. v. EPA,*[105] states:

> The meaning of "endanger" is, I hope, beyond dispute. Case law and dictionary definition agree that endanger means something less than actual harm. When one is endangered, harm is threatened; no actual injury need ever occur. "Endanger," . . . is not a standard prone to factual proof alone. Danger is a risk, and so can only be decided by assessment of risks.[106]

The *Ethyl* opinion went on to explain that "the 'will endanger' standard is precautionary in nature and does not require proof of actual harm before regulation is appropriate."[107]

The court discussed the need for effective regulation in the environmental field to take this approach:

> Undoubtedly, certainty is the scientific ideal—to the extent that even science can be certain of its truth. But certainty in the complexities of environmental medicine may be achievable only after the fact, when scientists have the opportunity for leisurely and isolated scrutiny of an entire mechanism. Awaiting certainty will often allow for only reactive, not preventive, regulation. Petitioners suggest that anything less than certainty, that any speculation, is irresponsible. But when statutes seek to avoid environmental catastrophe, can preventive, albeit uncertain, decisions legitimately be so labeled?[108]

. . . .

Who May Be Held Liable Under Section 7003?

Prior to the comprehensive amendment of RCRA in 1984, section 7003 authorized the EPA Administrator to bring suit against "any person" who is "contributing to" the "handling, storage, treatment, transportation or disposal of any solid waste or hazardous waste [which] may present an imminent and substantial endangerment to health or the environment."[109] The terms "person" and "contributing to" were left undefined in the statute itself, a situation which left for judicial resolution the scope and limitation of the class of parties who may be liable in enforcement actions pursuant to section 7003. This uncertainty was resolved in different ways by different federal courts, drawing upon relevant state common law, the somewhat fragmentary legislative history which bore on the issue, and varying judicial philosophies as to the appropriateness of broad or narrow interpretation of ambiguous regulatory legislation.

The 1984 amendments to section 7003 of RCRAin large measure settled the class of persons subject to liability under the provision. As noted earlier,[110] these amendments defined the words "any person" to include "any past or present generator, past or present transporter, or past or present owner or operator of a treatment, storage, or disposal facility."[111] A few questions still

---

[105] 541 F.2d 1, 17 (D.C. Cir.), *cert. denied,* 426 U.S. 941 (1976).

[106] 541 F.2d at 13.

[107] 541 F.2d at 17.

[108] 541 F.2d at 25.

[109] 42 U.S.C. § 6973(1982).

[110] [Footnote omitted.]

[111] 42 U.S.C. § 6973(Supp. II 1984).

remain, however, including the extent of liability of present site owners who purchase an abandoned hazardous waste site without knowledge of its previous use as a disposal area.

This section of the article will consider the potential liabilities of four sets of potential defendants in RCRA imminent hazard suits: generators of hazardous wastes, transporters of such wastes, and past and present owners of land which has been used as a hazardous waste dumping ground.

The Liability of Generators

As this section will explore, most of the court cases which preceded RCRA's amendment in 1984 concluded that section 7003 did not reach hazardous waste generators, particularly where they had produced their wastes in a different location from the site at which those wastes were disposed. Since the 1984 amendments, it has become apparent that these decisions are inconsistent with the intent of Congress.

In *United States v. Wade,*[112] a leading case prior to the 1984 amendments, the court took the position that "a court must look for clear legislative guidance before reading § 7003 to confer substantive liability upon so vast a class of potential defendants as off-site generators."[113] After reviewing the relevant legislative history, statutory language, and statutory structure, the *Wade* court failed to find such guidance.[114] It concluded that section 703 "may not in any case, be used to confer liability on non-negligent past off-site generators of hazardous waste."[115]

The *Wade* case was cited with approval in *United States v. Northeastern Pharmaceutical and Chemical Co.,*[116] where the court analyzed RCRA's wording and legislative history in a manner that closely mirrored the *Wade* court's approach. It, too, concluded that section 7003 does not impose liability upon past off-site generators who were not negligent.[117] Similarly, the court in *United States v. A & F Materials Co.*[118] dismissed the government's claims against generator defendants under section 7003 with the statement that "the court is aware of no case authority or contemporaneous legislative history which indicates that generators could be liable under RCRA."[119]

The notion that RCRA's imminent hazard provision did not reach generator defendants in section 7003 actions was by no means uniformly accepted. In

[112] 546 F. Supp. 785 (E.D. Pa. 1982).

[113] *Id.* at 790.

[114] The *Wade* court relied upon H. Rep. No. 1491, 94th Cong., 2d Sess. at 69, and S. Rep. No. 988, 94th Cong., 2d Sess. 16-17 (1976). It is noteworthy that the *Wade* court's analysis overlooked some relevant legislative history, including a House Committee Report which stated that "RCRA authorizes EPA to bring suit to force the cleanup of a hazardous waste problem if the generation . . . of the waste presents an imminent hazard to health or the environment." House Comm. On Interstate and Foreign Commerce, A Report on Hazardous Waste Disposal, H.R. Rep. No. 31, 96th Cong., 1st Sess. 6, 31 (1979). *See also* S. Rep. No. 172, 96th Cong., 2d Sess., which contains language to the same effect. *Accord* deC. Hinds, *Liability Under Federal Law for Hazardous Waste Injuries,* 6 Harv. Envtl. L. Rev. at 20 ("The legislative history of the 1980 amendments to RCRA suggests that, in some circumstances, the phrase 'person contributing to' also could include generators of hazardous wastes.").

[115] 546 F. Supp. at 790.

[116] 579 F. Supp. 823 (W.D. Mo. 1984).

[117] *Id.* at 833-37.

[118] 578 F. Supp. 1249 (S.D. Ill. 1984).

[119] *Id.* at 1258.

Jones v. Inmont Corp.,[120] for example, the court squarely declined to dismiss a RCRA imminent hazard suit against a generator defendant. It declared that "off-site generators are indeed among those who can be found to be 'contributing to' the activity that may present an imminent and substantial endangerment within the meaning of the statute."[121] When section 7003 was amended in 1984, Congress adopted the *Jones* court's position by including "past or present" generators in the list of parties subject to RCRA imminent hazard suits.[122] Any lingering doubt on the question was removed by RCRA's 1984 legislative history, which reiterates that both off-site and on-site hazardous waste generators are potentially subject to section 7003 liability.[123] Although RCRA's legislative history does not detail the policy considerations that favor generator liability, a variety of such considerations may be recognized.[124] One major consideration is that generators are normally in the best position to know or to investigate the hazardous properties of their waste. This access to information should allow generators to better appreciate and foresee the risks associated with improper disposal of the wastes.[125]

Likewise, there is every reason to assume that hazardous waste generators will have significant influence over the manner in which their wastes are disposed of by third parties if generators are subject to liability for hazardous waste endangerments. Just as no industrial entities are commonly in a position to demand materials and performances by others which conform to their specifications, hazardous waste generators can contract for careful and appropriate disposal of their wastes by disposal site operators. Generators can inspect conditions at disposal sites to make certain that their wastes are handled in accord with any contractual arrangements they make, and they can exert significant pressures on any parties managing the hazardous wastes.[126]

Furthermore, although generators are not always the cheapest risk bearer among the parties that handle hazardous wastes, they may often be in that

---

[120] 584 F. Supp. 1425 (S.D. Ohio 1984).

[121] *Id.* at 1435. The only other court to consider this question expressly reserved judgment with respect to it. *See* United States v. Conservation Chem. Corp., 589 F. Supp. 59, 62 (W.D. Mo. 1984).

[122] 42 U.S.C. § 6973(Supp. II 1984).

[123] H. R. Rep. No. 198, *supra* note 97; H.R. Conf. Rep. No. 1133, 98th Cong., 2d Sess.

[124] For arguments against imposing liability on generators in § 7003 actions, *see* Rodburg, *General Liability for Off-Site Disposal* in Hazardous Waste Litigation 87 (R. Mott ed. 1981). Essentially, Rodburg contends that the risks attendant to hazardous waste generation are not the same as those associated with waste disposal, and that this intrinsic difference between the activities merits treating the generator differently than the waste facility owner/operator. Rodburg rejects the premise that every generator can meaningfully affect the risks associated with hazardous waste disposal at distant facilities, and he asserts that the generator is not in every case the cheapest cost bearer. *Id.* at 124-26.

[125] *See* Ginsberg & Weiss, *Common Law Liability for Toxic Torts: A Phantom Remedy*, 9 Hofstra L. Rev. 859, 905-07, 911-13.

[126] In fact, Subtitle C of RCRA establishes "manifest requirements" which are designed to assure that generators have knowledge of the manner in which their wastes are disposed. It requires that any generator who transports, or offers for transport, any hazardous waste must prepare a manifest document. This document must designate the facility that is permitted to handle the waste. A transporter may not accept a shipment of hazardous waste unless it is accompanied by a proper manifest. Similarly, the designated facility may not accept any shipment of hazardous waste which is not accompanied by a manifest document. *See* 42 U.S.C. §§ 6922-6924(West Supp. 1986).

position. The chemical industry and other hazardous waste generating industries are typically larger, more financially viable, and more technically sophisticated than the firms which accept hazardous wastes for transportation or disposal. Generators can plan for the manner in which their hazardous wastes will be disposed, and may be able to pass on their waste disposal costs to the consumers of their products.[127]

Finally, generators benefit to the extent that disposal of their hazardous wastes is inexpensive. It thus seems fair to insist that generators be among the parties who are potentially liable when improper disposal of their wastes creates a perilous condition, rather than increasing the likelihood that heavy costs from such conditions will have to be borne by the public.[128]

The concept of generator liability in section 7003 enforcement cases, then, appears well supported by the language of the statute itself, its legislative history, and significant public policy concerns.

The Liability of Transporters

To a greater extent than generators, hazardous waste transporters have often proved the weak link in the chain of hazardous waste disposal. Historically, disposal companies have been small, under-capitalized operations, concerned with making a quick profit.[129] Some observers have also concluded that, at least in some parts of the United States, hazardous waste transporters are linked to organized crime, which profits from the mishandling of toxic chemical materials.[130] The question of whether hazardous waste transporters are potentially subject to section 7003 liability has received relatively scant judicial attention, despite the importance of that issue. One of the few section 7003 cases on this issue is the magistrate's opinion in *United States v. Waste Industries,*[131] written before the 1984 amendments. In that case, the government brought an action against a large number of defendants, including several parties that had hauled hazardous wastes onto a disposal site. In denying a motion by transporters for summary judgment, the magistrate emphasized that the transporters had "continually engaged in the use of the landfill."[132] Noting that the extent of contamination resulting from the haulers' use of the site was uncertain, the court indicated that "the extent of the use by the haulers is sufficient to avoid summary judgment on their behalf."[133] The magistrate's approach in *Waste Industries* is consistent with several court decisions holding transporters of hazardous substances liable for harm resulting from release.[134] It met with evident approval in the 1984

[127] *See* Ginsberg & Weiss, *supra* note 159, at 907-11; Note, *Allocating the Costs of Hazardous Waste Disposal,* 94 Harv. L. Rev. 584, 588-89 & n. 19 (1981).

[128] *See* Cohen & Derkies, *Financial Responsibility for Hazardous Waste Sites,* 9 Cap. U.L. Rev. 509, 510.

[129] This observation is based upon the author's experience and judgement while an EPA attorney and upon his continuing discussions with the EPA's professional staff.

[130] *See, e.g.,* Madonna, *Organized Crime in the Hazardous Waste Industry,* in Environmental Protection Report 1 (National Ass'n of Attorneys General 1983).

[131] No. 80-4-Civ.-7 (E.D. N.C. 1981) (Memorandum and Recommendation of the United States Magistrate).

[132] *Id.* at 159.

[133] *Id.*

[134] *See, e.g.,* Chavez v. Southern Pacific Transp. Co., 413 F. Supp. 1203 (E.D. Cal. 1976); Siegler v. Kuhlman, 81 Wash. 2d 448, 502 P.2d 1181 (1972).

RCRA amendments, which, as noted above,[135] listed past or present transporters as parties subject to imminent hazard liability.

The congressional decision to impose liability on transporters is supported by sound policy concerns. Like generators, hazardous waste transporters may be in a position to spread the costs of proper waste disposal by raising the price they charge customers for their hauling services. In addition, transporters are in a good position to ascertain how the hazardous wastes they ship are being disposed. And they, like generators, may obtain additional profit if they unload hazardous wastes at inexpensive, improper disposal sites. For these reasons transporters appear to be appropriate defendants in section 7003 enforcement cases, irrespective of whether their use of a dangerous hazardous waste site is "continual."[136] Even a single shipment of highly toxic or flammable chemicals to a site can, under certain circumstances, constitute an enormously significant "contribution" to an imminent hazard.[137]

Hence, like generator liability, the notion of transporter liability under section 7003 for shipment of hazardous wastes which are delivered to an improper disposal site is well grounded in both the language of the statute and sound policy.

The Liability of Past Owners of Hazardous Waste Disposal Sites

Past owners or operators of "a [hazardous waste] treatment, storage or disposal facility" are now clearly within the class of parties expressly subject to RCRA imminent hazard suits.[138] This clarification in the 1984 amendments generally comports with the limited body of case law which addresses the question.

The first section 7003 case to squarely consider this issue was *United States v. Price*.[139]

There, one set of defendants owned and operated a poorly managed hazardous waste landfill from 1969 through 1976. They sold the property in 1979 without taking measures to abate the hazardous condition which their disposal practices had created. Rejecting the defendants' motion for summary judgment, the court concluded that the defendants' sale of the property did not relieve them of their accountability under the statute.[140] The court based its judgment on two factors. First, it noted that the actions and omissions of the past landowners were "the primary case of the hazardous situation which now exists" and that it would be inequitable to require the present landowners to bear the entire burden of a situation created largely by others. Second, the court noted:

> [S]ociety's interests in deterring the improper disposal of hazardous wastes and in alleviating serious hazards as quickly as possible mandate that those responsible for the disposal of such wastes not be able to shirk

135 *See supra* text accompanying note 145.

136 [Footnote omitted.]

137 One example is a shipment of highly toxic chemical dioxin. This compound can apparently present a serious peril to health and the environment in even very small quantities.

138 42 U.S.C. § 6973(a)(Supp. II 1984).

139 523 F. Supp. 1055 (D.N.J. 1981).

140 *Id.* at 1072.

their statutory responsibilities by simply selling the property on which the wastes are stored.[141]

As noted above, *Price* was cited with approval in *Reilly Tar,* a case involving, *inter alia,* the potential liability of an on-site generator/disposer which had sold its former creosote refinery site in 1973 after manufacturing and using toxic substances there for 55 years. The *Reilly Tar* court stated that "[b]ecause of the *Price* holding, at this stage of the proceedings the court is not prepared to hold that § 7003 cannot be applied to prior owners of inactive sites."[142]

The *Price* decision is consistent with state court opinions which have considered similar issues. For example, in *State Department of Environmental Protection v. Exxon Corp.,*[143] a New Jersey court indicated in *dicta* that "[i]t is the general rule that the creator of a nuisance remains liable even after alienating his property."[144] Similarly, in *State Department of Environmental Protection v. Ventron Corp.*[145] it was held that "one who creates such a [hazardous waste] nuisance cannot avoid the responsibility therefore by saying that it is not on his land or that the land is no longer his."[146] There is some limited authority for the view that responsibility for a dangerous condition shifts to a new owner after he has had a reasonable opportunity to abate the problem;[147] however, a number of state courts have found that this principle does not apply where a former landowner has engaged in "affirmative acts" which have created the condition.[148]

The Liability of Present Owners of Hazardous Waste Disposal Sites

When Congress amended section 7003 in 1984, it left little doubt that liability under the provision attaches to owners of land who create an imminent and substantial danger on their land by accepting hazardous wastes for disposal and then dumping those wastes there in an unsafe fashion.[149]

---

141 *Id.*

142 546 F. Supp. at 1109. *Cf.* United States v. Waste Indus., 556 F. Supp. 1301, 1318 (E.D. N.C. 1982).

143 151 N.J. Super. 464, 376 A.2d 1339 (1977).

144 *Id.* at 485, 376 A.2d at 1349. *Compare* New York v. Shore Realty Corp., 759 F.2d 1032, 1044 (2d Cir. 1985), which took the view, in dicta, that CERCLA § 107(a)(2)must be interpreted to hold prior owners and operators of hazardous waste dumps liable only if they owned or operated such facilities "at the time of disposal of any hazardous substance."

145 No. C-2996-75 (N.J. Super. Ct. Ch. Div. 1979).

146 *Id.* slip op. at 52.

147 *See, e.g.,* Cavanaugh v. Pappas, 91 N.J. Super. 597, 602, 222 A.2d 34, 37 (1966); Tennessee Coal, Iron & R. Co. v. Hartline, 244 Ala. 116, 124, 11 So. 2d 833, 839 (1943); Kin v. Vicksburg Ry. & Light Co., 88 Miss. 456, 42 So. 204 (1906).

148 The best example is Merrick v. Murphy, 83 Misc. 2d 39, 41, 371 N.Y.S.2d 97, 100 (Sup. Ct. 1975) ("There is a distinction between mere negligent maintenance of property and affirmative acts of negligence in the actual creation of a nuisance or dangerous condition. In the latter instance, ownership or possession of the property upon which the condition is found is not necessarily a prerequisite to responsibility for injury or damage which results therefrom."). For a good discussion of an analogous legal issue, *see* Note, *Successor Corporate Liability for Improper Disposal of Hazardous Waste,* 7 W. New Eng. L. Rev. 909 (1985).

149 *See* H.R. Conf. Rep. No. 1133, 98th Cong., 2d Sess. 119 ("[P]ersons involved in the handling, storage . . . or disposal of hazardous wastes must share in the responsibility for the abatement of the hazards arising from their activities").

Regrettably, neither the amended version of section 7003 nor its legislative history appear to definitively resolve the more difficult question of whether current owners of land should be required to abate dangerous conditions created by their predecessors in interest (or by their lessees) to which the current owners did not contribute.[150]

In *United States v. Hooker Chemical & Plastics Corp.*,[151] the court concluded that present owners of land used for hazardous waste disposal are proper defendants in a section 7003 case. The court ordered New York State, the owner of a number of the Love Canal sites, joined in the action on the basis that they owned and had physical control of the sites, and that any order issued by the court would affect their land. For the *Hooker* court, the holder of land subject to a section 7003 action was a "quintessential party in interest" in the litigation.[152]

A similar view was taken in *United States v. Waste Industries.*[153] There the owners of land leased it to be used for a governmentally-approved landfill. When the leasehold was terminated, the land was returned to them "in a condition of contamination and nuisance." Although the magistrate exonerated the owners of any liability for contamination which might have occurred during the time the landfill was operated by the lessees, he ruled that liability attached to the landowners when the exclusive right of use of the entire property reverted to them.[154] This liability, he indicated, "arises only because they are the current owners of the property."[155]

United States v. Ottati & Goss, Inc.,[156] involved a set of facts similar to those in *Waste Industries.* A landowner leased his land to another who used it for the haphazard dumping of hazardous wastes. Upon the expiration of the lease, the landowner took no affirmative steps to abate the endangerment which has been created during the period of the lease. Denying the landowner's motion to dismiss, the court cited section 838 of the *Restatement (Second) of Torts*[157]

---

[150] A parallel question also arises under CERCLA. The issue was reached in New York v. Shore Realty Corp., 759 F.2d 1032 (2d Cir. 1983), where it was held that a purchaser of a hazardous waste site was responsible for its cleanup even though he neither owned the site at the time of disposal nor caused the presence of release of hazardous wastes at the site.

[151] Nos. Civ. 79-987, Civ. 79-9898 (W.D. N.Y. 1980).

[152] *Id.*, slip op. at 4. An important consideration in the *Hooker* court's opinion appears to be the fact that the permission of the current owner of an abandoned hazardous waste site is needed in order that the government or private parties may gain access to the site in order to carry out remedial activities. This represents a persuasive reason why present site owners should not be dismissed as parties in § 7003 cases. It should be noted, however, that the conclusion that a present site owner is a proper party in a § 7003 action is not necessarily dispositive of whether such an owner is to be held liable for the cleanup of an abandoned site to which he or she did not necessarily contribute hazardous wastes.

[153] No. Civ. 80-4-Civ. (E.D. N.C. 1980).

[154] *Id.*, slip. op. at 57.

[155] *Id.*, slip. op. at 58.

[156] No. 8-0225-L (D. N.H. 1980).

[157] Section 838 of the Restatement (Second) of Torts (1997) provides that:

> A possessor of land upon which a third person carries on an activity that causes a nuisance is subject to liability for the nuisance if it is otherwise actionable, and:
>
> (a) the possessor knows or has reason to know that the activity is being carried on and that it is causing or will involve an unreasonable risk of causing the nuisance, and
>
> (b) he consents to the activity or fails to exercise reasonable care to prevent the nuisance.

as support for the view that a "possessor of land" (including a landowner who is entitled to immediate occupation and control) is subject to liability under section 7003 of the RCRAfor an imminent hazard created by a third party if: (1) the possessor knew or had reason to know that a hazard-creating activity was being carried on, and (2) he consented to that activity, or failed to exercise reasonable care to prevent it.[158]

Other RCRA imminent hazard cases involved parties who purchased land after all hazardous waste dumping on the property had ceased, and who then took no measures to clean up the wastes. In general, the federal courts have resisted the argument that parties in this position have not "contributed to" the disposal of any hazardous wastes. In *United States v. Price*,[159] for example, the court held that the owners of a hazardous waste site were contributing to the disposal of wastes "merely by virtue of their studied indifference to the hazardous condition that now exists."[160] As in *Ottati & Goss,* the court seemed to be influenced by the fact that the landowners had actual or constructive[161] knowledge of the problem existing on their land, and that they did nothing to abate that danger.[162] Similarly, in *United States v. Midwest Solvent Recovery, Inc.*, a landowner was ordered to remove containers of hazardous wastes from its land, even though the containers had been improperly deposited there by another party without the landowner's consent.[163]

These section 7003 cases by no means provide a definitive, uniform resolution of that issue. Unfortunately, the common law of tort, rather than providing uniform guidance for federal courts hearing section 7003 matters, contains a diversity of views with regard to the circumstances under which such landowners are legally responsible for imminent hazards on their land which they have not created.

The strictest position on this question is taken by the first *Restatement of Torts.* Under this view a buyer is required, at his peril, to inspect his land before he takes possession of it. From the moment the purchaser of land takes possession, he assumes responsibility as to all artificial conditions which are not latent, regardless of whether he knows of the danger or has any opportunity to guard against it.[164] This position has been criticized as being unduly harsh by Prosser and other commentators,[165] and has not been widely accepted by the courts.[166] The Restatement (Second) of Torts has taken a less restrictive view of the obligations of present landowners with respect to nuisances or other artificial conditions on their land. As indicated above,

[158] No. 80-225-L, slip op. at 5-6.

[159] 523 F. Supp. 1055 (D. N.J. 1981).

[160] *Id.* at 1073.

[161] The court opined that "as sophisticated investors" the new landowners "had a duty to investigate the actual conditions that existed on the property or take it as it was." *Id.* The court's positing of this "duty to investigate" the condition of purchased land seems reasonable, particularly in the case of land used for waste disposal or industrial activities.

[162] *Id.*

[163] *See* 484 F. Supp. 138. *See also* United States v. Vertac Chem. Corp., 484 F. Supp. 138 (N.D. Ind. 1980) (court required a landowner to take a number of remedial measures with respect to endangerment on its property as to which previous owners and occupiers were partly or wholly the cause).

[164] Restatement of Torts § 366 (1938).

[165] *See* W. Prosser, D. Dobbs, R. Keeton & D. Owens, Prosser and Keeton on the Law of Torts § 64 (5th ed. 1984) [hereinafter Prosser & Keeton on Torts].

[166] *Id.* ("The weight of authority is heavily against this proposition.").

under this formulation, liability for a dangerous condition on his land only attaches to a landowner if he has been given actual or constructive notice of the condition and fails to correct it within a reasonable time.[167]

This position seems fair both to defendant landowners, who are properly excused from liability for conditions they could not have known about and corrected, and to plaintiffs, who justifiably expect prompt cleanup measures by persons who purchase land contaminated with hazardous materials.[168]

Regrettably, many of the state cases have not adopted the Restatement (Second) formulation.

A Pennsylvania case, *Commonwealth v. Wyeth Laboratories, Division of American Home Products Corp.*,[169] goes to considerable lengths to absolve a present landowner from liability. In this case, the defendant operated a chemical plant on land that had previously been used as a public dump at which both chemicals and domestic trash had been deposited. The groundwater under the plant became contaminated, which in turn polluted several surface water streams. The Commonwealth of Pennsylvania brought suit under its Clean Streams Law, a type of public nuisance statute, to force the defendant to abate the stream pollution. Rather than focus on the extent of the landowner's actual or constructive knowledge of the condition which existed on its land, the Pennsylvania Supreme Court put great stress on the fact that "throughout its ownership and use of said land," the defendant did "nothing affirmatively to aggravate the condition."[170]

Although the court did hold that the landowner was technically in violation of the Clean Streams Law, it placed a heavy burden on the Commonwealth to design a remedial plan and to prove the technical feasibility of the relief it recommended.

Other cases go further than *Wyeth* in extending judicial sympathy to the "innocent" owners of land containing hazardous wastes. In *State Department of Environmental Protection v. Exxon Corp.*,[171] for example, Exxon had owned

[167] Restatement (Second) of Torts §§ 366, 839 (1977). Although § 366 also provides that possessors of land are held to assume liability for an unreasonably dangerous condition on their land only after they know that it exists without the consent of those affected by it, this requirement clearly has no logical application in § 7003 cases. Such cases are analogous to public nuisance cases in which a request by an affected person that the landowner abate the nuisance is not a prerequisite to liability. *See* Prosser & Keeton on Torts, *supra* note 200, § 64.

[168] One important question which will arise, if this approach is followed in the context of § 7003 litigation, is what constitutes "constructive notice" to a landowner that his or her newly acquired land was previously used as a hazardous waste disposal site. In resolving this issue, the courts would do well to place the burden on a land purchaser to make reasonable inquiries as to the previous uses which were made of the land at issue. This could be simply accomplished by having purchasers' attorneys and title insurace companies expand their search for "clouds upon title" to include a review of the owners and types of enterprises which conducted industrial activities on the property in question at previous times. If this expanded search reveals that the land was once used by an industry known to generate or dispose of hazardous wastes, it would certainly be appropriate to conclude that the purchaser is "on notice" that the land he or she is buying may well have been used as a hazardous waste dump.

[169] 315 A.2d 648 (Pa. 1974).

[170] *Id.* at 654-55.

[171] 151 N.J. Super. 464, 376 A.2d 1339 (Ch. Div. 1977).

a parcel of property from 1898 through 1969 which it used as an oil refinery. During that period Exxon spilled massive quantities of oil onto the ground, creating a serious contamination of groundwaters near the property. In 1969, the land was sold to ICI American, Inc. (ICI), which did not engage in any activity that added oil to the polluted condition. The State of New Jersey brought suit against ICI on the theory that, by allowing a continuing leakage of oil from its land, ICI was "discharging" petroleum into the waters of the state in contravention of a New Jersey statute. The New Jersey Superior Court rejected this argument, refusing to examine the extent of ICI's knowledge of the existence of the contamination (either before or after it purchased the land). Rather, the court emphasized that ICI had not itself added oil to the land; it expressly declined to base liability on ICI's mere ownership of the land, stating:

> In this industrial age, ownership has no more relationship to the problems of pollution than did the theory of privity of contract to the problems of product liability . . . . It would be inequitable, if not a travesty of justice, to impose on ICI the burden of abating the pollution condition solely on the theory of ownership.[172]

Still another standard of liability for landowners who purchase property contaminated by hazardous wastes is enunciated in *Philadelphia Chewing Gum Corp. v. Commonwealth*.[173] The Philadelphia Chewing Gum Corp. ("Gum") and Clifford and Virginia Rogers ("Rogers") held title to adjoining tracks of land. Rogers leased part of its tract to Shell Oil Co. ("Shell"), which did not discharge any hazardous substances onto the land. Another part of the Rogers tract was let to Samuel Jacoby, who assigned his lease to a corporation he controlled. National Wood Preservers, Inc. ("Wood"). From 1947 to 1963, while operating a wood preservative business on its portion of the Rogers land, Wood discharged pentachlorophenol, a toxic chemical, into the ground. This compound leached into nearby groundwater and contaminated it. In 1963, Wood was sold to one Goldstein, who was assigned Jacoby's rights as a lessee. Goldstein had learned of the hazardous condition before he purchased from Wood. Based upon this knowledge, he negotiated a reduction in the purchase price of the agreement. Throughout this period, Gum held its own land, apparently unaware of the existence of any contamination on the adjoining property. Neither Goldstein, Rogers, Shell nor Gum actively contributed to the groundwater contamination.

In an action by the Commonwealth of Pennsylvania against Jacoby, Goldstein, Shell, Gum and Rogers, the Pennsylvania Commonwealth Court faced the task of defining a standard by which the liability of these parties could be measured. After noting the significant expenditures required to clean up the contamination, the court stated:

> Where the polluting condition is created by the conduct of an individual other than the owner or occupier, the owner or occupier of the land on

[172] *Id.* at 485, 376 A.2d at 1350. *See also* State Dep't of Envtl. Protection v. Ventron Corp., No. A-1395-79 (N.J. Super. App. Div. 1981), where the court dismissed an enforcement action against the purchaser of mercury-contaminated land on the basis that he had not received actual or constructive notice of the dangerous condition until well after he had purchased the property and the increment of mercury which he had added to the land was *de minimus*.

[173] 387 A.2d 142 (Pa. Commw. 1978).

> which the condition exists . . . can be ordered to take corrective measures . . . if he permitted or authorized the creation of the condition on his land. Such an owner or occupier can also be ordered to take corrective measures if he: 1) knows or should have know of the existence of the condition on the land; and 2) associates himself in some positive respect beyond mere ownership or occupancy, with the condition after its creation.[174]

The key element, according to the court, is whether an owner or occupier, after learning of a dangerous condition created on his land by a third party, "engages in some affirmative conduct indicating his adoption of the condition."[175]

Applying this standard, the *Philadelphia Chewing Gum* court held Jacoby liable for actively creating the contaminated condition. It held Goldstein liable on the basis that he had affirmatively adopted the condition by negotiating a lower price for the purchase of the property. And it ruled that Rogers had assumed liability by constructively knowing of the condition on its land and by collecting rent from Wood for over thirty years. Gum was dismissed from the suit because it did not have actual or constructive knowledge of the contamination prior to the lawsuit, and Shell was held not to be liable because it had never "engaged in any affirmative conduct indicating an association with or an adoption of the condition."[176]

Several aspects of this case are noteworthy. First, it declares a standard of liability which goes well beyond the Restatement (Second) of Torts by requiring a landowner to have "affirmatively associated himself" with a perilous condition created by another on his land before he can be held liable. The Restatement (Second), in contrast, holds a landowner liable where he merely knows of the condition and fails to abate it in a reasonable time. Second, the *Philadelphia Chewing Gum* court was inconsistent in its treatment of passive lessors (like Rogers) and passive lessees (like Shell). Both parties used the land for a profitable enterprise. Both knew of the perilous condition existing on or near the land, and both failed to take affirmative steps to correct it. Under these circumstances it seems that both should have been liable. Nonetheless, the court held only Rogers liable while exonerating Shell, a result which appears to unjustly reward Shell's passivity and to encourage a head-in-the-sand posture by others in Shell's position. Finally, the standard announced in *Philadelphia Chewing Gum* has not been followed by any other court, perhaps because of its excessive leniency to "innocent" bystanders. Its utility as a guide for the federal courts in deciding section 7003 cases thus appears minimal.

In sum, the courts still have not settled upon a uniform standard to determine the liability of landowners and other possessors of land for imminent hazards created on their property by third parties, and the 1984 amendments to RCRA have not squarely resolved the issue. Although the Restatement (Second) of Torts appears to enunciate the most fair and balanced standard, only the *Ottati and Goss* court has expressly applied it in the context of an imminent hazard case under RCRA.

---

[174] *Id.* at 150.

[175] *Id.*

[176] *Id.* at 150-52.

NOTES AND QUESTIONS

Notably, the approach taken by the Superfund Act towards passive or innocent landowners contrasts significantly with the approach taken by RCRA described above. Under CERCLA, a statute described more fully *infra,* parties who acquire contaminated real property are exempt from Superfund liability if, at the time of purchase, they "did not know and had no reason to know," of the prior disposal of hazardous substances on their property. To establish that they had no reason to know, such purchasers must have undertaken "all appropriate inquiry into the previous ownership and uses of the property consistent with good commercial or customary practices in an effort to minimize liability." *See* 42 U.S.C. § 9601(35)(A) and (B). Thus, in effect, CERCLA imposes a type of status liability which RCRA does not. In your view, which is the better statutory scheme?

UNITED STATES v. WASTE INDUSTRIES, INC.

United States Court of Appeals, Fourth Circuit (1984)
734 F.2d 159

SPROUSE, Circuit Judge.

[EPA brought action against Waste Industries and several other defendants ("the landfill group") regarding the Flemington landfill waste disposal site in North Carolina (the Flemington landfill).] The EPA demanded affirmative action by the landfill group under section 7003 of [RCRA] to abate alleged threats to public health and the environment posed by hazardous chemicals leaking from the Flemington landfill, to monitor the area for further contamination, to reimburse the EPA for money spent on the area, and to provide residents with a permanent potable water supply. . . .

. . . .

The district court . . . found that the EPA's claim for permanent injunctive relief failed to state a cause of action. It concluded that Waste Industries' failure to abate the leaching of contaminants was not actionable under section 7003 of the Act, because the provision was not intended to apply to past conduct that terminated before enforcement was sought. . . . .

On appeal, the EPA contends that the district court relied on erroneous premises to support its conclusion and argues that the broad remedial purposes of section 7003 can only be served by permitting actions such as this requiring malfeasant polluters to correct their past abuses of the environment. . . .

Section 7003 of the Act provides that

> [n]otwithstanding any other provision of this chapter, upon receipt of evidence that the handling, storage, treatment, transportation or disposal of any solid waste or hazardous waste may present an imminent and

> substantial endangerment to the health or the environment, the Administrator may bring suit on behalf of the United States in the appropriate District Court to immediately restrain any person contributing to such handling, storage, treatment, transportation, or disposal or to take such other action as may be necessary.

The landfill group contends, and the district court held, that this section does not authorize an action to correct hazardous conditions because it only regulates the wastes themselves before or as they are produced, not the conditions they later create. The fallacy of that contention is demonstrated by the indication of Congress that section 7003 remedies exist apart from the other provisions in the Act's structure. In addition, section 7003 stands apart from the other sections of the Act defining the EPA's regulatory authority. The regulatory scheme for hazardous wastes appears in subtitle C of the Act; the scheme for solid wastes, in subtitle D. In contrast, section 7003 appears in subtitle G, and it is designed to deal with situations in which the regulatory schemes break down or have been circumvented.

. . . .

[Section 7003)] is logically placed in the statutory structure to provide a remedy for environmental endangerment by hazardous or solid waste, whether or not those engaging in the endangering acts are subject to any other provision of the Act. Its application "notwithstanding any other provision of this chapter" indicates a congressional intent to include a broadly applicable section dealing with the concerns addressed by the statute as a whole.

The operative language of section 7003 authorizes the administrator to bring an action against any person contributing to the alleged disposal to stop such disposal "*or* to take such other action as may be necessary." 42 U.S.C. § 6973(a)(emphasis added). "Disposal" is defined in 42 U.S.C. § 6903(3)as follows:

> The term "disposal" means the discharge, deposit, injection, dumping, spilling, leaking, or placing of any solid waste or hazardous waste into or on any land or water so that such solid waste or hazardous waste or any constituent thereof may enter the environment or be emitted into the air or discharged into any waters, including ground waters.

The district court held, after a contextual analysis, that this language means only disposal by "active human conduct." We cannot agree. The term "disposal," it is true, is used throughout subtitle C in the sense that the Administrator can regulate current disposal of hazardous waste. In this way, the Act regulates current conduct of would-be polluters. But a strained reading of that term limiting its section 7003 meaning to active conduct would so frustrate the remedial purpose of the Act as to make it meaningless. Section 7003, unlike the provisions of the Act's subtitle C, does not regulate conduct but regulates and mitigates endangerments. The Administrator's intervention authorized by section 7003 is triggered by evidence that the "disposal of . . . hazardous waste *may present* an imminent and substantial endangerment." (emphasis added).

The inclusion of "leaking" as one of the diverse definitional components of "disposal" demonstrates that Congress intended "disposal" to have a range of meanings, including conduct, a physical state, and an occurrence. Discharging, dumping, and injection (conduct), hazardous waste reposing (a physical state) and movement of the waste after it has been placed in a state of repose (an occurrence) are all encompassed in the broad definition of disposal. "Leaking" ordinarily occurs when landfills are not constructed soundly or when drums and tank trucks filled with waste materials corrode, rust, or rot. Thus, "leaking" is an occurrence included in the meaning of "disposal."

The district court's statutory analysis relied heavily upon the present-tense definition of "disposal" as indicative of an intent to restrain only ongoing human conduct. The Act, however, permits a court to order a responsible party to "stop" activities "*or* to take such other action *as may be necessary*" (emphasis added) to abate the endangerment. Such grammatical niceties as tense may be useful in arriving at a narrowly-sculpted meaning, but they are of little help in interpreting remedial statutes in which actions such as "may be necessary" are contemplated in order to abate gross dangers to a community. Since the term "disposal" is used throughout the Act, its definition in section 6903(3) must necessarily be broad and general to encompass both routine regulatory and the less common emergency situations. Thus it includes such diverse characteristics as "deposit, injection, dumping, spilling, leaking, or placing" wastes. We must assume that Congress included "leaking" as a definitional component of "disposal" for a purpose. We conclude that Congress made "leaking" a part of the definition of "disposal" to meet the need to respond to the possibility of endangerment, among other reasons.

Congress expressly intended that this and other language of the Act close loopholes in environmental protection. Limiting the government's enforcement prerogatives to cases involving active human conduct would open a gaping hole in the overall protection of the environment envisioned by Congress, a protection designed to be responsive to unpredictable occurrences. Without a means to respond to disasters precipitated by earlier poor planning, our nation's resources could be "conserved" from further harm, as the title of [RCRA] suggests, but never "recovered" to their former wholesome condition.

The landfill group argues that section 7003 was designed to control pollution only in emergency situations . . . . We find this position unsupportable [sic], for the section's language stands in contrast to "emergency" type statutes. The language of section 7003 demonstrates that Congress contemplated circumstances in which the disposal of hazardous waste "*may present* an imminent and substantial endangerment" (emphasis added); therefore, the section's application is not specifically limited to an "emergency."

. . . .

The landfill group next contends, and the district court held, that section 7003 is solely jurisdictional, authorizing remedies or proceedings, not creating liabilities. Those liabilities, in this view, come only from the earlier, regulatory, portions of the Act. Again, we cannot agree.

Congress intended section 7003 to function both as a jurisdictional basis and a source of substantive liability. [The legislative history of the 1980 amendments to RCRA] states:

> § 7003 is essentially a codification of the common law public nuisance. . . .

> However, § 7003 should not be construed solely with respect to the common law. Some terms and concepts, such as persons "contributing to" disposal resulting in a substantial endangerment, are meant to be more liberal than their common law counterparts.

[Subcommittee on Oversight and Investigations of the Committee on Interstate and Foreign Commerce, Report on Hazardous Waste Disposal, H.R. Comm. Print No. 96-IFC 31, 96th Cong., 1st Sess. 31 (1979)]. Congress's intent, then was to establish a standard of liability by incorporating and expanding upon the common law.

The landfill group observes that some courts have held, by analogy to *City of Milwaukee v. Illinois,* 451 U.S. 304 (1981), that the regulatory provisions of the Act and CERCLA are the sole source of substantive standards in the field of solid and hazardous waste disposal. If true, this would leave no room for the application of common law principles. This, however, misreads the lesson of *City of Milwaukee.* In that case, the Supreme Court, interpreting the scope and effect of the Federal Water Pollution Control Act (FWPCA)amendments of 1972, held that federal courts were not free to apply nuisance principles in the area of water pollution control when Congress has occupied the field with a comprehensive regulatory scheme. The Court cautioned that the judiciary's power to apply common-law principles was not preempted by the FWPCA; it simply could not coexist with a statutory framework Congress devised to treat the same problems. The substantive duties created by the FWPCA, the Court emphasized, cannot be augmented or diminished by common law principles. *City of Milwaukee,* however, disapproved only of the courts' use of federal common law as a source for setting regulatory standards independent of those established by a comprehensive statutory scheme. The Court did not assail Congress's prerogative to empower the courts to apply common law principles as part of an ongoing regulatory scheme.

Section 7003 is a congressional mandate that the former common law of nuisance, as applied to situations in which a risk of harm from solid or hazardous wastes exists, shall include new terms and concepts which shall be developed in a liberal, not restrictive, manner. This ensures that problems that Congress could not have anticipated when passing the Act will be dealt with in a way minimizing the risk of harm to the environment and the public.

NOTES AND QUESTIONS

(1) One of the issues raised in *Waste Industries,* whether "disposal" occurs as a result of the passive leaking of hazardous waste from a landfill, has also arisen under the Superfund statute. In that context, it has been held that the passive discharge of hazardous waste that results from the leaching of hazardous substances does not give rise to liability for disposal. However, if the owner or operator of a landfill has engaged in activities that result in such discharges from existing deposits of hazardous waste, he or she may be liable as a responsible party under CERCLA. *See Joslyn Mfg. Co. v. T.L. James and Co.,* 696 F. Supp. 222 (W.D. La. 1988), *aff'd,* 893 F.2d 80 (5th Cir. 1990), *cert. denied,* 498 U.S. 1108 (1991); *United States v. CDMG Realty Co.,* 96 F.3d 706

(3d Cir. 1996). For additional analysis, *see* F. Grad, Treatise on Environmental Law, § 4A.02[1][f]. Which statutory arrangement is better, in your view?

(2)*Waste Industries* does not address the precise extent of contamination that must be present at a site before it will be considered to be an "imminent and substantial endangerment." By and large, the courts have given a broad interpretation to that phrase in subsequent decisions. *See, e.g., United States v. Conservation Chem. Co.,* 619 F. Supp. 162 (W.D. Mo. 1985), and *Dague v. City of Burlington,* 935 F.2d 1343 (2d Cir. 1991). *But compare Leister v. Black and Decker, Inc.,* 117 F.3d 1414 (4th Cir. 1997).

MEGHRIG v. KFC WESTERN, INC.

Supreme Court of the United States (1996)
516 U.S. 479, 116 S. Ct. 1251, 134 L. Ed. 2d 121

We consider whether § 7002 of the Resource Conservation and Recovery Act of 1976(RCRA), 42 U.S.C. § 6972(1988 ed.), authorizes a private cause of action to recover the prior cost of cleaning up toxic waste that does not, at the time of suit, continue to pose an endangerment to health or the environment. We conclude that it does not.

Respondent KFC Western, Inc. (KFC), owns and operates a "Kentucky Fried Chicken" restaurant on a parcel of property in Los Angeles. In 1988, KFC discovered during the course of a construction project that the property was contaminated with petroleum. The County of Los Angeles Department of Health Services ordered KFC to attend to the problem, and KFC spent $211,000 removing and disposing of the oil-tainted soil.

Three years later, KFC brought this suit under the citizen suit provision of RCRA, 90Stat. 2825, as amended, 42 U.S.C. § 6972(a)(1988 ed.), seeking to recover these cleanup costs from petitioners Alan and Margaret Meghrig.

KFC claimed that the contaminated soil was a "solid waste" covered by RCRA, *see* 42 U.S.C. § 6903(27)(1988 ed.), that it had previously posed an "imminent and substantial endangerment to health or the environment," *see* § 6972(a)(1)(B), and that the Meghrigs were responsible for "equitable restitution" of KFC's cleanup costs under § 6972(a) because, as prior owners of the property, they had contributed to the waste's "past or present handling, storage, treatment, transportation, or disposal." *See* App. 12-19 (first amended complaint).

The District Court held that § 6972(a) does not permit recovery of past cleanup costs and that § 6972(a)(1)(B) does not authorize a cause of action for the remediation of toxic waste that does not pose an "imminent and substantial endangerment to health or the environment," at the time suit is filed, and dismissed KFC's complaint. The Court of Appeals for the Ninth Circuit reversed, over a dissent, 49 F.3d 518, 724-528 (1995) (Brunetti, J.), finding that a district court had authority under § 6972(a) to award restitution of past cleanup costs, *id.,* at 521-523, and that a private party can proceed with a suit under § 6972(a)(1)(B) upon an allegation that the waste at issue presented an "imminent and substantial endangerment" at the time it was cleaned up. *Id.* at 520-521.

The Ninth Circuit's conclusion regarding the remedies available under RCRA conflicts with the decision of the Court of Appeals for the Eighth Circuit in *Furrer v. Brown*, 62 F.3d 1092, 1100-1101 (1995), and its interpretation of the "imminent endangerment" requirement represents a novel application of federal statutory law. We granted certiorari to address the conflict between the Circuits and to consider the correctness of the Ninth Circuit's interpretation of RCRA, 515U.S. 1192, 116 S.Ct. 41, 132 L.Ed.2d 922 (1995), and now reverse.

RCRA is a comprehensive environmental statute that governs the treatment, storage, and disposal of solid and hazardous waste. *See Chicago v. Environmental Defense Fund*, 511 U.S. 328, 114 S.Ct. 1588, 11590-1591, 128 L.Ed.2d 302 (1994). Unlike the Comprehensive Environmental Response, Compensation and Liability Act of 1980 (CERCLA), 94 Stat. 2767, as amended, 42 U.S.C. § 9601 *et seq.* (1988 ed. and Supp. V), RCRA is not principally designed to effectuate the cleanup of toxic waste sites or to compensate those who have attended to the remediation of environmental hazards. *Cf. General Electric Co. v. Litton Industrial Automation Systems, Inc.*, 920 F.2d 1415, 1422 (C.A.8 1990) (the "two . . . main purposes of CERCLA" are "prompt cleanup of hazardous waste sites and imposition of all cleanup costs on the responsible party"). RCRA's primary purpose, rather, is to reduce the generation of hazardous waste and to ensure the proper treatment, storage and disposal of that waste which is nonetheless generated, "so as to minimize the present and future threat to human health and the environment." 42 U.S.C. § 6902(b)(1988 ed).

Chief responsibility for the implementation and enforcement of RCRA rests with the Administrator of Environmental Protection Agency (EPA), *see* §§ 6928, 6973, but like other environmental laws, RCRA contains a citizen suit provision, § 6972, which permits private citizens to enforce its provisions in some circumstances.

Two requirements of § 6972(a) defeat KFC's suit against the Meghrigs. The first concerns the necessary timing of a citizen suit brought under § 6972(a)(1)(B): That section permits a private party to bring suit against certain responsible persons, including former owners, "who ha[ve] contributed or who [are] contributing to the past or present handling, storage, treatment, transportation, or disposal of any solid or hazardous waste which *may present* an *imminent* and substantial endangerment to health or the environment." (emphasis added). The second defines the remedies a district court can award in a suit brought under § 6972(a)(1)(B): Section 6972(a) authorizes district courts "*to restrain* any person who has contributed or who is contributing to the past or present handling, storage, treatment, transportation, or disposal of any solid or hazardous waste . . . , *to order such person to take such other action as may be necessary, or both.*" (emphasis added).

It is apparent from the two remedies described in § 6972(a) that RCRA's citizen suit provision is not directed at providing compensation for past cleanup efforts. Under a plain reading of this remedial scheme, a private citizen suing under § 6972(a)(1)(B) could seek a mandatory injunction, *i.e.*, one that orders a responsible party to "take action" by attending to the cleanup and proper disposal of toxic waste or a prohibitory injunction, *i.e.*, one that "restrains" a responsible party from further violating RCRA. Neither remedy, however, is susceptible of the interpretation adopted by the Ninth Circuit, as neither contemplates the award of past cleanup costs, whether these are denominated "damages" or "equitable restitution."

. . . .

That RCRA's citizen suit provision was not intended to provide a remedy for past cleanup costs is further apparent from the harm at which it is directed. Section 6972(a)(1)(B) permits a private party to bring suit only upon a showing that the solid or hazardous waste at issue "may present an imminent and substantial endangerment to health or the environment." The meaning of this timing restriction is plain: an endangerment can only be "imminent" if it "threaten[s] to occur immediately," Webster's New International Dictionary of English Language 1245 (2d ed. 1934), and the reference to waste which "may present" imminent harm quite clearly excludes waste that no longer presents such a danger. As the Ninth Circuit itself intimated in *Price v. United States Navy*, 39 F.3d 1011, 1019 (1994), this language "implies that there must be a threat which is present now, although the impact of the threat may not be felt until later." It follows that § 6972(a) was designed to provide a remedy that ameliorates present or obviates the risk of future "imminent" harms, not a remedy that compensates for past cleanup efforts. *Cf.* § 6902(b) (national policy behind RCRA is "to minimize the present and future threat to human health and the environment").

Other aspects of RCRA's enforcement scheme strongly support this conclusion. Unlike CERCLA, RCRA contains no statute of limitations, compare § 9613(g)(2) (limitations period in suits under CERCLA § 9607), and it does not require a showing that the response costs being sought are reasonable. Compare § 9607(a)(4)(A) and (B) (costs recovered under CERCLA must be "consistent with the national contingency plan"). If Congress had intended § 6972(a) to function as a cost-recovery mechanism, the absence of these provisions would be striking. Moreover, with one limited exception, *see Hallstrom v. Tillamook County,* 493 U.S. 20, 26-27, 110 S.Ct. 304, 309, 107 L. Ed. 2d 237 (1989) (noting exception to notice requirement "when there is a danger that hazardous waste will be discharged"), a private party may not bring suit under § 6972(a)(1)(B) without first giving 90 days' notice to the Administrator of the EPA, to "the State in which the alleged endangerment may occur," and to potential defendants. *See* §§ 6972(b)(2)(A)(i)-(iii). And no citizen suit can proceed if either the EPA or the State has commenced, and is diligently prosecuting, a separate enforcement action. *See* §§ 6972(b)(2)(B) and (C). Therefore, if RCRA were designed to compensate private parties for their past cleanup efforts, it would be a wholly irrational mechanism for doing so. Those parties with insubstantial problems, problems that neither the State nor the federal government feel compelled to address, could recover their response costs, whereas those parties whose waste problems were sufficiently severe as o attract the attention of government officials would be left without a recovery.

Though it agrees that KFC's complaint is defective for failing properly to allege an "imminent and substantial endangerment," the government (as amicus) nonetheless joins KFC in arguing that § 6972(a) does not in all circumstances preclude an award of past cleanup costs. *See* Brief for United States as Amicus Curiae 22-28. The government posits a situation in which suit is properly brought while the waste at issue continues to pose an imminent endangerment, and suggests that the plaintiff in such a case could seek equitable restitution of money previously spent on cleanup efforts. Echoing a similar argument made by KFC, *see* Brief for Respondent 11-19, the government does not rely on the remedies expressly provided in § 6972(a), but rather cites a line of cases holding that district courts retain inherent authority to award any equitable remedy that is not expressly taken away from them by Congress. *See, e.g., Porter v. Warner Holding Co.*, 328 U.S. 395, 66 S.Ct. 1086, 90 L.Ed. 2d 1332 (1946); *Wyandotte Transp. Co. v. United States,* 389 U.S. 191, 88 S. Ct. 379, 19 L.Ed. 2d 407 (1967); *Hecht Co. v. Bowles,* 321 U.S. 321, 64 S.Ct. 587, 88 L.Ed. 754 (1944). RCRA does not prevent a private party from recovering its cleanup costs under other federal or state laws, *see* § 6972(f) (preserving remedies under statutory and common law), but the limited remedies described in § 6972(a), along with the stark differences between the language of that section and the cost recovery provisions of CERCLA, amply demonstrate that Congress did not intend for a private citizen to be able to undertake a cleanup and then proceed to recover its costs under RCRA. As we explained in *Middlesex County Sewerage Authority v. National Sea Clammers Assn.,* 453 U.S. 1, 14, 101 S.Ct. 2615, 2623, 69 L.Ed. 2d 436 (1981), where Congress has provided "elaborate enforcement provisions" for remedying the violation of a federal statute, as Congress has done with RCRA and CERCLA, "it cannot be assumed that Congress intended to authorize by implication additional judicial remedies for private citizens" suing under the statute.

> [I]t is an elemental canon of statutory construction that where a statute expressly provides a particular remedy or remedies, a court must be chary of reading others into it. *Id.* at 14-15, 101 S.Ct. at 2623 (quoting *Transamerican Mortgage Advisors, Inc. v. Lewis,* 444 U.S. 11, 19, 100 S.Ct. 242, 247, 62 L.Ed. 2d 146 (1979)).

Without considering whether a private party could seek to obtain an injunction requiring another party to pay cleanup costs which arise after a RCRA citizen suit has been properly commenced, *cf. United States v. Price,* 688 F.2d 204, 211-213 (3d Cir.1982) (requiring funding of a diagnostic study is an appropriate form of relief in a suit brought by the Administrator under § 6973), or otherwise recover cleanup costs paid out after the invocation of RCRA's statutory process, we agree with the Meghrigs that a private party cannot recover the cost of a past cleanup effort under RCRA, and that KFC's complaint is defective for the reasons stated by the District Court. Section 6972(a) does not contemplate the award of past cleanup costs, and § 6972(a)(1)(B) permits a private party to bring suit only upon an allegation that the contaminated site presently poses an "imminent and substantial endangerment to health or the environment," and not upon an allegation that it posed such an endangerment at some time in the past. The judgment of the Ninth Circuit is reversed.

NOTES AND QUESTIONS

(1) Notice the Supreme Court's reliance on its 1981 decision, *Middlesex County Sewerage Auth. v. National Sea Clammers Ass'n,* 453 U.S. 1 (1981), for the view that where Congress has provided elaborate enforcement provisions, as in CERCLA and RCRA, it cannot be assumed that Congress intended to authorize, by implication, additional judicial remedies for private citizens suing under the statute. In fact, the courts have frequently looked askance at efforts to find implied remedies in environmental legislation, including but not limited to RCRA. For an insightful discussion of these decisions, *see* John E. Sullivan, *Implied Private Causes of Action and the Recoverability of Damages Under the RCRA Citizen Suit Provision,* 25 ELR 10408 (Aug. 1995).

(2) The *Mehgrig* case was significant, at least in part, because the Superfund Act contains a "petroleum exclusion" which excludes petroleum from that statute's definition of "hazardous substance," and thus from its entire liability scheme. *See* 42 U.S.C. § 9601(14), (33). Given this, up to the *Mehgrig* decision, recovery under RCRA § 7002appeared to be a viable possibility for the private recovery of clean up costs in areas afflicted by petroleum contamination. Should the Supreme Court have given that consideration greater weight in deciding *Mehgrig*?

[3] RCRA's Definition of Solid Waste and Hazardous Waste

AMERICAN MINING CONGRESS v. ENVIRONMENTAL PROTECTION AGENCY

United States Court of Appeals, District of Columbia Circuit (1987)
824 F.2d 1177

STARR, Circuit Judge:

. . . Petitioners, trade associations representing mining and oil refining interests, challenge regulations promulgated by EPA that amend the definition of "solid waste" to establish and define the agency's authority to regulate secondary materials reused within an industry's ongoing production process. In plain English, petitioners maintain that EPA has exceeded its regulatory authority in seeking to bring materials that are not discarded or otherwise disposed of within the compass of "waste."

. . . .

Congress' "overriding concern" in enacting RCRA was to establish the framework for a national system to insure the safe management of hazardous waste. . . .

RCRA includes two major parts: one deals with the nonhazardous solid waste management and the other with hazardous waste management. Under the latter, EPA is directed to promulgate regulations establishing a comprehensive management system. EPA's authority, however, extends only to the regulation of "hazardous waste." Because "hazardous waste" is defined as a subset of "solid waste," § 6903(5), the scope of EPA's jurisdiction is limited to those materials that constitute "solid waste." That pivotal term is defined by RCRA as:

> any garbage, refuse, sludge from a waste treatment plant, water supply treatment plant, or air pollution control facility *and other discarded material,* including solid, liquid, semisolid, or contained gaseous material, resulting from industrial, commercial, mining, and agricultural operations, and from community activities . . . . 42 U.S.C. § 6903(27)(emphasis added).

As will become evident, this case turns on the meaning of the phrase, "and other discarded materials," contained in the statute's definitional provisions.

EPA's interpretation of "solid waste" has evolved over time. On May 19, 1980, EPA issued interim regulations defining "solid waste" to include a material that is "a manufacturing or mining by-product and sometimes is discarded." 45 Fed. Reg. 33,119 (1980). This definition contained two terms needing elucidation: "by-product" and "sometimes discarded." In its definition of "a manufacturing or mining by-product," EPA expressly *excluded* "an intermediate manufacturing or mining product which results from one of the steps in a manufacturing or mining process and is typically processed through the next step of the process within a short time."

In 1983, the agency proposed narrowing amendments to the 1980 interim rule. The agency showed especial concern over *recycling* activities. In the preamble to the amendments, the agency observed that, in light of RCRA's legislative history, it was clear that "Congress indeed intended that materials being recycled or held for recycling can be wastes, and if hazardous, hazardous wastes." The agency also asserted that "not only can materials destined for recycling or being recycled be solid and hazardous wastes, but the Agency clearly has the authority to regulate recycling activities as hazardous waste management."

While asserting its interest in recycling activities (and materials being held for recycling), EPA's discussion left unclear whether the agency in fact believed its jurisdiction extended to materials recycled in an industry's ongoing production processes, or only to materials disposed of and recycled as part of a waste management program. In its preamble, EPA stated that "the revised definition of solid waste sets out the Agency's view of its jurisdiction over the recycling of hazardous waste . . . Proposed section 261.6 then contains exemptions from regulations for those hazardous waste recycling activities that we do not think require regulation." The amended regulatory description of "solid waste" itself, then, did not include materials "used or reused as effective substitutes for raw materials in processes using raw materials as principal feedstocks." EPA explained the exclusion as follows:

> [These] materials are being used essentially as raw materials and so ordinarily are not appropriate candidates for regulatory control. Moreover, when these materials are used to manufacture new products, the processes generally are normal manufacturing operations . . . . The Agency is reluctant to read the statue as regulating actual manufacturing processes.

This, then, seemed clear: EPA was drawing a line between discarding and ultimate recycling, on the one hand, and a continuous or ongoing manufacturing process with one-site "recycling," on the other. If the activity fell within the latter category, then the materials were not deemed to be "discarded."

After receiving extensive comments, EPA issued its final rule on January 4, 1985. Under the final rule, materials are considered "solid waste" if they are abandoned by being disposed of, burned, or incinerated; or stored, treated, or accumulated before or in lieu of those activities. In addition, certain recycling activities fall within EPA's definition. EPA determines whether a material is a RCRA solid waste when it is recycled by examining both the material or substance itself and the recycling activity involved. The final rule identifies five categories of "secondary materials" (spent materials, sludges, by-products, commercial chemical products, and scrap metal). These "secondary materials" constitute "solid waste" when they are disposed, burned for energy recovery or used to produce a fuel, reclaimed, or accumulated speculatively.[177] Under the final rule, if a material constitutes "solid waste," it is subject to RCRA regulation *unless* it is directly reused as an ingredient or as an effective substitute to its original manufacturing process.[178] In the jargon of the trade, the latter category is known as the "closed-loop" exception. In either case, the materials must not first be "reclaimed" (processed to recover a usable product or regenerated). EPA exempts these activities "because they are like ordinary usage of commercial products.

Petitioners, American Mining Congress ("AMC") and American Petroleum Institute ("API"), challenge the scope of EPA's final rule. Relying upon the statutory definition of "solid waste," petitioners contend that EPA's authority under RCRA is limited to controlling materials that are *discarded or intended for discard*. They argue that EPA's reuse and recycle rules, as applied to in-process secondary materials, regulate materials that have not been discarded, and therefore exceed EPA's jurisdiction.

[The court then describes the operation of petroleum refineries and the mining process. It further notes that under EPA's rule the materials recaptured by petroleum refineries and mining facilities are deemed "solid waste."]

. . . .

. . . Congress, it will be recalled, granted EPA power to regulate "solid waste." Congress specifically defined "solid waste" as "discarded material."

177 Under the final rule, a "use constituting disposal" is defined as direct placement on land of wastes or products containing or derived from wastes. A material is "accumulated speculatively" if it is accumulated prior to being recycled. If the accumulator can show that the materials feasibly can be recycled, and that during a one-year calendar period the amount of material recycled or transferred for recycling is 75% or more of the amount present at the beginning of the year, the materials are not considered solid wastes. A material is "reclaimed" if it is processed to recover a usable product, or if it is regenerated.

178 Specifically, the final rule excludes materials recycled by being: (1) [u]sed or reused as ingredients in an industrial process to make a product, *provided the materials are not being reclaimed*; or (2) [u]sed or reused as effective substitutes for comercial products; or (3) [r]eturned to the original process from which they are generated, without first being reclaimed." *Id.* (emphasis added). In the third category, the material must be returned to the original manufacturing process as a substitute for raw material feedstock, and the process must use raw materials as principal feedstocks.

EPA then defined "discarded material" to include materials destined for reuse in an industry's *ongoing* production processes. The challenge to EPA's jurisdictional reach is founded, again, on the proposition that in-process secondary materials are outside the bounds of EPA's lawful authority. Nothing has been *discarded,* the argument goes, and thus RCRA jurisdiction remains untriggered.

The first step in statutory interpretation is, of course, an analysis of the language itself. In pursuit of Congress' intent, we "start with the assumption that the legislative purpose is expressed by the ordinary meaning of the words used." Here, Congress defined "solid waste" as "discarded material." The ordinary plain-English meaning of the word "discarded" is "disposed of," "thrown away" or "abandoned." Encompassing materials retained for immediate reuse within the scope of "discarded material" strains, to say the least, the everyday usage of that term.

. . . .

The question we face, then, is whether, in light of the national legislature's expressly stated objectives and the underlying problems that motivated it to enact RCRA in the first instance, Congress was using the term "discarded" in its ordinary sense—"disposed of" or "abandoned"—or whether Congress was using it in a much more open-ended way, so as to encompass materials no longer useful in their original capacity though destined for immediate reuse in another phase of the industry's ongoing production process.

For the following reasons, we believe the former to be the case. RCRA was enacted, as the congressional objectives and findings make clear, in an effort to help states deal with the ever-increasing problem of solid waste *disposal* by encouraging the search for and use of alternatives to existing methods of disposal (including recycling) and protecting health and the environment by regulating hazardous wastes. To fulfill these purposes, it seems clear that EPA need not regulate "spent" materials that are recycled and reused in an *ongoing* manufacturing or industrial process. These materials have not yet become part of the waste disposal problem; rather, they are destined for beneficial reuse or recycling in a continuous process by the generating industry itself.

. . . .

. . . We are . . . not presented with a situation in which Congress likely intended that the pivotal jurisdictional term be read in its broadest sense, detached from everyday parlance; instead we have a situation in which Congress, perhaps through the process of legislative compromise which the courts must be loathe to tear asunder, employed a term with a widely accepted meaning to define the materials that EPA could regulate under RCRA. . . .

. . . .

We are constrained to conclude that, in light of the language and structure of RCRA, the problems animating Congress to enact it, and the relevant portions of the legislative history, Congress clearly and unambiguously expressed its intent that "solid waste" (and therefore EPA's regulatory authority) be limited to materials that are "discarded" by virtue of being disposed of, abandoned, or thrown away. While we do not lightly overturn an agency's reading of its own statute, we are persuaded that by regulating in-process secondary materials, EPA has acted in contravention of Congress' intent. Accordingly, the petition for review is granted.

MIKVA, CIRCUIT JUDGE, dissenting:

The court today strains to overturn the Environmental Protection Agency's interpretation of the Resource Conservation and Recovery Act to authorize the regulation of certain recycled industrial materials. Under today's decision, the EPA is prohibited from regulating in-process secondary materials that contribute to the ominous problem that Congress sought to eradicate passing the RCRA. In my opinion, the EPA has adequately demonstrated that its interpretation is a reasonable construction of an ambiguous term in a statute committed to the agency's administration. We therefore are obliged to defer to the agency's interpretation under the principles of *Chevron U.S.A., Inc. v. NRDC*, 467 U.S. 837, 104 S.Ct. 2778, 81 L.Ed. 2d 694 (1984), and *INS v. Cardoza-Fonseca*. 480 U.S. 421, 107 S.Ct. 1207, 94 L.Ed. 2d 434 (1987). . . .

. . . .

In my opinion, the EPA's interpretation of solid waste is completely reasonable in light of the language, policies, and legislative history of RCRA. Congress had broad remedial objectives in mind when it enacted RCRA, most notably to "regulat[e] the treatment, storage, transportation, and disposal of hazardous wastes which have adverse effects on the environment." The disposal problem Congress was combating encompassed more than just abandoned materials. RCRA makes this clear with its definition of the central statutory term "disposal":

> the discharge, deposit, injection, dumping, spilling, leaking or placing of any solid waste or hazardous waste into or on any land or water so that such solid waste or hazardous waste or any constituent thereof may enter the environment or be emitted into the air or discharged into any waters, including ground waters.

42 U.S.C. § 6903(3). This definition clearly encompasses more than the everyday meaning of disposal, which is a "discarding or throwing away." Webster's Third International Dictionary 654 (2d ed. 1981). The definition is *functional*: waste is disposed under this provision if it is put into contact with land or water in such a way as to pose the risks to health and the environment that animated Congress to pass RCRA. Whether the manufacturer subjectively intends to put the material to additional use is irrelevant to this definition, as indeed it should be, because the manufacturer's state of mind bears no necessary relation to the hazards of the industrial processes he employs.

Faithful to RCRA's functional approach, EPA reasonably concluded that regulation of certain in-process secondary materials was necessary to carry out its mandate. The materials at issue in this case can pose the same risks as abandoned wastes, whether or not the manufacturer intends eventually to put them to further beneficial use. As the agency explained, "[s]imply because a waste is likely to be recycled will not ensure that it will not be spilled or leaked before recycling occurs." The storage, transportation, and even recycling of in-process secondary materials can cause severe environmental harm. Indeed, the EPA documented environmental disasters caused by the handling or storage of such materials. It also pointed out the risk of damage from spills or leaks when certain in-process secondary materials are placed on land or in underground product storage. . . .

. . . .

. . . [I]n this case the EPA has interpreted solid waste in a manner that seems to expand the everyday usage of the word "discarded." Its conclusion, however, is fully supportable in light of the statutory scheme and legislative history of RCRA. The agency concluded that certain on-site recycled materials constitute an integral part of the waste disposal problem. This judgment is grounded in the EPA's technical expertise and is adequately supported by evidence in the record. The majority nevertheless reverses the agency because it believes that the materials at issue "have not yet become part of the waste disposal problem." This declaration is nothing more than a substitution of the majority's own conclusions for the sound technical judgment of the EPA. The EPA's interpretation is a reasonable construction of an ambiguous statutory provision and should be upheld.

NOTES AND QUESTIONS

(1) How persuasive was the critique of the majority opinion in this case contained in Judge Mikva's dissent? Should the D.C. Circuit have been more deferential to EPA's determination that on-site recycled materials contribute to the problem of waste disposal? Was such deference required by the Supreme Court's decision in the *Chevron USA* case?

(2) In light of the principal case, does EPA have the authority to regulate, as "solid waste" under RCRA, sewage treatment sludge which is stored in a surface impoundment if that sludge will be reprocessed for metals recovery at a future time? Distinguishing the *AMC I* decision, the D.C. Circuit held that the Agency has such authority. *See American Mining Congress v. EPA (AMC II),* 907 F.2d 1179 (D.C. Cir. 1990). The court stated that "[n]othing in *AMC* prevents the agency from treating as 'discarded' the wastes at issue in this case, which are managed in land disposal units that *are* part of wastewater treatment systems, which *have* therefore become 'part of the waste disposal problem,' and which are *not* part of ongoing industrial processes." (emphasis in original). *Id.* at 1186.

(3) The *AMC I* decision was also distinguished in *American Petroleum Institute v. EPA,* 906 F.2d 729 (D.C. Cir. 1990), in which the D.C. Circuit upheld a challenge by environmental organizations to an EPA determination that wastes which the agency had required to be treated through metals reclamation cease to be "solid wastes," for RCRA purposes, once they arrive at a reclamation facility. The court noted that the wastes in question had unquestionably been "discarded" before being subject to metals reclamation. Moreover, unlike the wastes at issue in *AMC I,* the materials at issue in the *American Petroleum Institute* case were "part of a mandatory waste treatment plan prescribed by EPA." *Id.* at 741. In view of the *AMC I* and *American Petroleum Institute* opinions, how much of a "loophole" did the *AMC I* decision actually create in EPA's RCRA solid waste regulations?

§ 4.04 Remediation of Hazardous Waste Landfills Under the Superfund Statute

[1] "Superfund"—The Comprehensive Environmental Response, Compensation, and Liability Act of 1980

On December 2, 1980, President Carter signed into law the so-called "Superfund" legislation, *i.e.*, the Comprehensive Environmental Response, Compensation, and Liability Act of 1980, "an Act to provide for liability compensation, cleanup, and emergency response for hazardous substances released into the environment and the cleanup of inactive waste disposal sites."[1]

The statute, which was substantially amended in 1986, is a very complex piece of legislation. It cross-refers and relies on other prior laws that deal with toxic and hazardous pollution. Moreover, the 1980 law had a stormy, contentious legislative history that left its mark on a hurried and technically imperfect draft of legislation. The draft adopted was not allowed to undergo technical revision for fear that such an effort would lead to its ultimate defeat.[2]

[a] Sections 101–103 Basic Requirements; Reporting

In brief summary, the law prohibits the release of a "reportable quantity" of a "hazardous substance," whether on land or on the navigable waters of the United States and waters of the contiguous zone.[3] The broad, general exception to this prohibition is any "federally permitted release,"[4] which is defined to include discharges under permit issued under the various pollution control acts, including the Clean Water[5] and Clean Air Acts,[6] the Marine Protection, Research and Sanctuaries Act,[7] the Safe Drinking Water Act,[8] the "Solid Waste Disposal Act (RCRA),"[9] and the Atomic Energy Act.[10]

"Hazardous substance" is defined to include substances designated pursuant to § 311(b)(2)(A) and toxic pollutants under § 307A of the Clean Water Act,[11] hazardous wastes so designated pursuant to § 3001 of RCRA,[12] and any

[1] Pub. Law No. 96-510, 94 Stat. 2767, 42 U.S.C. § 9601.

[2] *See* legislative history, F. Grad, Treatise on Environmental Law, § 4A.04[2].

[3] Comprehensive Environmental Response, Compensation, and Liability Act of 1980 (hereafter cited as "Superfund"), §§ 102-103.

[4] Superfund at § 101(10), 42 U.S.C. § 9601(10).

[5] CWA §§ 402, 404, 33 U.S.C. §§ 1342, 1344.

[6] "[A]ny emission into the air subject to a permit or control regulation under Section 111, Section 112, Title I Part C, Title I Part D, or state implementation plan submitted in accordance with section 110 of the Clean Air Act,. . . ."

[7] Marine Protection, Research and Sanctuaries Act of 1972, §§ 102-103, 33 U.S.C. §§ 1412, 1413.

[8] "[A]ny injection of fluids authorized . . . pursuant to Part C of the Safe Drinking Water Act . . . ."

[9] RCRA §§ 3005(a) through (d), 42 U.S.C. § 6925.

[10] "[A]ny release of source, special nuclear or byproduct material, as those terms are defined in the Atomic Energy Act of 1954, in compliance with a legally enforceable license, permit, regulation, or order issued pursuant to the Atomic Energy Act of 1954."

[11] 33 U.S.C. §§ 1317, 1321(b)(2)(A).

[12] 42 U.S.C. § 6921.

hazardous air pollutant listed under § 12 of the Clean Air Act.[13] Also included in the definition are hazardous chemical substances or mixtures under Section 7 of the Toxic Substances Control Act,[14] as well as substances so designated under Section 102 of the Superfund legislation itself. Substances designated under Section 102 are to include substances which, when released into the environment, may present substantial danger to the public health or welfare or the environment. EPA may, by regulation, establish reportable quantities of such substances and unless and until superseded by regulation, the reportable quantity shall be one pound of the substance or whatever quantity has been established pursuant to Section 311(b)(4) of the Federal Water Pollution Control Act.[15]

Section 103 of the Act establishes reporting requirements. The person in charge of any facility, onshore or offshore, must immediately report the release of a hazardous substance to the National Response Center established under the Clean Water Act. Failure to report as required subjects the person to criminal conviction and penalty of $10,000 or imprisonment up to one year. As under Section 311 of the Federal Water Pollution Control Act,notification pursuant to this section cannot be used in any criminal prosecution, though it will probably not shield against the imposition of civil penalties.[16]

Another reporting requirement under Section 103 requires any person who owns or operates or who at the time of disposal owned or operated a facility at which hazardous substances have been stored, treated, or disposed, as well as any transporter of hazardous wastes, to notify the Administrator of EPA of the existence of the facility. The person required to report must specify the amount and type of hazardous substance to be found there, and any known, suspected or likely release of such substances from the facility. This reporting requirement is not applicable, however, when the facility has a permit or has interim status under Subtitle C of the RCRA.[17] The Administrator has broad authority to require additional information as part of this registration process.

The section requires the retention of records regarding such facilities for 50 years. The destruction of such records is punishable by a fine of $20,000 or imprisonment of up to one year. Waivers of the requirements of this provision may be obtained from the Administrator upon application and a showing of good grounds. The Administrator may also require the retention of such records for more than 50 years.[18]

Knowing failure to notify the Administrator may result in a fine of $10,000 or imprisonment of up to one year. In addition, knowing failure to give the required notice has another consequence. The person who fails to report loses

---

[13] 43 U.S.C. § 7412.

[14] TOSCA § 107, 15 U.S.C. § 2606.

[15] Superfund § 102, 42 U.S.C. § 9606. On reportable quantities, see disposition of issue under Clean Water Act§ 311(b)(4), 33 U.S.C. § 1321(b)(4), in Manufacturing Chemists Association v. Costle, 451 F. Supp. 902 (W.D. La. 1978), and subsequent amendment of federal law, at F. Grad, Treatise on Environmental Law, § 3.03[8].

[16] Compare earlier disposition under § 311(b)(6) of the Clean Water Act, in United States v. Ward, 444 U.S. 1067, 100 S.Ct. 2636, 65 L.Ed. 2d 742 (1980).

[17] RCRA § 3001 *et seq.*, 42 U.S.C. § 6921 *et seq.*

[18] Superfund § 103(d)(2) to (4), 42 U.S.C. § 9603(d)(2) to (4).

the benefit of limited liability, as well as defenses to liability set forth in Section 107 of the Act.[19]

The section does not indicate whether a separate notification must be given to identify the site and to report releases from the site. It is also not clear whether filing late for interim status under RCRA[20] will relieve owners and operators of disposal sites from the requirement of reporting their sites under Section 103 of the Superfund legislation.[21]

[b] Response Authorities

Section 104 provides for response authorities.[22] EPA is given broad authority to undertake necessary actions to deal with the release or the threat of substantial release of hazardous substances into the environment. The President is authorized, consistent with the National Contingency Plan, to remove or to arrange for the removal and to provide for other remedial action relating to hazardous substances.[23] A distinction is made in the law—which was stressed in the course of the legislative history—between "removal," which covers immediate and essential cleanup operations, and "remedial action," which includes more far-reaching efforts to restore the environment and to repair the damage of releases of hazardous waste. The authority to undertake the necessary cleanup is generally similar to that provided for oil and hazardous waste pollution under Section 311 of the Clean Water Act.[24] Provision is made for notification of the affected states and for state participation and reimbursement for states' activities. However, no remedial action is to be provided by the federal government unless the state in which the release occurs first enters into a contract or cooperative agreement which provides for several specified assurances. The state must undertake to provide for the future maintenance of such wastes and must assure the availability of acceptable waste disposal facilities pursuant to Subtitle C of RCRA. The state must also agree to pay at least 10% of the total expenditures required, including subsequent maintenance, and 50% or more of the total expenditure if the state was in part responsible or owned or operated the facility in question.

The section also establishes an Agency for Toxic Substances and Disease Registry within the public health service to report directly to the Surgeon General. The Agency, with the cooperation of the states and of other listed environmental and public health agencies, is to establish and maintain a national registry of serious diseases and illnesses and a national registry of persons exposed to toxic substances. It is also required to collect other relevant information relating to toxic substances and areas which may be closed to the public because of the toxic substances contamination. In case of public health emergencies, the agency is also to provide medical care and testing services to exposed individuals. It is also to determine the relationships between exposure to toxic substances and illness.[25]

---

[19] Superfund at § 103(c); 42 U.S.C. § 9603(c).

[20] RCRA § 3005(e), 42 U.S.C. § 6925(e).

[21] 42 U.S.C. § 9603.

[22] 42 U.S.C. § 9604.

[23] The President had issued Executive Order 12286 (Jan. 19, 1981) to deal with "Responses to Environmental Damage," 46 Fed. Reg. 9901 (Jan. 30, 1981).

[24] 33 U.S.C. § 1321.

[25] Superfund § 104(i), 42 U.S.C. § 9604(i).

[c] Response Authorities Abatement Action

Section 106 covers abatement actions.[26] When the President determines that there is imminent and substantial endangerment, he may require the Attorney General to secure necessary relief. The district courts are granted jurisdiction for such abatement actions. The President may also issue such orders as may be necessary to protect the public health. Wilful violation or refusal to comply with a Presidential order may result in a fine of $5,000 per day for each day the violation continues. The legislative history, just before the passage of the bill in the Senate, indicated that to be liable for a penalty, the refusal would have to be without sufficient cause—*i.e.,* there could be such defenses as that the person ordered to comply was not the responsible party, under the Act, for the release of the hazardous substance or that the order was not in accordance with the National Contingency Plan. A detailed examination of the specific situation would be required before the penalty could be imposed for refusal to comply.[27]

Within six months after enactment of the law, guidelines are to be published by EPA after consultation with the Attorney General relating to the exercise of the imminent hazard enforcement power. The law provides for coordination with the exercise of imminent hazard enforcement powers under other pollution control legislation.[28]

[d] Liability

Section 107[29] provides broad liability for any person who owns or operates a facility where hazardous wastes are or were disposed of, or who arranges with a transporter for the disposal or treatment of such wastes, or any person who accepts or has previously accepted hazardous substances for transport to a disposal or treatment facility. Any such person is liable for the release or threatened release and for all costs of removal and remedial action incurred by the United States or a state or any other costs incurred consistent with the National Contingency Plan by any other person. In addition to liability for removal costs, such a person is also liable in damages for injury to or destruction of natural resources, including the costs of assessing such injury. However, only states or other units of government can sue for natural resource loss or damage on behalf of the public and to protect its interest.[30] The only available defenses include act of God, act of war, or third-party responsibility. In the case of the defense of third-party responsibility, the presumptively liable party must exhibit by a preponderance of evidence that he exercised due care and took precautions against such third-party acts or omissions. The legislative history indicates that the defense of third party acts or omissions may not be used to enable contractual arrangements to shield the responsible

[26] *See* Executive Order 12286, 46 Fed. Reg. 9901 (Jan. 30, 1981).

[27] *See* F. Grad, Treatise on Environmental Law, Legislative History, § 4A.04[2][f].

[28] CWA §§ 311(c)(2), 308, 309, 504(a), 33 U.S.C. §§ 1321, 1318, 1319, 1364; RCRA §§ 3007, 3008, 3013, 7003, 42 U.S.C. § 6927, 6928; SDWA §§ 1445, 1431, 42 U.S.C. § 300j-4, 300i; CAA §§ 113, 114, 303, 42 U.S.C. § 7413, 7414, 7603; TSCA § 7, 15 U.S.C. § 2606. *See* R. Skaff, *The Emergency Powers in Environmental Protection Statutes: A Suggestion for a Unified Emergency Provision,* 3 Harv. Envtl. L. Rev. 298 (1979).

[29] 42 U.S.C. § 9607.

[30] Superfund § 107(a), 42 U.S.C. § 3607(a).

party. For example, a potentially responsible owner/operator of hazardous wastes cannot relieve himself or herself of responsibility by letting someone else manage it.[31]

The liability under this section is unlimited for costs of remedy or removal, except in the case of vessel or vehicle owners or operators. There is a limit established per gross ton for vessels which carry hazardous substances ($5 million), and another limit for other vessels ($500,000). For motor vehicles, aircraft, pipelines and rolling stock, the limit is set at $50 million or such a lesser amount as the President may establish by regulation, but no less than $5 million, or, for release into navigable waters, $8 million.

Although there is no limit for facilities with respect to the total of cleanup costs—*i.e.,* all costs of response—there is a limit of $50 million for other damages under the Act—*i.e.,* damages to resources and to the environment.[32]

In the situation where limitations on liability for response costs would otherwise apply, *i.e.,* in the case of vessels, motor vehicles, aircrafts, etc., the full cost of response and damages will be the extent of the liability where the release or threatened release was the result of "willful misconduct or willful negligence," or where a person, otherwise subject to limited liability, fails to or refuses to provide reasonable cooperation and assistance in connection with response activities. The phrase in Section 311 of the Clean Water Actis "willful negligence or willful misconduct," but the legislative history indicates the express intention of Congress that the phrase, in spite of its reversal, have the same meaning as in Section 311.[33] Triple punitive damages are provided for failure to comply with an order for remedial action by the President pursuant to Section 106 of the Act. Triple damages are also provided under Section 104 of the Act, which may, however, be difficult to apply, because Section 104 does not provide for penalties![34]

The provision invalidates indemnification, hold harmless, or similar agreements which seek to shift the liability of the responsible person to another. However, insurance protection is expressly exempted from this restriction.[35]

Departments, agencies and instrumentalities of the three branches of the Federal government are required to comply with the Act to the same extent as non-government entities. Both procedural and substantive compliance by instrumentalities of the Federal government is required.[36]

Section 107 appears to establish strict liability for response costs and for damages to environmental resources. The definition of "liability" in Section 101(32)[37] refers to Section 311 of the Clean Water Act, and it is clear from

[31] Superfund § 107(b), 43 U.S.C. § 9607(b). *See* F. Grad, Treatise on Environmental Law, Legislative History § 4A.04[2][f], comments by Senator Randolph; *see also* § 4A.04[2][d], The Senate Committee Report, which had favored joint and several liability.

[32] Superfund § 107(c), 42 U.S.C. § 9607(c).

[33] Superfund § 107(c)(2), 42 U.S.C. § 9607(c)(2).

[34] Superfund § 107(c)(3), 42 U.S.C. § 9607(c)(3).

[35] Superfund § 107(e), 42 U.S.C. § 9607(e).

[36] Superfund § 107(g), 42 U.S.C. § 9607(g). Note that the extension of liability to federal agencies, etc., is not nearly as explicit as in other pollution control legislation. *See* F. Grad, Treatise on Environmental Law, §§ 2.03[4][b] and 3.03[7][f] for parallel provisions relating to air and water pollution.

[37] 42 U.S.C. § 9601(32).

the legislative history that strict liability was intended, even though the words "strict liability" were expressly excluded from the language of the statute. It is just as clear that joint and several liability was not intended and that the intention was to leave the decision of that issue to common law development or to other existing provisions under other laws.[38] The question of strict, joint and several liability was one of the most thoroughly debated issues in the consideration of the law.

[e] Financial Responsibility; Penalties

Financial responsibility requirements are imposed under § 108[39] on vessels which carry hazardous substances. Failure to comply will result in denial of clearance by the Secretary of the Treasury and in denial of entry into port or detention of vessels which do not meet the requirement.

Far more significant than the specific requirements for vessels is the authority granted to the President to promulgate requirements for the maintenance of financial responsibility for facilities which produce, transport, treat, store or dispose of hazardous substances. Such regulations were required to be promulgated not earlier than five years after the date of enactment of the law. Such regulations must incrementally impose financial responsibility requirements over a period of not less than three nor more than six years after their promulgation—*i.e.,* not less than eight nor more than 11 years after the date of enactment of the Superfund legislation. The financial responsibility requirements must generally be commensurate with the risk involved.

[f] Hazardous Substance Response Fund

Section 111[40] provides information on how the Hazardous Substance Response Fund established by Section 221 of the Act may be used.[41] In general, the Fund may be used for all costs of response and cleanup referred to earlier in the law. It may also be used for related purposes, such as necessary studies and investigations, and for the costs of assessing short-term and long-term injury to, and destruction of, natural resources resulting from the release of hazardous substances. To meet the primary obligation under the Fund, up to 85% of it is to be devoted to response costs, and the remainder to natural resource damages.

As noted in the discussion of liability, natural resource damage can only be claimed and recovered by a state or other unit of government, acting in the general interest of the public. The section provides in some detail information on how damages for particular purposes are to be assessed and on how and under what conditions the moneys are to be expended for the restoration and rehabilitation of the environment.[42] The law appears to permit foreign claimants to assert a claim for damages to natural resources to the same extent as United States claimants, if the release occurred in

[38] 33 U.S.C. § 1321.

[39] 42 U.S.C. § 9608.

[40] 42 U.S.C. § 9611.

[41] 42 U.S.C. § 9631.

[42] The duty to carry out the provisions of this section has been delegated by the President to the Director of the Office of Management and Budget (OMB); and certain other functions under the section are delegated, *inter alia,* to the Administrator of EPA, Executive Order 12286, 46 Fed. Reg. 9901 (Jan. 30, 1981).

navigable waters or on a territorial sea or adjacent shoreline of a foreign country, and if the claimant is not otherwise compensated for his loss, if the hazardous substance was released in connection with activities under the Outer Continental Shelflands Act,[43] and if recovery is authorized by treaty or executive agreement with the foreign country which affords comparable remedies to the United States government.

It is a major gap in the law that the section provides no remedy for personal injuries or property damage sustained by individuals in consequence of the release of hazardous substances or the earlier deposit of hazardous substances on waste disposal sites. Thus, the families and persons who suffer injuries or damage to property in such locations as Love Canal may not assert any claim under this Act.

[g] Miscellaneous Provisions; Litigations; Relations to Other Laws

Section 113, covering litigation, jurisdiction and venue,[44] provides for pre-enforcement review of regulations in the Circuit Court of Appeals for the District of Columbia within 90 days of promulgation. The United States District Courts have exclusive original jurisdiction over all controversies arising under the Act without regard to citizenship or to the amount in controversy. Venue lies in the district in which the release or damages occurred or where the defendant resides, is found, or has his principal office. The Act does not moot litigation commenced earlier concerning the release of any hazardous substance.

Section 114 covers the relationship with other laws.[45] The Act does not preempt the states from imposing additional liabilities with respect to the release of hazardous substances. It does, however, bar double recoveries under Superfund and other legislation relating to damages or claims for cleanup. Moreover, states may not create similar funds or similar taxes for the payment of compensation for claims for any costs of response or damage claims which may be compensated out of the Superfund.

This section also provides that no owner or operator of a vessel or facility who maintains evidence of financial responsibility under the Superfund law may be required under any state or local law, rule or regulation to maintain any other evidence of financial responsibility in connection with the release of a hazardous substance from such vessel or facility. Evidence of compliance with the Superfund legislation is to be accepted by a state in lieu of other requirements of financial responsibility for hazardous substance release.[46]

The legislative history shows that the purpose of Section 114 is mainly to avoid double taxation. States that have statutory schemes to collect taxes or fees from persons liable to pay under the law, for the purpose of covering the same costs, damages or injuries, will be preempted. However, if a state has

[43] 43 U.S.C. § 1331 *et seq.*

[44] Superfund § 113(b), 42 U.S.C. § 9613(b).

[45] 42 U.S.C. § 9614.

[46] Superfund § 114(c), (d), 42 U.S.C. § 9614(c)(d).

an oil spill fund, for instance, or a fund to cover damages not covered by the Superfund legislation, the state fund will not be affected in any way.[47]

[h] Hazardous Substance Response Revenue Act of 1980

Title II of the Superfund legislation is entitled "Hazardous Substance Response Revenue Act of 1980."[48] In form it is an amendment of the 1954 Internal Revenue Code. Briefly, it provides for the imposition of a tax of 79 cents on each barrel of crude oil. The law further imposes taxes in varying amounts on a list of chemical substances. The amount of taxes per ton appears to vary with the relative hazard created by each of the substances. The law provides that no tax is to be imposed on designated chemicals at any time when taxes are not imposed on crude oil.

Subtitle B, Section 221 of the Act[49] establishes the hazardous substance response trust fund. The trust fund referred to generally as the Response-Trust Fund consists of amounts appropriated and transferred as provided in the section.

[2] The Superfund Amendments and Reauthorization Act of 1986 (SARA)

After years of contentious debate, Congress amended Superfund in 1986 by enacting the Superfund Amendments and Reauthorization Act of 1986 (SARA). These amendments maintained intact the fundamental structure established in the Superfund statute, which was described in the preceding section. They also strengthened and clarified certain aspects of the Act with regard to the degree of cleanup to be attained at Superfund hazardous waste sites, the role of state agencies in the Superfund program, the redress of damage to natural resources, the settlement of enforcement cases, judicial review of the adequacy of response actions, and various other matters.

The following analysis, written shortly after SARA's passage, perceptively summarizes a number of its salient features:

Atkeson, Goldberg, Ellrod, and Connors, "AN ANNOTATED LEGISLATIVE HISTORY OF THE SUPERFUND AMENDMENTS AND REAUTHORIZATION ACT OF 1986 (SARA)"*

. . . .

SARA is the first major overhaul of CERCLA since that statute was enacted in 1980. This section attempts to summarize the main new developments SARA is likely to bring about in Superfund practice and to alert the practitioner to these changes. Its message is that SARA creates strong new

---

[47] *See* Legislative History in F. Grad, Treatise on Environmental Law, § 4A.02[2][g] text at N. 2, comments of Floor Manager of bill, Congressman Florio.

[48] Superfund § 201, Amendments to Internal Revenue Code of 1954, 26 U.S.C. §§ 4611, 4612, 4661.

[49] 42 U.S.C. § 9631.

incentives for private parties to begin active participation in the site assessment and negotiation process as early as possible. The new cleanup standards, settlement and enforcement provisions, and the much larger fund provide EPA with additional tools and greater leverage to achieve its goals. Only if PRPs [Potentially Responsible Parties] position themselves to have an early impact on remedy selection can they minimize the ultimate remediation cost.

Implications of New Cleanup Standards

The experience of PRPs under CERCLA has increasingly indicated that it is in their interest to become involved in site assessment early and to participate in the RI/FS [Remedial Investigation/Feasability Study] process in order to exert some measure of influence over the remedy. The new SARA cleanup standards provide even greater incentives in this direction. These standards are likely to be more onerous than they look.[50] Although it has been EPA's policy for some time to call for application of federal environmental standards that were legally "applicable or relevant and appropriate,"[51] in practice there has been room for discussion. The statutory cleanup standards in SARA compel EPA to apply the "legally applicable or relevant and appropriate" cleanup standard and will make cleanups more difficult for at least four reasons.

☐ *Detailed Federal Standards.* Many more detailed federal standards, particularly the recommended maximum contaminant levels (RMCLs) being developed under the Safe Drinking Water Act (SDWA)[52] (now designated under the 1986 amendments to the SDWA as "maximum contaminant level goals")[53] and the water quality criteria established under the Federal Water Pollution Control Act (FWPCA),[54] will now be applicable to the cleanup process.[55]

These stringent numerical standards will apply under SARA's general cleanup standard and could result in groundwater cleanups having to meet RMCLs that are 100 times purer than the requirements for tap water. In addition, other new federal standards will make SARA cleanup increasingly more costly. For example, EPA will be phasing in the land ban restrictions required by the 1984 amendments to the Resource Conservation and Recovery

[50] SARA § 121(a)adds a new § 121 to CERCLA requiring EPA to adhere to stringent requirements favoring permanent on-site treatment as the remedy for all sites. SARA § 121, CERCLA § 121, 42 U.S.C. § 9621, ELR Stat 44054. Under CERCLA § 121(b), EPA is required to conduct an assessment of permanent solutions and alternative treatment technologies at each site. The agency must select a remedy that protects human health and the environment, and that employs permanent solutions, alternative treatment technologies, or resource recovery technologies to the maximum extent practicable. *Id. See generally infra* text at 1.F (annotated section on cleanup standards.)

[51] Memorandum from J. Winston Porter, Assistant Administrator for Solid Waste and Emergency Response, EPA, to Regional Administrators, Regions I-IX, Re: CERCLA Compliance with Other Environmental Statutes (Oct. 2, 1985), ELR Admin. Materials 30066.

[52] 42 U.S.C. §§ 300f–300j-11, ELR Stat. 41101.

[53] SDWA § 1412(a)(2), 42 U.S.C. § 300g-1(a)(2), ELR Stat. 41102.

[54] FWPCA § 304(a), 33 U.S.C. § 1314(a), ELR Stat. 42126.

[55] SARA § 121(a), CERCLA § 121(d)(2)(A), 42 U.S.C. § 9621(d)(2)(A), ELR Stat. 44054.

Act (RCRA) over the next several years,[56] in part in response to the charge made during SARA enactment that it was creating new Superfund sites with the land disposal f wastes from the Superfund cleanups.[57]

The periodic issuance of new regulations implementing the 1984 RCRA amendments is also likely to have a heavy impact on future remedial action under CERCLA.

☐ *Applicability of State Standards.* The new SARA § 121requires that more stringent state standards be applied to CERCLA cleanups.[58]

Standards in a number of states[59] may make Superfund cleanups even more costly than if only federal standards were applied.[60]

☐ *Health Assessments.* The requirement that the Agency for Toxic Substances and Disease Registry (ATSDR) perform a health assessment on every site on the NPL [National Priorities List], with the goal of completing the health assessment before the RI/FS,[61] will put a red flag on every trace of toxicity at sites and will tend to alarm the surrounding community if anything (real, suspected, or possible) is identified as a potential health concern. This, in turn, will have a powerful effect on community comment on both the RI/FS and proposed remedial decision.[62] It also may trigger a citizen suit challenging the remedy selected in any ROD [Record of Decision] or consent decree.[63]

---

[56] The 1984 RCRA amendments prohibit land disposal of 12 categories of wastes effective November 8, 1986, unless EPA addresses safe land disposal by regulation before that date. *See* 51 Fed. Reg. 19300, 19304 (1986). On November 7, 1986, EPA published a final rule banning land disposal and establishing treatment standards for several categories of solvent wastes. As treatment technologies become available, land disposal bans will be broadened. 51 Fed. Reg. 40572 (1986).

[57] Senator Moynihan (D.N.Y.), during Senate floor debate on SARA, noted "a pattern of simply digging up toxic waste in one place and planting it in another." 131 Cong. Rec. S11864 (daily ed. Sept. 20, 1985).

[58] SARA §§ 121(a), CERCLA § 121(e) and (f), 42 U.S.C. § 9621(e) and (f), ELR Stat. 44056.

[59] For example, Proposition 54, known as the Toxic Initiative and approved by the voters in California this November, provides in effect that industry shall not release any toxic pollutant in any detectable amount. A New Jersey statute requires cleanup of an industrial site whenever it is closed or ownership is transferred. New Jersey Environmental Cleanup Responsibility Act, N.J. Stat. Ann. § 13:1K-6 *et seq.*

[60] SARA also provides for greater state participation in development and selection of remedial actions. EPA must issue regulations providing states an opportunity to object to any proposed remedial action that the state believes does not conform to applicable federal or state standards. SARA § 121, CERCLA § 121, 42 U.S.C. § 9621, ELR Stat. 44054.

[61] SARA requires the ATSDR to perform a health assessment on each site on the NPL, with priority given to sites where there is documented evidence of a release with potential risk to human health. SARA § 110(4), CERCLA § 104(i)(6), 42 U.S.C. § 9604(i)(6), ELR Stat. 44018. *See generally infra* text at 1.L (annotated section on health-related authorities).

[62] SARA requires public participation in the development of remedial actions. EPA is required to issue regulations providing, at a minimum, notice and an opportunity to comment on the proposed remedial action plan. SARA § 117, CERCLA § 117, 42 U.S.C. § 9617, ELR Stat. 44045. *See generally infra* text at 1.J (annotated section on public participation).

[63] SARA adds a new § 310 to CERCLA authorizing citizens to sue EPA, or any other person, alleged to be in violation of CERCLA or its regulations. This section also allows suits against EPA for failing to perform any nondiscretionary duty under the Act. *See generally infra* text at 11.I (annotated section on citizen suits).

☐ *Permanent Cleanups.* The emphasis in SARA § 121on permanent cleanups is new and based on very little engineering experience.[64] With EPA, the community, and the states expecting permanent solutions, PRPs will be pushed hard in this direction. Cleanup engineering firms will see much new business and stand ready to enter uncharted seas for handsome fees.

Because SARA's cleanup standards will make Superfund cleanups much more expensive, they place a premium on PRP participation. To the extent private parties can perform the RI/FS and otherwise run the cleanup, they can save money over what it would cost if EPA uses the Fund to do the job. Early and continuous participation will allow PRPs to exert some control over the selection of the remedy. This is the best opportunity the new statute gives the PRP to work toward greater cost-effectiveness. For example, the PRPs should concentrate on what is the most cost-effective solution, what waivers might be appropriate, and whether some alternative technology should be considered.

Settlements and Litigation Under SARA

SARA makes it much harder to postpone or challenge hard choices about remedial decisions. Under the new SARA procedure, EPA builds an administrative record, reaches a remedial decision, and then can implement that decision itself with ample resources from a replenished Superfund under § 104[65] or order the PRP to carry out that remedial decision under § 106.[66]

If EPA elects to do the cleanup itself, experience to date suggests it will be much more costly than if PRPs perform the work.[67] Also, SARA's preenforcement review limitations prevent the PRP from bringing any court challenge until the Department of Justice sues the PRP under § 106 or § 107.[68] To defend a § 107 response cost action or a § 106 enforcement proceeding, the PRP generally will have to how a busy court that some incredibly technical judgment, copiously documented by EPA, was arbitrary and capricious.[69] In other words, PRPs should be warned that litigation to challenge EPA cleanup decisions generally will take place years later, *after* EPA has incurred massive expenditures, and will impose upon PRPs a very difficult burden to overcome.

The SARA rules on deferral of judicial review provide additional incentives for PRPs to focus their use of expert opinions, data submission, and advocacy

64 *See, e.g.,* 132 Cong. Rec. H9603 (daily ed. Oct. 8, 1986) (statement of Rep. Henry (R-Mich.) Discussing the current lack of permanent treatment technologies, even the lack of standardized testing and demonstration protocols for such technologies).

65 CERCLA § 104, 42 U.S.C. § 9604, ELR Stat. 44011. The new Fund will contain $8.5 billion, compared with $1.6 billion Congress previously authorized. Conference Committee Report at 318, 320-21.

66 CERCLA § 106, 42 U.S.C. § 9606, ELR Stat. 44023; *See* SARA § 121, CERCLA § 121, ELR Stat. 44054.

67 *See, e.g.,* Anderson, *Negotiation and Informal Agency Action: The Case of Superfund,* 1985 Duke L.J. 261, 301-02 (EPA assessment and cleanup costs average 30 to 40 percent more than equivalent private cleanups).

68 SARA § 113(c)precludes preenforcement judicial review of any response action taken or ordered under § 104 or 106 of CERCLA. Review generally is available only in enforcement actions, and even then it is limited to the administrative record EPA has compiled supporting its decisions. SARA § 113(c), CERCLA § 113(h)(1), 42 U.S.C. § 9613(h)(1), ELR Stat. 44042. *See generally infra* text at 11.A (annotated section on judicial review).

69 SARA § 113(c), CERCLA § 113(j), 42 U.S.C. § 9613(j), ELR Stat. 44042.

as early as possible in the process. PRPs should concentrate on shaping the RI/FS and the administrative record of the remedial decision. Once the ROD is issued, it is likely to be too late to do anything to correct a bad or costly cleanup decision. EPA will issue important regulations on development of the administrative record for its RODs.[70] Significantly, SARA expressly states that these regulations need not provide an adjudicatory hearing before the ROD is finalized.[71]

Another aspect of paying early attention to CERCLA problems to minimize liability arises out of the SARA provision offering some hope to the "innocent landowner"[72] who exercised due diligence in purchasing property later found to be contaminated. This provision should guide the "due diligence" procedures private parties follow in acquiring property, and also should be considered in connection with acquisitions or mergers. SARA thus creates additional reasons to review real property transactions for potential CERCLA exposure before proceeding with a transaction, whether or not there is any pending EPA study or cleanup.

An essential element of organizing early on Superfund issues is identifying other PRPs likely to have significant involvement at the same site. SARA invites EPA to seek voluntary settlements.[73] It also encourages private conduct of both RI/FS work[74] and remedial action.[75] To facilitate settlement, SARA establishes a procedure for EPA to provide PRPs with information about a site and then allow a grace period for negotiations.[76] It takes time to educate the parties to cooperate on such problems, and practitioners should consider ways of accelerating and facilitating the distribution of he information that SARA authorizes EPA to acquire and share with PRPs. Private suits for response costs among PRPs under § 107 are becoming more numerous, and SARA lays an ample basis for extensive litigation about contribution among PRPs[77] if they choose not to cooperate. The Superfund practitioner should

[70] SARA § 113(c), CERCLA § 113(k), 42 U.S.C. § 9613(k), ELR Stat. 44043.

[71] *Id.*

[72] SARA provides some protection to landowners who purchase property without knowing that hazardous substances were present on it. A new definition adding § 101(35)(A) of CERCLAconfirms that a contract for sale of land or a deed establishes a contractual relationship for purposes of § 107 liability. However, landowners who acquired property without knowledge of contamination, and who had no reason to know of it, may have a defense under this provision.

[73] SARA § 122(a), CERCLA § 122, 42 U.S.C. § 9622, ELR Stat. 44058.

[74] SARA § 104(a)provides that private parties may conduct RI/FS provided that EPA approves the work and the private parties agree to reimburse EPA for the cost of retaining an EPA expert to oversee the study. SARA § 104(a), CERCLA § 122(a), 42 U.S.C. § 9622, ELR Stat. 44058.

[75] SARA § 122(a)authorizes EPA to enter into agreements with private parties to perform remedial work provided the work "will be done properly." Voluntary agreements are encouraged "to expedite effective remedial actions and minimize litigation." SARA § 122(a), CERCLA § 122, 42 U.S.C. § 9622, ELR Stat. 44058.

[76] SARA § 122(a)provides that EPA may provide PRPs with information on other PRPs, the volume and nature of wastes contributed, and a ranking by volume of wastes contributed. PRPs have 60 days from receipt of this information to make a proposal to EPA for voluntarily undertaking or funding the action under a consent agreement. EPA cannot commence an RI/FS for 90 days following notice, or an action under § 104 for 120 days. SARA § 111(a), CERCLA § 122, 42 U.S.C. § 9622(e), ELR Stat. 44059.

[77] Contribution actions are expressly provided for by SARA § 113(b). SARA § 113(b), CERCLA § 113(f), 42 U.S.C. § 9613(f), ELR Stat. 44041.

educate not only his own client, but also other PRPs, on the merits of cooperation as early as possible.

Once the client, the other PRPs, and EPA or the state are on the road to an understanding of the facts through the RI/FS, the Superfund practitioner will need to explore the aids to settlement authorized in SARA. These include mixed funding,[78] a request to EPA to give the parties its Nonbinding Preliminary Allocation of Responsibility (NPAR),[79] de minimis settlements with minor parties,[80] and possibly a covenant not to sue, though SARA greatly limits EPA's discretion with respect to the last.[81]

As a result of SARA, settlement will usually take the form of a consent decree.[82] The state in which the site is located and the public will be invited to comment.[83] The client's attention should be drawn to the fact that SARA requires a provision in the decree allowing fines of up to $25,000 a day for its violation.[84] The statute also provides penalties of up to $75,000 per day for the second and subsequent violations.[85] These penalties can be significant, particularly if there is a breakdown of PRP cooperation under consent decrees.

The greatly increased role given by SARA to states and the public will be an important new factor in Superfund cases. Not only must EPA be satisfied with the remedy selected, but input from these groups must be considered as well. And SARA authorizes EPA to provide $50,000 technical assistance grants from the Fund to community groups to aid their scrutiny of cleanup decisions.[86] Practitioners also should anticipate increased media attention on

---

[78] SARA § 122(a)authorizes EPA to agree to mixed funding settlements where the agency reimburses PRPs for tasks they have agreed to perform, but not to pay for. SARA § 122(a), CERCLA § 122(b)(1), 42 U.S.C. § 9622(b)(1), ELR Stat. 44058. This provision is designated to facilitate settlements where some responsible parties are unknown, insolvent, or refuse to settle. Conference Committee Report at 252.

[79] To encourage agreement on private funding on remedial action after completion of an RI/FS, SARA § 122(a)authorizes EPA to prepare a NPAR and provide it to the parties. SARA § 122(a), CERCLA § 122(e)(3), 42 U.S.C. § 9622(e)(3), ELR Stat. 44060. The NPAR is not admissible as evidence in any proceeding and is not subject to judicial review. The cost of preparing an NPAR is considered a response cost recoverable under § 107.

Assistant Attorrney General Henry Habicht, who handles EPA's Superfund litigation, stated in a recent talk that "[a]lthough performance of an NPAR is within the Administrator's discretion, we expect that such allocations will be prepared for a significant proportion of sites on the NPL, assuming that the parties want such an allocation." F. Henry Habicht II, Superfund Enforcement After Reauthorization: How Much Will the Process Change? (Oct. 23, 1986) (speech given at ALI-ABA Conference on Hazardous Wastes, Superfund, and Toxic Substances, Washington, D.C.).

[80] SARA authorizes EPA to enter into settlements with parties responsible for only a minor portion of response costs at facility, based upon volume and toxicity of waste contributed. SARA § 122(a), CERCLA § 122(g), 42 U.S.C. § 9622(g), ELR Stat. 44061.

[81] SARA § 122(a)authorizes EPA to enter into covenants not to sue with settling parties under certain, narrowly defined circumstances. SARA § 122(a), CERCLA § 122(f), 42 U.S.C. § 9622(f), ELR Stat. 44060. Generally, covenants can only be as effective as the remedy completed is permanent.

[82] SARA § 122(a), CERCLA § 122(c), 42 U.S.C. § 9622(c), ELR Stat. 44058. Subject to certain exceptions, SARA § 122(a)requires settlements with respect to remedial action to be in the form of consent decrees under CERCLA § 106.

[83] SARA §§ 117, 121(a), CERCLA §§ 117, 121(a), 42 U.S.C. §§ 9617, 9621(f), ELR Stat. 44045, 44054.

[84] SARA § 109(c), 42 U.S.C. § 9609, CERCLA § 109, ELR Stat. 44031.

[85] *Id.*

[86] *See* SARA § 117, CERCLA § 117, 42 U.S.C. § 9617, ELR Stat. 44045.

the cleanup process and take steps to ensure that media relations are properly addressed.

The previously mentioned SARA requirement for health assessments at each site on the NPL[87] means that the Superfund practitioner should pay careful attention to this aspect of the proceeding. Health concerns are one of the basic forces behind enactment of SARA.[88] A health assessment indicating a hazard is likely to trigger not only much more expensive cleanup but also toxic tort suits by area residents.[89] Early preparation and participation in this process to the fullest extent possible represent the best approach to this potential problem . . . .

[3] The 1990 National Contingency Plan

Starfield, "THE 1990 NATIONAL CONTINGENCY PLAN—MORE DETAIL AND MORE STRUCTURE, BUT STILL A BALANCING ACT"*

20 Environmental Law Reporter 10222, 10228-10229, 10236-10241 (1990)

Road Map to the CERCLA Site Response Process (Subpart E [of the NCP])

Site Discovery. The process begins with the discovery of a release by one of several possible mechanisms (*e.g.*, notification requirements under CERCLA § 103(a)or (b) or under other laws, a petition from a citizen, etc.). In the case of an emergency (*e.g.*, fire, explosion), a removal action will be taken to stabilize the site.

Removal Assessment. In non-emergency situations, the release is evaluated to determine if a removal action is appropriate based on a removal preliminary assessment (PA) and, if appropriate, a removal site inspection (SI).

Removal Action. Where necessary to protect human health and the environment, the Agency may initiate a removal action to prevent, mitigate, or minimize the threat posed by the release. This may involve removal of surface drums, fencing of the site, the provision of temporary drinking water supplies, etc. Removals may be emergency actions (taken within hours of discovery), time-critical actions, or non-time-critical actions.

---

87 SARA § 110, CERCLA § 104(i), 42 U.S.C. § 9604(i), ELR Stat. 44017. *See also supra* text accompanying note 20.

88 *See, e.g.*, SARA § 104(a), CERCLA § 104(a)(1), 42 U.S.C. § 9604(a)(1), ELR Stat. 44011. This section inserts a directive requiring that "the President shall give primary attention to those releases which the President deems may present a public health threat."

89 The toxic waste episode at Woburn, Massachusetts, with its extensive private damage claims, was as much a factor in congressional thinking about SARA as Love Canal was to CERCLA. *See* 132 Cong. Rec. S14932 (daily ed. Oct. 3, 1986) (statement of Sen. Kennedy (D. Mass.)).

Remedial Site Evaluations. A remedial PA (and SI, where appropriate) is conducted on all sites in the CERCLA Information System database (CERCLIS), to see if the site is a priority for long-term remedial response. These evaluations involve the collection of data for scoring the site under the hazard ranking system (HRS) model; sites scoring above the threshold in the HRS are placed on the national priorities list (NPL) for further evaluation and possible remedial action.

Remedial Priorities. The Agency evaluates releases for inclusion on the NPL based on the HRS score or one of the other methods for listing outlined in the NCP. The Agency may spend Fund monies for remedial action only at those sites that are on the NPL. ("Fund-financed remedial action" does not include removal action or enforcement action.)

Remedial Investigation/Feasibility Study. The Agency will undertake a remedial investigation and feasibility study (RI/FS) at sites that are, or appear to be, priorities for action (*i.e.*, that are on, or are proposed for listing on, the NPL). The RI/FS, like any other investigation conducted pursuant to CERCLA § 104(b), is a removal action under CERCLA § 101(23), despite the word remedial in its name.

During the RI, the nature and extent of the threat posed by the contamination is studied; concurrently, alternative approaches are developed as part of the FS for responding to and managing the site problem.

Preliminary Remediation Goal. The first step in developing alternatives during the FS is the establishment of a preliminary goal for the remediation of the site. This goal is initially based on readily available information, such as chemical-specific applicable, relevant and appropriate requirements of other environmental laws (ARARs) or the "point of departure" in the range of acceptable risk. Alternatives are then developed that are capable of attaining the preliminary remediation goal. (The goal may be modified as additional information is developed.)

Screening of Remedial Alternatives. A broad list of alternatives is then reviewed and screened, with the more extreme, impracticable options being eliminated before the detailed analysis of alternatives begins. Alternatives may be eliminated during screening based on effectiveness, implementability, or "grossly excessive" cost.

Analysis of Alternatives Using the Nine Criteria. The Agency then conducts a detailed analysis of the remaining alternatives (usually three to nine [of them], depending on the complexity of the problem). The advantages and disadvantages of the alternatives are studied and compared using the following nine remedy selection criteria:[90]

- Overall protection of human health and the environment;
- Compliance with (or waiver of) the ARARs of other laws;
- Long-term effectiveness and permanence;
- Reduction of toxicity, mobility, or volume through treatment;
- Short-term effectiveness;

[90] NCP § 300.430(e)(9).

- Implementability;
- Cost;
- State acceptance; and
- Community acceptance.

Selection of a Remedy. The nine criteria are then used to select the remedy by evaluating them in three functional categories (threshold, balancing, and modifying criteria), in order to reflect the nature and/or timing of their application. The first two criteria—protectiveness and compliance with ARARs—are identified as threshold criteria; only the alternatives that meet those criteria may be carried forward.

Protective, ARAR-compliant alternatives are then "balanced" (*i.e.*, used to evaluate tradeoffs) based on the middle five criteria (and the two modifying criteria, to the extent they are known). The Agency then attempts to select the remedial alternative that "utilizes permanent solutions and treatment . . . to the maximum extent practicable," and is "cost effective" based on a comparison of the appropriate balancing or modifying criteria. Alternatives are judged cost-effective if their costs are "in proportion" to their overall effectiveness; an alternative is found to achieve the maximum permanence and treatment practicable based on a balancing of the seven nonthreshold criteria, with an emphasis on the factors of "long-term effectiveness and permanence" and "reduction in mobility, toxicity or volume through treatment."

EPA and the state then discuss the remedial options and issue a proposed plan, which sets out the lead agency's recommended alternative. Consistent with CERCLA § 117, the public is afforded an opportunity to review and comment on the alternatives studied in the FS and the proposed plan. After review of and response to public comments, and formal consideration of the two modifying criteria (state and community acceptance), the final remedy selection is documented in a record of decision (ROD).

Remedial Design / Remedial Action and Operation and Maintenance. The lead agency then sets about designing, constructing, and implementing the selected remedy. Often, the remedial action plan set out in the ROD will need to be modified in light of information developed during the design phase (*e.g.*, the Agency may learn that more soil is contaminated and needs to be evacuated). If the remedial action to be taken differs "significantly" from the remedy selected in the ROD with respect to scope, performance, or cost, the lead agency will issue an explanation of significant differences (ESD). If the action to be taken "fundamentally alters" the basic features of the remedy selected in the ROD, the lead agency will propose and take comment on a ROD amendment.

Once the remedy is operational and functional (or later, for ground-water restoration remedies), the state undertakes responsibility for funding and carrying out operation and maintenance (O&M) of the remedy.

Deletion from the NPL, Five-Year Review. Once EPA has determined that no further response action is appropriate, the site may be proposed for deletion, or recategorized on the NPL, even where the O&M is continuing. Sites at which hazardous substances remain above levels that allow for unlimited use and unrestricted exposure must be reviewed at least every five years after the initiation of the remedy (not merely after completion), consistent with CERCLA § 121(c).

Major Issues/Changes in the 1990 NCP

ARARs Issues. There were several major changes and statements in the final NCP revisions relating to ARARs, the "applicable" or "relevant and appropriate" requirements of other environmental laws. How CERCLA actions comply with ARARs often determines the cleanup standard at a site or certain parameters that the remedial approach must fulfill. Thus, a discussion of major ARARs issues is an important starting point in a review of the final NCP.

Background. As defined in the final rule, "applicable" requirements are cleanup standards, standards of control, and other substantive environmental protection requirements, criteria, or limitations promulgated under federal environmental or state environmental or facility siting laws that specifically address a hazardous substance, pollutant, contaminant, remedial action, location, or other circumstance found at a CERCLA site.

A "relevant and appropriate" requirement is a *promulgated* standard that, while not applicable to the substance, location, or action, addresses problems or situations sufficiently similar to those encountered at a CERCLA site that its use is well suited to the particular site. One example is where a federal requirement has not been adopted by a state authorized to run the federal program. Such requirement may not be applicable in the state, but it could nevertheless be relevant and appropriate to management of the CERCLA waste at issue. In another example, RCRA waste management requirements may be relevant and appropriate to a CERCLA waste that is similar to a RCRA-listedhazardous waste but is not specifically listed in the RCRA regulations (and thus to which RCRA would not independently "apply").

The concept of requiring remedies to attain relevant and appropriate standards (*i.e.*, standards that do not independently apply as a matter of law) is unique to CERCLA and has generated controversy and confusion. (Indeed, it is somewhat counter-intuitive to be required to comply with requirements that do not apply as a matter of law.) To add some consistency to the process, the final rule offers several factors to consider in determining if a requirement is relevant and appropriate under the circumstances of the release (both findings must be made). However, the notion of what standards are appropriate is, almost by definition, a matter of judgment, subject to case-by-case variations. Thus, the Agency retains considerable discretion in making the ultimate decision of what standards a CERCLA remedy should attain based on potential relevance and appropriateness. (Of course, the decision that a remedy must attain a certain standard may be questioned during the comment period of the ROD.) This discretion is even broader in that the Agency may decide that only certain portions of a requirement are relevant and appropriate. The ability to find that a nonapplicable requirement is not appropriate has limited the instances in which statutory waivers are necessary for relevant and appropriate requirements.

There are four conditions that must be met for a requirement to be considered a potential ARAR, based either on applicability or relevance and appropriateness. First, the requirement must be promulgated (*i.e.*, "of general applicability and enforceable"). Second, it must be a substantive—rather than administrative—requirement. CERCLA actions are required to meet only the procedures set out in the NCP (additional procedures of other laws are met where appropriate, as a matter of policy.) Third, it must be a requirement of an "environmental" law, as provided in CERCLA § 121(d)(2)(A)(i) and (ii); the requirements and procedures of nonenvironmental laws are simply complied with to the extent they apply—they are not considered as part of the ARARs review process under CERCLA. Fourth, ARARs are limited to on-site actions, consistent with CERCLA § 121(d)(2)(A); where EPA sends wastes off site, that waste transfer must comply with the substantive and administrative requirements of applicable law (there would be no relevant and appropriate determination, and no waiver option).

. . . .

ARARs may be chemical-specific (*e.g.*, an established level for a specific chemical in groundwater), action-specific (*e.g.*, a land disposal restriction for RCRA hazardous wastes), or location-specific (*e.g.*, a restriction on actions that adversely affect wetlands). Thus, the concept is much broader than that of a specific cleanup level for a site.

. . . .

State ARARs Issues. The SARA amendments added the requirement that CERCLA remedial actions must comply with applicable or relevant and appropriate requirements of state environmental and facility siting laws (as well as federal environmental laws) where those requirements are promulgated, identified in a timely manner, and more stringent than those under federal law.

One of the most difficult state ARARs issues is the determination of whether legislated goals (*e.g.*, nondegradation standards under state law) constitute substantive requirements such that they should be considered ARARs. State laws setting general goals may be considered substantive ARARs if they are promulgated and enforceable, and "directive in intent," either on their face or through regulations. For example, if a state statute prohibits the degradation of surface water below a defined level, it is directive in nature and may be an ARAR. If a state law sets forth an anti-degradation goal without regulations or direction as to how to achieve it, the Agency must decide whether the goal constitutes an ARAR (*e.g.*, is it enforceable), and then may exercise flexibility in determining how to comply with the goal. In any case, even if a remedial response is found not to comply with a state anti-degradation ARAR during the response, an interim action waiver of the state standard may be appropriate if the ARAR will be satisfied upon completion of the total remedy for the site.

Risk Assessment and Risk Range

The NCP contemplates the use of risk assessments as an integral part of the process for developing remedial alternatives that are protective of human health and the environment.

Risk analysis begins during the early stages of the RI, when a "baseline risk assessment" is performed to evaluate the risk posed by a site in the absence of any remedial action. It is based on a comparison with this no-action risk level that the lead agency will target levels of risk that will be adequately protective of human health for a particular site. The baseline risk assessment also helps to provide justification for performing remedial action at the site.

Concurrently, the lead agency would begin to set a "preliminary remediation goal" as part of the FS. The preliminary remediation goal is an initial statement of the desired endpoint concentration or risk level, and alternatives are developed that are capable of meeting that goal. It is based on readily available information, such as chemical-specific ARARs (*e.g.*, a drinking water standard), concentrations associated with the reference doses or cancer potency factors, or the point of departure for the Agency's acceptable risk range, discussed below. . . .

. . . .

Where environmental effects are observed, EPA sets remediation goals based on environmental ARARs (where they exist) and levels based on a site-specific assessment of what is protective of the environment. For carcinogens, the establishment of an acceptable level of risk in cases where ARARs do not exist (or are not sufficiently protective) is especially sensitive, because such contaminants arguably pose a risk at almost any level of exposure (although that risk may be large or small depending on the amount and duration of the exposure and the type of carcinogen involved). Under the NCP, when remedies cannot entirely eliminate potential exposure to a carcinogen, the Agency may achieve protection of human health by selecting remedies that pose very small risks (*i.e.*, that are within an acceptable range of risk) based on a review of reliable cancer potency information such as EPA's cancer potency factors.

In the proposed NCP, the Agency had defined the acceptable risk range as being from 10-4 to 10-7, meaning that when the excess risk to an individual of contracting cancer due to a lifetime exposure to a certain concentration of a carcinogen falls between approximately 1 in 10,000 and 1 in 10 million, it is judged to be an acceptable exposure.[91] As a measure of additional protection, the proposal provided that there should be a "point of departure" of 10-6, toward the more protective end of the scale, that should be used in setting preliminary remediation goals; if conditions warranted, the final remedy could achieve a level elsewhere within the range.[92]

The final rule maintained the point of departure of 10-6, but narrowed the risk range to 10-4 through 10-6.[93] This action was taken in response to public comment and concerns that the Superfund range went below the accepted *de minimis* level used by other EPA programs and those of other federal agencies. It also reflects the limits of available analytical techniques, which cannot effectively verify for many contaminants that concentration levels corresponding to a risk of 10-6 have actually been attained.

[91] 53 Fed. Reg. 51425-26 (Dec. 21, 1988).

[92] Exposure factors, uncertainty factors, and technical factors may determine where to set remedial action goals within the risk range. *See* 55 Fed. Reg. 51426 (Mar. 8, 1990).

[93] NCP § 300.430(e)(i)(A)(2).

Although this change might appear to be a lessening of protection or a lessening of the Agency's commitment to protect, it is in fact likely to have minimal if any impact on the selection of remedies at Superfund sites for two reasons. First, no CERCLA remedies have selected 10-6 as a cleanup level to date (although one or two may have achieved it due to the efficacy of the technology). Second, the Agency has retained the discretion to select a cleanup level outside the range in appropriate circumstances (*e.g.*, where concerns about sensitive populations, synergistic effects among chemical mixtures, etc., suggest that the remedy should attain a level below 10-6).

The use of a range of acceptable risk is general practice for most government programs. As discussed below in the section on role of cost, it affords the Agency the flexibility to take into account different situations, different kinds of threats, and different kinds of technical remedies. If a single risk level had been adopted (*e.g.*, at the more stringent end of the risk range), fewer alternatives would be expected to pass the protectiveness threshold and qualify for consideration in the balancing phase of the remedy selection process.

. . . .

Role of Cost. The role of cost in remedy selection has been one of the most hotly disputed issues in the Superfund program. Many PRP groups argue that cost must be a major factor in deciding on an appropriate remedy and note that the requirement to select "cost-effective" remedies appears in CERCLA § 121(a) and (b). Many environmentalists and some legislators have argued that cost is given too much emphasis in remedy selection and have posited that cost should be considered only in determining the cost-efficient method for implementing a selected remedy. In effect, they argue that the proper cleanup level for a site should be set, and then a remedy should be selected to attain that level, without consideration of cost.

In the preamble to the final rule, EPA discussed the role of cost at great length. The Agency stated that it agrees that cost should not be considered in setting the protective level in situations where a specific ARAR defines the cleanup level that must be achieved at the site (*e.g.*, where an MCLG (maximum contaminant level goal) above zero is available for contaminants in drinkable groundwater). However, where ARARs are not available for the specific contaminants of concern (or where ARARs are not sufficiently protective), the Agency defines protectiveness in terms of the risk range, and several alternative remedial technologies may be capable of achieving protection within that range. Under such circumstances, cost may be one of the factors to consider in choosing among the available technologies.

It is important to note, however, that cost and other factors may be considered only to distinguish among alternatives that have been found to be protective of human health and the environment and in compliance with ARARs (or to have justified a waiver).

Cost is specifically considered during the final balancing process, as the Agency attempts to satisfy two statutory mandates of CERCLA § 121(b)(1)by identifying the remedial alternative that utilizes "permanent solutions and treatment . . . to the maximum extent practicable" while being cost-effective.

These determinations are intended to be made simultaneously; however, for ease of analysis, they are discussed separately in the NCP.

Cost-Effectiveness. The determination whether a proposed remedial alternative is cost-effective is based on an evaluation of several of the nine criteria. First, overall effectiveness is assessed based on: long-term effectiveness and permanence; reduction of mobility, toxicity, or volume through treatment; and short-term effectiveness. The overall effectiveness is then compared to the cost of the alternative to determine if they are "in proportion" to one another (*i.e.*, does the approach represent a reasonable value for the money?). In making this comparison, the decisionmaker is not directed by the NCP to place special emphasis on the factors of "reduction of toxicity, mobility or volume through treatment" and "long term effectiveness and permanence," as is required during the assessment of permanence and treatment to the maximum extent practicable (as provided in NCP § 300.430(f)(1)(ii)(E)). However, because "effectiveness" is measured based on those two factors (plus short-term effectiveness), an alternative that is high in treatment and permanence will be considered more effective and thus can justify a relatively higher cost (high effectiveness and high cost would be in proportion). The comparison of cost to effectiveness is performed for each alternative individually and for all the alternatives in relation to one another. This latter analysis allows the Agency to identify alternatives that produce an incremental increase in effectiveness for a reasonable increase in cost, based on a comparison of corresponding increases for other alternatives. Several alternatives may be found to be cost-effective.

Although the statute requires EPA to select cost-effective remedies, EPA has decided not to consider cost-effectiveness as a threshold criterion on a par with protectiveness and compliance with ARARs. This is based in part on the fact that unlike the "protectiveness" and "compliance with ARARs" determinations, which can be reached for each alternative individually, the cost effectiveness finding requires a comparison of each alternative in relation to other alternatives and the consideration of several factors during a balancing phase. (The same comment is true of the statutory mandate to utilize permanent solutions and treatment to the maximum extent practicable.) In addition, the preamble to the final rule suggests that reliable information on cost will not be generally available as early in the process as is information on a remedial technology's protectiveness, and thus cost should not be used too early in the final balancing process to eliminate viable alternatives.

Cost and Practicability. The statutory requirement to select the alternative (there is only one) that utilizes permanence and treatment to the maximum extent practicable is fulfilled by selecting the protective, ARAR-complaint alternative that provides the best balance or tradeoffs among alternatives based on a review of all the balancing and modifying criteria (if the latter are known). It is a subjective judgment, but the NCP sets out some parameters to help assure consistency in its application. Specifically, the NCP requires that during the balancing process, the factors of long-term effectiveness and permanence and reduction in toxicity, mobility, or volume should be emphasized, and that the "preference for treatment as a principal element" and the "bias against off-site land disposal of untreated wastes" must be considered.

This statutory determination is the final step in the process before a remedy is recommended in the proposed plan.

Although cost, as one of the nine criteria, is considered in making this determination, it is not expected to play a major role. The importance of almost every other criterion to this determination is emphasized by the NCP.

. . . .

Cost as a Screen. Cost may also be considered during one other aspect of the remedy selection process: screening, when alternatives that are deemed not to be viable are eliminated from more thorough consideration. The use of cost at this early stage, has also been the subject of considerable comment. Many were concerned that cost would be used to screen out appropriate remedial technologies early in the process before they were given a fair evaluation and without the benefit of public review and comment.

The final NCP has been revised to narrow the circumstances under which cost may be considered when screening alternatives at the start of the evaluation process. Specifically, the final rule provides that a given alternative may be eliminated during screening if it is determined that the cost of the alternative is "grossly excessive" compared with its effectiveness. This provision will allow the Agency to avoid the need to conduct resource-intensive analyses of extreme and unrealistic options, while at the same time not allowing cost to compromise consideration of viable options that may simply be more expensive than other alternatives.

. . . .

[4] A Note on Brownfield Programs: To Encourage the Reuse and Redevelopment of Contaminated Sites

A "brownfield" is an industrial site which has either been abandoned or remains undeveloped because its owners and operators fear the uncertainty of liability and the costly burden of environmental cleanups frequently associated with redevelopment. Former industrial sites often show evidence of soil and groundwater contamination, and are prime candidates for federal and state remedial investigations. Prospective purchasers and developers are reluctant to invest in brownfields because they subject themselves to potential cleanup liability merely by entering the chain of title, even if the contamination has been caused by previous owners and operators. Lenders are also reluctant to finance redevelopment of brownfields, and are criticized for "greenlining" or avoiding environmentally risky areas. Secured creditors and government entities which acquire brownfields involuntarily also shy away from redevelopment efforts due to the risk and uncertainty of cleanup liability.

Consequently, brownfields have become virtually unmarketable pieces of real estate in formerly industralized urban neighborhoods, and commercial businesses and industry have fled to the suburbs and rural areas surrounding cities. Industrial ghost towns, characterized by empty lots and silent factories, are also known by the severity of unemployment and economic devastation and loss of the tax base which industrial urban flight has brought about to many surrounding communities. The unremediated presence of soil and groundwater contamination at abandoned brownfields continues to threaten human health and the environment, while the industrialization of suburban and rural neighborhoods creates new environmental risks.

In response to increasing socio-economic and environmental concerns raised by abandoned industrial sites, EPA and several states have adopted "brownfield" programs which encourage the reuse and redevelopment of brownfields. These programs promote brownfield redevelopment by providing technical and economic remedial assistance to redevelopers and prospective purchasers, by limiting liability exposure through agency-initiated covenants not to sue, and by relaxing and streamlining cleanup standards to help reduce transaction costs.

In 1995, EPA launched its own "Brownfields Program" which is intended to be "a common sense, cost-effective way to redevelop contaminated land and return it to productive community use, create jobs and preserve the green areas outside our cities." EPA has announced its intent to fund fifty brownfield projects by providing redevelopment funds of up to $200,000 each, and as of February 1996, EPA had selected forty brownfield pilots. EPA has also lobbied regulated industries to participate in Brownfield programs, and EPA's "Common Sense Initiative" sector groups (CSI) are expected to sponsor select Brownfield pilot programs aimed at achieving "cleaner, cheaper, smarter" environmental protection.

In 1995, EPA also implemented two new "Brownfield" policies. The first policy, known as the "Guidance on Settlements with Prospective Purchasers of Contaminated Property," is EPA's most far-reaching effort to encourage brownfield redevelopment and reuse because it expands EPA's ability to enter into covenants not to sue with prospective purchasers of Superfund sites. The second policy, known as the "Final Policy Toward Owners of Property Containing Contaminated Aquifers," protects owners of property where contaminated water has migrated from off-site sources. If the owner has not contributed in any way to the contamination, EPA will not take enforcement actions against the landowner. Unlike the limited "innocent landowner" defense under CERCLA, the landowner is not required to investigate, contain or remediate the contamination in order to assert a "third-party" defense to CERCLA liability.

Finally, EPA has encouraged the states to develop their own brownfields programs. In February 1995, EPA removed 24,000 of the 38,000 sites listed on the Comprehensive Environmental Response, Compensation and Liability Identification Service (CERCLIS) database, which identifies sites to be evaluated for possible inclusion on the National Priorities List. As of April 1996, EPA had "delisted" 27,000 brownfield sites. In EPA's 1995 Guidance on Prospective Purchaser Agreements, EPA announced that federal enforcement actions at sites undergoing cleanups under state programs would be "extremely unlikely." Through these actions, EPA appears to have implicitly ceded jurisdiction over non-CERCLIS sites to state remediation and brownfield programs.

For in-depth coverage of issues that may arise in a brownfield transaction, see M. B. Gerrard, Brownfields Law and Practice: The Cleanup and

Redevelopment of Contaminated Land (Matthew Bender, 1995). *See also* F. Grad, Treatise on Environmental Law § 4A.02[1][bb].

[5] CERCLA's Definition of "Hazardous Substances"

EAGLE-PICHER INDUSTRIES v. EPA

United States Court of Appeals, District of Columbia Circuit (1985)
759 F.2d 922

STARR, Circuit Judge:

This case calls on us to examine the complex web of "Superfund" legislation passed by Congress in the waning days of 1980. Specifically, we are presented with contentions pressed by certain mining companies and an electric utility that their facilities were improperly included by the Environmental Protection Agency on a nationwide list of priority sites under the Comprehensive Environmental Response, Compensation and Liability Act of 1980. 42 U.S.C. §§ 9601 *et seq.* (1982) ("CERCLA" or "the Act").

CERCLA was designed to address the growing problem of inactive hazardous waste sites throughout the United States. The Act authorizes the Environmental Protection Agency ("EPA") to respond to the release of both "hazardous substances" and those "pollutants or contaminants" the release of which may present "an imminent and substantial danger to the public health or welfare," as those terms are defined in the Act. A response by EPA can be of two kinds: removal, or remedial action. Removal actions involve the actual cleanup of a release. 42 U.S.C. § 9601(23). Remedial actions are those actions consistent with a permanent remedy to prevent or minimize the release of hazardous substances. *Id.* § 9601(24).

To enable EPA to respond to those sites most urgently in need of cleanup, EPA is required under section 105(8)(B), 42 U.S.C. § 9605(8)(B), to compile the National Priorities List ("NPL") of releases or threatened releases throughout the United States. The petitioners in these consolidated cases object to the placement of their respective facilities on the NPL and advance various arguments as to why the EPA's actions were purportedly in error . . . . For the reasons that follow, we deny the petitions for review as to the specific contentions addressed herein.

. . . .

Petitioners first claim that mining wastes and fly ash are not "hazardous substances" within the meaning of CERCLA. The pivotal term "hazardous substance," is defined rather elaborately in section 101(14) of the Act, 42 U.S.C. § 9601(14):

> "[H]azardous substance" means (A) any substance designated pursuant to section 1321(b)(2)(A) of title 33, (B) any element, compound, mixture, solution, or substance designated pursuant to section 9602 of this title, (C) any hazardous waste having the characteristics identified under or listed pursuant to section 3001 of the Solid Waste Disposal Act[42 U.S.C. § 6921] (but not including any waste the regulation of which under the

> Solid Waste Disposal Act [42 U.S.C. § 6901 *et seq.*] has been suspended by Act of Congress), (D) any toxic pollutant listed under section 1317(a) of title 33, (E) any hazardous air pollutant listed under section 112 of the Clean Air Act[42 U.S.C. § 7412], and (F) any imminently hazardous chemical substance or mixture with respect to which the Administrator has taken action pursuant to section 2606 of title 15. The term does not include petroleum, including crude oil or any fraction thereof which is not otherwise specifically listed or designated as a hazardous substance under subparagraphs (A) through (F) of this paragraph, and the term does not include natural gas, natural gas liquids, liquefied natural gas, or synthetic gas usable for fuel (or mixtures of natural gas and such synthetic gas) . . . .

Petitioners ground their claim on the parenthetical clause found in subclause (C) of this complex provision, which expressly refers for its definitional purposes to several other federal statutes. That parenthetical clause applies by its terms to petitioners, inasmuch as both mining wastes and fly ash have been suspended from regulation under the Solid Waste Disposal Act (which includes the subsequently passed statute known as "RCRA"). *See* 42 U.S.C. §§ 6921(3)(A)(i), 6921(3)(A)(ii)(1982). From this exclusion, petitioners draw the conclusion that mining wastes and fly ash are thus excluded as well from CERCLA's definition of "hazardous substances."

Notwithstanding its superficial appeal, petitioners' arguments suffers from a mortal flaw, namely that their interpretation does not comport with the plain meaning of the entire statutory provision. As EPA notes, a substance is a "hazardous substance" within the meaning of CERCLA if it qualifies under *any* of the several subparagraphs of section 101(14). The exception for mining wastes and fly ash is found only in a parenthetical clause in subparagraph (C). The ordinary, straightforward reading of that exception is that it applies only to subparagraph (C), not to any of the other five subparagraphs. Had Congress intended to exempt mining wastes and fly ash from the entirety of section 101(14), it obviously could have placed the exemption at the beginning or end of the section, not in one of the several subparagraphs. Indeed, this is precisely what Congress did do with respect to other specific substances. At the conclusion of section 101(14), a *general exception* from the definition of "hazardous substance" is carved out for petroleum and natural gas products. Had Congress intended to create a similarly broad exception for mining wastes and fly ash, the Legislature readily could have placed that exception alongside the petroleum and natural gas exceptions.

Petitioners argue that such an interpretation must be rejected for two reasons: first, that the interpretation would render meaningless the exception in subparagraph (C), and second, that the legislative history of CERCLA clearly shows that the subparagraph (C) exception was meant to exempt totally such wastes from the term "hazardous substance."

As to the first argument, petitioners observe that EPA labels as "hazardous substances" the mining wastes and fly ash produced by petitioners because those wastes contain substances, such as arsenic, cadmium, and selenium, which are regulated under one or more of the several environmental statutes referred to in section 101(14). Petitioners claim that virtually all mining wastes and fly ash contain at least trace amounts of substances that qualify as "hazardous substances" under one of section 101(14)'s subparagraphs. Thus, they argue, EPA's interpretation would render all or virtually all mining wastes and fly ash CERCLA-covered"hazardous substances," with the effect of denuding the exception in subparagraph (C) of any efficacy whatsoever. Since, petitioners argue, courts should under settled principles reject a proffered statutory interpretation which renders any part of the statute meaningless where a reasonable alternative interpretation exists, we should be constrained to embrace their proposed construction which breathes life into all of CERCLA's definitional provisions.

Unfortunately for petitioners, they have cited nothing in CERCLA, its legislative history, or the record in this case demonstrating that all or virtually all mining wastes and fly ash have constituents which are "hazardous substances." We have nothing more than petitioners' bare assertions on this point. Likewise, petitioners have presented nothing demonstrating that Congress was of the view that all or almost all mining wastes and fly ash contain hazardous substances. It is quite possible that Congress was unconvinced that enough was known about mining wastes and fly ash for EPA to decide that those substances, as a general rule, posed a threat to the environment, but at the same time Congress may have been willing to bring any mining wastes and fly ash found to contain "hazardous substances" within the ambit of section 101(14). Without a showing that Congress believed that the regulation of mining wastes and fly ash under other subparagraphs of section 101(14) would render the exception in subparagraph (C) meaningless, we are disinclined to reject the plain meaning of section 101(14).

NOTES

(1) In certain respects the CERCLA definition of "hazardous substance" is more expansive than the concept of "hazardous waste," within the meaning of RCRA. *See Arizona v. Motorola, Inc.*, 774 F. Supp. 566 (D. Ariz. 1991).

(2) As the principal case mentions, CERCLA contains a "petroleum exclusion" that expressly excludes petroleum from the statutory definition of hazardous substance including "crude oil or any fraction thereof which is not specifically listed or designated as a hazardous substance." 42 U.S.C. § 9601(14), (33). This exclusion has been interpreted to be inapplicable to oil refining wastes that contain PCBs and sulfuric acid, which are not natural subcomponents of crude oil. *United States v. Gurley,* 43 F.3d 1188 (8th Cir. 1994). Similarly, the petroleum exclusion does not apply to jet fuel that contains benzene, toluene and xylene, *State of New York v. United States,* 620 F. Supp. 374 (E.D.N.Y. 1985), or to any separated water and oil accumulated at the bottom of a crude oil storage tank, *Cose v. Getty Oil Co.,* 4 F.3d 700 (9th Cir. 1993). On the other hand, however, the exclusion does apply to leaded gasoline, notwithstanding the fact that lead, standing alone, is a hazardous substance. *Wilshire Westwood Associates v. Atlantic Richfield Corp.,* 881 F.2d 801 (9th Cir. 1988).

[6] EPA's Settlement Procedures as to "De Minimis PRPs"

UNITED STATES v. CANNONS ENGINEERING CORP.

United States District Court for the District of Massachusetts (1989)
720 F. Supp. 1027

WOLF, J.

The United States, the Commonwealth of Massachusetts and the State of New Hampshire ("plaintiffs") brought these three consolidated actions under sections 107(a) and 113 of the Comprehensive Environmental Response, Compensation, and Liability Act ("CERCLA" or "Superfund"), 42 U.S.C. §§ 9607(a) and 9613, and under the applicable laws of Massachusetts and New Hampshire. Plaintiffs seek to recover the costs which they have incurred concerning four hazardous substance disposal sites and to obtain a declaration that the 84 defendants are liable for future environmental response costs at those sites. These defendants include parties who are alleged to be owners or operators of one or more of the sites, or generators or transporters of hazardous substances sent to one or more of the sites. Plaintiffs contend that these defendants are strictly, jointly and severally liable for the costs of cleaning-up each site with which they were involved.

Currently before this court are the plaintiffs' Motions for Entry of Two Partial Consent Decrees as Final Judgments involving 59 defendants. Under the proposed First Partial Consent Decree (the "Major PRP Consent Decree"), 47 settling defendants agree to undertake remedial actions at three of the four sites involved in this case, and to pay $18,855,000 to the United States and the State of New Hampshire to reimburse them for the environmental response costs incurred at two of the four sites. The settling defendants who have signed the Major PRP Consent Decree have agreed to accept the risk of increased costs of cleanup and may be liable for correcting undiscovered conditions at the sites. Approval of the Major PRP Consent Decree, and its entry as a final judgment, is opposed by seven non-settling defendants.

Under the proposed Second Partial Consent Decree (the "De Minimis PRP Consent Decree"), twelve other defendants agree to pay the United States, the Commonwealth of Massachusetts and the State of New Hampshire $792,000 to settle their liability for certain response costs already incurred. The non-settling defendants who oppose the Major PRP Consent Decree have not opposed approval of the De Minimis PRP Consent Decree. However, these non-settling defendants have raised questions about the fairness of the two Consent Decrees as they relate to one another.

MEMORANDUM AND ORDER

Section 122 of CERCLA. . . identifies several types of settlements which the United States may enter into with potentially responsible parties (PRPs) in a CERCLA action. 42 U.S.C. § 9622. Under § 122, the United States generally may enter into a Consent Decree which provides for the PRPs to reimburse the United States for response costs incurred, or under which the

PRPs agree to undertake response activities themselves. In such settlements, the United States may provide the settling parties with a covenant not to sue concerning their liability; however, except in extraordinary circumstances, that covenant will not extend to liability for unknown conditions discovered in the future. *See* 42 U.S.C. § 9622(f); *also see, e.g., Boeing Co. v. Northwest Steel,* No. C89-214M, (W.D. Wash., order of July 24, 1991), discussed at 6 Toxics L.Rep. 340 (1991). Once a settlement has been concluded between a PRP and the United States, that PRP is protected by operation of law from liability to any other PRP who may seek contribution from the settling party. *See* 42 U.S.C. § 9613(f)(2).

Section 122(g) of CERCLA, 42 U.S.C. § 9622(g), establishes special terms on which the United States may settle with *de minimis* PRPs. A *de minimis* PRP is one whose contribution is minimal both in the amount and toxicity of the hazardous substances involved. In such settlements, the United States may provide a complete covenant not to sue for all further liability with respect to the facility. § 9622(g)(2). PRPs who enter into *de minimis* settlements are also entitled to protection against suits for contribution by other PRPs, § 9622(g)(5).

The Administrative *De Minimis* Settlement

In 1987 and 1988, the United States and the States made a settlement proposal under the *de minimis* settlement provisions of § 122(g) to all the PRPs identified as generators of less than one percent of the waste that was sent to the four sites. The offer was based on PRP's "volumetric share"—the ratio of the volume of waste that each *de minimis* PRP sent to each of the four sites to the total amount of wastes sent to each of the four sites. A PRP's volumetric share was then multiplied by the estimated total of response costs for each site. Then, the United States and the States offered to settle with each *de minimis* PRP for 160 percent of its volumetric share of the estimated response costs.

The settlement figure of 160 percent of a PRP's volumetric share consisted of two components: (1) a revenue component equal to 100 percent of a PRP's volumetric share of estimated costs of cleanup of all four sites; and (2) a premium component equal to 60 percent of a PRP's volumetric share to cover any unexpected costs or unknown conditions which may be discovered in remediating the four sites. In return for this premium, the participants in this early settlement received a complete covenant not to sue to recover any additional amounts at a time when the plaintiffs had not completed environmental assessments for cleaning up at the sites and thus had not ascertained the final estimate of response costs at the sites. The settling defendants, therefore, obtained a complete limitation on their liability. The government plaintiffs, through the settlement premium, received a contribution to possible excess cleanup costs for known conditions and to cleanup costs of conditions which may be discovered at the sites in the future. The settling PRPs also paid an administrative charge.

In a cover letter accompanying the initial *de minimis* administrative settlement offer, the United States warned the eligible PRPs that:

> The government is anxious to achieve a high degree of participation in this *de minimis* settlement. Accordingly, the terms contained in this settlement offer are the most favorable terms that the government intends to make available to parties eligible for *de minimis* settlement in this case.

These terms were accepted by 300 PRPs and raised approximately $13,560,000. None of the 300 PRPS who joined these settlements are parties in this case.

The Major PRP Consent Decree

The Major PRP Consent Decree requires the settling parties to perform response actions at the Bridgewater, Plymouth and Londonderry sites, and to make payments with respect to the Plymouth and Nashua sites. More specifically, under this proposed settlement, the settling defendants would perform environmental response work at three sites with an estimated value of $15,940,000, and make payments totaling $18,855,000 to the United States, Massachusetts and New Hampshire. The settling defendants have also agreed to assume plaintiffs' costs of overseeing the defendants' response activities. Moreover, an additional $120,000 would be placed in escrow for use if further response actions are need at the Plymouth site.

In return, the United States, Massachusetts, and New Hampshire have provided a covenant not to sue these parties, qualified by specific re-opener provisions. With respect to response costs at the Bridgewater, Plymouth and Londonderry sites, the United States and the states agree not to sue the settling defendants, except if information or site conditions unknown to the United States at the time of settlement indicate that the remedies provided for by the settlement are not adequate to protect public health and the environment. With respect to the Nashua site, the United States and New Hampshire agree not to sue the settling defendants for response costs, unless plaintiffs spend more than $19,000,000 at that site after January 1, 1988.

Thus, the total liability of the PRPs who have accepted the Major PRP Consent Decree is still uncertain. These PRPs have agreed to accept the risk that the actual costs of cleanup may be higher than currently estimated. They may also be subject to liability for conditions discovered at these sites in the future which are currently unknown.

As indicated earlier, none of the settling parties may be sued for contribution by other PRPs for the subject matters covered by the settlement.§ 113(f)(2) of CERCLA, 42 U.S.C. § 9613(f)(2)

The *De Minimis* PRP Consent Decree

Beginning prior to filing this action, the plaintiffs offered another opportunity to settle to the PRPs who had been eligible to join the administrative *de minimis* settlement, but who had rejected the initial offer. This offer resulted in the *De Minimis* PRP Consent Decree now before the court. As with the administrative settlement, this settlement was offered to parties who had sent less than one percent of the volume of hazardous waste to the sites. § 9622(g).

Under terms of the *De Minimis* PRP Consent Decree, eligible [previously non-settling] PRPs may resolve their liability to the plaintiffs by paying 260 percent of their volumetric share of the estimated costs of the response actions at these sites. This settlement figure incorporated the 160 percent figure used in the earlier administrative settlement, increased by a surcharge of 100 percent of a settling PRP's volumetric share. The surcharge was designed to reward and encourage early settlement in this and other CERCLA cases. The surcharge will also further reduce the amounts sought by the plaintiffs from the major PRPs and the non-settling defendants.

Twelve *de minimis* generator defendants have agreed to the *De Minimis* PRP Consent Decree. Under this consent decree, the settling *de minimis* PRPs agree to pay a total of $792,000 in return for a covenant not to sue these defendants for response costs with respect to these sites. [They] are protected against suits for contribution brought by other PRPs.

Status of Non-Settling Defendants

Approval of the two pending proposed consent decrees, along with the prior administrative settlements, would resolve the claims of the United States, Massachusetts, and New Hampshire against 359 PRPs and result in a recovery, including the value of PRP performance and cash payments, with an estimated value of $48,000,000. The precise value of these settlements cannot be ascertained because the actual costs of cleanup for the Bridgewater and Londonderry sites cannot be determined until the agreed-upon remedies are implemented by the settling defendants and until it is determined whether the major PRPs will have financial responsibility for correcting any conditions which are now unknown.

Not all of the money previously spent at the four sites by plaintiffs would be recovered as a result of the settlements now proposed. The United States, Massachusetts and New Hampshire seek to recover the remainder of their past costs incurred from the 25 non-settling defendants in this action and to obtain a declaratory judgment against those defendants to establish their liability for future costs that are not covered by the re-opener provisions of the Major PRP Consent Decree.

. . . .

The Merits of the Proposed Consent Decrees: Standard of Review

Approval of a proposed consent decree is committed to the discretion of the district court. This discretion is to be exercised in light of the strong policy in favor of voluntary settlement of litigation. The presumption in favor of settlement is particularly strong where a consent decree has been negotiated by the Department of Justice on behalf of a federal administrative agency "specially equipped, trained or oriented in the field . . . ." EPA is such an agency.

In order to approve a consent decree, the court must determine that the settlement is fair, reasonable, and consistent with the Constitution and the mandate of Congress. Protection of the public interest is the key consideration in assessing these factors.

. . . .

In the instant case, the non-settling defendants challenged the Major PRP Consent Decree only on the basis of fairness and do not oppose approval of the *De Minimis* PRP Consent Decree. Nevertheless, the court must determine that each proposed consent decree conforms to all legal requirements and is reasonable.

. . . .

Fairness

In evaluating the fairness of a proposed consent decree, a court should examine both the procedural and substantive aspects of the decree. *See U.S. v. Hooker Chemical & Plastics Corp.*, 607 F. Supp. 1052, 1057 (W.D. N.Y.), *aff'd,* 776 F.2d 410 (2d Cir. 1985) (in determining whether the settlement is fair, court should look to factors such as "the good faith efforts of the negotiators, the opinions of counsel, and the possible risks involved in litigation if the settlement is not approved"). Fairness should be examined from the standpoint of signatories and non-parties to the decree. The effect on non-settlers should be considered, but is not determinative in the court's evaluation.

. . . .

Allocation of Costs Between Major and *De Minimis* Parties

The non-settling defendants argue that the court should not approve the Major PRP Consent Decree because it ignores the comparative fault of the various defendants by favoring the major PRPs.

Specifically, the non-settling defendants object to the 60 percent premium in the administrative *de minimis* settlement as allegedly being beyond any conceivable calculation of unforeseen costs. They also argue that the proposed *De Minimis* PRP Consent Decree, which charges a 100 percent penalty in addition to the 60 percent premium, constitutes a windfall to the major PRPs because the amount the *de minimis* generators will pay in excess of their volumetric shares will reduce the amount of the major PRPs' liability. Instead, the non-settling defendants seem to be arguing that liability should be based strictly on volumetric share.

The existence of different types of settlements in a single CERCLA action is not necessarily unfair. *See Seymour Recycling,* 554 F. Supp. at 1339. In *Seymour Recycling,* as in the instant case, there were two groups of defendants. One group agreed under a consent decree to undertake some of the remedial actions necessary at the site. Another group was settling on a "cash-out" basis and receiving a covenant not to sue. The court found nothing unfair in the United States' decision to structure the two settlements in different ways and to make separate settlement offers to different parties. As the court stated:

> While in total the sum being asked from those who are not a party to the Consent Decree is greater than the sum being paid by the 24 who are parties to the Decree, this does not render the government's approach unfair to any parties. Those who are parties to the Consent Decree took upon themselves the obligation to hire the subcontractor and to develop a work proposal by which the surface cleanup is to be completed without management (but with monitoring) by the United States and without respect to cost. Those companies who are not parties to the Decree have a number of choices. They may accept the government's offer for a cash settlement in return for a covenant not to sue; they may try to form a group of their own . . . .or they may choose to litigate with the United States . . . .

554 F. Supp. at 1339. *See also Acushner River & New Bedford Harbor: Proceedings re Alleged PCB Pollution,* 712 F. Supp. 1019, 1032 (D. Mass. 1989) ("Nor must this court ensure that the settlement is perfectly calibrated in terms of shares of liability so long as it is generally fair and reasonable").

In the instant case, the non-settling defendants' preoccupation with volumetric share is mistaken. In fact, neither Consent Decree is necessarily more attractive than the other. Comparing the settlements solely by volumetric calculation, as the non-settling defendants do, ignores the open-ended nature of the settling major PRPs' commitments under the Major PRP Consent Decree. The settlement contained in the Major PRP Consent Decree is based on requiring a group of parties to be jointly and severally liable for performance of the remedies to the plaintiffs' satisfaction at the Bridgewater, Plymouth and Londonderry sites,[94] as well as paying $17,920,000 toward the cleanup of the Nashua site and an additional $935,000 at the Plymouth site. Actual costs to the major PRPs cannot be ascertained until the cleanups are completed.[95] Remedial work at the Bridgewater and Londonderry sites has not even begun. The settling major PRPs have assumed the risk of encountering unknown environmental conditions or that the plaintiffs will require them to underake additional cleanup activities which may further drive up the costs.[96] In addition, they run the risk of future transaction and litigation costs if disputes arise as to the re-opener terms of the Major PRP Consent Decree.

[94] The Major PRP Consent Decree involves a settlement offer made collectively to a group, which could only have been accepted by the group as a whole, or by substantially all of the members of the group. Unlike the *de minimis* settlements, each settling party's share of the "mega-settlement" was not calculated by the plaintiffs. Rather, the settling parties agreed under para. 25 of the Major PRP Consent Decree to be jointly and severally liable for the total obligation of performing the work and making the payments, and entered into separate agreements among themselves as to how they would allocate the costs.

[95] This uncertainty in future costs is demonstrated by information submitted to the court since the May 9, 1989 hearing which indicates that the expected value of future costs at the Nashua site—the most advanced of the four clean-up efforts—has increased from $12.13 to $13.77 million.

[96] For example, at the Londonderry site the settling parties agreed to meet specified remediation goals concerning the soil and groundwater. They will have to pay for moving soil and pumping groundwater until those goals are met, regardless of the length of time it takes or the cost. They will also have to pay the cost of EPA's and New Hampshire's overseeing the project. They may have to pay stipulated penalties if their performance is delinquent, and EPA and New Hampshire retain the right to impose additional, and more costly, cleanup obligations if the performance standards are not achieved or if human health and

By contrast, under the *de minimis* settlement structure, contained in the initial administrative settlements and in the *De Minimis* PRP Consent Decree, eligible parties have an opportunity to obtain final resolution of liability in this case at a definite cost, which caps their exposure and saves them the cost of continued litigation.

. . . .

In view of the risks the major PRPs are continuing to assume, the 60 percent premium in the *de minimis* settlements is within the range of being fair and reasonable in order to cover unexpected costs or unknown conditions found at the sites. Indeed, plaintiffs and several major PRPs assert that during settlement negotiations some major PRPs objected that the United States and the States had charged a premium that was too low and made the settlement offer to too many parties.

The non-settling defendants point out that the uncertainty concerning costs could have been reduced if the plaintiffs had waited longer before making the initial administrative settlement offer. However, although the plaintiffs' costs estimates have increased since the time of the original *de minimis* settlement offer, final costs will not be established for many years. The prompt offer of settlement to *de minimis* parties was clearly intended by Congress when it enacted § 122(g). In this case, the plaintiffs accepted the recommendation of the *De Minimis* Subcommittee of the Cannons Steering Committee to offer a *de minimis* settlement to 300 *de minimis* parties as quickly as possible. This recommendation of prompt settlement reflects the strong view of most of the *de minimis* parties that finality in this case is extremely valuable and well worth the 60 percent premium. It would have been unfair to delay an administrative settlement that is consistent with congressional intent when 300 other *de minimis* parties wanted the plaintiffs to consummate that settlement expeditiously.

The 100 percent penalty under the *De Minimis* PRP Consent Decree is not unfair and certainly was not unforeseeable. As indicated earlier, in the cover letter accompanying the initial *de minimis* administrative settlement offer, the United States warned the eligible parties:

> The government is anxious to achieve a high degree of participation in this *de minimis* settlement. Accordingly, *the terms contained in this settlement offer are the most favorable terms that the government intends to make available to parties eligible for de minimis settlement in this case.* (Emphasis added.)

This warning was included to advise eligible *de minimis* parties that if they decided to reject the initial *de minimis* offer, they would face risks, particularly the risks of more costly settlements or joint and several liability. The plaintiffs point out that without such an incentive, few eligible parties would have accepted the administrative settlement. Although it is difficult to assess this

the environment are not adequately protected. The settling parties also agree to indemnify the governments against claims by third parties and assure that their contractors carry insurance. Instead of obtaining finality, these parties have undertaken risk. By contrast, the parties who joined the *de minimis* settlements have no obligation except to pay a specified sum and are protected from claims for future costs.

contention empirically, 300 *de minimis* parties evaluated the risks, determined the initial offer was fair, and accepted the settlement. In addition, 12 more *de minimis* generators have accepted the terms of the *De Minimis* PRP Consent Decree. The fact that a meaningful number of parties similarly situated to those who now object have agreed to the *De Minimis* PRP Consent Decree is added evidence of its fairness.

NOTES AND QUESTIONS

(1) The principal case typifies the approach that EPA has taken with respect to minor contributors of wastes at Superfund sites. The 1986 amendments encourage EPA settlements with those parties "whenever practicable and in the public interest." The Agency has acted in consonance with that Congressional guidance, while maintaining that its settlement obligations with respect to *de minimis* parties is essentially discretionary. *See* CERCLA § 122(g), 42 U.S.C. § 9622(g); U.S. Environmental Protection Agency, "Guidance on Settlement With *De Minimis* Waste Contributors Under CERCLA," 52 Fed. Reg. 24334 (1987). EPA's *de minimis* settlement policies also apply to property owners who did not have knowledge of the presence of hazardous substances on their property and did not contribute to the release of such substances. Under those policies, to be eligible for *de minimis* treatment, such landowners must exercise due care with respect to hazardous substances at the site. They must also allow EPA access to their property, and provide the Agency full cooperation as it implements response activities. *See* CERCLA § 122(g), 42 U.S.C. § 9622(g)(1)(B); EPA Guidance on Landowner Liability Under Section 170(a)(1) and *De Minimis* Settlements Under Section 122(g)(1)(B) of CERCLA and Settlements With Prospective Purchasers of Contaminated Property, June 6, 1989.

(2) Generally, as the *Cannons Engineering* case illustrates, courts tend to favor the voluntary settlement of disputes between defendants and government agencies in environmental cases, including but not limited to CERCLA matters. This policy can pose significant obstacles to third parties who seek to challenge the terms of environmental consent decrees. Is that appropriate?

(3) Another view of the judicial role in reviewing environmental consent decrees was stated by the U.S. District Court in *Kelley v. Thomas Solvent Co.*, 717 F. Supp. 507 (W.D. Mich. 1989):

> Review of a consent decree is committed to the informed discretion of the trial court. In its exercise of discretion, the trial court should consider the strong policy favoring voluntary settlement of litigation. The consent decree—as a judicial act—requires court approval. It may approve or reject the consent decree and, although it may suggest modifications, it can only approve or reject the consent decree. The controlling criterion is not what might have been agreed upon or what the court believes might have been the optimal settlement. Yet, the court must "eschew any rubber stamp approval" in favor of an independent evaluation. At the same time, a court must avoid the detailed investigation required if the parties were actually trying the case.

Does this reflect sound policy?

(4) Under the 1986 amendments to Superfund, EPA was given authority to assign non-binding allocations of responsibility (NBARs) among PRPs at the hazardous waste sites as a means of encouraging PRPs to develop settlement offers that allocate site clean-up costs among themselves in a fair and equitable way. *See* CERCLA § 122(e)(3), 42 U.S.C. § 9622(e)(3). The Agency has used this authority very sparingly, however.

The amendments also granted EPA discretion to enter into partial consent decrees, to use Superfund to pay "orphan shares" of hazardous waste site cleanups, and to finance certain other portions of site cleanup costs under so-called "mixed funding agreements." *See* CERCLA § 122(a) and (b); 42 U.S.C. § 9622(a) and (b). To what extent is it in the government's interest, and that of the public, for the EPA to employ these tools?

[7] CERCLA's Liability Standard

UNITED STATES v. CHEM-DYNE CORP.

United States District Court, Southern District of Ohio (1983)
572 F. Supp. 802

CARL B. RUBIN, Chief Judge.

. . . In order to expedite discovery and trial preparation, the defendants have moved for an early determination that they are not jointly and severally liable for the clean-up costs at Chem-Dyne.

A. Statutory Construction

. . . .

The liability section lists the classes of persons potentially liable under the Act for the costs incurred by government removal or remedial action. In contrast to plaintiff's assertion that joint and several liability is clear from the express statutory language, the Court finds the language ambiguous with regard to the scope of liability. Consequently, in an attempt to discern the Congressional intent, the Court will review and weigh the legislative history of the Act.

. . . .

As background, two different superfund bills proceeded simultaneously through the House and Senate. On November 24, 1980, the Senate made its final amendment to its bill, thereby eliminating the term strict, joint and several liability from its provisions. Subsequently, on December 3, 1980, the House struck the language in its bill and substituted the language of the Senate bill, which was later enacted. The defendants quote at length from Senator Helms' speech:

> Retention of joint and several liability in S. 1480 received intense and well-deserved criticism from a number of sources, since it could impose financial responsibility for massive costs and damages awards on persons who contributed only minimally (if at all) to a release or injury. Joint and

> several liability for costs and damages was especially pernicious in S. 1480, not only because of the exceedingly broad categories of persons subject to liability and the wide array of damages available, but also because it was coupled with an industry-based fund. Those contributing to the fund will frequently be paying for conditions they had no responsibility in creating or even contributing to. To adopt a joint and several liability scheme on top of this would have been grossly unfair.
>
> The drafters of the Stafford-Randolph substitute have recognized this unfairness, and the lack of wisdom in eliminating any meaningful link between culpable conduct and financial responsibility. Consequently, all references to joint and several liability in the bill have been deleted . . . .
>
> It is very clear from the language of the Stafford-Randolph substitute itself, from the legislative history, and from the liability provisions of section 311 of the Federal Water Pollution Control Act,that now the Stafford-Randolph bill does not in and of itself create joint and several liability.

This view of statutory construction is at odds with the guidelines provided by the Supreme Court. Senator Helms was an opponent of the bill. Accordingly, his statements are entitled to little weight in construing the statute.

Senator Stafford, sponsor of the bill, succinctly noted that there was an elimination of the term joint and several liability as well as an elimination of the scope of liability. Senator Randolph, sponsor, explained the significance of these modifications:

> We have kept strict liability in the compromise, specifying the standard of liability under section 311 of the Clean Water Act,but we have deleted any reference to joint and several liability, relying on common law principles to determine when parties should be severally liable . . . . The changes were made in recognition of the difficulty in prescribing in statutory terms liability standards which will be applicable in individual cases. The changes do not reflect a rejection of the standards in the earlier bill.
>
> . . . .
>
> It is intended that issues of liability not resolved by this act, if any, shall be governed by traditional and evolving principles of common law. An example is joint and several liability. Any reference to these terms has been deleted, and the liability of joint tortfeasors will be determined under common or previous statutory law.

. . . .

Statements of the legislation's sponsors are properly accorded substantial weight in interpreting the statute, although the remarks of a single legislator are not controlling. The fact that the term joint and several liability was deleted from a prior draft of the bill or that the term liability refers to the standard under 33 U.S.C. § 1321, in and of itself, is not dispositive of the scope of liability under CERCLA. Perhaps in other contexts, when Congress deletes certain language it "strongly militates against a judgment that Congress intended a result that it expressly declined to enact." This case, however, presents an exceptional situation. A reading of the entire legislative history in context reveals that the scope of liability and term joint and several liability were deleted to avoid a mandatory legislative standard applicable in all situations which might produce inequitable results in some cases. The deletion was not intended as a rejection of joint and several liability. Rather, the term was omitted in order to have the scope of liability determined under common law principles, where a court performing a case by case evaluation of the complex factual scenarios associated with multiple-generator waste sites will assess the propriety of applying joint and several liability on an individual basis.

B. Scope of Liability

Because the legislative history evinces the intent that the scope of liability under CERCLA, 42U.S.C. § 9607, be determined from traditional and evolving principles of common law, the next issue becomes whether state or federal common law should be applied. In situations where, as here, there is a lack of an express statutory provision selecting state or federal law, the inevitable incompleteness presented by all legislation means that interstitial federal lawmaking is a basic responsibility of the federal courts . . . .

State law as a rule of decision is not mandated under the Erie doctrine in this case because it falls within the exception provided for federal laws. 28 U.S.C. § 1652; *Erie v. Thompson*, 304 U.S. 64 (1938). Although *Erie* eliminated the power of federal courts to create federal general common law, the power to fashion federal specialized common law remains untouched when it is "necessary to protect uniquely federal interests."

The improper disposal or release of hazardous substances is an enormous and complex problem of national magnitude involving uniquely federal interests. Typically, an abandoned waste site will consist of waste produced by companies in several states within the area or region. The pollution of land, groundwater, surface water and air as a consequence of this dumping presents potentially interstate problems. A driving force toward the development of CERCLA was the recognition that a response to this pervasive condition at the state level was generally inadequate.

. . . .

Additionally, the superfund monies expended, for which the United States seeks reimbursement, are funded by general revenues and excise taxes. The degree to which the United States will be able to protect its financial interest in the trust fund is directly related to the scope of liability under CERCLA and is in no way dependent upon the laws of any state. When the United States derives its authority for reimbursement from the specific Act of Congress passed in the exercise of a constitutional function or power, its rights should also derive from federal common law.

. . . .

In conclusion, the rights, liabilities and responsibilities of the United States under 42 U.S.C. § 9607are governed by a federal rule of decision.

The question now becomes whether the scope of liability should be interpreted according to the incorporated state law of the forum state or a federally created uniform law. This determination is a matter of judicial policy dependent upon a variety of considerations relevant to the nature of the specific governmental interests and to the effects upon them of applying state law. Federal programs that by their nature are and must be uniform in character throughout the nation necessitate the formulation of federal rules of decision. CERCLA is such a federal program. . . . . A liability standard which varies in the different forum states would undermine the policies of the statute by encouraging illegal dumping in states with lax liability laws. There is no good reason why the United States' right to reimbursement should be subjected to the needless uncertainty and subsequent delay occasioned by diversified local disposition when this matter is appropriate for uniform national treatment.

Finding, then, that the delineation of a uniform federal rule of decision is consistent with the legislative history and policies of CERCLA and finding further that no compelling local interests mandate the incorporation of state law, a determination of the content of the federal rule is the final step in the analysis.

. . . .

Typically, as in this case, there will be numerous hazardous substance generators or transporters who have disposed of wastes at a particular site. The term joint and several liability was deleted from the express language of the statute in order to avoid its universal application to inappropriate circumstances. An examination of the common law reveals that when two or more persons acting independently caused a distinct or single harm for which there is a reasonable basis for division according to the contribution of each, each is subject to liability only for the portion of the total harm that he has himself caused. Restatement (Second) of Torts, §§ 433A, 881 (1976); Prosser, Law of Torts (4th ed. 1971), pp. 313-314. But where two or more persons cause a single and indivisible harm, each is subject to liability for the entire harm. Furthermore, where the conduct of two or more persons liable under § 9607 has combined to violate the statute, and one or more of the defendants seeks to limit his liability on the ground that the entire harm is capable of apportionment, the burden of proof as to apportionment is upon each defendant. These rules clearly enumerate the analysis to be undertaken when applying 42 U.S.C. § 9607 and are most likely to advance the legislative policies and objectives of the Act.

C. Summary Judgment

. . . .

The question of whether the defendants are jointly or severally liable for the clean-up costs turns on a fairly complex factual determination. Read in the light most favorable to the plaintiff, the following facts illustrate the nature of the problem. The Chem-Dyne facility contains a variety of hazardous waste from 289 generators or transporters, consisting of about 608,000 pounds of material. Some of the wastes have commingled but the identities of the sources of these wastes remain unascertained. The fact of the mixing of the wastes raises an issue as to the divisibility of the harm. Further, a dispute exists over which of the wastes have contaminated the ground water, the degree of their migration and concomitant health hazard. Finally, the volume of waste of a particular generator is not an accurate predictor of the risk associated with waste because the toxicity or migratory potential of a particular hazardous substance generally varies independently with the volume of the waste.

Because there are genuine issues of material fact concerning the divisibility of the harm and any potential apportionment, the defendants are not entitled to judgment as a matter of law.

NOTES AND QUESTIONS

(1) *Chem-Dyne* was a critical case that established the applicability of joint and several liability in Superfund cases. Do you concur in the approach taken by the court? What effect do you think the possibility of joint and several PRP liability will have on settlement negotiations, in CERCLA matters, between PRP defendants and government entities?

(2) In the aftermath of the *Chem-Dyne* decision, quite a few other federal courts agreed with the notion that CERCLA imposes joint and several liability on PRPs. *See, e.g.*, *O'Neil v. Picillo,* 883 F.2d 176 (1st Cir. 1989); *United States v. A. and F. Material Co.,* 578 F. Supp. 1249 (S.D. Ill. 1984); *United States v. R.W. Meyer, Inc.,* 889 F.2d 1497 (6th Cir. 1989); *United States v. Stringfellow,* 661 F. Supp. 1053 (C.D. Cal. 1987); *United States v. Northernaire Plating Co.,* 670 F. Supp. 742 (W.D. Mich. 1987); *United States v. South Carolina Recycling and Disposal, Inc.,* 653 F. Supp. 984 (D.S.C. 1986). For a general overview of these opinions *see* F. Grad, Treatise on Environmental Law § 4A.02[1][g][i].

UNITED STATES v. REILLY TAR & CHEMICAL CORP.

United States District Court, District of Minnesota (1982)
546 F. Supp. 1100

MAGNUSON, J.

. . . .

In 1917, Reilly Tar, an Indiana Corporation, began to operate a plant in St. Louis Park, Minnesota where it refined coal tar into creosote oil and other products, and treated wood products with creosote oil and other preservatives. For fifty-four years, until the plant ceased operations in 1972, Reilly Tar generated chemical wastes which were handled, stored, treated and disposed of at the Reilly Tar site.

In June 1973, the City of St. Louis Park purchased the Reilly Tar site and transferred its ownership to the Housing and Redevelopment Authority of St. Louis Park, a municipal corporation incorporated under the laws of Minnesota. From May 1978 through January 1980, defendants Oak Park Village

Associates, Rustic Oaks Condominium, Inc., and Philip's Investment Co. purchased part of the Reilly Tar site from the Housing and Redevelopment Authority. TCF Service Corporation is the successor in interest to Rustic Oaks Condominium, Inc. The United States and State of Minnesota named these entities as defendants only to insure that the remedial measures they seek can be fully implemented.

. . . .

Plaintiffs . . . allege that Reilly Tar spilled, leaked and discharged chemical wastes generated at the Reilly Tar site directly into the ground there, and that the wastes are in the ground at and surrounding the site. These chemicals have leached and migrated into the groundwater beneath and surrounding the site and will continue to do so.

The groundwater beneath the Reilly Tar site is part of a system of several aquifers which supplies water to St. Louis Park and other parts of the Minneapolis-St. Paul Metropolitan area. Many industrial and drinking water wells have been drilled into the aquifers. Inadequate groutings and casings in some of the wells permit further migration of the chemicals between the aquifers. One well at the Reilly Tar site is 909 feet deep, and is plugged with coal tar at a depth of approximately 590 feet.

St. Louis Park and Hopkins, as well as other municipalities, obtain drinking water for their residents from the system of aquifers extending beneath the Reilly Tar site. During 1978 and 1979, St. Louis Park closed five drinking water wells because the water was contaminated with chemicals from the Reilly Tar plant. In 1981, Hopkins closed a drinking water well for the same reason. Chemicals from the Reilly Tar operation have contaminated the groundwater in one aquifer at least two miles north of the site, and in another at least one and one-half miles east and southeast of the site. Unless preventive measures are taken, leaching and migration of groundwater will continue to move the chemicals from the Reilly Tar site through the aquifers and into the drinking water for the Minneapolis-St. Paul metropolitan area.

. . . .

The State, Hopkins, and St. Louis Park each allege that they have incurred substantial expenses because of Reilly Tar's conduct; that their costs and actions were consistent with the national contingency plan; that they have presented their claims to Reilly Tar under 42 U.S.C. § 9612(a)(Supp. IV 1980); and that Reilly Tar has denied liability and taken no action to satisfy their claims.

The United States alleges that since the passage of CERCLA, it has incurred and will continue to incur response costs in responding to the hazard created by the release and threatened release of hazardous substances from the site. It also alleges that Reilly Tar is liable to it for such costs.

Section 7003 of the Resource Conservation and Recovery Act(RCRA)

All plaintiffs have brought claims against Reilly Tar under Section 7003 of the Resource Conservation and Recovery Act of 1976. . . .

. . . .

Section 7003 is one of the several imminent hazard provisions that Congress has included in environmental statutes. *See* Section 1431 of the Safe Drinking Water Act, 42 U.S.C. § 3001(a); Section 504(a) of the Clean Water Act, 33 U.S.C. § 1364(a)(Supp. IV 1980); Section 303 of the Clean Air Act, 42 U.S.C. § 7603(Supp. IV 1980); Section 106(a) of the Comprehensive Environmental Response, Compensation and Liability Act, 42 U.S.C. § 9606(Supp. IV 1980). Congress broadly drafted these provisions to give appropriate government officials the right to seek judicial relief, or take other appropriate action to avert imminent and substantial threats to the environment or public health. *United States v. Price*, 523 F. Supp. 1053, 1070 (D.N.J. 1981).

Reilly Tar seeks dismissal of the section 7003 claims primarily on three grounds. First, it contends that section 7003 is jurisdictional only and provides no substantive standards for determining liability. *United States v. Midwest Solvent Recovery, Inc.*, 484 F. Supp. 138, 143 (N.D. Ind. 1980); *United States v. Ottati and Goss, Inc.* (D.N.H. Oct. 20, 1980). Liability under the statute, it argues, must be based on the federal common law of nuisance, which applies only to pollution having interstate effects. *Reserve Mining Company v. Environmental Protection Agency*, 514 F.2d 492, 520-522 (8th Cir. 1975). No interstate effects having been alleged in this case, Reilly Tar contends the section 7003 claim must be dismissed.

Not all courts have accepted the argument that section 7003 is jurisdictional only, and of those that have accepted the argument, some refuse to limit section 7003 to groundwater pollution having interstate effects. *United States v. Solvents Recovery Service of New England*, 496 F. Supp. 1127, 1135-38 (D. Conn. 1980). Congress did not intend to restrict section 7003 to the rare instance where groundwater pollution caused by hazardous waste disposal crosses state lines. Conditioning a section 7003 claim on an allegation of interstate effect would be inconsistent with the character of the pollution which is the target of the statute and incompatible with the nature and extent of the federal concern embodied in RCRA. Section 7003 requires the Administrator to give notice of the suit to "the affected State." Use of the singular "State" implies that Congress did not intend to limit the statute to imminent and substantial endangerments involving two or more states. The statute neither states nor implies that it is applicable only when the hazardous wastes have crossed state lines, and the Court will not so limit it.

Second, Reilly Tar asserts that section 7003 is limited to injunctive actions to restrain ongoing activities, and because it ceased operations in 1972 there is nothing to enjoin. It also contends the statue was not meant to apply to prior owners of inactive sites.

Although Reilly Tar no longer engages in ongoing activities at the site, this is no basis for dismissing the action. Other courts have held that a complaint based upon section 7003 need not contain an allegation of ongoing acts or disposal. *United States v. Solvents Recovery Service of New England*, 496 F. Supp. at 1139-41. The statute is aimed at the prevention or amelioration of harmful conditions, rather than the cessation of any particular human conduct. . . .

Nevertheless, there is some strength to Reilly Tar's argument that section 7003 cannot be invoked against *prior owners* of inactive sites. The section permits suits to "immediately restrain any person *contributing* to such handling or disposal to stop such handling . . . or disposal or to take such other action as may be necessary . . . " (emphasis added). It appears to apply only to persons "contributing to" the condition causing the endangerment. The use of the present tense suggests that the statute affects only those whose present conduct contributes to the threat. Reilly Tar, having sold the property ten years ago, no longer has control of its condition and does not appear to be, through its action or inaction, a person contributing to the condition giving rise to the endangerment; thus, it does not at first glance seem to be within the class of persons against whom the statute may be invoked.

The court, however, is not interpreting section 7003 in a vacuum and it cannot ignore constructions of the statute by other courts. On strikingly similar facts, the court in *United States v. Price*, 523 F. Supp. at 1072-73, held that section 7003 applied to the prior owner of a site whose waste disposal practices in the early 1970s caused present day groundwater contamination. Counsel for Reilly Tar conceded at the hearing that Price is indistinguishable. There the court said:

> We conclude that their sale of the property did not relieve them of their accountability under the statute. We reach this conclusion, in large part, because the actions and inaction of the Price defendants are the primary cause of the hazardous situation that now exists. Although the current owners of the property may well also have a duty to prevent the continued disposal of contaminants from the landfill, it would be inequitable to require them to bear the entire burden of a situation that was largely caused by others. *See Vertac Chem. Corp., supra,* 489 F. Supp. [870] at 877. More importantly, society's interests in deterring the improper disposal of hazardous wastes and in alleviating serious hazards as quickly as possible mandate that those responsible for the disposal of such wastes not be able to shirk their statutory responsibilities by simply selling the property on which the wastes are stored.
>
> Our conclusion that the Prices are proper defendants, notwithstanding their sale of the property, is supported, albeit indirectly, by the limited legislative history that is available. In adopting certain amendments to the statute, the Senate recently commented:
>
> > [S]ection 7003 should not be construed solely with respect to the common law. Some terms and concepts, such as persons "contributing to" disposal resulting in a substantial endangerment, are meant to be more liberal than their common law counterparts. For example, a company that *generated* hazardous waste might be someone "*contributing to*" an endangerment under section 7003 even where someone else deposited the waste in an improper disposal site . . . where the generator *had* knowledge of the illicit disposal or *failed* to exercise due care in selecting or instructing the entity actually conducting the disposal.
>
> S. Rep. No. 172, 96th Cong. 2d Sess. 5 (1980) (emphasis added). This legislative history reveals two noteworthy points: first, that Congress intended the phrase "contributing to" disposal to be interpreted in a liberal, not a restrictive, fashion; and second, that Congress realized that

past acts could presently be contributing to an endangerment and intended those acts to be within the ambit of the statute . . . .

Because of the Price holding, at this stage of the proceedings the court is not prepared to hold that section 7003 cannot be applied to prior owners of inactive sites.

Third, Reilly Tar argues that the facts alleged "do not amount to the sort of disastrous emergency situation required for invocation of a provision meant to deal with 'imminent and substantial endangerments.' " It contends that section 7003 may be invoked only in true emergency situations and not as a substitute procedure for chronic and recurring problems that may be dealt with under other statutes.

. . . .

The facts alleged in the complaints are sufficient to establish an imminent and substantial endangerment to health or the environment. Plaintiffs allege that many of the chemicals found in wastes disposed of by Reilly Tar are carcinogens and toxic. For over fifty-five years these wastes were spilled, leaked and discharged directly into the ground at the site, and from there entered and continue to enter the groundwater which is used as a water supply for the City of St. Louis Park and the surrounding area. The City of St. Louis Park has already closed five wells and the City of Hopkins has closed one. Unless preventative measures are taken, the contaminants will continue to move through the leaching and migration of groundwater into the drinking water for the Minneapolis-St. Paul metropolitan area.

The court should not grant a [motion for summary judgment] unless it appears beyond doubt that plaintiff is not entitled to relief under any set of facts that could be proved. The court must liberally construe the complaint in plaintiff's favor; take the facts alleged to be true; and give the plaintiff the benefit of all favorable inferences that may reasonably be drawn in his favor. Applying these rules to the facts alleged, and giving paramount importance to the objective of protection of the public health, the complaints are sufficient to establish an imminent and substantial endangerment to health or the environment under the statute. *United States v. Vertac Chemical Corp.* 489 F. Supp. 570, 884-85 (E.D. Ark. 1980); *United States v. Royal Hardage* (W.D. Okla. 1980).

Reilly Tar is correct in stating that section 7003 should not be used as a substitute procedure for chronic and recurring pollution problems that may be dealt with under other statutes. The House Report on section 108(k) of the Air Quality Act of 1967, the original imminent hazard provision, states that the provision is "not intended as a substitute procedure for chronic or generally recurring pollution problems, which should be dealt with under the other provisions of the act" H.R. Rep. No. 728, 90th Cong. 1st Sess. 119 (1967). Similarly, as indicated above, the House committee report discussion of the imminent hazard provision of the Safe Drinking Water Act states that the "Committee intends that this broad administrative authority not be used when the system of regulatory authorities provided elsewhere in the bill could be used adequately to protect the public health."

Although the alleged groundwater contamination in this case may be a recurring or chronic problem, it may also be, or develop into, one that presents an imminent and substantial endangerment to health or the environment. The legislative history Reilly Tar relies on indicates only that section 7003 should not be used as a substitute for other procedures. While section 7003 should not become a *substitute* for other reasonably available and adequate response authorities, it certainly may be used to *supplement* the response actions taken by government agencies under other environmental statutes. Even though response actions under other statutes may also be appropriate in this case, this does not mean that plaintiffs cannot resort to section 7003 as well.

The broad range of response authorities provided by Congress under RCRA and other statutes suggest that it intended to provide the EPA flexibility in tailoring its response actions to the particular problem with which it is dealing. The statutes do not require the EPA to elect either an imminent hazard provision or other statutory response authorities. The facts alleged in the complaint do not establish that other response mechanisms are reasonably available and adequate to meet the threat, or that the government is seeking to use section 7003 as a substitute for such other procedures.

Finally, Reilly Tar contends that the relief sought in the complaints is beyond that contemplated by section 7003, and requests that the prayers for relief be limited accordingly. The scope of the relief to which plaintiffs may be entitled under the statute is a matter more appropriately left to further proceedings.

. . . .

Section 106(a) CERCLAClaims

The United States asserts a second claim for relief based on section 106(a) of CERCLA. Section 106(a) is a broadly written imminent hazards provision. It permits the government to bring suit to obtain abatement action whenever the President determines there may be an imminent and substantial endangerment to the public health or welfare or the environment because of an actual or threatened release of a hazardous substance. This action gives the federal courts broad power to grant "such relief as the public interest and equities of the case may require." . . .

Reilly Tar first argues that the section 106(a) claim must be dismissed because the complaint does not allege that the President specifically authorized this suit.

A section 106(a) claim need not contain an allegation of specific presidential authorization for the suit. Section 115 of CERCLApermits the President to delegate or assign any duties or powers imposed upon or assigned to him under the Act. 42 U.S.C. § 9615. Section 3(b) of the Executive Order Number 12316 delegates to the Administrator of the Environmental Protection Agency "the functions vested in the President by Section 106(a) of the Act . . . ." Exec. Order No. 12316, 46 Fed. Reg. 42.237 at 42.238 (1961). Section 8(b) of the Order provides that "[n]otwithstanding any other provision of this Order, the President's authority under the Act to require the Attorney General to commence litigation is retained by the President." . . .

Reilly Tar also seeks dismissal of the section 106(a) claim on substantially the same grounds it raised for dismissal of the section 7003 RCRAclaims: (1)

the statute is jurisdictional only, therefore, liability must be based upon the federal common law of nuisance which applies only where an interstate effect is alleged; (2) the statute does not apply to prior owners of inactive sites; and (3) the complaint fails to allege sufficient facts to establish an imminent and substantial endangerment to the public health, welfare or the environment. Those arguments are without merit.

First, section 106(a) neither expressly nor impliedly states that it applies only where hazardous wastes cross state lines, nor should that requirement be read into it. The language of section 106(a), like that of section 7003 of RCRAsuggests a contrary conclusion. Section 106(a) refers to actions taken by "a state" and requires notice to "the affected state." The use of the singular "state" suggests that Congress did not intend the statute to apply only where two or more states are involved. Furthermore, as with section 7003, conditioning a section 106(a) groundwater claim on interstate effects would be inconsistent with the character of the pollution the statute applies to and with the nature and extent of the federal concern embodied in CERCLA.

Although the equitable principles of federal common law nuisance actions may apply to determine what remedies are appropriate,[97] Congress did not intend section 106(a) to incorporate the element of interstate effect required in federal common law nuisance actions. Cf. *United States v. Solvents Recovery Service of New England,* 496 F. Supp. at 1133-39 (incorporating federal common law nuisance into section 7003 but not requiring an allegation of interstate effect).

Second, nothing in the language of section 106(a) indicates that it cannot in appropriate circumstances be invoked against the prior owner of a disposal site. Section 106(a) is broader in scope than section 7003 of RCRA, and whatever concerns the court has regarding the applicability of section 7003 to *prior owners* of inactive sites do not apply to section 106(a). Section 106(a) of CERCLAcontains no limitations on the classes of persons within its reach. Nor does it contain language indicating that it applies only to present owners of waste disposal sites.

In addition, as noted above, section 106(a) empowers the federal courts to grant "such relief as the public interest and the equities of the case may require." *Id.* This broad grant of equitable power to the federal courts is not limited in its application to those who are the present owners of disposal sites. The equities of this case, as they appear in the complaints, do not suggest that Reilly Tar should escape the statute's reach. Cf. *United States v. Price,* 523 F. Supp. at 1072.

Third, there is no merit to Reilly Tar's argument that this case does not present the sort of emergency situation that section 106(a) was meant to cover. The earlier discussion on what constitutes an "imminent and substantial endangerment" under section 7003 is generally applicable here as well. Taking the facts alleged in the complaint as true, it cannot be said with positive

[97] The portion of the statute granting the court the power to grant such relief as "the equities of the case may require" may suggest that reference to federal common law nuisance principles is appropriate. Federal common law nuisance actions were clearly "equitable" in nature. Mugler v. Kansas, 123 U.S. 623, 673 (1887); Missouri v. Illinois & Chicago District, 180 U.S. 208, 244 (1900).

assurances that there exists no imminent and substantial endangerment to the public health, welfare or the environment.

The Court also notes that section 106(c) of the Act requires the Administrator of the EPA, after consultation with the Attorney General, to establish guidelines for using the imminent hazard, enforcement, and emergency response authorities of this section and other existing statutes to effectuate the responsibilities and powers created by the Act. These guidelines were published on May 13, 1962. The guidelines state that the particular authority or authorities to be used, and whether to precede court action with administrative action, will be determined on a case-by-case basis depending upon the most effective approach for achieving the desired site cleanup.

These guidelines, together with the wide variety of response actions available to the EPA under CERCLA and elsewhere, suggest that Congress intended to provide the EPA with flexibility to tailor response actions to fit the circumstances of the individual case. This flexibility clearly indicates that an imminent hazard provision such as section 106(a) may be used simultaneously with other statutory response authorities. While section 106(a) should not become a substitute for other reasonably available response mechanisms, the availability of other response authorities for dealing with chronic and recurring pollution problems does not preclude the simultaneous invocation of the imminent hazard provision of section 106.

Accordingly, Reilly Tar's motion to dismiss the section 106 claim is denied.

NOTES

(1) *Reilly Tar* was one of the first cases brought by EPA and the U.S. Department of Justice, in the early 1980s, to redress the well publicized problems caused by past misdisposal of hazardous wastes at industrial plants and abandoned dumps. The approach taken by the U.S. District Court in this case is fairly representative of the earliest Superfund decisions in these matters, in which the government achieved striking success in establishing the legal positions it advocated.

(2) Note the government's reliance on both § 7003 of the RCRA and § 106 of the Superfund in this case. This is especially typical of the first round of federal hazardous waste enforcement cases, which were filed prior to the passage of CERCLA on the basis of the RCRA imminent hazard provision. After the enactment of Superfund, the government amended its complaints in those cases to add CERCLA counts.

UNITED STATES v. NORTHEASTERN PHARMACEUTICAL & CHEMICAL CO. [NEPACCO]

United States Court of Appeals, Eighth Circuit (1986)
810 F.2d 726, cert. denied, 484 U.S. 848 (1988)

McMILLAN, J.

Northeastern Pharmaceutical & Chemical Co. [NEPACCO], Edwin Michaels, and John W. Lee appeal from a final judgment entered in the District Court for the Western District of Missouri finding them and Ronald Mills jointly and severally liable for response costs incurred by the government after December 11, 1980, and all future response costs relative to the cleanup of the Denney farm site that are not inconsistent with the national contingency plan [NCP] pursuant to §§ 104 and 107 of the Comprehensive Environmental Response, Compensation, and Liability Act of 1980 (CERCLA), 42 U.S.C. §§ 9604, 9607. . . .

. . . .

I. FACTS

The following statement of facts is taken in large part from the district court's excellent memorandum opinion. 579 F. Supp. 823 (W.D. Mo. 1984). NEPACCO was incorporated in 1966 . . . . Although NEPACCO's corporate charter was forfeited in 1976 for failure to maintain an agent for service of process, NEPACCO did not file a certificate or voluntary dissolution with the secretary of state of Delaware. In 1974 its corporate assets were liquidated, and the proceeds were used to pay corporate debts and then distributed to the shareholders. Michaels [had] formed NEPACCO, was a major shareholder and was its president. Lee was NEPACCO's vice-president, the supervisor of its manufacturing plant located in Verona, Missouri, and also a shareholder. Mills was employed as shift supervisor at NEPACCO's Verona plant.

From April 1970 to January 1972, NEPACCO manufactured the disinfectant hexachloraphene at its Verona plant. NEPACCO leased the plant from Syntex Agribusiness, Inc. [Syntex] . . . . Michaels and Lee knew that NEPACCO's manufacturing process produced various hazardous and toxic byproducts, including 2,4,5-trichlorophenol (TCP), 2,3,7,9-tetrachlorodibenzo-p-dioxin (TCDD or dioxin), and toluene. The waste byproducts were pumped into a holding tank which was periodically emptied by waste haulers. Occasionally, however, excess waste byproducts were sealed in 55-gallon drums and then stored at the plant.

In July 1971 Mills approached NEPACCO plant manager Bill Ray with a proposal to dispose of the waste-filled 55-gallon drums on a farm owned by James Denney located about seven miles south of Verona. Ray visited the Denney farm and discussed the proposal with Lee; Lee approved the use of Mills' services and the Denney farm as a disposal site. In mid-July 1971 Mills and Gerald Lechner dumped approximately 85 of the 55-gallon drums into a large trench on the Denney farm [Denney farm site] that had been excavated by Leon Vaughn. Vaughn then filled in the trench. Only NEPACCO drums were disposed of at the Denney farm site.

In October 1979 the Environmental Protection Agency (EPA) received an anonymous tip that hazardous wastes had been disposed of at the Denney farm. Subsequent EPA investigation confirmed that hazardous wastes had in fact been disposed of at the Denney farm and that the site was not geologically suitable for the disposal of hazardous wastes. Between January and April 1980 the EPA prepared a plan for the cleanup of the Denney farm site and constructed an access road and a security fence. During April 1980 the EPA conducted an on-site investigation, exposed and sampled 13 of the 55-gallon drums, which were found to be badly deteriorated, and took water and soil samples. The samples were found to contain "alarmingly" high concentrations of dioxin, TCP and toluene.

In July 1980 the EPA installed a temporary cap over the trench to prevent the runoff of surface water and to minimize contamination of the surrounding soil and groundwater . . . . The 55-gallon drums are now stored in a specially constructed concrete bunker on the Denney farm. The drums as stored do not present an imminent and substantial endangerment to health or the environment; however, no plan for permanent disposal has been developed, and the site will continue to require testing and monitoring in the future.

In August 1980 the government filed its initial complaint against NEPACCO, the generator of the hazardous substances; Michaels and Lee, the corporate officers responsible of arranging for the disposal of the hazardous substances; Mills, the transporter of the hazardous substances; and Syntex, the owner and lessor of the Verona plant, seeking injunctive relief and reimbursement of response costs pursuant to RCRA § 7003. In August 1982 the government filed an amended complaint adding counts for relief pursuant to CERCLA.

. . . .

III. CERCLA RETROACTIVITY

A. Application of CERCLA to Pre-1980 Acts

Appellants first argue the district court erred in applying CERCLA retroactively, that is, to impose liability for acts committed before its effective date, December 11, 1980. CERCLA § 302(a)provides that "[u]nless otherwise provided, all provisions of this chapter shall be effective on December 11, 1980." Appellants argue that CERCLA should not apply to pre-enactment conduct that was neither negligent nor unlawful when committed. Appellants argue that all the conduct at issue occurred in the early 1970s, well before CERCLA became effective. Appellants also argue that there is no language supporting retroactive application in CERCLA's liability section, or in the legislative history. Appellants further argue that because CERCLA imposes a new kind of liability, retroactive application of CERCLA violates due process and the taking clause. We disagree.

The district court correctly found Congress intended CERCLA to apply retroactively. We acknowledge there is a presumption against the retroactive application of statutes. We hold, however, that CERCLA § 302(a)is "merely a standard 'effective date' provision that indicates the date when an action can first be brought and when the time begins to run for issuing regulations and doing other future acts mandated by the statute."

Although CERCLA does not expressly provide for retroactivity, it is manifestly clear that Congress intended CERCLA to have retroactive effect. The language used in the key liability provision, CERCLA § 107, refers to actions and conditions in the past tense: "any person who at the time of disposal of any hazardous substances owned or operated," CERCLA § 107(a)(2), "any person who . . . arranged with a transporter for transport for disposal," CERCLA § 107(a)(3), and "any person who . . . accepted any hazardous substances for transport to . . . sites selected by any such person," CERCLA § 107(a)(4).

Further, the statutory scheme itself is overwhelmingly remedial and retroactive. CERCLA authorizes the EPA to force responsible parties to clean up inactive or abandoned hazardous substance sites, CERCLA § 106, and authorizes federal, state and local governments and private parties to clean up such sites and then seek recovery of their response costs from responsible parties, CERCLA §§ 104, 107. In order to be effective, CERCLA must reach past conduct. CERCLA's backward-looking focus is confirmed by the legislative history. *See generally* H.R.Rep. No. 1016, 96th Cong. 2d Sess., reprinted in 1980 U.S. Code Cong. & Ad. News 6119 (CERCLA House Report). Congress intended CERCLA "to initiate and establish a comprehensive response and financing mechanism to abate and control the vast problems associated with abandoned and inactive hazardous waste disposal sites."

The district court also correctly found that retroactive application of CERCLA does not violate due process. Appellants argue CERCLA creates a new form of liability that is designed to deter and punish those who, according to current standards, improperly disposed of hazardous substances in the past. We disagree.

It is by now well established that legislative Acts adjusting the burdens and benefits of economic life come to the court with a presumption of constitutionality and that the burden is on one complaining of a due process violation to establish that the legislature has acted in an arbitrary and irrational way. [L]egistation readjusting rights and burdens is not unlawful solely because it upsets otherwise settled expectations. This is true even though the effect of the legislation is to impose a new duty or liability based on past acts.

Due process is satisfied "simply by showing that the retroactive application of the legislation is itself justified by a rational legislative purpose." *Pension Benefit Guaranty Corp. v. R.A. Gray & Co.*, 467 U.S. 717, 730 (1984). Provided that the retroactive application of a statute is supported by a legitimate legislative purpose furthered by rational means, judgments about the wisdom of such legislation "remain within the exclusive province of the legislative and executive branches . . . ." *Id.* at 729.

Appellants failed to show that Congress acted in an arbitrary and irrational manner. Cleaning up inactive and abandoned hazardous waste disposal sites is a legitimate legislative purpose, and Congress acted in a rational manner in imposing liability for the cost of cleaning up such sites upon those parties who created and profited from the sites and upon the chemical industry as a whole. We hold retroactive application of CERCLA to impose liability upon responsible parties for acts committed before the effective date of the statute does not violate due process.

. . . .

V. SCOPE OF LIABILITY

The district court found NEPACCO liable as the "owner or operator" of a "facility" [the NEPACCO plant] under CERCLA § 107(a)(1) and as a "person" who arranged for the transportation and disposal of hazardous substances under CERCLA § 107(a)(3). The district court found Lee liable as a "person" who arranged for the disposal of hazardous substances under CERCLA § 107(a) and as an "owner or operator" of the NEPACCO plant under CERCLA § 107by "piercing the corporate veil." *Id.* at 848-49. The district court also found Michaels liable as an "owner or operator" of the NEPACCO plant under CERCLA § 107.

Appellants concede NEPACCO is liable under CERCLA § 107(a)(3)for arranging for the transportation and disposal or hazardous substances at the Denney farm site. Because NEPACCO's assets have already been liquidated and distributed to its shareholders however, it is unlikely that the government will be able to recover anything from NEPACCO.

Appellants argue (1) they cannot be held liable as "owners or operators" of a "facility" because they did not own or operate the Denney farm site, (2) Lee cannot be held individually liable for arranging for the transportation and disposal of hazardous substances because he did not "own or possess" the hazardous substances and because he made those arrangements as a corporate officer or employee acting on behalf of NEPACCO, and (3) the district court erred in finding Lee and Michaels individually liable by "piercing the corporate veil." Appellants have not claimed that any of CERCLA's limited affirmative defenses apply to them.

The government argues Lee can be held individually liable without "piercing the corporate veil," under CERCLA § 107(a)(3), and that Lee and Michaels can be held individually liable as "contributors" under RCRA § 7003(a). For the reasons discussed below, we agree with the government's liability arguments.

A. Liability under CERCLA § 107(a)(1)

First, appellants argue the district court erred in finding them liable under CERCLA § 107(a)(1)as "owners and operators" of a "facility" where hazardous substances are located. Appellants argue that, regardless of their relationship to the NEPACCO plant, they neither owned nor operated the Denney farm site, and that it is the Denney farm site, not the NEPACCO plant, that is a "facility" for purposes of "owner or operator" liability under CERCLA § 107(a)(1). We agree.

CERCLA defines the term "facility" in part as "any site or area where a hazardous substance has been deposited, stored, disposed of, or placed, or otherwise come to be located." CERCLA § 101(9)(B), *see New York v. Shore Realty Corp.,* 759 F.2d 1032, 1043 n.15 (2d Cir. 1985). The term "facility" should be construed very broadly to include "virtually any place at which hazardous wastes have been dumped, or otherwise disposed of." *United States v. Ward,* 618 F. Supp. At 895. In the present case, however, the place where the hazardous substances were disposed of and where the government has concentrated its cleanup efforts is the Denney farm site, not the NEPACCO plant. The Denney farm site is the "facility." Because NEPACCO, Lee and Michaels did not own or operate the Denney farm site, they cannot be held liable as the "owners or operators" of a "facility" where hazardous substances are located under CERCLA § 107(a)(1).

B. Individual Liability under CERCLA § 107(a)(3)

CERCLA § 107(a)(3)imposes strict liability upon "any person" who arranged for the disposal or transportation for disposal of hazardous substances. As defined by statute, the term "person" includes both individuals and corporations and does not exclude corporate officers or employees. Congress could have limited the statutory definition of "person" but chose not to do so. Compare CERCLA § 101(20)(A)limiting definition of "owner or operator." Moreover, construction of CERCLA to impose liability upon only the corporation and not the individual corporate officers and employees who are responsible for making corporate decisions about the handling and disposal of hazardous substances would open an enormous, and clearly unintended loophole in the statutory scheme.

First, Lee argues he cannot be held individually liable for having arranged for the transportation and disposal or hazardous substances under CERCLA § 107(a)(3)because he did not personally own or possess the hazardous substances. Lee argues NEPACCO owned or possessed the hazardous substances.

The government argues Lee "possessed" the hazardous substances within the meaning of CERCLA § 107(a)(3)because, as NEPACCO's plant supervisor, Lee had actual "control" over the NEPACCO plant's hazardous substances. We agree. It is the authority to control the handling and disposal of hazardous substances that is critical under the statutory scheme. The district court found that Lee, as plant supervisor, actually knew about, had immediate supervision over, and was directly responsible for arranging for the transportation and disposal of the NEPACCO plant's hazardous substances at the Denney farm site. We believe requiring proof of personal ownership or actual physical possession of hazardous substances as a precondition for liability under CERCLA § 107(a)(3)would be inconsistent with the broad remedial purposes of CERCLA.

Next, Lee argues that because he arranged for the transportation and disposal of the hazardous substances as a corporate officer or employee acting on behalf of NEPACCO, he cannot be held individually liable for NEPACCO's violations. Lee also argues the district court erred in disregarding the corporate entity by "piercing the corporate veil" because there was no evidence that NEPACCO was inadequately capitalized, the corporate formalities were not observed, individual and corporate interests were not separate, personal and corporate funds were commingled or corporate property was diverted, or the corporate form was used unjustly or fraudulently.

The government argues Lee can be held individually liable, without "piercing the corporate veil," because Lee personally arranged for the disposal or hazardous substances in violation of CERCLA § 107(a)(3). We agree. As discussed below, Lee can be held individually liable because he personally participated in conduct that violated CERCLA: this personal liability is distinct from the derivative liability that results from "piercing the corporate veil." "The effect of piercing a corporate veil is to hold the owner [of the corporation] liable. The rationale for piercing the corporate veil is that the corporation is something less than a bona fide independent entity." *Donsco, Inc. v. Casper Corp.,* 587 F.2d 602, 606 (3d Cir. 1978). Here, Lee is liable because he personally participated in the wrongful conduct and not because he is one of the owners of what may have been a less than bona fide corporation. For this reason, we need not decide whether the district court erred in piercing the corporate veil under these circumstances.

We now turn to Lee's basic argument. Lee argues that he cannot be held individually liable for NEPACCO's wrongful conduct because he acted solely as a corporate officer or employee on behalf of NEPACCO. The liability imposed upon Lee, however, was not derivative but personal. Liability was not premised solely upon Lee's status as a corporate officer or employee. Rather, Lee is individually liable under CERCLA § 107(a)(3)because he personally arranged for the transportation and disposal of hazardous substances on behalf of NEPACCO and thus actually participated in NEPACCO's CERCLA violations.

> A corporate officer is individually liable for the torts he or she personally commits [on behalf of the corporation] and cannot shield himself [or herself] behind a corporation when he [or she] is an actual participant in the tort. The fact that an officer is acting for a corporation also may make the corporation vicariously or secondarily liable under the doctrine of respondeat superior. It does not however relieve the individual of his [or her] responsibility.

Donsco, Inc. v. Casper Corp., 587 F.2d at 606. . . . Thus, Lee's personal involvement in NEPACCO's CERCLA violations made him individually liable.

. . . .

VII. BURDEN OF PROOF OF RESPONSE COSTS

The district court found appellants had the burden of proving the government's response costs were inconsistent with the NCP, and that response costs that are not inconsistent with the NCP are conclusively presumed to be reasonable and therefore recoverable. Appellants argue the district court erred in requiring them to prove the response costs were inconsistent with the NCP, not cost-effective or unnecessary. Appellants further argue the district court erred in assuming that all costs that are consistent with the NCP are conclusively presumed to be reasonable. Appellants note that the information and facts necessary to establish consistency with the NCP are matters within the possession of the government.

We believe the district court's analysis is correct. CERCLA § 107(a)(4)(A)states that the government may recover from responsible parties "all costs of removal or remedial action . . . not inconsistent with the [NCP]." The statutory language itself establishes an exception for costs that are inconsistent with the NCP, but appellants, as the parties claiming the benefit of the exception, have the burden of proving that certain costs are inconsistent with the NCP and, therefore, not recoverable.

. . . .

Because determining the appropriate removal and remedial action involves specialized knowledge and expertise, the choice is arbitrary and capricious. As explained in *United States v. Ward*:

> If [appellants] wish the court to review the consistency of [the government's] actions with the NCP, then they are essentially alleging that the EPA did not carry out its statutory duties. The statute provides liability except for costs "not inconsistent" with the NCP. This language requires deference by this court to the judgment of agency professionals. [Appellants], therefore, may not seek to have the court substitute its own judgment for that of the EPA. [Appellants] may only show that the EPA's decision about the method of cleanup was "inconsistent" with the NCP in that the EPA was arbitrary and capricious in the discharge of their duties under the NCP. 618 F. Supp. at 900.

Here, appellants failed to show that the government's response costs were inconsistent with the NCP. Appellants also failed to show that the EPA acted arbitrarily and capriciously in choosing the particular method it used to clean up the Denney farm site.

. . . .

NOTES AND QUESTIONS

(1) In *NEPACCO,* the Eighth Circuit recited what is now the prevailing view with regard to the retroactive applicability of most of the Superfund statute. *See also United States v. Olin Corp.,* 107 F.3d 1566 (11th Cir. 1997); *Virginia Properties, Inc. v. Home Ins. Co.,* 74 F.3d 1131 (11th Cir. 1996).

Is the natural resource damage claim aspect of CERCLA applicable to releases of hazardous substances that pre-date the statute's enactment? In fact, CERCLA itself resolves that question in the negative. At § 107(f)(1), 42 U.S.C. § 9607(f)(1) and § 111(d)(1), 42 U.S.C. § 9611(d)(1), the legislation prohibits natural resource damage claims as to hazardous substance releases which "occurred wholly" prior to the Superfund's effective date. Is there a logical reason to treat claims for natural resource damages differently from all other claims against Superfund with respect to the retroactive applicability of the statute?

(2) Perhaps the most significant aspect of the *NEPACCO* decision is the court's handling of the question of the individual CERCLA liability of corporate officers and employees.

Another leading decision in this area is *Kelley v. ARCO Industries,* 723 F. Supp. 1214 (W.D. Mich. 1989), which attempted to lay down a more precise and exacting legal standard as to corporate officers. In *Kelley,* the court determined that piercing the corporate veil is necessary, unless the court can determine that an individual was closely involved or had direct supervisory powers over the events that led to the wrongful conduct. An individual would be liable if he could have prevented or significantly abated the discharge of hazardous wastes. To make this determination, the courts must consider the individual's position in the company, whether he or she is a director or officer, and the percentage of shares that the individual owns. The courts must also take account of the nature of the individual's responsibility for waste disposal practices, as well as any affirmative steps that he or she took to prevent unlawful hazardous waste disposal.

(3) For further discussion of the CERCLA liability of corporate directors, officers and shareholders, *see* F. Grad, Treatise on Environmental Law § 4A.02[1][j]. *See also* Heidt, *Liability of Shareholders Under CERCLA,* 52 Ohio St. L. J. 133 (1991); Barber, *Piercing the Corporate Veil,* 17 Williamette L. Rev. 371 (1981); and Wallace, *Liability of Corporations and Corporate Officers, Directors and Shareholders Under Superfund: Should Corporate and Agency Law Concepts Apply?,* J. Corp. L. 839 (Summer, 1989).

STATE OF NEW YORK v. SHORE REALTY CORP.

United States Court of Appeals, Second Circuit (1985)
759 F.2d 1032

OAKES, C.J.:

This case involves several novel questions about the scope of the Comprehensive Environmental Response, Compensation, and Liability Act of 1980 ("CERCLA") 42 U.S.C. §§ 9601–9657 (1982), and the interplay between that statute and New York public nuisance law. CERCLA—adopted in the waning hours of the Ninety-sixth Congress, and signed by President Carter on December 11, 1980—was intended to provide means for cleaning up hazardous waste sites and spills, and may generally be known to the public as authorizing the so-called Superfund, the $1.6 billion Hazardous Substances Response Trust Fund, 42 U.S.C. §§ 9631-9633.

On February 29, 1984, the State of New York brought suit against Shore Realty Corp. ("Shore") and Donald LeoGrande, its officer and stockholder to clean up a hazardous waste disposal site at One Shore Road, Glennwood Landing, New York, which Shore had acquired for land development purposes. At the time of the acquisition, LeoGrande knew that hazardous waste was stored on the site and that cleanup would be expensive, though neither Shore nor LeoGrande had participated in the generation or transportation of the nearly 700,000 gallons of hazardous waste now on the premises. The State's suit under CERCLA for an injunction and damages was brought in the United States District Court for the Eastern District of New York, Henry Bramwell, Judge. The complaint also contained pendent state law nuisance claims based on both common law and N.Y. Real Prop. Acts. Law § 841, McKinney (1979). On October 15, 1984, the district court granted the State's motion for partial summary judgment. Apparently relying at least in part on CERCLA, it directed by permanent injunction that Shore and LeoGrande remove the hazardous waste stored on the property, subject to monitoring by the State, and held them liable for the State's "response costs." *See* 42 U.S.C.

§ 9607(a)(4)(A). In the alternative the court based the injunction on a finding that the Shore Road site was a public nuisance. Following a remand by this court on December 14, 1984, the district court on January 11, 1985, stated with more particularity the undisputed material facts underlying its decision finding defendants liable for the State's response costs and clarifying its earlier decision by basing the injunction solely on state public nuisance law. The court also modified its earlier decision by suggesting that CERCLA does not authorize injnctive relief in this case.

We affirm, concluding that Shore is liable under CERCLA for the State's response costs. We hold that Shore properly was found to be a covered person under 42 U.S.C. § 9607(a); that the nonlisting by the Environmental Protection Agency ("EPA") of the site on the National Priorities List ("NPL"), 42 U.S.C. § 9605(8)(B), is irrelevant to Shore's liability and that shore cannot rely on any of CERCLA's affirmative defenses . . . . Moreover, we hold LeoGrande jointly and severally liable under both CERCLA and New York Law.

Facts

Some of the most heated arguments on this appeal involve whether certain material facts are undisputed. After careful scrutiny of the record and the district court's supplemental memorandum, we base our decision on the following facts.

LeoGrande incorporated Shore solely for the purpose of purchasing the Shore Road property. All corporate decisions and actions were made, directed, and controlled by him. By contract dated July 14, 1983, Shore agreed to purchase the 3.2 acre site, a small peninsula surrounded on three sides by the waters of Hempstead Harbor and Moot Cove, for condominium development. Five large tanks in a field in the center of the site hold most of some 700,000 gallons of hazardous chemicals located there, though there are six smaller tanks both above and below ground containing hazardous waste, as well as some empty tanks, on the property. The tanks are connected by pipe to a tank truck loading rack and dockage facilities for loading by barge. Four roll-on/roll-off containers and one tank truck trailer hold additional waste. And before June 15, 1984, one of the two dilapidated masonry warehouses on the site contained over 400 drums of chemicals and contaminated solids, many of which were corroded and leaking.

It is beyond dispute that the tanks and drums contain "hazardous substances" within the meaning of CERCLA. 42 U.S.C. § 9601(4). The substances involved—including benzene, dichlorobenzenes, ethyl benzene, tetracholorethylene, trichloroethylene, 1, 1, 1-trichloroethene, chlordane, polychlorinated biphenyls (commonly known as PCBs), and bis (2-ethylhexyl) phtalate—are toxic, in some cases carcinogenic, and dangerous by way of contact, inhalation, or ingestion. These substances are present at the site in various combinations, some of which may cause the toxic effect to be synergistic.

The purchase agreement provided that it could be voided by Shore without penalty if after conducting an environmental study Shore had decided not to proceed. LeoGrande was fully aware that the tenants, Applied Environmental

Services, Inc., and Hazardous Waste Disposal, Inc., were then operating—illegally, it may be noted—a hazardous waste storage facility on the site. Shore's environmental consultant, WTM Management Corporation ("WTM"), prepared a detailed report in July, 1983, incorporated in the record and relied on by the district court for its findings. The report concluded that over the past several decades "the facility ha[d] received little if any preventive maintenance, the tanks (above ground and below ground), pipeline, loading rack, fire extinguishing system, and warehouse have deteriorated." WTM found that there had been several spills of hazardous waste at the site, including at least one large spill in 1978. Though there had been some attempts at cleanup, the WTM testing revealed that hazardous substances, such as benzene, were still leaching into the groundwater and the waters of the bay immediately adjacent to the bulkhead abutting Hempstead Harbor. After a site visit on July 18, 1983, WTM reported firsthand on the sorry state of the facility, observing, among other things, "seepage from the bulkhead," "corrosion" on all the tanks, signs of possible leakage from some of the tanks, deterioration of the pipeline and loading rack, and fifty to one hundred fifty-five gallon drums containing contaminated earth in one of the warehouses. The report concluded that if the current tenants "close up the operation and leave the material at the site," the owners would be left with a "potential time bomb." WTM estimated that the cost of environmental cleanup and monitoring would range from $650,00 to over $1 million before development could begin. After receiving this report Shore sought a waiver from the State Department of Envirnmental Conservation ("DEC") of liability as landowners for the disposal of the hazardous waste stored at the site. Although the DEC denied the waiver, Shore took title on October 13, 1983, and obtained certain rights over against the tenants, whom it subsequently evicted on January 5, 1984.

. . . .

Nevertheless, between October 13, 1983, and January 5, 1984, nearly 90,000 gallons of hazardous chemicals were added to the tanks. And during a state inspection on January 3, 1984, it became evident that the deteriorating and leaking drums of chemicals referred to above had also been brought onto the site. Needless to say, the tenants did not clean up the site before they left. Thus, conditions when Shore employees first entered the site were as bad as or worse than those described in the WTM report. As LeoGrande admitted by affidavit, "the various storage tanks, pipe lines and connections between these storage facilities were in a bad state of repair." While Shore claims to have made some improvements, such as sealing all the pipes and valves and continuing the cleanup of the damage from earlier spills, Shore did nothing about the hundreds of thousands of gallons of hazardous waste standing in deteriorating tanks. In addition, although a growing number of drums were leaking hazardous substances, Shore essentially ignored the problem until June, 1984.

On September 19, 1984, a DEC inspector observed one of the large tanks, which held over 300,000 gallons of hazardous materials, with rusting floor plates and tank walls, a pinhole leak, and a four-foot line of corrosion along one of the weld lines. On three other tanks, flakes of corroded metal "up to the size and thickness of a dime" were visible at the floorplate level. While defendants now claim that the large tank was not leaking, their denial is untimely; they did not formally dispute the fact before the district court rendered its October 15, 1984 order. Moreover, defendants' claim that the pinhole has been patched hardly makes the existence of the pinhole leak a triable issue of fact. In addition, defendants do not contest that Shore employees lack the knowledge to maintain safely the quantity of hazardous chemicals on the site. And, because LeoGrande has no intention of operating a hazardous waste storage facility, Shore has not and will not apply for a permit to do so. Nor do defendants contest that the State incurred certain costs in assessing the conditions at the site and supervising the removal of the drums of hazardous waste.

CERCLA

CERCLA's history reveals as much about the nature of the legislative process as about the nature of the legislation. In 1980, while the Senate considered one early version of CERCLA, the House considered and passed another. *See* H.R. 7020, 96th Cong., 2d Sess. (1980), reprinted in 2 Legislative History of the Comprehensive Environmental Response, Compensation, and Liability Act of 1980 (Superfund) 391-463 (Comm. Print 1983) [hereinafter cited as CERCLA Legislative History]; *see also* 126 Cong. Rec. 26, 757-99 (1980) (debate and passage of H.R. 7020), reprinted in 2 CERCLA Legislative History, *supra*, at 294-389. The version passed by both Houses, however, was an eleventh hour compromise put together primarily by Senate leaders and sponsors of the earlier Senate version. Unfortunately, we are without the benefit of committee reports concerning this compromise. Nevertheless, the evolution of the legislation provides useful guidance to Congress's intentions. The compromise contains many provisions closely resembling those from earlier versions of the legislation, and the House and Senate sponsors sought to articulate the differences between the compromise and earlier versions. One of the sponsors claimed that the version passed "embodie[d] those features of the Senate and House bills where there has been positive consensus" while "eliminat[ing] those provisions which were controversial." 126 Cong. Rec. 30,932 (statement of Sen. Randolph), reprinted in 1 CERCLA Legislative History, *supra*, at 685.

As explained in F. Anderson, D. Mandelker, & A. Tarlock, Environmental Protection: Law and Policy 568 (1984), CERCLA was designed "to bring order to the array of partly redundant, partly inadequate federal hazardous substances cleanup and compensation laws." It applies "primarily to the cleanup of leaking inactive or abandoned sites and to emergency responses to spills." And it distinguishes between two kinds of response: remedial actions—generally long-term or permanent containment or disposal programs and removal efforts—typically short-term cleanup arrangements.

. . . .

CERCLA authorizes the federal government to respond in several ways. EPA can use Superfund resources to clean up hazardous waste sites and spills. 42 U.S.C. § 9611. The National Contingency Plan ("NCP"), prepared by EPA pursuant to CERCLA, *id.* § 9605, governs cleanup efforts by "establish[ing] procedures and standards for responding to releases of hazardous substances." At the same time, EPA can sue for reimbursement of cleanup costs from any responsible parties it can locate, *id.* § 9607, allowing the federal government to respond immediately while later trying to shift financial responsibility to others. Thus, Superfund covers cleanup costs if the site has been abandoned, if the responsible parties elude detection, or if private resources are inadequate. *See* F. Andeson, D. Mandelker, & A. Tarlock, at 573. In addition, CERCLA authorizes EPA to seek an injunction in federal district court to force a responsible party to clean up any site or spill that presents an imminent and substantial danger to public health or welfare or the environment. 42 U.S.C. § 9606(a). In sum, CERCLA is not a regulatory standard-setting statute such as the Clean Air Act. *Id.* §§ 7401–7642. Rather, the government generally undertakes pollution abatement, and polluters pay for such abatement through tax and reimbursement liability. *See* F. Anderson, D. Mandelker, & A. Tarlock at 569.

Congress clearly did not intend, however, to leave clean up under CERCLA solely in the hands of the federal government. A state or political subdivision may enter into a contract or cooperative agreement with EPA, whereby both may take action on a cost-sharing basis. 42 U.S.C. §§ 9604(c),(d). And states, like EPA, can sue responsible parties for remedial and removal costs if such efforts are "not inconsistent with" the NCP. *Id.* § 9607(a)(4)(A). While CERCLA expressly does not preempt state law, *id.* § 9614(a), it precludes "recovering compensation for the same removal costs or damages or claims" under both CERCLA and state or other federal laws, *id.* § 9614(b), and prohibits states from requiring contributions to any fund "the purpose of which is to pay compensation for claims . . . which may be compensated under" CERCLA. *Id.* § 9614(c). Moreover, "any . . . person" who is acting consistently with the requirements of the NCP may recover "necessary costs of responses." *Id.* § 9607(a)(4)(B); *see also City of Philadelphia v. Stephan Chemical Co.*, 544 F. Supp. 1135, 1142-43 (D.C. E.D. Pa. 1982) (allowing a landowner to maintain a CERCLA action against a hazardous waste generator under section 9607(a)(4)(B)). Finally, responsible parties are liable for "damages for injury to, destruction of, or loss of natural resources, including the reasonable costs of assessing such injury, destruction, or loss resulting from such a release." 42 U.S.C. § 9607(a)(4)(C).

. . . .

Congress intended that responsible parties be held strictly liable, even though an explicit provision for strict liability was not included in the compromise. 33 U.S.C. § 1321. Section 9601 (32) provides that "liability" under CERCLA "shall be construed to be the standard of liability" under section 311 of the Clean Water Act, 33 U.S.C. § 1321, which courts have held to be strict liability, *see, e.g., Steuart Transportation Co. v. Allied Towing Corp.*, 596 F.2d 609, 613 (4th Cir. 1979), and which Congress understood to impose such liability. *See* S. Rep. No. 848, 96th Cong., 2d Sess. 34 (1980) (hereinafter cited as Senate Report), reprinted in 1 CERCLA Legislative History, *supra*, at 308, 341. Moreover, the sponsors of the compromise expressly stated that section 9607 provides for strict liability. *See* 126 Cong. Rec. 30,932 (statement of Sen. Randolph), reprinted in 1 CERCLA Legislative

History, *supra*, at 685; *Id.* at 31,964 (statement of Rep. Florio), reprinted in 1 CERCLA Legislative History, *supra*, at 777; *see also id.* at 31,966 (Department of Justice view of Senate compromise discussing strict liability), reprinted in 1 CERCLA Legislative History, *supra*, at 780-81. Strict liability under CERCLA, however, is not absolute; there are defenses for causation solely by an act of God, an act of war, or acts or omissions of a third party other than an employee or agent of the defendant or one whose act or omission occurs in connection with a contractual relationship with the defendant. 42 U.S.C. § 9607(b).

Discussion

A. Liability for Response Costs Under CERCLA

We hold that the district court properly awarded the state response costs under section 9607(a)(4)(A). The state's costs in assessing the conditions of the site and supervising the removal of the drums of hazardous waste squarely fall within CERCLA's definition of response costs, even though the state is not undertaking to do the removal. *See Id.* §§ 9601(23), (24), (25). Contrary to Shore's claim, the state's motion for summary judgment sought such costs, and Shore had ample opportunity for discovery. That a detailed accounting was submitted only at this court's request for supplemental findings is immaterial; Shore had an opportunity to contest the accounting but failed to make anything more than a perfunctory objection.

1. *Covered Persons.* CERCLA holds liable four classes of persons:

> (1) the owner and operator of a vessel (otherwise subject to the jurisdiction of the United States) or a facility;[98]
>
> (2) any person who at the time of disposal of any hazardous substance owned or operated any facility at which such hazardous substances were disposed of;
>
> (3) any person who by contract, agreement, or otherwise arranged for disposal or treatment, or arranged with a transporter for transport for disposal or treatment, of hazardous substances owned or possessed by such person, by any other party or entity, at any facility owned or operated by another party or entity and containing such hazardous substances; and
>
> (4) any person who accepts or accepted any hazardous substances for transport to disposal or treatment facilities or sites selected by such person. 42 U.S.C. § 9607(a).

As noted above, section 9607 makes these persons liable, if "there is a release, or a threatened release which causes the incurrence of response costs, of a hazardous substance" from the facility, among other things, "all costs of removal or remedial action incurred by the United States Government or a state not inconsistent with the national contingency plan."

Shore argues that it is not covered by section 9607(a) because it neither owned the site at the time of disposal nor caused the presence or the release

---

[98] CERCLA defines the term "facility" broadly to include any property at which hazardous substances have come to be located. *See* 42 U.S.C. § 9601(9).

of the hazardous waste at the facility. While section 9607(a)(1) appears to cover Shore, Shore attempts to infuse ambiguity into the statutory scheme, claiming that section 9607(a)(1) could not have been intended to include all owners, because the word "owned" in section 9607(a)(2) would be unnecessary since an owner "at the time of disposal" would necessarily be included in section 9607(a)(1). Shore claims that Congress intended that the scope of section 9607(a)(1) be no greater than that of section 9607(a)(2) and that both should be limited by the "at the time of disposal" language. By extension, Shore argues that both provisions should be interpreted as requiring a showing of causation. We agree with the state, however, that section 9607(a)(1) unequivocally imposes strict liability on the current owner of a facility from which there is a release or threat of release, with regard to causation.

Shore's claims of ambiguity are illusory; section 9607(a)'s structure is clear. Congress intended to cover different classes of persons differently. Section 9607(a)(1) applies to all current owners and operators, while section 9607(a)(2) primarily covers prior owners and operators. Moreover, section 9607(a)(2)'s scope is more limited than that of section 9607(a)(1). Prior owners and operators are liable only if they owned or operated the facility "at the time of disposal of any hazardous substance"; this limitation does not apply to current owners, like Shore. Thus, Shore's reliance on the holding of the district court in *Cadillac Fairview / California, Inc. v. Dow Chemical Co.,* 14 Envtl.L.Rep. (Envtl.L.Inst.) 20,376 (C.D. Cal. Mar. 5, 1984), is inappropriate. The *Cadillac Fairview* court was concerned with a prior owner and predicated its holding solely upon the words of section 9607(a)(2). *Id.* at 20, 378.

Shore's causation argument is also at odds with the structure of the statute. Interpreting section 9607(a)(1) as including a causation requirement makes superfluous the affirmative defenses provided in section 9607(b), each of which carves out from liability an exception based on causation. Without a clear congressional command otherwise, we will not construe a statute in any way that makes some of its provisions surplusage. *See, e.g., United States v. Mehrmanesh,* 689 F.2d 822, 829 (9th Cir. 1982); *National Insulation Transportation Committee v. ICC,* 683 F.2d 533, 537 (D.C. Cir. 1982). Moreover, Shore again improperly relies on *Cadillac Fairview.* There, the court did not interpret section 9607(a) to require causation, as defendants claim, but simply ownership "at the time of disposal." 14 Envtl.L.Rep. (Envtl.L.Inst.) at 20, 378. Several other district courts explicitly have declined to read a causation requirement into section 9607(a). *See, e.g., United States v. Cauffman,* No. CV 83-6318-KN (bx), slip op. at 2-3 (C.D. Cal. Oct. 23, 1984) (citing other cases).

Our interpretation draws further support from the legislative history. Congress specifically rejected including a causation requirement in section 9607(a). The early House version imposed liability only upon "any person who caused or contributed to the release or threatened release." H.R. 7020, 96th Cong., 2d Sess. § 3071(a), 126 Cong. Rec. 26, 779, reprinted in 2 CERCLA Legislative History, *supra* at 438. The compromise version, to which the House later agreed, *see* 126 Cong. Rec. 31,981-82, reprinted in 1 CERCLA Legislative History, *supra,* at 821-24, imposed liability on classes of persons without reference to whether they caused or contributed to the release or threat of release. *See also* S. 1480, 96th Cong., 2d Sess, § 4(a), 126 Cong. Rec. 30,900 (Senate version of legislation changed from imposing liability on an "owner or operator" and "any other person who caused or contributed . . . to such discharge, release, or disposal" to imposing liability on four classes of persons, the scheme adopted in the compromise version) reprinted in 1 CERCLA Legislative History, *supra* at 485-86. Thus, the remarks of Representatives Stockman and Gore describing the House version containing the causation language, *see* 126 Cong. Rec. 26,786-87, reprinted in 2 CERCLA Legislative History, *supra*, at 359-61, on which Shore relies, are inapposite.

Furthermore, as the state points out, accepting Shore's argument would open a huge loophole in CERCLA's coverage. It is quite clear that if the current owner of a site could avoid liability merely by having purchased the site after chemical dumping had ceased, waste sites certainly would be sold, following the cessation of dumping, to new owners who could avoid the liability otherwise required by CERCLA. Congress had well in mind that persons who dump or store hazardous waste sometimes cannot be located or may be deceased or judgment proof. *See, e.g.*, Senate Report, *supra*, at 16, reprinted in 1 CERCLA Legislative History, *supra*, at 323. We will not interpret section 9607(a) in any way that apparently frustrates the statute's goals, in the absence of a specific congressional intention otherwise. *See Capitano v. Secretary of Health and Human Services,* 732 F.2d 1066, 1076 (2d Cir. 1984); *Bartok v. Boosey & Hawkes, Inc.*, 523 F.2d 941, 947 (2d Cir. 1975).

Finally, we need not address whether Shore is also subject to liability under section 9607(a)(2) because some 90,000 gallons of waste were disposed of, apparently by unauthorized tenants, after Shore took title on October 13, 1983. Nor need we decide whether hazardous substances have been "disposed of" after Shore employees entered the property in January, 1984.

2. *Release or Threat of Release*. We reject Shore's repeated claims that it has put in dispute whether there has been a release or threat of release at the Shore Road site. The state has established that it was responding to "a release, or a threatened release" when it incurred its response costs. We hold that the leaking tanks and pipelines, the continuing leaching and seepage from the earlier spills, and the leaking drums all constitute "releases." 42 U.S.C. § 9601(22). Moreover, the corroding and deteriorating tanks, Shore's lack of expertise in handling hazardous waste, and even the failure to license the facility, amount to a threat of release.

In addition, Shore's suggestion that CERCLA does not impose liability for threatened releases is simply frivolous. Section 9607(a)(4)(A) imposes liability for "all costs of removal or remedial action." The definitions of "removal" and "remedial" explicitly refer to actions "taken in the event of the threat of release of hazardous substances." *See* Senate Report, *supra*, at 54, reprinted in 1 CERCLA Legislative History, *supra*, at 361.

. . . .

4. *Affirmative defense*. Shore also claims that it can assert an affirmative defense under CERCLA, which provides a limited exception to liability for a release or threat of release caused solely

> by an act or omission of a third party other than an employee or agent of the defendant, or than one whose act or omission occurs in connection with

a contractual relationship, existing directly or indirectly, with the defendant (except where the sole contractual arrangement arises from a published tariff and acceptance for carriage by a common carrier by rail), if the defendant establishes by a preponderance of the evidence that (a) he exercised due care with respect to the hazardous substance concerned, taking into consideration the characteristics of such hazardous substance, in light of all relevant facts and circumstances, and (b) he took precautions against foreseeable acts or omissions of any such third party and the consequence that could foreseeably result from such acts or omissions. 42 U.S.C. § 9607(b)(3).

We disagree. Shore argues that it had nothing to do with the transportation of the hazardous substances and that it has exercised due care since taking control of the site. Who the "third part(ies)" Shore claims were responsible is difficult to fathom. It is doubtful that a prior owner could be such, especially the prior owner here, since the acts or omissions referred to in the statute are doubtless those occurring during the ownership or operation of the defendant. Similarly, many of the acts and omissions of the prior tenants/operators fall outside the scope of section 9607(b)(3), because they occurred before Shore owned the property. In addition, we find that Shore cannot rely on the affirmative defense even with respect to the tenants' conduct during the period after Shore closed on the property and when Shore evicted the tenants. Shore was aware of the nature of the tenants' activities before the closing and could readily have foreseen that they would continue to dump hazardous waste at the site. In light of this knowledge, we cannot say that the releases and threats of release resulting of these activities were "caused solely" by the tenants or that Shore "took precautions against" these "foreseeable acts or omissions."

. . . .

D. LeoGrande's Personal Liability

We hold LeoGrande liable as an "operator" under CERCLA, 42U.S.C. § 9607, for the state's response costs. Under CERCLA "owner or operator" is defined to mean "any person owning or operating" an onshore facility, *id.* § 9601(20)(A), and "person" includes individuals as well as corporations. *Id.* § 9601(21). More important, the definition of "owner or operator" excludes "a person, who, without participating in the management of a . . . facility, holds indicia of ownership primarily to protect his security interest in the facility." *Id.* § 9601(20)(A). The use of this exception implies that an owning stockholder who manages the corporation, such as LeoGrande, is liable under CERCLA as an "owner or operator." That conclusion is consistent with that of other courts that have addressed the issue. *See, e.g., United States v. Carolawn, Co.*, 14 Envtl.L.Rep. (Envtl.L.Inst.) 20,699, 20,700 (D. S.C. June 15, 1984); *NEPACCO,* 579 F. Supp. at 847-48. In any event, LeoGrande is in charge of the operation of the facility in question, and as such is an "operator" within the meaning of CERCLA.

Turning to liability for abatement, it is debatable whether a New York court would hold LeoGrande personally liable by piercing the corporate veil. New

York courts disregard the corporate form "reluctantly," *see Gartner v. Snyder,* 607 F.2d 582, 586 (2d Cir. 1979), and while the state claims that LeoGrande dominated Shore and that Shore was undercapitalized, these allegations are probably insufficiently particularized. *See Walkovszky v. Carlton,* 18 N.Y.2d 414, 420, 223 N.E.2d 6, 10, 276 N.Y.S.2d 585, 590 (1966). Both the New York Court of Appeals and this court have been quite insistent that the corporate form will not be disregarded unless the opposing party shows that the corporate form is being used fraudulently or as a means of carrying on business for personal rather than corporate ends. *See Marine Midland Bank, N.A. v. Miller,* 664 F.2d 899, 903 (2d Cir. 1981); *Walkovszky,* 18 N.Y.2d at 418, 420, 223 N.E.2d at 8, 10, 276 N.Y.S.2d at 588-90. The state's claim has not at this stage risen to that level.

Nevertheless, we hold LeoGrande liable without piercing the corporate veil. New York courts have held that a corporate officer who controls corporate conduct and thus is an active individual participant in that conduct is liable for the torts of the corporation. *See State v. Ole Olsen, Ltd.*, 35 N.Y.2d 979, 324 N.E.2d 886, 365 N.Y.S.2d 528 (1975); *LaLumia v. Schwartz,* 23 A.D.2d 668, 669, 257 N.Y.S.2d 348, 350 (1965). We need not address whether he is liable merely as an officer of Shore, for it is beyond dispute that LeoGrande specifically directs, sanctions, and actively participates in Shore's maintenance of the nuisance. *See also Escude Cruz v. Ortho Pharmaceutical Corp.*, 619 F.2d 902, 907 (1st Cir. 1980) (citing federal cases pronouncing this rule of liability for corporate officers). This general rule is particularly appropriate in the public nuisance context where " 'everyone who . . . participates in the . . . maintenance . . . of a nuisance are liable jointly and severally.' " *Schenectady Chemicals,* 117 Misc. 2d at 966, 459 N.Y.S.2d at 976 (quoting 17 Carmody-Wait 2d, Actions for Waste, Nuisance and Trespass § 107:59, at 334 (1979)); *accord Caso v. District Council 37, American Federation of State, County & Municipal Employees,* 43 A.D.2d 159, 163, 350 N.Y.S.2d 173, 178 (1973).

. . . .

Judgment affirmed.

NOTES AND QUESTIONS

(1) Other courts have almost uniformly agreed with the *Shore Realty* court in its analysis of the CERCLA proof of causation issue. *See, e.g., United States v. Alcan Aluminum Corp.,* 964 F.2d 252 (3d Cir. 1992); *United States v. Monsanto,* 858 F.2d 160 (4th Cir.1988), *cert. denied,* 490 U.S. 1106 (1989).

(2) *Shore Realty* also reflects the clear majority view in its conclusion that CERCLA imposes strict liability on responsible parties, including present owners of hazardous waste sites. *See, e.g., Tanglewood-East Homeowners v. Charles-Thomas, Inc.,* 849 F.2d 1568 (5th Cir. 1988); *In re T.P. Long Chemical, Inc.,* 22 ERC 1547 (N.D. Ohio, 1985); *United States v. Price,* 577 F. Supp. 1103 (D.N.J. 1983). Is this standard too harsh where it is applied to hazardous waste generators who attempted, in good faith, to take careful precautions regarding the disposal of their waste materials? What considerations of public policy would favor the imposition of strict generator liability under those circumstances?

(3) In construing CERCLA, courts have generally held that present owners of hazardous waste sites may be liable for response costs that are attributable to the activities of their lessees. *See, e.g., United States v. Argent Corp.*, 21 ERC 1354 (D.N.M. 1984); *United States v. Monsanto Co.*, 858 F.2d 160 (4th Cir. 1988). Is that a fair and appropriate conclusion? Should it apply to lessors whose tenants have affirmatively misrepresented the nature of their activities?

UNITED STATES v. BESTFOODS, *et al.*

United States Supreme Court (1998)
524 U.S. 51, 118 S. Ct. 1876, 141 L. Ed. 2d 43

SOUTER, J.

The United States brought this action for the costs of cleaning up industrial waste generated by a chemical plant. The issue before us, under the Comprehensive Environmental Response, Compensation and Liability Act of 1980, CERCLA, 94Stat. 2767, as amended, 42 U.S.C. § 9601 *et seq.*, is whether a parent corporation that actively participated in, and exercised control over, the operations of a subsidiary may, without more, be held liable as an operator of a polluting facility owned or operated by the subsidiary. We answer no, unless the corporate veil may be pierced. But a corporate parent that actively participated in, and exercised control over, the operations of the facility itself may be held directly liable in its own right as an operator of the facility.

In 1980, CERCLA was enacted in response to the serious environmental and health risks posed by industrial pollution. *See Exxon Corp. v. Hunt,* 475 U.S. 355, 358-359, 106 S.Ct. 1103, 1107-1108, 89 L.Ed.2d 364 (1986). "As its name implies, CERCLA is a comprehensive statute that grants the President broad power to command government agencies and private parties to clean up hazardous waste sites." *Key Tronic Corp. v. United States,* 511 U.S. 809, 814, 114 S.Ct. 1960, 1964, 128 L.Ed.2d 797 (1984). If it satisfies certain statutory conditions, the United States may, for instance, use the "Hazardous Substance Superfund" to finance cleanup efforts, *see* 42 U.S.C. §§ 9601(11), 9604; 26 U.S.C. § 9507, which it may then replenish by suits brought under § 107 of the Act against, among others, "any person who at the time of disposal of any hazardous substance owned or operated any facility." 42 U.S.C. § 9607(a)(2). So, those actually "responsible for any damage, environmental harm, or injury from chemical poisons may be tagged with the cost of their actions." S. Rep. No. 96-848, pp. 6119, 13, U.S. Code Cong. & Admin. News 1980, p. 6119 (1980). The term "person" is defined in CERCLA to include corporations and other business organizations *see* § 9601(21), and the term "facility" enjoys a broad and detailed definition as well. *See* § 9601(9). The phrase "owner or operator" is defined only by tautology, however, as "any person owning or operating" a facility, § 9601(20)(A)(ii), and it is this bit of circularity that prompts our review. *Cf. Exxon Corp. v. Hunt, supra,* at 363,

106 S.Ct. at 1109 (CERCLA, "unfortunately, is not a model of legislative draftsmanship").

In 1957, Ott Chemical Co. (Ott I) began manufacturing chemicals at a plant near Muskegon, Michigan, and its intentional and unintentional dumping of hazardous substances significantly polluted the soil and ground water at the site. In 1965, respondent CPC International, Inc. incorporated a wholly owned subsidiary to buy Ott I's assets in exchange for CPC stock. The new company, also dubbed Ott Chemical Co. (Ott II), continued chemical manufacturing at the site, and continued to pollute its surroundings. CPC kept the managers of Ott I, including its founder, president, and principal shareholder, Arnold Ott, on board as officers of Ott II. Arnold Ott and several other Ott II officers and directors were also given positions at CPC, and they performed duties for both corporations.

In 1972, CPC sold Ott II to Story Chemical Company, which operated the Muskegon plant until its bankruptcy in 1977. Shortly thereafter, when respondent Michigan Department of Natural Resources (MDNR) examined the site for environmental damage, it found the land littered with thousands of leaking and even exploding drums of waste, and the soil and water saturated with noxious chemicals. MDNR sought a buyer for the property who would be willing to contribute towards its cleanup, and after extensive negotiations, respondent Aerojet-General Corp. arranged for transfer of the site from the Story bankruptcy trustee in 1977. Aerojet created a wholly owned California subsidiary, Cordova Chemical Company (Cordova/California), to purchase the property, and Cordova/California in turn created a wholly owned Michigan subsidiary, Cordova Chemical Company of Michigan (Cordova/Michigan), which manufactured chemicals at the site until 1986.

By 1981, the federal Environmental Protection Agency had undertaken to see the site cleaned up, and its long-term remedial plan called for expenditures well into the tens of millions of dollars. To recover some of that money, the United States filed this action under § 107 in 1989, naming five defendants as responsible parties: CPC, Aerojet, Cordova/California, Cordova/Michigan, and Arnold Ott. (By that time Ott I and Ott II were defunct). After the parties (and MDNR) had launched a flurry of contribution claims, counterclaims, and cross-claims, the District Court consolidated the cases for trial in three phases: liability, remedy, and insurance coverage. So far, only the first phase has been completed: in 1991, the District Court held a 15-day bench trial on the issue of liability. Because the parties stipulated that the Muskegon plant was a "facility" within the meaning of 42 U.S.C. § 9601(9), that hazardous substances had been released at the facility, and that the United States had incurred reimbursable response costs to clean up the site, the trial focused on the issues of whether CPC and Aerojet, as the parent corporations of Ott II and the Cordova companies, had "owned or operated" the facility within the meaning of § 107(a)(2).

The District Court said that operator liability may attach to a parent corporation both directly, when the parent itself operates the facility, and indirectly, when the corporate veil can be pierced under state law. *See CPC Int'l, Inc. v. Aerojet-General Corp.*, 777 F. Supp. 549, 752 (W.D. Mich. 1991). The court explained that, while CERCLA imposes direct liability in situations in which the corporate veil cannot be pierced under traditional concepts of corporate law, "the statute and its legislative history do not suggest that CERCLA rejects entirely the crucial limits to liability that are inherent to corporate law." *Id.* at 573. As the District Court put it,

> a parent corporation is directly liable under section 107(a)(2) as an operator only when it has exerted power or influence over its subsidiary by actively participating in and exercising control over the subsidiary's business during a period of disposal of hazardous waste. A parent's actual participation in and control over a subsidiary's functions and decision-making creates 'operator' liability under CERCLA; a parent's mere oversight of a subsidiary's business in a manner appropriate and consistent with the investment relationship between a parent and its wholly owned subsidiary does not. *Ibid.*

Applying that test to the facts of this case, the District Court held both CPC and Aerojet liable under § 107(a)(2) as operators. As to CPC, the court found it particularly telling that CPC selected Ott II's board of directors and populated its executive ranks with CPC officials, and that a CPC official, G.R.D. Williams, played a significant role in shaping Ott II's environmental compliance policy.

After a divided panel of the Court of Appeals for the Sixth Circuit reversed in part, *United States v. Cordova / Michigan,* 59 F.3d 584, that court granted rehearing en banc and vacated the panel decision. 67 F.3d 586 (1995). This time, 7 judges to 6, the court again reversed the District Court in part. 113 F.3d 572 (1997). The majority remarked on the possibility that a parent company might be held directly liable as an operator of a facility owned by its subsidiary: "At least conceivably, a parent might independently operate the facility in the stead of its subsidiary; or, as a sort of joint venturer, actually operate the facility alongside its subsidiary." *Id.* at 579. But the court refused to go any further and rejected the District Court's analysis with the explanation:

> that where a parent corporation is sought to be held liable as an operator pursuant to 42 U.S.C. § 9607(a)(2)based upon the extent of its control of its subsidiary which owns the facility, the parent will be liable only when the requirements necessary to pierce the corporate veil [under state law] are met. In other words, . . . whether the parent will be liable as an operator depends upon whether the degree to which it controls its subsidiary and the extent and manner of its involvement with the facility, amount to the abuse of the corporate form that will warrant piercing the corporate veil and disregarding the separate corporate entities of the parent and subsidiary. *Id.* at 580.

Applying Michigan veil-piercing law, the Court of Appeals decided that neither CPC nor Aeroject was liable for controlling the actions of its subsidiaries, since the parent and subsidiary corporations maintained separate personalities and the parents did not utilize the subsidiary corporate form to perpetrate fraud or subvert justice.

We granted certiorari, 522 U.S. ___, 118 S.Ct. 621, 139 L.Ed.2d 506 (1997), to resolve a conflict among the Circuits over the extent to which parent corporations may be held liable under CERCLA for operating facilities ostensibly under the control of their subsidiaries. We now vacate and remand.

. . . .

It is a general principle of corporate law deeply "ingrained in our economic and legal systems" that a parent corporation (so-called because of control through ownership of another corporation's stock) is not liable for the acts of its subsidiaries. Douglas & Shanks, *Insulation from Liability Through Subsidiary Corporations,* 39 Yale L.J. 193 (1929) (hereinafter Douglas). . . . . Thus, it is hornbook law that "the exercise of the 'control' which stock ownership gives to the stockholders . . . will not create liability beyond the assets of the subsidiary. That 'control' includes the election of directors, the making of by-laws . . . and the doing of all other acts incident to the legal status of stockholders. Nor will a duplication of some or all of the directors or executive officers be fatal." Although this respect for corporate distinctions when the subsidiary is a polluter has been severely criticized in the literature, *see, e.g.*, Note, *Liability of Parent Corporations for Hazardous Waste Cleanup and Damages,* 99 Harv. L. Rev. 986 (1986), nothing in CERCLA purports to reject this bedrock principle, and against this venerable common-law backdrop, the congressional silence is audible. *Cf. Edmonds v. Campagnie Generale Transatlantique,* 443 U.S. 256, 266-267, 99 S.Ct. 2753, 2759, 61 L.Ed.2d 521 (1979) ("silence is most eloquent, for such reticence while contemplating an important and controversial change in existing law is unlikely"). The Government has indeed made no claim that a corporate parent is liable as an owner or an operator under § 107 simply because its subsidiary is subject to liability for owning or operating a polluting facility.

But there is an equally fundamental principle of corporate law, applicable to the parent-subsidiary relationship as well as generally, that the corporate veil may be pierced and the shareholder held liable for the corporation's conduct when, inter alia, the corporate form would otherwise be misused to accomplish certain wrongful purposes, most notably fraud, on the shareholder's behalf.

. . . .

Nothing in CERCLA purports to rewrite this well-settled rule either. CERCLA is thus like many another congressional enactment in giving no indication "that the entire corpus of state corporation law is to be replaced simply because a plaintiff's cause of action is based upon a federal statute," *Burks v. Lasker*, 441 U.S. 471, 478, 99 S.Ct. 1831, 60 L.Ed.2d 404 (1979), and the failure of the statute to speak to a matter as fundamental as the liability implications of corporate ownership demands application of the rule that "[i]n order to abrogate a common-law principle, the statute must speak directly to the question addressed by the common law." *United States v. Texas*, 507 U.S. 529, 534, 113 S.Ct. 1631, 1634, 123 L.Ed.2d 245 (1993) (internal quotation marks omitted). The Court of Appeals was accordingly correct in holding that when (but only when) the corporate veil may be pierced, a parent corporation may be charged with derivative CERCLA liability for its subsidiary's action.

. . . .

If the act rested liability entirely on ownership of a polluting facility, this opinion might end here; but CERCLA liability may turn on operation as well as ownership, and nothing in the statute's terms bars a parent corporation from direct liability for its own actions in operating a facility owned by its subsidiary. As Justice (then-Professor) Douglas noted almost 70 years ago, derivative liability cases are to be distinguished from those in which "the alleged wrong can seemingly be traced to the parent through the conduit of its own personnel and management" and "the parent is directly a participant in the wrong complained of." Douglas, 207, 208. In such instances, the parent is directly liable for its own actions. *See* H. Henn & J. Alexander, Laws of Corporations 347 (3d ed. 1983) (hereinafter Henn & Alexander) ("Apart from corporation law principles, a shareholder, whether a natural person or a corporation, may be liable on the ground that such shareholder's activity resulted in the liability"). The fact that a corporate subsidiary happens to own a polluting facility operated by its parent does nothing, then, to displace the rule that the parent "corporation is [itself] responsible for the wrongs committed by its agents in the course of its business," *Mine Workers v. Coronado Coal Co.*, 259 U.S. 344, 395, 42 S.Ct. 570, 577, 66 L.Ed. 975 (1922), and whereas the rules of veil-piercing limit derivative liability for the actions of another corporation, CERCLA's "operator" provision is concerned primarily with direct liability for one's own actions. *See, e.g., Sidney S. Arst Co. v. Pipefitters Welfare Ed. Fund,* 25 F.3d 417, 420 (C.A. 7 1994) ("the direct, personal liability provided by CERCLA is distinct from the derivative liability that results from piercing the corporate veil") (internal quotation marks omitted). It is this direct liability that is properly seen as being at issue here.

Under the plain language of the statute, any person who operates a polluting facility is directly liable for the costs of cleaning up the pollution. *See* 42 U.S.C. § 9607(a)(2). This is so regardless of whether that person is the facility's owner, the owner's parent corporation or business partner, or even a saboteur who sneaks into the facility at night to discharge its poisons out of malice. If any such act of operating a corporate subsidiary's facility is done on behalf of a parent corporation, the existence of the parent-subsidiary relationship under state corporate law is simply irrelevant to the issue of direct liability.

. . . .

This much is easy to say; the difficulty comes in defining actions sufficient to constitute direct parental "operation." Here, of course, we may again rue the uselessness of CERCLA's definition of a facility's "operator" as "any person . . . operating" the facility, 42 U.S.C. § 9601(20)(A)(ii), which leaves us to do the best we can to give the term its "ordinary or natural meaning." *Bailey v. United States*, 516 U.S. 137, 145, 116 S.Ct. 501, 506, 133 L.Ed.2d 472 (1995) (internal quotation marks omitted). In a mechanical sense, to "operate" ordinarily means "[t]o control the functioning of; run; operate a sewing machine." American Heritage Dictionary 1268 (3d ed. 1992); *see also* Webster's New International Dictionary, 1707 (2d ed. 1958) ("to work; as, to operate a machine"). And in the organizational sense more obviously intended by CERCLA, the word ordinarily means "[t]o conduct the affairs of; manage: operate a business." American Heritage Dictionary, *supra* at 1268; *see also* Webster's New International Dictionary, *supra,* at 1707 ("to manage"). So, under CERCLA, an operator is simply someone who directs the workings of, manages, or conducts the affairs of a facility. To sharpen the definition for purposes of CERCLA's concern with environmental contamination, an operator must manage, direct, or conduct operations specifically related to pollution, that is, operations having to do with the leakage or disposal of hazardous waste, or decisions about compliance with environmental regulations.

With this understanding, we are satisfied that the Court of Appeals correctly rejected the District Court's analysis of direct liability. But we also think that the appeals court erred in limiting direct liability under the statute to a parent's sole or joint venture operation, so as to eliminate any possible finding that CPC is liable as an operator on the facts of this case. . . .

In imposing direct liability, the District Court failed to recognize that "it is entirely appropriate for directors of a parent corporation to serve as directors of its subsidiary, and that fact alone may not serve to expose the parent corporation to liability for its subsidiary's acts." *American Protein Corp. v. AB Volvo*, 844 F.2d 56, 57 (C.A. 2), *cert. denied,* 488 U.S. 852, 109 S.Ct. 136, 102 L.Ed.2d 109 (1988); *see also Kingston Dry Dock Co. v. Lake Champlain Transp. Co.*, 31 F.2d 265, 267 (C.A. 2 1929) (L. Hand, J.) ("Control through the ownership of shares does not fuse the corporations, even when the directors are common to each"); Henn & Alexander 355 (noting that it is "normal" for a parent and subsidiary to "have identical directors and officers").

This recognition that the corporate personalities remain distinct has its corollary in the "well established principle [of corporate law] that directors and officers holding positions with a parent and its subsidiary can and do 'change hats' to represent the two corporations separately, despite their common ownership." *Lusk v. Foxmeyer Health Corp.*, 129 F.3d 773, 779 (C.A. 5 1997); *see also Fisser v. International Bank,* 282 F.2d 231, 238 (C.A. 2 1960). Since courts generally presume "that the directors are wearing their 'subsidiary hats' and not their 'parent hats' when acting for the subsidiary," P. Blumberg, Law of Corporate Groups: Procedural Problems in the Law of Parent and Subsidiary Corporations § 1.02.1, at 12 (1983); *see, e.g., United States v. Jon-T Chemicals, Inc.*, 768 F.2d 686, 691 (C.A. 5 1985), cert. denied, 475 U.S. 1014, 106 S.Ct. 1194, 89 L.Ed.2d 309 (1986), it cannot be enough to establish liability here that dual officers and directors made policy decisions and supervised activities at the facility. The Government would have to show that, despite the general presumption to the contrary, the officers and directors were acting in their capacities as CPC officers and directors, and not as Ott II officers and directors, when they committed those acts. The District Court made no such enquiry here, however, disregarding entirely this time-honored common law rule.

In sum, the District Court's focus on the relationship between parent and subsidiary (rather than parent and facility), combined with its automatic attribution of the actions of dual officers and directors to the corporate parent, erroneously, even if unintentionally, treated CERCLA as though it displaced or fundamentally altered common law standards of limited liability. Indeed, if the evidence of common corporate personnel acting at management and directorial levels were enough to support a finding of a parent corporation's direct operator liability under CERCLA, then the possibility of resort to veil piercing to establish indirect, derivative liability for the subsidiary's violations would be academic. There would in essence be a relaxed, CERCLA-specificrule of derivative liability that would banish traditional standards and expectations from the law of CERCLA liability. But, as we have said, such a rule does not arise from congressional silence, and CERCLA's silence is dispositive.

We accordingly agree with the Court of Appeals that a participation-and-control test looking to the parent's supervision over the subsidiary, especially one that assumes that dual officers always act on behalf of the parent, cannot be used to identify operation of a facility resulting in direct parental liability. Nonetheless, a return to the ordinary meaning of the word "operate" in the organizational sense will indicate why we think that the Sixth Circuit stopped short when it confined its examples of direct parental operation to exclusive or joint ventures, and declined to find at least the possibility of direct operation by CPC in this case.

In our enquiry into the meaning Congress presumably had in mind when it used the verb "to operate," we recognized that the statute obviously meant something more than mere mechanical activation of pumps and valves, and must be read to contemplate "operation" as including the exercise of direction of the facility's activities. The Court of Appeals recognized this by indicating that a parent can be held directly liable when the parent operates the facility in the stead of its subsidiary or alongside the subsidiary in some sort of a joint venture. *See* 113 F.3d at 579. We anticipated a further possibility above, however, when we observed that a dual officer or director might depart so far from the norms of parental influence exercised through dual officeholding as to serve the parent, even when ostensibly acting on behalf of the subsidiary in operating the facility. Yet, another possibility, suggested by the facts of this case, is that an agent of the parent with no hat to wear but the parent's hat might manage or direct activities at the facility.

Identifying such an occurrence calls for line drawing yet again, since the acts of direct operation that give rise to parental liability must necessarily be distinguished from the interference that stems from the normal relationship between parent and subsidiary. Again norms of corporate behavior (undisturbed by any CERCLA provision) are crucial reference points.. . . .

The critical question is whether, in degree and detail, actions directed to the facility by an agent of the parent alone are eccentric under accepted norms of parental oversight of a subsidiary's facility.

There is, in fact, some evidence that CPC engaged in just this type and degree of activity at the Muskegon plant. The District Court's opinion speaks of an agent of CPC alone who played a conspicuous part in dealing with the toxic risks emanating from the operation of the plant. G.R.D. Williams worked only for CPC; he was not an employee, officer, or director of Ott II, and thus, his actions were of necessity taken only on behalf of CPC . . . .

We think that these findings are enough to raise an issue of CPC's operation of the facility through Williams's actions, though we would draw no ultimate conclusion from these findings at this point. Not only would we be deciding in the first instance an issue on which the trial and appellate courts did not focus, but the very fact that the District Court did not see the case as we do suggests that there may be still more to be known about Williams's activities.

Indeed, even as the factual findings stand, the trial court offered little in the way of concrete detail for its conclusions about Williams's role in Ott II's environmental affairs, and the parties vigorously dispute the extent of Williams's involvement. Prudence thus counsels us to remand, on the theory of direct operation set out here, for reevaluation of Williams's role, and of the role of any other CPC agent who might be said to have had a part in operating the Muskegon facility.

. . . .

The judgment of the Court of Appeals for the Sixth Circuit is vacated, and the case is remanded with instructions to return it to the District Court for further proceedings consistent with this opinion.

It is so ordered.

NOTES AND QUESTION

(1) Do you agree with the Court's analysis of CERCLA in this case? Is its reasoning consistent with the established notion that CERCLA is a strict liability statute? Does its conclusion detract from the achievement of the statute's environmental purposes?

(2) The principal case resolved a dispute among the lower federal courts as to the conditions under which a parent corporation may be liable for response costs necessitated by the activities of its subsidiary. Some courts had held that parent corporations may not be liable under CERCLA for response costs incurred by their subsidiaries. *See, e.g., Joslyn Corp. v. T.L. Jones and Co.,* 696 F. Supp. 222 (W.D. La. 1988); *In re Acushnet River and New Bedford Harbor Proceedings,* 675 F. Supp. 22 (D. Mass. 1987); *Aluminum Co. of Am. v. Beezer East, Inc.,* 124 F.2d 551 (3d Cir. 1987). Other courts evinced a willingness to hold parent corporations liable under CERCLA, at least under certain circumstances. *See, e.g., State of Idaho v. Bunker Hill,* 635 F. Supp. 665 (D. Idaho, 1986); *Rockwell Int'l. Corp. v. I U Int'l. Corp.,* 702 F. Supp. 1384 (N.D. Ill. 1988); *United States v. Kayser-Roth Corp.,* 910 F.2d 24 (1st Cir. 1990), *cert. denied,* 498 U.S. 1084 (1991); *United States v. Nicolet, Inc.,* 712 F. Supp. 1193 (E.D. Pa. 1989). For additional discussion of pre-*Bestfoods* caselaw, *see* F. Grad, Treatise on Environmental Law § 4A.02[1][j]. *See also,* Aronovsky and Fuller, *Liability of Parent Corporations for Hazardous Releases Under CERCLA,* 24 U.S.F. L. Rev. 421 (1990).

(3) One issue not reached by the United States Supreme Court in *Bestfoods* is whether, notwithstanding contrary provisions of state corporate law, dissolved corporations may be sued under CERCLA. At least one federal court has held that that is the case. *See United States v. Sharon Steel Corp.,* 681 F. Supp. 1492 (D. Utah 1987). Other courts disagree. *See, e.g., Levin Metals Corp. v. Parr-Richmond Terminal Co.,* 631 F. Supp. 303 (N.D. Cal. 1986), *aff'd,* 817 F.2d 1448 (9th Cir. 1987); *City of Philadelphia v. Stepan Chem. Co.,* 713 F. Supp. 1491 (E.D. Pa. 1989).

UNITED STATES v. MONSANTO COMPANY

United States Court of Appeals, Fourth Circuit (1988)
858 F.2d 160

SPROUSE, C.J.:

Oscar Seidenberg and Harvey Hutchinson (the site-owners) and Allied Corporation, Monsanto Company, and EM Industries, Inc. (the generator defendants), appeal from the district court's entry of summary judgment holding them liable to the United States and the State of South Carolina (the governments) under section 107(a) of the Comprehensive Environmental Response, Compensation, and Liability Act of 1980 (CERCLA). 42 U.S.C. § 9607(a)(West Supp. 1987). The court determined that the defendants were liable jointly and severally for $1,813,624 in response costs accrued from the partial removal of hazardous waste from a disposal facility located near Columbia, South Carolina.

In 1972, Seidenberg and Hutchinson leased a four-acre tract of land they owned to the Columbia Organic Chemical Company (COCC), a South Carolina chemical manufacturing corporation. The property, located along Bluff Road near Columbia, South Carolina, consisted of a small warehouse and surrounding areas. The lease was verbal, on a month-to-month basis, and according to the site-owners' deposition testimony, was executed for the sole purpose of allowing COCC to store raw materials and finished products in the warehouse. Seidenberg and Hutchinson received monthly lease payments of $200, which increased to $350 by 1980.

In the mid-1970s, COCC expanded its business to include the brokering and recycling of chemical waste generated by third parties. It used the Bluff Road site as a waste storage and disposal facility for its new operations. In 1976, COCC's principals incorporated South Carolina Recycling and Disposal Inc. (SCRDI), for the purpose of assuming COCC's waste-handling business, and the site-owners began accepting lease payments from SCRDI.

SCRDI contracted with numerous off-site waste producers for the transport, recycling, and disposal of chemical and other waste. Among these producers were agencies of the federal government and South Carolina, and various private entities including the three generator defendants in this litigation. Although SCRDI operated other disposal sites, it deposited much of the waste it received at the Bluff Road facility. The waste stored at Bluff Road contained many chemical substances that federal law defines as "hazardous."

Between 1976 and 1980, SCRDI haphazardly deposited more than 7,000 55-gallon drums of chemical waste on the four-acre Bluff Road site. It placed waste laden drums and containers wherever there was space, often without pallets to protect them from the damp ground. It stacked drums on top of one another without regard to the chemical compatibility of their contents. It maintained no documented safety procedures and kept no inventory of the stored chemicals. Over time many of the drums rusted, rotted, and otherwise deteriorated. Hazardous substances leaked from the decaying drums and oozed into the ground. The substances commingled with incompatible chemicals that had escaped from other containers, generating noxious fumes, fires, and explosions.

On October 26, 1977, a toxic cloud formed when chemicals leaking from rusted drums reacted with rainwater. Twelve responding firemen were hospitalized. Again, on July 24, 1979, an explosion and fire resulted when chemicals stored in glass jars leaked onto drums containing incompatible substances. SCRDI's site manager could not identify the substances that caused the explosion, making the fire difficult to extinguish.

In 1980, the Environmental Protection Agency (EPA) inspected the Bluff Road site. Its investigation revealed that the facility was filled well beyond its capacity with chemical waste. The number of drums and the reckless manner in which they were stacked precluded access to various areas in the site. Many of the drums observed were unlabeled, or their labels had become unreadable from exposure, rendering it impossible to identify their contents. The EPA concluded that the site posed "a major fire hazard."

Later that year, the United States filed suit under section 7003 of the Resource Conservation and Recovery Act, 42 U.S.C. § 6973, against SCRDI, COCC, and Oscar Seidenberg. The complaint was filed before the December 11, 1980, effective date of CERCLA, and it sought only injunctive relief. Thereafter, the State of South Carolina intervened as a plaintiff in the pending action.

In the course of discovery, the governments identified a number of waste generators, including the generator defendants in this appeal, that had contracted with SCRDI for waste disposal. The governments notified the generators that they were potentially responsible for the costs of cleanup at Bluff Road under section 107(a) of the newly-enacted CERCLA. As a result of these contacts, the governments executed individual settlement agreements with twelve of the identified off-site producers. The generator defendants, however, declined to settle.

. . . .

SITE-OWNERS' LIABILITY

In light of the strict liability imposed by § 107(a), we cannot agree with the site-owners' contention that they are not within the class of owners Congress intended to hold liable. The traditional elements of tort culpability on which the site-owners rely simply are absent from the statute. The plain language of § 107(a)(2) extends liability to owners of waste facilities regardless of their degree of participation in the subsequent disposal of hazardous waste.

Under § 107(a)(2), any person who owned a facility at a time when hazardous substances were deposited there may be held liable for all costs of removal or remedial action if a release or threatened release of a hazardous substance occurs. The site-owners do not dispute their ownership of the Bluff Road facility, or the fact that releases occurred there during their period of ownership. Under these circumstances, all the prerequisites to § 107(a) liability have been satisfied. *See New York v. Shore Realty,* 759 F.2d 1032, 1043-44 (2d Cir. 1985) (site-owner held liable under CERCLA § 107(a)(1)even though he did not contribute to the presence or cause the release of hazardous substances at the facility) . . . .

GENERATOR DEFENDANTS' LIABILITY

The generator defendants first contend that the district court misinterpreted § 107(a)(3) because it failed to read into the statute a requirement that the governments prove a nexus between the waste they sent to the site and resulting environmental harm. They maintain that the statutory phrase "containing such hazardous substances" requires proof that the specific substances they generated and sent to the site were present at the facility at the time of release. The district court held, however, that the statute was satisfied by proof that hazardous substances "like" those contained in the generator defendants' waste were found at the site. *United States v. South Carolina Recycling and Disposal, Inc.* 653 F. Supp. 984, 991-92 (D.S.C. 1986) (SCRDI). We agree with the district court's interpretation.

Reduced of surplus language, § 107(a)(3) and (4) impose liability on off-site waste generators who:

> arranged for disposal . . . of hazardous substances . . . at any facility . . . *containing such hazardous substances* . . . from which there is a release . . . of a hazardous substance . . . (emphasis supplied).

In our view the plain meaning of the adjective "such" in the phrase "containing such hazardous substances" is "[a]like, similar, or the like kind." Black's Law Dictionary 1284, 5th ed. (1979). As used in the statute, the phrase, "such hazardous substances" denotes hazardous substances alike, similar, or of a like kind to those that were present in a generator defendant's waste or that could have been produced by the mixture of the defendant's waste with other waste present at the site. It does not mean that the plaintiff must trace the ownership of each generic chemical compound found at a site. Absent proof that a generator defendant's specific waste remained at a facility at the time of release, a showing of chemical similarity between hazardous substances is sufficient.

The overall structure of CERCLA's liability provisions also militates against the generator defendants' "proof of ownership" argument. In *Shore Realty,* the Second Circuit held with respect to site-owners that requiring proof of ownership at any time later than the time of disposal would go far toward rendering the § 107(b) defenses superfluous. We agree with the court's reading of the statute and conclude that its reasoning applies equally to the generator defendants' contentions. As the statute provides—"[n]ot withstanding any other provision or rule of law"—liability under section 107(a) is "subject only to the defenses set forth" in section 107(b). Each of the three defenses established in § 107(b) "carves out from liability an exception based on causation." *Shore Realty,* 759 F.2d at 1044. Congress has therefore, allocated the burden of disproving causation to the defendant who profited from the generation and inexpensive disposal of hazardous waste. We decline to interpret the statute in a way that would neutralize the force of Congress' intent.

Finally, the purpose underlying CERCLA's liability provisions counsels against the generator defendants' argument. Throughout the statute's legislative history, there appears the recurring theme of facilitating prompt action to remedy the environmental blight of unscrupulous waste disposal. In deleting causation language from § 107(a), we assume as have many other courts that Congress knew of the synergistic and migratory capacities of leaking chemical waste and the technological infeasibility of tracing improperly disposed waste to its source. In view of this, we will not frustrate the statute's salutary goals by engrafting a "proof of ownership" requirement, which in practice, would be as onerous as the language Congress saw fit to delete. *See United States v. Wade,* 577 F. Supp. 1326, 1332 (E.D.Pa. 1983) ("To require a plaintiff under CERCLA to 'fingerprint' wastes is to eviscerate the statute.")

. . . .

NOTES AND QUESTIONS

(1) Do you agree with the Fourth Circuit's position as to proof of causation in this case? Should the court have required some showing of a causal link between particular generators' wastes and harm, or a risk of harm, posed at the site where those wastes were disposed? Should it have attempted to apply traditional tort law doctrines of causation-in-fact and proximate causation? What practical and policy considerations support the causation approach that the *Monsanto* court did take?

(2) A number of other federal courts have also held that, in CERCLA litigation, attenuated concepts of causation must be applied. *See, e.g., United States v. Bliss,* 667 F. Supp. 1298 (E.D. Mo. 1987); *Missouri v. Independent Petrochemical Corp.,* 610 F. Supp. 4 (E.D. Mo. 1985); *United States v. South Carolina Recycling and Disposal, Inc.,* 653 F. Supp. 984 (D.S.C. 1986); *Artesian Water Co. v. Government of New Castle County,* 659 F. Supp. 1269 (D. Del. 1987).

(3) In a portion of the *Monsanto* opinion that is not reproduced above, the Fourth Circuit rejected a contention of the generator defendants that their liability should have been apportioned on the basis of the volume of hazardous waste those parties had deposited at the Bluff Road site, as compared to the total volume of hazardous waste disposed of there by all parties. The court stated that the generator defendants had failed to present any evidence that demonstrated "a relationship between waste volume, the release of hazardous substances, and the harm at the site. Further, in light of the commingling of hazardous substances, the district court could not have reasonably apportioned liability without some evidence disclosing the individual and interactive qualities of the substances deposited there." *See United States v. Monsanto Co.,* 858 F.2d 160, 172-173 (4th Cir. 1988). Is the court's reasoning on this point persuasive?

[8] Private Cost Recovery Actions

CITY OF PHILADELPHIA v. STEPAN CHEMICAL CORP.

United States District Court, Eastern District of Pennsylvania (1982)
544 F. Supp. 1135

DITTER D.J.:

In this action, the City of Philadelphia ("the City") seeks to recover clean-up costs and consequential damages which resulted from the illegal dumping on city property of industrial waste generated by the defendants. The suit is predicated upon numerous federal and state environmental statutes as well as several common law theories of recovery. Defendants have filed a comprehensive motion for judgment on the pleadings under Fed. R. Civ. P. 12(c) asserting that the statutes upon which the City relies do not support its claim and that, as a matter of law, they cannot be held liable on any of the common law causes of action. For the reasons that follow, the motion will be granted in part and denied in part.

"In considering a motion for judgment on the pleadings, the trial court is required to view the facts presented in the light most favorable to the nonmoving party." *Chuy v. National Football League Players' Association,* 495 F. Supp. 137, 138 (E.D.Pa. 1980), *quoting* 5 C. Wright and A. Miller, Federal Practice and Procedure § 1368, at 690 (1969). A review of the pleadings in light of this standard reveals the following factual setting. Defendants are a number of concerns which generate industrial waste as a byproduct of their operations. At various times, each defendant contracted with either Lightman Drum Company ("Lightman") or ABM Disposal Service Company ("ABM") to haul and dispose of the waste. During 1974 and 1975, ABM and Lightman illegally dumped the waste at a landfill on Enterprise Avenue in Southwest Philadelphia ("the Enterprise site") which was owned by the City and intended for use only by the City. Access to the Enterprise site was gained by bribing two City employees. The existence of substantial quantities of waste on the Enterprise site was discovered by City officials in 1979. Criminal convictions were obtained against the employees who accepted the bribes and against Lightman and its president, Jerome Lightman. Charges are pending against the president of ABM, Ellis Barnhouse, who is presently a fugitive.

The City alleges that as a result of this illegal dumping, the soil at the Enterprise site has been contaminated and the adjacent Delaware River and groundwater underlying the site have been polluted. This has obligated the City to commence a comprehensive clean up program having an estimated cost of $10 million. In addition, a sewage sludge recycling center which is scheduled to be built on the Enterprise site has been postponed indefinitely, a delay which will increase construction costs by about $20 million. The City filed a nine-count complaint seeking to recover $30 million in damages as well as civil penalties. The complaint sets forth the following claims for relief: (1) liability under the Comprehensive Environmental Response, Compensation, and Liability Act, 42 U.S.C. § 9601 *et seq.* (CERCLA); (2) the citizen suit provision of the Clean Water Act, 33U.S.C. § 1365(a); (3) the federal common law of nuisance; (4) common law strict liability; (5) the Pennsylvania Solid Waste Management Act, 35 P.S. § 6018.10 *et seq.* (the SWMA); (6) the Pennsylvania Clean Streams Law, 35 P.S. § 691.1 *et seq.*; (7) common law trespass and nuisance; (8) common law negligence; and (9) various provisions of the Philadelphia Code. Jurisdiction is based upon 28 U.S.C. § 1331, 42 U.S.C. § 1331, 42 U.S.C. § 9613(b)(granting federal courts "exclusive original jurisdiction" of all controversies arising under CERCLA), and 33 U.S.C. § 1365(a)(granting federal courts jurisdiction over Clean Water Act actions). Jurisdiction over the state claims is pendent.

COUNT 1: COMPREHENSIVE ENVIRONMENTAL RESPONSE, COMPENSATION AND LIABILITY ACT

The City's CERCLA claim is predicated upon the statute's liability provision, 42 U.S.C. § 9607(a). That provision designates three categories of "responsible persons." They are (1) present and former owners of hazardous substances disposal sites; (2) transporters of hazardous substances, and (3) those who arrange for the transport or disposal of hazardous substances (normally generators). These responsible persons are liable for three types of costs which are incurred as the result of a release or threatened release of the hazardous substances: (1) governmental response costs, (2) private response costs incurred "by any other person" consistent with the national contingency plan, and (3) damage to natural resources. It can readily be seen that the three categories of "responsible persons" set forth in 42 U.S.C. § 9607(a)(1)-(4)encompass all of the principal actors in this litigation—the City owns and operates the landfill, defendants generated the hazardous substances and contracted for their disposal, and ABM and Lightman acted as transporters. Thus, had the federal or state government undertaken to clean up the Enterprise site, all of these parties arguably would be liable for the cost of removal or other remedial action under 42 U.S.C. § 9607(a)(4)(A).

However, that did not occur. Instead, the City, itself possibly subject to liability for governmental response costs, undertook the clean up and now contends that defendants are liable for its "necessary costs of response" under 42 U.S.C. § 9607(a)(4)(B). It is this anomaly which gives rise to defendants' primary argument in seeking judgment on the City's CERCLA claim. They contend that the term "any other person" as used in 42 U.S.C. § 9607(a)(4)(B)does not include a party which itself is subject to liability under the act. Although the statute's language does not explicitly support this construction, defendants assert that it is the only interpretation consistent with the act's structure and with the logical functioning of its many interrelated provisions. Specifically, they point to several inconsistencies in the administration of the Act's funding provisions which would result if the City may bring this action. Under 42 U.S.C. § 9611(a), the president is authorized to use money in the fund for payment of necessary response costs "incurred by any other person as a result of carrying out the national contingency plan . . . ." Defendants contend that if the term "any other person" includes those who are subject to liability under the act, responsible persons could claim against the fund and against other responsible parties. Because the government has subrogation rights for payments made from the fund, *see* 42 U.S.C.

§ 9612(c)(1), the City's interpretation would assertedly result in a merry go round of litigation with the government suing a responsible person which in turn could sue other responsible persons which in turn could claim against the fund and so forth. Defendants also point to the claims procedure under 42 U.S.C. § 9612as demonstrating the untenability of the City's position as a plaintiff. Under this section, a party making claim against the fund must first make demand for response costs upon known responsile persons and wait sixty days for satisfaction of demand. If reimbursement is not forthcoming, the claimant then has the choice of obtaining payment from the fund or suing the responsible person under 42 U.S.C. § 9607(a)(4)(B). Defendants argue that Congress could not have intended to give responsible parties the same right to claim against the fund and sue other responsible persons as does a nonculpable third party.

Concededly, defendants' approach possesses a degree of analytic neatness. Regardless of how tidy it may be, however, I cannot ignore the end result of their logic—that the City, which did not voluntarily allow the placement of the hazardous substances on its property and which sustained damages as the result of their illegal disposal, is precluded from recovering its clean-up costs from those parties who engaged in the very activities for which they can be held responsible under the act. Because such preclusion is not compelled by the language of the CERCLA, by its legislative history, or by the environmental objectives which it is designed to achieve, I will reject defendants' position and deny their motion for judgment on Count I of the complaint.

. . . Under 42 U.S.C. § 9601(21)both federal and state governments are subsumed under the definition of person. In the context in which it appears, then, the term "any other person" is quite conceivably designed to refer to persons other than federal or state governments and not, as defendants argue, to persons other than those made responsible under the act. Thus, although not a model of clarity, the provision does not specifically exclude parties who may be liable for the costs of governmental action nor does its language necessarily support such a construction.

Although the legislative history does little to clarify this question, it does demonstrate that defendants' position cuts directly against CERCLA's objectives and the environmental concerns which prompted its enactment. CERCLA was originally proposed by its sponsors in both Houses as "a multi-faceted federal regulatory scheme designed to provide an independent basis for environmental claims by both government and private parties." Dore, *The Standard of Civil Liability for Hazardous Waste Disposal Activity: Some Quirks of Superfund,* 57 Notre Dame Lawyer 260, 267 (1981). What was enacted and signed into law is a severely diminished piece of compromise legislation from which a number of significant features were deleted. However, it is clear from the discussions which preceded the passage of CERCLA that the statute is designed to achieve one key objective—to facilitate the prompt clean up of hazardous dumpsites by providing a means of financing both governmental and private responses and by placing the ultimate financial burden upon those responsible for the danger. The liability provision is an integral part of the statute's method of achieving this goal for it gives a private party the right to recover its response costs from responsible third parties which it may choose to pursue rather than claiming against the fund.

Viewing the statute in this context, I cannot attribute to Congress an intention to preclude the City from maintaining a CERCLA action in this case. While the City is admittedly the owner of the Enterprise site, and might have been liable to the federal or state governments had those entities commenced the clean up, the dispositive consideration is that the City did not operate a hazardous waste disposal facility on the premises and it asserts that it did not voluntarily permit the placement of the hazardous substances on its property. Moreover, it has undertaken to clean up the ensuing damage and now seeks to recover its response costs from parties which were allegedly involved in the illegal dumping and which are made expressly liable for response costs. I cannot conclude that the City's right to maintain this action is barred by the hypothetical possibility that had the federal or state government brought this suit, the City too would be liable. The parade of horrors posited by defendants does not counsel against such a result. The simple fact is that there has been no expenditure of superfund monies nor have the federal or state governments commenced an action against the City or anyone else. Rather, a party which has incurred response costs seeks to recover them from responsible parties, an action expressly authorized by CERCLA. This action is not barred because of some theoretical inconsistencies with statutory provisions which have not been made operative in this case.

. . . .

NOTES AND QUESTIONS

(1) As the principal case reflects, § 107 of CERCLAallows non-governmental entities that incur response costs at a facility which are consistent with the National Contingency Plan to recover those costs against PRPs. The plaintiffs in these matters are often current owners of contaminated properties whom the government has ordered to clean up the site. Typical defendants include generators who arranged to dispose of their hazardous wastes at the site, parties whose wastes have migrated to the site, or former occupiers of the property.

(2) In private § 107 actions, courts have not always been strict in their interpretation of the requirement that the plaintiff's response costs be "consistent" with the Superfund National Contingency Plan. *See, e.g., General Electric Co. v. Litton Industrial Automation Systems, Inc.,* 920 F.2d 1415 (8th Cir. 1990), *cert. denied,* 499 U.S. 937 (1991). ("The site evaluation does not have to comply strictly with the letter of the NCP, but only must be consistent with its requirements. It is not necessary that every factor mentioned by the NCP be dealt with explicitly." *Id.* at 1420).

(3) Section 113(f) of CERCLA authorizes persons who have been ordered to pay response costs to seek "contribution" from any other PRP. 42 U.S.C. § 9613(f). This provision, added to the Superfund Act in 1986, raises an issue which is discussed in some detail in the excerpt that follows: are PRPs limited to bringing contribution claims under § 113 when they pursue cost recovery against other PRPs or, alternatively, may they still pursue private cost recovery suits under § 107 in those circumstances?

Riesel and Bogin, "ALLOCATION OF ORPHAN SHARES AND OTHER PRIVATE PARTY CERCLA VAGARIES"*

Course Materials, 1998 ALI-ABA-ELI Course of Study in Environmental Law

I. Introduction

The focus of CERCLA[99] disputes may have shifted from the government versus private parties to one where private parties attempt to allocate response costs amongst themselves. Perhaps the starting point in examining this phenomenon is the frequently debated CERCLA issue relating to whether a PRP can pursue a § 107 cost recovery action[100] against other PRPs at a site, or whether it is limited to a contribution claim under § 113.[101]

The distinction between §§ 107 and 113 raises several issues that affect the rights and liabilities of PRPs. The significance of the distinction is most obvious where a plaintiff-PRP's contribution remedy is barred either because defendant-PRPs have received contribution protection as a result of settling with the government,[102] or because the 3-year statute of limitations for contribution claims has expired.[103]

However, several other, and perhaps more significant issues—such as burdens of proof and the allocation of "orphan share" liability—have increasingly been brought to the fore by recent decisions. These issues present uncertain consequences for PRPs, and add an element of complexity to burden a statutory scheme already riddled with complexities. As a result, many PRP's are now turning to Alternative Dispute Resolution ("ADR") techniques, such as arbitration or mediation, in an effort to reduce the transaction costs inherent in equitable apportionment litigation.

---

99 The Comprehensive Environmental Response, Compensation and Liability Act of 1980, 42 U.S.C. § 9601 *et seq.*

100 CERCLA § 107(a), 42 U.S.C. § 9607(a).

101 CERCLA § 113(f), 42 U.S.C. § 9613(f).

102 CERCLA § 113(f)(2)confers "contribution protection" upon a PRP who enters into a settlement with the government. *See* discussion at Section V, *infra.*

103 CERCLA § 113(g)creates a 3-year statute of limitations period for most § 113 contributions, and a 6-year statute of limitations for § 107 cost recovery actions. CERCLA § 113(g)(2), (3), 42 U.S.C. § 9613(g)(2),(3). *See United Technologies Corp. v. Browning-Ferris Industries, Inc.* ("United Technologies"), 33 F.3d 96, 103 (1st Cir. 1994), *cert. denied,* 513 U.S. 1183, 115 S.Ct. 1176 (1995). *But see Sun Co. Inc., v. Browning-Ferris, Inc.* ("Sun Co."), 124 F.3d 1187, 1192 (10th Cir. 1997) (petition for *certiorari* filed December 12, 1997) (6-year statute of limitations period under § 113(g)(2) applies to contribution claim by PRP that incurred response costs in any way except pursuant to a § 106 or § 107 government civil action because, in such cases, the PRP contribution action is itself the "initial action" under CERCLA).

II. Background—The 107/113 Distinction

CERCLA provides two distinct types of actions for private parties to recoup response costs: cost recovery actions under § 107(a) and contribution actions under § 113(f). These sections create different rights for plaintiff and defendant PRPs.

Under CERCLA § 107(a), liability is strict, joint and several,[104] subject to very limited defenses.[105] A defendant can be held responsible for all the harm at a site, regardless of whether the harm was caused by that defendant, absent a showing of divisibility of harm.[106] Under CERCLA § 113(f), on the other hand, liability is several, and each defendant is responsible only for the harm it caused at the site.[107] Moreover, in contribution proceedings, a court "may allocate response costs among liable parties using such equitable factors as [it] determines are appropriate."[108] Although CERCLA § 107clearly authorizes private parties to bring actions to recover response costs,[109] a question arises when the private party pursuing the § 107 action is itself liable under the section. May a PRP maintain a § 107 "cost recovery" action, or must a PRP proceed with a "contribution" action under § 113? While there is still a split of authority in the lower courts, "[e]very court of appeals that has examined this issue has come to the same conclusion: a § 107 action brought for recovery of costs may be brought only by *innocent* parties that have undertaken clean-ups, and a non-innocent PRP may only bring a § 113 action for contribution."[110]

The United States Courts of Appeals for the First, Third, Seventh, Ninth, Tenth and Eleventh Circuits have squarely confronted this issue, and have uniformly held that PRPs are limited to § 113 contribution actions.[111] The

---

104 *See, e.g., United States v. Rohm & Haas Co.,* 2 F.3d 1265, 1279-80 (3d Cir. 1993); *United States v. Monsanto Co. ("Monsanto"),* 858 F.2d 160, 168-70 (4th Cir. 1988), *cert. denied,* 490 U.S. 1106, 109 S.Ct. 3156 (1989); *United States v. Chem-Dyne Corp. ("Chem-Dyne"),* 572 F. Supp. 802, 806-08 (S.D. Ohio 1983).

105 Statutory defenses to § 107 are limited to: (1) acts of God; (2) acts of war; and (3) acts or omissions of unrelated third parties. 42 U.S.C. § 9607(b)(1)-(4).

106 *See United States v. Alcan Aluminum Corp.,* 964 F.2d 252, 270-71 (3d Cir. 1992) (*"Alcan I"*) (if a PRP can establish "that the harm [at a site] is divisible and that the damages are capable of some reasonable apportionment" that PRP "should be held liable only for the response costs relating to that portion of the harm to which it contributed"); *Matter of Bell Petroleum Services, Inc. ("Bell Petroleum"),* 3 F.3d 889, 902-03 (5th Cir. 1993) (defendant successfully proved harm was divisible and escaped joint and several liability).

107 *See, e.g., Pinal Creek Group v. Newmont Mining Corp. ("Pinal Creek"),* 118 F.3d 1298, 1301 (9th Cir. 1997) (petition for *certiorari* filed November 10, 1997); *United Technologies,* 33 F.3d at 103; *Akzo Coatings, Inc. v. Aigner Corp. ("Akzo Coatings"),* 30 F.3d 761, 764 (7th Cir. 1994). *But see* discussion at Section IV, *infra.*

108 42 U.S.C. § 9613(f)(1); *New Castle County v. Halliburton NUS Corp. ("New Castle"),* 111 F.3d 1116, 1121 (3d Cir. 1997). The "equitable factors" which courts and private allocators have applied in litigation and ADR are discussed, *infra.*

109 *See* CERCLA § 107(a)(4)(B), 42 U.S.C. § 9607(a)(4)(B). *See also Key Tronic Corp. v. United States ("Key Tronic"),* 511 U.S. 809, 812 n. 7, 114 S.Ct. 1960, 1965 n. 7 (1994); *In re Hemingway Transport, Inc.,* 993 F.2d 915, 931 (1st Cir.), *cert. denied,* 510 U.S. 914, 114 S. Ct. 303 (1993).

110 *New Castle,* 111 F.3d at 1120 (emphasis in original).

111 *See Pinal Creek, supra; New Castle, supra; Redwing Carriers, Inc. v. Saraland Apartments ("Redwing Carriers"),* 94 F.3d 1489 (11th Cir. 1996); *United States v. Colorado & Eastern R.R. Co. ("Colorado & Eastern R.R. Co."),* 50 F.3d 1530, 1536 (10th Cir. 1995); *United Tech-*

Fifth and Eighth Circuits, while not directly addressing the issue, have taken the same position.[112] And while the Second Circuit has not yet settled the question, it appears that it soon may do so.[113] These courts have reasoned that the very definition of contribution indicates that it is the only appropriate remedy for PRPs; that is, where a claim is "by and between jointly and severally liable parties for an appropriate division of the payment one of them has been compelled to make," it is a claim for contribution, and not cost recovery.[114] Some courts have found that the 1986 enactment of § 113 indicates that Congress intended contribution to be the exclusive remedy for PRPs,[115] and that to allow PRPs to recover cleanup costs under § 107 would render § 113 meaningless.[116] Others have insisted that the availability of § 107 actions should be limited to governmental or "innocent" PRPs for public policy reasons,[117] and that PRP-initiated § 107 actions would be "both procedurally unwieldy and substantively unfair.[118]

Curiously, the Supreme Court's decision in *Key Tronic* has not had much impact. In *Key Tronic,* the Supreme Court impliedly held that a PRP could bring a § 107 cost recovery action against other PRPs for response costs. The

---

nologies, supra; *Akzo Coatings,* 30 F.3d at 764; *but see Ninth Avenue Remedial Group v. Allis-Chalmers Corp. ("Ninth Avenue"),* 974 F. Supp. 684, 691 (N.D. Ind. 1997) (recognizing that *Akzo Coatings* and the foregoing precedents all "clearly state that a PRP can only sue for contribution," court nevertheless denies motion to dismiss § 107 cost recovery claim of PRP who has neither admitted nor been adjudicated liable under CERCLA; if the PRP is later found liable, however, it may only sue under § 113).

[112] *See Control Data Corp. v. S.C.S.C. Corp.,* 53 F.3d 930, 936 (8th Cir. 1995) (once a party is found liable under § 107, the focus shifts to contribution to determine its equitable share); *Amoco Oil Co. v. Borden, Inc.,* 889 F.2d 664, 672 (5th Cir. 1989) ("When one liable party sues another to recover its equitable share of the response costs, the action is one for contribution . . .").

[113] *See Cooper Industries, Inc. v. Agway, Inc.,* 1997 U.S. Dist. Lexis 19192, 20-21 (N.D. N.Y. 1997) (granting PRP-defendant's motio for interlocutory appeal to the Second Circuit on the lower court's ruling that "[PRPs] may bring cost recovery actions under CERCLA § 107. . .").

[114] *Colorado & Eastern R.R.Co.,* 50 F.3d at 1536 (a claim for reapportionment among PRPs is "the quintessential claim for contribution"); *United Technologies,* 33 F.3d at 99-101; *Akzo Coatings,* 30 F.3d at 764; *See also Matter of Reading Co.,* 900 F. Supp. 738, 748 (E.D. Pa. 1995), *aff'd,* 115 F.3d 111 (3d Cir. 1997) ("contribution" should be given its plain meaning); *Avnet, Inc. v. Allied-Signal, Inc. ("Avnet"),* 825 F. Supp. 1132 (D. R.I. 1992); *Transtech Industries, Inc. v. Z & Z Septic Clean,* 798 F. Supp. 1079 (D. N.J. 1992), *cert. denied,* 512 U.S. 1213, 114 S.Ct. 2692 (1994).

[115] *See, e.g., Reichold Chemicals, Inc. v. Textron, Inc.,* 888 F. Supp. 1116, 1123-24 (N.D. Fla. 1995).

[116] *See, e.g., Colorado & Eastern R.R. Co.,* 50 F.3d at 1536.

[117] *See, e.g., United Technologies,* 33 F.3d at 100.

[118] *SC Holdings, Inc. v. A.A.A. Realty Co. ("SC Holdings"),* 1996 U.S. Dist. Lexis 12428, 22 ("In a case involving multiple PRPs, [allowing a PRP § 107 action] could result in a chain reaction of multiple, and unnecessary lawsuits," and would provide an "unjustified windfall for the party who filed the first lawsuit"). *See also Stearns & Foster Bedding Co. v. Franklin Holding Corp. ("Stearns & Foster"),* 947 F. Supp. 790, 801 (D. N.J. 1996) (it is "fundamentally unfair" to impose joint and several liability "simply because the first PRP won the race to the courthouse door").

While agreeing that a private PRP may not bring a direct § 107 action, several courts have explained that §§ 107 and 113 should be read to work together—the first section establishing the claim for contribution and the second creating the mechanism for apportioning that § 107 liability among PRPs. *See, e.g., Pinal Creek,* 118 F.3d at 1302; *New Castle,* 111 F.3d at 1122 ("section 113 does not in itself create any new liabilities; rather it confirms the right of a [PRP] under section 107 to obtain contribution from other [PRPs]"); *United Technologies,* 33 F.3d at 102 (same).

Court's decision did not directly focus on the relationship between §§ 107 and 113, but instead addressed whether a PRP could recover attorneys fees as a "necessary cost of response" pursuant to § 107. Nevertheless, in the course of deciding this issue, the Court stated that CERCLA "expressly authorizes a cause of action for contribution in § 113 and impliedly authorizes a similar and somewhat overlapping remedy in § 107."[119] It further stated that § 107 "impliedly authorizes private parties to recover cleanup costs from *other* PRPs."[120] Nevertheless, courts have been reluctant to adhere to the Supreme Court's apparent authorization. Many courts distinguish *Key Tronic* on its facts,[121] or indicate that their decision to limit PRPs to contribution actions is, in actuality, consistent with the Court's decision.[122]

"Who, then, may bring a cost recovery action under section 107?"[123] The District Court decisions within circuits which have not yet ruled on the issue remain divided.[124]

Section 107 historically has been used by governments to recover the costs incurred in investigating and remediating hazardous substance sites. Some courts have reasoned that allowing "any other person"—including a PRP—to bring such an action is consistent with the plain language and express goals of CERCLA because it provides PRPs with an incentive to effectuate a prompt and voluntary cleanup.[125] Moreover, there is nothing in CERCLA that expressly precludes a PRP from maintaining a § 107 cost recovery action.[126] The recent spate of contrary Circuit Court decisions, however, may be signaling the end of this expansive view of § 107.[127]

---

119 511 U.S. at 816, 114 S.Ct. at 1966.

120 511 U.S. at 818, 114 S.Ct. at 1966-67 (emphasis added).

121 *United Technologies,* 33 F.3d at 103 n. 12 (noting that *Key Tronic* did not address the relation between §§ 107 and 113); *Stearns & Foster,* 947 F. Supp. at 795 (same).

122 *See, e.g., Pinal Creek,* 118 F.3d at 1303 ("[o]ur holding today is consistent with [*Key Tronic*] which implied that a claim "by a PRP against another PRP under . . . § 107 would be "for contribution against those treated as joint tortfeasors").

123 *New Castle,* 111 F.3d at 1123.

124 For example, within the Second Circuit, *see Idylwoods Associates v. Mader Capital,* 915 F. Supp. 1290, 1314 (W.D. N.Y. 1996) (holding PRPs may bring § 107 claims); *Town of New Windsor v. Tesa Tuck, Inc. ("Tesa Tuck"),* 919 F. Supp. 662, 679-81 (S.D. N.Y. 1996) (opposite); *Companies for Fair Allocation v. Axil Corp. ("Companies for Fair Allocation"),* 853 F. Supp. 575, 578-80 (D. Conn. 1994) (same); *See also* Michael v. Hernandez, *Cost Recovery or Contribution?: Resolving the Controversy Over CERCLA Claims Brought by Potentially Responsible Parties,* 21 Harv. Entl. L. Rev. 83 (1997) (discussing the inconsistent approaches taken by courts); *PRP Group Seeks High Court Review Of Question Who May Recover Costs,* 12 Tox. L. Rep. No. 27 at 750 (December 3, 1997) (*Pinal Creek* plaintiff-PRP's petition for a writ of *certiorari* on the § 107 versus § 113 issue because there is a disagreement in the district courts).

125 *See, e.g., Companies for Fair Allocation,* 853 F. Supp. at 579; *United States v. Kramer ("Kramer"),* 757 F. Supp. 397, 416-17 (D. N.J. 1991).

126 *See, e.g., Bethlehem Iron Works, Inc. v. Lewis Industries, Inc. ("Bethlehem Iron Works"),* 891 F. Supp. 221, 225 (E.D. Pa. 1995); *Chesapeake & Potomac Telephone Co. v. Peck Iron & Metal Co. ("Chesapeake & Potomac Telephone Co."),* 814 F. Supp. 1269, 1227 (E.D. Va. 1992); *Companies for Fair Allocation,* 853 F. Supp. at 579 (and cases cited therein) (the language of § 107 that allows "any other person" to maintain a cost recovery action, as well as the limited defenses to liability, indicates the broad sweep of § 107).

127 *See Pinal Creek,* 118 F.3d at 1303 (noting that, since 1995, four other Circuits have concluded "that a CERCLA claim by a PRP against another PRP is necessarily for contribution").

This apparent trend notwithstanding, several district and circuit courts have held that PRP's who are "innocent" may maintain a direct § 107 action "to recoup the whole of their expenditures" from defendant PRPs.[128] "Innocent" in this context may have varied meanings. Several courts have found that "parties who [are not] themselves liable" under CERCLA, *i.e.*, who can establish an "innocent landowner" defense under § 101(35) and § 107(b), are "innocent and so may bring direct § 107 actions."[129] Other courts suggest that an "innocent" party may not even need to meet the technicalities of such a complete defense. The First Circui, for example, has recognized that "[i]t is possible that, although falling outside the statutory parameters" of innocence "a PRP who spontaneously initiates a cleanup without government prodding" may be entitled to maintain a direct claim under § 107(b).[130] The Seventh Circuit also has recognized that a private land owner forced to remediate hazardous substances "that a third party spilled onto its property or that migrated there from adjacent lands" may be entitled to bring a direct § 107 action.[131] And while not expressing any particular opinion on the matter, the Third Circuit noted that the court in *AM International v. Datacard Corp.*,[132] recently found a landowner "innocent" for § 107 recovery purposes despite the fact that "the landowner . . . kn[ew] that it was buying into an expensive cleanup (and was therefore 'a little less "innocent" then the landowner described in *Akzo*' ".[133]

III. Burdens of Proof

The issue of "who must prove what" is straightforward in the case of a "typical" cost recovery action (*i.e.*, brought by the government or an innocent PRP) and a "typical" contribution claim. However, these clear rules appear to get a bit muddled in light of the 107/113 debate.

In a typical governmental § 107 cost recovery action, the plaintiff must first meet its burden of proving its prima facie case.[134] The burden then shifts to

---

[128] *See Rumpke of Indiana, Inc. v. Cummins Engine Co., Inc.* 107 F.3d 1235, 1239-42 (7th Cir. 1997); *See Pinal Creek*, 118 F.3d at 1303; *Redwing Carriers*, 94 F.3d at 1513; *United Technologies*, 33 F.3d at 99-100; *Akzo Coatings*, 30 F.3d at 764; *Boyce v. Bumb* ("*Boyce*"), 944 F. Supp. 807, 812 (N.D. Cal. 1996).

[129] *United Technologies*, 33 F.3d at 100; *see Redwing Carriers*, 94 F.3d at 1513 ("[p]arties who are not themselves liable or potentially liable for response costs under § 107(a) of CERCLAcan bring a cost recovery action directly under § 107(a) against potentially responsible parties"); *Boyce*, 944 F. Supp. at 812 ("although Plaintiffs here are presumptively PRPs by virtue of their current ownership of the Campisi Landfill, they are free to maintain a cost recovery action under § 9607(a) if they can prove themselves to be non-responsible 'innocent landowners' within the meaning of § 9601(35) and § 9607(b)").

[130] *United Technologies*, 33 F.3d at 764.

[131] *See Akzo Coatings*, 30 F.3d at 764.

[132] 106 F.3d 1342 (7th Cir. 1997).

[133] *New Castle*, 111 F.3d at 1123. This situation seems to describe a PRP who is not an "innocent landowner" under § 101(35) but who may still avail itself of CERCLA's "third party" defense under § 107(b). For a discussion of the difference between the two *see generally State of New York v. Lashins Arcade Co.*, 91 F.3d 353 (2d Cir. 1996).

[134] A defendant will be found liable under § 107(a) if the following 4 elements are met:

(1) the defendant falls within one of the 4 categories of "responsible parties";

(2) hazardous substances were disposed of at a "facility";

(3) there was a "release" or threat of release of hazardous substances into the environment; and

(4) the release caused "response costs" to be incurred.

Alcan I, 964 F.2d at 258-59.

the PRP, which can attempt to escape joint and several liability by showing that the harm is divisible.[135] The defendant has the burden of proving both that the harm at the site is divisible, and that there is a reasonable basis for apportioning liability for response costs.[136]

The burden of proving divisibility is a substantial one, and courts have had considerable difficulty in finding it satisfied.[137] The practical effect of placing the burden on defendants is that they have not frequently escaped joint and several liability.[138]

In a private PRP § 107 cost recovery action, the burden of proof determination is somewhat less clear since a defendant PRP can counterclaim for contributions. *See Kramer I,* 757 F. Supp. at 414-16. The Eastern District of Pennsylvania addressed this issue in *United States v. Atlas Minerals and Chemicals, Inc. ("Atlas Minerals"),* 41 Env't Rep. Case. (BNA) 1417 (E.D. Pa. 1995). In that case, the court held that where a private PRP sues under § 107, that PRP must only establish the defendants' status as "covered persons" under § 107 in order to impose joint and several liability. *Id.* at 1478. The burden then shifts to defendants to prove the plaintiff PRP's equitable share. *Id.*[139]

In a typical § 113 contribution action the plaintiff PRP first must demonstrate that the defendant is a "covered person" under § 107.[140]

Unlike a § 107 plaintiff, however, the § 113 plaintiff PRP then has the additional burden of proving each defendant's allocable share of damages.[141]

This is reflected in the legislative history of the SARA Amendments, which created the express right of contribution, and in which Congress stated: "[o]f course, the burden of proof is on the . . . party seeking apportionment to establish that it should be granted."[142]

---

[135] *See Bell Petroleum,* 3 F.3d at 902-03; *United States v. Alcan Aluminum Corp.,* 990 F.2d 711, 722 (2d Cir. 1993) (*"Alcan II"*); *Alcan I,* 964 F.2d at 270-71.

[136] *See, e.g., Alcan II,* 990 F.2d at 722; *Monsanto,* 858 F.2d at 172 (citing Restatement (Second) of Torts, § 433A); *Kelley v. Thomas Solvent Co.,* 727 F. Supp. 1532, 1552 (W.D. Mich. 1989); *Chem-Dyne,* 572 F. Supp. at 811.

[137] This is especially true where various hazardous substances are disposed of in one place for a long period of time. *See Colorado & Eastern R.R. Co.,* 50 F.3d at 1535 ("Due to the impossibility of determining the amount of environmental harm caused by each party where wastes of varying and unknown degrees of toxicity and migratory potential have mixed, the courts have been reluctant to apportion costs between PRPs . . ."). *Accord O'Neil v. Picillo ("O'Neil"),* 883 F.2d 176, 179 (1st Cir. 1989), *cert. denied,* 493 U.S. 1071, 110 S.Ct. 1115 (1990); *California v. Verticare,* 25 Chem. Waste Lit. Rep. 1137, 1140 (N.D. Cal. 1993); *United States v. Stringfellow,* 661 F. Supp. 1053, 1060 (C.D. Cal. 1987). *See also Arizona v. Motorola, Inc.,* 805 F. Supp. 749, 753 (D. Ariz. 1992).

[138] *See O'Neil,* 883 F.2d at 178.

[139] The court's holding is somewhat muddled because the PRP pursuing the § 107 action also sued for contribution under § 113. With respect to that latter claim, the PRP had the "additional burden of proving each [defendant's] equitable share." *Id.*

[140] *See Atlas Minterals,* 41 Env't l. Rep. Cas. (BNA) 1478.

[141] *See United States v. Taylor,* 909 F. Supp. 335, 361 and n. 4 (M.D. N.C. 1995); *Atlas Minerals,* 41 Env'tl. Rep. Cas. (BNA) at 1478. *Compare United States v. R.W. Meyer, Inc.,* 889 F.2d 1497, 1507-08 (6th Cir. 1989) (contribution plaintiff must demonstrate that the harm was divisible and that it paid more than its fair share).

[142] *See* H.R. Rep. No. 99-253 (Ill.), 99th Cong. 2nd Sess. 19 (1986), *reprinted* in 1986 U.S.C.C.A.N. 2835, 3038, 3042 (citing *Chem-Dyne Corp.*), 572 F. Supp. at 810).

A PRP's "defense" of a § 113 claim is also of a different character. Whereas a § 107 defendant PRP must prove a reasonable "apportionment of harm" to establish a divisibility defense to the imposition of joint and several liability, a § 113 defendant cannot be "allocated" more than its "equitable share" of several liability for the harm at a site.[143]

Therefore, even if a defendant cannot prove a reasonable basis for apportioning harm (within the meaning of *Alcan* or *Bell Petroleum*) as in a defense to § 107 liability, a court in a § 113 contribution proceeding can nevertheless consider any number of "equitable factors" to allocate that defendant only its fair share of response costs.[144]

At least one court has fashioned an additional "threshold" burden of proof for § 113 plaintiff PRPs to show at the outset of a § 113 action that a defendant PRP's equitable share of liability is substantial enough to "outweigh the public interest against recognizing causes of action the enforcement of which exceed the added resources that would be tapped for waste-site remediation."[145] To meet this burden, plaintiff PRPs must demonstrate "at the least, that the parties they elected to sue are among those responsible to some significant degree, as measured by an appropriately fashioned threshold-of-significance standard, for deposits of hazardous waste at the site."[146]

If plaintiff does satisfy this threshold burden, the burden then shifts back to defendant to demonstrate that "even though plaintiff has satisfied the threshold-of-significance burden, hazardous substances from defendant were so limited inquantity and nature in comparison with hazardous substances from other sources that, as a matter of law, that defendant's contributions were too small proportionately to warrant allocation of any shared responsibility under an 'equitable factors' test."[147]

---

[143] *See* David Montgomery Moore, "The Divisibility of Harm Defense to Joint and Several Liability Under CERCLA," 23 Envtl L. Rep., News & Analysis, No. 9 at 10529, 10532 (stressing the importance of distinguishing the apportionment of harm prong of a § 107 divisibility defense from the allocation of response costs in a § 113 contribution action); *see also United States v. Western Processing Co. ("Western Processing")*, 734 F. Supp. 930, 938 (W.D. Wash. 1990) ("the Court's discretion in allocating damages among the defendants during the contribution phase does not affect the defendant's liability").

[144] Courts have discretion to balance the equities in light of the totality of circumstances of each case. *See, e.g., United States v. R.W. Meyer, Inc. ("R.W. Meyer")*, 932 F.2d 568, 572-73 (6th Cir. 1991); *Environmental Transportation Systems v. Ensco, Inc. ("Ensco")*, 969 F.2d 503, 509 (7th Cir. 1992). However, their discretion is not unbridled. There are several different approaches which courts have applied in apportioning costs, such as *pro rata* comparative fault, comparative causation, and "Gore Factors" approaches. *See* discussion, *infra*.

[145] *See Acushnet Co. v. Coaters, Inc. ("Acushnet")*, 948 F. Supp. 128, 136 (D. Mass. 1996).

[146] 948 F. Supp. at 137. The court, however, did not define what "threshold-of-significance" was appropriate. However, it is certainly to show that a third-party defendant is responsible for more than a "de minimis contribution of hazardous substance to the site . . . ." *Id.*

[147] *Id.* at 141. If defendant satisfies that burden, the burden then shifts back to plaintiff and so on until someone "loses." Some have argued that this approach at the pre-trial stage could streamline litigation by eliminating minor PRPs early on. *See* William D. Evans, Jr., *New Castle County and Its Progeny: Defining Boundaries of Superfund Recoupment Litigation*, 12 Tox. L. Rep., Vol. 12, No. 30 at 846 (December 24, 1997). However, this evidentiary "ping pong" match would seemingly increase transaction costs in many cases.

Whether or not other courts adopt this "threshold-of-significance" burden remains to be seen.[148]

In any event, a court will ultimately apply equitable factors in apportioning response costs.[149] Therefore, a plaintiff PRP must, at bare minimum, be prepared to prove defendant PRPs' equitable shares of response costs and to defend its own, since a court may not free a plaintiff PRP from its share of liability merely because defendants fail to carry out their counterclaim burden.[150]

[9] The CERCLA Liability of Lenders

UNITED STATES v. MIRABILE

United States District Court, Eastern District of Pennsylvania (1985)
1985 U.S. Dist. LEXIS 15411, 15 ELR 20994

NEWCOMER, J.:

The United States commenced this civil action to recover costs incurred in the removal of allegedly hazardous waste from property presently owned by defendants Anna and Thomas Mirabile. The lawsuit was brought pursuant to the Comprehensive Environmental Response, Compensation, and Liability Act (CERCLA), 42 U.S.C. § 9601 *et seq.* Presently before me are motions for summary judgment filed by American Bank and Trust Company, Mellon Bank (East) National Association, and the United States (on behalf of the Small Business Administration). Each of these motions requires me to determine the circumstances under which CERCLA liability may be imposed upon parties that have been involved in financing the owner or operator of an alleged hazardous waste dumpsite. The parties agree that I am presented with issues of first impression.

Before proceeding to an analysis of the merits of these motions, an outline of the somewhat unusual posture of the parties is in order. The site at issue is located in Phoenixville, Pennsylvania, and will be referred to as the Turco site. The United States filed this action against, among others, the present owners of the Turco site, Anna and Thomas Mirabile. The Mirabiles, in turn, joined American Bank and Trust Company (ABT) and Mellon Bank (East) National Association (Mellon), amongst others, as third-party defendants. ABT and Mellon counterclaimed against the United States, relying on the alleged involvement of the Small Business Administration in creating the conditions existing at the site.

---

148 While not imposing such a threshold burden, other courts have clearly stated that "causation may be relevant in the allocation of costs under CERCLA's contribution provision." *Sean Lion, Inc. v. Wall Chemical Corp.*, 974 F. Supp. 589, 600 (S.D. Tex. 1996) (citing *Colorado & Eastern R.R. Co.*, 50 F.3d at 1534).

149 *See Atlas Minerals*, 41 Env't Rep. Cas. (BNA) at 1478-809; *Acushnet*, 948 F. Supp. at 134-35.

150 *See, e.g.*, Barry S. Neuman, "Litigating and Managing the Multi-Party Superfund Cost Recovery Case," ALI-ABA Course of Study Materials, p. 503 (1996). *See also United States v. Northernaire Plating Co.*, 18 Chem. Waste Lit. Rep. 1130, 1132 (W.D. Mich. 1989) (plain language of CERCLA places responsibility on owner simply by virtue of owning the site).

ABT, Mellon, and the SBA were each involved in financing the operations of Turco Coatings, Inc. (Turco), which operated a paint manufacturing business at the site at the time the allegedly hazardous condition was created. The Mirabiles contend that, by virtue of certain actions taken during the course of their financial dealings with Turco, Mellon and ABT became liable for creation of the hazardous conditions at the Turco site.

Mellon and ABT do not dispute the factual basis for this claim. Instead, they argue that a secured creditor's exercise of financial control over a debtor should not bring the creditor within the scope of CERCLA liability. In addition, Mellon and ABT do not contend with conviction that the factual basis underlying their claims against the SBA properly give rise to CERCLA liability. Instead, they argue that if their activities in connection with the Superior site provide a basis for the imposition of liability, then the SBA's activities provide an equally, if not more, compelling basis for liability. Thus, the major opposition to all three motions comes from the Mirabiles despite the fact that the Mirabiles have asserted no direct claim against the SBA.

Congress enacted CERCLA in 1980 in response to the growing problems caused by improper disposal of hazardous wastes. CERCLA authorizes the federal government, through the Environmental Protection Agency, to clean up hazardous waste dumpsites. Section 107 permits the United States to recover costs incurred from various parties involved in creation of the site. Potentially liable parties include those who owned or operated the site at the time the cleanup activities occurred, 42 U.S.C. § 9607(a)(1), and those who owned or operated the site at the time of disposal, 42 U.S.C. § 9607(a)(2). The lenders in this case are alleged to have acted as "owners or operators" within the meaning of the statute, thereby subjecting them to liability for cleanup costs.

Thus, the statutory definition of "owner or operator" becomes critical: "owner or operator" means ". . . (I) in the case of an onshore facility or an offshore facility, any person owning or operating such facility . . . . *Such term does not include a person, who, without participating in the management of a vessel or facility, holds indicia of ownership primarily to protect his security interest in the vessel or facility.*" 42 U.S.C. § 9601(20)(A). (Emphasis added.) Were it not for the underscored exemption from liability, the definition would be a hopeless tautology. Nevertheless, the exemption plainly suggests that provided a secured creditor does not become overly entangled in the affairs of the actual owner or operator of a facility, the creditor may not be held liable for cleanup costs. The difficulty arises, of course, in determining how far a secured creditor may go in protecting its financial interests before it can be said to have acted as an owner or operator within the meaning of the statute.

As noted previously, this issue has never been addressed; however, whether an individual involved in the management of a corporate disposer/defendant may interpose the corporate shield to protect himself from personal liability has been addressed. Courts have generally concluded that the exemption from liability gives rise to an inference that an individual who owns stock in a corporation and who actively participates in its management can be held liable for cleanup costs incurred as a result of improper disposal by the corporation. *State of New York v. Shore Realty Corp.*, No. 606—August Term, 1984, slip op. at 6 [15 ELR 20358] (2d Cir. April 4, 1985). *United States v. Carolawn,* 14 ELR 20699, 20700 (D.S.C. 1984); *United States v. Northeastern Pharmaceutical & Chemical Co.* (NEPACCO), 579 F. Supp. 823, 849 [14 ELR 20212] (W.D. Mo. 1984).

NEPACCO, Shore, and *Carolawn,* provide only limited guidance in the instant case because in each case the individual defendants were extremely active in the affairs of closely held corporations. Thus, while each court found active participants in day-to-day corporate affairs could be held liable, none provided any guidance on the issue with which I am presented—defining the point at which participation is too attenuated to permit the imposition of liability. In addition, each of those cases involved the liability of corporate officers and shareholders, as opposed to secured creditors. The courts were therefore confronted with individuals whose active participation in the management of the corporation plainly involved participation not only in financial aspects of management but also in the nuts-and-bolts, day-to-day production aspects of the business. In contrast, in the case before me, the participation of the creditors—at least, with respect to SBA and ABT—in the management of the corporation appears to have been limited to participation in financial decisions. In my view, the distinction is critical.

In *NEPACCO,* the court reasoned that imposition of liability on individuals who actively participate in corporate management was consistent with the Congressional intent "to insure, so far as possible, that the parties responsible for the creation of hazardous waste sites be liable for the response costs in cleaning them up." 579 F. Supp. At 848. The court also gleaned from the statutory scheme and its legislative history an intent to impose cleanup costs on those who bore the fruits of hazardous waste disposal and who were involved in the planning and implementation of the disposal practices. Similarly, another court has noted that "site control is an important consideration in determining who qualifies as an 'owner' under Section 107(a)." *United States v. SCRDI,* 21 ERC 1577, 1581 [14 ELR 20895] (D.S.C. 1984) (imposing liability on lessor of site).

This reasoning simply does not apply with the same force to secured creditors as it does to corporate officers and/or shareholders. In addition, I note that the exemption from liability is afforded to secured creditors who do not participate in the management of a "facility." "Facility" is defined as:

> (A) any building, structure, installation, equipment, pipe or pipeline (including any pipe into a sewer or publicly owned treatment works), well, pit, pond, lagoon, impoundment, ditch, landfill, storage container, motor vehicle, rolling stock, or aircraft, or (B) any site or area where a hazardous substance has been deposited, stored, disposed of, or placed, or otherwise come to be located; but does not include any consumer product in consumer use or any vessel; 42 U.S.C. § 9601(9). The reference to management of the "facility," as opposed to management of the affairs of the actual owner or operator of the facility, suggests once again that the participation which is critical is participation in operational, production, or waste disposal activities. Mere financial ability to control waste disposal practices of the sort possessed by the secured creditors in this case is not, in my view, sufficient for the imposition of liability.

That Congress intended to draw a distinction between parties involved in the actual operation of the facility and those who are involved in what may properly be characterized as the financial aspects of the business conducted at the facility finds some limited support in the legislative history:

In the case of the facility an "operator" is defined to be a person who is carrying out operational functions for the owner of the facility pursuant to an appropriate agreement. H.R. Rep. No. 172, 96th Cong., 2d Sess., reprinted in 1980 U.S. Code Cong.-Adm. News, 6160, 6180.

The facts adduced to date, and which are not in dispute, are as follows. During the 1970's defendant Arthur C. Mangels Industries, Inc. (Mangels) owned the Turco site. In February of 1973 ABT loaned a sum of money to Mangels, which operates a paint manufacturing facility on the site. The loan was secured, in part, by a mortgage on the Turco site. In 1976 defendant Turco acquired 96 of the outstanding shares of Mangels and shortly thereafter began to manufacture paint at the site. Turco filed a petition in bankruptcy under Chapter 11 of the Bankruptcy Code in January 1980. It ceased all operations at the site in December of 1980. ABT's mortgage remained in effect throughout this period.

In 1981 the Bankruptcy Court dismissed Turco's Chapter 11 petition. This enabled ABT to proceed with foreclosure on the Superior site. ABT was the highest bidder at the sheriff's sale held on August 21, 1981. It informed the Chester County Sheriff and tax department that it intended to take title to the property. Both before and after the sale ABT negotiated with other parties for purchase of the property. On December 15, 1981, ABT assigned its bid to defendant Thomas A. Mirabile who, together with his wife, defendant Anna Mirabile, accepted a sheriff's deed to the property.

In the period between the sheriff's sale and ABT's assignment of its bid to the Mirabiles, ABT took the following actions with respect to the property. It secured the building against vandalism by boarding up windows and changing locks, made inquiries as to the approximate cost of disposal for various drums located on the property, and, through its loan officer, Donald Hans, visited the property on various occasions for the purpose of showing it to prospective purchasers. All these activities occurred several months after Turco ceased its operations at the site.

In 1976 Girard Bank, the predecessor-in-interest of Mellon Bank, entered into a financing agreement with Turco whereby Girard would advance working capital to Turco. These advances were to be secured by the inventory and assets of Turco . . . .

After Turco ceased operations in late 1980 Girard, with the consent of Turco and approval of the Bankruptcy Court, took possession of Turco's inventory. A portion of the inventory was disposed of through private sales, with the balance being sold at a public auction in May of 1981.

In July of 1979 the SBA loaned $150,000 to Turco which was to be applied to specified debts. The loan was secured by a second lien security interest in Turco machinery and equipment, a second lien on inventory and accounts receivable, and a second mortgage on the real estate. The SBA also required a pledge of stock to secure its loan. SBA regulations in effect at the time of this loan required that the SBA provide management assistance to its borrowers. No evidence has been adduced to suggest that any such assistance was ever provided; however, SBA representatives visited the site three times during 1981 to monitor liquidation of assets. The loan agreement also required Turco to obtain SBA approval prior to the execution of any contracts for management consulting services. Turco never entered into any such contracts.

Finally, the loan agreement between Turco and the SBA contained certain restrictions on Turco's financial dealings. For example, the agreement placed specific limitations on the annual compensation of Turco's operating officers. In addition, the purchase of life insurance and payment of dividends or advances to Turco officers required prior written SBA consent.

I turn first to ABT's motion for summary judgment because I believe ABT's involvement with the site presents the most compelling case for the granting of such a motion. ABT's arguments are essentially twofold. First, it contends that under Pennsylvania law its successful bid at the sheriff's sale gave it only equitable title to the property which never evolved into legal title by virtue of its subsequent assignment of that bid to the Mirabiles. Second, ABT argues that its activities at the site were undertaken merely to protect its security interests in the property and that it never participated in the management of the site. The Mirabiles respond that ABT's equitable ownership of the property is sufficient to bring it within the statutory definition of "owner," and that its activities, outlined above, confirm that ABT acted as an owner or operator of the site.

I need not resolve the issue of whether, under Pennsylvania law, ABT's successful bid at the Sheriff's sale technically vested ABT with ownership as defined by the statute. Regardless of the nature of the title received by ABT, its actions with respect to the foreclosure were plainly undertaken in an effort to protect its security interest in the property. ABT made no effort to continue Turco's operations on the property, and indeed foreclosed some eight months after all operations had ceased.

In addition, I believe the statutory exemption for secured creditors is particularly applicable to ABT's limited activities at the property following foreclosure. The actions undertaken by ABT with respect to the site simply cannot be deemed to constitute participation in the management of the site. As noted above, in enacting CERCLA Congress manifested its intent to impose liability upon those who were responsible for and profited from improper disposal practices. Thus, it would appear that before a secured creditor such as ABT may be held liable, it must, at a minimum, participate in the day-to-day operational aspects of the site. In the instant case, ABT merely foreclosed on the property after all operations had ceased and thereafter took prudent and routine steps to secure the property against further depreciation.

Obviously, imposition of liability on secured creditors or lending institutions would enhance the government's chances of recovering its cleanup costs, given the fact that owners and operators of hazardous waste dumpsites are often elusive, defunct, or otherwise judgment proof. It may well be that the imposition of such liability would help to ensure more responsible management of such sites. The consideration of such policy matters, and the decision as to the imposition of such liability, however, lies with Congress. In enacting

CERCLA Congress singled out secured creditors for protection from liability under certain circumstances. Because I believe ABT has brought itself within that protection, ABT is entitled to the entry of summary judgment in its favor.

The SBA's motion is also compelling. At the time the motion was filed, the Mirabiles responded, in part, that the motion was premature because discovery had not then been completed. The discovery completion date has now passed. Since no party has supplemented the record I must conclude that the motion is now ripe for disposition.

Unlike ABT, the SBA never took either legal or equitable title to the site. In this respect, its case for summary judgment is stronger than that of ABT. The Mirabiles place principal reliance on the SBA's loan agreement with Turco which apparently contemplated some degree of involvement which could be characterized as participation in day-to-day management; however, this involvement apparently never occurred. The loan agreement also contained certain restrictions on Turco's finances which the Mirabiles contend are evidence of SBA participation in the management of Turco. They argue that in placing restrictions on the use of loan proceeds, the SBA "may have failed to prevent Turco from disposing of alleged hazardous substances on the site." I find nothing in the language of the statute or the case law under which it suggests that a lender must ensure that its loan proceeds are applied to clean up costs.

As noted above, I do not believe participation in purely financial aspects of operation, of the sort which occurred here, is sufficient to bring a lender within the scope of CERCLA liability. Furthermore, in the present case, many of the restrictions imposed by the SBA loan agreement limited the flow of corporate funds to principals of Turco. Thus, these restrictions do not support the Mirabiles' contention that the SBA precluded the use of its funds for cleanup activities and should therefore be held potentially liable. I will therefore enter summary judgment in favor of the SBA on all claims asserted against it.

NOTES

(1) The principal case was followed by other, somewhat consistent, judicial decisions. Collectively, these opinions left doubt as to the extent to which CERCLA's "secured creditor exemption" protected lenders who foreclose on contaminated properties.

In *United States v. Fleet Factors Corp.*, 901 F.2d 1150 (11th Cir. 1990), the Eleventh Circuit shocked the lending community when it held that a lender could be liable "without being an operator, by participating in the financial management of a facility to a degree indicating a *capacity to influence* the corporation's treatment of hazardous waste." The Supreme Court's subsequent refusal to grant certiorari review of *Fleet Factors,* 498 U.S. 1046 (1991), gave the lending community even more cause for alarm. In contrast, the Ninth Circuit refused to follow the Eleventh Circuit's "capacity to influence" standard, and instead held in *In re Bergsoe Metals Corp.,* 910 F.2d 668 (9th Cir. 1990), that "there must be *some* actual management of the facility before a secured creditor will fall outside the exemption."

The federal courts also failed to agree upon the extent to which lenders faced CERCLA liability when they foreclosed on contaminated property and became owners of title. A few courts agreed with the district court, in *Mirabile* that lenders were still exempt even after foreclosure. Other courts held that banks which foreclosed on contaminated properties ceased being "secured creditors" and became "owners and operators" subject to CERCLA liability. *See Guidice v. B.F.G. Electroplating and Mfg. Co.,* 732 F. Supp. 556 (W.D. Pa. 1989); *United States v. Maryland Bank and Trust Co.,* 532 F. Supp. 573 (D. Md. 1986).

(2) These uncertainties were resolved by Congress in the Asset Conservation, Lender Liability, and Deposit Insurance Protection Act of 1996 (ACA). *See* Sub-title E, The Omnibus Consolidated Appropriations Bill for Fiscal Year 1997, Pub. L. No. 104-208 (Sept. 30, 1996). Under this statute, a lender who holds indicia of ownership in a contaminated facility primarily to protect its security interest is not an "owner or operator," subject to CERCLA liability, so long as the lender does not "actually participate in the facility's management."

Lenders may now undertake a variety of activities relating to the facility to protect their security interests, without incurring liability (including providing financial advice to borrowers, performing site inspections, and requiring response actions of other parties). After foreclosure, a lender may maintain business at a contamination facility so long as it divests itself of the property "at the earliest practicable, commercially reasonable time, on commercially reasonable terms." Moreover, lenders are now protected from post-foreclosure liability when they undertake certain response actions to abate or prevent releases of hazardous substances.

For additional discussion of the ACA and its implications, *see* F. Grad, Treatise on Environmental Law § 4A.02[1][l]. *See also* William Buzbee, *CERCLA's New Safe Harbors For Banks, Lenders and Fiduciaries,* 25 ELR 10656 (Dec. 1996).

§ 4.05 Toxic Substances and Hazardous and Toxic Waste: An Overview of Other Major Legislation

[1] Private Cost Recovery Actions Introduction: The Differences in Regulatory Approach

Environmental protection legislation, such as *Air, Water*, and *Solid Waste* laws rely primarily on ambient standards to be achieved through the enforcement of emission and effluent controls. On the other hand, the Toxic Substances Control Act (TSCA)—similar in this respect to the Federal Food, Drug & Cosmetic Act and to the Federal Insecticide, Fungicide and Rodenticide Act (FIFRA), as amended by the Federal Environmental Pesticide Control Act—relies primarily on *product controls.*

[2] Comparison of Scope of Regulatory Controls

[a] Laws Emphasizing Product Controls

Toxic Substances Control Act of 1976, Pub. L. No. 94-469, 90 Stat. 2003 (1976), 15 U.S.C. § 2601 *et seq.*, is a product control law. TSCA regulates the manufacture, distribution and sale of chemical substances, and requires testing of new chemicals and of new uses of known chemicals which "*may present an unreasonable risk of injury to health or the environment.*" TSCA § 4.15, U.S.C. § 2604. Broad enforcement authority extends from labeling requirements to seizure of imminently hazardous substances. Advance notification, *i.e.*, in advance of marketing of new chemical substances, must be provided to EPA relating to chemical properties, manufacture, intended uses, and hazards. The burden of proof of safety is on the manufacturer or other proponent of registration. As a specific requirement, the Act required the Administrator to provide for the rapid phaseout and disposal of polychlorinated biphenyl. *See*, F. Grad, Treatise on Environmental Law, § 4B.02.

Federal Insecticide, Fungicide and Rodenticide Act (FIFRA), as amended by Federal Environmental Pesticide Act (FEPCA), 7 U.S.C. § 135 *et seq.*, controls manufacture, distribution and sale of economic poisons, including the registration of pesticides and their uses, and the regulation of persons who apply categories of pesticides as restricted to certain uses, and including, further, the testing of new pesticides before they are marketed. Only pesticides may be registered and used under the law which "*perform . . . intended function* [*i.e.*, to kill some target species of living organisms] *without unreasonable adverse effects on the environment . . .*," such adverse effects being defined to include adverse effects on human health. The registrant must overcome a rebuttable presumption against registration. FIFRA § 3(c), 5(c), 7 U.S.C. § 136a(c)(5)(C). *See, generally*, F. Grad, Treatise on Environmental Law, Ch. 8.

Federal Food, Drug and Cosmetic Act (FFDCA), 21 U.S.C. § 32 *et seq.*, regulates the manufacture, distribution and sale of food, drugs and cosmetics. In its regulation of products rather than emissions or effluents, it bears a certain similarity to TSCA, though in the area of food and cosmetics, *no premarketing demonstration of safety is required,* and the *burden is on the agency to show hazard or damage* before the distribution of a product may be limited.

The FFDCA was amended (together with FIFRA) in 1996 to prohibit the presence of pesticide residues on food unless a special tolerance or exemption has been issued by EPA. Such a tolerance or exemption must assure that the pesticide residue will be lower, by an ample margin of safety, than the level at which the residue will not cause or contribute to any known or anticipated harm to human health. *See* 7 U.S.C. § 136a-1(g)(2). For additional discussion of this amendment and its implications, see F. Grad, Treatise on Environmental Law § 8.03[1a].

Consumer Product Safety Act (CPSA), enacted in 1972, 15 U.S.C. § 2051 *et seq.*, authorizes the Consumer Product Safety Commission to ban products which pose an unreasonable risk of injury, or, short of such ban, to require changes in packaging or in the labeling of products so as to provide appropriate warnings. The Commission's jurisdiction includes products previously regulated under the Flammable Fabrics Act, the Federal Hazardous Substances Act, and the Poison Prevention Packaging Act. *No premarket testing of products* is required, and the *Commission has the burden of proving hazard or toxicity* before it may act. Examples of the exercise of the Commission's authority include the ban of tris, a fire retardant, in sleepwear when its carcinogenicity has been shown, the *ban on vinyl chloride* as an aerosol propellant in uses not within the jurisdiction of FDA, and the ban on asbestos for a variety of household and other uses.

[b] Laws Emphasizing Ambient Standards and Emission Controls

Clean Air Act, as last amended in 1977, 42 U.S.C. § 7401 *et seq.,* provides for national ambient air quality standards to protect "health" and "welfare," and provides for the regulation of emissions from stationary sources by the states through federally approved state implementation plans. The Act also provides for the direct regulation and for national emission standards for moving sources, for new stationary industrial sources, and notably, for *emissions of hazardous air pollutants.* C.A.A. § 112, 42 U.S.C. § 7412. Since both the "criteria pollutants" for which ambient standards are set, and the hazardous pollutants for which no such standards are set, are designed to protect health, there is little logical distinction between the two, though the latter are defined to include pollutants which in the judgment of the Administrator, "*may reasonable be anticipated to result in an increase in mortality or an increase in serious irreversible, or incapacitating reversible, illness.*" Moreover, standards for hazardous pollutants are to be set at a level which, in his judgment, provide "*an ample margin of safety . . . .*" The emission standards for such air pollutants that would certainly also meet the regulatory requirements of TSCA include asbestos, beryllium, mercury, vinyl chloride and benzene. (Lead, on the other hand, is a criteria pollutant with ambient standards.) In addition, the 1977 amendments to the Act make special provision for the protection of ozone and for steps to regulate fluorocarbons. C.A.A. §§ 150-159, 42 U.S.C. §§ 7450-7459. *See, generally,* F. Grad, Treatise on Environmental Law, § 2.03[1][b][iv].

Resource Conservation and Recovery Act of 1976 (RCRA), 42 U.S.C. § 6901 *et seq.,* provides for a comprehensive scheme of federal and state involvement in resource recovery and disposal of wastes. The federal government, however, exercises *preemptive power to issue regulations for the management of hazardous wastes,* though their actual administration may be delegated to the states. Hazardous wastes are defined as wastes which may cause or "*contribute to an increase in mortality, or an increase in serious irreversible, or incapacitating reversible, illness,*" or which may "*pose a substantial present or potential hazard to human health or the environment when improperly treated, stored . . . or otherwise managed.*" Excepted from the regulatory scope are nuclear wastes and certain wastes regulated under the Federal Water Pollution Control Act, though RCRA is greatly concerned with the protection of subsurface and other waters that may become contaminated from the disposal of wastes (*e.g.*, RCRA § 1002(b)(3), (4), 42 U.S.C. § 6901(b)(3), (4)). The Act provides for administration of RCRA by EPA consistent with other listed pollution control laws but does not refer to TSCA. RCRA seems to mirror TSCA in certain regulatory controls relating to a system of manifests to trace hazardous wastes from their production and transportation through disposal. *See generally*, F. Grad, Treatise on Environmental Law, § 4.02[3][b][ii] at Notes 59-109.

Federal Water Pollution Control Act, as last amended in 1977, 33 U.S.C. § 1151 *et seq.* The 1972 Act set zero pollution as its target and aimed at its eventual accomplishment in a variety of ways but primarily through national effluent limitations set by category of industry at progressively higher levels that effectively reflect the technological potential for the reduction of pollution ("best applicable technology . . ." "best available technology economically achievable . . .") FWPCA § 301, 33 U.S.C. § 1311. A different measure, however, is applied in the case of a *"toxic pollutant,"* which is defined to include substances that will, *"on the basis of information available to the Administration, cause death, disease, behavioral abnormalities, cancer, genetic mutations, physiological malfunctions (including malfunctions in reproduction) or physical deformations, in such organisms or their offspring."* FWPCA § 502(13), 33 U.S.C. § 1362. The obligation of the Administration to regulate "toxic pollutants" under FWPCA was substantially *broadened under the 1977 amendments, without* any reference, however, to TSCA. FWPCA § 307, 33 U.S.C. § 1317. FWPCA also regulates the *pollution of the marine environment* by prohibiting the discharge of oil or other *"hazardous substances,"* defined to include substances that present an imminent and substantial danger to the public health or welfare, and to fish, shellfish, and beaches. FWPCA § 311(b)(2)(A), 33 U.S.C. § 1321 (b)(2)(A). Other limitations of ocean discharge of hazardous and toxic materials are contained in the *Marine Protection Research and Sanctuaries Act of 1972,* generally referred to as the "Federal Ocean Dumping Act," which generally regulates the dumping of wastes into the sea, in part in carrying out U.S. obligations under international agreemens. The list of prohibitions includes such toxic substances as "radiological, chemical and biological warfare agents, radioactive materials; chemicals, biological and laboratory wastes . . ." 33 U.S.C. §§ 1401, 1402 *et seq. See generally,* F. Grad, Treatise on Environmental Law, § 3.03[4][b], § 4.02[4].

Safe Drinking Water Act of 1974, 42 U.S.C. § 300, provides for the eventual achievement of national drinking water standards. In working towards that goal, the Administrator is to set interim regulations, including *recommended* maximum levels for *toxic substances* that *"may have an adverse effect on the health of persons."* Such maximum contaminant levels have been recommended for a number of *inorganic toxics and for several persistent pesticides,* all regulated also under FIFRA, and for *chlorinated hydrocarbons* which are carcinogenic and which are produced by the chlorination of water that contains certain organic chemicals. The Act is also concerned with underground injection of wastes and the resulting risk of contamination of aquifers. As amended in 1996, the Act also requires public water systems to notify the public with respect to drinking water problems and calls for the assessment and improvement of the quality of "source water" later used for drinking purposes.

Occupational Safety and Health Act (OSHA), 29 U.S.C. § 651 *et seq.*, Pub. L. No. 91-596, 84 Stat. 1590 (1970), regulates health and safety in the workplace. The Occupational Safety and Health Administration in the U.S. Department of Labor has broad power to issue standards relating to occupational exposure to toxics. Permanent standards are to assure, "*to the extent feasible, on the basis of the best available evidence, that no employee will suffer material impairment of health or functional capacity even . . . [through]* regular exposure . . . for the period of his working life . . . ." OSHA § 6(b)(4), 29 U.S.C. § 656(b)(4). In addition, there is authority under OSHA for the promulgation of *emergency standards* if necessary for immediate employee protection. OSHA § 6(c)(1), 29 U.S.C. § 656(c)(1). Permanent standards promulgated under OSHA include limits for a number of carcinogens, and for asbestos, vinyl chloride and coke oven emissions. Standards for arsenic, beryllium and trichloroethylene, and for benzene have also been adopted. Since late 1977 OSHA has been moving in the direction of setting *generic standards* for certain categories of toxic substances—*e.g.*, "confirmed carcinogens," "suspected carcinogens," etc.

Chapter 5

THE NATIONAL ENVIRONMENTAL POLICY ACT OF 1969

§ 5.01 Background and Legislative History

[1] Contents and History of the Act

The National Environmental Policy Act and Environmental Litigation

The National Environmental Policy Act of 1969,[1] was signed in the closing days of that year. The essential provisions of the statute have changed little since then, and it has become the foundation of an enormous amount of environmental litigation.

Although litigation for the protection of the environment had begun somewhat earlier, the National Environmental Policy Act in many ways marked the beginning of environmental litigation as a force to be reckoned with by industry and developmental interests. The landmark *Scenic Hudson* case,[2] included in Chapter 8, *infra*, had been a breakthrough in overcoming the defense of lack of standing, which environmental litigators had faced earlier. Although, following *Scenic Hudson,* there were numerous cases in which environmentalists achieved standing and the right to litigate environmental issues, they scored relatively few notable successes. In instances where environmentalists were successful in compelling the consideration of environmental consequences before major projects could be undertaken, the basis for their success—such as in *Scenic Hudson*, in *Overton Park* and a few other cases—was the presence of existing legislation which addressed other primary purposes and which was extended to cover environmental interests. What was clearly needed, in addition to a procedurally sound basis for standing, was a sound basis for substantive intervention.

Prior to 1970, the situation of would-be environmental litigators in pollution control situations was even worse. Before the Clean Air Act Amendments of 1970 were enacted, the federal legislation which addressed pollution control had inadequate enforcement procedures and weak sanctions, and placed primary reliance on fairly inadequate state and local controls.[3] Moreover, there was no effective way for environmental interests to involve themselves in pollution control enforcement except possibly through private nuisance litigation and through cumbersome efforts to *mandamus* public officials. Beginning with the 1970 Clear Air Act Amendments, the situation changed

---

[1] Pub. L. No. 91-190, 83 Stat. 852, 42 U.S.C. § 4321 *et seq.*

[2] P. 1167 *infra*.

[3] *See* Chapters 2 and 3, *supra*.

drastically with the availability of the citizen suit to enforce air pollution controls.[4]

Prior to the enactment of the National Environmental Policy Act, there had been a period of some ten years when Congress with increasing frequency referred to environmental concerns and when a variety of efforts were undertaken to focus on legislation to bring about environmental improvement. A variety of bills were introduced and hearings held, starting in 1960, to establish bodies to serve as advisors to the President on environmental matters and to provide for environmental research and ecological surveys. In 1967, there had been a task force report to the Secretary of Health, Education, and Welfare entitled, "A Strategy for a Liveable Environment." In 1968, the Senate Committee on Interior and Insular Affairs and the House Committee on Science and Astronautics had sponsored a Joint House and Senate Colloquium to Discuss a National Policy for the Environment (90th Cong., 2d Sess. (1968)). A white paper was prepared by Dr. Lynton K. Caldwell of Indiana University and William J. Van Ness, Special Counsel to the Senate Committee on Interior and Insular Affairs, both of whom played a major role in the eventual development and passage of the National Environmental Policy Act of 1969.

The Act, which became effective on January 1, 1970, was a congressional response to continuing pressures for the creation of an agency that would provide an overview of environmental protection and conservation efforts generally, as well as a device for the integration and coordination of the variety of programs affecting environmental protection.

As ultimately enacted, the National Environmental Policy Act reflects a compromise of two rather drastically different bills introduced in the House and the Senate. Initially, the Senate bill contained only provisions to establish a strong council on environmental quality. Subsequently, during hearings on the bill[5] a new title was added which ultimately became Title I of NEPA. The changed emphasis was to draft an expanded statement of national environmental goals and to impose a mandate on federal agencies to consider the environmental consequences of agency action. The leading roles in this development were played by Senator Jackson and by Professor Caldwell who served as a consultant to the Committee and who had been the author, with Mr. Van Ness, of the *White Paper on a National Policy for the Environment*, referred to above.[6]

The House bill[7] merely created an independent advisory Council to the President. This council was to have broad and independent overview of current and long-term trends in the quality of the national environment, and was to advise the President, and through him the Congress, on steps needed to improve the environment. In the course of its floor debate of the bill, the House

---

[4] For a more detailed description of the pre-1970 state of environmental litigation, see F. Grad and L. Rockett, *Environmental Litigation—Where the Action Is?*, 10 Nat. Resources J. 742 (1970), which emphasized the need for substantive legislation to give environmentalists sound rights of action. *See also* H. Green, *The Role of Government in Environmental Conflict* in Baldwin, ed., Law and the Environment 235, 238-243 (1970).

[5] S. 1075, 91st Cong., 1st Sess. (1969).

[6] *See* 115 Cong. Rec. 29069 (1969).

[7] H.R. 6750, 91st Cong., 1st Sess.

rejected an amendment which would have incorporated Title I, which contained the § 102 environmental impact statement requirement.

As actually passed by both houses, the bill was written in the Conference Committee, and it was there amended to include both the Title I provisions emphasized by the Senate relating to agency obligation to review actions in the light of their environmental impact, and the provision contained in both bills relating to the establishment of a council on environmental quality. However, as passed, the Council on Environmental Quality was a somewhat weaker body than initially proposed in the Senate bill. In conference, too, the earlier provision of the Senate bill, which gave persons the *right* to clean and healthful environment, was amended to include the considerably weaker statement which eventually was passed. Major points of debate relating to the bill drafted in conference differed somewhat in the House and in the Senate.

In the House the major concern appeared to be the question of reconciling the agencies' primary obligations with their obligations to protect the environment pursuant to NEPA. Much of the debate in the Senate, on the other hand, dealt with matters of the scope of the bill in its application to agencies especially created for the protection of the environment. In particular, Senator Muskie was anxious to protect the jurisdiction of the federal water pollution control agency in view of the fact that his committee, the Committee on Public Works, had only recently been successful in securing the adoption of the Federal Water Quality Control Act of 1970 which had strengthened the authority of water pollution control authorities. The colloquies between Senators Jackson and Muskie became particularly significant in future applications of NEPA when questions arose whether agencies with authority to make and enforce environmental regulations were to be bound by the environmental impact statement requirement of § 102 of the Act.

In its finally enacted form, NEPA consists of a detailed, very elaborate and somewhat grandiloquent statement of national policy relating to the environment and a lengthy statement of purposes, which together take up about one-sixth of the length of the bill. The purposes of the bill are set out very broadly, and environmental protection is described in the widest of terms. The federal government must assume a continuing responsibility, consistent with other essential considerations of national policy, to advance environmental protection for a variety of purposes, including the responsibility of each generation as a trustee of the environment for succeeding generations. It is a stated policy of the federal government to use all practicable means and measures in cooperation with state and local governments and other concerned public and private organizations to create and maintain conditions "under which man and nature can exist in productive harmony, and fulfill the social economic and other requirements of present and future generations of Americans." Instead of the ringing declaration in an earlier version of the bill that each person is entitled to a clean and healthful environment, as finally passed the Act contains merely the statement that "each person should enjoy a healthful environment and that each person has a responsibility to contribute to the preservation and enhancement of the environment."

The most significant portion of the bill, and the only operational provision, is contained in § 102 which provides the congressional directive that to the fullest extent possible, the policy, regulations and laws of the United States are to be interpreted and administered in accordance with the policies of the National Environmental Policy Act. It also requires all agencies of federal government to apply a systematic interdisciplinary approach to insure the integrated use of the natural and social sciences and environmental design arts in planning and decision-making which may have an impact on man's environment. Agencies are further instructed, in consultation with the Council on Environmental Quality, to find ways to consider presently unquantified environmental amenities and values in the process of decision-making, along with economic and technical matters. Finally, and most importantly, the section provides that every agency "include in every recommendation or report on proposals for legislation and other major federal action significantly affecting the quality of the human environment a detailed statement by the responsible official on the environmental impact" of such action, specifying in some detail what the environmental impact statement is to consider. This requirement, commonly known as the Environmental Impact Statement (or "EIS") requirement, is the key "action forcing" provision of the statute. It is supplemented by an instruction to federal agencies to develop alternatives to recommended courses of action in any proposal which involves unresolved conflicts concerning alternative uses of resources.

The provisions of the National Environmental Policy Act with respect to agency obligations were first implemented by an Executive Order issued on March 5, 1970.[8] A very significant feature of that Executive Order was the imposition of the duty on the Council on Environmental Quality (CEQ) to promulgate guidelines for compliance with the environmental impact statement requirements. These guidelines were subsequently promulgated in the Federal Register as regulations.[9] The nature and scope of those regulations is well-described in a law review article by Dinah Bear, former general counsel of the CEQ, excerpts of which follow this note.

Most of the remainder of this chapter focuses on a set of critical issues that have arisen as federal courts, in resolving NEPA lawsuits, have struggled to "fill the gaps" in NEPA's statutory scheme. The development of these judge-made standards is analogous to the creation of "common law" standards in more traditional areas of the law. The chapter first considers what have sometimes been referred to as "the threshold issues" in NEPA law: under what circumstances is a federal agency or department required to prepare an environmental impact statement as to a proposed (or ongoing) activity or legislative proposal?

From there, we will examine the related question of the circumstances under which federal agencies and departments, may be exempt from the statute's EIS requirement. We will also consider the courts' treatment of the extent to which environmental impact statements must address region-wide activities of federal agencies and departments, the issues of whether NEPA's mandates apply outside the territorial borders of the United States, and the topics of who must prepare an EIS, what such a statement must contain, and what steps federal agencies must follow to comply with NEPA's provisions.

---

[8] 35 Red. Reg. 4247 (1970).

[9] *See* 40 C.F.R. parts 1500 to 1517.

At that point, this chapter moves to a consideration of which alternatives to proposed agency actions must be analyzed in the context of an EIS. It also considers the important (and now resolved) question of the extent to which NEPA imposes substantive, as opposed to merely procedural, obligations on federal agencies and departments; and it treats the issue of whether NEPA (in its current form as interpreted by judges and implemented within the federal executive branch) is a beneficial, effective statute or/and an enactment in need of reform.

Finally, this chapter examines, in brief fashion and by way of comparison and contrast, the environmental quality acts (sometimes referred to as "little NEPA's" or "SEQA's") that were passed by state legislatures, and implemented by state (and in some instances local) agencies, subsequent to the NEPA's enactment at the federal level.

[2] The Council on Environmental Quality (CEQ) and Its NEPA Regulations

Bear, "NEPA AT 19: A PRIMER ON AN 'OLD' LAW WITH SOLUTIONS TO NEW PROBLEMS"*

19 ELR 10060 (1989)

. . . .

CEQ Guidance and Regulations

Shortly after NEPA was signed into law, President Nixon issued Executive Order 11514 which, among other things, directed CEQ to issue guidelines on preparation of environmental impact statements. Beginning in 1970, CEQ issued a series of these guidelines, which addressed the basic requirements of environmental impact assessment and administratively interpreted the thrust of the considerable case law that was occurring throughout the 1970s.

While the guidelines were useful, the environmental impact assessment process, or "NEPA process," as it frequently is referred to in the federal establishment, acquired some unfortunate "barnacles" during the mid-1970s. The most frequent complaints were the length of EISs and the delays that the NEPA process was perceived to cause in the decisionmaking process. Observers believed that the lack of uniformity throughout the government and uncertainty about what was required accounted to a large degree for these problems. Consequently, in 1977 President Carter issued Executive Order 11991, directing CEQ to issue binding regulations to federal agencies in an effort to make the process more uniform and efficient. The regulations were to cover all procedural provisions of NEPA, and to include procedures for referral to CEQ of conflicts between agencies concerning the environmental impacts of proposed major federal actions.

Regulatory Structure

The CEQ regulations implementing the procedural provisions of NEPA apply to all federal agencies of the government, excluding Congress and any of its institutions, the judiciary, and the President, including the performance of staff functions for the President. The CEQ regulations are generic in nature, and do not address the applicability of the various procedural requirements to specific agency actions. Instead, each federal department and agency is required to prepare its own NEPA procedures that address that agency's compliance in relation to its particular mission. CEQ reviews and approves all agency procedures and amendments to those procedures.

The agency procedures are required to establish specific criteria for and identification of three classes of actions: those that require preparation of an environmental impact statement; those that require preparation of an environmental assessment; and those that are categorically excluded from further NEPA review. Additionally, agencies are required to address NEPA compliance for actions initiated outside of the federal government that require federal approval, the introduction of supplemental EISs into the administrative record, the integration of NEPA analysis into the agency decision making process, and to name a contact office for further information or documents prepared under NEPA.

Categorical Exclusions

"Categorical exclusions" refer to acts falling within a predesignated category of actions that do not individually or cumulatively have a significant effect on the human environment.[10] Thus, no documentation of environmental analysis is required. Agencies may list either very specific actions, or a broader class of actions with criteria and examples for guidance. However, federal officials must be alert to extraordinary circumstances in which a normally excluded action may have a significant environmental effect. A categorical exclusion is *not* an exemption from compliance with NEPA, but merely an administrative tool to avoid paperwork for those actions without significant environmental effects.

Environmental Assessments

An environmental assessment (EA) is supposed to be a concise public document[11] that may be prepared to achieve any of the following purposes: to provide sufficient evidence and analysis for determining whether to prepare an EIS; to aid an agency's compliance with NEPA when no EIS is necessary; and to facilitate preparation of an EIS if one is necessary. An EA should include a brief discussion of the need for the proposal, of alternatives as required by NEPA § 102(2)(E),[12] and of the environmental impacts of the

---

[10] 40 C.F.R. § 1508.4.

[11] CEQ's recommended length is 10 to 15 pages. *See*, Question 36a, "Forty Most Asked Questions Concerning CEQ's National Environmental Policy Act Regulations," 46 Fed. Reg. 18026, 18036, ELR Admin. Mat. 35020, 35029.

[12] Section 102(2)(E) requires federal agencies to, "Study, develop and describe appropriate alternatives to recommended courses of action in any proposal which involves unresolved conflicts concerning alternative uses of available resources." 42 U.S.C. § 4332(2)(E).

proposed action and alternatives. It should list agencies and persons consulted.[13] An EA is followed by one of two conclusions: either a Finding of No Significant Impact (FONSI) or a decision to prepare an EIS. A FONSI briefly presents the reasons why an action, not otherwise categorically excluded, will not have a significant effect on the human environment. It may include a summary of the EA, or simply be attached to the EA.[14] Neither EAs nor FONSIs are filed in a central location (unlike EISs which are filed with the Office of Federal Activities in the Environmental Protection Agency). However, they are public documents, and the agency responsible for their preparation must involve the public in an appropriate manner.[15] Agencies have discretion in selecting the appropriate level of public circulation of EAs and FONSIs, but there are two circumstances in which an agency is required to make a FONSI available for public review for 30 days. The first situation is when the proposed action is, or is closely similar to, an action which normally requires an EIS; the second case arises if the nature of the proposed action is without precedent in the agency's experience.[16]

While the EA and FONSI processes are a valuable and even essential tool, they have been subjected, far too often, to two types of abuse. On the one hand, some compliance has reduced the EA analysis to a one-page form that is so cursory that it is questionable whether the underlying decision about whether to prepare an EIS is sound. On the other hand, an EA all too frequently takes on the look, feel, and form of an EIS, complete with the same qualitative contents and volume and weight. There can be several reasons for this, but certainly one unfortunate rationale has been to avoid as much public involvement as an EIS would stimulate, while being prepared to turn the EA into an EIS rapidly if a court would so order. Agency officials thinking of that approach would be far better advised to simply proceed with circulation of the document as an EIS.

Environmental Impact Statements

The primary purpose of an EIS is to serve as an action-forcing device to ensure that the policies and goals defined in NEPA are infused into the ongoing programs and actions of the federal government. It must provide full and fair discussion of significant environmental impacts and shall inform decisionmakers and the public of the reasonable alternatives that would avoid or minimize adverse impacts or enhance the quality of the human environment. In preparing EISs, *agencies should focus on significant environmental issues and alternatives and reduce paperwork and the accumulation of extraneous background data*. Texts should be concise, clear, and to the point, and should be supported by evidence that the agency has made the necessary environmental analyses. An EIS is *more* than a disclosure document; it should be used by federal officials to plan actions and make decisions.

The threshold requirement for preparation of an EIS is, of course, the statutory threshold of a "major federal action significantly affecting the

[13] 40 C.F.R. § 1508.9.

[14] *See* 40 C.F.R. §§ 1500.3, 1500.5(1), 1501.4(e), 1504.1(a), 1508.13.

[15] 40 C.F.R. § 1506.6.

[16] 40 C.F.R. § 1501.4(e)(2)(i) and (ii).

quality of the human environment."[17] As interpreted by the CEQ regulations and case law, "major federal actions" include a wide range of actions, certainly much more than the construction projects most commonly associated with NEPA compliance. For example, "actions" include adoption of rules, regulations, and interpretations of policy under the Administrative Procedure Act (APA), legislative proposals, treaties and international conventions or agreements, and adoption of programs.[18] Actions include circumstances where the responsible official fails to act and that failure to act is reviewable by courts or administrative tribunals under the APA or other applicable law as agency action.[19] The only items specifically excluded as "actions" under NEPA are judicial or administrative enforcement actions (both civil and criminal) and funding assistance solely in the form of general revenue sharing funds distributed under the State and Local Financial Assistance Act of 1971, with no federal agency control over the subsequent use of such funds.[20]

The question of what is "significant," thus making EIS preparation necessary, has often been a difficult one. In fact, disagreement about whether a proposed action has "significant effects" has been the most frequent reason for NEPA litigation over the past 19 years. CEQ's regulations do not define which particular federal actions are "significant" for purposes of NEPA; rather, they provide a discussion of the factors that should be considered by each agency when drafting their own NEPA procedures and when considering proposed actions. The regulations emphasize the need to consider "significantly" in terms of both context and intensity.[21] "Context" means that the significance of the proposed action must be analyzed in relation to the societal and environmental framework in which the action would occur. Factors to be considered in evaluating "intensity" include the degree to which the proper action affects public health and safety, unique characteristics of the geographic area involved, the degree of controversy about the environmental impacts, the degree to which the possible effects on the human environment are highly uncertain or involve unique or unknown risks, the precedential value of the action, the presence of cumulative effects, the possible effects on historic, scientific, or cultural resources, the degree to which the action may adversely affect an endangered or threatened species or its habitat, and whether the proposed action would be a violation of a federal, state, or local law.[22] One frequently overlooked point is that the NEPA standard of significance applies to both *beneficial and adverse* impacts.[23]

Few federal courts have attempted to formulate a definition of the phrase "significantly affecting" that goes beyond the factual circumstances of a particular case. Instead, a review of the cases shows that almost all have been decided by the court determining whether the evidence in a given case pointed to the presence of potentially significant environmental effects and then deciding whether the agency's decision not to prepare an EIS was reasonable under the circumstances. Generally, however, the courts have rejected specific

[17] NEPA § 102(2)(C), 42 U.S.C. § 4332(2)(c). The statutory term is amplified in the regulations. *See* 41 C.F.R. § 1502.3.

[18] 40 C.F.R. § 1508.18(b).

[19] 40 C.F.R. § 1508.18.

[20] 40 C.F.R. § 1508.18(a).

[21] 40 C.F.R. § 1508.27(a) and (b).

[22] 40 C.F.R. § 1508.27(b)(1)-(10).

[23] 40 C.F.R. § 1508.27(b)(1).

size or monetary factors as a guide to determining the significance of an action.[24] Courts are also increasingly concerned with adequate consideration of cumulative and indirect effects.[25] Although social and economic impacts alone do *not* trigger the requirement to prepare an EIS under NEPA, the courts have required the inclusion of such impacts once the threshold requirement for preparation of an EIS has been reached.[26]

Two types of EISs that have received less attention than the typical project-specific EIS are the programmatic EIS and the legislative EIS. Programmatic EISs must be prepared prior to an agency's decision regarding a major program, plan, or policy with significant environmental impacts. It may be broad in scope, followed by site-specific EISs or EAs prepared at subsequent stages. The process of preparing a broad statement and subsequent, more narrowly focused NEPA documents is referred to as tiering.[27]

Legislative EISs meet the statutory requirement for a "detailed statement on proposals for legislation which would significantly affect the quality of the human environment."[28] Although there are some modifications, the procedures for preparation of legislative EISs are similar to EISs prepared for proposals for executive branch action.[29] Once the decision is made to prepare an EIS of any type, the proponent federal agency publishes a Notice of Intent (NOI) in the Federal Register. The NOI should describe the proper action and possible alternatives, the agency's intent to prepare an EIS, the agency's proposed scoping process, and any planned scoping meetings and the name and address of a contact person in the agency.[30]

The agency must then engage in the "scoping process," a process to determine the scope of issues to be addressed in the EIS and for identifying the significant issues related to a proposed action. Scoping may or may not include meetings, but the process should involve interested parties at all levels of government, and all interested private citizens and organizations. Scoping is also the appropriate point to allocate responsibilities among lead and cooperating agencies,[31] identify other environmental requirements that are applicable

---

[24] *Compare, e.g.,* the decisions in Forty-Seventh Street Improvement Ass'n. v. Volpe (D. Colo. 1973) (one-mile stretch of highway caused sufficient environmental impact to require preparation of an EIS) *with* James v. Tennessee Valley Authority, 538 F. Supp. 704 (E.D. Tenn. 1982) (TVA was not required to prepare an EIS before granting a permit for the construction of an inland coal-loading port even though the agency's own NEPA regulations indicated that port projects normally required an EIS).

[25] *See, e.g.,* Fritiofson v. Alexander, 772 F.2d 1225 (5th Cir. 1985); Conner v. Burford, 605 F. Supp. 107 (D. Mont. 1985).

[26] 40 C.F.R. § 1508.14; Hanly v. Mitchell, 460 F.2d 640 (2d Cir. 1972), and 471 F.2d 823 (2d Cir. 1972) (*sub nom.* Hanly v. Kleindienst).

[27] 40 C.F.R. §§ 1502.20, 1508.28. For CEQ guidance on programmatic EISs and the tiering concept, see "Guidance Regarding NEPA Regulations," 48 Fed. Reg. 34263, 34267 (1983) and Question 24, "Forty Most Asked Questions Concerning CEQ's National Environmental Policy Act Regulations," 46 Fed. Reg. 18026, 18033 (1981). *See also* California v. Block, 690 F.l2d 753 (9th Cir. 1982), and Foundation on Economic Trends v. Lyng, 817 F.2d 882 (D.C. Cir. 1987).

[28] NEPA § 102(2)(c), 42 U.S.C. § 4332(2)(C).

[29] *See* 40 C.F.R. § 1506.8for the applicable requirements.

[30] 40 C.F.R. § 1508.22.

[31] "Lead agency" and "cooperating agency" designations are used when there is more than one federal agency either proposing an action or involved in the same action or group of actions. Federal, state, or local agencies, including at least one federal agency, may act as joint lead agencies. For criteria and responsibilities of lead and cooperating agencies, see 40 C.F.R. §§ 1501.5 and 1501.6. For resolution of disputes over which agency should be lead agency, see 40 C.F.R. § 1501.5(c).

to the proposal, set any time and page limits, and, in general, structure the process in such a way that all identifiable participants are informed and involved at appropriate points. A well designed scoping process can have an extremely positive ripple effect throughout the rest of the NEPA process.

The next step is preparation of a draft EIS. The EIS may be prepared either by the lead agency, with assistance from any cooperating agencies, or by a contractor. However, if a contractor prepares the EIS, the contractor should be chosen by the agency and must execute a disclosure statement prepared by the lead agency, specifying that the contractor has no financial or other interest in the outcome of the project. The agency may accept information from any party, including the applicant, but it *always* has the duty to independently evaluate such information.

The content requirements of an EIS from cover sheet to appendices, are set out in the CEQ regulations. The "heart" of the EIS is the alternatives analysis, which inevitably leads to the question of which alternatives must be analyzed. The answer to that, like the answer to the question of what is "significant," is addressed on a case-by-case basis, with the key judicial standard being that of reasonableness.[32]

If the proposed action is the subject of a request for a federal permit or regulatory approval for a proposed action, the federal agency must consider both public and private purpose and need. Courts have stressed the need to consider the objectives of the permit applicant,[33] but they have also emphasized the requirement for the agency to exercise independent judgment as to the appropriate articulation of objective purpose and need.[34] Thus, NEPA requires the agency to consider both public and private purpose and need in formulating the alternatives to be examined in an EIS.

Once the draft EIS is prepared, it must be circulated for at least 45 days for public comment and review.[35] Federal agencies with jurisdiction by law or special expertise with respect to any of the relevant environmental impacts are expected to comment, although this may take the form of a "no comment" letter.[36] At the conclusion of the comment period, the agency must evaluate the comment letters and respond to the substantive comments in the final EIS.[37] The final EIS is sent to all parties who commented on the draft EIS. No decision may be made concerning the proposed action until at least 30 days

[32] *See* Vermont Yankee Nuclear Power Corp. v. Natural Resources Defense Council, Inc., 435 U.S. 519 (1978). Sometimes "reasonable alternatives" may include those outside the jurisdiction of the lead agency. Natural Resources Defense Council, Inc. v. Morton, 458 F.2d 827 (D.C. Cir. 1972).

[33] Roosevelt Campobello International Park Comm'n v. U.S. EPA, 684 F.2d 1034 (1st Cir. 1982).

[34] Van Abbema v. Fornell, 807 F.2d 633 (7th Cir. 1986).

[35] 40 C.F.R. § 1506.10(c). Both the draft and final EISs are filed with the Office of Federal Activities in the Environmental Protection Agency, which then publishes the official Notice of Availability for the EISs. Timing periods run from publication of the Notice of Availability for comments on EISs and for referrals to CEQ.

[36] 40 C.F.R. § 1503.2.

[37] 40 C.F.R. § 1503.4(b). The CEQ regulations state that the text to final EISs "shall normally be less than 150 pages; for proposals of unusual scope or complexity shall normally be less than 300 pages." 40 C.F.R. § 1502.7. All participants in the process would be better served if agencies would take serious efforts to comply with this standard.

after the Notice of Availability of the final EIS or 90 days after the publication of the Notice of Availability of the draft EIS, whichever is later.[38]

At the time of decision, the decisionmaker must sign a Record of Decision (ROD). The ROD states what the decision is, identifies which alternatives were considered by the agency in making the decision, specifies which alternatives were considered to be environmentally preferable, and discusses factors that were balanced by the decisionmaker. Further, the ROD states whether all practical methods to avoid or minimize environmental harm are being adopted, and if not, why not. The ROD also includes a description of any applicable enforcement and monitoring programs.[39]

The Referral Process

The referral process is a method for referring to CEQ those federal interagency disagreements concerning proposed major federal actions that might cause unsatisfactory environmental effects.[40] The head of a federal department or agency may refer a proposed major federal action to CEQ no later than 25 days after the Notice of Availability for the final EIS has been published by EPA. Under § 309 of the Clean Air Act,the Administrator of EPA has broader authority to refer to CEQ any proposed legislation, action, or regulation that he or she deems unsatisfactory from the standpoint of public health or welfare or environmental quality. The regulations provide guidance on procedures to be followed, criteria for referrals, contents of referring letters and supporting documents, responses by agencies, and involvement by the public. If CEQ accepts a referral, it has a number of options, including making recommendations to the President for action. However, most typically, CEQ publishes Findings and Recommendations regarding the issues under consideration. These recommendations are not binding on the lead agency, but they are most often accepted.

. . . .

NOTE

As the above excerpt alludes to, a number of federal agencies and departments initially resisted the adoption of NEPA's procedural mandates. Some delayed the implementation of the Act's EIS requirements. Others engaged in what has been described as administrative "overkill," by preparing statements that were so lengthy, detailed and unwieldy as to be virtually useless as an aid to decisionmaking. These problems were substantially ameliorated following the promulgation of CEQ's regulations.

---

[38] 40 C.F.R. § 1506.10. Agencies that have internal appeal procedures that provide a real opportunity to alter the ultimate decision may make and record the ultimate decision at the same time the EIS is published. 40 C.F.R. § 1506.10(b)(2).

[39] 40 C.F.R. § 1505.2.

[40] *See* 40 C.F.R. Part 1504 for full referral procedures.

§ 5.02 The Threshold Issue: When Is an EIS Required?

NEPA's requirement that an environmental impact statement be filed for major federal actions significantly affecting the quality of the human environment raises "threshold questions" as to whether the particular action proposed meets the statutory standard. In a sense, every agency faced with the issue faces a logical quandary in that it must determine whether its proposed action is "federal," is "major," and has "significant impact on the human environment," before it has actually had an opportunity to look into the full ramifications of the environmental impact via the Section 102 process. Nonetheless, the threshold determinations must be made, and agencies must prepare an analysis of the impact of the proposed action which is sufficiently detailed to support a conclusion, if necessary, that no environmental impact statement need be prepared.

The next several cases illustrate the ways in which federal courts have resolved these issues.

[1] What Is a "Major Federal Action?"

MARYLAND CONSERVATION COUNCIL, INC. v. GILCHRIST

United States Court of Appeals, Fourth Circuit (1986)
808 F.2d 1039

WINTER, C.J.:

The Maryland Conservation Council and two other citizens' groups sought to enjoin officials of Montgomery County, Maryland from authorizing further construction of a highway allegedly designed to pass through Seneca Creek State Park. The plaintiffs alleged, inter alia, that the County's construction program violated the National Environmental Policy Act (NEPA). 42 U.S.C. §§ 4331 *et seq.* (1982). Without hearing oral argument, the district court granted the defendants' motion to dismiss. We reverse in part and affirm in part.

. . . .

[F]or purposes of this appeal we treat as proved all facts well pleaded. They are as follows:

Seneca Creek State Park is located in Montgomery County, Maryland, near Gaithersburg and Germantown. It comprises over 6,000 acres and follows Great Seneca Creek for about 12 miles. The State of Maryland acquired much of the park land with federal funds, including $6.2 million received from the Department of the Interior. The area in which the park is located has existing and future deficits in day-use recreational facilities.

In 1971, Montgomery County began planning to construct the "Great Seneca Highway" through the park to relieve traffic congestion in the Gaithersburg-Germantown area. Because the project had been considered for federal-aid highway funds, the Department of Transportation and the County prepared a draft environmental impact statement (EIS) in 1983. The final EIS is still pending. Although the County received $245,000 in federal funds for planning the highway, there is no allegation that it has sought additional federal financing. There is, however, an allegation that additional federal funds may be sought, *i.e.*, that "additional Federal Aid will be pursued to the extent feasible."

The plaintiffs and other environmentalists concede that some highway access through the park is essential. Controversy exists, however, over which route, or "alignment," the highway should take. Environmentalists, the National Park Service, and the Environmental Protection Agency have urged that the County should upgrade existing highways so as to hold to a minimum damage to the park. The County did begin improvements on existing roads in the vicinity of the park, but it also began authorizing road construction along Alternate 2A, a route preferred by it that did not coincide with existing highways. If extended through the park, Alternate 2A would take three times as much park land as any other alternative route. Two federal agencies, the National Park Service and the Environmental Protection Agency, have expressed dissatisfaction with Alternate 2A, the National Park Service characterizing it as having "the most severe, negative effects" on the park.

Private real estate developers, who have undertaken to construct real property projects in the vicinity of Alternate 2A, have been required to develop the two segments of Alternate 2A entering and leaving the park, but not the middle segment, which would actually run through the park. The County has required them to dedicate to the County the right-of-way for that part of Alternate 2A passing through their properties and to design and grade four lanes and pave two lanes along the right-of-way. The County claims that this paving is merely for "access" to each subdivision. By this means, construction of approximately two miles, or 26% of the total, of Alternate 2A has already commenced on both sides of the park.

We turn first to plaintiffs' claim under NEPA. That statute requires an EIS for "major Federal actions" that significantly affect the environment, 42 U.S.C. § 4332(C), and authorizes the courts to enjoin federal actions that do not comply. The district court held that the Great Seneca Highway is not a "federal" action; it therefore dismissed the NEPA count for failure to state a claim.

A non-federal project is considered a "federal action" if it cannot "begin or continue without prior approval of a federal agency."

We conclude that the Great Seneca Highway is a federal action within the meaning of NEPA. Because the highway, wherever located, must inevitably cross Seneca Creek State Park, a park established with a grant of substantial federal funds, the approval of the Secretary of the Interior for conversion of park land to other than public outdoor recreation uses will be required. Conservation Act § 6(f), 16 U.S.C. § 4601-8(f)(3). In addition, it is alleged that the section of the highway that will cross the park will impinge on wetlands when it crosses Seneca Creek so that a permit from the Secretary of the Army to dredge wetlands will be required pursuant to the provisions of § 404 of the Water Act. 33 U.S.C. § 1344. Finally, if defendants seek additional federal funds for the construction of the highway, they will be required to obtain the approval of the Secretary of Transportation for the use of park land for a transportation program under § 4(f) of the Transportation Act. 49 U.S.C.

§ 303(c). In each instance, each Secretary will be required to consider a final EIS before exercising his or her authority. It is certain that this must be done by the Secretary of the Interior; it is almost certain that this must be done by the Secretary of the Army; and it is possible that this must be done by the Secretary of Transportation. Because of the inevitability of the need for at least one federal approval, we think that the construction of the highway will constitute a major federal action.

Because it is inevitable that the construction of the highway will involve a major federal action, it follows that compliance with NEPA is required before any portion of the road is built. This conclusion effectuates the purpose of NEPA. The decision of the Secretary of the Interior to approve the project, and the decision of any other Secretary whose authority may extend to the project, would inevitably be influenced if the County were allowed to construct major segments of the highway before issuance of a final EIS. It is precisely this sort of influence on federal decision-making that NEPA is designed to prevent. Non-federal actors may not be permitted to evade NEPA by completing a project without an EIS and then presenting the responsible federal agency with a *fait accompli.*

. . . .

MACHT v. SKINNER

United States Court of Appeals, District of Columbia Circuit (1990)
916 F.2d 13

WALD, C.J.:

Appellants Robert Macht, Lois Macht, and the Robert E. Lee Park Defense Fund, Inc. and its members, sued Samuel K. Skinner, Secretary of the United States Department of Transportation, and various other state and federal officials to enjoin construction of the Central Baltimore Light Rail Line, alleging that state and federal officials failed to comply with § 4(f) of the Department of Transportation Act, 49 U.S.C. § 303, and the National Environmental Policy Act ("NEPA"), 42 U.S.C. § 4321 *et seq.*, and rules and regulations promulgated thereunder. The district court denied the appellants' motion for summary judgment and granted the state and federal appellees' cross-motions for summary judgment.

. . . .

After preliminary analysis by the Maryland Mass Transit Administration ("MTA"), Maryland transit officials decided in December 1987 to build a 27-mile light rail transit system—the Central Baltimore Light Rail Line ("CLRT"). Maryland initially planned the CLRT to extend from Hunt Valley, in northern Baltimore County, through downtown Baltimore, to Baltimore-Washington International Airport ("BWI") and Dorsey Road in Anne Arundel County. Under the original plan, state and local governments were to finance $250 million of the estimated $290 million project, while the Urban Mass

Transportation Administration ("UMTA") was to contribute the remaining $40 million.

As the planning progressed, however, Maryland officials realized that they were required to comply with NEPA and § 4(f) in order to obtain UMTA funding. Because compliance with NEPA would delay construction of the CLRT, Maryland officials decided in late 1988 to withdraw their request for UMTA funding and build a smaller light rail line entirely with state and local funds. Under the modified Light Rail Project ("Light Rail Project" or "the Project"), Maryland is building a 22.5-mile baseline segment that will run from Dorsey Road in the south to Timonium Road in the north. In addition, Maryland is considering building three extensions with federal funds: (1) an extension from Timonium Road to Hunt Valley in the north, (2) a spur connecting BWI Airport to the Project in the south, and (3) a connection between Pennsylvania Station and either Cathedral Street or an area "north of the Mount Royal Station."

Maryland has begun construction on the 22.5-mile state segment. But thus far the only federal involvement in the Project has been a $2.5 million UMTA grant to help the state complete alternative analyses and draft environmental impact statements ("EIS") for the proposed extensions. Appellants brought suit in the district court to enjoin construction of the Light Rail Project, alleging that Maryland illegally divided the Project into a state segment and two federal extensions in order to avoid compliance with NEPA. In particular, appellants assert that the state segment under construction will have an adverse impact on the Robert E. Lee Park, and that Maryland is attempting to build the Light Rail Project through the park without doing the environmental analysis required by NEPA and § 4(f) of the Transportation Act.

. . . .

NEPA requires that federal agencies consider the environmental consequences of "major federal actions significantly affecting the quality of the human environment." 42 U.S.C. § 4332(2)(C). Thus, the threshold issue in this case is whether, at this point, there is sufficient federal involvement in the Light Rail Project to constitute major federal action affecting the environment under NEPA . . . . Appellants base their claim that the Project involves major federal action on two facts: (1) UMTA has given Maryland $2.5 million for preliminary engineering studies and environmental impact statements for the proposed extensions to the Light Rail Project; and (2) Maryland must obtain from the Army Corps of Engineers a wetlands permit pursuant to § 404 of the Clean Water Act and § 10 of the Rivers and Harbors Actin order to build the state segment. We hold that neither is sufficient to transform the entirely state-funded Light Rail Project into "major federal action" affecting the environment within the meaning of NEPA. . . .

A. UMTA Funding for Preliminary Studies

On September 29, 1989, UMTA granted MTA a maximum of $2,587,500 to perform an Alternative Analysis and Draft Environmental Impact Statement for the possible extensions to the Light Rail Project. Appellants argue that this federal expenditure makes the entire Light Rail Project—the 22.5-mile state segment under construction as well as the proposed extensions—"major federal action" affecting the environment within the meaning of NEPA. This argument is based on a misconception about NEPA's requirements.

NEPA requires federal agencies to prepare or evaluate an EIS for any proposed "major federal action" that will "significantly affect the quality of the human environment." 42 U.S.C. § 4332(2)(C). NEPA does not require UMTA to prepare an EIS until it proposes or decides to participate in a project that will affect the environment. In this case, UMTA has not yet decided to assist Maryland in the final design or construction of the proposed extensions to the Light Rail Project. As the district court aptly recognized, "[t]o argue that the federal funding . . . for the preliminary analysis studies constitutes major federal action in the proposed extensions would be putting the proverbial cart before the horse because until these studies are done a decision cannot be reached on what projects—if any—are to be developed."

Our holding that UMTA funding of preliminary studies in not major federal action within the meaning of NEPA is consistent with other circuit court precedent. In *Rapid Transit Advocates, Inc. v. Southern California Rapid Transit District*, 752 F.2d 373 (9th Cir. 1985) (per curiam), a group of homeowners sought to enjoin an UMTA grant to assist the local transit district in performing preliminary design and engineering studies for a proposed subway line, alleging that UMTA failed to comply with various provisions of the UMTA Act and NEPA. The Ninth Circuit rejected their claim, saying:

> Neither [UMTA's] decision nor the design and engineering work that will follow will have any impact upon appellants in and of themselves. The UMT Administration has explicitly disavowed any advance commitment to approve construction. The process may never be completed; the Wilshire Subway may never be funded. If it is, appellants' present objections can be raised and fully considered in a suit to review the agency's final action in light of then existing circumstances. 752 F.2d at 378-79; *see also Atlanta Coalition on the Transportation Crisis, Inc. v. Atlanta Regional Commission*, 599 F.2d 1333, 1347 (5th Cir. 1979) (development of regional transportation plan is not major federal action where the "federal financial assistance to the planning process in no way implies a commitment by any federal agency to fund any transportation project or projects or to undertake, fund or approve any action that directly affects the human environment").

Similarly in this case, UMTA's decision to fund preliminary studies, in and of itself, will have no impact on appellants or the environment. UMTA has expressly stated that its decision to provide funding for alternative analyses "is not a commitment to fund the construction of any project that may result." Letter from Alfred A. Dellibovi, Administrator of UMTA, to Ronald J. Hartman, Administrator of MTA (March 30, 1989). In fact, Maryland has not even decided to build the proposed extensions—with or without federal financial assistance. At this point, the federal involvement is not the firm commitment that could transform the so far entirely state-funded Light Rail Project into major federal action affecting the environment within the meaning of NEPA. *Cf. Defenders of Wildlife v. Andrus*, 627 F.2d 1238, 1243 (D.C. Cir. 1980) ("only when an agency reaches the point . . . where it is ready to propose a course of action need it be ready to produce an impact statement" pursuant to NEPA).

Nor are we persuaded that the Project involves major federal action because Maryland hopes to obtain a $40 million UMTA grant to build the extensions. The district court perceptively recognized that "in this era of federal fiscal shortcomings there is a wide gulf between what a state may want and what the federal government is willing to provide. The [appellants] have provided no evidence that the federal government is irretrievably committed to providing the funds for the proposed extensions." Absent such evidence, we cannot find major federal action in the Light Rail Project. *See Boston v. Volpe*, 464 F.2d 254, 258 (1st Cir. 1972) (state's "present intention eventually to seek federal funds for yet another stretch of [airport] taxiway" does not convert present state construction of taxiway into a federal project).

Because we hold that the Light Rail Project does not yet involve major federal action, we do not decide whether NEPA may require an environmental analysis if UMTA ultimately decides to fund construction of the extensions, or whether such a decision may constitute major federal action within the meaning of NEPA. *Cf. Indian Lookout Alliance v. Volpe*, 484 F.2d 11, 16 (8th Cir. 1973) ("any project for which federal funds have been approved or committed constitutes a major federal action bringing into play the requirements of NEPA"). If such an eventuality occurs, appellants may renew their claim that an EIS is required prior to the disbursement of federal funds or question the scope of the EIS, *i.e.*, whether it must encompass the baseline segment as well as the extensions. *See Kleppe v. Sierra Club*, 427 U.S. 390, 406 n. 15, 96 S.Ct. 2718, 2728 n. 15, 49 L.Ed.2d 576 (1976) ("the time at which a court enters the [NEPA] process is when the report or recommendation of the proposal [for major federal action] is made, and someone protests either the absence or the adequacy of the final impact statement"). An adequate EIS would, of course, be a necessary prerequisite for the expenditure of federal funds on the project.

B. The Army Corps of Engineers' Permit

Appellants also claim that even though the state segment is financed entirely with state funds, it is major federal action under NEPA because the Army Corps of Engineers must issue a wetlands permit pursuant to § 404 of the Clean Water Act, 33 U.S.C. § 1344, and § 10of the Rivers and Harbors Act, 33U.S.C. § 403. . . .

Appellants argue that because the Project has been "federalized," Maryland must comply with NEPA before it may construct the state segment. We disagree and take this opportunity to clarify what it means to "federalize" state or private action for purposes of NEPA.

NEPA requires *federal agencies*—not states or private parties—to consider the environmental impacts of their proposed actions. "[F]or any major federal action funded under a program of grants to States," however, NEPA allows a state agency to prepare an EIS for a federal agency if certain conditions are met. 42 U.S.C. § 4332(2)(D); *see also* 23 C.F.R. § 771.109(c)(UMTA regulations). Regardless of whether the EIS is prepared by a federal or state agency, the twofold purpose of NEPA is "to inject environmental considerations into the federal agency's deicionmaking process" and "to inform the public that the [federal] agency has considered environmental concerns in its decisionmaking process." *Weinberger v. Catholic Action of Hawaii/Peace Education Project*, 454 U.S. 139, 142, 102 S.Ct. 197, 201, 70 L.Ed.2d 298 (1981) (emphasis added).

Appellants correctly assert that federal involvement in a nonfederal project may be sufficient to "federalize" the project for purposes of NEPA. *See, e.g., Maryland Conservation Council, Inc. v. Gilchrist*, 808 F.2d 1039 (4th Cir. 1986); *Winnebago Tribe of Nebraska v. Ray*, 621 F.2d 269 (8th Cir.), *cert. denied*, 449 U.S. 836, 101 S.Ct. 110, 66 L.Ed.2d 43 (1980); *Sierra Club v. Hodel*, 544 F.2d 1036 (9th Cir. 1976). But contrary to appellants' argument, none of these cases stand for the proposition that a state must comply with NEPA if one of its projects is found to involve major federal action.

The cases instead fall into two categories. Cases in the first category involve allegations that a federal agency failed to comply with NEPA when it issued a permit allowing a nonfederal project to go forward. In these cases the question is usually whether the federal agency had to prepare an EIS before issuing the permit or whether the EIS prepared by the federal agency was sufficiently broad in scope. *See, e.g., Winnebago Tribe of Nebraska*, 621 F.2d at 272-73 (challenge to Army Corps' decision that issuance of wetlands permit would have no significant impact and thus EIS was not required); *Save the Bay, Inc. v. United States Corps of Engineers*, 610 F.2d 322 (5th Cir.) (challenge to Army Corps' decision that issuance of pipeline construction permit was not major federal action requiring compliance with NEPA), *cert. denied*, 449 U.S. 900, 101 S.Ct. 269, 99 L.Ed.2d 130 (1980). Because the Army Corps is not a party to this case and there is no allegation that the Army Corps has failed to comply with NEPA, these cases are not controlling on the issue before us. . . .

The issue in the second category of cases is whether state or private action on an entire project should be enjoined until the federal agencies that must approve particular portions of the project have complied with NEPA. The question in these cases is whether the federal participation in the project is so substantial that the state should not be allowed to go forward until all the federal approvals have been granted in accordance with NEPA. *See, e.g., Sierra Club v. Hodel*, 554 F.2d 1036 (9th Cir. 1976) (court enjoined construction of an ALCOA plant until the Bonneville Power Administration—a federal agency subject to NEPA—completed an EIS; by contracting to construct a transmission line and supply power to the ALOCA plant, the BPA federalized the entire project); *Dalsis v. Hills*, 424 F. Supp. 784, 787 (W.D.N.Y. 1976) (court enjoined construction of shopping mall until HUD prepared an EIS because HUD financed demolition of "substandard structures" on the site, and the developer "could not lawfully have started the redevelopment project without HUD's approval").

Maryland Conservation Council, Inc. v. Gilchrist, 808 F.2d 1039 (4th Cir. 1986), on which appellants primarily rely, falls in this latter category. Gilchrist involved an attempt to enjoin construction of a county highway designed to pass through a state park. The court found that the county highway project involved major federal action because: (1) the highway crossed a state park that had been purchased with a substantial federal grant; therefore, the county needed the approval of the Secretary of Interior, pursuant to § 6(f) of the Conservation Act, to convert the park land to other than recreational use; (2) the county needed a § 404 permit from the Army Corps to dredge a wetlands; and (3) the county might need the approval of the Secretary of Transportation to use park land for a transportation project under § 4(f) of the Transportation Act. 808 F.2d at 1042. On these facts, the court of appeals held that the district court should have considered the motion to enjoin the county's construction until the federal officials had complied with NEPA. *Id.* at 1403.

Gilchrist did not hold that the state had to comply with NEPA because the approval of several federal agencies was a necessary precondition to the state project. Instead, *Gilchrist* held that because the state needed permits and discretionary approval from several federal agencies in order to build a substantial part of the highway, the state could not construct any portion of the highway until the federal agencies had approved the project in compliance with NEPA. The reasoning of the Fourth Circuit in *Gilchrist* is sound: the state may not begin construction of any part of a project if the effect of such construction would be to limit significantly the options of the federal officials who have discretion over substantial portions of the project. Nevertheless, we decline to extend *Gilchrist* to this case where the only federal involvement is the issuance of a wetlands permit covering a maximum of 3.58 acres of the 22.5-mile Project.

First, and most significantly, the district court found that the Army Corps has discretion over only "a negligible portion of the entire project." This case is thus distinguishable from *Gilchrist* where several federal agencies had discretion over a substantial part of the highway project. *See also Sierra Club v. Alexander*, 484 F. Supp. 445, 472 (N.D. N.Y.), aff'd mem., 633 F.2d 206 (2d Cir. 1980) (court empowered to enjoin private construction of shopping mall until Army Corps complies with NEPA where completion of the project will require Army Corps approval to rechannel 2,000 linear feet of creek and fill 38 acres of wetlands).

Second, "the degree of federal involvement in the 22.5 mile Project is limited solely to the issuance of wetlands permits and no other federal activity is required for the Project's construction." Maryland has not, therefore, entered a "joint venture" with the federal government by contracting to obtain goods or services from a federal agency. *See Sierra Club v. Hodel*, 554 F.2d 1036 (9th Cir. 1976) (construction of ALCOA plant may be enjoined until federal agency prepares EIS because ALCOA federalized the project by contracting to have a federal agency construct a transmission line and supply power to the plant).

Finally, Maryland has not entered a financial "partnership" with the federal government because the district court found that "the federal government has given no direct—or indirect, for that matter—financial aid to the state for the Project." *Cf. Gilchrist*, 808 F.2d at 1042 (federal government provided indirect financial assistance because state highway would cross a park established with a "grant of substantial federal funds"); *Biderman v. Morton*, 497 F.2d 1141 (2d Cir. 1974) ("it is well settled that non-federal parties may be enjoined, pending completion of an EIS, where those non-federal entities have entered into a partnership or joint venture with the federal government and are thus recipients of federal funding"); *Foundation on Economic Trends v. Heckler*, 756 F.2d 143 (D.C. Cir. 1985) (enjoining University of California experiment that NIH approved and funded without complying with NEPA).

This is clearly not a case in which the state has entered a "partnership" or "joint venture" with the federal government by contracting with a federal agency to obtain goods, services, or financing. Nor is this a case where the federal government has discretion over substantial portions of the project. NEPA therefore provides no basis for enjoining Maryland's construction of the Light Rail Project.

. . . .

NOTES AND QUESTIONS

(1) Do you agree with these decisions? Are they consistent? On what basis did the *Macht* court attempt to distinguish the *Gilchrist* case from *Macht v. Skinner*? Was that distinction persuasive?

(2) Would the result in *Macht* have been different if the federal government had committed to funding all engineering work on the light rail project in issue, rather than merely preliminary engineering studies?

(3) In its NEPA regulations, the Council on Environmental Quality has provided the following definition of "major federal action":

40 C.F.R. § 1508.18Major Federal action

"Major Federal action" includes actions with effects that may be major and which are potentially subject to federal control and responsibility. Major reinforces but does not have a meaning independent of significantly (§ 1508.27). Actions include the circumstance where the responsible officials fail to act and that failure to act is reviewable by courts or administrative tribunals under the Administrative Procedure Act or other applicable law as agency action.

(a) Actions include new and continuing activities, including projects and programs entirely or partly financed, assisted,conducted, regulated, or approved by federal agencies; new or revised agency rules, regulations, plans, policies, or procedures; and legislative proposals (§§ 1506.8, 1508.17). Actions do not include funding assistance solely in the form of general revenue sharing funds, distributed under the state and federal Fiscal Assistance Act of 1972, 31 U.S.C. 1221 *et seq.*, with no federal agency control over the subsequent use of such funds. Actions do not include bringing judicial or administrative civil or criminal enforcement actions.

(b) Federal actions tend to fall within one of the following categories:

(1) Adoption of official policy, such as rules, regulations, and interpretations adopted pursuant to the Administrative Procedure Act, 5U.S.C. 551 *et seq.*; treaties and international conventions or agreements; formal documents establishing an agency's policies which will result in or substantially alter agency programs.

(2) Adoption of formal plans, such as official documents prepared or approved by federal agencies which guide or prescribe alternative uses of federal resources, upon which future agency actions will be based.

(3) Adoption of programs, such as a group of concerted actions to implement a specific policy or plan; systematic and connected agency decisions allocating agency resources to implement a specific statutory program or executive directive.

(4) Approval of specific projects, such as construction or management activities located in a defined geographic area. Projects include actions approved by permit or other regulatory decision as well as federal and federally assisted activities.

(4) In *Sierra Club v. Hodel*, 848 F.2d 1068, 1089-1090 (10th Cir. 1988), the court took an approach similar, in certain respects, to that of the Fourth Circuit in the *Gilchrist* case. It held that a proposed county road construction project passing through environmentally sensitive lands was a federal action, where the U.S. Department of Interior was obligated, by federal statute and regulation, to prevent the unnecessary destruction of wilderness areas in changes of rights-of-way. In the court's view, the "touchstone" for determining whether a major federal action existed was whether the federal agency had the "authority" to "influence significant nonfederal activity." Such influence, it opined, must be "more than the power to give nonbinding advice to the nonfederal influence." Instead, "the federal agency must possess actual power to control the nonfederal activity."

(5) As has been true with respect to many NEPA issues, the federal courts have not created uniform black-letter rules in determining when proposed projects constitute federal actions. For a sampling of other relevant cases, see *Atlanta Coalition on the Transportation Crisis, Inc. v. Atlanta Regional Commission*, 559 F.2d 1333, 1344-1447 (5th Cir. 1979) (federal funding assistance for local planning process is not major federal action where all planning decisions are "entrusted to state and local agencies"); *Ringsred v. City of Duluth*, 828 F.2d 1305 (8th Cir. 1987) (EIS was not required where federal action was not a legal condition precedent to construction of a local project); *Almond Hill High School v. U.S. Dept. of Agriculture*, 768 F.2d 1030, 1039 (9th Cir. 1985) (no federal action where federal officials constituted a minority on a state advisory board that had power to recommend, but not implement, pesticide spraying to combat a beetle infestation); *Monarch Chemical Works, Inc. v. Exon*, 452 F. Supp. 493 (D. Neb. 1978), *vacated* 466 F. Supp. 639, *aff'd*. 604 F.2d 1083 (8th Cir. 1979) (EIS required where, in acquiring site for a correctional facility, a "lengthy, extensive and close working relationship" was established between non-federal entity and a governmental unit acting as a federal agency); *Ramsey v. Kantor*, 96 F.3d 434 (9th Cir. 1996) (failure of U.S. Department of Commerce to disapprove state fish management council plans governing fishing off state coast constituted a major federal action). For an analysis of many of the pertinent decisions, *see* Ellis and Smith, *The Limits of Federal Responsibility and Control Under the National Environmental Policy Act*, 18 Envt'l. L. Rep. 10055 (1988).

[2] When Does A Major Federal Action "Significantly" Affect Environmental Quality?

HANLY v. KLEINDIENST ("HANLY II")

United States Court of Appeals, Second Circuit (1972)
471 F.2d 823

Mansfield, C.J.:

This case, which presents serious questions as to the interpretation of the National Environmental Policy Act of 1969, 42 U.S.C. §§ 4331 *et seq.* ("NEPA"), the language of which has been characterized as "opaque" and "woefully ambiguous," is here on appeal for the second time. Following the district court's denial for the second time of a preliminary injunction against construction of a jail and other facilities known as the Metropolitan Correction Center ("MCC") we are called upon to decide whether a redetermination by the General Services Administration ("GSA") that the MCC is not a facility "significantly affecting the quality of the human environment," made pursuant to this Court's decision remanding the case after the earlier appeal, *Hanly v. Mitchell*, 460 F.2d 640 (2d Cir. 1972) (Feinberg, J.), *cert. denied, Hanly v. Kleindienst,* 409 U.S. 990, 93 S.Ct. 313, 34 L.Ed.2d 256 (1972) (herein *"Hanly I")*, satisfies the requirements of NEPA and thus renders it unnecessary for GSA to follow the procedure prescribed by § 102(2)(C) of NEPA, 42 U.S.C. § 4332(2)(C), which requires a formal, detailed environmental impact statement. In view of the failure of the GSA, upon redetermination, to make findings with respect to certain relevant factors and to furnish an opportunity to appellants to submit relevant evidence, the case is again remanded.

Since the background of the action up to the date of our earlier remand is set forth in *Hanly I*, we limit ourselves to a brief summary. Appellants are members of groups residing or having their businesses in an area of lower Manhattan called "The Manhattan Civic Center" which comprises not only various courthouses, government buildings and businesses, but also residential housing, including cooperative apartments in two buildings close to the MCC and various similar apartments and tenements in nearby Chinatown. GSA, of which appellant Robert L. Kunzig was the Administrator, is engaged in the construction of an Annex to the United States Courthouse, Foley Square, Manhattan, located on a site to the east of the Courthouse and immediately to the south of Chinatown and the aforementioned two cooperative apartments. The Annex will consist of two buildings, each approximately 12 stories high, which will have a total of 345,601 gross square feet of space (214,264 net). One will be an office building for the staffs of the United States Attorney and the United States Marshall, presently located in the severely overcrowded main Courthouse building, and the other will be the MCC.

The MCC will serve, under the jurisdiction of the Bureau of Prisons, Department of Justice, as the detention center for approximately 449 persons awaiting trial or convicted of short term federal offenses. It will replace the present drastically overcrowded and inadequate facility on West Street, Manhattan, and will be large enough to provide space not only for incarceration but for diagnostic services, and medical, recreational and administrative facilities. Up to 48 of the detainees, mostly those scheduled for release within 30 to 90 days, may participate in a community treatment program whereby they will be permitted to spend part of each day in the city engaged in specific work or study activity, returning to the MCC after completion of each day's business. A new program will provide service for outpatient non-residents. The MCC will be serviced by approximately 130 employees, only 90 of whom will be present on the premises at any one time.

In February 1972, appellants sought injunctive relief against construction of the MCC on the ground that GSA had failed to comply with the mandates of § 102 of NEPA, 42 U.S.C. § 4332(2)(C), which requires the preparation of a detailed environmental impact statement with respect to major federal actions "significantly affecting the quality of the human environment." On March 22, 1972, the application was denied by the district court on the ground that GSA had concluded that the Annex would not have such an effect and that its findings were not "arbitrary" within the meaning of § 10 of the Administrative Procedure Act("APA"), 5 U.S.C. § 706. The Government concedes that construction of the Annex is a "major" federal action within the meaning of § 102 of NEPA.

Upon appeal this Court affirmed the district court's order as to the office building but reversed and remanded as to the detention center, the MCC, on the ground that the GSA's threshold determination, which had been set forth in a short memorandum entitled "Environmental Statement" dated February 23, 1971, was too meager to satisfy NEPA's requirements. That statement confined itself to a brief evaluation of the availability of utilities, the adequacy of mass transportation, the removal of trash, the absence of a relocation problem and the intention to comply with existing zoning regulations. In remanding the case this Court, although finding the GSA statement sufficient to support its threshold determination with respect to the proposed office building, concluded that the detention center "stands on a different footing," *Hanly I* at 646, and that the agency was required to give attention to other factors that might affect human environment in the area, including the possibility of riots and disturbances in the jail which might expose neighbors to additional noise, the dangers of crime to which neighbors might be exposed as the consequence of housing an out-patient treatment center in the building, possible traffic and parking problems that might be increased by trucks delivering food and supplies and by vans taking prisoners to and from the Eastern District and New Jersey District Courts, and the need for parking space for prison personnel and accommodations for visitors, including lawyers or members of the family. This Court concluded:

> "The Act must be construed to include protection of the quality of life for city residents. Noise, traffic, over-burdened mass transportation systems, crime, congestion and even availability of drugs all affect the urban 'environment' and are surely results of the 'profound influences of . . . high-density urbanization [and] industrial expansion.' " *Hanly I,* 460 F.2d at 647.

We further noted that in making the threshold determination authorized by § 102(2)(C) of NEPAthe agency must "affirmatively develop a reviewable environmental record" in lieu of limiting itself to perfunctory conclusions with respect to the MCC. This Court granted the injunction as to the MCC but after consideration of the balance of hardships stayed the order for a period of 30 days to enable GSA to make a new threshold determination which would take into account the factors set forth in the opinion.

Following the remand a new threshold determination in the form of a 25-page "Assessment of the Environmental Impact" ("Assessment" herein) was made by the GSA and submitted to the district court on June 15,1972. This document (to which photographs, architect's renditions and a letter of approval from the Director of the Office of Lower Manhattan Development, City of New York, are attached) reflects a detailed consideration of numerous relevant factors. Among other things, it analyzes the size, exact location, and proposed use of the MCC; its design features, construction, and aesthetic relationship to its surroundings; the extent to which its occupants and activities conducted in it will be visible by the community; the estimated effects of its operation upon traffic, public transit and parking facilities; its approximate population, including detainees and employees; its effect on the level of noise, smoke, dirt, obnoxious odors, sewage and solid waste removal; and its energy demands. It also sets forth possible alternatives, concluding that there is none that is satisfactory. Upon the basis of this Assessment the Acting Commissioner of the Public Building Service Division of the GSA, who is the responsible official in charge, concluded on June 7, 1972, that the MCC was not an action significantly affecting the quality of the human environment.

On August 2, 1972, appellants renewed their application to Judge Tenney for a preliminary injunction, arguing that the Assessment failed to comply with this Court's direction in *Hanly I*, that it amounted to nothing more than a rewrite of the earlier statement that had been found inadequate, and that some of its findings were incorrect or insufficient. Appellants further demanded a consolidation of the motion for preliminary relief with a jury trial of the issues. On August 8, 1972, Judge Tenney, in a careful opinion, denied appellants' motions, from which the present appeal was taken.

Decision

At the outset we accept and agree with the decision of the *Hanly I* panel that the agency in charge of a proposed federal action (in this case the GSA) is the party authorized to make the threshold determination whether an action is one "significantly affecting the quality of the human environment" as that phrase is used in § 102(2)(C). Judge Feinberg, speaking for the panel in *Hanly I*, recognized this screening function of agencies in upholding GSA's determination that the proposed office portion of the Annex building did not require a detailed impact statement. *Hanly I,* 460 F.2d at 644. This interpretation comports with the general pattern of NEPA, which contemplates that with respect to each major federal action the responsible official of the federal agency authorized to take the action is the person obligated to follow the "action-forcing" procedures prescribed by § 102(2)(C), and with guidelines issued by the Council on Environmental Quality (the "CEQ") and the GSA. *See, e.g.*, Council on Environmental Quality, Guidelines, 36 Fed. Reg. 7724 (April 23, 1971); Implementation Procedures attached to GSA order [PBS

1095.1A] issued December 2, 1971, by the Commissioner, Public Building Service, 1 Env.L.Rep. 46150-46152. Accordingly, we are satisfied that "GSA was the appropriate body to make the original determination as to environmental impact," *Hanly I*, 460 F.2d at 645.

We are next confronted with a question that was deferred in *Hanly I* —the standard of review that must be applied by us in reviewing GSA's action. The action involves both a question of law—the meaning of the word "significantly" in the statutory phrase "significantly affecting the quality of the human environment"—and a question of fact—whether the MCC will have a "significantly" adverse environmental impact. Strictly speaking, our function as a reviewing court is to determine *de novo* "all relevant questions of law," Administrative Procedure Act § 10(e), 6 U.S.C. § 706, *see* K. Davis, 4 Administrative Law Treatise § 29.01(1958) (herein "Davis") and, with respect to GSA's factual determinations, to abide by the Administrative Procedure Act, which limits us in matters not involving an agency's rule-making or adjudicatory function to determining whether its findings are "arbitrary, capricious, an abuse of discretion, or otherwise not in accordance with law" or "without observance of procedure required by law," APA § 10(e), 5 U.S.C. § 706(2)(A) and (D); *see Citizens to Preserve Overton Park v. Volpe*, 401 U.S. 402, 92 S.Ct. 814, 28 L.Ed.2d 136 (1971).

. . . .

[The Court notes that in similar instances of mixed questions of law and fact, the Supreme Court has authorized the application of the "rational basis" test—does the administrative decision have a warrant in the record and a reasonable basis in law. The Court decides, however, that the "arbitrary, capricious" standard as applied in *Overton Park* is more usual and appropriate.]

Upon attempting, according to the foregoing standard, to interpret the amorphous term "significantly," as it is used in § 102(2)(C), we are faced with the fact that almost every major federal action, no matter how limited in scope, has *some* adverse effect on the human environment. It is equally clear that an action which is environmentally important to one neighbor may be of no consequence to another. Congress could have decided that every major federal action must therefore be the subject of a detailed impact statement prepared according to the procedure prescribed by § 102(2)(C). By adding the word "significantly," however, it demonstrated that before the agency in charge triggered that procedure, it should conclude that a greater environmental impact would result than from "any major federal action." Yet the limits of the key term have not been adequately defined by Congress or by guidelines issued by the CEQ and other responsible federal agencies vested with broad discretionary powers under NEPA. Congress apparently was willing to depend principally upon the agency's good faith determination as to what conduct would be sufficiently serious from an ecological standpoint to require use of the full-scale procedure.

Guidelines issued by the CEQ, which are echoed in rules for implementation published by the Public Buildings Service, the branch of GSA concerned with the construction of the MCC, suggest that a formal impact statement should be prepared with respect to "proposed actions, the environmental impact of which is likely to be highly controversial." *See* Council on Environmental Quality, Statements on Proposed Federal Actions Affecting the Environment, Guidelines § 5(b), 36 Fed. Reg. 7724 (April 23, 1971); Public Buildings Service, Environmental Statements, Attachments § 1a(5) (Dec. 2, 1971), 1 Env.L.Rep. 46151. However, the term "controversial" apparently refers to cases where a substantial dispute exists as to size, nature or effect of the major federal action rather than to the existence of opposition to a use, the effect of which is relatively undisputed. This Court in *Hanly I*, for instance, did not require a formal impact statement with respect to the office building portion of the Annex despite the existence of neighborhood opposition to it. The suggestion that "controversial" must be equated with neighborhood opposition has also been rejected by others. *See Citizens for Reid State Park v. Laird*, 336 F. Supp. 783 (D.Me. 1972).[1]

In the absence of any Congressional or administrative interpretation of the term, we were persuaded that in deciding whether a major federal action will "significantly" affect the quality of the human environment the agency in charge, although vested with broad discretion, should normally be required to review the proposed action in the light of at least two relevant factors: (1) the extent to which the action will cause adverse environmental effects in excess of those created by existing uses in the area affected by it, and (2) the absolute quantitative adverse environmental effects of the action itself, including the cumulative harm that results from its contribution to existing adverse contributions or uses in the affected area. Where conduct conforms to existing uses, its adverse consequences will usually be less significant than when it represents a radical change. Absent some showing that an entire neighborhood is in the process of redevelopment, its existing environment, though frequently below an ideal standard, represents a norm that cannot be ignored. For instance, one more highway in an area honeycombed with roads usually has less of an adverse impact than if it were constructed through a roadless public park. *See e.g., Citizens to Preserve Overton Park v. Volpe*, 401 U.S. 402, 91 S.Ct. 814, 28 L.Ed.2d 136 (1971).

Although the existing environment of the area which is the site of a major federal action constitutes one criterion to be considered, it must be recognized that even a slight increase in adverse conditions that form an existing environmental milieu may sometimes threaten harm that is significant. One more factory polluting air and water in an area zoned for industrial use may represent the straw that breaks the back of the environmental camel. Hence the absolute, as well as comparative, effects of a major federal action must be considered. . . . .

Although this Court in *Hanly I* did not expressly articulate the standards we have used, its decision that the proposed office building portion of the Annex would not be environmentally significant conforms to the rationale. The

[1] To require an impact statement whenever a threshold determination dispensing with one is likely to face a court challenge, as the dissent suggests, would surrender the determination to opponents of a major federal action, no matter how insignificant its environmental effect when viewed objectively. Experience in local zoning disputes demonstrates that it is the rare case where some neighbors do not oppose a project, no matter how beneficial, and that their opposition is usually accompanied by threats of litigation.

office building would not differ substantially from the makeup of the surrounding area. Nor would it in absolute terms give rise to sizeable adverse environmental effects. Most of the employees occupying the building would merely be transferred from the existing Courthouse where the newly created space will be used primarily for courtrooms and desperately needed office space for court personnel. On the other hand, the proposed jail, for reasons set forth in detail in *Hanly I,* might have adverse effects differing both qualitatively and quantitatively from those associated with existing uses in the area. Moreover there was insufficient evidence that the absolute environmental effect with respect to the jail had been analyzed and considered by the GSA. Thus the matter was remanded for reappraisal. Now that the GSA has made and submitted its redetermination in the form of a 25-page "Assessment," our task is to determine (1) whether it satisfies the foregoing tests as to environmental significance, and (2) whether GSA, in making its assessment and determination, has observed "procedure required by law" as that term is used in § 10 of the APA, 5 U.S.C. § 706(2)(D). . . .

Appellants contend that the Assessment is merely a "rewrite" of GSA's earlier February 23, 1971 "Environmental Statement" found inadequate in *Hanly I*, and that GSA has failed to take into consideration certain adverse facts. A comparison of the 25-page detailed Assessment with the earlier statement reveals that the former is far more than a "rewrite" and that it furnishes detailed findings with respect to most of the relevant factors unmentioned in the earlier statement. On its face the Assessment indicates that GSA has redetermined the environmental impact of the MCC with care and thoroughness. In the absence of contrary factual proof, we would have no hesitancy in upholding it, whether it is reviewed by the "arbitrary, capricious" standard or the "rational basis" test. Judged by the comparative uses in the area and according to its quantitative environmental effects, the MCC should not have a significant effect upon the human environment.

Appellants offer little or no evidence to contradict the detailed facts found by the GSA. For the most part their opposition is based upon a psychological distaste for having a jail located so close to residential apartments, which is understandable enough. It is doubtful whether psychological and sociological effects upon neighbors constitute the type of factors that may be considered in making such a determination since they do not lend themselves to measurement. However we need not decide that issue because these apartments were constructed within two or three blocks of another existing jail, The Manhattan House of Detention for Men, which is much larger than the proposed MCC and houses approximately 1,200 prisoners. Furthermore the area in which the MCC is located has at all times been zoned by the City of New York as a commercial district designed to provide for a wide range of uses, *specifically including "Prisons."*

Despite the GSA's scrupulous efforts the appellants do present one or two factual issues that merit further consideration and findings by the GSA. One bears on the possibility that the MCC will substantially increase the risk of crime in the immediate area, a relevant factor as to which the Assessment fails to make an outright finding despite the direction to do so in *Hanly I.* Appellants urge that the Community Treatment Program and the program for observation and study of non-resident out-patients will endanger the health and safety of the immediate area by exposing neighbors and passersby to drug addicts visiting the MCC for drug maintenance and to drug pushers and hangers-on who would inevitably frequent the vicinity of a drug maintenance center. If the MCC were to be used as a drug treatment center, the potential increase in crime might tip the scales in favor of a mandatory detailed impact statement. The Government has assured us by post-argument letter addressed to the Court that:

> Neither the anticipated nonresident pre-sentence study program nor any program to be conducted within the Metropolitan Correction Center will include drug maintenance.

While we do not question the Government's good faith, a finding in the matter by GSA is essential, since the Assessment is ambiguous as to the scope of the non-resident out-patient observation program and makes no finding on the subject of whether the MCC will increase the risk of crime in the community.[2] In addition one of the appellants, Sien Wei Liu, has furnished to the district court an affidavit taking issue with certain facts found by the GSA, including the visibility of the jail's rear entrance from nearby apartment buildings, the distance of the MCC from the closest apartment, the possible use of nearby overcrowded community medical facilities by prisoners, and the claim that certain city officials are opposed to the location of the MCC.

Appellants further contend that they have never been given an opportunity to discuss the MCC with any governmental agency prior to GSA's submission of its Assessment, which raises the question whether the agency acted "without observance of procedure required by law," see *Citizens to Preserve Overton Park v. Volpe*, 401 U.S. 402, 91 S.Ct. 814, 28 L.Ed.2d 136 (1971) We do not share the Government's view that the procedural mandates of § 102(A), (B), and (D), 42 U.S.C. § 4332(2)(A), (B), and (D), apply only to actions found by the agency itself to have a significant environmental effect. While these sections are somewhat opaque, they are not expressly limited to "major Federal actions significantly affecting the quality of the human environment." Indeed if they were so limited § 102(D), which requires the agency to develop appropriate alternatives to the recommended course of action, would be duplicative since § 102(C), which does apply to actions "significantly affecting" the environment, specifies that the detailed impact statement must deal with "alternatives to the proposed action." 42 U.S.C. § 4332(2)(C)(iii). However, in our view the Assessment does, in fact, satisfy the requirement of § 102(2)(A) that an interdisciplinary approach taking into account the "natural and social sciences and the environmental design arts" be used. The GSA has retained architects familiar with the design requirements of the Civic Center and consulted with the Office of Lower Manhattan Development in an effort to harmonize the MCC with the Civic Center. The Assessment scrupulously takes into account the aesthetics and the tangible factors involved in the

[2] If the Government should later change the use of the premises to include a drug treatment center, or any other change that might significantly affect the quality of the human environment, then a detailed § 102(c) impact statement would be required at that time. *See* Council on Environmental Quality, Guidelines § 11, 36 Fed.Reg. 7724, 7727 (April 23, 1971); Public Buildings Service, Environmental Statements, Attachment B, § 1b(5) (Dec. 2,1971), 1 Env.L.Rep. 46150, 46151.

designing and planning of the MCC. Furthermore we find that § 102(2)(D) was complied with insofar as the GSA specifically considered the alternatives to continuing operation at the present facility at West Street and evaluated the selected site as compared with other specified possibilities. Although the assessment of the alternative sites was not as intensive as we might hope, its failure to analyze them in further detail does not warrant reversal. . . .

Where a proposed major federal action may affect the sensibilities of a neighborhood, the prudent course would be for the agency in charge, before making a threshold decision, to give notice to the community of the contemplated action and to accept all pertinent information proffered by concerned citizens with respect to it. Furthermore, in line with the procedure usually followed in zoning disputes, particularly where emotions are likely to be aroused by fears, or rumors or misinformation, a public hearing serves the dual purpose of enabling the agency to obtain all relevant data and to satisfy the community that its views are being considered. However, neither NEPA nor any other federal statute mandates the specific type of procedure to be followed by federal agencies. There is no statutory requirement that a public hearing be held before a site for a house of detention is selected by the Attorney General or construction of the facility is undertaken by the GSA. *See* 18 U.S.C. § 4003, 40 U.S.C. § 602–606. Although the Guidelines issued by the CEQ suggest that agencies "shall include, whenever appropriate, provision for public hearings, and shall provide the public with relevant information, including information on alternative courses of action," Council on Environmental Quality, Statements on Proposed Federal Actions Affecting the Environment, Guidelines § 10(e), 36 Fed.Reg. 7724, 7726 (April 23, 1971), these provisions apply only to the procedure for preparation of detailed impact statements *after* the preliminary determination of significance has been made.

Notwithstanding the absence of statutory or administrative provisions on the subject, this Court has already held in *Hanly I* at 647 that federal agencies must "affirmatively develop a reviewable environmental record . . . even for purposes of a threshold section 102(2)(C) determination." We now go further and hold that before a preliminary or threshold determination of significance is made the responsible agency must give notice to the public of the proposed major federal action and an opportunity to submit relevant facts which might bear upon the agency's threshold decision. We do not suggest that a full-fledged formal hearing must be provided before each such determination is made, although it should be apparent that in many cases such a hearing would be advisable for reasons already indicated. The necessity for a hearing will depend greatly upon the circumstances surrounding the particular proposed action and upon the likelihood that a hearing will be more effective than other methods in developing relevant information and an understanding of the proposed action. The precise procedural steps to be adopted are better left to the agency, which should be in a better position than the court to determine whether solution of the problems faced with respect to a specific major federal action can better be achieved through a hearing or by informal acceptance of relevant data.

In view of the Assessment's failure to make findings with respect to the possible existence of a drug maintenance program at the MCC, the increased risk of crime that might result from the operation of the MCC, and the fact that appellants have challenged certain findings of fact, we remand the case for the purpose of requiring the GSA to make a further investigation of these issues, with directions to accept from appellants and other concerned citizens such further evidence as they may proffer within a reasonable period, to make supplemental findings with respect to these issues, and to redetermine whether the MCC "significantly affects the quality of the human environment." If, as a result of such further investigation, the GSA determines that a detailed environmental impact statement is required, a preliminary injunction will be granted restraining further construction of the MCC until the agency has complied with the procedures required by § 102(2)(C) of NEPA. In the event that the GSA affirms its initial determination, the district court will determine, should a further request be made, whether preliminary injunctive relief is warranted . . . .

The case is remanded for further proceedings not inconsistent with this opinion. The mandate shall issue forthwith.

NOTES AND QUESTIONS

(1) In the aftermath of this opinion, the plaintiffs petitioned the U.S. Supreme Court for *certiorari*. That petition was denied at 412 U.S. 908 (1973). The case was remanded to the U.S. District Court which once again denied the plaintiffs' request for an injunction. The Second Circuit affirmed that District Court decision at 484 F.2d 448 (2d Cir. 1973). Concluding the lawsuit, the U.S. Supreme Court once again denied *certiorari* at 412 U.S. 936 (1974).

(2) Although the *Hanly II* decision is often referred to as the "leading case" with respect to the threshold issue it examined, its approach was not uniformly followed by other courts. A different holding on standards for judicial review was made in *Hiram Clarke Civic Club, Inc. v. Lynn*, 276 F.2d 421 (5th Cir. 1973).

That case involved a loan by HUD for the construction of a 272-unit apartment complex. The court found that HUD had properly issued a "negative declaration," finding that there was no significant environmental impact. The court upheld HUD in spite of the fact that there was some evidence that the project was of a controversial nature, and, in accordance with CEQ Guidelines then in effect, projects of a controversial nature should, in a doubtful case, be accompanied by an environmental impact statement. The court, however, took the position that HUD had acted in accordance with NEPA and its own regulations, and that compliance with the guidelines, if applicable, was not required since the Guidelines—unlike the current Regulations—did not have the force of law. The court refused to apply the "arbitrary and capricious standard" of review applied in the *Hanly* decision.

See also City of Davis v.Coleman, 521 F.2d 661 (9th Cir. 1975), where it was held that the standard of judicial review of the threshold determination does not require the courts to determine whether a challenged project *will in fact* have significant effects. Relying on *Save our Ten Acres v. Kreger*, 2 E.L.R. 20041 (S.D. Ala. 1972), *aff'd in part, rev'd in part* 472 F.2d 463 (5th Cir. 1973), the court held that it had to review "whether the responsible agency has 'reasonably concluded' that the project will have no significant adverse environmental consequences." However, in making this determination, the court must make sure that the agency has thoroughly studied the problem, and when "substantial questions are raised whether a project will have significant adverse impact" an environmental impact statement must be prepared "whenever a project *may* cause a significant degradation . . . ."

The debate among the lower courts was finally resolved by the U.S. Supreme Court in *Marsh v. Oregon Natural Resources*, 490 U.S. 360, 377 (1989). There the Court applied the arbitrary and capricious standard of review to a decision by the U.S. Army Corps of Engineers not to prepare a supplemental impact statement regarding a proposed dam in Southwest Oregon. The Court deferred to the Corps' expertise in analyzing the completeness, conclusiveness, and accuracy of scientific information regarding the likely effect of the dam on downstream water quality. At the same time, however, the Court cautioned that, in reviewing a decision not to supplement an EIS, "courts should not automatically defer to the agency's express reliance on an interest in finality without carefully reviewing the record and satisfying themselves that the agency has made a reasoned decision based on its evaluation of the significance—or lack of significance—of the new information. A contrary approach . . . would be contrary to the demand that courts ensure that agency decisions are founded on a reasoned evaluation of 'the relevant factors'." *Id.* at 1861.

Is *Marsh* a sound decision? Are the *Lynn* and *City of Davis* cases, referred to above, "good law" in view of it? Is *Hanly II* still good law?

(3) Chief Judge Friendly dissented in *Hanly II*. He opined that the majority's approach required too much of federal agencies, by requiring them to prepare burdensome "mini-impact statements" in situations where the proposed action in question is "truly minor or insignificant." At the same time however, in Friendly's view, the Second Circuit's approach raised higher than Congress had intended the floor of what constitutes "major Federal actions significantly affecting the quality of the human environment." Thus, he concluded, the court's analysis "gives these plaintiffs, and environmental advocates in future cases, both too little and too much."

(4) The CEQ's regulations, which are binding on all federal agencies, contain a number of provisions that bear on the question of when an environmental impact statement must be prepared. Among those provisions are the following:

40 C.F.R. § 1501.3When to prepare an environmental assessment

(a) Agencies shall prepare an environmental assessment (§ 1508.9) when necessary under the procedures adopted by individual agencies to supplement these regulations as described in § 1507.3. An assessment is not necessary if the agency has decided to prepare an environmental impact statement.

(b) Agencies may prepare an environmental assessment on any action at any time in order to assist agency planning and decisionmaking.

40 C.F.R. § 1501.4Whether to prepare an environmental impact statement

In determining whether to prepare an environmental impact statement the Federal agency shall:

(a) Determine under its procedures supplementing these regulations (described in § 1507.3) whether the proposal is one which:

(1) Normally requires an environmental impact statement, or

(2) Normally does not require either an environmental impact statement or an environmental assessment (categorical exclusion).

(b) If the proposed action is not covered by paragraph (a) of this section, prepare an environmental assessment (§ 1508.9). The agency shall involve environmental agencies, applicants, and the public, to the extent practicable, in preparing assessments required by § 1508.9(a)(1).

(c) Based on the environmental assessment make its determination whether to prepare an environmental impact statement.

(d) Commence the scoping process (§ 1507.7), if the agency will prepare an environmental impact statement.

(e) Prepare a finding of no significant impact (§ 1508.13), if the agency determines on the basis of the environmental assessment not to prepare a statement.

(1) The agency shall make the finding of no significant impact available to the affected public as specified in § 1506.6.

(2) In certain limited circumstances, which the agency may cover in its procedures under § 1507.3, the agency shall make the finding of no significant impact available for public review (including State and area-wide clearinghouses) for 30 days before the agency makes its final determination whether to prepare an environmental impact statement and before the action may begin. The circumstances are:

(i) The proposed action is, or is closely similar to, one which normally requires the preparation of an environmental impact statement under the procedures adopted by the agency pursuant to § 1507.3, or

(ii) The nature of the proposed action is one without precedent.

40 C.F.R. § 1508.7Cumulative Impact

"Cumulative impact" is the impact on the environment which results from the incremental impact of the action when added to other past, present, and reasonably foreseeable future actions regardless of what agency (Federal or non-Federal) or person undertakes such other actions. Cumulative impacts can result from individually minor but collectively significant actions taking place over a period of time.

40 C.F.R. § 1508.9Environmental assessment

"Environmental assessment":

(a) Means a concise public document for which a Federal agency is responsible that serves to:

(1) Briefly provide sufficient evidence and analysis for determining whether to prepare an environmental impact statement or a finding of no significant impact.

(2) Aid an agency's compliance with the Act when no environmental impact statement is necessary.

(3) Facilitate preparation of a statement when one is necessary.

(b) Shall include brief discussions of the need for the proposal, of alternatives as required by section 102(2)(E), of the environmental impacts of the proposed action and alternatives, and a listing of agencies and persons consulted.

40 C.F.R. § 1508.13Finding of no significant impact

"Finding of no significant impact" means a document by a Federal agency briefly presenting the reasons why an action, not otherwise excluded (§ 1508.4), will not have a significant effect on the human environment and for which an environmental impact statement therefore will not be prepared. It shall include the environmental assessment or a summary of it and shall note any other environmental documents related to it (§ 1501.7(a)(5)). If the assessment is included, the finding need not repeat any of the discussion in the assessment but may incorporate it by reference.

40 C.F.R. § 1508.27Significantly

"Significantly" as used in NEPA requires considerations of both context and intensity:

(a) *Context*. This means that the significance of an action must be analyzed in several contexts such as society as a whole (human, national), the affected region, the affected interests, and the locality. Significance varies with the setting of the proposed action. For instance, in the case of a site-specific action, significance would usually depend upon the effects in the locale rather than in the world as a whole. Both short-and long-term effects are relevant.

(b) *Intensity*. This refers to the severity of impact. Responsible officials must bear in mind that more than one agency may make decisions about partial aspects of a major action. The following should be considered in evaluating intensity:

(1) Impacts that may be both beneficial and adverse. A significant effect may exist even if the Federal agency believes that on balance the effect will be beneficial.

(2) The degree to which the proposed action affects public health or safety.

(3) Unique characteristics of the geographic area such as proximity to historic or cultural resources, park lands, prime farmlands, wetlands, wild and scenic rivers, or ecologically critical areas.

(4) The degree to which the effects on the quality of the human environment are likely to be highly controversial.

(5) The degree to which the possible effects on the human environment are highly uncertain or involve unique or unknown risks.

(6) The degree to which the action may establish a precedent for future actions with significant effects or represents a decision in principle about a future consideration.

(7) Whether the action is related to other actions with individually insignificant but cumulatively significant impact. Significance exists if it is reasonable to anticipate a cumulatively significant impact on the environment. Significance cannot be avoided by terming an action temporary or by breaking it down into small component parts.

(8) The degree to which the action may adversely affect districts, sites, highways, structures, or objects listed in or eligible for listing in the National Register of Historic Places or may cause loss or destruction of significant scientific, cultural, or historical resources.

(9) The degree to which the action may adversely affect an endangered or threatened species or its habitat that has been determined to be critical under the Endangered Species Act of 1973.

(10) Whether the action threatens a violation of Federal, State, or local law or requirements imposed for the protection of the environment.

(5) Why type of "effects" on the human environment require the preparation of an EIS? In *Metropolitan Edison Co. v. PANE*, 460 U.S. 766 (1983), the U.S. Supreme Court held that even though NEPA requires federal agencies to evaluate the risk that a proposed action will harm the *physical* environment, the potential *psychological* damage that may be caused to people who perceive such a risk is not a sufficient basis for requiring an EIS. In *PANE*, the Court specifically examined whether the Nuclear Regulatory Commission was required to consider if restarting a nuclear power plant, that was a companion to the damaged Three Mile Island reactor, would unacceptably harm the psychological well-being of neighboring residents. The Court concluded that, regardless of the severe psychological health damage that those residents feared, NEPA did not apply.

In *Nucleus of Chicago Homeowners v. Lynn*, 372 F. Supp. 147 (N.D. Ill. 1973), a non-profit homeowners organization brought suit to prevent what it referred to as "the damage to neighboring communities which will result if low-rent housing for low-income families is placed in working-class and middle-class neighborhoods of Chicago." The U.S. District Court dismissed the plaintiff's claims, declining to find that prospective low-income tenants would significantly affect the human environment. The Seventh Circuit affirmed. It, too, refused to hold that "the fears of neighbors of prospective public housing tenants" was the kind of "impact" that NEPA was intended to cover. In effect, the court concluded that "people are not pollution." 524 F.2d 225 (7th Cir. 1975).

Bicycle Trails of Marin v. Babbitt, 82 F.3d 1445 (9th Cir. 1996) involved a NEPA challenge by bicycle associations to U.S. Interior Department restrictions on the use of bicycles within national parks. Rejecting that challenge, the Ninth Circuit opined that "NEPA does not require that an agency take into account every conceivable impact of its actions, including impacts on citizens' subjective experiences. Rather, it requires agencies to take into account environmental impacts on the physical 'world around us.' Plaintiffs' argument that bicyclists being crowded onto fewer trails is such an environmental impact is incorrect . . . . The closing of certain trails to bicyclists [thus] did not mandate an EIS." *Id.* at 1466–1467.

(6) A related issue that has arisen in NEPA litigation is the extent to which the alleged or proven "controversiality" of a proposed project makes that project "significantly affect" the human environment. *See Town of Orangetown v. Gorsuch*, 718 F.2d 2929 (2d Cir. 1983), in which the Second Circuit held that the proposed expansion of a sewage treatment plant was not necessarily controversial, notwithstanding local opposition. *See also Foundation for Global Sustainability v. McConnell*, 829 F. Supp. 147, 153 (W.D.N.C. 1993) (to be deemed controversial a proposed project must involve a "substantial dispute," a "robust dissent" or a controversy of an "extraordinary nature").

(7) Proposals for Legislation. Section 102(2)(C) requires environmental impact statements to be filed with recommendations or reports on "proposals for legislation." Despite that language, there is little evidence that NEPA has had any significant effect on the legislative process. Although a number of Section 102 statements have been filed in connection with legislative proposals, the majority have involved administration plans to improve the environment, and thus their impact has been minimal. Obviously an environmental impact statement will be of little effect when it merely supports a legislative plan of action of agreed benefit to the environment. Few impact statements have been filed in the context of legislation that may have substantially adverse effects on the environment, and congressional committees are considering and approving legislation without prior preparation and filing by the appropriate federal agencies of § 102 statements.

§ 5.03 What Agencies Must File EISs?

PORTLAND CEMENT ASSOCIATION v. RUCKELSHAUS

United States Court of Appeals, D.C. Circuit (1973)
486 F.2d 375

. . . .

II. COMPLIANCE WITH NEPA

Petitioners argue that EPA acted contrary to the requirements of the National Environmental Policy Act of 1969, 42 U.S.C. §§ 4321-4335, in failing to file a "NEPA" statement in conjunction with the promulgation of the stationary standards. They draw particularly on the language of § 102(2)(C) of NEPAwhich states:

"The Congress authorizes and directs that, to the fullest extent possible: (1) the policies, regulations, and public laws of the United States shall be interpreted and administered in accordance with the policies set forth in this chapter, and (2) all agencies of the Federal Government shall—

". . . .

"(C) include in every recommendation or report on proposals for legislation and other major Federal actions significantly affecting the quality of the human environment, a detailed statement by the responsible official on—

"(i) the environmental impact of the proposed action . . . ."

1. Petitioners, in effect, predicate an EPA obligation to file an impact statement on this simple syllogism: (1) All federal agencies must file an impact statement; (2) EPA is a federal agency; (3) EPA must file an impact statement. Anaconda Copper Co. v. Ruckelshaus, 4 ERC 1817, 1828 (D. Col. 1972). If the premises be accepted, the logic is clear. But the argument is more simplistic than simple, for the premises require a more precise determination of legislative intent. In ascertaining congressional intent we begin with the language of a statute, but this is subject to an overriding requirement of looking to all sources including purpose and legislative history, to ascertain discernible legislative purpose. The question is whether EPA is a "federal agency" within the meaning of NEPA—whether, and to what extent, Congress intended it to be subject to the NEPA mandate concerning preparation of impact statements.

2. A primary purpose of NEPA, and specifically the impact statement requirement, was the design to coordinate disparate environmental policies of different federal agencies. At the time NEPA was enacted on January 1, 1970, EPA was not yet in existence. EPA was created by Reorganization Plan No. 3, submitted to Congress on July 9, 1970, which was designed to bring under one roof the major environmental federal programs which until that time had been scattered throughout different agencies of the government. It is by no means clear, as will appear, that NEPA's impact statement requirement was intended at time of passage of NEPA to be applicable to such environmental agencies as the National Air Pollution Control Administration of the Department of Health, Education and Welfare or the Federal Water Quality Administration of the Department of the Interior. But even assuming it was applicable to them, it does not necessarily follow that NEPA is applicable to EPA, which Congress did not have before it, and which in its own organization accomplished the purpose of coordination of environmental approach. In statutory interpretation, the courts must often, in effect, consider what answer the legislature would have made as to a problem that was neither discussed nor contemplated. . . .

3. The impact statement issue requires us to consider not only NEPA, but also the Clean Air Act and particularly the statutory scheme by which new stationary source standards are promulgated.

Section 111 of the Clean Air Actestablishes precise time schedules for the promulgation of new source standards. The Administrator was required to publish, 90 days after December 31, 1970, a list of categories of stationary sources which "contribute significantly to air pollution which causes or contributes to the endangerment of public health or welfare." Within 120 days of the inclusion of a category, the Administrator is required to proposed standards, and 90 days thereafter the standards are to go into effect. Obviously, a strong argument can be made that the Clean Air Act, and the provisions for unusual expedition in disposing of the complex environmental and other problems faced by the agency, assumed that the agency would not be subject to the additional time required to prepare a "detailed" proposal of an impact statement, circulate the statement to the agencies for comment and assess the comments made.

The time constraint of the Clean Air Act is perhaps not decisive but it is a substantial consideration and, as will be seen, an inter-related aspect of that Act reinforces the conclusion that NEPA is inapplicable to determinations under it.

Long Island Lighting Company argues that the Act could accommodate delay in the time allowed for publication of the list of categories of stationary sources until an impact statement had been duly prepared, in compliance with NEPA, and completed. This is at odds with the express language of the Act which specifies that any source which contributes to the endangerment of public health or welfare shall be placed on that list at the end of 90 days.

4. As we have already indicated, there is a serious question whether NEPA is applicable to environmentally protective regulatory agencies. There is no express exemption in the language of the Act or Committee Reports. However, such an exemption is set forth in a document entitled "Major Changes in S. 1075 as passed by the Senate" introduced into the Congressional Record by Senator Jackson during debate over approval of the Conference Report.

The document, in analyzing Section 102 of NEPA,detailing the procedures and requirements of an impact statement, stated that the provisions were "not designed to result in any change in the manner in which [environmental agencies] carry out their environmental protection authority." It stated immediately thereafter:

> "This provision is, however, clearly designed to assure consideration of environmental matters by all agencies in their planning and decision making—especially those agencies who now have little or no legislative authority to take environmental considerations into account."

Senator Muskie commented on this language as coming from his discussions with Senator Jackson, and then stated, in debate:

> "It is clear then, and this is the clear understanding of the Senator from Washington [Jackson] and his colleagues, and of those of us who serve on the Public Works Committee, that the agencies having authority in the environmental improvement field will continue to operate under their legislative mandates as previously established, and that those legislative mandates are not changed in any way by section 102-5."

Manifestly, the statements of these two Senators, who were among the most active in securing the passage of NEPA,[1] are entitled to weight in ascertaining legislative intent.

[1] Senator Jackson, floor manager of the debate on the Conference Report, was the sponsor of the original Senate bill on NEPA, S. 1075, chaired the Senate Committee on Interior and Insular Affairs, which considered the bill, and was a member of the Conference Committee. Senator Muskie was the Chairman of the Subcommittee on Air Pollution of the Committee on Public Works.

However, their understanding was not formalized by any statement in the Conference Report or in the section-by-section analysis of the bill as reported by the Conference Committee. Senator Allott, ranking minority member of the Interior Committee and of the Conference Committee, also a supporter of NEPA, stated:

> ". . . while the explanatory statements relative to the interpretation of the conference report language, as provided by the chairman, are useful, they have not been reviewed, agreed upon, and signed by the other Senate conferees. Only the conference report itself was signed by all the Senate conferees, and therefore, only it was agreed upon and is binding."

As for the House of Representatives, its action on the Conference Report was equally ambiguous. Representative Dingell submitted the Conference Report to the House on December 22, 1969, two days after the report had been submitted to the Senate by Senator Jackson. As part of his opening remarks, Rep. Dingell introduced into the record the text of answers to certain questions posed to him by Rep. Fallon, the Chairman of the Committee on Public Works. His answer to one of those questions tracked the language of the "Major Changes" document submitted to the Senate, indicating no intended change in requirements for "environmental control" agencies. There is no indication, however, of any debate or acceptance of Rep. Dingell's answer by any other member of the House.

5. We now turn to consideration of the import of subsequent congressional actions.

In the Federal Water Pollution Control Act Amendments of 1972 (FWPCA), Congress provided that NEPA did not control certain actions taken by EPA pursuant to their water pollution control activities.[2] The question arose in debate, and is carried on by the parties to this case, as to whether this was an "exemption"—in which case the assumption would be that prior law generally intended NEPA to be applicable—or an affirmative declaration that NEPA did apply to only a limited number of EPA activities specified in the amendments. Such debates of a later Congress have been described by the Supreme Court as offering a hazardous basis for inferring the intent of the earlier Congress; and this is borne out by our analysis.

Senator Muskie pointed during the 1972 debates to the Muskie-Jackson colloquy as expressing an intent to exempt EPA, and that the present legislation merely imposed some affirmative NEPA obligations, so as to narrow the exemption. Others, such as Senator Nelson, clearly perceived the water pollution control amendments as, in fact, exempting EPA from NEPA. Senator Jackson had doubts by 1972, as to the wisdom of his prior position on a broad exemption for "environmental control" agencies.

6. The matter resolves itself, as to this issue of exemption for environmental agencies, that we have items which are entitled to some weight as indicia of legislative intent, but cannot be taken as decisive. Here, again, we encounter

[2] Pub. L. No. 92-500, 86 Stat. 816 (1972). Section 511(c)(1) provides that NEPA is not applicable to EPA, at least as to impact statements, except in two cases: where grants are made for the construction of publicly owned waste treatment works and where the agency issues new source permits.

competing considerations reflecting the difficulty in resolving the question; but perhaps they point the way toward a resolution.

The policy thrust toward exemption of the environmental agency is discernible from these factors, taken in combination: (1) An exemption from NEPA is supportable on the basis that this best serves the objective of protecting the environment which is the purpose of NEPA. (2) This comes about because NEPA operates, in protection of the environment, by a broadly applicable measure that only provides a first step. The goal of protecting the environment requires more than NEPA provides, *i.e.*, specific assignment of duties to protection agencies, in certain areas identified by Congress as requiring extra protection. (3) The need in those areas for unusually expeditious decision would be thwarted by a NEPA impact statement requirement. (4) An impact statement requirement presents the danger that opponents of environmental protection would use the issue of compliance with any impact statement requirement as a tactic of litigation and delay.

The policies against a NEPA exemption embrace the endemic question of "Who shall police the police"? As Senator Jackson stated, "It cannot be assumed that EPA will always be the good guy." Concern was also voiced by petitioners in this case that EPA might wear blinders when promulgating standards protecting one resource as to effects on other resources, as is asserted in this case, that air standards may increase water pollution. Finally, it is argued that a NEPA statement's procedures, though burdensome, allow for needed input by other federal agencies and simultaneously open up the decision-making process to scrutiny by the public.

7. Our consideration of the complex questions raised by a broad exemption claim, reinforces our conclusion that these should not be decided in the present case, which may appropriately be determined upon the logic of a narrow exemption from NEPA applicable to determinations under section 111 of the Clean Air Act. What is decisive, ultimately, is the reality that, section 111 of the Clean Air Act,properly construed, requires the functional equivalent of a NEPA impact statement. Thus in this case, as in International Harvester v. Ruckelshaus (D.C. Cir. 1973), 155 U.S. App. D.C. 411, 446 n. 130, 478 F.2d 615, at 650 n. 130, we refrain from a determination of any broader claim of NEPA exemption.

Enlarging on our conclusion as to a narrower exemption, we note that section 111 of the Clean Air Actrequires a "standard of performance" which reflects "the best system of emission reduction," and requires the Administrator to take "into account the cost of achieving such reduction." These criteria require the Administrator to take into account counter-productive environmental effects of a proposed standard, as well as economic costs to the industry. The Act thus requires that the Administrator accompany a proposed standard with a statement of reasons that sets forth the environmental considerations, pro and con, which have been taken into account as required by the Act, and fulfillment of this requirement is reviewable directly by this Court.

Although the rule-making process may not import the complete advantages of the structured determinations of NEPA into the decision-making of EPA, it does, in our view strike a workable balance between some of the advantages and disadvantages of full application of NEPA. Without the problems of a NEPA delay conflicting with the constraints of the Clean Air Act, the ability of other agencies to make submissions to EPA concerning proposed rules, provides a channel for informed decision-making. These comments will be part of the record in the rule-making proceeding that EPA must take into account.

EPA's proposed rule, and reasons therefor, are inevitably an alert to environmental issues. The EPA's proposed rule and reasons may omit reference to adverse environmental consequences that another agency may discern, but a draft impact statement may likewise be marred by omission that another agency identifies. To the extent that EPA is aware of significant adverse environmental consequences of its proposal, good faith requires appropriate reference in its reasons for the proposal and its underlying balancing analysis. While there is more flexibility than NEPA's requirement of an impact statement, this court has stated, and EPA has recognized, that an EPA statement of reasons for standards and criteria requires a fuller presentation than the minimum rule-making requirement of the Administrative Procedure Act. Kennecott Cooper v. EPA, *supra*.

Similarly, EPA's proposed rule, and reasons therefor, are an alert to the public and the Congress who will have the opportunity to comment as to possible adverse environmental effects of the proposed rule, during the pendency of the rule making proceeding. And finally, the courts will be able to scrutinize the analysis of environmental considerations, in assuring that a reasoned decision has been reached.

The court's review guards against arbitrary disregard of environmental factors by EPA without significantly increasing the administrative burden on the agency. And since all environmental questions will have to be considered within the same review proceeding as other challenges to the validity of standards, the potential for incremental litigation delay is minimized.

As to the standard here at issue, petitioners raise possible adverse environmental impact questions in their briefs. But they have not indicated that these problems were brought to the attention of the agency. Since we are remanding the case for other reasons subsequently discussed, EPA should respond to these questions on remand.

We add, finally, a word of clarification: we establish a narrow exemption from NEPA, for EPA determination under section 111 of the Clean Air Act. NEPA must be accorded full vitality as to non-environmental agencies, as established by our outstanding precedents.

NOTES AND QUESTIONS

(1) How persuasive was the D.C. Circuit's reasoning in the *Portland Cement Association* case? Are there sound reasons for subjecting all federal agencies and departments to the NEPA EIS requirement? Do those reasons outweigh the considerations which led the court to decide *Portland Cement Association* as it did?

(2) For a consideration of the substantive provision (§ 111 of the Clean Air Act) at issue in this case, *see* Chapter 2, § 2.03[3][f], *supra*.

(3) In *Portland Cement Association*, EPA was primarily seen as an agency engaged in issuing and enforcing regulations for the protection of the environment. Are there situations where, consistent with the federal laws under which it operates, EPA functions as a "developmental agency," involved in advancing development and construction of physical structures and projects? Are those situations distinguishable from the principal case? Should EPA be made to prepare an EIS in those instances?

(4) *Portland Cement Association* is typical of a number of federal court decisions that resolved the question of whether NEPA applies to the activities of EPA. Today, no court has held that EPA is uniformly exempt from NEPA's EIS requirement. Rather, the issue has been dealt with on a case-by-case basis, with a specific inquiry—in each instance—as to whether the purpose and policy of NEPA would be served by requiring preparation of an impact statement. *See, e.g.*, *Western Nebraska Resources Council v. Environmental Protection Agency*, 943 F.2d 867 (8th Cir. 1991) (EPA is not required to comply with NEPA's formal requirements where environmental protection functions must be performed by the agency under other federal statutes); *Merrell v. Thomas*, 807 F.2d 776 (9th Cir. 1986) (NEPA is inapplicable to the pesticide registration process mandated by the Federal Insecticide Fungicide and Rodenticide Act); *State of Alabama v. Environmental Protection Agency*, 911 F.2d 499 (11th Cir. 1990) (No EIS is required where EPA issues a permit to a hazardous waste management facility pursuant to the Resource Conservation and Recovery Act, since the latter statute mandates a functionally equivalent "order and comprehensive" evaluation of environmental issues). *See also Indiana and Michigan Electric Co. v. EPA*, 508 F.2d 839, 7 ERC 1433 (7th Cir. 1975); *Getty Oil Co. v. Ruckelshaus*, 467 F.2d 349 (3d Cir. 1972), *cert. denied,* 409 U.S. 1125 (1972).

(5) Congress has not always left it to the federal courts to determine whether EPA is exempt from complying with NEPA's action-forcing duties. *See* Clean Water Act § 511(c)(1), 33 U.S.C. § 1371(c)(1), in which EPA is specifically exempted from NEPA compliance in carrying out its responsibilities under that statute *except* where the agency issues a permit to a new point source with regard to effluent discharges and/or provides federal financial assistance for the construction of a publicly owned treatment works.

(6) Other federal agencies and departments have sometimes been less successful than EPA has been in claiming exemption from NEPA on the basis that their statutorily mandated activities are the "functional equivalent" of an EIS. *See, e.g.*, *Texas Commission on Natural Resources v. Bergland*, 573 F.2d 201 (5th Cir. 1978), *cert. denied*, 439 U.S. 966 (1978) (Notwithstanding its environmental obligations under the National Forest Management Act, the National Forest Service is subject to NEPA); *Jones v. Gordon*, 621 F. Supp. 21 (D. Alaska, 1985) (The National Marine Fisheries Service must prepare an EIS notwithstanding the role it has been given in implementing a non-NEPA environmental statute). Compare, *Brooklyn Bridge Park Coalition v. Port Authority of New York and New Jersey*, 951 F. Supp. 383, 27 ELR 20788 (E.D. N.Y. 1997) (The Port Authority of New York and New Jersey was not obligated to comply with NEPA before leasing a waterfront pier in Brooklyn to a private company, for use as a corporate headquarters and building supply

facility, since the Port Authority was not properly viewed as an "agency of the Federal Government" for purposes of NEPA).

(7) Does NEPA's environmental impact statement requirement apply to activities of the U.S. Department of Defense that involve matters of national security? In *Weinberger v. Catholic Action of Hawaii*, 454 U.S. 139 (1981), the plaintiff brought suit to compel preparation of an EIS prior to the construction of new naval ammunition and weapons storage facilities in Hawaii, in which, it was claimed, nuclear weapons would be stored. The U.S. Navy took the position that, for national security reasons, it could neither admit nor deny that it would store nuclear weapons at the proposed facilities in question. Thus, it claimed, a federal court could not determine whether the Navy was proposing an action to which NEPA applied. The U.S. Supreme Court agreed in substantial part. Citing the Freedom of Information Act, 5 U.S.C. § 522, it ruled that classified national defense matters are exempt from public disclosure, and that information regarding the storage of nuclear weapons is within this category. At the same time, however, the Court stated that if the Navy did plan to store nuclear weapons at the proposed facilities the Department of Defense's own regulations may "fairly be read" to require that an EIS must be "prepared solely for internal purposes, even though such a document cannot be disclosed to the public."

§ 5.04 Divisible Projects: Issues of Segmentation, and Programmatic Impact Statements

The requirement of the National Environmental Policy Act that administrative agencies must, in the process of decision-making, weigh the environmental impact of any major project raises special problems in the case of long-range projects that may be divided into parts or segments. The recurring question in projects of this kind is at which point in time the total environmental impact of the project is to be considered. It would be possible to regard the decision to plan for a major network of highways as preliminary, because the real impact decisions will not be made until the precise route of a particular segment of the highway system is to be settled upon.[1] This may, however, circumvent the clear intent of the Act, because there would be no assessment of the environmental impact of the project taken as a whole.[2] An agency that wanted to circumvent the requirements of the Act would be able to point to the relatively minor environmental damage threatened by any one part of the project, ignoring the possibly major adverse impact of the project as a whole. The decision that a new highway system is needed should be subject to environmental impact considerations, just as the decision to build a particular stretch of the road.[3]

---

[1] *See* Indian Lookout Alliance v. Volpe, 345 F. Supp. 1167 (S.D. Iowa 1972)

[2] Guidelines § 1500.6(a).

[3] *See* San Antonio Conservation Society Members v. Texas Highway Department, 400 U.S. 968 (1970) (Dissenting opinion of Justices Black, Douglas and Brennan on denial of *certiorari*). *Also, see* 1606.84 Acres of Land v. United States, 400 U.S. 954 (1971) (Dissenting opinion of Justices Black and Douglas for denial of *certiorari*).

In Citizens for Responsible Area Growth v. Adams, 477 F. Supp. 994, 10 E.L.R. 20143 (D.N.H. 1979), the Farmers Home Administration, the Economic Development Administration and the Federal Aviation Administration

The problem presented by long-range projects, such as extensive road-building projects, extensive projects to construct flood control works to tame a particular river valley, extensive projects to build hydroelectric systems, or far-reaching plans to develop breeder reactor technology, all fall into this category. Since all of them require years, if not tens of years, for their completion, it is far easier to make environmental impact determinations from time to time as the work progresses. On the other hand, this neglects the very real problem of the total environmental impact of the project as a whole.

The intent of the law is best carried out by requiring a thorough, broadly gauged consideration of total environmental impact at the commencement of the entire project and further environmental impact statements with respect to each component part as it proceeds from planning to construction. The initial statement is to consider the environmental impact of the project as a whole in relation to the need for, and the benefits to be expected from, the completion of the large plan.[4] The shorter term impact statements must consider each segment of the plan and are to focus exclusively on the impact of the particular choices made with regard to that segment's execution. It is unnecessary to reconsider the initial broader impact statement that deals with the plan as a whole, unless, in the course of the execution of the project, changes occur that open up far-reaching alternative choices, or that cause such a change in the character of the project as to result in radically different effects on the environment from the ones initially anticipated. With a program or project that takes many years to complete, there is the additional responsibility that other intervening developments may require a reevaluation of the initial impact determination. To give but one example, if metropolitan growth or population density moves in directions not anticipated when the project was initially conceived, it is entirely possible that the need for particular highway links or for particular flood works may change radically and that

---

were all involved in assisting the City of Lebanon, N.H. to fund and develop a regional airport expansion and the expansion of other developments, including an industrial park. While at first the three federal agencies stressed the integrated nature of the plan, they each decided at some point that they were each funding a separate proposal or project, each of which, individually, was not large enough to require an impact statement. Issuing a preliminary injunction against further construction until the agencies had complied with NEPA, the court held that the project was an integrated one, both under the earlier CEQ guidelines and under CEQ regulations, 40 C.F.R. § 1508.25, having significant cumulative impact.

[4] Environmental Defense Fund, Inc. v. Corps of Engineers (Gillham Dam), 470 F.2d 289 (8th Cir. 1972), *cert. denied*, 412 U.S. 908 (1973).

The CEQ Regulations termed these types of federal activities "broad actions." Statements on proposals that involve broad actions, according to the Regulations, should be evaluated in one of the following ways:

> (1) Geographically, including actions occurring in the same general location, such as an ocean, region, or metropolitan area.
>
> (2) Generally, including actions which have relevant similarities, such as common timing, impacts, alternatives, methods of implementation, media, or subject matter.
>
> (3) By stage of technological development, including federal or federally assisted research, development or demonstration programs aimed at developing new technologies which, if applied, could significantly affect the quality of the human environment. Statements shall be prepared on such programs and shall be available before the program has reached a state of investment or commitment to implementation likely to determine subsequent development or restrict later alternatives.

40 C.F.R. § 1502.4(C)(1) to (4). *See also* § 1508.25 on the scope of the EIS to be prepared

alternative choices, far less costly or damaging, may become available, though they had not been at the program's inception.

The issue has been most frequently raised in the context of road building projects. The question of the time for consideration of the impact of an entire road system was given short shrift—and answered wrongly—in a district court decision in *Indian Lookout Alliance v. Volpe.*[5] The case involved a claim that separate impact statements should be prepared and filed for a new, 1,900-mile highway system for the State of Iowa, and for a particular 272-mile stretch of freeway. The need to file impact statements for segments of the road that were about to obtain federal approvals was conceded, and such a statement for a segment of a few miles had been prepared. The court focused on the fact that the plans called for construction over a period of twenty years, and that no federal approval had as yet been requested for the plans, nor had the plans progressed beyond the point of designating general corridors rather than specific routes. The court held that the plans had not as yet "reached the stage of being a 'major Federal action' " and that it would be impossible to prepare an environmental impact statement on the basis of the indefinite proposals available.

In the light of the intent of NEPA that considerations of environmental impact inform the planning process as early as possible so as to leave open the fullest range of options, decisions that require early consideration of the plan as a whole appear to state the better view of the law.

The segmentation of a major project for purposes of filing an environmental impact statement was expressly disapproved in *Thompson v. Fugate,*[6] where the court took the position that the absence of federal funding for a segment of highway that was part of a federally funded system did not exempt that segment from having to comply with the § 102 requirement of NEPA.

A similar position was advanced in *San Antonio Conservation Society v. Texas Highway Department,*[7] where the state had withdrawn its request for federal funds—shifting them to other eligible projects—in order to change the character of the road building enterprise from a federal to a state project. The court refused to accept this subterfuge and insisted on the preparation of an environmental impact statement. However, the court's decision in this case was subsequently overturned by act of Congress, which treated the San Antonio situation as unique and not as providing a precedent for the future.[8]

---

[5] 345 F. Supp. 1167 (S.D. Iowa 1972). To the same effect, see Northeast Welfare Rights Organization v. Volpe, 1 E.L.R. 20186 (D. Wash. 1970).

[6] 452 F.2d 57 (4th Cir. 1971); *on remand* 347 F. Supp. 120 (D.Va. 1972). To the same effect, Lathan v. Volpe, 455 F.2d 1111 (9th Cir. 1971), *on rehearing*, 455 F.2d 1122 (9th Cir. 1971). *See also* Scherr v. Volpe, 466 F.2d 1027 (7th Cir. 1972). The "piece-mealing" of highways was expressly disapproved in Appalachian Mountain Club v. Brinegar, 394 F. Supp. 105, 5 E.L.R. 20311 (D.N.H. 1975).

[7] 466 F.2d 1013 (5th Cir. 1971). Similar holding, Arlington Coalition on Transportation v. Volpe, 458 F.2d 1323 (4th Cir. 1972), *cert. denied,* 409 U.S. 1000 (1972).

For later developments in the Arlington Federation situation, see D.C. Federation v. Adams, 571 F.2d 1310, 11 E.R.C. 1461 (4th Cir. 1978), which upheld the earlier decision on Interstate 66, rejecting the claim that the development of D.C. METRO had not been taken into account.

[8] In Named Individual Members of the San Antonio Conservation Society v. Texas, 6 E.R.C. 1273 (W.D. Tex. 1973), *aff'd*, 496 F.2d 1017 (5th Cir., 1974), the San Antonio road

The "segmentation issue" has undergone a variety of approaches in cases involving highway projects decided since 1975. Thus, in *Coleman v. Conservation Society of Southern Vermont,*[9] the Second Circuit had found support in the requirement of NEPA that the environmental impact statement consider the relation between short and long-term uses of the environment for requiring an impact statement greater in scope than the specific project before the agency. However, upon appeal by the Federal Highway Administration, the Supreme Court, following the decision in *SCRAP II*, remanded the case[10] for "further consideration." Relying on *SCRAP II*,[11] the Second Circuit then stated that a federal agency must prepare its environmental impact statement at the time at which it makes a recommendation or report on a *proposal* for federal action, and pointed out that there was no overall federal plan for improving the entire Route 7 corridor into a superhighway. The court now found that inasmuch as the project at issue had local utility, it did *not* represent an irreversible or irretrievable commitment of federal funds for the entire corridor and therefore no obligation to prepare a corridor environmental impact statement existed. It should be noted that in its prior decision[12] the court had held that preparation of a NEPA impact statement on transportation systems within the entire Route 7 corridor in New England must precede federal funding of a reconstruction project for a twenty-mile segment of the highway.[13] Other cases which addressed the so-called "segmentation" issue hold that the "piece-mealing" of highways, without assessing the reasonable consequential environmental effects, violates the spirit and letter of NEPA.

For a more comprehensive treatment of this issue, see F. Grad, Treatise on Environmental Law § 9.02[2][c].

---

segment was held not to be a part of a federal highway project after it was congressionally removed from that status by the Federal Highway Act of 1973, Pub. L. No. 93-87, § 154, 93rd Cong., 1st Sess., 87 Stat. 250 (1973). The court in the Fifth Circuit opinion cites sections from the majority report of the Senate Public Works Committee, S. Rep. No. 93-61, 93rd Cong., 1st Sess. (1973), explaining the termination of the federal aid relationship of the San Antonio freeway. The thrust of these contentions by the Committee was that the project, being twice delayed by changes in the federal law, had cost the State of Texas $4,500,000 in damage claims and since the state and municipality were eager to finish the construction with local financing, it would be proper to allow them to do so.

The San Antonio exemption in the Federal Highway Act appeared in the Senate bill, S. Rep. No. 93-61, 93rd Cong., 1st Sess. (1973) at 23. The report stated that termination of federal involvement in such projects is not unprecedented, and that "the Committee recognizes that this is an unusual action and believes it is warranted only because of unusual circumstances." *Ibid.* The Senate report felt the only effect of this section of the legislation "would be to ratify the action of the Secretary of Transportation in accepting the funds already returned by the state and to terminate the federal-state relationship on the project." *Ibid.*

[9] 508 F.2d 927, 5 E.L.R. 20068 (2d Cir. 1974).

[10] Coleman v. Conservation Society of Southern Vermont, 423 U.S. 809, 6 E.L.R 20068 (1975).

[11] Abedeen & Rockfish R. Co. v. SCRAP, 422 U.S. 289, 95 S. Ct. 2336, 45 L. Ed. 2d 191 (1975).

[12] 508 F.2d 927, 5 E.L.R. 20068 (2d Cir. 1974).

[13] The court's decision on remand has been criticized as a misreading of *SCRAP II*. Comment, "Fallout From *SCRAP II* and the 1975 NEPA Amendments: Second Circuit Reverses Itself in Conservation Society," 6 E.L.R. 10081 (1976).

KLEPPE v. SIERRA CLUB

United States Supreme Court (1976)
427 U.S. 390, 96 S. Ct. 2718, 49 L. Ed. 2d 576

Mr. Justice Powell delivered the Opinion of the Court.

[Plaintiffs are organizations concerned with environmental protection. Defendants are officials of the Department of the Interior and other agencies responsible for issuing coal leases, approving mining plans, and for other actions necessary to enable private companies and public utilities to develop coal resources on public land in the Northern Great Plains region. Plaintiffs seek to enjoin further development without the preparation of a comprehensive environmental impact statement.]

The Northern Great Plains region identified in respondents' complaint encompasses portions of four States—northeastern Wyoming, eastern Montana, western North Dakota, and western South Dakota. There is no dispute about its richness in coal, nor about the waxing interest in developing that coal, nor about the crucial role the federal petitioners will play due to the significant percentage of the coal to which they control access. The Department has initiated, in this decade, three studies in areas either inclusive of or included within this region. The North Central Power Study was addressed to the potential for coordinated development of electric power in an area encompassing all or part of 15 States in the North Central United States. It aborted in 1972 for lack of interest on the part of electric utilities. The Montana-Wyoming Aqueducts Study, intended to recommend the best use of water resources for coal development in southeastern Montana and northeastern Wyoming, was suspended in 1972 with the initiation of the third study, the Northern Great Plains Resources Program (NGPRP).

While the record does not reveal the degree of concern with environmental matters in the first two studies, it is clear that the NGPRP was devoted entirely to the environment. It was carried out by an interagency, federal-state task force with public participation, and was designed "to assess the potential social, economic and environmental impacts" from resource development in five States—Montana, Wyoming, South Dakota, North Dakota, and Nebraska. Its primary objective was "to provide an analytical and informational framework for policy and planning decisions at all levels of government" by formulating several "scenarios" showing the probable consequences for the area's environment and culture from the various possible techniques and levels of resource development. The final interim report of the NGPRP was issued August 1, 1975, shortly after the decision of the Court of Appeals in this case.

In addition, since 1973 the Department has engaged in a complete review of its coal-leasing program for the entire Nation. On February 17 of that year the Secretary announced the review and announced also that during study a "short-term leasing policy" would prevail, under which new leasing would be restricted to narrowly defined circumstances and even then allowed only when an environmental impact statement had been prepared if required under NEPA. The purpose of the program review was to study the environmental impact of the Department's entire range of coal-related activities and to develop a planning system to guide the national leasing program. The impact statement, known as the "Coal Programmatic EIS," went through several drafts before issuing in final form on September 19, 1975—shortly before the petitions for certiorari were filed in this case. The Coal Programmatic EIS proposed a new leasing program based on a complex planning system called the Energy Minerals Activity Recommendation System (EMARS), and assessed the prospective environmental impact of the new program as well as the alternatives to it. We have been informed by the parties to this litigation that the Secretary is in the process of implementing the new program.

Against this factual background, we turn now to consider the issues raised by this case in the status in which it reached this Court.

III

The major issue remains the one with which the suit began: whether NEPA requires petitioners to prepare an environmental impact statement on the entire Northern Great Plains region. Petitioners, arguing the negative, rely squarely upon the facts of the case and the language of § 102(2)(C) of NEPA. We find their reliance well placed.

As noted in the first sentence of this opinion, § 102(2)(C) requires an impact statement "in every recommendation or report on proposals for legislation and other major Federal actions significantly affecting the quality of the human environment." Since no one has suggested that petitioners have proposed legislation on respondents' region, the controlling phrase in this section of the Act, for this case, is "major Federal actions." Respondents can prevail only if there has been a report or recommendation on a proposal for major federal action with respect to the Northern Great Plains region. Our statement of the relevant facts shows there has been none; instead, all proposals are for actions of either local or national scope.

The local actions are the decisions by the various petitioners to issue a lease, approve a mining plan, issue a right-of-way permit, or take other action to allow private activity at some point within the region identified by respondents. Several Courts of Appeals have held that an impact statement must be included in the report or recommendation on a proposal for such action if the private activity to be permitted is one "significantly affecting the quality of the human environment" within the meaning of § 102(2)(C). *See, e.g., Scientists' Institute for Public Information, Inc. v. AEC*, 156 U.S. App. D.C. 395, 404-405, 481 F.2d 1079, 1088-1089 (1973); *Davis v. Morton*, 469 F.2d 593 (CA10 1972).

. . . .

Quite apart from the fact that the statutory language requires an impact statement only in the event of a proposed action, respondents' desire for a regional environmental impact statement cannot be met for practical reasons. In the absence of a proposal for a regional plan of development, there is nothing that could be the subject of the analysis envisioned by the statute for an impact statement. Section 102(2)(C) requires that an impact statement contain, in essence, a detailed statement of the expected adverse environmental consequences of an action, the resource commitments involved in it, and the alternatives to it. Absent an overall plan for regional development, it is impossible to predict the level of coal-related activity that will occur in the region identified by respondents, and thus impossible to analyze the environmental consequences and the resource commitments involved in, and the alternatives to, such activity. A regional plan would define fairly precisely the scope and limits of the proposed development of the region. Where no such plan exists, any attempt to produce an impact statement would be little more than a study along the lines of the NGPRP, containing estimates of potential development and attendant environmental consequences. There would be no factual predicate for the production of an environmental impact statement of the type envisioned by NEPA.

We conclude that the Court of Appeals erred in both its factual assumptions and its interpretation of NEPA. We think the court was mistaken in concluding, on the record before it, that the petitioners were "contemplating" a regional development plan or program. . . .

Even had the record justified a finding that a regional program was contemplated by the petitioners, the legal conclusion drawn by the Court of Appeals cannot be squared with the Act. The court recognized that the mere "contemplation" of certain action is not sufficient to require an impact statement. But it believed the statute nevertheless empowers a court to require the preparation of an impact statement to begin at some point prior to the formal recommendation or report on a proposal. The Court of Appeals accordingly devised its own four-part "balancing" test for determining when, during the contemplation of a plan or other type of federal action, an agency must begin a statement. . . .

The Court's reasoning and action find no support in the language or legislative history of NEPA. The statute clearly states when an impact statement is required, and mentions nothing about a balancing of factors. Rather, as we noted last Term, under the first sentence of § 102(2)(C) the moment at which an agency must have a final statement ready "is the time at which it makes a recommendation or report on a *proposal* for federal action." *Aberdeen & Rockfish R. Co. v. SCRAP,* 422 U.S. 289, 320, 45 L.Ed.2d 191, 95 S.Ct. 2336 (1975) (SCRAP II) (emphasis in original). The procedural duty imposed upon agencies by this section is quite precise, and the role of the courts in enforcing that duty is similarly precise. A court has no authority to depart from the statutory language and, by a balancing of court-devised factors, determine a point during the germination process of a potential proposal at which an impact statement *should be prepared*. Such an assertion of judicial authority would leave the agencies uncertain as to their procedural duties under NEPA, would invite judicial involvement in the day-to-day decisionmaking process of the agencies, and would invite litigation. As the contemplation of a project and the accompanying study thereof do not necessarily result in a proposal for major federal action, it may be assumed that the balancing process devised by the Court of Appeals also would result in the preparation of a good many unnecessary impact statements.[14] [The Court holds that the injunction against the approval of the four mining plans would be error in any event because there had been no showing of irreparable harm and no balancing of the equities involved.]

Our discussion thus far has been addressed primarily to the decision of the Court of Appeals. It remains, however, to consider the contention now urged by respondents. They have not attempted to support the Court of Appeals' decision. Instead, respondents renew an argument they appear to have made to the Court of Appeals, but which that court did not reach. Respondents insist that, even without a comprehensive federal plan for the development of the Northern Great Plains, a "regional" impact statement nevertheless is required on all coal-related projects in the region because they are intimately related. . . .

We begin by stating our general agreement with respondents' basic premise that § 102(2)(C) may require a comprehensive impact statement in certain situations where several proposed actions are pending at the same time. NEPA announced a national policy of environmental protection and placed a responsibility upon the Federal Government to further specific environmental goals by "all practicable means, consistent with other essential considerations of national policy." NEPA § 101(b), 42 U.S.C. § 4331(b). Section 102(2)(C) is one of the "action-forcing" provisions intended as a directive to "all agencies to assure consideration of the environmental impact of their actions in decisionmaking." Conference Report on NEPA, 115Cong. Rec. 40416 (1969). By requiring an impact statement Congress intended to assure such consideration during the development of a proposal or—as in this case—during the formulation of a position on a proposal submitted by private parties. A comprehensive impact statement may be necessary in some cases for an agency to meet this duty. Thus, when several proposals for coal-related actions that will have cumulative or synergistic environmental impact upon a region are pending concurrently before an agency, their environmental consequences must be considered together. Only through comprehensive consideration of pending proposals can the agency evaluate different courses of action.[15]

[14] This is not to say that § 102(2)(C) imposes no duties upon an agency *prior* to its making a report or recommendation on a proposal for action. The section states that prior to preparing the impact statement the responsible official "shall consult with and obtain the comments of any Federal agency which has jurisdiction by law or special expertise with respect to any environmental impact involved." Thus, the section contemplates a consideration of environmental factors by agencies during the evolution of a report or recommendation on a proposal. But the time at which a court enters the process is when the report or recommendation on the proposal is made, and someone protests either the absence or the adequacy of the final impact statement. This is the point at which an agency's action has reached sufficient maturity to assure that judicial intervention will not hazard unnecessary disruption.

[15] Neither the statute nor its legislative history contemplates that the court should substitute its judgment for that of the agency as to the environmental consequences of its actions. *See* Scenic Hudson Preservation Conference v. FPC, 453 F.2d 463, 481 (CA2 1971), *cert. denied*, 407 U.S. 926, 32 L.Ed.2d 813, 92 S.Ct. 2453 (1972). The only role for a court is to insure that the agency has taken a "hard look" at environmental consequences; it cannot "interject itself within the area of discretion of the executive as to the choice of the action to be taken." Natural Resources Defense Council v. Morton, 148 U.S. App. D.C. 5, 16, 459 F.2d 827, 838 (1972).

Agreement to this extent with respondents' premise, however, does not require acceptance of their conclusion that all proposed coal-related actions in the Northern Great Plains region are so "related" as to require their analysis in a single comprehensive impact statement. Respondents informed us that the Secretary recently adopted an approach to impact statements on coal-related actions that provides:

> "A. As a general proposition, and as determined by the Secretary, when action is proposed involving coal development such as issuing several coal leases or approving mining plans in the same region, such actions will be covered by a single EIS rather than by multiple statements. In such cases, the region covered will be determined by basin boundaries, drainage areas, areas of common reclamation problems, administrative boundaries, areas of economic interdependence, and other relevant factors." Brief for Respondents App. 20a.

At another point, the document containing the Secretary's approach states that a "regional EIS" will be prepared "if a series of proposed actions with inter-related impacts are involved . . . unless a previous EIS has sufficiently analyzed the impacts of the proposed action(s)." *Id.*, at 20a-21a. Thus, the Department has decided to prepare comprehensive impact statements of the type contemplated by § 102(2)(C), although it has not deemed it appropriate to prepare such a statement on all proposed actions in the region identified by respondents.

. . . .

Respondents' basic argument is that one comprehensive statement on the Northern Great Plains is required because all coal-related activity in that region is "programmatically," "geographically," and "environmentally" related. Both the alleged "programmatic" relationship and the alleged "geographic" relationship resolve, ultimately, into an argument that the region is proper for a comprehensive impact statement because the petitioners themselves have approached environmental study in this area on a regional basis. Respondents point primarily to the NGPRP, which they claim—and petitioners deny—focused on the region described in the complaint. The precise region of the NGPRP is unimportant, for its irrelevance to the delineation of an appropriate area for analysis in a comprehensive impact statement has been well stated by the Secretary:

> "Resource studies [like the NGPRP] are one of many analytical tools employed by the Department to inform itself as to general resource availability, resource need and general environmental considerations so that it can intelligently determine the scope of environmental analysis and review specific actions it may take. Simply put, resource studies are a prelude to informed agency planning, and provide the data base on which the Department may decide to take specific actions for which impact statements are prepared. The scope of environmental impact statements seldom coincide with that of a given resource study, since the statements evolve from specific proposals for federal action while the studies simply provide an educational backdrop." Affidavit of Oct. 28, 1975, App 191.

As for the alleged "environmental" relationship, respondents contend that the coal-related projects "will produce a wide variety of cumulative environmental impacts" throughout the Northern Great Plains region. They described them as follows: diminished availability of water, air and water pollution, increases in population and industrial densities, and perhaps even climatic changes. Cumulative environmental impacts are, indeed, what require a comprehensive impact statement. But determination of the extent and effect of these factors, and particularly identification of the geographic area within which they may occur, is a task assigned to the special competency of the appropriate agencies. Petitioners dispute respondent's contentions that the interrelationship of environmental impacts is regionwide and, as respondents' own submissions indicate, petitioners appear to have determined that the appropriate scope of comprehensive statements should be based on basins, drainage areas, and other factors. *See supra*, at 410–411, 49 L.Ed.2d 591. We cannot say that petitioners' choices are arbitrary. Even if environmental interrelationships could be shown conclusively to extend across basins and drainage areas, practical considerations of feasibility might well necessitate restricting the scope of comprehensive statements.

In sum, respondents' contention as to the relationships between all proposed coal-related projects in the Northern Great Plain region does not require that petitioners prepare one comprehensive impact statement covering all before proceeding to approve specific pending applications.[16] As we already have determined that there exists no proposal for regionwide action that could require a regional impact statement, the judgment of the Court of Appeals must be reversed, and the judgment of the District Court reinstated and affirmed. The case is remanded for proceedings consistent with this opinion.

NOTES AND QUESTIONS

(1) Justice Marshall, joined by Justice Brennan, dissented in part in *Kleppe*. Marshall expressed concern that the *Kleppe* majority's decision unnecessarily limited the ability of the federal courts to effectuate the intent of NEPA. He noted that, since NEPA challenges are not usually made until after a federal agency or department has already made a decision to carry out an action "the courts have had to content themselves with the largely unsatisfactorily remedy of enjoining the proposed federal action and ordering the preparation of an impact statement." In Marshall's view this remedy is insufficient because, "except by deterrence, it does nothing to further early consideration of environmental factors." 424 U.S. at 415-16. Do you agree with that view?

(2) The *Kleppe* decision substantially set back judicial and scholarly support for an expanded use of programmatic EISs to compel agency consideration

---

[16] Nor is it necessary that petitioners always complete a comprehensive impact statement on all proposed actions in an appropriate region before approving any of the projects. As petitioners have emphasized, and respondents have not disputed, approval of one lease or mining plan does not commit the Secretary to approval of any others; nor, apparently, do single approvals by the other petitioners commit them to subsequent approvals. Thus, an agency could approve one pending project that is fully covered by an impact statement, then take into consideration the environmental effects of that existing project when preparing the comprehensive statement on the cumulative impact of the remaining proposals.

of environmental factors at an early stage of policy-making. *See* Comment, *NEPA Off the Top: The Supreme Court Interprets Impact Statement Requirements*, 5 ELR 10164 (1976); Note, *Kleppe v. Sierra Club: Addressing the Question of the Programmatic Impact Statement*, 55 N.C.L. Rev. 484 (1977). *But see National Wildlife Federation v. Benn*, 491 F. Supp. 1234 (S.D. N.Y. 1980).

The case received a critical reception. *See* F. Grad, Treatise on Environmental Law § 9.02; W. Rodgers, Environmental Law 924-28 (2d. ed) (1994); Note, *Program Environmental Impact Statements*, 75 Mich. L. Rev. 107 (1976); Comment, *The Scope of the Program EIS Requirement: The Need for a Coherent Judicial Approach*, 30 Stan. L. Rev. 767 (1978). These and other commentators have faulted *Kleppe* on several grounds, most notably that the decision defers too extensively to agency decisions, in contravention of the underlying policies of NEPA, and that it establishes a test that is mechanical, and unhelpful, since it assumes that it will always be clear whether an agency "proposal" exists. In your opinion, how persuasive are those criticisms?

For an extended analysis of *Kleppe*, see Johnston, *Kleppe v. Sierra Club: An Environmental Planning Catch-22?*, 1 Harv. Envtl. L. Rev. 182 (1976).

(3) As a practical matter, the program impact statement raises recurring questions for agencies. When a proposed program will be composed of individual projects, can the agency go ahead with interim actions (*e.g.*, the issuance of permits or licenses) based on its preparation of a series of individual project EISs (pending the preparation of a program EIS)? On the other hand, if the agency first prepares a thorough program EIS in these circumstances, is it then obliged to also draft individual, site-specific EISs for all consequent parts of the program? In the aftermath of *Kleppe v. Sierra Club*, the courts have largely based their answers to these questions on factual determinations as to whether an interim resolution would prejudice the ultimate determination (with respect to the program as a whole) or, in the alternative, whether individual projects have independent purposes, and are thus capable of being separated from the program as a whole for EIS purposes, without an irretrievable commitment of resources.

(4) The *Kleppe* opinion appears to have rejected the approach taken in *Scientists' Institute for Public Information, Inc. v. AEC* ("SIPI"), 481 F.2d 1079 (D.C. Cir. 1973), an earlier NEPA case in which the D.C. Circuit ruled that the Atomic Energy Commission must prepare a programmatic impact statement on the technology development program for the still unconstructed liquid fast metal nuclear breeder reactor. The court stated:

> In our view, the timing question can best be answered by reference to the underlying policies of NEPA in favor of meaningful, timely information on the effects of agency action. In the early states of research, when little is known about the technology and when future application of the technology is both doubtful and remote, it may well be impossible to draft a meaningful impact statement . . . . At the other end of the spectrum, by the time the commercial feasibility of the technology is conclusively demonstrated, and the effects of the application of the technology certain, the purposes of NEPA will already have been thwarted . . . . Any statement prepared at such a late date will no doubt be thorough, detailed and

> accurate, but it will be of little help in ensuring that decisions reflect environmental concerns. Thus we are pulled in two directions. Statements must be written late enough in the development process to contain meaningful information, but they must be written early enough so that whatever information is contained can practically serve as an input into the decision-making process. 481 F.2d at 1093-94.

(5) In the aftermath of the *Kleppe* decision, the Council on Environmental Quality amended its NEPA regulations to provide federal agencies with more explicit guidance on the issues of EIS "scope" and "timing" which the principal case concerns. Relevant portions of these regulations state:

40 C.F.R. § 1508.25Scope

Scope consists of the range of actions, alternatives, and impacts to be considered in an environmental impact statement. The scope of an individual statement may depend on its relationships to other statements (§§ 1502.20 and 1508.28). To determine the scope of environmental impact statements, agencies shall consider 3 types of actions, 3 types of alternatives, and 3 types of impacts. They include:

(a) Actions (other than unconnected single actions) which may be:

(1) Connected actions, which means that they are closely related and therefore should be discussed in the same impact statement. Actions are connected if they:

(i) Automatically trigger other actions which may require environmental impact statements.

(ii) Cannot or will not proceed unless other actions are taken previously or simultaneously.

(iii) Are interdependent parts of a larger action and depend on the larger action for their justification.

(2) Cumulative actions, which when viewed with other proposed actions have cumulatively significant impacts and should therefore be discussed in the same impact statement.

(3) Similar actions, which when viewed with other reasonably foreseeable or proposed agency actions, have similarities that provide a basis for evaluating their environmental consequences together, such as common timing or geography. An agency may wish to analyze these actions in the same impact statement. It should do so when the best way to assess adequately the combined impacts of similar actions or reasonable alternatives to such actions is to treat them in a single impact statement.

(b) Alternatives, which include: (1) No action alternative. (2) Other reasonable course of actions. (3) Mitigation measures (not in the proposed action).

(c) Impacts, which may be: (1) Direct. (2) Indirect. (3) Cumulative.

40 C.F.R. § 1502.5Timing

An agency shall commence preparation of an environmental impact statement as close as possible to the time the agency is developing or is presented with a proposal so that preparation can be complete in time for the final statement to be included in any recommendation or report on the proposal. The statement shall be prepared early enough so that it can serve practically as an important contribution to the decisionmaking process and will not be used to rationalize or justify decisions already made. For instance:

(a) For projects directly undertaken by Federal agencies the environmental impact statement shall be prepared at the feasibility analysis (go-no go) stage and may be supplemented at a later stage if necessary.

(b) For application to the agency appropriate environmental assessments or statements shall be commenced no later than immediately after the application is received. Federal agencies are encouraged to begin preparation of such assessments or statements earlier, preferably jointly with applicable State or local agencies.

(c) For adjudication, the final environmental impact statement shall normally precede the final staff recommendation and that portion of the public hearing related to the impact study. In appropriate circumstances the statement may follow preliminary hearings designed to gather information for use in statements.

(d) For informal rulemaking the draft environmental impact statement shall normally accompany the proposed rule.

40 C.F.R. § 1502.4(c)

When preparing statements on broad actions including proposals by more than one agency, agencies may find it useful to evaluate the proposal in one of the following ways:

(1) Geographically, including actions occurring in the same general location, such as a body of water, region, or metropolitan area.

(2) Generically, including actions which have relevant similarities, such as common timing, impacts, alternatives, methods of implementation, media, or subject matter.

(3) By stage of technological development including federal or federally assisted research, development or demonstration programs for new technologies which, if applied, could significantly affect the quality of the human environment. Statements shall be prepared on such programs, and shall be available before the program has reached a stage of investment or commitment to implementation likely to determine subsequent development or restrict later alternatives.

The CEQ regulations also define the term "proposal" as existing "at that stage in the development of an action when an Agency subject to the Act has a goal and is actively preparing to make a decision on one or more alternative means of accomplishing that goal and the effects can be meaningfully evaluated." *See* 40 C.F.R. § 1502.5.

(6) In *Blue Ocean Preservation Soc'y. v. Watkins*, 754 F. Supp. 1450, 21 ELR 20901 (D. Hawaii 1991), action was filed to compel the Department of Energy

to prepare a single EIS for a four-phase geothermal energy project, for which the DOE had provided substantial funding. Phases I and II of the project had been completed when action was filed. Phases I to III were devoted to drilling geothermal wells, demonstration projects, generic and site-specific surveys to determine feasibility of transmitting electricity by submarine cable systems. These activities would lay the foundation for the construction of a large 500 megawatt project in phase IV. Assuming that the project consisted of four distinct phases, each requiring a separate analysis under NEPA, the DOE moved for summary judgment, arguing that plaintiffs' suit was moot with respect to phases I and II, which were already complete, and not ripe for consideration, on grounds that no specific proposals for phases III and IV had been made.

The District Court denied the motion. Noting that there is no "bright line" rule to determine what constitutes a proposal, the court nonetheless ruled that since further decisions remained on the project in question, which could be influenced by an impact statement, preparation of such a statement would be required. Citing 40 C.F.R. § 1502.5(excerpted above), the court enjoined the commitment of further federal resources until the EIS was completed.

(7) CEQs regulations were also cited with approbation in *Thomas v. Peterson*, 753 F.2d 754 (9th Cir. 1985). There the National Forest Service proposed construction of a road that "would not be built but for . . . contemplated timber sales" in areas that the proposed timber road would serve. The Service declined to prepare an EIS for the road itself, nor was it willing to prepare such a statement regarding the related timber sales. Holding the proposed road and timbering activities to be "connected" and "cumulative" actions, the Ninth Circuit ordered preparation of an EIS that addressed their combined environmental impact. Is this decision consistent with *Kleppe*? For a somewhat critical analysis of the *Thomas* case, see Hapke, *Thomas v. Peterson: The Ninth Circuit Breathes New Life Into CEQ's Cumulative and Connected Actions Regulations*, 15 Envt'l. L. Rep. 10289 (1985). *See also Save the Yaak Comm. v. Block*, 840 F.2d 714 (9th Cir. 1988) (NEPA requires assessment of connected actions even if the environmental impact of any of them, standing alone, is not significant).

NAMED INDIVIDUAL MEMBERS, SAN ANTONIO CONSERVATION SOCIETY v. TEXAS HIGHWAY DEPARTMENT

United States Court of Appeals, Fifth Circuit (1974)
496 F.2d 1017

AINSWORTH, C.J.:

This much litigated and important environmental case has been in the courts for more than six years and is now before us for the second time. The complaint seeks to enjoin the construction of an expressway which would pass through parklands in the City of San Antonio, Texas. Plaintiffs are named individual members of the San Antonio Conservation Society, and defendants are The Texas Highway Department . . . [and the Federal Department of Transportation and a number of individual officers of each.]

The question for decision is whether the congressional enactment of section 154 of the Federal-Aid Highway Act of 1973, severing all federal connection with the San Antonio North Expressway, removes that project from the necessity for compliance with the provisions of the National Environmental Policy Act (NEPA) (42 U.S.C. § 4331 et seq.) and section 4(f) of the Department of Transportation Act (49 U.S.C. § 1653(f)).

Our prior decision (446 F.2d 1013 (1971)) reversed a summary judgment in favor of defendants and held that there had been a failure to comply with the provisions of NEPA and section 4(f) before proceeding with construction of the Expressway. We remanded the case with directions to the district court that it be held until the Secretary of Transportation had complied with his statutory responsibilities after which the district court was to conduct a full review of the matter. In the meanwhile, we ordered that "[c]onstruction shall not proceed until there has been full compliance with the law." *Id.* at 1029.

The San Antonio North Expressway has been projected since 1959. The disputed segment is approximately six miles long, running about north and south through the middle of the City of San Antonio, and extends between Interstate Loop 410 and Interstate Highway 35. The controversy arises out of the fact that it will traverse portions of the Brackenridge-Olmos Basin Parklands. Its proponents stress the imperative need to solve serious traffic problems of the city; its opponents do not wish it to go through the beautiful Parklands in mid San Antonio. Some time after our initial decision in this case, Congress enacted the Federal-Aid Highway Act of 1973. Section 154 of that Act is directly applicable to the Expressway here, and reads in full as follows:

> "Sec. 154. (a) Notwithstanding any other provisions of Federal law or any court decision to the contrary, the contractual relationship between the Federal and State Governments shall be ended with respect to all portions of the San Antonio North Expressway between Interstate Highway 35 and Interstate Loop 410, and the expressway shall cease to be a Federal-aid project.
>
> "(b) The amount of all Federal-aid highway funds paid on account of sections of the San Antonio North Expressway in Bexar County, Texas (Federal-aid projects numbered U 244(7), U 244(10), UG 244(9), U 244(8), and U 244(11), shall be repaid to the Treasurer of the United States and the amount so repaid shall be deposited to the credit of the appropriation for 'Federal-Aid Highways (Trust Fund)'. At the time of such repayment the Federal-aid projects with respect to which funds have been repaid and any other Federal-aid projects located on such expressway and programed for expenditure on such project, if any, shall be canceled and withdrawn from the Federal-aid highway program. Any amount so repaid, together with the unpaid balance of any amount programed for expenditure on any such project shall be credited to the unprogrammed balance of Federal-aid

highway funds of the same class last apportioned to the States, respectively. The amount so credited shall be available for expenditure in accordance with the provision of title 23, United States Code, as amended."

It is undisputed that in conformity with section 154 the State of Texas has returned to the Federal Government all federal-aid funds which it received on account of the Expressway and that it will receive no other federal funds in the future to aid in its construction. All funds received have been restored to the Federal Government and reapportioned among the States. By congressional enactment the Expressway is now entirely a state-financed project.

Upon the passage of section 154 the Federal Government and the State of Texas both moved the district court to dismiss plaintiffs' suit on the ground that removal of all federal funding by Congress exempted the project from compliance with the environmental provisions of NEPA and section 4(f). Plaintiffs contended, however, that passage of section 154 did not exempt the Expressway from the requirement that state and federal officials comply with federal environmental statutes specifically designed to protect parklands, especially NEPA and section 4(f). Plaintiffs argued that these statutory requirements are still applicable (1) because the Expressway would traverse an area in which U.S. Army Corps of Engineers' approval would be required, thus constituting a "major federal action" under 42 U.S.C. § 4332(2)(C) and necessitating an environmental impact statement; (2) because the Expressway was only a small portion of a larger federal-aid network and inextricably related thereto; (3) because it would cross the San Antonio River said to be navigable and for which a U.S. Coast Guard permit would be required, another "major federal action"; and (4) if section 154 did exempt the project, it violated the due process clause of the U.S. Constitution.

The district court ruled adversely to the plaintiffs on all of these issues and held that the San Antonio North Expressway was exempt from the requirements of the federal environmental laws by virtue of the congressional enactment of section 154, which was not unconstitutional. Summary judgment was granted in favor of defendants and plaintiffs bring this appeal. A large volume of evidence, affidavits, depositions, and exhibits was filed by the parties in connection with the motions, and there does not appear to be any serious dispute as to the facts. It is the law as to which the parties have stressed their principal arguments and on which they differ.

We stayed the district court order pending consideration of this appeal.

I.

Plaintiffs contend that section 154 does not in its terms specifically exempt the North Expressway from NEPA, section 4(f)or any other federal law, and the fact that the North Expressway is now exclusively a Texas state highway project is not dispositive of the environmental issues. They argue that if Congress intended this result it should have expressly stated it in section 154.

Following this premise the plaintiffs urge that the Expressway will pass through the San Antonio Channel Improvement Project over which the Army Corps of Engineers has jurisdiction, such as, for example the Olmos Dam and

Reservoir situated in the Olmos Basin Parklands which they aver are portions of the Channel Improvement Project. Plaintiffs contend that the State Highway Department must obtain the Army Corps' approval for the Expressway to cross the San Antonio River at Josephine Street and also to traverse the Olmos Dam and Reservoir area. They aver that the prior 1968 approval thereof by the Army Corps is outdated because there have been material changes in the design of the Expressway since that time. Finally they contend that the Army Corps' approval will constitute a "major federal action" and thereby trigger the provisions of NEPA relative to furnishing an environmental impact statement. The defendants, Federal and State Governments, respond that the plain language of section 154 as well as the legislative history make it clear that Congress intended to exempt the North Expressway from the environmental requirements of federal law. They contend that Army Corps' approval of the project insofar as the river crossing at Josephine Street and traversing the Olmos Dam and Reservoir are concerned is not required by statute, regulation, or otherwise and that the Corps has no authority to approve or disapprove the Expressway.

We agree with defendants. Section 154(a) clearly states that "*Notwithstanding any other provisions of Federal law* or any court decision to the contrary, the contractual relationship between the Federal and State Governments shall be ended . . . and the expressway shall cease to be a Federal-aid project." (Emphasis added.) If Congress had not intended to exempt the Expressway from the environmental statutes, there would have been no purpose in passing the legislation. We cannot believe that Congress intended a vain and useless act. Any doubt about the matter, however, is fully resolved by the legislative history which shows without question that Congress drew the bill with the evident purpose of exempting the Expressway from the provisions of federal environmental laws including NEPA and section 4(f).[17] The debates in the Senate and House disclose this unmistakably, as do the reports of the Senate and House Committees.[18] Federal control and involvement thus came to an end with enactment of section 154.

---

[17] Section 4(f) requirement is no longer in the case since section 154 eliminated all federal funds on the Expressway and approval of the Secretary of Transportation is thus no longer required. *See* Citizens to Preserve Overton Park, Inc. v. Volpe, 401 U.S. 402, 407, 411, 91 S.Ct. 814, 28 L.Ed.2d 136 (1971).

[18] *See* the Majority Report, Senate Public Works Committee, in pertinent part as follows:

TERMINATION OF FEDERAL-AID RELATIONSHIP, SAN ANTONIO FREEWAY

The San Antonio North Expressway would be terminated as a Federal-aid project and Federal funds programmed for the State of Texas for that project would be returned to the United States Department of Transportation for reapportionment among the States. While congressional termination of Federal involvement in such projects is not unprecedented, the Committee recognizes that this is an unusual action and believes it is warranted only because of unusual circumstances.

The project involves a non-Interstate urban expressway located wholly within the limits of the City of San Antonio which was planned and requested by that city in 1959. The State obtained initial route approval from the Federal Highway Administrator, purchased all rights-of-way, and completed all relocation with approximately $7 million in State and local funds prior to changes in Federal law which later involved it in legal controversy.

The Secretary approved the letting of construction contracts prior to recent Federal court decisions defining the standard by which the administrative approval was to be reviewed. Thus the project has been affected twice by subsequent changes in Federal law and proce-

Nor was approval of the Expressway by the Army Corps of Engineers necessary so as to constitute a "major federal action" and trigger the provisions of NEPA relative to the requirement of an environmental impact statement before the Expressway can proceed. The Olmos Dam and Reservoir areas and the Josephine Street crossing area are not within Corps jurisdiction or authority. No rights of way have been acquired in the area. As the Corps' witness testified, it would not be able to approve the Expressway plans because there is no Corps project there at the moment. . . .

II.

Plaintiff's second contention is that the Expressway is only a small portion of a larger federal-aid highway network and that even though this segment is to be constructed exclusively with state funds, NEPA must still be complied with by the state. Plaintiffs contend that practically every vehicle using the Expressway will enter or exit from the federal-aid route. Therefore, they argue that the North Expressway is basically a part of one federal-aid highway. Nevertheless, we cannot ignore the fact that Congress, by section 154, specifically determined the North Expressway was not to be a federal project. The court below also held that the North Expressway has an independent utility of its own. The Federal Government argues that the congressional enactment of section 154 answers and disposes of this issue since there has now been an express congressional determination that the North Expressway is not a part of a larger federal project. It is true that the Expressway connects with other federal interstate highways at the north and south ends thereof, but defendants point out that virtually every road in the country crosses or interchanges with federal-aid highways, and that there are many state-constructed roads which do not form a part of the federal network. The independent utility of the Expressway is found in its connection of downtown San Antonio with the airport and in its primary purpose to relieve the serious traffic problem in central San Antonio. Accordingly, we hold that the Expressway is properly considered independently of the interstate routes with which it connects.

. . . .

---

dures preventing its completion as a Federal-aid project.

As a result, $4 million in construction has been deteriorating and contractors have claimed an additional $4.5 million in damages against the State of Texas. Since the State and municipality have indicated the desire to complete the project with wholly local financing, the Committee believes that it would be proper to allow them to do so.

The Committee's recommendation is not intended to be an adverse comment on the Fifth Circuit Court of Appeals decision of August 5, 1971, setting forth the administrative procedures required of the Secretary of Transportation in approving Federal-aid projects, nor would it prevent future litigation in State court. Its only effect would be to ratify the action of the Secretary of Transportation in accepting the Federal funds already returned by the State and to terminate the Federal-State relationship on the project.

The Committee heard extensive evidence about the project, studied the proposed route and is satisfied that it would not involve significant damage to recreational areas. S. Rep. No., 93-61, 93d Cong., 1st Sess. 23, 54-56 (1973).

III.

The issue posed by plaintiffs on the navigability *vel non* of the San Antonio River is now moot. The Army Corps of Engineers made its determination on March 8, 1974 in which it concluded that the San Antonio River at the points involved in this case should not be regarded as a navigable water of the United States. Plaintiffs' contention that U.S. Coast Guard approval is required for a bridge to cross the river must, therefore, fail.

IV.

Plaintiffs finally contend that if Congress' enactment of section 154 did exempt the North Expressway such action violates the due process clause of the U.S. Constitution by arbitrarily discriminating against plaintiffs and depriving them of rights under federal environmental statutes. They argue that such fundamental federal rights are available to all other citizens in the nation in similar circumstances and that Congress has without any jurisdiction deprived them of such rights. They aver that there is no basis for treating the Expressway any differently "from any other federal-aid highway that threatens urban parklands." (Appellants' brief, p. 40.)

The short answer to this contention is that by virtue of section 154 the North Expressway is no longer a federal-aid highway and that the same Congress which enacted the environmental statutes to which plaintiffs refer concluded to exempt this segment of highway from these laws. The federal-aid highway program was established by Congress and there is no reason apparent why it cannot decide which roads of the nation shall be included in the system. The environmental statutes were designed to apply to federal projects. The Expressway is now a state highway, not a federal highway. Its former federal status has been terminated by act of Congress. Congress having spoken in the matter, we see no reason to attempt to override the solemn expression of its will found in the enactment of section 154.

CONCLUSION

This controversy has now "been resolved in the Halls of Congress, which is the proper place in our system of Government for priority decisions to be made." 446 F.2d at 1024. We therefore defer to the will of Congress and give effect to its solemn enactment. Here the litigation should end.

Affirmed.

NOTES

(1) For additional illustrations of the ways in which federal courts have resolved highway segmentation issues in NEPA cases, see *Swain v. Brinegar*, 542 F.2d 364 (7th Cir. 1976) (planned 15 mile highway segment lacked independent utility and was part of larger interstate highway); *Indiana Lookout Alliance v. Volpe*, 484 F.2d 11 (8th Cir. 1973) (EIS need not cover entire length of Iowa highway system); *Named Individual Members of the San Antonio Conservation Society v. Texas Highway Dep't. (I)*, 446 F.2d 1013 (5th

Cir. 1971) (where an entire highway is presented to the public as one entity, its components may not be segmented).

(2) Segmentation issues also frequently arise with respect to damage projects. *See, e.g., Atcheson, Topeka and Santa Fe Ry. Co. v. Callaway (I)*, 382 F. Supp. 610 (D.D.C. 1974); *Sierra Club v. Callaway*, 499 F.2d 982 (5th Cir. 1974); *Trout Unlimited v. Morton*, 509 F.2d 1276 (9th Cir. 1974).

(3) Other NEPA decisions have resolved segmentation questions with respect to proposed urban mass transit projects. *See Taxpayers Watchdog v. Stanley*, 810 F.2d 294 (D.C. Cir. 1987); *Dickman v. City of Santa Fe*, 724 F. Supp. 1341 (D.N.M. 1989).

§ 5.05 Does NEPA Apply Outside the United States?

ENVIRONMENTAL DEFENSE FUND, INC. v. MASSEY

United States Court of Appeals, District of Columbia Circuit (1993)
986 F.2d 528

MIKVA, C.J.:

The Environmental Defense Fund ("EDF") appeals the district court's order dismissing its action seeking declaratory and injunctive relief under the National Environmental Policy Act ("NEPA"). EDF alleges that the National Science Foundation ("NSF") violated NEPA by failing to prepare an environmental impact statement ("EIS") in accordance with Section 102(2)(C) before going forward with plans to incinerate food wastes in Antarctica. The district court dismissed EDF's action for lack of subject matter jurisdiction. The court explained that while Congress utilized broad language in NEPA, the statute nevertheless did not contain "a clear expression of legislative intent through a plain statement of extraterritorial statutory effect"; consequently, the court was compelled by the recent Supreme Court decision in *Equal Employment Opportunity Commission v. Arabian American Oil Co.*, 499 U.S. 244, 111 S.Ct. 1227, 113 L.Ed.2d 274 (1991) ("*Aramco*") to conclude that NEPA does not apply to NSF's decision to incinerate food wastes in Antarctica. *See Environmental Defense Fund, Inc. v. Massey*, 772 F. Supp. 1296, 1297 (D.D.C. 1991).

We reverse the district court's decision, and hold that the presumption against the extraterritorial application of statutes described in *Aramco* does not apply where the conduct regulated by the statute occurs primarily, if not exclusively, in the United States, and the alleged extraterritorial effect of the statute will be felt in Antarctica—a continent without a sovereign, and an area over which the United States has a great measure of legislative control. We therefore remand to the district court for a determination of whether NSF actually failed to comply with Section 102(2)(C) of NEPA,as EDF alleges in its complaint.

I.

As both parties readily acknowledge, Antarctica is not only a unique continent, but somewhat of an international anomaly. Antarctica is the only continent on earth which has never been, and is not now, subject to the sovereign rule of any nation. Since entry into force of the Antarctic Treaty in 1961, the United States and 39 other nations have agreed not to assert any territorial claims to the continent or to establish rights of sovereignty there. Hence, Antarctica is generally considered to be a "global common" and frequently analogized to outer space.

Under the auspices of the United States Antarctica Program, NSF operates the McMurdo Station research facility in Antarctica. McMurdo Station is one of three year-round installations that the United States has established in Antarctica, and over which NSF exercises exclusive control. All of the installations serve as platforms or logistic centers for U.S. scientific research; McMurdo Station is the largest of the three, with more than 100 buildings and a summer population of approximately 1200.

Over the years, NSF has burned food wastes at McMurdo Station in an open landfill as a means of disposal. In early 1991, NSF decided to improve its environmental practices in Antarctica by halting its practice of burning food wastes in the open by October, 1991. After discovering asbestos in the landfill, however, NSF decided to cease open burning in the landfill even earlier, and to develop quickly an alternative plan for disposal of its food waste. NSF stored the waste at McMurdo Station from February, 1991 to July, 1991, but subsequently decided to resume incineration in an "interim incinerator" until a state-of-the-art incinerator could be delivered to McMurdo Station. EDF contends that the planned incineration may produce highly toxic pollutants which could be hazardous to the environment, and that NSF failed to consider fully the consequences of its decision to resume incineration as required by the decision-making process established by NEPA.

Section 102(2)(C) of NEPArequires "all federal agencies" to prepare an EIS in connection with any proposal for a "major action significantly affecting the quality of the human environment." 42 U.S.C. § 4332(2)(C). The EIS requirement, along with the many other provisions in the statute, is designed to "promote efforts which will prevent or eliminate damage to the environment and biosphere." 42 U.S.C. § 4321. Following the passage of NEPA, NSF promulgated regulations applying the EIS requirement to its decisions regarding proposed actions in Antarctica. Since the issuance of Executive Order 12114, however, NSF has contended that proposed action affecting the environment in Antarctica is governed by the Executive Order, not NEPA. *See* Exec. Order 12114, 3 C.F.R. 356(1980) [hereinafter cited as E.O. 12114].

Executive Order 12114 declares that federal agencies are required to prepare environmental analyses for "major Federal actions significantly affecting the environment of the global commons outside the jurisdiction of any nation (*e.g.* the oceans or Antarctica)." E.O. 12114 § 2-3a. According to the Executive Order, major federal actions significantly affecting the environment of foreign countries may also require environmental analyses under certain circumstances. *Id.* Although the procedural requirements imposed by the Executive Order are analogous to those under NEPA, the Executive Order does not provide a cause of action to a plaintiff seeking agency compliance with the EIS requirement. The Executive Order explicitly states that the requirements contained therein are "solely for the purpose of establishing internal procedures for Federal agencies . . . and nothing in [the Order] shall be construed to create a cause of action." E.O. 12114 § 3-1. Thus, what is at stake in this litigation is whether a federal agency may decide to take actions significantly affecting the human environment in Antarctica without complying with NEPA and without being subject to judicial review.

II.

A. The Presumption Against Extraterritoriality

As the district court correctly noted, the Supreme Court recently reaffirmed the general presumption against the extraterritorial application of statutes in *Equal Employment Opportunity Commission v. Arabian American Oil Co.*, 113 L. Ed. 2d 274, 111 S. Ct. 1227 (1991) ("*Aramco*"). Extraterritoriality is essentially, and in common sense, a jurisdictional concept concerning the authority of a nation to adjudicate the rights of particular parties and to establish the norms of conduct applicable to events or persons outside its borders. More specifically, the extraterritoriality principle provides that "rules of the United States statutory law, whether prescribed by federal or state authority, apply only to conduct occurring within, or having effect within, the territory of the United States." As stated by the Supreme Court in *Aramco*, the primary purpose of this presumption against extraterritoriality is "to protect against the unintended clashes between our laws and those of other nations which could result in international discord."

An early example of the application of the extraterritoriality principle is *American Banana Co. v. United States Fruit Co.*, 213 U.S. 347, 53 L. Ed. 826, 29 S. Ct. 511 (1909). In that case, the plaintiff alleged that the defendant, a U.S. corporation, had violated United States antitrust laws by inducing a foreign government to take actions within its own territory which were adverse to the plaintiff's business. The Supreme Court refused, in the absence of a clear statement of extraterritorial scope, to infer congressional intent to apply the federal statute to the conduct of a foreign government because enforcement would have interfered with the exercise of foreign sovereignty. . . .

There are at least three general categories of cases for which the presumption against the extraterritorial application of statutes clearly does not apply. First, as made explicit in *Aramco*, the presumption will not apply where there is an "affirmative intention of the Congress clearly expressed" to extend the scope of the statute to conduct occurring within other sovereign nations.

Second, the presumption is generally not applied where the failure to extend the scope of the statute to a foreign setting will result in adverse effects within the United States. Two prime examples of this exception are the Sherman Anti-Trust Act, 15 U.S.C. §§ 1–7 (1976), and the Lanham Trade-mark Act, 15 U.S.C. § 1051(1976), which have both been applied extraterritorially where the failure to extend the statute's reach would have negative economic consequences within the United States.

Finally, the presumption against extraterritoriality is not applicable when the conduct regulated by the government occurs within the United States. By definition, an extraterritorial application of a statute involves the regulation of conduct beyond U.S. borders. Even where the significant effects of the regulated conduct are felt outside U.S. borders, the statute itself does not present a problem of extraterritoriality, so long as the conduct which Congress seeks to regulate occurs largely within the United States.

Despite these well-established exceptions to the presumption against extraterritoriality, the district court below by-passed the threshold question of whether the application of NEPA to agency actions in Antarctica presents an extraterritoriality problem at all. In particular, the court failed to determine whether the statute seeks to regulate conduct in the United States or in another sovereign country. It also declined to consider whether NEPA would create a potential for "clashes between our laws and those of other nations" if it was applied to the decision-making of federal agencies regarding proposed actions in Antarctica. *Aramco*, 111 S. Ct. at 1230. After a thorough review of these relevant factors, we conclude that this case does not present an issue of extraterritoriality.

B. Regulated Conduct Under NEPA

NEPA is designed to control the decisionmaking process of U.S. federal agencies, not the substance of agency decisions. By enacting NEPA, Congress exercised its statutory authority to determine the factors an agency must consider when exercising its discretion, and created a process whereby American officials, while acting within the United States, can reach enlightened policy decisions by taking into account environmental effects. In our view, such regulation of U.S. federal agencies and their decisionmaking process is a legitimate exercise of Congress' territoriality-based jurisdiction, and does not raise extraterritoriality concerns.

Section 102(2)(C) lies at the heart of NEPA and is often considered the "action-forcing" element of the statute. This section requires "all agencies of the Federal Government" to prepare a detailed environmental impact statement for every "major Federal action" which has the potential to significantly affect the human environment. 42 U.S.C. § 4332(2)(C). Section 102(2)(C) binds only American officials and controls the very essence of the government function: decisionmaking. Because the decisionmaking processes of federal agencies take place almost exclusively in this country and involve the workings of the United States government, they are uniquely domestic.

NEPA, unlike many environmental statutes, does not dictate agency policy or determine the fate of contemplated action. NEPA simply mandates a particular process that must be followed by a federal agency before taking action significantly affecting the human environment. After weighing environmental considerations, an agency decisionmaker remains free to subordinate the environmental concerns revealed in the EIS to other policy concerns. As this court observed almost two decades ago, the harm against which NEPA's impact statement requirement was directed was not solely or even primarily adverse consequences to the environment; such consequences may ensue despite the fullest compliance. Rather NEPA was intended to ensure that decisions about federal actions would be made only after responsible decisionmakers had fully adverted to the environmental consequences of the actions, and had decided that the public benefits flowing from the actions outweighed their environmental costs.

Moreover, NEPA would never require enforcement in a foreign forum or involve "choice of law" dilemmas. This factor alone is powerful evidence of the statute's domestic nature, and distinguishes NEPA from Title VII as well as the Federal Tort Claims Act—two statutes that have been limited in their effect by the presumption against extraterritoriality.

In sum, since NEPA is designed to regulate conduct occurring within the territory of the United States, and imposes no substantive requirements which could be interpreted to govern conduct abroad, the presumption against extraterritoriality does not apply to this case.

C. The Unique Status of Antarctica

Antarctica's unique status in the international arena further supports our conclusion that this case does not implicate the presumption against extraterritoriality. . . . [W]here the U.S. has some real measure of legislative control over the region at issue, the presumption against extraterritoriality is much weaker. And where there is no potential for conflict "between our laws and those of other nations," the purpose behind the presumption is eviscerated, and the presumption against extraterritoriality applies with significantly less force.

. . . [I]t cannot be seriously suggested that the United States lacks some real measure of legislative control over Antarctica. The United States controls all air transportation to Antarctica and conducts all search and rescue operations there. Moreover, the United States has exclusive legislative control over McMurdo Station and other research installations established there by the United States Antarctica Program. This legislative control, taken together with the status of Antarctica as a sovereignless continent, compels the conclusion that the presumption against extraterritoriality is particularly inappropriate under the circumstances presented in this case. . . .

D. Foreign Policy Considerations

Although NSF conceded that NEPA only seeks to regulate the decisionmaking process of federal agencies, and that this case does not present a conflict between U.S. and foreign sovereign law, NSF still contends that the presumption against extraterritoriality controls this case. In particular, NSF argues that the EIS requirement will interfere with U.S. efforts to work cooperatively with other nations toward solutions to environmental problems in Antarctica. In NSF's view, joint research and cooperative environmental assessment would be "placed at risk of NEPA injunctions, making the U.S. a doubtful partner for future international cooperation in Antarctica."

NSF also argues that the Protocol on Environmental Protection to the Antarctic Treaty, which was adopted and opened for signature on October 4, 1991, would, if adopted by all the proposed signatories, conflict with the procedural requirements adopted by Congress for the decisionmaking of federal agencies under NEPA. According to NSF, since NEPA requires the preparation of an EIS for actions with potentially "significant" impacts, while the

Protocol requires an environmental analysis even for actions with "minor or transitory" impacts on the Antarctic environment, the two regulatory schemes are incompatible and will result in international discord.

We find these arguments unpersuasive. First, it should be noted that the Protocol is not in effect in any form and is years away from ratification by the United States and all 26 signatories. Second, we are unable to comprehend the difficulty presented by the two standards of review. It is clear that NSF will have to perform fewer studies under NEPA than under the Protocol, and where an EIS is required under NEPA, it would not strain a researcher's intellect to indicate in a single document how the environmental impact of the proposed action is more than "minor" and also more than "significant."

. . . [T]he government may avoid the EIS requirement where U.S. foreign policy interests outweigh the benefits derived from preparing an EIS. Since NEPA imposes no substantive requirements, U.S. foreign policy interests in Antarctica will rarely be threatened, except perhaps where the time required to prepare an EIS would itself threaten international cooperation, or where the foreign policy interests at stake are particularly unique and delicate. Thus, contrary to NSF's assertions, where U.S. foreign policy interests outweigh the benefits of the EIS requirement, NSF's efforts to cooperate with foreign governments regarding environmental practices in Antarctica will not be frustrated by forced compliance with NEPA.

E. NEPA's Plain Language and Interpretation

NSF's final argument is that even if the presumption against extraterritoriality does not apply to this case, the plain language of Section 102(2)(C) precludes its application to NSF's decisionmaking regarding proposed agency action in Antarctica. We read the plain language differently.

Section 102(2)(C), on its face, is clearly not limited to actions of federal agencies that have significant environmental effects within U.S. borders. This Court has repeatedly taken note of the sweeping scope of NEPA and the EIS requirement.

Far from employing limiting language, Section 2 states that NEPA is intended to "encourage productive and enjoyable harmony between *man and his environment*" as well as to "promote effort which will prevent or eliminate damage to the environment and *biosphere*." 42 U.S.C. § 4321(emphasis added). Clearly, Congress painted with a far greater brush than NSF is willing to apply. . . .

Section 102(2)(F) further supports the conclusion that Congress, when enacting NEPA, was concerned with worldwide as well as domestic problems facing the environment. 42 U.S.C. § 4332(2)(F)(federal agencies required to "recognize the worldwide and long-range character of environmental problems"). NSF acknowledges that Section 102(2)(F) clearly addresses international environmental problems, but argues that this section announces Congress' only requirement for agencies pursuing action in the international arena.

We find nothing in the statute which supports the construction of Section 102 urged by NSF. Apparently, NSF has chosen to ignore the clear interrelationship between the Section 102 subsections and the Section 102 mandate as a whole. Section 102 lists several requirements under NEPA for "all Federal agencies." 42 U.S.C. § 4332(2). Compliance with one of the subsections can hardly be construed to relieve the agency from its duty to fulfill the obligations articulated in other subsections. For example, compliance with Section 102(2)(G), which requires agencies to make environmental information available to the states, does not excuse an agency from preparing an EIS under Section 102(2)(C).

We also note, that prior to the issuance of Executive Order 12114, the Council on Environmental Quality ("CEQ") maintained that NEPA applies to the decisionmaking process of federal agencies regarding actions in Antarctica. CEQ is the agency created by Congress to oversee the implementation of NEPA, and its interpretation of that statute is generally entitled to "substantial deference."

Conclusion

Applying the presumption against extraterritoriality here would result in a federal agency being allowed to undertake actions significantly affecting the human environment in Antarctica, an area over which the United States has substantial interest and authority, without ever being held accountable for its failure to comply with the decisionmaking procedures instituted by Congress—even though such accountability, if it was enforced, would result in no conflict with foreign law or threat to foreign policy. NSF has provided no support for its proposition that conduct occurring within the United States is rendered exempt from otherwise applicable statutes merely because the effects of its compliance would be felt in the global commons. We therefore reverse the district court's decision, and remand for a determination of whether the environmental analysis performed by NSF, prior to its decision to resume incineration, failed to comply with Section 102(2)(C) of NEPA.

We find it important to note, however, that we do not decide today how NEPA might apply to actions in a case involving an actual foreign sovereign or how other U.S. statutes might apply to Antarctica. We only hold that the alleged failure of NSF to comply with NEPA before resuming incineration in Antarctica does not implicate the presumption against extraterritoriality.

Reversed and remanded.

NOTES AND QUESTIONS

(1) How persuasive is the court's rationale in this case? Should its reasoning be employed in other cases to hold NEPA applicable to extra-territorial U.S. governmental activities outside of Antarctica?

(2) Other federal court decisions with respect to the application of NEPA outside of the United States have been mixed. Some courts, like the D.C. Circuit in *Massey*, have exhibited willingness to apply the statute's EIS requirement to international projects. *See, e.g.*, *Sierra Club v. Coleman*, 405 F. Supp. 53 (D.D.C. 1975) (Highway Administration may not proceed with construction of highway through Columbia and Panama without considering

foreign environmental impacts of the project); *Wilderness Society v. Morton*, 463 F.2d 1261 (D.C. Cir. 1972) (Department of Interior had to consider impact of American-built pipeline on the Canadian environment in making ultimate siting decision with respect to the pipeline); *People of Enetewak v. Laird*, 353 F. Supp. 811 (D. Hawaii 1973) ("NEPA is framed in expansive language that clearly evidences a concern for all persons subject to federal action which has a major impact on the environment—not merely United States' citizens located in the fifty states.") *Id.* at 816.

(3) Other courts have been more reluctant to apply NEPA outside of U.S. borders. Thus, in *Greenpeace USA v. Stone*, 748 F. Supp. 749 (D. Hawaii 1990), the court dismissed a challenge to the U.S. Army's decision not to prepare a comprehensive EIS regarding the potential environmental impacts of the transoceanic transportation of obsolete chemical munitions. The court held that NEPA only applied within the territorial jurisdiction of the United States and should not be implemented so as to interfere with the conduct of U.S. foreign policy.

In *Public Citizens v. United States Trade Representative*, 5 F.3d 549, 23 ELR 21471 (D.C. Cir. 1993), appellees (Public Citizens) had sued the Office of United States Trade Representatives (OTR) claiming that an environmental impact statement (EIS) was required for the North Atlantic Free Trade Agreement (NAFTA). The district court granted summary judgment in favor of the plaintiff and ordered that OTR prepare an EIS forthwith. Public Citizen rested its claim for judicial review on the Administrative Procedure Act (the APA) which provides for review only of "final agency action." Prior to the district court action, OTR had completed negotiations on NAFTA. Although President Clinton had signed and released a final draft of the agreement, the Trade Acts did not obligate him to submit the draft to Congress. The President indicated that he would not do so until negotiations had been completed on several side agreements.

The court reversed. Sidestepping the issue of Congressional intent, it held that OTR's completion of NAFTA negotiations was not "final agency action" because the agreement would have no effect on Public Citizens' members unless and until the President submitted it to Congress. According to *Franklin v. Massachusetts*, 112 S.Ct. 2767, 120 L.Ed.2d 636 (1992), agency action is final under the APA only when the result of the agency's decision-making process is one that will directly affect the parties. Because the President was not obligated to submit NAFTA to Congress, his action, and not that of OTR, would directly affect Public Citizen's members. Furthermore, the President's actions were not "agency action" and thus were not reviewable under the APA.

See also Gemeinschaft zum Schutz des Berliner Baumbesstandes v. Marienthal, 9 ELR 20011 (D.D.C. 1978) in which German environmentalists sued to enjoin the U.S. Army from constructing an apartment complex in West Berlin, without first preparing an EIS. The District Court ruled that the proposed apartment complex was a German governmental project, not a federal project, and thus NEPA did not apply to it. Finding serious foreign policy issues, and a failure to present a substantial case on the merits, the court denied a preliminary injunction.

For an overview of these cases, see generally F. Grad, Treatise on Environmental Law § 9.09; D. Mandelker, NEPA Law and Litigation § 5:18 (1984 and Supp.); and Gaines, *Environmental Effects Abroad of Major Federal Actions: An Executive Order Ordains a National Policy*, 3 Harv. L. Rev. 136 (1979).

(4) In *NEPA Coalition of Japan v. Aspin*, 837 F. Supp. 466, 24 ELR 20648 (D.C. Cir. 1993), the D.C. Circuit limited the holding in *Environmental Defense Fund v. Massey* by distinguishing the legal status of military bases in Japan, which were governed by complex and long-standing treaty arrangements with a sovereign power, from the status of research stations in Antarctica. The court held that, under the presumption against extraterritoriality, the U.S. Department of Defense (DOD) was not required to prepare environmental impact studies for U.S. military bases in Japan pursuant to NEPA. The presumption against extraterritoriality is reinforced by foreign policy and treaty interests since DOD's operations and the governance of military bases in Japan are controlled by a complex treaty arrangement which includes the establishment of a committee empowered to address the plaintiffs' concerns. In the absence of clear congressional intent to apply domestic regulations overseas, the presumption against extraterritoriality is particularly strong when there is great likelihood of affecting treaty relations. The court also held that even if NEPA did apply, no EISs would be required because U.S. foreign policy interests outweigh the benefits from preparation of EISs.

(5) The issue of the extraterritorial application of federal environmental legislation has also arisen with respect to the Endangered Species Act. In *Lujan v. Defenders of Wildlife*, 504 U.S. 555, 112 S. Ct. 2130, 119 L. Ed. 2d 351 (1992), environmental organizations challenged a rule, jointly promulgated under that Act by the Secretaries of the Interior and Commerce, that rendered the statute applicable only to federal agency actions that jeopardize the continued existence or habitat of endangered or threatened species within the United States or on the high seas. The U.S. Supreme Court held that the plaintiffs lacked standing to seek judicial review of the rule. The Court rejected the plaintiffs claim that they had suffered injury because the inapplicability of the Act to certain government funded activities abroad increased the rate of extinction of endangered species. While this constituted a cognizable injury for purposes of standing, the Court reasoned, it did not show injury in fact, *i.e.*, a concrete and particularized, actual or imminent invasion of a legally protected interest.

§ 5.06 NEPA's Requirements as to Internal Agency Decisionmaking

CALVERT CLIFFS' COORDINATING COMMITTEE, INC. v. U.S. ATOMIC ENERGY COMMISSION

United States Court of Appeals, District of Columbia Circuit (1971)
449 F.2d 1109

WRIGHT, C.J.:

These cases are only the beginning of what promises to become a flood of new litigation—litigation seeking judicial assistance in protecting our natural environment. Several recently enacted statutes attest to the commitment of the Government to control, at long last, the destructive engine of material "progress." But it remains to be seen whether the promise of this legislation will become a reality. Therein lies the judicial role. In these cases, we must for the first time interpret the broadest and perhaps most important of the recent statutes: the National Environmental Policy Act of 1969 (NEPA). We must assess claims that one of the agencies charged with its administration has failed to live up to the congressional mandate. Our duty, in short, is to see that important legislative purposes, heralded in the halls of Congress, are not lost or misdirected in the vast hallways of the federal bureaucracy. . . .

I.

We begin our analysis with an examination of NEPA's structure and approach and of the Atomic Energy Commission rules which are said to conflict with the requirements of the Act. The relevant portion of NEPA is Title I, consisting of five sections. Section 101 sets forth the Act's basic substantive policy: that the federal government "use all practicable means and measures" to protect environmental values. Congress did not establish environmental protection as an exclusive goal; rather, it desired a reordering of priorities, so that environmental costs and benefits will assume their proper place along with other considerations. In Section 101(b), imposing an explicit duty on federal officials the Act provides that "it is the continuing responsibility of the Federal Government to use all practicable means, consistent with other essential considerations of national policy," to avoid environmental degradation, preserve "historic, cultural, and natural" resources, and promote "the widest range of beneficial uses of the environment without . . . undesirable and unintended consequences."

Thus the general substantive policy of the Act is a flexible one. It leaves room for a responsible exercise of discretion and may not require particular substantive results in particular problematic instances. However, the Act also contains very important "procedural" provisions—provisions which are designed to see that all federal agencies do in fact exercise the substantive discretion given them. These provisions are not highly flexible. Indeed, they establish a strict standard of compliance.

NEPA, first of all, makes environmental protection a part of the mandate of every federal agency and department. The Atomic Energy Commission, for example, had continually asserted, prior to NEPA, that it had no statutory authority to concern itself with the adverse environmental effects of its actions. Now, however, its hands are no longer tied. It is not only permitted, but compelled, to take environmental values into account. Perhaps the greatest importance of NEPA is to require the Atomic Energy Commission and other agencies to *consider* environmental issues just as they consider other matters within their mandates. This compulsion is most plainly stated in Section 102. . . .

The sort of consideration of environmental values which NEPA compels is clarified in Section 102(2)(A) and (B). In general, all agencies must use a "systematic, interdisciplinary approach" to environmental planning and evaluation "in decisionmaking which may have an impact on man's environment." In order to include all possible environmental factors in the decisional equation, agencies must "identify and develop methods and procedures . . . which will insure that presently unquantified environmental amenities and values may be given appropriate consideration in decisionmaking along with economic and technical considerations." "Environmental amenities" will often be in conflict with "economic and technical considerations." To "consider" the former "along with" the latter must involve a balancing process. In some instances environmental costs may outweigh economic and technical benefits and in other instances they may not. But NEPA mandates a rather finely tuned and "systematic" balancing analysis in each instance.

To ensure that the balancing analysis is carried out and given full effect, Section 102(2)(C) requires that responsible officials of all agencies prepare a "detailed statement" covering the impact of particular actions on the environment, the environmental costs which might be avoided, and alternative measures which might alter the cost-benefit equation. The apparent purpose of the "detailed statement" is to aid in the agencies' own decision making process and to advise other interested agencies and the public of the environmental consequences of planned federal action. Beyond the "detailed statement," Section 102(2)(D) requires all agencies specifically to "study, develop, and describe appropriate alternatives to recommended courses of action in any proposal which involves unresolved conflicts concerning alternative uses of available resources." This requirement, like the "detailed statement" requirement, seeks to ensure that each agency decision maker has before him and takes into proper account all possible approaches to a particular project (including total abandonment of the project) which would alter the environmental impact and the cost-benefit balance. Only in that fashion is it likely that the most intelligent, optimally beneficial decision will ultimately be made. Moreover, by compelling a formal "detailed statement" and a description of alternatives, NEPA provides evidence that the mandated decision making process has in fact taken place and, most importantly, allows those removed from the initial process to evaluate and balance the factors on their own.

Of course, all of these Section 102 duties are qualified by the phrase "to the fullest extent possible." We must stress as forcefully as possible that this language does not provide an escape hatch for foot-dragging agencies; it does not make NEPA's procedural requirements somehow "discretionary." Congress did not intend the Act to be such a paper tiger. Indeed, the requirement of environmental consideration "to the fullest extent possible" sets a high standard for the agencies, a standard which must be rigorously enforced by the reviewing courts.

Unlike the substantive duties of Section 101(b), which require agencies to "use all practicable means consistent with other essential considerations," the procedural duties of Section 102 must be fulfilled to the "fullest extent possible." The contrast, in itself, is revealing. But the dispositive factor in our interpretation is the expressed views of the Senate and House conferees who wrote the "fullest extent possible" language into NEPA. They stated:

> ". . . The purpose of the new language is to make it clear that each agency of the Federal Government shall comply with the directives set out in

> . . . [Section 102(2)] unless the existing law applicable to such agency's operations expressly prohibits or makes full compliance with one of the directives impossible. . . . Thus, it is the intent of the conferees that the provision 'to the fullest extent possible' shall not be used by any Federal agency as a means of avoiding compliance with the directives set out in section 102. Rather, the language in section 102 is intended to assure that all agencies of the Federal Government shall comply with the directives set out in said section 'to the fullest extent possible' under their statutory authorizations and that no agency shall utilize an excessively narrow construction of its existing statutory authorizations to avoid compliance."

Thus the Section 102 duties are not inherently flexible. They must be complied with to the fullest extent, unless there is a clear conflict of *statutory* authority.[1] Considerations of administrative difficulty, delay or economic cost will not suffice to strip the section of its fundamental importance.

We conclude, then, that Section 102 of NEPAmandates a particular sort of careful and informed decisionmaking process and creates judicially enforceable duties. The reviewing courts probably cannot reverse a substantive decision on its merits, under Section 101, unless it be shown that the actual balance of costs and benefits that was struck was arbitrary or clearly gave insufficient weight to environmental values. But if the decision was reached procedurally without individualized consideration and balancing of environmental factors—conducted fully and in good faith—it is the responsibility of the courts to reverse. As one District Court has said of Section 102 requirements: "It is hard to imagine a clearer or stronger mandate to the Courts."

In the cases before us now, we do not have to review a particular decision by the Atomic Energy Commission granting a construction permit or an operating license. Rather, we must review the Commission's recently promulgated rules which govern consideration of environmental values in all such individual decisions. The rules were devised strictly in order to comply with the NEPA procedural requirements—but petitioners argue that they fall far short of the congressional mandate.

The period of the rules' gestation does not indicate overenthusiasm on the Commission's part. NEPA went into effect on January 1, 1970. On April 2,

---

[1] Section 104 of NEPAprovides that the Act does not eliminate any duties already imposed by other "specific statutory obligations." Only when such specific obligations conflict with NEPA do agencies have a right under § 104 and the "fullest extent possible" language to dilute their compliance with the full letter and spirit of the Act. *See* text at page 1123 *infra*. Sections 103 and 105 also support the general interpretation that the "fullest extent possible" language exempts agencies from full compliance only when there is a conflict of statutory obligations. Section 103 provides for agency review of existing obligations in order to discover and, if possible, correct any conflicts. And § 105 provides that "[t]he policies and goals set forth in this Act are supplementary to those set forth in existing authorization of Federal agencies." The report of the House conferees states that § 105 "does not . . . obviate the requirement that the Federal agencies conduct their activities in accordance with the provisions of this bill unless to do so would clearly violate their existing statutory obligations." 115 Cong. Rec. (Part 29) at 39703. The section-by-section analysis by the Senate conferees makes exactly the same point in slightly different language. 115 Cong. Rec. (Part 30) at 40418. The guidelines published by the Council on Environmental Quality state that "[t]he phrase 'to the fullest extent possible' . . . is meant to make clear that each agency of the Federal Government shall comply with the requirement unless existing law applicable to the agency's operations expressly prohibits or makes compliance impossible." 36 Fed. Reg. at 7724.

1970—three months later—the Commission issued its first, short policy statement on implementation of the Act's procedural provisions. After another span of two months, the Commission published a notice of proposed rule making in the Federal Register. Petitioners submitted substantial comments critical of the proposed rules. Finally, on December 3, 1970, the Commission terminated its long rule making proceeding by issuing a formal amendment, labeled Appendix D, to its governing regulations. Appendix D is a somewhat revised version of the earlier proposal and, at last, commits the Commission to consider environmental impact in its decision making process.

The procedure for environmental study and consideration set up by the Appendix D rules is as follows: Each applicant for an initial construction permit must submit to the Commission his own "environmental report," presenting his assessment of the environmental impact of the planned facility and possible alternatives which would alter the impact. When construction is completed and the applicant applies for a license to operate the new facility, he must again submit an "environmental report" noting any factors which have changed since the original report. At each stage, the Commission's regulatory staff must take the applicant's report and prepare its own "detailed statement" of environmental costs, benefits and alternatives. The statement will then be circulated to other interested and responsible agencies and made available to the public. After comments are received from those sources, the staff must prepare a final "detailed statement" and make a final recommendation on the application for a construction permit or operating license.

Up to this point in the Appendix D rules petitioners have raised no challenge. However, they do attack four other, specific parts of the rules which, they say, violate the requirements of Section 102 of NEPA. Each of these parts in some way limits full consideration and individualized balancing of environmental values in the Commission's decision making process. (1) Although environmental factors must be considered by the agency's regulatory staff under the rules, such factors need not be considered by the hearing board conducting an independent review of staff recommendations, unless affirmatively raised by outside parties or staff members. (2) Another part of the procedural rules prohibits any such party from raising nonradiological environmental issues at any hearing if the notice for that hearing appeared in the Federal Register before March 4, 1971. (3) Moreover, the hearing board is prohibited from conducting an independent evaluation and balancing of certain environmental factors if other responsible agencies have already certified that their own environmental standards are satisfied by the proposed federal action. (4) Finally, the Commission's rules provide that when a construction permit for a facility has been issued before NEPA compliance was required and when an operating license has yet to be issued, the agency will not formally consider environmental factors or require modifications in the proposed facility until the time of the issuance of the operating license. Each of these parts of the Commission's rules will be described at greater length and evaluated under NEPA in the following sections of this opinion.

NEPA makes only one specific reference to consideration of environmental values in agency review processes. Section 102(2)(C) provides that copies of the staff's "detailed statement" and comments thereon "shall accompany the proposal through the existing agency review processes." The Atomic Energy Commission's rules may seem in technical compliance with the letter of that provision. They state:

> "12. If any party to a proceeding . . . raises any [environmental] issue . . . the Applicant's Environmental Report and the Detailed Statement will be offered in evidence. The atomic safety and licensing board will make finding of fact on, and resolve, the matters in controversy among the parties with regard to those issues. Depending on the resolution of those issues, the permit or license may be granted, denied, or appropriately conditioned to protect environmental values.
>
> "13. When no party to a proceeding . . . raises any [environmental] issue . . . such issues will not be considered by the atomic safety and licensing board. Under such circumstances, although the Applicant's Environmental Report, comments thereon, and the Detailed Statement will accompany the application through the Commission's review processes, they will not be received in evidence, and the Commission's responsibilities under the National Environmental Policy Act of 1969 will be carried out in toto outside the hearing process."

The question here is whether the Commission is correct in thinking that its NEPA responsibilities may "be carried out in toto outside the hearing process"—whether it is enough that environmental data and evaluation merely "accompany" an application through the review process, but receive no consideration whatever from the hearing board.

We believe that the Commission's crabbed interpretation of NEPA makes a mockery of the Act. What possible purpose could there be in the Section 102(2)(C) requirement (that the "detailed statement" accompany proposals through agency review processes) if "accompany" means no more than physical proximity—mandating no more than the physical act of passing certain folders and papers, unopened, to reviewing officials along with other folders and papers? What possible purpose could there be in requiring the "detailed statement" to be before hearing boards, if the boards are free to ignore entirely the contents of the statement? NEPA was meant to do more than regulate the flow of papers in the federal bureaucracy. The word "accompany" in Section 102(2)(C) must not be read so narrowly as to make the Act ludicrous. It must, rather, be read to indicate a congressional intent that environmental factors, as compiled in the "detailed statement," be *considered* through agency review processes.[2] Beyond Section 102(2)(C), NEPA requires that agencies consider the environmental impact of their actions "to the fullest extent possible." The Act is addressed to agencies as a whole, not only to their professional staffs. Compliance to the "*fullest*" possible extent would seem to demand

[2] The guidelines issued by the Council on Environmental Quality emphasizes the importance of consideration of alternatives to staff recommendations during the agency review process: "A rigorous exploration and objective evaluation of alternative actions that might avoid some or all of the adverse environmental effects is essential. Sufficient analysis of such alternatives and their costs and impact on the environment should accompany the proposed action through the agency review process in order not to foreclose prematurely options which might have less detrimental effects." 36 Fed. Reg. at 7725. The Council also states that an objective of its guidelines is "to assist agencies in implementing not only the letter, but the spirit, of the Act." *Id.* at 7724.

that environmental issues be considered at every important stage in the decision making process concerning a particular action—at every stage where an overall balancing of environmental and nonenvironmental factors is appropriate and where alterations might be made in the proposed action to minimize environmental costs. Of course, consideration which is entirely duplicative is not necessarily required. But independent review of staff proposals by hearing boards is hardly a duplicative function. A truly independent review provides a crucial check on the staff's recommendations. The Commission's hearing boards automatically consider nonenvironmental factors, even though they have been previously studied by the staff. Clearly, the review process is an appropriate stage at which to balance conflicting factors against one another. And, just as clearly, it provides an important opportunity to reject or significantly modify the staff's recommended action. Environmental factors, therefore, should not be singled out and excluded, at this stage, from the proper balance of values envisioned by NEPA.

The Commission's regulations provide that in an uncontested proceeding the hearing board shall on its own "determine whether the application and the record of the proceeding contain sufficient information, and the review of the application by the Commission's regulatory staff has been adequate, to support affirmative findings on" various environmental factors. NEPA requires at least as much automatic consideration of environmental factors. In uncontested hearings, the board need not necessarily go over the same ground covered in the "detailed statement." But it must at least examine the statement carefully to determine whether "the review . . . by the Commission's regulatory staff has been adequate." And it must independently consider the final balance among conflicting factors that is struck in the staff's recommendation.

The rationale of the Commission's limitation of environmental issues to hearings in which parties affirmatively raise those issues may have been one of economy. It may have been supposed that, whenever there are serious environmental costs overlooked or uncorrected by the staff, some party will intervene to bring those costs to the hearing board's attention. Of course, independent review of the "detailed statement" and independent balancing of factors in an uncontested hearing will take some time. If it is done properly, it will take a significant amount of time. But all of the NEPA procedures take time. Such administrative costs are not enough to undercut the Act's requirement that environmental protection be considered "to the fullest extent possible". . . . It is, moreover, unrealistic to assume that there will always be an intervenor with the information, energy and money required to challenge a staff recommendation which ignores environmental costs. NEPA established environmental protection as an integral part of the Atomic Energy Commission's basic mandate. The primary responsibility for fulfilling that mandate lies with the Commission. Its responsibility is not simply to sit back, like an umpire, and resolve adversary contentions at the hearing stage. Rather, it must itself take the initiative of considering environmental values at every distinctive and comprehensive stage of the process beyond the staff's evaluation and recommendation.

III.

Congress passed the final version of NEPA in late 1969, and the Act went into full effect on January 1, 1970. Yet the Atomic Energy Commission's rules prohibit any consideration of environmental issues by its hearing boards at proceedings officially noted before March 4, 1971. This is 14 months after the effective date of NEPA. And the hearings affected may go on for as much as a year longer until final action is taken. The result is that major federal actions having a significant environmental impact may be taken by the Commission, without full NEPA compliance, more than two years after the Act's effective date. In view of the importance of environmental consideration during the agency review process, *see* Part II *supra*, such a time lag is shocking.

The Commission explained that its very long time lag was intended "to provide an orderly period of transition in the conduct of the Commission's regulatory proceedings and to avoid unreasonable delays in the construction and operation of nuclear power plants urgently needed to meet the national requirements for electric power." Before this court, it has claimed authority for its action, arguing that "the statute did not lay down detailed guidelines and inflexible timetables for its implementations, and we find in it no bar to agency provisions which are designed to accommodate transitional implementation problems."

Again, the Commission's approach to statutory interpretation is strange indeed—so strange that it seems to reveal a rather thorough-going reluctance to meet the NEPA procedural obligations in the agency review process, the stage at which deliberation is most open to public examination and subject to the participation of public intervenors. The Act, it is true, lacks an "inflexible timetable" for its implementation. But it does have a clear effective date, consistently enforced by reviewing courts up to now. Every federal court having faced the issues has held that the procedural requirements of NEPA must be met in order to uphold federal action taken after January 1, 1970. The absence of a "timetable" for compliance has never been held sufficient, in itself, to put off the date on which a congressional mandate takes effect. The absence of a "timetable," rather, indicates that compliance is required forthwith.

The only part of the Act which even implies that implementation may be subject, in some case, to some significant delay is Section 103. . . .

The actual review of existing statutory authority and regulations cannot be a particularly lengthy process for experienced counsel of a federal agency. Of course, the Atomic Energy Commission discovered no obstacle to NEPA implementation. Although it did not report its conclusion to the President until October 2, 1970, that nine-month delay (January to October) cannot justify so long a period of noncompliance with the Act. It certainly cannot justify a further delay of compliance until March 4, 1971.

No doubt the process of formulating procedural rules to implement NEPA takes some time. Congress cannot have expected that federal agencies would immediately begin considering environmental issues on January 1, 1970. But the effective date of the Act does set a time for agencies to begin adopting rules and it demands that they strive, "to the fullest extent possible," to be prompt in the process. The Atomic Energy Commission has failed in this regard. Consideration of environmental issues in the agency review process, for example, is quite clearly compelled by the Act. The Commission cannot justify its 11-month delay in adopting rules on this point as part of a difficult, discretionary effort to decide whether or not its hearing boards should deal with environmental questions at all.

Even if the long delay had been necessary, however, the Commission would not be relieved of all NEPA responsibility to hold public hearings on the environmental consequences of actions taken between January 1, 1970 and final adoption of the rules. Although the Act's effective date may not requre instant compliance, it must at least require that NEPA procedures, once established, be applied to consider prompt alterations in the plans or operations of facilities approved without compliance. Yet the Commission's rules contain no such provision. Indeed, they do not even apply to the hearings still being conducted at the time of their adoption on December 3, 1970—or, for that matter, to hearings initiated in the following three months. The delayed compliance date of March 4, 1971, then, cannot be justified by the Commission's long drawn out rule making process.

Strangely, the Commission has principally relied on more pragmatic arguments. It seems an unfortunate affliction of large organizations to resist new procedures and to envision massive roadblocks to their adoption. Hence the Commission's talk of the need for an "orderly transition" to the NEPA procedures. It is difficult to credit the Commission's argument that several months were needed to work the consideration of environmental values into its review process. Before the enactment of NEPA, the Commission already had regulations requiring that hearings include health, safety and radiological matters. The introduction of environmental matters cannot have presented a radically unsettling problem. And, in any event, the obvious sense of urgency on the part of Congress should make clear that a transition, however "orderly," must proceed at a pace faster than a funeral procession.

In the end, the Commission's long delay seems based upon what it believes to be a pressing national power crisis. Inclusion of environmental issues in pre-March 4, 1971 hearings might have held up the licensing of some power plants for a time. But the very purpose of NEPA was to tell federal agencies that environmental protection is as much a part of their responsibility as is protection and promotion of the industries they regulate. Whether or not the specter of a national power crisis is as real as the Commission apparently believes, it must not be used to create a blackout of environmental consideration in the agency review process. NEPA compels a case-by-case examination and balancing of discrete factors. Perhaps there may be cases in which the need for rapid licensing of a particular facility would justify a strict time limit on a hearing board's review of environmental issues; but a blanket banning of such issues until March 4, 1971 is impermissible under NEPA.

IV.

The sweep of NEPA is extraordinarily broad, compelling consideration of any and all types of environmental impact of federal action. However, the

Atomic Energy Commission's rules specifically exclude from full consideration a wide variety of environmental issues. First, they provide that no party may raise and the Commission may not independently examine any problem of water quality—perhaps the most significant impact of nuclear power plants. Rather, the Commission indicates that it will defer totally to water quality standards devised and administered by state agencies and approved by the federal government under the Federal Water Pollution Control Act. Secondly, the rules provide for similar abdication of NEPA authority to the standards of other agencies.

. . . .

VI.

We hold that, in the . . . respects detailed above, the Commission must revise its rules governing consideration of environmental issues. We do not impose a harsh burden on the Commission. For we require only an exercise of substantive discretion which will protect the environment "to the fullest extent possible." No less is required if the grand congressional purposes underlying NEPA are to become a reality.

Remanded for proceedings consistent with this opinion.

NOTES AND QUESTIONS

(1) *Calvert Cliffs* is a seminal case in NEPA law. It was the first major case to reach the courts following enactment of the statute, as well as the first attempt by a United States Court of Appeals to interpret NEPA's mandate. In part for that reason, Judge Wright's emphatic and frequently cited opinion was the major pronouncement on NEPA until the second half of the 1970's, when the U.S. Supreme Court began to construe the legislation. Did Judge Wright's opinion set an appropriate tone for judicial interpretation of NEPA? Do you agree with the distinction it makes between the procedural and the substantive duties that the statute establishes for federal agencies and departments?

(2) Who must take responsibility for the actual preparation of the EIS? The statute, in § 102, requires each agency to prepare the EIS and refers to "the responsible Federal official." From early on, the question of the permissibility of delegating the preparation of the EIS had been discussed, and a conflict of judicial views had developed on the subject. The holding that a delegation to another agency—such as a state power authority—was impermissible was pronounced in *Greene County Planning Board v. Federal Power Commission*, 455 F.2d 412 (2d Cir. 1972), *cert. denied*, 409 U.S. 849 (1972), which provided a thorough analysis of the subject, stressing the need for a coherent, comprehensive environmental analysis by the responsible agency itself. The *Greene* case and the split of authority led to an amendment to NEPA in 1975, Pub. L. No. 94-83, 89 Stat. 424, which added a new subdivision, § 102(1)(D), which permits the delegation of EIS preparation to a state agency of statewide jurisdiction which has authority over the action, if the responsible federal official furnishes guidance and participates in the preparation, and if the federal

official independently evaluates the statement prior to its approval and adoption.

(3) Delegation of EIS preparation to a private contractor is also permissible. *See Life of the Land v. Brinegar*, 485 F.2d 460 (9th Cir. 1973). In fact, such delegation is routine with respect to EIS preparation for a National Pollution Discharge Elimination System (NPDES) permit; usually the applicant allows EPA (which will ultimately review the EIS and the permit application) to select the consulting firm. In other cases, the agency solicits consultants itself. Federal procurement requirements do not apply. 40 C.F.R. § 1506.5. The consulting firm must disclose any financial interest it may have in the outcome of the EIS or the project. *See* CEQ, *Forty Most Asked Questions Concerning CEQ's National Environmental Policy Act Regulations*, reprinted in CEQ, *Environmental Quality—Twelfth Annual Report* 261 (Question 16, page 267) (1981). It is important to note that CEQ regulations are quite specific with respect to federal agency responsibility for an EIS prepared by a contractor. Section 1506.5(c) sates that "the responsible federal official shall furnish guidance and participate in the preparation and shall independently evaluate the statement prior to its approval and take responsibility for its scope and contents."

(4) *Lead Agency*. When more than one agency is involved in proposing or implementing an action, NEPA regulations provide for the designation of a "lead agency" (40 C.F.R. § 1501.5), with the designation decided by consensus, or in the case of dispute, with the aid of the Council on Environmental Quality (CEQ). The lead agency must solicit cooperation from other federal agencies that have legal authority or substantive expertise in the area of the proposed action and arrange for cooperation with state and local authorities as well. Cooperating agencies assume responsibility for allocating staff and resource information at the lead agency's request. 40 C.F.R. § 1501.6states that the "purpose of this section is to emphasize agency cooperation early in the NEPA process." If a cooperating agency is unable to allocate the needed resources, it may opt out of the EIS process, but only by agreeing to opt out of the project for federal action as well. 40 C.F.R. § 1501.6(c).

The lead agency is responsible for determining the depth and scope of the EIS. "Scoping," as explained in 40 C.F.R. § 1501.7, is a process by which the lead and cooperating agencies (and, by invitation and Federal Register Notice, any number of other agencies, state and local officials and interested parties) determine "the significant issues to be analyzed in depth in the environmental impact statement, identify and eliminate from detailed study the issues which are not significant or which have been covered by prior environmental review . . . allocate assignment for preparation of the environmental impact statement among the lead and cooperating agencies . . . indicate any public environmental assessments and other environmental impact statements which are being or will be prepared that are related to but are not part of the impact statement under consideration . . . ." Once a draft EIS is completed, cooperating agencies are obligated to comment on those issues within their jurisdiction by law or special expertise.

The federal agency is not relieved of its responsibilities for the scope, objectivity or content of the EIS. *See Conservation Society of Southern*

Vermont, Inc. v. Secretary of Transportation, 531 F.2d 637 (2d Cir. 1976); *Colony Federal Savings and Loan Association v. Harris*, 482 F. Supp. 296 (N.D. Pa. 1980).

(5) *Procedures*. Regulations promulgated by the Council on Environmental Quality (CEQ) set forth specific steps that federal agencies and departments must follow in complying with NEPA. Initially, the agency or department must determine the "scope" of the issues to be addressed by the EIS. 40 C.F.R. § 1501.7. It must then publish a "notice of intent" inviting participation in the EIS-process by interested persons, private proponents of the proposed action or project, Indian tribes, and interested federal, state and local agencies.

An EIS is then prepared in draft form and reviewed (and sometimes revised) internally. The draft EIS must be sent to the EPA, as well as to any other federal agencies with jurisdiction or special expertise on the environmental effects of the proposed action or project. 40 C.F.R. § 1503.1; Clean Air Act § 309; 42 U.S.C. § 7609. If EPA and/or another agency object to the draft EIS, and the proposing agency does not modify the document to accede to those intra-governmental objections, the objecting agency may refer the matter to the CEQ for resolution. 40 C.F.R. § 1504. This rarely occurs in practice, however.

The agency or department preparing an EIS is also obligated to seek comments from "those persons or organizations who may be interested or effected." 40 C.F.R. § 1503.1. These entities frequently include state and local governments, Indian tribes and environmental organizations, among others. Public participation is an important aspect of the EIS process and federal agencies and departments are required to "[e]ncourage and facilitate public involvement to the fullest extent possible." 40 C.F.R. § 1500.2(d). (*See also* 40 C.F.R. § 1506.6for the specific and detailed public notice and participation procedures required by CEQ's regulations).

In preparing a final EIS, the federal agency or department must take account of the comments it has received. Specifically, it must "discuss at appropriate points in the final statement any responsible opposing view which was not adequately discussed in the draft statement and . . . indicate the agency's response to the issues raised." 40 C.F.R. §§ 1502.9(b); 1503.4. Generally, before proceeding to a final EIS, the agency must allow at least 45 days for comments on its draft EIS. Moreover, it may not make a final decision on the proposed project or action until at least 90 days following publication of its notice of the draft EIS. 40 C.F.R. § 1506.10(b). The CEQ regulations also prescribe a minimum 30-day period for public comment on the final EIS. 40 C.F.R. § 1506.10(b)(2)(d).

Finally, after the agency or department has made a final decision to adopt the action or proposal in question, it must prepare a Record of Decision identifying alternatives to the action to be taken, and indicating "whether all practicable means to avoid or minimize environmental harm from the alternative selected have been adopted and, if not, why they were not." 40 C.F.R. § 1502.2.

(6) *Contents and Adequacy of the EIS*. Much NEPA litigation has involved judicial review of the adequacy of environmental impact statements prepared

by a federal department or agency. These cases involve judicial determinations as to whether the EIS in issue: "provides decision-makers with an environmental disclosure sufficiently detailed to aid in the substantive decision whether to proceed with the project in light of its environmental consequences." *Trout Unlimited v. Morton*, 509 F.2d 1276 (9th Cir. 1974).

Most courts place the burden on plaintiffs of proving affirmatively the inadequacy of any EIS they challenge; and, in general, the courts have been reluctant to remand final EISs back to the agencies that have prepared them on inadequacy grounds, particularly where those EISs have noted (and responded to) opposing viewpoints. *See, e.g.*, *Lange v. Brinegar*, 625 F.2d 812 (9th Cir. 1980); *Warm Springs Dam Task Force v. Gribble*, 621 F.2d 1017 (9th Cir. 1980); *National Indian Youth Council v. Andrus*, 501 F. Supp. 60 (D. N.M. 1980). On the other hand, however, some challenges to the adequacy of final EISs have been successful. *See, e.g.*, *Coalition for Canyon Preservation v. Bowers*, 632 F.2d 774 (9th Cir. 1980).

(7) Should agency violations of the procedural standards of NEPA be the basis for a preliminary injunction halting further work on the activity or project in issue until compliance is achieved? Increasingly, notwithstanding the D.C. Circuit's opinion in *Calvert Cliffs*, federal courts have been reluctant to delay the completion of federal actions on that basis. In your view, is this appropriate?

§ 5.07 Contents of EIS's; Consideration of Alternatives

ENVIRONMENTAL DEFENSE FUND v. CORPS OF ENGINEERS (GILLHAM DAM)

United States Court of Appeals, Eighth Circuit (1972)
470 F.2d 289

MATTHEWS, C.J.:

This is another of the rapidly increasing number of cases which are focused in large part upon, and result from the adoption of, the National Environmental Policy Act (NEPA), 42 U.S.C. §§ 4321–4347, which was passed by the Congress of the United States in December, 1969, and became effective January 1, 1970.

This litigation was triggered by the construction of a project known as Gillham Dam on the Cossatot River in Arkansas. The case is here on appeal by plaintiffs from the final order of the United States District Court, Eastern District of Arkansas, dissolving an injunction entered by that court on February 19, 1971, and dismissing the case.

I. HISTORY OF THE PROJECT

Judge Eisele has recorded a clear and graphic description of the Cossatot River and its environs, and we are not inclined to attempt to improve on what has been written. *See* 325 F. Supp. at 744–745. We are content to pinpoint the subject by making a few observations which lie at the heart of the controversy over the Gillham project.

During normal water stage the Cossatot, like many mountainous streams, is a valuable asset to man. The splendor of the scenery is magnificent. The clean water attracts many species of game fish, and wildlife abounds in the area. Fishermen, hunters and outdoor enthusiasts frequent the region; the rapids and pools challenge canoeists. But there is another side to the coin. When heavy rains descend in the Ouichita Mountain Range, as they have from time immemorial, the normal flow of water in the Cossatot becomes a raging torrent and the floods become an enemy to man. Thus, competing forces have aligned themselves for and against the dam. In part, the proponents are interested in controlling the floods, creating the recreational facilities and commercial development which accompany man-made lakes, and supplying pure water to the City of DeQueen, Arkansas. The opponents advance, among other arguments, the value of conserving one of the few remaining free-flowing rivers in southwest Arkansas, the sports of stream fishing and hunting, and the diversity of canoeing experiences.

Gillham Dam is a part of a massive flood control plan authorized by Congress in the Flood Control Act of 1958. The subject dam is one of seven authorized to be constructed in the Little River Basin. Of these, three have been completed, and three, including Gillham, are under construction. The Gillham project is designed to provide flood control, water supply and water quality control. Funds for construction were initially made available by the Public Works Appropriation Act of 1963. Work began in 1963, and Congress has since regularly funded the project, including appropriations of 1.5 million dollars for fiscal year 1973. As of September 1, 1970, the project was approximately two-thirds complete at a cost of 9.8 million dollars. Total project cost is estimated at 15.3 million dollars. While the spillway and outlet works have been substantially constructed, the dam itself remains to be built. At full flood control pool, which will occur on the average of once in twenty-five years, the reservoir created by the dam would inundate 13.5 miles of the Cossatot River and 4,680 acres of surrounding countryside. At top of conservation pool, sometimes referred to as "normal pool," the reservoir would inundate 7.7 miles of river and 1,370 acres of land.

II. HISTORY OF THE LITIGATION

The complaint was filed in the United States District Court on October 1, 1970.

. . . .

The district court dealt with the case in a series of six memorandum opinions filed over a period of one and one-half years. The first opinion held venue was proper. 325 F. Supp. 728 (Nov. 16, 1970). The second considered jurisdiction over the defendants and the subject matter, standing, and failure of the complaint to state a claim upon which relief could be granted. 325 F. Supp. 732 (Dec. 22, 1970). The third denied a preliminary injunction since plaintiffs had failed to demonstrate danger of imminent harm. 325 F. Supp. 737 (Dec. 22, 1970). In its fourth memorandum opinion, the court found that

NEPA was intended to be applied not only to contemplated agency action, but also to ongoing projects. 325 F. Supp. 741 (Jan. 21, 1971). The case was tried to the court on the merits on February 8, 9 and 10, 1971. In the fifth memorandum opinion, 325 F. Supp. 749 (Feb. 19, 1971), the court found that of the eleven claims for relief set forth in the complaint, only the two premised upon NEPA, claims one and eleven, were sufficient to grant relief. Accordingly, claims two through ten were dismissed. The court went on to find that defendants had not complied with the provisions of NEPA which require a detailed statement of the environmental impact of the project and a development of appropriate alternatives to the proposed course of action. Therefore, the court enjoined defendants from proceeding further with the Gillham Dam project unless and until they fully complied with the Act. Both parties appealed to this court, but the appeals were dismissed by agreement on July 22, 1971.

On January 13, 1972, defendants filed with the district court the new environmental impact statement (EIS) and simultaneously filed a motion for summary judgment in which they requested the court to dissolve and set aside the injunction theretofore granted. After an evidentiary hearing on April 27 and 28, 1972, the court approved the new impact statement, granted summary judgment for defendants and dissolved the injunction. The court's supporting opinion, the sixth one filed, is reported at 342 F. Supp. 1211 (May 5, 1972). It is from this final order that plaintiffs bring the present appeal.

Appellants contend that, contrary to the conclusion of the district court, appellees have not sufficiently complied with NEPA for the following reasons: (1) the objectivity of the final EIS was tainted by the alleged bias of its draftor; (2) the final EIS makes a less-than-full disclosure and contains important errors of fact; (3) the defendants have failed to study, develop and describe appropriate alternatives; and (4) the administrative determination by defendants that the dam should be constructed was reviewable by the court on the merits.

III. NATIONAL ENVIRONMENTAL POLICY ACT OF 1969

. . . .

IV. ADEQUACY OF THE FINAL ENVIRONMENTAL IMPACT STATEMENT

Appellants argue that the final EIS filed by the Corps falls short of the "detailed statement" required by § 102(2)(C) of NEPAfor two reasons: (1) the statement contains an inadequate and inaccurate disclosure of fact; and (2) the statement lacks objectivity either on its face or because of the alleged bias of the District Director responsible for its preparation. We disagree.

The final EIS submitted by the Corps of Engineers in this case was prepared at an alleged cost of approximately $250,000, and is 200 pages in length. Attached to the statements are six appendices containing an additional 1500 pages.

. . . .

We have read the statement and found it to contain a full and accurate disclosure of the information required by § 102(2)(C).

Nevertheless, appellants contend that the EIS is partial and biased, either on its face or as the work product of a biased agency official. The latter claim is based upon statements allegedly made by Colonel Vernon W. Pinkey, District Engineer in charge of preparing the EIS until his retirement, before a local Chamber of Commerce meeting, assuring his listeners that the Gillham Dam would definitely be built.

We agree with appellants, as did the district court, that NEPA "requires the agencies of the United States government to objectively evaluate their projects." 342 F. Supp. at 1222. However, we do not agree with the view implicit in the contentions of the appellants that NEPA requires agency officials to be subjectively impartial. The purpose of the procedural requirements of § 102 is:

> "to ensure that each agency decision maker has before him and takes into proper account all possible approaches to a particular project (including total abandonment of the project) which would alter the environmental impact and the cost-benefit balance. Only in that fashion is it likely that the most intelligent, optimally beneficial decision will ultimately be made. Moreover, by compelling a formal 'detailed statement' and a description of alternatives, NEPA provides evidence that the mandated decision making process has in fact taken place and, most importantly, allows those removed from the initial process to evaluate and balance the factors on their own." *Calvert Cliff's Coordinating Committee v. U.S. Atomic Energy Commission*, 449 F.2d 1109, 114 (D.C. Cir. 1971).

Thus, NEPA assumes as inevitable an institutional bias within an agency proposing a project and erects the procedural requirements of § 102 to insure that "there is no way [the decision maker] can fail to note the facts and understand the very serious arguments advanced by the plaintiffs if he carefully reviews the entire environmental impact statement." 342 F. Supp. at 1218. An institutional bias will most often be found when the project has been partially completed. Several courts have held that an agency involved in an ongoing federal project may approach the required compliance with § 102 differently from what might be required with respect to new projects. Here, the Gillham Dam project was almost two-thirds complete when the procedural requirements of NEPA went into effect on January 1, 1970. The federal funds expended, nearly ten million dollars, could not, in large part, be recouped if the project were abandoned. The Council on Environmental Quality (CEQ) has recognized that it may become impracticable to reassess the basic course of action where the project was initiated prior to the effective date of NEPA.[1] Accordingly, in the words of Judge Eisele:

---

[1] Guidelines for Federal Agencies under the National Environmental Policy Act, 36Fed. Reg. 7724, 7727 (1971):

> "11. *Application of section 102(2)(C) procedures to existing projects and programs.* To the maximum extent practicable the Section 102(2)(C) procedure should be applied to further major federal actions having a significant effect on the environment even though they arise from projects or programs initiated prior to enactment of the Act on January 1, 1970. Where it is not practicable to reassess the basic course of action, it is still important that further

"it is possible for federal officials and federal employees to comply in good faith with [NEPA] even though they personally oppose its philosophy, are 'anti-environmentalists,' and have unshakable, preconceived attitudes and opinions as to the 'rightness' of the project under consideration." 342 F. Supp. at 1223.

The test of compliance with § 102, then, is one of good faith objectivity rather than subjective impartiality.

Employing this standard, we are satisfied that the district court's findings and conclusions as to the objectivity of the EIS are supported by substantial evidence. Therefore we decline to hold that appellees have not complied in good faith with the procedural requirements of § 102(2)(C).

V. DEVELOPMENT OF ALTERNATIVES

Appellants also contend that appellees have failed to develop important and reasonable alternatives to the proposed dam project, in violation of § 102(2)(D) of NEPA. Section 102(2)(D) requires that the agency "study, develop, and describe appropriate alternatives to recommended courses of action in any proposal which involves unresolved conflicts concerning alternative uses of available resources." This provision follows and is in addition to the § 102(2)(C) requirement of a detailed statement discussing, *inter alia*, alternatives to the proposed action. This is not to suggest, however, that the more extensive treatment of alternatives required by § 102(2)(D) cannot be incorporated in the EIS. Indeed, "it is the essence and thrust of NEPA that the pertinent Statement serve to gather in one place a discussion of the relative environmental impact of alternatives." *National Resources Defense Council v. Morton*, 458 F.2d 827, 834 (D.C. Cir. 1972). So too, the guidelines to the federal agencies issued by the CEQ explain the import of § 102(2)(D) under the general heading "Content of Environmental Statement." 36 Fed. Reg. 7724, 7725 (1971). The guidelines suggest:

"A rigorous exploration and objective evaluation of alternative actions that might avoid some or all of the adverse environmental effects is essential. Sufficient analysis of such alternatives and their costs and impact on the environment should accompany the proposed action through the agency review process in order not to foreclose prematurely options which might have less detrimental effects."

Defendants have devoted thirty-seven pages of the 200-page impact statement to the discussion of alternatives, among them, total abandonment of the project. Particular attention is given to the suggestion that the Cossatot be preserved as a scenic river under the National Wild and Scenic Rivers Act. 16 U.S.C. § 1271 *et seq.* The economic benefits and environmental impact of each alternative are developed in great detail.

Again, we concur in the finding of the district court, implicit in its opinion, that the EIS contains the study, development and description of reasonable alternatives required by § 102(2)(D).

---

incremental major actions be shaped so as to minimize adverse environmental consequences. It is also important in further action that account be taken of the environmental consequences not fully evaluated at the outset of the project or program."

. . . .

We therefore affirm the judgment of the trial court for the reasons set forth in the opinion. Costs will be taxed equally to the parties.

NOTES AND QUESTIONS

(1) Do you agree with the Eighth Circuit's conclusion that the Corps of Engineers had complied with NEPA in the *Gillham Dam* case even though the Corps' District Engineer had publicly stated that Gillham Dam would "definitely be built?" Is the court's approach, on this point, consistent with the analysis given by the D.C. Circuit, in the *Calvert Cliffs'* case, regarding the obligation of federal agencies and departments to comply with NEPA's procedural directives "to the fullest extent possible?"

(2) NEPA stresses the exploration of alternatives to federal agency actions by referring to the subject twice within the Act. In addition to the mandate of § 102(2)(C)(iii) that environmental impact statements contain a discussion of "alternatives to the proposed action," § 102(2)(E) requires federal agencies and departments to "study, develop and describe appropriate alternatives to recommended courses of action in any proposal which involves unresolved conflicts concerning alternative uses of available resources." Some judicial decisions have given the latter requirement an independent effect. Can you see any reason why the statute includes two separate requirements that alternatives be considered?

(3) The question of alternatives is challenging because, as has been pointed out, they are potentially unlimited in number. Is "no action" a viable alternative that must be considered? As between a number of feasible alternatives, who ought to decide the one to rely on—the agency or the court? Under NEPA, is there any requirement that the optimum alternative be chosen, or is it merely required that a broad range of alternatives be considered?

(4) The CEQ's NEPA regulations provide federal agencies and departments with some direction as to how to analyze alternatives to proposed actions in EISs. They state, in relevant part:

40 C.F.R. § 1502.14Alternatives Including the Proposed Action

This section is the heart of the environmental impact statement. Based on the information and analysis presented in the sections on the Affected Environment (§ 1502.15) and the Environmental Consequences (§ 1502.16), it should present the environment impacts of the proposal and the alternatives in comparative form, thus sharply defining the issues and providing a clear basis for choice among options by the decisionmaker and the public. In this section agencies shall:

(a) Rigorously explore and objectively evaluate all reasonable alternatives, and for alternatives which were eliminated from detailed study, briefly discuss the reasons for their having been eliminated.

(b) Devote substantial treatment to each alternative considered in detail including the proposed action so that reviewers may evaluate their comparative merits.

(c) Include reasonable alternatives not within the jurisdiction of the lead agency.

(d) Include the alternative of no action.

(e) Identify the agency's preferred alternative or alternatives, if one or more exists, in the draft statement and identify such alternative in the final statement unless another law prohibits the expression of such a preference.

(f) Include appropriate mitigation measures not already included in the proposed action or alternatives.

NATURAL RESOURCES DEFENSE COUNCIL v. MORTON

United States Court of Appeals, District of Columbia Circuit (1972)
458 F.2d 827

[*NRDC v. Morton* concerned the proper range of alternatives to be considered by the Secretary of the Interior in the course of shaping a proposal for a general lease sale of offshore oil and gas tracts, pursuant to § 8 of the Outer Continental Shelf Lands Act. The proposal was finally structured to cover 10% of the available offshore tracts—some 380,000 acres—in order to implement rapidly the energy production policies announced in President Nixon's June 1971 Message on Supply of Energy and Clean Air. Offshore oil and gas exploration is a high-risk business; climatic conditions and technical limitations present a real risk of severe damage by oil spill and accumulated drilling debris to nearby fish and wildlife habitats important to the fishing and tourist industries, as well as loss of drilling equipment and capital funds. Conversely, offshore exploration can yield large amounts of oil and gas.

The case revolved around the issue of NEPA's directive that agencies should consider the "alternative ways of accomplishing the objectives of the proposed action and the results of not accomplishing the proposed action." The Secretary of the Interior contended that the agency's EIS need only consider alternatives it could actually implement. For example, the Secretary stated that considering the alternative of eliminating oil import quotas "involves complex factors and concepts, including national security, which are beyond the scope of this statement." The court rejected this argument, however, stating that:

> While we agree with so much of the Government's presentation as rests on the assumption that the alternatives required for discussion are those reasonably available, we do not agree that this requires a limitation to measures the agency or official can adopt . . . . The scope of this project is far broader than that of other proposed Federal actions discussed in impact statements, such as a single canal or dam. The Executive's proposed solution to a national problem, or a set of inter-related problems, may call for each of several departments or agencies to take a specific action. This cannot mean that the only discussion of alternatives required in the ensuing environmental impact statements would be the discussion

> by each department of the particular actions it could take as an alternative to the proposal underlying its impact statement. When the proposed action is an integral part of a coordinated plan to deal with a broad problem, the range of alternatives that must be evaluated is broadened. While the Department of Interior does not have the authority to eliminate or reduce oil import quotas, such action is within the purview of both Congress and the President, to whom the impact statement goes. The impact statement is not only for exposition of the thinking of the agency, but also for the guidance of those ultimate decision makers and must provide them with the environmental effects of both the proposal and the alternatives, for their consideration along with the various other elements of the public interest.

Although the court asserted that the only alternatives required for discussion are those "reasonably available," it nevertheless required full consideration of such alternatives as increasing nuclear energy development, as well as alternatives that may require legislative implementation. "The mere fact that an alternative requires legislative implementation does not automatically establish it was beyond the domain of what is required for discussion . . . ."

A vigorous dissent pointed out that the court's general language requires the impact statement to consider the environmental impact of: "1. meeting energy demands by federal legislation or administrative action, freeing current domestic production from state restriction on production; 2. changing the Federal Power Commission's policy with respect to the pricing of natural gas; 3. elimination of import quotas; 4. increasing onshore exploration and development; 5. development of oil shale; 6. increasing nuclear energy development; 7. increasing use of low sulfur coal and/or desulfurization of coal; 8. development of coal liquification and gasification; 9. development of geothermal resources; and 10. development of tar sands." The dissent read the majority opinion as holding that alternatives 5, 7, 8, 9 or 10 need not be discussed in any detail in the impact statement, that the impact statement is required to deal with 1, 2 and 6 to some extent, and 3 and 4 more fully. The dissent pointed out that:

> much of what is suggested by these so-called alternatives is already being done and is a matter of common knowledge. Some of the suggested alternatives would require immediate changes in existing federal laws and decisions of independent federal agencies; some are impractical because they would require officials to act in a manner that they have indicated is contrary to their declared intent; some suggest alternatives involving uncertain result, highly speculative probabilities, or experimental uncertainties; some suggest as alternatives, proposals that would not satisfy the same need; some would only be partial alternatives; and some involve ideas that are years away, if ever, from fruition. *None can be said to be realistic present alternatives.*

The dissent asserted that because of these circumstances, it would not find any of the suggestions to be alternatives within the meaning of the Act.]

NOTES AND QUESTIONS

(1) Six years following the *Morton* decision, the U.S. Supreme Court examined the question of alternatives under NEPA in *Vermont Yankee*

Nuclear Power Corp. v. Natural Resources Defense Council, 535 U.S. 519 (1978). There, the plaintiffs challenged the issuance of a license for a nuclear reactor on the basis that the accompanying EIS, prepared by the Nuclear Regulatory Commission, had declined to consider improved energy conservation as an alternative to constructing the nuclear plant in question. The Court upheld the Commission, finding that the phrase "energy conservation" was too broad to constitute a meaningful alternative. It stated:

> [A]s should be obvious even upon a moment's reflection, the term "alternatives" is not self-defining. To make an impact statement something more than an exercise in frivolous boilerplate the concept of alternatives must be bounded by some notion of feasibility. . . . Common sense also teaches us that the "detailed statement of alternatives" cannot be found wanting simply because the agency failed to include every alternative device and thought conceivable by the mind of man. Time and resources are simply too limited to hold that an impact statement fails because the agency failed to ferret out every possible alternative, regardless of how uncommon or unknown that alternative may have been at the time the project was approved.
>
> . . . [T]he concept of "alternatives" is an evolving one, requiring the agency to explore more or fewer alternatives as they become better known and understood.

Is this approach consistent with the D.C. Circuit's interpretation of NEPA's alternatives requirement? To what extent should environmental organizations that challenge a federal agency's EIS, in its consideration of alternatives to the proposed action, be required to demonstrate the feasibility of any alternative that was not, in their view, adequately considered in the EIS? What practical problems would such a rule pose for environmentalist plaintiffs?

(2) The *Vermont Yankee* decision was also notable as a precedent with respect to the authority of federal courts to review the decisionmaking procedures established by federal agencies. In that case, the Court of Appeals had held that, in the absence of what it considered effective rulemaking procedures, the Nuclear Regulatory Commission was obligated to consider, in individual licensing proceedings, the environmental impact of fuel processing and nuclear waste disposal. The U.S. Supreme Court reversed, holding that the Court of Appeals was wrong in imposing its own procedural notions on the Commission. Noting that administrative agencies should generally be free to fashion their own rules of procedure, the Supreme Court held that the Administrative Procedures Act defines the limits of judicial review of administrative procedure, and no greater procedural burdens may be imposed upon agencies by reviewing courts.

(3) For a critical analysis of the *Vermont Yankee* decision referred to in the preceding note, see Rogers, *A Hard Look At Vermont Yankee: Environmental Law Under Close Scrutiny*, 67 Geo. L.J. 699 (1979). *See also* Byse, *Vermont Yankee and the Evolution of Administrative Procedure: A Somewhat Different View*, 91 Harv. L. Rev. 1823 (1978); and Stewart, *Vermont Yankee and the Evolution of Administrative Procedure*, 91 Harv. L. Rev. 1805 (1978).

ROOSEVELT CAMPOBELLO INTERNATIONAL PARK COMMISSION v. U.S. ENVIRONMENTAL PROTECTION AGENCY

United States Court of Appeals, First Circuit (1982)
684 F.2d 1041

Coffin, C.J.:

In these three consolidated appeals petitioners challenge the final decision of the EPA Administrator to issue a National Pollutant Discharge Elimination System (NPDES) permit to the Pittston Company pursuant to § 402 of the Clean Water Act, 33 U.S.C. § 1342. The permit authorizes the Pittston Co. to construct and operate a 250,000 barrel per day oil refinery and associated deep water terminal at Eastport, Maine, in accordance with specified effluent limitations, monitoring requirements, and other conditions. Petitioners contend that EPA's actions violated the National Environmental Policy Act (NEPA), 42 U.S.C. § 4321 *et seq.*, the Endangered Species Act, 16U.S.C. § 1581, *et seq.*, and the Clean Water Act, 33U.S.C. § 1251 *et seq.*

Pittston proposes to construct an oil refinery and marine terminal in Eastport, Maine, a relatively pristine area of great natural beauty near the Canadian border. The area is known for being the foggiest on the East Coast, experiencing some 750-1000 hours of fog a year; daily tides approximate twenty feet. The plan contemplates that crude oil shipments will arrive several times a week in supertankers, or Very Large Crude Carriers (VLCCs), as long as four football fields, or slightly less than a quarter of a mile. The tankers will travel through Canadian waters around the northern tip of Campobello Island, where the Roosevelt Campobello International Park is located, *see* 16 U.S.C. § 1101 *et seq.*, down Head Harbor Passage to a refinery near Eastport where they will be turned and berthed. Numerous barges and small tankers will carry the refined product from Eastport to destination markets in the Northeast.

The protracted procedural history of this case begins in April 1973, when Pittston applied to the Maine Board of Environmental Protection (BEP) for permission to locate the refinery in Eastport. After public hearings, the BEP approved the proposal under the Maine Site Location of Development Law, 38 M.R.S.A. § 481 *et seq.*, subject to a number of pre-construction and pre-operation conditions designed primarily to reduce the risk of oil spills. Pittston subsequently filed an application with EPA to obtain an NPDES permit, and submitted an Environmental Assessment Report to aid EPA in its duty to prepare an Environmental Impact Statement (EIS) pursuant to NEPA. *See* 33 U.S.C. § 1371(c)(1); 42 U.S.C. § 4332(2)(C). EPA promulgated a draft EIS recommending issuance of the permit as conditioned by the Maine BEP, held a joint public hearing with the Army Corps. of Engineers in Eastport, and received approximately 600 responses during a public comment period. In

September 1977, the Maine Department of Environmental Protection certified, under § 401(a)(1) of the Clean Water Act, 33 U.S.C. § 1341(a)(1), that the proposed discharge would satisfy the appropriate requirements of state and federal law. In June 1978, the final EIS was issued, again recommending that the permit be issued pursuant to the BEP conditions.

Several months later, the National Marine Fisheries Service (NMFS) of the Department of Commerce and the Fish and Wildlife Service (FWS) of the Department of Interior initiated consultations with EPA concerning the proposed refinery's impact on endangered species—the right and humpback whales, and the northern bald eagle, respectively—under § 7 of the Endangered Species Act(ESA), 16 U.S.C. § 1586. In November, the NMFS issued a threshold determination that there were insufficient data to conclude that the project was not likely to jeopardize the continued existence of the endangered whales. In December, the FWS concluded that the project was likely to jeopardize the bald eagle. In light of these opinions and of the value of the natural resources in the Eastport area as noted in the EIS, EPA's Region I issued a notice of determination to deny Pittston's application for an NPDES permit in January 1979. Pittston thereafter sought an adjudicatory hearing and administrative review of this decision.

Prior to the hearing, extensive consultation between EPA, NMFS, FWS, and Pittston took place to consider mitigation measures proposed by Pittston. In May, NMFS concluded on the basis of the best scientific data available that EPA was unable to comply with the statutory mandate that it "insure that [the project] is not likely to jeopardize the continued existence of" endangered whales. 16 U.S.C. § 1536(a)(2). In June FWS reaffirmed its previous determination that the refinery was likely to jeopardize the bald eagle. EPA Region I amended its decision to include these new findings.

The adjudicatory hearing took place over five weeks in January and February of 1980. More than fifty witnesses testified and were cross-examined; several hundred exhibits were introduced. In January 1981, the ALJ rendered EPA's Initial Decision, overturning EPA Region I and ordering that the NPDES permit issue. He concluded that the EIS was adequate to comply with NEPA, and that no supplemental EIS was necessary; that the risk of oil spills was "minute" and that the refinery was therefore not likely to jeopardize any endangered species: and that the conditions imposed by the Maine BEP, and assumed by the EIS, were not required to be conditions of the federal permit. Petitioners subsequently sought review before the EPA Administrator, and also moved to reopen the record to admit a recent study showing an increased number of endangered whales in the Eastport region. Both motions were denied, and in September 1981 EPA Region I issued the NPDES permit to the Pittston Company. Petitioners now seek review in this court pursuant to § 509(b)(1)(F) of the Clean Water Act, 38 U.S.C. § 1389(b)(1)(F).

I. The National Environmental Policy Act

1. *The Standard of Review*

It is now well settled that there are two aspects to a court's review of agency action subject to the requirements of NEPA:

> First, the court makes a substantive review of the agency's action to determine if such action is arbitrary and capricious under the Administrative Procedure Act, 5U.S.C. § 706. This substantive review, although conducted on the basis of the entire administrative record, is quite narrow in scope. The court should only assure itself that the agency has given good faith consideration to the environmental consequences of its actions and should not pass judgment on the balance struck by the agency among competing concerns.
>
> Second, a reviewing court must assess the agency's compliance with the duties NEPA places upon it. These duties are essentially procedural. The primary procedural mechanism embodied in NEPA is the requirement that an agency prepare 'a detailed statement' discussing, inter alia, 'alternatives to the proposed action' 42 U.S.C. § 4332(2)(C). Requiring an agency to discuss alternatives within the EIS serves numerous goals. The detailed statement aids a reviewing court to ascertain whether the agency has given the good faith consideration to environmental concerns discussed above, provides environmental information to the public and to interested departments of government, and prevents stubborn problems or significant criticism from being shielded from internal and external scrutiny.

Grazing Fields Farm v. Goldschmidt, 626 F.2d 1068, 1072 (1st Cir. 1980) (citations & footnote omitted). *See also*, *Silva v. Lynn*, 482 F.2d 1282, 1283-84 (1st Cir. 1973).

2. *The Need for the Project*

In order to weigh the benefits of the project against the potential environmental costs, the EIS contained an analysis of the justification for the project and the anticipated economic benefits. The project was deemed consistent with a longstanding federal policy of encouraging the construction of domestic refining capacity in order to promote national security. New England, heavily dependent on imported oil, had no regional refining capacity. The project was designed to accommodate VLCCs, thus taking advantage of the cost saving offered by economies of scale. Constructing a refinery in the United States rather than abroad had the additional advantage of retaining jobs and investments in this country. Finally, the project was particularly attractive because it was designed to handle high sulfur crude oil and refine it into low sulfur fuels, thus facilitating compliance with new environmental standards. Such a refinery was "of an entirely different design" than most existing domestic refineries, which were built to handle domestic and steadily depleting sources of low sulfur crude.

Petitioners argue that the EIS was faulty because it failed to consider the possibility of conservation and the use of alternative fuels instead of the construction of additional oil refining capacity. We note first that petitioners failed to raise this concern in a meaningful way during the comment period. In any case, it is clear that at the time the EIS was drafted there was a forecasted need for the type of refinery planned by Pittston, and that it was federal policy to encourage the construction of such refineries. Nor are we persuaded by petitioners' argument that the discussion in the EIS of the need for the project is "totally outdated and of no present use." Even accepting their contention—based, we might add, primarily on statements of energy policy under President Carter, which might themselves be outdated—that there is no longer a strong need for additional refining capacity; it remains uncontested that there is still a demand for domestic refineries capable of processing high sulfur crude into low sulfur products. Given this continuing national and regional need, we see no need to supplement the EIS in order to accommodate the most recent data and federal policy shifts. *Cf. New England Coalition on Nuclear Pollution v. NRC*, 582 F.2d 87, 96-98 (1st Cir. 1978).

3. *Adequacy of Consideration of Alternatives*

Petitioners contend that the EIS failed to discuss adequately a number of alternatives to the proposed refinery at Eastport. First, they argue that EPA erred by conducting a less searching analysis of alternatives to this privately sponsored project than it would have had the project been publicly funded. Second, they urge that EPA unreasonably limited its consideration of alternative sites to three locations in Maine. Finally, they allege that EPA's comparison of the various sites was inadequate.

EPA's evaluation of alternatives was explicitly based on the premise that its role in reviewing privately sponsored projects "is to determine whether the proposed site is environmentally acceptable" and not, as in the case of a publicly funded project, "to undertake to locate what EPA would consider to be the optimum site for a new facility." Therefore, EPA considered its purpose in this case to be to search for alternatives "that would be substantially preferable from an environmental standpoint." EPA concluded that "[t]his different purpose affects the extent of the information on alternatives necessary to make a decision."

We are unable to fault EPA's reasoning. Petitioners concede that the substantive standard—"substantially preferable"—was correctly stated. *Cf. New England Coalition on Nuclear Pollution v. NRC,* 582 F.2d at 95-96 ("obvious superiority"). No purpose would be served by requiring EPA to study exhaustively all environmental impacts at each alternative site considered once it has reasonably concluded that none of the alternatives will be substantially preferable to the proposed site. Moreover, the guidelines adopted by EPA to limit its study of alternatives appears, in this case, to be consistent with the "rule of reason" by which a court measures federal agency compliance with NEPA's procedural requirements. *See, e.g., Grazing Fields Farm,* 628 F.2d at 1074; *Massachusetts v. Andrus*, 594 F.2d 872, 884 (1st Cir. 1979).

EPA's choice of alternative sites was focused by the primary objectives of the permit applicant, the Pittston Co. Pittston stated that its basic consideration was to find a port with deep water near shore in order to accommodate VLCCs. Only by using such supertankers could Pittston take advantage of economical scale, thereby making the project economically feasible. Therefore, after Pittston had reviewed and rejected a number of sites lacking such deep water, EPA limited its consideration to the only ports providing deep water access. Three alternative areas in Maine were considered: Portland, Machias, and Penobscot/Blue Hill.

EPA's duty under NEPA is to study all alternatives that "appear reasonable and appropriate for study at the time" of drafting the EIS, as well as "significant alternatives" suggested by other agencies or the public during the comment period. In order to preserve an alternatives issue for review, it is not enough simply to make a facially plausible suggestion: rather, an intervenor must offer tangible evidence that an alternative site might offer "a substantial measure of superiority" as a site. *See Seacoast Anti-Pollution League v. NRC,* 598 F.2d 1221, 1228-33 (1st Cir. 1979).

In light of this standard, petitioners' argument that EPA erred by restricting its consideration to alternative sites in Maine must fail, because they did not suggest any reasonable alternatives to EPA during the comment period. One alternative—a monobuoy off the mid-Atlantic coast—was raised for the first time at the adjudicatory hearing, too late for inclusion in the EIS. Although petitioners now contend that EPA *should* reasonably have been aware of such an alternative earlier, their citation to a 1976 study by the Office of Technology falls far short of persuading us; nor have they explained their failure to bring the report to EPA's attention in a timely manner. Another possibility, an offshore monobuoy in New England, was rejected by EPA in spite of its potential environmental benefits because of fierce public opposition to similar proposals off the coast of Massachusetts and New Hampshire. We cannot say that EPA acted unreasonably in concluding that such an option was not feasible. In short, we are not convinced that EPA failed to consider all alternatives which were feasible and reasonably apparent at the time of drafting the EIS.

Petitioners next urge that EPA's consideration of these alternative sites was inadequate. The EIS contained comparative analysis of the effects of the proposed project on air quality, water quality, present land and sea uses, terrestrial and aquatic flora and fauna, and aesthetics at the various sites. The Portland area was eliminated by Pittston because its shallow channel is unable to accommodate VLCCs and suitable land for a refinery site and marine terminal was not available. EPA considered an offshore monomooring system near Portland, but rejected it due to the vulnerability of the proposed location to the elements and the chronic spills associated with monomooring which would interfere with the nearby fishing and recreation industries. The Machias site was considered substantially similar to Eastport from an environmental perspective, but was eliminated by Pittston because suitable land was unavailable. EPA also noted that the harbor at Machias was more exposed to wind and weather than that at Eastport, thus making a tanker approach more hazardous. Heavy tourism at Penobscot/Blue Hill made a refinery undesirable; the area is also a center for Maine's lobster, clam and fishing industry. Finally, the tanker approach at the area is quite long with numerous islands, increasing the risk of mishap close to shore and inhabited areas. Consequently, EPA concluded that none of the alternative sites would provide a significantly greater degree of environmental protection than the Eastport site. Having carefully reviewed the record, we cannot say that EPA's consideration of these sites was inadequate, or that its conclusion to reject them was arbitrary and capricious.

We defer our consideration of additional NEPA issues raised by petitioners—the adequacy of the risk spill analysis in the EIS, and the need for a supplemental EIS—until after our discussion of the risk of oil spills in the context of the Endangered Species Act . . . . [The court then held that EPA's administrative law judge had run afoul of the federal Endangered Species Act, by failing to use the "best scientific and commercial data available" in determining that the proposed project would not jeopardize the continued existence of endangered species. The matter was remanded to EPA. Subsequently, Pittston Company abandoned its plan and no oil refinery/terminal was ever constructed in Eastport, Maine.]

NOTES AND QUESTIONS

(1) The court's opinion in this case appears to suggest that federal agencies and departments are justified in limiting their consideration of alternatives to a greater extent when they prepare EISs respecting proposals for private projects which they must approve or deny approval to, as opposed to projects to be constructed by the government agency or department itself. Is this a valid distinction? Is it consistent with the analysis of the D.C. Circuit in *NRDC v. Morton*, *supra*, p. 861.

(2) In some NEPA cases, the courts have limited the alternatives that agencies must consider to the statutory objectives of their actions. *See, e.g.*, *City of New York v. Department of Transportation*, 715 F.2d 732 (2d Cir. 1983), in which the court upheld a department's decision not to consider the alternatives of barge transportation of radioactive materials before promulgating a rule which authorized the highway transportation of such material. The court stated: "Statutory objectives provide a sensible compromise between unduly narrow objectives an agency might choose to identify to limit consideration of alternatives and hopelessly broad societal objectives that would unduly expand the range of relevant alternatives." *Id.* at 743. Is this a sound interpretation of NEPA?

(3) In *Citizens Against Burlington, Inc. v. Busey*, 938 F.2d 190 (D.C. Cir. 1991), the plaintiffs challenged a decision of the Federal Aviation Administration (FAA) to fund the expansion of a municipal airport in Toledo, Ohio without considering the relative environmental impact of expanding other airports in or outside of Toledo. The court upheld the FAA's approach, reasoning that the agency has a responsibility to define its goals and objectives in the decisionmaking process by taking account of the needs and objectives of applicants for federal permits or approvals. For a critique of this opinion, and an overview of the judicial decisions pertaining to NEPA's alternatives requirement, see F. Grad, Treatise on Environmental Law § 9.03[3][d].

§ 5.08 Does NEPA Create Substantive Duties or Require Mitigation of Environmental Impact?

STRYCKER'S BAY NEIGHBORHOOD COUNCIL v. KARLEN

United States Supreme Court (1980)
444 U.S. 223, 100 S. Ct. 497, 62 L. Ed. 2d 433

Per Curiam

The protracted nature of this litigation is perhaps best illustrated by the identity of the original federal defendant, "George Romney, Secretary of the Department of Housing and Urban Development." At the center of this dispute is the site of a proposed low-income housing project to be constructed on Manhattan's Upper West Side. In 1962, the New York City Planning Commission (Commission), acting in conjunction with the United States Department of Housing and Urban Development (HUD), began formulating a plan for the renewal of 20 square blocks known as the "West Side Urban Renewal Area" (WSURA) through a joint effort on the part of private parties and various government agencies. As originally written, the plan called for a mix of 70% middle-income housing and 30% low-income housing and designated the site at issue here as the location of one of the middle-income projects. In 1969, after substantial progress toward completion of the plan, local agencies in New York determined that the number of low-income units proposed for WSURA would be insufficient to satisfy an increased need for such units. In response to this shortage the Commission amended the plan to designate the site as the future location of a high-rise building containing 160 units of low-income housing. HUD approved this amendment in December 1972.

Meanwhile, in October 1971, the Trinity Episcopal School Corp. (Trinity), which had participated in the plan by building a combination school and middle-income housing development at a nearby location, sued in the United States District Court for the Southern District of New York to enjoin the Commission and HUD from constructing low-income housing on the site. The present respondents, Roland N. Karlen, Alvin C. Hudgins, and the Committee of Neighbors To Insure a Normal Urban Environment (CONTINUE), intervened as plaintiffs, while petitioner Strycker's Bay Neighborhood Council, Inc., intervened as a defendant.

The District Court entered judgment in favor of petitioners. *See Trinity Episcopal School Corp. v. Romney*, 387 F. Supp. 1044 (1974). It concluded, *inter alia*, that petitioners had not violated the National Environmental Policy Act of 1969 (NEPA), 83 Stat. 852, 42 U.S.C. § 4321 *et seq.*

On respondents' appeal the Second Circuit affirmed all but the District Court's treatment of the NEPA claim. *See Trinity Episcopal School Corp. v. Romney*, 523 F.2d 88 (1975). While the Court of Appeals agreed with the District Court that HUD was not required to prepare a full-scale environmental impact statement under § 102(2)(C) of NEPA, 42 U.S.C. § 4332(2)(C), it held that HUD had not complied with § 102(2)(E), which requires an agency to "study, develop, and describe appropriate alternatives to recommended courses of action in any proposal which involves unresolved conflicts concerning alternative uses of available resources." 42 U.S.C. § 4332(2)(E). *See* 523 F.2d, at 92–95. . . .

On remand, HUD prepared a lengthy report entitled Special Environmental Clearance (1977). After marshaling the data, the report asserted that, "while the choice of Site 30 for development as a 100 percent low-income project has raised valid questions about the potential social environmental impacts involved, the problems associated with the impact on social fabric and community structures are not considered so serious as to require that this component be rated as unacceptable." . . .

After soliciting the parties' comments on HUD's report, the District Court again entered judgment in favor of petitioners. *See Trinity Episcopal School Corp. v. Harris*, 445 F. Supp. 204 (1978). The court was "impressed with [HUD's analysis] as being thorough and exhaustive," *id.*, at 209-210, and found that "HUD's consideration of the alternatives was neither arbitrary nor capricious"; on the contrary, "[i]t was done in good faith and in full accordance with the law." *Id.*, at 220.

On appeal, the Second Circuit vacated and remanded again. *Karlen v. Harris,* 590 F.2d 39 (1978). The appellate court focused upon that part of HUD's report where the agency considered and rejected alternative sites, and in particular upon HUD's reliance on the delay such a relocation would entail. The Court of Appeals purported to recognize that its role in reviewing HUD's decision was defined by the Administrative Procedure Act (APA), 5 U.S.C. § 706(2)(A), which provides that agency actions should be set aside if found to be "arbitrary, capricious, an abuse of discretion, or otherwise not in accordance with the law . . . ." Additionally, however, the Court of Appeals looked to "[t]he provisions of NEPA" for "the substantive standards necessary to review the merits of agency decisions . . . ." 590 F.2d at 43. The Court of Appeals conceded that HUD had "given 'consideration' to alternatives" to redesignating the site. *Id.*, at 44. Nevertheless, the court believed that " 'consideration' is not an end in itself." *Ibid.* Concentrating on HUD's finding that development of an alternative location would entail an unacceptable delay, the appellate court held that such delay could not be "an overriding factor" in HUD's decision to proceed with the development. *Ibid.* According to the court, when HUD considers such projects, "environmental factors, such as crowding low-income housing into a concentrated area, should be given determinative weight." *Ibid.* The Court of Appeals therefore remanded the case to the District Court, instructing HUD to attack the shortage of low-income housing in a manner that would avoid the "concentration" of such housing on Site 30. *Id.*, at 45.

In *Vermont Yankee Nuclear Power Corp. v. NRDC*, 435 U.S. 519, 558 (1978), we stated that NEPA, while establishing "significant substantive goals for the Nation," imposes upon agencies duties that are "essentially procedural." As we stressed in that case, NEPA was designed "to insure a fully informed and well-considered decision," but not necessarily "a decision the judges of the Court of Appeals or of this Court would have reached had they been members of the decisionmaking unit of the agency." *Ibid. Vermont Yankee* cuts sharply against the Court of Appeals' conclusion that an agency, in selecting a course of action, must elevate environmental concerns over other appropriate considerations. On the contrary, once an agency has made a decision subject to NEPA's procedural requirements, the only role for a court is to insure that the agency has considered the environmental consequences; it cannot "interject itself within the area of discretion of the executive as to the choice of the action to be taken." *Kleppe v. Sierra Club,* 427 U.S. 390, 410 n. 21 (1976). *See also, FPC v. Transcontinental Gas Pipe Line Corp.*, 423 U.S. 326 (1976).[1] In the present case there is no doubt that HUD considered the environmental consequences of its decision to redesignate the proposed site for low-income housing. NEPA requires no more. The petitions for certiorari are granted, and the judgment of the Court of Appeals is therefore

Reversed

Mr. Justice Marshall, dissenting.

The issue raised by these cases is far more difficult than the *per curiam* opinion suggests. The Court of Appeals held that the Secretary of Housing and Urban Development (HUD) had acted arbitrarily in concluding that prevention of a delay in the construction process justified the selection of a housing site which could produce adverse social environmental effects, including racial and economic concentration. Today the majority responds that "once an agency has made a decision subject to NEPA's procedural requirements, the only role for a court is to insure that the agency has considered the environmental consequences," and that in this case "there is no doubt that HUD considered the environmental consequences of its decision to redesignate the proposed site for low-income housing. NEPA requires no more." The majority finds support for this conclusion in the closing paragraph of our decision in *Vermont Yankee Nuclear Power Corp. v. NRDC,* 435 U.S. 519, 558 (1978).

Vermont Yankee does not stand for the broad proposition that the majority advances today. The relevant passage in that opinion was meant to be only a "further observation of some relevance to this case," *Id.*, at 557. That "observation" was a response to this Court's perception that the Court of Appeals in that case was attempting "under the guise of judicial review of agency action" to assert its own policy judgment as to the desirability of developing nuclear energy as an energy source for this Nation, a judgment which is properly left to Congress. *Id.*, at 558. The Court of Appeals had remanded the case to the agency because of "a single alleged oversight on a peripheral issue, urged by parties who never fully cooperated or indeed raised the issue below," *ibid.* It was in this context that the Court remarked that "NEPA does set forth significant substantive goals for the Nation, but its mandate to the agencies is *essentially* procedural." *Ibid.* (emphasis supplied).

[1] If we could agree with the dissent that the Court of Appeals held that HUD had acted "arbitrarily" in redesignating the site for low-income housing, we might also agree that plenary review is warranted. But the District Court expressly concluded that HUD had not acted arbitrarily or capriciously and our reading of the opinion of the Court of Appeals satisfies us that it did not overturn that finding. Instead, the appellate court required HUD to elevate environmental concerns over other, admittedly legitimate considerations. Neither NEPA nor the APA provides any support for such a reordering of priorities by a reviewing court.

Accordingly, "[a]dministrative decisions should be set aside in this context, *as in every other*, only for substantial procedural or *substantive* reasons as mandated by statute," *ibid.* (emphasis supplied). Thus *Vermont Yankee* does not stand for the proposition that a court reviewing agency action under NEPA is limited solely to the factual issue of whether the agency "considered" environmental consequences. The agency's decision must still be set aside if it is "arbitrary, capricious, an abuse of discretion, or otherwise not in accordance with law," 5 U.S.C. § 706(2)(A), and the reviewing court must still insure that the agency "has taken a 'hard look' at environmental consequences," *Kleppe v. Sierra Club*, 427 U.S. 390, 410 n. 21 (1976).

In the present case, the Court of Appeals did not "substitute its judgment for that of the agency as to the environmental consequences of its actions," *ibid.*, for HUD in its Special Environmental Clearance Report acknowledged the adverse environmental consequences of its proposed action: . . . The report lists 10 ameliorative measures necessary to make the project acceptable. The report also discusses two alternatives, Sites 9 and 41, both of which are the appropriate size for the project and require "only minimal" amounts of relocation and clearance. Concerning Site 9 the report explicitly concludes that "[f]rom the standpoint of social environmental impact, this location would be superior to Site 30 for the development of low-rent public housing." The sole reason for rejecting the environmentally superior site was the fact that if the location were shifted to Site 9, there would be a projected delay of two years in the construction of the housing.

The issue before the Court of Appeals, therefore, was whether HUD was free under NEPA to reject an alternative acknowledged to be environmentally preferable solely on the ground that any change in sites would cause delay. This was hardly a "peripheral issue" in the case. Whether NEPA, which sets forth "significant substantive goals," *Vermont Yankee Nuclear Power Corp. v. NRDC, supra*, at 558 permits a projected 2-year time difference to be controlling over environmental superiority is by no means clear. Resolution of the issue, however, is certainly within the normal scope for review of agency action to determine if it is arbitrary, capricious, or an abuse of discretion. The question whether HUD can make delay the paramount concern over environmental superiority is essentially a restatement of the question whether HUD in considering the environmental consequences of its proposed action gave those consequences a "hard look," which is exactly the proper question for the reviewing court to ask. *Kleppe v. Sierra Club, supra*, at 410, n. 21.

The issue of whether the Secretary's decision was arbitrary or capricious is sufficiently difficult and important to merit plenary consideration in this Court. Further, I do not subscribe to the Court's apparent suggestion that *Vermont Yankee* limits the reviewing court to the essentially mindless task of determining whether an agency "considered" environmental factors even if that agency may have effectively decided to ignore those factors in reaching its conclusion. Indeed, I cannot believe that the Court would adhere to that position in a different factual setting. Our cases establish that the arbitrary or capricious standard prescribes a "searching and careful" judicial inquiry designed to ensure that the agency has not exercised its discretion in an unreasonable manner. *Citizens To Preserve Overton Park, Inc. v Volpe*, 401

U.S. 402, 416 (1971). Believing that today's summary reversal represents a departure from that principle, I respectfully dissent.

It is apparent to me that this is not the type of case for a summary disposition. We should at least have a plenary hearing.

NOTES AND QUESTIONS

(1) This decision set to rest a question that had been debated in the courts, in the classrooms and in the law journals for some ten years. It is now settled that NEPA is not a decision rule: whatever adverse effects the environmental impact statement shows, a court may not rely on NEPA to order the agency not to proceed with the project. To be sure, the demonstration of devastating environmental impact may dissuade the agency from proceeding. It may also provide political ammunition against funding the project, and/or it may even provide a basis for argument under the Atomic Energy Act, the Federal Power Act, the applicable federal housing legislation, the Federal Highway Act, or under whatever other legislation that authorizes the project, that the agency decision to proceed was arbitrary, capricious, an abuse of discretion or otherwise contrary to law. Nonetheless, in the wake of *Strycker's Bay*, such an argument must proceed under such other legislation, and not under NEPA. Is this an appropriate construction of NEPA? How persuasive are Justice Marshall's criticisms of the *Strycker's Bay* majority opinion?

(2) One aspect of the history of the *Strycker's Bay* controversy not reported in any of the judicial opinions that it spawned was the fact that, during the litigation, New York City and Trinity Episcopal School reached an understanding that the final version of the urban renewal project in question would not "tilt" the pre-existing racial make-up of the neighborhood in which the project was to be constructed. This understanding was probably known to the Second Circuit; and it may have affected that court's deliberations. Should the opinions in this case have reflected that agreement? If so, how should its existence have influenced the outcome of the case?

(3) Notice that the *Strycker's Bay* case was not decided under § 102(2)(C) of NEPA,the section that requires the preparation of an environmental impact statement, but under § 102(E), which requires agencies to "study, develop, and describe appropriate alternatives to recommended courses of action in any proposal which involves unresolved conflicts concerning alternative uses of available resources." The case did not involve a situation in which an EIS had to be prepared. It is clear that this distinction does not make a difference in the Court's opinion. Is that approach sound?

Moreover, in earlier considerations of the issue in a number of Courts of Appeals, the question had turned on whether there was "law to apply" in NEPA §§ 101 and 102for the court's review of the decision to proceed with the project. The "law to apply" issue is not even mentioned in *Strycker's Bay*, which relies only on the express language of NEPA, and which looks to the Administrative Procedure Act, as in other cases of nonstatutory review. Both the majority opinion and the Marshall dissent refer to the application of the "hard look" doctrine in the review of agency action taken pursuant to NEPA. It is clear under the Court's decision and the earlier cases cited that it is the

EIS that gets the "hard look" and not the ultimate decision to proceed with the project.

(4) The *Strycker's Bay* case raises, at least implicitly, some larger questions of institutional responsibility: Who should decide whether particular government agency projects (which may or may not have significant environmental consequences) should proceed? Is that the proper role of the proponent agency itself? Should Congress be the ultimate decisionmaker? What about the judiciary? Consider the extent to which the various judicial opinions in *Strycker's Bay* contribute to a sound resolution of these issues.

(5) Prior to *Strycker's Bay,* a number of commentators had argued that NEPA did create substantive duties that the courts should recognize. *See, e.g.*, Robie, *Recognition of Substantive Rights Under NEPA*, 7 Nat. Resources Law. 387 (1974); Arnold, *The Substantive Right to Environmental Quality Under the National Environmental Policy Act*, 3 ELR 50, 028 (1973); Wharton, *Judicially Enforceable Substantive Rights Under NEPA*, 10 U.S.C. L. Rev. 415 (1976); and Note, *The Least Adverse Alternative Approach to Substantive Review Under NEPA*, 88 Harv. L. Rev. 735 (1975). Several courts had adopted that view. *See Environmental Defense Fund, Inc. v. Corps of Engineers*, 470 F.2d 1123 (5th Cir. 1974); *Sierra Club v. Froehlke*, 345 F. Supp. 440 (W.D. Wis. 1972), *aff'd*, 486 F.2d 946 (7th Cir. 1973). *Compare National Helium Corp. v. Morton*,. 326 F. Supp. 151 (D. Kan. 1971), *aff'd*, 455 F.2d 650 (10th Cir. 1971).

ROBERTSON v. METHOW VALLEY CITIZENS COUNCIL

United States Supreme Court (1989)
409 U.S. 332, 109 S. Ct. 1835, 104 L. Ed. 2d 351

STEVENS. J.:

I

The Forest Service is authorized by statute to manage the national forests for "outdoor recreation, range, timber, watershed, and wildlife and fish purposes." 74 Stat. 215, 16 U.S.C. § 528. Pursuant to that authorization, the Forest Service has issued "special use" permits for the operation of approximately 170 alpine and nordic ski areas on federal lands.

The Forest Service permit process involves three separate stages. The Forest Service first examines the general environmental and financial feasibility of a proposed project and decides whether to issue a special use permit. *See* 36 C.F.R. § 152.54(f)(1988). Because that decision is a "major Federal action" within the meaning of NEPA, it must be preceded by the preparation of an Environmental Impact Statement (EIS). 42 U.S.C. § 4332. If the Service decides to issue a permit, it then proceeds to select a developer, formulate the basic terms of the arrangement with the selected party, and issue the permit. The special use permit does not, however, give the developer the right to begin construction. *See* 36 C.F.R. § 251.56(c)(1988). In a final stage of review, the Service evaluates the permitee's "master plan" for development, construction, and operation of the project. Construction may begin only after an additional environmental analysis (although it is not clear that a second EIS need always be prepared) and final approval of the developer's master plan. This case arises out of the Forest Service's decision to issue a special use permit authorizing the development of a major destination alpine ski resort at Sandy Butte in the North Cascade mountains.

Sandy Butte is a 6,000-foot mountain located in the Okanogan National Forest in Okanogan County, Washington. At present Sandy Butte, like the Methow Valley it overlooks, is an unspoiled, sparsely populated area that the district court characterized as "pristine." In 1968, Congress established the North Cascades National Park and directed the Secretaries of Interior and Agriculture to agree on the designation of areas within and adjacent to the park for public uses, including ski areas. 82 Stat. 926, 930, 16 U.S.C. §§ 90, 90d-3. A 1970 study conducted by the Forest Service pursuant to this congressional directive identified Sandy Butte as having the highest potential of any site in the State of Washington for development as a major downhill ski resort.

In 1978, Methow Recreation, Inc. (MRI) applied for a special use permit to develop and operate its proposed "Early Winters Ski Resort" on Sandy Butte and a 1,165 acre parcel of land it had acquired adjacent to the National Forest. The proposed development would make use of approximately 3,900 acres of Sandy Butte; would entice visitors to travel long distances to stay at the resort for several days at a time; and would stimulate extensive commercial and residential growth in the vicinity to accommodate both vacationers and staff.

In response to MRI's application, the Forest Service, in cooperation with state and county officials, prepared an EIS known as the Early Winters Alpine Winter Sports Study (Early Winters Study or Study).

The Early Winters Study is a printed document containing almost 150 pages of text and 12 appendices. It evaluated five alternative levels of development of Sandy Butte that might be authorized, the lowest being a "no action" alternative and the highest being development of a 16-lift ski area able to accommodate 10,500 skiers at one time. The Study considered the effect of each level of development on water resources, soil, wildlife, air quality, vegetation and visual quality, as well as land use and transportation in the Methow Valley, probable demographic shifts, the economic market for skiing and other summer and winter recreational activities in the Valley, and the energy requirements for the ski area and related developments. The Study's discussion of possible impacts was not limited to on-site effects, but also, as required by Council on Environmental Quality (CEQ) regulations, see 40 C.F.R. § 1502.16(b)(1987), addressed "off-site impacts that each alternative might have on community facilities, socio-economic and other environmental conditions in the Upper Methow Valley." As to off-site effects, the Study explained that "due to the uncertainty of where other public and private lands may become developed," it is difficult to evaluate off-site impacts, and thus the document's analysis is necessarily "not site-specific." Finally, the Study outlines certain steps that might be taken to mitigate adverse effects, both on Sandy Butte and in the neighboring Methow Valley, but indicated that these proposed steps are merely conceptual and "will be made more specific as part of the design and implementation stages of the planning process."

The effects of the proposed development on air quality and wildlife received particular attention in the Study. In the chapter on "Environmental Consequences," the first subject discussed is air quality. As is true of other subjects, the discussion included an analysis of cumulative impacts over several years resulting from actions on other lands as well as from the development of Sandy Butte itself. The Study concluded that although the construction, maintenance, and operation of the proposed ski area "will not have a measurable effect on existing or future air quality," the off-site development of private land under all five alternatives—including the "no action" alternative—"will have a significant effect on air quality during severe meteorological inversion periods." The burning of wood for space heat, the Study explained, would constitute the primary cause of diminished air quality and the damage would increase incrementally with each of the successive levels of proposed development. The Study cautioned that without efforts to mitigate these effects, even under the "no action" alternative, the increase in automobile, fireplace, and wood stove use would reduce air quality below state standards, but added that "[t]he numerous mitigation measures discussed" in the Study "will greatly reduce the impacts presented by the model."

In its discussion of air quality mitigation measures, the EIS identified actions that could be taken by the county government to mitigate the adverse effects of development, as well as those that the Forest Service itself could implement at the construction stage of the project. The Study suggested that Okanogan County develop an air quality management plan, requiring weatherization of new buildings, limiting the number of wood stoves and fireplaces, and adopting monitoring and enforcement measures. In addition, the Study suggested that the Forest Service require that the master plan include procedures to control dust and to comply with smoke management practices.

In a comment in response to the draft EIS, the Washington Department of Game voiced a special concern about potential losses to the State's largest migratory deer herd, which uses the Methow Valley as a critical winter range and as its migration route. The state agency estimated that the total population of mule deer in the area most likely to be affected was "better than 30,000 animals" and that "the ultimate impact on the Methow deer herd could exceed a 50 percent reduction in numbers." Ultimately, the Early Winters Study recommended the issuance of a permit for development at the second highest level considered—a 16-lift ski area able to accommodate 8,200 skiers at one time. On July 5, 1984, the Regional Forester decided to issue a special use permit as recommended by the Study. In his decision, the Regional Forester found that no major adverse effects would result directly from the federal action, but that secondary effects could include a degradation of existing air quality and a reduction of mule deer winter range. He therefore directed the supervisor of the Okanogan National Forest, both independently and in cooperation with local officials, to identify and implement certain mitigating measures.

Four organizations (respondents) opposing the decision to issue a permit appealed the Regional Forester's decision to the Chief of the Forest Service.

See 36 C.F.R. § 211.18(1988). After a hearing, he affirmed the Regional Forester's decision. Stressing that the decision, which simply approved the general concept of issuing a 30-year special use permit for development of Sandy Butte, did not authorize construction of a particular ski area and, in fact, did not even act on MRI's specific permit application, he concluded that the EIS's discussion of mitigation was "adequate for this stage in the review process."

Thereafter, respondents brought this action under the Administrative Procedure Act, 5U.S.C. §§ 701–706, to obtain judicial review of the Forest Service's decision. Their principal claim was that the Early Winters Study did not satisfy the requirements of NEPA, 42U.S.C. § 4332. With the consent of the parties, the case was assigned to a United States Magistrate. After a trial, the Magistrate filed a comprehensive written opinion and concluded that the EIS was adequate. Specifically, he found that the EIS had adequately disclosed the adverse impacts on the mule deer herd and on air quality and that there was no duty to prepare a "worst case analysis" because the relevant information essential to a reasoned decision was available. In concluding that the discussion of off-site, or secondary, impacts was adequate, the Magistrate stressed that courts apply a "rule of reason" in evaluating the adequacy of an EIS and "take the uncertainty and speculation involved with secondary impacts into account in passing on the adequacy of the discussion of secondary impacts." On the subject of mitigation, he explained that "[m]ere listing . . . is generally inadequate to satisfy the CEQ regulations," but found that "in this EIS there is more—not much more—but more than a mere listing of mitigation measures." Moreover, emphasizing the tiered nature of the Forest Service's decisional process, the Magistrate noted that additional mitigation strategies would be included in the master plan, that the Forest Service continues to develop mitigation plans as further information becomes available, and that the Regional Forester's decision conditioned issuance of the special use permit on execution of an agreement between the Forest Service, the State of Washington, and Okanogan County concerning mitigation.

Concluding that the Early Winters Study was inadequate as a matter of law, the Court of Appeals reversed. Methow Valley Citizens Council v. Regional Forester, 833 F.2d 810 (CA9 1987). The court held that the Forest Service could not rely on "the implementation of mitigation measures" to support its conclusion that the impact on the mule deer would be minor "since not only has the effectiveness of these mitigation measures not yet been assessed, but the mitigation measures themselves have yet to be developed." *Id.* at 817. It then added that if the agency had difficulty obtaining adequate information to make a reasoned assessment of the environmental impact on the herd, it had a duty to make a so-called "worst case analysis." Such an analysis is "'formulated on the basis of available information, using reasonable projections of the worst possible consequences of a proposed action.'"

The court found a similar defect in the EIS's treatment of air quality. Since the EIS made it clear that commercial development in the Methow Valley will result in violations of state air quality standards unless effective mitigation measures are put in place by the local governments and the private developer, the Court of Appeals concluded that the Forest Service had an affirmative duty to "develop the necessary mitigation measures *before* the permit is granted." *Id.* at 819 (emphasis in original) (footnote omitted). The court held that this duty was imposed by both the Forest Service's own regulations and § 102 of NEPA. *Ibid.* It read the statute as imposing a substantive requirement that "action be taken to mitigate the adverse effects of major federal actions." *Ibid.* (quoting Stop H-3 Assn. v. Brinegar, 389 F. Supp. 1102, 1111 (Haw. 1974), rev'd on other grounds, 533 F.2d 434 (CA9), cert. denied, 429 U.S. 999, 97 S.Ct. 526, 50 L.Ed.2d 610 (1976)). For this reason it concluded that "an EIS must include a fair discussion of measures to mitigate the adverse environmental impacts of a proposed action." 833 F.2d, at 819.

II

Section 101 of NEPAdeclares a broad national commitment to protecting and promoting environmental quality. 83 Stat. 852, 42 U.S.C. § 4331. To ensure that this commitment is "infused into the ongoing programs and actions of the Federal Government, the act also establishes some important 'action-forcing' procedures."

The statutory requirement that a federal agency contemplating a major action prepare such an environmental impact statement serves NEPA's "action-forcing" purpose in two important respects. It ensures that the agency, in reaching its decision, will have available and will carefully consider detailed information concerning significant environmental impacts; it also guarantees that the relevant information will be made available to the larger audience that may also play a role in both the decision making process and the implementation of that decision.

The sweeping policy goals announced in § 101 of NEPAare thus realized through a set of "action-forcing" procedures that require that agencies take a " 'hard look' at environmental consequences," and that provide for broad dissemination of relevant environmental information. Although these procedures are almost certain to affect the agency's substantive decision, it is now well settled that NEPA itself does not mandate particular results, but simply prescribes the necessary process. *See* Strycker's Bay Neighborhood Council, Inc. v. Karlen, 444 U.S. 223, 227-228, 100 S.Ct. 497, 499-500, 62 L.Ed.2d 433 (1980) (per curiam); Vermont Yankee Nuclear Power Corp. v. Natural Resource Defense Council, Inc., 435 U.S. 519, 558, 98 S.Ct. 1197, 1219, 55 L.Ed.2d 460 (1978). If the adverse environmental effects of the proposed action are adequately identified and evaluated, the agency is not constrained by NEPA from deciding that other values outweigh the environmental costs. In this case, for example, it would not have violated NEPA if the Forest Service, after complying with the Act's procedural prerequisites, had decided that the benefits to be derived from downhill skiing at Sandy Butte justified the issuance of a special use permit, notwithstanding the loss of 15 percent, 50 percent, or even 100 percent of the mule deer herd. Other statutes may impose substantive environmental obligations on federal agencies, but NEPA merely prohibits uninformed—rather than unwise—agency action.

To be sure, one important ingredient of an EIS is the discussion of steps that can be taken to mitigate adverse environmental consequences.[2] The requirement that an EIS contain a detailed discussion of possible mitigation measures flows from both the language of the Act and, more expressly, from CEQ's implementing regulations. Implicit in NEPA's demand that an agency prepare a detailed statement on "any adverse environmental effects which cannot be avoided should the proposal be implemented," 42 U.S.C. § 4332(C)(ii), is an understanding that the EIS will discuss the extent to which adverse effects can be avoided.

There is a fundamental distinction, however, between a requirement that mitigation be discussed in sufficient detail to ensure that environmental consequences have been fairly evaluated, on the one hand, and a substantive requirement that a complete mitigation plan be actually formulated and adopted, on the other. In this case, the off-site effects on air quality and on the mule deer herd cannot be mitigated unless nonfederal government agencies take appropriate action. Since it is those state and local governmental bodies that have jurisdiction over the area in which the adverse effects need be addressed and since they have the authority to mitigate them, it would be incongruous to conclude that the Forest Service has no power to act until the local agencies have reached a final conclusion on what mitigating measures they consider necessary. Even more significantly, it would be inconsistent with NEPA's reliance on procedural mechanisms—as opposed to substantive, result-based standards—to demand the presence of a fully developed plan that will mitigate environmental harm before an agency can act.

We thus conclude that the Court of Appeals erred, first, in assuming that "NEPA requires that 'action be taken to mitigate the adverse effects of major federal actions,'" and, second, in finding that this substantive requirement entails the further duty to include in every EIS "a detailed explanation of specific measures which *will* be employed to mitigate the adverse impacts of a proposed action."

III

The Court of Appeals also concluded that the Forest Service had an obligation to make a "worst case analysis" if it could not make a reasoned assessment of the impact of the Early Winters project on the mule deer herd. Such a "worst case analysis" was required at one time by CEQ regulations, but those regulations have since been amended. Moreover, although the prior regulations may well have expressed a permissible application of NEPA, the Act itself does not mandate that uncertainty in predicting environmental

---

[2] CEQ regulations define "mitigation" to include:

"(a) Avoiding the impact altogether by not taking a certain action or parts of an action.

(b) Minimizing impacts by limiting the degree or magnitude of the action and its implementation.

(c) Rectifying the impact by repairing, rehabilitating, or restoring the affected environment.

(d) Reducing or eliminating the impact over time by preservation and maintenance operations during the life of the action.

(e) Compensating for the impact by replacing or providing substitute resources or environments."

40 C.F.R. § 1508.20(1987).

harms be addressed exclusively in this manner. Accordingly, we conclude that the Court of Appeals also erred in requiring the "worst case" study.

In 1977, President Carter directed that CEQ promulgate binding regulations implementing the procedural provisions of NEPA. Exec. Order No. 11991, 3 C.F.R. 123(1977 Comp.). Pursuant to this presidential order, CEQ promulgated implementing regulations. Under § 1502.22 of these regulations—a provision which became known as the "worst case requirement"—CEQ provided that if certain information relevant to the agency's evaluation of the proposed action is either unavailable or too costly to obtain, the agency must include in the EIS a "worst case analysis and an indication of the probability or improbability of its occurrence." 40 C.F.R. § 1502.22(1985). In 1986, however, CEQ replaced the "worst case" requirement with a requirement that federal agencies, in the face of unavailable information concerning a reasonably foreseeable significant environmental consequence, prepare "a summary of existing credible scientific evidence which is relevant to evaluating the . . . adverse impacts" and prepare an "evaluation of such impacts based upon theoretical approaches or research methods generally accepted in the scientific community." 40 C.F.R. § 1502.22(b)(1987). The amended regulation thus "retains the duty to describe the consequences of a remote, but potentially severe impact, but grounds the duty in evaluation of scientific opinion rather than in the framework of a conjectural 'worst case analysis.'" 50 Fed. Reg. 32237 (1985).

The Court of Appeals recognized that the "worst case analysis" regulation has been superseded, yet held that "[t]his rescission . . . does not nullify the requirement . . . since the regulation was merely a codification of prior NEPA case law." 833 F.2d, at 817 n. 11. This conclusion, however, is erroneous in a number of respects. Most notably, review of NEPA case law reveals that the regulation, in fact, was not a codification of prior judicial decisions. The cases cited by the Court of Appeals ultimately rely on the Fifth Circuit's decision in Sierra Club v. Sigler, 695 F.2d 957 (1983). *Sigler*, however, simply recognized that the "worst case analysis" regulation codified the "judicially created principl[e]" that an EIS must "consider the probabilities of the occurrence of any environmental effects it discusses." *Id.* at 970-971. As CEQ recognized at the time it superseded the regulation, case law prior to the adoption of the "worst case analysis" provision did require agencies to describe environmental impacts even in the face of substantial uncertainty, but did not require that this obligation necessarily be met through the mechanism of a "worst case analysis." *See* 51 Fed. Reg. 15625 (1986). CEQ's abandonment of the "worst case analysis" provision, therefore, is not inconsistent with any previously established judicial interpretation of the statute.

Nor are we convinced that the new CEQ regulation is not controlling simply because it was preceded by a rule that was in some respects more demanding. In Andrus v. Sierra Club, 442 U.S., at 358, 99 S.Ct., at 2341, we held that CEQ regulations are entitled to substantial deference. In that case we recognized that although less deference may be in order in some cases in which the " 'administrative guidelines' " conflict " 'with earlier pronouncements of the agency,' " substantial deference is nonetheless appropriate if there appears to have been good reason for the change, 442 U.S., at 358, 99 S.Ct., at 2341.

Here, the amendment only came after the prior regulation had been subjected to considerable criticism. Moreover, the amendment was designed to better serve the twin functions of an EIS—requiring agencies to take a "hard look" at the consequences of the proposed action and providing important information to other groups and individuals. CEQ explained that by requiring that an EIS focus on reasonably foreseeable impacts, the new regulation "will generate information and discussion on those consequences of greatest concern to the public and greatest relevance to the agency's decision," 50 Fed. Reg. 32237 (1985), rather than distorting the decision making process by overemphasizing highly speculative harms, 51 Fed. Reg. 15624-15625 (1986); 50 Fed. Reg. 82236 (1985). In light of this well-considered basis for the change, the new regulation is entitled to substantial deference. Accordingly, the Court of Appeals erred in concluding that the Early Winters Study is inadequate because it failed to include a "worst case analysis."

. . . .

In sum, we conclude that NEPA does not require a fully developed plan detailing what steps *will* be taken to mitigate adverse environmental impacts and does not require a "worst case analysis." In addition, we hold that the Forest Service has adopted a permissible interpretation of its own regulations. The judgment of the Court of Appeals is accordingly reversed and the case is remanded for further proceedings consistent with this opinion.

NOTES AND QUESTIONS

(1) Prior to *Methow Valley*, some courts held that an agency's failure to consider mitigative measures in an EIS required remand. *See, e.g.*, *Louisiana Environmental Society, Inc. v. Coleman*, 437 F.2d 79 (5th Cir. 1976).

(2) The current CEQ regulation, which rescinded CEQ's worst-case regulation and was cited, with approbation, by the *Methow Valley* majority, provides in relevant part:

40 C.F.R. § 1502.22Incomplete or Unavailable Information

When an agency is evaluating reasonably foreseeable significant adverse effects on the human environment in an environmental impact statement and there is incomplete or unavailable information, the agency shall always make clear that such information is lacking.

(a) If the incomplete information relevant to reasonably foreseeable significant adverse impacts is essential to a reasoned choice among alternatives and the overall costs of obtaining it are not exorbitant, the agency shall include the information in the environmental impact statement.

(b) If the information relevant to reasonably foreseeable significant adverse impacts cannot be obtained because the overall costs of obtaining it are exorbitant or the means to obtain it are not known, the agency shall include within the environmental impact statement:

(1) a statement that such information is incomplete or unavailable;

(2) a statement of the relevance of the incomplete or unavailable information to evaluating reasonably foreseeable significant adverse impacts on the human environment;

(3) a summary of existing credible scientific evidence which is relevant to evaluating the reasonably foreseeable significant adverse impacts on the human environment;

(4) the agency's evaluation of such impacts based upon theoretical approaches or research methods generally accepted in the scientific community. For the purposes of this section, "reasonably foreseeable" includes impacts which have catastrophic consequences, even if their probability of occurrence is low, provided that the analysis of the impacts is supported by credible scientific evidence, is not based on pure conjecture, and is within the rule of reason.

Does this regulation reflect the most logical reading of NEPA?

(3) In *Methow Valley*, did the U.S. Supreme Court fail to consider NEPA's express policy that the federal government use "all practicable means" to carry out the Act? Is the decision consistent with the statute's directive that, in conducting their activities, federal agencies consider NEPA "to the fullest extent possible?"

(4) May an agency be held to account for failure to carry out mitigation measures it has promised to implement in a final EIS? In *Coeur D'Alene Lake v. Kiebert*, 790 F. Supp. 998 (D. Ida. 1992), environmental groups brought action against several federal agencies and the Idaho Transportation Department, alleging that the defendants had contravened NEPA by placing fill in a lake in violation of mitigation measures identified in the final EIS. The court dismissed the action. It held that NEPA is a procedural statute and a cause of action may not be based on the failure of a project to live up to commitments made in a final EIS. Did the U.S. Supreme Court's decision in *Methow Valley* compel that result?

§ 5.09 How Effective Is NEPA?

In the nearly three decades since its passage, NEPA has given rise to considerable commentary. The excerpt which follows, from a leading treatise on NEPA law, provides an overview of many of the leading assessments of the statute and its implementation.

Mandelker, "NEPA LAW AND LITIGATION," 11-1 to 11-12, 11-18 to 11-19 (1984/1997)*

Evaluating NEPA

Congress enacted the National Environmental Policy Act to compel federal agencies to broaden their decision making to include environmental values. How Congress expected NEPA to accomplish this change is not entirely clear,

* Reprinted with the permission of West Group, Inc.

and its failure to explain, much less understand, the impact NEPA was expected to have on federal agencies makes evaluation difficult.[1]

. . . .

Evaluations and studies of the effect of NEPA on federal agencies fall into two categories. In one category are evaluations based on personal experience or impressions that critically review NEPA's effects, either negatively or positively. Some of these evaluations appeared soon after NEPA's enactment. They expressed negative criticisms that have influenced attitudes toward NEPA, especially in the academic legal community. More positive evaluations came from observers outside the academic legal community who have been close to NEPA and its implementation.

Empirical studies of the effect of NEPA on federal agency decision-making are the second category of NEPA evaluations. These studies are inconclusive but not entirely negative. Some studies report that the impact statement requirement has influenced agency decision makers to give more emphasis to environmental values.

Negative Evaluations

Shortly after NEPA's enactment, articles authorized by leading law professors expert in administrative and environmental law considered the effect they expected NEPA to have on decision making by federal agencies. These articles took an almost universal negative view of NEPA's role and influence. They are worth reviewing because they continue to have an influence on evaluations of NEPA.

An early article by Professor Joseph Sax, now at the University of California Law School-Berkeley and a leading environmental academic, set the tone.[2] The Sax criticism is significant because he had published a pre-NEPA book advocating a statute authorizing citizen suits in which courts could set aside agency decisions that were harmful to the environment.[3] Sax was much less positive about NEPA in his article, even though judicial enforcement is a critical component of NEPA's implementation.

Although he admitted his views are "personal, impressionistic and limited," Professor Sax began his article by concluding that "the emphasis on the redemptive quality of procedural reform is about nine parts myth and one part coconut oil." He then stated the assumption behind NEPA's enactment, that the impact statement would encourage federal agencies to undertake program revisions in favor of "less environmentally damaging activities." He next indicated the "likely hypotheses" on which this assumption was based,

---

[1] *See* Bear, *The National Environmental Policy Act: Its Origins and Evolutions*, Natural Resources & Env't, Vol. 10, No. 2 at 3 (1995); Bear, *Using the National Environmental Policy Act to Protect Biological Diversity*, 76 Tul. Envtl. L. J. 77 (1994); Comment, *NEPA Business as Usual: The Weaknesses of the National Environmental Policy Act*, 59 J. Air. L. & Comm. 709 (1994); Pollack, *Reimagining NEPA: Choices for Environmentalists*, 9 Harv. Envtl. L. Rev. 359 (1985).

[2] Sax, *The (Unhappy) Truth About NEPA*, 26 Okla. L. Rev. 239 (1973).

[3] Sax, *Defending the Environment* (1970). The statute that Professor Sax proposed has been adopted in Michigan and several other states. For a critique of this legislation, *see* Bryden, *Environmental Rights in Theory and Practice*, 62 Minn. L. Rev. 163 (1978).

although he noted that the legislative history was unclear on this point. These hypotheses included the well-known arguments that environmental evaluation would act as a "road warning," that it would require environmentally knowledgeable staff, that it would alert the public to environmentally damaging programs, and that "the force of fact" would modify agency behavior.

To prove these hypotheses false, Professor Sax examined in detail an impact statement prepared for a new runway at Kennedy International Airport in New York City. The impact statement suggested a number of primary alternatives to the new runway that would make its construction unnecessary. These alternatives included the consolidation of flight schedules to eliminate congestion, improved air traffic control systems, reductions in noise exposure from the use of quieter airplanes and a heavy landing fee on private aircraft.

None of these alternatives were adopted, and Sax saw this outcome as a failure of the impact statement process. He attributed this failure to the scope of the airport agency's statutory authority, which did not include the power to implement these alternatives. Sax concluded that alternatives will not be recommended if they lack the certainty of traditional solutions. He also provided some rules of administrative behavior that were claimed to produce this result. These rules included the tendency to favor the solution whose financing is certain, political sensitivity, the ineffectiveness of public participation, and a failure on the part of agencies with authority to implement "no build" alternatives to take an interest in them.

Professor Sax made his case by concentrating on primary "no build" alternatives to proposed actions as NEPA's principal contribution to environmentally sensitive decision making. This view is a very limited conception of NEPA's environmental decision-making responsibilities. Sax also relied on the tendency of administrators to reject solutions outside their control to argue that NEPA was ineffective. Other legal scholars at the time based their criticisms of NEPA on similar assumptions about the administrative process as it was affected by the primary alternatives problem.

An early article by Professor Arthur Murphy of the Columbia Law School illustrates this complementary line of criticism.[4] Although Professor Murphy limited his article to the adjudicatory licensing proceedings of the federal nuclear regulatory agency, his criticisms apply generally to NEPA's implementation. Part of Murphy's criticism was based on an early landmark NEPA case[5] that required agencies to balance environmental against other values in their decision making. Murphy claimed that this ideal was unattainable because of "the requirement that the adjudicatory body make an independent determination of each issue coupled with the number of potential issues in each case." He quoted a leading authority on administrative behavior who argued that if an administrator must evaluate a decision "in terms of the whole range of human values . . . chaos would replace organization and responsibility would disappear."[6] Professor Murphy gave an example of a

---

[4] "The National Environmental Policy Act and the Licensing Process: Environmentalist Magna Carta or Agency Coup de Grace?," 72 Colum. L. Rev. 964 (1972).

[5] Calvert Cliffs' Coordinating Committee, Inc. v. Atomic Energy Comm'n, 449 F.2d 1109 (D.C. Cir. 1971).

[6] Simon, *Administrative Behavior* 17 (1957).

number of primary "no build" alternatives that were suggested for a nuclear power plant.[7]

Similar themes appeared in another early article by two administrative law experts, Roger Cramton and Richard Berg.[8] They admitted that NEPA had produced a number of beneficial effects but then proceeded to discuss "the dangers of excessive zeal" in its enforcement. Although it was not their only criticism, Cramton and Berg viewed the need to consider primary alternatives in a "balancing" process as one of the major dangers of "excessive zeal." They pointed out that the duty to consider primary alternatives required agencies to constantly reevaluate program values when they considered individual projects. The federal highway agency, for example, would be required to rethink the need for additional highways and whether funds available for highways should be spent for something else. This NEPA obligation required agencies to constantly rethink first principles, but the authors believed that "when program values are viewed as in constant and fluid competition with environmental values, first principles can never be very firmly established."

The concerns these critics expressed about agency responsibilities to consider primary alternatives have not materialized. The courts have limited the primary alternatives agencies are required to consider, and have upheld agency rejections of primary alternatives in most cases.

Cramton and Berg also questioned the ability of the courts to compel change in administrative policy, believing that "administrative agencies are needed to provide the motive power for necessary alternatives to the status quo." Cramton and another coauthor elaborated upon this theme in another early article[9] that considered a general proposal for citizens suits to enforce environmental standards. They questioned the legitimacy and technical competency of the courts as decision makers in environmental disputes, noting that "Rational resolution of environmental problems also involves benefit and resource-distribution judgments which affect broad segments of the economy and population, questions which are necessarily highly political in nature."[10]

The article argued that administrative agencies were better equipped to provide procedures in which competing interests could be heard. Courts should not "revise or reject" agency determinations if this political process were functioning wisely.

The NEPA criticisms that have been reviewed so far all assume a model of the administrative decision making process. This model states that administrators have limited decision-making capabilities, that they seek to preserve

[7] The proceeding in which these alternatives were proposed ultimately went to the Supreme Court, which rejected the most radical alternative.

[8] "On Leading a Horse to Water: NEPA and the Federal Bureaucracy," 71 Mich. L. Rev. 511 (1973). Cramton and Berg also believed that inherent limitations in the administrative process would prevent agencies from carrying out their responsibility to consider primary alternatives. Like Murphy, they believed that a requirement that agencies consider an excessive range of alternatives would paralyze the administrative process. They also noted that agencies could not easily consider alternatives that were outside their areas of expertise, and could not enforce the implementation of alternatives over which they had no jurisdiction.

[9] Cramton & Boyer, "Citizen Suits in the Environmental Field: Peril or Promise?," 2 Ecology L. Q. 407 (1972).

[10] *Id.* at 412.

and enhance the mission-directed activities of their agencies, and that they make decisions incrementally rather than through a rational review of alternatives.[11] The emphasis in these early criticisms was on the ability of the administrative process as portrayed in this model to handle its NEPA responsibilities. These critics did not apply this model to consider the equally important problem that would arise if agencies assumed a hostile attitude toward NEPA and avoided their environmental decision-making responsibilities.

A provocative article by Eugene Bardach and Lucian Pugliaresi,[12] who were responsible for preparing environmental impact statements in the Department of Interior, examined the noncompliance hypothesis. Although they did not adopt an explicit model of administrative decision making, Bardach and Pugliaresi concluded that federal agencies had adapted their programs to the necessities of environmental review through the impact statement. They also claimed that this adaptation did not provide the "hard look" NEPA was intended to guarantee because agency adaptation was largely defensive. This defensiveness prevented environmental analysis from being "penetrating or creative."

The authors gave a number of reasons for this conclusion. One was the "institutional pessimism" that pervaded impact statements. Agencies believed that too little pessimism could lead to "whitewashing" charges and a court order requiring the preparation of a new impact statement. Neither did agencies "wish the impact statement to have the appearance of a "balanced document lest environmental critics allege in a lawsuit that the balancing was incompetent or prejudicial to environmental interests." The desire to avoid an appearance of "balancing" often led an agency to discount the environmental benefits of a project.

Bardach and Pugliaresi also emphasized the potential for legal harassment in impact statement preparation. They claimed that litigating environmentalists made unjustified and exaggerated negative criticisms to advance their case in court. These two contentions—that NEPA produces defensively pessimistic impact statements and that judicial review is counterproductive—are important evaluative conclusions that have been challenged in other evaluations of NEPA's implementation.

. . . .

Positive Evaluations

Positive evaluations of NEPA's implementation by federal agencies appeared about ten years after NEPA's enactment. Richard Liroff, the author of a book[13] and other publications[14] on NEPA's implementation, summarized NEPA's impact on agency decision making in a 1980 article that reviewed ten

[11] An influential article adopting this point of view is Lindblom, "The Art of 'Muddling Through,'" 19 Pub. Admin. Rev. 79 (1959).

[12] "The Environmental-Impact Statement vs. The Real World," 49 Pub. Interest 22 (1979).

[13] Liroff, *A National Policy for the Environment* (1976).

[14] *E.g.*, Liroff, *The Environmental Impact Statement Process Under NEPA (III)* (Environmental Law Institute, 1978).

years of experience under the law.[15] Liroff concentrated on the "agents of change" that have modified agency consideration of environmental values. He believed the requirement for public comments on impact statements had produced positive changes in agency decision making. The openness of the commenting process and the threat of litigation had increased the "political capital" of the commenting process and had led to a greater reliance on environmental information. Change also has resulted from the recruitment of environmental analysts in federal agencies and the modification of organizational structures to promote greater consideration of environmental values.

Liroff concluded that NEPA "was instrumental in expanding the boundaries for conflict over environmental policy and natural resource use." The statute created new rules for "policy warfare and multiplied the arenas in which battles were fought." However, Liroff acknowledged that NEPA is a "blunt instrument." Some projects had been rejected because of an environmental analysis, but some had survived.

Professor Lynton Caldwell, the author of the impact statement requirement, defended NEPA in an article published about the same time.[16] Caldwell responded to negative criticisms that NEPA did not improve environmental decision making by federal agencies. Critics of NEPA also claimed that NEPA distorted the direction of scientific inquiry by shifting funding to applied rather than pure research. Caldwell answered that Congress, not NEPA, determined funding priorities for research and that the term "pure research" no longer was scientifically respectable.

Caldwell also answered the charge that NEPA unrealistically assumed a decision-making process characterized by abstract rationality and focused on a single decision maker unable to undertake the investigation of alternatives that NEPA requires. Caldwell claimed that the principal architects of NEPA consulted experienced students of public administration, were not committed to rational decision making models and were aware that a number of decision makers participated in agency decisions. He noted that many parties who could have contributed to a more balanced decision-making process had not been included prior to NEPA, which was precisely why NEPA required "the integrated use of the natural and social sciences and the environmental design arts"[17] in agency decision making.[18]

A more recent analysis of NEPA's effect on agency decision making by Professor Paul Culhane, who has long experience with NEPA environmental studies, takes a different view.[19] He believes the enactment of NEPA reflected several conflicting goals, but that one important goals was to reform what proponents viewed as a rational agency decision making process by requiring

[15] *NEPA—Where Have We Been and Where Are We Going?* 46 J. Am. Planning Ass'n 154 (1980).

[16] *Is NEPA Inherently Self-Defeating?* 9 ELR 50001 (1978).

[17] § 102(2)(A).

[18] For additional generally positive views of NEPA based on papers delivered at a 1975 symposium, *see* Cahn, *The Impact of NEPA on Public Perception of Environmental Issues,* 6 ELR 50010 (1976); Caldwell, *The National Environmental Policy Act: Retrospect and Prospect,* 6 ELR 50030 (1976); Miller, Anderson & Liroff, *The National Environmental Policy Act and Agency Policy: Neither Paper Tiger Nor Straightjacket,* 6 ELR 50020 (1976).

[19] *NEPA's Impacts on Federal Agencies, Anticipated and Unanticipated,* 20 Envtl. L. 681 (1990).

the identification of relevant alternatives and an analysis of environmental impacts. He cites Professor Caldwell as supporting, rather than opposing, this goal.[20] NEPA's "greatest impact on the federal bureaucracy, Culhane concludes, is that it provided a model for rational decision making and he believes this model dovetails with the professional training and ideology of environmentalists. But Culhane believes that the rational decision-making process NEPA created did not produce optimal decisions. Like other rational attempts at decision making, the NEPA process created interminable delays and litigation that led to the suspension and cancellation of many projects.

Professor Culhane, however, does not subscribe to a rationalist view of agency decision making. He prefers the incremental view of decision making that other critics of NEPA have also embraced. This view of decision making "describes the unpredictable decisions that emerge from 'organized anarchies'." He notes that NEPA did not mandate comprehensive administrative reform despite the concern with rational decision making, so that the statute was sufficiently open-ended to all policy entrepreneurs to read their pet ideas into agency procedures.

Culhane notes several important impacts NEPA had on the federal bureaucracy during its first two decades. These impacts were varied and unpredictable "as a natural result of the varied and often conflicting goals of those who sought to mold the NEPA process." NEPA's action-forcing requirements forced agencies to think about environmental impacts and to diversify staffs so that environmental specialists could take charge of environmental responsibilities. NEPA also increased participation in decision making. Culhane believes, however, that impact statements fall short of the standards for rational-comprehensive analysis that the drafters of NEPA intended, although he notes that precise and accurate impact assessment may simply be "difficult per se." Culhane concludes, despite his criticisms, that "NEPA has been a thoroughly beneficial reform."

. . . .

Studies of NEPA's Effect on Agency Decision Making

An Overview

Empirical studies of environmental decision making by federal agencies can provide an important supplement of impressionistic evaluations of NEPA. To put empirical studies in context, it is important to have criteria under which NEPA's impact can be evaluated. Because Congress expected NEPA to improve environmental decision making by federal agencies, NEPA can be considered successful if it has raised the environmental awareness of federal

[20] The other concerns were that environmental scientists believed that resource decisions did not recognize complex ecosystem relationships; congressmen and their staff were frustrated by the absence of alternatives in agency proposals and wanted a broader range of information for congressional oversight of the bureaucracy; legal reformers wanted to counteract the power conferred in broad delegations of rule making; environmental and citizen groups wanted more public participation in agency decision making; and federal agencies also supported public participation as a way of gaining public support for their decisions.

agencies, and if it has produced agency decisions which are environmentally more satisfactory.

If environmental decision making by federal agencies has improved, a second question is why this improvement has occurred. Both external and internal pressures should be considered. The courts provide important external pressures, for example. They are NEPA's principal enforcers and some commentators stress the importance of judicial enforcement in changing agency decision making.[21] Other commentators claim NEPA has internally reformed agency decision making and that the external pressure of litigation has not been critical.[22]

Comprehensive surveys of federal agencies that can provide answers to these two questions have not been conducted. The Council on Environmental Quality has regularly commissioned surveys of a number of agencies,[23] covering questions such as organization, staff resources, responsiveness, terminations, modifications, "clout" and involvement. The surveys are useful, but the information is too brief and anecdotal to provide a basis for firm conclusions.

A number of law review articles have also examined the effect of NEPA on federal agency programs and projects. Many of these articles appeared in the early years following NEPA's enactment, and articles that examine agency practices under NEPA continue to appear in the law reviews. These articles are useful and the more recent articles contain more sophisticated analysis, but they are usually limited to one agency, are often descriptive and do not prove a basis for a comprehensive evaluation of NEPA's impact.

More comprehensive studies of NEPA's impact have also been carried out.

. . . .

The CEQ NEPA Effectiveness Study

The Council on Environmental Quality carried out an effectiveness study of NEPA's first twenty-five years[24] that included organizations and individuals experienced in the application of NEPA. The report on the study described strengths and weaknesses in NEPA practice and suggested areas of improvement. It noted that while NEPA helps agencies to make better decisions,

---

[21] *E.g.*, Cortner, *A Case Analysis of Policy Implementation: The National Environmental Policy Act of 1969,* 16 Nat. Resources J. 323 (1976) (stressing that courts have ensured compliance with NEPA's procedural decision-making requirements).

[22] *See* Fairfax & Andrews, *Debate Within and Debate Without: NEPA and the Redefinition of the "Prudent Man" Rule,* 19 Nat. Resources J. 505 (1979).

[23] *E.g., NEPA in Action: Environmental Offices in Nineteen Federal Agencies* (Environmental Law Institute 1981). For a review of selected impact statements prepared by federal agencies, *see* Sewell, *The Quality of Scientific Considerations in Decisions Affecting the Environment* (Report to National Science Foundation, 1981). *See also Environmental Quality* 189-220 (21st Annual Report, Council on Envtl. Quality, 1990) (OCSLA and railroad abandonment proceedings).

[24] Council on Environmental Quality, The National Environmental Policy Act: A Study of Its Effectiveness After Twenty-Five Years (1997). For a companion international study, *see* Canadian Envt. Assessment Agency & Int'l Ass'n for Impact Assessment, International Study of the Effectiveness of Environmental Assessment, Final Report: Environmental Assessment in a Changing World (1996).

produce better results, and build trust in communities, it is often triggered too late to be fully effective. Participants in the study praised NEPA for opening up the federal decision-making process to public input and believed an open process improved project design effectiveness and implementation. The report noted, however, that the desired level of public participation was not always achieved.

Interagency coordination in the NEPA process helped to resolve conflicts, reduce duplication, and improve the environmental permitting process, but interagency coordination was hampered when agencies had different timetables, requirements, and public participation modes. The study found that effective use of NEPA requires integrated and interdisciplinary decision making, but that adequate environmental data and the techniques to use it are not always available. The study revealed, though, that federal agencies have been, and continue to improve their data base by developing environmental indicators, and new methods such as geographic information systems (GIS) help agencies to consider cumulative impacts and focus analysis.

Study participants also reported that agencies can improve environmental protection, initiate projects earlier, and dramatically reduce costs by monitoring and modifying project management rather than fully discussing environmental impacts before project approval. CEQ regulations require monitoring and enforcement of "any mitigation" when agencies prepare impact statements,[25] and also authorize agencies to "provide for monitoring to assure that their decisions are carried out and should do so in important cases."[26]

It has been apparent for some time that many more environmental assessments are written than impact statements, and the study noted that the environmental assessment "has evolved to the point where it is the predominant way agencies conduct NEPA analyses."[27] This reliance on assessments creates the danger of diminished public participation and the possibility that individual minor actions will have major adverse cumulative effects. It remains unclear, however, what level of public participation is required in preparing environmental assessments because the NEPA regulations and guidance are oriented primarily to preparing impact statements.

Another major trend is the preparation of mitigated Findings of No Significant Impact (FONSIs) following an environmental assessment. The reason for this trend's emergence is because agencies may discover impacts during the preparation of an assessment that are significant and may require preparation of an impact statement. To avoid the impact statement, agencies conclude the NEPA process by proposing mitigation measures that can remedy environmental impacts. The report cites mitigated FONSIs as a good way to integrate NEPA into planning, but some study participants asserted that FONSIs are sometimes based on less rigorous scientific evidence, little or no public participation, and consideration of fewer alternatives. The report also made suggestions for more effective information analysis and cumulative impact evaluations in impact statements.

---

[25] 40 C.F.R. § 1505.2(c).

[26] *Id.* § 1505.3.

[27] CEQ Effectiveness Report, at 19. *See also* Environmental Quality: 25th Anniversary Report of the Council on Environmental Quality (1997). The Report is available on the White House web site, http://www.whitehouse.gov/CEQ.

NOTES AND QUESTIONS

(1) Based on the materials you have read in this chapter, how would you evaluate the efficacy of NEPA? Should Congress amend the statute? If so, how?

(2) Two other "indirect benefits" of NEPA are also worthy of note: 1) As implemented, the statute has sometimes stimulated active public discussion (and governmental consideration) of the environmental consequences of proposed actions; and 2) at the federal level, compliance with the statute has resulted in a number of inter-agency and inter-departmental discussions of the merits of proposed projects with environmental implications. Are those desirable results? If so, how much weight should they be given in evaluating NEPA's utility?

§ 5.10 Environmental Justice: The Social and Demographic Impact of Environmental Choices

In the 1990s, a confluence of civil rights advocates and environmentalists began to make use of the courts to challenge the siting of polluting or risk creating facilities—especially hazardous waste disposal sites and new heavy industrial plants—in poor, racial minority communities. The three major grounds on which these "environmental justice" suits have been brought are: 1) the Equal Protection Clause of the Fourteenth Amendment of the U.S. Constitution; 2) civil rights laws (primarily Title VI of the Civil Rights Act of 1964); and 3) federal and state environmental laws. For an overview of the outcomes of this litigation to date and the obstacles encountered by its proponents, see F. Grad, Treatise on Environmental Law § 9.10.

Notably, the term environmental justice has also been used, in a broader sense, to refer to other problems including the alleged failure of federal, state and local environmental enforcement programs to respond to the needs of disadvantaged minority groups, the extent of the cleanup to be required at contaminated hazardous waste sites under the federal Superfund program, and the distribution of the cost of cleaning up contaminated waste sites among responsible parties. *See* Manaster, Environmental Protection and Justice, Chapter 4 (1995).

The concerns of environmental justice advocates have engendered a response in the executive branch of the federal government where, in 1992, the U.S. Environmental Protection Agency established an Office of Environmental Equity, to serve as a "point of outreach" for environmental justice, technical assistance, and information.

The following executive order represents an additional reaction by the executive branch to the views of the environmental justice movement.

Executive Order 12898 of February 11, 1994

59 Fed. Reg. 7629 (Feb. 16, 1994).

By the authority vested in me as President by the Constitution and the laws of the United States of America, it is hereby ordered as follows:

Section 1-1. Implementation

1-101. Agency Responsibilities. To the greatest extent practicable and permitted by law, and consistent with the principles set forth in the report on the National Performance Review, each Federal agency shall make achieving environmental justice part of its mission by identifying and addressing, as appropriate, disproportionately high and adverse human health or environmental effects of its programs, policies, and activities on minority populations and low-income populations in the United States and its territories and possessions, the District of Columbia, the Commonwealth of Puerto Rico, and the Commonwealth of the Mariana Islands.

1-102. Creation of an Interagency Working Group on Environmental Justice.

(a) Within 3 months of the date of this order, the Administrator of the Environmental Protection Agency ("Administrator") or the Administrator's designee shall convene an interagency Federal Working Group on Environmental Justice ("Working Group"). The Working Group shall comprise the heads of the following executive agencies and offices, or their designees: (a) Department of Defense; (b) Department of Health and Human Services; (c) Department of Housing and Urban Development; (d) Department of Labor; (e) Department of Agriculture; (f) Department of Transportation; (g) Department of Justice; (h) Department of the Interior; (i) Department of Commerce; (j) Department of Energy; (k) Environmental Protection Agency; (l) Office of Management and Budget; (m) Office of Science and Technology Policy; (n) Office of the Deputy Assistant to the President for Environmental Policy; (o) Office of the Assistant to the President for Domestic Policy; (p) National Economic Council; (q) Council of Economic Advisers; and (r) such other Government officials as the President may designate. The Working Group shall report to the President through the Deputy Assistant to the President for Environmental Policy and the Assistant to the President for Domestic Policy.

(b) The Working Group shall:

(1) provide guidance to Federal agencies on criteria for identifying disproportionately high and adverse human health or environmental effects on minority populations and low-income populations;

(2) coordinate with, provide guidance to, and serve as a clearing-house for, each Federal agency as it develops an environmental justice strategy as required by section 1-103 of this order, in order to ensure that the administration, interpretation and enforcement of programs, activities and policies are undertaken in a consistent manner;

(3) assist in coordinating research by, and stimulating cooperation among, the Environmental Protection Agency, the Department of Health and Human Services, the Department of Housing and Urban Development, and other agencies conducting research or other activities in accordance with section 3-3 of this order;

(4) assist in coordinating data collection, required by this order;

(5) examine existing data and studies on environmental justice;

(6) hold public meetings as required in section 5-502(d) of this order; and

(7) develop interagency model projects on environmental justice that evidence cooperation among Federal agencies.

1-103. Development of Agency Strategies.

(a) Except as provided in section 6-605 of this order, each Federal agency shall develop an agency-wide environmental justice strategy, as set forth in subsections (b)-(e) of this section that identifies and addresses disproportionately high and adverse human health or environmental effects of its programs, policies, and activities on minority populations and low-income populations. The environmental justice strategy shall list programs, policies, planning and public participation processes, enforcement, and/or rulemaking related to human health or the environment that should be revised to, at a minimum: (1) promote enforcement of all health and environmental statutes in areas with minority populations and low-income populations; (2) ensure greater public participation; (3) improve research and data collection relating to the health of and environment of minority populations and low-income populations; and (4) identify differential patterns of consumption of natural resources among minority populations and low-income populations. In addition, the environmental justice strategy shall include, where appropriate, a timetable for undertaking identified revisions and consideration of economic and social implications of the revisions.

(b) Within 4 months of the date of this order, each Federal agency shall identify an internal administrative process for developing its environmental justice strategy, and shall inform the Working Group of the process.

(c) Within 6 months of the date of this order, each Federal agency shall provide the Working Group with an outline of its proposed environmental justice strategy.

(d) Within 10 months of the date of this order, each Federal agency shall provide the Working Group with its proposed environmental justice strategy.

(e) Within 12 months of the date of this order, each Federal agency shall finalize its environmental justice strategy and provide a copy and written description of its strategy to the Working Group. During the 12 month period from the date of this order, each Federal agency, as part of its environmental justice strategy, shall identify several specific projects that can be promptly undertaken to address particular concerns identified during the development of the proposed environmental justice strategy, and a schedule for implementing those projects.

(f) Within 24 months of the date of this order, each Federal agency shall report to the Working Group on its progress in implementing its agency-wide environmental justice strategy.

(g) Federal agencies shall provide additional periodic reports to the Working Group as requested by the Working Group.

1-104. Reports to the President. Within 14 months of the date of this order, the Working Group shall submit to the President, through the Office of the Deputy Assistant to the President for Environmental Policy and the Office of the Assistant to the President for Domestic Policy, a report that describes the implementation of this order, and includes the final environmental justice strategies described in section 1-103(e) of this order.

Section 2-2. Federal Agency Responsibilities for Federal Programs

Each Federal agency shall conduct its programs, policies, and activities that substantially affect human health or the environment, in a manner that ensures that such programs, policies, and activities do not have the effect of excluding persons (including populations) from participating in, denying persons (including populations) the benefits of, or subjecting persons (including populations) to discrimination under, such programs, policies, and activities, because of their race, color, or national origin.

Section 3-3. Research, Data Collection, and Analysis

3-301. Human Health and Environmental Research and Analysis.

(a) Environmental human health research, whenever practicable and appropriate, shall include diverse segments of the population in epidemiological and clinical studies, including segments at high risk from environmental hazards, such as minority populations, low-income populations and workers who may be exposed to substantial environmental hazards.

(b) Environmental human health analyses, whenever practicable and appropriate, shall identify multiple and cumulative exposures.

(c) Federal agencies shall provide minority populations and low-income populations the opportunity to comment on the development and design of research strategies undertaken pursuant to this order.

3-302. Human Health and Environmental Data Collection and Analysis. To the extent permitted by existing law, including the Privacy Act, as amended (5 U.S.C. section 552a):

(a) Each Federal agency, whenever practicable and appropriate, shall collect, maintain, and analyze information assessing and comparing environmental and human health risks borne by populations identified by race, national origin, or income. To the extent practical and appropriate, Federal agencies shall use this information to determine whether their programs, policies, and activities have disproportionately high and adverse human health or environmental effects on minority populations and low-income populations;

(b) In connection with the development and implementation of agency strategies in section 1-103 of this order, each Federal agency, whenever practicable and appropriate, shall collect, maintain and analyze information on the race, national origin, income level, and other readily accessible and appropriate information for areas surrounding facilities or sites expected to have a substantial environmental, human health, or economic effect on the surrounding populations, when such facilities or sites become the subject of a substantial Federal environmental administrative or judicial action. Such information shall be made available to the public, unless prohibited by law; and

(c) Each Federal agency, whenever practicable and appropriate, shall collect, maintain, and analyze information on the race, national origin, income level, and other readily accessible and appropriate information for areas surrounding Federal facilities that are: (1) subject to the reporting requirements under the Emergency Planning and Community Right-to-Know Act, 42 U.S.C. section 11001-11050as mandated in Executive Order No. 12856; and (2) expected to have a substantial environmental, human health, or economic effect on surrounding populations. Such information shall be made available to the public, unless prohibited by law.

(d) In carrying out the responsibilities in this section, each Federal agency, whenever practicable and appropriate, shall share information and eliminate unnecessary duplication of efforts through the use of existing data systems and cooperative agreements among Federal agencies and with State, local, and tribal governments.

Section 4-4. Subsistence Consumption of Fish and Wildlife

4-401. Consumption Patterns. In order to assist in identifying the need for ensuring protection of populations with differential patterns of subsistence consumption of fish and wildlife, Federal agencies, whenever practicable and appropriate, shall collect, maintain, and analyze information on the consumption patterns of populations who principally rely on fish and/or wildlife for subsistence. Federal agencies shall communicate to the public the risks of those consumption patterns.

4-402. Guidance. Federal agencies, whenever practicable and appropriate, shall work in a coordinated manner to publish guidance reflecting the latest scientific information available concerning methods for evaluating the human health risks associated with the consumption of pollutant-bearing fish or wildlife. Agencies shall consider such guidance in developing their policies and rules.

Section 5-5. Public Participation and Access to Information

(a) The public may submit recommendations to Federal agencies relating to the incorporation of environmental justice principles into Federal agency programs or policies. Each Federal agency shall convey such recommendations to the Working Group.

(b) Each Federal agency may, whenever practicable and appropriate, translate crucial public documents, notices, and hearings relating to human health or the environment for limited English speaking populations.

(c) Each federal agency shall work to ensure that public documents, notices, and hearings relating to human health or the environment are concise, understandable, and readily accessible to the public.

(d) The Working Group shall hold public meetings, as appropriate, for the purpose of fact-finding, receiving public comments, and conducting inquiries concerning environmental justice. The Working Group shall prepare for public review a summary of the comments and recommendations discussed at the public meetings.

Section 6-6. General Provisions

6-601. Responsibility for Agency Implementation. The head of each Federal agency shall be responsible for ensuring compliance with this order. Each

Federal agency shall conduct internal reviews and take such other steps as may be necessary to monitor compliance with this order.

6-602. Executive Order No. 12250. This Executive Order is intended to supplement but not supercede Executive Order No. 12250, which requires consistent and effective implementation of various laws prohibiting discriminatory practices in programs receiving Federal financial assistance. Nothing herein shall limit the effect or mandate of Executive Order No. 12250.

6-603. Executive Order No. 12875. This Executive Order is not intended to limit the effect or mandate of Executive Order No. 12875.

6-604. Scope. For purposes of this order, Federal agency means any agency on the Working Group, and such other agencies as may be designated by the President, that conducts any Federal program or activity that substantially affects human health or the environment. Independent agencies are requested to comply with the provisions of this order.

6-605. Petitions for Exemptions. The head of a Federal agency may petition the President for an exemption from the requirements of this order on the grounds that all or some of the petitioning agency's programs or activities should not be subject to the requirements of this order.

6-606. Native American Programs. Each Federal agency responsibility set forth under this order shall apply equally to Native American programs. In addition, the Department of the Interior, in coordination with the Working Group, and, after consultation with tribal leaders, shall coordinate steps to be taken pursuant to this order that address Federally-recognized Indian Tribes.

6-607. Costs. Unless otherwise provided by law, Federal agencies shall assume the financial costs of complying with this order.

6-608. General. Federal agencies shall implement this order consistent with, and to the extent permitted by, existing law.

6-609. Judicial Review. This order is intended only to improve the internal management of the executive branch and is not intended to, nor does it create any right, benefit, or trust responsibility, substantive or procedural, enforceable at law or equity by a party against the United States, its agencies, its officers, or any person. This order shall not be construed to create any right to judicial review involving the compliance or non-compliance of the United States, its agencies, its officers, or any other person with this order.

/s/ WILLIAM J. CLINTON
THE WHITE HOUSE,
February 11, 1994.

NOTE

This Executive Order was the first federal initiative to address the concerns for environmental justice. It is recognized as a new and significant tool in the fight for environmental justice, because it adds environmental justice to the issues that must be considered when planning federal projects having a significant impact on the human environment.

There are criticisms, however, that the Order does not go far enough. In particular, it has been noted that the Order does not create a right of judicial review when there is no agency compliance. Moreover, the Order requires agencies to assess the financial costs of compliance. In failing to provide for judicial review, the agency follows NEPA, which does not articulate a right to judicial review either. Critics note, however, that lack of judicial review in this instance creates a problem because future administrations may be able to ignore the Executive Order's policies without taking any specific formal steps.[1]

It has also been noticed that minority interests may be underrepresented within government agencies, and that without any possibility for judicial review, the policy poses no enforceable duties and may do little more than to implement the personal policies of the president.[2] The Order has not been in effect long enough to have a major impact on environmental decisionmaking.[3] But there have been clear signs that there may be more far-reaching impacts in the future, because after the Order was signed, many agencies promptly complied with the Order's policies by promulgating their own agency environmental justice strategies.[4]

§ 5.11 State Environmental Quality Acts: "Little NEPAs"

NEPA's spillover effect on the individual states has been considerable. Environmental impact is now a major consideration of state agencies planning federally aided or federally regulated projects. Under this impetus, twenty-six states have imposed requirements relating to the filing of environmental impact statements and for the systematic review of state projects. Six states have proceeded by executive direction.[1] Fifteen states have enacted legislation of broad, general applicability,[2] and five have enacted laws to require environmental impact analysis in specified, limited situations.[3] One state, New Mexico, first enacted a law of general applicability and later repealed it.[4]

---

[1] *See* Graham & Grills, *Environmental Justice: A Survey of Federal and State Responses*, 8 Vill. Envtl. L.J. 237, 249 (1997). *See also* Hernandez, *Environmental Justice: Looking Beyond Executive Order No. 12898*, 14 UCLA J. Envtl. L. & Pol'y 181, 206 (1995/96).

[2] *See* Hernandez, *Environmental Justice: Looking Beyond Executive Order No. 12898*, 14 UCLA J. Envtl. L & Pol'y, 181, 207 (1995/96).

[3] *See* Manus, *The Owl, The Indian, The Feminist, and The Brother: Environmentalism Encounters the Social Justice Movement*, 23 B.C. Envtl. Aff. L. Rev. 249, 283 (1996).

[4] *See* Fahsbender, *An Analytical Approach to Defining the Affected Neighborhood in the Environmental Justice Context*, 5 N.Y.U. Envtl. L.J. 120, 175 (1996). John J. Fahsbender believes that most of the agencies' environmental strategies that he reviewed contained little specific guidance.

[1] Arizona: Game and Fish Commission Policy of July 2, 1971, Policy Memo, "Requirements for Environmental Impact Statements," June 9, 1971; Michigan Executive Directive 1974-4, issued by Governor May 3, 1974; Nebraska: Neb. Dept. of Roads, Dept. of Roads Action Plan (1973); New Jersey: N.J. Exec. Order No. 53 (Oct. 15, 1973) and Admin. Order No. 33 (Aug. 1, 1973); Texas: Policy for the Environment, adopted January 1, 1973; Utah: Executive Order of the Governor, Aug. 27, 1974.

[2] California, Connecticut, Hawaii, Indiana, Maryland, Massachusetts, Minnesota, Montana, New York, North Carolina, Puerto Rico, South Dakota, Virginia, Washington, Wisconsin.

[3] Delaware, Mississippi, Georgia, Nevada, North Dakota.

[4] N.M. Stat. Ann. § 12-20-1 *et seq.*, repealed by N.M. Laws 1974, ch. 46, § 1.

The majority of "little NEPAs" either make no mention of a body similar to CEQ or delegate similar duties to preexisting state agencies as, for example, does California. Of the established state councils none follows the federal pattern of a three-person appointed full-time body since Puerto Rico amended its legislation to include four ex-officio agency commissioners on the council, one of whom is to serve as chairperson. Each state includes at least one state official or employee, and states generally allow citizens or citizen advisors. Generally, a balance is maintained between official and citizen participation. The philosophy seems to be one of facilitating interagency coordination while providing for some citizen representation.[5]

While substantially similar to NEPA in many respects, state environmental policy legislation does differ from the federal statute in certain respects. Thus, in general, little NEPAs require greater substantive consideration of environmental values as well as, in many instances the affirmative mitigation of environmental impacts. For an overview of these provisions, see Renz, *The Coming of Age of State Environmental Policy Acts*, 5 Pub. Land L. Rev. 31, 49-52 (1984). It is also noteworthy that, since many little NEPAs apply to local governments, local land use decisions in many states—including rezonings, subdivision approvals, and other approvals of private development projects—are subject to an environmental review process. For a detailed and systematic analysis of one of the most important state statutes of this type (New York's SEQRA), *see* Gerrard, Ruzow and Weinberg, *Environmental Impact Review In New York* (Matthew Bender, 1996).

Note that the CEQ's Regulations require federal agencies to cooperate with state and local agencies to the fullest extent possible in reducing duplication in compliance with state and federal impact statement requirements. Joint planning and research is encouraged, as well as the preparation of a single document which complies with both NEPA and state law. The federal EIS must discuss any inconsistency between the proposal and state or local plans or laws, and the extent to which the federal agency will reconcile the conflict.

"Little NEPAs" in the Courts

Probably the most significant result of "little NEPA" litigation has been the courts' recognition of their relation to the parent act. *Keith v. Volpe* clearly established the power of federal courts to construe a state act in a joint action against federal and state defendants.[6] The California Environmental Quality Act's resemblance to NEPA was held "so uncanny" that the same liberal consideration of applicability need apply to both.[7] Similarly, NEPA guidelines and judicial construction have been held persuasive in interpreting CEQA. In *Friends of Mammoth v. Board of Supervisors of Mono County*,[8] the California Supreme Court found the timing, key provision, and much similar

[5] *See, e.g.,* Delaware (5 citizens appointees, 5 county planning commissioners), Minnesota (7 agency directors, 4 citizen advisors), Montana (4 senators, 4 representatives, 4 members of the public, the governor or his representative), Puerto Rico (3 citizen appointees, 4 commissioners), Virginia (3 citizen appointees, 2 state board chairmen).

[6] Keith v. Volpe, 352 F. Supp. 1324 (C.D. Cal. 1972).

[7] *Id.* at 1337.

[8] 8 Cal. 3d 277, 261 P.2d 1049, 1058, 104 Cal Rptr. 761, 770 (1972).

phraseology of both acts to indicate that the CEQA was "patterned on" NEPA. Accordingly in construing "project" in the state provisions, the definition of that word in the federal act and regulations becomes significant.

The California Court of Appeals elaborated:

> The two statutes are so parallel in context, so nearly identical in words, that judicial interpretation of the federal law is strongly pervasive in our deciding the meaning of our statute.[9]

These findings are significant in evaluating the scope of the majority of "little NEPAs" clearly modeled on the federal act. A state act containing a clear policy statement and no explicit provision to the contrary could easily be held to encompass private activity subject to state regulation or funding as does NEPA with respect to cognate federal involvement.

The issue most litigated with respect to "little NEPAs" is precisely the scope of the subject activity. Here it is important that the California courts have taken the lead in allowing their EQA the broadest possible interpretation based on the liberal intent of its policy statement.[10] Thus, regulated private activity,[11] ongoing projects where it is commercially feasible to do so,[12] and major modifications have been included in its reach.

The courts of Washington have likewise found that their Environmental Protection Act covers all "non-duplicative" discretionary determinations by a proper body concerning an action of requisite impact.[13] Washington also requires preliminary filings at the planning stage if feasible.[14] Ongoing projects were affected, however, only if hearings in the project continued beyond the Act's effective date.[15]

The standard of review for proper agency compliance with the statute has generally been set at "arbitrary or capricious" and judicial review has been reserved for questions of formal sufficiency as opposed to substantive validity as long as the agency itself is not empowered to determine the formal requirements.[16] However, California has held "acting with awareness" of environmental considerations can constitute sufficient compliance in lieu of a formal filing, where the agency in charge did not abuse its discretion.[17] Washington has demanded the formal findings.[18]

---

[9] Environmental Defense Fund, Inc. v. Coastside County Water District, 104 Cal. Rptr. 197, 200, 27 Cal. App. 3d 695, 701, supplemented, 104 Cal. Rptr. 714, 28 Cal. App. 3d 512 (1972). *See also* Inyo County v. Yorty, 108 Cal. Rptr. 377, 385, 32 Cal. App. 3d 795, 807 (Ct. App. Cal. 3d Dist. 1973). *See also*, Note, "State Environmental Impact Statements," 15 Washburn L. J. 64 (1976) (for a discussion of the provisions of the various "little NEPAs" and judicial decisions under them).

[10] *See* F. Grad, Treatise on Environmental Law § 9.08[3].

[11] Friends of Mammoth v. Board of Supervisors of Mono County, *supra* N. 9.

[12] Keith v. Volpe, 352 F. Supp. 1324 (C.D. Cal. 1972).

[13] Eastlake Community Council v. Roanoke Assoc., Inc., 82 Wash. 2d 475, 513 P.2d 36 (1973).

[14] Loveless v. Yantis, 82 Wash. 2d 754, 513 P.2d 1023 (1973).

[15] Stempel v. Department of Water Resources, 82 Wash. 2d 109, 508 P.2d 166 (1973).

[16] Environmental Defense Fund, Inc. v. Coastside County Water District, 104 Cal. Rptr. 197, 200, 27 Cal. App. 3d 695, 701, supplemented, 104 Cal. Rptr. 714, 28 Cal. App. 3d 512 (1972).

[17] No Oil, Inc. v. City of Los Angeles, 111 Cal. Rptr. 487, 36 Cal. App. 3d 149 (Ct. App. Cal. 2d Dist., Div. 3 1973).

[18] Merkel v. Port of Brownville, 8 Wash. App. 844, 509 P.2d 390 (1973).

In conclusion, the history of "little NEPA" litigation to date strongly suggests that the state courts will generally follow the federal courts in their interpretation of NEPA.

Chapter 6

PUBLIC LANDS AND CONSERVATION POLICIES

§ 6.01 Introduction: Public Lands and Conservation of Natural Resources

At the very end of the twentieth century, our thinking about public lands and the protection and conservation of the natural bounty of the nation immediately addresses the tension between developmental and conservational interests. Blessed or burdened with the wealth of a nation that sprawls a continent, we are compelled to make policy and political choices between husbanding our assets, our land and natural resources for another day and for future generations, or treating them as property ready to be spent, neither heedlessly nor particularly carefully because there appears to be so much of it around.

Public land, the land belonging to the nation, amounting to about one third of all the land in the nation, is our most valuable natural resource. Until the end of the nineteenth century there was little concern to plan or to manage the public lands. If there was any national policy relating to the public lands it was to dispose of it as quickly as possible for a variety of uses which seemed reasonable at the time without any stringent controls or constraints. Large amounts of land were conveyed to farmers and ranchers under various homestead acts. The open range in the West was used for grazing by privately owned cattle virtually without any controls. It was this acceptance of the private use of public land that is reflected also in the 1872 Hard Rock Mining Law, which, in the main unchanged, still casts a blight on planned resource development and serves as a reminder of earlier attitudes toward the uses of the public lands. It is more than a mere reminder, however; our inability to repeal this outrageous anachronism is still part of the current attitude, particularly prevalent in the western part of the United States, that the wealth of the nation is there for the taking by politically adept entrepreneurs.

Western politics has long asserted the right to exploit natural resources and to make use of public property at the lowest price possible, lawfully and without any substantial legal constraints. Nevertheless, some advances have been made. The second half of the twentieth century saw a great deal of progress in the planning and regulation of the uses of the national public lands, as well as major efforts to protect and conserve natural resources. But it is also clear that raw political power on the part of western legislators has all too often succeeded in thwarting, limiting or postponing regulatory efforts to protect public lands, public resources, and natural treasures which, once destroyed or wasted, can never be entirely reclaimed.

To provide just one example, note the case of *TVA v. Hill,* generally touted as a major victory for the Endangered Species Act and for the protection of an endangered species. It was certainly a great and principled victory, but it didn't last because when all the litigation was over, a group of legislators sneaked a brief amendment into an appropriation bill which specifically rendered the Endangered Species Act inapplicable to the completion of the Tellico Dam. So too, western legislators in the nineties defeated the effort to allow reasonable grazing fees to be set by regulation, protecting both the interests of western cattlemen and the interests of eastern hamburger joints. While the saga of the northern spotted owl, and the role it plays in protecting old growth lumber has not as yet played out, it is clear that ad hoc legislation designed to undo principled court decision enforcing existing laws is in the process of reversing many years of preservational efforts.

The contest between developmental interests and conservational interests to protect the integrity of valuable land and resources for the future is a continuing one. Though there have been environmental victories as well as setbacks, it is nonetheless clear that the rules of the game have been changed significantly, in terms of both substance and procedure, enabling environmental and conservational interests to get into court and raise the significant substantive issues which the laws now provide.

Legislation to protect the national interest in the public lands and procedural laws and regulations to enable environmental and protectionist interests to have their day in court have developed very recently in the history of the nation and in its growing concern for the protection of public lands. It was only in President Theodore Roosevelt's era at the turn of the century that conservational interests and awareness of the great national treasure of our public lands became part of the nation's consciousness. It took much longer for the law to provide the tools for the protection of conservational and preservational interests. Until the early part of the 1900s, the federal government acted primarily as a proprietor and not as a regulator. Early public land determinations were very difficult to challenge because they were regularly met by the defense of sovereign immunity, which came close to representing an absolute bar until 1976, when Section 702 of the Administrative Procedure Act (APA) was amended to provide that sovereign immunity would no longer be a bar to judicial review of any administrative action otherwise subject to review.[1]

Another barrier keeping preservationists from challenging actions affecting the public lands was the defense of lack of standing. That barrier was also removed through the APA grant of standing to persons who could show that they were aggrieved within the meaning of the Act. Standing barriers were also limited by judicial decisions holding that standing could be based on conservational, esthetic or environmental interests. Another recurring barrier to public interest actions involving public lands was the defense that the action challenged was not reviewable because it was "agency action committed to agency discretion by law" within the meaning of the APA. When this defense is asserted, courts normally look to see whether there is "law to apply." If so, the claim of discretion normally fails. The passage of the National Environmental Policy Act, effective in 1970, provided law to apply to most actions

[1] *See* Grad, Treatise on Environmental Law, § 12.02[2][b].

involving public lands. So too, the passage of other laws relating to the uses of the public lands as well as laws protective of designated environmental and conservational interests have narrowed the area in which agencies may assert that their action was committed to agency discretion by law, because there is now a great deal of law to apply, as will clearly appear from the array of public lands and conservation legislation passed in the last 30 years or so.[2]

The purpose of this chapter is to provide a significant overview of what comprises the federal lands and what agencies manage them. Congress exercises powers over the federal lands, and such powers are practically unlimited. It is essentially Congress that defines what lands are public lands and to what uses they may be put. Since the public lands comprise about one third of the nation's land, they represent substantial national wealth and their uses may fulfill various national policies and purposes.

Since 1960, and the enactment of the Multiple-Use Sustained Yield Act, the law provides for no dominant use of the public land but rather supports multiple uses and uses which will advance a sustained yield. The dominant piece of legislation for the management of federal lands is the 1976 Federal Land Policy and Management Act, which, while reaffirming multiple use and sustained yield, provides for a number of management controls relating to the acquisition, or regulation and use of the public lands. The agencies that manage the public lands include the Bureau of Land Management (BLM), which manages general public lands not otherwise designated. The BLM is part of the Department of the Interior and it manages some 340 million acres. The U.S. Forest Service, a part of the Department of Agriculture, manages the vast national forests, amounting to some 191 million acres. National wildlife refuges are managed by the U.S. Fish and Wildlife Service, also in the Department of the Interior, as are the national parks managed by the National Parks Service. There are also wilderness areas established under the Wilderness Act of 1964. Wilderness areas may be designated from lands managed by BLM, lands managed by the Forest Service, lands in national parks managed by the National Park Service or in national wildlife refuges managed by the U.S. Fish and Wildlife Service. The multiple use and sustained yield requirement for public lands applies both to the lands managed by BLM and to lands managed by the U.S. Forest Service.

Special laws cover particular uses. The National Forest Management Act of 1976 provides the general guidelines for forest management and other laws, notably the Taylor Act and its subsequent amendments, and laws such as the Forest and Rangeland Renewable Resources Planning Act of 1974 address the management of the range and grazing lands.

A significant use of the public lands is for mining and mineral resources. In addition to the 1872 Hard Rock Mining Law, an ancient fossil of legislation which still governs major mining activities on the public lands, oil, gas, coal and certain other named minerals may be mined or drilled for on public lands under the Mining Leasing Acts of 1920 and 1947, and on the continental shelf under the Outer Continental Shelf Lands Act of 1953. Another mining law, the Common Varieties Act of 1955, deals with other minerals, excluding sand,

---

[2] Grad, Treatise on Environmental Law, § 12.02[2][d].

stone, gravel, etc. In an effort to reconcile the administration of the mining laws, Congress enacted the Multiple Mineral Development Act in 1954. Following the enactment in 1970 of the one-section Mining and Minerals Policy Act of 1970, mining regulations began increasingly to reflect environmental concerns relating to mineral waste products and the reclamation of mined land, so as to lessen any adverse impact of mineral extraction upon the physical environment. The Mining and Minerals Policy Act of 1970 was the first law which in its legislative history reflected a concern for the conservation of natural resources, and for the protection of the health and safety of miners.

Another increasingly important use of the nation's lands are recreational uses, focused on the National Parks System and to some extent on the national forest system. Recreational uses have become increasingly important, with the National Parks System having an ever increasing problem of managing more visitors than the national parks can handle without damage to the very scenic and natural values which attract the visitors in the first place. Thus, recreational uses are constantly at war with preservational uses, not only in the national parks but also in the increasing number of wilderness areas which form a part of the national wilderness preservation system.

Selected areas of conservation legislation must also be referred to, particularly the protection of fish and wildlife under the Fish and Wildlife Coordination Act which is managed by the U.S. Fish and Wildlife Service, part of the Department of the Interior. In the protection of fish and wildlife, a dominant theme is the protection of habitat essential to the survival of many species.

A special area of protection which is treated at some length in this chapter is the protection of endangered species under the Endangered Species Act of 1975. It is treated in some detail because the protection of endangered species and the protection of their habitat has had a major impact on developmental activities, so that the ESA, in combination with the National Environmental Policy Act, has served as a major protection of critical habitats, a protection which has provided some necessary barriers to heedless developmental initiatives.

The review of litigation involving the Endangered Species Act—often in combination with the National Environmental Policy Act—provides an opportunity to examine legislative approaches not only to the preservation of endangered species, but also to the protection of environmental values generally and to the kinds of regulatory means appropriate to the effort of environmental protection generally.

§ 6.02 The Federal Lands and the Agencies That Manage Them

Constitution of the United States
Article IV, Section 3

The Congress shall have Power to dispose of and make all needful Rules and Regulations respecting the Territory or other Property belonging to the

United States; and nothing in this constitution shall be so construed as to Prejudice any Claims of the United States, or of any particular State.

GIBSON v. CHOUTEAU

80 U.S. (13 Wallace) 92, 99 (1871)

With respect to the public domain, the Constitution vests in Congress the power of disposition and of making all needful rules and regulations. That power is subject to no limitations. Congress has the absolute right to prescribe the times, the conditions, and the mode of transferring this property, or any part of it, and to designate the persons to whom the transfer shall be made. No State legislation can interfere with this right or embarrass its exercise; and to prevent the possibility of any attempted interference with it, a provision has been usually inserted in the compacts by which new States have been admitted into the Union, that such interference with the primary disposal of the soil of the United States shall never be made. . . .

Council on Environmental Quality First Annual Report, 165-167, 179-183

(transmitted to Congress, August 1970)

The 50 States comprise about 2.3 billion acres of land. Of that, 1.9 billion acres lie in the contiguous 48 States. Nearly 58 percent of the land area is used for crops and livestock. More than 22 percent is ungrazed forest land. Less than 3 percent is in urban and transportation uses, although it is increasing. Areas designated primarily for parks, recreation, wildlife refuges, and public installations and facilities account for about 5 percent. The rest—12 percent—is mainly desert, swamp, tundra, and other lands presently of limited use by man.

Almost 59 percent of the land is in private hands. Thirty-four percent is owned by the Federal Government. Some 94 percent of all Federal lands lie in the westernmost States—about half in Alaska alone. About 2 percent of the Nation's land is held by Indians. The rest—about 5 percent—is State, city, or county owned.

But land is not just acreage. Land embraces the complex biological systems of the soil and the plants and animals which are all part of a continuing life cycle. Man's understanding of these biological processes, particularly of the permanent damage that begins subtly with piecemeal alterations of the land, is still limited. Yet his dependence upon its stability is enormous.

In the Nation's early history, easy availability of land prodded millions to join the massive migrations west and along the major river basins. The wilderness was to be tamed, the trees cleared, and the soil put to crops. Much of the wilderness is now gone, and most of what is left is far distant from the three-quarters of the Nation that lives in the cities and the suburbs. The landscape visible to most Americans is cluttered with traffic, neon signs, power lines, and sprawl. Flood plains are not just for the river but are subjected to intense development. Open space, the elbow room for urban man, continues to dwindle. Unfortunately, traditions of land use have derived from an assumption that land is a limitless commodity—not a finite biological community.

Government spurs much of this land development by where it locates and how it designs airports and highways, insures home loans, permits filling of wetlands, and lays water and sewer lines. Local governments exercise the primary authority over land use. But effective public influence is hampered by a lack of agreement on objectives, by misplaced economic incentives, and by failure of local governments to harmonize land use.

The Federal lands

Management of most Federal natural lands falls under four agencies:

	Million acres
Department of the Interior:	
Bureau of Land Management	470.4
Fish and Wildlife Service	30.5
National Park Service	27.1
Department of Agriculture:	
Forest Service	186.9

Many other forests, parks, and recreation and conservation areas have also been set aside by State and local governments and by citizens groups with an interest in the natural environment.

Their management varies from protective preservation to multiple use. Most of the Federal lands are managed to combine outdoor recreation, range, timber, watershed, and fish and wildlife uses. Many of the management programs permit the extraction of oil, gas, and other minerals; others aim primarily at esthetic values. Although Federal land management is meant to maximize public benefit and not to reflect only economic gain, land management agencies have been criticized for policies that overemphasize developmental values.

As other natural areas are staked out for intensive resource development, they are bound to come into even more serious conflict with preservation and recreational interests. Statutory resolution of many of these potential conflicts may be necessary, as may administrative reforms by the Executive Branch.

. . . .

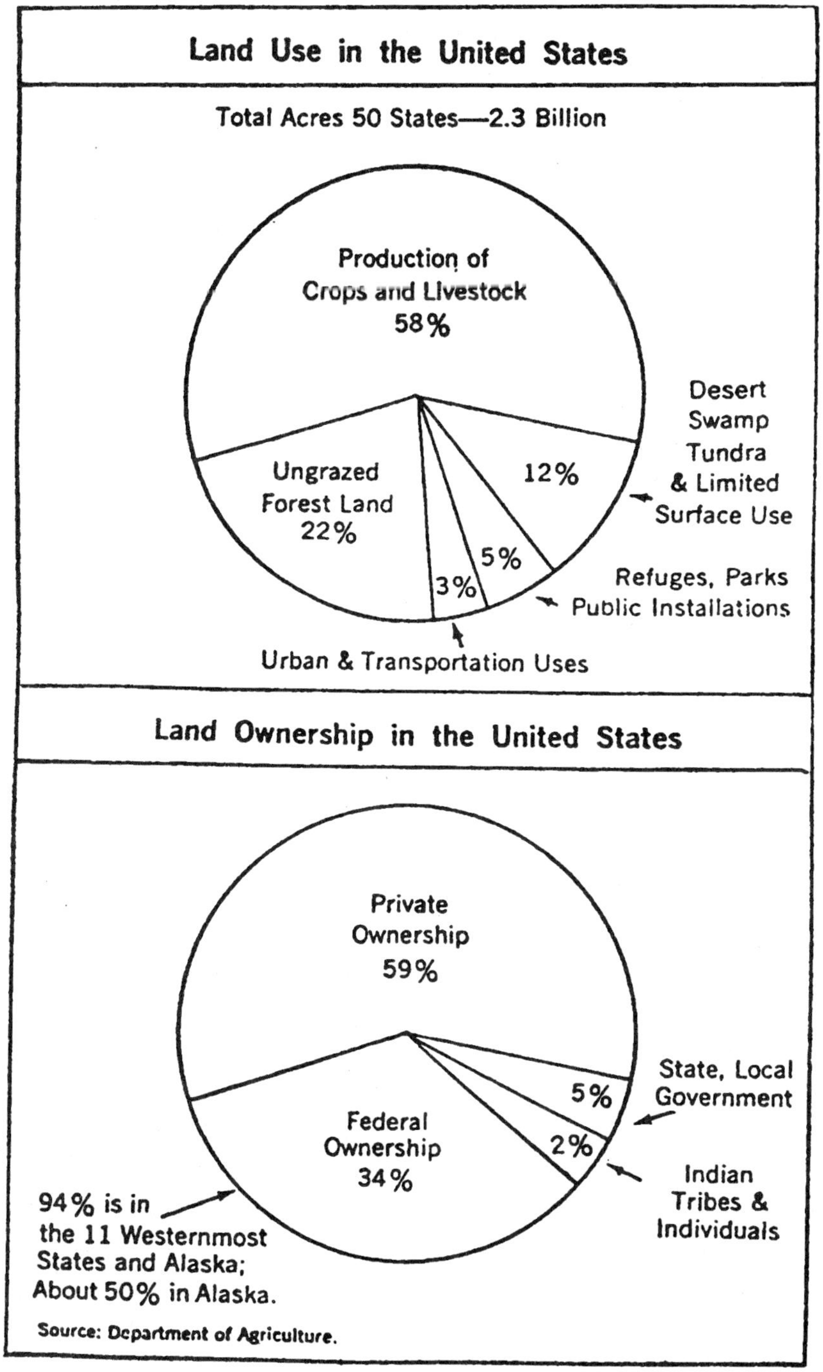

Federal lands managed primarily for the protection of their natural characteristics and the preservation of their fish and wildlife can take only so much use by man. Allowing people to enter these areas in large numbers must be weighed against their impact on the region's ecology. Protected areas must be managed so that constraints are placed on certain uses, including recreational uses requiring motorized transport.

The wilderness system

Some large areas under Federal control are expressly set aside as wilderness. The Wilderness Act of 1964 already protects approximately 10 million acres, although less than one percent of this is east of the Mississippi River. The Wilderness Act requires the Secretaries of Agriculture and the Interior to submit plans to Congress for including in the National Wilderness Preservation System additional natural areas having substantial wilderness qualities and presently managed by the Forest Service, the National Park Service, and the Fish and Wildlife Service. These areas are to be of sufficient size, permanently roadless, and without commercial development.

. . . .

Scattered throughout the Federal lands under various agencies are 336 "research natural areas"—a specific classification for lands left undisturbed for purposes of research and education. A number of ecosystems, however, such as the tall grass prairie of the Central Lowlands, are sparsely represented or are not included at all. Plans are now under consideration to add approximately 300 areas so that all major ecosystems will be represented.

Acquisition of natural areas

The major source of funds to purchase most Federal natural areas is the Land and Water Conservation Fund. Revenues for it comes primarily from a tax on motorboat fuel, sale of surplus Federal property, Treasury appropriations, user fees from Federal recreation areas, and—to bring the total to $200 million each year—Outer Continental Shelf mineral receipts . . .

The Migratory Bird Conservation Act of 1929 authorizes the Government to purchase additions to the 30-million acre National Wildlife Refuge System. Funds for this come mostly from the Migratory Bird Hunting Stamp Act of 1934, which requires all waterfowl hunters to purchase a Federal hunting stamp. Although about 25 million acres in the present 328-unit system are Federal lands which were withdrawn for refuge purposes, most of the national wildlife refuges acquired in the past 15 years have been bought with funds from sale of these "duckstamps."

Crowding

Natural areas under the direction of the National Park Service have become immensely popular with the millions who visit them each year. Yet the enjoyment diminishes as the number of tourists rises. Some of the more popular natural areas in our parklands have become clogged with traffic, noise, litter, smog, and most of the other elements of our technological society from which the visitors are trying to escape.

Exploitation

Timber is cut and sold from the national forests, and to a lesser extent, from lands administered by the Bureau of Land Management. This use is a growing one. Cattle and sheep are permitted to graze on approximately 273 million acres of Federal land. Mineral leasing, mostly oil and gas, now uses over 64 million acres. Most of the public lands are open for recreation in one form or another. Across all these lands are spread diverse habitats which support varied species of wildlife.

Overgrazing, widely practiced during the latter part of the 19th and early parts of the 20th century—and still a problem today—has dramatically affected these lands. The semiarid and arid climate of the West has added to the destruction. Dry years have usually coincided with falling market prices. And when that has happened, cattle and sheep ranchers short of cash have often overstocked already depleted ranges. Much of this land, particularly the vast public domain, remains today in desperate condition, as wind, rain, and drought have swept over them and eroded their exposed soils. Although the effects of overgrazing in rich pastures or prairie farmland can be quickly corrected, the process is often irreversible on the limited soils and arid climate of much of the public lands.

What overgrazing does to the soils and habitat of the vast range lands, poor lumbering practices do to the forests. Mismanagement of timber cutting, in addition to being an eyesore, can also damage natural systems far beyond the forests. Debris and erosion of the limited soils of the forested West often choke streambeds far downstream. The tendency toward monoculture for the benefit of lumber and pulp has its environmental results. Not the least of these is the loss of many native species. The greatest loss of timber is not from fire and disease but from insects, which can devastate large forests of single species. Widespread application of insecticides often follows.

NOTE

As the preceding excerpt from the Report of the Council on Environmental Quality points out, more than one-third of all the land in the United States is owned by the Federal Government. Of that land, 94 percent is in the eleven western states and Alaska; Alaska, indeed, contains half of all the land owned by the United States. Federal ownership extends from approximately 29 percent of the land of the state of Washington to more than 85 percent of the land of the state of Nevada. *See* Council on Environmental Quality, *Environmental Quality—Thirteenth Annual Report*, Table A-1 at 245 (1982). Thus, federal land ownership is capable of exerting enormous impact on the development and economic growth of the western states. If federal lands are not effectively utilized or if their utilization is in any way unbalanced, preferring one economic interest over another, or preferring resource exploitation over preservational purposes, the long-range effects of such federal policies will not only harm the ordinary development of the western states but will also have vast, and possibly irreversible impact on the ecology of the country as a whole.

Until the mid-seventies the public lands were administered under a vast miscellany of statutes passed from time to time from the beginning of the Republic and reflecting a variety of purposes depending on their time of passage and the particular economic and other interests involved in their sponsorship. The subject of public land management is a vast and important one and its economic ramifications go considerably beyond the scope of any work on environmental protection. While our consideration of public land management policies focuses primarily on their environmental impact, it is important to realize that decisions regarding land management, including judicial decisions, in areas that have no immediate environmental significance may have important value as precedents when environmental issues regarding public land management arise.

The importance of unified and coherent policies regarding the management of the vast federal lands has long been apparent. The materials that follow demonstrate the diverse policy considerations that enter into any decision affecting the disposal, rental, or use of public lands. The need for coherent policies had been apparent for some time when in 1963 Congressman Wayne N. Aspinall, Representative from the State of Colorado and Chairman of the House Committee on Interior and Insular Affairs, called for the enactment of a legislative program to obtain a reconsideration of the public land laws and their underlying policies in the light of contemporary conditions. He introduced the bill to establish the Public Land Law Review Commission, which was enacted into law on September 19, 1964 as Pub. L. No. 88-606, 78 Stat. 982, 43 U.S.C. §§ 1391-1400(1964). The purpose of the legislation as articulated in Section 2 of the Act was as follows:

> "Because the public land laws of the United States have developed over a long period of years through a series of Acts of Congress which are not fully correlated with each other and because those laws, or some of them, may be inadequate to meet the current and future needs of the American people and because administration of the public lands and the laws relating thereto has been divided among several agencies of the Federal Government, it is necessary to have a comprehensive review of those laws and the rules and regulations promulgated thereunder and to determine whether and to what extent revisions thereof are necessary."

The establishment of the Commission gave rise to hopes that some of the legislative and administrative confusion in public lands law would be resolved. Moreover, the Congressional reports pertaining to Public Law 88-606 indicated a number of urgent problems of a substantive nature. Basic policy on what public lands should be retained and which should be disposed of needed to be resolved. Conflicts of direction between the legislation and executive branches of the federal government needed to be dealt with, as well as conflicts on public land issues between the federal government and the several states. Some specific problems, such as the mining laws and the mineral leasing laws, needed to be reviewed, including the resolution of the anachronistic issues raised by the 1872 Hard Rock Mining Law. The formation of the Commission was considered a very significant legislative initiative, particularly from the point of view of the western states.[1]

The term of the Commission was initially set for three years and was extended to five years in 1967, when its appropriation was also increased to $7.39 million. Though it produced a lot of subsidiary studies, its final report, issued in June of 1970, settled few issues in public land management and created and aggravated some of the issues previously raised. It was disappointing in many of its anachronistic and lopsided policy choices. It wanted Congress to reassert its constitutional primacy in supervising the use of public lands and that it curb the president's power to shift public land from one use to another. It favored exploitative uses of the public lands over preservational ones. It reflected the usual view of western representatives that public land laws be revised to remove obstacles to such activities as mining, timber cutting and agriculture. In line with this recommendation was the proposal that the United States Forest Service be shifted from the Department of Agriculture to the Department of the Interior. It also recommended that land be made available to states for urban expansion. While recommending that there be no further large scale disposal of public lands, it also recommended that only such lands be removed from federal control as will yield maximum benefits for the public under nonfederal ownership. It recommended also that Congress establish guidelines and criteria to govern the management of public lands, replacing the broad authority presently delegated to executive agencies. In the Commission's view, Congress should have exclusive authority to set aside public lands for special uses, and in the absence of Congressional legislation it recommended express limits on the authority of the executive branch to designate such uses. The Presidents had been responsible, it should be remembered, for the creation of the National Forests, and for the reservation of the Wilderness Preservation System. Significantly, reflecting the largely western composition of the Commission's membership, the report championed "a maximum benefit" approach moving from a major emphasis on multiple use to a dominant use to yield maximum benefits. Though the report made a show of supporting the enhancement of environmental values, the major thrust of the report was to reassure private users of public lands. Some of the recommendations of the Commission relating to the use of public lands cannot stand detailed examination because of the recurring inconsistences between language that purports to be protective and language that presses maximum benefit and the protection of private interests.

The New York Times editorial comment is soundly based:

> Luckily for the country, the end product of five years of work by the Public Land Law Review Commission is a report, not yet a piece of legislation. As a study, curiously outmoded in tone, it can be read, pondered and put on the shelf. As an omnibus bill for the reform of American land policy it would

[1] For detailed accounts of the work of the Commission, *see* D.R. Phipps, *The Public Land Law Review Commission—A Challenge to the West,* 1 Land & Water L. Rev. 355, 357 (1966). For a running account of the Commission's work, *see* the following articles by the same author: *The Public Land Law Review Commission—Identifying and Defining the Problem*, 2 Land & Water L. Rev. 253 (1967); *The Public Land Law Review Commission—Status Report 1967-1968,* 3 Land & Water L. Rev. 301 (1968); and *The Public Land Law Review Commission—Status Report 1968-1969,* 4 Land & Water L. Rev. 318 (1969).

call for alarm signals from every conservation group in the land. *New York Times*, June 25, 1970, p. 44.

Continuing its comment, the Times expressed dismay at the fact that the report is "not encouraging to those who like to feel the country is moving away from the idea of the dollar sign as the measure of progress." The editorial comment expressly attacked the concept of "dominant use" to "yield maximum benefit," singling out for condemnation the recommendation that tracts promising a high timber yield, namely the nationally owned forests, be classified for commercial timber production. The editorial comment also raises the question whether expanding congressional authority over public lands is necessarily the answer—whether, indeed, the answer lies in concentrating control over public lands in congressional committees composed largely of Westerners whose political purpose has long been to advance the profitable use of natural resources.

It may be worth noting that the Commission's report was delivered in mid-1970, the year sometimes referred to as the year of the environment. When the Commission delivered its report, the National Environmental Policy Act had been enacted and was about to become effective. When the report was delivered to Congress, it had become an anachronism, because many determinations relating to the use of the public lands had become the subject of environmental impact review.

The Role of the Bureau of Land Management in the U.S. Department of the Interior

The function of the Bureau of Land Management (BLM) is described in its 1998 annual report from which the following materials have been drawn.[2] BLM manages 264 million acres of public lands, about one-eighth of the land area of the United States, and approximately 300 million additional acres of subsurface mineral estate. Most of the land acreage is in the western states and in Alaska. BLM manages more acreage of public land than any other agency. Among its varied responsibilities it lists stewardship for recreational opportunities on public lands; commercial activities on public lands; wildlife habitat; transportation systems, including roads, trails and bridges; paleontological localities and archaeological and historical sites; wild free-roaming horses and burros; wilderness and wilderness study areas; wild and scenic rivers; rare, vulnerable and representative habitats and ecosystems; and interpretive activities to meet scientific and educational needs.[3]

BLM administers 205,498 miles of fishable streams; 2.2 million acres of lakes and reservoirs; 6,600 miles of floatable rivers; over 500 boating access points; 64 national backcountry byways; and 300 watchable wildlife sites.

Among its commercial activities, BLM notes that during fiscal year 1998 the public lands produced 31% of the nation's coal, 11% of its natural gas,

[2] U.S. Department of the Interior, Bureau of Land Management, Your Lands, Your Legacy (1998 Annual Report). References in the notes that follow are to pages of the 1998 report.

[3] Page 4.

and 5% of its oil. National lands also produced a large portion of the nation's fertilizer minerals, mineral materials, gold, silver, and other metals. It also supervises mineral development on Indian lands. Livestock grazing on public lands is central to the economies and culture of many local communities. Each one dollar of grazing value, BLM notes, translates to $4.30 of economic benefit. The 1998 estimated market value of production occurring on the public lands was $11.8 billion, 99% of which was derived from energy and minerals. The direct and indirect economic impact of all commercial activities amounted to $26.3 billion.[4]

The report also lists major stewardship activities for national conservation areas, historic trails, scenic trails, national recreational areas and national natural landmarks, as well as research natural areas, five world heritage sites, three biosphere reserves, and two globally important bird areas.[5]

The report provides a detailed account of the 44,000 wild horses and burros in 201 herd management areas on the western public lands[6] as well as an account of its activities to protect threatened and endangered plants and animals.[7]

BLM provides an account of its stewardship of range lands, indicating that its count, some 6,057,599 acres of range lands, "meet all standards or are making significant progress towards meeting the standards" for ecologically sound range lands. Some 2,876,171 acres are not meeting all standards and are not making significant progress towards that goal, but action has been taken to ensure significant progress in the future. Only some 297,529 acres of range land are counted as not meeting all standards or not making significant progress towards meeting the standards.[8]

A significantly detailed account of BLM's activities in the area of water, riparian area and wetland health notes activity and significant progress. Its chart shows that about one third of riparian areas are in proper functioning condition, one third are functional at risk, and the remaining third appears to be in major measure unknown and in lesser measure non-functional.[9]

BLM also notes its major activities in broad areas of reforestation and forest stand treatment. The report details the agency's activities in different kinds of habitats, including riparian wetlands.[10] What is noteworthy, however, is that here as well as in other parts of its report, BLM makes no mention of the Department of Agriculture Forest Service, and on the face of the BLM report, there appears to be little connection between forest management by BLM and the National Forest Service. This is noteworthy because FLPMA, the Federal Land Policy and Management Act of 1976, which takes the role of an organic law for BLM, imposes parallel obligations on BLM and the Forest Service in the management of national forest lands. The absence of any mention of the National Forest Service is especially noteworthy because the BLM report stresses its multijurisdictional planning efforts and land use

[4] Page 11.

[5] Page 17.

[6] Page 18.

[7] Page 19.

[8] Page 26.

[9] Page 28.

[10] Pages 29-30.

planning issues for areas containing a mix of public and private land ownerships and overlapping government authorities.[11]

BLM refers to its application of the multiple use concept in its management of public lands, referring inter alia to range land. BLM manages 165 million acres of range land in the continental United States and another five million acres of reindeer range in Alaska. The report contains an analysis of the condition of rangelands noting that five million acres of Alaska reindeer range are in good condition and that 165 million acres of the continental U.S. range vary from excellent (29%), to fair (38%), and poor (12%), with some 16% being unclassified. Riparian areas and wetlands are largely properly functioning in Alaska, and in the lower 48 states are functioning in 36% of the acreage, functioning but at risk in 35%, nonfunctioning in 9% and unknown in 20%. Somewhat similar variations are noted in wetlands areas in the lower 48 states. In general it appears from the BLM evaluations that rangeland in Alaska is generally in much better shape than in the lower 48 states.[12]

The report notes that approximately one sixth of land under BLM jurisdiction is forest land, encompassing approximately 47 million acres, with 22 million acres in Alaska and the remaining 25 million in the 11 western states. The BLM forest lands are managed under the multiple use, sustained yield, and environmental quality protection required under the Federal Land Policy and Management Act (FLPMA). The report notes that of the 2.1 million acres of commercial forest land in western Oregon, about 492,000 acres are intensively managed for timber. The most valuable and intensively managed forest lands of the BLM are the 2.1 million acres in western Oregon known as the "Oregon and California (O&C) railroad grant lands" and the Coos Bay Wagon Road (CBWR) grant lands. These highly productive lands, managed under the Northwest Forest Plan, produce about 95% of the total value of timber harvested annually from BLM forests.[13]

Note that here too there is neither mention nor comparison with National Forest Service managed timberlands.

BLM notes the number and size of designated special management areas it is responsible for, including national wild and scenic rivers, wilderness areas, wilderness study areas, national conservation areas, a number of named recreation areas, national recreation trails, areas of critical environmental concern, as well as other specially designated areas including globally important bird areas.[14]

BLM provides a substantial account of its activities and involvements in a variety of special research and national landmark areas, noting its particular protective function and its value for research and scientific purposes.[15]

---

[11] Page 33. *Also see* page 41 which discusses the BLM management control program.

[12] Pages 80-81.

[13] Pages 92-93.

[14] Page 87.

[15] Pages 91-93.

Coggins, "OF SUCCOTASH SYNDROMES AND VACUOUS PLATITUDES: THE MEANING OF 'MULTIPLE USE, SUSTAINED YIELD' FOR PUBLIC LAND MANAGEMENT"*

53 U. Colo. L. Rev. 229 (1981)

B. The Land Management Agencies

In the course of the Nation's history, four different agencies charged with management of federal public lands have evolved. Two of these, the National Park Service and the Fish and Wildlife Service, can be roughly described as "dominant use" agencies. While each has a mission that involves production of several goods and services, both have primary management goals of recreation, preservation, and wildlife propagation.

The Forest Service and the Bureau of Land Management (BLM) are the primary multiple use management agencies. There are certain parallels in their operations, but the differences are more distinct. The Forest Service originally fell heir to the stewardship of approximately 150 million acres of relatively virgin wooded terrain. Even its later-acquired, agriculturally submarginal, eastern forests are still productive for silvaculture. For a half century the Service managed its timber in a custodial fashion as a sort of national reserve for the future. Consequently, its lands still contain large volumes of standing timber, especially in the remaining old-growth stands, and those lands produce large volumes of wildlife, forage, and recreational amenities.

The BLM, on the other hand, never had much to work with. Its predecessor agency was created to manage the newly formed grazing districts in 1934, but the lands that comprised those districts were in uniformly deplorable condition. Never very productive to start with, the rangelands had been subjected to fierce overgrazing and other abuses for the better part of a century; they were severely eroded and vegetatively depleted as compared to their historic capacity. The BLM thus never had the luxury of a custodial period and it still has no resource "cushion." Efforts at improvement are inherently more difficult on BLM lands, for forest ecosystems naturally tend to be more productive than western rangeland ecosystems. In terms of basic management problems, the BLM must cope with demands to improve the "poor" condition of its holdings while the Forest Service faces intense pressure to liquidate remaining old-growth stands.

A second major difference between the agencies is that no one is deemed to have a "right" to national forest resources. Some private ranchers, however, have acquired, through statutory preference and agency deference, a de facto "right" to grass on adjacent BLM lands, although there is little legal basis for it. The Forest Service has discretion whether or not to harvest any particular tract, and consequently, has considerable independent control over the resources entrusted to it. The BLM, however, has never enjoyed the esteem accorded the Forest Service, and it has never been able to gain an appreciable measure of independence.

The third difference lies in the nature of the primary economic resources managed by each agency. The BLM has devoted nearly all of its non-Alaskan lands to domestic livestock grazing (with some adjustment for rest-rotation, etc.). By contrast, only a very small fraction of the national forest area is being logged at any one time. Part of this, of course, is due to physical differences: a stand of timber can be clearcut only every fifty years or so, while grass does not retain its growth from one year to the next. Yet that is only part of the answer. The Forest Service has determined for a variety of reasons (such as distance from markets or marginal productive capacity) that no cutting will be allowed on some lands at all. The BLM, however, has seldom adopted a similar principle in its management. Instead, it seems to assume that virtually all lands under its jurisdiction are equally suited for livestock grazing. Given the demonstrable differences in ecosystem types, productive capacity, and site condition, such an assumption is at best questionable.

The fourth major difference is that, while both agencies actually devote most of their attention and resources to their respective major economic uses, the Forest Service is better at its version of dominant use than the BLM. Forest management theory and practice have far more ancient origins than do rangeland management and are far more advanced. The Forest Service also has had more experience with planning, a subject that the BLM seems unable to cope with, especially over a long period of time. While the Forest Service is projecting yields centuries ahead, the BLM has trouble predicting the trends for the following year.

This opinionated description of the multiple use agencies and their practices would not be complete without an explicit defense of public land managers. . . . The managers are the much-abused middlemen, contending with arrays of hostile, powerful interests, and often they are the scapegoats for unpopular decisions. They are quasi-scientists forced to be constituentless quasi-politicians who cannot possibly satisfy all of the diverse demands made on the resources under their jurisdiction. Their job is more difficult for lack of full information and reliable predictive mechanisms. . . .

§ 6.03 Public Lands and Their Uses

[1] Planning and Policy: In General

NATIONAL FOREST MANAGEMENT ACT OF 1976
16 U.S.C.
Chapter 2
The National Forests

§ 472. Laws affecting national forest lands

The Secretary of the Department of Agriculture shall execute or cause to be executed all laws affecting public lands reserved under the provisions of section 471 of this title, or sections supplemental to and amendatory thereof, subject to the provisions for national forests established under subdivision (b) of section 471 of this title, after such lands have been so reserved, excepting such laws as affect the surveying, prospecting, locating, appropriating, entering, relinquishing, reconveying, certifying, or patenting of any of such lands.

§ 475. Purposes for which national forests may be established and administered

All public lands designated and reserved prior to June 4, 1897, by the President of the United States under the provisions of section 471 of this title, the orders for which shall be and remain in full force and effect, unsuspended and unrevoked, and all public lands that may hereafter be set aside and reserved as national forests under said section, shall be as far as practicable controlled and administered in accordance with the following provisions. No national forest shall be established, except to improve and protect the forest within the boundaries, or for the purpose of securing favorable conditions of water flows, and to furnish a continuous supply of timber for the use and necessities of citizens of the United States; but it is not the purpose or intent of these provisions, or of said section, to authorize the inclusion therein of lands more valuable for the mineral therein, or for agricultural purposes, than for forest purposes.

§ 482. Mineral lands; restoration to public domain; location and entry

Upon the recommendation of the Secretary of the Interior, with the approval of the President, after sixty days' notice thereof, published in two papers of general circulation in the State or Territory wherein any national forest is situated, and near the said national forest, any public lands embraced within the limits of any such forest which, after due examination by personal inspection of a competent person appointed for that purpose by the Secretary of the Interior, shall be found better adapted for mining or for agricultural purposes than for forest usage, may be restored to the public domain. And any mineral lands in any national forest which have been or which may be shown to be such, and subject to entry under the existing mining laws of the United States and the rules and regulations applying thereto, shall continue to be subject to such location and entry, notwithstanding any provisions contained in sections 473–482 and 551 of this title.

§ 485. Exchange of lands in national forests; cutting timber in national forests in exchange for lands therein

When the public interests will be benefited thereby, the Secretary of the Interior is authorized in his discretion to accept on behalf of the United States title to any lands within the exterior boundaries of the national forests which, in the opinion of the Secretary of Agriculture, are chiefly valuable for national-forest purposes, and in exchange therefor may patent not to exceed an equal value of such national-forest land, in the same State, surveyed and non-mineral in character, or the Secretary of Agriculture may authorize the grantor to cut and remove an equal value of timber within the national forests of the same State; the values in each case to be determined by the Secretary of Agriculture. Before any such exchange is effected notice of the contemplated exchange reciting the lands involved shall be published once each week for four successive weeks in some newspaper published in any county in which may be situated any lands or timber to be given in such exchange. Timber given in such exchanges shall be cut and removed under the laws and regulations relating to the national forests, and under the direction and supervision and in accordance with the requirements of the Secretary of Agriculture. Lands conveyed to the United States under this section shall, upon acceptance of title, become parts of the national forest within whose exterior boundaries they are located.

NOTE

For other Renewable Resource Planning provisions, *see* Forest and Rangeland Renewable Resources Planning Acts of 1974 and 1978, and the Renewable Resources Extension Act of 1978.

For a series of discussions on national forest management, *see* Cartner and Schweitzer, *Institutional Limits to National Public Planning for Forest Resources: The Resources Planning Act*, 21 Nat. Res. J. 203 (1981); Mulhern, *The National Forest Management Act of 1976—A Critical Examination*, 7 B.C. Envtl. Aff. L. Rev. 99 (1978); Strong, *National Forest Management Act of 1976—What Impact on Federal Timber Management?*, 13 Idaho L. Rev. 263 (1977).

FEDERAL LAND POLICY AND MANAGEMENT ACT OF 1976

Authority to manage the public lands is dispersed among a number of agencies, which, as has been noted, carry out many similar responsibilities relating to public land uses for a variety of purposes. There is no single responsible agency, however, and there is no agency or body which is responsible for a national planning effort on the uses of the one-third of the nation's land.[1]

This situation was considerably improved, however, by the Federal Land Policy and Management Act of 1976,[2] passed in October of 1976, which represents a major step in public land management. The 1970 recommendations of the Public Land Law Commission recommended that some 3,000 public land laws enacted during the life of the country be consolidated. Prior to the adoption of the 1976 law, no single law set out a statement of purposes, goals or authority relating to the use of the public lands. The Federal Land Policy and Management Act (FLPMA)thus reflects a major effort at land law consolidation and at the establishment of a common policy for the management of public lands under the separate jurisdiction of the Department of the Interior, Bureau of Land Management, and the Forest Service in the Department of Agriculture.

In its general policies the FLPMA reaffirms multiple-use sustained-yield approaches and sets forth general purposes looking towards the establishment of regulations and plans to protect the environment on public lands as well as their valuable natural resources. It also sets forth as one of the purposes of the law the establishment of uniform procedures for the disposal of public lands, for the acquisition of non-federal land for public purposes, and for the exchange of public lands.[3]

Title II of the law establishes uniform procedures for sales, withdrawals, acquisitions and exchanges of land, and it grants the Bureau clear authority to engage in planning of public lands and in their designation (or classification) for particular purposes. It provides also for the reservation of mineral interests whenever public lands of the United States are disposed of. The procedures established in Title II apply both to Forest Service lands and BLM lands, with similar authority vested in the Secretaries of the Interior and of Agriculture. Title II takes the place of a vast mass of earlier legislation which had dealt separately with the subjects covered not only for each of the departments involved, but usually also for the particular area of public lands affected.[4]

Some of the most significant changes from prior law in Title II are the provisions dealing with the withdrawal of public lands. Withdrawal of public lands (which means the withholding of an area of federal land from settlement, sale, location or entry for the purpose of limiting activities so as to maintain other public values in the area or reserving the area for a particular public

---

1 This lack of overall planning authority and coordination was noted by the Public Land Law Review Commission, which recommended the establishment of inter-agency planning coordination, *One-Third of the Nation's Land* at 60-61, or, going beyond such a recommendation, the establishment of a new federal department of natural resources, to combine the responsibilities of the Department of the Interior with those of the Forest Service in the Department of Agriculture. *Id.* at 282, 283.

2 Pub. L. No. 94-579, 90 Stat. 2473, 43 U.S.C. § 1701 *et seq.* (FLPMA).

The constitutionality of FLPMA was upheld against a variety of challenges, including due process, void for vagueness, and obligation of contract claims, in Western Mining Council v. Watt, 643 F.2d 618 (9th Cir. 1981). In particular, the court upheld the "file or abandon" provisions.

3 FLPMA § 102, 43 U.S.C. § 1701.

4 FLPMA §§ 201-214, 43 U.S.C. §§ 1711-1722.

purpose or program) which previously was almost entirely a matter of executive authority exercised by the President or delegated by him, is now largely subjected to Congressional supervision. As to BLM lands, the Secretary of the Interior may make withdrawals of land in excess of 5,000 acres or more only for a period of not more than 20 years after notification of both houses of Congress which, under procedures set forth in the law, may disapprove the withdrawal.[5]

The provision was severely criticized in Congress by many Congressmen and Senators who viewed it as a yielding to special interest groups in dealing with the public lands, because each major withdrawal decision will be subjected to intense lobbying pressures, especially by mining interests who oppose withdrawal of the lands from the operation of the mining laws. Since withdrawal of public lands is generally viewed as an act of preservation, assertions were made in Congress that under the guise of an enlargement of Congressional authority relating to its oversight responsibilities, Congress had in fact yielded to special interest pressures which may well result in obstructing the withdrawal of lands for preservation and environmental protection purposes.[6]

Thus, although Title II represents a major formal advance in unifying and simplifying the public land laws, it may well represent a substantial retreat insofar as it subjects withdrawal decisions to substantial special interest pressures.

---

[5] FLPMA § 204, 43 U.S.C. § 1714.

Mountain States Legal Foundation v. Andrus, 499 F. Supp. 383 (D. Wyo. 1980) addressed the question of what constitutes a "withdrawal" as well as the issue of the need for Congressional approval of withdrawal. Plaintiffs, representing oil and gas interests, in their action against the Secretaries of the Interior and of Agriculture, asserted that their failure to act for several years on oil and gas lease applications relating to the million acre Western Overthrust Belt constituted a withdrawal of the lands from the operation of the Mineral Leasing Act of 1920, without submitting such withdrawal to Congress for approval as required by the Federal Land Policy Management Act, §§ 103(j), 204(c)(1), 43 U.S.C. §§ 1702(j), 1714(c)(1). Such a failure to act on oil and gas leases, plaintiffs asserted, also constituted a rule or regulation of the Departments of the Interior and Agriculture which was not promulgated as required by the Administrative Procedure Act, 5U.S.C. § 553(a). The court granted plaintiff's motion for summary judgment on both grounds, and ordered the two departments to promulgate rules and regulations on the basis of which oil and gas lease applications may be approved or denied, and "which relate to the principles on which cooperation between the Departments of Interior and Agriculture, with respect to such leasing activities is based." The court also ordered the Secretary of the Interior to report the withdrawal of the lands to Congress pursuant to 43 U.S.C. § 1714(c)or to cease withholding such lands from oil and gas leasing. Referring to the vast energy riches within the withheld area, the court indicated that the Secretaries of the Interior and Agriculture had each relied on their respective Roadless Area Review and Evaluation programs (RARE I and RARE II) for the evaluation and identification of areas for addition to the National Wilderness Preservation System. The court found, however, that Congress did not intend the desire for wilderness preservation to provide sufficient grounds for the withdrawal of such areas from mineral exploration and development without Congressional approval, as distinguished from lands already designated as wilderness areas, which will not be available for unlimited leasing until after December 31, 1983.

[6] *See* dissenting views of ten members of the House, H. Rept. No. 94-1163, Interior and Insular Affairs Committee, 94th Cong., 2d Sess 53 (1976).

For a different, later view which attributes aspects of the "sagebrush rebellion" to the more vigorous federal controls of FLPMA, *see* R.D. Clayton, *The Sagebrush Rebellion: Who Should Control the Public Lands?*, 1980 Utah L. Rev. 505 (1980).

Section 201 of FLPMA directs the Secretary of the Interior to conduct a one time review of the public domain for roadless tracts of at least 5000 acres with wilderness characteristics. The Secretary must recommend to the President lands to be included in the Wilderness Preservation System, and the President is directed to make his proposals to Congress (which alone has the power to classify lands as wilderness).

Section 603 of FLPMA controls the management of lands under consideration for wilderness status, *i.e.*, wilderness study areas. The provision attempts to protect both wilderness qualities pending designation and the economic activities already underway when FLPMA was enacted. The Solicitor of the Department of Interior initially interpreted the section to require severe restrictions on mining activities within the study areas. This interpretation prompted litigation which eventually upheld Interior's power to prohibit all activities which would impair wilderness qualities within study areas.[7]

Title III of the FLPMA provides an organic act for the Bureau of Land Management.[8]

The Bureau of Land Management, which controls some two-thirds of the public lands, previously had no unified charter of authority, deriving its authority from a variety of laws pertaining to the management of particular areas of the public lands. Indeed, its only unified source of authority had been the 1964 Multiple Use and Interim Classification Act which provided authority for land use decisions until the expiration of the term of the Public Land Law Commission in 1970.[9]

The provisions of Title III grant to BLM and to the Secretary of the Interior the exercise of the power referred to in Title II relating to planning, acquisitions and disposals of land, in addition to powers more directly concerned with the operations of BLM lands and the management of the Bureau, including the making of rules and regulations for land management, and their enforcement, as well as rules pertaining to mining claims.

In 1979, pursuant to the powers granted in Title III, BLM promulgated regulations to establish a process for "the development, approval, maintenance, amendment and revision of resource management plans" for public lands administered by BLM.[10]

The rules emphasize an interdisciplinary approach, consistent with the Multiple-Use, Sustained-Yield Act[11] calling for coordination of federal, state and local efforts.

Title IV of the Act provides for uniform rules relating to the management of the public range. The provisions relating to grazing leases and permits and to grazing advisory boards are unified for both the Forest Service and BLM.

---

[7] Utah v. Andrus, 486 F. Supp. 995 (D. Utah, 1980); Rocky Mountain Oil and Gas Association v. Andrus, 500 F. Supp. 1338 (D. Wyoming 1980), *rev'd sub nom.* Rocky Mountain Oil and Gas Association v. Watt, 13 Envtl. L. Rep. 20038 (10th Cir. Nov. 30, 1982). For further discussion, *see generally Tenth Circuit Approves Interior's Wilderness Protection Policies in Energy Rich Rocky Mountain Region*, 13 Envtl. L. Rep. 10004.

[8] FLPMA §§ 301-318, 43 U.S.C. §§ 1731-1748.

[9] Pub. L. No. 88-607, § 1, 78 Stat. 986, (Sept. 19, 1964).

[10] *Public Lands and Resources; Planning, Programming and Budgeting*, 46 Fed. Reg. 46386 (1979).

[11] N. 6 *supra*.

In addition, provision is made in the law for the uniform setting of grazing fees jointly by the Secretary of Agriculture and the Secretary of the Interior, and standards are set for the amount of the fees to be required.[12]

In Title V the law provides uniform requirements for the authorization and management of rights of way on public lands,[13] a subject previously dispersed in numerous separate provisions. Special provision is made in Title VI for certain larger management areas such as the California Desert conservation area and the King Range.[14]

The FLPMA repeals all earlier inconsistent laws,[15] but takes great care in its repeal provisions that existing mineral rights and existing prior interest acquired by use of public lands not be lost or adversely affected by the new law.[16]

Coggins, "THE LAW OF PUBLIC RANGELAND MANAGEMENT IV: FLPMA, PRIA, AND THE MULTIPLE USE MANDATE"*

14 Envtl. L. 1, 9-14 (1983)

1. The congressional policies

Section 1701(a) of FLPMA declares thirteen sweeping policies. Although it contains some apparent inconsistencies, the section is Congress's most thorough and unambiguous statement of public land policy. The statement is qualified by the proviso in section 1701(b) that FLPMA policies are not "effective" until specifically enacted in the Act itself or elsewhere. The courts faced with questions involving section 1701(a), however, have uniformly assumed that the policies are binding and effective in the absence of contrary provisions. Whatever their precise legal status, the congressional policies ought to serve as fundamental range management guidelines.

Congress first stated that the public lands will remain in federal ownership unless planning determines that the "national interest" requires disposal of "a particular parcel." The crux of this policy has been clear since 1934, and the 1981 dismissal of Nevada's claim of unconstitutional federal retention was affirmed in 1983.

The second policy is that "the national interest will be best realized if the public lands and their resources are periodically and systematically inventoried and their present and future use is projected through a land use planning

---

[12] FLPMA §§ 401-404, 43 U.S.C. §§ 1751-1753and 16 U.S.C. § 1338a.

[13] FLPMA § 501-511, 43 U.S.C. §§ 1761-1771.

[14] FLPMA §§ 601-603, 43 U.S.C. §§ 1781-1782and 16 U.S.C. § 460y-8.

[15] FLPMA §§ 702-706.

[16] FLPMA § 701, 43 U.S.C. § 1701. Note that legislation of similar scope to FLPMA has been enacted for the federal lands in Alaska. *See* Alaska National Interest Lands Conservation Act (ANILCO), Pub. Law No. 96-487, 24 Stat. 2371, 16 U.S.C. § 3101 *et seq.*

process coordinated with other Federal and State planning efforts." This policy was enacted in sections 1711 and 1712 of FLPMA. Inventorying and planning should become the central focus of public rangeland management.

Congress next called for review of all existing federal land classifications and then enacted the policy in the statute. Whether the fourth congressional policy of curbing and controlling the executive withdrawal power was enacted is open to question. In the fifth policy statement, Congress declared that

> in administering public land statutes and exercising discretionary authority granted by them, the Secretary [is] required to establish comprehensive rules and regulations after considering the views of the general public; and to structure adjudication procedures to assure adequate third party participation, objective administrative review of initial decisions, and expeditious decisionmaking.

The related sixth policy calls for judicial review of "public land adjudications." The need for a standard procedure arose from a longstanding habit of public land management agencies lagging far behind the procedural reforms made by or forced upon other organs of the federal government and from a longstanding tradition of judicial deference (if not abdication) to agency discretion in the public land circuits. Congress implemented the fifth policy in other sections of FLPMA; the Court of Appeals for the Ninth Circuit has implemented the sixth policy.

The seventh congressional statement should be, but has not yet become, the touchstone of public rangeland management. Congress declared that "goals and objectives be established by law as guidelines for public land use planning, and that management be on the basis of multiple use and sustained yield unless otherwise specified by law." Congress specifically enacted these general requirements, but the BLM has neither understood nor carried out these commands.

The eighth statement of policy is a radical departure from all prior rangeland management understanding. Congress required that

> the public lands be managed in a manner that will protect the quality of scientific, scenic, historical, ecological, environmental, air and atmospheric, water resource, and archeological values; that, where appropriate, will preserve and protect certain public lands in their natural condition; that will provide food and habitat for fish and wildlife and domestic animals; and that will provide for outdoor recreation and human occupancy and use.

Whether or to what extent Congress specifically enacted this goal is unclear. Some sections of FLPMA and other statutes support an argument that this policy binds public land managers, but all the statutory provisions are qualified in some way.

In its ninth policy, Congress sought "fair market value" for public land uses and resources "unless otherwise provided for by statute." This policy is definitely not law; not only are grazing fees set at a fraction of market value, but the United States probably does not receive full value for any of the nation's resources.

Congress's tenth policy statement calls for uniform procedures for disposal, exchange, or acquisition of public lands. This policy was enacted in other

FLPMA sections. The eleventh policy seeks rapid protection of "areas of critical environmental concern;" the statute provides that protection.

The twelfth congressional policy balances or counteracts the eighth by emphasizing use instead of preservation. Congress required that "[t]he public lands be managed in a manner which recognizes the Nation's need for domestic sources of minerals, food, timber, and fiber from the public lands including implementation of the Mining and Minerals Policy Act of 1970 . . . as it pertains to the public lands." Congress wrote this policy more tentatively than the preservation policy ("recognizes the Nation's need" versus "will protect"), but the statement reflects prior BLM management emphasis. The Mining and Minerals Policy Act, however, remains innocuous, to the distress of some commentators. Recognition of the need to produce domestic resources is reflected or enacted in scores of other statutes. The thirteenth and final policy calls for equitable reimbursement to states for the local tax burden caused by federal immunity from taxation. This policy was enacted in the Payment in Lieu of Taxes Act of 1976.

. . . .

NOTE

One of the significant advances for environmentalists and conservationists in FLPMA and the National Forest Management Act of 1976 (NFMA) is the opportunity provided to intervene in the decisionmaking process and to seek judicial review of environmentally questionable agency determinations. Prior to these statutory changes, the federal agencies involved often made decisions as if the lands involved were their private domain, and not public land in which the public generally held a vital interest. Litigants seeking review of public land decisions made by BLM or the Forest Service were routinely met with challenges to their standing, with defenses based on sovereign immunity, and with the assertion that the determination was not reviewable because it had been delegated to agency discretion as a matter of law. While FLPMA falls short of providing any clear right of intervention or citizen suit, its declaration of policy does require the Secretary "to structure adjudication procedures to assure adequate third party participation." In addition, the Act directs the Secretaries to hold hearings and create opportunities for public comment, where appropriate. Furthermore, the Act states as a policy that "judicial review of public land adjudication decisions be provided by law." Additional opportunities for public intervention may be available in those cases where NEPA requires that the land-use plan be accompanied by an environmental impact statement. On the problems earlier law presented to environmental litigants, *see* Reich, *Bureaucracy and the Forests;* Rogers, *The Need for Meaningful Control in the Management of Federally Owned Timberland*, 4 Land & Water L. Rev. 121 (1969).

For an overview of the purposes and effect of FLPMA, *see also* Clawson, *The Federal Land Policy Management Act of 1976 in a Broad Historical Perspective*, 21 Ariz. L. Rev. 585 (1980). Consider also the following progress notes, as presented to the 1980 report of the Council on Environmental Quality, 307-310:

> "The Federal Land Policy and Management Act of 1976 established a policy of multiple-use sustained-yield management for the 417 million acres of public land administered by the BLM. This Act requires the BLM to protect and manage these lands in an environmentally sound and cost-effective manner that will reserve the declining productivity of the public range and improve other resources.
>
> "'The President's 1979 Environmental Message included policy initiatives to achieve the goals set out in the FLPMA. He directed the Secretary of Interior to develop a comprehensive program development process—similar to the Forest Service RPA procedures—for BLM lands."

Environmental planning on the public lands will be affected most directly by the development of BLM's land use planning areas and the implementation of its multiple use planning regulations. The 1980 report by the Council on Environmental Quality stated that 80% of the public lands were already covered by pre-FLPMA Management Framework Plans, and that BLM regulations for land use "were based upon the best available information and sound planning principles." One commentator, however, remained unimpressed. "The BLM multiple use planning regulations under FLPMA illustrate the agency's disorganization and administrative problems more than they set precise guidelines for systematic planning. The BLM designed land use planning areas to be amenable to the agency's bureaucratic structure, without much regard for natural boundaries or geographic homogeneity." Coggins, *The Law of Public Rangeland Management IV: FLPMA, PRIA, and the Multiple-Use Mandate*, 14 Envtl. L. 1, 96 (1983).

QUESTIONS

(1) Is there any clear priority of uses expressed in the Classification and Sustained Yield Act? Existing classification and land use practices have been criticized because they give the Secretary of the Interior—or the Secretary of Agriculture—undue power to determine preferred uses. What is the argument in favor of executive as against legislative standard setting and rule making in this area? What dangers and difficulties are there in the Public Land Law Review Commission's general recommendation that Congress be given a freer hand in dealing with public lands? If classification and use decisions were to be left to Congress, who is most likely to make the specific determinations? Has the Federal Land Policy and Management Act of 1976 (FLPMA) fully resolved these issues? *See* 43 U.S.C. §§ 1701-1712.

(2) Assume that Congress decides to take a more active role in public land management. Assume further that instead of permitting the Secretary of the Interior to develop "regulations containing criteria" to determine which public lands are to be sold and which are to be retained and for what purpose, Congress itself enacts an identical set of provisions into law, thereby setting the criteria to be applied by a designated executive agency—the Secretary of

the Interior or some other officer specially delegated the task of public land management. Would such an arrangement limit the powers of the executive officer charged with applying the criteria to specific situations? As attorney for a group of conservationists who wish to challenge a particular classification decision, would it be easier or more difficult—or neither—to challenge the executive officer's determination made on the basis of legislative (rather than administrative) criteria? What light is cast on this question by the Congressional debates on the Federal Land Policy and Management Act of 1976? *See especially*, 123 Cong. Rec. 7599-7605. *See also* H. Rep. 94-1163, dissenting views.

(3) As a matter of permanent policy, could it be argued that the wisest course for Congress to follow is to make permanent the powers of the Secretary of the Interior to classify public lands under a set of regulations containing criteria which, for good and sufficient reason, the Secretary may review and amend from time to time after public hearings? Should a similar authority be extended to the Secretary in relation to reclassification by reason of changed circumstances of public lands previously classified? Could Congress under such permanent legislation permit the Secretary to make regulations containing criteria subject to some dominant legislative standard, such as for instance a legislative preference for multiple use over use for a dominant purpose yielding maximum gain? Would any such legislative innovation improve the conservationist's position in challenging particular classification decisions in the absence of procedural reform of administrative practices? To what extent are the issues here raised resolved in the Federal Land Policy and Management Act of 1976?

(4) The discretionary function doctrine is not limited to public land decisions. Barring obvious and palpable abuse of discretion, can a classification decision which is based on general criteria ever be reversed in judicial proceedings, assuming that the usual principles of administrative law or the review procedures under the Administrative Procedure Act are applied? What arguments can be made in favor of a review of classification decisions limited purely to the question of abuse of discretion? Would more general applicability of the Administrative Procedure Act necessarily broaden the scope of review of land use classification decisions?

(5) FLPMA § 704 attempts to abolish the executive's implied withdrawal power, as applied in *U.S. v. Midwest Oil*, 236 U.S. 459 (1915), and provides for comprehensive procedures for the withdrawal of BLM land. FLPMA, 43 U.S.C. § 1701. Is this repealer effective? Can it be undermined by silent Congressional acquiescence to executive withdrawals?

(6) FLPMA, 43 U.S.C. § 1714(d), subjects executive withdrawals of more than 5,000 acres to a Congressional veto. How is this affected by the Supreme Court decision in *Chadha v. INS*, 462 U.S. 919, 103 S. Ct. 2764, 77 L. Ed.2d 317 (1983)? An exception is made for emergency withdrawals. What constitutes an emergency? *See Alaska v. Carter*, 462 F. Supp. 1155 (1978).

(7) Do withdrawals under FLPMA constitute "major" federal actions "significantly affecting" the human environment? Do FLPMA's land use planning directives exempt it from NEPA's procedural requirements? *See N.R.D.C. v. Hughes*, 437 F. Supp. 981 (D.D.C. 1981) (federal coal leasing programs).

(8) Should NEPA apply to the rulemaking process by which BLM issues land use planning regulations? Are the priorities of FLPMA and NEPA the same?

[2] Multiple Use and Sustained Yield

[a] Forests and Timber

16 U.S.C., "MULTIPLE USE-SUSTAINED YIELD ACT OF 1960"

§ 528. Development and administration of renewable surface resources for multiple use and sustained yield of products and services—Congressional declaration of policy and purpose

It is the policy of the Congress that the national forests are established and shall be administered for outdoor recreation, range, timber, watershed, and wildlife and fish purposes. The purposes of sections 528–531 of this title are declared to be supplemental to, but not in derogation of, the purposes for which the national forests were established as set forth in section 475 of this title. Nothing herein shall be construed as affecting the jurisdiction or responsibilities of the several States with respect to wildlife and fish on the national forests. Nothing herein shall be construed so as to affect the use or administration of the mineral resources of national forest lands or to affect the use or administration of Federal lands not within national forests.

§ 529. Same; authorization; consideration to relative values of resources; areas of wilderness

The Secretary of Agriculture is authorized and directed to develop and administer the renewable surface resources of the national forests for multiple use and sustained yield of the several products and services obtained therefrom. In the administration of the national forests due consideration shall be given to the relative values of the various resources in particular areas. The establishment and maintenance of areas of wilderness are consistent with the purposes and provisions of sections 528–531 of this title.

§ 530. Same; cooperation with State and local governmental agencies and others

In the effectuation of sections 528–531 of this title the Secretary of Agriculture is authorized to cooperate with interested State and local governmental agencies and others in the development and management of the national forests.

§ 531. Same; definitions

As used in sections 528–531 of this title, the following terms shall have the following meanings:

(a) "Multiple use" means: The management of all the various renewable surface resources of the national forests so that they are utilized in the combination that will best meet the needs of the American people; making the most judicious use of the land for some or all of these resources or related services over areas large enough to provide sufficient latitude for periodic adjustments in use to conform to changing needs and conditions; that some land will be used for less than all of the resources; and harmonious and coordinated management of the various resources, each with the other, without impairment of the productivity of the land, with consideration being given to the relative values of the various resources, and not necessarily the combination of uses that will give the greatest dollar return or the greatest unit output.

(b) "Sustained yield of the several products and services" means the achievement and maintenance in perpetuity of a high-level annual or regular periodic output of the various renewable resources of the national forests without impairment of the productivity of the land.

NOTE

The Multiple-Use Sustained-Yield Act by its terms only applied to the forest reserve under Department of Agriculture management. The principle had been applied as well to the public lands under management of the Bureau of Land Management (BLM) in the Department of the Interior. The Multiple-Use Sustained-Yield approach was strongly reaffirmed in 1976 for BLM lands in the Federal Land Policy and Management Act of 1976, Pub. L. No. 94-579, § 302, 90 Stat. 2743, 43 U.S.C. § 1732, and for lands in the forest reserve in the National Forest Management Act of 1976, Pub. L. No. 94-588, 90 Stat. 2949, 16 U.S.C. § 1600 *et seq., infra.*

For an account of the legislative history and the conflicts sought to be resolved by the 1960 Act, *see* Note *Natural Resources—National Forest—The Multiple Use-Sustained Yield Act of 1960*, 41 Or. L. Rev. 49 (1961).

Coggins, "OF SUCCOTASH SYNDROMES AND VACUOUS PLATITUDES: THE MEANING OF 'MULTIPLE USE, SUSTAINED YIELD' FOR PUBLIC LAND MANAGEMENT"*

53 U. Colo. L. Rev. 229, 251–267 (1981)

A. *The 1960 Multiple-Use, Sustained-Yield Act*

The operative sections of the Multiple-Use, Sustained-Yield Act of 1960 are Title 16, sections 528, 529, and 531 of the United States Code.

Section 528 states "the policy of the Congress [is] that the national forests are established and shall be administered for outdoor recreation, range, timber, watershed, and wildlife and fish purposes." It also excludes mineral resources, disclaims interference with state wildlife jurisdiction, and declares the continuing validity of the 1897 Organic Act. Section 529 provides:

> The Secretary of Agriculture is authorized and directed to develop and administer the renewable surface resources of the national forests for multiple use and sustained yield of the several products and services obtained therefrom. In the administration of the national forests, due consideration shall be given to the relative values of the various resources in particular areas. The establishment and maintenance of areas of wilderness are consistent with the purposes and provisions of sections 528 and 531 of this title.

Section 531 is the most important provision for these purposes because, in defining the basic terms, it also defines the legal standards:

> As used in sections 528 to 531 of this title, the following terms shall have the following meanings:
>
> (a) "Multiple use" means: The management of all the various renewable surface resources of the national forests so that they are utilized in the combination that will best meet the needs of the American people; making the most judicious use of the land for some or all of these resources or related services over areas large enough to provide sufficient latitude for periodic adjustments in use to conform to changing needs and conditions; that some land will be used for less than all of the resources; and harmonious and coordinated management of the various resources, each with the other, without impairment of the productivity of the land, with consideration being given to the relative values of the various resources, and not necessarily the combination of uses that will give the greatest dollar return or the greatest unit output. (b) "Sustained yield of the several products and services" means the achievement and maintenance in perpetuity of a high-level annual or regular periodic output of the various renewable resources of the national forests without impairment of the productivity of the land.

What, precisely, did Congress intend for the Forest Service to do? How was the agency to go about reconciling uses or resolving conflicts? Did any uses have priority? These and other obvious questions are not answered directly by reference to the statute or to its legislative history. In fact, the statute came about in large part because of legislative disputes over pending wilderness bills: specifically, the Forest Service opposed congressionally-designated wilderness areas unless it got the broader organic authority it had already arrogated unto itself in prior theory and practice. It would be another four years until the Wilderness Act passed, but Congress in 1960 gave the Forest service—but not the forgotten BLM—the general authority it sought. The Act is not, however, a standardless delegation. In divining its meaning, the multiple uses themselves are a good starting point.

1. The Multiple Uses

The statute lists the resources to be managed in awkward alphabetical order: outdoor recreation, range, timber, watershed, and wildlife and fish.

Section 528 was thus worded in order to place recreation at the head of the list, emphasizing that each resource is equal and that timber has no priority. What are these "resources" precisely? In section 528 they are "purposes," in section 529 they are "renewable surface resources," and in section 531 they are "multiple uses" to be managed for "sustained yield." Each is considered a "renewable" resource, meaning that it regenerates in some biological or climatological fashion. Notably absent from the list are hardrock minerals, oil, gas, coal, and similar nonrenewable resources. These are governed by separate statutes. Hardrock mineral exploration and extraction had a clear legal priority over all other resource uses until 1976 and fuel mineral leasing enjoyed a similar, if merely de facto, preeminence. Also conspicuous by its absence from the list is the key resource, water itself. Congress evidently concluded, if it considered the matter at all, that water allocation was a matter for state law definition of rights. The location and uses of the federal lands dictated the functions of preserving water quality and quantity by enlightened upland management practices. Wilderness, or "preservation," is not listed as a resource use, but section 529 corrects the omission by providing that wilderness designation is compatible with the multiple use standard. Utilitarianism was either rejected outright by this provision or else elevated to a higher plane, depending on one's viewpoint. Congress neglected to define the five remaining resources.

. . . .

2. Multiple Use Management

The only explicit command to the agency in the MUSY Act reads: "The Secretary . . . is . . . directed to develop and administer the renewable surface resources . . . for multiple use and sustained yield of the several products and services obtained therefrom." This mandate by itself says very little, and neither the statute's history nor the judicial decisions add much to it. If that direction were all that the statute contained, the argument that it is a grant of virtually limitless authority, under which no individual decision could be found illegal or arbitrary, would be persuasive.

(a). Meeting the needs of the American people

The overall goal of the MUSY Act is primarily utilitarian: all of the listed resources are to be managed in the combination that best meets the needs of the American people. To give meaning to this variation on Pinchot's theme, one must work backwards, starting with the people's "needs." These, in the abstract, are infinite in variety and degree: food, clothing, and shelter are of course predominant; but health, prosperity, love, security, play, respect, beauty, culture, titillation, mobility, money, honor, happiness, and any number of other needs could be listed.

. . . .

Given that national, not regional, needs must be met and that those needs encompass all benefits, with and without ascertainable dollar values, how is the manager to accomplish a task of such magnitude? He is to do so by resource management in "combination," giving "due consideration" to "the relative value of the various resources."

. . . .

The seemingly vague mandate requires the manager to go through a certain rough thought process, with at least two major steps, before any "on-the-ground" decisions are possible. The usual label for such thinking is "planning." To consider relative values, one must know what values or resources are available for allocation or protection on the area in question. In science, this "fact-finding" function is known as the inventory phase. Following this semi-objective exercise (recall the difficulty in defining and identifying the listed resources), the manager must consider overall mixes of production. This is the essence of management planning, and planning is the essence of effective management.

. . . .

(b). Determining the appropriate unit planning size

An initial problem fundamental to planning involves the size of the appropriate planning unit. The national forests comprise 187 million acres divided into many forests, some with noncontiguous areas, all ranging greatly in size. The BLM grazing districts were established for reasons other than natural boundaries or geologic or biologic homogeneity. When the manager duly considers relative resource values, does he do so for the entire National Forest System, for each designated forest, for a subunit within the forest, or for each acre? The question is neither idle nor facetious. At the one-acre level, compatible combinations of resource uses are difficult, if not impossible; and at the entire System level, and perhaps even at the single forest level, combination planning is necessarily so general as to be virtually meaningless for resolution of individual resource questions.

. . . .

The importance of the unit size delineation for management becomes apparent when the question of "compatible combinations" is addressed. To environmentally oriented challengers of the agencies' decisions, the initial question will be whether the use of an overly large planning unit—by which means the agencies can avoid specific guidelines—could serve as the basis to invalidate subsequent decisions. The question has not been litigated, and no definitive answer is available.

. . . .

(c). Cautioning against economic optimality

The first noteworthy standard that emerges from a consideration of section 531(a), which defines "multiple use," is a caution: "greatest dollar return" or "greatest unit output" is not "necessarily" the primary management goal. This caution is a rejection of either gross production or net monetary return as the sole or primary forest management objective. The rejection is significant because it offers a partial answer to a question with which agencies have unsuccessfully struggled: "Management for what?" It represents a conscious choice to forego pure utilitarianism in favor of a broader approach to resource allocation.

. . . .

(d). Avoiding impairment of productivity

The second limitation in section 531(a) is the unqualified direction that management cannot cause "impairment of the productivity of the land." It is a fairly precise standard, and it ought to be enforceable. In a sense, it is a restatement of the watershed value, and, for emphasis, it is repeated in the definition of "sustained yield."

"Productivity" as measured by "renewable surface resources" must refer to the capacity of the land to support flora and fauna and to furnish "the several products and services obtained therefrom." The two key elements in such production are the soil and the water. . .. The nonimpairment standard imposes an affirmative duty on the land management agency to reclaim impaired lands, but its application can be measured only by particular circumstances.

That argumentative conclusion is founded, first, on a practical interpretation of the provision in light of the overall aims of Congress, and, second, on the entire context of statutory authority within which the multiple use agencies operate. . . .

(e). Planning for sustained yield

The most significant management limitation in the MUSY Act is derived from its definition of "sustained yield" in section 531(b). The phrase means *perpetual, high-level* resource outputs of *all* of the renewable resources annually, *without impairment.* It reinforces the nonimpairment conclusions above, in the ways mentioned. It is, in addition, a separate, binding ("*shall* administer") standard that makes continuing resource productivity the highest criterion. The plain meaning of sustained yield is that any administrative resource allocation which allows land deterioration or otherwise sacrifices future output of any renewable resource is illegal.

. . . .

It is obvious that specific provision for one resource has the potential to impede production of others. Thus the planning process must be one of conflict resolution by accommodation to the extent possible, giving priority to no one use—at least on the broad scale—and consideration to all. Failure to do so could leave multiple use decisions vulnerable to attack on sustained yield grounds.

The difficult part in implementing the standard is compatibility. The Act assumes that compatible use combinations can be worked out, but it must be recognized that some uses are simply incompatible with some others. Clearcutting, for instance, is compatible with the needs of a few wildlife species, but not of most, and it generally reduces habitat, impedes watershed protection, and conflicts with recreation resource uses. In practice, the BLM's emphasis on "range" has detracted from all other uses. Preservation has the same effect. All listed resources, in fact, conflict more than they get along.

In addition, each of the resources has potential for internal conflict. High-level watershed "production" can impede all other uses in the upper reaches of the stream while at the same time promoting them elsewhere. It is very difficult to accommodate both hikers and motorcyclists in one area even though they both are pursuing recreation. In short, more conflict than compatibility is likely to be encountered in the search for compatible use combinations at optimum production levels. The main means of multiple use decisionmaking will be conflict resolution, with all of the political problems it implies. But sustained yield in compatible combinations does resolve conflicts by forbidding—at least theoretically—the optimization of one resource if it is done at the expense of the others.

NOTE

The author of the preceding articles comments that very few courts have had occasion to interpret and apply the MUSY Act. Nevertheless, discussions of administrative discretion and consideration of conflicting uses and values in the area of mining can be found in *U.S. v. Curtis-Nevada Mines, Inc.*, 611 F.2d 1277 (9th Cir. 1980); *U.S. v. Richardson*, 599 F. 2d 290 (9th Cir. 1979); *Friends of the Earth v. Butz*, 406 F. Supp. 742 (D. Mont. 1975), *remanded as moot* 576 F. 2d 1377 (9th Cir. 1978). A typical problem in this area is the very deferential review courts give to agency decisions that purport to balance competing land uses. *See, e.g., Dorothy Thomas Foundation, Inc. v. Hardin*, 317 F. Supp. 1072 (W.D.N.C. 1970) (agency decision to use some national forest lands for timber rather than recreation is not arbitrary or capricious). This deferential standard of review was also used in *Sierra Club v. Hardin*, 325 F. Supp. 99 (D. Alaska 1971), when the District Court of Alaska was asked to review the Forest Service decision to sell nearly nine billion board feet, over a period of time, from the relatively virgin forests of southeastern Alaska. The Court stated that "[t]he Act requires that the Forest Service give 'due' consideration to the various competing uses. . . . 'Due' is impossible to define and merely indicates that Congress intended the Forest Service to apply their expertise to the problem after consideration of all relevant values." On appeal, the Ninth Circuit took a somewhat more rigorous view of the phrase "due consideration," a development that the author of the preceding article suggests may presage a new era in judicial review of multiple use decisions. In *Sierra Club v. Butz*, 3 E.L.R. 20292 (9th Cir. 1973) (not officially reported), the Ninth Circuit reversed the lower court and stated that "'due consideration' to us requires that the values in question be informedly and rationally taken into balance. This requirement can hardly be satisfied by a showing of knowledge of the consequences and a decision to ignore them." However, just six years later the same circuit considered a challenge by rancher plaintiffs to Forest Service reductions in the number of animals they were permitted to graze. In *Perkins v. Bergland*, 608 F.2d 803 (9th Cir. 1979), the Ninth Circuit stated that the phrase "due consideration" is language which "breathe[s] discretion at every pore . . . [T]he courts are not at liberty to . . . [choose] one theory of range management as superior to another. Thus, we conclude that only very narrow review is appropriate here. The district court should ascertain whether the agency's factual findings as to range conditions and carrying capacity are arbitrary and capricious. If not, the matter ends there." *See also* Grad, Treatise on Environmental Law § 12.03[1][a].

NATIONAL FOREST MANAGEMENT ACT OF 1976

Pub. L. No. 94-588, 90 Stat. 2949, 16 U.S.C. § 472a, § 1600 *et seq.*

A major clarification relating to the authority of the Forest Service in the management of the national forests was provided by the National Forest Management Act of 1976, passed in October of that year. In form an amendment of the Forest and Range Renewable Resources Planning Act, the law incorporates substantial guidelines for the management of the national forests and for the disposal of timber from forest lands.

The immediate occasion for the passage of the law was the decision in *Isaac Walton League v. Butz*, 522 F.2d 945 (4th Cir. 1975) which had interpreted the initial provision of the Forest Service Organic Act, to bar clear-cutting of national forests. The provision of the law, since repealed, was 16 U.S.C. § 476which provided that the Secretary of Agriculture, "under such rules and regulations as he shall prescribe, may cause to be designated and appraised so much of the dead, matured or large growth of trees . . . and may sell the same . . . which before being sold shall be marked and designated. . . ." The court, contrary to the "practical" interpretation given to the law previously, held that this meant that in the national forest only trees individually marked could be selected and harvested. The decision, subsequently followed in *Zieske v. Butz*, 406 F. Supp. 258 (D. Alaska 1975), threatened the very existence of the timber industry in the national forest. The Department of Agriculture estimated that the effectuation of the court's reading of the law would result in reducing the availability of soft wood supplies from the national forest by about one half, leading to a very major increase in the wholesale price of lumber. Faced with this prospect, the Congress enacted the National Forest Management Act of 1976. The first major law on the management of national forests since the Organic Act of 1897, 16 U.S.C. § 473 *et seq.*, and the Multiple Use Sustained Yield Act of 1960 (16 U.S.C. § 528 *et seq.*), the National Forest Management Act provides for a revised system of timber sales, 16 U.S.C. § 472a, and specifies the kind of cuts authorized in the national forests and the conditions which must be met for each. 16 U.S.C. § 1600 *et seq.* Clear-cutting is permitted only if it is determined to be the optimum method, and all cuts of the forest must be carried out in a manner consistent with the protection of soil, water shed, fish, wildlife, recreation and esthetic resources and the regeneration of timber resources. Other constraints on harvesting methods are set forth in the law relating to the topography and condition of the area, and with the provision that the harvesting system used is not selected primarily because it will give the greatest dollar return or the greatest unit output of timber. Substantial authority is provided for the making of rules and regulations under the Act. In spite of its protective provisions it is clear that the law for the first time provided authority—with certain safeguards—for the clear-cutting of national forests which had previously been conducted under some substantial doubt. For discussion and other sources on clear-cutting, see F. Grad, Treatise on Environmental Law § 12.03[1][c].

Coggins, "THE LAW OF PUBLIC RANGELAND MANAGEMENT IV: FLPMA, PRIA AND THE MULTIPLE USE MANDATE"*

14 Envtl Law 1, 61–63 (1983)

5. Managing for sustained yield

The most significant management limitation in FLPMA is the definition of "sustained yield" in section 1702(h). The phrase means *perpetual, high level* annual resource outputs of *all* renewable resources. Sustained yield is a separate, binding standard that makes continuing resource productivity the highest management criterion. The plain meaning of sustained yield in section 1702(h) is that administrators may not sacrifice the future output of any renewable resource in present resource allocations. The "permanent" impairment provision qualifies the sustained yield limitation by ensuring that only serious, longlasting damage is prohibited.

Even so, the sustained yield definition must be read together with the unit size provision, if for no other reason than a rigid, literal inter-resource interpretation would be absurd. In a literal interpretation, any grazing that severely impaired future recreation values would not be allowed, and, conversely, any recreation facilities that severely impaired future grazing would not be allowed. Also, just as nonimpairment is less restrictive than nondegradation, sustained annual yield does not mean precisely the same yield every year.

Sustained yield theory has developed primarily in the context of timber management. In its recent incarnation as "nondeclining even flow," sustained yield means roughly that the harvest must be limited to the volume of wood grown that year, with a few exceptions. As applied in timber management, the theory tends to be circular in that the predictive variables are unpredictably interrelated. Sustained yield theory is also much harder to apply to resources that are less easily quantified. Although timber growth is relatively constant from year to year, grass growth, rainfall, and wildlife propagation vary in unpredictable ways. Resources other than livestock and timber have never been successfully quantified, and BLM planning appears devoid of even a rudimentary or systematic attempt. Yet all resources are statutorily equal and deserving of more or less equal treatment. Thus, the statute demands an inventory of all resources, an estimate of sustainable high production levels for each resource, a restoration of the lands to high production levels where necessary, and a translation of the overall production levels into individual decisions. In other words, the agency must plan to accommodate recreation, timber, watershed, wildlife, and natural values, as well as grazing, at high levels in perpetuity, and then act according to that plan.

Historically, the livestock and timber industries have been among those public land users who overused their resources; when the private reserves were depleted, those industries turned to the public lands to meet demand—often on a subsidized basis. The sustained yield standard was enacted to ensure that public land managers do not repeat the mistakes of their private counterparts. Multiple use principles are fundamentally utilitarian, aimed largely at production of goods and services. But the sustained yield provision, more than any other, differentiates public from private land management. The private manager must discount future value; he deems benefits due more than a decade in the future currently valueless. The public entrepreneur may, and often must, take a longer view of profit potential. In imposing sustained yield as a primary management goal, FLPMA decrees that production of a unit a decade or a century from now will be just as valuable as a unit produced today.

NOTES AND QUESTIONS

(1) The Multiple Use-Sustained Yield Act of 1960 is regarded as one of the important developments for the environmental and conservational protections of the public lands. Is there anything in the Act itself which stresses environmental or conservation values? What precisely are the standards to be used in determining which of a variety of uses is the appropriate one in any particular instance? Even within the four corners of the Act, is there an indication that one particular use may still be preferred legislatively, in spite of the definition of "multiple use" which indicates that dollar return, or greatest unit output, is not to be determinative? Is "productivity of the land"—which is not to be impaired by multiple use—an aim which accords with that of strict conservationists or is it possible to argue that there may be no impairment of the productivity of the land in particular instances, even though, from the conservationist's point of view, a particular use causes environmental damage?

(2) The requirements of multiple use-sustained yield may lead to situations where incompatible uses may seem to be equally favored by the policies of the law. For an older, critical view of that problem, *see* Moses, *What Happened to Multiple-Purpose Resource Development—A Plea for Reasonableness*, 3 Land & Water L. Rev. 435 (1968), and for an excellent analytic approach, see E. Coggins, *The Law of Public Rangeland Management IV: FLPMA, PRIA, and the Multiple Use Mandate*, 14 Envtl. L. 1 (1983). *See* F. Grad, Treatise on Environmental Law § 12.03[1][a].

(3) Can an argument be made that eastern conservationists, who from their urban strongholds loudly advocate the need for wilderness preservation in the

far west, miss a large part of the western point of view? Review the location of most of the United States public lands—hardly any of them are located in the eastern part of the country. Can it be argued that western states must support the exploitation of resources on public lands simply to provide a sound tax base for state government? Assume the possibility of nonproductive uses of a substantial part of public lands in a state in which half or more of the land is publicly owned. What would provide the state's revenue?

[b] Range and Grazing

The materials that follow deal with two aspects of the exploitation of resources on federal lands. The two areas selected are grazing rights on public lands and exploitation of mineral resources on such lands under the mining laws. Several other areas could, of course, have been chosen and many of them reflect some of the same problems. The laws that deal with the development and exploitation of resources on public lands bear the stamp of the particular age that gave rise to them. In each instance, major economic interests are involved and environmental concerns have generally played a secondary role for most of the time of the laws' existence. The regulation of grazing lands, to some extent, carries out the tradition of the open range. Western development, of course, based predominantly on the acquisition and growth of large herds of cattle, depended greatly on the availability of public lands for grazing purposes. The laws regulating grazing rights thus reflect a contemporary balance of the need for grazing lands and the necessity on the part of the Federal Government to gain some, albeit limited, revenue from its lands. Such laws today also reflect the insight that the cow is the most effective mechanism to turn cheap grass into expensive proteins for the use of fast food hamburger joints, thus advancing both the interests of western cattle growers and eastern business interests, both of whom support low Congressionally set grazing fees. Grazing rights are not exclusive of other rights—including mining rights—and thus reflect an early acceptance of the multiple use pattern. Grazing rights legislation, beginning in 1934 with the Taylor Act, moreover, does not give permanent rights but merely provides permits for temporary, though long-term, use of grazing lands. The environmental issues are closely connected and probably dominated by the economic ones.

From the point of view of the cattle grower, the more cattle that can be successfully grazed in a given acreage, the more economically profitable the operation. From the environmental point of view, full economic exploitation of the range may well result in over-grazing with adverse and sometimes irreversible effects on the growth of plant coverage, and ultimately on erosion and runoff. Hence, the range regulations reflect economic as well as environmental considerations. *See also* F. Grad, Treatise on Environmental Law § 12.03[3], addressing some differences in grazing regulations on BLM and Forest Service lands.

For management purposes, the BLM lands are divided into grazing districts,[17] each supervised by a district manager.[18]

[17] 43 U.S.C. § 315.

[18] 43 C.F.R. § 4110.0-5(g).

Grazing permits are issued for the use of the land. The districts are to be managed "to enhance the productivity of the public rangelands by preventing overgrazing and soil deterioration; to provide for their orderly use, improvement and development; to stabilize the livestock industry dependent on the public range; provide for inventory and categorization of public rangelands on the basis of range conditions and trends; consistent with land-use plans, multiple use, sustained yield, environmental values, economic and other objectives stated in . . ." the Taylor Grazing Act as amended by FLPMA and the Public Rangelands Improvement Act of 1978.[19]

The Taylor Act provides for the organization into grazing districts of "vacant, unappropriated and unreserved" lands of the public domain.[20]

In a sense, these were left-over lands that had not been appropriated earlier for any other purpose. It has been suggested that these millions of acres had largely remained unappropriated because the country and the Congress could not agree on the method of disposition until after the crisis of the early thirties. But even then, the Taylor Act indicates, the use of the lands for grazing districts was considered a temporary arrangement of the unreserved "public lands . . . pending final disposal."[21]

The Act provided for the establishment of grazing districts following a public hearing, of which public notice had been given. The public notice also has "the effect of withdrawing all public lands within the exterior boundary of such proposed grazing districts from all forms of entry of settlement."[22]

Grazing districts are enormous in size, some covering millions of acres, and the question has been raised whether BLM personnel assigned to each district can possibly meet the task of policing the entire area.[23]

The regulations authorized under the Taylor Grazing Act are basically similar to the ones developed earlier by the Forest Service.[24]

Once a grazing district has been established, a grazier may obtain a permit for grazing a certain number of cattle or sheep on an allotted area,[25] and grazing without a permit is prohibited,[26] thus protecting holders of permits against trespassers. The imposition of a grazing fee is also authorized.[27]

The law is not very specific as to who is entitled to a permit—the Secretary of the Interior is authorized to have permits issued "to such bona fide settlers, residents, and other stock owners as under his rules and regulations are entitled to participate in the use of the range. . . ."[28]

The section also provides that

> Preference shall be given in the issuance of grazing permits to those within or near a district who are land owners engaged in the livestock business, bona fide occupants or settlers, or owners of water or water rights

---

[19] 43 C.F.R. § 4110.0-2.

[20] 43 U.S.C. § 315.

[21] 43 U.S.C. § 315.

[22] 43 U.S.C. § 315.

[23] Calef, Private Grazing and Public Lands 81 (1960).

[24] *See* discussion in F. Grad, Treatise on Environmental Law, § 12.03[3][b].

[25] 43 U.S.C. § 315b; 43 C.F.R. §§ 4111.1-1 to 4111.3-2.

[26] 43 C.F.R. § 4112.3-1(a).

[27] 43 U.S.C. § 315b.

[28] 43 U.S.C. § 315b.

as may be necessary to permit the proper use of lands, water or water rights owned, occupied or leased by them. . . .

The administration of the grazing lands under the Taylor Grazing Act thus constitutes a very considerable break with past traditions of open rangelands, unregulated and free for the taking. But although the Act has imposed a significant system of regulation where there had been none before, it has also perpetuated some of the practices existing prior to its enactment of the Act. Since one of the purposes of the Taylor Grazing Act was to stabilize the grazing industry, preference for grazing permits was given to those who had previously used the public land.[29]

This, coupled with the "base property" requirement which was adapted from the Forest Service regulations, gave the established operators a substantial advantage.

The established grazing interests also manage to maintain a degree of control over the administration of the lands. This control is exercised chiefly through the advisory boards.[30]

These boards vary in size from five to twelve members.[31]

The members of the board are usually elected with only those already holding grazing permits eligible to vote. While their statutory authority is only advisory, the actual power the members of the board wield in practice is rather substantial. They advise the district manager on topics ranging from base property qualifications, range capacity, consideration and improvement, to approval or cancellation of grazing permits and leases.[32]

There is evidence that the legal roles may be reversed in actuality, with the advisory board making most of the actual decisions, and the district manager largely acting as its agent. While the district manager may try to control the outcome of a board meeting through careful planning of the agenda or preparation of material to be discussed, he will rarely, if ever, reject an opinion of the board.[33]

Though the meetings must be open to the public, meetings at which the allocation of permits and licenses is determined may be held in executive session.[34]

BLM has land valuable for grazing situated outside of grazing districts. Such land is leased[35] (unlike the grazing districts which are administered through the permit system). In granting such leases, preference is accorded to prior users of the land.[36]

Such lands are also administered in accordance with multiple-use sustained-yield principles.[37]

The hazards of inadequate range management are clear. Overgrazing in an arid or semi-arid climate will create changes in the vegetation and may lead to major soil erosion and possibly irreversible dust bowl conditions. In

[29] 43 U.S.C. § 315b.

[30] 43 U.S.C. § 315o-1(a); 43 C.F.R. § 4114.1-5.

[31] 43 U.S.C. § 315o-1(a); 43 C.F.R. § 4114.1-1.

[32] 43 U.S.C. § 315o-1(b); 43 C.F.R. § 4114.1-5.

[33] Foss, Politics and Grass 107 (1960).

[34] 43 C.F.R. § 4114.1-4.

[35] 43 U.S.C. § 315m; 43 C.F.R. § 4121.1-2.

[36] 43 U.S.C. § 315m; 43 C.F.R. § 4121.1-2.

[37] 43 U.S.C. § 315m; 43 C.F.R. § 4122.1-1.

addition, overgrazing and inadequate management of water supplies will have disastrous effects on wildlife, because cattle and sheep on the range are in such competition with deer, antelope, and wild horses and burros that many wildlife species which share the range are in the threatened or endangered category. Though grazing regulations take into account the number of wild animals which graze in a particular area,[38] there is constant pressure from graziers to reduce the share reserved for them.

The public domain required no fee payments until 1934 when the Taylor Act was passed. Yielding to political pressures from western congressmen, Taylor Act fees remained low for many years to reflect only the cost of administering grazing permits—*not* the cost of maintaining the range.[39]

Grazing fees appear to be a permanent political issue in the West. In addition to indirect federal subsidies in the BLM and Forest Service grazing fee systems, other federal supports that have dubious environmental impact involve such matters as production and wildlife controls for the benefit of users of the range. There is a long-standing controversy over how much damage to cattle and sheep is caused by mountain lions, coyotes and other predators, but in response to demands for the protection of cattle and sheep, some of the predators have been decimated so as to be among the threatened or hazarded species. Their further destruction or extinction is likely to upset the ecological balance by allowing other wildlife—such as deer, antelope and elk—to propagate excessively, thereby again causing a greater potential for the depletion of range resources.[40]

For many years there had been little litigation for the vindication of ecological or conservational interests in rangelands, and there appears to have been no litigation for the application of the National Environmental Policy Act to grazing land determinations or to the granting of grazing permits covering vast areas of the range until the decision in 1974 in *National Resources Defense Council v. Morton.*[41]

The District Court of the District of Columbia found that NEPA was applicable to rangeland decisions, and noted that the requirement of filing an environmental impact statement depends not on the size of the geographical area, but on the severity of the impact of grazing on local environments.

In the settlement of the case, the Department of the Interior agreed to prepare environmental impact statements for grazing activities in each of the 200 grazing districts. These studies are in turn being used in the FLPMA-mandated Management Framework Plans for each district. One notable outcome, which recognizes both the decreased carrying capacity of the range and the increased emphasis on sharing cattle grazing with use of the range by wildlife, is the significant and widespread reduction in level of grazing allotted to livestock.

Congress responded to this situation in 1978 by imposing a one-year moratorium on increases in grazing fees, and by enacting the Public Rangeland Improvement Act.[42]

---

[38] *See, e.g.,* 43 C.F.R. § 4114.1-5(o).

[39] 43 U.S.C. § 315b.

[40] *See* discussion of protection of wildlife, F. Grad, Treatise on Environmental Law, § 12.04[1].

[41] 388 F. Supp. 829 (D.D.C. 1974).

[42] Pub. L. No. 95-514, 43 U.S.C. § 1901.

The Act set up a $360 million program to increase the productivity of the public rangelands over a 20-year period, relying heavily on such range improvements as fencing and weed and juniper control.

---

43 U.S.C.
Chapter 8A.—Grazing Lands [Taylor Act, enacted June 28, 1934]

§ 315. Grazing districts; establishment; restrictions; prior rights; rights-of-way; hearing and notice; hunting or fishing rights

In order to promote the highest use of the public lands pending its final disposal, the Secretary of the Interior is authorized, in his discretion, by order to establish grazing districts or additions thereto and/or to modify the boundaries thereof, of vacant, unappropriated, and unreserved lands from any part of the public domain of the United States (exclusive of Alaska), which are not in national forests, national parks and monuments, Indian reservations [and other listed exceptions] and which in his opinion are chiefly valuable for grazing and raising forage crops: *Provided*, That no lands withdrawn or reserved for any other purpose shall be included in any such district except with the approval of the head of the department having jurisdiction thereof. Nothing in this chapter shall be construed in any way to diminish, restrict, or impair any right which has been heretofore or may be hereafter initiated under existing law validly affecting the public lands, and which is maintained pursuant to such law except as otherwise expressly provided in this chapter, nor to affect any land heretofore or hereafter surveyed which, except for the provisions of this chapter, would be a part of any grant to any State, nor as limiting or restricting the power or authority of any State as to matters within its jurisdiction. Whenever any grazing district is established pursuant to this chapter, the Secretary shall grant to owners of land adjacent to such district, upon application of any such owner, such right-of-way over the lands included in such district for stock-driving purposes as may be necessary for the convenient access by any such owner to marketing facilities or to lands not within such district owned by such person or upon which such person has stock-grazing rights. Neither this chapter nor sections 291-301 of this title, commonly known as the "Stock Raising Homestead Act," shall be construed as limiting the authority or policy of Congress or the President to include in national forests public lands of the character described in section 471 of Title 16, for the purposes set forth in section 475 of Title 16, or such other purposes as Congress may specify. Before grazing districts are created in any State as herein provided, a hearing shall be held in the State, after public notice thereof shall have been given, at such location convenient for the attendance of State officials, and the settlers, residents, and livestock owners of the vicinity, as may be determined by the Secretary of the Interior. No such district shall be established until the expiration of ninety days after such notice shall have been given, nor until twenty days after such hearing shall be held: *Provided, however*, That the publication of such notice shall have the effect of withdrawing all public lands within the exterior boundary of such proposed grazing districts from all forms of entry of settlement. Nothing in this chapter shall be construed as in any way altering or restricting the right to hunt or fish within a grazing district in accordance with the laws of the United States or of any State, or as vesting in any permittee any right whatsoever to interfere with hunting or fishing within a grazing district.

§ 315a. Protection, administration, regulation, and improvement of districts; rules and regulations; study of erosion and flood control; offenses

[Provisions for the protection of the rangeland and its necessary rehabilitation and for the punishment of violations of rules.]

§ 315b. Grazing permits; fees; vested water rights; permits not to create right in land

The Secretary of the Interior is authorized to issue or cause to be issued permits to graze livestock on such grazing districts to such bona fide settlers, residents, and other stock owners as under his rules and regulations are entitled to participate in the use of the range, upon the payment annually of reasonable fees in each case to be fixed or determined from time to time in accordance with governing law. Grazing permits shall be issued only to citizens of the United States or to those who have filed the necessary declarations of intention to become such, as required by the naturalization laws, and to groups, associations, or corporations authorized to conduct business under the laws of the State in which the grazing district is located. Preference shall be given in the issuance of grazing permits to those within or near a district who are landowners engaged in the livestock business, bona fide occupants or settlers, or owners of water or water rights, as may be necessary to permit the proper use of lands, water or water rights owned, occupied, or leased by them, except that until July 1, 1935, no preference shall be given in the issuance of such permits to any such owner, occupant, or settler, whose rights were acquired between January 1, 1934, and December 31, 1934, both dates inclusive, except that no permittee complying with the rules and regulations laid down by the Secretary of the Interior shall be denied the renewal of such permit, if such denial will impair the value of the grazing unit of the permittee, when such unit is pledged as security for any bona fide loan. Such permits shall be for a period of not more than ten years, subject to the preference right of the permittees to renewal in the discretion of the Secretary of the Interior, who shall specify from time to time numbers of stock and seasons of use. During periods of range depletion due to severe drought or other natural causes, or in case of a general epidemic of disease, during the life of the permit, the Secretary of the Interior is authorized, in his discretion to remit, reduce, refund in whole or in part, or authorize postponement of payment of grazing fees for such depletion period so long as the emergency exists: *Provided further*, That nothing in this chapter shall be construed or administered in any way to diminish or impair any right to the possession and use of water for mining, agriculture, manufacture, or other purposes which has heretofore vested or accrued under existing law validly affecting the public lands or which may be hereafter initiated or acquired and maintained in accordance with such law. So far as consistent with the purposes and provisions of this chapter, grazing privileges recognized and acknowledged shall be adequately safeguarded, but the creation of a grazing district or the issuance of a permit pursuant to the provisions of this chapter shall not create any right, title, interest, or estate in or to the lands.

§ 315d. Grazing stock for domestic purposes; use of natural resources

The Secretary of the Interior shall permit, under regulations to be prescribed by him, the free grazing within such districts of livestock kept for domestic purposes; and provided that so far as authorized by existing law or laws hereinafter enacted, nothing contained in this chapter shall prevent the use of timber, stone, gravel, clay, coal, and other deposits by miners, prospectors for mineral, bona fide settlers and residents, for firewood, fencing, buildings, mining, prospecting, and domestic purposes within areas subject to the provisions of this chapter.

§ 315*l*. Lands under national-forest administration

The President of the United States is authorized to reserve by proclamation any place under national-forest administration in any State where national forests may be created or enlarged by Executive order any unappropriated public lands lying within watersheds forming a part of the national forests which, in his opinion, can best be administered, in connection with existing national-forest administration units, and to place under the Interior Department administration any lands within national forests, principally valuable for grazing, which, in his opinion, can best be administered under the provisions of this chapter: *Provided*, That such reservations or transfers shall not interfere with legal rights acquired under any public-land laws so long as such rights are legally maintained. Lands placed under the national-forest administration under the authority of this chapter shall be subject to all the laws and regulations relating to national forests, and lands placed under the Interior Department administration shall be subject to all public-land laws and regulations applicable to grazing districts created under authority of this chapter. Nothing in this section shall be construed so as to limit the power of the President (relating to reorganizations in the executive departments) granted by sections 124-132 of Title 5.

NOTE

The section of the Taylor Act, *supra*, relating to exchanges of public lands, interpreted in *LaRue v. Udall, infra*, was repealed in 1976. The subject of land exchanges has now been unified for both BLM lands and forest preserve lands in § 206 of the Federal Land Policy and Management Act of 1976, 43 U.S.C. 1716, as follows:

> Sec. 206. (a) A tract of public land or interests therein may be disposed of by exchange by the Secretary under this Act and a tract of land or interests therein within the National Forest System may be disposed of by exchange by the Secretary of Agriculture under applicable law where the Secretary concerned determines that the public interest will be well served by making that exchange: *Provided*, That when considering public interest the Secretary concerned shall give full consideration to better Federal land management and the needs of State and local people, including needs for lands for the economy, community expansion, recreation areas, food, fiber, minerals, and fish and wildlife and the Secretary concerned finds that the values and the objectives which Federal lands or interests to be conveyed may serve if retained in the Federal ownership are not more than the values of the non-Federal lands or interests and the public objectives they could serve if acquired.
>
> (b) In exercising the exchange authority granted by subsection (a) or by section 205(a) of this Act, the Secretary may accept title to any non-Federal land or interests therein in exchange for such land, or interests therein which he finds proper for transfer out of Federal ownership and which are located in the same State as the non-Federal land or interest to be acquired. For the purposes of this subsection, unsurveyed school sections which, upon survey by the Secretary, would become State lands, shall be considered as "non-Federal lands." The values of the lands exchanged by the Secretary under this Act and by the Secretary of Agriculture under applicable law relating to lands within the National Forest System either shall be equal, or if they are not equal, the values shall be equalized by the payment of money to the grantor or to the Secretary concerned as the circumstances require so long as payment does not exceed 25 per centum of the total value of the lands or interests transferred out of Federal ownership. The Secretary concerned shall try to reduce the amount of the payment of money to as small an amount as possible.
>
> (c) Lands acquired by exchange under this section by the Secretary which are within the boundaries of the National Forest System may be transferred to the Secretary of Agriculture and shall then become National Forest System lands and subject to all the laws, rules, and regulations applicable to the National Forest System. Lands acquired by exchange by the Secretary under this section which are within the boundaries of National Park, Wildlife Refuge, Wild and Scenic Rivers, Trails, or any other System established by Act of Congress may be transferred to the appropriate agency head for administration as part of such System and in accordance with the laws, rules, and regulations applicable to such System.

DIAMOND RING RANCH, INC. v. MORTON

United States Court of Appeals, Tenth Circuit (1976)
531 F.2d 1397

[The Department of the Interior imposed sanctions on Diamond Ring Ranch for violating the terms and conditions of a lease of government land under the Taylor Grazing Act. The violation consisted of alleged indiscriminatory spraying by Diamond Ring of sagebrush on government land used by Diamond Ring Ranch without obtaining the prior approval of the Bureau of Land Management. The effect of such spraying is to eradicate the sagebrush for some 8 to 10 years, thereby allowing the edible forage plants to grow. The defendant, Diamond Ring, had sought a subsidy from the Agriculture Department for spraying of approximately 5,000 acres of ranch company lands with herbicide 2, 4-D which defoliates plants. The government subsidy for the spraying of the land was obtained on a representation that only private land would be sprayed rather than public lands, which also contained areas used for hunting and fishing and for a reservoir. There was evidence to show that the spraying of the government land was willful in that Diamond Ring failed to supervise and instruct the pilot of the flying service that did the spraying as to the precise area to be sprayed. The spraying was clearly in violation of regulations of the Secretary of the Interior for the management of grazing lands. The court upheld the Secretary's power to suspend or revoke a grazing license for the violation of regulations and upheld the finding that the violation had indeed been willful. Since the statute involved was civil rather than criminal, questions of premeditation or specific intent did not enter into the decision and even if the violation on Diamond Ring's part was negligent, it was so grossly negligent as to support a determination of willfulness.

The court found that the action of the Secretary was reviewable under the Administrative Procedure Act, in the absence of any specific provisions for review under the Taylor Grazing Act itself. The court disagreed with the contention that this was a matter as to which discretion was rested entirely in the Secretary so as to preclude judicial review. The Department of Interior's trial examiner had imposed a sanction which denied the ranch all grazing privileges for a period of 3 years but then ordered that the sanction be suspended until a showing is made by BLM that a similar violation has occurred. The Interior Department of Land Appeals imposed a far more severe penalty suspending the permit or license entirely. On review, the court found that under the circumstances of the case the imposition of the more severe penalty was arbitrary and capricious, and remanded so that the lesser penalty imposed by the examiner could be reinstituted.]

LaRUE v. UDALL

United States Court of Appeals, District of Columbia Circuit (1963)
342 F.2d 428

[Ranchers licensed to graze cattle on federal lands contiguous to their ranch sought reversal of a decision of the Secretary of Interior to exchange this land for land owned by North American Aviation a substantial distance from their ranch. North American planned to use the land thus acquired in its program of development and manufacture of rocket engines and power plants. The majority opinion (which is omitted) held that the Secretary was authorized under the Act to exchange lands whenever the exchange would benefit the public interest. The ranchers had argued that the term "public interest" in the Act was restricted to grazing interests.]

BAZELON, Circuit Judge (concurring).

Under § 8(b) [now repealed] of the Taylor Grazing Act, 43 U.S.C. § 315g(b)(1958), any landowner may propose to exchange his land ["offered" lands] for federal land of equal value located within a grazing district ["selected" lands]; and the Secretary of the Interior may approve the exchange if "public interests will be benefited thereby." In this case, because the Secretary viewed the Taylor Act as a "multiple purpose" statute, he construed the term "public interests" as a broad reference to the general public interest, rather than being limited to grazing interests. In approving the exchange, the Secretary relied heavily on his finding that the exchange would benefit the general public interest, but he also found that the exchange would benefit grazing interests. This court holds that the exchange may be approved on either ground. I think approval can rest only on a finding of benefit to grazing interests.

The Taylor Grazing Act of 1934 closed the public domain, climaxing the reversal of earlier policy which had encouraged disposal of the public lands to private ownership. The policy of land conservation—retaining federal ownership and regulating land use to prevent depletion of natural resources—began with the creation of forest reserves after 1891. The Taylor Act extended this policy to the remaining 173,000,000 acres of public lands still unreserved by 1934. To prevent soil deterioration and stabilize the livestock industry which constituted the chief user of this public range, the Secretary of the Interior was authorized to reserve suitable lands for the creation of grazing districts and to regulate grazing within the districts by issuing permits. It was recognized however, that the existing checkerboard pattern of alternating public and private ownership, resulting from the course of land settlement during the nineteenth century, would make it difficult to administer the districts efficiently. To meet this problem, § 8 of the Act was designed to foster consolidation in the manner of earlier forest reserves legislation: the Secretary was authorized to accept land which would consolidate the grazing districts, either by gift or in exchange for other grazing land of equal value.

The legislative history of the Act shows that in authorizing the Secretary to convey public lands to private individuals as part of an exchange, § 8(b) was intended not as a new source of power to alienate federal lands, but simply to promote consolidation of the grazing districts. As such, I think that the determination that "public interests will be benefited [by an exchange]" includes only public interests in furtherance of the grazing and range stabilization policies which are the subject of the Act. The term was so construed in an opinion rendered by the Solicitor of the Department of the Interior shortly after the Act's passage, and there is no basis for the Secretary's suggestion that amendments since 1934 have changed the meaning of § 8.

QUESTIONS

(1) Grazing fees are set by the Secretary of the Interior, the BLM and the Secretary of Agriculture, on the lands within their respective control. Must they consider the actual costs ranchers incur when making capital investments on public land pastures? The investment made in grazing permits? *See Pankey Land & Cattle Co. v. Hardin*, 427 F.2d 43 (10th Cir. 1970). Does it matter that grazing fees are traditionally set lower than comparable rates for leasing public lands? What is the current effect of the Public Rangelands Improvement Act of 1978, 43 U.S.C. § 1905(a), which states that fees shall represent, within limits, "the economic value of the use of the land to the user."

(2) The case of *LaRue v. Udall* was generally considered a defeat for conservation forces. In view of the fact that the case primarily involved the conflicting rights of a grazing permit owner and of North American Aviation, Inc., to exchange certain properties under the Taylor Grazing Act, why are public conservation interests threatened? From the point of view of the rational development of public lands, can a counter argument be made that the decision of the court was right, and perhaps even an advance, on conservation grounds? Is the concurring opinion of Judge Bazelon more protective of conservation interests?

(3) Is there a hierarchy of uses implicit in the Taylor Grazing Act, particularly with respect to mining as against grazing rights, and generally with respect to other uses? Which appear to be the preferred uses and do they tend to favor conservation or economic exploitation policies?

[c] Mining and Minerals

The materials on the Mining Laws of 1872, which still govern most mining operations on public lands, reflect an even earlier approach to the use of public land resources. Essentially, the 1872 Act, which is a clear and outrageous anachronism today, regards the public land as available for the taking by anyone willing to expend some money and effort on its development. No attempt is made in the brief selections that follow to provide a general survey of the operation of the mining laws. The purpose here is merely to provide some indication of the profligacy of an earlier age in dealing with public lands, and with policies having environmental impact which the present has inherited. The selections that follow show the law's requirements and indicate that even under its recent interpretations it is still possible for a citizen to acquire title to major parcels of public lands by discovering mineral deposits of some economic value, by laying claim to them, commencing their exploitation, and then applying for a patent to the land. Though leasing of public lands for exploitation of oil and gas resources, as well as for certain other mineral deposits, is the pattern of more recent legislation (Public Lands Leasing Act, 41 Stat. 437 as amended 30 U.S.C. § 181 *et seq.*), the older pattern persists for most of the hard minerals and had even been extended to "building stones" (27 Stat. 348, 30 U.S.C. § 161). Though it is true that mining claims are presently being administered by the Department of the Interior with far greater stringency of regulation than was probably intended in the original Mining Law of 1872, and though judicial decisions would appear to place more stringent requirements on the claimant than they did more than 125 years ago, it is nonetheless true that it may still be possible for a claimant under the mining laws to acquire public lands, initially for mining purposes, but realistically with an eye to other exploitative and harmful uses. It should be noted that, aside from an obvious lack of direct concern for the alienation of valuable assets by the federal government, the original mining laws in 1872 made no provision for environmental protection or for the restoration of the environment to its earlier condition once mining operations had ceased. By its nature, of course, the Mining Act of 1872, which looked to the ultimate acquisition of the land by the locator of the mining claim, was not adapted to the imposition of conditions for environmental protection. The government in 1872 would not have been in any position to enforce any such condition once a patent to a mining claim had been obtained. The situation is a different one under the more modern lease arrangements, where continued adherence to provisions protecting the environment can be made a condition of the continuing lease term. In this area, as in others, the adoption of laws to provide adequately for long-range environmental protection meets head-on with economic interests that benefit from their reliance on an outmoded piece of legislation that has nothing but its age or the folklore of the hardy miner setting out in the wild with his burro to recommend it.

30 U.S.C.
Mining Laws of 1866 and 1872, *as amended.*

Act of July 4, 1866, c. 166, § 5 et seq., 14 Stat. 86;
Act of May 10, 1872, c. 152, § 2 et seq., 17 Stat. 91

§ 21. Mineral lands reserved

In all cases lands valuable for minerals shall be reserved from sale, except as otherwise expressly directed by law.

§ 22. Lands open to purchase by citizens

Except as otherwise provided, all valuable mineral deposits in lands belonging to the United States, both surveyed and unsurveyed, shall be free and open to exploration and purchase, and the lands in which they are found to occupation and purchase, by citizens of the United States and those who have declared their intention to become such, under regulations prescribed by law, and according to the local customs or rules of miners in the several mining districts, so far as the same are applicable and not inconsistent with the laws of the United States.

§ 26. Locators' rights of possession and enjoyment

The locators of all mining locations made on any mineral vein, lode, or ledge, situated on the public domain, their heirs and assigns, where no adverse claim existed on the 10th day of May 1872 so long as they comply with the laws of the United States, and with State, territorial, and local regulations not in conflict with the laws of the United States governing their possessory title, shall have the exclusive right of possession and enjoyment of all the surface included within the lines of their locations, and of all veins, lodes, and ledges throughout their entire depth, the top or apex of which lies inside of such surface lines extended downward vertically, although such veins, lodes, or ledges may so far depart from a perpendicular in their course downward as to extend outside the vertical side lines of such surface locations. But their right of possession to such outside parts of such veins or ledges shall be confined to such portions thereof as lie between vertical planes drawn downward as above described, through the end lines of their locations, so continued in their own direction that such planes will intersect such exterior parts of such veins or ledges. Nothing in this section shall authorize the locator or possessor of a vein or lode which extends in its downward course beyond the vertical lines of his claim to enter upon the surface of a claim owned or possessed by another.

§ 28. Mining district regulations by miners: location, recordation, and amount of work; marking of location on ground; records; annual labor or improvements on claims pending issue of patent; co-owner's succession in interest upon delinquency in contributing proportion of expenditures; tunnel as lode expenditure

The miners of each mining district may make regulations not in conflict with the laws of the United States, or with the laws of the State or Territory in which the district is situated, governing the location, manner of recording, amount of work necessary to hold possession of a mining claim, subject to the following requirements: The location must be distinctly marked on the ground so that its boundaries can be readily traced. All records of mining claims made after May 10, 1872, shall contain the name or names of the locators, the date of the location, and such a description of the claim or claims located by reference to some natural object or permanent monument as will identify the claim. On each claim located after the 10th day of May 1872, and until a patent has been issued therefor, not less than $100 worth of labor shall be performed or improvements made during each year. On all claims located prior to the 10th day of May 1872, $10 worth of labor shall be performed or improvements made each year, for each one hundred feet in length along the vein until a patent has been issued therefor; but where such claims are held in common, such expenditure may be made upon any one claim; and upon a failure to comply with these conditions, the claim or mine upon which such failure occurred shall be open to relocation in the same manner as if no location of the same had ever been made, provided that the original locators, their heirs, assigns, or legal representatives, have not resumed work upon the claim after failure and before such location. . . .

§ 29. Patents; procurement procedure; filing: application under oath, plat and field notes, notices, and affidavits; posting plat and notice on claim; publications and posting notice in office; certificate; adverse claims; payment per acre; objections; nonresident claimant's agent for execution of application and affidavits

A patent for any land claimed and located for valuable deposits may be obtained in the following manner: Any person, association, or corporation authorized to locate a claim under this chapter and sections 71 to 76 of this title, having claimed and located a piece of land for such purposes, who has, or have, complied with the terms of this chapter and sections 71 to 76 of this title, may file in the proper land office an application for a patent, under oath, showing such compliance, together with a plat and field notes of the claim or claims in common, made by or under the direction of the United States Chief Cadastral Engineer, showing accurately the boundaries of the claim or claims, which shall be distinctly marked by monuments on the ground, and shall post a copy of such plat, together with a notice of such application for a patent, in a conspicuous place on the land embraced in such plat previous to the filing of the application for a patent, and shall file an affidavit of at least two persons that such notice has been duly posted, and shall file a copy of the notice in such land office, and shall thereupon be entitled to a patent for the land, in the manner following. . . .

Letter from Stewart L. Udall, Secretary of the Interior, To the Public Land Law Review Commission

January 15, 1969

Dear Mr. Chairman and Members,

Public Land Law Review Commission:

Shortly I will complete my service as Secretary of the Interior. These eight years have been both challenging and rewarding. I take deep personal satisfaction in the progress this Nation has made in conservation, resource development, and in the efforts towards the orderly management of our public lands. The credit, of course, is due to many dedicated people—in the Congress, in the Executive Branch, and among our citizenry.

But there is much yet to be done; many new policies and laws are needed to put public land resource management on a sound foundation for the long-term future. After eight years in this office, I have come to the conclusion that the most important piece of unfinished business on the Nation's natural resource agenda is the complete replacement of the mining law of 1872.

This outmoded law has become the major obstacle to the wise conservation and effective management of the natural resources of our public lands. Many other problems in the administration of the public land laws are rooted in the mining law. For that reason I have decided to direct this communication to all the members of the Public Land Law Review Commission.

Put simply, this obsolete and outdated statute inhibits the best kind of multiple-use management. It operates as an outright giveaway of vital national resources. At the same time it harms the American mining industry. It not only fails to meet the needs of today's mining industry; it retards the industry's development. By its lack of security of tenure during the pre-discovery period, the mining law inhibits the use of highly sophisticated but expensive modern exploration techniques to probe for deep, hidden deposits. Its discovery requirement militates against the maintenance of rights in low-grade deposits as reserves for future development.

For almost 100 years the mining law has been a veritable jungle of legal uncertainties, such as extralateral rights, discovery, placer v. lode, and varying state requirements. It is the considered judgment of all my executives and experts that today the mining law obstructs rather than promotes the wise use of our mineral estate for the long-term future of the Nation. At the same time the law inhibits effective conservation, not only of our mineral resources but of other vital resources as well. It permits, indeed it encourages, uncontrolled despoliation of the public lands with irreparable damage to other resources. In far too many instances there is no justifying social or economic benefit from this destruction; far too often the damage results from compliance with purposeless laws, such as annual "assessment work" or the digging of "discovery" pits.

Needed measures designed to coordinate and harmonize mining with other land uses are either precluded or made meaningless by the 1872 act, for it gives the mining of mineral resources—regardless of their relative value—an overriding priority over all other conservation plans. With today's overlapping uses of the public lands there is a need for controlled exploration and development, the recordation with the federal government of mining claims, and for the safety and reclamation of mined-out lands. Our ability to exploit the environment has far outstripped our capacity for balanced use of our public resources keyed to the welfare of other generations of Americans.

In addition, the mining law contains strong incentives for abuses and fraud. The ease by which property rights may be obtained under the mining law, by merely "staking a claim," makes it a favorite tool to fraudulently appropriate public lands for non-mining purposes, such as timber, home sites, subdivisions, etc. Such abuses defeat the proper development of public lands for mining purposes and the orderly management and use of the land for other vital needs.

Finally, the mining law is a blatant give-away of resources that should be managed in the long-term national interest under laws that take into account modern resource management techniques. For only a token payment of $2.50

or $5.00 an acre, depending upon whether the claim is placer or lode, and the expenditure of a nominal $500 in "improvements" on the claim, title to the land and all of its resources passes to a locator who has made a discovery, and if he desires to take the minerals without obtaining the legal title to the land, the locator pays the government nothing. No private owner would countenance a system whereby he extends a continuing invitation to others, regardless of his own needs, to come onto his land without even notice to him, to search for and take out the minerals, to leave it despoiled, and to pay nothing. The time is long since past when the American people can afford such profligacy with their national heritage.

Such is the overriding applicability of the mining law that, except in special circumstances, the only way its harsh impact can be avoided is by the drastic step of complete withdrawal; that is, the complete closure of land to the law's applicability. Selectivity is impossible. Land cannot be left open for the mining of some minerals subject to the 1872 act but closed to others the mining of which is incompatible with what are, in a given case, more desirable land uses. Nor is there any practicable means of requiring observance of mining and prospecting practices designed to avoid or minimize damage to the lands themselves and their other resources of water, vegetation and animal life.

This state of affairs is, to put it mildly, not only undesirable in itself, it provokes needless conflict and controversy over the scope of authority to deal with the problem. This, in turn, leads to arguments over methodology which divert attention from consideration of the substantive issues of optimum land and resource management.

The reasons of public policy which led to the 1872 act have no validity today—indeed, they run counter to every lesson of 20th Century conservation. The needs of this Nation have changed drastically from what they were a century ago when this law was enacted. Today the demands for the orderly management and conservation of our natural resources are too important to allow any form of uncontrolled exploitation of our public lands to continue.

The deficiencies to which I have referred cannot be remedied by tinkering with the mining law; its inadequacies are too numerous—its rationale too outdated. The current consensus at Interior is that the mining law should be repealed outright and replaced with a modern system of mineral leasing keyed to the wise use of all resources of the public lands and the orderly availability of minerals on reasonable terms and conditions. I urge this not to lock up our mineral wealth or to frustrate the needs of our Nation to maintain a strong mineral industry in the interests of our own economic well-being and national defense. Rather this is the course we should now take in the interest of effective, efficient and balanced enjoyment of our public lands.

In 1920, the Congress had the courage and foresight to initiate a leasing system for such minerals as oil and gas, oil shale, coal, sodium, and phosphate. By coincidence, that action came forty-eight years after passage of the 1872 act. It is time now, after another forty-eight years have elapsed, to complete the job by placing all minerals under a leasing system. To aid you in your deliberations, I enclose a draft of a leasing bill, with section-by-section analysis. I offer it in the hope that it can serve as a vehicle for crystallizing discussion.

To conclude, I want to urge that the Commission give priority attention to this most urgent public lands problem.

Sincerely yours,
Stewart L. Udall
Secretary of the Interior

NOTE

The draft bill referred to in the Secretary's letter would have repealed the Mining Law of 1872, and provided that after its effective date all "hard rock minerals"—*i.e.*, all minerals except sulphur, would be governed by the provisions of the Mineral Leasing Act, 41 Stat. 437, 30 U.S.C. § 181 *et seq.* Provision was made for the conversion of existing rights under the 1872 law into rights under the leasing law. The Secretary's recommendation was not accepted by the Public Land Law Review Commission, and its failure to deal decisively with the 1872 mining law has been widely criticized.

The Regulation of Mining: Introduction

For more than a century, the interests of the prospector and miner have been accorded special protection and preferential status. This has often been at the expense of the environment, the effective use of other resources, and the public interest generally. The reasons for this preferential status are in part political, with powerful influences supporting exploitation, as well as historical, perpetuating not only the rather colorful traditions of the old West but also an earlier land ethic which viewed land as a free good, there for the taking, regardless of consequences. This earlier land ethic was reflected in the mining legislation of the early nineteenth century,[43] and which remains as a live witness to the past in mid-nineteenth century legislation which still remains the dominant law in the field.[44]

It is reflected in the preferential status given to mining in recent forest protection legislation[45] and in the 1970 report of the Public Land Law Review

---

[43] *See also* Swenson, "Legal Aspects of Mineral Resources Exploitation" in Gates, Ed., *History of Public Land Law Development* (U.S. Gov't Printing Office, 1968). Swenson cites the Lead Mines Act of 1807, 2 Stat. 448 (1807), which gave lead mines the privilege of leasing lands in Indiana. *See also* Lead Mines Act of 1829, 4 Stat. 364 (1829), Reserved Minerals Act of 1846, 9 Stat. 37 (1846).

[44] General Mining Law of 1872, May 10, 1872, ch. 152, 17 Stat. 91, 30 U.S.C. § 21 *et seq.*

[45] *E.g.*, the Wilderness Act, Pub. L. No. 88-577, Sept. 3, 1964, 78 Stat. 895, 16 U.S.C. §§ 1131-1136. The Act provides a special exemption for mining until 1984, 16 U.S.C. § 1133(d)(3). The Multiple-Use Sustained-Yield Act of 1960, Pub. L. No. 86-517, June 12, 1960, 74 Stat. 215, 16 U.S.C. §§ 528-530, provides that the forests are to be administered for certain specific purposes but nothing contained within the Act is to "be construed so as to affect the mineral resources of national forest lands" 16 U.S.C. § 528.

Commission.[46]

Mining on federal lands is authorized under three sets of laws, each of which was passed at a different time, addresses different kinds of resource exploitation, and has a different impact on other uses of the public lands. The oldest and most problematical is the Mining Law of 1872[47] which covers "hard rock" mining for metals. Oil, gas, coal and certain other named minerals may be mined or drilled for on public lands under the Mineral Leasing Acts of 1920 and 1947[48] (and on the Continental Shelf, under the Outer Continental Shelf Lands Act of 1953).[49]

Other minerals, including common varieties of sand, stone, gravel, etc., are excluded from the coverage of the other mining laws by the Common Varieties Act of 1955,[50] and may be purchased somewhat like timber, on competitive bids. To deal with the problem of different kinds of minerals in one area, and to reconcile the administration of the other laws, Congress in 1954 enacted the Multiple Mineral Development Act.[51]

As already indicated, the system makes up in variety for what it lacks in rationality.

Mining and Minerals Policy Act of 1970

The Mining and Minerals Policy Act of 1970,[52] a one-section law, was enacted the same year that the Public Land Law Review Commission made its report.

What is noteworthy is that the 1970 Act does not even approach the minimal modifications which the entire Public Land Law Review Commission had approved. Thus, it is an indication of how little in this area Congress can agree on, whether in 1970 or in 1999, in the face of industry opposition.

Viewed in this light, the Act's references to "reclaimable mineral resources" and the references to lessening of "any adverse impact . . . upon the physical environment that may result from mining or mineral activities,"[53] represent an advance, because they are rare references to environmental concerns in a body of mining law otherwise devoid of them.

---

[46] Public Land Law Review Comm'n, *One-Third of the Nation's Land*, A Report to the President and to Congress (U.S. Gov't Printing Office, 1970).

[47] The General Mining Law of 1872, May 10, 1872, ch. 152, 17 Stat. 91, 30 U.S.C. § 21 *et seq.*

[48] The Mineral Leasing Act of 1920, Feb. 25, 1920, ch. 85, 41 Stat. 437, 30 U.S.C. §§ 181-287. The Mineral Leasing Act of 1947, Aug. 7, 1947, ch. 513, 61 Stat. 913, 30 U.S.C. §§ 351-359.

[49] Outer Continental Shelf Lands Act of 1953, Aug. 7, 1953, ch. 345, 67 Stat. 462, 10 U.S.C. §§ 7421-7426, 43 U.S.C. §§ 1331note, 1331-1343.

[50] Common Varieties Act of 1955, July 23, 1955, c. 375, 69 Stat. 368, as amended Sept. 28, 1962, Pub. L. No. 87-713, § 1, 76 Stat. 652, 30 U.S.C. §§ 611-615.

[51] 30 U.S.C. §§ 523-531.

[52] Mining and Minerals Policy Act of 1970, Pub. L. No. 91-631, Dec. 31, 1970, 84 Stat. 1876, 30 U.S.C. § 21a.

[53] 30 U.S.C. § 21a.

Federal Agency Regulation

The National Forest Service

Mining in the national forests has presented certain problems traceable to the essential incompatibility of mining with forest preservation. Until the late 1960s, the Forest Service took the position that it had no authority to regulate mining on its lands.

It was not until 1974 that the Forest Service changed its position, and in 1974 promulgated a series of regulations to regulate mining for forest protection.[54]

Initially miners on land managed by the National Forest Service were thought to have the same rights as miners on BLM lands. In fact, the 1897 statute which created the national forests expressly excludes "lands more valuable for the mineral."[55]

And, free use of timber,[56] as well as free ingress and egress,[57] were granted miners and prospectors. The landmark case, *United States v. Rizenelli*,[58] held that it is the duty of the Secretary of the Interior to return lands valuable for minerals to the public domain. Even the Multiple-Use Sustained-Yield Act of 1960[59] safeguards miners from an interpretation of that law which would interfere with the mining laws. It provides that "nothing herein shall be construed so as to affect the use or administration of mineral resources of the national forest land."[60]

However, the Secretary of Agriculture derived authority for these regulations from two sources. One is in the Organic Act itself which provides that, though miners and prospectors must be allowed entrance into the national forests "for all proper and lawful purposes, including that of prospecting, locating, and developing the mineral resources thereof, such persons must comply with the rules and regulations covering such national forests."[61]

The second statute cited in the regulations as authority is in the Service and Management Act[62] which authorizes the Secretary of Agriculture to make such rules and regulations to "preserve the national forests from destruction." Other possible sources of authority that could have been cited are the 1955

---

[54] 30 C.F.R. Part 252. Miller, "Recordation and Surface Management Regulations Affecting Mining in the National Forests, the National Park System and on the Public Domain," 23 Rocky Mt. M. L. Inst. 841 (1977).

In fact, in 1980 the Supreme Court held that the grant of federal lease and drilling permits for oil exploration and extraction in the national forest preempts local regulation. Ventura County v. Gulf Oil Corp., 100 S. Ct. 1593, 445 U.S. 947 (1980), affirming 601 F.2d 1080 (9th Cir. 1979). The Forest Service Mining Regulations were upheld in United States v. Goldfield Deep Mines Co. of Nevada, 644 F.2d 1307 (9th Cir. 1981), where it was also held that the U.S. could obtain an injunction to halt destruction of forest lands without earlier validation of the administrative proceedings, as well as damages for earlier destruction.

The preferential status of prospectors and miners, however, has long survived other changes in the law.

[55] 16 U.S.C. § 475.

[56] 16 U.S.C. § 477.

[57] 16 U.S.C. § 478.

[58] 182 R. 675 (D. Idaho 1926). *See also* 16 U.S.C. § 482.

[59] Cited n. 3 *supra*.

[60] 16 U.S.C. § 528.

[61] 16 U.S.C. § 478.

[62] 16 U.S.C. § 551.

Common Varieties Act[63] and general environmental policies as reflected in NEPA[64] and in the Mining and Minerals Policy Act of 1970.[65]

Aside from their significance as environmental and conservation measures, these regulations are the first to provide for the registration of mining claims with an agency of the federal government. They came under severe criticism from the mining industry,[66] which expressed the fear that their "unreasonable" application would cause delays and add costs. It is clear that the mining industry was quite successful, because in many respects the statute places greater burdens on the Forest Service than it does on the mine operator. It is the Forest Service that is obliged to prepare environmental impact analyses,[67] and the burden of proof of violation is on the Service—the operator is hardly under any obligation to demonstrate compliance.[68]

The intent of the regulations was stated as protection of the surface resources on national forest system lands. In fact, as the regulations make explicit, "it is not the purpose of these regulations to provide for the management of mineral resources; the responsibility for managing such resources is in the Secretary of the Interior."[69]

The scope of the regulations is limited. They apply to all mining operations under the General Mining Law conducted on all national forest system lands.[70]

Before conducting operations that might cause disturbance of surface resources, the operator must submit a notice of intent, but only for operations which "will likely cause significant disturbance of surface resources"[71] to the district ranger. If the planned operation is minor,[72] entirely subsurface,[73] or restricted to vehicular use on existing roads,[74] a statement of intent but no further plan of operations is required.

The notice must contain information "sufficient to identify the area involved, the nature of the proposed operations, the route of access to the area of operations and the method of transport."[75]

In general, the regulations do not call for stringent enforcement, largely placing the burden to prove non-compliance on the ranger, rather than insisting that the operator demonstrate compliance with the requirements.[76]

The regulation is fairly specific as to what is to be done to control erosion, runoff, toxic materials, and to revegetate disturbed areas and rehabilitate fish and wildlife habitat.[77]

---

[63] 30 U.S.C. §§ 611-615, n. 8 *supra.*

[64] 42 U.S.C. §§ 4321-4347.

[65] 130 U.S.C. § 21a.

[66] 39 Fed. Reg. 31317 (1974).

[67] 36 C.F.R. § 252.4(f).

[68] 36 C.F.R. § 252.7(b); *see also* 36 C.F.R. §§ 252.4(e), 252.5(b).

[69] 36 C.F.R. § 252.1.

[70] 36 C.F.R. § 252.2.

[71] 36 C.F.R. § 252.4.

In United States v. Weiss, 642 F.2d 296 (9th Cir. 1981), the claimant was enjoined from conducting any mining activity which could result in surface disturbance until he complied with the Forest Service Mining Operating Permit Regulations, 36 C.F.R. 252. *See also* Bales v. Ruch, 522 F. Supp. 150 (E.D. Cal. 1981).

[72] 36 C.F.R. § 252.4(a)(i)-(iii).

[73] 36 C.F.R. § 252.4(a)(1)(v).

[74] 36 C.F.R. § 252.4(a)(1).

[75] 36 C.F.R. § 252.4.

[76] *See generally* Grad, Treatise on Environmental Law § 12.03[2][c][i].

[77] 36 C.F.R. § 252.8(h). *See* United States v. Goldfield Deep Mines Co. of Nevada, 644 F.2d 1307 (9th Cir. 1981), n. 12 *supra.*

But the regulation also states that

> Certification or other approval issued by State agencies of compliance with laws and regulations relating to mining operations will be accepted as compliance with similar or parallel requirements of these regulations.[78]

On the whole, there is little enforcement machinery for these regulations. Although the implication is that no operations may be commenced until a plan of operation is either approved or is found to be unnecessary, there is a provision that pending final approval of the plan—which may be delayed until a final environmental statement has been prepared—the authorized officer "*will* approve such operations as may be necessary for timely compliance with Federal or State laws" so long as operations are conducted so as to minimize environmental damage.[79]

The regulations are also applicable within national forest wilderness areas for as long as these areas remain open for mining. There are few special provisions applicable to such areas.

NOTES

(1) FLPMA sought to resolve the problem of uncertain claims and insecure titles to the land created by the filing practices under the General Mining Law of 1972. Under the law, claims were filed chronologically—together with other local documents relating to interests in land—with local or state land offices, county clerks' or other similar offices, depending on state law. In addition, the description of the areas covered by the claim, particularly for older claims, was likely to be inexact or inaccurate, and the visible marking of the boundaries of the claim was likely to disappear before long. But the claim was a possessory interest which passed by will or by the state laws of descent and distribution. Thus, there was no single way of determining how many unpatented claims were outstanding, what land was claimed, and who currently had a right to the claim—even assuming that the claim was valid to begin with. It had become a virtually insuperable task for the Forest Service and other public land agencies to clear the title to vast tracts of federal land. The best information available indicates that when FLPMA was enacted, 85 percent of all claims filed since the beginning of the law in 1872 were inactive.

The Federal Land Policy and Management Act made substantial contributions to remedying this uncertainty by requiring that all unpatented claims be filed both in the local office where the location notice or certificate is recorded and in the office of the Bureau designated by the Secretary of the Interior along with a notice of intention to hold the claim and the other proofs required for a Patent. If the requisite filing is not made within 3 years after the enactment of the Act and annually thereafter, the claim is conclusively deemed to have been abandoned.

(2) This "file or abandon" provision of FLPMA was upheld in *Western Mining Council v. Watt*, 643 F.2d 618 (9th Cir. 1981) against denial of due process and impairment of obligations of contract claims. *See also Topaz Beryllium*

[78] 36 C.F.R. § 252.8(h).

[79] 36 C.F.R. § 252.5(b).

Co. v. United States, 649 F.2d 775 (10th Cir. 1981), *aff'g* 479 F. Supp. 309 (D. Utah 1979), which upheld the BLM filing requirements, 43 C.F.R. Subpt. 3833 (as last amended April 5, 1979).[80]

(3) Fifty percent of the revenues that the Federal Government receives under the Mineral Leasing Act (as well as under the Federal Coal Leasing Amendments Act of 1975 and the Geothermal Steam Act of 1970) are returned to the states where the minerals are leased in the form of Community Impact Assistance. The state may utilize these funds for planning, construction and maintenance of public facilities, and provision of public service to the economically impacted areas. Forty percent of the revenues go to the reclamation fund established by the Reclamation Act. Alaska is exempted from the previous provisions and is entitled to receive a straight 90% return. Federal Land Policy and Management Act. Pub. L. No. 94-579 § 317, 90 Stat. 2770, 30 U.S.C. § 191. Excluding Alaska, of the 119.6 million dollars returned under this program in 1976, 88% went to five western states with Colorado, New Mexico and Wyoming taking the lion's share. Council on Environmental Quality, *Environmental Quality—Eighth Annual Report* 103 (1977). In *Watts v. Alaska*, 451 U.S. 259, 101 S. Ct. 1673, 68 L. Ed. 280 (1981), the Supreme Court decided an issue of statutory interpretation as to whether resources were to be distributed in accordance with § 35 of the Act, 30 U.S.C. § 191, or under § 401(c) of the Wildlife Refuge Revenue Sharing Act. Holding that the provisions of § 35 of the Mineral Leasing Act—which provides for payment of 90% of the revenue to Alaska, and 10% to the U.S. Treasury—applied, the Court found that the Wildlife Act—which benefits counties—made no reference to minerals in its list of refuge resources.

COLEMAN v. UNITED STATES

United States Court of Appeals, Ninth Circuit (1966)
363 F.2d 190, reversed, 390 U.S. 599 (1967)

[The case involved a recurring effort to assert claims for a patent based on a mining claim under the General Mining Law of 1872, involving mining for "ordinary building stones, essentially to use the property for the construction of a vacation home." This possibility was severely limited by the case in the interpretation of the Materials Act of 1947 as amended by the Common Varieties Act of 1955. Section 611 of Title 30 of the U.S. Code provides in part that "no deposit of common varieties of sand, stone, gravel, pumice, pumicite, or cinders shall be deemed a valuable mineral deposit within the meaning of the mining laws of the United States so as to give effective validity to any mining claim hereafter located under such mining laws. . . ." The claim had been granted by the Secretary, but was reversed by the Supreme Court, and calling the Secretary's determination that the deposits did not qualify as valuable because the stone could not be marketed at a profit, "an admirable

[80] For additional detail on the "file or abandon" provision of FLPMA and an analogous state law, see Grad, Treatise on Environmental Law § 12.03[2][a][i].

effort to identify with the greater precision and objectivity the factors relevant to a determination that a mineral deposit is 'valuable,'" and a "logical complement to the 'prudent-man test.' . . ." The Court interpreted § 611 to remove "common varieties" of building stone from the mining laws but leaving building stone that has "some property giving it distinct and special value" within it. In so holding, the Court relied on and upheld the Secretary's "marketability" test:

> The marketability test also has the advantage of throwing light on a claimant's intention, a matter which is inextricably bound together with valuableness. For evidence that a mineral deposit is not of economic value and cannot in all likelihood be operated at a profit may well suggest that a claimant seeks the land for other purposes. Indeed, as the Government points out, the facts of this case—the thousands of dollars and hours spent building a home on 720 acres in a highly scenic national forest located two hours from Los Angeles, the lack of an economically feasible market for the stone, and the immense quantities of identical stone found in the area outside the claims—might well be thought to raise a substantial question as to respondent Coleman's real intention.

Krueger v. Morton, 539 F.2d 235 (D.C. Cir. 1976).

Appellant Krueger had filed an application with BLM for a coal prospecting permit under the Mineral Leasing Act, 30 U.S.C. § 201(b). While the application was pending, the Secretary of the Interior issued an order indicating that he was rejecting all pending applications and withholding the issuance of further coal prospecting permits until further notice "in order to allow the preparation of a program for the more orderly development of coal resources upon the public lands . . . with proper regard for the protection of the environment." His order also stated that he had determined that the order was not major federal action significantly affecting the human environment, and therefore did not require the preparation of a NEPA environmental impact statement. Held, upholding the district court, that plaintiff's action was properly dismissed. Though the plaintiff had standing to raise the issue, and though the issue is reviewable, the order suspending further issuance of permits was not an abuse of discretion. Though the issue was not one strictly committed to agency discretion "by law," it was a matter that involved discretionary judgment concerning the manner of executing powers entrusted to the Secretary relating to the commitment of resources. The law is plain that he has authority to take a second look before making such commitments. On the issue of NEPA compliance, the court concluded that the subsequent issuance by the Secretary of detailed new environmentally protective regulations would render purposeless any belated requirement that the Secretary justify his initial determination.]

KLEPPE v. SIERRA CLUB

Text at Chapter 5, p. 820, *supra*.

NOTE

The case of *Kleppe v. Sierra Club* is one of the examples of the impact of the current energy problems on the public lands. A major issue affecting public lands is the extent to which large-scale coal mining activities are to be allowed, many of them involving major strip mining operations which will leave irremediable scars on the landscape particularly in the western and southwestern parts of the country where the range environment is relatively fragile. The issue of coal mining operations on public lands has been the subject of a number of cases and has been discussed in the literature. It has also given rise to significant federal/state issues. *See* Grad, Treatise on Environmental Law § 12.03[2][b].

QUESTIONS

(1) Mining interests have complained, sometimes vociferously, that the Department of the Interior—sometimes with the assistance of the Forest Service—has managed to undermine the clear intent of the 1872 mining laws and has managed to surround the language of the law with the burdensome and highly technical regulations that substitute contemporary administrative judgments for the original legislative intent of Congress. Examine the excerpt from the 1872 mining law in the context of the Court of Appeals' opinion in *Coleman* v. *United States*, as overruled by the Supreme Court, and the letter of Secretary of the Interior Udall, and consider whether there is any justification for the particular interpretation in the original statutory language. Assume that you are a witness appearing for the Department of the Interior at a congressional hearing in which your departmental policies in carrying out the 1872 mining laws are being criticized. What arguments can you make to support the assertion that the interpretation of the Department are not in violation of the intent of the 1872 law, or alternatively, that the question of their being in strict keeping with 1872 intent does not arise because of substantially changed circumstances which require administrative conformity with long-range federal purposes in public land management?

(2) The Mining Laws of 1872 allow prospecting on public lands without prior permit, though under present forest service regulations, administrative approval of certain activities must first be obtained. At which point of hard rock mineral exploitation do NEPA requirements attach? When is there "federal action" to require filing an impact statement, assuming the consequences of the action do result in significant impact on the human environment?

(3) Is water a "valuable mineral" under the 1872 Act? *See Andrus v. Charleston Stone Products Co., Inc.*, 553 F.2d 1209 (9th Cir. 1977), *rev'd*, 436 U.S. 604 (1978). Compare *United States v. Union Oil*, 549 F.2d 1271 (9th Cir. 1977), *cert. denied sub nom. Ottoboni v. United States*, 435 U.S. 911 (1978) (geothermal steam energy is a mineral for purposes of Stock-Raising Homestead Act of 1916).

[3] Recreational vs. Preservational Uses

One of the multiple uses protected under the Multiple Use Sustained Yield Act is the use of public lands for recreational purposes. In national park areas or national recreational areas under the direction of the National Parks Service, timber cutting or logging is permitted only for forest maintenance.[81] Mining also continues to be permitted, but it was terminated in wilderness areas after 1984.[82] Since recreational uses are incompatible with a variety of other, more exploitive uses of the land, the use of public land for outdoor recreation, including national parks, recreational areas or other outdoor facilities necessarily involve choices in resource allocation.

In addition to resource allocation problems, outdoor recreation has created significant problems of its own in overcrowding in national parks and other recreational areas which are overwhelmingly difficult to resolve. In its 1969 report, which has been discredited in many respects, the Public Land Law Review Commission[83] raised a number of issues which remain unresolved some 30 years later. The question of land use fees for purposes of rationing or access control is unresolved, as is a full definition of nonconforming uses in national parks and other recreation areas, even though there have been restrictions in some of the statutes establishing such areas. Access to many national parks and even to certain wilderness areas has reached such proportions as to endanger the very values for which these areas have been preserved. A fair basis for rationing access or for setting user fees is difficult to achieve. The expense of maintaining infrastructure developments in such areas has also raised significant issues, as has the question on what basis licenses to concessionaires should be granted.

Another recurring issue and one which has not been given as much attention as it deserves is that of competing recreational uses. Winter sports, and particularly ski slopes with their inevitable construction of access roads, funiculars, ski lifts of various kinds, and the necessary power lines to keep the machinery going, impose a significant burden on the environment, frequently requiring clearcutting for access to the ski slopes, both by ski lifts and power lines. In many parts of areas devoted to winter sports, it has become impossible to take a scenic photograph of the mountains which is not bifurcated by power lines and cables. There is a clear conflict between users of the public lands who look for a nature experience and those who want to have access without too much effort to the top of a hill in order to experience downhill schussing.[84] A recurring issue in the choice of recreational uses

[81] 16 U.S.C. § 3

[82] 16 U.S.C. § 11.33.

[83] Public Land Law Review Commission, One Third of the Nation's Land, A Report to the President and to the Congress (1970) at 203, 205-210.

[84] For an example that raises many allocation questions, see Sierra Club v. Hickel, 433 F.2d 24, reversed with respect to the standing issue not here covered by the Supreme Court in Sierra Club v. Morton, 405 U.S. 727 (1972), affirming Sierra Club v. Hickel, 433 F.2d 24 (9th Cir. 1970). The case involved an effort by the Sierra Club to obtain a preliminary injunction against the issuance by the Secretaries of the Department of Agriculture and Interior for construction of a large-scale commercial recreational development within the Sequoia National Forest in California. Injury to aesthetic and ecological interests were charged in the Mineral King area. Winter sports and other recreational uses were proposed in a Walt Disney development calling for a major hotel, a cog-assisted railway, and a two-lane access

reflects questions of economic discrimination, in that persons with substantial economic means will find it easier to have the equipment and transportation to visit remote and primitive areas for backpacking and mule packing which are not normally accessible to less well situated tourists and visitors.

---

16 U.S.C.
Chapter 23—National Wilderness Preservation System

§ 1131. National Wilderness Preservation System—Establishment; Congressional declaration of policy; wilderness areas; administration for public use and enjoyment, protection, preservation, and gathering and dissemination of information; provisions for designation as wilderness areas

(a) In order to assure that an increasing population, accompanied by expanding settlement and growing mechanization, does not occupy and modify all areas within the United States and its possessions, leaving no lands designated for preservation and protection in their natural condition, it is hereby declared to be the policy of the Congress to secure for the American people of present and future generations the benefits of an enduring resource of wilderness. For this purpose there is hereby established a National Wilderness Preservation System to be composed of federally owned areas designated by Congress as "wilderness areas," and these shall be administered for the use and enjoyment of the American people in such manner as will leave them unimpaired for future use and enjoyment as wilderness, and so as to provide for the protection of these areas, the preservation of their wilderness character, and for the gathering and dissemination of information regarding their use and enjoyment as wilderness; and no Federal lands shall be designated as "wilderness areas" except as provided for in this chapter or by a subsequent Act.

Management of area included in System; appropriations

(b) The inclusion of an area in the National Wilderness Preservation System notwithstanding, the area shall continue to be managed by the Department and agency having jurisdiction thereover immediately before its inclusion in the National Wilderness Preservation System unless otherwise provided by Act of Congress. . . .

---

highway, all done by extending a 30-year permit or lease for an 80-acre tract under a 30-year permit to allow the development of a much vaster tract of about 13,000 acres with ski lifts and other ski developments under a so-called revocable permit, using a permissible combination of long-term permits and revocable permits. The case not only involved recreational against conservational uses but also the question of the preference for a particular kind of winter sport use over other recreational uses. For further comment, *see* Grad, Treatise on Environmental Law § 12.03[4][d].

Definition of wilderness

(c) A wilderness, in contrast with those areas where man and his own works dominate the landscape, is hereby recognized as an area where the earth and its community of life are untrammeled by man, where man himself is a visitor who does not remain. An area of wilderness is further defined to mean in this chapter an area of undeveloped Federal land retaining its primeval character and influence, without permanent improvements or human habitation, which is protected and managed so as to preserve its natural conditions and which (1) generally appears to have been affected primarily by the forces of nature, with the imprint of man's work substantially unnoticeable; (2) has outstanding opportunities for solitude or a primitive and unconfined type of recreation; (3) has at least five thousand acres of land or is of sufficient size as to make practicable its preservation and use in an unimpaired condition; and (4) may also contain ecological, geological, or other features of scientific, educational, scenic, or historical value.

§ 1132. Extent of System—Designation of wilderness areas; filing of maps and descriptions with congressional committees; correction of errors; public records; availability of records in regional offices

. . . .

NOTE

For an account of the Wilderness Act, *See* Grad, Treatise on Environmental Law § 12.03[1][e].

PARKER v. UNITED STATES

United States District Court, D. Colorado (1970)
309 F. Supp. 508

[Suit to enjoin the Secretary of Agriculture from selling timber on federal land in a national forest which plaintiffs claim qualifies as wilderness under the Wilderness Act. The area in question is contiguous to land classified as a Primitive Area under the Multiple Use Act of 1960.]

WILLIAM E. DOYLE, District Judge:

The Gore Range-Eagles Nest Primitive Area . . . has a total area of about 61,000 acres. Included within it is about 30 miles of the so-called Gore Range of mountains, which is regarded as one of the most inaccessible ranges within the State of Colorado. . .. The East Meadow area is said to be sub-alpine. There are major streams and large lakes in the Gore area and a good many deer, elk, mountain sheep and small animals. There are no improvements other than a few abandoned cabins and temporary corrals. There are, however, extensive foot and horse trails maintained by the Forest Service.

East Meadow Creek area is, as we have indicated, contiguous to the Gore Primitive Region on the west. It consists of timbered valleys surrounded by timbered ridges. Within it are several parks, small grassy open areas from one acre to fifty acres surrounded by trees. On the average, the elevation of the East Meadow Creek region is about 10,000 feet, which is somewhat lower than the contiguous primitive area. It is located in what is known as the sub-alpine life zone. It is situated so that it may be used as an access route into the Gore Primitive Area.

The proposed sale area is located within the East Meadow Creek basin. . .. It consists of some 1,200 acres with an elevation between 9,200 and 10,500 feet. Deer and elk are found in the sale area throughout the summer and fall months and there is light recreation use in the region during the hunting season. The trees in the sale area consist mainly of Englemann Spruce and Lodgepole Pine, some of which are as much as 350 years old, and fir, the age of which ranges up to 120 years.

The East Meadow Creek region is generally untrammeled by man except for an access road which runs to a point about three-fourths of a mile inside the sale area. There is also a road known as the "bug road" which was constructed during the bark beetle control project in the early 1950's. This road is now blocked off and cannot be used by motorized vehicles. In some places the vegetation has camouflaged the "bug road" so that it is substantially unnoticeable. There are trails in the area.

The Denver Water Board is surveying, looking to possible use of the Meadow Creek drainage in connection with a water diversion project. There is also a possibility that a dam may be built at Piney Lake. These, however, are apparently in the early planning stages, and no definite decisions to undertake the projects have yet been made.

Substantial evidence has been presented as to the character of East Meadow Creek. The witnesses for plaintiff have testified that it is wild in that it is inhabited by animals, is thickly wooded, secluded and unspoiled. Witnesses who are familiar with wilderness say that a wilderness experience can be obtained in this area and that it is fairly accessible. They have also testified that this is an important tourist attraction which is a great source of value to Vail and which brings enjoyment to the tourists who visit it during the spring, summer and fall of each year.

Defendants' evidence does not create any serious dispute concerning the essential character of this area. Rather, they contend that their access road of itself prevents East Meadow from being classified as either primitive or wilderness, and that mining claims plus Denver Water Board surveys plus their own positive plans for the area make it more suitable for timber harvesting than for wilderness use.

It is crystal clear from the evidence that the consummation of the present sale will effectively take all of East Meadow Creek out of contention as a primitive or wilderness addition.

. . . .

The question presented is a limited and novel one. We are concerned not with whether the Secretary erred on his factual findings in ruling East Meadow Creek out as wilderness, but rather with whether there is sufficient evidence of its wilderness character so as to require study and submission to the President and Congress for determination of its character and whether acts which would change its character should be enjoined until the determination can be made.

The concept of preserving certain public lands in their natural state did not originate in the Wilderness Act. For many years primitive, wilderness and wild areas have been set aside by the Secretary of Agriculture and the Chief of the Forest Service. . .. However, prior to the Wilderness Act, the issue of what areas should be designated as wilderness, wild or primitive, and what uses might be made of such areas was entirely within the discretion of the Secretary of Agriculture and the Forest Service. Thus, the administrative decisions with respect to the suitability of an area for wild, wilderness or primitive classification, the need for preserving the natural state of such an area, and the relative values of various resources in the particular area were final and unreviewable. One of the major purposes of the Wilderness Act was to remove a great deal of this absolute discretion from the Secretary of Agriculture and the Forest Service by placing the ultimate responsibility for wilderness classification in Congress.

. . . .

We are called upon in this case to determine whether under the evidence presented there is a basis for determination by the President and Congress that the area in question is wilderness within the above definition. It is obvious, of course, that the area here involved does not encompass 5,000 acres. At the same time it is, as noted, contiguous to the Gore Range Wilderness Area which has been classified as such, and it is contended that the President and Congress should determine whether this contiguous area should be included.

See 16 U.S.C. § 1132(b)which provides as follows:

> The Secretary of Agriculture shall, within ten years after September 3, 1964, review, as to its suitability or nonsuitability for preservation as wilderness, each area in the national forests classified on September 3, 1964 by the Secretary of Agriculture or the Chief of the Forest Service as "primitive" and report his findings to the President. The President shall advise the United States Senate and House of Representatives of his recommendations with respect to the designation as "wilderness" or other reclassification of each area on which review has been completed together with maps and a definition of boundaries. . . . *Nothing herein contained shall limit the President in proposing, as part of his recommendations to Congress, the alteration of existing boundaries of primitive areas or recommending the addition of any contiguous area of national forest lands predominantly of wilderness value.* (Emphasis added.)

With respect to primitive areas, this provision of the Act quite clearly reserves the decision to classify as wilderness to the President and ultimately

Congress. The duty of the Secretary of Agriculture is to study and recommend, and this duty is mandatory.

East Meadow Creek, however, is not classified as a primitive region, but rather is *contiguous* to the Gore Primitive Area. With respect to such contiguous areas, the Act is less specific as to the division of responsibility between the Forest Service and Secretary of Agriculture on the one hand and the President and Congress on the other. Nevertheless, the last sentence of 16 U.S.C. § 1132(b)leaves no doubt that at least as to those contiguous areas which are predominantly of wilderness value, the decision to classify or not to classify them as wilderness *must remain open through the Presidential level.*

It follows from the above that

1. The Wilderness Act, § 1132(b), empowers the President to recommend to the Congress the addition of contiguous primitive area of national forest lands predominantly of wilderness value.

2. The Act contemplates that the President shall be in a position to exercise a meaningful decision with respect to contiguous areas.

3. The Act contemplates that the Secretary shall consider whether a contiguous area is to be included and that its determination is subject to review by the President and ultimately the Congress.

4. Where as here the contiguous area is shown by the evidence to have wilderness character, it thwarts the purpose and spirit of the Act to allow the Forest Service to take abortive action which effectively prevents a Presidential and Congressional decision.[85]

These basic rules which we have outlined above are fully supported by the regulations set forth in the Forest Service Manual.

. . . .

Defendants contend that the East Meadow Creek region was included in a study made pursuant to the Multiple Use-Sustained-Yield Act, 16 U.S.C. § 528 *et seq.* and was found not qualified for primitive, wild, or wilderness classification. Thus, it is claimed that the Forest Service has in effect also fulfilled its duty under the Wilderness Act and any further study of East Meadow Creek would be duplicitous. Again, this argument mistakes the function of the Forest Service with respect to wilderness area under the Wilderness Act as compared with the Multiple Use Act. Under the Multiple Use Act, the authority to classify as wilderness, primitive, or wild was vested solely in the Secretary of Agriculture or the Forest Service, and the decision on these matters was based not only on suitability, but also on availability and need. Since the Wilderness Act requires a study and report on those regions contiguous to primitive areas which merely meet the test of suitability, the Forest Service's conclusions under the Multiple Use Act are not conclusive

85 We are fully aware of the provision in 16 U.S.C. § 1132(b)which states, "Areas classified on September 3, 1964 shall continue to be administered under the rules and regulations affecting such areas on September 3,1964 until Congress has determined otherwise." Although this provision does vest some discretion in the Forest Service prior to the ultimate Congressional decision, we do not feel that it can or should be read so as to allow the Forest Service to change the basic character of the area. Such a broad reading of the above provision would allow the Forest Service to frustrate one of the major purposes of the Wilderness Act.

and indeed have little bearing on the question of whether East Meadow Creek must be included in the wilderness study report to the President and Congress.

. . . .

In conclusion, we hold that the East Meadow Creek region meets the minimum requirements of suitability for wilderness classification and must, therefore, be included in the study report to the President and Congress. Furthermore, we find that if the proposed sale and harvesting of timber proceeds, it will frustrate the purpose of the Wilderness Act to vest the ultimate decision as to wilderness classification in the President and Congress, rather than the Forest Service and Secretary of Agriculture. The Forest Service has been considering the proposed sale of timber in East Meadow Creek for several years. The decision to sell and harvest having now been made, the Service claims that the plans must proceed immediately. We must disagree. The interests of the plaintiffs and the public in maintaining the status quo until the requirements of the Act have been fulfilled far outweigh this desire to get the job done now—after more than ten years of delay.

We are not unmindful of the interests and equities of Kaibab Industries, but here again we cannot give effect to this interest, for the cutting of the trees, is as we have noted, too final and conclusive. It must await the processes of law.

We conclude then that the cause is a proper one for equitable intervention. We determine that the preliminary injunction heretofore entered be continued indefinitely or until a determination has been made by the President and Congress that East Meadow Creek is predominantly wilderness in character and should be made part of Gore Range-Eagles Nest or that it should not be.

Plaintiffs will submit an appropriate judgment for the Court's signature.

NOTE

Dorothy Thomas Foundation v. Hardin, 325 F. Supp. 99 (W.D.N.C. 1970), a suit by adjoining landowners for a preliminary injunction to prevent the Secretary of Agriculture from accepting bids for the sale of timber on national forest lands, illustrates the different treatment accorded federal lands under the Multiple Use and Sustained Yield, and the Wilderness Acts. Having found that defendants had considered the recreational qualities of the area as required by the Multiple Use Act, the court observed:

> The decision has been made, and this Court can only determine whether the action of the Secretary was "arbitrary, capricious, an abuse of discretion, or otherwise not in accordance with law," or that said action was "without observance of procedure required by law."
>
> The plaintiffs in this cause can only prevail if they can establish by clear and convincing proof that the action of the defendants is arbitrary, capricious, an abuse of discretion, or otherwise not in accordance with law. This they have failed to do thus far. There is no evidence in this record to show

any failure on the part of the defendants to consider all of the factors as required by law. The plaintiffs' evidence merely shows that they and their witnesses have a different opinion about how a national forest should be run and they desire that this Court restrain the sale of this timber pending the trial so that they may by the discovery process glean the defendants' records to see if they have failed in any respect to make this decision according to law. This Court cannot and should not interfere with this administrative procedure upon the evidence which has been offered.

NEW YORK STATE CONSTITUTION
Article XIV—Conservation

§1. [Forest preserve to be forever kept wild; certain uses and exceptions authorized]

"The lands of the state, now owned or hereafter acquired, constituting the forest preserve as now fixed by law, shall be forever kept as wild forest lands. They shall not be leased, sold or exchanged, or be taken by any corporation, public or private, nor shall the timber thereon be sold, removed or destroyed. Nothing herein contained shall prevent the state from constructing, completing and maintaining any highway heretofore specifically authorized by constitutional amendment, nor from constructing and maintaining to federal standards federal aid interstate highway route five hundred two from a point in the vicinity of the city of Glens Falls, thence northerly to the vicinity of the villages of Lake George and Warrensburg, the hamlets of South Horicon and Pottersville and thence northerly in a generally straight line on the west side of Schroon Lake . . ."

NOTE

The so-called "forever wild" provision of the New York Constitution then provides for other roads, the construction of ski trails, the construction of an airport landing strip for a small community, and other special exemptions. The protection of the "forever wild" provision is quite real, however, because special exemptions require a constitutional amendment, which in New York needs passage by two successive legislatures with one intervening general election, followed by a state-wide referendum. Since "forever wild" has great popular appeal, there is likely to be substantial debate over the amendment. Thus, the amendment does seem to prevent major raids—particularly by lumber interests—on the state forests.

ASSOCIATION FOR THE PROTECTION OF THE ADIRONDACKS v. MacDONALD

Court of Appeals of New York (1930)
253 N.Y. 234, 170 N.E. 902

CRANE, J.

By chapter 417 of the Laws of 1929 the Conservation Commissioner is authorized to construct and maintain a bobsleigh run or slide on state lands in the Forest Preserve in the town of North Elba, Essex county, on the western slope of the Sentinel range.

The act was passed for the purpose of providing facilities for the third Olympic winter games, which are to be held at or in the vicinity of Lake Placid, in the year 1932. . . . It is estimated that the construction will necessitate the removal of trees from about 4½ acres of land, or a total number of trees, large and small, estimated at 2,500. The Forest Preserve within the Adirondacks consists of 1,941,403 acres. The taking of 4 acres out of this vast acreage for this international sports' meet seems a very slight inroad upon the preserve for a matter of such public interest and benefit to the people of the state of New York and elsewhere. The Legislature, recognizing the benefits of an international gathering of this kind, has sought in the public interest, by the enactment of the above law, to provide appropriately and in the spirit of hospitality the necessary equipment and facilities for these games and contests, incident to winter sport, of which tobogganing is a large feature. . . .

Considering the distinction of having one of the beauty spots of New York state selected as appropriate for the International Olympic winter games and the advantages afforded by Lake Placid and its vicinity, together with the good will promoted in the recognition by the state, through its Legislature, of the event, what possible objection can there be to the above law permitting this toboggan slide to be constructed on state land? One objection, and one only—the Constitution of the state, which prevents the cutting of the trees. This objection has been raised by the Association for the Protection of the Adirondacks, which has sought and obtained an injunction restraining the conservation commission of this state and the superintendent of lands and forests from constructing and maintaining the bobsleigh run on the ground that chapter 417 of the Laws of 1929 is unconstitutional and void.

. . . .

[Held: Adirondack Park was to be preserved, not destroyed. Therefore all things necessary were permitted, such as measures to prevent forest fires, the repairs to roads and proper inspection, or the erection and maintenance of proper facilities for the use by the public which did not call for the removal of the timber to any material degree. The Forest Preserve is preserved for the public; its benefits are for the people of the state as a whole. Whatever the advantages may be of having wild forest lands preserved in their natural state, the advantages are for every one within the state and for the use of the people of the state. Unless prohibited by the constitutional provision, this use and preservation are subject to the reasonable regulations of the Legislature.]

. . . .

The Forest Preserve and the Adirondack Park within it are for the reasonable use and benefit of the public, as heretofore stated. A very considerable use may be made by campers and others without in any way interfering with this purpose of preserving them as wild forest lands. (*See* "The Problem of the Wilderness" by Robert Marshall in "The Scientific Monthly," Feb. 1930, p. 141.)

But the question still remains whether the construction of a toboggan slide, which requires the cutting of 2,500 trees, is such a reasonable use, or is forbidden by the Constitution.

Counsel for the appellants has very ably argued that, as the underlying purpose of all these restrictions upon the state lands is to preserve them for the free use of all the people for their health and pleasure, the erection of a toboggan slide for sport is within this purpose. He has pressed upon our attention the fact that outdoor sports do much to maintain the health, the happiness, and the welfare of the people of this state; and that, if a branch of these outdoor sports is to a minor extent permitted within the public lands, the very purpose which the framers of the Constitution of 1894 had in mind will be accomplished; that is the benefit to the people which this constitutional provision sought to preserve in the preservation of the forest. What can be more beneficial, asks counsel, than the establishment of forest sports, among which is classed this toboggan slide? We must admit much, if not all, that counsel has so eloquently pleaded in behalf of outdoor games. Perhaps much may be due to international sports, such as the Olympic games, lawn tennis, golf, even aviation, for creating good will among the nations, and a desire to establish those friendly relationships so vigorously claimed and earnestly sought for through treaties and world conferences. However tempting it may be to yield to the seductive influences of outdoor sports and international contests, we must not overlook the fact that constitutional provisions cannot always adjust themselves to the nice relationships of life. The framers of the Constitution, as before stated, intended to stop the willful destruction of trees upon the forest lands, and to preserve these in the wild state now existing; they adopted a measure forbidding the cutting down of these trees to any substantial extent for any purpose.

. . . .

. . . [C]hapter 417 of the Laws of 1929, permitting the erection of the bobsleigh slide and the destruction of the trees, is unconstitutional, and the judgment below is affirmed.

CARDOZO, C. J., and POUND, LEHMAN, KELLOGG, O'BRIEN, and HUBBS, JJ., concur.

NOTES AND QUESTIONS

(1) *Sierra Club v. Hickel* and the New York *Adirondack* case both involve the issue of recreational as against conservational uses, an issue which has become intensified by recreational developments that require changes in the landscape. A ski lift generally requires as much clear cutting of a mountain-side as does a powerline, and the construction of a ski jump may call for significant changes in the profile of a mountain. Yet construction for recreational purposes advances tourism, the sporting goods industry and other economic interests. Should the law take these into account in making alternative use decisions? Are these economic interests growing out of winter sports and other recreations taken into account under multiple use-sustained yield? To what extent must they be considered under NEPA?

(2) The assertion is sometimes heard that legislation to protect "wilderness" in its natural state prefers some socio-economic groups over others. Is there any support for this position in the materials presented? Is it likely that proposals for "permits" and general user fees or for mail reservations would make any real differences in the nature and frequency of recreational uses, or in the character of the population using the public lands?

(3) If a system of designated "dominant uses" to produce maximum benefit is to be adopted, is recreation—or retention as wilderness area—likely to acquire dominant use designation very often? Under what circumstances would such a designation be likely?

(4) Is government ownership the best way to insure adequate management of forest land? Consider the relative degree of control possible under government ownership as opposed to regulation, for instance, zoning provisions. What are the possibilities for private intervention in the decision-making processes under each? How could federal law be amended to provide for better representation of diverse views? Does the National Forest Management Act of 1976, 16 U.S.C. §§ 1600 *et seq.*, meet this requirement?

(5) Are decisions relating to the use of the national forests under the Wilderness Act, the Multiple-Use Sustained Yield Act and the National Forest Management Act of 1976 subject to the terms of the National Environmental Policy Act of 1969? What is the impact of NEPA on the discretionary nature of the various decisions involved?

(6) Aside from problems of interpretation, is a constitutional provision such as New York's a practical way of dealing with the problem of allocation? How does it affect the presentation of diverse views? Is it arguable that it confers standing on only one of the many appropriate interest groups?

§ 6.04 Protection of Fish and Wildlife

Introductory Note

Statutory treatment of wildlife conservation in the United States has traditionally been limited to hunting and fishing regulations protecting game species and the establishment and administration of wildlife refuges. In addition, state fish and game commissions have instituted programs of breeding and stocking of wildlife, primarily to insure and improve the commercial and recreational supply of game animals and fish.

In recent years the gradual shrinking of the wild environment has drawn attention to the necessity of preserving the habitat of wildlife as well as protecting game species against outright slaughter. This concern has, until quite recently, been limited to preservation of the natural character of wildlife refuges and national and state forests.

With the growing concern over the general condition of the environment, however, the effects of all forms of pollution on animals as well as humans has come to be recognized. Thus, the fight to preserve the wetlands, the remaining wild areas, and to prevent the use of pesticides such as DDT and the discharge of other pollutants which may have invisible effects on the food chain from lower to higher species of animal life, is in large part a fight to preserve the nation's wildlife. The reader should, therefore, keep the broader problems of environmental pollution in mind when considering the issue of wildlife preservation.

Kleppe v. New Mexico, 426 U.S. 529 (1976) raised the issue of the federal government's right to protect wild animals on public lands under the authority of the Wild Free-Roaming Horse and Burros Act, 16 U.S.C. §§ 1331–1340, in spite of assertion of rights to the animals under state law. The Court upheld the federal government's claim, as follows:

> Unquestionably the States have broad trustee and police powers over wild animals within their jurisdictions. *Toomer v. Witsell*, 334 U.S. 385, 402 (1948); *Lacoste v. Dept. of Conservation*, 263 U.S. 545, 549 (1924); *Geer v. Connecticut*, 161 U.S. 519, 528 (1896). But as *Geer v. Connecticut* cautions, those powers exist only "in so far as their exercise may not be incompatible with, or restrained by the rights conveyed to the Federal government by the Constitution." 161 U.S. at 528. "No doubt it is true that as between a State and its inhabitants the State may regulate the killing and sale of [wildlife], but it does not follow that its authority is exclusive of paramount powers." *Missouri v. Holland*, 252 U.S. 416, 434 (1920). Thus, the Privileges and Immunities Clause, U.S. Const., Art. IV, § 2, cl. 1, precludes a State from imposing prohibitory licensing fees on non-residents shrimping in its waters, *Toomer v. Witsell, supra;* the Treaty Clause, U.S. Const. Art. II, § 2, permits Congress to enter into and enforce a treaty to protect migratory birds despite state objections, *Missouri v. Holland, supra;* and the Property Clause gives Congress the power to thin overpopulated herds of deer on federal lands contrary to state law. *Hunt v. United States* (278 U.S. 96). We hold today that the Property Clause also gives Congress the power to protect wildlife on the public lands, state law notwithstanding.

Following *Kleppe*, the *Geer* doctrine, cited *supra*, continued to erode. For example, in *Douglas v. Seacoast Products, Inc.*, 431 U.S. 265, 97 S. Ct. 1740, 52 L. Ed. 2d 304 (1977), the Supreme Court expressly rejected the state ownership theory as a nineteenth century legal fiction and went on to hold that a federally granted fishing license preempted state police powers, even in state waters, because of the Commerce Clause:

> While appellant may be correct in arguing that at earlier times in our history, there was some doubt whether Congress had the power under the Commerce Clause to regulate the taking of fish in state waters, ... there can be no question today that such power exists where there is some effect on interstate commerce. The movement of vessels from one state to another in search of fish, and back again to processing plants, is certainly an activity which Congress could conclude affects interstate commerce.

The Supreme Court continued this line of reasoning in 1978, when it decided *Baldwin v. Montana Fish and Game Commission*, 436 U.S. 371, 98 S. Ct. 1852, 56 L. Ed. 2d 354 (1978). In that case, the Court upheld a state's power to charge a higher fee to nonresidents than to residents for purely recreational hunting licenses, but in general commented unfavorably on the state ownership doctrine of *Geer*. Finally, in 1979 the Court explicitly overruled *Geer* when it decided *Hughes v. Oklahoma*, 441 U.S. 322, 99 S. Ct. 1727, 60 L. Ed. 2d 250 (1979), which concerned a challenge to the Oklahoma prohibition against transporting or shipping for sale outside the state any minnows seined or procured within Oklahoma waters. Hughes had a commercial minnow business in Texas, and he purchased minnows from an Oklahoma dealer who obtained the fish from state waters. Finding the case indistinguishable from *Geer*, which had involved a Connecticut prohibition against transporting game birds outside the state, the Court held that while a state may have a legitimate interest in the preservation and regulation of fish and game within its borders, that interest cannot justify a burden on interstate commerce when alternative conservation measures exist:

> A state may no longer keep the property, if the sovereign so chooses, always within its jurisdiction for every purpose. The fiction of state ownership may no longer be used to force those outside the state to bear the full cost of "conserving" the wild animals within its borders when equally effective nondiscriminatory conservation measures are available. . .. The overruling of *Geer* does not leave the states powerless to protect and conserve wild animal life within their borders. Today's decision makes clear, however, that states may promote this legitimate purpose only in ways consistent with the basic principle that "our economic unit is the Nation," *H.P. Hood & Sons, Inc. v. Du Mond*, 336 U.S. at 537, and that when a wild animal "becomes an article of commerce . . . its use cannot be limited to the citizens of one state to the exclusion of citizens of another state." *Geer v. Connecticut*, 161 U.S. at 538 (Field, J., dissenting).

Federal legislation relating to the protection of fish and wildlife combines a number of purposes. Environmental protection, and the protection of threatened species (whether or not technically "endangered") is one of the purposes, but there are also other interests—to protect certain fish and animals as sources of food and as a source for the commercial fishing industry, and to provide fish and game for recreational hunting and fishing purposes, a mainstay of the sporting goods industry. The variety of interests protected is demonstrated by Chapter 9 of Title 16 which establishes the Fish and Wildlife Service:

> "whose basic function is preservation of the fishing industry. In furtherance of this function, the Service is authorized to make loans to the industry,

study the effects of chemicals (pesticides, herbicides) on fish, and make studies on the propagation of food fishes. Chapter 9A authorizes the Secretary of the Interior to maintain hatcheries for various types of fish and to conduct investigations."

Other interests are reflected in the predator control program, 7 U.S.C. § 426–426b which is designed to protect cattle and sheep interests, but that succeeded in putting a number of other wild animals, such as wolves and foxes, on the endangered species list.

Legislation for the protection of fish and wildlife follows two approaches, first, the protection of certain named or designated species, limiting the taking and dealing in specimens of the species; and second, the protection of the natural habitat of such threatened fish and wildlife. One of the most significant laws to protect habitat is the Fish and Wildlife Coordinations Act.

---

16 U.S.C.
Chapter 5A—Protection and Conservation of Wildlife

FISH AND WILDLIFE COORDINATION ACT

§ 661. Declaration of purpose; cooperation of agencies; surveys and investigations; donations

For the purpose of recognizing the vital contribution of our wildlife resources to the Nation, the increasing public interest and significance thereof due to expansion of our national economy and other factors, and to provide that wildlife conservation shall receive equal consideration and be coordinated with other features of water-resource development programs through the effectual and harmonious planning, development, maintenance, and coordination of wildlife conservation and rehabilitation for the purposes of sections 661-666c of this title in the United States, its Territories and possessions, the Secretary of the Interior is authorized (1) to provide assistance to, and cooperate with, Federal, State, and public or private agencies and organizations in the development, protection, rearing, and stocking of all species of wildlife, resources thereof, and their habitat, in controlling losses of the same from disease or other causes, in minimizing damages from overabundant species, in providing public shooting and fishing areas, including easements across public lands for access thereto, and in carrying out other measures necessary to effectuate the purposes of said sections; (2) to make surveys and investigations of the wildlife of the public domain, including lands and waters or interests therein acquired or controlled by any agency of the United States; and (3) to accept donations of land and contributions of funds in furtherance of the purposes of said sections.

Protection of Habitat

The relationship of fish and wildlife management and habitat to other developments is recognized in the Fish and Wildlife Coordination Act.[1]

The purpose of the law is to assure "that wildlife conservation will receive equal consideration and be coordinated with other features of water resource development programs through the effectual and harmonious planning, development, maintenance and coordination of wildlife conservation and rehabilitation. . . ."[2]

The further purpose of the law is to provide assistance to and cooperation with other governmental and private agencies and organizations in the development, protection, rearing and stocking of all species of wildlife and in protecting their habitat. Furthermore, the purpose is to protect against loss of wildlife from disease and other causes, and to minimize damages from overabundant species by providing public shooting and fishing areas. Other aims are to provide for the making of surveys and investigations of the wildlife in the public domain, including wildlife on lands and waters held by any agency of the United States.

The dependence of fish and wildlife on its natural habitat is recognized in a requirement that no body of water, including streams, may be impounded or modified in any way (by such methods as diversion or stream channelization) unless the agency of the United States which is undertaking the modification first consults with the U.S. Fish and Wildlife Service or with the head of the agency exercising administration over the wildlife resources of the particular state where the modification or impoundment is to take place. The same requirement of coordination applies in instances where the modification is not undertaken by an agency of the United States but by any public or private agency under a federal permit or license. The process anticipates NEPA impact statement requirements in significant ways.[3]

NOTE

Other legislation to protect habitat includes the National Wilderness Preservation System, *supra*, p. 964, and legislation relating to the establishment of National Wildlife and Game Refuges (referred to in *Sierra Club v. Hickel, supra* p. 963, n. 4).

Laws for the protection of designated species or kinds of fish and wildlife include the Wild Free-Roaming Horse and Burros Act, 16 U.S.C. §§ 1331–1340,

[1] Act of March 10, 1934, c. 55, 48 Stat. 401, 16 U.S.C. § 661 *et seq.* as amended.

[2] 16 U.S.C. § 661 *et seq.*

[3] For further analysis of the act and its relationship to NEPA, as well as to required coordination with other agencies, see Grad, Treatise on Environmental Law § 12.04[5][a].

and the Act to protect migratory game and insectivorous birds, 16 U.S.C. § 701 *et seq.*, which imposes a duty on the Department of the Interior to aid the preservation, restoration and propagation of "game birds and other wild birds." Migratory birds are also protected and their taking, sale and importation are prohibited under treaties with Great Britain and Mexico. 16 U.S.C. § 903. Other protected birds and animals include the bald or golden eagle, 16 U.S.C. § 668, and marine mammals. The Marine Mammal Protection Act (MMPA) 16U.S.C. §§ 1361–1407 was passed in 1972, about a year before the Endangered Species Act, and the protection it extends to marine mammals including whales, porpoises, seals, walruses, sea otters, polar bears and others is generally similar to that extended to endangered species under that act.

The Marine Mammal Protection Act of 1972 (MMPA), 16 U.S.C. § 1361, was addressed in part to the large number of porpoise deaths due to tuna fishing. Prior to 1960, the most common form of yellowfin tuna fishing was the use of pole, line and live bait. Soon, however, fishermen observed that yellowfin tuna habitually associate with porpoises. A new fishing technique, "purse-seine" fishing was developed—fisherman would set their nets over the porpoises, thus catching the porpoises and the tuna. Despite some efforts to dislodge trapped porpoises, between 100,000 and 300,000 deaths a year occurred in this endangered population of marine mammal.

The primary objective of the MMPA, as stated in § 1361, is "to maintain the health and stability of the marine ecosystem." However, the Act also states in the same section that mammals should be protected, "to the greatest extent feasible, commensurate with sound policies of resource management." To these ends, Congress mandated a two year moratorium on the taking and importation of all marine mammals, with a two year exemption with respect to incidental deaths in the course of commercial fishing. After expiration of the exemption in 1974, the Secretary of Commerce was authorized to issue permits for incidental takings, but only if consistent with the MMPA's directive that "it shall be the immediate goal that the incidental kill or incidental serious injury of marine mammals permitted in the course of commercial fishing operations be reduced to insignificant levels approaching a zero mortality and serious injury rate." The Act requires that such permits specify the number and kind of animals to be taken, that it comply with all applicable regulations, and that it be consistent with the purposes of the Act. The Secretary's regulations were to be issued after a rulemaking based on estimates of existing populations and theoretically optimal sustainable populations, and on findings of the impact the proposed regulations would have on the marine mammal population.

In *Committee for Humane Legislation v. Richardson*, 540 F.2d 1141 (D.C. Cir. 1976), plaintiffs challenged permits issued to tuna fishermen, allowing them to continue to take unspecified numbers of porpoises without any findings on the current populations or the impact such incidental takings might have on the species. The defendants argued that failure to issue the permits would cripple the tuna industry, a result not intended by Congress. The lower court found that the permits were invalid because the Secretary's regulations were not based on the requisite findings and because the fishermen's permit applications did not estimate impacts on the existing populations or otherwise display consistency with the purposes of the Act, which the lower court held were primarily the protection of marine mammals and not the protection of the tuna industry. The Court of Appeals agreed with the lower court, quoting testimony from a House Subcommittee hearing held subsequent to the lower court decision. In it, Rep. Robert Leggett, Chairman, stated that the Secretary must make a finding that incidental takings will not be detrimental to the marine mammal populations. "If he cannot make this finding, he cannot issue a permit. It is that simple . . . [T]he judge is interpreting the plain meaning of the law, and in order for the intention we want to be accomplished, that is to keep the tuna industry in business and still reach the objectives, we have to change the law. Because the law was rather explicit to what it required."

Subsequently the tuna fishermen brought an unsuccessful challenge to the constitutionality of MMPA. *See Motor Vessels Theresa Ann v. Richardson*, 9 Env't Rep. Cas. (BNA) 1510 and 1726 (S.D. Cal. 1977), injunction stayed *sub nom. M.V. Theresa Ann v. Kreps*, 548 F.2d 1832 (9th Cir. 1978). In 1981, the MMPA was amended to specify that the use of the best techniques that are economically and technologically feasible will satisfy the requirement to reduce porpoise mortality to levels "approaching zero." 16 U.S.C. § 1271(a)(2). In 1984, the Ninth Circuit held in *Balelo v. Baldridge*, 724 F.2d 753 (9th Cir. 1984) that the posting of federal inspectors on fishing boats to observe tuna catch techniques did not constitute an unconstitutional warrantless search.

Endangered Species Act of 1973

The federal laws to protect particular species or types of fish and wildlife were passed in response to particular needs and had little logic or plan to connect them. The Endangered Species Act of 1973, Pub. L. No. 92-205, 87 Stat. 884 (1973), as amended Pub. L. No. 96-159, 93 Stat. 1228 (1978), as further amended Pub. L. No. 92-304 (1982), 16 U.S.C. §§ 1531–1543, was the first comprehensive law to protect the increasing number of endangered species. In part, the Act, which followed earlier efforts to stop the extinction of species, responded to the Convention on International Trade in Endangered Species of Wild Fauna and Flora of 1973. The Convention was to regulate commercial and noncommercial international trade in endangered or potentially endangered species.

The Congressional purpose of the 1973 Act was similar to earlier, less effective acts designed to afford protection against the extinction of species. In addition, the Act notes the need for state cooperation, and stresses the importance of wildlife in the functioning of the ecosystem as a whole and the esthetic value of wildlife. Moreover, the basic enforcement mechanism has remained similar—to prohibit the "taking" and commercial activity in endangered species or products from such species. However, there are substantial changes in the scope of protection afforded by this Act. Most striking is the inclusion of plants among those species protected. The need for this coverage had become apparent with the extinction of a variety of domestic plants.

The definition of the Act also broadens the protection afforded to fish and wildlife. It has been broadened significantly by the inclusion of species not yet "endangered" but merely "threatened" with extinction. This provides the enforcement agencies with an opportunity to intervene earlier for the protection of species, before the situation becomes critical.

One of the deficiencies of the 1969 Act was that a species did not come under its protection if it was flourishing anywhere, even if it was becoming extinct within some other geographical area. The law now extends its authority to any species which is threatened or endangered throughout "all or a significant portion of its range." 16 U.S.C. at § 1533[14].

The law's broad coverage is evidenced by the wide definition of prohibited activities encompassed in the term "take." It is defined to mean "harass, harm, pursue, hunt, shoot, wound, kill, trap, capture, or collect, or attempt to engage in any such conduct."

The enforcement of the Endangered Species Act depends on the development and periodic updating of lists of endangered and threatened species. With respect to the listing of endangered species of plants, the Secretary of the Smithsonian Institute has been delegated a special responsibility. The responsibility for the listing of endangered or threatened fish and wildlife species is generally that of the Secretary of the Interior, but the Secretary of Commerce has a coordinate role with respect to migratory marine species of game fish. The Secretary is to designate endangered or threatened species by regulation, "because of any of the following factors:

(1) the present or threatened destruction, modification, or curtailment of its habitat or range;

(2) over-utilization for commercial, sporting, scientific, or educational purposes;

(3) disease or predation;

(4) the inadequacy of existing regulatory mechanisms; or

(5) other natural or man-made factors affecting its continued existence."

With respect to the species of marine game fish over which the Secretary of Interior exercises jurisdiction, the description must be given by him to the Secretary of Commerce, who must then put the species on the appropriate list. When the Secretary of Commerce wants to remove a species from the list or change its status, he must recommend this to the Secretary of the Interior, who shall take the recommended action if he concurs in the recommendation. The Secretary of the Interior, on the other hand, may not remove or change the listing of any species designated by the Commissioner of Commerce without the latter's concurrence. The clear result is to make it easier to list than to delist such migratory marine species of game fish.

Note that the 1982 amendments eliminated all economic considerations from the species listing process, although economic factors may be considered in the determinations of critical habitat. Pub. L. 97-304, 16 U.S.C. § 1533(1982).

The provisions for the listing of endangered and threatened species requires scientific judgment followed by elaborate notice requirement to governors of affected states, and Federal Register publication. The Secretary of State must also respond to foreign or international designations or limitations.

The Secretary may issue regulations to protect designated species, in accordance with APA, allowing 45 days for challenge and requests for public hearings. The Secretary must give the reasons for denial of requests and must also provide the factual basis for the regulations.

Perhaps the most controversial section of the Endangered Species Act is its Section 6, which provides for cooperation with the states. Aside from general provisions for consultation with a state prior to land acquisition therein for conservation purposes, and provisions for management agreements with states to assume the management of conservation areas, the law provides for "cooperative agreements." Such management agreements in effect provide for almost complete delegation of the administration and enforcement of the law to state agencies.

The Secretary may enter into such a cooperative agreement "with any state which establishes and maintains an adequate and active program for the conservation of endangered species and threatened species." The state submits such a program, and the Secretary must determine whether it meets the requirements. The Secretary must enter into an agreement "unless he determines . . . that the state program is not in accordance with this chapter." The requirements a state program must meet do not appear overly stringent:

> . . . the Secretary must find and annually thereafter reconfirm such finding, that under the state program:
>
> (1) authority resides in the State agency to conserve resident species of fish or wildlife determined by the State agency or the Secretary to be endangered or threatened;
>
> (2) the State agency has established acceptable conservation programs, consistent with the purposes and policies of this chapter, for all resident species of fish or wildlife in the State which are deemed by the Secretary to be endangered or threatened, and has furnished a copy of such plan and program together with all pertinent details, information, and data requested to the Secretary;
>
> (3) the State agency is authorized to conduct investigations to determine the status and requirements for survival of resident species of fish and wildlife;
>
> (4) the State agency is authorized to establish programs, including the acquisition of land or aquatic habitat or interests therein, for the conservation of resident endangered species or threatened species; and
>
> (5) provision is made for public participation in designating resident species of fish or wildlife as endangered or threatened.

When a state has entered into a cooperative agreement, it is eligible for a federal grant-in-aid of seventy-five percent of project cost, which is increased to ninety percent for two or more states acting together to protect a common interest.

The effects of a cooperative agreement on the applicability of federal law are very substantial. The prohibitions relating to the taking of endangered or threatened species under the federal law do not apply with respect to resident endangered or threatened species, other than to species covered under the Convention or specifically covered by treaty or other federal law. There is no indication that the Secretary may, on his own motion, take necessary protective action where a state under a cooperative agreement has failed to do so.

FEDERAL PROJECTS

As originally enacted, § 7 of the Endangered Species Actcontained a requirement of interagency cooperation, as well as a requirement of NEPA-like, general applicability which, in effect, prohibited the undertaking of any project that would jeopardize the existence of any endangered or threatened species, or that would result in the destruction or modification of its habitat. The section was significantly amended following its first, all too successful application in the case of the Tellico Dam.

In *TVA v. Hill*, 437 U.S. 153, 98 S. Ct. 2279, 57 L. Ed. 2d 117 (1978), *infra*, the Supreme Court held that the section imposes a firm duty on Federal agencies to take no action that will jeopardize an endangered species or its critical habitat. In *TVA v. Hill*, the critical habitat of the snail darter (a 3-inch, tannish-colored species of perch) would have been destroyed by the operation of the nearly completed, 78 million dollar Tellico Dam on the Tennessee River. The snail darter had been discovered only 4 months prior to the passage of the Endangered Species Act—well after the construction of the Dam had gotten underway. After the passage of the Act, the respondents in *TVA v. Hill* and others petitioned the Secretary of the Interior to list the snail darter as an endangered species. After following the mandated procedures, the Secretary listed the snail darter and identified the Tennessee River above the Tellico Dam as its critical habitat. This citizen suit to enjoin the operation of the Dam immediately followed. In affirming the grant of a permanent injunction, the Supreme Court rejected the TVA's interpretation—shared by both the House and Senate Committees which approved subsequent appropriations for the dam—that the Endangered Species Act did not apply to projects in progress and to the Tellico Dam in particular. The Court said that the language was clear and absolute, admitting of no exceptions. The Court cited the legislative history to show that Congress intended the protection of endangered species to have the "highest priorities." The Court also refused to imply a Congressional exemption from the passage of subsequent appropriations, nor did it find that any of the "hardship exemptions" applied.

Following the decision in *TVA v. Hill* a concerted and successful effort was made in Congress to prevent the recurrence of situations where major federal projects could be blocked in order to protect an endangered species, and regardless of the economic consequences. The 1978 amendment and a further amendment in 1980 establish a detailed procedure to permit exemptions, on a case-to-case basis, from the requirements of the Endangered Species Act when these requirements stand in the way of economic and other public interests in the execution of federal projects.

The very elaborate and detailed exemption process requires a judgment by the Endangered Species Committee (generally referred to as the God Squad) composed of six heads of federal agencies and designees of the governors of each affected state, that

(1) there are no reasonable and prudent alternatives to the agency action;

(2) the benefits of such action clearly outweigh the benefits of alternative courses of action consistent with conserving the species or its critical habitat, and such action is in the public interest; and

(3) the action is of regional or national significance. . . .

Any exemption granted must also require that reasonable mitigation measures, including live propagation, transplant and habitat acquisition, be adopted to minimize the adverse effects of the agency action. Denial of an exemption application is deemed a final agency action, and direct review is expressly provided in the appropriate federal court of appeals.

The enforcement of the Act is subject to a lengthy enumeration of prohibited acts. It is unlawful to "take" an endangered species of fish or wildlife within the United States or its territorial sea, or upon the high sea, or to possess, sell, deliver, etc., any species taken in violation of this prohibition, or to import or export, or carry on interstate commerce, or sell in foreign or interstate commerce any such *endangered* species, or to violate any regulation pertaining to endangered or *threatened* species.

A special exemption from the application of the Act is granted to Alaskan Indians, Aleuts or Eskimos or non-native permanent residents of an Alaskan native village. They may take endangered species for subsistence purposes, and they may sell or trade in inedible parts of such species in the form of "authentic native articles of handicrafts and clothing."

Civil penalties and criminal penalties are provided for, in a manner which is not entirely free from confusion. A person who "knowingly violates or who knowingly commits an act in the course of commercial activity which violates" the law or regulation issued under certain designated sections (except certain minor record keeping requirements), may be assessed a civil penalty up to $10,000 for each violation. Similar knowing violation of other provisions or regulations may be assessed a civil penalty up to $5,000 for each violation, and any "other" violation is subject to a $1,000 civil penalty. The penalty may be assessed after notice and opportunity for hearing; and hearings are to be conducted in accordance with the Administrative Procedure Act. Civil penalties may be mitigated or remitted by the Secretary.

Willful violation of the major designated prohibitions in the act give rise to a criminal fine of up to $20,000 and up to one year in prison, or both, and "other" willful violations are punishable by fines up to $5,000 or six months imprisonment, or both. In addition, upon conviction the person convicted may be deprived of any grazing permits he holds on public lands, and any federal hunting or fishing permits or stamps.

Enforcement by the Secretary of the Interior, Secretary of the Treasury, the Coast Guard or all of them is authorized. Detention for inspection of containers is permitted, and search warrants and arrest warrants or other process may be issued by any court of competent jurisdiction. Forfeiture of contraband is authorized, as is forfeiture of guns, traps, nets, vehicles, vessels, aircraft, etc., used in the taking or trading of fish, wildlife or plants in violation of the Act. *See, e.g., U.S. v. Species of Wildlife Consisting of a Fully Mounted Leopard*, 404 F. Supp. 1298 (E.D.N.Y. 1975).

The Act provides for citizen suits, imposing a sixty-day notice requirement, and providing that a court shall compel the Secretary to apply the prohibition sought if it finds that the allegation that an emergency exists is supported by substantial evidence.

NOTE

In states with endangered species legislation of their own, the question of conflict with federal law has arisen in spite of the federal provisions which leave some room for state initiatives. *See, e.g., Fooke Co. v. Brown*, 463 F. Supp. 1142 (E.D. Cal 1979) (conflict with ESA, Cal. law invalidated); *Fooke Co. v. Mandel*, 386 F. Supp. 1341 (D. Md. 1974) (conflict with MMPA, Md. law invalidated); *A.E. Nettleton Co. v. Diamond*, 27 N.Y.2d 182, 315 N.Y.S.2d 625, 264 N.E.2d 118 (1970) (conflict with ESA, N.Y. law upheld). Each of the cases involved the sale of hides or parts of protected animals.

TENNESSEE VALLEY AUTHORITY v. HILL

United States Supreme Court (1978)
437 U.S. 153, 98 S. Ct. 2279, 57 L. Ed. 2d 117

Mr. Chief Justice BURGER delivered the opinion of the Court.

The questions presented in this case are (a) whether the Endangered Species Act of 1973 requires a court to enjoin the operation of a virtually completed federal dam — which had been authorized prior to 1973 — when, pursuant to authority vested in him by Congress, the Secretary of the Interior has determined that operation of the dam would eradicate an endangered species; and (b) whether continued congressional appropriations for the dam after 1973 constituted an implied repeal of the Endangered Species Act, at least as to the particular dam.

I

The Little Tennessee River originates in the mountains of northern Georgia and flows through the national forest lands of North Carolina into Tennessee, where it converges with the Big Tennessee River near Knoxville. The lower 33 miles of the Little Tennessee takes the river's clear, free-flowing waters through an area of great natural beauty. Among other environmental amenities, this stretch of river is said to contain abundant trout. Considerable historical importance attaches to the areas immediately adjacent to this portion of the Little Tennessee's banks. To the south of the river's edge lies Fort Loudon, established in 1756 as England's southwestern outpost in the French and Indian War. Nearby are also the ancient sites of several native American villages, the archeological stores of which are to a large extent unexplored. These include the Cherokee towns of Echota and Tennase, the former being the sacred capital of the Cherokee Nation as early as the 16th century and the latter providing the linguistic basis from which the State of Tennessee derives its name.

In this area of the Little Tennessee River the Tennessee Valley Authority, a wholly owned public corporation of the United States, began constructing the Tellico Dam and Reservoir Project in 1967, shortly after Congress appropriated initial funds for its development. Tellico is a multipurpose regional development project designed principally to stimulate shoreline development, generate sufficient electric current to heat 20,000 homes, and provide flat-water recreation and flood control, as well as improve economic conditions in "an area characterized by underutilization of human resources and outmigration of young people." Hearings on Public Works for Power and Energy Research Appropriation Bill, 1977, before a Subcommittee of the House Committee on Appropriations, 94th Cong., 2d Sess., pt. 5, p. 261 (1976). Of particular relevance to this case is one aspect of the project, a dam which TVA determined to place on the Little Tennessee, a short distance from where the river's waters meet with the Big Tennessee. When fully operational, the dam would impound water covering some 16,500 acres — much of which represents valuable and productive farmland — thereby converting the river's shallow, fast-flowing waters into a deep reservoir over 30 miles in length.

The Tellico Dam has never opened, however, despite the fact that construction has been virtually completed and the dam is essentially ready for operation. Although Congress has appropriated monies for Tellico every year since 1967, progress was delayed, and ultimately stopped, by a tangle of lawsuits and administrative proceedings. After unsuccessfully urging TVA to consider alternatives to damming the Little Tennessee, local citizens and national conservation groups brought suit in the District Court, claiming that the project did not conform to the requirements of the National Environmental Policy Act of 1969 (NEPA), 83 Stat. 852, 42 U. S. C. § 4321 et seq. After finding TVA to be in violation of NEPA, the District Court enjoined the dam's completion pending the filing of an appropriate environmental impact statement. *Environmental Defense Fund v. TVA*, 339 F. Supp. 806 (ED Tenn.), aff'd, 468 F.2d 1164 (CA6 1972). The injunction remained in effect until late 1973, when the District Court concluded that TVA's final environmental impact statement for Tellico was in compliance with the law. *Environmental Defense Fund v. TVA*, 371 F. Supp. 1004 (ED Tenn. 1973), aff'd, 492 F.2d 466 (CA6 1974).[4]

A few months prior to the District Court's decision dissolving the NEPA injunction, a discovery was made in the waters of the Little Tennessee which

[4] The NEPA injunction was in effect some 21 months; when it was entered TVA had spent some $29 million on the project. Most of these funds have gone to purchase land, construct the concrete portions of the dam, and build a four-lane steel-span bridge to carry a state highway over the proposed reservoir. 339 F. Supp., at 808.

would profoundly affect the Tellico Project. Exploring the area around Coytee Springs, which is about seven miles from the mouth of the river, a University of Tennessee ichthyologist, Dr. David A. Etnier, found a previously unknown species of perch, the snail darter, or *Percina (Imostoma) tanasi*. This three-inch, tannish-colored fish, whose numbers are estimated to be in the range of 10,000 to 15,000, would soon engage the attention of environmentalists, the TVA, the Department of the Interior, the Congress of the United States, and ultimately the federal courts, as a new and additional basis to halt construction of the dam.

Until recently the finding of a new species of animal life would hardly generate a cause celebre. This is particularly so in the case of darters, of which there are approximately 130 known species, 8 to 10 of these having been identified only in the last five years. The moving force behind the snail darter's sudden fame came some four months after its discovery, when the Congress passed the Endangered Species Act of 1973 (Act), 87 Stat. 884, 16 U. S. C. § 1531 *et seq.* (1976 ed.). This legislation, among other things, authorizes the Secretary of the Interior to declare species of animal life "endangered" and to identify the "critical habitat"[5] of these creatures. When a species or its habitat is so listed, the following portion of the Act — relevant here — becomes effective:

> "The Secretary [of the Interior] shall review other programs administered by him and utilize such programs in furtherance of the purposes of this chapter. All other Federal departments and agencies shall, in consultation with and with the assistance of the Secretary, utilize their authorities in furtherance of the purposes of this chapter by carrying out programs for the conservation of endangered species and threatened species listed pursuant to section 1533 of this title and *by taking such action necessary to insure that actions authorized, funded, or carried out by them do not jeopardize the continued existence of such endangered species and threatened species or result in the destruction or modification of habitat of such species* which is determined by the Secretary, after consultation as appropriate with the affected States, to be critical." 16 U. S. C. § 1536 (1976 ed.) (emphasis added).

In January 1975, the respondents in this case and others petitioned the Secretary of the Interior to list the snail darter as an endangered species. After receiving comments from various interested parties, including TVA and the State of Tennessee, the Secretary formally listed the snail darter as an endangered species on October 8, 1975. 40 Fed. Reg. 47505–47506; *see* 50 CFR

[5] The Act does not define "critical habitat," but the Secretary of the Interior has administratively construed the term:

> "'Critical habitat' means any air, land, or water area (exclusive of those existing man-made structures or settlements which are not necessary to the survival and recovery of a listed species) and constituent elements thereof, the loss of which would appreciably decrease the likelihood of the survival and recovery of a listed species or a distinct segment of its population. The constituent elements of critical habitat include, but are not limited to: physical structures and topography, biota, climate, human activity, and the quality and chemical content of land, water, and air. Critical habitat may represent any portion of the present habitat of a listed species and may include additional areas for reasonable population expansion." 43 Fed. Reg. 874 (1978) (to be codified as 50 CFR § 402.02).

§ 17.11(i) (1976). In so acting, it was noted that "the snail darter is a living entity which is genetically distinct and reproductively isolated from other fishes." 40 Fed. Reg. 47505. More important for the purposes of this case, the Secretary determined that the snail darter apparently lives only in that portion of the Little Tennessee River which would be completely inundated by the reservoir created as a consequence of the Tellico Dam's completion. The Secretary went on to explain the significance of the dam to the habitat of the snail darter:

> "[The] snail darter occurs only in the swifter portions of shoals over clean gravel substrate in cool, low-turbidity water. Food of the snail darter is almost exclusively snails which require a clean gravel substrate for their survival. *The proposed impoundment of water behind the proposed Tellico Dam would result in total destruction of the snail darter's habitat.*" (emphasis added).

Subsequent to this determination, the Secretary declared the area of the Little Tennessee which would be affected by the Tellico Dam to be the "critical habitat" of the snail darter. 41 Fed. Reg. 13926–13928 (1976) (to be codified as 50 CFR § 17.81). Using these determinations as a predicate, and notwithstanding the near completion of the dam, the Secretary declared that pursuant to § 7 of the Act, "all Federal agencies must take such action as is necessary to insure that actions authorized, funded, or carried out by them do not result in the destruction or modification of this critical habitat area." 41 Fed. Reg. 13928 (1976) (to be codified as 50 CFR § 17.81(b)). This notice, of course, was pointedly directed at TVA and clearly aimed at halting completion or operation of the dam.

During the pendency of these administrative actions, other developments of relevance to the snail darter issue were transpiring. Communication was occurring between the Department of the Interior's Fish and Wildlife Service and TVA with a view toward settling the issue informally. These negotiations were to no avail, however, since TVA consistently took the position that the only available alternative was to attempt relocating the snail darter population to another suitable location. To this end, TVA conducted a search of alternative sites which might sustain the fish, culminating in the experimental transplantation of a number of snail darters to the nearby Hiwassee River. However, the Secretary of the Interior was not satisfied with the results of these efforts, finding that TVA had presented "little evidence that they have carefully studied the Hiwassee to determine whether or not" there were "biological and other factors in this river that [would] negate a successful transplant." 40 Fed. Reg. 47506 (1975).

Meanwhile, Congress had also become involved in the fate of the snail darter. Appearing before a Subcommittee of the House Committee on Appropriations in April 1975 — some seven months before the snail darter was listed as endangered — TVA representatives described the discovery of the fish and the relevance of the Endangered Species Act to the Tellico Project. Hearings on Public Works for Water and Power Development and Energy Research Appropriation Bill, 1976, before a Subcommittee of the House Committee on Appropriations, 94th Cong., 1st Sess., pt. 7, pp. 466-467 (1975); Hearings on H. R. 8122, Public Works for Water and Power Development and Energy

Research Appropriations for Fiscal Year 1976, before a Subcommittee of the Senate Committee on Appropriations, 94th Cong., 1st Sess., pt. 4, pp. 3775-3777 (1975). At that time TVA presented a position which it would advance in successive forums thereafter, namely, that the Act did not prohibit the completion of a project authorized, funded, and substantially constructed before the Act was passed. TVA also described its efforts to transplant the snail darter, but contended that the dam should be finished regardless of the experiment's success. Thereafter, the House Committee on Appropriations, in its June 20, 1975 Report, stated the following in the course of recommending that an additional $29 million be appropriated for Tellico:

> "The *Committee* directs that the project, for which an environmental impact statement has been completed and provided the Committee, should be completed as promptly as possible . . . ." H. R. Rep. No. 94-319, p. 76 (1975) (emphasis added).

Congress then approved the TVA general budget, which contained funds for continued construction of the Tellico Project. In December 1975, one month after the snail darter was declared an endangered species, the President signed the bill into law. Public Works for Water and Power Development and Energy Research Appropriation Act, 1976, 89 Stat. 1035, 1047.

In February 1976, pursuant to § 11(g) of the Endangered Species Act, 87 Stat. 900, 16 U. S. C. § 1540(g) (1976 ed.), respondents filed the case now under review, seeking to enjoin completion of the dam and impoundment of the reservoir on the ground that those actions would violate the Act by directly causing the extinction of the species *Percina (Imostoma) tanasi.* The District Court denied respondents' request for a preliminary injunction and set the matter for trial. Shortly thereafter the House and Senate held appropriations hearings which would include discussions of the Tellico budget.

At these hearings, TVA Chairman Wagner reiterated the agency's position that the Act did not apply to a project which was over 50% finished by the time the Act became effective and some 70% to 80% complete when the snail darter was officially listed as endangered. It also notified the Committees of the recently filed lawsuit's status and reported that TVA's efforts to transplant the snail darter had "been very encouraging." Hearings on Public Works for Water and Power Development and Energy Research Appropriation Bill, 1977, before a Subcommittee of the House Committee on Appropriations, 94th Cong., 2d Sess., pt. 5, pp. 261–262 (1976); Hearings on Public Works for Water and Power Development and Energy Research Appropriations for Fiscal Year 1977, before a Subcommittee of the Senate Committee on Appropriations, 94th Cong., 2d Sess., pt. 4, pp. 3096-3099 (1976).

Trial was held in the District Court on April 29 and 30, 1976, and on May 25, 1976, the court entered its memorandum opinion and order denying respondents their requested relief and dismissing the complaint. The District Court found that closure of the dam and the consequent impoundment of the reservoir would "result in the adverse modification, if not complete destruction, of the snail darter's critical habitat," making it "highly probable" that "the continued existence of the snail darter" would be "[jeopardized]." 419 F. Supp. 753, 757 (ED Tenn.). Despite these findings, the District Court declined to embrace the plaintiffs' position on the merits: that once a federal project was shown to jeopardize an endangered species, a court of equity is compelled to issue an injunction restraining violation of the Endangered Species Act.

In reaching this result, the District Court stressed that the entire project was then about 80% complete and, based on available evidence, "there [were] no alternatives to impoundment of the reservoir, short of scrapping the entire project." *Id.*, at 758. The District Court also found that if the Tellico Project was permanently enjoined, "some $53 million would be lost in nonrecoverable obligations," *id.*, at 759, meaning that a large portion of the $78 million already expended would be wasted. The court also noted that the Endangered Species Act of 1973 was passed some seven years after construction on the dam commenced and that Congress had continued appropriations for Tellico, with full awareness of the snail darter problem. Assessing these various factors, the District Court concluded:

> "At some point in time a federal project becomes so near completion and so incapable of modification that a court of equity should not apply a statute enacted long after inception of the project to produce an unreasonable result. . . . Where there has been an irreversible and irretrievable commitment of resources by Congress to a project over a span of almost a decade, the Court should proceed with a great deal of circumspection." *Id.*, at 760.

To accept the plaintiffs' position, the District Court argued, would inexorably lead to what it characterized as the absurd result of requiring "a court to halt impoundment of water behind a fully completed dam if an endangered species were discovered in the river on the day before such impoundment was scheduled to take place. We cannot conceive that Congress intended such a result." *Id.*, at 763.

Less than a month after the District Court decision, the Senate and House Appropriations Committees recommended the full budget request of $9 million for continued work on Tellico. *See* S. Rep. No. 94-960, p. 96 (1976); H. R. Rep. No. 94-1223, p. 83 (1976). In its Report accompanying the appropriations bill, the Senate Committee stated:

> "During subcommittee hearings, TVA was questioned about the relationship between the Tellico project's completion and the November 1975 listing of the snail darter (a small 3-inch fish which was discovered in 1973) as an endangered species under the Endangered Species Act. TVA informed the Committee that it was continuing its efforts to preserve the darter, while working towards the scheduled 1977 completion date. TVA repeated its view that the Endangered Species Act did not prevent the completion of the Tellico project, which has been under construction for nearly a decade. The subcommittee brought this matter, as well as the recent U.S. District Court's decision upholding TVA's decision to complete the project, to the attention of the full Committee. *The Committee does not view* the Endangered Species Act as prohibiting the completion of the Tellico project at its advanced stage and directs that this project be completed as promptly as possible in the public interest." S. Rep. No. 94-960, *supra*, at 96. (Emphasis added.)

On June 29, 1976, both Houses of Congress passed TVA's general budget, which included funds for Tellico; the President signed the bill on July 12, 1976.

Public Works for Water and Power Development and Energy Research Appropriation Act, 1977, 90 Stat. 889, 899.

Thereafter, in the Court of Appeals, respondents argued that the District Court had abused its discretion by not issuing an injunction in the face of "a blatant statutory violation." *Hill v. TVA*, 549 F.2d 1064, 1069 (CA6 1977). The Court of Appeals agreed, and on January 31, 1977, it reversed, remanding "with instructions that a permanent injunction issue halting all activities incident to the Tellico Project which may destroy or modify the critical habitat of the snail darter." *Id.*, at 1075. The Court of Appeals directed that the injunction "remain in effect until Congress, by appropriate legislation, exempts Tellico from compliance with the Act or the snail darter has been deleted from the list of endangered species or its critical habitat materially redefined." *Ibid.*

The Court of Appeals accepted the District Court's finding that closure of the dam would result in the known population of snail darters being "significantly reduced if not completely extirpated." *Id.*, at 1069. TVA, in fact, had conceded as much in the Court of Appeals, but argued that "closure of the Tellico Dam, as the last stage of a ten-year project, falls outside the legitimate purview of the Act if it is rationally construed." *Id.*, at 1070. Disagreeing, the Court of Appeals held that the record revealed a prima facie violation of § 7 of the Act, namely that TVA had failed to take "such action . . . necessary to insure" that its "actions" did not jeopardize the snail darter or its critical habitat.

The reviewing court thus rejected TVA's contention that the word "actions" in § 7 of the Act was not intended by Congress to encompass the terminal phases of ongoing projects. Not only could the court find no "positive reinforcement" for TVA's argument in the Act's legislative history, but also such an interpretation was seen as being "inimical to . . . its objectives." 549 F.2d, at 1070. By way of illustration, that court pointed out that "the detrimental impact of a project upon an endangered species may not always be clearly perceived before construction is well underway." *Id.*, at 1071. Given such a likelihood, the Court of Appeals was of the opinion that TVA's position would require the District Court, sitting as a chancellor, to balance the worth of an endangered species against the value of an ongoing public works measure, a result which the appellate court was not willing to accept. Emphasizing the limits on judicial power in this setting, the court stated:

> "Current project status cannot be translated into a workable standard of judicial review. Whether a dam is 50% or 90% completed is irrelevant in calculating the social and scientific costs attributable to the disappearance of a unique form of life. Courts are ill-equipped to calculate how many dollars must be invested before the value of a dam exceeds that of the endangered species. Our responsibility under § 1540(g)(1)(A) is merely to preserve the status quo where endangered species are threatened, thereby guaranteeing the legislative or executive branches sufficient opportunity to grapple with the alternatives." *Ibid.*

As far as the Court of Appeals was concerned, it made no difference that Congress had repeatedly approved appropriations for Tellico, referring to such legislative approval as an "advisory [opinion]" concerning the proper application of an existing statute. In that court's view, the only relevant legislation was the Act itself, "[the] meaning and spirit" of which was "clear on its face." *Id.*, at 1072.

Turning to the question of an appropriate remedy, the Court of Appeals ruled that the District Court had erred by not issuing an injunction. While recognizing the irretrievable loss of millions of dollars of public funds which would accompany injunctive relief, the court nonetheless decided that the Act explicitly commanded precisely that result:

> "It is conceivable that the welfare of an endangered species may weigh more heavily upon the public conscience, as expressed by the final will of Congress, than the writeoff of those millions of dollars already expended for Tellico in excess of its present salvageable value." *Id.*, at 1074.

Following the issuance of the permanent injunction, members of TVA's Board of Directors appeared before Subcommittees of the House and Senate Appropriations Committees to testify in support of continued appropriations for Tellico. The Subcommittees were apprised of all aspects of Tellico's status, including the Court of Appeals' decision. TVA reported that the dam stood "ready for the gates to be closed and the reservoir filled," Hearings on Public Works for Water and Power Development and Energy Research Appropriation Bill, 1978, before a Subcommittee of the House Committee on Appropriations, 95th Cong., 1st Sess., pt. 4, p. 234 (1977), and requested funds for completion of certain ancillary parts of the project, such as public use areas, roads, and bridges. As to the snail darter itself, TVA commented optimistically on its transplantation efforts, expressing the opinion that the relocated fish were "doing well and [had] reproduced." *Id.*, at 235, 261-262.

Both Appropriations Committees subsequently recommended the full amount requested for completion of the Tellico Project. In its June 2, 1977, Report, the House Appropriations Committee stated:

> "It is the *Committee's* view that the Endangered Species Act was not intended to halt projects such as these in their advanced stage of completion, and [the Committee] strongly recommends that these projects not be stopped because of misuse of the Act." H. R. Rep. No. 95-379, p. 104. (Emphasis added).

As a solution to the problem, the House Committee advised that TVA should cooperate with the Department of the Interior "to relocate the endangered species to another suitable habitat so as to permit the project to proceed as rapidly as possible." *Id.*, at 11. Toward this end, the Committee recommended a special appropriation of $2 million to facilitate relocation of the snail darter and other endangered species which threatened to delay or stop TVA projects. Much the same occurred on the Senate side, with its Appropriations Committee recommending both the amount requested to complete Tellico and the special appropriation for transplantation of endangered species. Reporting to the Senate on these measures, the Appropriations Committee took a particularly strong stand on the snail darter issue:

> "This *committee has not viewed* the Endangered Species Act as preventing the completion and use of these projects which were well under way at

> the time the affected species were listed as endangered. If the act has such an effect, which is contrary to the *Committee's understanding* of the intent of Congress in enacting the Endangered Species Act, funds should be appropriated to allow these projects to be completed and their benefits realized in the public interest, the Endangered Species Act notwithstanding." S. Rep. No. 95-301, p. 99 (1977). (Emphasis added).

TVA's budget, including funds for completion of Tellico and relocation of the snail darter, passed both Houses of Congress and was signed into law on August 7, 1977. Public Works for Water and Power Development and Energy Research Appropriation Act, 1978, 91 Stat. 797.

We granted certiorari, 434 U.S. 954 (1977), to review the judgment of the Court of Appeals.

II

We begin with the premise that operation of the Tellico Dam will either eradicate the known population of snail darters or destroy their critical habitat. Petitioner does not now seriously dispute this fact. In any event, under § 4(a)(1) of the Act, 87 Stat. 886, 16 U. S. C. § 1533(a)(1) (1976 ed.), the Secretary of the Interior is vested with exclusive authority to determine whether a species such as the snail darter is "endangered" or "threatened" and to ascertain the factors which have led to such a precarious existence. By § 4(d) Congress has authorized — indeed commanded — the Secretary to "issue such regulations as he deems necessary and advisable to provide for the conservation of such species." 16 U. S. C. § 1533(d) (1976 ed.). As we have seen, the Secretary promulgated regulations which declared the snail darter an endangered species whose critical habitat would be destroyed by creation of the Tellico Reservoir. Doubtless petitioner would prefer not to have these regulations on the books, but there is no suggestion that the Secretary exceeded his authority or abused his discretion in issuing the regulations. Indeed, no judicial review of the Secretary's determinations has ever been sought and hence the validity of his actions are not open to review in this Court.

Starting from the above premise, two questions are presented: (a) would TVA be in violation of the Act if it completed and operated the Tellico Dam as planned? (b) if TVA's actions would offend the Act, is an injunction the appropriate remedy for the violation? For the reasons stated hereinafter, we hold that both questions must be answered in the affirmative.

(A)

It may seem curious to some that the survival of a relatively small number of three-inch fish among all the countless millions of species extant would require the permanent halting of a virtually completed dam for which Congress has expended more than $100 million. The paradox is not minimized by the fact that Congress continued to appropriate large sums of public money for the project, even after congressional Appropriations Committees were apprised of its apparent impact upon the survival of the snail darter. We conclude, however, that the explicit provisions of the Endangered Species Act require precisely that result.

One would be hard pressed to find a statutory provision whose terms were any plainer than those in § 7 of the Endangered Species Act. Its very words affirmatively command all federal agencies "to *insure* that actions *authorized, funded*, or *carried out* by them do not *jeopardize* the continued existence" of an endangered species or "*result* in the destruction or modification of habitat of such species . . . ." 16 U. S. C. § 1536 (1976 ed.). (Emphasis added.) This language admits of no exception. Nonetheless, petitioner urges, as do the dissenters, that the Act cannot reasonably be interpreted as applying to a federal project which was well under way when Congress passed the Endangered Species Act of 1973. To sustain that position, however, we would be forced to ignore the ordinary meaning of plain language. It has not been shown, for example, how TVA can close the gates of the Tellico Dam without "carrying out" an action that has been "authorized" and "funded" by a federal agency. Nor can we understand how such action will "*insure*" that the snail darter's habitat is not disrupted. Accepting the Secretary's determinations, as we must, it is clear that TVA's proposed operation of the dam will have precisely the opposite effect, namely the *eradication* of an endangered species.

Concededly, this view of the Act will produce results requiring the sacrifice of the anticipated benefits of the project and of many millions of dollars in public funds. But examination of the language, history, and structure of the legislation under review here indicates beyond doubt that Congress intended endangered species to be afforded the highest of priorities.

When Congress passed the Act in 1973, it was not legislating on a clean slate. The first major congressional concern for the preservation of the endangered species had come with passage of the Endangered Species Act of 1966, 80 Stat. 926, repealed, 87 Stat. 903. In that legislation Congress gave the Secretary power to identify "the names of the species of native fish and wildlife found to be threatened with extinction," § 1(c), 80 Stat. 926, as well as authorization to purchase land for the conservation, protection, restoration, and propagation of "selected species" of "native fish and wildlife" threatened with extinction. §§ 2(a)-(c), 80 Stat. 926-927. Declaring the preservation of endangered species a national policy, the 1966 Act directed all federal agencies both to protect these species and "*insofar as is practicable and consistent with [their] primary purposes,*" § 1(b), 80 Stat. 926, "preserve the habitats of such threatened species on lands under their jurisdiction." *Ibid.* (Emphasis added). The 1966 statute was not a sweeping prohibition on the taking of endangered species, however, except on federal lands, § 4(c), 80 Stat. 928, and even in those federal areas the Secretary was authorized to allow the hunting and fishing of endangered species. § 4(d)(1), 80 Stat. 928.

In 1969 Congress enacted the Endangered Species Conservation Act, 83 Stat. 275, repealed, 87 Stat. 903, which continued the provisions of the 1966 Act while at the same time broadening federal involvement in the preservation of endangered species. Under the 1969 legislation, the Secretary was empowered to list species "threatened with worldwide extinction," § 3(a), 83 Stat. 275; in addition, the importation of any species so recognized into the United States was prohibited. § 2, 83 Stat. 275. An indirect approach to the taking of endangered species was also adopted in the Conservation Act by way of a ban on the transportation and sale of wildlife taken in violation of any federal, state, or foreign law. §§ 7(a)-(b), 83 Stat. 279.

Despite the fact that the 1966 and 1969 legislation represented "the most comprehensive of its type to be enacted by any nation" up to that time, Congress was soon persuaded that a more expansive approach was needed if the newly declared national policy of preserving endangered species was to be realized. By 1973, when Congress held hearings on what would later become the Endangered Species Act of 1973, it was informed that species were still being lost at the rate of about one per year, 1973 House Hearings 306 (statement of Stephen R. Seater, for Defenders of Wildlife), and "the pace of disappearance of species" appeared to be "accelerating." H. R. Rep. No. 93-412, p. 4 (1973). Moreover, Congress was also told that the primary cause of this trend was something other than the normal process of natural selection:

> "[Man] and his technology has [sic] continued at an ever-increasing rate to disrupt the natural ecosystem. This has resulted in a dramatic rise in the number and severity of the threats faced by the world's wildlife. The truth in this is apparent when one realizes that half of the recorded extinctions of mammals over the past 2,000 years have occurred in the most recent 50-year period." 1973 House Hearings 202 (statement of Assistant Secretary of the Interior).

That Congress did not view these developments lightly was stressed by one commentator:

> "The dominant theme pervading all Congressional discussion of the proposed [Endangered Species Act of 1973] was the overriding need to *devote whatever effort and resources were necessary* to avoid further diminution of national and worldwide wildlife resources. Much of the testimony at the hearings and much debate was devoted to the biological problem of extinction. Senators and Congressmen uniformly deplored the irreplaceable loss to aesthetics, science, ecology, and the national heritage should more species disappear." Coggins, Conserving Wildlife Resources: An Overview of the Endangered Species Act of 1973, 51 N. D. L. Rev. 315, 321 (1975). (Emphasis added).

The legislative proceedings in 1973 are, in fact, replete with expressions of concern over the risk that might lie in the loss of *any* endangered species. Typifying these sentiments is the Report of the House Committee on Merchant Marine and Fisheries on H. R. 37, a bill which contained the essential features of the subsequently enacted Act of 1973; in explaining the need for the legislation, the Report stated:

> "As we homogenize the habitats in which these plants and animals evolved, and as we increase the pressure for products that they are in a position to supply (usually unwillingly) we threaten their — and our own — genetic heritage.
>
> "*The value of this genetic heritage is, quite literally, incalculable. . . .*
>
> "From the most narrow possible point of view, it is in the best interests of mankind to minimize the losses of genetic variations. The reason is simple: they are potential resources. They are keys to puzzles which we

cannot solve, and may provide answers to questions which we have not yet learned to ask.

"To take a homely, but apt, example: one of the critical chemicals in the regulation of ovulations in humans was found in a common plant. Once discovered, and analyzed, humans could duplicate it synthetically, but had it never existed — or had it been driven out of existence before we knew its potentialities — we would never have tried to synthesize it in the first place.

"Who knows, or can say, what potential cures for cancer or other scourges, present or future, may lie locked up in the structures of plants which may yet be undiscovered, much less analyzed? . . . Sheer self-interest impels us to be cautious.

"*The institutionalization of that caution* lies at the heart of H. R. 37 . . . ." H. R. Rep. No. 93-412, pp. 4-5 (1973). (Emphasis added).

As the examples cited here demonstrate, Congress was concerned about the *unknown* uses that endangered species might have and about the *unforeseeable* place such creatures may have in the chain of life on this planet.

In shaping legislation to deal with the problem thus presented, Congress started from the finding that "[the] two major causes of extinction are hunting and destruction of natural habitat." S. Rep. No. 93-307, p. 2 (1973). Of these twin threats, Congress was informed that the greatest was destruction of natural habitats; *see* 1973 House Hearings 236 (statement of Associate Deputy Chief for National Forest System, Dept. of Agriculture); *id.*, at 241 (statement of Director of Mich. Dept. of Natural Resources); *id.*, at 306 (statement of Stephen R. Seater, Defenders of Wildlife); Lachenmeier, The Endangered Species Act of 1973: Preservation or Pandemonium?, 5 Environ. Law 29, 31 (1974). Witnesses recommended, among other things, that Congress require all land-managing agencies "to avoid damaging critical habitat for endangered species and to take positive steps to improve such habitat." 1973 House Hearings 241 (statement of Director of Mich. Dept. of Natural Resources). Virtually every bill introduced in Congress during the 1973 session responded to this concern by incorporating language similar, if not identical, to that found in the present § 7 of the Act. These provisions were designed, in the words of an administration witness, "for the first time [to] *prohibit* [a] federal agency from taking action which does jeopardize the status of endangered species," Hearings on S. 1592 and S. 1983 before the Subcommittee on Environment of the Senate Committee on Commerce, 93d Cong., 1st Sess., 68 (1973) (statement of Deputy Assistant Secretary of the Interior) (emphasis added); furthermore, the proposed bills would "[*direct*] all . . . Federal agencies to utilize their authorities for carrying out programs *for the protection* of endangered animals." 1973 House Hearings 205 (statement of Assistant Secretary of the Interior). (Emphasis added.)

As it was finally passed, the Endangered Species Act of 1973 represented the most comprehensive legislation for the preservation of endangered species ever enacted by any nation. Its stated purposes were "to provide a means whereby the ecosystems upon which endangered species and threatened species depend may be conserved," and "to provide a program for the conservation of such . . . species . . . ." 16 U. S. C. § 1531(b) (1976 ed.). In furtherance of these goals, Congress expressly stated in § 2(c) that "all Federal departments and agencies *shall* seek *to conserve endangered species* and threatened species. . . ." 16 U. S. C. § 1531(c) (1976 ed.). (Emphasis added.) Lest there be any ambiguity as to the meaning of this statutory directive, the Act specifically defined "conserve" as meaning "to use and the use of *all methods and procedures which are necessary to bring any endangered species or threatened species* to the point at which the measures provided pursuant to this chapter are no longer necessary." § 1532(2). (Emphasis added.) Aside from § 7, other provisions indicated the seriousness with which Congress viewed this issue: Virtually all dealings with endangered species, including taking, possession, transportation, and sale, were prohibited, 16 U. S. C. § 1538 (1976 ed.), except in extremely narrow circumstances, *see* § 1539(b). The Secretary was also given extensive power to develop regulations and programs for the preservation of endangered and threatened species. § 1533(d). Citizen involvement was encouraged by the Act, with provisions allowing interested persons to petition the Secretary to list a species as endangered or threatened, § 1533(c)(2), and bring civil suits in United States district courts to force compliance with any provision of the Act, §§ 1540(c) and (g).

Section 7 of the Act, which of course is relied upon by respondents in this case, provides a particularly good gauge of congressional intent. As we have seen, this provision had its genesis in the Endangered Species Act of 1966, but that legislation qualified the obligation of federal agencies by stating that they should seek to preserve endangered species only "*insofar as is practicable and consistent with [their] primary purposes* . . . ." Likewise, every bill introduced in 1973 contained a qualification similar to that found in the earlier statutes. Exemplary of these was the administration bill, H. R. 4758, which in § 2(b) would direct federal agencies to use their authorities to further the ends of the Act "*insofar as is practicable and consistent with [their] primary purposes* . . . ." (Emphasis added.) Explaining the idea behind this language, an administration spokesman told Congress that it "would further signal to all . . . agencies of the Government that this is the *first priority, consistent with their primary objectives.*" 1973 House Hearings 213 (statement of Deputy Assistant Secretary of the Interior). (Emphasis added.) This type of language did not go unnoticed by those advocating strong endangered species legislation. A representative of the Sierra Club, for example, attacked the use of the phrase "consistent with the primary purpose" in proposed H. R. 4758, cautioning that the qualification "could be construed to be a declaration of congressional policy that other agency purposes are necessarily more important than protection of endangered species and would always prevail if conflict were to occur." 1973 House Hearings 335 (statement of the chairman of the Sierra Club's National Wildlife Committee); *see id.*, at 251 (statement for the National Audubon Society).

What is very significant in this sequence is that the final version of the 1973 Act carefully omitted all of the reservations described above. In the bill which the Senate initially approved (S. 1983), however, the version of the current § 7 merely required federal agencies to "carry out such programs *as are practicable* for the protection of species listed . . . ." S. 1983, § 7(a). By way of contrast, the bill that originally passed the House, H. R. 37, contained a provision which was essentially a mirror image of the subsequently passed

§ 7 — indeed all phrases which might have qualified an agency's responsibilities had been omitted from the bill. In explaining the expected impact of this provision in H. R. 37 on federal agencies, the House Committee's Report states:

> "This subsection *requires* the Secretary and the heads of all other Federal departments and agencies to use their authorities in order to carry out programs for the protection of endangered species, and it further *requires* that those agencies take *the necessary action* that will *not jeopardize* the continuing existence of endangered species or result in the destruction of critical habitat of those species." H. R. Rep. No. 93-412, p. 14 (1973). (Emphasis added).

Resolution of this difference in statutory language, as well as other variations between the House and Senate bills, was the task of a Conference Committee. *See* 119 Cong. Rec. 30174-30175, 31183 (1973). The Conference Report, H. R. Conf. Rep. No. 93-740 (1973), basically adopted the Senate bill, S. 1983; but the conferees rejected the Senate version of § 7 and adopted the stringent, mandatory language in H. R. 37. While the Conference Report made no specific reference to this choice of provisions, the House manager of the bill, Representative Dingell, provided an interpretation of what the Conference bill would require, making it clear that the mandatory provisions of § 7 were not casually or inadvertently included:

> "[Section 7] substantially [amplifies] the obligation of [federal agencies] to take steps within their power to carry out the purposes of this act. A recent article . . . illustrates the problem which might occur absent this new language in the bill. It appears that the whooping cranes of this country, perhaps the best known of our endangered species, are being threatened by Air Force bombing activities along the gulf coast of Texas. Under existing law, the Secretary of Defense has some discretion as to whether or not he will take the necessary action to see that this threat disappears . . . . [Once] the bill is enacted, [the Secretary of Defense] *would be required* to take the proper steps . . . .
>
> "Another example . . . [has] to do with the continental population of grizzly bears which may or may not be endangered, but which is surely threatened . . . . Once this bill is enacted, the appropriate Secretary, whether of Interior, Agriculture or whatever, *will have to take action* to see that this situation is not permitted to worsen, and that these bears are not driven to extinction. The purposes of the bill included the conservation of the species and of the ecosystems upon which they depend, and *every agency of government is committed* to see that those purposes are carried out . . . . [The] agencies of Government can no longer plead that they can do nothing about it. They can, and they must. The law is clear." 119 Cong. Rec. 42913 (1973). (Emphasis added).

It is against this legislative background that we must measure TVA's claim that the Act was not intended to stop operation of a project which, like Tellico Dam, was near completion when an endangered species was discovered in its path. While there is no discussion in the legislative history of precisely this problem, the totality of congressional action makes it abundantly clear that the result we reach today is wholly in accord with both the words of the statute and the intent of Congress. The plain intent of Congress in enacting this statute was to halt and reverse the trend toward species extinction, whatever the cost. This is reflected not only in the stated policies of the Act, but in literally every section of the statute. All persons, including federal agencies, are specifically instructed not to "take" endangered species, meaning that no one is "to harass, harm, pursue, hunt, shoot, wound, kill, trap, capture, or collect" such life forms. 16 U. S. C. §§ 1532(14), 1538(a)(1)(B) (1976 ed.). Agencies in particular are directed by §§ 2(c) and 3(2) of the Act to "use . . . *all methods* and procedures which are necessary" to preserve endangered species. 16 U. S. C. §§ 1531(c), 1532(2) (1976 ed.) (emphasis added). In addition, the legislative history undergirding § 7 reveals an explicit congressional decision to require agencies to afford first priority to the declared national policy of saving endangered species. The pointed omission of the type of qualifying language previously included in endangered species legislation reveals a conscious decision by Congress to give endangered species priority over the "primary missions" of federal agencies.

It is not for us to speculate, much less act, on whether Congress would have altered its stance had the specific events of this case been anticipated. In any event, we discern no hint in the deliberations of Congress relating to the 1973 Act that would compel a different result than we reach here. Indeed, the repeated expressions of congressional concern over what it saw as the potentially enormous danger presented by the eradication of any endangered species suggest how the balance would have been struck had the issue been presented to Congress in 1973.

Furthermore, it is clear Congress foresaw that § 7 would, on occasion, require agencies to alter ongoing projects in order to fulfill the goals of the Act. Congressman Dingell's discussion of Air Force practice bombing, for instance, obviously pinpoints a particular activity — intimately related to the national defense — which a major federal department would be obliged to alter in deference to the strictures of § 7. A similar example is provided by the House Committee Report:

> "Under the authority of [§ 7], the Director of the Park Service would be required to *conform the practices of his agency* to the need for protecting the rapidly dwindling stock of grizzly bears within Yellowstone Park. These bears, which may be endangered, and are undeniably threatened, should at least be protected by supplying them with carcasses from excess elk within the park, *by curtailing the destruction of habitat by clearcutting National Forests surrounding the Park*, and by preventing hunting until their numbers have recovered sufficiently to withstand these pressures." H. R. Rep. No. 93-412, p. 14 (1973). (Emphasis added).

One might dispute the applicability of these examples to the Tellico Dam by saying that in this case the burden on the public through the loss of millions of unrecoverable dollars would greatly outweigh the loss of the snail darter. But neither the Endangered Species Act nor Art. III of the Constitution provides federal courts with authority to make such fine utilitarian calculations. On the contrary, the plain language of the Act, buttressed by its legislative history, shows clearly that Congress viewed the value of endangered species as "incalculable." Quite obviously, it would be difficult for a court to balance the loss of a sum certain — even $100 million — against a congressionally declared "incalculable" value, even assuming we had the power to engage in such a weighing process, which we emphatically do not.

In passing the Endangered Species Act of 1973, Congress was also aware of certain instances in which exceptions to the statute's broad sweep would be necessary. Thus, § 10, 16 U. S. C. § 1539 (1976 ed.), creates a number of limited "hardship exemptions," none of which would even remotely apply to the Tellico Project. In fact, there are no exemptions in the Endangered Species Act for federal agencies, meaning that under the maxim *expressio unius est exclusio alterius*, we must presume that these were the only "hardship cases" Congress intended to exempt. *Cf. National Railroad Passenger Corp. v. National Assn. of Railroad Passengers*, 414 U.S. 453, 458 (1974).

Notwithstanding Congress' expression of intent in 1973, we are urged to find that the continuing appropriations for Tellico Dam constitute an implied repeal of the 1973 Act, at least insofar as it applies to the Tellico Project. In support of this view, TVA points to the statements found in various House and Senate Appropriations Committees' Reports; as described in Part I, *supra*, those Reports generally reflected the attitude of the *Committees* either that the Act did not apply to Tellico or that the dam should be completed regardless of the provisions of the Act. Since we are unwilling to assume that these latter Committee statements constituted advice to ignore the provisions of a duly enacted law, we assume that these Committees believed that the Act simply was not applicable in this situation. But even under this interpretation of the Committees' actions, we are unable to conclude that the Act has been in any respect amended or repealed.

There is nothing in the appropriations measures, as passed, which states that the Tellico Project was to be completed irrespective of the requirements of the Endangered Species Act. These appropriations, in fact, represented relatively minor components of the lump-sum amounts for the entire TVA budget. To find a repeal of the Endangered Species Act under these circumstances would surely do violence to the "'cardinal rule . . . that repeals by implication are not favored.'" *Morton v. Mancari* , 417 U.S. 535, 549 (1974), quoting *Posadas v. National City Bank* , 296 U.S. 497, 503 (1936). In *Posadas* this Court held, in no uncertain terms, that "the intention of the legislature to repeal must be clear and manifest." *Ibid. See Georgia v. Pennsylvania R. Co.*, 324 U.S. 439, 456-457 (1945) ("Only a clear repugnancy between the old . . . and the new [law] results in the former giving way . . ."); *United States v. Borden Co.*, 308 U.S. 188, 198-199 (1939) ("[Intention] of the legislature to repeal 'must be clear and manifest.' . . . '[A] positive repugnancy [between the old and the new laws]'"); *Wood v. United States* , 16 Pet. 342, 363 (1842) ("[There] must be a positive repugnancy . . ."). In practical terms, this "cardinal rule" means that "[in] the absence of some affirmative showing of an intention to repeal, the only permissible justification for a repeal by implication is when the earlier and later statutes are irreconcilable." *Mancari, supra*, at 550. The doctrine disfavoring repeals by implication "applies with full vigor when . . . the subsequent legislation is an *appropriations* measure." *Committee for Nuclear Responsibility v. Seaborg* , 149 U. S. App. D. C. 380, 382, 463 F.2d 783, 785 (1971) (emphasis added); *Environmental Defense Fund v. Froehlke*, 473 F.2d 346, 355 (CA 8 1972). This is perhaps an understatement since it would be more accurate to say that the policy applies with even greater force when the claimed repeal rests solely on an Appropriations Act. We recognize that both substantive enactments and appropriations measures are "Acts of Congress," but the latter have the limited and specific purpose of providing funds for authorized programs. When voting on appropriations measures, legislators are entitled to operate under the assumption that the funds will be devoted to purposes which are lawful and not for any purpose forbidden. Without such an assurance, every appropriations measure would be pregnant with prospects of altering substantive legislation, repealing by implication any prior statute which might prohibit the expenditure. Not only would this lead to the absurd result of requiring Members to review exhaustively the background of every authorization before voting on an appropriation, but it would flout the very rules the Congress carefully adopted to avoid this need. House Rule XXI(2), for instance, specifically provides:

> "No appropriation shall be reported in any general appropriation bill, or be in order as an amendment thereto, for any expenditure not previously authorized by law, unless in continuation of appropriations for such public works as are already in progress. *Nor shall any provision in any such bill or amendment thereto changing existing law be in order.*" (Emphasis added.)

See also Standing Rules of the Senate, Rule 16.4. Thus, to sustain petitioner's position, we would be obliged to assume that Congress meant to repeal *pro tanto* § 7 of the Act by means of a procedure expressly prohibited under the rules of Congress.

Perhaps mindful of the fact that it is "swimming upstream" against a strong current of well-established precedent, TVA argues for an exception to the rule against implied repealers in a circumstance where, as here, Appropriations Committees have expressly stated their "understanding" that the earlier legislation would not prohibit the proposed expenditure. We cannot accept such a proposition. Expressions of committees dealing with requests for appropriations cannot be equated with statutes enacted by Congress, particularly not in the circumstances presented by this case. First, the Appropriations Committees had no jurisdiction over the subject of endangered species, much less did they conduct the type of extensive hearings which preceded passage of the earlier Endangered Species Acts, especially the 1973 Act. We venture to suggest that the House Committee on Merchant Marine and Fisheries and the Senate Committee on Commerce would be somewhat surprised to learn that their careful work on the substantive legislation had been undone by the simple — and brief — insertion of some inconsistent language in Appropriations Committees' Reports.

Second, there is no indication that Congress as a whole was aware of TVA's position, although the Appropriations Committees apparently agreed with petitioner's views. Only recently, in *SEC v. Sloan*, 436 U.S. 103 (1978), we declined to presume general congressional acquiescence in a 34-year-old practice of the Securities and Exchange Commission, despite the fact that the Senate Committee *having jurisdiction over the Commission's activities* had long expressed approval of the practice. Mr. Justice REHNQUIST, speaking for the Court, observed that we should be "extremely hesitant to presume general congressional awareness of the Commission's construction based only upon a few isolated statements in the thousands of pages of legislative documents." *Id.*, at 121. *A fortiori*, we should not assume that petitioner's views — and the Appropriations Committees' acceptance of them — were any better known, especially when the TVA is not the agency with primary responsibility for administering the Endangered Species Act. Quite apart from the foregoing factors, we would still be unable to find that in this case "the earlier and later statutes are irreconcilable," *Mancari*, 417 U.S., at 550; here it is entirely possible "to regard each as effective." *Id.*, at 551. The starting point in this analysis must be the legislative proceedings leading to the 1977 appropriations since the earlier funding of the dam occurred prior to the listing of the snail darter as an endangered species. In all successive years, TVA confidently reported to the Appropriations Committees that efforts to transplant the snail darter appeared to be successful; this surely gave those Committees some basis for the impression that there was no direct conflict between the Tellico Project and the Endangered Species Act. Indeed, the special appropriation for 1978 of $2 million for transplantation of endangered species supports the view that the Committees saw such relocation as the means whereby collision between Tellico and the Endangered Species Act could be avoided. It should also be noted that the Reports issued by the Senate and House Appropriations Committees in 1976 came within a month of the District Court's decision in this case, which hardly could have given the Members cause for concern over the possible applicability of the Act. This leaves only the 1978 appropriations, the Reports for which issued after the Court of Appeals' decision now before us. At that point very little remained to be accomplished on the project; the Committees understandably advised TVA to cooperate with the Department of the Interior "to relocate the endangered species to another suitable habitat so as to permit the project to proceed as rapidly as possible." H. R. Rep. No. 95-379, p. 11 (1977). It is true that the *Committees* repeated their earlier expressed "view" that the Act did not prevent completion of the Tellico Project. Considering these statements in context, however, it is evident that they " 'represent only the personal views of these legislators,' " and "however explicit, [they] cannot serve to change the legislative intent of Congress expressed before the Act's passage." *Regional Rail Reorganization Act Cases*, 419 U.S. 102, 132 (1974).

(B)

Having determined that there is an irreconcilable conflict between operation of the Tellico Dam and the explicit provisions of § 7 of the Endangered Species Act,we must now consider what remedy, if any, is appropriate. It is correct, of course, that a federal judge sitting as a chancellor is not mechanically obligated to grant an injunction for every violation of law. This Court made plain in *Hecht Co. v. Bowles*, 321 U.S. 321, 329 (1944), that "[a] grant of *jurisdiction* to issue compliance orders hardly suggests an absolute duty to do so under any and all circumstances." As a general matter it may be said that "[since] all or almost all equitable remedies are discretionary, the balancing of equities and hardships is appropriate in almost any case as a guide to the chancellor's discretion." D. Dobbs, Remedies 52 (1973). Thus, in *Hecht Co.* the Court refused to grant an injunction when it appeared from the District Court findings that "the issuance of an injunction would have 'no effect by way of insuring better compliance in the future' and would [have been] 'unjust' to [the] petitioner and not 'in the public interest.'" 321 U.S., at 326.

But these principles take a court only so far. Our system of government is, after all, a tripartite one, with each branch having certain defined functions delegated to it by the Constitution. While "[it] is emphatically the province and duty of the judicial department to say what the law is," *Marbury v. Madison*, 1 Cranch 137, 177 (1803), it is equally — and emphatically — the exclusive province of the Congress not only to formulate legislative policies and mandate programs and projects, but also to establish their relative priority for the Nation. Once Congress, exercising its delegated powers, has decided the order of priorities in a given area, it is for the Executive to administer the laws and for the courts to enforce them when enforcement is sought.

Here we are urged to view the Endangered Species Act "reasonably," and hence shape a remedy "that accords with some modicum of common sense and the public weal." Post, at 196. But is that our function? We have no expert knowledge on the subject of endangered species, much less do we have a mandate from the people to strike a balance of equities on the side of the Tellico Dam. Congress has spoken in the plainest of words, making it abundantly clear that the balance has been struck in favor of affording endangered species the highest of priorities, thereby adopting a policy which it described as "institutionalized caution."

Our individual appraisal of the wisdom or unwisdom of a particular course consciously selected by the Congress is to be put aside in the process of interpreting a statute. Once the meaning of an enactment is discerned and its constitutionality determined, the judicial process comes to an end. We do not sit as a committee of review, nor are we vested with the power of veto. The lines ascribed to Sir Thomas More by Robert Bolt are not without relevance here:

> "The law, Roper, the law. I know what's legal, not what's right. And I'll stick to what's legal . . . . I'm not God. The currents and eddies of right and wrong, which you find such plain-sailing, I can't navigate, I'm no voyager. But in the thickets of the law, oh there I'm a forester . . . . What would you do? Cut a great road through the law to get after the Devil? . . . And when the last law was down, and the Devil turned round on you — where would you hide, Roper, the laws all being flat? . . . This country's planted thick with laws from coast to coast — Man's laws, not God's — and if you cut them down . . . d'you really think you could stand upright in the winds that would blow then? . . . Yes, I'd give the Devil benefit of law, for my own safety's sake." R. Bolt, A Man for All Seasons, Act I, p. 147 (Three Plays, Heinemann ed. 1967).

We agree with the Court of Appeals that in our constitutional system the commitment to the separation of powers is too fundamental for us to pre-empt congressional action by judicially decreeing what accords with "common sense and the public weal." Our Constitution vests such responsibilities in the political branches.

Affirmed.

Mr. Justice POWELL, with whom Mr. Justice BLACKMUN joins, dissenting.

The Court today holds that § 7 of the Endangered Species Actrequires a federal court, for the purpose of protecting an endangered species or its habitat, to enjoin permanently the operation of any federal project, whether completed or substantially completed. This decision casts a long shadow over the operation of even the most important projects, serving vital needs of society and national defense, whenever it is determined that continued operation would threaten extinction of an endangered species or its habitat. This result is said to be required by the "plain intent of Congress" as well as by the language of the statute.

In my view § 7 cannot reasonably be interpreted as applying to a project that is completed or substantially completed when its threat to an endangered species is discovered. Nor can I believe that Congress could have intended this Act to produce the "absurd result" — in the words of the District Court — of this case. If it were clear from the language of the Act and its legislative history that Congress intended to authorize this result, this Court would be compelled to enforce it. It is not our province to rectify policy or political judgments by the Legislative Branch, however egregiously they may disserve the public interest. But where the statutory language and legislative history, as in this case, need not be construed to reach such a result, I view it as the duty of this Court to adopt a permissible construction that accords with some modicum of common sense and the public weal. . . .

Mr. Justice REHNQUIST, dissenting.

In the light of my Brother POWELL's dissenting opinion, I am far less convinced than is the Court that the Endangered Species Act of 1973, 16 U. S. C. § 1531 *et seq.* (1976 ed.), was intended to prohibit the completion of the Tellico Dam. But the very difficulty and doubtfulness of the correct answer to this legal question convinces me that the Act did *not* prohibit the District Court from refusing, in the exercise of its traditional equitable powers, to enjoin petitioner from completing the Dam. Section 11(g)(1) of the Act, 16 U. S. C. § 1540(g)(1) (1976 ed.), merely provides that "any person may commence a civil suit on his own behalf . . . to enjoin any person, including the United States and any other governmental instrumentality or agency . . . , who is alleged to be in violation of any provision of this chapter." It also grants the district courts "jurisdiction, without regard to the amount in controversy or the citizenship of the parties, to enforce any such provision."

. . . .

PALILA v. HAWAII DEPARTMENT OF LAND AND NATURAL RESOURCES

United States Court of Appeals, Ninth Circuit (1988)
852 F.2d 1106, 18 ELR 21199

Before O'SCANNLAIN, SCHROEDER, and NOONAN, Jr, Circuit Judges.

O'SCANNLAIN, Circuit Judge:

This is the fourth round of judicial activity involving a six-inch long finch-billed bird called palila, found only on the slopes of Mauna Kea on the Island of Hawaii.

As an endangered species under the Endangered Species Act ("Act"), 16 U.S.C. §§ 1531–43 (1982), the bird (*Loxioides bailleui*), a member of the Hawaiian honeycreeper family, also has legal status and wings its way into federal court as a plaintiff in its own right. The Palila (which has earned the right to be capitalized since it is a party to this proceeding) is represented by attorneys for the Sierra Club, Audubon Society, and other environmental parties who obtained an order directing the Hawaii Department of Land and Natural Resources ("Department") to remove mouflon sheep from its critical habitat. Sports hunters, represented by the Hawaii Rifle Association, among others, had intervened to dispute the contention that the Palila was "harmed" by the presence of mouflon sheep. Hence, these appeals. But, first, some history.

FACTS AND PROCEEDINGS

In 1978 the Sierra Club and others brought an action under the Act on behalf of the Palila, claiming that the Department's practice of maintaining feral goats and sheep (animals that originally were domesticated but were allowed to run wild) in the Palila's critical habitat constituted an unlawful "taking" under the Act. The district court agreed and ordered the Department to remove the animals because it found that the goats and sheep destroyed the mamane-naio woodlands upon which the Palila depend. *Palila v. Hawaii Dept. of Land & Natural Resources* ("*Palila I*"), 471 F. Supp. 985 (D. Haw. 1979). This court affirmed. *Palila v. Hawaii Dept. Land & Natural Resources* ("*Palila II*") 639 F.2d 495 (9th Cir. 1981).

In 1984 the Sierra Club reopened the 1978 proceeding by moving to amend its original complaint to add mouflon sheep as destructive animals to be removed from the Palila's habitat. The mouflon sheep had been introduced by the Department between 1962 and 1966 for the enjoyment of sport hunters. Apparently, they had not been the target of the original complaint because research into their effect upon the Palila's habitat had not been completed. The mouflon sheep, like the feral sheep and goats before them, feed on the mamane trees.

In November 1986 the district court ruled in favor of the Sierra Club. *Palila v. Hawaii Dept. of Land & Natural Resources* (*"Palila III"*), 649 F. Supp. 1070 (D. Haw. 1986). It found that presence of mouflon sheep "harmed" the Palila within the meaning of 50 C.F.R. § 17.3's definition of "harm" in two ways: (1) the eating habits of the sheep destroyed the mamane woodland and thus caused habitat degradation that could result in extinction; (2) were the mouflon to continue eating the mamane, the woodland would not regenerate and the Palila population would not recover to a point where it could be removed from the Endangered Species list.

The Department and intervenors filed timely appeals. We granted the United States *amicus curiae* status to represent the view of the Secretary that Judge King's order should be affirmed, but for reasons different than those stated in his opinion.

DISCUSSION

I

The Department argues that the district court construed the definition of "harm" in 50 C.F.R. § 17.3too broadly. The scope of the definition of harm is important because it in part sets the limit on what acts or omissions violate the Act's prohibition against "taking" an endangered species.

In making this argument, the Department suggests dichotomy between "actual" and "potential" harm. The Department believes that actual harm only includes those acts which result in the immediate destruction of the Palila's food sources; all other acts are "potential" harm no matter how clear the causal link and beyond the reach of the Act. Thus, the Department challenges the district court's finding that habitat destruction which could drive the Palila to extinction constitutes "harm."

We inquire whether the district court's interpretation is consistent with the Secretary's construction of the statute since he is charged with enforcing the Act, and entitled to deference if his regulation is reasonable and not in conflict with the intent of Congress.

While promulgating a revised definition of harm, the Secretary noted that harm includes not only direct physical injury, but also injury caused by impairment of essential behavior patterns via habitat modification that can have significant and permanent effects on a listed species. 46 Fed. Reg. 54748, 54750 (1981) (codified at 50 C.F.R. § 17.3). Moreover, in that same promulgation notice, the Secretary let stand the district court's construction of harm in *Palila I* . *Id.* at 54749-50. In *Palila I* , the district court construed harm to include habitat destruction that could result in the extinction of the Palila — exactly the same type of injury at issue here. *See generally Palila I* , 471 F. Supp. at 985. We conclude that the district court's inclusion within the definition of "harm" of habitat destruction that could drive the Palila to extinction falls within the Secretary's interpretation.

The Secretary's inclusion of habitat destruction that could result in extinction follows the plain language of the statute because it serves the overall purpose of the Act, which is "to provide a means whereby the ecosystems upon which endangered species and threatened species depend may be conserved...." 16 U.S.C. § 1531(b). The definition serves the overall purpose of the Act since it conserves the Palila's threatened ecosystem (the mamane-naio woodland).

The Secretary's construction of harm is also consistent with the policy of Congress evidenced by the legislative history. For example, in the Senate Report on the Act: " 'Take' is defined in . . . the broadest possible manner to include every conceivable way in which a person can 'take' or attempt to 'take' any fish or wildlife." S. Rep. No. 307, 93d Cong., 1st Sess. (1973), reprinted in 1973 U.S. Code Cong. & Admin. News 2989, 2995. The House Report said that the "harassment" form of taking would "allow, for example, the Secretary to regulate or prohibit the activities of birdwatchers where the effect of those activities might disturb the birds and make it difficult for them to hatch or raise their young." H.R. Rep. No. 412, 93d Cong., 1st Sess. (1973), reprinted in 4 House Miscellaneous Reports on Public Bills, 93d Cong., 1st Sess. 11 (1973). If the "harassment" form of taking includes activities so remote from actual injury to the bird as birdwatching, then the "harm" form of taking should include more direct activities, such as the mouflon sheep preventing any mamane from growing to maturity.

II

The Department contends that the district court erred when it found an unlawful "taking" within the meaning of section 9 of the Act. (Section 9—codified as 16 U.S.C. § 1538—lists the conduct prohibited by the Act). The Department argues that no taking exists because the evidence shows that (1) a huntable number of sheep (a flock large enough to sustain sports hunting) could co-exist with the Palila; and (2) the Palila are doing poorly because of the recently removed feral sheep and goats, not the mouflon sheep. Our review is for clear error. *Oregon Envtl. Council v. Kunzman*, 817 F.2d 484, 493 (9th Cir. 1987).

A. Co-existence

The Department's witnesses conceded that a large number of mouflon sheep in one area could significantly damage the mamane-naio woodlands and thereby drive the Palila to extinction. However, these witnesses maintained that a huntable number of mouflon sheep could co-exist with the Palila. In support of its co-existence thesis, the Department makes four arguments. First, since the removal of the feral sheep and goats, the mamane-naio woodland has regenerated. This regeneration will support both the mouflon sheep and the Palila. Second, the Department has begun a number of regeneration projects (replanting, fertilizing, etc.). Third, the mouflon sheep would not cause significant degradation if the Department controlled their density. Fourth, the population of the Palila has increased since January 1985.

The Sierra Club's witnesses controverted the Department's thesis of co-existence. First, although regeneration (new mamane seedlings and sprouts) has occurred in many areas, it takes twenty-five years for the mamane seedlings and sprouts to become mature trees capable of providing food and shelter for the Palila. However, for the first ten to fifteen years of this growth period, the mouflon sheep can kill the mamane trees and no significant regeneration would occur, at least not sufficient to sustain the Palila unless the trees survive to twenty-five years of age. Second, the Sierra Club's witnesses showed that the Department's additional programs as an alternative to removal of the mouflon sheep would not work. Third, they disagreed with the premise that the mouflon sheep population could co-exist with the Palila if the Department controlled their density. Fourth, the Sierra Club witnesses stated that the Palila's population, despite short-term fluctuations, has been static over the long term.

The Sierra Club witnesses put forth their own thesis: Because the grazing and browsing habits of the mouflon sheep destroy the mamane woodland upon which the Palila depend entirely for their existence, the sheep must be removed. This thesis received the support of one of the state's witnesses. This witness conceded that he believes that the mouflon sheep must be removed to ensure the survival of the Palila.

The Sierra Club's witnesses are not contradicted by the documentary evidence (*i.e.*, studies of the Palila, mouflon sheep, etc.), and the Sierra Club witnesses advanced a coherent and plausible thesis. On the issue of coexistence, then, the district court's decision to accept the Sierra Club's witnesses' testimony as more credible cannot be clearly erroneous.

B. Feral Sheep and Goats Versus Mouflon Sheep

The Department's witnesses asserted that there had been significant regeneration wherever the feral animals had been removed. The Sierra Club's witnesses agreed, but they went on to argue that where mouflon sheep have appeared, no significant regeneration has occurred.

On the question of which animals — the feral sheep and goats or the mouflon — damage the mamane, the district court again gave more credibility to the Sierra Club's witnesses; this preference cannot be clearly erroneous where the Sierra Club's witnesses were not contradicted by documentary evidence. Indeed, the testimony given by the Sierra Club witnesses — noticeable regeneration has occurred only where the feral animals have been removed and no mouflon sheep have appeared — is both plausible and consistent.

We affirm the district court's finding that the Department's permitting mouflon sheep in the area constitutes a "taking" of the Palila's habitat. The district court made its findings based on the testimony of the Sierra Club witnesses, which was not contradicted by extrinsic evidence. Therefore, the district court's findings should not be held clearly erroneous. *See Anderson v. City of Bessemer City* , N.C., 470 U.S. 564, 575, 84 L. Ed. 2d 518, 105 S. Ct. 1504 (1985) ("When a trial judge's finding is based on his decision to credit the testimony of one of two or more witnesses, each of whom has told a coherent and facially plausible story that is not contradicted by extrinsic evidence, that finding, if not internally inconsistent, can virtually never be clear error").

III

Under this resolution of the appeal, we do not reach the issue of whether harm includes habitat degradation that merely retards recovery. The district court's (and the Secretary's) interpretation of harm as including habitat destruction that could result in extinction, and findings to that effect are enough to sustain an order for the removal of the mouflon sheep.

CONCLUSION

The district court's finding of habitat degradation that could result in extinction constitutes "harm." The district court's finding of a "taking" was not clearly erroneous. We do not reach the issue of whether the district court properly found that harm included habitat degradation that prevents recovery of an endangered species.

AFFIRMED.

NORTHERN SPOTTED OWL v. HODEL

United States District Court, Western District of Washington (1988)
716 F. Supp. 479

ZILLY, District Judge.

A number of environmental organizations bring this action against the United States Fish & Wildlife Service ("Service") and others, alleging that the Service's decision not to list the northern spotted owl as endangered or threatened under the Endangered Species Act of 1973, as amended, 16 U.S.C. § 1531 *et seq.* ("ESA" or "the Act"), was arbitrary and capricious or contrary to law.

Since the 1970s the northern spotted owl has received much scientific attention, beginning with comprehensive studies of its natural history by Dr. Eric Forsman, whose most significant discovery was the close association between spotted owls and old-growth forests. This discovery raised concerns because the majority of remaining old-growth owl habitat is on public land available for harvest.

In January 1987, plaintiff Greenworld, pursuant to Sec. 4(b)(3) of the ESA, 16 U.S.C. § 1533(b)(3), petitioned the Service to list the northern spotted owl as endangered. In August 1987, 29 conservation organizations filed a second petition to list the owl as endangered both in the Olympic Peninsula in Washington and in the Oregon Coast Range, and as threatened throughout the rest of its range.

The ESA directs the Secretary of the Interior to determine whether any species have become endangered or threatened due to habitat destruction, overutilization, disease or predation, or other natural or manmade factors. 16 U.S.C. § 1533(a)(1). The Act was amended in 1982 to ensure that the decision whether to list a species as endangered or threatened was based solely on an evaluation of the biological risks faced by the species, to the exclusion of all other factors. *See* Conf. Report 97-835, 97th Cong. 2d Sess. (Sept. 17, 1982) at 19, reprinted in 1982 U.S. Code Cong. & Admin. News 2860.

The Service's role in deciding whether to list the northern spotted owl as endangered or threatened is to assess the technical and scientific data in the administrative record against the relevant listing criteria in section 4(a)(1) and then to exercise its own expert discretion in reaching its decision. *Cayman Turtle Farm, Ltd. v. Andrus*, 478 F. Supp. 125, 131 (D.C. Cir. 1979).

In July 1987, the Service announced that it would initiate a status review of the spotted owl and requested public comment. 52 Fed. Reg. 34396 (Sept. 11, 1987). The Service assembled a group of Service biologists, including Dr. Mark Shaffer, its staff expert on population viability, to conduct the review The Service charged Dr. Shaffer with analyzing current scientific information on the owl. Dr. Shaffer concluded that:

> the most reasonable interpretation of current data and knowledge indicate continued old growth harvesting is likely to lead to the extinction of the subspecies in the foreseeable future which argues strongly for listing the subspecies as threatened or endangered at this time.

M. Shaffer, letter of November 11, 1987, to Jay Gore, U.S. Fish and Wildlife Service, Region 1, Endangered Species, attached to *Final Assessment of Population Viability Projections for the Northern Spotted Owl* [Administrative Record at III.A.1].

The Service invited a peer review of Dr. Shaffer's analysis by a number of U.S. experts on population viability, all of whom agreed with Dr. Shaffer's prognosis for the owl, although each had some criticisms of his work.

The Service's decision is contained in its 1987 Status Review of the owl ("Status Review") [Administrative Record at II.C] and summarized in its Finding on Greenworld's petition ("Finding") [Administrative Record at I.D.1]. The Status Review was completed on December 14, 1987, and on December 17 the Service announced that listing the owl as endangered under the Act was not warranted at that time.[6] 52 Fed. Reg. 48552, 48554 (Dec. 23, 1987). This suit followed. . . .

. . . .

. . . Agency action is arbitrary and capricious where the agency has failed to "articulate a satisfactory explanation for its action including a 'rational connection between the facts found and the choice made.'" *Motor Vehicle Mfrs. Ass'n v. State Farm Mut. Auto Ins.*, 463 U.S. 29, 43, 77 L. Ed. 2d 443, 103 S. Ct. 2856 (1983) (citations omitted).

The Status Review and the Finding to the listing petition offer little insight into how the Service found that the owl currently has a viable population. Although the Status Review cites extensive empirical data and lists various conclusions, it fails to provide any analysis. The Service asserts that it is entitled to make its own decision, yet it provides no explanation for its

[6] The Service's Finding provides as follows:

> A finding is made that a proposed listing of the northern spotted owl is not warranted at this time. Due to the need for population trend information and other biological data, priority given by the Service to this species for further research and monitoring will continue to be high. Interagency agreements and Service initiatives support continued conservation efforts. This finding will be published in the Federal Register and the petitioner will be notified.

Finding at 5 [Administrative Record at I.D.1].

findings. An agency must set forth clearly the grounds on which it acted. *Atchison T. & S.F. Ry. v. Wichita Bd. of Trade*, 412 U.S. 800, 807, 37 L. Ed. 2d 350, 93 S. Ct. 2367 (1973). Judicial deference to agency expertise is proper, but the Court will not do so blindly. The Court finds that the Service has not set forth the grounds for its decision against listing the owl.

The Service's documents also lack any expert analysis supporting its conclusion. Rather, the expert opinion is entirely to the contrary. The only reference in the Status Review to an actual opinion that the owl does not face a significant likelihood of extinction is a mischaracterization of a conclusion of Dr. Mark Boyce:

> Boyce (1987) in his analysis of the draft preferred alternative concluded that there is a low probability that the spotted owls will go extinct. He does point out that population fragmentation appears to impose the greatest risks to extinction.

Status Review at 24 (footnote added). Dr. Boyce responded to the Service:

> I did not conclude that the Spotted Owl enjoys a low probability of extinction, and I would be very disappointed if efforts to preserve the Spotted Owl were in any way thwarted by a misinterpretation of something I wrote.

M. Boyce, letter of February 18, 1988, to Rolf Wallenstrom, U.S. Fish and Wildlife Service, Region 1, exhibit 7 to Complaint.

Numerous other experts on population viability contributed to or reviewed drafts of the Status Review, or otherwise assessed spotted owl viability. Some were employed by the Service; others were independent. None concluded that the northern spotted owl is not at risk of extinction. For example, as noted above, Dr. Shaffer evaluated the current data and knowledge and determined that continued logging of old growth likely would lead to the extinction of the owl in the foreseeable future. This risk, he concluded, argued strongly for immediate listing of the subspecies as threatened or endangered. M. Shaffer, *Final Assessment of Population Viability Projections for the Northern Spotted Owl*, Memorandum to Jay Gore, U.S. Fish and Wildlife Service, Region 1, Endangered Species (November 11, 1987) [Administrative Record at III.A.1].

The Service invited a peer review of Dr. Shaffer's analysis. Drs. Michael Soule, Bruce Wilcox, and Daniel Goodman, three leading U.S. experts on population viability, reviewed and agreed completely with Dr. Shaffer's prognosis for the owl.

For example, Dr. Soule, the acknowledged founder of the discipline of "conservation biology" (the study of species extinction), concluded:

> I completely concur with your conclusions, and the methods by which you reached them. The more one hears about *Strix occidentalis caurina*, the more concern one feels. Problems with the data base and in the models notwithstanding, and politics notwithstanding, I just can't see how a responsible biologist could reach any other conclusion than yours.

M. Soule, letter of November 1, 1987, to Dr. Mark Shaffer [Administrative Record at III.B.4].

The Court will reject conclusory assertions of agency "expertise" where the agency spurns unrebutted expert opinions without itself offering a credible alternative explanation. *See, e.g., American Tunaboat Ass'n v. Baldrige* , 738 F.2d 1013, 1016 (9th Cir. 1984). Here, the Service disregarded all the expert opinion on population viability, including that of its own expert, that the owl is facing extinction, and instead merely asserted its expertise in support of its conclusions.

The Service has failed to provide its own or other expert analysis supporting its conclusions. Such analysis is necessary to establish a rational connection between the evidence presented and the Service's decision. Accordingly, the United States Fish and Wildlife Service's decision not to list at this time the northern spotted owl as endangered or threatened under the Endangered Species Act was arbitrary and capricious and contrary to law.

The Court further finds that it is not possible from the record to determine that the Service considered the related issue of whether the northern spotted owl is a threatened species. This failure of the Service to review and make an express finding on the issue of threatened status is also arbitrary and capricious and contrary to law.

In deference to the Service's expertise and its role under the Endangered Species Act, the Court remands this matter to the Service, which has 90 days from the date of this order to provide an analysis for its decision that listing the northern spotted owl as threatened or endangered is not currently warranted. Further, the Service is ordered to supplement its Status Review and petition Finding consistent with this Court's ruling.

IT IS SO ORDERED.

BABBITT v. SWEET HOME CHAPTER OF COMMUNITIES FOR A GREAT OREGON

United States Supreme Court (1995)
515 U.S. 687, 115 S. Ct. 2407, 132 L. Ed. 2d 597

STEVENS, J., delivered the opinion of the Court, in which O'CONNOR, KENNEDY, SOUTER, GINSBURG, and BREYER, JJ., joined. O'CONNOR, J., filed a concurring opinion. SCALIA, J., filed a dissenting opinion, in which REHNQUIST, C. J., and THOMAS, J., joined.

The Endangered Species Act of 1973 (ESA or Act), 87 Stat. 884, 16 U.S.C. § 1531(1988 ed. and Supp. V), contains a variety of protections designed to save from extinction species that the Secretary of the Interior designates as endangered or threatened. Section 9 of the Act makes it unlawful for any person to "take" any endangered or threatened species. The Secretary has promulgated a regulation that defines the statute's prohibition on takings to include "significant habitat modification or degradation where it actually kills or injures wildlife." This case presents the question whether the Secretary exceeded his authority under the Act by promulgating that regulation.

I

Section 9(a)(1) of the Act provides the following protection for endangered species:

> "Except as provided in sections 1535(g)(2) and 1539 of this title, with respect to any endangered species of fish or wildlife listed pursuant to section 1533 of this title it is unlawful for any person subject to the jurisdiction of the United States to—
>
> . . . .
>
> "(B) take any such species within the United States or the territorial sea of the United States." 16 U.S.C. § 1538(a)(1).

Section 3(19) of the Act defines the statutory term "take":

> "The term 'take' means to harass, harm, pursue, hunt, shoot, wound, kill, trap, capture, or collect, or to attempt to engage in any such conduct." 16 U.S.C. § 1532(19).

The Act does not further define the terms it uses to define "take." The Interior Department regulations that implement the statute, however, define the statutory term "harm":

> "*Harm* in the definition of 'take' in the Act means an act which actually kills or injures wildlife. Such act may include significant habitat modification or degradation where it actually kills or injures wildlife by significantly impairing essential behavioral patterns, including breeding, feeding, or sheltering." 50 CFR § 17.3(1994).

This regulation has been in place since 1975.

A limitation on the § 9 "take" prohibition appears in § 10(a)(1)(B) of the Act, which Congress added by amendment in 1982. That section authorizes the Secretary to grant a permit for any taking otherwise prohibited by § 9(a)(1)(B) "if such taking is incidental to, and not the purpose of, the carrying out of an otherwise lawful activity." 16 U.S.C. § 1539(a)(1)(B).

In addition to the prohibition on takings, the Act provides several other protections for endangered species. Section 4, 16 U.S.C. § 1533, commands the Secretary to identify species of fish or wildlife that are in danger of extinction and to publish from time to time lists of all species he determines to be endangered or threatened. Section 5, 16 U.S.C. § 1534, authorizes the Secretary, in cooperation with the States, *see* § 1535, to acquire land to aid in preserving such species. Section 7 requires federal agencies to ensure that none of their activities, including the granting of licenses and permits, will jeopardize the continued existence of endangered species "or result in the destruction or adverse modification of habitat of such species which is determined by the Secretary . . . to be critical." 16 U.S.C. § 1536(a)(2).

Respondents in this action are small landowners, logging companies, and families dependent on the forest products industries in the Pacific Northwest and in the Southeast, and organizations that represent their interests. They brought this declaratory judgment action against petitioners, the Secretary of the Interior and the Director of the Fish and Wildlife Service, in the United States District Court for the District of Columbia to challenge the statutory validity of the Secretary's regulation defining "harm," particularly the inclusion of habitat modification and degradation in the definition. Respondents challenged the regulation on its face. Their complaint alleged that application of the "harm" regulation to the red-cockaded woodpecker, an endangered species, and the northern spotted owl, a threatened species, had injured them economically. App. 17-23.

Respondents advanced three arguments to support their submission that Congress did not intend the word "take" in § 9 to include habitat modification, as the Secretary's "harm" regulation provides. First, they correctly noted that language in the Senate's original version of the ESA would have defined "take" to include "destruction, modification, or curtailment of [the] habitat or range" of fish or wildlife, but the Senate deleted that language from the bill before enacting it. Second, respondents argued that Congress intended the Act's express authorization for the Federal Government to buy private land in order to prevent habitat degradation in § 5 to be the exclusive check against habitat modification on private property. Third, because the Senate added the term "harm" to the definition of "take" in a floor amendment without debate, respondents argued that the court should not interpret the term so expansively as to include habitat modification.

The District Court considered and rejected each of respondents' arguments, finding "that Congress intended an expansive interpretation of the word 'take,' an interpretation that encompasses habitat modification." 806 F. Supp. 279, 285 (1992). The court noted that in 1982, when Congress was aware of a judicial decision that had applied the Secretary's regulation, *see Palila v. Hawaii Dept. of Land and Natural Resources*, 639 F.2d 495 (CA9 1981) (*Palila I*), it amended the Act without using the opportunity to change the definition of "take." 806 F. Supp. at 284. The court stated that, even had it found the ESA " 'silent or ambiguous' " as to the authority for the Secretary's definition of "harm," it would nevertheless have upheld the regulation as a reasonable interpretation of the statute. *Id.*, at 285 (quoting *Chevron U.S.A. Inc. v. Natural Resources Defense Council, Inc.*, 467 U.S. 837, 843, 81 L. Ed. 2d 694, 104 S. Ct. 2778 (1984)). The District Court therefore entered summary judgment for petitioners and dismissed respondents' complaint.

A divided panel of the Court of Appeals initially affirmed the judgment of the District Court. 303 U.S. App. D.C. 42, 1 F.3d 1 (CADC 1993). After granting a petition for rehearing, however, the panel reversed. 305 U.S. App. D.C. 110, 17 F.3d 1463 (CADC 1994). Although acknowledging that "the potential breadth of the word 'harm' is indisputable," *Id.*, at 1464, the majority concluded that the immediate statutory context in which "harm" appeared counseled against a broad reading; like the other words in the definition of "take," the word "harm" should be read as applying only to "the perpetrator's direct application of force against the animal taken . . . . The forbidden acts fit, in ordinary language, the basic model 'A hit B.' " *Id.*, at 1465. The majority based its reasoning on a canon of statutory construction called *noscitur a sociis*, which holds that a word is known by the company it keeps. *See Neal v. Clark*, 95 U.S. 704, 708-709, 24 L. Ed. 586 (1878).

The majority claimed support for its construction from a decision of the Ninth Circuit that narrowly construed the word "harass" in the Marine

Mammal Protection Act of 1972, 16 U.S.C. § 1372(a)(2)(A), *see United States v. Hayashi* , 5 F.3d 1278, 1282 (1993); from the legislative history of the ESA; from its view that Congress must not have intended the purportedly broad curtailment of private property rights that the Secretary's interpretation permitted; and from the ESA's land acquisition provision in § 5 and restriction on federal agencies' activities regarding habitat in § 7, both of which the court saw as evidence that Congress had not intended the § 9 "take" prohibition to reach habitat modification. Most prominently, the court performed a lengthy analysis of the 1982 amendment to § 10 that provided for "incidental take permits" and concluded that the amendment did not change the meaning of the term "take" as defined in the 1973 statute.

Chief Judge Mikva, who had announced the panel's original decision, dissented. *See* 17 F.3d at 1473. In his view, a proper application of *Chevron* indicated that the Secretary had reasonably defined "harm," because respondents had failed to show that Congress unambiguously manifested its intent to exclude habitat modification from the ambit of "take." Chief Judge Mikva found the majority's reliance on *noscitur a sociis* inappropriate in light of the statutory language and unnecessary in light of the strong support in the legislative history for the Secretary's interpretation. He did not find the 1982 "incidental take permit" amendment alone sufficient to vindicate the Secretary's definition of "harm," but he believed the amendment provided additional support for that definition because it reflected Congress' view in 1982 that the definition was reasonable.

The Court of Appeals' decision created a square conflict with a 1988 decision of the Ninth Circuit that had upheld the Secretary's definition of "harm." *See Palila v. Hawaii Dept. of Land and Natural Resources* , 852 F.2d 1106 (1988) (*Palila II*). The Court of Appeals neither cited nor distinguished Palila II, despite the stark contrast between the Ninth Circuit's holding and its own. We granted certiorari to resolve the conflict. 513 U.S. 1072 (1995). Our consideration of the text and structure of the Act, its legislative history, and the significance of the 1982 amendment persuades us that the Court of Appeals' judgment should be reversed.

II

Because this case was decided on motions for summary judgment, we may appropriately make certain factual assumptions in order to frame the legal issue. First, we assume respondents have no desire to harm either the red-cockaded woodpecker or the spotted owl; they merely wish to continue logging activities that would be entirely proper if not prohibited by the ESA. On the other hand, we must assume, *arguendo*, that those activities will have the effect, even though unintended, of detrimentally changing the natural habitat of both listed species and that, as a consequence, members of those species will be killed or injured. Under respondents' view of the law, the Secretary's only means of forestalling that grave result—even when the actor knows it is certain to occur — is to use his § 5 authority to purchase the lands on which the survival of the species depends. The Secretary, on the other hand, submits that the § 9 prohibition on takings, which Congress defined to include "harm," places on respondents a duty to avoid harm that habitat alteration will cause the birds unless respondents first obtain a permit pursuant to § 10.

The text of the Act provides three reasons for concluding that the Secretary's interpretation is reasonable. First, an ordinary understanding of the word "harm" supports it. The dictionary definition of the verb form of "harm" is "to cause hurt or damage to: injure." Webster's Third New International Dictionary 1034 (1966). In the context of the ESA, that definition naturally encompasses habitat modification that results in actual injury or death to members of an endangered or threatened species.

Respondents argue that the Secretary should have limited the purview of "harm" to direct applications of force against protected species, but the dictionary definition does not include the word "directly" or suggest in any way that only direct or willful action that leads to injury constitutes "harm." Moreover, unless the statutory term "harm" encompasses indirect as well as direct injuries, the word has no meaning that does not duplicate the meaning of other words that § 3 uses to define "take." A reluctance to treat statutory terms as surplusage supports the reasonableness of the Secretary's interpretation. *See, e. g., Mackey v. Lanier Collection Agency & Service, Inc.*, 486 U.S. 825, 837, and n. 11, 100 L. Ed. 2d 836, 108 S. Ct. 2182 (1988).

Second, the broad purpose of the ESA supports the Secretary's decision to extend protection against activities that cause the precise harms Congress enacted the statute to avoid. In *TVA v. Hill*, 437 U.S. 153, 98 S. Ct. 2279, 57 L. Ed. 2d 117 (1978), we described the Act as "the most comprehensive legislation for the preservation of endangered species ever enacted by any nation." *Id.*, at 180. Whereas predecessor statutes enacted in 1966 and 1969 had not contained any sweeping prohibition against the taking of endangered species except on federal lands, *see id.*, at 175, the 1973 Act applied to all land in the United States and to the Nation's territorial seas. As stated in § 2 of the Act, among its central purposes is "to provide a means whereby the ecosystems upon which endangered species and threatened species depend may be conserved . . . ." 16 U.S.C. § 1531(b).

In *Hill*, we construed § 7 as precluding the completion of the Tellico Dam because of its predicted impact on the survival of the snail darter. *See* 437 U.S. at 193. Both our holding and the language in our opinion stressed the importance of the statutory policy. "The plain intent of Congress in enacting this statute," we recognized, "was to halt and reverse the trend toward species extinction, whatever the cost. This is reflected not only in the stated policies of the Act, but in literally every section of the statute." *Id.*, at 184. Although the § 9 "take" prohibition was not at issue in *Hill*, we took note of that prohibition, placing particular emphasis on the Secretary's inclusion of habitat modification in his definition of "harm." In light of that provision for habitat protection, we could "not understand how TVA intends to operate Tellico Dam without 'harming' the snail darter." *Id.*, at 184, n. 30. Congress' intent to provide comprehensive protection for endangered and threatened species supports the permissibility of the Secretary's "harm" regulation.

Respondents advance strong arguments that activities that cause minimal or unforeseeable harm will not violate the Act as construed in the "harm" regulation. Respondents, however, present a facial challenge to the regulation.

Cf. Anderson v. Edwards, 514 U.S. 143, 155-156, n. 6, 131 L. Ed. 2d 178, 115 S. Ct. 1291 (1995); *INS v. National Center for Immigrants' Rights, Inc.*, 502 U.S. 183, 188, 116 L. Ed. 2d 546, 112 S. Ct. 551 (1991). Thus, they ask us to invalidate the Secretary's understanding of "harm" in every circumstance, even when an actor knows that an activity, such as draining a pond, would actually result in the extinction of a listed species by destroying its habitat. Given Congress' clear expression of the ESA's broad purpose to protect endangered and threatened wildlife, the Secretary's definition of "harm" is reasonable.

Third, the fact that Congress in 1982 authorized the Secretary to issue permits for takings that § 9(a)(1)(B) would otherwise prohibit, "if such taking is incidental to, and not the purpose of, the carrying out of an otherwise lawful activity," 16 U.S.C. § 1539(a)(1)(B), strongly suggests that Congress understood § 9(a)(1)(B) to prohibit indirect as well as deliberate takings. *Cf. NLRB v. Bell Aerospace Co.*, 416 U.S. 267, 274-275, 40 L. Ed. 2d 134, 94 S. Ct. 1757 (1974). The permit process requires the applicant to prepare a "conservation plan" that specifies how he intends to "minimize and mitigate" the "impact" of his activity on endangered and threatened species, 16 U.S.C. § 1539(a)(2)(A), making clear that Congress had in mind foreseeable rather than merely accidental effects on listed species. No one could seriously request an "incidental" take permit to avert § 9 liability for direct, deliberate action against a member of an endangered or threatened species, but respondents would read "harm" so narrowly that the permit procedure would have little more than that absurd purpose. "When Congress acts to amend a statute, we presume it intends its amendment to have real and substantial effect." *Stone v. INS*, 514 U.S. 386, 397, 131 L. Ed. 2d 465, 115 S. Ct. 1537 (1995). Congress' addition of the § 10 permit provision supports the Secretary's conclusion that activities not intended to harm an endangered species, such as habitat modification, may constitute unlawful takings under the ESA unless the Secretary permits them.

The Court of Appeals made three errors in asserting that "harm" must refer to a direct application of force because the words around it do. First, the court's premise was flawed. Several of the words that accompany "harm" in the § 3 definition of "take," especially "harass," "pursue," "wound," and "kill," refer to actions or effects that do not require direct applications of force. Second, to the extent the court read a requirement of intent or purpose into the words used to define "take," it ignored § 11's express provision that a "knowing" action is enough to violate the Act. Third, the court employed *noscitur a sociis* to give "harm" essentially the same function as other words in the definition, thereby denying it independent meaning. The canon, to the contrary, counsels that a word "gathers meaning from the words around it." *Jarecki v. G. D. Searle & Co.*, 367 U.S. 303, 307, 6 L. Ed. 2d 859, 81 S. Ct. 1579 (1961). The statutory context of "harm" suggests that Congress meant that term to serve a particular function in the ESA, consistent with, but distinct from, the functions of the other verbs used to define "take." The Secretary's interpretation of "harm" to include indirectly injuring endangered animals through habitat modification permissibly interprets "harm" to have "a character of its own not to be submerged by its association." *Russell Motor Car Co. v. United States*, 261 U.S. 514, 519, 67 L. Ed. 778, 43 S. Ct. 428 (1923).

Nor does the Act's inclusion of the § 5 land acquisition authority and the § 7 directive to federal agencies to avoid destruction or adverse modification of critical habitat alter our conclusion. Respondents' argument that the Government lacks any incentive to purchase land under § 5 when it can simply prohibit takings under § 9 ignores the practical considerations that attend enforcement of the ESA. Purchasing habitat lands may well cost the Government less in many circumstances than pursuing civil or criminal penalties. In addition, the § 5 procedure allows for protection of habitat before the seller's activity has harmed any endangered animal, whereas the Government cannot enforce the § 9 prohibition until an animal has actually been killed or injured. The Secretary may also find the § 5 authority useful for preventing modification of land that is not yet but may in the future become habitat for an endangered or threatened species. The § 7 directive applies only to the Federal Government, whereas the § 9 prohibition applies to "any person." Section 7 imposes a broad, affirmative duty to avoid adverse habitat modifications that § 9 does not replicate, and § 7 does not limit its admonition to habitat modification that "actually kills or injures wildlife." Conversely, § 7 contains limitations that § 9 does not, applying only to actions "likely to jeopardize the continued existence of any endangered species or threatened species," 16 U.S.C. § 1536(a)(2), and to modifications of habitat that has been designated "critical" pursuant to § 4, 16 U.S.C. § 1533(b)(2). Any overlap that § 5 or § 7 may have with § 9 in particular cases is unexceptional, *see, e. g., Russello v. United States* , 464 U.S. 16, and n. 2, 24, 78 L. Ed. 2d 17, 104 S. Ct. 296 (1983), and simply reflects the broad purpose of the Act set out in § 2 and acknowledged in *TVA v. Hill.*

We need not decide whether the statutory definition of "take" compels the Secretary's interpretation of "harm," because our conclusions that Congress did not unambiguously manifest its intent to adopt respondents' view and that the Secretary's interpretation is reasonable suffice to decide this case. *See generally Chevron U.S.A. Inc. v. Natural Resources Defense Council, Inc.*, 467 U.S. 837, 81 L. Ed. 2d 694, 104 S. Ct. 2778 (1984). The latitude the ESA gives the Secretary in enforcing the statute, together with the degree of regulatory expertise necessary to its enforcement, establishes that we owe some degree of deference to the Secretary's reasonable interpretation. *See* Breyer, *Judicial Review of Questions of Law and Policy*, 38 Admin. L. Rev. 363, 373 (1986).

III

Our conclusion that the Secretary's definition of "harm" rests on a permissible construction of the ESA gains further support from the legislative history of the statute. The Committee Reports accompanying the bills that became the ESA do not specifically discuss the meaning of "harm," but they make clear that Congress intended "take" to apply broadly to cover indirect as well as purposeful actions. The Senate Report stressed that " 'take' is defined . . . in the broadest possible manner to include every conceivable way in which a person can 'take' or attempt to 'take' any fish or wildlife." S. Rep. No. 93-307, p. 7 (1973). The House Report stated that "the broadest possible terms" were used to define restrictions on takings. H. R. Rep. No. 93-412, p. 15 (1973). The House Report underscored the breadth of the "take" definition by noting that it included "harassment, *whether intentional or not.*" *Id.*, at 11 (emphasis added). The Report explained that the definition "would allow, for example, the Secretary to regulate or prohibit the activities of birdwatchers where the effect of those activities might disturb the birds and make it difficult for them to hatch or raise their young." *Ibid.* These comments, ignored in the dissent's welcome but selective foray into legislative history, support the Secretary's interpretation that the term "take" in § 9 reached far more than the deliberate actions of hunters and trappers.

Two endangered species bills, S. 1592 and S. 1983, were introduced in the Senate and referred to the Commerce Committee. Neither bill included the word "harm" in its definition of "take," although the definitions otherwise closely resembled the one that appeared in the bill as ultimately enacted. *See* Hearings on S. 1592 and S. 1983 before the Subcommittee on Environment of the Senate Committee on Commerce, 93d Cong., 1st Sess., pp. 7, 27 (1973) (hereinafter Hearings). Senator Tunney, the floor manager of the bill in the Senate, subsequently introduced a floor amendment that added "harm" to the definition, noting that this and accompanying amendments would "help to achieve the purposes of the bill." 119 Cong. Rec. 25683 (1973). Respondents argue that the lack of debate about the amendment that added "harm" counsels in favor of a narrow interpretation. We disagree. An obviously broad word that the Senate went out of its way to add to an important statutory definition is precisely the sort of provision that deserves a respectful reading. The definition of "take" that originally appeared in S. 1983 differed from the definition as ultimately enacted in one other significant respect: It included "the destruction, modification, or curtailment of [the] habitat or range" of fish and wildlife. Hearings, at 27. Respondents make much of the fact that the Commerce Committee removed this phrase from the "take" definition before S. 1983 went to the floor. *See* 119 Cong. Rec. 25663 (1973). We do not find that fact especially significant. The legislative materials contain no indication why the habitat protection provision was deleted. That provision differed greatly from the regulation at issue today. Most notably, the habitat protection provision in S. 1983 would have applied far more broadly than the regulation does because it made adverse habitat modification a categorical violation of the "take" prohibition, unbounded by the regulation's limitation to habitat modifications that actually kill or injure wildlife. The S. 1983 language also failed to qualify "modification" with the regulation's limiting adjective "significant." We do not believe the Senate's unelaborated disavowal of the provision in S. 1983 undermines the reasonableness of the more moderate habitat protection in the Secretary's "harm" regulation.[7]

---

[7] Respondents place heavy reliance for their argument that Congress intended the § 5 land acquisition provision and not § 9 to be the ESA's remedy for habitat modification on a floor statement by Senator Tunney:

> "Many species have been inadvertently exterminated by a negligent destruction of their habitat. Their habitats have been cut in size, polluted, or otherwise altered so that they are unsuitable environments for natural populations of fish and wildlife. Under this bill, we can take steps to make amends for our negligent encroachment. The Secretary would be empowered to use the land acquisition authority granted to him in certain existing legislation to acquire land for the use of the endangered species programs . . . . Through these land acquisition provisions, we will be able to conserve habitats necessary to protect fish and wildlife from further destruction.
>
> "Although most endangered species are

The history of the 1982 amendment that gave the Secretary authority to grant permits for "incidental" takings provides further support for his reading of the Act. The House Report expressly states that "by use of the word 'incidental' the Committee intends to cover situations in which it is known that a taking will occur if the other activity is engaged in but such taking is incidental to, and not the purpose of, the activity." H.R. Rep. No. 97-567, p. 31 (1982). This reference to the foreseeability of incidental takings undermines respondents' argument that the 1982 amendment covered only accidental killings of endangered and threatened animals that might occur in the course of hunting or trapping other animals. Indeed, Congress had habitat modification directly in mind: Both the Senate Report and the House Conference Report identified as the model for the permit process a cooperative state-federal response to a case in California where a development project threatened incidental harm to a species of endangered butterfly by modification of its habitat. *See* S. Rep. No. 97-418, p. 10 (1982); H. R. Conf. Rep. No. 97-835, pp. 30-32 (1982). Thus, Congress in 1982 focused squarely on the aspect of the "harm" regulation at issue in this litigation. Congress' implementation of a permit program is consistent with the Secretary's interpretation of the term "harm."

IV

When it enacted the ESA, Congress delegated broad administrative and interpretive power to the Secretary. *See* 16 U.S.C. §§ 1533, 1540(f). The task of defining and listing endangered and threatened species requires an expertise and attention to detail that exceeds the normal province of Congress. Fashioning appropriate standards for issuing permits under § 10 for takings that would otherwise violate § 9 necessarily requires the exercise of broad discretion. The proper interpretation of a term such as "harm" involves a complex policy choice. When Congress has entrusted the Secretary with broad discretion, we are especially reluctant to substitute our views of wise policy

---

> threatened primarily by the destruction of their natural habitats, a significant portion of these animals are subject to predation by man for commercial, sport, consumption, or other purposes. The provisions in S. 1983 would prohibit the commerce in or the importation, exportation, or taking of endangered species . . . ." 119 Cong. Rec. 25669 (1973).

Similarly, respondents emphasize a floor statement by Representative Sullivan, the House floor manager for the ESA:

> "For the most part, the principal threat to animals stems from destruction of their habitat . . . . H. R. 37 will meet this problem by providing funds for acquisition of critical habitat . . . . It will also enable the Department of Agriculture to cooperate with willing landowners who desire to assist in the protection of endangered species, but who are understandably unwilling to do so at excessive cost to themselves.
>
> "Another hazard to endangered species arises from those who would capture or kill them for pleasure or profit. There is no way that Congress can make it less pleasurable for a person to take an animal, but we can certainly make it less profitable for them to do so." *Id.*, at 30162.

Each of these statements merely explained features of the bills that Congress enacted in § 5 of the ESA and went on to discuss elements enacted in § 9. Neither statement even suggested that § 5 would be the Act's exclusive remedy for habitat modification by private landowners or that habitat modification by private landowners stood outside the ambit of § 9. Respondents' suggestion that these statements identified § 5 as the ESA's only response to habitat modification contradicts their emphasis elsewhere on the habitat protections in § 7. . . .

for his. *See Chevron*, 467 U.S. at 865-866. In this case, that reluctance accords with our conclusion, based on the text, structure, and legislative history of the ESA, that the Secretary reasonably construed the intent of Congress when he defined "harm" to include "significant habitat modification or degradation that actually kills or injures wildlife." In the elaboration and enforcement of the ESA, the Secretary and all persons who must comply with the law will confront difficult questions of proximity and degree; for, as all recognize, the Act encompasses a vast range of economic and social enterprises and endeavors. These questions must be addressed in the usual course of the law, through case-by-case resolution and adjudication.

The judgment of the Court of Appeals is reversed.

It is so ordered.

Justice O'CONNOR, concurring.

My agreement with the Court is founded on two understandings. First, the challenged regulation is limited to significant habitat modification that causes actual, as opposed to hypothetical or speculative, death or injury to identifiable protected animals. Second, even setting aside difficult questions of scienter, the regulation's application is limited by ordinary principles of proximate causation, which introduce notions of foreseeability. These limitations, in my view, call into question *Palila v. Hawaii Dept. of Land and Natural Resources*, 852 F.2d 1106 (CA9 1988) (*Palila II*), and with it, many of the applications derided by the dissent. Because there is no need to strike a regulation on a facial challenge out of concern that it is susceptible of erroneous application, however, and because there are many habitat-related circumstances in which the regulation might validly apply, I join the opinion of the Court.

In my view, the regulation is limited by its terms to actions that actually kill or injure individual animals. Justice SCALIA disagrees, arguing that the harm regulation "encompasses injury inflicted, not only upon individual animals, but upon populations of the protected species." . . . At one level, I could not reasonably quarrel with this observation; death to an individual animal always reduces the size of the population in which it lives, and in that sense, "injures" that population. But by its insight, the dissent means something else. Building upon the regulation's use of the word "breeding," Justice SCALIA suggests that the regulation facially bars significant habitat modification that actually kills or injures hypothetical animals (or, perhaps more aptly, causes potential additions to the population not to come into being). Because "impairment of breeding does not 'injure' living creatures," Justice SCALIA reasons, the regulation must contemplate application to "a population of animals which would otherwise have maintained or increased its numbers.". . . .

I disagree. As an initial matter, I do not find it as easy as Justice SCALIA does to dismiss the notion that significant impairment of breeding injures living creatures. . . .

This case, of course, comes to us as a facial challenge. We are charged with deciding whether the regulation on its face exceeds the agency's statutory mandate. I have identified at least one application of the regulation (*Palila II*) that is, in my view, inconsistent with the regulation's *own* limitations. That misapplication does not, however, call into question the validity of the regulation itself. One can doubtless imagine questionable applications of the regulation that test the limits of the agency's authority. However, it seems to me clear that the regulation does not on its terms exceed the agency's mandate, and that the regulation has innumerable valid habitat-related applications. Congress may, of course, see fit to revisit this issue. And nothing the Court says today prevents the agency itself from narrowing the scope of its regulation at a later date.

With this understanding, I join the Court's opinion.

Justice SCALIA, with whom the Chief Justice and Justice THOMAS join, dissenting.

I think it unmistakably clear that the legislation at issue here (1) forbade the hunting and killing of endangered animals, and (2) provided federal lands and federal funds *for the acquisition of private lands*, to preserve the habitat of endangered animals. The Court's holding that the hunting and killing prohibition incidentally preserves habitat on private lands imposes unfairness to the point of financial ruin—not just upon the rich, but upon the simplest farmer who finds his land conscripted to national zoological use. I respectfully dissent.

. . . .

NOTES AND QUESTIONS

(1) Consider the role of and opportunities for citizen involvement or intervention in the enforcement of the Endangered Species Act (a)in the designation of endangered or threatened species, (b) in the review of federal administrative action in the designation of endangered species, (c) in the protection of endangered or threatened species of plants. What are the differences between the treatment of animals and plants in the designation of endangered or threatened species?

(2) When is the use of citizen suits applicable to habitat designations?

(3) To what extent is private conduct regulated by the Endangered Species Act? Consider restrictions of private conduct (a) with respect to the sale of live or dead specimens; (b) with respect to the "taking" of endangered animals and of endangered plants; (c) as applied to habitat modification, particularly with respect to habitats in private ownership.

(4) In issuing its injunction in *TVA v. Hill,* did the Supreme Court undertake the balancing of interest commonly applied in the issuance of injunctions? Why not? Compare the Court's decision in *Weinberger v. Romero Barcelo*, at p. 1236, *infra*. Is the "God squad" required to balance equities or interests? Also consider whether the issue in *TVA v. Hill* could even have been raised prior to the enactment of the National Environmental Policy Act in 1969. It is interesting to consider the problems the Supreme Court faced in *TVA v. Hill,* which is described in some detail in Percival, *Environmental Law in the Supreme Court: Highlights from the Marshall Papers*, 23 Envtl. L. Rep. 10606, 10610–10611 (1993).

(5) Under what circumstances must an agency prepare a biological assessment as part of the designation of an endangered species? *See, e.g.*, *Palmers v. Peterson*, 753 F.2d 754 (9th Cir. 1985).

(6) How can Congress exempt a particular project from compliance with the Endangered Species Act? *See*, for example, the case of the endangered Mt. Graham red squirrel threatened by the location of major telescopes at Mt. Graham. *Mt. Graham Coalition v. Thomas*, 53 F.3d 970 (9th Cir. 1995).

(7) *See* Oliver Houck, *The Endangered Species Act and Its Implementation by the U.S. Departments of Interior and Commerce,* 64 U. Colo. L. Rev. 322 (1993), commenting on the rather relaxed attitudes of the Interior and Commerce Departments in making critical habitat designations.

(8) Consider the applicability of the Endangered Species Act to endangered species whose habitat is outside the United States. To what extent can you discern a Congressional purpose to protect species outside of the United States in the passage of such U.S. laws as the African Elephant Act? To what extent can U.S. law affect the taking of endangered African elephants outside the U.S. territory? How do we try to prevent the taking of African elephants by poachers inside Africa? *See also Defenders of Wildlife v. Lujan*, 911 F.2d 117 (8th Cir. 1990), holding that the Endangered Species Act applies extraterritorially. The decision was reversed by the Supreme Court in *Lujan v. Defenders of Wildlife*, 501 U.S. 555 (1992). The reversal was based on standing grounds, and did not address the merits of extraterritorial application. It would seem, however, that the general tenor of the majority of the Supreme Court displayed impatience and an adverse attitude to the assertion of the claim of extraterritorial application. The case involved the protection of the Nile crocodile and the Asian elephant. The decision has been read as inflicting major damage on the law of environmental standing. *See* F. Grad, Treatise on Environmental Law, § 12.04[7][j], U.S. Efforts to Protect Endangered Species Abroad; Citizen Suits To Affect Extraterritorial Application of the Endangered Species Act. For a general review of the Endangered Species Act, *see* F. Grad, Treatise on Environmental Law, § 12.04[7].

Chapter 7

LAND USE PLANNING AND ITS ENVIRONMENTAL IMPLICATIONS

§ 7.01 Introduction

As the twenty-first century begins, issues of land use planning, and the impacts of unplanned development on the natural environment are assuming greater political importance in the United States. Citizen concern over the results of "urban sprawl" and "leapfrog development" is growing; and lawmakers at all levels of government are responding with legal measures to control new growth, and limit its environmental consequences.

The idea of land use planning and land use controls is based on the proposition that properly constituted agencies of government, staffed by expert planners or expert environmentalists, are capable of making projections of future development for the public benefit. In a larger sense, land use planning and land use controls raise the question of who is capable of defining the public good and the public purpose. In a democratic system, the public interest is ultimately defined by the legislature, subject to correction at the polls from time to time.

The process of land use planning and the imposition of land use controls has sometimes been criticized as an exercise of government by experts,[1] and sometimes situations have arisen when the planners' definition of the public good and of desirable public purposes was at odds with the public good as conceived by particular groups in the neighborhood or in a given constituency. Whenever planners assert that they know what is best for a particular area or that they know better what is good for a particular area than the people who live there, they are likely to be met with the assertion that the people who live there have a right to determine their own future, and indeed, have a right to be wrong. A major effort of planning and land use development in a democratic society must be devoted to bridging the gap between the expert planner and the people affected by different constituencies.

People in a particular neighborhood may want a road to be built because they see considerable benefit from it, regardless of the fact that the road may cause damage to natural resources or to a neighboring trout stream.[2] If the question of planning for the road were put to the immediate area affected,

---

[1] For a detailed description of the planning profession and the variegated training of its members, *see* Williams, 1 American Land Planning Law 62-69. For a critical account of the planning professional, *see* Babcock, The Zoning Game (1966). For a selection of writings on the planner's role in a democratic society, *see* Haar, Land Use Planning 714-730, particularly Howard, *The Planner in a Democratic Society—A Credo,* at 727.

[2] *See, e.g.*, Pennsylvania Environmental Council v. Bartlett, 315 F. Supp. 238 (M.D. Pa. 1970). The facts showed that the people in the immediate area wanted the new road which a more broadly based group of environmentalists opposed.

the outcome might clearly be a vote for the road and against environmental interests. If, on the other hand, the question were put to the broader constituency of the region as a whole, the outcome might well be different. Thus, in every instance where planning and land use control regulations require the agreement to a plan or to particular controls by the community affected, the results of such a submission may well be subject to manipulation, depending on how the affected "community" is defined.

From the point of view of environmental protection, it is at least sometimes advantageous to rely on broader regional constituencies rather than on narrowly local constituencies whose parochial interests may outweigh the broader interests of environmental protection. The problem of the expert judgment and its possible opposition to the popular will, and the problem of the public interest as viewed by a narrower rather than a broader constituency affect almost all land use planning efforts. Their resolution may be the most difficult issue in the planning process.

The Federal Role

Because land use controls have traditionally been a state and local responsibility, the federal government has entered the field only by indirection. The Congress has thus far used two mechanisms to engage the federal government in land use decisions. The first of these is the use of the federal government's regulatory powers in areas clearly within federal jurisdiction in ways that impose an obligation on the states and municipalities to impose land use controls that will carry out the federal purposes within the federal regulatory ambit.[3] Examples of such exercises of federal power that impose obligations on the states can be found in the area of pollution control. The federal regulation of air pollution, water pollution and the disposal of solid wastes in turn impose obligations upon the states to deal with land use issues. The other exercise of federal power has been through the traditional grant-in-aid mechanism.[4] For instance, the federal government has imposed planning and land use requirements as a condition of the award of federal grants. Examples of this may be found in the highway and airport development area and in a variety of other areas that involve transportation or housing.

The federal government has exercised regulatory power in the land use field incidentally, as part of the exercise of clearly authorized regulatory powers, such as in the area of power plant licensing or the management of federal lands. Although Congress failed to pass a comprehensive federal land use act in the first half of the 1970s,[5] it is clear that the federal government has shown considerable interest in advancing land use planning and regulations. Indeed, much of the state and local initiative in developing more up-to-date land use approaches during the 1970s and 1980s was directly attributable to federal

[3] Based on the Commerce power, U.S. Const., Art. I, § 8, Cl. 3.

[4] Based on the power to tax and spend, Art. I, § 8, Cl. 1.

[5] H. 3354, 91st Cong., 2d Sess. (1970); S. 632, 92nd Cong., 1st Sess. (1971); S. 268, 93rd Cong., 1st Sess. (1973). Extensive hearings were held on each of these bills over a period of almost four years. For the legislative history, see U.S. Sen. Comm. On Interior and Insular Affairs, Report to Accompany S. 268, Land Use Policy and Planning Assistance Act, S. Rep. No. 93-197, 93d Cong., 1st Sess. (1973).

interest in the area and to developments relating to environmental law in the federal Congress.

Federal environmental legislation in the early 1970s had far-reaching land use implications, but the federal government had had substantial impact on state and local planning long before then. Federal highway planning and federal support for major national highway systems first constructed in the years following World War II, involved a major national commitment. In its fullest implications the federal highway network constitutes a national land use plan in setting the conditions, nationwide, for a whole range of future developments, population movements, and transportation choices. The impact of federal decisions on future land use is also apparent in a variety of other areas where federal choices condition major capital expenditures which constitute substantial commitments to particular land use choices. In sum, while federal decision making in land use control has not always been direct, it has nonetheless had a very significant impact.

One of the avenues of federal control of land use has been through pollution control legislation. The relationship of pollution control to land use is evident. In a sense, all pollution control laws are land use regulations. Particularly in the instance of emission controls, any limitation on pollution from a point source limits the uses of the property on which the point source is located. The prohibition on the emission of air or water pollution in excess of a fixed standard means that the particular area or locality cannot be used for industrial establishments that are likely to emit in excess of the standard. But even the setting of ambient standards—such as ambient air quality standards or ambient water standards—imposes limitations on land use, in that ambient standards are necessarily translated into emission standards which in turn allow a less intensive use of land than would otherwise be possible. From another point of view, an ambient air quality or water quality standard has implications for the land use of an entire region in that it may imply a less intensive, less growth-conscious use of the area for the future.

For additional discussion of the land use implications of federal pollution control laws, see F. Grad, Treatise on Environmental Law § 10.02.

The remainder of this chapter explores several aspects of environmental land use planning. It begins by examining an important component of the constitutional framework for governmental regulation of land use and the environment: the takings clause of the Fifth Amendment to the U.S. Constitution as interpreted by the U.S. Supreme Court. It then explores some of the legal techniques that state and local governments—sometimes in coordination with federal agencies and departments—have used to protect natural resources and environmental values: coastal zone management, agricultural land preservation, growth management and the transfer of development rights.

§ 7.02 The Constitutional Framework: Takings Litigation in Environmental Cases

W. Treanor, "THE ORIGINAL UNDERSTANDING OF THE TAKINGS CLAUSE"*

Environmental Policy Project, Georgetown University Law Center (1998)

The champions of the property rights movement claim that they are fighting to restore the original understanding of the Takings Clause of the Fifth Amendment. They invoke James Madison and other founding fathers as support for proposed statutes that require the federal government to pay property owners when it prevents them from harming the environment or jeopardizing the survival of endangered species. Wetlands regulations, it is often said, "take" property by diminishing its value, and the founders adopted the Takings Clause to ensure that, when government regulations diminished the value of property, the owner would receive compensation. Increasing numbers of lawsuits are being filed on the same theory. Established Supreme Court standards for resolving takings claims, litigants contend, are at odds with the founders' belief that property ownership was a natural right that the government could never limit. These suits urge courts to return to the founders' vision, and claim that, once that vision is revived, the judiciary will routinely invalidate local land use and environmental protection standards.

Widely shared and forcefully repeated, this conception of the original understanding has come to play a central role in the debate about the Takings Clause. But it is demonstrably and dramatically wrong. The original understanding of the Takings Clause was, very simply, that the federal government had to compensate the property owner when it physically took property—such as when it took land to build a fort. The clause did not require compensation for regulations under any circumstances. Property rights advocates ignore the plain language of the clause, the evidence about what the founders and other Americans in the early republic thought the clause actually meant, and the founders' views about property and democratic government. Claiming to rely on history, property rights advocates embrace, instead, a myth.

Despite the public prominence of the property rights argument, there is actually nothing novel or particularly controversial about the conclusion that the Takings Clause was limited to physical seizures. With some notable exceptions, prominent legal scholars of all shades of political opinion—including such leading conservatives as former Judge Robert Bork and former Solicitor General Charles Fried—support the conclusion that the property rights argument has no plausible foundation in the original understanding of the Takings Clause. Justice Scalia, the Supreme Court Justice who most consistently argues for a broad reading of the Takings Clause, has acknowledged that until well into the twentieth century "it was generally understood

* Originally published by the Environmental Policy Project, Georgetown University Law Center. Reprinted with permission.

that the Takings Clause reached only a 'direct appropriation' of property or [its] functional equivalent. . . ." *Lucas v. South Carolina Coastal Council,* 505 U.S. 1003, 1114 (1992). The only remarkable aspect of the original understanding of the Takings Clause is how rarely the original understanding of this clause is taken into account in political and legal debates over property rights.

Plain Language

Despite all the controversy about its meaning, the language of the Takings Clause—"nor shall private property be taken for public use, without just compensation"—is perfectly straightforward. Compensation is necessary only when property is "taken." In other words, the only time when government must compensate the property owner is when it physically seizes property. The text does not require compensation when regulations diminish the value of property. Indeed, the clause does not even mention regulations.

Proponents of a broad reading of the Takings Clause counter that, at the time of the ratification of the Takings Clause, "property" sometimes meant "anything of value." Thus, according to this view, whenever government diminishes the value of property through regulation, the Takings Clause can properly be read to require payment of compensation.

The problem with this view is that it ignores a critical part of the clause, the word "taken." "Take" means, and meant at the time the Fifth Amendment was ratified, "physically seize," not "diminish in value." All the debate among judges, scholars, policy-makers, and politicians about precisely what the Takings Clause means tends to obscure this obvious point, but it can be illustrated with a simple example. If I tell my daughter that she cannot play with her ball in the house, she has lost something of value—the right to play with the ball in the house. I have regulated what she can do with the ball, but I haven't "taken" it. She is still free to play with it outside. I only "take" her ball when I physically seize it. Only a child immersed in the literature of the property rights movement would argue otherwise. The plain language of the Takings Clause is to the same effect. Even if the word "property" is read to cover anything of value, compensation is owed only when property is "taken." Regulations, by their nature, are not "takings."

Original Understanding

The evidence of how the clause was originally understood leads to the same conclusion as analysis of its language: the Takings Clause applied only to physical takings.

While property rights advocates sometimes argue as if the founders believed that the Takings Clause was the central feature of the Constitution (or at least the Bill of Rights), the historical reality is almost the exact opposite. The state ratifying conventions that considered the Constitution proposed almost two hundred constitutional amendments. Not one, however, proposed a takings clause. The clause is part of the Constitution, not because there was a national demand for it, but because James Madison, the author of the Bill of Rights, unilaterally included it among the amendments he proposed in 1789. Madison did not explain what the clause meant when he presented it to Congress, and no debate in Congress about its meaning—if there was any debate—has been preserved. The language of Madison's proposal shows that he was concerned only with physical seizures: "No person shall be . . . obliged to relinquish his property, where it may be necessary for public use, without just compensation." This wording was altered in Congress to the current constitutional text. In the absence of recorded debates, we don't know why the change was made, but it is clear that the language eventually adopted was, like the language of Madison's initial proposal, the language of physical seizure. Indeed, the principal change was to highlight the physical action by the government. The focus is no longer on the individual's "relinquish[ing]"; it is on the government's "tak[ing]."

St. George Tucker, a Virginia judge, politician and legal educator, provided the first clear statement of the clause's meaning in 1803 when he wrote what became the early republic's preeminent constitutional law treatise. In that treatise, he observed that the Takings Clause "was probably intended to restrain the arbitrary and oppressive mode of obtaining supplies for the army, and other public uses, by impressment, as was too frequently practiced during the revolutionary war." Thus, according to Tucker, the purpose of the clause was to require compensation when the military seized civilian goods.

The other important early statements concerning the clause's scope are Madison's. In a 1792 newspaper essay criticizing Secretary of the Treasury Alexander Hamilton's economic policies, Madison attacked "arbitrary restrictions, exemptions, and monopolies [that] deny to part of [the nation's] citizens . . . free use of their faculties." Madison continued:

> "If there be a government then which prides itself in maintaining the inviolability of property; which provides that none shall be taken *directly* even for public use without indemnification to the owner, and yet . . . which *indirectly* violates their property, in their actual possessions, in the labor that acquires their very subsistence, and in the hallow remnant of time which ought to relive their fatigues and sooth their cares, . . . such a government is not a pattern for the United States."

Significantly, even as Madison in his essay is defending property interests, he demonstrates that the Takings Clause's prohibition is limited. In Madison's words, the clause provides that property "shall [not] be taken *directly*," It does not reach "*indirect*" violations—the "arbitrary restrictions, exemptions and violations" that Madison warns against, not as a matter of constitutional law, but as a matter of public policy.

Madison's other most significant writing about the Takings Clause reflects the same view of the clause's meaning. In a letter to an antislavery advocate, Madison proposed that the federal government purchase all slaves in order to free them. He observed, "Whatever may be the intrinsic character of that property [slavery], it is one known to the constitution and, as such, could not be constitutionally taken away without compensation." Again, compensation is necessary for Madison because the Government has physically "taken away" "property."

In drafting the clause, it appears that Madison sought to address very particular concerns. One type of government action during the revolutionary era that troubled him was the seizure of loyalist land. Such seizure had occurred on a scale of epic proportions: loyalist property worth more than twenty million dollars—one tenth the value of real property in the country—was confiscated. In addition, as a Virginian and slaveowner, he was worried that in the new republic the free states would band together in Congress and enact legislation that emancipated slaves without compensation. The Takings Clause, with its narrow ban on "direct" takings of physical property, precisely remedied these two problems.

In historical context, the narrow scope of the Takings Clause is hardly surprising. The clause provided greater protection for the property owner than the property owner had traditionally received. England's Magna Carta did not require compensation for government seizure of land. It only required compensation when the government took personal property. Thus, Crown officials were barred from "tak[ing] anyone's grain or other chattels, without immediately paying the money." Magna Carta, Art. 28. In contrast, the sole limitation on government seizure of land was one of procedural regularity: "No free man shall be dispossessed . . . except by the legal judgment of his peers or by the law of the land." Magna Carta, Art. 39. Early colonial charters were similarly limited in scope. Only the Massachusetts Body of Liberty, adopted in 1641, required compensation when personal property was taken. No colonial charter required compensation for the seizure of land. While property owners, in practice, commonly were paid when their land was seized, no colony had a constitutional obligation to do so, and, in fact, compensation was not always paid. Strikingly, except for Massachusetts, no colony paid compensation when it built roads on undeveloped land.

No colonial charter barred regulation that diminished the value or property, and colonial governments adopted innumerable regulations that constrained the use of property. In some respects colonial regulations, particularly pertaining to the permitted use and intensity of development, appear relatively rudimentary compared to modern regulations; other colonial regulations appear relatively stringent from a modern perspective. Land use statutes throughout the colonies limited where certain businesses—such as bakeries, slaughterhouses, and stills—could be located and what crops farmers could grow. Colonial laws regulated the permitted density of development; for example, a Connecticut building requirement limited the dispersion of development within the community, while a New Jersey law prohibited the subdivision of home lots to prevent overcrowding. Other colonial ordinances, such as in the colonies of New Amsterdam and Virginia, explicitly regulated the aesthetic features of development. An early Massachusetts Bay ordinance prohibited the construction of a dwelling unit more than half a mile from the meeting house.

Many colonial laws imposed affirmative obligations on residents to use their property for some specific purpose to advance the overall interests of the community. A Plymouth colony ordinance required those with rights in valuable minerals to exploit their rights or forfeit them. A Maryland law required owners of good mill sites to develop the sites or run the risk of losing their property to someone else who would develop the site. Similarly, when land was not developed or bridges fell into disuse, colonial governments took these properties from their owners and transferred them to someone else. Such forced transfers often occurred when the owner's initial grant contained provisions requiring use, but not always. New York's Governor Bellomont, for example, seized undeveloped land and, when confronted with the argument that he was not empowered to do so because the land grants had not explicitly required settlement, responded that the argument was inconsistent with royal authority and was "very presumptuous and unnatural."

The first state constitutions enacted after independence was declared did not require compensation when the government seized property. Instead, they left the decision to compensate or not to legislative discretion. As a Pennsylvania court stated, citizens "were bound to contribute as much of it [land] as, by the laws of the country, were deemed necessary for the public convenience." *M'Clenachan v. Curwin,* 3 Yeates 362, 373 (Pa. 1802). Similarly, South Carolina's Attorney General, in prevailing over a claimant who sought compensation for the taking of unimproved land, argued that such taking without payment was "one of the inherent prerogatives of the majesty of the people."

A compensation requirement began to win constitutional recognition during the revolutionary era, but only in a very limited way. Vermont—not one of the original thirteen states—broke from precedent in 1777 when it adopted the first constitutional provision requiring compensation "whenever any particular man's property is taken for the use of the public." Massachusetts adopted a similar restriction in its 1780 constitution. The Northwest Ordinance of 1787 was the third and final revolutionary era document to contain a compensation requirement. These constitutional provisions, however, were understood narrowly. None was read as a limit on government regulation. Indeed, an early court case construed the Northwest Ordinance's provision as applying only to military seizures, *Renthrop v. Bourg,* 4 Mart. 97, 132-33 (La. 1716), thus adopting a view similar to Tucker's view of the Takings Clause.

Until late in the nineteenth century, judicial constructions of the Takings Clause and of similar state constitutional provisions were consistently narrow. As one treatise writer observed in 1857, "It seems to be settled that, to be entitled to protection under this clause [the Takings Clause], the property must be actually taken in the physical sense of the word." Similarly, the Supreme Court declared in 1871:

> "[The Takings Clause] has always been understood as referring only to a direct appropriation . . . . It has never been supposed to have any bearing upon, or to inhibit laws that indirectly work harm and loss to individuals. A new tariff, an embargo, a draft, or a war may inevitably bring upon individuals great losses; may, indeed, render valuable property almost valueless. They may destroy the worth of contracts. But whoever supposed that, because of this, a tariff could not be changed, or a non-intercourse act, or an embargo be enacted, or a war be declared?"

Legal Tender Cases, 79 U.S. (12 Wall.) 457 (1871). In short, the Fifth Amendment's Takings Clause did not prevent regulations and statutes from restricting how property could be used nor did it prevent them from diminishing the value of property. The clause applied only to "a direct appropriation."

Current Supreme Court jurisprudence has dramatically departed from the original understanding. Since the 1890's, the Court has applied the clause to regulations (although its reading of the clause has still been much narrower than the reading favored by property rights advocates). Thus, the idea that regulations can violate the Takings Clause has a historical pedigree. But it is a pedigree that can be traced back only to the late nineteenth century, not to the framers of the Constitution.

Political Values

Finally, the limited scope of the Takings Clause reflects the basic political values of the founding fathers. Most fundamentally, the founders believed in democratic self-governance. They believed that, given the proper institutional framework, the people of this country could govern themselves wisely and well. The structure of the government the founders created embodied such a framework, one designed to ensure that debate on proposals would be fair, that elected officials who considered legislation were responsible leaders, and that statutes enacted into law enjoyed strong support—either from both houses of Congress and the President or two-thirds of both houses.

The Takings Clause was drafted narrowly, not because the founding fathers cared too little about property rights, but because they cared so much about representative democracy. The founders did not bring regulations within the ambit of the Takings Clause because they believed it was the appropriate responsibility of democratic decisionmakers to balance individual property interests against other community interests. Both in its wording and its theory of governance, the Constitution starts with "We the People," and the original meaning of the Takings Clause can only be understood in that larger context.

Proponents of a broad reading of the Takings Clause offer an alternative account. They assert that the founders were followers of the philosopher John Locke and therefore committed to the principle that the state can never diminish an individual's property. Sophisticated adherents of this view sometimes acknowledge that the founders favored certain statutes that caused the value of some private property to diminish. But, these proponents argue, the founders simply failed to see the tension between, say, their acceptance of state regulation in some circumstances and their general commitment to a Lockean conception of property. If we are to honor the original understanding, these proponents continue, we should honor the founders' general commitments, not their occasional blind spots.

This account is bad history. To start with, it misreads Locke, who did not see property rights as absolute. Far more important, regardless of whether or not the proponents of a broad reading of the Takings Clause have misread Locke, they have certainly misread the founders and their views on property. The founders were profoundly influenced by republicanism, the school of thought that contends that the essential role of the state is to promote individual virtue and commitment to the common good. Republicans treasured the institution of private property. Property gave the individual the independence he needed to participate responsibly in politics without fear of economic retribution. Because property was valued as a means, rather than as the end of the state, however, republicans believed that legislators could limit property interests in order to advance the common good.

The constitutionalization of a compensation requirement, first in several state constitutions, the Northwest Ordinance, and then in the Bill of Rights, reflected a break from this view, but only in a very limited way. During the revolutionary era, a range of Americans concluded that—with respect to the seizure of physical property—additional protection of private property was needed, even as their specific concerns varied dramatically. The movement for a compensation requirement began in Vermont and reflected the peculiarities of that state's history. The area that became Vermont had originally been a part of New Hampshire and then, in 1764, the English government had shifted the area to New York. The New York legislature subsequently invalidated the New Hampshire land titles. The Vermonters who declared their independence from New York included a Takings Clause in their constitution, presumably because their central grievance was the New York government's attempt to seize their land. Tucker's statement about the Fifth Amendment, as well as the court's holding in *Renthrop* interpreting the Northwest Ordinance, suggests that others supported constitutionalizing a compensation requirement because of their opposition to military seizure of civilian property. Madison's various political writings suggest that he was motivated by still other concerns: he feared that, because a majority would neither own land nor slaves, the interests of landowners and slaveowners were property interests that the political process was particularly unlikely to consider fairly. Moreover, while no one seems to have voiced objection to the constitutionalization of compensation requirement in the Takings Clause, there was not a strong movement in favor of it either. As noted, it is the one clause in the Bill of Rights that no state requested.

It is thus wrong to read the Takings Clause as embodying a fundamental rejection of majoritarian decision-making or republicanism. Its adoption reflected, instead, a congruence of concerns relating to the perceived need to protect particular forms of real property from state seizure. While it is true, as proponents of a broad reading of the Takings Clause often point out, that some of the actions of revolutionary era state governments—such as their confiscation of loyalist land—caused many of the founders to fear what unconstrained majorities, in the absence of appropriate checks and balances, might do, the founders were also worried about what wealthy property owners might do if they were not controlled. Thus, even a staunch conservative such as Pennsylvania's John Dickinson could declare at the constitutional convention that he "doubted the policy of interweaving into a Republican constitution a veneration for wealth [and] had always understood that a veneration for poverty & virtue, were the objects of republican encouragement."

The scope of the Takings Clause was limited, then, to physical seizures because most of the founders fundamentally believed in republicanism and believed, as well, that in most contexts majoritarian decision-making could appropriately limit property claims to advance the common good. John Adams described laws that caused "frequent division of landed property" as one of the five principal sources of liberty in New England. Madison in Federalist Ten recognized that governmental decisions necessarily involved creating economic winners and losers among competing interests: "A landed interest, a manufacturing interest, a mercantile interest, a moneyed interest, with many lesser interests, group of necessity in civilized nations. . . . The regulation of these various and interfering interests forms the principal task of modern legislation . . . ." Benjamin Franklin, however, offered perhaps the strongest statement of the relation between private property claims and the public good. He wrote, "Private Property . . . is a Creature of Society, and is subject to the Calls of that Society, whenever its Necessities shall require it, even to its last Farthing; its contribution to the public Exigencies are . . . to be considered . . . the Return of an obligation previously received, or the payment of a just debt." The limited scope of the Takings Clause was not, as proponents of a broad reading of the clause argue, the product of the founders' blindness. It was a product of their beliefs.

. . . .

Roger Pilon, "TAKING LIBERTIES WITH PROPERTY RIGHTS"*

Legal Times of Washington, May 25, 1998 at 21

. . . .

What then is the problem with Treanor's contention that government must compensate only "when it physically seizes property"? Quite simply, it begs the basic question. It assumes, for the purpose of interpreting the takings clause, that "property" should be defined more narrowly than it is in every other area of the law—indeed, so narrowly as to make a mockery of the very clause in which the term sits. The whole point of writing and ratifying the takings clause, after all, was to protect property rights. Yet, on Treanor's interpretation, the only property right that is protected is the right to possess. Every other property right is subject to extinction—to being taken—by the very government that the framers tells us was created to protect such rights.

What we have here, in short, is a monumental sleight of hand—perpetuated by the modern Court, to be sure—as a single example should make obvious. When David Lucas paid nearly $1 million for two parcels of land on the Outer Banks near Charleston, S.C., in 1986, he acquired all the rights of possession, use and exclusion that ran with the land—rights not unlike those his neighbors enjoyed. His "property," that is, was not simply the underlying estate but every estate that constituted it—the whole "bundle of sticks." On Day 1, he owned those rights, any one of which he might have sold, leased, bequeathed, what have you.

On Day 2, however, the South Carolina legislature, to promote tourism and provide its citizens with various amenities, effectively stripped Lucas of all such rights save one—the right to go on merely possessing "the property." That

* Reprinted with permission of the *Legal Times*, 1730 M St., N.W., Suite 802, Washington, D.C. 20036. Phone: 202-457-0686. Copyright, 1998.

made the property worthless, of course. But no compensable "taking" had occurred, according to Treanor, because "the property" had not been "physically seized." Only if the state had taken that final step, as it might have done on Day 3, would it have owed Lucas compensation? By then, however, the issue would have been moot, practically, for as of Day 2 the property was worthless.

Treanor would doubtless object that a court would see right through such a three-day ruse by the state. But that's not the point, is it? Rather, the point is that under Treanor's theory of the takings clause the state can accomplish all it wants and get out from under the clause's compensation requirement simply by leaving a worthless title with the owner. The state's aim, after all, was to provide the public with various goods—from wildlife habitat to lovely views—but to do so in a tax-free way. The public presumably wanted those goods; it just didn't want to pay for them. Fortunately for the legislature, there was Lucas, who had only one vote come election time, as against the many votes of the public. How convenient!

As we all know, Lucas did what every red-blooded American would do under those circumstances—he sued. The U.S. Supreme court ultimately ruled in his favor, 5-4, with an opinion that alarmed and outraged every regulator in the country. *Lucas v. South Carolina Coastal Council,* 505 U.S. 1003 (1992).Yet, in ruling, the Court only perpetuated the 70-odd years of ad hoc regulatory takings jurisprudence it had given us till then. Rather than articulate the principle of the matter—*all* regulations that take common law rights and cause losses not offset by equivalent benefits require compensation—the Court began at the other end: only if such regulations result in a complete wipeout is compensation required. To Justice Paul Stevens' query about why such an owner should recover in full while "[the] landowner whose property is diminished in value 95 percent recovers nothing," Justice Antonin Scalia could offer little more than the limp: "Takings law is full of these 'all or nothing' situations."

Treanor's misreading of the text—his crabbed, circular reading of "property"—is only compounded by the homely example he offers of his telling his daughter that she can play with her ball outside, but not in the house. "[S]he has lost something of value (to her)—the right to play with the ball in the house. I have regulated what she can do with the ball, but I haven't 'taken' it. . . . I only 'take' her ball when I physically seize it." Now really, no one is saying that the "it" Treanor's "regulation" took was his daughter's ball. What he took was her "*right*" (to play with the ball in the house). That was the "something" she "lost"—not the ball. (It should hardly need adding that her "right" was probably never held to begin with since Treanor sets the rules in his house: that's one of his property rights, which one imagines him loath to see taken.)

By plumbing the theory of the matter so little, then, Treanor has failed to grasp the analytical absurdity of his position, an absurdity the Court eliminated in *Lucas* in only the most absurd of cases—complete wipeouts resulting from regulatory takings of otherwise legitimate uses. But the historical account on which his contention primarily rests is hardly better. He seeks comfort, for example, in the Magna Carta's containing "no provision requiring compensation for the taking of land." And he adds that "the same is true for the charters of the original 13 colonies." One imagines 13th and 17th century zoning boards triumphant! . . . .

[W]hat is striking is how many of Treanor's supposedly contrary examples are taken from the colonial era. Has he forgotten that we fought a revolution to overthrow such tyranny? Perhaps not, but he certainly diminishes—and misstates—the point of that revolution, as with his contention that the takings clause was probably intended to restrain supplying the army through impressment.

But it is Treanor's reading of Madison's famous essay on "Property" in the 1792 National Gazette that wins the prize for tendentious history. Writing there, not of the federal government but of any government, Madison argues, in essence, that a government that prides itself on compensating owners when it directly takes their property, but then indirectly violates their rights in property, labor, and the like "is not a pattern for the United States." Incredibly, Treanor reads Madison as saying that "the prohibition in the [actual] takings clause is limited"; that the clause "applied only to physical takings: no property 'shall be taken *directly*' " without compensation; and that *indirect* violations should be resisted "on the basis of principle, not constitutional edict."

One simply despairs. As Professor James W. Ely, Jr. of Vanderbilt Law School wrote in a 1992 volume on the subject, "Madison's reference to indirect infringements indicates a generous understanding of the takings clause to encompass more than just the physical takings of property." Indeed, the very point of the passage is to condemn the artificial distinction between property and property rights, not to draw some narrow—and mistaken—legal distinction. Yet Treanor, with his final point, would have us conclude that it may be all right to commit "indirect" violations because they are a matter merely of principle, not constitutional edict. . . .

Treanor would leave it all to the political process: "Because property was primarily valued as a means . . . rather than as an end, the founding fathers believed that legislation could restrict property interests to advance the common good." Compare that with Madison:

> "Government is instituted to protect property of every sort; as well that which lies in the various rights of individuals, as that which the term particularly expresses. This being the end of government, that alone is *just* government, which *impartially* secures to every man, whatever is his own."

What we have in Treanor is neither theory nor history. It is politics parading as scholarship.

William Treanor, "FRAMERS TOOK NARROW VIEW OF SCOPE OF TAKINGS CLAUSE"*

Legal Times of Washington, June 8, 1998, at 25

The original understanding of many constitutional clauses is open to legitimate debate. Proponents of conflicting views can often point to different statements from the reports of the Constitutional Convention and state ratifying conventions, early case law, or early legal treatises that support their position. Notwithstanding Roger Pilon's heated response, however, the takings clause is not one of these clauses. As a result, his lengthy article is tellingly, but not surprisingly, short of historical evidence to support his views.

As I wrote, "[T]he takings clause was originally intended to apply only to outright physical seizures of property, and not to regulation of property under any circumstances." That doesn't mean that the regulatory takings doctrine—which the Supreme Court has consistently recognized for more than a century—is illegitimate. Constitutional doctrine in a host of areas has evolved away from the original understanding, and evolution in the takings area, as in other areas, is appropriate. But the issue of the legitimacy of constitutional change here should not obscure the fact that the modern case law represents a complete break with the way in which the clause was originally read. While Pilon attempts to dismiss my analysis, scholars and jurists across the political spectrum have reached the same conclusion that I have reached.

We have no record of debates in Congress concerning the takings clause when Madison proposed it, nor any records of ratification debates on the clause. Nonetheless, the evidence shows that the original understanding was that it applied to physical seizures, not government regulations. . . .

Pilon points to no statement from the ratification debates, no early treatise, and no case law to support his position. This failure is understandable because there is no such evidence. As a result, rather than actually looking to the original understanding, Pilon is forced to make an argument that is in part textualist and in part reflects his views of the framers' larger beliefs. He is, however, wrong here as well.

His textual argument is that, because the word "property" encompasses all common law rights, the clause means that "*all* regulations that take common law rights and cause losses not offset by equivalent benefit require compensation." This argument is without merit because it completely reads the word "take" out of the takings clause. "Take" meant (and means) "seize." As a result, the clause did not protect against government regulation of property. It prevented against seizure of property. . . .

Pilon's appeal to the framers' fundamental beliefs seems to reflect the premise that the founders had an absolute commitment to primacy of property

---

* Reprinted with permission of the *Legal Times*, 1730 M St., N.W., Suite 802, Washington, D.C. 20036. Phone: 202-457-0686. Copyright, 1998.

rights and, apparently, his belief that they favored activist judicial review to enforce those rights. He thus dismisses my reading of James Madison's essay "Property." In that essay, Madison is arguing against Alexander Hamilton's economic policy on the ground that it was inconsistent with the principles represented in the takings clause, not on the grounds that it actually violated the takings clause. The distinction, while lightly dismissed by Pilon, is critical, since it bears directly on the original understanding of the mandate established by the takings clause.

Pilon invokes the founders as he calls for judicial enforcement of the rule identified above—that any government regulation that limits common law rights without conferring offsetting benefits requires compensation. In effect, he is suggesting that the founders wanted broad-ranging judicial review that would allow courts to strike down legislation with redistributive consequences because it was at odds with their fundamental commitment to property rights. Such a view of the founders as uncomplicated libertarians is flatly inconsistent with historical scholarship. His view of judicial review is, if anything, even more obviously unfounded. The framing generation struggled with whether the then novel idea of judicial review was ever appropriate. The idea that the takings clause might be read as empowering courts to overturn any government regulation that affected "common law rights" would have made them gasp.

NOTES AND QUESTIONS

(1) Whose view of the "original intent" of the framers, with regard to the takings clause, did you find more persuasive, Treanor's or Pilon's? How much importance should the courts place on the framers' intentions when they interpret the Constitution?

(2) In addition to the discussions excerpted above, judicial construction of the takings clause has been the focus of extensive scholarly analysis. For a sampling of the pertinent literature, *See* Epstein, *Takings: Descent and Resurrection,* 1987 Sup. Ct. Rev. 1 (1987); Alexander, *Takings, Narratives and Power,* 88 Colum. L. Rev. 1752 (1988); Hill, Regulatory Takings: The Limits of Land Use Controls (1990); Lunney, *A Critical Reexamination of the Takings Jurisprudence,* 90 Mich. L. Rev. 1892 (1992); Kmiec, *The Original Understanding of the Takings Clause is Neither Weak Nor Obtuse,* 88 Colum. L. Rev. 1630 (1988); Michelman, *Takings, 1987,* 88 Colum. L. Rev. 1600 (1988); Rose-Ackerman, *Against Ad Hocery: A Comment on Michelman,* 88 Colum. L. Rev. 1697 (1988); Michelman, *A Reply To Susan Rose-Ackerman,* 88 Colum. L. Rev. 1712 (1988); and Humbach, *Evolving Thresholds of Nuisance and the Takings Clause,* 18 Colum. J. Envtl. L. 1 (1993).

(3) Please keep the perspectives of Treanor, Pilon and others in mind as you read the following U.S. Supreme Court interpretations of the Fifth Amendment's takings provision.

PENNSYLVANIA COAL CO. v. MAHON

United States Supreme Court (1922)
260 U.S. 393, 43 S. Ct. 158, 67 L. Ed. 322

HOLMES, J.:

This is a bill in equity brought by the defendants in error to prevent the Pennsylvania Coal Company from mining under their property in such ways as to remove the supports and cause a subsidence of the surface and of their house. The bill sets out a deed executed by the Coal Company in 1878, under which the plaintiffs claim. The deed conveys the surface but in express terms reserves the right to remove all the coal under the same and the grantee takes the premises with the risk and waives all claims for damages that may arise from mining out the coal. But the plaintiffs say that whatever may have been the Coal Company's rights, they were taken away by an Act of Pennsylvania, approved May 27, 1921 (P.L. 1198), commonly known there as the Kohler Act. . . .

The statute forbids the mining of anthracite coal in such a way as to cause the subsidence of, among other things, any structure used as a human habitation [*i.e.*, it forbade coal companies nearing the end of mining in underground coal seams from quarrying away parts of the supportive "pillars" of coal that had been kept in place to hold up the ceilings of the working mine if there were homes, public buildings, roads, lakes, or streams above] . . . . As applied to this case the statute is admitted to destroy previously existing rights of property and contract. The question is whether the police power can be stretched so far.

Government hardly could go on if to some extent values incident to property could not be diminished without paying for every such change in the general law. As long recognized some values are enjoyed under an implied limitation and must yield to the police power. But obviously the implied limitation must have its limits or the contract and due process clauses are gone. One fact for consideration in determining such limits is the extent of the diminution. When it reaches a certain magnitude, in most if not all cases, there must be an exercise of eminent domain and compensation to sustain the act. So the question depends upon the particular facts. The greatest weight is given to the judgment of the legislature but it always is open to interested parties to contend that the legislature has gone beyond its constitutional power. . . .

This is the case of a single private house. No doubt there is a public interest even in this, as there is in every purchase and sale and in all that happens within the commonwealth. Some existing rights may be modified even in such a case. *Rideout v. Knox,* 148 Mass. 368. But usually in ordinary private affairs the public interest does not warrant much of this kind of interference. A source of damage to such a house is not a public nuisance even if similar damage is inflicted on others in different places. The damage is not common or public. *Wesson v. Washburn Iron Co.,* 13 Allen, 195, 103. The extent of the public interest is shown by the statute to be limited, since the statute ordinarily does not apply to land when the surface is owned by the owner of the coal. Furthermore, it is not justified as a protection of personal safety. That could be provided for by notice. Indeed the very foundation of this bill is that the defendant gave timely notice of its intent to mine under the house. On the other hand, the extent of the taking is great. It purports to abolish what is recognized in Pennsylvania as an estate in land—a very valuable estate—and what is declared by the Court below to be a contract hitherto binding the plaintiffs. If we were called upon to deal with the plaintiffs' position alone, we should think it clear that the statute does not disclose a public interest sufficient to warrant so extensive a destruction of the defendant's constitutionally protected rights.

But the case has been treated as one in which the general validity of the act should be discussed. The Attorney General of the State, the City of Scranton, and the representatives of other extensive interests were allowed to take part in the argument below and have submitted their contentions here. It seems, therefore, to be our duty to go farther in the statement of our opinion, in order that it may be known at once, and that further suits should not be brought in vain.

It is our opinion that the act cannot be sustained as an exercise of the police power, so far as it affects the mining of coal under streets or cities in places where the right to mine such coal has been reserved. As said in a Pennsylvania case, "For practical purposes, the right to coal consists in the right to mine it." *Commonwealth v. Clearview Coal Co.,* 100 A. 820, 820 (Pa. 1917). What makes the right to mine coal valuable is that it can be exercised with profit. To make it commercially impractical to mine certain coals has nearly the same effect for constitutional purposes as appropriating or destroying it. This we think that we are warranted in assuming that the statute does.

. . . .

The protection of private property in the Fifth Amendment presupposes that it is wanted for public use, but provides that it shall not be taken for such use without compensation. A similar assumption is made in the decisions upon the Fourteenth Amendment. When this seemingly absolute protection is found to be qualified by the police power, the natural tendency of human nature is to extend the qualification more and more until at last private property disappears. But that cannot be accomplished in this way under the Constitution of the United States.

The general rule at least is that while property may be regulated to a certain extent, if regulation goes too far it will be recognized as a taking. It may be doubted how far exceptional cases, like the blowing up of a house to stop a conflagration, go—and if they go beyond the general rule, whether they do not stand as much upon tradition as upon principle. In general it is not plain that a man's misfortunes or necessities will justify his shifting the damages to his neighbor's shoulders. We are in danger of forgetting that a strong public desire to improve the public condition is not enough to warrant achieving the desire by a shorter cut than the constitutional way of paying for the change. As we already have said this is a question of degree—and therefore cannot be disposed of by general propositions. But we regard this as going beyond any of the cases decided by this Court. We assume, of course, that the statute was passed upon the conviction than an exigency existed that would warrant it, and we assume that an exigency exists that would warrant the exercise of eminent domain. But the question at bottom is upon whom the loss of the changes desired should fall. So far as private persons or communities have seen fit to take the risk of acquiring only surface rights, we cannot see that the fact that their risk has become a danger warrants the giving to them greater rights than they bought.

Decree reversed. THE ACT WAS OVERTURNED

BRANDEIS, J., dissenting.

. . . .

Coal in place is land, and the right of the owner to use his land is not absolute. He may not so use it as to create a public nuisance, and uses once harmless may, owing to changed conditions, seriously threaten the public welfare. Whenever they do, the Legislature has power to prohibit such uses without paying compensation; and the power to prohibit extends alike to the manner, the character and the purpose of the use.

Are we justified in declaring that the Legislature of Pennsylvania has, in restricting the right to mine anthracite, exercised this power so arbitrarily as to violate the Fourteenth Amendment? Every restriction upon the use of property imposed in the exercise of the police power deprives the owner of some right theretofore enjoyed, and is, in that sense, an abridgment by the state of rights in property without making compensation. But restriction imposed to protect the public health, safety or morals from dangers threatened is not a taking. The restriction here in question is merely the prohibition of a noxious use. . . . The state does not appropriate it or make any use of it. The state merely prevents the owner from making a use which interferes with paramount rights of the public. . . . The restriction upon the use of this property cannot, of course, be lawfully imposed, unless its purpose is to protect the public. But the purpose of a restriction does not cease to be public because incidentally some private persons may thereby receive gratuitously valuable special benefits. . . .

If by mining anthracite coal the owner would necessarily unloose poisonous gases, I suppose no one would doubt the power of the state to prevent the mining, without buying his coal fields. And why may not the state, likewise, without paying compensation, prohibit one from digging so deep or excavating so near the surface, as to expose the community to like dangers. In the latter case, as in the former, carrying on the business would be a public nuisance.

It is said that one fact for consideration in determining whether the limits of the police power have been exceeded is the extent of the resulting diminution in value, and that here the restriction destroys existing rights of property and contract. But values are relative. If we are to consider the value of the coal kept in place by the restriction, we should compare it with the value of the whole property. The rights of an owner as against the public are not increased by dividing the interests in his property into surface and subsoil. The sum of the rights in the parts cannot be greater than the rights in the whole. The estate of an owner in land is grandiloquently described as extending *ab orco usque ad coelum.* But I suppose no one would contend that by selling his interest above 100 feet from the surface he could prevent the state from limiting, by the police power, the height of structures in a city. And why should a sale of underground rights bar the state's power? For aught that appears the value of the coal kept in place by the restriction may be negligible as compared with the value of the whole property, or even as compared with that part of it which is represented by the coal remaining in place and which may be extracted despite the statute. . . .

A prohibition of mining which causes subsidence of such structures and facilities is obviously enacted for a public purpose; and it seems, likewise, clear that mere notice of intention to mine would not in this connection secure the public safety. Yet it is said that these provisions of the act cannot be sustained as an exercise of the police power where the right to mine such coal has been reserved. The conclusion seems to rest upon the assumption that in order to justify such exercise of the police power there must be "an average reciprocity of advantage" as between the owner of the property restricted and the rest of the community; and that here such reciprocity is absent. Reciprocity of advantage is an important consideration, and may even be an essential, where the state's power is exercised for the purpose of conferring benefits upon the property of a neighborhood, as in drainage projects. *Wurts v. Hoagland,* 114 U.S. 606, 5 S.Ct. 1086, 29 L.Ed. 229; *Fallbrook Irrigation District v. Bradley,* 164 U.S. 112, 17 S.Ct. 56, 41 L.Ed. 369; or upon adjoining owners, as by party wall provisions, *Jackman v. Rosenbaum Co.,* ante, 22. But where the police power is exercised, not to confer benefits upon property owners, but to protect the public from detriment and danger, there is, in my opinion, no room for considering reciprocity of advantage. . . .

NOTES AND QUESTIONS

(1) This decision was preceded by several other, quite different U.S. Supreme Court analyses of the takings clauses of the Fifth and Fourteenth Amendments. In *Mugler v. Kansas,* 123 U.S. 623 (1887), the Court upheld a Kansas statute that banned the manufacture of intoxicating liquors. In doing so, it stated that the constitutional principle that no person shall be deprived of life, liberty or property without due process of law "has never been regarded as incompatible with the principle, equally valid, because essential to the peace and safety of society, that all property in this country is held under the implied obligation that the owner's use of it shall not be injurious to the community." 123 U.S. at 669. Since the general use of intoxicating liquors may endanger public health, morals and safety it opined, Kansas' prohibition legislation was constitutionally sound.

Seven years following *Mugler,* in *Lawton v. Steele,* 152 U.S. 133 (1894), the Court let stand a New York statute that authorized governmental officials to seize and destroy illegal fishing nets without affording compensation to the owners of those nets. The Court stated that exercises of the police power do not run afoul of the due process/takings clause where it appears "first, the interests of the public require such interference; second, that the means are reasonably necessary for the accomplishment of the purpose, and not unduly oppressive on individuals." 152 U.S. at 137.

Additionally, in *Hadacheck v. Sebastian,* 239 U.S. 394 (1915), the Court upheld a Los Angeles ordinance that prohibited the operation of a brickyard in a section of the city, notwithstanding a brickyard owner's allegations that his land was worth $800,000 if used for brick-making purposes, but only worth $60,000 if used for any other purposes, and that enforcement of the ordinance would force him out of business. It opined: "We are dealing with one of the most essential powers of government, one that is the least limitable. It may indeed seem harsh in its exercise, usually is on some individual, but the imperative necessity for its existence precludes any limitation upon it when not exercised arbitrarily."

Is the majority opinion in the *Mahon* case consistent with these precedents?

(2) The principal case was the first U.S. Supreme Court decision to strike down an exercise of the police power on the basis that it affected a "regulatory taking," *i.e.*, a taking without a physical occupation of an owner's land. Is it consistent with Professor Treanor's historical analysis of the original understanding of the takings clause? How much weight, if any, should be given to the historical evidence Treanor presents? What "legal tests" are contained in Justice Holmes' opinion in *Mahon*? What are the strengths and shortcomings of those tests as you view them?

(3) How persuasive was Justice Brandeis' dissenting opinion in this case. Was Brandeis correct that the *Mahon* majority should have compared the value of the coal kept in place by the restriction in question with the value of all remaining parts of the coal company's real property, rather than examining its value standing alone?

PENN CENTRAL TRANSPORTATION CO. v. CITY OF NEW YORK

United States Supreme Court (1978)
438 U.S. 104, 98 S. Ct. 2646, 57 L. Ed. 2d 631

[Under New York City's Landmarks Preservation Law (the Landmarks Law), the Landmarks Preservation Commission (Commission) was authorized to designate a building to be a "landmark" on a particular "landmark site" or to designate an area to be an "historic district." The owner of the designated landmark was obligated to keep the building's exterior "in good repair" and to secure Commission approval before exterior alterations were made. Owners of landmark sites were allowed to transfer development rights from a landmark parcel to proximate lots.

Grand Central Terminal, which was owned by the Penn Central Transportation Co. (Penn Central), was designated a "landmark." Thereafter, Penn Central entered into a lease with UGP, whereby UGP was to construct a multistory office building over the Terminal. The Commission rejected appellants' plans for the building as destructive of the Terminal's historic and aesthetic features. Penn Central then brought suit in state court claiming that the application of the Landmarks Law had "taken" their property without just compensation in violation of the Fifth and Fourteenth Amendments and arbitrarily deprived them of their property without due process of law in violation of the Fourteenth Amendment.

The trial court granted relief. The New York Court of Appeals reversed, concluding that there was no "taking" since the Preservation law had not transferred control of the property to the City, but only restricted appellants' exploitation of it. The U.S. Supreme Court then granted certiorari.]

BRENNAN, J.:

. . . .

II

The issues presented by appellants are (1) whether the restrictions imposed by New York City's law upon appellants' exploitation of the Terminal site effect a "taking" of appellants' property for a public use within the meaning of the Fifth Amendment, which of course is made applicable to the States through the Fourteenth Amendment, and, (2) if so, whether the transferable development rights afforded appellants constitute "just compensation" within the meaning of the Fifth Amendment. We need only address the question whether a "taking" has occurred.[1]

A

Before considering appellants' specific contentions, it will be useful to review the factors that have shaped the jurisprudence of the Fifth Amendment injunction "nor shall private property be taken for public use, without just compensation." The question of what constitutes a "taking" for purposes of the Fifth Amendment has proved to be a problem of considerable difficulty. While this Court has recognized that the "Fifth Amendment's guarantee [is] designed to bar Government from forcing some people alone to bear public burdens which, in all fairness and justice, should be borne by the public as a whole," *Armstrong v. United States,* 364 U.S. 40, 49 (1960), this court, quite simply, has been unable to develop any "set formula" for determining when "justice and fairness" require that economic injuries caused by public action to be compensated by the Government, rather than remain disproportionately concentrated on a few persons. *See Goldblatt v. Hempstead,* 369 U.S. 590, 594 (1962). Indeed, we frequently observed that whether a particular restriction will be rendered invalid by the Government's failure to pay for any losses proximately caused by it depends largely "upon the particular circumstances [in that] case." *United States v. Central Eureka Mining Co.,* 357 U.S. 155, 169 (1958). CASE BY CASE ANALISIS.

In engaging in these essential ad hoc, factual inquiries, the Court's decisions have identified several factors that have particular significance. The economic impact of the regulation on the claimant and, particularly, the extent to which the regulation has interfered with distinct investment backed expectations are

[1] As is implicit in our opinion, we do not embrace the proposition that a "taking" can never occur unless Government has transferred physical control over a portion of a parcel.

of course relevant considerations. *See Goldblatt v. Hempstead, supra,* at 594. So too is the character of the governmental action. A "taking" may more readily be found when the interference with property can be characterized as a physical invasion by Government, *see, e.g., Causby v. United States,* 328 U.S. 256 (1946), than when interference arises from some public program adjusting the benefits and burdens of economic life to promote the common good.

"Government could hardly go on if to some extent values incident to property could not be diminished without paying for every such change in the general law." *Pennsylvania Coal Co. v. Mahon,* 260 U.S. 393, 413 (1922), and this Court has accordingly recognized, in a wide variety of contexts, that Government may execute laws or programs that adversely affect recognized economic values. Exercises of the taxing power are one obvious example. A second are the decisions in which this Court has dismissed "taking" challenges on the ground that, while the challenged Government action caused economic harm, it did not interfere with interests that were sufficiently bound up with the reasonable expectations of the claimant to constitute "property" for Fifth Amendment purposes. *See, e.g., United States v. Willow River Power Co.,* 324 U.S. 499 (1945) (interest in high water level of river for run off for tail waters to maintain power head is not property); *United States v. Chandler-Dunbar Water Power Co.,* 229 U.S. 53 (1913) (no property interest can exist in navigable waters); *see also* Sax, *Takings and the Police Power,* 74 Yale L.J. 36, 61-62 (1963).

More importantly for the present case, in instances in which a state tribunal reasonably concluded that "the health, safety, morals or general welfare" would be promoted by prohibiting particular contemplated uses of land, this Court has upheld land use regulations that destroyed or adversely affected recognized real property interests. Zoning laws are of course the classic example, *see Euclid v. Ambler Realty Co.,* 272 U.S. 365 (1926) (prohibition of industrial use); *Gorieb v. Fox,* 274 U.S. 603, 608 (1927) (requirement that portions of parcels be left unbuilt); *Welch v. Swasey,* 214 U.S. 91 (1909) (height restriction), which have been viewed as permissible government action even when prohibiting the most beneficial use of the property.

Zoning laws generally do not affect existing uses of real property, but taking challenges have also been held to be without merit in a wide variety of situations when the challenged governmental actions prohibited a beneficial use to which individual parcels had previously been devoted and thus caused substantial individualized harm. . . .

Pennsylvania Coal Co. v. Mahon, 260 U.S. 393 (1922), is the leading case for the proposition that a state statute that substantially furthers important public policies may so frustrate distinct investment-backed expectations as to amount to a "taking." There the claimant had sold the surface rights to particular parcels of property, but expressly reserved the right to remove the coal thereunder. A Pennsylvania statute, enacted after the transactions, forbade any mining of coal that caused the subsidence of any house, unless the house was the property of the owner of the underlying coal and was more than 150 feet from the improved property of another. Because the statute made it commercially impracticable to mine the coal, *id.,* at 414, and thus had nearly the same effect as the complete destruction of rights claimant had purchased from the owners of the surface land, *see id.,* at 414-415, the Court held that the statute was invalid as effecting a "taking" without just compensation. *See also Armstrong v. United States, supra* (government's complete destruction of a materialman's lien in certain property held a "taking); *Hudson Water Co. v. McCarter,* 209 U.S. 349, 355 (1908) (if height restriction makes property wholly useless "the right of property prevails over the public interest" and compensation is required). *See* generally Michelman, *Property, Utility and Fairness: Comments on the Ethical Foundations of "Just Compensation" Law,* 80 Harv. L. Rev. 1165, 1229-1234 (1967).

Finally, Government actions that may be characterized as acquisitions of resources to permit or facilitate uniquely public functions have often been held to constitute "takings." *Causby v. United States, supra,* is illustrative. In holding that direct overflights above the claimant's land, that destroyed the present use of the land as a chicken farm, constituted a "taking,"*Causby* emphasized that Government had not "merely destroyed property [but was] using a part of it for the flight of its planes." *Id.,* at 262-263, n. 7. *See also Griggs v. Allegheny County,* 369 U.S. 327 (1922) (United States' military installations repeated firing of guns over claimant's land is a taking); *United States v. Cress,* 243 U.S. 316 91917) (repeated floodings of land caused by water project is taking); *but see YMCA v. United States,* 395 U.S. 85 (1969) (damage caused to building when federal officers who were seeking to protect building were attacked by rioters held not a taking). *See generally* Michelman, 80 Harv. L. Rev. 1165, 1226-1229 (1967); Sax, 74 Yale L.J. 36 (1963).

B

In contending that the New York City law has "taken" their property in violation of the Fifth and Fourteenth Amendments, appellants make a series of arguments, which, while tailored to the facts of this case, essentially urge that any substantial restriction imposed pursuant to landmark law must be accompanied by just compensation if it is to be constitutional. Before considering these, we emphasize what is not in dispute. Because this Court has recognized, in a number of settings, that states and cities may enact land use restrictions or controls to enhance the quality of life by preserving the character and desirable aesthetic features of a city, see *New Orleans v. Dukes,* 427 U.S. 297 (1976); *Young v. American Mini Theatres, Inc.,* 427 U.S. 50 (1976); *Village of Belle Terre v. Borass,* 416 U.S. 1, 9-10 (1974); *Berman v. Parker,* 348 U.S. 26, 33 (1954); *Welch v. Swasey, supra* at 108, appellants do not contest that New York City's objective of preserving structures and areas with special historic, architectural, or cultural significance is an entirely permissible governmental goal. They also do not dispute that the restrictions imposed on its parcel are appropriate means of securing the purposes of New York City's law. Finally, appellants do not challenge any of the specific factual premises of the decision below. They accept for present purposes both that the parcel of land occupied by Grand Central Terminal must, in its present state, be regarded as capable of earning a reasonable return, and that the transferable development rights afforded appellants by virtue of the Terminal's designation as a landmark are valuable, even if not as valuable as the rights to construct above the Terminal. In appellant's view none of these factors derogate from their claim that New York City's law has effected a "taking."

. . . .

Stated boldly, appellants' position appears to be that the only means of ensuring that selected owners are not singled out to endure financial hardship for no reason is to hold that any restriction imposed on individual landmarks pursuant to the New York scheme is a "taking" requiring the payment of "just compensation." Agreement with this argument would of course invalidate not just New York City's law, but all comparable landmark legislation in the nation. We find no merit in it.

It is true, as appellants emphasize, that both historic district legislation and zoning laws regulate all properties within given physical communities whereas landmark laws apply only to selected parcels. But, contrary to appellants' suggestions, landmark laws are not like discriminatory, or "reverse spot," zoning: that is, a land use decision which arbitrarily singles out a particular parcel for different, less favorable treatment than the neighboring ones. In contrast to discriminatory zoning, which is the antithesis of land use control as part of some comprehensive plan, the New York City law embodies a comprehensive plan to preserve structures of historic or aesthetic interest wherever they might be found in the city,[2] and as noted, over 400 landmarks and 31 historic districts have been designated pursuant to this plan.

Equally without merit is the related argument that the decision to designate a structure as a landmark "is inevitably arbitrary or at least subjective because it basically is a matter of taste," Reply Brief of Appellant 22, thus unavoidably singling out individual landowners for disparate and unfair treatment. The argument has a particularly hollow ring in this case. For appellants not only did not seek judicial review of either the designation or of the denials of the certificates of appropriateness and of no exterior effect, but do not even now suggest that the Commission's decisions concerning the Terminal were in any sense arbitrary or unprincipled. But, in any event, a landmark owner has a right to judicial review of any Commission decision, and, quite simply, there is no basis whatsoever for a conclusion that courts will have any greater difficulty identifying arbitrary or discriminatory action in the context of landmark regulation than in the context of classic zoning or indeed in any other context.[3]

Next, appellants observe that New York City's law differs from zoning laws and historic district ordinances in that the Landmark Law does not impose

[2] Although the New York Court of Appeals contrasted the New York City Landmark Law with both zoning and historic district legislation and stated at one point that landmark laws do not "further a general community plan," 42 N.Y.2d at 330, it also emphasized that the implementation of the objectives of the landmark law constitutes an "acceptable reason to single out one particular parcel for different and less favorable treatment." *Ibid.* Therefore, we do not understand the New York Court of Appeals to disagree with our characterization of the Act.

[3] When a property owner challenges the application of a zoning ordinance to his property, the judicial inquiry focuses upon whether the challenged restriction can reasonably be deemed to promote the objectives of the community land use plan, and will include consideration of the treatment of similar parcels. *See generally Nectow v. Cambridge, supra.* When a property owner challenges a landmark designation or restriction as arbitrary or discriminatory, a similar inquiry presumably will occur.

identical or similar restrictions on all structures located in particular physical communities. It follows, they argue, that New York City's law is inherently incapable of producing the fair and equitable distribution of benefits and burdens of governmental action which is characteristic of zoning laws and historic district legislation and which they maintain is a constitutional requirement if "just compensation" is not to be afforded. It is of course true that the Landmark Law has a more severe impact on some landowners than on others, but that in itself does not mean that the law effects a "taking." Legislation designed to promote the general welfare commonly burdens some more than others. The owners of the brickyard in *Hadacheck*, of the cedar trees in *Miller v. Schoene*, and of the gravel and sand mine in *Goldblatt v. Hempstead,* were uniquely burdened by the legislation sustained in those cases.[4] Similarly, zoning laws often impact more severely on some property owners than others but have not been held to be invalid on that account. For example, the property owner in *Euclid* who wished to use his property for industrial purposes was affected far more severely by the ordinance than his neighbors who wished to use their land for residences.

In any event, appellants' repeated suggestions that they are solely burdened and unbenefitted is factually inaccurate. This contention overlooks the fact that the New York City law applies to vast numbers of structures in the city in addition to the Terminal—all the structures contained in the 31 historic districts and over 400 individual landmarks, many of which are close to the Terminal.[5] Unless we are to reject the judgment of the New York City Council that the preservation of landmarks benefits all New York citizens and all structures, both economically and by improving the quality of life in the city as a whole—which we are unwilling to do—we cannot conclude that the owners of the Terminal have in no sense been benefitted by the Landmark Law. Doubtless appellants believe they are more burdened than benefitted by the law, but that must have been true too of the property owners in *Miller, Hadacheck, Euclid, and Goldblatt.*[6]

Appellants' final broad-based attack would have us treat the law as an instance, like that in *United States v. Causby, supra,* in which Government, acting in an enterprise capacity, has appropriated part of their property for some strictly governmental purpose. Apart from the fact that *Causby* was a

---

[4] Appellants attempt to distinguish these cases on the ground that, in each, government was prohibiting a "noxious" use of land and that in the present case, in contrast, appellants' proposed construction above the Terminal would be beneficial. We observe that the uses in issue in *Hadacheck, Miller* and *Goldblatt* were perfectly lawful in themselves. They involved no "blameworthiness . . . moral wrongdoing, or conscious act of dangerous risk-taking which induced [society] to shift the cost to a particular individual." Sax, 74 Yale L.J. 36, 50 (1964). These cases are better understood as resting not on any supposed "noxious" quality of the prohibited uses but rather on the ground that the restrictions were reasonably related to the implementation of a policy—not unlike historic preservation—expected to produce a widespread public benefit and applicable to all similarly situated property.

[5] There are some 53 designated landmarks and three historic districts or scenic landmarks in Manhattan between 14th and 59th Streets. *See* Landmarks Preservation Commission, Landmarks and Historic Districts (1977).

[6] It is of course true that the fact the duties imposed by zoning and historic district legislation apply throughout particular physical communities provides assurances against arbitrariness, but the applicability of the landmarks law to large numbers of parcels in the city, in our view, provides comparable, if not identical, assurances.

case of invasion of airspace that destroyed the use of the farm beneath and this New York City law has in no wise impaired the present use of the Terminal, the Landmark Law neither exploits appellants' parcel for city purposes nor facilitates nor arises from any entrepreneurial operations of the city. The situation is not remotely like that in *Causby* when the airspace above the Terminal was in the flight pattern for military aircraft. The Landmarks Law's effect is simply to prohibit appellants or anyone else from occupying portions of the airspace above the Terminal, while permitting appellants to use the remainder of the parcel in a gainful fashion. This is no more an appropriation of property by Government for its own uses than is a zoning law prohibiting, for "aesthetic" reasons, two or more adult theatres within a specified area, *see Young v. American Mini Theatres, Inc, supra,* or a safety regulation prohibiting excavations below a certain level. *See Goldblatt v. City of Hempstead, supra.*

C

Rejection of appellants' broad arguments is not however the end of our inquiry, for all we thus far have established is that the New York law is not rendered invalid by its failure to provide "just compensation" whenever a landmark owner is restricted in the exploitation of property interests, such as air rights, to a greater extent than provided for under applicable zoning laws. We now must consider whether the interference with appellants' property is of such a magnitude that "there must be an exercise of eminent domain and compensation to sustain [it]." *Pennsylvania Coal Co. v. Mahon,* 260 U.S. at 413. That inquiry may be narrowed to the question of the severity of the impact of the law on appellants' parcel, and its resolution in turn requires a careful assessment of the impact of the regulation on the Terminal site.

Unlike the governmental acts in *Goldblatt, Miller, Causby, Griggs* and *Hadacheck,* the New York City law does not interfere in any way with the present uses of the Terminal. Its designation as a landmark not only permits but contemplates that appellants may continue to use the property precisely as it has for the past 65 years: as a railroad terminal containing office space and concessions. So the law does not interfere with what must be regarded as Penn Central's primary expectation concerning the use of the parcel. More importantly, on this record, we must regard the New York City law as permitting Penn Central not only to profit from the Terminal but to obtain a "reasonable return" on its investment.

Appellants, moreover, exaggerate the effect of the Act on its ability to make use of the air rights above the Terminal in two respects.[7] First, it simply cannot be maintained, on this record, that appellants have been prohibited from occupying *any* portion of the airspace above the Terminal. While the Commissions' actions in denying applications to construct an office building in excess of 50 stories above the Terminal may indicate that it will refuse to issue a certificate of appropriateness for any comparably sized structure,

[7] Appellants of course argue at length that the transferable development rights, while valuable, do not constitute "just compensation."

nothing the Commission has said or done suggests an intention to prohibit *any* construction above the Terminal.

Second, to the extent appellants have been denied the right to build above the Terminal, it is not literally accurate to say that they have been denied *all* use of even those pre-existing air rights. Their ability to use these rights has not been abrogated; they are made transferable to at least eight parcels in the vicinity of the Terminal, one or two of which have been found suitable for the construction of new office buildings. Although appellants and others have argued that New York City's transferable development rights program is far from ideal, the New York courts have supportably found that, at least in the case of the Terminal, the rights afforded are valuable. While these rights may well not have constituted "just compensation" if a "taking" had occurred, the rights nevertheless undoubtedly mitigate whatever financial burdens the law has imposed on appellants and, for that reason, are to be taken into account in considering the impact of regulation. Cf. *Goldblatt v. Hempstead, supra* at 594 n. 3.

On this record we conclude that the application of New York City's Landmark Preservation law has not affected a "taking" of appellants' property. The restrictions imposed are substantially related to the promotion of the general welfare and not only permit reasonable beneficial use of the landmark site but afford appellants opportunities further to enhance not only the Terminal site proper but also other properties.[8]

Affirmed.

JUSTICE REHNQUIST, with whom THE CHIEF JUSTICE and JUSTICE STEVENS join, dissenting.

. . . .

1

. . . .

Appellees are not prohibiting a nuisance. The record is clear that the proposed addition to the Grand Central Terminal would be in full compliance with zoning, height limitations, and other health and safety requirements. Instead, appellees are seeking to preserve what they believe to be an outstanding example of Beaux Arts architecture. Penn Central is prevented from further developing its property basically because it did *too good* of a job in designing and building it. The City of New York, because of its unadorned admiration for the design, has decided that the owners of the building must preserve it unchanged for the benefit of sightseeing New Yorkers and tourists.

Unlike in the case of land use regulations, appellees are not prohibiting Penn Central from using its property in a narrow sense. Instead, appellees have placed an affirmative duty on Penn Central to maintain the Terminal

[8] We emphasize that our holding today is on the present record which in turn is based on Penn Central's present ability to use the Terminal for its intended purposes and in a gainful fashion. The city conceded at oral argument that if appellants can demonstrate at some point in the future that circumstances have changed such that the Terminal ceases to be, in the city's counsel's words, "economically viable," appellants may obtain relief.

in its present state of "good repair." Appellants are not free to use their property as they see fit within broad outer boundaries but must strictly adhere to their past use except where appellees conclude that alternative uses would not detract from the Landmark. While Penn Central may continue to use the Terminal as it is presently designed, appellees otherwise "exercise complete dominion and control over the surface of the land," *United States v. Causby,* 328 U.S. 256, 262 (1946), and must compensate the owner for his gloss. . . .

2

Even where the government prohibits a noninjurious use, the Court has ruled that a taking does not take place if the prohibition applies over a broad cross section of land and thereby "secure[s] an average reciprocity of advantage." *Pennsylvania Coal Co. v. Mahon,* 260 U.S. 393, 415 (1922). While zoning at times reduces *individual* property values, the burden is shared relatively evenly and it is reasonable to conclude that on the whole an individual who is harmed by one aspect of the zoning will be benefitted by another.

Here, however, a multimillion dollar loss has been imposed on appellants; it is uniquely felt and is not offset by any benefits flowing from the preservation of some 500 other "Landmarks" in New York. Appellees have imposed a substantial cost on less than one-tenth of one percent of the buildings in New York for the general benefit of all its people. It is exactly this imposition of general costs on a few individuals at which the "taking" protection is directed. . . .

As Justice Homes pointed out in *Pennsylvania Coal Co. v. Mahon,* "the question at bottom" in an eminent domain case "is upon whom the loss of the changes desired should fall." 260 U.S. 416, 43 S.Ct. at 160. The benefits that appellees believe will flow from preservation of the Grand Central Terminal will accrue to all the citizens of New York. There is no reason to believe that appellants will enjoy a substantially greater share of these benefits. If the cost of preserving Grand Central Terminal were spread evenly across the entire population of the city of New York, the burden per person would be in cents per year—a minor cost appellees would surely concede for the benefit accrued. Instead, however, appellees would impose the entire cost of several million dollars per year on Penn Central. But it is precisely this sort of discrimination that the Fifth Amendment prohibits.

Appellees in response would argue that a taking only occurs where a property owner is denied *all* reasonable value of his property. The Court has frequently held that, even where a destruction of property rights would not *otherwise* constitute a taking, the inability of the owner to make a reasonable return on his property requires compensation under the Fifth Amendment. But the converse is not true. A taking does not become a noncompensable exercise of police power simply because the government in its graces allows the owner to make some "reasonable" use of his property. "[I]t is the character of the invasion, not the amount of damage resulting from it, so long as the damage is substantial, that determines the question whether it is a taking." *United States v. Cress,* 243 U.S. 316, 328 (1917); *United States v. Causby,* 328 U.S. 256, 266 (1946). . . .

NOTES AND QUESTIONS

(1) How do you assess the multiple takings tests that were referred to in the majority opinion in *Penn Central*? As Justice Brennan has interpreted the "average reciprocity of advantage test," is there any landowner who will not benefit (as a private citizen) from virtually any governmental action that affects his or her land? If so, is there anything left of the takings clause as a limit on governmental action?

(2) What is meant the by the phrase "investment backed expectation?" To what extent might real estate investors expect that their property values will decrease as a result of environmental regulations? Should this be taken into account in determining whether those regulations constitute a taking?

(3) In *Penn Central,* Justice Brennan opined that "[t]aking jurisprudence does not divide a single parcel into discrete segments and attempt to determine whether rights in a particular segment have been entirely abrogated." Instead, it focuses "both on the character of the action and on the nature and extent of the interference with rights in the parcel as a whole." Is that conclusion consistent with the majority opinion in the *Mahon* case?

(4) Citing *Causby v. United States,* 328 U.S. 256 (1946), the majority opinion in *Penn Central* observed that a taking "may more readily be found when the interference with property can be characterized as a physical invasion by government." This notion was reiterated and reinforced in *Loretta v. Teleprompter Manhattan CATV Corp.,* 458 U.S. 419 (1982), in which the Court struck down, as a "*per se* taking," a New York statute that required CATV carriers to run cables across, and attach cables to, apartment buildings. Notwithstanding the minimal extent to which the mandated cables interfered with the plaintiff's property rights—in fact, they occupied less than 1/8 of a cubic foot of space on the roof of his apartment building—the court found that an unconstitutional, "permanent physical occupation" had been created. It stated that, in such a situation, the "character of the governmental action is a determinative factor with regard to whether a taking has occurred." Compare *Yee v. City of Escondido,* 503 U.S. 519 (1992), where the Supreme Court rejected the argument that a statute that required mobile home park owners to roll back rents—and prohibited them from requiring the removal of a mobile home when it is sold—constituted a physical invasion of land.

KEYSTONE BITUMINOUS COAL ASS'N v. DeBENEDICTUS

United States Supreme Court (1987)
480 U.S. 470, 107 S. Ct. 1232, 94 L. Ed. 2d 472

STEVENS, J.:

In *Pennsylvania Coal Co. v. Mahon,* 260 U.S. 393 (1922), the Court reviewed the constitutionality of a Pennsylvania statute that admittedly destroyed "previously existing rights of property and contract." . . . In that case the "particular facts" led the Court to hold that the Pennsylvania Legislature had gone beyond its constitutional powers when it enacted a statute prohibiting the mining of anthracite coal in a manner that would cause the subsidence of land on which certain structures were located.

Now, 65 years later, we address a different set of "particular facts," involving the Pennsylvania Legislature's 1966 conclusion that the Commonwealth's existing mine subsidence legislation had failed to protect the public interest in safety, land conservation, preservation of affected municipalities' tax bases, and land development in the Commonwealth. Based on detailed findings, the legislature enacted the Bituminous Mine Subsidence and Land Conservation Act (the "Subsidence Act" or the "Act"), Pa. Stat. Ann., Tit. 52, § 1406.1 *et seq.* (Purdon Supp. 1986). Petitioners contend, relying heavily on our decision in *Pennsylvania Coal,* that § 4 and § 6 of the Act violates the Contracts Clause of the Federal Constitution. The District Court and the Court of appeals concluded that *Pennsylvania Coal* does not control for several reasons and that our subsequent cases make it clear that neither § 4 nor § 6 is unconstitutional on its face. We agree.

I

Coal mine subsidence is the lowering of strata overlying a coal mine, including the land surface, caused by the extraction of underground coal. This lowering of strata can have devastating effects. It often causes substantial damage to foundations, walls, other structural members, and the integrity of houses and buildings. Subsidence frequently causes sinkholes or troughs in land which make the land difficult or impossible to develop. Its effect on farming has been well documented—many subsided areas cannot be plowed or properly prepared. Subsidence can also cause the loss of groundwater and surface ponds. In short, it presents the type of environmental concern that has been the focus of so much federal, state, and local regulation in recent decades.[9]

. . . .

Pennsylvania's Subsidence Act authorizes the Pennsylvania Department of Environmental Resources (DER) to implement and enforce a comprehensive program to prevent or minimize subsidence and to regulate its consequences. Section 4 of the Subsidence Act, Pa. Stat. Ann., Tit. 52,§ 1406.4, prohibits mining that causes subsidence damage to three categories of structures that were in place on April 17, 1966: public buildings and noncommercial buildings generally used by the public; dwellings used for human habitation; and cemeteries. Since 1966 the DER has applied a formula that generally requires 50% of the coal beneath structures protected by § 4 to be kept in place as a means of providing surface support. Section 6 of the Subsidence Act, 52 Pa. Sta. Ann., Tit. 52, § 1406.6, authorizes the DER to revoke a mining permit if the removal of coal causes damage to a structure or area protected by § 4 and the operator has not within six months either repaired the damage,

[9] Indeed, in 1977, Congress passed the Federal Surface Mining Control and Reclamation Act, 91Stat. 445, 30 U.S.C. § 1201, *et seq.*, which includes regulation of subsidence caused by underground coal mining. *See* 30 U.S.C. § 1266.

satisfied any claim arising therefrom, or deposited a sum equal to the reasonable cost of repair with the DER as security.

II

In 1982, petitioners filed a civil rights action in the United States District Court for the Western District of Pennsylvania seeking to enjoin officials of the DER from enforcing the Subsidence Act and its implementing regulations. The petitioners are an association of coal mine operators, and four corporations that are engaged, either directly or through affiliates, in underground mining of bituminous coal in western Pennsylvania. The members of the association and the corporate petitioners own, lease or otherwise control substantial coal reserves beneath the surface of property affected by the Subsidence Act. The defendants in the action, respondents here, are the Secretary of the Commonwealth of Pennsylvania, the Chief of DER's Division of Mine Subsidence, and the Chief of DER's Section on Mine Subsidence Regulation.

The complaint alleges that Pennsylvania recognizes three separate estates in land: the mineral estate; the surface estate; and the "support estate." Beginning well over 100 years ago, land owners began severing title to underground coal and the right of surface support while retaining or conveying away ownership of the surface estate. It is stipulated that approximately 90% of the coal that is or will be mined by petitioners in western Pennsylvania was severed from the surface in the period between 1890 and 1920. When acquiring or retaining the mineral estate, petitioners or their predecessors typically acquired or retained certain additional rights that would enable them to extract and remove the coal. Thus, they acquired the right to deposit wastes, to provide for drainage and ventilation, and to erect facilities such as tipples, roads, or railroads, on the surface. Additionally, they typically acquired a waiver of any claims for damages that might result from the removal of the coal.

In the portions of the complaint that are relevant to us, petitioners alleged that both § 4 of the Subsidence Act, as implemented by the 50% rule, and § 6 of the Subsidence Act, constitute a taking of their private property without compensation in violation of the Fifth and Fourteenth Amendments. They also alleged that § 6 impairs their contractual agreements in violation of Article I, § 10 of the Constitution. The parties entered into a stipulation of facts pertaining to petitioners' facial challenge, and filed cross motions for summary judgment on the facial challenge. The District Court granted respondents' motion. . . . [The district court rejected the taking claim and the Court of Appeals affirmed.]

We granted certiorari, and now affirm.

III

Petitioners assert that disposition of their takings claim calls for no more than a straightforward application of the Court's decision in *Pennsylvania Coal Co. v. Mahon.* Although there are some obvious similarities between the cases, we agree with the Court of Appeals and the District Court that the similarities are far less significant than the differences, and that *Pennsylvania Coal* does not control this case. . . .

. . . .

The holdings and assumptions of the Court in *Pennsylvania Coal* provide obvious and necessary reasons for distinguishing *Pennsylvania Coal* from the case before us today. The two factors that the Court considered relevant, have become integral parts of our taking analysis. We have held that land use regulation can effect a taking of it "does not substantially advance legitimate state interests, . . . or denies an owner economically viable use of his land." *Agins v. Tiburon,* 447 U.S. 255, 260 (1980) (citations omitted); *see also Penn Central Transportation Co. v. New York City,* 438 U.S. 104, 124 (1978). Application of these tests to petitioners' challenge demonstrates that they have not satisfied their burden of showing that the Subsidence Act constitutes a taking. First, unlike the Kohler Act, the character of the government action involved here leans heavily against finding a taking; the Commonwealth of Pennsylvania has acted to arrest what is perceives to be a significant threat to the common welfare. Second, there is no reason in this case to support a finding, similar to the one the Court made in *Pennsylvania Coal,* that the Subsidence Act makes it impossible for petitioners to profitably engage in their business, or that there has been undue interference with their investment-backed expectations.

-THIS IS ALSO ALWAYS A TAKING ALONG W/ PHYS INVASION

The Public Purpose

Unlike the Kohler Act, which was passed upon in *Pennsylvania Coal,* the Subsidence Act does not merely involve a balancing of the private economic interests of coal companies against the private interests of the surface owners. The Pennsylvania legislature specifically found that important public interests are served by enforcing a policy that is designed to minimize subsidence in certain areas. Section 2 of the Subsidence Act provides:

> "This act shall be deemed to be an exercise of the police powers of the Commonwealth for the protection of the health, safety and general welfare of the people of the Commonwealth, by providing for the conservation of surface land areas which may be affected in the mining of bituminous coal by methods other than 'open pit' or 'strip' mining, to aid in the protection of the safety of the public, to enhance the value of such lands for taxation, to aid in the preservation of surface water drainage and public water supplies and generally to improve the use and enjoyment of such lands and to maintain primary jurisdiction over surface coal mining in Pennsylvania." Pa. Ann. Stat. Tit. 52, § 1406.2

The District Court and the Court of Appeals were both convinced that the legislative purposes set forth in the statute were genuine, substantial, and legitimate, and we have no reason to conclude otherwise.

None of the indicia of a statute enacted solely for the benefit of private parties identified in Justice Holmes' opinion are present here. First, Justice Holmes explained that the Kohler Act was a "private benefit" statute since it "ordinarily does not apply to land when the surface is owned by the owner of the coal." 260 U.S., at 414. The Subsidence Act, by contrast, has no such exception. The current surface owner may only waive the protection of the Act if the DER consents. *See* 25 Pa. Code § 89.145(b) (1983). Moreover, the Court was forced to reject the Commonwealth's safety justification for the Kohler Act because it found that the Commonwealth's interest in safety could as easily have been accomplished through a notice requirement to landowners. The Subsidence Act, by contrast, is designed to accomplish a number of widely varying interests, with reference to which petitioners have not suggested alternative methods through which the Commonwealth could proceed.

Petitioners argue that at least § 6, which requires coal companies to repair subsidence damage or pay damages to those who suffer subsidence damage, is unnecessary because the Commonwealth administers an insurance program that adequately reimburses surface owners for the cost of repairing their property. But this argument rests on the mistaken premise that the statute was motivated by a desire to protect private parties. In fact, however, the public purpose that motivated the enactment of the legislation is served by preventing the damage from occurring in the first place—in the words of the statute—"by providing for the conservation of the surface land areas." Pa. Stat. Ann., Tit. 52, § 1406.2. The requirement that the mine operator assume the financial responsibility for the repair of damaged structures deters the operator from causing the damage at all—the Commonwealth's main goal—whereas an insurance program would merely reimburse the surface owner after the damage occurs.[10]

Thus, the Subsidence Act differs from the Kohler Act in critical and dispositive respects. With regard to the Kohler Act, the Court believed that the Commonwealth had acted only to ensure against damage to some private landowners' homes. Justice Holmes stated that if the private individuals needed support for their structures, they should not have "take[n] the risk of acquiring only surface rights." 260 U.S., at 416. Here, by contrast, the Commonwealth is acting to protect the public interest in health, the environment, and the fiscal integrity of the area. That private individuals erred in taking a risk cannot estop the State from exercising its police power to abate activity akin to a public nuisance. The Subsidence Act is a prime example that "circumstances may so change in time . . . as to clothe with such a [public] interest that at other times . . . would be a matter of purely private concern." *Block v. Hirsh,* 265 U.S. 135, 155 (1921).

. . . .

[10] We do not suggest that courts have "a license to judge the effectiveness of legislation" [quoting language from the dissent of Justice REHNQUIST], or that courts are to undertake "least restrictive alternative" analysis in deciding whether a state regulatory scheme is designed to remedy a public harm or is instead intended to provide private benefits. That a land use regulation may be somewhat overinclusive or underinclusive is, of course, no justification for rejecting it. *See Euclid v. Amber Realty Co.,* 272 U.S. 365, 388-389 (1926). But, on the other hand, *Pennsylvania Coal* instructs courts to examine the operative provisions of a statute, not just its stated purpose, in assessing its true nature. In *Pennsylvania Coal,* that inquiry led the Court to reject the Pennsylvania Legislature's stated purpose for the statute, because the "extent of the public interest is shown by the statute to be limited." 260 U.S., at 413-414. In this case, we, the Court of Appeals, and the District Court, have conducted the same type of inquiry that the Court in *Pennsylvania Coal* conducted, and have determined that the details of the statute do not call the stated public purposes into question.

The Court's hesitance to find a taking when the state merely restrains uses of property that are tantamount to public nuisance is consistent with the notion of "reciprocity of advantage" that Justice Holmes referred to in *Pennsylvania Coal.*[11] Under our system of government, one of the state's primary ways of preserving the public weal is restricting the uses individuals can make of their property. While each of us is burdened somewhat by such restrictions, we, in turn, benefit greatly from the restrictions that are placed on others.[12] *See Penn Central Transportation Co. v. New York City,* 438 U.S., at 144-150 (Rehnquist, J., dissenting). These restrictions are "properly treated as part of the burden of common citizenship." *Kimball Laundry Co. v. United States,* 338 U.S. 1, 5 (1949). Long ago it was recognized that "all property in this country is held under the implied obligation that the owner's use of it shall not be injurious to the community." *Mugler v. Kansas,* 123 U.S., at 665, and the Takings Clause did not transform that principle to one that requires compensation whenever the State asserts its power to enforce it. . . .

As the cases discussed above demonstrate, the public interest in preventing activities similar to public nuisances is a substantial one, which in many instances has not required compensation. The Subsidence Act, unlike the Kohler Act, plainly seeks to further such an interest. Nonetheless, we need not rest our decision on this factor alone, because petitioners have also failed to make a showing of diminution of value sufficient to satisfy the test set forth in *Pennsylvania Coal* and our other regulatory takings cases.

Diminution of Value and Investment-Backed Expectations

The second factor that distinguishes this case from *Pennsylvania Coal* is the finding in that case that the Kohler Act made mining of "certain coal" commercially impracticable. In this case, by contrast, petitioners have not shown any deprivation significant enough to satisfy the heavy burden placed upon one alleging a regulatory taking. For this reason, their takings claim must fail.

. . . .

Petitioners thus face an uphill battle in making a facial attack on the Act as a taking.

The hill is made especially steep because petitioners have not claimed, at this stage, that the Act makes it commercially impracticable for them to continue mining their bituminous coal interest in western Pennsylvania.

---

[11] The special status of this type of state action can be understood on the simple theory that since no individual has a right to use his property so as to create a nuisance or otherwise harm others the state has not "taken" anything when it asserts its power to enjoin the nuisance-like activity.

However, as the current Chief Justice has explained: "The nuisance exception to the taking guarantee is not coterminous with the police power itself." Penn Central Transport Co., 438 U.S. at 145 (Rehnquist, J., dissenting). . . .

[12] The Takings Clause has never been read to require the States or the courts to calculate whether a specific individual has suffered burdens under this generic rule in excess of the benefits received. Not every individual gets a full dollar return in benefits for the taxes he or she pays; yet, no one suggests that an individual has a right to compensate for the difference between taxes paid and the dollar value of benefits received.

Indeed, petitioners have not even pointed to a single mine that can no longer be mined for profit. The only evidence available on the effect that the Subsidence Act has had on petitioners' mining operations comes from petitioners' answers to respondents' interrogatories. Petitioners described the effect that the Subsidence Act had from 1966-1982 on 13 mines that the various companies operate, and claimed that they have been required to leave a bit less than 27 million tons of coal in place to support § 4 areas. The total coal in those 13 mines amounts to over 1.46 billion tons. Thus § 4 requires them to leave less than 2% of their coal in place.[13] But, as we have indicated, nowhere near all of the underground coal is extractable even aside from the Subsidence Act. The categories of coal that must be left for § 4 purposes and other purposes are not necessarily distinct sets, and there is no information in the record as to how much coal is actually left in the ground solely because of § 4. We do know, however, that petitioners have never claimed that their mining operations, or even any specific mines, have been unprofitable since the Subsidence Act was passed. Nor is there evidence that mining in any specific location affected by the 50% rule has been unprofitable.

Instead, petitioners have sought to narrowly define certain segments of their property and assert that, when so defined, the Subsidence Act denies them economically viable use. They advance two alternative ways of carving their property in order to reach this conclusion. First, they focus on the specific tons of coal that they must leave in the ground under the Subsidence Act, and argue that the Commonwealth has effectively appropriated this coal since it has no other useful purpose if not mined. Second, they contend that the Commonwealth has taken their separate legal interest in property—the "support estate."

. . . .

The Coal in Place

The parties have stipulated that enforcement of the DER's 50% rule will require petitioners to leave approximately 27 million tons of coal in place. Because they own that coal but cannot mine it, they contend that Pennsylvania has appropriated it for public purposes described in the Subsidence Act.

This argument fails for the reason explained in *Penn Central* and *Andrus*. The 27 million tons of coal do not constitute a separate segment of property for takings law purposes. Many zoning ordinances place limits on the property owner's right to make profitable use of some segments of his property. A requirement that a building occupy no more than a specified percentage of the lot on which it is located could be characterized as a taking of the vacant area as readily as the requirement that coal pillars be left in place. Similarly, under petitioners' theory one could always argue that a set-back ordinance requiring that no structure be built within a certain distance from the property line constitutes a taking because the footage represents a distinct segment

[13] The percentage of the total that must be left in place under § 4 is not the same for every mine because of the wide variation in the extent of surface development in different areas. For 7 of the13 mines identified in the record, 1% or less of the coal must remain in place; for three others, less than 3% must be left in place; for the other three, the percentages are 4%, 7.8%, and 9.4%.

of property for takings law purposes. Cf. *Gorieb v. Fox,* 274 U.S. 603 (1927) (upholding validity of set-back ordinance) (per Homes, J.). There is no basis for treating the less than 2% of petitioners' coal as a separate parcel of property.

. . . .

The Support Estate

Pennsylvania property law is apparently unique in regarding the support estate as a separate interest in land that can be conveyed apart from either the mineral estate or the surface estate. Petitioners therefore argue that even if comparable legislation in other states would not constitute a taking, the Subsidence Act has that consequence because it entirely destroys the value of their unique support estate. It is clear, however, that our takings jurisprudence forecloses reliance on such legalistic distinctions within a bundle of property rights. For example, in *Penn Central,* the Court rejected the argument that the "air rights" above the terminal constituted a separate segment of property for Takings Clause purposes, 438 U.S., at 130. Likewise, in *Andrus v. Allard,* we viewed the right to sell property as just one element of the owner's property interest. 444 U.S., at 65-66. In neither case did the result turn on whether the state allowed the separate sale of the segment of property. . . .

The judgment of the Court of Appeals is affirmed. [CHIEF JUSTICE REHNQUIST, joined by JUSTICE POWELL, JUSTICE O'CONNOR, and JUSTICE SCALIA, dissented.]

NOTES AND QUESTIONS

(1) This decision, along with *Nollan v. California Coastal Commission* and *First English Evangelical Lutheran Church of Glendale v. County of Los Angeles, infra,* came to be known as the "takings trilogy": a set of significant interpretations of the Fifth Amendment takings clause handed down by the U.S. Supreme Court in 1987. Do you agree with the Court's distinction between the purposes of the Kohler Act (struck down in *Pennsylvania Coal Company v. Mahon*) and the Subsidence Act (upheld in *Keystone*)? Is the *Mahon* case still good law in the aftermath of the *Keystone* decision? If so, how much of that case has retained importance as a binding precedent?

(2) Chief Justice Rehnquist dissented in *Keystone.* He viewed the "support estate," *i.e.*, the 27 million tons of coal which the coal companies were not able to mine in Pennsylvania, as a result of the Subsidence Act, as a separate, identifiable property interest that had been "taken" by the legislation. Are you persuaded by that conclusion? To what extent should state law define which property segments may be "taken," as a matter of federal constitutional law?

NOLLAN v. CALIFORNIA COASTAL COMMISSION

United States Supreme Court (1987)
483 U.S. 825, 107 S. Ct. 3141, 97 L. Ed. 2d 677

SCALIA, J.:

James and Marilyn Nollan appealed from a decision of the California Court of Appeals ruling that the California Coastal Commission could condition its grant of permission to rebuild their house on their transfer to the public of an easement across their beachfront property. 223 Cal. Rptr. 28 (1986). The California Court rejected their claim that imposition of that condition violates the Takings Clause of the Fifth Amendment, as incorporated against the states by the Fourteenth Amendment. *Ibid.* We noted probable jurisdiction.

The Nollans own a beachfront lot in Ventura County, California. A quarter mile north of their property is Faria County Park, an oceanside public park with a public beach and recreation area. Another public beach area, known locally as "the Cove," lies 1,800 feet south of their lot. A concrete seawall approximately eight feet high separates the beach portion of the Nollans' property from the rest of the lot. The historic mean high tide line determines the lot's oceanside boundary.

The Nollans originally leased their property with an option to buy. The building on the lot was a small bungalow, totaling 504 square feet, which for a time they rented to summer vacationers. After years of rental use, however, the building had fallen into disrepair, and could no longer be rented out.

The Nollans' option to purchase was conditioned on their promise to demolish the bungalow and replace it. In order to do so, under California Public Resources Code §§ 30106, 30212, and 30600(West 1986), they were required to obtain a coastal development permit from the California Coastal Commission. On February 25, 1982, they submitted a permit application to the Commission in which they proposed to demolish the existing structure and replace it with a three-bedroom house in keeping with the rest of the neighborhood.

The Nollans were informed that their application had been placed on the administrative calendar, and that the Commission staff had recommended that the permit be granted subject to the condition that they allow the public an easement to pass across a portion of their property bounded by the mean high tide line on one side, and their seawall on the other side. This would make it easier for the public to get to Faria County Park and the Cove. The Nollans protested imposition of the condition, but the Commission overruled their objections and granted the permit subject to their recordation of a deed restriction granting the easement.

On June 3, 1982, the Nollans filed a petition for writ of administrative mandamus asking the Ventura County Superior Court to invalidate the access condition. They argued that the condition could not be imposed absent evidence that their proposed development would have a direct adverse impact on public access to the beach. The court agreed, and remanded the case to the Commission for a full evidentiary hearing on that issue.

On remand, the Commission held a public hearing, after which it made further factual findings and reaffirmed its imposition of the condition. . . .

. . . .

II

Had California simply required the Nollans to make an easement across their beachfront available to the public on a permanent basis in order to increase public access to the beach, rather than conditioning their permit to rebuild their house on their agreeing to do so, we have no doubt there would have been a taking. To say that the appropriation of a public easement across a landowner's premises does not constitute a taking of a property interest but rather (as Justice Brennan contends) "a mere restriction on its use," is to use words in a manner that deprives them of all their ordinary meaning. Indeed, one of the principal uses of the eminent domain power is to assure that the government be able to require conveyance of just such interests, so long as it pays for them. Perhaps because the point is so obvious, we have never been confronted with a controversy that required use to rule upon it, but our cases' analysis of the effect of other governmental action leads to the same conclusion. We have repeatedly held that, as to property reserved by its owner for private use, "the right to exclude [others is] one of the most essential sticks in the bundle of rights that are commonly characterized as 'property.'" *Loretto v. Teleprompter Manhattan CATV Corp.,* 458 U.S. 419, 433 (1982), quoting *Kaiser Aetna v. United States,* 444 U.S. 164, 176 (1979). In *Loretto* we observed that where governmental action results in "[a] permanent physical occupation" of the property, by the government itself or by others, *See* 458 U.S., at432-433, n. 9, "our cases uniformly have found a taking to the extent of the occupation, without regard to whether the action achieves an important public benefit or has only minimal economic impact on the owner." *id.*, at 434-435. We think a "permanent physical occupation" has occurred, for purposes of that rule, where individuals are given a permanent and continuous right to pass to and fro, so that the real property may continuously be traversed, even though no particular individual is permitted to station himself permanently upon the premises. . . .

- FOURTEENTH APPLYS OTHER THIRTEEN TO STATE GOV'T.

. . . .

Given, then, that requiring uncompensated conveyance of the easement outright would violate the Fourteenth Amendment, the question becomes whether requiring it to be conveyed as a condition for issuing a land use permit alters the outcome. We have long recognized that land use regulation does not effect a taking if it "substantially advance[s] legitimate state interests" and does not "den[y] an owner economically viable use of his land," *Agins v. Tiburon,* 447 U.S. 255, 260 (1980). *See also Penn Central Transportation Co. v. New York City,* 438 U.S. 104, 127 (1978) ("a use restriction may constitute a 'taking' if not reasonably necessary to the effectuation of a substantial government purpose"). Our cases have not elaborated on the standards for determining what constitutes a "legitimate state interest" or what type of connection between the regulation and the state interest satisfies the requirement that the former "substantially advance" the latter. They have made clear, however, that a broad range of governmental purposes and regulations satisfies these requirements. *See Agins v. Tiburon, supra,* at 260-262 (scenic zoning); *Penn Central Transportation Co. v. New York City, supra* (landmark preservation); *Euclid v. Ambler Realty Co.,* 272 U.S. 365 (1926) (residential zoning); Laitos and Westfall, Government Interference with Private Interests in Public Resources, 11 Harv. Envt'l. L. Rev. 1, 66 (1987). The Commission argues that among these permissible purposes are protecting the public's ability to see the beach, assisting the public in overcoming the "psychological barrier" to using the beach created by a developed shorefront, and preventing congestion on the public beaches. We assume, without deciding, that this is so—in which case the Commission unquestionably would be able to deny the Nollans their permit outright if their new house (alone, or by reason of the cumulative impact produced in conjunction with other construction) would substantially impede these purposes, unless the denial would interfere so drastically with the Nollans' use of their property as to constitute a taking. *See Penn Central Transportation Co. v. New York City, supra.* The Commission argues that a permit condition that serves the same legitimate police-power purpose as a refusal to issue the permit should not be found to be a taking if the refusal to issue the permit would not constitute a taking. We agree. Thus, if the Commission attached to the permit some condition that would have protected the public's ability to see the beach notwithstanding construction of a new house—for example, a height limitation, width restriction, or a ban on fences—so long as the Commission could have exercised its police power (as we have assumed it could) to forbid construction of the house altogether, imposition of the condition would also be constitutional. Moreover (and here we come closer to the facts of the present case), the condition would be constitutional even if it consisted of the requirement that the Nollans provide a viewing spot on their property for passersby with whose sighting of the ocean their new house would interfere. Although such a requirement, constituting a permanent grant of continuous access to the property, would have to be considered a taking if it were not attached to a development permit, the Commission's assumed power to forbid construction of the house in order to protect the public's view of the beach must surely include the power to condition construction upon some concession by the owner, even a concession of property rights, that serves the same end. If prohibition designed to accomplish that purpose would be a legitimate exercise of the police power rather than a taking, it would be strange to conclude that providing the owner an alternative to that prohibition which accomplishes the same purpose is not.

The evident constitutional property disappears, however, if the condition substituted for the prohibition utterly fails to further the end advanced as the justification for the prohibition. When that essential nexus is eliminated, the situation becomes the same as if California law forbade shouting fire in a crowded theater, but granted dispensations to those willing to contribute $100 to the state treasury. While a ban on shouting fire can be a core exercise of the state's police power to protect the public safety, and thus can meet even our stringent standards for regulation of speech, adding the unrelated condition alters the purpose to one which, while it may be legitimate, is inadequate to sustain the ban. Therefore, even though, in a sense, requiring a $100 tax contribution in order to shout fire is a lesser restriction on speech than an outright ban, it would not pass constitutional muster. Similarly, here, the lack of nexus between the condition and the original purpose of the building restriction converts the purpose to something other than what it was. The purpose then becomes, quite simply, the obtaining of an easement to serve some valid governmental purpose, but without payment of compensation. Whatever may be the outer limits of "legitimate state interests" in the takings and land use context, this is not one of them. In short, unless the permit condition serves the same governmental purpose as the development ban, the building restriction is not a valid regulation of land use but "an out-and-out plan of extortion." *J.E.D. Associates, Inc. v. Atkinson,* 432 A.2d 12, 14-15 (N.H. 1981). *See also Loretto v. Teleprompter Manhattan CATV Corp,* 458 U.S., at 439, n. 17.

III

The Commission claims that it concedes as much, and that we may sustain the condition at issue here by finding that it is reasonably related to the public need or burden that the Nollans' new house creates or to which it contributes. We can accept, for purposes of discussion, the Commission's proposed test as to how close a "fit" between the condition and the burden is required, because we find that this case does not meet even the most untailored standards. The Commission's principal contention to the contrary essentially turns on a play on the word "access." The Nollans' new house, the Commission found, will interfere with "visual access" to the beach. That in turn (along with other shorefront development), will interfere with the desire of people who drive past the Nollans' house to use the beach, thus creating a "psychological barrier" to "access." The Nollans' new house will also, by a process not altogether clear from the Commission's opinion but presumably potent enough to more than offset the effects of the psychological barrier, increase the use of the public beaches, thus creating the need for more "access." These burdens on "access" would be alleviated by a requirement that the Nollans provide "lateral access" to the beach.

Rewriting the argument to eliminate the play on words makes clear that there is nothing to it. It is quite impossible to understand how a requirement that people already on the public beaches be able to walk across the Nollans' property reduces any obstacles to viewing the beach created by the new house. It is also impossible to understand how it lowers any "psychological barrier" to using the public beaches, or how it helps to remedy any additional congestion on them caused by the construction of the Nollans' new house. We therefore find that the Commission's imposition of the permit condition cannot be treated as an exercise of its land use power for any of these purposes.[14]

[14] As Justice Brennan notes, the Commission also argued that the construction of the new house would "increases private use immediately adjacent to public tidelands," which in turn might result in more disputes between the Nollans and the public as to the location of the boundary. That risk of boundary disputes, however, is inherent in the right to exclude others from one's property, and the construction here can no more justify mandatory dedication of a

Our conclusion on this point is consistent with the approach taken by every other court that has considered the question, with the exception of the California state courts. . . .

. . . .

. . . We do not share Justice Brennan's confidence that the Commission "should have little difficulty in the future in utilizing its expertise to demonstrate a specific connection between provisions for access and burdens on access," that will avoid the effect of today's decision. We view the Fifth Amendment's property clause to be more than a pleading requirement, and compliance with it to be more than an exercise of cleverness and imagination. As indicated earlier, our cases describe the condition for abridgement of property rights through the police power as a "substantial advanc[ing]" of legitimate state interest. We are inclined to be particularly careful about the adjective where the actual conveyance of property is made on condition to the lifting of a land use restriction, since in that context there is a heightened risk that the purpose is avoidance of the compensation requirement, rather than the stated police power objective.

We are left, then, with the Commission's justification for the access requirement unrelated to land use regulation:

> Finally, the Commission notes that there are several existing provisions of pass and repass lateral access benefits already given by past Faria Beach Tract applicants as a result of prior coastal permit decisions. The access required as a condition of this permit is part of a comprehensive program to provide continuous public access along Faria Beach as the lots undergo development or redevelopment.

That is simply an expression of the Commission's belief that the public interest will be served by a continuous strip of publicly accessible beach along the coast. The Commission may well be right that it is a good idea, but that does not establish that the Nollans (and other coastal residents) alone can be compelled to contribute to its realization. Rather, California is free to advance its "comprehensive program," if it wishes, by using its power of eminent domain for this "public purpose," see U.S. Const., Amend. V; but if it wants an easement across the Nollans' property, it must pay for it.

Reversed. [JUSTICE BRENNAN, with whom JUSTICE MARSHALL joined, dissented. JUSTICES BLACKMUN and STEVENS also filed dissenting opinions.]

---

sort of "buffer zone" in order to avoid boundary disputes than can the construction of an addition to a single-family house near a public street. Moreover, a buffer zone has a boundary as well, and unless that zone is a "no-man's land" that is off-limits for both neighbors (which is of course not the case here) its creation achieves nothing except to shift the location of the boundary dispute further on to the private owner's land. It is true that in the distinctive situation of the Nollans' property the sea-wall could be established as a clear demarcation of the public easement. But since not all of the lands to which this land-use condition applies have such a convenient reference point, the avoidance of boundary disputes is, even more obviously than the others, a made-up purpose of the regulation.

NOTES AND QUESTIONS

(1) To what extent is this decision consistent with the *Keystone* case? Which of the two opinions is more consistent with the U.S. Supreme Court's decision in *Penn Central*?

(2) Is the "nexus text" a sound interpretation of the takings clause? Do you agree with Justice Scalia that the test was not satisfied on the facts in *Nollan*?

(3) Justice Brennan filed a vigorous dissent in the *Nollan* case. He reasoned that granting public access to a small strip of dry sand near the plaintiff's house would not diminish either the plaintiff's enjoyment of their property or its value. He also stated that the majority's decision imposed a standard of precision (for the exercise of the state's police power) that was unreasonably demanding and likely to hamper innovative governmental programs to protect natural resources. Additionally, Brennan opined that the permit under challenge in *Nollan* had provided valuable benefits to the plaintiffs, both as private landowners and as members of the public. It should thus be upheld, he stated, on the basis of the principle of "average reciprocity of advantage." How persuasive is Brennan's approach? In your opinion, is it more sound than the analysis offered by the *Nollan* majority?

LUCAS v. SOUTH CAROLINA COASTAL COUNCIL

United States Supreme Court (1992)
505 U.S. 1003, 112 S. Ct. 2886, 120 L. Ed. 2d 798

SCALIA, J.:

In 1986, petitioner David H. Lucas paid $975,000 for two residential lots on the Isle of Palms in Charleston County, South Carolina, on which he intended to build single-family homes. In 1988, however, the South Carolina Legislature enacted the Beachfront Management Act, S.C. Code § 48-39-250 *et seq.* (Supp. 1990) (Act), which had the direct effect of barring petitioner from erecting any permanent habitable structures on his two parcels. *See* § 48-39-290(A). A state trial court found that this prohibition rendered Lucas's parcels "valueless." This case requires us to decide whether the Act's dramatic effect on the economic value of Lucas's lots accomplished a taking of private property under the Fifth and Fourteenth Amendments requiring the payment of "just compensation." U.S. Const., Amend. 5.

I

A

South Carolina's expressed interest in intensively managing development activities in the so-called "coastal zone" dates from 1977 when, in the aftermath of Congress's passage of the federal Coastal Zone Management Act of 1972, 16 U.S.C. § 1451 *et seq.*, the legislature enacted a Coastal Zone

Management Act of its own. *See* S.C. Code § 48-39-10 *et seq.* (1987). In its original form, the South Carolina Act required owners of coastal zone land that qualified as a "critical area" (defined in the legislation to include beaches and immediately adjacent sand dunes, § 48-39-10(J)) to obtain a permit from the newly created South Carolina Coastal Council (respondent here) prior to committing the land to a "use other than the use the critical area was devoted to on [September 28, 1977]." § 48-39-130(A).

In the late 1970's, Lucas and others began extensive residential development of the Isle of Palms, a barrier island situated eastward of the City of Charleston. Toward the close of the development cycle for one residential subdivision known as "Beachwood East," Lucas in 1986 purchased the two lots at issue in this litigation for his own account. No portion of the lots, which were located approximately 300 feet from the beach, qualified as a "critical area" under the 1977 Act; accordingly, at the time Lucas acquired these parcels, he was not legally obliged to obtain a permit from the Council in advance of any development activity. His intention with respect to the lots was to do what the owners of the immediately adjacent parcels had already done: erect single-family residences. He commissioned architectural drawings for this purpose.

The Beachfront Management Act brought Lucas's plans to an abrupt end. Under that 1988 legislation, the Council was directed to establish a "baseline" connecting the landward-most "points of erosion . . . during the past forty years" in the region of the Isle of Palms that includes Lucas's lots. § 48-39-280(A)(2) (Supp. 1988). In action not challenged here, the Council fixed this baseline landward of Lucas's parcels. That was significant, for under the Act construction of occupiable improvements[15] was flatly prohibited seaward of a line drawn 20 feet landward of, and parallel to, the baseline, § 48-39-290(A) (Supp. 1988). The Act provided no exceptions.

B

Lucas promptly filed suit in the South Carolina Court of Common Pleas, contending that the Beachfront Management Act's construction bar effected a taking of his property without just compensation. Lucas did not take issue with the validity of the Act as a lawful exercise of South Carolina's police power, but contended that the Act's complete extinguishment of his property's value entitled him to compensation regardless of whether the legislature had acted in furtherance of legitimate police power objectives. Following a bench trial, the court agreed. Among its factual determinations was the finding that "at the time Lucas purchased the two lots, both were zoned for single-family residential construction and . . . there were no restrictions imposed upon such use of the property by either the State of South Carolina, the County of Charleston, or the Town of the Isle of Palms." The trial court further found that the Beachfront Management Act decreed a permanent ban on construction insofar as Lucas's lots were concerned, and that his prohibition "deprived

[15] The Act did allow the construction of certain nonhabitable improvements, *e.g.*, "wooden walkways no larger in width than six feet" and "small wooden decks no larger than one hundred forty-four square feet." §§ 48-39-290(A)(1) and (2) (Supp. 1988).

Lucas of any reasonable economic use of the lots, . . . eliminated the unrestricted right of use, and rendered them valueless." The court thus concluded that Lucas's properties had been "taken" by operation of the Act, and it ordered respondent to pay "just compensation" in the amount of $1,232,387.50.

The Supreme Court of South Carolina reversed. It found dispositive what it described as Lucas's concession "that the Beachfront Management Act [was] properly and validly designed to preserve . . . South Carolina's beaches." 404 S.E.2d 895, 896 (1991). Failing an attack on the validity of the statute as such, the court believed itself bound to accept the "uncontested . . . findings" of the South Carolina legislature that new construction in the coastal zone—such as petitioner intended—threatened this public resource. *Id.,* at 898. The Court ruled that when a regulation respecting the use of property is designed "to prevent serious public harm," *Id.,* at 899 (citing, *inter alia, Mugler v. Kansas,* 123 U.S. 623 (1887)), no compensation is owing under the Takings Clause regardless of the regulation's effect on the property's value.

Two justices dissented. They acknowledged that our *Mugler* line of cases recognized governmental power to prohibit "noxious" uses of property—*i.e.,* use of property akin to "public nuisances"—without having to pay compensation. But they would not have characterized the Beachfront Management Act's "*primary* purpose [as] the prevention of a nuisance." 404 S.E.2d at 906 (Harwell, J., dissenting). To the dissenters, the chief purposes of the legislation, among them the promotion of tourism and the creation of a "habitat for indigenous flora and fauna," could not fairly be compared to nuisance abatement. *Id.,* at 906. As a consequence, they would have affirmed the trial court's conclusion that the Act's obliteration of the value of petitioner's lots accomplished a taking.

We granted certiorari.

II

As a threshold matter, we must briefly address the Council's suggestion that this case is inappropriate for plenary review. After briefing and argument before the South Carolina Supreme Court, but prior to issuance of that court's opinion, the Beachfront Management Act was amended to authorize the Council, in certain circumstances, to issue "special permits" for the construction or reconstruction of habitable structures seaward of the baseline. *See* S.C. Code § 48-39-290(D)(1) (Supp. 1991). According to the Council, this amendment renders Lucas's claim of a permanent deprivation unripe, as Lucas may yet be able to secure permission to build on his property. "[T]he Court's cases," we are reminded, "uniformly reflect an insistence on knowing the nature and extent of permitted development before adjudicating the constitutionality of the regulations that purport to limit it." *MacDonald, Sommer & Frates v. County of Yolo,* 477 U.S. 340, 351 (1986). Because petitioner "has not yet obtained a final decision regarding how [he] will be allowed to develop [his] property," *Williamson County Regional Planning Comm'n of Johnson City v. Hamilton Bank,* 473 U.S. 172, 190 (1985), the Council argues that he is not yet entitled to definitive adjudication of his takings claim in this Court.

We think these considerations would preclude review had the South Carolina Supreme Court rested its judgment on ripeness grounds, as it was (essentially) invited to do by the Council, see Brief for Respondent 9, n. 3. The South Carolina Supreme Court shrugged off the possibility of further administrative and trial proceedings, however, preferring to dispose of Lucas's takings claim on the merits. Compare, *e.g., San Diego Gas & Electric Co.,* 450 U.S. 621, 631-632 (1981). This unusual disposition does not preclude Lucas from applying for a permit under the 1990 amendment for *future* construction, and challenging, on takings grounds, any denial. But it does preclude, both practically and legally, any takings claim with respect to Lucas's *past* deprivation, *i.e.,* for his having been denied construction rights during the period before the 1990 amendment. *See generally First English Evangelical Lutheran Church of Glendale v. County of Los Angeles,* 482 U.S. 304 (1987) (holding that temporary deprivations of use are compensable under the Takings Clause). Without even so much as commenting upon the consequences of the South Carolina Supreme Court's judgment in this respect, the Council insists that permitting Lucas to press his claim of past deprivation on this appeal would be improper, since "the issues of whether and to what extent [Lucas] has incurred a temporary taking . . . have simply never been addressed." Brief for Respondent 11. Yet Lucas had no reason to proceed on a "temporary taking" theory at trial, or even to seek remand for that purpose prior to submission of the case to the South Carolina Supreme Court, since as the Act then read, the taking was unconditional and permanent. Moreover, given the breadth of the South Carolina Supreme Court's holding and judgment, Lucas would plainly be unable (absent our intervention now) to obtain further state-court adjudication with respect to the 1988-1990 period.

In these circumstances, we think it would not accord with sound process to insist that Lucas pursue the late-created "special permit" procedure before his takings claim can be considered ripe. Lucas has properly alleged Article III injury-in-fact in this case, with respect to both the pre-1990 and post-1990 constraints placed on the use of his parcels by the Beachfront Management Act. That there is a discretionary "special permit" procedure by which he may regain—for the future, at least—beneficial use of his land goes only to the prudent "ripeness" of Lucas's challenge, and for the reasons discussed we do not think it prudent to apply that prudential requirement here. We leave for decision on remand, of course, the questions left unaddressed by the South Carolina Supreme court as a consequence of its categorical disposition.

III

A

Prior to Justice Holmes' exposition in *Pennsylvania Coal Co. v. Mahon,* 260 U.S. 393 (1922), it was generally thought that the Takings Clause reached only a "direct appropriation" of property, *Legal Tender Cases,* 12 Wall. 457, 551 (1871), or the functional equivalent of a "practical ouster of [the owner's] possession." *Transportation Co. v. Chicago,* 99 U.S. 634, 642 (1879). Justice Holmes recognized in *Mahon,* however, that if the protection against physical appropriations of private property was to be meaningfully enforced, the government's power to redefine the range of interests included in the ownership of property was necessarily constrained by constitutional limits. 260 U.S., at

414-415. If, instead, the uses of private property were subject to unbridled, uncompensated qualification under the police power, "the natural tendency of human nature [would be] to extend the qualification more and more until at last private property disappeared." *Id.,* at 415. These considerations gave birth in that case of the oft-cited maxim that "while property may be regulated to a certain extent, if regulation goes too far it will be recognized as a taking." *Ibid.*

Nevertheless, our decision in *Mahon* offered little insight into when, and under what circumstances, a given regulation would be seen as going "too far" for purposes of the Fifth Amendment. In 70-odd years of succeeding "regulatory takings" jurisprudence, we have generally eschewed any "set formula" for determining how far is too far, preferring to "engag[e] in . . . essentially ad hoc, factual inquires," *Penn Central Transportation Co. v. New York City,* 438 U.S. 104, 124 (1978) (quoting *Goldblatt v. Hempstead,* 369 U.S. 590, 594 (1962)). *See* Epstein, *Takings: Descent and Resurrection,* 1987 Sup. Ct. Rev. 1, 4. We have, however, described at least two discrete categories of regulatory action as compensable without case-specific inquiry into the public interest advanced in support of the restraint. The first encompasses regulations that compel the property owner to suffer physical "invasion" of his property. In general (at least with regard to permanent invasions), no matter how minute the intrusion, and no matter how weighty the public purpose behind it, we have required compensation. For example, in *Loretto v. Teleprompter Manhattan CATV Corp.,* 458 U.S. 419 (1982), we determined that New York's law requiring landlords to allow television cable companies to emplace cable facilities in their apartment buildings constituted a taking, *id.,* at 435-440, even though the facilities occupied at most only 1 cubic feet of the landlords' property, *see id.,* at 438, n. 16. *See also United States v. Causby,* 328 U.S. 256, 265, and n. 10 (1946) (physical invasions of airspace); cf. *Kaiser Aetna v. United States,* 444 U.S. 164 (1979) (imposition of navigational servitude upon private marina).

The second situation in which we have found categorical treatment appropriate is where regulation denies all economically beneficial or productive use of land. *See Agins,* 447 U.S., at 260. As we have said on numerous occasions, the Fifth Amendment is violated when land-use regulation "does not substantially advance legitimate state interests *or denies an owner economically viable use of his land.*" *Agins, supra,* at 260 (citations omitted) (emphasis added).

We have not set forth the justification for this rule. Perhaps it is simply, as Justice Brennan suggested, that total deprivation of beneficial use is, from the landowner's point of view, the equivalent of a physical appropriation. *See San Diego Gas & Electric Co. v. San Diego,* 450 U.S., at 652 (Brennan, J., dissenting). "[F]or what is the land but the profits thereof[?]" 1 E. Coke, Institutes ch. 1, § 1 (1st Am. ed. 1812). Surely, at least, in the extraordinary circumstance when *no* productive or economically beneficial use of land is permitted, it is less realistic to indulge our usual assumption that the legislature is simply "adjusting the benefits and burdens of economic life," *Penn Central Transportation Co.,* 438 U.S. at 124, in a manner that secures an "average reciprocity of advantage" to everyone concerned. *Pennsylvania*

Coal Co. v. Mahon, 260 U.S., at 415. And the *functional* basis for permitting the government, by regulation, to affect property values without compensation—that "Government hardly could go on if to some extent values incident to property could not be diminished without paying for every such change in the general law." *id.,* at 413—does not apply to the relatively rare situations where the government has deprived a landowner of all economically beneficial uses.

On the other side of the balance, affirmatively supporting a compensation requirement, is the fact that regulations that leave the owner of land without economically beneficial or productive options for its use—typically, as here, by requiring land to be left substantially in its natural state—carry with them a heightened risk that private property is being pressed into some form of public service under the guise of mitigating serious public harm. . . .

We think, in short, that there are good reasons for our frequently expressed belief that when the owner of real property has been called upon to sacrifice *all* economically beneficial uses in the name of the common good, that is, to leave his property economically idle, he has suffered a taking.

B

The trial court found Lucas's two beachfront lots to have been rendered valueless by respondent's enforcement of the coastal-zone construction ban. Under Lucas's theory of the case, which rested upon our "no economically viable use" statements, that finding entitled him to compensation. Lucas believed it unnecessary to take issue with either the purposes behind the Beachfront Management Act, or the means chosen by the South Carolina Legislature to effectuate those purposes. The South Carolina Supreme Court, however, thought otherwise. In its view, the Beachfront Management Act was no ordinary enactment, but involved an exercise of South Carolina's "police powers" to mitigate the harm to the public interest that petitioner's use of his land might occasion. 404 S.E.2d at 899. By neglecting to dispute the findings enumerated in the Act or otherwise to challenge the legislature's purposes, petitioner "conceded that the beach/dune area of South Carolina's shores is an extremely valuable public resource; that the erection of new construction, *inter alia,* contributes to the erosion and destruction of this public resource; and that discouraging new construction in close proximity to the beach/dune is necessary to prevent a great public harm." 404 S.E.2d., at 898. In the court's view, these concessions brought petitioner's challenge within a long line of this Court's cases sustaining against Due Process and Takings Clause challenges the state's use of its "police powers" to enjoin a property owner from activities akin to public nuisances. *See Mugler v. Kansas,* 123 U.S. 623 (1887) (law prohibiting manufacture of alcoholic beverages); *Hadacheck v. Sebastian,* 239 U.S. 394 (1915) (law barring operation of brick mill in residential area); *Miller v. Schoene,* 276 U.S. 272 (1928) (order to destroy diseased cedar trees to prevent infection of nearby orchards); *Goldblatt v. Hempstead,* 369 U.S. 590 (1962) (law effectively preventing continued operation of quarry in residential area).

It is correct that many of our prior opinions have suggested that "harmful or noxious uses" of property may be proscribed by government regulation without the requirement of compensation. For a number of reasons, however, we think the South Carolina Supreme Court was too quick to conclude that the principle decides the present case. . . .

. . . .

When it is understood that "prevention of harmful use" was merely our early formulation of the police power justification necessary to sustain (without compensation) *any* regulatory diminution in value; and that the distinction between regulation that "prevents harmful use" and that which "confers benefits" is difficult, if not impossible, to discern on an objective, value-free basis; it becomes self-evident that noxious-use logic cannot serve as a touchstone to distinguish regulatory "takings"—which require compensation—from regulatory deprivations that do not require compensation. A *fortiori* the legislature's recitation of a noxious-use justification cannot be the basis for departing from our categorical rule that total regulatory takings must be compensated. If it were, departure would virtually always be allowed. The South Carolina Supreme court's approach would essentially nullify *Mahon's* affirmation of limits to the noncompensable exercise of the police power. Our cases provide no support for this: None of them that employed the logic of "harmful use" prevention to sustain a regulation involved an allegation that the regulation wholly eliminated the value of the claimant's land. *See Keystone Bituminous Coal Assn.,* 480 U.S., at 513-514 (Rehnquist, C.J., dissenting).

Where the state seeks to sustain regulation that deprives land of all economically beneficial use, we think it may resist compensation only if the logically antecedent inquiry into the nature of the owner's estate shows that the proscribed use interests were not part of his title to being with. This accords, we think with our "takings" jurisprudence, which has traditionally been guided by the understandings of our citizens regarding the content of, and the state's power over, the "bundle of rights" that they acquire when they obtain title to property. It seems to us that the property owner necessarily expects the uses of his property to be restricted, from time to time, by various measures newly enacted by the state in legitimate exercise of its police powers: "[a]s long recognized, some values are enjoyed under an implied limitation and must yield to the police power." *Pennsylvania Coal Co. v. Mahon,* 260 U.S., at 413. And in the case of personal property, by reason of the state's traditionally high degree of control over commercial dealings, he ought to be aware of the possibility that new regulation might even render his property economically worthless (at least if the property's only economically productive use is sale or manufacture for sale), see *Andrus v. Allard,* 444 U.S. 51, 66-67 (1979) (prohibition on sale of eagle feathers). In the case of land, however, we think the notion pressed by the Council that title is somehow held subject to the "implied limitation" that the state may subsequently eliminate all economically valuable use is inconsistent with the historical compact recorded in the Takings Clause that has become part of our constitutional culture.

Where "permanent physical occupation" of land is concerned, we have refused to allow the government to decree it anew (without compensation), no matter how weighty the asserted "public interest" involved, *Loretto v. Teleprompter Manhattan CATV Corp.,* 458 U.S., at 426—though we assuredly *would* permit the government to assert a permanent easement that was a preexisting limitation upon the landowner's title. Compare *Scranton v. Wheeler,*

179 U.S. 141, 163 (1900) (interests of "riparian owner in the submerged lands . . . bordering on a public navigable water" held subject to Government's navigational servitude), with *Kaiser Aetna v. United States,* 444 U.S., at 178-180 (imposition of navigational servitude on marina created and rendered navigable at private expense held to constitute a taking). We believe similar treatment must be accorded confiscatory regulations, *i.e.,* regulations that prohibit all economically beneficial use of land: Any limitation so severe cannot be newly legislated or decreed (without compensation), but must inhere in the title itself, in the restrictions that background principles of the state's law of property and nuisance already place upon land ownership. A law or decree with such an effect must, in other words, do no more than duplicate the result that could have been achieved in the courts—by adjacent landowners (or other uniquely affected persons) under the state's law of private nuisance, or by the state under its complementary power to abate nuisances that affect the public generally, or otherwise. . . .

. . . .

The "total taking" inquiry we require today will ordinarily entail (as the application of state nuisance law ordinarily entails) analysis of, among other things, the degree of harm to public lands and resources, or adjacent private property, posed by the claimant's proposed activities, *see, e.g.,* Restatement (Second) of Torts §§ 826, 82, the social value of the claimant's activities and their suitability to the locality in question, *see e.g., id.,* §§ 828(a) and (b), 831, and the relative ease with which the alleged harm can be avoided through measures taken by the claimant and the government (or adjacent private landowners) alike, *see, e.g., id.,* §§ 827(e), 828(c), 830. The fact that a particular use has long been engaged in by similarly situated owners ordinarily imports a lack of any common-law prohibition (though changed circumstances or new knowledge may make what was previously permissible no longer so), *see* Restatement (Second) of Torts, *supra,* § 827, comment. So also does the fact that other landowners, similarly situated, are permitted to continue the use denied to the claimant.

It seems unlikely that common-law principles would have prevented the erection of any habitable or productive improvements on petitioner's land; they rarely support prohibition of the "essential use" of land, *Curtin v. Benson,* 222 U.S. 78, 86 (1911). The question, however, is one of state law to be dealt with on remand. We emphasize that to win its case South Carolina must do more than proffer the legislature's declaration that the uses Lucas desires are inconsistent with the public interest, or the conclusory assertion that they violate a common-law maxim such as *sic utere tuo ut alienum non laedas.* As we have said, a "state, by *ipse dixit,* may not transform private property into public property without compensation. . . ." *Webb's Fabulous Pharmacies, Inc. v. Beckwith,* 449 U.S. 155, 164 91980). Instead, as it would be required to do if it sought to restrain Lucas in a common-law action for public nuisance, South Carolina must identify background principles of nuisance and property law that prohibit the uses he now intends in the circumstances in which the property is presently found. Only on this showing can the state fairly claim that, in proscribing all such beneficial uses, the Beachfront Management Act is taking nothing.

The judgment is reversed and the cause remanded for proceedings not inconsistent with this opinion.

NOTES AND QUESTIONS

(1) Is the majority opinion in *Lucas* consistent with the *Penn Central* decision? Is it consistent with *Keystone*? Was the *Lucas* court correct in ignoring any "value" that Lucas might have enjoyed if, consistent with the Beachfront Management Act, he had used his land for camping or fishing?

(2) As you may have noticed, Justice Scalia's opinion in *Lucas* used varying terminology to describe the kind of loss that a landowner may suffer for a "total taking" to occur. He referred to loss of "economic use," "economically viable use," "economically beneficial use," "economically feasible use," "economically valuable use," and "economically beneficial or productive options for use." To what extent do these variations in language leave it unclear precisely when the principles of *Lucas* will apply in future cases?

(3) Justices Brennan and Stevens dissented in *Lucas* in separate opinions. Blackmun criticized the majority for "launching a missile to kill a mouse." He observed that the situation assumed to exist in *Lucas*—the prohibition of all economic uses of land—was likely to arise relatively rarely and had never arisen in the Court's previous cases. Stevens reiterated Blackmun's conclusions. He also expressed concern that, following *Lucas,* developers and investors would intentionally market specialized estates that would be rendered "valueless" by land use restrictions, thus entitling the developer/investor to compensation. Such arrangements, he opined, are neither desirable nor appropriate and represent "distortions of our takings jurisprudence."

(4) On remand, the South Carolina Supreme Court held that the Coastal Council did not possess the ability, under common law, to prohibit Mr. Lucas from constructing a habitable structure on his land. It also ruled that Lucas had suffered "a temporary taking, deserving of compensation." *Lucas v. South Carolina Coastal Council,* 424 S.E.2d 484 (1993). Following that, South Carolina settled with Mr. Lucas by purchasing his land for $1,575,000 and reselling it to another developer.

DOLAN v. CITY OF TIGARD

United States Supreme Court (1994)
512 U.S. 374, 114 S. Ct. 2309, 129 L. Ed. 2d 304

REHNQUIST, C.J.:

Petitioner challenges the decision of the Oregon Supreme Court which held that the city of Tigard could condition the approval of her building permit on the dedication of a portion of her property for flood control and traffic improvements. We granted certiorari to resolve a question left open by our decision in *Nollan v. California Coastal Comm'n,* of what is the required degree of connection between the exactions imposed by the city and the projected impacts of the proposed development.

I

The State of Oregon enacted a comprehensive land use management program in 1973. Ore. Rev. Stat. §§ 197.005–197.860 (1991). The program required all Oregon cities and counties to adopt new comprehensive land use plans that were consistent with the statewide planning goals. . . . [The city of Tigard] developed a comprehensive plan and codified it in its Community Development code (CDC). The CDC requires property owners in the area zoned Central Business District to comply with a 15% open space and landscaping requirement, which limits total site coverage, including all structures and paved parking, to 85% of the parcel. After the completion of a transportation study that identified congestion in the Central Business District as a particular problem, the city adopted a plan for a pedestrian/bicycle pathway intended to encourage alternatives to automobile transportation for short trips. . . .

The city also adopted a Master Drainage Plan (Drainage Plan). The Drainage Plan noted that flooding occurred in several areas long Fanno Creek, including areas near petitioner's property. The Drainage Plan suggested a series of improvements to the Fanno Creek Basin, including channel excavation in the area next to petitioner's property. . . . The Drainage Plan concluded that the cost of these improvements should be shared based on both direct and indirect benefits, with property owners along the waterways paying more due to the direct benefit that they would receive. . . .

Petitioner Florence Dolan owns a plumbing and electric supply store located on Main Street in the Central Business District of the city. The store covers approximately 9,700 square feet on the eastern side of a 1.67-acre parcel, which includes a gravel parking lot. Fanno Creek flows through the southwestern corner of the lot and along its western boundary. The year-round flow of the creek renders the area within the creek's 100-year floodplain virtually unusable for commercial development. The city's comprehensive plan includes the Fanno Creek floodplain as part of the city's greenway system.

Petitioner applied to the city for a permit to redevelop the site. Her proposed plans called for nearly doubling the size of the store to 17,600 square feet, and paving a 39-space parking lot. The existing store, located on the opposite side of the parcel, would be razed in sections as construction progressed on the new building. In the second phase of the project, petitioner proposed to build an additional structure on the northeast side of the site for complementary businesses, and to provide more parking. The proposed expansion and intensified use are consistent with the city's zoning scheme in the Central Business District.

The City Planning Commission granted petitioner's permit application subject to conditions imposed by the city's CDC [the Community Development Code, required by Oregon's comprehensive land use management statute]. The CDC establishes the following standard for site development review approval: "Where landfill and/or development is allowed within and adjacent to the 10-year floodplain, the city shall require the dedication of sufficient open land area for greenway adjoining and within the floodplain. This area shall include portions at a suitable elevation for the construction of a pedestrian/bicycle pathway within the floodplain in accordance with the adopted pedestrian/bicycle plan." . . . The dedication required by that condition encompasses approximately 7,000 square feet, or roughly 10% of the property. In accordance with city practice, petitioner could rely on the dedicated property to meet the 15% open space and landscaping of maintaining a landscaped buffer between the dedicated are and the new store. . . .

. . . .

II

The Takings Clause of the Fifth Amendment of the United States Constitution, made applicable to the states through the Fourteenth Amendment, *Chicago B. & Q.R. Co. v. Chicago,* 166 U.S. 226, 239 (1897), provides: "[N]or shall private property be taken for public use, without just compensation." One of the principal purposes of the Taking Clause is "to bar government from forcing some people alone to bear public burdens which, in all fairness and justice, should be borne by the public as a whole." *Armstrong v. United States,* 364 U.S. 40, 49 (1960). Without question, had the city simply required petitioner to dedicate a strip of land along Fanno Creek for public use, rather than conditioning the grant of her permit to redevelop her property on such a dedication, a taking would have occurred. *Nollan, supra,* at 831. Such public access would deprive petitioner of the right to exclude others, "one of the most essential sticks in the bundle of rights that are commonly characterized as property." *Kaiser Aetna v. United States,* 444 U.S. 164, 176 (1979).

On the other side of the ledger, the authority of state and local governments to engage in land use planning has been sustained against constitutional challenge as long ago as our decision in *Euclid v. Ambler Realty Co.,* 272 U.S. 365 (1926). "Government hardly could go on if to some extent values incident to property could not be diminished without paying for every such change in the general law." *Pennsylvania Coal Co. v. Mahon,* 260 U.S. 393, 413 (1922). A land use regulation does not effect a taking if it "substantially advance[s] legitimate state interests" and does not "den[y] an owner economically viable use of his land." *Agins v. Tiburon,* 447 U.S. 255, 260 (1980).[16]

The sorts of land use regulations discussed in the cases just cited, however, differ in two relevant particulars from the present case. First, they involved essentially legislative determinations classifying entire areas of the city, whereas here the city made an adjudicative decision to condition petitioner's application for a building permit on an individual parcel. Second, the conditions imposed were not simply a limitation on the use petitioner might make of her own parcel, but a requirement that she deed portions of the property to the city. In *Nollan, supra,* we held that governmental authority to exact such a condition was circumscribed by the Fifth and Fourteenth Amendments. Under the well-settled doctrine of "unconstitutional conditions," the government may not require a person to give up a constitutional right—here the right

[16] There can be no argument that the permit conditions would deprive petitioner "economically beneficial us[e]" of her property as she currently operates a retail store on the lot. Petitioner assuredly is able to derive some economic use from her property.

to receive just compensation when property is taken for a public use—in exchange for a discretionary benefit conferred by the government where the property sought has little or no relationship to the benefit. *See Perry v. Sindermann,* 480 U.S. 593 (1972); *Pickering v. Board of Ed. of Township High School Dist.,* 391 U.S. 563, 568 (1968).

Petitioner contends that the city has forced her to choose between the building permit and her right under the Fifth Amendment to just compensation for the public easement. Petitioner does not quarrel with the city's authority to exact some forms of dedication as a condition for the grant of a building permit, but challenges the showing made by the city to justify these exactions. She argues that the city has identified "no special benefits" conferred on her, and has not identified any "special quantifiable burdens" created by her new store that would justify the particular dedications required from her which are not required from the public at large.

III

In evaluating petitioner's claim, we must first determine whether the "essential nexus" exists between the "legitimate state interest" and the permit condition exacted by the city. *Nollan,* 483 U.S., at 837. If we find that a nexus exists, we must then decide the required degree of connection between the exactions and the projected impact of the proposed development. We were not required to reach this question in *Nollan* because we concluded that the connection did not meet even the loosest standard. Here, however, we must decide this question.

A

We addressed the essential nexus question in *Nollan.* [In that case, the] . . . absence of a nexus left the Coastal Commission in the position of simply trying to obtain an easement through gimmickry, which converted a valid regulation of land use into "an out-and-out plan of extortion." *Ibid,* quoting *J.E.D. Associates, Inc. v. Atkinson,* 432 A.2d 12, 14-15 (N.H. 1981).

No such gimmicks are associated with the permit conditions imposed by the city in this case. Undoubtedly, the prevention of flooding along Fanno Creek and the reduction of traffic congestion in the Central Business District qualify as the type of legitimate public purposes we have upheld. It seems equally obvious that a nexus exists between preventing flooding along Fanno Creek and limiting development within the creek's 100-year floodplain. Petitioner proposes to double the size of her retail store and to pave her now-gravel parking lot, thereby expanding the impervious surface on the property and increasing the amount of stormwater run-off into Fanno Creek.

The same may be said for the city's attempt to reduce traffic congestion by providing for alternative means of transportation. In theory, a pedestrian/bicycle pathway provides a useful alternative means of transportation for workers and shoppers: "Pedestrians and bicyclists occupying dedicated spaces for walking and/or bicycling . . . remove potential vehicles from streets, resulting in an overall improvement in total transportation system flow." A. Nelson, *Public Provision of Pedestrian and Bicycle Access Ways: Public Policy*

Rationale and the Nature of Private Benefits 11, Center for Planning Development, Georgia Institute of Technology, Working Paper Series (Jan. 1994). *See also*, Intermodal Surface Transportation Efficiency Act of 1991, Pub. L. 102-240, 150 Stat. 1914; (recognizing pedestrian and bicycle facilities as necessary components of any strategy to reduce traffic congestion).

B

The second part of our analysis requires us to determine whether the degree of the exactions demanded by the city's permit conditions bear the required relationship to the projected impact of petitioner's proposed development. *Nollan, supra,* at 834, quoting *Penn Central,* 438 U.S. 104, 127 (1978) ("'[A] use restriction may constitute a taking if not reasonably necessary to the effectuation of a substantial government purpose'"). Here the Oregon Supreme Court deferred to what it termed the "city's unchallenged factual findings" supporting the dedication conditions and found them to be reasonably related to the impact of the expansion of petitioner's business.

The city required that petitioner dedicate "to the city as greenway all portions of the site that fall within the existing 100-year floodplain [of Fanno Creek] . . . and all property 15 feet above [the floodplain] boundary." In addition, the city demanded that the retail store be designed so as not to intrude into the greenway area. The city relies on the Commission's rather tentative findings that increased stormwater flow from petitioner's property "can only add to the public need to manage the [floodplain] for drainage purposes" to support its conclusion that the "requirement of dedication of the floodplain area on the site is related to the applicant's plan to intensify development on the site."

The city made the following specific findings relevant to the pedestrian/bicycle pathway: "In addition, the proposed expanded use of this site is anticipated to generate additional vehicular traffic thereby increasing congestion."

The question for us is whether these findings are constitutionally sufficient to justify the conditions imposed by the city on petitioner's building permit. Since state courts have been dealing with this question a good deal longer than we have, we turn to representative decisions made by them.

. . . .

We think the "reasonable relationship" test adopted by a majority of the state courts is closer to the federal constitutional norm than either of those previously discussed. . . . But we do not adopt it as such, partly because the term "reasonable relationship" seems confusingly similar to the term "rational basis" which describes the minimal level of scrutiny under the Equal Protection Clause of the Fourteenth Amendment. We think a term such as "rough proportionality" best encapsulates what we hold to be the requirement of the Fifth Amendment. No precise mathematical calculation is required, but the city must make some sort of individualized determination that the required dedication is related both in nature and extent to the impact of the proposed development. . . .

. . . .

We turn now to analysis of whether the findings relied upon by the city here, first with respect to the floodplain easement, and second with respect to the pedestrian/bicycle path, satisfied these requirements.

It is axiomatic that increasing the amount of impervious surface will increase the quantity and rate of store-water flow from petitioner's property. Therefore, keeping the floodplain open and free from development would likely confine the pressures on Fanno Creek created by petitioner's development. In fact, because petitioner's property lies within the Central Business District, the Community Development Code already required that petitioner leave 15% of it as open space and the undeveloped floodplain would have nearly satisfied that requirement. But the city demanded more—it not only wanted petitioner not to build in the floodplain, but it also wanted petitioner's property along Fanno Creek for its greenway system. The city has never said why a public greenway, as opposed to a private one, was required in the interest of flood control.

The difference to petitioner, of course, is the loss of her ability to exclude others. As we have noted, this right to exclude others is "one of the most essential sticks in the bundle of rights that are commonly characterized as property." *Kaiser Aetna,* 444 U.S., at 176. It is difficult to see why recreational visitors trampling along petitioner's floodplain easement are sufficiently related to the city's legitimate interest in reducing flooding problems along Fanno Creek, and the city has not attempted to make any individualized determination to support this part of its request.

. . . .

If petitioner's proposed development had somehow encroached on existing greenway space in the city, it would have been reasonable to require petitioner to provide some alternative greenway space for the public either on her property or elsewhere. *See Nollan,* 483 U.S., at 836 ("Although such a requirement, constituting a permanent grant of continuous access to the property, would have to be considered a taking if it were not attached to a development permit, the Commission's assumed power to forbid construction of the house in order to protect the public's view of the beach must surely include the power to condition construction upon some concession by the owner, even a concession of property rights, that serves the same end.") But that is not the case here. We conclude that the findings upon which the city relies do not show the required reasonable relationship between the floodplain easement and the petitioner's proposed new building.

With respect to the pedestrian/bicycle pathway, we have no doubt that the city was correct in finding that the larger retail sales facility proposed by petitioner will increase traffic on the streets of the Central Business District. The city estimates that the proposed development would generate roughly 435 additional trips per day.[17] Dedications for streets, sidewalks, and other public ways are generally reasonable exactions to avoid excessive congestion from a proposed property use. But on the record before us, the city has not met

[17] The city uses a weekday average trip rate of 53.21 trips per 1000 square feet. Additional trips generated = 53.21 x (17,600 − 9720).

its burden of demonstrating that the additional number of vehicle and bicycle trips generated by the petitioner's development reasonably relate to the city's requirement for a dedication of the pedestrian/bicycle pathway easement. The city simply found that the creation of the pathway "could offset some of the traffic demand . . . and lessen the increase in traffic congestion."

As Justice Peterson of the Supreme Court of Oregon explained in his dissenting opinion, however, "[t]he findings of the fact that the bicycle pathway system '*could* offset some of the traffic demand' is a far cry from a finding that the bicycle pathway system *will,* or is *likely to,* offset some of the traffic demand." 854 P.2d, at 447 (emphasis in original). No precise mathematical calculation is required, but the city must make some effort to quantify its findings in support of the dedication for the pedestrian/bicycle pathway, beyond the conclusory statement that it could offset some of the traffic demand generated.

IV

Cities have long engaged in the commendable task of land use planning, made necessary by increasing urbanization particularly in metropolitan areas such as Portland. The city's goals of reducing flooding hazards and traffic congestion, and providing for public greenways, are laudable, but there are outer limits to how this may be done. "A strong public desire to improve the public condition [will not] warrant achieving the desire by a shorter cut than the constitutional way of paying for the change." *Pennsylvania Coal,* 260 U.S., at 416.

The judgment of the Supreme Court of Oregon is reversed, and the case is remanded for further proceedings consistent with this opinion.

Justice STEVENS, with whom Justice BLACKMUN and Justice GINSBURG join, dissenting.

. . . .

The Court has made a serious error by abandoning the traditional presumption of constitutionality and imposing a novel burden of proof on a city implementing an admittedly valid comprehensive land use plan. Even more consequential than its incorrect disposition of this case, however, is the Court's resurrection of a species of substantive due process analysis that it firmly rejected decades ago.

The Court begins its constitutional analysis by citing *Chicago, B. & Q. R. Co. v. Chicago,* [which] applied the same kind of substantive due process analysis more frequently identified with a better known case that accorded similar substantive protection to a baker's liberty interest in working 60 hours a week and 10 hours a day. *See Lochner v. New York,* 198 U.S. 45 (1905).[18] Later cases have interpreted the Fourteenth Amendment's substantive protection against uncompensated deprivations of private property by the States as

[18] The *Lochner* Court refused to presume that there was a reasonable connection between the regulation and the state interest in protecting the public health. 198 U.S., at 60-61. A similar refusal to identify a sufficient nexus between an enlarged building with a newly paved parking lot and the state interests in minimizing the risks of flooding and traffic congestion proves fatal to the city's permit conditions in this case under the Court's novel approach.

though it incorporated the text of the Fifth Amendment's Takings Clause. There was nothing problematic about that interpretation in cases enforcing the Fourteenth Amendment against state action that involved the actual physical invasion of private property. Justice Holmes charted a significant new course, however, when he opined that a state law making it "commercially impracticable to mine certain coal" had "very nearly the same effect for constitutional purposes as appropriating or destroying it." *Pennsylvania Coal Co. v. Mahon,* 260 U.S. 393, 414 (1922). The so-called "regulatory takings" doctrine that the Homes dictum kindled has an obvious kinship with the line of substantive due process cases that Lochner exemplified. Besides having similar ancestry, both doctrines are potentially open-ended sources of judicial power to invalidate state economic regulations that Members of this Court view as unwise or unfair.

This case inaugurates an even more recent judicial innovation than the regulatory takings doctrine: the application of the "unconstitutional conditions" label to a mutually beneficial transaction between a property owner and a city. The Court tells us that the city's refusal to grant Dolan a discretionary benefit infringes her right to receive just compensation for the property interests that she has refused to dedicate to the city "where the property sought has little or no relationship to the benefit." Although it is well settled that a government cannot deny a benefit on a basis that infringes constitutionally protected interests—"especially [one's] interest in freedom of speech," *Perry v. Sindermann,* 408 U.S. 593, 597 (1972)—the "unconstitutional conditions" doctrine provides an inadequate framework in which to analyze this case.[19] Dolan has no right to be compensated for a taking unless the city acquires the property interests that she has refused to surrender. Since no taking has yet occurred, there has not been any infringement of her constitutional right to compensation.

Even if Dolan should accept the city's conditions in exchange for the benefit that she seeks, it would not necessarily follow that she had been denied "just compensation" since it would be appropriate to consider the receipt of that benefit in any calculation of "just compensation." *See Pennsylvania Coal Co. v. Mahon,* 260 U.S. 393, 414 (1922) (noting that an "average reciprocity of advantage" was deemed to justify many laws); *Hodel v. Irving,* 481 U.S. 704, 715 (1987) (such "reciprocity of advantage" weighed in favor of a statute's constitutionality). Particularly in the absence of any evidence on the point, we should not presume that the discretionary benefit the city has offered is less valuable than the property interests that Dolan can retain or surrender

[19] Although it has a long history, *see Home Ins. Co. v. Morse,* 20 Wall. 445, 451 (1874), the "unconstitutional conditions" doctrine has for just as long suffered from notoriously inconsistent application: it has never been an overarching principle of constitutional law that operates with equal force regardless of the nature of the rights and power in question. *See, e.g.,* Sunstein, Why the Unconstitutional Conditions Doctrine is an Anachronism, 70 B.U.L. Rev. 593, 620 (1990) (doctrine is "too crude and too general to provide help in contested cases"); [Other citations omitted]. As the majority's case citations suggest, modern decisions invoking the doctrine have most frequently involved First Amendment liberties [citations omitted]. The necessary and traditional breadth of municipalities' power to regulate property development, together with the absence here of fragile and easily "chilled" constitutional rights such as that of free speech, make it quite clear that the Court is really writing on a clean slate rather than merely applying "well-settled" doctrine.

at her option. But even if that discretionary benefit were so trifling that it could not be considered just compensation when it has "little or no relationship" to the property, the Court fails to explain why the same value would suffice when the required nexus is present. In this respect, the Court's reliance on the "unconstitutional conditions" doctrine is assuredly novel, and arguably incoherent. The city's conditions are by no means immune from constitutional scrutiny. The level of scrutiny, however, does not approximate the kind of review that would apply if the city had insisted on a surrender of Dolan's First Amendment rights in exchange for a building permit. One can only hope that the Court's reliance today on First Amendment cases . . . [such as *Perry v. Sindermann*], and its candid disavowal of the term "rational basis" to describe its new standard of review, do not signify a reassertion of the kind of super legislative power the court exercised during the Lochner era.

. . . .

I respectfully dissent.

[The separate dissent of Justice Souter is omitted.]

NOTES AND QUESTIONS

(1) Was the Court correct in creating the "rough proportionality test" as a supplement to the "nexus test" announced in *Nollan*? Should the burden of demonstrating "rough proportionality" be placed on the city or should it be up to the plaintiff to demonstrate that it did not exist?

(2) One observer has suggested that, in takings cases, the courts should "avoid reading the *Dolan* test as establishing a rigid requirement, but instead interpret the circumstances of a dedication in terms of a general reasonableness standard, and applying heightened scrutiny to a dedication which is required as the result of an adjudicative or administrative determination." *See* Freilich, *Thou Shalt Not Take Title Without Adequate Planning: The Takings Equation After* Dolan v. City of Tigard, 27 Urb. Law. 187 (1995). Do you concur?

(3) In your view, was Justice Stevens on sound ground in likening the *Dolan* court's takings analysis to the *Lochner* line of cases, in which pre-New Deal social legislation was consistently struck down as violative of substantive due process limitations?

FIRST ENGLISH EVANGELICAL LUTHERAN CHURCH OF GLENDALE v. COUNTY OF LOS ANGELES

United States Supreme Court (1987)
482 U.S. 304, 107 S. Ct. 2378, 96 L. Ed.2d 250

REHNQUIST, C.J.:

In this case the California Court of Appeal held that a landowner who claims that his property has been "taken" by a land-use regulation may not recover damages for the time before it is finally determined that the regulation constitutes a "taking" of his property. We disagree, and conclude that in these circumstances the Fifth and Fourteenth Amendments to the United States Constitution would require compensation for that period.

In 1957, appellant First English Evangelical Lutheran Church purchases a 21-acre parcel of land in a canyon along the banks of the Middle Fork of Mill Creek in the Angeles National Forest. The Middle Fork is the natural drainage channel for a watershed area owned by the National Forest Service. Twelve of the acres owned by the church are flat land, and contained a dining hall, two bunkhouses, a caretaker's lodge, and outdoor chapel, and a footbridge across the creek. The church operated on the site a campground, known as "Lutherglen," as a retreat center and a recreational area for handicapped children.

In July 1977, a forest fire denuded the hills upstream from Lutherglen, destroying approximately 3,860 acres of the watershed area and creating a serious flood hazard. Such flooding occurred on February 9 and 10, 1978, when a storm dropped 11 inches of rain in the watershed. The runoff from the storm overflowed the banks of the Mill Creek, flooding Lutherglen and destroying its buildings.

In response to the flooding of the canyon, appellee County of Los Angeles adopted Interim Ordinance No. 11,855 in January 1979. The ordinance provided that "[a] person shall not construct, reconstruct, place or enlarge any building or structure, any portion of which is, or will be, located within the outer boundary lines of the interim flood protection area located in Mill Creek Canyon . . . ." The ordinance was effective immediately because the county determined that it was "required for the immediate preservation of the public health and safety . . . ." The interim flood protection area described by the ordinance included the flat areas on either side of Mill Creek on which Lutherglen had stood.

The church filed a complaint in the Superior Court of California a little more than a month after the ordinance was adopted. As subsequently amended, the complaint alleged two claims against the county and the Los Angeles County Flood Control District. The first alleged that the defendants were liable under Cal. Gov't Code Ann. § 835 (West 1980)[20] for dangerous conditions on their upstream properties that contributed to the flooding of Lutherglen. As a part of this claim, appellant also alleged that "Ordinance No. 11,855 denies [appellant] all use of Lutherglen." The second claim sought to recover from the Flood District in inverse condemnation and in tort for engaging in cloud seeding during the storm that flooded Lutherglen. Appellant sought damages under each count for loss of use of Lutherglen. The defendants moved to strike the portions of the complaint alleging that the county's ordinance denied all use of Lutherglen, on the view that the California Supreme Court's decision in *Agins v.Tiburon,* 598 P.2d 25 (Cal. 1979), aff'd on other grounds, 447 U.S. 255 (1980), rendered the allegation "entirely immaterial and irrelevant, [with] no bearing upon any conceivable cause of action herein." *See* Cal.

[20] Section 835 of the California Government Codeestablishes conditions under which a public entity may be liable "for injury caused by a dangerous condition of its property . . . ."

Civ. Proc. Code Ann. § 436 (West Supp. 1987) ("The court may . . . strike out any irrelevant, false, or improper matter inserted in any pleading").

In *Agins v. Tiburon, supra,* the Supreme Court of California decided that a landowner may not maintain an inverse condemnation suit in the courts of that state based upon a "regulator" taking. In the court's view, maintenance of such a suit would allow a landowner to force the legislature to exercise its powers of eminent domain. Under this decision, then, compensation is not required until the challenged regulation or ordinance has been held excessive in an action for declaratory relief or a writ of mandamus and the government has nevertheless decided to continue the regulation in effect. Based on this decision, the trial court in the present case granted the motion to strike the allegation that the church had been denied all use in Lutherglen. It explained that "a careful re-reading of the *Agins* case persuades the Court that when an ordinance, even a non-zoning ordinance, deprives a person of the total use of his lands, his challenge to the ordinance is by way of declaratory relief or possibly mandamus." Because the appellant alleged a regulatory taking and sought only damages, the allegation that the ordinance denied all use of Lutherglen was deemed irrelevant.

On appeal, the California Court of Appeals read the complaint as one seeking "damages for the uncompensated taking of all use of Lutherglen by County Ordinance, No. 11,855 . . . ." It too relied on the California Supreme Court's decision in *Agins* in rejecting the cause of action, declining appellant's invitation to reevaluate *Agins* in light of this Court's opinions in *San Diego Gas & Electric Co. v. San Diego,* 450 U.S. 621 (1981). The court found itself obligated to follow *Agins* "because the United States Supreme Court has not yet ruled on the question of whether a state may constitutionally limit the remedy for a taking to nonmonetary relief . . . ." It accordingly affirmed the trial court's decision to strike the allegations concerning appellee's ordinance. The Supreme Court of California denied review.

This appeal followed, and we noted probable jurisdiction. Appellant asks us to hold that the Supreme Court of California erred in *Agins v. Tiburon* in determining that the Fifth Amendment, as made applicable to the states through the Fourteenth Amendment, does not require compensation as a remedy for "temporary" regulatory takings—those regulatory takings which are ultimately invalidated by the courts. Four times this decade, we have considered similar claims and have found ourselves for one reason or another unable to consider the merits of the *Agins* rule. For the reasons explained below, however, we find the constitutional claims properly presented in this case, and hold that on these facts the California courts have decided the compensation question inconsistently with the requirements of the Fifth Amendment.

I

Concerns with finality left us unable to reach the remedial question in the earlier cases where we have been asked to consider the rule in *Agins.* In each of these cases, we concluded either that regulations considered to be in issue by the state court did not effect a taking, or that the factual disputes yet to be resolved by state authorities might still lead to the conclusion that no taking had occurred. Consideration of the remedial question in those circumstances, we concluded would be premature.

The posture of the present case is quite different. Appellant's complaint alleged that "Ordinance No. 11,855 denies [it] all use of Lutherglen," and sought damages for this deprivation. In affirming the decision to strike this allegation, the Court of Appeals assumed that the complaint sought "damages for the uncompensated *taking* of all use of Lutherglen by County Ordinance No. 11,855." (emphasis added). It relied on the California Supreme Court's *Agins* decision for the conclusion that "the remedy for a *taking* [is limited] to nonmonetary relief . . . ." (emphasis added). The disposition of the case on these grounds isolates the remedial question for our consideration. The rejection of appellant's allegations did not rest on the view that they were false. Nor did the court rely on the theory that regulatory measures such as Ordinance No. 11,855 may never constitute a taking in the constitutional sense. Instead, the claims were deemed irrelevant solely because of the California Supreme Court's decision in *Agins* that damages are unavailable to redress a "temporary" regulatory taking. The California Court of Appeal has thus held that regardless of the correctness of appellant's claim that the challenged ordinance denies it "all use of Lutherglen" appellant may not recover damages until the ordinance is finally declared unconstitutional, and then only for any period after that declaration for which the county seeks to enforce it. The constitutional question pretermitted in our earlier cases is therefore squarely presented here.[21]

We reject appellee's suggestion that, regardless of the state court's treatment of the question, we must independently evaluate the adequacy of the complaint and resolve the takings claim on the merits before we can reach the remedial question. However "cryptic"—to use appellee's description—the allegations with respect to the taking were, the California courts deemed them sufficient to present the issue. We accordingly have no occasion to decide whether the ordinance at issue actually denied appellant all use of its property or whether the county might avoid the conclusion that a compensable taking had occurred by establishing that the denial of all use was insulated as part of the State's authority to enact safety regulations. These questions, of course, remain open for decision on the remand we direct today. We now turn to the question of whether the Just Compensation Clause requires the government to pay for "temporary" regulatory takings.

II

Consideration of the compensation question must begin with direct reference to the language of the Fifth Amendment, which provides in relevant part that "private property [shall not] be taken for public use, without just

[21] Our cases have also required that one seeking compensation must "seek compensation through the procedures the state has provided for doing so" before the claim is ripe for review. *Williamson County Regional Planning Comm'n v. Hamilton Bank,* 473 U.S. 172, 194 (1985). It is clear that appellant met this requirement. Having assumed that a taking occurred, the California court's dismissal of the action establishes that "the inverse condemnation procedure is unavailable . . . ." *Id.,* at 197. The compensation claim is accordingly ripe for our consideration.

compensation." As its language indicates, and as the Court has frequently noted, this provision does not prohibit the taking of private property, but instead places a condition on the exercise of the power. This basic understanding of the Amendment makes clear that it is designed not to limit the governmental interference with property rights per se, but rather to secure compensation in the event of otherwise proper interference amounting to a taking. Thus, government action that works a taking of property rights necessarily implicates the "constitutional obligation to pay just compensation." *Armstrong v. United States,* 364 U.S. 40, 49 (1960).

We have recognized that a landowner is entitled to bring an action in inverse condemnation as a result of "the self-executing character of the constitutional provision with respect to compensation. . . ."

. . . .

It has also been established doctrine at least since Justice Holmes' opinion for the Court in *Pennsylvania Coal Co. v. Mahon,* 260 U.S. 393 (1922) that "[t]he general rule at least is, that while property may be regulated to a certain extent, if regulation goes too far it will be recognized as a taking." *Id.,* at 415. While the typical taking occurs when the government acts to condemn property in the exercise of its power of eminent domain, the entire doctrine of inverse condemnation is predicated on the proposition that a taking may occur without such formal proceedings. . . .

. . . .

While the Supreme Court of California may not have actually disavowed this general rule in *Agins,* we believe that it has truncated the rule by disallowing damages that occurred prior to the ultimate invalidation of the challenged regulation. The Supreme Court of California justified its conclusion at length in the *Agins* opinion, concluding that:

> "In combination, the need for preserving a degree of freedom in the land-use planning function, and the inhibiting financial force which inheres in the inverse condemnation remedy, persuade us that on balance mandamus, or declaratory relief rather than inverse condemnation is the appropriate relief under the circumstances." *Agins v. Tiburon,* 598 P.2d, at 31.

We, of course, are not unmindful of these considerations, but they must be evaluated in the light of the command of the Just Compensation Clause of the Fifth Amendment. The Court has recognized in more than one case that the government may elect to abandon its intrusion or discontinue regulations. *See, e.g., Kirby Forest Industries, Inc. v. United States,* 467 U.S. 1 (1984); *United States v. Dow,* 357 U.S. 17, 26 (1958). Similarly, a governmental body may acquiesce in a judicial declaration that one of its ordinances has affected an unconstitutional taking of property; the landowner has no right under the Just Compensation Clause to insist that a "temporary" taking be deemed a permanent taking. But we have not resolved whether abandonment by the government requires payment of compensation for the period of time during which regulations deny a landowner all use of his land.

In considering this question, we find substantial guidance in cases where the government has only temporary exercised its right to use private property. . . .

These cases reflect the fact that "temporary" takings which, as here, deny a landowner all use of his property, are not different in kind from permanent takings, for which the Constitution clearly requires compensation. Cf. *San Diego Gas & Electric Co.*, 450 U.S., at 657 (Brennan, J., dissenting) ("Nothing in the Just Compensation Clause suggests that 'takings' must be permanent and irrevocable"). It is axiomatic that the Fifth Amendment's just compensation provision is "designed to bar Government from forcing some people alone to bear public burdens which, in all fairness and justice, should be borne by the public as a whole." *Armstrong v. United States*, 364 U.S., at 49. In the present case the interim ordinance was adopted by the county of Los Angeles in January 1979, and became effective immediately. Appellant filed suit within a month after the effective date of the ordinance and yet when the Supreme Court of California denied a hearing in the case on October 17, 1985, the merits of appellant's claim had yet to be determined. The United States has been required to pay compensation for leasehold interests of shorter duration than this. The value of a leasehold interest in property for a period of years may be substantial, and the burden on the property owner in extinguishing such an interest for a period of years may be great indeed. *See, e.g., United States v. General Motors, supra.* Where this burden results from government action that amounted to a taking, the Just Compensation Clause of the Fifth Amendment requires that the government pay the landowner for the value of the use of the land during this period. Cf. *United States v. Causby,* 328 U.S., at 261 ("It is the owner's loss, not the taker's gain, which is the measure of the value of the property taken"). Invalidation of the ordinance or its successor ordinance after this period of time, though converting the taking into a "temporary" one, is not a sufficient remedy to meet the demands of the Just Compensation Clause.

Appellee argues that requiring compensation for denial of all use of land prior to invalidation is inconsistent with this Court's decisions in *Danforth v. United States,* 308 U.S. 271 (1939), and *Agins v. Tiburon,* 447 U.S. 255 (1980). In *Danforth,* the landowner contended that the "taking" of his property had occurred prior to the institution of condemnation proceedings, by reason of the enactment of the Flood Control Act itself. He claimed that the passage of that Act had diminished the value of his property because the plan embodied in the Act required condemnation of a flowage easement across his property. The Court held that in the context of condemnation proceedings a taking does not occur until compensation is determined and paid, and went on to say that "[a] reduction or increase in the value of property may occur by reason of legislation for or the beginning or completion of a project," but "[s]uch changes in the value are incidents of ownership. They cannot be considered as a 'taking' in the constitutional sense." *Danforth, supra,* at 285. *Agins* likewise rejected a claim that the city's preliminary activities constituted a taking, saying that "[m]ere fluctuations in value during the process of governmental decisionmaking, absent extraordinary delay, are 'incidents of ownership'." *See* 447 U.S., at 263, n. 9.

But these cases merely stand for the unexceptional proposition that the valuation of property which has been taken must be calculated as of the time of the taking, and that depreciation in value of the property by reason of preliminary activity is not chargeable to the government. Thus, in *Agins,* we concluded that the preliminary activity did not work a taking. It would require a considerable extension of these decisions to say that no compensable regulatory taking may occur until a challenged ordinance has ultimately been held invalid.

Nothing we say today is intended to abrogate the principle that the decision to exercise the power of eminent domain is a legislative function, "for Congress and Congress alone to determine." . . . We merely hold that where the government's activities have already worked a taking of all use of property, no subsequent action by the government can relieve it of the duty to provide compensation for the period during which the taking was effective.

We also point out that the allegation of the complaint which we treat as true for purposes of our decision was that the ordinance in question denied appellant all use of its property. We limit our holding to the facts presented, and of course do not deal with the quite different questions that would arise in the case of normal delays in obtaining building permits, changes in zoning ordinances, variances, and the like which are not before us. We realize that even our present holding will undoubtedly lessen to some extent the freedom and flexibility of land-use planners and governing bodies of municipal corporations when enacting land-use regulations. But such consequences necessarily flow from any decision upholding a claim of constitutional right; many of the provisions of the Constitution are designed to limit the flexibility and freedom of governmental authorities and the Just Compensation Clause of the Fifth Amendment is one of them. As Justice Holmes aptly noted more than 50 years ago, "a strong public desire to improve the public condition is not enough to warrant achieving the desire by a shorter cut than the constitutional way of paying for the change." *Pennsylvania Coal Co. v. Mahon,* 260 U.S., at 416.

Here we must assume that the Los Angeles County ordinances have denied appellant all use of its property for a considerable period of years, and we hold that invalidation of the ordinance without payment of fair value for the use of the property during this period of time would be a constitutionally insufficient remedy. The judgment of the California Court of Appeals is therefore reversed, and the case is remanded for further proceedings not inconsistent with this opinion.

NOTES AND QUESTIONS

(1) In a dissenting opinion in *First English,* Justice Stevens expressed the concern that the majority's decision would inhibit planners and local officials from imposing needed land-use restrictions on the basis that their actions might put their local governments at financial risk. Stevens opined that landowners should be made to rely upon the due process clause, rather than the takings clause, where they feel they have been unfairly denied an economic benefit as the result of a land use regulation; and he took the view that most temporary decreases in land values that result from land use restrictions do not amount to takings. How persuasive are those conclusions?

(2) How should the amount of monetary compensation be determined in "temporary takings" cases? Should it be measured by the amount which the value of the land in question decreased during the period of temporary taking?

Is the rental value of the land during that period a better measure? Does the *First English* decision shed light on these questions?

(3) On remand in this case, the California Court of Appeals dismissed the plaintiff's complaint. It determined that Los Angeles County's interim ordinance had substantially advanced a legitimate state purpose, and also that the ordinance had not denied the plaintiff all economically viable use of its property. Would the same result have been reached if the Court of Appeals had been bound by the "total takings" rule handed down in *Lucas v. South Carolina Coastal Council, supra*?

CITY OF MONTEREY v. DEL MONTE DUNES AT MONTEREY, LTD.

United States Supreme Court (1999)
526 U.S. 687, 119 S. Ct. 1624, 143 L. Ed. 2d 882

Justice Kennedy:

This case began with attempts by the respondent, Del Monte Dunes, and its predecessor in interest, to develop a parcel of land within the jurisdiction of the petitioner, the city of Monterey. The city, in a series of repeated rejections, denied proposals to develop the property, each time imposing more rigorous demands on the developers. Del Monte Dunes brought suit in the United States District Court for the Northern District of California, under Rev. Stat. § 1979, 42 U.S.C. § 1983. After protracted litigation, the case was submitted to the jury on Del Monte Dunes' theory that the city effected a regulatory taking or otherwise injured the property by unlawful acts, without paying compensation or providing an adequate post-deprivation remedy for the loss. The jury found for Del Monte Dunes, and the Court of Appeals affirmed.

The petitioner contends that the regulatory takings claim should not have been decided by the jury and that the Court of Appeals adopted an erroneous standard for regulatory takings liability. We need not decide all of the questions presented by the petitioner, nor need we examine each of the points given by the Court of Appeals in its decision to affirm. The controlling question is whether, given the city's apparent concession that the instructions were a correct statement of the law, the matter was properly submitted to the jury. We conclude that it was, and that the judgment of the Court of Appeals should be affirmed.

I

A

The property which respondent and its predecessor in interest (landowners) sought to develop was a 37.6 acre ocean-front parcel located in the city of

Monterey, at or near the city's boundary to the north, where Highway 1 enters. With the exception of the ocean and a state park located to the northeast, the parcel was virtually surrounded by a railroad right-of-way and properties devoted to industrial, commercial, and multifamily residential uses. The parcel itself was zoned for multifamily residential use under the city's general zoning ordinance.

The parcel had not been untouched by its urban and industrial proximities. A sewer line housed in 15-foot man-made dunes covered with jute matting and surrounded by snow fencing traversed the property. Trash, dumped in violation of the law, had accumulated on the premises. The parcel had been used for many years by an oil company as a terminal and tank farm where large quantities of oil were delivered, stored, and reshipped. When the company stopped using the site, it had removed its oil tanks but left behind tank pads, an industrial complex, pieces of pipe, broken concrete, and oil-soaked sand. The company had introduced nonnative ice plant to prevent erosion and to control soil conditions around the oil tanks. Ice plant secretes a substance that forces out other plants and is not compatible with the parcel's natural flora. By the time the landowners sought to develop the property, ice plant had spread to some 25 percent of the parcel, and, absent human intervention, would have continued to advance, endangering and perhaps eliminating the parcel's remaining natural vegetation.

The natural flow that the ice plant encroached upon included buckwheat, the natural habitat of the endangered Smith's Blue butterfly. The butterfly lives for one week, travels a maximum of 200 feet, and must land on a mature, flowering buckwheat plant to survive. Searches for the butterfly from 1981 through 1985 yielded but a single larva, discovered in 1984. No other specimens had been found on the property, and the parcel was quite isolated from other possible habitats of the butterfly.

B

In 1981 the landowners submitted an application to develop the property in conformance with the city's zoning and general plan requirements. Although the zoning requirements permitted the development of up to 29 housing units per acre, or more than 1,000 units for the entire parcel, the landowners' proposal was limited to 344 residential units. In 1982 the city's planning commission denied the application but stated that a proposal for 264 units would receive favorable consideration. In keeping with the suggestion, the landowners submitted a revised proposal for 264 units. In later 1983, however, the planning commission once more requested a reduction in the scale of the development, this time saying a plan for 224 units would be received with favor. The landowners returned to the drawing board and prepared a proposal for 224 units, which, its previous statements notwithstanding, the planning commission denied in 1984. The landowners appealed to the city council, which overruled the planning commission's denial and referred the project back to the commission, with instructions to consider a proposal for 190 units.

The landowners once again reduced the scope of their development proposal to comply with the city's request, and submitted four specific, detailed site plans, each for a total of 190 units for the whole parcel. Even so, the planning commission rejected the landowners' proposal later in 1984. Once more the landowners appealed to the city council. The council again overruled the commission, finding the proposal conceptually satisfactory and in conformance with the city's previous decisions regarding, *inter alia,* density, number of units, location on the property, and access. The council then approved one of the site plans, subject to various specific conditions, and granted an 18-month conditional use permit for the proposed development.

The landowners spent most of the next year revising their proposals and taking other steps to fulfill the city's conditions. Their final plan, submitted in 1985, devoted 17.9 of the 37.6 acres to public open space (including a public beach and areas for the restoration and preservation of the buckwheat habitat), 7.9 acres to open, landscaped areas, and 6.7 acres to public and private streets (including public parking and access to the beach). Only 5.1 acres were allocated to buildings and patios. The plan was designed, in accordance with the city's demands, to provide the public with a beach, a buffer-zone between the development and the adjoining sate park, and view corridors so the buildings would not be visible to motorists on the nearby highway; the proposal also called for restoring and preserving as much of the sand dune structure and buckwheat habitat as possible consistent with development and the city's requirements.

After detailed review of the proposed buildings, roads, and parking facilities, the city's architectural review committee approved the plan. Following hearings before the planning commission, the commission's professional staff found the final plan addressed and substantially satisfied the city's conditions. It proposed the planning commission make specific findings to this effect and recommended the plan be approved.

In January 1986, less than two months before the landowners' conditional use permit was to expire, the planning commission rejected the recommendation of its staff and denied the development plan. The landowners appealed to the city council, also requesting a 12-month extension of their permit to allow them time to attempt to comply with any additional requirements the council might impose. The permit was extended until a hearing could be held before the city council in June 1986. After the hearing, the city council denied the final plan, not only declining to specify measures the landowners could take to satisfy the concerns raised by the council but also refusing to extend the conditional use permit to allow time to address those concerns. The council's decision, moreover, came at a time when a sewer moratorium issued by another agency would have prevented or at least delayed development based on a new plan.

The council did not base its decision on the landowners' failure to meet any of the specific conditions earlier prescribed by the city. Rather, the council made general findings that the landowners had not provided adequate access for the development (even though the landowners had twice changed the specific access plans to comply with the city's demands and maintained they could satisfy the city's new objections if granted an extension), that the plan's layout would damage the environment (even though the location of the development of the property was necessitated by the city's demands for a public beach, view corridors, and a buffer zone next to the state park), and that the plan would disrupt the habitat of the Smith's Blue Butterfly (even though the plan would remove the encroaching ice plant and preserve or restore buckwheat habitat on almost half of the property, and even though only one larva had ever been found on the property).

C

After five years, five formal decisions, and 19 different site plans, respondent Del Monte Dunes decided the city would not permit development of the property under any circumstances. Del Monte Dunes commenced suit against the city in the United States District Court for the Northern District of California under 42 U.S.C. § 1983, alleging, *inter alia,* that denial of the final development proposal was a violation of the Due Process and Equal Protection provisions of the Fourteenth Amendment and an uncompensated, and so unconstitutional, regulatory taking.

The District Court dismissed the claims as unripe under *Williamson County Regional Planning Comm'n v. Hamilton Bank of Johnson City,* 473 U.S. 172 (1985), on the grounds that Del Monte Dunes had neither obtained a definitive decision as to the development the city would allow nor sought just compensation in state court. The Court of Appeals reversed, 920 F.2d 1496 (CA9 1990). . . .

On remand, the District Court determined, over the city's objections, to submit Del Monte Dunes' takings and equal protection claims to a jury but to reserve the substantive due process claim for decision by the court. Del Monte Dunes argued to the jury that, although the city had a right to regulate its property, the combined effect of the city's various demands—that the development be invisible from the highway, that a buffer be provided between the development and the state park, and that the public be provided with a beach—was to force development into the "bowl" area of the parcel. As a result, Del Monte Dunes argued, the city's subsequent decision that the bowl contained sensitive buckwheat habitat which could not be disturbed blocked the development of any portion of the property. While conceding the legitimacy of the city's stated regulatory purposes, Del Monte Dunes emphasized the tortuous and protracted history of attempts to develop the property, as well as the shifting and sometimes inconsistent positions taken by the city throughout the process, and argued that it had been treated in an unfair and irrational manner. Del Monte Dunes also submitted evidence designed to undermine the validity of the asserted factual premises for the city's denial of the final proposal and to suggest that the city had considered buying, or inducing the State to buy, the property for public use as early as 1979, reserving some money for this purpose but delaying or abandoning its plan for financial reasons. The State of California's purchase of the property during the pendency of the litigation may have bolstered the credibility of Del Monte Dunes' position.

At the close of argument, the District Court instructed the jury it should find for Del Monte Dunes if it found either that Del Monte Dunes had been denied all economically viable use of its property or that "the city's decision to reject the plaintiff's 190 unit development proposal did not substantially advance a legitimate public purpose." With respect to the first inquiry, the jury was instructed, in relevant part, as follows:

> "For the purpose of a taking claim, you will find that the plaintiff has been denied all economically viable use of its property, if, as the result of the city's regulatory decision there remains no permissible or beneficial use for that property. In proving whether the plaintiff has been denied all economically viable use of its property, it is not enough that the plaintiff show that after the challenged action by the city the property diminished in value or that it would suffer a serious economic loss as the result of the city's actions."

With respect to the second inquiry, the jury received the following instruction:

> "Public bodies, such as the city, have the authority to take actions which substantially advance legitimate public interest(s) and legitimate public interest(s) can include protecting the environment, preserving open space agriculture, protecting the health and safety of its citizens, and regulating the quality of the community by looking at development. So one of your jobs as jurors is to decide if the city's decision here substantially advanced any such legitimate public purpose.
>
> "The regulatory actions of the city or any agency substantially advanc[e] a legitimate public purpose if the action bears a reasonable relationship to that objective.
>
> "Now, if the preponderance of the evidence establishes that there was no reasonable relationship between the city's denial of the . . . proposal and legitimate public purpose, you should find in favor of the plaintiff. If you find that there existed a reasonable relationship between the city's decision and a legitimate public purpose, you should find in favor of the city. As long as the regulatory action by the city substantially advances their legitimate public purpose, . . . its underlying motives and reasons are not to be inquired into."

The essence of these instructions was proposed by the city.

The jury delivered a general verdict for Del Monte Dunes on its takings claim, a separate verdict for Del Monte Dunes on its equal protection claim, and a damages award of $1.45 million. After the jury's verdict, the District Court ruled for the city on the substantive due process claim, stating that its ruling was not inconsistent with the jury's verdict on the equal protection or the takings claim. The court later denied the city's motions for a new trial or for judgment as a matter of law.

The Court of Appeals affirmed. 95 F.3d 1422 (CA9 1996). . . .

The questions presented in the city's petition for certiorari were (1) whether issues of liability were properly submitted to the jury on Del Monte Dunes' regulatory takings claim, (2) whether the Court of Appeals impermissibly based its decision on a standard that allowed the jury to reweigh the reasonableness of the city's land-use decision, and (3) whether the Court of Appeals erred in assuming that the rough-proportionality standard of *Dolan v. City of Tigard,* 512 U.S. 374 (1994), applied to this case. We granted certiorari, 523 U.S. 1045 (1998), and now address these questions in reverse order.

II

In the course of holding a reasonable jury could have found the city's denial of the final proposal not substantially related to legitimate public interests, the Court of Appeals stated: "[e]ven if the City had a legitimate interest in denying Del Monte's development application, its action must be 'roughly proportional' to furthering that interest. . . . That is, the City's denial must be related 'both in nature and extent to the impact of the proposed development.'" 95 F.3d at 1430, quoting *Dolan, supra,* at 391.

Although in a general sense concerns for proportionality animate the Takings Clause, *see Armstrong v. United States,* 364 U.S. 40, 49 (1960) ("The Fifth Amendment's guarantee . . . was designed to bar the Government from forcing some people alone to bear public burdens which, in all fairness and justice, should be borne by the public as a whole"), we have not extended the rough-proportionality test of *Dolan* beyond the special context of exactions—land-use decisions conditioning approval of development on the dedication of property to public use. *See Dolan, supra* at 385; *Nollan v. California Coastal Comm'n,* 483 U.S. 825, 841 (1987). The rule applied in *Dolan* considers whether dedications demanded as conditions of development are proportional to the development's anticipated impacts. It was not designed to address, and is not readily applicable to, the much different questions arising where, as here, the landowner's challenge is based not on excessive exactions but on denial of development. We believe, accordingly, that the rough-proportionality test of *Dolan* is inapposite to a case such as this one.

The instructions given to the jury, however, did not mention proportionality, let alone require it to find for Del Monte Dunes unless the city's actions were roughly proportional to its asserted interests. The Court of Appeals' discussion of rough proportionality, we conclude, was unnecessary to its decision to sustain the jury's verdict. . . .

III

The city challenges the Court of Appeals' holding that the jury could have found the city's denial of the final development plan not reasonably related to legitimate public interests. Although somewhat obscure, the city's argument is not cast as a challenge to the sufficiency of the evidence; rather, the city maintains that the Court of Appeals adopted a legal standard for regulatory takings liability that allows juries to second-guess public land-use policy.

As the city itself proposed the essence of the instructions given to the jury, it cannot now contend that the instructions did not provide an accurate statement of law. In any event, although this Court has provided neither a definitive statement of the elements of a claim for a temporary regulatory taking nor a thorough explanation of the nature or applicability of the requirement that a regulation substantially advance legitimate public interests outside the context of required dedications or exactions, . . . we note that the trial court's instructions are consistent with our previous general discussions of regulatory takings liability. . . .

. . . .

. . . The jury was instructed to consider whether the city's denial of the final proposal was reasonably related to a legitimate public purpose. Even with regard to this issue, however, the jury was not given free rein to second-guess the city's land-use policies. Rather, the jury was instructed, in unmistakable terms, that the various purposes asserted by the city were legitimate public interests.

The jury, furthermore, was not asked to evaluate the city's decision in isolation but rather in context, and, in particular, in light of the tortuous and protracted history of attempts to develop the property. Although Del Monte Dunes was allowed to introduce evidence challenging the asserted factual bases for the city's decision, it also highlighted the shifting nature of the city's demands and in the inconsistency of its decision with the recommendation of its professional staff, as well as with its previous decisions. Del Monte Dunes also introduced evidence of the city's longstanding interest in acquiring the property for public use.

In short, the question submitted to the jury on this issue was confined to whether, in light of all the history and the context of the case, the city's particular decision to deny Del Monte Dunes' final development proposal was reasonably related to the city's proffered justifications. This question was couched, moreover, in an instruction that had been proposed in essence by the city, and as to which the city made no objection.

Thus, despite the protests of the city and its *amici,* it is clear that the Court of Appeals did not adopt a rule of takings law allowing wholesale interference by judge or jury with municipal land-use policies, laws, or routine regulatory decisions. . . .

IV

We next address whether it was proper for the District Court to submit the question of liability on Del Monte Dunes' regulatory takings claim to the jury. As the Court of Appeals recognized, the answer depends on whether Del Monte Dunes had a statutory or constitutional right to a jury trial, and, if it did, the nature and extent of the right. Del Monte Dunes asserts the right to a jury trial is conferred by § 1983 and by the Seventh Amendment. . . .

The character of § 1983 is vital to our Seventh Amendment analysis, but the statute does not itself confer the jury right. . . .

As a consequence, we must reach the constitutional question. The Seventh Amendment provides that "[i]n suits at common law, where the value in controversy shall exceed twenty dollars, the right of trial by jury shall be preserved . . . ." Consistent with the textual mandate that the jury right be preserved, our interpretation of the Amendment has been guided by historical analysis comprising two principal inquires. "[W]e ask, first, whether we are dealing with a cause of action that either was tried at law at the time of the founding or is at least analogous to one that was." *Markman v. Westview*

Instruments, Inc., 517 U.S. 370, 376 (1996). "If the action in question belongs in the law category, we then ask whether the particular trial decision must fall to the jury in order to preserve the substance of the common-law right as it existed in 1791." *Ibid.*

A

With respect to the first inquiry, we have recognized that "suits at common law" include "not merely suits, which the *common* law recognized among its old and settled proceedings, but [also] suits in which *legal* rights were to be ascertained and determined, in contradistinction to those where equitable rights alone were recognized, and equitable remedies were administered." *Parsons v. Bedford,* 3 pet. 433, 447 (1830). The Seventh Amendment thus applies not only to common-law causes of action but also to statutory causes of action " 'analogous to common-law causes of action ordinarily decided in English law courts in the late 18th century, as opposed to those customarily heard by courts of equity or admiralty.' " *Feltner, supra,* at 348 (quoting *Granfinanciera, S.A. v. Nordberg,* 492 U.S. 33, 42 (1989); accord *Curtis, supra,* at 193.

1

Del Monte Dunes brought this suit pursuant to § 1983 to vindicate its constitutional rights. We hold that a § 1983 suit seeking legal relief is an action at law within the meaning of the Seventh Amendment. . . .

It is undisputed that when the Seventh Amendment was adopted there was no action equivalent to § 1983, framed in specific terms for vindicating constitutional rights. It is settled law, however, that the Seventh Amendment jury guarantee extends to statutory claims unknown to the common law, so long as the claims can be said to "soun[d] basically in tort," and seek legal relief. *Curtis,* 415 U.S. at 195-196. . . .

. . . .

Here Del Monte Dunes sought legal relief. It was entitled to proceed in federal court under § 1983 because, at the time of the city's action, the State of California did not provide a compensatory remedy for temporary regulatory takings. *See First English,* 482 U.S. at 308-311. The constitutional injury alleged, therefore, is not that property was taken but that it was taken without just compensation. Had the city paid for the property or had an adequate post-deprivation remedy been made available, Del Monte Dunes would have suffered no constitutional injury from the taking alone. *See Williamson,* 473 U.S. at 194-195. Because its statutory action did not accrue until it was denied just compensation, in a strict sense Del Monte Dunes sought not just compensation *per se* but rather damages for the unconstitutional denial of such compensation. Damages for a constitutional violation are a legal remedy. *See, e.g., Teamsters v. Terry,* 494 U.S. 558, 570 (1990) ("Generally, an action for money damages was the 'the traditional form of relief offered in the courts of law' ") (quoting *Curtis, supra,* at 196).

Even when viewed as a simple suit for just compensation, we believe Del Monte Dunes' action sought essentially legal relief. . . . Because Del Monte

Dunes' statutory suit sounded in tort and sought legal relief, it was an action at law. . . .

. . . .

B

Having decided Del Monte Dunes' § 1983 claim was an action at law, we must determine whether the particular issues of liability were proper for determination by the jury. *See Markman v. Westview Instruments, Inc.*, 517 U.S. 370 (1996). In actions at law, issues that are proper for the jury must be submitted to it "to preserve the right to a jury's resolution of the ultimate dispute," as guaranteed by the Seventh Amendment. *Id.* at 377. We determine whether issues are proper for the jury, when possible, "by using the historical method, much as we do in characterizing the suits and actions within which [the issues] arise." *Id.* at 378. We look to history to determine whether the particular issues, or analogous ones, were decided by judge or by jury in suits at common law at the time the Seventh Amendment was adopted. Where history does not provide a clear answer, we look to precedent and functional considerations. *Id.* at 384.

1

Just as no exact analogue of Del Monte Dunes' § 1983 suit can be identified at common law, so also can we find no precise analogue for the specific test of liability submitted to the jury in this case. . . .

2

We look next to our existing precedents. Although this Court has decided many regulatory takings cases, none of our decisions has addressed the proper allocation of liability determinations between judge and jury in explicit terms. . . .

. . . .

. . . We turn next to considerations of process and function . . . .

. . . .

Almost from the inception of our regulatory takings doctrine, we have held that whether a regulation of property goes so far that "there must be an exercise of eminent domain and compensation to sustain the act . . . depends upon the particular facts." *Pennsylvania Coal Co. v. Mahon,* 260 U.S. 393, 413 (1922); accord *Keystone Bituminous Coal, supra,* at 473-74. Consistent with this understanding, we have described determinations of liability in regulatory takings cases as " 'essentially ad hoc, factual inquires.' " *Lucas, supra,* 1015 (quoting *Penn Central Transp. Co. v. New York City,* 438 U.S. 104, 124 (1978)), requiring "complex factual assessments of the purposes and economic effects of government actions," *Yee,* 503 U.S., at 523.

In accordance with these pronouncements, we hold that the issue whether a landowner has been deprived of all economically viable use of his property is a predominantly factual question. As our implied acknowledgment of the procedure in *Williamson, supra,* suggests, in actions at law otherwise within the purview of the Seventh Amendment, this question is for the jury.

The jury's role in determining whether a land-use decision substantially advances legitimate public interests within the meaning of our regulatory takings doctrine presents a more difficult question. Although our cases make clear that this inquiry involves an essential factual component, it no doubt has a legal aspect as well, and is probably best understood as a mixed question of fact and law.

In this case, the narrow question submitted to the jury was whether, when viewed in light of the context and protracted history of the development application process, the city's decision to reject a particular development plan bore a reasonable relationship to its proffered justifications. As the Court of Appeals recognized, this question was "essentially fact-bound [in] nature." 95 F.3d, at 1430 (internal quotation marks omitted) (alteration by Court of Appeals). Under these circumstances, we hold that it was proper to submit this narrow, factbound question to the jury.

C

We note the limitations of our Seventh Amendment holding. We do not address the jury's role in an ordinary inverse condemnation suit. The action here was brought under § 1983, a context in which the jury's role in vindicating constitutional rights has long been recognized by the federal courts. A federal court, moreover, cannot entertain a takings claim under § 1983 unless or until the complaining landowner has been denied an adequate post-deprivation remedy. Even the State of California, where this suit arose, now provides a facially adequate procedure for obtaining just compensation for temporary takings such as this one. Our decision is also circumscribed in its conceptual reach. The posture of the case does not present an appropriate occasion to define with precision the elements of a temporary regulatory takings claim; although the city objected to submitting issues of liability to the jury at all, it approved the instructions that were submitted to the jury and therefore has no basis to challenge them.

For these reasons, we do not attempt a precise demarcation of the respective provinces of judge and jury in determining whether a zoning decision substantially advances legitimate governmental interests. The city and its *amici* suggest that sustaining the judgment here will undermine the uniformity of the law and eviscerate state and local zoning authority by subjecting all land-use decisions to plenary, and potentially inconsistent, jury review. Our decision raises no such spectre. Del Monte Dunes did not bring a broad challenge to the constitutionality of the city's general land-use ordinances or policies, and our holding does not extend to a challenge of that sort. . . . Rather, to the extent Del Monte Dunes' challenge was premised on unreasonable governmental action, the theory argued and tried to the jury was that the city's denial of the final development permit was inconsistent not only with the city's general ordinances and policies but even with the shifting ad hoc restrictions previously imposed by the city. Del Monte Dunes' argument, in short, was not that the city had followed its zoning ordinances and policies but rather that it had not done so. As is often true in § 1983 actions, the disputed questions were whether the government had denied a constitutional right in acting outside the bounds of its authority, and, if so, the extent of any resulting damages. These were questions for the jury.

V

For the reasons stated, the judgment of the Court of Appeals is affirmed.

NOTES AND QUESTIONS

(1) Justice Scalia filed a concurring opinion in which he concluded that all § 1983 actions, including the plaintiff's suit in *Del Monte Dunes,* are analogous to tort actions for which a jury trial could have been provided at common law. Scalia agreed that it had been proper for the trial judge to remove from the jury's cognizance the question of whether the city's rejection of the development plans at issue represents a "legitimate state interest." Nonetheless, he asserted that the jury should have been allowed to consider a different subquestion: whether that legitimate state interest is "substantially furthered" by the challenged actions of the city.

(2) Justice Souter dissented in part, in an opinion joined by three other Justices (O'Connor, Ginsberg and Breyer). Souter viewed inverse condemnation proceedings as directly analogous to direct condemnation actions in which it has long been settled that there is no constitutional right to a jury trial. He was unpersuaded by the Court's analogy to tort-like § 1983 actions, noting that trial by jury is not a uniform feature of such actions, some of which seek only equitable relief; and he observed that it is illogical to confine the analogy to inverse condemnation actions alone. If the analogy were not so confined, however, he reasoned, it would need to include direct condemnation actions as well, in which, by prior decision, there is clearly no jury trial right. Finally, Justice Souter viewed the issue of whether an alleged taking makes no substantial contribution to a legitimate governmental purpose as closely related to similar issues in substantive due process property claims. Since the latter are routinely reserved for judicial determination it makes sense for them to also be questions for the court in regulatory takings cases.

(3) Were you persuaded by the Court's rationale in this case? Does its holding create a danger that juries will have a free hand to undercut the authority of local governments to pursue legitimate public objectives through land use regulations? In your view, are inverse condemnation cases more similar to direct condemnation actions or to tort cases? Should this distinction be dispositive as to whether plaintiffs who allege regulatory takings should have a constitutional right to a jury trial?

§ 7.03 Coastal Zone Management

The Coastal Zone Management Act of 1972[1] is the first federal law that

[1] Pub. L. No. 92-583, 86 Stat. 1280, *et seq.*, "A Guide for Federal Approval of State Coastal Zone Management Programs: A Working Paper," prepared for the Office of Coastal Environ-

was passed with clear national land use planning purposes in mind. The law advances the national purpose through grants-in-aid to the states and, similar to other grant-in-aid legislation, contains no federal enforcement powers other than the powers conditional on the states' acceptance of the grant. The law does, however, invite the states to develop plans for coastal zone management that meet some minimal federal guidelines, and it also provides a method for developing a uniform, nationwide system of identifying coastal zones, a coastal resource inventory, and a method for the consideration, in a systematic fashion, of the competing public and private interests in the coastal zone, including conservation and development goals, and the weighing of environmental and biophysical concerns against social and economic considerations.

Although the Coastal Zone Management Act provides little opportunity for direct federal regulatory land use controls, it may be viewed as a beginning of the assertion of a direct federal interest in such controls, and, if earlier federal grant-in-aid legislation in the environmental area is taken as a guide, it is likely that the Act will be used to test the efficacy of federal minimum planning standards, possibly in anticipation of broader, more general controls in the future.

Two basic determinations underlie the policy of the Coastal Zone Management Act. The Act notes that "There is a national interest in the effective management, beneficial use, protection and development of the coastal zone,"[2] and states that it is national policy to "preserve, protect, develop, and where possible, to restore or enhance, the resources of the Nation's coastal zone for this and succeeding generations."[3] Congress finds that the key to more effective protection and use of the land and water resources of the coastal zone is

> to encourage and assist the states to exercise effectively their responsibilities in the coastal zone through the development and implementation of management programs to achieve wise use of the land and water resources of the coastal zone giving full consideration to the ecological, cultural, historic and esthetic values as well as to needs for economic development.[4]

Thus, the law places primary responsibility for coastal zone management on states, within a general framework of planning based on environmental impact assessment. The federal government through the Secretary of Commerce, exercises its influence on coastal zone management by controlling the disbursement of grants to participating states. The incentive for state participation and for meeting the federal requirements is federal grant assistance (1) for setting up management programs[5] and (2) for the administration of

mental National Oceanic Atmospheric Administration, U.S. Department of Commerce, Nov. 30, 1973, at 1-8 (henceforth "CZMP Working Paper"). For a short summary of the Act see Council of State Governments, *The Land Use Puzzle* (1974) at 21, *et seq. See generally*, Robinson, *Environmental Regulation of Real Property*, ch. 17 (1985); 4 Rohan, *Zoning and Land Use Controls*, ch. 26 (1982, Supp. 1985).

[2] Coastal Zone Management Act (hereinafter "CZMA") § 302(a), 16 U.S.C. § 1451(a).

[3] CZMA § 303(1), 16 U.S.C. § 1452(1).

[4] CZMA § 303(2), 16 U.S.C. § 1452(2). *See* Conservation Law Foundation v. Watt, 560 F. Supp. 561 (D. Mass), *aff'd*, 716 F.2d 946 (1st Cir. 1983).

[5] CZMA § 305, 16 U.S.C. § 1454.

approved management programs[6] and, (3) following the 1976 amendment, for coastal energy impact programs.[7]

The coastal zone is defined to include "the non-federal coastal waters and non-federal lands beneath them, and adjacent non-federal shorelands," and includes the "transitional" and "intertidal" areas such as salt marshes, wetlands, and beaches.[8] Under the Coastal Zone Management Act, no state may assert management authority beyond the outer limits of the territorial sea, nor may a state management program interfere with rights under the Submerged Lands Act,[9] the Outer Continental Shelf Lands Act,[10] and acts creating national parks, forests, wildlife refuges, Indian Reservations and defense establishments.[11] State discretion in establishing the landward boundary of the coastal zone was also limited, so as to insure that "the zone extends inland from the shoreline only to the extent necessary to control shorelands, the use of which have a direct and significant impact on coastal waters."

The Senate Report explains the act's emphasis on primary state authority in coastal zone management, noting "considerable" existing local authority over this area. The problem, as the report viewed it, was not lack of state power, but the state's need for financial, planning, political and other assistance in resolving the conflict between commercial development and environmental protection in the coastal zone "so as to avert damage to natural values." The report also expressed the intent that existing commercial plans and programs that satisfied the act's requirements should continue to function under the state management program.[12] The Senate Report added that

> the states do have the resources, administrative machinery, enforcement powers and constitutional authority on which to build a sound coastal zone management program.[13]

State participation is entirely voluntary, however. The act does not create a federal enforcement mechanism to compel a state to submit coastal zone management programs for federal approval, or permitting the Administrator[14] to impose a plan on states that fail to submit a plan. A state that does not want to apply for a federal grant may decide to have no protection for coastal zones, or, using its own resources, it may adopt plans that would not meet the conditions of the act. It remains unclear whether a do-nothing state could be challenged by a neighboring coastal state alleging interference with management of its own conforming participatory and federally funded plan, on the basis of the act alone. Thus the act clearly does *not* follow the regulatory scheme or employ the enforcement mechanisms of such environmental protection statutes as the Federal Water Pollution Control Act Amendments of 1972[15] or the Clean Air Act Amendment of 1970.[16]

---

[6] CZMA § 306, 16 U.S.C. § 1455.

[7] 16 U.S.C. § 1456a.

[8] CZMA § 304(1), 16 U.S.C. § 1453(1); S. Rep. 92-753 at 4783.

[9] 43 U.S.C. § 1301 *et seq.*

[10] 43 U.S.C. § 1331 *et seq.*

[11] S. Rep. 92-753 at 4781.

[12] S. Rep. 92-753 at 4779.

[13] S. Rep. 92-753 at 4780.

[14] The Secretary of Commerce.

[15] 33 U.S.C. § 151 *et seq.*

[16] 42 U.S.C. § 7401 *et seq.* as amended in 1976.

The Coastal Zone Management Act was amended in 1976.[17] The stated purpose of the Coastal Zone Management Act Amendments of 1976 was to assist the states which face Outer Continental Shelf (OCS) oil and gas development, or other energy-related developments, including the construction of facilities, in meeting the effects of such developments on the coastal zone. The assistance takes the form of substantial planning grants and grants to reduce or compensate adverse impacts on the coastal zone, and to provide for public facilities and services made necessary by such coastal zone energy developments.[18] As the Congressional reports point out, major emphasis remains on the protection of coastal environmental and ecological resources. The CZMA was enacted in 1972, prior to the advent of the so-called energy crisis, and the 1976 amendment is thus a reflection of the pressures created on the coastal zones by the need for oil exploration and other energy development.[19] By the same token, the 1976 amendments do reflect some shift in priorities, in that federal grants will help not only to protect the coastal zone but also to aid the development of energy sources and facilities.[20]

The CZMA was amended again in 1980.[21] The purpose of the 1980 amendments was to "reaffirm the nation's commitment to the wise use and management of our coastal resources" during what President Carter endorsed as the "Year of the Coast."[22] The Act's declaration of policy section was expanded to provide for a higher level of protection for coastal resources of national significance defined as "any coastal wetland, beach, dune, barrier island, reef, estuary, or fish and wildlife habitat, if any such area is determined by a coastal state to be of substantial biological or natural storm protective value."[23] The administrative grants section was amended to link the award of federal funds more closely to a state's achievement of the national policy objectives of the Act.[24] In addition, a Coastal Resource Improvement Program was established to consolidate prior funding provisions of the act and provide increased funding to aid states in redeveloping urban waterfronts and parks and providing greater access to public beaches and coastal areas.[25] The Coastal Energy Impact Program provisions were also amended to provide greater funding to states to assist them in ameliorating the environmental impacts of increased coal transshipment, particularly in the area of the Great Lakes.[26]

For further explication of the Coastal Zone Management Act and its administration, *see* F. Grad, Treatise on Environmental Law § 10.04.

---

[17] Pub. L. No. 94-370, 90 Stat. 1013 (July 26, 1976).

[18] Senate Commerce Committee, Report to Accompany S.586, S. Rep. 94-277, 94th Cong., 2d Sess. 1-3 (1976).

[19] S. Rep. 94-277 at 3-19, House Conference Report No. 94-1298, 94th Cong. 2d Sess. 23-26 (1976).

[20] House Conference Report, N.19, *supra* at 24-25 (1976).

[21] Pub. L. No. 96-464, 94 Stat. 2060 (October 17, 1980).

[22] H. Rep. No. 1012, 96th Cong. 2d Sess., 14, *reprinted in* 1980 U.S. Code Cong. & Ad. News at 4362.

[23] 16 U.S.C. Sections 1542, 1453(2); Pub. L. No. 96-464, Sections 2-4, 94 Stat. 2060-62.

[24] 16 U.S.C. Section 1455; Pub. L. No. 96-464, Section 6, 94 Stat. 2062.

[25] 16 U.S.C. Section 1455a; Pub. L. No. 96-464, Section 6, 94 Stat. 2062-64.

[26] 16 U.S.C. Section 1456a; Pub. L. No. 96-464, Section 7, 94 Stat. 2064.

GHERINI v. CALIFORNIA COASTAL COMMISSION

California Court of Appeal for the Second District (1988)
204 Cal. App. 3d 699, 251 Cal. Rptr. 426

LUCAS, P.J.:

This appeal is taken from judgment denying appellants' petition for peremptory writ of administrative mandate and dismissing their complaint for inverse condemnation.

Facts

This case involves the unique natural characteristics of one of the Channel Islands and the application of the California Coastal Act (Act) to a land use plan for the Island.

Santa Cruz Island is located in the Santa Barbara Channel approximately 19 miles from the mainland. It is roughly 62,000 acres in size and is divided into two ranches and an ecological preserve. The Gherini Ranch owned by the appellants is on the eastern end of the island and is 6,700 acres in size. The Santa Cruz Island Company Ranch is a cattle ranch comprising 42,500 acres. The ecological preserve is currently 12,500 acres in size and is held by the Nature Conservancy. The Nature Conservancy also holds a conservation easement over the Santa Cruz Island Company Ranch and is scheduled to gain control over that land during the next 24 years, thereby controlling approximately 90 percent of the island.

Santa Cruz Island is one of five islands included in the Channel Islands National Park in order to protect its nationally significant natural, scenic, wildlife, marine, ecological, archaeological, cultural and scientific values. The waters within one nautical mile of Santa Cruz Island have been designated by the State Regional Water Quality Control Board as an "Area of Special Biological Significance" because of the location there of biological communities of extraordinary value.

In addition, an area extending six nautical miles in all directions from the island has been designated by the Secretary of Commerce as a marine sanctuary because of the extraordinary assemblage of marine mammals, endangered sea birds and important fishery resources in and around the island.

Under the Act (Pub. Resources Code, § 30000 *et seq.*), Santa Barbara County (County) was required to prepare a local coastal program, including a land use plan and a set of implementation maps and ordinances for all lands and waters within its jurisdiction which lay within the California coastal zone. This included Santa Cruz Island, Santa Rosa Island, which is another of the Channel Islands, and the mainland coastal areas within the County.

The local coastal program had to be submitted to the Coastal Commission (Commission) for review as to its compliance with the Act. (§ 30512.) The

County accordingly submitted a land use plan for review in January 1980. The portion of the plan relating to the Channel Islands would have permitted oil and gas development on Santa Cruz Island and would have allowed the Gherini and Santa Cruz Island Company ranches to be broken down into 320-acre "ranchettes." This portion of the plan was rejected by the Commission in December 1980 as inconsistent with the resource and agricultural protection policies of the Act.

In March 1981, the County resubmitted its land use plan to the Commission. As revised, the plan would have permitted oil and gas development on the island as a conditional use which could not occur unless the County could find, among other things, that the public would be better off with than without the proposed project. As to subdivision of the ranches, the County retained the 320-acre parcel size and allowed conversion of a portion of the land for coastal dependent industry, commercial visitor-serving uses, or public recreation if necessary to maintain continued agricultural use of the balance of the parcel. It also allowed application of a clustered residential land use proposal similar to a plan developed for a large mainland coastal ranch. This plan allowed residential development at a density of up to one unit per acre on 2 percent of the land, commercial visitor-serving and public recreational uses on 1 percent of the land and permanent reservation of the remaining 97 percent for agricultural and open space.

The Commission again found oil and gas development on Santa Cruz Island inconsistent with the Act and also rejected the higher density residential use as inconsistent with the protective policies of the Act. The Commission denied certification of the land use plan as submitted.

The Commission gave the County a set of changes it could make in the land use plan which would permit certification. The changes required prohibition of all energy development on the island and limited residential development to one principal residence per 320-acre parcel. All residential development on the island was to be clustered on no more than 2 percent of the gross area. As applied to the Gherini Ranch, this would permit only 21 dwelling units.

The Gherinis brought the within petition for writ of mandate challenging the Commission's decision to deny certification of the County's plan. Causes of action for declaratory relief and inverse condemnation were also included. The trial court upheld the Commission's decision and found that the Commission's actions did not constitute a taking or damaging of their property. Judgment was entered against the Gherinis from which this appeal is taken.

Authority of Coastal Commission

Appellants contend the Commission exceeded its authority under the Act in requiring the County to ban all oil and gas development on the Channel Islands in order for its land use plan to be certified. The trial court found the Commission acted within its jurisdiction, and that substantial evidence supported its decision. We agree.

. . . .

The Commission first found that hydrocarbon development on Santa Cruz Island would be inconsistent with the resource protection policies of the Act.

Such policies include section 30230, which requires that marine resources be maintained, enhanced and, if feasible, restored, and that special protection be given to areas and species of special biological or economic significance. (*See also* §§ 30231, 30240.)

The evidence before the Commission amply established the biological significance of Santa Cruz Island. For example, the State Regional Water Quality Control Board designated the waters surrounding the island as an area of special biological significance because they contain "biological communities of such extraordinary, even though unquantifiable, value that no acceptable risk of change in [its environment] as a result of man's activities can be entertained." Santa Cruz Island was included in the Channel Islands National Park to protect its significant natural, scenic, wildlife, marine, ecological, archaeological, cultural, and scientific values. Moreover, the area extending six nautical miles in all directions from Santa Cruz Island was designated by the Secretary of Commerce as a marine sanctuary because of the extraordinary assemblage of marine mammals, endangered seabirds and important fishery resources in and around the island.

Accepting this evidence of the biological significance of the area, the Commission determined that energy development on the island would be inconsistent with the resource protection policies of the Act. Appellants do not challenge this determination.

Their challenge is to the Commission's further determination that the energy development plan did not satisfy the standards for exception to the consistency requirement under section 30260. That section provides that even when coastal-dependent industrial facilities such as oil and gas development cannot feasiblely be accommodated consistently with the policies of the Act, "[T]hey may nonetheless be permitted in accordance with [§ 30260] and Sections 30261 and 30262 if (1) alternative locations are infeasible or more environmentally damaging; (2) to do otherwise would adversely affect the public welfare; and (3) adverse environmental effects are mitigated to the maximum extent feasible."

The Commission noted that a site probably could be found on the island for energy development in accordance with the first criterion of section 30260. However, the Commission found that the second criterion was not satisfied.

The second part of the test under section 30260 for permitting otherwise inconsistent coastal development is the determination that "to do otherwise would adversely affect the public welfare." Appellants claim the Commission improperly weighed environmental effects of development against public benefit in making this determination, rather than solely considering the adverse impact on the public welfare of prohibiting energy development. We do not read the section so narrowly.

In section 30001 of the Act, the Legislature expressly found the coastal zone to be "a distinct and valuable natural resource of vital and enduring interest to all the people" which "exists as a delicately balanced ecosystem." Permanent protection of the state's natural and scenic resources was therein declared to be a paramount concern to the residents of the state and nation. The Legislature further found that in order to promote the public safety, health and welfare, protect public and private property, wildlife, marine fisheries, ocean resources and the natural environment, "it is necessary to protect the ecological balance of the coastal zone and prevent its deterioration and destruction." The Legislature also recognized that existing developed uses and carefully planned future development consistent with the policies of the Act are essential to the economic and social well-being of the people of California. Implicit in these findings is the understanding that the public welfare involves both protection and preservation of natural coastal resources and the need for some coastal development. Further recognition of the competing needs for coastal preservation and coastal development is found in section 30001.2, in which the Legislature declared that although coastal-dependent development such as oil and gas development "may have significant adverse effects on coastal resources or coastal access, it may be necessary to locate such developments in the coastal zone in order to ensure that inland as well as coastal resources are preserved and that orderly economic development proceeds within the state."

It is clear from these express legislative findings that a determination of what will adversely affect the public welfare requires consideration of the preservation and protection of the state's natural resources and the ecological balance of the coastal zone as well as the need for a particular type of coastal-dependent development. The Commission quire properly balanced the risk of harm to the highly sensitive and unique natural resources in and around Santa Cruz Island against the public's need to permit oil and gas development in ascertaining whether refusal to permit such hydrocarbon development would adversely affect the public welfare.

As noted above, the biological significance and ecological sensitivity of the area was fully documented by its National Park and sanctuary designations by state and federal agencies. The Final Environmental Impact statement prepared on the proposed Channel Islands Marine Sanctuary contained extensive discussion of the potential adverse impact of hydrocarbon development on the marine, mammal and bird populations of the island and advocated a complete ban on such development. Much of that analysis was applicable to the island itself as well as the surrounding waters. Another report, entitled "Analysis of the Economic Impacts of the Proposed Channel Islands Sanctuary Regulations," prepared for the U.S. Department of Commerce in April 1980, evaluated the potential socioeconomic costs of failure to develop the hydrocarbon resources in the area.

Opinion evidence of experts in environmental planning may constitute substantial evidence upon which the Commission may base its decision. We find substantial evidence of this nature in the record to support the Commission's determination that, on balance, the public welfare would not be adversely affected by prohibition of energy development on Santa Cruz Island and thus that the second requirement for exception under section 30260 was not satisfied. In light of this finding, it is unnecessary to examine the Commission's determination as to the third criterion, the mitigation of adverse environmental effects to the maximum extent feasible.

Usurpation of Local Planning

Appellants argue that the Commission preempted the land use planning and implementation responsibilities of the County by banning all energy development. The only question the Commission should have considered, they claim, was whether the County's plan regulated energy development in conformity with section 30260 of the Act.

The Act clearly contemplates both local and statewide involvement in coastal planning. Section 30004 declares that "(a) To achieve maximum responsiveness to local conditions, accountability, and public accessibility, it is necessary to provide for continued state coastal planning and management through a state [C]oastal [C]ommission" in order to ensure conformity with the Act, provide maximum state involvement in federal activities, protect regional, state and national interests and coordinate the many agencies whose activities affect the coastal zone.

. . . .

The County plan in this case would have permitted energy development on Santa Cruz Island pursuant to a conditional use permit issuable if the County found the proposed project was consistent with the policies and requirements of sections 30260 and 30262. Such an arrangement would essentially bypass the Commission's review of the overall County plan for compliance with the Act, allowing the County to directly determine compliance of projects with the Act free of the Commission's statewide perspective. This approach would render the Commission's duty to consider and certify the local coastal programs meaningless.

We have found that substantial evidence supported the Commission's conclusion that a local plan permitting energy development on Santa Cruz Island could not meet the second requirement of section 30260. If the Commission's determination that any such development is inconsistent with the Act is to be meaningful, it must be held to override the County's attempt to retain full authority to determine the consistency of energy development proposals on a case-by-case basis. Therefore, the Commission properly refused to certify the portion of the proposed plan which would have allowed the County to permit energy development pursuant to issuance of a conditional use permit . . . .

Residential Development

The Commission also rejected the County's proposed plan for clustered residential development on Santa Cruz Island, although it certified an identical policy for coastal large ranch areas on the mainland. Appellants assert this was an abuse of discretion because the Commission's reasons for rejection were speculative and it reviewed the plan as if it were reviewing a specific permit application rather than a land use plan. We disagree. . . .

While approving the concept of clustered residential development on 2 percent of the island and public recreation or visitor services on 1 per cent of the island, the Commission rejected the proposed density of up to one dwelling per acre set forth in Policy 8-9. As in the County plan for energy development, this portion of the proposed plan would have permitted such projects only upon the County's making specific findings that the project was consistent with the policies of the Act.

The Commission found this portion of the plan inconsistent with the policies for marine resource protection (§ 30230), biological productivity and water quality protection (§ 30231), protection of sensitive habitat areas (§ 30240), and new development siting (§ 30250). Noting that Santa Cruz and Santa Rosa Islands are remote from existing developed areas, the Commission explained its concerns:

> The intensity of residential development allowed on the islands by Policy 8-9 would cause a substantial increase in boat or air traffic to the islands. Such activities, and facilities to serve additional traffic and residents, would disturb environmentally sensitive habitat areas. Grading and construction of residential structures, roads and service systems as well as noise and activities associated with such uses would degrade sensitive habitat areas. Many impacts of construction and continued use, such as landform alteration, traffic, the presence of people, etc. are similar to those discussed in the findings on Energy Development regarding marine habitats and the impacts of increased offshore activities on such habitats.

Appellants dispute the support for these findings regarding density, claiming there was no evidence showing that the increased density from 21 parcels under the approved 320-acre plan to the 134 parcels under the rejected Policy 8-9 would be excessive.

However, the land use plan did not just involve the 6,700 acre Gherini Ranch; it covered all of Santa Cruz Island, a total of 61,700 acres, as well as Santa Rosa Island, which is 53,600 acres. Thus, the 320-acre plan would permit a total of 193 parcels on all of Santa Cruz Island, and a total of 167 parcels on Santa Rosa Island, in contrast to 1,234 parcels on Santa Cruz and 1,072 on Santa Rosa under the one-acre development plan. The contrast is dramatic and illuminates the Commission's serious concern regarding the effect of the increased density proposed under the one-acre clustered development plan. The Commission's determination that an increase in density from 193 parcels to as many as 1,234 parcels was excessive in terms of the extreme sensitivity of the environment and remoteness of the island and therefore inconsistent with the policies of the Act is not mere speculation but a matter of common sense, strongly supported by evidence in the administrative record.

In the absence of countervailing evidence that the impact of the one-acre density plan would be consistent with the policies of the Act, the Commission properly denied certification of the one-acre development plan.

Such consistency was not established by the requirement in the plan that the County approve each proposed project for consistency with the Act. As we noted in regard to the energy development portion of the plan, it is for the Commission to decide in the first instance whether a proposed plan is consistent with the Act, and this determination cannot be sidestepped by a local government's plan which seeks to retain such decision making authority.

. . . .

NOTES AND QUESTIONS

(1) This case raises the issue of the proper division of responsibilities between state and local officials as to land use decisions that have environmental implications. Should federal legislation—and considerations of national interests—affect that division of responsibilities? In your view, did the California legislation referred to in *Gherini* allocate responsibilities among state and local authorities in an appropriate way? Was the *Gherini* court's construction of that statute reasonable and well-supported?

(2) In implementing the California Coastal Act, should the California Coastal Commission be permitted to consider the cumulative environmental impacts of proposed land use changes? In *Billings v. California Coastal Comn'n,* 103 Cal. App. 3d 729, 163 Cal. Rptr. 288 (1980), the court overturned the Commission's denial of a permit to sub-divide an existing farm into three smaller farms. Its decision was based, in part, on the conclusion that the Coastal Act did not authorize the Commission to take account of cumulative environmental impacts. The Act was subsequently amended to give the Commission the express authority to consider such impacts. *See* Cal. Pub. Res. Code. § 30105.5.

CALIFORNIA COASTAL COMMISSION v. GRANITE ROCK CO.

United States Supreme Court (1987)
480 U.S. 572, 107 S. Ct. 1419, 94 L. Ed. 2d 577

O'CONNOR, J.:

This case presents the question whether Forest Service Regulations, federal land use statutes and regulations, or the Coastal Zone Management Act of 1972 (CZMA), 16 U.S.C. § 1451 *et seq.* pre-empt the California Coastal Commission's imposition of a permit requirement on operation of an unpatented mining claim in a national forest.

Granite Rock Company is a privately owned firm that mines chemical and pharmaceutical grade white limestone. Under the Mining Act of 1872, 17 Stat. 91, as amended, 30 U.S.C. § 22 *et seq.*, a private citizen may enter federal lands to explore for mineral deposits, if a person locates a valuable mineral deposit on federal land, and perfects the claim by properly staking it and complying with other statutory requirements, the claimant "shall have the exclusive right of possession and enjoyment of all the surface included within the lines of their locations," 30 U.S.C. § 26, although the United States retains title to the land. The holder of a perfected mining claim may secure a patent to the land by complying with the requirements of the Mining Act and regulations promulgated thereunder, and, upon issuance of the patent, legal title to the land passes to the patent holder. Granite Rock holds unpatented mining claims on federally owned lands on and around Mount Pico Blanco in the Big Sur region of Los Padres National Forest.

From 1959 to 1980, Granite Rock removed small samples of limestone from this area for mineral analysis. In 1980, in accordance with federal regulations, Granite Rock submitted to the Forest Service a five-year plan of operations for the removal of substantial amounts of limestone. The plan discussed the location and appearance of the mining operation, including the size and shape of excavations, the location of all access roads, and the storage of any overburden. The Forest Service prepared an Environmental Assessment of the plan. The Assessment recommended modifications of the plan, and the responsible Forest Service Acting District Ranger approved the plan with the recommended modifications in 1981. Shortly after Forest Service approval of the modified plan of operations, Granite Rock began to mine.

Under the California Coastal Act (CCA), Cal. Pub. Res. Code Ann. § 30000 *et seq.*, any person undertaking any development, including mining, in the State's coastal zone must secure a permit from the California Coastal Commission. According to the CCA, the Coastal Commission exercises the State's police power and constitutes the State's coastal zone management program for purposes of the federal CZMA. In 1983 the Coastal Commission instructed Granite Rock to apply for a coastal development permit for any mining undertaken after the date of the Commission's letter.

Granite Rock immediately filed an action in the United States District Court for the Northern District of California seeking to enjoin officials of the Coastal Commission from compelling Granite Rock to comply with the Coastal Commission permit requirement and for declaratory relief. Granite Rock alleged that the Coastal Commission permit requirement was preempted by Forest Service regulations, by the Mining Act of 1872, and by the CZMA. Both sides agreed that there were no material facts in dispute. The District Court denied Granite Rock's motion for summary judgment and dismissed the action. 590 F. Supp. 1361 (1984). The Court of Appeals for the Ninth Circuit reversed. 768 F.2d 1077 (1985). The Court of Appeals held that the Coastal Commission permit requirement was pre-empted by the Mining Act of 1872 and Forest Service regulations. The Court of Appeals acknowledged that the statute and regulations do not "go so far as to occupy the field of establishing environmental standards," specifically noting that Forest Service regulations "recognize that a state may enact environmental regulations in addition to those established by federal agencies," and that the Forest Service "will apply [the state standards] in exercising its permit authority." 768 F.2d at 1083. However, the Court of Appeals held that "an independent state permit system to enforce state environmental standards would undermine the Forest Service's own permit authority and thus is pre-empted." *Ibid.*

The Coastal Commission appealed to this Court under 28 U.S.C. § 1254(2). . . .

. . . .

Granite Rock does not argue that the Coastal Commission has placed any particular conditions on the issuance of a permit that conflict with federal statutes or regulations. Indeed, the record does not disclose what conditions the Coastal Commission will place on the issuance of a permit. Rather, Granite Rock argues, as it must given the posture of the case, that there is no possible set of conditions the Coastal Commission could place on its permit that would not conflict with federal law—that any state permit requirement is per se pre-empted. The only issue in this case is this purely facial challenge to the Coastal Commission permit requirement.

The Property Clause provides that "Congress shall have Power to dispose of and make all needful Rules and Regulations respecting the Territory or other Property belonging to the United States." U.S. Const., Art. IV, § 3, cl. 2. This Court has "repeatedly observed" that " '[t]he power over the public land thus entrusted to Congress is without limitations.' " Granite Rock suggests that the Property Clause not only invests unlimited power in Congress over the use of federally owned lands, but also exempts federal lands from state regulation whether or not those regulations conflict with federal law. . . .

We agree with Granite Rock that the Property Clause gives Congress plenary power to legislate the use of the federal land on which Granite Rock holds its unpatented mining claim. The question in this case, however, is whether Congress has enacted legislation respecting this federal land that would pre-empt any requirement that Granite Rock obtain a California Coastal Commission permit. To answer this question we follow the pre-emption analysis by which the Court has been guided on numerous occasions:

> [S]tate law can be pre-empted in either of two general ways. If Congress evidences an intent to occupy a given field, any state law falling within that field is pre-empted. . . . If Congress has not entirely displaced state regulation over the matter in question, state law is still pre-empted to the extent it actually conflicts with federal law, that is, when it is impossible to comply with both state and federal law, or whether the state law stands as an obstacle to the accomplishment of the full purposes and objectives of Congress.

Granite Rock and the Solicitor General as *amicus* have made basically three arguments in support of a finding that any possible state permit requirement would be pre-empted. First, Granite Rock alleges that the Federal Government's environmental regulation of unpatented mining claims in national forests demonstrates an intent to pre-empt any state regulation. Second, Granite Rock and the Solicitor General assert that indications that state land use planning over unpatented mining claims in national forests is pre-empted should lead to the conclusion that the Coastal Commission permit requirement is pre-empted. Finally, Granite Rock and the Solicitor General assert that the CZMA, by excluding federal lands from its definition of the coastal zone, declared a legislative intent that federal lands be excluded from all state coastal zone regulation. We conclude that these federal statutes and regulations do not, either independently or in combination, justify a facial challenge to the Coastal Commission permit requirement.

. . . .

Upon examination, however, the Forest Service regulations that Granite Rock alleges pre-empt any state permit requirement not only are devoid of any expression of intent to pre-empt state law, but rather appear to assume that those submitting plans of operations will comply with state laws. The regulations explicitly require all operators within the national forests to comply with state air quality standards, 36 CFR § 228.8(a)(1986), state water quality standards, § 228.8(b), and state standards for the disposal and treatment of solid wastes, § 228.8(c). The regulations also provide that, pending final approval of the plan of operations, the Forest Service officer with authority to approve plans of operation "will approve such operations as may be necessary for timely compliance with the requirements of Federal and *State laws* . . . ." § 228.5(b) (emphasis added). Finally, the final subsection of § 228.8, "[r]equirements for environmental protection," provides:

> "[h] Certification or other approval issued by *State agencies* or other Federal agencies of compliance with laws and regulations relating to mining operations will be accepted as compliance with similar or parallel requirements of these regulations." (Emphasis supplied).

It is impossible to divine from these regulations, which expressly contemplate coincident compliance with state law as well as with federal law, an intention to pre-empt all state regulation of unpatented mining claims in national forests. Neither Granite Rock nor the Solicitor General contends that these Forest Service regulations are inconsistent with their authorizing statutes.

. . . .

The second argument proposed by Granite Rock is that federal land management statutes demonstrate a legislative intent to limit States to a purely advisory role in federal land management decisions, and that the Coastal Commission permit requirement is therefore pre-empted as an impermissible state land use regulation.

In 1976 two pieces of legislation were passed that called for the development of federal land use management plans affecting unpatented mining claims in national forests. Under the Federal Land Policy and Management Act of 1976 (FLPMA), 90 Stat. 2744, 43 U.S.C. § 1701 *et seq.,* the Department of the Interior's Bureau of Land Management is responsible for managing the mineral resources on federal forest lands; under the National Forest Management Act (NFMA), 90 Stat. 2949, 16 U.S.C. §§ 1600-1614, the Forest Service under the Secretary of Agriculture is responsible for the management of the surface impacts of mining on federal forest lands. Granite Rock, as well as the Solicitor General, point to aspects of these statutes indicating a legislative intent to limit States to an advisory role in federal land management decisions. For example, the NFMA directs the Secretary of Agriculture to "develop, maintain, and, as appropriate, revise land and resource management plans for units of the National Forest System, coordinated with the land and resource management planning processes of State and local governments and other Federal agencies," 16 U.S.C. § 1640(a). The FLPMA directs that land use plans developed by the Secretary of the Interior "shall be consistent with State and local plans to the maximum extent [the Secretary] finds consistent with Federal law," and calls for the Secretary, "to the extent he finds practical," to keep apprised of state land use plans, and to "assist in resolving, to the extent practical, inconsistencies between Federal and non-Federal Government plans." 43 U.S.C. § 1712(c)(9).

For purposes of this discussion and without deciding this issue, we may assume that the combination of the NFMA and the FLPMA pre-empts the extension of state land use plans onto unpatented mining claims in national forest lands. The Coastal Commission asserts that it will use permit conditions to impose environmental regulations.

While the CCA gives land use as well as environmental regulatory authority to the Coastal Commission, the state statute also gives the Coastal Commission the ability to limit the requirements it will place on the permit. . . . In the present case, the Coastal Commission has consistently maintained that it does not seek to prohibit mining of the unpatented claim on national forest land.

The line between environmental regulation and land use planning will not always be bright; for example, one may hypothesize a state environmental regulation so severe that a particular land use would become commercially impracticable. However, the core activity described by each phrase is undoubtedly different. Land use planning in essence chooses particular uses for the land; environmental regulation, at its core, does not mandate particular uses of the land but requires only that, however the land is used, damage to the environment is kept within prescribed limits. Congress has indicated its understanding of land use planning and environmental regulation as distinct activities. As noted above, 43 U.S.C. § 1712(c)(9)requires that the Secretary of the Interior's land use plans be consistent with state plans only "to the extent he finds practical." The immediately preceding subsection, however, requires that the Secretary's land use plans "provide for compliance with applicable pollution control laws, including State and Federal air, water, noise, or other pollution standards or implementation plans." § 1712(c)(8) . . . . Congress clearly envisioned that although environmental regulation and land use planning may hypothetically overlap in some instances, these two types of activity would in most cases be capable of differentiation. Considering the legislative understanding of environmental regulation and land use planning as distinct activities, it would be anomalous to maintain that Congress intended any state environmental regulation of unpatented mining claims in national forest to be *per se* pre-empted as an impermissible exercise of state land use planning. Congress' treatment of environmental regulation and land use planning as generally distinguishable calls for this Court to treat them as distinct, until an actual overlap between the two is demonstrated in a particular case.

Granite Rock suggests that the Coastal Commission's true purpose in enforcing a permit requirement is to prohibit Granite Rock's mining entirely. By choosing to seek injunctive and declaratory relief against the permit requirement before discovering what conditions the Coastal Commission would have placed on the permit, Granite Rock has lost the possibility of making this argument in this litigation. Granite Rock's case must stand or fall on the question whether *any possible* set of conditions attached to the Coastal Commission's permit requirements would be pre-empted. As noted in the previous section, the Forest Service regulations do not indicate a federal intent to pre-empt all state environmental regulation of unpatented mining claims in national forests. Whether or not state land use planning over unpatented mining claims in national forests is pre-empted, the Coastal Commission insists that its permit requirement is an exercise of environmental regulation rather than land use planning. In the present posture of this litigation, the Coastal Commission's identification of a possible set of permit conditions not pre-empted by federal law is sufficient to rebuff Granite Rock's facial challenge to the permit requirement. This analysis is not altered by the fact that the Coastal Commission chooses to impose its environmental regulation by means of a permit requirement. If the Federal Government occupied the field of environmental regulation of unpatented mining claims in national forests—concededly not the case—then state environmental regulation of Granite Rock's mining activity would be pre-empted, whether or not the regulation was implemented through a permit requirement. Conversely, if reasonable state environmental regulation is not pre-empted, then the use of a permit requirement to impose the state regulation does not create a conflict with federal law where none previously existed. The permit requirement itself is not talismanic.

Granite Rock's final argument involves the CZMA, 16 U.S.C. § 1451 *et seq.*, through which financial assistance is provided to States for the development of coastal zone management programs.

Granite Rock argues that the exclusion of "lands the use of which is by law subject solely to the discretion of or which is held in trust by the Federal Government, its officers or agents" excludes all federally owned land from the CZMA definition of a State's coastal zone, and demonstrates a congressional intent to pre-empt any possible Coastal Commission permit requirement as applied to the mining of Granite Rock's unpatented claim in the national forest land.

According to Granite Rock, because Granite Rock mines land owned by the Federal Government, the Coastal Commission's regulation of Granite Rock's mining operation must be limited to participation in a consistency review process detailed in the CZMA. Under the CZMA, once a state coastal zone management program has been approved by the Secretary of Commerce for federal administrative grants, "any applicant for a required Federal license or permit to conduct an activity affecting land or water uses in the coastal zone of that state shall provide in the application . . . a certification that the proposed activity complies with the state's approved program and that such activity will be conducted in a manner consistent with the [state] program." 16 U.S.C. § 1456(c)(3)(A). At the same time, the applicant must provide the State a copy of the certification. The State, after public notice and appropriate hearings, is to notify the federal agency concerned that the State concurs or objects to the certification. If the State fails to notify the federal agency within six months of receiving notification, it is presumed that the State concurs. If the State neither concurs nor is presumed to concur, the federal agency must reject the application, unless the Secretary of Commerce finds that the application is consistent with the objectives of the CZMA or is "otherwise necessary in the interest of national security." *Ibid.*

In order for an activity to be subject to CZMA consistency review, the activity must be on a list that the State provides federal agencies, which describes the type of federal permit and license applications the State wishes to review. 15 CFR § 930.53(1986). If the activity is unlisted, the State must within 30 days of receiving notice of the federal permit application inform the federal agency and federal permit applicant that the proposed activity requires CZMA consistency review. § 930.54. If the State does not provide timely notification, it waives the right to review the unlisted activity. In the present case, it appears that Granite Rock's proposed mining operations were not listed pursuant to § 930.53, and that the Coastal Commission did not timely notify the Forest Service or Granite Rock that Granite Rock's plan of operations required consistency review. App. 17. Therefore, the Coastal Commission waived its right to consistency review of the 1981-1986 plan of operations.

Absent any other expression of congressional intent regarding the pre-emptive effect of the CZMA, we would be required to decide, first, whether unpatented mining claims in national forests were meant to be excluded from the § 1453(1) definition of a State's coastal zone, and, second, whether this exclusion from the coastal zone definition was intended to pre-empt state regulations that were not pre-empted by any other federal statutes or regulations. Congress has provided several clear statements of its intent regarding the pre-emptive effect of the CZMA; those statements, which indicate that Congress clearly intended the CZMA not to be an independent cause of pre-emption except in cases of actual conflict, end our inquiry.

Title 16 U.S.C. § 1456(e)(1)provides:

> Nothing in this chapter shall be construed—
>
> (1) to diminish either Federal or state jurisdiction, responsibility or rights in the field of planning, development, or control of water resources, submerged lands, or navigable waters; nor to displace, supersede, limit, or modify any interstate compact or the jurisdiction or responsibility of any legally established joint or common agency of two or more states or of two or more states and the Federal Government; nor to limit the authority of Congress to authorize and fund projects. . . .

. . . .

The clearest statement of congressional intent as to the pre-emptive effect of the CZMA appears in the "Purpose" section of the Senate Report, quoted in full:

> [The CZMA] has as its main purpose the encouragement and assistance of States in preparing and implementing management programs to preserve, protect, develop and whenever possible restore the resources of the coastal zone of the United States. The bill authorizes Federal grants-in-aid to coastal states to develop coastal zone management programs. Additionally, it authorizes grants to help coastal states implement these management programs once approved, and States would be aided in the acquisition and operation of estuarine sanctuaries. Through the system of providing grants-in-aid, the States are provided financial incentives to undertake the responsibility for setting up management programs in the coastal zone. *There is no attempt to diminish state authority through federal preemption.* The intent of this legislation is to enhance state authority by encouraging and assisting the states to assume planning and regulatory powers over their coastal zones. S. Rep. No. 92-753, *supra,* at 1, U.S. Code Cong. & Admin. News 1972, p. 4776 (emphasis supplied).

Because Congress specifically disclaimed any intention to pre-empt pre-existing state authority in the CZMA, we conclude that even if all federal lands are excluded from the CZMA definition of "coastal zone," the CZMA does not automatically pre-empt all state regulation of activities on federal lands.

NOTES AND QUESTIONS

(1) This case also raises the general question of which level of government should have what type of responsibility for environmentally-related land use regulation. Following *Granite Rock,* how extensive is the authority of states to regulate federal lands in the coastal zone? How persuasive was Justice O'Connor's attempt to distinguish land use regulation from environmental regulation? Are those two forms of governmental control unavoidably intertwined?

(2) Justices Powell and Stevens filed a separate opinion in *Granite Rock,* concurring in part and dissenting in part. They took issue with the majority's conclusion that Congress has intended to allow California a state permit, opining that the Court's pre-emption analysis accorded insufficient weight to the fact that the mine was located in a national forest and to the comprehensive nature of the several federal statutes that had been the basis for Granite Rock's federal permit. In the view of Powell and Stevens, the state's regulation in this case was "intrusive," "duplicative," and likely to create "an intolerable conflict in decisionmaking."

(3) Justices Scalia and White dissented on different grounds. They disagreed with the Coastal Commission's characterization of its permit as "an exercise of environmental regulation." Instead they viewed that permit as purely a land-use control device plainly pre-empted by federal law.

(4) *Federal Consistency.* The Coastal Zone Management Act requires federal agencies that conduct or support "activities directly affecting the coastal zone" to carry out those activities "in a manner which is, to the maximum extent practicable, consistent with approved state management programs." 16 U.S.C. § 1456(c).

One significant issue that has arisen under this provision is the extent to which the Department of Interior's sale of oil and gas leases on the outer continental shelf is an activity directly affecting the coastal zone. In a controversial 5-4 decision, the U.S. Supreme Court answered that question in the negative, holding that only federal activities within the zone, as defined by the Act, have a direct effect. *See Secretary of Interior v. California,* 464 U.S. 313 (1984). This decision was overruled, however, when Congress amended the statute in 1990 to grant states the authority to limit federal and federally-approved land uses that conflict with the state's coastal zone management requirements. 16 U.S.C. § 1456(c)(1)(A).

§ 7.04 Agricultural Land Preservation

Coughlin and Keene, "THE PROTECTION OF FARMLAND: AN ANALYSIS OF VARIOUS STATE AND LOCAL APPROACHES"*

33 Land Use Law and Zoning Digest, No. 6., at 5 (1981)

. . . .

Land Use Controls

Agricultural zoning. One of the most surprising discoveries of the National Agricultural Lands Study project was that at least 270 local governments had enacted agricultural zoning ordinances to protect farmland in the last decade. Many of them were in California, Oregon, Wisconsin, and the Twin Cities area in Minnesota, where they were stimulated or required by integrated state agricultural land protection programs. We estimate that some 15 million acres of land are subject to such zoning in these four states alone. Significant activity also has occurred in South Dakota, Iowa, Illinois, Pennsylvania and Maryland.

The most important characteristic of agricultural zoning ordinances is the extent to which they limit the intrusion of new, nonagricultural uses (usually nonfarm dwellings) into established agricultural areas. We have divided these ordinances into two main categories, nonexclusive and exclusive agricultural zoning ordinances.

Nonexclusive agricultural zoning ordinances. The nonexclusive agricultural zoning ordinances are by far the most popular. Nonfarm dwellings are allowed, but agricultural uses are preferred. In these zones, nonfarm dwellings may be permitted conditionally or as of right. There are three main types.

(1) Large-lot ordinances, which require a substantial minimum lot size, ranging from as little as 10 acres to as much as 640 acres for one single-family dwelling.

(2) Area-based allocation ordinances, which allow owners to build one house for each unit of land of a specified area that they own. In some ordinances, the allowance is fixed, ranging in practice from one dwelling unit per 10 acres to one per 160 acres. No units are allowed for remainders of less than the specified number of acres. Thus, so-called "quarter/quarter" zoning ordinances allow a landowner to build one dwelling unit for each quarter of a quarter section, or 40 acres. The dwelling must be on a small building lot, typically of from one to three acres, leaving the rest of the land restricted to farm use. In other area-based allocation ordinances, the allocation is based on a sliding scale under which the number of dwellings permitted per acre decreases as farm size increases. The advantage of area-based allocation zones over large-lot zones is that they allow dwellings to be built on relatively small lots

---

* Reprinted with the permission of the American Planning Association.

clustered on one part of the farm. Thus, the rest of the farm is relatively distant from potentially conflicting residential uses.

(3) Conditional use zoning, which allows nonfarm dwellings as a conditional use if they meet specified criteria based on the compatibility of the proposed dwelling with surrounding agricultural uses. No large minimum lot size requirement is imposed. In theory, at least, conditional use zones tend to allow nonfarm development that is more compatible with the purpose of the agricultural zone than approaches that permit nonfarm dwellings of right.

Exclusive agricultural zoning ordinances. In exclusive agricultural zones, nonfarm dwellings are prohibited; a performance definition of farm or farm use is employed; and each request to build a farm dwelling requires individual review. The primary advantage of exclusive agricultural zoning is that the conflict between residential and farm uses is minimized because nonfarm dwellings are prohibited.

Studies in 10 communities that have enacted agricultural zoning ordinances suggest several conclusions regarding its effectiveness. After the enactment of zoning, agriculture is perceived as a long-term, permanent land use. Permitted densities have been greatly reduced, and those rezonings that have been granted generally apply only to lands that are not well suited to agriculture. Since initial adoption, most communities studied have revised their ordinances to strengthen the restrictions on nonfarm use, an indication that protection of agricultural land through zoning can sustain good political support. The effectiveness of the zoning has been reflected in the land market. Speculation for nonagricultural purposes has shifted from agricultural areas to designated development areas, and subdivision of agricultural land has greatly decreased.

Ordinances that rely on large-lot and fixed and sliding scale area-based allocation may temporarily deter nonagricultural development in agricultural areas, but, in the long run, the validity of these techniques is questionable, since they permit nonfarm uses as of right. Unless the acreage allowance per dwelling is at least as large as the typical farm in the locality, the solution to this long-term problem will most probably be found in either conditional use zoning, which requires a case-by-case evaluation of proposed dwellings in the agricultural area, or exclusive agricultural zoning premised on a performance definition of farm dwelling.

Purchase of interest in land. In certain situations, zoning may not be an appropriate technique for preventing the development of agricultural land. For example, it may prove politically infeasible and possibly unfair to enact an exclusive agricultural zoning ordinance, particularly in locations where development pressure is high and it is evidence that the zoning restrictions would deprive landowners of substantial value. Experience in many jurisdictions has shown that zoning regulations may be weakened to accommodate strong demands for development. In response to such concerns, many policy makers have turned to the idea of acquiring less-than-fee interests in land (including especially "conservation easements") in order to control its use . . . .

NOTES

(1) In other parts of their article Coughlin and Keene also summarize certain non-land use programs to preserve farmland. Those include tax incentives such as "preferential assessment," in which agricultural facilities are assessed for property tax purposes at agricultural use value (rather than at their "highest and best value"), and "deferred taxation," under which a "rollback" penalty is imposed when agricultural land is converted to a non-farm use after it has received a tax preference under a preferential assessment scheme.

An additional preservation technique is "agricultural districting." There farmers voluntarily form agricultural districts for fixed, renewable periods of time (usually ranging from 4 to 10 years). After these districts are approved by government officials, farms included within them are entitled to certain benefits and preferences, including, *e.g.*, limitations on public improvements for non-farm purposes, limits of special assessments, and freedom from administrative agency regulations that might interfere with farming or decrease its profitability.

(2) The following case considers the validity of a land use control device discussed above, area-based allocation zoning, that is still in effect in Pennsylvania and other jurisdictions.

BOUNDARY DRIVE ASSOCIATES v. SHREWSBURY TOWNSHIP BOARD OF SUPERVISORS

Supreme Court of Pennsylvania (1985)
507 Pa. 481, 491 A.2d 86

Hutchinson, J.:

This is an appeal from a Commonwealth Court order which affirmed an order entered by the Court of Common Pleas of York County. The Court of Common Pleas had affirmed a decision of the Shrewsbury Township Zoning Hearing Board denying appellant's request for a variance and rejecting its challenge to certain provisions of the Township's zoning ordinance designed to preserve agricultural land. On this appeal appellant argues that the provision in question is unconstitutional under the standards set forth in our opinion in *Hopewell Township Bd. of Supervisors v. Golla,* 499 Pa. 246, 452 A.2d 1337 (1982) (plurality opinion), and, additionally, that this Court should order approval of its subdivision plan. We hold that the challenged agricultural preservation provisions of Shrewsbury Township's zoning ordinance are constitutional both facially and as applied to appellant's property and, therefore, affirm Commonwealth Court.

Appellant, Boundary Drive Associates, owns thirty-nine acres of undeveloped prime farmland in Shrewsbury Township, York County, Pennsylvania. The tract originally comprised approximately forty-three acres when appellant purchased it in 1975.[1] At that time Shrewsbury had not enacted a zoning ordinance. However, a land development ordinance then in effect would have permitted appellant to subdivide the tract into half-acre residential lots provided that the new development was connected to New Freedom Borough's public sewer lines.[2] Appellant submitted a proposal to the Township to develop the tract into seventy-two lots. This proposal contemplated public sewer service and on-site water. It was effectively approved in July, 1976 when the Township failed to act on the plan. In November, 1976, the Township enacted its first zoning ordinance. Under it appellant's land was classified as agricultural. In September, 1978, the Township formally approved the subdivision proposal, at appellant's request. However, it attempted to qualify approval by stipulating that the Township would not assist appellant in securing connection to New Freedom Borough's public sewer system. Appellant was unsuccessful in its negotiations for sewer service with New Freedom Borough. Thereafter, Common Pleas found appellant abandoned efforts to implement this subdivision plan.

In 1979 the Township's Zoning Hearing Board approved appellant's proposal, consistent with the zoning ordinance, to sell three one-acre lots from its forty-three acre tract.[3] Those lots were sold. In October 1981 appellant submitted a second subdivision plan to the Board, proposing to develop its remaining thirty-nine acres into sixty-seven lots having on-site sewer and water systems. The Board determined that the second proposal was inconsistent with Sections 5.03(1)(1), 5.04(1) and 5.04(4) of Shrewsbury's zoning ordinance and refused to grant a validity variance from those provisions. Appellant appealed to the Court of Common Pleas of York County charging that the Board abused its discretion in denying the requested validity variance and, in the alternative, that the provision of Shrewsbury's zoning ordinance are exclusionary and confiscatory and therefore unconstitutional. Common Pleas affirmed the Zoning Hearing Board's substantive determinations. Commonwealth Court likewise held the challenged provisions constitutional, concluding that they "bear a rational relationship to the stated goal of agricultural preservation and do not effect irrational or discriminatory results." *Boundary Drive Associates v. Shrewsbury Township Board,* 81 Pa. Commonwealth Ct. 7, 15, 473 A.2d 706, 710 (1984).

Shrewsbury Township covers 28.6 square miles, seventy-eight percent of which is high quality farmland. Shrewsbury's leading industry is agriculture and, in fact, of all the communities in York County, the Township has one of the highest percentages of prime farmland.

The agricultural preservation provisions of Shrewsbury's zoning ordinance are designed to effectuate the Township's policies regarding farmland. These policies are set out in the Township's Comprehensive Plan:

---

[1] The entire tract purchased by Boundary Drive consisted of eighty acres, thirty-seven of which are located in adjoining New Freedom Borough.

[2] Shrewsbury's Subdivision and Land Use Ordinance permits 20,000 square foot residential lots only where public water or sewer service is available and requires all subdivision within 1000 feet of any existing public sewerage system to connect to that system.

[3] Under the zoning ordinance petitioner was permitted a total of four dwellings, each on a one-acre residential lot, on the original forty-three acre lot.

> In planning for agricultural land, it is the Township's policy not to consider agricultural land as "undeveloped farmland awaiting another use." Farmland must be considered as "developed land." It is being used to produce a product. Farming is a land-intensive manufacturing process which converts raw materials into a product, comparable to other industrial operations, with occasional accompanying nuisances of noise, odor and dust. The agricultural zone should not be considered a holding zone, but as a zone having a positive purpose of utilizing the Township's natural resources for the benefit of the entire community and the Township should protect the agricultural zone from interference by incompatible uses which break down the integrity of the zone and also interfere with normal and customary operations within the zone.

Specifically, the provisions of the zoning ordinance at issue here designate agricultural districts within the Township and regulate their use. Agricultural districts are further divided into three classifications based on soil capability.

The first category encompasses Class I, Class II, Class IIIe-1 and Class IIIe-2 soils. These soils represent the best farmland in the Township. Pursuant to the zoning ordinance, no non-agricultural use is permitted on such land except that, when necessary, a total of two dwellings may be located on a tract consisting entirely of this highest quality farmland.

The second category consists of soils in Classes IIIe-3 through IV-4. These too are highly suitable for agricultural use but slightly less productive than soils in the first three classes. Under the applicable zoning provisions, an owner may place on this less productive land the non-farm dwelling units allotted to him by an area-based density schedule. According to this schedule, the number of permissible dwellings increases with the size of the area owned, but not in direct linear proportion to that increase in area.

The third category consists of soils in Classes IVe-5 through VIIe-2. This land is not suitable for agricultural purposes either because of unfavorable topographical features or because the size or shape of contiguous or included suitable farmland precludes efficient use of modern farm equipment. Nevertheless, in order to avoid conflicts between residential and agricultural uses, the Township does not permit unlimited residential development of this type of land. Instead, land in this classification may be used for small farms, large homesites or a variety of uses permitted by special exception.

As stated previously, the Zoning Hearing Board determined that Sections 5.03(1)(1),[4] 5.04(4) of the zoning ordinance precluded appellant's subdivision plan. Section 5.04(1) allocates a permissible number of dwellings on parcels as they existed on November 10, 1976.[5] This provision, in turn, is subject to

---

[4] Section 5.03(1)(1) establishes a minimum residential lot area of 40,000 square feet or approximately one acre and a minium residential lot width of 200 feet. Appellant's proposed lot dimensions range from 20,000 to 35,000 square feet and thus are prohibited by Section 5.03(1)(1). Petitioner's argument that this provision is unrelated to the goal of agricultural preservation has no merit.

[5] The purpose of, in effect, freezing sizes for purposes of this provision is to eliminate the possibility of repeated subdivisions into smaller and smaller tracts each thereafter entitled to its own allotment of dwellings in accordance with the heavier density schedule available to smaller tracts, down to the limit of 40,000 square feet with a 200 foot front as prescribed by Section 5.03(1)(1). This differs from the Hopewell freeze in which all existing tracts were frozen at five residences without regard to tract size.

a qualification contained in Section 5.04(4) which limits the number of dwellings which can be located on the three classes in the first category of prime farmland. Under Section 5.04(1), dwellings are allotted according to a sliding scale which permits an increased number of homes as the tract size increases.

Size of Parcel	No. of Dwellings Permitted
0-5 acres	1
5-15 acres	2
15-30 acres	3
30-60 acres	4
60-90 acres	5
90-120 acres	6
120-150 acres	7
over 150 acres	8 plus 1 dwelling for each 30 acres over 150 acres

Section 5.04(4) requires that any dwellings constructed in accordance with the schedule set forth in Section 5.04(4)(1) be located in agricultural districts comprised of soils in Classes IIIe-3 through IIIe-6, IVe-1 through IVe-7, VI and VII. However, a maximum of two dwellings may be located in districts comprised exclusively of the best farmland, *i.e.*, soils in Classes I, II, IIIe-1 and IIIe-2.

The report of the Zoning Hearing Board states only that appellant's tract is "good" farmland. Based on the number of houses allotted, the original forty-three acre parcel apparently contained both soils which are first quality and those which are inferior but still highly suitable for farming. Since appellant has already subdivided and sold three one acre lots from its original forty-three acre tract, according to the provisions of the zoning ordinance, it may locate one additional dwelling on the remaining thirty-nine-acre parcel.

Appellant charges that Sections 5.03(1)(1), 5.04(1) and 5.04(4) are unconstitutional both facially and as applied to his property under the standards we enunciated in *Hopewell, supra.* Specifically, appellant argues that the fixed scale contained in Shrewsbury's zoning scheme which permits a maximum of two dwellings on tracts comprised exclusively of first quality farmland, regardless of original tract size, is more restrictive than the zoning scheme we struck down in *Hopewell* which allowed five residential lots per parcel without regard to tract size. In addition, appellant contends that the sliding scale set forth in Section 5.04(1) unreasonably discriminates in favor of owners of small tracts. Finally, appellant suggests that the one-acre minimum lot size requirement set forth in Section 5.03(1)(1) thwarts the Township's stated goal of agricultural land preservation; that smaller lot sizes would promote Shrewsbury's efforts to protect the farming industry.

In a zoning appeal, where the Court of Common Pleas has not taken additional evidence, appellate review is limited to a determination of whether the zoning hearing board committed an abuse of discretion or error of law. The reviewing court may not disturb the findings of the board if the record indicates the findings are supported by substantial evidence. 53 P.S. § 11010.

When presented with a challenge to a zoning ordinance, the reviewing court presumes the ordinance is valid. The burden of proving otherwise is on the challenging party.

A zoning ordinance is a valid exercise of the police power when it promotes public health, safety or welfare and its regulations are substantially related to the purpose the ordinance purports to serve. In applying that formulation, Pennsylvania courts use a substantive due process analysis which requires a reviewing court to balance the public interest served by the zoning ordinance against the confiscatory or exclusionary impact of regulation on individual rights. The party challenging the constitutionality of certain zoning provisions must establish that they are arbitrary, unreasonable and unrelated to the public health, safety, morals, and general welfare. Where their validity is debatable, the legislature's judgment must control.

Unquestionably, preservation of agricultural land is a legitimate governmental goal appropriately implemented by zoning regulations. *Hopewell,* 499 Pa. at 257, 452 A.2d at 1343. In recent years both Congress and Pennsylvania's General Assembly have instituted a variety of measures designed to protect farmland, in particular, and the agriculture industry, generally.[6] Moreover, Section 604(3) of Pennsylvania's Municipalities Planning Code specifically requires that zoning ordinance provisions be designed "to preserve prime agricultural and farmland considering topography, soil type and classification, and present use." 53 P.S. § 10604(3). Accordingly, the question which remains for our decision is whether, as appellant contends, Shrewsbury's agricultural preservation zoning provisions, particularly those which limit the number of permitted dwellings and relate dwellings to soil types, unreasonably restrict appellant's right to use its land as it wishes.

Appellant contends that Shrewsbury's zoning provisions do not pass constitutional muster under our decision in *Hopewell, supra.* The agricultural zoning ordinance there at issue essentially froze tract sizes as of June 5, 1974, the enactment's effective date, and permitted an owner of land in Hopewell's agricultural district, regardless of the size of his parcel, to establish up to five contiguous residential lots, each having one single family dwelling on a lot with a maximum size of one and one-half acres.

---

[6] *See, e.g.,* the Farmland Protection Policy Act, 7 U.S.C. § 4201 *et seq.* (Supp. 1984) (establishing procedures for maximizing the extent to which federal programs contribute to farmland conversion and for assuring that such programs are compatible with state, local and private efforts to protect such land); I.R.C. §§ 126, 175, 2032A, 6166(collectively providing tax incentives to inhibit conversion of farmland and to encourage soil conservation). *See also* the Agricultural Area Security Law, Act of June 30, 1981, P.L. 128, No. 43, 3 P.S.. § 901 *et seq.* (Supp. 1984-85) (declaring the Commonwealth's policy to conserve, protect and improve its agricultural land and providing various measures to implement that policy); The Right to Farm Law, Act of June 10, 1982, P.L. 454, No. 133, 3 P.S. § 951 *et seq.* (Supp. 1984-85) (limited the circumstances under which a farmer may be subjected to local nuisance regulations); Act of January 13, 1966, P.L. (1965) 1292 ("Act 515"), 16 P.S. § 11941 *et seq.* (Supp. 1984-85) and Act of December 19, 1974, P.L. 973, No. 319, 72 P.S. § 5490.3 (Supp. 1984-85) (authorizing assessment of eligible farmland at current use value for purposes of local property taxation); 72 Pa. C.S. § 1722 (Supp. 1984-85) (providing for the valuation of farmland at its current use value for state death tax purposes); Tax Reform Code of 1971, 72 P.S. § 7602.2 (Supp. 1984-85) (exempting family farm corporations from the ten-mill state capital stock franchise tax).

We ruled this zoning scheme constitutionally infirm on two grounds. First, we determined that:

> By limiting residential subdivisions in the prime agricultural zone of the Township to a maximum of five 1-1/2 acre plots *regardless* of the size of the original tract, an unreasonably severe limitation is placed upon permissible land uses.

499 Pa. At 258, 452 A.2d at 1343 (emphasis in original). Second, we noted that owners of smaller tracts could devote a greater percentage of their total acreage to single-family dwellings than owners of large tracts. We concluded that disparate treatment of large and small landowners was unreasonably discriminatory as it derived "from the mere circumstance of tract size on the effective date of the ordinance and from the limit of five residential lots which may be established without regard to the overall size of the tract." *Id.* at 259, 452 A.2d at 1344.

Unlike the *Hopewell* zoning scheme, Shrewsbury's ordinance relates residential development to tract size. Appellant suggests that our *Hopewell* decision requires regulation which provides for an increase in allowable dwellings in perfect straightline or linear proportion to tract size, *i.e.,* one dwelling for each X number of acres regardless of tract size. In *Hopewell* we stated that an ordinance permitting "the dedication of one 1-1/2 acre lot to a single-family residence per each X number of acres in the tract . . . would have a more equitable effect and would avoid impacting on landowners on an arbitrary basis." *Id.*

We do not read *Hopewell* as requiring a perfect linear relationship between residential lots and acreage. In fact, a zoning scheme requiring such absolute density equality would actually frustrate the objective of farmland preservation. For example, under a zoning scheme employing a strict linear proportion of one dwelling per acre, maximum allowable development would result in the location of 100 houses on every 100 acre tract. Clearly, meaningful preservation of agricultural land could not be achieved under this type of regulatory scheme. Moreover, a local legislative body could rationally conclude that an ordinance allowing one-half acre lots or so-called "clustering" of residential development would not serve the purpose of farmland preservation on the ground that a fifty-acre development of tract homes with attendant amenities could not co-exist compatibly with an adjacent productive farm. Such a conclusion could be based on the knowledge the members of that governing body had about the odors, noise and dust modern farming methods create.

Alternatively, a regulatory scheme based on dwelling allocation in linear proportion to area could, for example, allow one dwelling for every thirty acres of owned land. However, this linear scheme, if strictly adhered to, might severely and unnecessarily restrict residential and other non-agricultural use of tracts consisting of fewer than thirty acres. Such smaller tracts can be thought of as too small to support an economically viable, independent modern farm. Therefore, a legislative body could rationally conclude it would be unreasonable to prohibit greater densities on these tracts. Thus, while unfettered residential development might interfere with efforts to preserve farmland, the permission given a small landowner to subdivide his relatively small parcel into lots suitable for large homesteads or small, non-working farms is not rationally inconsistent with the legislative purpose of preserving prime farmland.

For the foregoing reasons, we must reject appellant's contention that Shrewsbury's zoning ordinance is unconstitutional because it does not employ a fixed area-based allocation method of regulation.

Appellant offers no additional reasons in support of its contention that Sections 5.03(1)(1), 5.04(1) and 5.04(4) of Shrewsbury's zoning ordinance are unduly restrictive and discriminatory when balanced against the public interest in protecting irreplaceable farmland. The sliding scale set forth in Section 5.04(1), which permits the permissible number of dwellings to increase with tract size, is substantially related to the goal of farmland preservation and is less restrictive than the fixed scale challenged in *Hopewell.* Furthermore, while the two-dwelling maximum allowed on prime farmland, regardless of tract size, is similar to the fixed scale we struck down in *Hopewell,* it is an integral part of a larger, comprehensive zoning scheme substantially related to the Township's goal of farmland preservation. Therefore, Sections 5.03(1)(1), 5.04(1) and 5.04(4) are not unduly restrictive.[7]

Similarly, the challenged provisions are not unreasonably discriminatory. The sliding scale allotment system does permit greater residential density on smaller tracts but, in so doing, eliminates certain deficiencies inherent in systems based on perfect linearity. Specifically, it accommodates the reasonable expectations of owners of small parcels by placing fewer restrictions on use and, at the same time, promotes the goal of farmland preservation by limiting residential density on larger tracts which can support productive working farms.[8] Therefore, the disparate treatment accorded large and small tract owners under Sections 5.04(1) has a rational basis.

Accordingly, Commonwealth Court correctly upheld the Zoning Hearing Board's determination that appellant's subdivision plan is precluded by Sections 5.03(1)(1), 5.04(1) and 5.04(4) of Shrewsbury's zoning ordinance.

NOTES AND QUESTIONS

(1) Were you persuaded by the Pennsylvania Supreme Court's interpretation of its earlier decision in *Hopewell Township Bd. of Supervisors v. Golla*? How effective is the area based allocation scheme at issue in *Boundary Drive Associates*? Should ordinances of this type be subject to case-by-case judicial review? How (if at all) may such review undercut the purposes of these measures?

---

[7] Today we hold only that those provisions of Shrewsbury's zoning ordinance at issue here are not unduly restrictive as applied to appellant's land. We, therefore, express no opinion as to whether the same or other provisions of the ordinance would pass constitutional muster when applied to other properties having different tract sizes and soil compositions.

[8] As evident from the discussion, *supra,* a straightline proportionality zoning scheme would either frustrate the reasonable expectations of owners of small parcels or the stated goal of preservation of agricultural land, depending on the ratio chosen.

(2) Justice Flaherty filed a concurring opinion in *Boundary Drive Associates.* In his view, the Shrewsbury Township zoning ordinance at issue in the case, *as applied*, did not violate the substantive due process test established by the Pennsylvania Supreme Court in the *Hopewell* case. Flaherty reserved judgment, however, "as to whether the zoning ordinance would be valid when applied to other properties having differing tract sizes and soil compositions[.]" In certain instances, he opined, such properties might be limited too far, in their potential for development, to pass constitutional muster.

LAUX v. CHOPIN LAND ASSOCIATES

Indiana Court of Appeals for the Third District (1990)
550 N.E.2d 100

GARRARD, JUDGE

The record discloses that in June 1986 Lauxes listed for sale with a local real estate dealer approximately 113 of the 123 acres they owned and farmed in Whitley County, Indiana. They intended to retain the remaining ten acres which surrounded their home.

In late July or early August Lauxes' sons purchased 29 feeder hogs and had them delivered to Lauxes' property. Initially the hogs were raised in a vacant implement shed. The size of the hog raising operation grew and at the time of sale closing in December 1986 Lauxes were feeding between 85 and 90 hogs. In March 1987 Lauxes commenced construction of a hog raising facility which was put into use in late May or early June 1987. During the summer of 1987 the number of hogs increased to between 300 and 350 in a farrow-to-finish operation.

Meanwhile, on August 14, 1986, several individuals had made a proposal to Lauxes to purchase the 113 acres being offered for sale. Negotiations continued through the fall, an agreement was reached and the sale was closed on December 2, 1986. Title was to be placed in the name of Chopin, which was subsequently incorporated in January 1987.

At all pertinent times the entire area was zoned for agricultural uses. While the purchasers advised Lauxes that they intended to use the land for the purpose of developing large residential tracts, the land has been actually used as a grain farm since the sale.

No tracts have been sold nor residences built, but Chopin lost an opportunity to sell a portion of the real estate to a physician because of odors produced by the hog raising operation.

Additionally, the trial court found that Mr. Popp of Chopin first learned of the hogs in late June of 1987 and protested to Lauxes. In August he caused a notice to be served upon them requesting abatement of a nuisance.

Chopin commenced suit on January 19, 1988, to abate the hog operation as a nuisance. Lauxes answered asserting inter alia that they were entitled to the protection of the Right-to-Farm Act, 1C 34-1-52-4.

The trial court, after hearing, entered its special findings of fact and conclusions thereon. It determined that the odor generated by the hog raising operation constituted a nuisance, and enjoined the Lauxes from maintaining, assisting or permitting the operation of any feeder hog operation on the 10.673 acres and to refrain from conducting or permitting any livestock raising operation on that real estate. This appeal followed.

In 1981 the Indiana legislature amended 1C 34-1-52-1 *et seq.* concerning actions for nuisance by adding a new section often referred to as the Right-to-Farm Act.

This section, 1C 34-1-52-4, declares the policy of this state to conserve, protect and encourage the development and improvement of its agricultural land for the production of food and other agricultural products. It further states the purpose of the section to be to reduce the loss to the state of its agricultural resources by limiting the circumstances under which agricultural operations may be deemed to be a nuisance, noting that when non-agricultural land uses extend into agricultural areas, nuisance suits against agricultural uses are often the result.

The critical provisions of the section state:

(f) No agricultural or industrial operation or any of its appurtenances shall be or become a nuisance, private or public, by any changed conditions in the vicinity of the locality after the agricultural or industrial operation, as the case may be, has been in operation continuously on the locality for more than one year, provided:

(1) There is no significant change in the hours of operation;

(2) There is no significant change in the type of operation; and

(3) The operation would not have been a nuisance at the time the agricultural or industrial operation, as the case may be, began on that locality.

(g) This section does not apply whenever a nuisance results from the negligent operation of an agricultural or industrial operation or its appurtenances.

The statute is essentially a non-claim statute. Thus, if the operation was not an actionable nuisance at the time it was begun, and if it is engaged in continuously for more than a year on that locality, then it will not become a nuisance because of any subsequent changed conditions in the vicinity. In other words, activities or uses subsequently "coming to the nuisance" will have no claim for its abatement.

The statute imposes three conditions, or limitations on that bar. Subsection (g) removes from the protection of the statute nuisances which result from negligent operation.

In addition, subsections (f)(1) and (2) remove the bar where there has been either a significant change in the hours of operation or a significant change in the type of operation. Because the language of the statute makes it applicable to any given point in time, the effect of a significant change in either hours of operation or type of operation is to again invoke the statutory conditions and recommence the running of the statutory clock. If then the operation was not an actionable nuisance when the change occurred (*i.e.*, went into effect), it will not become one by virtue of changed conditions in the vicinity which occur more than a year after the operation continuously exists in the changed form. *See* Hand, *Right-to-Farm Laws—Breaking New Ground in the Preservation of Farmland,* 45 U. Pitt. L. Rev. 289, 308-09.

In *Ebrich Products Co. v. Wills* (1987), Ind. App., 509 N.E.2d 850, our First District considered the statute's application to industrial operations. It determined that the burden of proof as to subsection (f) rested with the party claiming the benefit of that provision. It also determined that subsection (g) concerning negligent operation is an exception to subsection (f)'s application and the burden of proof for the exception rested upon the party opposing the application of the statutory defense. 509 N.E.2d at 858. The court in *Erbrich* was not directly concerned with which party bears the burden of proving the existence or non-existence of the three numbered provisos to subscription (f) that there be no significant change in hours of operation, and that the operation would not have been a nuisance at the time it began on that locality. Nevertheless, the reasoning employed by the court on general principles of evidence involving statutory exceptions clearly indicates that the court would have placed the burden of establishing compliance with the provisos upon the party claiming the benefit of the statute.

We therefore accept *Erbrich* as establishing the allocation of the burden of proof under the statute. . . .

In this case the court made no finding that Lauxes' hog raising operation would have been a nuisance absent any changes in the vicinity or that the facility was being operated negligently. Additionally, we note that Indiana has determined that the raising of hogs is not a nuisance *per se. Shatto v. McNulty* (1987), Ind. App., 509 N.E.2d 897; *Yeager and Sullian, Inc. v. O'Neill* (1975), 163 Ind. App. 466, 324 N.E.2d 846.

In its conclusions the trial court stated that the commencement of the hog raising operation constituted a significant change in the type of operation conducted by Lauxes "and increasing the operation from 29 hogs in August of 1986 to between two and three hundred by the summer of 1987 was another significant change."

In its findings (which were sustained by the evidence) the court determined that prior to August 1986, the land had been used for grain farming and in August the Lauxes commenced a hog raising operation. It also found that hog raising produced a distinctive and unpleasant odor. We agree that the findings sustain the conclusion that within the meaning of IC 34-1-52-4 the original change to a hog raising operation constituted a significant change in the type of operation.

The conclusion concerning a second change is much more troublesome. The requirement for invoking the statute is that there be no significant change in the *type of* operation. Since the statute supplies no definition of that term, we think it must be taken in its ordinary sense, as referring to qualities common to a number of items, individuals or activities which distinguish them as an identifiable class. It follows that merely increasing or decreasing the size or numbers of an operation will not serve to change the type of operation.

That is not to say, however, that other changes which occur as a part of or incidental to a change in size may not indeed work a change in the type of an operation. It does say that merely determining that numbers have increased is insufficient to support a conclusion that there has been a significant change in the type of an operation.

Here the only special findings to support the court's conclusion of a second significant change in the type of operation were its findings concerning the increase in the number of pigs and its findings that Lauxes constructed a facility for the hogs in the spring and summer of 1987. Those findings are not sufficient to sustain the conclusion of a significant change in the type of operation.

Another problem arises from the court's determination that IC 34-1-52-4 was inapplicable. The statute provides that no agricultural operation will become a nuisance "by any changed conditions in the vicinity . . . after the agricultural [operation] . . . has been in operation continuously on the locality for more than one (1) year. . . ."

The question then arises as to what constitutes a changed condition in the vicinity. Clearly, the principal scenario envisioned by the legislature arises when people build and move into residences close by a theretofore permissible agricultural or industrial operation. They then become disturbed over noise, odors, etc. and wish to have the offensive activity abated.

As already noted, the court's findings support the conclusion that there was a significant change in the type of agricultural operation conducted by Lauxes in August 1986. Since the court made no determination that their operation constituted an actionable nuisance at the time it began, we can assume for the purpose of analysis that the injurious effect (*see* IC 34-1-52-1 and 2) occurred because of the impact of the operation's odors on proposed residential development.

Yet during the one year period following August 1986, there were no residences built, no platting of a subdivision or change in the agricultural zoning. The court did find that due to the odor from the activity Chopin lost the opportunity to sell a portion of its real estate to a physician. That finding alone would appear insufficient to ground a determination that there had been such a change in conditions in the vicinity as to make hog raising an actionable nuisance and terminate the running of the statutory one year clock.

The court's other findings concerning the Chopin tract establish that Chopin paid more than the average market price for the land for agricultural purposes; that Lauxes were aware that Chopin was purchasing for residential development and sold the land for development purposes.

Such findings might be indicative of a basis for determining that Lauxes should be equitably estopped from claiming the benefit of the Right-to-Farm statute, but the court entered no findings or conclusions concerning estoppel. Therefore, we may not treat them on that basis. While they demonstrate an intention to change the conditions in the vicinity by beginning a residential development, we believe they are inadequate to demonstrate that such a change has in fact occurred so as to preclude the agricultural operator from establishing the one year continuous operation required by the statute.

Finally, we note that in all events the court's injunction prohibiting Lauxes from conducting or permitting "any livestock raising operation" on their land is overbroad. *See, e.g., Kuhn v. Wood* (1941) 34 Ohio L.Abs. 265, 268,36 N.E.2d 1006, 1008; *Cook v. Hatcher* (1932), 121 Cal.App. 398, 405-06, 9 P.2d 231, 234.

We realize that when the hearing was conducted herein neither the trial court nor the parties had available to them any detailed interpretation concerning the application of the Right-to-Farm Act. Under the circumstances it appears that fairness dictates that the parties should be entitled to develop their evidence in the light of our decision today. Therefore, we reverse and remand for a new hearing.

NOTES AND QUESTIONS

(1) As a matter of public policy, how sound are "right-to-farm" statutes like the legislation in issue in *Laux*? Should they be limited so as to provide farmers with a defense against nuisance suits only as to agricultural activities that are in compliance with applicable federal, state and local pollution control requirements? Is their utility as a means of protecting farming outweighed by the possibility that they may "license" continuing environmental degradation? For a provocative discussion of these laws, and their implications, see Hodas, *Private Actions for Public Nuisances: Common Law Citizen Suits for Relief From Environmental Harm*, 16 Ecology L.Q. 883 (1989).

(2) A number of right-to-farm statutes require that agricultural facilities be in operation for a one year period before they are entitled to an exemption from nuisance actions. Should that period of operation begin at least one year before conditions have changed in the surrounding community, or should it commence not less than one year prior to the institution of a nuisance suit? Many of the statutes provide no guidance on this issue.

SPUR INDUSTRIES, INC. v. DEL E. WEBB DEVELOPMENT CO.

Supreme Court of Arizona (1972)
108 Ariz. 178, 494 P.2d 700

CAMERON, Vice Chief Justice

From a judgment permanently enjoining the defendant, Spur Industries, Inc. ("Spur"), from operating a cattle feedlot near the plaintiff Del E. Webb Development Company's Sun City, Spur appeals. Webb cross-appeals. Although numerous issues are raised, we feel that it is necessary to answer only two questions. They are:

1. Where the operation of a business, such as a cattle feedlot is lawful in the first instance, but becomes a nuisance by reasons of a nearby residential area, may the feedlot operation be enjoined in an action brought by the developer of the residential area?

2. Assuming that the nuisance may be enjoined, may the developer of a completely new town or urban area in a previously agricultural area be required to indemnify the operator of the feedlot who must move or cease operation because of the presence of the residential area created by the developer?

[The facts of the case were that Spur Industries, the defendant cattle grower, had been in the area for many years, and had a herd of some 20 to 30 thousand head of cattle, on a substantial feedlot, producing about a million pounds of manure per day spread over 114 acres. The plaintiff developer, Webb Development Co., began a development in the area in the late fifties, which continued to expand southward until it came close to abutting on defendant's feedlot area. The development, a retirement community that had grown into an entire town, continued to grow until the southernmost lots, some 1,300 lots, were unfit for development because of the odor and fly problem from the feedlot, which affected the senior citizens in the southerly part of the development as well. The feedlot management and housekeeping practices of the defendant were admittedly good. There was evidence, too, that the plaintiff had purchased the area in question because farmland was far less expensive per acre than more urban land closer to Phoenix. The court noted that the purchasers of the lots—who were not parties to the suit—clearly had an action in private nuisance. The plaintiff developer sued in *public* nuisance.]

May Spur Be Enjoined?

The difference between a private nuisance and a public nuisance is generally one of degree. A private nuisance is one affecting a single individual or a definite small number of persons in the enjoyment of private rights not common to the public, while a public nuisance is one affecting the rights enjoyed by citizens as a part of the public. . . .

Where the injury is slight, the remedy for minor inconveniences lies in an action for damages rather than in one for an injunction. *Kubby v. Hammond,* 68 Ariz. 17, 198 P.2d 134 (1948). Moreover, some courts have held, in the "balancing of conveniences" cases, that damages may be the sole remedy. *See Boomer v. Atlantic Cement Co.,* 27 N.Y.2d, 309 N.Y.S.2d 312, 257 N.E.2d 870, 40 A.L.R.3d 590 (1970), and annotation comments, 40 A.L.R.3d 601.

Thus, it would appear from the admittedly incomplete record as developed in the trial court, that, at most, residents of Sun City would be entitled to damages rather than injunctive relief.

We have no difficulty, however, in agreeing with the conclusion of the trial court that Spur's operation was an enjoinable public nuisance as far as the people in the southern portion of Del Webb's Sun City were concerned. . . .

It is clear that as to the citizens of Sun City, the operation of Spur's feedlot was both a public and private nuisance. They could have successfully maintained an action to abate the nuisance. Del Webb, having shown a special injury in the loss of sales, had standing to bring suit to enjoin the nuisance. *Engle v. Clark,* 53 Ariz. 472, 90 P.2d 994 (1939); *City of Phoenix v. Johnson, supra.* The judgment of the trial court permanently enjoining the operation of the feedlot is affirmed.

Must Del Webb Indemnify Spur?

A suit to enjoin a nuisance sounds in equity and the courts have long recognized a special responsibility to the public when acting as a court of equity:

§ 104. Where public interest is involved:

"Courts of equity may, and frequently do, go much further both to give and withhold relief in furtherance of the public interest than they are accustomed to go when only private interests are involved. Accordingly, the granting or withholding of relief may properly be dependent upon considerations of public interest. . . ." 27 Am.Jur.2d, Equity, page 626.

In addition to protecting the public interest, however, courts of equity are concerned with protecting the operator of a lawfully, albeit noxious, business from the result of a knowing and willful encroachment by others near his business.

In the so-called "coming to the nuisance" cases, the courts have held that the residential landowner may not have relief if he knowingly came into a neighborhood reserved for industrial or agricultural endeavors and has been damaged thereby:

"Plaintiffs chose to live in an area uncontrolled by zoning laws or restrictive covenants and remote from urban development. In such an area plaintiffs cannot complain that legitimate agricultural pursuits carried on in the area depreciate the value of their homes. The area being *primarily agricultural,* any opinion reflecting the value of such property must take this factor into account. The standards affecting the value of the residence property in an urban setting, subject to zoning controls and controlled planning techniques, cannot be the standards by which agricultural properties are judged.

"People employed in a city who build their homes in suburban areas of the country beyond the limits of a city and zoning regulations do so for a reason. Some do so to avoid the high taxation rate imposed by cities, or to avoid special assessments for street, sewer, and water projects. They usually build on improved or hard surface highways, which have been built either at state or county expense and thereby avoid special assessments for these improvements. It may be that they desire to get away from the congestion of traffic, smoke, noise, foul air and the many other annoyances of city life. But with all these advantages in going beyond the area which is zoned and restricted to protect them in their homes, they must be prepared to take the disadvantages." *Dill v. Excel Packing Company,* 183 Kan. 513, 525, 526, 331 P.2d 539, 548, 549 (1958). *See also East St. Johns Shingle Co. v. City of Portland,* 195 Or. 505, 246 P.2d 554, 560-62 (1952).

And:

". . . a party cannot justly call upon the law to make that place suitable for his residence which was not so when he selected it. . . ." *Gilbert v. Showerman,* 23 Mich. 448, 455, 2 Brown 158 (1871).

Were Webb the only party injured, we would feel justified in holding that the doctrine of "coming to the nuisance" would have been a bar to the relief asked by Webb, and, on the other hand, had Spur located the feedlot near the outskirts of a city and had the city grown toward the feedlot, Spur would have to suffer the cost of abating the nuisance as to those people locating within the growth pattern of the expanding city:

> "The case affords, perhaps, an example where a business established at a place remote from population is gradually surrounded and becomes part of a populous center, so that a business which formerly was not an interference with the rights of others has become so by the encroachment of the population. . . ." *City of Ft. Smith v. Western Hide & Fur Co.,* 153 Ark. 99, 103, 239 S.W. 724, 726 (1922).

We agree, however, with the Massachusetts court that:

> "The law of nuisance affords no rigid rule to be applied in all instances. It is elastic. It undertakes to require only that which is fair and reasonable under all circumstances. In a commonwealth like this, which depends for its material prosperity so largely on the continued growth and enlargement of manufacturing of diverse varieties, 'extreme rights' cannot be enforced. . . ." *Stevens v. Rockport Granite Co.,* 216 Mass. 486, 488, 104 N.E. 371, 373 (1914).

There was no indication in the instant case at the time Spur and its predecessors located in western Maricopa County that a new city would spring up, full-blown, alongside the feeding operation and that the developer of that city would ask the court to order Spur to move because of the new city. Spur is required to move not because of any wrongdoing on the part of Spur, but because of a proper and legitimate regard of the courts for the rights and interests of the public.

Deb Webb, on the other hand, is entitled to the relief prayed for (a permanent injunction), not because Webb is blameless, but because of the damage to the people who have been encouraged to purchase homes in Sun City. It does not equitably or legally follow, however, that Webb, being entitled to the injunction, is then free of any liability to Spur if Webb has in fact been the cause of the damage Spur has sustained. It does not seem harsh to require a developer, who has taken advantage of the lesser land values in a rural area as well as the availability of large tracts of land on which to build and develop a new town or city in the area, to indemnify those who are forced to leave as a result.

Having brought people to the nuisance to the foreseeable detriment of Spur, Webb must indemnify Spur for a reasonable amount of the cost of moving or shutting down. It should be noted that this relief to Spur is limited to a case wherein a developer has, with foreseeability, brought into a previously agricultural or industrial area the population which makes necessary the granting of an injunction against a lawful business and for which the business has no adequate relief.

It is therefore the decision of this court that the matter be remanded to the trial court for a hearing upon the damages sustained by the defendant Spur as a reasonable and direct result of the granting of the permanent injunction.

Since the result of the appeal may appear novel and both sides have obtained a measure of relief, it is ordered that each side will bear its own costs.

Affirmed in part, reversed in part, and remanded for further proceedings consistent with this opinion.

QUESTIONS

(1) How would this case have come out if the "right-to-farm" statute in issue in the *Laux* case had applied in Arizona? What would the outcome have been in *Laux* if the approach taken in *Spur Industries* had been the prevailing view in Indiana at the time of the *Laux* decision?

(2) How sound is the "compensated injunction" remedy applied in the principal case? Should it be emulated in other states? What argument may be raised against such an approach?

§ 7.05 Growth Management

The relationship of growth, metropolitan development, and environmental and land use problems has been recounted often. Inadequate housing and transportation planning, combined with an American preference for living in single family homes in rural or semi-rural settings, have given rise to "urban sprawl." Suburban populations have grown dramatically in the years since World War II. This change in living patterns has been accompanied by higher costs for public services and facilities, loss of farmland, a decrease in public open space, increased air and water pollution, higher energy consumption, traffic problems, and the abandonment of the inner city to decay and to the erosion of its tax base.

To cope with rapid growth and its consequences, state and local governments have evolved a mix of temporary and permanent legal regulations, from quotas on new developments to requirements that development be prohibited unless adequate public facilities are available to attempts to prohibit development outside of pre-set "urban growth boundaries." These varied regulations, which have been generally grouped together under the rubric of "growth management," have proliferated and evolved over the past several decades.

The materials that follow illustrate some of the ways that states and communities have responded to growth and development, and the legal controversies their responses have spawned.

GOLDEN v. RAMAPO PLANNING BOARD

New York Court of Appeals (1972)
30 N.Y.2d 359, 285 N.E.2d 291

SCILEPPI, J.:

Both cases arise out of the 1969 amendments to the Town of Ramapo's Zoning Ordinance. In *Golden*, petitioners sought an order reviewing and annulling a decision and determination of the Planning Board of the Town of Ramapo which denied their application for preliminary approval of a residential subdivision plat because of an admitted failure to secure a special permit as required by section 46-13.1 of the Town zoning ordinance prohibiting subdivision approval except where the residential developer has secured, prior to the application for plat approval, a special permit or a variance pursuant to section F of the ordinance. . . .

The plaintiffs in *Rockland County Builders Association*, on the other hand, sought, in an action for declaratory judgment, to set aside the ordinance as unconstitutional and commenced the present action after the Planning Board had denied plaintiff Mildred Rhodes preliminary plat approval for her parcel of property because of a conceded failure on her part to obtain a special permit as required under the challenged ordinance. The remaining [are] Rockland County Builders Association, a membership corporation composed of builders engaged in the purchase of land and construction of residences of all types through the Town, as well as the Eldorado Developing Corporation, possessed of some 12 acres situated within the Town.

Experiencing the pressures of an increase in population and the ancillary problem of providing municipal facilities and services,[1] the Town of Ramapo, as early as 1964, made application for [a federal] grant . . . to develop a master plan. The plan's preparation included a four-volume study of the existing land uses, public facilities, transportation, industry and commerce, housing needs and projected population trends. The proposals appearing in the studies were subsequently adopted pursuant to section 272-a of the Town Law, in July, 1966 and implemented by way of a master plan. The master plan was followed by the adoption of a comprehensive zoning ordinance. Additional sewage district and drainage studies were undertaken which culminated in the adoption of a capital budget, providing for the development of the improvements specified in the master plan within the next six years. Pursuant to section 271 of the Town Law, authorizing comprehensive planning, and as a supplement to the capital budget, the Town Board adopted a capital program which provides for the location and sequence of additional capital improvements for the 12 years following the life of the capital budget. The two plans, covering a period of 18 years, detail the capital improvements projected for maximum development and conform to the specifications set forth in the master plan, the official map and drainage plan.

Based upon these criteria, the Town subsequently adopted the subject amendments for the alleged purpose of eliminating premature subdivision and urban sprawl. Residential development is to proceed according to the provision of adequate municipal facilities and services, with the assurance that any concomitant restraint upon property use is to be of a "temporary" nature and that other private uses, including the construction of individual housing, are authorized.

The amendments did not rezone or reclassify any land into different residential or use districts, but, for the purposes of implementing the proposals

[1] The Town's allegations that present facilities are inadequate to service increasing demands goes uncontested. We must assume, therefore, that the proposed improvements, both as to their nature and extent, reflect legitimate community needs and are not veiled efforts at exclusion.

appearing in the comprehensive plan, consist, in the main, of additions to the definitional sections of the ordinance, section 46-3, and the adoption of a new class of "Special Permit Uses," designated "Residential Development Use." "Residential Development Use" is defined as "The erection or construction of dwellings [on] any vacant plots, lots or parcels of land" (§ 46-3, as amd.); and, any person who acts so as to come within that definition, "shall be deemed to be engaged in residential development which shall be a separate use classification under this ordinance and subject to the requirement of obtaining a special permit from the Town Board" (§ 46-3, as amd.).

The standards for the issuance of special permits are framed in the terms of the availability to the proposed subdivision plat of five essential facilities or services; specifically (1) public sanitary sewers or approved substitutes; (2) drainage facilities; (3) improved public parks or recreation facilities, including public schools; (4) State, county or town roads—major, secondary or collector; and, (5) firehouses. No special permit shall issue unless the proposed residential development has accumulated 15 development points, to be computed on a sliding scale of values assigned to the specified improvements under the statute. Subdivision is thus a function of immediate availability to the proposed plat of certain municipal improvements; the avowed purpose of the amendments being to phase residential development to the Town's ability to provide the above facilities or services.

Certain savings and remedial provisions are designed to relieve of potentially unreasonable restrictions. Thus the board may issue special permits vesting a present right to proceed with residential development in such year as the development meets the required point minimum, but in no event later than the final year of the 18-year capital plan. The approved special use permit is fully assignable, and improvements scheduled for completion within one year from the date of an application are to be credited as though existing on the date of the application. A prospective developer may advance the date of subdivision approval by agreeing to provide those improvements which will bring the proposed plat within the number of development points required by the amendments. And applications are authorized to the "Development Easement Acquisition Commission" for a reduction of the assessed valuation. Finally, upon application to the Town Board the development point requirements may be varied should the board determine that such a variance or modification is consistent with the on-going development plan.

The undisputed effect of these integrated efforts in land use planning and development is to provide an over-all program of orderly growth and adequate facilities through a sequential development policy commensurate with progressing availability and capacity of public facilities. While its goals are clear and its purposes undisputably laudatory, serious questions are raised as to the manner in which these ends are to be effected, not the least of which relates to their legal viability under present zoning enabling legislation, particularly sections 261 and 263 of the Town Law. The owners of the subject premises argue, and the Appellate Division has sustained the proposition, that the primary purpose of the amending ordinance is to control or regulate population growth within the Town and as such is not within the authorized objectives of the zoning enabling legislation. We disagree.

In enacting the challenged amendments, the Town Board has sought to control subdivision in all residential districts, pending the provision (public or private) at some future date of various services and facilities. A reading of the relevant statutory provisions reveals that there is no specific authorization for the "sequential" and "timing" controls adopted here. That, of course, cannot be said to end the matter, for the additional inquiry remains as to whether the challenged amendments find their basis within the perimeters of the devices authorized and purposes sanctioned under current enabling legislation. Our concern is, as it should be, with the effects of the statutory scheme taken as a whole and its role in the propagation of a viable policy of land use and planning. . . .

. . . .

The power to restrict and regulate [conferred by the Town law includes] by way of necessary implication, the authority to direct the growth of population for the purposes indicated, within the confines of the township. It is the matrix of land use restrictions, common to each of the enumerated powers and sanctioned goals, a necessary concomitant to the municipalities' recognized authority to determine the lines along which local development shall proceed, though it may divert it from its natural course . . . .

. . . .

[T]o say that the Planning Board lacks the authority to deny subdivision rights is to mistake the nature of our inquiry which is essentially whether development may be conditioned pending the provision by the municipality of specified services and facilities. Whether it is the municipality or the developer who is to provide the improvements, the objective is the same—to provide adequate facilities, off-site and on-site; and in either case subdivision rights are conditioned, not denied.

Experience, over the last quarter century, however with greater technological integration and drastic shifts in population distribution has pointed up serious defects and community autonomy in land use controls has come under increasing attack by legal commentators, and students of urban problems alike, because of its pronounced insularism and its correlative role in producing distortions in metropolitan growth patterns, and perhaps more importantly, in crippling efforts toward regional and State-wide problem solving, be it pollution, decent housing, or public transportation.

Recognition of communal and regional interdependence, in turn, has resulted in proposals for schemes of regional and State-wide planning, in the hope that decisions would then correspond roughly to their level of impact. Yet, as salutary as such decisions may be, the power to zone under current law is vested in local municipalities, and we are constrained to resolve the issues accordingly. . . .

. . . .

Hence, unless we are to ignore the plain meaning of the statutory delegation, this much is clear: phased growth is well within the ambit of existing enabling legislation. And, of course, it is no answer to point to emergent problems to buttress the conclusion that such innovative schemes are beyond the perimeters of statutory authorization. These considerations, admittedly real, to the extent which they are relevant, bear solely upon the continued viability of "localism" in land use regulation; obviously, they can neither add nor detract from the initial grant of authority, obsolescent though it may be. The answer which Ramapo has posed can by no means be termed definitive; it is, however, a first practical step toward controlled growth achieved without forsaking broader social purposes.

The evolution of more sophisticated efforts to contend with the increasing complexities of urban and suburban growth has been met by a corresponding reluctance upon the part of the judiciary to substitute its judgment as to the plan's over-all effectiveness for the considered deliberations of its progenitors. Implicit in such a philosophy of judicial self-restraint is the growing awareness that matters of land use and development are peculiarly within the expertise of students of city and suburban planning, and thus well within the legislative prerogative, not lightly to be impeded. To this same end, we have afforded such regulations, the usual presumption of validity attending the exercise of the police power, and have cast the burden of proving their invalidity upon the party challenging their enactment. Deference in the matter of the regulations' over-all effectiveness, however, is not to be viewed as an abdication of judicial responsibility, and ours remains the function of defining the metes and bounds beyond which local regulations may not venture, regardless of their professedly beneficent purposes. . . .

. . . .

. . . The present amendments are the product of foresighted planning calculated to promote the welfare of the township. The Town has imposed temporary restrictions upon land use in residential areas while committing itself to a program of development. It has utilized its comprehensive plan to implement its timing controls and has coupled with these restrictions provisions for low and moderate income housing on a large scale. Considered as a whole, it represents both in its inception and implementation a reasonable attempt to provide for the sequential, orderly development of land in conjunction with the needs of the community, as well as individual parcels of land, while simultaneously obviating the blighted aftermath which the initial failure to provide needed facilities so often brings.

The proposed amendments have the effect of restricting development for onwards to 18 years in certain areas. Whether the subject parcels will be so restricted for the full term is not clear, for it is equally probable that the proposed facilities will be brought into these areas well before that time. Assuming, however, that the restrictions will remain outstanding for the life of the program, they still fall short of a confiscation within the meaning of the Constitution.

An ordinance which seeks to permanently restrict the use of property so that it may not be used for any reasonable purpose must be recognized as a taking: The only difference between the restriction and an outright taking in such a case "is that the restriction leaves the owner subject to the burden of payment of taxation, while outright confiscation would relieve him of that burden." (*Arverne Bay Constr. Co. v. Thatcher,* [15 N.E.2d 587 (N.Y. 1938).]) An appreciably different situation obtains where the restriction constitutes a *temporary* restriction, promising that the property may be put to a profitable use within a reasonable time. The hardship of holding unproductive property for some time might be compensated for by the ultimate benefit inuring to the individual owner in the form of a substantial increase in valuation; or, for that matter, the landowner might be compelled to chafe under the temporary restriction, without the benefit of such compensation, when that burden serves to promote the public good.

We are reminded, however, that these restrictions threaten to burden individual parcels for as long as a full generation and that such a restriction cannot, in any context, be viewed as a temporary expedient. The Town, on the other hand, contends that the landowner is not deprived of either the best use of his land or of numerous other appropriate uses, still permitted within various residential districts, including the construction of a single-family residence, and consequently, it cannot be deemed confiscatory. Although no proof has been submitted on reduction of value, the land owners point to obvious disparity between the value of the property, if limited in use by the subject amendments and its value for residential development purposes, and argue that the diminution is so considerable that for all intents and purposes the land cannot presently or in the near future be put to profitable or beneficial use, without violation of the restrictions.

Every restriction on the use of property entails hardships for some individual owners. Those difficulties are invariably the product of police regulation and the pecuniary profits of the individual must in the long run be subordinated to the needs of the community. The fact that the ordinance limits the use of, and may depreciate the value of the property will not render it unconstitutional, however, unless it can be shown that the measure is either unreasonable in terms of necessity or the diminution in value is such as to be tantamount to a confiscation. Diminution, in turn, is a relative factor and though its magnitude is an indicia of a taking, it does not of itself establish a confiscation.

Without a doubt restrictions upon the property in the present case are substantial in nature and duration. They are not, however, absolute. The amendments contemplate a definite term, as the development points are designed to operate for a maximum period of 18 years and during that period, the Town is committed to the construction and installation of capital improvements. The net result of the on-going development provision is that individual parcels may be committed to a residential development use prior to the expiration of the maximum period. Similarly, property owners under the terms of the amendments may elect to accelerate the date of development by installing, at their own expense, the necessary public services to bring the parcel within the required number of development points. While even the best of plans may not always be realized, in the absence of proof to the contrary, we must assume the Town will put its best effort forward in implementing the physical and fiscal timetable outlined under the plan. Should subsequent events prove this assumption unwarranted, or should the Town because of some unforeseen event fail in its primary obligation to these landowners, there will be ample opportunity to undo the restrictions upon default. For the present, at least, we are constrained to proceed upon the assumption that the program will be fully and timely implemented.

Thus, unlike the situation presented in *Arverne Bay Constr. Co. v. Thatcher,* the present amendments propose restrictions of a certain duration and founded upon estimate determined by fact. Prognostication on our part in upholding the ordinance proceeds upon the presently permissible inference that within a reasonable time the subject property will be put to the desired use at an appreciated value. In the interim assessed valuations for real estate tax purposes reflect the impact of the proposed restrictions. The proposed restraints, mitigated by the prospect of appreciated value and interim reductions in assessed value, and measured in terms of the nature and magnitude of the project undertaken, are within the limits of necessity.

In sum, where it is clear that the existing physical and financial resources of the community are inadequate to furnish the essential services and facilities which a substantial increase in population requires, there is a rational basis for "phased growth" and hence, the challenged ordinance is not violative of the Federal and State Constitutions.

NOTES AND QUESTIONS

(1) The *Golden* decision has been widely viewed as a leading case upholding the lawfulness of timing and phasing programs for the management of urban/suburban growth. Are you satisfied with the *Golden* court's analysis? To what extent is *Golden* consistent with the U.S. Supreme Court's takings decisions in the *Nollan, Dolan* and *Lucas* cases?

(2) To what extent is a local growth management program, like the one at issue in *Golden,* likely to shift new development to nearby communities that are not participating in the program? For a discussion of this and other issues raised by the Town of Ramapo's program, see S. Seidel, Housing Costs and Government Regulations: Confronting the Regulatory Maze, (1978). Additional discussion of the *Golden* case may be found in Bosselman, *Can the Town of Ramapo Pass A Law to Bind The Whole World?* 1 Fla. St. U. L. Rev. 234 (1973); O'Keefe, *Time Controls on Land Use: Prophyletic Law for Planners,* 57 Cornell L. Rev. 827 (1972); and Note, *Phased Zoning: Regulations of the Tempo and Sequence of Land Development,* 26 Stan. L. Rev. 585 (1974).

(3) Suppose that, in *Golden,* the Town subsequently falls behind in constructing the new public facilities necessary to support orderly growth. May the plaintiffs challenge the validity of Ramapo's ordinance in that event? In addition to what was said in the opinion with respect to that question, the *Golden* court also stated, in a footnote, that "should it arise at some future point in time that the Town must fail in its enterprise, an action for a declaratory judgment will indeed prove the most effective vehicle for relieving property owners of what would constitute absolute prohibitions."

(4) The "growth quota," a different type of municipal scheme for limiting growth from that employed in the *Golden* case was reviewed in *Construction Industry Association of Sonoma County v. City of Petaluma,* 375 F. Supp. 574 (N.D. Cal. 1974), *rev'd,* 522 F.2d 897 (9th Cir. 1975), *cert. denied,* 424 U.S. 934, 96 S. Ct. 1148 (1976). That case concerned the validity of a five-year-growth-limiting plan. Petaluma, a small town fifty miles from San Francisco, had enacted the plan in order to protect its small-town character and

surrounding open space. The major device for reducing the projected growth rate of the city was by means of a 500-unit yearly building limitation and by the use of an "urban extension line" to mark the ultimate outer boundary for expansion and an intention to refuse to annex or extend city facilities outside the extension line. The entire plan was to operate through a permit system for new construction. The district court held that the Petaluma plan constituted an interference with a basic constitutional right, namely the right to travel, relying on earlier cases.

On appeal to the Ninth Circuit, the district court's ruling was reversed; the appellate court found that the Construction Industry Association lacked standing on the right to travel issue because though it had been injured in fact by the plan, it did not have interests within the arguably protected zone of such interests of the constitutional right to travel. Only persons whose mobility was impaired by the plan could bring a suit based on the right to travel,[2] and the Association could not act as a third party on their behalf. However, the circuit court found that the Association *did* have standing to challenge the plan on other grounds, namely on grounds of unconstitutional taking and unreasonable burden on interstate commerce.

The court of appeals examined these issues for the first time, because they had not been discussed by the court below. The court concluded that the concept of public welfare was sufficiently broad to permit Petaluma to intervene to protect its small-town character and to impose order and sequence on its growth. The court cited decisions upholding zoning regulations designed to allow the preservation of quiet family neighborhoods and the preservation of rural environments in support of its opinion. These the court found to be legitimate state interests when implemented by a local zoning ordinance which did not have any exclusionary effect on any one income group or racial minority group. The court held that the plan, as a reasonable exercise of the police power, did not unduly burden, as a reasonable exercise of the police power, did not unduly burden interstate commerce.

BOARD OF COUNTY COMMISSIONERS OF BREVARD COUNTY v. SNYDER

Supreme Court of Florida (1993)
627 So. 2d 469

GRIMES, J.:

. . . Jack and Gail Snyder owned a one-half acre parcel of property on Merritt Island in the unincorporated area of Brevard County. The property is zoned GU (general use) which allows construction of a single-family residence. The Snyders filed an application to rezone their property to the RU-12-15 zoning classification which allows the construction of fifteen units per

---

[2] *See, e.g.*, Edwards v. California, 314 U.S. 160 (1941); Oregon v. Mitchell, 400 U.S. 112 (1969). *See also* Note, *Municipal Growth Limitations and the Right to Migration,* 52 S. Cal. L. Rev. 1239 (1979).

acre. The area is designated for residential use under the 1988 Brevard County Comprehensive Plan Future Land Use Map. Twenty-nine zoning classifications are considered potentially consistent with this land use designation, including both the GU and the RU-2-15 classifications.

After the application for rezoning was filed, the Brevard County Planning and Zoning staff reviewed the application and completed the county's standard "rezoning review worksheet." The worksheet indicated that the proposed multifamily use of the Snyders' property was consistent with all aspects of the comprehensive plan except for the fact that it was located in the one-hundred-year flood plain in which a maximum of only two units per acre was permitted. For this reason, the staff recommended that the request be denied.

At the planning and zoning board meeting, the county planning and zoning director indicated that when the property was developed the land elevation would be raised to the point where the one-hundred-year flood plain restriction would no longer be applicable. Thus, the director stated that the staff no longer opposed the application. The planning and zoning board voted to approve the Snyders' rezoning request.

When the matter came before the board of county commissioners, Snyder stated that he intended to build only five or six units on the property. However, a number of citizens spoke in opposition to the rezoning request. Their primary concern was the increase in traffic which would be caused by the development. Ultimately, the commission voted to deny the rezoning request without stating a reason for the denial.

The Snyders filed a petition for certiorari in the circuit court. Three circuit judges, sitting *en banc* reviewed the petition and denied it by a two-to-one decision. The Snyders then filed a petition for certiorari in the Fifth District Court of Appeal.

The district court of appeal acknowledged that zoning decisions have traditionally been considered legislative in nature. Therefore, courts were required to uphold them if they could be justified as being "fairly debatable." Drawing heavily on *Fasano v. Board of County Commissioners,* 507 P.2d 23 (Or. 1973), however, the court concluded that, unlike initial zoning enactments and comprehensive rezonings or rezonings affecting a large portion of the public, a rezoning action which entails the application of a general rule or policy to specific individuals, interests, or activities is quasi-judicial in nature. Under the latter circumstances, the court reasoned that a stricter standards of judicial review of the rezoning decision was required. The court went on to hold:

> (4) Since a property owner's right to own and use his property is constitutionally protected, review of any governmental action denying or abridging that right is subject to close judicial scrutiny. Effective judicial review, constitutional due process and other essential requirements of law, all necessitate that the governmental agency (by whatever name it may be characterized) applying legislated land use restrictions to particular parcels of privately owned lands, must state reasons for action that denies the owner the use of his land and must make findings of fact and a record of its proceedings, sufficient for judicial review of: the legal sufficiency

of the evidence to support the findings of fact made, the legal sufficiency of the findings of fact supporting the reasons given and the legal adequacy, under applicable law (*i.e.,* under general comprehensive zoning ordinances, applicable state and case law and state and federal constitutional provisions) of the reasons given for the result of the action taken.

(5) The initial burden is upon the landowner to demonstrate that his petition or application for use of privately owned lands, (rezoning, special exception, conditional use permit, variance, site plan approval, etc.) complies with the reasonable procedural requirements of the ordinance and that the use sought is consistent with the applicable comprehensive zoning plan. Upon such a showing the landowner is presumptively entitled to use his property in the manner he seeks unless the opposing governmental agency asserts and proves by clear and convincing evidence that a specifically stated public necessity requires a specified, more restrictive, use. After such a showing the burden shifts to the landowner to assert and prove that such specified more restrictive land use constitutes a taking of his property for public use for which he is entitled to compensation under the taking provisions of the state or federal constitutions.

Snyder v. Board of County Commissioners, 595 So. 2d [65] at 81 (footnotes omitted).

Applying these principles to the facts of the case, the court found (1) that the Snyders' petition for rezoning was consistent with the comprehensive plan; (2) that there was no assertion or evidence that a more restrictive zoning classification was necessary to protect the health, safety, morals, or welfare of the general public; and (3) that the denial of the requested zoning classification without reasons supported by facts was, as a matter of law, arbitrary and unreasonable. The court granted the petition for certiorari. . . .

Historically, local governments have exercised the zoning power pursuant to a broad delegation of state legislative power subject only to constitutional limitations. Both federal and state courts adopted a highly deferential standard of judicial review early in the history of local zoning. In *Village of Euclid v. Ambler Realty Co.,* 272 U.S. 365 (1926), the United States Supreme Court held that "if the validity of the legislative classification for zoning purposes be fairly debatable, the legislative judgment must be allowed to control," 272 U.S. at 388. This Court expressly adopted the fairly debatable principle in *City of Miami Beach v. Ocean & Inland Co.,* 3 So. 2d 364 (1941).

Inhibited only by the loose judicial scrutiny afforded by the fairly debatable rule, local zoning systems developed in a markedly inconsistent manner. Many land use experts and practitioners have been critical of the local zoning system. Richard Babcock deplored the effect of "neighborhoodism" and rank political influence on the local decision-making process. Richard F. Babcock, *The Zoning Game* (1966). Mandelker and Tarlock recently stated that "zoning decisions are too often ad hoc, sloppy and self-serving decisions with well-defined adverse consequences without off-setting benefits." Daniel R. Mandelker and A. Dan Tarlock, *Shifting the Presumption of Constitutionality in Land-Use Law,* 24 Urb. Law. 1, 2 (1992).

Professor Charles Haar, a leading proponent of zoning reform, was an early advocate of requiring that local land use regulation be consistent with a legally binding comprehensive plan which would serve long range goals, counteract local pressures for preferential treatment, and provide courts with a meaningful standard of review. Charles M. Haar, *"In Accordance With A Comprehensive Plan,"* 68 Harv. L. Rev.1154 (1955). In 1975, the American Law Institute adopted the Model Land Development Code, which provided for procedural and planning reforms at the local level and increased state participation in land use decision-making for developments of regional impact and areas of critical state concern.

Reacting to the increasing calls for reform, numerous states have adopted legislation to change the local land use decision-making process. As one of the leaders of this national reform, Florida adopted the Local Government Comprehensive Planning Act of 1975. Ch. 75-257, Laws of Fla. This law was substantially strengthened in 1985 by the Growth Management Act. Ch. 85-55, Laws of Fla.

Pursuant to the Growth Management Act, each county and municipality is required to prepare a comprehensive plan for approval by the Department of Community Affairs. The adopted local plan must include "principles, guidelines, and standards for the orderly and balanced future economic, social, physical, environmental, and fiscal development" of the local government's jurisdictional area. § 163.3177(1), Fla. Stat. (1991). At the minimum, the local plan must include elements covering future land use; capital improvements generally; sanitary sewer, solid waste, drainage, potable water, and natural ground water aquifer protection specifically; conservation; recreation and open space; housing; traffic circulation; intergovernmental coordination; coastal management (for local government in the coastal zone); and mass transit (for local jurisdictions with 50,000 or more people). *Id.* at § 163.3177(6).

Of special relevance to local rezoning actions, the future land use plan element of the local plan must contain both a future land use map and goals, policies, and measurable objectives to guide future land use decisions. This plan element must designate the "proposed future general distribution, location, and extent of the uses of land" for various purposes. *Id.* at § 163.3177(6)(a). It must include standards to be utilized in the control and distribution of densities and intensities of development. In addition, the future land use plan must be based on adequate data and analysis concerning the local jurisdiction, including the projected population, the amount of land needed to accommodate the estimated population, the availability of public services and facilities, and the character of undeveloped land. *Id.* at § 163.3177(6)(a).

The local plan must be implemented through the adoption of land development regulations that are consistent with the plan. *Id.* at § 163.3202. In addition, all development, both public and private, and all development orders approved by local governments must be consistent with the adopted local plan. *Id.* at § 163.3194(1)(a). Section 163.3194(3), Florida Statutes (1991), explains consistency as follows:

> (A) A development order or land development regulation shall be consistent with the comprehensive plan if the land uses, densities or intensities, and other aspects of development permitted by such order or regulation

> are compatible with and further the objectives, policies, land uses, and densities or intensities in the comprehensive plan and if it meets all other criteria enumerated by the local government.

Because an order granting or denying rezoning constitutes a development order and development orders must be consistent with the comprehensive plan [under the terms of the statute], it is clear that orders on rezoning applications must be consistent with the comprehensive plan.

The first issue we must decide is whether the Board's action on Snyder's rezoning application was legislative or quasi-judicial. A board's legislative action is subject to attack in circuit court. However, in deference to the policy-making function of a board when acting in a legislative capacity, its actions will be sustained as long as they are fairly debatable. On the other hand, the rulings of a board acting in its quasi-judicial capacity are subject to review by certiorari and will be upheld only if they are supported by substantial competent evidence.

Enactments of original zoning ordinances have always been considered legislative. . . .

It is the character of the hearing that determines whether or not board action is legislative or quasi-judicial. Generally speaking, legislative action results in the formulation of a general rule of policy, whereas judicial action results in the application of a general rule of policy. In *West Flagler Amusement Co. v. State Racing Commission,* 165 So. 2d 64, 65 (1935), we explained:

> A judicial or quasi-judicial act determines the rules of law applicable, and the rights affected by them, in relation to past transactions. On the other hand, a quasi-legislative or administrative order prescribes what the rule or requirement of administratively determined duty shall be with respect to transactions to be executed in the future, in order that same shall be considered lawful. But even so, quasi-legislative and quasi-executive orders, after they have already been entered, may have a quasi-judicial attribute if capable of being arrived at and provided by law to be declared by the administrative agency only after express statutory notice, hearing and consideration of evidence to be adduced as a basis for the making thereof.

Applying this criterion, it is evident that comprehensive rezonings affecting a large portion of the public are legislative in nature. However, we agree with the court below when it said:

> Rezoning actions which have an impact on a limited number of persons or property owners, on identifiable parties and interests, where the decision is contingent on a fact or facts arrived at from distinct alternatives presented at a hearing, and where the decision can be functionally viewed as policy application, rather than policy setting, are in the nature of . . . quasi-judicial action . . . . *Snyder,* 595 So. 2d at 78.

Therefore, the board's action on Snyder's application was in the nature of a quasi-judicial proceeding and properly reviewable by petition for certiorari.

We also agree with the court below that the review is subject to strict scrutiny. In practical effect, the review by strict scrutiny in zoning cases appears to be the same as that given in the review of other quasi-judicial decisions. *See Lee County v. Sunbelt Equities, II, Ltd. Partnership,* 619 So. 2d 996 (Fla. 2d DCA 1993) (The term "strict scrutiny" arises from the necessity of strict compliance with comprehensive plan.). This term as used in the review of land use decisions must be distinguished from the type of strict scrutiny review afforded in some constitutional cases.

At this point, we depart from the rationale of the court below. In the first place, the opinion overlooks the premise that the comprehensive plan is intended to provide for the future use of land, which contemplates a gradual and ordered growth. *See City of Jacksonville Beach,* 461 So. 2d at 163, in which the following statement from *Marracci v. City of Scappoose,* 552 P.2d 552, 553 (Or. Ct. App. 1976), was approved:

> [A] comprehensive plan only establishes a long-range maximum limit on the possible intensity of land use; a plan does not simultaneously establish an immediate minimum limit on the possible intensity of land use. The present use of land may, by zoning ordinance, continue to be more limited than the future use contemplated by the comprehensive plan.

Even where a denial of a zoning application would be inconsistent with the plan, the local government should have the discretion to decide that the maximum development density should not be allowed provided the governmental body approves some development that is consistent with the plan and the government's decision is supported by substantial, competent evidence.

Further, we cannot accept the proposition that once the landowner demonstrates that the proposed use is consistent with the comprehensive plan, he is presumptively entitled to this use unless the opposing governmental agency proves by clear and convincing evidence that specifically stated public necessity requires a more restricted use. We do not believe that a property owner is necessarily more entitled to relief by proving consistency when the board action is also consistent with the plan. . . .

This raises a question of whether the Growth Management Act provides any comfort to the landowner when the denial of the rezoning request is consistent with the comprehensive plan. It could be argued that the only recourse is to pursue the traditional remedy of attempting to prove that the denial of the application was arbitrary, discriminatory, or unreasonable. Yet, the fact that a proposed use is consistent with the plan means that the planners contemplated that that use would be acceptable at some point in the future. We do not believe the Growth Management Act was intended to preclude development but only to insure that it proceed in an orderly manner.

Upon consideration, we hold that a landowner seeking to rezone property has the burden of proving that the proposal is consistent with the comprehensive plan and complies with all procedural requirements of the zoning ordinance. At this point the burden shifts to the governmental board to demonstrate that maintaining the existing zoning classification with respect to the property accomplishes a legitimate public purpose. In effect, the landowners' traditional remedies will be subsumed within this rule, and the board will now have the burden of showing that the refusal to rezone the property is not arbitrary, discriminatory, or unreasonable. If the board carries its burden, a landowner's only remaining recourse will be to demonstrate that the existing zoning classification of the property is confiscatory and thereby constitutes a taking.

NOTES AND QUESTIONS

(1) As the *Snyder* case describes, in 1985 the State of Florida adopted a statute requiring each local government in the state to adopt a comprehensive plan. Individual development orders issued by local governments must be consistent with those comprehensive plans. Moreover, the legislation authorizes "any aggrieved or adversely affected party" to maintain a lawsuit to prevent local governments from taking actions on development orders that "materially [alter] the use or intensity of use on a particular piece of property that is not consistent with the comprehensive plan." Fla. Stat. § 163.3215(1). For a thorough summary of the Act, as interpreted, and a critique of its implementation by governmental officials in Florida, *see* Grosso, *Florida's Growth Management Act: How Far We Have Come and How Far Have We Yet To Go?* 20 Nova L. Rev. 589 (1996).

(2) Was the *Snyder* court correct in defining re-zoning decisions at quasi-judicial? Should re-zoning hearings require sworn testimony and cross-examination of witnesses? Do such procedures protect the interests of ordinary citizens? Might they discourage such citizens from becoming involved in land-use controversies?

(3) One impact of the *Snyder* decision was that it effectively prohibited *ex parte* contact between persons with an interest in particular zoning amendments and local elected officials. In 1996, the Florida legislature, under pressure from local governments, modified *Snyder*'s *ex parte* contact rule. *See* Fla. Stat. § 286.0115. Under the statute, counties and municipalities were authorized to adopt procedures removing the presumption of prejudice arising from *ex parte* communications in quasi-judicial proceedings. The substance of such communications, however, must be made a part of the public record "before or during the public meeting" at which a vote is taken on proposed zoning amendments, and persons with a contrary opinion must be given a reasonable opportunity to refute or respond to the *ex parte* communication. Is this a sound approach? Does it tend to favor developers or environmental organizations?

(4) Notwithstanding the *Snyder* decision, Florida's intermediate appellate courts have held that certain local land use decisions remain legislative, as opposed to quasi-judicial, in character. *See, e.g., Section 28 Partnership, Ltd. v. Martin County,* 642 So.2d 609 (Fla. 4th DCA 1994) which involved a challenge to a county's refusal to approve amendments to its comprehensive plan that would have permitted development on a 638-acre parcel adjacent to a National Park and a state nature preserve. The court opined that "considering the pristine nature of the land in the park and the river, and the use of the area by the public . . . the changes sought in this instance involved matters of policy and were subject to review under the 'fairly debatable' standard." *Id.* at 612. *See also City Environmental Services Landfill of Florida, Inc. v. Holmes County,* 677 So.2d 1327 (Fla. 1st DCA 1996).

§ 7.06 Transfer of Development Rights as an Environmental Protection Technique

The development of the idea of transferable development rights (TDRs) in the late 1960s was a response to the public need for the acquisition of certain lands in order to preserve them—or some of their aspects, historical, scenic or natural—for public enjoyment. This need to protect historic, scenic, natural or open areas by preventing their change in character through development for greater economic return can be met in a variety of ways.

The ingenious notion of the *transferable* development right, largely the work of Professor John J. Costonis,[1] is to find a way of avoiding payment for the owner's right to develop a particular piece of land by detaching these rights from the property itself and making them transferable—*i.e.*, available for use by the owner, or by some other person who has purchased these rights from the owner for use on another piece of land that is available for further development. In simplified form, the idea is that the owner of the property that is to be kept undeveloped has not been deprived of anything—*i.e.*, there is no taking—because he still has his development rights which are now transferable—available for sale or use elsewhere. In this way, TDRs, it is asserted, will accomplish the objective of protecting the resource from further development and that of compensating its owner for the loss of economic opportunity that the development potential represents.[2]

The TDR device has been suggested as a means of accomplishing several different land use objectives, namely the preservation of landmarks, historic urban areas and buildings; the preservation of certain nonurban, open or agricultural areas; and the achievement of certain comprehensive land use schemes. It is also used as a technique to preserve the environment.

With respect to the preservation of urban areas, two approaches predominate: the "New York Plan" and the "Chicago Plan."

The New York City Development Rights Transfer Program,[3] (the New York Plan) enacted by the Planning Commission in 1968, was intended to increase the chances of preserving the city's historic buildings.[4] Under the New York plan, the development potential of a landmark lot is represented by the amount of floor space which is authorized for that lot but which has not been built. A landmark owner may transfer his right to build this amount of floor area to the owner of a lot which is contiguous to, or across the street from, his own; under certain circumstances, he may also transfer it to a lot which forms part of a series connecting with his own.

The owner may continue to make transfers to one or more lots until his development rights have been exhausted; in many cases, a transfer of all development rights will require several transactions because, with some exceptions, the floor area of a transferee lot may not be increased by more than 20 percent of its authorized level. Each transfer must be approved by

---

[1] Costonis, *Development Rights Transfer: An Exploratory Essay,* 83 Yale L. J. 75, 77 (1973).

[2] Costonis, at 86.

[3] N.Y. Zoning Resolution, art. VII, ch. 4, § 74-79; art. IX, § 91-03.

[4] Richards, *Development Rights Transfer in New York City,* 82 Yale L. J. 338-372 (1972); also in Transfer of Development Rights 129 (J. Rose ed. 1975).

the Planning Commission and by the Board of Estimate. Transfers of development rights from publicly owned landmark sites are made contingent upon provision by the purchaser of a pedestrian circulation or transportation system improvement.[5]

An alternative TDR scheme for preserving historical buildings, represented by the "Chicago Plan," calls first for designation by the city council of "development rights transfer districts." The boundaries of each district are to include a number of the city's landmarks. A landmark owner within a given district would then be entitled to transfer the development potential of his lot to owners of non-landmark lots within that district; as under the New York plan, ceilings would be placed upon the permissible increase in development potential with respect to any individual transferee lot. In exchange for the city's authorization of a transfer, the landmark owner would be under an obligation to maintain his building in good condition and without alteration.[6]

The city would be empowered to condemn the development rights of landmark owners who resist the transfer device and demand compensation or the right to develop. Payment for these rights would come out of funds raised by sales made from a "development rights bank," which would consist of rights donated by other landmark owners, those transferred from publicly owned landmarks, and those which have been condemned.[7]

The architect of the Chicago plan, John J. Costonis, has indicated his belief that it represents a substantial improvement upon the New York TDR system for landmark preservation. Costonis is critical of the New York plan, primarily on the ground that it fails to assure with any substantial certainty that the landmark owner who refrains from demolition will be compensated for his decision. The Chicago plan, he argues, gives more security to the landmark owner. The use of transfer districts rather than adjacency requirements is intended to remove the uncertainty as to marketability of rights; rather than being dependent upon the amount of construction activity on particular adjacent sites, the existence of the Chicago plan market would be "governed instead by the general vigor of the construction and real estate markets in the particular municipality's central commercial and service areas."[8]

Much of the debate about the merits of TDRs centers on whether the device is either necessary or workable.

Proponents of the device as an aid in landmark preservation believe that the existing protection afforded by landmarks preservation legislation is inadequate. Costonis has expressed the view that the typical landmark ordinance is useful in preserving those buildings that are outside of high land value areas, but that it is inadequate to protect landmarks located in downtown areas, where challenge of development restrictions is much more

[5] Costonis, *The Chicago Plan: Inventive Zoning and the Preservation of Urban Landmarks*, 85 Harv. L. Rev. 574-631 (1972); also in Transfer of Development Rights 101 (J. Rose ed. 1975). For a detailed discussion of the implementation of New York City's plan, see Richards, *Transferable Development Rights: Corrective, Catastrophe, or Curiosity?*, 12 Real Est. J. 26 (1983).

[6] Costonis, N. 5 *supra*, Transfer of Development Rights (J. Rose ed. 1975).

[7] Costonis, N. 5 *supra*.

[8] Costonis, N. 5 *supra*, at 107.

common and where the cost to the city of acquiring and maintaining landmark structures would be prohibitive.[9]

Problems involved in the effective administration of TDR programs have been noted by supporters of the technique as well as by its opponents. A principal TDR proponent has pointed out that the success of a TDR scheme depends largely upon the accuracy with which planners can anticipate the economic demand for land development in certain areas.[10] The problem of maintaining, as well as that of anticipating, demand appears in all TDR discussions; the Chicago plan as noted above, attempts to deal with the market situation through the device of the development rights transfer district, but even under this plan the continued existence of a demand for development rights is not completely assured.

Problems of economic calculation have been noted with respect to the transferor end of the TDR system as well. Costonis points out that both the resource owner's loss, and the extent to which he is entitled to compensation for that loss, should be worked out accurately. While he does not anticipate difficulty in general in determining the loss, he believes that the compensation question is a troubling one because of the lack of an agreement on what kinds of economic expectations are justified. It is suggested that the economic experience of the administrative agency in charge of the transfer property may help promote an answer to this problem.[11]

For further discussion of TDR arrangements, *see* F. Grad, Treatise on Environmental Law § 10.03.

FRED F. FRENCH INVESTING CO. v. CITY OF NEW YORK

New York Court of Appeals (1976)
39 N.Y.2d 587, 350 N.E.2d 381

BREITEL, C.J.:

Plaintiff Fred F. French Investing Co., purchase money mortgagee of Tudor City, a Manhattan residential complex, brought this action to declare unconstitutional a 1972 amendment to the New York City Zoning Resolution and seeks compensation as for "inverse" taking by eminent domain. The amendment purported to create a "Special Park District," and rezoned two private parks in the Tudor City complex exclusively as parks open to the public. It further provided for the granting to the defendant property owners of transferable development (air) rights usable elsewhere. It created the transferable

---

[9] Costonis, N. 5 *supra* in Transfer of Development Rights 99-100 (J. Rose. ed. 1975).

[10] Rose, *Psychological, Legal and Administrative Problems of the Proposal to Use the Transfer of Development Rights as a Technique to Preserve Open Space,* Urb. Law., vol. 6, No. 4 (1974), in Transfer of Development Rights 297 (J. Rose ed. 1975). For an economic analysis of TDR by proponents of the technique, see, Berry and Steiker, *An Economic Analysis of Transfer of Development Rights,* 17 Nat. Resources J. 55 (1977).

[11] Costonis, *Development Rights Transfer: An Exploratory Essay,* 83 Yale L. J. 75, 122 (1973).

rights by severing the above-surface development rights from the surface development rights, a device of recent invention. . . .

Tudor City is a four-acre residential complex built on an elevated level above East 42nd Street, across First Avenue from the United Nations in mid-town Manhattan. Planned and developed as a residential community, Tudor City consists of 10 large apartment buildings housing approximately 8,000 people, a hotel, four brownstone buildings, and two 15,000 square-foot private parks, the parks, covering about 18-1/2% of the area of the complex, are elevated from grade and located on the north and south sides of East 42nd Street, with a connecting viaduct.

[The Tudor City property was conveyed and] the new owner announced plans to erect a building, said to be a 50-story tower, over East 42nd Street between First and Second Avenues. This plan would have required New York City Planning Commission approval of a shifting of development rights from the parks to the proposed adjoining site and a corresponding zoning change. Alternatively, the owner proposed to erect on each of the Tudor City park sites a building of maximum size permitted by the existing zoning regulations.

There was immediately an adverse public reaction to the owner's proposals, especially from Tudor City residents. After public hearings, the City Planning Commission recommended, over the dissent of one commissioner, and on December 7, 1972 the Board of Estimate approved, an amendment to the zoning resolution establishing Special Park District "P." By contemporaneous amendment to the zoning map, the two Tudor City parks were included within Special Park District "P."

Under the zoning amendment, "only passive recreational uses are permitted" in the Special Park District and improvements are limited to "structures incidental to passive recreational use." When the Special Park District would be mapped, the parks are required to be open daily to the public between 6:00 a.m. and 10:00 p.m.

The zoning amendment permits the transfer of development rights from a privately owned lot zoned as a Special Park District, denominated a "granting lot," to other areas in midtown Manhattan, bounded by 60th Street, Third Avenue, 38th Street and Eighth Avenue, denominated "receiving lots." Lots eligible to be receiving lots are those with a minimum lot size of 30,000 square feet and zoned to permit development at the maximum commercial density. The owner of a granting lot would be permitted to transfer part of his development rights to any eligible receiving lot, thereby increasing its maximum floor area up to 10%. Further increase in the receiving lot's floor area, limited to 20% of the maximum commercial density, is contingent upon a public hearing and approval by the City Planning Commission and the Board of Estimate. Development rights may be transferred by the owner directly to a receiving lot or to an individual or organization for later disposition to a receiving lot. Before development rights may be transferred, however, the Chairman of the City Planning Commission must certify the suitability of a plan for the continuing maintenance, at the owner's expense, of the granting lot as a park open to the public.

It is notable that the private parks become open to the public upon mapping of the Special Park District, and the opening does not depend upon the relocation and effective utilization of the transferable development rights. Indeed, the mapping occurred on December 7, 1972, and the development rights have never been marketed or used. . . .

In this case, the zoning amendment is unreasonable and, therefore, unconstitutional because, without due process of law, it deprives the owner of all his property rights, except the bare title and a dubious future reversion of full use. The amendment renders the park property unsuitable for any reasonable income productive or other private use for which it is adapted and thus destroys its economic value and deprives plaintiff of its security for its mortgages. Indeed, as Rathkopf has characterized it, the case is an "extreme example" of a deprivation (1 Rathkopf, Op. Cit., at p. 6-55; contra Marcus, *Mandatory Development Rights Transfer and the Taking Clause: The Case of Manhattan's Tudor City Parks*, 24 Buffalo L. Rev. 77, 93-94, 105).

It is recognized that the "value" of property is not a concrete or tangible attribute but an abstraction derived from the economic uses to which the property may be put. Thus, the development rights are an essential component of the value of the underlying property because they constitute some of the economic uses to which the property may be put. As such, they are a potentially valuable and even a transferable commodity and may not be disregarded in determining whether the ordinance has destroyed the economic value of the underlying property.

Of course, the development rights of the parks were not nullified by the city's action. In an attempt to preserve the rights they were severed from the real property and made transferable to another section of mid-Manhattan in the city, but not to any particular parcel or place. There was thus created floating development rights, utterly unusable until they could be attached to some accommodating real property, available by happenstance of prior ownership, or by grant, purchase, or devise, and subject to the contingent approvals of administrative agencies. In such case, the development rights, disembodied abstractions of man's ingenuity, float in a limbo until restored to reality by reattachment to tangible real property. Put another way, it is a tolerable abstraction to consider development rights apart from the solid land from which as a matter of zoning law they derive. But severed, the development rights are a double abstraction until they are actually attached to a receiving parcel, yet to be identified, acquired, and subject to the contingent future approvals of administrative agencies, events which may never happen because of the exigencies of the market and the contingencies and exigencies of administrative action. The acceptance of this contingency-ridden arrangement, however, was mandatory under the amendment.

The problem with this arrangement, as Mr. Justice Waltemade so wisely observed at Special Term, is that it fails to assure preservation of the very real economic value of the development rights as they existed when still attached to the underlying property. By compelling the owner to enter an unpredictable real estate market to find a suitable receiving lot for the rights, or a purchaser who would then share the same interest in using additional development rights, the amendment renders uncertain and thus severely impairs the value of the development rights before they were severed (*see*, Note, *The Unconstitutionality of Transferable Development Rights,* 84 Yale,

L.J. 1101, 1110-1111). Hence, when viewed in relation to both the value of the private parks after the amendment, and the value of the development rights detached from the private parks, the amendment destroyed the economic value of the property. It thus constituted a deprivation of property without due process of law.

None of this discussion of the effort to accomplish the highly beneficial purposes of creating additional park land in the teeming city bears any relation to other schemes, variously described as a "development bank" or the "Chicago Plan" (*see* Costonis, *The Chicago Plan: Incentive Zoning and the Preservation of Urban Landmarks,* 85 Harv. L.Rev. 574; Costonis, *Development Rights Transfer: An Exploratory Essay,* 83 Yale, L.J. 75, 86-87). For under such schemes or variations of them, the owner of the granting parcel may be allowed just compensation for his development rights, instantly and in money, and the acquired development rights are then placed in a "bank" from which enterprises may for a price purchase development rights to use on land owned by them. Insofar as the owner of the granting parcel is concerned, his development rights are taken by the State, straightforwardly, and he is paid just compensation for them in eminent domain. The appropriating governmental entity recoups its disbursements, when, as, and if it obtains a purchaser for those rights. In contrast, the 1972 zoning amendment short-circuits the double-tracked compensation scheme but to do this leaves the granting parcel's owner's development rights in limbo until the day of salvation, if ever it comes. . . .

It would be a misreading of the discussion above to conclude that the court is insensitive to the inescapable need for government to devise methods, other than by outright appropriation of the fee, to meet urgent environmental needs of a densely concentrated urban population. It would be equally simplistic to ignore modern recognition of the principle that no property has value except as the community contributes to that value. The obverse of this principle is, therefore, of first significance: no property is an economic island, free from contributing to the welfare of the whole of which it is but a dependent part. The limits are that unfair or disproportionate burdens may not, constitutionally, be placed on single properties or their owners. The possible solutions undoubtedly lie somewhere in the areas of general taxation, assessments for public benefit (but with an expansion of the traditional views with respect to what are assessable public benefits), horizontal eminent domain illustrated by a true "taking" of development rights with corresponding compensation, development banks, and other devices which will insure rudimentary fairness in the allocation of economic burdens.

Solutions must be reached for the problems of modern zoning, urban and rural conservation, and last but not least landmark preservations, whether by particular buildings or historical districts. Unfortunately, the land planners are now only at the beginning of the path to solution. In the process of traversing that path further, new ideas and new standards of constitutional tolerance must and will evolve. It is enough to say that the loose-ended transferable development rights in this case fall short of achieving a fair allocation of economic burden. Even though the development rights have not been nullified, their severance has rendered their value so uncertain and contingent, as to deprive the property owner of their practical usefulness, except under rare and perhaps coincidental circumstances.

The legislative and administrative efforts to solve the zoning and landmark problem in modern society demonstrate the presence of ingenuity. That ingenuity further pursued will in all likelihood achieve the goals without placing an impossible or unsuitable burden on the individual property owner, the public fisc, or the general taxpayer. These efforts are entitled to and will undoubtedly receive every encouragement. The task is difficult but not beyond management. The end is essential but the means must nevertheless conform to constitutional standards. . . .

NOTES AND QUESTIONS

(1) Would the TDR scheme at issue in this case have survived judicial scrutiny if the real estate market in Manhattan had been more robust at the time of the decision? Would the Chicago Plan for TDR, described *supra,* pass muster under the approach taken by the New York Court of Appeals in *French*? Is the *French* court's analysis consistent with the *Dolan* and *Lucas* decisions?

(2) After deciding the *French* case, the New York Court of Appeals revisited the constitutionality of TDR arrangements one year later in *Penn Central Transportation Co. v. City of New York,* 366 N.E.2d 1271 (N.Y. 1977). In that case, as part of its landmarks designation program, New York City had authorized the transfer of development rights from the preserved Grand Central Terminal site to other lots. Distinguishing *French,* the Court upheld the program:

> In *French,* the development rights on the original site were quite valuable. The regulations deprived the original site of any possibility of producing a reasonable return, since only park uses were permitted on the land. And, the transferrable development rights were left in legal limbo, due to a lack of common ownership of the rights and a suitable site for using them. Hence the plaintiffs were deprived of property without due process of law.
>
> The regulations of Grand Central Terminal, by contrast, permitted productive use of the terminal site as it had been used for more than half a century, as a railroad terminal. In addition, the development rights were made transferrable to numerous sites in the vicinity of the terminal, several owned by Penn Central, and at least one or two suitable for construction of office buildings. Since this regulation and substitution was reasonable, no due process violation resulted. *Id.* at 1278.

For contrasting commentary on these cases, compare Breitel, *A Judicial View of Transferrable Development Rights,* 33 Land Use L. and Zoning Dig., No. 2 at 5, 6 (1978) with Costonis, *The Disparity Issue: A Context for The Grand Central Terminal Decision,* 91 Harv. L. Rev. 402 (1977).

(3) Do TDRs satisfy the constitutional requirement of "just compensation"? Must a landowner, whose property decreases in value as a result of an environmental regulation, take steps to sell any TDR to which he or she is entitled before challenging the constitutionality of the regulation? Without

squarely reaching the first question, the U.S. Supreme Court decided the second issue in the negative in *Suitum v. Tahoe Regional Planning Agency,* 117 S. Ct. 1659 (1997). In *Suitum,* the plaintiff, who owned a parcel that had been placed in a "Stream Environmental Zone," had been given TDRs by the defendant agency. Reversing a contrary decision of the Ninth Circuit, the U.S. Supreme Court held that the agency's decision as to the classification of Suitum's land had been sufficiently "final" that her suit for damages for a regulatory taking could not be dismissed on ripeness grounds.

WEST MONTGOMERY COUNTY CITIZENS ASSOCIATION v. MARYLAND NATIONAL CAPITAL PARK & PLANNING COMMISSION

Court of Appeals of Maryland (1987)
309 Md. 183, 522 A.2d 1328

MCAULIFFE, J.

. . . .

A county enjoys no inherent power to zone or rezone, and may exercise zoning power only to the extent and in the manner directed by the State Legislature. The Regional District Act, Md. Code (1957, 1982 Repl. Vol.) Art. 28 § 8-101(b) grants zoning power to the Montgomery County Council sitting as a District Council. By that section, the Legislature specifically defines zoning power to include the right to regulate "the density and distribution of population" and authorizes the District Council to exercise that power by "amend[ing] the text of the zoning ordinance and . . . by . . . amend[ing] the map or maps accompanying the zoning ordinance text . . . ." By using the process of amending a Master Plan to effect a significant increase in the permissible density of development of residential zones, the District Council has run afoul of the state mandate that zoning changes be made by zoning procedures. Moreover, the alternative argument, that the density decisions were not made by the District Council but were made by the planning Board pursuant to a valid delegation of legislative power, is unavailing because of the breadth of the power involved and the failure of the District Council to establish sufficiently precise standards.

In October, 1980, the Functional Master Plan for the Preservation of Agriculture and Rural Open Space in Montgomery County ("Agricultural Preservation Plan") was approved and adopted. This plan recommended broad and innovative changes in the zoning text of Montgomery County, to be followed by dramatic zoning map changes that would directly affect one-fourth of the land in the County. The principal purpose of the plan was to preserve open space and agricultural land in the upper part of the County by restricting development of the land. An important adjunct of the plan was the recommendation that Montgomery County adopt and implement a system of transferable development rights ("TDRs"), to provide a form of compensation to owners whose rights to develop their properties would be significantly impaired by down-zoning, and to help ensure long term preservation of the agricultural use of the land.

The concept of TDRs is simple and straightforward. Ownership of land carries with it a bundle of rights, including the right to construct improvements on the land. These rights are subject to governmental regulation where reasonably required to accommodate public health, safety, or general welfare, and ordinarily these limitations of use may be imposed without the necessity of paying compensation to the land owner. There may arise situations, however, where the limitation of use imposed for the public good inflicts an economic impact on the landowner that, while not confiscatory, is so substantial as to prompt the government to provide some type of compensation. Cases involving the preservation of scenic easements and historic or architecturally valuable landmarks, preserving as they do benefits to the public that are largely cultural or aesthetic, yet concentrating the burden upon relatively few, have moved government officials to find ways to compensate the affected property owners. Maryland, recognizing the importance of agricultural land, and the efficacy of restricting the right to develop land as a means of accomplishing that objective, has developed a system for purchasing agricultural land preservation easements. *See* Md. Code (1974, 1985 Repl. Vol.) Agriculture Article, §§ 2-501 through 2-515. Purchasing development rights with public funds is not the exclusive method of providing compensation, however. Other jurisdictions have accomplished the desired objective by permitting the transfer of development rights from the burdened property to certain other properties in the political subdivision, and have given the value to this right by permitting a greater than normal intensity of development of the transferee or "receiving" property.

Montgomery County chose the latter course—the creation of a system of transferable development rights. In accordance with the recommendation of the Agricultural Preservation Plan, the District Council amended various provisions of the zoning text to provide for a new Rural Density Transfer zone ("RDT zone") having a base density of one single family dwelling unit for each 25 acres, and to create TDRs in favor of the owners of property placed in that classification. Montgomery County Code, 1984, §§ 59-C-11.2 thru 59-C-11.5. The owners of property down-zoned to the RDT zone are granted one TDR for each five acres, less one TDR for each existing dwelling unit. Other amendments to the zoning text provide that if the owners execute a covenant not to develop their land at its base density, the TDRs can be transferred to any property within a properly designed receiving zone, and under certain circumstances can be used to increase by one dwelling unit per TDR the density of development of the receiving property. The text provides that any property in six designated single family residential zones is eligible for designation as receiving areas for TDRs. The actual designation of the properties that would constitute the "receiving zone," i.e., those designated as available for more intense development through the use of TDRs, is to be made through the planning, rather than the zoning process. Section 59-C-1.39 provides:

> Any property in the RE-2C, RE-2, R-200, R-150, R-90 and R-60 zones that is located in a receiving area designated in an approved and adopted

> general, master, sector or functional plan may be developed at an increased density by the transfer of development rights in accordance with sections 59-A-6.1, and 59-C-11. . . .

Section 59-C-11.4 provides:

> In accordance with § 59-A-6.1 and in conformance with an approved and adopted general, master, sector or functional plan, residential density may be transferred at the rate of one development right per five (5) acres less one development right for each existing dwelling unit, from the rural density transfer zone to a duly designated receiving zone, pursuant to § 59-C-1.39.

The zoning text imposes no limitation on the ultimate density of development possible for a property placed in the receiving zone, but leaves this decision to the planning process as well. Thus, by General, Master, Sector or Functional Plan, the determination is to be made as to which single family residential properties will be placed in the receiving zone, and what limit of intensification of density will be assigned to each property so designated.

Finally, the zoning text provides that an owner of a designated receiving area property who wishes to intensify development through the use of TDRs must submit a preliminary subdivision plan and site plan detailing the proposed development of the property. These individual plans must conform to the development standards of the zone permitting a density nearest to the TDR density designated by the Master Plan Amendment. Upon approval of the site plan and preliminary plan of subdivision, an easement is recorded in favor of the County, restricting development of the property or properties from which the TDRs were obtained.

In addition to making the zoning text changes recommended by the Agricultural Preservation Plan, the District Council adopted a sectional map amendment, down-zoning 88,000 acres of land to the RDT zone, and thereby creating nearly 17,000 TDRs. It is the attempt by Appellees to utilize some of these TDRs to achieve density development of their property that has generated this controversy.

The principal questions presented by this appeal involve the validity of the process legislated by District Council for the classification of properties within the TDR receiving zone and the determination of the density limitation that shall apply to each property within the zone. . . .

We shall first address the question of whether the District Council validly exercised its zoning authority when it approved for adoption amendments to a master plan. At the outset, we state a basic proposition that is not contested by any of the parties—that the regulation of the density and the distribution of population is part of the zoning power and ordinarily is to be exercised by the District Council.

Next, we point out the very substantial distinction between the planning and zoning functions.

> "Master Plan" is not to be confused as a substitute for a comprehensive zoning or rezoning map, nor may it be equated with it in legal significance. . . . The zoning as recommended or proposed in the Master Plan

> may well become incorporated in a comprehensive zoning map for this area, but this will not be so until it is officially adopted and designated as such by the District Council. *Chapman v. Montgomery County,* 259 Md. 641, 643, 271 A.2d 156 (1970).

. . . .

A third major premise is that the County enjoys no inherent power to zone or rezone, and may exercise that power only to the extent and in the manner directed by the Legislature. That power has been granted to the County Council of Montgomery County, sitting as a District Council, and not to the Planning Commission or Planning Board. Art. 28, § 8-101. Thus, say Appellants, the classification and density decisions with respect to receiving area properties cannot be made by the adoption of a Master Plan because that plan is adopted by the Planning Commission and not the District Council. Appellees counter by arguing that enabling and implementing legislation places ultimate control of the Master Plan in the hands of the District Council, and thus the District Council's approval of a Master Plan constitutes the legislative decision required for the exercise of zoning power. Appellants dispute this, contending the District Council is without the necessary authority to initiate or complete the planning process, and that in any event the planning process fails to afford due process to those who might be aggrieved by the decision. Furthermore, they contend the enabling legislation that grants zoning power to the County specifically limits the manner of exercise of that power to the adoption and amendment of the zoning text and the accompanying zoning map.

We conclude, however, that this chartered county is precluded, by the express and unequivocal language of the statute that granted it zoning power, from exercising that power in any manner other than that specifically authorized—namely, by the zoning map and zoning text amendment procedures. At. 28, § 8-101(b) provides in pertinent part that:

> Each district council, respectively, in accordance with the conditions and procedures specified in this article, may by ordinance adopt and amend the text of the zoning ordinance and may by resolution or ordinance adopt and amend the map or maps accompanying the zoning ordinance text to regulate, in the portion of the regional district lying within its county . . .; (iv) the density and distribution of population; . . . .

The authority "to regulate . . . the density and distribution of population" is expressly to be accomplished by adoption and amendment of "the text of the zoning ordinance" and adoption and amendment of "the map or maps accompanying the zoning ordinance text." Thus, where the District Council purports to act in the exercise of its zoning authority, it must do so by adopting or changing the zoning text or zoning map.

As with all legislative grants, the zoning authority is circumscribed by any limitations established by the General Assembly in the enactment . . . . *Harbor Island Marina v. Calvert Co.,* 286 Md. 303, 309, 409 A.2d 738 (1979).

Because approval of amendments of the Master Plan does not come within the mandated procedures for legislative zoning action, this process cannot constitute a valid exercise of zoning authority. Accordingly, unless the procedure employed in this case can qualify as a valid delegation of zoning authority to the Planning Board, it cannot be sustained.

This Court has not been hesitant to approve a delegation of legislative power where that delegation is for the purpose of implementing a prior, specific legislative determination, and is accompanied by standards sufficient to limit and direct the exercise or discretion on the part of the agency or official to whom the power is delegated. We have applied these criteria to sustain carefully limited and directed delegations of zoning authority in a variety of cases.

Applying the established criteria to the facts of this case, we find the delegation of authority impermissible. No legislative determination was made to limit or define the optional densities that could or should be assigned to any property in the vast area involved. Nor did the Legislature establish precise standards by which the Planning Board might determine which properties should be placed in the TDR receiving zone, or what TDR density should be assigned to each. By contrast, the Planning Board in this case was given unlimited authority to select form a vast pool of residentially zoned property spread over the entire lower portion of the County, and to assign increased density potential to those properties without limitation.

In this case we note the absence of any effective zoning action by the District Council to generally classify properties within the TDR receiving zone. Virtually all of the single family residential properties in three-fourths of the County were declared eligible for that classification, but the ultimate decision of classification was left to the Planning Board. Additionally, there was no valid legislative action to assign different density classifications to properties within the receiving area, nor was there any ceiling on density established so as to leave the Planning Board with but limited authority to fix reduced densities.

The major deficiency in this entire process is the absence of the final step in the planning and zoning process—the amendment of the zoning map, and where necessary the zoning text, to implement the changes recommended by the Master Plan. Certainly comprehensive planning should form an integral part of the process of identifying TDR receiving areas and assigning density classifications. Once the planning has been accomplished and the recommendations made, however, it becomes the duty of the legislative authority to make any necessary changes in the zoning law. Ordinarily, these changes are accomplished through a sectional map amendment, which once proposed enjoys a strong presumption of validity and correctness, and requires no showing of change or mistake.

These deficiencies, although perhaps easily remedied by appropriate changes in the zoning text, are fatal to the designation and classification of TDR receiving areas in this case.

NOTES

(1) The analysis employed in the principal cases contrasts with that of the Ninth Circuit in *Barancik v. County of Marin,* 872 F.2d 834 (9th Cir. 1988). There the court rejected the plaintiff's claim that a countywide TDR plan

intended to preserve agricultural lands constituted a sale of "zoning dispensations." The court noted that the TDR scheme did not increase the total amount of development allowed in the county and that the county government had not attempted to control who carries out the development.

(2) Another celebrated TDR system for preserving natural resources was established by the New Jersey legislature in 1979 in the Pinelands Protection Act, N.J. Stat. Ann. §§ 13:18A-1 to 13:18 A-49. Under this statute, a Pineland Commissions was established and charged with responsibility for preparing a comprehensive management plan for the environmentally sensitive pinelands area, a unique coastal plain pine forest. Development within the pinelands area is severely restricted under this plan. However, landowners are entitled to transferrable pinelands development credits, which may be sold to those who wish to develop a particular area, so long as those purchasing credits agree to abide by covenants that restrict the use of their land consistent with the comprehensive plan. This arrangement, together with a related county development bank program, was upheld by the New Jersey courts. *See Matlack v. Board of Chosen Freeholders of County of Burlington,* 191 N.J. Super. 236, 466 A.2d 83 (1982), *aff'd,* 194 N.J. Super. 359, 476 A.2d 1262 (1984). *See also Gardner v. New Jersey Pinelands Comm'n,* 593 A.2d 251 (N.J. 1991).

(3) Owners of environmentally sensitive lands are also entitled to charitable deductions where they donate conservation easements to government agencies or qualified non-profit conservation organizations. *See* Internal Revenue Code § 170(h)(3) and (4).

Chapter 8

ENVIRONMENTAL LITIGATION AND ENFORCEMENT

§ 8.01 Introduction: Nature, Form and Categories of Environmental Litigation

Environmental litigation is generally regarded as a form of public interest litigation, and the plaintiffs in environmental cases are often such public interest groups as the Sierra Club Legal Defense Fund, the Environmental Defense Fund, the Natural Resources Defense Council and other national or local groups, sometimes specially formed to protect a particular environmental interest. Environmental defense efforts are a part of the large and diverse body of public interest law, and the development of the field of environmental law has in turn contributed to public interest law generally—as in the development of citizen suits, new standing rules, and other developments in administrative law.

On public interest law generally, see "Balancing the Scales of Justice, Financing Public Interest Law in America," A Report by the Council for Public Interest Law (1976). *See also*, Cappelletti, *Governmental and Private Advocates for the Public Interest in Civil Litigation: A Comparative Study,* 73 Mich. L. Rev. 793 (1975).

Environmental litigation involves knowledge and experience shared with other fields of litigation. It is specialized only in the sense that certain issues, questions and problems, both substantive and procedural, recur because of the nature of environmental law and the interests it seeks to protect. Needless to say, some of these are also of great significance in other kinds of litigation, but an effort has been made to draw examples from environmental cases and to analyze their importance to the environmental litigator. As used here, environmental litigation includes contested proceedings both in the courts and in administrative agencies.

Environmental litigation reflects great variety, as does the substantive law to protect environmental interests. While there are likely to be many situations which do not fit neatly into the following categories, it is still possible to categorize the recurring purposes and aims of environmental litigation. Normally, these actions pit environmental interests against developmental or industrial interests that create a risk of pollution. The character of environmental litigation is largely defined by recurring environmental problems and by the nature of the legislation enacted to deal with them.

[1] Litigation to Halt or to Modify Environmentally Damaging Development

When a government agency or a private developer undertakes a construction project or some other effort which will destroy or change environmental, scenic or other natural resources, litigation is used to halt or modify the project, on the grounds that it does not comply with the law under which it is being developed, or that it violates some requirement of law established to protect the environment—including the requirement under NEPA (Chapter 5, *supra*) that the agency must first prepare an environmental impact statement whenever the project constitutes major federal action with significant impact on the human environment.

The paradigmatic case for this kind of environmental litigation is, of course, the earliest major environmental litigation in *Scenic Hudson Preservation Conference v. Federal Power Commission,* p. 1167, *infra,* which raised environmental concerns based on the alleged violation of the requirements of the Federal Power Act in the proposed development of a pumped storage hydroelectric plant. Other instances, too, involve some of the leading cases here included, *i.e., Sierra Club v. Morton,* p. 1195, *infra,* involving the construction of a major recreational facility on public lands; *Citizens to Preserve Overton Park v. Volpe,* p. 1179, *infra,* to stop the construction of a highway on parkland, contrary to the Federal Aid Highway Act; and *Environmental Defense Fund v. Corps of Engineers,* (Gillham Dam), p. 855, *supra,* to halt the construction of a major dam before compliance with the NEPA requirement of the preparation of a full environmental impact statement. The substantive basis for the litigation is usually the federal statute under which the agency itself is proceeding with the development, or the federal statute under which the agency grants a permit to a private developer to proceed, as indeed in the *Scenic Hudson* case, and in the many cases involving permits from the Nuclear Regulatory Commission for the construction or operation of nuclear power plants.

One recurring aspect of this kind of litigation is that the development will proceed unless it is halted, and unless it is halted promptly, the very environmental resources sought to be protected may be destroyed or irredeemably damaged before the legal issues can be resolved. Immediate action to halt the development must be taken, because once the bulldozers move in there will be nothing more to protect or to litigate. The use of provisional remedies, and especially of *preliminary injunctions* is a recurring feature of this kind in environmental litigation. While regarded as the first step in a sequence of provisional remedies, in environmental litigation it may well be the entire case—it tests the soundness of the plaintiff's case, and if the motion for a preliminary injunction is lost, the development will probably proceed immediately, and the case will be over.

Preliminary injunctions are not granted lightly; plaintiffs must meet the burden of proof on four significant issues, as set forth in Rule 65 of the Federal Rules of Civil Procedure. The criteria for granting a preliminary injunction are as follows: (1) whether the plaintiffs will have an adequate remedy at law or will be irreparably harmed if an injunction is not issued; (2) whether the threatened injury to the plaintiff outweighs the harm the injunction may inflict on the defendant; (3) whether the plaintiff has at least a reasonable likelihood of success on the merits; and (4) whether granting the preliminary injunction will disserve the public interest.

In sum, Rule 65 requires first, a judgment that plaintiff may win on the merits, because otherwise there would be no point in stopping the defendant from proceeding with the planned development. Then, having decided that question affirmatively, the interests of the plaintiff, the defendant, and of the public must be weighed to determine whether to halt the project or to allow it to proceed. *See, e.g., Sierra Club v. Hickel,* 433 F.2d 24 (9th Cir. 1970), *aff'd,* 405 U.S. 727 (1970); *Consumers Power Co. v. Federal Energy Administration,* 413 F. Supp. (D. Mich. 1976).

Preliminary injunctions are often sought and granted to enforce compliance with the environmental impact statement requirement of NEPA. *See, e.g., Scherr v. Volpe,* 336 F. Supp. 882 (D. Wis. 1971), *aff'd,* 466 F.2d 1027 (7th Cir. 1972); compare *Conservation Law Foundation v. Andrus,* 617 F.2d 296 (1st Cir. 1979) (injunction against oil and gas lease sale denied; no irreparable harm since Secretary may protect environmental concerns even after sale). It seems that the showing of significant irreparable harm is very persuasive in the issuance of an injunction. *See, e.g., Environmental Defense Fund v. Corps of Engineers,* 331 F. Supp. 925 (D.D.C. 1971) (threatened destruction of wildlife—construction of Tombigbee River project); *United States v. Ray,* 281 F. Supp. 876 (S.D. Fla. 1965) (threatened destruction of coral reef). The issuance of a preliminary injunction leaves the situation unchanged until the legal issues can be adequately dealt with. It prevents the premature commitment of resources, and it also allows time for the development of less environmentally harmful alternative plans.

[2] Litigation Relating to the Adoption of Pollution Control Standards; Citizen Suits

An important source of litigation is the enforcement of pollution control standards, such as effluent limitations under the CWA, emission standards under the CAA, and so on. Enforcement litigation by EPA has been adverted to previously in connection with the discussion of air and water pollution control. Another aspect of enforcement litigation earlier referred to includes citizen suits for enforcement purposes. The parallel citizen suit provisions in the clean water, clear air and other pollution control laws allow the citizen to sue a polluter directly, after notice to EPA and to the appropriate state agency, and provide for the continuation of the enforcement action by EPA at its discretion, with the provision that the citizen may intervene in EPA's enforcement action, and EPA may in turn intervene in the citizen action as a matter of right. *See, e.g.,* CAA § 304, 42 U.S.C. § 7604; CWA § 505, 33 U.S.C. § 1365; RCRA § 7002, 42 U.S.C. § 6972. *See also*, Grad, Treatise on Environmental Law, §§ 2.03[19][c], 3.03[10][b].

As had long been the case with the remedy in mandamus, the precise limits on what are non-discretionary duties are hard to draw. In the landmark case of *Sierra Club v. Ruckelshaus,* p. 147, *supra,* the citizen suit was used to establish the legal requirement that the Administrator see to it that state implementation plans not set standards allowing the degradation of air quality. The decision was not only the beginning of regulations to prevent the significant deterioration of air quality; it was also a significant departure in the use of the mandamus-like citizen suit provision in that it found a non-discretionary obligation by necessary implication—at the time the non-degradation requirement was not an *express* requirement of the Clean Air Act.

A somewhat similar application of the citizen suit approach was involved in *Natural Resources Defense Council, Inc. v. Train,* p. 432, *supra,* in which NRDC challenged the very limited list of toxic effluents promulgated by the Administrator under the Federal Water Pollution Control Act, asserting that he was under a non-discretionary duty to promulgate a more substantial list in preparation of greater efforts in the control of toxic pollutants. The case had been brought under other provisions of the law in addition to the citizen suit provisions. While rejecting CWA § 509as a basis for jurisdiction, the court pursued the question raised by NRDC as a matter for review under the "arbitrary and capricious" standard of the Administrative Procedures Act § 10, 5 U.S.C. §§ 701–706, and found that the Administrator had not provided an adequate record to support his limited list. The decision was only the beginning of a lengthy litigation (*see* Chapter 2 at p. 438) to compel a full regulatory effort to control toxic effluents. But the suit had started as an effort to compel the Administrator to carry out his "nondiscretionary duties!" *See also Environmental Defense Fund, Inc. v. HEW,* 428 F.2d 1083 (D.C. Cir. 1970), noted in Brill, *The Citizen's Relief Against Inactive Federal Officials: Case Studies in Mandamus Actions*, 16 Akron L. Rev. 339, 384 (1983).

Thus a citizen suit is a litigation tool, first available in the 1970 Clean Air Act, to compel the administrator to bring enforcement actions, and to bring about his compliance with non-discretionary obligations. Note that the citizen suit provisions provide a method to compel the Administrator to get on with the job of standard setting and promulgation under the respective acts. The citizen suit does not provide a way of reviewing the standards already set. The challenge of standards already set is only cognizable in the course of a statutory review under the Clean Air Act § 307, Clean Water Act § 509, Resources Conservation and Recovery Act § 7006, and other pollution control statutes. *See* p. 1163, *infra*.

Once a regulation or standard has been adopted, there may be litigation to prevent it from becoming effective. This provides for another application of the preliminary injunctions under Rule 65 of the Federal Rules. A noteworthy use of the preliminary injunction in that situation was *Manufacturing Chemists Association v. Costle,* 455 F. Supp. 968 (W.D. La. 1978), reproduced in Chapter 3, at p. 573, *supra*. The case involved a successful effort to prevent the hazardous substance regulation under CWA § 311from coming into effect. The court analyzed the situation in accordance with Rule 65 criteria, concluding that the plaintiff would probably succeed on the merits because, in the court's view, the regulations were a violation of the statutory authorization, that the plaintiff chemical companies stood to lose more by a delay in the determinations than the public interest intervenors, and that there would be no significant injury to the public interest in delaying the effective date of the regulations. The review of the Regulations under the Administrative Procedures Act and the use of a preliminary injunction in this case was appropriate because standards set under § 311 of CWAare not reviewable under§ 509 of the Act which provides for statutory pre-enforcement review in the Court of Appeals of most other water standards set by the Administrator. The decision of the Court was short-lived because Congress, in a prompt corrective amendment of the law, reinstated, in effect, the Administrator's standards (*See* Chapter 3 at p. 580, *supra*).

The use of a preliminary injunction to prevent a standard or rule from becoming effective is limited, because most environmental standards promulgated under the Clear Air and Clean Water Acts, and other pollution control legislation, are subject to pre-enforcement review in the Court of Appeals, and a stay of the regulation pending judicial action will generally be granted. The availability of the preliminary injunction as a provisional remedy in nonstatutory review of standards under the Administrative Procedure Act should, however, be noted.

Notice that the citizen suit provisions may only be used by a private citizen to vindicate public rights. They may not be used to assert a private citizen's claim for damages, and a private citizen who sues to vindicate a public right may not combine this claim with a claim for damages. *See* Feller, *Private Enforcement of Federal Anti-Pollution Laws Through Citizen Suits: A Model,* 60 Denver L. J. 553 (1983).

[3] Judicial Review of Agency Action, Including Review of Agency Rulemaking in Setting Environmental Standards

Environmental litigation often takes the form of a lawsuit for the review of agency action. It is not necessary for purposes of this discussion to inquire whether there is any due process requirement of an opportunity for judicial review, but there have been numerous environmental cases that have referred to the usual presumption of reviewability. Unless there is an express statutory provision that makes certain agency actions unreviewable, reviewability is presumed. *See, e.g., Barlowe v. Collins,* 397 U.S. 159 (1970); *Natural Resources Defense Council, Inc. v. Train,* 519 F.2d 287 (D.C. Cir. 1975) Chapter 3, p. 432, *supra*. Even in instances where certain action is relegated to agency discretion as a matter of law, a court may normally review for abuse of discretion. *See, e.g., Citizens to Preserve Overton Park v. Volpe*, at p. 1179, *infra*; *Environmental Defense Fund v. Ruckelshaus,* 439 F.2d 584 (D.C. Cir. 1971).

Judicial review is said to be of two kinds, statutory and nonstatutory. In statutory review, the statute which authorizes the agency action also provides and sets the requirements for its judicial review. Typical examples of statutory review are found in the judicial review provisions of the Clean Air Act § 307(b)–(g); 42 U.S.C. § 7607(b); Clean Water Act § 509(b), 33 U.S.C. § 1319(b); Resource Conservation and Recovery Act § 7006, 42 U.S.C. § 9670. Nonstatutory review—which is an established misnomer—is review under another statute, namely the Administrative Procedure Act. It is "nonstatutory" in the sense that it is not provided for in the statute from which the agency derives its power to take the action which is being reviewed. A distinguishing factor is that nonstatutory review under APA is commenced by a plenary action in the district court.

As noted, most of the pollution control statutes provide for the review of certain agency action, notably action to promulgate effluent, emission and other standards. The nature of this statutory review has been referred to in the appropriate chapters *supra*. The usual pattern is to allow for direct judicial review of the standards by the Court of Appeals within a certain time period, and to prohibit the raising of any issues relating to the standards in an enforcement proceeding, if those issues could have been raised during judicial review and prior to enforcement. Judicial review of standards therefore take on special importance to environmental interests as well as to the industries which are subject to the new standards, and it is the rule rather than the exception that these interests take opposing sides in such a judicial review. *See e.g., Portland Cement Association v. Ruckelshaus,* Chapter 5 at p. 809, *supra,* (new source performance standards for the cement industry) where industry asserted that the standards were too stringent, and several environmental groups argued that they were not stringent enough. *See also Lead Industries Association, Inc. v. Environmental Protection Agency,* 647 F.2d 1130 (D.C. Cir.), Chapter 2 at p. 88 (national ambient air quality standards for lead); *Ethyl Corp. v. EPA,* 541 F.2d 1 (D.C. Cir. 1976) (regulation of lead content of gasoline; with industry in opposition and environmentalists for affirmation of the standards).

Nonstatutory review under the APA is usually addressed to the district court having venue and applies usually to public land use determinations. Even the most recent and most far-reaching of the public land laws, the Federal Land Planning and Management Act (FLPMA), does not provide for statutory review, though it states as a general policy that judicial review should be available. Thus, decisions relating to mining, timber and grazing on the public lands are first addressed in the district court, as are matters relating to oil and gas leases on the Outer Continental Shelf. In addition, nonstatutory review is also applicable to certain determinations under the pollution control laws for which no express statutory review provisions apply—as, for instance, the review of oil standards relating to dredge and fill operations under CWA § 404. Most notably, however, the review of compliance with NEPA is subject to APA review in the district court because NEPA does not expressly provide for judicial review of the agency obligation to prepare an environmental impact statement (EIS).

The subject of judicial review is complex, particularly when the courts must review determinations or standards that involve sophisticated questions of science and technology. It is this recurring problem, brought about also by statutes which necessarily grant to an Administrator rather broad authority to make regulatory judgments within a defined range of policies, that creates some special questions in the environmental field. Authorizations to fix effluent limitations at a level of "best practicable technology" or "best available technology," or to set standards so as "to provide an ample margin of safety" impose rather special burdens. Often in the construction of such statutes, the Administrator is called upon to make "essentially legislative policy judgments," as noted by Judge Wright and concurred with by Judge Bazelton in *Ethyl Corp. v. EPA,* 541 F.2d 1 (D.C. Cir. 1976). The characterization of issues in cases of review of technical standards generally defies the usual distinction between questions of law and fact. They are treated, generally without express reference to that distinction, as mixed questions, and therefore fully reviewable by the courts. *See* Sive, *Some Thoughts of an Environmental Lawyer in the Wilderness of Administrative Law . . . ,* 70 Colum. L. Rev. 612 (1970).

As noted in earlier chapters on air, water and waste pollution, the most frequent approach in judicial review of environmental determinations relating to standards and rules, *i.e.,* in notice and comment rulemaking, has been a review based on the "arbitrary and capricious . . . or otherwise not in accordance with the law" standard of the APA (as reflected in CAA § 307), with the gloss put on it by *Overton Park,* which requires evidence of consideration of all relevant facts and factors, and freedom from clear errors of judgment. Thus, as a number commentators have noted, this type of review falls short of that applied in formal rulemaking, where the courts examine whether the agency decision is supported by substantial evidence based on the record as a whole. Yet it goes beyond the older approach of a review which left most of the technical decisions entirely to the agency, as being singularly qualified to make them. This approach—with some judicial diversity to be noted—insists that the agency show how it arrived at its determination, and that there be a sufficient record for the court to review the consideration of relevant facts and factors. *See, e.g., Scenic Hudson Preservation Conference, infra; Portland Cement Association v. Ruckelshaus,* Chapter 5, p. 809, *supra*; *Lead Industries Association, Inc. v. EPA,* Chapter 2, at p. 88, *supra*; *Ethyl Corp. v. EPA. See also* Estreicher, *Pragmatic Justice: The Contributions of Judge Harold Leventhal to Administrative Law,* 80 Colum. L. Rev. 894 (1980).

The decisions in this area often demonstrate sound judicial concern over the proper judicial role. *See e.g.,* the various opinions following the *en banc* hearing in *Ethyl Corp. v. EPA,* in which Judges Leventhal and Bazelon reassert the differences in approach. Bazelon emphasizes the court's obligation to insist on strict and exacting procedures, even going beyond the requirements of APA (Judge Bazelon was reversed on that particular issue in *Vermont Yankee Nuclear Power Corp. v. NRDC, Inc.,* 435 U.S. 519 (1978)). Judge Leventhal, while respectful of the agency's expertise and regarding the court-agency relation as a "partnership," nonetheless believed that courts must steep themselves in technical and scientific knowledge, not in order to displace the agency's judgment in technical issues, but because, in his view, a court must be very knowledgeable to see whether all relevant facts and factors have been considered, and whether the agency's determination is free from clear errors of judgment. In his view, the court must itself know a great deal in order to review the agency determination. The split in the Leventhal-Bazelon approaches seems to be primarily one of emphasis, because during Judge Leventhal's lifetime he and Bazelon could usually be found on the same side of the decision, though differing on how best to get there.

Another recurring theory in judicial review of administrative action of all kinds has been the "hard look" requirement, which (together with the umpire calling balls and strikes, the crystal ball, and the court-administrative agency partnership) has entered the field of influential metaphors in environmental law. Initially it seems that the courts required the agency to take a hard look at the data and at the alternatives. Now it is not only the agencies that must give close scrutiny or take a hard look, but the court itself. The "hard look" approach expresses an attitude rather than a formal legal rule. It seems to mean that agencies and courts ought to do their job carefully. *See* Leventhal, *Environmental Decisionmaking in the Courts,* 122 Pa. L. Rev. 509 (1974); Rodgers, *A Hard Look at* Vermont Yankee: *Environmental Law Under Close Scrutiny,* 67 Geo. L. J. 699 (1979); Marcel, *The Role of Courts in a Legislative and Legal System: The Use of Hard Look Review in Environmental Litigation,* 62 Or. L. Rev. 403 (1983).

[4] The National Environmental Policy Act (NEPA) of 1969 as a Basis for Environmental Litigation

NEPA and its legal requirements and consequences form the subject of Chapter 5. In considering the subject of environmental litigation, the overwhelming impact of the Act on the nature of environmental litigation since its effective date in 1970 must be noted. NEPA imposes an additional general obligation on all federal agencies to consider environmental consequences, broadly defined, in carrying out their other delegated functions and obligations. It also imposes a specific obligation on agencies to prepare an environmental impact statement and to give it wide circulation for comment. Such an environmental impact statement must be prepared for all "major federal action significantly affecting the quality of the human environment . . . ."

Though generally referred to as a procedural statute, NEPA prescribes no specific procedures for its enforcement. As a result, a great deal of litigation has occurred to answer questions concerning whether particular actions were federal, major, had a significant impact, etc. (*i.e.* whether they were covered by the Act) and called for the preparation of an EIS. These questions, and the question of the adequacy of environmental consideration in the statement, as current a question now as it was in 1970, is considered in Chapter 5. Another issue, repeatedly litigated and disposed of in the case of *Strycker's Bay,* was whether courts could review the substantive agency decision to go ahead with a project on the basis of the EIS: could a court stop an agency from going ahead because in the court's view the environmental cost, shown by the EIS, was too high?

In addition to litigation growing directly out of the interpretation of NEPA, the Act's broader impact needs to be considered. Since federal permits and licenses are needed for most major private projects with environmental consequences—such as to build a power plant, drill for oil or to build or utilize resources on public land—NEPA's impact goes well beyond the usual "federal" projects. In the field of power plant construction, whether hydroelectric, nuclear or fossil fuel, ever since *Calvert Cliffs',* the issues have been as much NEPA issues as issues under the relevant federal statutes passed to advance power resource development. So, too, in the management and use of public lands, NEPA has created a new legal landscape. There were few opportunities for public interest litigators and environmentalists to involve themselves in land use issues and in questions relating to the use of resources—whether mineral, timber, range or recreational—on public lands until the advent of NEPA. An examination of the subject matter of NEPA decisions, compared to the earlier paucity of decisions relating to the public lands, shows that after NEPA the public lands could no longer be dealt with as the private domain of the Agriculture and Interior Departments.

§ 8.02 Judicial Review of Agency Action

SCENIC HUDSON PRESERVATION CONFERENCE v. FEDERAL POWER COMMISSION

United States Court of Appeals, Second Circuit (1965)
354 F.2d 608, cert. denied, 384 U.S. 941 (1966)

HAYS, Circuit Judge:

In this proceeding the petitioners are the Scenic Hudson Preservation Conference, an unincorporated association consisting of a number of non-profit, conservationist organizations, and the Towns of Cortland, Putnam Valley and Yorktown. Petitioners ask us, pursuant to § 313(b) of the Federal Power Act, 16 U.S.C. § 825(b), to set aside three orders of the respondent, the Federal Power Commission:[1]

a. An order of March 9, 1965 granting a license to the intervener, the Consolidated Edison Company of New York, Inc., to construct a pumped storage hydroelectric project on the west side of the Hudson River at Storm King Mountain in Cornwall, New York;

b. An order of May 6, 1965 denying petitioners' application for a rehearing of the March 9 order, and for the reopening of the proceeding to permit the introduction of additional evidence;

c. An order of May 6, 1965 denying joint motions filed by the petitioners to expand the scope of supplemental hearings to include consideration of the practicality and cost of underground transmission lines, and of the feasibility of *any* type of fish protection device.

A pumped storage plant generates electric energy for use during peak load periods,[2] using hydroelectric units driven by water from a head-water pool or reservoir. The contemplated Storm King project would be the largest of its kind in the world. Consolidated Edison has estimated its cost, including transmission facilities, at $162,000,000. The project would consist of three major components, a storage reservoir, a powerhouse, and transmission lines. The storage reservoir,[3] located over a thousand feet above the powerhouse,

[1] At oral argument petitioners made a motion to enlarge the record by including in it the supplemental hearings conducted before a Trial Examiner of the Federal Power Commission in May 1965. These hearings were limited to consideration of the routes of overhead transmission facilities and the design of fish protection devices. Petitioners allege that the May hearings divulge information which should have been developed and considered by the Commission at the time the license was granted. We are not being asked to review the October 4, 1965 order, setting forth the Commission's determination of the questions presented at the May hearings, but rather to consider evidence compiled at the May hearings as a convenient source of information from which inferences can be drawn about the completeness of the March 9 record. For this limited purpose we have granted petitioners' motion.

[2] Capacity for peak load periods is that part of a system's generating equipment which is operated intermittently for short periods during the hours of highest daily, weekly, or seasonal kilowatt demand.

[3] The project's reservoir would contain a surface area of 240 acres and a usable capacity of 25,000 acre-feet. A part of the space which it would occupy is now occupied by a reservoir providing part of the water supply for the Village of Cornwall. Another area consisting of approximately 70 acres of property within the

is to be connected to the powerhouse, located on the river front, by a tunnel 40 feet in diameter. The powerhouse, which is both a pumping and generating station, would be 800 feet long and contain eight pump generators.[4]

Transmission lines would run under the Hudson to the east bank and then underground for 1.6 miles to a switching station which Consolidated Edison would build at Nelsonville in the Town of Philipstown. Thereafter, overhead transmission lines would be placed on towers 100 to 150 feet high and these would require a path up to 125 feet wide[5] through Westchester and Putnam Counties for a distance of some 25 miles until they reached Consolidated Edison's main connections with New York City.[6]

During slack periods Consolidated Edison's conventional steam plants in New York City would provide electric power for the pumps at Storm King to force water up the mountain, through the tunnel, and into the upper reservoir. In peak periods water would be released to rush down the mountain and power the generators. Three kilowatts of power generated in New York City would be necessary to obtain two kilowatts from the Cornwall installation. When pumping the powerhouse would draw approximately 1,080,000 cubic feet of water per minute from the Hudson, and when generating would discharge up to 1,620,000 cubic feet of water per minute into the river. The installation would have a capacity of 2,000,000 kilowatts, but would be so constructed as to be capable of enlargement to a total of 3,000,000 kilowatts. The water in the upper reservoir may be regarded as the equivalent of stored electric energy; in effect, Consolidated Edison wishes to create a huge storage battery at Cornwall. *See* Federal Power Commission, National Power Survey 120-21 (1964).

The Storm King project has aroused grave concern among conservationist groups, adversely affected municipalities and various state and federal legislative units and administrative agencies.

To be licensed by the Commission a prospective project must meet the statutory test of being "best adapted to a comprehensive plan for improving or developing a waterway," Federal Power Act § 10(a), 16 U.S.C. § 803(a). In framing the issue before it, the Federal Power Commission properly noted:

> "[W]e must compare the Cornwall project with any alternatives that are available. If on this record Con Edison has available an alternative source for meeting its power needs which is better adapted to the development of the Hudson River for all beneficial uses, including scenic beauty, this application should be denied."

If the Commission is properly to discharge its duty in this regard, the record on which it bases its determination must be complete. The petitioners and

Black Rock Forest, a private forest reserve of Harvard University, would also be inundated by the proposed reservoir. Consolidated Edison has offered appropriate compensation for the acreage which would be used.

[4] According to plans presented to the Federal Power Commission three pumping generator units would be installed and go into operation in mid-1967 and the remaining five in 1968.

[5] However, the path might be even wider at corners, transportation points, access points, or points of an unusual character.

[6] As has already been noted we are not now concerned with the order of October 4, 1965 in which the Commission established the exact route of the transmission lines and the width of the right-of-way.

the public at large have a right to demand this completeness. It is our view, and we find, that the Commission has failed to compile a record which is sufficient to support its decision. The Commission has ignored certain relevant factors and failed to make a thorough study of possible alternatives to the Storm King project. While the courts have no authority to concern themselves with the policies of the Commission, it is their duty to see that the Commission's decisions receive that careful consideration which the statute contemplates. . . . Petitioners' application, pursuant to § 313(b), 16 U.S.C. § 825*l* (b), to adduce additional evidence is granted. We set aside the three orders of the Commission to which the petition is addressed and remand the case for further proceedings in accordance with this opinion.

I

The Storm King project is to be located in an area of unique beauty and major historical significance. The highlands and gorge of the Hudson offer one of the finest pieces of river scenery in the world. The great German traveler Baedeker called it "finer than the Rhine." Petitioners' contention that the Commission must take these factors into consideration in evaluating the Storm King project is justified by the history of the Federal Power Act.

The Federal Water Project Act of 1920, 41 Stat. 1063 (1920) (now Federal Power Act, 16U.S.C. § 791a *et seq.*), was the outgrowth of a widely supported effort on the part of conservationists to secure the enactment of a complete scheme of national regulation which would promote the comprehensive development of the nation's water resources. . . . It "was passed for the purpose of developing and preserving to the people the water power resources of the country." *United States ex rel. Chapman v. Federal Power Comm.*, 191 F.2d 796, 800 (4th Cir. 1951), aff'd, 345 U.S. 153, 73 S.Ct. 609, 97 L.Ed. 918 (1953).

Congress gave the Federal Power Commission sweeping authority and a specific planning responsibility.

Section 10(a) of the Federal Power Act, 16 U.S.C. § 803(a)reads:

> "§ 803. Conditions of license generally.
>
> All licenses issued under sections 792, 793, 795-818, and 820-823 of this title shall be on the following conditions:
>
> . . . .
>
> (a) That the project adopted, . . . shall be such as in the judgment of the Commission *will be best adapted to a comprehensive plan for improving or developing a waterway or waterways for the use or benefit of interstate or foreign commerce, for the improvement and utilization of water-power development, and for other beneficial public uses, including recreational purposes;* and if necessary in order to secure such plan the Commission shall have authority to require the modification of any project and of the plans and specifications of the project works before approval." (Emphasis added.)

"Recreational purposes" are expressly included among the beneficial public uses to which the statute refers. The phrase undoubtedly encompasses the conservation of natural resources, the maintenance of natural beauty, and the preservation of historic sites. *See Namekagon Hydro Co. v. Federal Power Comm.,* 216 F.2d 509, 511-512 (7th Cir. 1954). All of these "beneficial uses," the Supreme Court has observed, "while unregulated, might well be contradictory rather than harmonious." *Federal Power Comm. v. Union Electric Co.,* 381 U.S. 90, 98, 85 S.Ct. 1253, 1258 (1965). In licensing a project, it is the duty of the Federal Power Commission properly to weigh each factor.

In recent years the Commission has placed increasing emphasis on the right of the public to "out-door recreational resources." 1964 F.P.C. Report 69. Regulations issued in 1963, for the first time, required the inclusion of a recreation plan as part of a license application. F.P.C. Order No. 260-A, amending § 4.41 of Regulations under Federal Power Act, issued April 18, 1963, 29 F.P.C. 777, 28 Fed. Reg. 4092. The Commission has recognized generally that members of the public have rights in our recreational, historic and scenic resources under the Federal Power Act. *Namekagon Hydro Co.*, 12 F.P.C. 203, 206 (1954) ("the Commission realizes that in many cases where unique and most special types of recreation are encountered a dollar evaluation is inadequate as the public interest must be considered and it cannot be evaluated adequately only in dollars and cents"). In affirming *Namekagon* the Seventh Circuit upheld the Commission's denial of a license, to an otherwise economically feasible project, because fishing, canoeing and the scenic attraction of a "beautiful stretch of water" were threatened. *Namekagon Hydro Co. v. Federal Power Comm.,* 216 F.2d 509, 511-512 (7th Cir. 1954).

Commissioner Ross said in his dissent in the present case: "[I]t appears obvious that had this area of the 'Hudson Highlands' been declared a State or National Park, that is, had the people in the area already spoken, we probably would have listened and might well have refused to license it."

II

Respondent argues that "petitioners do not have standing to obtain review" because they "make no claim of any personal economic injury resulting from the Commission's action."

Section 313(b) of the Federal Power Act, 16 U.S.C. § 825*l* (b) reads:

> "(b) Any party to a proceeding under this chapter aggrieved by an order issued by the Commission in such proceeding may obtain a review of such order in the United States Court of Appeals for any circuit wherein the licensee or public utility to which the order relates is located . . . ."

The Commission takes a narrow view of the meaning of "aggrieved party" under the Act. The Supreme Court has observed that the law of standing is a "complicated specialty of federal jurisdiction, the solution of whose problems is in any event more or less determined by the specific circumstances of individual sections . . . ." *United States ex rel. Chapman v. Federal Power Comm.,* 345 U.S. 153, 156, 73 S.Ct. 609, 612, 97 L.Ed. 918 (1953). Although a "case" or "controversy" which is otherwise lacking cannot be created by statute, a statute may create new interests or rights and thus give standing to one who would otherwise be barred by the lack of a "case" or "controversy." The "case" or "controversy" requirement of Article III, § 2 of the Constitution does not require that an "aggrieved" or "adversely affected" party have a personal economic interest.

In *State of Washington Dept. of Game v. Federal Power Comm.*, 207 F.2d 391, 395 n. 11 (9th Cir. 1953), cert. denied, 347 U.S. 936, 74 S.Ct. 626 (1954), the Washington State Sportsmen's Council, Inc., a non-profit organization of residents, the State of Washington, Department of Game, and the State of Washington, Department of Fisheries, opposed the construction of a dam because it threatened to destroy fish. The Federal Power Commission granted the license; the intervenors applied for a rehearing which the Commission denied. Petitioners asked for review under § 313(b) and the court upheld their standing, noting:

> "All are 'parties aggrieved' since they claim that the Cowlitz Project will destroy fish in [sic] which they, among others, are interested in protecting." The Federal Power Act seeks to protect non-economic as well as economic interests. Indeed, the Commission recognized this in framing the issue in this very case:
>
> "The project is to be physically located in a general area of our nation steeped in the history of the American Revolution and of the colonial period. It is also a general area of great scenic beauty. The principal issue which must be decided is whether the project's effect on the scenic, historical and recreational values of the area are such that we should deny the application."

In order to insure that the Federal Power Commission will adequately protect the public interest in the aesthetic, conservational, and recreational aspects of power development, those who by their activities and conduct have exhibited a special interest in such areas, must be held to be included in the class of "aggrieved" parties under § 313(b). We hold that the Federal Power Act gives petitioners a legal right to protect their special interests . . . .

At an earlier point in these proceedings the Commission apparently accepted this view. Consolidated Edison strongly objected to the petitioners' standing, but the Commission did not deny their right to file an application for a rehearing under § 313(a) of the Act which also speaks in terms of "aggrieved parties."

Moreover, petitioners have sufficient economic interest to establish their standing. The New York-New Jersey Trail Conference, one of the two conservation groups that organized Scenic Hudson, has some seventeen miles of trailways in the area of Storm King Mountain. Portions of these trails would be inundated by the construction of the project's reservoir.

The primary transmission lines are an integral part of the Storm King project. *See* Federal Power Act § 3(11), 16 U.S.C. § 796(11). The towns that are co-petitioners with Scenic Hudson have standing because the transmission lines would cause a decrease in the proprietary value of publicly held land, reduce tax revenues collected from privately held land, and significantly interfere with long-range community planning. *See City of Pittsburgh v. Federal Power Comm.*, 99 U.S. App. D.C. 113, 237 F.2d 741, 748 (1956). Yorktown, for example, fears that the transmission lines would run over municipal land selected for a school site, greatly decreasing its value and interfering with school construction. Putnam Valley faces similar interference with local planning and a substantial decrease in land tax revenues.

We see no justification for the Commission's fear that our determination will encourage "literally thousands" to intervene and seek review in future proceedings. We rejected a similar contention in *Associated Industries, Inc. v. Ickes,* 134 F.2d 694, 707 (2d Cir.), vacated as moot, 320 U.S. 707, 64 S.Ct. 74 (1943), noting that "no such horrendous possibilities" exist. Our experience with public actions confirms the view that the expense and vexation of legal proceedings is not lightly undertaken.

In any case, the Federal Power Act creates no absolute right of intervention; § 308(a), 16 U.S.C. § 825g(a)reads:

> "In any proceeding before it, the Commission, in accordance with such rules and regulations as it may prescribe, may admit as a party any interested State, State commission, municipality, or any representative of interested consumers or security holders, or any competitor of a party to such proceeding, or any other person whose participation in the proceeding may be in the public interest."

Since the right to seek review under § 313(a) and (b) is limited to a "party" to the Commission proceeding, the Commission has ample authority reasonably to limit those eligible to intervene or to seek review. *See Alston Coal Co. v. Federal Power Comm.,* 137 F.2d 740, 742 (10th Cir. 1943). Representation of common interests by an organization such as Scenic Hudson serves to limit the number of those who might otherwise apply for intervention and serves to expedite the administrative process.

III

The Federal Power Act, § 313(b), 16 U.S.C. § 825*l* (b), reads in part:

> "(b) If any party shall apply to the court for leave to adduce additional evidence, and shall show to the satisfaction of the court that such additional evidence is material and that there were reasonable grounds for failure to adduce such evidence in the proceedings before the Commission, the court may order such additional evidence to be taken before the Commission and to be adduced upon the hearing in such manner and upon such terms and conditions as to the court may seem proper."

The Commission in its opinion recognized that in connection with granting a license to Consolidated Edison it "must compare the Cornwall Project with any alternatives that are available." There is no doubt that the Commission is under a statutory duty to give full consideration to alternative plans.

In *City of Pittsburgh,* three months after the hearings were closed, the petitioners attempted to present to the Commission memoranda supporting an alternative suggestion. The District of Columbia Circuit set aside the Commission's order and remanded the case with directions to reopen the record. It found that the Commission had improperly rejected as "untimely" evidence concerning the proposed alternative. The court stated that:

> "The existence of a more desirable alternative is one of the factors which enters into a determination of whether a particular proposal would serve

the public convenience and necessity. That the Commission has no authority to command the alternative does not mean that it cannot reject the [original] proposal." *City of Pittsburgh v. Federal Power Comm.*, 99 U.S. App. D.C. 113, 237 F.2d 741, 751 n. 28 (1956).

In the present case, the Commission heard oral argument on November 17, 1964, on the various exceptions to the Examiner's report. On January 7, 1965 the testimony of Mr. Alexander Lurkis, as to the feasibility of an alternative to the project, the use of gas turbines, was offered to the Commission by Hilltop Cooperative of Queens, a taxpayer and consumer group. The petition to intervene and present this new evidence was rejected on January 13, 1965, as not "timely." It was more than two months after the offer of this testimony, on March 9, 1965, that the Commission issued a license to Consolidated Edison. When Mr. Lurkis's testimony was subsequently reoffered by the petitioners on April 8, 1965, it was rejected because it represented "at best" a "disagreement between experts." On the other hand, we have found in the record no meaningful evidence which contradicts the proffered testimony supporting the gas turbine alternative.

Mr. Lurkis is a consulting engineer of thirty-nine years experience. He has served as Chief Engineer of the New York City Bureau of Gas and Electric, in charge of a staff of 400, and as Senior Engineer of the New York City Transit Authority, where he supervised the design and construction of power plants. The New York Joint Legislative Committee on Natural Resources, after holding hearings on the Storm King project on November 19 and 20, 1964, summarized Mr. Lurkis's testimony as follows:

"Mr. Alexander Lurkis . . . presented a detailed proposal for using gas turbines. This, he claimed, would meet the alleged peaking need of Con Ed and result in a saving for its customers of $132,000,000. The Committee has learned that similar gas turbine installations are now in use or proposed for use by a number of progressive electric utilities throughout the nation. In addition to meeting the alleged peak power needs and saving money for the ratepayer, the gas turbines proposed by Mr. Lurkis would have the following advantages:

1) Permit the company greater flexibility in meeting the power needs of its service area. Admittedly, technological developments in power production are changing and improving this field at such a rapid pace that it may well be entirely revolutionized in 10 to 15 years. There are obvious advantages in the gas turbine installations. Small installations can be added as needed to meet demand. This, in contrast to a single, giant, permanent installation such as Con Ed proposes at Storm King Mountain, which would tie the technology and investment of one company to a method of power production that might be obsolete in a few years.

2) Keep the power production facilities within New York City. This would not only avoid the desecration of the Hudson Gorge and Highlands, but, also, would eliminate the great swathe of destruction down through Putnam and Westchester Counties and their beautiful suburban communities." Preliminary Report at 6.

The Committee report, issued on February 16, 1965, three weeks before the license to Consolidated Edison was granted, concluded:

> "[T]he whole situation involved in the Consolidated Edison Storm King Mountain project, and the protection of the Hudson River and its shores, requires further and extensive study and investigation. . . .
>
> This Committee goes on record as opposing Con Ed's application until there has been adequate study of the points indicated in this report." Preliminary Report at 8.

Mr. Lurkis's analysis was based on an intensive study of the Consolidated Edison system, and of its parking needs projected year by year over a fifteen year period. He was prepared to make an economic comparison of a gas turbine system (including capital and fuel operating costs) and the Storm King pumped storage plant. Moreover, he was prepared to answer Consolidated Edison's objections to gas turbines by indicating:

1. that gas turbines could meet Consolidated Edison's reserve needs;
2. that the blackouts of 1959 and 1961 were caused by breakdowns in distribution, not by a lack of power;
3. that gas turbines would avoid the hazards of weather damage to high transmission lines involved in the Storm King project;
4. that since 3 kilowatts of power must be generated by steam plants in New York City in order to get 2 kilowatts of power from the Storm King project, gas turbines would be even more useful than the project in reducing air pollution;
5. that noise from the turbines would be at acceptable industrial levels.

Other benefits envisioned from gas turbines were higher reliability, increased system flexibility, and possible savings in transmission line investment.

Aside from self-serving general statements by officials of Consolidated Edison, the only testimony in the record bearing on the gas turbine alternative was offered by Ellery R. Fosdick. Fosdick's hastily prepared presentation considered turbines driven by steam and liquid fuel as well as gas; his direct testimony occupied less than ten pages of the record. Fosdick's testimony was too scanty to meet the requirement of a full consideration of alternatives. Indeed, under the circumstances, we must conclude that there was no significant attempt to develop evidence as to the gas turbine alternative; at least, there is no such evidence in the record.

The Commission argues that petitioners made "no attempt to secure additional testimony." Yet the record indicates that more than two months before the license was granted the Commission summarily rejected the offer of Mr. Lurkis's testimony.

It is not our present function to evaluate this evidence. Our focus is upon the action of the Commission. The fact that Lurkis's testimony was originally offered by a non-petitioner, Hilltop Cooperative, is irrelevant. A party acting as a "private attorney general" can raise issues that are not personal to it.

Especially in a case of this type, where public interest and concern is so great, the Commission's refusal to receive the Lurkis testimony, as well as proffered information on fish protection devices and underground transmission facilities, exhibits a disregard of the statute and of judicial mandates instructing the Commission to probe all feasible alternatives.

IV

The Federal Power Commission argues that having intervened "petitioners cannot impose an affirmative burden on the Commission." But, as we have pointed out, Congress gave the Federal Power Commission a specific planning responsibility. *See* Federal Power Act § 10(a), 16 U.S.C. § 803(a). The totality of a project's immediate and long-term range effects, and not merely the engineering and navigation aspects, are to be considered in a licensing proceeding. As Commissioner Ross said in his dissent:

> "I do feel the public is entitled to know on the record that no stone has been left unturned. How much better would it be if the public is clearly advised under oath and cross examination that there truly is no alternative? The thread running through this case has been that the applicant is entitled to a license upon making a prima facie case. My own personal regulatory philosophy compels me to reject this approach. This Commission of its own motion, should always seek to insure that a full and adequate record is presented to it. A regulatory commission can insure continuing confidence in its decisions only when it has used its staff and its own expertise in a manner not possible for the uninformed and poorly financed public. With our intimate knowledge of other systems and to a lesser extent of their plans, it should be possible to resolve all doubts as to alternative sources. This may have been done but the record doesn't speak. Let it do so."

In this case, as in many others, the Commission has claimed to be the representative of the public interest. This role does not permit it to act as an umpire blandly calling balls and strikes for adversaries appearing before it; the right of the public must receive active and affirmative protection at the hands of the Commission.

This Court cannot and should not attempt to substitute its judgment for that of the Commission. But we must decide whether the Commission has correctly discharged its duties, including the proper fulfillment of its planning function in deciding that the "licensing of the project would be in the overall public interest." The Commission must see to it that the record is complete. The Commission has an affirmative duty to inquire into and consider all relevant facts. [Citations omitted.]

In addition to the Commission's failure to receive or develop evidence concerning the gas turbine alternative, there are other instances where the Commission should have acted affirmatively in order to make a complete record.

The Commission neither investigated the use of interconnected power as a possible alternative to the Storm King project, nor required Consolidated Edison to supply such information. The record sets forth Consolidated Edison's interconnection with a vast network of other utilities, but the Commission dismissed this alternative by noting that "Con Edison is relying fully upon such interconnections in estimating its future available capacity." However, only ten pages later in its opinion the Commission conceded:

> "Of significant importance, in our opinion, is the absence in the record, or the inadequacy, of information in regard to Con Edison's future interconnection plans; its plans, if any, for upgrading existing transmission lines to higher voltages; and of its existing transmission line grid in this general area and its future plans."

Moreover, in its October 4, 1965 order, the Commission in explaining how Consolidated Edison would be able to send "substantial amounts" of Storm King power to upstate New York and New England power companies, each December, said:

> "ample spinning reserve would be available during the winter from the interconnected companies in New Jersey and Pennsylvania, including the 'mine-mouth' plants. Thus, even at time of the greatest diversion of Cornwall power, Con Edison would have other power sources immediately available to it for its peak requirements."

If interconnecting power can replace the Storm King project in December, why was it not considered as a permanent alternative?

Commissioner Ross in his dissent said:

> "In my opinion, the only true alternative that would likely be as economic as the proposed project would be purchased peaking power. There are two possibly differing sources; one would be purchasing pumped storage or normal hydro peaking which may be in the process of development in New England; or secondly, purchasing steam peaking power from new large scale thermal stations in Pennsylvania or in Appalachia."

There is no evidence in the record to indicate that either the Commission or Consolidated Edison ever seriously considered this alternative. Nor is there any evidence that a combination of devices, for example gas turbine and interconnections, were considered. Indeed, the Commission stated in its brief that it is "of doubtful relevance to the present case whether there are practical alternatives to an appropriate use of water power by which Con Ed could meet its anticipated needs for peaking power with generally comparable economy." The failure of the Commission to inform itself of these alternatives cannot be reconciled with its planning responsibility under the Federal Power Act.

In its March 9 opinion the Commission postponed a decision on the transmission routes to be chosen until the May 1965 hearings were completed. Inquiry into the cost of putting lines underground was precluded because the May hearings were limited to the question of overhead transmission routes. The petitioners' April 26, 1965 motion to enlarge the scope of the May hearing was denied. The Commission insisted that the question of underground costs had been "extensively considered." We find almost nothing in the record to support this statement.

Consolidated Edison estimated the cost of underground transmission at seven to twelve times that of overhead lines. These estimates were questioned by the Commission's own staff, which pointed out that Consolidated Edison's estimates incorrectly assumed that the underground route would be the same as the overhead; in fact, an underground route along the New York Central right-of-way would be clearly less costly than the estimate, since there are no large differences of elevation requiring special pumping facilities and no new cross-country right-of-way would be necessary. Moreover, the staff noted that the estimates were based on Consolidated Edison's experience in New York, where excavation and other costs are higher. The Examiner noted the staff's reservation in his opinion, but since no alternative figures had been presented, he accepted those submitted by Consolidated Edison, as did the Commission.

Consolidated Edison witnesses testified that the Storm King project would result in annual savings of $12,000,000 over a steam plant of equivalent capacity. Given these savings, the Commission should at least have inquired into the capital and annual cost of running segments of the transmission line underground in those areas where the overhead structures would cause the most serious scenic damage. We find no indication that the Commission seriously weighed the aesthetic advantages of underground transmission lines against the economic disadvantages.

At the time of its original hearings, there was sufficient evidence before the Commission concerning the danger to fish to warrant further inquiry. The evidence included a letter from Kenneth Holum, Assistant Secretary of the Department of the Interior, and a statement made for the record by Robert A. Cook, on behalf of the New York State Water Resources Commission in which Mr. Cook said: "[T]he possibility still exists that extensive losses of eggs and/or young of valuable species might occur after installation of the proposed screening devices."

Just after the Commission closed its proceedings in November the hearings held by the New York State Legislative Committee on Natural Resources alerted many fisherman groups to the threat posed by the Storm King project. On December 24 and 30, January 8, and February 3 each of four groups, concerned with fishing, petitioned for the right to intervene and present evidence. They wished to show that the major spawning grounds for the distinct race of Hudson River striped bass was in the immediate vicinity of the Storm King project and not "much farther upstream" as inferred by Dr. Perlmutter, the one expert witness called by Consolidated Edison; to attempt to prove that, contrary to the impression given by Dr. Perlmutter, bass eggs and larvae float in the water, at the mercy of currents; that due to the location of the spawning ground and the Hudson's tidal flow, the eggs and larvae would be directly subject to the influence of the plant and would be threatened with destruction; that "no screening device presently feasible would adequately protect these early stages of fish life" and that their loss would ultimately destroy the economically valuable fisheries. Their evidence also indicated that in the case of shad, the young migrate from their spawning grounds, down past Cornwall, and being smaller than the meshes of the contemplated fish screens, would be subject to the hazards already described. The Commission rejected all these petitions as "untimely," and seemingly placing great reliance on the testimony of Dr. Perlmutter, concluded:

> "The project will not adversely affect the fish resources of the Hudson River provided adequate protective facilities are installed."

Although an opportunity was made available at the May hearings for petitioners to submit evidence on protective designs, the question of the adequacy of *any* protective design was inexplicably excluded by the Commission.

Recent events illustrate other deficiencies in the Commission's record. In hearings before the House Subcommittee on Fisheries and Wildlife Studying the Hudson River Spawning Grounds, 89th Cong., 1st Sess., May 10, 11, 1965, Mr. James McBroom, representing the Department of the Interior, stated:

> "Practical screening methods are known which could prevent young-of-the-year striped bass and shad from being caught up in the [Storm King] project's pumps, but practical means of protection of eggs and larvae stages have yet to be devised. Furthermore the location of the proposed plant appears from available evidence to be at or very near the crucial spot as to potential for harm to the overall production of eggs and larvae of the Hudson River striped bass. The cumulative effect of unmitigated loss of eggs and larvae bass by this power project could have a serious effect on the Hudson River striped bass fishery and the dependent fisheries around Long Island and offshore."

Mr. E. L. Cheatum, representing the New York State Conservation Department, gave similar testimony. At the May hearings the testimony of Mr. Walburg and Mr. Wagner, witnesses for the Department of Interior, and Dr. Raney and Mr. Massmann, witnesses for Scenic Hudson, was substantially to the same effect. Indeed, the Commission in its October 4 order acknowledged that the protective device to which it had previously referred favorably (March 9 order) "may not be adequate to provide the protection required" (October 4 order).

On remand, the Commission should take the whole fisheries question into consideration before deciding whether the Storm King project is to be licensed.

The Commission should reexamine all questions on which we have found the record insufficient and all related matters. The Commission's renewed proceedings must include as a basic concern the preservation of natural beauty and of national historic shrines, keeping in mind that, in our affluent society, the cost of a project is only one of several factors to be considered. The record as it comes to us fails markedly to make out a case for the Storm King project on, among other matters, costs, public convenience and necessity, and absence of reasonable alternatives. Of course, the Commission should make every effort to expedite the new proceedings.

Petitioners' application, pursuant to Federal Power Act § 313(b), 16 U.S.C. § 825*l* (b), to adduce additional evidence concerning alternatives to the Storm King project and the cost and practicality of underground transmission facilities is granted.

The licensing order of March 9 and the two orders of May 6 are set aside, and the case remanded for further proceedings.

NOTES AND QUESTIONS

(1) After nearly two decades of controversy and litigation, representatives of eleven environmental, governmental and utility groups agreed to: (1) halt

construction at Storm King and dedicate the 500-acre site to Cornwall, N.Y. for park use; (2) reduce destruction of fish and other aquatic life at six other generators on the Hudson by minimizing water withdrawal and partially closing the plants during spawning season, when pumps suck fish and eggs into their pipelines; (3) build a hatchery to stock the Hudson River with stripped bass; (4) propose and build power plants on selected areas of the Hudson only if closed-cycle cooling systems can eliminate the environmental and fish life damage caused by cooling water uptake; (5) forgive the plants of any obligation to build cooling towers at selected sites, if partial closings are insufficient to prevent fish damage; (6) endow a new foundation to fund independent research on ways to lessen the impact on fish by power plants; and (7) drop all lawsuits and administrative proceedings among the parties. The settlement saved the utilities and their customers over $240 million in cooling-tower construction costs and $90 million a year in operating and carrying charges. Consolidated Edison estimated that the settlement cost the utilities less than a tenth of that amount. *See* Temple, "Peace at Storm King," 7 EPA Journal 28 (1981).

(2) *Scenic Hudson* was a classic environmental law case. The Scenic Hudson Preservation Conference was a forerunner of the Natural Resources Defense Council, now one of the leading national conservation organizations. One of the plaintiffs' attorneys, David Sive, went on to become a celebrated environmental lawyer.

(3) Notice the court's broad reading of the doctrine of standing-to-sue in this case—a view that presaged similar handling of the standing question by the U.S. Supreme Court in the 1970s. *See* § 8.03, *infra*. How persuasive is the *Scenic Hudson* court's opinion on this point?

(4) One critical aspect of the *Scenic Hudson* decision is the extent to which the Second Circuit required the Federal Power Commission to consider less environmentally harmful alternatives to the proposed hydroelectric project that was before it. Is that appropriate? Notably, this portion of the *Scenic Hudson* decision was a harbinger of the approach to the consideration of alternatives adopted by Congress in the National Environmental Policy Act of 1969.

CITIZENS TO PRESERVE OVERTON PARK v. VOLPE

United States Supreme Court (1971)
401 U.S. 402, 91 S. Ct. 814, 28 L. Ed. 2d 136

Mr. Justice Marshall delivered the opinion of the Court.

The growing public concern about the quality of our natural environment has prompted Congress in recent years to enact legislation designed to curb the accelerating destruction of our country's natural beauty. We are concerned in this case with § 4(f) of the Department of Transportation Act of 1966 and § 138 of the Federal-Aid Highway Act of 1968. These statutes prohibit the

Secretary of Transportation from authorizing the use of federal funds to finance the construction of highways through public parks if a "feasible and prudent" alternative route exists. If no such route is available, the statutes allow him to approve construction through parks only if there has been "all possible planning to minimize harm" to the park.

Petitioners, private citizens as well as local and national conservation organizations, contend that the Secretary has violated these statutes by authorizing the expenditure of federal funds for the construction of a six-lane interstate highway through a public park in Memphis Tennessee. Their claim was rejected by the District Court, which granted the Secretary's motion for summary judgment, and the Court of Appeals for the Sixth Circuit affirmed. After oral argument, the Court granted a stay that halted construction and, treating the application for the stay as a petition for certiorari, granted review. We now reverse the judgment below and remand for further proceedings in the District Court.

Overton Park is a 342-acre city park located near the center of Memphis. The park contains a zoo, a nine-hole municipal golf course, an outdoor theater, nature trails, a bridle path, an art academy, picnic areas, and 170 acres of forest. The proposed highway, which is to be a six-lane, high-speed, expressway,[7] will sever the zoo from the rest of the park. Although the roadway will be depressed below ground level except where it crosses a small creek, 26 acres of the park will be destroyed. The highway is to be a segment of Interstate Highway No. I-40, part of the National System of Interstate and Defense Highways. I-40 will provide Memphis with a major east-west expressway that will allow easier access to downtown Memphis from the residential areas on the eastern edge of the city.

Although the route through the park was approved by the Bureau of Public Roads in 1956 and by the Federal Highway Administrator in 1966, the enactment of § 4(f) of the Department of Transportation Act prevented distribution of federal funds for the section of the highway designated to go through Overton Park until the Secretary of Transportation determined whether the requirements of § 4(f) had been met. Federal funding for the rest of the project was, however, available; and the state acquired right-of-way on both sides of the park.[8] In April 1968, the Secretary announced that he concurred in the judgment of local officials that I-40 should be built through the park. And in September 1969 the State acquired the right-of-way inside Overton Park from the city.[9] Final approval for the project—the route as well as the design—was not announced until November 1969, after Congress had reiterated in § 138 of the Federal-Aid Highway Act that highway construction through public parks was to be restricted. Neither announcement approving the route and design of I-40 was accompanied by a statement of the Secretary's

[7] The proposed right-of-way will be 250 to 450 feet wide and will follow the route of a presently existing, nonaccess bus route, which carries occasional bus traffic along a 40-to 50-foot right-of-way.

[8] The Secretary approved these acquisitions in 1967 prior to the effective date of § 4(f).

[9] The State paid the City $2,000,000 for the 26-acre right-of-way and $206,000 to the Memphis Park Commission to replace park facilities that were to be destroyed by the highway. The City of Memphis has used $1,000,000 of these funds to pay for a new 160-acre park and it is anticipated that additional parkland will be acquired with the remaining money.

factual findings. He did not indicate why he believed there were no feasible and prudent alternative routes or why design changes could not be made to reduce the harm to the park.

Petitioners contend that the Secretary's action is invalid without such formal findings and that the Secretary did not make an independent determination but merely relied on the judgment of the Memphis City Council. They also contend that it would be "feasible and prudent" to route I-40 around Overton Park either to the north or to the south. And they argue that if these alternative routes are not "feasible and prudent," the present plan does not include "all possible" methods for reducing harm to the park. Petitioners claim that I-40 could be built under the park by using either of two possible tunneling methods, and they claim that, at a minimum, by using advanced drainage techniques the expressway could be depressed below ground level along the entire route through the park including the section that crosses the small creek.

Respondents argue that it was unnecessary for the Secretary to make formal findings and that he did, in fact, exercise his own independent judgment that was supported by the facts. In the District Court, respondents introduced affidavits, prepared specifically for this litigation, which indicated that the Secretary had made the decision and that the decision was supportable. These affidavits were contradicted by affidavits introduced by petitioners, who also sought to take the deposition of a former federal highway administrator who had participated in the decision to route I-40 through Overton Park.

The District Court and the Court of Appeals found that formal findings by the Secretary were not necessary and refused to order the deposition of the former Federal Highway Administrator because those courts believed that probing of the mental processes of an administrative decision maker was prohibited. And, believing that the Secretary's authority was wide and reviewing courts' authority narrow in the approval of highway routes, the lower courts held that the affidavits contained no basis for a determination that the Secretary had exceeded his authority.

We agree that formal findings were not required. But we do not believe that in this case judicial review based solely on litigation affidavits was adequate.

A threshold question—whether petitioners are entitled to any judicial review—is easily answered. Section 701 of the Administrative Procedure Act, 5 U.S.C. § 701(Supp. V), provides that the action of "each authority of the Government of the United States," which includes the Department of Transportation, is subject to judicial review except where there is a statutory prohibition on review or where "agency action is committed to agency discretion by law." 5 U.S.C. § 701(Supp. V). In this case, there is no indication that Congress sought to prohibit judicial review and there is most certainly no "showing of 'clear and convincing evidence' or a . . . legislative intent" to restrict access to judicial review. *Abbott Laboratories v. Gardner,* 387 U.S. 136, 141 (1967); *Brownell v. We Shung,* 352 U.S. 180, 185 (1956).

Similarly, the Secretary's decision here does not fall within the exception for action "committed to agency discretion." This is a very narrow exception. Berger, Administrative Arbitrariness and Judicial Review, 65 Col. L. Rev. 55

(1965). The legislative history of the Administrative Procedure Act indicates that it is applicable in those rare instances where "statutes are drawn in such broad terms that in a given case there is no law to apply." S. Rep. No. 758, Senate Committee on the Judiciary, 9th Cong., 1st Sess., 26 (1945).

Section 4(f) of the Department of Transportation Act and § 138 of the Federal-Aid Highway Act are clear and specific directives. Both the Department of Transportation Act and the Federal-Aid Highway Act provide that the Secretary "shall not approve any program or project" that requires the use of any public parkland "unless (1) there is no feasible and prudent alternative to the use of such land, and (2) such program includes all possible planning to minimize harm to such park . . . ." 23 U.S.C. § 138(Supp. V); 49 U.S.C. § 1653(f)(Supp. V). This language is a plain and explicit bar to the use of federal funds for construction of highways through parks—only the most unusual situations are exempted.

Despite the clarity of the statutory language, respondents argue that the Secretary has wide discretion. They recognize that the requirement that there be no "feasible" alternative route admits of little administrative discretion. For this exemption to apply the Secretary must find that as a matter of sound engineering it would not be feasible to build the highway along any other route. Respondents argue, however, that the requirement that there be no other "prudent" route requires the Secretary to engage in a wide-ranging balancing of competing interests. They contend that the Secretary should weigh the detriment resulting from the destruction of parkland against the cost of other routes, safety considerations, and other factors, and determine on the basis of the importance that he attaches to these other factors whether, on balance, alternative feasible routes would be "prudent."

But no such wide-ranging endeavor was intended. It is obvious that in most cases considerations of cost, directness of routes, and community disruption will indicate the parkland should be used for highway construction whenever possible. Although it may be necessary to transfer funds from one jurisdiction to another, there will always be a smaller outlay required from the public purse when parkland is used since the public already owns the land and there will be no need to pay for right-of-way. And since people do not live or work in parks, if a highway is built on parkland no one will have to leave his home or give up his business. Such factors are common to substantially all highway construction. Thus if Congress intended these factors to be on an equal footing with preservation of parkland there would have been no need for the statutes.

Congress clearly did not intend that cost and disruption of the community were to be ignored by the Secretary. But the very existence of the statute indicates that protection of parkland was to be given paramount importance. The few green havens that are public parks were not to be lost unless there were truly unusual factors present in a particular case or the cost or community disruption resulting from alternative routes reached extraordinary magnitudes. If the statutes are to have any meaning, the Secretary cannot approve the destruction of parkland unless he finds that alternative routes present unique problems.

Plainly, there is "law to apply" and thus the exemption for action "committed to agency discretion," is inapplicable. But the existence of judicial review is only the start: the standards for review must also be determined. For that we must look to § 706 of the Administrative Procedure Act, 5 U.S.C. § 706(Supp. V), which provides that a "reviewing court shall . . . hold unlawful and set aside agency action, findings and conclusions found" not to meet six separate standards. In all cases agency action must be set aside if the action was "arbitrary, capricious, an abuse of discretion, or otherwise not in accordance with law" or if the action failed to meet statutory, procedural, or constitutional requirements. 5 U.S.C. § 706(2)(A)(B)(C)(D)(Supp. V). In certain narrow, specifically limited situations, the agency action is to be set aside if the action was not supported by "substantial evidence." And in other equally narrow circumstances the reviewing court is to engage in a *de novo* review of the action and set it aside if it was "unwarranted by the facts." 5 U.S.C. § (2)(E)(F)(Supp. V).

Petitioners argue that the Secretary's approval of the construction of I-40 through Overton Park is subject to one or the other of these latter two standards of limited applicability. First, they contend that the "substantial evidence" standard of § 706(2)(E) must be applied. In the alternative, they claim that § 706(2)(F) applies and that there must be a *de novo* review to determine if the Secretary's action was "unwarranted by the facts." Neither of these standards is, however, applicable.

Review under the substantial evidence test is authorized only when the agency action is taken pursuant to a rulemaking provision of the Administrative Procedure Act itself, 5 U.S.C. § 553(Supp. V), or when the agency action is based on a public adjudicatory hearing. *See* 5 U.S.C. §§ 556, 557(Supp. V). The Secretary's decision to allow the expenditure of federal funds to build I-40 through Overton Park was plainly not an exercise of a rulemaking function.. . . And the only hearing that is required . . . is non-adjudicatory and not designed to produce a record that is to be the basis of agency action—the basic requirement for substantial evidence review . . . . The court is first required to decide whether the Secretary acted within the scope of his authority. *Schilling v. Rogers,* 363 U.S. 666, 676-677 (1960). This determination naturally begins with a delineation of the scope of the Secretary's authority and discretion. L. Jaffe, Judicial Control of Administrative Action 359 (1965). As has been shown, Congress has specified only a small range of choices that the Secretary can make. Also involved in this initial inquiry is a determination of whether on the facts the Secretary's decision can reasonably be said to be within that range. The reviewing court must consider whether the Secretary properly constructed his authority to approve the use of parkland as limited to situations where there are no feasible alternative routes or where feasible alternative routes involve uniquely difficult problems. And the reviewing court must be able to find that the Secretary could have reasonably believed that in this case there are no feasible alternatives or that alternatives do involve unique problems.

Scrutiny of the facts does not end, however, with the determination that the Secretary has acted within the scope of his statutory authority. Section 706(2)(A) requires a finding that the actual choice made was not "arbitrary, capricious, an abuse of discretion, or otherwise not in accordance with law." 5 U.S.C. § 706(2)(A)(Supp. V). To make this finding the court must consider whether the decision was based on a consideration of the relevant factors and whether there has been a clear error of judgment . . . .

Although this inquiry into the facts is to be searching and careful, the ultimate standard of review is a narrow one. The court is not empowered to substitute its judgment for that of the agency.

The final inquiry is whether the Secretary's action followed the necessary procedural requirements. Here the only procedural error alleged is the failure of the Secretary to make formal findings and state his reason for allowing the highway to be built through the park.

Undoubtedly, review of the Secretary's action is hampered by his failure to make such findings, but the absence of formal findings does not necessarily require that the case be remanded to the Secretary. Neither the Department of Transportation Act nor the Federal-Aid Highway Act requires such formal findings. . . .

Petitioners contend that although there may not be a statutory requirement that the Secretary make formal findings and even though this may not be a case for the reviewing court to impose a requirement that findings be made, Department of Transportation regulations require them. This argument is based on DOT Order 5610.1,[10] which requires the Secretary to make formal findings when he approves the use of parkland for highway construction but which was issued after the route for I-40 was approved.[11] Petitioners argue that even though the order was not in effect at the time approval was given to the Overton Park project and even though the order was not intended to have retrospective effect the order represents the law at the time of this Court's decision and under *Thorpe v. Housing Authority,* 393 U.S. 268, 281-282 (1969), should be applied to this case.

While we do not question that DOT Order 5610.1 constitutes the law in effect at the time of our decision, we do not believe that *Thorpe* compels us to remand for the Secretary to make formal findings.[12] Here, unlike the situation in *Thorpe,* there has been a change in circumstances—additional right-of-way has been cleared and the 26-acre right-of-way inside Overton Park has been purchased by the State. Moreover, there is an administrative record that allows the full, prompt review of the Secretary's action that is sought without additional delay which would result from having a remand to the Secretary.

That administrative record is not, however, before us. The lower courts based their review on the litigation affidavits that were presented. These affidavits were merely "*post hoc*" rationalizations, *Burlington Truck Lines v. United States,* 371 U.S. 156, 168-169 (1962), which have traditionally been found to be an inadequate basis for review. *Burlington Truck Lines v. United States, supra*; *SEC v. Chenery Corp.,* 318 U.S. 80, 87 (1943). And they clearly

[10] The regulation was promulgated pursuant to Executive Order 11514, dated March 5, 1970, which instructed all federal agencies to initiate procedures needed to direct their policies and programs toward meeting national environmental goals.

[11] DOT Order 5610.1 was issued on October 7, 1970.

[12] Even if formal findings by the Secretary were mandatory, the proper course would be to remand the case to the District Court directing that court to order the Secretary to make formal findings . . . .

do not constitute the "whole record" compiled by the agency: the basis for review required by § 706 of the Administrative Procedure Act. . . .

Thus it is necessary to remand this case to the District Court for plenary review of the Secretary's decision. That review is to be based on the full administrative record that was before the Secretary at the time he made his decision.[13] But since the bare record may not disclose the factors that were considered or the Secretary's construction of the evidence it may be necessary for the District Court to require some explanation in order to determine if the Secretary acted within the scope of his authority and if the Secretary's action was justifiable under the applicable standard. . . .

. . . .

Reversed and remanded.

Mr. Justice Douglas took no part in the consideration or decision of this case.

Separate opinion of Mr. Justice Black, with whom Mr. Justice Brennan joins.

I agree with the Court that the judgment of the Court of Appeals is wrong and that its action should be reversed. I do not agree that the whole matter should be remanded to the District Court. I think the case should be sent back to the Secretary of Transportation. It is apparent from the Court's opinion today that the Secretary of Transportation completely failed to comply with the duty imposed upon him by Congress not to permit a federally-financed public highway to run through a public park "unless (1) there is no feasible and prudent alternative to the use of such land, and (2) such program includes all possible planning to minimize harm to such park . . . ." 23 U.S.C. § 138; 49 U.S.C. § 1653(f). That congressional command should not be taken lightly by the Secretary or by this Court. It represents a solemn determination of the highest law-making body of this Nation that the beauty and health-giving facilities of our parks are not to be taken away for public roads without hearings, fact-findings and policy determinations under the supervision of a Cabinet officer—the Secretary of Transportation. The Act of Congress in connection with other Federal Highway Aid legislation, it seems to me, calls for hearings, hearings that a court can review, hearings that demonstrate more than mere arbitrary defiance by the Secretary. Whether the findings growing out of such hearings are labeled "formal" or "informal" appears to me to be no more than an exercise in semantics. Whatever the hearing requirements might be, the Department of Transportation failed to meet them in this case. I regret that I am compelled to conclude for myself that, except for some too-late formulations, apparently coming from the Solicitor General's Office, this record contains not one word to indicate that the Secretary raised even a finger to comply with the command of Congress. It is our duty, I believe, to remand this whole matter back to the Secretary of Transportation for him to give this mater the hearing it deserves in full good-faith obedience to the Act of Congress. That Act was obviously passed to protect our public parks from forays by road builders except in the most extraordinary and imperative

[13] The Solicitor General now urges that in order to avoid additional delay the proper course is to remand the case to the District Court for review of the full administrative record.

circumstances. This record does not demonstrate the existence of such circumstances. I dissent from the Court's failure to send the case back to the Secretary, whose duty has not yet been performed.

NOTES AND QUESTIONS

(1) *Overton Park* has been an influential decision, widely-cited by lower federal courts. Among other things, it stands for the principle that federal agencies must compile a written administrative record in informal "notice and comment" rulemaking proceedings. This has led many agencies, on the advice of their lawyers, to compile extensive decisional files that form a reviewable record in such proceedings.

One scholarly critic of this trend contends that it has resulted in an "ossification" of complex agency rulemaking:

> Because the agencies perceive that the reviewing courts are inconsistent in the degree to which they are deferential [to agency decisions], they are constrained to prepare for the worst-case scenario on judicial review. This can be extremely resource-intensive and time-consuming. Moreover, since the criteria for substantive judicial review are the same for repealing old rules as for promulgating new rules, the agencies are equally chary of revisiting old rules, even in the name of flexibility. McGarity, *Some Thoughts On "Deossifying" the Rulemaking Process*, 41 Duke L.J. 1419, 1420 (1992).

(2) Do you agree with Justice Marshall's conclusion that the Secretary of Transportation's decision, under § 4(f) of the Department of Transportation Act of 1966, was not "committed to agency discretion" under the Administrative Procedure Act? How much weight, if any, should the court have given to the Secretary's argument that § 4(f) enacted a balancing test? For provocative critiques of the result in *Overton Park,* see Strauss, *Considering Political Alternatives to "Hard Look" Review,* 1989 Duke L.J. 538, 544–547 and Strauss, *Revisiting* Overton Park: *Political and Judicial Controls Over Administrative Actions Affecting the Community*, 39 UCLA L. Rev. 1251 (1992).

(3) On remand, following a 25-day trial, the U.S. District Court reversed the Secretary of Transportation's decision and remanded the case to the Department. The Secretary then declined to find that there was no feasible or prudent alternative to building I-40 through Overton Park. That decision was subsequently upheld, on judicial review, and the road through the park was not built. *See Citizens to Preserve Overton Park v. Brinegar,* 357 F. Supp. 846 (W.D. Tenn. 1973), *rev'd*, 494 F.2d 1212 (6th Cir. 1974), *cert. denied*, 421 U.S. 991 (1975).

(4) The Supreme Court's *Overton Park* decision is frequently viewed as an example of "hard look" review, a term coined by Judge Harold Leventhal of the D.C. Circuit in *Greater Boston Television Corp. v. FCC,* 444 F.2d 841, 850 (D.C. Cir. 1970), *cert. denied* 403 U.S. 923 (1971) ("Its supervisory function calls on the court to intervene . . . if the court becomes aware, especially from a combination of danger signals, that the agency has not really taken a hard look at the salient problems, and has not genuinely engaged in reasoned decision-making."). For a spirited judicial defense of the "hard look" approach

in environmental matters, see Oakes, *The Judicial Role In Environmental Law,* 52 N.Y.U. L. Rev. 498 (1977). The scholarly debate on the merits of "hard look" review is summarized in Glicksman and Schroeder, *EPA and the Courts: Twenty Years of Law and Politics,* 54 Law and Contemp. Probs. 249 (1991).

(5) *Overton Park*'s strict approach to judicial review of informal agency decision-making was reinforced in *Motor Vehicle Mfrs. Ass'n. v. State Farm Mutual Automobile Ins. Co.,* 463 U.S. 29, 103 S. Ct. 2856, 77 L. Ed. 2d 443 (1983), in which the court overturned, as arbitrary and capricious, a decision by the National Highway Traffic Safety Administration not to require that cars produced after September 1982 be equipped with passive safety restraints. However, in a subsequent case, the Court ruled that an administrative agency's decision not to take enforcement action is "committed to agency discretion" and thus unsuitable for judicial review. *Heckler v. Chaney,* 470 U.S. 821, 105 S. Ct. 1649, 84 L. Ed. 2d 714 (1985). It has also been held that certain other species of informal agency action, including the issuance of general policy statements and interpretive statements, are not subject to the rulemaking requirements contemplated in § 553 of the Administrative Procedure Act and in the *Overton Park* decision. *See Morton v. Ruiz,* 415 U.S. 199 (1974) and *Pacific Gas and Electric Co. v. FPC,* 506 F.2d 33 (D.C. Cir. 1974).

(6) In light of *Overton Park,* may the federal courts require federal agencies to adopt rulemaking procedures that go beyond the straightforward notice and comment procedures prescribed by the Administrative Procedure Act? The U.S. Supreme Court resolved that question in the negative in *Vermont Yankee Nuclear Power Corp. v. Natural Resources Defense Council, Inc.,* 435 U.S. 519, 98 S. Ct. 1197, 55 L. Ed. 2d 460 (1978). Rejecting an attempt by the D.C. Circuit to impose "hybrid rulemaking" procedures on the Nuclear Regulatory Commission (in licensing proceedings regarding proposed nuclear power plants), the Court stated that where a court reviews administrative agency decisions which are accompanied by contemporaneous explanations, the court must not "stray beyond the judicial province to explore the procedural format or to impose upon the agency its own notion of which procedures are 'best' or most likely to further some vague, undefined public good."

CHEVRON U.S.A. INC. v. NATURAL RESOURCE DEFENSE COUNCIL et al.

United States Supreme Court (1984)
467 U.S. 839, 104 S. Ct. 2778, 81 L. Ed. 2d 694

Stevens, J.:

In the Clean Air Act Amendments of 1977, Congress enacted certain requirements applicable to States that had not achieved the national air quality standards . . . . The amended Clean Air Act required these "nonattainment" States to establish a permit program regulating "new or modified major stationary sources" of air pollution. Generally, a permit may not be issued for a new or modified major stationary source unless several stringent conditions are met. The EPA regulation promulgated to implement this permit requirement allows a State to adopt a plant wide definition of the term "stationary source." Under this definition, an existing plant that contains several pollution-emitting devices may install or modify one piece of equipment without meeting the permit conditions if the alteration will not increase the total emissions from the plant. The question presented by these cases is whether EPA's decision to allow States to treat all of the pollution-emitting devices within the same industrial grouping as though they were encased within a single "bubble" is based on a reasonable construction of the statutory term "stationary source."

The EPA regulations containing the plant wide definition of the term stationary source were promulgated on October 14, 1981. 46 Fed. Reg. 50766. Respondents filed a timely petition for review in the United States Court of Appeals for the District of Columbia Circuit pursuant to 42 U.S.C. § 7607(b)(1). The Court of Appeals set aside the regulations . . . .

The court observed that the relevant part of the amended Clean Air Act "does not explicitly define what Congress envisioned as a 'stationary source,' to which the permit program . . . should apply," and further stated that the precise issue was not "squarely addressed in the legislative history." *Id.,* at 273, 685 F.2d at 723. In light of its conclusion that the legislative history bearing on the question was "at best contradictory," it reasoned that "the purposes of the non-attainment program should guide our decision here." *Id.* at 276, n. 39, 685 F.2d, at 726, n.39. Based on two of its precedents concerning the applicability of the bubble concept to certain Clean Air Act programs, the court stated that the bubble concept was "mandatory" in programs designed merely to maintain existing air quality [PSD programs], but held that it was "inappropriate" in programs enacted to improve air quality. *Id.,* at 276, 685 F.2d, at 726. Since the purpose of the permit program—its *"raison d'etre,"* in the court's view—was to improve air quality [non-attainment programs], the court held that the bubble concept was inapplicable in these cases under its prior precedents. *Ibid.* It therefore set aside the regulations embodying the bubble concept as contrary to law. We granted certiorari to review that judgment . . ., and we now reverse.

The basic legal error of the Court of Appeals was to adopt a static judicial definition of the term "stationary source" when it had decided that Congress itself had not commanded that definition. Respondents do not defend the legal reasoning of the Court of Appeals. Nevertheless, since this Court reviews judgments, not opinions, we must determine whether the Court of Appeals' legal error resulted in an erroneous judgment on the validity of the regulations.

II

When a court reviews an agency's construction of the statute which it administers, it is confronted with two questions. First, always, is the question whether Congress has directly spoken to the precise question at issue. If the intent of Congress is clear, that is the end of the matter; for the court, as well as the agency, must give effect to the unambiguously expressed intent of Congress.[14] If, however, the court determines Congress has not directly addressed the precise question at issue, the court does not simply impose its own construction on the statute, as would be necessary in the absence of an administrative interpretation. Rather, if the statute is silent or ambiguous with respect to the specific issue, the question for the court is whether the agency's answer is based on a permissible construction of the statute.

"The power of an administrative agency to administer a congressionally created . . . program necessarily requires the formulation of policy and the making of rules to fill any gap left, implicitly or explicitly, by Congress." *Morton v. Ruiz,* 415 U.S. 199, 231 (1974). If Congress has explicitly left a gap for the agency to fill, there is an express delegation of authority to the agency to elucidate a specific provision of the statute by regulation. Such legislative regulations are given controlling weight unless they are arbitrary, capricious, or manifestly contrary to the statute. Sometimes the legislative delegation to an agency on a particular question is implicit rather than explicit. In such a case, a court may not substitute its own construction of a statutory provision for a reasonable interpretation made by the administrator of an agency.

We have long recognized that considerable weight should be accorded to an executive department's construction of a statutory scheme it is entrusted to administer, and the principle of deference to administrative interpretations

> has been consistently followed by this Court whenever decision as to the meaning or reach of a statute has involved reconciling conflicting policies, and a full understanding of the force of the statutory policy in the given situation has depended upon more than ordinary knowledge respecting the matters subjected to agency regulations . . . .
>
> . . . . If this choice represents a reasonable accommodation of conflicting policies that were committed to the agency's care by the statute, we should not disturb it unless it appears from the statute or its legislative history that the accommodation is not one that Congress would have sanctioned. *United States v. Shimer,* 367 U.S. 374, 382 383 (1961) . . . .

In light of these well-settled principles it is clear that the Court of Appeals misconceived the nature of its role in reviewing the regulations at issue. Once it determined, after its own examination of the legislation, that Congress did not actually have an intent regarding the applicability of the bubble concept to the permit program, the question before it was not whether in its view the concept is "inappropriate" in the general context of a program designed to improve air quality, but whether the Administrator's view that it is appropriate in the context of this particular program is a reasonable one. Based on the examination of the legislation and its history which follows, we agree with the Court of Appeals that Congress did not have a specific intention on the applicability of the bubble concept in these cases, and conclude that the EPA's use of that concept here is a reasonable policy choice for the agency to make.

[14] The Judiciary is the final authority on issues of statutory construction and must reject administrative constructions which are contrary to clear congressional intent . . . .

III

Section 111(a) defined the terms that are to be used in setting and enforcing standards of performance for new stationary sources. It provided:

For purposes of this section:

(3) The term "stationary source" means any building, structure, facility, or installation which emits or may emit any air pollutant. 84 Stat. 1683.

In the 1970 Amendments that definition was not only applicable to the NSPS program required by § 111, but also was made applicable to a requirement of § 110 that each state implementation plan contain a procedure for reviewing the location of any proposed new source and preventing its construction if it would preclude the attainment or maintenance of national air quality standards.

In due course, the EPA promulgated NAAQS's, approved SIP's, and adopted detailed regulations governing NSPS's for various categories of equipment. In one of its programs, the EPA used a plant wide definition of the term "stationary source." In 1974, it issued NSPS's for the nonferrous smelting industry that provided that the standards would not apply to the modification of major smelting units if their increased emissions were offset by reduction in other portions of the same plant.

Nonattainment

The 1970 legislation provided for the attainment of primary NAAQS's by 1975. In many areas of the country, particularly the most industrialized States, the statutory goals were not attained. In 1976, the 94th Congress was confronted with this fundamental problem, as well as many others respecting pollution control. As always in this area, the legislative struggle was basically between interests seeking strict schemes to reduce pollution rapidly to eliminate its social costs and interests advancing the economic concern that strict schemes would retard industrial development with attendant social costs. The 94th Congress, confronting these competing interests, was unable to agree on what response was in the public interest: legislative proposals to deal with nonattainment failed to command the necessary consensus.

In light of this situation, the EPA published an Emissions Offset Interpretative Ruling in December 1976, *see* 41 Fed. Reg. 55524, to "fill the gap," as respondents put it, until Congress acted . . . . The 1976 Ruling did not, however, explicitly adopt or reject the "bubble concept."

IV

The Clean Air Act Amendments of 1977 are a lengthy, detailed, technical, complex, and comprehensive response to a major social issue. A small portion of the statute—91 Stat. 745-751 (Part D of Title I of the amended Act, 42 U.S.C. §§ 7501-7508)—expressly deals with nonattainment areas. The focal point of this controversy is one phrase in that portion of the Amendments . . . .

Most significantly for our purposes, the statute provided that each plan shall

> "(6) require permits for the construction and operation of new or modified major stationary sources in accordance with section 173 . . . ." *Id.*, at 747
>
> . . .

The 1977 Amendments contain no specific reference to the "bubble concept." Nor do they contain a specific definition of the term "stationary source," though they did not disturb the definition of "stationary source" contained in § 111(a)(3), applicable by the terms of the Act to the NSPS program. Section 302(j), however, defines the term "major stationary source" as follows:

> (J) Except as otherwise expressly provided, the terms "major stationary source" and "major emitting facility" mean any stationary facility or source of air pollutants which directly emits, or has the potential to emit, one hundred tons per year or more of any air pollutant (including any major emitting facility or source of fugitive emissions of any such pollutant, as determined by rule by the Administrator). 91 Stat. 770.

V

The legislative history of the portion of the 1977 Amendments dealing with nonattainment areas does not contain any specific comment on the "bubble concept" or the question whether a plant wide definition of a stationary source is permissible under the permit program. It does, however, plainly disclose that in the permit program Congress sought to accommodate the conflict between the economic interest in permitting capital improvements to continue and the environmental interest in improving air quality . . . .

VI

As previously noted, prior to the 1977 Amendments, the EPA had adhered to a plant wide definition of the term "source" under a NSPS program. After adoption of the 1977 Amendments, proposals for a plant wide definition were considered in at least three formal proceedings . . . .

In 1981 a new administration took office and initiated a "Government-wide reexamination of regulatory burdens and complexities." 46 Fed. Reg. 16281. In the context of that review, the EPA reevaluated the various arguments that had been advanced in connection with the proper definition of the term "source" and concluded that the term should be given the same definition in both nonattainment areas and PSD areas.

In explaining its conclusions, the EPA first noted that the definitional issue was not squarely addressed in either the statute or its legislative history and therefore that the issue involved an agency "judgment as how to best carry out the Act." *Ibid.* It then set forth several reasons for concluding that the plant wide definition was more appropriate. It pointed out that the dual definition "can act as a disincentive to new investment and modernization by discouraging modifications to existing facilities" and "can actually retard progress in air pollution control by discouraging replacement of older, dirtier processes or pieces of equipment with new, cleaner ones." *Ibid.* Moreover, the new definition "would simplify EPA's rules by using the same definition of 'source' for PSD, nonattainment new source review and the construction moratorium. This reduces confusion and inconsistency." *Ibid.* Finally, the agency explained that additional requirements that remained in place would accomplish the fundamental purposes of achieving attainment with NAAQS's as expeditiously as possible.

VII

We are not persuaded that parsing of general terms in the text of the statute will reveal an actual intent of Congress. We know full well that this language is not dispositive; the terms are overlapping and the language is not precisely directed to the question of the applicability of a given term in the context of a larger operation. To the extent any congressional "intent" can be discerned from this language, it would appear that the listing of overlapping, illustrative terms was intended to enlarge, rather than to confine, the scope of the agency's power to regulate particular sources in order to effectuate the policies of the Act.

Legislative History

In addition, respondents argue that the legislative history and policies of the Act foreclose the plant wide definition, and that the EPA's interpretation is not entitled to deference because it represents a sharp break with prior interpretation of the Act.

Based on our examination of the legislative history, we agree with the Court of Appeals that it is unilluminating . . . . We find that the legislative history as a whole is silent on the precise issue before us. It is, however, consistent with the view that the EPA should have broad discretion in implementing the policies of the 1977 Amendments.

More importantly, that history plainly identifies the policy concerns that motivated the enactment; the plant wide definition is fully consistent with one of those concerns—the allowance of reasonable economic growth—and, whether or not we believe it most effectively implements the other, we must recognize that the EPA has advanced a reasonable explanation for its conclusion that the regulations serve the environmental objectives as well . . . . Indeed its reasoning is supported by the public record developed in the rulemaking process, as well as by certain private studies.

Our review of the EPA's varying interpretations of the word "source"—both before and after the 1977 Amendments—convinces us that the agency primarily responsible for administering this important legislation has consistently interpreted it flexibly—not in a sterile textual vacuum, but in the context of implementing policy decisions in a technical and complex arena. The fact that the agency has from time to time changed its interpretation of the term "source" does not, as respondents argue, lead us to conclude that no deference should be accorded the agency's interpretation of the statute. An initial agency interpretation is not instantly carved in stone. On the contrary, the agency, to engage in informed rulemaking, must consider varying interpretations and the wisdom of its policy on a continuing basis. Moreover, the fact that the agency has adopted different definitions in different contexts adds force to the argument that the definition itself is flexible, particularly since Congress has never indicated any disapproval of a flexible reading of the statute.

Significantly, it was not the agency in 1980, but rather the Court of Appeals that read the statute inflexibly to command a plant wide definition for programs designed to maintain clean air and to forbid such a definition for programs designed to improve air quality. The distinction the court drew may well be a sensible one, but our labored review of the problem has surely disclosed that it is not a distinction that Congress ever articulated itself, or one that the EPA found in the statute before the courts began to review the legislative work product . . . .

The arguments over policy that are advanced in the parties' briefs create the impression that respondents are now waging in a judicial forum a specific policy battle which they ultimately lost in the agency and in the 32 jurisdictions opting for the "bubble concept," but one which was never waged in Congress. Such policy arguments are more properly addressed to legislators or administrators, not to judges.

In these cases the Administrator's interpretation represents a reasonable accommodation of manifestly competing interests and is entitled to deference: the regulatory scheme is technical and complex, the agency considered the matter in a detailed and reasoned fashion, and the decision involves reconciling conflicting policies. Congress intended to accommodate both interests, but did not do so itself on the level of specificity presented by these cases. Perhaps that body consciously desired the Administrator to strike that balance at this level, thinking that those with great expertise and charged with responsibility for administering the provision would be in a better position to do so; perhaps it simply did not consider the question at this level; and perhaps Congress was unable to forge a coalition on either side of the question, and those on each side decided to take their chances with the scheme devised by the agency. For judicial purposes, it matters not which of these things occurred.

Judges are not experts in the field, and are not part of either political branch of the Government. Courts must, in some cases, reconcile competing political interests, but not on the basis of the judges' personal policy preferences. In contrast, an agency to which Congress has delegated policymaking may, within the limits of that delegation, properly rely upon the incumbent administration's views of wise policy to inform its judgments. While agencies are not directly accountable to the people, the Chief Executive is, and it is entirely appropriate for this political branch of the Government to make such policy choices—resolving the competing interests which Congress itself either inadvertently did not resolve, or intentionally left to be resolved by the agency charged with the administration of the statute in light of everyday realities.

When a challenge to an agency construction of a statutory provision, fairly conceptualized, really centers on the wisdom of the agency's policy, rather than whether it is a reasonable choice within a gap left open by Congress, the challenge must fail. In such a case, federal judges—who have no constituency—have a duty to respect legitimate policy choices made by those who do. The responsibilities for assessing the wisdom of such policy choices and resolving the struggle between competing views of the public interest are not judicial ones: "Our Constitution vests such responsibilities in the political branches." *TVA v. Hill,* 437 U.S. 153, 195 (1978).

We hold that the EPA's definition of the term "source" is a permissible construction of the statute which seeks to accommodate progress in reducing air pollution with economic growth. "The Regulations which the Administrator has adopted provide what the agency could allowably view as . . . [an] effective reconciliation of these twofold ends . . . ." *United States v. Shimer,* 367 U.S., at 383.

The judgment of the Court of Appeals is reversed.

NOTES AND QUESTIONS

(1) Was the Supreme Court correct in determining that courts should give conclusive weight to "permissible" statutory interpretations of administrative agencies with regard to ambiguous statutory provisions? Are agencies necessarily better situated than courts to perform that function? Is the Court's view in *Chevron* consistent with the Administrative Procedure Act? (That statute provides, in part, that reviewing courts are to "decide all relevant questions of law, interpret constitutional and statutory provisions, and determine the meaning or applicability of the terms of an agency action." *See* 5 U.S.C. § 706).

(2) The *Chevron* decision has been subject to scholarly and judicial criticism. In the view of one commentator: "Administrative agencies are constrained by statute, that is, law, and the mere fact that the statute is ambiguous shouldn't give the agency, of all people, the authority to decide on the meaning of the limitation. The cute way in which it's sometimes put is that foxes shouldn't guard henhouses. If *Chevron* is taken to mean that agencies judge the scope of their own authority, then one has precisely that problem." Sunstein, *Judicial Review of Administrative Action in A Conservative Era,* 39 Admin. L. Rev. 353, 362 (1987). Is this a fair evaluation of the *Chevron* doctrine? *See also* Breyer, *Judicial Review of Questions of Law and Policy,* 38 Admin. L. Rev. 363 (1986) (The *Chevron* doctrine is "seriously overbroad, counter productive and sometimes useless.").

(3) The *Chevron* decision has been widely cited by lower federal courts as a basis for deferring to agency decisions. Nonetheless, there is evidence that the case has often been ignored by the U.S. Supreme Court itself in its subsequent decisions. *See* Merrill, *Judicial Deference to Executive Precedent,* 101 Yale L. J. 969 (1992) and Merrill, *Textualism and the Future of the* Chevron *Doctrine,* 72 Wash. U. L. Q. 351 (1994).

(4) In its post-*Chevron* decisions, the U.S. Supreme Court has sometimes rejected administrative agency interpretations of statutory provisions. *See, e.g., Immigration and Naturalization Service v. Cardoza-Fonseca,* 408 U.S. 421 (1988), in which the Court declined to endorse the INS's construction of the phrase "well founded fear" of prosecution (as a determinant of when refugees are entitled to asylum). *See also Board of Governors v. Dimension Financial Corp.,* 474 U.S. 361 (1986), where the Court concluded that (notwithstanding a contrary interpretation by the Federal Reserve Board) the statutory term "book" is free from ambiguity.

(5) The *Chevron* case had considerable significance as a Clean Air Act precedent, as well as an administrative law decision. *See* Chapter 2, § 2.03.

§ 8.03 Standing-to-Sue in Environmental Law Suits

The Administrative Procedure Act

Pub. L. No. 89-554, 80 Stat. 392 (1966), 5 U.S.C. §§ 701, 702(Supp. V. 1965-69) as amended

§ 701. Application; definitions

(a) This chapter applies, according to the provisions thereof, except to the extent that—

(1) statutes preclude judicial review; or

(2) agency action is committed to agency discretion by law.

§ 702. Right of review

A person suffering legal wrong because of agency action, or adversely affected or aggrieved by agency action within the meaning of a relevant statute, is entitled to judicial review thereof. An action in a court of the United States seeking relief other than money damages and stating a claim that an agency or an officer or employee thereof acted or failed to act in an official capacity or under color of legal authority shall not be dismissed nor relief therein be denied on the ground that it is against the United States or that the United States is an indispensable party. The United States may be named as a defendant in any such action, and a judgment or decree may be entered against the United States. *Provided,* That any mandatory or injunctive decree shall specify the Federal officer or officers (by name or by title) and their successors in office, personally responsible for compliance. Nothing herein (1) affects other limitations on judicial review or the power or duty of the court to dismiss any action or deny relief on any other appropriate legal or equitable ground; or (2) confers authority to grant relief if any other statute that grants consent to suit expressly or impliedly forbids the relief which is sought. As amended Pub. L. 94-574, § 1, Oct. 21, 1976, 90 Stat. 2721.

SIERRA CLUB v. MORTON

United States Supreme Court (1972)
405 U.S. 727, 92 S. Ct. 1361, 31 L. Ed. 2d 636

Stewart, J.:

[The court restates the facts as given in the court below, at 433 F.2d 24 (9th Cir. 1970), *sub nom. Sierra Club v. Hickel.* Petitioners were seeking to enjoin the U.S. Forest Service from proceeding with a plan to turn Mineral King, an environmentally valuable area of great natural beauty in the Sierra

Nevada Mountains adjacent to Sequoia National Park, into a major recreational development complex of motels, restaurants, swimming pools, parking lots and other structures designed to accommodate 14,000 visitors daily. Other facilities were to include ski lifts, ski trails, cog assisted railways and utility installations. To provide access to the resort, the construction of a 20-mile highway was proposed which would traverse Sequoia National Park, as would a proposed high voltage power line needed to provide electricity for the recreational complex. The case antedated the enactment of NEPA.]

II

The first question presented is whether the Sierra Club has alleged facts that entitle it to obtain judicial review of the challenged action. Whether a party has a sufficient stake in an otherwise justiciable controversy to obtain judicial resolution of that controversy is what has traditionally been referred to as the question of standing to sue . . . .

The Sierra Club relies upon § 10 of the Administrative Procedure Act (APA), 80 Stat. 392, 5 U.S.C. § 702, which provides:

> "A person suffering legal wrong because of agency action, or adversely affected or aggrieved by agency action within the meaning of a relevant statute, is entitled to judicial review thereof . . . ."

In *Data Processing,* the injury claimed by the petitioners consisted of harm to their competitive position in the computer servicing market through a ruling by the Comptroller of the Currency that national banks might perform data processing services for their customers. In *Barlow,* the petitioners were tenant farmers who claimed that certain regulations of the Secretary of Agriculture adversely affected their economic position vis-a-vis their landlords. These palpable economic injuries have long been recognized as sufficient to lay the basis for standing, with or without a specific statutory provision for judicial review. Thus, neither *Data Processing* nor *Barlow* addressed itself to the question, which has arisen with increasing frequency in federal courts in recent years, as to what must be alleged by persons who claim injury of a noneconomic nature to interests that are widely shared. That question is presented in this case.

III

The injury alleged by the Sierra Club will be incurred entirely by reason of the change in the uses to which Mineral King will be put, and the attendant change in the aesthetics and ecology of the area. Thus, in referring to the road to be built through Sequoia National Park, the complaint alleged that the development "would destroy or otherwise affect the scenery, natural and historic objects and wildlife of the park and would impair the enjoyment of the park for future generations." We do not question that this type of harm may amount to an "injury in fact" sufficient to lay the basis for standing under § 10 of the APA. Aesthetic and environmental well-being, like economic well-being, are important ingredients of the quality of life in our society, and the fact that particular environmental interests are shared by the many rather than the few does not make them less deserving of legal protection through the judicial process. But the "injury in fact" test requires more than an injury to a cognizable interest. It requires that the party seeking review be himself among the injured.

The impact of the proposed changes in the environment of Mineral King will not fall indiscriminately upon every citizen. The alleged injury will be felt directly only by those who use Mineral King and Sequoia National Park, and for whom the aesthetic and recreational values of the area will be lessened by the highway and ski resort. The Sierra Club failed to allege that it or its members would be affected in any of their activities or pastimes by the Disney development. Nowhere in the pleadings or affidavits did the Club state that its members use Mineral King for any purpose, much less that they use it in any that would be significantly affected by the proposed actions of the respondents.

The Club apparently regarded any allegations of individualized injury as superfluous, on the theory that this was a "public" action involving questions as to the use of natural resources, and that the Club's longstanding concern with and expertise in such matters were sufficient to give it standing as "representative of the public."[1] This theory reflects a misunderstanding of our cases involving so-called "public actions" in the area of administrative law.

The origin of the theory advanced by the Sierra Club may be traced to a dictum in *Scripps-Howard Radio, Inc. v. FCC,* 316 U.S. 4, 62 S.Ct. 875, 86 L.Ed. 1229, in which the licensee of a radio station in Cincinnati, Ohio, sought a stay of an order of the FCC allowing another radio station in a nearby city to change its frequency and increase its range. In discussing its power to grant a stay, the Court noted that "these private litigants have standing only as representatives of the public interest." *Id.,* at 14, 62 S.Ct. at 882. But that observation did not describe the basis upon which the appellant was allowed to obtain judicial review as a "person aggrieved" within the meaning of the statute involved in that case, since *Scripps-Howard* was clearly "aggrieved" by reason of the economic injury that it would suffer as a result of the Commission's action. The Court's statement was rather directed to the theory upon which Congress had authorized judicial review of the Commission's actions. That theory had been described earlier in *FCC v. Sanders Bros. Radio Station,* 309 U.S. 470, 477, 60 S.Ct. 693, 698, 84 L.Ed. 869, as follows:

> Congress had some purpose in enacting section 402(b)(2). It may have been of opinion that one likely to be financially injured by the issue of a license would be the only person having a sufficient interest to bring to the attention of the appellate court errors of law in the action of the Commission in granting the license. It is within the power of Congress to confer such standing to prosecute an appeal.

Taken together, *Sanders* and *Scripps-Howard* thus established a dual proposition: the fact of economic injury is what gives a person standing to seek

[1] This approach to the question of standing was adopted by the Court of Appeals for the Second Circuit in Citizens Committee for Hudson Valley v. Volpe, 425 F.2d 97, 105:

"We hold, therefore, that the public interest in environmental resources—an interest created by statutes affecting the issuance of this permit—is a legally protected interest affording these plaintiffs, as responsible representatives of the public, standing to obtain judicial review of agency action alleged to be in contravention of that public interest."

judicial review under the statute, but once review is properly invoked, that person may argue the public interest in support of his claim that the agency has failed to comply with its statutory mandate. It was in the latter sense that the "standing" of the appellant in *Scripps-Howard* existed only as a "representative of the public interest." It is in a similar sense that we have used the phrase "private attorney general" to describe the function performed by persons upon whom Congress has conferred the right to seek judicial review of agency action. *See Data Processing, supra,* 397 U.S., at 154, 90 S.Ct., at 830.

The trend of cases arising under the APA and other statutes authorizing judicial review of federal agency action has been towards recognizing that injuries other than economic harm are sufficient to bring a person within the meaning of the statutory language, and towards discarding the notion that an injury that is widely shared is *ipso facto* not an injury sufficient to provide the basis for judicial review. We noted this development with approval in *Data Processing, supra,* at 154, 90 S.Ct., at 830, in saying that the interest alleged to have been injured "may reflect 'aesthetic, conservational, and recreational' as well as economic values." But broadening the categories of injury that may be alleged in support of standing is a different matter from abandoning the requirement that the party seeking review must have himself suffered an injury.

Some courts have indicated a willingness to take this latter step by conferring standing upon organizations that have demonstrated "an organizational interest in the problem" of environmental or consumer protection. *Environmental Defense Fund, Inc. v. Hardin,* 138 U.S. App. D.C. 391, 428 F.2d 1093, 1097. It is clear that an organization whose members are injured may represent those members in a proceeding for judicial review. *See, e.g., NAACP v. Button,* 371 U.S. 415, 428, 83 S.Ct. 328, 335, 9 L.Ed.2d 405. But a mere "interest in a problem," no matter how longstanding the interest and no matter how qualified the organization is in evaluating the problem, is not sufficient by itself to render the organization "adversely affected" or "aggrieved" within the meaning of the APA. The Sierra Club is a large and long-established organization, with an historic commitment to the cause of protecting our Nation's natural heritage from man's depredations. But if a "special interest" in this subject were enough to entitle the Sierra Club to commence this litigation, there would appear to be no objective basis upon which to disallow a suit by any other bona fide "special interest" organization however small or short-lived. And if any group with a bona fide "special interest" could initiate such litigation, it is difficult to perceive why any individual citizen with the same bona fide special interest would not also be entitled to do so.

The requirement that a party seeking review must allege facts showing that he is himself adversely affected does not insulate executive action from judicial review, nor does it prevent any public interests from being protected through the judicial process. It does serve as at least a rough attempt to put the decision as to whether review will be sought in the hands of those who have a direct stake in the outcome. That goal would be undermined were we to construe the APA to authorize judicial review at the behest of organizations or individuals who seek to do no more than vindicate their own value preferences through the judicial process. The principle that the Sierra Club would have us establish in this case would do just that.

As we conclude that the Court of Appeals was correct in its holding that the Sierra Club lacked standing to maintain this action, we do not reach any other questions presented in the petition, and we intimate no view on the merits of the complaint. The judgment is

Affirmed. Mr. Justice POWELL and Mr. Justice REHNQUIST took no part in the consideration or decision of this case. Mr. Justice DOUGLAS, dissenting.

I share the views of my Brother BLACKMUN and would reverse the judgement below.

The critical question of "standing" would be simplified and also put neatly in focus if we fashioned a federal rule that allowed environmental issues to be litigated before federal agencies or federal courts in the name of the inanimate object about to be despoiled, defaced, or invaded by roads and bulldozers and where injury is the subject of public outrage. Contemporary public concern for protecting nature's ecological equilibrium should lead to the conferral of standing upon environmental objects to sue for their own preservation . . . .

Inanimate objects are sometimes parties in litigation. A ship has a legal personality, a fiction found useful for maritime purposes. The corporation sole—a creature of ecclesiastical law—is an acceptable adversary and large fortunes ride on its cases. The ordinary corporation is a "person" for purposes of the adjudicatory processes, whether it represents proprietary, spiritual, aesthetic, or charitable causes.

So it should be as respects valleys, alpine meadows, rivers, lakes, estuaries, beaches, ridges, groves of trees, swampland, or even air that feels the destructive pressures of modern technology and modern life. The river, for example, is the living symbol of all the life it sustains or nourishes—fish, aquatic insects, water ouzels, otter, fisher, deer, elk, bear, and all other animals, including man, who are dependent on it or who enjoy it for its sight, its sound, or its life. The river as plaintiff speaks for the ecological unit of life that is part of it. Those people who have a meaningful relation to that body of water—whether it be a fisherman, a canoeist, a zoologist, or a logger—must be able to speak for the values which the river represents and which are threatened with destruction.

The voice of the inanimate object, therefore, should not be stilled. That does not mean that the judiciary takes over the managerial functions from the federal agency. It merely means that before these priceless bits of Americana (such as a valley, an alpine meadow, a river, or a lake) are forever lost or are so transformed as to be reduced to the eventual rubble of our urban environment, the voice of the existing beneficiaries of these environmental wonders should be heard . . . .

Those inarticulate members of the ecological group cannot speak. But those people who have so frequented the place as to know its values and wonders will be able to speak for the entire ecological community . . . .

That, as I see it, is the issue of "standing" in the present case and controversy. Mr. Justice Blackmun, dissenting . . . .

The ultimate result of the Court's decision today, I fear, and sadly so, is that the 35.3 million-dollar-complex, over 10 times greater than the Forest Service's suggested minimum, will now hastily proceed to completion; that serious opposition to it will recede in discouragement; and that Mineral King, the "area of great natural beauty nestled in the Sierra Nevada Mountains," to use the Court's words, will become defaced, at least in part, and, like so many other areas, will cease to be "uncluttered by the products of civilization."

Rather than pursue the course the Court has chosen to take by its affirmance of the judgment of the Court of Appeals, I would adopt one of two alternatives:

1. I would reverse that judgment and, instead, approve the judgment of the District Court which recognized standing in the Sierra Club and granted preliminary relief. I would be willing to do this on condition that the Sierra Club forthwith amend its complaint to meet the specifications the Court prescribes for standing. If Sierra Club fails or refuses to take that step, so be it; the case will then collapse. But if it does amend, the merits will be before the trial court once again . . . . [T]he issues on the merits are substantial and deserve resolution. They assay new ground. They are crucial to the future of Mineral King. They raise important ramifications for the quality of the country's public land management. They pose the propriety of the "dual permit" device as a means of avoiding the 80-acre "recreation and resort" limitation imposed by Congress in 16 U.S.C. § 497, an issue that apparently has never been litigated, and is clearly substantial in light of the congressional expansion of the limitation in 1956 arguably to put teeth into the old, unrealistic five-acre limitation. In fact, they concern the propriety of the 80-acre permit itself and the consistency of the entire, enormous development with the statutory purposes of the Sequoia Game Refuge of which the Valley is a part. In the context of this particular development, substantial questions are raised about the use of National Park area for Disney purposes for a new high speed road and a 66,000-volt power line to serve the complex. Lack of compliance with existing administrative regulations is also charged. These issues are not shallow or perfunctory.

2. Alternatively, I would permit an imaginative expansion of our traditional concepts of standing in order to enable an organization such as the Sierra Club, possessed, as it is, of pertinent, bona fide and well-recognized attributes and purposes in the area of environment, to litigate environmental issues. This incursion upon tradition need not be very extensive. Certainly, it should be no cause for alarm. It is no more progressive than was the decision in *Data Processing* itself. It need only recognize the interest of one who has a provable, sincere, dedicated, and established status. We need not fear that Pandora's box will be opened or that there will be no limit to the number of those who desire to participate in an environmental litigation. The courts will exercise appropriate restraints just as they have exercised them in the past. Who would have suspected 20 years ago that the concepts of standing enunciated in *Data Processing* and *Barlow* would be the measure for today? And Mr. Justice DOUGLAS, in his eloquent opinion, has imaginatively suggested another

means and one, in its own way, with obvious, appropriate and self-imposed limitations as to standing. As I read what he has written, he makes only one addition to the customary criteria (the existence of a genuine dispute; the assurance of adversariness; and a conviction that the party whose standing is challenged will adequately represent the interests he assets), that is, that the litigant be one who speaks knowingly for the environmental values he asserts . . . . (The dissenting opinion of Mr. Justice Brennan has been omitted.)

NOTES AND QUESTIONS

(1) Was the Supreme Court correct in making some use of controverted resources, by an environmental organization's members, a key factor in determining whether that organization should have standing to sue? Should other factors be given more weight? Might natural resources have value for persons who are never physically present on or near them?

(2) How do you evaluate the suggestion of Justice Douglas, in dissent, that standing to sue in environmental suits should be granted to persons who know the "values and wonders" of a place and who bring suit in the name of a threatened natural resource or inanimate object? Could "public interest organizations" that represent the perspective of business interests have standing to sue under that approach? Should they? In fact, Douglas' dissent contains a legal inaccuracy. Inanimate objects have never actually been the plaintiff in any litigation. In admiralty, and in other areas, such objects were made defendants (as opposed to plaintiffs) because the real defendant (*i.e.*, the owner of the object) was beyond the reach of the jurisdiction. To what extent does this mistake undercut the persuasiveness of Douglas' opinion?

(3) In his dissenting opinion, Justice Blackmun suggested that the court might have granted standing to the Sierra Club, in this case, based upon its "provable, sincere, dedicated and established status" as an environmental organization. Would Blackmun's suggestion rule out standing to sue for smaller, newer environmental groups and/or for ad hoc committees of neighbors who join together in opposition to what they perceive as an environmentally unsound projects? Is such a distinction justifiable?

(4) In a footnote to its opinion in *Sierra Club v. Morton,* the Supreme Court indicated that, when the case returned to the U.S. District Court, the Sierra Club was to be permitted to amend its complaint. On remand the Club did so, alleging that some of its individual members used the Mineral King area, and also adding a new claim based upon the National Environmental Policy Act. Following some further litigation—and the preparation of an environmental impact statement—the proposal to build a ski resort was abandoned and, in 1978, Mineral King was made part of the Sequoia National Park.

(5) To what extent should courts evaluate the motivations of individuals who make use of environmentally sensitive resources? *See Regional Ass'n of Concerned Environmentalists v. U.S. Dep't of Agriculture*, 765 F. Supp. 502 (S.D. Ill. 1990), in which the court denied standing to an individual who had previously made a dozen visits to a forested area on the basis that those visits were in pursuit of an "ongoing crusade of environmental activism," rather than being for recreational purposes. Is this a sound result?

UNITED STATES v. SCRAP

United States Supreme Court (1973)
412 U.S. 669, 93 S. Ct. 2405, 37 L. Ed. 2d 254

Stewart J.:

Under the Interstate Commerce Act, the initiative for rate increases remains with the railroads. But in the absence of special permission from the Interstate Commerce Commission, a railroad seeking an increase must provide at least 30 days notice to the Commission and the public before putting the new rate into effect. 49 U.S.C. § 6(3). During that 30-day period, the Commission may suspend the operation of the proposed rate for a maximum of seven months pending an investigation and decision on the lawfulness of the new rates. 49 U.S.C. § 15(7). At the end of the seven month period, the carrier may put the suspended rate into effect unless the Commission has earlier completed its investigation and found the rate unlawful.

Proceeding under this regulatory scheme, on December 13, 1971, substantially all of the railroads in the United States requested Commission authorization to file on 5 days' notice a 2.5% surcharge on nearly all freight rates. The railroads sought a January 1, 1972, effective date for the new rates. The surcharge was proposed as an interim emergency measure designed to produce some $246 million annually in increased revenues pending adoption of selective rate increases on a permanent basis.

As justification for the proposed surcharge, the railroads alleged increasing costs and severely inadequate revenues . . . . [The Court here summarizes facts tending to show the financial plight of the railroads, and recounts some intervening procedures before the ICC.]

On January 5, 1972, the railroads refiled the surcharge, to become effective on February 5, 1972. Shippers, competing carriers, and other interested persons requested the Commission to suspend the tariff for the statutory seven-month period. Various environmental groups, including Students Challenging Regulatory Agency Procedures (SCRAP) and the Environmental Defense Fund (EDF), two of the appellees here, protested that failure to suspend the surcharge would cause their members "economic, recreational and aesthetic harm." Specifically, they claimed that the rate structure would discourage the use of "recyclable" materials, and promote the use of new raw materials that compete with scrap, thereby adversely affecting the environment by encouraging unwarranted mining, lumbering, and other extractive activities. The members of these environmental groups were allegedly forced to pay more for finished products and their use of forests and streams was allegedly impaired because of unnecessary destruction of timber and extraction of raw materials, and the accumulation of otherwise recyclable solid and liquid waste materials. The railroads replied that since this was a general rate increase, recyclable materials would not be made any less competitive relative to other commodities, and that in the past general rate increases had not discouraged the movement of scrap materials.

The Commission issued an order on February 1, 1972, shortly before the surcharge would have automatically become effective. It recognized that "the railroads have a critical need for additional revenue from their interstate freight rates and charges to offset, in part, recently incurred increased operating costs," and announced its decision not to suspend the 2.5% surcharge for the seven-month statutory period. In anticipation of the proposed permanent selective increases to be filed by the railroads and to avoid further complications of the tariff rates, the Commission specified that its refusal to suspend was conditioned upon the carriers' setting an expiration date for the surcharge of no later than June 5, 1972. The Commission ordered the investigation into the railroads' rates which had been instituted by its December 21 order to be held in abeyance until the carriers requested permission to file the indicated permanent rate increases on a selective basis. With respect to the appellees' environmental arguments, the Commission found that "the involved general increase will have no significant adverse effect on the movement of traffic by railway or on the quality of the human environment within the meaning of the [National] Environmental Policy Act of 1969."

The proposed permanent selective increases, averaging 4.1%, were subsequently filed with the Commission, and various parties again requested that these proposed rates also be suspended. By order served March 6, 1972, the Commission did not grant the railroads' request to have the selective increases go into effect on April 1, 1972, as they had sought but it allowed the carriers to republish their rates to become effective on May 1, 1972, upon not less than 45 days' notice to the public. The carriers did republish the rates, and on April 24, 1972 the Commission entered an order suspending the proposed selective increase for the full seven-month period allowed by statute, up to and including November 30, 1972. The investigation into the increased rate was continued. Since the selective increases were to supplant the temporary surcharge, and since they had been suspended, the Commission modified its February 1 order and authorized the railroads to eliminate the June 5 expiration date for the surcharge and to continue collecting the surcharge until November 30, 1972.

I

On May 12, 1972, SCRAP filed the present suit against the United States and the Commission in the District Court for the District of Columbia seeking, along with other relief, a preliminary injunction to restrain enforcement of the Commission's February 1 and April 24 order allowing the railroads to collect the 2.5% surcharge.

SCRAP stated in its amended complaint that it was "an unincorporated association formed by five law students . . . in September, 1971. Its primary purpose is to enhance the quality of the human environment for its members, and for all citizens . . . ." To establish standing to bring this suit, SCRAP repeated many of the allegations it had made before the Commission in Ex parte 281. It claimed that each of its members "suffered economic, recreational and aesthetic harm directly as a result of the adverse environmental impact of the railroad freight structure, as modified by the Commission's actions to date in Ex parte 281." Specifically, SCRAP alleged that each of its members was caused to pay more for finished products, that each of its members "uses the forests, rivers, streams, mountains, and other natural resources surrounding the Washington Metropolitan area and at his legal residence, for camping, hiking, fishing, sightseeing, and other recreational [and] aesthetic purposes," and that these uses have been adversely affected by the increased freight rates, that each of its members breathes the air within the Washington metropolitan area and the area of his legal residence and that this air has suffered increased pollution caused by the modified rate structure, and that each member has been forced to pay increased taxes because of the sums which must be expended to dispose of otherwise reusable waste materials.

The main thrust of SCRAP's complaint was that the Commission's decisions of February 1 and April 24, insofar as they declined to suspend the 2.5% surcharge, were unlawful because the Commission had failed to include a detailed environmental impact statement as required by § 102(2)(C) of the National Environmental Policy Act of 1969 (NEPA), 42 U.S.C. § 4332(2)(C), NEPA requires such a statement in "every recommendation or report on proposals for legislation and other major Federal actions significantly affecting the quality of the human environment . . . ." *Ibid.* SCRAP contended that because of its alleged adverse impact upon recycling, the Commission's action with respect to the surcharge constituted a major federal action significantly affecting the environment.

Three additional environmental groups, also appellees here, were allowed to intervene as plaintiffs, and a group of railroads, appellants here, intervened as defendants to support the 2.5% surcharge. After a single district judge had denied the defendants' motion to dismiss and SCRAP's motion for a temporary restraining order, a statutory three-judge district court was convened pursuant to 28 U.S.C. §§ 2325, 2284, to decide the motion for a preliminary injunction and the cross-motion to dismiss the complaint.

On July 10, 1972, the District Court filed an opinion, 346 F. Supp. 189, and entered an injunction prohibiting the Commission "from permitting," and the railroads "from collecting" the 2.5% surcharge "insofar as that surcharge relates to goods being transported for purposes of recycling, pending further order of this court."

The court first rejected the contention that the appellees were without standing to sue because they allegedly had no more than "a general interest in seeing that the law is enforced," *id.,* at 195, and distinguished our recent decision in *Sierra Club v. Morton,* 405 U.S. 727, 31 L.Ed.2d 636, 92 S.Ct. 1361, on the basis that, unlike the petitioner in Sierra Club, the environmental groups here had alleged that their members used the forests, streams, mountains, and other resources in the Washington area and that this use was disturbed by the environmental impact caused by nonuse of recyclable goods.

Second, the court found that its power to grant an injunction was not barred by our decision in *Arrow Transportation Co. v. Southern R. Co.,* 372 U.S. 658, 667, 10 L.Ed.2d 52, 83 S.Ct. 984, where we held that in enacting 49 U.S.C. § 15(7), Congress had intentionally vested "in the Commission the sole and exclusive power to suspend and [withdrew] from the judiciary any pre-existing power to grant injunctive relief." The court reasoned that NEPA "implicitly confers authority on the federal courts to enjoin *any* federal action taken in violation of NEPA's procedural requirements so long as the review is confined to a determination as to whether the procedural requisites of NEPA have been followed." 346 F. Supp. at 197 and n. 11.

Finally, turning to the merits, the court concluded that the Commissioner's April 24 decision not to suspend the surcharge for the statutory seven-month period was a " 'major federal action significantly affecting the quality of the human environment.' " *Ibid.,* at 199. On the premise that an environmental impact statement is required "whenever the action *arguably* will have an adverse environmental impact," *id.,* at 201, the court held that "the danger of an adverse impact is sufficiently real to require a statement in this case." *Ibid*

The District Court declined to stay its injunctive order pending appeal to this Court, and on July 19, 1972, The Chief Justice, as Circuit Justice for the District of Columbia Circuit, denied applications to stay the preliminary injunction. 409 U.S. 1207, 34 L.Ed.2d 662, 93 S.Ct. 683.

II

The appellants challenge the appellees' standing to sue, arguing that the allegations in the pleadings as to standing were vague, unsubstantiated, and insufficient under our recent decision in *Sierra Club v. Morton, supra.* The appellees respond that, unlike the petitioner in Sierra Club, their pleadings sufficiently alleged that they were "adversely affected" or "aggrieved" within the meaning of the Administrative Procedure Act (APA), 5 U.S.C. § 702[2] and they point specifically to the allegations that their members used the forests, streams, mountains, and other resources in the Washington Metropolitan area for camping, hiking, fishing, and sightseeing, and that this use was disturbed by the adverse environmental impact caused by the nonuse of recyclable goods brought about by a rate increase on those commodities. The District Court found these allegations sufficient to withstand a motion to dismiss. We agree.

The petitioner in *Sierra Club,* "a large and long-established organization, with a historic commitment to the cause of protecting our Nation's natural heritage from man's depredations," 405 U.S., at 739, 31 L.Ed.2d 636, sought a declaratory judgment and an injunction to restrain federal officials from approving the creation of an extensive ski-resort development in the scenic Mineral King Valley of the Sequoia National Forest. The Sierra Club claimed standing to maintain its "public interest" lawsuit because it had " 'a special interest in the conservation and the sound maintenance of the national parks, game refuges and forests of the country . . . .' " *Id.,* at 730, 31 L.Ed.2d 636. We held those allegations insufficient.

---

[2] Like the petitioner in Sierra Club, the appellees here base their standing to sue upon the APA, 5 U.S.C. § 702, which provides:

"A person suffering legal wrong because of agency actions, or adversely affected or aggrieved by agency action within the meaning of a relevant statute, is entitled to judicial review thereof."

Relying upon our prior decisions in *Data Processing Service v. Camp,* 397 U.S. 150, 25 L.Ed.2d 184, 90 S.Ct. 827, and *Barlow v. Collins,* 397 U.S. 159, 25 L.Ed.2d 192, 90 S.Ct. 832, we held that § 702 of the APA conferred standing to obtain judicial review of agency action only upon those who could show "that the challenged action had caused them 'injury in fact,' and where the alleged injury was to an interest 'arguably within the zone of interests to be protected or regulated' by the statutes that the agencies were claimed to have violated." 405 U.S. at 733, 31 L.Ed.2d 636.[3]

In interpreting "injury in fact" we made it clear that standing was not confined to those who could show "economic harm," although both Data Processing and Barlow had involved that kind of injury. Nor, we said, could the fact that many persons shared the same injury be sufficient reason to disqualify from seeking review of an agency's action any person who had in fact suffered injury. Rather, we explained: "Aesthetic and environmental well-being, like economic well-being, are important ingredients of the quality of life in our society, and the fact that particular environmental interests are shared by the many rather than the few does not make them less deserving of legal protection through the judicial process." *Id.,* at 734, 31 L.Ed.2d 636. Consequently, neither the fact that the appellees here claimed only a harm to their use and enjoyment of the natural resources of the Washington area, nor the fact that all those who use those resources suffered the same harm, deprives them of standing.

In *Sierra Club,* though, we went on to stress the importance of demonstrating that the party seeking review be himself among the injured, for it is this requirement that gives a litigant a direct stake in the controversy and prevents the judicial process from becoming no more than a vehicle for the vindication of the value interests of concerned bystanders. No such specific injury was alleged in *Sierra Club.* In that case the asserted harm "will be felt directly only by those who use Mineral King and Sequoia National Park, and for whom the aesthetic and recreational values of the area will be lessened by the highway and ski resort," *id.* at 735, 31 L.Ed.2d 636. Yet "[t]he Sierra Club failed to allege that it or its members would be affected in any of their activities or pastimes by the . . . development." *Ibid.* Here, by contrast, the appellees claimed that the specific and allegedly illegal action of the Commission would directly harm them in their use of the natural resources of the Washington Metropolitan Area.

Unlike the specific and geographically limited federal action of which the petitioner complained in *Sierra Club,* the challenged agency action in this case is applicable to substantially all of the Nation's railroads, and thus allegedly has an adverse environmental impact on all the natural resources of the country. Rather than a limited group of persons who used a picturesque valley in California, all persons who utilize the scenic resources of the country, and indeed all who breathe its air, could claim harm similar to that alleged by

[3] As in Sierra Club, it is unnecessary to reach any question concerning the scope of the "zone of interests" test or its application to this case. It is undisputed that the "environmental interest" that the appellees seek to protect is within the interests to be protected by NEPA, and it is unnecessary to consider the various allegations of economic harm on which the appellees also relied in their pleadings and which the Government contends are outside the intended purposes of NEPA.

the environmental groups here. But we have already made it clear that standing is not to be denied simply because many people suffer the same injury. Indeed some of the cases on which we relied in *Sierra Club* demonstrated the patent fact that persons across the Nation could be adversely affected by the major governmental actions. *See, e.g., Environmental Defense Fund v. Hardin,* 428 F.2d 1093, 197 (interests of consumers affected by decision of Secretary of Agriculture refusing to suspend registration of certain pesticides containing DDT); *Reade v. Ewing,* 205 F.2d 630, 631-632 (interests of consumers of oleomargarine in fair labeling of product regulated by Federal Security Administration). To deny standing to persons who are in fact injured simply because many others are also injured, would mean that the most injurious and widespread Government actions could be questioned by nobody. We cannot accept that conclusion.

But the injury alleged here is also very different from that at issue in *Sierra Club* because here the alleged injury to the environment is far less direct and perceptible. The petitioner there complained about the construction of a specific project that would directly affect the Mineral King Valley. Here, the Court was asked to follow a far more attenuated line of causation to the eventual injury of which the appellees complained—a general rate increase would allegedly cause increased use of nonrecyclable commodities as compared to recyclable goods, thus resulting in the need to use more natural resources to produce such goods, some of which resources might be taken from the Washington area, and resulting in more refuse that might be discarded in national parks in the Washington area. The railroads protest that the appellees could never prove that a general increase in rates would have this effect, and they contend that these allegations were a ploy to avoid the need to show some injury in fact.

Of course, pleadings must be something more than an ingenious academic exercise in the conceivable. A plaintiff must allege that he has been or will in fact be perceptibly harmed by the challenged agency action, not that he can imagine circumstances in which he could be affected by the agency's action. And it is equally clear that the allegations must be true and capable of proof at trial. But we deal here simply with the pleadings in which the appellees alleged a specific and perceptible harm that distinguished them from other citizens who had not used the natural resources that were claimed to be affected.[4]

---

[4] The Government urges us to limit standing to those who have been "significantly" affected by agency action. But, even if we could begin to define what such a test would mean, we think it fundamentally misconceived. "Injury in fact" reflects the statutory requirement that a person be "adversely affected" or "aggrieved," and it serves to distinguish a person with a direct stake in the outcome of a litigation—even though small—from a person with a mere interest in the problem. We have allowed important interests to be vindicated by plaintiffs with no more at stake in the outcome of an action than a fraction of a vote, see Baker v. Carr, 369 U.S. 186, 7 L.Ed.2d 663, 82 S.Ct. 691; a five-dollar fine and costs, see McGowan v. Maryland, 366 U.S. 420, 6 L.Ed.2d 393, 81 S.Ct. 1101; and a $1.50 poll tax, Harper v. Virginia Bd. of Education, 383 U.S. 663, 16 L.Ed.2d 169, 87 S.Ct. 1079. While these cases were not dealing specifically with § 702 of the APA, we see no reason to adopt a more restrictive interpretation of "adversely affected" or "aggrieved." As Professor Davis has put it: "The basic idea that comes out in numerous cases is that an identifiable trifle is enough for standing to fight out a question of principle; the trifle is the basis for standing and the principle supplies the motivation." Davis, Standing: Taxpayers and Others, 35 U. Chi. L.Rev. 601, 613. *See also* K. Davis, Administrative Law Treatise §§ 22.09-5, 22.09-6 (Supp. 1970).

If, as the railroads now assert, these allegations were in fact untrue, then the appellants should have moved for summary judgment on the standing issue and demonstrated to the District Court that the allegations were sham and raised no genuine issue of fact. We cannot say on these pleadings that the appellees could not prove their allegations which, if proved, would place them squarely among those persons injured in fact by the Commission's action, and entitled under the clear import of *Sierra Club* to seek review. The District Court was correct in denying the appellants' motion to dismiss the complaint for failure to allege sufficient standing to bring this lawsuit. . . .

NOTES AND QUESTIONS

(1) Under the Supreme Court's approach in *SCRAP,* are environmental organizations nearly always able to make good-faith allegations sufficient to allow them to assert standing to sue in challenging the actions of a federal agency?

(2) In *SCRAP,* should the Supreme Court have given the broadest possible reading to the standing to sue doctrine, so as to allow virtually anyone to compel the preparation of an environmental impact statement required under the National Environmental Policy Act? For an argument to that effect, see Fletcher, *The Structure of Standing,* 98 Yale L. J. 221 (1988).

(3) As the other materials in this section suggest, the *SCRAP* case appears to be the "high water mark" in the Supreme Court's liberal approach to standing to sue in environmental suits. *See also Whitemore v. Arkansas,* 495 U.S. 149, 110 S. Ct., 1717, 109 L. Ed. 2d 135 (1990), in which the Court opined that *SCRAP* "surely went to the very outer limit of the law," and referred to the case as involving "[p]robably the most attenuated injury" that may serve as a foundational basis for standing. Please consider the extent to which *SCRAP* remains a viable decision as you read the following case.

LUJAN v. NATIONAL WILDLIFE FEDERATION

United States Supreme Court (1990)
497 U.S. 871, 110 S. Ct. 3177, 111 L. Ed. 2d 695

Scalia, J.:

In this case we must decide whether respondent, the National Wildlife Federation [hereinafter respondent], is a proper party to challenge actions of the Federal Government relating to certain public lands.

Respondent filed this action in 1985 in the United States District Court for the District of Columbia against petitioners the United States Department of Interior, the Secretary of Interior, and the Director of the Bureau of Land Management [BLM], an agency within the Department. In its amended complaint, respondent alleged that petitioners had violated the Federal Land Policy and Management Act of 1976 [FLPMA], 43 U.S.C. § 1701 *et seq.*, (1982 ed.), the National Environmental Policy Act of 1969 (NEPA), 42 U.S.C. § 4321 *et seq.*, and § 10(e) of the Administrative Procedure Act (APA), 5 U.S.C. § 706, in the course of administering what the complaint called the "land withdrawal review program" of the BLM . . . .

[T]he Secretary of the Interior and the President have statutory authority to classify lands for the purpose of either disposal or retention by the Federal Government. In 1976, Congress passed the FLPMA, which repealed many of the miscellaneous laws governing disposal of public land, 43 U.S.C. § 1701 *et seq.*, and established a policy in favor of retaining public lands for multiple use management. It directed the Secretary to "prepare and maintain on a continuing basis an inventory of all public lands and their resource and other values," § 1711(a), required land use planning for public lands, and established criteria to be used for that purpose, § 1712. It provided that existing classifications of public lands were subject to review in the land use planning process, and that the Secretary could "modify or terminate any such classification consistent with such land use plans." § 1712(d) . . . . Finally it directed the Secretary within 15 years to review withdrawals in existence in 1976 in 11 western States, § 1714(l)(1) . . . . The activities undertaken by the BLM to comply with these various provisions constitute what respondent's amended complaint styles the BLM's "land withdrawal review program," which is the subject of the current litigation.

In its complaint, respondent averred generally that the reclassification of some withdrawn lands and the return of others to the public domain would open the lands up to mining activities, thereby destroying their natural beauty. Respondent alleged that petitioners, in the course of administering the Nation's public lands, had violated the FLPMA by failing to "develop, maintain, and, when appropriate, revise land use plans which provide by tracts or areas for the use of the public lands," § 1712(a), failing to submit recommendations as to withdrawals in the 11 western States to the President, § 1714 (l); failing to consider multiple uses for the disputed lands, § 1732(a), focusing inordinately on such uses as mineral exploitation and development; and failing to provide public notice of decisions, §§ 1701(a)(5), 1712 (c)(9), 1712 (f), and 1739(e). Respondent also claimed that petitioners had violated the NEPA . . . . Finally, respondent alleged that all of the above actions were "arbitrary, capricious, an abuse of discretion, or otherwise not in accordance with law," and should therefore be set aside pursuant to § 10(e) of the APA, 5 U.S.C. § 706. Appended to the amended complaint was a schedule of specific land status determinations, which the complaint stated had been "taken by the defendants since January 1, 1981"; each was identified by a listing in the Federal Register.

In December 1985, the District Court granted respondent's motion for a preliminary injunction prohibiting petitioners from "[m]odifying, terminating or altering any withdrawal, classification, or other designation governing the protection of lands in the public domain that was in effect on January 1, 1981," and from "[t]aking any action inconsistent" with any such withdrawal, classification, or designation. In a subsequent order, the court denied petitioners' motion under Rule 12(b) of the Federal Rules of Civil Procedure to dismiss the complaint for failure to demonstrate standing to challenge petitioners' actions under the APA, 5 U.S.C. § 702. The Court of Appeals affirmed both orders. NWF v. Burford, 878 F.2d 422 (1989) . . . .

The Court of Appeals pointed to the affidavits of two of respondent's members, Peggy Kay Peterson and Richard Erman, which claimed used of land "in the vicinity" of the land covered by two of the listed actions. Thus, the Court of Appeals concluded, there was "concrete indication that [respondent's] members use specific lands covered by the agency's Program and will be adversely affected by the agency's actions," and the complaint was "sufficiently specific for purposes of a motion to dismiss." . . . .

Back before the District Court, petitioners again claimed, this time by means of a motion for summary judgment under Rule 56 of the Federal Rules of Civil Procedure(which motion had been outstanding during the proceedings before the Court of Appeals), that respondent had no standing to seek judicial review of petitioners' actions under the APA. After argument on this motion, and in purported response to the court's postargument request for additional briefing, respondent submitted four additional member affidavits pertaining to the issue of standing. The District Court rejected them as untimely, vacated the injunction, and granted the Rule 56 motion to dismiss . . . .

The Court of Appeals reversed. It both found the Peterson and Erman affidavits sufficient in themselves, and held that it was an abuse of discretion not to consider the four additional affidavits as well . . . .

We turn . . . to whether the specific facts alleged in the two affidavits considered by the District Court raised a genuine issue of fact as to whether an "agency action" taken by petitioners caused respondent to be "adversely affected or aggrieved . . . within the meaning of a relevant statute." We assume, since it has been uncontested, that the allegedly affected interests set forth in the affidavits—"recreational use and aesthetic enjoyment"—are sufficiently related to the purposes of respondent association that respondent meets the requirements of § 702 if any of its members do . . .

We also think that whatever "adverse effect" or "aggrievement" is established by the affidavits was "within the meaning of the relevant statute"—*i.e.*, met the "zone of interests" test . . . . The only issue, then, is whether the facts alleged in the affidavits showed that those interests *of Peterson and Erman* were actually affected.

The Peterson affidavit averred:

> My recreational use and aesthetic enjoyment of federal lands, particularly those in the vicinity of South Pass-Green Mountain, Wyoming have been and continue to be adversely affected in fact by the unlawful actions of the Bureau and the Department. In particular, the South Pass-Green Mountain area of Wyoming has been opened to the staking of mining claims and oil and gas leasing, an action which threatens the aesthetic beauty and wildlife habitat potential of these lands.

Erman's affidavit was substantially the same as Peterson's, with respect to all except the area involved; he claimed use of land "in the vicinity of Grand Canyon National Park, the Arizona Strip (Kanab Plateau) and the Kaibab National Forest." The District Court found the Peterson affidavit inadequate for the following reasons:

> Peterson . . . claims that she uses federal lands *in the vicinity* of the South Pass-Green Mountain area of Wyoming for recreational purposes and for aesthetic enjoyment and that her recreational and aesthetic environment has been and continues to be adversely affected as a result of the decision of BLM to open it to the staking of mining claims and oil and gas leasing . . . . This decision [W-6228] opened up to mining approximately 4500 acres within a two million acre area, the balance of which, with the exception of 2000 acres, has always been open to mineral leasing and mining . . . . There is no showing that Peterson's recreational use and enjoyment extends to the particular 4500 acres covered by the decision to terminate classification to the remainder of the two million acres affected by the termination. All she claims is that she uses land "in the vicinity." The affidavit on its face contains only a bare allegation of injury, and fails to show specific facts supporting the affiant's allegation. 699 F. Supp. at 331.

The District Court found the Erman affidavit "similarly flawed."

> The magnitude of Erman's claimed injury stretches the imagination . . . .[T]he Arizona Strip consists of all lands in Arizona north and west of the Colorado River on approximately 5.5 million acres, an area one-eighth the size of the State of Arizona.

The Court of Appeals disagreed with the District Court's assessment as to the Peterson affidavit (and thus found it unnecessary to consider the Erman affidavit) for the following reasons:

> If Peterson was not referring to lands in this 4500-acre affected area, her allegation of impairment to her use and enjoyment would be meaningless, or perjurious . . . . [T]he trial court overlooks the fact that unless Peterson's language is read to refer to the lands affected by the Program, the affidavit is, at best, a meaningless document.
>
> At a minimum [sic], Peterson's affidavit is ambiguous regarding whether the adversely affected lands are the ones she uses. When presented with ambiguity on a motion for summary judgment, a District Court must resolve any factual issues of controversy in favor of the non-moving party . . . .

In ruling upon a Rule 56 motion, "a District Court must resolve any factual issues of controversy in favor of the non-moving party" only in the sense that, where the facts specifically averred by that party contradict facts specifically averred by the movant, the motion must be denied. That is a world apart from assuming that general averments embrace the specific facts needed to sustain the complaint . . . .

At the margins here is some room for debate as to how "specific" must be the "specific facts" that Rule 56(e) requires in a particular case. But where the fact in question is the one put in issue by the § 702 challenge here—whether one of respondent's members has been, or is threatened to be, "adversely affected or aggrieved" by Government action—Rule 56(e) is assuredly not satisfied by averments which state only that one of respondent's members uses unspecified portions of an immense tract of territory, on some portions of which mining activity has occurred or probably will occur by virtue of the governmental action. It will not do to "presume" the missing facts because without them the affidavits would not establish the injury that they generally allege. That converts the operation of Rule 56 to a circular promenade: plaintiff's complaint makes general allegation of injury; defendant contests through Rule 56 existence of specific facts to support injury; plaintiff responds with affidavit containing general allegation of injury, which must be deemed to constitute averment of requisite specific facts since otherwise allegation of injury would be unsupported (which is precisely what defendant claims it is).

Respondent places great reliance, as did the Court of Appeals, upon our decision in United States v. Students Challenging Regulatory Agency Procedures (SCRAP), 412 U.S. 699 (1973). The SCRAP opinion, whose expansive expression of what would suffice for § 702 review under its particular facts has never since been emulated by this Court, is of no relevance here since it involved not a Rule 56 motion for summary judgment but a Rule12(b) motion to dismiss on the pleadings . . . .

Respondent alleges that violation of the law is rampant within this program—failure to revise land use plans in proper fashion, failure to submit certain recommendations to Congress, failure to consider multiple use, inordinate focus upon mineral exploitation, failure to provide adequate environmental impact statements. Perhaps so. But respondent cannot seek *wholesale* improvement of this program by court decree, rather than in the offices of the Department or the halls of Congress, where programmatic improvements are normally made . . . .

In the present case, the individual actions of the BLM identified in the six affidavits can be regarded as rules of general applicability (a "rule" is defined in the APA as agency action of "general or particular applicability *and future effect,*" 5 U.S.C. § 551(4)) announcing, with respect to vast expanses of territory that they cover, the agency's intent to grant requisite permission for certain activities, to decline to interfere with other activities, and to take other particular action if requested. It may well be, then, that even those individual actions will not be ripe for challenge until some further agency action or inaction more immediately harming the plaintiff occurs. But it is at least entirely certain that the flaws in the entire "program"—consisting principally of the many individual actions referenced in the complaint, and presumably actions yet to be taken as well—cannot be laid before the courts for wholesale correction under the APA, simply because one of them that is ripe for review adversely affects one of respondent's members.

The case-by-case approach that this requires is understandably frustrating to an organization such as respondent, which has as its objective across-the-board protection of our Nation's wildlife and the streams and forests that support it. But this is the traditional, and remains the normal, mode of operation of the courts. Except where Congress explicitly provides for our correction of the administrative process at a higher level of generality, we intervene in the administration of the laws only when, and to the extent that, a specific "final agency action" has an actual or immediately threatened effect. Such an intervention may ultimately have the effect of requiring a regulation, a series of regulations, or even a whole "program" to be revised by the agency in order to avoid the unlawful result that the court discerns. But it is assuredly not as swift or as immediately far-reaching a corrective process as those interested in systemic improvement would desire. Until confided to us, however, more sweeping actions are for the other Branches . . . .

JUSTICE BLACKMUN, with whom JUSTICE BRENNAN, JUSTICE MARSHALL, and JUSTICE STEVENS join, dissenting:

In my view, the affidavits of Peggy Kay Peterson and Richard Loren Erman, in conjunction with other record evidence before the District Court on the motions for summary judgment, were sufficient to establish the standing of the National Wildlife Federation (Federation or NWS) to bring this suit. I also conclude that the District Court abused its discretion by refusing to consider supplemental affidavits filed after the hearing on the parties' cross-motions for summary judgment. I therefore would affirm the judgment of the Court of Appeals. . . .

As the Court points out, the showing (whether as to standing or the merits) required to overcome a motion for summary judgment is more extensive than that required in the context of a motion to dismiss. The principal difference is that in the former context *evidence* is required, while in the latter setting the litigant may rest upon the allegations of his complaint. In addition, Rule 56(e) requires that the party opposing summary judgment "must set forth *specific* facts showing that there is a genuine issue for trial" (emphasis added). Thus, Courts of Appeals have reiterated that "conclusory" allegations unsupported by "specific" evidence will be insufficient to establish a genuine issue of fact.

The requirement that evidence be submitted is satisfied here: the Federation has offered the sworn statements of two of its members. There remains the question whether the allegations in these affidavits were sufficiently precise to satisfy the requirements of Rule 56(e). The line of demarcation between "specific" and "conclusory" allegations is hardly a bright one. But, to my mind, the allegations contained in the Peterson and Erman affidavits, in the context of the record as a whole, were adequate to defeat a motion for summary judgment. . . .

No contrary conclusion is compelled by the fact that Peterson alleged that she uses federal lands "in the vicinity of South Pass-Green Mountain, Wyoming," rather than averring that she uses the precise tract that was recently opened to mining. The agency itself has repeatedly referred to the "South Pass-Green Mountain area" in describing the region newly opened to mining. Peterson's assertion that her use and enjoyment of federal lands *have been* adversely affected by the agency's decision to permit more extensive mining is, as the Court of Appeals stated, "meaningless, or perjurious" if the lands she uses do not include those harmed by mining undertaken pursuant to termination order W-6228. To read particular assertions within the affidavit in light of the document as a whole is, as the majority might put it, "a world apart" from "presuming" facts that are neither stated nor implied simply because without them the plaintiff would lack standing. The Peterson and Erman affidavits doubtless could have been more artfully drafted, but they definitely were sufficient to withstand the Government's summary judgment motion. . . .

The Administrative Procedure Act permits suit to be brought by any person "adversely affected or aggrieved by agency action," 5 U.S.C. § 702. In some cases the "agency action" will consist of a rule of broad applicability; and if the plaintiff prevails, the result is that the rule is invalidated, not simply that the court forbids its application to a particular individual. Under these circumstances a single plaintiff, so long as he is injured by the rule, may obtain "programmatic" relief that affects the rights of parties not before the court. On the other hand, if a generally lawful policy is applied in an illegal manner on a particular occasion, one who is injured is not thereby entitled to challenge other applications of the rule.

Application of these principles to the instant case does not turn on whether, or how often, the Bureau's land-management policies have been described as a "program." In one sense, of course, there is no question that a "program" exists. Everyone associated with this lawsuit recognizes that the BLM, over the past decade, has attempted to develop and implement a comprehensive scheme for the termination of classifications and withdrawals. The real issue is whether the actions and omissions that NWF contends are illegal are themselves part of a plan or policy. For example: if the agency had published a regulation stating that an Environmental Impact Statement should never be developed prior to the termination of a classification or withdrawal, NWF could challenge the regulation (which would constitute an "agency action"). If the reviewing court then held that the statute required a pre-termination EIS, the relief (invalidation of the rule) would directly affect tracts other than the ones used by individual affiants. At the other extreme, if the applicable BLM regulation stated that an EIS *must* be developed, and NWF alleged that the administrator in charge of South Pass-Green Mountain had inexplicably failed to develop one, NWF should not be allowed (on the basis of the Peterson affidavit) to challenge a termination in Florida on the ground that an administrator there made the same mistake.

The majority, quoting the District Court, characterizes the Bureau's land management program as "1250 or so individual classification terminations and withdrawal revocations." The majority offers no argument in support of this conclusory assertion, and I am far from certain that the characterization is an accurate one. Since this issue bears on the scope of the relief ultimately to be awarded should the plaintiff prevail, rather than on the jurisdiction of the District Court to entertain the suit, I would allow the District Court to address the question on remand. . . .

NOTES AND QUESTIONS

(1) Was the Supreme Court on solid ground in requiring plaintiffs to allege injury in fact with the degree of specificity that the *Lujan* case requires? What practical problems, if any, may the Court's approach create for environmental organizations that wish to challenge the actions of government agencies?

(2) To what extent is *United States v. SCRAP* "good law" in the aftermath of *Lujan*? How, if at all, has its scope been limited?

(3) How persuasive is the *Lujan* court 's analysis of whether the challenged actions of the Bureau of Land Management constitute a "program" subject

to legal challenge? How does it contrast with the analysis of that question advanced by Justice Blackmun's dissenting opinion? What stumbling blocks may the court's approach create for environmentalist plaintiffs who seek judicial review of numerous, similar administrative agency decisions?

(4) To what extent does the *Lujan* opinion permit environmentalist plaintiffs to amend their pleadings in order to remedy insufficiently specific averments of injury-in-fact where all parties to the action are in agreement as to the areas or resources in dispute? *See Alaska Center for the Environment v. Browner,* 20 F.3d 981 (9th Cir. 1994) in which the plaintiff in a citizen suit challenging the EPA's failure to implement state water quality standards were required to allege that the program under challenge affected a representative number of the "interrelated" waterways that existed in the state.

BENNETT v. SPEAR

United States Supreme Court (1997)
520 U.S. 154, 117 S. Ct. 1154, 137 L. Ed. 2d 281

Scalia, J.:

This is a challenge to a biological opinion issued by the Fish and Wildlife Service in accordance with the Endangered Species Act of 1973 (ESA), 87 Stat. 884, as amended, 16 U.S.C. § 1531 *et seq.*, concerning the operation of the Klamath Irrigation Project by the Bureau of Reclamation, and the project's impact on two varieties of endangered fish. The question for decision is whether the petitioners, who have competing economic and other interests in Klamath Project water, have standing to seek judicial review of the biological opinion under the citizen-suit provision of the ESA, § 1540(g)(1), and the Administrative Procedure Act (APA), 80Stat. 392, as amended, 5 U.S.C. § 701 *et seq.*

I

The ESA requires the Secretary of the Interior to promulgate regulations listing those species of animals that are "threatened" or "endangered" under specified criteria, and to designate their "critical habitat." 16 U.S.C. § 1533. The ESA further requires each federal agency to "insure that any action authorized, funded or carried out by such agency . . . is not likely to jeopardize the continued existence of any endangered species or threatened species or result in the destruction or adverse modification of habitat of such species which is determined by the Secretary . . . to be critical." § 1536(a)(2). If an agency determines that action it proposes to take may adversely affect a listed species, it must engage in formal consultation with the Fish and Wildlife Service, as delegate of the Secretary, *ibid.*, 50 CFR § 402.14(1995), after which the Service must provide the agency with a written statement (the Biological Opinion) explaining how the proposed action will affect the species or its habitat, 16 U.S.C. § 1536(b)(3)(A). If the Service concludes that the proposed action will "jeopardize the continued existence of any [listed] species or result in the destruction or adverse modification of [critical habitat]," § 1536(a)(2), the Biological Opinion must outline any "reasonable and prudent alternatives" that the Service believes will avoid that consequence, § 1536(b)(3)(A). Additionally, if the Biological Opinion concludes that the agency action will not result in jeopardy or adverse habitat modification, or if it offers reasonable and prudent alternatives to avoid that consequence, the Service must provide the agency with a written statement (known as the "Incidental Take Statement") specifying the "impact of such incidental taking on the species," any "reasonable and prudent measures that the [Service] considers necessary or appropriate to minimize such impact," and setting forth "the terms and conditions . . . that must be compiled with by the Federal agency . . . to implement [those measures]." § 1536(b)(4).

The Klamath Project, one of the oldest federal reclamation schemes, is a series of lakes, rivers, dams and irrigation canals in northern California and southern Oregon. The project was undertaken by the Secretary of the Interior pursuant to the Reclamation Act of 1902, 32 Stat. 388, as amended, 43 U.S.C. § 371 *et seq.*, and the Act of Feb. 9, 1905, 33 Stat. 714, and is administered by the Bureau of Reclamation, which is under the Secretary's jurisdiction. In 1992, the Bureau notified the Service that operation of the project might affect the Lost River Sucker (Deltistes luxatus) and Shortnose Sucker (Chasmistes brevirostris), species of fish that were listed as endangered in 1988, *see* 53 Fed. Reg. 27130-27133 (1988). After formal consultation with the Bureau in accordance with 50 CFR § 402-14(1995), the Service issued a Biological Opinion which concluded the " 'long-term operation of the Klamath Project was likely to jeopardize the continued existence of the Lost River and shortnose suckers.' " The Biological Opinion identified "reasonable and prudent alternatives" the Service believed would avoid jeopardy, which included the maintenance of minimum water levels on Clear Lake and Gerber reservoirs. The Bureau later notified the Service that it intended to operate the project in compliance with the Biological Opinion.

Petitioners, two Oregon irrigation districts that receive Klamath Project water and the operators of two ranches within those districts, filed the present action against the director and regional director of the Service and the Secretary of the Interior. Neither the Bureau nor any of its officials is named as defendant. The complaint asserts that the Bureau "has been following essentially the same procedures for storing and releasing water from Clear Lake and Gerber reservoirs throughout the twentieth century"; that "there is no scientifically or commercially available evidence indicating that the populations of endangered suckers in Clear Lake and Gerber reservoirs have declined, are declining, or will decline as a result" of the Bureau's operation of the Klamath Project; that "there is no commercially or scientifically available evidence indicating that the restrictions on lake levels imposed in the Biological Opinion will have any beneficial effect on the . . . populations of suckers in the Clear Lake and Gerber reservoirs; and that the Bureau nonetheless "will abide by the restrictions imposed by the Biological Opinion."

Petitioners' complaint included three claims for relief that are relevant here. The first and second claims allege that the Service's jeopardy determination with respect to Clear Lake and Gerber reservoirs, and the ensuing imposition of minimum water levels, violated § 7 of the ESA, 16 U.S.C. § 1526. The third claim is that the imposition of minimum water elevations constituted an implicit determination of critical habitat for the suckers, which violated § 4 of the ESA, 16 U.S.C. § 1533(b)(2), because it failed to take into consideration the designation's economic impact. Each of the claims also states that the relevant action violated the APA's prohibition of agency action that is "arbitrary, capricious, an abuse of discretion, or otherwise not in accordance with law." 5 U.S.C. § 706(2)(A).

The complaint asserts that petitioners' use of the reservoirs and related waterways for "recreational, aesthetic and commercial purposes, as well as for their primary sources of irrigation water" will be "irreparably damaged" by the actions complained of, and that the restrictions on water delivery "recommended" by the Biological Opinion "adversely affect plaintiffs by substantially reducing the quantity of available irrigation water." In essence, petitioners claim a competing interest in the water the Biological Opinion declares necessary for the preservation of the suckers.

The District Court dismissed the complaint for lack of jurisdiction. It concluded that petitioners did not have standing because their "recreational, aesthetic, and commercial interests . . . do not fall within the zone of interest sought to be protected by ESA." The Court of Appeals for the Ninth Circuit affirmed. *Bennett v. Plenert,* 63 F.3d 915 (1995). It held that the "zone of interests" test limits the class of persons who may obtain judicial review not only under the APA, but also under the citizen-suit provision of the ESA, 16U.S.C. § 1540(g), and that "only plaintiffs who allege an interest in the preservation of endangered species fall within the zone of interests protected by the ESA," 63 F.3d at 919. We granted certiorari. 517 U.S. 1102 (1996).

In this Court, petitioners raise two questions: first, whether the prudential standing rule known as the "zone of interests" test applies to claims brought under the citizen-suit provision of the ESA; and second, if so, whether petitioners have standing under that test notwithstanding that the interests they seek to vindicate are economic rather than environmental. In this Court, the Government has made no effort to defend the reasoning of the Court of Appeals. Instead, it advances three alternative grounds for affirmance: (1) that petitioners fail to meet the standing requirements imposed by Article III of the Constitution; (2) that the ESA's citizen-suit provision does not authorize judicial review of the types of claims advanced by petitioners; and (3) that judicial review is unavailable under the APA because the Biological Opinion does not constitute final agency action.

II

We first turn to the question the Court of Appeals found dispositive: whether petitioners lack standing by virtue of the zone-of-interests test. Although petitioners contend that their claims lie both under the ESA and the APA, we look first at the ESA because it may permit petitioners to recover their litigation costs, *see* 16 U.S.C. § 1540(g)(4), and because the APA by its terms independently authorizes review only when "there is no other adequate remedy in a court," 5 U.S.C. § 704.

The question of standing "involves both constitutional limitations on federal-court jurisdiction and prudential limitations on its exercise." To satisfy the "case" or "controversy" requirement of Article III, which is the "irreducible constitutional minimum" of standing, a plaintiff must, generally speaking, demonstrate that he has suffered "injury in fact," that the injury is "fairly traceable" to the actions of the defendant, and that the injury will likely be redressed by a favorable decision. In addition to the immutable requirements of Article III, "the federal judiciary has also adhered to a set of prudential principles that bear on the question of standing." *Id.* at 474-475. Like their constitutional counterparts, these "judicially self-imposed limits on the exercise of federal jurisdiction," are "founded in concern about the proper—properly limited—role of the courts in a democratic society"; but unlike their constitutional counterparts, they can be modified or abrogated by Congress. Numbered among these prudential requirements is the doctrine of particular concern in this case: that a plaintiff's grievance must arguably fall within the zone of interests protected or regulated by the statutory provision or constitutional guarantee involved in the suit.

The "zone of interests" formulation was first employed in *Association of Data Processing Service Organizations, Inc. v. Camp,* 397 U.S. 150, 25 L.Ed.2d 184, 90 S.Ct. 827 (1970). There, certain data processors sought to invalidate a ruling by the Comptroller of the Currency authorizing national banks to sell data processing services on the ground that it violated, inter alia, § 4 of the Bank Service Corporation Act of 1962, 76 Stat. 1132, which prohibited bank service corporations from engaging in "any activity other than the performance of bank services for banks." . . . [In that case we] stated the applicable prudential standing requirement to be "whether the interest sought to be protected by the complainant is arguably within the zone of interests to be protected or regulated by the statute or constitutional guarantee in question." *Data Processing,* and its companion case, *Barlow v. Collins,* 397 U.S. 159, 25 L.Ed.2d 192, 90 S.Ct. 832 (1970), applied the zone-of-interests test to suits under the APA, but later cases have applied it also in suits not involving review of federal administrative action. We have made clear, however, that the breadth of the zone of interests varies according to the provisions of law at issue, so that what comes within the zone of interests of a statute for purposes of obtaining judicial review of administrative action under the "generous review provisions" of the APA may not do so for other purposes.

Congress legislates against the background of our prudential standing doctrine, which applies unless it is expressly negated. The first question in the present case is whether the ESA's citizen-suit provision negates the zone-of-interests test (or, perhaps more accurately, expands the zone of interests). We think it does. The first operative portion of the provision says that "any person may commence a civil suit"—an authorization of remarkable breadth when compared with the language Congress ordinarily uses. Even in some other environmental statutes, Congress has used more restrictive formulations, such as "[any person] having an interest which is or may be adversely affected," 33 U.S.C. § 1365(g)(Clear Water Act); *see also* 30 U.S.C. § 1270(a)(Surface Mining Control and Reclamation Act) (same); "any person suffering legal wrong," 15 U.S.C. § 797(b)(5)(Energy Supply and Environmental Coordination Act); or "any person having a valid legal interest which is or may be adversely affected . . . whenever such action constitutes a case or controversy," 42 U.S.C. § 9124(a)(Ocean Thermal Energy Conversion Act). And in contexts other than the environment, Congress has often been even more restrictive. In statutes concerning unfair trade practices and other commercial matters, for example, it has authorized suit only by "any person injured in his business or property," 7 U.S.C. § 2305(c); *see also* 15 U.S.C. § 72 (same), or only by "competitors, customers, or subsequent purchasers," § 298(b).

Our readiness to take the term "any person" at face value is greatly augmented by two interrelated considerations: that the overall subject matter of this legislation is the environment (a matter in which it is common to think all persons have an interest) and that the obvious purpose of the particular provision in question is to encourage enforcement by so-called "private attorneys general"—evidenced by its elimination of the usual amount-in-controversy and diversity-of-citizenship requirements, its provision for recovery of the costs of litigation (including even expert witness fees), and its reservation to the Government of a right of first refusal to pursue the action initially and a right to intervene later . . . .

It is true that the plaintiffs here are seeking to prevent application of environmental restrictions rather than to implement them. But the "any person" formulation applies to all the causes of action authorized by § 1540(g)—not only to actions against private violators of environmental restrictions, and not only to actions against the Secretary asserting under-enforcement restrictions under § 1533 but also to actions against the Secretary asserting over-enforcement under § 1533. As we shall discuss below, the citizen-suit provision does favor environmentalists in that it covers all private violations of the Act but not all failures of the Secretary to meet his administrative responsibilities; but there is no textual basis for saying that its expansion of standing requirements applies to environmentalists alone. The Court of Appeals therefore erred in concluding that petitioners lacked standing under the zone-of-interests test to bring their claims under the ESA's citizen-suit provision.

III

A

. . . The Government's first contention is that petitioners' complaint fails to satisfy the standing requirements imposed by the "case" or "controversy" provision of Article III. This "irreducible constitutional minimum" of standing requires: (1) that the plaintiff have suffered an "injury in fact"—an invasion of a judicially cognizable interest which is (a) concrete and particularized and (b) actual or imminent, not conjectural or hypothetical; (2) that there be a causal connection between the injury and the conduct complained of—the injury must be fairly traceable to the challenged action of the defendant, and not the result of the independent action of some third party not before the court; and (3) that it be likely, as opposed to merely speculative, that the injury will be redressed by a favorable decision.

Petitioners allege, among other things, that they currently receive irrigation water from Clear Lake, that the Bureau "will abide by the restrictions imposed by the Biological Opinion," and that "the restrictions on lake levels imposed in the Biological Opinion adversely affect [petitioners] by substantially reducing the quantity of available irrigation water." The Government contends, first, that these allegations fail to satisfy the "injury in fact" element of Article III standing because they demonstrate only a diminution in the aggregate amount of available water, and do not necessarily establish (absent information concerning the Bureau's water allocation practices) that the petitioners will receive less water. This contention overlooks, however, the proposition that each element of Article III standing "must be supported in the same way as any other matter on which the plaintiff bears the burden of proof, *i.e.*, with the manner and degree of evidence required at the successive stages of the litigation." Thus, while a plaintiff must "set forth" by affidavit or other evidence "specific facts," to survive a motion for summary judgment, Fed. Rule Civ. Proc. 56(e), and must ultimately support any contested facts with evidence adduced at trial, "at the pleading stage, general factual allegations of injury resulting from the defendant's conduct may suffice, for on a motion to dismiss we 'presume that general allegations embrace those specific facts that are necessary to support the claim.'" Given petitioners' allegation that the amount of available water will be reduced and that they will be adversely affected thereby, it is easy to presume specific facts under which petitioners will be injured—for example, the Bureau's distribution of the reduction pro rata among its customers. The complaint alleges the requisite injury in fact.

The Government also contests compliance with the second and third Article III standing requirements, contending that any injury suffered by petitioners is neither "fairly traceable" to the Service's Biological Opinion, nor "redressable" by a favorable judicial ruling, because the "action agency" (the Bureau) retains ultimate responsibility for determining whether and how a proposed action shall go forward. *See* 50 CFR § 402.15(a)(1995) ("Following the issuance of a biological opinion, the federal agency shall determine whether and in what manner to proceed with the action in light of its section 7 obligations and the Service's biological opinion"). "If the petitioners have suffered injury," the Government contends, "the proximate cause of their harm is an (as yet unidentified) decision by the Bureau regarding the volume of water allocated to petitioners, not the biological opinion itself." This wrongly equates injury "fairly traceable" to the defendant with injury as to which the defendant's actions are the very last step in the chain of causation. While, as we have said, it does not suffice if the injury complained of is "the result [of] the independent action of some third party not before the court," that does not exclude injury produced by determinative or coercive effect upon the action of someone else.

By the Government's own account, while the Service's Biological Opinion theoretically serves an "advisory function," 51 Fed. Reg. 19928 (1986), in reality it has a powerful coercive effect on the action agency:

> "The statutory scheme. . . presupposes that the biological opinion will play a central role in the action agency's decisionmaking process, and that

it will typically be based on an administrative record that is fully adequate for the action agency's decision insofar as ESA issues are concerned . . . . [A] federal agency that chooses to deviate from the recommendations contained in a biological opinion bears the burden of 'articulating in its administrative record its reasons for disagreeing with the conclusions of a biological opinion,' 51 Fed. Reg. 19,956 (1986). In the government's experience, action agencies very rarely choose to engage in conduct that the Service has concluded is likely to jeopardize the continued existence of a listed species."

What this concession omits to say, moreover, is that the action agency must not only articulate its reasons for disagreement (which ordinarily requires species and habitat investigations that are not within the action agency's expertise), but that it runs a substantial risk if its (inexpert) reasons turn out to be wrong. A Biological Opinion of the sort rendered here alters the legal regime to which the action agency is subject. When it "offers reasonable and prudent alternatives" to the proposed action, a Biological Opinion must include a so-called "Incidental Take Statement"—a written statement specifying, among other things, those "measures that the [Service] considers necessary or appropriate to minimize [the action's impact on the affected species]" and the "terms and conditions . . . that must be complied with by the federal agency . . . to implement [such] measures." 16 U.S.C. § 1536(b)(4). Any taking that is in compliance with these terms and conditions "shall not be considered to be a prohibited taking of the species concerned." § 1536(o)(2). Thus, the Biological Opinion's Incidental Take Statement constitutes a permit authorizing the action agency to "take" the endangered or threatened species so long as it respects the Service's "terms and conditions." The action agency is technically free to disregard the Biological Opinion and proceed with its proposed action, but it does so at its own peril (and that of its employees), for "any person" who knowingly "takes" an endangered or threatened species is subject to substantial civil and criminal penalties, including imprisonment.

The Service itself is, to put it mildly, keenly aware of the virtually determinative effect of its biological opinions. The Incidental Take Statement at issue in the present case begins by instructing the reader that any taking of a listed species is prohibited unless "such taking is in compliance with this incidental take statement," and warning that "measures described below are nondiscretionary, and must be taken by [the Bureau]." Given all of this, and given petitioners' allegation that the Bureau had, until issuance of the Biological Opinion, operated the Klamath Project in the same manner throughout the twentieth century, it is not difficult to conclude that petitioners have met their burden—which is relatively modest at this stage of the litigation—of alleging that their injury is "fairly traceable" to the Service's Biological Opinion and that it will "likely" be redressed—*i.e.*, the Bureau will not impose such water level restrictions—if the Biological Opinion is set aside.

B

Next, the Government contends that the ESA's citizen-suit provision does not authorize judicial review of petitioners' claims. The relevant portions of that provision provide that:

"any person may commence a civil suit on his own behalf—

"(A) to enjoin any person, including the United States and any other governmental instrumentality or agency . . . who is alleged to be in violation of any provision of this chapter or regulation issued under the authority thereof; or

. . . .

(C) against the Secretary [of Commerce or the Interior] where there is alleged a failure of the Secretary to perform any act or duty under section 1533 of this title which is not discretionary with the Secretary." 16 U.S.C. § 1540(g)(1).

The Government argues that judicial review is not available under subsection (A) because the Secretary is not "in violation" of the ESA, and under subsection (C) because the Secretary has not failed to perform any nondiscretionary duty under § 1533.

1

Turning first to subsection (C): that it covers only violations of § 1533 is clear and unambiguous. Petitioners' first and second claims, which assert that the Secretary has violated § 1536, are obviously not reviewable under this provision. However, as described above, the third claim alleges that the Biological Opinion implicitly determines critical habitat without complying with the mandate of § 1533(b)(2) that the Secretary "take into consideration the economic impact, and any other relevant impact, of specifying any particular area as critical habitat." This claim does come within subsection (C) . . . . [T]he terms of § 1533(b)(2) are plainly those of obligation rather then discretion . . . .

Having concluded that petitioners' § 1536 claims are not reviewable under subsection (C), we are left with the question whether they are reviewable under subsection (A), which authorizes injunctive actions against any person "who is alleged to be in violation" of the ESA or its implementing regulations. The Government contends that the Secretary's conduct in implementing or enforcing the ESA is not a "violation" of the ESA within the meaning of this provision. In its view, § 1540(g)(1)(A) is a means by which private parties may enforce the substantive provisions of the ESA against regulated parties—both private entities and Government agencies—but it is not an alternative avenue for judicial review of the Secretary's implementation of the statute. We agree.

. . . [T]he ESA uses the term "violation" elsewhere in contexts in which it is most unlikely to refer to failure by the Secretary or other federal officers and employees to perform their duties in administering the Act . . . . We know of no precedent for applying such a provision against those who administer (as opposed to those who are regulated by) a substantive law. Nor do we think it likely that the statute meant to subject the Secretary, his officers and employees to criminal liability . . . .

[I]nterpreting the term "violation" to include any errors on the part of the Secretary in administering the ESA would effect a wholesale abrogation of the APA's "final agency action" requirement. Any procedural default, even one that had not yet resulted in a final disposition of the matter at issue, would form the basis for a lawsuit. We are loathe to produce such an extraordinary regime without the clearest of statutory direction, which is hardly present here.

Viewed in the context of the entire statute, § 1540(g)(1)(A)'s reference to any "violation" of the ESA cannot be interpreted to include the Secretary's maladministration of the Act. Petitioners' claims are not subject to judicial review under § 1540(g)(1)(A).

IV

The foregoing analysis establishes that the principal statute invoked by petitioners, the ESA, does authorize review of their § 1533 claim, but does not support their claims based upon the Secretary's alleged failure to comply with § 1536. To complete our task, we must therefore inquire whether these § 1536 claims may nonetheless be brought under the Administrative Procedure Act, which authorizes a court to "set aside agency action, findings, and conclusions found to be . . . arbitrary, capricious, an abuse of discretion, or otherwise not in accordance with law," 5 U.S.C. § 706.

A

No one contends (and it would not be maintainable) that the causes of action against the Secretary set forth in the ESA's citizen-suit provision are exclusive, supplanting those provided by the APA. The APA, by its terms, provides a right to judicial review of all "final agency action for which there is no other adequate remedy in a court," 51 U.S.C. § 704, and applies universally "except to the extent that (1) statutes preclude judicial review; or (2) agency action is committed to agency discretion by law," § 701(a). Nothing in the ESA's citizen-suit provision expressly precludes review under the APA, nor do we detect anything in the statutory scheme suggesting a purpose to do so. And any contention that the relevant provision of 16 U.S.C. § 1536(a)(2)is discretionary would fly in the face of its text, which uses the imperative "shall."

In determining whether the petitioners have standing under the zone-of-interests test to bring their APA claims, we look not to the terms of the ESA's citizen-suit provision, but to the substantive provisions of the ESA, the alleged violations of which serve as the gravamen of the complaint. The classic formulation of the zone-of-interests test is . . . "whether the interest sought to be protected by the complainant is arguably within the zone of interests to be protected or regulated by the statute or constitutional guarantee in question." The Court of Appeals concluded that this test was not met here, since petitioners are neither directly regulated by the ESA nor seek to vindicate its overarching purpose of species preservation. That conclusion was error. . . .

In the claims that we have found not to be covered by the ESA's citizen suit provision, petitioners allege a violation of § 7 of the ESA, 16 U.S.C. § 1536, which requires, inter alia, that each agency "use their best scientific and commercial data available," § 1536(a)(2). Petitioners contend that the available scientific and commercial data show that the continued operation of the Klamath Project will not have a detrimental impact on the endangered suckers, that the imposition of minimum lake levels is not necessary to protect the fish, and that by issuing a Biological Opinion which makes unsubstantiated findings to the contrary the defendants have acted arbitrarily and in violation of § 1536(a)(2). The obvious purpose of the requirement that each agency "use the best scientific and commercial data available" is to ensure that the ESA not be implemented haphazardly, on the basis of speculation or surmise. While this no doubt serves to advance the ESA's overall goal of species preservation, we think it readily apparent that another objective (if not indeed the primary one) is to avoid needless economic dislocation produced by agency officials zealously but unintelligently pursuing their environmental objectives. That economic consequences are an explicit concern of the Act is evidenced by § 1536(h), which provides exemption from § 1536(a)(2)'s no-jeopardy mandate where there are no reasonable and prudent alternatives to the agency action and the benefits of the agency action clearly outweigh the benefits of any alternatives. We believe the "best scientific and commercial data" provision is similarly intended, at least in part, to prevent uneconomic (because erroneous) jeopardy determinations. Petitioners' claim that they are victims of such a mistake is plainly within the zone of interests that the provision protects . . . .

NOTES AND QUESTIONS

(1) Were you persuaded by the Supreme Court's interpretation of the purpose of the Endangered Species Act provision requiring use of "the best available scientific and commercial data available?" To what extent was a "primary goal" of that provision the avoidance of economic dislocation produced by zealous but unintelligent agency officials?

(2) Does *Bennett v. Spear* strengthen the position of environmental organizations when they assert standing to sue under the citizen suit provision of the Endangered Species Act and/or the citizen suit sections of other statutes?

(3) For another recent U.S. Supreme Court decision regarding, among other things, the standing-to-sue issue, see *Friends of the Earth, Inc. v. Laidlaw Environmental Services (TOC), Inc.*, p. 1326, *infra*.

§ 8.04 Attorneys Fees in Environmental Litigation

RUCKELSHAUS v. SIERRA CLUB

United States Supreme Court (1983)
463 U.S. 680, 103 S. Ct. 3274, 77 L. Ed. 2d 938

Rehnquist, J.:

In 1979, following a year of study and public comment, the Environmental Protection Agency (EPA) promulgated standards limiting the emission of sulfur dioxide by coal-burning powerplants. Both respondents in this case—the Environmental Defense Fund (EDF) and the Sierra Club—filed petitions for review of the agency's action in the United States Court of Appeals for the District of Columbia Circuit. EDF argued that the standards promulgated by the EPA were tainted by the agency's *ex parte* contacts with representatives of private industry, while the Sierra Club contended that EPA lacked authority under the Clean Air Act to issue the type of standards that it did. In a lengthy opinion, the Court of Appeals rejected all the claims of both EDF and the Sierra Club.

Notwithstanding their lack of success on the merits, EDF and the Sierra Club filed a request for attorney's fees incurred in the Sierra Club action. They relied on § 307(f) of the Clean Air Act, 42 U.S.C. § 7607(f)(1976 ed., Supp. V), which permits the award of attorney's fees in certain proceedings "whenever [the court] determines that such award is appropriate." Respondents argued that, despite their failure to obtain any of the relief they requested, it was "appropriate" for them to receive fees for their contributions to the goals of the Clean Air Act. The Court of Appeals agreed with respondents, ultimately awarding some $45,000 to the Sierra Club and some $46,000 to the EDF. We granted certiorari, to consider the important question decided by the Court of Appeals.

The question presented by this case is whether it is "appropriate," within the meaning of § 307(f) of the Clean Air Act, to award attorney's fees to a party that achieved no success on the merits of its claims. We conclude that the language of the section, read in the light of the historic principles of fee-shifting in this and other countries, requires the conclusion that some success on the merits be obtained before a party becomes eligible for a fee award under § 307(f).

Section 307(f) provides only that:

> "In any judicial proceeding under this section, the court may award costs of litigation (including reasonable attorney and expert witness fees) *whenever it determines that such award is appropriate.*" 42 U.S.C. § 7507(f)(1976 ed., Supp. V) (emphasis added).

It is difficult to draw any meaningful guidance from § 307(f)'s use of the word "appropriate," which means only "specially suitable: fit, proper." Webster's Third New International Dictionary 106 (1976). Obviously, in order to decide when fees should be awarded under § 307(f), a court first must decide *what* the award should be "specially suitable," "fit," or "proper" *for.* Section 307(f) alone does not begin to answer this question, and application of the provision thus requires reference to other sources, including fee-shifting rules developed in different contexts. As demonstrated below, inquiry into these sources shows that requiring a defendant, completely successful on all issues, to pay the unsuccessful plaintiff's legal fees would be a radical departure from long-standing fee-shifting principles adhered to in a wide variety of contexts.

Our basic point of reference is the "American Rule," *see Alyeska Pipeline Co. v. Wilderness Society,* 421 U.S. 240, 247 (1975), under which even "the *prevailing* litigant is ordinarily not entitled to collect a reasonable attorneys' fee from the *loser.*" It is clear that generations of American judges, lawyers, and legislators, with this rule as the point of departure, would regard it as quite "inappropriate" to award the "loser" an attorney's fee from the "prevailing litigant." Similarly, when Congress has chosen to depart from the American Rule by statute, virtually every one of the more than 150 existing federal fee-shifting provisions predicates fee awards on *some* success by the claimant; while these statutes contain varying standards as to the precise degree of success necessary for an award of fees—such as whether the fee claimant was the "prevailing party," the "substantially prevailing" party, or "successful"—the consistent rule is that complete failure will not justify shifting fees from the losing party to the winning party . . . . [Moreover], English courts have awarded counsel fees to *successful* litigants for 750 years, but they have never gone so far as to force a vindicated defendant to pay the plaintiff's legal expenses.

While the foregoing treatments of fee-shifting differ in many respects, they reflect one consistent, established rule: a successful party need not pay its unsuccessful adversary's fees. The uniform acceptance of this rule reflects, at least in part, intuitive notions of fairness to litigants. Put simply, ordinary conceptions of just returns reject the idea that a party who wrongly charges someone with violations of the law should be able to force that defendant to pay the costs of the wholly unsuccessful suit against it. Before we will conclude Congress abandoned this established principle that a successful party need not pay its unsuccessful adversary's fees—rooted as it is in intuitive notions of fairness and widely manifested in numerous different contexts—a clear showing that this result was intended is required.

Also relevant in deciding whether to accept the reading of "appropriate" urged by respondents is the fact that § 307(f) affects fee awards against the United States, as well as against private individuals. Except to the extent it has waived its immunity, the Government is immune from claims for attorney's fees, *Alyeska*, *supra*, at 267-268, and n. 42, 95 S.Ct., at 1626, and n. 42. Waivers of immunity must be "construed strictly in favor of the sovereign," and not "enlarge[d] . . . beyond what the language requires." In determining what sorts of fee awards are "appropriate," care must be taken not to "enlarge" § 307(f)'s waiver of immunity beyond what a fair reading of the language of the section requires.

Given all the foregoing, we fail to find in § 307(f) the requisite indication that Congress meant to abandon historic fee-shifting principles and intuitive notions of fairness when it enacted the section. Instead, we believe that the term "appropriate" modifies but does not completely reject the traditional rule that a fee claimant must "prevail" before it may recover attorney's fees. This result is the most reasonable interpretation of congressional intent.

Respondents make relatively little effort to dispute much of the foregoing, devoting their principal attention to the legislative history of § 307(f). Respondents' arguments rest primarily on the following excerpt from the 1977 House Report on § 307(f):

> "The committee bill also contains express authority for the courts to award attorneys' fees and expert witness fees in two situations. The judicial review proceedings under section 307 of the act [and] when the court determines such award is appropriate.
>
> "In the case of the section 307 judicial review litigation, the purposes of the authority to award fees are not only to discourage frivolous litigation, but also to encourage litigation which will assure proper

implementation and administration of the act or otherwise serve the public interest. *The committee did not intend that the court's discretion to award fees under this provision should be restricted to cases in which the party seeking fees was the 'prevailing party.'* In fact, such an amendment was expressly rejected by the committee . . . ." H.R. Rep. No. 95-294, p. 337 (1977) (emphasis added).

In determining the meaning of the Senate Report's rejection of the "prevailing party" standard it first is necessary to ascertain what this standard was understood to mean. When § 307(f) was enacted, the "prevailing party" standard had been interpreted in a variety of rather narrow ways. Some courts—although, to be sure, a minority—denied fees to plaintiffs who lacked a formal court order granting relief, while others required showings not just of some success, but "substantial" success. Indeed, even today, courts require that, to be a "prevailing party," one must succeed on the "central issue," or "essentially succeed in obtaining the relief he seeks in his claim on the merits[.]"

These various interpretations of the "prevailing party" standard provide a ready, and quite sensible, explanation for the Senate's Report's discussion of § 307(f). Section 307(f) was meant to expand the class of parties eligible for fee awards from prevailing parties to *partially prevailing* parties—parties achieving *some success,* even if not major success. Put differently, by enacting § 307(f), Congress intended to eliminate both the restrictive readings of "prevailing party" adopted in some of the cases cited above and the necessity for case-by-case scrutiny by federal courts into whether plaintiffs prevailed "essentially" on "central issues." . . . .

Section 304 suits may be brought against private businesses by any private citizen. Such suits frequently involve novel legal theories, theories that the EPA has rejected. After protracted litigation requiring payment of expensive legal fees and associated costs in both money and manpower, the private defendant may well succeed in refuting each charge against it—proving it was in complete compliance with every detail of the Clean Air Act. Yet, under respondents' view of the Act, the defendant's reward could be a second lawyer's bill—this one payable to those who wrongly accused it of violating the law. We simply do not believe that Congress would have intended such a result without clearly saying so . . . .

We conclude, therefore, that the language and legislative history of § 307(f) do not support respondent's argument that the section was intended as a radical departure from established principles requiring that a fee claimant attain some success on the merits before it may receive an award of fees. Instead, we are persuaded that if Congress intended such a novel result—which would require federal courts to make sensitive, difficult, and ultimately highly subjective determinations—it would have said so in far plainer language than that employed here. Hence, we hold that, absent some degree of success on the merits by the claimant, it is not "appropriate" for a federal court to award attorney's fees under § 307(f). Accordingly, the judgment of the Court of Appeals is reversed.

NOTES AND QUESTIONS

(1) To what extent might the Supreme Court's opinion in *Ruckelshaus* create practical barriers to the funding of environmental public interest litigation? How persuaded were you by the Court's invocation of the common law "American Rule" as to attorney's fees? Should it have mattered that, in § 307(f) of the Clean Air Act,Congress employed the phrase "whenever appropriate," rather than adopting the "prevailing or substantially prevailing party" standard that is used in the fee awards provision of other environmental statutes?

(2) In a dissenting opinion in *Ruckelshaus,* Justice Stevens, joined by three other Justices, noted that the Sierra Club had been the only party in the case to brief and argue a critically important issue, and that its participation may well have made a difference in the outcome of the litigation. After examining the legislative history of the Clean Air Act in some detail, he concluded that § 307(f) of that Act had been intended to be broader than a prevailing party standard, and that reviewing courts are bound to defer to the determinations of trial courts in these matters.

(3) In the aftermath of the *Ruckelshaus* decision, Congress has generally adopted the "prevailing or substantially prevailing party" standard in fashioning the attorney's fee award sections of other environmental litigation. *See, e.g.,* Resource Conservation and Recovery Act § 7002(e), 42 U.S.C. § 6972(e); Clean Water Act § 505(d), 33 U.S.C. § 1365(d); and Comprehensive Environmental Response, Compensation and Liability Act § 310(f), 42 U.S.C. § 9659(f).

PENNSYLVANIA v. DELAWARE VALLEY CITIZENS' COUNCIL FOR CLEAN AIR

United States Supreme Court (1986)
478 U.S. 546, 106 S. Ct. 3088, 92 L. Ed. 2d 439

White, J.:

The questions presented in this case are first, whether the Clean Air Act, 42U.S.C. § 7401 *et seq.,* authorizes attorney's fee awards for time spent by counsel participating in regulatory proceedings; second, whether a court may enhance an award to reflect superior quality of representation rendered by plaintiff's counsel; and third, whether enhancement of the fee is proper because of plaintiff's risk of not prevailing on the merits.

In 1977, the Delaware Valley Citizens' Council for Clean Air (Delaware Valley) and the United States each filed suit to compel the Commonwealth of Pennsylvania to implement a vehicle emission inspection and maintenance program (I/M program) as required by the Clean Air Act. Pursuant to a consent decree approved in 1978, the Commonwealth agreed to establish an I/M program for 10 counties in the Philadelphia and Pittsburgh areas by August

1, 1980. The decree called for the Pennsylvania Department of Transportation (PennDOT) to seek legislation instituting a franchise I/M system under which the Commonwealth would contract with garage owners for the establishment of inspection stations. If the legislature failed to approve such a system, then the decree required PennDOT to promulgate regulations allowing Pennsylvania to certify a number of private garage facilities to perform the inspections. In addition, the decree provided for Pennsylvania to pay Delaware Valley $30,000 for attorney's fees and costs incurred prior to the entry of the consent decree. . . . .

Section 304(d) of the Clean Air Act, 84 Stat. 1706, 42 U.S.C. § 7604(d), provides, in pertinent part, as follows:

> "The court, in issuing any final order in any action brought pursuant to subsection (a) of this section, may award costs of litigation (including reasonable attorney and expert witness fees) to any party, whenever the court determines such award is appropriate."

The Commonwealth argues that the plain language of the statute clearly limits the award of fees to "costs of litigation" for "action[s] brought" under the Act, and that the lower courts erred in awarding attorney's fees for Delaware Valley's activities in Phases II and IX, both of which involved the submission of comments on draft regulations to administrative agencies. The United States echoes these assertions, and contends that the "actions" contemplated by § 304(d) are judicial actions, not administrative proceedings. We reject these limiting constructions on the scope of § 304(d).

Although it is true that the proceedings involved in Phases II and IX were not "judicial" in the sense that they did not occur in a courtroom or involve "traditional" legal work such as examination of witnesses or selection of jurors for trial, the work done by counsel in these two phases was as necessary to the attainment of adequate relief for their client as was all of their earlier work in the courtroom which secured Delaware Valley's initial success in obtaining the consent decree. This case did not involve a single tortious act by the Commonwealth that resulted in a discrete injury to Delaware Valley, nor was the harm alleged the kind that could be remedied by a mere award of damages or the entry of declaratory relief. Instead, Delaware Valley filed suit to force the Commonwealth to comply with its obligations under the Clean Air Act to develop and implement an emissions inspection and maintenance program covering 10 counties surrounding two major metropolitan areas. To this end, the consent decree provided detailed instructions as to how the program was to be developed and the specific dates by which these tasks were to be accomplished.

Protection of the full scope of relief afforded by the consent decree was thus crucial to safeguard the interests asserted by Delaware Valley; and enforcement of the decree, whether in the courtroom before a judge, or in front of a regulatory agency with power to modify the substance of the program ordered by the court, involved the type of work which is properly compensable as a cost of litigation under § 304. In a case of this kind, measures necessary to enforce the remedy ordered by the District Court cannot be divorced from the matters upon which Delaware Valley prevailed in securing the consent decree. . . . .

It is well established that, under the "American Rule," "the prevailing litigant is ordinarily not entitled to collect a reasonable attorney's fee from the loser." *Alyeska Pipeline Co. v. Wilderness Society,* 421 U.S. 240, 247 (1975). There are exceptions to this principle, the major one being congressional authorization for the courts to require one party to award attorney's fees to the other. There are over 100 separate statutes providing for the award of attorney's fees; and although these provisions cover a wide variety of contexts and causes of action, the benchmark for the awards under nearly all of these statutes is that the attorney's fee must be "reasonable."

Courts have struggled to formulate the proper measure for determining the "reasonableness" of a particular fee award. One method, first employed by the Fifth Circuit in *Johnson v. Georgia Highway Express, Inc.,* 488 F.2d 714 (1974), involved consideration of 12 factors.[1] *Johnson* was widely followed by other courts, and was cited with approval by both the House and the Senate when § 1988 was enacted into law.

This approach required trial courts to consider the elements that go into determining the propriety of legal fees and was intended to provide appellate courts with more substantial and objective records on which to review trial court determinations. This mode of analysis, however, was not without its shortcomings. Its major fault was that it gave very little actual guidance to district courts. Setting attorney's fees by reference to a series of sometimes subjective factors placed unlimited discretion in trial judges and produced disparate results.

For this reason, the Third Circuit developed another method of calculating "reasonable" attorney's fees. This method, known as the "lodestar" approach, involved two steps. First, the court was to calculate the "lodestar," determined by multiplying the hours spent on a case by a reasonable hourly rate of compensation for each attorney involved. Second, using the lodestar figure as a starting point, the court could then make adjustments to this figure, in light of "(1) the contingent nature of the case, reflecting the likelihood that hours were invested and expenses incurred without assurance of compensation; and (2) the quality of the work performed as evidence by the work observed, the complexity of the issues and the recovery obtained." This formulation emphasized the amount of time expended by the attorneys, and provided a more analytical framework for lower courts to follow than the unguided "factors" approach provided by Johnson. On the other hand, allowing the courts to adjust the lodestar amount based on considerations of the "riskiness" of the lawsuit and the quality of the attorney's work could still produce inconsistent and arbitrary fee awards.

A strong presumption that the lodestar figure—the product of reasonable hours times a reasonable rate—represents a "reasonable" fee is wholly

[1] The 12 factors are: (1) the time and labor required; (2) the novelty and difficulty of the question; (3) the skill requisite to perform the legal service properly; (4) the preclusion of other employment by the attorney due to acceptance of the case; (5) the customary fee; (6) whether the fee is fixed or contingent; (7) time limitations imposed by the client or the circumstances; (8) the amount involved and the results obtained; (9) the experience, reputation, and ability of the attorney; (10) the "undesirability" of the case; (11) the nature and length of the professional relationship with the client; and (12) awards in similar cases. These factors were taken from the American Bar Association Code of Professional Responsibility, Discipline Rule 2-106 (1980).

consistent with the rationale behind the usual fee-shifting statute, including the one in the present case. These statutes were not designed as a form of economic relief to improve the financial lot of attorneys, nor were they intended to replicate exactly the fee an attorney could earn through a private fee arrangement with his client. Instead, the aim of such statutes was to enable private parties to obtain legal help in seeking redress for injuries resulting from the actual or threatened violation of specific federal laws. Hence, if plaintiffs, such as Delaware Valley, find it possible to engage a lawyer based on the statutory assurance that he will be paid a "reasonable fee," the purpose behind the fee-shifting statute has been satisfied.

Moreover, when an attorney first accepts a case and agrees to represent the client, he obligates himself to perform to the best of his ability and to produce the best possible results commensurate with his skill and his client's interests. Calculating the fee award in a manner that accounts for these factors, either in determining the reasonable number of hours expended on the litigation or in setting the reasonable hourly rate, thus adequately compensates the attorney, and leaves very little room for enhancing the award based on his post-engagement performance. In short, the lodestar figure includes most, if not all, of the relevant factors constituting a "reasonable" attorney's fee, and it is unnecessary to enhance the fee for superior performance in order to serve the statutory purpose of enabling plaintiffs to secure legal assistance. . . .

In sum, viewing the evidence submitted by Delaware Valley to support its petition for attorney's fees, there is no indication as to why the lodestar did not provide a reasonable fee award reflecting the quality of representation provided during Phase V of the litigation. Clearly, Delaware Valley was able to obtain counsel without any promise of reward for extraordinary performance. Furthermore, Delaware Valley presented no specific evidence as to what made the results it obtained during this phase so "outstanding," nor did it provide any indication that the lodestar figure for this portion of the case was far below awards made in similar cases where the court found equally superior quality of performance. Finally, neither the District Court nor the Court of Appeals made detailed findings as to why the lodestar amount was unreasonable, and in particular, as to why the quality of representation was not reflected in the product of the reasonable number of hours times the reasonable hourly rate. In the absence of such evidence and such findings, we find no reason to increase the fee award in Phase V for the quality of representation.

IV

There remains the question of upward adjustment, by way of multipliers or enhancement of the lodestar, based on the likelihood of success, or to put it another way, the risk of loss. This is the question that we left open in *Blum* and on which the Courts of Appeals are not entirely in accord. We are of the view that our resolution of the issue would be benefitted by reargument and hence we do not decide it now. Accordingly, an order will issue restoring the case to the argument docket insofar as it raises the question whether attorney's fees chargeable to a losing defendant under the Clean Air Act and the comparable statutes may be enhanced based on the risk of loss, and if so, to what extent.

The judgment below is therefore affirmed insofar as it upheld the award of attorney's fees for the work done in Phases II and IX and, except for the multiplier for risk, is otherwise reversed.

Justice Blackmun, with whom Justice Marshall joins, and with whom Justice Brennan joins as to Part II, concurring in part and dissenting in part:

I join only Parts I and II of the Court's opinion. In Part III, the Court purports to follow *Blum v. Stenson*, 466 U.S. 886, 104 S.Ct. 1541, 79 L.Ed.2d 891 (1984), in which we held that an adjustment for quality was available "in the rare case where the fee applicant offers specific evidence to show that the quality of service rendered was superior to that one reasonably should expect in light of the hourly rates charged and that the success was 'exceptional.'" *Id.*, at 899, 104 S.Ct., at 1549, citing *Hensley v. Eckerhart*, 461 U.S. 424, 435, 103 S.Ct. 1933, 1940, 76 L.Ed.2d 40 (1983). The Court today, however, improperly heightens the showing required to the point where it may be virtually impossible for a plaintiff to meet.

Although the District Court's decision was issued before *Blum*, its quality adjustment in Phase V was in full accord with the standards subsequently laid down in *Blum*, Compare 581 F. Supp. 1412, 1431 (E.D. Pa. 1984), with 465 U.S., at 899, 104 S.Ct., at 1549. The proper standard of review of an attorney's fee award is abuse of discretion. *Evans v. Jeff D.*, 475 U.S. 717, 742-743, 106 S.Ct. 1531, 1545, 89 L.Ed.2d 747 (1986); *Blum, supra*, 465 U.S., at 896, 104 S.Ct., at 1547. I do not think the District Court abused its discretion in multiplying by two the lodestar for Phase V in order to adjust for quality. If the majority applied the proper, deferential standard of review on the quality issue rather than substituting its judgment for that of the District Court, it may have reached the same result as I do.

NOTES AND QUESTIONS

(1) Was the Supreme Court justified in *Delaware Valley* in its reluctance to award attorney's fees in excess of the lodestar figure (*i.e.*, the product of reasonable hours times a reasonable rate)? Should the amount of attorney's fee awards also take into account the unpopularity of an attorney's client and/or his or her "opportunity costs" in not pursuing more lucrative cases?

(2) In a sequel to the principal case, *Pennsylvania v. Delaware Valley Citizens' Counsel for Clean Air (Delaware Valley II)*, 483 U.S. 711 (1987), the Supreme Court considered whether awards made to environmental attorneys under fee-shifting statutes should be increased to take account of the contingent risk of the attorneys of non-compensation in the event the case is lost. A divided Court rejected such an upward adjustment, declining to adopt the argument that doing so was necessary to attract competent counsel in environmental matters. *Accord, City of Burlington v. Degue,* 505 U.S. 557 (1992). But compare *Venegas v. Mitchell,* 495 U.S. 82 (1990), in which the Court allowed the prevailing plaintiffs in a civil rights case to contract for an attorney's fee in excess of the statutorily authorized amount in order to obtain the counsel of their choice.

(3) Are prevailing defendants entitled to attorney's fees in environmental cases? At least one federal court has held that that may only occur where the defeated plaintiff's suit was frivolous, meritless or vexatious. *See National Wildlife Federation v. Consumers Power Co.,* 729 F. Supp. 62 (W.D. Mich. 1989).

(4) The Equal Access to Justice Act provides additional avenues for the recovery of attorney's fees by prevailing plaintiffs in environmental cases. That federal statute authorizes the courts to award attorney's fees against the government "to the same extent that any party would be liable under the common law or the terms of any statute." 28 U.S.C. § 2412(b). It also allows awards to prevailing litigants, unless the government can prove that its position was "substantially justified" or that special circumstances would make an award of attorney's fees unjust. 28 U.S.C. § 2412(d). However, under a 1996 amendment to the Act, recovery pursuant to § 2412(d) is only available to the following categories of private parties:

1. individuals with a net worth less than $2 million at the time the civil action was filed;
2. businesses with a net worth less than $7 million and with fewer than 500 employees;
3. tax exempt organizations, as described in Section 501(c)(3) of the Internal Revenue Code,which are exempt from taxation under Section 501(a) of the Code, or a cooperative association as defined in Section 15(a) of the Agricultural Marketing Act, which may be a party regardless of the net worth of such organization or cooperative association; and
4. a small entity as defined in Section 601 of Title V of the U.S. Code.

For an analysis of this statute, see Grad, Treatise on Environmental Law § 14.03.

CITY OF BURLINGTON v. DAGUE

United States Supreme Court (1992)
505 U.S. 557, 112 S. Ct. 2638, 120 L. Ed. 2d 449

Scalia, J.:

This case presents the question whether a court, in determining an award of reasonable attorney's fees under § 7002(e) of the Solid Waste Disposal Act(SWDA), 90 Stat. 2826, as amended, 42 U.S.C. § 6972(e), or § 505(d) of the Federal Water Pollution Control Act(Clean Water Act (CWA)), 86 Stat. 889, as amended, 33 U.S.C. § 1365(d), may enhance the fee award above the "lodestar" amount in order to reflect the fact that the party's attorneys were retained on a contingent-fee basis and thus assumed the risk of receiving no payment at all for their services . . . .

I

Respondent Dague (whom we will refer to in place of all the respondents) owns land in Vermont adjacent to a landfill that was owned and operated by petitioner City of Burlington. Represented by attorneys retained on a contingent-fee basis, he sued Burlington over its operation of the landfill. The District Court ruled, *inter alia,* that Burlington had violated provisions of the SWDA and the CWA, and ordered Burlington to close the landfill by January 1, 1990. It also determined that Dague was a "substantially prevailing party" entitled to an award of attorney's fees under the Acts, *see* 42 U.S.C. § 6972(e); 33 U.S.C. § 1365(d).

In calculating the attorney's fees award, the District Court first found reasonable the figures advanced by Dague for his attorneys' hourly rates and for the number of hours expended by them, producing a resulting "lodestar" attorney's fee of $198,027.50. (What our cases have termed the "lodestar" is "the product of reasonable hours times a reasonable rate." *Pennsylvania v. Delaware Valley Citizens' Council for Clean Air,* 478 U.S. 546, 565 (1986) (*Delaware Valley I*)). Addressing Dague's request for a contingency enhancement, the court looked to Circuit precedent, which provided that "the rationale that should guide the court's discretion is whether "without the possibility of a fee enhancement . . . competent counsel might refuse to represent [environmental] clients thereby denying them effective access to the courts." [On this basis, the District Court increased the attorney's fee by 25%. The Court of Appeals affirmed.] . . . .

II

We first provide some background to the issue before us. Fees for legal services in litigation may be either "certain" or "contingent" (or some hybrid of the two). A fee is certain if it is payable without regard to the outcome of the suit; it is contingent if the obligation to pay depends on a particular result's being obtained. Under the most common contingent-fee contract for litigation, the attorney receives no payment for his services if his client loses. Under this arrangement, the attorney bears a contingent risk of non-payment that is the inverse of the case's prospects of success: if his client has an 80% chance of winning, the attorney's contingent risk is 20%.

III

Section 7002(e) of the SWDA and Section 505(d) of the CWAauthorize a court to "award costs of litigation (including *reasonable attorney . . . fees*)" to a "prevailing or substantially prevailing party." 42 U.S.C. § 6972(e)(emphasis added); 33 U.S.C. § 1365(d)(emphasis added). This language is similar to that of many other federal fee-shifting statutes, *see, e.g.,* 42 U.S.C. §§ 1988, 2000e-5(k), 7604(d); our case law construing what is a "reasonable" fee applies uniformly to all of them.

The "lodestar" figure has, as its name suggests, become the guiding light of our fee-shifting jurisprudence. We have established a "strong presumption" that the lodestar represents the "reasonable" fee, and have placed upon the fee applicant who seeks more than that the burden of showing that "such an adjustment is necessary to the determination of a reasonable fee." The Court of Appeals held, and Dague argues here, that a "reasonable" fee for attorneys who have been retained on a contingency-fee basis must go beyond the lodestar, to compensate for risk of loss and of consequent nonpayment. Fee-shifting statutes should be construed, he contends, to replicate the economic incentives that operate in the private legal market, where attorneys working on a contingency-fee basis can be expected to charge some premium over their ordinary hourly rates. Petitioner Burlington argues, by contrast, that the lodestar fee may not be enhanced for contingency.

We note at the outset that an enhancement for contingency would likely duplicate in substantial part factors already subsumed in the lodestar. The risk of loss in a particular case (and, therefore, the attorney's contingent risk) is the product of two factors: (1) the legal and factual merits of the claim, and (2) the difficulty of establishing those merits. The second factor, however, is ordinarily reflected in the lodestar—either in the higher number of hours expended to overcome the difficulty, or in the higher hourly rate of the attorney skilled and experienced enough to do so. Taking account of it again through lodestar enhancement amounts to double-counting.

The first factor (relative merits of the claim) is not reflected in the lodestar, but there are good reasons why it should play no part in the calculation of the award. It is, of course, a factor that *always* exists (no claim has a 100% chance of success), so that computation of the lodestar would never end the court's inquiry in contingent-fee cases. Moreover, the consequence of awarding contingency enhancement to take account of this "merits" factor would be to provide attorneys with the same incentive to bring relatively meritless claims as relatively meritorious ones . . . .

[W]e see a number of reasons for concluding that no contingency enhancement whatever is compatible with the fee-shifting statutes at issue. First, just as the statutory language limiting fees to prevailing (or substantially prevailing) parties bars a prevailing plaintiff from recovering fees relating to claims on which he lost, so should it bar a prevailing plaintiff from recovering for the risk of loss. An attorney operating on a contingency-fee basis pools the risks presented by his various cases: cases that turn out to be successful pay for the time he gambled on those that did not. To award a contingency enhancement under a fee-shifting statute would in effect pay for the attorney's time (or anticipated time) in cases where his client does *not* prevail.

Second . . . "we have generally turned away from the contingent-fee model"—which would make the fee award a percentage of the value of the relief awarded in the primary action—"to the lodestar model." We have done so, it must be noted, even though the lodestar model often (perhaps, generally) results in a larger fee award than the contingent-fee model . . . .

And finally, the interest in ready administrability that has underlain our adoption of the lodestar approach, and the related interest in avoiding burdensome satellite litigation, counsel strongly against adoption of contingency enhancement. Contingency enhancement would make the setting of fees more complex and arbitrary, hence more unpredictable, and hence more litigable. It is neither necessary nor even possible for application of the fee-shifting statutes to mimic the intricacies of the fee-paying market in every respect.

. . . [W]e hold that enhancement for contingency is not permitted under the fee-shifting statutes at issue. We reverse the Court of Appeals' judgment insofar as it affirmed the 25% enhancement of the lodestar.

§ 8.05 Injunctive Relief in Environmental Law Suits

WEINBERGER v. ROMERO-BARCELO

United States Supreme Court (1982)
456 U.S. 305, 102 S. Ct. 1798, 72 L. Ed. 2d 91

White, J.:

The issue in this case is whether the Federal Water Pollution Control Act (FWPCA or the Act), 86 Stat. 816, 33 U.S.C. § 1251 *et seq.* (1976 ed. and Supp. III), requires a district court to enjoin immediately all discharges of pollutants that do not comply with the Act's permit requirements or whether the district court retains discretion to order other relief to achieve compliance. The Court of Appeals for the First Circuit held that the Act withdrew the courts' equitable discretion. 643 F.2d 835 (1981). We reverse.

I

For many years, the Navy has used Vieques Island, a small island off the Puerto Rico coast, for weapons training. Currently all Atlantic Fleet vessels assigned to the Mediterranean and the Indian Ocean are required to complete their training at Vieques because it permits a full range of exercises under conditions similar to combat. During air-to-ground training, however, pilots sometimes miss land-based targets, and ordnance falls into the sea. That is, accidental bombings of the navigable waters and, occasionally, intentional bombings of water targets occur. The District Court found that these discharges have not harmed the quality of the water.

In 1978, respondents, who include the Governor of Puerto Rico and residents of the island, sued to enjoin the Navy's operations on the island. Their complaint alleged violations of numerous federal environmental statutes and various other acts. After an extensive hearing, the District Court found that under the explicit terms of the Act, the Navy had violated the Act by discharging ordnance into the waters surrounding the island without first obtaining a permit from the Environmental Protection Agency (EPA). 478 F. Supp. 646 (D PR 1979).

Under the FWPCA, the "discharge of any pollutant" requires a National Pollutant Discharge Elimination System (NPDES) permit. 33 U.S.C. § 1311(a), § 1323(a)(1976 ed. and Supp. III). The term "discharge of any pollutant" is defined as: ". . . any addition of any *pollutant* to the waters of the contiguous zone or the ocean from any *point source* other than a vessel or other floating craft." 33 U.S.C. § 1362(12)(emphasis added). Pollutant, in turn, means, ". . . dredged spoil, solid wastes, incinerator residue, sewage, garbage, sewage sludge, *munitions,* chemical wastes, biological materials, radioactive materials, heat, wrecked or discarded equipment, rock, sand, cellar dirt and industrial, municipal and agricultural waste discharged into water . . . ." 33 U.S.C. § 1362(6)(emphasis added).

And, under the Act, a "point source" is "any discernible, confined and discrete *conveyance,* including but not limited to any pipe, ditch, channel, tunnel, conduit, well, discrete fissure, container rolling stock, concentrated animal feeding operation, or *vessel* or other *floating craft from which pollutants are or may be discharged.* . . ." 33 U.S.C. § 1362(14)(emphasis added). Under the FWPCA, the EPA may not issue an NPDES without state certification that the permit conforms to state water quality standards. A state has the authority to deny certification of the permit application or attach conditions to the final permit. 33 U.S.C. § 1341.

As the District Court construed the FWPCA, the release of ordnance from aircraft or from ships into navigable waters is a discharge of pollutants, even though the Environmental Protection Agency, which administers the Act, had not promulgated any regulations setting effluent levels or providing for the issuance of a NPDES permit for this category of pollutants. Recognizing that violations of the Act "must be cured," 478 F. Supp., at 707, the District Court ordered the Navy to apply for a NPDES permit. It refused, however, to enjoin Navy operations pending consideration of the permit application. It explained that the Navy's "technical violations" were not causing any "appreciable harm" to the environment. *Id.* at 706 "Moreover, because of the importance of the island as a training center, the granting of the injunctive relief sought would cause grievous, and perhaps irreparable harm, not only to Defendant Navy, but to the general welfare of this Nation." *Ibid.* The District Court concluded that an injunction was not necessary to ensure suitably prompt compliance by the Navy. To support this conclusion, it emphasized an equity court's traditionally broad discretion in deciding appropriate relief and quoted from the classic description of injunctive relief in *Hecht v. Bowles,* 321 U.S. 321, 329-330 (1944): "The historic injunctive process was designed to deter, not to punish."

The Court of Appeals for the First Circuit vacated the District Court's order and remanded with instructions that the court order the Navy to cease the violation until it obtained a permit. 643 F.2d 835 (1981). Relying on *TVA v. Hill,* 437 U.S. 153 (1978), in which this Court held that an imminent violation of the Endangered Species Act required injunctive relief, the Court of Appeals concluded that the District Court erred in undertaking a traditional balancing of the parties' competing interests. "Whether or not the Navy's activities in fact harm the coastal waters, it has an absolute statutory obligation to stop any discharges of pollutant until the permit procedure has been followed and the Administrator of the Environmental Protection Agency, upon review of the evidence, has granted a permit." 643 F.2d, at 861. The court suggested that if the order would interfere significantly with military preparedness, the Navy should request that the President grant it an exemption from the requirements in the interest of national security.

Because this case posed an important question regarding the power of the federal courts to grant or withhold equitable relief for violations of the FWPCA, were granted certiorari. We now reverse.

II

It goes without saying that an injunction is an equitable remedy. It "is not a remedy which issues as of course," *Harrisonville v. U.S. Dickey Clay Mfg., Co.,* 289 U.S. 334, 338 (1933), or "to restrain an act the injurious consequences of which are merely trifling." *Consolidated Canal Co. v. Mesa Canal Co.,* 177 U.S. 296, 302 (1900). An injunction should issue only where the intervention of a court of equity "is essential in order effectually to protect property rights against injuries otherwise irremediable." *Cananaugh v. Looney,* 248 U.S. 453, 456 (1919). The Court has repeatedly held that the basis for injunctive relief in the federal courts has always been irreparable injury and the inadequacy of legal remedies. *Rondeau v. Mosinee Paper Corp.,* 422 U.S. 49, 61 (1975); *Sampson v. Murray,* 415 U.S. 61, 88 (1974); *Beacon Theaters, Inc. v. Westover,* 359 U.S. 500, 506-507 (1959); *Hecht Co. v. Bowles,* 321 U.S. 321, 329 (1944).

Where plaintiff and defendant present competing claims of injury, the traditional function of equity has been to arrive at a "nice adjustment and reconciliation" between the competing claims, *Hecht Co. v. Bowles, supra,* at 329. In such cases, the court "balances the conveniences of the parties and possible injuries to them according as they may be affected by the granting or withholding of the injunction." *Yakus v. United States,* 321 U.S. 414, 440 (1944). "The essence of equity has been the power of the chancellor to do equity and to mold each decree to the necessities of the particular case. Flexibility rather than rigidity has distinguished it. *Hecht Co. v. Bowles, supra,* at 329.

In exercising their sound discretion, courts of equity should pay particular regard for the public consequences in employing the extraordinary remedy of injunction. *Railroad Comm'n v. Pullman Co.,* 312 U.S. 496, 500 (1941). Thus, the Court has noted that "the award of an interlocutory injunction by courts of equity has never been regarded as strictly a matter of right, even though irreparable injury may otherwise result to the plaintiff," and that "where an injunction is asked which will adversely affect a public interest for whose impairment, even temporarily, an injunction bond cannot compensate, the court may in the public interest withhold relief until a final determination of the rights of the parties, though postponement may be burdensome to the plaintiff." *Yakus v. United States, supra,* at 440 (footnote omitted). The grant of jurisdiction to insure compliance with a statute hardly suggests an absolute duty to do so under any and all circumstances, and a federal judge sitting as chancellor is not mechanically obligated to grant an injunction for every violation of law. *TVA v. Hill,* 437 U.S. 153, 193 (1978); *Hecht Co. v. Bowles, supra,* at 329.

These commonplace considerations applicable to cases in which injunctions are sought in the federal courts reflect a "practice with a background of several hundred years of history," *Hecht Co. v. Bowles, supra,* at 329, a practice of which Congress is assuredly well aware. Of course, Congress may intervene and guide or control the exercise of the courts' discretion, but we do not lightly assume that Congress has intended to depart from established principles. *Hecht Co. v. Bowles, supra,* at 329. As the Court said in *Porter v. Warner Holding Co.,* 328 U.S. 395, 398 (1946):

> "Moreover, the comprehensiveness of this equitable jurisdiction is not to be denied or limited in the absence of a clear and valid legislative command. Unless a statute in so many words, or by a necessary and inescapable inference, restricts the court's jurisdiction in equity, the full scope of that jurisdiction is to be recognized and applied. 'The great principles of equity, securing complete justice, should not be yielded to light inferences, or doubtful construction.' *Brown v. Swann,* 10 Pet. 497, 503 . . . ."

In *TVA v. Hill,* we held that Congress had foreclosed the exercise of the usual discretion possessed by a court of equity. There, we thought that "one would be hard pressed to find a statutory provision whose terms were any plainer" than that before us. 437 U.S., at 173. The statute involved, the Endangered Species Act, 87Stat. 884, 16 U.S.C. § 1531 *et seq.,* required the district court to enjoin completion of the Tellico Dam in order to preserve the snail darter, a species of perch. The purpose and language of the statute under consideration in *Hill,* not the bare fact of a statutory violation, compelled that conclusion. Section 1536 of the Act requires federal agencies to "insure that actions authorized, funded, or carried out by them do not jeopardize the continued existence of [any] endangered species . . . or result in the destruction or habitat of such species which is determined . . . to be critical." The statute thus contains a flat ban on the destruction of critical habitats.

It was conceded in *Hill* that completion of the dam would eliminate an endangered species by destroying its critical habitat. Refusal to enjoin the action would have ignored the "explicit provisions of the Endangered Species Act." 437 U.S., at 173. Congress, it appeared to us, had chosen the snail darter over the dam. The purpose and language of the statute limited the remedies available to the district court; only an injunction could vindicate the objectives of the Act.

That is not the case here. An injunction is not the only means of ensuring compliance. The FWPCA itself, for example, provides for fines and criminal penalties. 33 U.S.C. § 1319(c) and (d). Respondents suggest that failure to enjoin the Navy will undermine the integrity of the permit process by allowing the statutory violation to continue. The integrity of the nation's waters, however, not the permit process, is the purpose of the FWPCA. As Congress explained, the objective of the FWPCA is to "restore and maintain the chemical, physical and biological integrity of the Nation's waters." 33 U.S.C. § 1251(a).

This purpose is to be achieved by compliance with the Act, including compliance with the permit requirements. Here, however, the discharge of ordnance had not polluted the waters, and, although the District Court declined to enjoin the discharges, it neither ignored the statutory violation nor undercut the purpose and function of the permit system. The court ordered the Navy to apply for a permit. It temporarily, not permanently, allowed the navy to continue its activities without a permit.

In *Hill,* we also noted that none of the limited "hardship exemptions" of the Endangered Species Act would "even remotely apply to the Tellico Project." 437 U.S. at 188. The prohibition of the FWPCA against discharge of pollutants, in contrast, can be overcome by the very permit the navy was ordered to seek. The Senate Report to the 1972 Amendments explains that it was enacting the Permit program because "the Committee recognizes the impracticality of any effort to halt all pollution immediately." S.Rep. 92-414, 92d Cong., 1st Sess. 43 (1971). That the scheme as a whole contemplates exercise of discretion and balancing of equities militates against the conclusion that Congress intended to deny courts their traditional equitable discretion in enforcing the statute.

Other aspects of the statutory scheme also suggest that Congress did not intend to deny courts the discretion to rely on remedies other than an immediate prohibitory injunction. Although the ultimate objective of the FWPCA is to eliminate all discharges of pollutants into the navigable waters by 1985, the statute sets forth a scheme of phased compliance. As enacted, it called for the achievement of the "best practicable control technology currently available" by July 1, 1977 and the "best available technology economically achievable" by July 1, 1983. 33 U.S.C. § 1311(b)(Supp. IV 1970). This scheme of phased compliance further suggests that this is a statute in which Congress envisioned, rather than curtailed, the exercise of discretion.

The FWPCA directs the Administrator of the EPA to seek an injunction to restrain immediately discharges of pollutants he finds to be presenting "an imminent and substantial endangerment of the health of persons or to the welfare of persons." 33 U.S.C.§ 1364(a). This rule of immediate cessation, however, is limited to the indicated class of violations. For other kinds of violations, the FWPCA authorizes the Administrator of the EPA "to commence a civil action for appropriate relief, including a permanent or temporary injunction, for any violation for which he is authorized to issue a compliance order . . . ." 33 U.S.C. § 1319(b). The provision makes clear that Congress did not anticipate that all discharges would be immediately enjoined. Consistent with this view, the administrative practice has not been to request immediate cessation orders. "Rather, enforcement actions typically result, by consent or otherwise, in a remedial order setting out a detailed schedule of compliance designed to cure the identified violation of the Act." Brief for United States 17. *See Milwaukee v. Illinois,* 451 U.S. 304, 320-322 (1981). Here, again, the statutory scheme contemplates equitable consideration . . . .

Like the language and structure of the Act, the legislative history does not suggest that Congress intended to deny courts their traditional equitable discretion. Congress passed the 1972 Amendments because it recognized that "the national effort to abate and control water pollution has been inadequate in every vital aspect." S. Rep. No. 92-914, 92d Cong., 1st Sess. 7. The past failings included enforcement efforts under the Rivers and Harbors Appropriations Act of 1899 (Refuse Act), 33 U.S.C. § 401 *et seq.* The "major purpose" of the 1972 Act was "to establish a comprehensive long-range policy for the elimination of water pollution." S. Rep. 92-914, at 95. The permit system was key to that policy. "The Amendments established a new system of regulation under which it is illegal for anyone to discharge pollutants into the Nation's waters except pursuant to a permit." *Milwaukee v. Illinois,* 451 U.S., at 310-311 (1981); *see generally EPA v. State Water Resources Control Board,* 426 U.S. 200 (1976). Nonetheless, "in writing the enforcement procedures involving the Federal Government the Committee drew extensively . . . upon the existing enforcement provisions of the Refuse Act of 1899." S. Rep. No. 92-414, at 63. Violations of the Refuse Act have not automatically led courts to issue injunctions.

III

This Court explained in *Hecht v. Bowles,* 321 U.S. 321 (1944), that a major departure from the long tradition of equity practice should not be lightly implied. As we did there, we construe the statue at issue "in favor of that interpretation which affords a full opportunity for equity courts to treat enforcement proceedings . . . in accordance with their traditional practices, as conditioned by the necessities of the public interest which Congress has sought to protect." 321 U.S. at 330. We do not read the FWPCA as foreclosing completely the exercise of the court's discretion. Rather than requiring a District Court to issue an injunction for any and all statutory violations, the FWPCA permits the District Court to order that relief it considers necessary to secure prompt compliance with the Act. That relief can include, but is not limited to, an order of immediate cessation.

The exercise of equitable discretion, which must include the ability to deny as well as grant injunctive relief, can fully protect the range of public interests at issue at this stage in the proceedings. The District Court did not face a situation in which a permit would very likely not issue and the requirements and objective of the statute could therefore not be vindicated if discharges were permitted to continue. Should it become clear that no permit will be issued and that compliance with the FWPCA will not be forthcoming, the statutory scheme and purpose would require the court to reconsider the balance it has struck.

Because Congress, in enacting the FWPCA, has not foreclosed the exercise of equitable discretion, the proper standard for appellate review is whether the district court abused its discretion in denying an immediate cessation order while the Navy applied for a permit. We reverse and remand to Court of Appeals for proceedings consistent with this opinion.

Justice Stevens, dissenting:

The appropriate remedy for the violation of a federal statute depends primarily on the terms of the statute and the character of the violation. Unless Congress specifically commands a particular form of relief, the question of remedy remains subject to a court's equitable discretion. Because the Federal Water Pollution Control Act does not specifically command the federal courts to issue an injunction every time an unpermitted discharge of a pollutant occurs, the Court today is obviously correct in asserting that such injunctions should not issue "automatically" or "mechanically" in every case. It is nevertheless equally clear that by enacting the 1972 amendments to the FWPCA Congress channeled the discretion of the federal judiciary much more narrowly than the Court's rather glib opinion suggests. Indeed, although there may well be situations in which the failure to obtain an NPDES permit would not require immediate cessation of all discharges, I am convinced that Congress has circumscribed the district courts' discretion on the question of remedy so narrowly that a general rule of immediate cessation must be applied in all but a narrow category of cases. The Court of Appeals was quite correct in holding that this case does not present the kind of exceptional situation that justifies a departure from the general rule.

The Court's mischaracterization of the Court of Appeals' holding is the premise for its essay on equitable discretion. This essay is analytically flawed because it overlooks the limitations on equitable discretion that apply in cases in which public interests are implicated and the defendant's violation of the law is ongoing. Of greater importance, the Court's opinion grants an open-ended license to federal judges to carve gaping holes in a reticulated statutory scheme designed by Congress to protect a precious natural resource from the consequences of ad hoc judgments about specific discharges of pollutants.

Contrary to the impression created by the Court's opinion, the Court of Appeals did not hold that the District Court was under an absolute duty to require compliance with the FWPCA "under any and all circumstances," *ante.* At 7, or that it was "mechanically obligated to grant an injunction for every violation of law," *ibid.* The only "absolute duty" that the Court of Appeals mentioned was the Navy's duty to obtain a permit before discharging pollutants into the waters off Vieques Island. In light of the Court's opinion the point is worth repeating—the Navy, like anyone else, must obey the law.

The Court of Appeals did not hold that the District Court had no discretion in formulating remedies for statutory violations. It merely "conclude[d] that the district court erred in undertaking a traditional balancing of the parties' competing interests." *Romero-Barcelo v. Brown,* 643 F.2d 835, 861 (CA 1 1981). The District Court was not free to disregard the "congressional ordering of priorities" and "the judiciary's 'responsibility to protect the integrity of the . . . process mandated by Congress.'" *Ibid.* (quoting *Jones v. Lynn,* 477 F.2d 885, 892 (CA1 1973)). The Court of Appeals distinguished a statutory violation that could be deemed merely "technical" from the Navy's "[utter disregard of] the statutory mandate." *Id.* at 861-862. It then pointed out that an order prohibiting any discharge of ordnance into the coastal waters off Vieques until an NPDES permit was obtained would not significantly affect the Navy's training operations because most, if not all, of the Navy's targets were land based. *Id.* at 862, n. 55. Finally, it noted that the statute authorized the Navy to obtain an exemption from the President if an injunction would have a significant effect on national security. *Id.,* at 862; *see* 33 U.S.C. § 1323(a).

The Court unfairly uses the Court of Appeals' opinion in this case as a springboard for a lecture on the principles of equitable remedies. The Court of Appeals' reasoning was correct in all respects. It recognized that the statute categorically prohibits discharges of pollutants without a permit. Unlike the Court, *see ante,* at 9, it recognized that the requested injunction was the only remedy that would bring the Navy into compliance with the statute on Congress' timetable. It then demonstrated that none of the reasons offered by the District Court for refusing injunctive relief was consistent with the statute or was compelling under the circumstances. The position of the Court of Appeals in effect was that the federal courts' equitable discretion is constrained by a strong presumption in favor of enforcing the law as Congress has written it. By reversing the Court casts doubt on the validity of that position. This doubt is especially dangerous in the environmental area, where the temptations to delay compliance are already substantial.

Our cases concerning equitable remedies have repeatedly identified two critical distinctions that the Court simply ignores today. The first is the distinction between cases in which only private interests are involved and those in which a requested injunction will implicate a public interest. Second, within the category of public interest cases, those cases in which there is no danger that a past violation of law will recur have always been treated differently from those in which an existing violation is certain to continue.

Yakus v. United States, 321 U.S. 441, illustrates the first distinction. The Court there held that Congress constitutionally could preclude a private party from obtaining an injunction against enforcement of federal price control regulations pending an adjudication of their validity. In any balancing process, the Court explained, special deference must be given to the public interest:

> Even in suits in which only private interests are involved the award is a matter of sound judicial discretion, in the exercise of which the court balances the conveniences of the parties and possible injuries to them according as they may be affected by the granting or withholding of the injunction. . . .
>
> But where an injunction is asked which will adversely affect a public interest for whose impairment, even temporarily, an injunction bond cannot compensate, the court may in the public interest withhold relief until a final determination of the rights of the parties, though the postponement may be burdensome to the plaintiff. *Id.,* at 440.

In that case, the public interest, reflected in an act of Congress, was in opposition to the availability of injunctive relief. The Court stated, however, that the public interest factor would have the same special weight if it flavored the granting of an injunction.

> This is but another application of the principle, declared in *Virginia Ry. Co. v. System Federation,* 300 U.S. 515, 552, that "Courts of equity may, and frequently do, go much farther both to give and withhold relief in furtherance of the public interest than they are accustomed to go when only private interests are involved." *Id.,* at 441.

Hecht Co. v. Bowles, 321 U.S. 321, which the Court repeatedly cites, did involve an attempt to obtain an injunction against future violations of a federal statute. That case fell into the category of cases in which a past violation of law had been found and the question was whether an injunction should issue to prevent future violations.

In contrast to the decision in *Hecht,* today the Court pays mere lip service to the statutory mandate and attaches no weight to the fact that the Navy's violation of law has not been corrected. The Court cites no precedent for its holding that an ongoing deliberate violation of a federal statute should be treated like any garden-variety private nuisance action in which the chancellor has the widest discretion in fashioning relief . . . .

The Court distinguishes *TVA v. Hill,* 437 U.S. 153, on the ground that the Endangered Species Act contained a "flat ban" on the destruction of critical habitats. *Ante,* at 8. But the statute involved in this case also contains a flat ban against discharges of pollutants into coastal waters without a permit. Surely the congressional directive to protect the Nation's waters from gradual but possibly irreversible contamination is no less clear than the command to protect the snail darter. To assume that Congress has placed a greater value on the protection of vanishing forms of animal life than on the protection of our water resources is to ignore the text, the legislative history, and the previously consistent interpretation of this statute.

It is true that in *TVA v. Hill* there was no room for compromise between the federal project and the statutory objective to preserve an endangered species; either the snail darter or the completion of the Tellico Dam had to be sacrificed. In the FWPCA, the Court tells us, the congressional objective is to protect the integrity of the Nation's waters, not to protect the integrity of the permit process. *Ante,* at 9. Therefore, the Court continues, *ante,* at 9, a federal court may compromise the process chosen by Congress to protect our waters as long as the court is content that the waters are not actually being harmed by the particular discharge of pollutants.

On analysis, however, this reasoning does not distinguish the two cases. Courts are in no better position to decide whether the permit process is necessary to achieve the objectives of the FWPCA than they are to decide whether the destruction of the snail darter is an acceptable cost of completing the Tellico Dam. Congress has made both decisions, and there is nothing in the respective statutes or legislative histories to suggest that Congress invited the federal courts to second-guess the former decision any more than the latter.

A disregard of the respective roles of the three branches of government also tarnishes the Court's other principal argument in favor of expansive equitable discretion in this area. The Court points out that Congress intended to halt water pollution gradually, not immediately, and that "the scheme as a whole contemplates the exercise of discretion and balancing of equities." *Ante,* at 10. In the Court's words, Congress enacted a "scheme of phased compliance." *Ante,* at 10. Equitable discretion in enforcing the statute, the Court states, is therefore consistent with the statutory scheme.

The Court's sophistry is premised on a gross misunderstanding of the statutory scheme. Naturally, in 1972 Congress did not expect dischargers to end pollution immediately. Rather, it entrusted to expert administrative agencies the task of establishing timetables by which dischargers could reach that ultimate goal. These timetables are determined by the agencies and included in the NPDES permits, the conditions in the permits constitute the terms by which compliance with the statute is measured. Quite obviously, then, the requirement that each discharger subject itself to the permit process is crucial to the operation of the "scheme of phased compliance." By requiring each discharger to obtain a permit *before* continuing its discharges of pollutants, Congress demonstrated an intolerance for delay in compliance with the statute. It is also obvious that the "exercise of discretion and balancing of equities" were tasks delegated by Congress to expert agencies, not to federal courts, yet the Court simply ignores the difference.

IV

The decision in *TVA v. Hill* did not depend on any peculiar or unique statutory language. Nor did it rest on any special interest in snail darters. The decision reflected a profound respect for the law and the proper allocation of lawmaking responsibilities in our government. There we refused to sit as a committee of review. Today the Court authorizes free thinking federal judges to do just that. Instead of requiring adherence to carefully integrated statutory procedures that assign to nonjudicial decisionmakers the responsibilities for evaluating potential harm to our water supply as well as potential harm to our national security, the Court unnecessarily and casually substitutes the chancellor's clumsy foot for the rule of law.

I respectfully dissent.

NOTES AND QUESTIONS

(1) In *TVA v. Hill,* 437 U.S. 153 (1978), a case referred to in *Weinberger,* the U.S. Supreme Court enjoined the operation of a "virtually completed" dam and reservoir project in Tennessee after it was discovered that operation of the dam would destroy the critical habitat of an endangered fish, the snail darter. The Court held that § 7 of the Endangered Species Act,which requires all federal agencies to insure that their actions do not "jeopardize" the continued existence of an endangered species, compelled the courts to issue an injunctive order. Do you agree with the majority opinion in *Weinberger* that *TVA v. Hill* was distinguishable from the principal case?

(2) Following the *Weinberger* decision, to what extent do trial courts now have discretion to permanently excuse compliance with requirements of environmental statutes? For a trenchant discussion of *Weinberger* and its implications, see Plater, *Statutory Violations and Equitable Discretion,* 70 Cal. L. Rev. 524 (1984). *See also* Farber, *Equitable Discretion, Legal Duties and Environmental Injunctions,* 45 U. Pitt. L. Rev. 513 (1984); and Note, *Injunctions for NEPA Violations: Balancing the Equities,* 59 U. Chi. L. Rev. 1263 (1992).

(3) In *Amoco Production Co. v. Village of Gambell, Alaska,* 480 U.S. 531 (1987), the U.S. Supreme Court affirmed a lower court's denial of a motion by Alaska native villages for a preliminary injunction halting the Secretary of Interior's sale of oil and gas leases on federally owned lands in the outer continental shelf. Relying on *Weinberger,* the Court refused to accept the plaintiffs' contention that violations of procedural safeguards contained in the Alaska National Interest Lands Conservation Act constituted an irreparable injury which justified a preliminary injunction. Nonetheless, *in dicta,* the Court appeared to retreat from *Weinberger,* to some extent, stating that "[e]nvironmental injury, by its nature, can seldom be adequately remedied by money damages and is often permanent or at least of long duration. If such injury is sufficiently likely, therefore, the balance of harms will usually favor the issuance of an injunction to protect the environment."

BOOMER v. ATLANTIC CEMENT CO.

Text at Chapter 2, p. 57, *supra*.

NOTES AND QUESTIONS

(1) Do you agree with the remedy selected by the majority in the *Boomer* case? Does an award of permanent damages create a disincentive for companies to develop technical solutions that will diminish or abate their pollution of the environment? Was the *Boomer* court correct that it is not appropriate for common law courts to "achieve direct public objectives" that go beyond the rights and interests of the parties before them?

(2) How do you react to Judge Jasen's view that the remedy imposed in *Boomer* amounts to "licensing a continuing wrong?" How sound is the dissent's conclusion that the court has effectively granted the defendant a power of inverse condemnation? Is the "technology forcing" relief suggested by Judge Jasen (*i.e.*, enjoining the cement company's dust emissions unless, within 18 months, the defendant abated its emissions) an appropriate and practical approach?

(3) Is the principal case distinguishable from *Weinberger v. Romero-Barcelo, infra* ? Should different considerations apply, in suits based upon public law and upon private law, with respect to the appropriateness of injunctive relief?

(4) There was, apparently, credible evidence introduced at trial that the plaintiffs in *Boomer* suffered from loud noise that resulted from very frequent blasting at the defendant's plant, and that the dust emitted by the defendant covered the plaintiff's property with a "plastic-like coating" that was nearly impossible for the plaintiffs to remove. *See* Farber, *Reassessing* Boomer: *Justice, Efficiency and Nuisance Law,* in Hay and Hoeflich, eds., Property Law and Legal Education, (1988). Should these facts have affected the outcome of the case?

RESERVE MINING CO. v. UNITED STATES

United States Court of Appeals, Eighth Circuit (1974)
498 F.2d 1073, 6 ERC 1609

Bright, C.J.:

Reserve Mining Company is a jointly owned subsidiary of Armco Steel Corporation and Republic Steel Corporation which mines low-grade iron ore, called "taconite," near Babbit, Minnesota. The taconite is shipped by rail to Reserve's "beneficiating" plant at Silver Bay, Minnesota, on the north shore of Lake Superior, where it is concentrated into "pellets" containing some 65 percent iron ore. The process involves crushing the taconite into fine granules, separating out the metallic iron with huge magnets, and flushing the residue into Lake Superior. Approximately 67,000 tons of this waste product, known as "tailings," are daily discharged into the lake.

The use of Lake Superior for this purpose was originally authorized by the State of Minnesota in 1947, and Reserve commenced operations in 1955. In granting this permit to Reserve, the State of Minnesota accepted Reserve's theory that the weight and velocity of the discharge would insure that the tailings would be deposited at a depth of approximately 900 feet in the "great trough" area of the lake, located offshore from Reserve's facility. The permit provides that:

> "[T]ailings shall not be discharged . . . so as to result in any material adverse effects on fish life or public water supplies or in any other material unlawful pollution of the waters of the lake . . . ."

This enforcement litigation was commenced after state and federal pollution control efforts dating from mid-1969 produced an unsuccessful series of administrative conferences and state court proceedings. On February 2, 1972, the United States Government—joined eventually by the States of Minnesota, Wisconsin and Michigan and by various environmental groups—filed a complaint alleging that Reserve's discharge of tailings into Lake Superior violated Section 13 of the 1899 Refuse Act (33 U.S.C. § 407), Section 10 of the Federal Water Pollution Control Act(33 U.S.C. § 1160), and the federal common law of public nuisance.

Until June 8, 1973, the case was essentially a water pollution abatement case, but on that date the focus of the controversy shifted to the public health impact of Reserve's discharge of asbestiform particles into the air and water. Hearings on a motion for preliminary injunction were consolidated with the trial on the merits, and on April 20, 1974, after 139 days of trial extending over a nine month period and after hearing more than 100 witnesses and examining over 1,600 exhibits, Judge Miles Lord of the United States District Court for the District of Minnesota entered an order closing Reserve's Silver Bay facility. In an abbreviated memorandum opinion, Judge Lord held that Reserve's water discharge violated federal water pollution laws and that its air emissions violated state air pollution regulations, and that both were common law nuisances. Most importantly to the question now before this court, Judge Lord concluded in Findings 9 and 10 of his opinion that:

9) The discharge into the air substantially endangers the health of the people of Silver Bay and surrounding communities as far away as the eastern shore of Wisconsin.

10) The discharge into the water substantially endangers the health of the people who procured their drinking water from the western arm of Lake Superior, including the communities of Silver Bay, Beaver Bay, Two Harbors, Cloquet, Duluth, and Superior, Wisconsin. Defendants Reserve, Armco, and Republic noticed their appeal to this court and moved for a stay of the district court's injunction pending the appeal. Judge Lord denied this request and Reserve applied to us for a stay.

Upon consideration of Judge Lord's opinion of April 20, 1974, the written motion and supporting documents presented by Reserve, and after hearing the arguments of counsel representing appellants and appellees, we entered our order on April 22, 1974, granting a short stay of the temporary injunction until the merits of the motion could be fully heard and decided upon full briefs and extended arguments by both sides. We scheduled a full hearing before the court on May 15, 1974, at the federal courthouse in St. Louis. We have now held that hearing and considered all material pertinent to the motion for stay, including Judge Lord's supplemental memorandum dated May 11, 1974, consisting of 109 typewritten pages of fact and conclusions of law, expanding on his April 20th opinion. The question now before us is whether, considering all facts and circumstances, the injunction order should be stayed pending Reserve's appeal. We grant the stay subject to certain conditions and limitations as stated herein.

I

A. *The Substance of the Controversy*

Although there is no dispute that significant amounts of waste tailings are discharged into the water and dust is discharged into the air by Reserve, the parties vigorously contest the precise nature of the discharge, its biological effects, and particularly with respect to the waters of Lake Superior, its ultimate destination. Plaintiffs contend that the mineral cummingtonite-grunerite, which Reserve admits to be a major component of its taconite wastes and a member of the mineral family known as amphiboles, is substantially identical in morphology (or shape and form) and similar in chemistry to amosite asbestos, a fibrous mineral which has been found, in certain occupational settings, to be carcinogenic. The plaintiffs further argue that the mineral fibers discharged represent a serious health threat, since they are present in the air of Silver Bay and surrounding communities and, by way of dispersion throughout Lake Superior, in the drinking water of Duluth and other communities drawing water from the lake.

Reserve has maintained throughout this litigation that its cummingtonite-grunerite does not have a fibrous form and is otherwise distinguishable from amosite asbestos. Reserve further maintains the tailings cannot be said to pose any health hazard and, in any event, with respect to its discharge into water, the tailings largely settle to the bottom of the lake in the "great trough" area within close range of the plant.

The evidence presented on these points was extensive and complex. There was testimony as to the comparisons of mineralogy between Reserve's cummingtonite-grunerite and amosite asbestos, based on electron microscope analysis of morphology, x-ray diffraction and analysis of crystal structure, and laboratory analysis of chemical composition. As for the dispersion through Lake Superior, there was considerable testimony as to whether Reserve was the sole source of cummingtonite-grunerite in the lake and whether the presence of the mineral could be used as a "tracer" for Reserve's discharge. The district court found, as plaintiffs contended, that Reserve discharged particles identical to and similar to amosite asbestos, and that the particles discharged into Lake Superior were dispersed widely.

The suggestion that particles of the cummingtonite-grunerite in Reserve's discharges are the equivalent to amosite asbestos raised an immediate health issue, since inhalation of amosite asbestos at occupational levels of exposure is a demonstrated health hazard resulting in asbestosis and various forms of cancer. However, the proof of a health hazard requires more than the mere fact of discharge, the discharge of an agent hazardous in one circumstance must be linked to some present or future likelihood of disease under the prevailing circumstances. An extraordinary amount of testimony was received on these issues, and the district court designated several court witnesses to serve as impartial sources of review and evaluation.

B. *What the Court Decided*

The district court's conclusion—that Reserve's discharge into Lake Superior and its emissions into the air created a common law nuisance under federal and state law, and violated state and federal pollution laws—made the discharges subject to abatement. In determining the proper remedy, the court concededly balanced the equities and considered the economic and technological feasibility of abatement and the protection of the public health. The course of the proceedings indicate that the rather drastic remedy ordered by the district court—the immediate closing of the plant—was a response to the finding of a substantial danger to the public health. This is clear from the court's initial memorandum, where Judge Lord notes:

> "The Court has no other alternative but to order an immediate halt to the discharge which threatens the lives of thousands. In that defendants have no plan to make the necessary modifications, there is no reason to delay any further the issuance of the injunction."

II

We come now to our limited review of the district court's injunction ordering Reserve Mining to cease immediately its discharges into the air and water. In considering whether our temporary stay of that injunction should remain in effect, we note the usual formulation of the applicable standards to be met by the party seeking a stay under Fed. R. Civ. P. 62 and Fed. R. App. P. 8: (1) a strong showing that he is likely to succeed on the merits of the appeal; (2) a showing that, unless a stay is granted, he will suffer irreparable injury; (3) a showing that no substantial harm will come to other interested parties; and (4) a showing that a stay will do no harm to the public interest. *See, e.g., Long v. Robinson,* 432 F.2d 977, 979 (4th Cir. 1970).

The first element goes to the sensible administration of justice: a stay should not ordinarily be granted if the court determines that the injunction will not ultimately take effect in any event. The other three elements, while distinguishable in some contexts, dissolve into a single equitable judgment: balancing the health and environmental demands of society at large against the economic well-being of those parties and local communities immediately affected. Of course, foremost consideration must be given to any demonstrable danger to the public health. *See United States v. Nutrition Service, Inc.*, 234 F. Supp. 578, 579 (W.D. Pa. 1964), *aff'd*, 347 F.2d 233 (3d Cir. 1965). Absent such demonstrated health danger, the public interest may arguably be served either way in environmental matters. In considering a stay application where no health hazard is shown, an appellate court must weigh, first, the seriousness of immediate harm to the environment which will result from allowing the alleged pollution to continue and, second, the economic and social dislocation to be suffered by the defendants and by the communities dependent upon them if the injunction immediately goes into effect . . . .

In relation to the motion for a stay, the parties have directed briefs and arguments almost exclusively to the health hazard issue. Given the concededly enormous economic impact that an immediate plant closure would have upon Reserve, given the personal impact on its approximately 3, 000 employees and their families, and given the social and economic impact upon the communities in which the employees live, we think that our preliminary resolution of the health hazard question should control our action as to whether to grant or deny a stay.

III

A. *Testimony Before the District Court*

The plaintiffs argue, and the district court found, that both Reserve's discharge into water and its discharge into air substantially endanger the health of residents in several communities around Lake Superior. We have reviewed the testimony on the health issue, giving careful and particular attention and weight, as we should at this interim stage of review, to the testimony of the impartial court witnesses and that of plaintiffs' chief medical witness, Dr. Irving Selikoff, Director of the Environmental Sciences Laboratory of Mt. Sinai School of Medicine. While not called upon at this stage to reach any final conclusion, our review suggests that this evidence does not support a finding of substantial danger and that, indeed, the testimony indicates that such a finding should not be made. In this regard, we conclude that Reserve appears likely to succeed on the merits of its appeal on the health issue. We proceed now to trace the outlines of the testimony supporting this view.

(1) Two Key Unknowns

The theory by which plaintiffs argue that the discharge presents a substantial danger is founded largely upon epidemiological studies of asbestos workers occupationally exposed to and inhaling high levels of asbestos dust. A study by Dr. Selikoff of workers at a New Jersey asbestos manufacturing plant demonstrated that occupational exposure to amosite asbestos poses a hazard of increased incidence of asbestosis and various forms of cancer. Similar studies in other occupational contexts leave no doubt that asbestos, at sufficiently high dosages, is injurious to health. However, in order to draw the conclusion that environmental exposure to Reserve's discharges presents a health threat in the instant case, it must be shown either that the circumstances of exposure are at least comparable to those in occupational settings, or, alternatively, that the occupational studies establish certain principles of asbestos-disease pathology which may be applied to predicting the occurrence of such disease in altered circumstances.

Initially, it must be observed that environmental exposure from Reserve's discharges into air and water is simply not comparable to that typical of occupational settings. The occupational studies involve direct exposure to and inhalation of asbestos dust in high concentrations and in confined spaces. This pattern of exposure cannot be equated with the discharge into the outside air of relatively low levels of asbestos fibers. While Dr. Taylor, a court-appointed witness, testified that there are statistically significant higher levels of fibers in the air of Silver Bay than in the air of St. Paul, these levels still only amounted to .0626 fibers per cubic centimeter of air, far below the five fibers per cc standard for permissible occupational exposure set by the Secretary of Labor under the Occupational Safety and Health Act. It is clear that the air of Silver Bay, though polluted by a statistically significant level of "excess" fibers, is not equivalent to the contaminated air found in an asbestos factory.

Nor can the occupational pattern of exposure be equated with the exposure resulting from the ingestion of fibers via the Duluth drinking water. This fact was confirmed by a tissue study, discussed in detail later in this opinion, in which the tissues of recently deceased Duluth residents were examined for asbestos fibers. The virtual absence of any fibers moved Dr. Brown, the principal court-appointed expert, to testify:

> "Q. [Dr. Pooley stated in his summary of the tissue analysis that:] 'There was no indication of an occupational exposure to asbestos dust.'
>
> A. I agree with that."

Thus, it cannot be said that either the discharge into the water or the discharge into the air results in circumstances of exposure comparable to those in an occupational context.

If this is true, no conclusions about health hazards in occupational settings may be utilized in the present situation except on the ground that certain principles of asbestos-disease pathology may be extrapolated from relevant medical knowledge and applied in altered circumstances. The principal altered circumstance is the lower lever of exposure. In order to make a prediction, based on the occupational studies, as to the likelihood of disease at lower levels of exposure, at least two key findings must be made. First, an attempt must be made to determine, with some precision, what that lower level of exposure is. Second, that lower level of exposure must be applied to the known pathology of asbestos-induced disease, *i.e.,* it must be determined whether the level of exposure is safe or unsafe.

Unfortunately, the testimony of Dr. Arnold Brown indicates that neither of these key determinations can be made. Dr. Brown testified that, with respect to both air and water, the level of fibers is not readily susceptible of measurement. This results from the relatively imprecise state of counting techniques and the wide margins of error which necessarily resulted, and is reflected in the widely divergent sample counts received by the court. We cite some of the relevant testimony by Dr. Brown:

> [I]t is reasonable to assume an error in the counts of the fibers in both water and air of at least nine times on the high-side to one-ninth on the low side.
>
> . . . .
>
> Well, in my thinking, Your Honor, as far as using the information that is supplied to the Court on counts, in view of the incredibly large errors associated with this procedure, I would have to assume virtually only a qualitative base for what is being reported. In other words, Your Honor, I do not recall having been exposed to a procedure with an error this large, and for which people have seriously proposed a number based on this very poor procedure.
>
> . . . .
>
> This [poor counting procedure] has somewhat wider implications, Your Honor, than just to the question of the presence of fibers in air and water.
>
> It has become, at least in my thinking, the kind of soft underbelly, if you will, of all of the research, much of the research, I should say, of the work that has been reported on asbestos in patients and in experimental animals.
>
> . . . .
>
> Well, I interpret the information that was obtained in the water study as indicating that there are amphibole fibers, certainly, in the water of Lake Superior and in the water supply in Duluth. But I have little confidence in the estimate of the numbers. Which is another way of saying, Your Honor, that I consider the counts that I have been exposed to as qualitative, not quantitative in their implications. The same to be true in air.
>
> . . . .
>
> Well, analytical tests are divided into two broad categories, one a qualitative test which is used merely to indicate the presence [or] absence of something. The quantitative kind of tests are used to quantify or measure with some degree of precision how much of that substance is present.

The testimony indicates that little more can be said about the level of fibers present in air or water other than that some fibers are present.

Even assuming that one could avoid imprecision and uncertainty in measuring the number of fibers at low levels, there remains vast uncertainty as to the medical consequences of low levels of exposure to asbestos fibers. In order to predict the likelihood and magnitude of disease resulting from exposure, one must have some idea of the relevant threshold value and dose-response relationships. Although there seems to be agreement that threshold values and dose-response relationships are observable with respect to cancer generally, the particular values and relationships associated with asbestos-induced cancer appear to be unknown. Regarding this, Dr. Brown testified:

> Q. What is your view on the dose-response relationship between asbestos and cancer?
>
> A. I would like to approach that from the general point of view first. It is my view that in virtually—well, I will strike the word "virtually"—in

> every carcinogen that I know in which it has been possible to study whether or not a dose-response relationship exists, there has, indeed, been such a dose-response relationship. That is the general statement.
>
> Proceeding from the general to the specific. I would have to say that there is no reason for me to believe that asbestos [is] other than like any other agent, chemical, that causes cancer. So in a hypothetical way I would say that, yes, there is a dose-response relationship between asbestos and the development of cancer. I haven't the foggiest idea, Your Honor, as to what that level might be, either in air or in water.

In commenting on the statement, "This suggests that there are levels of asbestos exposure that will not be associated with any detectable risk," Dr. Brown stated:

> "As a generalization, yes, I agree to that. But I must reiterate my view that I do not know what that level is."

(1) The Tissue Study

In the face of these two key unknowns in evaluating the risk of disease, we must now look to additional important evidence, a tissue study conducted at the request of the court and designed to measure the hazard to Duluth residents of ingesting fiber-contaminated water. This study was prompted by an almost complete lack of knowledge with respect to the human ingestion of asbestos fibers, since previous experiments had dealt largely with the effects of fiber inhalation, where interaction by asbestos with the respiratory tract was established. Any theory attempting to deal with the effects of ingestion of asbestos in liquid had to bridge the gap between the ingestion of fibers and the interaction by those fibers with the body tissues. If the fibers do not interact with the tissues but simply are eliminated by the body as wastes, presumably no disease will result. Accordingly, the court-appointed experts formulated a "protocol" or study plan designed to test whether people who drink Lake Superior waters accumulate asbestos-like fibers in body tissues from taconite.

This protocol involved analysis by electron microscope of the tissues of recently deceased Duluth residents who had ingested Duluth water for at least 15 years, that is, since the beginning of operations by Reserve. As a "control" check on results, samples were taken from the residents of Houston, Texas, where the water is free of asbestos fibers. Although this study was necessarily expedited, plaintiffs' principal medical witness, Dr. Selikoff, accepted its likely value:

> Q. And you regard that as a sound protocol which will provide significant information?
>
> A. I think so, sir.
>
> . . . .
>
> . . . I think that their study has great value and we certainly would like to see the results of it."

Those results, as explained to the court by one of its own experts, Dr. Pooley,[1] indicated that the tissues of Duluth residents were virtually free of any fibers which could be attributed to the Reserve discharge.[2] Dr. Brown summarized the results as follows:

> It's my conclusion, from the tissue study, that residents of Duluth have not been found to have asbestiform fibers in their tissues when compared with Houston.

The significance which may be attributed to these results is a matter of dispute. Before the results were in, Dr. Selikoff had no hesitancy in forecasting that negative results would possess substantial significance, and stated:

> Now, our feeling was that no matter what air samples show or water samples show or anything else, unless it is found that asbestos is in the tissues of people who have drunk this water . . . if we do not find it in the tissues in appreciable quantities, then I would risk a professional opinion that there is no danger, at least up to this point, to the population no matter what our samples show or water samples.

Moreover, Dr. Brown, while suggesting that the tissue study did not exonerate Reserve's operations as a hazard, did state:

> It does tell me that it is not an emergency situation, and that's about as far as I can go.

Plaintiffs, however, sought subsequently to discount the significance of these tissue studies. First, the argument was made, and was accepted by the district court, that the specimens of tissue from body organs surveyed were too minute, and thus fibers that were present may have been overlooked. However, this judgment must be balanced by the following exchange between the court and Dr. Selikoff, which occurred prior to the conclusion of the study:

> THE COURT: And if we examine those tissues and there are not fibers there, this operation is home-free as far as the health hazard goes?
>
> THE WITNESS [Dr. Selikoff]: I would think we should find some fibers there. We're looking for needles in a haystack, but that's all right, we should find needles in the haystack with all the difficulties of the study, the technical difficulties, if we examine sufficiently large numbers of samples in some instances we should find some fibers there.

As noted previously, Dr. Selikoff has stated his belief that the design of the protocol was sound and would yield significant information. The weight to be given the tissue study has also been challenged on collateral grounds, most notably by testimony as to the increased rate of gastro-intestinal cancer among

1 Dr. Frederick D. Pooley is a world-renowned scientist from Cardiff, Wales, Great Britain, and an expert in the field of identifying physical and chemical properties of asbestos and asbestos-like fibers. Dr. Selikoff, plaintiff's expert, described Dr. Pooley as the "one man who has competence and knowledge in this matter," *i.e.*, the scientific examination of tissue for the presence of asbestos or asbestos-like fibers.

2 Several aspects of Dr. Pooley's testimony regarding the tissue study should be noted. The few fibers which were found were not, in the main, "closely associated" with the tissue specimens, indicating that contamination was a likely source of the fibers. No "asbestos bodies," indicative of long-term residence of the fibers in the tissues, were found. Finally, there was no indication of occupational exposure characterized by very large numbers of fibers.

workers occupationally exposed to asbestos. This increased rate of gastro-intestinal cancer, it was theorized, is the result of asbestos workers' ingesting or swallowing particles during periods of exposure. However, a theory of ingestion is by no means the only basis for explaining the increased rates of gastro-intestinal cancer, and there is no scientific or medical certainty regarding the mechanism actually involved.

Although, based on our review of the testimony, we agree with Dr. Brown's statement that the ingestion of asbestos fibers cannot be exonerated as a hazard, we feel that, on any fair reading of the circumstances of the protocol, the results of the tissue study must weigh heavily against the assessment of any demonstrated hazard to health. We think it is clear that the tissue study raises a major obstacle to the proof that ingestion of Duluth water is hazardous. The study can only be overcome either by questioning the initial assessment, joined in by plaintiffs' chief medical witness, that the protocol was sound and would yield significant results, or by accepting the proposition that theoretical medical opinions alone may overcome direct evidence. Neither alone nor together can these two bases for attacking the study amount to affirmative evidence that ingestion of the water is harmful. At most, they only provide a theoretical but unsubstantiated basis for leaving the results of the study in doubt, and leaving the effects of ingestion unresolved.

B. *Evaluation of Testimony*

A fair review of this impartial testimony by the court's own witnesses—to which we necessarily must give great weight at this interim stage of review—clearly suggests that the discharges by Reserve can be characterized only as presenting an unquantifiable risk, *i.e.,* a health risk which either may be negligible or may be significant, but with any significance as yet based on unknowns. This conclusion is simply a logical deduction from the following facts: (1) that fiber levels are not at occupational levels; (2) that the low levels present cannot be expressed or measured as a health risk; and (3) that, in any event, threshold values and dose-response relationships are undetermined. In other words, it is not known what the level of fiber exposure is, other than that it is relatively low, and it is not known what level of exposure is safe or unsafe. Finally, no basis exists, save a theoretical one, for assuming that drinking water, otherwise pure but containing asbestos-like particles, is dangerous to health.

We are confirmed in our evaluation by the testimony of Dr. Brown:

> I suspect I have stated my opinion on this before, and I don't recall now the precise words that I used, but I suspect I could sum it up by saying that in my review of the scientific literature that I would be unable to predict from that information that there will be an adverse effect that will occur in the citizens of Duluth or Silver Bay based on the presence of fibers in their environment.

Moreover, we believe there is essential agreement with this point by Dr. Selikoff, plaintiffs' chief medical witness. Although perhaps more expressive than Dr. Brown of the medical concerns which are posed by the unknown risks of Reserve's discharges, Dr. Selikoff seems to recognize that the likelihood of increased disease attributable to the discharges cannot be estimated:

> [W]e have no quantitative information on the relationship between the burden in tissues and the possible health effects. . . .
>
> Q. You don't have evidence that fibers, if they were ingested with the drinking water of Duluth would, in fact, occasion a public health hazard?
>
> A. No . . . .

In the final analysis, Dr. Selikoff's vigorously expressed judgment that the discharges represent a danger reflects his underlying opinion that:

> I advocate that where, to the extent feasible, that carcinogenic substances should not be added to the environmental burden in which we live.

Dr. Brown expressed the same concern:

> [B]ecause asbestos is a known human carcinogen we have to know a lot more about it than we now know in order to establish safe limits for its presence. I have no expectations that our environment will ever be entirely free of asbestos. But until we know what safe limits are, as a physician, who would rather see well people than sick people, I have some sort of compulsion to protect ourselves against known agents that produce cancer until we know what the safe levels are. That is my entire base.

We think that Doctors Brown and Selikoff share a common medical concern, but are essentially in agreement that the discharges here simply have not been proven to be a demonstrable hazard.

Interestingly enough, although Judge Lord does on occasion speak of a substantial health danger, based on the presence of asbestiform fibers in the environment, a careful reading of his initial and supplemental memoranda reveals an acknowledgment, at least in certain instances, that any ill effects are simply beyond proof. This is indicated in the "negative" findings which Judge Lord sometimes makes. For example, Judge Lord responds to the small number of excess deaths from rectal cancer in the Duluth area by finding:

> [W]e cannot say that the increase seen, although small in number at this time, is not due to ingestion by these persons of asbestos from Reserve's taconite waste.

Of course, neither can the opposite be said. Perhaps the most revealing statement of all is contained in Judge Lord's initial memorandum:

> The state of the scientific and medical knowledge available in this area is in its early stages and there is insufficient knowledge upon which to base an opinion as to the magnitude of the risks associated with this exposure.

Considering all of the above, we think one conclusion is evident: although Reserve's discharges represent a possible medical danger, they have not in this case been proven to amount to a health hazard. The discharges may or may not result in detrimental health effects, but, for the present, that is simply unknown. The relevant legal question is thus what manner of judicial cognizance may be taken of the unknown.

We do not think that a bare risk of the unknown can amount to proof in this case. Plaintiffs have failed to prove that a demonstrable health hazard exists. This failure, we hasten to add, is not reflective of any weakness which it is within our power to cure, but rather, given the current state of medical and scientific knowledge, plaintiffs' case is based only on medical hypothesis and is simply beyond proof.

We believe that Judge Lord carried his analysis one step beyond the evidence. Since testimony clearly established that an assessment of the risk was made impossible by the absence of medical knowledge, Judge Lord apparently took the position that all uncertainties should be resolved in favor of health safety. Since the appropriate threshold level for safe toleration of fibers was unknown, the district court tipped the balance in favor of attempting to protect against the unknown and simply assumed that Reserve's discharge presents a health hazard. In doing so, he disregarded the tissue studies of his own experts which provided evidence to the contrary. If we are correct in our conclusion that evidence does not exist in the record on which to find Reserve's discharges to be unsafe, the district court's determination to resolve all doubts in favor of health safety represents a legislative policy judgment, not a judicial one . . . . We emphasize that our evaluation rests not on any view that the discharge exposes North Shore residents to no risk, but rather on the view that, given the evidence, no substantial danger has been, or could be proven. It cannot be said, other than as a matter of conjecture, that the discharges will result in any higher incidence of disease than that experienced by a general public not similarly exposed. Although we are sympathetic to the uncertainties facing the residents of the North Shore, we are a court of law, governed by rules of proof, and unknowns may not be substituted for proof of a demonstrable hazard to the public health.

IV

After our examination of the relevant portions of the lengthy record in this case, we come to these conclusions: (1) it is unlikely that Reserve will prevail on the merits of the pollution issue and overcome the trial court's determination that pollution of Lake Superior must be abated; (2) it is also unlikely that Reserve will overcome the trial court's determination that the air emission must be controlled; but (3) Reserve, as we have demonstrated, may well prevail in its contention that its emission into the air and water have not proven to be a substantial health hazard. If and when our court is called upon, on the appeal on the merits, to affirm or modify the terms of the injunction based upon the existence or nonexistence of a substantial health hazard, we can forecast, on the showing presently made, that Reserve will succeed on the health hazard issue. However, the district court's finding on the pollution aspects of this case appear to be based on sufficient evidence, apart from mere speculation, to withstand our initial scrutiny. Therefore, in the posture of this motion, we cannot forecast any success for Reserve in upsetting these findings relating to pollution, and are satisfied that the circumstances call for a stay conditioned upon assurances that there will be a speedy termination of Reserve's discharges into Lake Superior and control of its emission into the air.

The controversy between Reserve and governmental agencies over alleged pollution of Lake Superior has existed for more than five years. In retrospect, it must now be painfully clear to all who participated in the original decision to permit the discharge of tailings into Lake Superior, that such a decision amounted to a monumental environmental mistake. The actors in that decision, 25 years ago, included leading citizens and governmental officials of Minnesota as well as officials of Reserve, Armco, and Republic Steel. That decision obviously was made in good faith to create jobs, to provide other economic opportunities in an economically depressed area of northern Minnesota, and to utilize the almost unlimited supply of hitherto unusable, low-grade, taconite ore found in that area. To us there are neither heroes nor villains among the present participants in this lawsuit, nor among their predecessors in government, business, and society who were once allies in encouraging and creating a taconite industry in northern Minnesota. Nevertheless, the pollution of Lake Superior must cease as quickly as feasible under the circumstances.

Accordingly, our stay of the injunction will be conditioned upon Reserve taking prompt steps to abate its discharges into air and water. We invited Reserve to advise this court concerning plans for the on-land disposal of its tailings and the significant control of its air emissions. Reserve's counsel stated that the company envisioned a three and one-half year to five years "turn-around" time, but added that investigation continues in an effort to reduce further the time for achieving abatement.

Our stay of the injunction rests upon the good faith preparation and implementation of an acceptable plan. Therefore, we grant a 70-day stay upon these conditions. . . . .

SUMMARY

We summarize:

1) On appeal, Reserve is likely to prevail on the merits of whether the evidence supports the district court's finding that Reserve's emissions into the air and its discharges into the water substantially endanger the public health.

2) The plaintiffs (state and federal governments and environmental groups) are likely to prevail on the merits of whether the evidence establishes that Reserve's present operations otherwise pollute the air and water.

3) It is likely that abatement will ultimately be required upon reasonable terms that take into consideration the multiple environmental, social, and economic interests involved.

4) We grant a stay of injunction for 70 days upon conditions stated in item 5 herein, and as amplified in the opinion.

5) This stay is conditioned upon a showing by Reserve that it is taking prompt steps to prepare and implement an appropriate plan for abatement, which it has represented to the court that it is now ready to do.

6) We remand this case to the district court for the purpose of receiving its recommendation for continuance of the stay order, after it has considered Reserve's plan and plaintiffs' comments on that plan, and for the further purpose of assisting the parties in attempting to reach agreeable settlement of the controversy, such settlement to be consistent with the public interest.

NOTES AND QUESTIONS

(1) Was the Eighth Circuit correct in concluding that "unknowns may not be substituted for proof of a demonstrable hazard to the public health," in environmental disputes in which there is scientific uncertainty as to the existence of a health hazard? Which party should have the burden of proof on this issue? Should the potential economic impact of pollution abatement measures be considered pertinent to resolving these questions?

(2) Since the principal case was handed down scientists have done a good deal of research into the extent to which ingested asbestos causes cancer. In a 1983 survey of that research, the U.S. Environmental Protection Agency predicted that 3,300 excess deaths per year would occur in a city of one million people if the population of that city were exposed to 100 million asbestos fibers per liter of water over the entire course of their lifetimes. *See* Nicholson, *Human Cancer Risk From Ingested Asbestos, A Problem of Uncertainty,* 53 Envtl. Health Persp. 111 (1983). *See also* Farber, *Risk Regulations in Perspective: Reserve Mining Revisited,* 21 Envtl. Law 1321 (1991).

(3) Following this decision, litigation in this case continued for another six years. Much of the subsequent controversy concerned the location and scale of an on-land facility for the disposal of taconite tailing wastes from Reserve Mining's plant.

Shortly after the Eighth Circuit handed down its opinion, U.S. District Judge Miles Lord, who strongly disagreed with the Circuit Court's decision, held a series of hearings regarding the public health implications of the proposed on-land disposal facility. Additionally, Judge Lord ordered the defendant to pay $100,000 to Duluth to cover the city's water supply expenses.

On appeal, the Eighth Circuit dissolved Judge Lord's order. Viewing Lord's actions as an act of defiance, and concluding that he had "shed the role of the judge to assume the mantle of the advocate," the appellate court took the extraordinary step of ordering that Judge Lord be recused from further participation in this highly publicized case. *See Reserve Mining Co. v. Lord,* 529 F.2d 181, 185, 188–189 (8th Cir. 1976).

§ 8.06 Governmental Civil Enforcement of Environmental Requirements

Although federal environmental statutes differ from one another in the specific details of their enforcement provisions, nearly all of these provisions contain certain common elements. Such statutes typically authorize representatives of the U.S. Environmental Protection Agency (EPA) to enter onto premises which are sources of pollution (or in which records of pollution are kept), to sample discharges and emissions, inspect records and monitoring equipment, and to compel self-monitoring record keeping and the production of other pertinent information. *See, e.g.*, Clean Water Act § 308, 33 U.S.C. § 1318; Clean Air Act § 114, 42 U.S.C. § 7414; Resource Conservation and Recovery Act § 3007, 42 U.S.C. § 6927. Moreover, the statutes also generally provide EPA with a range of options for enforcing the requirements embodied in environmental standards and permits. Thus, the Agency may issue notices of violation and administrative compliance orders, assess administrative penalties, and initiate civil judicial actions seeking civil penalties and/or injunctive relief. *See, e.g.*, Clean Water Act § 309, 33 U.S.C. § 1319; Clean Air Act § 113, 42 U.S.C. § 7413; Resource Conservation and Recovery Act § 3008, 42 U.S.C. § 6928.

Additionally, the statutes frequently provide for parallel federal and state enforcement of pertinent requirements.

Beyond this, several environmental statutes contain additional sanctions, including mandatory and discretionary prohibitions on federal agency contracting with environmental violators, *see, e.g.,* Clean Water Act § 508, 33 U.S.C. § 1368; Clean Air Act § 306, 42 U.S.C. § 7606; and, in the case of the one statute, "non-compliance penalties" intended to remove any economic benefits that result from delayed compliance. *See* Clean Air Act § 120, 42 U.S.C. § 7420.

The materials in this section examine EPA's implementation of its civil environmental enforcement authorities, against the backdrop of judicial decisions that have clarified or conditioned, the Agency's enforcement activities.

Mintz, "ENFORCEMENT AT THE EPA: HIGH STAKES AND HARD CHOICES"*

(University of Texas, 1995)

. . . .

Enforcement occupies a central place in the administration of regulatory requirements. This is particularly so with regard to federal environmental laws. Laborious, technical, time-consuming, and suffused with tensions, the enforcement process of the U.S. Environmental Protection Agency is, in the words of one skillful, experienced participant, "where the rubber hits the road and everything else hits the fan."

For more than a century, following enactment of the Interstate Commerce Act of 1887, federal administrative regulation of economic activities has become an established fact of American life. In a variety of substantive areas (from aviation to securities to labor relations) Congress has culminated prolonged struggles for reform with the passage of broad legislation aimed at redressing significant public problems. Frequently, however, that culmination is more apparent than real. As students of federal regulation have noted, the first statutes which emerge from agitation for regulatory legislation are often imprecise compromises between social forces that favor regulation and powerful interests that oppose it.

Because regulatory legislation is generally broadly drafted, considerable discretion is often vested in federal administrative agencies. Those agencies are often charged with important responsibilities of establishing specific rules

* Reprinted courtesy of the University of Texas Press.

consistent with general policies and purposes of the regulatory statutes themselves and enforcing those specific rules in administrative and judicial proceedings. According to one knowledgeable observer, "They are like armies of occupation, left in the field to police the rule won by the victorious coalition."

From the perspective of some regulated industries, the enforcement of federal environmental laws represents another, perhaps final, opportunity to effectuate their longstanding policy preferences and views. Part of the reason for this is the sometimes indeterminate nature of environmental regulations. As Marc K. Landy and his co-authors have discovered:

> [R]egulations only reveal their true meaning through the enforcement process. The inevitably ambiguous language of the rules is defined only as decisions are made about what constitutes a violation in specific affairs. In that process, arcane technical specifications that spell out what [pollution control] devices are to be installed and how their operation is to be measured often have specific public policy implications. Given the variety of processes and settings that must be dealt with, even rules written in meticulous detail will not eliminate the need for case by case enforcement.

In view of this, firms who are subject to EPA enforcement actions will often attempt to persuade the agency to adopt case-specific interpretations of enforceable EPA regulations that are consistent with their own perceived needs, aims, and regulatory philosophies. At the same time, the enforcement process represents a continuing test of the effectiveness and vitality of the nation's environmental laws. Its outcome determines whether the lofty aims and purposes of federal environmental statutes will ultimately be realized and the public's interest served. In the insightful words of Marver Bernstein:

> The attitude of [an administrative agency] toward its enforcement responsibilities affects its entire regulatory program. Unless it demonstrates a capacity to enforce its regulations, they will be more honored in the breach than in the observance. Those who discover that violations go undetected and unpunished will have little respect for the [agency] and will violate regulations with impunity if it is to their financial or commercial advantage.

In a general sense, the enforcement activities of regulatory agencies can be seen as a sequential series of filtering operations. As Colin Diver has characterized it:

> The initial task is to identify . . . that set of activities involving an apparent violation of the underlying regulatory command. From this set of apparent violations, the enforcement agency must select those appropriate to serve as the basis for a demand for remedial action. The agency further distills this sub-set into a group of offenses warranting the imposition of punitive sanctions.

At EPA, enforcement cases typically go through three phases: inspection and information gathering, administrative case development, and (if the matter has not yet been resolved) formal litigation. In noncriminal cases, the agency has several primary sources of compliance information: self-monitoring, record keeping and reporting by individual sources of pollution, inspections by government personnel, and the specific complaints of concerned citizens.

Most EPA inspections are announced to the pollution source ahead of time to ensure the presence of vital plant personnel. Inspections may be either "for cause," that is, based on a reasonable suspicion that the inspected source is in violation, or else routinely conducted pursuant to a "neutral inspection scheme." Perhaps surprisingly, of the approximately 1,600 individuals who perform EPA inspections, more than 75 percent do so less than 20 percent of the time.

When the agency conducts an investigation on the basis of citizen information, that information may have come from a variety of individuals. Citizen informants often include, for example, disgruntled employees of suspected violators, neighbors, state or local inspectors, environmental citizens organizations, and suspected violators' economic competitors. In potential criminal matters, these sources of information may be replaced—or supplemented—by targeted inspections, conducted under color of search warrant, by EPA criminal investigators and/or special agents of the Federal Bureau of Investigation (FBI), as well as by grand jury proceedings under the auspices of the DOJ.

Once EPA (and/or DOJ) investigators have completed their information gathering, they must determine whether the source in question is in violation of applicable standards and, if so, what type of enforcement response the agency will make. Under most of the relevant federal environmental statutes, EPA has a range of options available to it. It may begin enforcement by issuing a notice of violation to the allegedly violating source, describing the violation and inviting the source to confer informally with agency enforcement personnel. Alternatively, EPA may issue the source an administrative order requiring compliance with applicable requirements and, in some cases, an assessed civil penalty. In addition, EPA is generally authorized to refer enforcement matters to the DOJ for civil action or criminal prosecution. If it deems the circumstances appropriate, the agency may defer to a planned or ongoing enforcement action by state or local environmental officials.

EPA decisions as to which of these various enforcement options to pursue are generally made at the regional level by technically trained personnel working in cooperation with enforcement attorneys. These determinations frequently take account of a number of factors. Regional officials typically consider, among other things, the degree to which the source's discharge or emission exceeds applicable legal requirements, the duration of the violation, the number of previous enforcement actions that have been taken successfully against the same source, any relevant national EPA enforcement policies, the potential deterrence value of the case, the resources available to the agency and DOJ at the time of the decision, EPA's working relationship with interested state and local officials, and the agency's estimation of the enforcement capability of those same officials. These calculations, which are usually made with little public knowledge or participation, have great administrative significance. As Colin Diver has written:

> Persons making these decisions—prosecutors, in the broad sense—occupy a very significant gatekeeping position in the regulatory process. Not only

must they ration their own scarce resources of time and energy among competing caseload demands, but they must also ration access to other institutions involved in the adjudication of violations.

One final factor is also of immense importance in the regulatory enforcement work of EPA and other administrative agencies: the clarity and legal enforceability of the written standards and regulations which provide the underpinning for all enforcement actions. Marver Bernstein and other observers have noted that in order to be enforceable, regulations must be understood by persons and firms subject to them. Such standards must set forth clearly what the individual or firm must do in order to comply. This conclusion has particular application to the voluminous set of requirements enforced by EPA, requirements designed to govern the conduct of hundreds of thousands of individuals, firms, and government entities. Regrettably, however, the performance of agency regulation writers has not always been adequate. In a number of instances, imprecise and/or incomprehensible regulatory drafting has precluded the successful initiation and completion of EPA enforcement activity.

In his provocative study of EPA implementation of the Clean Water Act, Peter Yeager has observed: "The [EPA] enforcement process is a deeply textured one. At subsurface levels, it is an uncertain mix of professional ambitions of (usually young) litigators, bureaucratic politics and changing priorities, and virtually constant negotiations with a host of recalcitrants." This complex process creates a number of inherent and all but intractable constraints for the agency's cadre of top and mid-level managers.

At the regional office level, enforcement duties are generally divided among senior career civil servants who head divisions that have responsibility for regulatory matters in one specific environmental medium (air, water, hazardous waste, etc.) as well as regional counsel. These officials report to more than one superior. On the one hand, they are all supervised by relatively autonomous regional administrators, senior officials whose appointments and outlooks are often heavily influenced by state governors and environmental officials. On the other hand, these same regional counsel and division directors are accountable to particular assistant administrators in EPA's headquarters who are appointed to their positions and subsequently confirmed by the U.S. Senate, with different kinds of political support. In view of their divergent power bases, it is not unusual for regional administrators and assistant administrators to disagree on particular matters of enforcement policy. When this occurs, regional division directors and regional counsel are often placed in an uncomfortable and difficult situation for reasons that are self-apparent.

These internal EPA conflicts are not the only constraints that regional managers must face as they carry out enforcement responsibilities. The same officials must maintain effective working relationships with managers and supervisors at the DOJ, an institution which, as we have seen, has primary responsibility for litigation of civil and criminal enforcement matters referred to it by EPA. They must also work cooperatively with state and local agency officials to encourage state and local enforcement actions consistent with agency policies and preferences. At the same time, they must initiate supplementary federal enforcement proceedings when a state or local government has taken an action that the agency deems grossly inadequate.

EPA headquarters executives face a separate set of managerial constraints. Since most EPA enforcement activity is carried out by regional office personnel, the agency's headquarters enforcement officials require the cooperation of regional managers (including regional administrators, regional counsel, and division directors) whose approaches to enforcement may conflict with the preferences of headquarters managers. In addition, headquarters executives must communicate effectively with their counterparts at the DOJ. Moreover, they must be responsive to the demands and criticisms of two frequently opposing institutions: members of Congress (and the staffs of congressional oversight and appropriations committees) and executive branch entities, such as the White House Office of Management and Budget (OMB).

All EPA enforcement managers, whether they sit in headquarters or a regional office, have a multitude of other responsibilities and concerns as well, ranging from hiring, training, overseeing, evaluating and retaining their staffs to preparing and justifying budget requests, relating to other managers at a peer level, responding to inquiries from investigative entities (such as the EPA Office of Inspector General and the GAO), and keeping abreast of the frequent changes in law, science, and policy that may have an impact on their enforcement work.

Finally, all EPA executives and managers with enforcement responsibilities face one additional constraint: the enforcement process itself is intrinsically and unavoidably difficult to supervise. As Marc K. Landy and his co-authors have observed:

> Because it involves such substantial discretion at the operational level, enforcement is notoriously hard to manage . . . . The great detail involved makes it difficult for bureaucratic superiors, even those with technical training, to know whether the requirements their staff proposes are adequate (or necessary) to meet cleanup objectives. It is equally difficult for them, as supervisors of an ongoing relationship, to know whether initiating coercive measures is defensible or wise. In addition, if enforcement decisions are to be technically appropriate and survive judicial review, engineers and lawyers must work together in their formulation. This creates immediate problems in managing the necessary integration.

In view of these various circumstances and constraints, EPA's enforcement managers face immense challenges. Under conflicting pressures, they must work effectively with a wide range of individuals to accomplish their missions in a timely, defensible way. Given their heavy workloads and the case-by-case nature of enforcement work, they must often rely extensively on the judgment, dedication, and skill of their professional staffs.

At EPA, as at many regulatory agencies and departments, enforcement work involves considerable bargaining. In most instances, bargaining serves the interests and goals of both the agency itself and the regulated enterprises that are subject to enforcement action. From EPA's point of view, the time and energy of its enforcement staff is limited. To accomplish its objectives, it is usually to the agency's advantage to resolve acceptably as many enforcement matters as possible, without resorting to expensive and resource-intensive litigation. Another consideration for agency officials is the bureaucratic wish to retain control over decisions within one's area of responsibility.

When compromise is not possible and EPA refers a matter to the DOJ for litigation, some of that control is inevitably relinquished to judges and DOJ attorneys and managers.

From the regulated enterprise's perspective, negotiation and compromise are equally useful. Vicki Masterman, an attorney who represents many private companies in EPA enforcement matters, explains:

> It's an unusual set of circumstances that need to be in place for a company to decide that it makes sense to litigate fully in defense of an [EPA] enforcement action. Even if you think you have a good case, even if you think the equities are in your favor, sometimes you just can't afford the team of lawyers and the years it would take to litigate, especially given the [other] implications it has for your business. Your lenders might require that some additional financial facilities be created to anticipate a loss in litigation. Your SEC [Securities and Exchange Commission] reporting might need to be changed . . . . And that's not to even mention the cloud that hangs over your [manufacturing production] processes if you think you're going to have to change one of [them] entirely.

Although a number of EPA enforcement cases implicate minor, routine violations that are amenable to prompt resolution, in other matters the enforcement process is laborious and time consuming. For all concerned, these more complex cases involve high stakes and hard choices.

For regulated enterprises, the risks of enforcement sanctions—including the possibility of monetary penalties, mandatory pollution control measures that may be expensive to install and maintain, and even, in some criminal cases, jail time for responsible corporate officials—are very great. As Vicki Masterman has observed, "Enforcement [by EPA] is a very real problem for industry. Threats of imprisonment and high penalties strike the deepest chords of fear in corporate environmental managers . . . . From industry's perspective enforcement is the key."

Beyond avoiding or minimizing sanctions, regulated industries have an interest in dispelling uncertainties about their future environmental responsibilities and the costs those responsibilities will entail. In many cases, they are also concerned with preserving (or repairing) their public image as responsible corporate citizens and in reassuring lenders, shareholders, and potential investors of their good faith and freedom from impending open-ended liability.

At the same time, regulated enterprises must take care that any settlement they enter into with EPA enforcement officials not harm their firm's competitive standing within its industry. Monies expended on pollution control measures and environmental penalties will not be available for investment in productive manufacturing equipment that can increase corporate profits. As they negotiate with regulators, representatives of industrial firms are thus often mindful of individuals within their companies who focus mostly on the bottom line and see little need for or benefit from corporate environmental expenditure.

For EPA's representatives there are difficult choices as well in enforcement negotiations. Any attempt at standardized decision-making by the EPA is confounded by the enormous variety of conditions and circumstances that individual cases involve. The agency's enforcement engineers and attorneys frequently face sensitive decisions with respect to the pollution control measures they will accept, the penalties they will assess, the amount of time they will allow a violator to come into compliance, the legal prerogatives and safeguards they will insist upon, and the appropriateness of avoiding, or terminating, negotiations and referring a matter to the Justice Department for civil or criminal action. These judgments are complex and demanding. As one of my own former colleagues at EPA once confided, "You know, we really have to be very reasonable when we're in the enforcement business. The problem is that a lot of times it's just damned difficult figuring out what being reasonable *means.*"

From the agency's point of view, one factor in the successfulness of enforcement staff work is the extent to which enforcement attorneys and engineers work together as a coordinated team. Two senior EPA managers, Dale Bryson and David Ullrich, have discussed this knowledgeably:

> Engineers and attorneys are often of different personality types and they "speak a different language." They have different approaches to problem-solving and perspectives on the issues. They bring very different skills to the enforcement process . . . . [T]he key for the enforcement managers and attorneys and engineers themselves is to overcome their differences and integrate their skills.

In addition to interdisciplinary coordination, successful enforcement staff work also demands persistence, patience, and tact. It requires an ability to communicate with a range of interested individuals and to keep higher-ranking officials (as well as DOJ attorneys) informed and supportive of negotiating strategies and positions. Above all, it requires firm and principled dedication to the public interest . . . .

QUESTIONS

Does EPA do an adequate job of distinguishing cases that call for civil enforcement from matters that should be dealt with through criminal prosecution? Some critics have accused the Agency, and its counterparts in the Department of Justice, with failing to do this on a consistent, credible basis. From the above description of EPA's enforcement structure and procedures, can you observe any institutional impediments to the kind of consistency sought by the Agency's critics? To the extent the Agency has been inconsistent in separating civil and criminal enforcement matters appropriately, what harm might that cause?

UNITED STATES v. SHARON STEEL CORPORATION

United States District Court, Northern District of Ohio (1989)
1989 U.S. Dist. LEXIS 16736, 30 ERC 1778

Manos, D.J.:

On March 30, 1987, the United States of America filed the above-captioned case against Sharon Steel Corporation ("Sharon"), alleging that Sharon discharged pollutants without authorization, in violation of § 301(a) of the Clean Water Act("CWA"), 33 U.S.C. § 1311(a). On January 10, 1989, the United States filed a supplemental complaint alleging that Sharon, after receiving authorization, continued to violate § 301(a) by discharging pollutants in excess of authorized levels. The United States has moved for partial summary judgment on the issue of Sharon's liability. For the following reasons, the motion is granted in part and denied in part.

I

"[T]he objective of the [CWA] . . . is to 'restore and maintain the chemical, physical, and biological integrity of the Nation's waters.' " *National Wildlife Fed'n v. Consumers Power Co.,* 862 F.2d 580, 582 (6th Cir. 1988) (quoting CWA § 101(a), 33 U.S.C. § 1251). This objective is implemented through § 301(a) of the CWAwhich prohibits all discharges of pollutants except as authorized pursuant to § 402. The § 402 exception establishes the national Pollutant Discharge Elimination System ("NPDES"). 33 U.S.C. § 1342. Under the NPDES, the Environmental Protection Agency ("EPA") issues permits to individual dischargers. The permits make the generally applicable effluent limitations and other water quality standards the individual obligation of the discharger. The [CWA] . . . provides that each discharger holding a NPDES permit shall monitor and report on its compliance with its permit. Each discharger must install, use, and maintain monitoring equipment and must sample its effluents. The discharger must report the results of its self-monitoring to the EPA. *Sierra Club v. Chevron U.S.A., Inc.,* 834 F.2d 1517, 1419 (9th Cir. 1987). Compliance with a NPDES permit is deemed compliance with § 301(a). CWA § 402(k), 33 U.S.C. 1342(k).

Although EPA "is principally responsible for administering the NPDES permit system, . . . it may lawfully delegate permit issuing authority to state government." *National Wildlife Fed'n,* 862 F.2d at 582 (citing CWA § 402(b), 33 U.S.C. § 1342(b)). Before such delegation can occur, a state must submit a proposed program to EPA which conforms to the federal program on substantive and enforcement matters. *See EPA v. California ex rel. State Water Resources Control Bd.,* 426 U.S. 200, 208 (1976). Once EPA approves a state program, it ceases to issue NPDES permits for discharges into navigable waters within the state's jurisdiction. *Id.* EPA approved Ohio's permit program on March 11, 1974. *See Peabody Coal Co. v. Train,* 518 F.2d 940, 942 [7 ERC 2125] (6th Cir. 1975).

"Even after [EPA] . . . has delegated authority over the NPDES system to a state, [it maintains] . . . close and continuing oversight and supervision of the state program . . . " *United States v. Cargill, Inc.,* 508 F. Supp. 734, 739-40 (D. Del. 1981). It retains review authority over permit applications and "it may withdraw approval of a state permit program which is not being administered in compliance with § 402." *State Water Resources Control Bd.,* 426 U.S. at 208. Additionally, EPA "must take independent action in the event that the state fails to fulfill its enforcement responsibility." *Sierra Club,* 834 F.2d at 1519.

II

Sharon owns and operates the Brainard Strapping Division, a steel producing plant located in Warren, Ohio. In conjunction with its manufacturing processes, the plant discharges waste water into two outfalls, 001 and 002. The waste water flows from the outfalls through a drainage pipe into the Red Run tributary of the Mahoning River.

On November 24, 1982, Sharon filed a NPDES permit application with the Ohio Environmental Protection Agency ("OEPA"). On August 31, 1987, OEPA issued a permit to Sharon. The following day, September 1, 1987, OEPA issued the Director's Final Findings and Orders ("DFFO"). On September 30, 1987, Sharon appealed both the permit and the DFFO to the Ohio Environmental Board of Review.

III

Summary judgment is appropriate when "there is no genuine issue as to any material fact and . . . the moving party is entitled to a judgment as a matter of law." Fed.R.Civ.P. 56(c). It "is [particularly] appropriate on the issue of liability for violations of the [CWA] . . . since NPDES enforcement actions are based on strict liability thus making intent and good faith irrelevant. . . ." *Student Pub. Interest Research Group, Inc. v. Monsanto Co.,* 600 F. Supp. 1479, 1485 (D. N.J. 1985). To establish a § 301(a) violation, the United States must prove two elements: (1) that a person discharged pollutants from a point source into navigable waters of the United States (2) without a NPDES or in violation of a permit.

A

It is undisputed that from April 16, 1973 until August 31, 1987, Sharon discharged pollutants from a point source into navigable waters of the United States without a NPDES permit. Hence, the United States seeks a judgment that Sharon violated the CWA during that period. Sharon raises four arguments in opposition to the United States' motion.

First, Sharon argues that it cannot be held liable for violations that occurred more than five years before the commencement of this action. It is well established that actions for civil penalties under the CWA are governed by the five-year federal statute of limitations, 28 U.S.C. § 2462. Accordingly, the United States' motion for partial summary judgment with respect to violations that occurred prior to March 30, 1982 is denied.

Second, Sharon argues that it is not liable for discharges which occurred during the pendency of its permit application—November 24, 1982 to August 31, 1987. Under § 309 of the CWA,EPA is authorized to bring an enforcement action and to recover civil penalties when a polluter is in violation of § 301(a). Sharon argues that its filing of a permit application amounts to compliance with § 301(a), thus shielding it from liability under § 309. This argument is predicated upon a portion of the legislative history of § 309:

> It should be noted that the Administrator is partially limited in acting under Section 301(a). The Administrator is precluded from acting where

> the allegation is for failure to acquire a necessary permit under Section 402, if the owner or operator of a discharge has filed an application for such required permit. . . .
>
> The distinction between enforcement for violation of an unlawful discharge and enforcement for operating without a required permit under Section 402 is intended to cause the Administrator to act expeditiously to issue permits under Section 402 . . . . S. Rep. No. 414 92d Cong., 2d Sess., reprinted in 1972 U.S. Code Cong. & Admin. News 3668, 3730 . . . .

The plain language of § 309 and § 301(a) is clear and unambiguous; "[a]ny discharge except pursuant to a permit is illegal." *Kitlutsisti v. Arco Alaska, Inc.,* 592 F. Supp. 832, 839 (D. Alaska 1984). In *United States v. Tom-Kat Dev.,* 614 F. Supp. 613 (D. Alaska 1985), the court reached the same conclusion. There, the polluter, citing the same legislative history, argued that EPA lacked standing to sue it because it had applied for a permit. The court rejected this argument, stating:

> Although the statements made in Senate Report No. 92-414 about § 309 considered in a vacuum might lead to the conclusion that Congress created a major loophole in the strict permit requirements set forth in § 402 of the Act, plain reading of § 309's statutory language reveals no such broad exception. *Id.,* at 615.

Further, when the legislative history is examined in light of § 402(k), 33 U.S.C. § 1342(k), Congress provided a limited liability shield for polluters who were discharging at the time of the CWA's enactment, October 18, 1972; until December 31, 1974, the discharge of any pollutant was not a violation of the CWA if the polluter applied for a permit within 180 days of the statute's enactment. *Natural Resources Defense Council, Inc. v. Train,* 510 F.2d 692, 695-96 (D.C. Cir. 1975). After December 31, 1974, Congress intended that liability attach to all discharges without a permit, regardless of whether the polluter had applied for one. *Id.* Thus Sharon's argument is without merit.

Third, Sharon argues that equitable considerations preclude liability for the period March 31, 1982 through November 23, 1982. It argues that any violation of the CWA prior to October 27, 1982 was unintentional because it had no knowledge that it was discharging pollutants into navigable waters. It also argues that laches may bar or mitigate the United States' claim for penalties.

Neither argument has merit. Strict liability is imposed for violations of the CWA; intent is irrelevant, "except in connection with the amount of the penalty imposed." *United States v. Amoco Oil Co.,* 580 F. Supp. 1042, 1050 (W.D. Mo. 1984). Further, "[t]he Supreme Court has consistently adhered to the principle that laches is not a defense against the sovereign." *Levy v. United States,* 477 F.2d 916, 918 (6th Cir. 1973) (citing *Costello v. United States,* 365 U.S. 265, 281 (1961); *Utah Power & Light Co. v. United States,* 243 U.S. 389, 409 (1917).

Accordingly the United States' motion for partial summary judgment is granted with respect to all CWA violations that occurred from March 30, 1982 until August 31, 1987.

B

Additionally, the United States seeks a judgment that Sharon violated the CWA by discharging in excess of the levels authorized by its NPDES permit which was issued on August 31, 1987. To establish these violations, the United States relies on monthly operating reports (MORs) submitted by Sharon to OEPA. The MORs indicate that Sharon's discharges exceeded permit limitations from October 1987 through January 1988. Since the MORs "are reports or records which are required to be kept by law, [they] . . . may be used as admissions to establish [Sharon's] . . . liability" for that period. *Chesapeake Bay Found. v. Bethlehem Steel Corp.,* 608 F. Supp. 440, 451 (D. Md. 1984).

Nevertheless, in one sentence of its brief, Sharon argues that summary judgment is improper because the DFFO, issued by OEPA on September 1, 1987, "did not require [it] . . . to adhere to the final discharge limitations set forth in the . . . [p]ermit." Sharon's Memorandum at 23. The DFFO is a three page document which states that Sharon "is not yet in compliance with its NPDES permit" and orders it to attain compliance, pursuant to a construction schedule, by September 1, 1988. Sharon's Memorandum, Ex. A. The United States argues that the terms of the DFFO suggest that no permit modification was intended and that for modification to occur, the DFFO must be issued under different statutory authority. In the absence of evidence that the DFFO suspended Sharon's obligation to comply with the permit under the CWA, Sharon's argument is without merit.

Alternatively, Sharon argues that under the doctrine of primary jurisdiction, the court should refrain from ruling until the Ohio Board of Environmental Review acts on its appeal of the permit and the DFFO.

Primary jurisdiction . . . comes into play whenever enforcement of the claim requires the resolution of issues which, under a regulatory scheme, have been placed within the special competence of an administrative body; in such a case the judicial process is suspended pending referral of such issues of the administrative body for its review. *United States v. Western Pac. R.R. Co.,* 352 U.S. 59, 63-64 (1956). Here, the court is not faced with complex technical issues, but rather "is asked to enforce the standards [OEPA] . . . has already determined are appropriate." Natural Resources Defense Council, Inc. v. Outboard Marine Corp., 692 F. Supp. 801, 809 (N.D. Ill. 1988). Since the court is able to determine whether Sharon has violated those standards, the doctrine of primary jurisdiction is inapplicable.

Accordingly the United State's motion for partial summary judgment is granted with respect to all CWA violations that occurred from October 1987 through January 1988.

IV

For the reasons stated above, the United State's motion for partial summary judgment is granted in part and denied in part. Sharon is liable for its CWA violations that occurred from March 30, 1982 until August 31, 1987 and from October 1987 through January 1988.

NOTES AND QUESTIONS

(1) This case illustrates a number of the issues raised in environmental civil judicial enforcement cases. Is the public being penalized in this case by EPA's delay in bringing an enforcement action? What might cause such a delay?

(2) Note the EPA's reliance, in this case, on Clean Water Act violations reported by Sharon Steel to the Ohio EPA in monthly operating reports (MORs) required to be submitted by the company's NPDES permit. Such reports, which may not be the basis for a criminal prosecution, are frequently used to prove civil violations. Is that appropriate? To what extent does this encourage dischargers to misrepresent the nature and extent of their discharges—or to fail to file reports where permit discharge limits have been exceeded? Does the government have any recourse in those situations?

DUQUESNE LIGHT CO. v. ENVIRONMENTAL PROTECTION AGENCY

United States Court of Appeals, District of Columbia Circuit (1983)
698 F.2d 456

Mikva, C.J.

To speed improvement of the nation's air quality, Congress adopted the Clean Air Act Amendments of 1977.

An innovative feature of the 1977 Amendments was the authorization of penalties to recoup the economic benefits derived by pollution sources that fail to comply with air pollution limitations. 1977 Amendments § 120.

In these twenty consolidated cases, industry petitioners seek review of a variety of aspects of the final rules [implementing section 120]. In nearly all respects, we find that EPA complied with the statutory mandate: to recover the economic benefits of continued noncompliance with air quality standards, swiftly but fairly.

. . . .

Section 120 is a unique federal experiment with economic penalties. It is designed to alter economic behavior by changing the costs of emitting pollutants in violation of applicable air quality standards. *See* H.R.Rep. No. 294, 95th Cong., 1st Sess. 72-79 (1977). Congress added section 120 to the Act because it anticipated that even the augmented civil and criminal penalty scheme would not create sufficient incentives for sources to comply with air quality standards. Congress also hoped that the section 120 penalties would increase administrative flexibility in enforcing the Act, by serving as a middle ground between stiff criminal sanctions or shutdown of noncomplying facilities. Equally important, by removing the economic benefits of noncompliance with the Act, Congress hoped to place polluters on the same economic footing as those who had limited their emissions through increased anti-pollution expenditures. . . .

Section 120 begins by specifying the sources made subject to noncompliance penalties. Under section 120(a)(2), penalties may be assessed against any major stationary source—defined as any source that emits or has the potential to emit one hundred or more tons of any pollutant per year, Act § 302(j), 42 U.S.C. § 7602(j)(Supp. IV 1980)—not in compliance with any applicable emission limitation. Such penalties also are to be assessed against other stationary sources not in compliance with federal new source performance standards or standards for hazardous pollutants. Finally, sources operating under certain types of delayed compliance orders allowed by the Act are to be assessed penalties if they fail to comply with the terms of such orders.

Sources meeting certain conditions, however, are to be exempted from the noncompliance penalties. For example, sources converting from petroleum to coal pursuant to orders issued under the Act, and complying with the terms of such orders, are exempt from noncompliance penalties. § 120(a)(2)(B)(i). So are sources experimenting with innovative technology under the Act, § 120(a)(2)(B)(ii), and certain sources unable to comply with emission limitations for reasons utterly beyond their control, § 120(a)(2)(B)(iv). These exemptions are mandatory, although the burden of demonstrating entitlement to any of them falls on the source. In addition, EPA may exempt sources from penalties for certain instances of noncompliance that are de minimis in nature and duration. § 120(a)(2)(C).

Penalties are to be assessed against noncomplying sources either by EPA or by the individual states. Section 120 directs EPA to promulgate regulations implementing the penalties after notice and opportunity for public hearing—the regulations we must evaluate here. Individual states may take over responsibility for administering the noncompliance penalty program if they submit plans approved by EPA, § 120(a)(1)(B)(i), in which case the penalties are paid to the states, § 120(d)(1). To date, however, states have shown little interest in taking responsibility for the program. In any event, the statute does not differentiate substantively between the penalty program as administered by EPA and by the states, and the discussion to follow will for convenience refer principally to EPA as administering the program.

Section 120 sets out carefully the procedures to be followed in assessing the noncompliance penalties. Sources not complying with applicable air quality standards are to be given "a brief but reasonably specific notice of noncompliance." § 120(b)(3). Upon receipt of a notice of noncompliance, a source must either calculate the amount of the penalty owed, which begins to accrue with the issuance of the notice of noncompliance, § 120(d)(3)(C)(ii), or submit a petition within forty-five days challenging the notice of noncompliance or asserting entitlement to an exemption. EPA is to provide a hearing on the record and to act on the petition within ninety days. § 120(b)(5). Should a source in receipt of a noncompliance notice fail to respond, EPA may contract for calculation of the penalty. § 120(c).

Penalties are to be calculated to reflect the projected economic value of noncompliance to a source. EPA is to promulgate regulations for calculating the penalty, which must include at least the quarterly equivalents of capital costs, operating costs, and maintenance expenses avoided as a result of noncompliance. § 120(d)(2)(A). The penalty is to be paid on a quarterly basis, in equal installments during the entire period of noncompliance, beginning with issuance of the notice of noncompliance and ending when the source comes into full compliance with applicable air quality standards. § 120(d)(3)(B), (C). Expenditures made during a quarter for the purpose of bringing the source into compliance with air quality standards, and not otherwise reflected in the calculation of the penalty amounts, are to be credited against the penalty assessment for that quarter. § 120(d)(2)(B). Credits not taken into account fully in a given quarter may be carried over and offset against the next quarter's penalty assessment. § 120(d)(2). When a source reaches full compliance with air quality standards, the penalty is to be recalculated to take into account the actual—rather than the projected—expenditures required to bring the source into compliance with air quality standards and the length of the actual period of delay in the expenditures. § 120(d)(4). Sources that have overpaid are entitled to reimbursement, at interest rates set by the United States Treasury (or by the state, if the state is administering the penalty program); sources that have underpaid are to be assessed the deficiency, again with interest. § 120(d)(4)(A), (B).

Initial penalty payments are due six months after issuance of the notice of noncompliance. A source may seek judicial review of a determination by EPA that penalizes the source under section 120, but the penalty is not stayed pending the review process, § 120(e). The penalties are in addition to other civil and criminal penalties under the Act, and do not alter a source's other obligations under the Act. § 120(f).

. . . .

[EPA's § 120 regulations] require non-compliance penalties to be assessed against major stationary sources operating under consent decrees. They explicitly provide that a major source is liable for failures to comply with emission limitations set for that source in the SIP of the state in which the source is located, even though the source has been sued for violation of the limitations in question, the suit has resulted in a consent decree, and the consent decree sets out a schedule for the source to come into compliance with the limitations in exchange for an agreement by EPA not to pursue the civil or criminal penalties set out in the enforcement section of the Act, § 113(c).

Industry petitioners concede that the statutory parenthetical "(whether or not such source is subject to a Federal or State consent decree)," § 120(a)(2)(A)(f), permits assessment of noncompliance penalties against some major sources operating under consent decrees. They contend, however, that such penalties may be assessed only in two kinds of cases: (1) if the source fails to comply with a different emission limitation that was not the subject of the consent decree and (2) if the source fails to comply with the terms of the consent decree itself. . . .

. . . .

We think that EPA's interpretation of the statute is sound. Section 120 distinguishes three categories in which noncompliance penalties are to be assessed. The disputed parenthetical language appears in the first of these—major sources failing to comply with any SIP limitations. Reference to consent decrees also appears in the third category, which provides for the assessment of penalties against sources failing to comply with the terms of consent decrees or other interim orders. Industry petitioners' reading of the parenthetical—that it principally indicates that penalties may be assessed against sources failing to comply with their consent decrees—accounts only for the reference to consent decrees in the third category. It would render the parenthetical superfluous, for the third category makes absolutely plain that sources failing to comply with consent decrees may be subject to penalties for that very failure. Thus the function of the initial parenthetical is to make clear that consent decrees do not bar the imposition of penalties against major sources in violation of any emission limitation.

The legislative history, although limited, also supports the interpretation of the parenthetical chosen by EPA. Section 120 as originally enacted did not include the disputed parenthetical. *See* Pub. L. No. 95-95, 91 Stat. 714 (1977). The parenthetical was added as one of a number of "technical" amendments to the Clean Air Act Amendments of 1977, in the Safe Drinking Water Amendments of 1977, Pub.L. No. 95-190, § 14(a)(28), 91 Stat. 1401. An item-by-item summary of the technical amendments offered to the House explained that the parenthetical:

> [c]larifies that a noncompliance penalty applies to any noncomplying source (which is not exempted) including a source which has received a Federal or State consent decree extending a final compliance date.

123 Cong. Rec. 36,331 (1977). The universal scope of the explanation—that penalties are to apply to *any* source, in spite of a consent decree—clearly expresses the understanding of the statute urged by EPA.

Moreover, EPA's interpretation furthers the statutory purpose of section 120: recouping the economic benefits of noncompliance. The legislative history of section 120 repeatedly emphasizes the goal of removing the benefits derived by sources from delayed compliance with the Act. A source under a consent decree reaps such benefits, although the benefits may be expected to shrink as the source follows the course of compliance set out under the decree. Industry petitioners are surely correct that sources would be encouraged to enter consent decrees if the decrees provided shelter from noncompliance penalties, but it does not follow that Congress meant the decrees to abrogate the penalties. The penalties are intended to provide a swift, even-handed, economic incentive for compliance with the Act's standards, but would not do so if sources could escape the penalty by means of consent decrees.

. . . .

Being in violation of an applicable legal requirement does not automatically subject a source to section 120 penalties. Five of these exemptions are mandatory, with the burden of proof on the source to show that it is entitled to the exemption it claims. § 120(a)(2)(B)(i)-(v). . . .

. . . .

Under the inability to comply exemption, a source is exempted from penalties if its failure to comply resulted, inter alia, from reasons entirely beyond its control. The statute does not list factors that are to trigger the exemption; it is entirely open-ended. . . .

EPA's regulation implementing section 120 enumerates seven factors that it will consider as beyond the control of a source:

(1) Act of God;

(2) Fire;

(3) Embargo;

(4) Strike;

(5) Inability to obtain capital, if that inability is the result of temporary market conditions;

(6) Failure of equipment to perform as designed, assuming expectations about performance were reasonable; and

(7) The complete inability of a supplier or contractor to furnish labor or materials.

. . . Only if a source can show that it meets one of these conditions will EPA grant it an exemption for inability to comply.

Industry petitioners object, first, that this list should be expanded to include technological impossibility as a factor. EPA based its refusal to grant a general exemption for technological incapacity on its understanding of the technology-forcing character of the Act. EPA recognized, however, the difficulties of assessing a penalty to reflect the economic benefits of noncompliance, when the technology was not yet available to outline the steps to be taken by the source to bring it into compliance. Estimating the costs of pollution control equipment, for example, may be impossible when it is not yet known what equipment will be necessary. EPA thus determined that:

> [w]here existing technology has not yet demonstrated compliance, the penalty will be based upon the cost of installing the best available controls as determined on a case-by-case basis, as well as a commitment to an appropriate research and development (R&D) program designed to develop the new means of emission control necessary to achieve the standards. Thus, a source that has taken and is continuing to take all possible steps to achieve compliance, including the installation of the best available controls and, where appropriate, participation in an appropriate R&D program, would be considered to be deriving no economic benefit from its failure to comply. . . .

EPA's approach, in other words, is to deny an exemption for technological impossibility but to calculate the penalties to ensure that sources doing their best to surmount existing technology will not be assessed any penalties. In EPA's judgment, this approach would provide the best mix of incentives to bring about the goals of the Clean Air Act: sources would be deterred from hiding their inadequate efforts behind the excuse of technological impossibility, and would be encouraged to take advantage of and build upon technological advances as they occur.

We agree with EPA that it is reasonable to exclude technological impossibility from the inability to comply exemption. At no time during the debates did Congress consider enumerating technological impossibility as one of the factors triggering the exemption, nor did Congress move towards the more flexible formulation of the exemption in order to incorporate technological impossibility. Indeed, Senator Muskie's explanation of the version of section 120 that emerged from the Senate and House conference stated explicitly that the exemption was not intended to cover a claim that needed technology is unavailable. Congress' emphasis that exemptions should be construed narrowly, to avoid diluting incentives created by the penalty provision, was repeated.

Furthermore, EPA's approach is a reasonable balance of statutory goals. Congress intended the Act to create incentives to develop the technology needed to abate air pollution. Perhaps the best that can be expected from sources in pursuit of this goal is use of the best available technology and continued efforts to develop better technology. EPA's treatment of technological impossibility encourages this progress, and we affirm such treatment.

. . . .

In 1977, Congress added section 120 to the Act to supplement the system of civil and criminal sanctions enacted in 1970. Section 120 establishes a penalty assessment system whereby sources not in compliance with the applicable legal requirements of the Act are fined in accordance with the economic value of that noncompliance. EPA was directed to and eventually did promulgate a series of regulations implementing this section of the statute.

. . . .

It is more than five years since Congress enacted this section; it is certainly time to put into operation the penalty assessment system Congress mandated.

NOTES AND QUESTIONS

(1) Did EPA and the D.C. Circuit reasonably interpret § 120 of the Clean Air Actin this case? To what extent is this decision consistent with the notion of "technology-forcing" that underlies a number of environmental statutes?

(2) Note the court's observation that "it is five years since Congress enacted" section 120 of the Clean Air Act. Is it appropriate for violators of the statute to benefit from litigation-induced delay when penalty assessment regulations are subjected to challenge in the courts? Could the statute have been fashioned to avoid that problem?

(3) In a sequel to the principal case, regulated utilities challenged the applicability of EPA's § 120 penalty assessment model to them. They noted that public utility regulatory bodies allowed utility expenditures on pollution control equipment to be "passed through" to the public, thus diminishing the financial impact on those companies of complying with Clean Air Act emission standards. At the same time, however, the same regulators typically did not allow pollution penalties to be passed through to rate payers by utilities. The D.C. Circuit dismissed these claims. It noted that § 120 states that penalties should be "no less" than the economic value of non-compliance, and that the statute specifically provides that "the capital costs of compliance" and "operation and maintenance costs foregone" are to be included in the § 120 penalties. *See Duquesne Light Co. v. EPA (Duquesne II),* 791 F.2d 959 (D.C. Cir. 1986).

(4) Does EPA have discretion not to assess a non-compliance penalty if a Clean Air Act violation falls within a designated category of Section 120? The Agency has answered that question in the affirmative. *See* 45 Fed. Reg. 50088 (1980). Is this position legally supportable? Is it sound policy?

IN THE MATTER OF SARA LEE CORP.

1993 EPA Consent LEXIS 180 (Nov. 4, 1993)

Consent Agreement and Consent Order

Environmental Appeals Judge, U.S. Environmental Protection Agency, Washington, D.C.

. . . .

C. EPCRA/CERCLA § 103(a)Compliance Audit

Sara Lee agrees that the internal audit conducted to review and report on the compliance of Sara Lee's continental U.S. manufacturing and food services distribution facilities with Sections 304, 311, 312 and 313 of EPCRA and Section 103(a) of CERCLAhas been and will be conducted as follows:

1. Scope of Audit: This audit, and the stipulated penalties identified in section V.C.7 below, shall apply only to Sara Lee's continental U.S. manufacturing and food services distribution facilities purchased and/or owned by Sara Lee during the three-year period preceding the execution of this Consent Agreement. However, for those facilities still owned or leased by Sara Lee and still in active operation at the time of the execution of this Consent Agreement, the audit shall cover the full three-year period, including the period prior to Sara Lee's ownership. "Active operation" means a facility which currently employs a paid staff and is engaged in some form of manufacturing or processing activities.

2. Independent Auditor: Sara Lee's EPCRA and CERCLA § 103audit activities have been and will continue to be conducted by independent third parties, *i.e.*, either trained outside consultants or trained in-house personnel who do not report to the management of the facility being audited. Oversight of auditing activities is provided by the Director of Environmental Affairs who is independent of any facility management personnel. The reports required under Paragraph V.C.4 of this Agreement shall be prepared and submitted by either the auditor or the Director of Environmental Affairs.

3. Audit Initiation/Termination: Auditing activities related to this CACO began in December of 1991 and shall be completed within 250 days of the date of execution of the Consent Order by the Environmental Appeals Board.

4. Reporting Requirements: Sara Lee agrees to submit the following reports during the course of the EPCRA/CERCLA § 103(a)audit:

(a) Initial Report. The initial report shall be submitted within 60 days of receipt of the executed Consent Order. The initial report shall list the Sara Lee facilities to be audited or already audited. The initial report shall also describe the records already audited and the procedures employed to audit such records ("the protocol"), and confirm that such audit procedures will encompass all the records necessary to comply with this Agreement.

(b) Final Report. The final report shall be submitted within 60 days following the completion of the audit. The final report shall provide in a cumulative fashion a list of the facilities and chemicals reviewed at each facility which meets Tier II and Form R threshold requirements for EPCRA and CERCLA § 103(a)reporting requirements, and a summary of the violations detected and the actions taken to remedy and mitigate the violations. The final report must also include: (1) a statement signed by a responsible corporate official certifying that the audit has been conducted and that the audit protocol was followed; and (2) to the extent practicable, an accounting for all costs incurred in conducting the audit, including all internal costs and all fees paid to consultants for audit-related work.

5. Immediately Reportable Events/Duty to Mitigate. Discovery of any of the following acts or omissions during the period covered by the audit shall constitute an immediately reportable event:

(a) failure to notify immediately the National Response Center of a release of a reportable quantity of a hazardous substance, or failure to provide all of the required information, as required by CERCLA § 103(a) and the applicable regulations.

(b) failure to notify immediately the State Emergency Response Commission and/or the Local Emergency Planning Committee of a release of a hazardous substance or an Extremely Hazardous Substance (EHS), as required by EPCRA § 304 and the applicable regulations.

(c) failure to provide written follow-up notification of an emergency release to the State Emergency Response Commission and/or the Local Emergency Planning Committee as soon as practicable, as required by EPCRA § 304(c) and the applicable regulations.

(d) failure to submit an MSDS as required by EPCRA § 311 and the applicable regulations.

(e) failure to submit emergency and hazardous chemical inventory forms as required by EPCRA § 312 and the applicable regulations; and

(f) failure to submit toxic chemical release forms ("Form Rs") timely as required by EPCRA § 313 and the applicable regulations.

Sara Lee is required to submit to EPA a written notice of each immediately reportable event discovered during the audit within 10 working days of confirmation of the event. The notice shall describe the nature and extent of the reportable event and indicate the steps taken, or being taken by Sara Lee to cure or mitigate the violation.

Sara Lee agrees to cure potential CERCLA § 103(a)violations by providing the required notification as specified in CERCLA § 103(a) and the applicable regulations. Sara Lee agrees to cure potential EPCRA § 304(a)violations by providing the required notification to the applicable authorities as specified in EPCRA § 304(a). Sara Lee agrees to cure potential EPCRA § 304(c)violations by providing written follow-up emergency notice to the applicable authorities as specified in EPCRA § 304(c) and the applicable regulations. Sara Lee agrees to cure potential EPCRA § 311, § 312, and § 313violations by submitting the required MSDS form, emergency and hazardous chemical inventory form, and/or toxic chemical release form to the applicable authorities as specified in the statute and accompanying regulations.

6. Reporting Period: The time periods to be covered by the audit shall be as follows:

(a) CERCLA § 103(a): Three years prior to the date of execution of this Consent Agreement.

(b) EPCRA § 304(c): Three years prior to the date of execution of this Consent Agreement.

(c) EPCRA § 311: Three years prior to the date of execution of this Consent Agreement.

(d) EPCRA § 312: Three years prior to the date of execution of this Consent Agreement.

(e) EPCRA § 313: Three years prior to the date of execution of this Consent Agreement.

7. Stipulated Penalties: The stipulated penalties set forth below shall apply for only those violations that are reported under the EPCRA/CERCLA § 103(a)compliance audit and which are remedied. Once a violation is reported and remedied, the stipulated penalty establishes the limit of Sara Lee's CERCLA § 103(a) and EPCRA § 304, § 311, § 312, and § 313liability for that violation. The amount assessed by EPA for a particular violation will depend upon the circumstances of the violation, however, per-day penalties will not be assessed. Otherwise, the applicable Enforcement Response Policy will serve as EPA's guide in calculating an appropriate penalty.

Sara Lee agrees to pay the following stipulated penalties:

a. Each violation of CERCLA § 103(a)shall be assessed on a per-violation basis. The penalty, under this section, shall not exceed $20,000 per violation.

b. Each violation of EPCRA § 304(a)shall be assessed on a per-violation basis. The penalty, under this section, shall not exceed $20,000 per violation; reporting to the LEPC, the SERC, or the local fire department constitute three separate points of compliance and therefore the failure to report to all three constitutes three separate violations.

c. Each violation of EPCRA § 304(a)shall be assessed on a per-violation basis. The penalty, under this section, shall not exceed $10,000 per violation; reporting to the LEPC, the SERC, or the local fire department constitutes three separate points of compliance and therefore the failure to report all three violations constitutes three separate violations.

d. Each violation of EPCRA § 311shall be assessed on a per-violation basis. The penalty, under this section, shall not exceed $8,000 per violation; reporting to the LEPC, the SERC, or the local fire department constitutes three separate points of compliance and therefore the failure to report all three violations constitutes three separate violations. However, for purposes only of this Consent Agreement and Consent Order, where all three points of compliance have been violated with respect to a given chemical, the total penalty for the three violations shall not exceed $20,000.

e. Each violation of EPCRA § 312shall be assessed on a per-violation basis. The penalty, under this section, shall not exceed $8,000 per violation; reporting to the LEPC, the SERC, or the local fire department constitutes three separate points of compliance and therefore the failure to report all three violations constitutes three separate violations. However, for purposes only of this Consent Agreement and Consent Order, where all three points of compliance have been violated with respect to a given chemical, the total penalty for the three violations shall not exceed $20,000.

f. Each late-reporting violation of EPCRA § 313shall be assessed on a per-violation basis. The penalty, under this section, shall not exceed $15,000 per chemical, per facility.

g. Each data-quality violation of EPCRA § 313shall be assessed on a per-violation basis. The penalty, under this section, shall not exceed $10,000 per violation.

8. Retention of Enforcement Authority: EPA reserves the right to take appropriate enforcement action, under the applicable enforcement response policy or penalty policy, for those CERCLA § 103(a) and EPCRA § 304, § 311, and § 313violations not reported to EPA under this audit, or for those violations reported under this audit but which are not remedied under the terms of this Agreement.

D. EPCRA and CERCLA § 103Compliance Program

The EPCRA and CERCLA § 103compliance program already developed and implemented by Sara Lee includes the following elements:

1. Educational and training efforts directed to specific employees which emphasize the importance of, and corporate procedures for, complying with EPCRA and the emergency release reporting requirements of CERCLA § 103. Such efforts stress EPCRA fundamentals and the fact that failure to comply with EPCRA may result in the interruption of manufacture or use of the substance, adversely affecting business operations. These employees include division vice presidents of operations, plant managers, division environmental coordinators, plant environmental coordinators, and other selected people.

2. The conduct of training involving at least eight (8) hours initially for the targeted employees, and eighty (80) hours initially for auditors, with sixteen (16) hours per year thereafter for auditors.

3. The development and distribution of manuals including EPCRA and CERCLA § 103compliance information, as a guide to the basic requirements of EPCRA and CERCLA § 103, with an explanation of reporting requirements under those statutes and applicable regulations. The Manual directs employees to those persons within Sara Lee with responsibility for compliance and reporting under EPCRA and CERCLA § 103.

4. A report describing a corporate training program, which has been submitted to EPA prior to signature of this Consent Agreement and Consent Order.

VI. Other Matters

A. This Agreement may be modified only upon written approval by EPA and Sara Lee.

B. Nothing in this Consent Agreement and Consent Order shall relieve Sara Lee of the duty to comply with all applicable EPCRA regulations or other applicable environmental statutes.

C. This Consent Agreement shall be binding upon the Parties to this action, as well as upon their successors and assigns. The undersigned representative of each Party of this Consent Agreement certifies that he or she is duly authorized by the Party whom he or she represents to enter into the terms and bind that Party to it.

D. This Consent Agreement shall take full effect upon the signing of the Consent Order by a member of EPA's Environmental Appeals Board or his or her designated representative.

E. Sara Lee's obligations under this Consent Agreement shall end when it has paid the civil penalty and any stipulated penalties in accordance with the Consent Agreement and Consent Order, and has completed the CERCLA § 103(a) and EPCRA § 304 and § 311, § 312, and § 313compliance audit specified in Paragraph V.C and V.D of this Agreement.

F. All of the terms and conditions of this Consent Agreement together comprise one Agreement, and each of the terms and conditions is in consideration for all of the other terms and conditions. In the event that this Consent Agreement (or one of more of its terms and conditions) is held invalid, or is not executed by all of the signatory parties in identical form, or is not approved in such identical form by a member of the EPA's Environmental Appeals Board or his or her designated representative, then the entire Consent Agreement shall be null and void.

G. This matter shall constitute a "history of prior violations" by Sara Lee Corporation's Forest, Mississippi facility, its Design Foods facility, Fort Worth, Texas, and its Hillshire Farm & Kahn's facility, New London, Wisconsin, as that phrase is used in the EPCRA § 313ERP and the EPCRA § 304/CERCLA § 103Penalty Policy.

H. Failure to remit the civil penalties provided herein will result in this matter being forwarded to the U.S. Department of Justice for collection of the amount due, plus stipulated penalties and interest at the statutory judgment rate proved for in 28 U.S.C. § 1961as in effect on the date of execution of the Consent Order.

I. Unless otherwise provided in the Agreement, whenever the Agreement requires notice or submission of reports, information or documents, such information shall be submitted to the following persons: . . . .

Consent Order

The United States Environmental Protection Agency as Complainant, and Sara Lee Corp. ("Sara Lee"), as Respondent, the Parties herein, having signed and consented to the entry of the Consent Agreement hereto attached and incorporated by reference into this Consent Order,

NOW, THEREFORE, IT IS ORDERED THAT:

1. Respondent Sara Lee Corporation shall comply with all terms of the Consent Agreement;

2. Respondent is assessed a civil penalty of $118,830;

3. Respondent shall, within thirty (30) calendar days of the date of this Order, forward a cashier's or certified check in the amount of $12,750 and payable to the order of the "EPA Hazardous Substance Superfund," to the following address:

U.S. Environmental Protection Agency Headquarters,
ATTENTION: Superfund Accounting
P.O. Box 360582M,
Pittsburgh, PA 15251

and

4. Respondent shall, within thirty (30) calendar days of the date of this Order, forward a certified or cashier's check in the amount of $106,080 and payable to the order of the "Treasurer of the United States of America," to the following address:

U.S. Environmental Protection Agency,
Hearing Clerk,
P.O. Box 360277M,
Pittsburgh, PA 15251

. . . .

NOTES AND QUESTIONS

(1) Many actual or potential EPA enforcement actions are resolved by Consent Decrees, or by consent orders like this one. What are the benefits and disadvantages of agreements of this kind for EPA and for regulated parties? To what extent is this agreement flawed by not requiring environmental auditing after 250 days following execution of the agreement?

(2) How might a company which conducts environmental auditing (as this agreement requires Sara Lee Corporation to do) ensure that such auditing

is truly "independent" of the company's staff? How critical is such independence to the accuracy and successfulness of the auditing?

EPA, Incentives for Self-Policing; Discovery, Disclosure, Correction and Prevention of Violations

60 Fed. Reg. 66, 706, 66, 711–766, 712 (1995)

C. Incentives for Self-Policing

1. No Gravity-Based Penalties

Where the regulated entity establishes that it satisfies all of the conditions of Section D of the policy, EPA will not seek gravity-based penalties for violations of federal environmental requirements.

2. Reduction of Gravity-based Penalties by 75%

EPA will reduce gravity-based penalties for violations of federal environmental requirements by 75% so long as the regulated entity satisfies all of the conditions of Section D(2) through D(9) below.

3. No Criminal Recommendations

(a) EPA will not recommend to the Department of Justice or other prosecuting authority that criminal charges be brought against a regulated entity where EPA determines that all of the conditions in Section D are satisfied, so long as the violation does not demonstrate or involve:

(i) a prevalent management philosophy or practice that concealed or condoned environmental violations; or

(ii) high-level corporate officials' or managers' conscious involvement in, or willful blindness to, the violations.

(b) Whether or not EPA refers the regulated entity for criminal prosecution under this section, the Agency reserves the right to recommend prosecution for the criminal acts of individual managers or employees under existing policies guiding the exercise of enforcement discretion.

4. No Routine Requests for Audits

EPA will not request or use an environmental audit report to initiate a civil or criminal investigation of the entity. For example, EPA will not request an environmental audit report in routine inspections. If the Agency has independent reason to believe that a violation has occurred, however, EPA may seek any information relevant to identifying violations or determining liability or extent of harm.

D. Conditions

1. Systematic Discovery

The violation was discovered through: (a) an environmental audit; or (b) an objective, documented, systematic procedure or practice reflecting the regulated entity's due diligence in preventing, detecting, and correcting violations. The regulated entity must provide accurate and complete documentation to the Agency as to how it exercises due diligence to prevent, detect and correct violations . . . ;

2. Voluntary Discovery

The violation was identified voluntarily, and not through a legally mandated monitoring or sampling requirement prescribed by statute, regulation, permit, judicial or administrative order, or consent agreement. For example, the policy does not apply to:

(a) emissions violations detected through a continuous emissions monitor (or alternative monitor established in a permit) where any such monitoring is required;

(b) violations of National Pollutant Discharge Elimination System (NPDES) discharge limits detected through required sampling or monitoring;

(c) violations discovered through a compliance audit required to be performed by the terms of a consent order or settlement agreement;

3. Prompt Disclosure

The regulated entity fully discloses a specific violation within 10 days (or such shorter period provided by law) after it has discovered that the violation has occurred, or may have occurred, in writing to EPA;

4. Discovery and Disclosure Independent of Government or Third Party Plaintiff

The violation must also be identified and disclosed by the regulated entity prior to:

(a) the commencement of a federal, state or local agency inspection or investigation, or the issuance by such agency of an information request to the regulated entity;

(b) notice of a citizen suit;

(c) the filing of a complaint by a third party;

(d) the reporting of the violation to EPA (or other government agency) by a "whistle blower" employee, rather than by one authorized to speak on behalf of the regulated entity; or

(c) imminent discovery of the violation by a regulatory agency;

5. Correction and Remediation

The regulated entity corrects the violation within 60 days, certifies in writing that violations have been corrected, and takes appropriate measures as determined by EPA to remedy any environmental or human harm due to the violation. If more than 60 days will be needed to correct the violation(s), the regulated entity must so notify EPA in writing before the 60-day period has passed. Where appropriate, EPA may require that to satisfy conditions 5 and 6, a regulated entity enter into a publicly available written agreement, administrative consent order or judicial consent decree, particularly where compliance or remedial measures are complex or a lengthy schedule for attaining and maintaining compliance or remediating harm is required;

6. Prevent Recurrence

The regulated entity agrees in writing to take steps to prevent a recurrence of the violation, which may include improvements to its environmental auditing or due diligence efforts;

7. No Repeat Violations

The specific violation (or closely related violation) has not occurred previously within the past three years at the same facility, or is not part of a pattern of federal, state or local violations by the facility's parent organization (if any), which have occurred within the past five years . . . ;

8. Other Violations Excluded

The violation is not one which (i) resulted in serious actual harm, or may have presented an imminent and substantial endangerment to, human health or the environment, or (ii) violates the specific terms of any judicial or administrative order or consent agreement;

9. Cooperation

The regulated entity cooperates as requested by EPA and provides such information as is necessary and requested by EPA to determine applicability of this policy. Cooperation includes, at a minimum, providing all requested documents and access to employees and assistance in investigating the violation, any noncompliance problems related to the disclosure, and any environmental consequences related to the violations.

E. Economic Benefit

EPA will retain its full discretion to recover any economic benefit gained as a result of noncompliance to preserve a "level playing field" in which violators do not gain a competitive advantage over regulated entities that do comply. EPA may forgive the entire penalty for violations which meet conditions 1 through 9 in section D and, in the Agency's opinion, do not merit any penalty due to the insignificant amount of any economic benefit.

NOTES AND QUESTIONS

(1) Does the EPA enforcement policy reflect sound policy? To what extent does it encourage regulated entities to conduct environmental audits? Is this a worthwhile goal?

(2) Should environmental regulatory violations that are discovered by regulated firms during environmental audits be completely exempted from enforcement actions? What arguments might be raised in favor of and in opposition to, such exemptions?

(3) In other portions of the same policy document, EPA has expressed firm opposition to statutory environmental audit privileges that shield evidence of violations—and thus undermine the public's right to know—as well as blanket immunities for violations that reflect criminal conduct, present serious threats to public health, allow a competitive economic advantage to non-complying companies or reflect repeated failure to comply.

(4) In contrast to EPA's policy, many state programs now provide some measure of administrative immunity from prosecution for environmental violations discovered during a voluntary self-audit. An even greater number of states have enacted environmental audit privilege laws that seek to protect information gathered during a voluntary self-audit from being disclosed to enforcement officials or admitted into evidence in court. For an overview and critique of the developments, see Grad, Treatise on Environmental Law § 17.04(6).

Mintz, "REBUTTAL: EPA ENFORCEMENT AND THE CHALLENGE OF CHANGE"*

26 ELR 10538

Over the past few years, regulated industry's criticism of the U.S. Environmental Protection Agency's (EPA's) approach to enforcing environmental requirements has increased. Perhaps emboldened by shifts in Congress' composition, the Agency's industrial critics have argued that EPA's arm's-length approach to enforcement, with an emphasis on sanctioning violators and deterring other parties from committing violations, is now anachronistic and unneeded.

One such critic is Bruce M. Diamond, a former EPA enforcement official. In his recent Dialogue, *Confessions of an Environmental Enforcer,* Diamond advocated "real changes" in the way enforcement activities are conducted at the Agency.[1] He contended that EPA's deference-based approach to enforcing environmental statutes should be replaced "in many, probably most situations" with "less adversarial" approaches that put a premium on cooperation

---

[1] Diamond, *Confessions of an Environmental Enforcer,* 26 ELR 10252 (May 1996).

between the Agency and regulated entities.[2] Noting changes of circumstance since the formative days of EPA enforcement, Diamond decried "political, bureaucratic, and psychological impediments to change."[3] While conceding that EPA's "traditional" enforcement activities have produced "much beneficial impact," and thus should not be completely abandoned, Diamond nonetheless contended that only "bold and comprehensive steps" away from such activities—and in the direction of greater governmental compliance assistance to regulated entities—can bring about a needed reformation of the environmental enforcement system.[4]

In substantial part, I disagree with Diamond's conclusions. For a number of reasons, in my view, a deterrent enforcement approach is at the core of an effective regulatory program. Moreover, such an approach is not necessarily a less efficient use of government resources than cooperative compliance assistance. Given the paucity of relevant records and statistics, no definitive comparison of the efficacy of these two governmental programs can be made.

At the same time, however, under appropriate circumstances, cooperative compliance assistance by EPA may have value. In addition, notwithstanding the Agency's chronic shortage of resources, EPA's deterrent enforcement efforts may be enhanced, at least incrementally, to improve both its effectiveness and its sensitivity to some concerns of regulated entities who have determined to "do the right thing." . . . .

Background: The Changed and Unchanged Context of EPA Enforcement

Much has certainly changed in the quarter century since EPA first began to enforce environmental laws. A fair evaluation of the usefulness of the Agency's traditional, deterrent enforcement approach requires keeping in mind the nature of the changes that have occurred at EPA, as well as some new and some long-existing aspects of the Agency's circumstances. Although a full account of the evolution of the Agency's enforcement approaches is beyond the scope of this Dialogue,[5] several developments and trends bear mention.

First, the scope of federal environmental regulation, and the number and variety of regulated entities, has grown gradually and immensely. Since the early 1970s, Congress has directed EPA to establish a great many environmental standards.[6] Moreover, in at least some industries and among some state and local governments, substantial progress has been made in remedying serious and significant environmental problems.[7] A number of companies

[2] *Id.* at 10252.

[3] *Id.* at 10254.

[4] *Id.* at 10252, 10254.

[5] For a more comprehensive description of the history of EPA's enforcement programs since 1971, *see* Joel A. Mintz, Enforcement at the EPA: High Stakes and Hard Choices (1995).

[6] By 1993, one widely used compendium of environmental statutes included 1,326 pages. In addition, some 12,120 pages of the *Code of Federal Regulations* pertained to the environment. *See Selected Environmental Law Statutes, 1993-1994 Educational Edition* (1993) and 40 C.F.R. pts. 1-1517 (West Publishing Company ed., 1995).

[7] The progress made in the 1970s in this regard was vividly described in U.S. EPA, National Accomplishments in Pollution Control: 1970-1980 (1980). Clearly, considerable further progress has been made since that time.

have created a new "infrastructure" of environmental managers charged with improving their organizations' environmental records. In some cases their diligent work, along with the efforts of their colleagues and co-workers, has resulted in genuine and needed improvements in environmental quality.[8]

The second relevant trend is that EPA's resources (for enforcement and nonenforcement work alike) have simply not kept pace with the ambitious requirements Congress has imposed on it. As the General Accounting Office (GAO) reported in March 1991:

> In constant (1982) dollars, EPA's operating budget, which covers all its programs except for the Superfund cleanup program and construction grants for sewage treatment plants, went from $1.7 billion in 1979 down to $1.0 billion in 1983 and rose back up to $1.7 billion again in 1991.
>
> Yet during this same period, EPA's responsibilities grew enormously. The 1984 amendments to the Resource Conservation and Recovery Act, for example, known as the Hazardous and Solid Waste Amendments, significantly broadened EPA's responsibilities for regulating the generation, treatment, storage and disposal of hazardous wastes. The amendments also directed EPA to set standards for responding to the presence of asbestos in school buildings, and to study the problems of asbestos in other public buildings. The 1980s also saw significant new responsibilities for the EPA under amendments to the Clean Water Act, the Federal Insecticide, Fungicide and Rodenticide Act, and Superfund legislation (In Title III, the Emergency Planning and Community-Right-To-Know Act).[9]

Regrettably, there is good reason to suspect that EPA's budget shortfalls existed even during the 1970s.[10] Moreover, since the GAO's information was reported to Congress, the size of the Agency's operating programs budget has decreased yet again.[11]

Third, in part as a result of its chronic and severe shortage of personnel and other resources, EPA has, until very recently, put little emphasis on keeping useful, internally accessible enforcement and compliance records. The Agency has recently begun to make some worthwhile improvement in its enforcement record keeping practices through the use of computer software specifically engineered to meet its needs. Nonetheless, in many cases,

[8] For a pragmatic discussion of how the work of these environmental managers may be most effectively approached, *see* Frank Friedman, Practical Guide to Environmental Management (6th ed. 1995).

[9] *Observations on the Environmental Protection Agency's Budget Request for Fiscal Year 1992, Hearing Before the U.S. Senate Comm. On Environment and Public Works,* 102d Cong., 1st Sess. (1991) (Statement of Richard L. Hembra, Director, Environmental Protection Issues, Resource, Community, and Economic Development Division, U.S. General Accounting Office).

[10] In 1980, John Quarles, EPA's former deputy administrator, stated: "In the nine years of EPA's existence, its manpower has roughly doubled while its program responsibilities have been multiplied by a factor of twenty . . . . Today, it cannot perform its workload." Steven A. Cohen, *EPA: A Qualified Success,* in Controversies in Environmental Policy 179 (Sheldon Kaminiecki et al. eds., 1986).

[11] In fiscal year 1996, Congress appropriated only $1.68 billion for EPA's Environmental Programs and Management (operating budget) account. *House Panel Reports Fiscal 1997 Funding of $6.55 Billion for EPA, With No Riders,* 27 Evn't Rep. (BNA) 399 (June 7, 1996)

obstacles to a well-organized, efficient enforcement and compliance record system appear to remain.[12]

Fourth, EPA has given relatively scant attention to the training and career development of its enforcement attorneys and engineers. Although some sporadic efforts have been made in this regard, there are few signs that the Agency has reexamined or substantially increased the training and career growth opportunities it affords to its professional staff.

Finally, on a fairly consistent basis, many EPA engineers and attorneys have chosen to leave the Agency after several years to pursue more lucrative opportunities in the private sector. In part, this "turnover" is an almost ineluctable result of the relatively lower salaries of EPA professionals, after a few years of government service, compared to the salaries of their counterparts in private firms and companies. It may also stem from the poor working conditions under which at least some of EPA's employees (professional and otherwise) must labor, as well as the limited professional training and career development opportunities mentioned above. Whatever its causes, however, the very frequent replacement of EPA enforcement personnel has substantially denied the Agency a firm foundation of experienced professional staff, as well as a reliable "institutional memory" that it can rely on as it pursues its enforcement work.

It is against this backdrop of constraints, shortcomings, and internal and external changes that EPA's deterrent enforcement approach and proposed alternatives to it must be assayed.

"If It Ain't Broke . . .": Is Deterrent EPA Enforcement Truly Outmoded and Inefficient?

Notwithstanding its inherent controversiality, one of the most striking characteristics of EPA's lengthy, deterrent enforcement program is its high level of success. As Kevin Gaynor has observed: "In fact, [EPA's] civil enforcement of many environmental programs is arguably quite good and may be the best kept secret."[13] Similarly, the Agency's criminal enforcement program has had a significant impact on the behavior of regulated corporate officers. In the words of one respected private environmental attorney: "The fact that there is a serious threat of criminal enforcement out there for serious violations has certainly gotten people's attention in the private sector. It has had a vast impact."[14]

To the extent that the incidence and impact of environmental pollution has diminished in recent years,[15] a good number of conscientious business managers, local government officials, and individuals certainly deserve to be commended. Nonetheless, it also seems reasonable to conclude that, in the words of no less staunch a critic of the Agency than Diamond, "EPA's traditional enforcement activities have produced much beneficial impact.

[12] For a critique of the Agency's problematic initial attempts to bring together data from different environmental programs, *see* U.S. GAO, GAO/MTEC-92-14, EPA's Management of Cross-Media Information (1992).

[13] Kevin Gaynor, *Too Many Cooks,* Envtl. F., Jan./Feb. 1989, at 9-10.

[14] Interview with David Buente, Sidley & Austin, Washington, D.C., (Mar. 22, 1991).

[15] *See supra* note 7.

There have been real environmental improvements and the enforcement program deserves much of the credit."[16]

Given this, one may well ask why a drastic change in EPA's deterrent enforcement methods would be urgently needed. In my opinion, the Agency's industrial critics have not, thus far, provided a sound and persuasive rationale for such a change.

One contention that EPA's opponents have made is that whatever its past shortcomings, the "regulated sector" has gradually altered its attitude toward regulatory compliance and environmental protection.[17] Without firm supporting evidence, this notion is difficult to credit. In fact, given the extraordinary number and diversity of American businesses and communities—and the frequent changes that characterize some of them—any sweeping statement as to the "general attitudes" of the multitude of entities regulated by EPA must be viewed with skepticism.

Some (or even many) businesses may well have come to realize that, in the words of former EPA Administrator William D. Ruckelshaus, "environmentalism is here to stay" and that "paying attention to the environmental impact of technology or processes benefits the bottom line."[18] On the other hand, others have undoubtedly not realized these things. Moreover, from the ketone contamination of the James River to the Love Canal and Bhopal, India, disasters to the *Exxon Valdez* oil spill, the still-recent history of environmental regulation illustrates that missteps by even a single company or its employees can do immense environmental harm. Thus, "general attitudes" of regulated entities, in and of themselves, may ultimately have little bearing on the overall impact and efficacy of environmental protection efforts.

In addition, even if one accepts the factual assumptions of EPA's enforcement critics regarding changes in "regulated sector attitudes," displacing or eliminating the Agency's deterrent approach in favor of compliance assistance or other "reforms" is not necessarily a logical response. As noted above, effective federal enforcement of environmental laws appears to have substantially encouraged many regulated entities to minimize or eliminate harm that they had been doing to the environment. Attitudes that have changed once may change again. The elimination or displacement of deterrent enforcement by EPA may well encourage entities that are presently complying with environmentally protective standards to continue to violate environmental standards. If that occurs, environmental protection will, over the long term, once again become a low priority for numerous entities with the capacity to pollute air, water, and land on a massive scale.

This grim scenario seems even more probable when one considers the thrust of EPA's "new partnership" with state environmental protection agencies. Under that approach, the Agency has encouraged (and deferred to) enforcement actions brought by state environmental protection agencies, rather than initiating independent federal enforcement cases, on the basis that the states have "primary" responsibility for enforcing environmental standards. In a

---

16 Diamond, *supra* note 1, at 10252.

17 *See, e.g., id.* at 10254.

18 William D. Ruckelshaus, *Stopping the Pendulum,* Envtl. F., Nov./Dec. 1995, at 25-26.

number of states, however, enforcement litigation is rarely brought or threatened. Instead, state officials gain negotiating "leverage" over environmental violators by threatening to step aside and turn the enforcement case over to federal authorities who will, presumably, take a firmer stance when dealing with the regulated entity in question.

To the extent that EPA is no longer prepared to pursue deterrent enforcement this "good cop, bad cop" technique will no longer be available to state enforcement officials. As a result, state agency representatives will be weakened in their settlement discussions with environmental violators, with long-term consequences for the effectiveness and credibility of state environmental enforcement programs.

A second argument advance by industrial critics is that EPA deterrent enforcement is inappropriately harsh, unduly penalizing companies that have failed to comply with environmental standards despite strenuous, good-faith efforts to do so. This contention is exaggerated. In most, if not nearly all, cases in which regulated entities take prudent, reasonable steps to comply with environmental requirements, their efforts succeed in achieving or exceeding regulatory compliance.[19]

Regulated companies may not always like the particular standards they are asked to meet. Nor are they always sanguine about the amount of money they will need to spend to achieve and maintain environmental compliance. Nonetheless, it was my experience at EPA that once such companies have decided to do what is necessary to meet applicable environmental requirements, they generally do so effectively. Moreover, when good-faith mistakes do occur, EPA enforcement officials often will quietly (and appropriately) decline to pursue enforcement action against the regulated entity in question—particularly when that company's noncompliance did not result in an economic savings or knowingly contribute to substantial environmental harm.

EPA's industrial enforcement critics also miss the mark in describing the Agency's enforcement staff as rigid, defensive, self-serving bureaucrats whose preference for deterrent enforcement is principally motivated by a search for personal satisfaction.[20] This characterization understates the adaptability and reasonableness of many EPA employees who do enforcement work. It fails to reveal the constant and conflicting pressures on EPA's enforcement staff, the frustrations they very frequently endure, and the intrinsic difficulty and thanklessness of their work. It also overlooks the possibility that EPA officials who favor a continuation of deterrent enforcement at the Agency are defending, in principled fashion, an approach for which there remains an objective, ongoing need.

---

[19] I do not wish to overstate this point. Credible observers have pointed out that the very complex regulatory requirements imposed by EPA's regulations under the Resource Conservation and Recovery Act, 42U.S.C. §§ 6901-6992k, ELR Stat. RCRA, and the 1990 Clean Air Act Amendments, Pub. L. No. 101-549, 104 Stat. 2399, *available in* ELR Stat. CAA, present formidable challenges for industrial environmental managers and their colleagues at facilities that have unusually complicated and variable production processes. Even in those exceptional instances, however, careful systematic in-house environmental protection programs seem likely to result in very substantial successful compliance with applicable environmental standards.

[20] *See, e.g.,* Diamond, *supra,* note 1, at 10253.

Another insupportable notion favored by opponents of deterrent EPA enforcement is that cooperative approaches are likely to produce environmental compliance more efficiently—and thus be more effective in protecting human health and the environment.[21] In fact, there is no persuasive evidence that nonadversarial compliance assistance will accomplish the Agency's environmental mission with less expenditure of time and effort on the EPA's part than would result from a continuation of deterrence-based techniques for reaching the same goal.

As Diamond has candidly written:

> In part because EPA has relied almost exclusively on punitive enforcement to encourage compliance, the Agency has no comparative basis for evaluating whether this is the best approach to improving environmental protection. Indeed, the Agency cannot say with any level of precision what impact its enforcement cases have had, either on compliance with environmental requirements or on the environment itself.[22]

Moreover, to date, EPA's experience with nonadversarial alternatives to deterrent enforcement has been highly limited, and the impact of nonadversarial approaches has not been measured.

Given this, it is difficult to credit any conclusion that the cooperative approach will encourage environmental protection more efficiently than a deterrent enforcement regime. In view of EPA's historically poor record keeping and the absence of reliable industry-wide compliance rate data, it seems more logical to conclude that the relative efficiency and effectiveness of deterrent enforcement and compliance assistance activities cannot be empirically shown.[23]

Diamond is certainly correct that adversarial enforcement actions may require considerable EPA resources and, as he stated, "even a few hard-fought administrative or judicial cases can act as a major multi year drain on government resources."[24] It seems entirely plausible, however, that the fact that the Agency is prepared to pursue such cases vigorously will tend to encourage many entities that might otherwise be tempted to ignore environmental standards to make sustained efforts to comply with them. Similarly, outreach, education, and improved EPA guidelines may assist a number of regulated entities in understanding how to correct existing environmental problems. Nevertheless, as noted above, to the extent such assistance supplants deterrent enforcement, instead of supplementing it, it may very well encourage regulated entities—whether presently complying with or violating environmental standards—to ignore or de-emphasize their environmental responsibilities in the press of other work . . . .

---

[21] *See id.* at 10254.

[22] *Id.* at 10252-53.

[23] This unfortunate situation makes it far more difficult for EPA to go about striking an appropriate balance between deterrent enforcement and cooperative assistance. It also makes it important for the Agency to make a sustained, serious effort to enhance its enforcement and compliance record keeping.

[24] Diamond, *supra* note 1, at 10253.

§ 8.07 Criminal Enforcement of Environmental Laws

In addition to the civil enforcement mechanisms treated in the last section of this chapter, most federal environmental legislation provides for criminal prosecution of environmental violators under certain circumstances. The statutes vary in the ways in which they define environmental crimes. Thus, for example, the Clean Water Act prescribes criminal penalties for persons who "negligently" violate certain enumerated statutory standards (or permit conditions or limitations that implement those standards), as well as more stringent penalties for those who "knowingly" violate the same standards, conditions, or limitations. Clean Water Act § 309(c); 33 U.S.C. § 1319(c). In contrast, the Clean Air Act only penalizes "knowing" violators of particular statutory requirements or limitations. Clean Air Act § 113(c); 42 U.S.C. § 7413(c). Nonetheless, the criminal penalty provisions of these and other environmental statutes also have considerable points of similarity.

The cases and materials in this section examine the interpretations courts have given to the "intent" requirements of environmental criminal laws, and discuss the larger policy implications of those standards.

UNITED STATES v. DEAN

United States Court of Appeals, Sixth Circuit (1992)
969 F.2d 187

Defendant Gale E. Dean appeals his convictions on one count of conspiracy to violate the Resource Conservation and Recovery Act (RCRA), 42 U.S.C. §§ 6901 *et seq.*, in violation of 18 U.S.C. § 371; one count of failure to file documentation of hazardous waste generation, storage, and disposal as required by 42 U.S.C. § 6928(d)(4); and one count of storage of spent chromic acid without a permit, one count of storage and disposal of chromic acid rinse water and wastewater sludges in a lagoon without a permit, and one count of disposal of paint sludge and solvent wastes in a pit without a permit, all in violation of 42 U.S.C. § 6928(2)(A).

I

Defendant's convictions arose out of the operation of the General Metal Fabricators, Inc. (GMF) facility in Erwin, Tennessee, which engaged in metal stamping, plating, and painting. The facility utilized hazardous chemicals and generated hazardous waste. The owners of GMF, Joseph and Jean Sanchez; as well as Dean, the production manager; and Clyde Griffith, the plant manager, were indicted for conspiracy to violate RCRA, and, individually, for violations of various sections of the statute. The district court granted defendant's motion to sever his trial from that of the other defendants.

RCRA provides a comprehensive system of oversight of hazardous materials, a system centered upon requirements that facilities utilizing such materials obtain permits, and maintain proper records of the treatment, storage, and disposal of hazardous substances. No permit was sought for the GMF facility. The hazardous waste disposal practices at GMF were discovered by chance by state waste-management authorities whose attention was caught, while driving to an appointment at another facility, by two 55-gallon drums abandoned among weeds on GMF's property.

As production manager, Dean had day-to-day supervision of GMF's production process and employees. Among his duties was the instruction of employees on hazardous waste handling and disposal. Numerous practices at GMF violated RCRA. GMF's plating operations utilized rinse baths, contaminated with hazardous chemicals, which were drained through a pipe into an earthen lagoon outside the facility. In addition, Dean instructed employees to shovel various kinds of solid wastes from the tanks into 55-gallon drums. Dean ordered the construction of a pit, concealed behind the facility, into which 38 drums of such hazardous waste were tossed. The contents spilled onto the soil from open or corroded drums. Chemical analyses of soil and solid wastes, entered by stipulation at trial, revealed that the lagoon and the pit were contaminated with chromium. In addition, the pit was contaminated with toluene and xylene solvents. All of these substances are hazardous. Drums of spent chromic acid solution were also illegally stored on the premises.

Defendant was familiar with the chemicals used in each of the tanks on the production lines, and described to authorities the manner in which the contents of the rinse tanks were deposited in the lagoon. Material Safety Data Sheets (MSDS) provided to GMF by the chemical manufacturer clearly stated that various chemicals in use at GMF were hazardous and were subject to state and federal pollution control laws. The MSDS were given to investigators by Dean, who demonstrated his knowledge of their contents. The MSDS delivered with the chromic acid made specific reference to RCRA and to related EPA regulations. Dean informed investigators that he "had read this RCRA waste code but thought it was a bunch of bullshit."

II

A

Dean assigns as error numerous aspects of the proceedings in the trial court. We shall address first a number of contentions going to the scope and elements of RCRA's criminal provisions, which we think of primary importance among the issues raised by defendant. The first of these issues arises in connection with defendant's contention that the trial court erred in denying his motion for an acquittal on County 4, because there was no evidence that defendant knew of RCRA's permit requirement. Defendant's characterization of the evidence is inaccurate; but moreover, we see no basis on the face of the statute for concluding that knowledge of the permit requirement is an element of the crime. The statute penalizes:

Any person who—

. . . .

> (2) knowingly treats, stores, or disposes of any hazardous waste identified or listed under this subchapter—
>
> (A) without a permit under this subchapter or pursuant to title I of the Marine Protection, Research, and Sanctuaries Act (86 Stat. 1052); or
>
> (B) in knowing violation of any material condition or requirement of such permit; or
>
> (C) in knowing violation of any material condition or requirement of any applicable interim status regulations or standards . . . .

42 U.S.C. § 6928(d)(2). Defendant was convicted of violating subsection 6928(d)(2)(A).

The question of interpretation presented by this provision is the familiar one of how far the initial "knowingly" travels. Other courts of appeals have divided on this question. In *United States v. Johnson & Towers, Inc.,* 741 F.2d 662 (3d Cir. 1984), *cert. denied., sub nom.,* the Court of Appeals for the Third Circuit concluded that knowledge of the permit requirement was an element of the crime, observing:

> Treatment, storage or disposal of hazardous waste in violation of any material condition or requirement of a permit must be "knowing," since the statute explicitly so states in subsection (B). It is unlikely that Congress could have intended to subject to criminal prosecution those persons who acted when no permit had been obtained irrespective of their knowledge (under subsection (A)), but not those persons who acted in violation of the terms of a permit unless that action was knowing (subsection (B)). Thus we are led to conclude either that the omission of the word "knowing" in (A) was inadvertent or that "knowingly" which introduces subsection (2) applies to subsection (A).

Id. at 668 (footnote omitted).

The Court of Appeals for the Ninth Circuit disagreed with the Third Circuit in *United States v. Hoflin,* 880 F.2d 1033 (9th Cir. 1989), *cert. denied,* 493 U.S. 1083, 107 L.Ed.2d 1047, 110 S.Ct. 1142 (1990). The Ninth circuit noted first the well-established principle of statutory construction that courts will "give effect, if possible, to every clause and word of a statute," *United States v. Menasche,* 348 U.S. 538-9, 99 L.Ed. 615, 75 S.Ct. 513 (citing *Inhabitants v. Ramsdell,* 107 U.S. 147, 152, 2 S.Ct. 391, 27 L.Ed. 431 (1883)), pointing out that the Third Circuit's reading of subsection 6928(d)(2)(A) would render mere surplusage the word "knowing" in subsections 6928(d)(2)(B) and (C). *Hoflin,* 880 F.2d at 1038. The Ninth Circuit also disagreed with the Third Circuit that there was anything illogical about reading subsections 6928(d)(2)(B) and (C) to have a knowledge requirement but subsection 6928(d)(2)(A) to have none. The Ninth Circuit observed that the permit requirement is intended to give the EPA notice that oversight of a facility is necessary (and, by implication, the force of the statutory scheme would be greatly diminished by exempting all who claimed ignorance of the statute's requirements). The difference in mens rea between the subsections signifies the relative importance, in the estimation of Congress, of the twin requirements of obtaining a permit and complying with the permit. This ranking is consistent with the greater likelihood that compliance with the permit will be monitored. The Court of Appeals for the Fourth Circuit agreed with the Ninth Circuit in *United States v. Dee,* 912 F.2d 741 (4th Cir. 1990), *cert. denied,* 499 U.S. 919, 111 S.Ct. 1307, 113 L.Ed.2d 242 (1991).

All of the courts to address this question have reasoned by analogy from the holding of the Supreme Court in *United States v. International Minerals & Chemical Corp.,* 402 U.S. 558, 29 L.Ed.2d 178, 91 S.Ct. 1697 (1971). In that case, the indictment was brought under 18 U.S.C. § 834(f), which penalizes knowing violation of any regulation. The regulation at issue, enacted by the Interstate Commerce Commission, required shipping papers to reflect certain information concerning corrosive liquids being shipped. The question before the Supreme Court was whether knowledge of existence of the regulation was an element of the crime. The Court held that it was not, turning its decision upon the maxim that ignorance of the law is no excuse. The Court concluded its opinion by stating, with equal force here, that when "dangerous or deleterious devices or products or obnoxious waste materials are involved, the probability of regulation is so great that anyone who is aware that he is in possession of them or dealing with them must be presumed to be aware of the regulation." *Id.* at 565. The Court of Appeals for the Third Circuit mitigated its holding in *Johnson & Towers* somewhat in light of *International Minerals,* holding that knowledge of RCRA would be imputed to employees above a certain level of responsibility (no guidance was given concerning the level of responsibility required, on grounds that there was insufficient evidence in the record on the responsibilities of the employees at issue).

We agree with the reasoning of the Court of Appeals for the Ninth Circuit in *Hoflin.* The "knowingly" which begins § 6928(d)(2) cannot be read as extending to the subsections without rendering nugatory the word "knowing" contained in subsections 6928(d)(2)(B) and (C). Subsection 6928(d)(2)(A) requires knowing treatment (or knowing storage, or knowing disposal) of hazardous waste. It also requires proof that the treatment, or storage, or disposal, was done without a permit. It does not require that the person charged have known that a permit was required, and that knowledge is not relevant.

As to subsections 6928(d)(2)(B) and (C), the requirements are different. Here, the statute clearly requires in addition that if one is to be charged under 6928(d)(2)(B) with violating the terms of a permit or under 6928(d)(2)(C) with violating regulations then one must be aware of the additional requirements of the permit or regulation. To us the statute is clear, makes sense, and does not contain the ambiguities or inconsistencies found by others.

The Court of Appeals for the Third Circuit hypothesized in the alternative that Congress inadvertently omitted the word "knowing" from subsection 6928(d)(2)(A), because, the court opined, the plain language reading of section 6928(d)(2) to which we adhere resulted in an "unlikely" statutory scheme. A general review of the reasonableness of legislative choices, however, is not among out statutory construction tools. The inquiry ends with a cogent means of reading the plain language of the statute, *United States Dep't of Energy v. Ohio,* 112 S.Ct., 1627, 1635, 118 L.Ed.2d 255 (1992). The *Hoflin* court, moreover, adequately addressed the reasons Congress might have had for crafting the statute in this manner. Finally, we note that statutes which are designed to protect the public health and safety (as is RCRA, *Johnson & Towers,* 741 F.2d at 668) have consistently been distinguished in Supreme Court precedent as more likely candidates for diminished mens rea requirements. *Liparota v. United States,* 471 U.S. 419, 433, 85 L.Ed.2d 434, 105 S.Ct. 2084 (1985).

We do not agree with the suggestion in *Johnson v. Towers* that section 6928(d)(2)(A) is in fact a strict liability crime if knowledge of the permit requirement need not be shown. The provision applies by its terms to any person who "*knowingly* treats, stores or disposes of hazardous waste." 42 U.S.C. § 6928(d)(2)(emphasis ours). The Supreme Court's pronouncement in *International Minerals,* quoted above, stands for the proposition that persons involved in hazardous waste handling have every reason to be aware that their activities are regulated by law, aside from the rule that ignorance of the law is no excuse. In this case, the documentation provided by the chemical manufacturer abundantly illustrates one means by which knowledge of hazardous waste laws is communicated. Accordingly, even absent the requirement of proof that defendant knew of RCRA's permit provisions, the statute does not impose strict liability. The district court did not err in declining to grant defendant's motion for acquittal based on his alleged ignorance of RCRA's permit requirement.

B

Defendant also contends that the district court should have granted his motion for acquittal because subsection 6928(d)(2)(A) was not intended to reach employees who are not "owners" or "operators" of facilities. By its terms, the provision applies to "any person." "Person" is a defined term meaning "an individual, trust, firm, joint stock company, corporation (including a government corporation), partnership, association, State, municipality, commission, political subdivision of a State, or any interstate body." 42 U.S.C. § 6903(15).

Defendant would be hard pressed to convince the court that he is not an "individual." He argues, however, that because only owners and operators of facilities are required to obtain permits, 42 U.S.C. § 6925, the penalty imposed for hazardous waste handling without a permit by subsection 6928(d)(2)(A) must apply only to owners and operators.

This contention is unpersuasive for numerous reasons. Of primary importance is the fact that it is contrary to the unambiguous language of the statute. *Cf. United States v. Northeastern Pharmaceutical & Chem. Co.,* 810 F.2d 726, 745 (8th Cir. 1986), *cert. denied,* 484 U.S. 484, 98 L.Ed.2d 102, 108 S.Ct. 146 (1987). We agree with the Third Circuit that "had Congress meant in § 6928(d)(2)(A) to take aim more narrowly, it could have used more narrow language." *United States v. Johnson & Towers, Inc.,* 741 F.2d 662 (3d Cir. 1984), *cert. denied, sub nom.* Second, while defendant's argument at first glance has logical appeal in relation to subsection 6928(d)(2)(A), the relevant language "any person" prefaces § 6928(d) generally. A number of separate crimes are set out in § 6928(d), several of them having nothing to do with the permit requirement (*e.g.*, failure to maintain requisite documentation or to comply with regulations). Defendant's argument would accordingly impose a limitation on all of the crimes set out in § 6928(d) on a ground relevant to few of them. Third, even the logical appeal of the assertion does not withstand scrutiny. The fact that Congress chose to impose the permit requirement upon owners and operators does not undercut the value of further assuring permit compliance by enacting criminal penalties which would lead others to make inquiry into the permit status of facilities. Given that "such wastes typically have no value, yet can only be safely disposed of at considerable cost," *United States v. Hoflin,* 880 F.2d 1033, 1038 (9th Cir. 1989), *cert. denied,* 493 U.S. 1083, 107 L.Ed.2d 1047, 110 S.Ct. 1143 (1990), facilities generating hazardous waste have a strong incentive to evade the law. Moreover, clean-up of the resulting environmental damage almost always involves far greater cost than proper disposal would have, and may be limited to containing the spread of the harm. Defendant argues hat employees are the least likely persons to know facilities' permit status. However, employees of a facility are more able to ascertain the relevant facts than the general public, which the statute is intended to protect. In light of these factors, it was entirely reasonable for Congress to have created broad criminal liability. Fourth, it is far from clear that defendant is in fact not an "operator" of GMF, a term defined in the regulations to mean "the person responsible for the overall operation of a facility." 40 CFR § 260.10(1991). Finally, we agree with the Court of Appeals for the Third Circuit that this result is also supported by the decision of the Supreme Court in *United States v. Dotterweich,* 320 U.S. 277, 88 L.Ed. 48, 64 S.Ct. 134 (1943), and by the legislative history. *See Johnson & Towers, Inc.,* 741 F.2d at 665-7. We conclude that employees may be criminally liable under § 6928(d).

C

Defendant contends that he should have been acquitted on Count 3 because the chromic acid at issue was not "hazardous waste" as required by 42 U.S.C. § 6928(d)(2)(A), set out above. The term "hazardous waste" is defined as:

> [A] solid waste, or combination of solid wastes, which because of its quantity, concentration, or physical, chemical, or infectious characteristics may—
>
> (A) cause, or significantly contribute to an increase in mortality or an increase in serious irreversible, or incapacitating irreversible, illness; or
>
> (B) pose a substantial present or potential hazard to human health or the environment when improperly treated, stored, transported, or disposed of, or otherwise managed.

42 U.S.C. § 6903(5). Count 3 involved spent chromic acid solution which was being stored in drums at the facility. Dean contends that the chromic acid was not "hazardous" within the meaning of § 6903(5), apparently on the ground that the chromic acid did not pose a danger to human health in the conditions under which it was being stored at GMF. *American Mining Congress v. EPA,* 907 F.2d 1179, 1191 (D.C. Cir. 1990), upon which defendant relies, contains nothing supporting this proposition, and is directed at an inapposite question of law.

Defendant does not deny that the "chemical . . . characteristics" of chromic acid involve a threat to human health, as was prominently stated in the MSDS provided by its vendor. It is not apparent from the plain language of the statute that it requires, as defendant would read it, that a hazardous waste present a threat to human health as a result of the manner in which it is being stored. We note that the definitions of "disposal" and "storage" under the statute are distinguished by the fact that the former is defined to mean placing the waste in a location where environmental contamination may result, while the latter is defined as "containment" of waste in a manner not constituting disposal, *i.e.*, such that environmental contamination will not result. *See,* 42 U.S.C. §§ 9603(3), 9603(33). A substance contained in a manner which does not threaten environmental contamination presumably would not present a threat to human health. Substances being "stored" would accordingly not be "hazardous," therefore storage could never be a predicate for a RCRA violation. This result is clearly contrary to the terms of the statute, and highlights the fallacy in defendant's argument.

Moreover, construing the statute to penalize storage of hazardous substances without a permit, without regard to whether the means of storage is itself unsafe, is in keeping with the statute's purposes. The requirement of a permit is intended to remedy the danger to the public health (underscored by the events in this case) presented by facilities whose generation of hazardous waste is unknown to authorities charged with monitoring the handling of wastes, for the protection of the environment. *Cf. United States v. Hoflin,* 880 F.2d 1033, 1038-9 (9th Cir. 1989), *cert. denied,* 493 U.S. 1083, 110 S.Ct. 1143, 107 L.Ed.2d 1047 (1990). . . .

Affirmed.

UNITED STATES v. WEITZENHOFF

United States Court of Appeals, Ninth Circuit (1994)
35 F.3d 1275

Fletcher, C.J.:

Michael H. Weitzenhoff and Thomas W. Mariani, who managed the East Honolulu Community Services Sewage Treatment Plant, appeal their convictions for violations of the Clean Water Act ("CWA"), 33 U.S.C. §§ 1251 *et seq.*, contending that the district court misconstrued the word "knowingly" under section 1319(c)(2) of the CWA. . . .

We affirm the convictions and the sentence.

Facts and Procedural History

In 1988 and 1989 Weitzenhoff was the manager and Mariani the assistant manager of the East Honolulu Community Service Sewage Treatment Plant ("the plant"), located not far from Sandy Beach, a popular swimming and surfing beach on Oahu. The plant is designed to treat some 4 million gallons of residential wastewater each day by removing the solids and other harmful pollutants from the sewage so that the resulting effluent can be safely discharged into the ocean. The plant operates under a permit issued pursuant to the national Pollution Discharge Elimination System ("NPDES"), which established the limits on the Total Suspended Solids ("TSS") and Biochemical Oxygen Demand ("BOD")—indicators of the solid and organic matter, respectively, in the effluent discharged at Sandy Beach. During the period in question, the permit limited the discharge of both the TSS and BOD to an average of 976 pounds per day over a 30-day period. It also imposed monitoring and sampling requirements on the plant's management.

The sewage treatment process that was overseen by Weitzenhoff and Mariani began with the removal of large inorganic items such as rags and coffee grounds from the incoming wastewater as it flowed through metal screens and a grit chamber at the head of the plant. The wastewater then entered large tanks known as primary clarifiers, where a portion of the organic solids settled to the bottom of the tanks. The solid material which settled in the primary clarifiers, known as primary sludge, was pumped to separate tanks, known as anaerobic digesters, to be further processed. Those solids that did not settle continued on to aeration basins, which contained microorganisms to feed on and remove the solids and other organic pollutants in the waste stream.

From the aeration basins the mixture flowed into final clarifiers, where the microorganisms settled out, producing a mixture that sank to the bottom of the clarifiers called activated sludge. The clarified stream then passed through a chlorine contact chamber, where the plant's sampling apparatus was, and emptied into the plant's outfall, a long underground pipe which discharged the plant's effluent into the ocean through diffusers 1,100 to 1,400 feet from shore (the "Sandy Beach outfall").

Meanwhile, the activated sludge that had settled in the final clarifiers was pumped from the bottom of the clarifiers. A certain portion was returned to the aeration basins, while the remainder, known as waste activated sludge ("WAS"), was pumped to the WAS holding tanks. From the holding tanks, the WAS could either be returned to other phases of the treatment process or hauled away to a different sewage treatment facility.

From March 1987 through March 1988, the excess WAS generated by the plant was hauled away to another treatment plant, the Sand Island Facility. In March 1988, certain improvements were made to the East Honolulu plant and the hauling was discontinued. Within a few weeks, however, the plant began experiencing a buildup of excess WAS. Rather than have the excess WAS hauled away as before, however, Weitzenhoff and Mariani instructed two employees at the plant to dispose of it on a regular basis by pumping it from the storage tanks directly into the outfall, that is, directly into the ocean. The WAS thereby bypassed the plant's effluent sampler so that the samples taken and reported to Hawaii's Department of Health ("DOH") and the EPA did not reflect its discharge.

The evidence produced by the government at trial showed that WAS was discharged directly into the ocean from the plant on about 40 separate occasions from April 1998 to June 1989, resulting in some 436,000 pounds of pollutant solids being discharged into the ocean, and that the discharges violated the plant's 30-day average effluent limit under the permit for most of the months during which they occurred. Most of the WAS discharges occurred during the night, and none was reported to the DOH or EPA. DOH inspectors contacted the plant on several occasions in 1988 in response to complaints by lifeguards at Sandy Beach that sewage was being emitted from the outfall, but Weitzenhoff and Mariani repeatedly denied that there was any problem at the plant. In one letter responding to a DOH inquiry in October 1988, Mariani stated that "the debris that was reported could not have been from the East Honolulu Wastewater Treatment facility, as our records of effluent quality up to this time will substantiate." One of the plant employees who participated in the dumping operation testified that Weitzenhoff instructed him not to say anything about the discharges, because if they all stuck together and did not reveal anything, "they [couldn't] do anything to us."

Following an FBI investigation, Weitzenhoff and Mariani were charged in a thirty-one count indictment with conspiracy and substantive violations of the Clean Water Act ("CWA"), 33 U.S.C. §§ 1251 *et seq.* At trial, Weitzenhoff and Mariani admitted having authorized the discharges, but claimed that their actions were justified under their interpretation of the NPDES permit. The jury found them guilty of six of the thirty-one counts.

Weitzenhoff was sentenced to twenty-one months and Mariani thirty-three months imprisonment. Each filed a timely notice of appeal.

Discussion

A. Intent Requirement

Section 1311(a) of the CWAprohibits the discharge of pollutants into navigable waters without an NPDES permit. 33 U.S.C. § 1311(a). Section 1319(c)(2) makes it a felony offense to "knowingly violate section 1311, 1312, 1316, 1317, 1318, 1321(b)(3), 1328 or 1345 . . . , or any permit condition or limitation implementing any of such sections in a permit issued under section 1342."

Prior to trial, the district court construed "knowingly" in section 1319(c)(2) as requiring only that Weitzenhoff and Mariani were aware that they were discharging the pollutants in question, not that they knew they were violating the terms of the statute or permit. According to appellants, the district court erred in its interpretation of the CWA and in instructing the jury that "the government is not required to prove that the defendant knew that his act or omissions were unlawful," as well as in rejecting their proposed instruction based on the defense that they mistakenly believed their conduct was authorized by the permit. Apparently, no Court of Appeals has confronted the issue raised by appellants.

We review a question of statutory construction de novo. United States v. Richison, 901 F.2d 778, 780 (9th Cir. 1990). "In construing statutes in a case of first impression, we first look to the language of the controlling statutes, and second to legislative history." Central Mont. Elec. Power Coop., Inc. v. Administrator of Booneville Power Admin., 840 F.2d 1472, 1477 (9th Cir.

1988). Whether a jury instruction misstates elements of a statutory crime is also a question of law reviewed de novo. United States v. Johnson, 956 F.2d 197, 199 (9th Cir. 1992). If the district court was correct in its interpretation of the statute, then it did not err in giving the instruction it did or refusing to submit appellants' mistake of law defense to the jury.

As with certain other criminal statutes that employ the term "knowingly" it is not apparent from the face of the statute whether "knowingly" means a knowing violation of the law or simply knowing conduct that is violative of the law. We turn, then, to the legislative history of the provision at issue to ascertain what Congress intended.

In 1987, Congress substantially amended the CWA, elevating the penalties for violations of the Act. *See* H.R. Conf. Rep. No. 1004, 99th Cong., 2d Sess. 138 (1986). Increased penalties were considered necessary to deter would-be polluters. S. Rep. No. 50, 99th Cong., 1st Sess. 29 (1985). With the 1987 amendments, Congress substituted "knowingly" for the earlier intent requirement of "willfully" that appeared in the predecessor to section 1319(c)(2). The Senate report accompanying the legislation explains that the changes in the penalty provisions were to ensure that "criminal liability shall . . . attach to any person who is not in compliance with all applicable federal, state, and local requirements and permits *and causes* a POTW [publicly owned treatment works] to violate any effluent limitation or condition in any permit issued to the treatment works." *Id.* (emphasis added). Similarly, the report accompanying the House version of the bill, which contained parallel provisions for enhancement of penalties, states that the proposed amendments were to "provide penalties for dischargers or individuals who knowingly or negligently violate *or cause the violation of* certain of the Act's requirements." H.R. Rep. No. 189, 99th Cong., 1st Sess. 29-30 (1985) (emphasis added). Because they speak in terms of "causing" a violation, the congressional explanations of the new penalty provisions strongly suggest that criminal sanctions are to be imposed on an individual who knowingly engages in conduct that results in a permit violation, regardless of whether the polluter is cognizant of the requirements or even the existence of the permit.

Our conclusion that "knowingly" does not refer to the legal violation is fortified by decisions interpreting analogous public welfare statutes. The leading case in this area is United States v. International Minerals & Chem. Corp., 402 U.S. 558 (1971). In *International Minerals,* the Supreme Court construed a statue which made it a crime to "knowingly violate any . . . regulation" promulgated by the [Interstate Commerce Commission] pursuant to 18 U.S.C. § 834(a), a provision authorizing the agency to formulate regulations for the safe transport of corrosive liquids, *Id.* at 559. The Court held that the term "knowingly" referred to the acts made criminal rather than a violation of the regulation, and that "regulation" was a shorthand designation for the specific acts or omissions contemplated by the act. *Id.* at 560-62. "Where . . . dangerous or deleterious devices or products or obnoxious waste materials are involved, the probability of regulation is so great that anyone who is aware that he is in possession of them or dealing with them must be presumed to be aware of the regulation." *id.* at 565.

This court followed *International Minerals* in United States v. Hoflin, 880 F.2d 1033 (9th Cir. 1989), cert. denied, 493 U.S. 1083 (1990), when it held that knowledge of the absence of a permit is not an element of the offense defined by 42 U.S.C. § 6928(d)(2)(A), part of the Resource Conservation and Recovery Act ("RCRA"). *Id.* at 1039. "There can be little question that RCRA's purposes, like those of the Food and Drug Act . . . touch phases of the lives and health of people which, in the circumstances of modern industrialism, are largely beyond self-protection." *Id.* at 1038, quoting United States v. Dotterweich, 320 U.S. 277, 280 (1943) (construing Food, Drug and Cosmetic Act); *see also* United States v. Sherbondy, 865 F.2d 996, 1001-03 (9th Cir. 1988) (use of word "knowingly" in 18 U.S.C. §§ 922(g), 924(A)(1)(B), part of Firearms Owners' Protection Act, does not require proof that defendant knew he was violating law). Other courts have also followed *International Minerals* by similarly construing the knowledge requirement in statutes that regulate deleterious devices or obnoxious waste material.

Appellants seek to rely on the Supreme Court's decision in Liparota v. United States, 471 U.S. 419 (1985), to support their alternative reading of the intent requirement. *Liparota* concerned 7 U.S.C. § 2024(b)(1), which provides that anyone who "knowingly uses, transfers, acquires, alters, or possesses [food stamp] coupons or authorization cards in any manner not authorized by [the statute] or regulations" is subject to a fine or imprisonment. *Id.* at 420. The Court, noting that the conduct at issue did not constitute a public welfare offense, distinguished the *International Minerals* line of cases and held that the government must prove the defendant knew that his acquisition or possession of food stamps was in a manner unauthorized by statute or regulations. *Id.* at 432-33.

Subsequent to the filing of the original opinion in this case, the Supreme Court decided two cases which Weitzenhoff contends call our analysis into question. *See* Ratzlaf v. United States, 114 S.Ct. 655 (1994); Staples v. United States, 114 S.Ct. 1793 (1994). We disagree.

The statute in *Ratzlaf* does not deal with a public welfare offense, but rather with violations of the banking statutes. The Court construed the term "willfully" in the anti-structuring provisions of the Bank Secrecy Act to require both that the defendant knew he was structuring transactions to avoid reporting requirements and that he knew his acts were unlawful. The Court recognized that the money structuring provisions are not directed at conduct which a reasonable person necessarily should know is subject to strict public regulation and that the structuring offense applied to all persons with more than $10,000, many of whom could be engaged in structuring for innocent reasons. *Ratzlaf,* 114 S.Ct. at 660-62. In contrast, parties such as Weitzenhoff are closely regulated and are discharging waste materials that affect public health. The *International Minerals* rationale requires that we impute to these parties knowledge of their operating permit. This was recognized by the Court in *Staples.*

The specific holding in *Staples* was that the government is required to prove that a defendant charged with possession of a machine gun knew that the weapon he possessed had the characteristics that brought it within the statutory definition of a machine gun. But the Court took pains to contrast the gun laws to other regulatory regimes, specifically those regulations that govern the handling of "obnoxious waste materials." *See Staples,* 114 S.Ct. at 1798.

It noted that the mere innocent ownership of guns is not a public welfare offense. *Id.* at 1804. The Court focused on the long tradition of widespread gun ownership in this country and, recognizing that approximately 50% of American homes contain a firearm, *id.* at 1801, acknowledged that mere ownership of a gun is not sufficient to place people on notice that the act of owning an unregistered firearm is not innocent under the law.

Staples thus explicitly contrasted the mere possession of guns to public welfare offenses, which include statutes that regulate "dangerous or deleterious devices or products or obnoxious waste materials," *id.* at 1800, and confirmed the continued vitality of statutes covering public welfare offenses, which "regulate potentially harmful or injurious items" and place a defendant on notice that he is dealing with a device or substance "that places him in 'responsible relation to a public danger.' " *Id.* "In such cases Congress intended to place the burden on the defendant to ascertain at his peril whether [his conduct] comes within the inhibition of the statute." *Id.* at 1798 (citations and internal quotations omitted).

Unlike "guns [which] in general are not 'deleterious devices or products or obnoxious waste materials,'*International Minerals, supra*, . . . that put their owners on notice that they stand 'in responsible relation to a public danger[,]' *Dotterweich,* 320 U.S. at 281," *Staples,* 114 S.Ct. at 1800, the dumping of sewage and other pollutants into our nation's waters is precisely the type of activity that puts the discharger on notice that his acts may pose a public danger. Like other public welfare offenses that regulate the discharge of pollutants into the air, the disposal of hazardous wastes, the undocumented shipping of acids, and the use of pesticides on our food, the improper and excessive discharge of sewage causes cholera, hepatitis, and other serious illnesses, and can have serious repercussions for public health and welfare.

The criminal provisions of the CWA are clearly designed to protect the public at large from the potentially dire consequences of water pollution, *see* S. Rep. No. 99-50, 99th Cong., 1st Sess. 29 (1985), and as such fall within the category of public welfare legislation. *International Minerals* rather than *Liparota* controls the case at hand. The government did not need to prove that Weitzenhoff and Mariani knew that their acts violated the permit or the CWA. . . .

KLEINFIELD, Circuit Judge, with whom Circuit Judges REINHARDT, KOZINSKI, TROTT, and T.G. NELSON join, dissenting from the order rejecting the suggestion for rehearing en banc:

I respectfully dissent from our decision to reject the suggestion for rehearing en banc.

Most of us vote against most such petitions and suggestions even when we think the panel decision is mistaken. We do so because federal courts of appeals decide case in three judge panels. En banc review is extraordinary, and is generally reserved for conflicting precedent within the circuit which makes application of the law by district courts unduly difficult, and egregious errors in important cases. In my view, this is a case of exceptional importance, for two reasons. First, it impairs a fundamental purpose of criminal justice, sorting out the innocent from the guilty before imposing punishment. Second, it does so in the context of the Clean Water Act. This statute has tremendous sweep. Most statutes permit anything except what is prohibited, but this one prohibits all regulated conduct involving waters and wetlands except what is permitted. 33 U.S.C. § 1311(a); United States v. Riverside Bayview Homes, Inc., 474 U.S. 121 (1985). Much more ordinary, innocent, productive activity is regulated by this law than people not versed in environmental law might imagine.

The harm our mistaken decision may do is not necessarily limited to Clean Water Act cases. Dilution of the traditional requirement of a criminal state of mind, and application of the criminal law to innocent conduct, reduces the moral authority of our system of criminal law. If we use prison to achieve social goals regardless of the moral innocence of those we incarcerate, then imprisonment loses its moral opprobrium and our criminal law becomes morally arbitrary.

We have now made felons of a large number of innocent people doing socially valuable work. They are innocent, because the one thing which makes their conduct felonious is something they do not know. It is we, and not Congress, who have made them felons. The statute, read in an ordinary way, does not. If we are fortunate, sewer plant workers around the circuit will continue to perform their vitally important work despite our decision. If they knew they risk three years in prison, some might decide that their pay, though sufficient inducement for processing the public's wastes, is not enough to risk prison for doing their jobs. We have decided that they should go to prison if, unbeknownst to them, their plant discharges exceed permit limits. Likewise for power plant operators who discharge warm water into rivers near their plants, and for all sorts of other dischargers in public and private life. If they know they are discharging into water, have a permit for the discharges, think they are conforming to their permits, but unknowingly violate their permit conditions, into prison they go with the violent criminals.

The statute does not say that. The statute at issue makes it a felony, subject to three years of imprisonment, to "knowingly violate . . . any permit condition or limitation." 33 U.S.C. § 1319(c)(2)(A).[1]

. . . In this case, the defendant, sewage plant operators, had a permit to discharge sewage into the ocean, but exceeded the permit limitations. The legal issue for the panel was what knowledge would turn innocently or negligently violating a permit into "knowingly" violating a permit. Were the plant operators felons if they knew they were discharging sewage, but did not know that they were violating their permit: Or did they also have to know that they were violating their permit? Ordinary English grammar, common sense, and precedent, all compel the latter construction.

As the panel opinion states the facts, these two defendants were literally "midnight dumpers." They managed a sewer plant and told their employees to dump 436,000 pounds of sewage into the ocean, mostly at night, fouling a nearby beach. Their conduct, as set out in the panel opinion, suggests that they must have known they were violating their National Pollution Discharge

[1] A 1987 amendment raised the crime from a misdemeanor to a felony, and changed the intent requirement from "willfully" to "knowingly." Pub. L. N. 100-4, § 312, 101 Stat. 42 (1987).

Elimination System (NPDES) permit. United States v. Weitzenhoff, 1 F.3d 1523, 1527-28 (9th Cir. 1993). But we cannot decide the case on that basis, because the jury did not. The court instructed the jury that the government did not have to prove the defendants knew their conduct was unlawful, and refused to instruct the jury that a mistaken belief that the discharge was authorized by the permit would be a defense. Because of the way the jury was instructed, its verdict is consistent with the proposition that the defendants honestly and reasonably believed that their NPDES permit authorized the discharges.

This proposition could be true. NPDES permits are often difficult to understand and obey. The EPA had licensed the defendants' plant to discharge 976 pounds of waste per day, or about 409,920 pounds over the fourteen months covered by the indictment, into the ocean. The wrongful conduct is not discharging waste into the ocean. That was socially desirable conduct by which the defendants protected the people of their city from sewage-borne disease and earned their pay. The wrongful conduct was violating the NPDES permit by discharging 26,000 more pounds of waste than the permit authorized during the fourteen months. Whether these defendants were innocent or not, in the sense of knowing that they were exceeding their permit limitation, the panel's holding will make innocence irrelevant in other permit violation cases where the defendants had no idea that they were exceeding permit limits. The only thing they have to know to be guilty is that they were dumping sewage into the ocean, yet that was a lawful activity expressly authorized by their federal permit.

The statute says "knowingly violates . . . any permit condition or limitation." "Knowingly" is an adverb. It modifies the verb "violates." The object of the verb is "any permit condition or limitation." The word "knowingly" is placed before "violates" to "explain its meaning in the case at hand more clearly." 1 George O. Curme. A Grammar of the English Language 72 (1935). Congress has distinguished those who knowingly violate permit conditions, and are thereby felons, from those who unknowingly violate permit conditions, so are not. The panel reads the statute as though it says "knowingly discharges pollutants." It does not. If we read the statute on the assumption that Congress used the English language in an ordinary way, the state of mind required is knowledge that one is violating a permit condition.

This approach has the virtue of attributing common sense and a rational purpose to Congress. Cf. Longview Fibre Co. v. Rasmussen, 980 F.2d 1307, 1311 (9th Cir. 1992); United States v. Martinez-Cano, 6 F.3d 1400, 1405 (9th Cir. 1993) (dissent). It is one thing to defy a permit limitation, but quite another to violate it without reading that one is violating it. Congress promulgated a parallel statute making it a misdemeanor "negligently" to violate a permit condition or limitation. 33 U.S.C. § 1319(c)(1)(A). If negligent violation is a misdemeanor, why would Congress want to make it a felony to violate the permit without negligence and without even knowing that the discharge exceeded the permit limit? That does not make any sense. It would deter people from working in sewer plants, instead of deterring people from violating permits. All dischargers acting lawfully pursuant to a permit know that they are discharging pollutants. The presence or absence of that knowledge, which is the only mental element determining guilt under the panel's decision, has no bearing on any conduct Congress could have meant to turn into a felony. The only knowledge which could have mattered to Congress, the only knowledge which distinguishes good conduct from bad, is knowledge that the discharge violates the permit. That is what the statute says, "knowingly violates," not "knowingly discharges." There is no sensible reason to doubt that Congress meant what it said and said what it meant.

The panel reaches its surprising result in surprising ways. First, it says that the statute is ambiguous. "As with certain other criminal statutes that employ the term 'knowingly,' it is not apparent from the face of the statute whether 'knowingly' means a knowing violation of the law or simply knowing conduct that is violative of the law." *Weitzenhoff,* 1 F.3d at 1529. As explained above, a grammatical and sensible reading of the statute leaves no room for ambiguity. But for the sake of discussion, suppose that the statute is ambiguous, as the panel says. Then the rule of lenity requires that the construction allowing the defendant more liberty rather than less be applied by the courts . . . .

The panel then tries to bolster its construction by categorizing the offense as a "public welfare offense," as though that justified more aggressive criminalization without a plain statutory command. This category is a modernized version of "malum prohibitum." Traditionally the criminal law distinguishes between malum in se, conduct wrong upon principles of natural moral law, and malum prohibitum, conduct not inherently immoral but wrong because prohibited by law. Black's Law Dictionary 1112 (4th ed. 1951). To put this in plain, modern terms, any normal person knows murder, rape and robbery are wrong, and they would be wrong even in a place with no sovereign and no law. Discharging 6% more pollutants than one's permit allows is wrong only because the law says so. Substitution of the modern term "public welfare offense" for the traditional one, malum prohibitum, allows for confusion by rhetorical suggestion. The new term suggests that other offenses might merely be private in their impact, and therefore less serious. The older set of terms made it clear that murder was more vile than violating a federal regulation. The category of malum prohibitum, or public welfare offenses, makes the rule of lenity especially important, more particularly for felons, because persons of good conscience may not recognize the wrongfulness of the conduct when they engage in it . . . .

The panel, finally, asserts that as a matter of policy, the Clean Water Act crimes "are clearly designed to protect the public at large from the dire consequences of water pollution." That is true, but the panel does not explain how the public is to be protected by making felons of sewer workers who unknowingly violate their plants' permits. Provision for sanitary sewage disposal is among the most ancient laws of civilization. Deuteronomy 23:12-13. Sewage workers perform essential work of great social value. Probably nothing has prevented more infant mortality, or freed more people from cholera, hepatitis, typhoid fever, and other diseases, than the development in the last two centuries of municipal sewer systems. *See* W.H. Corfield, The Treatment and Utilization of Sewage 17-27 (1871). Sewage utility workers perform their difficult work in malodorous and dangerous environments. We have now imposed on these vitally important public servants, a massive legal risk, unjustified by law or precedent, if they unknowingly violate their permit conditions.

Nor is the risk of prison limited to sewage plant workers. It applies to anyone who discharges pollutants pursuant to a permit, and unknowingly violates the permit . . . .

We undermine the foundation of criminal law when we so vitiate the requirements of a criminal state of knowledge and intention as to make felons of the morally innocent.

NOTES AND QUESTIONS

(1) Have the Sixth and Ninth Circuits appropriately construed the criminal intent requirements of RCRA and the Clean Water Act? Should RCRA, a statute that is aimed, in part, at the regulation of hazardous and toxic wastes, be distinguished from the Clean Water Act in this context?

(2) How persuasive is Judge Kleinfield's dissent in the *Weitzenhoff* case? Do you agree with his conclusion that the majority opinion in that case has "made felons of a large number of innocent people doing socially valuable work?" To what extent would the narrower interpretation he favors undercut the deterrent effect of the statute's criminal penalty provision?

(3) In recent years, EPA and the U.S. Department of Justice have relied upon criminal prosecution of environmental violations to an increased extent. There is some evidence that, in response to this trend, a number of U.S. corporations have re-organized their internal structures to enhance their levels of environmental compliance. *See* "Giving the Environment Teeth," New York Times, March 3, 1991, at Section 3, p. 29.

Lazarus, "MEETING THE DEMANDS OF INTEGRATION IN THE EVOLUTION OF ENVIRONMENTAL LAW: REFORMING ENVIRONMENTAL CRIMINAL LAW"*

83 Geo. L.J. 2407 (1995)

Legal assimilation denotes the process by which a new set of priorities and information simultaneously influence different legal sectors, restriking equilibria that underlie a host of legal rules in disparate contexts. By contrast, integration describes the evolutionary process within any one discrete area of law. It involves an initial period of confrontation between one body of law's assumptions, values, and goals and those underlying other intersecting areas of law. Confrontation is followed by accommodation and reconciliation as the two areas of law interact and inform each other in a process of mutual evolution . . . .

This article's thesis is that this process of integration, necessary to law's consistency and coherence, has not yet occurred in environmental criminal law. This is not to say that other areas of the law are currently in a state of equilibrium; it is unlikely this will ever occur, given the dynamic nature of environmental policy, science, and law. Yet for reasons discussed below, the process of integration is far less mature in environmental criminal law than in virtually any other area that intersects with environmental law—including some of the most controversial, like property law.

Better integration is, however, simultaneously more important in environmental criminal law than in other areas of the law. The fundamental fairness of the criminal incarceration sanction—one of the most severe imposed by the law—is undercut by any incoherence and inconsistency in its imposition. They sap the sanction of its legitimacy and invite, just as has happened in environmental criminal law, accusations of government abuse both when those sanctions are imposed and when they are not. Such claims of government abuse can, to be sure, provide the impetus necessary to prompt a thoughtful effort to address the underlying problem. The risk, however, is that the emotions of the moment, which are generally high in both the environmental and criminal contexts, will instead prompt misdirected surficial changes that fail to address the source of the problem and ultimately make matters worse. That is precisely the risk presented now by the federal environmental crimes program, as it is increasingly attacked by those on either end of the political spectrum . . . .

Even the most cursory review of the competing features of environmental law and criminal law reveals several obvious tensions confronting the development of an environmental criminal program. Criminal law requires more demanding proof to convict, but environmental law makes such a showing problematic because of scientific uncertainties and fragmented decisionmaking authority. Criminal law emphasizes settled norms, while environmental law constantly changes and aspires for fundamental and dramatic change. And, although criminal law requires clear, determinate, and readily accessible legal standards, familiar to the general public, environmental law is replete with obscure, indeterminate, and highly technical standards, the meaning of which few can claim genuine mastery.

None of these tensions means that there is something "wrong" with environmental law; most of its features are justifiable. There are legitimate, often unavoidable, reasons for this conflict inherent in both the subject of environmental pollution and this nation's institutional structure for lawmaking. But regardless of the merits of their origins, the above tensions testify to the need for reconciliation and some mutual accommodation of competing interests in the development of environmental criminal law. Each presents a distinct challenge.

Nor is any of these tensions totally unique to environmental criminal law. Undoubtedly, there are other regulatory schemes with criminal sanctions that present problems of complexity, especially indeterminacy and obscurity, and that are also dynamic in character. Food and drug law, securities regulation, and the tax code (which is also marked by pervasiveness in its application) are obvious examples. Few other regulatory areas, however, present as many of these features in combination as does environmental law. Environmental law is likely unparalleled in the intensity of the conflicts that have resulted from its criminalization. But even more important, those in government responsible for resolution of these kinds of tensions have done so more successfully in other areas of law than in environmental criminal law. Criminal law applicable to securities regulation and the tax code, for example, reflects more concerted integrative efforts in the initial definition, interpretation, and enforcement than environmental criminal law. And problems that might be posed in food and drug regulation have likely not been as acute because the applicable penalties are so low.

In the environmental criminal area, all three branches of government have not met the challenges that are presented by the need to integrate environmental and criminal law: Congress, in drafting the relevant statutory provisions; the Executive Branch, in prosecuting environmental crimes; and, finally, the Courts, in construing the relevant language—all share responsibility for this lapse. No branch has appreciated how these tensions bear on its respective role . . . .

Providing for a meaningful debate in the environmental crimes context is especially difficult. The environmental criminal penalty provisions can attract support from both the more liberal pro-environmental protection legislators and the more conservative "law-and-order" representatives. Both "environmental protection" and "criminal prosecution" enjoy a rhetorical advantage that masks the difficult policy issues underlying their scope and application—and that, unfortunately, render difficult the thoughtful public debate of the policy implications of different options. There is little political advantage for either liberal or conservative legislators to gain through concern for potential overreaching. It is far easier just to assume away those issues and rely on the exercise of prosecutorial discretion—a result naturally supported, notwithstanding the associated pitfalls, by the executive branch agency that wants its programs dignified by criminal sanctions and by a Justice Department that prefers maximum discretion. Consequently, the prospects for legislative or executive branch reform of the existing program are bleak, despite the tremendous need for such reform.

The political realities of reform should not, however, chill its discussion. Concrete examples of the kinds of reform possible and comparison of the environmental criminal penalty provisions with criminal law elsewhere can reduce existing misapprehensions. Reform of the environmental criminal penalty provisions is not tantamount to a retreat from environmental protection or from its strict enforcement. The substitution of program coherence and integrity for existing statutory rhetoric offers instead an opportunity to create an effective criminal enforcement effort.

Congress presents simultaneously the forum most resistant to reform and most appropriate to bring about this reform. There are also significant integrative functions to be performed by the other two branches—executive and judicial—in descending order of priority.

The challenge Congress faces is to amend the existing environmental criminal penalty provisions to account better for the natural tensions that exist between environmental and criminal law. Congress needs to identify and define more carefully those states of mind and types of conduct that warrant the moral stigma of a felony conviction and a substantial term of incarceration. There is no one "correct" way for Congress to do so. Congress must strike a balance between competing concerns—ranging from the need to define felonies in a manner consistent with their associated moral stigma to the obvious deterrent advantages of the threat of criminal prosecution. How Congress strikes that balance is ultimately a matter of policy and (yes) politics.

But there are limits. Some of the more obvious boundaries are supplied by the Constitution itself. The law cannot, of course, be so vague as to violate due process. And there are constitutional limits on Congress's ability to create strict liability felony offenses . . . .

My own view is that a reasonable accommodation of the competing demands of environmental and criminal law can strike a proper balance long before embracing the extreme result of noncriminalization. Criminal law can reasonably accommodate environmental law's need to define injuries in terms of risk, rather than actual harm. And, given the irreversible and ultimately noncompensable adverse human health and environmental effects on future generations that environmental laws seek to avoid, environmental law's need for deterrence beyond mere liability rules is likewise worthy of accommodation through to the extent of a complete substitution of deterrence for moral blameworthiness. In short, violations of federal environmental laws can involve the kind of morally culpable behavior warranting felony sanctions. The challenge is to define the sanctions in a manner more consistent with that culpability touchstone, rather than either, at one extreme, basing crimes on deterrence needs alone or, at the other extreme, jettisoning the entire enterprise of criminalization as misguided from conception.

For example, at least those persons who know the relevant environmental standard and the associated human health and environmental risks of noncompliance and, notwithstanding that knowledge, engage in conduct that they know amounts to a violation, can be properly subjected to a felony sanction. Their knowledge of the risks they create is sufficient to establish the level of moral culpability that criminal law has traditionally sought prior to the imposition of felony sanctions. . . .

Congress should . . . consider the harder mens rea issue of the facts a defendant must know to have committed a felony offense. The baseline rule for environmental cases should be that, like other kinds of felony offenses, the government must prove the defendant's knowledge of all of the legally relevant facts. Congress must then justify any departure from that default principle . . . .

There are . . . a number of middle ground options worth detailed legislative consideration. Congress could, for instance, dictate that the defendant must know only a few limited critical facts that Congress believes sufficient to establish the defendant's moral culpability. Once that threshold knowledge is established (*e.g.*, the toxic nature of the material), the government need not prove the defendant's knowledge of all the technical details related to his or her conduct (*e.g.*, the precise extent of the leaching of contaminants under specified conditions), notwithstanding their relevance to the applicable legal standard.

Another opinion would be to provide for a lesser mens rea requirement—such as recklessness—in certain narrowly defined circumstances, for example, when heightened irreversible health or environmental risks are created. Most environmental violations would not meet this standard. But for those that do, the need for additional deterrence could justify a reduced showing of mens rea. One feature of environmental law—the fragmentation of authority in corporate decisionmaking—would certainly support the need for such a reduction in a narrowly defined set of cases. Otherwise, it may be too difficult to hold accountable those in large corporations who seek to insulate themselves from knowledge of pollution activities.

A distinct, yet related option would be to include a "stand-alone" criminal sanction. Such a provision would depart from the administrative law model that currently dominates environmental criminal law and be more like a traditional criminal endangerment provision. The criminal sanction would not depend on proof of a violation of any underlying environmental regulation, but would instead turn on proof of mens rea and either actual serious harm to human health or the environment or, perhaps, a substantial threat of such harm. Virtually all of the major federal environmental laws currently include an analogous civil enforcement provision that provides for civil enforcement based on the presence of an imminent and substantial endangerment, without the need for a showing that any environmental standard has been violated.

The advantage of such a provision is that it would avoid having the success of a felony prosecution turn on the government's ability to prove the defendant's knowledge of the very obtuse and rarified facts that frequently determine whether a particular environmental regulation has been violated. But, to maintain the propriety of such a felony sanction in the absence of such proof, the endangerment provision would need to provide an alternative justification. Such a justification could be, as it is in criminal endangerment provisions generally, based on a showing of the defendant's awareness of the environmental and human health risks created by her conduct. Congress could also draft the provision, as it has in a host of other areas of criminal law, to impose especially high sanctions when that threat is realized and actual serious harm occurs. Although the defendant's state of mind is the same regardless of whether the harm threatened is actually realized, society has long drawn that distinction in imposing heightened criminal penalties.

Finally, as with mistakes about the applicable law, an affirmative mistake of fact defense as to certain types of facts might well be an appropriate accommodation of the competing demands of environmental and criminal law. The burden would not be on the government to prove the defendant's knowledge of all the legally relevant obscure facts; there would instead be a threshold presumption of such knowledge. But, unlike under current case law, the defendant would be allowed to rebut that presumption. The burden would be on the defendant, not the government, but the possibility of such a defense would exist. The defense could be written either in terms of good faith mistakes of fact or, more likely, objectively reasonable mistakes of fact. And, as with a reasonable mistake of law defense, this defense could be made applicable only to substantial terms of imprisonment . . . .

The executive branch could also pursue several possible reforms. The single most important is the establishment of guidelines for deciding whether a particular case warrants civil or criminal enforcement. These guidelines should not be drafted in an open-ended, indeterminate fashion. They should force policymakers to make the tough policy decisions that can best be made prospectively on a generic basis, rather than in a hurried, and ad hoc fashion. The latter context simply does not allow for the kind of considered and reasoned decisionmaking that the underlying policy issues require.

The guidelines also need to be drafted in coordination with all the major participants in environmental enforcement, at least at the federal level. These include EPA's Office of Enforcement (both civil and criminal offices) and the Department of Justice (both Main Justice and the United States Attorney Offices). The drafting process will be difficult, but that is precisely why it needs to be done: both to rationalize the decisionmaking process and to build the bridges between the policymakers necessary to promote greater understanding and acceptance of each other's decisions . . . .

As previously described, the courts' integrative opportunities lie principally within the realm of statutory construction. It will require the abandonment of canons of statutory construction that are based on assumptions that cannot fairly be applied to many of the environmental criminal felony penalty provisions . . . .

Congress should endeavor to speak directly and clearly to the policy considerations underlying the identification of actors who deserve significant terms of incarceration for violating environmental protection laws. But when Congress has not done so—or when the environmental protection requirements upon which those violations are based are too obscure or indeterminate—the applicable law should be read in a light more favorable to the criminal defendant. That is the central teaching of the rule of lenity, consistent with the aims and limits of criminal law. There is no sound reason why environmental laws should be exempted from the application of that rule. Indeed, for reasons outlined in this article, there is good reason to assume that the problems intended to be redressed by the rule of lenity are especially pronounced in the environmental law context.

Finally, there may be innovative ways in which courts can take a more proactive role in serving an integrative function should both Congress and the executive branch fail to do so. For instance, the courts could, on their own initiative, create affirmative defenses . . . .

Schiffer and Simon, "THE REALITY OF PROSECUTING ENVIRONMENTAL CRIMINALS: A RESPONSE TO PROFESSOR LAZARUS"*

83 Geo. L.J. 2531 (1995)

In his article, Meeting the Demands of Integration in the Evolution of Environmental Law: Reforming Environmental Criminal Law, Richard Lazarus provides a provocative review of federal environmental criminal enforcement. The article contains many interesting points that warrant a longer discussion than is permitted here. However, we fundamentally disagree with significant aspects of the analysis. This response focuses on two weaknesses of Professor Lazarus' analysis: (1) the problems that he identifies are more theoretical than real; and (2) the proposed changes—the consequences of which are largely unconsidered in the article—would seriously undermine legitimate law enforcement . . . .

I. The Article Mischaracterizes Federal Environmental Criminal Enforcement

We disagree with the arguments in Professor Lazarus' article that, in the area of environmental law, prosecutions are brought to punish conduct that does not violate "traditional norms of moral culpability" evident in other types of criminal cases. In fact, criminal environmental cases are brought to punish egregious and plainly wrongful conduct. Some examples of the types of conduct recently prosecuted include the following: intentionally discharging pollutants in violation of specific water quality permit requirements; unpermitted discharging of raw sewage into rivers and streams through a bypass pipe without reporting it to the Environmental Protection Agency (EPA); falsifying sample test results required to be reported to the government; surreptitious dumping of chemical wastes on the ground or beside a creek; and failing to follow well-known and easily understood procedures in the removal of asbestos. In all of these cases, the defendants did not need extraordinary expertise in science, engineering, or economics to understand the criminal nature of their conduct.

For environmental crimes, as in other prosecutions, there are incentives and controls—largely overlooked in the article—that guide prosecutors to pursue the most egregious types of violations. For example, federal prosecutors are governed in their exercise of discretion by the Principles of Federal Prosecution, which seek to ensure that all federal laws, regardless of their complexity, are enforced in a fair and reasonable manner. Moreover, in each case, the prosecutor must be prepared to persuade a judge and jury that the defendant committed serious criminal conduct. Prosecutors naturally want to be successful in their cases, and thus have an incentive to investigate and prosecute conduct that is illegal for reasons that are clear and evident, rather than cloudy, overly technical, or arcane.

Partly for these reasons, cases prosecuted as environmental crimes strongly resemble prosecutions in other areas. One measure of this similarity is that some prosecutions that relate to environmental violations also include charges under more generic criminal provisions, such as the proscriptions against making false statements, or committing mail fraud or perjury.

II. Professor Lazarus' Article Fails to Establish the Need for Changes Proposed

The article argues that certain aspects of environmental law are difficult to "integrate" with criminal law. For example, the article identifies environmental law's "aspirational quality" (the tendency to set ambitious goals for environmental quality) and complexity as characteristics that are problematic for criminal enforcement. In practice, however, prosecutions are not brought for failure to meet aspirations, but rather for specific bad conduct as measured against specific and definite standards. Such conduct includes: failing to comply with permits requiring well-understood treatment systems; stealthy dumping of waste that is known to be noxious; and making knowingly false statements.

Moreover, with respect to complexity, it is important to distinguish the occasionally complex types of proof that are required at trial from the far more straightforward facts confronted by the actors involved in the conduct at issue. For example, the government may require complex laboratory documentation and expert testimony to identify a particular substance and thereby prove that it satisfies the definition of hazardous waste under the Resource Conservation and Recovery Act (RCRA). By contrast, defendants who arrange to dump hazardous waste unlawfully in a ravine may have had no trouble identifying the material, because they may have purchased it, or used it on a day-to-day basis, or routinely disposed of it . . . .

III. Professor Lazarus' Proposals Would Create Serious Obstacles to Effective Environmental Law Enforcement

Professor Lazarus makes . . . suggestions for substantive legal changes that would make criminal prosecutions more difficult, and in some cases allow people guilty of egregious, culpable conduct to go free.

The article first proposes a specific intent, or "willfulness," standard which would require the government to prove that the defendant had knowledge of the law that was being violated. In an environmental context, such a requirement might require proof of knowledge of permit requirements or specific regulations, making it difficult to obtain a conviction against offenders who have reason to know that their conduct is wrongful, but who do not have specific knowledge of the law. For example, consider the above hypothetical trucker who dumped drums of wastes in fields and vacant lots in a rural area.

Although the trucker had reasons to know the wastes were dangerous, he cannot be shown to have been aware of RCRA statutory and regulatory requirements. Under a willfulness standard, the trucker might avoid conviction by arguing that he lacked knowledge that the wastes were "hazardous wastes" subject to federal regulation. Significantly, Professor Lazarus acknowledges that in environmental law "[a] willfulness standard may be much too demanding."

Moreover, a specific intent requirement could jeopardize the public health and welfare. Environmental crimes, like other general intent crimes, apply the well-established principle that ignorance of the law is no defense. That doctrine applies with particular strength in cases of laws to protect public health and welfare, of which environmental laws are classic examples . . . .

A second proposal in the article is to replace current environmental criminal provisions with "stand-alone" sections. These provisions would proscribe certain types of conduct, undertaken either knowingly or willfully or both, that causes actual harm or threatens substantial harm to human health or the environment.

Legislation enacting such stand-alone provisions in lieu of the existing statutory framework would have a highly deleterious effect on the environmental criminal enforcement program. The article itself explains why requiring proof of harm would immunize many egregious violations from enforcement. In many cases, there is a long latency period between the conduct and any discernible harm. In addition, proving cause and effect is often problematic . . . .

There are additional problems with the stand-alone approach. For example, the cumulative impact of multiple violations by multiple parties poses significant risk in many environmental cases. It would be difficult under the "stand-alone" approach to prosecute an individual who contributes to the cumulative harm but whose individual actions cannot be proven to be harmful by themselves. To illustrate, enforcement actions, including criminal prosecutions, may be brought for unlawful discharges into city sewers, even though individual discharges cause no provable harm. The cumulative effect of widespread noncompliance could disable or severely damage a sewage treatment plant and pose a safety hazard for sewage plant workers.

The article also proposes the creation of new affirmative defenses: "mistake of fact" and "mistake of law." A "mistake of fact" defense, however, is unnecessary because, as noted, under current federal environmental laws a defendant who can show an honest mistake of material fact avoids prosecution by negating the intent required for a felony conviction. A "mistake of law" defense merely recasts the same issue as legislating specific intent, and would cause the same problems for law enforcement.

IV. Conclusion

Environmental crimes are real crimes with real victims, and as Professor Lazarus recognizes, criminal enforcement is critical for an effective environmental protection program. The article greatly exaggerates the problems with environmental criminal enforcement. It fails to offer any compelling reasons to change an otherwise effective program. Moreover, rather than improving environmental criminal law, the proposed solutions would create serious problems for maintaining a fair, effective program of environmental prosecutions as one means of assuring a clean and healthy environmental for the American public.

QUESTIONS

(1) How persuaded were you by the proposed reforms of environmental criminal law proposed by Professor Lazarus? Would the relevant statutes be improved if they specified the critical facts that defendants must be proven to know to establish their moral culpability? Are lesser mens rea standards (such as recklessness) appropriate? Has Lazarus overstated the extent to which environmental criminal cases turn upon technical, complex and obscure questions?

(2) To what extent have Simon and Schiffer demonstrated that Lazarus' suggestions "would create serious obstacles to effective law enforcement"? Have they given appropriate weight to the need to integrate environmental criminal law with intersecting fields of law?

§ 8.08 Citizen Suit Enforcement

Since 1970, Congress has included citizen suit provisions in most environmental statutes. These provisions which generally authorize "any person" or "any citizen" to institute suit against "any person" alleged to be in violation of enumerated statutory standards, have been said to allow citizens to serve as "private attorneys general." They typically require plaintiffs to give at least sixty days notice, to federal and state officials as well as to the alleged violator, prior to the initiation of litigation. They also generally bar citizen suits where federal or state authorities are "diligently prosecuting" governmental enforcement actions. However, citizens have a right to intervene in federal civil suits under those circumstances.

The citizen suit sections of environmental statutes also authorize actions against the Administrator of the U.S. Environmental Protection Agency for failure to perform a "non-discretionary" act or duty prescribed by the legislation.

ATLANTIC TERMINAL URBAN RENEWAL AREA COALITION v. NEW YORK CITY DEPARTMENT OF ENVIRONMENTAL PROTECTION

United States District Court, Southern District of New York (1989)
705 F. Supp. 988

Lasker, J.

Atlantic Terminal Urban Renewal Area Coalition and several individuals (collectively "ATURA") who live in the vicinity of the proposed Atlantic Terminal and Brooklyn Center Projects ("the Project") move to amend their complaint to add three claims . . . . The underlying suit, as well as the proposed amendments, address the effect of the Project on the quality of the surrounding air and, more specifically, the effect of the Project on the concentration of carbon monoxide in the environs . . . .

The United States Environmental Protection Agency and its Administrator William K. Reilly (collectively "EPA") oppose ATURA's motion for leave to amend to add claim six, which alleges a violation of § 113(a)(1) of the Clean Air Act("CAA"), 42 U.S.C. § 7413(a)(1). Section 113(a)(1) states: "Whenever, on the basis of any information available to him, the Administrator finds that any person is in violation of any requirement of an applicable implementation plan, the Administrator shall notify the person in violation of the plan and the state in which the plan applies of such finding. If such violation extends beyond the 30th day after the date of the Administrator's notification, the Administrator may issue an order requiring such person to comply with the requirements of such plan or he may bring a civil action in accordance with subsection (b) of this section." Although the Administrator has not made a formal finding, ATURA contends that he has found that the City of New York violated para. 3.6(A) of New York's State Implementation Plan ("SIP"), which provides in relevant part that: "if an EIS [Environmental Impact Statement] for a project proposal identifies a violation or exacerbation of the carbon monoxide standard, then the City commits to assure that mitigating measures will be implemented by the project sponsor or City, so as to provide for attainment of the standard by December 31, 1987 and maintenance of it thereafter." ATURA contends that the City is in violation of para. 3.6(A) because the Final Environmental Impact Statement ("FEIS") for the Project indicates that, even with mitigation measures, the locations surrounding the Project will not comply with the carbon monoxide standard by December 31, 1987. ATURA also relies for support of its allegation that the EPA has found a violation on a letter dated October 16, 1986 from Barbara Pastalove, Chief of the Environmental Impacts Branch of Region II of the EPA, to Michael P.M. Spies, Assistant Vice President of he New York City Public Development Corporation, which states in relevant part that the mitigation plans for the Project "do not meet Clean Air Act requirements and could not receive EPA approval if submitted as control measures for the [carbon monoxide] hot spots identified by the EISs."

The EPA contends that ATURA has done no more than establish that the agency has before it information that may enable it to make a finding that the City is in violation of the SIP. However, the EPA argues that it has not made such a finding nor can it be compelled to do so, because the duty to make such a finding is discretionary. It is not disputed that § 304 of the CAA, 42 U.S.C. § 7604(a)(2), confers subject matter jurisdiction on the court only to compel the Administrator to perform a mandatory duty. Council of Commuter Org. v. Metropolitan Transp. Auth., 683 F.2d 663, 665 (2d Cir. 1982).

At issue is the nature of the Administrator's duty as specified in § 113(a)(1) of the Act to "find" the existence of a violation. For a number of reasons, I find more persuasive the reasoning of those courts that have construed the duty to "find" a violation under § 113 and parallel provisions of the Federal Water Pollution Control Act ("FWPCA") as discretionary more persuasive than those that have found the duty mandatory. Compare Dubois v. Thomas, 820 F.2d 943, 947 (8th Cir. 1987) (holding duty to find a permit violation under § 309(a)(3) of FWPCA, 33 U.S.C. § 1319(a)(3), not mandatory); Harmon Cove Condominium Ass'n v. Marsh, 815 F.2d 949, 953 (3rd Cir. 1987) (duty of Secretary under § 404 of FWPCA, 33 U.S.C. § 1344, to find a violation is discretionary); Seabrook v. Costle, 659 F.2d 1371, 1375 (5th Cir. 1981) (section 113(a) of the CAA"does not impose a nondiscretionary duty to make a finding on every alleged violation of a SIP"); Council of Commuter Org. v. Metropolitan Transp. Auth., 524 F. Supp. 90, 92 (S.D. N.Y. 1981) (duty to issue notices of violation arises only after Administrator "makes a discretionary finding that such violations have occurred"), aff'd [on other grounds], 683 F.2d 663 (2nd Cir. 1982) with New England Legal Found. v. Costle, 475 F. Supp. 425, 433 (D. Conn. 1979) (the Administrator has been held "to make . . . a finding [of a SIP violation pursuant to § 113(a)(1) when information regarding an alleged violation is presented to him"), aff'd in part and reversed in part, 632 F.2d 936 (2d Cir. 1980); Wisconsin's Envtl. Decade, Inc. v. Wisconsin Power and Light Co., 395 F. Supp. 313, 320 (W.D. Wisc. 1975) ("when presented with evidence indicating that a violation may exist [under § 113(a)(1)], the Administrator must make a finding that a violation does or does not exist"); Marinoff v. EPA, No. 78-3042 (S.D. N.Y. Nov. 22, 1978) (citing language of Wisconsin but finding that neither party indicated whether Administrator has been presented with evidence of a violation).

First, the language of § 113 does not compel a holding that the Administrator must make a finding whenever he or she is informed of an alleged violation. As is true of the language of § 309(a)(3) of the FWPCA, the language of § 113(a)(1) "makes no mention whatever of a duty to make findings, much less a duty to carry out an investigation of each and every citizen complaint." Dubois v. Thomas, 820 F.2d at 947.

Second, a construction of the statute, like that of Wisconsin and New England Legal Foundation, requiring the Administrator to determine whether a violation exists each time an allegation is made, could frustrate the purpose of the Act. Although investigations of every alleged violation may be ideal, limited time and resources constrain the Administrator; as the court in Seabrook reasoned, a rule requiring investigations at the drop of an allegation would more likely than not divert resources from efficient and effective investigations of violations appearing most egregious. 659 F.2d at 1375. *See also* Dubois v. Thomas, 820 F.2d at 947 (holding that goal of FWPCA would be frustrated were Secretary to have mandatory duty to investigate and find permit violations because agency would not be able to concentrate its energies on those claims considered more egregious).

Third, § 113 involves questions of the Administrator's prosecutorial discretion, which should be limited only if the language of the statute or the congressional history were to indicate more clearly a mandatory duty. As Seabrook, Dubois, and Harmon Cove have held, decisions to take enforcement activity are generally committed to agency discretion in the absence of statutory language or legislative history to the contrary, and the "principle of almost absolute discretion in initiating enforcement action should apply with equal force to the decision to take the preliminary investigatory steps that would provide the basis for enforcement action." Seabrook, 659 F.2d at 1374.

Of course, it can be argued, as in Wisconsin, that "[b]ecause . . . Congress made a deliberate decision that the duty to issue notices of violation should be non-discretionary, I cannot accept an interpretation of the language of § 113(a) which would make this duty an empty one by permitting the Administrator to make a finding or not to make a finding as he or she sees fit." 395 F. Supp. at 320. However, other language in § 113 belies this interpretation. Section 113 provides that if the violation continues after the notice is issued: "the Administrator may issue an order requiring such person to comply with the requirements of such plan or he may bring a civil action." This language has been interpreted to give the Administrator discretion not only as to the form the enforcement may take, but also whether to take any enforcement action . . . . [H]olding the Administrator's duty to make a finding to be discretionary will not undermine or thwart the purpose of § 113.

Finally, as is apparent in this case, the statutory scheme supports, although it does not compel, the holding that the Administrator's duty to find a violation is discretionary. In this case, the Regional Administrator of the EPA has notified Governor Cuomo that the air in the New York City metropolitan area failed to comply with the national ambient air quality standards for ozone and carbon monoxide and that the SIP accordingly requires revision pursuant to § 110 of the CAA. ATURA's construction of the statute would require the Administrator, in each instance in which SIP revision is required because of nonattainment in a region, to issue a notice of violation. It would thereby prevent the EPA from selecting among a range of remedies available to address nonattainment and choosing, as it has in this case, to initiate the SIP revision process, rather than to pursue individual violations.

The construction of the Administrator's duty to make a finding when informed of an alleged violation as discretionary comports with, rather than frustrates, not only § 113, but the Act as well. Plaintiffs in this action are not left without a remedy; alleged violations of an applicable SIP need not, as a result of this decision, go unaddressed. Section 304(a)(1) of the Act provides for a citizen suit "against any person . . . who is alleged to be in violation of (A) an emission standard or limitation under this chapter or (B) an order issued by the Administrator or a state with respect to such a standard or limitation . . . ." Plaintiff can, as it has already done in claim one of this action, bring suit against the responsible agencies and officers of the City of New York for this alleged violation of para. 3.6(A) of the SIP.

NOTES AND QUESTIONS

(1) In your view is this case correctly decided? To what extent should EPA (and other governmental enforcement agencies) have unfettered discretion to decide whether to "find" violations of environmental standards? What kinds of considerations should guide EPA's exercise of enforcement discretion?

(2) As the principal case itself indicates the courts have been divided as to whether the EPA Administrator is under a mandatory obligation to find the existence of a violation where evidence of such a violation is before him or her. Even when such an EPA finding has been made, however, several courts have held that the Agency still has discretion as to whether to proceed with an enforcement action. *See, e.g.*, *Thompson v. Thomas,* 680 F. Supp. 1 (D. D.C. 1987); *Sierra Club v. Train,* 557 F.2d 485 (5th Cir. 1977); *Ringbolt Farms Homeowners Ass'n v. Town of Hull,* 714 F. Supp. 1246 (D. Mass. 1989). Is that a sound conclusion?

GWALTNEY OF SMITHFIELD, LTD. v. CHESAPEAKE BAY FOUNDATION, INC.

United States Supreme Court (1987)
484 U.S. 49, 108 S. Ct. 376, 98 L. Ed. 2d 306

Marshall, J.:

In this case, we must decide whether § 505(a) of the Clean Water Act,also known as the Federal Water Pollution Control Act, 33U.S.C. § 1365(a), confers federal jurisdiction over citizen suits for wholly past violations.

The Clean Water Act (Act)was enacted in 1972 "to restore and maintain the chemical, physical, and biological integrity of the nation's waters." § 1251(a). In order to achieve these goals, § 301(a) of the Act makes unlawful the discharge of any pollutant into navigable waters except as authorized by specified sections of the Act.

One of these specified sections is § 402, which establishes the National Pollutant Discharge Elimination System (NPDES). Pursuant to § 402(a), the Administrator of the Environmental Protection Agency (EPA) may issue permits authorizing the discharge of pollutants in accordance with specified conditions. Pursuant to § 402(b), each state may establish and administer its own permit program if the program conforms to federal guidelines and is approved by the Administrator. The Act calls for the Administrator to suspend the issuance of federal permits as to waters subject to an approved state program. § 1342(c)(1).

The holder of a federal NPDES permit is subject to enforcement action by the Administrator for failure to comply with the conditions of the permit. The Administrator's enforcement arsenal includes administrative, civil, and criminal sanctions. § 1319. The holder of a state NPDES permit is subject to both federal and state enforcement action for failure to comply. §§ 1319, 1342(b)(7). In the absence of federal or state enforcement, private citizens may commence civil actions against any person "alleged to be in violation of" the conditions of either a federal or state NPDES permit. § 1365(a)(1). If the citizen prevails in such an action, the court may order injunctive relief and/or impose civil penalties payable to the United States Treasury. § 1365(a).

. . . .

Between 1981 and 1984, petitioner repeatedly violated the conditions of [its NPDES] permit by exceeding effluent limitations on five of the seven pollutants covered. These violations are chronicled in the Discharge Monitoring Reports (DMRs) that the permit required petitioner to maintain. Petitioner installed new equipment to improve its chlorination system in March 1982, and its last reported chlorine violation occurred in October 1982. The new chlorination system also helped to control the discharge of fecal coliform, and the last recorded fecal coliform violation occurred in February 1984. Petitioner installed an upgraded wastewater treatment system in October 1983, and its last reported TKN violation occurred on May 15, 1984.

Respondents Chesapeake Bay Foundation and Natural Resources Defense Council, two nonprofit corporations dedicated to the protection of natural resources, sent notice in February 1984, to Gwaltney, the Administrator of EPA, and the Virginia State Water Control Board, indicating respondents' intention to commence a citizen suit under the Act based on petitioner's violations of its permit conditions. Respondents proceeded to file this suit in June 1984, alleging that petitioner "has violated . . . (and) will continue to violate its NPDES permit." Respondents requested that the District Court provide declaratory and injunctive relief, impose civil penalties, and award attorney's fees and costs. The District Court granted partial summary judgment for respondents in August 1984, declaring Gwaltney "to have violated and to be in violation" of the Act. The District Court then held a trial to determine the appropriate remedy.

Before the District Court reached a decision, Gwaltney moved, in May 1985, for dismissal of the action for want of subject-matter jurisdiction under the Act. Gwaltney argued that the language of § 505(a), which permits private citizens to bring suit against any person "alleged to be in violation" of the Act, requires that a defendant be violating the Act at the time of suit . . . . Gwaltney contended that because its last recorded violation occurred several weeks before respondents filed their complaint, the District Court lacked subject-matter jurisdiction over respondents' action.

The District Court rejected Gwaltney's argument, concluding that § 505 authorizes citizens to bring enforcement actions on the basis of wholly past violations . . . . The District Court held in the alternative that respondents satisfied the jurisdictional requirements of § 505 because their complaint alleged in good faith that Gwaltney was continuing to violate its permit at the time the suit was filed.

The Court of Appeals affirmed . . . .

. . . .

It is well settled that "the starting point for interpreting a statute is the language of the statute itself." *Consumer Product Safety Comm'n v. GTE Sylvania, Inc.*, 447 U.S. 102, 108, 100 S.Ct. 2051, 2056, 64 L.Ed.2d 766 (1980). The Court of Appeals concluded that the "to be in violation" language of § 505 is ambiguous, whereas petitioner asserts that it plainly precludes the construction adopted below. We must agree with the Court of Appeals that § 505 is not a provision in which Congress' limpid prose put an end to all dispute. But to acknowledge ambiguity is not to conclude that all interpretations are equally plausible. The most natural reading of "to be in violation" is a requirement that citizen-plaintiffs allege a state of either continuous or intermittent violation—that is, a reasonable likelihood that a past polluter will continue to pollute in the future. Congress could have phrased its requirement in language that looked to the past ("to have violated"), but it did not choose this readily available option.

Respondents urge that the choice of the phrase "to be in violation" rather than phrasing more clearly directed to the past, is a "careless accident," the result of a "debatable lapse of syntactical precision." But the prospective orientation of that phrase could not have escaped Congress' attention. Congress used identical language in the citizen suit provisions of several other environmental statutes that authorize only prospective relief. Moreover, Congress has demonstrated in yet other statutory provisions that is knows how to avoid this prospective implication by using language that explicitly targets wholly past violations.

Respondents seek to counter this reasoning by observing that Congress also used the phrase "is in violation" in § 309(a) of the Act, which authorizes the Administrator of EPA to issue compliance orders. That language is incorporated by reference in § 309(b), which authorizes the Administrator to bring civil enforcement actions. Because it is little questioned that the Administrator may bring enforcement actions to recover civil penalties for wholly past violations, respondents contend, the parallel language of § 309(a) and § 505(a) must mean that citizens, too, may maintain such actions.

Although this argument has some initial plausibility, it cannot withstand close scrutiny and comparison of the two statutory provisions. The Administrator's ability to seek civil penalties is not discussed in either § 309(a) or § 309(b); civil penalties are not mentioned until § 309(d), which does not contain the "is in violation" language. This Court recently has recognized that § 309(d) constitutes a separate grant of enforcement authority:

> "Section 1319 does not intertwine equitable relief with the imposition of civil penalties. Instead each kind of relief is separably authorized in a separate and distinct statutory provision. Subsection (b), providing injunctive relief, is independent of subsection (d), which provides only for civil penalties." Tull v. United States, 481 U.S. 412, 107 S.Ct. 1831, 95 L.Ed.2d 365 (1987).

In contrast, § 505 of the Act does not authorize civil penalties separately from injunctive relief; rather, the two forms of relief are referred to in the same subsection, even in the same sentence. The citizen suit provision suggests a connection between injunctive relief and civil penalties that is noticeably absent from the provisions authorizing agency enforcement. A comparison of § 309 and § 505 thus supports rather than refutes our conclusion that citizens, unlike the Administrator, may seek civil penalties only in a suit brought to enjoin or otherwise abate an ongoing violation.

Our reading of the "to be in violation" language of § 505(a) is bolstered by the language and structure of the rest of the citizen suit provisions in § 505 of the Act. These provisions together make plain that the interest of the citizen-plaintiff is primarily forward-looking.

One of the most striking indicia of the prospective orientation of the citizen suit is the pervasive use of the present tense throughout § 505. A citizen suit may be brought only for violation of a permit limitation "which is in effect" under the Act. 33 U.S.C. § 1365(f). Citizen-plaintiffs must give notice to the alleged violator, the Administrator of EPA, and the state in which the alleged violation "occurs." § 1365(b)(1)(A). A Governor of a state may sue as a citizen when the Administrator fails to enforce an effluent limitation "the violation of which is occurring in another state and is causing an adverse effect on the public health or welfare in his state." § 165(h). The most telling use of the present tense is in the definition of "citizen" as "a person . . . having an interest which is or may be adversely affected" by the defendant's violations of the Act. § 1365(g). This definition makes plain what the undeviating use of the present tense strongly suggests: the harm sought to be addressed by the citizen suit lies in the present or the future, not in the past.

Any other conclusion would render incomprehensible § 505's notice provision, which requires citizens to give 60 days notice of their intent to sue to the alleged violator as well as to the Administrator and the state. § 1365(b)(1)(A). If the Administrator or the state commences enforcement actions within that 60 day period, the citizen suit is barred, presumably because the governmental action has rendered it unnecessary. § 1365(b)(1)(B). It follows logically that the purpose of notice to the alleged violator is to give it an opportunity to bring itself into complete compliance with the Act and thus likewise render unnecessary a citizen suit. If we assume, as respondents urge, that citizen suits may target wholly past violations, the requirement of notice to the alleged violator becomes gratuitous. Indeed, respondents, in propounding their interpretation of the Act, can think of no reasons for Congress to require such notice other than that "it seemed right" to inform an alleged violator that it was about to be sued.

Adopting respondents' interpretation of § 505's jurisdictional grant would create a second and even more disturbing anomaly. The bar on citizen suits when governmental enforcement action is underway suggests that the citizen suit is meant to supplement rather than to supplant governmental action. The legislative history of the Act reinforces this view of the role of the citizen suit. The Senate Report noted that "(t)he Committee intends the great volume of enforcement actions (to) be brought by the state," and that citizen suits are proper only "if the federal, state and local agencies fail to exercise their enforcement responsibility." Permitting citizen suits for wholly past violations of the Act could undermine the supplementary role envisioned for the citizen suit. This danger is best illustrated by an example. Suppose that the Administrator identified a violator of the Act and issued a compliance order under § 309(a). Suppose further that the Administrator agreed not to assess or otherwise seek civil penalties on the condition that the violator take some extreme corrective action, such as to install particularly effective but expensive machinery, that it otherwise would not be obliged to take. If citizens could file suit, months or years later, in order to seek the civil penalties that the Administrator chose to forgo, then the Administrator's discretion to enforce the Act in the public interest would be curtailed considerably. The same might be said of the discretion of state enforcement authorities. Respondents' interpretation of the scope of the citizen suit would change the nature of the citizens' role from interstitial to potentially intrusive. We cannot agree that Congress intended such a result.

. . . .

Our conclusion that § 505 does not permit citizen suits for wholly past violations does not necessarily dispose of this lawsuit, as both lower courts recognized. The Court of Appeals acknowledged . . . that "(a) very sound argument can be made that (respondents') allegations of continuing violation were made in good faith," but expressly declined to rule on this alternative holding. Because we agree that § 505 confers jurisdiction over citizen suits when the citizen-plaintiffs make a good-faith allegation of continuous or intermittent violation, we remand the case to the Court of Appeals for further consideration. . . .

Petitioner also worries that our construction of § 505 would permit citizen-plaintiffs, if their allegations of ongoing noncompliance become false at some later point in the litigation because the defendant begins to comply with the Act, to continue nonetheless to press their suit to conclusion. According to petitioner, such a result would contravene both the prospective purpose of the citizen suit provisions and the "case or controversy" requirements of Article III. Longstanding principles of mootness, however, prevent the maintenance of suit when "there is no reasonable expectation that the wrong will be repeated." *United States v. W.T. Grant Co.,* 345 U.S. 629, 633, 73 S.Ct. 894, 897, 97 L.Ed. 1303 (1953) (quoting *United States v. Aluminum Co. of America,* 148 F.2d 416, 448 (CA2 1945)). In seeking to have a case dismissed as moot, however, the defendant's burden "is a heavy one." 345 U.S. at 633, 73 S.Ct. at 897. The defendants must demonstrate that it is "*absolutely clear* that the allegedly wrongful behavior could not reasonably be expected to recur." *United States v. Phosphate Export Assn., Inc.,* 393 U.S. 199, 203, 89 S.Ct. 361, 364, 21 L.Ed.2d 344 (1968) (emphasis added). Mootness doctrine thus protects defendants from the maintenance of suit under the Clean Air Act based solely on violations wholly unconnected to any present or future wrongdoing, while it also protects plaintiffs from defendants who seek to evade sanction by predictable "protestations of repentance and reform." *United States v. Oregon State Medical Society,* 343 U.S. 326, 333, 72 S.Ct. 690, 696, 96 L.Ed. 978 (1952).

Because the court below erroneously concluded that respondents could maintain an action based on wholly past violations of the Act, it declined to decide whether respondents' complaint contained a good-faith allegation of ongoing violation by petitioner. We therefore remand the case for consideration of this question. The judgment of the Court of Appeals is vacated, and the case is remanded for further proceedings consistent with this opinion.

NOTES AND QUESTIONS

(1) Are you persuaded that allowing citizen suits to redress wholly past violations of environmental laws would constitute undue interference with the enforcement discretion of federal and state officials? Is there a sound reason for EPA and the states to have more unfettered enforcement discretion as to past environmental violations than they do with respect to ongoing or continuing exceedances?

(2) On remand in *Gwaltney,* the U.S. District Court found that trial testimony in the case had "established without question that at least some reasonable likelihood of a recurrence in intermittent violations existed." It thus retained jurisdiction. *Chesapeake Bay Foundation, Inc. v. Gwaltney of Smithfield, Ltd.,* 688 F. Supp. 1078, 1079 (E.D. Va. 1988), *aff'd,* 890 F.2d 690 (4th Cir. 1989).

(3) May the defendant in a citizen suit avoid liability by completing remedial activities after a complaint is filed but prior to the rendering of a final judgment? Several courts have held that post-complaint remediation can moot claims for injunctive relief, but not claims for civil penalties. *See Chesapeake Bay Foundation, Inc. v. Gwaltney of Smithfield, Ltd.,* 890 F.2d 690, 696-697 (4th Cir. 1989); *Atlantic States Legal Foundation v. Tyson Foods, Inc.,* 897 F.2d 1127 (11th Cir. 1990). Notably, the citizen suit provisions of environmental statutes have been held not to authorize awards of compensatory damages. *See, e.g., City of Philadelphia v. Stepan Chem. Co.,* 544 F. Supp. 1135 (E.D. Pa. 1982); *Connecticut v. LILCO,* 535 F. Supp. 546 (E.D.N.Y. 1982).

(4) The issue of whether citizen suits may be instituted as to past environmental violations took on a constitutional dimension in *The Steel Company v. Citizens for a Better Environment,* 523 U.S. 83, 118 S. Ct. 1003, 140 L. Ed. 2d 210 (1998). There an environmental citizens organization filed suit under the citizen suit provision of the Emergency Planning and Community Right to Know Act of 1986 (EPCRA), alleging that the defendant steel company had failed to file timely toxic and hazardous chemical storage and emission reports, as required by the Act. The Court held that the plaintiff lacked standing to maintain the suit, since the relief it was seeking—declaratory judgment, injunctive relief, civil penalties and attorney's fees—would not serve to reimburse the plaintiff for any losses it incurred as a result of the defendant's late reporting, or eliminate any effects upon the plaintiff of the defendant's tardiness.

FRIENDS OF THE EARTH, INC. v. LAIDLAW ENVIRONMENTAL SERVICES (TOC), INC.

United States Supreme Court (2000)
__ U.S. __, 120 S. Ct. 693, 145 L. Ed. 2d 610

Justice GINSBURG delivered the opinion of the Court.

This case presents an important question concerning the operation of the citizen-suit provisions of the Clean Water Act. Congress authorized the federal district courts to entertain Clean Water Act suits initiated by "a person or persons having an interest which is or may be adversely affected." 33 U.S.C. §§ 1365(a), (g). To impel future compliance with the Act, a district court may prescribe injunctive relief in such a suit; additionally or alternatively, the court may impose civil penalties payable to the United States Treasury. § 1365(a). In the Clean Water Act citizen suit now before us, the District Court determined that injunctive relief was inappropriate because the defendant, after the institution of the litigation, achieved substantial compliance with the terms of its discharge permit. 956 F. Supp. 588, 611 [44 ERC 1232] (SC 1997). The court did, however, assess a civil penalty of $405,800. Id., at 610. The "total deterrent effect" of the penalty would be adequate to forestall future violations, the court reasoned, taking into account that the defendant "will be required to reimburse plaintiffs for a significant amount of legal fees and has, itself, incurred significant legal expenses." Id., at 610-611.

The Court of Appeals vacated the District Court's order. 149 F.3d 303 (CA4 1998). The case became moot, the appellate court declared, once the defendant fully complied with the terms of its permit and the plaintiff failed to appeal the denial of equitable relief. "[C]ivil penalties payable to the government," the Court of Appeals stated, "would not redress any injury Plaintiffs have suffered." Id., at 307. Nor were attorneys' fees in order, the Court of Appeals noted, because absent relief on the merits, plaintiffs could not qualify as prevailing parties. Id., at 307, n. 5.

We reverse the judgment of the Court of Appeals. The appellate court erred in concluding that a citizen suitor's claim for civil penalties must be dismissed as moot when the defendant, albeit after commencement of the litigation, has come into compliance. In directing dismissal of the suit on grounds of mootness, the Court of Appeals incorrectly conflated our case law on initial standing to bring suit, *see, e.g., Steel Co. v. Citizens for a Better Environment*, 523 U.S. 83 (1998), with our case law on post-commencement mootness, *see, e.g., City of Mesquite v. Aladdin's Castle, Inc.*, 455 U.S. 283 (1982). A defendant's voluntary cessation of allegedly unlawful conduct ordinarily does not suffice to moot a case. The Court of Appeals also misperceived the remedial potential of civil penalties. Such penalties may serve, as an alternative to an injunction, to deter further violations and thereby redress the injuries that prompted a citizen suitor to commence litigation.

I

A

In 1972, Congress enacted the Clean Water Act (Act), also known as the Federal Water Pollution Control Act, 86Stat. 816, as amended, 33 U.S.C. § 1251 et seq. Section 402of the Act, 33 U.S.C. § 1342, provides for the issuance, by the Administrator of the Environmental Protection Agency (EPA) or by authorized States, of National Pollutant Discharge Elimination System (NPDES) permits. NPDES permits impose limitations on the discharge of pollutants, and establish related monitoring and reporting requirements, in order to improve the cleanliness and safety of the Nation's waters. Noncompliance with a permit constitutes a violation of the Act. § 1342(h).

Under § 505(a) of the Act, a suit to enforce any limitation in an NPDES permit may be brought by any "citizen," defined as "a person or persons having an interest which is or may be adversely affected." 33 U.S.C. §§ 1365(a), (g). Sixty days before initiating a citizen suit, however, the would-be plaintiff must give notice of the alleged violation to the EPA, the State in which the alleged violation occurred, and the alleged violator. § 1365 (b)(1)(A). "[T]he purpose of notice to the alleged violator is to give it an opportunity to bring itself into complete compliance with the Act and thus . . . render unnecessary a citizen suit." *Gwaltney of Smithfield, Ltd. v. Chesapeake Bay Foundation, Inc.*, 484 U.S. 49, 60 (1987). Accordingly, we have held that citizens lack statutory standing under § 505(a) to sue for violations that have ceased by the time the complaint is filed. Id., at 56-63. The Act also bars a citizen from suing if the EPA or the State has already commenced, and is "diligently prosecuting," an enforcement action. 33 U.S.C. § 1365(b)(1)(B).

The Act authorizes district courts in citizen-suit proceedings to enter injunctions and to assess civil penalties, which are payable to the United States Treasury. § 1365(a). In determining the amount of any civil penalty, the district court must take into account "the seriousness of the violation or violations, the economic benefit (if any) resulting from the violation, any history of such violations, any good-faith efforts to comply with the applicable requirements, the economic impact of the penalty on the violator, and such other matters as justice may require." § 1319(d). In addition, the court "may award costs of litigation (including reasonable attorney and expert witness fees) to any prevailing or substantially prevailing party, whenever the court determines such award is appropriate." § 1365(d).

B

In 1986, defendant-respondent Laidlaw Environmental Services (TOC), Inc., bought a hazardous waste incinerator facility in Roebuck, South Carolina, that included a wastewater treatment plant. (The company has since changed its name to Safety-Kleen (Roebuck), Inc., but for simplicity we will refer to it as "Laidlaw" throughout.) Shortly after Laidlaw acquired the facility, the South Carolina Department of Health and Environmental Control (DHEC), acting under 33 U.S.C. § 1342(a)(1), granted Laidlaw an NPDES permit authorizing the company to discharge treated water into the North Tyger River. The permit, which became effective on January 1, 1987, placed limits on Laidlaw's discharge of several pollutants into the river, including—of particular relevance to this case—mercury, an extremely toxic pollutant. The permit also regulated the flow, temperature, toxicity, and pH of the effluent from the facility, and imposed monitoring and reporting obligations.

Once it received its permit, Laidlaw began to discharge various pollutants into the waterway; repeatedly, Laidlaw's discharges exceeded the limits set by the permit. In particular, despite experimenting with several technological fixes, Laidlaw consistently failed to meet the permit's stringent 1.3 ppb (parts per billion) daily average limit on mercury discharges. The District Court later found that Laidlaw had violated the mercury limits on 489 occasions between 1987 and 1995. 956 F. Supp., at 613-621.

On April 10, 1992, plaintiff-petitioners Friends of the Earth (FOE) and Citizens Local Environmental Action Network, Inc. (CLEAN) (referred to collectively in this opinion, together with later joined plaintiff-petitioner, Sierra Club, as "FOE") took the preliminary step necessary to the institution of litigation. They sent a letter to Laidlaw notifying the company of their intention to file a citizen suit against it under § 505(a) of the Act after the expiration of the requisite 60-day notice period, i.e., on or after June 10, 1992. Laidlaw's lawyer then contacted DHEC to ask whether DHEC would consider filing a lawsuit against Laidlaw. The District Court later found that Laidlaw's reason for requesting that DHEC file a lawsuit against it was to bar FOE's proposed citizen suit through the operation of 33 U.S.C. § 1365(b)(1)(B). 890 F. Supp. 470, 478 (SC 1995). DHEC agreed to file a lawsuit against Laidlaw; the company's lawyer then drafted the complaint for DHEC and paid the filing fee. On June 9, 1992, the last day before FOE's 60-day notice period expired, DHEC and Laidlaw reached a settlement requiring Laidlaw to pay $100,000 in civil penalties and to make " 'every effort' " to comply with its permit obligations. 890 F. Supp., at 479

On June 12, 1992, FOE filed this citizen suit against Laidlaw under § 505(a) of the Act, alleging noncompliance with the NPDES permit and seeking declaratory and injunctive relief and an award of civil penalties. Laidlaw moved for summary judgment on the ground that FOE had failed to present evidence demonstrating injury in fact, and therefore lacked Article III standing to bring the lawsuit. Record, Doc. No. 43. In opposition to this motion, FOE submitted affidavits and deposition testimony from members of the plaintiff organizations. Record, Doc. No. 71 (Exhs. 41-51). The record before the District Court also included affidavits from the organizations' members submitted by FOE in support of an earlier motion for preliminary injunctive relief. Record, Doc. No. 21 (Exhs. 5-10). After examining this evidence, the District Court denied Laidlaw's summary judgment motion, finding—albeit "by the very slimmest of margins"—that FOE had standing to bring the suit. App. In No. 97-1246 (CA4), pp. 207-208 (Tr. Of Hearing 39-40 (June 30, 1993)).

Laidlaw also moved to dismiss the action on the ground that the citizen suit was barred under 33 U.C.S. § 1365(b)(1)(B) by DHEC's prior action against the company. The United States, appearing as *amicus curiae*, joined FOE in opposing the motion. After an extensive analysis of the Laidlaw-DHEC settlement and the circumstances under which it was reached, the District Court held that DHEC's action against Laidlaw had not been "diligently prosecuted"; consequently, the court allowed FOE's citizen suit to proceed, 890 F. Supp., at 499. The record indicates that after FOE initiated the suit, but before the District Court rendered judgment, Laidlaw violated the mercury discharge limitation in its permit 13 times. 956 F. Supp., at 621. The District Court also found that Laidlaw had committed 13 monitoring and 10 reporting violations during this period. Id., at 601. The last recorded mercury discharge violation occurred in January, 1995, long after the complaint was filed but about two years before judgment was rendered. Id., at 621.

On January 22, 1997, the District Court issued its judgment. 956 F. Supp. 588 (SC 1997). It found that Laidlaw had gained a total economic benefit of $1,092,581 as a result of its extended period of noncompliance with the mercury discharge limit in its permit. Id., at 603. The court concluded, however, that a civil penalty of $405,800 was adequate in light of the guiding factors listed in 33 U.S.C. § 1319(d). 956 F. Supp., at 610. In particular, the District Court stated that the lesser penalty was appropriate taking into account the judgment's "total deterrent effect." In reaching this determination, the court "considered that Laidlaw will be required to reimburse plaintiffs for a significant amount of legal fees." Id., at 610-611. The court declined to grant FOE's request for injunctive relief, stating that an injunction was inappropriate because "Laidlaw has been in substantial compliance with all parameters in its NPDES permit since at least August 1992." Id., at 611.

FOE appealed the District Court's civil penalty judgment, arguing that the penalty was inadequate, but did not appeal the denial of declaratory or injunctive relief. Laidlaw cross-appealed, arguing, among other things, that FOE lacked standing to bring the suit and that DHEC's action qualified as a diligent prosecution precluding FOE's litigation. The United States continued to participate as *amicus curiae* in support of FOE.

On July 16, 1998, the Court of Appeals for the Fourth Circuit issued its judgment. 149 F.3d 303. The Court of Appeals assumed without deciding that FOE initially had standing to bring the action, id., at 306, n. 3, but went on to hold that the case had become moot. The appellate court stated, first, that the elements of Article III standing—injury, causation, and redressability—must persist at every stage of review, or else the action becomes moot. Id., at 306. Citing our decision in *Steel Co.*, the Court of Appeals reasoned that the case had become moot because "the only remedy currently available to [FOE]—civil penalties payable to the government—would not redress any injury [FOE has] suffered." Id., at 306-307. The court therefore vacated the District Court's order and remanded with instructions to dismiss the action. In a footnote, the Court of Appeals added that FOE's "failure to obtain relief on the merits of [its] claims precludes any recovery of attorneys' fees or other litigation costs because such an award is available only to a 'prevailing or substantially prevailing party.'" Id., at 307, n. 5 (quoting 33 U.S.C. § 1365(d)).

According to Laidlaw, after the Court of Appeals issued its decision but before this Court granted certiorari, the entire incinerator facility in Roebuck was permanently closed, dismantled, and put up for sale, and all discharges from the facility permanently ceased. Respondent's Suggestion of Mootness 3.

We granted certiorari, 525 U.S. 1176 (1999), to resolve the inconsistency between the Fourth Circuit's decision in this case and the decisions of several other Courts of Appeals, which have held that a defendant's compliance with its permit after the commencement of litigation does not moot claims for civil penalties under the Act. *See, e.g.*, *Atlantic States Legal Foundation, Inc. v. Stroh Die Casting Co.*, 116 F.3d 814, 820 (CA7), cert. denied, 522 U.S. 981 (1997); *Natural Resources Defense Council, Inc. v. Texaco Rfg. And Mktg., Inc.*, 2 F.3d 493, 503-504(CA3 1993); *Atlantic States Legal Foundation, Inc. v. Pan American Tanning Corp.*, 993 F.2d 1017, 1020-1021 (CA2 1993); *Atlantic States Legal Foundation, Inc. v. Tyson Foods, Inc.*, 897 F.2d 1128, 1135-1136 (CA11 1990).

II

A

The Constitution's case-or-controversy limitation on federal judicial authority, Art. III, § 2, underpins both our standing and our mootness jurisprudence, but the two inquiries differ in respects critical to the proper resolution of this case, so we address them separately. Because the Court of Appeals was persuaded that the case had become moot and so held, it simply assumed without deciding that FOE had initial standing. *See Arizonans for Official English v. Arizona*, 520 U.S. 43, 66-67 (1997) (court may assume without deciding that standing exists in order to analyze mootness). But because we hold that the Court of Appeals erred in declaring the case moot, we have an obligation to assure ourselves that FOE had Article III standing at the outset of the litigation. We therefore address the question of standing before turning to mootness.

In *Lujan v. Defenders of Wildlife*, 504 U.S. 555, 560-561 [34 ERC 1785] (1992), we held that, to satisfy Article III's standing requirements, a plaintiff must show (1) it has suffered an "injury in fact" that is (a) concrete and particularized and (b) actual or imminent, not conjectural or hypothetical; (2) the injury is fairly traceable to the challenged action of the defendant; and (3) it is likely, as opposed to merely speculative, that the injury will be redressed by a favorable decision. An association has standing to bring suit on behalf of its members when its members would otherwise have standing to sue in their own right, the interests at stake are germane to the organization's purpose, and neither the claim asserted nor the relief requested requires the participation of individual members in the lawsuit. *Hunt v. Washington State Apple Advertising Comm'n*, 432 U.S. 333, 343 (1977).

Laidlaw contends first that FOE lacked standing from the outset even to seek injunctive relief, because the plaintiff organizations failed to show that any of their members had sustained or faced the threat of any "injury in fact" from Laidlaw's activities. In support of this contention Laidlaw points to the District Court's finding, made in the course of setting the penalty amount, that there had been "no demonstrated proof of harm to the environment" for Laidlaw's mercury discharge violations. 956 F. Supp., at 602; see also *ibid.* ("[T]he NPDES permit violations at issue in this citizen suit did not result in any health risk or environmental harm.").

The relevant showing for purposes of Article III standing, however, is not injury to the environment but injury to the plaintiff. To insist upon the former rather than the latter as part of the standing inquiry (as the dissent in essence does) is to raise the standing hurdle higher than the necessary showing for success on the merits in an action alleging noncompliance with an NPDES permit. Focusing properly on injury to the plaintiff, the District Court found that FOE had demonstrated sufficient injury to establish standing. App. In No. 97-1246 (CA4), pp. 207-208 (Tr. of Hearing 39-40 (June 30, 1993)). For example, FOE member Kenneth Lee Curtis averred in affidavits that he lived a half-mile from Laidlaw's facility; that he occasionally drove over the North Tyger River, and that it looked and smelled polluted; and that he would like to fish, camp, swim, and picnic in and near the river between 3 and 15 miles downstream from the facility, as he did when he was a teenager, but would not do so because he was concerned that the water was polluted by Laidlaw's discharges. Record, Doc. No. 71 (Exhs. 41, 42). Curtis reaffirmed these statements in extensive deposition testimony. For example, he testified that he would like to fish in the river at a specific spot he used as a boy, but that he would not do so now because of his concerns about Laidlaw's discharges. Ibid. (Exh. 43, at 52-53; Exh. 44, at 33).

Other members presented evidence to similar effect . . . .

These sworn testimonies, as the District Court determined, adequately documented injury in fact. We have held that environmental plaintiffs adequately allege injury in fact when they aver that they use the affected area and are persons "for whom the aesthetic and recreational values of the area will be lessened" by the challenged activity. *Sierra Club v. Morton*, 405 U.S. 727, 735 [1 ERC 1669] (1972). *See also Defenders of Wildlife*, 504 U.S., at 562-563 ("Of course, the desire to use or observe an animal species, even for purely esthetic purposes, is undeniably a cognizable interest for purposes of standing.").

Our decision in *Lujan v. National Wildlife Federation*, 497 U.S. 871 [31 ERC 1553] (1990), is not to the contrary. In that case an environmental organization assailed the Bureau of Land Management's "land withdrawal review program," a program covering millions of acres, alleging that the program illegally opened up public lands to mining activities. The defendants moved for summary judgment, challenging the plaintiff organization's standing to initiate the action under the Administrative Procedure Act, 5U.S.C. § 702. We held that the plaintiff could not survive the summary judgment motion merely by offering "averments which state only that one of [the organization's] members uses unspecified portions of an immense tract of territory, on some portions of which mining activity has occurred or probably will occur by virtue of the governmental action." 497 U.S., at 889.

In contrast, the affidavits and testimony presented by FOE in this case assert that Laidlaw's discharges, and the affiant members' reasonable concerns about the effects of those discharges, directly affected those affiants' recreational, aesthetic, and economic interests. These submissions present dispositively more than the mere "general averments" and "conclusory allegations" found inadequate in *National Wildlife Federation*, Id., at 888. Nor can the affiants' conditional statements—that they would use the nearby North Tyger River for recreation if Laidlaw were not discharging pollutants into it—be equated with the speculative " 'some day' intentions" to visit endangered species halfway around the world that we held insufficient to show injury in fact in *Defenders of Wildlife*. 504 U.S., at 564.

Los Angeles v. Lyons, 461 U.S. 95 (1983), relied on by the dissent, does not weigh against standing in this case. In *Lyons*, we held that a plaintiff lacked standing to seek an injunction against the enforcement of a police chokehold policy because he could not credibly allege that he faced a realistic threat from the policy. 461 U.S., at 107, n. 7. In the footnote from *Lyons* cited by the dissent, we noted that "[t]he reasonableness of Lyons' fear is dependent upon the likelihood of a recurrence of the allegedly unlawful conduct," and that his "subjective apprehensions" that such a recurrence would even *take place* were not enough to support standing. Id., at 108, n. 8. Here, in contrast, it is undisputed that Laidlaw's unlawful conduct—discharging pollutants in excess of permit limits—was occurring at the time the complaint was filed. Under *Lyons*, then, the only "subjective" issue here is "[t]he reasonableness of [the] fear" that led the affiants to respond to that concededly ongoing conduct by refraining from use of the North Tyger River and surrounding areas. Unlike the dissent, we see nothing "improbable" about the proposition that a company's continuous and pervasive illegal discharges of pollutants into a river would cause nearby residents to curtail their recreational use of that waterway and would subject them to other economic and aesthetic harms. The proposition is entirely reasonable, the District Court found it was true in this case, and that is enough for injury in fact.

Laidlaw argues next that even if FOE had standing to seek injunctive relief, it lacked standing to seek civil penalties. Here the asserted defect is not injury but redressability. Civil penalties offer no redress to private plaintiffs, Laidlaw argues, because they are paid to the government, and therefore a citizen plaintiff can never have standing to seek them.

Laidlaw is right to insist that a plaintiff must demonstrate standing separately for each form of relief sought. *See, e.g., Lyons*, 461 U.S., at 109 (notwithstanding the fact that plaintiff had standing to pursue damages, he lacked standing to pursue injunctive relief); *see also Lewis v. Casey*, 518 U.S. 343, 358, n. 6 (1996) ("[S]tanding is not dispensed in gross."). But it is wrong to maintain that citizen plaintiffs facing ongoing violations never have standing to seek civil penalties.

We have recognized on numerous occasions that "all civil penalties have some deterrent effect." *Hudson v. United States*, 522 U.S. 93, 102 (1997); *see also, e.g., Department of Revenue of Mont. v. Kurth Ranch*, 511 U.S. 767, 778 (1994). More specifically, Congress has found that civil penalties in Clean Water Act cases do more than promote immediate compliance by limiting the defendant's economic incentive to delay its attainment of permit limits; they also deter future violations. This congressional determination warrants judicial attention and respect. "The legislative history of the Act reveals that Congress wanted the district court to consider the need for retribution and deterrence, in addition to restitution, when it imposed civil penalties. . . . [The district court may] seek to deter future violations by basing the penalty on its economic impact." *Tull v. United States*, 481 U.S. 412, 422-423 (1987).

It can scarcely be doubted that, for a plaintiff who is injured or faces the threat of future injury due to illegal conduct ongoing at the time of suit, a sanction that effectively abates that conduct and prevents its recurrence provides a form of redress. Civil penalties can fit that description. To the extent that they encourage defendants to discontinue current violations and deter them from committing future ones, they afford redress to citizen plaintiffs who are injured or threatened with injury as a consequence of ongoing unlawful conduct . . . .

In this case we need not explore the outer limits of the principle that civil penalties provide sufficient deterrence to support redressability. Here, the civil penalties sought by FOE carried with them a deterrent effect that made it likely, as opposed to merely speculative, that the penalties would redress FOE's injuries by abating current violations and preventing future ones—as the District Court reasonably found when it assessed a penalty of $405,800. 956 F. Supp., at 610-611.

Laidlaw contends that the reasoning of our decision in *Steel Co.* directs the conclusion that citizen plaintiffs have no standing to seek civil penalties under the Act. We disagree. *Steel Co.* established that citizen suitors lack standing to seek civil penalties for violations that have abated by the time of suit. 523 U.S., at 106-107. We specifically noted in that case that there was no allegation in the complaint of any continuing or imminent violation, and that no basis for such an allegation appeared to exist. Id., at 108; *see also Gwaltney*, 484 U.S., at 59 ("the harm sought to be addressed by the citizen suit lies in the present or the future, not in the past"). In short, *Steel Co.* held that private plaintiffs, unlike the Federal Government, may not sue to assess penalties for wholly past violations, but our decision in that case did not reach the issue of standing to seek penalties for violations that are ongoing at the time of the complaint and that could continue into the future if undeterred.

B

Satisfied that FOE had standing under Article III to bring this action, we turn to the question of mootness.

The only conceivable basis for a finding of mootness in this case is Laidlaw's voluntary conduct—either its achievement by August 1992 of substantial compliance with its NPDES permit or its more recent shutdown of the Roebuck facility. It is well settled that "a defendant's voluntary cessation of a challenged practice does not deprive a federal court of its power to determine the legality of the practice." *City of Mesquite*, 455 U.S., at 289. "[I]f it did, the courts would be compelled to leave '[t]he defendant . . . free to return to his old ways.'" Id. at 289, n. 10 (citing *United States v. W. T. Grant Co.*, 345 U.S. 629, 632 (1953)). In accordance with this principle, the standard we have announced for determining whether a case has been mooted by the defendant's voluntary conduct is stringent: "A case might become moot if subsequent events made it absolutely clear that the allegedly wrongful behavior could not reasonably be expected to recur." *United States v. Concentrated Phosphate Export Assn., Inc.*, 393 U.S. 199, 203 (1968). The "heavy burden of persua[ding]" the court that the challenged conduct cannot reasonably be expected to start up again lies with the party asserting mootness. Ibid.

The Court of Appeals justified its mootness disposition by reference to *Steel Co.*, which held that citizen plaintiffs lack standing to seek civil penalties for wholly past violations. In relying on *Steel Co.*, the Court of Appeals confused mootness with standing. The confusion is understandable, given this Court's repeated statements that the doctrine of mootness can be described as "the doctrine of standing set in a time frame: The requisite personal interest that must exist at the commencement of the litigation (standing) must continue throughout its existence (mootness)." *Arizonans for Official English*, 520 U.S., at 68, n. 22 (quoting *United States Parole Comm'n v. Geraghty*, 445 U.S. 388, 397 (1980), in turn quoting Monaghan, Constitutional Adjudication: The Who and When, 82 Yale L. J. 1363, 1384 (1973)) (internal quotation marks omitted).

Careful reflection on the long-recognized exceptions to mootness, however, reveals that the description of mootness as "standing set in a time frame" is not comprehensive. As just noted, a defendant claiming that its voluntary compliance moots a case bears the formidable burden of showing that it is absolutely clear the allegedly wrongful behavior could not reasonably be expected to recur. *Concentrated Phosphate Export Assn.*, 393 U.S., at 203. By contrast, in a lawsuit brought to force compliance, it is the plaintiff's burden to establish standing by demonstrating that, if unchecked by the litigation, the defendant's allegedly wrongful behavior will likely occur or continue, and that the "threatened injury [is] certainly impending." *Whitmore v. Arkansas*, 495 U.S. 149, 158 (1990) (citations and internal quotation marks omitted). . . . The plain lesson of these cases is that there are circumstances in which the prospect that a defendant will engage in (or resume) harmful conduct may be too speculative to support standing, but not too speculative to overcome mootness . . . .

Standing doctrine functions to ensure, among other things, that the scarce resources of the federal courts are devoted to those disputes in which the parties have a concrete stake. In contrast, by the time mootness is an issue, the case has been brought and litigated, often (as here) for years. To abandon the case at an advanced stage may prove more wasteful than frugal. This argument from sunk costs does not license courts to retain jurisdiction over cases in which one or both of the parties plainly lacks a continuing interest, as when the parties have settled or a plaintiff pursuing a nonsurviving claim has died . . . .

In its brief, Laidlaw appears to argue that, regardless of the effect of Laidlaw's compliance, FOE doomed its own civil penalty claim to mootness by failing to appeal the District Court's denial of injunctive relief. Brief for Respondent 14-17. This argument misconceives the statutory scheme. Under § 1365(a), the district court has discretion to determine which form of relief is best suited, in the particular case, to abate current violations and deter future ones. "[A] federal judge sitting as chancellor is not mechanically obligated to grant an injunction for every violation of law." *Weinberger v. Romero-Barcelo*, 456 U.S. 305, 313 (1982). Denial of injunctive relief does not necessarily mean that the district court had concluded there is no prospect of future violations for civil penalties to deter. Indeed, it meant no such thing in this case. The District Court denied injunctive relief, but expressly based its award of civil penalties on the need for deterrence. *See* 956 F. Supp., at 610-611. As the dissent notes, *post*, at 8, federal courts should aim to ensure " 'the framing of relief no broader than required by the precise facts.' " *Schlesinger v. Reservists Comm. to Stop the War*, 418 U.S. 208, 222 (1974). In accordance with this aim, a district Court in a Clean Water Act citizen suit properly may conclude that an injunction would be an excessively intrusive remedy, because it could entail continuing superintendence of the permit holder's activities by a federal court—a process burdensome to court and permit holder alike. *See City of Mesquite*, 455 U.S., at 289 (although the defendant's voluntary cessation of the challenged practice does not moot the case, "[s]uch abandonment is an important factor bearing on the question whether a court should exercise its power to enjoin the defendant from renewing the practice"

Laidlaw also asserts, in a supplemental suggestion of mootness, that the closure of its Roebuck facility, which took place after the Court of Appeals issued its decision, mooted the case. The facility closure, like Laidlaw's earlier achievement of substantial compliance with its permit requirements, might moot the case, but—we once more reiterate—only if one or the other of these events made it absolutely clear that Laidlaw's permit violations could not reasonably be expected to recur. *Concentrated Phosphate Export Assn.*, 393 U.S., at 203. The effect of both Laidlaw's compliance and the facility closure on the prospect of future violations is a disputed factual matter. FOE points out, for example—and Laidlaw does not appear to contest—that Laidlaw retains its NPDES permit. These issues have not been aired in the lower courts; they remain open for consideration on remand.

. . . .

For the reasons stated, the judgment of the United States Court of Appeals for the Fourth Circuit is reversed, and the case is remanded for further proceedings consistent with this opinion.

It is so ordered.

NOTES AND QUESTIONS

(1) Were you persuaded by the majority's reasoning in this case? Is this decision consistent with the Court's earlier decision in *The Steel Co. v. Citizens for a Better Environment*? If the Court had ruled for the defendants, on the issues of mootness and standing-to-sue, what types of environmental citizen suits (if any) could still have been maintained by environmental citizen groups?

(2) Justice Stevens wrote a separate concurring opinion in *Laidlaw*. In his view, no post-judgment conduct of the respondent would warrant a vacation of the civil penalty that the District Court had assessed against the defendant. Thus, the case could not be moot—even if it were absolutely clear that the respondent posed no threat of future permit violations.

(3) Justice Kennedy also concurred. Kennedy opined that "difficult and fundamental questions" are raised as to whether exactions of public fines by private litigants constitute a permissible delegation of executive power. In his view, however, those issues are "best reserved for a later case." To what extent does this represent a valid concern? Under what kinds of factual circumstances might defendants in citizen suits seek to raise a non-delegation defense?

(4) Justices Scalia and Thomas dissented in the *Laidlaw* case. They reasoned that the plaintiff's affidavits were too "short on specific facts" to satisfy the plaintiff's burden of demonstrating injury-in-fact. Moreover, they opined, a plaintiff's desire to benefit from the deterrent effect of a public penalty for a polluter's past misconduct can never suffice to establish a "case or controversy" for purposes of standing-to-sue. The Court's discussion of that point, in their view, has thus "promulgated a revolutionary new doctrine of standing that will permit the entire body of public civil penalties to be handed over to enforcement by private interests."

TABLE OF CASES

[Principal cases appear in capitals; references are to pages.]

A

[Principal cases appear in capitals; references are to pages.]

[Principal cases appear in capitals; references are to pages.]

[Principal cases appear in capitals; references are to pages.]

[Principal cases appear in capitals; references are to pages.]

[Principal cases appear in capitals; references are to pages.]

[Principal cases appear in capitals; references are to pages.]

[Principal cases appear in capitals; references are to pages.]

[Principal cases appear in capitals; references are to pages.]

[Principal cases appear in capitals; references are to pages.]

D

[Principal cases appear in capitals; references are to pages.]

[Principal cases appear in capitals; references are to pages.]

[Principal cases appear in capitals; references are to pages.]

[Principal cases appear in capitals; references are to pages.]

[Principal cases appear in capitals; references are to pages.]

[Principal cases appear in capitals; references are to pages.]

H

[Principal cases appear in capitals; references are to pages.]

[Principal cases appear in capitals; references are to pages.]

I

J

[Principal cases appear in capitals; references are to pages.]

[Principal cases appear in capitals; references are to pages.]

L

[Principal cases appear in capitals; references are to pages.]

M

[Principal cases appear in capitals; references are to pages.]

[Principal cases appear in capitals; references are to pages.]

N

[Principal cases appear in capitals; references are to pages.]

[Principal cases appear in capitals; references are to pages.]

O

[Principal cases appear in capitals; references are to pages.]

[Principal cases appear in capitals; references are to pages.]

[Principal cases appear in capitals; references are to pages.]

[Principal cases appear in capitals; references are to pages.]

S

[Principal cases appear in capitals; references are to pages.]

[Principal cases appear in capitals; references are to pages.]

[Principal cases appear in capitals; references are to pages.]

T

[Principal cases appear in capitals; references are to pages.]

[Principal cases appear in capitals; references are to pages.]

U

[Principal cases appear in capitals; references are to pages.]

[Principal cases appear in capitals; references are to pages.]

[Principal cases appear in capitals; references are to pages.]

[Principal cases appear in capitals; references are to pages.]

[Principal cases appear in capitals; references are to pages.]

Y

Z

INDEX

[References are to pages.]

A

[References are to pages.]

C

[References are to pages.]

[References are to pages.]

[References are to pages.]

[References are to pages.]

[References are to pages.]

[References are to pages.]

O

P

[References are to pages.]

[References are to pages.]